THE UNIVERSAL BIBLE

OF THE PROTESTANT, CATHOLIC, ORTHODOX, ETHIOPIC, SYRIAC, AND SAMARITAN CHURCH

THE UNIVERSAL BIBLE
OF THE PROTESTANT, CATHOLIC, ORTHODOX, ETHIOPIC, SYRIAC, AND SAMARITAN CHURCH

Fifth Estate Publishers,
Post Office Box 116, Blountsville, AL 35031.

First Printing, 2010

Cover Design by An Quigley

Printed on acid-free paper

Library of Congress Control No: 2010924985

ISBN 13: 9781933580937

Fifth Estate, 2010

List of Churches and their Canon of Scripture
(1) Samaritan (2) Hebrew (3) Orthodox (4) Catholic (5) Syriac (6) Ethiopian (7) Protestant

Book	1	2	3	4	5	6	7
Genesis	■	■	■	■	■	■	■
Exodus	■	■	■	■	■	■	■
Leviticus	■	■	■	■	■	■	■
Numbers	■	■	■	■	■	■	■
Deuteronomy	■	■	■	■	■	■	■
Joshua	■	■	■	■	■	■	■
Judges		■	■	■	■	■	■
Ruth		■	■	■	■	■	■
1 Samuel		■	■	■	■	■	■
2 Samuel		■	■	■	■	■	■
1 Kings		■	■	■	■	■	■
2 Kings		■	■	■	■	■	■
1 Chronicles		■	■	■	■	■	■
2 Chronicles		■	■	■	■	■	■
1 Esdras			■	■	■	■	
2 Esdras			■	■		■	
Ezra		■	■	■	■	■	■
Nehemiah		■	■	■	■	■	■
Esther		■	■	■	■	■	■
Judith			■	■	■	■	
Tobit			■	■	■	■	
1 Maccabees			■	■	■	■	
2 Maccabees			■	■	■	■	
3 Maccabees			■		■	■	
4 Maccabees			■		■		
Psalms		■	■	■	■	■	■
Odes			■		■		
Prayer of Manasseh			■	■		■	
Proverbs		■	■	■	■	■	■
Ecclesiastes		■	■	■	■	■	■
Song of Songs		■	■	■	■	■	■
Job		■	■	■	■	■	■

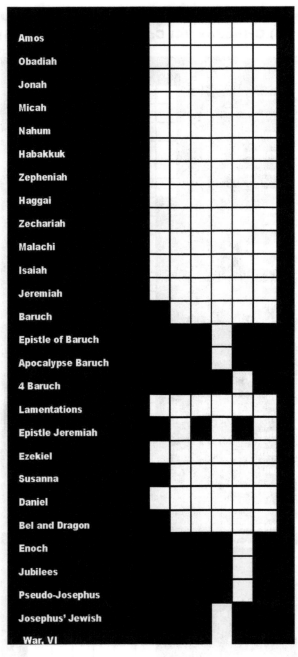

Amos
Obadiah
Jonah
Micah
Nahum
Habakkuk
Zepheniah
Haggai
Zechariah
Malachi
Isaiah
Jeremiah
Baruch
Epistle of Baruch
Apocalypse Baruch
4 Baruch
Lamentations
Epistle Jeremiah
Ezekiel
Susanna
Daniel
Bel and Dragon
Enoch
Jubilees
Pseudo-Josephus
Josephus' Jewish War, VI

(1) Samaritan (2) Hebrew (3) Orthodox (4) Catholic (5) Syriac (6) Ethiopian (7) Protestant

Matthew					
Mark					
Luke					
John					
Acts					
Romans					
1 Corinthians					
2 Corinthians					
Galatians					
Ephesians					
Philippians					
Colossians					
1 Thessalonians					
2 Thessalonians					
1 Timothy					
2 Timothy					
Titus					
Philemon					
Hebrews					
James					
1 Peter					
2 Peter					
1 John					
2 John					
3 John					
Jude					
Revelation					
Epistle - Laodiceans					
Acts of Paul - Thecla					
3 Corinthians					
Sinodos					
Clement					
The Book Covenant					
Ethiopian Didascalia					
Shepherd of Hermas					
Ascension of Isaiah					

Sinodos, Book of the Covenant, and Didascalia outline the order and procedures of worship and are specific to certain churches. These are contained in the Broad Ethiopian Canon. They are not included here.

Old Testament

THE FIRST BOOK OF MOSES,
CALLED
GENESIS.

CHAPTER 1

IN the beginning God created the heaven and the earth.

2 And the earth was without form, and void; and darkness was upon the face of the deep. And the Spirit of God moved upon the face of the waters.

3 And God said, Let there be light: and there was light.

4 And God saw the light, that it was good: and God divided the light from the darkness.

5 And God called the light Day, and the darkness he called Night. And the evening and the morning were the first day.

6And God said, Let there be a firmament in the midst of the waters, and let it divide the waters from the waters.

7 And God made the firmament, and divided the waters which were under the firmament from the waters which were above the firmament: and it was so.

8 And God called the firmament Heaven. And the evening and the morning were the second day.

9And God said, Let the waters under the heaven be gathered together unto one place, and let the dry land appear: and it was so.

10 And God called the dry land Earth; and the gathering together of the waters called he Seas: and God saw that it was good.

11 And God said, Let the earth bring forth grass, the herb yielding seed, and the fruit tree yielding fruit after his kind, whose seed is in itself, upon the earth: and it was so.

12 And the earth brought forth grass, and herb yielding seed after his kind, and the tree yielding fruit, whose seed was in itself, after his kind: and God saw that it was good.

13 And the evening and the morning were the third day.

14And God said, Let there be lights in the firmament of the heaven to divide the day from the night; and let them be for signs, and for seasons, and for days, and years:

15 And let them be for lights in the firmament of the heaven to give light upon the earth: and it was so.

16 And God made two great lights; the greater light to rule the day, and the lesser light to rule the night: he made the stars also.

17 And God set them in the firmament of the heaven to give light upon the earth,

18 And to rule over the day and over the night, and to divide the light from the darkness: and God saw that it was good.

19 And the evening and the morning were the fourth day.

20 And God said, Let the waters bring forth abundantly the moving creature that has life, and fowl that may fly above the earth in the open firmament of heaven.

21 And God created great whales, and every living creature that moveth, which the waters brought forth abundantly, after their kind, and every winged fowl after his kind: and God saw that it was good.

22 And God blessed them, saying, Be fruitful, and multiply, and fill the waters in the seas, and let fowl multiply in the earth.

23 And the evening and the morning were the fifth day.

24And God said, Let the earth bring forth the living creature after his kind, cattle, and creeping thing, and beast of the earth after his kind: and it was so.

25 And God made the beast of the earth after his kind, and cattle after their kind, and every thing that creepeth upon the earth after his kind: and God saw that it was good.

26And God said, Let us make man in our image, after our likeness: and let them have dominion over the fish of the sea, and over the fowl of the air, and over the cattle, and over all the earth, and over every creeping thing that creepeth upon the earth.

27 So God created man in his own image, in the image of God created he him; male and female created he them.

28 And God blessed them, and God said unto them, Be fruitful, and multiply, and replenish the earth, and subdue it: and have dominion over the fish of the sea, and over the fowl of the air, and over every living thing that moveth upon the earth.

29And God said, Behold, I have given you every herb bearing seed, which is upon the face of all the earth, and every tree, in the which is the fruit of a tree yielding seed; to you it shall be for meat.

30 And to every beast of the earth, and to every fowl of the air, and to every thing that creepeth upon the earth, wherein there is life, I have given every green herb for meat: and it was so.

31 And God saw every thing that he had made, and, behold, it was very good. And the evening and the morning were the sixth day.

CHAPTER 2

THUS the heavens and the earth were finished, and all the host of them.

2 And on the seventh day God ended his work which he had made; and he rested on the seventh day from all his work which he had made.

3 And God blessed the seventh day, and sanctified it: because that in it he had rested from all his work which God created and made.

4These are the generations of the heavens and of the earth when they were created, in the day that the LORD God made the earth and the heavens,

5 And every plant of the field before it was in the earth, and every herb of the field before it grew: for the LORD God had not caused it to rain upon the earth, and there was not a man to till the ground.

6 But there went up a mist from the earth, and watered the whole face of the ground.

7 And the LORD God formed man of the dust of the ground, and breathed into his nostrils the breath of life; and man became a living soul.

8And the LORD God planted a garden eastward in Eden; and there he put the man whom he had formed.

9 And out of the ground made the LORD God to grow every tree that is pleasant to the sight, and good for food; the tree of life also in the midst of the garden, and the tree of knowledge of good and evil.

10 And a river went out of Eden to water the garden; and from thence it was parted, and became into four heads.

11 The name of the first is Pison: that is it which compasseth the whole land of Havilah, where there is gold;

12 And the gold of that land is good: there is bdellium and the onyx stone.

13 And the name of the second river is Gihon: the same is it that compasseth the whole land of Ethiopia.

14 And the name of the third river is Hiddekel: that is it which goeth toward the east of Assyria. And the fourth river is Euphrates.

15 And the LORD God took the man, and put him into the garden of Eden to dress it and to keep it.

16 And the LORD God commanded the man, saying, Of every tree of the garden you mayest freely eat:

17 But of the tree of the knowledge of good and evil, you shalt not eat of it: for in the day that you eatest thereof you shalt surely die.

18And the LORD God said, It is not good that the man should be alone; I will make him an help meet for him.

19 And out of the ground the LORD God formed every beast of the field, and every fowl of the air; and brought them unto Adam to see what he would call them: and whatsoever Adam called every living creature, that was the name thereof.

20 And Adam gave names to all cattle, and to the fowl of the air, and to every beast of the field; but for Adam there was not found an help meet for him.

21 And the LORD God caused a deep sleep to fall upon Adam, and he slept: and he took one of his ribs, and closed up the flesh instead thereof;

22 And the rib, which the LORD God had taken from man, made he a woman, and brought her unto the man.

23 And Adam said, This is now bone of my bones, and flesh of my flesh: she shall be called Woman, because she was taken out of Man.

24 Therefore shall a man leave his father and his mother, and shall cleave unto his wife: and they shall be one flesh.

25 And they were both naked, the man and his wife, and were not ashamed.

CHAPTER 3

NOW the serpent was more subtil than any beast of the field which the LORD God had made. And he said unto the woman, Yea, has God said, You shall not eat of every tree of the garden?

2 And the woman said unto the serpent, We may eat of the fruit of the trees of the garden:

3 But of the fruit of the tree which is in the midst of the garden, God has said, You shall not eat of it, neither shall you touch it, lest you die.

4 And the serpent said unto the woman, You shall not surely die:

5 For God doth know that in the day you eat thereof, then your eyes shall be opened, and you shall be as gods, knowing good and evil.

6 And when the woman saw that the tree was good for food, and that it was pleasant to the eyes, and a tree to be desired to make one wise, she took of the fruit thereof, and did eat, and gave also unto her husband with her; and he did eat.

7 And the eyes of them both were opened, and they knew that they were naked; and they sewed fig leaves together, and made themselves aprons.

8 And they heard the voice of the LORD God walking in the garden in the cool of the day: and Adam and his wife hid themselves from the presence of the LORD God amongst the trees of the garden.

9 And the LORD God called unto Adam, and said unto him, Where art you ?

10 And he said, I heard your voice in the garden, and I was afraid, because I was naked; and I hid myself.

11 And he said, Who told you that you wast naked? Have you eaten of the tree, whereof I commanded you that you shouldest not eat?

12 And the man said, The woman whom you gavest to be with me, she gave me of the tree, and I did eat.

13 And the LORD God said unto the woman, What is this that you have done? And the woman said, The serpent beguiled me, and I did eat.

14 And the LORD God said unto the serpent, Because you have done this, you are cursed above all cattle, and above every beast of the field; upon your belly shalt you go, and dust shalt you eat all the days of your life:

15 And I will put enmity between you and the woman, and between your seed and her seed; it shall bruise your head, and you shalt bruise his heel.

16 Unto the woman he said, I will greatly multiply your sorrow and your conception; in sorrow you shalt bring forth children; and your desire shall be to your husband, and he shall rule over you.

17 And unto Adam he said, Because you have hearkened unto the voice of your wife, and have eaten of the tree, of which I commanded you, saying, You shalt not eat of it: cursed is the ground for your sake; in sorrow shalt you eat of it all the days of your life;

18 Thorns also and thistles shall it bring forth to you; and you shalt eat the herb of the field;

19 In the sweat of your face shalt you eat bread, till you return unto the ground; for out of it wast you taken: for dust you are, and unto dust shalt you return.

20 And Adam called his wife's name Eve; because she was the mother of all living.

21 Unto Adam also and to his wife did the LORD God make coats of skins, and clothed them.

22 And the LORD God said, Behold, the man is become as one of us, to know good and evil: and now, lest he put forth his hand, and take also of the tree of life, and eat, and live for ever:

23 Therefore the LORD God sent him forth from the garden of Eden, to till the ground from whence he was taken.

24 So he drove out the man; and he placed at the east of the garden of Eden Cherubims, and a flaming sword which turned every way, to keep the way of the tree of life.

CHAPTER 4

AND Adam knew Eve his wife; and she conceived, and bare Cain, and said, I have gotten a man from the LORD.

2 And she again bare his brother Abel. And Abel was a keeper of sheep, but Cain was a tiller of the ground.

3 And in process of time it came to pass, that Cain brought of the fruit of the ground an offering unto the LORD.

4 And Abel, he also brought of the firstlings of his flock and of the fat thereof. And the LORD had respect unto Abel and to his offering:

5 But unto Cain and to his offering he had not respect. And Cain was very wroth, and his countenance fell.

6 And the LORD said unto Cain, Why are you wroth? and why is your countenance fallen?

7 If you doest well, shalt you not be accepted? and if you doest not well, sin lies at the door. And unto you shall be his desire, and you shalt rule over him.

8 And Cain talked with Abel his brother: and it came to pass, when they were in the field, that Cain rose up against Abel his brother, and slew him.

9 And the LORD said unto Cain, Where is Abel your brother? And he said, I know not: Am I my brother's keeper?

10 And he said, What have you done? the voice of your brother's blood crieth unto me from the ground.

11 And now are you cursed from the earth, which has opened her mouth to receive your brother's blood from your hand;

12 When you tillest the ground, it shall not henceforth yield unto you her strength; a fugitive and a vagabond shalt you be in the earth.

13 And Cain said unto the LORD, My punishment is greater than I can bear.

14 Behold, you have driven me out this day from the face of the earth; and from your face shall I be hid; and I shall be a fugitive and a vagabond in the earth; and it shall come to pass, that every one that findeth me shall slay me.

15 And the LORD said unto him, Therefore whosoever slayeth Cain, vengeance shall be taken on him sevenfold. And the LORD set a mark upon Cain, lest any finding him should kill him.

16 And Cain went out from the presence of the LORD, and dwelt in the land of Nod, on the east of Eden.

17 And Cain knew his wife; and she conceived, and bare Enoch: and he builded a city, and called the name of the city, after the name of his son, Enoch.

18 And unto Enoch was born Irad: and Irad begat Mehujael: and Mehujael begat Methusael: and Methusael begat Lamech.

19 And Lamech took unto him two wives: the name of the one was Adah, and the name of the other Zillah.

20 And Adah bare Jabal: he was the father of such as dwell in tents, and of such as have cattle.

21 And his brother's name was Jubal: he was the father of all such as handle the harp and organ.

22 And Zillah, she also bare Tubal-cain, an instructer of every artificer in brass and iron: and the sister of Tubal-cain was Naamah.

23 And Lamech said unto his wives, Adah and Zillah, Hear my voice; you wives of Lamech, hearken unto my speech: for I have slain a man to my wounding, and a young man to my hurt.

24 If Cain shall be avenged sevenfold, truly Lamech seventy and sevenfold.

25 And Adam knew his wife again; and she bare a son, and called his name Seth: For God, said she, has appointed me another seed instead of Abel, whom Cain slew.

26 And to Seth, to him also there was born a son; and he called his name Enos: then began men to call upon the name of the LORD.

CHAPTER 5

THIS is the book of the generations of Adam. In the day that God created man, in the likeness of God made he him;

2 Male and female created he them; and blessed them, and called their name Adam, in the day when they were created.

3 And Adam lived an hundred and thirty years, and begat a son in his own likeness, after his image; and called his name Seth:

4 And the days of Adam after he had begotten Seth were eight hundred years: and he begat sons and daughters:

5 And all the days that Adam lived were nine hundred and thirty years: and he died.

6 And Seth lived an hundred and five years, and begat Enos:

7 And Seth lived after he begat Enos eight hundred and seven years, and begat sons and daughters:

8 And all the days of Seth were nine hundred and twelve years: and he died.

9 And Enos lived ninety years, and begat Cainan:

10 And Enos lived after he begat Cainan eight hundred and fifteen years, and begat sons and daughters:

11 And all the days of Enos were nine hundred and five years: and he died.

12 And Cainan lived seventy years, and begat Mahalaleel:

13 And Cainan lived after he begat Mahalaleel eight hundred and forty years, and begat sons and daughters:

14 And all the days of Cainan were nine hundred and ten years: and he died.

15 And Mahalaleel lived sixty and five years, and begat Jared:

16 And Mahalaleel lived after he begat Jared eight hundred and thirty years, and begat sons and daughters:

17 And all the days of Mahalaleel were eight hundred ninety and five years: and he died.

18 And Jared lived an hundred sixty and two years, and he begat Enoch:

19 And Jared lived after he begat Enoch eight hundred years, and begat sons and daughters:

20 And all the days of Jared were nine hundred sixty and two years: and he died.

21 And Enoch lived sixty and five years, and begat Methuselah:

22 And Enoch walked with God after he begat Methuselah three hundred years, and begat sons and daughters:

23 And all the days of Enoch were three hundred sixty and five years:

24 And Enoch walked with God: and he was not; for God took him.

25 And Methuselah lived an hundred eighty and seven years, and begat Lamech:

26 And Methuselah lived after he begat Lamech seven hundred eighty and two years, and begat sons and daughters:

27 And all the days of Methuselah were nine hundred sixty and nine years: and he died.

28 And Lamech lived an hundred eighty and two years, and begat a son:

29 And he called his name Noah, saying, This same shall comfort us concerning our work and toil of our hands, because of the ground which the LORD has cursed.

30 And Lamech lived after he begat Noah five hundred ninety and five years, and begat sons and daughters:

31 And all the days of Lamech were seven hundred seventy and seven years: and he died.

32 And Noah was five hundred years old: and Noah begat Shem, Ham, and Japheth.

CHAPTER 6

AND it came to pass, when men began to multiply on the face of the earth, and daughters were born unto them,

2 That the sons of God saw the daughters of men that they were fair; and they took them wives of all which they chose.

3 And the LORD said, My spirit shall not always strive with man, for that he also is flesh: yet his days shall be an hundred and twenty years.

4 There were giants in the earth in those days; and also after that, when the sons of God came in unto the daughters of men, and they bare children to them, the same became mighty men which were of old, men of renown.

5And GOD saw that the wickedness of man was great in the earth, and that every imagination of the thoughts of his heart was only evil continually.

6 And it repented the LORD that he had made man on the earth, and it grieved him at his heart.

7 And the LORD said, I will destroy man whom I have created from the face of the earth; both man, and beast, and the creeping thing, and the fowls of the air; for it repenteth me that I have made them.

8 But Noah found grace in the eyes of the LORD.

9These are the generations of Noah: Noah was a just man and perfect in his generations, and Noah walked with God.

10 And Noah begat three sons, Shem, Ham, and Japheth.

11 The earth also was corrupt before God, and the earth was filled with violence.

12 And God looked upon the earth, and, behold, it was corrupt; for all flesh had corrupted his way upon the earth.

13 And God said unto Noah, The end of all flesh is come before me; for the earth is filled with violence through them; and, behold, I will destroy them with the earth.

14Make you an ark of gopher wood; rooms shalt you make in the ark, and shalt pitch it within and without with pitch.

15 And this is the fashion which you shalt make it of: The length of the ark shall be three hundred cubits, the breadth of it fifty cubits, and the height of it thirty cubits.

16 A window shalt you make to the ark, and in a cubit shalt you finish it above; and the door of the ark shalt you set in the side thereof; with lower, second, and third stories shalt you make it.

17 And, behold, I, even I, do bring a flood of waters upon the earth, to destroy all flesh, wherein is the breath of life, from under heaven; and every thing that is in the earth shall die.

18 But with you will I establish my covenant; and you shalt come into the ark, you , and your sons, and your wife, and your sons' wives with you.

19 And of every living thing of all flesh, two of every sort shalt you bring into the ark, to keep them alive with you; they shall be male and female.

20 Of fowls after their kind, and of cattle after their kind, of every creeping thing of the earth after his kind, two of every sort shall come unto you, to keep them alive.

21 And take you unto you of all food that is eaten, and you shalt gather it to you; and it shall be for food for you, and for them.

22 Thus did Noah; according to all that God commanded him, so did he.

CHAPTER 7

AND the LORD said unto Noah, Come you and all your house into the ark; for you have I seen righteous before me in this generation.

2 Of every clean beast you shalt take to you by sevens, the male and his female: and of beasts that are not clean by two, the male and his female.

3 Of fowls also of the air by sevens, the male and the female; to keep seed alive upon the face of all the earth.

4 For yet seven days, and I will cause it to rain upon the earth forty days and forty nights; and every living substance that I have made will I destroy from off the face of the earth.

5 And Noah did according unto all that the LORD commanded him.

6 And Noah was six hundred years old when the flood of waters was upon the earth.

7And Noah went in, and his sons, and his wife, and his sons' wives with him, into the ark, because of the waters of the flood.

8 Of clean beasts, and of beasts that are not clean, and of fowls, and of every thing that creepeth upon the earth,

9 There went in two and two unto Noah into the ark, the male and the female, as God had commanded Noah.

10 And it came to pass after seven days, that the waters of the flood were upon the earth.

11In the six hundredth year of Noah's life, in the second month, the seventeenth day of the month, the same day were all the fountains of the great deep broken up, and the windows of heaven were opened.

12 And the rain was upon the earth forty days and forty nights.

13 In the selfsame day entered Noah, and Shem, and Ham, and Japheth, the sons of Noah, and Noah's wife, and the three wives of his sons with them, into the ark;

14 They, and every beast after his kind, and all the cattle after their kind, and every creeping thing that creepeth upon the earth after his kind, and every fowl after his kind, every bird of every sort.

15 And they went in unto Noah into the ark, two and two of all flesh, wherein is the breath of life.

16 And they that went in, went in male and female of all flesh, as God had commanded him: and the LORD shut him in.

17 And the flood was forty days upon the earth; and the waters increased, and bare up the ark, and it was lift up above the earth.

18 And the waters prevailed, and were increased greatly upon the earth; and the ark went upon the face of the waters.

19 And the waters prevailed exceedingly upon the earth; and all the high hills, that were under the whole heaven, were covered.

20 Fifteen cubits upward did the waters prevail; and the mountains were covered.

21 And all flesh died that moved upon the earth, both of fowl, and of cattle, and of beast, and of every creeping thing that creepeth upon the earth, and every man:

22 All in whose nostrils was the breath of life, of all that was in the dry land, died.

23 And every living substance was destroyed which was upon the face of the ground, both man, and cattle, and the creeping things, and the fowl of the heaven; and they were destroyed from the earth: and Noah only remained alive, and they that were with him in the ark.

24 And the waters prevailed upon the earth an hundred and fifty days.

CHAPTER 8

AND God remembered Noah, and every living thing, and all the cattle that was with him in the ark: and God made a wind to pass over the earth, and the waters asswaged;

2 The fountains also of the deep and the windows of heaven were stopped, and the rain from heaven was restrained;

3 And the waters returned from off the earth continually: and after the end of the hundred and fifty days the waters were abated.

4 And the ark rested in the seventh month, on the seventeenth day of the month, upon the mountains of Ararat.

5 And the waters decreased continually until the tenth month: in the tenth month, on the first day of the month, were the tops of the mountains seen.

6And it came to pass at the end of forty days, that Noah opened the window of the ark which he had made:

7 And he sent forth a raven, which went forth to and fro, until the waters were dried up from off the earth.

8 Also he sent forth a dove from him, to see if the waters were abated from off the face of the ground;

9 But the dove found no rest for the sole of her foot, and she returned unto him into the ark, for the waters were on the face of the whole earth: then he put forth his hand, and took her, and pulled her in unto him into the ark.

10 And he stayed yet other seven days; and again he sent forth the dove out of the ark;

11 And the dove came in to him in the evening; and, lo, in her mouth was an olive leaf pluckt off: so Noah knew that the waters were abated from off the earth.

12 And he stayed yet other seven days; and sent forth the dove; which returned not again unto him any more.

13And it came to pass in the six hundredth and first year, in the first month, the first day of the month, the waters were dried up from off the earth: and Noah removed the covering of the ark, and looked, and, behold, the face of the ground was dry.

14 And in the second month, on the seven and twentieth day of the month, was the earth dried.

15And God spake unto Noah, saying,

16 Go forth of the ark, you , and your wife, and your sons, and your sons' wives with you.

17 Bring forth with you every living thing that is with you, of all flesh, both of fowl, and of cattle, and of every creeping thing that creepeth upon the earth; that they may breed abundantly in the earth, and be fruitful, and multiply upon the earth.

18 And Noah went forth, and his sons, and his wife, and his sons' wives with him:

19 Every beast, every creeping thing, and every fowl, and whatsoever creepeth upon the earth, after their kinds, went forth out of the ark.

20And Noah builded an altar unto the LORD; and took of every clean beast, and of every clean fowl, and offered burnt offerings on the altar.

21 And the LORD smelled a sweet savour; and the LORD said in his heart, I will not again curse the ground any more for man's sake; for the imagination of man's heart is evil from his youth; neither will I again strike any more every thing living, as I have done.

22 While the earth remaineth, seedtime and harvest, and cold and heat, and summer and winter, and day and night shall not cease.

CHAPTER 9

AND God blessed Noah and his sons, and said unto them, Be fruitful, and multiply, and replenish the earth.

2 And the fear of you and the dread of you shall be upon every beast of the earth, and upon every fowl of the air, upon all that moveth upon the earth, and upon all the fishes of the sea; into your hand are they delivered.

3 Every moving thing that liveth shall be meat for you; even as the green herb have I given you all things.

4 But flesh with the life thereof, which is the blood thereof, shall you not eat.

5 And surely your blood of your lives will I require; at the hand of every beast will I require it, and at the hand of man; at the hand of every man's brother will I require the life of man.

6 Whoso sheddeth man's blood, by man shall his blood be shed: for in the image of God made he man.

7 And you, be you fruitful, and multiply; bring forth abundantly in the earth, and multiply therein.

8And God spake unto Noah, and to his sons with him, saying,

9 And I, behold, I establish my covenant with you, and with your seed after you;

10 And with every living creature that is with you, of the fowl, of the cattle, and of every beast of the earth with you; from all that go out of the ark, to every beast of the earth.

11 And I will establish my covenant with you; neither shall all flesh be cut off any more by the waters of a flood; neither shall there any more be a flood to destroy the earth.

12 And God said, This is the token of the covenant which I make between me and you and every living creature that is with you, for perpetual generations:

13 I do set my bow in the cloud, and it shall be for a token of a covenant between me and the earth.

14 And it shall come to pass, when I bring a cloud over the earth, that the bow shall be seen in the cloud:

15 And I will remember my covenant, which is between me and you and every living creature of all flesh; and the waters shall no more become a flood to destroy all flesh.

16 And the bow shall be in the cloud; and I will look upon it, that I may remember the everlasting covenant between God and every living creature of all flesh that is upon the earth.

17 And God said unto Noah, This is the token of the covenant, which I have established between me and all flesh that is upon the earth.

18And the sons of Noah, that went forth of the ark, were Shem, and Ham, and Japheth: and Ham is the father of Canaan.

19 These are the three sons of Noah: and of them was the whole earth overspread.

20 And Noah began to be an husbandman, and he planted a vineyard:

21 And he drank of the wine, and was drunken; and he was uncovered within his tent.

22 And Ham, the father of Canaan, saw the nakedness of his father, and told his two brethren without.

23 And Shem and Japheth took a garment, and laid it upon both their shoulders, and went backward, and covered the nakedness of their father; and their faces were backward, and they saw not their father's nakedness.

24 And Noah awoke from his wine, and knew what his younger son had done unto him.

25 And he said, Cursed be Canaan; a servant of servants shall he be unto his brethren.

26 And he said, Blessed be the LORD God of Shem; and Canaan shall be his servant.

27 God shall enlarge Japheth, and he shall dwell in the tents of Shem; and Canaan shall be his servant.

28And Noah lived after the flood three hundred and fifty years.

29 And all the days of Noah were nine hundred and fifty years: and he died.

CHAPTER 10

NOW these are the generations of the sons of Noah, Shem, Ham, and Japheth: and unto them were sons born after the flood.

2 The sons of Japheth; Gomer, and Magog, and Madai, and Javan, and Tubal, and Meshech, and Tiras.

3 And the sons of Gomer; Ashkenaz, and Riphath, and Togarmah.

4 And the sons of Javan; Elishah, and Tarshish, Kittim, and Dodanim.

5 By these were the isles of the Gentiles divided in their lands; every one after his tongue, after their families, in their nations.

6And the sons of Ham; Cush, and Mizraim, and Phut, and Canaan.

7 And the sons of Cush; Seba, and Havilah, and Sabtah, and Raamah, and Sabtecha: and the sons of Raamah; Sheba, and Dedan.

8 And Cush begat Nimrod: he began to be a mighty one in the earth.

9 He was a mighty hunter before the LORD: wherefore it is said, Even as Nimrod the mighty hunter before the LORD.

10 And the beginning of his kingdom was Babel, and Erech, and Accad, and Calneh, in the land of Shinar.

11 Out of that land went forth Asshur, and builded Nineveh, and the city Rehoboth, and Calah,

12 And Resen between Nineveh and Calah: the same is a great city.

13 And Mizraim begat Ludim, and Anamim, and Lehabim, and Naphtuhim,

14 And Pathrusim, and Casluhim, (out of whom came Philistim,) and Caphtorim.

15And Canaan begat Sidon his firstborn, and Heth,

16 And the Jebusite, and the Amorite, and the Girgasite,

17 And the Hivite, and the Arkite, and the Sinite,

18 And the Arvadite, and the Zemarite, and the Hamathite: and afterward were the families of the Canaanites spread abroad.

19 And the border of the Canaanites was from Sidon, as you comest to Gerar, unto Gaza; as you go, unto Sodom, and Gomorrah, and Admah, and Zeboim, even unto Lasha.

20 These are the sons of Ham, after their families, after their tongues, in their countries, and in their nations.

21Unto Shem also, the father of all the children of Eber, the brother of Japheth the elder, even to him were children born.

22 The children of Shem; Elam, and Asshur, and Arphaxad, and Lud, and Aram.

23 And the children of Aram; Uz, and Hul, and Gether, and Mash.

24 And Arphaxad begat Salah; and Salah begat Eber.

25 And unto Eber were born two sons: the name of one was Peleg; for in his days was the earth divided; and his brother's name was Joktan.

26 And Joktan begat Almodad, and Sheleph, and Hazarmaveth, and Jerah,

27 And Hadoram, and Uzal, and Diklah,

28 And Obal, and Abimael, and Sheba,

29 And Ophir, and Havilah, and Jobab: all these were the sons of Joktan.

30 And their dwelling was from Mesha, as you go unto Sephar a mount of the east.

31 These are the sons of Shem, after their families, after their tongues, in their lands, after their nations.

32 These are the families of the sons of Noah, after their generations, in their nations: and by these were the nations divided in the earth after the flood.

CHAPTER 11

AND the whole earth was of one language, and of one speech.

2 And it came to pass, as they journeyed from the east, that they found a plain in the land of Shinar; and they dwelt there.

3 And they said one to another, Go to, let us make brick, and burn them throughly. And they had brick for stone, and slime had they for morter.

4 And they said, Go to, let us build us a city and a tower, whose top may reach unto heaven; and let us make us a name, lest we be scattered abroad upon the face of the whole earth.

5 And the LORD came down to see the city and the tower, which the children of men builded.

6 And the LORD said, Behold, the people is one, and they have all one language; and this they begin to do: and now nothing will be restrained from them, which they have imagined to do.

7 Go to, let us go down, and there confound their language, that they may not understand one another's speech.

8 So the LORD scattered them abroad from thence upon the face of all the earth: and they left off to build the city.

9 Therefore is the name of it called Babel; because the LORD did there confound the language of all the earth: and from thence did the LORD scatter them abroad upon the face of all the earth.

10These are the generations of Shem: Shem was an hundred years old, and begat Arphaxad two years after the flood:

11 And Shem lived after he begat Arphaxad five hundred years, and begat sons and daughters.

12 And Arphaxad lived five and thirty years, and begat Salah:

13 And Arphaxad lived after he begat Salah four hundred and three years, and begat sons and daughters.

14 And Salah lived thirty years, and begat Eber:

15 And Salah lived after he begat Eber four hundred and three years, and begat sons and daughters.

16 And Eber lived four and thirty years, and begat Peleg:

17 And Eber lived after he begat Peleg four hundred and thirty years, and begat sons and daughters.

18 And Peleg lived thirty years, and begat Reu:

19 And Peleg lived after he begat Reu two hundred and nine years, and begat sons and daughters.

20 And Reu lived two and thirty years, and begat Serug:

21 And Reu lived after he begat Serug two hundred and seven years, and begat sons and daughters.

22 And Serug lived thirty years, and begat Nahor:

23 And Serug lived after he begat Nahor two hundred years, and begat sons and daughters.

24 And Nahor lived nine and twenty years, and begat Terah:

25 And Nahor lived after he begat Terah an hundred and nineteen years, and begat sons and daughters.

26 And Terah lived seventy years, and begat Abram, Nahor, and Haran.

27Now these are the generations of Terah: Terah begat Abram, Nahor, and Haran; and Haran begat Lot.

28 And Haran died before his father Terah in the land of his nativity, in Ur of the Chaldees.

29 And Abram and Nahor took them wives: the name of Abram's wife was Sarai; and the name of Nahor's wife, Milcah, the daughter of Haran, the father of Milcah, and the father of Iscah.

30 But Sarai was barren; she had no child.

31 And Terah took Abram his son, and Lot the son of Haran his son's son, and Sarai his daughter in law, his son Abram's wife; and they went forth with them from Ur of the Chaldees, to go into the land of Canaan; and they came unto Haran, and dwelt there.

32 And the days of Terah were two hundred and five years: and Terah died in Haran.

CHAPTER 12

NOW the LORD had said unto Abram, Get you out of your country, and from your kindred, and from your father's house, unto a land that I will shew you:

2 And I will make of you a great nation, and I will bless you, and make your name great; and you shalt be a blessing:

3 And I will bless them that bless you, and curse him that curseth you: and in you shall all families of the earth be blessed.

4 So Abram departed, as the LORD had spoken unto him; and Lot went with him: and Abram was seventy and five years old when he departed out of Haran.

5 And Abram took Sarai his wife, and Lot his brother's son, and all their substance that they had gathered, and the souls that they had gotten in Haran; and they went forth to go into the land of Canaan; and into the land of Canaan they came.

6And Abram passed through the land unto the place of Sichem, unto the plain of Moreh. And the Canaanite was then in the land.

7 And the LORD appeared unto Abram, and said, Unto your seed will I give this land: and there builded he an altar unto the LORD, who appeared unto him.

8 And he removed from thence unto a mountain on the east of Beth-el, and pitched his tent, having Beth-el on the west, and Hai on the east: and there he builded an altar unto the LORD, and called upon the name of the LORD.

9 And Abram journeyed, going on still toward the south.

10And there was a famine in the land: and Abram went down into Egypt to sojourn there; for the famine was grievous in the land.

11 And it came to pass, when he was come near to enter into Egypt, that he said unto Sarai his wife, Behold now, I know that you are a fair woman to look upon:

12 Therefore it shall come to pass, when the Egyptians shall see you, that they shall say, This is his wife: and they will kill me, but they will save you alive.

13 Say, I pray you, you are my sister: that it may be well with me for your sake; and my soul shall live because of you.

14And it came to pass, that, when Abram was come into Egypt, the Egyptians beheld the woman that she was very fair.

15 The princes also of Pharaoh saw her, and commended her before Pharaoh: and the woman was taken into Pharaoh's house.

16 And he entreated Abram well for her sake: and he had sheep, and oxen, and he asses, and menservants, and maidservants, and she asses, and camels.

17 And the LORD plagued Pharaoh and his house with great plagues because of Sarai Abram's wife.

18 And Pharaoh called Abram, and said, What is this that you have done unto me? why did you not tell me that she was your wife?

19 Why saidst you , She is my sister? so I might have taken her to me to wife: now therefore behold your wife, take her, and go your way.

20 And Pharaoh commanded his men concerning him: and they sent him away, and his wife, and all that he had.

CHAPTER 13

AND Abram went up out of Egypt, he, and his wife, and all that he had, and Lot with him, into the south.

2 And Abram was very rich in cattle, in silver, and in gold.

3 And he went on his journeys from the south even to Beth-el, unto the place where his tent had been at the beginning, between Beth-el and Hai;

4 Unto the place of the altar, which he had made there at the first: and there Abram called on the name of the LORD.

5And Lot also, which went with Abram, had flocks, and herds, and tents.

6 And the land was not able to bear them, that they might dwell together: for their substance was great, so that they could not dwell together.

7 And there was a strife between the herdmen of Abram's cattle and the herdmen of Lot's cattle: and the Canaanite and the Perizzite dwelled then in the land.

8 And Abram said unto Lot, Let there be no strife, I pray you, between me and you, and between my herdmen and your herdmen; for we be brethren.

9 Is not the whole land before you? separate yourself, I pray you, from me: if you will take the left hand, then I will go to the right; or if you depart to the right hand, then I will go to the left.

10 And Lot lifted up his eyes, and beheld all the plain of Jordan, that it was well watered every where, before the LORD destroyed Sodom and Gomorrah, even as the garden of the LORD, like the land of Egypt, as you comest unto Zoar.

11 Then Lot chose him all the plain of Jordan; and Lot journeyed east: and they separated themselves the one from the other.

12 Abram dwelled in the land of Canaan, and Lot dwelled in the cities of the plain, and pitched his tent toward Sodom.

13 But the men of Sodom were wicked and sinners before the LORD exceedingly.

14And the LORD said unto Abram, after that Lot was separated from him, Lift up now yours eyes, and look from the place where you are northward, and southward, and eastward, and westward:

15 For all the land which you seest, to you will I give it, and to your seed for ever.

16 And I will make your seed as the dust of the earth: so that if a man can number the dust of the earth, then shall your seed also be numbered.

17 Arise, walk through the land in the length of it and in the breadth of it; for I will give it unto you.

18 Then Abram removed his tent, and came and dwelt in the plain of Mamre, which is in Hebron, and built there an altar unto the LORD.

CHAPTER 14

AND it came to pass in the days of Amraphel king of Shinar, Arioch king of Ellasar, Chedorlaomer king of Elam, and Tidal king of nations;

2 That these made war with Bera king of Sodom, and with Birsha king of Gomorrah, Shinab king of Admah, and Shemeber king of Zeboiim, and the king of Bela, which is Zoar.

3 All these were joined together in the vale of Siddim, which is the salt sea.

4 Twelve years they served Chedorlaomer, and in the thirteenth year they rebelled.

5 And in the fourteenth year came Chedorlaomer, and the kings that were with him, and struck the Rephaims in Ashteroth Karnaim, and the Zuzims in Ham, and the Emims in Shaveh Kiriathaim,

6 And the Horites in their mount Seir, unto El-paran, which is by the wilderness.

7 And they returned, and came to En-mishpat, which is Kadesh, and struck all the country of the Amalekites, and also the Amorites, that dwelt in Hazezon-tamar.

8 And there went out the king of Sodom, and the king of Gomorrah, and the king of Admah, and the king of Zeboiim, and the king of Bela (the same is Zoar;) and they joined battle with them in the vale of Siddim;

9 With Chedorlaomer the king of Elam, and with Tidal king of nations, and Amraphel king of Shinar, and Arioch king of Ellasar; four kings with five.

10 And the vale of Siddim was full of slimepits; and the kings of Sodom and Gomorrah fled, and fell there; and they that remained fled to the mountain.

11 And they took all the goods of Sodom and Gomorrah, and all their victuals, and went their way.

12 And they took Lot, Abram's brother's son, who dwelt in Sodom, and his goods, and departed.

13 And there came one that had escaped, and told Abram the Hebrew; for he dwelt in the plain of Mamre the Amorite, brother of Eshcol, and brother of Aner: and these were confederate with Abram.

14 And when Abram heard that his brother was taken captive, he armed his trained servants, born in his own house, three hundred and eighteen, and pursued them unto Dan.

15 And he divided himself against them, he and his servants, by night, and struck them, and pursued them unto Hobah, which is on the left hand of Damascus.

16 And he brought back all the goods, and also brought again his brother Lot, and his goods, and the women also, and the people.

17 And the king of Sodom went out to meet him after his return from the slaughter of Chedorlaomer, and of the kings that were with him, at the valley of Shaveh, which is the king's dale.

18 And Melchizedek king of Salem brought forth bread and wine: and he was the priest of the most high God.

19 And he blessed him, and said, Blessed be Abram of the most high God, possessor of heaven and earth:

20 And blessed be the most high God, which has delivered yours enemies into your hand. And he gave him tithes of all.

21 And the king of Sodom said unto Abram, Give me the persons, and take the goods to yourself.

22 And Abram said to the king of Sodom, I have lift up my hand unto the LORD, the most high God, the possessor of heaven and earth,

23 That I will not take from a thread even to a shoelatchet, and that I will not take any thing that is yours, lest you shouldest say, I have made Abram rich:

24 Save only that which the young men have eaten, and the portion of the men which went with me, Aner, Eshcol, and Mamre; let them take their portion.

CHAPTER 15

AFTER these things the word of the LORD came unto Abram in a vision, saying, Fear not, Abram: I am your shield, and your exceeding great reward.

2 And Abram said, Lord GOD, what will you give me, seeing I go childless, and the steward of my house is this Eliezer of Damascus?

3 And Abram said, Behold, to me you have given no seed: and, lo, one born in my house is my heir.

4 And, behold, the word of the LORD came unto him, saying, This shall not be yours heir; but he that shall come forth out of yours own bowels shall be yours heir.

5 And he brought him forth abroad, and said, Look now toward heaven, and tell the stars, if you be able to number them: and he said unto him, So shall your seed be.

6 And he believed in the LORD; and he counted it to him for righteousness.

7 And he said unto him, I am the LORD that brought you out of Ur of the Chaldees, to give you this land to inherit it.

8 And he said, Lord GOD, whereby shall I know that I shall inherit it?

9 And he said unto him, Take me an heifer of three years old, and a she goat of three years old, and a ram of three years old, and a turtledove, and a young pigeon.

10 And he took unto him all these, and divided them in the midst, and laid each piece one against another: but the birds divided he not.

11 And when the fowls came down upon the carcases, Abram drove them away.

12 And when the sun was going down, a deep sleep fell upon Abram; and, lo, an horror of great darkness fell upon him.

13 And he said unto Abram, Know of a surety that your seed shall be a stranger in a land that is not theirs, and shall serve them; and they shall afflict them four hundred years;

14 And also that nation, whom they shall serve, will I judge: and afterward shall they come out with great substance.

15 And you shalt go to your fathers in peace; you shalt be buried in a good old age.

16 But in the fourth generation they shall come hither again: for the iniquity of the Amorites is not yet full.

17 And it came to pass, that, when the sun went down, and it was dark, behold a smoking furnace, and a burning lamp that passed between those pieces.

18 In the same day the LORD made a covenant with Abram, saying, Unto your seed have I given this land, from the river of Egypt unto the great river, the river Euphrates:

19 The Kenites, and the Kenizzites, and the Kadmonites,

20 And the Hittites, and the Perizzites, and the Rephaims,

21 And the Amorites, and the Canaanites, and the Girgashites, and the Jebusites.

CHAPTER 16

NOW Sarai Abram's wife bare him no children: and she had an handmaid, an Egyptian, whose name was Hagar.

2 And Sarai said unto Abram, Behold now, the LORD has restrained me from bearing: I pray you, go in unto my maid; it may be that I may obtain children by her. And Abram hearkened to the voice of Sarai.

3 And Sarai Abram's wife took Hagar her maid the Egyptian, after Abram had dwelt ten years in the land of Canaan, and gave her to her husband Abram to be his wife.

4 And he went in unto Hagar, and she conceived: and when she saw that she had conceived, her mistress was despised in her eyes.

5 And Sarai said unto Abram, My wrong be upon you: I have given my maid into your bosom; and when she saw that she had conceived, I was despised in her eyes: the LORD judge between me and you.

6 But Abram said unto Sarai, Behold, your maid is in your hand; do to her as it pleases you. And when Sarai dealt hardly with her, she fled from her face.

7 And the angel of the LORD found her by a fountain of water in the wilderness, by the fountain in the way to Shur.

8 And he said, Hagar, Sarai's maid, whence camest you ? and whither will you go? And she said, I flee from the face of my mistress Sarai.

9 And the angel of the LORD said unto her, Return to your mistress, and submit yourself under her hands.

10 And the angel of the LORD said unto her, I will multiply your seed exceedingly, that it shall not be numbered for multitude.

11 And the angel of the LORD said unto her, Behold, you are with child, and shalt bear a son, and shalt call his name Ishmael; because the LORD has heard your affliction.

12 And he will be a wild man; his hand will be against every man, and every man's hand against him; and he shall dwell in the presence of all his brethren.

13 And she called the name of the LORD that spake unto her, You God seest me: for she said, Have I also here looked after him that seeth me?

14 Wherefore the well was called Beer-lahai-roi; behold, it is between Kadesh and Bered.

15 And Hagar bare Abram a son: and Abram called his son's name, which Hagar bare, Ishmael.

16 And Abram was fourscore and six years old, when Hagar bare Ishmael to Abram.

CHAPTER 17

AND when Abram was ninety years old and nine, the LORD appeared to Abram, and said unto him, I am the Almighty God; walk before me, and be you perfect.

2 And I will make my covenant between me and you, and will multiply you exceedingly.

3 And Abram fell on his face: and God talked with him, saying,

4 As for me, behold, my covenant is with you, and you shalt be a father of many nations.

5 Neither shall your name any more be called Abram, but your name shall be Abraham; for a father of many nations have I made you.

6 And I will make you exceeding fruitful, and I will make nations of you, and kings shall come out of you.

7 And I will establish my covenant between me and you and your seed after you in their generations for an everlasting covenant, to be a God unto you, and to your seed after you.

8 And I will give unto you, and to your seed after you, the land wherein you are a stranger, all the land of Canaan, for an everlasting possession; and I will be their God.

9 And God said unto Abraham, You shalt keep my covenant therefore, you , and your seed after you in their generations.

10 This is my covenant, which you shall keep, between me and you and your seed after you; Every man child among you shall be circumcised.

11 And you shall circumcise the flesh of your foreskin; and it shall be a token of the covenant betwixt me and you.

12 And he that is eight days old shall be circumcised among you, every man child in your generations, he that is born in the house, or bought with money of any stranger, which is not of your seed.

13 He that is born in your house, and he that is bought with your money, must needs be circumcised: and my covenant shall be in your flesh for an everlasting covenant.

14 And the uncircumcised man child whose flesh of his foreskin is not circumcised, that soul shall be cut off from his people; he has broken my covenant.

15 And God said unto Abraham, As for Sarai your wife, you shalt not call her name Sarai, but Sarah shall her name be.

16 And I will bless her, and give you a son also of her: yea, I will bless her, and she shall be a mother of nations; kings of people shall be of her.

17 Then Abraham fell upon his face, and laughed, and said in his heart, Shall a child be born unto him that is an hundred years old? and shall Sarah, that is ninety years old, bear?

18 And Abraham said unto God, O that Ishmael might live before you!

19 And God said, Sarah your wife shall bear you a son indeed; and you shalt call his name Isaac: and I will establish my covenant with him for an everlasting covenant, and with his seed after him.

20 And as for Ishmael, I have heard you: Behold, I have blessed him, and will make him fruitful, and will multiply him exceedingly; twelve princes shall he beget, and I will make him a great nation.

21 But my covenant will I establish with Isaac, which Sarah shall bear unto you at this set time in the next year.

22 And he left off talking with him, and God went up from Abraham.

23 And Abraham took Ishmael his son, and all that were born in his house, and all that were bought with his money, every male among the men of Abraham's house; and circumcised the flesh of their foreskin in the selfsame day, as God had said unto him.

24 And Abraham was ninety years old and nine, when he was circumcised in the flesh of his foreskin.

25 And Ishmael his son was thirteen years old, when he was circumcised in the flesh of his foreskin.

26 In the selfsame day was Abraham circumcised, and Ishmael his son.

27 And all the men of his house, born in the house, and bought with money of the stranger, were circumcised with him.

CHAPTER 18

AND the LORD appeared unto him in the plains of Mamre: and he sat in the tent door in the heat of the day;

2 And he lift up his eyes and looked, and, lo, three men stood by him: and when he saw them, he ran to meet them from the tent door, and bowed himself toward the ground,

3 And said, My Lord, if now I have found favour in your sight, pass not away, I pray you, from your servant:

4 Let a little water, I pray you, be fetched, and wash your feet, and rest yourselves under the tree:

5 And I will fetch a morsel of bread, and comfort you your hearts; after that you shall pass on: for therefore are you come to your servant. And they said, So do, as you have said.

6 And Abraham hastened into the tent unto Sarah, and said, Make ready quickly three measures of fine meal, knead it, and make cakes upon the hearth.

7 And Abraham ran unto the herd, and fetcht a calf tender and good, and gave it unto a young man; and he hasted to dress it.

8 And he took butter, and milk, and the calf which he had dressed, and set it before them; and he stood by them under the tree, and they did eat.

9 And they said unto him, Where is Sarah your wife? And he said, Behold, in the tent.

10 And he said, I will certainly return unto you according to the time of life; and, lo, Sarah your wife shall have a son. And Sarah heard it in the tent door, which was behind him.

11 Now Abraham and Sarah were old and well stricken in age; and it ceased to be with Sarah after the manner of women.

12 Therefore Sarah laughed within herself, saying, After I am waxed old shall I have pleasure, my lord being old also?

13 And the LORD said unto Abraham, Wherefore did Sarah laugh, saying, Shall I of a surety bear a child, which am old?

14 Is any thing too hard for the LORD? At the time appointed I will return unto you, according to the time of life, and Sarah shall have a son.

15 Then Sarah denied, saying, I laughed not; for she was afraid. And he said, Nay; but you did laugh.

16 And the men rose up from thence, and looked toward Sodom: and Abraham went with them to bring them on the way.

17 And the LORD said, Shall I hide from Abraham that thing which I do;

18 Seeing that Abraham shall surely become a great and mighty nation, and all the nations of the earth shall be blessed in him?

19 For I know him, that he will command his children and his household after him, and they shall keep the way of the LORD, to do justice and judgment; that the LORD may bring upon Abraham that which he has spoken of him.

20 And the LORD said, Because the cry of Sodom and Gomorrah is great, and because their sin is very grievous;

21 I will go down now, and see whether they have done altogether according to the cry of it, which is come unto me; and if not, I will know.

22 And the men turned their faces from thence, and went toward Sodom: but Abraham stood yet before the LORD.

23 And Abraham drew near, and said, Will you also destroy the righteous with the wicked?

24 What if there be fifty righteous within the city: will you also destroy and not spare the place for the fifty righteous that are therein?

25 That be far from you to do after this manner, to slay the righteous with the wicked: and that the righteous should be as the wicked, that be far from you: Shall not the Judge of all the earth do right?

26 And the LORD said, If I find in Sodom fifty righteous within the city, then I will spare all the place for their sakes.

27 And Abraham answered and said, Behold now, I have taken upon me to speak unto the Lord, which am but dust and ashes:

28 What if there shall lack five of the fifty righteous: will you destroy all the city for lack of five? And he said, If I find there forty and five, I will not destroy it.

29 And he spake unto him yet again, and said, What if there shall be forty found there. And he said, I will not do it for forty's sake.

30 And he said unto him, Oh let not the Lord be angry, and I will speak: What if there shall thirty be found there. And he said, I will not do it, if I find thirty there.

31 And he said, Behold now, I have taken upon me to speak unto the Lord: What if there shall be twenty found there. And he said, I will not destroy it for twenty's sake.

32 And he said, Oh let not the Lord be angry, and I will speak yet but this once: What if ten shall be found there. And he said, I will not destroy it for ten's sake.

33 And the LORD went his way, as soon as he had left communing with Abraham: and Abraham returned unto his place.

CHAPTER 19

AND there came two angels to Sodom at even; and Lot sat in the gate of Sodom: and Lot seeing them rose up to meet them; and he bowed himself with his face toward the ground;

2 And he said, Behold now, my lords, turn in, I pray you, into your servant's house, and tarry all night, and wash your feet, and you shall rise up early, and go on your ways. And they said, Nay; but we will abide in the street all night.

3 And he pressed upon them greatly; and they turned in unto him, and entered into his house; and he made them a feast, and did bake unleavened bread, and they did eat.

4 But before they lay down, the men of the city, even the men of Sodom, compassed the house round, both old and young, all the people from every quarter:

5 And they called unto Lot, and said unto him, Where are the men which came in to you this night? bring them out unto us, that we may know them.

6 And Lot went out at the door unto them, and shut the door after him,

7 And said, I pray you, brethren, do not so wickedly.

8 Behold now, I have two daughters which have not known man; let me, I pray you, bring them out unto you, and do you to them as is good in your eyes: only unto these men do nothing; for therefore came they under the shadow of my roof.

9 And they said, Stand back. And they said again, This one fellow came in to sojourn, and he will needs be a judge: now will we deal worse with you, than with them. And they pressed sore upon the man, even Lot, and came near to break the door.

10 But the men put forth their hand, and pulled Lot into the house to them, and shut to the door.

11 And they struck the men that were at the door of the house with blindness, both small and great: so that they wearied themselves to find the door.

12 And the men said unto Lot, Have you here any besides? son in law, and your sons, and your daughters, and whatsoever you have in the city, bring them out of this place:

13 For we will destroy this place, because the cry of them is waxen great before the face of the LORD; and the LORD has sent us to destroy it.

14 And Lot went out, and spake unto his sons in law, which married his daughters, and said, Up, get you out of this place; for the LORD will destroy this city. But he seemed as one that mocked unto his sons in law.

15 And when the morning arose, then the angels hastened Lot, saying, Arise, take your wife, and your two daughters, which are here; lest you be consumed in the iniquity of the city.

16 And while he lingered, the men laid hold upon his hand, and upon the hand of his wife, and upon the hand of his two daughters; the LORD being merciful unto him: and they brought him forth, and set him without the city.

17 And it came to pass, when they had brought them forth abroad, that he said, Escape for your life; look not behind you, neither stay you in all the plain; escape to the mountain, lest you be consumed.

18 And Lot said unto them, Oh, not so, my Lord:

19 Behold now, your servant has found grace in your sight, and you have magnified your mercy, which you have shewed unto me in saving my life; and I cannot escape to the mountain, lest some evil take me, and I die:

20 Behold now, this city is near to flee unto, and it is a little one: Oh, let me escape thither, (is it not a little one?) and my soul shall live.

21 And he said unto him, See, I have accepted you concerning this thing also, that I will not overthrow this city, for the which you have spoken.

22 Haste you, escape thither; for I cannot do any thing till you be come thither. Therefore the name of the city was called Zoar.

23 The sun was risen upon the earth when Lot entered into Zoar.

24 Then the LORD rained upon Sodom and upon Gomorrah brimstone and fire from the LORD out of heaven;

25 And he overthrew those cities, and all the plain, and all the inhabitants of the cities, and that which grew upon the ground.

26 But his wife looked back from behind him, and she became a pillar of salt.

27 And Abraham gat up early in the morning to the place where he stood before the LORD:

28 And he looked toward Sodom and Gomorrah, and toward all the land of the plain, and beheld, and, lo, the smoke of the country went up as the smoke of a furnace.

29 And it came to pass, when God destroyed the cities of the plain, that God remembered Abraham, and sent Lot out of the midst of the overthrow, when he overthrew the cities in the which Lot dwelt.

30 And Lot went up out of Zoar, and dwelt in the mountain, and his two daughters with him; for he feared to dwell in Zoar: and he dwelt in a cave, he and his two daughters.

31 And the firstborn said unto the younger, Our father is old, and there is not a man in the earth to come in unto us after the manner of all the earth:

32 Come, let us make our father drink wine, and we will lie with him, that we may preserve seed of our father.

33 And they made their father drink wine that night: and the firstborn went in, and lay with her father; and he perceived not when she lay down, nor when she arose.

34 And it came to pass on the morrow, that the firstborn said unto the younger, Behold, I lay yesternight with my father: let us make him drink wine this night also; and go you in, and lie with him, that we may preserve seed of our father.

35 And they made their father drink wine that night also: and the younger arose, and lay with him; and he perceived not when she lay down, nor when she arose.

36 Thus were both the daughters of Lot with child by their father.

37 And the firstborn bare a son, and called his name Moab: the same is the father of the Moabites unto this day.

38 And the younger, she also bare a son, and called his name Ben-ammi: the same is the father of the children of Ammon unto this day.

CHAPTER 20

AND Abraham journeyed from thence toward the south country, and dwelled between Kadesh and Shur, and sojourned in Gerar.

2 And Abraham said of Sarah his wife, She is my sister: and Abimelech king of Gerar sent, and took Sarah.

3 But God came to Abimelech in a dream by night, and said to him, Behold, you are but a dead man, for the woman which you have taken; for she is a man's wife.

4 But Abimelech had not come near her: and he said, Lord, will you slay also a righteous nation?

5 Said he not unto me, She is my sister? and she, even she herself said, He is my brother: in the integrity of my heart and innocency of my hands have I done this.

6 And God said unto him in a dream, Yea, I know that you did this in the integrity of your heart; for I also withheld you from sinning against me: therefore suffered I you not to touch her.

7 Now therefore restore the man his wife; for he is a prophet, and he shall pray for you, and you shalt live: and if you restore her not, know you that you shalt surely die, you , and all that are yours.

8 Therefore Abimelech rose early in the morning, and called all his servants, and told all these things in their ears: and the men were sore afraid.

9 Then Abimelech called Abraham, and said unto him, What have you done unto us? and what have I offended you, that you have brought on me and on my kingdom a great sin? you have done deeds unto me that ought not to be done.

10 And Abimelech said unto Abraham, What sawest you , that you have done this thing?

11 And Abraham said, Because I thought, Surely the fear of God is not in this place; and they will slay me for my wife's sake.

12 And yet indeed she is my sister; she is the daughter of my father, but not the daughter of my mother; and she became my wife.

13 And it came to pass, when God caused me to wander from my father's house, that I said unto her, This is your kindness which you shalt shew unto me; at every place whither we shall come, say of me, He is my brother.

14 And Abimelech took sheep, and oxen, and menservants, and womenservants, and gave them unto Abraham, and restored him Sarah his wife.

15 And Abimelech said, Behold, my land is before you: dwell where it pleases you.

16 And unto Sarah he said, Behold, I have given your brother a thousand pieces of silver: behold, he is to you a covering of the eyes, unto all that are with you, and with all other: thus she was reproved.

17 So Abraham prayed unto God: and God healed Abimelech, and his wife, and his maidservants; and they bare children.

18 For the LORD had fast closed up all the wombs of the house of Abimelech, because of Sarah Abraham's wife.

CHAPTER 21

AND the LORD visited Sarah as he had said, and the LORD did unto Sarah as he had spoken.

2 For Sarah conceived, and bare Abraham a son in his old age, at the set time of which God had spoken to him.

3 And Abraham called the name of his son that was born unto him, whom Sarah bare to him, Isaac.

4 And Abraham circumcised his son Isaac being eight days old, as God had commanded him.

5 And Abraham was an hundred years old, when his son Isaac was born unto him.

6 And Sarah said, God has made me to laugh, so that all that hear will laugh with me.

7 And she said, Who would have said unto Abraham, that Sarah should have given children suck? for I have born him a son in his old age.

8 And the child grew, and was weaned: and Abraham made a great feast the same day that Isaac was weaned.

9 And Sarah saw the son of Hagar the Egyptian, which she had born unto Abraham, mocking.

10 Wherefore she said unto Abraham, Cast out this bondwoman and her son: for the son of this bondwoman shall not be heir with my son, even with Isaac.

11 And the thing was very grievous in Abraham's sight because of his son.

12 And God said unto Abraham, Let it not be grievous in your sight because of the lad, and because of your bondwoman; in all that Sarah has said unto you, hearken unto her voice; for in Isaac shall your seed be called.

13 And also of the son of the bondwoman will I make a nation, because he is your seed.

14 And Abraham rose up early in the morning, and took bread, and a bottle of water, and gave it unto Hagar, putting it on her shoulder, and the child, and sent her away: and she departed, and wandered in the wilderness of Beer-sheba.

15 And the water was spent in the bottle, and she cast the child under one of the shrubs.

16 And she went, and sat her down over against him a good way off, as it were a bowshot: for she said, Let me not see the death of the child. And she sat over against him, and lift up her voice, and wept.

17 And God heard the voice of the lad; and the angel of God called to Hagar out of heaven, and said unto her, What aileth you, Hagar? fear not; for God has heard the voice of the lad where he is.

18 Arise, lift up the lad, and hold him in yours hand; for I will make him a great nation.

19 And God opened her eyes, and she saw a well of water; and she went, and filled the bottle with water, and gave the lad drink.

20 And God was with the lad; and he grew, and dwelt in the wilderness, and became an archer.

21 And he dwelt in the wilderness of Paran: and his mother took him a wife out of the land of Egypt.

22 And it came to pass at that time, that Abimelech and Phichol the chief captain of his host spake unto Abraham, saying, God is with you in all that you doest:

23 Now therefore swear unto me here by God that you will not deal falsely with me, nor with my son, nor with my son's son: but according to the kindness that I have done unto you, you shalt do unto me, and to the land wherein you have sojourned.

24 And Abraham said, I will swear.

25 And Abraham reproved Abimelech because of a well of water, which Abimelech's servants had violently taken away.

26 And Abimelech said, I wot not who has done this thing: neither did you tell me, neither yet heard I of it, but to day.

27 And Abraham took sheep and oxen, and gave them unto Abimelech; and both of them made a covenant.

28 And Abraham set seven ewe lambs of the flock by themselves.

29 And Abimelech said unto Abraham, What mean these seven ewe lambs which you have set by themselves?

30 And he said, For these seven ewe lambs shalt you take of my hand, that they may be a witness unto me, that I have digged this well.

31 Wherefore he called that place Beer-sheba; because there they sware both of them.

32 Thus they made a covenant at Beer-sheba: then Abimelech rose up, and Phichol the chief captain of his host, and they returned into the land of the Philistines.

33 And Abraham planted a grove in Beer-sheba, and called there on the name of the LORD, the everlasting God.

34 And Abraham sojourned in the Philistines' land many days.

CHAPTER 22

AND it came to pass after these things, that God did tempt Abraham, and said unto him, Abraham: and he said, Behold, here I am.

2 And he said, Take now your son, yours only son Isaac, whom you lovest, and get you into the land of Moriah; and offer him there for a burnt offering upon one of the mountains which I will tell you of.

3 And Abraham rose up early in the morning, and saddled his ass, and took two of his young men with him, and Isaac his son, and clave the wood for the burnt offering, and rose up, and went unto the place of which God had told him.

4 Then on the third day Abraham lifted up his eyes, and saw the place afar off.

5 And Abraham said unto his young men, Abide you here with the ass; and I and the lad will go yonder and worship, and come again to you.

6 And Abraham took the wood of the burnt offering, and laid it upon Isaac his son; and he took the fire in his hand, and a knife; and they went both of them together.

7 And Isaac spake unto Abraham his father, and said, My father: and he said, Here am I, my son. And he said, Behold the fire and the wood: but where is the lamb for a burnt offering?

8 And Abraham said, My son, God will provide himself a lamb for a burnt offering: so they went both of them together.

9 And they came to the place which God had told him of; and Abraham built an altar there, and laid the wood in order, and bound Isaac his son, and laid him on the altar upon the wood.

10 And Abraham stretched forth his hand, and took the knife to slay his son.

11 And the angel of the LORD called unto him out of heaven, and said, Abraham, Abraham: and he said, Here am I.

12 And he said, Lay not yours hand upon the lad, neither do you any thing unto him: for now I know that you fearest God, seeing you have not withheld your son, yours only son from me.

13 And Abraham lifted up his eyes, and looked, and behold behind him a ram caught in a thicket by his horns: and Abraham went and took the ram, and offered him up for a burnt offering in the stead of his son.

14 And Abraham called the name of that place Jehovah-jireh: as it is said to this day, In the mount of the LORD it shall be seen.

15 And the angel of the LORD called unto Abraham out of heaven the second time,

16 And said, By myself have I sworn, saith the LORD, for because you have done this thing, and have not withheld your son, yours only son:

17 That in blessing I will bless you, and in multiplying I will multiply your seed as the stars of the heaven, and as the sand which is upon the sea shore; and your seed shall possess the gate of his enemies;

18 And in your seed shall all the nations of the earth be blessed; because you have obeyed my voice.

19 So Abraham returned unto his young men, and they rose up and went together to Beer-sheba; and Abraham dwelt at Beer-sheba.

20 And it came to pass after these things, that it was told Abraham, saying, Behold, Milcah, she has also born children unto your brother Nahor;

21 Huz his firstborn, and Buz his brother, and Kemuel the father of Aram,

22 And Chesed, and Hazo, and Pildash, and Jidlaph, and Bethuel.

23 And Bethuel begat Rebekah: these eight Milcah did bear to Nahor, Abraham's brother.

24 And his concubine, whose name was Reumah, she bare also Tebah, and Gaham, and Thahash, and Maachah.

CHAPTER 23

AND Sarah was an hundred and seven and twenty years old: these were the years of the life of Sarah.

2 And Sarah died in Kirjath-arba; the same is Hebron in the land of Canaan: and Abraham came to mourn for Sarah, and to weep for her.

3 And Abraham stood up from before his dead, and spake unto the sons of Heth, saying,

4 I am a stranger and a sojourner with you: give me a possession of a buryingplace with you, that I may bury my dead out of my sight.

5 And the children of Heth answered Abraham, saying unto him,

6 Hear us, my lord: you are a mighty prince among us: in the choice of our sepulchres bury your dead; none of us shall withhold from you his sepulchre, but that you mayest bury your dead.

7 And Abraham stood up, and bowed himself to the people of the land, even to the children of Heth.

8 And he communed with them, saying, If it be your mind that I should bury my dead out of my sight; hear me, and intreat for me to Ephron the son of Zohar,

9 That he may give me the cave of Machpelah, which he has, which is in the end of his field; for as much money as it is worth he shall give it me for a possession of a buryingplace amongst you.

10 And Ephron dwelt among the children of Heth: and Ephron the Hittite answered Abraham in the audience of the children of Heth, even of all that went in at the gate of his city, saying,

11 Nay, my lord, hear me: the field give I you, and the cave that is therein, I give it you; in the presence of the sons of my people give I it you: bury your dead.

12 And Abraham bowed down himself before the people of the land.

13 And he spake unto Ephron in the audience of the people of the land, saying, But if you will give it, I pray you, hear me: I will give you money for the field; take it of me, and I will bury my dead there.

14 And Ephron answered Abraham, saying unto him,

15 My lord, hearken unto me: the land is worth four hundred shekels of silver; what is that betwixt me and you? bury therefore your dead.

16 And Abraham hearkened unto Ephron; and Abraham weighed to Ephron the silver, which he had named in the audience of the sons of Heth, four hundred shekels of silver, current money with the merchant.

17 And the field of Ephron, which was in Machpelah, which was before Mamre, the field, and the cave which was therein, and all the trees that were in the field, that were in all the borders round about, were made sure

18 Unto Abraham for a possession in the presence of the children of Heth, before all that went in at the gate of his city.

19 And after this, Abraham buried Sarah his wife in the cave of the field of Machpelah before Mamre: the same is Hebron in the land of Canaan.

20 And the field, and the cave that is therein, were made sure unto Abraham for a possession of a buryingplace by the sons of Heth.

CHAPTER 24

AND Abraham was old, and well stricken in age: and the LORD had blessed Abraham in all things.

2 And Abraham said unto his eldest servant of his house, that ruled over all that he had, Put, I pray you, your hand under my thigh:

3 And I will make you swear by the LORD, the God of heaven, and the God of the earth, that you shalt not take a wife unto my son of the daughters of the Canaanites, among whom I dwell:

4 But you shalt go unto my country, and to my kindred, and take a wife unto my son Isaac.

5 And the servant said unto him, What if the woman will not be willing to follow me unto this land: must I needs bring your son again unto the land from whence you camest?

6 And Abraham said unto him, Beware you that you bring not my son thither again.

7 The LORD God of heaven, which took me from my father's house, and from the land of my kindred, and which spake unto me, and that sware unto me, saying, Unto your seed will I give this land; he shall send his angel before you, and you shalt take a wife unto my son from thence.

8 And if the woman will not be willing to follow you, then you shalt be clear from this my oath: only bring not my son thither again.

9 And the servant put his hand under the thigh of Abraham his master, and sware to him concerning that matter.

10 And the servant took ten camels of the camels of his master, and departed; for all the goods of his master were in his hand: and he arose, and went to Mesopotamia, unto the city of Nahor.

11 And he made his camels to kneel down without the city by a well of water at the time of the evening, even the time that women go out to draw water.

12 And he said, O LORD God of my master Abraham, I pray you, send me good speed this day, and shew kindness unto my master Abraham.

13 Behold, I stand here by the well of water; and the daughters of the men of the city come out to draw water:

14 And let it come to pass, that the damsel to whom I shall say, Let down your pitcher, I pray you, that I may drink; and she shall say, Drink, and I will give your camels drink also: let the same be she that you have appointed for your servant Isaac; and thereby shall I know that have shewed kindness unto my master.

15 And it came to pass, before he had done speaking, that, behold, Rebekah came out, who was born to Bethuel, son of Milcah, the wife of Nahor, Abraham's brother, with her pitcher upon her shoulder.

16 And the damsel was very fair to look upon, a virgin, neither had any man known her: and she went down to the well, and filled her pitcher, and came up.

17 And the servant ran to meet her, and said, Let me, I pray you, drink a little water of your pitcher.

18 And she said, Drink, my lord: and she hasted, and let down her pitcher upon her hand, and gave him drink.

19 And when she had done giving him drink, she said, I will draw water for your camels also, until they have done drinking.

20 And she hasted, and emptied her pitcher into the trough, and ran again unto the well to draw water, and drew for all his camels.

21 And the man wondering at her held his peace, to wit whether the LORD had made his journey prosperous or not.

22 And it came to pass, as the camels had done drinking, that the man took a golden earring of half a shekel weight, and two bracelets for her hands of ten shekels weight of gold;

23 And said, Whose daughter are you ? tell me, I pray you: is there room in your father's house for us to lodge in?

24 And she said unto him, I am the daughter of Bethuel the son of Milcah, which she bare unto Nahor.

25 She said moreover unto him, We have both straw and provender enough, and room to lodge in.

26 And the man bowed down his head, and worshipped the LORD.

27 And he said, Blessed be the LORD God of my master Abraham, who has not left destitute my master of his mercy and his truth: I being in the way, the LORD led me to the house of my master's brethren.

28 And the damsel ran, and told them of her mother's house these things.

29 And Rebekah had a brother, and his name was Laban: and Laban ran out unto the man, unto the well.

30 And it came to pass, when he saw the earring and bracelets upon his sister's hands, and when he heard the words of Rebekah his sister, saying, Thus spake the man unto me; that he came unto the man; and, behold, he stood by the camels at the well.

31 And he said, Come in, you blessed of the LORD; wherefore standest you without? for I have prepared the house, and room for the camels.

32 And the man came into the house: and he ungirded his camels, and gave straw and provender for the camels, and water to wash his feet, and the men's feet that were with him.

33 And there was set meat before him to eat: but he said, I will not eat, until I have told my errand. And he said, Speak on.

34 And he said, I am Abraham's servant.

35 And the LORD has blessed my master greatly; and he is become great: and he has given him flocks, and herds, and silver, and gold, and menservants, and maidservants, and camels, and asses.

36 And Sarah my master's wife bare a son to my master when she was old: and unto him has he given all that he has.

37 And my master made me swear, saying, You shalt not take a wife to my son of the daughters of the Canaanites, in whose land I dwell:

38 But you shalt go unto my father's house, and to my kindred, and take a wife unto my son.

39 And I said unto my master, What if the woman will not follow me.

40 And he said unto me, The LORD, before whom I walk, will send his angel with you, and prosper your way; and you shalt take a wife for my son of my kindred, and of my father's house:

41 Then shalt you be clear from this my oath, when you comest to my kindred; and if they give not you one, you shalt be clear from my oath.

42 And I came this day unto the well, and said, O LORD God of my master Abraham, if now you do prosper my way which I go:

43 Behold, I stand by the well of water; and it shall come to pass, that when the virgin comes forth to draw water, and I say to her, Give me, I pray you, a little water of your pitcher to drink;

44 And she say to me, Both drink you , and I will also draw for your camels: let the same be the woman whom the LORD has appointed out for my master's son.

45 And before I had done speaking in my heart, behold, Rebekah came forth with her pitcher on her shoulder; and she went down unto the well, and drew water: and I said unto her, Let me drink, I pray you.

46 And she made haste, and let down her pitcher from her shoulder, and said, Drink, and I will give your camels drink also: so I drank, and she made the camels drink also.

47 And I asked her, and said, Whose daughter are you ? And she said, The daughter of Bethuel, Nahor's son, whom Milcah bare unto him: and I put the earring upon her face, and the bracelets upon her hands.

48 And I bowed down my head, and worshipped the LORD, and blessed the LORD God of my master Abraham, which had led me in the right way to take my master's brother's daughter unto his son.

49 And now if you will deal kindly and truly with my master, tell me: and if not, tell me; that I may turn to the right hand, or to the left.

50 Then Laban and Bethuel answered and said, The thing proceedeth from the LORD: we cannot speak unto you bad or good.

51 Behold, Rebekah is before you, take her, and go, and let her be your master's son's wife, as the LORD has spoken.

52 And it came to pass, that, when Abraham's servant heard their words, he worshipped the LORD, bowing himself to the earth.

53 And the servant brought forth jewels of silver, and jewels of gold, and raiment, and gave them to Rebekah: he gave also to her brother and to her mother precious things.

54 And they did eat and drink, he and the men that were with him, and tarried all night; and they rose up in the morning, and he said, Send me away unto my master.

55 And her brother and her mother said, Let the damsel abide with us a few days, at the least ten; after that she shall go.

56 And he said unto them, Hinder me not, seeing the LORD has prospered my way; send me away that I may go to my master.

57 And they said, We will call the damsel, and inquire at her mouth.

58 And they called Rebekah, and said unto her, Will you go with this man? And she said, I will go.

59 And they sent away Rebekah their sister, and her nurse, and Abraham's servant, and his men.

60 And they blessed Rebekah, and said unto her, You are our sister, be you the mother of thousands of millions, and let your seed possess the gate of those which hate them.

61 And Rebekah arose, and her damsels, and they rode upon the camels, and followed the man: and the servant took Rebekah, and went his way.

62 And Isaac came from the way of the well Lahai-roi; for he dwelt in the south country.

63 And Isaac went out to meditate in the field at the eventide: and he lifted up his eyes, and saw, and, behold, the camels were coming.

64 And Rebekah lifted up her eyes, and when she saw Isaac, she lighted off the camel.

65 For she had said unto the servant, What man is this that walketh in the field to meet us? And the servant had said, It is my master: therefore she took a vail, and covered herself.

66 And the servant told Isaac all things that he had done.

67 And Isaac brought her into his mother Sarah's tent, and took Rebekah, and she became his wife; and he loved her: and Isaac was comforted after his mother's death.

CHAPTER 25

THEN again Abraham took a wife, and her name was Keturah.

2 And she bare him Zimran, and Jokshan, and Medan, and Midian, and Ishbak, and Shuah.

3 And Jokshan begat Sheba, and Dedan. And the sons of Dedan were Asshurim, and Letushim, and Leummim.

4 And the sons of Midian; Ephah, and Epher, and Hanoch, and Abida, and Eldaah. All these were the children of Keturah.

5 And Abraham gave all that he had unto Isaac.

6 But unto the sons of the concubines, which Abraham had, Abraham gave gifts, and sent them away from Isaac his son, while he yet lived, eastward, unto the east country.

7 And these are the days of the years of Abraham's life which he lived, an hundred threescore and fifteen years.

8 Then Abraham gave up the ghost, and died in a good old age, an old man, and full of years; and was gathered to his people.

9 And his sons Isaac and Ishmael buried him in the cave of Machpelah, in the field of Ephron the son of Zohar the Hittite, which is before Mamre;

10 The field which Abraham purchased of the sons of Heth: there was Abraham buried, and Sarah his wife.

11 And it came to pass after the death of Abraham, that God blessed his son Isaac; and Isaac dwelt by the well Lahai-roi.

12 Now these are the generations of Ishmael, Abraham's son, whom Hagar the Egyptian, Sarah's handmaid, bare unto Abraham:

13 And these are the names of the sons of Ishmael, by their names, according to their generations: the firstborn of Ishmael, Nebajoth; and Kedar, and Adbeel, and Mibsam,

14 And Mishma, and Dumah, and Massa,

15 Hadar, and Tema, Jetur, Naphish, and Kedemah:

16 These are the sons of Ishmael, and these are their names, by their towns, and by their castles; twelve princes according to their nations.

17 And these are the years of the life of Ishmael, an hundred and thirty and seven years: and he gave up the ghost and died; and was gathered unto his people.

18 And they dwelt from Havilah unto Shur, that is before Egypt, as you go toward Assyria: and he died in the presence of all his brethren.

19 And these are the generations of Isaac, Abraham's son: Abraham begat Isaac:

20 And Isaac was forty years old when he took Rebekah to wife, the daughter of Bethuel the Syrian of Padan-aram, the sister to Laban the Syrian.

21 And Isaac intreated the LORD for his wife, because she was barren: and the LORD was intreated of him, and Rebekah his wife conceived.

22 And the children struggled together within her; and she said, If it be so, why am I thus? And she went to inquire of the LORD.

23 And the LORD said unto her, Two nations are in your womb, and two manner of people shall be separated from your bowels; and the one people shall be stronger than the other people; and the elder shall serve the younger.

24 And when her days to be delivered were fulfilled, behold, there were twins in her womb.

25 And the first came out red, all over like an hairy garment; and they called his name Esau.

26 And after that came his brother out, and his hand took hold on Esau's heel; and his name was called Jacob: and Isaac was threescore years old when she bare them.

27 And the boys grew: and Esau was a cunning hunter, a man of the field; and Jacob was a plain man, dwelling in tents.

28 And Isaac loved Esau, because he did eat of his venison: but Rebekah loved Jacob.

29 And Jacob sod pottage: and Esau came from the field, and he was faint:

30 And Esau said to Jacob, Feed me, I pray you, with that same red pottage; for I am faint: therefore was his name called Edom.

31 And Jacob said, Sell me this day your birthright.

32 And Esau said, Behold, I am at the point to die: and what profit shall this birthright do to me?

33 And Jacob said, Swear to me this day; and he sware unto him: and he sold his birthright unto Jacob.

34 Then Jacob gave Esau bread and pottage of lentiles; and he did eat and drink, and rose up, and went his way: thus Esau despised his birthright.

CHAPTER 26

AND there was a famine in the land, beside the first famine that was in the days of Abraham. And Isaac went unto Abimelech king of the Philistines unto Gerar.

2 And the LORD appeared unto him, and said, Go not down into Egypt; dwell in the land which I shall tell you of:

3 Sojourn in this land, and I will be with you, and will bless you; for unto you, and unto your seed, I will give all these countries, and I will perform the oath which I sware unto Abraham your father;

4 And I will make your seed to multiply as the stars of heaven, and will give unto your seed all these countries; and in your seed shall all the nations of the earth be blessed;

5 Because that Abraham obeyed my voice, and kept my charge, my commandments, my statutes, and my laws.

6 And Isaac dwelt in Gerar:

7 And the men of the place asked him of his wife; and he said, She is my sister: for he feared to say, She is my wife; lest, said he, the men of the place should kill me for Rebekah; because she was fair to look upon.

8 And it came to pass, when he had been there a long time, that Abimelech king of the Philistines looked out at a window, and saw, and, behold, Isaac was sporting with Rebekah his wife.

9 And Abimelech called Isaac, and said, Behold, of a surety she is your wife: and how saidst you , She is my sister? And Isaac said unto him, Because I said, Lest I die for her.

10 And Abimelech said, What is this you have done unto us? one of the people might lightly have lien with your wife, and you shouldest have brought guiltiness upon us.

11 And Abimelech charged all his people, saying, He that toucheth this man or his wife shall surely be put to death.

12 Then Isaac sowed in that land, and received in the same year an hundredfold: and the LORD blessed him.

13 And the man waxed great, and went forward, and grew until he became very great:

14 For he had possession of flocks, and possession of herds, and great store of servants: and the Philistines envied him.

15 For all the wells which his father's servants had digged in the days of Abraham his father, the Philistines had stopped them, and filled them with earth.

16 And Abimelech said unto Isaac, Go from us; for you are much mightier than we.

17 And Isaac departed thence, and pitched his tent in the valley of Gerar, and dwelt there.

18 And Isaac digged again the wells of water, which they had digged in the days of Abraham his father; for the Philistines had stopped them after the death of Abraham: and he called their names after the names by which his father had called them.

19 And Isaac's servants digged in the valley, and found there a well of springing water.

20 And the herdmen of Gerar did strive with Isaac's herdmen, saying, The water is ours: and he called the name of the well Esek; because they strove with him.

21 And they digged another well, and strove for that also: and he called the name of it Sitnah.

22 And he removed from thence, and digged another well; and for that they strove not: and he called the name of it Rehoboth; and he said, For now the LORD has made room for us, and we shall be fruitful in the land.

23 And he went up from thence to Beer-sheba.

24 And the LORD appeared unto him the same night, and said, I am the God of Abraham your father: fear not, for I am with you, and will bless you, and multiply your seed for my servant Abraham's sake.

25 And he builded an altar there, and called upon the name of the LORD, and pitched his tent there: and there Isaac's servants digged a well.

26 Then Abimelech went to him from Gerar, and Ahuzzath one of his friends, and Phichol the chief captain of his army.

27 And Isaac said unto them, Wherefore come you to me, seeing you hate me, and have sent me away from you?

28 And they said, We saw certainly that the LORD was with you: and we said, Let there be now an oath betwixt us, even betwixt us and you, and let us make a covenant with you;

29 That you will do us no hurt, as we have not touched you, and as we have done unto you nothing but good, and have sent you away in peace: you are now the blessed of the LORD.

30 And he made them a feast, and they did eat and drink.

31 And they rose up betimes in the morning, and sware one to another: and Isaac sent them away, and they departed from him in peace.

32 And it came to pass the same day, that Isaac's servants came, and told him concerning the well which they had digged, and said unto him, We have found water.

33 And he called it Shebah: therefore the name of the city is Beer-sheba unto this day.

34 And Esau was forty years old when he took to wife Judith the daughter of Beeri the Hittite, and Bashemath the daughter of Elon the Hittite:

35 Which were a grief of mind unto Isaac and to Rebekah.

CHAPTER 27

AND it came to pass, that when Isaac was old, and his eyes were dim, so that he could not see, he called Esau his eldest son, and said unto him, My son: and he said unto him, Behold, here am I.

2 And he said, Behold now, I am old, I know not the day of my death:

3 Now therefore take, I pray you, your weapons, your quiver and your bow, and go out to the field, and take me some venison;

4 And make me savoury meat, such as I love, and bring it to me, that I may eat; that my soul may bless you before I die.

5 And Rebekah heard when Isaac spake to Esau his son. And Esau went to the field to hunt for venison, and to bring it.

6 And Rebekah spake unto Jacob her son, saying, Behold, I heard your father speak unto Esau your brother, saying,

7 Bring me venison, and make me savoury meat, that I may eat, and bless you before the LORD before my death.

8 Now therefore, my son, obey my voice according to that which I command you.

9 Go now to the flock, and fetch me from thence two good kids of the goats; and I will make them savoury meat for your father, such as he loveth:

10 And you shalt bring it to your father, that he may eat, and that he may bless you before his death.

11 And Jacob said to Rebekah his mother, Behold, Esau my brother is a hairy man, and I am a smooth man:

12 My father what if will feel me, and I shall seem to him as a deceiver; and I shall bring a curse upon me, and not a blessing.

13 And his mother said unto him, Upon me be your curse, my son: only obey my voice, and go fetch me them.

14 And he went, and fetched, and brought them to his mother: and his mother made savoury meat, such as his father loved.

15 And Rebekah took goodly raiment of her eldest son Esau, which were with her in the house, and put them upon Jacob her younger son:

16 And she put the skins of the kids of the goats upon his hands, and upon the smooth of his neck:

17 And she gave the savoury meat and the bread, which she had prepared, into the hand of her son Jacob.

18And he came unto his father, and said, My father: and he said, Here am I; who are you , my son?

19 And Jacob said unto his father, I am Esau your firstborn; I have done according as you badest me: arise, I pray you, sit and eat of my venison, that your soul may bless me.

20 And Isaac said unto his son, How is it that you have found it so quickly, my son? And he said, Because the LORD your God brought it to me.

21 And Isaac said unto Jacob, Come near, I pray you, that I may feel you, my son, whether you be my very son Esau or not.

22 And Jacob went near unto Isaac his father; and he felt him, and said, The voice is Jacob's voice, but the hands are the hands of Esau.

23 And he discerned him not, because his hands were hairy, as his brother Esau's hands: so he blessed him.

24 And he said, Are you my very son Esau? And he said, I am.

25 And he said, Bring it near to me, and I will eat of my son's venison, that my soul may bless you. And he brought it near to him, and he did eat: and he brought him wine, and he drank.

26 And his father Isaac said unto him, Come near now, and kiss me, my son.

27 And he came near, and kissed him: and he smelled the smell of his raiment, and blessed him, and said, See, the smell of my son is as the smell of a field which the LORD has blessed:

28 Therefore God give you of the dew of heaven, and the fatness of the earth, and plenty of corn and wine:

29 Let people serve you, and nations bow down to you: be lord over your brethren, and let your mother's sons bow down to you: cursed be every one that curseth you, and blessed be he that blesseth you.

30And it came to pass, as soon as Isaac had made an end of blessing Jacob, and Jacob was yet scarce gone out from the presence of Isaac his father, that Esau his brother came in from his hunting.

31 And he also had made savoury meat, and brought it unto his father, and said unto his father, Let my father arise, and eat of his son's venison, that your soul may bless me.

32 And Isaac his father said unto him, Who are you ? And he said, I am your son, your firstborn Esau.

33 And Isaac trembled very exceedingly, and said, Who? where is he that has taken venison, and brought it me, and I have eaten of all before you camest, and have blessed him? yea, and he shall be blessed.

34 And when Esau heard the words of his father, he cried with a great and exceeding bitter cry, and said unto his father, Bless me, even me also, O my father.

35 And he said, Your brother came with subtilty, and has taken away your blessing.

36 And he said, Is not he rightly named Jacob? for he has supplanted me these two times: he took away my birthright; and, behold, now he has taken away my blessing. And he said, Have you not reserved a blessing for me?

37 And Isaac answered and said unto Esau, Behold, I have made him your lord, and all his brethren have I given to him for servants; and with corn and wine have I sustained him: and what shall I do now unto you, my son?

38 And Esau said unto his father, Have you but one blessing, my father? bless me, even me also, O my father. And Esau lifted up his voice, and wept.

39 And Isaac his father answered and said unto him, Behold, your dwelling shall be the fatness of the earth, and of the dew of heaven from above;

40 And by your sword shalt you live, and shalt serve your brother; and it shall come to pass when you shalt have the dominion, that you shalt break his yoke from off your neck.

41And Esau hated Jacob because of the blessing wherewith his father blessed him: and Esau said in his heart, The days of mourning for my father are at hand; then will I slay my brother Jacob.

42 And these words of Esau her elder son were told to Rebekah: and she sent and called Jacob her younger son, and said unto him, Behold, your brother Esau, as touching you, doth comfort himself, purposing to kill you.

43 Now therefore, my son, obey my voice; and arise, flee you to Laban my brother to Haran;

44 And tarry with him a few days, until your brother's fury turn away;

45 Until your brother's anger turn away from you, and he forget that which you have done to him: then I will send, and fetch you from thence: why should I be deprived also of you both in one day?

46 And Rebekah said to Isaac, I am weary of my life because of the daughters of Heth: if Jacob take a wife of the daughters of Heth, such as these which are of the daughters of the land, what good shall my life do me?

CHAPTER 28

AND Isaac called Jacob, and blessed him, and charged him, and said unto him, You shalt not take a wife of the daughters of Canaan.

2 Arise, go to Padan-aram, to the house of Bethuel your mother's father; and take you a wife from thence, the daughters of Laban your mother's brother.

3 And God Almighty bless you, and make you fruitful, and multiply you, that you mayest be a multitude of people;

4 And give you the blessing of Abraham, to you, and to your seed with you; that you mayest inherit the land wherein you are a stranger, which God gave unto Abraham.

5 And Isaac sent away Jacob: and he went to Padan-aram unto Laban, son of Bethuel the Syrian, the brother of Rebekah, Jacob's and Esau's mother.

6When Esau saw that Isaac had blessed Jacob, and sent him away to Padan-aram, to take him a wife from thence; and that as he blessed him he gave him a charge, saying, You shalt not take a wife of the daughters of Canaan;

7 And that Jacob obeyed his father and his mother, and was gone to Padan-aram;

8 And Esau seeing that the daughters of Canaan pleased not Isaac his father;

9 Then went Esau unto Ishmael, and took unto the wives which he had Mahalath the daughter of Ishmael Abraham's son, the sister of Nebajoth, to be his wife.

10And Jacob went out from Beer-sheba, and went toward Haran.

11 And he lighted upon a certain place, and tarried there all night, because the sun was set; and he took of the stones of that place, and put them for his pillows, and lay down in that place to sleep.

12 And he dreamed, and behold a ladder set up on the earth, and the top of it reached to heaven: and behold the angels of God ascending and descending on it.

13 And, behold, the LORD stood above it, and said, I am the LORD God of Abraham your father, and the God of Isaac: the land whereon you liest, to you will I give it, and to your seed;

14 And your seed shall be as the dust of the earth, and you shalt spread abroad to the west, and to the east, and to the north, and to the south: and in you and in your seed shall all the families of the earth be blessed.

15 And, behold, I am with you, and will keep you in all places whither you go, and will bring you again into this land; for I will not leave you, until I have done that which I have spoken to you of.

16And Jacob awaked out of his sleep, and he said, Surely the LORD is in this place; and I knew it not.

17 And he was afraid, and said, How dreadful is this place! this is none other but the house of God, and this is the gate of heaven.

18 And Jacob rose up early in the morning, and took the stone that he had put for his pillows, and set it up for a pillar, and poured oil upon the top of it.

19 And he called the name of that place Beth-el: but the name of that city was called Luz at the first.

20 And Jacob vowed a vow, saying, If God will be with me, and will keep me in this way that I go, and will give me bread to eat, and raiment to put on,

21 So that I come again to my father's house in peace; then shall the LORD be my God:

22 And this stone, which I have set for a pillar, shall be God's house: and of all that you shalt give me I will surely give the tenth unto you.

CHAPTER 29

THEN Jacob went on his journey, and came into the land of the people of the east.

2 And he looked, and behold a well in the field, and, lo, there were three flocks of sheep lying by it; for out of that well they watered the flocks: and a great stone was upon the well's mouth.

3 And thither were all the flocks gathered: and they rolled the stone from the well's mouth, and watered the sheep, and put the stone again upon the well's mouth in his place.

4 And Jacob said unto them, My brethren, whence be you ? And they said, Of Haran are we.

5 And he said unto them, Know you Laban the son of Nahor? And they said, We know him.

6 And he said unto them, Is he well? And they said, He is well: and, behold, Rachel his daughter comes with the sheep.

7 And he said, Lo, it is yet high day, neither is it time that the cattle should be gathered together: water you the sheep, and go and feed them.

8 And they said, We cannot, until all the flocks be gathered together, and till they roll the stone from the well's mouth; then we water the sheep.

9 And while he yet spake with them, Rachel came with her father's sheep: for she kept them.

10 And it came to pass, when Jacob saw Rachel the daughter of Laban his mother's brother, and the sheep of Laban his mother's brother, that Jacob went near, and rolled the stone from the well's mouth, and watered the flock of Laban his mother's brother.

11 And Jacob kissed Rachel, and lifted up his voice, and wept.

12 And Jacob told Rachel that he was her father's brother, and that he was Rebekah's son: and she ran and told her father.

13 And it came to pass, when Laban heard the tidings of Jacob his sister's son, that he ran to meet him, and embraced him, and kissed him, and brought him to his house. And he told Laban all these things.

14 And Laban said to him, Surely you are my bone and my flesh. And he abode with him the space of a month.

15 And Laban said unto Jacob, Because you are my brother, shouldest you therefore serve me for nought? tell me, what shall your wages be?

16 And Laban had two daughters: the name of the elder was Leah, and the name of the younger was Rachel.

17 Leah was tender eyed; but Rachel was beautiful and well favoured.

18 And Jacob loved Rachel; and said, I will serve you seven years for Rachel your younger daughter.

19 And Laban said, It is better that I give her to you, than that I should give her to another man: abide with me.

20 And Jacob served seven years for Rachel; and they seemed unto him but a few days, for the love he had to her.

21 And Jacob said unto Laban, Give me my wife, for my days are fulfilled, that I may go in unto her.

22 And Laban gathered together all the men of the place, and made a feast.

23 And it came to pass in the evening, that he took Leah his daughter, and brought her to him; and he went in unto her.

24 And Laban gave unto his daughter Leah Zilpah his maid for an handmaid.

25 And it came to pass, that in the morning, behold, it was Leah: and he said to Laban, What is this you have done unto me? did not I serve with you for Rachel? wherefore then have you beguiled me?

26 And Laban said, It must not be so done in our country, to give the younger before the firstborn.

27 Fulfil her week, and we will give you this also for the service which you shalt serve with me yet seven other years.

28 And Jacob did so, and fulfilled her week: and he gave him Rachel his daughter to wife also.

29 And Laban gave to Rachel his daughter Bilhah his handmaid to be her maid.

30 And he went in also unto Rachel, and he loved also Rachel more than Leah, and served with him yet seven other years.

31 And when the LORD saw that Leah was hated, he opened her womb: but Rachel was barren.

32 And Leah conceived, and bare a son, and she called his name Reuben: for she said, Surely the LORD has looked upon my affliction; now therefore my husband will love me.

33 And she conceived again, and bare a son; and said, Because the LORD has heard that I was hated, he has therefore given me this son also: and she called his name Simeon.

34 And she conceived again, and bare a son; and said, Now this time will my husband be joined unto me, because I have born him three sons: therefore was his name called Levi.

35 And she conceived again, and bare a son: and she said, Now will I praise the LORD: therefore she called his name Judah; and left bearing.

CHAPTER 30

AND when Rachel saw that she bare Jacob no children, Rachel envied her sister; and said unto Jacob, Give me children, or else I die.

2 And Jacob's anger was kindled against Rachel: and he said, Am I in God's stead, who has withheld from you the fruit of the womb?

3 And she said, Behold my maid Bilhah, go in unto her; and she shall bear upon my knees, that I may also have children by her.

4 And she gave him Bilhah her handmaid to wife: and Jacob went in unto her.

5 And Bilhah conceived, and bare Jacob a son.

6 And Rachel said, God has judged me, and has also heard my voice, and has given me a son: therefore called she his name Dan.

7 And Bilhah Rachel's maid conceived again, and bare Jacob a second son.

8 And Rachel said, With great wrestlings have I wrestled with my sister, and I have prevailed: and she called his name Naphtali.

9 When Leah saw that she had left bearing, she took Zilpah her maid, and gave her Jacob to wife.

10 And Zilpah Leah's maid bare Jacob a son.

11 And Leah said, A troop comes: and she called his name Gad.

12 And Zilpah Leah's maid bare Jacob a second son.

13 And Leah said, Happy am I, for the daughters will call me blessed: and she called his name Asher.

14 And Reuben went in the days of wheat harvest, and found mandrakes in the field, and brought them unto his mother Leah. Then Rachel said to Leah, Give me, I pray you, of your son's mandrakes.

15 And she said unto her, Is it a small matter that you have taken my husband? and wouldest you take away my son's mandrakes also? And Rachel said, Therefore he shall lie with you to night for your son's mandrakes.

16 And Jacob came out of the field in the evening, and Leah went out to meet him, and said, You must come in unto me; for surely I have hired you with my son's mandrakes. And he lay with her that night.

17 And God hearkened unto Leah, and she conceived, and bare Jacob the fifth son.

18 And Leah said, God has given me my hire, because I have given my maiden to my husband: and she called his name Issachar.

19 And Leah conceived again, and bare Jacob the sixth son.

20 And Leah said, God has endued me with a good dowry; now will my husband dwell with me, because I have born him six sons: and she called his name Zebulun.

21 And afterwards she bare a daughter, and called her name Dinah.

22 And God remembered Rachel, and God hearkened to her, and opened her womb.

23 And she conceived, and bare a son; and said, God has taken away my reproach:

24 And she called his name Joseph; and said, The LORD shall add to me another son.

25 And it came to pass, when Rachel had born Joseph, that Jacob said unto Laban, Send me away, that I may go unto my own place, and to my country.

26 Give me my wives and my children, for whom I have served you, and let me go: for you knowest my service which I have done you.

27 And Laban said unto him, I pray you, if I have found favour in yours eyes, tarry: for I have learned by experience that the LORD has blessed me for your sake.

28 And he said, Appoint me your wages, and I will give it.

29 And he said unto him, You knowest how I have served you, and how your cattle was with me.

30 For it was little which you hadst before I came, and it is now increased unto a multitude; and the LORD has blessed you since my coming: and now when shall I provide for my own house also?

31 And he said, What shall I give you? And Jacob said, You shalt not give me any thing: if you will do this thing for me, I will again feed and keep your flock:

32 I will pass through all your flock to day, removing from thence all the speckled and spotted cattle, and all the brown cattle among the sheep, and the spotted and speckled among the goats: and of such shall be my hire.

33 So shall my righteousness answer for me in time to come, when it shall come for my hire before your face: every one that is not speckled and spotted among the goats, and brown among the sheep, that shall be counted stolen with me.

34 And Laban said, Behold, I would it might be according to your word.

35 And he removed that day the he goats that were ringstraked and spotted, and all the she goats that were speckled and spotted, and every one that had some white in it, and all the brown among the sheep, and gave them into the hand of his sons.

36 And he set three days' journey betwixt himself and Jacob: and Jacob fed the rest of Laban's flocks.

37 And Jacob took him rods of green poplar, and of the hazel and chesnut tree; and pilled white strakes in them, and made the white appear which was in the rods.

38 And he set the rods which he had pilled before the flocks in the gutters in the watering troughs when the flocks came to drink, that they should conceive when they came to drink.

39 And the flocks conceived before the rods, and brought forth cattle ringstraked, speckled, and spotted.

40 And Jacob did separate the lambs, and set the faces of the flocks toward the ringstraked, and all the brown in the flock of Laban; and he put his own flocks by themselves, and put them not unto Laban's cattle.

41 And it came to pass, whensoever the stronger cattle did conceive, that Jacob laid the rods before the eyes of the cattle in the gutters, that they might conceive among the rods.

42 But when the cattle were feeble, he put them not in: so the feebler were Laban's, and the stronger Jacob's.

43 And the man increased exceedingly, and had much cattle, and maidservants, and menservants, and camels, and asses.

CHAPTER 31

AND he heard the words of Laban's sons, saying, Jacob has taken away all that was our father's; and of that which was our father's has he gotten all this glory.

2 And Jacob beheld the countenance of Laban, and, behold, it was not toward him as before.

3 And the LORD said unto Jacob, Return unto the land of your fathers, and to your kindred; and I will be with you.

4 And Jacob sent and called Rachel and Leah to the field unto his flock,

5 And said unto them, I see your father's countenance, that it is not toward me as before; but the God of my father has been with me.

6 And you know that with all my power I have served your father.

7 And your father has deceived me, and changed my wages ten times; but God suffered him not to hurt me.

8 If he said thus, The speckled shall be your wages; then all the cattle bare speckled: and if he said thus, The ringstraked shall be your hire; then bare all the cattle ringstraked.

9 Thus God has taken away the cattle of your father, and given them to me.

10 And it came to pass at the time that the cattle conceived, that I lifted up my eyes, and saw in a dream, and, behold, the rams which leaped upon the cattle were ringstraked, speckled, and grisled.

11 And the angel of God spake unto me in a dream, saying, Jacob: And I said, Here am I.

12 And he said, Lift up now yours eyes, and see, all the rams which leap upon the cattle are ringstraked, speckled, and grisled: for I have seen all that Laban doeth unto you.

13 I am the God of Beth-el, where you anointedst the pillar, and where you vowedst a vow unto me: now arise, get you out from this land, and return unto the land of your kindred.

14 And Rachel and Leah answered and said unto him, Is there yet any portion or inheritance for us in our father's house?

15 Are we not counted of him strangers? for he has sold us, and has quite devoured also our money.

16 For all the riches which God has taken from our father, that is ours, and our children's: now then, whatsoever God has said unto you, do.

17 Then Jacob rose up, and set his sons and his wives upon camels;

18 And he carried away all his cattle, and all his goods which he had gotten, the cattle of his getting, which he had gotten in Padan-aram, for to go to Isaac his father in the land of Canaan.

19 And Laban went to shear his sheep: and Rachel had stolen the images that were her father's.

20 And Jacob stole away unawares to Laban the Syrian, in that he told him not that he fled.

21 So he fled with all that he had; and he rose up, and passed over the river, and set his face toward the mount Gilead.

22 And it was told Laban on the third day that Jacob was fled.

23 And he took his brethren with him, and pursued after him seven days' journey; and they overtook him in the mount Gilead.

24 And God came to Laban the Syrian in a dream by night, and said unto him, Take heed that you speak not to Jacob either good or bad.

25 Then Laban overtook Jacob. Now Jacob had pitched his tent in the mount: and Laban with his brethren pitched in the mount of Gilead.

26 And Laban said to Jacob, What have you done, that you have stolen away unawares to me, and carried away my daughters, as captives taken with the sword?

27 Wherefore did you flee away secretly, and steal away from me; and did not tell me, that I might have sent you away with mirth, and with songs, with tabret, and with harp?

28 And have not suffered me to kiss my sons and my daughters? you have now done foolishly in so doing.

29 It is in the power of my hand to do you hurt: but the God of your father spake unto me yesternight, saying, Take you heed that you speak not to Jacob either good or bad.

30 And now, though you wouldest needs be gone, because you sore longedst after your father's house, yet wherefore have you stolen my gods?

31 And Jacob answered and said to Laban, Because I was afraid: for I said, What if you wouldest take by force your daughters from me.

32 With whomsoever you findest your gods, let him not live: before our brethren discern you what is yours with me, and take it to you. For Jacob knew not that Rachel had stolen them.

33 And Laban went into Jacob's tent, and into Leah's tent, and into the two maidservants' tents; but he found them not. Then went he out of Leah's tent, and entered into Rachel's tent.

34 Now Rachel had taken the images, and put them in the camel's furniture, and sat upon them. And Laban searched all the tent, but found them not.

35 And she said to her father, Let it not displease my lord that I cannot rise up before you; for the custom of women is upon me. And he searched, but found not the images.

36 And Jacob was wroth, and chode with Laban: and Jacob answered and said to Laban, What is my trespass? what is my sin, that you have so hotly pursued after me?

37 Whereas you have searched all my stuff, what have you found of all your household stuff? set it here before my brethren and your brethren, that they may judge betwixt us both.

38 This twenty years have I been with you; your ewes and your she goats have not cast their young, and the rams of your flock have I not eaten.

39 That which was torn of beasts I brought not unto you; I bare the loss of it; of my hand did you require it, whether stolen by day, or stolen by night.

40 Thus I was; in the day the drought consumed me, and the frost by night; and my sleep departed from my eyes.

41 Thus have I been twenty years in your house; I served you fourteen years for your two daughters, and six years for your cattle: and you have changed my wages ten times.

42 Except the God of my father, the God of Abraham, and the fear of Isaac, had been with me, surely you hadst sent me away now empty. God has seen my affliction and the labour of my hands, and rebuked you yesternight.

43 And Laban answered and said unto Jacob, These daughters are my daughters, and these children are my children, and these cattle are my cattle, and all that you seest is my: and what can I do this day unto these my daughters, or unto their children which they have born?

44 Now therefore come you , let us make a covenant, I and you ; and let it be for a witness between me and you.

45 And Jacob took a stone, and set it up for a pillar.

46 And Jacob said unto his brethren, Gather stones; and they took stones, and made an heap: and they did eat there upon the heap.

47 And Laban called it Jegar-sahadutha: but Jacob called it Galeed.

48 And Laban said, This heap is a witness between me and you this day. Therefore was the name of it called Galeed;

49 And Mizpah; for he said, The LORD watch between me and you, when we are absent one from another.

50 If you shalt afflict my daughters, or if you shalt take other wives beside my daughters, no man is with us; see, God is witness betwixt me and you.

51 And Laban said to Jacob, Behold this heap, and behold this pillar, which I have cast betwixt me and you;

52 This heap be witness, and this pillar be witness, that I will not pass over this heap to you, and that you shalt not pass over this heap and this pillar unto me, for harm.

53 The God of Abraham, and the God of Nahor, the God of their father, judge betwixt us. And Jacob sware by the fear of his father Isaac.

54 Then Jacob offered sacrifice upon the mount, and called his brethren to eat bread: and they did eat bread, and tarried all night in the mount.

55 And early in the morning Laban rose up, and kissed his sons and his daughters, and blessed them: and Laban departed, and returned unto his place.

CHAPTER 32

AND Jacob went on his way, and the angels of God met him.

2 And when Jacob saw them, he said, This is God's host: and he called the name of that place Mahanaim.

3 And Jacob sent messengers before him to Esau his brother unto the land of Seir, the country of Edom.

4 And he commanded them, saying, Thus shall you speak unto my lord Esau; Your servant Jacob saith thus, I have sojourned with Laban, and stayed there until now:

5 And I have oxen, and asses, flocks, and menservants, and womenservants: and I have sent to tell my lord, that I may find grace in your sight.

6 And the messengers returned to Jacob, saying, We came to your brother Esau, and also he comes to meet you, and four hundred men with him.

7 Then Jacob was greatly afraid and distressed: and he divided the people that was with him, and the flocks, and herds, and the camels, into two bands;

8 And said, If Esau come to the one company, and strike it, then the other company which is left shall escape.

9 And Jacob said, O God of my father Abraham, and God of my father Isaac, the LORD which saidst unto me, Return unto your country, and to your kindred, and I will deal well with you:

10 I am not worthy of the least of all the mercies, and of all the truth, which you have shewed unto your servant; for with my staff I passed over this Jordan; and now I am become two bands.

11 Deliver me, I pray you, from the hand of my brother, from the hand of Esau: for I fear him, lest he will come and strike me, and the mother with the children.

12 And you saidst, I will surely do you good, and make your seed as the sand of the sea, which cannot be numbered for multitude.

13 And he lodged there that same night; and took of that which came to his hand a present for Esau his brother;

14 Two hundred she goats, and twenty he goats, two hundred ewes, and twenty rams,

15 Thirty milch camels with their colts, forty kine, and ten bulls, twenty she asses, and ten foals.

16 And he delivered them into the hand of his servants, every drove by themselves; and said unto his servants, Pass over before me, and put a space betwixt drove and drove.

17 And he commanded the foremost, saying, When Esau my brother meeteth you, and asketh you, saying, Whose are you? and whither go you? and whose are these before you?

18 Then you shalt say, They be your servant Jacob's; it is a present sent unto my lord Esau: and, behold, also he is behind us.

19 And so commanded he the second, and the third, and all that followed the droves, saying, On this manner shall you speak unto Esau, when you find him.

20 And say you moreover, Behold, your servant Jacob is behind us. For he said, I will appease him with the present that goeth before me, and afterward I will see his face; what if he will accept of me.

21 So went the present over before him: and himself lodged that night in the company.

22 And he rose up that night, and took his two wives, and his two womenservants, and his eleven sons, and passed over the ford Jabbok.

23 And he took them, and sent them over the brook, and sent over that he had.

24 And Jacob was left alone; and there wrestled a man with him until the breaking of the day.

25 And when he saw that he prevailed not against him, he touched the hollow of his thigh; and the hollow of Jacob's thigh was out of joint, as he wrestled with him.

26 And he said, Let me go, for the day breaketh. And he said, I will not let you go, except you bless me.

27 And he said unto him, What is your name? And he said, Jacob.

28 And he said, Your name shall be called no more Jacob, but Israel: for as a prince have you power with God and with men, and have prevailed.

29 And Jacob asked him, and said, Tell me, I pray you, your name. And he said, Wherefore is it that you dost ask after my name? And he blessed him there.

30 And Jacob called the name of the place Peniel: for I have seen God face to face, and my life is preserved.

31 And as he passed over Penuel the sun rose upon him, and he halted upon his thigh.

32 Therefore the children of Israel eat not of the sinew which shrank, which is upon the hollow of the thigh, unto this day: because he touched the hollow of Jacob's thigh in the sinew that shrank.

CHAPTER 33

AND Jacob lifted up his eyes, and looked, and, behold, Esau came, and with him four hundred men. And he divided the children unto Leah, and unto Rachel, and unto the two handmaids.

2 And he put the handmaids and their children foremost, and Leah and her children after, and Rachel and Joseph hindermost.

3 And he passed over before them, and bowed himself to the ground seven times, until he came near to his brother.

4 And Esau ran to meet him, and embraced him, and fell on his neck, and kissed him: and they wept.

5 And he lifted up his eyes, and saw the women and the children; and said, Who are those with you? And he said, The children which God has graciously given your servant.

6 Then the handmaidens came near, they and their children, and they bowed themselves.

7 And Leah also with her children came near, and bowed themselves: and after came Joseph near and Rachel, and they bowed themselves.

8 And he said, What meanest you by all this drove which I met? And he said, These are to find grace in the sight of my lord.

9 And Esau said, I have enough, my brother; keep that you have unto yourself.

10 And Jacob said, Nay, I pray you, if now I have found grace in your sight, then receive my present at my hand: for therefore I have seen your face, as though I had seen the face of God, and you wast pleased with me.

11 Take, I pray you, my blessing that is brought to you; because God has dealt graciously with me, and because I have enough. And he urged him, and he took it.

12 And he said, Let us take our journey, and let us go, and I will go before you.

13 And he said unto him, My lord knoweth that the children are tender, and the flocks and herds with young are with me: and if men should overdrive them one day, all the flock will die.

14 Let my lord, I pray you, pass over before his servant: and I will lead on softly, according as the cattle that goeth before me and the children be able to endure, until I come unto my lord unto Seir.

15 And Esau said, Let me now leave with you some of the folk that are with me. And he said, What needeth it? let me find grace in the sight of my lord.

16 So Esau returned that day on his way unto Seir.

17 And Jacob journeyed to Succoth, and built him an house, and made booths for his cattle: therefore the name of the place is called Succoth.

18 And Jacob came to Shalem, a city of Shechem, which is in the land of Canaan, when he came from Padan-aram; and pitched his tent before the city.

19 And he bought a parcel of a field, where he had spread his tent, at the hand of the children of Hamor, Shechem's father, for an hundred pieces of money.

20 And he erected there an altar, and called it El-elohe-Israel.

CHAPTER 34

AND Dinah the daughter of Leah, which she bare unto Jacob, went out to see the daughters of the land.

2 And when Shechem the son of Hamor the Hivite, prince of the country, saw her, he took her, and lay with her, and defiled her.

3 And his soul clave unto Dinah the daughter of Jacob, and he loved the damsel, and spake kindly unto the damsel.

4 And Shechem spake unto his father Hamor, saying, Get me this damsel to wife.

5 And Jacob heard that he had defiled Dinah his daughter: now his sons were with his cattle in the field: and Jacob held his peace until they were come.

6 And Hamor the father of Shechem went out unto Jacob to commune with him.

7 And the sons of Jacob came out of the field when they heard it: and the men were grieved, and they were very wroth, because he had created folly in Israel in lying with Jacob's daughter; which thing ought not to be done.

8 And Hamor communed with them, saying, The soul of my son Shechem longeth for your daughter: I pray you give her him to wife.

9 And make you marriages with us, and give your daughters unto us, and take our daughters unto you.

10 And you shall dwell with us: and the land shall be before you; dwell and trade you therein, and get you possessions therein.

11 And Shechem said unto her father and unto her brethren, Let me find grace in your eyes, and what you shall say unto me I will give.

12 Ask me never so much dowry and gift, and I will give according as you shall say unto me: but give me the damsel to wife.

13 And the sons of Jacob answered Shechem and Hamor his father deceitfully, and said, because he had defiled Dinah their sister:

14 And they said unto them, We cannot do this thing, to give our sister to one that is uncircumcised; for that were a reproach unto us:

15 But in this will we consent unto you: If you will be as we be, that every male of you be circumcised;

16 Then will we give our daughters unto you, and we will take your daughters to us, and we will dwell with you, and we will become one people.

17 But if you will not hearken unto us, to be circumcised; then will we take our daughter, and we will be gone.

18 And their words pleased Hamor, and Shechem Hamor's son.

19 And the young man deferred not to do the thing, because he had delight in Jacob's daughter: and he was more honourable than all the house of his father.

20 And Hamor and Shechem his son came unto the gate of their city, and communed with the men of their city, saying,

21 These men are peaceable with us; therefore let them dwell in the land, and trade therein; for the land, behold, it is large enough for them; let us take their daughters to us for wives, and let us give them our daughters.

22 Only herein will the men consent unto us for to dwell with us, to be one people, if every male among us be circumcised, as they are circumcised.

23 Shall not their cattle and their substance and every beast of theirs be ours? only let us consent unto them, and they will dwell with us.

24 And unto Hamor and unto Shechem his son hearkened all that went out of the gate of his city; and every male was circumcised, all that went out of the gate of his city.

25And it came to pass on the third day, when they were sore, that two of the sons of Jacob, Simeon and Levi, Dinah's brethren, took each man his sword, and came upon the city boldly, and slew all the males.

26 And they slew Hamor and Shechem his son with the edge of the sword, and took Dinah out of Shechem's house, and went out.

27 The sons of Jacob came upon the slain, and spoiled the city, because they had defiled their sister.

28 They took their sheep, and their oxen, and their asses, and that which was in the city, and that which was in the field,

29 And all their wealth, and all their little ones, and their wives took they captive, and spoiled even all that was in the house.

30 And Jacob said to Simeon and Levi, You have troubled me to make me to stink among the inhabitants of the land, among the Canaanites and the Perizzites: and I being few in number, they shall gather themselves together against me, and slay me; and I shall be destroyed, I and my house.

31 And they said, Should he deal with our sister as with an harlot?

CHAPTER 35

AND God said unto Jacob, Arise, go up to Beth-el, and dwell there: and make there an altar unto God, that appeared unto you when you fled from the face of Esau your brother.

2 Then Jacob said unto his household, and to all that were with him, Put away the strange gods that are among you, and be clean, and change your garments:

3 And let us arise, and go up to Beth-el; and I will make there an altar unto God, who answered me in the day of my distress, and was with me in the way which I went.

4 And they gave unto Jacob all the strange gods which were in their hand, and all their earrings which were in their ears; and Jacob hid them under the oak which was by Shechem.

5 And they journeyed: and the terror of God was upon the cities that were round about them, and they did not pursue after the sons of Jacob.

6So Jacob came to Luz, which is in the land of Canaan, that is, Beth-el, he and all the people that were with him.

7 And he built there an altar, and called the place El-beth-el: because there God appeared unto him, when he fled from the face of his brother.

8 But Deborah Rebekah's nurse died, and she was buried beneath Beth-el under an oak: and the name of it was called Allon-bachuth.

9And God appeared unto Jacob again, when he came out of Padan-aram, and blessed him.

10 And God said unto him, Your name is Jacob: your name shall not be called any more Jacob, but Israel shall be your name: and he called his name Israel.

11 And God said unto him, I am God Almighty: be fruitful and multiply; a nation and a company of nations shall be of you, and kings shall come out of your loins;

12 And the land which I gave Abraham and Isaac, to you I will give it, and to your seed after you will I give the land.

13 And God went up from him in the place where he talked with him.

14 And Jacob set up a pillar in the place where he talked with him, even a pillar of stone: and he poured a drink offering thereon, and he poured oil thereon.

15 And Jacob called the name of the place where God spake with him, Beth-el.

16And they journeyed from Beth-el; and there was but a little way to come to Ephrath: and Rachel travailed, and she had hard labour.

17 And it came to pass, when she was in hard labour, that the midwife said unto her, Fear not; you shalt have this son also.

18 And it came to pass, as her soul was in departing, (for she died) that she called his name Ben-oni: but his father called him Benjamin.

19 And Rachel died, and was buried in the way to Ephrath, which is Beth-lehem.

20 And Jacob set a pillar upon her grave: that is the pillar of Rachel's grave unto this day.

21And Israel journeyed, and spread his tent beyond the tower of Edar.

22 And it came to pass, when Israel dwelt in that land, that Reuben went and lay with Bilhah his father's concubine: and Israel heard it. Now the sons of Jacob were twelve:

23 The sons of Leah; Reuben, Jacob's firstborn, and Simeon, and Levi, and Judah, and Issachar, and Zebulun:

24 The sons of Rachel; Joseph, and Benjamin:

25 And the sons of Bilhah, Rachel's handmaid; Dan, and Naphtali:

26 And the sons of Zilpah, Leah's handmaid; Gad, and Asher: these are the sons of Jacob, which were born to him in Padan-aram.

27And Jacob came unto Isaac his father unto Mamre, unto the city of Arbah, which is Hebron, where Abraham and Isaac sojourned.

28 And the days of Isaac were an hundred and fourscore years.

29 And Isaac gave up the ghost, and died, and was gathered unto his people, being old and full of days: and his sons Esau and Jacob buried him.

CHAPTER 36

NOW these are the generations of Esau, who is Edom.

2 Esau took his wives of the daughters of Canaan; Adah the daughter of Elon the Hittite, and Aholibamah the daughter of Anah the daughter of Zibeon the Hivite;

3 And Bashemath Ishmael's daughter, sister of Nebajoth.

4 And Adah bare to Esau Eliphaz; and Bashemath bare Reuel;

5 And Aholibamah bare Jeush, and Jaalam, and Korah: these are the sons of Esau, which were born unto him in the land of Canaan.

6 And Esau took his wives, and his sons, and his daughters, and all the persons of his house, and his cattle, and all his beasts, and all his substance, which he had got in the land of Canaan; and went into the country from the face of his brother Jacob.

7 For their riches were more than that they might dwell together; and the land wherein they were strangers could not bear them because of their cattle.

8 Thus dwelt Esau in mount Seir: Esau is Edom.

9And these are the generations of Esau the father of the Edomites in mount Seir:

10 These are the names of Esau's sons; Eliphaz the son of Adah the wife of Esau, Reuel the son of Bashemath the wife of Esau.

11 And the sons of Eliphaz were Teman, Omar, Zepho, and Gatam, and Kenaz.

12 And Timna was concubine to Eliphaz Esau's son; and she bare to Eliphaz Amalek: these were the sons of Adah Esau's wife.

13 And these are the sons of Reuel; Nahath, and Zerah, Shammah, and Mizzah: these were the sons of Bashemath Esau's wife.

14And these were the sons of Aholibamah, the daughter of Anah the daughter of Zibeon, Esau's wife: and she bare to Esau Jeush, and Jaalam, and Korah.

15These were dukes of the sons of Esau: the sons of Eliphaz the firstborn son of Esau; duke Teman, duke Omar, duke Zepho, duke Kenaz,

16 Duke Korah, duke Gatam, and duke Amalek: these are the dukes that came of Eliphaz in the land of Edom; these were the sons of Adah.

17And these are the sons of Reuel Esau's son; duke Nahath, duke Zerah, duke Shammah, duke Mizzah: these are the dukes that came of Reuel in the land of Edom; these are the sons of Bashemath Esau's wife.

18And these are the sons of Aholibamah Esau's wife; duke Jeush, duke Jaalam, duke Korah: these were the dukes that came of Aholibamah the daughter of Anah, Esau's wife.

19 These are the sons of Esau, who is Edom, and these are their dukes.

20These are the sons of Seir the Horite, who inhabited the land; Lotan, and Shobal, and Zibeon, and Anah,

21 And Dishon, and Ezer, and Dishan: these are the dukes of the Horites, the children of Seir in the land of Edom.

22 And the children of Lotan were Hori and Hemam; and Lotan's sister was Timna.

23 And the children of Shobal were these; Alvan, and Manahath, and Ebal, Shepho, and Onam.

24 And these are the children of Zibeon; both Ajah, and Anah: this was that Anah that found the mules in the wilderness, as he fed the asses of Zibeon his father.

25 And the children of Anah were these; Dishon, and Aholibamah the daughter of Anah.

26 And these are the children of Dishon; Hemdan, and Eshban, and Ithran, and Cheran.

27 The children of Ezer are these; Bilhan, and Zaavan, and Akan.

28 The children of Dishan are these; Uz, and Aran.

29 These are the dukes that came of the Horites; duke Lotan, duke Shobal, duke Zibeon, duke Anah,

30 Duke Dishon, duke Ezer, duke Dishan: these are the dukes that came of Hori, among their dukes in the land of Seir.

31And these are the kings that reigned in the land of Edom, before there reigned any king over the children of Israel.

32 And Bela the son of Beor reigned in Edom: and the name of his city was Dinhabah.

33 And Bela died, and Jobab the son of Zerah of Bozrah reigned in his stead.

34 And Jobab died, and Husham of the land of Temani reigned in his stead.

35 And Husham died, and Hadad the son of Bedad, who struck Midian in the field of Moab, reigned in his stead: and the name of his city was Avith.

36 And Hadad died, and Samlah of Masrekah reigned in his stead.

37 And Samlah died, and Saul of Rehoboth by the river reigned in his stead.

38 And Saul died, and Baal-hanan the son of Achbor reigned in his stead.

39 And Baal-hanan the son of Achbor died, and Hadar reigned in his stead: and the name of his city was Pau; and his wife's name was Mehetabel, the daughter of Matred, the daughter of Mezahab.

40 And these are the names of the dukes that came of Esau, according to their families, after their places, by their names; duke Timnah, duke Alvah, duke Jetheth,

41 Duke Aholibamah, duke Elah, duke Pinon,

42 Duke Kenaz, duke Teman, duke Mibzar,

43 Duke Magdiel, duke Iram: these be the dukes of Edom, according to their habitations in the land of their possession: he is Esau the father of the Edomites.

CHAPTER 37

AND Jacob dwelt in the land wherein his father was a stranger, in the land of Canaan.

2 These are the generations of Jacob. Joseph, being seventeen years old, was feeding the flock with his brethren; and the lad was with the sons of Bilhah, and with the sons of Zilpah, his father's wives: and Joseph brought unto his father their evil report.

3 Now Israel loved Joseph more than all his children, because he was the son of his old age: and he made him a coat of many colours.

4 And when his brethren saw that their father loved him more than all his brethren, they hated him, and could not speak peaceably unto him.

5 And Joseph dreamed a dream, and he told it his brethren: and they hated him yet the more.

6 And he said unto them, Hear, I pray you, this dream which I have dreamed:

7 For, behold, we were binding sheaves in the field, and, lo, my sheaf arose, and also stood upright; and, behold, your sheaves stood round about, and made obeisance to my sheaf.

8 And his brethren said to him, Shalt you indeed reign over us? or shalt you indeed have dominion over us? And they hated him yet the more for his dreams, and for his words.

9 And he dreamed yet another dream, and told it his brethren, and said, Behold, I have dreamed a dream more; and, behold, the sun and the moon and the eleven stars made obeisance to me.

10 And he told it to his father, and to his brethren: and his father rebuked him, and said unto him, What is this dream that you have dreamed? Shall I and your mother and your brethren indeed come to bow down ourselves to you to the earth?

11 And his brethren envied him; but his father observed the saying.

12 And his brethren went to feed their father's flock in Shechem.

13 And Israel said unto Joseph, Do not your brethren feed the flock in Shechem? come, and I will send you unto them. And he said to him, Here am I.

14 And he said to him, Go, I pray you, see whether it be well with your brethren, and well with the flocks; and bring me word again. So he sent him out of the vale of Hebron, and he came to Shechem.

15 And a certain man found him, and, behold, he was wandering in the field: and the man asked him, saying, What seekest you ?

16 And he said, I seek my brethren: tell me, I pray you, where they feed their flocks.

17 And the man said, They are departed hence; for I heard them say, Let us go to Dothan. And Joseph went after his brethren, and found them in Dothan.

18 And when they saw him afar off, even before he came near unto them, they conspired against him to slay him.

19 And they said one to another, Behold, this dreamer comes.

20 Come now therefore, and let us slay him, and cast him into some pit, and we will say, Some evil beast has devoured him: and we shall see what will become of his dreams.

21 And Reuben heard it, and he delivered him out of their hands; and said, Let us not kill him.

22 And Reuben said unto them, Shed no blood, but cast him into this pit that is in the wilderness, and lay no hand upon him; that he might rid him out of their hands, to deliver him to his father again.

23 And it came to pass, when Joseph was come unto his brethren, that they stript Joseph out of his coat, his coat of many colours that was on him;

24 And they took him, and cast him into a pit: and the pit was empty, there was no water in it.

25 And they sat down to eat bread: and they lifted up their eyes and looked, and, behold, a company of Ishmeelites came from Gilead with their camels bearing spicery and balm and myrrh, going to carry it down to Egypt.

26 And Judah said unto his brethren, What profit is it if we slay our brother, and conceal his blood?

27 Come, and let us sell him to the Ishmeelites, and let not our hand be upon him; for he is our brother and our flesh. And his brethren were content.

28 Then there passed by Midianites merchantmen; and they drew and lifted up Joseph out of the pit, and sold Joseph to the Ishmeelites for twenty pieces of silver: and they brought Joseph into Egypt.

29 And Reuben returned unto the pit; and, behold, Joseph was not in the pit; and he rent his clothes.

30 And he returned unto his brethren, and said, The child is not; and I, whither shall I go?

31 And they took Joseph's coat, and killed a kid of the goats, and dipped the coat in the blood;

32 And they sent the coat of many colours, and they brought it to their father; and said, This have we found: know now whether it be your son's coat or no.

33 And he knew it, and said, It is my son's coat; an evil beast has devoured him; Joseph is without doubt rent in pieces.

34 And Jacob rent his clothes, and put sackcloth upon his loins, and mourned for his son many days.

35 And all his sons and all his daughters rose up to comfort him; but he refused to be comforted; and he said, For I will go down into the grave unto my son mourning. Thus his father wept for him.

36 And the Midianites sold him into Egypt unto Potiphar, an officer of Pharaoh's, and captain of the guard.

CHAPTER 38

AND it came to pass at that time, that Judah went down from his brethren, and turned in to a certain Adullamite, whose name was Hirah.

2 And Judah saw there a daughter of a certain Canaanite, whose name was Shuah; and he took her, and went in unto her.

3 And she conceived, and bare a son; and he called his name Er.

4 And she conceived again, and bare a son; and she called his name Onan.

5 And she yet again conceived, and bare a son; and called his name Shelah: and he was at Chezib, when she bare him.

6 And Judah took a wife for Er his firstborn, whose name was Tamar.

7 And Er, Judah's firstborn, was wicked in the sight of the LORD; and the LORD slew him.

8 And Judah said unto Onan, Go in unto your brother's wife, and marry her, and raise up seed to your brother.

9 And Onan knew that the seed should not be his; and it came to pass, when he went in unto his brother's wife, that he spilled it on the ground, lest that he should give seed to his brother.

10 And the thing which he did displeased the LORD: wherefore he slew him also.

11 Then said Judah to Tamar his daughter in law, Remain a widow at your father's house, till Shelah my son be grown: for he said, Lest what if he die also, as his brethren did. And Tamar went and dwelt in her father's house.

12 And in process of time the daughter of Shuah Judah's wife died; and Judah was comforted, and went up unto his sheepshearers to Timnath, he and his friend Hirah the Adullamite.

13 And it was told Tamar, saying, Behold your father in law goeth up to Timnath to shear his sheep.

14 And she put her widow's garments off from her, and covered her with a vail, and wrapped herself, and sat in an open place, which is by the way to Timnath; for she saw that Shelah was grown, and she was not given unto him to wife.

15 When Judah saw her, he thought her to be an harlot; because she had covered her face.

16 And he turned unto her by the way, and said, Go to, I pray you, let me come in unto you; (for he knew not that she was his daughter in law.) And she said, What will you give me, that you mayest come in unto me?

17 And he said, I will send you a kid from the flock. And she said, Will you give me a pledge, till you send it?

18 And he said, What pledge shall I give you? And she said, Your signet, and your bracelets, and your staff that is in yours hand. And he gave it her, and came in unto her, and she conceived by him.

19 And she arose, and went away, and laid by her vail from her, and put on the garments of her widowhood.

20 And Judah sent the kid by the hand of his friend the Adullamite, to receive his pledge from the woman's hand: but he found her not.

21 Then he asked the men of that place, saying, Where is the harlot, that was openly by the way side? And they said, There was no harlot in this place.

22 And he returned to Judah, and said, I cannot find her; and also the men of the place said, that there was no harlot in this place.

23 And Judah said, Let her take it to her, lest we be shamed: behold, I sent this kid, and you have not found her.

24And it came to pass about three months after, that it was told Judah, saying, Tamar your daughter in law has played the harlot; and also, behold, she is with child by whoredom. And Judah said, Bring her forth, and let her be burnt.

25 When she was brought forth, she sent to her father in law, saying, By the man, whose these are, am I with child: and she said, Discern, I pray you, whose are these, the signet, and bracelets, and staff.

26 And Judah acknowledged them, and said, She has been more righteous than I; because that I gave her not to Shelah my son. And he knew her again no more.

27And it came to pass in the time of her travail, that, behold, twins were in her womb.

28 And it came to pass, when she travailed, that the one put out his hand: and the midwife took and bound upon his hand a scarlet thread, saying, This came out first.

29 And it came to pass, as he drew back his hand, that, behold, his brother came out: and she said, How have you broken forth? this breach be upon you: therefore his name was called Pharez.

30 And afterward came out his brother, that had the scarlet thread upon his hand: and his name was called Zarah.

CHAPTER 39

AND Joseph was brought down to Egypt; and Potiphar, an officer of Pharaoh, captain of the guard, an Egyptian, bought him of the hands of the Ishmeelites, which had brought him down thither.

2 And the LORD was with Joseph, and he was a prosperous man; and he was in the house of his master the Egyptian.

3 And his master saw that the LORD was with him, and that the LORD made all that he did to prosper in his hand.

4 And Joseph found grace in his sight, and he served him: and he made him overseer over his house, and all that he had he put into his hand.

5 And it came to pass from the time that he had made him overseer in his house, and over all that he had, that the LORD blessed the Egyptian's house for Joseph's sake; and the blessing of the LORD was upon all that he had in the house, and in the field.

6 And he left all that he had in Joseph's hand; and he knew not ought he had, save the bread which he did eat. And Joseph was a goodly person, and well favoured.

7And it came to pass after these things, that his master's wife cast her eyes upon Joseph; and she said, Lie with me.

8 But he refused, and said unto his master's wife, Behold, my master wotteth not what is with me in the house, and he has committed all that he has to my hand;

9 There is none greater in this house than I; neither has he kept back any thing from me but you, because you are his wife: how then can I do this great wickedness, and sin against God?

10 And it came to pass, as she spake to Joseph day by day, that he hearkened not unto her, to lie by her, or to be with her.

11 And it came to pass about this time, that Joseph went into the house to do his business; and there was none of the men of the house there within.

12 And she caught him by his garment, saying, Lie with me: and he left his garment in her hand, and fled, and got him out.

13 And it came to pass, when she saw that he had left his garment in her hand, and was fled forth,

14 That she called unto the men of her house, and spake unto them, saying, See, he has brought in an Hebrew unto us to mock us; he came in unto me to lie with me, and I cried with a loud voice:

15 And it came to pass, when he heard that I lifted up my voice and cried, that he left his garment with me, and fled, and got him out.

16 And she laid up his garment by her, until his lord came home.

17 And she spake unto him according to these words, saying, The Hebrew servant, which you have brought unto us, came in unto me to mock me:

18 And it came to pass, as I lifted up my voice and cried, that he left his garment with me, and fled out.

19 And it came to pass, when his master heard the words of his wife, which she spake unto him, saying, After this manner did your servant to me; that his wrath was kindled.

20 And Joseph's master took him, and put him into the prison, a place where the king's prisoners were bound: and he was there in the prison.

21But the LORD was with Joseph, and shewed him mercy, and gave him favour in the sight of the keeper of the prison.

22 And the keeper of the prison committed to Joseph's hand all the prisoners that were in the prison; and whatsoever they did there, he was the doer of it.

23 The keeper of the prison looked not to any thing that was under his hand; because the LORD was with him, and that which he did, the LORD made it to prosper.

CHAPTER 40

AND it came to pass after these things, that the butler of the king of Egypt and his baker had offended their lord the king of Egypt.

2 And Pharaoh was wroth against two of his officers, against the chief of the butlers, and against the chief of the bakers.

3 And he put them in ward in the house of the captain of the guard, into the prison, the place where Joseph was bound.

4 And the captain of the guard charged Joseph with them, and he served them: and they continued a season in ward.

5And they dreamed a dream both of them, each man his dream in one night, each man according to the interpretation of his dream, the butler and the baker of the king of Egypt, which were bound in the prison.

6 And Joseph came in unto them in the morning, and looked upon them, and, behold, they were sad.

7 And he asked Pharaoh's officers that were with him in the ward of his lord's house, saying, Wherefore look you so sadly to day?

8 And they said unto him, We have dreamed a dream, and there is no interpreter of it. And Joseph said unto them, Do not interpretations belong to God? tell me them, I pray you.

9 And the chief butler told his dream to Joseph, and said to him, In my dream, behold, a vine was before me;

10 And in the vine were three branches: and it was as though it budded, and her blossoms shot forth; and the clusters thereof brought forth ripe grapes:

11 And Pharaoh's cup was in my hand: and I took the grapes, and pressed them into Pharaoh's cup, and I gave the cup into Pharaoh's hand.

12 And Joseph said unto him, This is the interpretation of it: The three branches are three days:

13 Yet within three days shall Pharaoh lift up yours head, and restore you unto your place: and you shalt deliver Pharaoh's cup into his hand, after the former manner when you wast his butler.

14 But think on me when it shall be well with you, and shew kindness, I pray you, unto me, and make mention of me unto Pharaoh, and bring me out of this house:

15 For indeed I was stolen away out of the land of the Hebrews: and here also have I done nothing that they should put me into the dungeon.

16 When the chief baker saw that the interpretation was good, he said unto Joseph, I also was in my dream, and, behold, I had three white baskets on my head:

17 And in the uppermost basket there was of all manner of bakemeats for Pharaoh; and the birds did eat them out of the basket upon my head.

18 And Joseph answered and said, This is the interpretation thereof: The three baskets are three days:

19 Yet within three days shall Pharaoh lift up your head from off you, and shall hang you on a tree; and the birds shall eat your flesh from off you.

20And it came to pass the third day, which was Pharaoh's birthday, that he made a feast unto all his servants: and he lifted up the head of the chief butler and of the chief baker among his servants.

21 And he restored the chief butler unto his butlership again; and he gave the cup into Pharaoh's hand:

22 But he hanged the chief baker: as Joseph had interpreted to them.

23 Yet did not the chief butler remember Joseph, but forgat him.

CHAPTER 41

AND it came to pass at the end of two full years, that Pharaoh dreamed: and, behold, he stood by the river.

2 And, behold, there came up out of the river seven well favoured kine and fatfleshed; and they fed in a meadow.

3 And, behold, seven other kine came up after them out of the river, ill favoured and leanfleshed; and stood by the other kine upon the brink of the river.

4 And the ill favoured and leanfleshed kine did eat up the seven well favoured and fat kine. So Pharaoh awoke.

5 And he slept and dreamed the second time: and, behold, seven ears of corn came up upon one stalk, rank and good.

6 And, behold, seven thin ears and blasted with the east wind sprung up after them.

7 And the seven thin ears devoured the seven rank and full ears. And Pharaoh awoke, and, behold, it was a dream.

8 And it came to pass in the morning that his spirit was troubled; and he sent and called for all the magicians of Egypt, and all the wise men thereof: and Pharaoh told them his dream; but there was none that could interpret them unto Pharaoh.

9 Then spake the chief butler unto Pharaoh, saying, I do remember my faults this day:

10 Pharaoh was wroth with his servants, and put me in ward in the captain of the guard's house, both me and the chief baker:

11 And we dreamed a dream in one night, I and he; we dreamed each man according to the interpretation of his dream.

12 And there was there with us a young man, an Hebrew, servant to the captain of the guard; and we told him, and he interpreted to us our dreams; to each man according to his dream he did interpret.

13 And it came to pass, as he interpreted to us, so it was; me he restored unto my office, and him he hanged.

14 Then Pharaoh sent and called Joseph, and they brought him hastily out of the dungeon: and he shaved himself, and changed his raiment, and came in unto Pharaoh.

15 And Pharaoh said unto Joseph, I have dreamed a dream, and there is none that can interpret it: and I have heard say of you, that you can understand a dream to interpret it.

16 And Joseph answered Pharaoh, saying, It is not in me: God shall give Pharaoh an answer of peace.

17 And Pharaoh said unto Joseph, In my dream, behold, I stood upon the bank of the river:

18 And, behold, there came up out of the river seven kine, fatfleshed and well favoured; and they fed in a meadow:

19 And, behold, seven other kine came up after them, poor and very ill favoured and leanfleshed, such as I never saw in all the land of Egypt for badness:

20 And the lean and the ill favoured kine did eat up the first seven fat kine:

21 And when they had eaten them up, it could not be known that they had eaten them; but they were still ill favoured, as at the beginning. So I awoke.

22 And I saw in my dream, and, behold, seven ears came up in one stalk, full and good:

23 And, behold, seven ears, withered, thin, and blasted with the east wind, sprung up after them:

24 And the thin ears devoured the seven good ears: and I told this unto the magicians; but there was none that could declare it to me.

25 And Joseph said unto Pharaoh, The dream of Pharaoh is one: God has shewed Pharaoh what he is about to do.

26 The seven good kine are seven years; and the seven good ears are seven years: the dream is one.

27 And the seven thin and ill favoured kine that came up after them are seven years; and the seven empty ears blasted with the east wind shall be seven years of famine.

28 This is the thing which I have spoken unto Pharaoh: What God is about to do he sheweth unto Pharaoh.

29 Behold, there come seven years of great plenty throughout all the land of Egypt:

30 And there shall arise after them seven years of famine; and all the plenty shall be forgotten in the land of Egypt; and the famine shall consume the land;

31 And the plenty shall not be known in the land by reason of that famine following; for it shall be very grievous.

32 And for that the dream was doubled unto Pharaoh twice; it is because the thing is established by God, and God will shortly bring it to pass.

33 Now therefore let Pharaoh look out a man discreet and wise, and set him over the land of Egypt.

34 Let Pharaoh do this, and let him appoint officers over the land, and take up the fifth part of the land of Egypt in the seven plenteous years.

35 And let them gather all the food of those good years that come, and lay up corn under the hand of Pharaoh, and let them keep food in the cities.

36 And that food shall be for store to the land against the seven years of famine, which shall be in the land of Egypt; that the land perish not through the famine.

37 And the thing was good in the eyes of Pharaoh, and in the eyes of all his servants.

38 And Pharaoh said unto his servants, Can we find such a one as this is, a man in whom the Spirit of God is?

39 And Pharaoh said unto Joseph, Forasmuch as God has shewed you all this, there is none so discreet and wise as you are:

40 You shalt be over my house, and according unto your word shall all my people be ruled: only in the throne will I be greater than you .

41 And Pharaoh said unto Joseph, See, I have set you over all the land of Egypt.

42 And Pharaoh took off his ring from his hand, and put it upon Joseph's hand, and arrayed him in vestures of fine linen, and put a gold chain about his neck;

43 And he made him to ride in the second chariot which he had; and they cried before him, Bow the knee: and he made him ruler over all the land of Egypt.

44 And Pharaoh said unto Joseph, I am Pharaoh, and without you shall no man lift up his hand or foot in all the land of Egypt.

45 And Pharaoh called Joseph's name Zaphnath-paaneah; and he gave him to wife Asenath the daughter of Poti-pherah priest of On. And Joseph went out over all the land of Egypt.

46 And Joseph was thirty years old when he stood before Pharaoh king of Egypt. And Joseph went out from the presence of Pharaoh, and went throughout all the land of Egypt.

47 And in the seven plenteous years the earth brought forth by handfuls.

48 And he gathered up all the food of the seven years, which were in the land of Egypt, and laid up the food in the cities: the food of the field, which was round about every city, laid he up in the same.

49 And Joseph gathered corn as the sand of the sea, very much, until he left numbering; for it was without number.

50 And unto Joseph were born two sons before the years of famine came, which Asenath the daughter of Poti-pherah priest of On bare unto him.

51 And Joseph called the name of the firstborn Manasseh: For God, said he, has made me forget all my toil, and all my father's house.

52 And the name of the second called he Ephraim: For God has caused me to be fruitful in the land of my affliction.

53 And the seven years of plenteousness, that was in the land of Egypt, were ended.

54 And the seven years of dearth began to come, according as Joseph had said: and the dearth was in all lands; but in all the land of Egypt there was bread.

55 And when all the land of Egypt was famished, the people cried to Pharaoh for bread: and Pharaoh said unto all the Egyptians, Go unto Joseph; what he saith to you, do.

56 And the famine was over all the face of the earth: And Joseph opened all the storehouses, and sold unto the Egyptians; and the famine waxed sore in the land of Egypt.

57 And all countries came into Egypt to Joseph for to buy corn; because that the famine was so sore in all lands.

CHAPTER 42

NOW when Jacob saw that there was corn in Egypt, Jacob said unto his sons, Why do you look one upon another?

2 And he said, Behold, I have heard that there is corn in Egypt: get you down thither, and buy for us from thence; that we may live, and not die.

3 And Joseph's ten brethren went down to buy corn in Egypt.

4 But Benjamin, Joseph's brother, Jacob sent not with his brethren; for he said, Lest what if mischief befall him.

5 And the sons of Israel came to buy corn among those that came: for the famine was in the land of Canaan.

6 And Joseph was the governor over the land, and he it was that sold to all the people of the land: and Joseph's brethren came, and bowed down themselves before him with their faces to the earth.

7 And Joseph saw his brethren, and he knew them, but made himself strange unto them, and spake roughly unto them; and he said unto them, Whence come you ? And they said, From the land of Canaan to buy food.

8 And Joseph knew his brethren, but they knew not him.

9 And Joseph remembered the dreams which he dreamed of them, and said unto them, You are spies; to see the nakedness of the land you are come.

10 And they said unto him, Nay, my lord, but to buy food are your servants come.

11 We are all one man's sons; we are true men, your servants are no spies.

12 And he said unto them, Nay, but to see the nakedness of the land you are come.

13 And they said, Your servants are twelve brethren, the sons of one man in the land of Canaan; and, behold, the youngest is this day with our father, and one is not.

14 And Joseph said unto them, That is it that I spake unto you, saying, You are spies:

15 Hereby you shall be proved: By the life of Pharaoh you shall not go forth hence, except your youngest brother come hither.

16 Send one of you, and let him fetch your brother, and you shall be kept in prison, that your words may be proved, whether there be any truth in you: or else by the life of Pharaoh surely you are spies.

17 And he put them all together into ward three days.

18 And Joseph said unto them the third day, This do, and live; for I fear God:

19 If you be true men, let one of your brethren be bound in the house of your prison: go you , carry corn for the famine of your houses:

20 But bring your youngest brother unto me; so shall your words be verified, and you shall not die. And they did so.

21 And they said one to another, We are verily guilty concerning our brother, in that we saw the anguish of his soul, when he besought us, and we would not hear; therefore is this distress come upon us.

22 And Reuben answered them, saying, Spake I not unto you, saying, Do not sin against the child; and you would not hear? therefore, behold, also his blood is required.

23 And they knew not that Joseph understood them; for he spake unto them by an interpreter.

24 And he turned himself about from them, and wept; and returned to them again, and communed with them, and took from them Simeon, and bound him before their eyes.

25 Then Joseph commanded to fill their sacks with corn, and to restore every man's money into his sack, and to give them provision for the way: and thus did he unto them.

26 And they laded their asses with the corn, and departed thence.

27 And as one of them opened his sack to give his ass provender in the inn, he espied his money; for, behold, it was in his sack's mouth.

28 And he said unto his brethren, My money is restored; and, lo, it is even in my sack: and their heart failed them, and they were afraid, saying one to another, What is this that God has done unto us?

29 And they came unto Jacob their father unto the land of Canaan, and told him all that befell unto them; saying,

30 The man, who is the lord of the land, spake roughly to us, and took us for spies of the country.

31 And we said unto him, We are true men; we are no spies:

32 We be twelve brethren, sons of our father; one is not, and the youngest is this day with our father in the land of Canaan.

33 And the man, the lord of the country, said unto us, Hereby shall I know that you are true men; leave one of your brethren here with me, and take food for the famine of your households, and be gone:

34 And bring your youngest brother unto me: then shall I know that you are no spies, but that you are true men: so will I deliver you your brother, and you shall traffick in the land.

35 And it came to pass as they emptied their sacks, that, behold, every man's bundle of money was in his sack: and when both they and their father saw the bundles of money, they were afraid.

36 And Jacob their father said unto them, Me have you bereaved of my children: Joseph is not, and Simeon is not, and you will take Benjamin away: all these things are against me.

37 And Reuben spake unto his father, saying, Slay my two sons, if I bring him not to you: deliver him into my hand, and I will bring him to you again.

38 And he said, My son shall not go down with you; for his brother is dead, and he is left alone: if mischief befall him by the way in the which you go, then shall you bring down my gray hairs with sorrow to the grave.

CHAPTER 43

AND the famine was sore in the land.

2 And it came to pass, when they had eaten up the corn which they had brought out of Egypt, their father said unto them, Go again, buy us a little food.

3 And Judah spake unto him, saying, The man did solemnly protest unto us, saying, You shall not see my face, except your brother be with you.

4 If you will send our brother with us, we will go down and buy you food:

5 But if you will not send him, we will not go down: for the man said unto us, You shall not see my face, except your brother be with you.

6 And Israel said, Wherefore dealt you so ill with me, as to tell the man whether you had yet a brother?

7 And they said, The man asked us straitly of our state, and of our kindred, saying, Is your father yet alive? have you another brother? and we told him according to the tenor of these words: could we certainly know that he would say, Bring your brother down?

8 And Judah said unto Israel his father, Send the lad with me, and we will arise and go; that we may live, and not die, both we, and you , and also our little ones.

9 I will be surety for him; of my hand shalt you require him: if I bring him not unto you, and set him before you, then let me bear the blame for ever:

10 For except we had lingered, surely now we had returned this second time.

11 And their father Israel said unto them, If it must be so now, do this; take of the best fruits in the land in your vessels, and carry down the man a present, a little balm, and a little honey, spices, and myrrh, nuts, and almonds:

12 And take double money in your hand; and the money that was brought again in the mouth of your sacks, carry it again in your hand; what if it was an oversight:

13 Take also your brother, and arise, go again unto the man:

14 And God Almighty give you mercy before the man, that he may send away your other brother, and Benjamin. If I be bereaved of my children, I am bereaved.

15 And the men took that present, and they took double money in their hand, and Benjamin; and rose up, and went down to Egypt, and stood before Joseph.

16 And when Joseph saw Benjamin with them, he said to the ruler of his house, Bring these men home, and slay, and make ready; for these men shall dine with me at noon.

17 And the man did as Joseph bade; and the man brought the men into Joseph's house.

18 And the men were afraid, because they were brought into Joseph's house; and they said, Because of the money that was returned in our sacks at the first time are we brought in; that he may seek occasion against us, and fall upon us, and take us for bondmen, and our asses.

19 And they came near to the steward of Joseph's house, and they communed with him at the door of the house,

20 And said, O sir, we came indeed down at the first time to buy food:

21 And it came to pass, when we came to the inn, that we opened our sacks, and, behold, every man's money was in the mouth of his sack, our money in full weight: and we have brought it again in our hand.

22 And other money have we brought down in our hands to buy food: we cannot tell who put our money in our sacks.

23 And he said, Peace be to you, fear not: your God, and the God of your father, has given you treasure in your sacks: I had your money. And he brought Simeon out unto them.

24 And the man brought the men into Joseph's house, and gave them water, and they washed their feet; and he gave their asses provender.

25 And they made ready the present against Joseph came at noon: for they heard that they should eat bread there.

26 And when Joseph came home, they brought him the present which was in their hand into the house, and bowed themselves to him to the earth.

27 And he asked them of their welfare, and said, Is your father well, the old man of whom you spake? Is he yet alive?

28 And they answered, Your servant our father is in good health, he is yet alive. And they bowed down their heads, and made obeisance.

29 And he lifted up his eyes, and saw his brother Benjamin, his mother's son, and said, Is this your younger brother, of whom you spake unto me? And he said, God be gracious unto you, my son.

30 And Joseph made haste; for his bowels did yearn upon his brother: and he sought where to weep; and he entered into his chamber, and wept there.

31 And he washed his face, and went out, and refrained himself, and said, Set on bread.

32 And they set on for him by himself, and for them by themselves, and for the Egyptians, which did eat with him, by themselves: because the Egyptians might not eat bread with the Hebrews; for that is an abomination unto the Egyptians.

33 And they sat before him, the firstborn according to his birthright, and the youngest according to his youth: and the men marvelled one at another.

34 And he took and sent messes unto them from before him: but Benjamin's mess was five times so much as any of theirs. And they drank, and were merry with him.

CHAPTER 44

AND he commanded the steward of his house, saying, Fill the men's sacks with food, as much as they can carry, and put every man's money in his sack's mouth.

2 And put my cup, the silver cup, in the sack's mouth of the youngest, and his corn money. And he did according to the word that Joseph had spoken.

3 As soon as the morning was light, the men were sent away, they and their asses.

4 And when they were gone out of the city, and not yet far off, Joseph said unto his steward, Up, follow after the men; and when you dost overtake them, say unto them, Wherefore have you rewarded evil for good?

5 Is not this it in which my lord drinketh, and whereby indeed he divineth? you have done evil in so doing.

6 And he overtook them, and he spake unto them these same words.

7 And they said unto him, Wherefore saith my lord these words? God forbid that your servants should do according to this thing:

8 Behold, the money, which we found in our sacks' mouths, we brought again unto you out of the land of Canaan: how then should we steal out of your lord's house silver or gold?

9 With whomsoever of your servants it be found, both let him die, and we also will be my lord's bondmen.

10 And he said, Now also let it be according unto your words: he with whom it is found shall be my servant; and you shall be blameless.

11 Then they speedily took down every man his sack to the ground, and opened every man his sack.

12 And he searched, and began at the eldest, and left at the youngest: and the cup was found in Benjamin's sack.

13 Then they rent their clothes, and laded every man his ass, and returned to the city.

14 And Judah and his brethren came to Joseph's house; for he was yet there: and they fell before him on the ground.

15 And Joseph said unto them, What deed is this that you have done? wot you not that such a man as I can certainly divine?

16 And Judah said, What shall we say unto my lord? what shall we speak? or how shall we clear ourselves? God has found out the iniquity of your servants: behold, we are my lord's servants, both we, and he also with whom the cup is found.

17 And he said, God forbid that I should do so: but the man in whose hand the cup is found, he shall be my servant; and as for you, get you up in peace unto your father.

18 Then Judah came near unto him, and said, Oh my lord, let your servant, I pray you, speak a word in my lord's ears, and let not yours anger burn against your servant: for you are even as Pharaoh.

19 My lord asked his servants, saying, Have you a father, or a brother?

20 And we said unto my lord, We have a father, an old man, and a child of his old age, a little one; and his brother is dead, and he alone is left of his mother, and his father loveth him.

21 And you saidst unto your servants, Bring him down unto me, that I may set my eyes upon him.

22 And we said unto my lord, The lad cannot leave his father: for if he should leave his father, his father would die.

23 And you saidst unto your servants, Except your youngest brother come down with you, you shall see my face no more.

24 And it came to pass when we came up unto your servant my father, we told him the words of my lord.

25 And our father said, Go again, and buy us a little food.

26 And we said, We cannot go down: if our youngest brother be with us, then will we go down: for we may not see the man's face, except our youngest brother be with us.

27 And your servant my father said unto us, You know that my wife bare me two sons:

28 And the one went out from me, and I said, Surely he is torn in pieces; and I saw him not since:

29 And if you take this also from me, and mischief befall him, you shall bring down my gray hairs with sorrow to the grave.

30 Now therefore when I come to your servant my father, and the lad be not with us; seeing that his life is bound up in the lad's life;

31 It shall come to pass, when he seeth that the lad is not with us, that he will die: and your servants shall bring down the gray hairs of your servant our father with sorrow to the grave.

32 For your servant became surety for the lad unto my father, saying, If I bring him not unto you, then I shall bear the blame to my father for ever.

33 Now therefore, I pray you, let your servant abide instead of the lad a bondman to my lord; and let the lad go up with his brethren.

34 For how shall I go up to my father, and the lad be not with me? lest what if I see the evil that shall come on my father.

CHAPTER 45

THEN Joseph could not refrain himself before all them that stood by him; and he cried, Cause every man to go out from me. And there stood no man with him, while Joseph made himself known unto his brethren.

2 And he wept aloud: and the Egyptians and the house of Pharaoh heard.

3 And Joseph said unto his brethren, I am Joseph; doth my father yet live? And his brethren could not answer him; for they were troubled at his presence.

4 And Joseph said unto his brethren, Come near to me, I pray you. And they came near. And he said, I am Joseph your brother, whom you sold into Egypt.

5 Now therefore be not grieved, nor angry with yourselves, that you sold me hither: for God did send me before you to preserve life.

6 For these two years has the famine been in the land: and yet there are five years, in the which there shall neither be earing nor harvest.

7 And God sent me before you to preserve you a posterity in the earth, and to save your lives by a great deliverance.

8 So now it was not you that sent me hither, but God: and he has made me a father to Pharaoh, and lord of all his house, and a ruler throughout all the land of Egypt.

9 Haste you , and go up to my father, and say unto him, Thus saith your son Joseph, God has made me lord of all Egypt: come down unto me, tarry not:

10 And you shalt dwell in the land of Goshen, and you shalt be near unto me, you , and your children, and your children's children, and your flocks, and your herds, and all that you have:

11 And there will I nourish you; for yet there are five years of famine; lest you , and your household, and all that you have, come to poverty.

12 And, behold, your eyes see, and the eyes of my brother Benjamin, that it is my mouth that speaketh unto you.

13 And you shall tell my father of all my glory in Egypt, and of all that you have seen; and you shall haste and bring down my father hither.

14 And he fell upon his brother Benjamin's neck, and wept; and Benjamin wept upon his neck.

15 Moreover he kissed all his brethren, and wept upon them: and after that his brethren talked with him.

16 And the fame thereof was heard in Pharaoh's house, saying, Joseph's brethren are come: and it pleased Pharaoh well, and his servants.

17 And Pharaoh said unto Joseph, Say unto your brethren, This do you ; lade your beasts, and go, get you unto the land of Canaan;

18 And take your father and your households, and come unto me: and I will give you the good of the land of Egypt, and you shall eat the fat of the land.

19 Now you are commanded, this do you ; take you wagons out of the land of Egypt for your little ones, and for your wives, and bring your father, and come.

20 Also regard not your stuff; for the good of all the land of Egypt is yours.

21 And the children of Israel did so: and Joseph gave them wagons, according to the commandment of Pharaoh, and gave them provision for the way.

22 To all of them he gave each man changes of raiment; but to Benjamin he gave three hundred pieces of silver, and five changes of raiment.

23 And to his father he sent after this manner; ten asses laden with the good things of Egypt, and ten she asses laden with corn and bread and meat for his father by the way.

24 So he sent his brethren away, and they departed: and he said unto them, See that you fall not out by the way.

25 And they went up out of Egypt, and came into the land of Canaan unto Jacob their father,

26 And told him, saying, Joseph is yet alive, and he is governor over all the land of Egypt. And Jacob's heart fainted, for he believed them not.

27 And they told him all the words of Joseph, which he had said unto them: and when he saw the wagons which Joseph had sent to carry him, the spirit of Jacob their father revived:

28 And Israel said, It is enough; Joseph my son is yet alive: I will go and see him before I die.

CHAPTER 46

AND Israel took his journey with all that he had, and came to Beer-sheba, and offered sacrifices unto the God of his father Isaac.

2 And God spake unto Israel in the visions of the night, and said, Jacob, Jacob. And he said, Here am I.

3 And he said, I am God, the God of your father: fear not to go down into Egypt; for I will there make of you a great nation:

4 I will go down with you into Egypt; and I will also surely bring you up again: and Joseph shall put his hand upon yours eyes.

5 And Jacob rose up from Beer-sheba: and the sons of Israel carried Jacob their father, and their little ones, and their wives, in the wagons which Pharaoh had sent to carry him.

6 And they took their cattle, and their goods, which they had gotten in the land of Canaan, and came into Egypt, Jacob, and all his seed with him:

7 His sons, and his sons' sons with him, his daughters, and his sons' daughters, and all his seed brought he with him into Egypt.

8 And these are the names of the children of Israel, which came into Egypt, Jacob and his sons: Reuben, Jacob's firstborn.

9 And the sons of Reuben; Hanoch, and Phallu, and Hezron, and Carmi.

10 And the sons of Simeon; Jemuel, and Jamin, and Ohad, and Jachin, and Zohar, and Shaul the son of a Canaanitish woman.

11 And the sons of Levi; Gershon, Kohath, and Merari.

12And the sons of Judah; Er, and Onan, and Shelah, and Pharez, and Zerah: but Er and Onan died in the land of Canaan. And the sons of Pharez were Hezron and Hamul.

13And the sons of Issachar; Tola, and Phuvah, and Job, and Shimron.

14And the sons of Zebulun; Sered, and Elon, and Jahleel.

15 These be the sons of Leah, which she bare unto Jacob in Padan-aram, with his daughter Dinah: all the souls of his sons and his daughters were thirty and three.

16And the sons of Gad; Ziphion, and Haggi, Shuni, and Ezbon, Eri, and Arodi, and Areli.

17And the sons of Asher; Jimnah, and Ishuah, and Isui, and Beriah, and Serah their sister: and the sons of Beriah; Heber, and Malchiel.

18 These are the sons of Zilpah, whom Laban gave to Leah his daughter, and these she bare unto Jacob, even sixteen souls.

19 The sons of Rachel Jacob's wife; Joseph, and Benjamin.

20And unto Joseph in the land of Egypt were born Manasseh and Ephraim, which Asenath the daughter of Poti-pherah priest of On bare unto him.

21And the sons of Benjamin were Belah, and Becher, and Ashbel, Gera, and Naaman, Ehi, and Rosh, Muppim, and Huppim, and Ard.

22 These are the sons of Rachel, which were born to Jacob: all the souls were fourteen.

23And the sons of Dan; Hushim.

24And the sons of Naphtali; Jahzeel, and Guni, and Jezer, and Shillem.

25 These are the sons of Bilhah, which Laban gave unto Rachel his daughter, and she bare these unto Jacob: all the souls were seven.

26 All the souls that came with Jacob into Egypt, which came out of his loins, besides Jacob's sons' wives, all the souls were threescore and six;

27 And the sons of Joseph, which were born him in Egypt, were two souls: all the souls of the house of Jacob, which came into Egypt, were threescore and ten.

28And he sent Judah before him unto Joseph, to direct his face unto Goshen; and they came into the land of Goshen.

29 And Joseph made ready his chariot, and went up to meet Israel his father, to Goshen, and presented himself unto him; and he fell on his neck, and wept on his neck a good while.

30 And Israel said unto Joseph, Now let me die, since I have seen your face, because you are yet alive.

31 And Joseph said unto his brethren, and unto his father's house, I will go up, and shew Pharaoh, and say unto him, My brethren, and my father's house, which were in the land of Canaan, are come unto me;

32 And the men are shepherds, for their trade has been to feed cattle; and they have brought their flocks, and their herds, and all that they have.

33 And it shall come to pass, when Pharaoh shall call you, and shall say, What is your occupation?

34 That you shall say, Your servants' trade has been about cattle from our youth even until now, both we, and also our fathers: that you may dwell in the land of Goshen; for every shepherd is an abomination unto the Egyptians.

CHAPTER 47

THEN Joseph came and told Pharaoh, and said, My father and my brethren, and their flocks, and their herds, and all that they have, are come out of the land of Canaan; and, behold, they are in the land of Goshen.

2 And he took some of his brethren, even five men, and presented them unto Pharaoh.

3 And Pharaoh said unto his brethren, What is your occupation? And they said unto Pharaoh, Your servants are shepherds, both we, and also our fathers.

4 They said moreover unto Pharaoh, For to sojourn in the land are we come; for your servants have no pasture for their flocks; for the famine is sore in the land of Canaan: now therefore, we pray you, let your servants dwell in the land of Goshen.

5 And Pharaoh spake unto Joseph, saying, Your father and your brethren are come unto you:

6 The land of Egypt is before you; in the best of the land make your father and brethren to dwell; in the land of Goshen let them dwell: and if you knowest any men of activity among them, then make them rulers over my cattle.

7 And Joseph brought in Jacob his father, and set him before Pharaoh: and Jacob blessed Pharaoh.

8 And Pharaoh said unto Jacob, How old are you ?

9 And Jacob said unto Pharaoh, The days of the years of my pilgrimage are an hundred and thirty years: few and evil have the days of the years of my life been, and have not attained unto the days of the years of the life of my fathers in the days of their pilgrimage.

10 And Jacob blessed Pharaoh, and went out from before Pharaoh.

11And Joseph placed his father and his brethren, and gave them a possession in the land of Egypt, in the best of the land, in the land of Rameses, as Pharaoh had commanded.

12 And Joseph nourished his father, and his brethren, and all his father's household, with bread, according to their families.

13And there was no bread in all the land; for the famine was very sore, so that the land of Egypt and all the land of Canaan fainted by reason of the famine.

14 And Joseph gathered up all the money that was found in the land of Egypt, and in the land of Canaan, for the corn which they bought: and Joseph brought the money into Pharaoh's house.

15 And when money failed in the land of Egypt, and in the land of Canaan, all the Egyptians came unto Joseph, and said, Give us bread: for why should we die in your presence? for the money faileth.

16 And Joseph said, Give your cattle; and I will give you for your cattle, if money fail.

17 And they brought their cattle unto Joseph: and Joseph gave them bread in exchange for horses, and for the flocks, and for the cattle of the herds, and for the asses: and he fed them with bread for all their cattle for that year.

18 When that year was ended, they came unto him the second year, and said unto him, We will not hide it from my lord, how that our money is spent; my lord also has our herds of cattle; there is not ought left in the sight of my lord, but our bodies, and our lands:

19 Wherefore shall we die before yours eyes, both we and our land? buy us and our land for bread, and we and our land will be servants unto Pharaoh: and give us seed, that we may live, and not die, that the land be not desolate.

20 And Joseph bought all the land of Egypt for Pharaoh; for the Egyptians sold every man his field, because the famine prevailed over them: so the land became Pharaoh's.

21 And as for the people, he removed them to cities from one end of the borders of Egypt even to the other end thereof.

22 Only the land of the priests bought he not; for the priests had a portion assigned them of Pharaoh, and did eat their portion which Pharaoh gave them: wherefore they sold not their lands.

23 Then Joseph said unto the people, Behold, I have bought you this day and your land for Pharaoh: lo, here is seed for you, and you shall sow the land.

24 And it shall come to pass in the increase, that you shall give the fifth part unto Pharaoh, and four parts shall be your own, for seed of the field, and for your food, and for them of your households, and for food for your little ones.

25 And they said, You have saved our lives: let us find grace in the sight of my lord, and we will be Pharaoh's servants.

26 And Joseph made it a law over the land of Egypt unto this day, that Pharaoh should have the fifth part; except the land of the priests only, which became not Pharaoh's.

27And Israel dwelt in the land of Egypt, in the country of Goshen; and they had possessions therein, and grew, and multiplied exceedingly.

28 And Jacob lived in the land of Egypt seventeen years: so the whole age of Jacob was an hundred forty and seven years.

29 And the time drew nigh that Israel must die: and he called his son Joseph, and said unto him, If now I have found grace in your sight, put, I pray you, your hand under my thigh, and deal kindly and truly with me; bury me not, I pray you, in Egypt:

30 But I will lie with my fathers, and you shalt carry me out of Egypt, and bury me in their buryingplace. And he said, I will do as you have said.

31 And he said, Swear unto me. And he sware unto him. And Israel bowed himself upon the bed's head.

CHAPTER 48

AND it came to pass after these things, that one told Joseph, Behold, your father is sick: and he took with him his two sons, Manasseh and Ephraim.

2 And one told Jacob, and said, Behold, your son Joseph comes unto you: and Israel strengthened himself, and sat upon the bed.

3 And Jacob said unto Joseph, God Almighty appeared unto me at Luz in the land of Canaan, and blessed me,

4 And said unto me, Behold, I will make you fruitful, and multiply you, and I will make of you a multitude of people; and will give this land to your seed after you for an everlasting possession.

5And now your two sons, Ephraim and Manasseh, which were born unto you in the land of Egypt before I came unto you into Egypt, are my; as Reuben and Simeon, they shall be my.

6 And your issue, which you begettest after them, shall be yours, and shall be called after the name of their brethren in their inheritance.

7 And as for me, when I came from Padan, Rachel died by me in the land of Canaan in the way, when yet there was but a little way to come unto Ephrath: and I buried her there in the way of Ephrath; the same is Beth-lehem.

8 And Israel beheld Joseph's sons, and said, Who are these?

9 And Joseph said unto his father, They are my sons, whom God has given me in this place. And he said, Bring them, I pray you, unto me, and I will bless them.

10 Now the eyes of Israel were dim for age, so that he could not see. And he brought them near unto him; and he kissed them, and embraced them.

11 And Israel said unto Joseph, I had not thought to see your face: and, lo, God has shewed me also your seed.

12 And Joseph brought them out from between his knees, and he bowed himself with his face to the earth.

13 And Joseph took them both, Ephraim in his right hand toward Israel's left hand, and Manasseh in his left hand toward Israel's right hand, and brought them near unto him.

14 And Israel stretched out his right hand, and laid it upon Ephraim's head, who was the younger, and his left hand upon Manasseh's head, guiding his hands wittingly; for Manasseh was the firstborn.

15 And he blessed Joseph, and said, God, before whom my fathers Abraham and Isaac did walk, the God which fed me all my life long unto this day,

16 The Angel which redeemed me from all evil, bless the lads; and let my name be named on them, and the name of my fathers Abraham and Isaac; and let them grow into a multitude in the midst of the earth.

17 And when Joseph saw that his father laid his right hand upon the head of Ephraim, it displeased him: and he held up his father's hand, to remove it from Ephraim's head unto Manasseh's head.

18 And Joseph said unto his father, Not so, my father: for this is the firstborn; put your right hand upon his head.

19 And his father refused, and said, I know it, my son, I know it: he also shall become a people, and he also shall be great: but truly his younger brother shall be greater than he, and his seed shall become a multitude of nations.

20 And he blessed them that day, saying, In you shall Israel bless, saying, God make you as Ephraim and as Manasseh: and he set Ephraim before Manasseh.

21 And Israel said unto Joseph, Behold, I die: but God shall be with you, and bring you again unto the land of your fathers.

22 Moreover I have given to you one portion above your brethren, which I took out of the hand of the Amorite with my sword and with my bow.

CHAPTER 49

AND Jacob called unto his sons, and said, Gather yourselves together, that I may tell you that which shall befall you in the last days.

2 Gather yourselves together, and hear, you sons of Jacob; and hearken unto Israel your father.

3 Reuben, you are my firstborn, my might, and the beginning of my strength, the excellency of dignity, and the excellency of power:

4 Unstable as water, you shalt not excel; because you wentest up to your father's bed; then defiledst you it: he went up to my couch.

5 Simeon and Levi are brethren; instruments of cruelty are in their habitations.

6 O my soul, come not you into their secret; unto their assembly, my honour, be not you united: for in their anger they slew a man, and in their selfwill they digged down a wall.

7 Cursed be their anger, for it was fierce; and their wrath, for it was cruel: I will divide them in Jacob, and scatter them in Israel.

8 Judah, you are he whom your brethren shall praise: your hand shall be in the neck of yours enemies; your father's children shall bow down before you.

9 Judah is a lion's whelp: from the prey, my son, you are gone up: he stooped down, he couched as a lion, and as an old lion; who shall rouse him up?

10 The sceptre shall not depart from Judah, nor a lawgiver from between his feet, until Shiloh come; and unto him shall the gathering of the people be.

11 Binding his foal unto the vine, and his ass's colt unto the choice vine; he washed his garments in wine, and his clothes in the blood of grapes:

12 His eyes shall be red with wine, and his teeth white with milk.

13 Zebulun shall dwell at the haven of the sea; and he shall be for an haven of ships; and his border shall be unto Zidon.

14 Issachar is a strong ass couching down between two burdens:

15 And he saw that rest was good, and the land that it was pleasant; and bowed his shoulder to bear, and became a servant unto tribute.

16 Dan shall judge his people, as one of the tribes of Israel.

17 Dan shall be a serpent by the way, an adder in the path, that biteth the horse heels, so that his rider shall fall backward.

18 I have waited for your salvation, O LORD.

19 Gad, a troop shall overcome him: but he shall overcome at the last.

20 Out of Asher his bread shall be fat, and he shall yield royal dainties.

21 Naphtali is a hind let loose: he giveth goodly words.

22 Joseph is a fruitful bough, even a fruitful bough by a well; whose branches run over the wall:

23 The archers have sorely grieved him, and shot at him, and hated him:

24 But his bow abode in strength, and the arms of his hands were made strong by the hands of the mighty God of Jacob; (from thence is the shepherd, the stone of Israel:)

25 Even by the God of your father, who shall help you; and by the Almighty, who shall bless you with blessings of heaven above, blessings of the deep that lies under, blessings of the breasts, and of the womb:

26 The blessings of your father have prevailed above the blessings of my progenitors unto the utmost bound of the everlasting hills: they shall be on the head of Joseph, and on the crown of the head of him that was separate from his brethren.

27 Benjamin shall ravin as a wolf: in the morning he shall devour the prey, and at night he shall divide the spoil.

28 All these are the twelve tribes of Israel: and this is it that their father spake unto them, and blessed them; every one according to his blessing he blessed them.

29 And he charged them, and said unto them, I am to be gathered unto my people: bury me with my fathers in the cave that is in the field of Ephron the Hittite,

30 In the cave that is in the field of Machpelah, which is before Mamre, in the land of Canaan, which Abraham bought with the field of Ephron the Hittite for a possession of a buryingplace.

31 There they buried Abraham and Sarah his wife; there they buried Isaac and Rebekah his wife; and there I buried Leah.

32 The purchase of the field and of the cave that is therein was from the children of Heth.

33 And when Jacob had made an end of commanding his sons, he gathered up his feet into the bed, and yielded up the ghost, and was gathered unto his people.

CHAPTER 50

AND Joseph fell upon his father's face, and wept upon him, and kissed him.

2 And Joseph commanded his servants the physicians to embalm his father: and the physicians embalmed Israel.

3 And forty days were fulfilled for him; for so are fulfilled the days of those which are embalmed: and the Egyptians mourned for him threescore and ten days.

4 And when the days of his mourning were past, Joseph spake unto the house of Pharaoh, saying, If now I have found grace in your eyes, speak, I pray you, in the ears of Pharaoh, saying,

5 My father made me swear, saying, Lo, I die: in my grave which I have digged for me in the land of Canaan, there shalt you bury me. Now therefore let me go up, I pray you, and bury my father, and I will come again.

6 And Pharaoh said, Go up, and bury your father, according as he made you swear.

7 And Joseph went up to bury his father: and with him went up all the servants of Pharaoh, the elders of his house, and all the elders of the land of Egypt,

8 And all the house of Joseph, and his brethren, and his father's house: only their little ones, and their flocks, and their herds, they left in the land of Goshen.

9 And there went up with him both chariots and horsemen: and it was a very great company.

10 And they came to the threshingfloor of Atad, which is beyond Jordan, and there they mourned with a great and very sore lamentation: and he made a mourning for his father seven days.

11 And when the inhabitants of the land, the Canaanites, saw the mourning in the floor of Atad, they said, This is a grievous mourning to the Egyptians: wherefore the name of it was called Abel-mizraim, which is beyond Jordan.

12 And his sons did unto him according as he commanded them:

13 For his sons carried him into the land of Canaan, and buried him in the cave of the field of Machpelah, which Abraham bought with the field for a possession of a buryingplace of Ephron the Hittite, before Mamre.

14 And Joseph returned into Egypt, he, and his brethren, and all that went up with him to bury his father, after he had buried his father.

15 And when Joseph's brethren saw that their father was dead, they said, Joseph will what if hate us, and will certainly requite us all the evil which we did unto him.

16 And they sent a messenger unto Joseph, saying, Your father did command before he died, saying,

17 So shall you say unto Joseph, Forgive, I pray you now, the trespass of your brethren, and their sin; for they did unto you evil: and now, we pray you, forgive the trespass of the servants of the God of your father. And Joseph wept when they spake unto him.

18 And his brethren also went and fell down before his face; and they said, Behold, we be your servants.

19 And Joseph said unto them, Fear not: for am I in the place of God?

20 But as for you, you thought evil against me; but God meant it unto good, to bring to pass, as it is this day, to save much people alive.

21 Now therefore fear you not: I will nourish you, and your little ones. And he comforted them, and spake kindly unto them.

22 And Joseph dwelt in Egypt, he, and his father's house: and Joseph lived an hundred and ten years.

23 And Joseph saw Ephraim's children of the third generation: the children also of Machir the son of Manasseh were brought up upon Joseph's knees.

24 And Joseph said unto his brethren, I die: and God will surely visit you, and bring you out of this land unto the land which he sware to Abraham, to Isaac, and to Jacob.

25 And Joseph took an oath of the children of Israel, saying, God will surely visit you, and you shall carry up my bones from hence.

26 So Joseph died, being an hundred and ten years old: and they embalmed him, and he was put in a coffin in Egypt.

THE SECOND BOOK OF MOSES,
CALLED
EXODUS.

CHAPTER 1

NOW these are the names of the children of Israel, which came into Egypt; every man and his household came with Jacob.

2 Reuben, Simeon, Levi, and Judah,

3 Issachar, Zebulun, and Benjamin,

4 Dan, and Naphtali, Gad, and Asher.

5 And all the souls that came out of the loins of Jacob were seventy souls: for Joseph was in Egypt already.

6 And Joseph died, and all his brethren, and all that generation.

7And the children of Israel were fruitful, and increased abundantly, and multiplied, and waxed exceeding mighty; and the land was filled with them.

8 Now there arose up a new king over Egypt, which knew not Joseph.

9 And he said unto his people, Behold, the people of the children of Israel are more and mightier than we:

10 Come on, let us deal wisely with them; lest they multiply, and it come to pass, that, when there falleth out any war, they join also unto our enemies, and fight against us, and so get them up out of the land.

11 Therefore they did set over them taskmasters to afflict them with their burdens. And they built for Pharaoh treasure cities, Pithom and Raamses.

12 But the more they afflicted them, the more they multiplied and grew. And they were grieved because of the children of Israel.

13 And the Egyptians made the children of Israel to serve with rigour:

14 And they made their lives bitter with hard bondage, in morter, and in brick, and in all manner of service in the field: all their service, wherein they made them serve, was with rigour.

15And the king of Egypt spake to the Hebrew midwives, of which the name of the one was Shiphrah, and the name of the other Puah:

16 And he said, When you do the office of a midwife to the Hebrew women, and see them upon the stools; if it be a son, then you shall kill him: but if it be a daughter, then she shall live.

17 But the midwives feared God, and did not as the king of Egypt commanded them, but saved the men children alive.

18 And the king of Egypt called for the midwives, and said unto them, Why have you done this thing, and have saved the men children alive?

19 And the midwives said unto Pharaoh, Because the Hebrew women are not as the Egyptian women; for they are lively, and are delivered ere the midwives come in unto them.

20 Therefore God dealt well with the midwives: and the people multiplied, and waxed very mighty.

21 And it came to pass, because the midwives feared God, that he made them houses.

22 And Pharaoh charged all his people, saying, Every son that is born you shall cast into the river, and every daughter you shall save alive.

CHAPTER 2

AND there went a man of the house of Levi, and took to wife a daughter of Levi.

2 And the woman conceived, and bare a son: and when she saw him that he was a goodly child, she hid him three months.

3 And when she could not longer hide him, she took for him an ark of bulrushes, and daubed it with slime and with pitch, and put the child therein; and she laid it in the flags by the river's brink.

4 And his sister stood afar off, to wit what would be done to him.

5And the daughter of Pharaoh came down to wash herself at the river; and her maidens walked along by the river's side; and when she saw the ark among the flags, she sent her maid to fetch it.

6 And when she had opened it, she saw the child: and, behold, the babe wept. And she had compassion on him, and said, This is one of the Hebrews' children.

7 Then said his sister to Pharaoh's daughter, Shall I go and call to you a nurse of the Hebrew women, that she may nurse the child for you?

8 And Pharaoh's daughter said to her, Go. And the maid went and called the child's mother.

9 And Pharaoh's daughter said unto her, Take this child away, and nurse it for me, and I will give you your wages. And the woman took the child, and nursed it.

10 And the child grew, and she brought him unto Pharaoh's daughter, and he became her son. And she called his name Moses: and she said, Because I drew him out of the water.

11And it came to pass in those days, when Moses was grown, that he went out unto his brethren, and looked on their burdens: and he spied an Egyptian striking an Hebrew, one of his brethren.

12 And he looked this way and that way, and when he saw that there was no man, he slew the Egyptian, and hid him in the sand.

13 And when he went out the second day, behold, two men of the Hebrews strove together: and he said to him that did the wrong, Wherefore smitest you your fellow?

14 And he said, Who made you a prince and a judge over us? intendest you to kill me, as you killedst the Egyptian? And Moses feared, and said, Surely this thing is known.

15 Now when Pharaoh heard this thing, he sought to slay Moses. But Moses fled from the face of Pharaoh, and dwelt in the land of Midian: and he sat down by a well.

16 Now the priest of Midian had seven daughters: and they came and drew water, and filled the troughs to water their father's flock.

17 And the shepherds came and drove them away: but Moses stood up and helped them, and watered their flock.

18 And when they came to Reuel their father, he said, How is it that you are come so soon to day?

19 And they said, An Egyptian delivered us out of the hand of the shepherds, and also drew water enough for us, and watered the flock.

20 And he said unto his daughters, And where is he? why is it that you have left the man? call him, that he may eat bread.

21 And Moses was content to dwell with the man: and he gave Moses Zipporah his daughter.

22 And she bare him a son, and he called his name Gershom: for he said, I have been a stranger in a strange land.

23And it came to pass in process of time, that the king of Egypt died: and the children of Israel sighed by reason of the bondage, and they cried, and their cry came up unto God by reason of the bondage.

24 And God heard their groaning, and God remembered his covenant with Abraham, with Isaac, and with Jacob.

25 And God looked upon the children of Israel, and God had respect unto them.

CHAPTER 3

NOW Moses kept the flock of Jethro his father in law, the priest of Midian: and he led the flock to the backside of the desert, and came to the mountain of God, even to Horeb.

2 And the angel of the LORD appeared unto him in a flame of fire out of the midst of a bush: and he looked, and, behold, the bush burned with fire, and the bush was not consumed.

3 And Moses said, I will now turn aside, and see this great sight, why the bush is not burnt.

4 And when the LORD saw that he turned aside to see, God called unto him out of the midst of the bush, and said, Moses, Moses. And he said, Here am I.

5 And he said, Draw not nigh hither: put off your shoes from off your feet, for the place whereon you standest is holy ground.

6 Moreover he said, I am the God of your father, the God of Abraham, the God of Isaac, and the God of Jacob. And Moses hid his face; for he was afraid to look upon God.

7And the LORD said, I have surely seen the affliction of my people which are in Egypt, and have heard their cry by reason of their taskmasters; for I know their sorrows;

8 And I am come down to deliver them out of the hand of the Egyptians, and to bring them up out of that land unto a good land and a large, unto a land flowing with milk and honey; unto the place of the Canaanites, and the Hittites, and the Amorites, and the Perizzites, and the Hivites, and the Jebusites.

9 Now therefore, behold, the cry of the children of Israel is come unto me: and I have also seen the oppression wherewith the Egyptians oppress them.

10 Come now therefore, and I will send you unto Pharaoh, that you mayest bring forth my people the children of Israel out of Egypt.

11And Moses said unto God, Who am I, that I should go unto Pharaoh, and that I should bring forth the children of Israel out of Egypt?

12 And he said, Certainly I will be with you; and this shall be a token unto you, that I have sent you: When you have brought forth the people out of Egypt, you shall serve God upon this mountain.

13 And Moses said unto God, Behold, when I come unto the children of Israel, and shall say unto them, The God of your fathers has sent me unto you; and they shall say to me, What is his name? what shall I say unto them?

14 And God said unto Moses, I AM THAT I AM: and he said, Thus shalt you say unto the children of Israel, I AM has sent me unto you.

15 And God said moreover unto Moses, Thus shalt you say unto the children of Israel, The LORD God of your fathers, the God of Abraham, the God of Isaac, and the God of Jacob, has sent me unto you: this is my name for ever, and this is my memorial unto all generations.

16 Go, and gather the elders of Israel together, and say unto them, The LORD God of your fathers, the God of Abraham, of Isaac, and of Jacob, appeared unto me, saying, I have surely visited you, and seen that which is done to you in Egypt:

17 And I have said, I will bring you up out of the affliction of Egypt unto the land of the Canaanites, and the Hittites, and the Amorites, and the Perizzites, and the Hivites, and the Jebusites, unto a land flowing with milk and honey.

18 And they shall hearken to your voice: and you shalt come, you and the elders of Israel, unto the king of Egypt, and you shall say unto him, The LORD God of the Hebrews has met with us: and now let us go, we beseech you, three days' journey into the wilderness, that we may sacrifice to the LORD our God.

19And I am sure that the king of Egypt will not let you go, no, not by a mighty hand.

20 And I will stretch out my hand, and strike Egypt with all my wonders which I will do in the midst thereof: and after that he will let you go.

21 And I will give this people favour in the sight of the Egyptians: and it shall come to pass, that, when you go, you shall not go empty:

22 But every woman shall borrow of her neighbour, and of her that sojourneth in her house, jewels of silver, and jewels of gold, and raiment: and you shall put them upon your sons, and upon your daughters; and you shall spoil the Egyptians.

CHAPTER 4

AND Moses answered and said, But, behold, they will not believe me, nor hearken unto my voice: for they will say, The LORD has not appeared unto you.

2 And the LORD said unto him, What is that in yours hand? And he said, A rod.

3 And he said, Cast it on the ground. And he cast it on the ground, and it became a serpent; and Moses fled from before it.

4 And the LORD said unto Moses, Put forth yours hand, and take it by the tail. And he put forth his hand, and caught it, and it became a rod in his hand:

5 That they may believe that the LORD God of their fathers, the God of Abraham, the God of Isaac, and the God of Jacob, has appeared unto you.

6And the LORD said furthermore unto him, Put now yours hand into your bosom. And he put his hand into his bosom: and when he took it out, behold, his hand was leprous as snow.

7 And he said, Put yours hand into your bosom again. And he put his hand into his bosom again; and plucked it out of his bosom, and, behold, it was turned again as his other flesh.

8 And it shall come to pass, if they will not believe you, neither hearken to the voice of the first sign, that they will believe the voice of the latter sign.

9 And it shall come to pass, if they will not believe also these two signs, neither hearken unto your voice, that you shalt take of the water of the river, and pour it upon the dry land: and the water which you takest out of the river shall become blood upon the dry land.

10And Moses said unto the LORD, O my Lord, I am not eloquent, neither heretofore, nor since you have spoken unto your servant: but I am slow of speech, and of a slow tongue.

11 And the LORD said unto him, Who has made man's mouth? or who maketh the dumb, or deaf, or the seeing, or the blind? have not I the LORD?

12 Now therefore go, and I will be with your mouth, and teach you what you shalt say.

13 And he said, O my Lord, send, I pray you, by the hand of him whom you will send.

14 And the anger of the LORD was kindled against Moses, and he said, Is not Aaron the Levite your brother? I know that he can speak well. And also, behold, he comes forth to meet you: and when he seeth you, he will be glad in his heart.

15 And you shalt speak unto him, and put words in his mouth: and I will be with your mouth, and with his mouth, and will teach you what you shall do.

16 And he shall be your spokesman unto the people: and he shall be, even he shall be to you instead of a mouth, and you shalt be to him instead of God.

17 And you shalt take this rod in yours hand, wherewith you shalt do signs.

18And Moses went and returned to Jethro his father in law, and said unto him, Let me go, I pray you, and return unto my brethren which are in Egypt, and see whether they be yet alive. And Jethro said to Moses, Go in peace.

19 And the LORD said unto Moses in Midian, Go, return into Egypt: for all the men are dead which sought your life.

20 And Moses took his wife and his sons, and set them upon an ass, and he returned to the land of Egypt: and Moses took the rod of God in his hand.

21 And the LORD said unto Moses, When you go to return into Egypt, see that you do all those wonders before Pharaoh, which I have put in yours hand: but I will harden his heart, that he shall not let the people go.

22 And you shalt say unto Pharaoh, Thus saith the LORD, Israel is my son, even my firstborn:

23 And I say unto you, Let my son go, that he may serve me: and if you refuse to let him go, behold, I will slay your son, even your firstborn.

24And it came to pass by the way in the inn, that the LORD met him, and sought to kill him.

25 Then Zipporah took a sharp stone, and cut off the foreskin of her son, and cast it at his feet, and said, Surely a bloody husband are you to me.

26 So he let him go: then she said, A bloody husband you are, because of the circumcision.

27And the LORD said to Aaron, Go into the wilderness to meet Moses. And he went, and met him in the mount of God, and kissed him.

28 And Moses told Aaron all the words of the LORD who had sent him, and all the signs which he had commanded him.

29And Moses and Aaron went and gathered together all the elders of the children of Israel:

30 And Aaron spake all the words which the LORD had spoken unto Moses, and did the signs in the sight of the people.

31 And the people believed: and when they heard that the LORD had visited the children of Israel, and that he had looked upon their affliction, then they bowed their heads and worshipped.

CHAPTER 5

AND afterward Moses and Aaron went in, and told Pharaoh, Thus saith the LORD God of Israel, Let my people go, that they may hold a feast unto me in the wilderness.

2 And Pharaoh said, Who is the LORD, that I should obey his voice to let Israel go? I know not the LORD, neither will I let Israel go.

3 And they said, The God of the Hebrews has met with us: let us go, we pray you, three days' journey into the desert, and sacrifice unto the LORD our God; lest he fall upon us with pestilence, or with the sword.

4 And the king of Egypt said unto them, Wherefore do you , Moses and Aaron, let the people from their works? get you unto your burdens.

5 And Pharaoh said, Behold, the people of the land now are many, and you make them rest from their burdens.

6 And Pharaoh commanded the same day the taskmasters of the people, and their officers, saying,

7 You shall no more give the people straw to make brick, as heretofore: let them go and gather straw for themselves.

8 And the tale of the bricks, which they did make heretofore, you shall lay upon them; you shall not diminish ought thereof: for they be idle; therefore they cry, saying, Let us go and sacrifice to our God.

9 Let there more work be laid upon the men, that they may labour therein; and let them not regard vain words.

10And the taskmasters of the people went out, and their officers, and they spake to the people, saying, Thus saith Pharaoh, I will not give you straw.

11 Go you , get you straw where you can find it: yet not ought of your work shall be diminished.

12 So the people were scattered abroad throughout all the land of Egypt to gather stubble instead of straw.

13 And the taskmasters hasted them, saying, Fulfil your works, your daily tasks, as when there was straw.

14 And the officers of the children of Israel, which Pharaoh's taskmasters had set over them, were beaten, and demanded, Wherefore have you not fulfilled your task in making brick both yesterday and to day, as heretofore?

15Then the officers of the children of Israel came and cried unto Pharaoh, saying, Wherefore dealest you thus with your servants?

16 There is no straw given unto your servants, and they say to us, Make brick: and, behold, your servants are beaten; but the fault is in yours own people.

17 But he said, You are idle, you are idle: therefore you say, Let us go and do sacrifice to the LORD.

18 Go therefore now, and work; for there shall no straw be given you, yet shall you deliver the tale of bricks.

19 And the officers of the children of Israel did see that they were in evil case, after it was said, You shall not minish ought from your bricks of your daily task.

20And they met Moses and Aaron, who stood in the way, as they came forth from Pharaoh:

21 And they said unto them, The LORD look upon you, and judge; because you have made our savour to be abhorred in the eyes of Pharaoh, and in the eyes of his servants, to put a sword in their hand to slay us.

22 And Moses returned unto the LORD, and said, Lord, wherefore have you so evil entreated this people? why is it that you have sent me?

23 For since I came to Pharaoh to speak in your name, he has done evil to this people; neither have you delivered your people at all.

CHAPTER 6

THEN the LORD said unto Moses, Now shalt you see what I will do to Pharaoh: for with a strong hand shall he let them go, and with a strong hand shall he drive them out of his land.

2 And God spake unto Moses, and said unto him, I am the LORD:

3 And I appeared unto Abraham, unto Isaac, and unto Jacob, by the name of God Almighty, but by my name JEHOVAH was I not known to them.

4 And I have also established my covenant with them, to give them the land of Canaan, the land of their pilgrimage, wherein they were strangers.

5 And I have also heard the groaning of the children of Israel, whom the Egyptians keep in bondage; and I have remembered my covenant.

6 Wherefore say unto the children of Israel, I am the LORD, and I will bring you out from under the burdens of the Egyptians, and I will rid you out of their bondage, and I will redeem you with a stretched out arm, and with great judgments:

7 And I will take you to me for a people, and I will be to you a God: and you shall know that I am the LORD your God, which bringeth you out from under the burdens of the Egyptians.

8 And I will bring you in unto the land, concerning the which I did swear to give it to Abraham, to Isaac, and to Jacob; and I will give it you for an heritage: I am the LORD.

9And Moses spake so unto the children of Israel: but they hearkened not unto Moses for anguish of spirit, and for cruel bondage.

10 And the LORD spake unto Moses, saying,

11 Go in, speak unto Pharaoh king of Egypt, that he let the children of Israel go out of his land.

12 And Moses spake before the LORD, saying, Behold, the children of Israel have not hearkened unto me; how then shall Pharaoh hear me, who am of uncircumcised lips?

13 And the LORD spake unto Moses and unto Aaron, and gave them a charge unto the children of Israel, and unto Pharaoh king of Egypt, to bring the children of Israel out of the land of Egypt.

14These be the heads of their fathers' houses: The sons of Reuben the firstborn of Israel; Hanoch, and Pallu, Hezron, and Carmi: these be the families of Reuben.

15 And the sons of Simeon; Jemuel, and Jamin, and Ohad, and Jachin, and Zohar, and Shaul the son of a Canaanitish woman: these are the families of Simeon.

16And these are the names of the sons of Levi according to their generations; Gershon, and Kohath, and Merari: and the years of the life of Levi were an hundred thirty and seven years.

17 The sons of Gershon; Libni, and Shimi, according to their families.

18 And the sons of Kohath; Amram, and Izhar, and Hebron, and Uzziel: and the years of the life of Kohath were an hundred thirty and three years.

19 And the sons of Merari; Mahali and Mushi: these are the families of Levi according to their generations.

20 And Amram took him Jochebed his father's sister to wife; and she bare him Aaron and Moses: and the years of the life of Amram were an hundred and thirty and seven years.

21And the sons of Izhar; Korah, and Nepheg, and Zichri.

22 And the sons of Uzziel; Mishael, and Elzaphan, and Zithri.

23 And Aaron took him Elisheba, daughter of Amminadab, sister of Naashon, to wife; and she bare him Nadab, and Abihu, Eleazar, and Ithamar.

24 And the sons of Korah; Assir, and Elkanah, and Abiasaph: these are the families of the Korhites.

25 And Eleazar Aaron's son took him one of the daughters of Putiel to wife; and she bare him Phinehas: these are the heads of the fathers of the Levites according to their families.

26 These are that Aaron and Moses, to whom the LORD said, Bring out the children of Israel from the land of Egypt according to their armies.

27 These are they which spake to Pharaoh king of Egypt, to bring out the children of Israel from Egypt: these are that Moses and Aaron.

28And it came to pass on the day when the LORD spake unto Moses in the land of Egypt,

29 That the LORD spake unto Moses, saying, I am the LORD: speak you unto Pharaoh king of Egypt all that I say unto you.

30 And Moses said before the LORD, Behold, I am of uncircumcised lips, and how shall Pharaoh hearken unto me?

CHAPTER 7

AND the LORD said unto Moses, See, I have made you a god to Pharaoh: and Aaron your brother shall be your prophet.

2 You shalt speak all that I command you: and Aaron your brother shall speak unto Pharaoh, that he send the children of Israel out of his land.

3 And I will harden Pharaoh's heart, and multiply my signs and my wonders in the land of Egypt.

4 But Pharaoh shall not hearken unto you, that I may lay my hand upon Egypt, and bring forth my armies, and my people the children of Israel, out of the land of Egypt by great judgments.

5 And the Egyptians shall know that I am the LORD, when I stretch forth my hand upon Egypt, and bring out the children of Israel from among them.

6 And Moses and Aaron did as the LORD commanded them, so did they.

7 And Moses was fourscore years old, and Aaron fourscore and three years old, when they spake unto Pharaoh.

8And the LORD spake unto Moses and unto Aaron, saying,

9 When Pharaoh shall speak unto you, saying, Shew a miracle for you: then you shalt say unto Aaron, Take your rod, and cast it before Pharaoh, and it shall become a serpent.

10And Moses and Aaron went in unto Pharaoh, and they did so as the LORD had commanded: and Aaron cast down his rod before Pharaoh, and before his servants, and it became a serpent.

11 Then Pharaoh also called the wise men and the sorcerers: now the magicians of Egypt, they also did in like manner with their enchantments.

12 For they cast down every man his rod, and they became serpents: but Aaron's rod swallowed up their rods.

13 And he hardened Pharaoh's heart, that he hearkened not unto them; as the LORD had said.

14And the LORD said unto Moses, Pharaoh's heart is hardened, he refuseth to let the people go.

15 Get you unto Pharaoh in the morning; lo, he goeth out unto the water; and you shalt stand by the river's brink against he come; and the rod which was turned to a serpent shalt you take in yours hand.

16 And you shalt say unto him, The LORD God of the Hebrews has sent me unto you, saying, Let my people go, that they may serve me in the wilderness: and, behold, hitherto you wouldest not hear.

17 Thus saith the LORD, In this you shalt know that I am the LORD: behold, I will strike with the rod that is in my hand upon the waters which are in the river, and they shall be turned to blood.

18 And the fish that is in the river shall die, and the river shall stink; and the Egyptians shall lothe to drink of the water of the river.

19And the LORD spake unto Moses, Say unto Aaron, Take your rod, and stretch out yours hand upon the waters of Egypt, upon their streams, upon their rivers, and upon their ponds, and upon all their pools of water, that they may become blood; and that there may be blood throughout all the land of Egypt, both in vessels of wood, and in vessels of stone.

20 And Moses and Aaron did so, as the LORD commanded; and he lifted up the rod, and struck the waters that were in the river, in the sight of Pharaoh, and in the sight of his servants; and all the waters that were in the river were turned to blood.

21 And the fish that was in the river died; and the river stank, and the Egyptians could not drink of the water of the river; and there was blood throughout all the land of Egypt.

22 And the magicians of Egypt did so with their enchantments: and Pharaoh's heart was hardened, neither did he hearken unto them; as the LORD had said.

23 And Pharaoh turned and went into his house, neither did he set his heart to this also.

24 And all the Egyptians digged round about the river for water to drink; for they could not drink of the water of the river.

25 And seven days were fulfilled, after that the LORD had smitten the river.

CHAPTER 8

AND the LORD spake unto Moses, Go unto Pharaoh, and say unto him, Thus saith the LORD, Let my people go, that they may serve me.

2 And if you refuse to let them go, behold, I will strike all your borders with frogs:

3 And the river shall bring forth frogs abundantly, which shall go up and come into yours house, and into your bedchamber, and upon your bed, and into the house of your servants, and upon your people, and into yours ovens, and into your kneadingtroughs:

4 And the frogs shall come up both on you, and upon your people, and upon all your servants.

5And the LORD spake unto Moses, Say unto Aaron, Stretch forth yours hand with your rod over the streams, over the rivers, and over the ponds, and cause frogs to come up upon the land of Egypt.

6 And Aaron stretched out his hand over the waters of Egypt; and the frogs came up, and covered the land of Egypt.

7 And the magicians did so with their enchantments, and brought up frogs upon the land of Egypt.

8 Then Pharaoh called for Moses and Aaron, and said, Intreat the LORD, that he may take away the frogs from me, and from my people; and I will let the people go, that they may do sacrifice unto the LORD.

9 And Moses said unto Pharaoh, Glory over me: when shall I intreat for you, and for your servants, and for your people, to destroy the frogs from you and your houses, that they may remain in the river only?

10 And he said, To morrow. And he said, Be it according to your word: that you mayest know that there is none like unto the LORD our God.

11 And the frogs shall depart from you, and from your houses, and from your servants, and from your people; they shall remain in the river only.

12 And Moses and Aaron went out from Pharaoh: and Moses cried unto the LORD because of the frogs which he had brought against Pharaoh.

13 And the LORD did according to the word of Moses; and the frogs died out of the houses, out of the villages, and out of the fields.

14 And they gathered them together upon heaps: and the land stank.

15 But when Pharaoh saw that there was respite, he hardened his heart, and hearkened not unto them; as the LORD had said.

16 And the LORD said unto Moses, Say unto Aaron, Stretch out your rod, and strike the dust of the land, that it may become lice throughout all the land of Egypt.

17 And they did so; for Aaron stretched out his hand with his rod, and struck the dust of the earth, and it became lice in man, and in beast; all the dust of the land became lice throughout all the land of Egypt.

18 And the magicians did so with their enchantments to bring forth lice, but they could not: so there were lice upon man, and upon beast.

19 Then the magicians said unto Pharaoh, This is the finger of God: and Pharaoh's heart was hardened, and he hearkened not unto them; as the LORD had said.

20 And the LORD said unto Moses, Rise up early in the morning, and stand before Pharaoh; lo, he comes forth to the water; and say unto him, Thus saith the LORD, Let my people go, that they may serve me.

21 Else, if you will not let my people go, behold, I will send swarms of flies upon you, and upon your servants, and upon your people, and into your houses: and the houses of the Egyptians shall be full of swarms of flies, and also the ground whereon they are.

22 And I will sever in that day the land of Goshen, in which my people dwell, that no swarms of flies shall be there; to the end you mayest know that I am the LORD in the midst of the earth.

23 And I will put a division between my people and your people: to morrow shall this sign be.

24 And the LORD did so; and there came a grievous swarm of flies into the house of Pharaoh, and into his servants' houses, and into all the land of Egypt: the land was corrupted by reason of the swarm of flies.

25 And Pharaoh called for Moses and for Aaron, and said, Go you, sacrifice to your God in the land.

26 And Moses said, It is not meet so to do; for we shall sacrifice the abomination of the Egyptians to the LORD our God: lo, shall we sacrifice the abomination of the Egyptians before their eyes, and will they not stone us?

27 We will go three days' journey into the wilderness, and sacrifice to the LORD our God, as he shall command us.

28 And Pharaoh said, I will let you go, that you may sacrifice to the LORD your God in the wilderness; only you shall not go very far away: intreat for me.

29 And Moses said, Behold, I go out from you, and I will intreat the LORD that the swarms of flies may depart from Pharaoh, from his servants, and from his people, to morrow: but let not Pharaoh deal deceitfully any more in not letting the people go to sacrifice to the LORD.

30 And Moses went out from Pharaoh, and intreated the LORD.

31 And the LORD did according to the word of Moses; and he removed the swarms of flies from Pharaoh, from his servants, and from his people; there remained not one.

32 And Pharaoh hardened his heart at this time also, neither would he let the people go.

CHAPTER 9

THEN the LORD said unto Moses, Go in unto Pharaoh, and tell him, Thus saith the LORD God of the Hebrews, Let my people go, that they may serve me.

2 For if you refuse to let them go, and will hold them still,

3 Behold, the hand of the LORD is upon your cattle which is in the field, upon the horses, upon the asses, upon the camels, upon the oxen, and upon the sheep: there shall be a very grievous murrain.

4 And the LORD shall sever between the cattle of Israel and the cattle of Egypt: and there shall nothing die of all that is the children's of Israel.

5 And the LORD appointed a set time, saying, To morrow the LORD shall do this thing in the land.

6 And the LORD did that thing on the morrow, and all the cattle of Egypt died: but of the cattle of the children of Israel died not one.

7 And Pharaoh sent, and, behold, there was not one of the cattle of the Israelites dead. And the heart of Pharaoh was hardened, and he did not let the people go.

8 And the LORD said unto Moses and unto Aaron, Take to you handfuls of ashes of the furnace, and let Moses sprinkle it toward the heaven in the sight of Pharaoh.

9 And it shall become small dust in all the land of Egypt, and shall be a boil breaking forth with pustules upon man, and upon beast, throughout all the land of Egypt.

10 And they took ashes of the furnace, and stood before Pharaoh; and Moses sprinkled it up toward heaven; and it became a boil breaking forth with pustules upon man, and upon beast.

11 And the magicians could not stand before Moses because of the boils; for the boil was upon the magicians, and upon all the Egyptians.

12 And the LORD hardened the heart of Pharaoh, and he hearkened not unto them; as the LORD had spoken unto Moses.

13 And the LORD said unto Moses, Rise up early in the morning, and stand before Pharaoh, and say unto him, Thus saith the LORD God of the Hebrews, Let my people go, that they may serve me.

14 For I will at this time send all my plagues upon yours heart, and upon your servants, and upon your people; that you mayest know that there is none like me in all the earth.

15 For now I will stretch out my hand, that I may strike you and your people with pestilence; and you shalt be cut off from the earth.

16 And in very deed for this cause have I raised you up, for to shew in you my power; and that my name may be declared throughout all the earth.

17 As yet exaltest you yourself against my people, that you will not let them go?

18 Behold, to morrow about this time I will cause it to rain a very grievous hail, such as has not been in Egypt since the foundation thereof even until now.

19 Send therefore now, and gather your cattle, and all that you have in the field; for upon every man and beast which shall be found in the field, and shall not be brought home, the hail shall come down upon them, and they shall die.

20 He that feared the word of the LORD among the servants of Pharaoh made his servants and his cattle flee into the houses:

21 And he that regarded not the word of the LORD left his servants and his cattle in the field.

22 And the LORD said unto Moses, Stretch forth yours hand toward heaven, that there may be hail in all the land of Egypt, upon man, and upon beast, and upon every herb of the field, throughout the land of Egypt.

23 And Moses stretched forth his rod toward heaven: and the LORD sent thunder and hail, and the fire ran along upon the ground; and the LORD rained hail upon the land of Egypt.

24 So there was hail, and fire mingled with the hail, very grievous, such as there was none like it in all the land of Egypt since it became a nation.

25 And the hail struck throughout all the land of Egypt all that was in the field, both man and beast; and the hail struck every herb of the field, and brake every tree of the field.

26 Only in the land of Goshen, where the children of Israel were, was there no hail.

27 And Pharaoh sent, and called for Moses and Aaron, and said unto them, I have sinned this time: the LORD is righteous, and I and my people are wicked.

28 Intreat the LORD (for it is enough) that there be no more mighty thunderings and hail; and I will let you go, and you shall stay no longer.

29 And Moses said unto him, As soon as I am gone out of the city, I will spread abroad my hands unto the LORD; and the thunder shall cease, neither shall there be any more hail; that you mayest know how that the earth is the LORD's.

30 But as for you and your servants, I know that you will not yet fear the LORD God.

31 And the flax and the barley was smitten: for the barley was in the ear, and the flax was bolled.

32 But the wheat and the rie were not smitten: for they were not grown up.

33 And Moses went out of the city from Pharaoh, and spread abroad his hands unto the LORD: and the thunders and hail ceased, and the rain was not poured upon the earth.

34 And when Pharaoh saw that the rain and the hail and the thunders were ceased, he sinned yet more, and hardened his heart, he and his servants.

35 And the heart of Pharaoh was hardened, neither would he let the children of Israel go; as the LORD had spoken by Moses.

CHAPTER 10

AND the LORD said unto Moses, Go in unto Pharaoh: for I have hardened his heart, and the heart of his servants, that I might shew these my signs before him:

2 And that you mayest tell in the ears of your son, and of your son's son, what things I have created in Egypt, and my signs which I have done among them; that you may know how that I am the LORD.

3 And Moses and Aaron came in unto Pharaoh, and said unto him, Thus saith the LORD God of the Hebrews, How long will you refuse to humble yourself before me? let my people go, that they may serve me.

4 Else, if you refuse to let my people go, behold, to morrow will I bring the locusts into your coast:

5 And they shall cover the face of the earth, that one cannot be able to see the earth: and they shall eat the residue of that which is escaped, which remaineth unto you from the hail, and shall eat every tree which groweth for you out of the field:

6 And they shall fill your houses, and the houses of all your servants, and the houses of all the Egyptians; which neither your fathers, nor your fathers' fathers have seen, since the day that they were upon the earth unto this day. And he turned himself, and went out from Pharaoh.

7 And Pharaoh's servants said unto him, How long shall this man be a snare unto us? let the men go, that they may serve the LORD their God: knowest you not yet that Egypt is destroyed?

8 And Moses and Aaron were brought again unto Pharaoh: and he said unto them, Go, serve the LORD your God: but who are they that shall go?

9 And Moses said, We will go with our young and with our old, with our sons and with our daughters, with our flocks and with our herds will we go; for we must hold a feast unto the LORD.

10 And he said unto them, Let the LORD be so with you, as I will let you go, and your little ones: look to it; for evil is before you.

11 Not so: go now you that are men, and serve the LORD; for that you did desire. And they were driven out from Pharaoh's presence.

12 And the LORD said unto Moses, Stretch out yours hand over the land of Egypt for the locusts, that they may come up upon the land of Egypt, and eat every herb of the land, even all that the hail has left.

13 And Moses stretched forth his rod over the land of Egypt, and the LORD brought an east wind upon the land all that day, and all that night; and when it was morning, the east wind brought the locusts.

14 And the locusts went up over all the land of Egypt, and rested in all the coasts of Egypt: very grievous were they; before them there were no such locusts as they, neither after them shall be such.

15 For they covered the face of the whole earth, so that the land was darkened; and they did eat every herb of the land, and all the fruit of the trees which the hail had left: and there remained not any green thing in the trees, or in the herbs of the field, through all the land of Egypt.

16 Then Pharaoh called for Moses and Aaron in haste; and he said, I have sinned against the LORD your God, and against you.

17 Now therefore forgive, I pray you, my sin only this once, and intreat the LORD your God, that he may take away from me this death only.

18 And he went out from Pharaoh, and intreated the LORD.

19 And the LORD turned a mighty strong west wind, which took away the locusts, and cast them into the Red sea; there remained not one locust in all the coasts of Egypt.

20 But the LORD hardened Pharaoh's heart, so that he would not let the children of Israel go.

21 And the LORD said unto Moses, Stretch out yours hand toward heaven, that there may be darkness over the land of Egypt, even darkness which may be felt.

22 And Moses stretched forth his hand toward heaven; and there was a thick darkness in all the land of Egypt three days:

23 They saw not one another, neither rose any from his place for three days: but all the children of Israel had light in their dwellings.

24 And Pharaoh called unto Moses, and said, Go you, serve the LORD; only let your flocks and your herds be stayed: let your little ones also go with you.

25 And Moses said, You must give us also sacrifices and burnt offerings, that we may sacrifice unto the LORD our God.

26 Our cattle also shall go with us; there shall not an hoof be left behind; for thereof must we take to serve the LORD our God; and we know not with what we must serve the LORD, until we come thither.

27 But the LORD hardened Pharaoh's heart, and he would not let them go.

28 And Pharaoh said unto him, Get you from me, take heed to yourself, see my face no more; for in that day you seest my face you shalt die.

29 And Moses said, You have spoken well, I will see your face again no more.

CHAPTER 11

AND the LORD said unto Moses, Yet will I bring one plague more upon Pharaoh, and upon Egypt; afterwards he will let you go hence: when he shall let you go, he shall surely thrust you out hence altogether.

2 Speak now in the ears of the people, and let every man borrow of his neighbour, and every woman of her neighbour, jewels of silver, and jewels of gold.

3 And the LORD gave the people favour in the sight of the Egyptians. Moreover the man Moses was very great in the land of Egypt, in the sight of Pharaoh's servants, and in the sight of the people.

4 And Moses said, Thus saith the LORD, About midnight will I go out into the midst of Egypt:

5 And all the firstborn in the land of Egypt shall die, from the firstborn of Pharaoh that sitteth upon his throne, even unto the firstborn of the maidservant that is behind the mill; and all the firstborn of beasts.

6 And there shall be a great cry throughout all the land of Egypt, such as there was none like it, nor shall be like it any more.

7 But against any of the children of Israel shall not a dog move his tongue, against man or beast: that you may know how that the LORD doth put a difference between the Egyptians and Israel.

8 And all these your servants shall come down unto me, and bow down themselves unto me, saying, Get you out, and all the people that follow you: and after that I will go out. And he went out from Pharaoh in a great anger.

9 And the LORD said unto Moses, Pharaoh shall not hearken unto you; that my wonders may be multiplied in the land of Egypt.

10 And Moses and Aaron did all these wonders before Pharaoh: and the LORD hardened Pharaoh's heart, so that he would not let the children of Israel go out of his land.

CHAPTER 12

AND the LORD spake unto Moses and Aaron in the land of Egypt, saying,

2 This month shall be unto you the beginning of months: it shall be the first month of the year to you.

3 Speak you unto all the congregation of Israel, saying, In the tenth day of this month they shall take to them every man a lamb, according to the house of their fathers, a lamb for an house:

4 And if the household be too little for the lamb, let him and his neighbour next unto his house take it according to the number of the souls; every man according to his eating shall make your count for the lamb.

5 Your lamb shall be without blemish, a male of the first year: you shall take it out from the sheep, or from the goats:

6 And you shall keep it up until the fourteenth day of the same month: and the whole assembly of the congregation of Israel shall kill it in the evening.

7 And they shall take of the blood, and strike it on the two side posts and on the upper door post of the houses, wherein they shall eat it.

8 And they shall eat the flesh in that night, roast with fire, and unleavened bread; and with bitter herbs they shall eat it.

9 Eat not of it raw, nor sodden at all with water, but roast with fire; his head with his legs, and with the purtenance thereof.

10 And you shall let nothing of it remain until the morning; and that which remaineth of it until the morning you shall burn with fire.

11 And thus shall you eat it; with your loins girded, your shoes on your feet, and your staff in your hand; and you shall eat it in haste: it is the LORD's passover.

12 For I will pass through the land of Egypt this night, and will strike all the firstborn in the land of Egypt, both man and beast; and against all the gods of Egypt I will execute judgment: I am the LORD.

13 And the blood shall be to you for a token upon the houses where you are: and when I see the blood, I will pass over you, and the plague shall not be upon you to destroy you, when I strike the land of Egypt.

14 And this day shall be unto you for a memorial; and you shall keep it a feast to the LORD throughout your generations; you shall keep it a feast by an ordinance for ever.

15 Seven days shall you eat unleavened bread; even the first day you shall put away leaven out of your houses: for whosoever eateth leavened bread from the first day until the seventh day, that soul shall be cut off from Israel.

16 And in the first day there shall be an holy convocation, and in the seventh day there shall be an holy convocation to you; no manner of work shall be done in them, save that which every man must eat, that only may be done of you.

17 And you shall observe the feast of unleavened bread; for in this selfsame day have I brought your armies out of the land of Egypt: therefore shall you observe this day in your generations by an ordinance for ever.

18 In the first month, on the fourteenth day of the month at even, you shall eat unleavened bread, until the one and twentieth day of the month at even.

19 Seven days shall there be no leaven found in your houses: for whosoever eateth that which is leavened, even that soul shall be cut off from the congregation of Israel, whether he be a stranger, or born in the land.

20 You shall eat nothing leavened; in all your habitations shall you eat unleavened bread.

21 Then Moses called for all the elders of Israel, and said unto them, Draw out and take you a lamb according to your families, and kill the passover.

22 And you shall take a bunch of hyssop, and dip it in the blood that is in the bason, and strike the lintel and the two side posts with the blood that is in the bason; and none of you shall go out at the door of his house until the morning.

23 For the LORD will pass through to strike the Egyptians; and when he seeth the blood upon the lintel, and on the two side posts, the LORD will pass over the door, and will not suffer the destroyer to come in unto your houses to strike you.

24 And you shall observe this thing for an ordinance to you and to your sons for ever.

25 And it shall come to pass, when you be come to the land which the LORD will give you, according as he has promised, that you shall keep this service.

26 And it shall come to pass, when your children shall say unto you, What mean you by this service?

27 That you shall say, It is the sacrifice of the LORD's passover, who passed over the houses of the children of Israel in Egypt, when he struck the Egyptians, and delivered our houses. And the people bowed the head and worshipped.

28 And the children of Israel went away, and did as the LORD had commanded Moses and Aaron, so did they.

29 And it came to pass, that at midnight the LORD struck all the firstborn in the land of Egypt, from the firstborn of Pharaoh that sat on his throne unto the firstborn of the captive that was in the dungeon; and all the firstborn of cattle.

30 And Pharaoh rose up in the night, he, and all his servants, and all the Egyptians; and there was a great cry in Egypt; for there was not a house where there was not one dead.

31 And he called for Moses and Aaron by night, and said, Rise up, and get you forth from among my people, both you and the children of Israel; and go, serve the LORD, as you have said.

32 Also take your flocks and your herds, as you have said, and be gone; and bless me also.

33 And the Egyptians were urgent upon the people, that they might send them out of the land in haste; for they said, We be all dead men.

34 And the people took their dough before it was leavened, their kneadingtroughs being bound up in their clothes upon their shoulders.

35 And the children of Israel did according to the word of Moses; and they borrowed of the Egyptians jewels of silver, and jewels of gold, and raiment:

36 And the LORD gave the people favour in the sight of the Egyptians, so that they lent unto them such things as they required. And they spoiled the Egyptians.

37 And the children of Israel journeyed from Rameses to Succoth, about six hundred thousand on foot that were men, beside children.

38 And a mixed multitude went up also with them; and flocks, and herds, even very much cattle.

39 And they baked unleavened cakes of the dough which they brought forth out of Egypt, for it was not leavened; because they were thrust out of Egypt, and could not tarry, neither had they prepared for themselves any victual.

40 Now the sojourning of the children of Israel, who dwelt in Egypt, was four hundred and thirty years.

41 And it came to pass at the end of the four hundred and thirty years, even the selfsame day it came to pass, that all the hosts of the LORD went out from the land of Egypt.

42 It is a night to be much observed unto the LORD for bringing them out from the land of Egypt: this is that night of the LORD to be observed of all the children of Israel in their generations.

43 And the LORD said unto Moses and Aaron, This is the ordinance of the passover: There shall no stranger eat thereof:

44 But every man's servant that is bought for money, when you have circumcised him, then shall he eat thereof.

45 A foreigner and an hired servant shall not eat thereof.

46 In one house shall it be eaten; you shalt not carry forth ought of the flesh abroad out of the house; neither shall you break a bone thereof.

47 All the congregation of Israel shall keep it.

48 And when a stranger shall sojourn with you, and will keep the passover to the LORD, let all his males be circumcised, and then let him come near and keep it; and he shall be as one that is born in the land: for no uncircumcised person shall eat thereof.

49 One law shall be to him that is homeborn, and unto the stranger that sojourneth among you.

50 Thus did all the children of Israel; as the LORD commanded Moses and Aaron, so did they.

51 And it came to pass the selfsame day, that the LORD did bring the children of Israel out of the land of Egypt by their armies.

CHAPTER 13

AND the LORD spake unto Moses, saying,

2 Sanctify unto me all the firstborn, whatsoever openeth the womb among the children of Israel, both of man and of beast: it is my.

3 And Moses said unto the people, Remember this day, in which you came out from Egypt, out of the house of bondage; for by strength of hand the LORD brought you out from this place: there shall no leavened bread be eaten.

4 This day came you out in the month Abib.

5 And it shall be when the LORD shall bring you into the land of the Canaanites, and the Hittites, and the Amorites, and the Hivites, and the Jebusites, which he sware unto your fathers to give you, a land flowing with milk and honey, that you shalt keep this service in this month.

6 Seven days you shalt eat unleavened bread, and in the seventh day shall be a feast to the LORD.

7 Unleavened bread shall be eaten seven days; and there shall no leavened bread be seen with you, neither shall there be leaven seen with you in all your quarters.

8 And you shalt shew your son in that day, saying, This is done because of that which the LORD did unto me when I came forth out of Egypt.

9 And it shall be for a sign unto you upon yours hand, and for a memorial between yours eyes, that the LORD's law may be in your mouth: for with a strong hand has the LORD brought you out of Egypt.

10 You shalt therefore keep this ordinance in his season from year to year.

11 And it shall be when the LORD shall bring you into the land of the Canaanites, as he sware unto you and to your fathers, and shall give it you,

12 That you shalt set apart unto the LORD all that openeth the matrix, and every firstling that comes of a beast which you have; the males shall be the LORD's.

13 And every firstling of an ass you shalt redeem with a lamb; and if you will not redeem it, then you shalt break his neck: and all the firstborn of man among your children shalt you redeem.

14 And it shall be when your son asketh you in time to come, saying, What is this? that you shalt say unto him, By strength of hand the LORD brought us out from Egypt, from the house of bondage:

15 And it came to pass, when Pharaoh would hardly let us go, that the LORD slew all the firstborn in the land of Egypt, both the firstborn of man, and the firstborn of beast: therefore I sacrifice to the LORD all that openeth the matrix, being males; but all the firstborn of my children I redeem.

16 And it shall be for a token upon yours hand, and for frontlets between yours eyes: for by strength of hand the LORD brought us forth out of Egypt.

17 And it came to pass, when Pharaoh had let the people go, that God led them not through the way of the land of the Philistines, although that was near; for God said, Lest what if the people repent when they see war, and they return to Egypt:

18 But God led the people about, through the way of the wilderness of the Red sea: and the children of Israel went up harnessed out of the land of Egypt.

19 And Moses took the bones of Joseph with him: for he had straitly sworn the children of Israel, saying, God will surely visit you; and you shall carry up my bones away hence with you.

20 And they took their journey from Succoth, and encamped in Etham, in the edge of the wilderness.

21 And the LORD went before them by day in a pillar of a cloud, to lead them the way; and by night in a pillar of fire, to give them light; to go by day and night:

22 He took not away the pillar of the cloud by day, nor the pillar of fire by night, from before the people.

CHAPTER 14

AND the LORD spake unto Moses, saying,

2 Speak unto the children of Israel, that they turn and encamp before Pi-hahiroth, between Migdol and the sea, over against Baal-zephon: before it shall you encamp by the sea.

3 For Pharaoh will say of the children of Israel, They are entangled in the land, the wilderness has shut them in.

4 And I will harden Pharaoh's heart, that he shall follow after them; and I will be honoured upon Pharaoh, and upon all his host; that the Egyptians may know that I am the LORD. And they did so.

5And it was told the king of Egypt that the people fled: and the heart of Pharaoh and of his servants was turned against the people, and they said, Why have we done this, that we have let Israel go from serving us?

6 And he made ready his chariot, and took his people with him:

7 And he took six hundred chosen chariots, and all the chariots of Egypt, and captains over every one of them.

8 And the LORD hardened the heart of Pharaoh king of Egypt, and he pursued after the children of Israel: and the children of Israel went out with an high hand.

9 But the Egyptians pursued after them, all the horses and chariots of Pharaoh, and his horsemen, and his army, and overtook them encamping by the sea, beside Pi-hahiroth, before Baal-zephon.

10And when Pharaoh drew nigh, the children of Israel lifted up their eyes, and, behold, the Egyptians marched after them; and they were sore afraid: and the children of Israel cried out unto the LORD.

11 And they said unto Moses, Because there were no graves in Egypt, have you taken us away to die in the wilderness? wherefore have you dealt thus with us, to carry us forth out of Egypt?

12 Is not this the word that we did tell you in Egypt, saying, Let us alone, that we may serve the Egyptians? For it had been better for us to serve the Egyptians, than that we should die in the wilderness.

13And Moses said unto the people, Fear you not, stand still, and see the salvation of the LORD, which he will shew to you to day: for the Egyptians whom you have seen to day, you shall see them again no more for ever.

14 The LORD shall fight for you, and you shall hold your peace.

15And the LORD said unto Moses, Wherefore criest you unto me? speak unto the children of Israel, that they go forward:

16 But lift you up your rod, and stretch out yours hand over the sea, and divide it: and the children of Israel shall go on dry ground through the midst of the sea.

17 And I, behold, I will harden the hearts of the Egyptians, and they shall follow them: and I will get me honour upon Pharaoh, and upon all his host, upon his chariots, and upon his horsemen.

18 And the Egyptians shall know that I am the LORD, when I have gotten me honour upon Pharaoh, upon his chariots, and upon his horsemen.

19And the angel of God, which went before the camp of Israel, removed and went behind them; and the pillar of the cloud went from before their face, and stood behind them:

20 And it came between the camp of the Egyptians and the camp of Israel; and it was a cloud and darkness to them, but it gave light by night to these: so that the one came not near the other all the night.

21 And Moses stretched out his hand over the sea; and the LORD caused the sea to go back by a strong east wind all that night, and made the sea dry land, and the waters were divided.

22 And the children of Israel went into the midst of the sea upon the dry ground: and the waters were a wall unto them on their right hand, and on their left.

23And the Egyptians pursued, and went in after them to the midst of the sea, even all Pharaoh's horses, his chariots, and his horsemen.

24 And it came to pass, that in the morning watch the LORD looked unto the host of the Egyptians through the pillar of fire and of the cloud, and troubled the host of the Egyptians,

25 And took off their chariot wheels, that they drave them heavily: so that the Egyptians said, Let us flee from the face of Israel; for the LORD fighteth for them against the Egyptians.

26And the LORD said unto Moses, Stretch out yours hand over the sea, that the waters may come again upon the Egyptians, upon their chariots, and upon their horsemen.

27 And Moses stretched forth his hand over the sea, and the sea returned to his strength when the morning appeared; and the Egyptians fled against it; and the LORD overthrew the Egyptians in the midst of the sea.

28 And the waters returned, and covered the chariots, and the horsemen, and all the host of Pharaoh that came into the sea after them; there remained not so much as one of them.

29 But the children of Israel walked upon dry land in the midst of the sea; and the waters were a wall unto them on their right hand, and on their left.

30 Thus the LORD saved Israel that day out of the hand of the Egyptians; and Israel saw the Egyptians dead upon the sea shore.

31 And Israel saw that great work which the LORD did upon the Egyptians: and the people feared the LORD, and believed the LORD, and his servant Moses.

CHAPTER 15

THEN sang Moses and the children of Israel this song unto the LORD, and spake, saying, I will sing unto the LORD, for he has triumphed gloriously: the horse and his rider has he thrown into the sea.

2 The LORD is my strength and song, and he is become my salvation: he is my God, and I will prepare him an habitation; my father's God, and I will exalt him.

3 The LORD is a man of war: the LORD is his name.

4 Pharaoh's chariots and his host has he cast into the sea: his chosen captains also are drowned in the Red sea.

5 The depths have covered them: they sank into the bottom as a stone.

6 Your right hand, O LORD, is become glorious in power: your right hand, O LORD, has dashed in pieces the enemy.

7 And in the greatness of yours excellency you have overthrown them that rose up against you: you sentest forth your wrath, which consumed them as stubble.

8 And with the blast of your nostrils the waters were gathered together, the floods stood upright as an heap, and the depths were congealed in the heart of the sea.

9 The enemy said, I will pursue, I will overtake, I will divide the spoil; my lust shall be satisfied upon them; I will draw my sword, my hand shall destroy them.

10 You did blow with your wind, the sea covered them: they sank as lead in the mighty waters.

11 Who is like unto you, O LORD, among the gods? who is like you, glorious in holiness, fearful in praises, doing wonders?

12 You stretchedst out your right hand, the earth swallowed them.

13 You in your mercy have led forth the people which you have redeemed: you have guided them in your strength unto your holy habitation.

14 The people shall hear, and be afraid: sorrow shall take hold on the inhabitants of Palestina.

15 Then the dukes of Edom shall be amazed; the mighty men of Moab, trembling shall take hold upon them; all the inhabitants of Canaan shall melt away.

16 Fear and dread shall fall upon them; by the greatness of yours arm they shall be as still as a stone; till your people pass over, O LORD, till the people pass over, which you have purchased.

17 You shalt bring them in, and plant them in the mountain of yours inheritance, in the place, O LORD, which you have made for you to dwell in, in the Sanctuary, O Lord, which your hands have established.

18 The LORD shall reign for ever and ever.

19 For the horse of Pharaoh went in with his chariots and with his horsemen into the sea, and the LORD brought again the waters of the sea upon them; but the children of Israel went on dry land in the midst of the sea.

20And Miriam the prophetess, the sister of Aaron, took a timbrel in her hand; and all the women went out after her with timbrels and with dances.

21 And Miriam answered them, Sing you to the LORD, for he has triumphed gloriously; the horse and his rider has he thrown into the sea.

22 So Moses brought Israel from the Red sea, and they went out into the wilderness of Shur; and they went three days in the wilderness, and found no water.

23And when they came to Marah, they could not drink of the waters of Marah, for they were bitter: therefore the name of it was called Marah.

24 And the people murmured against Moses, saying, What shall we drink?

25 And he cried unto the LORD; and the LORD shewed him a tree, which when he had cast into the waters, the waters were made sweet: there he made for them a statute and an ordinance, and there he proved them,

26 And said, If you will diligently hearken to the voice of the LORD your God, and will do that which is right in his sight, and will give ear to his commandments, and keep all his statutes, I will put none of these diseases upon you, which I have brought upon the Egyptians: for I am the LORD that healeth you.

27And they came to Elim, where were twelve wells of water, and threescore and ten palm trees: and they encamped there by the waters.

CHAPTER 16

AND they took their journey from Elim, and all the congregation of the children of Israel came unto the wilderness of Sin, which is between Elim and Sinai, on the fifteenth day of the second month after their departing out of the land of Egypt.

2 And the whole congregation of the children of Israel murmured against Moses and Aaron in the wilderness:

3 And the children of Israel said unto them, Would to God we had died by the hand of the LORD in the land of Egypt, when we sat by the flesh pots, and when we did eat bread to the full; for you have brought us forth into this wilderness, to kill this whole assembly with hunger.

4Then said the LORD unto Moses, Behold, I will rain bread from heaven for you; and the people shall go out and gather a certain rate every day, that I may prove them, whether they will walk in my law, or no.

5 And it shall come to pass, that on the sixth day they shall prepare that which they bring in; and it shall be twice as much as they gather daily.

6 And Moses and Aaron said unto all the children of Israel, At even, then you shall know that the LORD has brought you out from the land of Egypt:

7 And in the morning, then you shall see the glory of the LORD; for that he heareth your murmurings against the LORD: and what are we, that you murmur against us?

8 And Moses said, This shall be, when the LORD shall give you in the evening flesh to eat, and in the morning bread to the full; for that the LORD heareth your murmurings which you murmur against him: and what are we? your murmurings are not against us, but against the LORD.

9 And Moses spake unto Aaron, Say unto all the congregation of the children of Israel, Come near before the LORD: for he has heard your murmurings.

10 And it came to pass, as Aaron spake unto the whole congregation of the children of Israel, that they looked toward the wilderness, and, behold, the glory of the LORD appeared in the cloud.

11 And the LORD spake unto Moses, saying,

12 I have heard the murmurings of the children of Israel: speak unto them, saying, At even you shall eat flesh, and in the morning you shall be filled with bread; and you shall know that I am the LORD your God.

13 And it came to pass, that at even the quails came up, and covered the camp: and in the morning the dew lay round about the host.

14 And when the dew that lay was gone up, behold, upon the face of the wilderness there lay a small round thing, as small as the hoar frost on the ground.

15 And when the children of Israel saw it, they said one to another, It is manna: for they wist not what it was. And Moses said unto them, This is the bread which the LORD has given you to eat.

16 This is the thing which the LORD has commanded, Gather of it every man according to his eating, an omer for every man, according to the number of your persons; take you every man for them which are in his tents.

17 And the children of Israel did so, and gathered, some more, some less.

18 And when they did mete it with an omer, he that gathered much had nothing over, and he that gathered little had no lack; they gathered every man according to his eating.

19 And Moses said, Let no man leave of it till the morning.

20 Notwithstanding they hearkened not unto Moses; but some of them left of it until the morning, and it bred worms, and stank: and Moses was wroth with them.

21 And they gathered it every morning, every man according to his eating: and when the sun waxed hot, it melted.

22 And it came to pass, that on the sixth day they gathered twice as much bread, two omers for one man: and all the rulers of the congregation came and told Moses.

23 And he said unto them, This is that which the LORD has said, To morrow is the rest of the holy sabbath unto the LORD: bake that which you will bake to day, and seethe that you will seethe; and that which remaineth over lay up for you to be kept until the morning.

24 And they laid it up till the morning, as Moses bade: and it did not stink, neither was there any worm therein.

25 And Moses said, Eat that to day; for to day is a sabbath unto the LORD: to day you shall not find it in the field.

26 Six days you shall gather it; but on the seventh day, which is the sabbath, in it there shall be none.

27 And it came to pass, that there went out some of the people on the seventh day for to gather, and they found none.

28 And the LORD said unto Moses, How long refuse you to keep my commandments and my laws?

29 See, for that the LORD has given you the sabbath, therefore he giveth you on the sixth day the bread of two days; abide you every man in his place, let no man go out of his place on the seventh day.

30 So the people rested on the seventh day.

31 And the house of Israel called the name thereof Manna: and it was like coriander seed, white; and the taste of it was like wafers made with honey.

32 And Moses said, This is the thing which the LORD commandeth, Fill an omer of it to be kept for your generations; that they may see the bread wherewith I have fed you in the wilderness, when I brought you forth from the land of Egypt.

33 And Moses said unto Aaron, Take a pot, and put an omer full of manna therein, and lay it up before the LORD, to be kept for your generations.

34 As the LORD commanded Moses, so Aaron laid it up before the Testimony, to be kept.

35 And the children of Israel did eat manna forty years, until they came to a land inhabited; they did eat manna, until they came unto the borders of the land of Canaan.

36 Now an omer is the tenth part of an ephah.

CHAPTER 17

AND all the congregation of the children of Israel journeyed from the wilderness of Sin, after their journeys, according to the commandment of the LORD, and pitched in Rephidim: and there was no water for the people to drink.

2 Wherefore the people did chide with Moses, and said, Give us water that we may drink. And Moses said unto them, Why chide you with me? wherefore do you tempt the LORD?

3 And the people thirsted there for water; and the people murmured against Moses, and said, Wherefore is this that you have brought us up out of Egypt, to kill us and our children and our cattle with thirst?

4 And Moses cried unto the LORD, saying, What shall I do unto this people? they be almost ready to stone me.

5 And the LORD said unto Moses, Go on before the people, and take with you of the elders of Israel; and your rod, wherewith you smotest the river, take in yours hand, and go.

6 Behold, I will stand before you there upon the rock in Horeb; and you shalt strike the rock, and there shall come water out of it, that the people may drink. And Moses did so in the sight of the elders of Israel.

7 And he called the name of the place Massah, and Meribah, because of the chiding of the children of Israel, and because they tempted the LORD, saying, Is the LORD among us, or not?

8 Then came Amalek, and fought with Israel in Rephidim.

9 And Moses said unto Joshua, Choose us out men, and go out, fight with Amalek: to morrow I will stand on the top of the hill with the rod of God in my hand.

10 So Joshua did as Moses had said to him, and fought with Amalek: and Moses, Aaron, and Hur went up to the top of the hill.

11 And it came to pass, when Moses held up his hand, that Israel prevailed: and when he let down his hand, Amalek prevailed.

12 But Moses' hands were heavy; and they took a stone, and put it under him, and he sat thereon; and Aaron and Hur stayed up his hands, the one on the one side, and the other on the other side; and his hands were steady until the going down of the sun.

13 And Joshua discomfited Amalek and his people with the edge of the sword.

14 And the LORD said unto Moses, Write this for a memorial in a book, and rehearse it in the ears of Joshua: for I will utterly put out the remembrance of Amalek from under heaven.

15 And Moses built an altar, and called the name of it Jehovah-nissi:

16 For he said, Because the LORD has sworn that the LORD will have war with Amalek from generation to generation.

CHAPTER 18

WHEN Jethro, the priest of Midian, Moses' father in law, heard of all that God had done for Moses, and for Israel his people, and that the LORD had brought Israel out of Egypt;

2 Then Jethro, Moses' father in law, took Zipporah, Moses' wife, after he had sent her back,

3 And her two sons; of which the name of the one was Gershom; for he said, I have been an alien in a strange land:

4 And the name of the other was Eliezer; for the God of my father, said he, was my help, and delivered me from the sword of Pharaoh:

5 And Jethro, Moses' father in law, came with his sons and his wife unto Moses into the wilderness, where he encamped at the mount of God:

6 And he said unto Moses, I your father in law Jethro am come unto you, and your wife, and her two sons with her.

7 And Moses went out to meet his father in law, and did obeisance, and kissed him; and they asked each other of their welfare; and they came into the tent.

8 And Moses told his father in law all that the LORD had done unto Pharaoh and to the Egyptians for Israel's sake, and all the travail that had come upon them by the way, and how the LORD delivered them.

9 And Jethro rejoiced for all the goodness which the LORD had done to Israel, whom he had delivered out of the hand of the Egyptians.

10 And Jethro said, Blessed be the LORD, who has delivered you out of the hand of the Egyptians, and out of the hand of Pharaoh, who has delivered the people from under the hand of the Egyptians.

11 Now I know that the LORD is greater than all gods: for in the thing wherein they dealt proudly he was above them.

12 And Jethro, Moses' father in law, took a burnt offering and sacrifices for God: and Aaron came, and all the elders of Israel, to eat bread with Moses' father in law before God.

13 And it came to pass on the morrow, that Moses sat to judge the people: and the people stood by Moses from the morning unto the evening.

14 And when Moses' father in law saw all that he did to the people, he said, What is this thing that you doest to the people? why sittest you yourself alone, and all the people stand by you from morning unto even?

15 And Moses said unto his father in law, Because the people come unto me to inquire of God:

16 When they have a matter, they come unto me; and I judge between one and another, and I do make them know the statutes of God, and his laws.

17 And Moses' father in law said unto him, The thing that you doest is not good.

18 You will surely wear away, both you , and this people that is with you: for this thing is too heavy for you; you are not able to perform it yourself alone.

19 Hearken now unto my voice, I will give you counsel, and God shall be with you: Be you for the people to God-ward, that you mayest bring the causes unto God:

20 And you shalt teach them ordinances and laws, and shalt shew them the way wherein they must walk, and the work that they must do.

21 Moreover you shalt provide out of all the people able men, such as fear God, men of truth, hating covetousness; and place such over them, to be rulers of thousands, and rulers of hundreds, rulers of fifties, and rulers of tens:

22 And let them judge the people at all seasons: and it shall be, that every great matter they shall bring unto you, but every small matter they shall judge: so shall it be easier for yourself, and they shall bear the burden with you.

23 If you shalt do this thing, and God command you so, then you shalt be able to endure, and all this people shall also go to their place in peace.

24 So Moses hearkened to the voice of his father in law, and did all that he had said.

25 And Moses chose able men out of all Israel, and made them heads over the people, rulers of thousands, rulers of hundreds, rulers of fifties, and rulers of tens.

26 And they judged the people at all seasons: the hard causes they brought unto Moses, but every small matter they judged themselves.

27 And Moses let his father in law depart; and he went his way into his own land.

CHAPTER 19

IN the third month, when the children of Israel were gone forth out of the land of Egypt, the same day came they into the wilderness of Sinai.

2 For they were departed from Rephidim, and were come to the desert of Sinai, and had pitched in the wilderness; and there Israel camped before the mount.

3 And Moses went up unto God, and the LORD called unto him out of the mountain, saying, Thus shalt you say to the house of Jacob, and tell the children of Israel;

4 You have seen what I did unto the Egyptians, and how I bare you on eagles' wings, and brought you unto myself.

5 Now therefore, if you will obey my voice indeed, and keep my covenant, then you shall be a peculiar treasure unto me above all people: for all the earth is my:

6 And you shall be unto me a kingdom of priests, and an holy nation. These are the words which you shalt speak unto the children of Israel.

7 And Moses came and called for the elders of the people, and laid before their faces all these words which the LORD commanded him.

8 And all the people answered together, and said, All that the LORD has spoken we will do. And Moses returned the words of the people unto the LORD.

9 And the LORD said unto Moses, Lo, I come unto you in a thick cloud, that the people may hear when I speak with you, and believe you for ever. And Moses told the words of the people unto the LORD.

10 And the LORD said unto Moses, Go unto the people, and sanctify them to day and to morrow, and let them wash their clothes,

11 And be ready against the third day: for the third day the LORD will come down in the sight of all the people upon mount Sinai.

12 And you shalt set bounds unto the people round about, saying, Take heed to yourselves, that you go not up into the mount, or touch the border of it: whosoever toucheth the mount shall be surely put to death:

13 There shall not an hand touch it, but he shall surely be stoned, or shot through; whether it be beast or man, it shall not live: when the trumpet soundeth long, they shall come up to the mount.

14 And Moses went down from the mount unto the people, and sanctified the people; and they washed their clothes.

15 And he said unto the people, Be ready against the third day: come not at your wives.

16 And it came to pass on the third day in the morning, that there were thunders and lightnings, and a thick cloud upon the mount, and the voice of the trumpet exceeding loud; so that all the people that was in the camp trembled.

17 And Moses brought forth the people out of the camp to meet with God; and they stood at the nether part of the mount.

18 And mount Sinai was altogether on a smoke, because the LORD descended upon it in fire: and the smoke thereof ascended as the smoke of a furnace, and the whole mount quaked greatly.

19 And when the voice of the trumpet sounded long, and waxed louder and louder, Moses spake, and God answered him by a voice.

20 And the LORD came down upon mount Sinai, on the top of the mount: and the LORD called Moses up to the top of the mount; and Moses went up.

21 And the LORD said unto Moses, Go down, charge the people, lest they break through unto the LORD to gaze, and many of them perish.

22 And let the priests also, which come near to the LORD, sanctify themselves, lest the LORD break forth upon them.

23 And Moses said unto the LORD, The people cannot come up to mount Sinai: for you chargedst us, saying, Set bounds about the mount, and sanctify it.

24 And the LORD said unto him, Away, get you down, and you shalt come up, you , and Aaron with you: but let not the priests and the people break through to come up unto the LORD, lest he break forth upon them.

25 So Moses went down unto the people, and spake unto them.

CHAPTER 20

AND God spake all these words, saying,

2 I am the LORD your God, which have brought you out of the land of Egypt, out of the house of bondage.

3 You shalt have no other gods before me.

4 You shalt not make unto you any graven image, or any likeness of any thing that is in heaven above, or that is in the earth beneath, or that is in the water under the earth:

5 You shalt not bow down yourself to them, nor serve them: for I the LORD your God am a jealous God, visiting the iniquity of the fathers upon the children unto the third and fourth generation of them that hate me;

6 And shewing mercy unto thousands of them that love me, and keep my commandments.

7 You shalt not take the name of the LORD your God in vain; for the LORD will not hold him guiltless that taketh his name in vain.

8 Remember the sabbath day, to keep it holy.

9 Six days shalt you labour, and do all your work:

10 But the seventh day is the sabbath of the LORD your God: in it you shalt not do any work, you , nor your son, nor your daughter, your manservant, nor your maidservant, nor your cattle, nor your stranger that is within your gates:

11 For in six days the LORD made heaven and earth, the sea, and all that in them is, and rested the seventh day: wherefore the LORD blessed the sabbath day, and hallowed it.

12 Honour your father and your mother: that your days may be long upon the land which the LORD your God giveth you.

13 You shalt not kill.

14 You shalt not commit adultery.

15 You shalt not steal.

16 You shalt not bear false witness against your neighbour.

17 You shalt not covet your neighbour's house, you shalt not covet your neighbour's wife, nor his manservant, nor his maidservant, nor his ox, nor his ass, nor any thing that is your neighbour's.

18 And all the people saw the thunderings, and the lightnings, and the noise of the trumpet, and the mountain smoking: and when the people saw it, they removed, and stood afar off.

19 And they said unto Moses, Speak you with us, and we will hear: but let not God speak with us, lest we die.

20 And Moses said unto the people, Fear not: for God is come to prove you, and that his fear may be before your faces, that you sin not.

21 And the people stood afar off, and Moses drew near unto the thick darkness where God was.

22 And the LORD said unto Moses, Thus you shalt say unto the children of Israel, You have seen that I have talked with you from heaven.

23 You shall not make with me gods of silver, neither shall you make unto you gods of gold.

24An altar of earth you shalt make unto me, and shalt sacrifice thereon your burnt offerings, and your peace offerings, your sheep, and yours oxen: in all places where I record my name I will come unto you, and I will bless you.

25 And if you will make me an altar of stone, you shalt not build it of hewn stone: for if you lift up your tool upon it, you have polluted it.

26 Neither shalt you go up by steps unto my altar, that your nakedness be not discovered thereon.

CHAPTER 21

NOW these are the judgments which you shalt set before them.

2 If you buy an Hebrew servant, six years he shall serve: and in the seventh he shall go out free for nothing.

3 If he came in by himself, he shall go out by himself: if he were married, then his wife shall go out with him.

4 If his master have given him a wife, and she have born him sons or daughters; the wife and her children shall be her master's, and he shall go out by himself.

5 And if the servant shall plainly say, I love my master, my wife, and my children; I will not go out free:

6 Then his master shall bring him unto the judges; he shall also bring him to the door, or unto the door post; and his master shall bore his ear through with an aul; and he shall serve him for ever.

7And if a man sell his daughter to be a maidservant, she shall not go out as the menservants do.

8 If she please not her master, who has betrothed her to himself, then shall he let her be redeemed: to sell her unto a strange nation he shall have no power, seeing he has dealt deceitfully with her.

9 And if he have betrothed her unto his son, he shall deal with her after the manner of daughters.

10 If he take him another wife; her food, her raiment, and her duty of marriage, shall he not diminish.

11 And if he do not these three unto her, then shall she go out free without money.

12He that smiteth a man, so that he die, shall be surely put to death.

13 And if a man lie not in wait, but God deliver him into his hand; then I will appoint you a place whither he shall flee.

14 But if a man come presumptuously upon his neighbour, to slay him with guile; you shalt take him from my altar, that he may die.

15And he that smiteth his father, or his mother, shall be surely put to death.

16And he that stealeth a man, and selleth him, or if he be found in his hand, he shall surely be put to death.

17And he that curseth his father, or his mother, shall surely be put to death.

18And if men strive together, and one strike another with a stone, or with his fist, and he die not, but keepeth his bed:

19 If he rise again, and walk abroad upon his staff, then shall he that struck him be quit: only he shall pay for the loss of his time, and shall cause him to be thoroughly healed.

20And if a man strike his servant, or his maid, with a rod, and he die under his hand; he shall be surely punished.

21 Notwithstanding, if he continue a day or two, he shall not be punished: for he is his money.

22If men strive, and hurt a woman with child, so that her fruit depart from her, and yet no mischief follow: he shall be surely punished, according as the woman's husband will lay upon him; and he shall pay as the judges determine.

23 And if any mischief follow, then you shalt give life for life,

24 Eye for eye, tooth for tooth, hand for hand, foot for foot,

25 Burning for burning, wound for wound, stripe for stripe.

26And if a man strike the eye of his servant, or the eye of his maid, that it perish; he shall let him go free for his eye's sake.

27 And if he strike out his manservant's tooth, or his maidservant's tooth; he shall let him go free for his tooth's sake.

28If an ox gore a man or a woman, that they die: then the ox shall be surely stoned, and his flesh shall not be eaten; but the owner of the ox shall be quit.

29 But if the ox were wont to push with his horn in time past, and it has been testified to his owner, and he has not kept him in, but that he has killed a man or a woman; the ox shall be stoned, and his owner also shall be put to death.

30 If there be laid on him a sum of money, then he shall give for the ransom of his life whatsoever is laid upon him.

31 Whether he have gored a son, or have gored a daughter, according to this judgment shall it be done unto him.

32 If the ox shall push a manservant or a maidservant; he shall give unto their master thirty shekels of silver, and the ox shall be stoned.

33And if a man shall open a pit, or if a man shall dig a pit, and not cover it, and an ox or an ass fall therein;

34 The owner of the pit shall make it good, and give money unto the owner of them; and the dead beast shall be his.

35And if one man's ox hurt another's, that he die; then they shall sell the live ox, and divide the money of it; and the dead ox also they shall divide.

36 Or if it be known that the ox has used to push in time past, and his owner has not kept him in; he shall surely pay ox for ox; and the dead shall be his own.

CHAPTER 22

IF a man shall steal an ox, or a sheep, and kill it, or sell it; he shall restore five oxen for an ox, and four sheep for a sheep.

2If a thief be found breaking up, and be smitten that he die, there shall no blood be shed for him.

3 If the sun be risen upon him, there shall be blood shed for him; for he should make full restitution; if he have nothing, then he shall be sold for his theft.

4 If the theft be certainly found in his hand alive, whether it be ox, or ass, or sheep; he shall restore double.

5If a man shall cause a field or vineyard to be eaten, and shall put in his beast, and shall feed in another man's field; of the best of his own field, and of the best of his own vineyard, shall he make restitution.

6If fire break out, and catch in thorns, so that the stacks of corn, or the standing corn, or the field, be consumed therewith; he that kindled the fire shall surely make restitution.

7If a man shall deliver unto his neighbour money or stuff to keep, and it be stolen out of the man's house; if the thief be found, let him pay double.

8 If the thief be not found, then the master of the house shall be brought unto the judges, to see whether he have put his hand unto his neighbour's goods.

9 For all manner of trespass, whether it be for ox, for ass, for sheep, for raiment, or for any manner of lost thing, which another challengeth to be his, the cause of both parties shall come before the judges; and whom the judges shall condemn, he shall pay double unto his neighbour.

10 If a man deliver unto his neighbour an ass, or an ox, or a sheep, or any beast, to keep; and it die, or be hurt, or driven away, no man seeing it:

11 Then shall an oath of the LORD be between them both, that he has not put his hand unto his neighbour's goods; and the owner of it shall accept thereof, and he shall not make it good.

12 And if it be stolen from him, he shall make restitution unto the owner thereof.

13 If it be torn in pieces, then let him bring it for witness, and he shall not make good that which was torn.

14And if a man borrow ought of his neighbour, and it be hurt, or die, the owner thereof being not with it, he shall surely make it good.

15 But if the owner thereof be with it, he shall not make it good: if it be an hired thing, it came for his hire.

16And if a man entice a maid that is not betrothed, and lie with her, he shall surely endow her to be his wife.

17 If her father utterly refuse to give her unto him, he shall pay money according to the dowry of virgins.

18You shalt not suffer a witch to live.

19Whosoever lies with a beast shall surely be put to death.

20He that sacrificeth unto any god, save unto the LORD only, he shall be utterly destroyed.

21You shalt neither vex a stranger, nor oppress him: for you were strangers in the land of Egypt.

22You shall not afflict any widow, or fatherless child.

23 If you afflict them in any wise, and they cry at all unto me, I will surely hear their cry;

24 And my wrath shall wax hot, and I will kill you with the sword; and your wives shall be widows, and your children fatherless.

25If you lend money to any of my people that is poor by you, you shalt not be to him as an usurer, neither shalt you lay upon him usury.

26 If you at all take your neighbour's raiment to pledge, you shalt deliver it unto him by that the sun goeth down:

27 For that is his covering only, it is his raiment for his skin: wherein shall he sleep? and it shall come to pass, when he crieth unto me, that I will hear; for I am gracious.

28You shalt not revile the gods, nor curse the ruler of your people.

29You shalt not delay to offer the first of your ripe fruits, and of your liquors: the firstborn of your sons shalt you give unto me.

30 Likewise shalt you do with yours oxen, and with your sheep: seven days it shall be with his dam; on the eighth day you shalt give it me.

31 And you shall be holy men unto me: neither shall you eat any flesh that is torn of beasts in the field; you shall cast it to the dogs.

CHAPTER 23

YOU shalt not raise a false report: put not yours hand with the wicked to be an unrighteous witness.

2 You shalt not follow a multitude to do evil; neither shalt you speak in a cause to decline after many to wrest judgment:

3 Neither shalt you countenance a poor man in his cause.

4 If you meet yours enemy's ox or his ass going astray, you shalt surely bring it back to him again.

5 If you see the ass of him that hateth you lying under his burden, and wouldest forbear to help him, you shalt surely help with him.

6 You shalt not wrest the judgment of your poor in his cause.

7 Keep you far from a false matter; and the innocent and righteous slay you not: for I will not justify the wicked.

8 And you shalt take no gift: for the gift blindeth the wise, and perverteth the words of the righteous.

9 Also you shalt not oppress a stranger: for you know the heart of a stranger, seeing you were strangers in the land of Egypt.

10 And six years you shalt sow your land, and shalt gather in the fruits thereof:

11 But the seventh year you shalt let it rest and lie still; that the poor of your people may eat: and what they leave the beasts of the field shall eat. In like manner you shalt deal with your vineyard, and with your oliveyard.

12 Six days you shalt do your work, and on the seventh day you shalt rest: that yours ox and yours ass may rest, and the son of your handmaid, and the stranger, may be refreshed.

13 And in all things that I have said unto you be circumspect: and make no mention of the name of other gods, neither let it be heard out of your mouth.

14 Three times you shalt keep a feast unto me in the year.

15 You shalt keep the feast of unleavened bread: (you shalt eat unleavened bread seven days, as I commanded you, in the time appointed of the month Abib; for in it you camest out from Egypt: and none shall appear before me empty:)

16 And the feast of harvest, the firstfruits of your labours, which you have sown in the field: and the feast of ingathering, which is in the end of the year, when you have gathered in your labours out of the field.

17 Three times in the year all your males shall appear before the Lord GOD.

18 You shalt not offer the blood of my sacrifice with leavened bread; neither shall the fat of my sacrifice remain until the morning.

19 The first of the firstfruits of your land you shalt bring into the house of the LORD your God. You shalt not seethe a kid in his mother's milk.

20 Behold, I send an Angel before you, to keep you in the way, and to bring you into the place which I have prepared.

21 Beware of him, and obey his voice, provoke him not; for he will not pardon your transgressions: for my name is in him.

22 But if you shalt indeed obey his voice, and do all that I speak; then I will be an enemy unto yours enemies, and an adversary unto yours adversaries.

23 For my Angel shall go before you, and bring you in unto the Amorites, and the Hittites, and the Perizzites, and the Canaanites, and the Hivites, and the Jebusites: and I will cut them off.

24 You shalt not bow down to their gods, nor serve them, nor do after their works: but you shalt utterly overthrow them, and quite break down their images.

25 And you shall serve the LORD your God, and he shall bless your bread, and your water; and I will take sickness away from the midst of you.

26 There shall nothing cast their young, nor be barren, in your land: the number of your days I will fulfil.

27 I will send my fear before you, and will destroy all the people to whom you shalt come, and I will make all yours enemies turn their backs unto you.

28 And I will send hornets before you, which shall drive out the Hivite, the Canaanite, and the Hittite, from before you.

29 I will not drive them out from before you in one year; lest the land become desolate, and the beast of the field multiply against you.

30 By little and little I will drive them out from before you, until you be increased, and inherit the land.

31 And I will set your bounds from the Red sea even unto the sea of the Philistines, and from the desert unto the river: for I will deliver the inhabitants of the land into your hand; and you shalt drive them out before you.

32 You shalt make no covenant with them, nor with their gods.

33 They shall not dwell in your land, lest they make you sin against me: for if you serve their gods, it will surely be a snare unto you.

CHAPTER 24

AND he said unto Moses, Come up unto the LORD, you , and Aaron, Nadab, and Abihu, and seventy of the elders of Israel; and worship you afar off.

2 And Moses alone shall come near the LORD: but they shall not come nigh; neither shall the people go up with him.

3 And Moses came and told the people all the words of the LORD, and all the judgments: and all the people answered with one voice, and said, All the words which the LORD has said will we do.

4 And Moses wrote all the words of the LORD, and rose up early in the morning, and builded an altar under the hill, and twelve pillars, according to the twelve tribes of Israel.

5 And he sent young men of the children of Israel, which offered burnt offerings, and sacrificed peace offerings of oxen unto the LORD.

6 And Moses took half of the blood, and put it in basons; and half of the blood he sprinkled on the altar.

7 And he took the book of the covenant, and read in the audience of the people: and they said, All that the LORD has said will we do, and be obedient.

8 And Moses took the blood, and sprinkled it on the people, and said, Behold the blood of the covenant, which the LORD has made with you concerning all these words.

9 Then went up Moses, and Aaron, Nadab, and Abihu, and seventy of the elders of Israel:

10 And they saw the God of Israel: and there was under his feet as it were a paved work of a sapphire stone, and as it were the body of heaven in his clearness.

11 And upon the nobles of the children of Israel he laid not his hand: also they saw God, and did eat and drink.

12 And the LORD said unto Moses, Come up to me into the mount, and be there: and I will give you tables of stone, and a law, and commandments which I have written; that you mayest teach them.

13 And Moses rose up, and his minister Joshua: and Moses went up into the mount of God.

14 And he said unto the elders, Tarry you here for us, until we come again unto you: and, behold, Aaron and Hur are with you: if any man have any matters to do, let him come unto them.

15 And Moses went up into the mount, and a cloud covered the mount.

16 And the glory of the LORD abode upon mount Sinai, and the cloud covered it six days: and the seventh day he called unto Moses out of the midst of the cloud.

17 And the sight of the glory of the LORD was like devouring fire on the top of the mount in the eyes of the children of Israel.

18 And Moses went into the midst of the cloud, and gat him up into the mount: and Moses was in the mount forty days and forty nights.

CHAPTER 25

AND the LORD spake unto Moses, saying,

2 Speak unto the children of Israel, that they bring me an offering: of every man that giveth it willingly with his heart you shall take my offering.

3 And this is the offering which you shall take of them; gold, and silver, and brass,

4 And blue, and purple, and scarlet, and fine linen, and goats' hair,

5 And rams' skins dyed red, and badgers' skins, and shittim wood,

6 Oil for the light, spices for anointing oil, and for sweet incense,

7 Onyx stones, and stones to be set in the ephod, and in the breastplate.

8 And let them make me a sanctuary; that I may dwell among them.

9 According to all that I shew you, after the pattern of the tabernacle, and the pattern of all the instruments thereof, even so shall you make it.

10 And they shall make an ark of shittim wood: two cubits and a half shall be the length thereof, and a cubit and a half the breadth thereof, and a cubit and a half the height thereof.

11 And you shalt overlay it with pure gold, within and without shalt you overlay it, and shalt make upon it a crown of gold round about.

12 And you shalt cast four rings of gold for it, and put them in the four corners thereof; and two rings shall be in the one side of it, and two rings in the other side of it.

13 And you shalt make staves of shittim wood, and overlay them with gold.

14 And you shalt put the staves into the rings by the sides of the ark, that the ark may be borne with them.

15 The staves shall be in the rings of the ark: they shall not be taken from it.

16 And you shalt put into the ark the testimony which I shall give you.

17 And you shalt make a mercy seat of pure gold: two cubits and a half shall be the length thereof, and a cubit and a half the breadth thereof.

18 And you shalt make two cherubims of gold, of beaten work shalt you make them, in the two ends of the mercy seat.

19 And make one cherub on the one end, and the other cherub on the other end: even of the mercy seat shall you make the cherubims on the two ends thereof.

20 And the cherubims shall stretch forth their wings on high, covering the mercy seat with their wings, and their faces shall look one to another; toward the mercy seat shall the faces of the cherubims be.

21 And you shalt put the mercy seat above upon the ark; and in the ark you shalt put the testimony that I shall give you.

22 And there I will meet with you, and I will commune with you from above the mercy seat, from between the two cherubims which are upon the ark of the testimony, of all things which I will give you in commandment unto the children of Israel.

23 You shalt also make a table of shittim wood: two cubits shall be the length thereof, and a cubit the breadth thereof, and a cubit and a half the height thereof.

24 And you shalt overlay it with pure gold, and make thereto a crown of gold round about.

25 And you shalt make unto it a border of an hand breadth round about, and you shalt make a golden crown to the border thereof round about.

26 And you shalt make for it four rings of gold, and put the rings in the four corners that are on the four feet thereof.

27 Over against the border shall the rings be for places of the staves to bear the table.

28 And you shalt make the staves of shittim wood, and overlay them with gold, that the table may be borne with them.

29 And you shalt make the dishes thereof, and spoons thereof, and covers thereof, and bowls thereof, to cover withal: of pure gold shalt you make them.

30 And you shalt set upon the table shewbread before me alway.

31 And you shalt make a candlestick of pure gold: of beaten work shall the candlestick be made: his shaft, and his branches, his bowls, his knops, and his flowers, shall be of the same.

32 And six branches shall come out of the sides of it; three branches of the candlestick out of the one side, and three branches of the candlestick out of the other side:

33 Three bowls made like unto almonds, with a knop and a flower in one branch; and three bowls made like almonds in the other branch, with a knop and a flower: so in the six branches that come out of the candlestick.

34 And in the candlestick shall be four bowls made like unto almonds, with their knops and their flowers.

35 And there shall be a knop under two branches of the same, and a knop under two branches of the same, and a knop under two branches of the same, according to the six branches that proceed out of the candlestick.

36 Their knops and their branches shall be of the same: all it shall be one beaten work of pure gold.

37 And you shalt make the seven lamps thereof: and they shall light the lamps thereof, that they may give light over against it.

38 And the tongs thereof, and the snuffdishes thereof, shall be of pure gold.

39 Of a talent of pure gold shall he make it, with all these vessels.

40 And look that you make them after their pattern, which was shewed you in the mount.

CHAPTER 26

MOREOVER you shalt make the tabernacle with ten curtains of fine twined linen, and blue, and purple, and scarlet: with cherubims of cunning work shalt you make them.

2 The length of one curtain shall be eight and twenty cubits, and the breadth of one curtain four cubits: and every one of the curtains shall have one measure.

3 The five curtains shall be coupled together one to another; and other five curtains shall be coupled one to another.

4 And you shalt make loops of blue upon the edge of the one curtain from the selvedge in the coupling; and likewise shalt you make in the uttermost edge of another curtain, in the coupling of the second.

5 Fifty loops shalt you make in the one curtain, and fifty loops shalt you make in the edge of the curtain that is in the coupling of the second; that the loops may take hold one of another.

6 And you shalt make fifty taches of gold, and couple the curtains together with the taches: and it shall be one tabernacle.

7 And you shalt make curtains of goats' hair to be a covering upon the tabernacle: eleven curtains shalt you make.

8 The length of one curtain shall be thirty cubits, and the breadth of one curtain four cubits: and the eleven curtains shall be all of one measure.

9 And you shalt couple five curtains by themselves, and six curtains by themselves, and shalt double the sixth curtain in the forefront of the tabernacle.

10 And you shalt make fifty loops on the edge of the one curtain that is outmost in the coupling, and fifty loops in the edge of the curtain which coupleth the second.

11 And you shalt make fifty taches of brass, and put the taches into the loops, and couple the tent together, that it may be one.

12 And the remnant that remaineth of the curtains of the tent, the half curtain that remaineth, shall hang over the backside of the tabernacle.

13 And a cubit on the one side, and a cubit on the other side of that which remaineth in the length of the curtains of the tent, it shall hang over the sides of the tabernacle on this side and on that side, to cover it.

14 And you shalt make a covering for the tent of rams' skins dyed red, and a covering above of badgers' skins.

15 And you shalt make boards for the tabernacle of shittim wood standing up.

16 Ten cubits shall be the length of a board, and a cubit and a half shall be the breadth of one board.

17 Two tenons shall there be in one board, set in order one against another: thus shalt you make for all the boards of the tabernacle.

18 And you shalt make the boards for the tabernacle, twenty boards on the south side southward.

19 And you shalt make forty sockets of silver under the twenty boards; two sockets under one board for his two tenons, and two sockets under another board for his two tenons.

20 And for the second side of the tabernacle on the north side there shall be twenty boards:

21 And their forty sockets of silver; two sockets under one board, and two sockets under another board.

22 And for the sides of the tabernacle westward you shalt make six boards.

23 And two boards shalt you make for the corners of the tabernacle in the two sides.

24 And they shall be coupled together beneath, and they shall be coupled together above the head of it unto one ring: thus shall it be for them both; they shall be for the two corners.

25 And they shall be eight boards, and their sockets of silver, sixteen sockets; two sockets under one board, and two sockets under another board.

26 And you shalt make bars of shittim wood; five for the boards of the one side of the tabernacle,

27 And five bars for the boards of the other side of the tabernacle, and five bars for the boards of the side of the tabernacle, for the two sides westward.

28 And the middle bar in the midst of the boards shall reach from end to end.

29 And you shalt overlay the boards with gold, and make their rings of gold for places for the bars: and you shalt overlay the bars with gold.

30 And you shalt rear up the tabernacle according to the fashion thereof which was shewed you in the mount.

31 And you shalt make a vail of blue, and purple, and scarlet, and fine twined linen of cunning work: with cherubims shall it be made:

32 And you shalt hang it upon four pillars of shittim wood overlaid with gold: their hooks shall be of gold, upon the four sockets of silver.

33 And you shalt hang up the vail under the taches, that you mayest bring in thither within the vail the ark of the testimony: and the vail shall divide unto you between the holy place and the most holy.

34 And you shalt put the mercy seat upon the ark of the testimony in the most holy place.

35 And you shalt set the table without the vail, and the candlestick over against the table on the side of the tabernacle toward the south: and you shalt put the table on the north side.

36 And you shalt make an hanging for the door of the tent, of blue, and purple, and scarlet, and fine twined linen, created with needlework.

37 And you shalt make for the hanging five pillars of shittim wood, and overlay them with gold, and their hooks shall be of gold: and you shalt cast five sockets of brass for them.

CHAPTER 27

AND you shalt make an altar of shittim wood, five cubits long, and five cubits broad; the altar shall be foursquare: and the height thereof shall be three cubits.

44

2 And you shalt make the horns of it upon the four corners thereof: his horns shall be of the same: and you shalt overlay it with brass.

3 And you shalt make his pans to receive his ashes, and his shovels, and his basons, and his fleshhooks, and his firepans: all the vessels thereof you shalt make of brass.

4 And you shalt make for it a grate of network of brass; and upon the net shalt you make four brasen rings in the four corners thereof.

5 And you shalt put it under the compass of the altar beneath, that the net may be even to the midst of the altar.

6 And you shalt make staves for the altar, staves of shittim wood, and overlay them with brass.

7 And the staves shall be put into the rings, and the staves shall be upon the two sides of the altar, to bear it.

8 Hollow with boards shalt you make it: as it was shewed you in the mount, so shall they make it.

9 And you shalt make the court of the tabernacle: for the south side southward there shall be hangings for the court of fine twined linen of an hundred cubits long for one side:

10 And the twenty pillars thereof and their twenty sockets shall be of brass; the hooks of the pillars and their fillets shall be of silver.

11 And likewise for the north side in length there shall be hangings of an hundred cubits long, and his twenty pillars and their twenty sockets of brass; the hooks of the pillars and their fillets of silver.

12 And for the breadth of the court on the west side shall be hangings of fifty cubits: their pillars ten, and their sockets ten.

13 And the breadth of the court on the east side eastward shall be fifty cubits.

14 The hangings of one side of the gate shall be fifteen cubits: their pillars three, and their sockets three.

15 And on the other side shall be hangings fifteen cubits: their pillars three, and their sockets three.

16 And for the gate of the court shall be an hanging of twenty cubits, of blue, and purple, and scarlet, and fine twined linen, created with needlework: and their pillars shall be four, and their sockets four.

17 All the pillars round about the court shall be filleted with silver; their hooks shall be of silver, and their sockets of brass.

18 The length of the court shall be an hundred cubits, and the breadth fifty every where, and the height five cubits of fine twined linen, and their sockets of brass.

19 All the vessels of the tabernacle in all the service thereof, and all the pins thereof, and all the pins of the court, shall be of brass.

20 And you shalt command the children of Israel, that they bring you pure oil olive beaten for the light, to cause the lamp to burn always.

21 In the tabernacle of the congregation without the vail, which is before the testimony, Aaron and his sons shall order it from evening to morning before the LORD: it shall be a statute for ever unto their generations on the behalf of the children of Israel.

CHAPTER 28

AND take you unto you Aaron your brother, and his sons with him, from among the children of Israel, that he may minister unto me in the priest's office, even Aaron, Nadab and Abihu, Eleazar and Ithamar, Aaron's sons.

2 And you shalt make holy garments for Aaron your brother for glory and for beauty.

3 And you shalt speak unto all that are wise hearted, whom I have filled with the spirit of wisdom, that they may make Aaron's garments to consecrate him, that he may minister unto me in the priest's office.

4 And these are the garments which they shall make; a breastplate, and an ephod, and a robe, and a broidered coat, a mitre, and a girdle: and they shall make holy garments for Aaron your brother, and his sons, that he may minister unto me in the priest's office.

5 And they shall take gold, and blue, and purple, and scarlet, and fine linen.

6 And they shall make the ephod of gold, of blue, and of purple, of scarlet, and fine twined linen, with cunning work.

7 It shall have the two shoulderpieces thereof joined at the two edges thereof; and so it shall be joined together.

8 And the curious girdle of the ephod, which is upon it, shall be of the same, according to the work thereof; even of gold, of blue, and purple, and scarlet, and fine twined linen.

9 And you shalt take two onyx stones, and grave on them the names of the children of Israel:

10 Six of their names on one stone, and the other six names of the rest on the other stone, according to their birth.

11 With the work of an engraver in stone, like the engravings of a signet, shalt you engrave the two stones with the names of the children of Israel: you shalt make them to be set in ouches of gold.

12 And you shalt put the two stones upon the shoulders of the ephod for stones of memorial unto the children of Israel: and Aaron shall bear their names before the LORD upon his two shoulders for a memorial.

13 And you shalt make ouches of gold;

14 And two chains of pure gold at the ends; of wreathen work shalt you make them, and fasten the wreathen chains to the ouches.

15 And you shalt make the breastplate of judgment with cunning work; after the work of the ephod you shalt make it; of gold, of blue, and of purple, and of scarlet, and of fine twined linen, shalt you make it.

16 Foursquare it shall be being doubled; a span shall be the length thereof, and a span shall be the breadth thereof.

17 And you shalt set in it settings of stones, even four rows of stones: the first row shall be a sardius, a topaz, and a carbuncle: this shall be the first row.

18 And the second row shall be an emerald, a sapphire, and a diamond.

19 And the third row a ligure, an agate, and an amethyst.

20 And the fourth row a beryl, and an onyx, and a jasper: they shall be set in gold in their inclosings.

21 And the stones shall be with the names of the children of Israel, twelve, according to their names, like the engravings of a signet; every one with his name shall they be according to the twelve tribes.

22 And you shalt make upon the breastplate chains at the ends of wreathen work of pure gold.

23 And you shalt make upon the breastplate two rings of gold, and shalt put the two rings on the two ends of the breastplate.

24 And you shalt put the two wreathen chains of gold in the two rings which are on the ends of the breastplate.

25 And the other two ends of the two wreathen chains you shalt fasten in the two ouches, and put them on the shoulderpieces of the ephod before it.

26 And you shalt make two rings of gold, and you shalt put them upon the two ends of the breastplate in the border thereof, which is in the side of the ephod inward.

27 And two other rings of gold you shalt make, and shalt put them on the two sides of the ephod underneath, toward the forepart thereof, over against the other coupling thereof, above the curious girdle of the ephod.

28 And they shall bind the breastplate by the rings thereof unto the rings of the ephod with a lace of blue, that it may be above the curious girdle of the ephod, and that the breastplate be not loosed from the ephod.

29 And Aaron shall bear the names of the children of Israel in the breastplate of judgment upon his heart, when he goeth in unto the holy place, for a memorial before the LORD continually.

30 And you shalt put in the breastplate of judgment the Urim and the Thummim; and they shall be upon Aaron's heart, when he goeth in before the LORD: and Aaron shall bear the judgment of the children of Israel upon his heart before the LORD continually.

31 And you shalt make the robe of the ephod all of blue.

32 And there shall be an hole in the top of it, in the midst thereof: it shall have a binding of woven work round about the hole of it, as it were the hole of an habergeon, that it be not rent.

33 And beneath upon the hem of it you shalt make pomegranates of blue, and of purple, and of scarlet, round about the hem thereof; and bells of gold between them round about:

34 A golden bell and a pomegranate, a golden bell and a pomegranate, upon the hem of the robe round about.

35 And it shall be upon Aaron to minister: and his sound shall be heard when he goeth in unto the holy place before the LORD, and when he comes out, that he die not.

36 And you shalt make a plate of pure gold, and grave upon it, like the engravings of a signet, HOLINESS TO THE LORD.

37 And you shalt put it on a blue lace, that it may be upon the mitre; upon the forefront of the mitre it shall be.

38 And it shall be upon Aaron's forehead, that Aaron may bear the iniquity of the holy things, which the children of Israel shall hallow in all their holy gifts; and it shall be always upon his forehead, that they may be accepted before the LORD.

39 And you shalt embroider the coat of fine linen, and you shalt make the mitre of fine linen, and you shalt make the girdle of needlework.

40 And for Aaron's sons you shalt make coats, and you shalt make for them girdles, and bonnets shalt you make for them, for glory and for beauty.

41 And you shalt put them upon Aaron your brother, and his sons with him; and shalt anoint them, and consecrate them, and sanctify them, that they may minister unto me in the priest's office.

42 And you shalt make them linen breeches to cover their nakedness; from the loins even unto the thighs they shall reach:

43 And they shall be upon Aaron, and upon his sons, when they come in unto the tabernacle of the congregation, or when they come near unto the altar to minister in the holy place; that they bear not iniquity, and die: it shall be a statute for ever unto him and his seed after him.

CHAPTER 29

AND this is the thing that you shalt do unto them to hallow them, to minister unto me in the priest's office: Take one young bullock, and two rams without blemish,

2 And unleavened bread, and cakes unleavened tempered with oil, and wafers unleavened anointed with oil: of wheaten flour shalt you make them.

3 And you shalt put them into one basket, and bring them in the basket, with the bullock and the two rams.

4 And Aaron and his sons you shalt bring unto the door of the tabernacle of the congregation, and shalt wash them with water.

5 And you shalt take the garments, and put upon Aaron the coat, and the robe of the ephod, and the ephod, and the breastplate, and gird him with the curious girdle of the ephod:

6 And you shalt put the mitre upon his head, and put the holy crown upon the mitre.

7 Then shalt you take the anointing oil, and pour it upon his head, and anoint him.

8 And you shalt bring his sons, and put coats upon them.

9 And you shalt gird them with girdles, Aaron and his sons, and put the bonnets on them: and the priest's office shall be theirs for a perpetual statute: and you shalt consecrate Aaron and his sons.

10 And you shalt cause a bullock to be brought before the tabernacle of the congregation: and Aaron and his sons shall put their hands upon the head of the bullock.

11 And you shalt kill the bullock before the LORD, by the door of the tabernacle of the congregation.

12 And you shalt take of the blood of the bullock, and put it upon the horns of the altar with your finger, and pour all the blood beside the bottom of the altar.

13 And you shalt take all the fat that covers the inwards, and the caul that is above the liver, and the two kidneys, and the fat that is upon them, and burn them upon the altar.

14 But the flesh of the bullock, and his skin, and his dung, shalt you burn with fire without the camp: it is a sin offering.

15 You shalt also take one ram; and Aaron and his sons shall put their hands upon the head of the ram.

16 And you shalt slay the ram, and you shalt take his blood, and sprinkle it round about upon the altar.

17 And you shalt cut the ram in pieces, and wash the inwards of him, and his legs, and put them unto his pieces, and unto his head.

18 And you shalt burn the whole ram upon the altar: it is a burnt offering unto the LORD: it is a sweet savour, an offering made by fire unto the LORD.

19 And you shalt take the other ram; and Aaron and his sons shall put their hands upon the head of the ram.

20 Then shalt you kill the ram, and take of his blood, and put it upon the tip of the right ear of Aaron, and upon the tip of the right ear of his sons, and upon the thumb of their right hand, and upon the great toe of their right foot, and sprinkle the blood upon the altar round about.

21 And you shalt take of the blood that is upon the altar, and of the anointing oil, and sprinkle it upon Aaron, and upon his garments, and upon his sons, and upon the garments of his sons with him: and he shall be hallowed, and his garments, and his sons, and his sons' garments with him.

22 Also you shalt take of the ram the fat and the rump, and the fat that covers the inwards, and the caul above the liver, and the two kidneys, and the fat that is upon them, and the right shoulder; for it is a ram of consecration:

23 And one loaf of bread, and one cake of oiled bread, and one wafer out of the basket of the unleavened bread that is before the LORD:

24 And you shalt put all in the hands of Aaron, and in the hands of his sons; and shalt wave them for a wave offering before the LORD.

25 And you shalt receive them of their hands, and burn them upon the altar for a burnt offering, for a sweet savour before the LORD: it is an offering made by fire unto the LORD.

26 And you shalt take the breast of the ram of Aaron's consecration, and wave it for a wave offering before the LORD: and it shall be your part.

27 And you shalt sanctify the breast of the wave offering, and the shoulder of the heave offering, which is waved, and which is heaved up, of the ram of the consecration, even of that which is for Aaron, and of that which is for his sons:

28 And it shall be Aaron's and his sons' by a statute for ever from the children of Israel: for it is an heave offering: and it shall be an heave offering from the children of Israel of the sacrifice of their peace offerings, even their heave offering unto the LORD.

29 And the holy garments of Aaron shall be his sons' after him, to be anointed therein, and to be consecrated in them.

30 And that son that is priest in his stead shall put them on seven days, when he comes into the tabernacle of the congregation to minister in the holy place.

31 And you shalt take the ram of the consecration, and seethe his flesh in the holy place.

32 And Aaron and his sons shall eat the flesh of the ram, and the bread that is in the basket, by the door of the tabernacle of the congregation.

33 And they shall eat those things wherewith the atonement was made, to consecrate and to sanctify them: but a stranger shall not eat thereof, because they are holy.

34 And if ought of the flesh of the consecrations, or of the bread, remain unto the morning, then you shalt burn the remainder with fire: it shall not be eaten, because it is holy.

35 And thus shalt you do unto Aaron, and to his sons, according to all things which I have commanded you: seven days shalt you consecrate them.

36 And you shalt offer every day a bullock for a sin offering for atonement: and you shalt cleanse the altar, when you have made an atonement for it, and you shalt anoint it, to sanctify it.

37 Seven days you shalt make an atonement for the altar, and sanctify it; and it shall be an altar most holy: whatsoever toucheth the altar shall be holy.

38 Now this is that which you shalt offer upon the altar; two lambs of the first year day by day continually.

39 The one lamb you shalt offer in the morning; and the other lamb you shalt offer at even:

40 And with the one lamb a tenth deal of flour mingled with the fourth part of an hin of beaten oil; and the fourth part of an hin of wine for a drink offering.

41 And the other lamb you shalt offer at even, and shalt do thereto according to the meat offering of the morning, and according to the drink offering thereof, for a sweet savour, an offering made by fire unto the LORD.

42 This shall be a continual burnt offering throughout your generations at the door of the tabernacle of the congregation before the LORD: where I will meet you, to speak there unto you.

43 And there I will meet with the children of Israel, and the tabernacle shall be sanctified by my glory.

44 And I will sanctify the tabernacle of the congregation, and the altar: I will sanctify also both Aaron and his sons, to minister to me in the priest's office.

45 And I will dwell among the children of Israel, and will be their God.

46 And they shall know that I am the LORD their God, that brought them forth out of the land of Egypt, that I may dwell among them: I am the LORD their God.

CHAPTER 30

AND you shalt make an altar to burn incense upon: of shittim wood shalt you make it.

2 A cubit shall be the length thereof, and a cubit the breadth thereof; foursquare shall it be: and two cubits shall be the height thereof: the horns thereof shall be of the same.

3 And you shalt overlay it with pure gold, the top thereof, and the sides thereof round about, and the horns thereof; and you shalt make unto it a crown of gold round about.

4 And two golden rings shalt you make to it under the crown of it, by the two corners thereof, upon the two sides of it shalt you make it; and they shall be for places for the staves to bear it withal.

5 And you shalt make the staves of shittim wood, and overlay them with gold.

6 And you shalt put it before the vail that is by the ark of the testimony, before the mercy seat that is over the testimony, where I will meet with you.

7 And Aaron shall burn thereon sweet incense every morning: when he dresseth the lamps, he shall burn incense upon it.

8 And when Aaron lighteth the lamps at even, he shall burn incense upon it, a perpetual incense before the LORD throughout your generations.

9 You shall offer no strange incense thereon, nor burnt sacrifice, nor meat offering; neither shall you pour drink offering thereon.

10 And Aaron shall make an atonement upon the horns of it once in a year with the blood of the sin offering of atonements: once in the year shall he make atonement upon it throughout your generations: it is most holy unto the LORD.

11 And the LORD spake unto Moses, saying,

12 When you takest the sum of the children of Israel after their number, then shall they give every man a ransom for his soul unto the LORD, when you numberest them; that there be no plague among them, when you numberest them.

13 This they shall give, every one that passes among them that are numbered, half a shekel after the shekel of the sanctuary: (a shekel is twenty gerahs:) an half shekel shall be the offering of the LORD.

14 Every one that passes among them that are numbered, from twenty years old and above, shall give an offering unto the LORD.

15 The rich shall not give more, and the poor shall not give less than half a shekel, when they give an offering unto the LORD, to make an atonement for your souls.

16 And you shalt take the atonement money of the children of Israel, and shalt appoint it for the service of the tabernacle of the congregation; that it may be a memorial unto the children of Israel before the LORD, to make an atonement for your souls.

17 And the LORD spake unto Moses, saying,

18 You shalt also make a laver of brass, and his foot also of brass, to wash withal: and you shalt put it between the tabernacle of the congregation and the altar, and you shalt put water therein.

19 For Aaron and his sons shall wash their hands and their feet thereat:

20 When they go into the tabernacle of the congregation, they shall wash with water, that they die not; or when they come near to the altar to minister, to burn offering made by fire unto the LORD:

21 So they shall wash their hands and their feet, that they die not: and it shall be a statute for ever to them, even to him and to his seed throughout their generations.

22 Moreover the LORD spake unto Moses, saying,

23 Take you also unto you principal spices, of pure myrrh five hundred shekels, and of sweet cinnamon half so much, even two hundred and fifty shekels, and of sweet calamus two hundred and fifty shekels,

24 And of cassia five hundred shekels, after the shekel of the sanctuary, and of oil olive an hin:

25 And you shalt make it an oil of holy ointment, an ointment compound after the are of the apothecary: it shall be an holy anointing oil.

26 And you shalt anoint the tabernacle of the congregation therewith, and the ark of the testimony,

27 And the table and all his vessels, and the candlestick and his vessels, and the altar of incense,

28 And the altar of burnt offering with all his vessels, and the laver and his foot.

29 And you shalt sanctify them, that they may be most holy: whatsoever toucheth them shall be holy.

30 And you shalt anoint Aaron and his sons, and consecrate them, that they may minister unto me in the priest's office.

31 And you shalt speak unto the children of Israel, saying, This shall be an holy anointing oil unto me throughout your generations.

32 Upon man's flesh shall it not be poured, neither shall you make any other like it, after the composition of it: it is holy, and it shall be holy unto you.

33 Whosoever compoundeth any like it, or whosoever putteth any of it upon a stranger, shall even be cut off from his people.

34 And the LORD said unto Moses, Take unto you sweet spices, stacte, and onycha, and galbanum; these sweet spices with pure frankincense: of each shall there be a like weight:

35 And you shalt make it a perfume, a confection after the are of the apothecary, tempered together, pure and holy:

36 And you shalt beat some of it very small, and put of it before the testimony in the tabernacle of the congregation, where I will meet with you: it shall be unto you most holy.

37 And as for the perfume which you shalt make, you shall not make to yourselves according to the composition thereof: it shall be unto you holy for the LORD.

38 Whosoever shall make like unto that, to smell thereto, shall even be cut off from his people.

CHAPTER 31

AND the LORD spake unto Moses, saying,

2 See, I have called by name Bezaleel the son of Uri, the son of Hur, of the tribe of Judah:

3 And I have filled him with the spirit of God, in wisdom, and in understanding, and in knowledge, and in all manner of workmanship,

4 To devise cunning works, to work in gold, and in silver, and in brass,

5 And in cutting of stones, to set them, and in carving of timber, to work in all manner of workmanship.

6 And I, behold, I have given with him Aholiab, the son of Ahisamach, of the tribe of Dan: and in the hearts of all that are wise hearted I have put wisdom, that they may make all that I have commanded you;

7 The tabernacle of the congregation, and the ark of the testimony, and the mercy seat that is thereupon, and all the furniture of the tabernacle,

8 And the table and his furniture, and the pure candlestick with all his furniture, and the altar of incense,

9 And the altar of burnt offering with all his furniture, and the laver and his foot,

10 And the cloths of service, and the holy garments for Aaron the priest, and the garments of his sons, to minister in the priest's office,

11 And the anointing oil, and sweet incense for the holy place: according to all that I have commanded you shall they do.

12 And the LORD spake unto Moses, saying,

13 Speak you also unto the children of Israel, saying, Verily my sabbaths you shall keep: for it is a sign between me and you throughout your generations; that you may know that I am the LORD that doth sanctify you.

14 You shall keep the sabbath therefore; for it is holy unto you: every one that defileth it shall surely be put to death: for whosoever doeth any work therein, that soul shall be cut off from among his people.

15 Six days may work be done; but in the seventh is the sabbath of rest, holy to the LORD: whosoever doeth any work in the sabbath day, he shall surely be put to death.

16 Wherefore the children of Israel shall keep the sabbath, to observe the sabbath throughout their generations, for a perpetual covenant.

17 It is a sign between me and the children of Israel for ever: for in six days the LORD made heaven and earth, and on the seventh day he rested, and was refreshed.

18 And he gave unto Moses, when he had made an end of communing with him upon mount Sinai, two tables of testimony, tables of stone, written with the finger of God.

CHAPTER 32

AND when the people saw that Moses delayed to come down out of the mount, the people gathered themselves together unto Aaron, and said unto him, Up, make us gods, which shall go before us; for as for this Moses, the man that brought us up out of the land of Egypt, we wot not what is become of him.

2 And Aaron said unto them, Break off the golden earrings, which are in the ears of your wives, of your sons, and of your daughters, and bring them unto me.

3 And all the people brake off the golden earrings which were in their ears, and brought them unto Aaron.

4 And he received them at their hand, and fashioned it with a graving tool, after he had made it a molten calf: and they said, These be your gods, O Israel, which brought you up out of the land of Egypt.

5 And when Aaron saw it, he built an altar before it; and Aaron made proclamation, and said, To morrow is a feast to the LORD.

6 And they rose up early on the morrow, and offered burnt offerings, and brought peace offerings; and the people sat down to eat and to drink, and rose up to play.

7 And the LORD said unto Moses, Go, get you down; for your people, which you broughtest out of the land of Egypt, have corrupted themselves:

8 They have turned aside quickly out of the way which I commanded them: they have made them a molten calf, and have worshipped it, and have sacrificed thereunto, and said, These be your gods, O Israel, which have brought you up out of the land of Egypt.

9 And the LORD said unto Moses, I have seen this people, and, behold, it is a stiffnecked people:

10 Now therefore let me alone, that my wrath may wax hot against them, and that I may consume them: and I will make of you a great nation.

11 And Moses besought the LORD his God, and said, LORD, why doth your wrath wax hot against your people, which you have brought forth out of the land of Egypt with great power, and with a mighty hand?

12 Wherefore should the Egyptians speak, and say, For mischief did he bring them out, to slay them in the mountains, and to consume them from the face of the earth? Turn from your fierce wrath, and repent of this evil against your people.

13 Remember Abraham, Isaac, and Israel, your servants, to whom you swarest by yours own self, and saidst unto them, I will multiply your seed as the stars of heaven, and all this land that I have spoken of will I give unto your seed, and they shall inherit it for ever.

14 And the LORD repented of the evil which he thought to do unto his people.

15 And Moses turned, and went down from the mount, and the two tables of the testimony were in his hand: the tables were written on both their sides; on the one side and on the other were they written.

16 And the tables were the work of God, and the writing was the writing of God, graven upon the tables.

17 And when Joshua heard the noise of the people as they shouted, he said unto Moses, There is a noise of war in the camp.

18 And he said, It is not the voice of them that shout for mastery, neither is it the voice of them that cry for being overcome: but the noise of them that sing do I hear.

19 And it came to pass, as soon as he came nigh unto the camp, that he saw the calf, and the dancing: and Moses' anger waxed hot, and he cast the tables out of his hands, and brake them beneath the mount.

20 And he took the calf which they had made, and burnt it in the fire, and ground it to powder, and strawed it upon the water, and made the children of Israel drink of it.

21 And Moses said unto Aaron, What did this people unto you, that you have brought so great a sin upon them?

22 And Aaron said, Let not the anger of my lord wax hot: you knowest the people, that they are set on mischief.

23 For they said unto me, Make us gods, which shall go before us: for as for this Moses, the man that brought us up out of the land of Egypt, we wot not what is become of him.

24 And I said unto them, Whosoever has any gold, let them break it off. So they gave it me: then I cast it into the fire, and there came out this calf.

25 And when Moses saw that the people were naked; (for Aaron had made them naked unto their shame among their enemies:)

26 Then Moses stood in the gate of the camp, and said, Who is on the LORD's side? let him come unto me. And all the sons of Levi gathered themselves together unto him.

27 And he said unto them, Thus saith the LORD God of Israel, Put every man his sword by his side, and go in and out from gate to gate throughout the camp, and slay every man his brother, and every man his companion, and every man his neighbour.

28 And the children of Levi did according to the word of Moses: and there fell of the people that day about three thousand men.

29 For Moses had said, Consecrate yourselves to day to the LORD, even every man upon his son, and upon his brother; that he may bestow upon you a blessing this day.

30 And it came to pass on the morrow, that Moses said unto the people, You have sinned a great sin: and now I will go up unto the LORD; what if I shall make an atonement for your sin.

31 And Moses returned unto the LORD, and said, Oh, this people have sinned a great sin, and have made them gods of gold.

32 Yet now, if you will forgive their sin-; and if not, blot me, I pray you, out of your book which you have written.

33 And the LORD said unto Moses, Whosoever has sinned against me, him will I blot out of my book.

34 Therefore now go, lead the people unto the place of which I have spoken unto you: behold, my Angel shall go before you: nevertheless in the day when I visit I will visit their sin upon them.

35 And the LORD plagued the people, because they made the calf, which Aaron made.

CHAPTER 33

AND the LORD said unto Moses, Depart, and go up hence, you and the people which you have brought up out of the land of Egypt, unto the land which I sware unto Abraham, to Isaac, and to Jacob, saying, Unto your seed will I give it:

2 And I will send an angel before you; and I will drive out the Canaanite, the Amorite, and the Hittite, and the Perizzite, the Hivite, and the Jebusite:

3 Unto a land flowing with milk and honey: for I will not go up in the midst of you; for you are a stiffnecked people: lest I consume you in the way.

4 And when the people heard these evil tidings, they mourned: and no man did put on him his ornaments.

5 For the LORD had said unto Moses, Say unto the children of Israel, You are a stiffnecked people: I will come up into the midst of you in a moment, and consume you: therefore now put off your ornaments from you, that I may know what to do unto you.

6 And the children of Israel stripped themselves of their ornaments by the mount Horeb.

7 And Moses took the tabernacle, and pitched it without the camp, afar off from the camp, and called it the Tabernacle of the congregation. And it came to pass, that every one which sought the LORD went out unto the tabernacle of the congregation, which was without the camp.

8 And it came to pass, when Moses went out unto the tabernacle, that all the people rose up, and stood every man at his tent door, and looked after Moses, until he was gone into the tabernacle.

9 And it came to pass, as Moses entered into the tabernacle, the cloudy pillar descended, and stood at the door of the tabernacle, and the LORD talked with Moses.

10 And all the people saw the cloudy pillar stand at the tabernacle door: and all the people rose up and worshipped, every man in his tent door.

11 And the LORD spake unto Moses face to face, as a man speaketh unto his friend. And he turned again into the camp: but his servant Joshua, the son of Nun, a young man, departed not out of the tabernacle.

12 And Moses said unto the LORD, See, you say unto me, Bring up this people: and you have not let me know whom you will send with me. Yet you have said, I know you by name, and you have also found grace in my sight.

13 Now therefore, I pray you, if I have found grace in your sight, shew me now your way, that I may know you, that I may find grace in your sight: and consider that this nation is your people.

14 And he said, My presence shall go with you, and I will give you rest.

15 And he said unto him, If your presence go not with me, carry us not up hence.

16 For wherein shall it be known here that I and your people have found grace in your sight? is it not in that you go with us? so shall we be separated, I and your people, from all the people that are upon the face of the earth.

17 And the LORD said unto Moses, I will do this thing also that you have spoken: for you have found grace in my sight, and I know you by name.

18 And he said, I beseech you, shew me your glory.

19 And he said, I will make all my goodness pass before you, and I will proclaim the name of the LORD before you; and will be gracious to whom I will be gracious, and will shew mercy on whom I will shew mercy.

20 And he said, You can not see my face: for there shall no man see me, and live.

21 And the LORD said, Behold, there is a place by me, and you shalt stand upon a rock:

22 And it shall come to pass, while my glory passes by, that I will put you in a clift of the rock, and will cover you with my hand while I pass by:

23 And I will take away my hand, and you shalt see my back parts: but my face shall not be seen.

CHAPTER 34

AND the LORD said unto Moses, Hew you two tables of stone like unto the first: and I will write upon these tables the words that were in the first tables, which you brakest.

2 And be ready in the morning, and come up in the morning unto mount Sinai, and present yourself there to me in the top of the mount.

3 And no man shall come up with you, neither let any man be seen throughout all the mount; neither let the flocks nor herds feed before that mount.

4 And he hewed two tables of stone like unto the first; and Moses rose up early in the morning, and went up unto mount Sinai, as the LORD had commanded him, and took in his hand the two tables of stone.

5 And the LORD descended in the cloud, and stood with him there, and proclaimed the name of the LORD.

6 And the LORD passed by before him, and proclaimed, The LORD, The LORD God, merciful and gracious, longsuffering, and abundant in goodness and truth,

7 Keeping mercy for thousands, forgiving iniquity and transgression and sin, and that will by no means clear the guilty; visiting the iniquity of the fathers upon the children, and upon the children's children, unto the third and to the fourth generation.

8 And Moses made haste, and bowed his head toward the earth, and worshipped.

9 And he said, If now I have found grace in your sight, O Lord, let my Lord, I pray you, go among us; for it is a stiffnecked people; and pardon our iniquity and our sin, and take us for yours inheritance.

10 And he said, Behold, I make a covenant: before all your people I will do marvels, such as have not been done in all the earth, nor in any nation: and all the people among which you are shall see the work of the LORD: for it is a terrible thing that I will do with you.

11 Observe you that which I command you this day: behold, I drive out before you the Amorite, and the Canaanite, and the Hittite, and the Perizzite, and the Hivite, and the Jebusite.

12 Take heed to yourself, lest you make a covenant with the inhabitants of the land whither you go, lest it be for a snare in the midst of you:

13 But you shall destroy their altars, break their images, and cut down their groves:

14 For you shalt worship no other god: for the LORD, whose name is Jealous, is a jealous God:

15 Lest you make a covenant with the inhabitants of the land, and they go a whoring after their gods, and do sacrifice unto their gods, and one call you, and you eat of his sacrifice;

16 And you take of their daughters unto your sons, and their daughters go a whoring after their gods, and make your sons go a whoring after their gods.

17 You shalt make you no molten gods.

18 The feast of unleavened bread shalt you keep. Seven days you shalt eat unleavened bread, as I commanded you, in the time of the month Abib: for in the month Abib you camest out from Egypt.

19 All that openeth the matrix is my; and every firstling among your cattle, whether ox or sheep, that is male.

20 But the firstling of an ass you shalt redeem with a lamb: and if you redeem him not, then shalt you break his neck. All the firstborn of your sons you shalt redeem. And none shall appear before me empty.

21 Six days you shalt work, but on the seventh day you shalt rest: in earing time and in harvest you shalt rest.

22 And you shalt observe the feast of weeks, of the firstfruits of wheat harvest, and the feast of ingathering at the year's end.

23 Thrice in the year shall all your men children appear before the Lord GOD, the God of Israel.

24 For I will cast out the nations before you, and enlarge your borders: neither shall any man desire your land, when you shalt go up to appear before the LORD your God thrice in the year.

25 You shalt not offer the blood of my sacrifice with leaven; neither shall the sacrifice of the feast of the passover be left unto the morning.

26 The first of the firstfruits of your land you shalt bring unto the house of the LORD your God. You shalt not seethe a kid in his mother's milk.

27 And the LORD said unto Moses, Write you these words: for after the tenor of these words I have made a covenant with you and with Israel.

28 And he was there with the LORD forty days and forty nights; he did neither eat bread, nor drink water. And he wrote upon the tables the words of the covenant, the ten commandments.

29 And it came to pass, when Moses came down from mount Sinai with the two tables of testimony in Moses' hand, when he came down from the mount, that Moses wist not that the skin of his face shone while he talked with him.

30 And when Aaron and all the children of Israel saw Moses, behold, the skin of his face shone; and they were afraid to come nigh him.

31 And Moses called unto them; and Aaron and all the rulers of the congregation returned unto him: and Moses talked with them.

32 And afterward all the children of Israel came nigh: and he gave them in commandment all that the LORD had spoken with him in mount Sinai.

33 And till Moses had done speaking with them, he put a vail on his face.

34 But when Moses went in before the LORD to speak with him, he took the vail off, until he came out. And he came out, and spake unto the children of Israel that which he was commanded.

35 And the children of Israel saw the face of Moses, that the skin of Moses' face shone: and Moses put the vail upon his face again, until he went in to speak with him.

CHAPTER 35

AND Moses gathered all the congregation of the children of Israel together, and said unto them, These are the words which the LORD has commanded, that you should do them.

2 Six days shall work be done, but on the seventh day there shall be to you an holy day, a sabbath of rest to the LORD: whosoever doeth work therein shall be put to death.

3 You shall kindle no fire throughout your habitations upon the sabbath day.

4 And Moses spake unto all the congregation of the children of Israel, saying, This is the thing which the LORD commanded, saying,

5 Take you from among you an offering unto the LORD: whosoever is of a willing heart, let him bring it, an offering of the LORD; gold, and silver, and brass,

6 And blue, and purple, and scarlet, and fine linen, and goats' hair,

7 And rams' skins dyed red, and badgers' skins, and shittim wood,

8 And oil for the light, and spices for anointing oil, and for the sweet incense,

9 And onyx stones, and stones to be set for the ephod, and for the breastplate.

10 And every wise hearted among you shall come, and make all that the LORD has commanded;

11 The tabernacle, his tent, and his covering, his taches, and his boards, his bars, his pillars, and his sockets,

12 The ark, and the staves thereof, with the mercy seat, and the vail of the covering,

13 The table, and his staves, and all his vessels, and the shewbread,

14 The candlestick also for the light, and his furniture, and his lamps, with the oil for the light,

15 And the incense altar, and his staves, and the anointing oil, and the sweet incense, and the hanging for the door at the entering in of the tabernacle,

16 The altar of burnt offering, with his brasen grate, his staves, and all his vessels, the laver and his foot,

17 The hangings of the court, his pillars, and their sockets, and the hanging for the door of the court,

18 The pins of the tabernacle, and the pins of the court, and their cords,

19 The cloths of service, to do service in the holy place, the holy garments for Aaron the priest, and the garments of his sons, to minister in the priest's office.

20 And all the congregation of the children of Israel departed from the presence of Moses.

21 And they came, every one whose heart stirred him up, and every one whom his spirit made willing, and they brought the LORD's offering to the work of the tabernacle of the congregation, and for all his service, and for the holy garments.

22 And they came, both men and women, as many as were willing hearted, and brought bracelets, and earrings, and rings, and tablets, all jewels of gold: and every man that offered offered an offering of gold unto the LORD.

23 And every man, with whom was found blue, and purple, and scarlet, and fine linen, and goats' hair, and red skins of rams, and badgers' skins, brought them.

24 Every one that did offer an offering of silver and brass brought the LORD's offering: and every man, with whom was found shittim wood for any work of the service, brought it.

25 And all the women that were wise hearted did spin with their hands, and brought that which they had spun, both of blue, and of purple, and of scarlet, and of fine linen.

26 And all the women whose heart stirred them up in wisdom spun goats' hair.

27 And the rulers brought onyx stones, and stones to be set, for the ephod, and for the breastplate;

28 And spice, and oil for the light, and for the anointing oil, and for the sweet incense.

29 The children of Israel brought a willing offering unto the LORD, every man and woman, whose heart made them willing to bring for all manner of work, which the LORD had commanded to be made by the hand of Moses.

30 And Moses said unto the children of Israel, See, the LORD has called by name Bezaleel the son of Uri, the son of Hur, of the tribe of Judah;

31 And he has filled him with the spirit of God, in wisdom, in understanding, and in knowledge, and in all manner of workmanship;

32 And to devise curious works, to work in gold, and in silver, and in brass,

33 And in the cutting of stones, to set them, and in carving of wood, to make any manner of cunning work.

34 And he has put in his heart that he may teach, both he, and Aholiab, the son of Ahisamach, of the tribe of Dan.

35 Them has he filled with wisdom of heart, to work all manner of work, of the engraver, and of the cunning workman, and of the embroiderer, in blue, and in purple, in scarlet, and in fine linen, and of the weaver, even of them that do any work, and of those that devise cunning work.

CHAPTER 36

THEN created Bezaleel and Aholiab, and every wise hearted man, in whom the LORD put wisdom and understanding to know how to work all manner of work for the service of the sanctuary, according to all that the LORD had commanded.

2 And Moses called Bezaleel and Aholiab, and every wise hearted man, in whose heart the LORD had put wisdom, even every one whose heart stirred him up to come unto the work to do it:

3 And they received of Moses all the offering, which the children of Israel had brought for the work of the service of the sanctuary, to make it withal. And they brought yet unto him free offerings every morning.

4 And all the wise men, that created all the work of the sanctuary, came every man from his work which they made;

5 And they spake unto Moses, saying, The people bring much more than enough for the service of the work, which the LORD commanded to make.

6 And Moses gave commandment, and they caused it to be proclaimed throughout the camp, saying, Let neither man nor woman make any more work for the offering of the sanctuary. So the people were restrained from bringing.

7 For the stuff they had was sufficient for all the work to make it, and too much.

8 And every wise hearted man among them that created the work of the tabernacle made ten curtains of fine twined linen, and blue, and purple, and scarlet: with cherubims of cunning work made he them.

9 The length of one curtain was twenty and eight cubits, and the breadth of one curtain four cubits: the curtains were all of one size.

10 And he coupled the five curtains one unto another: and the other five curtains he coupled one unto another.

11 And he made loops of blue on the edge of one curtain from the selvedge in the coupling: likewise he made in the uttermost side of another curtain, in the coupling of the second.

12 Fifty loops made he in one curtain, and fifty loops made he in the edge of the curtain which was in the coupling of the second: the loops held one curtain to another.

13 And he made fifty taches of gold, and coupled the curtains one unto another with the taches: so it became one tabernacle.

14 And he made curtains of goats' hair for the tent over the tabernacle: eleven curtains he made them.

15 The length of one curtain was thirty cubits, and four cubits was the breadth of one curtain: the eleven curtains were of one size.

16 And he coupled five curtains by themselves, and six curtains by themselves.

17 And he made fifty loops upon the uttermost edge of the curtain in the coupling, and fifty loops made he upon the edge of the curtain which coupleth the second.

18 And he made fifty taches of brass to couple the tent together, that it might be one.

19 And he made a covering for the tent of rams' skins dyed red, and a covering of badgers' skins above that.

20And he made boards for the tabernacle of shittim wood, standing up.

21 The length of a board was ten cubits, and the breadth of a board one cubit and a half.

22 One board had two tenons, equally distant one from another: thus did he make for all the boards of the tabernacle.

23 And he made boards for the tabernacle; twenty boards for the south side southward:

24 And forty sockets of silver he made under the twenty boards; two sockets under one board for his two tenons, and two sockets under another board for his two tenons.

25 And for the other side of the tabernacle, which is toward the north corner, he made twenty boards,

26 And their forty sockets of silver; two sockets under one board, and two sockets under another board.

27 And for the sides of the tabernacle westward he made six boards.

28 And two boards made he for the corners of the tabernacle in the two sides.

29 And they were coupled beneath, and coupled together at the head thereof, to one ring: thus he did to both of them in both the corners.

30 And there were eight boards; and their sockets were sixteen sockets of silver, under every board two sockets.

31And he made bars of shittim wood; five for the boards of the one side of the tabernacle,

32 And five bars for the boards of the other side of the tabernacle, and five bars for the boards of the tabernacle for the sides westward.

33 And he made the middle bar to shoot through the boards from the one end to the other.

34 And he overlaid the boards with gold, and made their rings of gold to be places for the bars, and overlaid the bars with gold.

35And he made a vail of blue, and purple, and scarlet, and fine twined linen: with cherubims made he it of cunning work.

36 And he made thereunto four pillars of shittim wood, and overlaid them with gold: their hooks were of gold; and he cast for them four sockets of silver.

37And he made an hanging for the tabernacle door of blue, and purple, and scarlet, and fine twined linen, of needlework;

38 And the five pillars of it with their hooks: and he overlaid their chapiters and their fillets with gold: but their five sockets were of brass.

CHAPTER 37

AND Bezaleel made the ark of shittim wood: two cubits and a half was the length of it, and a cubit and a half the breadth of it, and a cubit and a half the height of it:

2 And he overlaid it with pure gold within and without, and made a crown of gold to it round about.

3 And he cast for it four rings of gold, to be set by the four corners of it; even two rings upon the one side of it, and two rings upon the other side of it.

4 And he made staves of shittim wood, and overlaid them with gold.

5 And he put the staves into the rings by the sides of the ark, to bear the ark.

6And he made the mercy seat of pure gold: two cubits and a half was the length thereof, and one cubit and a half the breadth thereof.

7 And he made two cherubims of gold, beaten out of one piece made he them, on the two ends of the mercy seat;

8 One cherub on the end on this side, and another cherub on the other end on that side: out of the mercy seat made he the cherubims on the two ends thereof.

9 And the cherubims spread out their wings on high, and covered with their wings over the mercy seat, with their faces one to another; even to the mercy seatward were the faces of the cherubims.

10And he made the table of shittim wood: two cubits was the length thereof, and a cubit the breadth thereof, and a cubit and a half the height thereof:

11 And he overlaid it with pure gold, and made thereunto a crown of gold round about.

12 Also he made thereunto a border of an handbreadth round about; and made a crown of gold for the border thereof round about.

13 And he cast for it four rings of gold, and put the rings upon the four corners that were in the four feet thereof.

14 Over against the border were the rings, the places for the staves to bear the table.

15 And he made the staves of shittim wood, and overlaid them with gold, to bear the table.

16 And he made the vessels which were upon the table, his dishes, and his spoons, and his bowls, and his covers to cover withal, of pure gold.

17And he made the candlestick of pure gold: of beaten work made he the candlestick; his shaft, and his branch, his bowls, his knops, and his flowers, were of the same:

18 And six branches going out of the sides thereof; three branches of the candlestick out of the one side thereof, and three branches of the candlestick out of the other side thereof:

19 Three bowls made after the fashion of almonds in one branch, a knop and a flower; and three bowls made like almonds in another branch, a knop and a flower: so throughout the six branches going out of the candlestick.

20 And in the candlestick were four bowls made like almonds, his knops, and his flowers:

21 And a knop under two branches of the same, and a knop under two branches of the same, and a knop under two branches of the same, according to the six branches going out of it.

22 Their knops and their branches were of the same: all of it was one beaten work of pure gold.

23 And he made his seven lamps, and his snuffers, and his snuffdishes, of pure gold.

24 Of a talent of pure gold made he it, and all the vessels thereof.

25And he made the incense altar of shittim wood: the length of it was a cubit, and the breadth of it a cubit; it was foursquare; and two cubits was the height of it; the horns thereof were of the same.

26 And he overlaid it with pure gold, both the top of it, and the sides thereof round about, and the horns of it: also he made unto it a crown of gold round about.

27 And he made two rings of gold for it under the crown thereof, by the two corners of it, upon the two sides thereof, to be places for the staves to bear it withal.

28 And he made the staves of shittim wood, and overlaid them with gold.

29And he made the holy anointing oil, and the pure incense of sweet spices, according to the work of the apothecary.

CHAPTER 38

AND he made the altar of burnt offering of shittim wood: five cubits was the length thereof, and five cubits the breadth thereof; it was foursquare; and three cubits the height thereof.

2 And he made the horns thereof on the four corners of it; the horns thereof were of the same: and he overlaid it with brass.

3 And he made all the vessels of the altar, the pots, and the shovels, and the basons, and the fleshhooks, and the firepans: all the vessels thereof made he of brass.

4 And he made for the altar a brasen grate of network under the compass thereof beneath unto the midst of it.

5 And he cast four rings for the four ends of the grate of brass, to be places for the staves.

6 And he made the staves of shittim wood, and overlaid them with brass.

7 And he put the staves into the rings on the sides of the altar, to bear it withal; he made the altar hollow with boards.

8And he made the laver of brass, and the foot of it of brass, of the lookingglasses of the women assembling, which assembled at the door of the tabernacle of the congregation.

9And he made the court: on the south side southward the hangings of the court were of fine twined linen, an hundred cubits:

10 Their pillars were twenty, and their brasen sockets twenty; the hooks of the pillars and their fillets were of silver.

11 And for the north side the hangings were an hundred cubits, their pillars were twenty, and their sockets of brass twenty; the hooks of the pillars and their fillets of silver.

12 And for the west side were hangings of fifty cubits, their pillars ten, and their sockets ten; the hooks of the pillars and their fillets of silver.

13 And for the east side eastward fifty cubits.

14 The hangings of the one side of the gate were fifteen cubits; their pillars three, and their sockets three.

15 And for the other side of the court gate, on this hand and that hand, were hangings of fifteen cubits; their pillars three, and their sockets three.

16 All the hangings of the court round about were of fine twined linen.

17 And the sockets for the pillars were of brass; the hooks of the pillars and their fillets of silver; and the overlaying of their chapiters of silver; and all the pillars of the court were filleted with silver.

18 And the hanging for the gate of the court was needlework, of blue, and purple, and scarlet, and fine twined linen: and twenty cubits was the length, and the height in the breadth was five cubits, answerable to the hangings of the court.

19 And their pillars were four, and their sockets of brass four; their hooks of silver, and the overlaying of their chapiters and their fillets of silver.

20 And all the pins of the tabernacle, and of the court round about, were of brass.

21 This is the sum of the tabernacle, even of the tabernacle of testimony, as it was counted, according to the commandment of Moses, for the service of the Levites, by the hand of Ithamar, son to Aaron the priest.

22 And Bezaleel the son of Uri, the son of Hur, of the tribe of Judah, made all that the LORD commanded Moses.

23 And with him was Aholiab, son of Ahisamach, of the tribe of Dan, an engraver, and a cunning workman, and an embroiderer in blue, and in purple, and in scarlet, and fine linen.

24 All the gold that was occupied for the work in all the work of the holy place, even the gold of the offering, was twenty and nine talents, and seven hundred and thirty shekels, after the shekel of the sanctuary.

25 And the silver of them that were numbered of the congregation was an hundred talents, and a thousand seven hundred and threescore and fifteen shekels, after the shekel of the sanctuary:

26 A bekah for every man, that is, half a shekel, after the shekel of the sanctuary, for every one that went to be numbered, from twenty years old and upward, for six hundred thousand and three thousand and five hundred and fifty men.

27 And of the hundred talents of silver were cast the sockets of the sanctuary, and the sockets of the vail; an hundred sockets of the hundred talents, a talent for a socket.

28 And of the thousand seven hundred seventy and five shekels he made hooks for the pillars, and overlaid their chapiters, and filleted them.

29 And the brass of the offering was seventy talents, and two thousand and four hundred shekels.

30 And therewith he made the sockets to the door of the tabernacle of the congregation, and the brasen altar, and the brasen grate for it, and all the vessels of the altar,

31 And the sockets of the court round about, and the sockets of the court gate, and all the pins of the tabernacle, and all the pins of the court round about.

CHAPTER 39

AND of the blue, and purple, and scarlet, they made cloths of service, to do service in the holy place, and made the holy garments for Aaron; as the LORD commanded Moses.

2 And he made the ephod of gold, blue, and purple, and scarlet, and fine twined linen.

3 And they did beat the gold into thin plates, and cut it into wires, to work it in the blue, and in the purple, and in the scarlet, and in the fine linen, with cunning work.

4 They made shoulderpieces for it, to couple it together: by the two edges was it coupled together.

5 And the curious girdle of his ephod, that was upon it, was of the same, according to the work thereof; of gold, blue, and purple, and scarlet, and fine twined linen; as the LORD commanded Moses.

6 And they created onyx stones inclosed in ouches of gold, graven, as signets are graven, with the names of the children of Israel.

7 And he put them on the shoulders of the ephod, that they should be stones for a memorial to the children of Israel; as the LORD commanded Moses.

8 And he made the breastplate of cunning work, like the work of the ephod; of gold, blue, and purple, and scarlet, and fine twined linen.

9 It was foursquare; they made the breastplate double: a span was the length thereof, and a span the breadth thereof, being doubled.

10 And they set in it four rows of stones: the first row was a sardius, a topaz, and a carbuncle: this was the first row.

11 And the second row, an emerald, a sapphire, and a diamond.

12 And the third row, a ligure, an agate, and an amethyst.

13 And the fourth row, a beryl, an onyx, and a jasper: they were inclosed in ouches of gold in their inclosings.

14 And the stones were according to the names of the children of Israel, twelve, according to their names, like the engravings of a signet, every one with his name, according to the twelve tribes.

15 And they made upon the breastplate chains at the ends, of wreathen work of pure gold.

16 And they made two ouches of gold, and two gold rings; and put the two rings in the two ends of the breastplate.

17 And they put the two wreathen chains of gold in the two rings on the ends of the breastplate.

18 And the two ends of the two wreathen chains they fastened in the two sockets, and put them on the shoulderpieces of the ephod, before it.

19 And they made two rings of gold, and put them on the two ends of the breastplate, upon the border of it, which was on the side of the ephod inward.

20 And they made two other golden rings, and put them on the two sides of the ephod underneath, toward the forepart of it, over against the other coupling thereof, above the curious girdle of the ephod.

21 And they did bind the breastplate by his rings unto the rings of the ephod with a lace of blue, that it might be above the curious girdle of the ephod, and that the breastplate might not be loosed from the ephod; as the LORD commanded Moses.

22 And he made the robe of the ephod of woven work, all of blue.

23 And there was an hole in the midst of the robe, as the hole of an habergeon, with a band round about the hole, that it should not rend.

24 And they made upon the hems of the robe pomegranates of blue, and purple, and scarlet, and twined linen.

25 And they made bells of pure gold, and put the bells between the pomegranates upon the hem of the robe, round about between the pomegranates;

26 A bell and a pomegranate, a bell and a pomegranate, round about the hem of the robe to minister in; as the LORD commanded Moses.

27 And they made coats of fine linen of woven work for Aaron, and for his sons,

28 And a mitre of fine linen, and goodly bonnets of fine linen, and linen breeches of fine twined linen,

29 And a girdle of fine twined linen, and blue, and purple, and scarlet, of needlework; as the LORD commanded Moses.

30 And they made the plate of the holy crown of pure gold, and wrote upon it a writing, like to the engravings of a signet, HOLINESS TO THE LORD.

31 And they tied unto it a lace of blue, to fasten it on high upon the mitre; as the LORD commanded Moses.

32 Thus was all the work of the tabernacle of the tent of the congregation finished: and the children of Israel did according to all that the LORD commanded Moses, so did they.

33 And they brought the tabernacle unto Moses, the tent, and all his furniture, his taches, his boards, his bars, and his pillars, and his sockets,

34 And the covering of rams' skins dyed red, and the covering of badgers' skins, and the vail of the covering,

35 The ark of the testimony, and the staves thereof, and the mercy seat,

36 The table, and all the vessels thereof, and the shewbread,

37 The pure candlestick, with the lamps thereof, even with the lamps to be set in order, and all the vessels thereof, and the oil for light,

38 And the golden altar, and the anointing oil, and the sweet incense, and the hanging for the tabernacle door,

39 The brasen altar, and his grate of brass, his staves, and all his vessels, the laver and his foot,

40 The hangings of the court, his pillars, and his sockets, and the hanging for the court gate, his cords, and his pins, and all the vessels of the service of the tabernacle, for the tent of the congregation,

41 The cloths of service to do service in the holy place, and the holy garments for Aaron the priest, and his sons' garments, to minister in the priest's office.

42 According to all that the LORD commanded Moses, so the children of Israel made all the work.

43 And Moses did look upon all the work, and, behold, they had done it as the LORD had commanded, even so had they done it: and Moses blessed them.

CHAPTER 40

AND the LORD spake unto Moses, saying,

2 On the first day of the first month shalt you set up the tabernacle of the tent of the congregation.

3 And you shalt put therein the ark of the testimony, and cover the ark with the vail.

4 And you shalt bring in the table, and set in order the things that are to be set in order upon it; and you shalt bring in the candlestick, and light the lamps thereof.

5 And you shalt set the altar of gold for the incense before the ark of the testimony, and put the hanging of the door to the tabernacle.

6 And you shalt set the altar of the burnt offering before the door of the tabernacle of the tent of the congregation.

7 And you shalt set the laver between the tent of the congregation and the altar, and shalt put water therein.

8 And you shalt set up the court round about, and hang up the hanging at the court gate.

9 And you shalt take the anointing oil, and anoint the tabernacle, and all that is therein, and shalt hallow it, and all the vessels thereof: and it shall be holy.

10 And you shalt anoint the altar of the burnt offering, and all his vessels, and sanctify the altar: and it shall be an altar most holy.

11 And you shalt anoint the laver and his foot, and sanctify it.

12 And you shalt bring Aaron and his sons unto the door of the tabernacle of the congregation, and wash them with water.

13 And you shalt put upon Aaron the holy garments, and anoint him, and sanctify him; that he may minister unto me in the priest's office.

14 And you shalt bring his sons, and clothe them with coats:

15 And you shalt anoint them, as you did anoint their father, that they may minister unto me in the priest's office: for their anointing shall surely be an everlasting priesthood throughout their generations.

16 Thus did Moses: according to all that the LORD commanded him, so did he.

17And it came to pass in the first month in the second year, on the first day of the month, that the tabernacle was reared up.

18 And Moses reared up the tabernacle, and fastened his sockets, and set up the boards thereof, and put in the bars thereof, and reared up his pillars.

19 And he spread abroad the tent over the tabernacle, and put the covering of the tent above upon it; as the LORD commanded Moses.

20And he took and put the testimony into the ark, and set the staves on the ark, and put the mercy seat above upon the ark:

21 And he brought the ark into the tabernacle, and set up the vail of the covering, and covered the ark of the testimony; as the LORD commanded Moses.

22And he put the table in the tent of the congregation, upon the side of the tabernacle northward, without the vail.

23 And he set the bread in order upon it before the LORD; as the LORD had commanded Moses.

24And he put the candlestick in the tent of the congregation, over against the table, on the side of the tabernacle southward.

25 And he lighted the lamps before the LORD; as the LORD commanded Moses.

26And he put the golden altar in the tent of the congregation before the vail:

27 And he burnt sweet incense thereon; as the LORD commanded Moses.

28And he set up the hanging at the door of the tabernacle.

29 And he put the altar of burnt offering by the door of the tabernacle of the tent of the congregation, and offered upon it the burnt offering and the meat offering; as the LORD commanded Moses.

30And he set the laver between the tent of the congregation and the altar, and put water there, to wash withal.

31 And Moses and Aaron and his sons washed their hands and their feet thereat:

32 When they went into the tent of the congregation, and when they came near unto the altar, they washed; as the LORD commanded Moses.

33 And he reared up the court round about the tabernacle and the altar, and set up the hanging of the court gate. So Moses finished the work.

34Then a cloud covered the tent of the congregation, and the glory of the LORD filled the tabernacle.

35 And Moses was not able to enter into the tent of the congregation, because the cloud abode thereon, and the glory of the LORD filled the tabernacle.

36 And when the cloud was taken up from over the tabernacle, the children of Israel went onward in all their journeys:

37 But if the cloud were not taken up, then they journeyed not till the day that it was taken up.

38 For the cloud of the LORD was upon the tabernacle by day, and fire was on it by night, in the sight of all the house of Israel, throughout all their journeys.

THE THIRD BOOK OF MOSES,
CALLED
LEVITICUS.

CHAPTER 1

AND the LORD called unto Moses, and spake unto him out of the tabernacle of the congregation, saying,

2 Speak unto the children of Israel, and say unto them, If any man of you bring an offering unto the LORD, you shall bring your offering of the cattle, even of the herd, and of the flock.

3 If his offering be a burnt sacrifice of the herd, let him offer a male without blemish: he shall offer it of his own voluntary will at the door of the tabernacle of the congregation before the LORD.

4 And he shall put his hand upon the head of the burnt offering; and it shall be accepted for him to make atonement for him.

5 And he shall kill the bullock before the LORD: and the priests, Aaron's sons, shall bring the blood, and sprinkle the blood round about upon the altar that is by the door of the tabernacle of the congregation.

6 And he shall flay the burnt offering, and cut it into his pieces.

7 And the sons of Aaron the priest shall put fire upon the altar, and lay the wood in order upon the fire:

8 And the priests, Aaron's sons, shall lay the parts, the head, and the fat, in order upon the wood that is on the fire which is upon the altar:

9 But his inwards and his legs shall he wash in water: and the priest shall burn all on the altar, to be a burnt sacrifice, an offering made by fire, of a sweet savour unto the LORD.

10 And if his offering be of the flocks, namely, of the sheep, or of the goats, for a burnt sacrifice; he shall bring it a male without blemish.

11 And he shall kill it on the side of the altar northward before the LORD: and the priests, Aaron's sons, shall sprinkle his blood round about upon the altar.

12 And he shall cut it into his pieces, with his head and his fat: and the priest shall lay them in order on the wood that is on the fire which is upon the altar:

13 But he shall wash the inwards and the legs with water: and the priest shall bring it all, and burn it upon the altar: it is a burnt sacrifice, an offering made by fire, of a sweet savour unto the LORD.

14 And if the burnt sacrifice for his offering to the LORD be of fowls, then he shall bring his offering of turtledoves, or of young pigeons.

15 And the priest shall bring it unto the altar, and wring off his head, and burn it on the altar; and the blood thereof shall be wrung out at the side of the altar:

16 And he shall pluck away his crop with his feathers, and cast it beside the altar on the east part, by the place of the ashes:

17 And he shall cleave it with the wings thereof, but shall not divide it asunder: and the priest shall burn it upon the altar, upon the wood that is upon the fire: it is a burnt sacrifice, an offering made by fire, of a sweet savour unto the LORD.

CHAPTER 2

AND when any will offer a meat offering unto the LORD, his offering shall be of fine flour; and he shall pour oil upon it, and put frankincense thereon:

2 And he shall bring it to Aaron's sons the priests: and he shall take thereout his handful of the flour thereof, and of the oil thereof, with all the frankincense thereof; and the priest shall burn the memorial of it upon the altar, to be an offering made by fire, of a sweet savour unto the LORD:

3 And the remnant of the meat offering shall be Aaron's and his sons': it is a thing most holy of the offerings of the LORD made by fire.

4 And if you bring an oblation of a meat offering baken in the oven, it shall be unleavened cakes of fine flour mingled with oil, or unleavened wafers anointed with oil.

5 And if your oblation be a meat offering baken in a pan, it shall be of fine flour unleavened, mingled with oil.

6 You shalt part it in pieces, and pour oil thereon: it is a meat offering.

7 And if your oblation be a meat offering baken in the fryingpan, it shall be made of fine flour with oil.

8 And you shalt bring the meat offering that is made of these things unto the LORD: and when it is presented unto the priest, he shall bring it unto the altar.

9 And the priest shall take from the meat offering a memorial thereof, and shall burn it upon the altar: it is an offering made by fire, of a sweet savour unto the LORD.

10 And that which is left of the meat offering shall be Aaron's and his sons': it is a thing most holy of the offerings of the LORD made by fire.

11 No meat offering, which you shall bring unto the LORD, shall be made with leaven: for you shall burn no leaven, nor any honey, in any offering of the LORD made by fire.

12 As for the oblation of the firstfruits, you shall offer them unto the LORD: but they shall not be burnt on the altar for a sweet savour.

13 And every oblation of your meat offering shalt you season with salt; neither shalt you suffer the salt of the covenant of your God to be lacking from your meat offering: with all yours offerings you shalt offer salt.

14 And if you offer a meat offering of your firstfruits unto the LORD, you shalt offer for the meat offering of your firstfruits green ears of corn dried by the fire, even corn beaten out of full ears.

15 And you shalt put oil upon it, and lay frankincense thereon: it is a meat offering.

16 And the priest shall burn the memorial of it, part of the beaten corn thereof, and part of the oil thereof, with all the frankincense thereof: it is an offering made by fire unto the LORD.

CHAPTER 3

AND if his oblation be a sacrifice of peace offering, if he offer it of the herd; whether it be a male or female, he shall offer it without blemish before the LORD.

2 And he shall lay his hand upon the head of his offering, and kill it at the door of the tabernacle of the congregation: and Aaron's sons the priests shall sprinkle the blood upon the altar round about.

3 And he shall offer of the sacrifice of the peace offering an offering made by fire unto the LORD; the fat that covers the inwards, and all the fat that is upon the inwards,

4 And the two kidneys, and the fat that is on them, which is by the flanks, and the caul above the liver, with the kidneys, it shall he take away.

5 And Aaron's sons shall burn it on the altar upon the burnt sacrifice, which is upon the wood that is on the fire: it is an offering made by fire, of a sweet savour unto the LORD.

6 And if his offering for a sacrifice of peace offering unto the LORD be of the flock; male or female, he shall offer it without blemish.

7 If he offer a lamb for his offering, then shall he offer it before the LORD.

8 And he shall lay his hand upon the head of his offering, and kill it before the tabernacle of the congregation: and Aaron's sons shall sprinkle the blood thereof round about upon the altar.

9 And he shall offer of the sacrifice of the peace offering an offering made by fire unto the LORD; the fat thereof, and the whole rump, it shall he take off hard by the backbone; and the fat that covers the inwards, and all the fat that is upon the inwards,

10 And the two kidneys, and the fat that is upon them, which is by the flanks, and the caul above the liver, with the kidneys, it shall he take away.

11 And the priest shall burn it upon the altar: it is the food of the offering made by fire unto the LORD.

12 And if his offering be a goat, then he shall offer it before the LORD.

13 And he shall lay his hand upon the head of it, and kill it before the tabernacle of the congregation: and the sons of Aaron shall sprinkle the blood thereof upon the altar round about.

14 And he shall offer thereof his offering, even an offering made by fire unto the LORD; the fat that covers the inwards, and all the fat that is upon the inwards,

15 And the two kidneys, and the fat that is upon them, which is by the flanks, and the caul above the liver, with the kidneys, it shall he take away.

16 And the priest shall burn them upon the altar: it is the food of the offering made by fire for a sweet savour: all the fat is the LORD's.

17 It shall be a perpetual statute for your generations throughout all your dwellings, that you eat neither fat nor blood.

CHAPTER 4

AND the LORD spake unto Moses, saying,

2 Speak unto the children of Israel, saying, If a soul shall sin through ignorance against any of the commandments of the LORD concerning things which ought not to be done, and shall do against any of them:

3 If the priest that is anointed do sin according to the sin of the people; then let him bring for his sin, which he has sinned, a young bullock without blemish unto the LORD for a sin offering.

4 And he shall bring the bullock unto the door of the tabernacle of the congregation before the LORD; and shall lay his hand upon the bullock's head, and kill the bullock before the LORD.

5 And the priest that is anointed shall take of the bullock's blood, and bring it to the tabernacle of the congregation:

6 And the priest shall dip his finger in the blood, and sprinkle of the blood seven times before the LORD, before the vail of the sanctuary.

7 And the priest shall put some of the blood upon the horns of the altar of sweet incense before the LORD, which is in the tabernacle of the congregation; and shall pour all the blood of the bullock at the bottom of the altar of the burnt offering, which is at the door of the tabernacle of the congregation.

8 And he shall take off from it all the fat of the bullock for the sin offering; the fat that covers the inwards, and all the fat that is upon the inwards,

9 And the two kidneys, and the fat that is upon them, which is by the flanks, and the caul above the liver, with the kidneys, it shall he take away,

10 As it was taken off from the bullock of the sacrifice of peace offerings: and the priest shall burn them upon the altar of the burnt offering.

11 And the skin of the bullock, and all his flesh, with his head, and with his legs, and his inwards, and his dung,

12 Even the whole bullock shall he carry forth without the camp unto a clean place, where the ashes are poured out, and burn him on the wood with fire: where the ashes are poured out shall he be burnt.

13 And if the whole congregation of Israel sin through ignorance, and the thing be hid from the eyes of the assembly, and they have done somewhat against any of the commandments of the LORD concerning things which should not be done, and are guilty;

14 When the sin, which they have sinned against it, is known, then the congregation shall offer a young bullock for the sin, and bring him before the tabernacle of the congregation.

15 And the elders of the congregation shall lay their hands upon the head of the bullock before the LORD: and the bullock shall be killed before the LORD.

16 And the priest that is anointed shall bring of the bullock's blood to the tabernacle of the congregation:

17 And the priest shall dip his finger in some of the blood, and sprinkle it seven times before the LORD, even before the vail.

18 And he shall put some of the blood upon the horns of the altar which is before the LORD, that is in the tabernacle of the congregation, and shall pour out all the blood at the bottom of the altar of the burnt offering, which is at the door of the tabernacle of the congregation.

19 And he shall take all his fat from him, and burn it upon the altar.

20 And he shall do with the bullock as he did with the bullock for a sin offering, so shall he do with this: and the priest shall make an atonement for them, and it shall be forgiven them.

21 And he shall carry forth the bullock without the camp, and burn him as he burned the first bullock: it is a sin offering for the congregation.

22 When a ruler has sinned, and done somewhat through ignorance against any of the commandments of the LORD his God concerning things which should not be done, and is guilty;

23 Or if his sin, wherein he has sinned, come to his knowledge; he shall bring his offering, a kid of the goats, a male without blemish:

24 And he shall lay his hand upon the head of the goat, and kill it in the place where they kill the burnt offering before the LORD: it is a sin offering.

25 And the priest shall take of the blood of the sin offering with his finger, and put it upon the horns of the altar of burnt offering, and shall pour out his blood at the bottom of the altar of burnt offering.

26 And he shall burn all his fat upon the altar, as the fat of the sacrifice of peace offerings: and the priest shall make an atonement for him as concerning his sin, and it shall be forgiven him.

27 And if any one of the common people sin through ignorance, while he doeth somewhat against any of the commandments of the LORD concerning things which ought not to be done, and be guilty;

28 Or if his sin, which he has sinned, come to his knowledge: then he shall bring his offering, a kid of the goats, a female without blemish, for his sin which he has sinned.

29 And he shall lay his hand upon the head of the sin offering, and slay the sin offering in the place of the burnt offering.

30 And the priest shall take of the blood thereof with his finger, and put it upon the horns of the altar of burnt offering, and shall pour out all the blood thereof at the bottom of the altar.

31 And he shall take away all the fat thereof, as the fat is taken away from off the sacrifice of peace offerings; and the priest shall burn it upon the altar for a sweet savour unto the LORD; and the priest shall make an atonement for him, and it shall be forgiven him.

32 And if he bring a lamb for a sin offering, he shall bring it a female without blemish.

33 And he shall lay his hand upon the head of the sin offering, and slay it for a sin offering in the place where they kill the burnt offering.

34 And the priest shall take of the blood of the sin offering with his finger, and put it upon the horns of the altar of burnt offering, and shall pour out all the blood thereof at the bottom of the altar:

35 And he shall take away all the fat thereof, as the fat of the lamb is taken away from the sacrifice of the peace offerings; and the priest shall burn them upon the altar, according to the offerings made by fire unto the LORD: and the priest shall make an atonement for his sin that he has committed, and it shall be forgiven him.

CHAPTER 5

AND if a soul sin, and hear the voice of swearing, and is a witness, whether he has seen or known of it; if he do not utter it, then he shall bear his iniquity.

2 Or if a soul touch any unclean thing, whether it be a carcase of an unclean beast, or a carcase of unclean cattle, or the carcase of unclean creeping things, and if it be hidden from him; he also shall be unclean, and guilty.

3 Or if he touch the uncleanness of man, whatsoever uncleanness it be that a man shall be defiled withal, and it be hid from him; when he knoweth of it, then he shall be guilty.

4 Or if a soul swear, pronouncing with his lips to do evil, or to do good, whatsoever it be that a man shall pronounce with an oath, and it be hid from him; when he knoweth of it, then he shall be guilty in one of these.

5 And it shall be, when he shall be guilty in one of these things, that he shall confess that he has sinned in that thing:

6 And he shall bring his trespass offering unto the LORD for his sin which he has sinned, a female from the flock, a lamb or a kid of the goats, for a sin offering; and the priest shall make an atonement for him concerning his sin.

7 And if he be not able to bring a lamb, then he shall bring for his trespass, which he has committed, two turtledoves, or two young pigeons, unto the LORD; one for a sin offering, and the other for a burnt offering.

8 And he shall bring them unto the priest, who shall offer that which is for the sin offering first, and wring off his head from his neck, but shall not divide it asunder:

9 And he shall sprinkle of the blood of the sin offering upon the side of the altar; and the rest of the blood shall be wrung out at the bottom of the altar: it is a sin offering.

10 And he shall offer the second for a burnt offering, according to the manner: and the priest shall make an atonement for him for his sin which he has sinned, and it shall be forgiven him.

11 But if he be not able to bring two turtledoves, or two young pigeons, then he that sinned shall bring for his offering the tenth part of an ephah of fine flour for a sin offering; he shall put no oil upon it, neither shall he put any frankincense thereon: for it is a sin offering.

12 Then shall he bring it to the priest, and the priest shall take his handful of it, even a memorial thereof, and burn it on the altar, according to the offerings made by fire unto the LORD: it is a sin offering.

13 And the priest shall make an atonement for him as touching his sin that he has sinned in one of these, and it shall be forgiven him: and the remnant shall be the priest's, as a meat offering.

14 And the LORD spake unto Moses, saying,

15 If a soul commit a trespass, and sin through ignorance, in the holy things of the LORD; then he shall bring for his trespass unto the LORD a ram without blemish out of the flocks, with your estimation by shekels of silver, after the shekel of the sanctuary, for a trespass offering:

16 And he shall make amends for the harm that he has done in the holy thing, and shall add the fifth part thereto, and give it unto the priest: and the priest shall make an atonement for him with the ram of the trespass offering, and it shall be forgiven him.

17 And if a soul sin, and commit any of these things which are forbidden to be done by the commandments of the LORD; though he wist it not, yet is he guilty, and shall bear his iniquity.

18 And he shall bring a ram without blemish out of the flock, with your estimation, for a trespass offering, unto the priest: and the priest shall make an atonement for him concerning his ignorance wherein he erred and wist it not, and it shall be forgiven him.

19 It is a trespass offering: he has certainly trespassed against the LORD.

CHAPTER 6

AND the LORD spake unto Moses, saying,

2 If a soul sin, and commit a trespass against the LORD, and lie unto his neighbour in that which was delivered him to keep, or in fellowship, or in a thing taken away by violence, or has deceived his neighbour;

3 Or have found that which was lost, and lies concerning it, and sweareth falsely; in any of all these that a man doeth, sinning therein:

4 Then it shall be, because he has sinned, and is guilty, that he shall restore that which he took violently away, or the thing which he has deceitfully gotten, or that which was delivered him to keep, or the lost thing which he found,

5 Or all that about which he has sworn falsely; he shall even restore it in the principal, and shall add the fifth part more thereto, and give it unto him to whom it appertaineth, in the day of his trespass offering.

6 And he shall bring his trespass offering unto the LORD, a ram without blemish out of the flock, with your estimation, for a trespass offering, unto the priest:

7 And the priest shall make an atonement for him before the LORD: and it shall be forgiven him for any thing of all that he has done in trespassing therein.

8 And the LORD spake unto Moses, saying,

9 Command Aaron and his sons, saying, This is the law of the burnt offering: It is the burnt offering, because of the burning upon the altar all night unto the morning, and the fire of the altar shall be burning in it.

10 And the priest shall put on his linen garment, and his linen breeches shall he put upon his flesh, and take up the ashes which the fire has consumed with the burnt offering on the altar, and he shall put them beside the altar.

11 And he shall put off his garments, and put on other garments, and carry forth the ashes without the camp unto a clean place.

12 And the fire upon the altar shall be burning in it; it shall not be put out: and the priest shall burn wood on it every morning, and lay the burnt offering in order upon it; and he shall burn thereon the fat of the peace offerings.

13 The fire shall ever be burning upon the altar; it shall never go out.

14 And this is the law of the meat offering: the sons of Aaron shall offer it before the LORD, before the altar.

15 And he shall take of it his handful, of the flour of the meat offering, and of the oil thereof, and all the frankincense which is upon the meat offering, and shall burn it upon the altar for a sweet savour, even the memorial of it, unto the LORD.

16 And the remainder thereof shall Aaron and his sons eat: with unleavened bread shall it be eaten in the holy place; in the court of the tabernacle of the congregation they shall eat it.

17 It shall not be baken with leaven. I have given it unto them for their portion of my offerings made by fire; it is most holy, as is the sin offering, and as the trespass offering.

18 All the males among the children of Aaron shall eat of it. It shall be a statute for ever in your generations concerning the offerings of the LORD made by fire: every one that toucheth them shall be holy.

19 And the LORD spake unto Moses, saying,

20 This is the offering of Aaron and of his sons, which they shall offer unto the LORD in the day when he is anointed; the tenth part of an ephah of fine flour for a meat offering perpetual, half of it in the morning, and half thereof at night.

21 In a pan it shall be made with oil; and when it is baken, you shalt bring it in: and the baken pieces of the meat offering shalt you offer for a sweet savour unto the LORD.

22 And the priest of his sons that is anointed in his stead shall offer it: it is a statute for ever unto the LORD; it shall be wholly burnt.

23 For every meat offering for the priest shall be wholly burnt: it shall not be eaten.

24 And the LORD spake unto Moses, saying,

25 Speak unto Aaron and to his sons, saying, This is the law of the sin offering: In the place where the burnt offering is killed shall the sin offering be killed before the LORD: it is most holy.

26 The priest that offereth it for sin shall eat it: in the holy place shall it be eaten, in the court of the tabernacle of the congregation.

27 Whatsoever shall touch the flesh thereof shall be holy: and when there is sprinkled of the blood thereof upon any garment, you shalt wash that whereon it was sprinkled in the holy place.

28 But the earthen vessel wherein it is sodden shall be broken: and if it be sodden in a brasen pot, it shall be both scoured, and rinsed in water.

29 All the males among the priests shall eat thereof: it is most holy.

30 And no sin offering, whereof any of the blood is brought into the tabernacle of the congregation to reconcile withal in the holy place, shall be eaten: it shall be burnt in the fire.

CHAPTER 7

LIKEWISE this is the law of the trespass offering: it is most holy.

2 In the place where they kill the burnt offering shall they kill the trespass offering: and the blood thereof shall he sprinkle round about upon the altar.

3 And he shall offer of it all the fat thereof; the rump, and the fat that covers the inwards,

4 And the two kidneys, and the fat that is on them, which is by the flanks, and the caul that is above the liver, with the kidneys, it shall he take away:

5 And the priest shall burn them upon the altar for an offering made by fire unto the LORD: it is a trespass offering.

6 Every male among the priests shall eat thereof: it shall be eaten in the holy place: it is most holy.

7 As the sin offering is, so is the trespass offering: there is one law for them: the priest that maketh atonement therewith shall have it.

8 And the priest that offereth any man's burnt offering, even the priest shall have to himself the skin of the burnt offering which he has offered.

9 And all the meat offering that is baken in the oven, and all that is dressed in the fryingpan, and in the pan, shall be the priest's that offereth it.

10 And every meat offering, mingled with oil, and dry, shall all the sons of Aaron have, one as much as another.

11 And this is the law of the sacrifice of peace offerings, which he shall offer unto the LORD.

12 If he offer it for a thanksgiving, then he shall offer with the sacrifice of thanksgiving unleavened cakes mingled with oil, and unleavened wafers anointed with oil, and cakes mingled with oil, of fine flour, fried.

13 Besides the cakes, he shall offer for his offering leavened bread with the sacrifice of thanksgiving of his peace offerings.

14 And of it he shall offer one out of the whole oblation for an heave offering unto the LORD, and it shall be the priest's that sprinkleth the blood of the peace offerings.

15 And the flesh of the sacrifice of his peace offerings for thanksgiving shall be eaten the same day that it is offered; he shall not leave any of it until the morning.

16 But if the sacrifice of his offering be a vow, or a voluntary offering, it shall be eaten the same day that he offereth his sacrifice: and on the morrow also the remainder of it shall be eaten:

17 But the remainder of the flesh of the sacrifice on the third day shall be burnt with fire.

18 And if any of the flesh of the sacrifice of his peace offerings be eaten at all on the third day, it shall not be accepted, neither shall it be imputed unto him that offereth it: it shall be an abomination, and the soul that eateth of it shall bear his iniquity.

19 And the flesh that toucheth any unclean thing shall not be eaten; it shall be burnt with fire: and as for the flesh, all that be clean shall eat thereof.

20 But the soul that eateth of the flesh of the sacrifice of peace offerings, that pertain unto the LORD, having his uncleanness upon him, even that soul shall be cut off from his people.

21 Moreover the soul that shall touch any unclean thing, as the uncleanness of man, or any unclean beast, or any abominable unclean thing, and eat of the flesh of the sacrifice of peace offerings, which pertain unto the LORD, even that soul shall be cut off from his people.

22 And the LORD spake unto Moses, saying,

23 Speak unto the children of Israel, saying, You shall eat no manner of fat, of ox, or of sheep, or of goat.

24 And the fat of the beast that dieth of itself, and the fat of that which is torn with beasts, may be used in any other use: but you shall in no wise eat of it.

25 For whosoever eateth the fat of the beast, of which men offer an offering made by fire unto the LORD, even the soul that eateth it shall be cut off from his people.

26 Moreover you shall eat no manner of blood, whether it be of fowl or of beast, in any of your dwellings.

27 Whatsoever soul it be that eateth any manner of blood, even that soul shall be cut off from his people.

28 And the LORD spake unto Moses, saying,

29 Speak unto the children of Israel, saying, He that offereth the sacrifice of his peace offerings unto the LORD shall bring his oblation unto the LORD of the sacrifice of his peace offerings.

30 His own hands shall bring the offerings of the LORD made by fire, the fat with the breast, it shall he bring, that the breast may be waved for a wave offering before the LORD.

31 And the priest shall burn the fat upon the altar: but the breast shall be Aaron's and his sons'.

32 And the right shoulder shall you give unto the priest for an heave offering of the sacrifices of your peace offerings.

33 He among the sons of Aaron, that offereth the blood of the peace offerings, and the fat, shall have the right shoulder for his part.

34 For the wave breast and the heave shoulder have I taken of the children of Israel from off the sacrifices of their peace offerings, and have given them unto Aaron the priest and unto his sons by a statute for ever from among the children of Israel.

35 This is the portion of the anointing of Aaron, and of the anointing of his sons, out of the offerings of the LORD made by fire, in the day when he presented them to minister unto the LORD in the priest's office;

36 Which the LORD commanded to be given them of the children of Israel, in the day that he anointed them, by a statute for ever throughout their generations.

37 This is the law of the burnt offering, of the meat offering, and of the sin offering, and of the trespass offering, and of the consecrations, and of the sacrifice of the peace offerings;

38 Which the LORD commanded Moses in mount Sinai, in the day that he commanded the children of Israel to offer their oblations unto the LORD, in the wilderness of Sinai.

CHAPTER 8

AND the LORD spake unto Moses, saying,

2 Take Aaron and his sons with him, and the garments, and the anointing oil, and a bullock for the sin offering, and two rams, and a basket of unleavened bread;

3 And gather you all the congregation together unto the door of the tabernacle of the congregation.

4 And Moses did as the LORD commanded him; and the assembly was gathered together unto the door of the tabernacle of the congregation.

5 And Moses said unto the congregation, This is the thing which the LORD commanded to be done.

6 And Moses brought Aaron and his sons, and washed them with water.

7 And he put upon him the coat, and girded him with the girdle, and clothed him with the robe, and put the ephod upon him, and he girded him with the curious girdle of the ephod, and bound it unto him therewith.

8 And he put the breastplate upon him: also he put in the breastplate the Urim and the Thummim.

9 And he put the mitre upon his head; also upon the mitre, even upon his forefront, did he put the golden plate, the holy crown; as the LORD commanded Moses.

10 And Moses took the anointing oil, and anointed the tabernacle and all that was therein, and sanctified them.

11 And he sprinkled thereof upon the altar seven times, and anointed the altar and all his vessels, both the laver and his foot, to sanctify them.

12 And he poured of the anointing oil upon Aaron's head, and anointed him, to sanctify him.

13 And Moses brought Aaron's sons, and put coats upon them, and girded them with girdles, and put bonnets upon them; as the LORD commanded Moses.

14 And he brought the bullock for the sin offering: and Aaron and his sons laid their hands upon the head of the bullock for the sin offering.

15 And he slew it; and Moses took the blood, and put it upon the horns of the altar round about with his finger, and purified the altar, and poured the blood at the bottom of the altar, and sanctified it, to make reconciliation upon it.

16 And he took all the fat that was upon the inwards, and the caul above the liver, and the two kidneys, and their fat, and Moses burned it upon the altar.

17 But the bullock, and his hide, his flesh, and his dung, he burnt with fire without the camp; as the LORD commanded Moses.

18 And he brought the ram for the burnt offering: and Aaron and his sons laid their hands upon the head of the ram.

19 And he killed it; and Moses sprinkled the blood upon the altar round about.

20 And he cut the ram into pieces; and Moses burnt the head, and the pieces, and the fat.

21 And he washed the inwards and the legs in water; and Moses burnt the whole ram upon the altar: it was a burnt sacrifice for a sweet savour, and an offering made by fire unto the LORD; as the LORD commanded Moses.

22 And he brought the other ram, the ram of consecration: and Aaron and his sons laid their hands upon the head of the ram.

23 And he slew it; and Moses took of the blood of it, and put it upon the tip of Aaron's right ear, and upon the thumb of his right hand, and upon the great toe of his right foot.

24 And he brought Aaron's sons, and Moses put of the blood upon the tip of their right ear, and upon the thumbs of their right hands, and upon the great toes of their right feet: and Moses sprinkled the blood upon the altar round about.

25 And he took the fat, and the rump, and all the fat that was upon the inwards, and the caul above the liver, and the two kidneys, and their fat, and the right shoulder:

26 And out of the basket of unleavened bread, that was before the LORD, he took one unleavened cake, and a cake of oiled bread, and one wafer, and put them on the fat, and upon the right shoulder:

27 And he put all upon Aaron's hands, and upon his sons' hands, and waved them for a wave offering before the LORD.

28 And Moses took them from off their hands, and burnt them on the altar upon the burnt offering: they were consecrations for a sweet savour: it is an offering made by fire unto the LORD.

29 And Moses took the breast, and waved it for a wave offering before the LORD: for of the ram of consecration it was Moses' part; as the LORD commanded Moses.

30 And Moses took of the anointing oil, and of the blood which was upon the altar, and sprinkled it upon Aaron, and upon his garments, and upon his sons, and upon his sons' garments with him; and sanctified Aaron, and his garments, and his sons, and his sons' garments with him.

31 And Moses said unto Aaron and to his sons, Boil the flesh at the door of the tabernacle of the congregation: and there eat it with the bread that is in the basket of consecrations, as I commanded, saying, Aaron and his sons shall eat it.

32 And that which remaineth of the flesh and of the bread shall you burn with fire.

33 And you shall not go out of the door of the tabernacle of the congregation in seven days, until the days of your consecration be at an end: for seven days shall he consecrate you.

34 As he has done this day, so the LORD has commanded to do, to make an atonement for you.

35 Therefore shall you abide at the door of the tabernacle of the congregation day and night seven days, and keep the charge of the LORD, that you die not: for so I am commanded.

36 So Aaron and his sons did all things which the LORD commanded by the hand of Moses.

CHAPTER 9

AND it came to pass on the eighth day, that Moses called Aaron and his sons, and the elders of Israel;

2 And he said unto Aaron, Take you a young calf for a sin offering, and a ram for a burnt offering, without blemish, and offer them before the LORD.

3 And unto the children of Israel you shalt speak, saying, Take you a kid of the goats for a sin offering; and a calf and a lamb, both of the first year, without blemish, for a burnt offering;

4 Also a bullock and a ram for peace offerings, to sacrifice before the LORD; and a meat offering mingled with oil: for to day the LORD will appear unto you.

5 And they brought that which Moses commanded before the tabernacle of the congregation: and all the congregation drew near and stood before the LORD.

6 And Moses said, This is the thing which the LORD commanded that you should do: and the glory of the LORD shall appear unto you.

7 And Moses said unto Aaron, Go unto the altar, and offer your sin offering, and your burnt offering, and make an atonement for yourself, and for the people: and offer the offering of the people, and make an atonement for them; as the LORD commanded.

8 Aaron therefore went unto the altar, and slew the calf of the sin offering, which was for himself.

9 And the sons of Aaron brought the blood unto him: and he dipped his finger in the blood, and put it upon the horns of the altar, and poured out the blood at the bottom of the altar:

10 But the fat, and the kidneys, and the caul above the liver of the sin offering, he burnt upon the altar; as the LORD commanded Moses.

11 And the flesh and the hide he burnt with fire without the camp.

12 And he slew the burnt offering; and Aaron's sons presented unto him the blood, which he sprinkled round about upon the altar.

13 And they presented the burnt offering unto him, with the pieces thereof, and the head: and he burnt them upon the altar.

14 And he did wash the inwards and the legs, and burnt them upon the burnt offering on the altar.

15 And he brought the people's offering, and took the goat, which was the sin offering for the people, and slew it, and offered it for sin, as the first.

16 And he brought the burnt offering, and offered it according to the manner.

17 And he brought the meat offering, and took an handful thereof, and burnt it upon the altar, beside the burnt sacrifice of the morning.

18 He slew also the bullock and the ram for a sacrifice of peace offerings, which was for the people: and Aaron's sons presented unto him the blood, which he sprinkled upon the altar round about,

19 And the fat of the bullock and of the ram, the rump, and that which covers the inwards, and the kidneys, and the caul above the liver:

20 And they put the fat upon the breasts, and he burnt the fat upon the altar:

21 And the breasts and the right shoulder Aaron waved for a wave offering before the LORD; as Moses commanded.

22 And Aaron lifted up his hand toward the people, and blessed them, and came down from offering of the sin offering, and the burnt offering, and peace offerings.

23 And Moses and Aaron went into the tabernacle of the congregation, and came out, and blessed the people: and the glory of the LORD appeared unto all the people.

24 And there came a fire out from before the LORD, and consumed upon the altar the burnt offering and the fat: which when all the people saw, they shouted, and fell on their faces.

CHAPTER 10

AND Nadab and Abihu, the sons of Aaron, took either of them his censer, and put fire therein, and put incense thereon, and offered strange fire before the LORD, which he commanded them not.

2 And there went out fire from the LORD, and devoured them, and they died before the LORD.

3 Then Moses said unto Aaron, This is it that the LORD spake, saying, I will be sanctified in them that come nigh me, and before all the people I will be glorified. And Aaron held his peace.

4 And Moses called Mishael and Elzaphan, the sons of Uzziel the uncle of Aaron, and said unto them, Come near, carry your brethren from before the sanctuary out of the camp.

5 So they went near, and carried them in their coats out of the camp; as Moses had said.

6 And Moses said unto Aaron, and unto Eleazar and unto Ithamar, his sons, Uncover not your heads, neither rend your clothes; lest you die, and lest wrath come upon all the people: but let your brethren, the whole house of Israel, bewail the burning which the LORD has kindled.

7 And you shall not go out from the door of the tabernacle of the congregation, lest you die: for the anointing oil of the LORD is upon you. And they did according to the word of Moses.

8 And the LORD spake unto Aaron, saying,

9 Do not drink wine nor strong drink, you , nor your sons with you, when you go into the tabernacle of the congregation, lest you die: it shall be a statute for ever throughout your generations:

10 And that you may put difference between holy and unholy, and between unclean and clean;

11 And that you may teach the children of Israel all the statutes which the LORD has spoken unto them by the hand of Moses.

12 And Moses spake unto Aaron, and unto Eleazar and unto Ithamar, his sons that were left, Take the meat offering that remaineth of the offerings of the LORD made by fire, and eat it without leaven beside the altar: for it is most holy:

13 And you shall eat it in the holy place, because it is your due, and your sons' due, of the sacrifices of the LORD made by fire: for so I am commanded.

14 And the wave breast and heave shoulder shall you eat in a clean place; you , and your sons, and your daughters with you: for they be your due, and your sons' due, which are given out of the sacrifices of peace offerings of the children of Israel.

15 The heave shoulder and the wave breast shall they bring with the offerings made by fire of the fat, to wave it for a wave offering before the LORD; and it shall be yours, and your sons' with you, by a statute for ever; as the LORD has commanded.

16 And Moses diligently sought the goat of the sin offering, and, behold, it was burnt: he was angry with Eleazar and Ithamar, the sons of Aaron which were left alive, saying,

17 Wherefore have you not eaten the sin offering in the holy place, seeing it is most holy, and God has given it you to bear the iniquity of the congregation, to make atonement for them before the LORD?

18 Behold, the blood of it was not brought in within the holy place: you should indeed have eaten it in the holy place, as I commanded.

19 And Aaron said unto Moses, Behold, this day have they offered their sin offering and their burnt offering before the LORD; and such things have befallen me: and if I had eaten the sin offering to day, should it have been accepted in the sight of the LORD?

20 And when Moses heard that, he was content.

CHAPTER 11

AND the LORD spake unto Moses and to Aaron, saying unto them,

2 Speak unto the children of Israel, saying, These are the beasts which you shall eat among all the beasts that are on the earth.

3 Whatsoever parteth the hoof, and is clovenfooted, and cheweth the cud, among the beasts, that shall you eat.

4 Nevertheless these shall you not eat of them that chew the cud, or of them that divide the hoof: as the camel, because he cheweth the cud, but divideth not the hoof; he is unclean unto you.

5 And the coney, because he cheweth the cud, but divideth not the hoof; he is unclean unto you.

6 And the hare, because he cheweth the cud, but divideth not the hoof; he is unclean unto you.

7 And the swine, though he divide the hoof, and be clovenfooted, yet he cheweth not the cud; he is unclean to you.

8 Of their flesh shall you not eat, and their carcase shall you not touch; they are unclean to you.

9 These shall you eat of all that are in the waters: whatsoever has fins and scales in the waters, in the seas, and in the rivers, them shall you eat.

10 And all that have not fins and scales in the seas, and in the rivers, of all that move in the waters, and of any living thing which is in the waters, they shall be an abomination unto you:

11 They shall be even an abomination unto you; you shall not eat of their flesh, but you shall have their carcases in abomination.

12 Whatsoever has no fins nor scales in the waters, that shall be an abomination unto you.

13 And these are they which you shall have in abomination among the fowls; they shall not be eaten, they are an abomination: the eagle, and the ossifrage, and the ospray,

14 And the vulture, and the kite after his kind;

15 Every raven after his kind;

16 And the owl, and the night hawk, and the cuckow, and the hawk after his kind,

17 And the little owl, and the cormorant, and the great owl,

18 And the swan, and the pelican, and the gier eagle,

19 And the stork, the heron after her kind, and the lapwing, and the bat.

20 All fowls that creep, going upon all four, shall be an abomination unto you.

21 Yet these may you eat of every flying creeping thing that goeth upon all four, which have legs above their feet, to leap withal upon the earth;

22 Even these of them you may eat; the locust after his kind, and the bald locust after his kind, and the beetle after his kind, and the grasshopper after his kind.

23 But all other flying creeping things, which have four feet, shall be an abomination unto you.

24 And for these you shall be unclean: whosoever toucheth the carcase of them shall be unclean until the even.

25 And whosoever beareth ought of the carcase of them shall wash his clothes, and be unclean until the even.

26 The carcases of every beast which divideth the hoof, and is not clovenfooted, nor cheweth the cud, are unclean unto you: every one that toucheth them shall be unclean.

27 And whatsoever goeth upon his paws, among all manner of beasts that go on all four, those are unclean unto you: whoso toucheth their carcase shall be unclean until the even.

28 And he that beareth the carcase of them shall wash his clothes, and be unclean until the even: they are unclean unto you.

29 These also shall be unclean unto you among the creeping things that creep upon the earth; the weasel, and the mouse, and the tortoise after his kind,

30 And the ferret, and the chameleon, and the lizard, and the snail, and the mole.

31 These are unclean to you among all that creep: whosoever doth touch them, when they be dead, shall be unclean until the even.

32 And upon whatsoever any of them, when they are dead, doth fall, it shall be unclean; whether it be any vessel of wood, or raiment, or skin, or sack, whatsoever vessel it be, wherein any work is done, it must be put into water, and it shall be unclean until the even; so it shall be cleansed.

33 And every earthen vessel, whereinto any of them falleth, whatsoever is in it shall be unclean; and you shall break it.

34 Of all meat which may be eaten, that on which such water comes shall be unclean: and all drink that may be drunk in every such vessel shall be unclean.

35 And every thing whereupon any part of their carcase falleth shall be unclean; whether it be oven, or ranges for pots, they shall be broken down: for they are unclean, and shall be unclean unto you.

36 Nevertheless a fountain or pit, wherein there is plenty of water, shall be clean: but that which toucheth their carcase shall be unclean.

37 And if any part of their carcase fall upon any sowing seed which is to be sown, it shall be clean.

38 But if any water be put upon the seed, and any part of their carcase fall thereon, it shall be unclean unto you.

39 And if any beast, of which you may eat, die; he that toucheth the carcase thereof shall be unclean until the even.

40 And he that eateth of the carcase of it shall wash his clothes, and be unclean until the even: he also that beareth the carcase of it shall wash his clothes, and be unclean until the even.

41 And every creeping thing that creepeth upon the earth shall be an abomination; it shall not be eaten.

42 Whatsoever goeth upon the belly, and whatsoever goeth upon all four, or whatsoever has more feet among all creeping things that creep upon the earth, them you shall not eat; for they are an abomination.

43 You shall not make yourselves abominable with any creeping thing that creepeth, neither shall you make yourselves unclean with them, that you should be defiled thereby.

44 For I am the LORD your God: you shall therefore sanctify yourselves, and you shall be holy; for I am holy: neither shall you defile yourselves with any manner of creeping thing that creepeth upon the earth.

45 For I am the LORD that bringeth you up out of the land of Egypt, to be your God: you shall therefore be holy, for I am holy.

46 This is the law of the beasts, and of the fowl, and of every living creature that moveth in the waters, and of every creature that creepeth upon the earth:

47 To make a difference between the unclean and the clean, and between the beast that may be eaten and the beast that may not be eaten.

CHAPTER 12

AND the LORD spake unto Moses, saying,

2 Speak unto the children of Israel, saying, If a woman have conceived seed, and born a man child: then she shall be unclean seven days; according to the days of the separation for her infirmity shall she be unclean.

3 And in the eighth day the flesh of his foreskin shall be circumcised.

4 And she shall then continue in the blood of her purifying three and thirty days; she shall touch no hallowed thing, nor come into the sanctuary, until the days of her purifying be fulfilled.

5 But if she bear a maid child, then she shall be unclean two weeks, as in her separation: and she shall continue in the blood of her purifying threescore and six days.

6 And when the days of her purifying are fulfilled, for a son, or for a daughter, she shall bring a lamb of the first year for a burnt offering, and a young pigeon, or a turtledove, for a sin offering, unto the door of the tabernacle of the congregation, unto the priest:

7 Who shall offer it before the LORD, and make an atonement for her; and she shall be cleansed from the issue of her blood. This is the law for her that has born a male or a female.

8 And if she be not able to bring a lamb, then she shall bring two turtles, or two young pigeons; the one for the burnt offering, and the other for a sin offering: and the priest shall make an atonement for her, and she shall be clean.

CHAPTER 13

AND the LORD spake unto Moses and Aaron, saying,

2 When a man shall have in the skin of his flesh a rising, a scab, or bright spot, and it be in the skin of his flesh like the plague of leprosy; then he shall be brought unto Aaron the priest, or unto one of his sons the priests:

3 And the priest shall look on the plague in the skin of the flesh: and when the hair in the plague is turned white, and the plague in sight be deeper than the skin of his flesh, it is a plague of leprosy: and the priest shall look on him, and pronounce him unclean.

4 If the bright spot be white in the skin of his flesh, and in sight not deeper than the skin, and the hair thereof be not turned white; then the priest shall shut up him that has the plague seven days:

5 And the priest shall look on him the seventh day: and, behold, if the plague in his sight be at a stay, and the plague spread not in the skin; then the priest shall shut him up seven days more:

6 And the priest shall look on him again the seventh day: and, behold, if the plague be somewhat dark, and the plague spread not in the skin, the priest shall pronounce him clean: it is but a scab: and he shall wash his clothes, and be clean.

7 But if the scab spread much abroad in the skin, after that he has been seen of the priest for his cleansing, he shall be seen of the priest again:

8 And if the priest see that, behold, the scab spreadeth in the skin, then the priest shall pronounce him unclean: it is a leprosy.

9 When the plague of leprosy is in a man, then he shall be brought unto the priest;

10 And the priest shall see him: and, behold, if the rising be white in the skin, and it have turned the hair white, and there be quick raw flesh in the rising;

11 It is an old leprosy in the skin of his flesh, and the priest shall pronounce him unclean, and shall not shut him up: for he is unclean.

12 And if a leprosy break out abroad in the skin, and the leprosy cover all the skin of him that has the plague from his head even to his foot, wheresoever the priest looketh;

13 Then the priest shall consider: and, behold, if the leprosy have covered all his flesh, he shall pronounce him clean that has the plague: it is all turned white: he is clean.

14 But when raw flesh appeareth in him, he shall be unclean.

15 And the priest shall see the raw flesh, and pronounce him to be unclean: for the raw flesh is unclean: it is a leprosy.

16 Or if the raw flesh turn again, and be changed unto white, he shall come unto the priest;

17 And the priest shall see him: and, behold, if the plague be turned into white; then the priest shall pronounce him clean that has the plague: he is clean.

18 The flesh also, in which, even in the skin thereof, was a boil, and is healed,

19 And in the place of the boil there be a white rising, or a bright spot, white, and somewhat reddish, and it be shewed to the priest;

20 And if, when the priest seeth it, behold, it be in sight lower than the skin, and the hair thereof be turned white; the priest shall pronounce him unclean: it is a plague of leprosy broken out of the boil.

21 But if the priest look on it, and, behold, there be no white hairs therein, and if it be not lower than the skin, but be somewhat dark; then the priest shall shut him up seven days:

22 And if it spread much abroad in the skin, then the priest shall pronounce him unclean: it is a plague.

23 But if the bright spot stay in his place, and spread not, it is a burning boil; and the priest shall pronounce him clean.

24 Or if there be any flesh, in the skin whereof there is a hot burning, and the quick flesh that burneth have a white bright spot, somewhat reddish, or white;

25 Then the priest shall look upon it: and, behold, if the hair in the bright spot be turned white, and it be in sight deeper than the skin; it is a leprosy broken out of the burning: wherefore the priest shall pronounce him unclean: it is the plague of leprosy.

26 But if the priest look on it, and, behold, there be no white hair in the bright spot, and it be no lower than the other skin, but be somewhat dark; then the priest shall shut him up seven days:

27 And the priest shall look upon him the seventh day: and if it be spread much abroad in the skin, then the priest shall pronounce him unclean: it is the plague of leprosy.

28 And if the bright spot stay in his place, and spread not in the skin, but it be somewhat dark; it is a rising of the burning, and the priest shall pronounce him clean: for it is an inflammation of the burning.

29 If a man or woman have a plague upon the head or the beard;

30 Then the priest shall see the plague: and, behold, if it be in sight deeper than the skin; and there be in it a yellow thin hair; then the priest shall pronounce him unclean: it is a dry scall, even a leprosy upon the head or beard.

31 And if the priest look on the plague of the scall, and, behold, it be not in sight deeper than the skin, and that there is no black hair in it; then the priest shall shut up him that has the plague of the scall seven days:

32 And in the seventh day the priest shall look on the plague: and, behold, if the scall spread not, and there be in it no yellow hair, and the scall be not in sight deeper than the skin;

33 He shall be shaven, but the scall shall he not shave; and the priest shall shut up him that has the scall seven days more:

34 And in the seventh day the priest shall look on the scall: and, behold, if the scall be not spread in the skin, nor be in sight deeper than the skin; then the priest shall pronounce him clean: and he shall wash his clothes, and be clean.

35 But if the scall spread much in the skin after his cleansing;

36 Then the priest shall look on him: and, behold, if the scall be spread in the skin, the priest shall not seek for yellow hair; he is unclean.

37 But if the scall be in his sight at a stay, and that there is black hair grown up therein; the scall is healed, he is clean: and the priest shall pronounce him clean.

38 If a man also or a woman have in the skin of their flesh bright spots, even white bright spots;

39 Then the priest shall look: and, behold, if the bright spots in the skin of their flesh be darkish white; it is a freckled spot that groweth in the skin; he is clean.

40 And the man whose hair is fallen off his head, he is bald; yet is he clean.

41 And he that has his hair fallen off from the part of his head toward his face, he is forehead bald: yet is he clean.

42 And if there be in the bald head, or bald forehead, a white reddish sore; it is a leprosy sprung up in his bald head, or his bald forehead.

43 Then the priest shall look upon it: and, behold, if the rising of the sore be white reddish in his bald head, or in his bald forehead, as the leprosy appeareth in the skin of the flesh;

44 He is a leprous man, he is unclean: the priest shall pronounce him utterly unclean; his plague is in his head.

45 And the leper in whom the plague is, his clothes shall be rent, and his head bare, and he shall put a covering upon his upper lip, and shall cry, Unclean, unclean.

46 All the days wherein the plague shall be in him he shall be defiled; he is unclean: he shall dwell alone; without the camp shall his habitation be.

47 The garment also that the plague of leprosy is in, whether it be a woollen garment, or a linen garment;

48 Whether it be in the warp, or woof; of linen, or of woollen; whether in a skin, or in any thing made of skin;

49 And if the plague be greenish or reddish in the garment, or in the skin, either in the warp, or in the woof, or in any thing of skin; it is a plague of leprosy, and shall be shewed unto the priest:

50 And the priest shall look upon the plague, and shut up it that has the plague seven days:

51 And he shall look on the plague on the seventh day: if the plague be spread in the garment, either in the warp, or in the woof, or in a skin, or in any work that is made of skin; the plague is a fretting leprosy; it is unclean.

52 He shall therefore burn that garment, whether warp or woof, in woollen or in linen, or any thing of skin, wherein the plague is: for it is a fretting leprosy; it shall be burnt in the fire.

53 And if the priest shall look, and, behold, the plague be not spread in the garment, either in the warp, or in the woof, or in any thing of skin;

54 Then the priest shall command that they wash the thing wherein the plague is, and he shall shut it up seven days more:

55 And the priest shall look on the plague, after that it is washed: and, behold, if the plague have not changed his colour, and the plague be not spread; it is unclean; you shalt burn it in the fire; it is fret inward, whether it be bare within or without.

56 And if the priest look, and, behold, the plague be somewhat dark after the washing of it; then he shall rend it out of the garment, or out of the skin, or out of the warp, or out of the woof:

57 And if it appear still in the garment, either in the warp, or in the woof, or in any thing of skin; it is a spreading plague: you shalt burn that wherein the plague is with fire.

58 And the garment, either warp, or woof, or whatsoever thing of skin it be, which you shalt wash, if the plague be departed from them, then it shall be washed the second time, and shall be clean.

59 This is the law of the plague of leprosy in a garment of woollen or linen, either in the warp, or woof, or any thing of skins, to pronounce it clean, or to pronounce it unclean.

CHAPTER 14

AND the LORD spake unto Moses, saying,

2 This shall be the law of the leper in the day of his cleansing: He shall be brought unto the priest:

3 And the priest shall go forth out of the camp; and the priest shall look, and, behold, if the plague of leprosy be healed in the leper;

4 Then shall the priest command to take for him that is to be cleansed two birds alive and clean, and cedar wood, and scarlet, and hyssop:

5 And the priest shall command that one of the birds be killed in an earthen vessel over running water:

6 As for the living bird, he shall take it, and the cedar wood, and the scarlet, and the hyssop, and shall dip them and the living bird in the blood of the bird that was killed over the running water:

7 And he shall sprinkle upon him that is to be cleansed from the leprosy seven times, and shall pronounce him clean, and shall let the living bird loose into the open field.

8 And he that is to be cleansed shall wash his clothes, and shave off all his hair, and wash himself in water, that he may be clean: and after that he shall come into the camp, and shall tarry abroad out of his tent seven days.

9 But it shall be on the seventh day, that he shall shave all his hair off his head and his beard and his eyebrows, even all his hair he shall shave off: and he shall wash his clothes, also he shall wash his flesh in water, and he shall be clean.

10 And on the eighth day he shall take two he lambs without blemish, and one ewe lamb of the first year without blemish, and three tenth deals of fine flour for a meat offering, mingled with oil, and one log of oil.

11 And the priest that maketh him clean shall present the man that is to be made clean, and those things, before the LORD, at the door of the tabernacle of the congregation:

12 And the priest shall take one he lamb, and offer him for a trespass offering, and the log of oil, and wave them for a wave offering before the LORD:

13 And he shall slay the lamb in the place where he shall kill the sin offering and the burnt offering, in the holy place: for as the sin offering is the priest's, so is the trespass offering: it is most holy:

14 And the priest shall take some of the blood of the trespass offering, and the priest shall put it upon the tip of the right ear of him that is to be cleansed, and upon the thumb of his right hand, and upon the great toe of his right foot:

15 And the priest shall take some of the log of oil, and pour it into the palm of his own left hand:

16 And the priest shall dip his right finger in the oil that is in his left hand, and shall sprinkle of the oil with his finger seven times before the LORD:

17 And of the rest of the oil that is in his hand shall the priest put upon the tip of the right ear of him that is to be cleansed, and upon the thumb of his right hand, and upon the great toe of his right foot, upon the blood of the trespass offering:

18 And the remnant of the oil that is in the priest's hand he shall pour upon the head of him that is to be cleansed: and the priest shall make an atonement for him before the LORD.

19 And the priest shall offer the sin offering, and make an atonement for him that is to be cleansed from his uncleanness; and afterward he shall kill the burnt offering:

20 And the priest shall offer the burnt offering and the meat offering upon the altar: and the priest shall make an atonement for him, and he shall be clean.

21 And if he be poor, and cannot get so much; then he shall take one lamb for a trespass offering to be waved, to make an atonement for him, and one tenth deal of fine flour mingled with oil for a meat offering, and a log of oil;

22 And two turtledoves, or two young pigeons, such as he is able to get; and the one shall be a sin offering, and the other a burnt offering.

23 And he shall bring them on the eighth day for his cleansing unto the priest, unto the door of the tabernacle of the congregation, before the LORD.

24 And the priest shall take the lamb of the trespass offering, and the log of oil, and the priest shall wave them for a wave offering before the LORD:

25 And he shall kill the lamb of the trespass offering, and the priest shall take some of the blood of the trespass offering, and put it upon the tip of the right ear of him that is to be cleansed, and upon the thumb of his right hand, and upon the great toe of his right foot:

26 And the priest shall pour of the oil into the palm of his own left hand:

27 And the priest shall sprinkle with his right finger some of the oil that is in his left hand seven times before the LORD:

28 And the priest shall put of the oil that is in his hand upon the tip of the right ear of him that is to be cleansed, and upon the thumb of his right hand, and upon the great toe of his right foot, upon the place of the blood of the trespass offering:

29 And the rest of the oil that is in the priest's hand he shall put upon the head of him that is to be cleansed, to make an atonement for him before the LORD.

30 And he shall offer the one of the turtledoves, or of the young pigeons, such as he can get;

31 Even such as he is able to get, the one for a sin offering, and the other for a burnt offering, with the meat offering: and the priest shall make an atonement for him that is to be cleansed before the LORD.

32 This is the law of him in whom is the plague of leprosy, whose hand is not able to get that which pertaineth to his cleansing.

33 And the LORD spake unto Moses and unto Aaron, saying,

34 When you be come into the land of Canaan, which I give to you for a possession, and I put the plague of leprosy in a house of the land of your possession;

35 And he that owneth the house shall come and tell the priest, saying, It seemeth to me there is as it were a plague in the house:

36 Then the priest shall command that they empty the house, before the priest go into it to see the plague, that all that is in the house be not made unclean: and afterward the priest shall go in to see the house:

37 And he shall look on the plague, and, behold, if the plague be in the walls of the house with hollow strakes, greenish or reddish, which in sight are lower than the wall;

38 Then the priest shall go out of the house to the door of the house, and shut up the house seven days:

39 And the priest shall come again the seventh day, and shall look: and, behold, if the plague be spread in the walls of the house;

40 Then the priest shall command that they take away the stones in which the plague is, and they shall cast them into an unclean place without the city:

41 And he shall cause the house to be scraped within round about, and they shall pour out the dust that they scrape off without the city into an unclean place:

42 And they shall take other stones, and put them in the place of those stones; and he shall take other morter, and shall plaister the house.

43 And if the plague come again, and break out in the house, after that he has taken away the stones, and after he has scraped the house, and after it is plaistered;

44 Then the priest shall come and look, and, behold, if the plague be spread in the house, it is a fretting leprosy in the house: it is unclean.

45 And he shall break down the house, the stones of it, and the timber thereof, and all the morter of the house; and he shall carry them forth out of the city into an unclean place.

46 Moreover he that goeth into the house all the while that it is shut up shall be unclean until the even.

47 And he that lies in the house shall wash his clothes; and he that eateth in the house shall wash his clothes.

48 And if the priest shall come in, and look upon it, and, behold, the plague has not spread in the house, after the house was plaistered: then the priest shall pronounce the house clean, because the plague is healed.

49 And he shall take to cleanse the house two birds, and cedar wood, and scarlet, and hyssop:

50 And he shall kill the one of the birds in an earthen vessel over running water:

51 And he shall take the cedar wood, and the hyssop, and the scarlet, and the living bird, and dip them in the blood of the slain bird, and in the running water, and sprinkle the house seven times:

52 And he shall cleanse the house with the blood of the bird, and with the running water, and with the living bird, and with the cedar wood, and with the hyssop, and with the scarlet:

53 But he shall let go the living bird out of the city into the open fields, and make an atonement for the house: and it shall be clean.

54 This is the law for all manner of plague of leprosy, and scall,

55 And for the leprosy of a garment, and of a house,

56 And for a rising, and for a scab, and for a bright spot:

57 To teach when it is unclean, and when it is clean: this is the law of leprosy.

CHAPTER 15

AND the LORD spake unto Moses and to Aaron, saying,

2 Speak unto the children of Israel, and say unto them, When any man has a running issue out of his flesh, because of his issue he is unclean.

3 And this shall be his uncleanness in his issue: whether his flesh run with his issue, or his flesh be stopped from his issue, it is his uncleanness.

4 Every bed, whereon he lies that has the issue, is unclean: and every thing, whereon he sitteth, shall be unclean.

5 And whosoever toucheth his bed shall wash his clothes, and bathe himself in water, and be unclean until the even.

6 And he that sitteth on any thing whereon he sat that has the issue shall wash his clothes, and bathe himself in water, and be unclean until the even.

7 And he that toucheth the flesh of him that has the issue shall wash his clothes, and bathe himself in water, and be unclean until the even.

8 And if he that has the issue spit upon him that is clean; then he shall wash his clothes, and bathe himself in water, and be unclean until the even.

9 And what saddle soever he rideth upon that has the issue shall be unclean.

10 And whosoever toucheth any thing that was under him shall be unclean until the even: and he that beareth any of those things shall wash his clothes, and bathe himself in water, and be unclean until the even.

11 And whomsoever he toucheth that has the issue, and has not rinsed his hands in water, he shall wash his clothes, and bathe himself in water, and be unclean until the even.

12 And the vessel of earth, that he toucheth which has the issue, shall be broken: and every vessel of wood shall be rinsed in water.

13 And when he that has an issue is cleansed of his issue; then he shall number to himself seven days for his cleansing, and wash his clothes, and bathe his flesh in running water, and shall be clean.

14 And on the eighth day he shall take to him two turtledoves, or two young pigeons, and come before the LORD unto the door of the tabernacle of the congregation, and give them unto the priest:

15 And the priest shall offer them, the one for a sin offering, and the other for a burnt offering; and the priest shall make an atonement for him before the LORD for his issue.

16 And if any man's seed of copulation go out from him, then he shall wash all his flesh in water, and be unclean until the even.

17 And every garment, and every skin, whereon is the seed of copulation, shall be washed with water, and be unclean until the even.

18 The woman also with whom man shall lie with seed of copulation, they shall both bathe themselves in water, and be unclean until the even.

19 And if a woman have an issue, and her issue in her flesh be blood, she shall be put apart seven days: and whosoever toucheth her shall be unclean until the even.

20 And every thing that she lies upon in her separation shall be unclean: every thing also that she sitteth upon shall be unclean.

21 And whosoever toucheth her bed shall wash his clothes, and bathe himself in water, and be unclean until the even.

22 And whosoever toucheth any thing that she sat upon shall wash his clothes, and bathe himself in water, and be unclean until the even.

23 And if it be on her bed, or on any thing whereon she sitteth, when he toucheth it, he shall be unclean until the even.

24 And if any man lie with her at all, and her flowers be upon him, he shall be unclean seven days; and all the bed whereon he lies shall be unclean.

25 And if a woman have an issue of her blood many days out of the time of her separation, or if it run beyond the time of her separation; all the days of the issue of her uncleanness shall be as the days of her separation: she shall be unclean.

26 Every bed whereon she lies all the days of her issue shall be unto her as the bed of her separation: and whatsoever she sitteth upon shall be unclean, as the uncleanness of her separation.

27 And whosoever toucheth those things shall be unclean, and shall wash his clothes, and bathe himself in water, and be unclean until the even.

28 But if she be cleansed of her issue, then she shall number to herself seven days, and after that she shall be clean.

29 And on the eighth day she shall take unto her two turtles, or two young pigeons, and bring them unto the priest, to the door of the tabernacle of the congregation.

30 And the priest shall offer the one for a sin offering, and the other for a burnt offering; and the priest shall make an atonement for her before the LORD for the issue of her uncleanness.

31 Thus shall you separate the children of Israel from their uncleanness; that they die not in their uncleanness, when they defile my tabernacle that is among them.

32 This is the law of him that has an issue, and of him whose seed goeth from him, and is defiled therewith;

33 And of her that is sick of her flowers, and of him that has an issue, of the man, and of the woman, and of him that lies with her that is unclean.

CHAPTER 16

AND the LORD spake unto Moses after the death of the two sons of Aaron, when they offered before the LORD, and died;

2 And the LORD said unto Moses, Speak unto Aaron your brother, that he come not at all times into the holy place within the vail before the mercy seat, which is upon the ark; that he die not: for I will appear in the cloud upon the mercy seat.

3 Thus shall Aaron come into the holy place: with a young bullock for a sin offering, and a ram for a burnt offering.

4 He shall put on the holy linen coat, and he shall have the linen breeches upon his flesh, and shall be girded with a linen girdle, and with the linen mitre shall he be attired: these are holy garments; therefore shall he wash his flesh in water, and so put them on.

5 And he shall take of the congregation of the children of Israel two kids of the goats for a sin offering, and one ram for a burnt offering.

6 And Aaron shall offer his bullock of the sin offering, which is for himself, and make an atonement for himself, and for his house.

7 And he shall take the two goats, and present them before the LORD at the door of the tabernacle of the congregation.

8 And Aaron shall cast lots upon the two goats; one lot for the LORD, and the other lot for the scapegoat.

9 And Aaron shall bring the goat upon which the LORD's lot fell, and offer him for a sin offering.

10 But the goat, on which the lot fell to be the scapegoat, shall be presented alive before the LORD, to make an atonement with him, and to let him go for a scapegoat into the wilderness.

11 And Aaron shall bring the bullock of the sin offering, which is for himself, and shall make an atonement for himself, and for his house, and shall kill the bullock of the sin offering which is for himself:

12 And he shall take a censer full of burning coals of fire from off the altar before the LORD, and his hands full of sweet incense beaten small, and bring it within the vail:

13 And he shall put the incense upon the fire before the LORD, that the cloud of the incense may cover the mercy seat that is upon the testimony, that he die not:

14 And he shall take of the blood of the bullock, and sprinkle it with his finger upon the mercy seat eastward; and before the mercy seat shall he sprinkle of the blood with his finger seven times.

15 Then shall he kill the goat of the sin offering, that is for the people, and bring his blood within the vail, and do with that blood as he did with the blood of the bullock, and sprinkle it upon the mercy seat, and before the mercy seat:

16 And he shall make an atonement for the holy place, because of the uncleanness of the children of Israel, and because of their transgressions in all their sins: and so shall he do for the tabernacle of the congregation, that remaineth among them in the midst of their uncleanness.

17 And there shall be no man in the tabernacle of the congregation when he goeth in to make an atonement in the holy place, until he come out, and have made an atonement for himself, and for his household, and for all the congregation of Israel.

18 And he shall go out unto the altar that is before the LORD, and make an atonement for it; and shall take of the blood of the bullock, and of the blood of the goat, and put it upon the horns of the altar round about.

19 And he shall sprinkle of the blood upon it with his finger seven times, and cleanse it, and hallow it from the uncleanness of the children of Israel.

20And when he has made an end of reconciling the holy place, and the tabernacle of the congregation, and the altar, he shall bring the live goat:

21 And Aaron shall lay both his hands upon the head of the live goat, and confess over him all the iniquities of the children of Israel, and all their transgressions in all their sins, putting them upon the head of the goat, and shall send him away by the hand of a fit man into the wilderness:

22 And the goat shall bear upon him all their iniquities unto a land not inhabited: and he shall let go the goat in the wilderness.

23 And Aaron shall come into the tabernacle of the congregation, and shall put off the linen garments, which he put on when he went into the holy place, and shall leave them there:

24 And he shall wash his flesh with water in the holy place, and put on his garments, and come forth, and offer his burnt offering, and the burnt offering of the people, and make an atonement for himself, and for the people.

25 And the fat of the sin offering shall he burn upon the altar.

26 And he that let go the goat for the scapegoat shall wash his clothes, and bathe his flesh in water, and afterward come into the camp.

27 And the bullock for the sin offering, and the goat for the sin offering, whose blood was brought in to make atonement in the holy place, shall one carry forth without the camp; and they shall burn in the fire their skins, and their flesh, and their dung.

28 And he that burneth them shall wash his clothes, and bathe his flesh in water, and afterward he shall come into the camp.

29And this shall be a statute for ever unto you: that in the seventh month, on the tenth day of the month, you shall afflict your souls, and do no work at all, whether it be one of your own country, or a stranger that sojourneth among you:

30 For on that day shall the priest make an atonement for you, to cleanse you, that you may be clean from all your sins before the LORD.

31 It shall be a sabbath of rest unto you, and you shall afflict your souls, by a statute for ever.

32 And the priest, whom he shall anoint, and whom he shall consecrate to minister in the priest's office in his father's stead, shall make the atonement, and shall put on the linen clothes, even the holy garments:

33 And he shall make an atonement for the holy sanctuary, and he shall make an atonement for the tabernacle of the congregation, and for the altar, and he shall make an atonement for the priests, and for all the people of the congregation.

34 And this shall be an everlasting statute unto you, to make an atonement for the children of Israel for all their sins once a year. And he did as the LORD commanded Moses.

CHAPTER 17

AND the LORD spake unto Moses, saying,

2 Speak unto Aaron, and unto his sons, and unto all the children of Israel, and say unto them; This is the thing which the LORD has commanded, saying,

3 What man soever there be of the house of Israel, that killeth an ox, or lamb, or goat, in the camp, or that killeth it out of the camp,

4 And bringeth it not unto the door of the tabernacle of the congregation, to offer an offering unto the LORD before the tabernacle of the LORD; blood shall be imputed unto that man; he has shed blood; and that man shall be cut off from among his people:

5 To the end that the children of Israel may bring their sacrifices, which they offer in the open field, even that they may bring them unto the LORD, unto the door of the tabernacle of the congregation, unto the priest, and offer them for peace offerings unto the LORD.

6 And the priest shall sprinkle the blood upon the altar of the LORD at the door of the tabernacle of the congregation, and burn the fat for a sweet savour unto the LORD.

7 And they shall no more offer their sacrifices unto devils, after whom they have gone a whoring. This shall be a statute for ever unto them throughout their generations.

8And you shalt say unto them, Whatsoever man there be of the house of Israel, or of the strangers which sojourn among you, that offereth a burnt offering or sacrifice,

9 And bringeth it not unto the door of the tabernacle of the congregation, to offer it unto the LORD; even that man shall be cut off from among his people.

10And whatsoever man there be of the house of Israel, or of the strangers that sojourn among you, that eateth any manner of blood; I will even set my face against that soul that eateth blood, and will cut him off from among his people.

11 For the life of the flesh is in the blood: and I have given it to you upon the altar to make an atonement for your souls: for it is the blood that maketh an atonement for the soul.

12 Therefore I said unto the children of Israel, No soul of you shall eat blood, neither shall any stranger that sojourneth among you eat blood.

13 And whatsoever man there be of the children of Israel, or of the strangers that sojourn among you, which hunteth and catcheth any beast or fowl that may be eaten; he shall even pour out the blood thereof, and cover it with dust.

14 For it is the life of all flesh; the blood of it is for the life thereof: therefore I said unto the children of Israel, You shall eat the blood of no manner of flesh: for the life of all flesh is the blood thereof: whosoever eateth it shall be cut off.

15 And every soul that eateth that which died of itself, or that which was torn with beasts, whether it be one of your own country, or a stranger, he shall both wash his clothes, and bathe himself in water, and be unclean until the even: then shall he be clean.

16 But if he wash them not, nor bathe his flesh; then he shall bear his iniquity.

CHAPTER 18

AND the LORD spake unto Moses, saying,

2 Speak unto the children of Israel, and say unto them, I am the LORD your God.

3 After the doings of the land of Egypt, wherein you dwelt, shall you not do: and after the doings of the land of Canaan, whither I bring you, shall you not do: neither shall you walk in their ordinances.

4 You shall do my judgments, and keep my ordinances, to walk therein: I am the LORD your God.

5 You shall therefore keep my statutes, and my judgments: which if a man do, he shall live in them: I am the LORD.

6None of you shall approach to any that is near of kin to him, to uncover their nakedness: I am the LORD.

7 The nakedness of your father, or the nakedness of your mother, shalt you not uncover: she is your mother; you shalt not uncover her nakedness.

8 The nakedness of your father's wife shalt you not uncover: it is your father's nakedness.

9 The nakedness of your sister, the daughter of your father, or daughter of your mother, whether she be born at home, or born abroad, even their nakedness you shalt not uncover.

10 The nakedness of your son's daughter, or of your daughter's daughter, even their nakedness you shalt not uncover: for theirs is yours own nakedness.

11 The nakedness of your father's wife's daughter, begotten of your father, she is your sister, you shalt not uncover her nakedness.

12 You shalt not uncover the nakedness of your father's sister: she is your father's near kinswoman.

13 You shalt not uncover the nakedness of your mother's sister: for she is your mother's near kinswoman.

14 You shalt not uncover the nakedness of your father's brother, you shalt not approach to his wife: she is yours aunt.

15 You shalt not uncover the nakedness of your daughter in law: she is your son's wife; you shalt not uncover her nakedness.

16 You shalt not uncover the nakedness of your brother's wife: it is your brother's nakedness.

17 You shalt not uncover the nakedness of a woman and her daughter, neither shalt you take her son's daughter, or her daughter's daughter, to uncover her nakedness; for they are her near kinswomen: it is wickedness.

18 Neither shalt you take a wife to her sister, to vex her, to uncover her nakedness, beside the other in her life time.

19 Also you shalt not approach unto a woman to uncover her nakedness, as long as she is put apart for her uncleanness.

20 Moreover you shalt not lie carnally with your neighbour's wife, to defile yourself with her.

21 And you shalt not let any of your seed pass through the fire to Molech, neither shalt you profane the name of your God: I am the LORD.

22 You shalt not lie with mankind, as with womankind: it is abomination.

23 Neither shalt you lie with any beast to defile yourself therewith: neither shall any woman stand before a beast to lie down thereto: it is confusion.

24 Defile not you yourselves in any of these things: for in all these the nations are defiled which I cast out before you:

25 And the land is defiled: therefore I do visit the iniquity thereof upon it, and the land itself vomiteth out her inhabitants.

26 You shall therefore keep my statutes and my judgments, and shall not commit any of these abominations; neither any of your own nation, nor any stranger that sojourneth among you:

27 (For all these abominations have the men of the land done, which were before you, and the land is defiled;)

28 That the land spue not you out also, when you defile it, as it spued out the nations that were before you.

29 For whosoever shall commit any of these abominations, even the souls that commit them shall be cut off from among their people.

30 Therefore shall you keep my ordinance, that you commit not any one of these abominable customs, which were committed before you, and that you defile not yourselves therein: I am the LORD your God.

CHAPTER 19

AND the LORD spake unto Moses, saying,

2 Speak unto all the congregation of the children of Israel, and say unto them, You shall be holy: for I the LORD your God am holy.

3 You shall fear every man his mother, and his father, and keep my sabbaths: I am the LORD your God.

4 Turn you not unto idols, nor make to yourselves molten gods: I am the LORD your God.

5 And if you offer a sacrifice of peace offerings unto the LORD, you shall offer it at your own will.

6 It shall be eaten the same day you offer it, and on the morrow: and if ought remain until the third day, it shall be burnt in the fire.

7 And if it be eaten at all on the third day, it is abominable; it shall not be accepted.

8 Therefore every one that eateth it shall bear his iniquity, because he has profaned the hallowed thing of the LORD: and that soul shall be cut off from among his people.

9 And when you reap the harvest of your land, you shalt not wholly reap the corners of your field, neither shalt you gather the gleanings of your harvest.

10 And you shalt not glean your vineyard, neither shalt you gather every grape of your vineyard; you shalt leave them for the poor and stranger: I am the LORD your God.

11 You shall not steal, neither deal falsely, neither lie one to another.

12 And you shall not swear by my name falsely, neither shalt you profane the name of your God: I am the LORD.

13 You shalt not defraud your neighbour, neither rob him: the wages of him that is hired shall not abide with you all night until the morning.

14 You shalt not curse the deaf, nor put a stumblingblock before the blind, but shalt fear your God: I am the LORD.

15 You shall do no unrighteousness in judgment: you shalt not respect the person of the poor, nor honour the person of the mighty: but in righteousness shalt you judge your neighbour.

16 You shalt not go up and down as a talebearer among your people: neither shalt you stand against the blood of your neighbour: I am the LORD.

17 You shalt not hate your brother in yours heart: you shalt in any wise rebuke your neighbour, and not suffer sin upon him.

18 You shalt not avenge, nor bear any grudge against the children of your people, but you shalt love your neighbour as yourself: I am the LORD.

19 You shall keep my statutes. You shalt not let your cattle gender with a diverse kind: you shalt not sow your field with mingled seed: neither shall a garment mingled of linen and woollen come upon you.

20 And whosoever lies carnally with a woman, that is a bondmaid, betrothed to an husband, and not at all redeemed, nor freedom given her; she shall be scourged; they shall not be put to death, because she was not free.

21 And he shall bring his trespass offering unto the LORD, unto the door of the tabernacle of the congregation, even a ram for a trespass offering.

22 And the priest shall make an atonement for him with the ram of the trespass offering before the LORD for his sin which he has done: and the sin which he has done shall be forgiven him.

23 And when you shall come into the land, and shall have planted all manner of trees for food, then you shall count the fruit thereof as uncircumcised: three years shall it be as uncircumcised unto you: it shall not be eaten of.

24 But in the fourth year all the fruit thereof shall be holy to praise the LORD withal.

25 And in the fifth year shall you eat of the fruit thereof, that it may yield unto you the increase thereof: I am the LORD your God.

26 You shall not eat any thing with the blood: neither shall you use enchantment, nor observe times.

27 You shall not round the corners of your heads, neither shalt you mar the corners of your beard.

28 You shall not make any cuttings in your flesh for the dead, nor print any marks upon you: I am the LORD.

29 Do not prostitute your daughter, to cause her to be a whore; lest the land fall to whoredom, and the land become full of wickedness.

30 You shall keep my sabbaths, and reverence my sanctuary: I am the LORD.

31 Regard not them that have familiar spirits, neither seek after wizards, to be defiled by them: I am the LORD your God.

32 You shalt rise up before the hoary head, and honour the face of the old man, and fear your God: I am the LORD.

33 And if a stranger sojourn with you in your land, you shall not vex him.

34 But the stranger that dwelleth with you shall be unto you as one born among you, and you shalt love him as yourself; for you were strangers in the land of Egypt: I am the LORD your God.

35 You shall do no unrighteousness in judgment, in meteyard, in weight, or in measure.

36 Just balances, just weights, a just ephah, and a just hin, shall you have: I am the LORD your God, which brought you out of the land of Egypt.

37 Therefore shall you observe all my statutes, and all my judgments, and do them: I am the LORD.

CHAPTER 20

AND the LORD spake unto Moses, saying,

2 Again, you shalt say to the children of Israel, Whosoever he be of the children of Israel, or of the strangers that sojourn in Israel, that giveth any of his seed unto Molech; he shall surely be put to death: the people of the land shall stone him with stones.

3 And I will set my face against that man, and will cut him off from among his people; because he has given of his seed unto Molech, to defile my sanctuary, and to profane my holy name.

4 And if the people of the land do any ways hide their eyes from the man, when he giveth of his seed unto Molech, and kill him not:

5 Then I will set my face against that man, and against his family, and will cut him off, and all that go a whoring after him, to commit whoredom with Molech, from among their people.

6 And the soul that turneth after such as have familiar spirits, and after wizards, to go a whoring after them, I will even set my face against that soul, and will cut him off from among his people.

7 Sanctify yourselves therefore, and be you holy: for I am the LORD your God.

8 And you shall keep my statutes, and do them: I am the LORD which sanctify you.

9 For every one that curseth his father or his mother shall be surely put to death: he has cursed his father or his mother; his blood shall be upon him.

10 And the man that committeth adultery with another man's wife, even he committeth adultery with his neighbour's wife, the adulterer and the adulteress shall surely be put to death.

11 And the man that lies with his father's wife has uncovered his father's nakedness: both of them shall surely be put to death; their blood shall be upon them.

12 And if a man lie with his daughter in law, both of them shall surely be put to death: they have created confusion; their blood shall be upon them.

13 If a man also lie with mankind, as he lies with a woman, both of them have committed an abomination: they shall surely be put to death; their blood shall be upon them.

14 And if a man take a wife and her mother, it is wickedness: they shall be burnt with fire, both he and they; that there be no wickedness among you.

15 And if a man lie with a beast, he shall surely be put to death: and you shall slay the beast.

16 And if a woman approach unto any beast, and lie down thereto, you shalt kill the woman, and the beast: they shall surely be put to death; their blood shall be upon them.

17 And if a man shall take his sister, his father's daughter, or his mother's daughter, and see her nakedness, and she see his nakedness; it is a wicked thing; and they shall be cut off in the sight of their people: he has uncovered his sister's nakedness; he shall bear his iniquity.

18 And if a man shall lie with a woman having her sickness, and shall uncover her nakedness; he has discovered her fountain, and she has uncovered the fountain of her blood: and both of them shall be cut off from among their people.

19 And you shalt not uncover the nakedness of your mother's sister, nor of your father's sister: for he uncovereth his near kin: they shall bear their iniquity.

20 And if a man shall lie with his uncle's wife, he has uncovered his uncle's nakedness: they shall bear their sin; they shall die childless.

21 And if a man shall take his brother's wife, it is an unclean thing: he has uncovered his brother's nakedness; they shall be childless.

22 You shall therefore keep all my statutes, and all my judgments, and do them: that the land, whither I bring you to dwell therein, spue you not out.

23 And you shall not walk in the manners of the nation, which I cast out before you: for they committed all these things, and therefore I abhorred them.

24 But I have said unto you, You shall inherit their land, and I will give it unto you to possess it, a land that floweth with milk and honey: I am the LORD your God, which have separated you from other people.

25 You shall therefore put difference between clean beasts and unclean, and between unclean fowls and clean: and you shall not make your souls abominable by beast, or by fowl, or by any manner of living thing that creepeth on the ground, which I have separated from you as unclean.

26 And you shall be holy unto me: for I the LORD am holy, and have severed you from other people, that you should be my.

27 A man also or woman that has a familiar spirit, or that is a wizard, shall surely be put to death: they shall stone them with stones: their blood shall be upon them.

CHAPTER 21

AND the LORD said unto Moses, Speak unto the priests the sons of Aaron, and say unto them, There shall none be defiled for the dead among his people:

2 But for his kin, that is near unto him, that is, for his mother, and for his father, and for his son, and for his daughter, and for his brother,

3 And for his sister a virgin, that is nigh unto him, which has had no husband; for her may he be defiled.

4 But he shall not defile himself, being a chief man among his people, to profane himself.

5 They shall not make baldness upon their head, neither shall they shave off the corner of their beard, nor make any cuttings in their flesh.

6 They shall be holy unto their God, and not profane the name of their God: for the offerings of the LORD made by fire, and the bread of their God, they do offer: therefore they shall be holy.

7 They shall not take a wife that is a whore, or profane; neither shall they take a woman put away from her husband: for he is holy unto his God.

8 You shalt sanctify him therefore; for he offereth the bread of your God: he shall be holy unto you: for I the LORD, which sanctify you, am holy.

9 And the daughter of any priest, if she profane herself by playing the whore, she profaneth her father: she shall be burnt with fire.

10 And he that is the high priest among his brethren, upon whose head the anointing oil was poured, and that is consecrated to put on the garments, shall not uncover his head, nor rend his clothes;

11 Neither shall he go in to any dead body, nor defile himself for his father, or for his mother;

12 Neither shall he go out of the sanctuary, nor profane the sanctuary of his God; for the crown of the anointing oil of his God is upon him: I am the LORD.

13 And he shall take a wife in her virginity.

14 A widow, or a divorced woman, or profane, or an harlot, these shall he not take: but he shall take a virgin of his own people to wife.

15 Neither shall he profane his seed among his people: for I the LORD do sanctify him.

16 And the LORD spake unto Moses, saying,

17 Speak unto Aaron, saying, Whosoever he be of your seed in their generations that has any blemish, let him not approach to offer the bread of his God.

18 For whatsoever man he be that has a blemish, he shall not approach: a blind man, or a lame, or he that has a flat nose, or any thing superfluous,

19 Or a man that is brokenfooted, or brokenhanded,

20 Or crookbackt, or a dwarf, or that has a blemish in his eye, or be scurvy, or scabbed, or has his stones broken;

21 No man that has a blemish of the seed of Aaron the priest shall come nigh to offer the offerings of the LORD made by fire: he has a blemish; he shall not come nigh to offer the bread of his God.

22 He shall eat the bread of his God, both of the most holy, and of the holy.

23 Only he shall not go in unto the vail, nor come nigh unto the altar, because he has a blemish; that he profane not my sanctuaries: for I the LORD do sanctify them.

24 And Moses told it unto Aaron, and to his sons, and unto all the children of Israel.

CHAPTER 22

AND the LORD spake unto Moses, saying,

2 Speak unto Aaron and to his sons, that they separate themselves from the holy things of the children of Israel, and that they profane not my holy name in those things which they hallow unto me: I am the LORD.

3 Say unto them, Whosoever he be of all your seed among your generations, that goeth unto the holy things, which the children of Israel hallow unto the LORD, having his uncleanness upon him, that soul shall be cut off from my presence: I am the LORD.

4 What man soever of the seed of Aaron is a leper, or has a running issue; he shall not eat of the holy things, until he be clean. And whoso toucheth any thing that is unclean by the dead, or a man whose seed goeth from him;

5 Or whosoever toucheth any creeping thing, whereby he may be made unclean, or a man of whom he may take uncleanness, whatsoever uncleanness he has;

6 The soul which has touched any such shall be unclean until even, and shall not eat of the holy things, unless he wash his flesh with water.

7 And when the sun is down, he shall be clean, and shall afterward eat of the holy things; because it is his food.

8 That which dieth of itself, or is torn with beasts, he shall not eat to defile himself therewith: I am the LORD.

9 They shall therefore keep my ordinance, lest they bear sin for it, and die therefore, if they profane it: I the LORD do sanctify them.

10 There shall no stranger eat of the holy thing: a sojourner of the priest, or an hired servant, shall not eat of the holy thing.

11 But if the priest buy any soul with his money, he shall eat of it, and he that is born in his house: they shall eat of his meat.

12 If the priest's daughter also be married unto a stranger, she may not eat of an offering of the holy things.

13 But if the priest's daughter be a widow, or divorced, and have no child, and is returned unto her father's house, as in her youth, she shall eat of her father's meat: but there shall no stranger eat thereof.

14 And if a man eat of the holy thing unwittingly, then he shall put the fifth part thereof unto it, and shall give it unto the priest with the holy thing.

15 And they shall not profane the holy things of the children of Israel, which they offer unto the LORD;

16 Or suffer them to bear the iniquity of trespass, when they eat their holy things: for I the LORD do sanctify them.

17 And the LORD spake unto Moses, saying,

18 Speak unto Aaron, and to his sons, and unto all the children of Israel, and say unto them, Whatsoever he be of the house of Israel, or of the strangers in Israel, that will offer his oblation for all his vows, and for all his freewill offerings, which they will offer unto the LORD for a burnt offering;

19 You shall offer at your own will a male without blemish, of the beeves, of the sheep, or of the goats.

20 But whatsoever has a blemish, that shall you not offer: for it shall not be acceptable for you.

21 And whosoever offereth a sacrifice of peace offerings unto the LORD to accomplish his vow, or a freewill offering in beeves or sheep, it shall be perfect to be accepted; there shall be no blemish therein.

22 Blind, or broken, or maimed, or having a wen, or scurvy, or scabbed, you shall not offer these unto the LORD, nor make an offering by fire of them upon the altar unto the LORD.

23 Either a bullock or a lamb that has any thing superfluous or lacking in his parts, that mayest you offer for a freewill offering; but for a vow it shall not be accepted.

24 You shall not offer unto the LORD that which is bruised, or crushed, or broken, or cut; neither shall you make any offering thereof in your land.

25 Neither from a stranger's hand shall you offer the bread of your God of any of these; because their corruption is in them, and blemishes be in them: they shall not be accepted for you.

26 And the LORD spake unto Moses, saying,

27 When a bullock, or a sheep, or a goat, is brought forth, then it shall be seven days under the dam; and from the eighth day and thenceforth it shall be accepted for an offering made by fire unto the LORD.

28 And whether it be cow or ewe, you shall not kill it and her young both in one day.

29 And when you will offer a sacrifice of thanksgiving unto the LORD, offer it at your own will.

30 On the same day it shall be eaten up; you shall leave none of it until the morrow: I am the LORD.

31 Therefore shall you keep my commandments, and do them: I am the LORD.

32 Neither shall you profane my holy name; but I will be hallowed among the children of Israel: I am the LORD which hallow you,

33 That brought you out of the land of Egypt, to be your God: I am the LORD.

CHAPTER 23

AND the LORD spake unto Moses, saying,

2 Speak unto the children of Israel, and say unto them, Concerning the feasts of the LORD, which you shall proclaim to be holy convocations, even these are my feasts.

3 Six days shall work be done: but the seventh day is the sabbath of rest, an holy convocation; you shall do no work therein: it is the sabbath of the LORD in all your dwellings.

4 These are the feasts of the LORD, even holy convocations, which you shall proclaim in their seasons.

5 In the fourteenth day of the first month at even is the LORD's passover.

6 And on the fifteenth day of the same month is the feast of unleavened bread unto the LORD: seven days you must eat unleavened bread.

7 In the first day you shall have an holy convocation: you shall do no servile work therein.

8 But you shall offer an offering made by fire unto the LORD seven days: in the seventh day is an holy convocation: you shall do no servile work therein.

9 And the LORD spake unto Moses, saying,

10 Speak unto the children of Israel, and say unto them, When you be come into the land which I give unto you, and shall reap the harvest thereof, then you shall bring a sheaf of the firstfruits of your harvest unto the priest:

11 And he shall wave the sheaf before the LORD, to be accepted for you: on the morrow after the sabbath the priest shall wave it.

12 And you shall offer that day when you wave the sheaf an he lamb without blemish of the first year for a burnt offering unto the LORD.

13 And the meat offering thereof shall be two tenth deals of fine flour mingled with oil, an offering made by fire unto the LORD for a sweet savour: and the drink offering thereof shall be of wine, the fourth part of an hin.

14 And you shall eat neither bread, nor parched corn, nor green ears, until the selfsame day that you have brought an offering unto your God: it shall be a statute for ever throughout your generations in all your dwellings.

15 And you shall count unto you from the morrow after the sabbath, from the day that you brought the sheaf of the wave offering; seven sabbaths shall be complete:

16 Even unto the morrow after the seventh sabbath shall you number fifty days; and you shall offer a new meat offering unto the LORD.

17 You shall bring out of your habitations two wave loaves of two tenth deals: they shall be of fine flour; they shall be baken with leaven; they are the firstfruits unto the LORD.

18 And you shall offer with the bread seven lambs without blemish of the first year, and one young bullock, and two rams: they shall be for a burnt offering unto the LORD, with their meat offering, and their drink offerings, even an offering made by fire, of sweet savour unto the LORD.

19 Then you shall sacrifice one kid of the goats for a sin offering, and two lambs of the first year for a sacrifice of peace offerings.

20 And the priest shall wave them with the bread of the firstfruits for a wave offering before the LORD, with the two lambs: they shall be holy to the LORD for the priest.

21 And you shall proclaim on the selfsame day, that it may be an holy convocation unto you: you shall do no servile work therein: it shall be a statute for ever in all your dwellings throughout your generations.

22 And when you reap the harvest of your land, you shalt not make clean riddance of the corners of your field when you reapest, neither shalt you gather any gleaning of your harvest: you shalt leave them unto the poor, and to the stranger: I am the LORD your God.

23 And the LORD spake unto Moses, saying,

24 Speak unto the children of Israel, saying, In the seventh month, in the first day of the month, shall you have a sabbath, a memorial of blowing of trumpets, an holy convocation.

25 You shall do no servile work therein: but you shall offer an offering made by fire unto the LORD.

26 And the LORD spake unto Moses, saying,

27 Also on the tenth day of this seventh month there shall be a day of atonement: it shall be an holy convocation unto you; and you shall afflict your souls, and offer an offering made by fire unto the LORD.

28 And you shall do no work in that same day: for it is a day of atonement, to make an atonement for you before the LORD your God.

29 For whatsoever soul it be that shall not be afflicted in that same day, he shall be cut off from among his people.

30 And whatsoever soul it be that doeth any work in that same day, the same soul will I destroy from among his people.

31 You shall do no manner of work: it shall be a statute for ever throughout your generations in all your dwellings.

32 It shall be unto you a sabbath of rest, and you shall afflict your souls: in the ninth day of the month at even, from even unto even, shall you celebrate your sabbath.

33 And the LORD spake unto Moses, saying,

34 Speak unto the children of Israel, saying, The fifteenth day of this seventh month shall be the feast of tabernacles for seven days unto the LORD.

35 On the first day shall be an holy convocation: you shall do no servile work therein.

36 Seven days you shall offer an offering made by fire unto the LORD: on the eighth day shall be an holy convocation unto you; and you shall offer an offering made by fire unto the LORD: it is a solemn assembly; and you shall do no servile work therein.

37 These are the feasts of the LORD, which you shall proclaim to be holy convocations, to offer an offering made by fire unto the LORD, a burnt offering, and a meat offering, a sacrifice, and drink offerings, every thing upon his day:

38 Beside the sabbaths of the LORD, and beside your gifts, and beside all your vows, and beside all your freewill offerings, which you give unto the LORD.

39 Also in the fifteenth day of the seventh month, when you have gathered in the fruit of the land, you shall keep a feast unto the LORD seven days: on the first day shall be a sabbath, and on the eighth day shall be a sabbath.

40 And you shall take you on the first day the boughs of goodly trees, branches of palm trees, and the boughs of thick trees, and willows of the brook; and you shall rejoice before the LORD your God seven days.

41 And you shall keep it a feast unto the LORD seven days in the year. It shall be a statute for ever in your generations: you shall celebrate it in the seventh month.

42 You shall dwell in booths seven days; all that are Israelites born shall dwell in booths:

43 That your generations may know that I made the children of Israel to dwell in booths, when I brought them out of the land of Egypt: I am the LORD your God.

44 And Moses declared unto the children of Israel the feasts of the LORD.

CHAPTER 24

AND the LORD spake unto Moses, saying,

2 Command the children of Israel, that they bring unto you pure oil olive beaten for the light, to cause the lamps to burn continually.

3 Without the vail of the testimony, in the tabernacle of the congregation, shall Aaron order it from the evening unto the morning before the LORD continually: it shall be a statute for ever in your generations.

4 He shall order the lamps upon the pure candlestick before the LORD continually.

5 And you shalt take fine flour, and bake twelve cakes thereof: two tenth deals shall be in one cake.

6 And you shalt set them in two rows, six on a row, upon the pure table before the LORD.

7 And you shalt put pure frankincense upon each row, that it may be on the bread for a memorial, even an offering made by fire unto the LORD.

8 Every sabbath he shall set it in order before the LORD continually, being taken from the children of Israel by an everlasting covenant.

9 And it shall be Aaron's and his sons'; and they shall eat it in the holy place: for it is most holy unto him of the offerings of the LORD made by fire by a perpetual statute.

10 And the son of an Israelitish woman, whose father was an Egyptian, went out among the children of Israel: and this son of the Israelitish woman and a man of Israel strove together in the camp;

11 And the Israelitish woman's son blasphemed the name of the LORD, and cursed. And they brought him unto Moses: (and his mother's name was Shelomith, the daughter of Dibri, of the tribe of Dan:)

12 And they put him in ward, that the mind of the LORD might be shewed them.

13 And the LORD spake unto Moses, saying,

14 Bring forth him that has cursed without the camp; and let all that heard him lay their hands upon his head, and let all the congregation stone him.

15 And you shalt speak unto the children of Israel, saying, Whosoever curseth his God shall bear his sin.

16 And he that blasphemeth the name of the LORD, he shall surely be put to death, and all the congregation shall certainly stone him: as well the stranger, as he that is born in the land, when he blasphemeth the name of the LORD, shall be put to death.

17 And he that killeth any man shall surely be put to death.

18 And he that killeth a beast shall make it good; beast for beast.

19 And if a man cause a blemish in his neighbour; as he has done, so shall it be done to him;

20 Breach for breach, eye for eye, tooth for tooth: as he has caused a blemish in a man, so shall it be done to him again.

21 And he that killeth a beast, he shall restore it: and he that killeth a man, he shall be put to death.

22 You shall have one manner of law, as well for the stranger, as for one of your own country: for I am the LORD your God.

23 And Moses spake to the children of Israel, that they should bring forth him that had cursed out of the camp, and stone him with stones. And the children of Israel did as the LORD commanded Moses.

CHAPTER 25

AND the LORD spake unto Moses in mount Sinai, saying,

2 Speak unto the children of Israel, and say unto them, When you come into the land which I give you, then shall the land keep a sabbath unto the LORD.

3 Six years you shalt sow your field, and six years you shalt prune your vineyard, and gather in the fruit thereof;

4 But in the seventh year shall be a sabbath of rest unto the land, a sabbath for the LORD: you shalt neither sow your field, nor prune your vineyard.

5 That which groweth of its own accord of your harvest you shalt not reap, neither gather the grapes of your vine undressed: for it is a year of rest unto the land.

6 And the sabbath of the land shall be meat for you; for you, and for your servant, and for your maid, and for your hired servant, and for your stranger that sojourneth with you,

7 And for your cattle, and for the beast that are in your land, shall all the increase thereof be meat.

8 And you shalt number seven sabbaths of years unto you, seven times seven years; and the space of the seven sabbaths of years shall be unto you forty and nine years.

9 Then shalt you cause the trumpet of the jubile to sound on the tenth day of the seventh month, in the day of atonement shall you make the trumpet sound throughout all your land.

10 And you shall hallow the fiftieth year, and proclaim liberty throughout all the land unto all the inhabitants thereof: it shall be a jubile unto you; and you shall return every man unto his possession, and you shall return every man unto his family.

11 A jubile shall that fiftieth year be unto you: you shall not sow, neither reap that which groweth of itself in it, nor gather the grapes in it of your vine undressed.

12 For it is the jubile; it shall be holy unto you: you shall eat the increase thereof out of the field.

13 In the year of this jubile you shall return every man unto his possession.

14 And if you sell ought unto your neighbour, or buyest ought of your neighbour's hand, you shall not oppress one another:

15 According to the number of years after the jubile you shalt buy of your neighbour, and according unto the number of years of the fruits he shall sell unto you:

16 According to the multitude of years you shalt increase the price thereof, and according to the fewness of years you shalt diminish the price of it: for according to the number of the years of the fruits doth he sell unto you.

17 You shall not therefore oppress one another; but you shalt fear your God: for I am the LORD your God.

18 Wherefore you shall do my statutes, and keep my judgments, and do them; and you shall dwell in the land in safety.

19 And the land shall yield her fruit, and you shall eat your fill, and dwell therein in safety.

20 And if you shall say, What shall we eat the seventh year? behold, we shall not sow, nor gather in our increase:

21 Then I will command my blessing upon you in the sixth year, and it shall bring forth fruit for three years.

22 And you shall sow the eighth year, and eat yet of old fruit until the ninth year; until her fruits come in you shall eat of the old store.

23 The land shall not be sold for ever: for the land is my; for you are strangers and sojourners with me.

24 And in all the land of your possession you shall grant a redemption for the land.

25 If your brother be waxen poor, and has sold away some of his possession, and if any of his kin come to redeem it, then shall he redeem that which his brother sold.

26 And if the man have none to redeem it, and himself be able to redeem it;

27 Then let him count the years of the sale thereof, and restore the overplus unto the man to whom he sold it; that he may return unto his possession.

28 But if he be not able to restore it to him, then that which is sold shall remain in the hand of him that has bought it until the year of jubile: and in the jubile it shall go out, and he shall return unto his possession.

29 And if a man sell a dwelling house in a walled city, then he may redeem it within a whole year after it is sold; within a full year may he redeem it.

30 And if it be not redeemed within the space of a full year, then the house that is in the walled city shall be established for ever to him that bought it throughout his generations: it shall not go out in the jubile.

31 But the houses of the villages which have no wall round about them shall be counted as the fields of the country: they may be redeemed, and they shall go out in the jubile.

32 Notwithstanding the cities of the Levites, and the houses of the cities of their possession, may the Levites redeem at any time.

33 And if a man purchase of the Levites, then the house that was sold, and the city of his possession, shall go out in the year of jubile: for the houses of the cities of the Levites are their possession among the children of Israel.

34 But the field of the suburbs of their cities may not be sold; for it is their perpetual possession.

35 And if your brother be waxen poor, and fallen in decay with you; then you shalt relieve him: yea, though he be a stranger, or a sojourner; that he may live with you.

36 Take you no usury of him, or increase: but fear your God; that your brother may live with you.

37 You shalt not give him your money upon usury, nor lend him your victuals for increase.

38 I am the LORD your God, which brought you forth out of the land of Egypt, to give you the land of Canaan, and to be your God.

39 And if your brother that dwelleth by you be waxen poor, and be sold unto you; you shalt not compel him to serve as a bondservant:

40 But as an hired servant, and as a sojourner, he shall be with you, and shall serve you unto the year of jubile:

41 And then shall he depart from you, both he and his children with him, and shall return unto his own family, and unto the possession of his fathers shall he return.

42 For they are my servants, which I brought forth out of the land of Egypt: they shall not be sold as bondmen.

43 You shalt not rule over him with rigour; but shalt fear your God.

44 Both your bondmen, and your bondmaids, which you shalt have, shall be of the heathen that are round about you; of them shall you buy bondmen and bondmaids.

45 Moreover of the children of the strangers that do sojourn among you, of them shall you buy, and of their families that are with you, which they begat in your land: and they shall be your possession.

46 And you shall take them as an inheritance for your children after you, to inherit them for a possession; they shall be your bondmen for ever: but over your brethren the children of Israel, you shall not rule one over another with rigour.

47 And if a sojourner or stranger wax rich by you, and your brother that dwelleth by him wax poor, and sell himself unto the stranger or sojourner by you, or to the stock of the stranger's family:

48 After that he is sold he may be redeemed again; one of his brethren may redeem him:

49 Either his uncle, or his uncle's son, may redeem him, or any that is nigh of kin unto him of his family may redeem him; or if he be able, he may redeem himself.

50 And he shall reckon with him that bought him from the year that he was sold to him unto the year of jubile: and the price of his sale shall be according unto the number of years, according to the time of an hired servant shall it be with him.

51 If there be yet many years behind, according unto them he shall give again the price of his redemption out of the money that he was bought for.

52 And if there remain but few years unto the year of jubile, then he shall count with him, and according unto his years shall he give him again the price of his redemption.

53 And as a yearly hired servant shall he be with him: and the other shall not rule with rigour over him in your sight.

54 And if he be not redeemed in these years, then he shall go out in the year of jubile, both he, and his children with him.

55 For unto me the children of Israel are servants; they are my servants whom I brought forth out of the land of Egypt: I am the LORD your God.

CHAPTER 26

YOU shall make you no idols nor graven image, neither rear you up a standing image, neither shall you set up any image of stone in your land, to bow down unto it: for I am the LORD your God.

2 You shall keep my sabbaths, and reverence my sanctuary: I am the LORD.

3 If you walk in my statutes, and keep my commandments, and do them;

4 Then I will give you rain in due season, and the land shall yield her increase, and the trees of the field shall yield their fruit.

5 And your threshing shall reach unto the vintage, and the vintage shall reach unto the sowing time: and you shall eat your bread to the full, and dwell in your land safely.

6 And I will give peace in the land, and you shall lie down, and none shall make you afraid: and I will rid evil beasts out of the land, neither shall the sword go through your land.

7 And you shall chase your enemies, and they shall fall before you by the sword.

8 And five of you shall chase an hundred, and an hundred of you shall put ten thousand to flight: and your enemies shall fall before you by the sword.

9 For I will have respect unto you, and make you fruitful, and multiply you, and establish my covenant with you.

10 And you shall eat old store, and bring forth the old because of the new.

11 And I will set my tabernacle among you: and my soul shall not abhor you.

12 And I will walk among you, and will be your God, and you shall be my people.

13 I am the LORD your God, which brought you forth out of the land of Egypt, that you should not be their bondmen; and I have broken the bands of your yoke, and made you go upright.

14 But if you will not hearken unto me, and will not do all these commandments;

15 And if you shall despise my statutes, or if your soul abhor my judgments, so that you will not do all my commandments, but that you break my covenant:

16 I also will do this unto you; I will even appoint over you terror, consumption, and the burning ague, that shall consume the eyes, and cause sorrow of heart: and you shall sow your seed in vain, for your enemies shall eat it.

17 And I will set my face against you, and you shall be slain before your enemies: they that hate you shall reign over you; and you shall flee when none pursueth you.

18 And if you will not yet for all this hearken unto me, then I will punish you seven times more for your sins.

19 And I will break the pride of your power; and I will make your heaven as iron, and your earth as brass:

20 And your strength shall be spent in vain: for your land shall not yield her increase, neither shall the trees of the land yield their fruits.

21 And if you walk contrary unto me, and will not hearken unto me; I will bring seven times more plagues upon you according to your sins.

22 I will also send wild beasts among you, which shall rob you of your children, and destroy your cattle, and make you few in number; and your high ways shall be desolate.

23 And if you will not be reformed by me by these things, but will walk contrary unto me;

24 Then will I also walk contrary unto you, and will punish you yet seven times for your sins.

25 And I will bring a sword upon you, that shall avenge the quarrel of my covenant: and when you are gathered together within your cities, I will send the pestilence among you; and you shall be delivered into the hand of the enemy.

26 And when I have broken the staff of your bread, ten women shall bake your bread in one oven, and they shall deliver you your bread again by weight: and you shall eat, and not be satisfied.

27 And if you will not for all this hearken unto me, but walk contrary unto me;

28 Then I will walk contrary unto you also in fury; and I, even I, will chastise you seven times for your sins.

29 And you shall eat the flesh of your sons, and the flesh of your daughters shall you eat.

30 And I will destroy your high places, and cut down your images, and cast your carcases upon the carcases of your idols, and my soul shall abhor you.

31 And I will make your cities waste, and bring your sanctuaries unto desolation, and I will not smell the savour of your sweet odours.

32 And I will bring the land into desolation: and your enemies which dwell therein shall be astonished at it.

33 And I will scatter you among the heathen, and will draw out a sword after you: and your land shall be desolate, and your cities waste.

34 Then shall the land enjoy her sabbaths, as long as it lies desolate, and you be in your enemies' land; even then shall the land rest, and enjoy her sabbaths.

35 As long as it lies desolate it shall rest; because it did not rest in your sabbaths, when you dwelt upon it.

36 And upon them that are left alive of you I will send a faintness into their hearts in the lands of their enemies; and the sound of a shaken leaf shall chase them; and they shall flee, as fleeing from a sword; and they shall fall when none pursueth.

37 And they shall fall one upon another, as it were before a sword, when none pursueth: and you shall have no power to stand before your enemies.

38 And you shall perish among the heathen, and the land of your enemies shall eat you up.

39 And they that are left of you shall pine away in their iniquity in your enemies' lands; and also in the iniquities of their fathers shall they pine away with them.

40 If they shall confess their iniquity, and the iniquity of their fathers, with their trespass which they trespassed against me, and that also they have walked contrary unto me;

41 And that I also have walked contrary unto them, and have brought them into the land of their enemies; if then their uncircumcised hearts be humbled, and they then accept of the punishment of their iniquity:

42 Then will I remember my covenant with Jacob, and also my covenant with Isaac, and also my covenant with Abraham will I remember; and I will remember the land.

43 The land also shall be left of them, and shall enjoy her sabbaths, while she lies desolate without them: and they shall accept of the punishment of their iniquity: because, even because they despised my judgments, and because their soul abhorred my statutes.

44 And yet for all that, when they be in the land of their enemies, I will not cast them away, neither will I abhor them, to destroy them utterly, and to break my covenant with them: for I am the LORD their God.

45 But I will for their sakes remember the covenant of their ancestors, whom I brought forth out of the land of Egypt in the sight of the heathen, that I might be their God: I am the LORD.

46 These are the statutes and judgments and laws, which the LORD made between him and the children of Israel in mount Sinai by the hand of Moses.

CHAPTER 27

AND the LORD spake unto Moses, saying,

2 Speak unto the children of Israel, and say unto them, When a man shall make a singular vow, the persons shall be for the LORD by your estimation.

3 And your estimation shall be of the male from twenty years old even unto sixty years old, even your estimation shall be fifty shekels of silver, after the shekel of the sanctuary.

4 And if it be a female, then your estimation shall be thirty shekels.

5 And if it be from five years old even unto twenty years old, then your estimation shall be of the male twenty shekels, and for the female ten shekels.

6 And if it be from a month old even unto five years old, then your estimation shall be of the male five shekels of silver, and for the female your estimation shall be three shekels of silver.

7 And if it be from sixty years old and above; if it be a male, then your estimation shall be fifteen shekels, and for the female ten shekels.

8 But if he be poorer than your estimation, then he shall present himself before the priest, and the priest shall value him; according to his ability that vowed shall the priest value him.

9 And if it be a beast, whereof men bring an offering unto the LORD, all that any man giveth of such unto the LORD shall be holy.

10 He shall not alter it, nor change it, a good for a bad, or a bad for a good: and if he shall at all change beast for beast, then it and the exchange thereof shall be holy.

11 And if it be any unclean beast, of which they do not offer a sacrifice unto the LORD, then he shall present the beast before the priest:

12 And the priest shall value it, whether it be good or bad: as you valuest it, who are the priest, so shall it be.

13 But if he will at all redeem it, then he shall add a fifth part thereof unto your estimation.

14 And when a man shall sanctify his house to be holy unto the LORD, then the priest shall estimate it, whether it be good or bad: as the priest shall estimate it, so shall it stand.

15 And if he that sanctified it will redeem his house, then he shall add the fifth part of the money of your estimation unto it, and it shall be his.

16 And if a man shall sanctify unto the LORD some part of a field of his possession, then your estimation shall be according to the seed thereof: an homer of barley seed shall be valued at fifty shekels of silver.

17 If he sanctify his field from the year of jubile, according to your estimation it shall stand.

18 But if he sanctify his field after the jubile, then the priest shall reckon unto him the money according to the years that remain, even unto the year of the jubile, and it shall be abated from your estimation.

19 And if he that sanctified the field will in any wise redeem it, then he shall add the fifth part of the money of your estimation unto it, and it shall be assured to him.

20 And if he will not redeem the field, or if he have sold the field to another man, it shall not be redeemed any more.

21 But the field, when it goeth out in the jubile, shall be holy unto the LORD, as a field devoted; the possession thereof shall be the priest's.

22 And if a man sanctify unto the LORD a field which he has bought, which is not of the fields of his possession;

23 Then the priest shall reckon unto him the worth of your estimation, even unto the year of the jubile: and he shall give yours estimation in that day, as a holy thing unto the LORD.

24 In the year of the jubile the field shall return unto him of whom it was bought, even to him to whom the possession of the land did belong.

25 And all your estimations shall be according to the shekel of the sanctuary: twenty gerahs shall be the shekel.

26 Only the firstling of the beasts, which should be the LORD's firstling, no man shall sanctify it; whether it be ox, or sheep: it is the LORD's.

27 And if it be of an unclean beast, then he shall redeem it according to yours estimation, and shall add a fifth part of it thereto: or if it be not redeemed, then it shall be sold according to your estimation.

28 Notwithstanding no devoted thing, that a man shall devote unto the LORD of all that he has, both of man and beast, and of the field of his possession, shall be sold or redeemed: every devoted thing is most holy unto the LORD.

29 None devoted, which shall be devoted of men, shall be redeemed; but shall surely be put to death.

30 And all the tithe of the land, whether of the seed of the land, or of the fruit of the tree, is the LORD's: it is holy unto the LORD.

31 And if a man will at all redeem ought of his tithes, he shall add thereto the fifth part thereof.

32 And concerning the tithe of the herd, or of the flock, even of whatsoever passes under the rod, the tenth shall be holy unto the LORD.

33 He shall not search whether it be good or bad, neither shall he change it: and if he change it at all, then both it and the change thereof shall be holy; it shall not be redeemed.

34 These are the commandments, which the LORD commanded Moses for the children of Israel in mount Sinai.

THE FOURTH BOOK OF MOSES,
CALLED
NUMBERS.

CHAPTER 1

AND the LORD spake unto Moses in the wilderness of Sinai, in the tabernacle of the congregation, on the first day of the second month, in the second year after they were come out of the land of Egypt, saying,

2 Take you the sum of all the congregation of the children of Israel, after their families, by the house of their fathers, with the number of their names, every male by their polls;

3 From twenty years old and upward, all that are able to go forth to war in Israel: you and Aaron shall number them by their armies.

4 And with you there shall be a man of every tribe; every one head of the house of his fathers.

5 And these are the names of the men that shall stand with you: of the tribe of Reuben; Elizur the son of Shedeur.

6 Of Simeon; Shelumiel the son of Zurishaddai.

7 Of Judah; Nahshon the son of Amminadab.

8 Of Issachar; Nethaneel the son of Zuar.

9 Of Zebulun; Eliab the son of Helon.

10 Of the children of Joseph: of Ephraim; Elishama the son of Ammihud: of Manasseh; Gamaliel the son of Pedahzur.

11 Of Benjamin; Abidan the son of Gideoni.

12 Of Dan; Ahiezer the son of Ammishaddai.

13 Of Asher; Pagiel the son of Ocran.

14 Of Gad; Eliasaph the son of Deuel.

15 Of Naphtali; Ahira the son of Enan.

16 These were the renowned of the congregation, princes of the tribes of their fathers, heads of thousands in Israel.

17 And Moses and Aaron took these men which are expressed by their names:

18 And they assembled all the congregation together on the first day of the second month, and they declared their pedigrees after their families, by the house of their fathers, according to the number of the names, from twenty years old and upward, by their polls.

19 As the LORD commanded Moses, so he numbered them in the wilderness of Sinai.

20 And the children of Reuben, Israel's eldest son, by their generations, after their families, by the house of their fathers, according to the number of the names, by their polls, every male from twenty years old and upward, all that were able to go forth to war;

21 Those that were numbered of them, even of the tribe of Reuben, were forty and six thousand and five hundred.

22 Of the children of Simeon, by their generations, after their families, by the house of their fathers, those that were numbered of them, according to the number of the names, by their polls, every male from twenty years old and upward, all that were able to go forth to war;

23 Those that were numbered of them, even of the tribe of Simeon, were fifty and nine thousand and three hundred.

24 Of the children of Gad, by their generations, after their families, by the house of their fathers, according to the number of the names, from twenty years old and upward, all that were able to go forth to war;

25 Those that were numbered of them, even of the tribe of Gad, were forty and five thousand six hundred and fifty.

26 Of the children of Judah, by their generations, after their families, by the house of their fathers, according to the number of the names, from twenty years old and upward, all that were able to go forth to war;

27 Those that were numbered of them, even of the tribe of Judah, were threescore and fourteen thousand and six hundred.

28 Of the children of Issachar, by their generations, after their families, by the house of their fathers, according to the number of the names, from twenty years old and upward, all that were able to go forth to war;

29 Those that were numbered of them, even of the tribe of Issachar, were fifty and four thousand and four hundred.

30 Of the children of Zebulun, by their generations, after their families, by the house of their fathers, according to the number of the names, from twenty years old and upward, all that were able to go forth to war;

31 Those that were numbered of them, even of the tribe of Zebulun, were fifty and seven thousand and four hundred.

32 Of the children of Joseph, namely, of the children of Ephraim, by their generations, after their families, by the house of their fathers, according to the number of the names, from twenty years old and upward, all that were able to go forth to war;

33 Those that were numbered of them, even of the tribe of Ephraim, were forty thousand and five hundred.

34 Of the children of Manasseh, by their generations, after their families, by the house of their fathers, according to the number of the names, from twenty years old and upward, all that were able to go forth to war;

35 Those that were numbered of them, even of the tribe of Manasseh, were thirty and two thousand and two hundred.

36 Of the children of Benjamin, by their generations, after their families, by the house of their fathers, according to the number of the names, from twenty years old and upward, all that were able to go forth to war;

37 Those that were numbered of them, even of the tribe of Benjamin, were thirty and five thousand and four hundred.

38 Of the children of Dan, by their generations, after their families, by the house of their fathers, according to the number of the names, from twenty years old and upward, all that were able to go forth to war;

39 Those that were numbered of them, even of the tribe of Dan, were threescore and two thousand and seven hundred.

40 Of the children of Asher, by their generations, after their families, by the house of their fathers, according to the number of the names, from twenty years old and upward, all that were able to go forth to war;

41 Those that were numbered of them, even of the tribe of Asher, were forty and one thousand and five hundred.

42 Of the children of Naphtali, throughout their generations, after their families, by the house of their fathers, according to the number of the names, from twenty years old and upward, all that were able to go forth to war;

43 Those that were numbered of them, even of the tribe of Naphtali, were fifty and three thousand and four hundred.

44 These are those that were numbered, which Moses and Aaron numbered, and the princes of Israel, being twelve men: each one was for the house of his fathers.

45 So were all those that were numbered of the children of Israel, by the house of their fathers, from twenty years old and upward, all that were able to go forth to war in Israel;

46 Even all they that were numbered were six hundred thousand and three thousand and five hundred and fifty.

47 But the Levites after the tribe of their fathers were not numbered among them.

48 For the LORD had spoken unto Moses, saying,

49 Only you shalt not number the tribe of Levi, neither take the sum of them among the children of Israel:

50 But you shalt appoint the Levites over the tabernacle of testimony, and over all the vessels thereof, and over all things that belong to it: they shall bear the tabernacle, and all the vessels thereof; and they shall minister unto it, and shall encamp round about the tabernacle.

51 And when the tabernacle setteth forward, the Levites shall take it down: and when the tabernacle is to be pitched, the Levites shall set it up: and the stranger that comes nigh shall be put to death.

52 And the children of Israel shall pitch their tents, every man by his own camp, and every man by his own standard, throughout their hosts.

53 But the Levites shall pitch round about the tabernacle of testimony, that there be no wrath upon the congregation of the children of Israel: and the Levites shall keep the charge of the tabernacle of testimony.

54 And the children of Israel did according to all that the LORD commanded Moses, so did they.

CHAPTER 2

AND the LORD spake unto Moses and unto Aaron, saying,

2 Every man of the children of Israel shall pitch by his own standard, with the ensign of their father's house: far off about the tabernacle of the congregation shall they pitch.

3 And on the east side toward the rising of the sun shall they of the standard of the camp of Judah pitch throughout their armies: and Nahshon the son of Amminadab shall be captain of the children of Judah.

4 And his host, and those that were numbered of them, were threescore and fourteen thousand and six hundred.

5 And those that do pitch next unto him shall be the tribe of Issachar: and Nethaneel the son of Zuar shall be captain of the children of Issachar.

6 And his host, and those that were numbered thereof, were fifty and four thousand and four hundred.

7 Then the tribe of Zebulun: and Eliab the son of Helon shall be captain of the children of Zebulun.

8 And his host, and those that were numbered thereof, were fifty and seven thousand and four hundred.

9 All that were numbered in the camp of Judah were an hundred thousand and fourscore thousand and six thousand and four hundred, throughout their armies. These shall first set forth.

10 On the south side shall be the standard of the camp of Reuben according to their armies: and the captain of the children of Reuben shall be Elizur the son of Shedeur.

11 And his host, and those that were numbered thereof, were forty and six thousand and five hundred.

12 And those which pitch by him shall be the tribe of Simeon: and the captain of the children of Simeon shall be Shelumiel the son of Zurishaddai.

13 And his host, and those that were numbered of them, were fifty and nine thousand and three hundred.

14 Then the tribe of Gad: and the captain of the sons of Gad shall be Eliasaph the son of Reuel.

15 And his host, and those that were numbered of them, were forty and five thousand and six hundred and fifty.

16 All that were numbered in the camp of Reuben were an hundred thousand and fifty and one thousand and four hundred and fifty, throughout their armies. And they shall set forth in the second rank.

17 Then the tabernacle of the congregation shall set forward with the camp of the Levites in the midst of the camp: as they encamp, so shall they set forward, every man in his place by their standards.

18 On the west side shall be the standard of the camp of Ephraim according to their armies: and the captain of the sons of Ephraim shall be Elishama the son of Ammihud.

19 And his host, and those that were numbered of them, were forty thousand and five hundred.

20 And by him shall be the tribe of Manasseh: and the captain of the children of Manasseh shall be Gamaliel the son of Pedahzur.

21 And his host, and those that were numbered of them, were thirty and two thousand and two hundred.

22 Then the tribe of Benjamin: and the captain of the sons of Benjamin shall be Abidan the son of Gideoni.

23 And his host, and those that were numbered of them, were thirty and five thousand and four hundred.

24 All that were numbered of the camp of Ephraim were an hundred thousand and eight thousand and an hundred, throughout their armies. And they shall go forward in the third rank.

25 The standard of the camp of Dan shall be on the north side by their armies: and the captain of the children of Dan shall be Ahiezer the son of Ammishaddai.

26 And his host, and those that were numbered of them, were threescore and two thousand and seven hundred.

27 And those that encamp by him shall be the tribe of Asher: and the captain of the children of Asher shall be Pagiel the son of Ocran.

28 And his host, and those that were numbered of them, were forty and one thousand and five hundred.

29 Then the tribe of Naphtali: and the captain of the children of Naphtali shall be Ahira the son of Enan.

30 And his host, and those that were numbered of them, were fifty and three thousand and four hundred.

31 All they that were numbered in the camp of Dan were an hundred thousand and fifty and seven thousand and six hundred. They shall go hindmost with their standards.

32 These are those which were numbered of the children of Israel by the house of their fathers: all those that were numbered of the camps throughout their hosts were six hundred thousand and three thousand and five hundred and fifty.

33 But the Levites were not numbered among the children of Israel; as the LORD commanded Moses.

34 And the children of Israel did according to all that the LORD commanded Moses: so they pitched by their standards, and so they set forward, every one after their families, according to the house of their fathers.

CHAPTER 3

THESE also are the generations of Aaron and Moses in the day that the LORD spake with Moses in mount Sinai.

2 And these are the names of the sons of Aaron; Nadab the firstborn, and Abihu, Eleazar, and Ithamar.

3 These are the names of the sons of Aaron, the priests which were anointed, whom he consecrated to minister in the priest's office.

4 And Nadab and Abihu died before the LORD, when they offered strange fire before the LORD, in the wilderness of Sinai, and they had no children: and Eleazar and Ithamar ministered in the priest's office in the sight of Aaron their father.

5 And the LORD spake unto Moses, saying,

6 Bring the tribe of Levi near, and present them before Aaron the priest, that they may minister unto him.

7 And they shall keep his charge, and the charge of the whole congregation before the tabernacle of the congregation, to do the service of the tabernacle.

8 And they shall keep all the instruments of the tabernacle of the congregation, and the charge of the children of Israel, to do the service of the tabernacle.

9 And you shalt give the Levites unto Aaron and to his sons: they are wholly given unto him out of the children of Israel.

10 And you shalt appoint Aaron and his sons, and they shall wait on their priest's office: and the stranger that comes nigh shall be put to death.

11 And the LORD spake unto Moses, saying,

12 And I, behold, I have taken the Levites from among the children of Israel instead of all the firstborn that openeth the matrix among the children of Israel: therefore the Levites shall be my;

13 Because all the firstborn are my; for on the day that I struck all the firstborn in the land of Egypt I hallowed unto me all the firstborn in Israel, both man and beast: my shall they be: I am the LORD.

14 And the LORD spake unto Moses in the wilderness of Sinai, saying,

15 Number the children of Levi after the house of their fathers, by their families: every male from a month old and upward shalt you number them.

16 And Moses numbered them according to the word of the LORD, as he was commanded.

17 And these were the sons of Levi by their names; Gershon, and Kohath, and Merari.

18 And these are the names of the sons of Gershon by their families; Libni, and Shimei.

19 And the sons of Kohath by their families; Amram, and Izehar, Hebron, and Uzziel.

20 And the sons of Merari by their families; Mahli, and Mushi. These are the families of the Levites according to the house of their fathers.

21 Of Gershon was the family of the Libnites, and the family of the Shimites: these are the families of the Gershonites.

22 Those that were numbered of them, according to the number of all the males, from a month old and upward, even those that were numbered of them were seven thousand and five hundred.

23 The families of the Gershonites shall pitch behind the tabernacle westward.

24 And the chief of the house of the father of the Gershonites shall be Eliasaph the son of Lael.

25 And the charge of the sons of Gershon in the tabernacle of the congregation shall be the tabernacle, and the tent, the covering thereof, and the hanging for the door of the tabernacle of the congregation,

26 And the hangings of the court, and the curtain for the door of the court, which is by the tabernacle, and by the altar round about, and the cords of it for all the service thereof.

27 And of Kohath was the family of the Amramites, and the family of the Izeharites, and the family of the Hebronites, and the family of the Uzzielites: these are the families of the Kohathites.

28 In the number of all the males, from a month old and upward, were eight thousand and six hundred, keeping the charge of the sanctuary.

29 The families of the sons of Kohath shall pitch on the side of the tabernacle southward.

30 And the chief of the house of the father of the families of the Kohathites shall be Elizaphan the son of Uzziel.

31 And their charge shall be the ark, and the table, and the candlestick, and the altars, and the vessels of the sanctuary wherewith they minister, and the hanging, and all the service thereof.

32 And Eleazar the son of Aaron the priest shall be chief over the chief of the Levites, and have the oversight of them that keep the charge of the sanctuary.

33 Of Merari was the family of the Mahlites, and the family of the Mushites: these are the families of Merari.

34 And those that were numbered of them, according to the number of all the males, from a month old and upward, were six thousand and two hundred.

35 And the chief of the house of the father of the families of Merari was Zuriel the son of Abihail: these shall pitch on the side of the tabernacle northward.

36 And under the custody and charge of the sons of Merari shall be the boards of the tabernacle, and the bars thereof, and the pillars thereof, and the sockets thereof, and all the vessels thereof, and all that serveth thereto,

37 And the pillars of the court round about, and their sockets, and their pins, and their cords.

38 But those that encamp before the tabernacle toward the east, even before the tabernacle of the congregation eastward, shall be Moses, and Aaron and his sons, keeping the charge of the sanctuary for the charge of the children of Israel; and the stranger that comes nigh shall be put to death.

39 All that were numbered of the Levites, which Moses and Aaron numbered at the commandment of the LORD, throughout their families, all the males from a month old and upward, were twenty and two thousand.

40 And the LORD said unto Moses, Number all the firstborn of the males of the children of Israel from a month old and upward, and take the number of their names.

41 And you shalt take the Levites for me (I am the LORD) instead of all the firstborn among the children of Israel; and the cattle of the Levites instead of all the firstlings among the cattle of the children of Israel.

42 And Moses numbered, as the LORD commanded him, all the firstborn among the children of Israel.

43 And all the firstborn males by the number of names, from a month old and upward, of those that were numbered of them, were twenty and two thousand two hundred and threescore and thirteen.

44 And the LORD spake unto Moses, saying,

45 Take the Levites instead of all the firstborn among the children of Israel, and the cattle of the Levites instead of their cattle; and the Levites shall be my: I am the LORD.

46 And for those that are to be redeemed of the two hundred and threescore and thirteen of the firstborn of the children of Israel, which are more than the Levites;

47 You shalt even take five shekels apiece by the poll, after the shekel of the sanctuary shalt you take them: (the shekel is twenty gerahs:)

48 And you shalt give the money, wherewith the odd number of them is to be redeemed, unto Aaron and to his sons.

49 And Moses took the redemption money of them that were over and above them that were redeemed by the Levites:

50 Of the firstborn of the children of Israel took he the money; a thousand three hundred and threescore and five shekels, after the shekel of the sanctuary:

51 And Moses gave the money of them that were redeemed unto Aaron and to his sons, according to the word of the LORD, as the LORD commanded Moses.

CHAPTER 4

AND the LORD spake unto Moses and unto Aaron, saying,

2 Take the sum of the sons of Kohath from among the sons of Levi, after their families, by the house of their fathers,

3 From thirty years old and upward even until fifty years old, all that enter into the host, to do the work in the tabernacle of the congregation.

4 This shall be the service of the sons of Kohath in the tabernacle of the congregation, about the most holy things:

5 And when the camp setteth forward, Aaron shall come, and his sons, and they shall take down the covering vail, and cover the ark of testimony with it:

6 And shall put thereon the covering of badgers' skins, and shall spread over it a cloth wholly of blue, and shall put in the staves thereof.

7 And upon the table of shewbread they shall spread a cloth of blue, and put thereon the dishes, and the spoons, and the bowls, and covers to cover withal: and the continual bread shall be thereon:

8 And they shall spread upon them a cloth of scarlet, and cover the same with a covering of badgers' skins, and shall put in the staves thereof.

9 And they shall take a cloth of blue, and cover the candlestick of the light, and his lamps, and his tongs, and his snuffdishes, and all the oil vessels thereof, wherewith they minister unto it:

10 And they shall put it and all the vessels thereof within a covering of badgers' skins, and shall put it upon a bar.

11 And upon the golden altar they shall spread a cloth of blue, and cover it with a covering of badgers' skins, and shall put to the staves thereof:

12 And they shall take all the instruments of ministry, wherewith they minister in the sanctuary, and put them in a cloth of blue, and cover them with a covering of badgers' skins, and shall put them on a bar:

13 And they shall take away the ashes from the altar, and spread a purple cloth thereon:

14 And they shall put upon it all the vessels thereof, wherewith they minister about it, even the censers, the fleshhooks, and the shovels, and the basons, all the vessels of the altar; and they shall spread upon it a covering of badgers' skins, and put to the staves of it.

15 And when Aaron and his sons have made an end of covering the sanctuary, and all the vessels of the sanctuary, as the camp is to set forward; after that, the sons of Kohath shall come to bear it: but they shall not touch any holy thing, lest they die. These things are the burden of the sons of Kohath in the tabernacle of the congregation.

16 And to the office of Eleazar the son of Aaron the priest pertaineth the oil for the light, and the sweet incense, and the daily meat offering, and the anointing oil, and the oversight of all the tabernacle, and of all that therein is, in the sanctuary, and in the vessels thereof.

17 And the LORD spake unto Moses and unto Aaron, saying,

18 Cut you not off the tribe of the families of the Kohathites from among the Levites:

19 But thus do unto them, that they may live, and not die, when they approach unto the most holy things: Aaron and his sons shall go in, and appoint them every one to his service and to his burden:

20 But they shall not go in to see when the holy things are covered, lest they die.

21 And the LORD spake unto Moses, saying,

22 Take also the sum of the sons of Gershon, throughout the houses of their fathers, by their families;

23 From thirty years old and upward until fifty years old shalt you number them; all that enter in to perform the service, to do the work in the tabernacle of the congregation.

24 This is the service of the families of the Gershonites, to serve, and for burdens:

25 And they shall bear the curtains of the tabernacle, and the tabernacle of the congregation, his covering, and the covering of the badgers' skins that is above upon it, and the hanging for the door of the tabernacle of the congregation,

26 And the hangings of the court, and the hanging for the door of the gate of the court, which is by the tabernacle and by the altar round about, and their cords, and all the instruments of their service, and all that is made for them: so shall they serve.

27 At the appointment of Aaron and his sons shall be all the service of the sons of the Gershonites, in all their burdens, and in all their service: and you shall appoint unto them in charge all their burdens.

28 This is the service of the families of the sons of Gershon in the tabernacle of the congregation: and their charge shall be under the hand of Ithamar the son of Aaron the priest.

29 As for the sons of Merari, you shalt number them after their families, by the house of their fathers;

30 From thirty years old and upward even unto fifty years old shalt you number them, every one that entereth into the service, to do the work of the tabernacle of the congregation.

31 And this is the charge of their burden, according to all their service in the tabernacle of the congregation; the boards of the tabernacle, and the bars thereof, and the pillars thereof, and sockets thereof,

32 And the pillars of the court round about, and their sockets, and their pins, and their cords, with all their instruments, and with all their service: and by name you shall reckon the instruments of the charge of their burden.

33 This is the service of the families of the sons of Merari, according to all their service, in the tabernacle of the congregation, under the hand of Ithamar the son of Aaron the priest.

34 And Moses and Aaron and the chief of the congregation numbered the sons of the Kohathites after their families, and after the house of their fathers,

35 From thirty years old and upward even unto fifty years old, every one that entereth into the service, for the work in the tabernacle of the congregation:

36 And those that were numbered of them by their families were two thousand seven hundred and fifty.

37 These were they that were numbered of the families of the Kohathites, all that might do service in the tabernacle of the congregation, which Moses and Aaron did number according to the commandment of the LORD by the hand of Moses.

38 And those that were numbered of the sons of Gershon, throughout their families, and by the house of their fathers,

39 From thirty years old and upward even unto fifty years old, every one that entereth into the service, for the work in the tabernacle of the congregation,

40 Even those that were numbered of them, throughout their families, by the house of their fathers, were two thousand and six hundred and thirty.

41 These are they that were numbered of the families of the sons of Gershon, of all that might do service in the tabernacle of the congregation, whom Moses and Aaron did number according to the commandment of the LORD.

42 And those that were numbered of the families of the sons of Merari, throughout their families, by the house of their fathers,

43 From thirty years old and upward even unto fifty years old, every one that entereth into the service, for the work in the tabernacle of the congregation,

44 Even those that were numbered of them after their families, were three thousand and two hundred.

45 These be those that were numbered of the families of the sons of Merari, whom Moses and Aaron numbered according to the word of the LORD by the hand of Moses.

46 All those that were numbered of the Levites, whom Moses and Aaron and the chief of Israel numbered, after their families, and after the house of their fathers,

47 From thirty years old and upward even unto fifty years old, every one that came to do the service of the ministry, and the service of the burden in the tabernacle of the congregation,

48 Even those that were numbered of them, were eight thousand and five hundred and fourscore.

49 According to the commandment of the LORD they were numbered by the hand of Moses, every one according to his service, and according to his burden: thus were they numbered of him, as the LORD commanded Moses.

CHAPTER 5

AND the LORD spake unto Moses, saying,

2 Command the children of Israel, that they put out of the camp every leper, and every one that has an issue, and whosoever is defiled by the dead:

3 Both male and female shall you put out, without the camp shall you put them; that they defile not their camps, in the midst whereof I dwell.

4 And the children of Israel did so, and put them out without the camp: as the LORD spake unto Moses, so did the children of Israel.

5 And the LORD spake unto Moses, saying,

6 Speak unto the children of Israel, When a man or woman shall commit any sin that men commit, to do a trespass against the LORD, and that person be guilty;

7 Then they shall confess their sin which they have done: and he shall recompense his trespass with the principal thereof, and add unto it the fifth part thereof, and give it unto him against whom he has trespassed.

8 But if the man have no kinsman to recompense the trespass unto, let the trespass be recompensed unto the LORD, even to the priest; beside the ram of the atonement, whereby an atonement shall be made for him.

9 And every offering of all the holy things of the children of Israel, which they bring unto the priest, shall be his.

10 And every man's hallowed things shall be his: whatsoever any man giveth the priest, it shall be his.

11 And the LORD spake unto Moses, saying,

12 Speak unto the children of Israel, and say unto them, If any man's wife go aside, and commit a trespass against him,

13 And a man lie with her carnally, and it be hid from the eyes of her husband, and be kept close, and she be defiled, and there be no witness against her, neither she be taken with the manner;

14 And the spirit of jealousy come upon him, and he be jealous of his wife, and she be defiled: or if the spirit of jealousy come upon him, and he be jealous of his wife, and she be not defiled:

15 Then shall the man bring his wife unto the priest, and he shall bring her offering for her, the tenth part of an ephah of barley meal; he shall pour no oil upon it, nor put frankincense thereon; for it is an offering of jealousy, an offering of memorial, bringing iniquity to remembrance.

16 And the priest shall bring her near, and set her before the LORD:

17 And the priest shall take holy water in an earthen vessel; and of the dust that is in the floor of the tabernacle the priest shall take, and put it into the water:

18 And the priest shall set the woman before the LORD, and uncover the woman's head, and put the offering of memorial in her hands, which is the jealousy offering: and the priest shall have in his hand the bitter water that causeth the curse:

19 And the priest shall charge her by an oath, and say unto the woman, If no man have lain with you, and if you have not gone aside to uncleanness with another instead of your husband, be you free from this bitter water that causeth the curse:

20 But if you have gone aside to another instead of your husband, and if you be defiled, and some man have lain with you beside yours husband:

21 Then the priest shall charge the woman with an oath of cursing, and the priest shall say unto the woman, The LORD make you a curse and an oath among your people, when the LORD doth make your thigh to rot, and your belly to swell;

22 And this water that causeth the curse shall go into your bowels, to make your belly to swell, and your thigh to rot: And the woman shall say, Amen, amen.

23 And the priest shall write these curses in a book, and he shall blot them out with the bitter water:

24 And he shall cause the woman to drink the bitter water that causeth the curse: and the water that causeth the curse shall enter into her, and become bitter.

25 Then the priest shall take the jealousy offering out of the woman's hand, and shall wave the offering before the LORD, and offer it upon the altar:

26 And the priest shall take an handful of the offering, even the memorial thereof, and burn it upon the altar, and afterward shall cause the woman to drink the water.

27 And when he has made her to drink the water, then it shall come to pass, that, if she be defiled, and have done trespass against her husband, that the water that causeth the curse shall enter into her, and become bitter, and her belly shall swell, and her thigh shall rot: and the woman shall be a curse among her people.

28 And if the woman be not defiled, but clean; then she shall be free, and shall conceive seed.

29 This is the law of jealousies, when a wife goeth aside to another instead of her husband, and is defiled;

30 Or when the spirit of jealousy comes upon him, and he be jealous over his wife, and shall set the woman before the LORD, and the priest shall execute upon her all this law.

31 Then shall the man be guiltless from iniquity, and this woman shall bear her iniquity.

CHAPTER 6

AND the LORD spake unto Moses, saying,

2 Speak unto the children of Israel, and say unto them, When either man or woman shall separate themselves to vow a vow of a Nazarite, to separate themselves unto the LORD:

3 He shall separate himself from wine and strong drink, and shall drink no vinegar of wine, or vinegar of strong drink, neither shall he drink any liquor of grapes, nor eat moist grapes, or dried.

4 All the days of his separation shall he eat nothing that is made of the vine tree, from the kernels even to the husk.

5 All the days of the vow of his separation there shall no rasor come upon his head: until the days be fulfilled, in the which he separateth himself unto the LORD, he shall be holy, and shall let the locks of the hair of his head grow.

6 All the days that he separateth himself unto the LORD he shall come at no dead body.

7 He shall not make himself unclean for his father, or for his mother, for his brother, or for his sister, when they die: because the consecration of his God is upon his head.

8 All the days of his separation he is holy unto the LORD.

9 And if any man die very suddenly by him, and he has defiled the head of his consecration; then he shall shave his head in the day of his cleansing, on the seventh day shall he shave it.

10 And on the eighth day he shall bring two turtles, or two young pigeons, to the priest, to the door of the tabernacle of the congregation:

11 And the priest shall offer the one for a sin offering, and the other for a burnt offering, and make an atonement for him, for that he sinned by the dead, and shall hallow his head that same day.

12 And he shall consecrate unto the LORD the days of his separation, and shall bring a lamb of the first year for a trespass offering: but the days that were before shall be lost, because his separation was defiled.

13 And this is the law of the Nazarite, when the days of his separation are fulfilled: he shall be brought unto the door of the tabernacle of the congregation:

14 And he shall offer his offering unto the LORD, one he lamb of the first year without blemish for a burnt offering, and one ewe lamb of the first year without blemish for a sin offering, and one ram without blemish for peace offerings,

15 And a basket of unleavened bread, cakes of fine flour mingled with oil, and wafers of unleavened bread anointed with oil, and their meat offering, and their drink offerings.

16 And the priest shall bring them before the LORD, and shall offer his sin offering, and his burnt offering:

17 And he shall offer the ram for a sacrifice of peace offerings unto the LORD, with the basket of unleavened bread: the priest shall offer also his meat offering, and his drink offering.

18 And the Nazarite shall shave the head of his separation at the door of the tabernacle of the congregation, and shall take the hair of the head of his separation, and put it in the fire which is under the sacrifice of the peace offerings.

19 And the priest shall take the sodden shoulder of the ram, and one unleavened cake out of the basket, and one unleavened wafer, and shall put them upon the hands of the Nazarite, after the hair of his separation is shaven:

20 And the priest shall wave them for a wave offering before the LORD: this is holy for the priest, with the wave breast and heave shoulder: and after that the Nazarite may drink wine.

21 This is the law of the Nazarite who has vowed, and of his offering unto the LORD for his separation, beside that that his hand shall get: according to the vow which he vowed, so he must do after the law of his separation.

22 And the LORD spake unto Moses, saying,

23 Speak unto Aaron and unto his sons, saying, On this wise you shall bless the children of Israel, saying unto them,

24 The LORD bless you, and keep you:

25 The LORD make his face shine upon you, and be gracious unto you:

26 The LORD lift up his countenance upon you, and give you peace.

27 And they shall put my name upon the children of Israel; and I will bless them.

CHAPTER 7

AND it came to pass on the day that Moses had fully set up the tabernacle, and had anointed it, and sanctified it, and all the instruments thereof, both the altar and all the vessels thereof, and had anointed them, and sanctified them;

2 That the princes of Israel, heads of the house of their fathers, who were the princes of the tribes, and were over them that were numbered, offered:

3 And they brought their offering before the LORD, six covered wagons, and twelve oxen; a wagon for two of the princes, and for each one an ox: and they brought them before the tabernacle.

4 And the LORD spake unto Moses, saying,

5 Take it of them, that they may be to do the service of the tabernacle of the congregation; and you shalt give them unto the Levites, to every man according to his service.

6 And Moses took the wagons and the oxen, and gave them unto the Levites.

7 Two wagons and four oxen he gave unto the sons of Gershon, according to their service:

8 And four wagons and eight oxen he gave unto the sons of Merari, according unto their service, under the hand of Ithamar the son of Aaron the priest.

9 But unto the sons of Kohath he gave none: because the service of the sanctuary belonging unto them was that they should bear upon their shoulders.

10 And the princes offered for dedicating of the altar in the day that it was anointed, even the princes offered their offering before the altar.

11 And the LORD said unto Moses, They shall offer their offering, each prince on his day, for the dedicating of the altar.

12 And he that offered his offering the first day was Nahshon the son of Amminadab, of the tribe of Judah:

13 And his offering was one silver charger, the weight thereof was an hundred and thirty shekels, one silver bowl of seventy shekels, after the shekel of the sanctuary; both of them were full of fine flour mingled with oil for a meat offering:

14 One spoon of ten shekels of gold, full of incense:

15 One young bullock, one ram, one lamb of the first year, for a burnt offering:

16 One kid of the goats for a sin offering:

17 And for a sacrifice of peace offerings, two oxen, five rams, five he goats, five lambs of the first year: this was the offering of Nahshon the son of Amminadab.

18 On the second day Nethaneel the son of Zuar, prince of Issachar, did offer:

19 He offered for his offering one silver charger, the weight whereof was an hundred and thirty shekels, one silver bowl of seventy shekels, after the shekel of the sanctuary; both of them full of fine flour mingled with oil for a meat offering:

20 One spoon of gold of ten shekels, full of incense:

21 One young bullock, one ram, one lamb of the first year, for a burnt offering:

22 One kid of the goats for a sin offering:

23 And for a sacrifice of peace offerings, two oxen, five rams, five he goats, five lambs of the first year: this was the offering of Nethaneel the son of Zuar.

24 On the third day Eliab the son of Helon, prince of the children of Zebulun, did offer:

25 His offering was one silver charger, the weight whereof was an hundred and thirty shekels, one silver bowl of seventy shekels, after the shekel of the sanctuary; both of them full of fine flour mingled with oil for a meat offering:

26 One golden spoon of ten shekels, full of incense:

27 One young bullock, one ram, one lamb of the first year, for a burnt offering:

28 One kid of the goats for a sin offering:

29 And for a sacrifice of peace offerings, two oxen, five rams, five he goats, five lambs of the first year: this was the offering of Eliab the son of Helon.

30 On the fourth day Elizur the son of Shedeur, prince of the children of Reuben, did offer:

31 His offering was one silver charger of the weight of an hundred and thirty shekels, one silver bowl of seventy shekels, after the shekel of the sanctuary; both of them full of fine flour mingled with oil for a meat offering:

32 One golden spoon of ten shekels, full of incense:

33 One young bullock, one ram, one lamb of the first year, for a burnt offering:

34 One kid of the goats for a sin offering:

35 And for a sacrifice of peace offerings, two oxen, five rams, five he goats, five lambs of the first year: this was the offering of Elizur the son of Shedeur.

36 On the fifth day Shelumiel the son of Zurishaddai, prince of the children of Simeon, did offer:

37 His offering was one silver charger, the weight whereof was an hundred and thirty shekels, one silver bowl of seventy shekels, after the shekel of the sanctuary; both of them full of fine flour mingled with oil for a meat offering:

38 One golden spoon of ten shekels, full of incense:

39 One young bullock, one ram, one lamb of the first year, for a burnt offering:

40 One kid of the goats for a sin offering:

41 And for a sacrifice of peace offerings, two oxen, five rams, five he goats, five lambs of the first year: this was the offering of Shelumiel the son of Zurishaddai.

42 On the sixth day Eliasaph the son of Deuel, prince of the children of Gad, offered:

43 His offering was one silver charger of the weight of an hundred and thirty shekels, a silver bowl of seventy shekels, after the shekel of the sanctuary; both of them full of fine flour mingled with oil for a meat offering:

44 One golden spoon of ten shekels, full of incense:

45 One young bullock, one ram, one lamb of the first year, for a burnt offering:

46 One kid of the goats for a sin offering:

47 And for a sacrifice of peace offerings, two oxen, five rams, five he goats, five lambs of the first year: this was the offering of Eliasaph the son of Deuel.

48 On the seventh day Elishama the son of Ammihud, prince of the children of Ephraim, offered:

49 His offering was one silver charger, the weight whereof was an hundred and thirty shekels, one silver bowl of seventy shekels, after the shekel of the sanctuary; both of them full of fine flour mingled with oil for a meat offering:

50 One golden spoon of ten shekels, full of incense:

51 One young bullock, one ram, one lamb of the first year, for a burnt offering:

52 One kid of the goats for a sin offering:

53 And for a sacrifice of peace offerings, two oxen, five rams, five he goats, five lambs of the first year: this was the offering of Elishama the son of Ammihud.

54 On the eighth day offered Gamaliel the son of Pedahzur, prince of the children of Manasseh:

55 His offering was one silver charger of the weight of an hundred and thirty shekels, one silver bowl of seventy shekels, after the shekel of the sanctuary; both of them full of fine flour mingled with oil for a meat offering:

56 One golden spoon of ten shekels, full of incense:

57 One young bullock, one ram, one lamb of the first year, for a burnt offering:

58 One kid of the goats for a sin offering:

59 And for a sacrifice of peace offerings, two oxen, five rams, five he goats, five lambs of the first year: this was the offering of Gamaliel the son of Pedahzur.

60 On the ninth day Abidan the son of Gideoni, prince of the children of Benjamin, offered:

61 His offering was one silver charger, the weight whereof was an hundred and thirty shekels, one silver bowl of seventy shekels, after the shekel of the sanctuary; both of them full of fine flour mingled with oil for a meat offering:

62 One golden spoon of ten shekels, full of incense:

63 One young bullock, one ram, one lamb of the first year, for a burnt offering:

64 One kid of the goats for a sin offering:

65 And for a sacrifice of peace offerings, two oxen, five rams, five he goats, five lambs of the first year: this was the offering of Abidan the son of Gideoni.

66 On the tenth day Ahiezer the son of Ammishaddai, prince of the children of Dan, offered:

67 His offering was one silver charger, the weight whereof was an hundred and thirty shekels, one silver bowl of seventy shekels, after the shekel of the sanctuary; both of them full of fine flour mingled with oil for a meat offering:

68 One golden spoon of ten shekels, full of incense:

69 One young bullock, one ram, one lamb of the first year, for a burnt offering:

70 One kid of the goats for a sin offering:

71 And for a sacrifice of peace offerings, two oxen, five rams, five he goats, five lambs of the first year: this was the offering of Ahiezer the son of Ammishaddai.

72 On the eleventh day Pagiel the son of Ocran, prince of the children of Asher, offered:

73 His offering was one silver charger, the weight whereof was an hundred and thirty shekels, one silver bowl of seventy shekels, after the shekel of the sanctuary; both of them full of fine flour mingled with oil for a meat offering:

74 One golden spoon of ten shekels, full of incense:

75 One young bullock, one ram, one lamb of the first year, for a burnt offering:

76 One kid of the goats for a sin offering:

77 And for a sacrifice of peace offerings, two oxen, five rams, five he goats, five lambs of the first year: this was the offering of Pagiel the son of Ocran.

78 On the twelfth day Ahira the son of Enan, prince of the children of Naphtali, offered:

79 His offering was one silver charger, the weight whereof was an hundred and thirty shekels, one silver bowl of seventy shekels, after the shekel of the sanctuary; both of them full of fine flour mingled with oil for a meat offering:

80 One golden spoon of ten shekels, full of incense:

81 One young bullock, one ram, one lamb of the first year, for a burnt offering:

82 One kid of the goats for a sin offering:

83 And for a sacrifice of peace offerings, two oxen, five rams, five he goats, five lambs of the first year: this was the offering of Ahira the son of Enan.

84 This was the dedication of the altar, in the day when it was anointed, by the princes of Israel: twelve chargers of silver, twelve silver bowls, twelve spoons of gold:

85 Each charger of silver weighing an hundred and thirty shekels, each bowl seventy: all the silver vessels weighed two thousand and four hundred shekels, after the shekel of the sanctuary:

86 The golden spoons were twelve, full of incense, weighing ten shekels apiece, after the shekel of the sanctuary: all the gold of the spoons was an hundred and twenty shekels.

87 All the oxen for the burnt offering were twelve bullocks, the rams twelve, the lambs of the first year twelve, with their meat offering: and the kids of the goats for sin offering twelve.

88 And all the oxen for the sacrifice of the peace offerings were twenty and four bullocks, the rams sixty, the he goats sixty, the lambs of the first year sixty. This was the dedication of the altar, after that it was anointed.

89 And when Moses was gone into the tabernacle of the congregation to speak with him, then he heard the voice of one speaking unto him from off the mercy seat that was upon the ark of testimony, from between the two cherubims: and he spake unto him.

CHAPTER 8

AND the LORD spake unto Moses, saying,

2 Speak unto Aaron, and say unto him, When you lightest the lamps, the seven lamps shall give light over against the candlestick.

3 And Aaron did so; he lighted the lamps thereof over against the candlestick, as the LORD commanded Moses.

4 And this work of the candlestick was of beaten gold, unto the shaft thereof, unto the flowers thereof, was beaten work: according unto the pattern which the LORD had shewed Moses, so he made the candlestick.

5 And the LORD spake unto Moses, saying,

6 Take the Levites from among the children of Israel, and cleanse them.

7 And thus shalt you do unto them, to cleanse them: Sprinkle water of purifying upon them, and let them shave all their flesh, and let them wash their clothes, and so make themselves clean.

8 Then let them take a young bullock with his meat offering, even fine flour mingled with oil, and another young bullock shalt you take for a sin offering.

9 And you shalt bring the Levites before the tabernacle of the congregation: and you shalt gather the whole assembly of the children of Israel together:

10 And you shalt bring the Levites before the LORD: and the children of Israel shall put their hands upon the Levites:

11 And Aaron shall offer the Levites before the LORD for an offering of the children of Israel, that they may execute the service of the LORD.

12 And the Levites shall lay their hands upon the heads of the bullocks: and you shalt offer the one for a sin offering, and the other for a burnt offering, unto the LORD, to make an atonement for the Levites.

13 And you shalt set the Levites before Aaron, and before his sons, and offer them for an offering unto the LORD.

14 Thus shalt you separate the Levites from among the children of Israel: and the Levites shall be my.

15 And after that shall the Levites go in to do the service of the tabernacle of the congregation: and you shalt cleanse them, and offer them for an offering.

16 For they are wholly given unto me from among the children of Israel; instead of such as open every womb, even instead of the firstborn of all the children of Israel, have I taken them unto me.

17 For all the firstborn of the children of Israel are my, both man and beast: on the day that I struck every firstborn in the land of Egypt I sanctified them for myself.

18 And I have taken the Levites for all the firstborn of the children of Israel.

19 And I have given the Levites as a gift to Aaron and to his sons from among the children of Israel, to do the service of the children of Israel in the tabernacle of the congregation, and to make an atonement for the children of Israel: that there be no plague among the children of Israel, when the children of Israel come nigh unto the sanctuary.

20 And Moses, and Aaron, and all the congregation of the children of Israel, did to the Levites according unto all that the LORD commanded Moses concerning the Levites, so did the children of Israel unto them.

21 And the Levites were purified, and they washed their clothes; and Aaron offered them as an offering before the LORD; and Aaron made an atonement for them to cleanse them.

22 And after that went the Levites in to do their service in the tabernacle of the congregation before Aaron, and before his sons: as the LORD had commanded Moses concerning the Levites, so did they unto them.

23 And the LORD spake unto Moses, saying,

24 This is it that belongeth unto the Levites: from twenty and five years old and upward they shall go in to wait upon the service of the tabernacle of the congregation:

25 And from the age of fifty years they shall cease waiting upon the service thereof, and shall serve no more:

26 But shall minister with their brethren in the tabernacle of the congregation, to keep the charge, and shall do no service. Thus shalt you do unto the Levites touching their charge.

CHAPTER 9

AND the LORD spake unto Moses in the wilderness of Sinai, in the first month of the second year after they were come out of the land of Egypt, saying,

2 Let the children of Israel also keep the passover at his appointed season.

3 In the fourteenth day of this month, at even, you shall keep it in his appointed season: according to all the rites of it, and according to all the ceremonies thereof, shall you keep it.

4 And Moses spake unto the children of Israel, that they should keep the passover.

5 And they kept the passover on the fourteenth day of the first month at even in the wilderness of Sinai: according to all that the LORD commanded Moses, so did the children of Israel.

6 And there were certain men, who were defiled by the dead body of a man, that they could not keep the passover on that day: and they came before Moses and before Aaron on that day:

7 And those men said unto him, We are defiled by the dead body of a man: wherefore are we kept back, that we may not offer an offering of the LORD in his appointed season among the children of Israel?

8 And Moses said unto them, Stand still, and I will hear what the LORD will command concerning you.

9 And the LORD spake unto Moses, saying,

10 Speak unto the children of Israel, saying, If any man of you or of your posterity shall be unclean by reason of a dead body, or be in a journey afar off, yet he shall keep the passover unto the LORD.

11 The fourteenth day of the second month at even they shall keep it, and eat it with unleavened bread and bitter herbs.

12 They shall leave none of it unto the morning, nor break any bone of it: according to all the ordinances of the passover they shall keep it.

13 But the man that is clean, and is not in a journey, and forbeareth to keep the passover, even the same soul shall be cut off from among his people: because he brought not the offering of the LORD in his appointed season, that man shall bear his sin.

14 And if a stranger shall sojourn among you, and will keep the passover unto the LORD; according to the ordinance of the passover, and according to the manner thereof, so shall he do: you shall have one ordinance, both for the stranger, and for him that was born in the land.

15 And on the day that the tabernacle was reared up the cloud covered the tabernacle, namely, the tent of the testimony: and at even there was upon the tabernacle as it were the appearance of fire, until the morning.

16 So it was alway: the cloud covered it by day, and the appearance of fire by night.

17 And when the cloud was taken up from the tabernacle, then after that the children of Israel journeyed: and in the place where the cloud abode, there the children of Israel pitched their tents.

18 At the commandment of the LORD the children of Israel journeyed, and at the commandment of the LORD they pitched: as long as the cloud abode upon the tabernacle they rested in their tents.

19 And when the cloud tarried long upon the tabernacle many days, then the children of Israel kept the charge of the LORD, and journeyed not.

20 And so it was, when the cloud was a few days upon the tabernacle; according to the commandment of the LORD they abode in their tents, and according to the commandment of the LORD they journeyed.

21 And so it was, when the cloud abode from even unto the morning, and that the cloud was taken up in the morning, then they journeyed: whether it was by day or by night that the cloud was taken up, they journeyed.

22 Or whether it were two days, or a month, or a year, that the cloud tarried upon the tabernacle, remaining thereon, the children of Israel abode in their tents, and journeyed not: but when it was taken up, they journeyed.

23 At the commandment of the LORD they rested in the tents, and at the commandment of the LORD they journeyed: they kept the charge of the LORD, at the commandment of the LORD by the hand of Moses.

CHAPTER 10

AND the LORD spake unto Moses, saying,

2 Make you two trumpets of silver; of a whole piece shalt you make them: that you mayest use them for the calling of the assembly, and for the journeying of the camps.

3 And when they shall blow with them, all the assembly shall assemble themselves to you at the door of the tabernacle of the congregation.

4 And if they blow but with one trumpet, then the princes, which are heads of the thousands of Israel, shall gather themselves unto you.

5 When you blow an alarm, then the camps that lie on the east parts shall go forward.

6 When you blow an alarm the second time, then the camps that lie on the south side shall take their journey: they shall blow an alarm for their journeys.

7 But when the congregation is to be gathered together, you shall blow, but you shall not sound an alarm.

8 And the sons of Aaron, the priests, shall blow with the trumpets; and they shall be to you for an ordinance for ever throughout your generations.

9 And if you go to war in your land against the enemy that oppresseth you, then you shall blow an alarm with the trumpets; and you shall be remembered before the LORD your God, and you shall be saved from your enemies.

10 Also in the day of your gladness, and in your solemn days, and in the beginnings of your months, you shall blow with the trumpets over your burnt offerings, and over the sacrifices of your peace offerings; that they may be to you for a memorial before your God: I am the LORD your God.

11 And it came to pass on the twentieth day of the second month, in the second year, that the cloud was taken up from off the tabernacle of the testimony.

12 And the children of Israel took their journeys out of the wilderness of Sinai; and the cloud rested in the wilderness of Paran.

13 And they first took their journey according to the commandment of the LORD by the hand of Moses.

14 In the first place went the standard of the camp of the children of Judah according to their armies: and over his host was Nahshon the son of Amminadab.

15 And over the host of the tribe of the children of Issachar was Nethaneel the son of Zuar.

16 And over the host of the tribe of the children of Zebulun was Eliab the son of Helon.

17 And the tabernacle was taken down; and the sons of Gershon and the sons of Merari set forward, bearing the tabernacle.

18 And the standard of the camp of Reuben set forward according to their armies: and over his host was Elizur the son of Shedeur.

19 And over the host of the tribe of the children of Simeon was Shelumiel the son of Zurishaddai.

20 And over the host of the tribe of the children of Gad was Eliasaph the son of Deuel.

21 And the Kohathites set forward, bearing the sanctuary: and the other did set up the tabernacle against they came.

22 And the standard of the camp of the children of Ephraim set forward according to their armies: and over his host was Elishama the son of Ammihud.

23 And over the host of the tribe of the children of Manasseh was Gamaliel the son of Pedahzur.

24 And over the host of the tribe of the children of Benjamin was Abidan the son of Gideoni.

25 And the standard of the camp of the children of Dan set forward, which was the rereward of all the camps throughout their hosts: and over his host was Ahiezer the son of Ammishaddai.

26 And over the host of the tribe of the children of Asher was Pagiel the son of Ocran.

27 And over the host of the tribe of the children of Naphtali was Ahira the son of Enan.

28 Thus were the journeyings of the children of Israel according to their armies, when they set forward.

29 And Moses said unto Hobab, the son of Raguel the Midianite, Moses' father in law, We are journeying unto the place of which the LORD said, I will give it you: come you with us, and we will do you good: for the LORD has spoken good concerning Israel.

30 And he said unto him, I will not go; but I will depart to my own land, and to my kindred.

31 And he said, Leave us not, I pray you; forasmuch as you knowest how we are to encamp in the wilderness, and you mayest be to us instead of eyes.

32 And it shall be, if you go with us, yea, it shall be, that what goodness the LORD shall do unto us, the same will we do unto you.

33 And they departed from the mount of the LORD three days' journey: and the ark of the covenant of the LORD went before them in the three days' journey, to search out a resting place for them.

34 And the cloud of the LORD was upon them by day, when they went out of the camp.

35 And it came to pass, when the ark set forward, that Moses said, Rise up, LORD, and let yours enemies be scattered; and let them that hate you flee before you.

36 And when it rested, he said, Return, O LORD, unto the many thousands of Israel.

CHAPTER 11

AND when the people complained, it displeased the LORD: and the LORD heard it; and his anger was kindled; and the fire of the LORD burnt among them, and consumed them that were in the uttermost parts of the camp.

2 And the people cried unto Moses; and when Moses prayed unto the LORD, the fire was quenched.

3 And he called the name of the place Taberah: because the fire of the LORD burnt among them.

4 And the mixt multitude that was among them fell a lusting: and the children of Israel also wept again, and said, Who shall give us flesh to eat?

5 We remember the fish, which we did eat in Egypt freely; the cucumbers, and the melons, and the leeks, and the onions, and the garlick:

6 But now our soul is dried away: there is nothing at all, beside this manna, before our eyes.

7 And the manna was as coriander seed, and the colour thereof as the colour of bdellium.

8 And the people went about, and gathered it, and ground it in mills, or beat it in a mortar, and baked it in pans, and made cakes of it: and the taste of it was as the taste of fresh oil.

9 And when the dew fell upon the camp in the night, the manna fell upon it.

10 Then Moses heard the people weep throughout their families, every man in the door of his tent: and the anger of the LORD was kindled greatly; Moses also was displeased.

11 And Moses said unto the LORD, Wherefore have you afflicted your servant? and wherefore have I not found favour in your sight, that you layest the burden of all this people upon me?

12 Have I conceived all this people? have I begotten them, that you shouldest say unto me, Carry them in your bosom, as a nursing father beareth the sucking child, unto the land which you swarest unto their fathers?

13 Whence should I have flesh to give unto all this people? for they weep unto me, saying, Give us flesh, that we may eat.

14 I am not able to bear all this people alone, because it is too heavy for me.

15 And if you deal thus with me, kill me, I pray you, out of hand, if I have found favour in your sight; and let me not see my wretchedness.

16 And the LORD said unto Moses, Gather unto me seventy men of the elders of Israel, whom you knowest to be the elders of the people, and officers over them; and bring them unto the tabernacle of the congregation, that they may stand there with you.

17 And I will come down and talk with you there: and I will take of the spirit which is upon you, and will put it upon them; and they shall bear the burden of the people with you, that you bear it not yourself alone.

18 And say you unto the people, Sanctify yourselves against to morrow, and you shall eat flesh: for you have wept in the ears of the LORD, saying, Who shall give us flesh to eat? for it was well with us in Egypt: therefore the LORD will give you flesh, and you shall eat.

19 You shall not eat one day, nor two days, nor five days, neither ten days, nor twenty days;

20 But even a whole month, until it come out at your nostrils, and it be loathsome unto you: because that you have despised the LORD which is among you, and have wept before him, saying, Why came we forth out of Egypt?

21 And Moses said, The people, among whom I am, are six hundred thousand footmen; and you have said, I will give them flesh, that they may eat a whole month.

22 Shall the flocks and the herds be slain for them, to suffice them? or shall all the fish of the sea be gathered together for them, to suffice them?

23 And the LORD said unto Moses, Is the LORD's hand waxed short? you shalt see now whether my word shall come to pass unto you or not.

24And Moses went out, and told the people the words of the LORD, and gathered the seventy men of the elders of the people, and set them round about the tabernacle.

25 And the LORD came down in a cloud, and spake unto him, and took of the spirit that was upon him, and gave it unto the seventy elders: and it came to pass, that, when the spirit rested upon them, they prophesied, and did not cease.

26 But there remained two of the men in the camp, the name of the one was Eldad, and the name of the other Medad: and the spirit rested upon them; and they were of them that were written, but went not out unto the tabernacle: and they prophesied in the camp.

27 And there ran a young man, and told Moses, and said, Eldad and Medad do prophesy in the camp.

28 And Joshua the son of Nun, the servant of Moses, one of his young men, answered and said, My lord Moses, forbid them.

29 And Moses said unto him, Enviest you for my sake? would God that all the LORD's people were prophets, and that the LORD would put his spirit upon them!

30 And Moses gat him into the camp, he and the elders of Israel.

31And there went forth a wind from the LORD, and brought quails from the sea, and let them fall by the camp, as it were a day's journey on this side, and as it were a day's journey on the other side, round about the camp, and as it were two cubits high upon the face of the earth.

32 And the people stood up all that day, and all that night, and all the next day, and they gathered the quails: he that gathered least gathered ten homers: and they spread them all abroad for themselves round about the camp.

33 And while the flesh was yet between their teeth, ere it was chewed, the wrath of the LORD was kindled against the people, and the LORD struck the people with a very great plague.

34 And he called the name of that place Kibroth-hattaavah: because there they buried the people that lusted.

35 And the people journeyed from Kibroth-hattaavah unto Hazeroth; and abode at Hazeroth.

CHAPTER 12

AND Miriam and Aaron spake against Moses because of the Ethiopian woman whom he had married: for he had married an Ethiopian woman.

2 And they said, Has the LORD indeed spoken only by Moses? has he not spoken also by us? And the LORD heard it.

3 (Now the man Moses was very meek, above all the men which were upon the face of the earth.)

4 And the LORD spake suddenly unto Moses, and unto Aaron, and unto Miriam, Come out you three unto the tabernacle of the congregation. And they three came out.

5 And the LORD came down in the pillar of the cloud, and stood in the door of the tabernacle, and called Aaron and Miriam: and they both came forth.

6 And he said, Hear now my words: If there be a prophet among you, I the LORD will make myself known unto him in a vision, and will speak unto him in a dream.

7 My servant Moses is not so, who is faithful in all my house.

8 With him will I speak mouth to mouth, even apparently, and not in dark speeches; and the similitude of the LORD shall he behold: wherefore then were you not afraid to speak against my servant Moses?

9 And the anger of the LORD was kindled against them; and he departed.

10 And the cloud departed from off the tabernacle; and, behold, Miriam became leprous, white as snow: and Aaron looked upon Miriam, and, behold, she was leprous.

11 And Aaron said unto Moses, Alas, my lord, I beseech you, lay not the sin upon us, wherein we have done foolishly, and wherein we have sinned.

12 Let her not be as one dead, of whom the flesh is half consumed when he comes out of his mother's womb.

13 And Moses cried unto the LORD, saying, Heal her now, O God, I beseech you.

14And the LORD said unto Moses, If her father had but spit in her face, should she not be ashamed seven days? let her be shut out from the camp seven days, and after that let her be received in again.

15 And Miriam was shut out from the camp seven days: and the people journeyed not till Miriam was brought in again.

16 And afterward the people removed from Hazeroth, and pitched in the wilderness of Paran.

CHAPTER 13

AND the LORD spake unto Moses, saying,

2 Send you men, that they may search the land of Canaan, which I give unto the children of Israel: of every tribe of their fathers shall you send a man, every one a ruler among them.

3 And Moses by the commandment of the LORD sent them from the wilderness of Paran: all those men were heads of the children of Israel.

4 And these were their names: of the tribe of Reuben, Shammua the son of Zaccur.

5 Of the tribe of Simeon, Shaphat the son of Hori.

6 Of the tribe of Judah, Caleb the son of Jephunneh.

7 Of the tribe of Issachar, Igal the son of Joseph.

8 Of the tribe of Ephraim, Oshea the son of Nun.

9 Of the tribe of Benjamin, Palti the son of Raphu.

10 Of the tribe of Zebulun, Gaddiel the son of Sodi.

11 Of the tribe of Joseph, namely, of the tribe of Manasseh, Gaddi the son of Susi.

12 Of the tribe of Dan, Ammiel the son of Gemalli.

13 Of the tribe of Asher, Sethur the son of Michael.

14 Of the tribe of Naphtali, Nahbi the son of Vophsi.

15 Of the tribe of Gad, Geuel the son of Machi.

16 These are the names of the men which Moses sent to spy out the land. And Moses called Oshea the son of Nun Jehoshua.

17And Moses sent them to spy out the land of Canaan, and said unto them, Get you up this way southward, and go up into the mountain:

18 And see the land, what it is; and the people that dwelleth therein, whether they be strong or weak, few or many;

19 And what the land is that they dwell in, whether it be good or bad; and what cities they be that they dwell in, whether in tents, or in strong holds;

20 And what the land is, whether it be fat or lean, whether there be wood therein, or not. And be you of good courage, and bring of the fruit of the land. Now the time was the time of the firstripe grapes.

21So they went up, and searched the land from the wilderness of Zin unto Rehob, as men come to Hamath.

22 And they ascended by the south, and came unto Hebron; where Ahiman, Sheshai, and Talmai, the children of Anak, were. (Now Hebron was built seven years before Zoan in Egypt.)

23 And they came unto the brook of Eshcol, and cut down from thence a branch with one cluster of grapes, and they bare it between two upon a staff; and they brought of the pomegranates, and of the figs.

24 The place was called the brook Eshcol, because of the cluster of grapes which the children of Israel cut down from thence.

25 And they returned from searching of the land after forty days.

26And they went and came to Moses, and to Aaron, and to all the congregation of the children of Israel, unto the wilderness of Paran, to Kadesh; and brought back word unto them, and unto all the congregation, and shewed them the fruit of the land.

27 And they told him, and said, We came unto the land whither you sentest us, and surely it floweth with milk and honey; and this is the fruit of it.

28 Nevertheless the people be strong that dwell in the land, and the cities are walled, and very great: and moreover we saw the children of Anak there.

29 The Amalekites dwell in the land of the south: and the Hittites, and the Jebusites, and the Amorites, dwell in the mountains: and the Canaanites dwell by the sea, and by the coast of Jordan.

30 And Caleb stilled the people before Moses, and said, Let us go up at once, and possess it; for we are well able to overcome it.

31 But the men that went up with him said, We be not able to go up against the people; for they are stronger than we.

32 And they brought up an evil report of the land which they had searched unto the children of Israel, saying, The land, through which we have gone to search it, is a land that eateth up the inhabitants thereof; and all the people that we saw in it are men of a great stature.

33 And there we saw the giants, the sons of Anak, which come of the giants: and we were in our own sight as grasshoppers, and so we were in their sight.

CHAPTER 14

AND all the congregation lifted up their voice, and cried; and the people wept that night.

2 And all the children of Israel murmured against Moses and against Aaron: and the whole congregation said unto them, Would God that we had died in the land of Egypt! or would God we had died in this wilderness!

3 And wherefore has the LORD brought us unto this land, to fall by the sword, that our wives and our children should be a prey? were it not better for us to return into Egypt?

4 And they said one to another, Let us make a captain, and let us return into Egypt.

5 Then Moses and Aaron fell on their faces before all the assembly of the congregation of the children of Israel.

6And Joshua the son of Nun, and Caleb the son of Jephunneh, which were of them that searched the land, rent their clothes:

7 And they spake unto all the company of the children of Israel, saying, The land, which we passed through to search it, is an exceeding good land.

8 If the LORD delight in us, then he will bring us into this land, and give it us; a land which floweth with milk and honey.

9 Only rebel not you against the LORD, neither fear you the people of the land; for they are bread for us: their defence is departed from them, and the LORD is with us: fear them not.

10 But all the congregation bade stone them with stones. And the glory of the LORD appeared in the tabernacle of the congregation before all the children of Israel.

11And the LORD said unto Moses, How long will this people provoke me? and how long will it be ere they believe me, for all the signs which I have shewed among them?

12 I will strike them with the pestilence, and disinherit them, and will make of you a greater nation and mightier than they.

13And Moses said unto the LORD, Then the Egyptians shall hear it, (for you broughtest up this people in your might from among them;)

14 And they will tell it to the inhabitants of this land: for they have heard that you LORD are among this people, that you LORD are seen face to face, and that your cloud standeth over them, and that you go before them, by day time in a pillar of a cloud, and in a pillar of fire by night.

15Now if you shalt kill all this people as one man, then the nations which have heard the fame of you will speak, saying,

16 Because the LORD was not able to bring this people into the land which he sware unto them, therefore he has slain them in the wilderness.

17 And now, I beseech you, let the power of my Lord be great, according as you have spoken, saying,

18 The LORD is longsuffering, and of great mercy, forgiving iniquity and transgression, and by no means clearing the guilty, visiting the iniquity of the fathers upon the children unto the third and fourth generation.

19 Pardon, I beseech you, the iniquity of this people according unto the greatness of your mercy, and as you have forgiven this people, from Egypt even until now.

20 And the LORD said, I have pardoned according to your word:

21 But as truly as I live, all the earth shall be filled with the glory of the LORD.

22 Because all those men which have seen my glory, and my miracles, which I did in Egypt and in the wilderness, and have tempted me now these ten times, and have not hearkened to my voice;

23 Surely they shall not see the land which I sware unto their fathers, neither shall any of them that provoked me see it:

24 But my servant Caleb, because he had another spirit with him, and has followed me fully, him will I bring into the land whereinto he went; and his seed shall possess it.

25 (Now the Amalekites and the Canaanites dwelt in the valley.) To morrow turn you, and get you into the wilderness by the way of the Red sea.

26And the LORD spake unto Moses and unto Aaron, saying,

27 How long shall I bear with this evil congregation, which murmur against me? I have heard the murmurings of the children of Israel, which they murmur against me.

28 Say unto them, As truly as I live, saith the LORD, as you have spoken in my ears, so will I do to you:

29 Your carcases shall fall in this wilderness; and all that were numbered of you, according to your whole number, from twenty years old and upward, which have murmured against me,

30 Doubtless you shall not come into the land, concerning which I sware to make you dwell therein, save Caleb the son of Jephunneh, and Joshua the son of Nun.

31 But your little ones, which you said should be a prey, them will I bring in, and they shall know the land which you have despised.

32 But as for you, your carcases, they shall fall in this wilderness.

33 And your children shall wander in the wilderness forty years, and bear your whoredoms, until your carcases be wasted in the wilderness.

34 After the number of the days in which you searched the land, even forty days, each day for a year, shall you bear your iniquities, even forty years, and you shall know my breach of promise.

35 I the LORD have said, I will surely do it unto all this evil congregation, that are gathered together against me: in this wilderness they shall be consumed, and there they shall die.

36 And the men, which Moses sent to search the land, who returned, and made all the congregation to murmur against him, by bringing up a slander upon the land,

37 Even those men that did bring up the evil report upon the land, died by the plague before the LORD.

38 But Joshua the son of Nun, and Caleb the son of Jephunneh, which were of the men that went to search the land, lived still.

39 And Moses told these sayings unto all the children of Israel: and the people mourned greatly.

40And they rose up early in the morning, and gat them up into the top of the mountain, saying, Lo, we be here, and will go up unto the place which the LORD has promised: for we have sinned.

41 And Moses said, Wherefore now do you transgress the commandment of the LORD? but it shall not prosper.

42 Go not up, for the LORD is not among you; that you be not smitten before your enemies.

43 For the Amalekites and the Canaanites are there before you, and you shall fall by the sword: because you are turned away from the LORD, therefore the LORD will not be with you.

44 But they presumed to go up unto the hill top: nevertheless the ark of the covenant of the LORD, and Moses, departed not out of the camp.

45 Then the Amalekites came down, and the Canaanites which dwelt in that hill, and struck them, and discomfited them, even unto Hormah.

CHAPTER 15

AND the LORD spake unto Moses, saying,

2 Speak unto the children of Israel, and say unto them, When you be come into the land of your habitations, which I give unto you,

3 And will make an offering by fire unto the LORD, a burnt offering, or a sacrifice in performing a vow, or in a freewill offering, or in your solemn feasts, to make a sweet savour unto the LORD, of the herd, or of the flock:

4 Then shall he that offereth his offering unto the LORD bring a meat offering of a tenth deal of flour mingled with the fourth part of an hin of oil.

5 And the fourth part of an hin of wine for a drink offering shalt you prepare with the burnt offering or sacrifice, for one lamb.

6 Or for a ram, you shalt prepare for a meat offering two tenth deals of flour mingled with the third part of an hin of oil.

7 And for a drink offering you shalt offer the third part of an hin of wine, for a sweet savour unto the LORD.

8 And when you preparest a bullock for a burnt offering, or for a sacrifice in performing a vow, or peace offerings unto the LORD:

9 Then shall he bring with a bullock a meat offering of three tenth deals of flour mingled with half an hin of oil.

10 And you shalt bring for a drink offering half an hin of wine, for an offering made by fire, of a sweet savour unto the LORD.

11 Thus shall it be done for one bullock, or for one ram, or for a lamb, or a kid.

12 According to the number that you shall prepare, so shall you do to every one according to their number.

13 All that are born of the country shall do these things after this manner, in offering an offering made by fire, of a sweet savour unto the LORD.

14 And if a stranger sojourn with you, or whosoever be among you in your generations, and will offer an offering made by fire, of a sweet savour unto the LORD; as you do, so he shall do.

15 One ordinance shall be both for you of the congregation, and also for the stranger that sojourneth with you, an ordinance for ever in your generations: as you are, so shall the stranger be before the LORD.

16 One law and one manner shall be for you, and for the stranger that sojourneth with you.

17And the LORD spake unto Moses, saying,

18 Speak unto the children of Israel, and say unto them, When you come into the land whither I bring you,

19 Then it shall be, that, when you eat of the bread of the land, you shall offer up an heave offering unto the LORD.

20 You shall offer up a cake of the first of your dough for an heave offering: as you do the heave offering of the threshingfloor, so shall you heave it.

21 Of the first of your dough you shall give unto the LORD an heave offering in your generations.

22And if you have erred, and not observed all these commandments, which the LORD has spoken unto Moses,

23 Even all that the LORD has commanded you by the hand of Moses, from the day that the LORD commanded Moses, and henceforward among your generations;

24 Then it shall be, if ought be committed by ignorance without the knowledge of the congregation, that all the congregation shall offer one young bullock for a burnt offering, for a sweet savour unto the LORD, with his meat offering, and his drink offering, according to the manner, and one kid of the goats for a sin offering.

25 And the priest shall make an atonement for all the congregation of the children of Israel, and it shall be forgiven them; for it is ignorance: and they shall bring their offering, a sacrifice made by fire unto the LORD, and their sin offering before the LORD, for their ignorance:

26 And it shall be forgiven all the congregation of the children of Israel, and the stranger that sojourneth among them; seeing all the people were in ignorance.

27 And if any soul sin through ignorance, then he shall bring a she goat of the first year for a sin offering.

28 And the priest shall make an atonement for the soul that sinneth ignorantly, when he sinneth by ignorance before the LORD, to make an atonement for him; and it shall be forgiven him.

29 You shall have one law for him that sinneth through ignorance, both for him that is born among the children of Israel, and for the stranger that sojourneth among them.

30 But the soul that doeth ought presumptuously, whether he be born in the land, or a stranger, the same reproacheth the LORD; and that soul shall be cut off from among his people.

31 Because he has despised the word of the LORD, and has broken his commandment, that soul shall utterly be cut off; his iniquity shall be upon him.

32 And while the children of Israel were in the wilderness, they found a man that gathered sticks upon the sabbath day.

33 And they that found him gathering sticks brought him unto Moses and Aaron, and unto all the congregation.

34 And they put him in ward, because it was not declared what should be done to him.

35 And the LORD said unto Moses, The man shall be surely put to death: all the congregation shall stone him with stones without the camp.

36 And all the congregation brought him without the camp, and stoned him with stones, and he died; as the LORD commanded Moses.

37 And the LORD spake unto Moses, saying,

38 Speak unto the children of Israel, and bid them that they make them fringes in the borders of their garments throughout their generations, and that they put upon the fringe of the borders a ribband of blue:

39 And it shall be unto you for a fringe, that you may look upon it, and remember all the commandments of the LORD, and do them; and that you seek not after your own heart and your own eyes, after which you use to go a whoring:

40 That you may remember, and do all my commandments, and be holy unto your God.

41 I am the LORD your God, which brought you out of the land of Egypt, to be your God: I am the LORD your God.

CHAPTER 16

NOW Korah, the son of Izhar, the son of Kohath, the son of Levi, and Dathan and Abiram, the sons of Eliab, and On, the son of Peleth, sons of Reuben, took men:

2 And they rose up before Moses, with certain of the children of Israel, two hundred and fifty princes of the assembly, famous in the congregation, men of renown:

3 And they gathered themselves together against Moses and against Aaron, and said unto them, You take too much upon you, seeing all the congregation are holy, every one of them, and the LORD is among them: wherefore then lift you up yourselves above the congregation of the LORD?

4 And when Moses heard it, he fell upon his face:

5 And he spake unto Korah and unto all his company, saying, Even to morrow the LORD will shew who are his, and who is holy; and will cause him to come near unto him: even him whom he has chosen will he cause to come near unto him.

6 This do; Take you censers, Korah, and all his company;

7 And put fire therein, and put incense in them before the LORD to morrow: and it shall be that the man whom the LORD doth choose, he shall be holy: you take too much upon you, you sons of Levi.

8 And Moses said unto Korah, Hear, I pray you, you sons of Levi:

9 Seemeth it but a small thing unto you, that the God of Israel has separated you from the congregation of Israel, to bring you near to himself to do the service of the tabernacle of the LORD, and to stand before the congregation to minister unto them?

10 And he has brought you near to him, and all your brethren the sons of Levi with you: and seek you the priesthood also?

11 For which cause both you and all your company are gathered together against the LORD: and what is Aaron, that you murmur against him?

12 And Moses sent to call Dathan and Abiram, the sons of Eliab: which said, We will not come up:

13 Is it a small thing that you have brought us up out of a land that floweth with milk and honey, to kill us in the wilderness, except you make yourself altogether a prince over us?

14 Moreover you have not brought us into a land that floweth with milk and honey, or given us inheritance of fields and vineyards: will you put out the eyes of these men? we will not come up.

15 And Moses was very wroth, and said unto the LORD, Respect not you their offering: I have not taken one ass from them, neither have I hurt one of them.

16 And Moses said unto Korah, Be you and all your company before the LORD, you , and they, and Aaron, to morrow:

17 And take every man his censer, and put incense in them, and bring you before the LORD every man his censer, two hundred and fifty censers; you also, and Aaron, each of you his censer.

18 And they took every man his censer, and put fire in them, and laid incense thereon, and stood in the door of the tabernacle of the congregation with Moses and Aaron.

19 And Korah gathered all the congregation against them unto the door of the tabernacle of the congregation: and the glory of the LORD appeared unto all the congregation.

20 And the LORD spake unto Moses and unto Aaron, saying,

21 Separate yourselves from among this congregation, that I may consume them in a moment.

22 And they fell upon their faces, and said, O God, the God of the spirits of all flesh, shall one man sin, and will you be wroth with all the congregation?

23 And the LORD spake unto Moses, saying,

24 Speak unto the congregation, saying, Get you up from about the tabernacle of Korah, Dathan, and Abiram.

25 And Moses rose up and went unto Dathan and Abiram; and the elders of Israel followed him.

26 And he spake unto the congregation, saying, Depart, I pray you, from the tents of these wicked men, and touch nothing of theirs, lest you be consumed in all their sins.

27 So they gat up from the tabernacle of Korah, Dathan, and Abiram, on every side: and Dathan and Abiram came out, and stood in the door of their tents, and their wives, and their sons, and their little children.

28 And Moses said, Hereby you shall know that the LORD has sent me to do all these works; for I have not done them of my own mind.

29 If these men die the common death of all men, or if they be visited after the visitation of all men; then the LORD has not sent me.

30 But if the LORD make a new thing, and the earth open her mouth, and swallow them up, with all that appertain unto them, and they go down quick into the pit; then you shall understand that these men have provoked the LORD.

31 And it came to pass, as he had made an end of speaking all these words, that the ground clave asunder that was under them:

32 And the earth opened her mouth, and swallowed them up, and their houses, and all the men that appertained unto Korah, and all their goods.

33 They, and all that appertained to them, went down alive into the pit, and the earth closed upon them: and they perished from among the congregation.

34 And all Israel that were round about them fled at the cry of them: for they said, Lest the earth swallow us up also.

35 And there came out a fire from the LORD, and consumed the two hundred and fifty men that offered incense.

36 And the LORD spake unto Moses, saying,

37 Speak unto Eleazar the son of Aaron the priest, that he take up the censers out of the burning, and scatter you the fire yonder; for they are hallowed.

38 The censers of these sinners against their own souls, let them make them broad plates for a covering of the altar: for they offered them before the LORD, therefore they are hallowed: and they shall be a sign unto the children of Israel.

39 And Eleazar the priest took the brasen censers, wherewith they that were burnt had offered; and they were made broad plates for a covering of the altar:

40 To be a memorial unto the children of Israel, that no stranger, which is not of the seed of Aaron, come near to offer incense before the LORD; that he be not as Korah, and as his company: as the LORD said to him by the hand of Moses.

41 But on the morrow all the congregation of the children of Israel murmured against Moses and against Aaron, saying, You have killed the people of the LORD.

42 And it came to pass, when the congregation was gathered against Moses and against Aaron, that they looked toward the tabernacle of the congregation: and, behold, the cloud covered it, and the glory of the LORD appeared.

43 And Moses and Aaron came before the tabernacle of the congregation.

44 And the LORD spake unto Moses, saying,

45 Get you up from among this congregation, that I may consume them as in a moment. And they fell upon their faces.

46 And Moses said unto Aaron, Take a censer, and put fire therein from off the altar, and put on incense, and go quickly unto the congregation, and make an atonement for them: for there is wrath gone out from the LORD; the plague is begun.

47 And Aaron took as Moses commanded, and ran into the midst of the congregation; and, behold, the plague was begun among the people: and he put on incense, and made an atonement for the people.

48 And he stood between the dead and the living; and the plague was stayed.

49 Now they that died in the plague were fourteen thousand and seven hundred, beside them that died about the matter of Korah.

50 And Aaron returned unto Moses unto the door of the tabernacle of the congregation: and the plague was stayed.

CHAPTER 17

AND the LORD spake unto Moses, saying,

2 Speak unto the children of Israel, and take of every one of them a rod according to the house of their fathers, of all their princes according to the house of their fathers twelve rods: write you every man's name upon his rod.

3 And you shalt write Aaron's name upon the rod of Levi: for one rod shall be for the head of the house of their fathers.

4 And you shalt lay them up in the tabernacle of the congregation before the testimony, where I will meet with you.

5 And it shall come to pass, that the man's rod, whom I shall choose, shall blossom: and I will make to cease from me the murmurings of the children of Israel, whereby they murmur against you.

6 And Moses spake unto the children of Israel, and every one of their princes gave him a rod apiece, for each prince one, according to their fathers' houses, even twelve rods: and the rod of Aaron was among their rods.

7 And Moses laid up the rods before the LORD in the tabernacle of witness.

8 And it came to pass, that on the morrow Moses went into the tabernacle of witness; and, behold, the rod of Aaron for the house of Levi was budded, and brought forth buds, and bloomed blossoms, and yielded almonds.

9 And Moses brought out all the rods from before the LORD unto all the children of Israel: and they looked, and took every man his rod.

10 And the LORD said unto Moses, Bring Aaron's rod again before the testimony, to be kept for a token against the rebels; and you shalt quite take away their murmurings from me, that they die not.

11 And Moses did so: as the LORD commanded him, so did he.

12 And the children of Israel spake unto Moses, saying, Behold, we die, we perish, we all perish.

13 Whosoever comes any thing near unto the tabernacle of the LORD shall die: shall we be consumed with dying?

CHAPTER 18

AND the LORD said unto Aaron, You and your sons and your father's house with you shall bear the iniquity of the sanctuary: and you and your sons with you shall bear the iniquity of your priesthood.

2 And your brethren also of the tribe of Levi, the tribe of your father, bring you with you, that they may be joined unto you, and minister unto you: but you and your sons with you shall minister before the tabernacle of witness.

3 And they shall keep your charge, and the charge of all the tabernacle: only they shall not come nigh the vessels of the sanctuary and the altar, that neither they, nor you also, die.

4 And they shall be joined unto you, and keep the charge of the tabernacle of the congregation, for all the service of the tabernacle: and a stranger shall not come nigh unto you.

5 And you shall keep the charge of the sanctuary, and the charge of the altar: that there be no wrath any more upon the children of Israel.

6 And I, behold, I have taken your brethren the Levites from among the children of Israel: to you they are given as a gift for the LORD, to do the service of the tabernacle of the congregation.

7 Therefore you and your sons with you shall keep your priest's office for every thing of the altar, and within the vail; and you shall serve: I have given your priest's office unto you as a service of gift: and the stranger that comes nigh shall be put to death.

8 And the LORD spake unto Aaron, Behold, I also have given you the charge of my heave offerings of all the hallowed things of the children of Israel; unto you have I given them by reason of the anointing, and to your sons, by an ordinance for ever.

9 This shall be yours of the most holy things, reserved from the fire: every oblation of theirs, every meat offering of theirs, and every sin offering of theirs, and every trespass offering of theirs, which they shall render unto me, shall be most holy for you and for your sons.

10 In the most holy place shalt you eat it; every male shall eat it: it shall be holy unto you.

11 And this is yours; the heave offering of their gift, with all the wave offerings of the children of Israel: I have given them unto you, and to your sons and to your daughters with you, by a statute for ever: every one that is clean in your house shall eat of it.

12 All the best of the oil, and all the best of the wine, and of the wheat, the firstfruits of them which they shall offer unto the LORD, them have I given you.

13 And whatsoever is first ripe in the land, which they shall bring unto the LORD, shall be yours; every one that is clean in yours house shall eat of it.

14 Every thing devoted in Israel shall be yours.

15 Every thing that openeth the matrix in all flesh, which they bring unto the LORD, whether it be of men or beasts, shall be yours: nevertheless the firstborn of man shalt you surely redeem, and the firstling of unclean beasts shalt you redeem.

16 And those that are to be redeemed from a month old shalt you redeem, according to yours estimation, for the money of five shekels, after the shekel of the sanctuary, which is twenty gerahs.

17 But the firstling of a cow, or the firstling of a sheep, or the firstling of a goat, you shalt not redeem; they are holy: you shalt sprinkle their blood upon the altar, and shalt burn their fat for an offering made by fire, for a sweet savour unto the LORD.

18 And the flesh of them shall be yours, as the wave breast and as the right shoulder are yours.

19 All the heave offerings of the holy things, which the children of Israel offer unto the LORD, have I given you, and your sons and your daughters with you, by a statute for ever: it is a covenant of salt for ever before the LORD unto you and to your seed with you.

20 And the LORD spake unto Aaron, You shalt have no inheritance in their land, neither shalt you have any part among them: I am your part and yours inheritance among the children of Israel.

21 And, behold, I have given the children of Levi all the tenth in Israel for an inheritance, for their service which they serve, even the service of the tabernacle of the congregation.

22 Neither must the children of Israel henceforth come nigh the tabernacle of the congregation, lest they bear sin, and die.

23 But the Levites shall do the service of the tabernacle of the congregation, and they shall bear their iniquity: it shall be a statute for ever throughout your generations, that among the children of Israel they have no inheritance.

24 But the tithes of the children of Israel, which they offer as an heave offering unto the LORD, I have given to the Levites to inherit: therefore I have said unto them, Among the children of Israel they shall have no inheritance.

25 And the LORD spake unto Moses, saying,

26 Thus speak unto the Levites, and say unto them, When you take of the children of Israel the tithes which I have given you from them for your inheritance, then you shall offer up an heave offering of it for the LORD, even a tenth part of the tithe.

27 And this your heave offering shall be reckoned unto you, as though it were the corn of the threshingfloor, and as the fulness of the winepress.

28 Thus you also shall offer an heave offering unto the LORD of all your tithes, which you receive of the children of Israel; and you shall give thereof the LORD's heave offering to Aaron the priest.

29 Out of all your gifts you shall offer every heave offering of the LORD, of all the best thereof, even the hallowed part thereof out of it.

30 Therefore you shalt say unto them, When you have heaved the best thereof from it, then it shall be counted unto the Levites as the increase of the threshingfloor, and as the increase of the winepress.

31 And you shall eat it in every place, you and your households: for it is your reward for your service in the tabernacle of the congregation.

32 And you shall bear no sin by reason of it, when you have heaved from it the best of it: neither shall you pollute the holy things of the children of Israel, lest you die.

CHAPTER 19

AND the LORD spake unto Moses and unto Aaron, saying,

2 This is the ordinance of the law which the LORD has commanded, saying, Speak unto the children of Israel, that they bring you a red heifer without spot, wherein is no blemish, and upon which never came yoke:

3 And you shall give her unto Eleazar the priest, that he may bring her forth without the camp, and one shall slay her before his face:

4 And Eleazar the priest shall take of her blood with his finger, and sprinkle of her blood directly before the tabernacle of the congregation seven times:

5 And one shall burn the heifer in his sight; her skin, and her flesh, and her blood, with her dung, shall he burn:

6 And the priest shall take cedar wood, and hyssop, and scarlet, and cast it into the midst of the burning of the heifer.

7 Then the priest shall wash his clothes, and he shall bathe his flesh in water, and afterward he shall come into the camp, and the priest shall be unclean until the even.

8 And he that burneth her shall wash his clothes in water, and bathe his flesh in water, and shall be unclean until the even.

9 And a man that is clean shall gather up the ashes of the heifer, and lay them up without the camp in a clean place, and it shall be kept for the congregation of the children of Israel for a water of separation: it is a purification for sin.

10 And he that gathereth the ashes of the heifer shall wash his clothes, and be unclean until the even: and it shall be unto the children of Israel, and unto the stranger that sojourneth among them, for a statute for ever.

11 He that toucheth the dead body of any man shall be unclean seven days.

12 He shall purify himself with it on the third day, and on the seventh day he shall be clean: but if he purify not himself the third day, then the seventh day he shall not be clean.

13 Whosoever toucheth the dead body of any man that is dead, and purifieth not himself, defileth the tabernacle of the LORD; and that soul shall be cut off from Israel: because the water of separation was not sprinkled upon him, he shall be unclean; his uncleanness is yet upon him.

14 This is the law, when a man dieth in a tent: all that come into the tent, and all that is in the tent, shall be unclean seven days.

15 And every open vessel, which has no covering bound upon it, is unclean.

16 And whosoever toucheth one that is slain with a sword in the open fields, or a dead body, or a bone of a man, or a grave, shall be unclean seven days.

17 And for an unclean person they shall take of the ashes of the burnt heifer of purification for sin, and running water shall be put thereto in a vessel:

18 And a clean person shall take hyssop, and dip it in the water, and sprinkle it upon the tent, and upon all the vessels, and upon the persons that were there, and upon him that touched a bone, or one slain, or one dead, or a grave:

19 And the clean person shall sprinkle upon the unclean on the third day, and on the seventh day: and on the seventh day he shall purify himself, and wash his clothes, and bathe himself in water, and shall be clean at even.

20 But the man that shall be unclean, and shall not purify himself, that soul shall be cut off from among the congregation, because he has defiled the sanctuary of the LORD: the water of separation has not been sprinkled upon him; he is unclean.

21 And it shall be a perpetual statute unto them, that he that sprinkleth the water of separation shall wash his clothes; and he that toucheth the water of separation shall be unclean until even.

22 And whatsoever the unclean person toucheth shall be unclean; and the soul that toucheth it shall be unclean until even.

CHAPTER 20

THEN came the children of Israel, even the whole congregation, into the desert of Zin in the first month: and the people abode in Kadesh; and Miriam died there, and was buried there.

2 And there was no water for the congregation: and they gathered themselves together against Moses and against Aaron.

3 And the people chode with Moses, and spake, saying, Would God that we had died when our brethren died before the LORD!

4 And why have you brought up the congregation of the LORD into this wilderness, that we and our cattle should die there?

5 And wherefore have you made us to come up out of Egypt, to bring us in unto this evil place? it is no place of seed, or of figs, or of vines, or of pomegranates; neither is there any water to drink.

6 And Moses and Aaron went from the presence of the assembly unto the door of the tabernacle of the congregation, and they fell upon their faces: and the glory of the LORD appeared unto them.

7 And the LORD spake unto Moses, saying,

8 Take the rod, and gather you the assembly together, you , and Aaron your brother, and speak you unto the rock before their eyes; and it shall give forth his water, and you shalt bring forth to them water out of the rock: so you shalt give the congregation and their beasts drink.

9 And Moses took the rod from before the LORD, as he commanded him.

10 And Moses and Aaron gathered the congregation together before the rock, and he said unto them, Hear now, you rebels; must we fetch you water out of this rock?

11 And Moses lifted up his hand, and with his rod he struck the rock twice: and the water came out abundantly, and the congregation drank, and their beasts also.

12 And the LORD spake unto Moses and Aaron, Because you believed me not, to sanctify me in the eyes of the children of Israel, therefore you shall not bring this congregation into the land which I have given them.

13 This is the water of Meribah; because the children of Israel strove with the LORD, and he was sanctified in them.

14 And Moses sent messengers from Kadesh unto the king of Edom, Thus saith your brother Israel, You knowest all the travail that has befallen us:

15 How our fathers went down into Egypt, and we have dwelt in Egypt a long time; and the Egyptians vexed us, and our fathers:

16 And when we cried unto the LORD, he heard our voice, and sent an angel, and has brought us forth out of Egypt: and, behold, we are in Kadesh, a city in the uttermost of your border:

17 Let us pass, I pray you, through your country: we will not pass through the fields, or through the vineyards, neither will we drink of the water of the wells: we will go by the king's high way, we will not turn to the right hand nor to the left, until we have passed your borders.

18 And Edom said unto him, You shalt not pass by me, lest I come out against you with the sword.

19 And the children of Israel said unto him, We will go by the high way: and if I and my cattle drink of your water, then I will pay for it: I will only, without doing any thing else, go through on my feet.

20 And he said, You shalt not go through. And Edom came out against him with much people, and with a strong hand.

21 Thus Edom refused to give Israel passage through his border: wherefore Israel turned away from him.

22 And the children of Israel, even the whole congregation, journeyed from Kadesh, and came unto mount Hor.

23 And the LORD spake unto Moses and Aaron in mount Hor, by the coast of the land of Edom, saying,

24 Aaron shall be gathered unto his people: for he shall not enter into the land which I have given unto the children of Israel, because you rebelled against my word at the water of Meribah.

25 Take Aaron and Eleazar his son, and bring them up unto mount Hor:

26 And strip Aaron of his garments, and put them upon Eleazar his son: and Aaron shall be gathered unto his people, and shall die there.

27 And Moses did as the LORD commanded: and they went up into mount Hor in the sight of all the congregation.

28 And Moses stripped Aaron of his garments, and put them upon Eleazar his son; and Aaron died there in the top of the mount: and Moses and Eleazar came down from the mount.

29 And when all the congregation saw that Aaron was dead, they mourned for Aaron thirty days, even all the house of Israel.

CHAPTER 21

AND when king Arad the Canaanite, which dwelt in the south, heard tell that Israel came by the way of the spies; then he fought against Israel, and took some of them prisoners.

2 And Israel vowed a vow unto the LORD, and said, If you will indeed deliver this people into my hand, then I will utterly destroy their cities.

3 And the LORD hearkened to the voice of Israel, and delivered up the Canaanites; and they utterly destroyed them and their cities: and he called the name of the place Hormah.

4 And they journeyed from mount Hor by the way of the Red sea, to compass the land of Edom: and the soul of the people was much discouraged because of the way.

5 And the people spake against God, and against Moses, Wherefore have you brought us up out of Egypt to die in the wilderness? for there is no bread, neither is there any water; and our soul loatheth this light bread.

6 And the LORD sent fiery serpents among the people, and they bit the people; and much people of Israel died.

7 Therefore the people came to Moses, and said, We have sinned, for we have spoken against the LORD, and against you; pray unto the LORD, that he take away the serpents from us. And Moses prayed for the people.

8 And the LORD said unto Moses, Make you a fiery serpent, and set it upon a pole: and it shall come to pass, that every one that is bitten, when he looketh upon it, shall live.

9 And Moses made a serpent of brass, and put it upon a pole, and it came to pass, that if a serpent had bitten any man, when he beheld the serpent of brass, he lived.

10And the children of Israel set forward, and pitched in Oboth.

11 And they journeyed from Oboth, and pitched at Ije-abarim, in the wilderness which is before Moab, toward the sunrising.

12From thence they removed, and pitched in the valley of Zared.

13 From thence they removed, and pitched on the other side of Arnon, which is in the wilderness that comes out of the coasts of the Amorites: for Arnon is the border of Moab, between Moab and the Amorites.

14 Wherefore it is said in the book of the wars of the LORD, What he did in the Red sea, and in the brooks of Arnon,

15 And at the stream of the brooks that goeth down to the dwelling of Ar, and lies upon the border of Moab.

16 And from thence they went to Beer: that is the well whereof the LORD spake unto Moses, Gather the people together, and I will give them water.

17Then Israel sang this song, Spring up, O well; sing you unto it:

18 The princes digged the well, the nobles of the people digged it, by the direction of the lawgiver, with their staves. And from the wilderness they went to Mattanah:

19 And from Mattanah to Nahaliel: and from Nahaliel to Bamoth:

20 And from Bamoth in the valley, that is in the country of Moab, to the top of Pisgah, which looketh toward Jeshimon.

21And Israel sent messengers unto Sihon king of the Amorites, saying,

22 Let me pass through your land: we will not turn into the fields, or into the vineyards; we will not drink of the waters of the well: but we will go along by the king's high way, until we be past your borders.

23 And Sihon would not suffer Israel to pass through his border: but Sihon gathered all his people together, and went out against Israel into the wilderness: and he came to Jahaz, and fought against Israel.

24 And Israel struck him with the edge of the sword, and possessed his land from Arnon unto Jabbok, even unto the children of Ammon: for the border of the children of Ammon was strong.

25 And Israel took all these cities: and Israel dwelt in all the cities of the Amorites, in Heshbon, and in all the villages thereof.

26 For Heshbon was the city of Sihon the king of the Amorites, who had fought against the former king of Moab, and taken all his land out of his hand, even unto Arnon.

27 Wherefore they that speak in proverbs say, Come into Heshbon, let the city of Sihon be built and prepared:

28 For there is a fire gone out of Heshbon, a flame from the city of Sihon: it has consumed Ar of Moab, and the lords of the high places of Arnon.

29 Woe to you, Moab! you are undone, O people of Chemosh: he has given his sons that escaped, and his daughters, into captivity unto Sihon king of the Amorites.

30 We have shot at them; Heshbon is perished even unto Dibon, and we have laid them waste even unto Nophah, which reacheth unto Medeba.

31Thus Israel dwelt in the land of the Amorites.

32 And Moses sent to spy out Jaazer, and they took the villages thereof, and drove out the Amorites that were there.

33And they turned and went up by the way of Bashan: and Og the king of Bashan went out against them, he, and all his people, to the battle at Edrei.

34 And the LORD said unto Moses, Fear him not: for I have delivered him into your hand, and all his people, and his land; and you shalt do to him as you did unto Sihon king of the Amorites, which dwelt at Heshbon.

35 So they struck him, and his sons, and all his people, until there was none left him alive: and they possessed his land.

CHAPTER 22

AND the children of Israel set forward, and pitched in the plains of Moab on this side Jordan by Jericho.

2And Balak the son of Zippor saw all that Israel had done to the Amorites.

3 And Moab was sore afraid of the people, because they were many: and Moab was distressed because of the children of Israel.

4 And Moab said unto the elders of Midian, Now shall this company lick up all that are round about us, as the ox licketh up the grass of the field. And Balak the son of Zippor was king of the Moabites at that time.

5 He sent messengers therefore unto Balaam the son of Beor to Pethor, which is by the river of the land of the children of his people, to call him, saying, Behold, there is a people come out from Egypt: behold, they cover the face of the earth, and they abide over against me:

6 Come now therefore, I pray you, curse me this people; for they are too mighty for me: what if I shall prevail, that we may strike them, and that I may drive them out of the land: for I wot that he whom you blessest is blessed, and he whom you cursest is cursed.

7 And the elders of Moab and the elders of Midian departed with the rewards of divination in their hand; and they came unto Balaam, and spake unto him the words of Balak.

8 And he said unto them, Lodge here this night, and I will bring you word again, as the LORD shall speak unto me: and the princes of Moab abode with Balaam.

9 And God came unto Balaam, and said, What men are these with you?

10 And Balaam said unto God, Balak the son of Zippor, king of Moab, has sent unto me, saying,

11 Behold, there is a people come out of Egypt, which covers the face of the earth: come now, curse me them; what if I shall be able to overcome them, and drive them out.

12 And God said unto Balaam, You shalt not go with them; you shalt not curse the people: for they are blessed.

13 And Balaam rose up in the morning, and said unto the princes of Balak, Get you into your land: for the LORD refuseth to give me leave to go with you.

14 And the princes of Moab rose up, and they went unto Balak, and said, Balaam refuseth to come with us.

15And Balak sent yet again princes, more, and more honourable than they.

16 And they came to Balaam, and said to him, Thus saith Balak the son of Zippor, Let nothing, I pray you, hinder you from coming unto me:

17 For I will promote you unto very great honour, and I will do whatsoever you say unto me: come therefore, I pray you, curse me this people.

18 And Balaam answered and said unto the servants of Balak, If Balak would give me his house full of silver and gold, I cannot go beyond the word of the LORD my God, to do less or more.

19 Now therefore, I pray you, tarry you also here this night, that I may know what the LORD will say unto me more.

20 And God came unto Balaam at night, and said unto him, If the men come to call you, rise up, and go with them; but yet the word which I shall say unto you, that shalt you do.

21 And Balaam rose up in the morning, and saddled his ass, and went with the princes of Moab.

22And God's anger was kindled because he went: and the angel of the LORD stood in the way for an adversary against him. Now he was riding upon his ass, and his two servants were with him.

23 And the ass saw the angel of the LORD standing in the way, and his sword drawn in his hand: and the ass turned aside out of the way, and went into the field: and Balaam struck the ass, to turn her into the way.

24 But the angel of the LORD stood in a path of the vineyards, a wall being on this side, and a wall on that side.

25 And when the ass saw the angel of the LORD, she thrust herself unto the wall, and crushed Balaam's foot against the wall: and he struck her again.

26 And the angel of the LORD went further, and stood in a narrow place, where was no way to turn either to the right hand or to the left.

27 And when the ass saw the angel of the LORD, she fell down under Balaam: and Balaam's anger was kindled, and he struck the ass with a staff.

28 And the LORD opened the mouth of the ass, and she said unto Balaam, What have I done unto you, that you have smitten me these three times?

29 And Balaam said unto the ass, Because you have mocked me: I would there were a sword in my hand, for now would I kill you.

30 And the ass said unto Balaam, Am not I yours ass, upon which you have ridden ever since I was yours unto this day? was I ever wont to do so unto you? And he said, Nay.

31 Then the LORD opened the eyes of Balaam, and he saw the angel of the LORD standing in the way, and his sword drawn in his hand: and he bowed down his head, and fell flat on his face.

32 And the angel of the LORD said unto him, Wherefore have you smitten yours ass these three times? behold, I went out to withstand you, because your way is perverse before me:

33 And the ass saw me, and turned from me these three times: unless she had turned from me, surely now also I had slain you, and saved her alive.

34 And Balaam said unto the angel of the LORD, I have sinned; for I knew not that you stoodest in the way against me: now therefore, if it displease you, I will get me back again.

35 And the angel of the LORD said unto Balaam, Go with the men: but only the word that I shall speak unto you, that you shalt speak. So Balaam went with the princes of Balak.

36And when Balak heard that Balaam was come, he went out to meet him unto a city of Moab, which is in the border of Arnon, which is in the utmost coast.

37 And Balak said unto Balaam, Did I not earnestly send unto you to call you? wherefore camest you not unto me? am I not able indeed to promote you to honour?

38 And Balaam said unto Balak, Lo, I am come unto you: have I now any power at all to say any thing? the word that God putteth in my mouth, that shall I speak.

39 And Balaam went with Balak, and they came unto Kirjath-huzoth.

40 And Balak offered oxen and sheep, and sent to Balaam, and to the princes that were with him.

41 And it came to pass on the morrow, that Balak took Balaam, and brought him up into the high places of Baal, that thence he might see the utmost part of the people.

CHAPTER 23

AND Balaam said unto Balak, Build me here seven altars, and prepare me here seven oxen and seven rams.

2 And Balak did as Balaam had spoken; and Balak and Balaam offered on every altar a bullock and a ram.

3 And Balaam said unto Balak, Stand by your burnt offering, and I will go: what if the LORD will come to meet me: and whatsoever he sheweth me I will tell you. And he went to an high place.

4 And God met Balaam: and he said unto him, I have prepared seven altars, and I have offered upon every altar a bullock and a ram.

5 And the LORD put a word in Balaam's mouth, and said, Return unto Balak, and thus you shalt speak.

6 And he returned unto him, and, lo, he stood by his burnt sacrifice, he, and all the princes of Moab.

7 And he took up his parable, and said, Balak the king of Moab has brought me from Aram, out of the mountains of the east, saying, Come, curse me Jacob, and come, defy Israel.

8 How shall I curse, whom God has not cursed? or how shall I defy, whom the LORD has not defied?

9 For from the top of the rocks I see him, and from the hills I behold him: lo, the people shall dwell alone, and shall not be reckoned among the nations.

10 Who can count the dust of Jacob, and the number of the fourth part of Israel? Let me die the death of the righteous, and let my last end be like his!

11 And Balak said unto Balaam, What have you done unto me? I took you to curse my enemies, and, behold, you have blessed them altogether.

12 And he answered and said, Must I not take heed to speak that which the LORD has put in my mouth?

13 And Balak said unto him, Come, I pray you, with me unto another place, from whence you mayest see them: you shalt see but the utmost part of them, and shalt not see them all: and curse me them from thence.

14And he brought him into the field of Zophim, to the top of Pisgah, and built seven altars, and offered a bullock and a ram on every altar.

15 And he said unto Balak, Stand here by your burnt offering, while I meet the LORD yonder.

16 And the LORD met Balaam, and put a word in his mouth, and said, Go again unto Balak, and say thus.

17 And when he came to him, behold, he stood by his burnt offering, and the princes of Moab with him. And Balak said unto him, What has the LORD spoken?

18 And he took up his parable, and said, Rise up, Balak, and hear; hearken unto me, you son of Zippor:

19 God is not a man, that he should lie; neither the son of man, that he should repent: has he said, and shall he not do it? or has he spoken, and shall he not make it good?

20 Behold, I have received commandment to bless: and he has blessed; and I cannot reverse it.

21 He has not beheld iniquity in Jacob, neither has he seen perverseness in Israel: the LORD his God is with him, and the shout of a king is among them.

22 God brought them out of Egypt; he has as it were the strength of an unicorn.

23 Surely there is no enchantment against Jacob, neither is there any divination against Israel: according to this time it shall be said of Jacob and of Israel, What has God created!

24 Behold, the people shall rise up as a great lion, and lift up himself as a young lion: he shall not lie down until he eat of the prey, and drink the blood of the slain.

25And Balak said unto Balaam, Neither curse them at all, nor bless them at all.

26 But Balaam answered and said unto Balak, Told not I you, saying, All that the LORD speaketh, that I must do?

27And Balak said unto Balaam, Come, I pray you, I will bring you unto another place; what if it will please God that you mayest curse me them from thence.

28 And Balak brought Balaam unto the top of Peor, that looketh toward Jeshimon.

29 And Balaam said unto Balak, Build me here seven altars, and prepare me here seven bullocks and seven rams.

30 And Balak did as Balaam had said, and offered a bullock and a ram on every altar.

CHAPTER 24

AND when Balaam saw that it pleased the LORD to bless Israel, he went not, as at other times, to seek for enchantments, but he set his face toward the wilderness.

2 And Balaam lifted up his eyes, and he saw Israel abiding in his tents according to their tribes; and the spirit of God came upon him.

3 And he took up his parable, and said, Balaam the son of Beor has said, and the man whose eyes are open has said:

4 He has said, which heard the words of God, which saw the vision of the Almighty, falling into a trance, but having his eyes open:

5 How goodly are your tents, O Jacob, and your tabernacles, O Israel!

6 As the valleys are they spread forth, as gardens by the river's side, as the trees of lign aloes which the LORD has planted, and as cedar trees beside the waters.

7 He shall pour the water out of his buckets, and his seed shall be in many waters, and his king shall be higher than Agag, and his kingdom shall be exalted.

8 God brought him forth out of Egypt; he has as it were the strength of an unicorn: he shall eat up the nations his enemies, and shall break their bones, and pierce them through with his arrows.

9 He couched, he lay down as a lion, and as a great lion: who shall stir him up? Blessed is he that blesseth you, and cursed is he that curseth you.

10And Balak's anger was kindled against Balaam, and he struck his hands together: and Balak said unto Balaam, I called you to curse my enemies, and, behold, you have altogether blessed them these three times.

11 Therefore now flee you to your place: I thought to promote you unto great honour; but, lo, the LORD has kept you back from honour.

12 And Balaam said unto Balak, Spake I not also to your messengers which you sentest unto me, saying,

13 If Balak would give me his house full of silver and gold, I cannot go beyond the commandment of the LORD, to do either good or bad of my own mind; but what the LORD saith, that will I speak?

14 And now, behold, I go unto my people: come therefore, and I will advertise you what this people shall do to your people in the latter days.

15And he took up his parable, and said, Balaam the son of Beor has said, and the man whose eyes are open has said:

16 He has said, which heard the words of God, and knew the knowledge of the most High, which saw the vision of the Almighty, falling into a trance, but having his eyes open:

17 I shall see him, but not now: I shall behold him, but not nigh: there shall come a Star out of Jacob, and a Sceptre shall rise out of Israel, and shall strike the corners of Moab, and destroy all the children of Sheth.

18 And Edom shall be a possession, Seir also shall be a possession for his enemies; and Israel shall do valiantly.

19 Out of Jacob shall come he that shall have dominion, and shall destroy him that remaineth of the city.

20And when he looked on Amalek, he took up his parable, and said, Amalek was the first of the nations; but his latter end shall be that he perish for ever.

21 And he looked on the Kenites, and took up his parable, and said, Strong is your dwellingplace, and you puttest your nest in a rock.

22 Nevertheless the Kenite shall be wasted, until Asshur shall carry you away captive.

23 And he took up his parable, and said, Alas, who shall live when God doeth this!

24 And ships shall come from the coast of Chittim, and shall afflict Asshur, and shall afflict Eber, and he also shall perish for ever.

25 And Balaam rose up, and went and returned to his place: and Balak also went his way.

CHAPTER 25

AND Israel abode in Shittim, and the people began to commit whoredom with the daughters of Moab.

2 And they called the people unto the sacrifices of their gods: and the people did eat, and bowed down to their gods.

3 And Israel joined himself unto Baal-peor: and the anger of the LORD was kindled against Israel.

4 And the LORD said unto Moses, Take all the heads of the people, and hang them up before the LORD against the sun, that the fierce anger of the LORD may be turned away from Israel.

5 And Moses said unto the judges of Israel, Slay you every one his men that were joined unto Baal-peor.

6And, behold, one of the children of Israel came and brought unto his brethren a Midianitish woman in the sight of Moses, and in the sight of all the congregation of the children of Israel, who were weeping before the door of the tabernacle of the congregation.

7 And when Phinehas, the son of Eleazar, the son of Aaron the priest, saw it, he rose up from among the congregation, and took a javelin in his hand;

8 And he went after the man of Israel into the tent, and thrust both of them through, the man of Israel, and the woman through her belly. So the plague was stayed from the children of Israel.

9 And those that died in the plague were twenty and four thousand.

10And the LORD spake unto Moses, saying,

11 Phinehas, the son of Eleazar, the son of Aaron the priest, has turned my wrath away from the children of Israel, while he was zealous for my sake among them, that I consumed not the children of Israel in my jealousy.

12 Wherefore say, Behold, I give unto him my covenant of peace:

13 And he shall have it, and his seed after him, even the covenant of an everlasting priesthood; because he was zealous for his God, and made an atonement for the children of Israel.

14 Now the name of the Israelite that was slain, even that was slain with the Midianitish woman, was Zimri, the son of Salu, a prince of a chief house among the Simeonites.

15 And the name of the Midianitish woman that was slain was Cozbi, the daughter of Zur; he was head over a people, and of a chief house in Midian.

16And the LORD spake unto Moses, saying,

17 Vex the Midianites, and strike them:

18 For they vex you with their wiles, wherewith they have beguiled you in the matter of Peor, and in the matter of Cozbi, the daughter of a prince of Midian, their sister, which was slain in the day of the plague for Peor's sake.

CHAPTER 26

AND it came to pass after the plague, that the LORD spake unto Moses and unto Eleazar the son of Aaron the priest, saying,

2 Take the sum of all the congregation of the children of Israel, from twenty years old and upward, throughout their fathers' house, all that are able to go to war in Israel.

3 And Moses and Eleazar the priest spake with them in the plains of Moab by Jordan near Jericho, saying,

4 Take the sum of the people, from twenty years old and upward; as the LORD commanded Moses and the children of Israel, which went forth out of the land of Egypt.

5Reuben, the eldest son of Israel: the children of Reuben; Hanoch, of whom comes the family of the Hanochites: of Pallu, the family of the Palluites:

6 Of Hezron, the family of the Hezronites: of Carmi, the family of the Carmites.

7 These are the families of the Reubenites: and they that were numbered of them were forty and three thousand and seven hundred and thirty.

8 And the sons of Pallu; Eliab.

9 And the sons of Eliab; Nemuel, and Dathan, and Abiram. This is that Dathan and Abiram, which were famous in the congregation, who strove against Moses and against Aaron in the company of Korah, when they strove against the LORD:

10 And the earth opened her mouth, and swallowed them up together with Korah, when that company died, what time the fire devoured two hundred and fifty men: and they became a sign.

11 Notwithstanding the children of Korah died not.

12The sons of Simeon after their families: of Nemuel, the family of the Nemuelites: of Jamin, the family of the Jaminites: of Jachin, the family of the Jachinites:

13 Of Zerah, the family of the Zarhites: of Shaul, the family of the Shaulites.

14 These are the families of the Simeonites, twenty and two thousand and two hundred.

15The children of Gad after their families: of Zephon, the family of the Zephonites: of Haggi, the family of the Haggites: of Shuni, the family of the Shunites:

16 Of Ozni, the family of the Oznites: of Eri, the family of the Erites:

17 Of Arod, the family of the Arodites: of Areli, the family of the Arelites.

18 These are the families of the children of Gad according to those that were numbered of them, forty thousand and five hundred.

19The sons of Judah were Er and Onan: and Er and Onan died in the land of Canaan.

20 And the sons of Judah after their families were; of Shelah, the family of the Shelanites: of Pharez, the family of the Pharzites: of Zerah, the family of the Zarhites.

21 And the sons of Pharez were; of Hezron, the family of the Hezronites: of Hamul, the family of the Hamulites.

22 These are the families of Judah according to those that were numbered of them, threescore and sixteen thousand and five hundred.

23Of the sons of Issachar after their families: of Tola, the family of the Tolaites: of Pua, the family of the Punites:

24 Of Jashub, the family of the Jashubites: of Shimron, the family of the Shimronites.

25 These are the families of Issachar according to those that were numbered of them, threescore and four thousand and three hundred.

26Of the sons of Zebulun after their families: of Sered, the family of the Sardites: of Elon, the family of the Elonites: of Jahleel, the family of the Jahleelites.

27 These are the families of the Zebulunites according to those that were numbered of them, threescore thousand and five hundred.

28The sons of Joseph after their families were Manasseh and Ephraim.

29 Of the sons of Manasseh: of Machir, the family of the Machirites: and Machir begat Gilead: of Gilead come the family of the Gileadites.

30 These are the sons of Gilead: of Jeezer, the family of the Jeezerites: of Helek, the family of the Helekites:

31 And of Asriel, the family of the Asrielites: and of Shechem, the family of the Shechemites:

32 And of Shemida, the family of the Shemidaites: and of Hepher, the family of the Hepherites.

33And Zelophehad the son of Hepher had no sons, but daughters: and the names of the daughters of Zelophehad were Mahlah, and Noah, Hoglah, Milcah, and Tirzah.

34 These are the families of Manasseh, and those that were numbered of them, fifty and two thousand and seven hundred.

35These are the sons of Ephraim after their families: of Shuthelah, the family of the Shuthalhites: of Becher, the family of the Bachrites: of Tahan, the family of the Tahanites.

36 And these are the sons of Shuthelah: of Eran, the family of the Eranites.

37 These are the families of the sons of Ephraim according to those that were numbered of them, thirty and two thousand and five hundred. These are the sons of Joseph after their families.

38The sons of Benjamin after their families: of Bela, the family of the Belaites: of Ashbel, the family of the Ashbelites: of Ahiram, the family of the Ahiramites:

39 Of Shupham, the family of the Shuphamites: of Hupham, the family of the Huphamites.

40 And the sons of Bela were Ard and Naaman: of Ard, the family of the Ardites: and of Naaman, the family of the Naamites.

41 These are the sons of Benjamin after their families: and they that were numbered of them were forty and five thousand and six hundred.

42These are the sons of Dan after their families: of Shuham, the family of the Shuhamites. These are the families of Dan after their families.

43 All the families of the Shuhamites, according to those that were numbered of them, were threescore and four thousand and four hundred.

44Of the children of Asher after their families: of Jimna, the family of the Jimnites: of Jesui, the family of the Jesuites: of Beriah, the family of the Beriites.

45 Of the sons of Beriah: of Heber, the family of the Heberites: of Malchiel, the family of the Malchielites.

46 And the name of the daughter of Asher was Sarah.

47 These are the families of the sons of Asher according to those that were numbered of them; who were fifty and three thousand and four hundred.

48Of the sons of Naphtali after their families: of Jahzeel, the family of the Jahzeelites: of Guni, the family of the Gunites:

49 Of Jezer, the family of the Jezerites: of Shillem, the family of the Shillemites.

50 These are the families of Naphtali according to their families: and they that were numbered of them were forty and five thousand and four hundred.

51 These were the numbered of the children of Israel, six hundred thousand and a thousand seven hundred and thirty.

52And the LORD spake unto Moses, saying,

53 Unto these the land shall be divided for an inheritance according to the number of names.

54 To many you shalt give the more inheritance, and to few you shalt give the less inheritance: to every one shall his inheritance be given according to those that were numbered of him.

55 Notwithstanding the land shall be divided by lot: according to the names of the tribes of their fathers they shall inherit.

56 According to the lot shall the possession thereof be divided between many and few.

57And these are they that were numbered of the Levites after their families: of Gershon, the family of the Gershonites: of Kohath, the family of the Kohathites: of Merari, the family of the Merarites.

58 These are the families of the Levites: the family of the Libnites, the family of the Hebronites, the family of the Mahlites, the family of the Mushites, the family of the Korathites. And Kohath begat Amram.

59 And the name of Amram's wife was Jochebed, the daughter of Levi, whom her mother bare to Levi in Egypt: and she bare unto Amram Aaron and Moses, and Miriam their sister.

60 And unto Aaron was born Nadab, and Abihu, Eleazar, and Ithamar.

61 And Nadab and Abihu died, when they offered strange fire before the LORD.

62 And those that were numbered of them were twenty and three thousand, all males from a month old and upward: for they were not numbered among the children of Israel, because there was no inheritance given them among the children of Israel.

63 These are they that were numbered by Moses and Eleazar the priest, who numbered the children of Israel in the plains of Moab by Jordan near Jericho.

64 But among these there was not a man of them whom Moses and Aaron the priest numbered, when they numbered the children of Israel in the wilderness of Sinai.

65 For the LORD had said of them, They shall surely die in the wilderness. And there was not left a man of them, save Caleb the son of Jephunneh, and Joshua the son of Nun.

CHAPTER 27

THEN came the daughters of Zelophehad, the son of Hepher, the son of Gilead, the son of Machir, the son of Manasseh, of the families of Manasseh the son of Joseph: and these are the names of his daughters; Mahlah, Noah, and Hoglah, and Milcah, and Tirzah.

2 And they stood before Moses, and before Eleazar the priest, and before the princes and all the congregation, by the door of the tabernacle of the congregation, saying,

3 Our father died in the wilderness, and he was not in the company of them that gathered themselves together against the LORD in the company of Korah; but died in his own sin, and had no sons.

4 Why should the name of our father be done away from among his family, because he has no son? Give unto us therefore a possession among the brethren of our father.

5 And Moses brought their cause before the LORD.

6 And the LORD spake unto Moses, saying,

7 The daughters of Zelophehad speak right: you shalt surely give them a possession of an inheritance among their father's brethren; and you shalt cause the inheritance of their father to pass unto them.

8 And you shalt speak unto the children of Israel, saying, If a man die, and have no son, then you shall cause his inheritance to pass unto his daughter.

9 And if he have no daughter, then you shall give his inheritance unto his brethren.

10 And if he have no brethren, then you shall give his inheritance unto his father's brethren.

11 And if his father have no brethren, then you shall give his inheritance unto his kinsman that is next to him of his family, and he shall possess it: and it shall be unto the children of Israel a statute of judgment, as the LORD commanded Moses.

12 And the LORD said unto Moses, Get you up into this mount Abarim, and see the land which I have given unto the children of Israel.

13 And when you have seen it, you also shalt be gathered unto your people, as Aaron your brother was gathered.

14 For you rebelled against my commandment in the desert of Zin, in the strife of the congregation, to sanctify me at the water before their eyes: that is the water of Meribah in Kadesh in the wilderness of Zin.

15 And Moses spake unto the LORD, saying,

16 Let the LORD, the God of the spirits of all flesh, set a man over the congregation,

17 Which may go out before them, and which may go in before them, and which may lead them out, and which may bring them in; that the congregation of the LORD be not as sheep which have no shepherd.

18 And the LORD said unto Moses, Take you Joshua the son of Nun, a man in whom is the spirit, and lay yours hand upon him;

19 And set him before Eleazar the priest, and before all the congregation; and give him a charge in their sight.

20 And you shalt put some of yours honour upon him, that all the congregation of the children of Israel may be obedient.

21 And he shall stand before Eleazar the priest, who shall ask counsel for him after the judgment of Urim before the LORD: at his word shall they go out, and at his word they shall come in, both he, and all the children of Israel with him, even all the congregation.

22 And Moses did as the LORD commanded him: and he took Joshua, and set him before Eleazar the priest, and before all the congregation:

23 And he laid his hands upon him, and gave him a charge, as the LORD commanded by the hand of Moses.

CHAPTER 28

AND the LORD spake unto Moses, saying,

2 Command the children of Israel, and say unto them, My offering, and my bread for my sacrifices made by fire, for a sweet savour unto me, shall you observe to offer unto me in their due season.

3 And you shalt say unto them, This is the offering made by fire which you shall offer unto the LORD; two lambs of the first year without spot day by day, for a continual burnt offering.

4 The one lamb shalt you offer in the morning, and the other lamb shalt you offer at even;

5 And a tenth part of an ephah of flour for a meat offering, mingled with the fourth part of an hin of beaten oil.

6 It is a continual burnt offering, which was ordained in mount Sinai for a sweet savour, a sacrifice made by fire unto the LORD.

7 And the drink offering thereof shall be the fourth part of an hin for the one lamb: in the holy place shalt you cause the strong wine to be poured unto the LORD for a drink offering.

8 And the other lamb shalt you offer at even: as the meat offering of the morning, and as the drink offering thereof, you shalt offer it, a sacrifice made by fire, of a sweet savour unto the LORD.

9 And on the sabbath day two lambs of the first year without spot, and two tenth deals of flour for a meat offering, mingled with oil, and the drink offering thereof:

10 This is the burnt offering of every sabbath, beside the continual burnt offering, and his drink offering.

11 And in the beginnings of your months you shall offer a burnt offering unto the LORD; two young bullocks, and one ram, seven lambs of the first year without spot;

12 And three tenth deals of flour for a meat offering, mingled with oil, for one bullock; and two tenth deals of flour for a meat offering, mingled with oil, for one ram;

13 And a several tenth deal of flour mingled with oil for a meat offering unto one lamb; for a burnt offering of a sweet savour, a sacrifice made by fire unto the LORD.

14 And their drink offerings shall be half an hin of wine unto a bullock, and the third part of an hin unto a ram, and a fourth part of an hin unto a lamb: this is the burnt offering of every month throughout the months of the year.

15 And one kid of the goats for a sin offering unto the LORD shall be offered, beside the continual burnt offering, and his drink offering.

16 And in the fourteenth day of the first month is the passover of the LORD.

17 And in the fifteenth day of this month is the feast: seven days shall unleavened bread be eaten.

18 In the first day shall be an holy convocation; you shall do no manner of servile work therein:

19 But you shall offer a sacrifice made by fire for a burnt offering unto the LORD; two young bullocks, and one ram, and seven lambs of the first year: they shall be unto you without blemish:

20 And their meat offering shall be of flour mingled with oil: three tenth deals shall you offer for a bullock, and two tenth deals for a ram;

21 A several tenth deal shalt you offer for every lamb, throughout the seven lambs:

22 And one goat for a sin offering, to make an atonement for you.

23 You shall offer these beside the burnt offering in the morning, which is for a continual burnt offering.

24 After this manner you shall offer daily, throughout the seven days, the meat of the sacrifice made by fire, of a sweet savour unto the LORD: it shall be offered beside the continual burnt offering, and his drink offering.

25 And on the seventh day you shall have an holy convocation; you shall do no servile work.

26 Also in the day of the firstfruits, when you bring a new meat offering unto the LORD, after your weeks be out, you shall have an holy convocation; you shall do no servile work:

27 But you shall offer the burnt offering for a sweet savour unto the LORD; two young bullocks, one ram, seven lambs of the first year;

28 And their meat offering of flour mingled with oil, three tenth deals unto one bullock, two tenth deals unto one ram,

29 A several tenth deal unto one lamb, throughout the seven lambs;

30 And one kid of the goats, to make an atonement for you.

31 You shall offer them beside the continual burnt offering, and his meat offering, (they shall be unto you without blemish) and their drink offerings.

CHAPTER 29

AND in the seventh month, on the first day of the month, you shall have an holy convocation; you shall do no servile work: it is a day of blowing the trumpets unto you.

2 And you shall offer a burnt offering for a sweet savour unto the LORD; one young bullock, one ram, and seven lambs of the first year without blemish:

3 And their meat offering shall be of flour mingled with oil, three tenth deals for a bullock, and two tenth deals for a ram,

4 And one tenth deal for one lamb, throughout the seven lambs:

5 And one kid of the goats for a sin offering, to make an atonement for you:

6 Beside the burnt offering of the month, and his meat offering, and the daily burnt offering, and his meat offering, and their drink offerings, according unto their manner, for a sweet savour, a sacrifice made by fire unto the LORD.

7 And you shall have on the tenth day of this seventh month an holy convocation; and you shall afflict your souls: you shall not do any work therein:

8 But you shall offer a burnt offering unto the LORD for a sweet savour; one young bullock, one ram, and seven lambs of the first year; they shall be unto you without blemish:

9 And their meat offering shall be of flour mingled with oil, three tenth deals to a bullock, and two tenth deals to one ram,

10 A several tenth deal for one lamb, throughout the seven lambs:

11 One kid of the goats for a sin offering; beside the sin offering of atonement, and the continual burnt offering, and the meat offering of it, and their drink offerings.

12 And on the fifteenth day of the seventh month you shall have an holy convocation; you shall do no servile work, and you shall keep a feast unto the LORD seven days:

13 And you shall offer a burnt offering, a sacrifice made by fire, of a sweet savour unto the LORD; thirteen young bullocks, two rams, and fourteen lambs of the first year; they shall be without blemish:

14 And their meat offering shall be of flour mingled with oil, three tenth deals unto every bullock of the thirteen bullocks, two tenth deals to each ram of the two rams,

15 And a several tenth deal to each lamb of the fourteen lambs:

16 And one kid of the goats for a sin offering; beside the continual burnt offering, his meat offering, and his drink offering.

17 And on the second day you shall offer twelve young bullocks, two rams, fourteen lambs of the first year without spot:

18 And their meat offering and their drink offerings for the bullocks, for the rams, and for the lambs, shall be according to their number, after the manner:

19 And one kid of the goats for a sin offering; beside the continual burnt offering, and the meat offering thereof, and their drink offerings.

20 And on the third day eleven bullocks, two rams, fourteen lambs of the first year without blemish;

21 And their meat offering and their drink offerings for the bullocks, for the rams, and for the lambs, shall be according to their number, after the manner:

22 And one goat for a sin offering; beside the continual burnt offering, and his meat offering, and his drink offering.

23 And on the fourth day ten bullocks, two rams, and fourteen lambs of the first year without blemish:

24 Their meat offering and their drink offerings for the bullocks, for the rams, and for the lambs, shall be according to their number, after the manner:

25 And one kid of the goats for a sin offering; beside the continual burnt offering, his meat offering, and his drink offering.

26 And on the fifth day nine bullocks, two rams, and fourteen lambs of the first year without spot:

27 And their meat offering and their drink offerings for the bullocks, for the rams, and for the lambs, shall be according to their number, after the manner:

28 And one goat for a sin offering; beside the continual burnt offering, and his meat offering, and his drink offering.

29 And on the sixth day eight bullocks, two rams, and fourteen lambs of the first year without blemish:

30 And their meat offering and their drink offerings for the bullocks, for the rams, and for the lambs, shall be according to their number, after the manner:

31 And one goat for a sin offering; beside the continual burnt offering, his meat offering, and his drink offering.

32 And on the seventh day seven bullocks, two rams, and fourteen lambs of the first year without blemish:

33 And their meat offering and their drink offerings for the bullocks, for the rams, and for the lambs, shall be according to their number, after the manner:

34 And one goat for a sin offering; beside the continual burnt offering, his meat offering, and his drink offering.

35 On the eighth day you shall have a solemn assembly: you shall do no servile work therein:

36 But you shall offer a burnt offering, a sacrifice made by fire, of a sweet savour unto the LORD: one bullock, one ram, seven lambs of the first year without blemish:

37 Their meat offering and their drink offerings for the bullock, for the ram, and for the lambs, shall be according to their number, after the manner:

38 And one goat for a sin offering; beside the continual burnt offering, and his meat offering, and his drink offering.

39 These things you shall do unto the LORD in your set feasts, beside your vows, and your freewill offerings, for your burnt offerings, and for your meat offerings, and for your drink offerings, and for your peace offerings.

40 And Moses told the children of Israel according to all that the LORD commanded Moses.

CHAPTER 30

AND Moses spake unto the heads of the tribes concerning the children of Israel, saying, This is the thing which the LORD has commanded.

2 If a man vow a vow unto the LORD, or swear an oath to bind his soul with a bond; he shall not break his word, he shall do according to all that proceedeth out of his mouth.

3 If a woman also vow a vow unto the LORD, and bind herself by a bond, being in her father's house in her youth;

4 And her father hear her vow, and her bond wherewith she has bound her soul, and her father shall hold his peace at her: then all her vows shall stand, and every bond wherewith she has bound her soul shall stand.

5 But if her father disallow her in the day that he heareth; not any of her vows, or of her bonds wherewith she has bound her soul, shall stand: and the LORD shall forgive her, because her father disallowed her.

6 And if she had at all an husband, when she vowed, or uttered ought out of her lips, wherewith she bound her soul;

7 And her husband heard it, and held his peace at her in the day that he heard it: then her vows shall stand, and her bonds wherewith she bound her soul shall stand.

8 But if her husband disallowed her on the day that he heard it; then he shall make her vow which she vowed, and that which she uttered with her lips, wherewith she bound her soul, of none effect: and the LORD shall forgive her.

9 But every vow of a widow, and of her that is divorced, wherewith they have bound their souls, shall stand against her.

10 And if she vowed in her husband's house, or bound her soul by a bond with an oath;

11 And her husband heard it, and held his peace at her, and disallowed her not: then all her vows shall stand, and every bond wherewith she bound her soul shall stand.

12 But if her husband has utterly made them void on the day he heard them; then whatsoever proceeded out of her lips concerning her vows, or concerning the bond of her soul, shall not stand: her husband has made them void; and the LORD shall forgive her.

13 Every vow, and every binding oath to afflict the soul, her husband may establish it, or her husband may make it void.

14 But if her husband altogether hold his peace at her from day to day; then he establisheth all her vows, or all her bonds, which are upon her: he confirmeth them, because he held his peace at her in the day that he heard them.

15 But if he shall any ways make them void after that he has heard them; then he shall bear her iniquity.

16 These are the statutes, which the LORD commanded Moses, between a man and his wife, between the father and his daughter, being yet in her youth in her father's house.

CHAPTER 31

AND the LORD spake unto Moses, saying,

2 Avenge the children of Israel of the Midianites: afterward shalt you be gathered unto your people.

3 And Moses spake unto the people, saying, Arm some of yourselves unto the war, and let them go against the Midianites, and avenge the LORD of Midian.

4 Of every tribe a thousand, throughout all the tribes of Israel, shall you send to the war.

5 So there were delivered out of the thousands of Israel, a thousand of every tribe, twelve thousand armed for war.

6 And Moses sent them to the war, a thousand of every tribe, them and Phinehas the son of Eleazar the priest, to the war, with the holy instruments, and the trumpets to blow in his hand.

7 And they warred against the Midianites, as the LORD commanded Moses; and they slew all the males.

8 And they slew the kings of Midian, beside the rest of them that were slain; namely, Evi, and Rekem, and Zur, and Hur, and Reba, five kings of Midian: Balaam also the son of Beor they slew with the sword.

9 And the children of Israel took all the women of Midian captives, and their little ones, and took the spoil of all their cattle, and all their flocks, and all their goods.

10 And they burnt all their cities wherein they dwelt, and all their goodly castles, with fire.

11 And they took all the spoil, and all the prey, both of men and of beasts.

12 And they brought the captives, and the prey, and the spoil, unto Moses, and Eleazar the priest, and unto the congregation of the children of Israel, unto the camp at the plains of Moab, which are by Jordan near Jericho.

13 And Moses, and Eleazar the priest, and all the princes of the congregation, went forth to meet them without the camp.

14 And Moses was wroth with the officers of the host, with the captains over thousands, and captains over hundreds, which came from the battle.

15 And Moses said unto them, Have you saved all the women alive?

16 Behold, these caused the children of Israel, through the counsel of Balaam, to commit trespass against the LORD in the matter of Peor, and there was a plague among the congregation of the LORD.

17 Now therefore kill every male among the little ones, and kill every woman that has known man by lying with him.

18 But all the women children, that have not known a man by lying with him, keep alive for yourselves.

19 And do you abide without the camp seven days: whosoever has killed any person, and whosoever has touched any slain, purify both yourselves and your captives on the third day, and on the seventh day.

20 And purify all your raiment, and all that is made of skins, and all work of goats' hair, and all things made of wood.

21 And Eleazar the priest said unto the men of war which went to the battle, This is the ordinance of the law which the LORD commanded Moses;

22 Only the gold, and the silver, the brass, the iron, the tin, and the lead,

23 Every thing that may abide the fire, you shall make it go through the fire, and it shall be clean: nevertheless it shall be purified with the water of separation: and all that abideth not the fire you shall make go through the water.

24 And you shall wash your clothes on the seventh day, and you shall be clean, and afterward you shall come into the camp.

25 And the LORD spake unto Moses, saying,

26 Take the sum of the prey that was taken, both of man and of beast, you , and Eleazar the priest, and the chief fathers of the congregation:

27 And divide the prey into two parts; between them that took the war upon them, who went out to battle, and between all the congregation:

28 And levy a tribute unto the LORD of the men of war which went out to battle: one soul of five hundred, both of the persons, and of the beeves, and of the asses, and of the sheep:

29 Take it of their half, and give it unto Eleazar the priest, for an heave offering of the LORD.

30 And of the children of Israel's half, you shalt take one portion of fifty, of the persons, of the beeves, of the asses, and of the flocks, of all manner of beasts, and give them unto the Levites, which keep the charge of the tabernacle of the LORD.

31 And Moses and Eleazar the priest did as the LORD commanded Moses.

32 And the booty, being the rest of the prey which the men of war had caught, was six hundred thousand and seventy thousand and five thousand sheep,

33 And threescore and twelve thousand beeves,

34 And threescore and one thousand asses,

35 And thirty and two thousand persons in all, of women that had not known man by lying with him.

36 And the half, which was the portion of them that went out to war, was in number three hundred thousand and seven and thirty thousand and five hundred sheep:

37 And the LORD's tribute of the sheep was six hundred and threescore and fifteen.

38 And the beeves were thirty and six thousand; of which the LORD's tribute was threescore and twelve.

39 And the asses were thirty thousand and five hundred; of which the LORD's tribute was threescore and one.

40 And the persons were sixteen thousand; of which the LORD's tribute was thirty and two persons.

41 And Moses gave the tribute, which was the LORD's heave offering, unto Eleazar the priest, as the LORD commanded Moses.

42 And of the children of Israel's half, which Moses divided from the men that warred,

43 (Now the half that pertained unto the congregation was three hundred thousand and thirty thousand and seven thousand and five hundred sheep,

44 And thirty and six thousand beeves,

45 And thirty thousand asses and five hundred,

46 And sixteen thousand persons;)

47 Even of the children of Israel's half, Moses took one portion of fifty, both of man and of beast, and gave them unto the Levites, which kept the charge of the tabernacle of the LORD; as the LORD commanded Moses.

48 And the officers which were over thousands of the host, the captains of thousands, and captains of hundreds, came near unto Moses:

49 And they said unto Moses, Your servants have taken the sum of the men of war which are under our charge, and there lacketh not one man of us.

50 We have therefore brought an oblation for the LORD, what every man has gotten, of jewels of gold, chains, and bracelets, rings, earrings, and tablets, to make an atonement for our souls before the LORD.

51 And Moses and Eleazar the priest took the gold of them, even all created jewels.

52 And all the gold of the offering that they offered up to the LORD, of the captains of thousands, and of the captains of hundreds, was sixteen thousand seven hundred and fifty shekels.

53 (For the men of war had taken spoil, every man for himself.)

54 And Moses and Eleazar the priest took the gold of the captains of thousands and of hundreds, and brought it into the tabernacle of the congregation, for a memorial for the children of Israel before the LORD.

CHAPTER 32

NOW the children of Reuben and the children of Gad had a very great multitude of cattle: and when they saw the land of Jazer, and the land of Gilead, that, behold, the place was a place for cattle;

2 The children of Gad and the children of Reuben came and spake unto Moses, and to Eleazar the priest, and unto the princes of the congregation, saying,

3 Ataroth, and Dibon, and Jazer, and Nimrah, and Heshbon, and Elealeh, and Shebam, and Nebo, and Beon,

4 Even the country which the LORD struck before the congregation of Israel, is a land for cattle, and your servants have cattle:

5 Wherefore, said they, if we have found grace in your sight, let this land be given unto your servants for a possession, and bring us not over Jordan.

6 And Moses said unto the children of Gad and to the children of Reuben, Shall your brethren go to war, and shall you sit here?

7 And wherefore discourage you the heart of the children of Israel from going over into the land which the LORD has given them?

8 Thus did your fathers, when I sent them from Kadesh-barnea to see the land.

9 For when they went up unto the valley of Eshcol, and saw the land, they discouraged the heart of the children of Israel, that they should not go into the land which the LORD had given them.

10 And the LORD's anger was kindled the same time, and he sware, saying,

11 Surely none of the men that came up out of Egypt, from twenty years old and upward, shall see the land which I sware unto Abraham, unto Isaac, and unto Jacob; because they have not wholly followed me:

12 Save Caleb the son of Jephunneh the Kenezite, and Joshua the son of Nun: for they have wholly followed the LORD.

13 And the LORD's anger was kindled against Israel, and he made them wander in the wilderness forty years, until all the generation, that had done evil in the sight of the LORD, was consumed.

14 And, behold, you are risen up in your fathers' stead, an increase of sinful men, to augment yet the fierce anger of the LORD toward Israel.

15 For if you turn away from after him, he will yet again leave them in the wilderness; and you shall destroy all this people.

16 And they came near unto him, and said, We will build sheepfolds here for our cattle, and cities for our little ones:

17 But we ourselves will go ready armed before the children of Israel, until we have brought them unto their place: and our little ones shall dwell in the fenced cities because of the inhabitants of the land.

18 We will not return unto our houses, until the children of Israel have inherited every man his inheritance.

19 For we will not inherit with them on yonder side Jordan, or forward; because our inheritance is fallen to us on this side Jordan eastward.

20 And Moses said unto them, If you will do this thing, if you will go armed before the LORD to war,

21 And will go all of you armed over Jordan before the LORD, until he has driven out his enemies from before him,

22 And the land be subdued before the LORD: then afterward you shall return, and be guiltless before the LORD, and before Israel; and this land shall be your possession before the LORD.

23 But if you will not do so, behold, you have sinned against the LORD: and be sure your sin will find you out.

24 Build you cities for your little ones, and folds for your sheep; and do that which has proceeded out of your mouth.

25 And the children of Gad and the children of Reuben spake unto Moses, saying, Your servants will do as my lord commandeth.

26 Our little ones, our wives, our flocks, and all our cattle, shall be there in the cities of Gilead:

27 But your servants will pass over, every man armed for war, before the LORD to battle, as my lord saith.

28 So concerning them Moses commanded Eleazar the priest, and Joshua the son of Nun, and the chief fathers of the tribes of the children of Israel:

29 And Moses said unto them, If the children of Gad and the children of Reuben will pass with you over Jordan, every man armed to battle, before the LORD, and the land shall be subdued before you; then you shall give them the land of Gilead for a possession:

30 But if they will not pass over with you armed, they shall have possessions among you in the land of Canaan.

31 And the children of Gad and the children of Reuben answered, saying, As the LORD has said unto your servants, so will we do.

32 We will pass over armed before the LORD into the land of Canaan, that the possession of our inheritance on this side Jordan may be ours.

33 And Moses gave unto them, even to the children of Gad, and to the children of Reuben, and unto half the tribe of Manasseh the son of Joseph, the kingdom of Sihon king of the Amorites, and the kingdom of Og king of Bashan, the land, with the cities thereof in the coasts, even the cities of the country round about.

34 And the children of Gad built Dibon, and Ataroth, and Aroer,

35 And Atroth, Shophan, and Jaazer, and Jogbehah,

36 And Beth-nimrah, and Beth-haran, fenced cities: and folds for sheep.

37 And the children of Reuben built Heshbon, and Elealeh, and Kirjathaim,

38 And Nebo, and Baal-meon, (their names being changed,) and Shibmah: and gave other names unto the cities which they builded.

39 And the children of Machir the son of Manasseh went to Gilead, and took it, and dispossessed the Amorite which was in it.

40 And Moses gave Gilead unto Machir the son of Manasseh; and he dwelt therein.

41 And Jair the son of Manasseh went and took the small towns thereof, and called them Havoth-jair.

42 And Nobah went and took Kenath, and the villages thereof, and called it Nobah, after his own name.

CHAPTER 33

THESE are the journeys of the children of Israel, which went forth out of the land of Egypt with their armies under the hand of Moses and Aaron.

2 And Moses wrote their goings out according to their journeys by the commandment of the LORD: and these are their journeys according to their goings out.

3 And they departed from Rameses in the first month, on the fifteenth day of the first month; on the morrow after the passover the children of Israel went out with an high hand in the sight of all the Egyptians.

4 For the Egyptians buried all their firstborn, which the LORD had smitten among them: upon their gods also the LORD executed judgments.

5 And the children of Israel removed from Rameses, and pitched in Succoth.

6 And they departed from Succoth, and pitched in Etham, which is in the edge of the wilderness.

7 And they removed from Etham, and turned again unto Pi-hahiroth, which is before Baal-zephon: and they pitched before Migdol.

8 And they departed from before Pi-hahiroth, and passed through the midst of the sea into the wilderness, and went three days' journey in the wilderness of Etham, and pitched in Marah.

9 And they removed from Marah, and came unto Elim: and in Elim were twelve fountains of water, and threescore and ten palm trees; and they pitched there.

10 And they removed from Elim, and encamped by the Red sea.

11 And they removed from the Red sea, and encamped in the wilderness of Sin.

12 And they took their journey out of the wilderness of Sin, and encamped in Dophkah.

13 And they departed from Dophkah, and encamped in Alush.

14 And they removed from Alush, and encamped at Rephidim, where was no water for the people to drink.

15 And they departed from Rephidim, and pitched in the wilderness of Sinai.

16 And they removed from the desert of Sinai, and pitched at Kibroth-hattaavah.

17 And they departed from Kibroth-hattaavah, and encamped at Hazeroth.

18 And they departed from Hazeroth, and pitched in Rithmah.

19 And they departed from Rithmah, and pitched at Rimmon-parez.

20 And they departed from Rimmon-parez, and pitched in Libnah.

21 And they removed from Libnah, and pitched at Rissah.

22 And they journeyed from Rissah, and pitched in Kehelathah.

23 And they went from Kehelathah, and pitched in mount Shapher.

24 And they removed from mount Shapher, and encamped in Haradah.

25 And they removed from Haradah, and pitched in Makheloth.

26 And they removed from Makheloth, and encamped at Tahath.

27 And they departed from Tahath, and pitched at Tarah.

28 And they removed from Tarah, and pitched in Mithcah.

29 And they went from Mithcah, and pitched in Hashmonah.

30 And they departed from Hashmonah, and encamped at Moseroth.

31 And they departed from Moseroth, and pitched in Bene-jaakan.

32 And they removed from Bene-jaakan, and encamped at Hor-hagidgad.

33 And they went from Hor-hagidgad, and pitched in Jotbathah.

34 And they removed from Jotbathah, and encamped at Ebronah.

35 And they departed from Ebronah, and encamped at Ezion-gaber.

36 And they removed from Ezion-gaber, and pitched in the wilderness of Zin, which is Kadesh.

37 And they removed from Kadesh, and pitched in mount Hor, in the edge of the land of Edom.

38 And Aaron the priest went up into mount Hor at the commandment of the LORD, and died there, in the fortieth year after the children of Israel were come out of the land of Egypt, in the first day of the fifth month.

39 And Aaron was an hundred and twenty and three years old when he died in mount Hor.

40 And king Arad the Canaanite, which dwelt in the south in the land of Canaan, heard of the coming of the children of Israel.

41 And they departed from mount Hor, and pitched in Zalmonah.

42 And they departed from Zalmonah, and pitched in Punon.

43 And they departed from Punon, and pitched in Oboth.

44 And they departed from Oboth, and pitched in Ije-abarim, in the border of Moab.

45 And they departed from Iim, and pitched in Dibon-gad.

46 And they removed from Dibon-gad, and encamped in Almon-diblathaim.

47 And they removed from Almon-diblathaim, and pitched in the mountains of Abarim, before Nebo.

48 And they departed from the mountains of Abarim, and pitched in the plains of Moab by Jordan near Jericho.

49 And they pitched by Jordan, from Beth-jesimoth even unto Abel-shittim in the plains of Moab.

50 And the LORD spake unto Moses in the plains of Moab by Jordan near Jericho, saying,

51 Speak unto the children of Israel, and say unto them, When you are passed over Jordan into the land of Canaan;

52 Then you shall drive out all the inhabitants of the land from before you, and destroy all their pictures, and destroy all their molten images, and quite pluck down all their high places:

53 And you shall dispossess the inhabitants of the land, and dwell therein: for I have given you the land to possess it.

54 And you shall divide the land by lot for an inheritance among your families: and to the more you shall give the more inheritance, and to the fewer you shall give the less inheritance: every man's inheritance shall be in the place where his lot falleth; according to the tribes of your fathers you shall inherit.

55 But if you will not drive out the inhabitants of the land from before you; then it shall come to pass, that those which you let remain of them shall be pricks in your eyes, and thorns in your sides, and shall vex you in the land wherein you dwell.

56 Moreover it shall come to pass, that I shall do unto you, as I thought to do unto them.

CHAPTER 34

AND the LORD spake unto Moses, saying,

2 Command the children of Israel, and say unto them, When you come into the land of Canaan; (this is the land that shall fall unto you for an inheritance, even the land of Canaan with the coasts thereof:)

3 Then your south quarter shall be from the wilderness of Zin along by the coast of Edom, and your south border shall be the outmost coast of the salt sea eastward:

4 And your border shall turn from the south to the ascent of Akrabbim, and pass on to Zin: and the going forth thereof shall be from the south to Kadesh-barnea, and shall go on to Hazar-addar, and pass on to Azmon:

5 And the border shall fetch a compass from Azmon unto the river of Egypt, and the goings out of it shall be at the sea.

6 And as for the western border, you shall even have the great sea for a border: this shall be your west border.

7 And this shall be your north border: from the great sea you shall point out for you mount Hor:

8 From mount Hor you shall point out your border unto the entrance of Hamath; and the goings forth of the border shall be to Zedad:

9 And the border shall go on to Ziphron, and the goings out of it shall be at Hazar-enan: this shall be your north border.

10 And you shall point out your east border from Hazar-enan to Shepham:

11 And the coast shall go down from Shepham to Riblah, on the east side of Ain; and the border shall descend, and shall reach unto the side of the sea of Chinnereth eastward:

12 And the border shall go down to Jordan, and the goings out of it shall be at the salt sea: this shall be your land with the coasts thereof round about.

13 And Moses commanded the children of Israel, saying, This is the land which you shall inherit by lot, which the LORD commanded to give unto the nine tribes, and to the half tribe:

14 For the tribe of the children of Reuben according to the house of their fathers, and the tribe of the children of Gad according to the house of their fathers, have received their inheritance; and half the tribe of Manasseh have received their inheritance:

15 The two tribes and the half tribe have received their inheritance on this side Jordan near Jericho eastward, toward the sunrising.

16 And the LORD spake unto Moses, saying,

17 These are the names of the men which shall divide the land unto you: Eleazar the priest, and Joshua the son of Nun.

18 And you shall take one prince of every tribe, to divide the land by inheritance.

19 And the names of the men are these: Of the tribe of Judah, Caleb the son of Jephunneh.

20 And of the tribe of the children of Simeon, Shemuel the son of Ammihud.

21 Of the tribe of Benjamin, Elidad the son of Chislon.

22 And the prince of the tribe of the children of Dan, Bukki the son of Jogli.

23 The prince of the children of Joseph, for the tribe of the children of Manasseh, Hanniel the son of Ephod.

24 And the prince of the tribe of the children of Ephraim, Kemuel the son of Shiphtan.

25 And the prince of the tribe of the children of Zebulun, Elizaphan the son of Parnach.

26 And the prince of the tribe of the children of Issachar, Paltiel the son of Azzan.

27 And the prince of the tribe of the children of Asher, Ahihud the son of Shelomi.

28 And the prince of the tribe of the children of Naphtali, Pedahel the son of Ammihud.

29 These are they whom the LORD commanded to divide the inheritance unto the children of Israel in the land of Canaan.

CHAPTER 35

AND the LORD spake unto Moses in the plains of Moab by Jordan near Jericho, saying,

2 Command the children of Israel, that they give unto the Levites of the inheritance of their possession cities to dwell in; and you shall give also unto the Levites suburbs for the cities round about them.

3 And the cities shall they have to dwell in; and the suburbs of them shall be for their cattle, and for their goods, and for all their beasts.

4 And the suburbs of the cities, which you shall give unto the Levites, shall reach from the wall of the city and outward a thousand cubits round about.

5 And you shall measure from without the city on the east side two thousand cubits, and on the south side two thousand cubits, and on the west side two thousand cubits, and on the north side two thousand cubits; and the city shall be in the midst: this shall be to them the suburbs of the cities.

6 And among the cities which you shall give unto the Levites there shall be six cities for refuge, which you shall appoint for the manslayer, that he may flee thither: and to them you shall add forty and two cities:

7 So all the cities which you shall give to the Levites shall be forty and eight cities: them shall you give with their suburbs.

8 And the cities which you shall give shall be of the possession of the children of Israel: from them that have many you shall give many; but from them that have few you shall give few: every one shall give of his cities unto the Levites according to his inheritance which he inheriteth.

9 And the LORD spake unto Moses, saying,

10 Speak unto the children of Israel, and say unto them, When you be come over Jordan into the land of Canaan;

11 Then you shall appoint you cities to be cities of refuge for you; that the slayer may flee thither, which killeth any person at unawares.

12 And they shall be unto you cities for refuge from the avenger; that the manslayer die not, until he stand before the congregation in judgment.

13 And of these cities which you shall give six cities shall you have for refuge.

14 You shall give three cities on this side Jordan, and three cities shall you give in the land of Canaan, which shall be cities of refuge.

15 These six cities shall be a refuge, both for the children of Israel, and for the stranger, and for the sojourner among them: that every one that killeth any person unawares may flee thither.

16 And if he strike him with an instrument of iron, so that he die, he is a murderer: the murderer shall surely be put to death.

17 And if he strike him with throwing a stone, wherewith he may die, and he die, he is a murderer: the murderer shall surely be put to death.

18 Or if he strike him with an hand weapon of wood, wherewith he may die, and he die, he is a murderer: the murderer shall surely be put to death.

19 The revenger of blood himself shall slay the murderer: when he meeteth him, he shall slay him.

20 But if he thrust him of hatred, or hurl at him by laying of wait, that he die;

21 Or in enmity strike him with his hand, that he die: he that struck him shall surely be put to death; for he is a murderer: the revenger of blood shall slay the murderer, when he meeteth him.

22 But if he thrust him suddenly without enmity, or have cast upon him any thing without laying of wait,

23 Or with any stone, wherewith a man may die, seeing him not, and cast it upon him, that he die, and was not his enemy, neither sought his harm:

24 Then the congregation shall judge between the slayer and the revenger of blood according to these judgments:

25 And the congregation shall deliver the slayer out of the hand of the revenger of blood, and the congregation shall restore him to the city of his refuge, whither he was fled: and he shall abide in it unto the death of the high priest, which was anointed with the holy oil.

26 But if the slayer shall at any time come without the border of the city of his refuge, whither he was fled;

27 And the revenger of blood find him without the borders of the city of his refuge, and the revenger of blood kill the slayer; he shall not be guilty of blood:

28 Because he should have remained in the city of his refuge until the death of the high priest: but after the death of the high priest the slayer shall return into the land of his possession.

29 So these things shall be for a statute of judgment unto you throughout your generations in all your dwellings.

30 Whoso killeth any person, the murderer shall be put to death by the mouth of witnesses: but one witness shall not testify against any person to cause him to die.

31 Moreover you shall take no satisfaction for the life of a murderer, which is guilty of death: but he shall be surely put to death.

32 And you shall take no satisfaction for him that is fled to the city of his refuge, that he should come again to dwell in the land, until the death of the priest.

33 So you shall not pollute the land wherein you are: for blood it defileth the land: and the land cannot be cleansed of the blood that is shed therein, but by the blood of him that shed it.

34 Defile not therefore the land which you shall inhabit, wherein I dwell: for I the LORD dwell among the children of Israel.

CHAPTER 36

AND the chief fathers of the families of the children of Gilead, the son of Machir, the son of Manasseh, of the families of the sons of Joseph, came near, and spake before Moses, and before the princes, the chief fathers of the children of Israel:

2 And they said, The LORD commanded my lord to give the land for an inheritance by lot to the children of Israel: and my lord was commanded by the LORD to give the inheritance of Zelophehad our brother unto his daughters.

3 And if they be married to any of the sons of the other tribes of the children of Israel, then shall their inheritance be taken from the inheritance of our fathers, and shall be put to the inheritance of the tribe whereunto they are received: so shall it be taken from the lot of our inheritance.

4 And when the jubile of the children of Israel shall be, then shall their inheritance be put unto the inheritance of the tribe whereunto they are received: so shall their inheritance be taken away from the inheritance of the tribe of our fathers.

5 And Moses commanded the children of Israel according to the word of the LORD, saying, The tribe of the sons of Joseph has said well.

6 This is the thing which the LORD doth command concerning the daughters of Zelophehad, saying, Let them marry to whom they think best; only to the family of the tribe of their father shall they marry.

7 So shall not the inheritance of the children of Israel remove from tribe to tribe: for every one of the children of Israel shall keep himself to the inheritance of the tribe of his fathers.

8 And every daughter, that possesseth an inheritance in any tribe of the children of Israel, shall be wife unto one of the family of the tribe of her father, that the children of Israel may enjoy every man the inheritance of his fathers.

9 Neither shall the inheritance remove from one tribe to another tribe; but every one of the tribes of the children of Israel shall keep himself to his own inheritance.

10 Even as the LORD commanded Moses, so did the daughters of Zelophehad:

11 For Mahlah, Tirzah, and Hoglah, and Milcah, and Noah, the daughters of Zelophehad, were married unto their father's brothers' sons:

12 And they were married into the families of the sons of Manasseh the son of Joseph, and their inheritance remained in the tribe of the family of their father.

13 These are the commandments and the judgments, which the LORD commanded by the hand of Moses unto the children of Israel in the plains of Moab by Jordan near Jericho.

THE FIFTH BOOK OF MOSES,
CALLED
DEUTERONOMY.

CHAPTER 1

THESE be the words which Moses spake unto all Israel on this side Jordan in the wilderness, in the plain over against the Red sea, between Paran, and Tophel, and Laban, and Hazeroth, and Dizahab.

2 (There are eleven days' journey from Horeb by the way of mount Seir unto Kadesh-barnea.)

3 And it came to pass in the fortieth year, in the eleventh month, on the first day of the month, that Moses spake unto the children of Israel, according unto all that the LORD had given him in commandment unto them;

4 After he had slain Sihon the king of the Amorites, which dwelt in Heshbon, and Og the king of Bashan, which dwelt at Astaroth in Edrei:

5 On this side Jordan, in the land of Moab, began Moses to declare this law, saying,

6 The LORD our God spake unto us in Horeb, saying, You have dwelt long enough in this mount:

7 Turn you, and take your journey, and go to the mount of the Amorites, and unto all the places nigh thereunto, in the plain, in the hills, and in the vale, and in the south, and by the sea side, to the land of the Canaanites, and unto Lebanon, unto the great river, the river Euphrates.

8 Behold, I have set the land before you: go in and possess the land which the LORD sware unto your fathers, Abraham, Isaac, and Jacob, to give unto them and to their seed after them.

9And I spake unto you at that time, saying, I am not able to bear you myself alone:

10 The LORD your God has multiplied you, and, behold, you are this day as the stars of heaven for multitude.

11 (The LORD God of your fathers make you a thousand times so many more as you are, and bless you, as he has promised you!)

12 How can I myself alone bear your cumbrance, and your burden, and your strife?

13 Take you wise men, and understanding, and known among your tribes, and I will make them rulers over you.

14 And you answered me, and said, The thing which you have spoken is good for us to do.

15 So I took the chief of your tribes, wise men, and known, and made them heads over you, captains over thousands, and captains over hundreds, and captains over fifties, and captains over tens, and officers among your tribes.

16 And I charged your judges at that time, saying, Hear the causes between your brethren, and judge righteously between every man and his brother, and the stranger that is with him.

17 You shall not respect persons in judgment; but you shall hear the small as well as the great; you shall not be afraid of the face of man; for the judgment is God's: and the cause that is too hard for you, bring it unto me, and I will hear it.

18 And I commanded you at that time all the things which you should do.

19And when we departed from Horeb, we went through all that great and terrible wilderness, which you saw by the way of the mountain of the Amorites, as the LORD our God commanded us; and we came to Kadesh-barnea.

20 And I said unto you, You are come unto the mountain of the Amorites, which the LORD our God doth give unto us.

21 Behold, the LORD your God has set the land before you: go up and possess it, as the LORD God of your fathers has said unto you; fear not, neither be discouraged.

22And you came near unto me every one of you, and said, We will send men before us, and they shall search us out the land, and bring us word again by what way we must go up, and into what cities we shall come.

23 And the saying pleased me well: and I took twelve men of you, one of a tribe:

24 And they turned and went up into the mountain, and came unto the valley of Eshcol, and searched it out.

25 And they took of the fruit of the land in their hands, and brought it down unto us, and brought us word again, and said, It is a good land which the LORD our God doth give us.

26 Notwithstanding you would not go up, but rebelled against the commandment of the LORD your God:

27 And you murmured in your tents, and said, Because the LORD hated us, he has brought us forth out of the land of Egypt, to deliver us into the hand of the Amorites, to destroy us.

28 Whither shall we go up? our brethren have discouraged our heart, saying, The people is greater and taller than we; the cities are great and walled up to heaven; and moreover we have seen the sons of the Anakims there.

29 Then I said unto you, Dread not, neither be afraid of them.

30 The LORD your God which goeth before you, he shall fight for you, according to all that he did for you in Egypt before your eyes;

31 And in the wilderness, where you have seen how that the LORD your God bare you, as a man doth bear his son, in all the way that you went, until you came into this place.

32 Yet in this thing you did not believe the LORD your God,

33 Who went in the way before you, to search you out a place to pitch your tents in, in fire by night, to shew you by what way you should go, and in a cloud by day.

34 And the LORD heard the voice of your words, and was wroth, and sware, saying,

35 Surely there shall not one of these men of this evil generation see that good land, which I sware to give unto your fathers,

36 Save Caleb the son of Jephunneh; he shall see it, and to him will I give the land that he has trodden upon, and to his children, because he has wholly followed the LORD.

37 Also the LORD was angry with me for your sakes, saying, You also shalt not go in thither.

38 But Joshua the son of Nun, which standeth before you, he shall go in thither: encourage him: for he shall cause Israel to inherit it.

39 Moreover your little ones, which you said should be a prey, and your children, which in that day had no knowledge between good and evil, they shall go in thither, and unto them will I give it, and they shall possess it.

40 But as for you, turn you, and take your journey into the wilderness by the way of the Red sea.

41 Then you answered and said unto me, We have sinned against the LORD, we will go up and fight, according to all that the LORD our God commanded us. And when you had girded on every man his weapons of war, you were ready to go up into the hill.

42 And the LORD said unto me, Say unto them, Go not up, neither fight; for I am not among you; lest you be smitten before your enemies.

43 So I spake unto you; and you would not hear, but rebelled against the commandment of the LORD, and went presumptuously up into the hill.

44 And the Amorites, which dwelt in that mountain, came out against you, and chased you, as bees do, and destroyed you in Seir, even unto Hormah.

45 And you returned and wept before the LORD; but the LORD would not hearken to your voice, nor give ear unto you.

46 So you abode in Kadesh many days, according unto the days that you abode there.

CHAPTER 2

THEN we turned, and took our journey into the wilderness by the way of the Red sea, as the LORD spake unto me: and we compassed mount Seir many days.

2 And the LORD spake unto me, saying,

3 You have compassed this mountain long enough: turn you northward.

4 And command you the people, saying, You are to pass through the coast of your brethren the children of Esau, which dwell in Seir; and they shall be afraid of you: take you good heed unto yourselves therefore:

5 Meddle not with them; for I will not give you of their land, no, not so much as a foot breadth; because I have given mount Seir unto Esau for a possession.

6 You shall buy meat of them for money, that you may eat; and you shall also buy water of them for money, that you may drink.

7 For the LORD your God has blessed you in all the works of your hand: he knoweth your walking through this great wilderness: these forty years the LORD your God has been with you; you have lacked nothing.

8 And when we passed by from our brethren the children of Esau, which dwelt in Seir, through the way of the plain from Elath, and from Ezion-gaber, we turned and passed by the way of the wilderness of Moab.

9 And the LORD said unto me, Distress not the Moabites, neither contend with them in battle: for I will not give you of their land for a possession; because I have given Ar unto the children of Lot for a possession.

10 The Emims dwelt therein in times past, a people great, and many, and tall, as the Anakims;

11 Which also were accounted giants, as the Anakims; but the Moabites call them Emims.

12 The Horims also dwelt in Seir beforetime; but the children of Esau succeeded them, when they had destroyed them from before them, and dwelt in their stead; as Israel did unto the land of his possession, which the LORD gave unto them.

13 Now rise up, said I, and get you over the brook Zered. And we went over the brook Zered.

14 And the space in which we came from Kadesh-barnea, until we were come over the brook Zered, was thirty and eight years; until all the generation of the men of war were wasted out from among the host, as the LORD sware unto them.

15 For indeed the hand of the LORD was against them, to destroy them from among the host, until they were consumed.

16 So it came to pass, when all the men of war were consumed and dead from among the people,

17 That the LORD spake unto me, saying,

18 You are to pass over through Ar, the coast of Moab, this day:

19 And when you comest nigh over against the children of Ammon, distress them not, nor meddle with them: for I will not give you of the land of the children of Ammon any possession; because I have given it unto the children of Lot for a possession.

20 (That also was accounted a land of giants: giants dwelt therein in old time; and the Ammonites call them Zamzummims;

21 A people great, and many, and tall, as the Anakims; but the LORD destroyed them before them; and they succeeded them, and dwelt in their stead:

22 As he did to the children of Esau, which dwelt in Seir, when he destroyed the Horims from before them; and they succeeded them, and dwelt in their stead even unto this day:

23 And the Avims which dwelt in Hazerim, even unto Azzah, the Caphtorims, which came forth out of Caphtor, destroyed them, and dwelt in their stead.)

24 Rise you up, take your journey, and pass over the river Arnon: behold, I have given into yours hand Sihon the Amorite, king of Heshbon, and his land: begin to possess it, and contend with him in battle.

25 This day will I begin to put the dread of you and the fear of you upon the nations that are under the whole heaven, who shall hear report of you, and shall tremble, and be in anguish because of you.

26 And I sent messengers out of the wilderness of Kedemoth unto Sihon king of Heshbon with words of peace, saying,

27 Let me pass through your land: I will go along by the high way, I will neither turn unto the right hand nor to the left.

28 You shalt sell me meat for money, that I may eat; and give me water for money, that I may drink: only I will pass through on my feet;

29 (As the children of Esau which dwell in Seir, and the Moabites which dwell in Ar, did unto me;) until I shall pass over Jordan into the land which the LORD our God giveth us.

30 But Sihon king of Heshbon would not let us pass by him: for the LORD your God hardened his spirit, and made his heart obstinate, that he might deliver him into your hand, as appeareth this day.

31 And the LORD said unto me, Behold, I have begun to give Sihon and his land before you: begin to possess, that you mayest inherit his land.

32 Then Sihon came out against us, he and all his people, to fight at Jahaz.

33 And the LORD our God delivered him before us; and we struck him, and his sons, and all his people.

34 And we took all his cities at that time, and utterly destroyed the men, and the women, and the little ones, of every city, we left none to remain:

35 Only the cattle we took for a prey unto ourselves, and the spoil of the cities which we took.

36 From Aroer, which is by the brink of the river of Arnon, and from the city that is by the river, even unto Gilead, there was not one city too strong for us: the LORD our God delivered all unto us:

37 Only unto the land of the children of Ammon you camest not, nor unto any place of the river Jabbok, nor unto the cities in the mountains, nor unto whatsoever the LORD our God forbad us.

CHAPTER 3

THEN we turned, and went up the way to Bashan: and Og the king of Bashan came out against us, he and all his people, to battle at Edrei.

2 And the LORD said unto me, Fear him not: for I will deliver him, and all his people, and his land, into your hand; and you shalt do unto him as you did unto Sihon king of the Amorites, which dwelt at Heshbon.

3 So the LORD our God delivered into our hands Og also, the king of Bashan, and all his people: and we struck him until none was left to him remaining.

4 And we took all his cities at that time, there was not a city which we took not from them, threescore cities, all the region of Argob, the kingdom of Og in Bashan.

5 All these cities were fenced with high walls, gates, and bars; beside unwalled towns a great many.

6 And we utterly destroyed them, as we did unto Sihon king of Heshbon, utterly destroying the men, women, and children, of every city.

7 But all the cattle, and the spoil of the cities, we took for a prey to ourselves.

8 And we took at that time out of the hand of the two kings of the Amorites the land that was on this side Jordan, from the river of Arnon unto mount Hermon;

9 (Which Hermon the Sidonians call Sirion; and the Amorites call it Shenir;)

10 All the cities of the plain, and all Gilead, and all Bashan, unto Salchah and Edrei, cities of the kingdom of Og in Bashan.

11 For only Og king of Bashan remained of the remnant of giants; behold, his bedstead was a bedstead of iron; is it not in Rabbath of the children of Ammon? nine cubits was the length thereof, and four cubits the breadth of it, after the cubit of a man.

12 And this land, which we possessed at that time, from Aroer, which is by the river Arnon, and half mount Gilead, and the cities thereof, gave I unto the Reubenites and to the Gadites.

13 And the rest of Gilead, and all Bashan, being the kingdom of Og, gave I unto the half tribe of Manasseh; all the region of Argob, with all Bashan, which was called the land of giants.

14 Jair the son of Manasseh took all the country of Argob unto the coasts of Geshuri and Maachathi; and called them after his own name, Bashan-havoth-jair, unto this day.

15 And I gave Gilead unto Machir.

16 And unto the Reubenites and unto the Gadites I gave from Gilead even unto the river Arnon half the valley, and the border even unto the river Jabbok, which is the border of the children of Ammon;

17 The plain also, and Jordan, and the coast thereof, from Chinnereth even unto the sea of the plain, even the salt sea, under Ashdoth-pisgah eastward.

18 And I commanded you at that time, saying, The LORD your God has given you this land to possess it: you shall pass over armed before your brethren the children of Israel, all that are meet for the war.

19 But your wives, and your little ones, and your cattle, (for I know that you have much cattle,) shall abide in your cities which I have given you;

20 Until the LORD have given rest unto your brethren, as well as unto you, and until they also possess the land which the LORD your God has given them beyond Jordan: and then shall you return every man unto his possession, which I have given you.

21 And I commanded Joshua at that time, saying, Yours eyes have seen all that the LORD your God has done unto these two kings: so shall the LORD do unto all the kingdoms whither you passest.

22 You shall not fear them: for the LORD your God he shall fight for you.

23 And I besought the LORD at that time, saying,

24 O Lord GOD, you have begun to shew your servant your greatness, and your mighty hand: for what God is there in heaven or in earth, that can do according to your works, and according to your might?

25 I pray you, let me go over, and see the good land that is beyond Jordan, that goodly mountain, and Lebanon.

26 But the LORD was wroth with me for your sakes, and would not hear me: and the LORD said unto me, Let it suffice you; speak no more unto me of this matter.

27 Get you up into the top of Pisgah, and lift up yours eyes westward, and northward, and southward, and eastward, and behold it with yours eyes: for you shalt not go over this Jordan.

28 But charge Joshua, and encourage him, and strengthen him: for he shall go over before this people, and he shall cause them to inherit the land which you shalt see.

29 So we abode in the valley over against Beth-peor.

CHAPTER 4

NOW therefore hearken, O Israel, unto the statutes and unto the judgments, which I teach you, for to do them, that you may live, and go in and possess the land which the LORD God of your fathers giveth you.

2 You shall not add unto the word which I command you, neither shall you diminish ought from it, that you may keep the commandments of the LORD your God which I command you.

3 Your eyes have seen what the LORD did because of Baal-peor: for all the men that followed Baal-peor, the LORD your God has destroyed them from among you.

4 But you that did cleave unto the LORD your God are alive every one of you this day.

5 Behold, I have taught you statutes and judgments, even as the LORD my God commanded me, that you should do so in the land whither you go to possess it.

6 Keep therefore and do them; for this is your wisdom and your understanding in the sight of the nations, which shall hear all these statutes, and say, Surely this great nation is a wise and understanding people.

7 For what nation is there so great, who has God so nigh unto them, as the LORD our God is in all things that we call upon him for?

8 And what nation is there so great, that has statutes and judgments so righteous as all this law, which I set before you this day?

9 Only take heed to yourself, and keep your soul diligently, lest you forget the things which yours eyes have seen, and lest they depart from your heart all the days of your life: but teach them your sons, and your sons' sons;

10 Specially the day that you stoodest before the LORD your God in Horeb, when the LORD said unto me, Gather me the people together, and I will make them hear my words, that they may learn to fear me all the days that they shall live upon the earth, and that they may teach their children.

11 And you came near and stood under the mountain; and the mountain burned with fire unto the midst of heaven, with darkness, clouds, and thick darkness.

12 And the LORD spake unto you out of the midst of the fire: you heard the voice of the words, but saw no similitude; only you heard a voice.

13 And he declared unto you his covenant, which he commanded you to perform, even ten commandments; and he wrote them upon two tables of stone.

14 And the LORD commanded me at that time to teach you statutes and judgments, that you might do them in the land whither you go over to possess it.

15 Take you therefore good heed unto yourselves; for you saw no manner of similitude on the day that the LORD spake unto you in Horeb out of the midst of the fire:

16 Lest you corrupt yourselves, and make you a graven image, the similitude of any figure, the likeness of male or female,

17 The likeness of any beast that is on the earth, the likeness of any winged fowl that flieth in the air,

18 The likeness of any thing that creepeth on the ground, the likeness of any fish that is in the waters beneath the earth:

19 And lest you lift up yours eyes unto heaven, and when you seest the sun, and the moon, and the stars, even all the host of heaven, shouldest be driven to worship them, and serve them, which the LORD your God has divided unto all nations under the whole heaven.

20 But the LORD has taken you, and brought you forth out of the iron furnace, even out of Egypt, to be unto him a people of inheritance, as you are this day.

21 Furthermore the LORD was angry with me for your sakes, and sware that I should not go over Jordan, and that I should not go in unto that good land, which the LORD your God giveth you for an inheritance:

22 But I must die in this land, I must not go over Jordan: but you shall go over, and possess that good land.

23 Take heed unto yourselves, lest you forget the covenant of the LORD your God, which he made with you, and make you a graven image, or the likeness of any thing, which the LORD your God has forbidden you.

24 For the LORD your God is a consuming fire, even a jealous God.

25 When you shalt beget children, and children's children, and you shall have remained long in the land, and shall corrupt yourselves, and make a graven image, or the likeness of any thing, and shall do evil in the sight of the LORD your God, to provoke him to anger:

26 I call heaven and earth to witness against you this day, that you shall soon utterly perish from off the land whereunto you go over Jordan to possess it; you shall not prolong your days upon it, but shall utterly be destroyed.

27 And the LORD shall scatter you among the nations, and you shall be left few in number among the heathen, whither the LORD shall lead you.

28 And there you shall serve gods, the work of men's hands, wood and stone, which neither see, nor hear, nor eat, nor smell.

29 But if from thence you shalt seek the LORD your God, you shalt find him, if you seek him with all your heart and with all your soul.

30 When you are in tribulation, and all these things are come upon you, even in the latter days, if you turn to the LORD your God, and shalt be obedient unto his voice;

31 (For the LORD your God is a merciful God;) he will not forsake you, neither destroy you, nor forget the covenant of your fathers which he sware unto them.

32 For ask now of the days that are past, which were before you, since the day that God created man upon the earth, and ask from the one side of heaven unto the other, whether there has been any such thing as this great thing is, or has been heard like it?

33 Did ever people hear the voice of God speaking out of the midst of the fire, as you have heard, and live?

34 Or has God assayed to go and take him a nation from the midst of another nation, by temptations, by signs, and by wonders, and by war, and by a mighty hand, and by a stretched out arm, and by great terrors, according to all that the LORD your God did for you in Egypt before your eyes?

35 Unto you it was shewed, that you mightest know that the LORD he is God; there is none else beside him.

36 Out of heaven he made you to hear his voice, that he might instruct you: and upon earth he shewed you his great fire; and you heardest his words out of the midst of the fire.

37 And because he loved your fathers, therefore he chose their seed after them, and brought you out in his sight with his mighty power out of Egypt;

38 To drive out nations from before you greater and mightier than you are, to bring you in, to give you their land for an inheritance, as it is this day.

39 Know therefore this day, and consider it in yours heart, that the LORD he is God in heaven above, and upon the earth beneath: there is none else.

40 You shalt keep therefore his statutes, and his commandments, which I command you this day, that it may go well with you, and with your children after you, and that you mayest prolong your days upon the earth, which the LORD your God giveth you, for ever.

41 Then Moses severed three cities on this side Jordan toward the sunrising;

42 That the slayer might flee thither, which should kill his neighbour unawares, and hated him not in times past; and that fleeing unto one of these cities he might live:

43 Namely, Bezer in the wilderness, in the plain country, of the Reubenites; and Ramoth in Gilead, of the Gadites; and Golan in Bashan, of the Manassites.

44 And this is the law which Moses set before the children of Israel:

45 These are the testimonies, and the statutes, and the judgments, which Moses spake unto the children of Israel, after they came forth out of Egypt,

46 On this side Jordan, in the valley over against Beth-peor, in the land of Sihon king of the Amorites, who dwelt at Heshbon, whom Moses and the children of Israel struck, after they were come forth out of Egypt:

47 And they possessed his land, and the land of Og king of Bashan, two kings of the Amorites, which were on this side Jordan toward the sunrising;

48 From Aroer, which is by the bank of the river Arnon, even unto mount Sion, which is Hermon,

49 And all the plain on this side Jordan eastward, even unto the sea of the plain, under the springs of Pisgah.

CHAPTER 5

AND Moses called all Israel, and said unto them, Hear, O Israel, the statutes and judgments which I speak in your ears this day, that you may learn them, and keep, and do them.

2 The LORD our God made a covenant with us in Horeb.

3 The LORD made not this covenant with our fathers, but with us, even us, who are all of us here alive this day.

4 The LORD talked with you face to face in the mount out of the midst of the fire,

5 (I stood between the LORD and you at that time, to shew you the word of the LORD: for you were afraid by reason of the fire, and went not up into the mount;) saying,

6 I am the LORD your God, which brought you out of the land of Egypt, from the house of bondage.

7 You shalt have none other gods before me.

8 You shalt not make you any graven image, or any likeness of any thing that is in heaven above, or that is in the earth beneath, or that is in the waters beneath the earth:

9 You shalt not bow down yourself unto them, nor serve them: for I the LORD your God am a jealous God, visiting the iniquity of the fathers upon the children unto the third and fourth generation of them that hate me,

10 And shewing mercy unto thousands of them that love me and keep my commandments.

11 You shalt not take the name of the LORD your God in vain: for the LORD will not hold him guiltless that taketh his name in vain.

12 Keep the sabbath day to sanctify it, as the LORD your God has commanded you.

13 Six days you shalt labour, and do all your work:

14 But the seventh day is the sabbath of the LORD your God: in it you shalt not do any work, you , nor your son, nor your daughter, nor your manservant, nor your maidservant, nor yours ox, nor yours ass, nor any of your cattle, nor your stranger that is within your gates; that your manservant and your maidservant may rest as well as you .

15 And remember that you wast a servant in the land of Egypt, and that the LORD your God brought you out thence through a mighty hand and by a stretched out arm: therefore the LORD your God commanded you to keep the sabbath day.

16 Honour your father and your mother, as the LORD your God has commanded you; that your days may be prolonged, and that it may go well with you, in the land which the LORD your God giveth you.

17 You shalt not kill.

18 Neither shalt you commit adultery.

19 Neither shalt you steal.

20 Neither shalt you bear false witness against your neighbour.

21 Neither shalt you desire your neighbour's wife, neither shalt you covet your neighbour's house, his field, or his manservant, or his maidservant, his ox, or his ass, or any thing that is your neighbour's.

22 These words the LORD spake unto all your assembly in the mount out of the midst of the fire, of the cloud, and of the thick darkness, with a great voice: and he added no more. And he wrote them in two tables of stone, and delivered them unto me.

23 And it came to pass, when you heard the voice out of the midst of the darkness, (for the mountain did burn with fire,) that you came near unto me, even all the heads of your tribes, and your elders;

24 And you said, Behold, the LORD our God has shewed us his glory and his greatness, and we have heard his voice out of the midst of the fire: we have seen this day that God doth talk with man, and he liveth.

25 Now therefore why should we die? for this great fire will consume us: if we hear the voice of the LORD our God any more, then we shall die.

26 For who is there of all flesh, that has heard the voice of the living God speaking out of the midst of the fire, as we have, and lived?

27 Go you near, and hear all that the LORD our God shall say: and speak you unto us all that the LORD our God shall speak unto you; and we will hear it, and do it.

28 And the LORD heard the voice of your words, when you spake unto me; and the LORD said unto me, I have heard the voice of the words of this people, which they have spoken unto you: they have well said all that they have spoken.

29 O that there were such an heart in them, that they would fear me, and keep all my commandments always, that it might be well with them, and with their children for ever!

30 Go say to them, Get you into your tents again.

31 But as for you, stand you here by me, and I will speak unto you all the commandments, and the statutes, and the judgments, which you shalt teach them, that they may do them in the land which I give them to possess it.

32 You shall observe to do therefore as the LORD your God has commanded you: you shall not turn aside to the right hand or to the left.

33 You shall walk in all the ways which the LORD your God has commanded you, that you may live, and that it may be well with you, and that you may prolong your days in the land which you shall possess.

CHAPTER 6

NOW these are the commandments, the statutes, and the judgments, which the LORD your God commanded to teach you, that you might do them in the land whither you go to possess it:

2 That you mightest fear the LORD your God, to keep all his statutes and his commandments, which I command you, you , and your son, and your son's son, all the days of your life; and that your days may be prolonged.

3 Hear therefore, O Israel, and observe to do it; that it may be well with you, and that you may increase mightily, as the LORD God of your fathers has promised you, in the land that floweth with milk and honey.

4 Hear, O Israel: The LORD our God is one LORD:

5 And you shalt love the LORD your God with all yours heart, and with all your soul, and with all your might.

6 And these words, which I command you this day, shall be in yours heart:

7 And you shalt teach them diligently unto your children, and shalt talk of them when you sittest in yours house, and when you walkest by the way, and when you liest down, and when you risest up.

8 And you shalt bind them for a sign upon yours hand, and they shall be as frontlets between yours eyes.

9 And you shalt write them upon the posts of your house, and on your gates.

10 And it shall be, when the LORD your God shall have brought you into the land which he sware unto your fathers, to Abraham, to Isaac, and to Jacob, to give you great and goodly cities, which you buildedst not,

11 And houses full of all good things, which you filledst not, and wells digged, which you diggedst not, vineyards and olive trees, which you plantedst not; when you shalt have eaten and be full;

12 Then beware lest you forget the LORD, which brought you forth out of the land of Egypt, from the house of bondage.

13 You shalt fear the LORD your God, and serve him, and shalt swear by his name.

14 You shall not go after other gods, of the gods of the people which are round about you;

15 (For the LORD your God is a jealous God among you) lest the anger of the LORD your God be kindled against you, and destroy you from off the face of the earth.

16 You shall not tempt the LORD your God, as you tempted him in Massah.

17 You shall diligently keep the commandments of the LORD your God, and his testimonies, and his statutes, which he has commanded you.

18 And you shalt do that which is right and good in the sight of the LORD: that it may be well with you, and that you mayest go in and possess the good land which the LORD sware unto your fathers,

19 To cast out all yours enemies from before you, as the LORD has spoken.

20 And when your son asketh you in time to come, saying, What mean the testimonies, and the statutes, and the judgments, which the LORD our God has commanded you?

21 Then you shalt say unto your son, We were Pharaoh's bondmen in Egypt; and the LORD brought us out of Egypt with a mighty hand:

22 And the LORD shewed signs and wonders, great and sore, upon Egypt, upon Pharaoh, and upon all his household, before our eyes:

23 And he brought us out from thence, that he might bring us in, to give us the land which he sware unto our fathers.

24 And the LORD commanded us to do all these statutes, to fear the LORD our God, for our good always, that he might preserve us alive, as it is at this day.

25 And it shall be our righteousness, if we observe to do all these commandments before the LORD our God, as he has commanded us.

CHAPTER 7

WHEN the LORD your God shall bring you into the land whither you go to possess it, and has cast out many nations before you, the Hittites, and the Girgashites, and the Amorites, and the Canaanites, and the Perizzites, and the Hivites, and the Jebusites, seven nations greater and mightier than you ;

2 And when the LORD your God shall deliver them before you; you shalt strike them, and utterly destroy them; you shalt make no covenant with them, nor shew mercy unto them:

3 Neither shalt you make marriages with them; your daughter you shalt not give unto his son, nor his daughter shalt you take unto your son.

4 For they will turn away your son from following me, that they may serve other gods: so will the anger of the LORD be kindled against you, and destroy you suddenly.

5 But thus shall you deal with them; you shall destroy their altars, and break down their images, and cut down their groves, and burn their graven images with fire.

6 For you are an holy people unto the LORD your God: the LORD your God has chosen you to be a special people unto himself, above all people that are upon the face of the earth.

7 The LORD did not set his love upon you, nor choose you, because you were more in number than any people; for you were the fewest of all people:

8 But because the LORD loved you, and because he would keep the oath which he had sworn unto your fathers, has the LORD brought you out with a mighty hand, and redeemed you out of the house of bondmen, from the hand of Pharaoh king of Egypt.

9 Know therefore that the LORD your God, he is God, the faithful God, which keepeth covenant and mercy with them that love him and keep his commandments to a thousand generations;

10 And repayeth them that hate him to their face, to destroy them: he will not be slack to him that hateth him, he will repay him to his face.

11 You shalt therefore keep the commandments, and the statutes, and the judgments, which I command you this day, to do them.

12 Wherefore it shall come to pass, if you hearken to these judgments, and keep, and do them, that the LORD your God shall keep unto you the covenant and the mercy which he sware unto your fathers:

13 And he will love you, and bless you, and multiply you: he will also bless the fruit of your womb, and the fruit of your land, your corn, and your wine, and yours oil, the increase of your kine, and the flocks of your sheep, in the land which he sware unto your fathers to give you.

14 You shalt be blessed above all people: there shall not be male or female barren among you, or among your cattle.

15 And the LORD will take away from you all sickness, and will put none of the evil diseases of Egypt, which you knowest, upon you; but will lay them upon all them that hate you.

16 And you shalt consume all the people which the LORD your God shall deliver you; yours eye shall have no pity upon them: neither shalt you serve their gods; for that will be a snare unto you.

17 If you shalt say in yours heart, These nations are more than I; how can I dispossess them?

18 You shalt not be afraid of them: but shalt well remember what the LORD your God did unto Pharaoh, and unto all Egypt;

19 The great temptations which yours eyes saw, and the signs, and the wonders, and the mighty hand, and the stretched out arm, whereby the LORD your God brought you out: so shall the LORD your God do unto all the people of whom you are afraid.

20 Moreover the LORD your God will send the hornet among them, until they that are left, and hide themselves from you, be destroyed.

21 You shalt not be affrighted at them: for the LORD your God is among you, a mighty God and terrible.

22 And the LORD your God will put out those nations before you by little and little: you mayest not consume them at once, lest the beasts of the field increase upon you.

23 But the LORD your God shall deliver them unto you, and shall destroy them with a mighty destruction, until they be destroyed.

24 And he shall deliver their kings into yours hand, and you shalt destroy their name from under heaven: there shall no man be able to stand before you, until you have destroyed them.

25 The graven images of their gods shall you burn with fire: you shalt not desire the silver or gold that is on them, nor take it unto you, lest you be snared therein: for it is an abomination to the LORD your God.

26 Neither shalt you bring an abomination into yours house, lest you be a cursed thing like it: but you shalt utterly detest it, and you shalt utterly abhor it; for it is a cursed thing.

CHAPTER 8

ALL the commandments which I command you this day shall you observe to do, that you may live, and multiply, and go in and possess the land which the LORD sware unto your fathers.

2 And you shalt remember all the way which the LORD your God led you these forty years in the wilderness, to humble you, and to prove you, to know what was in yours heart, whether you wouldest keep his commandments, or no.

3 And he humbled you, and suffered you to hunger, and fed you with manna, which you knewest not, neither did your fathers know; that he might make you know that man doth not live by bread only, but by every word that proceedeth out of the mouth of the LORD doth man live.

4 Your raiment waxed not old upon you, neither did your foot swell, these forty years.

5 You shalt also consider in yours heart, that, as a man chasteneth his son, so the LORD your God chasteneth you.

6 Therefore you shalt keep the commandments of the LORD your God, to walk in his ways, and to fear him.

7 For the LORD your God bringeth you into a good land, a land of brooks of water, of fountains and depths that spring out of valleys and hills;

8 A land of wheat, and barley, and vines, and fig trees, and pomegranates; a land of oil olive, and honey;

9 A land wherein you shalt eat bread without scarceness, you shalt not lack any thing in it; a land whose stones are iron, and out of whose hills you mayest dig brass.

10 When you have eaten and are full, then you shalt bless the LORD your God for the good land which he has given you.

11 Beware that you forget not the LORD your God, in not keeping his commandments, and his judgments, and his statutes, which I command you this day:

12 Lest when you have eaten and are full, and have built goodly houses, and dwelt therein;

13 And when your herds and your flocks multiply, and your silver and your gold is multiplied, and all that you have is multiplied;

14 Then yours heart be lifted up, and you forget the LORD your God, which brought you forth out of the land of Egypt, from the house of bondage;

15 Who led you through that great and terrible wilderness, wherein were fiery serpents, and scorpions, and drought, where there was no water; who brought you forth water out of the rock of flint;

16 Who fed you in the wilderness with manna, which your fathers knew not, that he might humble you, and that he might prove you, to do you good at your latter end;

17 And you say in yours heart, My power and the might of my hand has gotten me this wealth.

18 But you shalt remember the LORD your God: for it is he that giveth you power to get wealth, that he may establish his covenant which he sware unto your fathers, as it is this day.

19 And it shall be, if you do at all forget the LORD your God, and walk after other gods, and serve them, and worship them, I testify against you this day that you shall surely perish.

20 As the nations which the LORD destroyeth before your face, so shall you perish; because you would not be obedient unto the voice of the LORD your God.

CHAPTER 9

HEAR, O Israel: You are to pass over Jordan this day, to go in to possess nations greater and mightier than yourself, cities great and fenced up to heaven,

2 A people great and tall, the children of the Anakims, whom you knewest, and of whom you have heard say, Who can stand before the children of Anak!

3 Understand therefore this day, that the LORD your God is he which goeth over before you; as a consuming fire he shall destroy them, and he shall bring them down before your face: so shalt you drive them out, and destroy them quickly, as the LORD has said unto you.

4 Speak not you in yours heart, after that the LORD your God has cast them out from before you, saying, For my righteousness the LORD has brought me in to possess this land: but for the wickedness of these nations the LORD doth drive them out from before you.

5 Not for your righteousness, or for the uprightness of yours heart, dost you go to possess their land: but for the wickedness of these nations the LORD your God doth drive them out from before you, and that he may perform the word which the LORD sware unto your fathers, Abraham, Isaac, and Jacob.

6 Understand therefore, that the LORD your God giveth you not this good land to possess it for your righteousness; for you are a stiffnecked people.

7 Remember, and forget not, how you provokedst the LORD your God to wrath in the wilderness: from the day that you did depart out of the land of Egypt, until you came unto this place, you have been rebellious against the LORD.

8 Also in Horeb you provoked the LORD to wrath, so that the LORD was angry with you to have destroyed you.

9 When I was gone up into the mount to receive the tables of stone, even the tables of the covenant which the LORD made with you, then I abode in the mount forty days and forty nights, I neither did eat bread nor drink water:

10 And the LORD delivered unto me two tables of stone written with the finger of God; and on them was written according to all the words, which the LORD spake with you in the mount out of the midst of the fire in the day of the assembly.

11 And it came to pass at the end of forty days and forty nights, that the LORD gave me the two tables of stone, even the tables of the covenant.

12 And the LORD said unto me, Arise, get you down quickly from hence; for your people which you have brought forth out of Egypt have corrupted themselves; they are quickly turned aside out of the way which I commanded them; they have made them a molten image.

13 Furthermore the LORD spake unto me, saying, I have seen this people, and, behold, it is a stiffnecked people:

14 Let me alone, that I may destroy them, and blot out their name from under heaven: and I will make of you a nation mightier and greater than they.

15 So I turned and came down from the mount, and the mount burned with fire: and the two tables of the covenant were in my two hands.

16 And I looked, and, behold, you had sinned against the LORD your God, and had made you a molten calf: you had turned aside quickly out of the way which the LORD had commanded you.

17 And I took the two tables, and cast them out of my two hands, and brake them before your eyes.

18 And I fell down before the LORD, as at the first, forty days and forty nights: I did neither eat bread, nor drink water, because of all your sins which you sinned, in doing wickedly in the sight of the LORD, to provoke him to anger.

19 For I was afraid of the anger and hot displeasure, wherewith the LORD was wroth against you to destroy you. But the LORD hearkened unto me at that time also.

20 And the LORD was very angry with Aaron to have destroyed him: and I prayed for Aaron also the same time.

21 And I took your sin, the calf which you had made, and burnt it with fire, and stamped it, and ground it very small, even until it was as small as dust: and I cast the dust thereof into the brook that descended out of the mount.

22 And at Taberah, and at Massah, and at Kibroth-hattaavah, you provoked the LORD to wrath.

23 Likewise when the LORD sent you from Kadesh-barnea, saying, Go up and possess the land which I have given you; then you rebelled against the commandment of the LORD your God, and you believed him not, nor hearkened to his voice.

24 You have been rebellious against the LORD from the day that I knew you.

25 Thus I fell down before the LORD forty days and forty nights, as I fell down at the first; because the LORD had said he would destroy you.

26 I prayed therefore unto the LORD, and said, O Lord GOD, destroy not your people and yours inheritance, which you have redeemed through your greatness, which you have brought forth out of Egypt with a mighty hand.

27 Remember your servants, Abraham, Isaac, and Jacob; look not unto the stubbornness of this people, nor to their wickedness, nor to their sin:

28 Lest the land whence you broughtest us out say, Because the LORD was not able to bring them into the land which he promised them, and because he hated them, he has brought them out to slay them in the wilderness.

29 Yet they are your people and yours inheritance, which you broughtest out by your mighty power and by your stretched out arm.

CHAPTER 10

AT that time the LORD said unto me, Hew you two tables of stone like unto the first, and come up unto me into the mount, and make you an ark of wood.

2 And I will write on the tables the words that were in the first tables which you brakest, and you shalt put them in the ark.

3 And I made an ark of shittim wood, and hewed two tables of stone like unto the first, and went up into the mount, having the two tables in my hand.

4 And he wrote on the tables, according to the first writing, the ten commandments, which the LORD spake unto you in the mount out of the midst of the fire in the day of the assembly: and the LORD gave them unto me.

5 And I turned myself and came down from the mount, and put the tables in the ark which I had made; and there they be, as the LORD commanded me.

6And the children of Israel took their journey from Beeroth of the children of Jaakan to Mosera: there Aaron died, and there he was buried; and Eleazar his son ministered in the priest's office in his stead.

7 From thence they journeyed unto Gudgodah; and from Gudgodah to Jotbath, a land of rivers of waters.

8At that time the LORD separated the tribe of Levi, to bear the ark of the covenant of the LORD, to stand before the LORD to minister unto him, and to bless in his name, unto this day.

9 Wherefore Levi has no part nor inheritance with his brethren; the LORD is his inheritance, according as the LORD your God promised him.

10 And I stayed in the mount, according to the first time, forty days and forty nights; and the LORD hearkened unto me at that time also, and the LORD would not destroy you.

11 And the LORD said unto me, Arise, take your journey before the people, that they may go in and possess the land, which I sware unto their fathers to give unto them.

12And now, Israel, what doth the LORD your God require of you, but to fear the LORD your God, to walk in all his ways, and to love him, and to serve the LORD your God with all your heart and with all your soul,

13 To keep the commandments of the LORD, and his statutes, which I command you this day for your good?

14 Behold, the heaven and the heaven of heavens is the LORD's your God, the earth also, with all that therein is.

15 Only the LORD had a delight in your fathers to love them, and he chose their seed after them, even you above all people, as it is this day.

16 Circumcise therefore the foreskin of your heart, and be no more stiffnecked.

17 For the LORD your God is God of gods, and Lord of lords, a great God, a mighty, and a terrible, which regardeth not persons, nor taketh reward:

18 He doth execute the judgment of the fatherless and widow, and loveth the stranger, in giving him food and raiment.

19 Love you therefore the stranger: for you were strangers in the land of Egypt.

20 You shalt fear the LORD your God; him shalt you serve, and to him shalt you cleave, and swear by his name.

21 He is your praise, and he is your God, that has done for you these great and terrible things, which yours eyes have seen.

22 Your fathers went down into Egypt with threescore and ten persons; and now the LORD your God has made you as the stars of heaven for multitude.

CHAPTER 11

THEREFORE you shalt love the LORD your God, and keep his charge, and his statutes, and his judgments, and his commandments, alway.

2 And know you this day: for I speak not with your children which have not known, and which have not seen the chastisement of the LORD your God, his greatness, his mighty hand, and his stretched out arm,

3 And his miracles, and his acts, which he did in the midst of Egypt unto Pharaoh the king of Egypt, and unto all his land;

4 And what he did unto the army of Egypt, unto their horses, and to their chariots; how he made the water of the Red sea to overflow them as they pursued after you, and how the LORD has destroyed them unto this day;

5 And what he did unto you in the wilderness, until you came into this place;

6 And what he did unto Dathan and Abiram, the sons of Eliab, the son of Reuben: how the earth opened her mouth, and swallowed them up, and their households, and their tents, and all the substance that was in their possession, in the midst of all Israel:

7 But your eyes have seen all the great acts of the LORD which he did.

8 Therefore shall you keep all the commandments which I command you this day, that you may be strong, and go in and possess the land, whither you go to possess it;

9 And that you may prolong your days in the land, which the LORD sware unto your fathers to give unto them and to their seed, a land that floweth with milk and honey.

10For the land, whither you go in to possess it, is not as the land of Egypt, from whence you came out, where you sowedst your seed, and wateredst it with your foot, as a garden of herbs:

11 But the land, whither you go to possess it, is a land of hills and valleys, and drinketh water of the rain of heaven:

12 A land which the LORD your God careth for: the eyes of the LORD your God are always upon it, from the beginning of the year even unto the end of the year.

13And it shall come to pass, if you shall hearken diligently unto my commandments which I command you this day, to love the LORD your God, and to serve him with all your heart and with all your soul,

14 That I will give you the rain of your land in his due season, the first rain and the latter rain, that you mayest gather in your corn, and your wine, and yours oil.

15 And I will send grass in your fields for your cattle, that you mayest eat and be full.

16 Take heed to yourselves, that your heart be not deceived, and you turn aside, and serve other gods, and worship them;

17 And then the LORD's wrath be kindled against you, and he shut up the heaven, that there be no rain, and that the land yield not her fruit; and lest you perish quickly from off the good land which the LORD giveth you.

18Therefore shall you lay up these my words in your heart and in your soul, and bind them for a sign upon your hand, that they may be as frontlets between your eyes.

19 And you shall teach them your children, speaking of them when you sittest in yours house, and when you walkest by the way, when you liest down, and when you risest up.

20 And you shalt write them upon the door posts of yours house, and upon your gates:

21 That your days may be multiplied, and the days of your children, in the land which the LORD sware unto your fathers to give them, as the days of heaven upon the earth.

22For if you shall diligently keep all these commandments which I command you, to do them, to love the LORD your God, to walk in all his ways, and to cleave unto him;

23 Then will the LORD drive out all these nations from before you, and you shall possess greater nations and mightier than yourselves.

24 Every place whereon the soles of your feet shall tread shall be yours: from the wilderness and Lebanon, from the river, the river Euphrates, even unto the uttermost sea shall your coast be.

25 There shall no man be able to stand before you: for the LORD your God shall lay the fear of you and the dread of you upon all the land that you shall tread upon, as he has said unto you.

26Behold, I set before you this day a blessing and a curse;

27 A blessing, if you obey the commandments of the LORD your God, which I command you this day:

28 And a curse, if you will not obey the commandments of the LORD your God, but turn aside out of the way which I command you this day, to go after other gods, which you have not known.

29 And it shall come to pass, when the LORD your God has brought you in unto the land whither you go to possess it, that you shalt put the blessing upon mount Gerizim, and the curse upon mount Ebal.

30 Are they not on the other side Jordan, by the way where the sun goeth down, in the land of the Canaanites, which dwell in the champaign over against Gilgal, beside the plains of Moreh?

31 For you shall pass over Jordan to go in to possess the land which the LORD your God giveth you, and you shall possess it, and dwell therein.

32 And you shall observe to do all the statutes and judgments which I set before you this day.

CHAPTER 12

THESE are the statutes and judgments, which you shall observe to do in the land, which the LORD God of your fathers giveth you to possess it, all the days that you live upon the earth.

2 You shall utterly destroy all the places, wherein the nations which you shall possess served their gods, upon the high mountains, and upon the hills, and under every green tree:

3 And you shall overthrow their altars, and break their pillars, and burn their groves with fire; and you shall hew down the graven images of their gods, and destroy the names of them out of that place.

4 You shall not do so unto the LORD your God.

5 But unto the place which the LORD your God shall choose out of all your tribes to put his name there, even unto his habitation shall you seek, and thither you shalt come:

6 And thither you shall bring your burnt offerings, and your sacrifices, and your tithes, and heave offerings of your hand, and your vows, and your freewill offerings, and the firstlings of your herds and of your flocks:

7 And there you shall eat before the LORD your God, and you shall rejoice in all that you put your hand unto, you and your households, wherein the LORD your God has blessed you.

8 You shall not do after all the things that we do here this day, every man whatsoever is right in his own eyes.

9 For you are not as yet come to the rest and to the inheritance, which the LORD your God giveth you.

10 But when you go over Jordan, and dwell in the land which the LORD your God giveth you to inherit, and when he giveth you rest from all your enemies round about, so that you dwell in safety;

11 Then there shall be a place which the LORD your God shall choose to cause his name to dwell there; thither shall you bring all that I command you; your burnt offerings, and your sacrifices, your tithes, and the heave offering of your hand, and all your choice vows which you vow unto the LORD:

12 And you shall rejoice before the LORD your God, you , and your sons, and your daughters, and your menservants, and your maidservants, and the Levite that is within your gates; forasmuch as he has no part nor inheritance with you.

13 Take heed to yourself that you offer not your burnt offerings in every place that you seest:

14 But in the place which the LORD shall choose in one of your tribes, there you shalt offer your burnt offerings, and there you shalt do all that I command you.

15 Notwithstanding you mayest kill and eat flesh in all your gates, whatsoever your soul lusteth after, according to the blessing of the LORD your God which he has given you: the unclean and the clean may eat thereof, as of the roebuck, and as of the hart.

16 Only you shall not eat the blood; you shall pour it upon the earth as water.

17 You mayest not eat within your gates the tithe of your corn, or of your wine, or of your oil, or the firstlings of your herds or of your flock, nor any of your vows which you vowest, nor your freewill offerings, or heave offering of yours hand:

18 But you must eat them before the LORD your God in the place which the LORD your God shall choose, you , and your son, and your daughter, and your manservant, and your maidservant, and the Levite that is within your gates: and you shalt rejoice before the LORD your God in all that you puttest yours hands unto.

19 Take heed to yourself that you forsake not the Levite as long as you livest upon the earth.

20 When the LORD your God shall enlarge your border, as he has promised you, and you shalt say, I will eat flesh, because your soul longeth to eat flesh; you mayest eat flesh, whatsoever your soul lusteth after.

21 If the place which the LORD your God has chosen to put his name there be too far from you, then you shalt kill of your herd and of your flock, which the LORD has given you, as I have commanded you, and you shalt eat in your gates whatsoever your soul lusteth after.

22 Even as the roebuck and the hart is eaten, so you shalt eat them: the unclean and the clean shall eat of them alike.

23 Only be sure that you eat not the blood: for the blood is the life; and you mayest not eat the life with the flesh.

24 You shalt not eat it; you shalt pour it upon the earth as water.

25 You shalt not eat it; that it may go well with you, and with your children after you, when you shalt do that which is right in the sight of the LORD.

26 Only your holy things which you have, and your vows, you shalt take, and go unto the place which the LORD shall choose:

27 And you shalt offer your burnt offerings, the flesh and the blood, upon the altar of the LORD your God: and the blood of your sacrifices shall be poured out upon the altar of the LORD your God, and you shalt eat the flesh.

28 Observe and hear all these words which I command you, that it may go well with you, and with your children after you for ever, when you doest that which is good and right in the sight of the LORD your God.

29 When the LORD your God shall cut off the nations from before you, whither you go to possess them, and you succeedest them, and dwellest in their land;

30 Take heed to yourself that you be not snared by following them, after that they be destroyed from before you; and that you inquire not after their gods, saying, How did these nations serve their gods? even so will I do likewise.

31 You shalt not do so unto the LORD your God: for every abomination to the LORD, which he hateth, have they done unto their gods; for even their sons and their daughters they have burnt in the fire to their gods.

32 What thing soever I command you, observe to do it: you shalt not add thereto, nor diminish from it.

CHAPTER 13

IF there arise among you a prophet, or a dreamer of dreams, and giveth you a sign or a wonder,

2 And the sign or the wonder come to pass, whereof he spake unto you, saying, Let us go after other gods, which you have not known, and let us serve them;

3 You shalt not hearken unto the words of that prophet, or that dreamer of dreams: for the LORD your God proveth you, to know whether you love the LORD your God with all your heart and with all your soul.

4 You shall walk after the LORD your God, and fear him, and keep his commandments, and obey his voice, and you shall serve him, and cleave unto him.

5 And that prophet, or that dreamer of dreams, shall be put to death; because he has spoken to turn you away from the LORD your God, which brought you out of the land of Egypt, and redeemed you out of the house of bondage, to thrust you out of the way which the LORD your God commanded you to walk in. So shalt you put the evil away from the midst of you.

6 If your brother, the son of your mother, or your son, or your daughter, or the wife of your bosom, or your friend, which is as yours own soul, entice you secretly, saying, Let us go and serve other gods, which you have not known, you , nor your fathers;

7 Namely, of the gods of the people which are round about you, nigh unto you, or far off from you, from the one end of the earth even unto the other end of the earth;

8 You shalt not consent unto him, nor hearken unto him; neither shall yours eye pity him, neither shalt you spare, neither shalt you conceal him:

9 But you shalt surely kill him; yours hand shall be first upon him to put him to death, and afterwards the hand of all the people.

10 And you shalt stone him with stones, that he die; because he has sought to thrust you away from the LORD your God, which brought you out of the land of Egypt, from the house of bondage.

11 And all Israel shall hear, and fear, and shall do no more any such wickedness as this is among you.

12 If you shalt hear say in one of your cities, which the LORD your God has given you to dwell there, saying,

13 Certain men, the children of Belial, are gone out from among you, and have withdrawn the inhabitants of their city, saying, Let us go and serve other gods, which you have not known;

14 Then shalt you inquire, and make search, and ask diligently; and, behold, if it be truth, and the thing certain, that such abomination is created among you;

15 You shalt surely strike the inhabitants of that city with the edge of the sword, destroying it utterly, and all that is therein, and the cattle thereof, with the edge of the sword.

16 And you shalt gather all the spoil of it into the midst of the street thereof, and shalt burn with fire the city, and all the spoil thereof every whit, for the LORD your God: and it shall be an heap for ever; it shall not be built again.

17 And there shall cleave nought of the cursed thing to yours hand: that the LORD may turn from the fierceness of his anger, and shew you mercy, and have compassion upon you, and multiply you, as he has sworn unto your fathers;

18 When you shalt hearken to the voice of the LORD your God, to keep all his commandments which I command you this day, to do that which is right in the eyes of the LORD your God.

CHAPTER 14

YOU are the children of the LORD your God: you shall not cut yourselves, nor make any baldness between your eyes for the dead.

2 For you are an holy people unto the LORD your God, and the LORD has chosen you to be a peculiar people unto himself, above all the nations that are upon the earth.

3 You shall not eat any abominable thing.

4 These are the beasts which you shall eat: the ox, the sheep, and the goat,

5 The hart, and the roebuck, and the fallow deer, and the wild goat, and the pygarg, and the wild ox, and the chamois.

6 And every beast that parteth the hoof, and cleaveth the cleft into two claws, and cheweth the cud among the beasts, that you shall eat.

7 Nevertheless these you shall not eat of them that chew the cud, or of them that divide the cloven hoof; as the camel, and the hare, and the coney: for they chew the cud, but divide not the hoof; therefore they are unclean unto you.

8 And the swine, because it divideth the hoof, yet cheweth not the cud, it is unclean unto you: you shall not eat of their flesh, nor touch their dead carcase.

9 These you shall eat of all that are in the waters: all that have fins and scales shall you eat:

10 And whatsoever has not fins and scales you may not eat; it is unclean unto you.

95

11 Of all clean birds you shall eat.

12 But these are they of which you shall not eat: the eagle, and the ossifrage, and the ospray,

13 And the glede, and the kite, and the vulture after his kind,

14 And every raven after his kind,

15 And the owl, and the night hawk, and the cuckow, and the hawk after his kind,

16 The little owl, and the great owl, and the swan,

17 And the pelican, and the gier eagle, and the cormorant,

18 And the stork, and the heron after her kind, and the lapwing, and the bat.

19 And every creeping thing that flieth is unclean unto you: they shall not be eaten.

20 But of all clean fowls you may eat.

21 You shall not eat of any thing that dieth of itself: you shalt give it unto the stranger that is in your gates, that he may eat it; or you mayest sell it unto an alien: for you are an holy people unto the LORD your God. You shalt not seethe a kid in his mother's milk.

22 You shalt truly tithe all the increase of your seed, that the field bringeth forth year by year.

23 And you shalt eat before the LORD your God, in the place which he shall choose to place his name there, the tithe of your corn, of your wine, and of yours oil, and the firstlings of your herds and of your flocks; that you mayest learn to fear the LORD your God always.

24 And if the way be too long for you, so that you are not able to carry it; or if the place be too far from you, which the LORD your God shall choose to set his name there, when the LORD your God has blessed you:

25 Then shalt you turn it into money, and bind up the money in yours hand, and shalt go unto the place which the LORD your God shall choose:

26 And you shalt bestow that money for whatsoever your soul lusteth after, for oxen, or for sheep, or for wine, or for strong drink, or for whatsoever your soul desireth: and you shalt eat there before the LORD your God, and you shalt rejoice, you , and yours household,

27 And the Levite that is within your gates; you shalt not forsake him; for he has no part nor inheritance with you.

28 At the end of three years you shalt bring forth all the tithe of yours increase the same year, and shalt lay it up within your gates:

29 And the Levite, (because he has no part nor inheritance with you,) and the stranger, and the fatherless, and the widow, which are within your gates, shall come, and shall eat and be satisfied; that the LORD your God may bless you in all the work of yours hand which you doest.

CHAPTER 15

AT the end of every seven years you shalt make a release.

2 And this is the manner of the release: Every creditor that lendeth ought unto his neighbour shall release it; he shall not exact it of his neighbour, or of his brother; because it is called the LORD's release.

3 Of a foreigner you mayest exact it again: but that which is yours with your brother yours hand shall release;

4 Save when there shall be no poor among you; for the LORD shall greatly bless you in the land which the LORD your God giveth you for an inheritance to possess it:

5 Only if you carefully hearken unto the voice of the LORD your God, to observe to do all these commandments which I command you this day.

6 For the LORD your God blesseth you, as he promised you: and you shalt lend unto many nations, but you shalt not borrow; and you shalt reign over many nations, but they shall not reign over you.

7 If there be among you a poor man of one of your brethren within any of your gates in your land which the LORD your God giveth you, you shalt not harden yours heart, nor shut yours hand from your poor brother:

8 But you shalt open yours hand wide unto him, and shalt surely lend him sufficient for his need, in that which he wanteth.

9 Beware that there be not a thought in your wicked heart, saying, The seventh year, the year of release, is at hand; and yours eye be evil against your poor brother, and you givest him nought; and he cry unto the LORD against you, and it be sin unto you.

10 You shalt surely give him, and yours heart shall not be grieved when you givest unto him: because that for this thing the LORD your God shall bless you in all your works, and in all that you puttest yours hand unto.

11 For the poor shall never cease out of the land: therefore I command you, saying, You shalt open yours hand wide unto your brother, to your poor, and to your needy, in your land.

12 And if your brother, an Hebrew man, or an Hebrew woman, be sold unto you, and serve you six years; then in the seventh year you shalt let him go free from you.

13 And when you sendest him out free from you, you shalt not let him go away empty:

14 You shalt furnish him liberally out of your flock, and out of your floor, and out of your winepress: of that wherewith the LORD your God has blessed you you shalt give unto him.

15 And you shalt remember that you wast a bondman in the land of Egypt, and the LORD your God redeemed you: therefore I command you this thing to day.

16 And it shall be, if he say unto you, I will not go away from you; because he loveth you and yours house, because he is well with you;

17 Then you shalt take an aul, and thrust it through his ear unto the door, and he shall be your servant for ever. And also unto your maidservant you shalt do likewise.

18 It shall not seem hard unto you, when you sendest him away free from you; for he has been worth a double hired servant to you, in serving you six years: and the LORD your God shall bless you in all that you doest.

19 All the firstling males that come of your herd and of your flock you shalt sanctify unto the LORD your God: you shalt do no work with the firstling of your bullock, nor shear the firstling of your sheep.

20 You shalt eat it before the LORD your God year by year in the place which the LORD shall choose, you and your household.

21 And if there be any blemish therein, as if it be lame, or blind, or have any ill blemish, you shalt not sacrifice it unto the LORD your God.

22 You shalt eat it within your gates: the unclean and the clean person shall eat it alike, as the roebuck, and as the hart.

23 Only you shalt not eat the blood thereof; you shalt pour it upon the ground as water.

CHAPTER 16

OBSERVE the month of Abib, and keep the passover unto the LORD your God: for in the month of Abib the LORD your God brought you forth out of Egypt by night.

2 You shalt therefore sacrifice the passover unto the LORD your God, of the flock and the herd, in the place which the LORD shall choose to place his name there.

3 You shalt eat no leavened bread with it; seven days shalt you eat unleavened bread therewith, even the bread of affliction; for you camest forth out of the land of Egypt in haste: that you mayest remember the day when you camest forth out of the land of Egypt all the days of your life.

4 And there shall be no leavened bread seen with you in all your coast seven days; neither shall there any thing of the flesh, which you sacrificedst the first day at even, remain all night until the morning.

5 You mayest not sacrifice the passover within any of your gates, which the LORD your God giveth you:

6 But at the place which the LORD your God shall choose to place his name in, there you shalt sacrifice the passover at even, at the going down of the sun, at the season that you camest forth out of Egypt.

7 And you shalt roast and eat it in the place which the LORD your God shall choose: and you shalt turn in the morning, and go unto your tents.

8 Six days you shalt eat unleavened bread: and on the seventh day shall be a solemn assembly to the LORD your God: you shalt do no work therein.

9 Seven weeks shalt you number unto you: begin to number the seven weeks from such time as you beginnest to put the sickle to the corn.

10 And you shalt keep the feast of weeks unto the LORD your God with a tribute of a freewill offering of yours hand, which you shalt give unto the LORD your God, according as the LORD your God has blessed you:

11 And you shalt rejoice before the LORD your God, you , and your son, and your daughter, and your manservant, and your maidservant, and the Levite that is within your gates, and the stranger, and the fatherless, and the widow, that are among you, in the place which the LORD your God has chosen to place his name there.

12 And you shalt remember that you wast a bondman in Egypt: and you shalt observe and do these statutes.

13 You shalt observe the feast of tabernacles seven days, after that you have gathered in your corn and your wine:

14 And you shalt rejoice in your feast, you , and your son, and your daughter, and your manservant, and your maidservant, and the Levite, the stranger, and the fatherless, and the widow, that are within your gates.

15 Seven days shalt you keep a solemn feast unto the LORD your God in the place which the LORD shall choose: because the LORD your God shall bless you in all yours increase, and in all the works of yours hands, therefore you shalt surely rejoice.

16 Three times in a year shall all your males appear before the LORD your God in the place which he shall choose; in the feast of unleavened bread, and in the feast of weeks, and in the feast of tabernacles: and they shall not appear before the LORD empty:

17 Every man shall give as he is able, according to the blessing of the LORD your God which he has given you.

18 Judges and officers shalt you make you in all your gates, which the LORD your God giveth you, throughout your tribes: and they shall judge the people with just judgment.

19 You shalt not wrest judgment; you shalt not respect persons, neither take a gift: for a gift doth blind the eyes of the wise, and pervert the words of the righteous.

20 That which is altogether just shalt you follow, that you mayest live, and inherit the land which the LORD your God giveth you.

21 You shalt not plant you a grove of any trees near unto the altar of the LORD your God, which you shalt make you.

22 Neither shalt you set you up any image; which the LORD your God hateth.

CHAPTER 17

YOU shalt not sacrifice unto the LORD your God any bullock, or sheep, wherein is blemish, or any evilfavouredness: for that is an abomination unto the LORD your God.

2 If there be found among you, within any of your gates which the LORD your God giveth you, man or woman, that has created wickedness in the sight of the LORD your God, in transgressing his covenant,

3 And has gone and served other gods, and worshipped them, either the sun, or moon, or any of the host of heaven, which I have not commanded;

4 And it be told you, and you have heard of it, and inquired diligently, and, behold, it be true, and the thing certain, that such abomination is created in Israel:

5 Then shalt you bring forth that man or that woman, which have committed that wicked thing, unto your gates, even that man or that woman, and shalt stone them with stones, till they die.

6 At the mouth of two witnesses, or three witnesses, shall he that is worthy of death be put to death; but at the mouth of one witness he shall not be put to death.

7 The hands of the witnesses shall be first upon him to put him to death, and afterward the hands of all the people. So you shalt put the evil away from among you.

8 If there arise a matter too hard for you in judgment, between blood and blood, between plea and plea, and between stroke and stroke, being matters of controversy within your gates: then shalt you arise, and get you up into the place which the LORD your God shall choose;

9 And you shalt come unto the priests the Levites, and unto the judge that shall be in those days, and inquire; and they shall shew you the sentence of judgment:

10 And you shalt do according to the sentence, which they of that place which the LORD shall choose shall shew you; and you shalt observe to do according to all that they inform you:

11 According to the sentence of the law which they shall teach you, and according to the judgment which they shall tell you, you shalt do: you shalt not decline from the sentence which they shall shew you, to the right hand, nor to the left.

12 And the man that will do presumptuously, and will not hearken unto the priest that standeth to minister there before the LORD your God, or unto the judge, even that man shall die: and you shalt put away the evil from Israel.

13 And all the people shall hear, and fear, and do no more presumptuously.

14 When you are come unto the land which the LORD your God giveth you, and shalt possess it, and shalt dwell therein, and shalt say, I will set a king over me, like as all the nations that are about me;

15 You shalt in any wise set him king over you, whom the LORD your God shall choose: one from among your brethren shalt you set king over you: you mayest not set a stranger over you, which is not your brother.

16 But he shall not multiply horses to himself, nor cause the people to return to Egypt, to the end that he should multiply horses: forasmuch as the LORD has said unto you, You shall henceforth return no more that way.

17 Neither shall he multiply wives to himself, that his heart turn not away: neither shall he greatly multiply to himself silver and gold.

18 And it shall be, when he sitteth upon the throne of his kingdom, that he shall write him a copy of this law in a book out of that which is before the priests the Levites:

19 And it shall be with him, and he shall read therein all the days of his life: that he may learn to fear the LORD his God, to keep all the words of this law and these statutes, to do them:

20 That his heart be not lifted up above his brethren, and that he turn not aside from the commandment, to the right hand, or to the left: to the end that he may prolong his days in his kingdom, he, and his children, in the midst of Israel.

CHAPTER 18

THE priests the Levites, and all the tribe of Levi, shall have no part nor inheritance with Israel: they shall eat the offerings of the LORD made by fire, and his inheritance.

2 Therefore shall they have no inheritance among their brethren: the LORD is their inheritance, as he has said unto them.

3 And this shall be the priest's due from the people, from them that offer a sacrifice, whether it be ox or sheep; and they shall give unto the priest the shoulder, and the two cheeks, and the maw.

4 The firstfruit also of your corn, of your wine, and of yours oil, and the first of the fleece of your sheep, shalt you give him.

5 For the LORD your God has chosen him out of all your tribes, to stand to minister in the name of the LORD, him and his sons for ever.

6 And if a Levite come from any of your gates out of all Israel, where he sojourned, and come with all the desire of his mind unto the place which the LORD shall choose;

7 Then he shall minister in the name of the LORD his God, as all his brethren the Levites do, which stand there before the LORD.

8 They shall have like portions to eat, beside that which comes of the sale of his patrimony.

9 When you are come into the land which the LORD your God giveth you, you shalt not learn to do after the abominations of those nations.

10 There shall not be found among you any one that maketh his son or his daughter to pass through the fire, or that useth divination, or an observer of times, or an enchanter, or a witch,

11 Or a charmer, or a consulter with familiar spirits, or a wizard, or a necromancer.

12 For all that do these things are an abomination unto the LORD: and because of these abominations the LORD your God doth drive them out from before you.

13 You shalt be perfect with the LORD your God.

14 For these nations, which you shalt possess, hearkened unto observers of times, and unto diviners: but as for you, the LORD your God has not suffered you so to do.

15 The LORD your God will raise up unto you a Prophet from the midst of you, of your brethren, like unto me; unto him you shall hearken;

16 According to all that you desiredst of the LORD your God in Horeb in the day of the assembly, saying, Let me not hear again the voice of the LORD my God, neither let me see this great fire any more, that I die not.

17 And the LORD said unto me, They have well spoken that which they have spoken.

18 I will raise them up a Prophet from among their brethren, like unto you, and will put my words in his mouth; and he shall speak unto them all that I shall command him.

19 And it shall come to pass, that whosoever will not hearken unto my words which he shall speak in my name, I will require it of him.

20 But the prophet, which shall presume to speak a word in my name, which I have not commanded him to speak, or that shall speak in the name of other gods, even that prophet shall die.

21 And if you say in yours heart, How shall we know the word which the LORD has not spoken?

22 When a prophet speaketh in the name of the LORD, if the thing follow not, nor come to pass, that is the thing which the LORD has not spoken, but the prophet has spoken it presumptuously: you shalt not be afraid of him.

CHAPTER 19

WHEN the LORD your God has cut off the nations, whose land the LORD your God giveth you, and you succeedest them, and dwellest in their cities, and in their houses;

2 You shalt separate three cities for you in the midst of your land, which the LORD your God giveth you to possess it.

3 You shalt prepare you a way, and divide the coasts of your land, which the LORD your God giveth you to inherit, into three parts, that every slayer may flee thither.

4 And this is the case of the slayer, which shall flee thither, that he may live: Whoso killeth his neighbour ignorantly, whom he hated not in time past;

5 As when a man goeth into the wood with his neighbour to hew wood, and his hand fetcheth a stroke with the axe to cut down the tree, and the head slippeth from the helve, and lighteth upon his neighbour, that he die; he shall flee unto one of those cities, and live:

6 Lest the avenger of the blood pursue the slayer, while his heart is hot, and overtake him, because the way is long, and slay him; whereas he was not worthy of death, inasmuch as he hated him not in time past.

7 Wherefore I command you, saying, You shalt separate three cities for you.

8 And if the LORD your God enlarge your coast, as he has sworn unto your fathers, and give you all the land which he promised to give unto your fathers;

9 If you shalt keep all these commandments to do them, which I command you this day, to love the LORD your God, and to walk ever in his ways; then shalt you add three cities more for you, beside these three:

10 That innocent blood be not shed in your land, which the LORD your God giveth you for an inheritance, and so blood be upon you.

11 But if any man hate his neighbour, and lie in wait for him, and rise up against him, and strike him mortally that he die, and fleeth into one of these cities:

12 Then the elders of his city shall send and fetch him thence, and deliver him into the hand of the avenger of blood, that he may die.

13 Yours eye shall not pity him, but you shalt put away the guilt of innocent blood from Israel, that it may go well with you.

14 You shalt not remove your neighbour's landmark, which they of old time have set in yours inheritance, which you shalt inherit in the land that the LORD your God giveth you to possess it.

15 One witness shall not rise up against a man for any iniquity, or for any sin, in any sin that he sinneth: at the mouth of two witnesses, or at the mouth of three witnesses, shall the matter be established.

16 If a false witness rise up against any man to testify against him that which is wrong;

17 Then both the men, between whom the controversy is, shall stand before the LORD, before the priests and the judges, which shall be in those days;

18 And the judges shall make diligent inquisition: and, behold, if the witness be a false witness, and has testified falsely against his brother;

19 Then shall you do unto him, as he had thought to have done unto his brother: so shalt you put the evil away from among you.

20 And those which remain shall hear, and fear, and shall henceforth commit no more any such evil among you.

21 And yours eye shall not pity; but life shall go for life, eye for eye, tooth for tooth, hand for hand, foot for foot.

CHAPTER 20

WHEN you go out to battle against yours enemies, and seest horses, and chariots, and a people more than you , be not afraid of them: for the LORD your God is with you, which brought you up out of the land of Egypt.

2 And it shall be, when you are come nigh unto the battle, that the priest shall approach and speak unto the people,

3 And shall say unto them, Hear, O Israel, you approach this day unto battle against your enemies: let not your hearts faint, fear not, and do not tremble, neither be you terrified because of them;

4 For the LORD your God is he that goeth with you, to fight for you against your enemies, to save you.

5 And the officers shall speak unto the people, saying, What man is there that has built a new house, and has not dedicated it? let him go and return to his house, lest he die in the battle, and another man dedicate it.

6 And what man is he that has planted a vineyard, and has not yet eaten of it? let him also go and return unto his house, lest he die in the battle, and another man eat of it.

7 And what man is there that has betrothed a wife, and has not taken her? let him go and return unto his house, lest he die in the battle, and another man take her.

8 And the officers shall speak further unto the people, and they shall say, What man is there that is fearful and fainthearted? let him go and return unto his house, lest his brethren's heart faint as well as his heart.

9 And it shall be, when the officers have made an end of speaking unto the people, that they shall make captains of the armies to lead the people.

10 When you comest nigh unto a city to fight against it, then proclaim peace unto it.

11 And it shall be, if it make you answer of peace, and open unto you, then it shall be, that all the people that is found therein shall be tributaries unto you, and they shall serve you.

12 And if it will make no peace with you, but will make war against you, then you shalt besiege it:

13 And when the LORD your God has delivered it into yours hands, you shalt strike every male thereof with the edge of the sword:

14 But the women, and the little ones, and the cattle, and all that is in the city, even all the spoil thereof, shalt you take unto yourself; and you shalt eat the spoil of yours enemies, which the LORD your God has given you.

15 Thus shalt you do unto all the cities which are very far off from you, which are not of the cities of these nations.

16 But of the cities of these people, which the LORD your God doth give you for an inheritance, you shalt save alive nothing that breatheth:

17 But you shalt utterly destroy them; namely, the Hittites, and the Amorites, the Canaanites, and the Perizzites, the Hivites, and the Jebusites; as the LORD your God has commanded you:

18 That they teach you not to do after all their abominations, which they have done unto their gods; so should you sin against the LORD your God.

19 When you shalt besiege a city a long time, in making war against it to take it, you shalt not destroy the trees thereof by forcing an axe against them: for you mayest eat of them, and you shalt not cut them down (for the tree of the field is man's life) to employ them in the siege:

20 Only the trees which you knowest that they be not trees for meat, you shalt destroy and cut them down; and you shalt build bulwarks against the city that maketh war with you, until it be subdued.

CHAPTER 21

IF one be found slain in the land which the LORD your God giveth you to possess it, lying in the field, and it be not known who has slain him:

2 Then your elders and your judges shall come forth, and they shall measure unto the cities which are round about him that is slain:

3 And it shall be, that the city which is next unto the slain man, even the elders of that city shall take an heifer, which has not been created with, and which has not drawn in the yoke;

4 And the elders of that city shall bring down the heifer unto a rough valley, which is neither eared nor sown, and shall strike off the heifer's neck there in the valley:

5 And the priests the sons of Levi shall come near; for them the LORD your God has chosen to minister unto him, and to bless in the name of the LORD; and by their word shall every controversy and every stroke be tried:

6 And all the elders of that city, that are next unto the slain man, shall wash their hands over the heifer that is beheaded in the valley:

7 And they shall answer and say, Our hands have not shed this blood, neither have our eyes seen it.

8 Be merciful, O LORD, unto your people Israel, whom you have redeemed, and lay not innocent blood unto your people of Israel's charge. And the blood shall be forgiven them.

9 So shalt you put away the guilt of innocent blood from among you, when you shalt do that which is right in the sight of the LORD.

10 When you go forth to war against yours enemies, and the LORD your God has delivered them into yours hands, and you have taken them captive,

11 And seest among the captives a beautiful woman, and have a desire unto her, that you wouldest have her to your wife;

12 Then you shalt bring her home to yours house; and she shall shave her head, and pare her nails;

13 And she shall put the raiment of her captivity from off her, and shall remain in yours house, and bewail her father and her mother a full month: and after that you shalt go in unto her, and be her husband, and she shall be your wife.

14 And it shall be, if you have no delight in her, then you shalt let her go whither she will; but you shalt not sell her at all for money, you shalt not make merchandise of her, because you have humbled her.

15 If a man have two wives, one beloved, and another hated, and they have born him children, both the beloved and the hated; and if the firstborn son be hers that was hated:

16 Then it shall be, when he maketh his sons to inherit that which he has, that he may not make the son of the beloved firstborn before the son of the hated, which is indeed the firstborn:

17 But he shall acknowledge the son of the hated for the firstborn, by giving him a double portion of all that he has: for he is the beginning of his strength; the right of the firstborn is his.

18 If a man have a stubborn and rebellious son, which will not obey the voice of his father, or the voice of his mother, and that, when they have chastened him, will not hearken unto them:

19 Then shall his father and his mother lay hold on him, and bring him out unto the elders of his city, and unto the gate of his place;

20 And they shall say unto the elders of his city, This our son is stubborn and rebellious, he will not obey our voice; he is a glutton, and a drunkard.

21 And all the men of his city shall stone him with stones, that he die: so shalt you put evil away from among you; and all Israel shall hear, and fear.

22 And if a man have committed a sin worthy of death, and he be to be put to death, and you hang him on a tree:

23 His body shall not remain all night upon the tree, but you shalt in any wise bury him that day; (for he that is hanged is accursed of God;) that your land be not defiled, which the LORD your God giveth you for an inheritance.

CHAPTER 22

YOU shalt not see your brother's ox or his sheep go astray, and hide yourself from them: you shalt in any case bring them again unto your brother.

2 And if your brother be not nigh unto you, or if you know him not, then you shalt bring it unto yours own house, and it shall be with you until your brother seek after it, and you shalt restore it to him again.

3 In like manner shalt you do with his ass; and so shalt you do with his raiment; and with all lost thing of your brother's, which he has lost, and you have found, shalt you do likewise: you mayest not hide yourself.

4 You shalt not see your brother's ass or his ox fall down by the way, and hide yourself from them: you shalt surely help him to lift them up again.

5 The woman shall not wear that which pertaineth unto a man, neither shall a man put on a woman's garment: for all that do so are abomination unto the LORD your God.

6 If a bird's nest chance to be before you in the way in any tree, or on the ground, whether they be young ones, or eggs, and the dam sitting upon the young, or upon the eggs, you shalt not take the dam with the young:

7 But you shalt in any wise let the dam go, and take the young to you; that it may be well with you, and that you mayest prolong your days.

8 When you buildest a new house, then you shalt make a battlement for your roof, that you bring not blood upon yours house, if any man fall from thence.

9 You shalt not sow your vineyard with divers seeds: lest the fruit of your seed which you have sown, and the fruit of your vineyard, be defiled.

10 You shalt not plow with an ox and an ass together.

11 You shalt not wear a garment of divers sorts, as of woollen and linen together.

12 You shalt make you fringes upon the four quarters of your vesture, wherewith you coverest yourself.

13 If any man take a wife, and go in unto her, and hate her,

14 And give occasions of speech against her, and bring up an evil name upon her, and say, I took this woman, and when I came to her, I found her not a maid:

15 Then shall the father of the damsel, and her mother, take and bring forth the tokens of the damsel's virginity unto the elders of the city in the gate:

16 And the damsel's father shall say unto the elders, I gave my daughter unto this man to wife, and he hateth her;

17 And, lo, he has given occasions of speech against her, saying, I found not your daughter a maid; and yet these are the tokens of my daughter's virginity. And they shall spread the cloth before the elders of the city.

18 And the elders of that city shall take that man and chastise him;

19 And they shall amerce him in an hundred shekels of silver, and give them unto the father of the damsel, because he has brought up an evil name upon a virgin of Israel: and she shall be his wife; he may not put her away all his days.

20 But if this thing be true, and the tokens of virginity be not found for the damsel:

21 Then they shall bring out the damsel to the door of her father's house, and the men of her city shall stone her with stones that she die: because she has created folly in Israel, to play the whore in her father's house: so shalt you put evil away from among you.

22 If a man be found lying with a woman married to an husband, then they shall both of them die, both the man that lay with the woman, and the woman: so shalt you put away evil from Israel.

23 If a damsel that is a virgin be betrothed unto an husband, and a man find her in the city, and lie with her;

24 Then you shall bring them both out unto the gate of that city, and you shall stone them with stones that they die; the damsel, because she cried not, being in the city; and the man, because he has humbled his neighbour's wife: so you shalt put away evil from among you.

25 But if a man find a betrothed damsel in the field, and the man force her, and lie with her: then the man only that lay with her shall die:

26 But unto the damsel you shalt do nothing; there is in the damsel no sin worthy of death: for as when a man riseth against his neighbour, and slayeth him, even so is this matter:

27 For he found her in the field, and the betrothed damsel cried, and there was none to save her.

28 If a man find a damsel that is a virgin, which is not betrothed, and lay hold on her, and lie with her, and they be found;

29 Then the man that lay with her shall give unto the damsel's father fifty shekels of silver, and she shall be his wife; because he has humbled her, he may not put her away all his days.

30 A man shall not take his father's wife, nor discover his father's skirt.

CHAPTER 23

HE that is wounded in the stones, or has his privy member cut off, shall not enter into the congregation of the LORD.

2 A bastard shall not enter into the congregation of the LORD; even to his tenth generation shall he not enter into the congregation of the LORD.

3 An Ammonite or Moabite shall not enter into the congregation of the LORD; even to their tenth generation shall they not enter into the congregation of the LORD for ever:

4 Because they met you not with bread and with water in the way, when you came forth out of Egypt; and because they hired against you Balaam the son of Beor of Pethor of Mesopotamia, to curse you.

5 Nevertheless the LORD your God would not hearken unto Balaam; but the LORD your God turned the curse into a blessing unto you, because the LORD your God loved you.

6 You shalt not seek their peace nor their prosperity all your days for ever.

7 You shalt not abhor an Edomite; for he is your brother: you shalt not abhor an Egyptian; because you wast a stranger in his land.

8 The children that are begotten of them shall enter into the congregation of the LORD in their third generation.

9 When the host goeth forth against yours enemies, then keep you from every wicked thing.

10 If there be among you any man, that is not clean by reason of uncleanness that chanceth him by night, then shall he go abroad out of the camp, he shall not come within the camp:

11 But it shall be, when evening comes on, he shall wash himself with water: and when the sun is down, he shall come into the camp again.

12 You shalt have a place also without the camp, whither you shalt go forth abroad:

13 And you shalt have a paddle upon your weapon; and it shall be, when you will ease yourself abroad, you shalt dig therewith, and shalt turn back and cover that which comes from you:

14 For the LORD your God walketh in the midst of your camp, to deliver you, and to give up yours enemies before you; therefore shall your camp be holy: that he see no unclean thing in you, and turn away from you.

15 You shalt not deliver unto his master the servant which is escaped from his master unto you:

16 He shall dwell with you, even among you, in that place which he shall choose in one of your gates, where it liketh him best: you shalt not oppress him.

17 There shall be no whore of the daughters of Israel, nor a sodomite of the sons of Israel.

18 You shalt not bring the hire of a whore, or the price of a dog, into the house of the LORD your God for any vow: for even both these are abomination unto the LORD your God.

19 You shalt not lend upon usury to your brother; usury of money, usury of victuals, usury of any thing that is lent upon usury:

20 Unto a stranger you mayest lend upon usury; but unto your brother you shalt not lend upon usury: that the LORD your God may bless you in all that you settest yours hand to in the land whither you go to possess it.

21 When you shalt vow a vow unto the LORD your God, you shalt not slack to pay it: for the LORD your God will surely require it of you; and it would be sin in you.

22 But if you shalt forbear to vow, it shall be no sin in you.

23 That which is gone out of your lips you shalt keep and perform; even a freewill offering, according as you have vowed unto the LORD your God, which you have promised with your mouth.

24 When you comest into your neighbour's vineyard, then you mayest eat grapes your fill at yours own pleasure; but you shalt not put any in your vessel.

25 When you comest into the standing corn of your neighbour, then you mayest pluck the ears with yours hand; but you shalt not move a sickle unto your neighbour's standing corn.

CHAPTER 24

WHEN a man has taken a wife, and married her, and it come to pass that she find no favour in his eyes, because he has found some uncleanness in her: then let him write her a bill of divorcement, and give it in her hand, and send her out of his house.

2 And when she is departed out of his house, she may go and be another man's wife.

3 And if the latter husband hate her, and write her a bill of divorcement, and giveth it in her hand, and sendeth her out of his house; or if the latter husband die, which took her to be his wife;

4 Her former husband, which sent her away, may not take her again to be his wife, after that she is defiled; for that is abomination before the LORD: and you shalt not cause the land to sin, which the LORD your God giveth you for an inheritance.

5When a man has taken a new wife, he shall not go out to war, neither shall he be charged with any business: but he shall be free at home one year, and shall cheer up his wife which he has taken.

6No man shall take the nether or the upper millstone to pledge: for he taketh a man's life to pledge.

7If a man be found stealing any of his brethren of the children of Israel, and maketh merchandise of him, or selleth him; then that thief shall die; and you shalt put evil away from among you.

8Take heed in the plague of leprosy, that you observe diligently, and do according to all that the priests the Levites shall teach you: as I commanded them, so you shall observe to do.

9 Remember what the LORD your God did unto Miriam by the way, after that you were come forth out of Egypt.

10When you dost lend your brother any thing, you shalt not go into his house to fetch his pledge.

11 You shalt stand abroad, and the man to whom you dost lend shall bring out the pledge abroad unto you.

12 And if the man be poor, you shalt not sleep with his pledge:

13 In any case you shalt deliver him the pledge again when the sun goeth down, that he may sleep in his own raiment, and bless you: and it shall be righteousness unto you before the LORD your God.

14You shalt not oppress an hired servant that is poor and needy, whether he be of your brethren, or of your strangers that are in your land within your gates:

15 At his day you shalt give him his hire, neither shall the sun go down upon it; for he is poor, and setteth his heart upon it: lest he cry against you unto the LORD, and it be sin unto you.

16 The fathers shall not be put to death for the children, neither shall the children be put to death for the fathers: every man shall be put to death for his own sin.

17You shalt not pervert the judgment of the stranger, nor of the fatherless; nor take a widow's raiment to pledge:

18 But you shalt remember that you wast a bondman in Egypt, and the LORD your God redeemed you thence: therefore I command you to do this thing.

19When you cuttest down yours harvest in your field, and have forgot a sheaf in the field, you shalt not go again to fetch it: it shall be for the stranger, for the fatherless, and for the widow: that the LORD your God may bless you in all the work of yours hands.

20 When you beatest yours olive tree, you shalt not go over the boughs again: it shall be for the stranger, for the fatherless, and for the widow.

21 When you gatherest the grapes of your vineyard, you shalt not glean it afterward: it shall be for the stranger, for the fatherless, and for the widow.

22 And you shalt remember that you wast a bondman in the land of Egypt: therefore I command you to do this thing.

CHAPTER 25

IF there be a controversy between men, and they come unto judgment, that the judges may judge them; then they shall justify the righteous, and condemn the wicked.

2 And it shall be, if the wicked man be worthy to be beaten, that the judge shall cause him to lie down, and to be beaten before his face, according to his fault, by a certain number.

3 Forty stripes he may give him, and not exceed: lest, if he should exceed, and beat him above these with many stripes, then your brother should seem vile unto you.

4You shalt not muzzle the ox when he treadeth out the corn.

5If brethren dwell together, and one of them die, and have no child, the wife of the dead shall not marry without unto a stranger: her husband's brother shall go in unto her, and take her to him to wife, and perform the duty of an husband's brother unto her.

6 And it shall be, that the firstborn which she beareth shall succeed in the name of his brother which is dead, that his name be not put out of Israel.

7 And if the man like not to take his brother's wife, then let his brother's wife go up to the gate unto the elders, and say, My husband's brother refuseth to raise up unto his brother a name in Israel, he will not perform the duty of my husband's brother.

8 Then the elders of his city shall call him, and speak unto him: and if he stand to it, and say, I like not to take her;

9 Then shall his brother's wife come unto him in the presence of the elders, and loose his shoe from off his foot, and spit in his face, and shall answer and say, So shall it be done unto that man that will not build up his brother's house.

10 And his name shall be called in Israel, The house of him that has his shoe loosed.

11When men strive together one with another, and the wife of the one draweth near for to deliver her husband out of the hand of him that smiteth him, and putteth forth her hand, and taketh him by the secrets:

12 Then you shalt cut off her hand, yours eye shall not pity her.

13You shalt not have in your bag divers weights, a great and a small.

14 You shalt not have in yours house divers measures, a great and a small.

15 But you shalt have a perfect and just weight, a perfect and just measure shalt you have: that your days may be lengthened in the land which the LORD your God giveth you.

16 For all that do such things, and all that do unrighteously, are an abomination unto the LORD your God.

17Remember what Amalek did unto you by the way, when you were come forth out of Egypt;

18 How he met you by the way, and struck the hindmost of you, even all that were feeble behind you, when you wast faint and weary; and he feared not God.

19 Therefore it shall be, when the LORD your God has given you rest from all yours enemies round about, in the land which the LORD your God giveth you for an inheritance to possess it, that you shalt blot out the remembrance of Amalek from under heaven; you shalt not forget it.

CHAPTER 26

AND it shall be, when you are come in unto the land which the LORD your God giveth you for an inheritance, and possessest it, and dwellest therein;

2 That you shalt take of the first of all the fruit of the earth, which you shalt bring of your land that the LORD your God giveth you, and shalt put it in a basket, and shalt go unto the place which the LORD your God shall choose to place his name there.

3 And you shalt go unto the priest that shall be in those days, and say unto him, I profess this day unto the LORD your God, that I am come unto the country which the LORD sware unto our fathers for to give us.

4 And the priest shall take the basket out of yours hand, and set it down before the altar of the LORD your God.

5 And you shalt speak and say before the LORD your God, A Syrian ready to perish was my father, and he went down into Egypt, and sojourned there with a few, and became there a nation, great, mighty, and populous:

6 And the Egyptians evil entreated us, and afflicted us, and laid upon us hard bondage:

7 And when we cried unto the LORD God of our fathers, the LORD heard our voice, and looked on our affliction, and our labour, and our oppression:

8 And the LORD brought us forth out of Egypt with a mighty hand, and with an outstretched arm, and with great terribleness, and with signs, and with wonders:

9 And he has brought us into this place, and has given us this land, even a land that floweth with milk and honey.

10 And now, behold, I have brought the firstfruits of the land, which you , O LORD, have given me. And you shalt set it before the LORD your God, and worship before the LORD your God:

11 And you shalt rejoice in every good thing which the LORD your God has given unto you, and unto yours house, you , and the Levite, and the stranger that is among you.

12When you have made an end of tithing all the tithes of yours increase the third year, which is the year of tithing, and have given it unto the Levite, the stranger, the fatherless, and the widow, that they may eat within your gates, and be filled;

13 Then you shalt say before the LORD your God, I have brought away the hallowed things out of my house, and also have given them unto the Levite, and unto the stranger, to the fatherless, and to the widow, according to all your commandments which you have commanded me: I have not transgressed your commandments, neither have I forgotten them:

14 I have not eaten thereof in my mourning, neither have I taken away ought thereof for any unclean use, nor given ought thereof for the dead: but I have hearkened to the voice of the LORD my God, and have done according to all that you have commanded me.

15 Look down from your holy habitation, from heaven, and bless your people Israel, and the land which you have given us, as you swarest unto our fathers, a land that floweth with milk and honey.

16This day the LORD your God has commanded you to do these statutes and judgments: you shalt therefore keep and do them with all yours heart, and with all your soul.

17 You have avouched the LORD this day to be your God, and to walk in his ways, and to keep his statutes, and his commandments, and his judgments, and to hearken unto his voice:

18 And the LORD has avouched you this day to be his peculiar people, as he has promised you, and that you shouldest keep all his commandments;

19 And to make you high above all nations which he has made, in praise, and in name, and in honour; and that you mayest be an holy people unto the LORD your God, as he has spoken.

CHAPTER 27

AND Moses with the elders of Israel commanded the people, saying, Keep all the commandments which I command you this day.

2 And it shall be on the day when you shall pass over Jordan unto the land which the LORD your God giveth you, that you shalt set you up great stones, and plaister them with plaister:

3 And you shalt write upon them all the words of this law, when you are passed over, that you mayest go in unto the land which the LORD your God giveth you, a land that floweth with milk and honey; as the LORD God of your fathers has promised you.

4 Therefore it shall be when you be gone over Jordan, that you shall set up these stones, which I command you this day, in mount Ebal, and you shalt plaister them with plaister.

5 And there shalt you build an altar unto the LORD your God, an altar of stones: you shalt not lift up any iron tool upon them.

6 You shalt build the altar of the LORD your God of whole stones: and you shalt offer burnt offerings thereon unto the LORD your God:

7 And you shalt offer peace offerings, and shalt eat there, and rejoice before the LORD your God.

8 And you shalt write upon the stones all the words of this law very plainly.

9 And Moses and the priests the Levites spake unto all Israel, saying, Take heed, and hearken, O Israel; this day you are become the people of the LORD your God.

10 You shalt therefore obey the voice of the LORD your God, and do his commandments and his statutes, which I command you this day.

11 And Moses charged the people the same day, saying,

12 These shall stand upon mount Gerizim to bless the people, when you are come over Jordan; Simeon, and Levi, and Judah, and Issachar, and Joseph, and Benjamin:

13 And these shall stand upon mount Ebal to curse; Reuben, Gad, and Asher, and Zebulun, Dan, and Naphtali.

14 And the Levites shall speak, and say unto all the men of Israel with a loud voice,

15 Cursed be the man that maketh any graven or molten image, an abomination unto the LORD, the work of the hands of the craftsman, and putteth it in a secret place. And all the people shall answer and say, Amen.

16 Cursed be he that setteth light by his father or his mother. And all the people shall say, Amen.

17 Cursed be he that removeth his neighbour's landmark. And all the people shall say, Amen.

18 Cursed be he that maketh the blind to wander out of the way. And all the people shall say, Amen.

19 Cursed be he that perverteth the judgment of the stranger, fatherless, and widow. And all the people shall say, Amen.

20 Cursed be he that lies with his father's wife; because he uncovereth his father's skirt. And all the people shall say, Amen.

21 Cursed be he that lies with any manner of beast. And all the people shall say, Amen.

22 Cursed be he that lies with his sister, the daughter of his father, or the daughter of his mother. And all the people shall say, Amen.

23 Cursed be he that lies with his mother in law. And all the people shall say, Amen.

24 Cursed be he that smiteth his neighbour secretly. And all the people shall say, Amen.

25 Cursed be he that taketh reward to slay an innocent person. And all the people shall say, Amen.

26 Cursed be he that confirmeth not all the words of this law to do them. And all the people shall say, Amen.

CHAPTER 28

AND it shall come to pass, if you shalt hearken diligently unto the voice of the LORD your God, to observe and to do all his commandments which I command you this day, that the LORD your God will set you on high above all nations of the earth:

2 And all these blessings shall come on you, and overtake you, if you shalt hearken unto the voice of the LORD your God.

3 Blessed shalt you be in the city, and blessed shalt you be in the field.

4 Blessed shall be the fruit of your body, and the fruit of your ground, and the fruit of your cattle, the increase of your kine, and the flocks of your sheep.

5 Blessed shall be your basket and your store.

6 Blessed shalt you be when you comest in, and blessed shalt you be when you go out.

7 The LORD shall cause yours enemies that rise up against you to be smitten before your face: they shall come out against you one way, and flee before you seven ways.

8 The LORD shall command the blessing upon you in your storehouses, and in all that you settest yours hand unto; and he shall bless you in the land which the LORD your God giveth you.

9 The LORD shall establish you an holy people unto himself, as he has sworn unto you, if you shalt keep the commandments of the LORD your God, and walk in his ways.

10 And all people of the earth shall see that you are called by the name of the LORD; and they shall be afraid of you.

11 And the LORD shall make you plenteous in goods, in the fruit of your body, and in the fruit of your cattle, and in the fruit of your ground, in the land which the LORD sware unto your fathers to give you.

12 The LORD shall open unto you his good treasure, the heaven to give the rain unto your land in his season, and to bless all the work of yours hand: and you shalt lend unto many nations, and you shalt not borrow.

13 And the LORD shall make you the head, and not the tail; and you shalt be above only, and you shalt not be beneath; if that you hearken unto the commandments of the LORD your God, which I command you this day, to observe and to do them:

14 And you shalt not go aside from any of the words which I command you this day, to the right hand, or to the left, to go after other gods to serve them.

15 But it shall come to pass, if you will not hearken unto the voice of the LORD your God, to observe to do all his commandments and his statutes which I command you this day; that all these curses shall come upon you, and overtake you:

16 Cursed shalt you be in the city, and cursed shalt you be in the field.

17 Cursed shall be your basket and your store.

18 Cursed shall be the fruit of your body, and the fruit of your land, the increase of your kine, and the flocks of your sheep.

19 Cursed shalt you be when you comest in, and cursed shalt you be when you go out.

20 The LORD shall send upon you cursing, vexation, and rebuke, in all that you settest yours hand unto for to do, until you be destroyed, and until you perish quickly; because of the wickedness of your doings, whereby you have forsaken me.

21 The LORD shall make the pestilence cleave unto you, until he have consumed you from off the land, whither you go to possess it.

22 The LORD shall strike you with a consumption, and with a fever, and with an inflammation, and with an extreme burning, and with the sword, and with blasting, and with mildew; and they shall pursue you until you perish.

23 And your heaven that is over your head shall be brass, and the earth that is under you shall be iron.

24 The LORD shall make the rain of your land powder and dust: from heaven shall it come down upon you, until you be destroyed.

25 The LORD shall cause you to be smitten before yours enemies: you shalt go out one way against them, and flee seven ways before them: and shalt be removed into all the kingdoms of the earth.

26 And your carcase shall be meat unto all fowls of the air, and unto the beasts of the earth, and no man shall fray them away.

27 The LORD will strike you with the botch of Egypt, and with the emerods, and with the scab, and with the itch, whereof you can not be healed.

28 The LORD shall strike you with madness, and blindness, and astonishment of heart:

29 And you shalt grope at noonday, as the blind gropeth in darkness, and you shalt not prosper in your ways: and you shalt be only oppressed and spoiled evermore, and no man shall save you.

30 You shalt betroth a wife, and another man shall lie with her: you shalt build an house, and you shalt not dwell therein: you shalt plant a vineyard, and shalt not gather the grapes thereof.

31 Yours ox shall be slain before yours eyes, and you shalt not eat thereof: yours ass shall be violently taken away from before your face, and shall not be restored to you: your sheep shall be given unto yours enemies, and you shalt have none to rescue them.

32 Your sons and your daughters shall be given unto another people, and yours eyes shall look, and fail with longing for them all the day long: and there shall be no might in yours hand.

33 The fruit of your land, and all your labours, shall a nation which you knowest not eat up; and you shalt be only oppressed and crushed alway:

34 So that you shalt be mad for the sight of yours eyes which you shalt see.

35 The LORD shall strike you in the knees, and in the legs, with a sore botch that cannot be healed, from the sole of your foot unto the top of your head.

36 The LORD shall bring you, and your king which you shalt set over you, unto a nation which neither you nor your fathers have known; and there shalt you serve other gods, wood and stone.

37 And you shalt become an astonishment, a proverb, and a byword, among all nations whither the LORD shall lead you.

38 You shalt carry much seed out into the field, and shalt gather but little in; for the locust shall consume it.

39 You shalt plant vineyards, and dress them, but shalt neither drink of the wine, nor gather the grapes; for the worms shall eat them.

40 You shalt have olive trees throughout all your coasts, but you shalt not anoint yourself with the oil; for yours olive shall cast his fruit.

41 You shalt beget sons and daughters, but you shalt not enjoy them; for they shall go into captivity.

42 All your trees and fruit of your land shall the locust consume.

43 The stranger that is within you shall get up above you very high; and you shalt come down very low.

44 He shall lend to you, and you shalt not lend to him: he shall be the head, and you shalt be the tail.

45 Moreover all these curses shall come upon you, and shall pursue you, and overtake you, till you be destroyed; because you hearkenedst not unto the voice of the LORD your God, to keep his commandments and his statutes which he commanded you:

46 And they shall be upon you for a sign and for a wonder, and upon your seed for ever.

47 Because you servedst not the LORD your God with joyfulness, and with gladness of heart, for the abundance of all things;

48 Therefore shalt you serve yours enemies which the LORD shall send against you, in hunger, and in thirst, and in nakedness, and in want of all things: and he shall put a yoke of iron upon your neck, until he have destroyed you.

49 The LORD shall bring a nation against you from far, from the end of the earth, as swift as the eagle flieth; a nation whose tongue you shalt not understand;

50 A nation of fierce countenance, which shall not regard the person of the old, nor shew favour to the young:

51 And he shall eat the fruit of your cattle, and the fruit of your land, until you be destroyed: which also shall not leave you either corn, wine, or oil, or the increase of your kine, or flocks of your sheep, until he have destroyed you.

52 And he shall besiege you in all your gates, until your high and fenced walls come down, wherein you trustedst, throughout all your land: and he shall besiege you in all your gates throughout all your land, which the LORD your God has given you.

53 And you shalt eat the fruit of yours own body, the flesh of your sons and of your daughters, which the LORD your God has given you, in the siege, and in the straitness, wherewith yours enemies shall distress you:

54 So that the man that is tender among you, and very delicate, his eye shall be evil toward his brother, and toward the wife of his bosom, and toward the remnant of his children which he shall leave:

55 So that he will not give to any of them of the flesh of his children whom he shall eat: because he has nothing left him in the siege, and in the straitness, wherewith yours enemies shall distress you in all your gates.

56 The tender and delicate woman among you, which would not adventure to set the sole of her foot upon the ground for delicateness and tenderness, her eye shall be evil toward the husband of her bosom, and toward her son, and toward her daughter,

57 And toward her young one that comes out from between her feet, and toward her children which she shall bear: for she shall eat them for want of all things secretly in the siege and straitness, wherewith yours enemy shall distress you in your gates.

58 If you will not observe to do all the words of this law that are written in this book, that you mayest fear this glorious and fearful name, THE LORD YOUR GOD;

59 Then the LORD will make your plagues wonderful, and the plagues of your seed, even great plagues, and of long continuance, and sore sicknesses, and of long continuance.

60 Moreover he will bring upon you all the diseases of Egypt, which you wast afraid of; and they shall cleave unto you.

61 Also every sickness, and every plague, which is not written in the book of this law, them will the LORD bring upon you, until you be destroyed.

62 And you shall be left few in number, whereas you were as the stars of heaven for multitude; because you wouldest not obey the voice of the LORD your God.

63 And it shall come to pass, that as the LORD rejoiced over you to do you good, and to multiply you; so the LORD will rejoice over you to destroy you, and to bring you to nought; and you shall be plucked from off the land whither you go to possess it.

64 And the LORD shall scatter you among all people, from the one end of the earth even unto the other; and there you shalt serve other gods, which neither you nor your fathers have known, even wood and stone.

65 And among these nations shalt you find no ease, neither shall the sole of your foot have rest: but the LORD shall give you there a trembling heart, and failing of eyes, and sorrow of mind:

66 And your life shall hang in doubt before you; and you shalt fear day and night, and shalt have none assurance of your life:

67 In the morning you shalt say, Would God it were even! and at even you shalt say, Would God it were morning! for the fear of yours heart wherewith you shalt fear, and for the sight of yours eyes which you shalt see.

68 And the LORD shall bring you into Egypt again with ships, by the way whereof I spake unto you, You shalt see it no more again: and there you shall be sold unto your enemies for bondmen and bondwomen, and no man shall buy you.

CHAPTER 29

THESE are the words of the covenant, which the LORD commanded Moses to make with the children of Israel in the land of Moab, beside the covenant which he made with them in Horeb.

2And Moses called unto all Israel, and said unto them, You have seen all that the LORD did before your eyes in the land of Egypt unto Pharaoh, and unto all his servants, and unto all his land;

3 The great temptations which yours eyes have seen, the signs, and those great miracles:

4 Yet the LORD has not given you an heart to perceive, and eyes to see, and ears to hear, unto this day.

5 And I have led you forty years in the wilderness: your clothes are not waxen old upon you, and your shoe is not waxen old upon your foot.

6 You have not eaten bread, neither have you drunk wine or strong drink: that you might know that I am the LORD your God.

7 And when you came unto this place, Sihon the king of Heshbon, and Og the king of Bashan, came out against us unto battle, and we struck them:

8 And we took their land, and gave it for an inheritance unto the Reubenites, and to the Gadites, and to the half tribe of Manasseh.

9 Keep therefore the words of this covenant, and do them, that you may prosper in all that you do.

10You stand this day all of you before the LORD your God; your captains of your tribes, your elders, and your officers, with all the men of Israel,

11 Your little ones, your wives, and your stranger that is in your camp, from the hewer of your wood unto the drawer of your water:

12 That you shouldest enter into covenant with the LORD your God, and into his oath, which the LORD your God maketh with you this day:

13 That he may establish you to day for a people unto himself, and that he may be unto you a God, as he has said unto you, and as he has sworn unto your fathers, to Abraham, to Isaac, and to Jacob.

14 Neither with you only do I make this covenant and this oath;

15 But with him that standeth here with us this day before the LORD our God, and also with him that is not here with us this day:

16 (For you know how we have dwelt in the land of Egypt; and how we came through the nations which you passed by;

17 And you have seen their abominations, and their idols, wood and stone, silver and gold, which were among them:)

18 Lest there should be among you man, or woman, or family, or tribe, whose heart turneth away this day from the LORD our God, to go and serve the gods of these nations; lest there should be among you a root that beareth gall and wormwood;

19 And it come to pass, when he heareth the words of this curse, that he bless himself in his heart, saying, I shall have peace, though I walk in the imagination of my heart, to add drunkenness to thirst:

20 The LORD will not spare him, but then the anger of the LORD and his jealousy shall smoke against that man, and all the curses that are written in this book shall lie upon him, and the LORD shall blot out his name from under heaven.

21 And the LORD shall separate him unto evil out of all the tribes of Israel, according to all the curses of the covenant that are written in this book of the law:

22 So that the generation to come of your children that shall rise up after you, and the stranger that shall come from a far land, shall say, when they see the plagues of that land, and the sicknesses which the LORD has laid upon it;

23 And that the whole land thereof is brimstone, and salt, and burning, that it is not sown, nor beareth, nor any grass groweth therein, like the overthrow of Sodom, and Gomorrah, Admah, and Zeboim, which the LORD overthrew in his anger, and in his wrath:

24 Even all nations shall say, Wherefore has the LORD done thus unto this land? what meaneth the heat of this great anger?

25 Then men shall say, Because they have forsaken the covenant of the LORD God of their fathers, which he made with them when he brought them forth out of the land of Egypt:

26 For they went and served other gods, and worshipped them, gods whom they knew not, and whom he had not given unto them:

27 And the anger of the LORD was kindled against this land, to bring upon it all the curses that are written in this book:

28 And the LORD rooted them out of their land in anger, and in wrath, and in great indignation, and cast them into another land, as it is this day.

29 The secret things belong unto the LORD our God: but those things which are revealed belong unto us and to our children for ever, that we may do all the words of this law.

CHAPTER 30

AND it shall come to pass, when all these things are come upon you, the blessing and the curse, which I have set before you, and you shalt call them to mind among all the nations, whither the LORD your God has driven you,

2 And shalt return unto the LORD your God, and shalt obey his voice according to all that I command you this day, you and your children, with all yours heart, and with all your soul;

3 That then the LORD your God will turn your captivity, and have compassion upon you, and will return and gather you from all the nations, whither the LORD your God has scattered you.

4 If any of yours be driven out unto the outmost parts of heaven, from thence will the LORD your God gather you, and from thence will he fetch you:

5 And the LORD your God will bring you into the land which your fathers possessed, and you shalt possess it; and he will do you good, and multiply you above your fathers.

6 And the LORD your God will circumcise yours heart, and the heart of your seed, to love the LORD your God with all yours heart, and with all your soul, that you mayest live.

7 And the LORD your God will put all these curses upon yours enemies, and on them that hate you, which persecuted you.

8 And you shalt return and obey the voice of the LORD, and do all his commandments which I command you this day.

9 And the LORD your God will make you plenteous in every work of yours hand, in the fruit of your body, and in the fruit of your cattle, and in the fruit of your land, for good: for the LORD will again rejoice over you for good, as he rejoiced over your fathers:

10 If you shalt hearken unto the voice of the LORD your God, to keep his commandments and his statutes which are written in this book of the law, and if you turn unto the LORD your God with all yours heart, and with all your soul.

11 For this commandment which I command you this day, it is not hidden from you, neither is it far off.

12 It is not in heaven, that you shouldest say, Who shall go up for us to heaven, and bring it unto us, that we may hear it, and do it?

13 Neither is it beyond the sea, that you shouldest say, Who shall go over the sea for us, and bring it unto us, that we may hear it, and do it?

14 But the word is very nigh unto you, in your mouth, and in your heart, that you mayest do it.

15 See, I have set before you this day life and good, and death and evil;

16 In that I command you this day to love the LORD your God, to walk in his ways, and to keep his commandments and his statutes and his judgments, that you mayest live and multiply: and the LORD your God shall bless you in the land whither you go to possess it.

17 But if yours heart turn away, so that you will not hear, but shalt be drawn away, and worship other gods, and serve them;

18 I denounce unto you this day, that you shall surely perish, and that you shall not prolong your days upon the land, whither you passest over Jordan to go to possess it.

19 I call heaven and earth to record this day against you, that I have set before you life and death, blessing and cursing: therefore choose life, that both you and your seed may live:

20 That you mayest love the LORD your God, and that you mayest obey his voice, and that you mayest cleave unto him: for he is your life, and the length of your days: that you mayest dwell in the land which the LORD sware unto your fathers, to Abraham, to Isaac, and to Jacob, to give them.

CHAPTER 31

AND Moses went and spake these words unto all Israel.

2 And he said unto them, I am an hundred and twenty years old this day; I can no more go out and come in: also the LORD has said unto me, You shalt not go over this Jordan.

3 The LORD your God, he will go over before you, and he will destroy these nations from before you, and you shalt possess them: and Joshua, he shall go over before you, as the LORD has said.

4 And the LORD shall do unto them as he did to Sihon and to Og, kings of the Amorites, and unto the land of them, whom he destroyed.

5 And the LORD shall give them up before your face, that you may do unto them according unto all the commandments which I have commanded you.

6 Be strong and of a good courage, fear not, nor be afraid of them: for the LORD your God, he it is that doth go with you; he will not fail you, nor forsake you.

7 And Moses called unto Joshua, and said unto him in the sight of all Israel, Be strong and of a good courage: for you must go with this people unto the land which the LORD has sworn unto their fathers to give them; and you shalt cause them to inherit it.

8 And the LORD, he it is that doth go before you; he will be with you, he will not fail you, neither forsake you: fear not, neither be dismayed.

9 And Moses wrote this law, and delivered it unto the priests the sons of Levi, which bare the ark of the covenant of the LORD, and unto all the elders of Israel.

10 And Moses commanded them, saying, At the end of every seven years, in the solemnity of the year of release, in the feast of tabernacles,

11 When all Israel is come to appear before the LORD your God in the place which he shall choose, you shalt read this law before all Israel in their hearing.

12 Gather the people together, men, and women, and children, and your stranger that is within your gates, that they may hear, and that they may learn, and fear the LORD your God, and observe to do all the words of this law:

13 And that their children, which have not known any thing, may hear, and learn to fear the LORD your God, as long as you live in the land whither you go over Jordan to possess it.

14 And the LORD said unto Moses, Behold, your days approach that you must die: call Joshua, and present yourselves in the tabernacle of the congregation, that I may give him a charge. And Moses and Joshua went, and presented themselves in the tabernacle of the congregation.

15 And the LORD appeared in the tabernacle in a pillar of a cloud: and the pillar of the cloud stood over the door of the tabernacle.

16 And the LORD said unto Moses, Behold, you shalt sleep with your fathers; and this people will rise up, and go a whoring after the gods of the strangers of the land, whither they go to be among them, and will forsake me, and break my covenant which I have made with them.

17 Then my anger shall be kindled against them in that day, and I will forsake them, and I will hide my face from them, and they shall be devoured, and many evils and troubles shall befall them; so that they will say in that day, Are not these evils come upon us, because our God is not among us?

18 And I will surely hide my face in that day for all the evils which they shall have created, in that they are turned unto other gods.

19 Now therefore write you this song for you, and teach it the children of Israel: put it in their mouths, that this song may be a witness for me against the children of Israel.

20 For when I shall have brought them into the land which I sware unto their fathers, that floweth with milk and honey; and they shall have eaten and filled themselves, and waxen fat; then will they turn unto other gods, and serve them, and provoke me, and break my covenant.

21 And it shall come to pass, when many evils and troubles are befallen them, that this song shall testify against them as a witness; for it shall not be forgotten out of the mouths of their seed: for I know their imagination which they go about, even now, before I have brought them into the land which I sware.

22 Moses therefore wrote this song the same day, and taught it the children of Israel.

23 And he gave Joshua the son of Nun a charge, and said, Be strong and of a good courage: for you shalt bring the children of Israel into the land which I sware unto them: and I will be with you.

24 And it came to pass, when Moses had made an end of writing the words of this law in a book, until they were finished,

25 That Moses commanded the Levites, which bare the ark of the covenant of the LORD, saying,

26 Take this book of the law, and put it in the side of the ark of the covenant of the LORD your God, that it may be there for a witness against you.

27 For I know your rebellion, and your stiff neck: behold, while I am yet alive with you this day, you have been rebellious against the LORD; and how much more after my death?

28 Gather unto me all the elders of your tribes, and your officers, that I may speak these words in their ears, and call heaven and earth to record against them.

29 For I know that after my death you will utterly corrupt yourselves, and turn aside from the way which I have commanded you; and evil will befall you in the latter days; because you will do evil in the sight of the LORD, to provoke him to anger through the work of your hands.

30 And Moses spake in the ears of all the congregation of Israel the words of this song, until they were ended.

CHAPTER 32

GIVE ear, O you heavens, and I will speak; and hear, O earth, the words of my mouth.

2 My doctrine shall drop as the rain, my speech shall distil as the dew, as the small rain upon the tender herb, and as the showers upon the grass:

3 Because I will publish the name of the LORD: ascribe you greatness unto our God.

4 He is the Rock, his work is perfect: for all his ways are judgment: a God of truth and without iniquity, just and right is he.

5 They have corrupted themselves, their spot is not the spot of his children: they are a perverse and crooked generation.

6 Do you thus requite the LORD, O foolish people and unwise? is not he your father that has bought you? has he not made you, and established you?

7Remember the days of old, consider the years of many generations: ask your father, and he will shew you; your elders, and they will tell you.

8 When the most High divided to the nations their inheritance, when he separated the sons of Adam, he set the bounds of the people according to the number of the children of Israel.

9 For the LORD's portion is his people; Jacob is the lot of his inheritance.

10 He found him in a desert land, and in the waste howling wilderness; he led him about, he instructed him, he kept him as the apple of his eye.

11 As an eagle stirreth up her nest, fluttereth over her young, spreadeth abroad her wings, taketh them, beareth them on her wings:

12 So the LORD alone did lead him, and there was no strange god with him.

13 He made him ride on the high places of the earth, that he might eat the increase of the fields; and he made him to suck honey out of the rock, and oil out of the flinty rock;

14 Butter of kine, and milk of sheep, with fat of lambs, and rams of the breed of Bashan, and goats, with the fat of kidneys of wheat; and you did drink the pure blood of the grape.

15But Jeshurun waxed fat, and kicked: you are waxen fat, you are grown thick, you are covered with fatness; then he forsook God which made him, and lightly esteemed the Rock of his salvation.

16 They provoked him to jealousy with strange gods, with abominations provoked they him to anger.

17 They sacrificed unto devils, not to God; to gods whom they knew not, to new gods that came newly up, whom your fathers feared not.

18 Of the Rock that begat you you are unmindful, and have forgotten God that formed you.

19 And when the LORD saw it, he abhorred them, because of the provoking of his sons, and of his daughters.

20 And he said, I will hide my face from them, I will see what their end shall be: for they are a very froward generation, children in whom is no faith.

21 They have moved me to jealousy with that which is not God; they have provoked me to anger with their vanities: and I will move them to jealousy with those which are not a people; I will provoke them to anger with a foolish nation.

22 For a fire is kindled in my anger, and shall burn unto the lowest hell, and shall consume the earth with her increase, and set on fire the foundations of the mountains.

23 I will heap mischiefs upon them; I will spend my arrows upon them.

24 They shall be burnt with hunger, and devoured with burning heat, and with bitter destruction: I will also send the teeth of beasts upon them, with the poison of serpents of the dust.

25 The sword without, and terror within, shall destroy both the young man and the virgin, the suckling also with the man of gray hairs.

26 I said, I would scatter them into corners, I would make the remembrance of them to cease from among men:

27 Were it not that I feared the wrath of the enemy, lest their adversaries should behave themselves strangely, and lest they should say, Our hand is high, and the LORD has not done all this.

28 For they are a nation void of counsel, neither is there any understanding in them.

29 O that they were wise, that they understood this, that they would consider their latter end!

30 How should one chase a thousand, and two put ten thousand to flight, except their Rock had sold them, and the LORD had shut them up?

31 For their rock is not as our Rock, even our enemies themselves being judges.

32 For their vine is of the vine of Sodom, and of the fields of Gomorrah: their grapes are grapes of gall, their clusters are bitter:

33 Their wine is the poison of dragons, and the cruel venom of asps.

34 Is not this laid up in store with me, and sealed up among my treasures?

35 To me belongeth vengeance, and recompence; their foot shall slide in due time: for the day of their calamity is at hand, and the things that shall come upon them make haste.

36 For the LORD shall judge his people, and repent himself for his servants, when he seeth that their power is gone, and there is none shut up, or left.

37 And he shall say, Where are their gods, their rock in whom they trusted,

38 Which did eat the fat of their sacrifices, and drank the wine of their drink offerings? let them rise up and help you, and be your protection.

39 See now that I, even I, am he, and there is no god with me: I kill, and I make alive; I wound, and I heal: neither is there any that can deliver out of my hand.

40 For I lift up my hand to heaven, and say, I live for ever.

41 If I whet my glittering sword, and my hand take hold on judgment; I will render vengeance to my enemies, and will reward them that hate me.

42 I will make my arrows drunk with blood, and my sword shall devour flesh; and that with the blood of the slain and of the captives, from the beginning of revenges upon the enemy.

43 Rejoice, O you nations, with his people: for he will avenge the blood of his servants, and will render vengeance to his adversaries, and will be merciful unto his land, and to his people.

44And Moses came and spake all the words of this song in the ears of the people, he, and Hoshea the son of Nun.

45 And Moses made an end of speaking all these words to all Israel:

46 And he said unto them, Set your hearts unto all the words which I testify among you this day, which you shall command your children to observe to do, all the words of this law.

47 For it is not a vain thing for you; because it is your life: and through this thing you shall prolong your days in the land, whither you go over Jordan to possess it.

48 And the LORD spake unto Moses that selfsame day, saying,

49 Get you up into this mountain Abarim, unto mount Nebo, which is in the land of Moab, that is over against Jericho; and behold the land of Canaan, which I give unto the children of Israel for a possession:

50 And die in the mount whither you go up, and be gathered unto your people; as Aaron your brother died in mount Hor, and was gathered unto his people:

51 Because you trespassed against me among the children of Israel at the waters of Meribah-Kadesh, in the wilderness of Zin; because you sanctified me not in the midst of the children of Israel.

52 Yet you shalt see the land before you; but you shalt not go thither unto the land which I give the children of Israel.

CHAPTER 33

AND this is the blessing, wherewith Moses the man of God blessed the children of Israel before his death.

2 And he said, The LORD came from Sinai, and rose up from Seir unto them; he shined forth from mount Paran, and he came with ten thousands of saints: from his right hand went a fiery law for them.

3 Yea, he loved the people; all his saints are in your hand: and they sat down at your feet; every one shall receive of your words.

4 Moses commanded us a law, even the inheritance of the congregation of Jacob.

5 And he was king in Jeshurun, when the heads of the people and the tribes of Israel were gathered together.

6Let Reuben live, and not die; and let not his men be few.

7And this is the blessing of Judah: and he said, Hear, LORD, the voice of Judah, and bring him unto his people: let his hands be sufficient for him; and be you an help to him from his enemies.

8And of Levi he said, Let your Thummim and your Urim be with your holy one, whom you did prove at Massah, and with whom you did strive at the waters of Meribah;

9 Who said unto his father and to his mother, I have not seen him; neither did he acknowledge his brethren, nor knew his own children: for they have observed your word, and kept your covenant.

10 They shall teach Jacob your judgments, and Israel your law: they shall put incense before you, and whole burnt sacrifice upon yours altar.

11 Bless, LORD, his substance, and accept the work of his hands: strike through the loins of them that rise against him, and of them that hate him, that they rise not again.

12And of Benjamin he said, The beloved of the LORD shall dwell in safety by him; and the LORD shall cover him all the day long, and he shall dwell between his shoulders.

13And of Joseph he said, Blessed of the LORD be his land, for the precious things of heaven, for the dew, and for the deep that coucheth beneath,

14 And for the precious fruits brought forth by the sun, and for the precious things put forth by the moon,

15 And for the chief things of the ancient mountains, and for the precious things of the lasting hills,

16 And for the precious things of the earth and fulness thereof, and for the good will of him that dwelt in the bush: let the blessing come upon the head of Joseph, and upon the top of the head of him that was separated from his brethren.

17 His glory is like the firstling of his bullock, and his horns are like the horns of unicorns: with them he shall push the people together to the ends of the earth: and they are the ten thousands of Ephraim, and they are the thousands of Manasseh.

18And of Zebulun he said, Rejoice, Zebulun, in your going out; and, Issachar, in your tents.

19 They shall call the people unto the mountain; there they shall offer sacrifices of righteousness: for they shall suck of the abundance of the seas, and of treasures hid in the sand.

20And of Gad he said, Blessed be he that enlargeth Gad: he dwelleth as a lion, and teareth the arm with the crown of the head.

21 And he provided the first part for himself, because there, in a portion of the lawgiver, was he seated; and he came with the heads of the people, he executed the justice of the LORD, and his judgments with Israel.

22And of Dan he said, Dan is a lion's whelp: he shall leap from Bashan.

23And of Naphtali he said, O Naphtali, satisfied with favour, and full with the blessing of the LORD: possess you the west and the south.

24And of Asher he said, Let Asher be blessed with children; let him be acceptable to his brethren, and let him dip his foot in oil.

25 Your shoes shall be iron and brass; and as your days, so shall your strength be.

26There is none like unto the God of Jeshurun, who rideth upon the heaven in your help, and in his excellency on the sky.

27 The eternal God is your refuge, and underneath are the everlasting arms: and he shall thrust out the enemy from before you; and shall say, Destroy them.

28 Israel then shall dwell in safety alone: the fountain of Jacob shall be upon a land of corn and wine; also his heavens shall drop down dew.

29 Happy are you , O Israel: who is like unto you, O people saved by the LORD, the shield of your help, and who is the sword of your excellency! and yours enemies shall be found liars unto you; and you shalt tread upon their high places.

CHAPTER 34

AND Moses went up from the plains of Moab unto the mountain of Nebo, to the top of Pisgah, that is over against Jericho. And the LORD shewed him all the land of Gilead, unto Dan,

2 And all Naphtali, and the land of Ephraim, and Manasseh, and all the land of Judah, unto the utmost sea,

3 And the south, and the plain of the valley of Jericho, the city of palm trees, unto Zoar.

4 And the LORD said unto him, This is the land which I sware unto Abraham, unto Isaac, and unto Jacob, saying, I will give it unto your seed: I have caused you to see it with yours eyes, but you shalt not go over thither.

5So Moses the servant of the LORD died there in the land of Moab, according to the word of the LORD.

6 And he buried him in a valley in the land of Moab, over against Beth-peor: but no man knoweth of his sepulchre unto this day.

7And Moses was an hundred and twenty years old when he died: his eye was not dim, nor his natural force abated.

8And the children of Israel wept for Moses in the plains of Moab thirty days: so the days of weeping and mourning for Moses were ended.

9And Joshua the son of Nun was full of the spirit of wisdom; for Moses had laid his hands upon him: and the children of Israel hearkened unto him, and did as the LORD commanded Moses.

10And there arose not a prophet since in Israel like unto Moses, whom the LORD knew face to face,

11 In all the signs and the wonders, which the LORD sent him to do in the land of Egypt to Pharaoh, and to all his servants, and to all his land,

12 And in all that mighty hand, and in all the great terror which Moses shewed in the sight of all Israel.

THE BOOK OF JOSHUA.

CHAPTER 1

NOW after the death of Moses the servant of the LORD it came to pass, that the LORD spake unto Joshua the son of Nun, Moses' minister, saying,

2 Moses my servant is dead; now therefore arise, go over this Jordan, you , and all this people, unto the land which I do give to them, even to the children of Israel.

3 Every place that the sole of your foot shall tread upon, that have I given unto you, as I said unto Moses.

4 From the wilderness and this Lebanon even unto the great river, the river Euphrates, all the land of the Hittites, and unto the great sea toward the going down of the sun, shall be your coast.

5 There shall not any man be able to stand before you all the days of your life: as I was with Moses, so I will be with you: I will not fail you, nor forsake you.

6 Be strong and of a good courage: for unto this people shalt you divide for an inheritance the land, which I sware unto their fathers to give them.

7 Only be you strong and very courageous, that you mayest observe to do according to all the law, which Moses my servant commanded you: turn not from it to the right hand or to the left, that you mayest prosper whithersoever you go.

8 This book of the law shall not depart out of your mouth; but you shalt meditate therein day and night, that you mayest observe to do according to all that is written therein: for then you shalt make your way prosperous, and then you shalt have good success.

9 Have not I commanded you? Be strong and of a good courage; be not afraid, neither be you dismayed: for the LORD your God is with you whithersoever you go.

10Then Joshua commanded the officers of the people, saying,

11 Pass through the host, and command the people, saying, Prepare you victuals; for within three days you shall pass over this Jordan, to go in to possess the land, which the LORD your God giveth you to possess it.

12And to the Reubenites, and to the Gadites, and to half the tribe of Manasseh, spake Joshua, saying,

13 Remember the word which Moses the servant of the LORD commanded you, saying, The LORD your God has given you rest, and has given you this land.

14 Your wives, your little ones, and your cattle, shall remain in the land which Moses gave you on this side Jordan; but you shall pass before your brethren armed, all the mighty men of valour, and help them;

15 Until the LORD have given your brethren rest, as he has given you, and they also have possessed the land which the LORD your God giveth them: then you shall return unto the land of your possession, and enjoy it, which Moses the LORD's servant gave you on this side Jordan toward the sunrising.

16And they answered Joshua, saying, All that you commandest us we will do, and whithersoever you sendest us, we will go.

17 According as we hearkened unto Moses in all things, so will we hearken unto you: only the LORD your God be with you, as he was with Moses.

18 Whosoever he be that doth rebel against your commandment, and will not hearken unto your words in all that you commandest him, he shall be put to death: only be strong and of a good courage.

CHAPTER 2

AND Joshua the son of Nun sent out of Shittim two men to spy secretly, saying, Go view the land, even Jericho. And they went, and came into an harlot's house, named Rahab, and lodged there.

2 And it was told the king of Jericho, saying, Behold, there came men in hither to night of the children of Israel to search out the country.

3 And the king of Jericho sent unto Rahab, saying, Bring forth the men that are come to you, which are entered into yours house: for they be come to search out all the country.

4 And the woman took the two men, and hid them, and said thus, There came men unto me, but I wist not whence they were:

5 And it came to pass about the time of shutting of the gate, when it was dark, that the men went out: whither the men went I wot not: pursue after them quickly; for you shall overtake them.

6 But she had brought them up to the roof of the house, and hid them with the stalks of flax, which she had laid in order upon the roof.

7 And the men pursued after them the way to Jordan unto the fords: and as soon as they which pursued after them were gone out, they shut the gate.

8And before they were laid down, she came up unto them upon the roof;

9 And she said unto the men, I know that the LORD has given you the land, and that your terror is fallen upon us, and that all the inhabitants of the land faint because of you.

10 For we have heard how the LORD dried up the water of the Red sea for you, when you came out of Egypt; and what you did unto the two kings of the Amorites, that were on the other side Jordan, Sihon and Og, whom you utterly destroyed.

11 And as soon as we had heard these things, our hearts did melt, neither did there remain any more courage in any man, because of you: for the LORD your God, he is God in heaven above, and in earth beneath.

12 Now therefore, I pray you, swear unto me by the LORD, since I have shewed you kindness, that you will also shew kindness unto my father's house, and give me a true token:

13 And that you will save alive my father, and my mother, and my brethren, and my sisters, and all that they have, and deliver our lives from death.

14 And the men answered her, Our life for yours, if you utter not this our business. And it shall be, when the LORD has given us the land, that we will deal kindly and truly with you.

15 Then she let them down by a cord through the window: for her house was upon the town wall, and she dwelt upon the wall.

16 And she said unto them, Get you to the mountain, lest the pursuers meet you; and hide yourselves there three days, until the pursuers be returned: and afterward may you go your way.

17 And the men said unto her, We will be blameless of this yours oath which you have made us swear.

18 Behold, when we come into the land, you shalt bind this line of scarlet thread in the window which you did let us down by: and you shalt bring your father, and your mother, and your brethren, and your father's household, home unto you.

19 And it shall be, that whosoever shall go out of the doors of your house into the street, his blood shall be upon his head, and we will be guiltless: and whosoever shall be with you in the house, his blood shall be on our head, if any hand be upon him.

20 And if you utter this our business, then we will be quit of yours oath which you have made us swear.

21 And she said, According unto your words, so be it. And she sent them away, and they departed: and she bound the scarlet line in the window.

22 And they went, and came unto the mountain, and abode there three days, until the pursuers were returned: and the pursuers sought them throughout all the way, but found them not.

23So the two men returned, and descended from the mountain, and passed over, and came to Joshua the son of Nun, and told him all things that befell them:

24 And they said unto Joshua, Truly the LORD has delivered into our hands all the land; for even all the inhabitants of the country do faint because of us.

CHAPTER 3

AND Joshua rose early in the morning; and they removed from Shittim, and came to Jordan, he and all the children of Israel, and lodged there before they passed over.

2 And it came to pass after three days, that the officers went through the host;

3 And they commanded the people, saying, When you see the ark of the covenant of the LORD your God, and the priests the Levites bearing it, then you shall remove from your place, and go after it.

4 Yet there shall be a space between you and it, about two thousand cubits by measure: come not near unto it, that you may know the way by which you must go: for you have not passed this way heretofore.

5 And Joshua said unto the people, Sanctify yourselves: for to morrow the LORD will do wonders among you.

6 And Joshua spake unto the priests, saying, Take up the ark of the covenant, and pass over before the people. And they took up the ark of the covenant, and went before the people.

7And the LORD said unto Joshua, This day will I begin to magnify you in the sight of all Israel, that they may know that, as I was with Moses, so I will be with you.

8 And you shalt command the priests that bear the ark of the covenant, saying, When you are come to the brink of the water of Jordan, you shall stand still in Jordan.

9And Joshua said unto the children of Israel, Come hither, and hear the words of the LORD your God.

10 And Joshua said, Hereby you shall know that the living God is among you, and that he will without fail drive out from before you the Canaanites, and the Hittites, and the Hivites, and the Perizzites, and the Girgashites, and the Amorites, and the Jebusites.

11 Behold, the ark of the covenant of the Lord of all the earth passes over before you into Jordan.

12 Now therefore take you twelve men out of the tribes of Israel, out of every tribe a man.

13 And it shall come to pass, as soon as the soles of the feet of the priests that bear the ark of the LORD, the Lord of all the earth, shall rest in the waters of Jordan, that the waters of Jordan shall be cut off from the waters that come down from above; and they shall stand upon an heap.

14And it came to pass, when the people removed from their tents, to pass over Jordan, and the priests bearing the ark of the covenant before the people;

15 And as they that bare the ark were come unto Jordan, and the feet of the priests that bare the ark were dipped in the brim of the water, (for Jordan overfloweth all his banks all the time of harvest,)

16 That the waters which came down from above stood and rose up upon an heap very far from the city Adam, that is beside Zaretan: and those that came down toward the sea of the plain, even the salt sea, failed, and were cut off: and the people passed over right against Jericho.

17 And the priests that bare the ark of the covenant of the LORD stood firm on dry ground in the midst of Jordan, and all the Israelites passed over on dry ground, until all the people were passed clean over Jordan.

CHAPTER 4

AND it came to pass, when all the people were clean passed over Jordan, that the LORD spake unto Joshua, saying,

2 Take you twelve men out of the people, out of every tribe a man,

3 And command you them, saying, Take you hence out of the midst of Jordan, out of the place where the priests' feet stood firm, twelve stones, and you shall carry them over with you, and leave them in the lodging place, where you shall lodge this night.

4 Then Joshua called the twelve men, whom he had prepared of the children of Israel, out of every tribe a man:

5 And Joshua said unto them, Pass over before the ark of the LORD your God into the midst of Jordan, and take you up every man of you a stone upon his shoulder, according unto the number of the tribes of the children of Israel:

6 That this may be a sign among you, that when your children ask their fathers in time to come, saying, What mean you by these stones?

7 Then you shall answer them, That the waters of Jordan were cut off before the ark of the covenant of the LORD; when it passed over Jordan, the waters of Jordan were cut off: and these stones shall be for a memorial unto the children of Israel for ever.

8 And the children of Israel did so as Joshua commanded, and took up twelve stones out of the midst of Jordan, as the LORD spake unto Joshua, according to the number of the tribes of the children of Israel, and carried them over with them unto the place where they lodged, and laid them down there.

9 And Joshua set up twelve stones in the midst of Jordan, in the place where the feet of the priests which bare the ark of the covenant stood: and they are there unto this day.

10For the priests which bare the ark stood in the midst of Jordan, until every thing was finished that the LORD commanded Joshua to speak unto the people, according to all that Moses commanded Joshua: and the people hasted and passed over.

11 And it came to pass, when all the people were clean passed over, that the ark of the LORD passed over, and the priests, in the presence of the people.

12 And the children of Reuben, and the children of Gad, and half the tribe of Manasseh, passed over armed before the children of Israel, as Moses spake unto them:

13 About forty thousand prepared for war passed over before the LORD unto battle, to the plains of Jericho.

14On that day the LORD magnified Joshua in the sight of all Israel; and they feared him, as they feared Moses, all the days of his life.

15 And the LORD spake unto Joshua, saying,

16 Command the priests that bear the ark of the testimony, that they come up out of Jordan.

17 Joshua therefore commanded the priests, saying, Come you up out of Jordan.

18 And it came to pass, when the priests that bare the ark of the covenant of the LORD were come up out of the midst of Jordan, and the soles of the priests' feet were lifted up unto the dry land, that the waters of Jordan returned unto their place, and flowed over all his banks, as they did before.

19And the people came up out of Jordan on the tenth day of the first month, and encamped in Gilgal, in the east border of Jericho.

20 And those twelve stones, which they took out of Jordan, did Joshua pitch in Gilgal.

21 And he spake unto the children of Israel, saying, When your children shall ask their fathers in time to come, saying, What mean these stones?

22 Then you shall let your children know, saying, Israel came over this Jordan on dry land.

23 For the LORD your God dried up the waters of Jordan from before you, until you were passed over, as the LORD your God did to the Red sea, which he dried up from before us, until we were gone over:

24 That all the people of the earth might know the hand of the LORD, that it is mighty: that you might fear the LORD your God for ever.

CHAPTER 5

AND it came to pass, when all the kings of the Amorites, which were on the side of Jordan westward, and all the kings of the Canaanites, which were by the sea, heard that the LORD had dried up the waters of Jordan from before the children of Israel, until we were passed over, that their heart melted, neither was there spirit in them any more, because of the children of Israel.

2At that time the LORD said unto Joshua, Make you sharp knives, and circumcise again the children of Israel the second time.

3 And Joshua made him sharp knives, and circumcised the children of Israel at the hill of the foreskins.

4 And this is the cause why Joshua did circumcise: All the people that came out of Egypt, that were males, even all the men of war, died in the wilderness by the way, after they came out of Egypt.

5 Now all the people that came out were circumcised: but all the people that were born in the wilderness by the way as they came forth out of Egypt, them they had not circumcised.

6 For the children of Israel walked forty years in the wilderness, till all the people that were men of war, which came out of Egypt, were consumed, because they obeyed not the voice of the LORD: unto whom the LORD sware that he would not shew them the land, which the LORD sware unto their fathers that he would give us, a land that floweth with milk and honey.

7 And their children, whom he raised up in their stead, them Joshua circumcised: for they were uncircumcised, because they had not circumcised them by the way.

8 And it came to pass, when they had done circumcising all the people, that they abode in their places in the camp, till they were whole.

9 And the LORD said unto Joshua, This day have I rolled away the reproach of Egypt from off you. Wherefore the name of the place is called Gilgal unto this day.

10And the children of Israel encamped in Gilgal, and kept the passover on the fourteenth day of the month at even in the plains of Jericho.

11 And they did eat of the old corn of the land on the morrow after the passover, unleavened cakes, and parched corn in the selfsame day.

12And the manna ceased on the morrow after they had eaten of the old corn of the land; neither had the children of Israel manna any more; but they did eat of the fruit of the land of Canaan that year.

13And it came to pass, when Joshua was by Jericho, that he lifted up his eyes and looked, and, behold, there stood a man over against him with his sword drawn in his hand: and Joshua went unto him, and said unto him, Are you for us, or for our adversaries?

14 And he said, Nay; but as captain of the host of the LORD am I now come. And Joshua fell on his face to the earth, and did worship, and said unto him, What saith my lord unto his servant?

15 And the captain of the LORD's host said unto Joshua, Loose your shoe from off your foot; for the place whereon you standest is holy. And Joshua did so.

CHAPTER 6

NOW Jericho was straitly shut up because of the children of Israel: none went out, and none came in.

2 And the LORD said unto Joshua, See, I have given into yours hand Jericho, and the king thereof, and the mighty men of valour.

3 And you shall compass the city, all you men of war, and go round about the city once. Thus shalt you do six days.

4 And seven priests shall bear before the ark seven trumpets of rams' horns: and the seventh day you shall compass the city seven times, and the priests shall blow with the trumpets.

5 And it shall come to pass, that when they make a long blast with the ram's horn, and when you hear the sound of the trumpet, all the people shall shout with a great shout; and the wall of the city shall fall down flat, and the people shall ascend up every man straight before him.

6And Joshua the son of Nun called the priests, and said unto them, Take up the ark of the covenant, and let seven priests bear seven trumpets of rams' horns before the ark of the LORD.

7 And he said unto the people, Pass on, and compass the city, and let him that is armed pass on before the ark of the LORD.

8And it came to pass, when Joshua had spoken unto the people, that the seven priests bearing the seven trumpets of rams' horns passed on before the LORD, and blew with the trumpets: and the ark of the covenant of the LORD followed them.

9And the armed men went before the priests that blew with the trumpets, and the rereward came after the ark, the priests going on, and blowing with the trumpets.

10 And Joshua had commanded the people, saying, You shall not shout, nor make any noise with your voice, neither shall any word proceed out of your mouth, until the day I bid you shout; then shall you shout.

11 So the ark of the LORD compassed the city, going about it once: and they came into the camp, and lodged in the camp.

12And Joshua rose early in the morning, and the priests took up the ark of the LORD.

13 And seven priests bearing seven trumpets of rams' horns before the ark of the LORD went on continually, and blew with the trumpets: and the armed men went before them; but the rereward came after the ark of the LORD, the priests going on, and blowing with the trumpets.

14 And the second day they compassed the city once, and returned into the camp: so they did six days.

15 And it came to pass on the seventh day, that they rose early about the dawning of the day, and compassed the city after the same manner seven times: only on that day they compassed the city seven times.

16 And it came to pass at the seventh time, when the priests blew with the trumpets, Joshua said unto the people, Shout; for the LORD has given you the city.

17And the city shall be accursed, even it, and all that are therein, to the LORD: only Rahab the harlot shall live, she and all that are with her in the house, because she hid the messengers that we sent.

18 And you , in any wise keep yourselves from the accursed thing, lest you make yourselves accursed, when you take of the accursed thing, and make the camp of Israel a curse, and trouble it.

19 But all the silver, and gold, and vessels of brass and iron, are consecrated unto the LORD: they shall come into the treasury of the LORD.

20 So the people shouted when the priests blew with the trumpets: and it came to pass, when the people heard the sound of the trumpet, and the people shouted with a great shout, that the wall fell down flat, so that the people went up into the city, every man straight before him, and they took the city.

21 And they utterly destroyed all that was in the city, both man and woman, young and old, and ox, and sheep, and ass, with the edge of the sword.

22 But Joshua had said unto the two men that had spied out the country, Go into the harlot's house, and bring out thence the woman, and all that she has, as you sware unto her.

23 And the young men that were spies went in, and brought out Rahab, and her father, and her mother, and her brethren, and all that she had; and they brought out all her kindred, and left them without the camp of Israel.

24 And they burnt the city with fire, and all that was therein: only the silver, and the gold, and the vessels of brass and of iron, they put into the treasury of the house of the LORD.

25 And Joshua saved Rahab the harlot alive, and her father's household, and all that she had; and she dwelleth in Israel even unto this day; because she hid the messengers, which Joshua sent to spy out Jericho.

26And Joshua adjured them at that time, saying, Cursed be the man before the LORD, that riseth up and buildeth this city Jericho: he shall lay the foundation thereof in his firstborn, and in his youngest son shall he set up the gates of it.

27 So the LORD was with Joshua; and his fame was noised throughout all the country.

CHAPTER 7

BUT the children of Israel committed a trespass in the accursed thing: for Achan, the son of Carmi, the son of Zabdi, the son of Zerah, of the tribe of Judah, took of the accursed thing: and the anger of the LORD was kindled against the children of Israel.

2 And Joshua sent men from Jericho to Ai, which is beside Beth-aven, on the east side of Beth-el, and spake unto them, saying, Go up and view the country. And the men went up and viewed Ai.

3 And they returned to Joshua, and said unto him, Let not all the people go up; but let about two or three thousand men go up and strike Ai; and make not all the people to labour thither; for they are but few.

4 So there went up thither of the people about three thousand men: and they fled before the men of Ai.

5 And the men of Ai struck of them about thirty and six men: for they chased them from before the gate even unto Shebarim, and struck them in the going down: wherefore the hearts of the people melted, and became as water.

6And Joshua rent his clothes, and fell to the earth upon his face before the ark of the LORD until the eventide, he and the elders of Israel, and put dust upon their heads.

7 And Joshua said, Alas, O Lord GOD, wherefore have you at all brought this people over Jordan, to deliver us into the hand of the Amorites, to destroy us? would to God we had been content, and dwelt on the other side Jordan!

8 O Lord, what shall I say, when Israel turneth their backs before their enemies!

9 For the Canaanites and all the inhabitants of the land shall hear of it, and shall environ us round, and cut off our name from the earth: and what will you do unto your great name?

10And the LORD said unto Joshua, Get you up; wherefore liest you thus upon your face?

11 Israel has sinned, and they have also transgressed my covenant which I commanded them: for they have even taken of the accursed thing, and have also stolen, and dissembled also, and they have put it even among their own stuff.

12 Therefore the children of Israel could not stand before their enemies, but turned their backs before their enemies, because they were accursed: neither will I be with you any more, except you destroy the accursed from among you.

13 Up, sanctify the people, and say, Sanctify yourselves against to morrow: for thus saith the LORD God of Israel, There is an accursed thing in the midst of you, O Israel: you can not stand before yours enemies, until you take away the accursed thing from among you.

14 In the morning therefore you shall be brought according to your tribes: and it shall be, that the tribe which the LORD taketh shall come according to the families thereof; and the family which the LORD shall take shall come by households; and the household which the LORD shall take shall come man by man.

15 And it shall be, that he that is taken with the accursed thing shall be burnt with fire, he and all that he has: because he has transgressed the covenant of the LORD, and because he has created folly in Israel.

16So Joshua rose up early in the morning, and brought Israel by their tribes; and the tribe of Judah was taken:

17 And he brought the family of Judah; and he took the family of the Zarhites: and he brought the family of the Zarhites man by man; and Zabdi was taken:

18 And he brought his household man by man; and Achan, the son of Carmi, the son of Zabdi, the son of Zerah, of the tribe of Judah, was taken.

19 And Joshua said unto Achan, My son, give, I pray you, glory to the LORD God of Israel, and make confession unto him; and tell me now what you have done; hide it not from me.

20 And Achan answered Joshua, and said, Indeed I have sinned against the LORD God of Israel, and thus and thus have I done:

21 When I saw among the spoils a goodly Babylonish garment, and two hundred shekels of silver, and a wedge of gold of fifty shekels weight, then I coveted them, and took them; and, behold, they are hid in the earth in the midst of my tent, and the silver under it.

22So Joshua sent messengers, and they ran unto the tent; and, behold, it was hid in his tent, and the silver under it.

23 And they took them out of the midst of the tent, and brought them unto Joshua, and unto all the children of Israel, and laid them out before the LORD.

24 And Joshua, and all Israel with him, took Achan the son of Zerah, and the silver, and the garment, and the wedge of gold, and his sons, and his daughters, and his oxen, and his asses, and his sheep, and his tent, and all that he had: and they brought them unto the valley of Achor.

25 And Joshua said, Why have you troubled us? the LORD shall trouble you this day. And all Israel stoned him with stones, and burned them with fire, after they had stoned them with stones.

26 And they raised over him a great heap of stones unto this day. So the LORD turned from the fierceness of his anger. Wherefore the name of that place was called, The valley of Achor, unto this day.

CHAPTER 8

AND the LORD said unto Joshua, Fear not, neither be you dismayed: take all the people of war with you, and arise, go up to Ai: see, I have given into your hand the king of Ai, and his people, and his city, and his land:

2 And you shalt do to Ai and her king as you did unto Jericho and her king: only the spoil thereof, and the cattle thereof, shall you take for a prey unto yourselves: lay you an ambush for the city behind it.

3So Joshua arose, and all the people of war, to go up against Ai: and Joshua chose out thirty thousand mighty men of valour, and sent them away by night.

4 And he commanded them, saying, Behold, you shall lie in wait against the city, even behind the city: go not very far from the city, but be you all ready:

5 And I, and all the people that are with me, will approach unto the city: and it shall come to pass, when they come out against us, as at the first, that we will flee before them,

6 (For they will come out after us) till we have drawn them from the city; for they will say, They flee before us, as at the first: therefore we will flee before them.

7 Then you shall rise up from the ambush, and seize upon the city: for the LORD your God will deliver it into your hand.

8 And it shall be, when you have taken the city, that you shall set the city on fire: according to the commandment of the LORD shall you do. See, I have commanded you.

9Joshua therefore sent them forth: and they went to lie in ambush, and abode between Beth-el and Ai, on the west side of Ai: but Joshua lodged that night among the people.

10 And Joshua rose up early in the morning, and numbered the people, and went up, he and the elders of Israel, before the people to Ai.

11 And all the people, even the people of war that were with him, went up, and drew nigh, and came before the city, and pitched on the north side of Ai: now there was a valley between them and Ai.

12 And he took about five thousand men, and set them to lie in ambush between Beth-el and Ai, on the west side of the city.

13 And when they had set the people, even all the host that was on the north of the city, and their liers in wait on the west of the city, Joshua went that night into the midst of the valley.

14And it came to pass, when the king of Ai saw it, that they hasted and rose up early, and the men of the city went out against Israel to battle, he and all his people, at a time appointed, before the plain; but he wist not that there were liers in ambush against him behind the city.

15 And Joshua and all Israel made as if they were beaten before them, and fled by the way of the wilderness.

16 And all the people that were in Ai were called together to pursue after them: and they pursued after Joshua, and were drawn away from the city.

17 And there was not a man left in Ai or Beth-el, that went not out after Israel: and they left the city open, and pursued after Israel.

18 And the LORD said unto Joshua, Stretch out the spear that is in your hand toward Ai; for I will give it into yours hand. And Joshua stretched out the spear that he had in his hand toward the city.

19 And the ambush arose quickly out of their place, and they ran as soon as he had stretched out his hand: and they entered into the city, and took it, and hasted and set the city on fire.

20 And when the men of Ai looked behind them, they saw, and, behold, the smoke of the city ascended up to heaven, and they had no power to flee this way or that way: and the people that fled to the wilderness turned back upon the pursuers.

21 And when Joshua and all Israel saw that the ambush had taken the city, and that the smoke of the city ascended, then they turned again, and slew the men of Ai.

22 And the other issued out of the city against them; so they were in the midst of Israel, some on this side, and some on that side: and they struck them, so that they let none of them remain or escape.

23 And the king of Ai they took alive, and brought him to Joshua.

24 And it came to pass, when Israel had made an end of slaying all the inhabitants of Ai in the field, in the wilderness wherein they chased them, and when they were all fallen on the edge of the sword, until they were consumed, that all the Israelites returned unto Ai, and struck it with the edge of the sword.

25 And so it was, that all that fell that day, both of men and women, were twelve thousand, even all the men of Ai.

26 For Joshua drew not his hand back, wherewith he stretched out the spear, until he had utterly destroyed all the inhabitants of Ai.

27 Only the cattle and the spoil of that city Israel took for a prey unto themselves, according unto the word of the LORD which he commanded Joshua.

28 And Joshua burnt Ai, and made it an heap for ever, even a desolation unto this day.

29 And the king of Ai he hanged on a tree until eventide: and as soon as the sun was down, Joshua commanded that they should take his carcase down from the tree, and cast it at the entering of the gate of the city, and raise thereon a great heap of stones, that remaineth unto this day.

30Then Joshua built an altar unto the LORD God of Israel in mount Ebal,

31 As Moses the servant of the LORD commanded the children of Israel, as it is written in the book of the law of Moses, an altar of whole stones, over which no man has lift up any iron: and they offered thereon burnt offerings unto the LORD, and sacrificed peace offerings.

32And he wrote there upon the stones a copy of the law of Moses, which he wrote in the presence of the children of Israel.

33 And all Israel, and their elders, and officers, and their judges, stood on this side the ark and on that side before the priests the Levites, which bare the ark of the covenant of the LORD, as well the stranger, as he that was born among them; half of them over against mount Gerizim, and half of them over against mount Ebal; as Moses the servant of the LORD had commanded before, that they should bless the people of Israel.

34 And afterward he read all the words of the law, the blessings and cursings, according to all that is written in the book of the law.

35 There was not a word of all that Moses commanded, which Joshua read not before all the congregation of Israel, with the women, and the little ones, and the strangers that were conversant among them.

CHAPTER 9

AND it came to pass, when all the kings which were on this side Jordan, in the hills, and in the valleys, and in all the coasts of the great sea over against Lebanon, the Hittite, and the Amorite, the Canaanite, the Perizzite, the Hivite, and the Jebusite, heard thereof;

2 That they gathered themselves together, to fight with Joshua and with Israel, with one accord.

3And when the inhabitants of Gibeon heard what Joshua had done unto Jericho and to Ai,

4 They did work wilily, and went and made as if they had been ambassadors, and took old sacks upon their asses, and wine bottles, old, and rent, and bound up;

5 And old shoes and clouted upon their feet, and old garments upon them; and all the bread of their provision was dry and mouldy.

6 And they went to Joshua unto the camp at Gilgal, and said unto him, and to the men of Israel, We be come from a far country: now therefore make you a league with us.

7 And the men of Israel said unto the Hivites, What if you dwell among us; and how shall we make a league with you?

8 And they said unto Joshua, We are your servants. And Joshua said unto them, Who are you ? and from whence come you ?

9 And they said unto him, From a very far country your servants are come because of the name of the LORD your God: for we have heard the fame of him, and all that he did in Egypt,

10 And all that he did to the two kings of the Amorites, that were beyond Jordan, to Sihon king of Heshbon, and to Og king of Bashan, which was at Ashtaroth.

11 Wherefore our elders and all the inhabitants of our country spake to us, saying, Take victuals with you for the journey, and go to meet them, and say unto them, We are your servants: therefore now make you a league with us.

12 This our bread we took hot for our provision out of our houses on the day we came forth to go unto you; but now, behold, it is dry, and it is mouldy:

13 And these bottles of wine, which we filled, were new; and, behold, they be rent: and these our garments and our shoes are become old by reason of the very long journey.

14 And the men took of their victuals, and asked not counsel at the mouth of the LORD.

15 And Joshua made peace with them, and made a league with them, to let them live: and the princes of the congregation sware unto them.

16And it came to pass at the end of three days after they had made a league with them, that they heard that they were their neighbours, and that they dwelt among them.

17 And the children of Israel journeyed, and came unto their cities on the third day. Now their cities were Gibeon, and Chephirah, and Beeroth, and Kirjath-jearim.

18 And the children of Israel struck them not, because the princes of the congregation had sworn unto them by the LORD God of Israel. And all the congregation murmured against the princes.

19 But all the princes said unto all the congregation, We have sworn unto them by the LORD God of Israel: now therefore we may not touch them.

20 This we will do to them; we will even let them live, lest wrath be upon us, because of the oath which we sware unto them.

21 And the princes said unto them, Let them live; but let them be hewers of wood and drawers of water unto all the congregation; as the princes had promised them.

22And Joshua called for them, and he spake unto them, saying, Wherefore have you beguiled us, saying, We are very far from you; when you dwell among us?

23 Now therefore you are cursed, and there shall none of you be freed from being bondmen, and hewers of wood and drawers of water for the house of my God.

24 And they answered Joshua, and said, Because it was certainly told your servants, how that the LORD your God commanded his servant Moses to give you all the land, and to destroy all the inhabitants of the land from before you, therefore we were sore afraid of our lives because of you, and have done this thing.

25 And now, behold, we are in yours hand: as it seemeth good and right unto you to do unto us, do.

26 And so did he unto them, and delivered them out of the hand of the children of Israel, that they slew them not.

27 And Joshua made them that day hewers of wood and drawers of water for the congregation, and for the altar of the LORD, even unto this day, in the place which he should choose.

CHAPTER 10

NOW it came to pass, when Adoni-zedek king of Jerusalem had heard how Joshua had taken Ai, and had utterly destroyed it; as he had done to Jericho and her king, so he had done to Ai and her king; and how the inhabitants of Gibeon had made peace with Israel, and were among them;

2 That they feared greatly, because Gibeon was a great city, as one of the royal cities, and because it was greater than Ai, and all the men thereof were mighty.

3 Wherefore Adoni-zedek king of Jerusalem sent unto Hoham king of Hebron, and unto Piram king of Jarmuth, and unto Japhia king of Lachish, and unto Debir king of Eglon, saying,

4 Come up unto me, and help me, that we may strike Gibeon: for it has made peace with Joshua and with the children of Israel.

5 Therefore the five kings of the Amorites, the king of Jerusalem, the king of Hebron, the king of Jarmuth, the king of Lachish, the king of Eglon, gathered themselves together, and went up, they and all their hosts, and encamped before Gibeon, and made war against it.

6 And the men of Gibeon sent unto Joshua to the camp to Gilgal, saying, Slack not your hand from your servants; come up to us quickly, and save us, and help us: for all the kings of the Amorites that dwell in the mountains are gathered together against us.

7 So Joshua ascended from Gilgal, he, and all the people of war with him, and all the mighty men of valour.

8 And the LORD said unto Joshua, Fear them not: for I have delivered them into yours hand; there shall not a man of them stand before you.

9 Joshua therefore came unto them suddenly, and went up from Gilgal all night.

10 And the LORD discomfited them before Israel, and slew them with a great slaughter at Gibeon, and chased them along the way that goeth up to Beth-horon, and struck them to Azekah, and unto Makkedah.

11 And it came to pass, as they fled from before Israel, and were in the going down to Beth-horon, that the LORD cast down great stones from heaven upon them unto Azekah, and they died: they were more which died with hailstones than they whom the children of Israel slew with the sword.

12 Then spake Joshua to the LORD in the day when the LORD delivered up the Amorites before the children of Israel, and he said in the sight of Israel, Sun, stand you still upon Gibeon; and you , Moon, in the valley of Ajalon.

13 And the sun stood still, and the moon stayed, until the people had avenged themselves upon their enemies. Is not this written in the book of Jasher? So the sun stood still in the midst of heaven, and hasted not to go down about a whole day.

14 And there was no day like that before it or after it, that the LORD hearkened unto the voice of a man: for the LORD fought for Israel.

15 And Joshua returned, and all Israel with him, unto the camp to Gilgal.

16 But these five kings fled, and hid themselves in a cave at Makkedah.

17 And it was told Joshua, saying, The five kings are found hid in a cave at Makkedah.

18 And Joshua said, Roll great stones upon the mouth of the cave, and set men by it for to keep them:

19 And stay you not, but pursue after your enemies, and strike the hindmost of them; suffer them not to enter into their cities: for the LORD your God has delivered them into your hand.

20 And it came to pass, when Joshua and the children of Israel had made an end of slaying them with a very great slaughter, till they were consumed, that the rest which remained of them entered into fenced cities.

21 And all the people returned to the camp to Joshua at Makkedah in peace: none moved his tongue against any of the children of Israel.

22 Then said Joshua, Open the mouth of the cave, and bring out those five kings unto me out of the cave.

23 And they did so, and brought forth those five kings unto him out of the cave, the king of Jerusalem, the king of Hebron, the king of Jarmuth, the king of Lachish, and the king of Eglon.

24 And it came to pass, when they brought out those kings unto Joshua, that Joshua called for all the men of Israel, and said unto the captains of the men of war which went with him, Come near, put your feet upon the necks of these kings. And they came near, and put their feet upon the necks of them.

25 And Joshua said unto them, Fear not, nor be dismayed, be strong and of good courage: for thus shall the LORD do to all your enemies against whom you fight.

26 And afterward Joshua struck them, and slew them, and hanged them on five trees: and they were hanging upon the trees until the evening.

27 And it came to pass at the time of the going down of the sun, that Joshua commanded, and they took them down off the trees, and cast them into the cave wherein they had been hid, and laid great stones in the cave's mouth, which remain until this very day.

28 And that day Joshua took Makkedah, and struck it with the edge of the sword, and the king thereof he utterly destroyed, them, and all the souls that were therein; he let none remain: and he did to the king of Makkedah as he did unto the king of Jericho.

29 Then Joshua passed from Makkedah, and all Israel with him, unto Libnah, and fought against Libnah:

30 And the LORD delivered it also, and the king thereof, into the hand of Israel; and he struck it with the edge of the sword, and all the souls that were therein; he let none remain in it; but did unto the king thereof as he did unto the king of Jericho.

31 And Joshua passed from Libnah, and all Israel with him, unto Lachish, and encamped against it, and fought against it:

32 And the LORD delivered Lachish into the hand of Israel, which took it on the second day, and struck it with the edge of the sword, and all the souls that were therein, according to all that he had done to Libnah.

33 Then Horam king of Gezer came up to help Lachish; and Joshua struck him and his people, until he had left him none remaining.

34 And from Lachish Joshua passed unto Eglon, and all Israel with him; and they encamped against it, and fought against it:

35 And they took it on that day, and struck it with the edge of the sword, and all the souls that were therein he utterly destroyed that day, according to all that he had done to Lachish.

36 And Joshua went up from Eglon, and all Israel with him, unto Hebron; and they fought against it:

37 And they took it, and struck it with the edge of the sword, and the king thereof, and all the cities thereof, and all the souls that were therein; he left none remaining, according to all that he had done to Eglon; but destroyed it utterly, and all the souls that were therein.

38 And Joshua returned, and all Israel with him, to Debir; and fought against it:

39 And he took it, and the king thereof, and all the cities thereof; and they struck them with the edge of the sword, and utterly destroyed all the souls that were therein; he left none remaining: as he had done to Hebron, so he did to Debir, and to the king thereof; as he had done also to Libnah, and to her king.

40 So Joshua struck all the country of the hills, and of the south, and of the vale, and of the springs, and all their kings: he left none remaining, but utterly destroyed all that breathed, as the LORD God of Israel commanded.

41 And Joshua struck them from Kadesh-barnea even unto Gaza, and all the country of Goshen, even unto Gibeon.

42 And all these kings and their land did Joshua take at one time, because the LORD God of Israel fought for Israel.

43 And Joshua returned, and all Israel with him, unto the camp to Gilgal.

CHAPTER 11

AND it came to pass, when Jabin king of Hazor had heard those things, that he sent to Jobab king of Madon, and to the king of Shimron, and to the king of Achshaph,

2 And to the kings that were on the north of the mountains, and of the plains south of Chinneroth, and in the valley, and in the borders of Dor on the west,

3 And to the Canaanite on the east and on the west, and to the Amorite, and the Hittite, and the Perizzite, and the Jebusite in the mountains, and to the Hivite under Hermon in the land of Mizpeh.

4 And they went out, they and all their hosts with them, much people, even as the sand that is upon the sea shore in multitude, with horses and chariots very many.

5 And when all these kings were met together, they came and pitched together at the waters of Merom, to fight against Israel.

6 And the LORD said unto Joshua, Be not afraid because of them: for to morrow about this time will I deliver them up all slain before Israel: you shalt hough their horses, and burn their chariots with fire.

7 So Joshua came, and all the people of war with him, against them by the waters of Merom suddenly; and they fell upon them.

8 And the LORD delivered them into the hand of Israel, who struck them, and chased them unto great Zidon, and unto Misrephoth-maim, and unto the valley of Mizpeh eastward; and they struck them, until they left them none remaining.

9 And Joshua did unto them as the LORD bade him: he houghed their horses, and burnt their chariots with fire.

10 And Joshua at that time turned back, and took Hazor, and struck the king thereof with the sword: for Hazor beforetime was the head of all those kingdoms.

11 And they struck all the souls that were therein with the edge of the sword, utterly destroying them: there was not any left to breathe: and he burnt Hazor with fire.

12 And all the cities of those kings, and all the kings of them, did Joshua take, and struck them with the edge of the sword, and he utterly destroyed them, as Moses the servant of the LORD commanded.

13 But as for the cities that stood still in their strength, Israel burned none of them, save Hazor only; that did Joshua burn.

14 And all the spoil of these cities, and the cattle, the children of Israel took for a prey unto themselves; but every man they struck with the edge of the sword, until they had destroyed them, neither left they any to breathe.

15 As the LORD commanded Moses his servant, so did Moses command Joshua, and so did Joshua; he left nothing undone of all that the LORD commanded Moses.

16 So Joshua took all that land, the hills, and all the south country, and all the land of Goshen, and the valley, and the plain, and the mountain of Israel, and the valley of the same;

17 Even from the mount Halak, that goeth up to Seir, even unto Baal-gad in the valley of Lebanon under mount Hermon: and all their kings he took, and struck them, and slew them.

18 Joshua made war a long time with all those kings.

19 There was not a city that made peace with the children of Israel, save the Hivites the inhabitants of Gibeon: all other they took in battle.

20 For it was of the LORD to harden their hearts, that they should come against Israel in battle, that he might destroy them utterly, and that they might have no favour, but that he might destroy them, as the LORD commanded Moses.

21And at that time came Joshua, and cut off the Anakims from the mountains, from Hebron, from Debir, from Anab, and from all the mountains of Judah, and from all the mountains of Israel: Joshua destroyed them utterly with their cities.

22 There was none of the Anakims left in the land of the children of Israel: only in Gaza, in Gath, and in Ashdod, there remained.

23 So Joshua took the whole land, according to all that the LORD said unto Moses; and Joshua gave it for an inheritance unto Israel according to their divisions by their tribes. And the land rested from war.

CHAPTER 12

NOW these are the kings of the land, which the children of Israel struck, and possessed their land on the other side Jordan toward the rising of the sun, from the river Arnon unto mount Hermon, and all the plain on the east:

2 Sihon king of the Amorites, who dwelt in Heshbon, and ruled from Aroer, which is upon the bank of the river Arnon, and from the middle of the river, and from half Gilead, even unto the river Jabbok, which is the border of the children of Ammon;

3 And from the plain to the sea of Chinneroth on the east, and unto the sea of the plain, even the salt sea on the east, the way to Beth-jeshimoth; and from the south, under Ashdoth-pisgah:

4And the coast of Og king of Bashan, which was of the remnant of the giants, that dwelt at Ashtaroth and at Edrei,

5 And reigned in mount Hermon, and in Salcah, and in all Bashan, unto the border of the Geshurites and the Maachathites, and half Gilead, the border of Sihon king of Heshbon.

6 Them did Moses the servant of the LORD and the children of Israel strike: and Moses the servant of the LORD gave it for a possession unto the Reubenites, and the Gadites, and the half tribe of Manasseh.

7And these are the kings of the country which Joshua and the children of Israel struck on this side Jordan on the west, from Baal-gad in the valley of Lebanon even unto the mount Halak, that goeth up to Seir; which Joshua gave unto the tribes of Israel for a possession according to their divisions;

8 In the mountains, and in the valleys, and in the plains, and in the springs, and in the wilderness, and in the south country; the Hittites, the Amorites, and the Canaanites, the Perizzites, the Hivites, and the Jebusites:

9The king of Jericho, one; the king of Ai, which is beside Beth-el, one;

10 The king of Jerusalem, one; the king of Hebron, one;

11 The king of Jarmuth, one; the king of Lachish, one;

12 The king of Eglon, one; the king of Gezer, one;

13 The king of Debir, one; the king of Geder, one;

14 The king of Hormah, one; the king of Arad, one;

15 The king of Libnah, one; the king of Adullam, one;

16 The king of Makkedah, one; the king of Beth-el, one;

17 The king of Tappuah, one; the king of Hepher, one;

18 The king of Aphek, one; the king of Lasharon, one;

19 The king of Madon, one; the king of Hazor, one;

20 The king of Shimron-meron, one; the king of Achshaph, one;

21 The king of Taanach, one; the king of Megiddo, one;

22 The king of Kedesh, one; the king of Jokneam of Carmel, one;

23 The king of Dor in the coast of Dor, one; the king of the nations of Gilgal, one;

24 The king of Tirzah, one: all the kings thirty and one.

CHAPTER 13

NOW Joshua was old and stricken in years; and the LORD said unto him, You are old and stricken in years, and there remaineth yet very much land to be possessed.

2 This is the land that yet remaineth: all the borders of the Philistines, and all Geshuri,

3 From Sihor, which is before Egypt, even unto the borders of Ekron northward, which is counted to the Canaanite: five lords of the Philistines; the Gazathites, and the Ashdothites, the Eshkalonites, the Gittites, and the Ekronites; also the Avites:

4 From the south, all the land of the Canaanites, and Mearah that is beside the Sidonians, unto Aphek, to the borders of the Amorites:

5 And the land of the Giblites, and all Lebanon, toward the sunrising, from Baal-gad under mount Hermon unto the entering into Hamath.

6 All the inhabitants of the hill country from Lebanon unto Misrephoth-maim, and all the Sidonians, them will I drive out from before the children of Israel: only divide you it by lot unto the Israelites for an inheritance, as I have commanded you.

7 Now therefore divide this land for an inheritance unto the nine tribes, and the half tribe of Manasseh,

8 With whom the Reubenites and the Gadites have received their inheritance, which Moses gave them, beyond Jordan eastward, even as Moses the servant of the LORD gave them;

9 From Aroer, that is upon the bank of the river Arnon, and the city that is in the midst of the river, and all the plain of Medeba unto Dibon;

10 And all the cities of Sihon king of the Amorites, which reigned in Heshbon, unto the border of the children of Ammon;

11 And Gilead, and the border of the Geshurites and Maachathites, and all mount Hermon, and all Bashan unto Salcah;

12 All the kingdom of Og in Bashan, which reigned in Ashtaroth and in Edrei, who remained of the remnant of the giants: for these did Moses strike, and cast them out.

13 Nevertheless the children of Israel expelled not the Geshurites, nor the Maachathites: but the Geshurites and the Maachathites dwell among the Israelites until this day.

14 Only unto the tribe of Levi he gave none inheritance; the sacrifices of the LORD God of Israel made by fire are their inheritance, as he said unto them.

15And Moses gave unto the tribe of the children of Reuben inheritance according to their families.

16 And their coast was from Aroer, that is on the bank of the river Arnon, and the city that is in the midst of the river, and all the plain by Medeba;

17 Heshbon, and all her cities that are in the plain; Dibon, and Bamoth-baal, and Beth-baal-meon,

18 And Jahazah, and Kedemoth, and Mephaath,

19 And Kirjathaim, and Sibmah, and Zareth-shahar in the mount of the valley,

20 And Beth-peor, and Ashdoth-pisgah, and Beth-jeshimoth,

21 And all the cities of the plain, and all the kingdom of Sihon king of the Amorites, which reigned in Heshbon, whom Moses struck with the princes of Midian, Evi, and Rekem, and Zur, and Hur, and Reba, which were dukes of Sihon, dwelling in the country.

22Balaam also the son of Beor, the soothsayer, did the children of Israel slay with the sword among them that were slain by them.

23 And the border of the children of Reuben was Jordan, and the border thereof. This was the inheritance of the children of Reuben after their families, the cities and the villages thereof.

24 And Moses gave inheritance unto the tribe of Gad, even unto the children of Gad according to their families.

25 And their coast was Jazer, and all the cities of Gilead, and half the land of the children of Ammon, unto Aroer that is before Rabbah;

26 And from Heshbon unto Ramath-mizpeh, and Betonim; and from Mahanaim unto the border of Debir;

27 And in the valley, Beth-aram, and Beth-nimrah, and Succoth, and Zaphon, the rest of the kingdom of Sihon king of Heshbon, Jordan and his border, even unto the edge of the sea of Chinnereth on the other side Jordan eastward.

28 This is the inheritance of the children of Gad after their families, the cities, and their villages.

29And Moses gave inheritance unto the half tribe of Manasseh: and this was the possession of the half tribe of the children of Manasseh by their families.

30 And their coast was from Mahanaim, all Bashan, all the kingdom of Og king of Bashan, and all the towns of Jair, which are in Bashan, threescore cities:

31 And half Gilead, and Ashtaroth, and Edrei, cities of the kingdom of Og in Bashan, were pertaining unto the children of Machir the son of Manasseh, even to the one half of the children of Machir by their families.

32 These are the countries which Moses did distribute for inheritance in the plains of Moab, on the other side Jordan, by Jericho, eastward.

33 But unto the tribe of Levi Moses gave not any inheritance: the LORD God of Israel was their inheritance, as he said unto them.

CHAPTER 14

AND these are the countries which the children of Israel inherited in the land of Canaan, which Eleazar the priest, and Joshua the son of Nun, and the heads of the fathers of the tribes of the children of Israel, distributed for inheritance to them.

2 By lot was their inheritance, as the LORD commanded by the hand of Moses, for the nine tribes, and for the half tribe.

3 For Moses had given the inheritance of two tribes and an half tribe on the other side Jordan: but unto the Levites he gave none inheritance among them.

4 For the children of Joseph were two tribes, Manasseh and Ephraim: therefore they gave no part unto the Levites in the land, save cities to dwell in, with their suburbs for their cattle and for their substance.

5 As the LORD commanded Moses, so the children of Israel did, and they divided the land.

6 Then the children of Judah came unto Joshua in Gilgal: and Caleb the son of Jephunneh the Kenezite said unto him, You knowest the thing that the LORD said unto Moses the man of God concerning me and you in Kadesh-barnea.

7 Forty years old was I when Moses the servant of the LORD sent me from Kadesh-barnea to espy out the land; and I brought him word again as it was in my heart.

8 Nevertheless my brethren that went up with me made the heart of the people melt: but I wholly followed the LORD my God.

9 And Moses sware on that day, saying, Surely the land whereon your feet have trodden shall be yours inheritance, and your children's for ever, because you have wholly followed the LORD my God.

10 And now, behold, the LORD has kept me alive, as he said, these forty and five years, even since the LORD spake this word unto Moses, while the children of Israel wandered in the wilderness: and now, lo, I am this day fourscore and five years old.

11 As yet I am as strong this day as I was in the day that Moses sent me: as my strength was then, even so is my strength now, for war, both to go out, and to come in.

12 Now therefore give me this mountain, whereof the LORD spake in that day; for you heardest in that day how the Anakims were there, and that the cities were great and fenced: if so be the LORD will be with me, then I shall be able to drive them out, as the LORD said.

13 And Joshua blessed him, and gave unto Caleb the son of Jephunneh Hebron for an inheritance.

14 Hebron therefore became the inheritance of Caleb the son of Jephunneh the Kenezite unto this day, because that he wholly followed the LORD God of Israel.

15 And the name of Hebron before was Kirjath-arba; which Arba was a great man among the Anakims. And the land had rest from war.

CHAPTER 15

THIS then was the lot of the tribe of the children of Judah by their families; even to the border of Edom the wilderness of Zin southward was the uttermost part of the south coast.

2 And their south border was from the shore of the salt sea, from the bay that looketh southward:

3 And it went out to the south side to Maaleh-acrabbim, and passed along to Zin, and ascended up on the south side unto Kadesh-barnea, and passed along to Hezron, and went up to Adar, and fetched a compass to Karkaa:

4 From thence it passed toward Azmon, and went out unto the river of Egypt; and the goings out of that coast were at the sea: this shall be your south coast.

5 And the east border was the salt sea, even unto the end of Jordan. And their border in the north quarter was from the bay of the sea at the uttermost part of Jordan:

6 And the border went up to Beth-hogla, and passed along by the north of Beth-arabah; and the border went up to the stone of Bohan the son of Reuben:

7 And the border went up toward Debir from the valley of Achor, and so northward, looking toward Gilgal, that is before the going up to Adummim, which is on the south side of the river: and the border passed toward the waters of En-shemesh, and the goings out thereof were at En-rogel:

8 And the border went up by the valley of the son of Hinnom unto the south side of the Jebusite; the same is Jerusalem: and the border went up to the top of the mountain that lies before the valley of Hinnom westward, which is at the end of the valley of the giants northward:

9 And the border was drawn from the top of the hill unto the fountain of the water of Nephtoah, and went out to the cities of mount Ephron; and the border was drawn to Baalah, which is Kirjath-jearim:

10 And the border compassed from Baalah westward unto mount Seir, and passed along unto the side of mount Jearim, which is Chesalon, on the north side, and went down to Beth-shemesh, and passed on to Timnah:

11 And the border went out unto the side of Ekron northward: and the border was drawn to Shicron, and passed along to mount Baalah, and went out unto Jabneel; and the goings out of the border were at the sea.

12 And the west border was to the great sea, and the coast thereof. This is the coast of the children of Judah round about according to their families.

13 And unto Caleb the son of Jephunneh he gave a part among the children of Judah, according to the commandment of the LORD to Joshua, even the city of Arba the father of Anak, which city is Hebron.

14 And Caleb drove thence the three sons of Anak, Sheshai, and Ahiman, and Talmai, the children of Anak.

15 And he went up thence to the inhabitants of Debir: and the name of Debir before was Kirjath-sepher.

16 And Caleb said, He that smiteth Kirjath-sepher, and taketh it, to him will I give Achsah my daughter to wife.

17 And Othniel the son of Kenaz, the brother of Caleb, took it: and he gave him Achsah his daughter to wife.

18 And it came to pass, as she came unto him, that she moved him to ask of her father a field: and she lighted off her ass; and Caleb said unto her, What wouldest you ?

19 Who answered, Give me a blessing; for you have given me a south land; give me also springs of water. And he gave her the upper springs, and the nether springs.

20 This is the inheritance of the tribe of the children of Judah according to their families.

21 And the uttermost cities of the tribe of the children of Judah toward the coast of Edom southward were Kabzeel, and Eder, and Jagur,

22 And Kinah, and Dimonah, and Adadah,

23 And Kedesh, and Hazor, and Ithnan,

24 Ziph, and Telem, and Bealoth,

25 And Hazor, Hadattah, and Kerioth, and Hezron, which is Hazor,

26 Amam, and Shema, and Moladah,

27 And Hazar-gaddah, and Heshmon, and Beth-palet,

28 And Hazar-shual, and Beer-sheba, and Bizjothjah,

29 Baalah, and Iim, and Azem,

30 And Eltolad, and Chesil, and Hormah,

31 And Ziklag, and Madmannah, and Sansannah,

32 And Lebaoth, and Shilhim, and Ain, and Rimmon: all the cities are twenty and nine, with their villages:

33 And in the valley, Eshtaol, and Zoreah, and Ashnah,

34 And Zanoah, and En-gannim, Tappuah, and Enam,

35 Jarmuth, and Adullam, Socoh, and Azekah,

36 And Sharaim, and Adithaim, and Gederah, and Gederothaim; fourteen cities with their villages:

37 Zenan, and Hadashah, and Migdal-gad,

38 And Dilean, and Mizpeh, and Joktheel,

39 Lachish, and Bozkath, and Eglon,

40 And Cabbon, and Lahmam, and Kithlish,

41 And Gederoth, Beth-dagon, and Naamah, and Makkedah; sixteen cities with their villages:

42 Libnah, and Ether, and Ashan,

43 And Jiphtah, and Ashnah, and Nezib,

44 And Keilah, and Achzib, and Mareshah; nine cities with their villages:

45 Ekron, with her towns and her villages:

46 From Ekron even unto the sea, all that lay near Ashdod, with their villages:

47 Ashdod with her towns and her villages, Gaza with her towns and her villages, unto the river of Egypt, and the great sea, and the border thereof:

48 And in the mountains, Shamir, and Jattir, and Socoh,

49 And Dannah, and Kirjath-sannah, which is Debir,

50 And Anab, and Eshtemoh, and Anim,

51 And Goshen, and Holon, and Giloh; eleven cities with their villages:

52 Arab, and Dumah, and Eshean,

53 And Janum, and Beth-tappuah, and Aphekah,

54 And Humtah, and Kirjath-arba, which is Hebron, and Zior; nine cities with their villages:

55 Maon, Carmel, and Ziph, and Juttah,

56 And Jezreel, and Jokdeam, and Zanoah,

57 Cain, Gibeah, and Timnah; ten cities with their villages:

58 Halhul, Beth-zur, and Gedor,

59 And Maarath, and Beth-anoth, and Eltekon; six cities with their villages:

60 Kirjath-baal, which is Kirjath-jearim, and Rabbah; two cities with their villages:

61 In the wilderness, Beth-arabah, Middin, and Secacah,

62 And Nibshan, and the city of Salt, and En-gedi; six cities with their villages:

63 As for the Jebusites the inhabitants of Jerusalem, the children of Judah could not drive them out: but the Jebusites dwell with the children of Judah at Jerusalem unto this day.

CHAPTER 16

AND the lot of the children of Joseph fell from Jordan by Jericho, unto the water of Jericho on the east, to the wilderness that goeth up from Jericho throughout mount Beth-el,

2 And goeth out from Beth-el to Luz, and passes along unto the borders of Archi to Ataroth,

3 And goeth down westward to the coast of Japhleti, unto the coast of Beth-horon the nether, and to Gezer: and the goings out thereof are at the sea.

4 So the children of Joseph, Manasseh and Ephraim, took their inheritance.

5And the border of the children of Ephraim according to their families was thus: even the border of their inheritance on the east side was Ataroth-addar, unto Beth-horon the upper;

6 And the border went out toward the sea to Michmethah on the north side; and the border went about eastward unto Taanath-shiloh, and passed by it on the east to Janohah;

7 And it went down from Janohah to Ataroth, and to Naarath, and came to Jericho, and went out at Jordan.

8 The border went out from Tappuah westward unto the river Kanah; and the goings out thereof were at the sea. This is the inheritance of the tribe of the children of Ephraim by their families.

9 And the separate cities for the children of Ephraim were among the inheritance of the children of Manasseh, all the cities with their villages.

10 And they drave not out the Canaanites that dwelt in Gezer: but the Canaanites dwell among the Ephraimites unto this day, and serve under tribute.

CHAPTER 17

THERE was also a lot for the tribe of Manasseh; for he was the firstborn of Joseph; to wit, for Machir the firstborn of Manasseh, the father of Gilead: because he was a man of war, therefore he had Gilead and Bashan.

2 There was also a lot for the rest of the children of Manasseh by their families; for the children of Abiezer, and for the children of Helek, and for the children of Asriel, and for the children of Shechem, and for the children of Hepher, and for the children of Shemida: these were the male children of Manasseh the son of Joseph by their families.

3But Zelophehad, the son of Hepher, the son of Gilead, the son of Machir, the son of Manasseh, had no sons, but daughters: and these are the names of his daughters, Mahlah, and Noah, Hoglah, Milcah, and Tirzah.

4 And they came near before Eleazar the priest, and before Joshua the son of Nun, and before the princes, saying, The LORD commanded Moses to give us an inheritance among our brethren. Therefore according to the commandment of the LORD he gave them an inheritance among the brethren of their father.

5 And there fell ten portions to Manasseh, beside the land of Gilead and Bashan, which were on the other side Jordan;

6 Because the daughters of Manasseh had an inheritance among his sons: and the rest of Manasseh's sons had the land of Gilead.

7And the coast of Manasseh was from Asher to Michmethah, that lies before Shechem; and the border went along on the right hand unto the inhabitants of En-tappuah.

8 Now Manasseh had the land of Tappuah: but Tappuah on the border of Manasseh belonged to the children of Ephraim;

9 And the coast descended unto the river Kanah, southward of the river: these cities of Ephraim are among the cities of Manasseh: the coast of Manasseh also was on the north side of the river, and the outgoings of it were at the sea:

10 Southward it was Ephraim's, and northward it was Manasseh's, and the sea is his border; and they met together in Asher on the north, and in Issachar on the east.

11 And Manasseh had in Issachar and in Asher Beth-shean and her towns, and Ibleam and her towns, and the inhabitants of Dor and her towns, and the inhabitants of Endor and her towns, and the inhabitants of Taanach and her towns, and the inhabitants of Megiddo and her towns, even three countries.

12 Yet the children of Manasseh could not drive out the inhabitants of those cities; but the Canaanites would dwell in that land.

13 Yet it came to pass, when the children of Israel were waxen strong, that they put the Canaanites to tribute; but did not utterly drive them out.

14 And the children of Joseph spake unto Joshua, saying, Why have you given me but one lot and one portion to inherit, seeing I am a great people, forasmuch as the LORD has blessed me hitherto?

15 And Joshua answered them, If you be a great people, then get you up to the wood country, and cut down for yourself there in the land of the Perizzites and of the giants, if mount Ephraim be too narrow for you.

16 And the children of Joseph said, The hill is not enough for us: and all the Canaanites that dwell in the land of the valley have chariots of iron, both they who are of Beth-shean and her towns, and they who are of the valley of Jezreel.

17 And Joshua spake unto the house of Joseph, even to Ephraim and to Manasseh, saying, You are a great people, and have great power: you shalt not have one lot only:

18 But the mountain shall be yours; for it is a wood, and you shalt cut it down: and the outgoings of it shall be yours: for you shalt drive out the Canaanites, though they have iron chariots, and though they be strong.

CHAPTER 18

AND the whole congregation of the children of Israel assembled together at Shiloh, and set up the tabernacle of the congregation there. And the land was subdued before them.

2 And there remained among the children of Israel seven tribes, which had not yet received their inheritance.

3 And Joshua said unto the children of Israel, How long are you slack to go to possess the land, which the LORD God of your fathers has given you?

4 Give out from among you three men for each tribe: and I will send them, and they shall rise, and go through the land, and describe it according to the inheritance of them; and they shall come again to me.

5 And they shall divide it into seven parts: Judah shall abide in their coast on the south, and the house of Joseph shall abide in their coasts on the north.

6 You shall therefore describe the land into seven parts, and bring the description hither to me, that I may cast lots for you here before the LORD our God.

7 But the Levites have no part among you; for the priesthood of the LORD is their inheritance: and Gad, and Reuben, and half the tribe of Manasseh, have received their inheritance beyond Jordan on the east, which Moses the servant of the LORD gave them.

8And the men arose, and went away: and Joshua charged them that went to describe the land, saying, Go and walk through the land, and describe it, and come again to me, that I may here cast lots for you before the LORD in Shiloh.

9 And the men went and passed through the land, and described it by cities into seven parts in a book, and came again to Joshua to the host at Shiloh.

10And Joshua cast lots for them in Shiloh before the LORD: and there Joshua divided the land unto the children of Israel according to their divisions.

11And the lot of the tribe of the children of Benjamin came up according to their families: and the coast of their lot came forth between the children of Judah and the children of Joseph.

12 And their border on the north side was from Jordan; and the border went up to the side of Jericho on the north side, and went up through the mountains westward; and the goings out thereof were at the wilderness of Beth-aven.

13 And the border went over from thence toward Luz, to the side of Luz, which is Beth-el, southward; and the border descended to Ataroth-adar, near the hill that lies on the south side of the nether Beth-horon.

14 And the border was drawn thence, and compassed the corner of the sea southward, from the hill that lies before Beth-horon southward; and the goings out thereof were at Kirjath-baal, which is Kirjath-jearim, a city of the children of Judah: this was the west quarter.

15 And the south quarter was from the end of Kirjath-jearim, and the border went out on the west, and went out to the well of waters of Nephtoah:

16 And the border came down to the end of the mountain that lies before the valley of the son of Hinnom, and which is in the valley of the giants on the north, and descended to the valley of Hinnom, to the side of Jebusi on the south, and descended to En-rogel,

17 And was drawn from the north, and went forth to En-shemesh, and went forth toward Geliloth, which is over against the going up of Adummim, and descended to the stone of Bohan the son of Reuben,

18 And passed along toward the side over against Arabah northward, and went down unto Arabah:

19 And the border passed along to the side of Beth-hoglah northward: and the outgoings of the border were at the north bay of the salt sea at the south end of Jordan: this was the south coast.

20 And Jordan was the border of it on the east side. This was the inheritance of the children of Benjamin, by the coasts thereof round about, according to their families.

21 Now the cities of the tribe of the children of Benjamin according to their families were Jericho, and Beth-hoglah, and the valley of Keziz,

22 And Beth-arabah, and Zemaraim, and Beth-el,

23 And Avim, and Parah, and Ophrah,

24 And Chephar-haammonai, and Ophni, and Gaba; twelve cities with their villages:

25 Gibeon, and Ramah, and Beeroth,

26 And Mizpeh, and Chephirah, and Mozah,

27 And Rekem, and Irpeel, and Taralah,

28 And Zelah, Eleph, and Jebusi, which is Jerusalem, Gibeath, and Kirjath; fourteen cities with their villages. This is the inheritance of the children of Benjamin according to their families.

CHAPTER 19

AND the second lot came forth to Simeon, even for the tribe of the children of Simeon according to their families: and their inheritance was within the inheritance of the children of Judah.

2 And they had in their inheritance Beer-sheba, or Sheba, and Moladah,

3 And Hazar-shual, and Balah, and Azem,

4 And Eltolad, and Bethul, and Hormah,

5 And Ziklag, and Beth-marcaboth, and Hazar-susah,

6 And Beth-lebaoth, and Sharuhen; thirteen cities and their villages:

7 Ain, Remmon, and Ether, and Ashan; four cities and their villages:

8 And all the villages that were round about these cities to Baalath-beer, Ramath of the south. This is the inheritance of the tribe of the children of Simeon according to their families.

9 Out of the portion of the children of Judah was the inheritance of the children of Simeon: for the part of the children of Judah was too much for them: therefore the children of Simeon had their inheritance within the inheritance of them.

10 And the third lot came up for the children of Zebulun according to their families: and the border of their inheritance was unto Sarid:

11 And their border went up toward the sea, and Maralah, and reached to Dabbasheth, and reached to the river that is before Jokneam;

12 And turned from Sarid eastward toward the sunrising unto the border of Chisloth-tabor, and then goeth out to Daberath, and goeth up to Japhia,

13 And from thence passes on along on the east to Gittah-hepher, to Ittah-kazin, and goeth out to Remmon-methoar to Neah;

14 And the border compasseth it on the north side to Hannathon: and the outgoings thereof are in the valley of Jiphthah-el:

15 And Kattath, and Nahallal, and Shimron, and Idalah, and Beth-lehem: twelve cities with their villages.

16 This is the inheritance of the children of Zebulun according to their families, these cities with their villages.

17 And the fourth lot came out to Issachar, for the children of Issachar according to their families.

18 And their border was toward Jezreel, and Chesulloth, and Shunem,

19 And Hapharaim, and Shion, and Anaharath,

20 And Rabbith, and Kishion, and Abez,

21 And Remeth, and En-gannim, and En-haddah, and Beth-pazzez;

22 And the coast reacheth to Tabor, and Shahazimah, and Beth-shemesh; and the outgoings of their border were at Jordan: sixteen cities with their villages.

23 This is the inheritance of the tribe of the children of Issachar according to their families, the cities and their villages.

24 And the fifth lot came out for the tribe of the children of Asher according to their families.

25 And their border was Helkath, and Hali, and Beten, and Achshaph,

26 And Alammelech, and Amad, and Misheal; and reacheth to Carmel westward, and to Shihor-libnath;

27 And turneth toward the sunrising to Beth-dagon, and reacheth to Zebulun, and to the valley of Jiphthah-el toward the north side of Beth-emek, and Neiel, and goeth out to Cabul on the left hand,

28 And Hebron, and Rehob, and Hammon, and Kanah, even unto great Zidon;

29 And then the coast turneth to Ramah, and to the strong city Tyre; and the coast turneth to Hosah; and the outgoings thereof are at the sea from the coast to Achzib:

30 Ummah also, and Aphek, and Rehob: twenty and two cities with their villages.

31 This is the inheritance of the tribe of the children of Asher according to their families, these cities with their villages.

32 The sixth lot came out to the children of Naphtali, even for the children of Naphtali according to their families.

33 And their coast was from Heleph, from Allon to Zaanannim, and Adami, Nekeb, and Jabneel, unto Lakum; and the outgoings thereof were at Jordan:

34 And then the coast turneth westward to Aznoth-tabor, and goeth out from thence to Hukkok, and reacheth to Zebulun on the south side, and reacheth to Asher on the west side, and to Judah upon Jordan toward the sunrising.

35 And the fenced cities are Ziddim, Zer, and Hammath, Rakkath, and Chinnereth,

36 And Adamah, and Ramah, and Hazor,

37 And Kedesh, and Edrei, and En-hazor,

38 And Iron, and Migdal-el, Horem, and Beth-anath, and Beth-shemesh; nineteen cities with their villages.

39 This is the inheritance of the tribe of the children of Naphtali according to their families, the cities and their villages.

40 And the seventh lot came out for the tribe of the children of Dan according to their families.

41 And the coast of their inheritance was Zorah, and Eshtaol, and Ir-shemesh,

42 And Shaalabbin, and Ajalon, and Jethlah,

43 And Elon, and Thimnathah, and Ekron,

44 And Eltekeh, and Gibbethon, and Baalath,

45 And Jehud, and Bene-berak, and Gath-rimmon,

46 And Me-jarkon, and Rakkon, with the border before Japho.

47 And the coast of the children of Dan went out too little for them: therefore the children of Dan went up to fight against Leshem, and took it, and struck it with the edge of the sword, and possessed it, and dwelt therein, and called Leshem, Dan, after the name of Dan their father.

48 This is the inheritance of the tribe of the children of Dan according to their families, these cities with their villages.

49 When they had made an end of dividing the land for inheritance by their coasts, the children of Israel gave an inheritance to Joshua the son of Nun among them:

50 According to the word of the LORD they gave him the city which he asked, even Timnath-serah in mount Ephraim: and he built the city, and dwelt therein.

51 These are the inheritances, which Eleazar the priest, and Joshua the son of Nun, and the heads of the fathers of the tribes of the children of Israel, divided for an inheritance by lot in Shiloh before the LORD, at the door of the tabernacle of the congregation. So they made an end of dividing the country.

CHAPTER 20

THE LORD also spake unto Joshua, saying,

2 Speak to the children of Israel, saying, Appoint out for you cities of refuge, whereof I spake unto you by the hand of Moses:

3 That the slayer that killeth any person unawares and unwittingly may flee thither: and they shall be your refuge from the avenger of blood.

4 And when he that doth flee unto one of those cities shall stand at the entering of the gate of the city, and shall declare his cause in the ears of the elders of that city, they shall take him into the city unto them, and give him a place, that he may dwell among them.

5 And if the avenger of blood pursue after him, then they shall not deliver the slayer up into his hand; because he struck his neighbour unwittingly, and hated him not beforetime.

6 And he shall dwell in that city, until he stand before the congregation for judgment, and until the death of the high priest that shall be in those days: then shall the slayer return, and come unto his own city, and unto his own house, unto the city from whence he fled.

7 And they appointed Kedesh in Galilee in mount Naphtali, and Shechem in mount Ephraim, and Kirjath-arba, which is Hebron, in the mountain of Judah.

8 And on the other side Jordan by Jericho eastward, they assigned Bezer in the wilderness upon the plain out of the tribe of Reuben, and Ramoth in Gilead out of the tribe of Gad, and Golan in Bashan out of the tribe of Manasseh.

9 These were the cities appointed for all the children of Israel, and for the stranger that sojourneth among them, that whosoever killeth any person at unawares might flee thither, and not die by the hand of the avenger of blood, until he stood before the congregation.

CHAPTER 21

THEN came near the heads of the fathers of the Levites unto Eleazar the priest, and unto Joshua the son of Nun, and unto the heads of the fathers of the tribes of the children of Israel;

2 And they spake unto them at Shiloh in the land of Canaan, saying, The LORD commanded by the hand of Moses to give us cities to dwell in, with the suburbs thereof for our cattle.

3 And the children of Israel gave unto the Levites out of their inheritance, at the commandment of the LORD, these cities and their suburbs.

4 And the lot came out for the families of the Kohathites: and the children of Aaron the priest, which were of the Levites, had by lot out of the tribe of Judah, and out of the tribe of Simeon, and out of the tribe of Benjamin, thirteen cities.

5 And the rest of the children of Kohath had by lot out of the families of the tribe of Ephraim, and out of the tribe of Dan, and out of the half tribe of Manasseh, ten cities.

6 And the children of Gershon had by lot out of the families of the tribe of Issachar, and out of the tribe of Asher, and out of the tribe of Naphtali, and out of the half tribe of Manasseh in Bashan, thirteen cities.

7 The children of Merari by their families had out of the tribe of Reuben, and out of the tribe of Gad, and out of the tribe of Zebulun, twelve cities.

8 And the children of Israel gave by lot unto the Levites these cities with their suburbs, as the LORD commanded by the hand of Moses.

9And they gave out of the tribe of the children of Judah, and out of the tribe of the children of Simeon, these cities which are here mentioned by name,

10 Which the children of Aaron, being of the families of the Kohathites, who were of the children of Levi, had: for theirs was the first lot.

11 And they gave them the city of Arba the father of Anak, which city is Hebron, in the hill country of Judah, with the suburbs thereof round about it.

12 But the fields of the city, and the villages thereof, gave they to Caleb the son of Jephunneh for his possession.

13Thus they gave to the children of Aaron the priest Hebron with her suburbs, to be a city of refuge for the slayer; and Libnah with her suburbs,

14 And Jattir with her suburbs, and Eshtemoa with her suburbs,

15 And Holon with her suburbs, and Debir with her suburbs,

16 And Ain with her suburbs, and Juttah with her suburbs, and Beth-shemesh with her suburbs; nine cities out of those two tribes.

17 And out of the tribe of Benjamin, Gibeon with her suburbs, Geba with her suburbs,

18 Anathoth with her suburbs, and Almon with her suburbs; four cities.

19 All the cities of the children of Aaron, the priests, were thirteen cities with their suburbs.

20And the families of the children of Kohath, the Levites which remained of the children of Kohath, even they had the cities of their lot out of the tribe of Ephraim.

21 For they gave them Shechem with her suburbs in mount Ephraim, to be a city of refuge for the slayer; and Gezer with her suburbs,

22 And Kibzaim with her suburbs, and Beth-horon with her suburbs; four cities.

23 And out of the tribe of Dan, Eltekeh with her suburbs, Gibbethon with her suburbs,

24 Aijalon with her suburbs, Gath-rimmon with her suburbs; four cities.

25 And out of the half tribe of Manasseh, Tanach with her suburbs, and Gath-rimmon with her suburbs; two cities.

26 All the cities were ten with their suburbs for the families of the children of Kohath that remained.

27And unto the children of Gershon, of the families of the Levites, out of the other half tribe of Manasseh they gave Golan in Bashan with her suburbs, to be a city of refuge for the slayer; and Beesh-terah with her suburbs; two cities.

28 And out of the tribe of Issachar, Kishon with her suburbs, Dabareh with her suburbs,

29 Jarmuth with her suburbs, En-gannim with her suburbs; four cities.

30 And out of the tribe of Asher, Mishal with her suburbs, Abdon with her suburbs,

31 Helkath with her suburbs, and Rehob with her suburbs; four cities.

32 And out of the tribe of Naphtali, Kedesh in Galilee with her suburbs, to be a city of refuge for the slayer; and Hammoth-dor with her suburbs, and Kartan with her suburbs; three cities.

33 All the cities of the Gershonites according to their families were thirteen cities with their suburbs.

34And unto the families of the children of Merari, the rest of the Levites, out of the tribe of Zebulun, Jokneam with her suburbs, and Kartah with her suburbs,

35 Dimnah with her suburbs, Nahalal with her suburbs; four cities.

36 And out of the tribe of Reuben, Bezer with her suburbs, and Jahazah with her suburbs,

37 Kedemoth with her suburbs, and Mephaath with her suburbs; four cities.

38 And out of the tribe of Gad, Ramoth in Gilead with her suburbs, to be a city of refuge for the slayer; and Mahanaim with her suburbs,

39 Heshbon with her suburbs, Jazer with her suburbs; four cities in all.

40 So all the cities for the children of Merari by their families, which were remaining of the families of the Levites, were by their lot twelve cities.

41 All the cities of the Levites within the possession of the children of Israel were forty and eight cities with their suburbs.

42 These cities were every one with their suburbs round about them: thus were all these cities.

43And the LORD gave unto Israel all the land which he sware to give unto their fathers; and they possessed it, and dwelt therein.

44 And the LORD gave them rest round about, according to all that he sware unto their fathers: and there stood not a man of all their enemies before them; the LORD delivered all their enemies into their hand.

45 There failed not ought of any good thing which the LORD had spoken unto the house of Israel; all came to pass.

CHAPTER 22

THEN Joshua called the Reubenites, and the Gadites, and the half tribe of Manasseh,

2 And said unto them, You have kept all that Moses the servant of the LORD commanded you, and have obeyed my voice in all that I commanded you:

3 You have not left your brethren these many days unto this day, but have kept the charge of the commandment of the LORD your God.

4 And now the LORD your God has given rest unto your brethren, as he promised them: therefore now return you , and get you unto your tents, and unto the land of your possession, which Moses the servant of the LORD gave you on the other side Jordan.

5 But take diligent heed to do the commandment and the law, which Moses the servant of the LORD charged you, to love the LORD your God, and to walk in all his ways, and to keep his commandments, and to cleave unto him, and to serve him with all your heart and with all your soul.

6 So Joshua blessed them, and sent them away: and they went unto their tents.

7Now to the one half of the tribe of Manasseh Moses had given possession in Bashan: but unto the other half thereof gave Joshua among their brethren on this side Jordan westward. And when Joshua sent them away also unto their tents, then he blessed them,

8 And he spake unto them, saying, Return with much riches unto your tents, and with very much cattle, with silver, and with gold, and with brass, and with iron, and with very much raiment: divide the spoil of your enemies with your brethren.

9And the children of Reuben and the children of Gad and the half tribe of Manasseh returned, and departed from the children of Israel out of Shiloh, which is in the land of Canaan, to go unto the country of Gilead, to the land of their possession, whereof they were possessed, according to the word of the LORD by the hand of Moses.

10And when they came unto the borders of Jordan, that are in the land of Canaan, the children of Reuben and the children of Gad and the half tribe of Manasseh built there an altar by Jordan, a great altar to see to.

11And the children of Israel heard say, Behold, the children of Reuben and the children of Gad and the half tribe of Manasseh have built an altar over against the land of Canaan, in the borders of Jordan, at the passage of the children of Israel.

12 And when the children of Israel heard of it, the whole congregation of the children of Israel gathered themselves together at Shiloh, to go up to war against them.

13 And the children of Israel sent unto the children of Reuben, and to the children of Gad, and to the half tribe of Manasseh, into the land of Gilead, Phinehas the son of Eleazar the priest,

14 And with him ten princes, of each chief house a prince throughout all the tribes of Israel; and each one was an head of the house of their fathers among the thousands of Israel.

15And they came unto the children of Reuben, and to the children of Gad, and to the half tribe of Manasseh, unto the land of Gilead, and they spake with them, saying,

16 Thus saith the whole congregation of the LORD, What trespass is this that you have committed against the God of Israel, to turn away this day from following the LORD, in that you have builded you an altar, that you might rebel this day against the LORD?

17 Is the iniquity of Peor too little for us, from which we are not cleansed until this day, although there was a plague in the congregation of the LORD,

18 But that you must turn away this day from following the LORD? and it will be, seeing you rebel to day against the LORD, that to morrow he will be wroth with the whole congregation of Israel.

19 Notwithstanding, if the land of your possession be unclean, then pass you over unto the land of the possession of the LORD, wherein the LORD's tabernacle dwelleth, and take possession among us: but rebel not against the LORD, nor rebel against us, in building you an altar beside the altar of the LORD our God.

20 Did not Achan the son of Zerah commit a trespass in the accursed thing, and wrath fell on all the congregation of Israel? and that man perished not alone in his iniquity.

21Then the children of Reuben and the children of Gad and the half tribe of Manasseh answered, and said unto the heads of the thousands of Israel,

22 The LORD God of gods, the LORD God of gods, he knoweth, and Israel he shall know; if it be in rebellion, or if in transgression against the LORD, (save us not this day,)

23 That we have built us an altar to turn from following the LORD, or if to offer thereon burnt offering or meat offering, or if to offer peace offerings thereon, let the LORD himself require it;

24 And if we have not rather done it for fear of this thing, saying, In time to come your children might speak unto our children, saying, What have you to do with the LORD God of Israel?

25 For the LORD has made Jordan a border between us and you, you children of Reuben and children of Gad; you have no part in the LORD: so shall your children make our children cease from fearing the LORD.

26 Therefore we said, Let us now prepare to build us an altar, not for burnt offering, nor for sacrifice:

27 But that it may be a witness between us, and you, and our generations after us, that we might do the service of the LORD before him with our burnt offerings, and with our sacrifices, and with our peace offerings; that your children may not say to our children in time to come, You have no part in the LORD.

28 Therefore said we, that it shall be, when they should so say to us or to our generations in time to come, that we may say again, Behold the pattern of the altar of the LORD, which our fathers made, not for burnt offerings, nor for sacrifices; but it is a witness between us and you.

29 God forbid that we should rebel against the LORD, and turn this day from following the LORD, to build an altar for burnt offerings, for meat offerings, or for sacrifices, beside the altar of the LORD our God that is before his tabernacle.

30And when Phinehas the priest, and the princes of the congregation and heads of the thousands of Israel which were with him, heard the words that the children of Reuben and the children of Gad and the children of Manasseh spake, it pleased them.

31 And Phinehas the son of Eleazar the priest said unto the children of Reuben, and to the children of Gad, and to the children of Manasseh, This day we perceive that the LORD is among us, because you have not committed this trespass against the LORD: now you have delivered the children of Israel out of the hand of the LORD.

32And Phinehas the son of Eleazar the priest, and the princes, returned from the children of Reuben, and from the children of Gad, out of the land of Gilead, unto the land of Canaan, to the children of Israel, and brought them word again.

33 And the thing pleased the children of Israel; and the children of Israel blessed God, and did not intend to go up against them in battle, to destroy the land wherein the children of Reuben and Gad dwelt.

34 And the children of Reuben and the children of Gad called the altar Ed: for it shall be a witness between us that the LORD is God.

CHAPTER 23

AND it came to pass a long time after that the LORD had given rest unto Israel from all their enemies round about, that Joshua waxed old and stricken in age.

2 And Joshua called for all Israel, and for their elders, and for their heads, and for their judges, and for their officers, and said unto them, I am old and stricken in age:

3 And you have seen all that the LORD your God has done unto all these nations because of you; for the LORD your God is he that has fought for you.

4 Behold, I have divided unto you by lot these nations that remain, to be an inheritance for your tribes, from Jordan, with all the nations that I have cut off, even unto the great sea westward.

5 And the LORD your God, he shall expel them from before you, and drive them from out of your sight; and you shall possess their land, as the LORD your God has promised unto you.

6 Be you therefore very courageous to keep and to do all that is written in the book of the law of Moses, that you turn not aside therefrom to the right hand or to the left;

7 That you come not among these nations, these that remain among you; neither make mention of the name of their gods, nor cause to swear by them, neither serve them, nor bow yourselves unto them:

8 But cleave unto the LORD your God, as you have done unto this day.

9 For the LORD has driven out from before you great nations and strong: but as for you, no man has been able to stand before you unto this day.

10 One man of you shall chase a thousand: for the LORD your God, he it is that fighteth for you, as he has promised you.

11 Take good heed therefore unto yourselves, that you love the LORD your God.

12 Else if you do in any wise go back, and cleave unto the remnant of these nations, even these that remain among you, and shall make marriages with them, and go in unto them, and they to you:

13 Know for a certainty that the LORD your God will no more drive out any of these nations from before you; but they shall be snares and traps unto you, and scourges in your sides, and thorns in your eyes, until you perish from off this good land which the LORD your God has given you.

14 And, behold, this day I am going the way of all the earth: and you know in all your hearts and in all your souls, that not one thing has failed of all the good things which the LORD your God spake concerning you; all are come to pass unto you, and not one thing has failed thereof.

15 Therefore it shall come to pass, that as all good things are come upon you, which the LORD your God promised you; so shall the LORD bring upon you all evil things, until he have destroyed you from off this good land which the LORD your God has given you.

16 When you have transgressed the covenant of the LORD your God, which he commanded you, and have gone and served other gods, and bowed yourselves to them; then shall the anger of the LORD be kindled against you, and you shall perish quickly from off the good land which he has given unto you.

CHAPTER 24

AND Joshua gathered all the tribes of Israel to Shechem, and called for the elders of Israel, and for their heads, and for their judges, and for their officers; and they presented themselves before God.

2 And Joshua said unto all the people, Thus saith the LORD God of Israel, Your fathers dwelt on the other side of the flood in old time, even Terah, the father of Abraham, and the father of Nachor: and they served other gods.

3 And I took your father Abraham from the other side of the flood, and led him throughout all the land of Canaan, and multiplied his seed, and gave him Isaac.

4 And I gave unto Isaac Jacob and Esau: and I gave unto Esau mount Seir, to possess it; but Jacob and his children went down into Egypt.

5 I sent Moses also and Aaron, and I plagued Egypt, according to that which I did among them: and afterward I brought you out.

6 And I brought your fathers out of Egypt: and you came unto the sea; and the Egyptians pursued after your fathers with chariots and horsemen unto the Red sea.

7 And when they cried unto the LORD, he put darkness between you and the Egyptians, and brought the sea upon them, and covered them; and your eyes have seen what I have done in Egypt: and you dwelt in the wilderness a long season.

8 And I brought you into the land of the Amorites, which dwelt on the other side Jordan; and they fought with you: and I gave them into your hand, that you might possess their land; and I destroyed them from before you.

9 Then Balak the son of Zippor, king of Moab, arose and warred against Israel, and sent and called Balaam the son of Beor to curse you:

10 But I would not hearken unto Balaam; therefore he blessed you still: so I delivered you out of his hand.

11 And you went over Jordan, and came unto Jericho: and the men of Jericho fought against you, the Amorites, and the Perizzites, and the Canaanites, and the Hittites, and the Girgashites, the Hivites, and the Jebusites; and I delivered them into your hand.

12 And I sent the hornet before you, which drave them out from before you, even the two kings of the Amorites; but not with your sword, nor with your bow.

13 And I have given you a land for which you did not labour, and cities which you built not, and you dwell in them; of the vineyards and oliveyards which you planted not do you eat.

14Now therefore fear the LORD, and serve him in sincerity and in truth: and put away the gods which your fathers served on the other side of the flood, and in Egypt; and serve you the LORD.

15 And if it seem evil unto you to serve the LORD, choose you this day whom you will serve; whether the gods which your fathers served that were on the other side of the flood, or the gods of the Amorites, in whose land you dwell: but as for me and my house, we will serve the LORD.

16 And the people answered and said, God forbid that we should forsake the LORD, to serve other gods;

17 For the LORD our God, he it is that brought us up and our fathers out of the land of Egypt, from the house of bondage, and which did those great signs in our sight, and preserved us in all the way wherein we went, and among all the people through whom we passed:

18 And the LORD drave out from before us all the people, even the Amorites which dwelt in the land: therefore will we also serve the LORD; for he is our God.

19 And Joshua said unto the people, You cannot serve the LORD: for he is an holy God; he is a jealous God; he will not forgive your transgressions nor your sins.

20 If you forsake the LORD, and serve strange gods, then he will turn and do you hurt, and consume you, after that he has done you good.

21 And the people said unto Joshua, Nay; but we will serve the LORD.

22 And Joshua said unto the people, You are witnesses against yourselves that you have chosen you the LORD, to serve him. And they said, We are witnesses.

23 Now therefore put away, said he, the strange gods which are among you, and incline your heart unto the LORD God of Israel.

24 And the people said unto Joshua, The LORD our God will we serve, and his voice will we obey.

25 So Joshua made a covenant with the people that day, and set them a statute and an ordinance in Shechem.

26 And Joshua wrote these words in the book of the law of God, and took a great stone, and set it up there under an oak, that was by the sanctuary of the LORD.

27 And Joshua said unto all the people, Behold, this stone shall be a witness unto us; for it has heard all the words of the LORD which he spake unto us: it shall be therefore a witness unto you, lest you deny your God.

28 So Joshua let the people depart, every man unto his inheritance.

29 And it came to pass after these things, that Joshua the son of Nun, the servant of the LORD, died, being an hundred and ten years old.

30 And they buried him in the border of his inheritance in Timnath-serah, which is in mount Ephraim, on the north side of the hill of Gaash.

31 And Israel served the LORD all the days of Joshua, and all the days of the elders that overlived Joshua, and which had known all the works of the LORD, that he had done for Israel.

32 And the bones of Joseph, which the children of Israel brought up out of Egypt, buried they in Shechem, in a parcel of ground which Jacob bought of the sons of Hamor the father of Shechem for an hundred pieces of silver: and it became the inheritance of the children of Joseph.

33 And Eleazar the son of Aaron died; and they buried him in a hill that pertained to Phinehas his son, which was given him in mount Ephraim.

THE BOOK OF JUDGES.

CHAPTER 1

NOW after the death of Joshua it came to pass, that the children of Israel asked the LORD, saying, Who shall go up for us against the Canaanites first, to fight against them?

2 And the LORD said, Judah shall go up: behold, I have delivered the land into his hand.

3 And Judah said unto Simeon his brother, Come up with me into my lot, that we may fight against the Canaanites; and I likewise will go with you into your lot. So Simeon went with him.

4 And Judah went up; and the LORD delivered the Canaanites and the Perizzites into their hand: and they slew of them in Bezek ten thousand men.

5 And they found Adoni-bezek in Bezek: and they fought against him, and they slew the Canaanites and the Perizzites.

6 But Adoni-bezek fled; and they pursued after him, and caught him, and cut off his thumbs and his great toes.

7 And Adoni-bezek said, Threescore and ten kings, having their thumbs and their great toes cut off, gathered their meat under my table: as I have done, so God has requited me. And they brought him to Jerusalem, and there he died.

8 Now the children of Judah had fought against Jerusalem, and had taken it, and smitten it with the edge of the sword, and set the city on fire.

9 And afterward the children of Judah went down to fight against the Canaanites, that dwelt in the mountain, and in the south, and in the valley.

10 And Judah went against the Canaanites that dwelt in Hebron: (now the name of Hebron before was Kirjath-arba:) and they slew Sheshai, and Ahiman, and Talmai.

11 And from thence he went against the inhabitants of Debir: and the name of Debir before was Kirjath-sepher:

12 And Caleb said, He that smiteth Kirjath-sepher, and taketh it, to him will I give Achsah my daughter to wife.

13 And Othniel the son of Kenaz, Caleb's younger brother, took it: and he gave him Achsah his daughter to wife.

14 And it came to pass, when she came to him, that she moved him to ask of her father a field: and she lighted from off her ass; and Caleb said unto her, What will you ?

15 And she said unto him, Give me a blessing: for you have given me a south land; give me also springs of water. And Caleb gave her the upper springs and the nether springs.

16 And the children of the Kenite, Moses' father in law, went up out of the city of palm trees with the children of Judah into the wilderness of Judah, which lies in the south of Arad; and they went and dwelt among the people.

17 And Judah went with Simeon his brother, and they slew the Canaanites that inhabited Zephath, and utterly destroyed it. And the name of the city was called Hormah.

18 Also Judah took Gaza with the coast thereof, and Askelon with the coast thereof, and Ekron with the coast thereof.

19 And the LORD was with Judah; and he drave out the inhabitants of the mountain; but could not drive out the inhabitants of the valley, because they had chariots of iron.

20 And they gave Hebron unto Caleb, as Moses said: and he expelled thence the three sons of Anak.

21 And the children of Benjamin did not drive out the Jebusites that inhabited Jerusalem; but the Jebusites dwell with the children of Benjamin in Jerusalem unto this day.

22 And the house of Joseph, they also went up against Beth-el: and the LORD was with them.

23 And the house of Joseph sent to descry Beth-el. (Now the name of the city before was Luz.)

24 And the spies saw a man come forth out of the city, and they said unto him, Shew us, we pray you, the entrance into the city, and we will shew you mercy.

25 And when he shewed them the entrance into the city, they struck the city with the edge of the sword; but they let go the man and all his family.

26 And the man went into the land of the Hittites, and built a city, and called the name thereof Luz: which is the name thereof unto this day.

27 Neither did Manasseh drive out the inhabitants of Beth-shean and her towns, nor Taanach and her towns, nor the inhabitants of Dor and her towns, nor the inhabitants of Ibleam and her towns, nor the inhabitants of Megiddo and her towns: but the Canaanites would dwell in that land.

28 And it came to pass, when Israel was strong, that they put the Canaanites to tribute, and did not utterly drive them out.

29 Neither did Ephraim drive out the Canaanites that dwelt in Gezer; but the Canaanites dwelt in Gezer among them.

30 Neither did Zebulun drive out the inhabitants of Kitron, nor the inhabitants of Nahalol; but the Canaanites dwelt among them, and became tributaries.

31 Neither did Asher drive out the inhabitants of Accho, nor the inhabitants of Zidon, nor of Ahlab, nor of Achzib, nor of Helbah, nor of Aphik, nor of Rehob:

32 But the Asherites dwelt among the Canaanites, the inhabitants of the land: for they did not drive them out.

33 Neither did Naphtali drive out the inhabitants of Beth-shemesh, nor the inhabitants of Beth-anath; but he dwelt among the Canaanites, the inhabitants of the land: nevertheless the inhabitants of Beth-shemesh and of Beth-anath became tributaries unto them.

34 And the Amorites forced the children of Dan into the mountain: for they would not suffer them to come down to the valley:

35 But the Amorites would dwell in mount Heres in Aijalon, and in Shaalbim: yet the hand of the house of Joseph prevailed, so that they became tributaries.

36 And the coast of the Amorites was from the going up to Akrabbim, from the rock, and upward.

CHAPTER 2

AND an angel of the LORD came up from Gilgal to Bochim, and said, I made you to go up out of Egypt, and have brought you unto the land which I sware unto your fathers; and I said, I will never break my covenant with you.

2 And you shall make no league with the inhabitants of this land; you shall throw down their altars: but you have not obeyed my voice: why have you done this?

3 Wherefore I also said, I will not drive them out from before you; but they shall be as thorns in your sides, and their gods shall be a snare unto you.

4 And it came to pass, when the angel of the LORD spake these words unto all the children of Israel, that the people lifted up their voice, and wept.

5 And they called the name of that place Bochim: and they sacrificed there unto the LORD.

6 And when Joshua had let the people go, the children of Israel went every man unto his inheritance to possess the land.

7 And the people served the LORD all the days of Joshua, and all the days of the elders that outlived Joshua, who had seen all the great works of the LORD, that he did for Israel.

8 And Joshua the son of Nun, the servant of the LORD, died, being an hundred and ten years old.

9 And they buried him in the border of his inheritance in Timnath-heres, in the mount of Ephraim, on the north side of the hill Gaash.

10 And also all that generation were gathered unto their fathers: and there arose another generation after them, which knew not the LORD, nor yet the works which he had done for Israel.

11 And the children of Israel did evil in the sight of the LORD, and served Baalim:

12 And they forsook the LORD God of their fathers, which brought them out of the land of Egypt, and followed other gods, of the gods of the people that were round about them, and bowed themselves unto them, and provoked the LORD to anger.

13 And they forsook the LORD, and served Baal and Ashtaroth.

14 And the anger of the LORD was hot against Israel, and he delivered them into the hands of spoilers that spoiled them, and he sold them into the hands of their enemies round about, so that they could not any longer stand before their enemies.

15 Whithersoever they went out, the hand of the LORD was against them for evil, as the LORD had said, and as the LORD had sworn unto them: and they were greatly distressed.

16 Nevertheless the LORD raised up judges, which delivered them out of the hand of those that spoiled them.

17 And yet they would not hearken unto their judges, but they went a whoring after other gods, and bowed themselves unto them: they turned quickly out of the way which their fathers walked in, obeying the commandments of the LORD; but they did not so.

18 And when the LORD raised them up judges, then the LORD was with the judge, and delivered them out of the hand of their enemies all the days of the judge: for it repented the LORD because of their groanings by reason of them that oppressed them and vexed them.

19 And it came to pass, when the judge was dead, that they returned, and corrupted themselves more than their fathers, in following other gods to serve them, and to bow down unto them; they ceased not from their own doings, nor from their stubborn way.

20 And the anger of the LORD was hot against Israel; and he said, Because that this people has transgressed my covenant which I commanded their fathers, and have not hearkened unto my voice;

21 I also will not henceforth drive out any from before them of the nations which Joshua left when he died:

22 That through them I may prove Israel, whether they will keep the way of the LORD to walk therein, as their fathers did keep it, or not.

23 Therefore the LORD left those nations, without driving them out hastily; neither delivered he them into the hand of Joshua.

CHAPTER 3

NOW these are the nations which the LORD left, to prove Israel by them, even as many of Israel as had not known all the wars of Canaan;

2 Only that the generations of the children of Israel might know, to teach them war, at the least such as before knew nothing thereof;

3 Namely, five lords of the Philistines, and all the Canaanites, and the Sidonians, and the Hivites that dwelt in mount Lebanon, from mount Baal-hermon unto the entering in of Hamath.

4 And they were to prove Israel by them, to know whether they would hearken unto the commandments of the LORD, which he commanded their fathers by the hand of Moses.

5 And the children of Israel dwelt among the Canaanites, Hittites, and Amorites, and Perizzites, and Hivites, and Jebusites:

6 And they took their daughters to be their wives, and gave their daughters to their sons, and served their gods.

7 And the children of Israel did evil in the sight of the LORD, and forgat the LORD their God, and served Baalim and the groves.

8 Therefore the anger of the LORD was hot against Israel, and he sold them into the hand of Chushan-rishathaim king of Mesopotamia: and the children of Israel served Chushan-rishathaim eight years.

9 And when the children of Israel cried unto the LORD, the LORD raised up a deliverer to the children of Israel, who delivered them, even Othniel the son of Kenaz, Caleb's younger brother.

10 And the Spirit of the LORD came upon him, and he judged Israel, and went out to war: and the LORD delivered Chushan-rishathaim king of Mesopotamia into his hand; and his hand prevailed against Chushan-rishathaim.

11 And the land had rest forty years. And Othniel the son of Kenaz died.

12 And the children of Israel did evil again in the sight of the LORD: and the LORD strengthened Eglon the king of Moab against Israel, because they had done evil in the sight of the LORD.

13 And he gathered unto him the children of Ammon and Amalek, and went and struck Israel, and possessed the city of palm trees.

14 So the children of Israel served Eglon the king of Moab eighteen years.

15 But when the children of Israel cried unto the LORD, the LORD raised them up a deliverer, Ehud the son of Gera, a Benjamite, a man lefthanded: and by him the children of Israel sent a present unto Eglon the king of Moab.

16 But Ehud made him a dagger which had two edges, of a cubit length; and he did gird it under his raiment upon his right thigh.

17 And he brought the present unto Eglon king of Moab: and Eglon was a very fat man.

18 And when he had made an end to offer the present, he sent away the people that bare the present.

19 But he himself turned again from the quarries that were by Gilgal, and said, I have a secret errand unto you, O king: who said, Keep silence. And all that stood by him went out from him.

20 And Ehud came unto him; and he was sitting in a summer parlour, which he had for himself alone. And Ehud said, I have a message from God unto you. And he arose out of his seat.

21 And Ehud put forth his left hand, and took the dagger from his right thigh, and thrust it into his belly:

22 And the haft also went in after the blade; and the fat closed upon the blade, so that he could not draw the dagger out of his belly; and the dirt came out.

23 Then Ehud went forth through the porch, and shut the doors of the parlour upon him, and locked them.

24 When he was gone out, his servants came; and when they saw that, behold, the doors of the parlour were locked, they said, Surely he covers his feet in his summer chamber.

25 And they tarried till they were ashamed: and, behold, he opened not the doors of the parlour; therefore they took a key, and opened them: and, behold, their lord was fallen down dead on the earth.

26 And Ehud escaped while they tarried, and passed beyond the quarries, and escaped unto Seirath.

27 And it came to pass, when he was come, that he blew a trumpet in the mountain of Ephraim, and the children of Israel went down with him from the mount, and he before them.

28 And he said unto them, Follow after me: for the LORD has delivered your enemies the Moabites into your hand. And they went down after him, and took the fords of Jordan toward Moab, and suffered not a man to pass over.

29 And they slew of Moab at that time about ten thousand men, all lusty, and all men of valour; and there escaped not a man.

30 So Moab was subdued that day under the hand of Israel. And the land had rest fourscore years.

31 And after him was Shamgar the son of Anath, which slew of the Philistines six hundred men with an ox goad: and he also delivered Israel.

CHAPTER 4

AND the children of Israel again did evil in the sight of the LORD, when Ehud was dead.

2 And the LORD sold them into the hand of Jabin king of Canaan, that reigned in Hazor; the captain of whose host was Sisera, which dwelt in Harosheth of the Gentiles.

3 And the children of Israel cried unto the LORD: for he had nine hundred chariots of iron; and twenty years he mightily oppressed the children of Israel.

4 And Deborah, a prophetess, the wife of Lapidoth, she judged Israel at that time.

5 And she dwelt under the palm tree of Deborah between Ramah and Beth-el in mount Ephraim: and the children of Israel came up to her for judgment.

6 And she sent and called Barak the son of Abinoam out of Kedesh-naphtali, and said unto him, Has not the LORD God of Israel commanded, saying, Go and draw toward mount Tabor, and take with you ten thousand men of the children of Naphtali and of the children of Zebulun?

7 And I will draw unto you to the river Kishon Sisera, the captain of Jabin's army, with his chariots and his multitude; and I will deliver him into yours hand.

8 And Barak said unto her, If you will go with me, then I will go: but if you will not go with me, then I will not go.

9 And she said, I will surely go with you: notwithstanding the journey that you takest shall not be for yours honour; for the LORD shall sell Sisera into the hand of a woman. And Deborah arose, and went with Barak to Kedesh.

10 And Barak called Zebulun and Naphtali to Kedesh; and he went up with ten thousand men at his feet: and Deborah went up with him.

11 Now Heber the Kenite, which was of the children of Hobab the father in law of Moses, had severed himself from the Kenites, and pitched his tent unto the plain of Zaanaim, which is by Kedesh.

12 And they shewed Sisera that Barak the son of Abinoam was gone up to mount Tabor.

13 And Sisera gathered together all his chariots, even nine hundred chariots of iron, and all the people that were with him, from Harosheth of the Gentiles unto the river of Kishon.

14 And Deborah said unto Barak, Up; for this is the day in which the LORD has delivered Sisera into yours hand: is not the LORD gone out before you? So Barak went down from mount Tabor, and ten thousand men after him.

15 And the LORD discomfited Sisera, and all his chariots, and all his host, with the edge of the sword before Barak; so that Sisera lighted down off his chariot, and fled away on his feet.

16 But Barak pursued after the chariots, and after the host, unto Harosheth of the Gentiles: and all the host of Sisera fell upon the edge of the sword; and there was not a man left.

17 Howbeit Sisera fled away on his feet to the tent of Jael the wife of Heber the Kenite: for there was peace between Jabin the king of Hazor and the house of Heber the Kenite.

18 And Jael went out to meet Sisera, and said unto him, Turn in, my lord, turn in to me; fear not. And when he had turned in unto her into the tent, she covered him with a mantle.

19 And he said unto her, Give me, I pray you, a little water to drink; for I am thirsty. And she opened a bottle of milk, and gave him drink, and covered him.

20 Again he said unto her, Stand in the door of the tent, and it shall be, when any man doth come and inquire of you, and say, Is there any man here? that you shalt say, No.

21 Then Jael Heber's wife took a nail of the tent, and took an hammer in her hand, and went softly unto him, and struck the nail into his temples, and fastened it into the ground: for he was fast asleep and weary. So he died.

22 And, behold, as Barak pursued Sisera, Jael came out to meet him, and said unto him, Come, and I will shew you the man whom you seekest. And when he came into her tent, behold, Sisera lay dead, and the nail was in his temples.

23 So God subdued on that day Jabin the king of Canaan before the children of Israel.

24 And the hand of the children of Israel prospered, and prevailed against Jabin the king of Canaan, until they had destroyed Jabin king of Canaan.

CHAPTER 5

THEN sang Deborah and Barak the son of Abinoam on that day, saying,

2 Praise you the LORD for the avenging of Israel, when the people willingly offered themselves.

3 Hear, O you kings; give ear, O you princes; I, even I, will sing unto the LORD; I will sing praise to the LORD God of Israel.

4 LORD, when you wentest out of Seir, when you marchedst out of the field of Edom, the earth trembled, and the heavens dropped, the clouds also dropped water.

5 The mountains melted from before the LORD, even that Sinai from before the LORD God of Israel.

6 In the days of Shamgar the son of Anath, in the days of Jael, the highways were unoccupied, and the travellers walked through byways.

7 The inhabitants of the villages ceased, they ceased in Israel, until that I Deborah arose, that I arose a mother in Israel.

8 They chose new gods; then was war in the gates: was there a shield or spear seen among forty thousand in Israel?

9 My heart is toward the governors of Israel, that offered themselves willingly among the people. Bless you the LORD.

10 Speak, you that ride on white asses, you that sit in judgment, and walk by the way.

11 They that are delivered from the noise of archers in the places of drawing water, there shall they rehearse the righteous acts of the LORD, even the righteous acts toward the inhabitants of his villages in Israel: then shall the people of the LORD go down to the gates.

12 Awake, awake, Deborah: awake, awake, utter a song: arise, Barak, and lead your captivity captive, you son of Abinoam.

13 Then he made him that remaineth have dominion over the nobles among the people: the LORD made me have dominion over the mighty.

14 Out of Ephraim was there a root of them against Amalek; after you, Benjamin, among your people; out of Machir came down governors, and out of Zebulun they that handle the pen of the writer.

15 And the princes of Issachar were with Deborah; even Issachar, and also Barak: he was sent on foot into the valley. For the divisions of Reuben there were great thoughts of heart.

16 Why abodest you among the sheepfolds, to hear the bleatings of the flocks? For the divisions of Reuben there were great searchings of heart.

17 Gilead abode beyond Jordan: and why did Dan remain in ships? Asher continued on the sea shore, and abode in his breaches.

18 Zebulun and Naphtali were a people that jeoparded their lives unto the death in the high places of the field.

19 The kings came and fought, then fought the kings of Canaan in Taanach by the waters of Megiddo; they took no gain of money.

20 They fought from heaven; the stars in their courses fought against Sisera.

21 The river of Kishon swept them away, that ancient river, the river Kishon. O my soul, you have trodden down strength.

22 Then were the horsehoofs broken by the means of the pransings, the pransings of their mighty ones.

23 Curse you Meroz, said the angel of the LORD, curse you bitterly the inhabitants thereof; because they came not to the help of the LORD, to the help of the LORD against the mighty.

24 Blessed above women shall Jael the wife of Heber the Kenite be, blessed shall she be above women in the tent.

25 He asked water, and she gave him milk; she brought forth butter in a lordly dish.

26 She put her hand to the nail, and her right hand to the workmen's hammer; and with the hammer she struck Sisera, she struck off his head, when she had pierced and stricken through his temples.

27 At her feet he bowed, he fell, he lay down: at her feet he bowed, he fell: where he bowed, there he fell down dead.

28 The mother of Sisera looked out at a window, and cried through the lattice, Why is his chariot so long in coming? why tarry the wheels of his chariots?

29 Her wise ladies answered her, yea, she returned answer to herself,

30 Have they not sped? have they not divided the prey; to every man a damsel or two; to Sisera a prey of divers colours, a prey of divers colours of needlework, of divers colours of needlework on both sides, meet for the necks of them that take the spoil?

31 So let all yours enemies perish, O LORD: but let them that love him be as the sun when he goeth forth in his might. And the land had rest forty years.

CHAPTER 6

AND the children of Israel did evil in the sight of the LORD: and the LORD delivered them into the hand of Midian seven years.

2 And the hand of Midian prevailed against Israel: and because of the Midianites the children of Israel made them the dens which are in the mountains, and caves, and strong holds.

3 And so it was, when Israel had sown, that the Midianites came up, and the Amalekites, and the children of the east, even they came up against them;

4 And they encamped against them, and destroyed the increase of the earth, till you come unto Gaza, and left no sustenance for Israel, neither sheep, nor ox, nor ass.

5 For they came up with their cattle and their tents, and they came as grasshoppers for multitude; for both they and their camels were without number: and they entered into the land to destroy it.

6 And Israel was greatly impoverished because of the Midianites; and the children of Israel cried unto the LORD.

7 And it came to pass, when the children of Israel cried unto the LORD because of the Midianites,

8 That the LORD sent a prophet unto the children of Israel, which said unto them, Thus saith the LORD God of Israel, I brought you up from Egypt, and brought you forth out of the house of bondage;

9 And I delivered you out of the hand of the Egyptians, and out of the hand of all that oppressed you, and drave them out from before you, and gave you their land;

10 And I said unto you, I am the LORD your God; fear not the gods of the Amorites, in whose land you dwell: but you have not obeyed my voice.

11 And there came an angel of the LORD, and sat under an oak which was in Ophrah, that pertained unto Joash the Abi-ezrite: and his son Gideon threshed wheat by the winepress, to hide it from the Midianites.

12 And the angel of the LORD appeared unto him, and said unto him, The LORD is with you, you mighty man of valour.

13 And Gideon said unto him, Oh my Lord, if the LORD be with us, why then is all this befallen us? and where be all his miracles which our fathers told us of, saying, Did not the LORD bring us up from Egypt? but now the LORD has forsaken us, and delivered us into the hands of the Midianites.

14 And the LORD looked upon him, and said, Go in this your might, and you shalt save Israel from the hand of the Midianites: have not I sent you?

15 And he said unto him, Oh my Lord, wherewith shall I save Israel? behold, my family is poor in Manasseh, and I am the least in my father's house.

16 And the LORD said unto him, Surely I will be with you, and you shalt strike the Midianites as one man.

17 And he said unto him, If now I have found grace in your sight, then shew me a sign that you talkest with me.

18 Depart not hence, I pray you, until I come unto you, and bring forth my present, and set it before you. And he said, I will tarry until you come again.

19 And Gideon went in, and made ready a kid, and unleavened cakes of an ephah of flour: the flesh he put in a basket, and he put the broth in a pot, and brought it out unto him under the oak, and presented it.

20 And the angel of God said unto him, Take the flesh and the unleavened cakes, and lay them upon this rock, and pour out the broth. And he did so.

21 Then the angel of the LORD put forth the end of the staff that was in his hand, and touched the flesh and the unleavened cakes; and there rose up fire out of the rock, and consumed the flesh and the unleavened cakes. Then the angel of the LORD departed out of his sight.

22 And when Gideon perceived that he was an angel of the LORD, Gideon said, Alas, O Lord GOD! for because I have seen an angel of the LORD face to face.

23 And the LORD said unto him, Peace be unto you; fear not: you shalt not die.

24 Then Gideon built an altar there unto the LORD, and called it Jehovah-shalom: unto this day it is yet in Ophrah of the Abi-ezrites.

25 And it came to pass the same night, that the LORD said unto him, Take your father's young bullock, even the second bullock of seven years old, and throw down the altar of Baal that your father has, and cut down the grove that is by it:

26 And build an altar unto the LORD your God upon the top of this rock, in the ordered place, and take the second bullock, and offer a burnt sacrifice with the wood of the grove which you shalt cut down.

27 Then Gideon took ten men of his servants, and did as the LORD had said unto him: and so it was, because he feared his father's household, and the men of the city, that he could not do it by day, that he did it by night.

28 And when the men of the city arose early in the morning, behold, the altar of Baal was cast down, and the grove was cut down that was by it, and the second bullock was offered upon the altar that was built.

29 And they said one to another, Who has done this thing? And when they inquired and asked, they said, Gideon the son of Joash has done this thing.

30 Then the men of the city said unto Joash, Bring out your son, that he may die: because he has cast down the altar of Baal, and because he has cut down the grove that was by it.

31 And Joash said unto all that stood against him, Will you plead for Baal? will you save him? he that will plead for him, let him be put to death whilst it is yet morning: if he be a god, let him plead for himself, because one has cast down his altar.

32 Therefore on that day he called him Jerubbaal, saying, Let Baal plead against him, because he has thrown down his altar.

33 Then all the Midianites and the Amalekites and the children of the east were gathered together, and went over, and pitched in the valley of Jezreel.

34 But the Spirit of the LORD came upon Gideon, and he blew a trumpet; and Abi-ezer was gathered after him.

35 And he sent messengers throughout all Manasseh; who also was gathered after him: and he sent messengers unto Asher, and unto Zebulun, and unto Naphtali; and they came up to meet them.

36 And Gideon said unto God, If you will save Israel by my hand, as you have said,

37 Behold, I will put a fleece of wool in the floor; and if the dew be on the fleece only, and it be dry upon all the earth beside, then shall I know that you will save Israel by my hand, as you have said.

38 And it was so: for he rose up early on the morrow, and thrust the fleece together, and wringed the dew out of the fleece, a bowl full of water.

39 And Gideon said unto God, Let not yours anger be hot against me, and I will speak but this once: let me prove, I pray you, but this once with the fleece; let it now be dry only upon the fleece, and upon all the ground let there be dew.

40 And God did so that night: for it was dry upon the fleece only, and there was dew on all the ground.

CHAPTER 7

THEN Jerubbaal, who is Gideon, and all the people that were with him, rose up early, and pitched beside the well of Harod: so that the host of the Midianites were on the north side of them, by the hill of Moreh, in the valley.

2 And the LORD said unto Gideon, The people that are with you are too many for me to give the Midianites into their hands, lest Israel vaunt themselves against me, saying, My own hand has saved me.

3 Now therefore go to, proclaim in the ears of the people, saying, Whosoever is fearful and afraid, let him return and depart early from mount Gilead. And there returned of the people twenty and two thousand; and there remained ten thousand.

4 And the LORD said unto Gideon, The people are yet too many; bring them down unto the water, and I will try them for you there: and it shall be, that of whom I say unto you, This shall go with you, the same shall go with you; and of whomsoever I say unto you, This shall not go with you, the same shall not go.

5 So he brought down the people unto the water: and the LORD said unto Gideon, Every one that lappeth of the water with his tongue, as a dog lappeth, him shalt you set by himself; likewise every one that boweth down upon his knees to drink.

6 And the number of them that lapped, putting their hand to their mouth, were three hundred men: but all the rest of the people bowed down upon their knees to drink water.

7 And the LORD said unto Gideon, By the three hundred men that lapped will I save you, and deliver the Midianites into yours hand: and let all the other people go every man unto his place.

8 So the people took victuals in their hand, and their trumpets: and he sent all the rest of Israel every man unto his tent, and retained those three hundred men: and the host of Midian was beneath him in the valley.

9 And it came to pass the same night, that the LORD said unto him, Arise, get you down unto the host; for I have delivered it into yours hand.

10 But if you fear to go down, go you with Phurah your servant down to the host:

11 And you shalt hear what they say; and afterward shall yours hands be strengthened to go down unto the host. Then went he down with Phurah his servant unto the outside of the armed men that were in the host.

12 And the Midianites and the Amalekites and all the children of the east lay along in the valley like grasshoppers for multitude; and their camels were without number, as the sand by the sea side for multitude.

13 And when Gideon was come, behold, there was a man that told a dream unto his fellow, and said, Behold, I dreamed a dream, and, lo, a cake of barley bread tumbled into the host of Midian, and came unto a tent, and struck it that it fell, and overturned it, that the tent lay along.

14 And his fellow answered and said, This is nothing else save the sword of Gideon the son of Joash, a man of Israel: for into his hand has God delivered Midian, and all the host.

15 And it was so, when Gideon heard the telling of the dream, and the interpretation thereof, that he worshipped, and returned into the host of Israel, and said, Arise; for the LORD has delivered into your hand the host of Midian.

16 And he divided the three hundred men into three companies, and he put a trumpet in every man's hand, with empty pitchers, and lamps within the pitchers.

17 And he said unto them, Look on me, and do likewise: and, behold, when I come to the outside of the camp, it shall be that, as I do, so shall you do.

18 When I blow with a trumpet, I and all that are with me, then blow you the trumpets also on every side of all the camp, and say, The sword of the LORD, and of Gideon.

19 So Gideon, and the hundred men that were with him, came unto the outside of the camp in the beginning of the middle watch; and they had but newly set the watch: and they blew the trumpets, and brake the pitchers that were in their hands.

20 And the three companies blew the trumpets, and brake the pitchers, and held the lamps in their left hands, and the trumpets in their right hands to blow withal: and they cried, The sword of the LORD, and of Gideon.

21 And they stood every man in his place round about the camp: and all the host ran, and cried, and fled.

22 And the three hundred blew the trumpets, and the LORD set every man's sword against his fellow, even throughout all the host: and the host fled to Beth-shittah in Zererath, and to the border of Abel-meholah, unto Tabbath.

23 And the men of Israel gathered themselves together out of Naphtali, and out of Asher, and out of all Manasseh, and pursued after the Midianites.

24 And Gideon sent messengers throughout all mount Ephraim, saying, Come down against the Midianites, and take before them the waters unto Beth-barah and Jordan. Then all the men of Ephraim gathered themselves together, and took the waters unto Beth-barah and Jordan.

25 And they took two princes of the Midianites, Oreb and Zeeb; and they slew Oreb upon the rock Oreb, and Zeeb they slew at the winepress of Zeeb, and pursued Midian, and brought the heads of Oreb and Zeeb to Gideon on the other side Jordan.

CHAPTER 8

AND the men of Ephraim said unto him, Why have you served us thus, that you calledst us not, when you wentest to fight with the Midianites? And they did chide with him sharply.

2 And he said unto them, What have I done now in comparison of you? Is not the gleaning of the grapes of Ephraim better than the vintage of Abi-ezer?

3 God has delivered into your hands the princes of Midian, Oreb and Zeeb: and what was I able to do in comparison of you? Then their anger was abated toward him, when he had said that.

4 And Gideon came to Jordan, and passed over, he, and the three hundred men that were with him, faint, yet pursuing them.

5 And he said unto the men of Succoth, Give, I pray you, loaves of bread unto the people that follow me; for they be faint, and I am pursuing after Zebah and Zalmunna, kings of Midian.

6 And the princes of Succoth said, Are the hands of Zebah and Zalmunna now in yours hand, that we should give bread unto yours army?

7 And Gideon said, Therefore when the LORD has delivered Zebah and Zalmunna into my hand, then I will tear your flesh with the thorns of the wilderness and with briers.

8 And he went up thence to Penuel, and spake unto them likewise: and the men of Penuel answered him as the men of Succoth had answered him.

9 And he spake also unto the men of Penuel, saying, When I come again in peace, I will break down this tower.

10 Now Zebah and Zalmunna were in Karkor, and their hosts with them, about fifteen thousand men, all that were left of all the hosts of the children of the east: for there fell an hundred and twenty thousand men that drew sword.

11 And Gideon went up by the way of them that dwelt in tents on the east of Nobah and Jogbehah, and struck the host: for the host was secure.

12 And when Zebah and Zalmunna fled, he pursued after them, and took the two kings of Midian, Zebah and Zalmunna, and discomfited all the host.

13 And Gideon the son of Joash returned from battle before the sun was up,

14 And caught a young man of the men of Succoth, and inquired of him: and he described unto him the princes of Succoth, and the elders thereof, even threescore and seventeen men.

15 And he came unto the men of Succoth, and said, Behold Zebah and Zalmunna, with whom you did upbraid me, saying, Are the hands of Zebah and Zalmunna now in yours hand, that we should give bread unto your men that are weary?

16 And he took the elders of the city, and thorns of the wilderness and briers, and with them he taught the men of Succoth.

17 And he beat down the tower of Penuel, and slew the men of the city.

18 Then said he unto Zebah and Zalmunna, What manner of men were they whom you slew at Tabor? And they answered, As you are, so were they; each one resembled the children of a king.

19 And he said, They were my brethren, even the sons of my mother: as the LORD liveth, if you had saved them alive, I would not slay you.

20 And he said unto Jether his firstborn, Up, and slay them. But the youth drew not his sword: for he feared, because he was yet a youth.

21 Then Zebah and Zalmunna said, Rise you , and fall upon us: for as the man is, so is his strength. And Gideon arose, and slew Zebah and Zalmunna, and took away the ornaments that were on their camels' necks.

22 Then the men of Israel said unto Gideon, Rule you over us, both you , and your son, and your son's son also: for you have delivered us from the hand of Midian.

23 And Gideon said unto them, I will not rule over you, neither shall my son rule over you: the LORD shall rule over you.

24 And Gideon said unto them, I would desire a request of you, that you would give me every man the earrings of his prey. (For they had golden earrings, because they were Ishmaelites.)

25 And they answered, We will willingly give them. And they spread a garment, and did cast therein every man the earrings of his prey.

26 And the weight of the golden earrings that he requested was a thousand and seven hundred shekels of gold; beside ornaments, and collars, and purple raiment that was on the kings of Midian, and beside the chains that were about their camels' necks.

27 And Gideon made an ephod thereof, and put it in his city, even in Ophrah: and all Israel went thither a whoring after it: which thing became a snare unto Gideon, and to his house.

28 Thus was Midian subdued before the children of Israel, so that they lifted up their heads no more. And the country was in quietness forty years in the days of Gideon.

29 And Jerubbaal the son of Joash went and dwelt in his own house.

30 And Gideon had threescore and ten sons of his body begotten: for he had many wives.

31 And his concubine that was in Shechem, she also bare him a son, whose name he called Abimelech.

32 And Gideon the son of Joash died in a good old age, and was buried in the sepulchre of Joash his father, in Ophrah of the Abi-ezrites.

33 And it came to pass, as soon as Gideon was dead, that the children of Israel turned again, and went a whoring after Baalim, and made Baal-berith their god.

34 And the children of Israel remembered not the LORD their God, who had delivered them out of the hands of all their enemies on every side:

35 Neither shewed they kindness to the house of Jerubbaal, namely, Gideon, according to all the goodness which he had shewed unto Israel.

CHAPTER 9

AND Abimelech the son of Jerubbaal went to Shechem unto his mother's brethren, and communed with them, and with all the family of the house of his mother's father, saying,

2 Speak, I pray you, in the ears of all the men of Shechem, Whether is better for you, either that all the sons of Jerubbaal, which are threescore and ten persons, reign over you, or that one reign over you? remember also that I am your bone and your flesh.

3 And his mother's brethren spake of him in the ears of all the men of Shechem all these words: and their hearts inclined to follow Abimelech; for they said, He is our brother.

4 And they gave him threescore and ten pieces of silver out of the house of Baal-berith, wherewith Abimelech hired vain and light persons, which followed him.

5 And he went unto his father's house at Ophrah, and slew his brethren the sons of Jerubbaal, being threescore and ten persons, upon one stone: notwithstanding yet Jotham the youngest son of Jerubbaal was left; for he hid himself.

6 And all the men of Shechem gathered together, and all the house of Millo, and went, and made Abimelech king, by the plain of the pillar that was in Shechem.

7 And when they told it to Jotham, he went and stood in the top of mount Gerizim, and lifted up his voice, and cried, and said unto them, Hearken unto me, you men of Shechem, that God may hearken unto you.

8 The trees went forth on a time to anoint a king over them; and they said unto the olive tree, Reign you over us.

9 But the olive tree said unto them, Should I leave my fatness, wherewith by me they honour God and man, and go to be promoted over the trees?

10 And the trees said to the fig tree, Come you , and reign over us.

11 But the fig tree said unto them, Should I forsake my sweetness, and my good fruit, and go to be promoted over the trees?

12 Then said the trees unto the vine, Come you , and reign over us.

13 And the vine said unto them, Should I leave my wine, which cheereth God and man, and go to be promoted over the trees?

14 Then said all the trees unto the bramble, Come you , and reign over us.

15 And the bramble said unto the trees, If in truth you anoint me king over you, then come and put your trust in my shadow: and if not, let fire come out of the bramble, and devour the cedars of Lebanon.

16 Now therefore, if you have done truly and sincerely, in that you have made Abimelech king, and if you have dealt well with Jerubbaal and his house, and have done unto him according to the deserving of his hands;

17 (For my father fought for you, and adventured his life far, and delivered you out of the hand of Midian:

18 And you are risen up against my father's house this day, and have slain his sons, threescore and ten persons, upon one stone, and have made Abimelech, the son of his maidservant, king over the men of Shechem, because he is your brother;)

19 If you then have dealt truly and sincerely with Jerubbaal and with his house this day, then rejoice you in Abimelech, and let him also rejoice in you:

20 But if not, let fire come out from Abimelech, and devour the men of Shechem, and the house of Millo; and let fire come out from the men of Shechem, and from the house of Millo, and devour Abimelech.

21 And Jotham ran away, and fled, and went to Beer, and dwelt there, for fear of Abimelech his brother.

22 When Abimelech had reigned three years over Israel,

23 Then God sent an evil spirit between Abimelech and the men of Shechem; and the men of Shechem dealt treacherously with Abimelech:

24 That the cruelty done to the threescore and ten sons of Jerubbaal might come, and their blood be laid upon Abimelech their brother, which slew them; and upon the men of Shechem, which aided him in the killing of his brethren.

25 And the men of Shechem set liers in wait for him in the top of the mountains, and they robbed all that came along that way by them: and it was told Abimelech.

26 And Gaal the son of Ebed came with his brethren, and went over to Shechem: and the men of Shechem put their confidence in him.

27 And they went out into the fields, and gathered their vineyards, and trode the grapes, and made merry, and went into the house of their god, and did eat and drink, and cursed Abimelech.

28 And Gaal the son of Ebed said, Who is Abimelech, and who is Shechem, that we should serve him? is not he the son of Jerubbaal? and Zebul his officer? serve the men of Hamor the father of Shechem: for why should we serve him?

29 And would to God this people were under my hand! then would I remove Abimelech. And he said to Abimelech, Increase yours army, and come out.

30 And when Zebul the ruler of the city heard the words of Gaal the son of Ebed, his anger was kindled.

31 And he sent messengers unto Abimelech privily, saying, Behold, Gaal the son of Ebed and his brethren be come to Shechem; and, behold, they fortify the city against you.

32 Now therefore up by night, you and the people that is with you, and lie in wait in the field:

33 And it shall be, that in the morning, as soon as the sun is up, you shalt rise early, and set upon the city: and, behold, when he and the people that is with him come out against you, then mayest you do to them as you shalt find occasion.

34 And Abimelech rose up, and all the people that were with him, by night, and they laid wait against Shechem in four companies.

35 And Gaal the son of Ebed went out, and stood in the entering of the gate of the city: and Abimelech rose up, and the people that were with him, from lying in wait.

36 And when Gaal saw the people, he said to Zebul, Behold, there come people down from the top of the mountains. And Zebul said unto him, You seest the shadow of the mountains as if they were men.

37 And Gaal spake again and said, See there come people down by the middle of the land, and another company come along by the plain of Meonenim.

38 Then said Zebul unto him, Where is now your mouth, wherewith you saidst, Who is Abimelech, that we should serve him? is not this the people that you have despised? go out, I pray now, and fight with them.

39 And Gaal went out before the men of Shechem, and fought with Abimelech.

40 And Abimelech chased him, and he fled before him, and many were overthrown and wounded, even unto the entering of the gate.

41 And Abimelech dwelt at Arumah: and Zebul thrust out Gaal and his brethren, that they should not dwell in Shechem.

42 And it came to pass on the morrow, that the people went out into the field; and they told Abimelech.

43 And he took the people, and divided them into three companies, and laid wait in the field, and looked, and, behold, the people were come forth out of the city; and he rose up against them, and struck them.

44 And Abimelech, and the company that was with him, rushed forward, and stood in the entering of the gate of the city: and the two other companies ran upon all the people that were in the fields, and slew them.

45 And Abimelech fought against the city all that day; and he took the city, and slew the people that was therein, and beat down the city, and sowed it with salt.

46 And when all the men of the tower of Shechem heard that, they entered into an hold of the house of the god Berith.

47 And it was told Abimelech, that all the men of the tower of Shechem were gathered together.

48 And Abimelech gat him up to mount Zalmon, he and all the people that were with him; and Abimelech took an axe in his hand, and cut down a bough from the trees, and took it, and laid it on his shoulder, and said unto the people that were with him, What you have seen me do, make haste, and do as I have done.

49 And all the people likewise cut down every man his bough, and followed Abimelech, and put them to the hold, and set the hold on fire upon them; so that all the men of the tower of Shechem died also, about a thousand men and women.

50 Then went Abimelech to Thebez, and encamped against Thebez, and took it.

51 But there was a strong tower within the city, and thither fled all the men and women, and all they of the city, and shut it to them, and gat them up to the top of the tower.

52 And Abimelech came unto the tower, and fought against it, and went hard unto the door of the tower to burn it with fire.

53 And a certain woman cast a piece of a millstone upon Abimelech's head, and all to brake his skull.

54 Then he called hastily unto the young man his armourbearer, and said unto him, Draw your sword, and slay me, that men say not of me, A woman slew him. And his young man thrust him through, and he died.

55 And when the men of Israel saw that Abimelech was dead, they departed every man unto his place.

56 Thus God rendered the wickedness of Abimelech, which he did unto his father, in slaying his seventy brethren:

57 And all the evil of the men of Shechem did God render upon their heads: and upon them came the curse of Jotham the son of Jerubbaal.

CHAPTER 10

AND after Abimelech there arose to defend Israel Tola the son of Puah, the son of Dodo, a man of Issachar; and he dwelt in Shamir in mount Ephraim.

2 And he judged Israel twenty and three years, and died, and was buried in Shamir.

3 And after him arose Jair, a Gileadite, and judged Israel twenty and two years.

4 And he had thirty sons that rode on thirty ass colts, and they had thirty cities, which are called Havoth-jair unto this day, which are in the land of Gilead.

5 And Jair died, and was buried in Camon.

6 And the children of Israel did evil again in the sight of the LORD, and served Baalim, and Ashtaroth, and the gods of Syria, and the gods of Zidon, and the gods of Moab, and the gods of the children of Ammon, and the gods of the Philistines, and forsook the LORD, and served not him.

7 And the anger of the LORD was hot against Israel, and he sold them into the hands of the Philistines, and into the hands of the children of Ammon.

8 And that year they vexed and oppressed the children of Israel: eighteen years, all the children of Israel that were on the other side Jordan in the land of the Amorites, which is in Gilead.

9 Moreover the children of Ammon passed over Jordan to fight also against Judah, and against Benjamin, and against the house of Ephraim; so that Israel was sore distressed.

10 And the children of Israel cried unto the LORD, saying, We have sinned against you, both because we have forsaken our God, and also served Baalim.

11 And the LORD said unto the children of Israel, Did not I deliver you from the Egyptians, and from the Amorites, from the children of Ammon, and from the Philistines?

12 The Zidonians also, and the Amalekites, and the Maonites, did oppress you; and you cried to me, and I delivered you out of their hand.

13 Yet you have forsaken me, and served other gods: wherefore I will deliver you no more.

14 Go and cry unto the gods which you have chosen; let them deliver you in the time of your tribulation.

15 And the children of Israel said unto the LORD, We have sinned: do you unto us whatsoever seemeth good unto you; deliver us only, we pray you, this day.

16 And they put away the strange gods from among them, and served the LORD: and his soul was grieved for the misery of Israel.

17 Then the children of Ammon were gathered together, and encamped in Gilead. And the children of Israel assembled themselves together, and encamped in Mizpeh.

18 And the people and princes of Gilead said one to another, What man is he that will begin to fight against the children of Ammon? he shall be head over all the inhabitants of Gilead.

CHAPTER 11

NOW Jephthah the Gileadite was a mighty man of valour, and he was the son of an harlot: and Gilead begat Jephthah.

2 And Gilead's wife bare him sons; and his wife's sons grew up, and they thrust out Jephthah, and said unto him, You shalt not inherit in our father's house; for you are the son of a strange woman.

3 Then Jephthah fled from his brethren, and dwelt in the land of Tob: and there were gathered vain men to Jephthah, and went out with him.

4 And it came to pass in process of time, that the children of Ammon made war against Israel.

5 And it was so, that when the children of Ammon made war against Israel, the elders of Gilead went to fetch Jephthah out of the land of Tob:

6 And they said unto Jephthah, Come, and be our captain, that we may fight with the children of Ammon.

7 And Jephthah said unto the elders of Gilead, Did not you hate me, and expel me out of my father's house? and why are you come unto me now when you are in distress?

8 And the elders of Gilead said unto Jephthah, Therefore we turn again to you now, that you mayest go with us, and fight against the children of Ammon, and be our head over all the inhabitants of Gilead.

9 And Jephthah said unto the elders of Gilead, If you bring me home again to fight against the children of Ammon, and the LORD deliver them before me, shall I be your head?

10 And the elders of Gilead said unto Jephthah, The LORD be witness between us, if we do not so according to your words.

11 Then Jephthah went with the elders of Gilead, and the people made him head and captain over them: and Jephthah uttered all his words before the LORD in Mizpeh.

12 And Jephthah sent messengers unto the king of the children of Ammon, saying, What have you to do with me, that you are come against me to fight in my land?

13 And the king of the children of Ammon answered unto the messengers of Jephthah, Because Israel took away my land, when they came up out of Egypt, from Arnon even unto Jabbok, and unto Jordan: now therefore restore those lands again peaceably.

14 And Jephthah sent messengers again unto the king of the children of Ammon:

15 And said unto him, Thus saith Jephthah, Israel took not away the land of Moab, nor the land of the children of Ammon:

16 But when Israel came up from Egypt, and walked through the wilderness unto the Red sea, and came to Kadesh;

17 Then Israel sent messengers unto the king of Edom, saying, Let me, I pray you, pass through your land: but the king of Edom would not hearken thereto. And in like manner they sent unto the king of Moab: but he would not consent: and Israel abode in Kadesh.

18 Then they went along through the wilderness, and compassed the land of Edom, and the land of Moab, and came by the east side of the land of Moab, and pitched on the other side of Arnon, but came not within the border of Moab: for Arnon was the border of Moab.

19 And Israel sent messengers unto Sihon king of the Amorites, the king of Heshbon; and Israel said unto him, Let us pass, we pray you, through your land into my place.

20 But Sihon trusted not Israel to pass through his coast: but Sihon gathered all his people together, and pitched in Jahaz, and fought against Israel.

21 And the LORD God of Israel delivered Sihon and all his people into the hand of Israel, and they struck them: so Israel possessed all the land of the Amorites, the inhabitants of that country.

22 And they possessed all the coasts of the Amorites, from Arnon even unto Jabbok, and from the wilderness even unto Jordan.

23 So now the LORD God of Israel has dispossessed the Amorites from before his people Israel, and shouldest you possess it?

24 Will not you possess that which Chemosh your god giveth you to possess? So whomsoever the LORD our God shall drive out from before us, them will we possess.

25 And now are you any thing better than Balak the son of Zippor, king of Moab? did he ever strive against Israel, or did he ever fight against them,

26 While Israel dwelt in Heshbon and her towns, and in Aroer and her towns, and in all the cities that be along by the coasts of Arnon, three hundred years? why therefore did you not recover them within that time?

27 Wherefore I have not sinned against you, but you doest me wrong to war against me: the LORD the Judge be judge this day between the children of Israel and the children of Ammon.

28 Howbeit the king of the children of Ammon hearkened not unto the words of Jephthah which he sent him.

29 Then the Spirit of the LORD came upon Jephthah, and he passed over Gilead, and Manasseh, and passed over Mizpeh of Gilead, and from Mizpeh of Gilead he passed over unto the children of Ammon.

30 And Jephthah vowed a vow unto the LORD, and said, If you shalt without fail deliver the children of Ammon into my hands,

31 Then it shall be, that whatsoever comes forth of the doors of my house to meet me, when I return in peace from the children of Ammon, shall surely be the LORD's, and I will offer it up for a burnt offering.

32 So Jephthah passed over unto the children of Ammon to fight against them; and the LORD delivered them into his hands.

33 And he struck them from Aroer, even till you come to Minnith, even twenty cities, and unto the plain of the vineyards, with a very great slaughter. Thus the children of Ammon were subdued before the children of Israel.

34 And Jephthah came to Mizpeh unto his house, and, behold, his daughter came out to meet him with timbrels and with dances: and she was his only child; beside her he had neither son nor daughter.

35 And it came to pass, when he saw her, that he rent his clothes, and said, Alas, my daughter! you have brought me very low, and you are one of them that trouble me: for I have opened my mouth unto the LORD, and I cannot go back.

36 And she said unto him, My father, if you have opened your mouth unto the LORD, do to me according to that which has proceeded out of your mouth; forasmuch as the LORD has taken vengeance for you of yours enemies, even of the children of Ammon.

37 And she said unto her father, Let this thing be done for me: let me alone two months, that I may go up and down upon the mountains, and bewail my virginity, I and my fellows.

38 And he said, Go. And he sent her away for two months: and she went with her companions, and bewailed her virginity upon the mountains.

39 And it came to pass at the end of two months, that she returned unto her father, who did with her according to his vow which he had vowed: and she knew no man. And it was a custom in Israel,

40 That the daughters of Israel went yearly to lament the daughter of Jephthah the Gileadite four days in a year.

CHAPTER 12

AND the men of Ephraim gathered themselves together, and went northward, and said unto Jephthah, Wherefore passed you over to fight against the children of Ammon, and did not call us to go with you? we will burn yours house upon you with fire.

2 And Jephthah said unto them, I and my people were at great strife with the children of Ammon; and when I called you, you delivered me not out of their hands.

3 And when I saw that you delivered me not, I put my life in my hands, and passed over against the children of Ammon, and the LORD delivered them into my hand: wherefore then are you come up unto me this day, to fight against me?

4 Then Jephthah gathered together all the men of Gilead, and fought with Ephraim: and the men of Gilead struck Ephraim, because they said, You Gileadites are fugitives of Ephraim among the Ephraimites, and among the Manassites.

5 And the Gileadites took the passages of Jordan before the Ephraimites: and it was so, that when those Ephraimites which were escaped said, Let me go over; that the men of Gilead said unto him, Are you an Ephraimite? If he said, Nay;

6 Then said they unto him, Say now Shibboleth: and he said Sibboleth: for he could not frame to pronounce it right. Then they took him, and slew him at the passages of Jordan: and there fell at that time of the Ephraimites forty and two thousand.

7 And Jephthah judged Israel six years. Then died Jephthah the Gileadite, and was buried in one of the cities of Gilead.

8 And after him Ibzan of Beth-lehem judged Israel.

9 And he had thirty sons, and thirty daughters, whom he sent abroad, and took in thirty daughters from abroad for his sons. And he judged Israel seven years.

10 Then died Ibzan, and was buried at Beth-lehem.

11 And after him Elon, a Zebulonite, judged Israel; and he judged Israel ten years.

12 And Elon the Zebulonite died, and was buried in Aijalon in the country of Zebulun.

13 And after him Abdon the son of Hillel, a Pirathonite, judged Israel.

14 And he had forty sons and thirty nephews, that rode on threescore and ten ass colts: and he judged Israel eight years.

15 And Abdon the son of Hillel the Pirathonite died, and was buried in Pirathon in the land of Ephraim, in the mount of the Amalekites.

CHAPTER 13

AND the children of Israel did evil again in the sight of the LORD; and the LORD delivered them into the hand of the Philistines forty years.

2 And there was a certain man of Zorah, of the family of the Danites, whose name was Manoah; and his wife was barren, and bare not.

3 And the angel of the LORD appeared unto the woman, and said unto her, Behold now, you are barren, and bearest not: but you shalt conceive, and bear a son.

4 Now therefore beware, I pray you, and drink not wine nor strong drink, and eat not any unclean thing:

5 For, lo, you shalt conceive, and bear a son; and no rasor shall come on his head: for the child shall be a Nazarite unto God from the womb: and he shall begin to deliver Israel out of the hand of the Philistines.

6 Then the woman came and told her husband, saying, A man of God came unto me, and his countenance was like the countenance of an angel of God, very terrible: but I asked him not whence he was, neither told he me his name:

7 But he said unto me, Behold, you shalt conceive, and bear a son; and now drink no wine nor strong drink, neither eat any unclean thing: for the child shall be a Nazarite to God from the womb to the day of his death.

8 Then Manoah intreated the LORD, and said, O my Lord, let the man of God which you did send come again unto us, and teach us what we shall do unto the child that shall be born.

9 And God hearkened to the voice of Manoah; and the angel of God came again unto the woman as she sat in the field: but Manoah her husband was not with her.

10 And the woman made haste, and ran, and shewed her husband, and said unto him, Behold, the man has appeared unto me, that came unto me the other day.

11 And Manoah arose, and went after his wife, and came to the man, and said unto him, Are you the man that spakest unto the woman? And he said, I am.

12 And Manoah said, Now let your words come to pass. How shall we order the child, and how shall we do unto him?

13 And the angel of the LORD said unto Manoah, Of all that I said unto the woman let her beware.

14 She may not eat of any thing that comes of the vine, neither let her drink wine or strong drink, nor eat any unclean thing: all that I commanded her let her observe.

15 And Manoah said unto the angel of the LORD, I pray you, let us detain you, until we shall have made ready a kid for you.

16 And the angel of the LORD said unto Manoah, Though you detain me, I will not eat of your bread: and if you will offer a burnt offering, you must offer it unto the LORD. For Manoah knew not that he was an angel of the LORD.

17 And Manoah said unto the angel of the LORD, What is your name, that when your sayings come to pass we may do you honour?

18 And the angel of the LORD said unto him, Why askest you thus after my name, seeing it is secret?

19 So Manoah took a kid with a meat offering, and offered it upon a rock unto the LORD: and the angel did wondrously; and Manoah and his wife looked on.

20 For it came to pass, when the flame went up toward heaven from off the altar, that the angel of the LORD ascended in the flame of the altar. And Manoah and his wife looked on it, and fell on their faces to the ground.

21 But the angel of the LORD did no more appear to Manoah and to his wife. Then Manoah knew that he was an angel of the LORD.

22 And Manoah said unto his wife, We shall surely die, because we have seen God.

23 But his wife said unto him, If the LORD were pleased to kill us, he would not have received a burnt offering and a meat offering at our hands, neither would he have shewed us all these things, nor would as at this time have told us such things as these.

24 And the woman bare a son, and called his name Samson: and the child grew, and the LORD blessed him.

25 And the Spirit of the LORD began to move him at times in the camp of Dan between Zorah and Eshtaol.

CHAPTER 14

AND Samson went down to Timnath, and saw a woman in Timnath of the daughters of the Philistines.

2 And he came up, and told his father and his mother, and said, I have seen a woman in Timnath of the daughters of the Philistines: now therefore get her for me to wife.

3 Then his father and his mother said unto him, Is there never a woman among the daughters of your brethren, or among all my people, that you go to take a wife of the uncircumcised Philistines? And Samson said unto his father, Get her for me; for she pleases me well.

4 But his father and his mother knew not that it was of the LORD, that he sought an occasion against the Philistines: for at that time the Philistines had dominion over Israel.

5 Then went Samson down, and his father and his mother, to Timnath, and came to the vineyards of Timnath: and, behold, a young lion roared against him.

6 And the Spirit of the LORD came mightily upon him, and he rent him as he would have rent a kid, and he had nothing in his hand: but he told not his father or his mother what he had done.

7 And he went down, and talked with the woman; and she pleased Samson well.

8 And after a time he returned to take her, and he turned aside to see the carcase of the lion: and, behold, there was a swarm of bees and honey in the carcase of the lion.

9 And he took thereof in his hands, and went on eating, and came to his father and mother, and he gave them, and they did eat: but he told not them that he had taken the honey out of the carcase of the lion.

10 So his father went down unto the woman: and Samson made there a feast; for so used the young men to do.

11 And it came to pass, when they saw him, that they brought thirty companions to be with him.

12 And Samson said unto them, I will now put forth a riddle unto you: if you can certainly declare it me within the seven days of the feast, and find it out, then I will give you thirty sheets and thirty change of garments:

13 But if you cannot declare it me, then shall you give me thirty sheets and thirty change of garments. And they said unto him, Put forth your riddle, that we may hear it.

14 And he said unto them, Out of the eater came forth meat, and out of the strong came forth sweetness. And they could not in three days expound the riddle.

15 And it came to pass on the seventh day, that they said unto Samson's wife, Entice your husband, that he may declare unto us the riddle, lest we burn you and your father's house with fire: have you called us to take that we have? is it not so?

16 And Samson's wife wept before him, and said, You dost but hate me, and lovest me not: you have put forth a riddle unto the children of my people, and have not told it me. And he said unto her, Behold, I have not told it my father nor my mother, and shall I tell it you?

17 And she wept before him the seven days, while their feast lasted: and it came to pass on the seventh day, that he told her, because she lay sore upon him: and she told the riddle to the children of her people.

18 And the men of the city said unto him on the seventh day before the sun went down, What is sweeter than honey? and what is stronger than a lion? And he said unto them, If you had not plowed with my heifer, you had not found out my riddle.

19 And the Spirit of the LORD came upon him, and he went down to Ashkelon, and slew thirty men of them, and took their spoil, and gave change of garments unto them which expounded the riddle. And his anger was kindled, and he went up to his father's house.

20 But Samson's wife was given to his companion, whom he had used as his friend.

CHAPTER 15

BUT it came to pass within a while after, in the time of wheat harvest, that Samson visited his wife with a kid; and he said, I will go in to my wife into the chamber. But her father would not suffer him to go in.

2 And her father said, I verily thought that you hadst utterly hated her; therefore I gave her to your companion: is not her younger sister fairer than she? take her, I pray you, instead of her.

3 And Samson said concerning them, Now shall I be more blameless than the Philistines, though I do them a displeasure.

4 And Samson went and caught three hundred foxes, and took firebrands, and turned tail to tail, and put a firebrand in the midst between two tails.

5 And when he had set the brands on fire, he let them go into the standing corn of the Philistines, and burnt up both the shocks, and also the standing corn, with the vineyards and olives.

6 Then the Philistines said, Who has done this? And they answered, Samson, the son in law of the Timnite, because he had taken his wife, and given her to his companion. And the Philistines came up, and burnt her and her father with fire.

7 And Samson said unto them, Though you have done this, yet will I be avenged of you, and after that I will cease.

8 And he struck them hip and thigh with a great slaughter: and he went down and dwelt in the top of the rock Etam.

9 Then the Philistines went up, and pitched in Judah, and spread themselves in Lehi.

10 And the men of Judah said, Why are you come up against us? And they answered, To bind Samson are we come up, to do to him as he has done to us.

11 Then three thousand men of Judah went to the top of the rock Etam, and said to Samson, Knowest you not that the Philistines are rulers over us? what is this that you have done unto us? And he said unto them, As they did unto me, so have I done unto them.

12 And they said unto him, We are come down to bind you, that we may deliver you into the hand of the Philistines. And Samson said unto them, Swear unto me, that you will not fall upon me yourselves.

13 And they spake unto him, saying, No; but we will bind you fast, and deliver you into their hand: but surely we will not kill you. And they bound him with two new cords, and brought him up from the rock.

14 And when he came unto Lehi, the Philistines shouted against him: and the Spirit of the LORD came mightily upon him, and the cords that were upon his arms became as flax that was burnt with fire, and his bands loosed from off his hands.

15 And he found a new jawbone of an ass, and put forth his hand, and took it, and slew a thousand men therewith.

16 And Samson said, With the jawbone of an ass, heaps upon heaps, with the jaw of an ass have I slain a thousand men.

17 And it came to pass, when he had made an end of speaking, that he cast away the jawbone out of his hand, and called that place Ramath-lehi.

18 And he was sore athirst, and called on the LORD, and said, You have given this great deliverance into the hand of your servant: and now shall I die for thirst, and fall into the hand of the uncircumcised?

19 But God clave an hollow place that was in the jaw, and there came water thereout; and when he had drunk, his spirit came again, and he revived: wherefore he called the name thereof En-hakkore, which is in Lehi unto this day.

20 And he judged Israel in the days of the Philistines twenty years.

CHAPTER 16

THEN went Samson to Gaza, and saw there an harlot, and went in unto her.

2 And it was told the Gazites, saying, Samson is come hither. And they compassed him in, and laid wait for him all night in the gate of the city, and were quiet all the night, saying, In the morning, when it is day, we shall kill him.

3 And Samson lay till midnight, and arose at midnight, and took the doors of the gate of the city, and the two posts, and went away with them, bar and all, and put them upon his shoulders, and carried them up to the top of an hill that is before Hebron.

4 And it came to pass afterward, that he loved a woman in the valley of Sorek, whose name was Delilah.

5 And the lords of the Philistines came up unto her, and said unto her, Entice him, and see wherein his great strength lies, and by what means we may prevail against him, that we may bind him to afflict him: and we will give you every one of us eleven hundred pieces of silver.

6 And Delilah said to Samson, Tell me, I pray you, wherein your great strength lies, and wherewith you mightest be bound to afflict you.

7 And Samson said unto her, If they bind me with seven green withs that were never dried, then shall I be weak, and be as another man.

8 Then the lords of the Philistines brought up to her seven green withs which had not been dried, and she bound him with them.

9 Now there were men lying in wait, abiding with her in the chamber. And she said unto him, The Philistines be upon you, Samson. And he brake the withs, as a thread of tow is broken when it toucheth the fire. So his strength was not known.

10 And Delilah said unto Samson, Behold, you have mocked me, and told me lies: now tell me, I pray you, wherewith you mightest be bound.

11 And he said unto her, If they bind me fast with new ropes that never were occupied, then shall I be weak, and be as another man.

12 Delilah therefore took new ropes, and bound him therewith, and said unto him, The Philistines be upon you, Samson. And there were liers in wait abiding in the chamber. And he brake them from off his arms like a thread.

13 And Delilah said unto Samson, Hitherto you have mocked me, and told me lies: tell me wherewith you mightest be bound. And he said unto her, If you weavest the seven locks of my head with the web.

14 And she fastened it with the pin, and said unto him, The Philistines be upon you, Samson. And he awaked out of his sleep, and went away with the pin of the beam, and with the web.

15And she said unto him, How can you say, I love you, when yours heart is not with me? you have mocked me these three times, and have not told me wherein your great strength lies.

16 And it came to pass, when she pressed him daily with her words, and urged him, so that his soul was vexed unto death;

17 That he told her all his heart, and said unto her, There has not come a rasor upon my head; for I have been a Nazarite unto God from my mother's womb: if I be shaven, then my strength will go from me, and I shall become weak, and be like any other man.

18 And when Delilah saw that he had told her all his heart, she sent and called for the lords of the Philistines, saying, Come up this once, for he has shewed me all his heart. Then the lords of the Philistines came up unto her, and brought money in their hand.

19 And she made him sleep upon her knees; and she called for a man, and she caused him to shave off the seven locks of his head; and she began to afflict him, and his strength went from him.

20 And she said, The Philistines be upon you, Samson. And he awoke out of his sleep, and said, I will go out as at other times before, and shake myself. And he wist not that the LORD was departed from him.

21But the Philistines took him, and put out his eyes, and brought him down to Gaza, and bound him with fetters of brass; and he did grind in the prison house.

22 Howbeit the hair of his head began to grow again after he was shaven.

23 Then the lords of the Philistines gathered them together for to offer a great sacrifice unto Dagon their god, and to rejoice: for they said, Our god has delivered Samson our enemy into our hand.

24 And when the people saw him, they praised their god: for they said, Our god has delivered into our hands our enemy, and the destroyer of our country, which slew many of us.

25 And it came to pass, when their hearts were merry, that they said, Call for Samson, that he may make us sport. And they called for Samson out of the prison house; and he made them sport: and they set him between the pillars.

26 And Samson said unto the lad that held him by the hand, Suffer me that I may feel the pillars whereupon the house standeth, that I may lean upon them.

27 Now the house was full of men and women; and all the lords of the Philistines were there; and there were upon the roof about three thousand men and women, that beheld while Samson made sport.

28 And Samson called unto the LORD, and said, O Lord GOD, remember me, I pray you, and strengthen me, I pray you, only this once, O God, that I may be at once avenged of the Philistines for my two eyes.

29 And Samson took hold of the two middle pillars upon which the house stood, and on which it was borne up, of the one with his right hand, and of the other with his left.

30 And Samson said, Let me die with the Philistines. And he bowed himself with all his might; and the house fell upon the lords, and upon all the people that were therein. So the dead which he slew at his death were more than they which he slew in his life.

31 Then his brethren and all the house of his father came down, and took him, and brought him up, and buried him between Zorah and Eshtaol in the buryingplace of Manoah his father. And he judged Israel twenty years.

CHAPTER 17

AND there was a man of mount Ephraim, whose name was Micah.

2 And he said unto his mother, The eleven hundred shekels of silver that were taken from you, about which you cursedst, and spakest of also in my ears, behold, the silver is with me; I took it. And his mother said, Blessed be you of the LORD, my son.

3 And when he had restored the eleven hundred shekels of silver to his mother, his mother said, I had wholly dedicated the silver unto the LORD from my hand for my son, to make a graven image and a molten image: now therefore I will restore it unto you.

4 Yet he restored the money unto his mother; and his mother took two hundred shekels of silver, and gave them to the founder, who made thereof a graven image and a molten image: and they were in the house of Micah.

5 And the man Micah had an house of gods, and made an ephod, and teraphim, and consecrated one of his sons, who became his priest.

6 In those days there was no king in Israel, but every man did that which was right in his own eyes.

7And there was a young man out of Beth-lehem-judah of the family of Judah, who was a Levite, and he sojourned there.

8 And the man departed out of the city from Beth-lehem-judah to sojourn where he could find a place: and he came to mount Ephraim to the house of Micah, as he journeyed.

9 And Micah said unto him, Whence comest you ? And he said unto him, I am a Levite of Beth-lehem-judah, and I go to sojourn where I may find a place.

10 And Micah said unto him, Dwell with me, and be unto me a father and a priest, and I will give you ten shekels of silver by the year, and a suit of apparel, and your victuals. So the Levite went in.

11 And the Levite was content to dwell with the man; and the young man was unto him as one of his sons.

12 And Micah consecrated the Levite; and the young man became his priest, and was in the house of Micah.

13 Then said Micah, Now know I that the LORD will do me good, seeing I have a Levite to my priest.

CHAPTER 18

IN those days there was no king in Israel: and in those days the tribe of the Danites sought them an inheritance to dwell in; for unto that day all their inheritance had not fallen unto them among the tribes of Israel.

2 And the children of Dan sent of their family five men from their coasts, men of valour, from Zorah, and from Eshtaol, to spy out the land, and to search it; and they said unto them, Go, search the land: who when they came to mount Ephraim, to the house of Micah, they lodged there.

3 When they were by the house of Micah, they knew the voice of the young man the Levite: and they turned in thither, and said unto him, Who brought you hither? and what makest you in this place? and what have you here?

4 And he said unto them, Thus and thus dealeth Micah with me, and has hired me, and I am his priest.

5 And they said unto him, Ask counsel, we pray you, of God, that we may know whether our way which we go shall be prosperous.

6 And the priest said unto them, Go in peace: before the LORD is your way wherein you go.

7Then the five men departed, and came to Laish, and saw the people that were therein, how they dwelt careless, after the manner of the Zidonians, quiet and secure; and there was no magistrate in the land, that might put them to shame in any thing; and they were far from the Zidonians, and had no business with any man.

8 And they came unto their brethren to Zorah and Eshtaol: and their brethren said unto them, What say you ?

9 And they said, Arise, that we may go up against them: for we have seen the land, and, behold, it is very good: and are you still? be not slothful to go, and to enter to possess the land.

10 When you go, you shall come unto a people secure, and to a large land: for God has given it into your hands; a place where there is no want of any thing that is in the earth.

11And there went from thence of the family of the Danites, out of Zorah and out of Eshtaol, six hundred men appointed with weapons of war.

12 And they went up, and pitched in Kirjath-jearim, in Judah: wherefore they called that place Mahaneh-dan unto this day: behold, it is behind Kirjath-jearim.

13 And they passed thence unto mount Ephraim, and came unto the house of Micah.

14Then answered the five men that went to spy out the country of Laish, and said unto their brethren, Do you know that there is in these houses an ephod, and teraphim, and a graven image, and a molten image? now therefore consider what you have to do.

15 And they turned thitherward, and came to the house of the young man the Levite, even unto the house of Micah, and saluted him.

16 And the six hundred men appointed with their weapons of war, which were of the children of Dan, stood by the entering of the gate.

17 And the five men that went to spy out the land went up, and came in thither, and took the graven image, and the ephod, and the teraphim, and the molten image: and the priest stood in the entering of the gate with the six hundred men that were appointed with weapons of war.

18 And these went into Micah's house, and fetched the carved image, the ephod, and the teraphim, and the molten image. Then said the priest unto them, What do you ?

19 And they said unto him, Hold your peace, lay yours hand upon your mouth, and go with us, and be to us a father and a priest: is it better for you to be a priest unto the house of one man, or that you be a priest unto a tribe and a family in Israel?

20 And the priest's heart was glad, and he took the ephod, and the teraphim, and the graven image, and went in the midst of the people.

21 So they turned and departed, and put the little ones and the cattle and the carriage before them.

22And when they were a good way from the house of Micah, the men that were in the houses near to Micah's house were gathered together, and overtook the children of Dan.

23 And they cried unto the children of Dan. And they turned their faces, and said unto Micah, What aileth you, that you comest with such a company?

24 And he said, You have taken away my gods which I made, and the priest, and you are gone away: and what have I more? and what is this that you say unto me, What aileth you?

25 And the children of Dan said unto him, Let not your voice be heard among us, lest angry fellows run upon you, and you lose your life, with the lives of your household.

26 And the children of Dan went their way: and when Micah saw that they were too strong for him, he turned and went back unto his house.

27 And they took the things which Micah had made, and the priest which he had, and came unto Laish, unto a people that were at quiet and secure: and they struck them with the edge of the sword, and burnt the city with fire.

28 And there was no deliverer, because it was far from Zidon, and they had no business with any man; and it was in the valley that lies by Beth-rehob. And they built a city, and dwelt therein.

29 And they called the name of the city Dan, after the name of Dan their father, who was born unto Israel: howbeit the name of the city was Laish at the first.

30 And the children of Dan set up the graven image: and Jonathan, the son of Gershom, the son of Manasseh, he and his sons were priests to the tribe of Dan until the day of the captivity of the land.

31 And they set them up Micah's graven image, which he made, all the time that the house of God was in Shiloh.

CHAPTER 19

AND it came to pass in those days, when there was no king in Israel, that there was a certain Levite sojourning on the side of mount Ephraim, who took to him a concubine out of Beth-lehem-judah.

2 And his concubine played the whore against him, and went away from him unto her father's house to Beth-lehem-judah, and was there four whole months.

3 And her husband arose, and went after her, to speak friendly unto her, and to bring her again, having his servant with him, and a couple of asses: and she brought him into her father's house: and when the father of the damsel saw him, he rejoiced to meet him.

4 And his father in law, the damsel's father, retained him; and he abode with him three days: so they did eat and drink, and lodged there.

5 And it came to pass on the fourth day, when they arose early in the morning, that he rose up to depart: and the damsel's father said unto his son in law, Comfort yours heart with a morsel of bread, and afterward go your way.

6 And they sat down, and did eat and drink both of them together: for the damsel's father had said unto the man, Be content, I pray you, and tarry all night, and let yours heart be merry.

7 And when the man rose up to depart, his father in law urged him: therefore he lodged there again.

8 And he arose early in the morning on the fifth day to depart: and the damsel's father said, Comfort yours heart, I pray you. And they tarried until afternoon, and they did eat both of them.

9 And when the man rose up to depart, he, and his concubine, and his servant, his father in law, the damsel's father, said unto him, Behold, now the day draweth toward evening, I pray you tarry all night: behold, the day groweth to an end, lodge here, that yours heart may be merry; and to morrow get you early on your way, that you mayest go home.

10 But the man would not tarry that night, but he rose up and departed, and came over against Jebus, which is Jerusalem; and there were with him two asses saddled, his concubine also was with him.

11 And when they were by Jebus, the day was far spent; and the servant said unto his master, Come, I pray you, and let us turn in into this city of the Jebusites, and lodge in it.

12 And his master said unto him, We will not turn aside hither into the city of a stranger, that is not of the children of Israel; we will pass over to Gibeah.

13 And he said unto his servant, Come, and let us draw near to one of these places to lodge all night, in Gibeah, or in Ramah.

14 And they passed on and went their way; and the sun went down upon them when they were by Gibeah, which belongeth to Benjamin.

15 And they turned aside thither, to go in and to lodge in Gibeah: and when he went in, he sat him down in a street of the city: for there was no man that took them into his house to lodging.

16 And, behold, there came an old man from his work out of the field at even, which was also of mount Ephraim; and he sojourned in Gibeah: but the men of the place were Benjamites.

17 And when he had lifted up his eyes, he saw a wayfaring man in the street of the city: and the old man said, Whither go you ? and whence comest you ?

18 And he said unto him, We are passing from Beth-lehem-judah toward the side of mount Ephraim; from thence am I: and I went to Beth-lehem-judah, but I am now going to the house of the LORD; and there is no man that receiveth me to house.

19 Yet there is both straw and provender for our asses; and there is bread and wine also for me, and for your handmaid, and for the young man which is with your servants: there is no want of any thing.

20 And the old man said, Peace be with you; howsoever let all your wants lie upon me; only lodge not in the street.

21 So he brought him into his house, and gave provender unto the asses: and they washed their feet, and did eat and drink.

22 Now as they were making their hearts merry, behold, the men of the city, certain sons of Belial, beset the house round about, and beat at the door, and spake to the master of the house, the old man, saying, Bring forth the man that came into yours house, that we may know him.

23 And the man, the master of the house, went out unto them, and said unto them, Nay, my brethren, nay, I pray you, do not so wickedly; seeing that this man is come into my house, do not this folly.

24 Behold, here is my daughter a maiden, and his concubine; them I will bring out now, and humble you them, and do with them what seemeth good unto you: but unto this man do not so vile a thing.

25 But the men would not hearken to him: so the man took his concubine, and brought her forth unto them; and they knew her, and abused her all the night until the morning: and when the day began to spring, they let her go.

26 Then came the woman in the dawning of the day, and fell down at the door of the man's house where her lord was, till it was light.

27 And her lord rose up in the morning, and opened the doors of the house, and went out to go his way: and, behold, the woman his concubine was fallen down at the door of the house, and her hands were upon the threshold.

28 And he said unto her, Up, and let us be going. But none answered. Then the man took her up upon an ass, and the man rose up, and gat him unto his place.

29 And when he was come into his house, he took a knife, and laid hold on his concubine, and divided her, together with her bones, into twelve pieces, and sent her into all the coasts of Israel.

30 And it was so, that all that saw it said, There was no such deed done nor seen from the day that the children of Israel came up out of the land of Egypt unto this day: consider of it, take advice, and speak your minds.

CHAPTER 20

THEN all the children of Israel went out, and the congregation was gathered together as one man, from Dan even to Beer-sheba, with the land of Gilead, unto the LORD in Mizpeh.

2 And the chief of all the people, even of all the tribes of Israel, presented themselves in the assembly of the people of God, four hundred thousand footmen that drew sword.

3 (Now the children of Benjamin heard that the children of Israel were gone up to Mizpeh.) Then said the children of Israel, Tell us, how was this wickedness?

4 And the Levite, the husband of the woman that was slain, answered and said, I came into Gibeah that belongeth to Benjamin, I and my concubine, to lodge.

5 And the men of Gibeah rose against me, and beset the house round about upon me by night, and thought to have slain me: and my concubine have they forced, that she is dead.

6 And I took my concubine, and cut her in pieces, and sent her throughout all the country of the inheritance of Israel: for they have committed lewdness and folly in Israel.

7 Behold, you are all children of Israel; give here your advice and counsel.

8 And all the people arose as one man, saying, We will not any of us go to his tent, neither will we any of us turn into his house.

9 But now this shall be the thing which we will do to Gibeah; we will go up by lot against it;

10 And we will take ten men of an hundred throughout all the tribes of Israel, and an hundred of a thousand, and a thousand out of ten thousand, to fetch victual for the people, that they may do, when they come to Gibeah of Benjamin, according to all the folly that they have created in Israel.

11 So all the men of Israel were gathered against the city, knit together as one man.

12 And the tribes of Israel sent men through all the tribe of Benjamin, saying, What wickedness is this that is done among you?

13 Now therefore deliver us the men, the children of Belial, which are in Gibeah, that we may put them to death, and put away evil from Israel. But the children of Benjamin would not hearken to the voice of their brethren the children of Israel:

14 But the children of Benjamin gathered themselves together out of the cities unto Gibeah, to go out to battle against the children of Israel.

15 And the children of Benjamin were numbered at that time out of the cities twenty and six thousand men that drew sword, beside the inhabitants of Gibeah, which were numbered seven hundred chosen men.

16 Among all this people there were seven hundred chosen men lefthanded; every one could sling stones at an hair breadth, and not miss.

17 And the men of Israel, beside Benjamin, were numbered four hundred thousand men that drew sword: all these were men of war.

18And the children of Israel arose, and went up to the house of God, and asked counsel of God, and said, Which of us shall go up first to the battle against the children of Benjamin? And the LORD said, Judah shall go up first.

19 And the children of Israel rose up in the morning, and encamped against Gibeah.

20 And the men of Israel went out to battle against Benjamin; and the men of Israel put themselves in array to fight against them at Gibeah.

21 And the children of Benjamin came forth out of Gibeah, and destroyed down to the ground of the Israelites that day twenty and two thousand men.

22 And the people the men of Israel encouraged themselves, and set their battle again in array in the place where they put themselves in array the first day.

23 (And the children of Israel went up and wept before the LORD until even, and asked counsel of the LORD, saying, Shall I go up again to battle against the children of Benjamin my brother? And the LORD said, Go up against him.)

24 And the children of Israel came near against the children of Benjamin the second day.

25 And Benjamin went forth against them out of Gibeah the second day, and destroyed down to the ground of the children of Israel again eighteen thousand men; all these drew the sword.

26Then all the children of Israel, and all the people, went up, and came unto the house of God, and wept, and sat there before the LORD, and fasted that day until even, and offered burnt offerings and peace offerings before the LORD.

27 And the children of Israel inquired of the LORD, (for the ark of the covenant of God was there in those days,

28 And Phinehas, the son of Eleazar, the son of Aaron, stood before it in those days,) saying, Shall I yet again go out to battle against the children of Benjamin my brother, or shall I cease? And the LORD said, Go up; for to morrow I will deliver them into yours hand.

29 And Israel set liers in wait round about Gibeah.

30 And the children of Israel went up against the children of Benjamin on the third day, and put themselves in array against Gibeah, as at other times.

31 And the children of Benjamin went out against the people, and were drawn away from the city; and they began to strike of the people, and kill, as at other times, in the highways, of which one goeth up to the house of God, and the other to Gibeah in the field, about thirty men of Israel.

32 And the children of Benjamin said, They are smitten down before us, as at the first. But the children of Israel said, Let us flee, and draw them from the city unto the highways.

33 And all the men of Israel rose up out of their place, and put themselves in array at Baal-tamar: and the liers in wait of Israel came forth out of their places, even out of the meadows of Gibeah.

34 And there came against Gibeah ten thousand chosen men out of all Israel, and the battle was sore: but they knew not that evil was near them.

35 And the LORD struck Benjamin before Israel: and the children of Israel destroyed of the Benjamites that day twenty and five thousand and an hundred men: all these drew the sword.

36 So the children of Benjamin saw that they were smitten: for the men of Israel gave place to the Benjamites, because they trusted unto the liers in wait which they had set beside Gibeah.

37 And the liers in wait hasted, and rushed upon Gibeah; and the liers in wait drew themselves along, and struck all the city with the edge of the sword.

38 Now there was an appointed sign between the men of Israel and the liers in wait, that they should make a great flame with smoke rise up out of the city.

39 And when the men of Israel retired in the battle, Benjamin began to strike and kill of the men of Israel about thirty persons: for they said, Surely they are smitten down before us, as in the first battle.

40 But when the flame began to arise up out of the city with a pillar of smoke, the Benjamites looked behind them, and, behold, the flame of the city ascended up to heaven.

41 And when the men of Israel turned again, the men of Benjamin were amazed: for they saw that evil was come upon them.

42 Therefore they turned their backs before the men of Israel unto the way of the wilderness; but the battle overtook them; and them which came out of the cities they destroyed in the midst of them.

43 Thus they inclosed the Benjamites round about, and chased them, and trode them down with ease over against Gibeah toward the sunrising.

44 And there fell of Benjamin eighteen thousand men; all these were men of valour.

45 And they turned and fled toward the wilderness unto the rock of Rimmon: and they gleaned of them in the highways five thousand men; and pursued hard after them unto Gidom, and slew two thousand men of them.

46 So that all which fell that day of Benjamin were twenty and five thousand men that drew the sword; all these were men of valour.

47 But six hundred men turned and fled to the wilderness unto the rock Rimmon, and abode in the rock Rimmon four months.

48 And the men of Israel turned again upon the children of Benjamin, and struck them with the edge of the sword, as well the men of every city, as the beast, and all that came to hand: also they set on fire all the cities that they came to.

CHAPTER 21

NOW the men of Israel had sworn in Mizpeh, saying, There shall not any of us give his daughter unto Benjamin to wife.

2 And the people came to the house of God, and abode there till even before God, and lifted up their voices, and wept sore;

3 And said, O LORD God of Israel, why is this come to pass in Israel, that there should be to day one tribe lacking in Israel?

4 And it came to pass on the morrow, that the people rose early, and built there an altar, and offered burnt offerings and peace offerings.

5 And the children of Israel said, Who is there among all the tribes of Israel that came not up with the congregation unto the LORD? For they had made a great oath concerning him that came not up to the LORD to Mizpeh, saying, He shall surely be put to death.

6 And the children of Israel repented them for Benjamin their brother, and said, There is one tribe cut off from Israel this day.

7 How shall we do for wives for them that remain, seeing we have sworn by the LORD that we will not give them of our daughters to wives?

8And they said, What one is there of the tribes of Israel that came not up to Mizpeh to the LORD? And, behold, there came none to the camp from Jabesh-gilead to the assembly.

9 For the people were numbered, and, behold, there were none of the inhabitants of Jabesh-gilead there.

10 And the congregation sent thither twelve thousand men of the valiantest, and commanded them, saying, Go and strike the inhabitants of Jabesh-gilead with the edge of the sword, with the women and the children.

11 And this is the thing that you shall do, You shall utterly destroy every male, and every woman that has lain by man.

12 And they found among the inhabitants of Jabesh-gilead four hundred young virgins, that had known no man by lying with any male: and they brought them unto the camp to Shiloh, which is in the land of Canaan.

13 And the whole congregation sent some to speak to the children of Benjamin that were in the rock Rimmon, and to call peaceably unto them.

14 And Benjamin came again at that time; and they gave them wives which they had saved alive of the women of Jabesh-gilead: and yet so they sufficed them not.

15 And the people repented them for Benjamin, because that the LORD had made a breach in the tribes of Israel.

16Then the elders of the congregation said, How shall we do for wives for them that remain, seeing the women are destroyed out of Benjamin?

17 And they said, There must be an inheritance for them that be escaped of Benjamin, that a tribe be not destroyed out of Israel.

18 Howbeit we may not give them wives of our daughters: for the children of Israel have sworn, saying, Cursed be he that giveth a wife to Benjamin.

19 Then they said, Behold, there is a feast of the LORD in Shiloh yearly in a place which is on the north side of Beth-el, on the east side of the highway that goeth up from Beth-el to Shechem, and on the south of Lebonah.

20 Therefore they commanded the children of Benjamin, saying, Go and lie in wait in the vineyards;

21 And see, and, behold, if the daughters of Shiloh come out to dance in dances, then come you out of the vineyards, and catch you every man his wife of the daughters of Shiloh, and go to the land of Benjamin.

22 And it shall be, when their fathers or their brethren come unto us to complain, that we will say unto them, Be favourable unto them for our sakes: because we reserved not to each man his wife in the war: for you did not give unto them at this time, that you should be guilty.

23 And the children of Benjamin did so, and took them wives, according to their number, of them that danced, whom they caught: and they went and returned unto their inheritance, and repaired the cities, and dwelt in them.

24 And the children of Israel departed thence at that time, every man to his tribe and to his family, and they went out from thence every man to his inheritance.

25 In those days there was no king in Israel: every man did that which was right in his own eyes.

THE BOOK OF RUTH.

CHAPTER 1

NOW it came to pass in the days when the judges ruled, that there was a famine in the land. And a certain man of Beth-lehem-judah went to sojourn in the country of Moab, he, and his wife, and his two sons.

2 And the name of the man was Elimelech, and the name of his wife Naomi, and the name of his two sons Mahlon and Chilion, Ephrathites of Beth-lehem-judah. And they came into the country of Moab, and continued there.

3 And Elimelech Naomi's husband died; and she was left, and her two sons.

4 And they took them wives of the women of Moab; the name of the one was Orpah, and the name of the other Ruth: and they dwelled there about ten years.

5 And Mahlon and Chilion died also both of them; and the woman was left of her two sons and her husband.

6 Then she arose with her daughters in law, that she might return from the country of Moab: for she had heard in the country of Moab how that the LORD had visited his people in giving them bread.

7 Wherefore she went forth out of the place where she was, and her two daughters in law with her; and they went on the way to return unto the land of Judah.

8 And Naomi said unto her two daughters in law, Go, return each to her mother's house: the LORD deal kindly with you, as you have dealt with the dead, and with me.

9 The LORD grant you that you may find rest, each of you in the house of her husband. Then she kissed them; and they lifted up their voice, and wept.

10 And they said unto her, Surely we will return with you unto your people.

11 And Naomi said, Turn again, my daughters: why will you go with me? are there yet any more sons in my womb, that they may be your husbands?

12 Turn again, my daughters, go your way; for I am too old to have an husband. If I should say, I have hope, if I should have an husband also to night, and should also bear sons;

13 Would you tarry for them till they were grown? would you stay for them from having husbands? nay, my daughters; for it grieveth me much for your sakes that the hand of the LORD is gone out against me.

14 And they lifted up their voice, and wept again: and Orpah kissed her mother in law; but Ruth clave unto her.

15 And she said, Behold, your sister in law is gone back unto her people, and unto her gods: return you after your sister in law.

16 And Ruth said, Intreat me not to leave you, or to return from following after you: for whither you go, I will go; and where you lodgest, I will lodge: your people shall be my people, and your God my God:

17 Where you diest, will I die, and there will I be buried: the LORD do so to me, and more also, if ought but death part you and me.

18 When she saw that she was stedfastly minded to go with her, then she left speaking unto her.

19 So they two went until they came to Beth-lehem. And it came to pass, when they were come to Beth-lehem, that all the city was moved about them, and they said, Is this Naomi?

20 And she said unto them, Call me not Naomi, call me Mara: for the Almighty has dealt very bitterly with me.

21 I went out full, and the LORD has brought me home again empty: why then call you me Naomi, seeing the LORD has testified against me, and the Almighty has afflicted me?

22 So Naomi returned, and Ruth the Moabitess, her daughter in law, with her, which returned out of the country of Moab: and they came to Beth-lehem in the beginning of barley harvest.

CHAPTER 2

AND Naomi had a kinsman of her husband's, a mighty man of wealth, of the family of Elimelech; and his name was Boaz.

2 And Ruth the Moabitess said unto Naomi, Let me now go to the field, and glean ears of corn after him in whose sight I shall find grace. And she said unto her, Go, my daughter.

3 And she went, and came, and gleaned in the field after the reapers: and her hap was to light on a part of the field belonging unto Boaz, who was of the kindred of Elimelech.

4 And, behold, Boaz came from Beth-lehem, and said unto the reapers, The LORD be with you. And they answered him, The LORD bless you.

5 Then said Boaz unto his servant that was set over the reapers, Whose damsel is this?

6 And the servant that was set over the reapers answered and said, It is the Moabitish damsel that came back with Naomi out of the country of Moab:

7 And she said, I pray you, let me glean and gather after the reapers among the sheaves: so she came, and has continued even from the morning until now, that she tarried a little in the house.

8 Then said Boaz unto Ruth, Hearest you not, my daughter? Go not to glean in another field, neither go from hence, but abide here fast by my maidens:

9 Let yours eyes be on the field that they do reap, and go you after them: have I not charged the young men that they shall not touch you? and when you are athirst, go unto the vessels, and drink of that which the young men have drawn.

10 Then she fell on her face, and bowed herself to the ground, and said unto him, Why have I found grace in yours eyes, that you shouldest take knowledge of me, seeing I am a stranger?

11 And Boaz answered and said unto her, It has fully been shewed me, all that you have done unto your mother in law since the death of yours husband: and how you have left your father and your mother, and the land of your nativity, and are come unto a people which you knewest not heretofore.

12 The LORD recompense your work, and a full reward be given you of the LORD God of Israel, under whose wings you are come to trust.

13 Then she said, Let me find favour in your sight, my lord; for that you have comforted me, and for that you have spoken friendly unto yours handmaid, though I be not like unto one of yours handmaidens.

14 And Boaz said unto her, At mealtime come you hither, and eat of the bread, and dip your morsel in the vinegar. And she sat beside the reapers: and he reached her parched corn, and she did eat, and was sufficed, and left.

15 And when she was risen up to glean, Boaz commanded his young men, saying, Let her glean even among the sheaves, and reproach her not:

16 And let fall also some of the handfuls of purpose for her, and leave them, that she may glean them, and rebuke her not.

17 So she gleaned in the field until even, and beat out that she had gleaned: and it was about an ephah of barley.

18 And she took it up, and went into the city: and her mother in law saw what she had gleaned: and she brought forth, and gave to her that she had reserved after she was sufficed.

19 And her mother in law said unto her, Where have you gleaned to day? and where wroughtest you? blessed be he that did take knowledge of you. And she shewed her mother in law with whom she had created, and said, The man's name with whom I created to day is Boaz.

20 And Naomi said unto her daughter in law, Blessed be he of the LORD, who has not left off his kindness to the living and to the dead. And Naomi said unto her, The man is near of kin unto us, one of our next kinsmen.

21 And Ruth the Moabitess said, He said unto me also, You shalt keep fast by my young men, until they have ended all my harvest.

22 And Naomi said unto Ruth her daughter in law, It is good, my daughter, that you go out with his maidens, that they meet you not in any other field.

23 So she kept fast by the maidens of Boaz to glean unto the end of barley harvest and of wheat harvest; and dwelt with her mother in law.

CHAPTER 3

THEN Naomi her mother in law said unto her, My daughter, shall I not seek rest for you, that it may be well with you?

2 And now is not Boaz of our kindred, with whose maidens you wast? Behold, he winnoweth barley to night in the threshingfloor.

3 Wash yourself therefore, and anoint you, and put your raiment upon you, and get you down to the floor: but make not yourself known unto the man, until he shall have done eating and drinking.

4 And it shall be, when he lies down, that you shalt mark the place where he shall lie, and you shalt go in, and uncover his feet, and lay you down; and he will tell you what you shalt do.

5 And she said unto her, All that you say unto me I will do.

6 And she went down unto the floor, and did according to all that her mother in law bade her.

7 And when Boaz had eaten and drunk, and his heart was merry, he went to lie down at the end of the heap of corn: and she came softly, and uncovered his feet, and laid her down.

8 And it came to pass at midnight, that the man was afraid, and turned himself: and, behold, a woman lay at his feet.

9 And he said, Who are you? And she answered, I am Ruth yours handmaid: spread therefore your skirt over yours handmaid; for you are a near kinsman.

10 And he said, Blessed be you of the LORD, my daughter: for you have shewed more kindness in the latter end than at the beginning, inasmuch as you followedst not young men, whether poor or rich.

11 And now, my daughter, fear not; I will do to you all that you requirest: for all the city of my people doth know that you are a virtuous woman.

12 And now it is true that I am your near kinsman: howbeit there is a kinsman nearer than I.

13 Tarry this night, and it shall be in the morning, that if he will perform unto you the part of a kinsman, well; let him do the kinsman's part: but if he will not do the part of a kinsman to you, then will I do the part of a kinsman to you, as the LORD liveth: lie down until the morning.

14 And she lay at his feet until the morning: and she rose up before one could know another. And he said, Let it not be known that a woman came into the floor.

15 Also he said, Bring the vail that you have upon you, and hold it. And when she held it, he measured six measures of barley, and laid it on her: and she went into the city.

16 And when she came to her mother in law, she said, Who are you , my daughter? And she told her all that the man had done to her.

17 And she said, These six measures of barley gave he me; for he said to me, Go not empty unto your mother in law.

18 Then said she, Sit still, my daughter, until you know how the matter will fall: for the man will not be in rest, until he have finished the thing this day.

CHAPTER 4

THEN went Boaz up to the gate, and sat him down there: and, behold, the kinsman of whom Boaz spake came by; unto whom he said, Ho, such a one! turn aside, sit down here. And he turned aside, and sat down.

2 And he took ten men of the elders of the city, and said, Sit you down here. And they sat down.

3 And he said unto the kinsman, Naomi, that is come again out of the country of Moab, selleth a parcel of land, which was our brother Elimelech's:

4 And I thought to advertise you, saying, Buy it before the inhabitants, and before the elders of my people. If you will redeem it, redeem it: but if you will not redeem it, then tell me, that I may know: for there is none to redeem it beside you; and I am after you. And he said, I will redeem it.

5 Then said Boaz, What day you buyest the field of the hand of Naomi, you must buy it also of Ruth the Moabitess, the wife of the dead, to raise up the name of the dead upon his inheritance.

6 And the kinsman said, I cannot redeem it for myself, lest I mar my own inheritance: redeem you my right to yourself; for I cannot redeem it.

7 Now this was the manner in former time in Israel concerning redeeming and concerning changing, for to confirm all things; a man plucked off his shoe, and gave it to his neighbour: and this was a testimony in Israel.

8 Therefore the kinsman said unto Boaz, Buy it for you. So he drew off his shoe.

9 And Boaz said unto the elders, and unto all the people, You are witnesses this day, that I have bought all that was Elimelech's, and all that was Chilion's and Mahlon's, of the hand of Naomi.

10 Moreover Ruth the Moabitess, the wife of Mahlon, have I purchased to be my wife, to raise up the name of the dead upon his inheritance, that the name of the dead be not cut off from among his brethren, and from the gate of his place: you are witnesses this day.

11 And all the people that were in the gate, and the elders, said, We are witnesses. The LORD make the woman that is come into yours house like Rachel and like Leah, which two did build the house of Israel: and do you worthily in Ephratah, and be famous in Beth-lehem:

12 And let your house be like the house of Pharez, whom Tamar bare unto Judah, of the seed which the LORD shall give you of this young woman.

13 So Boaz took Ruth, and she was his wife: and when he went in unto her, the LORD gave her conception, and she bare a son.

14 And the women said unto Naomi, Blessed be the LORD, which has not left you this day without a kinsman, that his name may be famous in Israel.

15 And he shall be unto you a restorer of your life, and a nourisher of yours old age: for your daughter in law, which loveth you, which is better to you than seven sons, has born him.

16 And Naomi took the child, and laid it in her bosom, and became nurse unto it.

17 And the women her neighbours gave it a name, saying, There is a son born to Naomi; and they called his name Obed: he is the father of Jesse, the father of David.

18 Now these are the generations of Pharez: Pharez begat Hezron,

19 And Hezron begat Ram, and Ram begat Amminadab,

20 And Amminadab begat Nahshon, and Nahshon begat Salmon,

21 And Salmon begat Boaz, and Boaz begat Obed,

22 And Obed begat Jesse, and Jesse begat David.

THE
FIRST BOOK OF SAMUEL,
OTHERWISE CALLED,
THE FIRST BOOK OF THE KINGS.

CHAPTER 1

NOW there was a certain man of Ramathaim-zophim, of mount Ephraim, and his name was Elkanah, the son of Jeroham, the son of Elihu, the son of Tohu, the son of Zuph, an Ephrathite:

2 And he had two wives; the name of the one was Hannah, and the name of the other Peninnah: and Peninnah had children, but Hannah had no children.

3 And this man went up out of his city yearly to worship and to sacrifice unto the LORD of hosts in Shiloh. And the two sons of Eli, Hophni and Phinehas, the priests of the LORD, were there.

4And when the time was that Elkanah offered, he gave to Peninnah his wife, and to all her sons and her daughters, portions:

5 But unto Hannah he gave a worthy portion; for he loved Hannah: but the LORD had shut up her womb.

6 And her adversary also provoked her sore, for to make her fret, because the LORD had shut up her womb.

7 And as he did so year by year, when she went up to the house of the LORD, so she provoked her; therefore she wept, and did not eat.

8 Then said Elkanah her husband to her, Hannah, why weepest you ? and why eatest you not? and why is your heart grieved? am not I better to you than ten sons?

9So Hannah rose up after they had eaten in Shiloh, and after they had drunk. Now Eli the priest sat upon a seat by a post of the temple of the LORD.

10 And she was in bitterness of soul, and prayed unto the LORD, and wept sore.

11 And she vowed a vow, and said, O LORD of hosts, if you will indeed look on the affliction of yours handmaid, and remember me, and not forget yours handmaid, but will give unto yours handmaid a man child, then I will give him unto the LORD all the days of his life, and there shall no rasor come upon his head.

12 And it came to pass, as she continued praying before the LORD, that Eli marked her mouth.

13 Now Hannah, she spake in her heart; only her lips moved, but her voice was not heard: therefore Eli thought she had been drunken.

14 And Eli said unto her, How long will you be drunken? put away your wine from you.

15 And Hannah answered and said, No, my lord, I am a woman of a sorrowful spirit: I have drunk neither wine nor strong drink, but have poured out my soul before the LORD.

16 Count not yours handmaid for a daughter of Belial: for out of the abundance of my complaint and grief have I spoken hitherto.

17 Then Eli answered and said, Go in peace: and the God of Israel grant you your petition that you have asked of him.

18 And she said, Let yours handmaid find grace in your sight. So the woman went her way, and did eat, and her countenance was no more sad.

19And they rose up in the morning early, and worshipped before the LORD, and returned, and came to their house to Ramah: and Elkanah knew Hannah his wife; and the LORD remembered her.

20 Wherefore it came to pass, when the time was come about after Hannah had conceived, that she bare a son, and called his name Samuel, saying, Because I have asked him of the LORD.

21 And the man Elkanah, and all his house, went up to offer unto the LORD the yearly sacrifice, and his vow.

22 But Hannah went not up; for she said unto her husband, I will not go up until the child be weaned, and then I will bring him, that he may appear before the LORD, and there abide for ever.

23 And Elkanah her husband said unto her, Do what seemeth you good; tarry until you have weaned him; only the LORD establish his word. So the woman abode, and gave her son suck until she weaned him.

24And when she had weaned him, she took him up with her, with three bullocks, and one ephah of flour, and a bottle of wine, and brought him unto the house of the LORD in Shiloh: and the child was young.

25 And they slew a bullock, and brought the child to Eli.

26 And she said, Oh my lord, as your soul liveth, my lord, I am the woman that stood by you here, praying unto the LORD.

27 For this child I prayed; and the LORD has given me my petition which I asked of him:

28 Therefore also I have lent him to the LORD; as long as he liveth he shall be lent to the LORD. And he worshipped the LORD there.

CHAPTER 2

AND Hannah prayed, and said, My heart rejoiceth in the LORD, my horn is exalted in the LORD: my mouth is enlarged over my enemies; because I rejoice in your salvation.

2 There is none holy as the LORD: for there is none beside you: neither is there any rock like our God.

3 Talk no more so exceeding proudly; let not arrogancy come out of your mouth: for the LORD is a God of knowledge, and by him actions are weighed.

4 The bows of the mighty men are broken, and they that stumbled are girded with strength.

5 They that were full have hired out themselves for bread; and they that were hungry ceased: so that the barren has born seven; and she that has many children is waxed feeble.

6 The LORD killeth, and maketh alive: he bringeth down to the grave, and bringeth up.

7 The LORD maketh poor, and maketh rich: he bringeth low, and lifteth up.

8 He raiseth up the poor out of the dust, and lifteth up the beggar from the dunghill, to set them among princes, and to make them inherit the throne of glory: for the pillars of the earth are the LORD's, and he has set the world upon them.

9 He will keep the feet of his saints, and the wicked shall be silent in darkness; for by strength shall no man prevail.

10 The adversaries of the LORD shall be broken to pieces; out of heaven shall he thunder upon them: the LORD shall judge the ends of the earth; and he shall give strength unto his king, and exalt the horn of his anointed.

11 And Elkanah went to Ramah to his house. And the child did minister unto the LORD before Eli the priest.

12Now the sons of Eli were sons of Belial; they knew not the LORD.

13 And the priests' custom with the people was, that, when any man offered sacrifice, the priest's servant came, while the flesh was in seething, with a fleshhook of three teeth in his hand;

14 And he struck it into the pan, or kettle, or caldron, or pot; all that the fleshhook brought up the priest took for himself. So they did in Shiloh unto all the Israelites that came thither.

15 Also before they burnt the fat, the priest's servant came, and said to the man that sacrificed, Give flesh to roast for the priest; for he will not have sodden flesh of you, but raw.

16 And if any man said unto him, Let them not fail to burn the fat presently, and then take as much as your soul desireth; then he would answer him, Nay; but you shalt give it me now: and if not, I will take it by force.

17 Wherefore the sin of the young men was very great before the LORD: for men abhorred the offering of the LORD.

18But Samuel ministered before the LORD, being a child, girded with a linen ephod.

19 Moreover his mother made him a little coat, and brought it to him from year to year, when she came up with her husband to offer the yearly sacrifice.

20And Eli blessed Elkanah and his wife, and said, The LORD give you seed of this woman for the loan which is lent to the LORD. And they went unto their own home.

21 And the LORD visited Hannah, so that she conceived, and bare three sons and two daughters. And the child Samuel grew before the LORD.

22Now Eli was very old, and heard all that his sons did unto all Israel; and how they lay with the women that assembled at the door of the tabernacle of the congregation.

23 And he said unto them, Why do you such things? for I hear of your evil dealings by all this people.

24 Nay, my sons; for it is no good report that I hear: you make the LORD's people to transgress.

25 If one man sin against another, the judge shall judge him: but if a man sin against the LORD, who shall intreat for him? Notwithstanding they hearkened not unto the voice of their father, because the LORD would slay them.

26 And the child Samuel grew on, and was in favour both with the LORD, and also with men.

27And there came a man of God unto Eli, and said unto him, Thus saith the LORD, Did I plainly appear unto the house of your father, when they were in Egypt in Pharaoh's house?

28 And did I choose him out of all the tribes of Israel to be my priest, to offer upon my altar, to burn incense, to wear an ephod before me? and did I give unto the house of your father all the offerings made by fire of the children of Israel?

29 Wherefore kick you at my sacrifice and at my offering, which I have commanded in my habitation; and honourest your sons above me, to make yourselves fat with the chiefest of all the offerings of Israel my people?

30 Wherefore the LORD God of Israel saith, I said indeed that your house, and the house of your father, should walk before me for ever: but now the LORD saith, Be it far from me; for them that honour me I will honour, and they that despise me shall be lightly esteemed.

31 Behold, the days come, that I will cut off yours arm, and the arm of your father's house, that there shall not be an old man in yours house.

32 And you shalt see an enemy in my habitation, in all the wealth which God shall give Israel: and there shall not be an old man in yours house for ever.

33 And the man of yours, whom I shall not cut off from my altar, shall be to consume yours eyes, and to grieve yours heart: and all the increase of yours house shall die in the flower of their age.

34 And this shall be a sign unto you, that shall come upon your two sons, on Hophni and Phinehas; in one day they shall die both of them.

35 And I will raise me up a faithful priest, that shall do according to that which is in my heart and in my mind: and I will build him a sure house; and he shall walk before my anointed for ever.

36 And it shall come to pass, that every one that is left in yours house shall come and crouch to him for a piece of silver and a morsel of bread, and shall say, Put me, I pray you, into one of the priests' offices, that I may eat a piece of bread.

CHAPTER 3

AND the child Samuel ministered unto the LORD before Eli. And the word of the LORD was precious in those days; there was no open vision.

2 And it came to pass at that time, when Eli was laid down in his place, and his eyes began to wax dim, that he could not see;

3 And ere the lamp of God went out in the temple of the LORD, where the ark of God was, and Samuel was laid down to sleep;

4 That the LORD called Samuel: and he answered, Here am I.

5 And he ran unto Eli, and said, Here am I; for you calledst me. And he said, I called not; lie down again. And he went and lay down.

6 And the LORD called yet again, Samuel. And Samuel arose and went to Eli, and said, Here am I; for you did call me. And he answered, I called not, my son; lie down again.

7 Now Samuel did not yet know the LORD, neither was the word of the LORD yet revealed unto him.

8 And the LORD called Samuel again the third time. And he arose and went to Eli, and said, Here am I; for you did call me. And Eli perceived that the LORD had called the child.

9 Therefore Eli said unto Samuel, Go, lie down: and it shall be, if he call you, that you shalt say, Speak, LORD; for your servant heareth. So Samuel went and lay down in his place.

10 And the LORD came, and stood, and called as at other times, Samuel, Samuel. Then Samuel answered, Speak; for your servant heareth.

11 And the LORD said to Samuel, Behold, I will do a thing in Israel, at which both the ears of every one that heareth it shall tingle.

12 In that day I will perform against Eli all things which I have spoken concerning his house: when I begin, I will also make an end.

13 For I have told him that I will judge his house for ever for the iniquity which he knoweth; because his sons made themselves vile, and he restrained them not.

14 And therefore I have sworn unto the house of Eli, that the iniquity of Eli's house shall not be purged with sacrifice nor offering for ever.

15 And Samuel lay until the morning, and opened the doors of the house of the LORD. And Samuel feared to shew Eli the vision.

16 Then Eli called Samuel, and said, Samuel, my son. And he answered, Here am I.

17 And he said, What is the thing that the LORD has said unto you? I pray you hide it not from me: God do so to you, and more also, if you hide any thing from me of all the things that he said unto you.

18 And Samuel told him every whit, and hid nothing from him. And he said, It is the LORD: let him do what seemeth him good.

19 And Samuel grew, and the LORD was with him, and did let none of his words fall to the ground.

20 And all Israel from Dan even to Beer-sheba knew that Samuel was established to be a prophet of the LORD.

21 And the LORD appeared again in Shiloh: for the LORD revealed himself to Samuel in Shiloh by the word of the LORD.

CHAPTER 4

AND the word of Samuel came to all Israel. Now Israel went out against the Philistines to battle, and pitched beside Eben-ezer: and the Philistines pitched in Aphek.

2 And the Philistines put themselves in array against Israel: and when they joined battle, Israel was smitten before the Philistines: and they slew of the army in the field about four thousand men.

3 And when the people were come into the camp, the elders of Israel said, Wherefore has the LORD smitten us to day before the Philistines? Let us fetch the ark of the covenant of the LORD out of Shiloh unto us, that, when it comes among us, it may save us out of the hand of our enemies.

4 So the people sent to Shiloh, that they might bring from thence the ark of the covenant of the LORD of hosts, which dwelleth between the cherubims: and the two sons of Eli, Hophni and Phinehas, were there with the ark of the covenant of God.

5 And when the ark of the covenant of the LORD came into the camp, all Israel shouted with a great shout, so that the earth rang again.

6 And when the Philistines heard the noise of the shout, they said, What meaneth the noise of this great shout in the camp of the Hebrews? And they understood that the ark of the LORD was come into the camp.

7 And the Philistines were afraid, for they said, God is come into the camp. And they said, Woe unto us! for there has not been such a thing heretofore.

8 Woe unto us! who shall deliver us out of the hand of these mighty Gods? these are the Gods that struck the Egyptians with all the plagues in the wilderness.

9 Be strong, and quit yourselves like men, O you Philistines, that you be not servants unto the Hebrews, as they have been to you: quit yourselves like men, and fight.

10 And the Philistines fought, and Israel was smitten, and they fled every man into his tent: and there was a very great slaughter; for there fell of Israel thirty thousand footmen.

11 And the ark of God was taken; and the two sons of Eli, Hophni and Phinehas, were slain.

12 And there ran a man of Benjamin out of the army, and came to Shiloh the same day with his clothes rent, and with earth upon his head.

13 And when he came, lo, Eli sat upon a seat by the wayside watching: for his heart trembled for the ark of God. And when the man came into the city, and told it, all the city cried out.

14 And when Eli heard the noise of the crying, he said, What meaneth the noise of this tumult? And the man came in hastily, and told Eli.

15 Now Eli was ninety and eight years old; and his eyes were dim, that he could not see.

16 And the man said unto Eli, I am he that came out of the army, and I fled to day out of the army. And he said, What is there done, my son?

17 And the messenger answered and said, Israel is fled before the Philistines, and there has been also a great slaughter among the people, and your two sons also, Hophni and Phinehas, are dead, and the ark of God is taken.

18 And it came to pass, when he made mention of the ark of God, that he fell from off the seat backward by the side of the gate, and his neck brake, and he died: for he was an old man, and heavy. And he had judged Israel forty years.

19 And his daughter in law, Phinehas' wife, was with child, near to be delivered: and when she heard the tidings that the ark of God was taken, and that her father in law and her husband were dead, she bowed herself and travailed; for her pains came upon her.

20 And about the time of her death the women that stood by her said unto her, Fear not; for you have born a son. But she answered not, neither did she regard it.

21 And she named the child I-chabod, saying, The glory is departed from Israel: because the ark of God was taken, and because of her father in law and her husband.

22 And she said, The glory is departed from Israel: for the ark of God is taken.

CHAPTER 5

AND the Philistines took the ark of God, and brought it from Eben-ezer unto Ashdod.

2 When the Philistines took the ark of God, they brought it into the house of Dagon, and set it by Dagon.

3 And when they of Ashdod arose early on the morrow, behold, Dagon was fallen upon his face to the earth before the ark of the LORD. And they took Dagon, and set him in his place again.

4 And when they arose early on the morrow morning, behold, Dagon was fallen upon his face to the ground before the ark of the LORD; and the head of Dagon and both the palms of his hands were cut off upon the threshold; only the stump of Dagon was left to him.

5 Therefore neither the priests of Dagon, nor any that come into Dagon's house, tread on the threshold of Dagon in Ashdod unto this day.

6 But the hand of the LORD was heavy upon them of Ashdod, and he destroyed them, and struck them with emerods, even Ashdod and the coasts thereof.

7 And when the men of Ashdod saw that it was so, they said, The ark of the God of Israel shall not abide with us: for his hand is sore upon us, and upon Dagon our god.

8 They sent therefore and gathered all the lords of the Philistines unto them, and said, What shall we do with the ark of the God of Israel? And they answered, Let the ark of the God of Israel be carried about unto Gath. And they carried the ark of the God of Israel about thither.

9 And it was so, that, after they had carried it about, the hand of the LORD was against the city with a very great destruction: and he struck the men of the city, both small and great, and they had emerods in their secret parts.

10Therefore they sent the ark of God to Ekron. And it came to pass, as the ark of God came to Ekron, that the Ekronites cried out, saying, They have brought about the ark of the God of Israel to us, to slay us and our people.

11 So they sent and gathered together all the lords of the Philistines, and said, Send away the ark of the God of Israel, and let it go again to his own place, that it slay us not, and our people: for there was a deadly destruction throughout all the city; the hand of God was very heavy there.

12 And the men that died not were smitten with the emerods: and the cry of the city went up to heaven.

CHAPTER 6

AND the ark of the LORD was in the country of the Philistines seven months.

2 And the Philistines called for the priests and the diviners, saying, What shall we do to the ark of the LORD? tell us wherewith we shall send it to his place.

3 And they said, If you send away the ark of the God of Israel, send it not empty; but in any wise return him a trespass offering: then you shall be healed, and it shall be known to you why his hand is not removed from you.

4 Then said they, What shall be the trespass offering which we shall return to him? They answered, Five golden emerods, and five golden mice, according to the number of the lords of the Philistines: for one plague was on you all, and on your lords.

5 Wherefore you shall make images of your emerods, and images of your mice that mar the land; and you shall give glory unto the God of Israel: what if he will lighten his hand from off you, and from off your gods, and from off your land.

6 Wherefore then do you harden your hearts, as the Egyptians and Pharaoh hardened their hearts? when he had created wonderfully among them, did they not let the people go, and they departed?

7 Now therefore make a new cart, and take two milch kine, on which there has come no yoke, and tie the kine to the cart, and bring their calves home from them:

8 And take the ark of the LORD, and lay it upon the cart; and put the jewels of gold, which you return him for a trespass offering, in a coffer by the side thereof; and send it away, that it may go.

9 And see, if it goeth up by the way of his own coast to Beth-shemesh, then he has done us this great evil: but if not, then we shall know that it is not his hand that struck us; it was a chance that happened to us.

10And the men did so; and took two milch kine, and tied them to the cart, and shut up their calves at home:

11 And they laid the ark of the LORD upon the cart, and the coffer with the mice of gold and the images of their emerods.

12 And the kine took the straight way to the way of Beth-shemesh, and went along the highway, lowing as they went, and turned not aside to the right hand or to the left; and the lords of the Philistines went after them unto the border of Beth-shemesh.

13 And they of Beth-shemesh were reaping their wheat harvest in the valley: and they lifted up their eyes, and saw the ark, and rejoiced to see it.

14 And the cart came into the field of Joshua, a Beth-shemite, and stood there, where there was a great stone: and they clave the wood of the cart, and offered the kine a burnt offering unto the LORD.

15 And the Levites took down the ark of the LORD, and the coffer that was with it, wherein the jewels of gold were, and put them on the great stone: and the men of Beth-shemesh offered burnt offerings and sacrificed sacrifices the same day unto the LORD.

16 And when the five lords of the Philistines had seen it, they returned to Ekron the same day.

17 And these are the golden emerods which the Philistines returned for a trespass offering unto the LORD; for Ashdod one, for Gaza one, for Askelon one, for Gath one, for Ekron one;

18 And the golden mice, according to the number of all the cities of the Philistines belonging to the five lords, both of fenced cities, and of country villages, even unto the great stone of Abel, whereon they set down the ark of the LORD: which stone remaineth unto this day in the field of Joshua, the Beth-shemite.

19And he struck the men of Beth-shemesh, because they had looked into the ark of the LORD, even he struck of the people fifty thousand and threescore and ten men: and the people lamented, because the LORD had smitten many of the people with a great slaughter.

20 And the men of Beth-shemesh said, Who is able to stand before this holy LORD God? and to whom shall he go up from us?

21And they sent messengers to the inhabitants of Kirjath-jearim, saying, The Philistines have brought again the ark of the LORD; come you down, and fetch it up to you.

CHAPTER 7

AND the men of Kirjath-jearim came, and fetched up the ark of the LORD, and brought it into the house of Abinadab in the hill, and sanctified Eleazar his son to keep the ark of the LORD.

2 And it came to pass, while the ark abode in Kirjath-jearim, that the time was long; for it was twenty years: and all the house of Israel lamented after the LORD.

3And Samuel spake unto all the house of Israel, saying, If you do return unto the LORD with all your hearts, then put away the strange gods and Ashtaroth from among you, and prepare your hearts unto the LORD, and serve him only: and he will deliver you out of the hand of the Philistines.

4 Then the children of Israel did put away Baalim and Ashtaroth, and served the LORD only.

5 And Samuel said, Gather all Israel to Mizpeh, and I will pray for you unto the LORD.

6 And they gathered together to Mizpeh, and drew water, and poured it out before the LORD, and fasted on that day, and said there, We have sinned against the LORD. And Samuel judged the children of Israel in Mizpeh.

7 And when the Philistines heard that the children of Israel were gathered together to Mizpeh, the lords of the Philistines went up against Israel. And when the children of Israel heard it, they were afraid of the Philistines.

8 And the children of Israel said to Samuel, Cease not to cry unto the LORD our God for us, that he will save us out of the hand of the Philistines.

9And Samuel took a sucking lamb, and offered it for a burnt offering wholly unto the LORD: and Samuel cried unto the LORD for Israel; and the LORD heard him.

10 And as Samuel was offering up the burnt offering, the Philistines drew near to battle against Israel: but the LORD thundered with a great thunder on that day upon the Philistines, and discomfited them; and they were smitten before Israel.

11 And the men of Israel went out of Mizpeh, and pursued the Philistines, and struck them, until they came under Beth-car.

12 Then Samuel took a stone, and set it between Mizpeh and Shen, and called the name of it Eben-ezer, saying, Hitherto has the LORD helped us.

13So the Philistines were subdued, and they came no more into the coast of Israel: and the hand of the LORD was against the Philistines all the days of Samuel.

14 And the cities which the Philistines had taken from Israel were restored to Israel, from Ekron even unto Gath; and the coasts thereof did Israel deliver out of the hands of the Philistines. And there was peace between Israel and the Amorites.

15 And Samuel judged Israel all the days of his life.

16 And he went from year to year in circuit to Beth-el, and Gilgal, and Mizpeh, and judged Israel in all those places.

17 And his return was to Ramah; for there was his house; and there he judged Israel; and there he built an altar unto the LORD.

CHAPTER 8

AND it came to pass, when Samuel was old, that he made his sons judges over Israel.

2 Now the name of his firstborn was Joel; and the name of his second, Abiah: they were judges in Beer-sheba.

3 And his sons walked not in his ways, but turned aside after lucre, and took bribes, and perverted judgment.

4 Then all the elders of Israel gathered themselves together, and came to Samuel unto Ramah,

5 And said unto him, Behold, you are old, and your sons walk not in your ways: now make us a king to judge us like all the nations.

6But the thing displeased Samuel, when they said, Give us a king to judge us. And Samuel prayed unto the LORD.

7 And the LORD said unto Samuel, Hearken unto the voice of the people in all that they say unto you: for they have not rejected you, but they have rejected me, that I should not reign over them.

8 According to all the works which they have done since the day that I brought them up out of Egypt even unto this day, wherewith they have forsaken me, and served other gods, so do they also unto you.

9 Now therefore hearken unto their voice: howbeit yet protest solemnly unto them, and shew them the manner of the king that shall reign over them.

10And Samuel told all the words of the LORD unto the people that asked of him a king.

11 And he said, This will be the manner of the king that shall reign over you: He will take your sons, and appoint them for himself, for his chariots, and to be his horsemen; and some shall run before his chariots.

12 And he will appoint him captains over thousands, and captains over fifties; and will set them to ear his ground, and to reap his harvest, and to make his instruments of war, and instruments of his chariots.

13 And he will take your daughters to be confectionaries, and to be cooks, and to be bakers.

14 And he will take your fields, and your vineyards, and your oliveyards, even the best of them, and give them to his servants.

15 And he will take the tenth of your seed, and of your vineyards, and give to his officers, and to his servants.

16 And he will take your menservants, and your maidservants, and your goodliest young men, and your asses, and put them to his work.

17 He will take the tenth of your sheep: and you shall be his servants.

18 And you shall cry out in that day because of your king which you shall have chosen you; and the LORD will not hear you in that day.

19 Nevertheless the people refused to obey the voice of Samuel; and they said, Nay; but we will have a king over us;

20 That we also may be like all the nations; and that our king may judge us, and go out before us, and fight our battles.

21 And Samuel heard all the words of the people, and he rehearsed them in the ears of the LORD.

22 And the LORD said to Samuel, Hearken unto their voice, and make them a king. And Samuel said unto the men of Israel, Go you every man unto his city.

CHAPTER 9

NOW there was a man of Benjamin, whose name was Kish, the son of Abiel, the son of Zeror, the son of Bechorath, the son of Aphiah, a Benjamite, a mighty man of power.

2 And he had a son, whose name was Saul, a choice young man, and a goodly: and there was not among the children of Israel a goodlier person than he: from his shoulders and upward he was higher than any of the people.

3 And the asses of Kish Saul's father were lost. And Kish said to Saul his son, Take now one of the servants with you, and arise, go seek the asses.

4 And he passed through mount Ephraim, and passed through the land of Shalisha, but they found them not: then they passed through the land of Shalim, and there they were not: and he passed through the land of the Benjamites, but they found them not.

5 And when they were come to the land of Zuph, Saul said to his servant that was with him, Come, and let us return; lest my father leave caring for the asses, and take thought for us.

6 And he said unto him, Behold now, there is in this city a man of God, and he is an honourable man; all that he saith comes surely to pass: now let us go thither; what if he can shew us our way that we should go.

7 Then said Saul to his servant, But, behold, if we go, what shall we bring the man? for the bread is spent in our vessels, and there is not a present to bring to the man of God: what have we?

8 And the servant answered Saul again, and said, Behold, I have here at hand the fourth part of a shekel of silver: that will I give to the man of God, to tell us our way.

9 (Beforetime in Israel, when a man went to inquire of God, thus he spake, Come, and let us go to the seer: for he that is now called a Prophet was beforetime called a Seer.)

10 Then said Saul to his servant, Well said; come, let us go. So they went unto the city where the man of God was.

11 And as they went up the hill to the city, they found young maidens going out to draw water, and said unto them, Is the seer here?

12 And they answered them, and said, He is; behold, he is before you: make haste now, for he came to day to the city; for there is a sacrifice of the people to day in the high place:

13 As soon as you be come into the city, you shall straightway find him, before he go up to the high place to eat: for the people will not eat until he come, because he doth bless the sacrifice; and afterwards they eat that be bidden. Now therefore get you up; for about this time you shall find him.

14 And they went up into the city: and when they were come into the city, behold, Samuel came out against them, for to go up to the high place.

15 Now the LORD had told Samuel in his ear a day before Saul came, saying,

16 To morrow about this time I will send you a man out of the land of Benjamin, and you shalt anoint him to be captain over my people Israel, that he may save my people out of the hand of the Philistines: for I have looked upon my people, because their cry is come unto me.

17 And when Samuel saw Saul, the LORD said unto him, Behold the man whom I spake to you of! this same shall reign over my people.

18 Then Saul drew near to Samuel in the gate, and said, Tell me, I pray you, where the seer's house is.

19 And Samuel answered Saul, and said, I am the seer: go up before me unto the high place; for you shall eat with me to day, and to morrow I will let you go, and will tell you all that is in yours heart.

20 And as for yours asses that were lost three days ago, set not your mind on them; for they are found. And on whom is all the desire of Israel? Is it not on you, and on all your father's house?

21 And Saul answered and said, Am not I a Benjamite, of the smallest of the tribes of Israel? and my family the least of all the families of the tribe of Benjamin? wherefore then speakest you so to me?

22 And Samuel took Saul and his servant, and brought them into the parlour, and made them sit in the chiefest place among them that were bidden, which were about thirty persons.

23 And Samuel said unto the cook, Bring the portion which I gave you, of which I said unto you, Set it by you.

24 And the cook took up the shoulder, and that which was upon it, and set it before Saul. And Samuel said, Behold that which is left! set it before you, and eat: for unto this time has it been kept for you since I said, I have invited the people. So Saul did eat with Samuel that day.

25 And when they were come down from the high place into the city, Samuel communed with Saul upon the top of the house.

26 And they arose early: and it came to pass about the spring of the day, that Samuel called Saul to the top of the house, saying, Up, that I may send you away. And Saul arose, and they went out both of them, he and Samuel, abroad.

27 And as they were going down to the end of the city, Samuel said to Saul, Bid the servant pass on before us, (and he passed on,) but stand you still a while, that I may shew you the word of God.

CHAPTER 10

THEN Samuel took a vial of oil, and poured it upon his head, and kissed him, and said, Is it not because the LORD has anointed you to be captain over his inheritance?

2 When you are departed from me to day, then you shalt find two men by Rachel's sepulchre in the border of Benjamin at Zelzah; and they will say unto you, The asses which you wentest to seek are found: and, lo, your father has left the care of the asses, and sorroweth for you, saying, What shall I do for my son?

3 Then shalt you go on forward from thence, and you shalt come to the plain of Tabor, and there shall meet you three men going up to God to Beth-el, one carrying three kids, and another carrying three loaves of bread, and another carrying a bottle of wine:

4 And they will salute you, and give you two loaves of bread; which you shalt receive of their hands.

5 After that you shalt come to the hill of God, where is the garrison of the Philistines: and it shall come to pass, when you are come thither to the city, that you shalt meet a company of prophets coming down from the high place with a psaltery, and a tabret, and a pipe, and a harp, before them; and they shall prophesy:

6 And the Spirit of the LORD will come upon you, and you shalt prophesy with them, and shalt be turned into another man.

7 And let it be, when these signs are come unto you, that you do as occasion serve you; for God is with you.

8 And you shalt go down before me to Gilgal; and, behold, I will come down unto you, to offer burnt offerings, and to sacrifice sacrifices of peace offerings: seven days shalt you tarry, till I come to you, and shew you what you shalt do.

9 And it was so, that when he had turned his back to go from Samuel, God gave him another heart: and all those signs came to pass that day.

10 And when they came thither to the hill, behold, a company of prophets met him; and the Spirit of God came upon him, and he prophesied among them.

11 And it came to pass, when all that knew him beforetime saw that, behold, he prophesied among the prophets, then the people said one to another, What is this that is come unto the son of Kish? Is Saul also among the prophets?

12 And one of the same place answered and said, But who is their father? Therefore it became a proverb, Is Saul also among the prophets?

13 And when he had made an end of prophesying, he came to the high place.

14 And Saul's uncle said unto him and to his servant, Whither went you? And he said, To seek the asses: and when we saw that they were no where, we came to Samuel.

15 And Saul's uncle said, Tell me, I pray you, what Samuel said unto you.

16 And Saul said unto his uncle, He told us plainly that the asses were found. But of the matter of the kingdom, whereof Samuel spake, he told him not.

17 And Samuel called the people together unto the LORD to Mizpeh;

18 And said unto the children of Israel, Thus saith the LORD God of Israel, I brought up Israel out of Egypt, and delivered you out of the hand of the Egyptians, and out of the hand of all kingdoms, and of them that oppressed you:

19 And you have this day rejected your God, who himself saved you out of all your adversities and your tribulations; and you have said unto him, Nay, but set a king over us. Now therefore present yourselves before the LORD by your tribes, and by your thousands.

20 And when Samuel had caused all the tribes of Israel to come near, the tribe of Benjamin was taken.

21 When he had caused the tribe of Benjamin to come near by their families, the family of Matri was taken, and Saul the son of Kish was taken: and when they sought him, he could not be found.

22 Therefore they inquired of the LORD further, if the man should yet come thither. And the LORD answered, Behold, he has hid himself among the stuff.

23 And they ran and fetched him thence: and when he stood among the people, he was higher than any of the people from his shoulders and upward.

24 And Samuel said to all the people, See you him whom the LORD has chosen, that there is none like him among all the people? And all the people shouted, and said, God save the king.

25 Then Samuel told the people the manner of the kingdom, and wrote it in a book, and laid it up before the LORD. And Samuel sent all the people away, every man to his house.

26 And Saul also went home to Gibeah; and there went with him a band of men, whose hearts God had touched.

27 But the children of Belial said, How shall this man save us? And they despised him, and brought him no presents. But he held his peace.

CHAPTER 11

THEN Nahash the Ammonite came up, and encamped against Jabesh-gilead: and all the men of Jabesh said unto Nahash, Make a covenant with us, and we will serve you.

2 And Nahash the Ammonite answered them, On this condition will I make a covenant with you, that I may thrust out all your right eyes, and lay it for a reproach upon all Israel.

3 And the elders of Jabesh said unto him, Give us seven days' respite, that we may send messengers unto all the coasts of Israel: and then, if there be no man to save us, we will come out to you.

4 Then came the messengers to Gibeah of Saul, and told the tidings in the ears of the people: and all the people lifted up their voices, and wept.

5 And, behold, Saul came after the herd out of the field; and Saul said, What aileth the people that they weep? And they told him the tidings of the men of Jabesh.

6 And the Spirit of God came upon Saul when he heard those tidings, and his anger was kindled greatly.

7 And he took a yoke of oxen, and hewed them in pieces, and sent them throughout all the coasts of Israel by the hands of messengers, saying, Whosoever comes not forth after Saul and after Samuel, so shall it be done unto his oxen. And the fear of the LORD fell on the people, and they came out with one consent.

8 And when he numbered them in Bezek, the children of Israel were three hundred thousand, and the men of Judah thirty thousand.

9 And they said unto the messengers that came, Thus shall you say unto the men of Jabesh-gilead, To morrow, by that time the sun be hot, you shall have help. And the messengers came and shewed it to the men of Jabesh; and they were glad.

10 Therefore the men of Jabesh said, To morrow we will come out unto you, and you shall do with us all that seemeth good unto you.

11 And it was so on the morrow, that Saul put the people in three companies; and they came into the midst of the host in the morning watch, and slew the Ammonites until the heat of the day: and it came to pass, that they which remained were scattered, so that two of them were not left together.

12 And the people said unto Samuel, Who is he that said, Shall Saul reign over us? bring the men, that we may put them to death.

13 And Saul said, There shall not a man be put to death this day: for to day the LORD has created salvation in Israel.

14 Then said Samuel to the people, Come, and let us go to Gilgal, and renew the kingdom there.

15 And all the people went to Gilgal; and there they made Saul king before the LORD in Gilgal; and there they sacrificed sacrifices of peace offerings before the LORD; and there Saul and all the men of Israel rejoiced greatly.

CHAPTER 12

AND Samuel said unto all Israel, Behold, I have hearkened unto your voice in all that you said unto me, and have made a king over you.

2 And now, behold, the king walketh before you: and I am old and grayheaded; and, behold, my sons are with you: and I have walked before you from my childhood unto this day.

3 Behold, here I am: witness against me before the LORD, and before his anointed: whose ox have I taken? or whose ass have I taken? or whom have I defrauded? whom have I oppressed? or of whose hand have I received any bribe to blind my eyes therewith? and I will restore it you.

4 And they said, You have not defrauded us, nor oppressed us, neither have you taken ought of any man's hand.

5 And he said unto them, The LORD is witness against you, and his anointed is witness this day, that you have not found ought in my hand. And they answered, He is witness.

6 And Samuel said unto the people, It is the LORD that advanced Moses and Aaron, and that brought your fathers up out of the land of Egypt.

7 Now therefore stand still, that I may reason with you before the LORD of all the righteous acts of the LORD, which he did to you and to your fathers.

8 When Jacob was come into Egypt, and your fathers cried unto the LORD, then the LORD sent Moses and Aaron, which brought forth your fathers out of Egypt, and made them dwell in this place.

9 And when they forgat the LORD their God, he sold them into the hand of Sisera, captain of the host of Hazor, and into the hand of the Philistines, and into the hand of the king of Moab, and they fought against them.

10 And they cried unto the LORD, and said, We have sinned, because we have forsaken the LORD, and have served Baalim and Ashtaroth: but now deliver us out of the hand of our enemies, and we will serve you.

11 And the LORD sent Jerubbaal, and Bedan, and Jephthah, and Samuel, and delivered you out of the hand of your enemies on every side, and you dwelled safe.

12 And when you saw that Nahash the king of the children of Ammon came against you, you said unto me, Nay; but a king shall reign over us: when the LORD your God was your king.

13 Now therefore behold the king whom you have chosen, and whom you have desired! and, behold, the LORD has set a king over you.

14 If you will fear the LORD, and serve him, and obey his voice, and not rebel against the commandment of the LORD, then shall both you and also the king that reigneth over you continue following the LORD your God:

15 But if you will not obey the voice of the LORD, but rebel against the commandment of the LORD, then shall the hand of the LORD be against you, as it was against your fathers.

16 Now therefore stand and see this great thing, which the LORD will do before your eyes.

17 Is it not wheat harvest to day? I will call unto the LORD, and he shall send thunder and rain; that you may perceive and see that your wickedness is great, which you have done in the sight of the LORD, in asking you a king.

18 So Samuel called unto the LORD; and the LORD sent thunder and rain that day: and all the people greatly feared the LORD and Samuel.

19 And all the people said unto Samuel, Pray for your servants unto the LORD your God, that we die not: for we have added unto all our sins this evil, to ask us a king.

20 And Samuel said unto the people, Fear not: you have done all this wickedness: yet turn not aside from following the LORD, but serve the LORD with all your heart;

21 And turn you not aside: for then should you go after vain things, which cannot profit nor deliver; for they are vain.

22 For the LORD will not forsake his people for his great name's sake: because it has pleased the LORD to make you his people.

23 Moreover as for me, God forbid that I should sin against the LORD in ceasing to pray for you: but I will teach you the good and the right way:

24 Only fear the LORD, and serve him in truth with all your heart: for consider how great things he has done for you.

25 But if you shall still do wickedly, you shall be consumed, both you and your king.

CHAPTER 13

SAUL reigned one year; and when he had reigned two years over Israel,

2 Saul chose him three thousand men of Israel; whereof two thousand were with Saul in Michmash and in mount Beth-el, and a thousand were with Jonathan in Gibeah of Benjamin: and the rest of the people he sent every man to his tent.

3 And Jonathan struck the garrison of the Philistines that was in Geba, and the Philistines heard of it. And Saul blew the trumpet throughout all the land, saying, Let the Hebrews hear.

4 And all Israel heard say that Saul had smitten a garrison of the Philistines, and that Israel also was had in abomination with the Philistines. And the people were called together after Saul to Gilgal.

5 And the Philistines gathered themselves together to fight with Israel, thirty thousand chariots, and six thousand horsemen, and people as the sand which is on the sea shore in multitude: and they came up, and pitched in Michmash, eastward from Beth-aven.

6 When the men of Israel saw that they were in a strait, (for the people were distressed,) then the people did hide themselves in caves, and in thickets, and in rocks, and in high places, and in pits.

7 And some of the Hebrews went over Jordan to the land of Gad and Gilead. As for Saul, he was yet in Gilgal, and all the people followed him trembling.

8 And he tarried seven days, according to the set time that Samuel had appointed: but Samuel came not to Gilgal; and the people were scattered from him.

9 And Saul said, Bring hither a burnt offering to me, and peace offerings. And he offered the burnt offering.

10 And it came to pass, that as soon as he had made an end of offering the burnt offering, behold, Samuel came; and Saul went out to meet him, that he might salute him.

11 And Samuel said, What have you done? And Saul said, Because I saw that the people were scattered from me, and that you camest not within the days appointed, and that the Philistines gathered themselves together at Michmash;

12 Therefore said I, The Philistines will come down now upon me to Gilgal, and I have not made supplication unto the LORD: I forced myself therefore, and offered a burnt offering.

13 And Samuel said to Saul, You have done foolishly: you have not kept the commandment of the LORD your God, which he commanded you: for now would the LORD have established your kingdom upon Israel for ever.

14 But now your kingdom shall not continue: the LORD has sought him a man after his own heart, and the LORD has commanded him to be captain over his people, because you have not kept that which the LORD commanded you.

15 And Samuel arose, and gat him up from Gilgal unto Gibeah of Benjamin. And Saul numbered the people that were present with him, about six hundred men.

16 And Saul, and Jonathan his son, and the people that were present with them, abode in Gibeah of Benjamin: but the Philistines encamped in Michmash.

17 And the spoilers came out of the camp of the Philistines in three companies: one company turned unto the way that leadeth to Ophrah, unto the land of Shual:

18 And another company turned the way to Beth-horon: and another company turned to the way of the border that looketh to the valley of Zeboim toward the wilderness.

19 Now there was no smith found throughout all the land of Israel: for the Philistines said, Lest the Hebrews make them swords or spears:

20 But all the Israelites went down to the Philistines, to sharpen every man his share, and his coulter, and his axe, and his mattock.

21 Yet they had a file for the mattocks, and for the coulters, and for the forks, and for the axes, and to sharpen the goads.

22 So it came to pass in the day of battle, that there was neither sword nor spear found in the hand of any of the people that were with Saul and Jonathan: but with Saul and with Jonathan his son was there found.

23 And the garrison of the Philistines went out to the passage of Michmash.

CHAPTER 14

NOW it came to pass upon a day, that Jonathan the son of Saul said unto the young man that bare his armour, Come, and let us go over to the Philistines' garrison, that is on the other side. But he told not his father.

2 And Saul tarried in the uttermost part of Gibeah under a pomegranate tree which is in Migron: and the people that were with him were about six hundred men;

3 And Ahiah, the son of Ahitub, I-chabod's brother, the son of Phinehas, the son of Eli, the LORD's priest in Shiloh, wearing an ephod. And the people knew not that Jonathan was gone.

4 And between the passages, by which Jonathan sought to go over unto the Philistines' garrison, there was a sharp rock on the one side, and a sharp rock on the other side: and the name of the one was Bozez, and the name of the other Seneh.

5 The forefront of the one was situate northward over against Michmash, and the other southward over against Gibeah.

6 And Jonathan said to the young man that bare his armour, Come, and let us go over unto the garrison of these uncircumcised: it may be that the LORD will work for us: for there is no restraint to the LORD to save by many or by few.

7 And his armourbearer said unto him, Do all that is in yours heart: turn you; behold, I am with you according to your heart.

8 Then said Jonathan, Behold, we will pass over unto these men, and we will discover ourselves unto them.

9 If they say thus unto us, Tarry until we come to you; then we will stand still in our place, and will not go up unto them.

10 But if they say thus, Come up unto us; then we will go up: for the LORD has delivered them into our hand: and this shall be a sign unto us.

11 And both of them discovered themselves unto the garrison of the Philistines: and the Philistines said, Behold, the Hebrews come forth out of the holes where they had hid themselves.

12 And the men of the garrison answered Jonathan and his armourbearer, and said, Come up to us, and we will shew you a thing. And Jonathan said unto his armourbearer, Come up after me: for the LORD has delivered them into the hand of Israel.

13 And Jonathan climbed up upon his hands and upon his feet, and his armourbearer after him: and they fell before Jonathan; and his armourbearer slew after him.

14 And that first slaughter, which Jonathan and his armourbearer made, was about twenty men, within as it were an half acre of land, which a yoke of oxen might plow.

15 And there was trembling in the host, in the field, and among all the people: the garrison, and the spoilers, they also trembled, and the earth quaked: so it was a very great trembling.

16 And the watchmen of Saul in Gibeah of Benjamin looked; and, behold, the multitude melted away, and they went on beating down one another.

17 Then said Saul unto the people that were with him, Number now, and see who is gone from us. And when they had numbered, behold, Jonathan and his armourbearer were not there.

18 And Saul said unto Ahiah, Bring hither the ark of God. For the ark of God was at that time with the children of Israel.

19 And it came to pass, while Saul talked unto the priest, that the noise that was in the host of the Philistines went on and increased: and Saul said unto the priest, Withdraw yours hand.

20 And Saul and all the people that were with him assembled themselves, and they came to the battle: and, behold, every man's sword was against his fellow, and there was a very great discomfiture.

21 Moreover the Hebrews that were with the Philistines before that time, which went up with them into the camp from the country round about, even they also turned to be with the Israelites that were with Saul and Jonathan.

22 Likewise all the men of Israel which had hid themselves in mount Ephraim, when they heard that the Philistines fled, even they also followed hard after them in the battle.

23 So the LORD saved Israel that day: and the battle passed over unto Beth-aven.

24 And the men of Israel were distressed that day: for Saul had adjured the people, saying, Cursed be the man that eateth any food until evening, that I may be avenged on my enemies. So none of the people tasted any food.

25 And all they of the land came to a wood; and there was honey upon the ground.

26 And when the people were come into the wood, behold, the honey dropped; but no man put his hand to his mouth: for the people feared the oath.

27 But Jonathan heard not when his father charged the people with the oath: wherefore he put forth the end of the rod that was in his hand, and dipped it in an honeycomb, and put his hand to his mouth; and his eyes were enlightened.

28 Then answered one of the people, and said, Your father straitly charged the people with an oath, saying, Cursed be the man that eateth any food this day. And the people were faint.

29 Then said Jonathan, My father has troubled the land: see, I pray you, how my eyes have been enlightened, because I tasted a little of this honey.

30 How much more, if haply the people had eaten freely to day of the spoil of their enemies which they found? for had there not been now a much greater slaughter among the Philistines?

31 And they struck the Philistines that day from Michmash to Aijalon: and the people were very faint.

32 And the people flew upon the spoil, and took sheep, and oxen, and calves, and slew them on the ground: and the people did eat them with the blood.

33 Then they told Saul, saying, Behold, the people sin against the LORD, in that they eat with the blood. And he said, You have transgressed: roll a great stone unto me this day.

34 And Saul said, Disperse yourselves among the people, and say unto them, Bring me hither every man his ox, and every man his sheep, and slay them here, and eat; and sin not against the LORD in eating with the blood. And all the people brought every man his ox with him that night, and slew them there.

35 And Saul built an altar unto the LORD: the same was the first altar that he built unto the LORD.

36 And Saul said, Let us go down after the Philistines by night, and spoil them until the morning light, and let us not leave a man of them. And they said, Do whatsoever seemeth good unto you. Then said the priest, Let us draw near hither unto God.

37 And Saul asked counsel of God, Shall I go down after the Philistines? will you deliver them into the hand of Israel? But he answered him not that day.

38 And Saul said, Draw you near hither, all the chief of the people: and know and see wherein this sin has been this day.

39 For, as the LORD liveth, which saveth Israel, though it be in Jonathan my son, he shall surely die. But there was not a man among all the people that answered him.

40 Then said he unto all Israel, Be you on one side, and I and Jonathan my son will be on the other side. And the people said unto Saul, Do what seemeth good unto you.

41 Therefore Saul said unto the LORD God of Israel, Give a perfect lot. And Saul and Jonathan were taken: but the people escaped.

42 And Saul said, Cast lots between me and Jonathan my son. And Jonathan was taken.

43 Then Saul said to Jonathan, Tell me what you have done. And Jonathan told him, and said, I did but taste a little honey with the end of the rod that was in my hand, and, lo, I must die.

44 And Saul answered, God do so and more also: for you shalt surely die, Jonathan.

45 And the people said unto Saul, Shall Jonathan die, who has created this great salvation in Israel? God forbid: as the LORD liveth, there shall not one hair of his head fall to the ground; for he has created with God this day. So the people rescued Jonathan, that he died not.

46 Then Saul went up from following the Philistines: and the Philistines went to their own place.

47 So Saul took the kingdom over Israel, and fought against all his enemies on every side, against Moab, and against the children of Ammon, and against Edom, and against the kings of Zobah, and against the Philistines: and whithersoever he turned himself, he vexed them.

48 And he gathered an host, and struck the Amalekites, and delivered Israel out of the hands of them that spoiled them.

49 Now the sons of Saul were Jonathan, and Ishui, and Melchi-shua: and the names of his two daughters were these; the name of the firstborn Merab, and the name of the younger Michal:

50 And the name of Saul's wife was Ahinoam, the daughter of Ahimaaz: and the name of the captain of his host was Abner, the son of Ner, Saul's uncle.

51 And Kish was the father of Saul; and Ner the father of Abner was the son of Abiel.

52 And there was sore war against the Philistines all the days of Saul: and when Saul saw any strong man, or any valiant man, he took him unto him.

CHAPTER 15

SAMUEL also said unto Saul, The LORD sent me to anoint you to be king over his people, over Israel: now therefore hearken you unto the voice of the words of the LORD.

2 Thus saith the LORD of hosts, I remember that which Amalek did to Israel, how he laid wait for him in the way, when he came up from Egypt.

3 Now go and strike Amalek, and utterly destroy all that they have, and spare them not; but slay both man and woman, infant and suckling, ox and sheep, camel and ass.

4 And Saul gathered the people together, and numbered them in Telaim, two hundred thousand footmen, and ten thousand men of Judah.

5 And Saul came to a city of Amalek, and laid wait in the valley.

6 And Saul said unto the Kenites, Go, depart, get you down from among the Amalekites, lest I destroy you with them: for you shewed kindness to all the children of Israel, when they came up out of Egypt. So the Kenites departed from among the Amalekites.

7 And Saul struck the Amalekites from Havilah until you comest to Shur, that is over against Egypt.

8 And he took Agag the king of the Amalekites alive, and utterly destroyed all the people with the edge of the sword.

9 But Saul and the people spared Agag, and the best of the sheep, and of the oxen, and of the fatlings, and the lambs, and all that was good, and would not utterly destroy them: but every thing that was vile and refuse, that they destroyed utterly.

10 Then came the word of the LORD unto Samuel, saying,

11 It repenteth me that I have set up Saul to be king: for he is turned back from following me, and has not performed my commandments. And it grieved Samuel; and he cried unto the LORD all night.

12 And when Samuel rose early to meet Saul in the morning, it was told Samuel, saying, Saul came to Carmel, and, behold, he set him up a place, and is gone about, and passed on, and gone down to Gilgal.

13 And Samuel came to Saul: and Saul said unto him, Blessed be you of the LORD: I have performed the commandment of the LORD.

14 And Samuel said, What meaneth then this bleating of the sheep in my ears, and the lowing of the oxen which I hear?

15 And Saul said, They have brought them from the Amalekites: for the people spared the best of the sheep and of the oxen, to sacrifice unto the LORD your God; and the rest we have utterly destroyed.

16 Then Samuel said unto Saul, Stay, and I will tell you what the LORD has said to me this night. And he said unto him, Say on.

17 And Samuel said, When you wast little in yours own sight, wast you not made the head of the tribes of Israel, and the LORD anointed you king over Israel?

18 And the LORD sent you on a journey, and said, Go and utterly destroy the sinners the Amalekites, and fight against them until they be consumed.

19 Wherefore then did you not obey the voice of the LORD, but did fly upon the spoil, and did evil in the sight of the LORD?

20 And Saul said unto Samuel, Yea, I have obeyed the voice of the LORD, and have gone the way which the LORD sent me, and have brought Agag the king of Amalek, and have utterly destroyed the Amalekites.

21 But the people took of the spoil, sheep and oxen, the chief of the things which should have been utterly destroyed, to sacrifice unto the LORD your God in Gilgal.

22 And Samuel said, Has the LORD as great delight in burnt offerings and sacrifices, as in obeying the voice of the LORD? Behold, to obey is better than sacrifice, and to hearken than the fat of rams.

23 For rebellion is as the sin of witchcraft, and stubbornness is as iniquity and idolatry. Because you have rejected the word of the LORD, he has also rejected you from being king.

24 And Saul said unto Samuel, I have sinned: for I have transgressed the commandment of the LORD, and your words: because I feared the people, and obeyed their voice.

25 Now therefore, I pray you, pardon my sin, and turn again with me, that I may worship the LORD.

26 And Samuel said unto Saul, I will not return with you: for you have rejected the word of the LORD, and the LORD has rejected you from being king over Israel.

27 And as Samuel turned about to go away, he laid hold upon the skirt of his mantle, and it rent.

28 And Samuel said unto him, The LORD has rent the kingdom of Israel from you this day, and has given it to a neighbour of yours, that is better than you .

29 And also the Strength of Israel will not lie nor repent: for he is not a man, that he should repent.

30 Then he said, I have sinned: yet honour me now, I pray you, before the elders of my people, and before Israel, and turn again with me, that I may worship the LORD your God.

31 So Samuel turned again after Saul; and Saul worshipped the LORD.

32 Then said Samuel, Bring you hither to me Agag the king of the Amalekites. And Agag came unto him delicately. And Agag said, Surely the bitterness of death is past.

33 And Samuel said, As your sword has made women childless, so shall your mother be childless among women. And Samuel hewed Agag in pieces before the LORD in Gilgal.

34 Then Samuel went to Ramah; and Saul went up to his house to Gibeah of Saul.

35 And Samuel came no more to see Saul until the day of his death: nevertheless Samuel mourned for Saul: and the LORD repented that he had made Saul king over Israel.

CHAPTER 16

AND the LORD said unto Samuel, How long will you mourn for Saul, seeing I have rejected him from reigning over Israel? fill yours horn with oil, and go, I will send you to Jesse the Beth-lehemite: for I have provided me a king among his sons.

2 And Samuel said, How can I go? if Saul hear it, he will kill me. And the LORD said, Take an heifer with you, and say, I am come to sacrifice to the LORD.

3 And call Jesse to the sacrifice, and I will shew you what you shalt do: and you shalt anoint unto me him whom I name unto you.

4 And Samuel did that which the LORD spake, and came to Beth-lehem. And the elders of the town trembled at his coming, and said, Comest you peaceably?

5 And he said, Peaceably: I am come to sacrifice unto the LORD: sanctify yourselves, and come with me to the sacrifice. And he sanctified Jesse and his sons, and called them to the sacrifice.

6 And it came to pass, when they were come, that he looked on Eliab, and said, Surely the LORD's anointed is before him.

7 But the LORD said unto Samuel, Look not on his countenance, or on the height of his stature; because I have refused him: for the LORD seeth not as man seeth; for man looketh on the outward appearance, but the LORD looketh on the heart.

8 Then Jesse called Abinadab, and made him pass before Samuel. And he said, Neither has the LORD chosen this.

9 Then Jesse made Shammah to pass by. And he said, Neither has the LORD chosen this.

10 Again, Jesse made seven of his sons to pass before Samuel. And Samuel said unto Jesse, The LORD has not chosen these.

11 And Samuel said unto Jesse, Are here all your children? And he said, There remaineth yet the youngest, and, behold, he keepeth the sheep. And Samuel said unto Jesse, Send and fetch him: for we will not sit down till he come hither.

12 And he sent, and brought him in. Now he was ruddy, and withal of a beautiful countenance, and goodly to look to. And the LORD said, Arise, anoint him: for this is he.

13 Then Samuel took the horn of oil, and anointed him in the midst of his brethren: and the Spirit of the LORD came upon David from that day forward. So Samuel rose up, and went to Ramah.

14 But the Spirit of the LORD departed from Saul, and an evil spirit from the LORD troubled him.

15 And Saul's servants said unto him, Behold now, an evil spirit from God troubleth you.

16 Let our lord now command your servants, which are before you, to seek out a man, who is a cunning player on an harp: and it shall come to pass, when the evil spirit from God is upon you, that he shall play with his hand, and you shalt be well.

17 And Saul said unto his servants, Provide me now a man that can play well, and bring him to me.

18 Then answered one of the servants, and said, Behold, I have seen a son of Jesse the Beth-lehemite, that is cunning in playing, and a mighty valiant man, and a man of war, and prudent in matters, and a comely person, and the LORD is with him.

19 Wherefore Saul sent messengers unto Jesse, and said, Send me David your son, which is with the sheep.

20 And Jesse took an ass laden with bread, and a bottle of wine, and a kid, and sent them by David his son unto Saul.

21 And David came to Saul, and stood before him: and he loved him greatly; and he became his armourbearer.

22 And Saul sent to Jesse, saying, Let David, I pray you, stand before me; for he has found favour in my sight.

23 And it came to pass, when the evil spirit from God was upon Saul, that David took an harp, and played with his hand: so Saul was refreshed, and was well, and the evil spirit departed from him.

CHAPTER 17

NOW the Philistines gathered together their armies to battle, and were gathered together at Shochoh, which belongeth to Judah, and pitched between Shochoh and Azekah, in Ephes-dammim.

2 And Saul and the men of Israel were gathered together, and pitched by the valley of Elah, and set the battle in array against the Philistines.

3 And the Philistines stood on a mountain on the one side, and Israel stood on a mountain on the other side: and there was a valley between them.

4 And there went out a champion out of the camp of the Philistines, named Goliath, of Gath, whose height was six cubits and a span.

5 And he had an helmet of brass upon his head, and he was armed with a coat of mail; and the weight of the coat was five thousand shekels of brass.

6 And he had greaves of brass upon his legs, and a target of brass between his shoulders.

7 And the staff of his spear was like a weaver's beam; and his spear's head weighed six hundred shekels of iron: and one bearing a shield went before him.

8 And he stood and cried unto the armies of Israel, and said unto them, Why are you come out to set your battle in array? am not I a Philistine, and you servants to Saul? choose you a man for you, and let him come down to me.

9 If he be able to fight with me, and to kill me, then will we be your servants: but if I prevail against him, and kill him, then shall you be our servants, and serve us.

10 And the Philistine said, I defy the armies of Israel this day; give me a man, that we may fight together.

11 When Saul and all Israel heard those words of the Philistine, they were dismayed, and greatly afraid.

12 Now David was the son of that Ephrathite of Beth-lehem-judah, whose name was Jesse; and he had eight sons: and the man went among men for an old man in the days of Saul.

13 And the three eldest sons of Jesse went and followed Saul to the battle: and the names of his three sons that went to the battle were Eliab the firstborn, and next unto him Abinadab, and the third Shammah.

14 And David was the youngest: and the three eldest followed Saul.

15 But David went and returned from Saul to feed his father's sheep at Beth-lehem.

16 And the Philistine drew near morning and evening, and presented himself forty days.

17 And Jesse said unto David his son, Take now for your brethren an ephah of this parched corn, and these ten loaves, and run to the camp to your brethren;

18 And carry these ten cheeses unto the captain of their thousand, and look how your brethren fare, and take their pledge.

19 Now Saul, and they, and all the men of Israel, were in the valley of Elah, fighting with the Philistines.

20 And David rose up early in the morning, and left the sheep with a keeper, and took, and went, as Jesse had commanded him; and he came to the trench, as the host was going forth to the fight, and shouted for the battle.

21 For Israel and the Philistines had put the battle in array, army against army.

22 And David left his carriage in the hand of the keeper of the carriage, and ran into the army, and came and saluted his brethren.

23 And as he talked with them, behold, there came up the champion, the Philistine of Gath, Goliath by name, out of the armies of the Philistines, and spake according to the same words: and David heard them.

24 And all the men of Israel, when they saw the man, fled from him, and were sore afraid.

25 And the men of Israel said, Have you seen this man that is come up? surely to defy Israel is he come up: and it shall be, that the man who killeth him, the king will enrich him with great riches, and will give him his daughter, and make his father's house free in Israel.

26 And David spake to the men that stood by him, saying, What shall be done to the man that killeth this Philistine, and taketh away the reproach from Israel? for who is this uncircumcised Philistine, that he should defy the armies of the living God?

27 And the people answered him after this manner, saying, So shall it be done to the man that killeth him.

28 And Eliab his eldest brother heard when he spake unto the men; and Eliab's anger was kindled against David, and he said, Why camest you down hither? and with whom have you left those few sheep in the wilderness? I know your pride, and the naughtiness of yours heart; for you are come down that you mightest see the battle.

29 And David said, What have I now done? Is there not a cause?

30 And he turned from him toward another, and spake after the same manner: and the people answered him again after the former manner.

31 And when the words were heard which David spake, they rehearsed them before Saul: and he sent for him.

32 And David said to Saul, Let no man's heart fail because of him; your servant will go and fight with this Philistine.

33 And Saul said to David, You are not able to go against this Philistine to fight with him: for you are but a youth, and he a man of war from his youth.

34 And David said unto Saul, Your servant kept his father's sheep, and there came a lion, and a bear, and took a lamb out of the flock:

35 And I went out after him, and struck him, and delivered it out of his mouth: and when he arose against me, I caught him by his beard, and struck him, and slew him.

36 Your servant slew both the lion and the bear: and this uncircumcised Philistine shall be as one of them, seeing he has defied the armies of the living God.

37 David said moreover, The LORD that delivered me out of the paw of the lion, and out of the paw of the bear, he will deliver me out of the hand of this Philistine. And Saul said unto David, Go, and the LORD be with you.

38 And Saul armed David with his armour, and he put an helmet of brass upon his head; also he armed him with a coat of mail.

39 And David girded his sword upon his armour, and he assayed to go; for he had not proved it. And David said unto Saul, I cannot go with these; for I have not proved them. And David put them off him.

40 And he took his staff in his hand, and chose him five smooth stones out of the brook, and put them in a shepherd's bag which he had, even in a scrip; and his sling was in his hand: and he drew near to the Philistine.

41 And the Philistine came on and drew near unto David; and the man that bare the shield went before him.

42 And when the Philistine looked about, and saw David, he disdained him: for he was but a youth, and ruddy, and of a fair countenance.

43 And the Philistine said unto David, Am I a dog, that you comest to me with staves? And the Philistine cursed David by his gods.

44 And the Philistine said to David, Come to me, and I will give your flesh unto the fowls of the air, and to the beasts of the field.

45 Then said David to the Philistine, You comest to me with a sword, and with a spear, and with a shield: but I come to you in the name of the LORD of hosts, the God of the armies of Israel, whom you have defied.

46 This day will the LORD deliver you into my hand; and I will strike you, and take yours head from you; and I will give the carcases of the host of the Philistines this day unto the fowls of the air, and to the wild beasts of the earth; that all the earth may know that there is a God in Israel.

47 And all this assembly shall know that the LORD saveth not with sword and spear: for the battle is the LORD's, and he will give you into our hands.

48 And it came to pass, when the Philistine arose, and came and drew nigh to meet David, that David hasted, and ran toward the army to meet the Philistine.

49 And David put his hand in his bag, and took thence a stone, and slang it, and struck the Philistine in his forehead, that the stone sunk into his forehead; and he fell upon his face to the earth.

50 So David prevailed over the Philistine with a sling and with a stone, and struck the Philistine, and slew him; but there was no sword in the hand of David.

51 Therefore David ran, and stood upon the Philistine, and took his sword, and drew it out of the sheath thereof, and slew him, and cut off his head therewith. And when the Philistines saw their champion was dead, they fled.

52 And the men of Israel and of Judah arose, and shouted, and pursued the Philistines, until you come to the valley, and to the gates of Ekron. And the wounded of the Philistines fell down by the way to Shaaraim, even unto Gath, and unto Ekron.

53 And the children of Israel returned from chasing after the Philistines, and they spoiled their tents.

54 And David took the head of the Philistine, and brought it to Jerusalem; but he put his armour in his tent.

55And when Saul saw David go forth against the Philistine, he said unto Abner, the captain of the host, Abner, whose son is this youth? And Abner said, As your soul liveth, O king, I cannot tell.

56 And the king said, Inquire you whose son the stripling is.

57 And as David returned from the slaughter of the Philistine, Abner took him, and brought him before Saul with the head of the Philistine in his hand.

58 And Saul said to him, Whose son are you , you young man? And David answered, I am the son of your servant Jesse the Beth-lehemite.

CHAPTER 18

AND it came to pass, when he had made an end of speaking unto Saul, that the soul of Jonathan was knit with the soul of David, and Jonathan loved him as his own soul.

2 And Saul took him that day, and would let him go no more home to his father's house.

3 Then Jonathan and David made a covenant, because he loved him as his own soul.

4 And Jonathan stripped himself of the robe that was upon him, and gave it to David, and his garments, even to his sword, and to his bow, and to his girdle.

5And David went out whithersoever Saul sent him, and behaved himself wisely: and Saul set him over the men of war, and he was accepted in the sight of all the people, and also in the sight of Saul's servants.

6 And it came to pass as they came, when David was returned from the slaughter of the Philistine, that the women came out of all cities of Israel, singing and dancing, to meet king Saul, with tabrets, with joy, and with instruments of musick.

7 And the women answered one another as they played, and said, Saul has slain his thousands, and David his ten thousands.

8 And Saul was very wroth, and the saying displeased him; and he said, They have ascribed unto David ten thousands, and to me they have ascribed but thousands: and what can he have more but the kingdom?

9 And Saul eyed David from that day and forward.

10And it came to pass on the morrow, that the evil spirit from God came upon Saul, and he prophesied in the midst of the house: and David played with his hand, as at other times: and there was a javelin in Saul's hand.

11 And Saul cast the javelin; for he said, I will strike David even to the wall with it. And David avoided out of his presence twice.

12And Saul was afraid of David, because the LORD was with him, and was departed from Saul.

13 Therefore Saul removed him from him, and made him his captain over a thousand; and he went out and came in before the people.

14 And David behaved himself wisely in all his ways; and the LORD was with him.

15 Wherefore when Saul saw that he behaved himself very wisely, he was afraid of him.

16 But all Israel and Judah loved David, because he went out and came in before them.

17And Saul said to David, Behold my elder daughter Merab, her will I give you to wife: only be you valiant for me, and fight the LORD's battles. For Saul said, Let not my hand be upon him, but let the hand of the Philistines be upon him.

18 And David said unto Saul, Who am I? and what is my life, or my father's family in Israel, that I should be son in law to the king?

19 But it came to pass at the time when Merab Saul's daughter should have been given to David, that she was given unto Adriel the Meholathite to wife.

20 And Michal Saul's daughter loved David: and they told Saul, and the thing pleased him.

21 And Saul said, I will give him her, that she may be a snare to him, and that the hand of the Philistines may be against him. Wherefore Saul said to David, You shalt this day be my son in law in the one of the twain.

22And Saul commanded his servants, saying, Commune with David secretly, and say, Behold, the king has delight in you, and all his servants love you: now therefore be the king's son in law.

23 And Saul's servants spake those words in the ears of David. And David said, Seemeth it to you a light thing to be a king's son in law, seeing that I am a poor man, and lightly esteemed?

24 And the servants of Saul told him, saying, On this manner spake David.

25 And Saul said, Thus shall you say to David, The king desireth not any dowry, but an hundred foreskins of the Philistines, to be avenged of the king's enemies. But Saul thought to make David fall by the hand of the Philistines.

26 And when his servants told David these words, it pleased David well to be the king's son in law: and the days were not expired.

27 Wherefore David arose and went, he and his men, and slew of the Philistines two hundred men; and David brought their foreskins, and they gave them in full tale to the king, that he might be the king's son in law. And Saul gave him Michal his daughter to wife.

28And Saul saw and knew that the LORD was with David, and that Michal Saul's daughter loved him.

29 And Saul was yet the more afraid of David; and Saul became David's enemy continually.

30 Then the princes of the Philistines went forth: and it came to pass, after they went forth, that David behaved himself more wisely than all the servants of Saul; so that his name was much set by.

CHAPTER 19

AND Saul spake to Jonathan his son, and to all his servants, that they should kill David.

2 But Jonathan Saul's son delighted much in David: and Jonathan told David, saying, Saul my father seeketh to kill you: now therefore, I pray you, take heed to yourself until the morning, and abide in a secret place, and hide yourself:

3 And I will go out and stand beside my father in the field where you are, and I will commune with my father of you; and what I see, that I will tell you.

4And Jonathan spake good of David unto Saul his father, and said unto him, Let not the king sin against his servant, against David; because he has not sinned against you, and because his works have been to you-ward very good:

5 For he did put his life in his hand, and slew the Philistine, and the LORD created a great salvation for all Israel: you sawest it, and did rejoice: wherefore then will you sin against innocent blood, to slay David without a cause?

6 And Saul hearkened unto the voice of Jonathan: and Saul sware, As the LORD liveth, he shall not be slain.

7 And Jonathan called David, and Jonathan shewed him all those things. And Jonathan brought David to Saul, and he was in his presence, as in times past.

8And there was war again: and David went out, and fought with the Philistines, and slew them with a great slaughter; and they fled from him.

9 And the evil spirit from the LORD was upon Saul, as he sat in his house with his javelin in his hand: and David played with his hand.

10 And Saul sought to strike David even to the wall with the javelin; but he slipped away out of Saul's presence, and he struck the javelin into the wall: and David fled, and escaped that night.

11 Saul also sent messengers unto David's house, to watch him, and to slay him in the morning: and Michal David's wife told him, saying, If you save not your life to night, to morrow you shalt be slain.

12So Michal let David down through a window: and he went, and fled, and escaped.

13 And Michal took an image, and laid it in the bed, and put a pillow of goats' hair for his bolster, and covered it with a cloth.

14 And when Saul sent messengers to take David, she said, He is sick.

15 And Saul sent the messengers again to see David, saying, Bring him up to me in the bed, that I may slay him.

16 And when the messengers were come in, behold, there was an image in the bed, with a pillow of goats' hair for his bolster.

17 And Saul said unto Michal, Why have you deceived me so, and sent away my enemy, that he is escaped? And Michal answered Saul, He said unto me, Let me go; why should I kill you?

18 So David fled, and escaped, and came to Samuel to Ramah, and told him all that Saul had done to him. And he and Samuel went and dwelt in Naioth.

19 And it was told Saul, saying, Behold, David is at Naioth in Ramah.

20 And Saul sent messengers to take David: and when they saw the company of the prophets prophesying, and Samuel standing as appointed over them, the Spirit of God was upon the messengers of Saul, and they also prophesied.

21 And when it was told Saul, he sent other messengers, and they prophesied likewise. And Saul sent messengers again the third time, and they prophesied also.

22 Then went he also to Ramah, and came to a great well that is in Sechu: and he asked and said, Where are Samuel and David? And one said, Behold, they be at Naioth in Ramah.

23 And he went thither to Naioth in Ramah: and the Spirit of God was upon him also, and he went on, and prophesied, until he came to Naioth in Ramah.

24 And he stripped off his clothes also, and prophesied before Samuel in like manner, and lay down naked all that day and all that night. Wherefore they say, Is Saul also among the prophets?

CHAPTER 20

AND David fled from Naioth in Ramah, and came and said before Jonathan, What have I done? what is my iniquity? and what is my sin before your father, that he seeketh my life?

2 And he said unto him, God forbid; you shalt not die: behold, my father will do nothing either great or small, but that he will shew it me: and why should my father hide this thing from me? it is not so.

3 And David sware moreover, and said, Your father certainly knoweth that I have found grace in yours eyes; and he saith, Let not Jonathan know this, lest he be grieved: but truly as the LORD liveth, and as your soul liveth, there is but a step between me and death.

4 Then said Jonathan unto David, Whatsoever your soul desireth, I will even do it for you.

5 And David said unto Jonathan, Behold, to morrow is the new moon, and I should not fail to sit with the king at meat: but let me go, that I may hide myself in the field unto the third day at even.

6 If your father at all miss me, then say, David earnestly asked leave of me that he might run to Beth-lehem his city: for there is a yearly sacrifice there for all the family.

7 If he say thus, It is well; your servant shall have peace: but if he be very wroth, then be sure that evil is determined by him.

8 Therefore you shalt deal kindly with your servant; for you have brought your servant into a covenant of the LORD with you: notwithstanding, if there be in me iniquity, slay me yourself; for why shouldest you bring me to your father?

9 And Jonathan said, Far be it from you: for if I knew certainly that evil were determined by my father to come upon you, then would not I tell it you?

10 Then said David to Jonathan, Who shall tell me? or what if your father answer you roughly?

11 And Jonathan said unto David, Come, and let us go out into the field. And they went out both of them into the field.

12 And Jonathan said unto David, O LORD God of Israel, when I have sounded my father about to morrow any time, or the third day, and, behold, if there be good toward David, and I then send not unto you, and shew it you;

13 The LORD do so and much more to Jonathan: but if it please my father to do you evil, then I will shew it you, and send you away, that you mayest go in peace: and the LORD be with you, as he has been with my father.

14 And you shalt not only while yet I live shew me the kindness of the LORD, that I die not:

15 But also you shalt not cut off your kindness from my house for ever: no, not when the LORD has cut off the enemies of David every one from the face of the earth.

16 So Jonathan made a covenant with the house of David, saying, Let the LORD even require it at the hand of David's enemies.

17 And Jonathan caused David to swear again, because he loved him: for he loved him as he loved his own soul.

18 Then Jonathan said to David, To morrow is the new moon: and you shalt be missed, because your seat will be empty.

19 And when you have stayed three days, then you shalt go down quickly, and come to the place where you did hide yourself when the business was in hand, and shalt remain by the stone Ezel.

20 And I will shoot three arrows on the side thereof, as though I shot at a mark.

21 And, behold, I will send a lad, saying, Go, find out the arrows. If I expressly say unto the lad, Behold, the arrows are on this side of you, take them; then come you : for there is peace to you, and no hurt; as the LORD liveth.

22 But if I say thus unto the young man, Behold, the arrows are beyond you; go your way: for the LORD has sent you away.

23 And as touching the matter which you and I have spoken of, behold, the LORD be between you and me for ever.

24 So David hid himself in the field: and when the new moon was come, the king sat him down to eat meat.

25 And the king sat upon his seat, as at other times, even upon a seat by the wall: and Jonathan arose, and Abner sat by Saul's side, and David's place was empty.

26 Nevertheless Saul spake not any thing that day: for he thought, Something has befallen him, he is not clean; surely he is not clean.

27 And it came to pass on the morrow, which was the second day of the month, that David's place was empty: and Saul said unto Jonathan his son, Wherefore comes not the son of Jesse to meat, neither yesterday, nor to day?

28 And Jonathan answered Saul, David earnestly asked leave of me to go to Beth-lehem:

29 And he said, Let me go, I pray you; for our family has a sacrifice in the city; and my brother, he has commanded me to be there: and now, if I have found favour in yours eyes, let me get away, I pray you, and see my brethren. Therefore he comes not unto the king's table.

30 Then Saul's anger was kindled against Jonathan, and he said unto him, You son of the perverse rebellious woman, do not I know that you have chosen the son of Jesse to yours own confusion, and unto the confusion of your mother's nakedness?

31 For as long as the son of Jesse liveth upon the ground, you shalt not be established, nor your kingdom. Wherefore now send and fetch him unto me, for he shall surely die.

32 And Jonathan answered Saul his father, and said unto him, Wherefore shall he be slain? what has he done?

33 And Saul cast a javelin at him to strike him: whereby Jonathan knew that it was determined of his father to slay David.

34 So Jonathan arose from the table in fierce anger, and did eat no meat the second day of the month: for he was grieved for David, because his father had done him shame.

35 And it came to pass in the morning, that Jonathan went out into the field at the time appointed with David, and a little lad with him.

36 And he said unto his lad, Run, find out now the arrows which I shoot. And as the lad ran, he shot an arrow beyond him.

37 And when the lad was come to the place of the arrow which Jonathan had shot, Jonathan cried after the lad, and said, Is not the arrow beyond you?

38 And Jonathan cried after the lad, Make speed, haste, stay not. And Jonathan's lad gathered up the arrows, and came to his master.

39 But the lad knew not any thing: only Jonathan and David knew the matter.

40 And Jonathan gave his artillery unto his lad, and said unto him, Go, carry them to the city.

41 And as soon as the lad was gone, David arose out of a place toward the south, and fell on his face to the ground, and bowed himself three times: and they kissed one another, and wept one with another, until David exceeded.

42 And Jonathan said to David, Go in peace, forasmuch as we have sworn both of us in the name of the LORD, saying, The LORD be between me and you, and between my seed and your seed for ever. And he arose and departed: and Jonathan went into the city.

CHAPTER 21

THEN came David to Nob to Ahimelech the priest: and Ahimelech was afraid at the meeting of David, and said unto him, Why are you alone, and no man with you?

2 And David said unto Ahimelech the priest, The king has commanded me a business, and has said unto me, Let no man know any thing of the business whereabout I send you, and what I have commanded you: and I have appointed my servants to such and such a place.

3 Now therefore what is under yours hand? give me five loaves of bread in my hand, or what there is present.

4 And the priest answered David, and said, There is no common bread under my hand, but there is hallowed bread; if the young men have kept themselves at least from women.

5 And David answered the priest, and said unto him, Of a truth women have been kept from us about these three days, since I came out, and the vessels of the young men are holy, and the bread is in a manner common, yea, though it were sanctified this day in the vessel.

6 So the priest gave him hallowed bread: for there was no bread there but the shewbread, that was taken from before the LORD, to put hot bread in the day when it was taken away.

7 Now a certain man of the servants of Saul was there that day, detained before the LORD; and his name was Doeg, an Edomite, the chiefest of the herdmen that belonged to Saul.

8And David said unto Ahimelech, And is there not here under yours hand spear or sword? for I have neither brought my sword nor my weapons with me, because the king's business required haste.

9 And the priest said, The sword of Goliath the Philistine, whom you slewest in the valley of Elah, behold, it is here wrapped in a cloth behind the ephod: if you will take that, take it: for there is no other save that here. And David said, There is none like that; give it me.

10And David arose, and fled that day for fear of Saul, and went to Achish the king of Gath.

11 And the servants of Achish said unto him, Is not this David the king of the land? did they not sing one to another of him in dances, saying, Saul has slain his thousands, and David his ten thousands?

12 And David laid up these words in his heart, and was sore afraid of Achish the king of Gath.

13 And he changed his behaviour before them, and feigned himself mad in their hands, and scrabbled on the doors of the gate, and let his spittle fall down upon his beard.

14 Then said Achish unto his servants, Lo, you see the man is mad: wherefore then have you brought him to me?

15 Have I need of mad men, that you have brought this fellow to play the mad man in my presence? shall this fellow come into my house?

CHAPTER 22

DAVID therefore departed thence, and escaped to the cave Adullam: and when his brethren and all his father's house heard it, they went down thither to him.

2 And every one that was in distress, and every one that was in debt, and every one that was discontented, gathered themselves unto him; and he became a captain over them: and there were with him about four hundred men.

3And David went thence to Mizpeh of Moab: and he said unto the king of Moab, Let my father and my mother, I pray you, come forth, and be with you, till I know what God will do for me.

4 And he brought them before the king of Moab: and they dwelt with him all the while that David was in the hold.

5And the prophet Gad said unto David, Abide not in the hold; depart, and get you into the land of Judah. Then David departed, and came into the forest of Hareth.

6When Saul heard that David was discovered, and the men that were with him, (now Saul abode in Gibeah under a tree in Ramah, having his spear in his hand, and all his servants were standing about him;)

7 Then Saul said unto his servants that stood about him, Hear now, you Benjamites; will the son of Jesse give every one of you fields and vineyards, and make you all captains of thousands, and captains of hundreds;

8 That all of you have conspired against me, and there is none that sheweth me that my son has made a league with the son of Jesse, and there is none of you that is sorry for me, or sheweth unto me that my son has stirred up my servant against me, to lie in wait, as at this day?

9Then answered Doeg the Edomite, which was set over the servants of Saul, and said, I saw the son of Jesse coming to Nob, to Ahimelech the son of Ahitub.

10 And he inquired of the LORD for him, and gave him victuals, and gave him the sword of Goliath the Philistine.

11 Then the king sent to call Ahimelech the priest, the son of Ahitub, and all his father's house, the priests that were in Nob: and they came all of them to the king.

12 And Saul said, Hear now, you son of Ahitub. And he answered, Here I am, my lord.

13 And Saul said unto him, Why have you conspired against me, you and the son of Jesse, in that you have given him bread, and a sword, and have inquired of God for him, that he should rise against me, to lie in wait, as at this day?

14 Then Ahimelech answered the king, and said, And who is so faithful among all your servants as David, which is the king's son in law, and goeth at your bidding, and is honourable in yours house?

15 Did I then begin to inquire of God for him? be it far from me: let not the king impute any thing unto his servant, nor to all the house of my father: for your servant knew nothing of all this, less or more.

16 And the king said, You shalt surely die, Ahimelech, you , and all your father's house.

17And the king said unto the footmen that stood about him, Turn, and slay the priests of the LORD; because their hand also is with David, and because they knew when he fled, and did not shew it to me. But the servants of the king would not put forth their hand to fall upon the priests of the LORD.

18 And the king said to Doeg, Turn you , and fall upon the priests. And Doeg the Edomite turned, and he fell upon the priests, and slew on that day fourscore and five persons that did wear a linen ephod.

19 And Nob, the city of the priests, struck he with the edge of the sword, both men and women, children and sucklings, and oxen, and asses, and sheep, with the edge of the sword.

20And one of the sons of Ahimelech the son of Ahitub, named Abiathar, escaped, and fled after David.

21 And Abiathar shewed David that Saul had slain the LORD's priests.

22 And David said unto Abiathar, I knew it that day, when Doeg the Edomite was there, that he would surely tell Saul: I have occasioned the death of all the persons of your father's house.

23 Abide you with me, fear not: for he that seeketh my life seeketh your life: but with me you shalt be in safeguard.

CHAPTER 23

THEN they told David, saying, Behold, the Philistines fight against Keilah, and they rob the threshingfloors.

2 Therefore David inquired of the LORD, saying, Shall I go and strike these Philistines? And the LORD said unto David, Go, and strike the Philistines, and save Keilah.

3 And David's men said unto him, Behold, we be afraid here in Judah: how much more then if we come to Keilah against the armies of the Philistines?

4 Then David inquired of the LORD yet again. And the LORD answered him and said, Arise, go down to Keilah; for I will deliver the Philistines into yours hand.

5 So David and his men went to Keilah, and fought with the Philistines, and brought away their cattle, and struck them with a great slaughter. So David saved the inhabitants of Keilah.

6 And it came to pass, when Abiathar the son of Ahimelech fled to David to Keilah, that he came down with an ephod in his hand.

7And it was told Saul that David was come to Keilah. And Saul said, God has delivered him into my hand; for he is shut in, by entering into a town that has gates and bars.

8 And Saul called all the people together to war, to go down to Keilah, to besiege David and his men.

9And David knew that Saul secretly practised mischief against him; and he said to Abiathar the priest, Bring hither the ephod.

10 Then said David, O LORD God of Israel, your servant has certainly heard that Saul seeketh to come to Keilah, to destroy the city for my sake.

11 Will the men of Keilah deliver me up into his hand? will Saul come down, as your servant has heard? O LORD God of Israel, I beseech you, tell your servant. And the LORD said, He will come down.

12 Then said David, Will the men of Keilah deliver me and my men into the hand of Saul? And the LORD said, They will deliver you up.

13Then David and his men, which were about six hundred, arose and departed out of Keilah, and went whithersoever they could go. And it was told Saul that David was escaped from Keilah; and he forbare to go forth.

14 And David abode in the wilderness in strong holds, and remained in a mountain in the wilderness of Ziph. And Saul sought him every day, but God delivered him not into his hand.

15 And David saw that Saul was come out to seek his life: and David was in the wilderness of Ziph in a wood.

16And Jonathan Saul's son arose, and went to David into the wood, and strengthened his hand in God.

17 And he said unto him, Fear not: for the hand of Saul my father shall not find you; and you shalt be king over Israel, and I shall be next unto you; and that also Saul my father knoweth.

18 And they two made a covenant before the LORD: and David abode in the wood, and Jonathan went to his house.

19Then came up the Ziphites to Saul to Gibeah, saying, Doth not David hide himself with us in strong holds in the wood, in the hill of Hachilah, which is on the south of Jeshimon?

20 Now therefore, O king, come down according to all the desire of your soul to come down; and our part shall be to deliver him into the king's hand.

21 And Saul said, Blessed be you of the LORD; for you have compassion on me.

22 Go, I pray you, prepare yet, and know and see his place where his haunt is, and who has seen him there: for it is told me that he dealeth very subtilly.

23 See therefore, and take knowledge of all the lurking places where he hideth himself, and come you again to me with the certainty, and I will go with you: and it shall come to pass, if he be in the land, that I will search him out throughout all the thousands of Judah.

24 And they arose, and went to Ziph before Saul: but David and his men were in the wilderness of Maon, in the plain on the south of Jeshimon.

25 Saul also and his men went to seek him. And they told David: wherefore he came down into a rock, and abode in the wilderness of Maon. And when Saul heard that, he pursued after David in the wilderness of Maon.

26 And Saul went on this side of the mountain, and David and his men on that side of the mountain: and David made haste to get away for fear of Saul; for Saul and his men compassed David and his men round about to take them.

27But there came a messenger unto Saul, saying, Haste you, and come; for the Philistines have invaded the land.

28 Wherefore Saul returned from pursuing after David, and went against the Philistines: therefore they called that place Sela-hammahlekoth.

29And David went up from thence, and dwelt in strong holds at En-gedi.

CHAPTER 24

AND it came to pass, when Saul was returned from following the Philistines, that it was told him, saying, Behold, David is in the wilderness of En-gedi.

2 Then Saul took three thousand chosen men out of all Israel, and went to seek David and his men upon the rocks of the wild goats.

3 And he came to the sheepcotes by the way, where was a cave; and Saul went in to cover his feet: and David and his men remained in the sides of the cave.

4 And the men of David said unto him, Behold the day of which the LORD said unto you, Behold, I will deliver yours enemy into yours hand, that you mayest do to him as it shall seem good unto you. Then David arose, and cut off the skirt of Saul's robe privily.

5 And it came to pass afterward, that David's heart struck him, because he had cut off Saul's skirt.

6 And he said unto his men, The LORD forbid that I should do this thing unto my master, the LORD's anointed, to stretch forth my hand against him, seeing he is the anointed of the LORD.

7 So David stayed his servants with these words, and suffered them not to rise against Saul. But Saul rose up out of the cave, and went on his way.

8 David also arose afterward, and went out of the cave, and cried after Saul, saying, My lord the king. And when Saul looked behind him, David stooped with his face to the earth, and bowed himself.

9And David said to Saul, Wherefore hearest you men's words, saying, Behold, David seeketh your hurt?

10 Behold, this day yours eyes have seen how that the LORD had delivered you to day into my hand in the cave: and some bade me kill you: but my eye spared you; and I said, I will not put forth my hand against my lord; for he is the LORD's anointed.

11 Moreover, my father, see, yea, see the skirt of your robe in my hand: for in that I cut off the skirt of your robe, and killed you not, know you and see that there is neither evil nor transgression in my hand, and I have not sinned against you; yet you huntest my soul to take it.

12 The LORD judge between me and you, and the LORD avenge me of you: but my hand shall not be upon you.

13 As saith the proverb of the ancients, Wickedness proceedeth from the wicked: but my hand shall not be upon you.

14 After whom is the king of Israel come out? after whom dost you pursue? after a dead dog, after a flea.

15 The LORD therefore be judge, and judge between me and you, and see, and plead my cause, and deliver me out of yours hand.

16And it came to pass, when David had made an end of speaking these words unto Saul, that Saul said, Is this your voice, my son David? And Saul lifted up his voice, and wept.

17 And he said to David, You are more righteous than I: for you have rewarded me good, whereas I have rewarded you evil.

18 And you have shewed this day how that you have dealt well with me: forasmuch as when the LORD had delivered me into yours hand, you killedst me not.

19 For if a man find his enemy, will he let him go well away? wherefore the LORD reward you good for that you have done unto me this day.

20 And now, behold, I know well that you shalt surely be king, and that the kingdom of Israel shall be established in yours hand.

21 Swear now therefore unto me by the LORD, that you will not cut off my seed after me, and that you will not destroy my name out of my father's house.

22 And David sware unto Saul. And Saul went home; but David and his men gat them up unto the hold.

CHAPTER 25

AND Samuel died; and all the Israelites were gathered together, and lamented him, and buried him in his house at Ramah. And David arose, and went down to the wilderness of Paran.

2 And there was a man in Maon, whose possessions were in Carmel; and the man was very great, and he had three thousand sheep, and a thousand goats: and he was shearing his sheep in Carmel.

3 Now the name of the man was Nabal; and the name of his wife Abigail: and she was a woman of good understanding, and of a beautiful countenance: but the man was churlish and evil in his doings; and he was of the house of Caleb.

4And David heard in the wilderness that Nabal did shear his sheep.

5 And David sent out ten young men, and David said unto the young men, Get you up to Carmel, and go to Nabal, and greet him in my name:

6 And thus shall you say to him that liveth in prosperity, Peace be both to you, and peace be to yours house, and peace be unto all that you have.

7 And now I have heard that you have shearers: now your shepherds which were with us, we hurt them not, neither was there ought missing unto them, all the while they were in Carmel.

8 Ask your young men, and they will shew you. Wherefore let the young men find favour in yours eyes: for we come in a good day: give, I pray you, whatsoever comes to yours hand unto your servants, and to your son David.

9 And when David's young men came, they spake to Nabal according to all those words in the name of David, and ceased.

10And Nabal answered David's servants, and said, Who is David? and who is the son of Jesse? there be many servants now a days that break away every man from his master.

11 Shall I then take my bread, and my water, and my flesh that I have killed for my shearers, and give it unto men, whom I know not whence they be?

12 So David's young men turned their way, and went again, and came and told him all those sayings.

13 And David said unto his men, Gird you on every man his sword. And they girded on every man his sword; and David also girded on his sword: and there went up after David about four hundred men; and two hundred abode by the stuff.

14But one of the young men told Abigail, Nabal's wife, saying, Behold, David sent messengers out of the wilderness to salute our master; and he railed on them.

15 But the men were very good unto us, and we were not hurt, neither missed we any thing, as long as we were conversant with them, when we were in the fields:

16 They were a wall unto us both by night and day, all the while we were with them keeping the sheep.

17 Now therefore know and consider what you will do; for evil is determined against our master, and against all his household: for he is such a son of Belial, that a man cannot speak to him.

18Then Abigail made haste, and took two hundred loaves, and two bottles of wine, and five sheep ready dressed, and five measures of parched corn, and an hundred clusters of raisins, and two hundred cakes of figs, and laid them on asses.

19 And she said unto her servants, Go on before me; behold, I come after you. But she told not her husband Nabal.

20 And it was so, as she rode on the ass, that she came down by the covert of the hill, and, behold, David and his men came down against her; and she met them.

21 Now David had said, Surely in vain have I kept all that this fellow has in the wilderness, so that nothing was missed of all that pertained unto him: and he has requited me evil for good.

22 So and more also do God unto the enemies of David, if I leave of all that pertain to him by the morning light any that pisseth against the wall.

23 And when Abigail saw David, she hasted, and lighted off the ass, and fell before David on her face, and bowed herself to the ground,

24 And fell at his feet, and said, Upon me, my lord, upon me let this iniquity be: and let yours handmaid, I pray you, speak in yours audience, and hear the words of yours handmaid.

25 Let not my lord, I pray you, regard this man of Belial, even Nabal: for as his name is, so is he; Nabal is his name, and folly is with him: but I yours handmaid saw not the young men of my lord, whom you did send.

26 Now therefore, my lord, as the LORD liveth, and as your soul liveth, seeing the LORD has withholden you from coming to shed blood, and from avenging yourself with yours own hand, now let yours enemies, and they that seek evil to my lord, be as Nabal.

27 And now this blessing which yours handmaid has brought unto my lord, let it even be given unto the young men that follow my lord.

28 I pray you, forgive the trespass of yours handmaid: for the LORD will certainly make my lord a sure house; because my lord fighteth the battles of the LORD, and evil has not been found in you all your days.

29 Yet a man is risen to pursue you, and to seek your soul: but the soul of my lord shall be bound in the bundle of life with the LORD your God; and the souls of yours enemies, them shall he sling out, as out of the middle of a sling.

30 And it shall come to pass, when the LORD shall have done to my lord according to all the good that he has spoken concerning you, and shall have appointed you ruler over Israel;

31 That this shall be no grief unto you, nor offence of heart unto my lord, either that you have shed blood causeless, or that my lord has avenged himself: but when the LORD shall have dealt well with my lord, then remember yours handmaid.

32And David said to Abigail, Blessed be the LORD God of Israel, which sent you this day to meet me:

33 And blessed be your advice, and blessed be you , which have kept me this day from coming to shed blood, and from avenging myself with my own hand.

34 For in very deed, as the LORD God of Israel liveth, which has kept me back from hurting you, except you hadst hasted and come to meet me, surely there had not been left unto Nabal by the morning light any that pisseth against the wall.

35 So David received of her hand that which she had brought him, and said unto her, Go up in peace to yours house; see, I have hearkened to your voice, and have accepted your person.

36And Abigail came to Nabal; and, behold, he held a feast in his house, like the feast of a king; and Nabal's heart was merry within him, for he was very drunken: wherefore she told him nothing, less or more, until the morning light.

37 But it came to pass in the morning, when the wine was gone out of Nabal, and his wife had told him these things, that his heart died within him, and he became as a stone.

38 And it came to pass about ten days after, that the LORD struck Nabal, that he died.

39And when David heard that Nabal was dead, he said, Blessed be the LORD, that has pleaded the cause of my reproach from the hand of Nabal, and has kept his servant from evil: for the LORD has returned the wickedness of Nabal upon his own head. And David sent and communed with Abigail, to take her to him to wife.

40 And when the servants of David were come to Abigail to Carmel, they spake unto her, saying, David sent us unto you, to take you to him to wife.

41 And she arose, and bowed herself on her face to the earth, and said, Behold, let yours handmaid be a servant to wash the feet of the servants of my lord.

42 And Abigail hasted, and arose, and rode upon an ass, with five damsels of hers that went after her; and she went after the messengers of David, and became his wife.

43 David also took Ahinoam of Jezreel; and they were also both of them his wives.

44But Saul had given Michal his daughter, David's wife, to Phalti the son of Laish, which was of Gallim.

CHAPTER 26

AND the Ziphites came unto Saul to Gibeah, saying, Doth not David hide himself in the hill of Hachilah, which is before Jeshimon?

2 Then Saul arose, and went down to the wilderness of Ziph, having three thousand chosen men of Israel with him, to seek David in the wilderness of Ziph.

3 And Saul pitched in the hill of Hachilah, which is before Jeshimon, by the way. But David abode in the wilderness, and he saw that Saul came after him into the wilderness.

4 David therefore sent out spies, and understood that Saul was come in very deed.

5And David arose, and came to the place where Saul had pitched: and David beheld the place where Saul lay, and Abner the son of Ner, the captain of his host: and Saul lay in the trench, and the people pitched round about him.

6 Then answered David and said to Ahimelech the Hittite, and to Abishai the son of Zeruiah, brother to Joab, saying, Who will go down with me to Saul to the camp? And Abishai said, I will go down with you.

7 So David and Abishai came to the people by night: and, behold, Saul lay sleeping within the trench, and his spear stuck in the ground at his bolster: but Abner and the people lay round about him.

8 Then said Abishai to David, God has delivered yours enemy into yours hand this day: now therefore let me strike him, I pray you, with the spear even to the earth at once, and I will not strike him the second time.

9 And David said to Abishai, Destroy him not: for who can stretch forth his hand against the LORD's anointed, and be guiltless?

10 David said furthermore, As the LORD liveth, the LORD shall strike him; or his day shall come to die; or he shall descend into battle, and perish.

11 The LORD forbid that I should stretch forth my hand against the LORD's anointed: but, I pray you, take you now the spear that is at his bolster, and the cruse of water, and let us go.

12 So David took the spear and the cruse of water from Saul's bolster; and they gat them away, and no man saw it, nor knew it, neither awaked: for they were all asleep; because a deep sleep from the LORD was fallen upon them.

13Then David went over to the other side, and stood on the top of an hill afar off; a great space being between them:

14 And David cried to the people, and to Abner the son of Ner, saying, Answerest you not, Abner? Then Abner answered and said, Who are you that criest to the king?

15 And David said to Abner, Are not you a valiant man? and who is like to you in Israel? wherefore then have you not kept your lord the king? for there came one of the people in to destroy the king your lord.

16 This thing is not good that you have done. As the LORD liveth, you are worthy to die, because you have not kept your master, the LORD's anointed. And now see where the king's spear is, and the cruse of water that was at his bolster.

17 And Saul knew David's voice, and said, Is this your voice, my son David? And David said, It is my voice, my lord, O king.

18 And he said, Wherefore doth my lord thus pursue after his servant? for what have I done? or what evil is in my hand?

19 Now therefore, I pray you, let my lord the king hear the words of his servant. If the LORD have stirred you up against me, let him accept an offering: but if they be the children of men, cursed be they before the LORD; for they have driven me out this day from abiding in the inheritance of the LORD, saying, Go, serve other gods.

20 Now therefore, let not my blood fall to the earth before the face of the LORD: for the king of Israel is come out to seek a flea, as when one doth hunt a partridge in the mountains.

21Then said Saul, I have sinned: return, my son David: for I will no more do you harm, because my soul was precious in yours eyes this day: behold, I have played the fool, and have erred exceedingly.

22 And David answered and said, Behold the king's spear! and let one of the young men come over and fetch it.

23 The LORD render to every man his righteousness and his faithfulness: for the LORD delivered you into my hand to day, but I would not stretch forth my hand against the LORD's anointed.

24 And, behold, as your life was much set by this day in my eyes, so let my life be much set by in the eyes of the LORD, and let him deliver me out of all tribulation.

25 Then Saul said to David, Blessed be you , my son David: you shalt both do great things, and also shalt still prevail. So David went on his way, and Saul returned to his place.

CHAPTER 27

AND David said in his heart, I shall now perish one day by the hand of Saul: there is nothing better for me than that I should speedily escape into the land of the Philistines; and Saul shall despair of me, to seek me any more in any coast of Israel: so shall I escape out of his hand.

2 And David arose, and he passed over with the six hundred men that were with him unto Achish, the son of Maoch, king of Gath.

3 And David dwelt with Achish at Gath, he and his men, every man with his household, even David with his two wives, Ahinoam the Jezreelitess, and Abigail the Carmelitess, Nabal's wife.

4 And it was told Saul that David was fled to Gath: and he sought no more again for him.

5And David said unto Achish, If I have now found grace in yours eyes, let them give me a place in some town in the country, that I may dwell there: for why should your servant dwell in the royal city with you?

6 Then Achish gave him Ziklag that day: wherefore Ziklag pertaineth unto the kings of Judah unto this day.

7 And the time that David dwelt in the country of the Philistines was a full year and four months.

8And David and his men went up, and invaded the Geshurites, and the Gezrites, and the Amalekites: for those nations were of old the inhabitants of the land, as you go to Shur, even unto the land of Egypt.

9 And David struck the land, and left neither man nor woman alive, and took away the sheep, and the oxen, and the asses, and the camels, and the apparel, and returned, and came to Achish.

10 And Achish said, Whither have you made a road to day? And David said, Against the south of Judah, and against the south of the Jerahmeelites, and against the south of the Kenites.

11 And David saved neither man nor woman alive, to bring tidings to Gath, saying, Lest they should tell on us, saying, So did David, and so will be his manner all the while he dwelleth in the country of the Philistines.

12 And Achish believed David, saying, He has made his people Israel utterly to abhor him; therefore he shall be my servant for ever.

CHAPTER 28

AND it came to pass in those days, that the Philistines gathered their armies together for warfare, to fight with Israel. And Achish said unto David, Know you assuredly, that you shalt go out with me to battle, you and your men.

2 And David said to Achish, Surely you shalt know what your servant can do. And Achish said to David, Therefore will I make you keeper of my head for ever.

3Now Samuel was dead, and all Israel had lamented him, and buried him in Ramah, even in his own city. And Saul had put away those that had familiar spirits, and the wizards, out of the land.

4 And the Philistines gathered themselves together, and came and pitched in Shunem: and Saul gathered all Israel together, and they pitched in Gilboa.

5 And when Saul saw the host of the Philistines, he was afraid, and his heart greatly trembled.

6 And when Saul inquired of the LORD, the LORD answered him not, neither by dreams, nor by Urim, nor by prophets.

7 Then said Saul unto his servants, Seek me a woman that has a familiar spirit, that I may go to her, and inquire of her. And his servants said to him, Behold, there is a woman that has a familiar spirit at Endor.

8 And Saul disguised himself, and put on other raiment, and he went, and two men with him, and they came to the woman by night: and he said, I pray you, divine unto me by the familiar spirit, and bring me him up, whom I shall name unto you.

9 And the woman said unto him, Behold, you knowest what Saul has done, how he has cut off those that have familiar spirits, and the wizards, out of the land: wherefore then layest you a snare for my life, to cause me to die?

10 And Saul sware to her by the LORD, saying, As the LORD liveth, there shall no punishment happen to you for this thing.

11 Then said the woman, Whom shall I bring up unto you? And he said, Bring me up Samuel.

12 And when the woman saw Samuel, she cried with a loud voice: and the woman spake to Saul, saying, Why have you deceived me? for you are Saul.

13 And the king said unto her, Be not afraid: for what sawest you ? And the woman said unto Saul, I saw gods ascending out of the earth.

14 And he said unto her, What form is he of? And she said, An old man comes up; and he is covered with a mantle. And Saul perceived that it was Samuel, and he stooped with his face to the ground, and bowed himself.

15 And Samuel said to Saul, Why have you disquieted me, to bring me up? And Saul answered, I am sore distressed; for the Philistines make war against me, and God is departed from me, and answereth me no more, neither by prophets, nor by dreams: therefore I have called you, that you mayest make known unto me what I shall do.

16 Then said Samuel, Wherefore then dost you ask of me, seeing the LORD is departed from you, and is become yours enemy?

17 And the LORD has done to him, as he spake by me: for the LORD has rent the kingdom out of yours hand, and given it to your neighbour, even to David:

18 Because you obeyedst not the voice of the LORD, nor executedst his fierce wrath upon Amalek, therefore has the LORD done this thing unto you this day.

19 Moreover the LORD will also deliver Israel with you into the hand of the Philistines: and to morrow shalt you and your sons be with me: the LORD also shall deliver the host of Israel into the hand of the Philistines.

20 Then Saul fell straightway all along on the earth, and was sore afraid, because of the words of Samuel: and there was no strength in him; for he had eaten no bread all the day, nor all the night.

21 And the woman came unto Saul, and saw that he was sore troubled, and said unto him, Behold, yours handmaid has obeyed your voice, and I have put my life in my hand, and have hearkened unto your words which you spakest unto me.

22 Now therefore, I pray you, hearken you also unto the voice of yours handmaid, and let me set a morsel of bread before you; and eat, that you mayest have strength, when you go on your way.

23 But he refused, and said, I will not eat. But his servants, together with the woman, compelled him; and he hearkened unto their voice. So he arose from the earth, and sat upon the bed.

24 And the woman had a fat calf in the house; and she hasted, and killed it, and took flour, and kneaded it, and did bake unleavened bread thereof:

25 And she brought it before Saul, and before his servants; and they did eat. Then they rose up, and went away that night.

CHAPTER 29

NOW the Philistines gathered together all their armies to Aphek: and the Israelites pitched by a fountain which is in Jezreel.

2 And the lords of the Philistines passed on by hundreds, and by thousands: but David and his men passed on in the rereward with Achish.

3 Then said the princes of the Philistines, What do these Hebrews here? And Achish said unto the princes of the Philistines, Is not this David, the servant of Saul the king of Israel, which has been with me these days, or these years, and I have found no fault in him since he fell unto me unto this day?

4 And the princes of the Philistines were wroth with him; and the princes of the Philistines said unto him, Make this fellow return, that he may go again to his place which you have appointed him, and let him not go down with us to battle, lest in the battle he be an adversary to us: for wherewith should he reconcile himself unto his master? should it not be with the heads of these men?

5 Is not this David, of whom they sang one to another in dances, saying, Saul slew his thousands, and David his ten thousands?

6 Then Achish called David, and said unto him, Surely, as the LORD liveth, you have been upright, and your going out and your coming in with me in the host is good in my sight: for I have not found evil in you since the day of your coming unto me unto this day: nevertheless the lords favour you not.

7 Wherefore now return, and go in peace, that you displease not the lords of the Philistines.

8 And David said unto Achish, But what have I done? and what have you found in your servant so long as I have been with you unto this day, that I may not go fight against the enemies of my lord the king?

9 And Achish answered and said to David, I know that you are good in my sight, as an angel of God: notwithstanding the princes of the Philistines have said, He shall not go up with us to the battle.

10 Wherefore now rise up early in the morning with your master's servants that are come with you: and as soon as you be up early in the morning, and have light, depart.

11 So David and his men rose up early to depart in the morning, to return into the land of the Philistines. And the Philistines went up to Jezreel.

CHAPTER 30

AND it came to pass, when David and his men were come to Ziklag on the third day, that the Amalekites had invaded the south, and Ziklag, and smitten Ziklag, and burned it with fire;

2 And had taken the women captives, that were therein: they slew not any, either great or small, but carried them away, and went on their way.

3 So David and his men came to the city, and, behold, it was burned with fire; and their wives, and their sons, and their daughters, were taken captives.

4 Then David and the people that were with him lifted up their voice and wept, until they had no more power to weep.

5 And David's two wives were taken captives, Ahinoam the Jezreelitess, and Abigail the wife of Nabal the Carmelite.

6 And David was greatly distressed; for the people spake of stoning him, because the soul of all the people was grieved, every man for his sons and for his daughters: but David encouraged himself in the LORD his God.

7 And David said to Abiathar the priest, Ahimelech's son, I pray you, bring me hither the ephod. And Abiathar brought thither the ephod to David.

8 And David inquired at the LORD, saying, Shall I pursue after this troop? shall I overtake them? And he answered him, Pursue: for you shalt surely overtake them, and without fail recover all.

9 So David went, he and the six hundred men that were with him, and came to the brook Besor, where those that were left behind stayed.

10 But David pursued, he and four hundred men: for two hundred abode behind, which were so faint that they could not go over the brook Besor.

11 And they found an Egyptian in the field, and brought him to David, and gave him bread, and he did eat; and they made him drink water;

12 And they gave him a piece of a cake of figs, and two clusters of raisins: and when he had eaten, his spirit came again to him: for he had eaten no bread, nor drunk any water, three days and three nights.

13 And David said unto him, To whom belongest you ? and whence are you ? And he said, I am a young man of Egypt, servant to an Amalekite; and my master left me, because three days agone I fell sick.

14 We made an invasion upon the south of the Cherethites, and upon the coast which belongeth to Judah, and upon the south of Caleb; and we burned Ziklag with fire.

15 And David said to him, Can you bring me down to this company? And he said, Swear unto me by God, that you will neither kill me, nor deliver me into the hands of my master, and I will bring you down to this company.

16 And when he had brought him down, behold, they were spread abroad upon all the earth, eating and drinking, and dancing, because of all the great spoil that they had taken out of the land of the Philistines, and out of the land of Judah.

17 And David struck them from the twilight even unto the evening of the next day: and there escaped not a man of them, save four hundred young men, which rode upon camels, and fled.

18 And David recovered all that the Amalekites had carried away: and David rescued his two wives.

19 And there was nothing lacking to them, neither small nor great, neither sons nor daughters, neither spoil, nor any thing that they had taken to them: David recovered all.

20 And David took all the flocks and the herds, which they drave before those other cattle, and said, This is David's spoil.

21 And David came to the two hundred men, which were so faint that they could not follow David, whom they had made also to abide at the brook Besor: and they went forth to meet David, and to meet the people that were with him: and when David came near to the people, he saluted them.

22 Then answered all the wicked men and men of Belial, of those that went with David, and said, Because they went not with us, we will not give them ought of the spoil that we have recovered, save to every man his wife and his children, that they may lead them away, and depart.

23 Then said David, You shall not do so, my brethren, with that which the LORD has given us, who has preserved us, and delivered the company that came against us into our hand.

24 For who will hearken unto you in this matter? but as his part is that goeth down to the battle, so shall his part be that tarrieth by the stuff: they shall part alike.

25 And it was so from that day forward, that he made it a statute and an ordinance for Israel unto this day.

26 And when David came to Ziklag, he sent of the spoil unto the elders of Judah, even to his friends, saying, Behold a present for you of the spoil of the enemies of the LORD;

27 To them which were in Beth-el, and to them which were in south Ramoth, and to them which were in Jattir,

28 And to them which were in Aroer, and to them which were in Siphmoth, and to them which were in Eshtemoa,

29 And to them which were in Rachal, and to them which were in the cities of the Jerahmeelites, and to them which were in the cities of the Kenites,

30 And to them which were in Hormah, and to them which were in Chor-ashan, and to them which were in Athach,

31 And to them which were in Hebron, and to all the places where David himself and his men were wont to haunt.

CHAPTER 31

NOW the Philistines fought against Israel: and the men of Israel fled from before the Philistines, and fell down slain in mount Gilboa.

2 And the Philistines followed hard upon Saul and upon his sons; and the Philistines slew Jonathan, and Abinadab, and Malchi-shua, Saul's sons.

3 And the battle went sore against Saul, and the archers hit him; and he was sore wounded of the archers.

4 Then said Saul unto his armourbearer, Draw your sword, and thrust me through therewith; lest these uncircumcised come and thrust me through, and abuse me. But his armourbearer would not; for he was sore afraid. Therefore Saul took a sword, and fell upon it.

5 And when his armourbearer saw that Saul was dead, he fell likewise upon his sword, and died with him.

6 So Saul died, and his three sons, and his armourbearer, and all his men, that same day together.

7 And when the men of Israel that were on the other side of the valley, and they that were on the other side Jordan, saw that the men of Israel fled, and that Saul and his sons were dead, they forsook the cities, and fled; and the Philistines came and dwelt in them.

8 And it came to pass on the morrow, when the Philistines came to strip the slain, that they found Saul and his three sons fallen in mount Gilboa.

9 And they cut off his head, and stripped off his armour, and sent into the land of the Philistines round about, to publish it in the house of their idols, and among the people.

10 And they put his armour in the house of Ashtaroth: and they fastened his body to the wall of Beth-shan.

11 And when the inhabitants of Jabesh-gilead heard of that which the Philistines had done to Saul;

12 All the valiant men arose, and went all night, and took the body of Saul and the bodies of his sons from the wall of Beth-shan, and came to Jabesh, and burnt them there.

13 And they took their bones, and buried them under a tree at Jabesh, and fasted seven days.

THE
SECOND BOOK OF SAMUEL,
OTHERWISE CALLED,
THE SECOND BOOK OF THE KINGS.

CHAPTER 1

NOW it came to pass after the death of Saul, when David was returned from the slaughter of the Amalekites, and David had abode two days in Ziklag;

2 It came even to pass on the third day, that, behold, a man came out of the camp from Saul with his clothes rent, and earth upon his head: and so it was, when he came to David, that he fell to the earth, and did obeisance.

3 And David said unto him, From whence comest you ? And he said unto him, Out of the camp of Israel am I escaped.

4 And David said unto him, How went the matter? I pray you, tell me. And he answered, That the people are fled from the battle, and many of the people also are fallen and dead; and Saul and Jonathan his son are dead also.

5 And David said unto the young man that told him, How knowest you that Saul and Jonathan his son be dead?

6 And the young man that told him said, As I happened by chance upon mount Gilboa, behold, Saul leaned upon his spear; and, lo, the chariots and horsemen followed hard after him.

7 And when he looked behind him, he saw me, and called unto me. And I answered, Here am I.

8 And he said unto me, Who are you ? And I answered him, I am an Amalekite.

9 He said unto me again, Stand, I pray you, upon me, and slay me: for anguish is come upon me, because my life is yet whole in me.

10 So I stood upon him, and slew him, because I was sure that he could not live after that he was fallen: and I took the crown that was upon his head, and the bracelet that was on his arm, and have brought them hither unto my lord.

11 Then David took hold on his clothes, and rent them; and likewise all the men that were with him:

12 And they mourned, and wept, and fasted until even, for Saul, and for Jonathan his son, and for the people of the LORD, and for the house of Israel; because they were fallen by the sword.

13 And David said unto the young man that told him, Whence are you ? And he answered, I am the son of a stranger, an Amalekite.

14 And David said unto him, How wast you not afraid to stretch forth yours hand to destroy the LORD's anointed?

15 And David called one of the young men, and said, Go near, and fall upon him. And he struck him that he died.

16 And David said unto him, Your blood be upon your head; for your mouth has testified against you, saying, I have slain the LORD's anointed.

17 And David lamented with this lamentation over Saul and over Jonathan his son:

18 (Also he bade them teach the children of Judah the use of the bow: behold, it is written in the book of Jasher.)

19 The beauty of Israel is slain upon your high places: how are the mighty fallen!

20 Tell it not in Gath, publish it not in the streets of Askelon; lest the daughters of the Philistines rejoice, lest the daughters of the uncircumcised triumph.

21 You mountains of Gilboa, let there be no dew, neither let there be rain, upon you, nor fields of offerings: for there the shield of the mighty is vilely cast away, the shield of Saul, as though he had not been anointed with oil.

22 From the blood of the slain, from the fat of the mighty, the bow of Jonathan turned not back, and the sword of Saul returned not empty.

23 Saul and Jonathan were lovely and pleasant in their lives, and in their death they were not divided: they were swifter than eagles, they were stronger than lions.

24 You daughters of Israel, weep over Saul, who clothed you in scarlet, with other delights, who put on ornaments of gold upon your apparel.

25 How are the mighty fallen in the midst of the battle! O Jonathan, you wast slain in yours high places.

26 I am distressed for you, my brother Jonathan: very pleasant have you been unto me: your love to me was wonderful, passing the love of women.

27 How are the mighty fallen, and the weapons of war perished!

CHAPTER 2

AND it came to pass after this, that David inquired of the LORD, saying, Shall I go up into any of the cities of Judah? And the LORD said unto him, Go up. And David said, Whither shall I go up? And he said, Unto Hebron.

2 So David went up thither, and his two wives also, Ahinoam the Jezreelitess, and Abigail Nabal's wife the Carmelite.

3 And his men that were with him did David bring up, every man with his household: and they dwelt in the cities of Hebron.

4 And the men of Judah came, and there they anointed David king over the house of Judah. And they told David, saying, That the men of Jabesh-gilead were they that buried Saul.

5And David sent messengers unto the men of Jabesh-gilead, and said unto them, Blessed be you of the LORD, that you have shewed this kindness unto your lord, even unto Saul, and have buried him.

6 And now the LORD shew kindness and truth unto you: and I also will requite you this kindness, because you have done this thing.

7 Therefore now let your hands be strengthened, and be you valiant: for your master Saul is dead, and also the house of Judah have anointed me king over them.

8But Abner the son of Ner, captain of Saul's host, took Ish-bosheth the son of Saul, and brought him over to Mahanaim;

9 And made him king over Gilead, and over the Ashurites, and over Jezreel, and over Ephraim, and over Benjamin, and over all Israel.

10 Ish-bosheth Saul's son was forty years old when he began to reign over Israel, and reigned two years. But the house of Judah followed David.

11 And the time that David was king in Hebron over the house of Judah was seven years and six months.

12And Abner the son of Ner, and the servants of Ish-bosheth the son of Saul, went out from Mahanaim to Gibeon.

13 And Joab the son of Zeruiah, and the servants of David, went out, and met together by the pool of Gibeon: and they sat down, the one on the one side of the pool, and the other on the other side of the pool.

14 And Abner said to Joab, Let the young men now arise, and play before us. And Joab said, Let them arise.

15 Then there arose and went over by number twelve of Benjamin, which pertained to Ish-bosheth the son of Saul, and twelve of the servants of David.

16 And they caught every one his fellow by the head, and thrust his sword in his fellow's side; so they fell down together: wherefore that place was called Helkath-hazzurim, which is in Gibeon.

17 And there was a very sore battle that day; and Abner was beaten, and the men of Israel, before the servants of David.

18And there were three sons of Zeruiah there, Joab, and Abishai, and Asahel: and Asahel was as light of foot as a wild roe.

19 And Asahel pursued after Abner; and in going he turned not to the right hand nor to the left from following Abner.

20 Then Abner looked behind him, and said, Are you Asahel? And he answered, I am.

21 And Abner said to him, Turn you aside to your right hand or to your left, and lay you hold on one of the young men, and take you his armour. But Asahel would not turn aside from following of him.

22 And Abner said again to Asahel, Turn you aside from following me: wherefore should I strike you to the ground? how then should I hold up my face to Joab your brother?

23 Howbeit he refused to turn aside: wherefore Abner with the hinder end of the spear struck him under the fifth rib, that the spear came out behind him; and he fell down there, and died in the same place: and it came to pass, that as many as came to the place where Asahel fell down and died stood still.

24 Joab also and Abishai pursued after Abner: and the sun went down when they were come to the hill of Ammah, that lies before Giah by the way of the wilderness of Gibeon.

25And the children of Benjamin gathered themselves together after Abner, and became one troop, and stood on the top of an hill.

26 Then Abner called to Joab, and said, Shall the sword devour for ever? knowest you not that it will be bitterness in the latter end? how long shall it be then, ere you bid the people return from following their brethren?

27 And Joab said, As God liveth, unless you hadst spoken, surely then in the morning the people had gone up every one from following his brother.

28 So Joab blew a trumpet, and all the people stood still, and pursued after Israel no more, neither fought they any more.

29 And Abner and his men walked all that night through the plain, and passed over Jordan, and went through all Bithron, and they came to Mahanaim.

30 And Joab returned from following Abner: and when he had gathered all the people together, there lacked of David's servants nineteen men and Asahel.

31 But the servants of David had smitten of Benjamin, and of Abner's men, so that three hundred and threescore men died.

32And they took up Asahel, and buried him in the sepulchre of his father, which was in Beth-lehem. And Joab and his men went all night, and they came to Hebron at break of day.

CHAPTER 3

NOW there was long war between the house of Saul and the house of David: but David waxed stronger and stronger, and the house of Saul waxed weaker and weaker.

2And unto David were sons born in Hebron: and his firstborn was Amnon, of Ahinoam the Jezreelitess;

3 And his second, Chileab, of Abigail the wife of Nabal the Carmelite; and the third, Absalom the son of Maacah the daughter of Talmai king of Geshur;

4 And the fourth, Adonijah the son of Haggith; and the fifth, Shephatiah the son of Abital;

5 And the sixth, Ithream, by Eglah David's wife. These were born to David in Hebron.

6And it came to pass, while there was war between the house of Saul and the house of David, that Abner made himself strong for the house of Saul.

7 And Saul had a concubine, whose name was Rizpah, the daughter of Aiah: and Ish-bosheth said to Abner, Wherefore have you gone in unto my father's concubine?

8 Then was Abner very wroth for the words of Ish-bosheth, and said, Am I a dog's head, which against Judah do shew kindness this day unto the house of Saul your father, to his brethren, and to his friends, and have not delivered you into the hand of David, that you chargest me to day with a fault concerning this woman?

9 So do God to Abner, and more also, except, as the LORD has sworn to David, even so I do to him;

10 To translate the kingdom from the house of Saul, and to set up the throne of David over Israel and over Judah, from Dan even to Beer-sheba.

11 And he could not answer Abner a word again, because he feared him.

12And Abner sent messengers to David on his behalf, saying, Whose is the land? saying also, Make your league with me, and, behold, my hand shall be with you, to bring about all Israel unto you.

13And he said, Well; I will make a league with you: but one thing I require of you, that is, You shalt not see my face, except you first bring Michal Saul's daughter, when you comest to see my face.

14 And David sent messengers to Ish-bosheth Saul's son, saying, Deliver me my wife Michal, which I espoused to me for an hundred foreskins of the Philistines.

15 And Ish-bosheth sent, and took her from her husband, even from Phaltiel the son of Laish.

16 And her husband went with her along weeping behind her to Bahurim. Then said Abner unto him, Go, return. And he returned.

17And Abner had communication with the elders of Israel, saying, You sought for David in times past to be king over you:

18 Now then do it: for the LORD has spoken of David, saying, By the hand of my servant David I will save my people Israel out of the hand of the Philistines, and out of the hand of all their enemies.

19 And Abner also spake in the ears of Benjamin: and Abner went also to speak in the ears of David in Hebron all that seemed good to Israel, and that seemed good to the whole house of Benjamin.

20 So Abner came to David to Hebron, and twenty men with him. And David made Abner and the men that were with him a feast.

21 And Abner said unto David, I will arise and go, and will gather all Israel unto my lord the king, that they may make a league with you, and that you mayest reign over all that yours heart desireth. And David sent Abner away; and he went in peace.

22And, behold, the servants of David and Joab came from pursuing a troop, and brought in a great spoil with them: but Abner was not with David in Hebron; for he had sent him away, and he was gone in peace.

23 When Joab and all the host that was with him were come, they told Joab, saying, Abner the son of Ner came to the king, and he has sent him away, and he is gone in peace.

24 Then Joab came to the king, and said, What have you done? behold, Abner came unto you; why is it that you have sent him away, and he is quite gone?

25 You knowest Abner the son of Ner, that he came to deceive you, and to know your going out and your coming in, and to know all that you doest.

26 And when Joab was come out from David, he sent messengers after Abner, which brought him again from the well of Sirah: but David knew it not.

27 And when Abner was returned to Hebron, Joab took him aside in the gate to speak with him quietly, and struck him there under the fifth rib, that he died, for the blood of Asahel his brother.

28And afterward when David heard it, he said, I and my kingdom are guiltless before the LORD for ever from the blood of Abner the son of Ner:

29 Let it rest on the head of Joab, and on all his father's house; and let there not fail from the house of Joab one that has an issue, or that is a leper, or that leaneth on a staff, or that falleth on the sword, or that lacketh bread.

30 So Joab and Abishai his brother slew Abner, because he had slain their brother Asahel at Gibeon in the battle.

31And David said to Joab, and to all the people that were with him, Rend your clothes, and gird you with sackcloth, and mourn before Abner. And king David himself followed the bier.

32 And they buried Abner in Hebron: and the king lifted up his voice, and wept at the grave of Abner; and all the people wept.

33 And the king lamented over Abner, and said, Died Abner as a fool dieth?

34 Your hands were not bound, nor your feet put into fetters: as a man falleth before wicked men, so fellest you . And all the people wept again over him.

35 And when all the people came to cause David to eat meat while it was yet day, David sware, saying, So do God to me, and more also, if I taste bread, or ought else, till the sun be down.

36 And all the people took notice of it, and it pleased them: as whatsoever the king did pleased all the people.

37 For all the people and all Israel understood that day that it was not of the king to slay Abner the son of Ner.

38 And the king said unto his servants, Know you not that there is a prince and a great man fallen this day in Israel?

39 And I am this day weak, though anointed king; and these men the sons of Zeruiah be too hard for me: the LORD shall reward the doer of evil according to his wickedness.

CHAPTER 4

AND when Saul's son heard that Abner was dead in Hebron, his hands were feeble, and all the Israelites were troubled.

2 And Saul's son had two men that were captains of bands: the name of the one was Baanah, and the name of the other Rechab, the sons of Rimmon a Beerothite, of the children of Benjamin: (for Beeroth also was reckoned to Benjamin:

3 And the Beerothites fled to Gittaim, and were sojourners there until this day.)

4 And Jonathan, Saul's son, had a son that was lame of his feet. He was five years old when the tidings came of Saul and Jonathan out of Jezreel, and his nurse took him up, and fled: and it came to pass, as she made haste to flee, that he fell, and became lame. And his name was Mephibosheth.

5 And the sons of Rimmon the Beerothite, Rechab and Baanah, went, and came about the heat of the day to the house of Ish-bosheth, who lay on a bed at noon.

6 And they came thither into the midst of the house, as though they would have fetched wheat; and they struck him under the fifth rib: and Rechab and Baanah his brother escaped.

7 For when they came into the house, he lay on his bed in his bedchamber, and they struck him, and slew him, and beheaded him, and took his head, and gat them away through the plain all night.

8 And they brought the head of Ish-bosheth unto David to Hebron, and said to the king, Behold the head of Ish-bosheth the son of Saul yours enemy, which sought your life; and the LORD has avenged my lord the king this day of Saul, and of his seed.

9And David answered Rechab and Baanah his brother, the sons of Rimmon the Beerothite, and said unto them, As the LORD liveth, who has redeemed my soul out of all adversity,

10 When one told me, saying, Behold, Saul is dead, thinking to have brought good tidings, I took hold of him, and slew him in Ziklag, who thought that I would have given him a reward for his tidings:

11 How much more, when wicked men have slain a righteous person in his own house upon his bed? shall I not therefore now require his blood of your hand, and take you away from the earth?

12 And David commanded his young men, and they slew them, and cut off their hands and their feet, and hanged them up over the pool in Hebron. But they took the head of Ish-bosheth, and buried it in the sepulchre of Abner in Hebron.

CHAPTER 5

THEN came all the tribes of Israel to David unto Hebron, and spake, saying, Behold, we are your bone and your flesh.

2 Also in time past, when Saul was king over us, you wast he that leddest out and broughtest in Israel: and the LORD said to you, You shalt feed my people Israel, and you shalt be a captain over Israel.

3 So all the elders of Israel came to the king to Hebron; and king David made a league with them in Hebron before the LORD: and they anointed David king over Israel.

4David was thirty years old when he began to reign, and he reigned forty years.

5 In Hebron he reigned over Judah seven years and six months: and in Jerusalem he reigned thirty and three years over all Israel and Judah.

6And the king and his men went to Jerusalem unto the Jebusites, the inhabitants of the land: which spake unto David, saying, Except you take away the blind and the lame, you shalt not come in hither: thinking, David cannot come in hither.

7 Nevertheless David took the strong hold of Zion: the same is the city of David.

8 And David said on that day, Whosoever getteth up to the gutter, and smiteth the Jebusites, and the lame and the blind, that are hated of David's soul, he shall be chief and captain. Wherefore they said, The blind and the lame shall not come into the house.

9 So David dwelt in the fort, and called it the city of David. And David built round about from Millo and inward.

10 And David went on, and grew great, and the LORD God of hosts was with him.

11And Hiram king of Tyre sent messengers to David, and cedar trees, and carpenters, and masons: and they built David an house.

12 And David perceived that the LORD had established him king over Israel, and that he had exalted his kingdom for his people Israel's sake.

13And David took him more concubines and wives out of Jerusalem, after he was come from Hebron: and there were yet sons and daughters born to David.

14 And these be the names of those that were born unto him in Jerusalem; Shammua, and Shobab, and Nathan, and Solomon,

15 Ibhar also, and Elishua, and Nepheg, and Japhia,

16 And Elishama, and Eliada, and Eliphalet.

17But when the Philistines heard that they had anointed David king over Israel, all the Philistines came up to seek David; and David heard of it, and went down to the hold.

18 The Philistines also came and spread themselves in the valley of Rephaim.

19 And David inquired of the LORD, saying, Shall I go up to the Philistines? will you deliver them into my hand? And the LORD said unto David, Go up: for I will doubtless deliver the Philistines into yours hand.

20 And David came to Baal-perazim, and David struck them there, and said, The LORD has broken forth upon my enemies before me, as the breach of waters. Therefore he called the name of that place Baal-perazim.

21 And there they left their images, and David and his men burned them.

22And the Philistines came up yet again, and spread themselves in the valley of Rephaim.

23 And when David inquired of the LORD, he said, You shalt not go up; but fetch a compass behind them, and come upon them over against the mulberry trees.

24 And let it be, when you hearest the sound of a going in the tops of the mulberry trees, that then you shalt bestir yourself: for then shall the LORD go out before you, to strike the host of the Philistines.

25 And David did so, as the LORD had commanded him; and struck the Philistines from Geba until you come to Gazer.

CHAPTER 6

AGAIN, David gathered together all the chosen men of Israel, thirty thousand.

2 And David arose, and went with all the people that were with him from Baale of Judah, to bring up from thence the ark of God, whose name is called by the name of the LORD of hosts that dwelleth between the cherubims.

3 And they set the ark of God upon a new cart, and brought it out of the house of Abinadab that was in Gibeah: and Uzzah and Ahio, the sons of Abinadab, drave the new cart.

4 And they brought it out of the house of Abinadab which was at Gibeah, accompanying the ark of God: and Ahio went before the ark.

5 And David and all the house of Israel played before the LORD on all manner of instruments made of fir wood, even on harps, and on psalteries, and on timbrels, and on cornets, and on cymbals.

6And when they came to Nachon's threshingfloor, Uzzah put forth his hand to the ark of God, and took hold of it; for the oxen shook it.

7 And the anger of the LORD was kindled against Uzzah; and God struck him there for his error; and there he died by the ark of God.

8 And David was displeased, because the LORD had made a breach upon Uzzah: and he called the name of the place Perez-uzzah to this day.

9 And David was afraid of the LORD that day, and said, How shall the ark of the LORD come to me?

10 So David would not remove the ark of the LORD unto him into the city of David: but David carried it aside into the house of Obed-edom the Gittite.

11 And the ark of the LORD continued in the house of Obed-edom the Gittite three months: and the LORD blessed Obed-edom, and all his household.

12And it was told king David, saying, The LORD has blessed the house of Obed-edom, and all that pertaineth unto him, because of the ark of God. So David went and brought up the ark of God from the house of Obed-edom into the city of David with gladness.

13 And it was so, that when they that bare the ark of the LORD had gone six paces, he sacrificed oxen and fatlings.

14 And David danced before the LORD with all his might; and David was girded with a linen ephod.

15 So David and all the house of Israel brought up the ark of the LORD with shouting, and with the sound of the trumpet.

16 And as the ark of the LORD came into the city of David, Michal Saul's daughter looked through a window, and saw king David leaping and dancing before the LORD; and she despised him in her heart.

17And they brought in the ark of the LORD, and set it in his place, in the midst of the tabernacle that David had pitched for it: and David offered burnt offerings and peace offerings before the LORD.

18 And as soon as David had made an end of offering burnt offerings and peace offerings, he blessed the people in the name of the LORD of hosts.

19 And he dealt among all the people, even among the whole multitude of Israel, as well to the women as men, to every one a cake of bread, and a good piece of flesh, and a flagon of wine. So all the people departed every one to his house.

20Then David returned to bless his household. And Michal the daughter of Saul came out to meet David, and said, How glorious was the king of Israel to day, who uncovered himself to day in the eyes of the handmaids of his servants, as one of the vain fellows shamelessly uncovereth himself!

21 And David said unto Michal, It was before the LORD, which chose me before your father, and before all his house, to appoint me ruler over the people of the LORD, over Israel: therefore will I play before the LORD.

22 And I will yet be more vile than thus, and will be base in my own sight: and of the maidservants which you have spoken of, of them shall I be had in honour.

23 Therefore Michal the daughter of Saul had no child unto the day of her death.

CHAPTER 7

AND it came to pass, when the king sat in his house, and the LORD had given him rest round about from all his enemies;

2 That the king said unto Nathan the prophet, See now, I dwell in an house of cedar, but the ark of God dwelleth within curtains.

3 And Nathan said to the king, Go, do all that is in yours heart; for the LORD is with you.

4And it came to pass that night, that the word of the LORD came unto Nathan, saying,

5 Go and tell my servant David, Thus saith the LORD, Shalt you build me an house for me to dwell in?

6 Whereas I have not dwelt in any house since the time that I brought up the children of Israel out of Egypt, even to this day, but have walked in a tent and in a tabernacle.

7 In all the places wherein I have walked with all the children of Israel spake I a word with any of the tribes of Israel, whom I commanded to feed my people Israel, saying, Why build you not me an house of cedar?

8 Now therefore so shalt you say unto my servant David, Thus saith the LORD of hosts, I took you from the sheepcote, from following the sheep, to be ruler over my people, over Israel:

9 And I was with you whithersoever you wentest, and have cut off all yours enemies out of your sight, and have made you a great name, like unto the name of the great men that are in the earth.

10 Moreover I will appoint a place for my people Israel, and will plant them, that they may dwell in a place of their own, and move no more; neither shall the children of wickedness afflict them any more, as beforetime,

11 And as since the time that I commanded judges to be over my people Israel, and have caused you to rest from all yours enemies. Also the LORD telleth you that he will make you an house.

12And when your days be fulfilled, and you shalt sleep with your fathers, I will set up your seed after you, which shall proceed out of your bowels, and I will establish his kingdom.

13 He shall build an house for my name, and I will stablish the throne of his kingdom for ever.

14 I will be his father, and he shall be my son. If he commit iniquity, I will chasten him with the rod of men, and with the stripes of the children of men:

15 But my mercy shall not depart away from him, as I took it from Saul, whom I put away before you.

16 And yours house and your kingdom shall be established for ever before you: your throne shall be established for ever.

17 According to all these words, and according to all this vision, so did Nathan speak unto David.

18 Then went king David in, and sat before the LORD, and he said, Who am I, O Lord GOD? and what is my house, that you have brought me hitherto?

19 And this was yet a small thing in your sight, O Lord GOD; but you have spoken also of your servant's house for a great while to come. And is this the manner of man, O Lord GOD?

20 And what can David say more unto you? for you , Lord GOD, knowest your servant.

21 For your word's sake, and according to yours own heart, have you done all these great things, to make your servant know them.

22 Wherefore you are great, O LORD God: for there is none like you, neither is there any God beside you, according to all that we have heard with our ears.

23 And what one nation in the earth is like your people, even like Israel, whom God went to redeem for a people to himself, and to make him a name, and to do for you great things and terrible, for your land, before your people, which you redeemedst to you from Egypt, from the nations and their gods?

24 For you have confirmed to yourself your people Israel to be a people unto you for ever: and you , LORD, are become their God.

25 And now, O LORD God, the word that you have spoken concerning your servant, and concerning his house, establish it for ever, and do as you have said.

26 And let your name be magnified for ever, saying, The LORD of hosts is the God over Israel: and let the house of your servant David be established before you.

27 For you , O LORD of hosts, God of Israel, have revealed to your servant, saying, I will build you an house: therefore has your servant found in his heart to pray this prayer unto you.

28 And now, O Lord GOD, you are that God, and your words be true, and you have promised this goodness unto your servant:

29 Therefore now let it please you to bless the house of your servant, that it may continue for ever before you: for you , O Lord GOD, have spoken it: and with your blessing let the house of your servant be blessed for ever.

CHAPTER 8

AND after this it came to pass, that David struck the Philistines, and subdued them: and David took Metheg-ammah out of the hand of the Philistines.

2 And he struck Moab, and measured them with a line, casting them down to the ground; even with two lines measured he to put to death, and with one full line to keep alive. And so the Moabites became David's servants, and brought gifts.

3 David struck also Hadadezer, the son of Rehob, king of Zobah, as he went to recover his border at the river Euphrates.

4 And David took from him a thousand chariots, and seven hundred horsemen, and twenty thousand footmen: and David houghed all the chariot horses, but reserved of them for an hundred chariots.

5 And when the Syrians of Damascus came to succour Hadadezer king of Zobah, David slew of the Syrians two and twenty thousand men.

6 Then David put garrisons in Syria of Damascus: and the Syrians became servants to David, and brought gifts. And the LORD preserved David whithersoever he went.

7 And David took the shields of gold that were on the servants of Hadadezer, and brought them to Jerusalem.

8 And from Betah, and from Berothai, cities of Hadadezer, king David took exceeding much brass.

9 When Toi king of Hamath heard that David had smitten all the host of Hadadezer,

10 Then Toi sent Joram his son unto king David, to salute him, and to bless him, because he had fought against Hadadezer, and smitten him: for Hadadezer had wars with Toi. And Joram brought with him vessels of silver, and vessels of gold, and vessels of brass:

11 Which also king David did dedicate unto the LORD, with the silver and gold that he had dedicated of all nations which he subdued;

12 Of Syria, and of Moab, and of the children of Ammon, and of the Philistines, and of Amalek, and of the spoil of Hadadezer, son of Rehob, king of Zobah.

13 And David gat him a name when he returned from striking of the Syrians in the valley of salt, being eighteen thousand men.

14 And he put garrisons in Edom; throughout all Edom put he garrisons, and all they of Edom became David's servants. And the LORD preserved David whithersoever he went.

15 And David reigned over all Israel; and David executed judgment and justice unto all his people.

16 And Joab the son of Zeruiah was over the host; and Jehoshaphat the son of Ahilud was recorder;

17 And Zadok the son of Ahitub, and Ahimelech the son of Abiathar, were the priests; and Seraiah was the scribe;

18 And Benaiah the son of Jehoiada was over both the Cherethites and the Pelethites; and David's sons were chief rulers.

CHAPTER 9

AND David said, Is there yet any that is left of the house of Saul, that I may shew him kindness for Jonathan's sake?

2 And there was of the house of Saul a servant whose name was Ziba. And when they had called him unto David, the king said unto him, Are you Ziba? And he said, Your servant is he.

3 And the king said, Is there not yet any of the house of Saul, that I may shew the kindness of God unto him? And Ziba said unto the king, Jonathan has yet a son, which is lame on his feet.

4 And the king said unto him, Where is he? And Ziba said unto the king, Behold, he is in the house of Machir, the son of Ammiel, in Lo-debar.

5 Then king David sent, and fetched him out of the house of Machir, the son of Ammiel, from Lo-debar.

6 Now when Mephibosheth, the son of Jonathan, the son of Saul, was come unto David, he fell on his face, and did reverence. And David said, Mephibosheth. And he answered, Behold your servant!

7 And David said unto him, Fear not: for I will surely shew you kindness for Jonathan your father's sake, and will restore you all the land of Saul your father; and you shalt eat bread at my table continually.

8 And he bowed himself, and said, What is your servant, that you shouldest look upon such a dead dog as I am?

9 Then the king called to Ziba, Saul's servant, and said unto him, I have given unto your master's son all that pertained to Saul and to all his house.

10 You therefore, and your sons, and your servants, shall till the land for him, and you shalt bring in the fruits, that your master's son may have food to eat: but Mephibosheth your master's son shall eat bread alway at my table. Now Ziba had fifteen sons and twenty servants.

11 Then said Ziba unto the king, According to all that my lord the king has commanded his servant, so shall your servant do. As for Mephibosheth, said the king, he shall eat at my table, as one of the king's sons.

12 And Mephibosheth had a young son, whose name was Micha. And all that dwelt in the house of Ziba were servants unto Mephibosheth.

13 So Mephibosheth dwelt in Jerusalem: for he did eat continually at the king's table; and was lame on both his feet.

CHAPTER 10

AND it came to pass after this, that the king of the children of Ammon died, and Hanun his son reigned in his stead.

2 Then said David, I will shew kindness unto Hanun the son of Nahash, as his father shewed kindness unto me. And David sent to comfort him by the hand of his servants for his father. And David's servants came into the land of the children of Ammon.

3 And the princes of the children of Ammon said unto Hanun their lord, Thinkest you that David doth honour your father, that he has sent comforters unto you? has not David rather sent his servants unto you, to search the city, and to spy it out, and to overthrow it?

4 Wherefore Hanun took David's servants, and shaved off the one half of their beards, and cut off their garments in the middle, even to their buttocks, and sent them away.

5 When they told it unto David, he sent to meet them, because the men were greatly ashamed: and the king said, Tarry at Jericho until your beards be grown, and then return.

6 And when the children of Ammon saw that they stank before David, the children of Ammon sent and hired the Syrians of Beth-rehob, and the Syrians of Zoba, twenty thousand footmen, and of king Maacah a thousand men, and of Ish-tob twelve thousand men.

7 And when David heard of it, he sent Joab, and all the host of the mighty men.

8 And the children of Ammon came out, and put the battle in array at the entering in of the gate: and the Syrians of Zoba, and of Rehob, and Ish-tob, and Maacah, were by themselves in the field.

9 When Joab saw that the front of the battle was against him before and behind, he chose of all the choice men of Israel, and put them in array against the Syrians:

10 And the rest of the people he delivered into the hand of Abishai his brother, that he might put them in array against the children of Ammon.

11 And he said, If the Syrians be too strong for me, then you shalt help me: but if the children of Ammon be too strong for you, then I will come and help you.

12 Be of good courage, and let us play the men for our people, and for the cities of our God: and the LORD do that which seemeth him good.

13 And Joab drew nigh, and the people that were with him, unto the battle against the Syrians: and they fled before him.

14 And when the children of Ammon saw that the Syrians were fled, then fled they also before Abishai, and entered into the city. So Joab returned from the children of Ammon, and came to Jerusalem.

15And when the Syrians saw that they were smitten before Israel, they gathered themselves together.

16 And Hadarezer sent, and brought out the Syrians that were beyond the river: and they came to Helam; and Shobach the captain of the host of Hadarezer went before them.

17 And when it was told David, he gathered all Israel together, and passed over Jordan, and came to Helam. And the Syrians set themselves in array against David, and fought with him.

18 And the Syrians fled before Israel; and David slew the men of seven hundred chariots of the Syrians, and forty thousand horsemen, and struck Shobach the captain of their host, who died there.

19 And when all the kings that were servants to Hadarezer saw that they were smitten before Israel, they made peace with Israel, and served them. So the Syrians feared to help the children of Ammon any more.

CHAPTER 11

AND it came to pass, after the year was expired, at the time when kings go forth to battle, that David sent Joab, and his servants with him, and all Israel; and they destroyed the children of Ammon, and besieged Rabbah. But David tarried still at Jerusalem.

2And it came to pass in an eveningtide, that David arose from off his bed, and walked upon the roof of the king's house: and from the roof he saw a woman washing herself; and the woman was very beautiful to look upon.

3 And David sent and inquired after the woman. And one said, Is not this Bath-sheba, the daughter of Eliam, the wife of Uriah the Hittite?

4 And David sent messengers, and took her; and she came in unto him, and he lay with her; for she was purified from her uncleanness: and she returned unto her house.

5 And the woman conceived, and sent and told David, and said, I am with child.

6And David sent to Joab, saying, Send me Uriah the Hittite. And Joab sent Uriah to David.

7 And when Uriah was come unto him, David demanded of him how Joab did, and how the people did, and how the war prospered.

8 And David said to Uriah, Go down to your house, and wash your feet. And Uriah departed out of the king's house, and there followed him a mess of meat from the king.

9 But Uriah slept at the door of the king's house with all the servants of his lord, and went not down to his house.

10 And when they had told David, saying, Uriah went not down unto his house, David said unto Uriah, Camest you not from your journey? why then did you not go down unto yours house?

11 And Uriah said unto David, The ark, and Israel, and Judah, abide in tents; and my lord Joab, and the servants of my lord, are encamped in the open fields; shall I then go into my house, to eat and to drink, and to lie with my wife? as you livest, and as your soul liveth, I will not do this thing.

12 And David said to Uriah, Tarry here to day also, and to morrow I will let you depart. So Uriah abode in Jerusalem that day, and the morrow.

13 And when David had called him, he did eat and drink before him; and he made him drunk: and at even he went out to lie on his bed with the servants of his lord, but went not down to his house.

14And it came to pass in the morning, that David wrote a letter to Joab, and sent it by the hand of Uriah.

15 And he wrote in the letter, saying, Set you Uriah in the forefront of the hottest battle, and retire you from him, that he may be smitten, and die.

16 And it came to pass, when Joab observed the city, that he assigned Uriah unto a place where he knew that valiant men were.

17 And the men of the city went out, and fought with Joab: and there fell some of the people of the servants of David; and Uriah the Hittite died also.

18Then Joab sent and told David all the things concerning the war;

19 And charged the messenger, saying, When you have made an end of telling the matters of the war unto the king,

20 And if so be that the king's wrath arise, and he say unto you, Wherefore approached you so nigh unto the city when you did fight? knew you not that they would shoot from the wall?

21 Who struck Abimelech the son of Jerubbesheth? did not a woman cast a piece of a millstone upon him from the wall, that he died in Thebez? why went you nigh the wall? then say you , Your servant Uriah the Hittite is dead also.

22So the messenger went, and came and shewed David all that Joab had sent him for.

23 And the messenger said unto David, Surely the men prevailed against us, and came out unto us into the field, and we were upon them even unto the entering of the gate.

24 And the shooters shot from off the wall upon your servants; and some of the king's servants be dead, and your servant Uriah the Hittite is dead also.

25 Then David said unto the messenger, Thus shalt you say unto Joab, Let not this thing displease you, for the sword devoureth one as well as another: make your battle more strong against the city, and overthrow it: and encourage you him.

26And when the wife of Uriah heard that Uriah her husband was dead, she mourned for her husband.

27 And when the mourning was past, David sent and fetched her to his house, and she became his wife, and bare him a son. But the thing that David had done displeased the LORD.

CHAPTER 12

AND the LORD sent Nathan unto David. And he came unto him, and said unto him, There were two men in one city; the one rich, and the other poor.

2 The rich man had exceeding many flocks and herds:

3 But the poor man had nothing, save one little ewe lamb, which he had bought and nourished up: and it grew up together with him, and with his children; it did eat of his own meat, and drank of his own cup, and lay in his bosom, and was unto him as a daughter.

4 And there came a traveller unto the rich man, and he spared to take of his own flock and of his own herd, to dress for the wayfaring man that was come unto him; but took the poor man's lamb, and dressed it for the man that was come to him.

5 And David's anger was greatly kindled against the man; and he said to Nathan, As the LORD liveth, the man that has done this thing shall surely die:

6 And he shall restore the lamb fourfold, because he did this thing, and because he had no pity.

7And Nathan said to David, You are the man. Thus saith the LORD God of Israel, I anointed you king over Israel, and I delivered you out of the hand of Saul;

8 And I gave you your master's house, and your master's wives into your bosom, and gave you the house of Israel and of Judah; and if that had been too little, I would moreover have given unto you such and such things.

9 Wherefore have you despised the commandment of the LORD, to do evil in his sight? you have killed Uriah the Hittite with the sword, and have taken his wife to be your wife, and have slain him with the sword of the children of Ammon.

10 Now therefore the sword shall never depart from yours house; because you have despised me, and have taken the wife of Uriah the Hittite to be your wife.

11 Thus saith the LORD, Behold, I will raise up evil against you out of yours own house, and I will take your wives before yours eyes, and give them unto your neighbour, and he shall lie with your wives in the sight of this sun.

12 For you did it secretly: but I will do this thing before all Israel, and before the sun.

13 And David said unto Nathan, I have sinned against the LORD. And Nathan said unto David, The LORD also has put away your sin; you shalt not die.

14 Howbeit, because by this deed you have given great occasion to the enemies of the LORD to blaspheme, the child also that is born unto you shall surely die.

15And Nathan departed unto his house. And the LORD struck the child that Uriah's wife bare unto David, and it was very sick.

16 David therefore besought God for the child; and David fasted, and went in, and lay all night upon the earth.

17 And the elders of his house arose, and went to him, to raise him up from the earth: but he would not, neither did he eat bread with them.

18 And it came to pass on the seventh day, that the child died. And the servants of David feared to tell him that the child was dead: for they said, Behold, while the child was yet alive, we spake unto him, and he would not hearken unto our voice: how will he then vex himself, if we tell him that the child is dead?

19 But when David saw that his servants whispered, David perceived that the child was dead: therefore David said unto his servants, Is the child dead? And they said, He is dead.

20 Then David arose from the earth, and washed, and anointed himself, and changed his apparel, and came into the house of the LORD, and worshipped: then he came to his own house; and when he required, they set bread before him, and he did eat.

21 Then said his servants unto him, What thing is this that you have done? you did fast and weep for the child, while it was alive; but when the child was dead, you did rise and eat bread.

22 And he said, While the child was yet alive, I fasted and wept: for I said, Who can tell whether GOD will be gracious to me, that the child may live?

23 But now he is dead, wherefore should I fast? can I bring him back again? I shall go to him, but he shall not return to me.

24 And David comforted Bath-sheba his wife, and went in unto her, and lay with her: and she bare a son, and he called his name Solomon: and the LORD loved him.

25 And he sent by the hand of Nathan the prophet; and he called his name Jedidiah, because of the LORD.

26 And Joab fought against Rabbah of the children of Ammon, and took the royal city.

27 And Joab sent messengers to David, and said, I have fought against Rabbah, and have taken the city of waters.

28 Now therefore gather the rest of the people together, and encamp against the city, and take it: lest I take the city, and it be called after my name.

29 And David gathered all the people together, and went to Rabbah, and fought against it, and took it.

30 And he took their king's crown from off his head, the weight whereof was a talent of gold with the precious stones: and it was set on David's head. And he brought forth the spoil of the city in great abundance.

31 And he brought forth the people that were therein, and put them under saws, and under harrows of iron, and under axes of iron, and made them pass through the brickkiln: and thus did he unto all the cities of the children of Ammon. So David and all the people returned unto Jerusalem.

CHAPTER 13

AND it came to pass after this, that Absalom the son of David had a fair sister, whose name was Tamar; and Amnon the son of David loved her.

2 And Amnon was so vexed, that he fell sick for his sister Tamar; for she was a virgin; and Amnon thought it hard for him to do any thing to her.

3 But Amnon had a friend, whose name was Jonadab, the son of Shimeah David's brother: and Jonadab was a very subtil man.

4 And he said unto him, Why are you , being the king's son, lean from day to day? will you not tell me? And Amnon said unto him, I love Tamar, my brother Absalom's sister.

5 And Jonadab said unto him, Lay you down on your bed, and make yourself sick: and when your father comes to see you, say unto him, I pray you, let my sister Tamar come, and give me meat, and dress the meat in my sight, that I may see it, and eat it at her hand.

6 So Amnon lay down, and made himself sick: and when the king was come to see him, Amnon said unto the king, I pray you, let Tamar my sister come, and make me a couple of cakes in my sight, that I may eat at her hand.

7 Then David sent home to Tamar, saying, Go now to your brother Amnon's house, and dress him meat.

8 So Tamar went to her brother Amnon's house; and he was laid down. And she took flour, and kneaded it, and made cakes in his sight, and did bake the cakes.

9 And she took a pan, and poured them out before him; but he refused to eat. And Amnon said, Have out all men from me. And they went out every man from him.

10 And Amnon said unto Tamar, Bring the meat into the chamber, that I may eat of yours hand. And Tamar took the cakes which she had made, and brought them into the chamber to Amnon her brother.

11 And when she had brought them unto him to eat, he took hold of her, and said unto her, Come lie with me, my sister.

12 And she answered him, Nay, my brother, do not force me; for no such thing ought to be done in Israel: do not you this folly.

13 And I, whither shall I cause my shame to go? and as for you, you shalt be as one of the fools in Israel. Now therefore, I pray you, speak unto the king; for he will not withhold me from you.

14 Howbeit he would not hearken unto her voice: but, being stronger than she, forced her, and lay with her.

15 Then Amnon hated her exceedingly; so that the hatred wherewith he hated her was greater than the love wherewith he had loved her. And Amnon said unto her, Arise, be gone.

16 And she said unto him, There is no cause: this evil in sending me away is greater than the other that you did unto me. But he would not hearken unto her.

17 Then he called his servant that ministered unto him, and said, Put now this woman out from me, and bolt the door after her.

18 And she had a garment of divers colours upon her: for with such robes were the king's daughters that were virgins apparelled. Then his servant brought her out, and bolted the door after her.

19 And Tamar put ashes on her head, and rent her garment of divers colours that was on her, and laid her hand on her head, and went on crying.

20 And Absalom her brother said unto her, Has Amnon your brother been with you? but hold now your peace, my sister: he is your brother; regard not this thing. So Tamar remained desolate in her brother Absalom's house.

21 But when king David heard of all these things, he was very wroth.

22 And Absalom spake unto his brother Amnon neither good nor bad: for Absalom hated Amnon, because he had forced his sister Tamar.

23 And it came to pass after two full years, that Absalom had sheepshearers in Baal-hazor, which is beside Ephraim: and Absalom invited all the king's sons.

24 And Absalom came to the king, and said, Behold now, your servant has sheepshearers; let the king, I beseech you, and his servants go with your servant.

25 And the king said to Absalom, Nay, my son, let us not all now go, lest we be chargeable unto you. And he pressed him: howbeit he would not go, but blessed him.

26 Then said Absalom, If not, I pray you, let my brother Amnon go with us. And the king said unto him, Why should he go with you?

27 But Absalom pressed him, that he let Amnon and all the king's sons go with him.

28 Now Absalom had commanded his servants, saying, Mark you now when Amnon's heart is merry with wine, and when I say unto you, Strike Amnon; then kill him, fear not: have not I commanded you? be courageous, and be valiant.

29 And the servants of Absalom did unto Amnon as Absalom had commanded. Then all the king's sons arose, and every man gat him up upon his mule, and fled.

30 And it came to pass, while they were in the way, that tidings came to David, saying, Absalom has slain all the king's sons, and there is not one of them left.

31 Then the king arose, and tare his garments, and lay on the earth; and all his servants stood by with their clothes rent.

32 And Jonadab, the son of Shimeah David's brother, answered and said, Let not my lord suppose that they have slain all the young men the king's sons; for Amnon only is dead: for by the appointment of Absalom this has been determined from the day that he forced his sister Tamar.

33 Now therefore let not my lord the king take the thing to his heart, to think that all the king's sons are dead: for Amnon only is dead.

34 But Absalom fled. And the young man that kept the watch lifted up his eyes, and looked, and, behold, there came much people by the way of the hill side behind him.

35 And Jonadab said unto the king, Behold, the king's sons come: as your servant said, so it is.

36 And it came to pass, as soon as he had made an end of speaking, that, behold, the king's sons came, and lifted up their voice and wept: and the king also and all his servants wept very sore.

37 But Absalom fled, and went to Talmai, the son of Ammihud, king of Geshur. And David mourned for his son every day.

38 So Absalom fled, and went to Geshur, and was there three years.

39 And the soul of king David longed to go forth unto Absalom: for he was comforted concerning Amnon, seeing he was dead.

CHAPTER 14

NOW Joab the son of Zeruiah perceived that the king's heart was toward Absalom.

2 And Joab sent to Tekoah, and fetched thence a wise woman, and said unto her, I pray you, feign yourself to be a mourner, and put on now mourning apparel, and anoint not yourself with oil, but be as a woman that had a long time mourned for the dead:

3 And come to the king, and speak on this manner unto him. So Joab put the words in her mouth.

4 And when the woman of Tekoah spake to the king, she fell on her face to the ground, and did obeisance, and said, Help, O king.

5 And the king said unto her, What aileth you? And she answered, I am indeed a widow woman, and my husband is dead.

6 And your handmaid had two sons, and they two strove together in the field, and there was none to part them, but the one struck the other, and slew him.

7 And, behold, the whole family is risen against yours handmaid, and they said, Deliver him that struck his brother, that we may kill him, for the life of his brother whom he slew; and we will destroy the heir also: and so they shall quench my coal which is left, and shall not leave to my husband neither name nor remainder upon the earth.

8 And the king said unto the woman, Go to yours house, and I will give charge concerning you.

9 And the woman of Tekoah said unto the king, My lord, O king, the iniquity be on me, and on my father's house: and the king and his throne be guiltless.

10 And the king said, Whosoever saith ought unto you, bring him to me, and he shall not touch you any more.

11 Then said she, I pray you, let the king remember the LORD your God, that you wouldest not suffer the revengers of blood to destroy any more, lest they destroy my son. And he said, As the LORD liveth, there shall not one hair of your son fall to the earth.

12 Then the woman said, Let yours handmaid, I pray you, speak one word unto my lord the king. And he said, Say on.

13 And the woman said, Wherefore then have you thought such a thing against the people of God? for the king doth speak this thing as one which is faulty, in that the king doth not fetch home again his banished.

14 For we must needs die, and are as water spilt on the ground, which cannot be gathered up again; neither doth God respect any person: yet doth he devise means, that his banished be not expelled from him.

15 Now therefore that I am come to speak of this thing unto my lord the king, it is because the people have made me afraid: and your handmaid said, I will now speak unto the king; it may be that the king will perform the request of his handmaid.

16 For the king will hear, to deliver his handmaid out of the hand of the man that would destroy me and my son together out of the inheritance of God.

17 Then yours handmaid said, The word of my lord the king shall now be comfortable: for as an angel of God, so is my lord the king to discern good and bad: therefore the LORD your God will be with you.

18 Then the king answered and said unto the woman, Hide not from me, I pray you, the thing that I shall ask you. And the woman said, Let my lord the king now speak.

19 And the king said, Is not the hand of Joab with you in all this? And the woman answered and said, As your soul liveth, my lord the king, none can turn to the right hand or to the left from ought that my lord the king has spoken: for your servant Joab, he bade me, and he put all these words in the mouth of yours handmaid:

20 To fetch about this form of speech has your servant Joab done this thing: and my lord is wise, according to the wisdom of an angel of God, to know all things that are in the earth.

21And the king said unto Joab, Behold now, I have done this thing: go therefore, bring the young man Absalom again.

22 And Joab fell to the ground on his face, and bowed himself, and thanked the king: and Joab said, To day your servant knoweth that I have found grace in your sight, my lord, O king, in that the king has fulfilled the request of his servant.

23 So Joab arose and went to Geshur, and brought Absalom to Jerusalem.

24 And the king said, Let him turn to his own house, and let him not see my face. So Absalom returned to his own house, and saw not the king's face.

25But in all Israel there was none to be so much praised as Absalom for his beauty: from the sole of his foot even to the crown of his head there was no blemish in him.

26 And when he polled his head, (for it was at every year's end that he polled it: because the hair was heavy on him, therefore he polled it:) he weighed the hair of his head at two hundred shekels after the king's weight.

27 And unto Absalom there were born three sons, and one daughter, whose name was Tamar: she was a woman of a fair countenance.

28So Absalom dwelt two full years in Jerusalem, and saw not the king's face.

29 Therefore Absalom sent for Joab, to have sent him to the king; but he would not come to him: and when he sent again the second time, he would not come.

30 Therefore he said unto his servants, See, Joab's field is near my, and he has barley there; go and set it on fire. And Absalom's servants set the field on fire.

31 Then Joab arose, and came to Absalom unto his house, and said unto him, Wherefore have your servants set my field on fire?

32 And Absalom answered Joab, Behold, I sent unto you, saying, Come hither, that I may send you to the king, to say, Wherefore am I come from Geshur? it had been good for me to have been there still: now therefore let me see the king's face; and if there be any iniquity in me, let him kill me.

33 So Joab came to the king, and told him: and when he had called for Absalom, he came to the king, and bowed himself on his face to the ground before the king: and the king kissed Absalom.

CHAPTER 15

AND it came to pass after this, that Absalom prepared him chariots and horses, and fifty men to run before him.

2 And Absalom rose up early, and stood beside the way of the gate: and it was so, that when any man that had a controversy came to the king for judgment, then Absalom called unto him, and said, Of what city are you ? And he said, Your servant is of one of the tribes of Israel.

3 And Absalom said unto him, See, your matters are good and right; but there is no man deputed of the king to hear you.

4 Absalom said moreover, Oh that I were made judge in the land, that every man which has any suit or cause might come unto me, and I would do him justice!

5 And it was so, that when any man came nigh to him to do him obeisance, he put forth his hand, and took him, and kissed him.

6 And on this manner did Absalom to all Israel that came to the king for judgment: so Absalom stole the hearts of the men of Israel.

7And it came to pass after forty years, that Absalom said unto the king, I pray you, let me go and pay my vow, which I have vowed unto the LORD, in Hebron.

8 For your servant vowed a vow while I abode at Geshur in Syria, saying, If the LORD shall bring me again indeed to Jerusalem, then I will serve the LORD.

9 And the king said unto him, Go in peace. So he arose, and went to Hebron.

10But Absalom sent spies throughout all the tribes of Israel, saying, As soon as you hear the sound of the trumpet, then you shall say, Absalom reigneth in Hebron.

11 And with Absalom went two hundred men out of Jerusalem, that were called; and they went in their simplicity, and they knew not any thing.

12 And Absalom sent for Ahithophel the Gilonite, David's counseller, from his city, even from Giloh, while he offered sacrifices. And the conspiracy was strong; for the people increased continually with Absalom.

13And there came a messenger to David, saying, The hearts of the men of Israel are after Absalom.

14 And David said unto all his servants that were with him at Jerusalem, Arise, and let us flee; for we shall not else escape from Absalom: make speed to depart, lest he overtake us suddenly, and bring evil upon us, and strike the city with the edge of the sword.

15 And the king's servants said unto the king, Behold, your servants are ready to do whatsoever my lord the king shall appoint.

16 And the king went forth, and all his household after him. And the king left ten women, which were concubines, to keep the house.

17 And the king went forth, and all the people after him, and tarried in a place that was far off.

18 And all his servants passed on beside him; and all the Cherethites, and all the Pelethites, and all the Gittites, six hundred men which came after him from Gath, passed on before the king.

19Then said the king to Ittai the Gittite, Wherefore go you also with us? return to your place, and abide with the king: for you are a stranger, and also an exile.

20 Whereas you camest but yesterday, should I this day make you go up and down with us? seeing I go whither I may, return you , and take back your brethren: mercy and truth be with you.

21 And Ittai answered the king, and said, As the LORD liveth, and as my lord the king liveth, surely in what place my lord the king shall be, whether in death or life, even there also will your servant be.

22 And David said to Ittai, Go and pass over. And Ittai the Gittite passed over, and all his men, and all the little ones that were with him.

23 And all the country wept with a loud voice, and all the people passed over: the king also himself passed over the brook Kidron, and all the people passed over, toward the way of the wilderness.

24And lo Zadok also, and all the Levites were with him, bearing the ark of the covenant of God: and they set down the ark of God; and Abiathar went up, until all the people had done passing out of the city.

25 And the king said unto Zadok, Carry back the ark of God into the city: if I shall find favour in the eyes of the LORD, he will bring me again, and shew me both it, and his habitation:

26 But if he thus say, I have no delight in you; behold, here am I, let him do to me as seemeth good unto him.

27 The king said also unto Zadok the priest, Are not you a seer? return into the city in peace, and your two sons with you, Ahimaaz your son, and Jonathan the son of Abiathar.

28 See, I will tarry in the plain of the wilderness, until there come word from you to certify me.

29 Zadok therefore and Abiathar carried the ark of God again to Jerusalem: and they tarried there.

30And David went up by the ascent of mount Olivet, and wept as he went up, and had his head covered, and he went barefoot: and all the people that was with him covered every man his head, and they went up, weeping as they went up.

31And one told David, saying, Ahithophel is among the conspirators with Absalom. And David said, O LORD, I pray you, turn the counsel of Ahithophel into foolishness.

32And it came to pass, that when David was come to the top of the mount, where he worshipped God, behold, Hushai the Archite came to meet him with his coat rent, and earth upon his head:

33 Unto whom David said, If you passest on with me, then you shalt be a burden unto me:

34 But if you return to the city, and say unto Absalom, I will be your servant, O king; as I have been your father's servant hitherto, so will I now also be your servant: then mayest you for me defeat the counsel of Ahithophel.

35 And have you not there with you Zadok and Abiathar the priests? therefore it shall be, that what thing soever you shalt hear out of the king's house, you shalt tell it to Zadok and Abiathar the priests.

36 Behold, they have there with them their two sons, Ahimaaz Zadok's son, and Jonathan Abiathar's son; and by them you shall send unto me every thing that you can hear.

37 So Hushai David's friend came into the city, and Absalom came into Jerusalem.

CHAPTER 16

AND when David was a little past the top of the hill, behold, Ziba the servant of Mephibosheth met him, with a couple of asses saddled, and upon them two hundred loaves of bread, and an hundred bunches of raisins, and an hundred of summer fruits, and a bottle of wine.

2 And the king said unto Ziba, What meanest you by these? And Ziba said, The asses be for the king's household to ride on; and the bread and summer fruit for the young men to eat; and the wine, that such as be faint in the wilderness may drink.

3 And the king said, And where is your master's son? And Ziba said unto the king, Behold, he abideth at Jerusalem: for he said, To day shall the house of Israel restore me the kingdom of my father.

4 Then said the king to Ziba, Behold, yours are all that pertained unto Mephibosheth. And Ziba said, I humbly beseech you that I may find grace in your sight, my lord, O king.

5And when king David came to Bahurim, behold, thence came out a man of the family of the house of Saul, whose name was Shimei, the son of Gera: he came forth, and cursed still as he came.

6 And he cast stones at David, and at all the servants of king David: and all the people and all the mighty men were on his right hand and on his left.

7 And thus said Shimei when he cursed, Come out, come out, you bloody man, and you man of Belial:

8 The LORD has returned upon you all the blood of the house of Saul, in whose stead you have reigned; and the LORD has delivered the kingdom into the hand of Absalom your son: and, behold, you are taken in your mischief, because you are a bloody man.

9Then said Abishai the son of Zeruiah unto the king, Why should this dead dog curse my lord the king? let me go over, I pray you, and take off his head.

10 And the king said, What have I to do with you, you sons of Zeruiah? so let him curse, because the LORD has said unto him, Curse David. Who shall then say, Wherefore have you done so?

11 And David said to Abishai, and to all his servants, Behold, my son, which came forth of my bowels, seeketh my life: how much more now may this Benjamite do it? let him alone, and let him curse; for the LORD has bidden him.

12 It may be that the LORD will look on my affliction, and that the LORD will requite me good for his cursing this day.

13 And as David and his men went by the way, Shimei went along on the hill's side over against him, and cursed as he went, and threw stones at him, and cast dust.

14 And the king, and all the people that were with him, came weary, and refreshed themselves there.

15And Absalom, and all the people the men of Israel, came to Jerusalem, and Ahithophel with him.

16 And it came to pass, when Hushai the Archite, David's friend, was come unto Absalom, that Hushai said unto Absalom, God save the king, God save the king.

17 And Absalom said to Hushai, Is this your kindness to your friend? why wentest you not with your friend?

18 And Hushai said unto Absalom, Nay; but whom the LORD, and this people, and all the men of Israel, choose, his will I be, and with him will I abide.

19 And again, whom should I serve? should I not serve in the presence of his son? as I have served in your father's presence, so will I be in your presence.

20Then said Absalom to Ahithophel, Give counsel among you what we shall do.

21 And Ahithophel said unto Absalom, Go in unto your father's concubines, which he has left to keep the house; and all Israel shall hear that you are abhorred of your father: then shall the hands of all that are with you be strong.

22 So they spread Absalom a tent upon the top of the house; and Absalom went in unto his father's concubines in the sight of all Israel.

23 And the counsel of Ahithophel, which he counselled in those days, was as if a man had inquired at the oracle of God: so was all the counsel of Ahithophel both with David and with Absalom.

CHAPTER 17

MOREOVER Ahithophel said unto Absalom, Let me now choose out twelve thousand men, and I will arise and pursue after David this night:

2 And I will come upon him while he is weary and weak handed, and will make him afraid: and all the people that are with him shall flee; and I will strike the king only:

3 And I will bring back all the people unto you: the man whom you seekest is as if all returned: so all the people shall be in peace.

4 And the saying pleased Absalom well, and all the elders of Israel.

5 Then said Absalom, Call now Hushai the Archite also, and let us hear likewise what he saith.

6 And when Hushai was come to Absalom, Absalom spake unto him, saying, Ahithophel has spoken after this manner: shall we do after his saying? if not; speak you .

7 And Hushai said unto Absalom, The counsel that Ahithophel has given is not good at this time.

8 For, said Hushai, you knowest your father and his men, that they be mighty men, and they be chafed in their minds, as a bear robbed of her whelps in the field: and your father is a man of war, and will not lodge with the people.

9 Behold, he is hid now in some pit, or in some other place: and it will come to pass, when some of them be overthrown at the first, that whosoever heareth it will say, There is a slaughter among the people that follow Absalom.

10 And he also that is valiant, whose heart is as the heart of a lion, shall utterly melt: for all Israel knoweth that your father is a mighty man, and they which be with him are valiant men.

11 Therefore I counsel that all Israel be generally gathered unto you, from Dan even to Beer-sheba, as the sand that is by the sea for multitude; and that you go to battle in yours own person.

12 So shall we come upon him in some place where he shall be found, and we will light upon him as the dew falleth on the ground: and of him and of all the men that are with him there shall not be left so much as one.

13 Moreover, if he be gotten into a city, then shall all Israel bring ropes to that city, and we will draw it into the river, until there be not one small stone found there.

14 And Absalom and all the men of Israel said, The counsel of Hushai the Archite is better than the counsel of Ahithophel. For the LORD had appointed to defeat the good counsel of Ahithophel, to the intent that the LORD might bring evil upon Absalom.

15Then said Hushai unto Zadok and to Abiathar the priests, Thus and thus did Ahithophel counsel Absalom and the elders of Israel; and thus and thus have I counselled.

16 Now therefore send quickly, and tell David, saying, Lodge not this night in the plains of the wilderness, but speedily pass over; lest the king be swallowed up, and all the people that are with him.

17 Now Jonathan and Ahimaaz stayed by En-rogel; for they might not be seen to come into the city: and a wench went and told them; and they went and told king David.

18 Nevertheless a lad saw them, and told Absalom: but they went both of them away quickly, and came to a man's house in Bahurim, which had a well in his court; whither they went down.

19 And the woman took and spread a covering over the well's mouth, and spread ground corn thereon; and the thing was not known.

20 And when Absalom's servants came to the woman to the house, they said, Where is Ahimaaz and Jonathan? And the woman said unto them, They be gone over the brook of water. And when they had sought and could not find them, they returned to Jerusalem.

21 And it came to pass, after they were departed, that they came up out of the well, and went and told king David, and said unto David, Arise, and pass quickly over the water: for thus has Ahithophel counselled against you.

22 Then David arose, and all the people that were with him, and they passed over Jordan: by the morning light there lacked not one of them that was not gone over Jordan.

23And when Ahithophel saw that his counsel was not followed, he saddled his ass, and arose, and gat him home to his house, to his city, and put his household in order, and hanged himself, and died, and was buried in the sepulchre of his father.

24 Then David came to Mahanaim. And Absalom passed over Jordan, he and all the men of Israel with him.

25And Absalom made Amasa captain of the host instead of Joab: which Amasa was a man's son, whose name was Ithra an Israelite, that went in to Abigail the daughter of Nahash, sister to Zeruiah Joab's mother.

26 So Israel and Absalom pitched in the land of Gilead.

27And it came to pass, when David was come to Mahanaim, that Shobi the son of Nahash of Rabbah of the children of Ammon, and Machir the son of Ammiel of Lo-debar, and Barzillai the Gileadite of Rogelim,

28 Brought beds, and basons, and earthen vessels, and wheat, and barley, and flour, and parched corn, and beans, and lentiles, and parched pulse,

29 And honey, and butter, and sheep, and cheese of kine, for David, and for the people that were with him, to eat: for they said, The people is hungry, and weary, and thirsty, in the wilderness.

CHAPTER 18

AND David numbered the people that were with him, and set captains of thousands and captains of hundreds over them.

2 And David sent forth a third part of the people under the hand of Joab, and a third part under the hand of Abishai the son of Zeruiah, Joab's brother, and a third part under the hand of Ittai the Gittite. And the king said unto the people, I will surely go forth with you myself also.

3 But the people answered, You shalt not go forth: for if we flee away, they will not care for us; neither if half of us die, will they care for us: but now you are worth ten thousand of us: therefore now it is better that you succour us out of the city.

4 And the king said unto them, What seemeth you best I will do. And the king stood by the gate side, and all the people came out by hundreds and by thousands.

5 And the king commanded Joab and Abishai and Ittai, saying, Deal gently for my sake with the young man, even with Absalom. And all the people heard when the king gave all the captains charge concerning Absalom.

6 So the people went out into the field against Israel: and the battle was in the wood of Ephraim;

7 Where the people of Israel were slain before the servants of David, and there was there a great slaughter that day of twenty thousand men.

8 For the battle was there scattered over the face of all the country: and the wood devoured more people that day than the sword devoured.

9 And Absalom met the servants of David. And Absalom rode upon a mule, and the mule went under the thick boughs of a great oak, and his head caught hold of the oak, and he was taken up between the heaven and the earth; and the mule that was under him went away.

10 And a certain man saw it, and told Joab, and said, Behold, I saw Absalom hanged in an oak.

11 And Joab said unto the man that told him, And, behold, you sawest him, and why did you not strike him there to the ground? and I would have given you ten shekels of silver, and a girdle.

12 And the man said unto Joab, Though I should receive a thousand shekels of silver in my hand, yet would I not put forth my hand against the king's son: for in our hearing the king charged you and Abishai and Ittai, saying, Beware that none touch the young man Absalom.

13 Otherwise I should have created falsehood against my own life: for there is no matter hid from the king, and you yourself wouldest have set yourself against me.

14 Then said Joab, I may not tarry thus with you. And he took three darts in his hand, and thrust them through the heart of Absalom, while he was yet alive in the midst of the oak.

15 And ten young men that bare Joab's armour compassed about and struck Absalom, and slew him.

16 And Joab blew the trumpet, and the people returned from pursuing after Israel: for Joab held back the people.

17 And they took Absalom, and cast him into a great pit in the wood, and laid a very great heap of stones upon him: and all Israel fled every one to his tent.

18 Now Absalom in his lifetime had taken and reared up for himself a pillar, which is in the king's dale: for he said, I have no son to keep my name in remembrance: and he called the pillar after his own name: and it is called unto this day, Absalom's place.

19 Then said Ahimaaz the son of Zadok, Let me now run, and bear the king tidings, how that the LORD has avenged him of his enemies.

20 And Joab said unto him, You shalt not bear tidings this day, but you shalt bear tidings another day: but this day you shalt bear no tidings, because the king's son is dead.

21 Then said Joab to Cushi, Go tell the king what you have seen. And Cushi bowed himself unto Joab, and ran.

22 Then said Ahimaaz the son of Zadok yet again to Joab, But howsoever, let me, I pray you, also run after Cushi. And Joab said, Wherefore will you run, my son, seeing that you have no tidings ready?

23 But howsoever, said he, let me run. And he said unto him, Run. Then Ahimaaz ran by the way of the plain, and overran Cushi.

24 And David sat between the two gates: and the watchman went up to the roof over the gate unto the wall, and lifted up his eyes, and looked, and behold a man running alone.

25 And the watchman cried, and told the king. And the king said, If he be alone, there is tidings in his mouth. And he came apace, and drew near.

26 And the watchman saw another man running: and the watchman called unto the porter, and said, Behold another man running alone. And the king said, He also bringeth tidings.

27 And the watchman said, Me thinketh the running of the foremost is like the running of Ahimaaz the son of Zadok. And the king said, He is a good man, and comes with good tidings.

28 And Ahimaaz called, and said unto the king, All is well. And he fell down to the earth upon his face before the king, and said, Blessed be the LORD your God, which has delivered up the men that lifted up their hand against my lord the king.

29 And the king said, Is the young man Absalom safe? And Ahimaaz answered, When Joab sent the king's servant, and me your servant, I saw a great tumult, but I knew not what it was.

30 And the king said unto him, Turn aside, and stand here. And he turned aside, and stood still.

31 And, behold, Cushi came; and Cushi said, Tidings, my lord the king: for the LORD has avenged you this day of all them that rose up against you.

32 And the king said unto Cushi, Is the young man Absalom safe? And Cushi answered, The enemies of my lord the king, and all that rise against you to do you hurt, be as that young man is.

33 And the king was much moved, and went up to the chamber over the gate, and wept: and as he went, thus he said, O my son Absalom, my son, my son Absalom! would God I had died for you, O Absalom, my son, my son!

CHAPTER 19

AND it was told Joab, Behold, the king weepeth and mourneth for Absalom.

2 And the victory that day was turned into mourning unto all the people: for the people heard say that day how the king was grieved for his son.

3 And the people gat them by stealth that day into the city, as people being ashamed steal away when they flee in battle.

4 But the king covered his face, and the king cried with a loud voice, O my son Absalom, O Absalom, my son, my son!

5 And Joab came into the house to the king, and said, You have shamed this day the faces of all your servants, which this day have saved your life, and the lives of your sons and of your daughters, and the lives of your wives, and the lives of your concubines;

6 In that you lovest yours enemies, and hatest your friends. For you have declared this day, that you regardest neither princes nor servants: for this day I perceive, that if Absalom had lived, and all we had died this day, then it had pleased you well.

7 Now therefore arise, go forth, and speak comfortably unto your servants: for I swear by the LORD, if you go not forth, there will not tarry one with you this night: and that will be worse unto you than all the evil that befell you from your youth until now.

8 Then the king arose, and sat in the gate. And they told unto all the people, saying, Behold, the king doth sit in the gate. And all the people came before the king: for Israel had fled every man to his tent.

9 And all the people were at strife throughout all the tribes of Israel, saying, The king saved us out of the hand of our enemies, and he delivered us out of the hand of the Philistines; and now he is fled out of the land for Absalom.

10 And Absalom, whom we anointed over us, is dead in battle. Now therefore why speak you not a word of bringing the king back?

11 And king David sent to Zadok and to Abiathar the priests, saying, Speak unto the elders of Judah, saying, Why are you the last to bring the king back to his house? seeing the speech of all Israel is come to the king, even to his house.

12 You are my brethren, you are my bones and my flesh: wherefore then are you the last to bring back the king?

13 And say you to Amasa, Are you not of my bone, and of my flesh? God do so to me, and more also, if you be not captain of the host before me continually in the room of Joab.

14 And he bowed the heart of all the men of Judah, even as the heart of one man; so that they sent this word unto the king, Return you , and all your servants.

15 So the king returned, and came to Jordan. And Judah came to Gilgal, to go to meet the king, to conduct the king over Jordan.

16 And Shimei the son of Gera, a Benjamite, which was of Bahurim, hasted and came down with the men of Judah to meet king David.

17 And there were a thousand men of Benjamin with him, and Ziba the servant of the house of Saul, and his fifteen sons and his twenty servants with him; and they went over Jordan before the king.

18 And there went over a ferry boat to carry over the king's household, and to do what he thought good. And Shimei the son of Gera fell down before the king, as he was come over Jordan;

19 And said unto the king, Let not my lord impute iniquity unto me, neither do you remember that which your servant did perversely the day that my lord the king went out of Jerusalem, that the king should take it to his heart.

20 For your servant doth know that I have sinned: therefore, behold, I am come the first this day of all the house of Joseph to go down to meet my lord the king.

21 But Abishai the son of Zeruiah answered and said, Shall not Shimei be put to death for this, because he cursed the LORD's anointed?

22 And David said, What have I to do with you, you sons of Zeruiah, that you should this day be adversaries unto me? shall there any man be put to death this day in Israel? for do not I know that I am this day king over Israel?

23 Therefore the king said unto Shimei, You shalt not die. And the king sware unto him.

24 And Mephibosheth the son of Saul came down to meet the king, and had neither dressed his feet, nor trimmed his beard, nor washed his clothes, from the day the king departed until the day he came again in peace.

25 And it came to pass, when he was come to Jerusalem to meet the king, that the king said unto him, Wherefore wentest not you with me, Mephibosheth?

26 And he answered, My lord, O king, my servant deceived me: for your servant said, I will saddle me an ass, that I may ride thereon, and go to the king; because your servant is lame.

27 And he has slandered your servant unto my lord the king; but my lord the king is as an angel of God: do therefore what is good in yours eyes.

28 For all of my father's house were but dead men before my lord the king: yet did you set your servant among them that did eat at yours own table. What right therefore have I yet to cry any more unto the king?

29 And the king said unto him, Why speakest you any more of your matters? I have said, You and Ziba divide the land.

30 And Mephibosheth said unto the king, Yea, let him take all, forasmuch as my lord the king is come again in peace unto his own house.

31 And Barzillai the Gileadite came down from Rogelim, and went over Jordan with the king, to conduct him over Jordan.

32 Now Barzillai was a very aged man, even fourscore years old: and he had provided the king of sustenance while he lay at Mahanaim; for he was a very great man.

33 And the king said unto Barzillai, Come you over with me, and I will feed you with me in Jerusalem.

34 And Barzillai said unto the king, How long have I to live, that I should go up with the king unto Jerusalem?

35 I am this day fourscore years old: and can I discern between good and evil? can your servant taste what I eat or what I drink? can I hear any more the voice of singing men and singing women? wherefore then should your servant be yet a burden unto my lord the king?

36 Your servant will go a little way over Jordan with the king: and why should the king recompense it me with such a reward?

37 Let your servant, I pray you, turn back again, that I may die in my own city, and be buried by the grave of my father and of my mother. But behold your servant Chimham; let him go over with my lord the king; and do to him what shall seem good unto you.

38 And the king answered, Chimham shall go over with me, and I will do to him that which shall seem good unto you: and whatsoever you shalt require of me, that will I do for you.

39 And all the people went over Jordan. And when the king was come over, the king kissed Barzillai, and blessed him; and he returned unto his own place.

40 Then the king went on to Gilgal, and Chimham went on with him: and all the people of Judah conducted the king, and also half the people of Israel.

41 And, behold, all the men of Israel came to the king, and said unto the king, Why have our brethren the men of Judah stolen you away, and have brought the king, and his household, and all David's men with him, over Jordan?

42 And all the men of Judah answered the men of Israel, Because the king is near of kin to us: wherefore then be you angry for this matter? have we eaten at all of the king's cost? or has he given us any gift?

43 And the men of Israel answered the men of Judah, and said, We have ten parts in the king, and we have also more right in David than you : why then did you despise us, that our advice should not be first had in bringing back our king? And the words of the men of Judah were fiercer than the words of the men of Israel.

CHAPTER 20

AND there happened to be there a man of Belial, whose name was Sheba, the son of Bichri, a Benjamite: and he blew a trumpet, and said, We have no part in David, neither have we inheritance in the son of Jesse: every man to his tents, O Israel.

2 So every man of Israel went up from after David, and followed Sheba the son of Bichri: but the men of Judah clave unto their king, from Jordan even to Jerusalem.

3 And David came to his house at Jerusalem; and the king took the ten women his concubines, whom he had left to keep the house, and put them in ward, and fed them, but went not in unto them. So they were shut up unto the day of their death, living in widowhood.

4 Then said the king to Amasa, Assemble me the men of Judah within three days, and be you here present.

5 So Amasa went to assemble the men of Judah: but he tarried longer than the set time which he had appointed him.

6 And David said to Abishai, Now shall Sheba the son of Bichri do us more harm than did Absalom: take you your lord's servants, and pursue after him, lest he get him fenced cities, and escape us.

7 And there went out after him Joab's men, and the Cherethites, and the Pelethites, and all the mighty men: and they went out of Jerusalem, to pursue after Sheba the son of Bichri.

8 When they were at the great stone which is in Gibeon, Amasa went before them. And Joab's garment that he had put on was girded unto him, and upon it a girdle with a sword fastened upon his loins in the sheath thereof; and as he went forth it fell out.

9 And Joab said to Amasa, Are you in health, my brother? And Joab took Amasa by the beard with the right hand to kiss him.

10 But Amasa took no heed to the sword that was in Joab's hand: so he struck him therewith in the fifth rib, and shed out his bowels to the ground, and struck him not again; and he died. So Joab and Abishai his brother pursued after Sheba the son of Bichri.

11 And one of Joab's men stood by him, and said, He that favoureth Joab, and he that is for David, let him go after Joab.

12 And Amasa wallowed in blood in the midst of the highway. And when the man saw that all the people stood still, he removed Amasa out of the highway into the field, and cast a cloth upon him, when he saw that every one that came by him stood still.

13 When he was removed out of the highway, all the people went on after Joab, to pursue after Sheba the son of Bichri.

14 And he went through all the tribes of Israel unto Abel, and to Beth-maachah, and all the Berites: and they were gathered together, and went also after him.

15 And they came and besieged him in Abel of Beth-maachah, and they cast up a bank against the city, and it stood in the trench: and all the people that were with Joab battered the wall, to throw it down.

16 Then cried a wise woman out of the city, Hear, hear; say, I pray you, unto Joab, Come near hither, that I may speak with you.

17 And when he was come near unto her, the woman said, Are you Joab? And he answered, I am he. Then she said unto him, Hear the words of yours handmaid. And he answered, I do hear.

18 Then she spake, saying, They were wont to speak in old time, saying, They shall surely ask counsel at Abel: and so they ended the matter.

19 I am one of them that are peaceable and faithful in Israel: you seekest to destroy a city and a mother in Israel: why will you swallow up the inheritance of the LORD?

20 And Joab answered and said, Far be it, far be it from me, that I should swallow up or destroy.

21 The matter is not so: but a man of mount Ephraim, Sheba the son of Bichri by name, has lifted up his hand against the king, even against David: deliver him only, and I will depart from the city. And the woman said unto Joab, Behold, his head shall be thrown to you over the wall.

22 Then the woman went unto all the people in her wisdom. And they cut off the head of Sheba the son of Bichri, and cast it out to Joab. And he blew a trumpet, and they retired from the city, every man to his tent. And Joab returned to Jerusalem unto the king.

23 Now Joab was over all the host of Israel: and Benaiah the son of Jehoiada was over the Cherethites and over the Pelethites:

24 And Adoram was over the tribute: and Jehoshaphat the son of Ahilud was recorder:

25 And Sheva was scribe: and Zadok and Abiathar were the priests:

26 And Ira also the Jairite was a chief ruler about David.

CHAPTER 21

THEN there was a famine in the days of David three years, year after year; and David inquired of the LORD. And the LORD answered, It is for Saul, and for his bloody house, because he slew the Gibeonites.

2 And the king called the Gibeonites, and said unto them; (now the Gibeonites were not of the children of Israel, but of the remnant of the Amorites; and the children of Israel had sworn unto them: and Saul sought to slay them in his zeal to the children of Israel and Judah.)

3 Wherefore David said unto the Gibeonites, What shall I do for you? and wherewith shall I make the atonement, that you may bless the inheritance of the LORD?

4 And the Gibeonites said unto him, We will have no silver nor gold of Saul, nor of his house; neither for us shalt you kill any man in Israel. And he said, What you shall say, that will I do for you.

5 And they answered the king, The man that consumed us, and that devised against us that we should be destroyed from remaining in any of the coasts of Israel,

6 Let seven men of his sons be delivered unto us, and we will hang them up unto the LORD in Gibeah of Saul, whom the LORD did choose. And the king said, I will give them.

7 But the king spared Mephibosheth, the son of Jonathan the son of Saul, because of the LORD's oath that was between them, between David and Jonathan the son of Saul.

8 But the king took the two sons of Rizpah the daughter of Aiah, whom she bare unto Saul, Armoni and Mephibosheth; and the five sons of Michal the daughter of Saul, whom she brought up for Adriel the son of Barzillai the Meholathite:

9 And he delivered them into the hands of the Gibeonites, and they hanged them in the hill before the LORD: and they fell all seven together, and were put to death in the days of harvest, in the first days, in the beginning of barley harvest.

10 And Rizpah the daughter of Aiah took sackcloth, and spread it for her upon the rock, from the beginning of harvest until water dropped upon them out of heaven, and suffered neither the birds of the air to rest on them by day, nor the beasts of the field by night.

11 And it was told David what Rizpah the daughter of Aiah, the concubine of Saul, had done.

12 And David went and took the bones of Saul and the bones of Jonathan his son from the men of Jabesh-gilead, which had stolen them from the street of Beth-shan, where the Philistines had hanged them, when the Philistines had slain Saul in Gilboa:

13 And he brought up from thence the bones of Saul and the bones of Jonathan his son; and they gathered the bones of them that were hanged.

14 And the bones of Saul and Jonathan his son buried they in the country of Benjamin in Zelah, in the sepulchre of Kish his father: and they performed all that the king commanded. And after that God was intreated for the land.

15 Moreover the Philistines had yet war again with Israel; and David went down, and his servants with him, and fought against the Philistines: and David waxed faint.

16 And Ishbi-benob, which was of the sons of the giant, the weight of whose spear weighed three hundred shekels of brass in weight, he being girded with a new sword, thought to have slain David.

17 But Abishai the son of Zeruiah succoured him, and struck the Philistine, and killed him. Then the men of David sware unto him, saying, You shalt go no more out with us to battle, that you quench not the light of Israel.

18 And it came to pass after this, that there was again a battle with the Philistines at Gob: then Sibbechai the Hushathite slew Saph, which was of the sons of the giant.

19 And there was again a battle in Gob with the Philistines, where Elhanan the son of Jaare-oregim, a Beth-lehemite, slew the brother of Goliath the Gittite, the staff of whose spear was like a weaver's beam.

20 And there was yet a battle in Gath, where was a man of great stature, that had on every hand six fingers, and on every foot six toes, four and twenty in number; and he also was born to the giant.

21 And when he defied Israel, Jonathan the son of Shimea the brother of David slew him.

22 These four were born to the giant in Gath, and fell by the hand of David, and by the hand of his servants.

CHAPTER 22

AND David spake unto the LORD the words of this song in the day that the LORD had delivered him out of the hand of all his enemies, and out of the hand of Saul:

2 And he said, The LORD is my rock, and my fortress, and my deliverer;

3 The God of my rock; in him will I trust: he is my shield, and the horn of my salvation, my high tower, and my refuge, my saviour; you savest me from violence.

4 I will call on the LORD, who is worthy to be praised: so shall I be saved from my enemies.

5 When the waves of death compassed me, the floods of ungodly men made me afraid;

6 The sorrows of hell compassed me about; the snares of death prevented me;

7 In my distress I called upon the LORD, and cried to my God: and he did hear my voice out of his temple, and my cry did enter into his ears.

8 Then the earth shook and trembled; the foundations of heaven moved and shook, because he was wroth.

9 There went up a smoke out of his nostrils, and fire out of his mouth devoured: coals were kindled by it.

10 He bowed the heavens also, and came down; and darkness was under his feet.

11 And he rode upon a cherub, and did fly: and he was seen upon the wings of the wind.

12 And he made darkness pavilions round about him, dark waters, and thick clouds of the skies.

13 Through the brightness before him were coals of fire kindled.

14 The LORD thundered from heaven, and the most High uttered his voice.

15 And he sent out arrows, and scattered them; lightning, and discomfited them.

16 And the channels of the sea appeared, the foundations of the world were discovered, at the rebuking of the LORD, at the blast of the breath of his nostrils.

17 He sent from above, he took me; he drew me out of many waters;

18 He delivered me from my strong enemy, and from them that hated me: for they were too strong for me.

19 They prevented me in the day of my calamity: but the LORD was my stay.

20 He brought me forth also into a large place: he delivered me, because he delighted in me.

21 The LORD rewarded me according to my righteousness: according to the cleanness of my hands has he recompensed me.

22 For I have kept the ways of the LORD, and have not wickedly departed from my God.

23 For all his judgments were before me: and as for his statutes, I did not depart from them.

24 I was also upright before him, and have kept myself from my iniquity.

25 Therefore the LORD has recompensed me according to my righteousness; according to my cleanness in his eye sight.

26 With the merciful you will shew yourself merciful, and with the upright man you will shew yourself upright.

27 With the pure you will shew yourself pure; and with the froward you will shew yourself unsavoury.

28 And the afflicted people you will save: but yours eyes are upon the haughty, that you mayest bring them down.

29 For you are my lamp, O LORD: and the LORD will lighten my darkness.

30 For by you I have run through a troop: by my God have I leaped over a wall.

31 As for God, his way is perfect; the word of the LORD is tried: he is a buckler to all them that trust in him.

32 For who is God, save the LORD? and who is a rock, save our God?

33 God is my strength and power: and he maketh my way perfect.

34 He maketh my feet like hinds' feet: and setteth me upon my high places.

35 He teacheth my hands to war; so that a bow of steel is broken by my arms.

36 You have also given me the shield of your salvation: and your gentleness has made me great.

37 You have enlarged my steps under me; so that my feet did not slip.

38 I have pursued my enemies, and destroyed them; and turned not again until I had consumed them.

39 And I have consumed them, and wounded them, that they could not arise: yea, they are fallen under my feet.

40 For you have girded me with strength to battle: them that rose up against me have you subdued under me.

41 You have also given me the necks of my enemies, that I might destroy them that hate me.

42 They looked, but there was none to save; even unto the LORD, but he answered them not.

43 Then did I beat them as small as the dust of the earth, I did stamp them as the mire of the street, and did spread them abroad.

44 You also have delivered me from the strivings of my people, you have kept me to be head of the heathen: a people which I knew not shall serve me.

45 Strangers shall submit themselves unto me: as soon as they hear, they shall be obedient unto me.

46 Strangers shall fade away, and they shall be afraid out of their close places.

47 The LORD liveth; and blessed be my rock; and exalted be the God of the rock of my salvation.

48 It is God that avengeth me, and that bringeth down the people under me,

49 And that bringeth me forth from my enemies: you also have lifted me up on high above them that rose up against me: you have delivered me from the violent man.

50 Therefore I will give thanks unto you, O LORD, among the heathen, and I will sing praises unto your name.

51 He is the tower of salvation for his king: and sheweth mercy to his anointed, unto David, and to his seed for evermore.

CHAPTER 23

NOW these be the last words of David. David the son of Jesse said, and the man who was raised up on high, the anointed of the God of Jacob, and the sweet psalmist of Israel, said,

2 The Spirit of the LORD spake by me, and his word was in my tongue.

3 The God of Israel said, the Rock of Israel spake to me, He that ruleth over men must be just, ruling in the fear of God.

4 And he shall be as the light of the morning, when the sun riseth, even a morning without clouds; as the tender grass springing out of the earth by clear shining after rain.

5 Although my house be not so with God; yet he has made with me an everlasting covenant, ordered in all things, and sure: for this is all my salvation, and all my desire, although he make it not to grow.

6But the sons of Belial shall be all of them as thorns thrust away, because they cannot be taken with hands:

7 But the man that shall touch them must be fenced with iron and the staff of a spear; and they shall be utterly burned with fire in the same place.

8These be the names of the mighty men whom David had: The Tachmonite that sat in the seat, chief among the captains; the same was Adino the Eznite: he lift up his spear against eight hundred, whom he slew at one time.

9 And after him was Eleazar the son of Dodo the Ahohite, one of the three mighty men with David, when they defied the Philistines that were there gathered together to battle, and the men of Israel were gone away:

10 He arose, and struck the Philistines until his hand was weary, and his hand clave unto the sword: and the LORD created a great victory that day; and the people returned after him only to spoil.

11 And after him was Shammah the son of Agee the Hararite. And the Philistines were gathered together into a troop, where was a piece of ground full of lentiles: and the people fled from the Philistines.

12 But he stood in the midst of the ground, and defended it, and slew the Philistines: and the LORD created a great victory.

13 And three of the thirty chief went down, and came to David in the harvest time unto the cave of Adullam: and the troop of the Philistines pitched in the valley of Rephaim.

14 And David was then in an hold, and the garrison of the Philistines was then in Beth-lehem.

15 And David longed, and said, Oh that one would give me drink of the water of the well of Beth-lehem, which is by the gate!

16 And the three mighty men brake through the host of the Philistines, and drew water out of the well of Beth-lehem, that was by the gate, and took it, and brought it to David: nevertheless he would not drink thereof, but poured it out unto the LORD.

17 And he said, Be it far from me, O LORD, that I should do this: is not this the blood of the men that went in jeopardy of their lives? therefore he would not drink it. These things did these three mighty men.

18 And Abishai, the brother of Joab, the son of Zeruiah, was chief among three. And he lifted up his spear against three hundred, and slew them, and had the name among three.

19 Was he not most honourable of three? therefore he was their captain: howbeit he attained not unto the first three.

20 And Benaiah the son of Jehoiada, the son of a valiant man, of Kabzeel, who had done many acts, he slew two lionlike men of Moab: he went down also and slew a lion in the midst of a pit in time of snow:

21 And he slew an Egyptian, a goodly man: and the Egyptian had a spear in his hand; but he went down to him with a staff, and plucked the spear out of the Egyptian's hand, and slew him with his own spear.

22 These things did Benaiah the son of Jehoiada, and had the name among three mighty men.

23 He was more honourable than the thirty, but he attained not to the first three. And David set him over his guard.

24 Asahel the brother of Joab was one of the thirty; Elhanan the son of Dodo of Beth-lehem,

25 Shammah the Harodite, Elika the Harodite,

26 Helez the Paltite, Ira the son of Ikkesh the Tekoite,

27 Abiezer the Anethothite, Mebunnai the Hushathite,

28 Zalmon the Ahohite, Maharai the Netophathite,

29 Heleb the son of Baanah, a Netophathite, Ittai the son of Ribai out of Gibeah of the children of Benjamin,

30 Benaiah the Pirathonite, Hiddai of the brooks of Gaash,

31 Abi-albon the Arbathite, Azmaveth the Barhumite,

32 Eliahba the Shaalbonite, of the sons of Jashen, Jonathan,

33 Shammah the Hararite, Ahiam the son of Sharar the Hararite,

34 Eliphelet the son of Ahasbai, the son of the Maachathite, Eliam the son of Ahithophel the Gilonite,

35 Hezrai the Carmelite, Paarai the Arbite,

36 Igal the son of Nathan of Zobah, Bani the Gadite,

37 Zelek the Ammonite, Naharai the Beerothite, armourbearer to Joab the son of Zeruiah,

38 Ira an Ithrite, Gareb an Ithrite,

39 Uriah the Hittite: thirty and seven in all.

CHAPTER 24

AND again the anger of the LORD was kindled against Israel, and he moved David against them to say, Go, number Israel and Judah.

2 For the king said to Joab the captain of the host, which was with him, Go now through all the tribes of Israel, from Dan even to Beer-sheba, and number you the people, that I may know the number of the people.

3 And Joab said unto the king, Now the LORD your God add unto the people, how many soever they be, an hundredfold, and that the eyes of my lord the king may see it: but why doth my lord the king delight in this thing?

4 Notwithstanding the king's word prevailed against Joab, and against the captains of the host. And Joab and the captains of the host went out from the presence of the king, to number the people of Israel.

5And they passed over Jordan, and pitched in Aroer, on the right side of the city that lies in the midst of the river of Gad, and toward Jazer:

6 Then they came to Gilead, and to the land of Tahtim-hodshi; and they came to Dan-jaan, and about to Zidon,

7 And came to the strong hold of Tyre, and to all the cities of the Hivites, and of the Canaanites: and they went out to the south of Judah, even to Beer-sheba.

8 So when they had gone through all the land, they came to Jerusalem at the end of nine months and twenty days.

9 And Joab gave up the sum of the number of the people unto the king: and there were in Israel eight hundred thousand valiant men that drew the sword; and the men of Judah were five hundred thousand men.

10And David's heart struck him after that he had numbered the people. And David said unto the LORD, I have sinned greatly in that I have done: and now, I beseech you, O LORD, take away the iniquity of your servant; for I have done very foolishly.

11 For when David was up in the morning, the word of the LORD came unto the prophet Gad, David's seer, saying,

12 Go and say unto David, Thus saith the LORD, I offer you three things; choose you one of them, that I may do it unto you.

13 So Gad came to David, and told him, and said unto him, Shall seven years of famine come unto you in your land? or will you flee three months before yours enemies, while they pursue you? or that there be three days' pestilence in your land? now advise, and see what answer I shall return to him that sent me.

14 And David said unto Gad, I am in a great strait: let us fall now into the hand of the LORD; for his mercies are great: and let me not fall into the hand of man.

15So the LORD sent a pestilence upon Israel from the morning even to the time appointed: and there died of the people from Dan even to Beer-sheba seventy thousand men.

16 And when the angel stretched out his hand upon Jerusalem to destroy it, the LORD repented him of the evil, and said to the angel that destroyed the people, It is enough: stay now yours hand. And the angel of the LORD was by the threshingplace of Araunah the Jebusite.

17 And David spake unto the LORD when he saw the angel that struck the people, and said, Lo, I have sinned, and I have done wickedly: but these sheep, what have they done? let yours hand, I pray you, be against me, and against my father's house.

18And Gad came that day to David, and said unto him, Go up, rear an altar unto the LORD in the threshingfloor of Araunah the Jebusite.

19 And David, according to the saying of Gad, went up as the LORD commanded.

20 And Araunah looked, and saw the king and his servants coming on toward him: and Araunah went out, and bowed himself before the king on his face upon the ground.

21 And Araunah said, Wherefore is my lord the king come to his servant? And David said, To buy the threshingfloor of you, to build an altar unto the LORD, that the plague may be stayed from the people.

22 And Araunah said unto David, Let my lord the king take and offer up what seemeth good unto him: behold, here be oxen for burnt sacrifice, and threshing instruments and other instruments of the oxen for wood.

23 All these things did Araunah, as a king, give unto the king. And Araunah said unto the king, The LORD your God accept you.

24 And the king said unto Araunah, Nay; but I will surely buy it of you at a price: neither will I offer burnt offerings unto the LORD my God of that which doth cost me nothing. So David bought the threshingfloor and the oxen for fifty shekels of silver.

25 And David built there an altar unto the LORD, and offered burnt offerings and peace offerings. So the LORD was intreated for the land, and the plague was stayed from Israel.

THE FIRST
BOOK OF THE KINGS,
COMMONLY CALLED,
THE THIRD BOOK OF THE KINGS.

CHAPTER 1

NOW king David was old and stricken in years; and they covered him with clothes, but he gat no heat.

2 Wherefore his servants said unto him, Let there be sought for my lord the king a young virgin: and let her stand before the king, and let her cherish him, and let her lie in your bosom, that my lord the king may get heat.

3 So they sought for a fair damsel throughout all the coasts of Israel, and found Abishag a Shunammite, and brought her to the king.

4 And the damsel was very fair, and cherished the king, and ministered to him: but the king knew her not.

5 Then Adonijah the son of Haggith exalted himself, saying, I will be king: and he prepared him chariots and horsemen, and fifty men to run before him.

6 And his father had not displeased him at any time in saying, Why have you done so? and he also was a very goodly man; and his mother bare him after Absalom.

7 And he conferred with Joab the son of Zeruiah, and with Abiathar the priest: and they following Adonijah helped him.

8 But Zadok the priest, and Benaiah the son of Jehoiada, and Nathan the prophet, and Shimei, and Rei, and the mighty men which belonged to David, were not with Adonijah.

9 And Adonijah slew sheep and oxen and fat cattle by the stone of Zoheleth, which is by En-rogel, and called all his brethren the king's sons, and all the men of Judah the king's servants:

10 But Nathan the prophet, and Benaiah, and the mighty men, and Solomon his brother, he called not.

11 Wherefore Nathan spake unto Bath-sheba the mother of Solomon, saying, Have you not heard that Adonijah the son of Haggith doth reign, and David our lord knoweth it not?

12 Now therefore come, let me, I pray you, give you counsel, that you mayest save yours own life, and the life of your son Solomon.

13 Go and get you in unto king David, and say unto him, Did not you , my lord, O king, swear unto yours handmaid, saying, Assuredly Solomon your son shall reign after me, and he shall sit upon my throne? why then doth Adonijah reign?

14 Behold, while you yet talkest there with the king, I also will come in after you, and confirm your words.

15 And Bath-sheba went in unto the king into the chamber: and the king was very old; and Abishag the Shunammite ministered unto the king.

16 And Bath-sheba bowed, and did obeisance unto the king. And the king said, What wouldest you ?

17 And she said unto him, My lord, you swarest by the LORD your God unto yours handmaid, saying, Assuredly Solomon your son shall reign after me, and he shall sit upon my throne.

18 And now, behold, Adonijah reigneth; and now, my lord the king, you knowest it not:

19 And he has slain oxen and fat cattle and sheep in abundance, and has called all the sons of the king, and Abiathar the priest, and Joab the captain of the host: but Solomon your servant has he not called.

20 And you , my lord, O king, the eyes of all Israel are upon you, that you shouldest tell them who shall sit on the throne of my lord the king after him.

21 Otherwise it shall come to pass, when my lord the king shall sleep with his fathers, that I and my son Solomon shall be counted offenders.

22 And, lo, while she yet talked with the king, Nathan the prophet also came in.

23 And they told the king, saying, Behold Nathan the prophet. And when he was come in before the king, he bowed himself before the king with his face to the ground.

24 And Nathan said, My lord, O king, have you said, Adonijah shall reign after me, and he shall sit upon my throne?

25 For he is gone down this day, and has slain oxen and fat cattle and sheep in abundance, and has called all the king's sons, and the captains of the host, and Abiathar the priest; and, behold, they eat and drink before him, and say, God save king Adonijah.

26 But me, even me your servant, and Zadok the priest, and Benaiah the son of Jehoiada, and your servant Solomon, has he not called.

27 Is this thing done by my lord the king, and you have not shewed it unto your servant, who should sit on the throne of my lord the king after him?

28 Then king David answered and said, Call me Bath-sheba. And she came into the king's presence, and stood before the king.

29 And the king sware, and said, As the LORD liveth, that has redeemed my soul out of all distress,

30 Even as I sware unto you by the LORD God of Israel, saying, Assuredly Solomon your son shall reign after me, and he shall sit upon my throne in my stead; even so will I certainly do this day.

31 Then Bath-sheba bowed with her face to the earth, and did reverence to the king, and said, Let my lord king David live for ever.

32 And king David said, Call me Zadok the priest, and Nathan the prophet, and Benaiah the son of Jehoiada. And they came before the king.

33 The king also said unto them, Take with you the servants of your lord, and cause Solomon my son to ride upon my own mule, and bring him down to Gihon:

34 And let Zadok the priest and Nathan the prophet anoint him there king over Israel: and blow you with the trumpet, and say, God save king Solomon.

35 Then you shall come up after him, that he may come and sit upon my throne; for he shall be king in my stead: and I have appointed him to be ruler over Israel and over Judah.

36 And Benaiah the son of Jehoiada answered the king, and said, Amen: the LORD God of my lord the king say so too.

37 As the LORD has been with my lord the king, even so be he with Solomon, and make his throne greater than the throne of my lord king David.

38 So Zadok the priest, and Nathan the prophet, and Benaiah the son of Jehoiada, and the Cherethites, and the Pelethites, went down, and caused Solomon to ride upon king David's mule, and brought him to Gihon.

39 And Zadok the priest took an horn of oil out of the tabernacle, and anointed Solomon. And they blew the trumpet; and all the people said, God save king Solomon.

40 And all the people came up after him, and the people piped with pipes, and rejoiced with great joy, so that the earth rent with the sound of them.

41 And Adonijah and all the guests that were with him heard it as they had made an end of eating. And when Joab heard the sound of the trumpet, he said, Wherefore is this noise of the city being in an uproar?

42 And while he yet spake, behold, Jonathan the son of Abiathar the priest came: and Adonijah said unto him, Come in; for you are a valiant man, and bringest good tidings.

43 And Jonathan answered and said to Adonijah, Verily our lord king David has made Solomon king.

44 And the king has sent with him Zadok the priest, and Nathan the prophet, and Benaiah the son of Jehoiada, and the Cherethites, and the Pelethites, and they have caused him to ride upon the king's mule:

45 And Zadok the priest and Nathan the prophet have anointed him king in Gihon: and they are come up from thence rejoicing, so that the city rang again. This is the noise that you have heard.

46 And also Solomon sitteth on the throne of the kingdom.

47 And moreover the king's servants came to bless our lord king David, saying, God make the name of Solomon better than your name, and make his throne greater than your throne. And the king bowed himself upon the bed.

48 And also thus said the king, Blessed be the LORD God of Israel, which has given one to sit on my throne this day, my eyes even seeing it.

49 And all the guests that were with Adonijah were afraid, and rose up, and went every man his way.

50 And Adonijah feared because of Solomon, and arose, and went, and caught hold on the horns of the altar.

51 And it was told Solomon, saying, Behold, Adonijah feareth king Solomon: for, lo, he has caught hold on the horns of the altar, saying, Let king Solomon swear unto me to day that he will not slay his servant with the sword.

52 And Solomon said, If he will shew himself a worthy man, there shall not an hair of him fall to the earth: but if wickedness shall be found in him, he shall die.

53 So king Solomon sent, and they brought him down from the altar. And he came and bowed himself to king Solomon: and Solomon said unto him, Go to yours house.

CHAPTER 2

NOW the days of David drew nigh that he should die; and he charged Solomon his son, saying,

2 I go the way of all the earth: be you strong therefore, and shew yourself a man;

3 And keep the charge of the LORD your God, to walk in his ways, to keep his statutes, and his commandments, and his judgments, and his testimonies, as it is written in the law of Moses, that you mayest prosper in all that you doest, and whithersoever you turnest yourself:

4 That the LORD may continue his word which he spake concerning me, saying, If your children take heed to their way, to walk before me in truth with all their heart and with all their soul, there shall not fail you (said he) a man on the throne of Israel.

5 Moreover you knowest also what Joab the son of Zeruiah did to me, and what he did to the two captains of the hosts of Israel, unto Abner the son of Ner, and unto Amasa the son of Jether, whom he slew, and shed the blood of war in peace, and put the blood of war upon his girdle that was about his loins, and in his shoes that were on his feet.

6 Do therefore according to your wisdom, and let not his hoar head go down to the grave in peace.

7 But shew kindness unto the sons of Barzillai the Gileadite, and let them be of those that eat at your table: for so they came to me when I fled because of Absalom your brother.

8 And, behold, you have with you Shimei the son of Gera, a Benjamite of Bahurim, which cursed me with a grievous curse in the day when I went to Mahanaim: but he came down to meet me at Jordan, and I sware to him by the LORD, saying, I will not put you to death with the sword.

9 Now therefore hold him not guiltless: for you are a wise man, and knowest what you oughtest to do unto him; but his hoar head bring you down to the grave with blood.

10 So David slept with his fathers, and was buried in the city of David.

11 And the days that David reigned over Israel were forty years: seven years reigned he in Hebron, and thirty and three years reigned he in Jerusalem.

12 Then sat Solomon upon the throne of David his father; and his kingdom was established greatly.

13 And Adonijah the son of Haggith came to Bath-sheba the mother of Solomon. And she said, Comest you peaceably? And he said, Peaceably.

14 He said moreover, I have somewhat to say unto you. And she said, Say on.

15 And he said, You knowest that the kingdom was my, and that all Israel set their faces on me, that I should reign: howbeit the kingdom is turned about, and is become my brother's: for it was his from the LORD.

16 And now I ask one petition of you, deny me not. And she said unto him, Say on.

17 And he said, Speak, I pray you, unto Solomon the king, (for he will not say you nay,) that he give me Abishag the Shunammite to wife.

18 And Bath-sheba said, Well; I will speak for you unto the king.

19 Bath-sheba therefore went unto king Solomon, to speak unto him for Adonijah. And the king rose up to meet her, and bowed himself unto her, and sat down on his throne, and caused a seat to be set for the king's mother; and she sat on his right hand.

20 Then she said, I desire one small petition of you; I pray you, say me not nay. And the king said unto her, Ask on, my mother: for I will not say you nay.

21 And she said, Let Abishag the Shunammite be given to Adonijah your brother to wife.

22 And king Solomon answered and said unto his mother, And why dost you ask Abishag the Shunammite for Adonijah? ask for him the kingdom also; for he is my elder brother; even for him, and for Abiathar the priest, and for Joab the son of Zeruiah.

23 Then king Solomon sware by the LORD, saying, God do so to me, and more also, if Adonijah have not spoken this word against his own life.

24 Now therefore, as the LORD liveth, which has established me, and set me on the throne of David my father, and who has made me an house, as he promised, Adonijah shall be put to death this day.

25 And king Solomon sent by the hand of Benaiah the son of Jehoiada; and he fell upon him that he died.

26 And unto Abiathar the priest said the king, Get you to Anathoth, unto yours own fields; for you are worthy of death: but I will not at this time put you to death, because you barest the ark of the Lord GOD before David my father, and because you have been afflicted in all wherein my father was afflicted.

27 So Solomon thrust out Abiathar from being priest unto the LORD; that he might fulfil the word of the LORD, which he spake concerning the house of Eli in Shiloh.

28 Then tidings came to Joab: for Joab had turned after Adonijah, though he turned not after Absalom. And Joab fled unto the tabernacle of the LORD, and caught hold on the horns of the altar.

29 And it was told king Solomon that Joab was fled unto the tabernacle of the LORD; and, behold, he is by the altar. Then Solomon sent Benaiah the son of Jehoiada, saying, Go, fall upon him.

30 And Benaiah came to the tabernacle of the LORD, and said unto him, Thus saith the king, Come forth. And he said, Nay; but I will die here. And Benaiah brought the king word again, saying, Thus said Joab, and thus he answered me.

31 And the king said unto him, Do as he has said, and fall upon him, and bury him; that you mayest take away the innocent blood, which Joab shed, from me, and from the house of my father.

32 And the LORD shall return his blood upon his own head, who fell upon two men more righteous and better than he, and slew them with the sword, my father David not knowing thereof, to wit, Abner the son of Ner, captain of the host of Israel, and Amasa the son of Jether, captain of the host of Judah.

33 Their blood shall therefore return upon the head of Joab, and upon the head of his seed for ever: but upon David, and upon his seed, and upon his house, and upon his throne, shall there be peace for ever from the LORD.

34 So Benaiah the son of Jehoiada went up, and fell upon him, and slew him: and he was buried in his own house in the wilderness.

35 And the king put Benaiah the son of Jehoiada in his room over the host: and Zadok the priest did the king put in the room of Abiathar.

36 And the king sent and called for Shimei, and said unto him, Build you an house in Jerusalem, and dwell there, and go not forth thence any whither.

37 For it shall be, that on the day you go out, and passest over the brook Kidron, you shalt know for certain that you shalt surely die: your blood shall be upon yours own head.

38 And Shimei said unto the king, The saying is good: as my lord the king has said, so will your servant do. And Shimei dwelt in Jerusalem many days.

39 And it came to pass at the end of three years, that two of the servants of Shimei ran away unto Achish son of Maachah king of Gath. And they told Shimei, saying, Behold, your servants be in Gath.

40 And Shimei arose, and saddled his ass, and went to Gath to Achish to seek his servants: and Shimei went, and brought his servants from Gath.

41 And it was told Solomon that Shimei had gone from Jerusalem to Gath, and was come again.

42 And the king sent and called for Shimei, and said unto him, Did I not make you to swear by the LORD, and protested unto you, saying, Know for a certain, on the day you go out, and walkest abroad any whither, that you shalt surely die? and you saidst unto me, The word that I have heard is good.

43 Why then have you not kept the oath of the LORD, and the commandment that I have charged you with?

44 The king said moreover to Shimei, You knowest all the wickedness which yours heart is privy to, that you did to David my father: therefore the LORD shall return your wickedness upon yours own head;

45 And king Solomon shall be blessed, and the throne of David shall be established before the LORD for ever.

46 So the king commanded Benaiah the son of Jehoiada; which went out, and fell upon him, that he died. And the kingdom was established in the hand of Solomon.

CHAPTER 3

AND Solomon made affinity with Pharaoh king of Egypt, and took Pharaoh's daughter, and brought her into the city of David, until he had made an end of building his own house, and the house of the LORD, and the wall of Jerusalem round about.

2 Only the people sacrificed in high places, because there was no house built unto the name of the LORD, until those days.

3 And Solomon loved the LORD, walking in the statutes of David his father: only he sacrificed and burnt incense in high places.

4 And the king went to Gibeon to sacrifice there; for that was the great high place: a thousand burnt offerings did Solomon offer upon that altar.

5 In Gibeon the LORD appeared to Solomon in a dream by night: and God said, Ask what I shall give you.

6 And Solomon said, You have shewed unto your servant David my father great mercy, according as he walked before you in truth, and in righteousness, and in uprightness of heart with you; and you have kept for him this great kindness, that you have given him a son to sit on his throne, as it is this day.

7 And now, O LORD my God, you have made your servant king instead of David my father: and I am but a little child: I know not how to go out or come in.

8 And your servant is in the midst of your people which you have chosen, a great people, that cannot be numbered nor counted for multitude.

9 Give therefore your servant an understanding heart to judge your people, that I may discern between good and bad: for who is able to judge this your so great a people?

10 And the speech pleased the Lord, that Solomon had asked this thing.

11 And God said unto him, Because you have asked this thing, and have not asked for yourself long life; neither have asked riches for yourself, nor have asked the life of yours enemies; but have asked for yourself understanding to discern judgment;

12 Behold, I have done according to your words: lo, I have given you a wise and an understanding heart; so that there was none like you before you, neither after you shall any arise like unto you.

13 And I have also given you that which you have not asked, both riches, and honour: so that there shall not be any among the kings like unto you all your days.

14 And if you will walk in my ways, to keep my statutes and my commandments, as your father David did walk, then I will lengthen your days.

15 And Solomon awoke; and, behold, it was a dream. And he came to Jerusalem, and stood before the ark of the covenant of the LORD, and offered up burnt offerings, and offered peace offerings, and made a feast to all his servants.

16 Then came there two women, that were harlots, unto the king, and stood before him.

17 And the one woman said, O my lord, I and this woman dwell in one house; and I was delivered of a child with her in the house.

18 And it came to pass the third day after that I was delivered, that this woman was delivered also: and we were together; there was no stranger with us in the house, save we two in the house.

19 And this woman's child died in the night; because she overlaid it.

20 And she arose at midnight, and took my son from beside me, while yours handmaid slept, and laid it in her bosom, and laid her dead child in my bosom.

21 And when I rose in the morning to give my child suck, behold, it was dead: but when I had considered it in the morning, behold, it was not my son, which I did bear.

22 And the other woman said, Nay; but the living is my son, and the dead is your son. And this said, No; but the dead is your son, and the living is my son. Thus they spake before the king.

23 Then said the king, The one saith, This is my son that liveth, and your son is the dead: and the other saith, Nay; but your son is the dead, and my son is the living.

24 And the king said, Bring me a sword. And they brought a sword before the king.

25 And the king said, Divide the living child in two, and give half to the one, and half to the other.

26 Then spake the woman whose the living child was unto the king, for her bowels yearned upon her son, and she said, O my lord, give her the living child, and in no wise slay it. But the other said, Let it be neither my nor yours, but divide it.

27 Then the king answered and said, Give her the living child, and in no wise slay it: she is the mother thereof.

28 And all Israel heard of the judgment which the king had judged; and they feared the king: for they saw that the wisdom of God was in him, to do judgment.

CHAPTER 4

SO king Solomon was king over all Israel.

2 And these were the princes which he had; Azariah the son of Zadok the priest,

3 Elihoreph and Ahiah, the sons of Shisha, scribes; Jehoshaphat the son of Ahilud, the recorder.

4 And Benaiah the son of Jehoiada was over the host: and Zadok and Abiathar were the priests:

5 And Azariah the son of Nathan was over the officers: and Zabud the son of Nathan was principal officer, and the king's friend:

6 And Ahishar was over the household: and Adoniram the son of Abda was over the tribute.

7 And Solomon had twelve officers over all Israel, which provided victuals for the king and his household: each man his month in a year made provision.

8 And these are their names: The son of Hur, in mount Ephraim:

9 The son of Dekar, in Makaz, and in Shaalbim, and Beth-shemesh, and Elon-beth-hanan:

10 The son of Hesed, in Aruboth; to him pertained Sochoh, and all the land of Hepher:

11 The son of Abinadab, in all the region of Dor; which had Taphath the daughter of Solomon to wife:

12 Baana the son of Ahilud; to him pertained Taanach and Megiddo, and all Beth-shean, which is by Zartanah beneath Jezreel, from Beth-shean to Abel-meholah, even unto the place that is beyond Jokneam:

13 The son of Geber, in Ramoth-gilead; to him pertained the towns of Jair the son of Manasseh, which are in Gilead; to him also pertained the region of Argob, which is in Bashan, threescore great cities with walls and brasen bars:

14 Ahinadab the son of Iddo had Mahanaim:

15 Ahimaaz was in Naphtali; he also took Basmath the daughter of Solomon to wife:

16 Baanah the son of Hushai was in Asher and in Aloth:

17 Jehoshaphat the son of Paruah, in Issachar:

18 Shimei the son of Elah, in Benjamin:

19 Geber the son of Uri was in the country of Gilead, in the country of Sihon king of the Amorites, and of Og king of Bashan; and he was the only officer which was in the land.

20 Judah and Israel were many, as the sand which is by the sea in multitude, eating and drinking, and making merry.

21 And Solomon reigned over all kingdoms from the river unto the land of the Philistines, and unto the border of Egypt: they brought presents, and served Solomon all the days of his life.

22 And Solomon's provision for one day was thirty measures of fine flour, and threescore measures of meal,

23 Ten fat oxen, and twenty oxen out of the pastures, and an hundred sheep, beside harts, and roebucks, and fallowdeer, and fatted fowl.

24 For he had dominion over all the region on this side the river, from Tiphsah even to Azzah, over all the kings on this side the river: and he had peace on all sides round about him.

25 And Judah and Israel dwelt safely, every man under his vine and under his fig tree, from Dan even to Beer-sheba, all the days of Solomon.

26 And Solomon had forty thousand stalls of horses for his chariots, and twelve thousand horsemen.

27 And those officers provided victual for king Solomon, and for all that came unto king Solomon's table, every man in his month: they lacked nothing.

28 Barley also and straw for the horses and dromedaries brought they unto the place where the officers were, every man according to his charge.

29 And God gave Solomon wisdom and understanding exceeding much, and largeness of heart, even as the sand that is on the sea shore.

30 And Solomon's wisdom excelled the wisdom of all the children of the east country, and all the wisdom of Egypt.

31 For he was wiser than all men; than Ethan the Ezrahite, and Heman, and Chalcol, and Darda, the sons of Mahol: and his fame was in all nations round about.

32 And he spake three thousand proverbs: and his songs were a thousand and five.

33 And he spake of trees, from the cedar tree that is in Lebanon even unto the hyssop that springeth out of the wall: he spake also of beasts, and of fowl, and of creeping things, and of fishes.

34 And there came of all people to hear the wisdom of Solomon, from all kings of the earth, which had heard of his wisdom.

CHAPTER 5

AND Hiram king of Tyre sent his servants unto Solomon; for he had heard that they had anointed him king in the room of his father: for Hiram was ever a lover of David.

2 And Solomon sent to Hiram, saying,

3 You knowest how that David my father could not build an house unto the name of the LORD his God for the wars which were about him on every side, until the LORD put them under the soles of his feet.

4 But now the LORD my God has given me rest on every side, so that there is neither adversary nor evil occurrent.

5 And, behold, I purpose to build an house unto the name of the LORD my God, as the LORD spake unto David my father, saying, Your son, whom I will set upon your throne in your room, he shall build an house unto my name.

6 Now therefore command you that they hew me cedar trees out of Lebanon; and my servants shall be with your servants: and unto you will I give hire for your servants according to all that you shalt appoint: for you knowest that there is not among us any that can skill to hew timber like unto the Sidonians.

7 And it came to pass, when Hiram heard the words of Solomon, that he rejoiced greatly, and said, Blessed be the LORD this day, which has given unto David a wise son over this great people.

8 And Hiram sent to Solomon, saying, I have considered the things which you sentest to me for: and I will do all your desire concerning timber of cedar, and concerning timber of fir.

9 My servants shall bring them down from Lebanon unto the sea: and I will convey them by sea in floats unto the place that you shalt appoint me, and will cause them to be discharged there, and you shalt receive them: and you shalt accomplish my desire, in giving food for my household.

10 So Hiram gave Solomon cedar trees and fir trees according to all his desire.

11 And Solomon gave Hiram twenty thousand measures of wheat for food to his household, and twenty measures of pure oil: thus gave Solomon to Hiram year by year.

12 And the LORD gave Solomon wisdom, as he promised him: and there was peace between Hiram and Solomon; and they two made a league together.

13 And king Solomon raised a levy out of all Israel; and the levy was thirty thousand men.

14 And he sent them to Lebanon, ten thousand a month by courses: a month they were in Lebanon, and two months at home: and Adoniram was over the levy.

15 And Solomon had threescore and ten thousand that bare burdens, and fourscore thousand hewers in the mountains;

16 Beside the chief of Solomon's officers which were over the work, three thousand and three hundred, which ruled over the people that created in the work.

17 And the king commanded, and they brought great stones, costly stones, and hewed stones, to lay the foundation of the house.

18 And Solomon's builders and Hiram's builders did hew them, and the stonesquarers: so they prepared timber and stones to build the house.

CHAPTER 6

AND it came to pass in the four hundred and eightieth year after the children of Israel were come out of the land of Egypt, in the fourth year of Solomon's reign over Israel, in the month Zif, which is the second month, that he began to build the house of the LORD.

2 And the house which king Solomon built for the LORD, the length thereof was threescore cubits, and the breadth thereof twenty cubits, and the height thereof thirty cubits.

3 And the porch before the temple of the house, twenty cubits was the length thereof, according to the breadth of the house; and ten cubits was the breadth thereof before the house.

4 And for the house he made windows of narrow lights.

5And against the wall of the house he built chambers round about, against the walls of the house round about, both of the temple and of the oracle: and he made chambers round about:

6 The nethermost chamber was five cubits broad, and the middle was six cubits broad, and the third was seven cubits broad: for without in the wall of the house he made narrowed rests round about, that the beams should not be fastened in the walls of the house.

7 And the house, when it was in building, was built of stone made ready before it was brought thither: so that there was neither hammer nor axe nor any tool of iron heard in the house, while it was in building.

8 The door for the middle chamber was in the right side of the house: and they went up with winding stairs into the middle chamber, and out of the middle into the third.

9 So he built the house, and finished it; and covered the house with beams and boards of cedar.

10 And then he built chambers against all the house, five cubits high: and they rested on the house with timber of cedar.

11And the word of the LORD came to Solomon, saying,

12 Concerning this house which you are in building, if you will walk in my statutes, and execute my judgments, and keep all my commandments to walk in them; then will I perform my word with you, which I spake unto David your father:

13 And I will dwell among the children of Israel, and will not forsake my people Israel.

14 So Solomon built the house, and finished it.

15 And he built the walls of the house within with boards of cedar, both the floor of the house, and the walls of the cieling: and he covered them on the inside with wood, and covered the floor of the house with planks of fir.

16 And he built twenty cubits on the sides of the house, both the floor and the walls with boards of cedar: he even built them for it within, even for the oracle, even for the most holy place.

17 And the house, that is, the temple before it, was forty cubits long.

18 And the cedar of the house within was carved with knops and open flowers: all was cedar; there was no stone seen.

19 And the oracle he prepared in the house within, to set there the ark of the covenant of the LORD.

20 And the oracle in the forepart was twenty cubits in length, and twenty cubits in breadth, and twenty cubits in the height thereof: and he overlaid it with pure gold; and so covered the altar which was of cedar.

21 So Solomon overlaid the house within with pure gold: and he made a partition by the chains of gold before the oracle; and he overlaid it with gold.

22 And the whole house he overlaid with gold, until he had finished all the house: also the whole altar that was by the oracle he overlaid with gold.

23And within the oracle he made two cherubims of olive tree, each ten cubits high.

24 And five cubits was the one wing of the cherub, and five cubits the other wing of the cherub: from the uttermost part of the one wing unto the uttermost part of the other were ten cubits.

25 And the other cherub was ten cubits: both the cherubims were of one measure and one size.

26 The height of the one cherub was ten cubits, and so was it of the other cherub.

27 And he set the cherubims within the inner house: and they stretched forth the wings of the cherubims, so that the wing of the one touched the one wall, and the wing of the other cherub touched the other wall; and their wings touched one another in the midst of the house.

28 And he overlaid the cherubims with gold.

29 And he carved all the walls of the house round about with carved figures of cherubims and palm trees and open flowers, within and without.

30 And the floor of the house he overlaid with gold, within and without.

31And for the entering of the oracle he made doors of olive tree: the lintel and side posts were a fifth part of the wall.

32 The two doors also were of olive tree; and he carved upon them carvings of cherubims and palm trees and open flowers, and overlaid them with gold, and spread gold upon the cherubims, and upon the palm trees.

33 So also made he for the door of the temple posts of olive tree, a fourth part of the wall.

34 And the two doors were of fir tree: the two leaves of the one door were folding, and the two leaves of the other door were folding.

35 And he carved thereon cherubims and palm trees and open flowers: and covered them with gold fitted upon the carved work.

36And he built the inner court with three rows of hewed stone, and a row of cedar beams.

37In the fourth year was the foundation of the house of the LORD laid, in the month Zif:

38 And in the eleventh year, in the month Bul, which is the eighth month, was the house finished throughout all the parts thereof, and according to all the fashion of it. So was he seven years in building it.

CHAPTER 7

BUT Solomon was building his own house thirteen years, and he finished all his house.

2He built also the house of the forest of Lebanon; the length thereof was an hundred cubits, and the breadth thereof fifty cubits, and the height thereof thirty cubits, upon four rows of cedar pillars, with cedar beams upon the pillars.

3 And it was covered with cedar above upon the beams, that lay on forty five pillars, fifteen in a row.

4 And there were windows in three rows, and light was against light in three ranks.

5 And all the doors and posts were square, with the windows: and light was against light in three ranks.

6And he made a porch of pillars; the length thereof was fifty cubits, and the breadth thereof thirty cubits: and the porch was before them: and the other pillars and the thick beam were before them.

7Then he made a porch for the throne where he might judge, even the porch of judgment: and it was covered with cedar from one side of the floor to the other.

8And his house where he dwelt had another court within the porch, which was of the like work. Solomon made also an house for Pharaoh's daughter, whom he had taken to wife, like unto this porch.

9 All these were of costly stones, according to the measures of hewed stones, sawed with saws, within and without, even from the foundation unto the coping, and so on the outside toward the great court.

10 And the foundation was of costly stones, even great stones, stones of ten cubits, and stones of eight cubits.

11 And above were costly stones, after the measures of hewed stones, and cedars.

12 And the great court round about was with three rows of hewed stones, and a row of cedar beams, both for the inner court of the house of the LORD, and for the porch of the house.

13And king Solomon sent and fetched Hiram out of Tyre.

14 He was a widow's son of the tribe of Naphtali, and his father was a man of Tyre, a worker in brass: and he was filled with wisdom, and understanding, and cunning to work all works in brass. And he came to king Solomon, and created all his work.

15 For he cast two pillars of brass, of eighteen cubits high apiece: and a line of twelve cubits did compass either of them about.

16 And he made two chapiters of molten brass, to set upon the tops of the pillars: the height of the one chapiter was five cubits, and the height of the other chapiter was five cubits:

17 And nets of checker work, and wreaths of chain work, for the chapiters which were upon the top of the pillars; seven for the one chapiter, and seven for the other chapiter.

18 And he made the pillars, and two rows round about upon the one network, to cover the chapiters that were upon the top, with pomegranates: and so did he for the other chapiter.

19 And the chapiters that were upon the top of the pillars were of lily work in the porch, four cubits.

20 And the chapiters upon the two pillars had pomegranates also above, over against the belly which was by the network: and the pomegranates were two hundred in rows round about upon the other chapiter.

21 And he set up the pillars in the porch of the temple: and he set up the right pillar, and called the name thereof Jachin: and he set up the left pillar, and called the name thereof Boaz.

22 And upon the top of the pillars was lily work: so was the work of the pillars finished.

23And he made a molten sea, ten cubits from the one brim to the other: it was round all about, and his height was five cubits: and a line of thirty cubits did compass it round about.

24 And under the brim of it round about there were knops compassing it, ten in a cubit, compassing the sea round about: the knops were cast in two rows, when it was cast.

25 It stood upon twelve oxen, three looking toward the north, and three looking toward the west, and three looking toward the south, and three looking toward the east: and the sea was set above upon them, and all their hinder parts were inward.

26 And it was an hand breadth thick, and the brim thereof was created like the brim of a cup, with flowers of lilies: it contained two thousand baths.

27And he made ten bases of brass; four cubits was the length of one base, and four cubits the breadth thereof, and three cubits the height of it.

28 And the work of the bases was on this manner: they had borders, and the borders were between the ledges:

29 And on the borders that were between the ledges were lions, oxen, and cherubims: and upon the ledges there was a base above: and beneath the lions and oxen were certain additions made of thin work.

30 And every base had four brasen wheels, and plates of brass: and the four corners thereof had undersetters: under the laver were undersetters molten, at the side of every addition.

31 And the mouth of it within the chapiter and above was a cubit: but the mouth thereof was round after the work of the base, a cubit and an half: and also upon the mouth of it were gravings with their borders, foursquare, not round.

32 And under the borders were four wheels; and the axletrees of the wheels were joined to the base: and the height of a wheel was a cubit and half a cubit.

33 And the work of the wheels was like the work of a chariot wheel: their axletrees, and their naves, and their felloes, and their spokes, were all molten.

34 And there were four undersetters to the four corners of one base: and the undersetters were of the very base itself.

35 And in the top of the base was there a round compass of half a cubit high: and on the top of the base the ledges thereof and the borders thereof were of the same.

36 For on the plates of the ledges thereof, and on the borders thereof, he graved cherubims, lions, and palm trees, according to the proportion of every one, and additions round about.

37 After this manner he made the ten bases: all of them had one casting, one measure, and one size.

38Then made he ten lavers of brass: one laver contained forty baths: and every laver was four cubits: and upon every one of the ten bases one laver.

39 And he put five bases on the right side of the house, and five on the left side of the house: and he set the sea on the right side of the house eastward over against the south.

40And Hiram made the lavers, and the shovels, and the basons. So Hiram made an end of doing all the work that he made king Solomon for the house of the LORD:

41 The two pillars, and the two bowls of the chapiters that were on the top of the two pillars; and the two networks, to cover the two bowls of the chapiters which were upon the top of the pillars;

42 And four hundred pomegranates for the two networks, even two rows of pomegranates for one network, to cover the two bowls of the chapiters that were upon the pillars;

43 And the ten bases, and ten lavers on the bases;

44 And one sea, and twelve oxen under the sea;

45 And the pots, and the shovels, and the basons: and all these vessels, which Hiram made to king Solomon for the house of the LORD, were of bright brass.

46 In the plain of Jordan did the king cast them, in the clay ground between Succoth and Zarthan.

47 And Solomon left all the vessels unweighed, because they were exceeding many: neither was the weight of the brass found out.

48 And Solomon made all the vessels that pertained unto the house of the LORD: the altar of gold, and the table of gold, whereupon the shewbread was,

49 And the candlesticks of pure gold, five on the right side, and five on the left, before the oracle, with the flowers, and the lamps, and the tongs of gold,

50 And the bowls, and the snuffers, and the basons, and the spoons, and the censers of pure gold; and the hinges of gold, both for the doors of the inner house, the most holy place, and for the doors of the house, to wit, of the temple.

51 So was ended all the work that king Solomon made for the house of the LORD. And Solomon brought in the things which David his father had dedicated; even the silver, and the gold, and the vessels, did he put among the treasures of the house of the LORD.

CHAPTER 8

THEN Solomon assembled the elders of Israel, and all the heads of the tribes, the chief of the fathers of the children of Israel, unto king Solomon in Jerusalem, that they might bring up the ark of the covenant of the LORD out of the city of David, which is Zion.

2 And all the men of Israel assembled themselves unto king Solomon at the feast in the month Ethanim, which is the seventh month.

3 And all the elders of Israel came, and the priests took up the ark.

4 And they brought up the ark of the LORD, and the tabernacle of the congregation, and all the holy vessels that were in the tabernacle, even those did the priests and the Levites bring up.

5 And king Solomon, and all the congregation of Israel, that were assembled unto him, were with him before the ark, sacrificing sheep and oxen, that could not be told nor numbered for multitude.

6 And the priests brought in the ark of the covenant of the LORD unto his place, into the oracle of the house, to the most holy place, even under the wings of the cherubims.

7 For the cherubims spread forth their two wings over the place of the ark, and the cherubims covered the ark and the staves thereof above.

8 And they drew out the staves, that the ends of the staves were seen out in the holy place before the oracle, and they were not seen without: and there they are unto this day.

9 There was nothing in the ark save the two tables of stone, which Moses put there at Horeb, when the LORD made a covenant with the children of Israel, when they came out of the land of Egypt.

10 And it came to pass, when the priests were come out of the holy place, that the cloud filled the house of the LORD,

11 So that the priests could not stand to minister because of the cloud: for the glory of the LORD had filled the house of the LORD.

12Then spake Solomon, The LORD said that he would dwell in the thick darkness.

13 I have surely built you an house to dwell in, a settled place for you to abide in for ever.

14 And the king turned his face about, and blessed all the congregation of Israel: (and all the congregation of Israel stood;)

15 And he said, Blessed be the LORD God of Israel, which spake with his mouth unto David my father, and has with his hand fulfilled it, saying,

16 Since the day that I brought forth my people Israel out of Egypt, I chose no city out of all the tribes of Israel to build an house, that my name might be therein; but I chose David to be over my people Israel.

17 And it was in the heart of David my father to build an house for the name of the LORD God of Israel.

18 And the LORD said unto David my father, Whereas it was in yours heart to build an house unto my name, you did well that it was in yours heart.

19 Nevertheless you shalt not build the house; but your son that shall come forth out of your loins, he shall build the house unto my name.

20 And the LORD has performed his word that he spake, and I am risen up in the room of David my father, and sit on the throne of Israel, as the LORD promised, and have built an house for the name of the LORD God of Israel.

21 And I have set there a place for the ark, wherein is the covenant of the LORD, which he made with our fathers, when he brought them out of the land of Egypt.

22And Solomon stood before the altar of the LORD in the presence of all the congregation of Israel, and spread forth his hands toward heaven:

23 And he said, LORD God of Israel, there is no God like you, in heaven above, or on earth beneath, who keepest covenant and mercy with your servants that walk before you with all their heart:

24 Who have kept with your servant David my father that you promisedst him: you spakest also with your mouth, and have fulfilled it with yours hand, as it is this day.

25 Therefore now, LORD God of Israel, keep with your servant David my father that you promisedst him, saying, There shall not fail you a man in my sight to sit on the throne of Israel; so that your children take heed to their way, that they walk before me as you have walked before me.

26 And now, O God of Israel, let your word, I pray you, be verified, which you spakest unto your servant David my father.

27 But will God indeed dwell on the earth? behold, the heaven and heaven of heavens cannot contain you; how much less this house that I have builded?

28 Yet have you respect unto the prayer of your servant, and to his supplication, O LORD my God, to hearken unto the cry and to the prayer, which your servant prayeth before you to day:

29 That yours eyes may be open toward this house night and day, even toward the place of which you have said, My name shall be there: that you mayest hearken unto the prayer which your servant shall make toward this place.

30 And hearken you to the supplication of your servant, and of your people Israel, when they shall pray toward this place: and hear you in heaven your dwelling place: and when you hearest, forgive.

31If any man trespass against his neighbour, and an oath be laid upon him to cause him to swear, and the oath come before yours altar in this house:

32 Then hear you in heaven, and do, and judge your servants, condemning the wicked, to bring his way upon his head; and justifying the righteous, to give him according to his righteousness.

33When your people Israel be smitten down before the enemy, because they have sinned against you, and shall turn again to you, and confess your name, and pray, and make supplication unto you in this house:

34 Then hear you in heaven, and forgive the sin of your people Israel, and bring them again unto the land which you gavest unto their fathers.

35When heaven is shut up, and there is no rain, because they have sinned against you; if they pray toward this place, and confess your name, and turn from their sin, when you afflictest them:

36 Then hear you in heaven, and forgive the sin of your servants, and of your people Israel, that you teach them the good way wherein they should walk, and give rain upon your land, which you have given to your people for an inheritance.

37If there be in the land famine, if there be pestilence, blasting, mildew, locust, or if there be caterpiller; if their enemy besiege them in the land of their cities; whatsoever plague, whatsoever sickness there be;

38 What prayer and supplication soever be made by any man, or by all your people Israel, which shall know every man the plague of his own heart, and spread forth his hands toward this house:

39 Then hear you in heaven your dwelling place, and forgive, and do, and give to every man according to his ways, whose heart you knowest; (for you , even you only, knowest the hearts of all the children of men;)

40 That they may fear you all the days that they live in the land which you gavest unto our fathers.

41 Moreover concerning a stranger, that is not of your people Israel, but comes out of a far country for your name's sake;

42 (For they shall hear of your great name, and of your strong hand, and of your stretched out arm;) when he shall come and pray toward this house;

43 Hear you in heaven your dwelling place, and do according to all that the stranger calleth to you for: that all people of the earth may know your name, to fear you, as do your people Israel; and that they may know that this house, which I have builded, is called by your name.

44If your people go out to battle against their enemy, whithersoever you shalt send them, and shall pray unto the LORD toward the city which you have chosen, and toward the house that I have built for your name:

45 Then hear you in heaven their prayer and their supplication, and maintain their cause.

46 If they sin against you, (for there is no man that sinneth not,) and you be angry with them, and deliver them to the enemy, so that they carry them away captives unto the land of the enemy, far or near;

47 Yet if they shall bethink themselves in the land whither they were carried captives, and repent, and make supplication unto you in the land of them that carried them captives, saying, We have sinned, and have done perversely, we have committed wickedness;

48 And so return unto you with all their heart, and with all their soul, in the land of their enemies, which led them away captive, and pray unto you toward their land, which you gavest unto their fathers, the city which you have chosen, and the house which I have built for your name:

49 Then hear you their prayer and their supplication in heaven your dwelling place, and maintain their cause,

50 And forgive your people that have sinned against you, and all their transgressions wherein they have transgressed against you, and give them compassion before them who carried them captive, that they may have compassion on them:

51 For they be your people, and yours inheritance, which you broughtest forth out of Egypt, from the midst of the furnace of iron:

52 That yours eyes may be open unto the supplication of your servant, and unto the supplication of your people Israel, to hearken unto them in all that they call for unto you.

53 For you did separate them from among all the people of the earth, to be yours inheritance, as you spakest by the hand of Moses your servant, when you broughtest our fathers out of Egypt, O Lord GOD.

54 And it was so, that when Solomon had made an end of praying all this prayer and supplication unto the LORD, he arose from before the altar of the LORD, from kneeling on his knees with his hands spread up to heaven.

55 And he stood, and blessed all the congregation of Israel with a loud voice, saying,

56 Blessed be the LORD, that has given rest unto his people Israel, according to all that he promised: there has not failed one word of all his good promise, which he promised by the hand of Moses his servant.

57 The LORD our God be with us, as he was with our fathers: let him not leave us, nor forsake us:

58 That he may incline our hearts unto him, to walk in all his ways, and to keep his commandments, and his statutes, and his judgments, which he commanded our fathers.

59 And let these my words, wherewith I have made supplication before the LORD, be nigh unto the LORD our God day and night, that he maintain the cause of his servant, and the cause of his people Israel at all times, as the matter shall require:

60 That all the people of the earth may know that the LORD is God, and that there is none else.

61 Let your heart therefore be perfect with the LORD our God, to walk in his statutes, and to keep his commandments, as at this day.

62And the king, and all Israel with him, offered sacrifice before the LORD.

63 And Solomon offered a sacrifice of peace offerings, which he offered unto the LORD, two and twenty thousand oxen, and an hundred and twenty thousand sheep. So the king and all the children of Israel dedicated the house of the LORD.

64 The same day did the king hallow the middle of the court that was before the house of the LORD: for there he offered burnt offerings, and meat offerings, and the fat of the peace offerings: because the brasen altar that was before the LORD was too little to receive the burnt offerings, and meat offerings, and the fat of the peace offerings.

65 And at that time Solomon held a feast, and all Israel with him, a great congregation, from the entering in of Hamath unto the river of Egypt, before the LORD our God, seven days and seven days, even fourteen days.

66 On the eighth day he sent the people away: and they blessed the king, and went unto their tents joyful and glad of heart for all the goodness that the LORD had done for David his servant, and for Israel his people.

CHAPTER 9

AND it came to pass, when Solomon had finished the building of the house of the LORD, and the king's house, and all Solomon's desire which he was pleased to do,

2 That the LORD appeared to Solomon the second time, as he had appeared unto him at Gibeon.

3 And the LORD said unto him, I have heard your prayer and your supplication, that you have made before me: I have hallowed this house, which you have built, to put my name there for ever; and my eyes and my heart shall be there perpetually.

4 And if you will walk before me, as David your father walked, in integrity of heart, and in uprightness, to do according to all that I have commanded you, and will keep my statutes and my judgments:

5 Then I will establish the throne of your kingdom upon Israel for ever, as I promised to David your father, saying, There shall not fail you a man upon the throne of Israel.

6 But if you shall at all turn from following me, you or your children, and will not keep my commandments and my statutes which I have set before you, but go and serve other gods, and worship them:

7 Then will I cut off Israel out of the land which I have given them; and this house, which I have hallowed for my name, will I cast out of my sight; and Israel shall be a proverb and a byword among all people:

8 And at this house, which is high, every one that passes by it shall be astonished, and shall hiss; and they shall say, Why has the LORD done thus unto this land, and to this house?

9 And they shall answer, Because they forsook the LORD their God, who brought forth their fathers out of the land of Egypt, and have taken hold upon other gods, and have worshipped them, and served them: therefore has the LORD brought upon them all this evil.

10And it came to pass at the end of twenty years, when Solomon had built the two houses, the house of the LORD, and the king's house,

11 (Now Hiram the king of Tyre had furnished Solomon with cedar trees and fir trees, and with gold, according to all his desire,) that then king Solomon gave Hiram twenty cities in the land of Galilee.

12 And Hiram came out from Tyre to see the cities which Solomon had given him; and they pleased him not.

13 And he said, What cities are these which you have given me, my brother? And he called them the land of Cabul unto this day.

14 And Hiram sent to the king sixscore talents of gold.

15And this is the reason of the levy which king Solomon raised; for to build the house of the LORD, and his own house, and Millo, and the wall of Jerusalem, and Hazor, and Megiddo, and Gezer.

16 For Pharaoh king of Egypt had gone up, and taken Gezer, and burnt it with fire, and slain the Canaanites that dwelt in the city, and given it for a present unto his daughter, Solomon's wife.

17 And Solomon built Gezer, and Beth-horon the nether,

18 And Baalath, and Tadmor in the wilderness, in the land,

19 And all the cities of store that Solomon had, and cities for his chariots, and cities for his horsemen, and that which Solomon desired to build in Jerusalem, and in Lebanon, and in all the land of his dominion.

20 And all the people that were left of the Amorites, Hittites, Perizzites, Hivites, and Jebusites, which were not of the children of Israel,

21 Their children that were left after them in the land, whom the children of Israel also were not able utterly to destroy, upon those did Solomon levy a tribute of bondservice unto this day.

22 But of the children of Israel did Solomon make no bondmen: but they were men of war, and his servants, and his princes, and his captains, and rulers of his chariots, and his horsemen.

23 These were the chief of the officers that were over Solomon's work, five hundred and fifty, which bare rule over the people that created in the work.

24 But Pharaoh's daughter came up out of the city of David unto her house which Solomon had built for her: then did he build Millo.

25 And three times in a year did Solomon offer burnt offerings and peace offerings upon the altar which he built unto the LORD, and he burnt incense upon the altar that was before the LORD. So he finished the house.

26 And king Solomon made a navy of ships in Ezion-geber, which is beside Eloth, on the shore of the Red sea, in the land of Edom.

27 And Hiram sent in the navy his servants, shipmen that had knowledge of the sea, with the servants of Solomon.

28 And they came to Ophir, and fetched from thence gold, four hundred and twenty talents, and brought it to king Solomon.

CHAPTER 10

AND when the queen of Sheba heard of the fame of Solomon concerning the name of the LORD, she came to prove him with hard questions.

2 And she came to Jerusalem with a very great train, with camels that bare spices, and very much gold, and precious stones: and when she was come to Solomon, she communed with him of all that was in her heart.

3 And Solomon told her all her questions: there was not any thing hid from the king, which he told her not.

4 And when the queen of Sheba had seen all Solomon's wisdom, and the house that he had built,

5 And the meat of his table, and the sitting of his servants, and the attendance of his ministers, and their apparel, and his cupbearers, and his ascent by which he went up unto the house of the LORD; there was no more spirit in her.

6 And she said to the king, It was a true report that I heard in my own land of your acts and of your wisdom.

7 Howbeit I believed not the words, until I came, and my eyes had seen it: and, behold, the half was not told me: your wisdom and prosperity exceedeth the fame which I heard.

8 Happy are your men, happy are these your servants, which stand continually before you, and that hear your wisdom.

9 Blessed be the LORD your God, which delighted in you, to set you on the throne of Israel: because the LORD loved Israel for ever, therefore made he you king, to do judgment and justice.

10 And she gave the king an hundred and twenty talents of gold, and of spices very great store, and precious stones: there came no more such abundance of spices as these which the queen of Sheba gave to king Solomon.

11 And the navy also of Hiram, that brought gold from Ophir, brought in from Ophir great plenty of almug trees, and precious stones.

12 And the king made of the almug trees pillars for the house of the LORD, and for the king's house, harps also and psalteries for singers: there came no such almug trees, nor were seen unto this day.

13 And king Solomon gave unto the queen of Sheba all her desire, whatsoever she asked, beside that which Solomon gave her of his royal bounty. So she turned and went to her own country, she and her servants.

14 Now the weight of gold that came to Solomon in one year was six hundred threescore and six talents of gold,

15 Beside that he had of the merchantmen, and of the traffick of the spice merchants, and of all the kings of Arabia, and of the governors of the country.

16 And king Solomon made two hundred targets of beaten gold: six hundred shekels of gold went to one target.

17 And he made three hundred shields of beaten gold; three pound of gold went to one shield: and the king put them in the house of the forest of Lebanon.

18 Moreover the king made a great throne of ivory, and overlaid it with the best gold.

19 The throne had six steps, and the top of the throne was round behind: and there were stays on either side on the place of the seat, and two lions stood beside the stays.

20 And twelve lions stood there on the one side and on the other upon the six steps: there was not the like made in any kingdom.

21 And all king Solomon's drinking vessels were of gold, and all the vessels of the house of the forest of Lebanon were of pure gold; none were of silver: it was nothing accounted of in the days of Solomon.

22 For the king had at sea a navy of Tharshish with the navy of Hiram: once in three years came the navy of Tharshish, bringing gold, and silver, ivory, and apes, and peacocks.

23 So king Solomon exceeded all the kings of the earth for riches and for wisdom.

24 And all the earth sought to Solomon, to hear his wisdom, which God had put in his heart.

25 And they brought every man his present, vessels of silver, and vessels of gold, and garments, and armour, and spices, horses, and mules, a rate year by year.

26 And Solomon gathered together chariots and horsemen: and he had a thousand and four hundred chariots, and twelve thousand horsemen, whom he bestowed in the cities for chariots, and with the king at Jerusalem.

27 And the king made silver to be in Jerusalem as stones, and cedars made he to be as the sycomore trees that are in the vale, for abundance.

28 And Solomon had horses brought out of Egypt, and linen yarn: the king's merchants received the linen yarn at a price.

29 And a chariot came up and went out of Egypt for six hundred shekels of silver, and an horse for an hundred and fifty: and so for all the kings of the Hittites, and for the kings of Syria, did they bring them out by their means.

CHAPTER 11

BUT king Solomon loved many strange women, together with the daughter of Pharaoh, women of the Moabites, Ammonites, Edomites, Zidonians, and Hittites;

2 Of the nations concerning which the LORD said unto the children of Israel, You shall not go in to them, neither shall they come in unto you: for surely they will turn away your heart after their gods: Solomon clave unto these in love.

3 And he had seven hundred wives, princesses, and three hundred concubines: and his wives turned away his heart.

4 For it came to pass, when Solomon was old, that his wives turned away his heart after other gods: and his heart was not perfect with the LORD his God, as was the heart of David his father.

5 For Solomon went after Ashtoreth the goddess of the Zidonians, and after Milcom the abomination of the Ammonites.

6 And Solomon did evil in the sight of the LORD, and went not fully after the LORD, as did David his father.

7 Then did Solomon build an high place for Chemosh, the abomination of Moab, in the hill that is before Jerusalem, and for Molech, the abomination of the children of Ammon.

8 And likewise did he for all his strange wives, which burnt incense and sacrificed unto their gods.

9 And the LORD was angry with Solomon, because his heart was turned from the LORD God of Israel, which had appeared unto him twice,

10 And had commanded him concerning this thing, that he should not go after other gods: but he kept not that which the LORD commanded.

11 Wherefore the LORD said unto Solomon, Forasmuch as this is done of you, and you have not kept my covenant and my statutes, which I have commanded you, I will surely rend the kingdom from you, and will give it to your servant.

12 Notwithstanding in your days I will not do it for David your father's sake: but I will rend it out of the hand of your son.

13 Howbeit I will not rend away all the kingdom; but will give one tribe to your son for David my servant's sake, and for Jerusalem's sake which I have chosen.

14 And the LORD stirred up an adversary unto Solomon, Hadad the Edomite: he was of the king's seed in Edom.

15 For it came to pass, when David was in Edom, and Joab the captain of the host was gone up to bury the slain, after he had smitten every male in Edom;

16 (For six months did Joab remain there with all Israel, until he had cut off every male in Edom:)

17 That Hadad fled, he and certain Edomites of his father's servants with him, to go into Egypt; Hadad being yet a little child.

18 And they arose out of Midian, and came to Paran: and they took men with them out of Paran, and they came to Egypt, unto Pharaoh king of Egypt; which gave him an house, and appointed him victuals, and gave him land.

19 And Hadad found great favour in the sight of Pharaoh, so that he gave him to wife the sister of his own wife, the sister of Tahpenes the queen.

20 And the sister of Tahpenes bare him Genubath his son, whom Tahpenes weaned in Pharaoh's house: and Genubath was in Pharaoh's household among the sons of Pharaoh.

21 And when Hadad heard in Egypt that David slept with his fathers, and that Joab the captain of the host was dead, Hadad said to Pharaoh, Let me depart, that I may go to my own country.

22 Then Pharaoh said unto him, But what have you lacked with me, that, behold, you seekest to go to yours own country? And he answered, Nothing: howbeit let me go in any wise.

23 And God stirred him up another adversary, Rezon the son of Eliadah, which fled from his lord Hadadezer king of Zobah:

24 And he gathered men unto him, and became captain over a band, when David slew them of Zobah: and they went to Damascus, and dwelt therein, and reigned in Damascus.

25 And he was an adversary to Israel all the days of Solomon, beside the mischief that Hadad did: and he abhorred Israel, and reigned over Syria.

26 And Jeroboam the son of Nebat, an Ephrathite of Zereda, Solomon's servant, whose mother's name was Zeruah, a widow woman, even he lifted up his hand against the king.

27 And this was the cause that he lifted up his hand against the king: Solomon built Millo, and repaired the breaches of the city of David his father.

28 And the man Jeroboam was a mighty man of valour: and Solomon seeing the young man that he was industrious, he made him ruler over all the charge of the house of Joseph.

29 And it came to pass at that time when Jeroboam went out of Jerusalem, that the prophet Ahijah the Shilonite found him in the way; and he had clad himself with a new garment; and they two were alone in the field:

30 And Ahijah caught the new garment that was on him, and rent it in twelve pieces:

31 And he said to Jeroboam, Take you ten pieces: for thus saith the LORD, the God of Israel, Behold, I will rend the kingdom out of the hand of Solomon, and will give ten tribes to you:

32 (But he shall have one tribe for my servant David's sake, and for Jerusalem's sake, the city which I have chosen out of all the tribes of Israel:)

33 Because that they have forsaken me, and have worshipped Ashtoreth the goddess of the Zidonians, Chemosh the god of the Moabites, and Milcom the god of the children of Ammon, and have not walked in my ways, to do that which is right in my eyes, and to keep my statutes and my judgments, as did David his father.

34 Howbeit I will not take the whole kingdom out of his hand: but I will make him prince all the days of his life for David my servant's sake, whom I chose, because he kept my commandments and my statutes:

35 But I will take the kingdom out of his son's hand, and will give it unto you, even ten tribes.

36 And unto his son will I give one tribe, that David my servant may have a light alway before me in Jerusalem, the city which I have chosen me to put my name there.

37 And I will take you, and you shalt reign according to all that your soul desireth, and shalt be king over Israel.

38 And it shall be, if you will hearken unto all that I command you, and will walk in my ways, and do that is right in my sight, to keep my statutes and my commandments, as David my servant did; that I will be with you, and build you a sure house, as I built for David, and will give Israel unto you.

39 And I will for this afflict the seed of David, but not for ever.

40 Solomon sought therefore to kill Jeroboam. And Jeroboam arose, and fled into Egypt, unto Shishak king of Egypt, and was in Egypt until the death of Solomon.

41 And the rest of the acts of Solomon, and all that he did, and his wisdom, are they not written in the book of the acts of Solomon?

42 And the time that Solomon reigned in Jerusalem over all Israel was forty years.

43 And Solomon slept with his fathers, and was buried in the city of David his father: and Rehoboam his son reigned in his stead.

CHAPTER 12

AND Rehoboam went to Shechem: for all Israel were come to Shechem to make him king.

2 And it came to pass, when Jeroboam the son of Nebat, who was yet in Egypt, heard of it, (for he was fled from the presence of king Solomon, and Jeroboam dwelt in Egypt;)

3 That they sent and called him. And Jeroboam and all the congregation of Israel came, and spake unto Rehoboam, saying,

4 Your father made our yoke grievous: now therefore make you the grievous service of your father, and his heavy yoke which he put upon us, lighter, and we will serve you.

5 And he said unto them, Depart yet for three days, then come again to me. And the people departed.

6 And king Rehoboam consulted with the old men, that stood before Solomon his father while he yet lived, and said, How do you advise that I may answer this people?

7 And they spake unto him, saying, If you will be a servant unto this people this day, and will serve them, and answer them, and speak good words to them, then they will be your servants for ever.

8 But he forsook the counsel of the old men, which they had given him, and consulted with the young men that were grown up with him, and which stood before him:

9 And he said unto them, What counsel give you that we may answer this people, who have spoken to me, saying, Make the yoke which your father did put upon us lighter?

10 And the young men that were grown up with him spake unto him, saying, Thus shalt you speak unto this people that spake unto you, saying, Your father made our yoke heavy, but make you it lighter unto us; thus shalt you say unto them, My little finger shall be thicker than my father's loins.

11 And now whereas my father did lade you with a heavy yoke, I will add to your yoke: my father has chastised you with whips, but I will chastise you with scorpions.

12 So Jeroboam and all the people came to Rehoboam the third day, as the king had appointed, saying, Come to me again the third day.

13 And the king answered the people roughly, and forsook the old men's counsel that they gave him;

14 And spake to them after the counsel of the young men, saying, My father made your yoke heavy, and I will add to your yoke: my father also chastised you with whips, but I will chastise you with scorpions.

15 Wherefore the king hearkened not unto the people; for the cause was from the LORD, that he might perform his saying, which the LORD spake by Ahijah the Shilonite unto Jeroboam the son of Nebat.

16 So when all Israel saw that the king hearkened not unto them, the people answered the king, saying, What portion have we in David? neither have we inheritance in the son of Jesse: to your tents, O Israel: now see to yours own house, David. So Israel departed unto their tents.

17 But as for the children of Israel which dwelt in the cities of Judah, Rehoboam reigned over them.

18 Then king Rehoboam sent Adoram, who was over the tribute; and all Israel stoned him with stones, that he died. Therefore king Rehoboam made speed to get him up to his chariot, to flee to Jerusalem.

19 So Israel rebelled against the house of David unto this day.

20 And it came to pass, when all Israel heard that Jeroboam was come again, that they sent and called him unto the congregation, and made him king over all Israel: there was none that followed the house of David, but the tribe of Judah only.

21 And when Rehoboam was come to Jerusalem, he assembled all the house of Judah, with the tribe of Benjamin, an hundred and fourscore thousand chosen men, which were warriors, to fight against the house of Israel, to bring the kingdom again to Rehoboam the son of Solomon.

22 But the word of God came unto Shemaiah the man of God, saying,

23 Speak unto Rehoboam, the son of Solomon, king of Judah, and unto all the house of Judah and Benjamin, and to the remnant of the people, saying,

24 Thus saith the LORD, You shall not go up, nor fight against your brethren the children of Israel: return every man to his house; for this thing is from me. They hearkened therefore to the word of the LORD, and returned to depart, according to the word of the LORD.

25 Then Jeroboam built Shechem in mount Ephraim, and dwelt therein; and went out from thence, and built Penuel.

26 And Jeroboam said in his heart, Now shall the kingdom return to the house of David:

27 If this people go up to do sacrifice in the house of the LORD at Jerusalem, then shall the heart of this people turn again unto their lord, even unto Rehoboam king of Judah, and they shall kill me, and go again to Rehoboam king of Judah.

28 Whereupon the king took counsel, and made two calves of gold, and said unto them, It is too much for you to go up to Jerusalem: behold your gods, O Israel, which brought you up out of the land of Egypt.

29 And he set the one in Beth-el, and the other put he in Dan.

30 And this thing became a sin: for the people went to worship before the one, even unto Dan.

31 And he made an house of high places, and made priests of the lowest of the people, which were not of the sons of Levi.

32 And Jeroboam ordained a feast in the eighth month, on the fifteenth day of the month, like unto the feast that is in Judah, and he offered upon the altar. So did he in Beth-el, sacrificing unto the calves that he had made: and he placed in Beth-el the priests of the high places which he had made.

33 So he offered upon the altar which he had made in Beth-el the fifteenth day of the eighth month, even in the month which he had devised of his own heart; and ordained a feast unto the children of Israel: and he offered upon the altar, and burnt incense.

CHAPTER 13

AND, behold, there came a man of God out of Judah by the word of the LORD unto Beth-el: and Jeroboam stood by the altar to burn incense.

2 And he cried against the altar in the word of the LORD, and said, O altar, altar, thus saith the LORD; Behold, a child shall be born unto the house of David, Josiah by name; and upon you shall he offer the priests of the high places that burn incense upon you, and men's bones shall be burnt upon you.

3 And he gave a sign the same day, saying, This is the sign which the LORD has spoken; Behold, the altar shall be rent, and the ashes that are upon it shall be poured out.

4 And it came to pass, when king Jeroboam heard the saying of the man of God, which had cried against the altar in Beth-el, that he put forth his hand from the altar, saying, Lay hold on him. And his hand, which he put forth against him, dried up, so that he could not pull it in again to him.

5 The altar also was rent, and the ashes poured out from the altar, according to the sign which the man of God had given by the word of the LORD.

6 And the king answered and said unto the man of God, Intreat now the face of the LORD your God, and pray for me, that my hand may be restored me again. And the man of God besought the LORD, and the king's hand was restored him again, and became as it was before.

7 And the king said unto the man of God, Come home with me, and refresh yourself, and I will give you a reward.

8 And the man of God said unto the king, If you will give me half yours house, I will not go in with you, neither will I eat bread nor drink water in this place:

9 For so was it charged me by the word of the LORD, saying, Eat no bread, nor drink water, nor turn again by the same way that you camest.

10 So he went another way, and returned not by the way that he came to Beth-el.

11 Now there dwelt an old prophet in Beth-el; and his sons came and told him all the works that the man of God had done that day in Beth-el: the words which he had spoken unto the king, them they told also to their father.

12 And their father said unto them, What way went he? For his sons had seen what way the man of God went, which came from Judah.

13 And he said unto his sons, Saddle me the ass. So they saddled him the ass: and he rode thereon,

14 And went after the man of God, and found him sitting under an oak: and he said unto him, Are you the man of God that camest from Judah? And he said, I am.

15 Then he said unto him, Come home with me, and eat bread.

16 And he said, I may not return with you, nor go in with you: neither will I eat bread nor drink water with you in this place:

17 For it was said to me by the word of the LORD, You shalt eat no bread nor drink water there, nor turn again to go by the way that you camest.

18 He said unto him, I am a prophet also as you are; and an angel spake unto me by the word of the LORD, saying, Bring him back with you into yours house, that he may eat bread and drink water. But he lied unto him.

19 So he went back with him, and did eat bread in his house, and drank water.

20 And it came to pass, as they sat at the table, that the word of the LORD came unto the prophet that brought him back:

21 And he cried unto the man of God that came from Judah, saying, Thus saith the LORD, Forasmuch as you have disobeyed the mouth of the LORD, and have not kept the commandment which the LORD your God commanded you,

22 But camest back, and have eaten bread and drunk water in the place, of the which the LORD did say to you, Eat no bread, and drink no water; your carcase shall not come unto the sepulchre of your fathers.

23 And it came to pass, after he had eaten bread, and after he had drunk, that he saddled for him the ass, to wit, for the prophet whom he had brought back.

24 And when he was gone, a lion met him by the way, and slew him: and his carcase was cast in the way, and the ass stood by it, the lion also stood by the carcase.

25 And, behold, men passed by, and saw the carcase cast in the way, and the lion standing by the carcase: and they came and told it in the city where the old prophet dwelt.

26 And when the prophet that brought him back from the way heard thereof, he said, It is the man of God, who was disobedient unto the word of the LORD: therefore the LORD has delivered him unto the lion, which has torn him, and slain him, according to the word of the LORD, which he spake unto him.

27 And he spake to his sons, saying, Saddle me the ass. And they saddled him.

28 And he went and found his carcase cast in the way, and the ass and the lion standing by the carcase: the lion had not eaten the carcase, nor torn the ass.

29 And the prophet took up the carcase of the man of God, and laid it upon the ass, and brought it back: and the old prophet came to the city, to mourn and to bury him.

30 And he laid his carcase in his own grave; and they mourned over him, saying, Alas, my brother!

31 And it came to pass, after he had buried him, that he spake to his sons, saying, When I am dead, then bury me in the sepulchre wherein the man of God is buried; lay my bones beside his bones:

32 For the saying which he cried by the word of the LORD against the altar in Beth-el, and against all the houses of the high places which are in the cities of Samaria, shall surely come to pass.

33 After this thing Jeroboam returned not from his evil way, but made again of the lowest of the people priests of the high places: whosoever would, he consecrated him, and he became one of the priests of the high places.

34 And this thing became sin unto the house of Jeroboam, even to cut it off, and to destroy it from off the face of the earth.

CHAPTER 14

AT that time Abijah the son of Jeroboam fell sick.

2 And Jeroboam said to his wife, Arise, I pray you, and disguise yourself, that you be not known to be the wife of Jeroboam; and get you to Shiloh: behold, there is Ahijah the prophet, which told me that I should be king over this people.

3 And take with you ten loaves, and cracknels, and a cruse of honey, and go to him: he shall tell you what shall become of the child.

4 And Jeroboam's wife did so, and arose, and went to Shiloh, and came to the house of Ahijah. But Ahijah could not see; for his eyes were set by reason of his age.

5 And the LORD said unto Ahijah, Behold, the wife of Jeroboam comes to ask a thing of you for her son; for he is sick: thus and thus shalt you say unto her: for it shall be, when she comes in, that she shall feign herself to be another woman.

6 And it was so, when Ahijah heard the sound of her feet, as she came in at the door, that he said, Come in, you wife of Jeroboam; why feignest you yourself to be another? for I am sent to you with heavy tidings.

7 Go, tell Jeroboam, Thus saith the LORD God of Israel, Forasmuch as I exalted you from among the people, and made you prince over my people Israel,

8 And rent the kingdom away from the house of David, and gave it you: and yet you have not been as my servant David, who kept my commandments, and who followed me with all his heart, to do that only which was right in my eyes;

9 But have done evil above all that were before you: for you have gone and made you other gods, and molten images, to provoke me to anger, and have cast me behind your back:

10 Therefore, behold, I will bring evil upon the house of Jeroboam, and will cut off from Jeroboam him that pisseth against the wall, and him that is shut up and left in Israel, and will take away the remnant of the house of Jeroboam, as a man taketh away dung, till it be all gone.

11 Him that dieth of Jeroboam in the city shall the dogs eat; and him that dieth in the field shall the fowls of the air eat: for the LORD has spoken it.

12 Arise you therefore, get you to yours own house: and when your feet enter into the city, the child shall die.

13 And all Israel shall mourn for him, and bury him: for he only of Jeroboam shall come to the grave, because in him there is found some good thing toward the LORD God of Israel in the house of Jeroboam.

14 Moreover the LORD shall raise him up a king over Israel, who shall cut off the house of Jeroboam that day: but what? even now.

15 For the LORD shall strike Israel, as a reed is shaken in the water, and he shall root up Israel out of this good land, which he gave to their fathers, and shall scatter them beyond the river, because they have made their groves, provoking the LORD to anger.

16 And he shall give Israel up because of the sins of Jeroboam, who did sin, and who made Israel to sin.

17 And Jeroboam's wife arose, and departed, and came to Tirzah: and when she came to the threshold of the door, the child died;

18 And they buried him; and all Israel mourned for him, according to the word of the LORD, which he spake by the hand of his servant Ahijah the prophet.

19 And the rest of the acts of Jeroboam, how he warred, and how he reigned, behold, they are written in the book of the chronicles of the kings of Israel.

20 And the days which Jeroboam reigned were two and twenty years: and he slept with his fathers, and Nadab his son reigned in his stead.

21 And Rehoboam the son of Solomon reigned in Judah. Rehoboam was forty and one years old when he began to reign, and he reigned seventeen years in Jerusalem, the city which the LORD did choose out of all the tribes of Israel, to put his name there. And his mother's name was Naamah an Ammonitess.

22 And Judah did evil in the sight of the LORD, and they provoked him to jealousy with their sins which they had committed, above all that their fathers had done.

23 For they also built them high places, and images, and groves, on every high hill, and under every green tree.

24 And there were also sodomites in the land: and they did according to all the abominations of the nations which the LORD cast out before the children of Israel.

25And it came to pass in the fifth year of king Rehoboam, that Shishak king of Egypt came up against Jerusalem:

26 And he took away the treasures of the house of the LORD, and the treasures of the king's house; he even took away all: and he took away all the shields of gold which Solomon had made.

27 And king Rehoboam made in their stead brasen shields, and committed them unto the hands of the chief of the guard, which kept the door of the king's house.

28 And it was so, when the king went into the house of the LORD, that the guard bare them, and brought them back into the guard chamber.

29Now the rest of the acts of Rehoboam, and all that he did, are they not written in the book of the chronicles of the kings of Judah?

30 And there was war between Rehoboam and Jeroboam all their days.

31 And Rehoboam slept with his fathers, and was buried with his fathers in the city of David. And his mother's name was Naamah an Ammonitess. And Abijam his son reigned in his stead.

CHAPTER 15

NOW in the eighteenth year of king Jeroboam the son of Nebat reigned Abijam over Judah.

2 Three years reigned he in Jerusalem. And his mother's name was Maachah, the daughter of Abishalom.

3 And he walked in all the sins of his father, which he had done before him: and his heart was not perfect with the LORD his God, as the heart of David his father.

4 Nevertheless for David's sake did the LORD his God give him a lamp in Jerusalem, to set up his son after him, and to establish Jerusalem:

5 Because David did that which was right in the eyes of the LORD, and turned not aside from any thing that he commanded him all the days of his life, save only in the matter of Uriah the Hittite.

6 And there was war between Rehoboam and Jeroboam all the days of his life.

7 Now the rest of the acts of Abijam, and all that he did, are they not written in the book of the chronicles of the kings of Judah? And there was war between Abijam and Jeroboam.

8 And Abijam slept with his fathers; and they buried him in the city of David: and Asa his son reigned in his stead.

9And in the twentieth year of Jeroboam king of Israel reigned Asa over Judah.

10 And forty and one years reigned he in Jerusalem. And his mother's name was Maachah, the daughter of Abishalom.

11 And Asa did that which was right in the eyes of the LORD, as did David his father.

12 And he took away the sodomites out of the land, and removed all the idols that his fathers had made.

13 And also Maachah his mother, even her he removed from being queen, because she had made an idol in a grove; and Asa destroyed her idol, and burnt it by the brook Kidron.

14 But the high places were not removed: nevertheless Asa's heart was perfect with the LORD all his days.

15 And he brought in the things which his father had dedicated, and the things which himself had dedicated, into the house of the LORD, silver, and gold, and vessels.

16And there was war between Asa and Baasha king of Israel all their days.

17 And Baasha king of Israel went up against Judah, and built Ramah, that he might not suffer any to go out or come in to Asa king of Judah.

18 Then Asa took all the silver and the gold that were left in the treasures of the house of the LORD, and the treasures of the king's house, and delivered them into the hand of his servants: and king Asa sent them to Ben-hadad, the son of Tabrimon, the son of Hezion, king of Syria, that dwelt at Damascus, saying,

19 There is a league between me and you, and between my father and your father: behold, I have sent unto you a present of silver and gold; come and break your league with Baasha king of Israel, that he may depart from me.

20 So Ben-hadad hearkened unto king Asa, and sent the captains of the hosts which he had against the cities of Israel, and struck Ijon, and Dan, and Abel-beth-maachah, and all Cinneroth, with all the land of Naphtali.

21 And it came to pass, when Baasha heard thereof, that he left off building of Ramah, and dwelt in Tirzah.

22 Then king Asa made a proclamation throughout all Judah; none was exempted: and they took away the stones of Ramah, and the timber thereof, wherewith Baasha had builded; and king Asa built with them Geba of Benjamin, and Mizpah.

23 The rest of all the acts of Asa, and all his might, and all that he did, and the cities which he built, are they not written in the book of the chronicles of the kings of Judah? Nevertheless in the time of his old age he was diseased in his feet.

24 And Asa slept with his fathers, and was buried with his fathers in the city of David his father: and Jehoshaphat his son reigned in his stead.

25And Nadab the son of Jeroboam began to reign over Israel in the second year of Asa king of Judah, and reigned over Israel two years.

26 And he did evil in the sight of the LORD, and walked in the way of his father, and in his sin wherewith he made Israel to sin.

27And Baasha the son of Ahijah, of the house of Issachar, conspired against him; and Baasha struck him at Gibbethon, which belonged to the Philistines; for Nadab and all Israel laid siege to Gibbethon.

28 Even in the third year of Asa king of Judah did Baasha slay him, and reigned in his stead.

29 And it came to pass, when he reigned, that he struck all the house of Jeroboam; he left not to Jeroboam any that breathed, until he had destroyed him, according unto the saying of the LORD, which he spake by his servant Ahijah the Shilonite:

30 Because of the sins of Jeroboam which he sinned, and which he made Israel sin, by his provocation wherewith he provoked the LORD God of Israel to anger.

31Now the rest of the acts of Nadab, and all that he did, are they not written in the book of the chronicles of the kings of Israel?

32 And there was war between Asa and Baasha king of Israel all their days.

33 In the third year of Asa king of Judah began Baasha the son of Ahijah to reign over all Israel in Tirzah, twenty and four years.

34 And he did evil in the sight of the LORD, and walked in the way of Jeroboam, and in his sin wherewith he made Israel to sin.

CHAPTER 16

THEN the word of the LORD came to Jehu the son of Hanani against Baasha, saying,

2 Forasmuch as I exalted you out of the dust, and made you prince over my people Israel; and you have walked in the way of Jeroboam, and have made my people Israel to sin, to provoke me to anger with their sins;

3 Behold, I will take away the posterity of Baasha, and the posterity of his house; and will make your house like the house of Jeroboam the son of Nebat.

4 Him that dieth of Baasha in the city shall the dogs eat; and him that dieth of his in the fields shall the fowls of the air eat.

5 Now the rest of the acts of Baasha, and what he did, and his might, are they not written in the book of the chronicles of the kings of Israel?

6 So Baasha slept with his fathers, and was buried in Tirzah: and Elah his son reigned in his stead.

7 And also by the hand of the prophet Jehu the son of Hanani came the word of the LORD against Baasha, and against his house, even for all the evil that he did in the sight of the LORD, in provoking him to anger with the work of his hands, in being like the house of Jeroboam; and because he killed him.

8In the twenty and sixth year of Asa king of Judah began Elah the son of Baasha to reign over Israel in Tirzah, two years.

9 And his servant Zimri, captain of half his chariots, conspired against him, as he was in Tirzah, drinking himself drunk in the house of Arza steward of his house in Tirzah.

10 And Zimri went in and struck him, and killed him, in the twenty and seventh year of Asa king of Judah, and reigned in his stead.

11And it came to pass, when he began to reign, as soon as he sat on his throne, that he slew all the house of Baasha: he left him not one that pisseth against a wall, neither of his kinsfolks, nor of his friends.

12 Thus did Zimri destroy all the house of Baasha, according to the word of the LORD, which he spake against Baasha by Jehu the prophet,

13 For all the sins of Baasha, and the sins of Elah his son, by which they sinned, and by which they made Israel to sin, in provoking the LORD God of Israel to anger with their vanities.

14 Now the rest of the acts of Elah, and all that he did, are they not written in the book of the chronicles of the kings of Israel?

15In the twenty and seventh year of Asa king of Judah did Zimri reign seven days in Tirzah. And the people were encamped against Gibbethon, which belonged to the Philistines.

16 And the people that were encamped heard say, Zimri has conspired, and has also slain the king: wherefore all Israel made Omri, the captain of the host, king over Israel that day in the camp.

17 And Omri went up from Gibbethon, and all Israel with him, and they besieged Tirzah.

18 And it came to pass, when Zimri saw that the city was taken, that he went into the palace of the king's house, and burnt the king's house over him with fire, and died,

19 For his sins which he sinned in doing evil in the sight of the LORD, in walking in the way of Jeroboam, and in his sin which he did, to make Israel to sin.

20 Now the rest of the acts of Zimri, and his treason that he created, are they not written in the book of the chronicles of the kings of Israel?

21 Then were the people of Israel divided into two parts: half of the people followed Tibni the son of Ginath, to make him king; and half followed Omri.

22 But the people that followed Omri prevailed against the people that followed Tibni the son of Ginath: so Tibni died, and Omri reigned.

23 In the thirty and first year of Asa king of Judah began Omri to reign over Israel, twelve years: six years reigned he in Tirzah.

24 And he bought the hill Samaria of Shemer for two talents of silver, and built on the hill, and called the name of the city which he built, after the name of Shemer, owner of the hill, Samaria.

25 But Omri created evil in the eyes of the LORD, and did worse than all that were before him.

26 For he walked in all the way of Jeroboam the son of Nebat, and in his sin wherewith he made Israel to sin, to provoke the LORD God of Israel to anger with their vanities.

27 Now the rest of the acts of Omri which he did, and his might that he shewed, are they not written in the book of the chronicles of the kings of Israel?

28 So Omri slept with his fathers, and was buried in Samaria: and Ahab his son reigned in his stead.

29 And in the thirty and eighth year of Asa king of Judah began Ahab the son of Omri to reign over Israel: and Ahab the son of Omri reigned over Israel in Samaria twenty and two years.

30 And Ahab the son of Omri did evil in the sight of the LORD above all that were before him.

31 And it came to pass, as if it had been a light thing for him to walk in the sins of Jeroboam the son of Nebat, that he took to wife Jezebel the daughter of Ethbaal king of the Zidonians, and went and served Baal, and worshipped him.

32 And he reared up an altar for Baal in the house of Baal, which he had built in Samaria.

33 And Ahab made a grove; and Ahab did more to provoke the LORD God of Israel to anger than all the kings of Israel that were before him.

34 In his days did Hiel the Beth-elite build Jericho: he laid the foundation thereof in Abiram his firstborn, and set up the gates thereof in his youngest son Segub, according to the word of the LORD, which he spake by Joshua the son of Nun.

CHAPTER 17

AND Elijah the Tishbite, who was of the inhabitants of Gilead, said unto Ahab, As the LORD God of Israel liveth, before whom I stand, there shall not be dew nor rain these years, but according to my word.

2 And the word of the LORD came unto him, saying,

3 Get you hence, and turn you eastward, and hide yourself by the brook Cherith, that is before Jordan.

4 And it shall be, that you shalt drink of the brook; and I have commanded the ravens to feed you there.

5 So he went and did according unto the word of the LORD: for he went and dwelt by the brook Cherith, that is before Jordan.

6 And the ravens brought him bread and flesh in the morning, and bread and flesh in the evening; and he drank of the brook.

7 And it came to pass after a while, that the brook dried up, because there had been no rain in the land.

8 And the word of the LORD came unto him, saying,

9 Arise, get you to Zarephath, which belongeth to Zidon, and dwell there: behold, I have commanded a widow woman there to sustain you.

10 So he arose and went to Zarephath. And when he came to the gate of the city, behold, the widow woman was there gathering of sticks: and he called to her, and said, Fetch me, I pray you, a little water in a vessel, that I may drink.

11 And as she was going to fetch it, he called to her, and said, Bring me, I pray you, a morsel of bread in yours hand.

12 And she said, As the LORD your God liveth, I have not a cake, but an handful of meal in a barrel, and a little oil in a cruse: and, behold, I am gathering two sticks, that I may go in and dress it for me and my son, that we may eat it, and die.

13 And Elijah said unto her, Fear not; go and do as you have said: but make me thereof a little cake first, and bring it unto me, and after make for you and for your son.

14 For thus saith the LORD God of Israel, The barrel of meal shall not waste, neither shall the cruse of oil fail, until the day that the LORD sendeth rain upon the earth.

15 And she went and did according to the saying of Elijah: and she, and he, and her house, did eat many days.

16 And the barrel of meal wasted not, neither did the cruse of oil fail, according to the word of the LORD, which he spake by Elijah.

17 And it came to pass after these things, that the son of the woman, the mistress of the house, fell sick; and his sickness was so sore, that there was no breath left in him.

18 And she said unto Elijah, What have I to do with you, O you man of God? are you come unto me to call my sin to remembrance, and to slay my son?

19 And he said unto her, Give me your son. And he took him out of her bosom, and carried him up into a loft, where he abode, and laid him upon his own bed.

20 And he cried unto the LORD, and said, O LORD my God, have you also brought evil upon the widow with whom I sojourn, by slaying her son?

21 And he stretched himself upon the child three times, and cried unto the LORD, and said, O LORD my God, I pray you, let this child's soul come into him again.

22 And the LORD heard the voice of Elijah; and the soul of the child came into him again, and he revived.

23 And Elijah took the child, and brought him down out of the chamber into the house, and delivered him unto his mother: and Elijah said, See, your son liveth.

24 And the woman said to Elijah, Now by this I know that you are a man of God, and that the word of the LORD in your mouth is truth.

CHAPTER 18

AND it came to pass after many days, that the word of the LORD came to Elijah in the third year, saying, Go, shew yourself unto Ahab; and I will send rain upon the earth.

2 And Elijah went to shew himself unto Ahab. And there was a sore famine in Samaria.

3 And Ahab called Obadiah, which was the governor of his house. (Now Obadiah feared the LORD greatly:

4 For it was so, when Jezebel cut off the prophets of the LORD, that Obadiah took an hundred prophets, and hid them by fifty in a cave, and fed them with bread and water.)

5 And Ahab said unto Obadiah, Go into the land, unto all fountains of water, and unto all brooks: what if we may find grass to save the horses and mules alive, that we lose not all the beasts.

6 So they divided the land between them to pass throughout it: Ahab went one way by himself, and Obadiah went another way by himself.

7 And as Obadiah was in the way, behold, Elijah met him: and he knew him, and fell on his face, and said, Are you that my lord Elijah?

8 And he answered him, I am: go, tell your lord, Behold, Elijah is here.

9 And he said, What have I sinned, that you wouldest deliver your servant into the hand of Ahab, to slay me?

10 As the LORD your God liveth, there is no nation or kingdom, whither my lord has not sent to seek you: and when they said, He is not there; he took an oath of the kingdom and nation, that they found you not.

11 And now you say, Go, tell your lord, Behold, Elijah is here.

12 And it shall come to pass, as soon as I am gone from you, that the Spirit of the LORD shall carry you whither I know not; and so when I come and tell Ahab, and he cannot find you, he shall slay me: but I your servant fear the LORD from my youth.

13 Was it not told my lord what I did when Jezebel slew the prophets of the LORD, how I hid an hundred men of the LORD's prophets by fifty in a cave, and fed them with bread and water?

14 And now you say, Go, tell your lord, Behold, Elijah is here: and he shall slay me.

15 And Elijah said, As the LORD of hosts liveth, before whom I stand, I will surely shew myself unto him to day.

16 So Obadiah went to meet Ahab, and told him: and Ahab went to meet Elijah.

17 And it came to pass, when Ahab saw Elijah, that Ahab said unto him, Are you he that troubleth Israel?

18 And he answered, I have not troubled Israel; but you , and your father's house, in that you have forsaken the commandments of the LORD, and you have followed Baalim.

19 Now therefore send, and gather to me all Israel unto mount Carmel, and the prophets of Baal four hundred and fifty, and the prophets of the groves four hundred, which eat at Jezebel's table.

20 So Ahab sent unto all the children of Israel, and gathered the prophets together unto mount Carmel.

21 And Elijah came unto all the people, and said, How long halt you between two opinions? if the LORD be God, follow him: but if Baal, then follow him. And the people answered him not a word.

22 Then said Elijah unto the people, I, even I only, remain a prophet of the LORD; but Baal's prophets are four hundred and fifty men.

23 Let them therefore give us two bullocks; and let them choose one bullock for themselves, and cut it in pieces, and lay it on wood, and put no fire under: and I will dress the other bullock, and lay it on wood, and put no fire under:

24 And call you on the name of your gods, and I will call on the name of the LORD: and the God that answereth by fire, let him be God. And all the people answered and said, It is well spoken.

25 And Elijah said unto the prophets of Baal, Choose you one bullock for yourselves, and dress it first; for you are many; and call on the name of your gods, but put no fire under.

26 And they took the bullock which was given them, and they dressed it, and called on the name of Baal from morning even until noon, saying, O Baal, hear us. But there was no voice, nor any that answered. And they leaped upon the altar which was made.

27 And it came to pass at noon, that Elijah mocked them, and said, Cry aloud: for he is a god; either he is talking, or he is pursuing, or he is in a journey, or what if he sleepeth, and must be awaked.

28 And they cried aloud, and cut themselves after their manner with knives and lancets, till the blood gushed out upon them.

29 And it came to pass, when midday was past, and they prophesied until the time of the offering of the evening sacrifice, that there was neither voice, nor any to answer, nor any that regarded.

30 And Elijah said unto all the people, Come near unto me. And all the people came near unto him. And he repaired the altar of the LORD that was broken down.

31 And Elijah took twelve stones, according to the number of the tribes of the sons of Jacob, unto whom the word of the LORD came, saying, Israel shall be your name:

32 And with the stones he built an altar in the name of the LORD: and he made a trench about the altar, as great as would contain two measures of seed.

33 And he put the wood in order, and cut the bullock in pieces, and laid him on the wood, and said, Fill four barrels with water, and pour it on the burnt sacrifice, and on the wood.

34 And he said, Do it the second time. And they did it the second time. And he said, Do it the third time. And they did it the third time.

35 And the water ran round about the altar; and he filled the trench also with water.

36 And it came to pass at the time of the offering of the evening sacrifice, that Elijah the prophet came near, and said, LORD God of Abraham, Isaac, and of Israel, let it be known this day that you are God in Israel, and that I am your servant, and that I have done all these things at your word.

37 Hear me, O LORD, hear me, that this people may know that you are the LORD God, and that you have turned their heart back again.

38 Then the fire of the LORD fell, and consumed the burnt sacrifice, and the wood, and the stones, and the dust, and licked up the water that was in the trench.

39 And when all the people saw it, they fell on their faces: and they said, The LORD, he is the God; the LORD, he is the God.

40 And Elijah said unto them, Take the prophets of Baal; let not one of them escape. And they took them: and Elijah brought them down to the brook Kishon, and slew them there.

41 And Elijah said unto Ahab, Get you up, eat and drink; for there is a sound of abundance of rain.

42 So Ahab went up to eat and to drink. And Elijah went up to the top of Carmel; and he cast himself down upon the earth, and put his face between his knees,

43 And said to his servant, Go up now, look toward the sea. And he went up, and looked, and said, There is nothing. And he said, Go again seven times.

44 And it came to pass at the seventh time, that he said, Behold, there ariseth a little cloud out of the sea, like a man's hand. And he said, Go up, say unto Ahab, Prepare your chariot, and get you down, that the rain stop you not.

45 And it came to pass in the mean while, that the heaven was black with clouds and wind, and there was a great rain. And Ahab rode, and went to Jezreel.

46 And the hand of the LORD was on Elijah; and he girded up his loins, and ran before Ahab to the entrance of Jezreel.

CHAPTER 19

AND Ahab told Jezebel all that Elijah had done, and withal how he had slain all the prophets with the sword.

2 Then Jezebel sent a messenger unto Elijah, saying, So let the gods do to me, and more also, if I make not your life as the life of one of them by to morrow about this time.

3 And when he saw that, he arose, and went for his life, and came to Beer-sheba, which belongeth to Judah, and left his servant there.

4 But he himself went a day's journey into the wilderness, and came and sat down under a juniper tree: and he requested for himself that he might die; and said, It is enough; now, O LORD, take away my life; for I am not better than my fathers.

5 And as he lay and slept under a juniper tree, behold, then an angel touched him, and said unto him, Arise and eat.

6 And he looked, and, behold, there was a cake baken on the coals, and a cruse of water at his head. And he did eat and drink, and laid him down again.

7 And the angel of the LORD came again the second time, and touched him, and said, Arise and eat; because the journey is too great for you.

8 And he arose, and did eat and drink, and went in the strength of that meat forty days and forty nights unto Horeb the mount of God.

9 And he came thither unto a cave, and lodged there; and, behold, the word of the LORD came to him, and he said unto him, What doest you here, Elijah?

10 And he said, I have been very jealous for the LORD God of hosts: for the children of Israel have forsaken your covenant, thrown down yours altars, and slain your prophets with the sword; and I, even I only, am left; and they seek my life, to take it away.

11 And he said, Go forth, and stand upon the mount before the LORD. And, behold, the LORD passed by, and a great and strong wind rent the mountains, and brake in pieces the rocks before the LORD; but the LORD was not in the wind: and after the wind an earthquake; but the LORD was not in the earthquake:

12 And after the earthquake a fire; but the LORD was not in the fire: and after the fire a still small voice.

13 And it was so, when Elijah heard it, that he wrapped his face in his mantle, and went out, and stood in the entering in of the cave. And, behold, there came a voice unto him, and said, What doest you here, Elijah?

14 And he said, I have been very jealous for the LORD God of hosts: because the children of Israel have forsaken your covenant, thrown down yours altars, and slain your prophets with the sword; and I, even I only, am left; and they seek my life, to take it away.

15 And the LORD said unto him, Go, return on your way to the wilderness of Damascus: and when you comest, anoint Hazael to be king over Syria:

16 And Jehu the son of Nimshi shalt you anoint to be king over Israel: and Elisha the son of Shaphat of Abel-meholah shalt you anoint to be prophet in your room.

17 And it shall come to pass, that him that escapeth the sword of Hazael shall Jehu slay: and him that escapeth from the sword of Jehu shall Elisha slay.

18 Yet I have left me seven thousand in Israel, all the knees which have not bowed unto Baal, and every mouth which has not kissed him.

19 So he departed thence, and found Elisha the son of Shaphat, who was plowing with twelve yoke of oxen before him, and he with the twelfth: and Elijah passed by him, and cast his mantle upon him.

20 And he left the oxen, and ran after Elijah, and said, Let me, I pray you, kiss my father and my mother, and then I will follow you. And he said unto him, Go back again: for what have I done to you?

21 And he returned back from him, and took a yoke of oxen, and slew them, and boiled their flesh with the instruments of the oxen, and gave unto the people, and they did eat. Then he arose, and went after Elijah, and ministered unto him.

CHAPTER 20

AND Ben-hadad the king of Syria gathered all his host together: and there were thirty and two kings with him, and horses, and chariots: and he went up and besieged Samaria, and warred against it.

2 And he sent messengers to Ahab king of Israel into the city, and said unto him, Thus saith Ben-hadad,

3 Your silver and your gold is my; your wives also and your children, even the goodliest, are my.

4 And the king of Israel answered and said, My lord, O king, according to your saying, I am yours, and all that I have.

5 And the messengers came again, and said, Thus speaketh Ben-hadad, saying, Although I have sent unto you, saying, You shalt deliver me your silver, and your gold, and your wives, and your children;

6 Yet I will send my servants unto you to morrow about this time, and they shall search yours house, and the houses of your servants; and it shall be, that whatsoever is pleasant in yours eyes, they shall put it in their hand, and take it away.

7 Then the king of Israel called all the elders of the land, and said, Mark, I pray you, and see how this man seeketh mischief: for he sent unto me for my wives, and for my children, and for my silver, and for my gold; and I denied him not.

8 And all the elders and all the people said unto him, Hearken not unto him, nor consent.

9 Wherefore he said unto the messengers of Ben-hadad, Tell my lord the king, All that you did send for to your servant at the first I will do: but this thing I may not do. And the messengers departed, and brought him word again.

10 And Ben-hadad sent unto him, and said, The gods do so unto me, and more also, if the dust of Samaria shall suffice for handfuls for all the people that follow me.

11 And the king of Israel answered and said, Tell him, Let not him that girdeth on his harness boast himself as he that putteth it off.

12 And it came to pass, when Ben-hadad heard this message, as he was drinking, he and the kings in the pavilions, that he said unto his servants, Set yourselves in array. And they set themselves in array against the city.

13 And, behold, there came a prophet unto Ahab king of Israel, saying, Thus saith the LORD, Have you seen all this great multitude? behold, I will deliver it into yours hand this day; and you shalt know that I am the LORD.

14 And Ahab said, By whom? And he said, Thus saith the LORD, Even by the young men of the princes of the provinces. Then he said, Who shall order the battle? And he answered, You .

15 Then he numbered the young men of the princes of the provinces, and they were two hundred and thirty two: and after them he numbered all the people, even all the children of Israel, being seven thousand.

16 And they went out at noon. But Ben-hadad was drinking himself drunk in the pavilions, he and the kings, the thirty and two kings that helped him.

17 And the young men of the princes of the provinces went out first; and Ben-hadad sent out, and they told him, saying, There are men come out of Samaria.

18 And he said, Whether they be come out for peace, take them alive; or whether they be come out for war, take them alive.

19 So these young men of the princes of the provinces came out of the city, and the army which followed them.

20 And they slew every one his man: and the Syrians fled; and Israel pursued them: and Ben-hadad the king of Syria escaped on an horse with the horsemen.

21 And the king of Israel went out, and struck the horses and chariots, and slew the Syrians with a great slaughter.

22 And the prophet came to the king of Israel, and said unto him, Go, strengthen yourself, and mark, and see what you doest: for at the return of the year the king of Syria will come up against you.

23 And the servants of the king of Syria said unto him, Their gods are gods of the hills; therefore they were stronger than we; but let us fight against them in the plain, and surely we shall be stronger than they.

24 And do this thing, Take the kings away, every man out of his place, and put captains in their rooms:

25 And number you an army, like the army that you have lost, horse for horse, and chariot for chariot: and we will fight against them in the plain, and surely we shall be stronger than they. And he hearkened unto their voice, and did so.

26 And it came to pass at the return of the year, that Ben-hadad numbered the Syrians, and went up to Aphek, to fight against Israel.

27 And the children of Israel were numbered, and were all present, and went against them: and the children of Israel pitched before them like two little flocks of kids; but the Syrians filled the country.

28 And there came a man of God, and spake unto the king of Israel, and said, Thus saith the LORD, Because the Syrians have said, The LORD is God of the hills, but he is not God of the valleys, therefore will I deliver all this great multitude into yours hand, and you shall know that I am the LORD.

29 And they pitched one over against the other seven days. And so it was, that in the seventh day the battle was joined: and the children of Israel slew of the Syrians an hundred thousand footmen in one day.

30 But the rest fled to Aphek, into the city; and there a wall fell upon twenty and seven thousand of the men that were left. And Ben-hadad fled, and came into the city, into an inner chamber.

31 And his servants said unto him, Behold now, we have heard that the kings of the house of Israel are merciful kings: let us, I pray you, put sackcloth on our loins, and ropes upon our heads, and go out to the king of Israel: what if he will save your life.

32 So they girded sackcloth on their loins, and put ropes on their heads, and came to the king of Israel, and said, Your servant Ben-hadad saith, I pray you, let me live. And he said, Is he yet alive? he is my brother.

33 Now the men did diligently observe whether any thing would come from him, and did hastily catch it: and they said, Your brother Ben-hadad. Then he said, Go you , bring him. Then Ben-hadad came forth to him; and he caused him to come up into the chariot.

34 And Ben-hadad said unto him, The cities, which my father took from your father, I will restore; and you shalt make streets for you in Damascus, as my father made in Samaria. Then said Ahab, I will send you away with this covenant. So he made a covenant with him, and sent him away.

35 And a certain man of the sons of the prophets said unto his neighbour in the word of the LORD, Strike me, I pray you. And the man refused to strike him.

36 Then said he unto him, Because you have not obeyed the voice of the LORD, behold, as soon as you are departed from me, a lion shall slay you. And as soon as he was departed from him, a lion found him, and slew him.

37 Then he found another man, and said, Strike me, I pray you. And the man struck him, so that in striking he wounded him.

38 So the prophet departed, and waited for the king by the way, and disguised himself with ashes upon his face.

39 And as the king passed by, he cried unto the king: and he said, Your servant went out into the midst of the battle; and, behold, a man turned aside, and brought a man unto me, and said, Keep this man: if by any means he be missing, then shall your life be for his life, or else you shalt pay a talent of silver.

40 And as your servant was busy here and there, he was gone. And the king of Israel said unto him, So shall your judgment be; yourself have decided it.

41 And he hasted, and took the ashes away from his face; and the king of Israel discerned him that he was of the prophets.

42 And he said unto him, Thus saith the LORD, Because you have let go out of your hand a man whom I appointed to utter destruction, therefore your life shall go for his life, and your people for his people.

43 And the king of Israel went to his house heavy and displeased, and came to Samaria.

CHAPTER 21

AND it came to pass after these things, that Naboth the Jezreelite had a vineyard, which was in Jezreel, hard by the palace of Ahab king of Samaria.

2 And Ahab spake unto Naboth, saying, Give me your vineyard, that I may have it for a garden of herbs, because it is near unto my house: and I will give you for it a better vineyard than it; or, if it seem good to you, I will give you the worth of it in money.

3 And Naboth said to Ahab, The LORD forbid it me, that I should give the inheritance of my fathers unto you.

4 And Ahab came into his house heavy and displeased because of the word which Naboth the Jezreelite had spoken to him: for he had said, I will not give you the inheritance of my fathers. And he laid him down upon his bed, and turned away his face, and would eat no bread.

5 But Jezebel his wife came to him, and said unto him, Why is your spirit so sad, that you eatest no bread?

6 And he said unto her, Because I spake unto Naboth the Jezreelite, and said unto him, Give me your vineyard for money; or else, if it please you, I will give you another vineyard for it: and he answered, I will not give you my vineyard.

7 And Jezebel his wife said unto him, Dost you now govern the kingdom of Israel? arise, and eat bread, and let yours heart be merry: I will give you the vineyard of Naboth the Jezreelite.

8 So she wrote letters in Ahab's name, and sealed them with his seal, and sent the letters unto the elders and to the nobles that were in his city, dwelling with Naboth.

9 And she wrote in the letters, saying, Proclaim a fast, and set Naboth on high among the people:

10 And set two men, sons of Belial, before him, to bear witness against him, saying, You did blaspheme God and the king. And then carry him out, and stone him, that he may die.

11 And the men of his city, even the elders and the nobles who were the inhabitants in his city, did as Jezebel had sent unto them, and as it was written in the letters which she had sent unto them.

12 They proclaimed a fast, and set Naboth on high among the people.

13 And there came in two men, children of Belial, and sat before him: and the men of Belial witnessed against him, even against Naboth, in the presence of the people, saying, Naboth did blaspheme God and the king. Then they carried him forth out of the city, and stoned him with stones, that he died.

14 Then they sent to Jezebel, saying, Naboth is stoned, and is dead.

15 And it came to pass, when Jezebel heard that Naboth was stoned, and was dead, that Jezebel said to Ahab, Arise, take possession of the vineyard of Naboth the Jezreelite, which he refused to give you for money: for Naboth is not alive, but dead.

16 And it came to pass, when Ahab heard that Naboth was dead, that Ahab rose up to go down to the vineyard of Naboth the Jezreelite, to take possession of it.

17 And the word of the LORD came to Elijah the Tishbite, saying,

18 Arise, go down to meet Ahab king of Israel, which is in Samaria: behold, he is in the vineyard of Naboth, whither he is gone down to possess it.

19 And you shalt speak unto him, saying, Thus saith the LORD, Have you killed, and also taken possession? And you shalt speak unto him, saying, Thus saith the LORD, In the place where dogs licked the blood of Naboth shall dogs lick your blood, even yours.

20 And Ahab said to Elijah, Have you found me, O my enemy? And he answered, I have found you: because you have sold yourself to work evil in the sight of the LORD.

21 Behold, I will bring evil upon you, and will take away your posterity, and will cut off from Ahab him that pisseth against the wall, and him that is shut up and left in Israel,

22 And will make yours house like the house of Jeroboam the son of Nebat, and like the house of Baasha the son of Ahijah, for the provocation wherewith you have provoked me to anger, and made Israel to sin.

23 And of Jezebel also spake the LORD, saying, The dogs shall eat Jezebel by the wall of Jezreel.

24 Him that dieth of Ahab in the city the dogs shall eat; and him that dieth in the field shall the fowls of the air eat.

25But there was none like unto Ahab, which did sell himself to work wickedness in the sight of the LORD, whom Jezebel his wife stirred up.

26 And he did very abominably in following idols, according to all things as did the Amorites, whom the LORD cast out before the children of Israel.

27 And it came to pass, when Ahab heard those words, that he rent his clothes, and put sackcloth upon his flesh, and fasted, and lay in sackcloth, and went softly.

28 And the word of the LORD came to Elijah the Tishbite, saying,

29 Seest you how Ahab humbleth himself before me? because he humbleth himself before me, I will not bring the evil in his days: but in his son's days will I bring the evil upon his house.

CHAPTER 22

AND they continued three years without war between Syria and Israel.

2 And it came to pass in the third year, that Jehoshaphat the king of Judah came down to the king of Israel.

3 And the king of Israel said unto his servants, Know you that Ramoth in Gilead is ours, and we be still, and take it not out of the hand of the king of Syria?

4 And he said unto Jehoshaphat, Will you go with me to battle to Ramoth-gilead? And Jehoshaphat said to the king of Israel, I am as you are, my people as your people, my horses as your horses.

5 And Jehoshaphat said unto the king of Israel, Inquire, I pray you, at the word of the LORD to day.

6 Then the king of Israel gathered the prophets together, about four hundred men, and said unto them, Shall I go against Ramoth-gilead to battle, or shall I forbear? And they said, Go up; for the Lord shall deliver it into the hand of the king.

7 And Jehoshaphat said, Is there not here a prophet of the LORD besides, that we might inquire of him?

8 And the king of Israel said unto Jehoshaphat, There is yet one man, Micaiah the son of Imlah, by whom we may inquire of the LORD: but I hate him; for he doth not prophesy good concerning me, but evil. And Jehoshaphat said, Let not the king say so.

9 Then the king of Israel called an officer, and said, Hasten hither Micaiah the son of Imlah.

10 And the king of Israel and Jehoshaphat the king of Judah sat each on his throne, having put on their robes, in a void place in the entrance of the gate of Samaria; and all the prophets prophesied before them.

11 And Zedekiah the son of Chenaanah made him horns of iron: and he said, Thus saith the LORD, With these shalt you push the Syrians, until you have consumed them.

12 And all the prophets prophesied so, saying, Go up to Ramoth-gilead, and prosper: for the LORD shall deliver it into the king's hand.

13 And the messenger that was gone to call Micaiah spake unto him, saying, Behold now, the words of the prophets declare good unto the king with one mouth: let your word, I pray you, be like the word of one of them, and speak that which is good.

14 And Micaiah said, As the LORD liveth, what the LORD saith unto me, that will I speak.

15So he came to the king. And the king said unto him, Micaiah, shall we go against Ramoth-gilead to battle, or shall we forbear? And he answered him, Go, and prosper: for the LORD shall deliver it into the hand of the king.

16 And the king said unto him, How many times shall I adjure you that you tell me nothing but that which is true in the name of the LORD?

17 And he said, I saw all Israel scattered upon the hills, as sheep that have not a shepherd: and the LORD said, These have no master: let them return every man to his house in peace.

18 And the king of Israel said unto Jehoshaphat, Did I not tell you that he would prophesy no good concerning me, but evil?

19 And he said, Hear you therefore the word of the LORD: I saw the LORD sitting on his throne, and all the host of heaven standing by him on his right hand and on his left.

20 And the LORD said, Who shall persuade Ahab, that he may go up and fall at Ramoth-gilead? And one said on this manner, and another said on that manner.

21 And there came forth a spirit, and stood before the LORD, and said, I will persuade him.

22 And the LORD said unto him, Wherewith? And he said, I will go forth, and I will be a lying spirit in the mouth of all his prophets. And he said, You shalt persuade him, and prevail also: go forth, and do so.

23 Now therefore, behold, the LORD has put a lying spirit in the mouth of all these your prophets, and the LORD has spoken evil concerning you.

24 But Zedekiah the son of Chenaanah went near, and struck Micaiah on the cheek, and said, Which way went the Spirit of the LORD from me to speak unto you?

25 And Micaiah said, Behold, you shalt see in that day, when you shalt go into an inner chamber to hide yourself.

26 And the king of Israel said, Take Micaiah, and carry him back unto Amon the governor of the city, and to Joash the king's son;

27 And say, Thus saith the king, Put this fellow in the prison, and feed him with bread of affliction and with water of affliction, until I come in peace.

28 And Micaiah said, If you return at all in peace, the LORD has not spoken by me. And he said, Hearken, O people, every one of you.

29 So the king of Israel and Jehoshaphat the king of Judah went up to Ramoth-gilead.

30 And the king of Israel said unto Jehoshaphat, I will disguise myself, and enter into the battle; but put you on your robes. And the king of Israel disguised himself, and went into the battle.

31 But the king of Syria commanded his thirty and two captains that had rule over his chariots, saying, Fight neither with small nor great, save only with the king of Israel.

32 And it came to pass, when the captains of the chariots saw Jehoshaphat, that they said, Surely it is the king of Israel. And they turned aside to fight against him: and Jehoshaphat cried out.

33 And it came to pass, when the captains of the chariots perceived that it was not the king of Israel, that they turned back from pursuing him.

34 And a certain man drew a bow at a venture, and struck the king of Israel between the joints of the harness: wherefore he said unto the driver of his chariot, Turn yours hand, and carry me out of the host; for I am wounded.

35 And the battle increased that day: and the king was stayed up in his chariot against the Syrians, and died at even: and the blood ran out of the wound into the midst of the chariot.

36 And there went a proclamation throughout the host about the going down of the sun, saying, Every man to his city, and every man to his own country.

37So the king died, and was brought to Samaria; and they buried the king in Samaria.

38 And one washed the chariot in the pool of Samaria; and the dogs licked up his blood; and they washed his armour; according unto the word of the LORD which he spake.

39 Now the rest of the acts of Ahab, and all that he did, and the ivory house which he made, and all the cities that he built, are they not written in the book of the chronicles of the kings of Israel?

40 So Ahab slept with his fathers; and Ahaziah his son reigned in his stead.

41And Jehoshaphat the son of Asa began to reign over Judah in the fourth year of Ahab king of Israel.

42 Jehoshaphat was thirty and five years old when he began to reign; and he reigned twenty and five years in Jerusalem. And his mother's name was Azubah the daughter of Shilhi.

43 And he walked in all the ways of Asa his father; he turned not aside from it, doing that which was right in the eyes of the LORD: nevertheless the high places were not taken away; for the people offered and burnt incense yet in the high places.

44 And Jehoshaphat made peace with the king of Israel.

45 Now the rest of the acts of Jehoshaphat, and his might that he shewed, and how he warred, are they not written in the book of the chronicles of the kings of Judah?

46 And the remnant of the sodomites, which remained in the days of his father Asa, he took out of the land.

47 There was then no king in Edom: a deputy was king.

48 Jehoshaphat made ships of Tharshish to go to Ophir for gold: but they went not; for the ships were broken at Ezion-geber.

49 Then said Ahaziah the son of Ahab unto Jehoshaphat, Let my servants go with your servants in the ships. But Jehoshaphat would not.

50And Jehoshaphat slept with his fathers, and was buried with his fathers in the city of David his father: and Jehoram his son reigned in his stead.

51 Ahaziah the son of Ahab began to reign over Israel in Samaria the seventeenth year of Jehoshaphat king of Judah, and reigned two years over Israel.

52 And he did evil in the sight of the LORD, and walked in the way of his father, and in the way of his mother, and in the way of Jeroboam the son of Nebat, who made Israel to sin:

53 For he served Baal, and worshipped him, and provoked to anger the LORD God of Israel, according to all that his father had done.

THE SECOND
BOOK OF THE KINGS,
COMMONLY CALLED,
THE FOURTH BOOK OF THE KINGS.

CHAPTER 1

THEN Moab rebelled against Israel after the death of Ahab.

2 And Ahaziah fell down through a lattice in his upper chamber that was in Samaria, and was sick: and he sent messengers, and said unto them, Go, inquire of Baal-zebub the god of Ekron whether I shall recover of this disease.

3 But the angel of the LORD said to Elijah the Tishbite, Arise, go up to meet the messengers of the king of Samaria, and say unto them, Is it not because there is not a God in Israel, that you go to inquire of Baal-zebub the god of Ekron?

4 Now therefore thus saith the LORD, You shalt not come down from that bed on which you are gone up, but shalt surely die. And Elijah departed.

5And when the messengers turned back unto him, he said unto them, Why are you now turned back?

6 And they said unto him, There came a man up to meet us, and said unto us, Go, turn again unto the king that sent you, and say unto him, Thus saith the LORD, Is it not because there is not a God in Israel, that you sendest to inquire of Baal-zebub the god of Ekron? therefore you shalt not come down from that bed on which you are gone up, but shalt surely die.

7 And he said unto them, What manner of man was he which came up to meet you, and told you these words?

8 And they answered him, He was an hairy man, and girt with a girdle of leather about his loins. And he said, It is Elijah the Tishbite.

9 Then the king sent unto him a captain of fifty with his fifty. And he went up to him: and, behold, he sat on the top of an hill. And he spake unto him, You man of God, the king has said, Come down.

10 And Elijah answered and said to the captain of fifty, If I be a man of God, then let fire come down from heaven, and consume you and your fifty. And there came down fire from heaven, and consumed him and his fifty.

11 Again also he sent unto him another captain of fifty with his fifty. And he answered and said unto him, O man of God, thus has the king said, Come down quickly.

12 And Elijah answered and said unto them, If I be a man of God, let fire come down from heaven, and consume you and your fifty. And the fire of God came down from heaven, and consumed him and his fifty.

13And he sent again a captain of the third fifty with his fifty. And the third captain of fifty went up, and came and fell on his knees before Elijah, and besought him, and said unto him, O man of God, I pray you, let my life, and the life of these fifty your servants, be precious in your sight.

14 Behold, there came fire down from heaven, and burnt up the two captains of the former fifties with their fifties: therefore let my life now be precious in your sight.

15 And the angel of the LORD said unto Elijah, Go down with him: be not afraid of him. And he arose, and went down with him unto the king.

16 And he said unto him, Thus saith the LORD, Forasmuch as you have sent messengers to inquire of Baal-zebub the god of Ekron, is it not because there is no God in Israel to inquire of his word? therefore you shalt not come down off that bed on which you are gone up, but shalt surely die.

17So he died according to the word of the LORD which Elijah had spoken. And Jehoram reigned in his stead in the second year of Jehoram the son of Jehoshaphat king of Judah; because he had no son.

18 Now the rest of the acts of Ahaziah which he did, are they not written in the book of the chronicles of the kings of Israel?

CHAPTER 2

AND it came to pass, when the LORD would take up Elijah into heaven by a whirlwind, that Elijah went with Elisha from Gilgal.

2 And Elijah said unto Elisha, Tarry here, I pray you; for the LORD has sent me to Beth-el. And Elisha said unto him, As the LORD liveth, and as your soul liveth, I will not leave you. So they went down to Beth-el.

3 And the sons of the prophets that were at Beth-el came forth to Elisha, and said unto him, Knowest you that the LORD will take away your master from your head to day? And he said, Yea, I know it; hold you your peace.

4 And Elijah said unto him, Elisha, tarry here, I pray you; for the LORD has sent me to Jericho. And he said, As the LORD liveth, and as your soul liveth, I will not leave you. So they came to Jericho.

5 And the sons of the prophets that were at Jericho came to Elisha, and said unto him, Knowest you that the LORD will take away your master from your head to day? And he answered, Yea, I know it; hold you your peace.

6 And Elijah said unto him, Tarry, I pray you, here; for the LORD has sent me to Jordan. And he said, As the LORD liveth, and as your soul liveth, I will not leave you. And they two went on.

7 And fifty men of the sons of the prophets went, and stood to view afar off: and they two stood by Jordan.

8 And Elijah took his mantle, and wrapped it together, and struck the waters, and they were divided hither and thither, so that they two went over on dry ground.

9And it came to pass, when they were gone over, that Elijah said unto Elisha, Ask what I shall do for you, before I be taken away from you. And Elisha said, I pray you, let a double portion of your spirit be upon me.

10 And he said, You have asked a hard thing: nevertheless, if you see me when I am taken from you, it shall be so unto you; but if not, it shall not be so.

11 And it came to pass, as they still went on, and talked, that, behold, there appeared a chariot of fire, and horses of fire, and parted them both asunder; and Elijah went up by a whirlwind into heaven.

12And Elisha saw it, and he cried, My father, my father, the chariot of Israel, and the horsemen thereof. And he saw him no more: and he took hold of his own clothes, and rent them in two pieces.

13 He took up also the mantle of Elijah that fell from him, and went back, and stood by the bank of Jordan;

14 And he took the mantle of Elijah that fell from him, and struck the waters, and said, Where is the LORD God of Elijah? and when he also had smitten the waters, they parted hither and thither: and Elisha went over.

15 And when the sons of the prophets which were to view at Jericho saw him, they said, The spirit of Elijah doth rest on Elisha. And they came to meet him, and bowed themselves to the ground before him.

16And they said unto him, Behold now, there be with your servants fifty strong men; let them go, we pray you, and seek your master: lest what if the Spirit of the LORD has taken him up, and cast him upon some mountain, or into some valley. And he said, You shall not send.

17 And when they urged him till he was ashamed, he said, Send. They sent therefore fifty men; and they sought three days, but found him not.

18 And when they came again to him, (for he tarried at Jericho,) he said unto them, Did I not say you, Go not?

19And the men of the city said unto Elisha, Behold, I pray you, the situation of this city is pleasant, as my lord seeth: but the water is naught, and the ground barren.

20 And he said, Bring me a new cruse, and put salt therein. And they brought it to him.

21 And he went forth unto the spring of the waters, and cast the salt in there, and said, Thus saith the LORD, I have healed these waters; there shall not be from thence any more death or barren land.

22 So the waters were healed unto this day, according to the saying of Elisha which he spake.

23And he went up from thence unto Beth-el: and as he was going up by the way, there came forth little children out of the city, and mocked him, and said unto him, Go up, you bald head; go up, you bald head.

24 And he turned back, and looked on them, and cursed them in the name of the LORD. And there came forth two she bears out of the wood, and tare forty and two children of them.

25 And he went from thence to mount Carmel, and from thence he returned to Samaria.

CHAPTER 3

NOW Jehoram the son of Ahab began to reign over Israel in Samaria the eighteenth year of Jehoshaphat king of Judah, and reigned twelve years.

2 And he created evil in the sight of the LORD; but not like his father, and like his mother: for he put away the image of Baal that his father had made.

3 Nevertheless he cleaved unto the sins of Jeroboam the son of Nebat, which made Israel to sin; he departed not therefrom.

4And Mesha king of Moab was a sheepmaster, and rendered unto the king of Israel an hundred thousand lambs, and an hundred thousand rams, with the wool.

5 But it came to pass, when Ahab was dead, that the king of Moab rebelled against the king of Israel.

6And king Jehoram went out of Samaria the same time, and numbered all Israel.

7 And he went and sent to Jehoshaphat the king of Judah, saying, The king of Moab has rebelled against me: will you go with me against Moab to battle? And he said, I will go up: I am as you are, my people as your people, and my horses as your horses.

8 And he said, Which way shall we go up? And he answered, The way through the wilderness of Edom.

9 So the king of Israel went, and the king of Judah, and the king of Edom: and they fetched a compass of seven days' journey: and there was no water for the host, and for the cattle that followed them.

10 And the king of Israel said, Alas! that the LORD has called these three kings together, to deliver them into the hand of Moab!

11 But Jehoshaphat said, Is there not here a prophet of the LORD, that we may inquire of the LORD by him? And one of the king of Israel's servants answered and said, Here is Elisha the son of Shaphat, which poured water on the hands of Elijah.

12 And Jehoshaphat said, The word of the LORD is with him. So the king of Israel and Jehoshaphat and the king of Edom went down to him.

13 And Elisha said unto the king of Israel, What have I to do with you? get you to the prophets of your father, and to the prophets of your mother. And the king of Israel said unto him, Nay: for the LORD has called these three kings together, to deliver them into the hand of Moab.

14 And Elisha said, As the LORD of hosts liveth, before whom I stand, surely, were it not that I regard the presence of Jehoshaphat the king of Judah, I would not look toward you, nor see you.

15 But now bring me a minstrel. And it came to pass, when the minstrel played, that the hand of the LORD came upon him.

16 And he said, Thus saith the LORD, Make this valley full of ditches.

17 For thus saith the LORD, You shall not see wind, neither shall you see rain; yet that valley shall be filled with water, that you may drink, both you , and your cattle, and your beasts.

18 And this is but a light thing in the sight of the LORD: he will deliver the Moabites also into your hand.

19 And you shall strike every fenced city, and every choice city, and shall fell every good tree, and stop all wells of water, and mar every good piece of land with stones.

20 And it came to pass in the morning, when the meat offering was offered, that, behold, there came water by the way of Edom, and the country was filled with water.

21 And when all the Moabites heard that the kings were come up to fight against them, they gathered all that were able to put on armour, and upward, and stood in the border.

22 And they rose up early in the morning, and the sun shone upon the water, and the Moabites saw the water on the other side as red as blood:

23 And they said, This is blood: the kings are surely slain, and they have smitten one another: now therefore, Moab, to the spoil.

24 And when they came to the camp of Israel, the Israelites rose up and struck the Moabites, so that they fled before them: but they went forward striking the Moabites, even in their country.

25 And they beat down the cities, and on every good piece of land cast every man his stone, and filled it; and they stopped all the wells of water, and felled all the good trees: only in Kir-haraseth left they the stones thereof; howbeit the slingers went about it, and struck it.

26 And when the king of Moab saw that the battle was too sore for him, he took with him seven hundred men that drew swords, to break through even unto the king of Edom: but they could not.

27 Then he took his eldest son that should have reigned in his stead, and offered him for a burnt offering upon the wall. And there was great indignation against Israel: and they departed from him, and returned to their own land.

CHAPTER 4

NOW there cried a certain woman of the wives of the sons of the prophets unto Elisha, saying, Your servant my husband is dead; and you knowest that your servant did fear the LORD: and the creditor is come to take unto him my two sons to be bondmen.

2 And Elisha said unto her, What shall I do for you? tell me, what have you in the house? And she said, Yours handmaid has not any thing in the house, save a pot of oil.

3 Then he said, Go, borrow you vessels abroad of all your neighbours, even empty vessels; borrow not a few.

4 And when you are come in, you shalt shut the door upon you and upon your sons, and shalt pour out into all those vessels, and you shalt set aside that which is full.

5 So she went from him, and shut the door upon her and upon her sons, who brought the vessels to her; and she poured out.

6 And it came to pass, when the vessels were full, that she said unto her son, Bring me yet a vessel. And he said unto her, There is not a vessel more. And the oil stayed.

7 Then she came and told the man of God. And he said, Go, sell the oil, and pay your debt, and live you and your children of the rest.

8 And it fell on a day, that Elisha passed to Shunem, where was a great woman; and she constrained him to eat bread. And so it was, that as oft as he passed by, he turned in thither to eat bread.

9 And she said unto her husband, Behold now, I perceive that this is an holy man of God, which passes by us continually.

10 Let us make a little chamber, I pray you, on the wall; and let us set for him there a bed, and a table, and a stool, and a candlestick: and it shall be, when he comes to us, that he shall turn in thither.

11 And it fell on a day, that he came thither, and he turned into the chamber, and lay there.

12 And he said to Gehazi his servant, Call this Shunammite. And when he had called her, she stood before him.

13 And he said unto him, Say now unto her, Behold, you have been careful for us with all this care; what is to be done for you? wouldest you be spoken for to the king, or to the captain of the host? And she answered, I dwell among my own people.

14 And he said, What then is to be done for her? And Gehazi answered, Verily she has no child, and her husband is old.

15 And he said, Call her. And when he had called her, she stood in the door.

16 And he said, About this season, according to the time of life, you shalt embrace a son. And she said, Nay, my lord, you man of God, do not lie unto yours handmaid.

17 And the woman conceived, and bare a son at that season that Elisha had said unto her, according to the time of life.

18 And when the child was grown, it fell on a day, that he went out to his father to the reapers.

19 And he said unto his father, My head, my head. And he said to a lad, Carry him to his mother.

20 And when he had taken him, and brought him to his mother, he sat on her knees till noon, and then died.

21 And she went up, and laid him on the bed of the man of God, and shut the door upon him, and went out.

22 And she called unto her husband, and said, Send me, I pray you, one of the young men, and one of the asses, that I may run to the man of God, and come again.

23 And he said, Wherefore will you go to him to day? it is neither new moon, nor sabbath. And she said, It shall be well.

24 Then she saddled an ass, and said to her servant, Drive, and go forward; slack not your riding for me, except I bid you.

25 So she went and came unto the man of God to mount Carmel. And it came to pass, when the man of God saw her afar off, that he said to Gehazi his servant, Behold, yonder is that Shunammite:

26 Run now, I pray you, to meet her, and say unto her, Is it well with you? is it well with your husband? is it well with the child? And she answered, It is well.

27 And when she came to the man of God to the hill, she caught him by the feet: but Gehazi came near to thrust her away. And the man of God said, Let her alone; for her soul is vexed within her: and the LORD has hid it from me, and has not told me.

28 Then she said, Did I desire a son of my lord? did I not say, Do not deceive me?

29 Then he said to Gehazi, Gird up your loins, and take my staff in yours hand, and go your way: if you meet any man, salute him not; and if any salute you, answer him not again: and lay my staff upon the face of the child.

30 And the mother of the child said, As the LORD liveth, and as your soul liveth, I will not leave you. And he arose, and followed her.

31 And Gehazi passed on before them, and laid the staff upon the face of the child; but there was neither voice, nor hearing. Wherefore he went again to meet him, and told him, saying, The child is not awaked.

32 And when Elisha was come into the house, behold, the child was dead, and laid upon his bed.

33 He went in therefore, and shut the door upon them twain, and prayed unto the LORD.

34 And he went up, and lay upon the child, and put his mouth upon his mouth, and his eyes upon his eyes, and his hands upon his hands: and he stretched himself upon the child; and the flesh of the child waxed warm.

35 Then he returned, and walked in the house to and fro; and went up, and stretched himself upon him: and the child sneezed seven times, and the child opened his eyes.

36 And he called Gehazi, and said, Call this Shunammite. So he called her. And when she was come in unto him, he said, Take up your son.

37 Then she went in, and fell at his feet, and bowed herself to the ground, and took up her son, and went out.

38 And Elisha came again to Gilgal: and there was a dearth in the land; and the sons of the prophets were sitting before him: and he said unto his servant, Set on the great pot, and seethe pottage for the sons of the prophets.

39 And one went out into the field to gather herbs, and found a wild vine, and gathered thereof wild gourds his lap full, and came and shred them into the pot of pottage: for they knew them not.

40 So they poured out for the men to eat. And it came to pass, as they were eating of the pottage, that they cried out, and said, O you man of God, there is death in the pot. And they could not eat thereof.

41 But he said, Then bring meal. And he cast it into the pot; and he said, Pour out for the people, that they may eat. And there was no harm in the pot.

42And there came a man from Baal-shalisha, and brought the man of God bread of the firstfruits, twenty loaves of barley, and full ears of corn in the husk thereof. And he said, Give unto the people, that they may eat.

43 And his servitor said, What, should I set this before an hundred men? He said again, Give the people, that they may eat: for thus saith the LORD, They shall eat, and shall leave thereof.

44 So he set it before them, and they did eat, and left thereof, according to the word of the LORD.

CHAPTER 5

NOW Naaman, captain of the host of the king of Syria, was a great man with his master, and honourable, because by him the LORD had given deliverance unto Syria: he was also a mighty man in valour, but he was a leper.

2 And the Syrians had gone out by companies, and had brought away captive out of the land of Israel a little maid; and she waited on Naaman's wife.

3 And she said unto her mistress, Would God my lord were with the prophet that is in Samaria! for he would recover him of his leprosy.

4 And one went in, and told his lord, saying, Thus and thus said the maid that is of the land of Israel.

5 And the king of Syria said, Go to, go, and I will send a letter unto the king of Israel. And he departed, and took with him ten talents of silver, and six thousand pieces of gold, and ten changes of raiment.

6 And he brought the letter to the king of Israel, saying, Now when this letter is come unto you, behold, I have therewith sent Naaman my servant to you, that you mayest recover him of his leprosy.

7 And it came to pass, when the king of Israel had read the letter, that he rent his clothes, and said, Am I God, to kill and to make alive, that this man doth send unto me to recover a man of his leprosy? wherefore consider, I pray you, and see how he seeketh a quarrel against me.

8And it was so, when Elisha the man of God had heard that the king of Israel had rent his clothes, that he sent to the king, saying, Wherefore have you rent your clothes? let him come now to me, and he shall know that there is a prophet in Israel.

9 So Naaman came with his horses and with his chariot, and stood at the door of the house of Elisha.

10 And Elisha sent a messenger unto him, saying, Go and wash in Jordan seven times, and your flesh shall come again to you, and you shalt be clean.

11 But Naaman was wroth, and went away, and said, Behold, I thought, He will surely come out to me, and stand, and call on the name of the LORD his God, and strike his hand over the place, and recover the leper.

12 Are not Abana and Pharpar, rivers of Damascus, better than all the waters of Israel? may I not wash in them, and be clean? So he turned and went away in a rage.

13 And his servants came near, and spake unto him, and said, My father, if the prophet had bid you do some great thing, wouldest you not have done it? how much rather then, when he saith to you, Wash, and be clean?

14 Then went he down, and dipped himself seven times in Jordan, according to the saying of the man of God: and his flesh came again like unto the flesh of a little child, and he was clean.

15And he returned to the man of God, he and all his company, and came, and stood before him: and he said, Behold, now I know that there is no God in all the earth, but in Israel: now therefore, I pray you, take a blessing of your servant.

16 But he said, As the LORD liveth, before whom I stand, I will receive none. And he urged him to take it; but he refused.

17 And Naaman said, Shall there not then, I pray you, be given to your servant two mules' burden of earth? for your servant will henceforth offer neither burnt offering nor sacrifice unto other gods, but unto the LORD.

18 In this thing the LORD pardon your servant, that when my master goeth into the house of Rimmon to worship there, and he leaneth on my hand, and I bow myself in the house of Rimmon: when I bow down myself in the house of Rimmon, the LORD pardon your servant in this thing.

19 And he said unto him, Go in peace. So he departed from him a little way.

20But Gehazi, the servant of Elisha the man of God, said, Behold, my master has spared Naaman this Syrian, in not receiving at his hands that which he brought: but, as the LORD liveth, I will run after him, and take somewhat of him.

21 So Gehazi followed after Naaman. And when Naaman saw him running after him, he lighted down from the chariot to meet him, and said, Is all well?

22 And he said, All is well. My master has sent me, saying, Behold, even now there be come to me from mount Ephraim two young men of the sons of the prophets: give them, I pray you, a talent of silver, and two changes of garments.

23 And Naaman said, Be content, take two talents. And he urged him, and bound two talents of silver in two bags, with two changes of garments, and laid them upon two of his servants; and they bare them before him.

24 And when he came to the tower, he took them from their hand, and bestowed them in the house: and he let the men go, and they departed.

25 But he went in, and stood before his master. And Elisha said unto him, Whence comest you , Gehazi? And he said, Your servant went no whither.

26 And he said unto him, Went not my heart with you, when the man turned again from his chariot to meet you? Is it a time to receive money, and to receive garments, and oliveyards, and vineyards, and sheep, and oxen, and menservants, and maidservants?

27 The leprosy therefore of Naaman shall cleave unto you, and unto your seed for ever. And he went out from his presence a leper as white as snow.

CHAPTER 6

AND the sons of the prophets said unto Elisha, Behold now, the place where we dwell with you is too strait for us.

2 Let us go, we pray you, unto Jordan, and take thence every man a beam, and let us make us a place there, where we may dwell. And he answered, Go you .

3 And one said, Be content, I pray you, and go with your servants. And he answered, I will go.

4 So he went with them. And when they came to Jordan, they cut down wood.

5 But as one was felling a beam, the axe head fell into the water: and he cried, and said, Alas, master! for it was borrowed.

6 And the man of God said, Where fell it? And he shewed him the place. And he cut down a stick, and cast it in thither; and the iron did swim.

7 Therefore said he, Take it up to you. And he put out his hand, and took it.

8Then the king of Syria warred against Israel, and took counsel with his servants, saying, In such and such a place shall be my camp.

9 And the man of God sent unto the king of Israel, saying, Beware that you pass not such a place; for thither the Syrians are come down.

10 And the king of Israel sent to the place which the man of God told him and warned him of, and saved himself there, not once nor twice.

11 Therefore the heart of the king of Syria was sore troubled for this thing; and he called his servants, and said unto them, Will you not shew me which of us is for the king of Israel?

12 And one of his servants said, None, my lord, O king: but Elisha, the prophet that is in Israel, telleth the king of Israel the words that you speakest in your bedchamber.

13And he said, Go and spy where he is, that I may send and fetch him. And it was told him, saying, Behold, he is in Dothan.

14 Therefore sent he thither horses, and chariots, and a great host: and they came by night, and compassed the city about.

15 And when the servant of the man of God was risen early, and gone forth, behold, an host compassed the city both with horses and chariots. And his servant said unto him, Alas, my master! how shall we do?

16 And he answered, Fear not: for they that be with us are more than they that be with them.

17 And Elisha prayed, and said, LORD, I pray you, open his eyes, that he may see. And the LORD opened the eyes of the young man; and he saw: and, behold, the mountain was full of horses and chariots of fire round about Elisha.

18 And when they came down to him, Elisha prayed unto the LORD, and said, Strike this people, I pray you, with blindness. And he struck them with blindness according to the word of Elisha.

19And Elisha said unto them, This is not the way, neither is this the city: follow me, and I will bring you to the man whom you seek. But he led them to Samaria.

20 And it came to pass, when they were come into Samaria, that Elisha said, LORD, open the eyes of these men, that they may see. And the LORD opened their eyes, and they saw; and, behold, they were in the midst of Samaria.

21 And the king of Israel said unto Elisha, when he saw them, My father, shall I strike them? shall I strike them?

22 And he answered, You shalt not strike them: wouldest you strike those whom you have taken captive with your sword and with your bow? set bread and water before them, that they may eat and drink, and go to their master.

23 And he prepared great provision for them: and when they had eaten and drunk, he sent them away, and they went to their master. So the bands of Syria came no more into the land of Israel.

24And it came to pass after this, that Ben-hadad king of Syria gathered all his host, and went up, and besieged Samaria.

25 And there was a great famine in Samaria: and, behold, they besieged it, until an ass's head was sold for fourscore pieces of silver, and the fourth part of a cab of dove's dung for five pieces of silver.

26 And as the king of Israel was passing by upon the wall, there cried a woman unto him, saying, Help, my lord, O king.

27 And he said, If the LORD do not help you, whence shall I help you? out of the barnfloor, or out of the winepress?

28 And the king said unto her, What aileth you? And she answered, This woman said unto me, Give your son, that we may eat him to day, and we will eat my son to morrow.

29 So we boiled my son, and did eat him: and I said unto her on the next day, Give your son, that we may eat him: and she has hid her son.

30And it came to pass, when the king heard the words of the woman, that he rent his clothes; and he passed by upon the wall, and the people looked, and, behold, he had sackcloth within upon his flesh.

31 Then he said, God do so and more also to me, if the head of Elisha the son of Shaphat shall stand on him this day.

32 But Elisha sat in his house, and the elders sat with him; and the king sent a man from before him: but ere the messenger came to him, he said to the elders, See you how this son of a murderer has sent to take away my head? look, when the messenger comes, shut the door, and hold him fast at the door: is not the sound of his master's feet behind him?

33 And while he yet talked with them, behold, the messenger came down unto him: and he said, Behold, this evil is of the LORD; what should I wait for the LORD any longer?

CHAPTER 7

THEN Elisha said, Hear you the word of the LORD; Thus saith the LORD, To morrow about this time shall a measure of fine flour be sold for a shekel, and two measures of barley for a shekel, in the gate of Samaria.

2 Then a lord on whose hand the king leaned answered the man of God, and said, Behold, if the LORD would make windows in heaven, might this thing be? And he said, Behold, you shalt see it with yours eyes, but shalt not eat thereof.

3And there were four leprous men at the entering in of the gate: and they said one to another, Why sit we here until we die?

4 If we say, We will enter into the city, then the famine is in the city, and we shall die there: and if we sit still here, we die also. Now therefore come, and let us fall unto the host of the Syrians: if they save us alive, we shall live; and if they kill us, we shall but die.

5 And they rose up in the twilight, to go unto the camp of the Syrians: and when they were come to the uttermost part of the camp of Syria, behold, there was no man there.

6 For the Lord had made the host of the Syrians to hear a noise of chariots, and a noise of horses, even the noise of a great host: and they said one to another, Lo, the king of Israel has hired against us the kings of the Hittites, and the kings of the Egyptians, to come upon us.

7 Wherefore they arose and fled in the twilight, and left their tents, and their horses, and their asses, even the camp as it was, and fled for their life.

8 And when these lepers came to the uttermost part of the camp, they went into one tent, and did eat and drink, and carried thence silver, and gold, and raiment, and went and hid it; and came again, and entered into another tent, and carried thence also, and went and hid it.

9 Then they said one to another, We do not well: this day is a day of good tidings, and we hold our peace: if we tarry till the morning light, some mischief will come upon us: now therefore come, that we may go and tell the king's household.

10 So they came and called unto the porter of the city: and they told them, saying, We came to the camp of the Syrians, and, behold, there was no man there, neither voice of man, but horses tied, and asses tied, and the tents as they were.

11 And he called the porters; and they told it to the king's house within.

12And the king arose in the night, and said unto his servants, I will now shew you what the Syrians have done to us. They know that we be hungry; therefore are they gone out of the camp to hide themselves in the field, saying, When they come out of the city, we shall catch them alive, and get into the city.

13 And one of his servants answered and said, Let some take, I pray you, five of the horses that remain, which are left in the city, (behold, they are as all the multitude of Israel that are left in it: behold, I say, they are even as all the multitude of the Israelites that are consumed:) and let us send and see.

14 They took therefore two chariot horses; and the king sent after the host of the Syrians, saying, Go and see.

15 And they went after them unto Jordan: and, lo, all the way was full of garments and vessels, which the Syrians had cast away in their haste. And the messengers returned, and told the king.

16 And the people went out, and spoiled the tents of the Syrians. So a measure of fine flour was sold for a shekel, and two measures of barley for a shekel, according to the word of the LORD.

17And the king appointed the lord on whose hand he leaned to have the charge of the gate: and the people trode upon him in the gate, and he died, as the man of God had said, who spake when the king came down to him.

18 And it came to pass as the man of God had spoken to the king, saying, Two measures of barley for a shekel, and a measure of fine flour for a shekel, shall be to morrow about this time in the gate of Samaria:

19 And that lord answered the man of God, and said, Now, behold, if the LORD should make windows in heaven, might such a thing be? And he said, Behold, you shalt see it with yours eyes, but shalt not eat thereof.

20 And so it fell out unto him: for the people trode upon him in the gate, and he died.

CHAPTER 8

THEN spake Elisha unto the woman, whose son he had restored to life, saying, Arise, and go you and yours household, and sojourn wheresoever you can sojourn: for the LORD has called for a famine; and it shall also come upon the land seven years.

2 And the woman arose, and did after the saying of the man of God: and she went with her household, and sojourned in the land of the Philistines seven years.

3 And it came to pass at the seven years' end, that the woman returned out of the land of the Philistines: and she went forth to cry unto the king for her house and for her land.

4 And the king talked with Gehazi the servant of the man of God, saying, Tell me, I pray you, all the great things that Elisha has done.

5 And it came to pass, as he was telling the king how he had restored a dead body to life, that, behold, the woman, whose son he had restored to life, cried to the king for her house and for her land. And Gehazi said, My lord, O king, this is the woman, and this is her son, whom Elisha restored to life.

6 And when the king asked the woman, she told him. So the king appointed unto her a certain officer, saying, Restore all that was hers, and all the fruits of the field since the day that she left the land, even until now.

7And Elisha came to Damascus; and Ben-hadad the king of Syria was sick; and it was told him, saying, The man of God is come hither.

8 And the king said unto Hazael, Take a present in yours hand, and go, meet the man of God, and inquire of the LORD by him, saying, Shall I recover of this disease?

9 So Hazael went to meet him, and took a present with him, even of every good thing of Damascus, forty camels' burden, and came and stood before him, and said, Your son Ben-hadad king of Syria has sent me to you, saying, Shall I recover of this disease?

10 And Elisha said unto him, Go, say unto him, You mayest certainly recover: howbeit the LORD has shewed me that he shall surely die.

11 And he settled his countenance stedfastly, until he was ashamed: and the man of God wept.

12 And Hazael said, Why weepeth my lord? And he answered, Because I know the evil that you will do unto the children of Israel: their strong holds will you set on fire, and their young men will you slay with the sword, and will dash their children, and rip up their women with child.

13 And Hazael said, But what, is your servant a dog, that he should do this great thing? And Elisha answered, The LORD has shewed me that you shalt be king over Syria.

14 So he departed from Elisha, and came to his master; who said to him, What said Elisha to you? And he answered, He told me that you shouldest surely recover.

15 And it came to pass on the morrow, that he took a thick cloth, and dipped it in water, and spread it on his face, so that he died: and Hazael reigned in his stead.

16And in the fifth year of Joram the son of Ahab king of Israel, Jehoshaphat being then king of Judah, Jehoram the son of Jehoshaphat king of Judah began to reign.

17 Thirty and two years old was he when he began to reign; and he reigned eight years in Jerusalem.

18 And he walked in the way of the kings of Israel, as did the house of Ahab: for the daughter of Ahab was his wife: and he did evil in the sight of the LORD.

19 Yet the LORD would not destroy Judah for David his servant's sake, as he promised him to give him alway a light, and to his children.

20In his days Edom revolted from under the hand of Judah, and made a king over themselves.

21 So Joram went over to Zair, and all the chariots with him: and he rose by night, and struck the Edomites which compassed him about, and the captains of the chariots: and the people fled into their tents.

22 Yet Edom revolted from under the hand of Judah unto this day. Then Libnah revolted at the same time.

23 And the rest of the acts of Joram, and all that he did, are they not written in the book of the chronicles of the kings of Judah?

24 And Joram slept with his fathers, and was buried with his fathers in the city of David: and Ahaziah his son reigned in his stead.

25 In the twelfth year of Joram the son of Ahab king of Israel did Ahaziah the son of Jehoram king of Judah begin to reign.

26 Two and twenty years old was Ahaziah when he began to reign; and he reigned one year in Jerusalem. And his mother's name was Athaliah, the daughter of Omri king of Israel.

27 And he walked in the way of the house of Ahab, and did evil in the sight of the LORD, as did the house of Ahab: for he was the son in law of the house of Ahab.

28 And he went with Joram the son of Ahab to the war against Hazael king of Syria in Ramoth-gilead; and the Syrians wounded Joram.

29 And king Joram went back to be healed in Jezreel of the wounds which the Syrians had given him at Ramah, when he fought against Hazael king of Syria. And Ahaziah the son of Jehoram king of Judah went down to see Joram the son of Ahab in Jezreel, because he was sick.

CHAPTER 9

AND Elisha the prophet called one of the children of the prophets, and said unto him, Gird up your loins, and take this box of oil in yours hand, and go to Ramoth-gilead:

2 And when you comest thither, look out there Jehu the son of Jehoshaphat the son of Nimshi, and go in, and make him arise up from among his brethren, and carry him to an inner chamber;

3 Then take the box of oil, and pour it on his head, and say, Thus saith the LORD, I have anointed you king over Israel. Then open the door, and flee, and tarry not.

4 So the young man, even the young man the prophet, went to Ramoth-gilead.

5 And when he came, behold, the captains of the host were sitting; and he said, I have an errand to you, O captain. And Jehu said, Unto which of all us? And he said, To you, O captain.

6 And he arose, and went into the house; and he poured the oil on his head, and said unto him, Thus saith the LORD God of Israel, I have anointed you king over the people of the LORD, even over Israel.

7 And you shalt strike the house of Ahab your master, that I may avenge the blood of my servants the prophets, and the blood of all the servants of the LORD, at the hand of Jezebel.

8 For the whole house of Ahab shall perish: and I will cut off from Ahab him that pisseth against the wall, and him that is shut up and left in Israel:

9 And I will make the house of Ahab like the house of Jeroboam the son of Nebat, and like the house of Baasha the son of Ahijah:

10 And the dogs shall eat Jezebel in the portion of Jezreel, and there shall be none to bury her. And he opened the door, and fled.

11 Then Jehu came forth to the servants of his lord: and one said unto him, Is all well? wherefore came this mad fellow to you? And he said unto them, You know the man, and his communication.

12 And they said, It is false; tell us now. And he said, Thus and thus spake he to me, saying, Thus saith the LORD, I have anointed you king over Israel.

13 Then they hasted, and took every man his garment, and put it under him on the top of the stairs, and blew with trumpets, saying, Jehu is king.

14 So Jehu the son of Jehoshaphat the son of Nimshi conspired against Joram. (Now Joram had kept Ramoth-gilead, he and all Israel, because of Hazael king of Syria.

15 But king Joram was returned to be healed in Jezreel of the wounds which the Syrians had given him, when he fought with Hazael king of Syria.) And Jehu said, If it be your minds, then let none go forth nor escape out of the city to go to tell it in Jezreel.

16 So Jehu rode in a chariot, and went to Jezreel; for Joram lay there. And Ahaziah king of Judah was come down to see Joram.

17 And there stood a watchman on the tower in Jezreel, and he spied the company of Jehu as he came, and said, I see a company. And Joram said, Take an horseman, and send to meet them, and let him say, Is it peace?

18 So there went one on horseback to meet them, and said, Thus saith the king, Is it peace? And Jehu said, What have you to do with peace? turn you behind me. And the watchman told, saying, The messenger came to them, but he comes not again.

19 Then he sent out a second on horseback, which came to them, and said, Thus saith the king, Is it peace? And Jehu answered, What have you to do with peace? turn you behind me.

20 And the watchman told, saying, He came even unto them, and comes not again: and the driving is like the driving of Jehu the son of Nimshi; for he driveth furiously.

21 And Joram said, Make ready. And his chariot was made ready. And Joram king of Israel and Ahaziah king of Judah went out, each in his chariot, and they went out against Jehu, and met him in the portion of Naboth the Jezreelite.

22 And it came to pass, when Joram saw Jehu, that he said, Is it peace, Jehu? And he answered, What peace, so long as the whoredoms of your mother Jezebel and her witchcrafts are so many?

23 And Joram turned his hands, and fled, and said to Ahaziah, There is treachery, O Ahaziah.

24 And Jehu drew a bow with his full strength, and struck Jehoram between his arms, and the arrow went out at his heart, and he sunk down in his chariot.

25 Then said Jehu to Bidkar his captain, Take up, and cast him in the portion of the field of Naboth the Jezreelite: for remember how that, when I and you rode together after Ahab his father, the LORD laid this burden upon him;

26 Surely I have seen yesterday the blood of Naboth, and the blood of his sons, saith the LORD; and I will requite you in this plat, saith the LORD. Now therefore take and cast him into the plat of ground, according to the word of the LORD.

27 But when Ahaziah the king of Judah saw this, he fled by the way of the garden house. And Jehu followed after him, and said, Strike him also in the chariot. And they did so at the going up to Gur, which is by Ibleam. And he fled to Megiddo, and died there.

28 And his servants carried him in a chariot to Jerusalem, and buried him in his sepulchre with his fathers in the city of David.

29 And in the eleventh year of Joram the son of Ahab began Ahaziah to reign over Judah.

30 And when Jehu was come to Jezreel, Jezebel heard of it; and she painted her face, and tired her head, and looked out at a window.

31 And as Jehu entered in at the gate, she said, Had Zimri peace, who slew his master?

32 And he lifted up his face to the window, and said, Who is on my side? who? And there looked out to him two or three eunuchs.

33 And he said, Throw her down. So they threw her down: and some of her blood was sprinkled on the wall, and on the horses: and he trode her under foot.

34 And when he was come in, he did eat and drink, and said, Go, see now this cursed woman, and bury her: for she is a king's daughter.

35 And they went to bury her: but they found no more of her than the skull, and the feet, and the palms of her hands.

36 Wherefore they came again, and told him. And he said, This is the word of the LORD, which he spake by his servant Elijah the Tishbite, saying, In the portion of Jezreel shall dogs eat the flesh of Jezebel:

37 And the carcase of Jezebel shall be as dung upon the face of the field in the portion of Jezreel; so that they shall not say, This is Jezebel.

CHAPTER 10

AND Ahab had seventy sons in Samaria. And Jehu wrote letters, and sent to Samaria, unto the rulers of Jezreel, to the elders, and to them that brought up Ahab's children, saying,

2 Now as soon as this letter comes to you, seeing your master's sons are with you, and there are with you chariots and horses, a fenced city also, and armour;

3 Look even out the best and meetest of your master's sons, and set him on his father's throne, and fight for your master's house.

4 But they were exceedingly afraid, and said, Behold, two kings stood not before him: how then shall we stand?

5 And he that was over the house, and he that was over the city, the elders also, and the bringers up of the children, sent to Jehu, saying, We are your servants, and will do all that you shalt bid us; we will not make any king: do you that which is good in yours eyes.

6 Then he wrote a letter the second time to them, saying, If you be my, and if you will hearken unto my voice, take you the heads of the men your master's sons, and come to me to Jezreel by to morrow this time. Now the king's sons, being seventy persons, were with the great men of the city, which brought them up.

7 And it came to pass, when the letter came to them, that they took the king's sons, and slew seventy persons, and put their heads in baskets, and sent him them to Jezreel.

8 And there came a messenger, and told him, saying, They have brought the heads of the king's sons. And he said, Lay you them in two heaps at the entering in of the gate until the morning.

9 And it came to pass in the morning, that he went out, and stood, and said to all the people, You be righteous: behold, I conspired against my master, and slew him: but who slew all these?

10 Know now that there shall fall unto the earth nothing of the word of the LORD, which the LORD spake concerning the house of Ahab: for the LORD has done that which he spake by his servant Elijah.

11 So Jehu slew all that remained of the house of Ahab in Jezreel, and all his great men, and his kinsfolks, and his priests, until he left him none remaining.

12 And he arose and departed, and came to Samaria. And as he was at the shearing house in the way,

13 Jehu met with the brethren of Ahaziah king of Judah, and said, Who are you ? And they answered, We are the brethren of Ahaziah; and we go down to salute the children of the king and the children of the queen.

14 And he said, Take them alive. And they took them alive, and slew them at the pit of the shearing house, even two and forty men; neither left he any of them.

15 And when he was departed thence, he lighted on Jehonadab the son of Rechab coming to meet him: and he saluted him, and said to him, Is yours heart right, as my heart is with your heart? And Jehonadab answered, It is. If it be, give me yours hand. And he gave him his hand; and he took him up to him into the chariot.

16 And he said, Come with me, and see my zeal for the LORD. So they made him ride in his chariot.

17 And when he came to Samaria, he slew all that remained unto Ahab in Samaria, till he had destroyed him, according to the saying of the LORD, which he spake to Elijah.

18 And Jehu gathered all the people together, and said unto them, Ahab served Baal a little; but Jehu shall serve him much.

19 Now therefore call unto me all the prophets of Baal, all his servants, and all his priests; let none be wanting: for I have a great sacrifice to do to Baal; whosoever shall be wanting, he shall not live. But Jehu did it in subtilty, to the intent that he might destroy the worshippers of Baal.

20 And Jehu said, Proclaim a solemn assembly for Baal. And they proclaimed it.

21 And Jehu sent through all Israel: and all the worshippers of Baal came, so that there was not a man left that came not. And they came into the house of Baal; and the house of Baal was full from one end to another.

22 And he said unto him that was over the vestry, Bring forth vestments for all the worshippers of Baal. And he brought them forth vestments.

23 And Jehu went, and Jehonadab the son of Rechab, into the house of Baal, and said unto the worshippers of Baal, Search, and look that there be here with you none of the servants of the LORD, but the worshippers of Baal only.

24 And when they went in to offer sacrifices and burnt offerings, Jehu appointed fourscore men without, and said, If any of the men whom I have brought into your hands escape, he that letteth him go, his life shall be for the life of him.

25 And it came to pass, as soon as he had made an end of offering the burnt offering, that Jehu said to the guard and to the captains, Go in, and slay them; let none come forth. And they struck them with the edge of the sword; and the guard and the captains cast them out, and went to the city of the house of Baal.

26 And they brought forth the images out of the house of Baal, and burned them.

27 And they brake down the image of Baal, and brake down the house of Baal, and made it a draught house unto this day.

28 Thus Jehu destroyed Baal out of Israel.

29 Howbeit from the sins of Jeroboam the son of Nebat, who made Israel to sin, Jehu departed not from after them, to wit, the golden calves that were in Beth-el, and that were in Dan.

30 And the LORD said unto Jehu, Because you have done well in executing that which is right in my eyes, and have done unto the house of Ahab according to all that was in my heart, your children of the fourth generation shall sit on the throne of Israel.

31 But Jehu took no heed to walk in the law of the LORD God of Israel with all his heart: for he departed not from the sins of Jeroboam, which made Israel to sin.

32 In those days the LORD began to cut Israel short: and Hazael struck them in all the coasts of Israel;

33 From Jordan eastward, all the land of Gilead, the Gadites, and the Reubenites, and the Manassites, from Aroer, which is by the river Arnon, even Gilead and Bashan.

34 Now the rest of the acts of Jehu, and all that he did, and all his might, are they not written in the book of the chronicles of the kings of Israel?

35 And Jehu slept with his fathers: and they buried him in Samaria. And Jehoahaz his son reigned in his stead.

36 And the time that Jehu reigned over Israel in Samaria was twenty and eight years.

CHAPTER 11

AND when Athaliah the mother of Ahaziah saw that her son was dead, she arose and destroyed all the seed royal.

2 But Jehosheba, the daughter of king Joram, sister of Ahaziah, took Joash the son of Ahaziah, and stole him from among the king's sons which were slain; and they hid him, even him and his nurse, in the bedchamber from Athaliah, so that he was not slain.

3 And he was with her hid in the house of the LORD six years. And Athaliah did reign over the land.

4 And the seventh year Jehoiada sent and fetched the rulers over hundreds, with the captains and the guard, and brought them to him into the house of the LORD, and made a covenant with them, and took an oath of them in the house of the LORD, and shewed them the king's son.

5 And he commanded them, saying, This is the thing that you shall do; A third part of you that enter in on the sabbath shall even be keepers of the watch of the king's house;

6 And a third part shall be at the gate of Sur; and a third part at the gate behind the guard: so shall you keep the watch of the house, that it be not broken down.

7 And two parts of all you that go forth on the sabbath, even they shall keep the watch of the house of the LORD about the king.

8 And you shall compass the king round about, every man with his weapons in his hand: and he that comes within the ranges, let him be slain: and be you with the king as he goeth out and as he comes in.

9 And the captains over the hundreds did according to all things that Jehoiada the priest commanded: and they took every man his men that were to come in on the sabbath, with them that should go out on the sabbath, and came to Jehoiada the priest.

10 And to the captains over hundreds did the priest give king David's spears and shields, that were in the temple of the LORD.

11 And the guard stood, every man with his weapons in his hand, round about the king, from the right corner of the temple to the left corner of the temple, along by the altar and the temple.

12 And he brought forth the king's son, and put the crown upon him, and gave him the testimony; and they made him king, and anointed him; and they clapped their hands, and said, God save the king.

13 And when Athaliah heard the noise of the guard and of the people, she came to the people into the temple of the LORD.

14 And when she looked, behold, the king stood by a pillar, as the manner was, and the princes and the trumpeters by the king, and all the people of the land rejoiced, and blew with trumpets: and Athaliah rent her clothes, and cried, Treason, Treason.

15 But Jehoiada the priest commanded the captains of the hundreds, the officers of the host, and said unto them, Have her forth without the ranges: and him that followeth her kill with the sword. For the priest had said, Let her not be slain in the house of the LORD.

16 And they laid hands on her; and she went by the way by the which the horses came into the king's house: and there was she slain.

17 And Jehoiada made a covenant between the LORD and the king and the people, that they should be the LORD's people; between the king also and the people.

18 And all the people of the land went into the house of Baal, and brake it down; his altars and his images brake they in pieces thoroughly, and slew Mattan the priest of Baal before the altars. And the priest appointed officers over the house of the LORD.

19 And he took the rulers over hundreds, and the captains, and the guard, and all the people of the land; and they brought down the king from the house of the LORD, and came by the way of the gate of the guard to the king's house. And he sat on the throne of the kings.

20 And all the people of the land rejoiced, and the city was in quiet: and they slew Athaliah with the sword beside the king's house.

21 Seven years old was Jehoash when he began to reign.

CHAPTER 12

IN the seventh year of Jehu Jehoash began to reign; and forty years reigned he in Jerusalem. And his mother's name was Zibiah of Beer-sheba.

2 And Jehoash did that which was right in the sight of the LORD all his days wherein Jehoiada the priest instructed him.

3 But the high places were not taken away: the people still sacrificed and burnt incense in the high places.

4 And Jehoash said to the priests, All the money of the dedicated things that is brought into the house of the LORD, even the money of every one that passes the account, the money that every man is set at, and all the money that comes into any man's heart to bring into the house of the LORD,

5 Let the priests take it to them, every man of his acquaintance: and let them repair the breaches of the house, wheresoever any breach shall be found.

6 But it was so, that in the three and twentieth year of king Jehoash the priests had not repaired the breaches of the house.

7 Then king Jehoash called for Jehoiada the priest, and the other priests, and said unto them, Why repair you not the breaches of the house? now therefore receive no more money of your acquaintance, but deliver it for the breaches of the house.

8 And the priests consented to receive no more money of the people, neither to repair the breaches of the house.

9 But Jehoiada the priest took a chest, and bored a hole in the lid of it, and set it beside the altar, on the right side as one comes into the house of the LORD: and the priests that kept the door put therein all the money that was brought into the house of the LORD.

10 And it was so, when they saw that there was much money in the chest, that the king's scribe and the high priest came up, and they put up in bags, and told the money that was found in the house of the LORD.

11 And they gave the money, being told, into the hands of them that did the work, that had the oversight of the house of the LORD: and they laid it out to the carpenters and builders, that created upon the house of the LORD,

12 And to masons, and hewers of stone, and to buy timber and hewed stone to repair the breaches of the house of the LORD, and for all that was laid out for the house to repair it.

13 Howbeit there were not made for the house of the LORD bowls of silver, snuffers, basons, trumpets, any vessels of gold, or vessels of silver, of the money that was brought into the house of the LORD:

14 But they gave that to the workmen, and repaired therewith the house of the LORD.

15 Moreover they reckoned not with the men, into whose hand they delivered the money to be bestowed on workmen: for they dealt faithfully.

16 The trespass money and sin money was not brought into the house of the LORD: it was the priests'.

17 Then Hazael king of Syria went up, and fought against Gath, and took it: and Hazael set his face to go up to Jerusalem.

18 And Jehoash king of Judah took all the hallowed things that Jehoshaphat, and Jehoram, and Ahaziah, his fathers, kings of Judah, had dedicated, and his own hallowed things, and all the gold that was found in the treasures of the house of the LORD, and in the king's house, and sent it to Hazael king of Syria: and he went away from Jerusalem.

19 And the rest of the acts of Joash, and all that he did, are they not written in the book of the chronicles of the kings of Judah?

20 And his servants arose, and made a conspiracy, and slew Joash in the house of Millo, which goeth down to Silla.

21 For Jozachar the son of Shimeath, and Jehozabad the son of Shomer, his servants, struck him, and he died; and they buried him with his fathers in the city of David: and Amaziah his son reigned in his stead.

CHAPTER 13

IN the three and twentieth year of Joash the son of Ahaziah king of Judah Jehoahaz the son of Jehu began to reign over Israel in Samaria, and reigned seventeen years.

2 And he did that which was evil in the sight of the LORD, and followed the sins of Jeroboam the son of Nebat, which made Israel to sin; he departed not therefrom.

3 And the anger of the LORD was kindled against Israel, and he delivered them into the hand of Hazael king of Syria, and into the hand of Ben-hadad the son of Hazael, all their days.

4 And Jehoahaz besought the LORD, and the LORD hearkened unto him: for he saw the oppression of Israel, because the king of Syria oppressed them.

5 (And the LORD gave Israel a saviour, so that they went out from under the hand of the Syrians: and the children of Israel dwelt in their tents, as beforetime.

6 Nevertheless they departed not from the sins of the house of Jeroboam, who made Israel sin, but walked therein: and there remained the grove also in Samaria.)

7 Neither did he leave of the people to Jehoahaz but fifty horsemen, and ten chariots, and ten thousand footmen; for the king of Syria had destroyed them, and had made them like the dust by threshing.

8 Now the rest of the acts of Jehoahaz, and all that he did, and his might, are they not written in the book of the chronicles of the kings of Israel?

9 And Jehoahaz slept with his fathers; and they buried him in Samaria: and Joash his son reigned in his stead.

10 In the thirty and seventh year of Joash king of Judah began Jehoash the son of Jehoahaz to reign over Israel in Samaria, and reigned sixteen years.

11 And he did that which was evil in the sight of the LORD; he departed not from all the sins of Jeroboam the son of Nebat, who made Israel sin: but he walked therein.

12 And the rest of the acts of Joash, and all that he did, and his might wherewith he fought against Amaziah king of Judah, are they not written in the book of the chronicles of the kings of Israel?

13 And Joash slept with his fathers; and Jeroboam sat upon his throne: and Joash was buried in Samaria with the kings of Israel.

14 Now Elisha was fallen sick of his sickness whereof he died. And Joash the king of Israel came down unto him, and wept over his face, and said, O my father, my father, the chariot of Israel, and the horsemen thereof.

15 And Elisha said unto him, Take bow and arrows. And he took unto him bow and arrows.

16 And he said to the king of Israel, Put yours hand upon the bow. And he put his hand upon it: and Elisha put his hands upon the king's hands.

17 And he said, Open the window eastward. And he opened it. Then Elisha said, Shoot. And he shot. And he said, The arrow of the LORD's deliverance, and the arrow of deliverance from Syria: for you shalt strike the Syrians in Aphek, till you have consumed them.

18 And he said, Take the arrows. And he took them. And he said unto the king of Israel, Strike upon the ground. And he struck thrice, and stayed.

19 And the man of God was wroth with him, and said, You shouldest have smitten five or six times; then hadst you smitten Syria till you hadst consumed it: whereas now you shalt strike Syria but thrice.

20 And Elisha died, and they buried him. And the bands of the Moabites invaded the land at the coming in of the year.

21 And it came to pass, as they were burying a man, that, behold, they spied a band of men; and they cast the man into the sepulchre of Elisha: and when the man was let down, and touched the bones of Elisha, he revived, and stood up on his feet.

22 But Hazael king of Syria oppressed Israel all the days of Jehoahaz.

23 And the LORD was gracious unto them, and had compassion on them, and had respect unto them, because of his covenant with Abraham, Isaac, and Jacob, and would not destroy them, neither cast he them from his presence as yet.

24 So Hazael king of Syria died; and Ben-hadad his son reigned in his stead.

25 And Jehoash the son of Jehoahaz took again out of the hand of Ben-hadad the son of Hazael the cities, which he had taken out of the hand of Jehoahaz his father by war. Three times did Joash beat him, and recovered the cities of Israel.

CHAPTER 14

IN the second year of Joash son of Jehoahaz king of Israel reigned Amaziah the son of Joash king of Judah.

2 He was twenty and five years old when he began to reign, and reigned twenty and nine years in Jerusalem. And his mother's name was Jehoaddan of Jerusalem.

3 And he did that which was right in the sight of the LORD, yet not like David his father: he did according to all things as Joash his father did.

4 Howbeit the high places were not taken away: as yet the people did sacrifice and burnt incense on the high places.

5 And it came to pass, as soon as the kingdom was confirmed in his hand, that he slew his servants which had slain the king his father.

6 But the children of the murderers he slew not: according unto that which is written in the book of the law of Moses, wherein the LORD commanded, saying, The fathers shall not be put to death for the children, nor the children be put to death for the fathers; but every man shall be put to death for his own sin.

7 He slew of Edom in the valley of salt ten thousand, and took Selah by war, and called the name of it Joktheel unto this day.

8 Then Amaziah sent messengers to Jehoash, the son of Jehoahaz son of Jehu, king of Israel, saying, Come, let us look one another in the face.

9 And Jehoash the king of Israel sent to Amaziah king of Judah, saying, The thistle that was in Lebanon sent to the cedar that was in Lebanon, saying, Give your daughter to my son to wife: and there passed by a wild beast that was in Lebanon, and trode down the thistle.

10 You have indeed smitten Edom, and yours heart has lifted you up: glory of this, and tarry at home: for why shouldest you meddle to your hurt, that you shouldest fall, even you , and Judah with you?

11 But Amaziah would not hear. Therefore Jehoash king of Israel went up; and he and Amaziah king of Judah looked one another in the face at Beth-shemesh, which belongeth to Judah.

12 And Judah was put to the worse before Israel; and they fled every man to their tents.

13 And Jehoash king of Israel took Amaziah king of Judah, the son of Jehoash the son of Ahaziah, at Beth-shemesh, and came to Jerusalem, and brake down the wall of Jerusalem from the gate of Ephraim unto the corner gate, four hundred cubits.

14 And he took all the gold and silver, and all the vessels that were found in the house of the LORD, and in the treasures of the king's house, and hostages, and returned to Samaria.

15 Now the rest of the acts of Jehoash which he did, and his might, and how he fought with Amaziah king of Judah, are they not written in the book of the chronicles of the kings of Israel?

16 And Jehoash slept with his fathers, and was buried in Samaria with the kings of Israel; and Jeroboam his son reigned in his stead.

17 And Amaziah the son of Joash king of Judah lived after the death of Jehoash son of Jehoahaz king of Israel fifteen years.

18 And the rest of the acts of Amaziah, are they not written in the book of the chronicles of the kings of Judah?

19 Now they made a conspiracy against him in Jerusalem: and he fled to Lachish; but they sent after him to Lachish, and slew him there.

20 And they brought him on horses: and he was buried at Jerusalem with his fathers in the city of David.

21 And all the people of Judah took Azariah, which was sixteen years old, and made him king instead of his father Amaziah.

22 He built Elath, and restored it to Judah, after that the king slept with his fathers.

23 In the fifteenth year of Amaziah the son of Joash king of Judah Jeroboam the son of Joash king of Israel began to reign in Samaria, and reigned forty and one years.

24 And he did that which was evil in the sight of the LORD: he departed not from all the sins of Jeroboam the son of Nebat, who made Israel to sin.

25 He restored the coast of Israel from the entering of Hamath unto the sea of the plain, according to the word of the LORD God of Israel, which he spake by the hand of his servant Jonah, the son of Amittai, the prophet, which was of Gath-hepher.

26 For the LORD saw the affliction of Israel, that it was very bitter: for there was not any shut up, nor any left, nor any helper for Israel.

27 And the LORD said not that he would blot out the name of Israel from under heaven: but he saved them by the hand of Jeroboam the son of Joash.

28 Now the rest of the acts of Jeroboam, and all that he did, and his might, how he warred, and how he recovered Damascus, and Hamath, which belonged to Judah, for Israel, are they not written in the book of the chronicles of the kings of Israel?

29 And Jeroboam slept with his fathers, even with the kings of Israel; and Zachariah his son reigned in his stead.

CHAPTER 15

IN the twenty and seventh year of Jeroboam king of Israel began Azariah son of Amaziah king of Judah to reign.

2 Sixteen years old was he when he began to reign, and he reigned two and fifty years in Jerusalem. And his mother's name was Jecholiah of Jerusalem.

3 And he did that which was right in the sight of the LORD, according to all that his father Amaziah had done;

4 Save that the high places were not removed: the people sacrificed and burnt incense still on the high places.

5 And the LORD struck the king, so that he was a leper unto the day of his death, and dwelt in a several house. And Jotham the king's son was over the house, judging the people of the land.

6 And the rest of the acts of Azariah, and all that he did, are they not written in the book of the chronicles of the kings of Judah?

7 So Azariah slept with his fathers; and they buried him with his fathers in the city of David: and Jotham his son reigned in his stead.

8 In the thirty and eighth year of Azariah king of Judah did Zachariah the son of Jeroboam reign over Israel in Samaria six months.

9 And he did that which was evil in the sight of the LORD, as his fathers had done: he departed not from the sins of Jeroboam the son of Nebat, who made Israel to sin.

10 And Shallum the son of Jabesh conspired against him, and struck him before the people, and slew him, and reigned in his stead.

11 And the rest of the acts of Zachariah, behold, they are written in the book of the chronicles of the kings of Israel.

12 This was the word of the LORD which he spake unto Jehu, saying, Your sons shall sit on the throne of Israel unto the fourth generation. And so it came to pass.

13 Shallum the son of Jabesh began to reign in the nine and thirtieth year of Uzziah king of Judah; and he reigned a full month in Samaria.

14 For Menahem the son of Gadi went up from Tirzah, and came to Samaria, and struck Shallum the son of Jabesh in Samaria, and slew him, and reigned in his stead.

15 And the rest of the acts of Shallum, and his conspiracy which he made, behold, they are written in the book of the chronicles of the kings of Israel.

16 Then Menahem struck Tiphsah, and all that were therein, and the coasts thereof from Tirzah: because they opened not to him, therefore he struck it; and all the women therein that were with child he ripped up.

17 In the nine and thirtieth year of Azariah king of Judah began Menahem the son of Gadi to reign over Israel, and reigned ten years in Samaria.

18 And he did that which was evil in the sight of the LORD: he departed not all his days from the sins of Jeroboam the son of Nebat, who made Israel to sin.

19 And Pul the king of Assyria came against the land: and Menahem gave Pul a thousand talents of silver, that his hand might be with him to confirm the kingdom in his hand.

20 And Menahem exacted the money of Israel, even of all the mighty men of wealth, of each man fifty shekels of silver, to give to the king of Assyria. So the king of Assyria turned back, and stayed not there in the land.

21 And the rest of the acts of Menahem, and all that he did, are they not written in the book of the chronicles of the kings of Israel?

22 And Menahem slept with his fathers; and Pekahiah his son reigned in his stead.

23 In the fiftieth year of Azariah king of Judah Pekahiah the son of Menahem began to reign over Israel in Samaria, and reigned two years.

24 And he did that which was evil in the sight of the LORD: he departed not from the sins of Jeroboam the son of Nebat, who made Israel to sin.

25 But Pekah the son of Remaliah, a captain of his, conspired against him, and struck him in Samaria, in the palace of the king's house, with Argob and Arieh, and with him fifty men of the Gileadites: and he killed him, and reigned in his room.

26 And the rest of the acts of Pekahiah, and all that he did, behold, they are written in the book of the chronicles of the kings of Israel.

27 In the two and fiftieth year of Azariah king of Judah Pekah the son of Remaliah began to reign over Israel in Samaria, and reigned twenty years.

28 And he did that which was evil in the sight of the LORD: he departed not from the sins of Jeroboam the son of Nebat, who made Israel to sin.

29 In the days of Pekah king of Israel came Tiglath-pileser king of Assyria, and took Ijon, and Abel-beth-maachah, and Janoah, and Kedesh, and Hazor, and Gilead, and Galilee, all the land of Naphtali, and carried them captive to Assyria.

30 And Hoshea the son of Elah made a conspiracy against Pekah the son of Remaliah, and struck him, and slew him, and reigned in his stead, in the twentieth year of Jotham the son of Uzziah.

31 And the rest of the acts of Pekah, and all that he did, behold, they are written in the book of the chronicles of the kings of Israel.

32 In the second year of Pekah the son of Remaliah king of Israel began Jotham the son of Uzziah king of Judah to reign.

33 Five and twenty years old was he when he began to reign, and he reigned sixteen years in Jerusalem. And his mother's name was Jerusha, the daughter of Zadok.

34 And he did that which was right in the sight of the LORD: he did according to all that his father Uzziah had done.

35 Howbeit the high places were not removed: the people sacrificed and burned incense still in the high places. He built the higher gate of the house of the LORD.

36 Now the rest of the acts of Jotham, and all that he did, are they not written in the book of the chronicles of the kings of Judah?

37 In those days the LORD began to send against Judah Rezin the king of Syria, and Pekah the son of Remaliah.

38 And Jotham slept with his fathers, and was buried with his fathers in the city of David his father: and Ahaz his son reigned in his stead.

CHAPTER 16

IN the seventeenth year of Pekah the son of Remaliah Ahaz the son of Jotham king of Judah began to reign.

2 Twenty years old was Ahaz when he began to reign, and reigned sixteen years in Jerusalem, and did not that which was right in the sight of the LORD his God, like David his father.

3 But he walked in the way of the kings of Israel, yea, and made his son to pass through the fire, according to the abominations of the heathen, whom the LORD cast out from before the children of Israel.

4 And he sacrificed and burnt incense in the high places, and on the hills, and under every green tree.

5 Then Rezin king of Syria and Pekah son of Remaliah king of Israel came up to Jerusalem to war: and they besieged Ahaz, but could not overcome him.

6 At that time Rezin king of Syria recovered Elath to Syria, and drave the Jews from Elath: and the Syrians came to Elath, and dwelt there unto this day.

7 So Ahaz sent messengers to Tiglath-pileser king of Assyria, saying, I am your servant and your son: come up, and save me out of the hand of the king of Syria, and out of the hand of the king of Israel, which rise up against me.

8 And Ahaz took the silver and gold that was found in the house of the LORD, and in the treasures of the king's house, and sent it for a present to the king of Assyria.

9 And the king of Assyria hearkened unto him: for the king of Assyria went up against Damascus, and took it, and carried the people of it captive to Kir, and slew Rezin.

10 And king Ahaz went to Damascus to meet Tiglath-pileser king of Assyria, and saw an altar that was at Damascus: and king Ahaz sent to Urijah the priest the fashion of the altar, and the pattern of it, according to all the workmanship thereof.

11 And Urijah the priest built an altar according to all that king Ahaz had sent from Damascus: so Urijah the priest made it against king Ahaz came from Damascus.

12 And when the king was come from Damascus, the king saw the altar: and the king approached to the altar, and offered thereon.

13 And he burnt his burnt offering and his meat offering, and poured his drink offering, and sprinkled the blood of his peace offerings, upon the altar.

14 And he brought also the brasen altar, which was before the LORD, from the forefront of the house, from between the altar and the house of the LORD, and put it on the north side of the altar.

15 And king Ahaz commanded Urijah the priest, saying, Upon the great altar burn the morning burnt offering, and the evening meat offering, and the king's burnt sacrifice, and his meat offering, with the burnt offering of all the people of the land, and their meat offering, and their drink offerings; and sprinkle upon it all the blood of the burnt offering, and all the blood of the sacrifice: and the brasen altar shall be for me to inquire by.

16 Thus did Urijah the priest, according to all that king Ahaz commanded.

17 And king Ahaz cut off the borders of the bases, and removed the laver from off them; and took down the sea from off the brasen oxen that were under it, and put it upon a pavement of stones.

18 And the covert for the sabbath that they had built in the house, and the king's entry without, turned he from the house of the LORD for the king of Assyria.

19 Now the rest of the acts of Ahaz which he did, are they not written in the book of the chronicles of the kings of Judah?

20 And Ahaz slept with his fathers, and was buried with his fathers in the city of David: and Hezekiah his son reigned in his stead.

CHAPTER 17

IN the twelfth year of Ahaz king of Judah began Hoshea the son of Elah to reign in Samaria over Israel nine years.

2 And he did that which was evil in the sight of the LORD, but not as the kings of Israel that were before him.

3 Against him came up Shalmaneser king of Assyria; and Hoshea became his servant, and gave him presents.

4 And the king of Assyria found conspiracy in Hoshea: for he had sent messengers to So king of Egypt, and brought no present to the king of Assyria, as he had done year by year: therefore the king of Assyria shut him up, and bound him in prison.

5 Then the king of Assyria came up throughout all the land, and went up to Samaria, and besieged it three years.

6 In the ninth year of Hoshea the king of Assyria took Samaria, and carried Israel away into Assyria, and placed them in Halah and in Habor by the river of Gozan, and in the cities of the Medes.

7 For so it was, that the children of Israel had sinned against the LORD their God, which had brought them up out of the land of Egypt, from under the hand of Pharaoh king of Egypt, and had feared other gods,

8 And walked in the statutes of the heathen, whom the LORD cast out from before the children of Israel, and of the kings of Israel, which they had made.

9 And the children of Israel did secretly those things that were not right against the LORD their God, and they built them high places in all their cities, from the tower of the watchmen to the fenced city.

10 And they set them up images and groves in every high hill, and under every green tree:

11 And there they burnt incense in all the high places, as did the heathen whom the LORD carried away before them; and created wicked things to provoke the LORD to anger:

12 For they served idols, whereof the LORD had said unto them, You shall not do this thing.

13 Yet the LORD testified against Israel, and against Judah, by all the prophets, and by all the seers, saying, Turn you from your evil ways, and keep my commandments and my statutes, according to all the law which I commanded your fathers, and which I sent to you by my servants the prophets.

14 Notwithstanding they would not hear, but hardened their necks, like to the neck of their fathers, that did not believe in the LORD their God.

15 And they rejected his statutes, and his covenant that he made with their fathers, and his testimonies which he testified against them; and they followed vanity, and became vain, and went after the heathen that were round about them, concerning whom the LORD had charged them, that they should not do like them.

16 And they left all the commandments of the LORD their God, and made them molten images, even two calves, and made a grove, and worshipped all the host of heaven, and served Baal.

17 And they caused their sons and their daughters to pass through the fire, and used divination and enchantments, and sold themselves to do evil in the sight of the LORD, to provoke him to anger.

18 Therefore the LORD was very angry with Israel, and removed them out of his sight: there was none left but the tribe of Judah only.

19 Also Judah kept not the commandments of the LORD their God, but walked in the statutes of Israel which they made.

20 And the LORD rejected all the seed of Israel, and afflicted them, and delivered them into the hand of spoilers, until he had cast them out of his sight.

21 For he rent Israel from the house of David; and they made Jeroboam the son of Nebat king: and Jeroboam drave Israel from following the LORD, and made them sin a great sin.

22 For the children of Israel walked in all the sins of Jeroboam which he did; they departed not from them;

23 Until the LORD removed Israel out of his sight, as he had said by all his servants the prophets. So was Israel carried away out of their own land to Assyria unto this day.

24 And the king of Assyria brought men from Babylon, and from Cuthah, and from Ava, and from Hamath, and from Sepharvaim, and placed them in the cities of Samaria instead of the children of Israel: and they possessed Samaria, and dwelt in the cities thereof.

25 And so it was at the beginning of their dwelling there, that they feared not the LORD: therefore the LORD sent lions among them, which slew some of them.

26 Wherefore they spake to the king of Assyria, saying, The nations which you have removed, and placed in the cities of Samaria, know not the manner of the God of the land: therefore he has sent lions among them, and, behold, they slay them, because they know not the manner of the God of the land.

27 Then the king of Assyria commanded, saying, Carry thither one of the priests whom you brought from thence; and let them go and dwell there, and let him teach them the manner of the God of the land.

28 Then one of the priests whom they had carried away from Samaria came and dwelt in Beth-el, and taught them how they should fear the LORD.

29 Howbeit every nation made gods of their own, and put them in the houses of the high places which the Samaritans had made, every nation in their cities wherein they dwelt.

30 And the men of Babylon made Succoth-benoth, and the men of Cuth made Nergal, and the men of Hamath made Ashima,

31 And the Avites made Nibhaz and Tartak, and the Sepharvites burnt their children in fire to Adrammelech and Anammelech, the gods of Sepharvaim.

32 So they feared the LORD, and made unto themselves of the lowest of them priests of the high places, which sacrificed for them in the houses of the high places.

33 They feared the LORD, and served their own gods, after the manner of the nations whom they carried away from thence.

34 Unto this day they do after the former manners: they fear not the LORD, neither do they after their statutes, or after their ordinances, or after the law and commandment which the LORD commanded the children of Jacob, whom he named Israel;

35 With whom the LORD had made a covenant, and charged them, saying, You shall not fear other gods, nor bow yourselves to them, nor serve them, nor sacrifice to them:

36 But the LORD, who brought you up out of the land of Egypt with great power and a stretched out arm, him shall you fear, and him shall you worship, and to him shall you do sacrifice.

37 And the statutes, and the ordinances, and the law, and the commandment, which he wrote for you, you shall observe to do for evermore; and you shall not fear other gods.

38 And the covenant that I have made with you you shall not forget; neither shall you fear other gods.

39 But the LORD your God you shall fear; and he shall deliver you out of the hand of all your enemies.

40 Howbeit they did not hearken, but they did after their former manner.

41 So these nations feared the LORD, and served their graven images, both their children, and their children's children: as did their fathers, so do they unto this day.

CHAPTER 18

NOW it came to pass in the third year of Hoshea son of Elah king of Israel, that Hezekiah the son of Ahaz king of Judah began to reign.

2 Twenty and five years old was he when he began to reign; and he reigned twenty and nine years in Jerusalem. His mother's name also was Abi, the daughter of Zachariah.

3 And he did that which was right in the sight of the LORD, according to all that David his father did.

4He removed the high places, and brake the images, and cut down the groves, and brake in pieces the brasen serpent that Moses had made: for unto those days the children of Israel did burn incense to it: and he called it Nehushtan.

5 He trusted in the LORD God of Israel; so that after him was none like him among all the kings of Judah, nor any that were before him.

6 For he clave to the LORD, and departed not from following him, but kept his commandments, which the LORD commanded Moses.

7 And the LORD was with him; and he prospered whithersoever he went forth: and he rebelled against the king of Assyria, and served him not.

8 He struck the Philistines, even unto Gaza, and the borders thereof, from the tower of the watchmen to the fenced city.

9And it came to pass in the fourth year of king Hezekiah, which was the seventh year of Hoshea son of Elah king of Israel, that Shalmaneser king of Assyria came up against Samaria, and besieged it.

10 And at the end of three years they took it: even in the sixth year of Hezekiah, that is the ninth year of Hoshea king of Israel, Samaria was taken.

11 And the king of Assyria did carry away Israel unto Assyria, and put them in Halah and in Habor by the river of Gozan, and in the cities of the Medes:

12 Because they obeyed not the voice of the LORD their God, but transgressed his covenant, and all that Moses the servant of the LORD commanded, and would not hear them, nor do them.

13Now in the fourteenth year of king Hezekiah did Sennacherib king of Assyria come up against all the fenced cities of Judah, and took them.

14 And Hezekiah king of Judah sent to the king of Assyria to Lachish, saying, I have offended; return from me: that which you puttest on me will I bear. And the king of Assyria appointed unto Hezekiah king of Judah three hundred talents of silver and thirty talents of gold.

15 And Hezekiah gave him all the silver that was found in the house of the LORD, and in the treasures of the king's house.

16 At that time did Hezekiah cut off the gold from the doors of the temple of the LORD, and from the pillars which Hezekiah king of Judah had overlaid, and gave it to the king of Assyria.

17And the king of Assyria sent Tartan and Rabsaris and Rab-shakeh from Lachish to king Hezekiah with a great host against Jerusalem. And they went up and came to Jerusalem. And when they were come up, they came and stood by the conduit of the upper pool, which is in the highway of the fuller's field.

18 And when they had called to the king, there came out to them Eliakim the son of Hilkiah, which was over the household, and Shebna the scribe, and Joah the son of Asaph the recorder.

19 And Rab-shakeh said unto them, Speak you now to Hezekiah, Thus saith the great king, the king of Assyria, What confidence is this wherein you trustest?

20 You say, (but they are but vain words,) I have counsel and strength for the war. Now on whom dost you trust, that you rebellest against me?

21 Now, behold, you trustest upon the staff of this bruised reed, even upon Egypt, on which if a man lean, it will go into his hand, and pierce it: so is Pharaoh king of Egypt unto all that trust on him.

22 But if you say unto me, We trust in the LORD our God: is not that he, whose high places and whose altars Hezekiah has taken away, and has said to Judah and Jerusalem, You shall worship before this altar in Jerusalem?

23 Now therefore, I pray you, give pledges to my lord the king of Assyria, and I will deliver you two thousand horses, if you be able on your part to set riders upon them.

24 How then will you turn away the face of one captain of the least of my master's servants, and put your trust on Egypt for chariots and for horsemen?

25 Am I now come up without the LORD against this place to destroy it? The LORD said to me, Go up against this land, and destroy it.

26 Then said Eliakim the son of Hilkiah, and Shebna, and Joah, unto Rab-shakeh, Speak, I pray you, to your servants in the Syrian language; for we understand it: and talk not with us in the Jews' language in the ears of the people that are on the wall.

27 But Rab-shakeh said unto them, Has my master sent me to your master, and to you, to speak these words? has he not sent me to the men which sit on the wall, that they may eat their own dung, and drink their own piss with you?

28 Then Rab-shakeh stood and cried with a loud voice in the Jews' language, and spake, saying, Hear the word of the great king, the king of Assyria:

29 Thus saith the king, Let not Hezekiah deceive you: for he shall not be able to deliver you out of his hand:

30 Neither let Hezekiah make you trust in the LORD, saying, The LORD will surely deliver us, and this city shall not be delivered into the hand of the king of Assyria.

31 Hearken not to Hezekiah: for thus saith the king of Assyria, Make an agreement with me by a present, and come out to me, and then eat you every man of his own vine, and every one of his fig tree, and drink you every one the waters of his cistern:

32 Until I come and take you away to a land like your own land, a land of corn and wine, a land of bread and vineyards, a land of oil olive and of honey, that you may live, and not die: and hearken not unto Hezekiah, when he persuadeth you, saying, The LORD will deliver us.

33 Has any of the gods of the nations delivered at all his land out of the hand of the king of Assyria?

34 Where are the gods of Hamath, and of Arpad? where are the gods of Sepharvaim, Hena, and Ivah? have they delivered Samaria out of my hand?

35 Who are they among all the gods of the countries, that have delivered their country out of my hand, that the LORD should deliver Jerusalem out of my hand?

36 But the people held their peace, and answered him not a word: for the king's commandment was, saying, Answer him not.

37 Then came Eliakim the son of Hilkiah, which was over the household, and Shebna the scribe, and Joah the son of Asaph the recorder, to Hezekiah with their clothes rent, and told him the words of Rab-shakeh.

CHAPTER 19

AND it came to pass, when king Hezekiah heard it, that he rent his clothes, and covered himself with sackcloth, and went into the house of the LORD.

2 And he sent Eliakim, which was over the household, and Shebna the scribe, and the elders of the priests, covered with sackcloth, to Isaiah the prophet the son of Amoz.

3 And they said unto him, Thus saith Hezekiah, This day is a day of trouble, and of rebuke, and blasphemy: for the children are come to the birth, and there is not strength to bring forth.

4 It may be the LORD your God will hear all the words of Rab-shakeh, whom the king of Assyria his master has sent to reproach the living God; and will reprove the words which the LORD your God has heard: wherefore lift up your prayer for the remnant that are left.

5 So the servants of king Hezekiah came to Isaiah.

6And Isaiah said unto them, Thus shall you say to your master, Thus saith the LORD, Be not afraid of the words which you have heard, with which the servants of the king of Assyria have blasphemed me.

7 Behold, I will send a blast upon him, and he shall hear a rumour, and shall return to his own land; and I will cause him to fall by the sword in his own land.

8So Rab-shakeh returned, and found the king of Assyria warring against Libnah: for he had heard that he was departed from Lachish.

9 And when he heard say of Tirhakah king of Ethiopia, Behold, he is come out to fight against you: he sent messengers again unto Hezekiah, saying,

10 Thus shall you speak to Hezekiah king of Judah, saying, Let not your God in whom you trustest deceive you, saying, Jerusalem shall not be delivered into the hand of the king of Assyria.

11 Behold, you have heard what the kings of Assyria have done to all lands, by destroying them utterly: and shalt you be delivered?

12 Have the gods of the nations delivered them which my fathers have destroyed; as Gozan, and Haran, and Rezeph, and the children of Eden which were in Thelasar?

13 Where is the king of Hamath, and the king of Arpad, and the king of the city of Sepharvaim, of Hena, and Ivah?

14And Hezekiah received the letter of the hand of the messengers, and read it: and Hezekiah went up into the house of the LORD, and spread it before the LORD.

15 And Hezekiah prayed before the LORD, and said, O LORD God of Israel, which dwellest between the cherubims, you are the God, even you alone, of all the kingdoms of the earth; you have made heaven and earth.

16 LORD, bow down yours ear, and hear: open, LORD, yours eyes, and see: and hear the words of Sennacherib, which has sent him to reproach the living God.

17 Of a truth, LORD, the kings of Assyria have destroyed the nations and their lands,

18 And have cast their gods into the fire: for they were no gods, but the work of men's hands, wood and stone: therefore they have destroyed them.

19 Now therefore, O LORD our God, I beseech you, save you us out of his hand, that all the kingdoms of the earth may know that you are the LORD God, even you only.

20Then Isaiah the son of Amoz sent to Hezekiah, saying, Thus saith the LORD God of Israel, That which you have prayed to me against Sennacherib king of Assyria I have heard.

21 This is the word that the LORD has spoken concerning him; The virgin the daughter of Zion has despised you, and laughed you to scorn; the daughter of Jerusalem has shaken her head at you.

22 Whom have you reproached and blasphemed? and against whom have you exalted your voice, and lifted up yours eyes on high? even against the Holy One of Israel.

23 By your messengers you have reproached the Lord, and have said, With the multitude of my chariots I am come up to the height of the mountains, to the sides of Lebanon, and will cut down the tall cedar trees thereof, and the choice fir trees thereof: and I will enter into the lodgings of his borders, and into the forest of his Carmel.

24 I have digged and drunk strange waters, and with the sole of my feet have I dried up all the rivers of besieged places.

25 Have you not heard long ago how I have done it, and of ancient times that I have formed it? now have I brought it to pass, that you shouldest be to lay waste fenced cities into ruinous heaps.

26 Therefore their inhabitants were of small power, they were dismayed and confounded; they were as the grass of the field, and as the green herb, as the grass on the housetops, and as corn blasted before it be grown up.

27 But I know your abode, and your going out, and your coming in, and your rage against me.

28 Because your rage against me and your tumult is come up into my ears, therefore I will put my hook in your nose, and my bridle in your lips, and I will turn you back by the way by which you camest.

29 And this shall be a sign unto you, You shall eat this year such things as grow of themselves, and in the second year that which springeth of the same; and in the third year sow you , and reap, and plant vineyards, and eat the fruits thereof.

30 And the remnant that is escaped of the house of Judah shall yet again take root downward, and bear fruit upward.

31 For out of Jerusalem shall go forth a remnant, and they that escape out of mount Zion: the zeal of the LORD of hosts shall do this.

32 Therefore thus saith the LORD concerning the king of Assyria, He shall not come into this city, nor shoot an arrow there, nor come before it with shield, nor cast a bank against it.

33 By the way that he came, by the same shall he return, and shall not come into this city, saith the LORD.

34 For I will defend this city, to save it, for my own sake, and for my servant David's sake.

35And it came to pass that night, that the angel of the LORD went out, and struck in the camp of the Assyrians an hundred fourscore and five thousand: and when they arose early in the morning, behold, they were all dead corpses.

36 So Sennacherib king of Assyria departed, and went and returned, and dwelt at Nineveh.

37 And it came to pass, as he was worshipping in the house of Nisroch his god, that Adrammelech and Sharezer his sons struck him with the sword: and they escaped into the land of Armenia. And Esarhaddon his son reigned in his stead.

CHAPTER 20

IN those days was Hezekiah sick unto death. And the prophet Isaiah the son of Amoz came to him, and said unto him, Thus saith the LORD, Set yours house in order; for you shalt die, and not live.

2 Then he turned his face to the wall, and prayed unto the LORD, saying,

3 I beseech you, O LORD, remember now how I have walked before you in truth and with a perfect heart, and have done that which is good in your sight. And Hezekiah wept sore.

4 And it came to pass, afore Isaiah was gone out into the middle court, that the word of the LORD came to him, saying,

5 Turn again, and tell Hezekiah the captain of my people, Thus saith the LORD, the God of David your father, I have heard your prayer, I have seen your tears: behold, I will heal you: on the third day you shalt go up unto the house of the LORD.

6 And I will add unto your days fifteen years; and I will deliver you and this city out of the hand of the king of Assyria; and I will defend this city for my own sake, and for my servant David's sake.

7 And Isaiah said, Take a lump of figs. And they took and laid it on the boil, and he recovered.

8And Hezekiah said unto Isaiah, What shall be the sign that the LORD will heal me, and that I shall go up into the house of the LORD the third day?

9 And Isaiah said, This sign shalt you have of the LORD, that the LORD will do the thing that he has spoken: shall the shadow go forward ten degrees, or go back ten degrees?

10 And Hezekiah answered, It is a light thing for the shadow to go down ten degrees: nay, but let the shadow return backward ten degrees.

11 And Isaiah the prophet cried unto the LORD: and he brought the shadow ten degrees backward, by which it had gone down in the dial of Ahaz.

12At that time Berodach-baladan, the son of Baladan, king of Babylon, sent letters and a present unto Hezekiah: for he had heard that Hezekiah had been sick.

13 And Hezekiah hearkened unto them, and shewed them all the house of his precious things, the silver, and the gold, and the spices, and the precious ointment, and all the house of his armour, and all that was found in his treasures: there was nothing in his house, nor in all his dominion, that Hezekiah shewed them not.

14Then came Isaiah the prophet unto king Hezekiah, and said unto him, What said these men? and from whence came they unto you? And Hezekiah said, They are come from a far country, even from Babylon.

15 And he said, What have they seen in yours house? And Hezekiah answered, All the things that are in my house have they seen: there is nothing among my treasures that I have not shewed them.

16 And Isaiah said unto Hezekiah, Hear the word of the LORD.

17 Behold, the days come, that all that is in yours house, and that which your fathers have laid up in store unto this day, shall be carried into Babylon: nothing shall be left, saith the LORD.

18 And of your sons that shall issue from you, which you shalt beget, shall they take away; and they shall be eunuchs in the palace of the king of Babylon.

19 Then said Hezekiah unto Isaiah, Good is the word of the LORD which you have spoken. And he said, Is it not good, if peace and truth be in my days?

20And the rest of the acts of Hezekiah, and all his might, and how he made a pool, and a conduit, and brought water into the city, are they not written in the book of the chronicles of the kings of Judah?

21 And Hezekiah slept with his fathers: and Manasseh his son reigned in his stead.

CHAPTER 21

MANASSEH was twelve years old when he began to reign, and reigned fifty and five years in Jerusalem. And his mother's name was Hephzi-bah.

2 And he did that which was evil in the sight of the LORD, after the abominations of the heathen, whom the LORD cast out before the children of Israel.

3 For he built up again the high places which Hezekiah his father had destroyed; and he reared up altars for Baal, and made a grove, as did Ahab king of Israel; and worshipped all the host of heaven, and served them.

4 And he built altars in the house of the LORD, of which the LORD said, In Jerusalem will I put my name.

5 And he built altars for all the host of heaven in the two courts of the house of the LORD.

6 And he made his son pass through the fire, and observed times, and used enchantments, and dealt with familiar spirits and wizards: he created much wickedness in the sight of the LORD, to provoke him to anger.

7 And he set a graven image of the grove that he had made in the house, of which the LORD said to David, and to Solomon his son, In this house, and in Jerusalem, which I have chosen out of all tribes of Israel, will I put my name for ever:

8 Neither will I make the feet of Israel move any more out of the land which I gave their fathers; only if they will observe to do according to all that I have commanded them, and according to all the law that my servant Moses commanded them.

9 But they hearkened not: and Manasseh seduced them to do more evil than did the nations whom the LORD destroyed before the children of Israel.

10And the LORD spake by his servants the prophets, saying,

11 Because Manasseh king of Judah has done these abominations, and has done wickedly above all that the Amorites did, which were before him, and has made Judah also to sin with his idols:

12 Therefore thus saith the LORD God of Israel, Behold, I am bringing such evil upon Jerusalem and Judah, that whosoever heareth of it, both his ears shall tingle.

13 And I will stretch over Jerusalem the line of Samaria, and the plummet of the house of Ahab: and I will wipe Jerusalem as a man wipeth a dish, wiping it, and turning it upside down.

14 And I will forsake the remnant of my inheritance, and deliver them into the hand of their enemies; and they shall become a prey and a spoil to all their enemies;

15 Because they have done that which was evil in my sight, and have provoked me to anger, since the day their fathers came forth out of Egypt, even unto this day.

16 Moreover Manasseh shed innocent blood very much, till he had filled Jerusalem from one end to another; beside his sin wherewith he made Judah to sin, in doing that which was evil in the sight of the LORD.

17 Now the rest of the acts of Manasseh, and all that he did, and his sin that he sinned, are they not written in the book of the chronicles of the kings of Judah?

18 And Manasseh slept with his fathers, and was buried in the garden of his own house, in the garden of Uzza: and Amon his son reigned in his stead.

19 Amon was twenty and two years old when he began to reign, and he reigned two years in Jerusalem. And his mother's name was Meshullemeth, the daughter of Haruz of Jotbah.

20 And he did that which was evil in the sight of the LORD, as his father Manasseh did.

21 And he walked in all the way that his father walked in, and served the idols that his father served, and worshipped them:

22 And he forsook the LORD God of his fathers, and walked not in the way of the LORD.

23 And the servants of Amon conspired against him, and slew the king in his own house.

24 And the people of the land slew all them that had conspired against king Amon; and the people of the land made Josiah his son king in his stead.

25 Now the rest of the acts of Amon which he did, are they not written in the book of the chronicles of the kings of Judah?

26 And he was buried in his sepulchre in the garden of Uzza: and Josiah his son reigned in his stead.

CHAPTER 22

JOSIAH was eight years old when he began to reign, and he reigned thirty and one years in Jerusalem. And his mother's name was Jedidah, the daughter of Adaiah of Boscath.

2 And he did that which was right in the sight of the LORD, and walked in all the way of David his father, and turned not aside to the right hand or to the left.

3 And it came to pass in the eighteenth year of king Josiah, that the king sent Shaphan the son of Azaliah, the son of Meshullam, the scribe, to the house of the LORD, saying,

4 Go up to Hilkiah the high priest, that he may sum the silver which is brought into the house of the LORD, which the keepers of the door have gathered of the people:

5 And let them deliver it into the hand of the doers of the work, that have the oversight of the house of the LORD: and let them give it to the doers of the work which is in the house of the LORD, to repair the breaches of the house,

6 Unto carpenters, and builders, and masons, and to buy timber and hewn stone to repair the house.

7 Howbeit there was no reckoning made with them of the money that was delivered into their hand, because they dealt faithfully.

8 And Hilkiah the high priest said unto Shaphan the scribe, I have found the book of the law in the house of the LORD. And Hilkiah gave the book to Shaphan, and he read it.

9 And Shaphan the scribe came to the king, and brought the king word again, and said, Your servants have gathered the money that was found in the house, and have delivered it into the hand of them that do the work, that have the oversight of the house of the LORD.

10 And Shaphan the scribe shewed the king, saying, Hilkiah the priest has delivered me a book. And Shaphan read it before the king.

11 And it came to pass, when the king had heard the words of the book of the law, that he rent his clothes.

12 And the king commanded Hilkiah the priest, and Ahikam the son of Shaphan, and Achbor the son of Michaiah, and Shaphan the scribe, and Asahiah a servant of the king's, saying,

13 Go you , inquire of the LORD for me, and for the people, and for all Judah, concerning the words of this book that is found: for great is the wrath of the LORD that is kindled against us, because our fathers have not hearkened unto the words of this book, to do according unto all that which is written concerning us.

14 So Hilkiah the priest, and Ahikam, and Achbor, and Shaphan, and Asahiah, went unto Huldah the prophetess, the wife of Shallum the son of Tikvah, the son of Harhas, keeper of the wardrobe; (now she dwelt in Jerusalem in the college;) and they communed with her.

15 And she said unto them, Thus saith the LORD God of Israel, Tell the man that sent you to me,

16 Thus saith the LORD, Behold, I will bring evil upon this place, and upon the inhabitants thereof, even all the words of the book which the king of Judah has read:

17 Because they have forsaken me, and have burned incense unto other gods, that they might provoke me to anger with all the works of their hands; therefore my wrath shall be kindled against this place, and shall not be quenched.

18 But to the king of Judah which sent you to inquire of the LORD, thus shall you say to him, Thus saith the LORD God of Israel, As touching the words which you have heard;

19 Because yours heart was tender, and you have humbled yourself before the LORD, when you heardest what I spake against this place, and against the inhabitants thereof, that they should become a desolation and a curse, and have rent your clothes, and wept before me; I also have heard you, saith the LORD.

20 Behold therefore, I will gather you unto your fathers, and you shalt be gathered into your grave in peace; and yours eyes shall not see all the evil which I will bring upon this place. And they brought the king word again.

CHAPTER 23

AND the king sent, and they gathered unto him all the elders of Judah and of Jerusalem.

2 And the king went up into the house of the LORD, and all the men of Judah and all the inhabitants of Jerusalem with him, and the priests, and the prophets, and all the people, both small and great: and he read in their ears all the words of the book of the covenant which was found in the house of the LORD.

3 And the king stood by a pillar, and made a covenant before the LORD, to walk after the LORD, and to keep his commandments and his testimonies and his statutes with all their heart and all their soul, to perform the words of this covenant that were written in this book. And all the people stood to the covenant.

4 And the king commanded Hilkiah the high priest, and the priests of the second order, and the keepers of the door, to bring forth out of the temple of the LORD all the vessels that were made for Baal, and for the grove, and for all the host of heaven: and he burned them without Jerusalem in the fields of Kidron, and carried the ashes of them unto Beth-el.

5 And he put down the idolatrous priests, whom the kings of Judah had ordained to burn incense in the high places in the cities of Judah, and in the places round about Jerusalem; them also that burned incense unto Baal, to the sun, and to the moon, and to the planets, and to all the host of heaven.

6 And he brought out the grove from the house of the LORD, without Jerusalem, unto the brook Kidron, and burned it at the brook Kidron, and stamped it small to powder, and cast the powder thereof upon the graves of the children of the people.

7 And he brake down the houses of the sodomites, that were by the house of the LORD, where the women wove hangings for the grove.

8 And he brought all the priests out of the cities of Judah, and defiled the high places where the priests had burned incense, from Geba to Beer-sheba, and brake down the high places of the gates that were in the entering in of the gate of Joshua the governor of the city, which were on a man's left hand at the gate of the city.

9 Nevertheless the priests of the high places came not up to the altar of the LORD in Jerusalem, but they did eat of the unleavened bread among their brethren.

10 And he defiled Topheth, which is in the valley of the children of Hinnom, that no man might make his son or his daughter to pass through the fire to Molech.

11 And he took away the horses that the kings of Judah had given to the sun, at the entering in of the house of the LORD, by the chamber of Nathan-melech the chamberlain, which was in the suburbs, and burned the chariots of the sun with fire.

12 And the altars that were on the top of the upper chamber of Ahaz, which the kings of Judah had made, and the altars which Manasseh had made in the two courts of the house of the LORD, did the king beat down, and brake them down from thence, and cast the dust of them into the brook Kidron.

13 And the high places that were before Jerusalem, which were on the right hand of the mount of corruption, which Solomon the king of Israel had builded for Ashtoreth the abomination of the Zidonians, and for Chemosh the abomination of the Moabites, and for Milcom the abomination of the children of Ammon, did the king defile.

14 And he brake in pieces the images, and cut down the groves, and filled their places with the bones of men.

15 Moreover the altar that was at Beth-el, and the high place which Jeroboam the son of Nebat, who made Israel to sin, had made, both that altar and the high place he brake down, and burned the high place, and stamped it small to powder, and burned the grove.

16 And as Josiah turned himself, he spied the sepulchres that were there in the mount, and sent, and took the bones out of the sepulchres, and burned them upon the altar, and polluted it, according to the word of the LORD which the man of God proclaimed, who proclaimed these words.

17 Then he said, What title is that that I see? And the men of the city told him, It is the sepulchre of the man of God, which came from Judah, and proclaimed these things that you have done against the altar of Beth-el.

18 And he said, Let him alone; let no man move his bones. So they let his bones alone, with the bones of the prophet that came out of Samaria.

19 And all the houses also of the high places that were in the cities of Samaria, which the kings of Israel had made to provoke the LORD to anger, Josiah took away, and did to them according to all the acts that he had done in Beth-el.

20 And he slew all the priests of the high places that were there upon the altars, and burned men's bones upon them, and returned to Jerusalem.

21And the king commanded all the people, saying, Keep the passover unto the LORD your God, as it is written in the book of this covenant.

22 Surely there was not holden such a passover from the days of the judges that judged Israel, nor in all the days of the kings of Israel, nor of the kings of Judah;

23 But in the eighteenth year of king Josiah, wherein this passover was holden to the LORD in Jerusalem.

24Moreover the workers with familiar spirits, and the wizards, and the images, and the idols, and all the abominations that were spied in the land of Judah and in Jerusalem, did Josiah put away, that he might perform the words of the law which were written in the book that Hilkiah the priest found in the house of the LORD.

25 And like unto him was there no king before him, that turned to the LORD with all his heart, and with all his soul, and with all his might, according to all the law of Moses; neither after him arose there any like him.

26Notwithstanding the LORD turned not from the fierceness of his great wrath, wherewith his anger was kindled against Judah, because of all the provocations that Manasseh had provoked him withal.

27 And the LORD said, I will remove Judah also out of my sight, as I have removed Israel, and will cast off this city Jerusalem which I have chosen, and the house of which I said, My name shall be there.

28 Now the rest of the acts of Josiah, and all that he did, are they not written in the book of the chronicles of the kings of Judah?

29In his days Pharaoh-nechoh king of Egypt went up against the king of Assyria to the river Euphrates: and king Josiah went against him; and he slew him at Megiddo, when he had seen him.

30 And his servants carried him in a chariot dead from Megiddo, and brought him to Jerusalem, and buried him in his own sepulchre. And the people of the land took Jehoahaz the son of Josiah, and anointed him, and made him king in his father's stead.

31Jehoahaz was twenty and three years old when he began to reign; and he reigned three months in Jerusalem. And his mother's name was Hamutal, the daughter of Jeremiah of Libnah.

32 And he did that which was evil in the sight of the LORD, according to all that his fathers had done.

33 And Pharaoh-nechoh put him in bands at Riblah in the land of Hamath, that he might not reign in Jerusalem; and put the land to a tribute of an hundred talents of silver, and a talent of gold.

34 And Pharaoh-nechoh made Eliakim the son of Josiah king in the room of Josiah his father, and turned his name to Jehoiakim, and took Jehoahaz away: and he came to Egypt, and died there.

35 And Jehoiakim gave the silver and the gold to Pharaoh; but he taxed the land to give the money according to the commandment of Pharaoh: he exacted the silver and the gold of the people of the land, of every one according to his taxation, to give it unto Pharaoh-nechoh.

36Jehoiakim was twenty and five years old when he began to reign; and he reigned eleven years in Jerusalem. And his mother's name was Zebudah, the daughter of Pedaiah of Rumah.

37 And he did that which was evil in the sight of the LORD, according to all that his fathers had done.

CHAPTER 24

IN his days Nebuchadnezzar king of Babylon came up, and Jehoiakim became his servant three years: then he turned and rebelled against him.

2 And the LORD sent against him bands of the Chaldees, and bands of the Syrians, and bands of the Moabites, and bands of the children of Ammon, and sent them against Judah to destroy it, according to the word of the LORD, which he spake by his servants the prophets.

3 Surely at the commandment of the LORD came this upon Judah, to remove them out of his sight, for the sins of Manasseh, according to all that he did;

4 And also for the innocent blood that he shed: for he filled Jerusalem with innocent blood; which the LORD would not pardon.

5Now the rest of the acts of Jehoiakim, and all that he did, are they not written in the book of the chronicles of the kings of Judah?

6 So Jehoiakim slept with his fathers: and Jehoiachin his son reigned in his stead.

7 And the king of Egypt came not again any more out of his land: for the king of Babylon had taken from the river of Egypt unto the river Euphrates all that pertained to the king of Egypt.

8Jehoiachin was eighteen years old when he began to reign, and he reigned in Jerusalem three months. And his mother's name was Nehushta, the daughter of Elnathan of Jerusalem.

9 And he did that which was evil in the sight of the LORD, according to all that his father had done.

10At that time the servants of Nebuchadnezzar king of Babylon came up against Jerusalem, and the city was besieged.

11 And Nebuchadnezzar king of Babylon came against the city, and his servants did besiege it.

12 And Jehoiachin the king of Judah went out to the king of Babylon, he, and his mother, and his servants, and his princes, and his officers: and the king of Babylon took him in the eighth year of his reign.

13 And he carried out thence all the treasures of the house of the LORD, and the treasures of the king's house, and cut in pieces all the vessels of gold which Solomon king of Israel had made in the temple of the LORD, as the LORD had said.

14 And he carried away all Jerusalem, and all the princes, and all the mighty men of valour, even ten thousand captives, and all the craftsmen and smiths: none remained, save the poorest sort of the people of the land.

15 And he carried away Jehoiachin to Babylon, and the king's mother, and the king's wives, and his officers, and the mighty of the land, those carried he into captivity from Jerusalem to Babylon.

16 And all the men of might, even seven thousand, and craftsmen and smiths a thousand, all that were strong and apt for war, even them the king of Babylon brought captive to Babylon.

17And the king of Babylon made Mattaniah his father's brother king in his stead, and changed his name to Zedekiah.

18 Zedekiah was twenty and one years old when he began to reign, and he reigned eleven years in Jerusalem. And his mother's name was Hamutal, the daughter of Jeremiah of Libnah.

19 And he did that which was evil in the sight of the LORD, according to all that Jehoiakim had done.

20 For through the anger of the LORD it came to pass in Jerusalem and Judah, until he had cast them out from his presence, that Zedekiah rebelled against the king of Babylon.

CHAPTER 25

AND it came to pass in the ninth year of his reign, in the tenth month, in the tenth day of the month, that Nebuchadnezzar king of Babylon came, he, and all his host, against Jerusalem, and pitched against it; and they built forts against it round about.

2 And the city was besieged unto the eleventh year of king Zedekiah.

3 And on the ninth day of the fourth month the famine prevailed in the city, and there was no bread for the people of the land.

4And the city was broken up, and all the men of war fled by night by the way of the gate between two walls, which is by the king's garden: (now the Chaldees were against the city round about:) and the king went the way toward the plain.

5 And the army of the Chaldees pursued after the king, and overtook him in the plains of Jericho: and all his army were scattered from him.

6 So they took the king, and brought him up to the king of Babylon to Riblah; and they gave judgment upon him.

7 And they slew the sons of Zedekiah before his eyes, and put out the eyes of Zedekiah, and bound him with fetters of brass, and carried him to Babylon.

8And in the fifth month, on the seventh day of the month, which is the nineteenth year of king Nebuchadnezzar king of Babylon, came Nebuzar-adan, captain of the guard, a servant of the king of Babylon, unto Jerusalem:

9 And he burnt the house of the LORD, and the king's house, and all the houses of Jerusalem, and every great man's house burnt he with fire.

10 And all the army of the Chaldees, that were with the captain of the guard, brake down the walls of Jerusalem round about.

11 Now the rest of the people that were left in the city, and the fugitives that fell away to the king of Babylon, with the remnant of the multitude, did Nebuzar-adan the captain of the guard carry away.

12 But the captain of the guard left of the poor of the land to be vinedressers and husbandmen.

13 And the pillars of brass that were in the house of the LORD, and the bases, and the brasen sea that was in the house of the LORD, did the Chaldees break in pieces, and carried the brass of them to Babylon.

14 And the pots, and the shovels, and the snuffers, and the spoons, and all the vessels of brass wherewith they ministered, took they away.

15 And the firepans, and the bowls, and such things as were of gold, in gold, and of silver, in silver, the captain of the guard took away.

16 The two pillars, one sea, and the bases which Solomon had made for the house of the LORD; the brass of all these vessels was without weight.

17 The height of the one pillar was eighteen cubits, and the chapiter upon it was brass: and the height of the chapiter three cubits; and the wreathen work, and pomegranates upon the chapiter round about, all of brass: and like unto these had the second pillar with wreathen work.

18 And the captain of the guard took Seraiah the chief priest, and Zephaniah the second priest, and the three keepers of the door:

19 And out of the city he took an officer that was set over the men of war, and five men of them that were in the king's presence, which were found in the city, and the principal scribe of the host, which mustered the people of the land, and threescore men of the people of the land that were found in the city:

20 And Nebuzar-adan captain of the guard took these, and brought them to the king of Babylon to Riblah:

21 And the king of Babylon struck them, and slew them at Riblah in the land of Hamath. So Judah was carried away out of their land.

22 And as for the people that remained in the land of Judah, whom Nebuchadnezzar king of Babylon had left, even over them he made Gedaliah the son of Ahikam, the son of Shaphan, ruler.

23 And when all the captains of the armies, they and their men, heard that the king of Babylon had made Gedaliah governor, there came to Gedaliah to Mizpah, even Ishmael the son of Nethaniah, and Johanan the son of Careah, and Seraiah the son of Tanhumeth the Netophathite, and Jaazaniah the son of a Maachathite, they and their men.

24 And Gedaliah sware to them, and to their men, and said unto them, Fear not to be the servants of the Chaldees: dwell in the land, and serve the king of Babylon; and it shall be well with you.

25 But it came to pass in the seventh month, that Ishmael the son of Nethaniah, the son of Elishama, of the seed royal, came, and ten men with him, and struck Gedaliah, that he died, and the Jews and the Chaldees that were with him at Mizpah.

26 And all the people, both small and great, and the captains of the armies, arose, and came to Egypt: for they were afraid of the Chaldees.

27 And it came to pass in the seven and thirtieth year of the captivity of Jehoiachin king of Judah, in the twelfth month, on the seven and twentieth day of the month, that Evil-merodach king of Babylon in the year that he began to reign did lift up the head of Jehoiachin king of Judah out of prison;

28 And he spake kindly to him, and set his throne above the throne of the kings that were with him in Babylon;

29 And changed his prison garments: and he did eat bread continually before him all the days of his life.

30 And his allowance was a continual allowance given him of the king, a daily rate for every day, all the days of his life.

THE FIRST BOOK OF THE CHRONICLES.

CHAPTER 1

ADAM, Sheth, Enosh,

2 Kenan, Mahalaleel, Jered,

3 Henoch (Enoch), Methuselah, Lamech,

4 Noah, Shem, Ham, and Japheth.

5 The sons of Japheth; Gomer, and Magog, and Madai, and Javan, and Tubal, and Meshech, and Tiras.

6 And the sons of Gomer; Ashchenaz, and Riphath, and Togarmah.

7 And the sons of Javan; Elishah, and Tarshish, Kittim, and Dodanim.

8 The sons of Ham; Cush, and Mizraim, Put, and Canaan.

9 And the sons of Cush; Seba, and Havilah, and Sabta, and Raamah, and Sabtecha. And the sons of Raamah; Sheba, and Dedan.

10 And Cush begat Nimrod: he began to be mighty upon the earth.

11 And Mizraim begat Ludim, and Anamim, and Lehabim, and Naphtuhim,

12 And Pathrusim, and Casluhim, (of whom came the Philistines,) and Caphthorim.

13 And Canaan begat Zidon his firstborn, and Heth,

14 The Jebusite also, and the Amorite, and the Girgashite,

15 And the Hivite, and the Arkite, and the Sinite,

16 And the Arvadite, and the Zemarite, and the Hamathite.

17 The sons of Shem; Elam, and Asshur, and Arphaxad, and Lud, and Aram, and Uz, and Hul, and Gether, and Meshech.

18 And Arphaxad begat Shelah, and Shelah begat Eber.

19 And unto Eber were born two sons: the name of the one was Peleg; because in his days the earth was divided: and his brother's name was Joktan.

20 And Joktan begat Almodad, and Sheleph, and Hazarmaveth, and Jerah,

21 Hadoram also, and Uzal, and Diklah,

22 And Ebal, and Abimael, and Sheba,

23 And Ophir, and Havilah, and Jobab. All these were the sons of Joktan.

24 Shem, Arphaxad, Shelah,

25 Eber, Peleg, Reu,

26 Serug, Nahor, Terah,

27 Abram; the same is Abraham.

28 The sons of Abraham; Isaac, and Ishmael.

29 These are their generations: The firstborn of Ishmael, Nebaioth; then Kedar, and Adbeel, and Mibsam,

30 Mishma, and Dumah, Massa, Hadad, and Tema,

31 Jetur, Naphish, and Kedemah. These are the sons of Ishmael.

32 Now the sons of Keturah, Abraham's concubine: she bare Zimran, and Jokshan, and Medan, and Midian, and Ishbak, and Shuah. And the sons of Jokshan; Sheba, and Dedan.

33 And the sons of Midian; Ephah, and Epher, and Henoch, and Abida, and Eldaah. All these are the sons of Keturah.

34 And Abraham begat Isaac. The sons of Isaac; Esau and Israel.

35 The sons of Esau; Eliphaz, Reuel, and Jeush, and Jaalam, and Korah.

36 The sons of Eliphaz; Teman, and Omar, Zephi, and Gatam, Kenaz, and Timna, and Amalek.

37 The sons of Reuel; Nahath, Zerah, Shammah, and Mizzah.

38 And the sons of Seir; Lotan, and Shobal, and Zibeon, and Anah, and Dishon, and Ezer, and Dishan.

39 And the sons of Lotan; Hori, and Homam: and Timna was Lotan's sister.

40 The sons of Shobal; Alian, and Manahath, and Ebal, Shephi, and Onam. And the sons of Zibeon; Aiah, and Anah.

41 The sons of Anah; Dishon. And the sons of Dishon; Amram, and Eshban, and Ithran, and Cheran.

42 The sons of Ezer; Bilhan, and Zavan, and Jakan. The sons of Dishan; Uz, and Aran.

43 Now these are the kings that reigned in the land of Edom before any king reigned over the children of Israel; Bela the son of Beor: and the name of his city was Dinhabah.

44 And when Bela was dead, Jobab the son of Zerah of Bozrah reigned in his stead.

45 And when Jobab was dead, Husham of the land of the Temanites reigned in his stead.

46 And when Husham was dead, Hadad the son of Bedad, which struck Midian in the field of Moab, reigned in his stead: and the name of his city was Avith.

47 And when Hadad was dead, Samlah of Masrekah reigned in his stead.

48 And when Samlah was dead, Shaul of Rehoboth by the river reigned in his stead.

49 And when Shaul was dead, Baal-hanan the son of Achbor reigned in his stead.

50 And when Baal-hanan was dead, Hadad reigned in his stead: and the name of his city was Pai; and his wife's name was Mehetabel, the daughter of Matred, the daughter of Mezahab.

51 Hadad died also. And the dukes of Edom were; duke Timnah, duke Aliah, duke Jetheth,

52 Duke Aholibamah, duke Elah, duke Pinon,

53 Duke Kenaz, duke Teman, duke Mibzar,

54 Duke Magdiel, duke Iram. These are the dukes of Edom.

CHAPTER 2

THESE are the sons of Israel; Reuben, Simeon, Levi, and Judah, Issachar, and Zebulun,

2 Dan, Joseph, and Benjamin, Naphtali, Gad, and Asher.

3 The sons of Judah; Er, and Onan, and Shelah: which three were born unto him of the daughter of Shua the Canaanitess. And Er, the firstborn of Judah, was evil in the sight of the LORD; and he slew him.

4 And Tamar his daughter in law bare him Pharez and Zerah. All the sons of Judah were five.

5 The sons of Pharez; Hezron, and Hamul.

6 And the sons of Zerah; Zimri, and Ethan, and Heman, and Calcol, and Dara: five of them in all.

7 And the sons of Carmi; Achar, the troubler of Israel, who transgressed in the thing accursed.

8 And the sons of Ethan; Azariah.

9 The sons also of Hezron, that were born unto him; Jerahmeel, and Ram, and Chelubai.

10 And Ram begat Amminadab; and Amminadab begat Nahshon, prince of the children of Judah;

11 And Nahshon begat Salma, and Salma begat Boaz,

12 And Boaz begat Obed, and Obed begat Jesse,

13 And Jesse begat his firstborn Eliab, and Abinadab the second, and Shimma the third,

14 Nethaneel the fourth, Raddai the fifth,

15 Ozem the sixth, David the seventh:

16 Whose sisters were Zeruiah, and Abigail. And the sons of Zeruiah; Abishai, and Joab, and Asahel, three.

17 And Abigail bare Amasa: and the father of Amasa was Jether the Ishmeelite.

18 And Caleb the son of Hezron begat children of Azubah his wife, and of Jerioth: her sons are these; Jesher, and Shobab, and Ardon.

19 And when Azubah was dead, Caleb took unto him Ephrath, which bare him Hur.

20 And Hur begat Uri, and Uri begat Bezaleel.

21 And afterward Hezron went in to the daughter of Machir the father of Gilead, whom he married when he was threescore years old; and she bare him Segub.

22 And Segub begat Jair, who had three and twenty cities in the land of Gilead.

23 And he took Geshur, and Aram, with the towns of Jair, from them, with Kenath, and the towns thereof, even threescore cities. All these belonged to the sons of Machir the father of Gilead.

24 And after that Hezron was dead in Caleb-ephratah, then Abiah Hezron's wife bare him Ashur the father of Tekoa.

25 And the sons of Jerahmeel the firstborn of Hezron were, Ram the firstborn, and Bunah, and Oren, and Ozem, and Ahijah.

26 Jerahmeel had also another wife, whose name was Atarah; she was the mother of Onam.

27 And the sons of Ram the firstborn of Jerahmeel were, Maaz, and Jamin, and Eker.

28 And the sons of Onam were, Shammai, and Jada. And the sons of Shammai; Nadab, and Abishur.

29 And the name of the wife of Abishur was Abihail, and she bare him Ahban, and Molid.

30 And the sons of Nadab; Seled, and Appaim: but Seled died without children.

31 And the sons of Appaim; Ishi. And the sons of Ishi; Sheshan. And the children of Sheshan; Ahlai.

32 And the sons of Jada the brother of Shammai; Jether, and Jonathan: and Jether died without children.

33 And the sons of Jonathan; Peleth, and Zaza. These were the sons of Jerahmeel.

34 Now Sheshan had no sons, but daughters. And Sheshan had a servant, an Egyptian, whose name was Jarha.

35 And Sheshan gave his daughter to Jarha his servant to wife; and she bare him Attai.

36 And Attai begat Nathan, and Nathan begat Zabad,

37 And Zabad begat Ephlal, and Ephlal begat Obed,

38 And Obed begat Jehu, and Jehu begat Azariah,

39 And Azariah begat Helez, and Helez begat Eleasah,

40 And Eleasah begat Sisamai, and Sisamai begat Shallum,

41 And Shallum begat Jekamiah, and Jekamiah begat Elishama.

42 Now the sons of Caleb the brother of Jerahmeel were, Mesha his firstborn, which was the father of Ziph; and the sons of Mareshah the father of Hebron.

43 And the sons of Hebron; Korah, and Tappuah, and Rekem, and Shema.

44 And Shema begat Raham, the father of Jorkoam: and Rekem begat Shammai.

45 And the son of Shammai was Maon: and Maon was the father of Beth-zur.

46 And Ephah, Caleb's concubine, bare Haran, and Moza, and Gazez: and Haran begat Gazez.

47 And the sons of Jahdai; Regem, and Jotham, and Geshan, and Pelet, and Ephah, and Shaaph.

48 Maachah, Caleb's concubine, bare Sheber, and Tirhanah.

49 She bare also Shaaph the father of Madmannah, Sheva the father of Machbenah, and the father of Gibea: and the daughter of Caleb was Achsah.

50 These were the sons of Caleb the son of Hur, the firstborn of Ephratah; Shobal the father of Kirjath-jearim,

51 Salma the father of Beth-lehem, Hareph the father of Beth-gader.

52 And Shobal the father of Kirjath-jearim had sons; Haroeh, and half of the Manahethites.

53 And the families of Kirjath-jearim; the Ithrites, and the Puhites, and the Shumathites, and the Mishraites; of them came the Zareathites, and the Eshtaulites.

54 The sons of Salma; Beth-lehem, and the Netophathites, Ataroth, the house of Joab, and half of the Manahethites, the Zorites.

55 And the families of the scribes which dwelt at Jabez; the Tirathites, the Shimeathites, and Suchathites. These are the Kenites that came of Hemath, the father of the house of Rechab.

CHAPTER 3

NOW these were the sons of David, which were born unto him in Hebron; the firstborn Amnon, of Ahinoam the Jezreelitess; the second Daniel, of Abigail the Carmelitess:

2 The third, Absalom the son of Maachah the daughter of Talmai king of Geshur: the fourth, Adonijah the son of Haggith:

3 The fifth, Shephatiah of Abital: the sixth, Ithream by Eglah his wife.

4 These six were born unto him in Hebron; and there he reigned seven years and six months: and in Jerusalem he reigned thirty and three years.

5 And these were born unto him in Jerusalem; Shimea, and Shobab, and Nathan, and Solomon, four, of Bath-shua the daughter of Ammiel:

6 Ibhar also, and Elishama, and Eliphelet,

7 And Nogah, and Nepheg, and Japhia,

8 And Elishama, and Eliada, and Eliphelet, nine.

9 These were all the sons of David, beside the sons of the concubines, and Tamar their sister.

10 And Solomon's son was Rehoboam, Abia his son, Asa his son, Jehoshaphat his son,

11 Joram his son, Ahaziah his son, Joash his son,

12 Amaziah his son, Azariah his son, Jotham his son,

13 Ahaz his son, Hezekiah his son, Manasseh his son,

14 Amon his son, Josiah his son.

15 And the sons of Josiah were, the firstborn Johanan, the second Jehoiakim, the third Zedekiah, the fourth Shallum.

16 And the sons of Jehoiakim: Jeconiah his son, Zedekiah his son.

17 And the sons of Jeconiah; Assir, Salathiel his son,

18 Malchiram also, and Pedaiah, and Shenazar, Jecamiah, Hoshama, and Nedabiah.

19 And the sons of Pedaiah were, Zerubbabel, and Shimei: and the sons of Zerubbabel; Meshullam, and Hananiah, and Shelomith their sister:

20 And Hashubah, and Ohel, and Berechiah, and Hasadiah, Jushab-hesed, five.

21 And the sons of Hananiah; Pelatiah, and Jesaiah: the sons of Rephaiah, the sons of Arnan, the sons of Obadiah, the sons of Shechaniah.

22 And the sons of Shechaniah; Shemaiah: and the sons of Shemaiah; Hattush, and Igeal, and Bariah, and Neariah, and Shaphat, six.

23 And the sons of Neariah; Elioenai, and Hezekiah, and Azrikam, three.

24 And the sons of Elioenai were, Hodaiah, and Eliashib, and Pelaiah, and Akkub, and Johanan, and Dalaiah, and Anani, seven.

CHAPTER 4

THE sons of Judah; Pharez, Hezron, and Carmi, and Hur, and Shobal.

2 And Reaiah the son of Shobal begat Jahath; and Jahath begat Ahumai, and Lahad. These are the families of the Zorathites.

3 And these were of the father of Etam; Jezreel, and Ishma, and Idbash: and the name of their sister was Hazelelponi:

4 And Penuel the father of Gedor, and Ezer the father of Hushah. These are the sons of Hur, the firstborn of Ephratah, the father of Beth-lehem.

5 And Ashur the father of Tekoa had two wives, Helah and Naarah.

6 And Naarah bare him Ahuzam, and Hepher, and Temeni, and Haahashtari. These were the sons of Naarah.

7 And the sons of Helah were, Zereth, and Jezoar, and Ethnan.

8 And Coz begat Anub, and Zobebah, and the families of Aharhel the son of Harum.

9 And Jabez was more honourable than his brethren: and his mother called his name Jabez, saying, Because I bare him with sorrow.

10 And Jabez called on the God of Israel, saying, Oh that you wouldest bless me indeed, and enlarge my coast, and that yours hand might be with me, and that you wouldest keep me from evil, that it may not grieve me! And God granted him that which he requested.

11 And Chelub the brother of Shuah begat Mehir, which was the father of Eshton.

12 And Eshton begat Beth-rapha, and Paseah, and Tehinnah the father of Ir-nahash. These are the men of Rechah.

13 And the sons of Kenaz; Othniel, and Seraiah: and the sons of Othniel; Hathath.

14 And Meonothai begat Ophrah: and Seraiah begat Joab, the father of the valley of Charashim; for they were craftsmen.

15 And the sons of Caleb the son of Jephunneh; Iru, Elah, and Naam: and the sons of Elah, even Kenaz.

16 And the sons of Jehaleleel; Ziph, and Ziphah, Tiria, and Asareel.

17 And the sons of Ezra were, Jether, and Mered, and Epher, and Jalon: and she bare Miriam, and Shammai, and Ishbah the father of Eshtemoa.

18 And his wife Jehudijah bare Jered the father of Gedor, and Heber the father of Socho, and Jekuthiel the father of Zanoah. And these are the sons of Bithiah the daughter of Pharaoh, which Mered took.

19 And the sons of his wife Hodiah the sister of Naham, the father of Keilah the Garmite, and Eshtemoa the Maachathite.

20 And the sons of Shimon were, Amnon, and Rinnah, Ben-hanan, and Tilon. And the sons of Ishi were, Zoheth, and Ben-zoheth.

21 The sons of Shelah the son of Judah were, Er the father of Lecah, and Laadah the father of Mareshah, and the families of the house of them that created fine linen, of the house of Ashbea,

22 And Jokim, and the men of Chozeba, and Joash, and Saraph, who had the dominion in Moab, and Jashubi-lehem. And these are ancient things.

23 These were the potters, and those that dwelt among plants and hedges: there they dwelt with the king for his work.

24 The sons of Simeon were, Nemuel, and Jamin, Jarib, Zerah, and Shaul:

25 Shallum his son, Mibsam his son, Mishma his son.

26 And the sons of Mishma; Hamuel his son, Zacchur his son, Shimei his son.

27 And Shimei had sixteen sons and six daughters; but his brethren had not many children, neither did all their family multiply, like to the children of Judah.

28 And they dwelt at Beer-sheba, and Moladah, and Hazar-shual,

29 And at Bilhah, and at Ezem, and at Tolad,

30 And at Bethuel, and at Hormah, and at Ziklag,

31 And at Beth-marcaboth, and Hazar-susim, and at Beth-birei, and at Shaaraim. These were their cities unto the reign of David.

32 And their villages were, Etam, and Ain, Rimmon, and Tochen, and Ashan, five cities:

33 And all their villages that were round about the same cities, unto Baal. These were their habitations, and their genealogy.

34 And Meshobab, and Jamlech, and Joshah the son of Amaziah,

35 And Joel, and Jehu the son of Josibiah, the son of Seraiah, the son of Asiel,

36 And Elioenai, and Jaakobah, and Jeshohaiah, and Asaiah, and Adiel, and Jesimiel, and Benaiah,

37 And Ziza the son of Shiphi, the son of Allon, the son of Jedaiah, the son of Shimri, the son of Shemaiah;

38 These mentioned by their names were princes in their families: and the house of their fathers increased greatly.

39 And they went to the entrance of Gedor, even unto the east side of the valley, to seek pasture for their flocks.

40 And they found fat pasture and good, and the land was wide, and quiet, and peaceable; for they of Ham had dwelt there of old.

41 And these written by name came in the days of Hezekiah king of Judah, and struck their tents, and the habitations that were found there, and destroyed them utterly unto this day, and dwelt in their rooms: because there was pasture there for their flocks.

42 And some of them, even of the sons of Simeon, five hundred men, went to mount Seir, having for their captains Pelatiah, and Neariah, and Rephaiah, and Uzziel, the sons of Ishi.

43 And they struck the rest of the Amalekites that were escaped, and dwelt there unto this day.

CHAPTER 5

NOW the sons of Reuben the firstborn of Israel, (for he was the firstborn; but, forasmuch as he defiled his father's bed, his birthright was given unto the sons of Joseph the son of Israel: and the genealogy is not to be reckoned after the birthright.

2 For Judah prevailed above his brethren, and of him came the chief ruler; but the birthright was Joseph's:)

3 The sons, I say, of Reuben the firstborn of Israel were, Hanoch, and Pallu, Hezron, and Carmi.

4 The sons of Joel; Shemaiah his son, Gog his son, Shimei his son,

5 Micah his son, Reaia his son, Baal his son,

6 Beerah his son, whom Tilgath-pilneser king of Assyria carried away captive: he was prince of the Reubenites.

7 And his brethren by their families, when the genealogy of their generations was reckoned, were the chief, Jeiel, and Zechariah,

8 And Bela the son of Azaz, the son of Shema, the son of Joel, who dwelt in Aroer, even unto Nebo and Baal-meon:

9 And eastward he inhabited unto the entering in of the wilderness from the river Euphrates: because their cattle were multiplied in the land of Gilead.

10 And in the days of Saul they made war with the Hagarites, who fell by their hand: and they dwelt in their tents throughout all the east land of Gilead.

11 And the children of Gad dwelt over against them, in the land of Bashan unto Salchah:

12 Joel the chief, and Shapham the next, and Jaanai, and Shaphat in Bashan.

13 And their brethren of the house of their fathers were, Michael, and Meshullam, and Sheba, and Jorai, and Jachan, and Zia, and Heber, seven.

14 These are the children of Abihail the son of Huri, the son of Jaroah, the son of Gilead, the son of Michael, the son of Jeshishai, the son of Jahdo, the son of Buz;

15 Ahi the son of Abdiel, the son of Guni, chief of the house of their fathers.

16 And they dwelt in Gilead in Bashan, and in her towns, and in all the suburbs of Sharon, upon their borders.

17 All these were reckoned by genealogies in the days of Jotham king of Judah, and in the days of Jeroboam king of Israel.

18 The sons of Reuben, and the Gadites, and half the tribe of Manasseh, of valiant men, men able to bear buckler and sword, and to shoot with bow, and skilful in war, were four and forty thousand seven hundred and threescore, that went out to the war.

19 And they made war with the Hagarites, with Jetur, and Nephish, and Nodab.

20 And they were helped against them, and the Hagarites were delivered into their hand, and all that were with them: for they cried to God in the battle, and he was intreated of them; because they put their trust in him.

21 And they took away their cattle; of their camels fifty thousand, and of sheep two hundred and fifty thousand, and of asses two thousand, and of men an hundred thousand.

22 For there fell down many slain, because the war was of God. And they dwelt in their steads until the captivity.

23 And the children of the half tribe of Manasseh dwelt in the land: they increased from Bashan unto Baal-hermon and Senir, and unto mount Hermon.

24 And these were the heads of the house of their fathers, even Epher, and Ishi, and Eliel, and Azriel, and Jeremiah, and Hodaviah, and Jahdiel, mighty men of valour, famous men, and heads of the house of their fathers.

25 And they transgressed against the God of their fathers, and went a whoring after the gods of the people of the land, whom God destroyed before them.

26 And the God of Israel stirred up the spirit of Pul king of Assyria, and the spirit of Tilgath-pilneser king of Assyria, and he carried them away, even the Reubenites, and the Gadites, and the half tribe of Manasseh, and brought them unto Halah, and Habor, and Hara, and to the river Gozan, unto this day.

CHAPTER 6

THE sons of Levi; Gershon, Kohath, and Merari.

2 And the sons of Kohath; Amram, Izhar, and Hebron, and Uzziel.

3 And the children of Amram; Aaron, and Moses, and Miriam. The sons also of Aaron; Nadab, and Abihu, Eleazar, and Ithamar.

4 Eleazar begat Phinehas, Phinehas begat Abishua,

5 And Abishua begat Bukki, and Bukki begat Uzzi,

6 And Uzzi begat Zerahiah, and Zerahiah begat Meraioth,

7 Meraioth begat Amariah, and Amariah begat Ahitub,

8 And Ahitub begat Zadok, and Zadok begat Ahimaaz,

9 And Ahimaaz begat Azariah, and Azariah begat Johanan,

10 And Johanan begat Azariah, (he it is that executed the priest's office in the temple that Solomon built in Jerusalem:)

11 And Azariah begat Amariah, and Amariah begat Ahitub,

12 And Ahitub begat Zadok, and Zadok begat Shallum,

13 And Shallum begat Hilkiah, and Hilkiah begat Azariah,

14 And Azariah begat Seraiah, and Seraiah begat Jehozadak,

15 And Jehozadak went into captivity, when the LORD carried away Judah and Jerusalem by the hand of Nebuchadnezzar.

16 The sons of Levi; Gershom, Kohath, and Merari.

17 And these be the names of the sons of Gershom; Libni, and Shimei.

18 And the sons of Kohath were, Amram, and Izhar, and Hebron, and Uzziel.

19 The sons of Merari; Mahli, and Mushi. And these are the families of the Levites according to their fathers.

20 Of Gershom; Libni his son, Jahath his son, Zimmah his son,

21 Joah his son, Iddo his son, Zerah his son, Jeaterai his son.

22 The sons of Kohath; Amminadab his son, Korah his son, Assir his son,

23 Elkanah his son, and Ebiasaph his son, and Assir his son,

24 Tahath his son, Uriel his son, Uzziah his son, and Shaul his son.

25 And the sons of Elkanah; Amasai, and Ahimoth.

26 As for Elkanah: the sons of Elkanah; Zophai his son, and Nahath his son,

27 Eliab his son, Jeroham his son, Elkanah his son.

28 And the sons of Samuel; the firstborn Vashni, and Abiah.

29 The sons of Merari; Mahli, Libni his son, Shimei his son, Uzza his son,

30 Shimea his son, Haggiah his son, Asaiah his son.

31 And these are they whom David set over the service of song in the house of the LORD, after that the ark had rest.

32 And they ministered before the dwelling place of the tabernacle of the congregation with singing, until Solomon had built the house of the LORD in Jerusalem: and then they waited on their office according to their order.

33 And these are they that waited with their children. Of the sons of the Kohathites: Heman a singer, the son of Joel, the son of Shemuel,

34 The son of Elkanah, the son of Jeroham, the son of Eliel, the son of Toah,

35 The son of Zuph, the son of Elkanah, the son of Mahath, the son of Amasai,

36 The son of Elkanah, the son of Joel, the son of Azariah, the son of Zephaniah,

37 The son of Tahath, the son of Assir, the son of Ebiasaph, the son of Korah,

38 The son of Izhar, the son of Kohath, the son of Levi, the son of Israel.

39 And his brother Asaph, who stood on his right hand, even Asaph the son of Berachiah, the son of Shimea,

40 The son of Michael, the son of Baaseiah, the son of Malchiah,

41 The son of Ethni, the son of Zerah, the son of Adaiah,

42 The son of Ethan, the son of Zimmah, the son of Shimei,

43 The son of Jahath, the son of Gershom, the son of Levi.

44 And their brethren the sons of Merari stood on the left hand: Ethan the son of Kishi, the son of Abdi, the son of Malluch,

45 The son of Hashabiah, the son of Amaziah, the son of Hilkiah,

46 The son of Amzi, the son of Bani, the son of Shamer,

47 The son of Mahli, the son of Mushi, the son of Merari, the son of Levi.

48 Their brethren also the Levites were appointed unto all manner of service of the tabernacle of the house of God.

49 But Aaron and his sons offered upon the altar of the burnt offering, and on the altar of incense, and were appointed for all the work of the place most holy, and to make an atonement for Israel, according to all that Moses the servant of God had commanded.

50 And these are the sons of Aaron; Eleazar his son, Phinehas his son, Abishua his son,

51 Bukki his son, Uzzi his son, Zerahiah his son,

52 Meraioth his son, Amariah his son, Ahitub his son,

53 Zadok his son, Ahimaaz his son.

54 Now these are their dwelling places throughout their castles in their coasts, of the sons of Aaron, of the families of the Kohathites: for theirs was the lot.

55 And they gave them Hebron in the land of Judah, and the suburbs thereof round about it.

56 But the fields of the city, and the villages thereof, they gave to Caleb the son of Jephunneh.

57 And to the sons of Aaron they gave the cities of Judah, namely, Hebron, the city of refuge, and Libnah with her suburbs, and Jattir, and Eshtemoa, with their suburbs,

58 And Hilen with her suburbs, Debir with her suburbs,

59 And Ashan with her suburbs, and Beth-shemesh with her suburbs:

60 And out of the tribe of Benjamin; Geba with her suburbs, and Alemeth with her suburbs, and Anathoth with her suburbs. All their cities throughout their families were thirteen cities.

61 And unto the sons of Kohath, which were left of the family of that tribe, were cities given out of the half tribe, namely, out of the half tribe of Manasseh, by lot, ten cities.

62 And to the sons of Gershom throughout their families out of the tribe of Issachar, and out of the tribe of Asher, and out of the tribe of Naphtali, and out of the tribe of Manasseh in Bashan, thirteen cities.

63 Unto the sons of Merari were given by lot, throughout their families, out of the tribe of Reuben, and out of the tribe of Gad, and out of the tribe of Zebulun, twelve cities.

64 And the children of Israel gave to the Levites these cities with their suburbs.

65 And they gave by lot out of the tribe of the children of Judah, and out of the tribe of the children of Simeon, and out of the tribe of the children of Benjamin, these cities, which are called by their names.

66 And the residue of the families of the sons of Kohath had cities of their coasts out of the tribe of Ephraim.

67 And they gave unto them, of the cities of refuge, Shechem in mount Ephraim with her suburbs; they gave also Gezer with her suburbs,

68 And Jokmeam with her suburbs, and Beth-horon with her suburbs,

69 And Aijalon with her suburbs, and Gath-rimmon with her suburbs:

70 And out of the half tribe of Manasseh; Aner with her suburbs, and Bileam with her suburbs, for the family of the remnant of the sons of Kohath.

71 Unto the sons of Gershom were given out of the family of the half tribe of Manasseh, Golan in Bashan with her suburbs, and Ashtaroth with her suburbs:

72 And out of the tribe of Issachar; Kedesh with her suburbs, Daberath with her suburbs,

73 And Ramoth with her suburbs, and Anem with her suburbs:

74 And out of the tribe of Asher; Mashal with her suburbs, and Abdon with her suburbs,

75 And Hukok with her suburbs, and Rehob with her suburbs:

76 And out of the tribe of Naphtali; Kedesh in Galilee with her suburbs, and Hammon with her suburbs, and Kirjathaim with her suburbs.

77 Unto the rest of the children of Merari were given out of the tribe of Zebulun, Rimmon with her suburbs, Tabor with her suburbs:

78 And on the other side Jordan by Jericho, on the east side of Jordan, were given them out of the tribe of Reuben, Bezer in the wilderness with her suburbs, and Jahzah with her suburbs,

79 Kedemoth also with her suburbs, and Mephaath with her suburbs:

80 And out of the tribe of Gad; Ramoth in Gilead with her suburbs, and Mahanaim with her suburbs,

81 And Heshbon with her suburbs, and Jazer with her suburbs.

CHAPTER 7

NOW the sons of Issachar were, Tola, and Puah, Jashub, and Shimron, four.

2 And the sons of Tola; Uzzi, and Rephaiah, and Jeriel, and Jahmai, and Jibsam, and Shemuel, heads of their father's house, to wit, of Tola: they were valiant men of might in their generations; whose number was in the days of David two and twenty thousand and six hundred.

3 And the sons of Uzzi; Izrahiah: and the sons of Izrahiah; Michael, and Obadiah, and Joel, Ishiah, five: all of them chief men.

4 And with them, by their generations, after the house of their fathers, were bands of soldiers for war, six and thirty thousand men: for they had many wives and sons.

5 And their brethren among all the families of Issachar were valiant men of might, reckoned in all by their genealogies fourscore and seven thousand.

6 The sons of Benjamin; Bela, and Becher, and Jediael, three.

7 And the sons of Bela; Ezbon, and Uzzi, and Uzziel, and Jerimoth, and Iri, five; heads of the house of their fathers, mighty men of valour; and were reckoned by their genealogies twenty and two thousand and thirty and four.

8 And the sons of Becher; Zemira, and Joash, and Eliezer, and Elioenai, and Omri, and Jerimoth, and Abiah, and Anathoth, and Alameth. All these are the sons of Becher.

9 And the number of them, after their genealogy by their generations, heads of the house of their fathers, mighty men of valour, was twenty thousand and two hundred.

10 The sons also of Jediael; Bilhan: and the sons of Bilhan; Jeush, and Benjamin, and Ehud, and Chenaanah, and Zethan, and Tharshish, and Ahishahar.

11 All these the sons of Jediael, by the heads of their fathers, mighty men of valour, were seventeen thousand and two hundred soldiers, fit to go out for war and battle.

12 Shuppim also, and Huppim, the children of Ir, and Hushim, the sons of Aher.

13 The sons of Naphtali; Jahziel, and Guni, and Jezer, and Shallum, the sons of Bilhah.

14 The sons of Manasseh; Ashriel, whom she bare: (but his concubine the Aramitess bare Machir the father of Gilead:

15 And Machir took to wife the sister of Huppim and Shuppim, whose sister's name was Maachah;) and the name of the second was Zelophehad: and Zelophehad had daughters.

16 And Maachah the wife of Machir bare a son, and she called his name Peresh; and the name of his brother was Sheresh; and his sons were Ulam and Rakem.

17 And the sons of Ulam; Bedan. These were the sons of Gilead, the son of Machir, the son of Manasseh.

18 And his sister Hammoleketh bare Ishod, and Abiezer, and Mahalah.

19 And the sons of Shemida were, Ahian, and Shechem, and Likhi, and Aniam.

20 And the sons of Ephraim; Shuthelah, and Bered his son, and Tahath his son, and Eladah his son, and Tahath his son,

21 And Zabad his son, and Shuthelah his son, and Ezer, and Elead, whom the men of Gath that were born in that land slew, because they came down to take away their cattle.

22 And Ephraim their father mourned many days, and his brethren came to comfort him.

23 And when he went in to his wife, she conceived, and bare a son, and he called his name Beriah, because it went evil with his house.

24 (And his daughter was Sherah, who built Beth-horon the nether, and the upper, and Uzzen-sherah.)

25 And Rephah was his son, also Resheph, and Telah his son, and Tahan his son,

26 Laadan his son, Ammihud his son, Elishama his son,

27 Non his son, Jehoshua his son.

28 And their possessions and habitations were, Beth-el and the towns thereof, and eastward Naaran, and westward Gezer, with the towns thereof; Shechem also and the towns thereof, unto Gaza and the towns thereof:

29 And by the borders of the children of Manasseh, Beth-shean and her towns, Taanach and her towns, Megiddo and her towns, Dor and her towns. In these dwelt the children of Joseph the son of Israel.

30 The sons of Asher; Imnah, and Isuah, and Ishuai, and Beriah, and Serah their sister.

31 And the sons of Beriah; Heber, and Malchiel, who is the father of Birzavith.

32 And Heber begat Japhlet, and Shomer, and Hotham, and Shua their sister.

33 And the sons of Japhlet; Pasach, and Bimhal, and Ashvath. These are the children of Japhlet.

34 And the sons of Shamer; Ahi, and Rohgah, Jehubbah, and Aram.

35 And the sons of his brother Helem; Zophah, and Imna, and Shelesh, and Amal.

36 The sons of Zophah; Suah, and Harnepher, and Shual, and Beri, and Imrah,

37 Bezer, and Hod, and Shamma, and Shilshah, and Ithran, and Beera.

38 And the sons of Jether; Jephunneh, and Pispah, and Ara.

39 And the sons of Ulla; Arah, and Haniel, and Rezia.

40 All these were the children of Asher, heads of their father's house, choice and mighty men of valour, chief of the princes. And the number throughout the genealogy of them that were apt to the war and to battle was twenty and six thousand men.

CHAPTER 8

NOW Benjamin begat Bela his firstborn, Ashbel the second, and Aharah the third,

2 Nohah the fourth, and Rapha the fifth.

3 And the sons of Bela were, Addar, and Gera, and Abihud,

4 And Abishua, and Naaman, and Ahoah,

5 And Gera, and Shephuphan, and Huram.

6 And these are the sons of Ehud: these are the heads of the fathers of the inhabitants of Geba, and they removed them to Manahath:

7 And Naaman, and Ahiah, and Gera, he removed them, and begat Uzza, and Ahihud.

8 And Shaharaim begat children in the country of Moab, after he had sent them away; Hushim and Baara were his wives.

9 And he begat of Hodesh his wife, Jobab, and Zibia, and Mesha, and Malcham,

10 And Jeuz, and Shachia, and Mirma. These were his sons, heads of the fathers.

11 And of Hushim he begat Abitub, and Elpaal.

12 The sons of Elpaal; Eber, and Misham, and Shamed, who built Ono, and Lod, with the towns thereof:

13 Beriah also, and Shema, who were heads of the fathers of the inhabitants of Aijalon, who drove away the inhabitants of Gath:

14 And Ahio, Shashak, and Jeremoth,

15 And Zebadiah, and Arad, and Ader,

16 And Michael, and Ispah, and Joha, the sons of Beriah;

17 And Zebadiah, and Meshullam, and Hezeki, and Heber,

18 Ishmerai also, and Jezliah, and Jobab, the sons of Elpaal;

19 And Jakim, and Zichri, and Zabdi,

20 And Elienai, and Zilthai, and Eliel,

21 And Adaiah, and Beraiah, and Shimrath, the sons of Shimhi;

22 And Ishpan, and Heber, and Eliel,

23 And Abdon, and Zichri, and Hanan,

24 And Hananiah, and Elam, and Antothijah,

25 And Iphedeiah, and Penuel, the sons of Shashak;

26 And Shamsherai, and Shehariah, and Athaliah,

27 And Jaresiah, and Eliah, and Zichri, the sons of Jeroham.

28 These were heads of the fathers, by their generations, chief men. These dwelt in Jerusalem.

29 And at Gibeon dwelt the father of Gibeon; whose wife's name was Maachah:

30 And his firstborn son Abdon, and Zur, and Kish, and Baal, and Nadab,

31 And Gedor, and Ahio, and Zacher.

32 And Mikloth begat Shimeah. And these also dwelt with their brethren in Jerusalem, over against them.

33 And Ner begat Kish, and Kish begat Saul, and Saul begat Jonathan, and Malchi-shua, and Abinadab, and Esh-baal.

34 And the son of Jonathan was Merib-baal; and Merib-baal begat Micah.

35 And the sons of Micah were, Pithon, and Melech, and Tarea, and Ahaz.

36 And Ahaz begat Jehoadah; and Jehoadah begat Alemeth, and Azmaveth, and Zimri; and Zimri begat Moza,

37 And Moza begat Binea: Rapha was his son, Eleasah his son, Azel his son:

38 And Azel had six sons, whose names are these, Azrikam, Bocheru, and Ishmael, and Sheariah, and Obadiah, and Hanan. All these were the sons of Azel.

39 And the sons of Eshek his brother were, Ulam his firstborn, Jehush the second, and Eliphelet the third.

40 And the sons of Ulam were mighty men of valour, archers, and had many sons, and sons' sons, an hundred and fifty. All these are of the sons of Benjamin.

CHAPTER 9

SO all Israel were reckoned by genealogies; and, behold, they were written in the book of the kings of Israel and Judah, who were carried away to Babylon for their transgression.

2 Now the first inhabitants that dwelt in their possessions in their cities were, the Israelites, the priests, Levites, and the Nethinims.

3 And in Jerusalem dwelt of the children of Judah, and of the children of Benjamin, and of the children of Ephraim, and Manasseh;

4 Uthai the son of Ammihud, the son of Omri, the son of Imri, the son of Bani, of the children of Pharez the son of Judah.

5 And of the Shilonites; Asaiah the firstborn, and his sons.

6 And of the sons of Zerah; Jeuel, and their brethren, six hundred and ninety.

7 And of the sons of Benjamin; Sallu the son of Meshullam, the son of Hodaviah, the son of Hasenuah,

8 And Ibneiah the son of Jeroham, and Elah the son of Uzzi, the son of Michri, and Meshullam the son of Shephathiah, the son of Reuel, the son of Ibnijah;

9 And their brethren, according to their generations, nine hundred and fifty and six. All these men were chief of the fathers in the house of their fathers.

10 And of the priests; Jedaiah, and Jehoiarib, and Jachin,

11 And Azariah the son of Hilkiah, the son of Meshullam, the son of Zadok, the son of Meraioth, the son of Ahitub, the ruler of the house of God;

12 And Adaiah the son of Jeroham, the son of Pashur, the son of Malchijah, and Maasiai the son of Adiel, the son of Jahzerah, the son of Meshullam, the son of Meshillemith, the son of Immer;

13 And their brethren, heads of the house of their fathers, a thousand and seven hundred and threescore; very able men for the work of the service of the house of God.

14 And of the Levites; Shemaiah the son of Hasshub, the son of Azrikam, the son of Hashabiah, of the sons of Merari;

15 And Bakbakkar, Heresh, and Galal, and Mattaniah the son of Micah, the son of Zichri, the son of Asaph;

16 And Obadiah the son of Shemaiah, the son of Galal, the son of Jeduthun, and Berechiah the son of Asa, the son of Elkanah, that dwelt in the villages of the Netophathites.

17 And the porters were, Shallum, and Akkub, and Talmon, and Ahiman, and their brethren: Shallum was the chief;

18 Who hitherto waited in the king's gate eastward: they were porters in the companies of the children of Levi.

19 And Shallum the son of Kore, the son of Ebiasaph, the son of Korah, and his brethren, of the house of his father, the Korahites, were over the work of the service, keepers of the gates of the tabernacle: and their fathers, being over the host of the LORD, were keepers of the entry.

20 And Phinehas the son of Eleazar was the ruler over them in time past, and the LORD was with him.

21 And Zechariah the son of Meshelemiah was porter of the door of the tabernacle of the congregation.

22 All these which were chosen to be porters in the gates were two hundred and twelve. These were reckoned by their genealogy in their villages, whom David and Samuel the seer did ordain in their set office.

23 So they and their children had the oversight of the gates of the house of the LORD, namely, the house of the tabernacle, by wards.

24 In four quarters were the porters, toward the east, west, north, and south.

25 And their brethren, which were in their villages, were to come after seven days from time to time with them.

26 For these Levites, the four chief porters, were in their set office, and were over the chambers and treasuries of the house of God.

27 And they lodged round about the house of God, because the charge was upon them, and the opening thereof every morning pertained to them.

28 And certain of them had the charge of the ministering vessels, that they should bring them in and out by tale.

29 Some of them also were appointed to oversee the vessels, and all the instruments of the sanctuary, and the fine flour, and the wine, and the oil, and the frankincense, and the spices.

30 And some of the sons of the priests made the ointment of the spices.

31 And Mattithiah, one of the Levites, who was the firstborn of Shallum the Korahite, had the set office over the things that were made in the pans.

32 And other of their brethren, of the sons of the Kohathites, were over the shewbread, to prepare it every sabbath.

33 And these are the singers, chief of the fathers of the Levites, who remaining in the chambers were free: for they were employed in that work day and night.

34 These chief fathers of the Levites were chief throughout their generations; these dwelt at Jerusalem.

35 And in Gibeon dwelt the father of Gibeon, Jehiel, whose wife's name was Maachah:

36 And his firstborn son Abdon, then Zur, and Kish, and Baal, and Ner, and Nadab,

37 And Gedor, and Ahio, and Zechariah, and Mikloth.

38 And Mikloth begat Shimeam. And they also dwelt with their brethren at Jerusalem, over against their brethren.

39 And Ner begat Kish; and Kish begat Saul; and Saul begat Jonathan, and Malchi-shua, and Abinadab, and Esh-baal.

40 And the son of Jonathan was Merib-baal: and Merib-baal begat Micah.

41 And the sons of Micah were, Pithon, and Melech, and Tahrea, and Ahaz.

42 And Ahaz begat Jarah; and Jarah begat Alemeth, and Azmaveth, and Zimri; and Zimri begat Moza;

43 And Moza begat Binea; and Rephaiah his son, Eleasah his son, Azel his son.

44 And Azel had six sons, whose names are these, Azrikam, Bocheru, and Ishmael, and Sheariah, and Obadiah, and Hanan: these were the sons of Azel.

CHAPTER 10

NOW the Philistines fought against Israel; and the men of Israel fled from before the Philistines, and fell down slain in mount Gilboa.

2 And the Philistines followed hard after Saul, and after his sons; and the Philistines slew Jonathan, and Abinadab, and Malchi-shua, the sons of Saul.

3 And the battle went sore against Saul, and the archers hit him, and he was wounded of the archers.

4 Then said Saul to his armourbearer, Draw your sword, and thrust me through therewith; lest these uncircumcised come and abuse me. But his armourbearer would not; for he was sore afraid. So Saul took a sword, and fell upon it.

5 And when his armourbearer saw that Saul was dead, he fell likewise on the sword, and died.

6 So Saul died, and his three sons, and all his house died together.

7 And when all the men of Israel that were in the valley saw that they fled, and that Saul and his sons were dead, then they forsook their cities, and fled: and the Philistines came and dwelt in them.

8 And it came to pass on the morrow, when the Philistines came to strip the slain, that they found Saul and his sons fallen in mount Gilboa.

9 And when they had stripped him, they took his head, and his armour, and sent into the land of the Philistines round about, to carry tidings unto their idols, and to the people.

10 And they put his armour in the house of their gods, and fastened his head in the temple of Dagon.

11 And when all Jabesh-gilead heard all that the Philistines had done to Saul,

12 They arose, all the valiant men, and took away the body of Saul, and the bodies of his sons, and brought them to Jabesh, and buried their bones under the oak in Jabesh, and fasted seven days.

13 So Saul died for his transgression which he committed against the LORD, even against the word of the LORD, which he kept not, and also for asking counsel of one that had a familiar spirit, to inquire of it;

14 And inquired not of the LORD: therefore he slew him, and turned the kingdom unto David the son of Jesse.

CHAPTER 11

THEN all Israel gathered themselves to David unto Hebron, saying, Behold, we are your bone and your flesh.

2 And moreover in time past, even when Saul was king, you wast he that leddest out and broughtest in Israel: and the LORD your God said unto you, You shalt feed my people Israel, and you shalt be ruler over my people Israel.

3 Therefore came all the elders of Israel to the king to Hebron; and David made a covenant with them in Hebron before the LORD; and they anointed David king over Israel, according to the word of the LORD by Samuel.

4 And David and all Israel went to Jerusalem, which is Jebus; where the Jebusites were, the inhabitants of the land.

5 And the inhabitants of Jebus said to David, You shalt not come hither. Nevertheless David took the castle of Zion, which is the city of David.

6 And David said, Whosoever smiteth the Jebusites first shall be chief and captain. So Joab the son of Zeruiah went first up, and was chief.

7 And David dwelt in the castle; therefore they called it the city of David.

8 And he built the city round about, even from Millo round about: and Joab repaired the rest of the city.

9 So David waxed greater and greater: for the LORD of hosts was with him.

10 These also are the chief of the mighty men whom David had, who strengthened themselves with him in his kingdom, and with all Israel, to make him king, according to the word of the LORD concerning Israel.

11 And this is the number of the mighty men whom David had; Jashobeam, an Hachmonite, the chief of the captains: he lifted up his spear against three hundred slain by him at one time.

12 And after him was Eleazar the son of Dodo, the Ahohite, who was one of the three mighties.

13 He was with David at Pas-dammim, and there the Philistines were gathered together to battle, where was a parcel of ground full of barley; and the people fled from before the Philistines.

14 And they set themselves in the midst of that parcel, and delivered it, and slew the Philistines; and the LORD saved them by a great deliverance.

15 Now three of the thirty captains went down to the rock to David, into the cave of Adullam; and the host of the Philistines encamped in the valley of Rephaim.

16 And David was then in the hold, and the Philistines' garrison was then at Beth-lehem.

17 And David longed, and said, Oh that one would give me drink of the water of the well of Beth-lehem, that is at the gate!

18 And the three brake through the host of the Philistines, and drew water out of the well of Beth-lehem, that was by the gate, and took it, and brought it to David: but David would not drink of it, but poured it out to the LORD,

19 And said, My God forbid it me, that I should do this thing: shall I drink the blood of these men that have put their lives in jeopardy? for with the jeopardy of their lives they brought it. Therefore he would not drink it. These things did these three mightiest.

20 And Abishai the brother of Joab, he was chief of the three: for lifting up his spear against three hundred, he slew them, and had a name among the three.

21 Of the three, he was more honourable than the two; for he was their captain: howbeit he attained not to the first three.

22 Benaiah the son of Jehoiada, the son of a valiant man of Kabzeel, who had done many acts; he slew two lionlike men of Moab: also he went down and slew a lion in a pit in a snowy day.

23 And he slew an Egyptian, a man of great stature, five cubits high; and in the Egyptian's hand was a spear like a weaver's beam; and he went down to him with a staff, and plucked the spear out of the Egyptian's hand, and slew him with his own spear.

24 These things did Benaiah the son of Jehoiada, and had the name among the three mighties.

25 Behold, he was honourable among the thirty, but attained not to the first three: and David set him over his guard.

26 Also the valiant men of the armies were, Asahel the brother of Joab, Elhanan the son of Dodo of Beth-lehem,

27 Shammoth the Harorite, Helez the Pelonite,

28 Ira the son of Ikkesh the Tekoite, Abi-ezer the Antothite,

29 Sibbecai the Hushathite, Ilai the Ahohite,

30 Maharai the Netophathite, Heled the son of Baanah the Netophathite,

31 Ithai the son of Ribai of Gibeah, that pertained to the children of Benjamin, Benaiah the Pirathonite,

32 Hurai of the brooks of Gaash, Abiel the Arbathite,

33 Azmaveth the Baharumite, Eliahba the Shaalbonite,

34 The sons of Hashem the Gizonite, Jonathan the son of Shage the Hararite,

35 Ahiam the son of Sacar the Hararite, Eliphal the son of Ur,

36 Hepher the Mecherathite, Ahijah the Pelonite,

37 Hezro the Carmelite, Naarai the son of Ezbai,

38 Joel the brother of Nathan, Mibhar the son of Haggeri,

39 Zelek the Ammonite, Naharai the Berothite, the armourbearer of Joab the son of Zeruiah,

40 Ira the Ithrite, Gareb the Ithrite,

41 Uriah the Hittite, Zabad the son of Ahlai,

42 Adina the son of Shiza the Reubenite, a captain of the Reubenites, and thirty with him,

43 Hanan the son of Maachah, and Joshaphat the Mithnite,

44 Uzzia the Ashterathite, Shama and Jehiel the sons of Hothan the Aroerite,

45 Jediael the son of Shimri, and Joha his brother, the Tizite,

46 Eliel the Mahavite, and Jeribai, and Joshaviah, the sons of Elnaam, and Ithmah the Moabite,

47 Eliel, and Obed, and Jasiel the Mesobaite.

CHAPTER 12

NOW these are they that came to David to Ziklag, while he yet kept himself close because of Saul the son of Kish: and they were among the mighty men, helpers of the war.

2 They were armed with bows, and could use both the right hand and the left in hurling stones and shooting arrows out of a bow, even of Saul's brethren of Benjamin.

3 The chief was Ahiezer, then Joash, the sons of Shemaah the Gibeathite; and Jeziel, and Pelet, the sons of Azmaveth; and Berachah, and Jehu the Antothite,

4 And Ismaiah the Gibeonite, a mighty man among the thirty, and over the thirty; and Jeremiah, and Jahaziel, and Johanan, and Josabad the Gederathite,

5 Eluzai, and Jerimoth, and Bealiah, and Shemariah, and Shephatiah the Haruphite,

6 Elkanah, and Jesiah, and Azareel, and Joezer, and Jashobeam, the Korhites,

7 And Joelah, and Zebadiah, the sons of Jeroham of Gedor.

8 And of the Gadites there separated themselves unto David into the hold to the wilderness men of might, and men of war fit for the battle, that could handle shield and buckler, whose faces were like the faces of lions, and were as swift as the roes upon the mountains;

9 Ezer the first, Obadiah the second, Eliab the third,

10 Mishmannah the fourth, Jeremiah the fifth,

11 Attai the sixth, Eliel the seventh,

12 Johanan the eighth, Elzabad the ninth,

13 Jeremiah the tenth, Machbanai the eleventh.

14 These were of the sons of Gad, captains of the host: one of the least was over an hundred, and the greatest over a thousand.

15 These are they that went over Jordan in the first month, when it had overflown all his banks; and they put to flight all them of the valleys, both toward the east, and toward the west.

16 And there came of the children of Benjamin and Judah to the hold unto David.

17 And David went out to meet them, and answered and said unto them, If you be come peaceably unto me to help me, my heart shall be knit unto you: but if you be come to betray me to my enemies, seeing there is no wrong in my hands, the God of our fathers look thereon, and rebuke it.

18 Then the spirit came upon Amasai, who was chief of the captains, and he said, Yours are we, David, and on your side, you son of Jesse: peace, peace be unto you, and peace be to yours helpers; for your God helpeth you. Then David received them, and made them captains of the band.

19 And there fell some of Manasseh to David, when he came with the Philistines against Saul to battle: but they helped them not: for the lords of the Philistines upon advisement sent him away, saying, He will fall to his master Saul to the jeopardy of our heads.

20 As he went to Ziklag, there fell to him of Manasseh, Adnah, and Jozabad, and Jediael, and Michael, and Jozabad, and Elihu, and Zilthai, captains of the thousands that were of Manasseh.

21 And they helped David against the band of the rovers: for they were all mighty men of valour, and were captains in the host.

22 For at that time day by day there came to David to help him, until it was a great host, like the host of God.

23 And these are the numbers of the bands that were ready armed to the war, and came to David to Hebron, to turn the kingdom of Saul to him, according to the word of the LORD.

24 The children of Judah that bare shield and spear were six thousand and eight hundred, ready armed to the war.

25 Of the children of Simeon, mighty men of valour for the war, seven thousand and one hundred.

26 Of the children of Levi four thousand and six hundred.

27 And Jehoiada was the leader of the Aaronites, and with him were three thousand and seven hundred;

28 And Zadok, a young man mighty of valour, and of his father's house twenty and two captains.

29 And of the children of Benjamin, the kindred of Saul, three thousand: for hitherto the greatest part of them had kept the ward of the house of Saul.

30 And of the children of Ephraim twenty thousand and eight hundred, mighty men of valour, famous throughout the house of their fathers.

31 And of the half tribe of Manasseh eighteen thousand, which were expressed by name, to come and make David king.

32 And of the children of Issachar, which were men that had understanding of the times, to know what Israel ought to do; the heads of them were two hundred; and all their brethren were at their commandment.

33 Of Zebulun, such as went forth to battle, expert in war, with all instruments of war, fifty thousand, which could keep rank: they were not of double heart.

34 And of Naphtali a thousand captains, and with them with shield and spear thirty and seven thousand.

35 And of the Danites expert in war twenty and eight thousand and six hundred.

36 And of Asher, such as went forth to battle, expert in war, forty thousand.

37 And on the other side of Jordan, of the Reubenites, and the Gadites, and of the half tribe of Manasseh, with all manner of instruments of war for the battle, an hundred and twenty thousand.

38 All these men of war, that could keep rank, came with a perfect heart to Hebron, to make David king over all Israel: and all the rest also of Israel were of one heart to make David king.

39 And there they were with David three days, eating and drinking: for their brethren had prepared for them.

40 Moreover they that were nigh them, even unto Issachar and Zebulun and Naphtali, brought bread on asses, and on camels, and on mules, and on oxen, and meat, meal, cakes of figs, and bunches of raisins, and wine, and oil, and oxen, and sheep abundantly: for there was joy in Israel.

CHAPTER 13

AND David consulted with the captains of thousands and hundreds, and with every leader.

2 And David said unto all the congregation of Israel, If it seem good unto you, and that it be of the LORD our God, let us send abroad unto our brethren every where, that are left in all the land of Israel, and with them also to the priests and Levites which are in their cities and suburbs, that they may gather themselves unto us:

3 And let us bring again the ark of our God to us: for we inquired not at it in the days of Saul.

4 And all the congregation said that they would do so: for the thing was right in the eyes of all the people.

5 So David gathered all Israel together, from Shihor of Egypt even unto the entering of Hemath, to bring the ark of God from Kirjath-jearim.

6 And David went up, and all Israel, to Baalah, that is, to Kirjath-jearim, which belonged to Judah, to bring up thence the ark of God the LORD, that dwelleth between the cherubims, whose name is called on it.

7 And they carried the ark of God in a new cart out of the house of Abinadab: and Uzza and Ahio drave the cart.

8 And David and all Israel played before God with all their might, and with singing, and with harps, and with psalteries, and with timbrels, and with cymbals, and with trumpets.

9 And when they came unto the threshingfloor of Chidon, Uzza put forth his hand to hold the ark; for the oxen stumbled.

10 And the anger of the LORD was kindled against Uzza, and he struck him, because he put his hand to the ark: and there he died before God.

11 And David was displeased, because the LORD had made a breach upon Uzza: wherefore that place is called Perez-uzza to this day.

12 And David was afraid of God that day, saying, How shall I bring the ark of God home to me?

13 So David brought not the ark home to himself to the city of David, but carried it aside into the house of Obed-edom the Gittite.

14 And the ark of God remained with the family of Obed-edom in his house three months. And the LORD blessed the house of Obed-edom, and all that he had.

CHAPTER 14

NOW Hiram king of Tyre sent messengers to David, and timber of cedars, with masons and carpenters, to build him an house.

2 And David perceived that the LORD had confirmed him king over Israel, for his kingdom was lifted up on high, because of his people Israel.

3 And David took more wives at Jerusalem: and David begat more sons and daughters.

4 Now these are the names of his children which he had in Jerusalem; Shammua, and Shobab, Nathan, and Solomon,

5 And Ibhar, and Elishua, and Elpalet,

6 And Nogah, and Nepheg, and Japhia,

7 And Elishama, and Beeliada, and Eliphalet.

8 And when the Philistines heard that David was anointed king over all Israel, all the Philistines went up to seek David. And David heard of it, and went out against them.

9 And the Philistines came and spread themselves in the valley of Rephaim.

10 And David inquired of God, saying, Shall I go up against the Philistines? and will you deliver them into my hand? And the LORD said unto him, Go up; for I will deliver them into yours hand.

11 So they came up to Baal-perazim; and David struck them there. Then David said, God has broken in upon my enemies by my hand like the breaking forth of waters: therefore they called the name of that place Baal-perazim.

12 And when they had left their gods there, David gave a commandment, and they were burned with fire.

13 And the Philistines yet again spread themselves abroad in the valley.

14 Therefore David inquired again of God; and God said unto him, Go not up after them; turn away from them, and come upon them over against the mulberry trees.

15 And it shall be, when you shalt hear a sound of going in the tops of the mulberry trees, that then you shalt go out to battle: for God is gone forth before you to strike the host of the Philistines.

16 David therefore did as God commanded him: and they struck the host of the Philistines from Gibeon even to Gazer.

17 And the fame of David went out into all lands; and the LORD brought the fear of him upon all nations.

CHAPTER 15

AND David made him houses in the city of David, and prepared a place for the ark of God, and pitched for it a tent.

2 Then David said, None ought to carry the ark of God but the Levites: for them has the LORD chosen to carry the ark of God, and to minister unto him for ever.

3 And David gathered all Israel together to Jerusalem, to bring up the ark of the LORD unto his place, which he had prepared for it.

4 And David assembled the children of Aaron, and the Levites:

5 Of the sons of Kohath; Uriel the chief, and his brethren an hundred and twenty:

6 Of the sons of Merari; Asaiah the chief, and his brethren two hundred and twenty:

7 Of the sons of Gershom; Joel the chief, and his brethren an hundred and thirty:

8 Of the sons of Elizaphan; Shemaiah the chief, and his brethren two hundred:

9 Of the sons of Hebron; Eliel the chief, and his brethren fourscore:

10 Of the sons of Uzziel; Amminadab the chief, and his brethren an hundred and twelve.

11 And David called for Zadok and Abiathar the priests, and for the Levites, for Uriel, Asaiah, and Joel, Shemaiah, and Eliel, and Amminadab,

12 And said unto them, You are the chief of the fathers of the Levites: sanctify yourselves, both you and your brethren, that you may bring up the ark of the LORD God of Israel unto the place that I have prepared for it.

13 For because you did it not at the first, the LORD our God made a breach upon us, for that we sought him not after the due order.

14 So the priests and the Levites sanctified themselves to bring up the ark of the LORD God of Israel.

15 And the children of the Levites bare the ark of God upon their shoulders with the staves thereon, as Moses commanded according to the word of the LORD.

16 And David spake to the chief of the Levites to appoint their brethren to be the singers with instruments of musick, psalteries and harps and cymbals, sounding, by lifting up the voice with joy.

17 So the Levites appointed Heman the son of Joel; and of his brethren, Asaph the son of Berechiah; and of the sons of Merari their brethren, Ethan the son of Kushaiah;

18 And with them their brethren of the second degree, Zechariah, Ben, and Jaaziel, and Shemiramoth, and Jehiel, and Unni, Eliab, and Benaiah, and Maaseiah, and Mattithiah, and Elipheleh, and Mikneiah, and Obed-edom, and Jeiel, the porters.

19 So the singers, Heman, Asaph, and Ethan, were appointed to sound with cymbals of brass;

20 And Zechariah, and Aziel, and Shemiramoth, and Jehiel, and Unni, and Eliab, and Maaseiah, and Benaiah, with psalteries on Alamoth;

21 And Mattithiah, and Elipheleh, and Mikneiah, and Obed-edom, and Jeiel, and Azaziah, with harps on the Sheminith to excel.

22 And Chenaniah, chief of the Levites, was for song: he instructed about the song, because he was skilful.

23 And Berechiah and Elkanah were doorkeepers for the ark.

24 And Shebaniah, and Jehoshaphat, and Nethaneel, and Amasai, and Zechariah, and Benaiah, and Eliezer, the priests, did blow with the trumpets before the ark of God: and Obed-edom and Jehiah were doorkeepers for the ark.

25 So David, and the elders of Israel, and the captains over thousands, went to bring up the ark of the covenant of the LORD out of the house of Obed-edom with joy.

26 And it came to pass, when God helped the Levites that bare the ark of the covenant of the LORD, that they offered seven bullocks and seven rams.

27 And David was clothed with a robe of fine linen, and all the Levites that bare the ark, and the singers, and Chenaniah the master of the song with the singers: David also had upon him an ephod of linen.

28 Thus all Israel brought up the ark of the covenant of the LORD with shouting, and with sound of the cornet, and with trumpets, and with cymbals, making a noise with psalteries and harps.

29 And it came to pass, as the ark of the covenant of the LORD came to the city of David, that Michal the daughter of Saul looking out at a window saw king David dancing and playing: and she despised him in her heart.

CHAPTER 16

SO they brought the ark of God, and set it in the midst of the tent that David had pitched for it: and they offered burnt sacrifices and peace offerings before God.

2 And when David had made an end of offering the burnt offerings and the peace offerings, he blessed the people in the name of the LORD.

3 And he dealt to every one of Israel, both man and woman, to every one a loaf of bread, and a good piece of flesh, and a flagon of wine.

4 And he appointed certain of the Levites to minister before the ark of the LORD, and to record, and to thank and praise the LORD God of Israel:

5 Asaph the chief, and next to him Zechariah, Jeiel, and Shemiramoth, and Jehiel, and Mattithiah, and Eliab, and Benaiah, and Obed-edom: and Jeiel with psalteries and with harps; but Asaph made a sound with cymbals;

6 Benaiah also and Jahaziel the priests with trumpets continually before the ark of the covenant of God.

7 Then on that day David delivered first this psalm to thank the LORD into the hand of Asaph and his brethren.

8 Give thanks unto the LORD, call upon his name, make known his deeds among the people.

9 Sing unto him, sing psalms unto him, talk you of all his wondrous works.

10 Glory you in his holy name: let the heart of them rejoice that seek the LORD.

11 Seek the LORD and his strength, seek his face continually.

12 Remember his marvellous works that he has done, his wonders, and the judgments of his mouth;

13 O you seed of Israel his servant, you children of Jacob, his chosen ones.

14 He is the LORD our God; his judgments are in all the earth.

15 Be you mindful always of his covenant; the word which he commanded to a thousand generations;

16 Even of the covenant which he made with Abraham, and of his oath unto Isaac;

17 And has confirmed the same to Jacob for a law, and to Israel for an everlasting covenant,

18 Saying, Unto you will I give the land of Canaan, the lot of your inheritance;

19 When you were but few, even a few, and strangers in it.

20 And when they went from nation to nation, and from one kingdom to another people;

21 He suffered no man to do them wrong: yea, he reproved kings for their sakes,

22 Saying, Touch not my anointed, and do my prophets no harm.

23 Sing unto the LORD, all the earth; shew forth from day to day his salvation.

24 Declare his glory among the heathen; his marvellous works among all nations.

25 For great is the LORD, and greatly to be praised: he also is to be feared above all gods.

26 For all the gods of the people are idols: but the LORD made the heavens.

27 Glory and honour are in his presence; strength and gladness are in his place.

28 Give unto the LORD, you kindreds of the people, give unto the LORD glory and strength.

29 Give unto the LORD the glory due unto his name: bring an offering, and come before him: worship the LORD in the beauty of holiness.

30 Fear before him, all the earth: the world also shall be stable, that it be not moved.

31 Let the heavens be glad, and let the earth rejoice: and let men say among the nations, The LORD reigneth.

32 Let the sea roar, and the fulness thereof: let the fields rejoice, and all that is therein.

33 Then shall the trees of the wood sing out at the presence of the LORD, because he comes to judge the earth.

34 O give thanks unto the LORD; for he is good; for his mercy endureth for ever.

35 And say you , Save us, O God of our salvation, and gather us together, and deliver us from the heathen, that we may give thanks to your holy name, and glory in your praise.

36 Blessed be the LORD God of Israel for ever and ever. And all the people said, Amen, and praised the LORD.

37 So he left there before the ark of the covenant of the LORD Asaph and his brethren, to minister before the ark continually, as every day's work required:

38 And Obed-edom with their brethren, threescore and eight; Obed-edom also the son of Jeduthun and Hosah to be porters:

39 And Zadok the priest, and his brethren the priests, before the tabernacle of the LORD in the high place that was at Gibeon,

40 To offer burnt offerings unto the LORD upon the altar of the burnt offering continually morning and evening, and to do according to all that is written in the law of the LORD, which he commanded Israel;

41 And with them Heman and Jeduthun, and the rest that were chosen, who were expressed by name, to give thanks to the LORD, because his mercy endureth for ever;

42 And with them Heman and Jeduthun with trumpets and cymbals for those that should make a sound, and with musical instruments of God. And the sons of Jeduthun were porters.

43 And all the people departed every man to his house: and David returned to bless his house.

CHAPTER 17

NOW it came to pass, as David sat in his house, that David said to Nathan the prophet, Lo, I dwell in an house of cedars, but the ark of the covenant of the LORD remaineth under curtains.

2 Then Nathan said unto David, Do all that is in yours heart; for God is with you.

3 And it came to pass the same night, that the word of God came to Nathan, saying,

4 Go and tell David my servant, Thus saith the LORD, You shalt not build me an house to dwell in:

5 For I have not dwelt in an house since the day that I brought up Israel unto this day; but have gone from tent to tent, and from one tabernacle to another.

6 Wheresoever I have walked with all Israel, spake I a word to any of the judges of Israel, whom I commanded to feed my people, saying, Why have you not built me an house of cedars?

7 Now therefore thus shalt you say unto my servant David, Thus saith the LORD of hosts, I took you from the sheepcote, even from following the sheep, that you shouldest be ruler over my people Israel:

8 And I have been with you whithersoever you have walked, and have cut off all yours enemies from before you, and have made you a name like the name of the great men that are in the earth.

9 Also I will ordain a place for my people Israel, and will plant them, and they shall dwell in their place, and shall be moved no more; neither shall the children of wickedness waste them any more, as at the beginning,

10 And since the time that I commanded judges to be over my people Israel. Moreover I will subdue all yours enemies. Furthermore I tell you that the LORD will build you an house.

11And it shall come to pass, when your days be expired that you must go to be with your fathers, that I will raise up your seed after you, which shall be of your sons; and I will establish his kingdom.

12 He shall build me an house, and I will stablish his throne for ever.

13 I will be his father, and he shall be my son: and I will not take my mercy away from him, as I took it from him that was before you:

14 But I will settle him in my house and in my kingdom for ever: and his throne shall be established for evermore.

15 According to all these words, and according to all this vision, so did Nathan speak unto David.

16And David the king came and sat before the LORD, and said, Who am I, O LORD God, and what is my house, that you have brought me hitherto?

17 And yet this was a small thing in yours eyes, O God; for you have also spoken of your servant's house for a great while to come, and have regarded me according to the estate of a man of high degree, O LORD God.

18 What can David speak more to you for the honour of your servant? for you knowest your servant.

19 O LORD, for your servant's sake, and according to yours own heart, have you done all this greatness, in making known all these great things.

20 O LORD, there is none like you, neither is there any God beside you, according to all that we have heard with our ears.

21 And what one nation in the earth is like your people Israel, whom God went to redeem to be his own people, to make you a name of greatness and terribleness, by driving out nations from before your people, whom you have redeemed out of Egypt?

22 For your people Israel did you make yours own people for ever; and you , LORD, becamest their God.

23 Therefore now, LORD, let the thing that you have spoken concerning your servant and concerning his house be established for ever, and do as you have said.

24 Let it even be established, that your name may be magnified for ever, saying, The LORD of hosts is the God of Israel, even a God to Israel: and let the house of David your servant be established before you.

25 For you , O my God, have told your servant that you will build him an house: therefore your servant has found in his heart to pray before you.

26 And now, LORD, you are God, and have promised this goodness unto your servant:

27 Now therefore let it please you to bless the house of your servant, that it may be before you for ever: for you blessest, O LORD, and it shall be blessed for ever.

CHAPTER 18

NOW after this it came to pass, that David struck the Philistines, and subdued them, and took Gath and her towns out of the hand of the Philistines.

2 And he struck Moab; and the Moabites became David's servants, and brought gifts.

3And David struck Hadarezer king of Zobah unto Hamath, as he went to stablish his dominion by the river Euphrates.

4 And David took from him a thousand chariots, and seven thousand horsemen, and twenty thousand footmen: David also houghed all the chariot horses, but reserved of them an hundred chariots.

5 And when the Syrians of Damascus came to help Hadarezer king of Zobah, David slew of the Syrians two and twenty thousand men.

6 Then David put garrisons in Syria-damascus; and the Syrians became David's servants, and brought gifts. Thus the LORD preserved David whithersoever he went.

7 And David took the shields of gold that were on the servants of Hadarezer, and brought them to Jerusalem.

8 Likewise from Tibhath, and from Chun, cities of Hadarezer, brought David very much brass, wherewith Solomon made the brasen sea, and the pillars, and the vessels of brass.

9Now when Tou king of Hamath heard how David had smitten all the host of Hadarezer king of Zobah;

10 He sent Hadoram his son to king David, to inquire of his welfare, and to congratulate him, because he had fought against Hadarezer, and smitten him; (for Hadarezer had war with Tou;) and with him all manner of vessels of gold and silver and brass.

11Them also king David dedicated unto the LORD, with the silver and the gold that he brought from all these nations; from Edom, and from Moab, and from the children of Ammon, and from the Philistines, and from Amalek.

12 Moreover Abishai the son of Zeruiah slew of the Edomites in the valley of salt eighteen thousand.

13And he put garrisons in Edom; and all the Edomites became David's servants. Thus the LORD preserved David whithersoever he went.

14So David reigned over all Israel, and executed judgment and justice among all his people.

15 And Joab the son of Zeruiah was over the host; and Jehoshaphat the son of Ahilud, recorder.

16 And Zadok the son of Ahitub, and Abimelech the son of Abiathar, were the priests; and Shavsha was scribe;

17 And Benaiah the son of Jehoiada was over the Cherethites and the Pelethites; and the sons of David were chief about the king.

CHAPTER 19

NOW it came to pass after this, that Nahash the king of the children of Ammon died, and his son reigned in his stead.

2 And David said, I will shew kindness unto Hanun the son of Nahash, because his father shewed kindness to me. And David sent messengers to comfort him concerning his father. So the servants of David came into the land of the children of Ammon to Hanun, to comfort him.

3 But the princes of the children of Ammon said to Hanun, Thinkest you that David doth honour your father, that he has sent comforters unto you? are not his servants come unto you for to search, and to overthrow, and to spy out the land?

4 Wherefore Hanun took David's servants, and shaved them, and cut off their garments in the midst hard by their buttocks, and sent them away.

5 Then there went certain, and told David how the men were served. And he sent to meet them: for the men were greatly ashamed. And the king said, Tarry at Jericho until your beards be grown, and then return.

6And when the children of Ammon saw that they had made themselves odious to David, Hanun and the children of Ammon sent a thousand talents of silver to hire them chariots and horsemen out of Mesopotamia, and out of Syria-maachah, and out of Zobah.

7 So they hired thirty and two thousand chariots, and the king of Maachah and his people; who came and pitched before Medeba. And the children of Ammon gathered themselves together from their cities, and came to battle.

8 And when David heard of it, he sent Joab, and all the host of the mighty men.

9 And the children of Ammon came out, and put the battle in array before the gate of the city: and the kings that were come were by themselves in the field.

10 Now when Joab saw that the battle was set against him before and behind, he chose out of all the choice of Israel, and put them in array against the Syrians.

11 And the rest of the people he delivered unto the hand of Abishai his brother, and they set themselves in array against the children of Ammon.

12 And he said, If the Syrians be too strong for me, then you shalt help me: but if the children of Ammon be too strong for you, then I will help you.

13 Be of good courage, and let us behave ourselves valiantly for our people, and for the cities of our God: and let the LORD do that which is good in his sight.

14 So Joab and the people that were with him drew nigh before the Syrians unto the battle; and they fled before him.

15 And when the children of Ammon saw that the Syrians were fled, they likewise fled before Abishai his brother, and entered into the city. Then Joab came to Jerusalem.

16And when the Syrians saw that they were put to the worse before Israel, they sent messengers, and drew forth the Syrians that were beyond the river: and Shophach the captain of the host of Hadarezer went before them.

17 And it was told David; and he gathered all Israel, and passed over Jordan, and came upon them, and set the battle in array against them. So when David had put the battle in array against the Syrians, they fought with him.

18 But the Syrians fled before Israel; and David slew of the Syrians seven thousand men which fought in chariots, and forty thousand footmen, and killed Shophach the captain of the host.

19 And when the servants of Hadarezer saw that they were put to the worse before Israel, they made peace with David, and became his servants: neither would the Syrians help the children of Ammon any more.

CHAPTER 20

AND it came to pass, that after the year was expired, at the time that kings go out to battle, Joab led forth the power of the army, and wasted the country of the children of Ammon, and came and besieged Rabbah. But David tarried at Jerusalem. And Joab struck Rabbah, and destroyed it.

2 And David took the crown of their king from off his head, and found it to weigh a talent of gold, and there were precious stones in it; and it was set upon David's head: and he brought also exceeding much spoil out of the city.

3 And he brought out the people that were in it, and cut them with saws, and with harrows of iron, and with axes. Even so dealt David with all the cities of the children of Ammon. And David and all the people returned to Jerusalem.

4And it came to pass after this, that there arose war at Gezer with the Philistines; at which time Sibbechai the Hushathite slew Sippai, that was of the children of the giant: and they were subdued.

5 And there was war again with the Philistines; and Elhanan the son of Jair slew Lahmi the brother of Goliath the Gittite, whose spear staff was like a weaver's beam.

6 And yet again there was war at Gath, where was a man of great stature, whose fingers and toes were four and twenty, six on each hand, and six on each foot: and he also was the son of the giant.

7 But when he defied Israel, Jonathan the son of Shimea David's brother slew him.

8 These were born unto the giant in Gath; and they fell by the hand of David, and by the hand of his servants.

CHAPTER 21

AND Satan stood up against Israel, and provoked David to number Israel.

2 And David said to Joab and to the rulers of the people, Go, number Israel from Beer-sheba even to Dan; and bring the number of them to me, that I may know it.

3 And Joab answered, The LORD make his people an hundred times so many more as they be: but, my lord the king, are they not all my lord's servants? why then doth my lord require this thing? why will he be a cause of trespass to Israel?

4 Nevertheless the king's word prevailed against Joab. Wherefore Joab departed, and went throughout all Israel, and came to Jerusalem.

5And Joab gave the sum of the number of the people unto David. And all they of Israel were a thousand thousand and an hundred thousand men that drew sword: and Judah was four hundred threescore and ten thousand men that drew sword.

6 But Levi and Benjamin counted he not among them: for the king's word was abominable to Joab.

7 And God was displeased with this thing; therefore he struck Israel.

8 And David said unto God, I have sinned greatly, because I have done this thing: but now, I beseech you, do away the iniquity of your servant; for I have done very foolishly.

9And the LORD spake unto Gad, David's seer, saying,

10 Go and tell David, saying, Thus saith the LORD, I offer you three things: choose you one of them, that I may do it unto you.

11 So Gad came to David, and said unto him, Thus saith the LORD, Choose you

12 Either three years' famine; or three months to be destroyed before your foes, while that the sword of yours enemies overtaketh you; or else three days the sword of the LORD, even the pestilence, in the land, and the angel of the LORD destroying throughout all the coasts of Israel. Now therefore advise yourself what word I shall bring again to him that sent me.

13 And David said unto Gad, I am in a great strait: let me fall now into the hand of the LORD; for very great are his mercies: but let me not fall into the hand of man.

14So the LORD sent pestilence upon Israel: and there fell of Israel seventy thousand men.

15 And God sent an angel unto Jerusalem to destroy it: and as he was destroying, the LORD beheld, and he repented him of the evil, and said to the angel that destroyed, It is enough, stay now yours hand. And the angel of the LORD stood by the threshingfloor of Ornan the Jebusite.

16 And David lifted up his eyes, and saw the angel of the LORD stand between the earth and the heaven, having a drawn sword in his hand stretched out over Jerusalem. Then David and the elders of Israel, who were clothed in sackcloth, fell upon their faces.

17 And David said unto God, Is it not I that commanded the people to be numbered? even I it is that have sinned and done evil indeed; but as for these sheep, what have they done? let yours hand, I pray you, O LORD my God, be on me, and on my father's house; but not on your people, that they should be plagued.

18Then the angel of the LORD commanded Gad to say to David, that David should go up, and set up an altar unto the LORD in the threshingfloor of Ornan the Jebusite.

19 And David went up at the saying of Gad, which he spake in the name of the LORD.

20 And Ornan turned back, and saw the angel; and his four sons with him hid themselves. Now Ornan was threshing wheat.

21 And as David came to Ornan, Ornan looked and saw David, and went out of the threshingfloor, and bowed himself to David with his face to the ground.

22 Then David said to Ornan, Grant me the place of this threshingfloor, that I may build an altar therein unto the LORD: you shalt grant it me for the full price: that the plague may be stayed from the people.

23 And Ornan said unto David, Take it to you, and let my lord the king do that which is good in his eyes: lo, I give you the oxen also for burnt offerings, and the threshing instruments for wood, and the wheat for the meat offering; I give it all.

24 And king David said to Ornan, Nay; but I will verily buy it for the full price: for I will not take that which is yours for the LORD, nor offer burnt offerings without cost.

25 So David gave to Ornan for the place six hundred shekels of gold by weight.

26 And David built there an altar unto the LORD, and offered burnt offerings and peace offerings, and called upon the LORD; and he answered him from heaven by fire upon the altar of burnt offering.

27 And the LORD commanded the angel; and he put up his sword again into the sheath thereof.

28At that time when David saw that the LORD had answered him in the threshingfloor of Ornan the Jebusite, then he sacrificed there.

29 For the tabernacle of the LORD, which Moses made in the wilderness, and the altar of the burnt offering, were at that season in the high place at Gibeon.

30 But David could not go before it to inquire of God: for he was afraid because of the sword of the angel of the LORD.

CHAPTER 22

THEN David said, This is the house of the LORD God, and this is the altar of the burnt offering for Israel.

2 And David commanded to gather together the strangers that were in the land of Israel; and he set masons to hew created stones to build the house of God.

3 And David prepared iron in abundance for the nails for the doors of the gates, and for the joinings; and brass in abundance without weight;

4 Also cedar trees in abundance: for the Zidonians and they of Tyre brought much cedar wood to David.

5 And David said, Solomon my son is young and tender, and the house that is to be builded for the LORD must be exceeding magnifical, of fame and of glory throughout all countries: I will therefore now make preparation for it. So David prepared abundantly before his death.

6Then he called for Solomon his son, and charged him to build an house for the LORD God of Israel.

7 And David said to Solomon, My son, as for me, it was in my mind to build an house unto the name of the LORD my God:

8 But the word of the LORD came to me, saying, You have shed blood abundantly, and have made great wars: you shalt not build an house unto my name, because you have shed much blood upon the earth in my sight.

9 Behold, a son shall be born to you, who shall be a man of rest; and I will give him rest from all his enemies round about: for his name shall be Solomon, and I will give peace and quietness unto Israel in his days.

10 He shall build an house for my name; and he shall be my son, and I will be his father; and I will establish the throne of his kingdom over Israel for ever.

11 Now, my son, the LORD be with you; and prosper you , and build the house of the LORD your God, as he has said of you.

12 Only the LORD give you wisdom and understanding, and give you charge concerning Israel, that you mayest keep the law of the LORD your God.

13 Then shalt you prosper, if you takest heed to fulfil the statutes and judgments which the LORD charged Moses with concerning Israel: be strong, and of good courage; dread not, nor be dismayed.

14 Now, behold, in my trouble I have prepared for the house of the LORD an hundred thousand talents of gold, and a thousand thousand talents of silver; and of brass and iron without weight; for it is in abundance: timber also and stone have I prepared; and you mayest add thereto.

15 Moreover there are workmen with you in abundance, hewers and workers of stone and timber, and all manner of cunning men for every manner of work.

16 Of the gold, the silver, and the brass, and the iron, there is no number. Arise therefore, and be doing, and the LORD be with you.

17David also commanded all the princes of Israel to help Solomon his son, saying,

18 Is not the LORD your God with you? and has he not given you rest on every side? for he has given the inhabitants of the land into my hand; and the land is subdued before the LORD, and before his people.

19 Now set your heart and your soul to seek the LORD your God; arise therefore, and build you the sanctuary of the LORD God, to bring the ark of the covenant of the LORD, and the holy vessels of God, into the house that is to be built to the name of the LORD.

CHAPTER 23

SO when David was old and full of days, he made Solomon his son king over Israel.

2And he gathered together all the princes of Israel, with the priests and the Levites.

3 Now the Levites were numbered from the age of thirty years and upward: and their number by their polls, man by man, was thirty and eight thousand.

4 Of which, twenty and four thousand were to set forward the work of the house of the LORD; and six thousand were officers and judges:

5 Moreover four thousand were porters; and four thousand praised the LORD with the instruments which I made, said David, to praise therewith.

6 And David divided them into courses among the sons of Levi, namely, Gershon, Kohath, and Merari.

7Of the Gershonites were, Laadan, and Shimei.

8 The sons of Laadan; the chief was Jehiel, and Zetham, and Joel, three.

9 The sons of Shimei; Shelomith, and Haziel, and Haran, three. These were the chief of the fathers of Laadan.

10 And the sons of Shimei were, Jahath, Zina, and Jeush, and Beriah. These four were the sons of Shimei.

11 And Jahath was the chief, and Zizah the second: but Jeush and Beriah had not many sons; therefore they were in one reckoning, according to their father's house.

12The sons of Kohath; Amram, Izhar, Hebron, and Uzziel, four.

13 The sons of Amram; Aaron and Moses: and Aaron was separated, that he should sanctify the most holy things, he and his sons for ever, to burn incense before the LORD, to minister unto him, and to bless in his name for ever.

14 Now concerning Moses the man of God, his sons were named of the tribe of Levi.

15 The sons of Moses were, Gershom, and Eliezer.

16 Of the sons of Gershom, Shebuel was the chief.

17 And the sons of Eliezer were, Rehabiah the chief. And Eliezer had none other sons; but the sons of Rehabiah were very many.

18 Of the sons of Izhar; Shelomith the chief.

19 Of the sons of Hebron; Jeriah the first, Amariah the second, Jahaziel the third, and Jekameam the fourth.

20 Of the sons of Uzziel; Michah the first, and Jesiah the second.

21The sons of Merari; Mahli, and Mushi. The sons of Mahli; Eleazar, and Kish.

22 And Eleazar died, and had no sons, but daughters: and their brethren the sons of Kish took them.

23 The sons of Mushi; Mahli, and Eder, and Jeremoth, three.

24These were the sons of Levi after the house of their fathers; even the chief of the fathers, as they were counted by number of names by their polls, that did the work for the service of the house of the LORD, from the age of twenty years and upward.

25 For David said, The LORD God of Israel has given rest unto his people, that they may dwell in Jerusalem for ever:

26 And also unto the Levites; they shall no more carry the tabernacle, nor any vessels of it for the service thereof.

27 For by the last words of David the Levites were numbered from twenty years old and above:

28 Because their office was to wait on the sons of Aaron for the service of the house of the LORD, in the courts, and in the chambers, and in the purifying of all holy things, and the work of the service of the house of God;

29 Both for the shewbread, and for the fine flour for meat offering, and for the unleavened cakes, and for that which is baked in the pan, and for that which is fried, and for all manner of measure and size;

30 And to stand every morning to thank and praise the LORD, and likewise at even;

31 And to offer all burnt sacrifices unto the LORD in the sabbaths, in the new moons, and on the set feasts, by number, according to the order commanded unto them, continually before the LORD:

32 And that they should keep the charge of the tabernacle of the congregation, and the charge of the holy place, and the charge of the sons of Aaron their brethren, in the service of the house of the LORD.

CHAPTER 24

NOW these are the divisions of the sons of Aaron. The sons of Aaron; Nadab, and Abihu, Eleazar, and Ithamar.

2 But Nadab and Abihu died before their father, and had no children: therefore Eleazar and Ithamar executed the priest's office.

3 And David distributed them, both Zadok of the sons of Eleazar, and Ahimelech of the sons of Ithamar, according to their offices in their service.

4 And there were more chief men found of the sons of Eleazar than of the sons of Ithamar; and thus were they divided. Among the sons of Eleazar there were sixteen chief men of the house of their fathers, and eight among the sons of Ithamar according to the house of their fathers.

5 Thus were they divided by lot, one sort with another; for the governors of the sanctuary, and governors of the house of God, were of the sons of Eleazar, and of the sons of Ithamar.

6 And Shemaiah the son of Nethaneel the scribe, one of the Levites, wrote them before the king, and the princes, and Zadok the priest, and Ahimelech the son of Abiathar, and before the chief of the fathers of the priests and Levites: one principal household being taken for Eleazar, and one taken for Ithamar.

7 Now the first lot came forth to Jehoiarib, the second to Jedaiah,

8 The third to Harim, the fourth to Seorim,

9 The fifth to Malchijah, the sixth to Mijamin,

10 The seventh to Hakkoz, the eighth to Abijah,

11 The ninth to Jeshua, the tenth to Shecaniah,

12 The eleventh to Eliashib, the twelfth to Jakim,

13 The thirteenth to Huppah, the fourteenth to Jeshebeab,

14 The fifteenth to Bilgah, the sixteenth to Immer,

15 The seventeenth to Hezir, the eighteenth to Aphses,

16 The nineteenth to Pethahiah, the twentieth to Jehezekel,

17 The one and twentieth to Jachin, the two and twentieth to Gamul,

18 The three and twentieth to Delaiah, the four and twentieth to Maaziah.

19 These were the orderings of them in their service to come into the house of the LORD, according to their manner, under Aaron their father, as the LORD God of Israel had commanded him.

20And the rest of the sons of Levi were these: Of the sons of Amram; Shubael: of the sons of Shubael; Jehdeiah.

21 Concerning Rehabiah: of the sons of Rehabiah, the first was Isshiah.

22 Of the Izharites; Shelomoth: of the sons of Shelomoth; Jahath.

23 And the sons of Hebron; Jeriah the first, Amariah the second, Jahaziel the third, Jekameam the fourth.

24 Of the sons of Uzziel; Michah: of the sons of Michah; Shamir.

25 The brother of Michah was Isshiah: of the sons of Isshiah; Zechariah.

26 The sons of Merari were Mahli and Mushi: the sons of Jaaziah; Beno.

27The sons of Merari by Jaaziah; Beno, and Shoham, and Zaccur, and Ibri.

28 Of Mahli came Eleazar, who had no sons.

29 Concerning Kish: the son of Kish was Jerahmeel.

30 The sons also of Mushi; Mahli, and Eder, and Jerimoth. These were the sons of the Levites after the house of their fathers.

31 These likewise cast lots over against their brethren the sons of Aaron in the presence of David the king, and Zadok, and Ahimelech, and the chief of the fathers of the priests and Levites, even the principal fathers over against their younger brethren.

CHAPTER 25

MOREOVER David and the captains of the host separated to the service of the sons of Asaph, and of Heman, and of Jeduthun, who should prophesy with harps, with psalteries, and with cymbals: and the number of the workmen according to their service was:

2 Of the sons of Asaph; Zaccur, and Joseph, and Nethaniah, and Asarelah, the sons of Asaph under the hands of Asaph, which prophesied according to the order of the king.

3 Of Jeduthun: the sons of Jeduthun; Gedaliah, and Zeri, and Jeshaiah, Hashabiah, and Mattithiah, six, under the hands of their father Jeduthun, who prophesied with a harp, to give thanks and to praise the LORD.

4 Of Heman: the sons of Heman; Bukkiah, Mattaniah, Uzziel, Shebuel, and Jerimoth, Hananiah, Hanani, Eliathah, Giddalti, and Romamti-ezer, Joshbekashah, Mallothi, Hothir, and Mahazioth:

5 All these were the sons of Heman the king's seer in the words of God, to lift up the horn. And God gave to Heman fourteen sons and three daughters.

6 All these were under the hands of their father for song in the house of the LORD, with cymbals, psalteries, and harps, for the service of the house of God, according to the king's order to Asaph, Jeduthun, and Heman.

7 So the number of them, with their brethren that were instructed in the songs of the LORD, even all that were cunning, was two hundred fourscore and eight.

8And they cast lots, ward against ward, as well the small as the great, the teacher as the scholar.

9 Now the first lot came forth for Asaph to Joseph: the second to Gedaliah, who with his brethren and sons were twelve:

10 The third to Zaccur, he, his sons, and his brethren, were twelve:

11 The fourth to Izri, he, his sons, and his brethren, were twelve:

12 The fifth to Nethaniah, he, his sons, and his brethren, were twelve:

13 The sixth to Bukkiah, he, his sons, and his brethren, were twelve:

14 The seventh to Jesharelah, he, his sons, and his brethren, were twelve:

15 The eighth to Jeshaiah, he, his sons, and his brethren, were twelve:

16 The ninth to Mattaniah, he, his sons, and his brethren, were twelve:

17 The tenth to Shimei, he, his sons, and his brethren, were twelve:

18 The eleventh to Azareel, he, his sons, and his brethren, were twelve:

19 The twelfth to Hashabiah, he, his sons, and his brethren, were twelve:

20 The thirteenth to Shubael, he, his sons, and his brethren, were twelve:

21 The fourteenth to Mattithiah, he, his sons, and his brethren, were twelve:

22 The fifteenth to Jeremoth, he, his sons, and his brethren, were twelve:

23 The sixteenth to Hananiah, he, his sons, and his brethren, were twelve:

24 The seventeenth to Joshbekashah, he, his sons, and his brethren, were twelve:

25 The eighteenth to Hanani, he, his sons, and his brethren, were twelve:

26 The nineteenth to Mallothi, he, his sons, and his brethren, were twelve:

27 The twentieth to Eliathah, he, his sons, and his brethren, were twelve:

28 The one and twentieth to Hothir, he, his sons, and his brethren, were twelve:

29 The two and twentieth to Giddalti, he, his sons, and his brethren, were twelve:

30 The three and twentieth to Mahazioth, he, his sons, and his brethren, were twelve:

31 The four and twentieth to Romamti-ezer, he, his sons, and his brethren, were twelve.

CHAPTER 26

CONCERNING the divisions of the porters: Of the Korhites was Meshelemiah the son of Kore, of the sons of Asaph.

2 And the sons of Meshelemiah were, Zechariah the firstborn, Jediael the second, Zebadiah the third, Jathniel the fourth,

3 Elam the fifth, Jehohanan the sixth, Elioenai the seventh.

4 Moreover the sons of Obed-edom were, Shemaiah the firstborn, Jehozabad the second, Joah the third, and Sacar the fourth, and Nethaneel the fifth,

5 Ammiel the sixth, Issachar the seventh, Peulthai the eighth: for God blessed him.

6 Also unto Shemaiah his son were sons born, that ruled throughout the house of their father: for they were mighty men of valour.

7 The sons of Shemaiah; Othni, and Rephael, and Obed, Elzabad, whose brethren were strong men, Elihu, and Semachiah.

8 All these of the sons of Obed-edom: they and their sons and their brethren, able men for strength for the service, were threescore and two of Obed-edom.

9 And Meshelemiah had sons and brethren, strong men, eighteen.

10 Also Hosah, of the children of Merari, had sons; Simri the chief, (for though he was not the firstborn, yet his father made him the chief;)

11 Hilkiah the second, Tebaliah the third, Zechariah the fourth: all the sons and brethren of Hosah were thirteen.

12 Among these were the divisions of the porters, even among the chief men, having wards one against another, to minister in the house of the LORD.

13And they cast lots, as well the small as the great, according to the house of their fathers, for every gate.

14 And the lot eastward fell to Shelemiah. Then for Zechariah his son, a wise counseller, they cast lots; and his lot came out northward.

15 To Obed-edom southward; and to his sons the house of Asuppim.

16 To Shuppim and Hosah the lot came forth westward, with the gate Shallecheth, by the causeway of the going up, ward against ward.

17 Eastward were six Levites, northward four a day, southward four a day, and toward Asuppim two and two.

18 At Parbar westward, four at the causeway, and two at Parbar.

19 These are the divisions of the porters among the sons of Kore, and among the sons of Merari.

20And of the Levites, Ahijah was over the treasures of the house of God, and over the treasures of the dedicated things.

21 As concerning the sons of Laadan; the sons of the Gershonite Laadan, chief fathers, even of Laadan the Gershonite, were Jehieli.

22 The sons of Jehieli; Zetham, and Joel his brother, which were over the treasures of the house of the LORD.

23 Of the Amramites, and the Izharites, the Hebronites, and the Uzzielites:

24 And Shebuel the son of Gershom, the son of Moses, was ruler of the treasures.

25 And his brethren by Eliezer; Rehabiah his son, and Jeshaiah his son, and Joram his son, and Zichri his son, and Shelomith his son.

26 Which Shelomith and his brethren were over all the treasures of the dedicated things, which David the king, and the chief fathers, the captains over thousands and hundreds, and the captains of the host, had dedicated.

27 Out of the spoils won in battles did they dedicate to maintain the house of the LORD.

28 And all that Samuel the seer, and Saul the son of Kish, and Abner the son of Ner, and Joab the son of Zeruiah, had dedicated; and whosoever had dedicated any thing, it was under the hand of Shelomith, and of his brethren.

29Of the Izharites, Chenaniah and his sons were for the outward business over Israel, for officers and judges.

30 And of the Hebronites, Hashabiah and his brethren, men of valour, a thousand and seven hundred, were officers among them of Israel on this side Jordan westward in all the business of the LORD, and in the service of the king.

31 Among the Hebronites was Jerijah the chief, even among the Hebronites, according to the generations of his fathers. In the fortieth year of the reign of David they were sought for, and there were found among them mighty men of valour at Jazer of Gilead.

32 And his brethren, men of valour, were two thousand and seven hundred chief fathers, whom king David made rulers over the Reubenites, the Gadites, and the half tribe of Manasseh, for every matter pertaining to God, and affairs of the king.

CHAPTER 27

NOW the children of Israel after their number, to wit, the chief fathers and captains of thousands and hundreds, and their officers that served the king in any matter of the courses, which came in and went out month by month throughout all the months of the year, of every course were twenty and four thousand.

2 Over the first course for the first month was Jashobeam the son of Zabdiel: and in his course were twenty and four thousand.

3 Of the children of Perez was the chief of all the captains of the host for the first month.

4 And over the course of the second month was Dodai an Ahohite, and of his course was Mikloth also the ruler: in his course likewise were twenty and four thousand.

5 The third captain of the host for the third month was Benaiah the son of Jehoiada, a chief priest: and in his course were twenty and four thousand.

6 This is that Benaiah, who was mighty among the thirty, and above the thirty: and in his course was Ammizabad his son.

7 The fourth captain for the fourth month was Asahel the brother of Joab, and Zebadiah his son after him: and in his course were twenty and four thousand.

8 The fifth captain for the fifth month was Shamhuth the Izrahite: and in his course were twenty and four thousand.

9 The sixth captain for the sixth month was Ira the son of Ikkesh the Tekoite: and in his course were twenty and four thousand.

10 The seventh captain for the seventh month was Helez the Pelonite, of the children of Ephraim: and in his course were twenty and four thousand.

11 The eighth captain for the eighth month was Sibbecai the Hushathite, of the Zarhites: and in his course were twenty and four thousand.

12 The ninth captain for the ninth month was Abiezer the Anetothite, of the Benjamites: and in his course were twenty and four thousand.

13 The tenth captain for the tenth month was Maharai the Netophathite, of the Zarhites: and in his course were twenty and four thousand.

14 The eleventh captain for the eleventh month was Benaiah the Pirathonite, of the children of Ephraim: and in his course were twenty and four thousand.

15 The twelfth captain for the twelfth month was Heldai the Netophathite, of Othniel: and in his course were twenty and four thousand.

16Furthermore over the tribes of Israel: the ruler of the Reubenites was Eliezer the son of Zichri: of the Simeonites, Shephatiah the son of Maachah:

17 Of the Levites, Hashabiah the son of Kemuel: of the Aaronites, Zadok:

18 Of Judah, Elihu, one of the brethren of David: of Issachar, Omri the son of Michael:

19 Of Zebulun, Ishmaiah the son of Obadiah: of Naphtali, Jerimoth the son of Azriel:

20 Of the children of Ephraim, Hoshea the son of Azaziah: of the half tribe of Manasseh, Joel the son of Pedaiah:

21 Of the half tribe of Manasseh in Gilead, Iddo the son of Zechariah: of Benjamin, Jaasiel the son of Abner:

22 Of Dan, Azareel the son of Jeroham. These were the princes of the tribes of Israel.

23But David took not the number of them from twenty years old and under: because the LORD had said he would increase Israel like to the stars of the heavens.

24 Joab the son of Zeruiah began to number, but he finished not, because there fell wrath for it against Israel; neither was the number put in the account of the chronicles of king David.

25And over the king's treasures was Azmaveth the son of Adiel: and over the storehouses in the fields, in the cities, and in the villages, and in the castles, was Jehonathan the son of Uzziah:

26 And over them that did the work of the field for tillage of the ground was Ezri the son of Chelub:

27 And over the vineyards was Shimei the Ramathite: over the increase of the vineyards for the wine cellars was Zabdi the Shiphmite:

28 And over the olive trees and the sycomore trees that were in the low plains was Baal-hanan the Gederite: and over the cellars of oil was Joash:

29 And over the herds that fed in Sharon was Shitrai the Sharonite: and over the herds that were in the valleys was Shaphat the son of Adlai:

30 Over the camels also was Obil the Ishmaelite: and over the asses was Jehdeiah the Meronothite:

31 And over the flocks was Jaziz the Hagerite. All these were the rulers of the substance which was king David's.

32 Also Jonathan David's uncle was a counsellor, a wise man, and a scribe: and Jehiel the son of Hachmoni was with the king's sons:

33 And Ahithophel was the king's counseller: and Hushai the Archite was the king's companion:

34 And after Ahithophel was Jehoiada the son of Benaiah, and Abiathar: and the general of the king's army was Joab.

CHAPTER 28

AND David assembled all the princes of Israel, the princes of the tribes, and the captains of the companies that ministered to the king by course, and the captains over the thousands, and captains over the hundreds, and the stewards over all the substance and possession of the king, and of his sons, with the officers, and with the mighty men, and with all the valiant men, unto Jerusalem.

2 Then David the king stood up upon his feet, and said, Hear me, my brethren, and my people: As for me, I had in my heart to build an house of rest for the ark of the covenant of the LORD, and for the footstool of our God, and had made ready for the building:

3 But God said unto me, You shalt not build an house for my name, because you have been a man of war, and have shed blood.

4 Howbeit the LORD God of Israel chose me before all the house of my father to be king over Israel for ever: for he has chosen Judah to be the ruler; and of the house of Judah, the house of my father; and among the sons of my father he liked me to make me king over all Israel:

5 And of all my sons, (for the LORD has given me many sons,) he has chosen Solomon my son to sit upon the throne of the kingdom of the LORD over Israel.

6 And he said unto me, Solomon your son, he shall build my house and my courts: for I have chosen him to be my son, and I will be his father.

7 Moreover I will establish his kingdom for ever, if he be constant to do my commandments and my judgments, as at this day.

8 Now therefore in the sight of all Israel the congregation of the LORD, and in the audience of our God, keep and seek for all the commandments of the LORD your God: that you may possess this good land, and leave it for an inheritance for your children after you for ever.

9And you , Solomon my son, know you the God of your father, and serve him with a perfect heart and with a willing mind: for the LORD searches all hearts, and understands all the imaginations of the thoughts: if you seek him, he will be found of you; but if you forsake him, he will cast you off for ever.

10 Take heed now; for the LORD has chosen you to build an house for the sanctuary: be strong, and do it.

11Then David gave to Solomon his son the pattern of the porch, and of the houses thereof, and of the treasuries thereof, and of the upper chambers thereof, and of the inner parlours thereof, and of the place of the mercy seat,

12 And the pattern of all that he had by the spirit, of the courts of the house of the LORD, and of all the chambers round about, of the treasuries of the house of God, and of the treasuries of the dedicated things:

13 Also for the courses of the priests and the Levites, and for all the work of the service of the house of the LORD, and for all the vessels of service in the house of the LORD.

14 He gave of gold by weight for things of gold, for all instruments of all manner of service; silver also for all instruments of silver by weight, for all instruments of every kind of service:

15 Even the weight for the candlesticks of gold, and for their lamps of gold, by weight for every candlestick, and for the lamps thereof: and for the candlesticks of silver by weight, both for the candlestick, and also for the lamps thereof, according to the use of every candlestick.

16 And by weight he gave gold for the tables of shewbread, for every table; and likewise silver for the tables of silver:

17 Also pure gold for the fleshhooks, and the bowls, and the cups: and for the golden basons he gave gold by weight for every bason; and likewise silver by weight for every bason of silver:

18 And for the altar of incense refined gold by weight; and gold for the pattern of the chariot of the cherubims, that spread out their wings, and covered the ark of the covenant of the LORD.

19 All this, said David, the LORD made me understand in writing by his hand upon me, even all the works of this pattern.

20 And David said to Solomon his son, Be strong and of good courage, and do it: fear not, nor be dismayed: for the LORD God, even my God, will be with you; he will not fail you, nor forsake you, until you have finished all the work for the service of the house of the LORD.

21 And, behold, the courses of the priests and the Levites, even they shall be with you for all the service of the house of God: and there shall be with you for all manner of workmanship every willing skilful man, for any manner of service: also the princes and all the people will be wholly at your commandment.

CHAPTER 29

FURTHERMORE David the king said unto all the congregation, Solomon my son, whom alone God has chosen, is yet young and tender, and the work is great: for the palace is not for man, but for the LORD God.

2 Now I have prepared with all my might for the house of my God the gold for things to be made of gold, and the silver for things of silver, and the brass for things of brass, the iron for things of iron, and wood for things of wood; onyx stones, and stones to be set, glistering stones, and of divers colours, and all manner of precious stones, and marble stones in abundance.

3 Moreover, because I have set my affection to the house of my God, I have of my own proper good, of gold and silver, which I have given to the house of my God, over and above all that I have prepared for the holy house,

4 Even three thousand talents of gold, of the gold of Ophir, and seven thousand talents of refined silver, to overlay the walls of the houses withal:

5 The gold for things of gold, and the silver for things of silver, and for all manner of work to be made by the hands of artificers. And who then is willing to consecrate his service this day unto the LORD?

6Then the chief of the fathers and princes of the tribes of Israel, and the captains of thousands and of hundreds, with the rulers of the king's work, offered willingly,

7 And gave for the service of the house of God of gold five thousand talents and ten thousand drams, and of silver ten thousand talents, and of brass eighteen thousand talents, and one hundred thousand talents of iron.

8 And they with whom precious stones were found gave them to the treasure of the house of the LORD, by the hand of Jehiel the Gershonite.

9 Then the people rejoiced, for that they offered willingly, because with perfect heart they offered willingly to the LORD: and David the king also rejoiced with great joy.

10Wherefore David blessed the LORD before all the congregation: and David said, Blessed be you , LORD God of Israel our father, for ever and ever.

11 Yours, O LORD, is the greatness, and the power, and the glory, and the victory, and the majesty: for all that is in the heaven and in the earth is yours; yours is the kingdom, O LORD, and you are exalted as head above all.

12 Both riches and honour come of you, and you reignest over all; and in yours hand is power and might; and in yours hand it is to make great, and to give strength unto all.

13 Now therefore, our God, we thank you, and praise your glorious name.

14 But who am I, and what is my people, that we should be able to offer so willingly after this sort? for all things come of you, and of yours own have we given you.

15 For we are strangers before you, and sojourners, as were all our fathers: our days on the earth are as a shadow, and there is none abiding.

16 O LORD our God, all this store that we have prepared to build you an house for yours holy name comes of yours hand, and is all yours own.

17 I know also, my God, that you triest the heart, and have pleasure in uprightness. As for me, in the uprightness of my heart I have willingly offered all these things: and now have I seen with joy your people, which are present here, to offer willingly unto you.

18 O LORD God of Abraham, Isaac, and of Israel, our fathers, keep this for ever in the imagination of the thoughts of the heart of your people, and prepare their heart unto you:

19 And give unto Solomon my son a perfect heart, to keep your commandments, your testimonies, and your statutes, and to do all these things, and to build the palace, for the which I have made provision.

20 And David said to all the congregation, Now bless the LORD your God. And all the congregation blessed the LORD God of their fathers, and bowed down their heads, and worshipped the LORD, and the king.

21 And they sacrificed sacrifices unto the LORD, and offered burnt offerings unto the LORD, on the morrow after that day, even a thousand bullocks, a thousand rams, and a thousand lambs, with their drink offerings, and sacrifices in abundance for all Israel:

22 And did eat and drink before the LORD on that day with great gladness. And they made Solomon the son of David king the second time, and anointed him unto the LORD to be the chief governor, and Zadok to be priest.

23 Then Solomon sat on the throne of the LORD as king instead of David his father, and prospered; and all Israel obeyed him.

24 And all the princes, and the mighty men, and all the sons likewise of king David, submitted themselves unto Solomon the king.

25 And the LORD magnified Solomon exceedingly in the sight of all Israel, and bestowed upon him such royal majesty as had not been on any king before him in Israel.

26 Thus David the son of Jesse reigned over all Israel.

27 And the time that he reigned over Israel was forty years; seven years reigned he in Hebron, and thirty and three years reigned he in Jerusalem.

28 And he died in a good old age, full of days, riches, and honour: and Solomon his son reigned in his stead.

29 Now the acts of David the king, first and last, behold, they are written in the book of Samuel the seer, and in the book of Nathan the prophet, and in the book of Gad the seer,

30 With all his reign and his might, and the times that went over him, and over Israel, and over all the kingdoms of the countries.

THE SECOND BOOK OF THE CHRONICLES.

CHAPTER 1

AND Solomon the son of David was strengthened in his kingdom, and the LORD his God was with him, and magnified him exceedingly.

2 Then Solomon spake unto all Israel, to the captains of thousands and of hundreds, and to the judges, and to every governor in all Israel, the chief of the fathers.

3 So Solomon, and all the congregation with him, went to the high place that was at Gibeon; for there was the tabernacle of the congregation of God, which Moses the servant of the LORD had made in the wilderness.

4 But the ark of God had David brought up from Kirjath-jearim to the place which David had prepared for it: for he had pitched a tent for it at Jerusalem.

5 Moreover the brasen altar, that Bezaleel the son of Uri, the son of Hur, had made, he put before the tabernacle of the LORD: and Solomon and the congregation sought unto it.

6 And Solomon went up thither to the brasen altar before the LORD, which was at the tabernacle of the congregation, and offered a thousand burnt offerings upon it.

7 In that night did God appear unto Solomon, and said unto him, Ask what I shall give you.

8 And Solomon said unto God, You have shewed great mercy unto David my father, and have made me to reign in his stead.

9 Now, O LORD God, let your promise unto David my father be established: for you have made me king over a people like the dust of the earth in multitude.

10 Give me now wisdom and knowledge, that I may go out and come in before this people: for who can judge this your people, that is so great?

11 And God said to Solomon, Because this was in yours heart, and you have not asked riches, wealth, or honour, nor the life of yours enemies, neither yet have asked long life; but have asked wisdom and knowledge for yourself, that you mayest judge my people, over whom I have made you king:

12 Wisdom and knowledge is granted unto you; and I will give you riches, and wealth, and honour, such as none of the kings have had that have been before you, neither shall there any after you have the like.

13 Then Solomon came from his journey to the high place that was at Gibeon to Jerusalem, from before the tabernacle of the congregation, and reigned over Israel.

14 And Solomon gathered chariots and horsemen: and he had a thousand and four hundred chariots, and twelve thousand horsemen, which he placed in the chariot cities, and with the king at Jerusalem.

15 And the king made silver and gold at Jerusalem as plenteous as stones, and cedar trees made he as the sycomore trees that are in the vale for abundance.

16 And Solomon had horses brought out of Egypt, and linen yarn: the king's merchants received the linen yarn at a price.

17 And they fetched up, and brought forth out of Egypt a chariot for six hundred shekels of silver, and an horse for an hundred and fifty: and so brought they out horses for all the kings of the Hittites, and for the kings of Syria, by their means.

CHAPTER 2

AND Solomon determined to build an house for the name of the LORD, and an house for his kingdom.

2 And Solomon told out threescore and ten thousand men to bear burdens, and fourscore thousand to hew in the mountain, and three thousand and six hundred to oversee them.

3 And Solomon sent to Huram the king of Tyre, saying, As you did deal with David my father, and did send him cedars to build him an house to dwell therein, even so deal with me.

4 Behold, I build an house to the name of the LORD my God, to dedicate it to him, and to burn before him sweet incense, and for the continual shewbread, and for the burnt offerings morning and evening, on the sabbaths, and on the new moons, and on the solemn feasts of the LORD our God. This is an ordinance for ever to Israel.

5 And the house which I build is great: for great is our God above all gods.

6 But who is able to build him an house, seeing the heaven and heaven of heavens cannot contain him? who am I then, that I should build him an house, save only to burn sacrifice before him?

7 Send me now therefore a man cunning to work in gold, and in silver, and in brass, and in iron, and in purple, and crimson, and blue, and that can skill to grave with the cunning men that are with me in Judah and in Jerusalem, whom David my father did provide.

8 Send me also cedar trees, fir trees, and algum trees, out of Lebanon: for I know that your servants can skill to cut timber in Lebanon; and, behold, my servants shall be with your servants,

9 Even to prepare me timber in abundance: for the house which I am about to build shall be wonderful great.

10 And, behold, I will give to your servants, the hewers that cut timber, twenty thousand measures of beaten wheat, and twenty thousand measures of barley, and twenty thousand baths of wine, and twenty thousand baths of oil.

11 Then Huram the king of Tyre answered in writing, which he sent to Solomon, Because the LORD has loved his people, he has made you king over them.

12 Huram said moreover, Blessed be the LORD God of Israel, that made heaven and earth, who has given to David the king a wise son, endued with prudence and understanding, that might build an house for the LORD, and an house for his kingdom.

13 And now I have sent a cunning man, endued with understanding, of Huram my father's,

14 The son of a woman of the daughters of Dan, and his father was a man of Tyre, skilful to work in gold, and in silver, in brass, in iron, in stone, and in timber, in purple, in blue, and in fine linen, and in crimson; also to grave any manner of graving, and to find out every device which shall be put to him, with your cunning men, and with the cunning men of my lord David your father.

15 Now therefore the wheat, and the barley, the oil, and the wine, which my lord has spoken of, let him send unto his servants:

16 And we will cut wood out of Lebanon, as much as you shalt need: and we will bring it to you in floats by sea to Joppa; and you shalt carry it up to Jerusalem.

17 And Solomon numbered all the strangers that were in the land of Israel, after the numbering wherewith David his father had numbered them; and they were found an hundred and fifty thousand and three thousand and six hundred.

18 And he set threescore and ten thousand of them to be bearers of burdens, and fourscore thousand to be hewers in the mountain, and three thousand and six hundred overseers to set the people a work.

CHAPTER 3

THEN Solomon began to build the house of the LORD at Jerusalem in mount Moriah, where the LORD appeared unto David his father, in the place that David had prepared in the threshingfloor of Ornan the Jebusite.

2 And he began to build in the second day of the second month, in the fourth year of his reign.

3 Now these are the things wherein Solomon was instructed for the building of the house of God. The length by cubits after the first measure was threescore cubits, and the breadth twenty cubits.

4 And the porch that was in the front of the house, the length of it was according to the breadth of the house, twenty cubits, and the height was an hundred and twenty: and he overlaid it within with pure gold.

5 And the greater house he cieled with fir tree, which he overlaid with fine gold, and set thereon palm trees and chains.

6 And he garnished the house with precious stones for beauty: and the gold was gold of Parvaim.

7 He overlaid also the house, the beams, the posts, and the walls thereof, and the doors thereof, with gold; and graved cherubims on the walls.

8 And he made the most holy house, the length whereof was according to the breadth of the house, twenty cubits, and the breadth thereof twenty cubits: and he overlaid it with fine gold, amounting to six hundred talents.

9 And the weight of the nails was fifty shekels of gold. And he overlaid the upper chambers with gold.

10 And in the most holy house he made two cherubims of image work, and overlaid them with gold.

11 And the wings of the cherubims were twenty cubits long: one wing of the one cherub was five cubits, reaching to the wall of the house: and the other wing was likewise five cubits, reaching to the wing of the other cherub.

12 And one wing of the other cherub was five cubits, reaching to the wall of the house: and the other wing was five cubits also, joining to the wing of the other cherub.

13 The wings of these cherubims spread themselves forth twenty cubits: and they stood on their feet, and their faces were inward.

14 And he made the vail of blue, and purple, and crimson, and fine linen, and created cherubims thereon.

15 Also he made before the house two pillars of thirty and five cubits high, and the chapiter that was on the top of each of them was five cubits.

16 And he made chains, as in the oracle, and put them on the heads of the pillars; and made an hundred pomegranates, and put them on the chains.

17 And he reared up the pillars before the temple, one on the right hand, and the other on the left; and called the name of that on the right hand Jachin, and the name of that on the left Boaz.

CHAPTER 4

MOREOVER he made an altar of brass, twenty cubits the length thereof, and twenty cubits the breadth thereof, and ten cubits the height thereof.

2Also he made a molten sea of ten cubits from brim to brim, round in compass, and five cubits the height thereof; and a line of thirty cubits did compass it round about.

3 And under it was the similitude of oxen, which did compass it round about: ten in a cubit, compassing the sea round about. Two rows of oxen were cast, when it was cast.

4 It stood upon twelve oxen, three looking toward the north, and three looking toward the west, and three looking toward the south, and three looking toward the east: and the sea was set above upon them, and all their hinder parts were inward.

5 And the thickness of it was an handbreadth, and the brim of it like the work of the brim of a cup, with flowers of lilies; and it received and held three thousand baths.

6He made also ten lavers, and put five on the right hand, and five on the left, to wash in them: such things as they offered for the burnt offering they washed in them; but the sea was for the priests to wash in.

7 And he made ten candlesticks of gold according to their form, and set them in the temple, five on the right hand, and five on the left.

8 He made also ten tables, and placed them in the temple, five on the right side, and five on the left. And he made an hundred basons of gold.

9Furthermore he made the court of the priests, and the great court, and doors for the court, and overlaid the doors of them with brass.

10 And he set the sea on the right side of the east end, over against the south.

11 And Huram made the pots, and the shovels, and the basons. And Huram finished the work that he was to make for king Solomon for the house of God;

12 To wit, the two pillars, and the pommels, and the chapiters which were on the top of the two pillars, and the two wreaths to cover the two pommels of the chapiters which were on the top of the pillars;

13 And four hundred pomegranates on the two wreaths; two rows of pomegranates on each wreath, to cover the two pommels of the chapiters which were upon the pillars.

14 He made also bases, and lavers made he upon the bases;

15 One sea, and twelve oxen under it.

16 The pots also, and the shovels, and the fleshhooks, and all their instruments, did Huram his father make to king Solomon for the house of the LORD of bright brass.

17 In the plain of Jordan did the king cast them, in the clay ground between Succoth and Zeredathah.

18 Thus Solomon made all these vessels in great abundance: for the weight of the brass could not be found out.

19And Solomon made all the vessels that were for the house of God, the golden altar also, and the tables whereon the shewbread was set;

20 Moreover the candlesticks with their lamps, that they should burn after the manner before the oracle, of pure gold;

21 And the flowers, and the lamps, and the tongs, made he of gold, and that perfect gold;

22 And the snuffers, and the basons, and the spoons, and the censers, of pure gold: and the entry of the house, the inner doors thereof for the most holy place, and the doors of the house of the temple, were of gold.

CHAPTER 5

THUS all the work that Solomon made for the house of the LORD was finished: and Solomon brought in all the things that David his father had dedicated; and the silver, and the gold, and all the instruments, put he among the treasures of the house of God.

2Then Solomon assembled the elders of Israel, and all the heads of the tribes, the chief of the fathers of the children of Israel, unto Jerusalem, to bring up the ark of the covenant of the LORD out of the city of David, which is Zion.

3 Wherefore all the men of Israel assembled themselves unto the king in the feast which was in the seventh month.

4 And all the elders of Israel came; and the Levites took up the ark.

5 And they brought up the ark, and the tabernacle of the congregation, and all the holy vessels that were in the tabernacle, these did the priests and the Levites bring up.

6 Also king Solomon, and all the congregation of Israel that were assembled unto him before the ark, sacrificed sheep and oxen, which could not be told nor numbered for multitude.

7 And the priests brought in the ark of the covenant of the LORD unto his place, to the oracle of the house, into the most holy place, even under the wings of the cherubims:

8 For the cherubims spread forth their wings over the place of the ark, and the cherubims covered the ark and the staves thereof above.

9 And they drew out the staves of the ark, that the ends of the staves were seen from the ark before the oracle; but they were not seen without. And there it is unto this day.

10 There was nothing in the ark save the two tables which Moses put therein at Horeb, when the LORD made a covenant with the children of Israel, when they came out of Egypt.

11And it came to pass, when the priests were come out of the holy place: (for all the priests that were present were sanctified, and did not then wait by course:

12 Also the Levites which were the singers, all of them of Asaph, of Heman, of Jeduthun, with their sons and their brethren, being arrayed in white linen, having cymbals and psalteries and harps, stood at the east end of the altar, and with them an hundred and twenty priests sounding with trumpets:)

13 It came even to pass, as the trumpeters and singers were as one, to make one sound to be heard in praising and thanking the LORD; and when they lifted up their voice with the trumpets and cymbals and instruments of musick, and praised the LORD, saying, For he is good; for his mercy endureth for ever: that then the house was filled with a cloud, even the house of the LORD;

14 So that the priests could not stand to minister by reason of the cloud: for the glory of the LORD had filled the house of God.

CHAPTER 6

THEN said Solomon, The LORD has said that he would dwell in the thick darkness.

2 But I have built an house of habitation for you, and a place for your dwelling for ever.

3 And the king turned his face, and blessed the whole congregation of Israel: and all the congregation of Israel stood.

4 And he said, Blessed be the LORD God of Israel, who has with his hands fulfilled that which he spake with his mouth to my father David, saying,

5 Since the day that I brought forth my people out of the land of Egypt I chose no city among all the tribes of Israel to build an house in, that my name might be there; neither chose I any man to be a ruler over my people Israel:

6 But I have chosen Jerusalem, that my name might be there; and have chosen David to be over my people Israel.

7 Now it was in the heart of David my father to build an house for the name of the LORD God of Israel.

8 But the LORD said to David my father, Forasmuch as it was in yours heart to build an house for my name, you did well in that it was in yours heart:

9 Notwithstanding you shalt not build the house; but your son which shall come forth out of your loins, he shall build the house for my name.

10 The LORD therefore has performed his word that he has spoken: for I am risen up in the room of David my father, and am set on the throne of Israel, as the LORD promised, and have built the house for the name of the LORD God of Israel.

11 And in it have I put the ark, wherein is the covenant of the LORD, that he made with the children of Israel.

12And he stood before the altar of the LORD in the presence of all the congregation of Israel, and spread forth his hands:

13 For Solomon had made a brasen scaffold, of five cubits long, and five cubits broad, and three cubits high, and had set it in the midst of the court: and upon it he stood, and kneeled down upon his knees before all the congregation of Israel, and spread forth his hands toward heaven,

14 And said, O LORD God of Israel, there is no God like you in the heaven, nor in the earth; which keepest covenant, and shewest mercy unto your servants, that walk before you with all their hearts:

15 You which have kept with your servant David my father that which you have promised him; and spakest with your mouth, and have fulfilled it with yours hand, as it is this day.

16 Now therefore, O LORD God of Israel, keep with your servant David my father that which you have promised him, saying, There shall not fail you a man in my sight to sit upon the throne of Israel; yet so that your children take heed to their way to walk in my law, as you have walked before me.

17 Now then, O LORD God of Israel, let your word be verified, which you have spoken unto your servant David.

18 But will God in very deed dwell with men on the earth? behold, heaven and the heaven of heavens cannot contain you; how much less this house which I have built!

19 Have respect therefore to the prayer of your servant, and to his supplication, O LORD my God, to hearken unto the cry and the prayer which your servant prayeth before you:

20 That yours eyes may be open upon this house day and night, upon the place whereof you have said that you wouldest put your name there; to hearken unto the prayer which your servant prayeth toward this place.

21 Hearken therefore unto the supplications of your servant, and of your people Israel, which they shall make toward this place: hear you from your dwelling place, even from heaven; and when you hearest, forgive.

22 If a man sin against his neighbour, and an oath be laid upon him to make him swear, and the oath come before yours altar in this house;

23 Then hear you from heaven, and do, and judge your servants, by requiting the wicked, by recompensing his way upon his own head; and by justifying the righteous, by giving him according to his righteousness.

24 And if your people Israel be put to the worse before the enemy, because they have sinned against you; and shall return and confess your name, and pray and make supplication before you in this house;

25 Then hear you from the heavens, and forgive the sin of your people Israel, and bring them again unto the land which you gavest to them and to their fathers.

26 When the heaven is shut up, and there is no rain, because they have sinned against you; yet if they pray toward this place, and confess your name, and turn from their sin, when you dost afflict them;

27 Then hear you from heaven, and forgive the sin of your servants, and of your people Israel, when you have taught them the good way, wherein they should walk; and send rain upon your land, which you have given unto your people for an inheritance.

28 If there be dearth in the land, if there be pestilence, if there be blasting, or mildew, locusts, or caterpillers; if their enemies besiege them in the cities of their land; whatsoever sore or whatsoever sickness there be:

29 Then what prayer or what supplication soever shall be made of any man, or of all your people Israel, when every one shall know his own sore and his own grief, and shall spread forth his hands in this house:

30 Then hear you from heaven your dwelling place, and forgive, and render unto every man according unto all his ways, whose heart you knowest; (for you only knowest the hearts of the children of men:)

31 That they may fear you, to walk in your ways, so long as they live in the land which you gavest unto our fathers.

32 Moreover concerning the stranger, which is not of your people Israel, but is come from a far country for your great name's sake, and your mighty hand, and your stretched out arm; if they come and pray in this house;

33 Then hear you from the heavens, even from your dwelling place, and do according to all that the stranger calleth to you for; that all people of the earth may know your name, and fear you, as doth your people Israel, and may know that this house which I have built is called by your name.

34 If your people go out to war against their enemies by the way that you shalt send them, and they pray unto you toward this city which you have chosen, and the house which I have built for your name;

35 Then hear you from the heavens their prayer and their supplication, and maintain their cause.

36 If they sin against you, (for there is no man which sinneth not,) and you be angry with them, and deliver them over before their enemies, and they carry them away captives unto a land far off or near;

37 Yet if they bethink themselves in the land whither they are carried captive, and turn and pray unto you in the land of their captivity, saying, We have sinned, we have done amiss, and have dealt wickedly;

38 If they return to you with all their heart and with all their soul in the land of their captivity, whither they have carried them captives, and pray toward their land, which you gavest unto their fathers, and toward the city which you have chosen, and toward the house which I have built for your name:

39 Then hear you from the heavens, even from your dwelling place, their prayer and their supplications, and maintain their cause, and forgive your people which have sinned against you.

40 Now, my God, let, I beseech you, yours eyes be open, and let yours ears be attent unto the prayer that is made in this place.

41 Now therefore arise, O LORD God, into your resting place, you , and the ark of your strength: let your priests, O LORD God, be clothed with salvation, and let your saints rejoice in goodness.

42 O LORD God, turn not away the face of yours anointed: remember the mercies of David your servant.

CHAPTER 7

NOW when Solomon had made an end of praying, the fire came down from heaven, and consumed the burnt offering and the sacrifices; and the glory of the LORD filled the house.

2 And the priests could not enter into the house of the LORD, because the glory of the LORD had filled the LORD's house.

3 And when all the children of Israel saw how the fire came down, and the glory of the LORD upon the house, they bowed themselves with their faces to the ground upon the pavement, and worshipped, and praised the LORD, saying, For he is good; for his mercy endureth for ever.

4 Then the king and all the people offered sacrifices before the LORD.

5 And king Solomon offered a sacrifice of twenty and two thousand oxen, and an hundred and twenty thousand sheep: so the king and all the people dedicated the house of God.

6 And the priests waited on their offices: the Levites also with instruments of musick of the LORD, which David the king had made to praise the LORD, because his mercy endureth for ever, when David praised by their ministry; and the priests sounded trumpets before them, and all Israel stood.

7 Moreover Solomon hallowed the middle of the court that was before the house of the LORD: for there he offered burnt offerings, and the fat of the peace offerings, because the brasen altar which Solomon had made was not able to receive the burnt offerings, and the meat offerings, and the fat.

8 Also at the same time Solomon kept the feast seven days, and all Israel with him, a very great congregation, from the entering in of Hamath unto the river of Egypt.

9 And in the eighth day they made a solemn assembly: for they kept the dedication of the altar seven days, and the feast seven days.

10 And on the three and twentieth day of the seventh month he sent the people away into their tents, glad and merry in heart for the goodness that the LORD had shewed unto David, and to Solomon, and to Israel his people.

11 Thus Solomon finished the house of the LORD, and the king's house: and all that came into Solomon's heart to make in the house of the LORD, and in his own house, he prosperously effected.

12 And the LORD appeared to Solomon by night, and said unto him, I have heard your prayer, and have chosen this place to myself for an house of sacrifice.

13 If I shut up heaven that there be no rain, or if I command the locusts to devour the land, or if I send pestilence among my people;

14 If my people, which are called by my name, shall humble themselves, and pray, and seek my face, and turn from their wicked ways; then will I hear from heaven, and will forgive their sin, and will heal their land.

15 Now my eyes shall be open, and my ears attent unto the prayer that is made in this place.

16 For now have I chosen and sanctified this house, that my name may be there for ever: and my eyes and my heart shall be there perpetually.

17 And as for you, if you will walk before me, as David your father walked, and to according to all that I have commanded you, and shalt observe my statutes and my judgments;

18 Then will I stablish the throne of your kingdom, according as I have covenanted with David your father, saying, There shall not fail you a man to be ruler in Israel.

19 But if you turn away, and forsake my statutes and my commandments, which I have set before you, and shall go and serve other gods, and worship them;

20 Then will I pluck them up by the roots out of my land which I have given them; and this house, which I have sanctified for my name, will I cast out of my sight, and will make it to be a proverb and a byword among all nations.

21 And this house, which is high, shall be an astonishment to every one that passes by it; so that he shall say, Why has the LORD done thus unto this land, and unto this house?

22 And it shall be answered, Because they forsook the LORD God of their fathers, which brought them forth out of the land of Egypt, and laid hold on other gods, and worshipped them, and served them: therefore has he brought all this evil upon them.

CHAPTER 8

AND it came to pass at the end of twenty years, wherein Solomon had built the house of the LORD, and his own house,

2 That the cities which Huram had restored to Solomon, Solomon built them, and caused the children of Israel to dwell there.

3 And Solomon went to Hamath-zobah, and prevailed against it.

4 And he built Tadmor in the wilderness, and all the store cities, which he built in Hamath.

5 Also he built Beth-horon the upper, and Beth-horon the nether, fenced cities, with walls, gates, and bars;

6 And Baalath, and all the store cities that Solomon had, and all the chariot cities, and the cities of the horsemen, and all that Solomon desired to build in Jerusalem, and in Lebanon, and throughout all the land of his dominion.

7 As for all the people that were left of the Hittites, and the Amorites, and the Perizzites, and the Hivites, and the Jebusites, which were not of Israel,

8 But of their children, who were left after them in the land, whom the children of Israel consumed not, them did Solomon make to pay tribute until this day.

9 But of the children of Israel did Solomon make no servants for his work; but they were men of war, and chief of his captains, and captains of his chariots and horsemen.

10 And these were the chief of king Solomon's officers, even two hundred and fifty, that bare rule over the people.

11 And Solomon brought up the daughter of Pharaoh out of the city of David unto the house that he had built for her: for he said, My wife shall not dwell in the house of David king of Israel, because the places are holy, whereunto the ark of the LORD has come.

12 Then Solomon offered burnt offerings unto the LORD on the altar of the LORD, which he had built before the porch,

13 Even after a certain rate every day, offering according to the commandment of Moses, on the sabbaths, and on the new moons, and on the solemn feasts, three times in the year, even in the feast of unleavened bread, and in the feast of weeks, and in the feast of tabernacles.

14 And he appointed, according to the order of David his father, the courses of the priests to their service, and the Levites to their charges, to praise and minister before the priests, as the duty of every day required: the porters also by their courses at every gate: for so had David the man of God commanded.

15 And they departed not from the commandment of the king unto the priests and Levites concerning any matter, or concerning the treasures.

16 Now all the work of Solomon was prepared unto the day of the foundation of the house of the LORD, and until it was finished. So the house of the LORD was perfected.

17 Then went Solomon to Ezion-geber, and to Eloth, at the sea side in the land of Edom.

18 And Huram sent him by the hands of his servants ships, and servants that had knowledge of the sea; and they went with the servants of Solomon to Ophir, and took thence four hundred and fifty talents of gold, and brought them to king Solomon.

CHAPTER 9

AND when the queen of Sheba heard of the fame of Solomon, she came to prove Solomon with hard questions at Jerusalem, with a very great company, and camels that bare spices, and gold in abundance, and precious stones: and when she was come to Solomon, she communed with him of all that was in her heart.

2 And Solomon told her all her questions: and there was nothing hid from Solomon which he told her not.

3 And when the queen of Sheba had seen the wisdom of Solomon, and the house that he had built,

4 And the meat of his table, and the sitting of his servants, and the attendance of his ministers, and their apparel; his cupbearers also, and their apparel; and his ascent by which he went up into the house of the LORD; there was no more spirit in her.

5 And she said to the king, It was a true report which I heard in my own land of yours acts, and of your wisdom:

6 Howbeit I believed not their words, until I came, and my eyes had seen it: and, behold, the one half of the greatness of your wisdom was not told me: for you exceedest the fame that I heard.

7 Happy are your men, and happy are these your servants, which stand continually before you, and hear your wisdom.

8 Blessed be the LORD your God, which delighted in you to set you on his throne, to be king for the LORD your God: because your God loved Israel, to establish them for ever, therefore made he you king over them, to do judgment and justice.

9 And she gave the king an hundred and twenty talents of gold, and of spices great abundance, and precious stones: neither was there any such spice as the queen of Sheba gave king Solomon.

10 And the servants also of Huram, and the servants of Solomon, which brought gold from Ophir, brought algum trees and precious stones.

11 And the king made of the algum trees terraces to the house of the LORD, and to the king's palace, and harps and psalteries for singers: and there were none such seen before in the land of Judah.

12 And king Solomon gave to the queen of Sheba all her desire, whatsoever she asked, beside that which she had brought unto the king. So she turned, and went away to her own land, she and her servants.

13 Now the weight of gold that came to Solomon in one year was six hundred and threescore and six talents of gold;

14 Beside that which chapmen and merchants brought. And all the kings of Arabia and governors of the country brought gold and silver to Solomon.

15 And king Solomon made two hundred targets of beaten gold: six hundred shekels of beaten gold went to one target.

16 And three hundred shields made he of beaten gold: three hundred shekels of gold went to one shield. And the king put them in the house of the forest of Lebanon.

17 Moreover the king made a great throne of ivory, and overlaid it with pure gold.

18 And there were six steps to the throne, with a footstool of gold, which were fastened to the throne, and stays on each side of the sitting place, and two lions standing by the stays:

19 And twelve lions stood there on the one side and on the other upon the six steps. There was not the like made in any kingdom.

20 And all the drinking vessels of king Solomon were of gold, and all the vessels of the house of the forest of Lebanon were of pure gold: none were of silver; it was not any thing accounted of in the days of Solomon.

21 For the king's ships went to Tarshish with the servants of Huram: every three years once came the ships of Tarshish bringing gold, and silver, ivory, and apes, and peacocks.

22 And king Solomon passed all the kings of the earth in riches and wisdom.

23 And all the kings of the earth sought the presence of Solomon, to hear his wisdom, that God had put in his heart.

24 And they brought every man his present, vessels of silver, and vessels of gold, and raiment, harness, and spices, horses, and mules, a rate year by year.

25 And Solomon had four thousand stalls for horses and chariots, and twelve thousand horsemen; whom he bestowed in the chariot cities, and with the king at Jerusalem.

26 And he reigned over all the kings from the river even unto the land of the Philistines, and to the border of Egypt.

27 And the king made silver in Jerusalem as stones, and cedar trees made he as the sycomore trees that are in the low plains in abundance.

28 And they brought unto Solomon horses out of Egypt, and out of all lands.

29 Now the rest of the acts of Solomon, first and last, are they not written in the book of Nathan the prophet, and in the prophecy of Ahijah the Shilonite, and in the visions of Iddo the seer against Jeroboam the son of Nebat?

30 And Solomon reigned in Jerusalem over all Israel forty years.

31 And Solomon slept with his fathers, and he was buried in the city of David his father: and Rehoboam his son reigned in his stead.

CHAPTER 10

AND Rehoboam went to Shechem: for to Shechem were all Israel come to make him king.

2 And it came to pass, when Jeroboam the son of Nebat, who was in Egypt, whither he had fled from the presence of Solomon the king, heard it, that Jeroboam returned out of Egypt.

3 And they sent and called him. So Jeroboam and all Israel came and spake to Rehoboam, saying,

4 Your father made our yoke grievous: now therefore ease you somewhat the grievous servitude of your father, and his heavy yoke that he put upon us, and we will serve you.

5 And he said unto them, Come again unto me after three days. And the people departed.

6 And king Rehoboam took counsel with the old men that had stood before Solomon his father while he yet lived, saying, What counsel give you me to return answer to this people?

7 And they spake unto him, saying, If you be kind to this people, and please them, and speak good words to them, they will be your servants for ever.

8 But he forsook the counsel which the old men gave him, and took counsel with the young men that were brought up with him, that stood before him.

9 And he said unto them, What advice give you that we may return answer to this people, which have spoken to me, saying, Ease somewhat the yoke that your father did put upon us?

10 And the young men that were brought up with him spake unto him, saying, Thus shalt you answer the people that spake unto you, saying, Your father made our yoke heavy, but make you it somewhat lighter for us; thus shalt you say unto them, My little finger shall be thicker than my father's loins.

11 For whereas my father put a heavy yoke upon you, I will put more to your yoke: my father chastised you with whips, but I will chastise you with scorpions.

12 So Jeroboam and all the people came to Rehoboam on the third day, as the king bade, saying, Come again to me on the third day.

13 And the king answered them roughly; and king Rehoboam forsook the counsel of the old men,

14 And answered them after the advice of the young men, saying, My father made your yoke heavy, but I will add thereto: my father chastised you with whips, but I will chastise you with scorpions.

15 So the king hearkened not unto the people: for the cause was of God, that the LORD might perform his word, which he spake by the hand of Ahijah the Shilonite to Jeroboam the son of Nebat.

16 And when all Israel saw that the king would not hearken unto them, the people answered the king, saying, What portion have we in David? and we have none inheritance in the son of Jesse: every man to your tents, O Israel: and now, David, see to yours own house. So all Israel went to their tents.

17 But as for the children of Israel that dwelt in the cities of Judah, Rehoboam reigned over them.

18 Then king Rehoboam sent Hadoram that was over the tribute; and the children of Israel stoned him with stones, that he died. But king Rehoboam made speed to get him up to his chariot, to flee to Jerusalem.

19 And Israel rebelled against the house of David unto this day.

CHAPTER 11

AND when Rehoboam was come to Jerusalem, he gathered of the house of Judah and Benjamin an hundred and fourscore thousand chosen men, which were warriors, to fight against Israel, that he might bring the kingdom again to Rehoboam.

2 But the word of the LORD came to Shemaiah the man of God, saying,

3 Speak unto Rehoboam the son of Solomon, king of Judah, and to all Israel in Judah and Benjamin, saying,

4 Thus saith the LORD, You shall not go up, nor fight against your brethren: return every man to his house: for this thing is done of me. And they obeyed the words of the LORD, and returned from going against Jeroboam.

5And Rehoboam dwelt in Jerusalem, and built cities for defence in Judah.

6 He built even Beth-lehem, and Etam, and Tekoa,

7 And Beth-zur, and Shoco, and Adullam,

8 And Gath, and Mareshah, and Ziph,

9 And Adoraim, and Lachish, and Azekah,

10 And Zorah, and Aijalon, and Hebron, which are in Judah and in Benjamin fenced cities.

11 And he fortified the strong holds, and put captains in them, and store of victual, and of oil and wine.

12 And in every several city he put shields and spears, and made them exceeding strong, having Judah and Benjamin on his side.

13And the priests and the Levites that were in all Israel resorted to him out of all their coasts.

14 For the Levites left their suburbs and their possession, and came to Judah and Jerusalem: for Jeroboam and his sons had cast them off from executing the priest's office unto the LORD:

15 And he ordained him priests for the high places, and for the devils, and for the calves which he had made.

16 And after them out of all the tribes of Israel such as set their hearts to seek the LORD God of Israel came to Jerusalem, to sacrifice unto the LORD God of their fathers.

17 So they strengthened the kingdom of Judah, and made Rehoboam the son of Solomon strong, three years: for three years they walked in the way of David and Solomon.

18And Rehoboam took him Mahalath the daughter of Jerimoth the son of David to wife, and Abihail the daughter of Eliab the son of Jesse;

19 Which bare him children; Jeush, and Shamariah, and Zaham.

20 And after her he took Maachah the daughter of Absalom; which bare him Abijah, and Attai, and Ziza, and Shelomith.

21 And Rehoboam loved Maachah the daughter of Absalom above all his wives and his concubines: (for he took eighteen wives, and threescore concubines; and begat twenty and eight sons, and threescore daughters.)

22 And Rehoboam made Abijah the son of Maachah the chief, to be ruler among his brethren: for he thought to make him king.

23 And he dealt wisely, and dispersed of all his children throughout all the countries of Judah and Benjamin, unto every fenced city: and he gave them victual in abundance. And he desired many wives.

CHAPTER 12

AND it came to pass, when Rehoboam had established the kingdom, and had strengthened himself, he forsook the law of the LORD, and all Israel with him.

2 And it came to pass, that in the fifth year of king Rehoboam Shishak king of Egypt came up against Jerusalem, because they had transgressed against the LORD,

3 With twelve hundred chariots, and threescore thousand horsemen: and the people were without number that came with him out of Egypt; the Lubims, the Sukkiims, and the Ethiopians.

4 And he took the fenced cities which pertained to Judah, and came to Jerusalem.

5Then came Shemaiah the prophet to Rehoboam, and to the princes of Judah, that were gathered together to Jerusalem because of Shishak, and said unto them, Thus saith the LORD, You have forsaken me, and therefore have I also left you in the hand of Shishak.

6 Whereupon the princes of Israel and the king humbled themselves; and they said, The LORD is righteous.

7 And when the LORD saw that they humbled themselves, the word of the LORD came to Shemaiah, saying, They have humbled themselves; therefore I will not destroy them, but I will grant them some deliverance; and my wrath shall not be poured out upon Jerusalem by the hand of Shishak.

8 Nevertheless they shall be his servants; that they may know my service, and the service of the kingdoms of the countries.

9 So Shishak king of Egypt came up against Jerusalem, and took away the treasures of the house of the LORD, and the treasures of the king's house; he took all: he carried away also the shields of gold which Solomon had made.

10 Instead of which king Rehoboam made shields of brass, and committed them to the hands of the chief of the guard, that kept the entrance of the king's house.

11 And when the king entered into the house of the LORD, the guard came and fetched them, and brought them again into the guard chamber.

12 And when he humbled himself, the wrath of the LORD turned from him, that he would not destroy him altogether: and also in Judah things went well.

13So king Rehoboam strengthened himself in Jerusalem, and reigned: for Rehoboam was one and forty years old when he began to reign, and he reigned seventeen years in Jerusalem, the city which the LORD had chosen out of all the tribes of Israel, to put his name there. And his mother's name was Naamah an Ammonitess.

14 And he did evil, because he prepared not his heart to seek the LORD.

15 Now the acts of Rehoboam, first and last, are they not written in the book of Shemaiah the prophet, and of Iddo the seer concerning genealogies? And there were wars between Rehoboam and Jeroboam continually.

16 And Rehoboam slept with his fathers, and was buried in the city of David: and Abijah his son reigned in his stead.

CHAPTER 13

NOW in the eighteenth year of king Jeroboam began Abijah to reign over Judah.

2 He reigned three years in Jerusalem. His mother's name also was Michaiah the daughter of Uriel of Gibeah. And there was war between Abijah and Jeroboam.

3 And Abijah set the battle in array with an army of valiant men of war, even four hundred thousand chosen men: Jeroboam also set the battle in array against him with eight hundred thousand chosen men, being mighty men of valour.

4And Abijah stood up upon mount Zemaraim, which is in mount Ephraim, and said, Hear me, you Jeroboam, and all Israel;

5 Ought you not to know that the LORD God of Israel gave the kingdom over Israel to David for ever, even to him and to his sons by a covenant of salt?

6 Yet Jeroboam the son of Nebat, the servant of Solomon the son of David, is risen up, and has rebelled against his lord.

7 And there are gathered unto him vain men, the children of Belial, and have strengthened themselves against Rehoboam the son of Solomon, when Rehoboam was young and tenderhearted, and could not withstand them.

8 And now you think to withstand the kingdom of the LORD in the hand of the sons of David; and you be a great multitude, and there are with you golden calves, which Jeroboam made you for gods.

9 Have you not cast out the priests of the LORD, the sons of Aaron, and the Levites, and have made you priests after the manner of the nations of other lands? so that whosoever comes to consecrate himself with a young bullock and seven rams, the same may be a priest of them that are no gods.

10 But as for us, the LORD is our God, and we have not forsaken him; and the priests, which minister unto the LORD, are the sons of Aaron, and the Levites wait upon their business:

11 And they burn unto the LORD every morning and every evening burnt sacrifices and sweet incense: the shewbread also set they in order upon the pure table; and the candlestick of gold with the lamps thereof, to burn every evening: for we keep the charge of the LORD our God; but you have forsaken him.

12 And, behold, God himself is with us for our captain, and his priests with sounding trumpets to cry alarm against you. O children of Israel, fight you not against the LORD God of your fathers; for you shall not prosper.

13But Jeroboam caused an ambushment to come about behind them: so they were before Judah, and the ambushment was behind them.

14 And when Judah looked back, behold, the battle was before and behind: and they cried unto the LORD, and the priests sounded with the trumpets.

15 Then the men of Judah gave a shout: and as the men of Judah shouted, it came to pass, that God struck Jeroboam and all Israel before Abijah and Judah.

16 And the children of Israel fled before Judah: and God delivered them into their hand.

17 And Abijah and his people slew them with a great slaughter: so there fell down slain of Israel five hundred thousand chosen men.

18 Thus the children of Israel were brought under at that time, and the children of Judah prevailed, because they relied upon the LORD God of their fathers.

19 And Abijah pursued after Jeroboam, and took cities from him, Beth-el with the towns thereof, and Jeshanah with the towns thereof, and Ephrain with the towns thereof.

20 Neither did Jeroboam recover strength again in the days of Abijah: and the LORD struck him, and he died.

21 But Abijah waxed mighty, and married fourteen wives, and begat twenty and two sons, and sixteen daughters.

22 And the rest of the acts of Abijah, and his ways, and his sayings, are written in the story of the prophet Iddo.

CHAPTER 14

SO Abijah slept with his fathers, and they buried him in the city of David: and Asa his son reigned in his stead. In his days the land was quiet ten years.

2 And Asa did that which was good and right in the eyes of the LORD his God:

3 For he took away the altars of the strange gods, and the high places, and brake down the images, and cut down the groves:

4 And commanded Judah to seek the LORD God of their fathers, and to do the law and the commandment.

5 Also he took away out of all the cities of Judah the high places and the images: and the kingdom was quiet before him.

6 And he built fenced cities in Judah: for the land had rest, and he had no war in those years; because the LORD had given him rest.

7 Therefore he said unto Judah, Let us build these cities, and make about them walls, and towers, gates, and bars, while the land is yet before us; because we have sought the LORD our God, we have sought him, and he has given us rest on every side. So they built and prospered.

8 And Asa had an army of men that bare targets and spears, out of Judah three hundred thousand; and out of Benjamin, that bare shields and drew bows, two hundred and fourscore thousand: all these were mighty men of valour.

9 And there came out against them Zerah the Ethiopian with a host of a thousand thousand, and three hundred chariots; and came unto Mareshah.

10 Then Asa went out against him, and they set the battle in array in the valley of Zephathah at Mareshah.

11 And Asa cried unto the LORD his God, and said, LORD, it is nothing with you to help, whether with many, or with them that have no power: help us, O LORD our God; for we rest on you, and in your name we go against this multitude. O LORD, you are our God; let not man prevail against you.

12 So the LORD struck the Ethiopians before Asa, and before Judah; and the Ethiopians fled.

13 And Asa and the people that were with him pursued them unto Gerar: and the Ethiopians were overthrown, that they could not recover themselves; for they were destroyed before the LORD, and before his host; and they carried away very much spoil.

14 And they struck all the cities round about Gerar; for the fear of the LORD came upon them: and they spoiled all the cities; for there was exceeding much spoil in them.

15 They struck also the tents of cattle, and carried away sheep and camels in abundance, and returned to Jerusalem.

CHAPTER 15

AND the Spirit of God came upon Azariah the son of Oded:

2 And he went out to meet Asa, and said unto him, Hear you me, Asa, and all Judah and Benjamin; The LORD is with you, while you be with him; and if you seek him, he will be found of you; but if you forsake him, he will forsake you.

3 Now for a long season Israel has been without the true God, and without a teaching priest, and without law.

4 But when they in their trouble did turn unto the LORD God of Israel, and sought him, he was found of them.

5 And in those times there was no peace to him that went out, nor to him that came in, but great vexations were upon all the inhabitants of the countries.

6 And nation was destroyed of nation, and city of city: for God did vex them with all adversity.

7 Be you strong therefore, and let not your hands be weak: for your work shall be rewarded.

8 And when Asa heard these words, and the prophecy of Oded the prophet, he took courage, and put away the abominable idols out of all the land of Judah and Benjamin, and out of the cities which he had taken from mount Ephraim, and renewed the altar of the LORD, that was before the porch of the LORD.

9 And he gathered all Judah and Benjamin, and the strangers with them out of Ephraim and Manasseh, and out of Simeon: for they fell to him out of Israel in abundance, when they saw that the LORD his God was with him.

10 So they gathered themselves together at Jerusalem in the third month, in the fifteenth year of the reign of Asa.

11 And they offered unto the LORD the same time, of the spoil which they had brought, seven hundred oxen and seven thousand sheep.

12 And they entered into a covenant to seek the LORD God of their fathers with all their heart and with all their soul;

13 That whosoever would not seek the LORD God of Israel should be put to death, whether small or great, whether man or woman.

14 And they sware unto the LORD with a loud voice, and with shouting, and with trumpets, and with cornets.

15 And all Judah rejoiced at the oath: for they had sworn with all their heart, and sought him with their whole desire; and he was found of them: and the LORD gave them rest round about.

16 And also concerning Maachah the mother of Asa the king, he removed her from being queen, because she had made an idol in a grove: and Asa cut down her idol, and stamped it, and burnt it at the brook Kidron.

17 But the high places were not taken away out of Israel: nevertheless the heart of Asa was perfect all his days.

18 And he brought into the house of God the things that his father had dedicated, and that he himself had dedicated, silver, and gold, and vessels.

19 And there was no more war unto the five and thirtieth year of the reign of Asa.

CHAPTER 16

IN the six and thirtieth year of the reign of Asa Baasha king of Israel came up against Judah, and built Ramah, to the intent that he might let none go out or come in to Asa king of Judah.

2 Then Asa brought out silver and gold out of the treasures of the house of the LORD and of the king's house, and sent to Ben-hadad king of Syria, that dwelt at Damascus, saying,

3 There is a league between me and you, as there was between my father and your father: behold, I have sent you silver and gold; go, break your league with Baasha king of Israel, that he may depart from me.

4 And Ben-hadad hearkened unto king Asa, and sent the captains of his armies against the cities of Israel; and they struck Ijon, and Dan, and Abel-maim, and all the store cities of Naphtali.

5 And it came to pass, when Baasha heard it, that he left off building of Ramah, and let his work cease.

6 Then Asa the king took all Judah; and they carried away the stones of Ramah, and the timber thereof, wherewith Baasha was building; and he built therewith Geba and Mizpah.

7 And at that time Hanani the seer came to Asa king of Judah, and said unto him, Because you have relied on the king of Syria, and not relied on the LORD your God, therefore is the host of the king of Syria escaped out of yours hand.

8 Were not the Ethiopians and the Lubims a huge host, with very many chariots and horsemen? yet, because you did rely on the LORD, he delivered them into yours hand.

9 For the eyes of the LORD run to and fro throughout the whole earth, to shew himself strong in the behalf of them whose heart is perfect toward him. Herein you have done foolishly: therefore from henceforth you shalt have wars.

10 Then Asa was wroth with the seer, and put him in a prison house; for he was in a rage with him because of this thing. And Asa oppressed some of the people the same time.

11 And, behold, the acts of Asa, first and last, lo, they are written in the book of the kings of Judah and Israel.

12 And Asa in the thirty and ninth year of his reign was diseased in his feet, until his disease was exceeding great: yet in his disease he sought not to the LORD, but to the physicians.

13 And Asa slept with his fathers, and died in the one and fortieth year of his reign.

14 And they buried him in his own sepulchres, which he had made for himself in the city of David, and laid him in the bed which was filled with sweet odours and divers kinds of spices prepared by the apothecaries' are: and they made a very great burning for him.

CHAPTER 17

AND Jehoshaphat his son reigned in his stead, and strengthened himself against Israel.

2 And he placed forces in all the fenced cities of Judah, and set garrisons in the land of Judah, and in the cities of Ephraim, which Asa his father had taken.

3 And the LORD was with Jehoshaphat, because he walked in the first ways of his father David, and sought not unto Baalim:

4 But sought to the LORD God of his father, and walked in his commandments, and not after the doings of Israel.

5 Therefore the LORD stablished the kingdom in his hand; and all Judah brought to Jehoshaphat presents; and he had riches and honour in abundance.

6 And his heart was lifted up in the ways of the LORD: moreover he took away the high places and groves out of Judah.

7 Also in the third year of his reign he sent to his princes, even to Ben-hail, and to Obadiah, and to Zechariah, and to Nethaneel, and to Michaiah, to teach in the cities of Judah.

8 And with them he sent Levites, even Shemaiah, and Nethaniah, and Zebadiah, and Asahel, and Shemiramoth, and Jehonathan, and Adonijah, and Tobijah, and Tob-adonijah, Levites; and with them Elishama and Jehoram, priests.

9 And they taught in Judah, and had the book of the law of the LORD with them, and went about throughout all the cities of Judah, and taught the people.

10 And the fear of the LORD fell upon all the kingdoms of the lands that were round about Judah, so that they made no war against Jehoshaphat.

11 Also some of the Philistines brought Jehoshaphat presents, and tribute silver; and the Arabians brought him flocks, seven thousand and seven hundred rams, and seven thousand and seven hundred he goats.

12 And Jehoshaphat waxed great exceedingly; and he built in Judah castles, and cities of store.

13 And he had much business in the cities of Judah: and the men of war, mighty men of valour, were in Jerusalem.

14 And these are the numbers of them according to the house of their fathers: Of Judah, the captains of thousands; Adnah the chief, and with him mighty men of valour three hundred thousand.

15 And next to him was Jehohanan the captain, and with him two hundred and fourscore thousand.

16 And next him was Amasiah the son of Zichri, who willingly offered himself unto the LORD; and with him two hundred thousand mighty men of valour.

17 And of Benjamin; Eliada a mighty man of valour, and with him armed men with bow and shield two hundred thousand.

18 And next him was Jehozabad, and with him an hundred and fourscore thousand ready prepared for the war.

19 These waited on the king, beside those whom the king put in the fenced cities throughout all Judah.

CHAPTER 18

NOW Jehoshaphat had riches and honour in abundance, and joined affinity with Ahab.

2 And after certain years he went down to Ahab to Samaria. And Ahab killed sheep and oxen for him in abundance, and for the people that he had with him, and persuaded him to go up with him to Ramoth-gilead.

3 And Ahab king of Israel said unto Jehoshaphat king of Judah, Will you go with me to Ramoth-gilead? And he answered him, I am as you are, and my people as your people; and we will be with you in the war.

4 And Jehoshaphat said unto the king of Israel, Inquire, I pray you, at the word of the LORD to day.

5 Therefore the king of Israel gathered together of prophets four hundred men, and said unto them, Shall we go to Ramoth-gilead to battle, or shall I forbear? And they said, Go up; for God will deliver it into the king's hand.

6 But Jehoshaphat said, Is there not here a prophet of the LORD besides, that we might inquire of him?

7 And the king of Israel said unto Jehoshaphat, There is yet one man, by whom we may inquire of the LORD: but I hate him; for he never prophesied good unto me, but always evil: the same is Micaiah the son of Imla. And Jehoshaphat said, Let not the king say so.

8 And the king of Israel called for one of his officers, and said, Fetch quickly Micaiah the son of Imla.

9 And the king of Israel and Jehoshaphat king of Judah sat either of them on his throne, clothed in their robes, and they sat in a void place at the entering in of the gate of Samaria; and all the prophets prophesied before them.

10 And Zedekiah the son of Chenaanah had made him horns of iron, and said, Thus saith the LORD, With these you shalt push Syria until they be consumed.

11 And all the prophets prophesied so, saying, Go up to Ramoth-gilead, and prosper: for the LORD shall deliver it into the hand of the king.

12 And the messenger that went to call Micaiah spake to him, saying, Behold, the words of the prophets declare good to the king with one assent; let your word therefore, I pray you, be like one of theirs, and speak you good.

13 And Micaiah said, As the LORD liveth, even what my God saith, that will I speak.

14 And when he was come to the king, the king said unto him, Micaiah, shall we go to Ramoth-gilead to battle, or shall I forbear? And he said, Go you up, and prosper, and they shall be delivered into your hand.

15 And the king said to him, How many times shall I adjure you that you say nothing but the truth to me in the name of the LORD?

16 Then he said, I did see all Israel scattered upon the mountains, as sheep that have no shepherd: and the LORD said, These have no master; let them return therefore every man to his house in peace.

17 And the king of Israel said to Jehoshaphat, Did I not tell you that he would not prophesy good unto me, but evil?

18 Again he said, Therefore hear the word of the LORD; I saw the LORD sitting upon his throne, and all the host of heaven standing on his right hand and on his left.

19 And the LORD said, Who shall entice Ahab king of Israel, that he may go up and fall at Ramoth-gilead? And one spake saying after this manner, and another saying after that manner.

20 Then there came out a spirit, and stood before the LORD, and said, I will entice him. And the LORD said unto him, Wherewith?

21 And he said, I will go out, and be a lying spirit in the mouth of all his prophets. And the LORD said, You shalt entice him, and you shalt also prevail: go out, and do even so.

22 Now therefore, behold, the LORD has put a lying spirit in the mouth of these your prophets, and the LORD has spoken evil against you.

23 Then Zedekiah the son of Chenaanah came near, and struck Micaiah upon the cheek, and said, Which way went the Spirit of the LORD from me to speak unto you?

24 And Micaiah said, Behold, you shalt see on that day when you shalt go into an inner chamber to hide yourself.

25 Then the king of Israel said, Take you Micaiah, and carry him back to Amon the governor of the city, and to Joash the king's son;

26 And say, Thus saith the king, Put this fellow in the prison, and feed him with bread of affliction and with water of affliction, until I return in peace.

27 And Micaiah said, If you certainly return in peace, then has not the LORD spoken by me. And he said, Hearken, all you people.

28 So the king of Israel and Jehoshaphat the king of Judah went up to Ramoth-gilead.

29 And the king of Israel said unto Jehoshaphat, I will disguise myself, and will go to the battle; but put you on your robes. So the king of Israel disguised himself; and they went to the battle.

30 Now the king of Syria had commanded the captains of the chariots that were with him, saying, Fight you not with small or great, save only with the king of Israel.

31 And it came to pass, when the captains of the chariots saw Jehoshaphat, that they said, It is the king of Israel. Therefore they compassed about him to fight: but Jehoshaphat cried out, and the LORD helped him; and God moved them to depart from him.

32 For it came to pass, that, when the captains of the chariots perceived that it was not the king of Israel, they turned back again from pursuing him.

33 And a certain man drew a bow at a venture, and struck the king of Israel between the joints of the harness: therefore he said to his chariot man, Turn yours hand, that you mayest carry me out of the host; for I am wounded.

34 And the battle increased that day: howbeit the king of Israel stayed himself up in his chariot against the Syrians until the even: and about the time of the sun going down he died.

CHAPTER 19

AND Jehoshaphat the king of Judah returned to his house in peace to Jerusalem.

2 And Jehu the son of Hanani the seer went out to meet him, and said to king Jehoshaphat, Shouldest you help the ungodly, and love them that hate the LORD? therefore is wrath upon you from before the LORD.

3 Nevertheless there are good things found in you, in that you have taken away the groves out of the land, and have prepared yours heart to seek God.

4 And Jehoshaphat dwelt at Jerusalem: and he went out again through the people from Beer-sheba to mount Ephraim, and brought them back unto the LORD God of their fathers.

5 And he set judges in the land throughout all the fenced cities of Judah, city by city,

6 And said to the judges, Take heed what you do: for you judge not for man, but for the LORD, who is with you in the judgment.

7 Wherefore now let the fear of the LORD be upon you; take heed and do it: for there is no iniquity with the LORD our God, nor respect of persons, nor taking of gifts.

8 Moreover in Jerusalem did Jehoshaphat set of the Levites, and of the priests, and of the chief of the fathers of Israel, for the judgment of the LORD, and for controversies, when they returned to Jerusalem.

9 And he charged them, saying, Thus shall you do in the fear of the LORD, faithfully, and with a perfect heart.

10 And what cause soever shall come to you of your brethren that dwell in their cities, between blood and blood, between law and commandment, statutes and judgments, you shall even warn them that they trespass not against the LORD, and so wrath come upon you, and upon your brethren: this do, and you shall not trespass.

11 And, behold, Amariah the chief priest is over you in all matters of the LORD; and Zebadiah the son of Ishmael, the ruler of the house of Judah, for all the king's matters: also the Levites shall be officers before you. Deal courageously, and the LORD shall be with the good.

CHAPTER 20

IT came to pass after this also, that the children of Moab, and the children of Ammon, and with them other beside the Ammonites, came against Jehoshaphat to battle.

2 Then there came some that told Jehoshaphat, saying, There comes a great multitude against you from beyond the sea on this side Syria; and, behold, they be in Hazazon-tamar, which is En-gedi.

3 And Jehoshaphat feared, and set himself to seek the LORD, and proclaimed a fast throughout all Judah.

4 And Judah gathered themselves together, to ask help of the LORD: even out of all the cities of Judah they came to seek the LORD.

5 And Jehoshaphat stood in the congregation of Judah and Jerusalem, in the house of the LORD, before the new court,

6 And said, O LORD God of our fathers, are not you God in heaven? and rulest not you over all the kingdoms of the heathen? and in yours hand is there not power and might, so that none is able to withstand you?

7 Are not you our God, who did drive out the inhabitants of this land before your people Israel, and gavest it to the seed of Abraham your friend for ever?

8 And they dwelt therein, and have built you a sanctuary therein for your name, saying,

9 If, when evil comes upon us, as the sword, judgment, or pestilence, or famine, we stand before this house, and in your presence, (for your name is in this house,) and cry unto you in our affliction, then you will hear and help.

10 And now, behold, the children of Ammon and Moab and mount Seir, whom you wouldest not let Israel invade, when they came out of the land of Egypt, but they turned from them, and destroyed them not;

11 Behold, I say, how they reward us, to come to cast us out of your possession, which you have given us to inherit.

12 O our God, will you not judge them? for we have no might against this great company that comes against us; neither know we what to do: but our eyes are upon you.

13 And all Judah stood before the LORD, with their little ones, their wives, and their children.

14 Then upon Jahaziel the son of Zechariah, the son of Benaiah, the son of Jeiel, the son of Mattaniah, a Levite of the sons of Asaph, came the Spirit of the LORD in the midst of the congregation;

15 And he said, Hearken you , all Judah, and you inhabitants of Jerusalem, and you king Jehoshaphat, Thus saith the LORD unto you, Be not afraid nor dismayed by reason of this great multitude; for the battle is not yours, but God's.

16 To morrow go you down against them: behold, they come up by the cliff of Ziz; and you shall find them at the end of the brook, before the wilderness of Jeruel.

17 You shall not need to fight in this battle: set yourselves, stand you still, and see the salvation of the LORD with you, O Judah and Jerusalem: fear not, nor be dismayed; to morrow go out against them: for the LORD will be with you.

18 And Jehoshaphat bowed his head with his face to the ground: and all Judah and the inhabitants of Jerusalem fell before the LORD, worshipping the LORD.

19 And the Levites, of the children of the Kohathites, and of the children of the Korhites, stood up to praise the LORD God of Israel with a loud voice on high.

20 And they rose early in the morning, and went forth into the wilderness of Tekoa: and as they went forth, Jehoshaphat stood and said, Hear me, O Judah, and you inhabitants of Jerusalem; Believe in the LORD your God, so shall you be established; believe his prophets, so shall you prosper.

21 And when he had consulted with the people, he appointed singers unto the LORD, and that should praise the beauty of holiness, as they went out before the army, and to say, Praise the LORD; for his mercy endureth for ever.

22 And when they began to sing and to praise, the LORD set ambushments against the children of Ammon, Moab, and mount Seir, which were come against Judah; and they were smitten.

23 For the children of Ammon and Moab stood up against the inhabitants of mount Seir, utterly to slay and destroy them: and when they had made an end of the inhabitants of Seir, every one helped to destroy another.

24 And when Judah came toward the watch tower in the wilderness, they looked unto the multitude, and, behold, they were dead bodies fallen to the earth, and none escaped.

25 And when Jehoshaphat and his people came to take away the spoil of them, they found among them in abundance both riches with the dead bodies, and precious jewels, which they stripped off for themselves, more than they could carry away: and they were three days in gathering of the spoil, it was so much.

26 And on the fourth day they assembled themselves in the valley of Berachah; for there they blessed the LORD: therefore the name of the same place was called, The valley of Berachah, unto this day.

27 Then they returned, every man of Judah and Jerusalem, and Jehoshaphat in the forefront of them, to go again to Jerusalem with joy; for the LORD had made them to rejoice over their enemies.

28 And they came to Jerusalem with psalteries and harps and trumpets unto the house of the LORD.

29 And the fear of God was on all the kingdoms of those countries, when they had heard that the LORD fought against the enemies of Israel.

30 So the realm of Jehoshaphat was quiet: for his God gave him rest round about.

31 And Jehoshaphat reigned over Judah: he was thirty and five years old when he began to reign, and he reigned twenty and five years in Jerusalem. And his mother's name was Azubah the daughter of Shilhi.

32 And he walked in the way of Asa his father, and departed not from it, doing that which was right in the sight of the LORD.

33 Howbeit the high places were not taken away: for as yet the people had not prepared their hearts unto the God of their fathers.

34 Now the rest of the acts of Jehoshaphat, first and last, behold, they are written in the book of Jehu the son of Hanani, who is mentioned in the book of the kings of Israel.

35 And after this did Jehoshaphat king of Judah join himself with Ahaziah king of Israel, who did very wickedly:

36 And he joined himself with him to make ships to go to Tarshish: and they made the ships in Ezion-geber.

37 Then Eliezer the son of Dodavah of Mareshah prophesied against Jehoshaphat, saying, Because you have joined yourself with Ahaziah, the LORD has broken your works. And the ships were broken, that they were not able to go to Tarshish.

CHAPTER 21

NOW Jehoshaphat slept with his fathers, and was buried with his fathers in the city of David. And Jehoram his son reigned in his stead.

2 And he had brethren the sons of Jehoshaphat, Azariah, and Jehiel, and Zechariah, and Azariah, and Michael, and Shephatiah: all these were the sons of Jehoshaphat king of Israel.

3 And their father gave them great gifts of silver, and of gold, and of precious things, with fenced cities in Judah: but the kingdom gave he to Jehoram; because he was the firstborn.

4 Now when Jehoram was risen up to the kingdom of his father, he strengthened himself, and slew all his brethren with the sword, and divers also of the princes of Israel.

5 Jehoram was thirty and two years old when he began to reign, and he reigned eight years in Jerusalem.

6 And he walked in the way of the kings of Israel, like as did the house of Ahab: for he had the daughter of Ahab to wife: and he created that which was evil in the eyes of the LORD.

7 Howbeit the LORD would not destroy the house of David, because of the covenant that he had made with David, and as he promised to give a light to him and to his sons for ever.

8 In his days the Edomites revolted from under the dominion of Judah, and made themselves a king.

9 Then Jehoram went forth with his princes, and all his chariots with him: and he rose up by night, and struck the Edomites which compassed him in, and the captains of the chariots.

10 So the Edomites revolted from under the hand of Judah unto this day. The same time also did Libnah revolt from under his hand; because he had forsaken the LORD God of his fathers.

11 Moreover he made high places in the mountains of Judah, and caused the inhabitants of Jerusalem to commit fornication, and compelled Judah thereto.

12And there came a writing to him from Elijah the prophet, saying, Thus saith the LORD God of David your father, Because you have not walked in the ways of Jehoshaphat your father, nor in the ways of Asa king of Judah,

13 But have walked in the way of the kings of Israel, and have made Judah and the inhabitants of Jerusalem to go a whoring, like to the whoredoms of the house of Ahab, and also have slain your brethren of your father's house, which were better than yourself:

14 Behold, with a great plague will the LORD strike your people, and your children, and your wives, and all your goods:

15 And you shalt have great sickness by disease of your bowels, until your bowels fall out by reason of the sickness day by day.

16Moreover the LORD stirred up against Jehoram the spirit of the Philistines, and of the Arabians, that were near the Ethiopians:

17 And they came up into Judah, and brake into it, and carried away all the substance that was found in the king's house, and his sons also, and his wives; so that there was never a son left him, save Jehoahaz, the youngest of his sons.

18And after all this the LORD struck him in his bowels with an incurable disease.

19 And it came to pass, that in process of time, after the end of two years, his bowels fell out by reason of his sickness: so he died of sore diseases. And his people made no burning for him, like the burning of his fathers.

20 Thirty and two years old was he when he began to reign, and he reigned in Jerusalem eight years, and departed without being desired. Howbeit they buried him in the city of David, but not in the sepulchres of the kings.

CHAPTER 22

AND the inhabitants of Jerusalem made Ahaziah his youngest son king in his stead: for the band of men that came with the Arabians to the camp had slain all the eldest. So Ahaziah the son of Jehoram king of Judah reigned.

2 Forty and two years old was Ahaziah when he began to reign, and he reigned one year in Jerusalem. His mother's name also was Athaliah the daughter of Omri.

3 He also walked in the ways of the house of Ahab: for his mother was his counseller to do wickedly.

4 Wherefore he did evil in the sight of the LORD like the house of Ahab: for they were his counsellers after the death of his father to his destruction.

5He walked also after their counsel, and went with Jehoram the son of Ahab king of Israel to war against Hazael king of Syria at Ramoth-gilead: and the Syrians struck Joram.

6 And he returned to be healed in Jezreel because of the wounds which were given him at Ramah, when he fought with Hazael king of Syria. And Azariah the son of Jehoram king of Judah went down to see Jehoram the son of Ahab at Jezreel, because he was sick.

7 And the destruction of Ahaziah was of God by coming to Joram: for when he was come, he went out with Jehoram against Jehu the son of Nimshi, whom the LORD had anointed to cut off the house of Ahab.

8 And it came to pass, that, when Jehu was executing judgment upon the house of Ahab, and found the princes of Judah, and the sons of the brethren of Ahaziah, that ministered to Ahaziah, he slew them.

9 And he sought Ahaziah: and they caught him, (for he was hid in Samaria,) and brought him to Jehu: and when they had slain him, they buried him: Because, said they, he is the son of Jehoshaphat, who sought the LORD with all his heart. So the house of Ahaziah had no power to keep still the kingdom.

10But when Athaliah the mother of Ahaziah saw that her son was dead, she arose and destroyed all the seed royal of the house of Judah.

11 But Jehoshabeath, the daughter of the king, took Joash the son of Ahaziah, and stole him from among the king's sons that were slain, and put him and his nurse in a bedchamber. So Jehoshabeath, the daughter of king Jehoram, the wife of Jehoiada the priest, (for she was the sister of Ahaziah,) hid him from Athaliah, so that she slew him not.

12 And he was with them hid in the house of God six years: and Athaliah reigned over the land.

CHAPTER 23

AND in the seventh year Jehoiada strengthened himself, and took the captains of hundreds, Azariah the son of Jeroham, and Ishmael the son of Jehohanan, and Azariah the son of Obed, and Maaseiah the son of Adaiah, and Elishaphat the son of Zichri, into covenant with him.

2 And they went about in Judah, and gathered the Levites out of all the cities of Judah, and the chief of the fathers of Israel, and they came to Jerusalem.

3 And all the congregation made a covenant with the king in the house of God. And he said unto them, Behold, the king's son shall reign, as the LORD has said of the sons of David.

4 This is the thing that you shall do; A third part of you entering on the sabbath, of the priests and of the Levites, shall be porters of the doors;

5 And a third part shall be at the king's house; and a third part at the gate of the foundation: and all the people shall be in the courts of the house of the LORD.

6 But let none come into the house of the LORD, save the priests, and they that minister of the Levites; they shall go in, for they are holy: but all the people shall keep the watch of the LORD.

7 And the Levites shall compass the king round about, every man with his weapons in his hand; and whosoever else comes into the house, he shall be put to death: but be you with the king when he comes in, and when he goeth out.

8 So the Levites and all Judah did according to all things that Jehoiada the priest had commanded, and took every man his men that were to come in on the sabbath, with them that were to go out on the sabbath: for Jehoiada the priest dismissed not the courses.

9 Moreover Jehoiada the priest delivered to the captains of hundreds spears, and bucklers, and shields, that had been king David's, which were in the house of God.

10 And he set all the people, every man having his weapon in his hand, from the right side of the temple to the left side of the temple, along by the altar and the temple, by the king round about.

11 Then they brought out the king's son, and put upon him the crown, and gave him the testimony, and made him king. And Jehoiada and his sons anointed him, and said, God save the king.

12Now when Athaliah heard the noise of the people running and praising the king, she came to the people into the house of the LORD:

13 And she looked, and, behold, the king stood at his pillar at the entering in, and the princes and the trumpets by the king: and all the people of the land rejoiced, and sounded with trumpets, also the singers with instruments of musick, and such as taught to sing praise. Then Athaliah rent her clothes, and said, Treason, Treason.

14 Then Jehoiada the priest brought out the captains of hundreds that were set over the host, and said unto them, Have her forth of the ranges: and whoso followeth her, let him be slain with the sword. For the priest said, Slay her not in the house of the LORD.

15 So they laid hands on her; and when she was come to the entering of the horse gate by the king's house, they slew her there.

16And Jehoiada made a covenant between him, and between all the people, and between the king, that they should be the LORD's people.

17 Then all the people went to the house of Baal, and brake it down, and brake his altars and his images in pieces, and slew Mattan the priest of Baal before the altars.

18 Also Jehoiada appointed the offices of the house of the LORD by the hand of the priests the Levites, whom David had distributed in the house of the LORD, to offer the burnt offerings of the LORD, as it is written in the law of Moses, with rejoicing and with singing, as it was ordained by David.

19 And he set the porters at the gates of the house of the LORD, that none which was unclean in any thing should enter in.

20 And he took the captains of hundreds, and the nobles, and the governors of the people, and all the people of the land, and brought down the king from the house of the LORD: and they came through the high gate into the king's house, and set the king upon the throne of the kingdom.

21 And all the people of the land rejoiced: and the city was quiet, after that they had slain Athaliah with the sword.

CHAPTER 24

JOASH was seven years old when he began to reign, and he reigned forty years in Jerusalem. His mother's name also was Zibiah of Beer-sheba.

2 And Joash did that which was right in the sight of the LORD all the days of Jehoiada the priest.

3 And Jehoiada took for him two wives; and he begat sons and daughters.

4And it came to pass after this, that Joash was minded to repair the house of the LORD.

5 And he gathered together the priests and the Levites, and said to them, Go out unto the cities of Judah, and gather of all Israel money to repair the house of your God from year to year, and see that you hasten the matter. Howbeit the Levites hastened it not.

6 And the king called for Jehoiada the chief, and said unto him, Why have you not required of the Levites to bring in out of Judah and out of Jerusalem the collection, according to the commandment of Moses the servant of the LORD, and of the congregation of Israel, for the tabernacle of witness?

7 For the sons of Athaliah, that wicked woman, had broken up the house of God; and also all the dedicated things of the house of the LORD did they bestow upon Baalim.

8 And at the king's commandment they made a chest, and set it without at the gate of the house of the LORD.

9 And they made a proclamation through Judah and Jerusalem, to bring in to the LORD the collection that Moses the servant of God laid upon Israel in the wilderness.

10 And all the princes and all the people rejoiced, and brought in, and cast into the chest, until they had made an end.

11 Now it came to pass, that at what time the chest was brought unto the king's office by the hand of the Levites, and when they saw that there was much money, the king's scribe and the high priest's officer came and emptied the chest, and took it, and carried it to his place again. Thus they did day by day, and gathered money in abundance.

12 And the king and Jehoiada gave it to such as did the work of the service of the house of the LORD, and hired masons and carpenters to repair the house of the LORD, and also such as created iron and brass to mend the house of the LORD.

13 So the workmen created, and the work was perfected by them, and they set the house of God in his state, and strengthened it.

14 And when they had finished it, they brought the rest of the money before the king and Jehoiada, whereof were made vessels for the house of the LORD, even vessels to minister, and to offer withal, and spoons, and vessels of gold and silver. And they offered burnt offerings in the house of the LORD continually all the days of Jehoiada.

15 But Jehoiada waxed old, and was full of days when he died; an hundred and thirty years old was he when he died.

16 And they buried him in the city of David among the kings, because he had done good in Israel, both toward God, and toward his house.

17 Now after the death of Jehoiada came the princes of Judah, and made obeisance to the king. Then the king hearkened unto them.

18 And they left the house of the LORD God of their fathers, and served groves and idols: and wrath came upon Judah and Jerusalem for this their trespass.

19 Yet he sent prophets to them, to bring them again unto the LORD; and they testified against them: but they would not give ear.

20 And the Spirit of God came upon Zechariah the son of Jehoiada the priest, which stood above the people, and said unto them, Thus saith God, Why transgress you the commandments of the LORD, that you cannot prosper? because you have forsaken the LORD, he has also forsaken you.

21 And they conspired against him, and stoned him with stones at the commandment of the king in the court of the house of the LORD.

22 Thus Joash the king remembered not the kindness which Jehoiada his father had done to him, but slew his son. And when he died, he said, The LORD look upon it, and require it.

23 And it came to pass at the end of the year, that the host of Syria came up against him: and they came to Judah and Jerusalem, and destroyed all the princes of the people from among the people, and sent all the spoil of them unto the king of Damascus.

24 For the army of the Syrians came with a small company of men, and the LORD delivered a very great host into their hand, because they had forsaken the LORD God of their fathers. So they executed judgment against Joash.

25 And when they were departed from him, (for they left him in great diseases,) his own servants conspired against him for the blood of the sons of Jehoiada the priest, and slew him on his bed, and he died: and they buried him in the city of David, but they buried him not in the sepulchres of the kings.

26 And these are they that conspired against him; Zabad the son of Shimeath an Ammonitess, and Jehozabad the son of Shimrith a Moabitess.

27 Now concerning his sons, and the greatness of the burdens laid upon him, and the repairing of the house of God, behold, they are written in the story of the book of the kings. And Amaziah his son reigned in his stead.

CHAPTER 25

AMAZIAH was twenty and five years old when he began to reign, and he reigned twenty and nine years in Jerusalem. And his mother's name was Jehoaddan of Jerusalem.

2 And he did that which was right in the sight of the LORD, but not with a perfect heart.

3 Now it came to pass, when the kingdom was established to him, that he slew his servants that had killed the king his father.

4 But he slew not their children, but did as it is written in the law in the book of Moses, where the LORD commanded, saying, The fathers shall not die for the children, neither shall the children die for the fathers, but every man shall die for his own sin.

5 Moreover Amaziah gathered Judah together, and made them captains over thousands, and captains over hundreds, according to the houses of their fathers, throughout all Judah and Benjamin: and he numbered them from twenty years old and above, and found them three hundred thousand choice men, able to go forth to war, that could handle spear and shield.

6 He hired also an hundred thousand mighty men of valour out of Israel for an hundred talents of silver.

7 But there came a man of God to him, saying, O king, let not the army of Israel go with you; for the LORD is not with Israel, to wit, with all the children of Ephraim.

8 But if you will go, do it, be strong for the battle: God shall make you fall before the enemy: for God has power to help, and to cast down.

9 And Amaziah said to the man of God, But what shall we do for the hundred talents which I have given to the army of Israel? And the man of God answered, The LORD is able to give you much more than this.

10 Then Amaziah separated them, to wit, the army that was come to him out of Ephraim, to go home again: wherefore their anger was greatly kindled against Judah, and they returned home in great anger.

11 And Amaziah strengthened himself, and led forth his people, and went to the valley of salt, and struck of the children of Seir ten thousand.

12 And other ten thousand left alive did the children of Judah carry away captive, and brought them unto the top of the rock, and cast them down from the top of the rock, that they all were broken in pieces.

13 But the soldiers of the army which Amaziah sent back, that they should not go with him to battle, fell upon the cities of Judah, from Samaria even unto Beth-horon, and struck three thousand of them, and took much spoil.

14 Now it came to pass, after that Amaziah was come from the slaughter of the Edomites, that he brought the gods of the children of Seir, and set them up to be his gods, and bowed down himself before them, and burned incense unto them.

15 Wherefore the anger of the LORD was kindled against Amaziah, and he sent unto him a prophet, which said unto him, Why have you sought after the gods of the people, which could not deliver their own people out of yours hand?

16 And it came to pass, as he talked with him, that the king said unto him, Are you made of the king's counsel? forbear; why shouldest you be smitten? Then the prophet forbare, and said, I know that God has determined to destroy you, because you have done this, and have not hearkened unto my counsel.

17 Then Amaziah king of Judah took advice, and sent to Joash, the son of Jehoahaz, the son of Jehu, king of Israel, saying, Come, let us see one another in the face.

18 And Joash king of Israel sent to Amaziah king of Judah, saying, The thistle that was in Lebanon sent to the cedar that was in Lebanon, saying, Give your daughter to my son to wife: and there passed by a wild beast that was in Lebanon, and trode down the thistle.

19 You say, Lo, you have smitten the Edomites; and yours heart lifteth you up to boast: abide now at home; why shouldest you meddle to yours hurt, that you shouldest fall, even you , and Judah with you?

20 But Amaziah would not hear; for it came of God, that he might deliver them into the hand of their enemies, because they sought after the gods of Edom.

21 So Joash the king of Israel went up; and they saw one another in the face, both he and Amaziah king of Judah, at Beth-shemesh, which belongeth to Judah.

22 And Judah was put to the worse before Israel, and they fled every man to his tent.

23 And Joash the king of Israel took Amaziah king of Judah, the son of Joash, the son of Jehoahaz, at Beth-shemesh, and brought him to Jerusalem, and brake down the wall of Jerusalem from the gate of Ephraim to the corner gate, four hundred cubits.

24 And he took all the gold and the silver, and all the vessels that were found in the house of God with Obed-edom, and the treasures of the king's house, the hostages also, and returned to Samaria.

25 And Amaziah the son of Joash king of Judah lived after the death of Joash son of Jehoahaz king of Israel fifteen years.

26 Now the rest of the acts of Amaziah, first and last, behold, are they not written in the book of the kings of Judah and Israel?

27 Now after the time that Amaziah did turn away from following the LORD they made a conspiracy against him in Jerusalem; and he fled to Lachish: but they sent to Lachish after him, and slew him there.

28 And they brought him upon horses, and buried him with his fathers in the city of Judah.

CHAPTER 26

THEN all the people of Judah took Uzziah, who was sixteen years old, and made him king in the room of his father Amaziah.

2 He built Eloth, and restored it to Judah, after that the king slept with his fathers.

3 Sixteen years old was Uzziah when he began to reign, and he reigned fifty and two years in Jerusalem. His mother's name also was Jecoliah of Jerusalem.

4 And he did that which was right in the sight of the LORD, according to all that his father Amaziah did.

5 And he sought God in the days of Zechariah, who had understanding in the visions of God: and as long as he sought the LORD, God made him to prosper.

6 And he went forth and warred against the Philistines, and brake down the wall of Gath, and the wall of Jabneh, and the wall of Ashdod, and built cities about Ashdod, and among the Philistines.

7 And God helped him against the Philistines, and against the Arabians that dwelt in Gur-baal, and the Mehunims.

8 And the Ammonites gave gifts to Uzziah: and his name spread abroad even to the entering in of Egypt; for he strengthened himself exceedingly.

9 Moreover Uzziah built towers in Jerusalem at the corner gate, and at the valley gate, and at the turning of the wall, and fortified them.

10 Also he built towers in the desert, and digged many wells: for he had much cattle, both in the low country, and in the plains: husbandmen also, and vine dressers in the mountains, and in Carmel: for he loved husbandry.

11 Moreover Uzziah had an host of fighting men, that went out to war by bands, according to the number of their account by the hand of Jeiel the scribe and Maaseiah the ruler, under the hand of Hananiah, one of the king's captains.

12 The whole number of the chief of the fathers of the mighty men of valour were two thousand and six hundred.

13 And under their hand was an army, three hundred thousand and seven thousand and five hundred, that made war with mighty power, to help the king against the enemy.

14 And Uzziah prepared for them throughout all the host shields, and spears, and helmets, and habergeons, and bows, and slings to cast stones.

15 And he made in Jerusalem engines, invented by cunning men, to be on the towers and upon the bulwarks, to shoot arrows and great stones withal. And his name spread far abroad; for he was marvellously helped, till he was strong.

16 But when he was strong, his heart was lifted up to his destruction: for he transgressed against the LORD his God, and went into the temple of the LORD to burn incense upon the altar of incense.

17 And Azariah the priest went in after him, and with him fourscore priests of the LORD, that were valiant men:

18 And they withstood Uzziah the king, and said unto him, It appertaineth not unto you, Uzziah, to burn incense unto the LORD, but to the priests the sons of Aaron, that are consecrated to burn incense: go out of the sanctuary; for you have trespassed; neither shall it be for yours honour from the LORD God.

19 Then Uzziah was wroth, and had a censer in his hand to burn incense: and while he was wroth with the priests, the leprosy even rose up in his forehead before the priests in the house of the LORD, from beside the incense altar.

20 And Azariah the chief priest, and all the priests, looked upon him, and, behold, he was leprous in his forehead, and they thrust him out from thence; yea, himself hasted also to go out, because the LORD had smitten him.

21 And Uzziah the king was a leper unto the day of his death, and dwelt in a several house, being a leper; for he was cut off from the house of the LORD: and Jotham his son was over the king's house, judging the people of the land.

22 Now the rest of the acts of Uzziah, first and last, did Isaiah the prophet, the son of Amoz, write.

23 So Uzziah slept with his fathers, and they buried him with his fathers in the field of the burial which belonged to the kings; for they said, He is a leper: and Jotham his son reigned in his stead.

CHAPTER 27

JOTHAM was twenty and five years old when he began to reign, and he reigned sixteen years in Jerusalem. His mother's name also was Jerushah, the daughter of Zadok.

2 And he did that which was right in the sight of the LORD, according to all that his father Uzziah did: howbeit he entered not into the temple of the LORD. And the people did yet corruptly.

3 He built the high gate of the house of the LORD, and on the wall of Ophel he built much.

4 Moreover he built cities in the mountains of Judah, and in the forests he built castles and towers.

5 He fought also with the king of the Ammonites, and prevailed against them. And the children of Ammon gave him the same year an hundred talents of silver, and ten thousand measures of wheat, and ten thousand of barley. So much did the children of Ammon pay unto him, both the second year, and the third.

6 So Jotham became mighty, because he prepared his ways before the LORD his God.

7 Now the rest of the acts of Jotham, and all his wars, and his ways, lo, they are written in the book of the kings of Israel and Judah.

8 He was five and twenty years old when he began to reign, and reigned sixteen years in Jerusalem.

9 And Jotham slept with his fathers, and they buried him in the city of David: and Ahaz his son reigned in his stead.

CHAPTER 28

AHAZ was twenty years old when he began to reign, and he reigned sixteen years in Jerusalem: but he did not that which was right in the sight of the LORD, like David his father:

2 For he walked in the ways of the kings of Israel, and made also molten images for Baalim.

3 Moreover he burnt incense in the valley of the son of Hinnom, and burnt his children in the fire, after the abominations of the heathen whom the LORD had cast out before the children of Israel.

4 He sacrificed also and burnt incense in the high places, and on the hills, and under every green tree.

5 Wherefore the LORD his God delivered him into the hand of the king of Syria; and they struck him, and carried away a great multitude of them captives, and brought them to Damascus. And he was also delivered into the hand of the king of Israel, who struck him with a great slaughter.

6 For Pekah the son of Remaliah slew in Judah an hundred and twenty thousand in one day, which were all valiant men; because they had forsaken the LORD God of their fathers.

7 And Zichri, a mighty man of Ephraim, slew Maaseiah the king's son, and Azrikam the governor of the house, and Elkanah that was next to the king.

8 And the children of Israel carried away captive of their brethren two hundred thousand, women, sons, and daughters, and took also away much spoil from them, and brought the spoil to Samaria.

9 But a prophet of the LORD was there, whose name was Oded: and he went out before the host that came to Samaria, and said unto them, Behold, because the LORD God of your fathers was wroth with Judah, he has delivered them into your hand, and you have slain them in a rage that reacheth up unto heaven.

10 And now you purpose to keep under the children of Judah and Jerusalem for bondmen and bondwomen unto you: but are there not with you, even with you, sins against the LORD your God?

11 Now hear me therefore, and deliver the captives again, which you have taken captive of your brethren: for the fierce wrath of the LORD is upon you.

12 Then certain of the heads of the children of Ephraim, Azariah the son of Johanan, Berechiah the son of Meshillemoth, and Jehizkiah the son of Shallum, and Amasa the son of Hadlai, stood up against them that came from the war,

13 And said unto them, You shall not bring in the captives hither: for whereas we have offended against the LORD already, you intend to add more to our sins and to our trespass: for our trespass is great, and there is fierce wrath against Israel.

14 So the armed men left the captives and the spoil before the princes and all the congregation.

15 And the men which were expressed by name rose up, and took the captives, and with the spoil clothed all that were naked among them, and arrayed them, and shod them, and gave them to eat and to drink, and anointed them, and carried all the feeble of them upon asses, and brought them to Jericho, the city of palm trees, to their brethren: then they returned to Samaria.

16 At that time did king Ahaz send unto the kings of Assyria to help him.

17 For again the Edomites had come and smitten Judah, and carried away captives.

18 The Philistines also had invaded the cities of the low country, and of the south of Judah, and had taken Beth-shemesh, and Ajalon, and Gederoth, and Shocho with the villages thereof, and Timnah with the villages thereof, Gimzo also and the villages thereof: and they dwelt there.

19 For the LORD brought Judah low because of Ahaz king of Israel; for he made Judah naked, and transgressed sore against the LORD.

20 And Tilgath-pilneser king of Assyria came unto him, and distressed him, but strengthened him not.

21 For Ahaz took away a portion out of the house of the LORD, and out of the house of the king, and of the princes, and gave it unto the king of Assyria: but he helped him not.

22 And in the time of his distress did he trespass yet more against the LORD: this is that king Ahaz.

23 For he sacrificed unto the gods of Damascus, which struck him: and he said, Because the gods of the kings of Syria help them, therefore will I sacrifice to them, that they may help me. But they were the ruin of him, and of all Israel.

24 And Ahaz gathered together the vessels of the house of God, and cut in pieces the vessels of the house of God, and shut up the doors of the house of the LORD, and he made him altars in every corner of Jerusalem.

25 And in every several city of Judah he made high places to burn incense unto other gods, and provoked to anger the LORD God of his fathers.

26 Now the rest of his acts and of all his ways, first and last, behold, they are written in the book of the kings of Judah and Israel.

27 And Ahaz slept with his fathers, and they buried him in the city, even in Jerusalem: but they brought him not into the sepulchres of the kings of Israel: and Hezekiah his son reigned in his stead.

CHAPTER 29

HEZEKIAH began to reign when he was five and twenty years old, and he reigned nine and twenty years in Jerusalem. And his mother's name was Abijah, the daughter of Zechariah.

2 And he did that which was right in the sight of the LORD, according to all that David his father had done.

3He in the first year of his reign, in the first month, opened the doors of the house of the LORD, and repaired them.

4 And he brought in the priests and the Levites, and gathered them together into the east street,

5 And said unto them, Hear me, you Levites, sanctify now yourselves, and sanctify the house of the LORD God of your fathers, and carry forth the filthiness out of the holy place.

6 For our fathers have trespassed, and done that which was evil in the eyes of the LORD our God, and have forsaken him, and have turned away their faces from the habitation of the LORD, and turned their backs.

7 Also they have shut up the doors of the porch, and put out the lamps, and have not burned incense nor offered burnt offerings in the holy place unto the God of Israel.

8 Wherefore the wrath of the LORD was upon Judah and Jerusalem, and he has delivered them to trouble, to astonishment, and to hissing, as you see with your eyes.

9 For, lo, our fathers have fallen by the sword, and our sons and our daughters and our wives are in captivity for this.

10 Now it is in my heart to make a covenant with the LORD God of Israel, that his fierce wrath may turn away from us.

11 My sons, be not now negligent: for the LORD has chosen you to stand before him, to serve him, and that you should minister unto him, and burn incense.

12Then the Levites arose, Mahath the son of Amasai, and Joel the son of Azariah, of the sons of the Kohathites: and of the sons of Merari, Kish the son of Abdi, and Azariah the son of Jehalelel: and of the Gershonites; Joah the son of Zimmah, and Eden the son of Joah:

13 And of the sons of Elizaphan; Shimri, and Jeiel: and of the sons of Asaph; Zechariah, and Mattaniah:

14 And of the sons of Heman; Jehiel, and Shimei: and of the sons of Jeduthun; Shemaiah, and Uzziel.

15 And they gathered their brethren, and sanctified themselves, and came, according to the commandment of the king, by the words of the LORD, to cleanse the house of the LORD.

16 And the priests went into the inner part of the house of the LORD, to cleanse it, and brought out all the uncleanness that they found in the temple of the LORD into the court of the house of the LORD. And the Levites took it, to carry it out abroad into the brook Kidron.

17 Now they began on the first day of the first month to sanctify, and on the eighth day of the month came they to the porch of the LORD: so they sanctified the house of the LORD in eight days; and in the sixteenth day of the first month they made an end.

18 Then they went in to Hezekiah the king, and said, We have cleansed all the house of the LORD, and the altar of burnt offering, with all the vessels thereof, and the shewbread table, with all the vessels thereof.

19 Moreover all the vessels, which king Ahaz in his reign did cast away in his transgression, have we prepared and sanctified, and, behold, they are before the altar of the LORD.

20Then Hezekiah the king rose early, and gathered the rulers of the city, and went up to the house of the LORD.

21 And they brought seven bullocks, and seven rams, and seven lambs, and seven he goats, for a sin offering for the kingdom, and for the sanctuary, and for Judah. And he commanded the priests the sons of Aaron to offer them on the altar of the LORD.

22 So they killed the bullocks, and the priests received the blood, and sprinkled it on the altar: likewise, when they had killed the rams, they sprinkled the blood upon the altar: they killed also the lambs, and they sprinkled the blood upon the altar.

23 And they brought forth the he goats for the sin offering before the king and the congregation; and they laid their hands upon them:

24 And the priests killed them, and they made reconciliation with their blood upon the altar, to make an atonement for all Israel: for the king commanded that the burnt offering and the sin offering should be made for all Israel.

25 And he set the Levites in the house of the LORD with cymbals, with psalteries, and with harps, according to the commandment of David, and of Gad the king's seer, and Nathan the prophet: for so was the commandment of the LORD by his prophets.

26 And the Levites stood with the instruments of David, and the priests with the trumpets.

27 And Hezekiah commanded to offer the burnt offering upon the altar. And when the burnt offering began, the song of the LORD began also with the trumpets, and with the instruments ordained by David king of Israel.

28 And all the congregation worshipped, and the singers sang, and the trumpeters sounded: and all this continued until the burnt offering was finished.

29 And when they had made an end of offering, the king and all that were present with him bowed themselves, and worshipped.

30 Moreover Hezekiah the king and the princes commanded the Levites to sing praise unto the LORD with the words of David, and of Asaph the seer. And they sang praises with gladness, and they bowed their heads and worshipped.

31 Then Hezekiah answered and said, Now you have consecrated yourselves unto the LORD, come near and bring sacrifices and thank offerings into the house of the LORD. And the congregation brought in sacrifices and thank offerings; and as many as were of a free heart burnt offerings.

32 And the number of the burnt offerings, which the congregation brought, was threescore and ten bullocks, an hundred rams, and two hundred lambs: all these were for a burnt offering to the LORD.

33 And the consecrated things were six hundred oxen and three thousand sheep.

34 But the priests were too few, so that they could not flay all the burnt offerings: wherefore their brethren the Levites did help them, till the work was ended, and until the other priests had sanctified themselves: for the Levites were more upright in heart to sanctify themselves than the priests.

35 And also the burnt offerings were in abundance, with the fat of the peace offerings, and the drink offerings for every burnt offering. So the service of the house of the LORD was set in order.

36 And Hezekiah rejoiced, and all the people, that God had prepared the people: for the thing was done suddenly.

CHAPTER 30

AND Hezekiah sent to all Israel and Judah, and wrote letters also to Ephraim and Manasseh, that they should come to the house of the LORD at Jerusalem, to keep the passover unto the LORD God of Israel.

2 For the king had taken counsel, and his princes, and all the congregation in Jerusalem, to keep the passover in the second month.

3 For they could not keep it at that time, because the priests had not sanctified themselves sufficiently, neither had the people gathered themselves together to Jerusalem.

4 And the thing pleased the king and all the congregation.

5 So they established a decree to make proclamation throughout all Israel, from Beer-sheba even to Dan, that they should come to keep the passover unto the LORD God of Israel at Jerusalem: for they had not done it of a long time in such sort as it was written.

6 So the posts went with the letters from the king and his princes throughout all Israel and Judah, and according to the commandment of the king, saying, You children of Israel, turn again unto the LORD God of Abraham, Isaac, and Israel, and he will return to the remnant of you, that are escaped out of the hand of the kings of Assyria.

7 And be not you like your fathers, and like your brethren, which trespassed against the LORD God of their fathers, who therefore gave them up to desolation, as you see.

8 Now be you not stiffnecked, as your fathers were, but yield yourselves unto the LORD, and enter into his sanctuary, which he has sanctified for ever: and serve the LORD your God, that the fierceness of his wrath may turn away from you.

9 For if you turn again unto the LORD, your brethren and your children shall find compassion before them that lead them captive, so that they shall come again into this land: for the LORD your God is gracious and merciful, and will not turn away his face from you, if you return unto him.

10 So the posts passed from city to city through the country of Ephraim and Manasseh even unto Zebulun: but they laughed them to scorn, and mocked them.

11 Nevertheless divers of Asher and Manasseh and of Zebulun humbled themselves, and came to Jerusalem.

12 Also in Judah the hand of God was to give them one heart to do the commandment of the king and of the princes, by the word of the LORD.

13And there assembled at Jerusalem much people to keep the feast of unleavened bread in the second month, a very great congregation.

14 And they arose and took away the altars that were in Jerusalem, and all the altars for incense took they away, and cast them into the brook Kidron.

15 Then they killed the passover on the fourteenth day of the second month: and the priests and the Levites were ashamed, and sanctified themselves, and brought in the burnt offerings into the house of the LORD.

16 And they stood in their place after their manner, according to the law of Moses the man of God: the priests sprinkled the blood, which they received of the hand of the Levites.

17 For there were many in the congregation that were not sanctified: therefore the Levites had the charge of the killing of the passovers for every one that was not clean, to sanctify them unto the LORD.

18 For a multitude of the people, even many of Ephraim, and Manasseh, Issachar, and Zebulun, had not cleansed themselves, yet did they eat the passover otherwise than it was written. But Hezekiah prayed for them, saying, The good LORD pardon every one

19 That prepareth his heart to seek God, the LORD God of his fathers, though he be not cleansed according to the purification of the sanctuary.

20 And the LORD hearkened to Hezekiah, and healed the people.

21 And the children of Israel that were present at Jerusalem kept the feast of unleavened bread seven days with great gladness: and the Levites and the priests praised the LORD day by day, singing with loud instruments unto the LORD.

22 And Hezekiah spake comfortably unto all the Levites that taught the good knowledge of the LORD: and they did eat throughout the feast seven days, offering peace offerings, and making confession to the LORD God of their fathers.

23 And the whole assembly took counsel to keep other seven days: and they kept other seven days with gladness.

24 For Hezekiah king of Judah did give to the congregation a thousand bullocks and seven thousand sheep; and the princes gave to the congregation a thousand bullocks and ten thousand sheep: and a great number of priests sanctified themselves.

25 And all the congregation of Judah, with the priests and the Levites, and all the congregation that came out of Israel, and the strangers that came out of the land of Israel, and that dwelt in Judah, rejoiced.

26 So there was great joy in Jerusalem: for since the time of Solomon the son of David king of Israel there was not the like in Jerusalem.

27 Then the priests the Levites arose and blessed the people: and their voice was heard, and their prayer came up to his holy dwelling place, even unto heaven.

CHAPTER 31

NOW when all this was finished, all Israel that were present went out to the cities of Judah, and brake the images in pieces, and cut down the groves, and threw down the high places and the altars out of all Judah and Benjamin, in Ephraim also and Manasseh, until they had utterly destroyed them all. Then all the children of Israel returned, every man to his possession, into their own cities.

2 And Hezekiah appointed the courses of the priests and the Levites after their courses, every man according to his service, the priests and Levites for burnt offerings and for peace offerings, to minister, and to give thanks, and to praise in the gates of the tents of the LORD.

3 He appointed also the king's portion of his substance for the burnt offerings, to wit, for the morning and evening burnt offerings, and the burnt offerings for the sabbaths, and for the new moons, and for the set feasts, as it is written in the law of the LORD.

4 Moreover he commanded the people that dwelt in Jerusalem to give the portion of the priests and the Levites, that they might be encouraged in the law of the LORD.

5 And as soon as the commandment came abroad, the children of Israel brought in abundance the firstfruits of corn, wine, and oil, and honey, and of all the increase of the field; and the tithe of all things brought they in abundantly.

6 And concerning the children of Israel and Judah, that dwelt in the cities of Judah, they also brought in the tithe of oxen and sheep, and the tithe of holy things which were consecrated unto the LORD their God, and laid them by heaps.

7 In the third month they began to lay the foundation of the heaps, and finished them in the seventh month.

8 And when Hezekiah and the princes came and saw the heaps, they blessed the LORD, and his people Israel.

9 Then Hezekiah questioned with the priests and the Levites concerning the heaps.

10 And Azariah the chief priest of the house of Zadok answered him, and said, Since the people began to bring the offerings into the house of the LORD, we have had enough to eat, and have left plenty: for the LORD has blessed his people; and that which is left is this great store.

11 Then Hezekiah commanded to prepare chambers in the house of the LORD; and they prepared them,

12 And brought in the offerings and the tithes and the dedicated things faithfully: over which Cononiah the Levite was ruler, and Shimei his brother was the next.

13 And Jehiel, and Azaziah, and Nahath, and Asahel, and Jerimoth, and Jozabad, and Eliel, and Ismachiah, and Mahath, and Benaiah, were overseers under the hand of Cononiah and Shimei his brother, at the commandment of Hezekiah the king, and Azariah the ruler of the house of God.

14 And Kore the son of Imnah the Levite, the porter toward the east, was over the freewill offerings of God, to distribute the oblations of the LORD, and the most holy things.

15 And next him were Eden, and Miniamin, and Jeshua, and Shemaiah, Amariah, and Shecaniah, in the cities of the priests, in their set office, to give to their brethren by courses, as well to the great as to the small:

16 Beside their genealogy of males, from three years old and upward, even unto every one that entereth into the house of the LORD, his daily portion for their service in their charges according to their courses;

17 Both to the genealogy of the priests by the house of their fathers, and the Levites from twenty years old and upward, in their charges by their courses;

18 And to the genealogy of all their little ones, their wives, and their sons, and their daughters, through all the congregation: for in their set office they sanctified themselves in holiness:

19 Also of the sons of Aaron the priests, which were in the fields of the suburbs of their cities, in every several city, the men that were expressed by name, to give portions to all the males among the priests, and to all that were reckoned by genealogies among the Levites.

20 And thus did Hezekiah throughout all Judah, and created that which was good and right and truth before the LORD his God.

21 And in every work that he began in the service of the house of God, and in the law, and in the commandments, to seek his God, he did it with all his heart, and prospered.

CHAPTER 32

AFTER these things, and the establishment thereof, Sennacherib king of Assyria came, and entered into Judah, and encamped against the fenced cities, and thought to win them for himself.

2 And when Hezekiah saw that Sennacherib was come, and that he was purposed to fight against Jerusalem,

3 He took counsel with his princes and his mighty men to stop the waters of the fountains which were without the city: and they did help him.

4 So there was gathered much people together, who stopped all the fountains, and the brook that ran through the midst of the land, saying, Why should the kings of Assyria come, and find much water?

5 Also he strengthened himself, and built up all the wall that was broken, and raised it up to the towers, and another wall without, and repaired Millo in the city of David, and made darts and shields in abundance.

6 And he set captains of war over the people, and gathered them together to him in the street of the gate of the city, and spake comfortably to them, saying,

7 Be strong and courageous, be not afraid nor dismayed for the king of Assyria, nor for all the multitude that is with him: for there be more with us than with him:

8 With him is an arm of flesh; but with us is the LORD our God to help us, and to fight our battles. And the people rested themselves upon the words of Hezekiah king of Judah.

9 After this did Sennacherib king of Assyria send his servants to Jerusalem, (but he himself laid siege against Lachish, and all his power with him,) unto Hezekiah king of Judah, and unto all Judah that were at Jerusalem, saying,

10 Thus saith Sennacherib king of Assyria, Whereon do you trust, that you abide in the siege in Jerusalem?

11 Doth not Hezekiah persuade you to give over yourselves to die by famine and by thirst, saying, The LORD our God shall deliver us out of the hand of the king of Assyria?

12 Has not the same Hezekiah taken away his high places and his altars, and commanded Judah and Jerusalem, saying, You shall worship before one altar, and burn incense upon it?

13 Know you not what I and my fathers have done unto all the people of other lands? were the gods of the nations of those lands any ways able to deliver their lands out of my hand?

14 Who was there among all the gods of those nations that my fathers utterly destroyed, that could deliver his people out of my hand, that your God should be able to deliver you out of my hand?

15 Now therefore let not Hezekiah deceive you, nor persuade you on this manner, neither yet believe him: for no god of any nation or kingdom was able to deliver his people out of my hand, and out of the hand of my fathers: how much less shall your God deliver you out of my hand?

16 And his servants spake yet more against the LORD God, and against his servant Hezekiah.

17 He wrote also letters to rail on the LORD God of Israel, and to speak against him, saying, As the gods of the nations of other lands have not delivered their people out of my hand, so shall not the God of Hezekiah deliver his people out of my hand.

18 Then they cried with a loud voice in the Jews' speech unto the people of Jerusalem that were on the wall, to affright them, and to trouble them; that they might take the city.

19 And they spake against the God of Jerusalem, as against the gods of the people of the earth, which were the work of the hands of man.

20 And for this cause Hezekiah the king, and the prophet Isaiah the son of Amoz, prayed and cried to heaven.

21And the LORD sent an angel, which cut off all the mighty men of valour, and the leaders and captains in the camp of the king of Assyria. So he returned with shame of face to his own land. And when he was come into the house of his god, they that came forth of his own bowels slew him there with the sword.

22 Thus the LORD saved Hezekiah and the inhabitants of Jerusalem from the hand of Sennacherib the king of Assyria, and from the hand of all other, and guided them on every side.

23 And many brought gifts unto the LORD to Jerusalem, and presents to Hezekiah king of Judah: so that he was magnified in the sight of all nations from thenceforth.

24In those days Hezekiah was sick to the death, and prayed unto the LORD: and he spake unto him, and he gave him a sign.

25 But Hezekiah rendered not again according to the benefit done unto him; for his heart was lifted up: therefore there was wrath upon him, and upon Judah and Jerusalem.

26 Notwithstanding Hezekiah humbled himself for the pride of his heart, both he and the inhabitants of Jerusalem, so that the wrath of the LORD came not upon them in the days of Hezekiah.

27And Hezekiah had exceeding much riches and honour: and he made himself treasuries for silver, and for gold, and for precious stones, and for spices, and for shields, and for all manner of pleasant jewels;

28 Storehouses also for the increase of corn, and wine, and oil; and stalls for all manner of beasts, and cotes for flocks.

29 Moreover he provided him cities, and possessions of flocks and herds in abundance: for God had given him substance very much.

30 This same Hezekiah also stopped the upper watercourse of Gihon, and brought it straight down to the west side of the city of David. And Hezekiah prospered in all his works.

31Howbeit in the business of the ambassadors of the princes of Babylon, who sent unto him to inquire of the wonder that was done in the land, God left him, to try him, that he might know all that was in his heart.

32Now the rest of the acts of Hezekiah, and his goodness, behold, they are written in the vision of Isaiah the prophet, the son of Amoz, and in the book of the kings of Judah and Israel.

33 And Hezekiah slept with his fathers, and they buried him in the chiefest of the sepulchres of the sons of David: and all Judah and the inhabitants of Jerusalem did him honour at his death. And Manasseh his son reigned in his stead.

CHAPTER 33

MANASSEH was twelve years old when he began to reign, and he reigned fifty and five years in Jerusalem:

2 But did that which was evil in the sight of the LORD, like unto the abominations of the heathen, whom the LORD had cast out before the children of Israel.

3For he built again the high places which Hezekiah his father had broken down, and he reared up altars for Baalim, and made groves, and worshipped all the host of heaven, and served them.

4 Also he built altars in the house of the LORD, whereof the LORD had said, In Jerusalem shall my name be for ever.

5 And he built altars for all the host of heaven in the two courts of the house of the LORD.

6 And he caused his children to pass through the fire in the valley of the son of Hinnom: also he observed times, and used enchantments, and used witchcraft, and dealt with a familiar spirit, and with wizards: he created much evil in the sight of the LORD, to provoke him to anger.

7 And he set a carved image, the idol which he had made, in the house of God, of which God had said to David and to Solomon his son, In this house, and in Jerusalem, which I have chosen before all the tribes of Israel, will I put my name for ever:

8 Neither will I any more remove the foot of Israel from out of the land which I have appointed for your fathers; so that they will take heed to do all that I have commanded them, according to the whole law and the statutes and the ordinances by the hand of Moses.

9 So Manasseh made Judah and the inhabitants of Jerusalem to err, and to do worse than the heathen, whom the LORD had destroyed before the children of Israel.

10 And the LORD spake to Manasseh, and to his people: but they would not hearken.

11Wherefore the LORD brought upon them the captains of the host of the king of Assyria, which took Manasseh among the thorns, and bound him with fetters, and carried him to Babylon.

12 And when he was in affliction, he besought the LORD his God, and humbled himself greatly before the God of his fathers,

13 And prayed unto him: and he was intreated of him, and heard his supplication, and brought him again to Jerusalem into his kingdom. Then Manasseh knew that the LORD he was God.

14 Now after this he built a wall without the city of David, on the west side of Gihon, in the valley, even to the entering in at the fish gate, and compassed about Ophel, and raised it up a very great height, and put captains of war in all the fenced cities of Judah.

15 And he took away the strange gods, and the idol out of the house of the LORD, and all the altars that he had built in the mount of the house of the LORD, and in Jerusalem, and cast them out of the city.

16 And he repaired the altar of the LORD, and sacrificed thereon peace offerings and thank offerings, and commanded Judah to serve the LORD God of Israel.

17 Nevertheless the people did sacrifice still in the high places, yet unto the LORD their God only.

18Now the rest of the acts of Manasseh, and his prayer unto his God, and the words of the seers that spake to him in the name of the LORD God of Israel, behold, they are written in the book of the kings of Israel.

19 His prayer also, and how God was intreated of him, and all his sin, and his trespass, and the places wherein he built high places, and set up groves and graven images, before he was humbled: behold, they are written among the sayings of the seers.

20So Manasseh slept with his fathers, and they buried him in his own house: and Amon his son reigned in his stead.

21Amon was two and twenty years old when he began to reign, and reigned two years in Jerusalem.

22 But he did that which was evil in the sight of the LORD, as did Manasseh his father: for Amon sacrificed unto all the carved images which Manasseh his father had made, and served them;

23 And humbled not himself before the LORD, as Manasseh his father had humbled himself; but Amon trespassed more and more.

24 And his servants conspired against him, and slew him in his own house.

25But the people of the land slew all them that had conspired against king Amon; and the people of the land made Josiah his son king in his stead.

CHAPTER 34

JOSIAH was eight years old when he began to reign, and he reigned in Jerusalem one and thirty years.

2 And he did that which was right in the sight of the LORD, and walked in the ways of David his father, and declined neither to the right hand, nor to the left.

3For in the eighth year of his reign, while he was yet young, he began to seek after the God of David his father: and in the twelfth year he began to purge Judah and Jerusalem from the high places, and the groves, and the carved images, and the molten images.

4 And they brake down the altars of Baalim in his presence; and the images, that were on high above them, he cut down; and the groves, and the carved images, and the molten images, he brake in pieces, and made dust of them, and strowed it upon the graves of them that had sacrificed unto them.

5 And he burnt the bones of the priests upon their altars, and cleansed Judah and Jerusalem.

6 And so did he in the cities of Manasseh, and Ephraim, and Simeon, even unto Naphtali, with their mattocks round about.

7 And when he had broken down the altars and the groves, and had beaten the graven images into powder, and cut down all the idols throughout all the land of Israel, he returned to Jerusalem.

8Now in the eighteenth year of his reign, when he had purged the land, and the house, he sent Shaphan the son of Azaliah, and Maaseiah the governor of the city, and Joah the son of Joahaz the recorder, to repair the house of the LORD his God.

9 And when they came to Hilkiah the high priest, they delivered the money that was brought into the house of God, which the Levites that kept the doors had gathered of the hand of Manasseh and Ephraim, and of all the remnant of Israel, and of all Judah and Benjamin; and they returned to Jerusalem.

10 And they put it in the hand of the workmen that had the oversight of the house of the LORD, and they gave it to the workmen that created in the house of the LORD, to repair and amend the house:

11 Even to the artificers and builders gave they it, to buy hewn stone, and timber for couplings, and to floor the houses which the kings of Judah had destroyed.

12 And the men did the work faithfully: and the overseers of them were Jahath and Obadiah, the Levites, of the sons of Merari; and Zechariah and Meshullam, of the sons of the Kohathites, to set it forward; and other of the Levites, all that could skill of instruments of musick.

13 Also they were over the bearers of burdens, and were overseers of all that created the work in any manner of service: and of the Levites there were scribes, and officers, and porters.

14And when they brought out the money that was brought into the house of the LORD, Hilkiah the priest found a book of the law of the LORD given by Moses.

15 And Hilkiah answered and said to Shaphan the scribe, I have found the book of the law in the house of the LORD. And Hilkiah delivered the book to Shaphan.

16 And Shaphan carried the book to the king, and brought the king word back again, saying, All that was committed to your servants, they do it.

17 And they have gathered together the money that was found in the house of the LORD, and have delivered it into the hand of the overseers, and to the hand of the workmen.

18 Then Shaphan the scribe told the king, saying, Hilkiah the priest has given me a book. And Shaphan read it before the king.

19 And it came to pass, when the king had heard the words of the law, that he rent his clothes.

20 And the king commanded Hilkiah, and Ahikam the son of Shaphan, and Abdon the son of Micah, and Shaphan the scribe, and Asaiah a servant of the king's, saying,

21 Go, inquire of the LORD for me, and for them that are left in Israel and in Judah, concerning the words of the book that is found: for great is the wrath of the LORD that is poured out upon us, because our fathers have not kept the word of the LORD, to do after all that is written in this book.

22 And Hilkiah, and they that the king had appointed, went to Huldah the prophetess, the wife of Shallum the son of Tikvath, the son of Hasrah, keeper of the wardrobe; (now she dwelt in Jerusalem in the college:) and they spake to her to that effect.

23 And she answered them, Thus saith the LORD God of Israel, Tell you the man that sent you to me,

24 Thus saith the LORD, Behold, I will bring evil upon this place, and upon the inhabitants thereof, even all the curses that are written in the book which they have read before the king of Judah:

25 Because they have forsaken me, and have burned incense unto other gods, that they might provoke me to anger with all the works of their hands; therefore my wrath shall be poured out upon this place, and shall not be quenched.

26 And as for the king of Judah, who sent you to inquire of the LORD, so shall you say unto him, Thus saith the LORD God of Israel concerning the words which you have heard;

27 Because yours heart was tender, and you did humble yourself before God, when you heardest his words against this place, and against the inhabitants thereof, and humbledst yourself before me, and did rend your clothes, and weep before me; I have even heard you also, saith the LORD.

28 Behold, I will gather you to your fathers, and you shalt be gathered to your grave in peace, neither shall yours eyes see all the evil that I will bring upon this place, and upon the inhabitants of the same. So they brought the king word again.

29 Then the king sent and gathered together all the elders of Judah and Jerusalem.

30 And the king went up into the house of the LORD, and all the men of Judah, and the inhabitants of Jerusalem, and the priests, and the Levites, and all the people, great and small: and he read in their ears all the words of the book of the covenant that was found in the house of the LORD.

31 And the king stood in his place, and made a covenant before the LORD, to walk after the LORD, and to keep his commandments, and his testimonies, and his statutes, with all his heart, and with all his soul, to perform the words of the covenant which are written in this book.

32 And he caused all that were present in Jerusalem and Benjamin to stand to it. And the inhabitants of Jerusalem did according to the covenant of God, the God of their fathers.

33 And Josiah took away all the abominations out of all the countries that pertained to the children of Israel, and made all that were present in Israel to serve, even to serve the LORD their God. And all his days they departed not from following the LORD, the God of their fathers.

CHAPTER 35

MOREOVER Josiah kept a passover unto the LORD in Jerusalem: and they killed the passover on the fourteenth day of the first month.

2 And he set the priests in their charges, and encouraged them to the service of the house of the LORD,

3 And said unto the Levites that taught all Israel, which were holy unto the LORD, Put the holy ark in the house which Solomon the son of David king of Israel did build; it shall not be a burden upon your shoulders: serve now the LORD your God, and his people Israel,

4 And prepare yourselves by the houses of your fathers, after your courses, according to the writing of David king of Israel, and according to the writing of Solomon his son.

5 And stand in the holy place according to the divisions of the families of the fathers of your brethren the people, and after the division of the families of the Levites.

6 So kill the passover, and sanctify yourselves, and prepare your brethren, that they may do according to the word of the LORD by the hand of Moses.

7 And Josiah gave to the people, of the flock, lambs and kids, all for the passover offerings, for all that were present, to the number of thirty thousand, and three thousand bullocks: these were of the king's substance.

8 And his princes gave willingly unto the people, to the priests, and to the Levites: Hilkiah and Zechariah and Jehiel, rulers of the house of God, gave unto the priests for the passover offerings two thousand and six hundred small cattle, and three hundred oxen.

9 Conaniah also, and Shemaiah and Nethaneel, his brethren, and Hashabiah and Jeiel and Jozabad, chief of the Levites, gave unto the Levites for passover offerings five thousand small cattle, and five hundred oxen.

10 So the service was prepared, and the priests stood in their place, and the Levites in their courses, according to the king's commandment.

11 And they killed the passover, and the priests sprinkled the blood from their hands, and the Levites flayed them.

12 And they removed the burnt offerings, that they might give according to the divisions of the families of the people, to offer unto the LORD, as it is written in the book of Moses. And so did they with the oxen.

13 And they roasted the passover with fire according to the ordinance: but the other holy offerings sod they in pots, and in caldrons, and in pans, and divided them speedily among all the people.

14 And afterward they made ready for themselves, and for the priests: because the priests the sons of Aaron were busied in offering of burnt offerings and the fat until night; therefore the Levites prepared for themselves, and for the priests the sons of Aaron.

15 And the singers the sons of Asaph were in their place, according to the commandment of David, and Asaph, and Heman, and Jeduthun the king's seer; and the porters waited at every gate; they might not depart from their service; for their brethren the Levites prepared for them.

16 So all the service of the LORD was prepared the same day, to keep the passover, and to offer burnt offerings upon the altar of the LORD, according to the commandment of king Josiah.

17 And the children of Israel that were present kept the passover at that time, and the feast of unleavened bread seven days.

18 And there was no passover like to that kept in Israel from the days of Samuel the prophet; neither did all the kings of Israel keep such a passover as Josiah kept, and the priests, and the Levites, and all Judah and Israel that were present, and the inhabitants of Jerusalem.

19 In the eighteenth year of the reign of Josiah was this passover kept.

20 After all this, when Josiah had prepared the temple, Necho king of Egypt came up to fight against Carchemish by Euphrates: and Josiah went out against him.

21 But he sent ambassadors to him, saying, What have I to do with you, you king of Judah? I come not against you this day, but against the house wherewith I have war: for God commanded me to make haste: forbear you from meddling with God, who is with me, that he destroy you not.

22 Nevertheless Josiah would not turn his face from him, but disguised himself, that he might fight with him, and hearkened not unto the words of Necho from the mouth of God, and came to fight in the valley of Megiddo.

23 And the archers shot at king Josiah; and the king said to his servants, Have me away; for I am sore wounded.

24 His servants therefore took him out of that chariot, and put him in the second chariot that he had; and they brought him to Jerusalem, and he died, and was buried in one of the sepulchres of his fathers. And all Judah and Jerusalem mourned for Josiah.

25 And Jeremiah lamented for Josiah: and all the singing men and the singing women spake of Josiah in their lamentations to this day, and made them an ordinance in Israel: and, behold, they are written in the lamentations.

26 Now the rest of the acts of Josiah, and his goodness, according to that which was written in the law of the LORD,

27 And his deeds, first and last, behold, they are written in the book of the kings of Israel and Judah.

CHAPTER 36

THEN the people of the land took Jehoahaz the son of Josiah, and made him king in his father's stead in Jerusalem.

2 Jehoahaz was twenty and three years old when he began to reign, and he reigned three months in Jerusalem.

3 And the king of Egypt put him down at Jerusalem, and condemned the land in an hundred talents of silver and a talent of gold.

4 And the king of Egypt made Eliakim his brother king over Judah and Jerusalem, and turned his name to Jehoiakim. And Necho took Jehoahaz his brother, and carried him to Egypt.

5 Jehoiakim was twenty and five years old when he began to reign, and he reigned eleven years in Jerusalem: and he did that which was evil in the sight of the LORD his God.

6 Against him came up Nebuchadnezzar king of Babylon, and bound him in fetters, to carry him to Babylon.

7 Nebuchadnezzar also carried of the vessels of the house of the LORD to Babylon, and put them in his temple at Babylon.

8 Now the rest of the acts of Jehoiakim, and his abominations which he did, and that which was found in him, behold, they are written in the book of the kings of Israel and Judah: and Jehoiachin his son reigned in his stead.

9Jehoiachin was eight years old when he began to reign, and he reigned three months and ten days in Jerusalem: and he did that which was evil in the sight of the LORD.

10 And when the year was expired, king Nebuchadnezzar sent, and brought him to Babylon, with the goodly vessels of the house of the LORD, and made Zedekiah his brother king over Judah and Jerusalem.

11Zedekiah was one and twenty years old when he began to reign, and reigned eleven years in Jerusalem.

12 And he did that which was evil in the sight of the LORD his God, and humbled not himself before Jeremiah the prophet speaking from the mouth of the LORD.

13 And he also rebelled against king Nebuchadnezzar, who had made him swear by God: but he stiffened his neck, and hardened his heart from turning unto the LORD God of Israel.

14Moreover all the chief of the priests, and the people, transgressed very much after all the abominations of the heathen; and polluted the house of the LORD which he had hallowed in Jerusalem.

15 And the LORD God of their fathers sent to them by his messengers, rising up betimes, and sending; because he had compassion on his people, and on his dwelling place:

16 But they mocked the messengers of God, and despised his words, and misused his prophets, until the wrath of the LORD arose against his people, till there was no remedy.

17 Therefore he brought upon them the king of the Chaldees, who slew their young men with the sword in the house of their sanctuary, and had no compassion upon young man or maiden, old man, or him that stooped for age: he gave them all into his hand.

18 And all the vessels of the house of God, great and small, and the treasures of the house of the LORD, and the treasures of the king, and of his princes; all these he brought to Babylon.

19 And they burnt the house of God, and brake down the wall of Jerusalem, and burnt all the palaces thereof with fire, and destroyed all the goodly vessels thereof.

20 And them that had escaped from the sword carried he away to Babylon; where they were servants to him and his sons until the reign of the kingdom of Persia:

21 To fulfil the word of the LORD by the mouth of Jeremiah, until the land had enjoyed her sabbaths: for as long as she lay desolate she kept sabbath, to fulfil threescore and ten years.

22Now in the first year of Cyrus king of Persia, that the word of the LORD spoken by the mouth of Jeremiah might be accomplished, the LORD stirred up the spirit of Cyrus king of Persia, that he made a proclamation throughout all his kingdom, and put it also in writing, saying,

23 Thus saith Cyrus king of Persia, All the kingdoms of the earth has the LORD God of heaven given me; and he has charged me to build him an house in Jerusalem, which is in Judah. Who is there among you of all his people? The LORD his God be with him, and let him go up.

EZRA.

CHAPTER 1

NOW in the first year of Cyrus king of Persia, that the word of the LORD by the mouth of Jeremiah might be fulfilled, the LORD stirred up the spirit of Cyrus king of Persia, that he made a proclamation throughout all his kingdom, and put it also in writing, saying,

2 Thus saith Cyrus king of Persia, The LORD God of heaven has given me all the kingdoms of the earth; and he has charged me to build him an house at Jerusalem, which is in Judah.

3 Who is there among you of all his people? his God be with him, and let him go up to Jerusalem, which is in Judah, and build the house of the LORD God of Israel, (he is the God,) which is in Jerusalem.

4 And whosoever remaineth in any place where he sojourneth, let the men of his place help him with silver, and with gold, and with goods, and with beasts, beside the freewill offering for the house of God that is in Jerusalem.

5 Then rose up the chief of the fathers of Judah and Benjamin, and the priests, and the Levites, with all them whose spirit God had raised, to go up to build the house of the LORD which is in Jerusalem.

6 And all they that were about them strengthened their hands with vessels of silver, with gold, with goods, and with beasts, and with precious things, beside all that was willingly offered.

7 Also Cyrus the king brought forth the vessels of the house of the LORD, which Nebuchadnezzar had brought forth out of Jerusalem, and had put them in the house of his gods;

8 Even those did Cyrus king of Persia bring forth by the hand of Mithredath the treasurer, and numbered them unto Sheshbazzar, the prince of Judah.

9 And this is the number of them: thirty chargers of gold, a thousand chargers of silver, nine and twenty knives,

10 Thirty basons of gold, silver basons of a second sort four hundred and ten, and other vessels a thousand.

11 All the vessels of gold and of silver were five thousand and four hundred. All these did Sheshbazzar bring up with them of the captivity that were brought up from Babylon unto Jerusalem.

CHAPTER 2

NOW these are the children of the province that went up out of the captivity, of those which had been carried away, whom Nebuchadnezzar the king of Babylon had carried away unto Babylon, and came again unto Jerusalem and Judah, every one unto his city;

2 Which came with Zerubbabel: Jeshua, Nehemiah, Seraiah, Reelaiah, Mordecai, Bilshan, Mispar, Bigvai, Rehum, Baanah. The number of the men of the people of Israel:

3 The children of Parosh, two thousand an hundred seventy and two.

4 The children of Shephatiah, three hundred seventy and two.

5 The children of Arah, seven hundred seventy and five.

6 The children of Pahath-moab, of the children of Jeshua and Joab, two thousand eight hundred and twelve.

7 The children of Elam, a thousand two hundred fifty and four.

8 The children of Zattu, nine hundred forty and five.

9 The children of Zaccai, seven hundred and threescore.

10 The children of Bani, six hundred forty and two.

11 The children of Bebai, six hundred twenty and three.

12 The children of Azgad, a thousand two hundred twenty and two.

13 The children of Adonikam, six hundred sixty and six.

14 The children of Bigvai, two thousand fifty and six.

15 The children of Adin, four hundred fifty and four.

16 The children of Ater of Hezekiah, ninety and eight.

17 The children of Bezai, three hundred twenty and three.

18 The children of Jorah, an hundred and twelve.

19 The children of Hashum, two hundred twenty and three.

20 The children of Gibbar, ninety and five.

21 The children of Beth-lehem, an hundred twenty and three.

22 The men of Netophah, fifty and six.

23 The men of Anathoth, an hundred twenty and eight.

24 The children of Azmaveth, forty and two.

25 The children of Kirjath-arim, Chephirah, and Beeroth, seven hundred and forty and three.

26 The children of Ramah and Geba, six hundred twenty and one.

27 The men of Michmas, an hundred twenty and two.

28 The men of Beth-el and Ai, two hundred twenty and three.

29 The children of Nebo, fifty and two.

30 The children of Magbish, an hundred fifty and six.

31 The children of the other Elam, a thousand two hundred fifty and four.

32 The children of Harim, three hundred and twenty.

33 The children of Lod, Hadid, and Ono, seven hundred twenty and five.

34 The children of Jericho, three hundred forty and five.

35 The children of Senaah, three thousand and six hundred and thirty.

36 The priests: the children of Jedaiah, of the house of Jeshua, nine hundred seventy and three.

37 The children of Immer, a thousand fifty and two.

38 The children of Pashur, a thousand two hundred forty and seven.

39 The children of Harim, a thousand and seventeen.

40 The Levites: the children of Jeshua and Kadmiel, of the children of Hodaviah, seventy and four.

41 The singers: the children of Asaph, an hundred twenty and eight.

42 The children of the porters: the children of Shallum, the children of Ater, the children of Talmon, the children of Akkub, the children of Hatita, the children of Shobai, in all an hundred thirty and nine.

43 The Nethinims: the children of Ziha, the children of Hasupha, the children of Tabbaoth,

44 The children of Keros, the children of Siaha, the children of Padon,

45 The children of Lebanah, the children of Hagabah, the children of Akkub,

46 The children of Hagab, the children of Shalmai, the children of Hanan,

47 The children of Giddel, the children of Gahar, the children of Reaiah,

48 The children of Rezin, the children of Nekoda, the children of Gazzam,

49 The children of Uzza, the children of Paseah, the children of Besai,

50 The children of Asnah, the children of Mehunim, the children of Nephusim,

51 The children of Bakbuk, the children of Hakupha, the children of Harhur,

52 The children of Bazluth, the children of Mehida, the children of Harsha,

53 The children of Barkos, the children of Sisera, the children of Thamah,

54 The children of Neziah, the children of Hatipha.

55 The children of Solomon's servants: the children of Sotai, the children of Sophereth, the children of Peruda,

56 The children of Jaalah, the children of Darkon, the children of Giddel,

57 The children of Shephatiah, the children of Hattil, the children of Pochereth of Zebaim, the children of Ami.

58 All the Nethinims, and the children of Solomon's servants, were three hundred ninety and two.

59 And these were they which went up from Tel-melah, Tel-harsa, Cherub, Addan, and Immer: but they could not shew their father's house, and their seed, whether they were of Israel:

60 The children of Delaiah, the children of Tobiah, the children of Nekoda, six hundred fifty and two.

61 And of the children of the priests: the children of Habaiah, the children of Koz, the children of Barzillai; which took a wife of the daughters of Barzillai the Gileadite, and was called after their name:

62 These sought their register among those that were reckoned by genealogy, but they were not found: therefore were they, as polluted, put from the priesthood.

63 And the Tirshatha said unto them, that they should not eat of the most holy things, till there stood up a priest with Urim and with Thummim.

64 The whole congregation together was forty and two thousand three hundred and threescore,

65 Beside their servants and their maids, of whom there were seven thousand three hundred thirty and seven: and there were among them two hundred singing men and singing women.

66 Their horses were seven hundred thirty and six; their mules, two hundred forty and five;

67 Their camels, four hundred thirty and five; their asses, six thousand seven hundred and twenty.

68 And some of the chief of the fathers, when they came to the house of the LORD which is at Jerusalem, offered freely for the house of God to set it up in his place:

69 They gave after their ability unto the treasure of the work threescore and one thousand drams of gold, and five thousand pound of silver, and one hundred priests' garments.

70 So the priests, and the Levites, and some of the people, and the singers, and the porters, and the Nethinims, dwelt in their cities, and all Israel in their cities.

CHAPTER 3

AND when the seventh month was come, and the children of Israel were in the cities, the people gathered themselves together as one man to Jerusalem.

2 Then stood up Jeshua the son of Jozadak, and his brethren the priests, and Zerubbabel the son of Shealtiel, and his brethren, and builded the altar of the God of Israel, to offer burnt offerings thereon, as it is written in the law of Moses the man of God.

3 And they set the altar upon his bases; for fear was upon them because of the people of those countries: and they offered burnt offerings thereon unto the LORD, even burnt offerings morning and evening.

4 They kept also the feast of tabernacles, as it is written, and offered the daily burnt offerings by number, according to the custom, as the duty of every day required;

5 And afterward offered the continual burnt offering, both of the new moons, and of all the set feasts of the LORD that were consecrated, and of every one that willingly offered a freewill offering unto the LORD.

6 From the first day of the seventh month began they to offer burnt offerings unto the LORD. But the foundation of the temple of the LORD was not yet laid.

7 They gave money also unto the masons, and to the carpenters; and meat, and drink, and oil, unto them of Zidon, and to them of Tyre, to bring cedar trees from Lebanon to the sea of Joppa, according to the grant that they had of Cyrus king of Persia.

8 Now in the second year of their coming unto the house of God at Jerusalem, in the second month, began Zerubbabel the son of Shealtiel, and Jeshua the son of Jozadak, and the remnant of their brethren the priests and the Levites, and all they that were come out of the captivity unto Jerusalem; and appointed the Levites, from twenty years old and upward, to set forward the work of the house of the LORD.

9 Then stood Jeshua with his sons and his brethren, Kadmiel and his sons, the sons of Judah, together, to set forward the workmen in the house of God: the sons of Henadad, with their sons and their brethren the Levites.

10 And when the builders laid the foundation of the temple of the LORD, they set the priests in their apparel with trumpets, and the Levites the sons of Asaph with cymbals, to praise the LORD, after the ordinance of David king of Israel.

11 And they sang together by course in praising and giving thanks unto the LORD; because he is good, for his mercy endureth for ever toward Israel. And all the people shouted with a great shout, when they praised the LORD, because the foundation of the house of the LORD was laid.

12 But many of the priests and Levites and chief of the fathers, who were ancient men, that had seen the first house, when the foundation of this house was laid before their eyes, wept with a loud voice; and many shouted aloud for joy:

13 So that the people could not discern the noise of the shout of joy from the noise of the weeping of the people: for the people shouted with a loud shout, and the noise was heard afar off.

CHAPTER 4

NOW when the adversaries of Judah and Benjamin heard that the children of the captivity builded the temple unto the LORD God of Israel;

2 Then they came to Zerubbabel, and to the chief of the fathers, and said unto them, Let us build with you: for we seek your God, as you do; and we do sacrifice unto him since the days of Esar-haddon king of Assur, which brought us up hither.

3 But Zerubbabel, and Jeshua, and the rest of the chief of the fathers of Israel, said unto them, You have nothing to do with us to build an house unto our God; but we ourselves together will build unto the LORD God of Israel, as king Cyrus the king of Persia has commanded us.

4 Then the people of the land weakened the hands of the people of Judah, and troubled them in building,

5 And hired counsellers against them, to frustrate their purpose, all the days of Cyrus king of Persia, even until the reign of Darius king of Persia.

6 And in the reign of Ahasuerus, in the beginning of his reign, wrote they unto him an accusation against the inhabitants of Judah and Jerusalem.

7 And in the days of Artaxerxes wrote Bishlam, Mithredath, Tabeel, and the rest of their companions, unto Artaxerxes king of Persia; and the writing of the letter was written in the Syrian tongue, and interpreted in the Syrian tongue.

8 Rehum the chancellor and Shimshai the scribe wrote a letter against Jerusalem to Artaxerxes the king in this sort:

9 Then wrote Rehum the chancellor, and Shimshai the scribe, and the rest of their companions; the Dinaites, the Apharsathchites, the Tarpelites, the Apharsites, the Archevites, the Babylonians, the Susanchites, the Dehavites, and the Elamites,

10 And the rest of the nations whom the great and noble Asnappar brought over, and set in the cities of Samaria, and the rest that are on this side the river, and at such a time.

11 This is the copy of the letter that they sent unto him, even unto Artaxerxes the king; Your servants the men on this side the river, and at such a time.

12 Be it known unto the king, that the Jews which came up from you to us are come unto Jerusalem, building the rebellious and the bad city, and have set up the walls thereof, and joined the foundations.

13 Be it known now unto the king, that, if this city be builded, and the walls set up again, then will they not pay toll, tribute, and custom, and so you shalt endamage the revenue of the kings.

14 Now because we have maintenance from the king's palace, and it was not meet for us to see the king's dishonour, therefore have we sent and certified the king;

15 That search may be made in the book of the records of your fathers: so shalt you find in the book of the records, and know that this city is a rebellious city, and hurtful unto kings and provinces, and that they have moved sedition within the same of old time: for which cause was this city destroyed.

16 We certify the king that, if this city be builded again, and the walls thereof set up, by this means you shalt have no portion on this side the river.

17 Then sent the king an answer unto Rehum the chancellor, and to Shimshai the scribe, and to the rest of their companions that dwell in Samaria, and unto the rest beyond the river, Peace, and at such a time.

18 The letter which you sent unto us has been plainly read before me.

19 And I commanded, and search has been made, and it is found that this city of old time has made insurrection against kings, and that rebellion and sedition have been made therein.

20 There have been mighty kings also over Jerusalem, which have ruled over all countries beyond the river; and toll, tribute, and custom, was paid unto them.

21 Give you now commandment to cause these men to cease, and that this city be not builded, until another commandment shall be given from me.

22 Take heed now that you fail not to do this: why should damage grow to the hurt of the kings?

23 Now when the copy of king Artaxerxes' letter was read before Rehum, and Shimshai the scribe, and their companions, they went up in haste to Jerusalem unto the Jews, and made them to cease by force and power.

24 Then ceased the work of the house of God which is at Jerusalem. So it ceased unto the second year of the reign of Darius king of Persia.

CHAPTER 5

THEN the prophets, Haggai the prophet, and Zechariah the son of Iddo, prophesied unto the Jews that were in Judah and Jerusalem in the name of the God of Israel, even unto them.

2 Then rose up Zerubbabel the son of Shealtiel, and Jeshua the son of Jozadak, and began to build the house of God which is at Jerusalem: and with them were the prophets of God helping them.

3 At the same time came to them Tatnai, governor on this side the river, and Shethar-boznai, and their companions, and said thus unto them, Who has commanded you to build this house, and to make up this wall?

4 Then said we unto them after this manner, What are the names of the men that make this building?

5 But the eye of their God was upon the elders of the Jews, that they could not cause them to cease, till the matter came to Darius: and then they returned answer by letter concerning this matter.

6 The copy of the letter that Tatnai, governor on this side the river, and Shethar-boznai, and his companions the Apharsachites, which were on this side the river, sent unto Darius the king:

7 They sent a letter unto him, wherein was written thus; Unto Darius the king, all peace.

8 Be it known unto the king, that we went into the province of Judea, to the house of the great God, which is builded with great stones, and timber is laid in the walls, and this work goeth fast on, and prospereth in their hands.

9 Then asked we those elders, and said unto them thus, Who commanded you to build this house, and to make up these walls?

10 We asked their names also, to certify you, that we might write the names of the men that were the chief of them.

11 And thus they returned us answer, saying, We are the servants of the God of heaven and earth, and build the house that was builded these many years ago, which a great king of Israel builded and set up.

12 But after that our fathers had provoked the God of heaven unto wrath, he gave them into the hand of Nebuchadnezzar the king of Babylon, the Chaldean, who destroyed this house, and carried the people away into Babylon.

13 But in the first year of Cyrus the king of Babylon the same king Cyrus made a decree to build this house of God.

14 And the vessels also of gold and silver of the house of God, which Nebuchadnezzar took out of the temple that was in Jerusalem, and brought them into the temple of Babylon, those did Cyrus the king take out of the temple of Babylon, and they were delivered unto one, whose name was Sheshbazzar, whom he had made governor;

15 And said unto him, Take these vessels, go, carry them into the temple that is in Jerusalem, and let the house of God be builded in his place.

16 Then came the same Sheshbazzar, and laid the foundation of the house of God which is in Jerusalem: and since that time even until now has it been in building, and yet it is not finished.

17 Now therefore, if it seem good to the king, let there be search made in the king's treasure house, which is there at Babylon, whether it be so, that a decree was made of Cyrus the king to build this house of God at Jerusalem, and let the king send his pleasure to us concerning this matter.

CHAPTER 6

THEN Darius the king made a decree, and search was made in the house of the rolls, where the treasures were laid up in Babylon.

2 And there was found at Achmetha, in the palace that is in the province of the Medes, a roll, and therein was a record thus written:

3 In the first year of Cyrus the king the same Cyrus the king made a decree concerning the house of God at Jerusalem, Let the house be builded, the place where they offered sacrifices, and let the foundations thereof be strongly laid; the height thereof threescore cubits, and the breadth thereof threescore cubits;

4 With three rows of great stones, and a row of new timber: and let the expences be given out of the king's house:

5 And also let the golden and silver vessels of the house of God, which Nebuchadnezzar took forth out of the temple which is at Jerusalem, and brought unto Babylon, be restored, and brought again unto the temple which is at Jerusalem, every one to his place, and place them in the house of God.

6 Now therefore, Tatnai, governor beyond the river, Shethar-boznai, and your companions the Apharsachites, which are beyond the river, be you far from thence:

7 Let the work of this house of God alone; let the governor of the Jews and the elders of the Jews build this house of God in his place.

8 Moreover I make a decree what you shall do to the elders of these Jews for the building of this house of God: that of the king's goods, even of the tribute beyond the river, forthwith expences given unto these men, that they be not hindered.

9 And that which they have need of, both young bullocks, and rams, and lambs, for the burnt offerings of the God of heaven, wheat, salt, wine, and oil, according to the appointment of the priests which are at Jerusalem, let it be given them day by day without fail:

10 That they may offer sacrifices of sweet savours unto the God of heaven, and pray for the life of the king, and of his sons.

11 Also I have made a decree, that whosoever shall alter this word, let timber be pulled down from his house, and being set up, let him be hanged thereon; and let his house be made a dunghill for this.

12 And the God that has caused his name to dwell there destroy all kings and people, that shall put to their hand to alter and to destroy this house of God which is at Jerusalem. I Darius have made a decree; let it be done with speed.

13 Then Tatnai, governor on this side the river, Shethar-boznai, and their companions, according to that which Darius the king had sent, so they did speedily.

14 And the elders of the Jews builded, and they prospered through the prophesying of Haggai the prophet and Zechariah the son of Iddo. And they builded, and finished it, according to the commandment of the God of Israel, and according to the commandment of Cyrus, and Darius, and Artaxerxes king of Persia.

15 And this house was finished on the third day of the month Adar, which was in the sixth year of the reign of Darius the king.

16 And the children of Israel, the priests, and the Levites, and the rest of the children of the captivity, kept the dedication of this house of God with joy,

17 And offered at the dedication of this house of God an hundred bullocks, two hundred rams, four hundred lambs; and for a sin offering for all Israel, twelve he goats, according to the number of the tribes of Israel.

18 And they set the priests in their divisions, and the Levites in their courses, for the service of God, which is at Jerusalem; as it is written in the book of Moses.

19 And the children of the captivity kept the passover upon the fourteenth day of the first month.

20 For the priests and the Levites were purified together, all of them were pure, and killed the passover for all the children of the captivity, and for their brethren the priests, and for themselves.

21 And the children of Israel, which were come again out of captivity, and all such as had separated themselves unto them from the filthiness of the heathen of the land, to seek the LORD God of Israel, did eat,

22 And kept the feast of unleavened bread seven days with joy: for the LORD had made them joyful, and turned the heart of the king of Assyria unto them, to strengthen their hands in the work of the house of God, the God of Israel.

CHAPTER 7

NOW after these things, in the reign of Artaxerxes king of Persia, Ezra the son of Seraiah, the son of Azariah, the son of Hilkiah,

2 The son of Shallum, the son of Zadok, the son of Ahitub,

3 The son of Amariah, the son of Azariah, the son of Meraioth,

4 The son of Zerahiah, the son of Uzzi, the son of Bukki,

5 The son of Abishua, the son of Phinehas, the son of Eleazar, the son of Aaron the chief priest:

6 This Ezra went up from Babylon; and he was a ready scribe in the law of Moses, which the LORD God of Israel had given: and the king granted him all his request, according to the hand of the LORD his God upon him.

7 And there went up some of the children of Israel, and of the priests, and the Levites, and the singers, and the porters, and the Nethinims, unto Jerusalem, in the seventh year of Artaxerxes the king.

8 And he came to Jerusalem in the fifth month, which was in the seventh year of the king.

9 For upon the first day of the first month began he to go up from Babylon, and on the first day of the fifth month came he to Jerusalem, according to the good hand of his God upon him.

10 For Ezra had prepared his heart to seek the law of the LORD, and to do it, and to teach in Israel statutes and judgments.

11 Now this is the copy of the letter that the king Artaxerxes gave unto Ezra the priest, the scribe, even a scribe of the words of the commandments of the LORD, and of his statutes to Israel.

12 Artaxerxes, king of kings, unto Ezra the priest, a scribe of the law of the God of heaven, perfect peace, and at such a time.

13 I make a decree, that all they of the people of Israel, and of his priests and Levites, in my realm, which are minded of their own freewill to go up to Jerusalem, go with you.

14 Forasmuch as you are sent of the king, and of his seven counsellors, to inquire concerning Judah and Jerusalem, according to the law of your God which is in yours hand;

15 And to carry the silver and gold, which the king and his counsellors have freely offered unto the God of Israel, whose habitation is in Jerusalem,

16 And all the silver and gold that you can find in all the province of Babylon, with the freewill offering of the people, and of the priests, offering willingly for the house of their God which is in Jerusalem:

17 That you mayest buy speedily with this money bullocks, rams, lambs, with their meat offerings and their drink offerings, and offer them upon the altar of the house of your God which is in Jerusalem.

18 And whatsoever shall seem good to you, and to your brethren, to do with the rest of the silver and the gold, that do after the will of your God.

19 The vessels also that are given you for the service of the house of your God, those deliver you before the God of Jerusalem.

20 And whatsoever more shall be needful for the house of your God, which you shalt have occasion to bestow, bestow it out of the king's treasure house.

21 And I, even I Artaxerxes the king, do make a decree to all the treasurers which are beyond the river, that whatsoever Ezra the priest, the scribe of the law of the God of heaven, shall require of you, it be done speedily,

22 Unto an hundred talents of silver, and to an hundred measures of wheat, and to an hundred baths of wine, and to an hundred baths of oil, and salt without prescribing how much.

23 Whatsoever is commanded by the God of heaven, let it be diligently done for the house of the God of heaven: for why should there be wrath against the realm of the king and his sons?

24 Also we certify you, that touching any of the priests and Levites, singers, porters, Nethinims, or ministers of this house of God, it shall not be lawful to impose toll, tribute, or custom, upon them.

25 And you , Ezra, after the wisdom of your God, that is in yours hand, set magistrates and judges, which may judge all the people that are beyond the river, all such as know the laws of your God; and teach you them that know them not.

26 And whosoever will not do the law of your God, and the law of the king, let judgment be executed speedily upon him, whether it be unto death, or to banishment, or to confiscation of goods, or to imprisonment.

27 Blessed be the LORD God of our fathers, which has put such a thing as this in the king's heart, to beautify the house of the LORD which is in Jerusalem:

28 And has extended mercy unto me before the king, and his counsellors, and before all the king's mighty princes. And I was strengthened as the hand of the LORD my God was upon me, and I gathered together out of Israel chief men to go up with me.

CHAPTER 8

THESE are now the chief of their fathers, and this is the genealogy of them that went up with me from Babylon, in the reign of Artaxerxes the king.

2 Of the sons of Phinehas; Gershom: of the sons of Ithamar; Daniel: of the sons of David; Hattush.

3 Of the sons of Shechaniah, of the sons of Pharosh; Zechariah: and with him were reckoned by genealogy of the males an hundred and fifty.

4 Of the sons of Pahath-moab; Elihoenai the son of Zerahiah, and with him two hundred males.

5 Of the sons of Shechaniah; the son of Jahaziel, and with him three hundred males.

6 Of the sons also of Adin; Ebed the son of Jonathan, and with him fifty males.

7 And of the sons of Elam; Jeshaiah the son of Athaliah, and with him seventy males.

8 And of the sons of Shephatiah; Zebadiah the son of Michael, and with him fourscore males.

9 Of the sons of Joab; Obadiah the son of Jehiel, and with him two hundred and eighteen males.

10 And of the sons of Shelomith; the son of Josiphiah, and with him an hundred and threescore males.

11 And of the sons of Bebai; Zechariah the son of Bebai, and with him twenty and eight males.

12 And of the sons of Azgad; Johanan the son of Hakkatan, and with him an hundred and ten males.

13 And of the last sons of Adonikam, whose names are these, Eliphelet, Jeiel, and Shemaiah, and with them threescore males.

14 Of the sons also of Bigvai; Uthai, and Zabbud, and with them seventy males.

15And I gathered them together to the river that runneth to Ahava; and there abode we in tents three days: and I viewed the people, and the priests, and found there none of the sons of Levi.

16 Then sent I for Eliezer, for Ariel, for Shemaiah, and for Elnathan, and for Jarib, and for Elnathan, and for Nathan, and for Zechariah, and for Meshullam, chief men; also for Joiarib, and for Elnathan, men of understanding.

17 And I sent them with commandment unto Iddo the chief at the place Casiphia, and I told them what they should say unto Iddo, and to his brethren the Nethinims, at the place Casiphia, that they should bring unto us ministers for the house of our God.

18 And by the good hand of our God upon us they brought us a man of understanding, of the sons of Mahli, the son of Levi, the son of Israel; and Sherebiah, with his sons and his brethren, eighteen;

19 And Hashabiah, and with him Jeshaiah of the sons of Merari, his brethren and their sons, twenty;

20 Also of the Nethinims, whom David and the princes had appointed for the service of the Levites, two hundred and twenty Nethinims: all of them were expressed by name.

21Then I proclaimed a fast there, at the river of Ahava, that we might afflict ourselves before our God, to seek of him a right way for us, and for our little ones, and for all our substance.

22 For I was ashamed to require of the king a band of soldiers and horsemen to help us against the enemy in the way: because we had spoken unto the king, saying, The hand of our God is upon all them for good that seek him; but his power and his wrath is against all them that forsake him.

23 So we fasted and besought our God for this: and he was intreated of us.

24Then I separated twelve of the chief of the priests, Sherebiah, Hashabiah, and ten of their brethren with them,

25 And weighed unto them the silver, and the gold, and the vessels, even the offering of the house of our God, which the king, and his counsellers, and his lords, and all Israel there present, had offered:

26 I even weighed unto their hand six hundred and fifty talents of silver, and silver vessels an hundred talents, and of gold an hundred talents;

27 Also twenty basons of gold, of a thousand drams; and two vessels of fine copper, precious as gold.

28 And I said unto them, You are holy unto the LORD; the vessels are holy also; and the silver and the gold are a freewill offering unto the LORD God of your fathers.

29 Watch you , and keep them, until you weigh them before the chief of the priests and the Levites, and chief of the fathers of Israel, at Jerusalem, in the chambers of the house of the LORD.

30 So took the priests and the Levites the weight of the silver, and the gold, and the vessels, to bring them to Jerusalem unto the house of our God.

31Then we departed from the river of Ahava on the twelfth day of the first month, to go unto Jerusalem: and the hand of our God was upon us, and he delivered us from the hand of the enemy, and of such as lay in wait by the way.

32 And we came to Jerusalem, and abode there three days.

33Now on the fourth day was the silver and the gold and the vessels weighed in the house of our God by the hand of Meremoth the son of Uriah the priest; and with him was Eleazar the son of Phinehas; and with them was Jozabad the son of Jeshua, and Noadiah the son of Binnui, Levites;

34 By number and by weight of every one: and all the weight was written at that time.

35 Also the children of those that had been carried away, which were come out of the captivity, offered burnt offerings unto the God of Israel, twelve bullocks for all Israel, ninety and six rams, seventy and seven lambs, twelve he goats for a sin offering: all this was a burnt offering unto the LORD.

36And they delivered the king's commissions unto the king's lieutenants, and to the governors on this side the river: and they furthered the people, and the house of God.

CHAPTER 9

NOW when these things were done, the princes came to me, saying, The people of Israel, and the priests, and the Levites, have not separated themselves from the people of the lands, doing according to their abominations, even of the Canaanites, the Hittites, the Perizzites, the Jebusites, the Ammonites, the Moabites, the Egyptians, and the Amorites.

2 For they have taken of their daughters for themselves, and for their sons: so that the holy seed have mingled themselves with the people of those lands: yea, the hand of the princes and rulers has been chief in this trespass.

3 And when I heard this thing, I rent my garment and my mantle, and plucked off the hair of my head and of my beard, and sat down astonied.

4 Then were assembled unto me every one that trembled at the words of the God of Israel, because of the transgression of those that had been carried away; and I sat astonied until the evening sacrifice.

5And at the evening sacrifice I arose up from my heaviness; and having rent my garment and my mantle, I fell upon my knees, and spread out my hands unto the LORD my God,

6 And said, O my God, I am ashamed and blush to lift up my face to you, my God: for our iniquities are increased over our head, and our trespass is grown up unto the heavens.

7 Since the days of our fathers have we been in a great trespass unto this day; and for our iniquities have we, our kings, and our priests, been delivered into the hand of the kings of the lands, to the sword, to captivity, and to a spoil, and to confusion of face, as it is this day.

8 And now for a little space grace has been shewed from the LORD our God, to leave us a remnant to escape, and to give us a nail in his holy place, that our God may lighten our eyes, and give us a little reviving in our bondage.

9 For we were bondmen; yet our God has not forsaken us in our bondage, but has extended mercy unto us in the sight of the kings of Persia, to give us a reviving, to set up the house of our God, and to repair the desolations thereof, and to give us a wall in Judah and in Jerusalem.

10 And now, O our God, what shall we say after this? for we have forsaken your commandments,

11 Which you have commanded by your servants the prophets, saying, The land, unto which you go to possess it, is an unclean land with the filthiness of the people of the lands, with their abominations, which have filled it from one end to another with their uncleanness.

12 Now therefore give not your daughters unto their sons, neither take their daughters unto your sons, nor seek their peace or their wealth for ever: that you may be strong, and eat the good of the land, and leave it for an inheritance to your children for ever.

13 And after all that is come upon us for our evil deeds, and for our great trespass, seeing that you our God have punished us less than our iniquities deserve, and have given us such deliverance as this;

14 Should we again break your commandments, and join in affinity with the people of these abominations? wouldest not you be angry with us till you hadst consumed us, so that there should be no remnant nor escaping?

15 O LORD God of Israel, you are righteous: for we remain yet escaped, as it is this day: behold, we are before you in our trespasses: for we cannot stand before you because of this.

CHAPTER 10

NOW when Ezra had prayed, and when he had confessed, weeping and casting himself down before the house of God, there assembled unto him out of Israel a very great congregation of men and women and children: for the people wept very sore.

2 And Shechaniah the son of Jehiel, one of the sons of Elam, answered and said unto Ezra, We have trespassed against our God, and have taken strange wives of the people of the land: yet now there is hope in Israel concerning this thing.

3 Now therefore let us make a covenant with our God to put away all the wives, and such as are born of them, according to the counsel of my lord, and of those that tremble at the commandment of our God; and let it be done according to the law.

4 Arise; for this matter belongeth unto you: we also will be with you: be of good courage, and do it.

5 Then arose Ezra, and made the chief priests, the Levites, and all Israel, to swear that they should do according to this word. And they sware.

6Then Ezra rose up from before the house of God, and went into the chamber of Johanan the son of Eliashib: and when he came thither, he did eat no bread, nor drink water: for he mourned because of the transgression of them that had been carried away.

7 And they made proclamation throughout Judah and Jerusalem unto all the children of the captivity, that they should gather themselves together unto Jerusalem;

8 And that whosoever would not come within three days, according to the counsel of the princes and the elders, all his substance should be forfeited, and himself separated from the congregation of those that had been carried away.

9Then all the men of Judah and Benjamin gathered themselves together unto Jerusalem within three days. It was the ninth month, on the twentieth day of the month; and all the people sat in the street of the house of God, trembling because of this matter, and for the great rain.

10 And Ezra the priest stood up, and said unto them, You have transgressed, and have taken strange wives, to increase the trespass of Israel.

11 Now therefore make confession unto the LORD God of your fathers, and do his pleasure: and separate yourselves from the people of the land, and from the strange wives.

12 Then all the congregation answered and said with a loud voice, As you have said, so must we do.

13 But the people are many, and it is a time of much rain, and we are not able to stand without, neither is this a work of one day or two: for we are many that have transgressed in this thing.

14 Let now our rulers of all the congregation stand, and let all them which have taken strange wives in our cities come at appointed times, and with them the elders of every city, and the judges thereof, until the fierce wrath of our God for this matter be turned from us.

15Only Jonathan the son of Asahel and Jahaziah the son of Tikvah were employed about this matter: and Meshullam and Shabbethai the Levite helped them.

16 And the children of the captivity did so. And Ezra the priest, with certain chief of the fathers, after the house of their fathers, and all of them by their names, were separated, and sat down in the first day of the tenth month to examine the matter.

17 And they made an end with all the men that had taken strange wives by the first day of the first month.

18And among the sons of the priests there were found that had taken strange wives: namely, of the sons of Jeshua the son of Jozadak, and his brethren; Maaseiah, and Eliezer, and Jarib, and Gedaliah.

19 And they gave their hands that they would put away their wives; and being guilty, they offered a ram of the flock for their trespass.

20 And of the sons of Immer; Hanani, and Zebadiah.

21 And of the sons of Harim; Maaseiah, and Elijah, and Shemaiah, and Jehiel, and Uzziah.

22 And of the sons of Pashur; Elioenai, Maaseiah, Ishmael, Nethaneel, Jozabad, and Elasah.

23 Also of the Levites; Jozabad, and Shimei, and Kelaiah, (the same is Kelita,) Pethahiah, Judah, and Eliezer.

24 Of the singers also; Eliashib: and of the porters; Shallum, and Telem, and Uri.

25 Moreover of Israel: of the sons of Parosh; Ramiah, and Jeziah, and Malchiah, and Miamin, and Eleazar, and Malchijah, and Benaiah.

26 And of the sons of Elam; Mattaniah, Zechariah, and Jehiel, and Abdi, and Jeremoth, and Eliah.

27 And of the sons of Zattu; Elioenai, Eliashib, Mattaniah, and Jeremoth, and Zabad, and Aziza.

28 Of the sons also of Bebai; Jehohanan, Hananiah, Zabbai, and Athlai.

29 And of the sons of Bani; Meshullam, Malluch, and Adaiah, Jashub, and Sheal, and Ramoth.

30 And of the sons of Pahath-moab; Adna, and Chelal, Benaiah, Maaseiah, Mattaniah, Bezaleel, and Binnui, and Manasseh.

31 And of the sons of Harim; Eliezer, Ishijah, Malchiah, Shemaiah, Shimeon,

32 Benjamin, Malluch, and Shemariah.

33 Of the sons of Hashum; Mattenai, Mattathah, Zabad, Eliphelet, Jeremai, Manasseh, and Shimei.

34 Of the sons of Bani; Maadai, Amram, and Uel,

35 Benaiah, Bedeiah, Chelluh,

36 Vaniah, Meremoth, Eliashib,

37 Mattaniah, Mattenai, and Jaasau,

38 And Bani, and Binnui, Shimei,

39 And Shelemiah, and Nathan, and Adaiah,

40 Machnadebai, Shashai, Sharai,

41 Azareel, and Shelemiah, Shemariah,

42 Shallum, Amariah, and Joseph.

43 Of the sons of Nebo; Jeiel, Mattithiah, Zabad, Zebina, Jadau, and Joel, Benaiah.

44 All these had taken strange wives: and some of them had wives by whom they had children.

THE
BOOK OF NEHEMIAH.

CHAPTER 1

THE words of Nehemiah the son of Hachaliah. And it came to pass in the month Chisleu, in the twentieth year, as I was in Shushan the palace,

2 That Hanani, one of my brethren, came, he and certain men of Judah; and I asked them concerning the Jews that had escaped, which were left of the captivity, and concerning Jerusalem.

3 And they said unto me, The remnant that are left of the captivity there in the province are in great affliction and reproach: the wall of Jerusalem also is broken down, and the gates thereof are burned with fire.

4 And it came to pass, when I heard these words, that I sat down and wept, and mourned certain days, and fasted, and prayed before the God of heaven,

5 And said, I beseech you, O LORD God of heaven, the great and terrible God, that keepeth covenant and mercy for them that love him and observe his commandments:

6 Let yours ear now be attentive, and yours eyes open, that you mayest hear the prayer of your servant, which I pray before you now, day and night, for the children of Israel your servants, and confess the sins of the children of Israel, which we have sinned against you: both I and my father's house have sinned.

7 We have dealt very corruptly against you, and have not kept the commandments, nor the statutes, nor the judgments, which you commandedst your servant Moses.

8 Remember, I beseech you, the word that you commandedst your servant Moses, saying, If you transgress, I will scatter you abroad among the nations:

9 But if you turn unto me, and keep my commandments, and do them; though there were of you cast out unto the uttermost part of the heaven, yet will I gather them from thence, and will bring them unto the place that I have chosen to set my name there.

10 Now these are your servants and your people, whom you have redeemed by your great power, and by your strong hand.

11 O Lord, I beseech you, let now yours ear be attentive to the prayer of your servant, and to the prayer of your servants, who desire to fear your name: and prosper, I pray you, your servant this day, and grant him mercy in the sight of this man. For I was the king's cupbearer.

CHAPTER 2

AND it came to pass in the month Nisan, in the twentieth year of Artaxerxes the king, that wine was before him: and I took up the wine, and gave it unto the king. Now I had not been beforetime sad in his presence.

2 Wherefore the king said unto me, Why is your countenance sad, seeing you are not sick? this is nothing else but sorrow of heart. Then I was very sore afraid,

3 And said unto the king, Let the king live for ever: why should not my countenance be sad, when the city, the place of my fathers' sepulchres, lies waste, and the gates thereof are consumed with fire?

4 Then the king said unto me, For what dost you make request? So I prayed to the God of heaven.

5 And I said unto the king, If it please the king, and if your servant have found favour in your sight, that you wouldest send me unto Judah, unto the city of my fathers' sepulchres, that I may build it.

6 And the king said unto me, (the queen also sitting by him,) For how long shall your journey be? and when will you return? So it pleased the king to send me; and I set him a time.

7 Moreover I said unto the king, If it please the king, let letters be given me to the governors beyond the river, that they may convey me over till I come into Judah;

8 And a letter unto Asaph the keeper of the king's forest, that he may give me timber to make beams for the gates of the palace which appertained to the house, and for the wall of the city, and for the house that I shall enter into. And the king granted me, according to the good hand of my God upon me.

9 Then I came to the governors beyond the river, and gave them the king's letters. Now the king had sent captains of the army and horsemen with me.

10 When Sanballat the Horonite, and Tobiah the servant, the Ammonite, heard of it, it grieved them exceedingly that there was come a man to seek the welfare of the children of Israel.

11 So I came to Jerusalem, and was there three days.

12 And I arose in the night, I and some few men with me; neither told I any man what my God had put in my heart to do at Jerusalem: neither was there any beast with me, save the beast that I rode upon.

13 And I went out by night by the gate of the valley, even before the dragon well, and to the dung port, and viewed the walls of Jerusalem, which were broken down, and the gates thereof were consumed with fire.

14 Then I went on to the gate of the fountain, and to the king's pool: but there was no place for the beast that was under me to pass.

15 Then went I up in the night by the brook, and viewed the wall, and turned back, and entered by the gate of the valley, and so returned.

16 And the rulers knew not whither I went, or what I did; neither had I as yet told it to the Jews, nor to the priests, nor to the nobles, nor to the rulers, nor to the rest that did the work.

17 Then said I unto them, You see the distress that we are in, how Jerusalem lies waste, and the gates thereof are burned with fire: come, and let us build up the wall of Jerusalem, that we be no more a reproach.

18 Then I told them of the hand of my God which was good upon me; as also the king's words that he had spoken unto me. And they said, Let us rise up and build. So they strengthened their hands for this good work.

19 But when Sanballat the Horonite, and Tobiah the servant, the Ammonite, and Geshem the Arabian, heard it, they laughed us to scorn, and despised us, and said, What is this thing that you do? will you rebel against the king?

20 Then answered I them, and said unto them, The God of heaven, he will prosper us; therefore we his servants will arise and build: but you have no portion, nor right, nor memorial, in Jerusalem.

CHAPTER 3

THEN Eliashib the high priest rose up with his brethren the priests, and they builded the sheep gate; they sanctified it, and set up the doors of it; even unto the tower of Meah they sanctified it, unto the tower of Hananeel.

2 And next unto him builded the men of Jericho. And next to them builded Zaccur the son of Imri.

3 But the fish gate did the sons of Hassenaah build, who also laid the beams thereof, and set up the doors thereof, the locks thereof, and the bars thereof.

4 And next unto them repaired Meremoth the son of Urijah, the son of Koz. And next unto them repaired Meshullam the son of Berechiah, the son of Meshezabeel. And next unto them repaired Zadok the son of Baana.

5 And next unto them the Tekoites repaired; but their nobles put not their necks to the work of their Lord.

6 Moreover the old gate repaired Jehoiada the son of Paseah, and Meshullam the son of Besodeiah; they laid the beams thereof, and set up the doors thereof, and the locks thereof, and the bars thereof.

7 And next unto them repaired Melatiah the Gibeonite, and Jadon the Meronothite, the men of Gibeon, and of Mizpah, unto the throne of the governor on this side the river.

8 Next unto him repaired Uzziel the son of Harhaiah, of the goldsmiths. Next unto him also repaired Hananiah the son of one of the apothecaries, and they fortified Jerusalem unto the broad wall.

9 And next unto them repaired Rephaiah the son of Hur, the ruler of the half part of Jerusalem.

10 And next unto them repaired Jedaiah the son of Harumaph, even over against his house. And next unto him repaired Hattush the son of Hashabniah.

11 Malchijah the son of Harim, and Hashub the son of Pahath-moab, repaired the other piece, and the tower of the furnaces.

12 And next unto him repaired Shallum the son of Halohesh, the ruler of the half part of Jerusalem, he and his daughters.

13 The valley gate repaired Hanun, and the inhabitants of Zanoah; they built it, and set up the doors thereof, the locks thereof, and the bars thereof, and a thousand cubits on the wall unto the dung gate.

14 But the dung gate repaired Malchiah the son of Rechab, the ruler of part of Beth-haccerem; he built it, and set up the doors thereof, the locks thereof, and the bars thereof.

15 But the gate of the fountain repaired Shallun the son of Col-hozeh, the ruler of part of Mizpah; he built it, and covered it, and set up the doors thereof, the locks thereof, and the bars thereof, and the wall of the pool of Siloah by the king's garden, and unto the stairs that go down from the city of David.

16 After him repaired Nehemiah the son of Azbuk, the ruler of the half part of Beth-zur, unto the place over against the sepulchres of David, and to the pool that was made, and unto the house of the mighty.

17 After him repaired the Levites, Rehum the son of Bani. Next unto him repaired Hashabiah, the ruler of the half part of Keilah, in his part.

18 After him repaired their brethren, Bavai the son of Henadad, the ruler of the half part of Keilah.

19 And next to him repaired Ezer the son of Jeshua, the ruler of Mizpah, another piece over against the going up to the armoury at the turning of the wall.

20 After him Baruch the son of Zabbai earnestly repaired the other piece, from the turning of the wall unto the door of the house of Eliashib the high priest.

21 After him repaired Meremoth the son of Urijah the son of Koz another piece, from the door of the house of Eliashib even to the end of the house of Eliashib.

22 And after him repaired the priests, the men of the plain.

23 After him repaired Benjamin and Hashub over against their house. After him repaired Azariah the son of Maaseiah the son of Ananiah by his house.

24 After him repaired Binnui the son of Henadad another piece, from the house of Azariah unto the turning of the wall, even unto the corner.

25 Palal the son of Uzai, over against the turning of the wall, and the tower which lies out from the king's high house, that was by the court of the prison. After him Pedaiah the son of Parosh.

26 Moreover the Nethinims dwelt in Ophel, unto the place over against the water gate toward the east, and the tower that lies out.

27 After them the Tekoites repaired another piece, over against the great tower that lies out, even unto the wall of Ophel.

28 From above the horse gate repaired the priests, every one over against his house.

29 After them repaired Zadok the son of Immer over against his house. After him repaired also Shemaiah the son of Shechaniah, the keeper of the east gate.

30 After him repaired Hananiah the son of Shelemiah, and Hanun the sixth son of Zalaph, another piece. After him repaired Meshullam the son of Berechiah over against his chamber.

31 After him repaired Malchiah the goldsmith's son unto the place of the Nethinims, and of the merchants, over against the gate Miphkad, and to the going up of the corner.

32 And between the going up of the corner unto the sheep gate repaired the goldsmiths and the merchants.

CHAPTER 4

BUT it came to pass, that when Sanballat heard that we builded the wall, he was wroth, and took great indignation, and mocked the Jews.

2 And he spake before his brethren and the army of Samaria, and said, What do these feeble Jews? will they fortify themselves? will they sacrifice? will they make an end in a day? will they revive the stones out of the heaps of the rubbish which are burned?

3 Now Tobiah the Ammonite was by him, and he said, Even that which they build, if a fox go up, he shall even break down their stone wall.

4 Hear, O our God; for we are despised: and turn their reproach upon their own head, and give them for a prey in the land of captivity:

5 And cover not their iniquity, and let not their sin be blotted out from before you: for they have provoked you to anger before the builders.

6 So built we the wall; and all the wall was joined together unto the half thereof: for the people had a mind to work.

7 But it came to pass, that when Sanballat, and Tobiah, and the Arabians, and the Ammonites, and the Ashdodites, heard that the walls of Jerusalem were made up, and that the breaches began to be stopped, then they were very wroth,

8 And conspired all of them together to come and to fight against Jerusalem, and to hinder it.

9 Nevertheless we made our prayer unto our God, and set a watch against them day and night, because of them.

10 And Judah said, The strength of the bearers of burdens is decayed, and there is much rubbish; so that we are not able to build the wall.

11 And our adversaries said, They shall not know, neither see, till we come in the midst among them, and slay them, and cause the work to cease.

12 And it came to pass, that when the Jews which dwelt by them came, they said unto us ten times, From all places whence you shall return unto us they will be upon you.

13 Therefore set I in the lower places behind the wall, and on the higher places, I even set the people after their families with their swords, their spears, and their bows.

14 And I looked, and rose up, and said unto the nobles, and to the rulers, and to the rest of the people, Be not you afraid of them: remember the Lord, which is great and terrible, and fight for your brethren, your sons, and your daughters, your wives, and your houses.

15 And it came to pass, when our enemies heard that it was known unto us, and God had brought their counsel to nought, that we returned all of us to the wall, every one unto his work.

16 And it came to pass from that time forth, that the half of my servants created in the work, and the other half of them held both the spears, the shields, and the bows, and the habergeons; and the rulers were behind all the house of Judah.

17 They which builded on the wall, and they that bare burdens, with those that laded, every one with one of his hands created in the work, and with the other hand held a weapon.

18 For the builders, every one had his sword girded by his side, and so builded. And he that sounded the trumpet was by me.

19 And I said unto the nobles, and to the rulers, and to the rest of the people, The work is great and large, and we are separated upon the wall, one far from another.

20 In what place therefore you hear the sound of the trumpet, resort you thither unto us: our God shall fight for us.

21 So we laboured in the work: and half of them held the spears from the rising of the morning till the stars appeared.

22 Likewise at the same time said I unto the people, Let every one with his servant lodge within Jerusalem, that in the night they may be a guard to us, and labour on the day.

23 So neither I, nor my brethren, nor my servants, nor the men of the guard which followed me, none of us put off our clothes, saving that every one put them off for washing.

CHAPTER 5

AND there was a great cry of the people and of their wives against their brethren the Jews.

2 For there were that said, We, our sons, and our daughters, are many: therefore we take up corn for them, that we may eat, and live.

3 Some also there were that said, We have mortgaged our lands, vineyards, and houses, that we might buy corn, because of the dearth.

4 There were also that said, We have borrowed money for the king's tribute, and that upon our lands and vineyards.

5 Yet now our flesh is as the flesh of our brethren, our children as their children: and, lo, we bring into bondage our sons and our daughters to be servants, and some of our daughters are brought unto bondage already: neither is it in our power to redeem them; for other men have our lands and vineyards.

6 And I was very angry when I heard their cry and these words.

7 Then I consulted with myself, and I rebuked the nobles, and the rulers, and said unto them, You exact usury, every one of his brother. And I set a great assembly against them.

8 And I said unto them, We after our ability have redeemed our brethren the Jews, which were sold unto the heathen; and will you even sell your brethren? or shall they be sold unto us? Then held they their peace, and found nothing to answer.

9 Also I said, It is not good that you do: ought you not to walk in the fear of our God because of the reproach of the heathen our enemies?

10 I likewise, and my brethren, and my servants, might exact of them money and corn: I pray you, let us leave off this usury.

11 Restore, I pray you, to them, even this day, their lands, their vineyards, their oliveyards, and their houses, also the hundredth part of the money, and of the corn, the wine, and the oil, that you exact of them.

12 Then said they, We will restore them, and will require nothing of them; so will we do as you say. Then I called the priests, and took an oath of them, that they should do according to this promise.

13 Also I shook my lap, and said, So God shake out every man from his house, and from his labour, that performeth not this promise, even thus be he shaken out, and emptied. And all the congregation said, Amen, and praised the LORD. And the people did according to this promise.

14 Moreover from the time that I was appointed to be their governor in the land of Judah, from the twentieth year even unto the two and thirtieth year of Artaxerxes the king, that is, twelve years, I and my brethren have not eaten the bread of the governor.

15 But the former governors that had been before me were chargeable unto the people, and had taken of them bread and wine, beside forty shekels of silver; yea, even their servants bare rule over the people: but so did not I, because of the fear of God.

16 Yea, also I continued in the work of this wall, neither bought we any land: and all my servants were gathered thither unto the work.

17 Moreover there were at my table an hundred and fifty of the Jews and rulers, beside those that came unto us from among the heathen that are about us.

18 Now that which was prepared for me daily was one ox and six choice sheep; also fowls were prepared for me, and once in ten days store of all sorts of wine: yet for all this required not I the bread of the governor, because the bondage was heavy upon this people.

19 Think upon me, my God, for good, according to all that I have done for this people.

CHAPTER 6

NOW it came to pass, when Sanballat, and Tobiah, and Geshem the Arabian, and the rest of our enemies, heard that I had builded the wall, and that there was no breach left therein; (though at that time I had not set up the doors upon the gates;)

2 That Sanballat and Geshem sent unto me, saying, Come, let us meet together in some one of the villages in the plain of Ono. But they thought to do me mischief.

3 And I sent messengers unto them, saying, I am doing a great work, so that I cannot come down: why should the work cease, whilst I leave it, and come down to you?

4 Yet they sent unto me four times after this sort; and I answered them after the same manner.

5 Then sent Sanballat his servant unto me in like manner the fifth time with an open letter in his hand;

6 Wherein was written, It is reported among the heathen, and Gashmu saith it, that you and the Jews think to rebel: for which cause you buildest the wall, that you mayest be their king, according to these words.

7 And you have also appointed prophets to preach of you at Jerusalem, saying, There is a king in Judah: and now shall it be reported to the king according to these words. Come now therefore, and let us take counsel together.

8 Then I sent unto him, saying, There are no such things done as you say, but you feignest them out of yours own heart.

9 For they all made us afraid, saying, Their hands shall be weakened from the work, that it be not done. Now therefore, O God, strengthen my hands.

10 Afterward I came unto the house of Shemaiah the son of Delaiah the son of Mehetabeel, who was shut up; and he said, Let us meet together in the house of God, within the temple, and let us shut the doors of the temple: for they will come to slay you; yea, in the night will they come to slay you.

11 And I said, Should such a man as I flee? and who is there, that, being as I am, would go into the temple to save his life? I will not go in.

12 And, lo, I perceived that God had not sent him; but that he pronounced this prophecy against me: for Tobiah and Sanballat had hired him.

13 Therefore was he hired, that I should be afraid, and do so, and sin, and that they might have matter for an evil report, that they might reproach me.

14 My God, think you upon Tobiah and Sanballat according to these their works, and on the prophetess Noadiah, and the rest of the prophets, that would have put me in fear.

15 So the wall was finished in the twenty and fifth day of the month Elul, in fifty two days.

16 And it came to pass, that when all our enemies heard thereof, and all the heathen that were about us saw these things, they were much cast down in their own eyes: for they perceived that this work was created of our God.

17 Moreover in those days the nobles of Judah sent many letters unto Tobiah, and the letters of Tobiah came unto them.

18 For there were many in Judah sworn unto him, because he was the son in law of Shechaniah the son of Arah; and his son Johanan had taken the daughter of Meshullam the son of Berechiah.

19 Also they reported his good deeds before me, and uttered my words to him. And Tobiah sent letters to put me in fear.

CHAPTER 7

NOW it came to pass, when the wall was built, and I had set up the doors, and the porters and the singers and the Levites were appointed,

2 That I gave my brother Hanani, and Hananiah the ruler of the palace, charge over Jerusalem: for he was a faithful man, and feared God above many.

3 And I said unto them, Let not the gates of Jerusalem be opened until the sun be hot; and while they stand by, let them shut the doors, and bar them: and appoint watches of the inhabitants of Jerusalem, every one in his watch, and every one to be over against his house.

4 Now the city was large and great: but the people were few therein, and the houses were not builded.

5 And my God put into my heart to gather together the nobles, and the rulers, and the people, that they might be reckoned by genealogy. And I found a register of the genealogy of them which came up at the first, and found written therein,

6 These are the children of the province, that went up out of the captivity, of those that had been carried away, whom Nebuchadnezzar the king of Babylon had carried away, and came again to Jerusalem and to Judah, every one unto his city;

7 Who came with Zerubbabel, Jeshua, Nehemiah, Azariah, Raamiah, Nahamani, Mordecai, Bilshan, Mispereth, Bigvai, Nehum, Baanah. The number, I say, of the men of the people of Israel was this;

8 The children of Parosh, two thousand an hundred seventy and two.

9 The children of Shephatiah, three hundred seventy and two.

10 The children of Arah, six hundred fifty and two.

11 The children of Pahath-moab, of the children of Jeshua and Joab, two thousand and eight hundred and eighteen.

12 The children of Elam, a thousand two hundred fifty and four.

13 The children of Zattu, eight hundred forty and five.

14 The children of Zaccai, seven hundred and threescore.

15 The children of Binnui, six hundred forty and eight.

16 The children of Bebai, six hundred twenty and eight.

17 The children of Azgad, two thousand three hundred twenty and two.

18 The children of Adonikam, six hundred threescore and seven.

19 The children of Bigvai, two thousand threescore and seven.

20 The children of Adin, six hundred fifty and five.

21 The children of Ater of Hezekiah, ninety and eight.

22 The children of Hashum, three hundred twenty and eight.

23 The children of Bezai, three hundred twenty and four.

24 The children of Hariph, an hundred and twelve.

25 The children of Gibeon, ninety and five.

26 The men of Beth-lehem and Netophah, an hundred fourscore and eight.

27 The men of Anathoth, an hundred twenty and eight.

28 The men of Beth-azmaveth, forty and two.

29 The men of Kirjath-jearim, Chephirah, and Beeroth, seven hundred forty and three.

30 The men of Ramah and Geba, six hundred twenty and one.

31 The men of Michmas, an hundred and twenty and two.

32 The men of Beth-el and Ai, an hundred twenty and three.

33 The men of the other Nebo, fifty and two.

34 The children of the other Elam, a thousand two hundred fifty and four.

35 The children of Harim, three hundred and twenty.

36 The children of Jericho, three hundred forty and five.

37 The children of Lod, Hadid, and Ono, seven hundred twenty and one.

38 The children of Senaah, three thousand nine hundred and thirty.

39 The priests: the children of Jedaiah, of the house of Jeshua, nine hundred seventy and three.

40 The children of Immer, a thousand fifty and two.

41 The children of Pashur, a thousand two hundred forty and seven.

42 The children of Harim, a thousand and seventeen.

43 The Levites: the children of Jeshua, of Kadmiel, and of the children of Hodevah, seventy and four.

44 The singers: the children of Asaph, an hundred forty and eight.

45 The porters: the children of Shallum, the children of Ater, the children of Talmon, the children of Akkub, the children of Hatita, the children of Shobai, an hundred thirty and eight.

46 The Nethinims: the children of Ziha, the children of Hashupha, the children of Tabbaoth,

47 The children of Keros, the children of Sia, the children of Padon,

48 The children of Lebana, the children of Hagaba, the children of Shalmai,

49 The children of Hanan, the children of Giddel, the children of Gahar,

50 The children of Reaiah, the children of Rezin, the children of Nekoda,

51 The children of Gazzam, the children of Uzza, the children of Phaseah,

52 The children of Besai, the children of Meunim, the children of Nephishesim,

53 The children of Bakbuk, the children of Hakupha, the children of Harhur,

54 The children of Bazlith, the children of Mehida, the children of Harsha,

55 The children of Barkos, the children of Sisera, the children of Tamah,

56 The children of Neziah, the children of Hatipha.

57 The children of Solomon's servants: the children of Sotai, the children of Sophereth, the children of Perida,

58 The children of Jaala, the children of Darkon, the children of Giddel,

59 The children of Shephatiah, the children of Hattil, the children of Pochereth of Zebaim, the children of Amon.

60 All the Nethinims, and the children of Solomon's servants, were three hundred ninety and two.

61 And these were they which went up also from Tel-melah, Tel-haresha, Cherub, Addon, and Immer: but they could not shew their father's house, nor their seed, whether they were of Israel.

62 The children of Delaiah, the children of Tobiah, the children of Nekoda, six hundred forty and two.

63 And of the priests: the children of Habaiah, the children of Koz, the children of Barzillai, which took one of the daughters of Barzillai the Gileadite to wife, and was called after their name.

64 These sought their register among those that were reckoned by genealogy, but it was not found: therefore were they, as polluted, put from the priesthood.

65 And the Tirshatha said unto them, that they should not eat of the most holy things, till there stood up a priest with Urim and Thummim.

66 The whole congregation together was forty and two thousand three hundred and threescore,

67 Beside their manservants and their maidservants, of whom there were seven thousand three hundred thirty and seven: and they had two hundred forty and five singing men and singing women.

68 Their horses, seven hundred thirty and six: their mules, two hundred forty and five:

69 Their camels, four hundred thirty and five: six thousand seven hundred and twenty asses.

70 And some of the chief of the fathers gave unto the work. The Tirshatha gave to the treasure a thousand drams of gold, fifty basons, five hundred and thirty priests' garments.

71 And some of the chief of the fathers gave to the treasure of the work twenty thousand drams of gold, and two thousand and two hundred pound of silver.

72 And that which the rest of the people gave was twenty thousand drams of gold, and two thousand pound of silver, and threescore and seven priests' garments.

73 So the priests, and the Levites, and the porters, and the singers, and some of the people, and the Nethinims, and all Israel, dwelt in their cities; and when the seventh month came, the children of Israel were in their cities.

CHAPTER 8

AND all the people gathered themselves together as one man into the street that was before the water gate; and they spake unto Ezra the scribe to bring the book of the law of Moses, which the LORD had commanded to Israel.

2 And Ezra the priest brought the law before the congregation both of men and women, and all that could hear with understanding, upon the first day of the seventh month.

3 And he read therein before the street that was before the water gate from the morning until midday, before the men and the women, and those that could understand; and the ears of all the people were attentive unto the book of the law.

4 And Ezra the scribe stood upon a pulpit of wood, which they had made for the purpose; and beside him stood Mattithiah, and Shema, and Anaiah, and Urijah, and Hilkiah, and Maaseiah, on his right hand; and on his left hand, Pedaiah, and Mishael, and Malchiah, and Hashum, and Hashbadana, Zechariah, and Meshullam.

5 And Ezra opened the book in the sight of all the people; (for he was above all the people;) and when he opened it, all the people stood up:

6 And Ezra blessed the LORD, the great God. And all the people answered, Amen, Amen, with lifting up their hands: and they bowed their heads, and worshipped the LORD with their faces to the ground.

7 Also Jeshua, and Bani, and Sherebiah, Jamin, Akkub, Shabbethai, Hodijah, Maaseiah, Kelita, Azariah, Jozabad, Hanan, Pelaiah, and the Levites, caused the people to understand the law: and the people stood in their place.

8 So they read in the book in the law of God distinctly, and gave the sense, and caused them to understand the reading.

9 And Nehemiah, which is the Tirshatha, and Ezra the priest the scribe, and the Levites that taught the people, said unto all the people, This day is holy unto the LORD your God; mourn not, nor weep. For all the people wept, when they heard the words of the law.

10 Then he said unto them, Go your way, eat the fat, and drink the sweet, and send portions unto them for whom nothing is prepared: for this day is holy unto our Lord: neither be you sorry; for the joy of the LORD is your strength.

11 So the Levites stilled all the people, saying, Hold your peace, for the day is holy; neither be you grieved.

12 And all the people went their way to eat, and to drink, and to send portions, and to make great mirth, because they had understood the words that were declared unto them.

13 And on the second day were gathered together the chief of the fathers of all the people, the priests, and the Levites, unto Ezra the scribe, even to understand the words of the law.

14 And they found written in the law which the LORD had commanded by Moses, that the children of Israel should dwell in booths in the feast of the seventh month:

15 And that they should publish and proclaim in all their cities, and in Jerusalem, saying, Go forth unto the mount, and fetch olive branches, and pine branches, and myrtle branches, and palm branches, and branches of thick trees, to make booths, as it is written.

16 So the people went forth, and brought them, and made themselves booths, every one upon the roof of his house, and in their courts, and in the courts of the house of God, and in the street of the water gate, and in the street of the gate of Ephraim.

17 And all the congregation of them that were come again out of the captivity made booths, and sat under the booths: for since the days of Jeshua the son of Nun unto that day had not the children of Israel done so. And there was very great gladness.

18 Also day by day, from the first day unto the last day, he read in the book of the law of God. And they kept the feast seven days; and on the eighth day was a solemn assembly, according unto the manner.

CHAPTER 9

NOW in the twenty and fourth day of this month the children of Israel were assembled with fasting, and with sackclothes, and earth upon them.

2 And the seed of Israel separated themselves from all strangers, and stood and confessed their sins, and the iniquities of their fathers.

3 And they stood up in their place, and read in the book of the law of the LORD their God one fourth part of the day; and another fourth part they confessed, and worshipped the LORD their God.

4 Then stood up upon the stairs, of the Levites, Jeshua, and Bani, Kadmiel, Shebaniah, Bunni, Sherebiah, Bani, and Chenani, and cried with a loud voice unto the LORD their God.

5 Then the Levites, Jeshua, and Kadmiel, Bani, Hashabniah, Sherebiah, Hodijah, Shebaniah, and Pethahiah, said, Stand up and bless the LORD your God for ever and ever: and blessed be your glorious name, which is exalted above all blessing and praise.

6 You , even you , are LORD alone; you have made heaven, the heaven of heavens, with all their host, the earth, and all things that are therein, the seas, and all that is therein, and you preservest them all; and the host of heaven worshippeth you.

7 You are the LORD the God, who did choose Abram, and broughtest him forth out of Ur of the Chaldees, and gavest him the name of Abraham;

8 And foundest his heart faithful before you, and madest a covenant with him to give the land of the Canaanites, the Hittites, the Amorites, and the Perizzites, and the Jebusites, and the Girgashites, to give it, I say, to his seed, and have performed your words; for you are righteous:

9 And did see the affliction of our fathers in Egypt, and heardest their cry by the Red sea;

10 And shewedst signs and wonders upon Pharaoh, and on all his servants, and on all the people of his land: for you knewest that they dealt proudly against them. So did you get you a name, as it is this day.

11 And you did divide the sea before them, so that they went through the midst of the sea on the dry land; and their persecutors you threwest into the deeps, as a stone into the mighty waters.

12 Moreover you leddest them in the day by a cloudy pillar; and in the night by a pillar of fire, to give them light in the way wherein they should go.

13 You camest down also upon mount Sinai, and spakest with them from heaven, and gavest them right judgments, and true laws, good statutes and commandments:

14 And madest known unto them your holy sabbath, and commandedst them precepts, statutes, and laws, by the hand of Moses your servant:

15 And gavest them bread from heaven for their hunger, and broughtest forth water for them out of the rock for their thirst, and promisedst them that they should go in to possess the land which you hadst sworn to give them.

16 But they and our fathers dealt proudly, and hardened their necks, and hearkened not to your commandments,

17 And refused to obey, neither were mindful of your wonders that you did among them; but hardened their necks, and in their rebellion appointed a captain to return to their bondage: but you are a God ready to pardon, gracious and merciful, slow to anger, and of great kindness, and forsookest them not.

18 Yea, when they had made them a molten calf, and said, This is your God that brought you up out of Egypt, and had created great provocations;

19 Yet you in your manifold mercies forsookest them not in the wilderness: the pillar of the cloud departed not from them by day, to lead them in the way; neither the pillar of fire by night, to shew them light, and the way wherein they should go.

20 You gavest also your good spirit to instruct them, and withheldest not your manna from their mouth, and gavest them water for their thirst.

21 Yea, forty years did you sustain them in the wilderness, so that they lacked nothing; their clothes waxed not old, and their feet swelled not.

22 Moreover you gavest them kingdoms and nations, and did divide them into corners: so they possessed the land of Sihon, and the land of the king of Heshbon, and the land of Og king of Bashan.

23 Their children also multipliedst you as the stars of heaven, and broughtest them into the land, concerning which you hadst promised to their fathers, that they should go in to possess it.

24 So the children went in and possessed the land, and you subduedst before them the inhabitants of the land, the Canaanites, and gavest them into their hands, with their kings, and the people of the land, that they might do with them as they would.

25 And they took strong cities, and a fat land, and possessed houses full of all goods, wells digged, vineyards, and oliveyards, and fruit trees in abundance: so they did eat, and were filled, and became fat, and delighted themselves in your great goodness.

26 Nevertheless they were disobedient, and rebelled against you, and cast your law behind their backs, and slew your prophets which testified against them to turn them to you, and they created great provocations.

27 Therefore you deliveredst them into the hand of their enemies, who vexed them: and in the time of their trouble, when they cried unto you, you heardest them from heaven; and according to your manifold mercies you gavest them saviours, who saved them out of the hand of their enemies.

28 But after they had rest, they did evil again before you: therefore leftest you them in the hand of their enemies, so that they had the dominion over them: yet when they returned, and cried unto you, you heardest them from heaven; and many times did you deliver them according to your mercies;

29 And testifiedst against them, that you mightest bring them again unto your law: yet they dealt proudly, and hearkened not unto your commandments, but sinned against your judgments, (which if a man do, he shall live in them;) and withdrew the shoulder, and hardened their neck, and would not hear.

30 Yet many years did you forbear them, and testifiedst against them by your spirit in your prophets: yet would they not give ear: therefore gavest you them into the hand of the people of the lands.

31 Nevertheless for your great mercies' sake you did not utterly consume them, nor forsake them; for you are a gracious and merciful God.

32 Now therefore, our God, the great, the mighty, and the terrible God, who keepest covenant and mercy, let not all the trouble seem little before you, that has come upon us, on our kings, on our princes, and on our priests, and on our prophets, and on our fathers, and on all your people, since the time of the kings of Assyria unto this day.

33 Howbeit you are just in all that is brought upon us; for you have done right, but we have done wickedly:

34 Neither have our kings, our princes, our priests, nor our fathers, kept your law, nor hearkened unto your commandments and your testimonies, wherewith you did testify against them.

35 For they have not served you in their kingdom, and in your great goodness that you gavest them, and in the large and fat land which you gavest before them, neither turned they from their wicked works.

36 Behold, we are servants this day, and for the land that you gavest unto our fathers to eat the fruit thereof and the good thereof, behold, we are servants in it:

37 And it yieldeth much increase unto the kings whom you have set over us because of our sins: also they have dominion over our bodies, and over our cattle, at their pleasure, and we are in great distress.

38 And because of all this we make a sure covenant, and write it; and our princes, Levites, and priests, seal unto it.

CHAPTER 10

NOW those that sealed were, Nehemiah, the Tirshatha, the son of Hachaliah, and Zidkijah,

2 Seraiah, Azariah, Jeremiah,

3 Pashur, Amariah, Malchijah,

4 Hattush, Shebaniah, Malluch,

5 Harim, Meremoth, Obadiah,

6 Daniel, Ginnethon, Baruch,

7 Meshullam, Abijah, Mijamin,

8 Maaziah, Bilgai, Shemaiah: these were the priests.

9 And the Levites: both Jeshua the son of Azaniah, Binnui of the sons of Henadad, Kadmiel;

10 And their brethren, Shebaniah, Hodijah, Kelita, Pelaiah, Hanan,

11 Micha, Rehob, Hashabiah,

12 Zaccur, Sherebiah, Shebaniah,

13 Hodijah, Bani, Beninu.

14 The chief of the people; Parosh, Pahath-moab, Elam, Zatthu, Bani,

15 Bunni, Azgad, Bebai,

16 Adonijah, Bigvai, Adin,

17 Ater, Hizkijah, Azzur,

18 Hodijah, Hashum, Bezai,

19 Hariph, Anathoth, Nebai,

20 Magpiash, Meshullam, Hezir,

21 Meshezabeel, Zadok, Jaddua,

22 Pelatiah, Hanan, Anaiah,

23 Hoshea, Hananiah, Hashub,

24 Hallohesh, Pileha, Shobek,

25 Rehum, Hashabnah, Maaseiah,

26 And Ahijah, Hanan, Anan,

27 Malluch, Harim, Baanah.

28 And the rest of the people, the priests, the Levites, the porters, the singers, the Nethinims, and all they that had separated themselves from the people of the lands unto the law of God, their wives, their sons, and their daughters, every one having knowledge, and having understanding;

29 They clave to their brethren, their nobles, and entered into a curse, and into an oath, to walk in God's law, which was given by Moses the servant of God, and to observe and do all the commandments of the LORD our Lord, and his judgments and his statutes;

30 And that we would not give our daughters unto the people of the land, nor take their daughters for our sons:

31 And if the people of the land bring ware or any victuals on the sabbath day to sell, that we would not buy it of them on the sabbath, or on the holy day: and that we would leave the seventh year, and the exaction of every debt.

32 Also we made ordinances for us, to charge ourselves yearly with the third part of a shekel for the service of the house of our God;

33 For the shewbread, and for the continual meat offering, and for the continual burnt offering, of the sabbaths, of the new moons, for the set feasts, and for the holy things, and for the sin offerings to make an atonement for Israel, and for all the work of the house of our God.

34 And we cast the lots among the priests, the Levites, and the people, for the wood offering, to bring it into the house of our God, after the houses of our fathers, at times appointed year by year, to burn upon the altar of the LORD our God, as it is written in the law:

35 And to bring the firstfruits of our ground, and the firstfruits of all fruit of all trees, year by year, unto the house of the LORD:

36 Also the firstborn of our sons, and of our cattle, as it is written in the law, and the firstlings of our herds and of our flocks, to bring to the house of our God, unto the priests that minister in the house of our God:

37 And that we should bring the firstfruits of our dough, and our offerings, and the fruit of all manner of trees, of wine and of oil, unto the priests, to the chambers of the house of our God; and the tithes of our ground unto the Levites, that the same Levites might have the tithes in all the cities of our tillage.

38 And the priest the son of Aaron shall be with the Levites, when the Levites take tithes: and the Levites shall bring up the tithe of the tithes unto the house of our God, to the chambers, into the treasure house.

39 For the children of Israel and the children of Levi shall bring the offering of the corn, of the new wine, and the oil, unto the chambers, where are the vessels of the sanctuary, and the priests that minister, and the porters, and the singers: and we will not forsake the house of our God.

CHAPTER 11

AND the rulers of the people dwelt at Jerusalem: the rest of the people also cast lots, to bring one of ten to dwell in Jerusalem the holy city, and nine parts to dwell in other cities.

2 And the people blessed all the men, that willingly offered themselves to dwell at Jerusalem.

3 Now these are the chief of the province that dwelt in Jerusalem: but in the cities of Judah dwelt every one in his possession in their cities, to wit, Israel, the priests, and the Levites, and the Nethinims, and the children of Solomon's servants.

4 And at Jerusalem dwelt certain of the children of Judah, and of the children of Benjamin. Of the children of Judah; Athaiah the son of Uzziah, the son of Zechariah, the son of Amariah, the son of Shephatiah, the son of Mahalaleel, of the children of Perez;

5 And Maaseiah the son of Baruch, the son of Col-hozeh, the son of Hazaiah, the son of Adaiah, the son of Joiarib, the son of Zechariah, the son of Shiloni.

6 All the sons of Perez that dwelt at Jerusalem were four hundred threescore and eight valiant men.

7 And these are the sons of Benjamin; Sallu the son of Meshullam, the son of Joed, the son of Pedaiah, the son of Kolaiah, the son of Maaseiah, the son of Ithiel, the son of Jesaiah.

8 And after him Gabbai, Sallai, nine hundred twenty and eight.

9 And Joel the son of Zichri was their overseer: and Judah the son of Senuah was second over the city.

10 Of the priests: Jedaiah the son of Joiarib, Jachin.

11 Seraiah the son of Hilkiah, the son of Meshullam, the son of Zadok, the son of Meraioth, the son of Ahitub, was the ruler of the house of God.

12 And their brethren that did the work of the house were eight hundred twenty and two: and Adaiah the son of Jeroham, the son of Pelaliah, the son of Amzi, the son of Zechariah, the son of Pashur, the son of Malchiah,

13 And his brethren, chief of the fathers, two hundred forty and two: and Amashai the son of Azareel, the son of Ahasai, the son of Meshillemoth, the son of Immer,

14 And their brethren, mighty men of valour, an hundred twenty and eight: and their overseer was Zabdiel, the son of one of the great men.

15 Also of the Levites: Shemaiah the son of Hashub, the son of Azrikam, the son of Hashabiah, the son of Bunni;

16 And Shabbethai and Jozabad, of the chief of the Levites, had the oversight of the outward business of the house of God.

17 And Mattaniah the son of Micha, the son of Zabdi, the son of Asaph, was the principal to begin the thanksgiving in prayer: and Bakbukiah the second among his brethren, and Abda the son of Shammua, the son of Galal, the son of Jeduthun.

18 All the Levites in the holy city were two hundred fourscore and four.

19 Moreover the porters, Akkub, Talmon, and their brethren that kept the gates, were an hundred seventy and two.

20 And the residue of Israel, of the priests, and the Levites, were in all the cities of Judah, every one in his inheritance.

21 But the Nethinims dwelt in Ophel: and Ziha and Gispa were over the Nethinims.

22 The overseer also of the Levites at Jerusalem was Uzzi the son of Bani, the son of Hashabiah, the son of Mattaniah, the son of Micha. Of the sons of Asaph, the singers were over the business of the house of God.

23 For it was the king's commandment concerning them, that a certain portion should be for the singers, due for every day.

24 And Pethahiah the son of Meshezabeel, of the children of Zerah the son of Judah, was at the king's hand in all matters concerning the people.

25 And for the villages, with their fields, some of the children of Judah dwelt at Kirjath-arba, and in the villages thereof, and at Dibon, and in the villages thereof, and at Jekabzeel, and in the villages thereof,

26 And at Jeshua, and at Moladah, and at Beth-phelet,

27 And at Hazar-shual, and at Beer-sheba, and in the villages thereof,

28 And at Ziklag, and at Mekonah, and in the villages thereof,

29 And at En-rimmon, and at Zareah, and at Jarmuth,

30 Zanoah, Adullam, and in their villages, at Lachish, and the fields thereof, at Azekah, and in the villages thereof. And they dwelt from Beer-sheba unto the valley of Hinnom.

31 The children also of Benjamin from Geba dwelt at Michmash, and Aija, and Beth-el, and in their villages,

32 And at Anathoth, Nob, Ananiah,

33 Hazor, Ramah, Gittaim,

34 Hadid, Zeboim, Neballat,

35 Lod, and Ono, the valley of craftsmen.

36 And of the Levites were divisions in Judah, and in Benjamin.

CHAPTER 12

NOW these are the priests and the Levites that went up with Zerubbabel the son of Shealtiel, and Jeshua: Seraiah, Jeremiah, Ezra,

2 Amariah, Malluch, Hattush,

3 Shechaniah, Rehum, Meremoth,

4 Iddo, Ginnetho, Abijah,

5 Miamin, Maadiah, Bilgah,

6 Shemaiah, and Joiarib, Jedaiah,

7 Sallu, Amok, Hilkiah, Jedaiah. These were the chief of the priests and of their brethren in the days of Jeshua.

8 Moreover the Levites: Jeshua, Binnui, Kadmiel, Sherebiah, Judah, and Mattaniah, which was over the thanksgiving, he and his brethren.

9 Also Bakbukiah and Unni, their brethren, were over against them in the watches.

10 And Jeshua begat Joiakim, Joiakim also begat Eliashib, and Eliashib begat Joiada,

11 And Joiada begat Jonathan, and Jonathan begat Jaddua.

12 And in the days of Joiakim were priests, the chief of the fathers: of Seraiah, Meraiah; of Jeremiah, Hananiah;

13 Of Ezra, Meshullam; of Amariah, Jehohanan;

14 Of Melicu, Jonathan; of Shebaniah, Joseph;

15 Of Harim, Adna; of Meraioth, Helkai;

16 Of Iddo, Zechariah; of Ginnethon, Meshullam;

17 Of Abijah, Zichri; of Miniamin, of Moadiah, Piltai;

18 Of Bilgah, Shammua; of Shemaiah, Jehonathan;

19 And of Joiarib, Mattenai; of Jedaiah, Uzzi;

20 Of Sallai, Kallai; of Amok, Eber;

21 Of Hilkiah, Hashabiah; of Jedaiah, Nethaneel.

22 The Levites in the days of Eliashib, Joiada, and Johanan, and Jaddua, were recorded chief of the fathers: also the priests, to the reign of Darius the Persian.

23 The sons of Levi, the chief of the fathers, were written in the book of the chronicles, even until the days of Johanan the son of Eliashib.

24 And the chief of the Levites: Hashabiah, Sherebiah, and Jeshua the son of Kadmiel, with their brethren over against them, to praise and to give thanks, according to the commandment of David the man of God, ward over against ward.

25 Mattaniah, and Bakbukiah, Obadiah, Meshullam, Talmon, Akkub, were porters keeping the ward at the thresholds of the gates.

26 These were in the days of Joiakim the son of Jeshua, the son of Jozadak, and in the days of Nehemiah the governor, and of Ezra the priest, the scribe.

27 And at the dedication of the wall of Jerusalem they sought the Levites out of all their places, to bring them to Jerusalem, to keep the dedication with gladness, both with thanksgivings, and with singing, with cymbals, psalteries, and with harps.

28 And the sons of the singers gathered themselves together, both out of the plain country round about Jerusalem, and from the villages of Netophathi;

29 Also from the house of Gilgal, and out of the fields of Geba and Azmaveth: for the singers had builded them villages round about Jerusalem.

30 And the priests and the Levites purified themselves, and purified the people, and the gates, and the wall.

31 Then I brought up the princes of Judah upon the wall, and appointed two great companies of them that gave thanks, whereof one went on the right hand upon the wall toward the dung gate:

32 And after them went Hoshaiah, and half of the princes of Judah,

33 And Azariah, Ezra, and Meshullam,

34 Judah, and Benjamin, and Shemaiah, and Jeremiah,

35 And certain of the priests' sons with trumpets; namely, Zechariah the son of Jonathan, the son of Shemaiah, the son of Mattaniah, the son of Michaiah, the son of Zaccur, the son of Asaph:

36 And his brethren, Shemaiah, and Azarael, Milalai, Gilalai, Maai, Nethaneel, and Judah, Hanani, with the musical instruments of David the man of God, and Ezra the scribe before them.

37 And at the fountain gate, which was over against them, they went up by the stairs of the city of David, at the going up of the wall, above the house of David, even unto the water gate eastward.

38 And the other company of them that gave thanks went over against them, and I after them, and the half of the people upon the wall, from beyond the tower of the furnaces even unto the broad wall;

39 And from above the gate of Ephraim, and above the old gate, and above the fish gate, and the tower of Hananeel, and the tower of Meah, even unto the sheep gate: and they stood still in the prison gate.

40 So stood the two companies of them that gave thanks in the house of God, and I, and the half of the rulers with me:

41 And the priests; Eliakim, Maaseiah, Miniamin, Michaiah, Elioenai, Zechariah, and Hananiah, with trumpets;

42 And Maaseiah, and Shemaiah, and Eleazar, and Uzzi, and Jehohanan, and Malchijah, and Elam, and Ezer. And the singers sang loud, with Jezrahiah their overseer.

43 Also that day they offered great sacrifices, and rejoiced: for God had made them rejoice with great joy: the wives also and the children rejoiced: so that the joy of Jerusalem was heard even afar off.

44 And at that time were some appointed over the chambers for the treasures, for the offerings, for the firstfruits, and for the tithes, to gather into them out of the fields of the cities the portions of the law for the priests and Levites: for Judah rejoiced for the priests and for the Levites that waited.

45 And both the singers and the porters kept the ward of their God, and the ward of the purification, according to the commandment of David, and of Solomon his son.

46 For in the days of David and Asaph of old there were chief of the singers, and songs of praise and thanksgiving unto God.

47 And all Israel in the days of Zerubbabel, and in the days of Nehemiah, gave the portions of the singers and the porters, every day his portion: and they sanctified holy things unto the Levites; and the Levites sanctified them unto the children of Aaron.

CHAPTER 13

ON that day they read in the book of Moses in the audience of the people; and therein was found written, that the Ammonite and the Moabite should not come into the congregation of God for ever;

2 Because they met not the children of Israel with bread and with water, but hired Balaam against them, that he should curse them: howbeit our God turned the curse into a blessing.

3 Now it came to pass, when they had heard the law, that they separated from Israel all the mixed multitude.

4 And before this, Eliashib the priest, having the oversight of the chamber of the house of our God, was allied unto Tobiah:

5 And he had prepared for him a great chamber, where aforetime they laid the meat offerings, the frankincense, and the vessels, and the tithes of the corn, the new wine, and the oil, which was commanded to be given to the Levites, and the singers, and the porters; and the offerings of the priests.

6 But in all this time was not I at Jerusalem: for in the two and thirtieth year of Artaxerxes king of Babylon came I unto the king, and after certain days obtained I leave of the king:

7 And I came to Jerusalem, and understood of the evil that Eliashib did for Tobiah, in preparing him a chamber in the courts of the house of God.

8 And it grieved me sore: therefore I cast forth all the household stuff of Tobiah out of the chamber.

9 Then I commanded, and they cleansed the chambers: and thither brought I again the vessels of the house of God, with the meat offering and the frankincense.

10 And I perceived that the portions of the Levites had not been given them: for the Levites and the singers, that did the work, were fled every one to his field.

11 Then contended I with the rulers, and said, Why is the house of God forsaken? And I gathered them together, and set them in their place.

12 Then brought all Judah the tithe of the corn and the new wine and the oil unto the treasuries.

13 And I made treasurers over the treasuries, Shelemiah the priest, and Zadok the scribe, and of the Levites, Pedaiah: and next to them was Hanan the son of Zaccur, the son of Mattaniah: for they were counted faithful, and their office was to distribute unto their brethren.

14 Remember me, O my God, concerning this, and wipe not out my good deeds that I have done for the house of my God, and for the offices thereof.

15 In those days saw I in Judah some treading wine presses on the sabbath, and bringing in sheaves, and lading asses; as also wine, grapes, and figs, and all manner of burdens, which they brought into Jerusalem on the sabbath day: and I testified against them in the day wherein they sold victuals.

16 There dwelt men of Tyre also therein, which brought fish, and all manner of ware, and sold on the sabbath unto the children of Judah, and in Jerusalem.

17 Then I contended with the nobles of Judah, and said unto them, What evil thing is this that you do, and profane the sabbath day?

18 Did not your fathers thus, and did not our God bring all this evil upon us, and upon this city? yet you bring more wrath upon Israel by profaning the sabbath.

19 And it came to pass, that when the gates of Jerusalem began to be dark before the sabbath, I commanded that the gates should be shut, and charged that they should not be opened till after the sabbath: and some of my servants set I at the gates, that there should no burden be brought in on the sabbath day.

20 So the merchants and sellers of all kind of ware lodged without Jerusalem once or twice.

21 Then I testified against them, and said unto them, Why lodge you about the wall? if you do so again, I will lay hands on you. From that time forth came they no more on the sabbath.

22 And I commanded the Levites that they should cleanse themselves, and that they should come and keep the gates, to sanctify the sabbath day. Remember me, O my God, concerning this also, and spare me according to the greatness of your mercy.

23 In those days also saw I Jews that had married wives of Ashdod, of Ammon, and of Moab:

24 And their children spake half in the speech of Ashdod, and could not speak in the Jews' language, but according to the language of each people.

25 And I contended with them, and cursed them, and struck certain of them, and plucked off their hair, and made them swear by God, saying, You shall not give your daughters unto their sons, nor take their daughters unto your sons, or for yourselves.

26 Did not Solomon king of Israel sin by these things? yet among many nations was there no king like him, who was beloved of his God, and God made him king over all Israel: nevertheless even him did outlandish women cause to sin.

27 Shall we then hearken unto you to do all this great evil, to transgress against our God in marrying strange wives?

28 And one of the sons of Joiada, the son of Eliashib the high priest, was son in law to Sanballat the Horonite: therefore I chased him from me.

29 Remember them, O my God, because they have defiled the priesthood, and the covenant of the priesthood, and of the Levites.

30 Thus cleansed I them from all strangers, and appointed the wards of the priests and the Levites, every one in his business;

31 And for the wood offering, at times appointed, and for the firstfruits. Remember me, O my God, for good.

THE
BOOK OF ESTHER.

CHAPTER 1

NOW it came to pass in the days of Ahasuerus, (this is Ahasuerus which reigned, from India even unto Ethiopia, over an hundred and seven and twenty provinces:)

2 That in those days, when the king Ahasuerus sat on the throne of his kingdom, which was in Shushan the palace,

3 In the third year of his reign, he made a feast unto all his princes and his servants; the power of Persia and Media, the nobles and princes of the provinces, being before him:

4 When he shewed the riches of his glorious kingdom and the honour of his excellent majesty many days, even an hundred and fourscore days.

5 And when these days were expired, the king made a feast unto all the people that were present in Shushan the palace, both unto great and small, seven days, in the court of the garden of the king's palace;

6 Where were white, green, and blue, hangings, fastened with cords of fine linen and purple to silver rings and pillars of marble: the beds were of gold and silver, upon a pavement of red, and blue, and white, and black, marble.

7 And they gave them drink in vessels of gold, (the vessels being diverse one from another,) and royal wine in abundance, according to the state of the king.

8 And the drinking was according to the law; none did compel: for so the king had appointed to all the officers of his house, that they should do according to every man's pleasure.

9 Also Vashti the queen made a feast for the women in the royal house which belonged to king Ahasuerus.

10 On the seventh day, when the heart of the king was merry with wine, he commanded Mehuman, Biztha, Harbona, Bigtha, and Abagtha, Zethar, and Carcas, the seven chamberlains that served in the presence of Ahasuerus the king,

11 To bring Vashti the queen before the king with the crown royal, to shew the people and the princes her beauty: for she was fair to look on.

12 But the queen Vashti refused to come at the king's commandment by his chamberlains: therefore was the king very wroth, and his anger burned in him.

13 Then the king said to the wise men, which knew the times, (for so was the king's manner toward all that knew law and judgment:

14 And the next unto him was Carshena, Shethar, Admatha, Tarshish, Meres, Marsena, and Memucan, the seven princes of Persia and Media, which saw the king's face, and which sat the first in the kingdom;)

15 What shall we do unto the queen Vashti according to law, because she has not performed the commandment of the king Ahasuerus by the chamberlains?

16 And Memucan answered before the king and the princes, Vashti the queen has not done wrong to the king only, but also to all the princes, and to all the people that are in all the provinces of the king Ahasuerus.

17 For this deed of the queen shall come abroad unto all women, so that they shall despise their husbands in their eyes, when it shall be reported, The king Ahasuerus commanded Vashti the queen to be brought in before him, but she came not.

18 Likewise shall the ladies of Persia and Media say this day unto all the king's princes, which have heard of the deed of the queen. Thus shall there arise too much contempt and wrath.

19 If it please the king, let there go a royal commandment from him, and let it be written among the laws of the Persians and the Medes, that it be not altered, That Vashti come no more before king Ahasuerus; and let the king give her royal estate unto another that is better than she.

20 And when the king's decree which he shall make shall be published throughout all his empire, (for it is great,) all the wives shall give to their husbands honour, both to great and small.

21 And the saying pleased the king and the princes; and the king did according to the word of Memucan:

22 For he sent letters into all the king's provinces, into every province according to the writing thereof, and to every people after their language, that every man should bear rule in his own house, and that it should be published according to the language of every people.

CHAPTER 2

AFTER these things, when the wrath of king Ahasuerus was appeased, he remembered Vashti, and what she had done, and what was decreed against her.

2 Then said the king's servants that ministered unto him, Let there be fair young virgins sought for the king:

3 And let the king appoint officers in all the provinces of his kingdom, that they may gather together all the fair young virgins unto Shushan the palace, to the house of the women, unto the custody of Hege the king's chamberlain, keeper of the women; and let their things for purification be given them:

4 And let the maiden which pleases the king be queen instead of Vashti. And the thing pleased the king; and he did so.

5 Now in Shushan the palace there was a certain Jew, whose name was Mordecai, the son of Jair, the son of Shimei, the son of Kish, a Benjamite;

6 Who had been carried away from Jerusalem with the captivity which had been carried away with Jeconiah king of Judah, whom Nebuchadnezzar the king of Babylon had carried away.

7 And he brought up Hadassah, that is, Esther, his uncle's daughter: for she had neither father nor mother, and the maid was fair and beautiful; whom Mordecai, when her father and mother were dead, took for his own daughter.

8 So it came to pass, when the king's commandment and his decree was heard, and when many maidens were gathered together unto Shushan the palace, to the custody of Hegai, that Esther was brought also unto the king's house, to the custody of Hegai, keeper of the women.

9 And the maiden pleased him, and she obtained kindness of him; and he speedily gave her her things for purification, with such things as belonged to her, and seven maidens, which were meet to be given her, out of the king's house: and he preferred her and her maids unto the best place of the house of the women.

10 Esther had not shewed her people nor her kindred: for Mordecai had charged her that she should not shew it.

11 And Mordecai walked every day before the court of the women's house, to know how Esther did, and what should become of her.

12 Now when every maid's turn was come to go in to king Ahasuerus, after that she had been twelve months, according to the manner of the women, (for so were the days of their purifications accomplished, to wit, six months with oil of myrrh, and six months with sweet odours, and with other things for the purifying of the women;)

13 Then thus came every maiden unto the king; whatsoever she desired was given her to go with her out of the house of the women unto the king's house.

14 In the evening she went, and on the morrow she returned into the second house of the women, to the custody of Shaashgaz, the king's chamberlain, which kept the concubines: she came in unto the king no more, except the king delighted in her, and that she were called by name.

15 Now when the turn of Esther, the daughter of Abihail the uncle of Mordecai, who had taken her for his daughter, was come to go in unto the king, she required nothing but what Hegai the king's chamberlain, the keeper of the women, appointed. And Esther obtained favour in the sight of all them that looked upon her.

16 So Esther was taken unto king Ahasuerus into his house royal in the tenth month, which is the month Tebeth, in the seventh year of his reign.

17 And the king loved Esther above all the women, and she obtained grace and favour in his sight more than all the virgins; so that he set the royal crown upon her head, and made her queen instead of Vashti.

18 Then the king made a great feast unto all his princes and his servants, even Esther's feast; and he made a release to the provinces, and gave gifts, according to the state of the king.

19 And when the virgins were gathered together the second time, then Mordecai sat in the king's gate.

20 Esther had not yet shewed her kindred nor her people; as Mordecai had charged her: for Esther did the commandment of Mordecai, like as when she was brought up with him.

21 In those days, while Mordecai sat in the king's gate, two of the king's chamberlains, Bigthan and Teresh, of those which kept the door, were wroth, and sought to lay hand on the king Ahasuerus.

22 And the thing was known to Mordecai, who told it unto Esther the queen; and Esther certified the king thereof in Mordecai's name.

23 And when inquisition was made of the matter, it was found out; therefore they were both hanged on a tree: and it was written in the book of the chronicles before the king.

CHAPTER 3

AFTER these things did king Ahasuerus promote Haman the son of Hammedatha the Agagite, and advanced him, and set his seat above all the princes that were with him.

2 And all the king's servants, that were in the king's gate, bowed, and reverenced Haman: for the king had so commanded concerning him. But Mordecai bowed not, nor did him reverence.

3 Then the king's servants, which were in the king's gate, said unto Mordecai, Why transgressest you the king's commandment?

4 Now it came to pass, when they spake daily unto him, and he hearkened not unto them, that they told Haman, to see whether Mordecai's matters would stand: for he had told them that he was a Jew.

5 And when Haman saw that Mordecai bowed not, nor did him reverence, then was Haman full of wrath.

6 And he thought scorn to lay hands on Mordecai alone; for they had shewed him the people of Mordecai: wherefore Haman sought to destroy all the Jews that were throughout the whole kingdom of Ahasuerus, even the people of Mordecai.

7 In the first month, that is, the month Nisan, in the twelfth year of king Ahasuerus, they cast Pur, that is, the lot, before Haman from day to day, and from month to month, to the twelfth month, that is, the month Adar.

8 And Haman said unto king Ahasuerus, There is a certain people scattered abroad and dispersed among the people in all the provinces of your kingdom; and their laws are diverse from all people; neither keep they the king's laws: therefore it is not for the king's profit to suffer them.

9 If it please the king, let it be written that they may be destroyed: and I will pay ten thousand talents of silver to the hands of those that have the charge of the business, to bring it into the king's treasuries.

10 And the king took his ring from his hand, and gave it unto Haman the son of Hammedatha the Agagite, the Jews' enemy.

11 And the king said unto Haman, The silver is given to you, the people also, to do with them as it seemeth good to you.

12 Then were the king's scribes called on the thirteenth day of the first month, and there was written according to all that Haman had commanded unto the king's lieutenants, and to the governors that were over every province, and to the rulers of every people of every province according to the writing thereof, and to every people after their language; in the name of king Ahasuerus was it written, and sealed with the king's ring.

13 And the letters were sent by posts into all the king's provinces, to destroy, to kill, and to cause to perish, all Jews, both young and old, little children and women, in one day, even upon the thirteenth day of the twelfth month, which is the month Adar, and to take the spoil of them for a prey.

14 The copy of the writing for a commandment to be given in every province was published unto all people, that they should be ready against that day.

15 The posts went out, being hastened by the king's commandment, and the decree was given in Shushan the palace. And the king and Haman sat down to drink; but the city Shushan was perplexed.

CHAPTER 4

WHEN Mordecai perceived all that was done, Mordecai rent his clothes, and put on sackcloth with ashes, and went out into the midst of the city, and cried with a loud and a bitter cry;

2 And came even before the king's gate: for none might enter into the king's gate clothed with sackcloth.

3 And in every province, whithersoever the king's commandment and his decree came, there was great mourning among the Jews, and fasting, and weeping, and wailing; and many lay in sackcloth and ashes.

4 So Esther's maids and her chamberlains came and told it her. Then was the queen exceedingly grieved; and she sent raiment to clothe Mordecai, and to take away his sackcloth from him: but he received it not.

5 Then called Esther for Hatach, one of the king's chamberlains, whom he had appointed to attend upon her, and gave him a commandment to Mordecai, to know what it was, and why it was.

6 So Hatach went forth to Mordecai unto the street of the city, which was before the king's gate.

7 And Mordecai told him of all that had happened unto him, and of the sum of the money that Haman had promised to pay to the king's treasuries for the Jews, to destroy them.

8 Also he gave him the copy of the writing of the decree that was given at Shushan to destroy them, to shew it unto Esther, and to declare it unto her, and to charge her that she should go in unto the king, to make supplication unto him, and to make request before him for her people.

9 And Hatach came and told Esther the words of Mordecai.

10 Again Esther spake unto Hatach, and gave him commandment unto Mordecai;

11 All the king's servants, and the people of the king's provinces, do know, that whosoever, whether man or woman, shall come unto the king into the inner court, who is not called, there is one law of his to put him to death, except such to whom the king shall hold out the golden sceptre, that he may live: but I have not been called to come in unto the king these thirty days.

12 And they told to Mordecai Esther's words.

13 Then Mordecai commanded to answer Esther, Think not with yourself that you shalt escape in the king's house, more than all the Jews.

14 For if you altogether holdest your peace at this time, then shall there enlargement and deliverance arise to the Jews from another place; but you and your father's house shall be destroyed: and who knoweth whether you are come to the kingdom for such a time as this?

15 Then Esther bade them return Mordecai this answer,

16 Go, gather together all the Jews that are present in Shushan, and fast you for me, and neither eat nor drink three days, night or day: I also and my maidens will fast likewise; and so will I go in unto the king, which is not according to the law: and if I perish, I perish.

17 So Mordecai went his way, and did according to all that Esther had commanded him.

CHAPTER 5

NOW it came to pass on the third day, that Esther put on her royal apparel, and stood in the inner court of the king's house, over against the king's house: and the king sat upon his royal throne in the royal house, over against the gate of the house.

2 And it was so, when the king saw Esther the queen standing in the court, that she obtained favour in his sight: and the king held out to Esther the golden sceptre that was in his hand. So Esther drew near, and touched the top of the sceptre.

3 Then said the king unto her, What will you , queen Esther? and what is your request? it shall be even given you to the half of the kingdom.

4 And Esther answered, If it seem good unto the king, let the king and Haman come this day unto the banquet that I have prepared for him.

5 Then the king said, Cause Haman to make haste, that he may do as Esther has said. So the king and Haman came to the banquet that Esther had prepared.

6 And the king said unto Esther at the banquet of wine, What is your petition? and it shall be granted you: and what is your request? even to the half of the kingdom it shall be performed.

7 Then answered Esther, and said, My petition and my request is;

8 If I have found favour in the sight of the king, and if it please the king to grant my petition, and to perform my request, let the king and Haman come to the banquet that I shall prepare for them, and I will do to morrow as the king has said.

9 Then went Haman forth that day joyful and with a glad heart: but when Haman saw Mordecai in the king's gate, that he stood not up, nor moved for him, he was full of indignation against Mordecai.

10 Nevertheless Haman refrained himself: and when he came home, he sent and called for his friends, and Zeresh his wife.

11 And Haman told them of the glory of his riches, and the multitude of his children, and all the things wherein the king had promoted him, and how he had advanced him above the princes and servants of the king.

12 Haman said moreover, Yea, Esther the queen did let no man come in with the king unto the banquet that she had prepared but myself; and to morrow am I invited unto her also with the king.

13 Yet all this availeth me nothing, so long as I see Mordecai the Jew sitting at the king's gate.

14 Then said Zeresh his wife and all his friends unto him, Let a gallows be made of fifty cubits high, and to morrow speak you unto the king that Mordecai may be hanged thereon: then go you in merrily with the king unto the banquet. And the thing pleased Haman; and he caused the gallows to be made.

CHAPTER 6

ON that night could not the king sleep, and he commanded to bring the book of records of the chronicles; and they were read before the king.

2 And it was found written, that Mordecai had told of Bigthana and Teresh, two of the king's chamberlains, the keepers of the door, who sought to lay hand on the king Ahasuerus.

3 And the king said, What honour and dignity has been done to Mordecai for this? Then said the king's servants that ministered unto him, There is nothing done for him.

4 And the king said, Who is in the court? Now Haman was come into the outward court of the king's house, to speak unto the king to hang Mordecai on the gallows that he had prepared for him.

5 And the king's servants said unto him, Behold, Haman standeth in the court. And the king said, Let him come in.

6 So Haman came in. And the king said unto him, What shall be done unto the man whom the king delighteth to honour? Now Haman thought in his heart, To whom would the king delight to do honour more than to myself?

7 And Haman answered the king, For the man whom the king delighteth to honour,

8 Let the royal apparel be brought which the king useth to wear, and the horse that the king rideth upon, and the crown royal which is set upon his head:

9 And let this apparel and horse be delivered to the hand of one of the king's most noble princes, that they may array the man withal whom the king delighteth to honour, and bring him on horseback through the street of the city, and proclaim before him, Thus shall it be done to the man whom the king delighteth to honour.

10 Then the king said to Haman, Make haste, and take the apparel and the horse, as you have said, and do even so to Mordecai the Jew, that sitteth at the king's gate: let nothing fail of all that you have spoken.

11 Then took Haman the apparel and the horse, and arrayed Mordecai, and brought him on horseback through the street of the city, and proclaimed before him, Thus shall it be done unto the man whom the king delighteth to honour.

12And Mordecai came again to the king's gate. But Haman hasted to his house mourning, and having his head covered.

13 And Haman told Zeresh his wife and all his friends every thing that had befallen him. Then said his wise men and Zeresh his wife unto him, If Mordecai be of the seed of the Jews, before whom you have begun to fall, you shalt not prevail against him, but shalt surely fall before him.

14 And while they were yet talking with him, came the king's chamberlains, and hasted to bring Haman unto the banquet that Esther had prepared.

CHAPTER 7

SO the king and Haman came to banquet with Esther the queen.

2 And the king said again unto Esther on the second day at the banquet of wine, What is your petition, queen Esther? and it shall be granted you: and what is your request? and it shall be performed, even to the half of the kingdom.

3 Then Esther the queen answered and said, If I have found favour in your sight, O king, and if it please the king, let my life be given me at my petition, and my people at my request:

4 For we are sold, I and my people, to be destroyed, to be slain, and to perish. But if we had been sold for bondmen and bondwomen, I had held my tongue, although the enemy could not countervail the king's damage.

5Then the king Ahasuerus answered and said unto Esther the queen, Who is he, and where is he, that durst presume in his heart to do so?

6 And Esther said, The adversary and enemy is this wicked Haman. Then Haman was afraid before the king and the queen.

7And the king arising from the banquet of wine in his wrath went into the palace garden: and Haman stood up to make request for his life to Esther the queen; for he saw that there was evil determined against him by the king.

8 Then the king returned out of the palace garden into the place of the banquet of wine; and Haman was fallen upon the bed whereon Esther was. Then said the king, Will he force the queen also before me in the house? As the word went out of the king's mouth, they covered Haman's face.

9 And Harbonah, one of the chamberlains, said before the king, Behold also, the gallows fifty cubits high, which Haman had made for Mordecai, who had spoken good for the king, standeth in the house of Haman. Then the king said, Hang him thereon.

10 So they hanged Haman on the gallows that he had prepared for Mordecai. Then was the king's wrath pacified.

CHAPTER 8

ON that day did the king Ahasuerus give the house of Haman the Jews' enemy unto Esther the queen. And Mordecai came before the king; for Esther had told what he was unto her.

2 And the king took off his ring, which he had taken from Haman, and gave it unto Mordecai. And Esther set Mordecai over the house of Haman.

3And Esther spake yet again before the king, and fell down at his feet, and besought him with tears to put away the mischief of Haman the Agagite, and his device that he had devised against the Jews.

4 Then the king held out the golden sceptre toward Esther. So Esther arose, and stood before the king,

5 And said, If it please the king, and if I have found favour in his sight, and the thing seem right before the king, and I be pleasing in his eyes, let it be written to reverse the letters devised by Haman the son of Hammedatha the Agagite, which he wrote to destroy the Jews which are in all the king's provinces:

6 For how can I endure to see the evil that shall come unto my people? or how can I endure to see the destruction of my kindred?

7Then the king Ahasuerus said unto Esther the queen and to Mordecai the Jew, Behold, I have given Esther the house of Haman, and him they have hanged upon the gallows, because he laid his hand upon the Jews.

8 Write you also for the Jews, as it liketh you, in the king's name, and seal it with the king's ring: for the writing which is written in the king's name, and sealed with the king's ring, may no man reverse.

9 Then were the king's scribes called at that time in the third month, that is, the month Sivan, on the three and twentieth day thereof; and it was written according to all that Mordecai commanded unto the Jews, and to the lieutenants, and the deputies and rulers of the provinces which are from India unto

Ethiopia, an hundred twenty and seven provinces, unto every province according to the writing thereof, and unto every people after their language, and to the Jews according to their writing, and according to their language.

10 And he wrote in the king Ahasuerus' name, and sealed it with the king's ring, and sent letters by posts on horseback, and riders on mules, camels, and young dromedaries:

11 Wherein the king granted the Jews which were in every city to gather themselves together, and to stand for their life, to destroy, to slay, and to cause to perish, all the power of the people and province that would assault them, both little ones and women, and to take the spoil of them for a prey,

12 Upon one day in all the provinces of king Ahasuerus, namely, upon the thirteenth day of the twelfth month, which is the month Adar.

13 The copy of the writing for a commandment to be given in every province was published unto all people, and that the Jews should be ready against that day to avenge themselves on their enemies.

14 So the posts that rode upon mules and camels went out, being hastened and pressed on by the king's commandment. And the decree was given at Shushan the palace.

15And Mordecai went out from the presence of the king in royal apparel of blue and white, and with a great crown of gold, and with a garment of fine linen and purple: and the city of Shushan rejoiced and was glad.

16 The Jews had light, and gladness, and joy, and honour.

17 And in every province, and in every city, whithersoever the king's commandment and his decree came, the Jews had joy and gladness, a feast and a good day. And many of the people of the land became Jews; for the fear of the Jews fell upon them.

CHAPTER 9

NOW in the twelfth month, that is, the month Adar, on the thirteenth day of the same, when the king's commandment and his decree drew near to be put in execution, in the day that the enemies of the Jews hoped to have power over them, (though it was turned to the contrary, that the Jews had rule over them that hated them;)

2 The Jews gathered themselves together in their cities throughout all the provinces of the king Ahasuerus, to lay hand on such as sought their hurt: and no man could withstand them; for the fear of them fell upon all people.

3 And all the rulers of the provinces, and the lieutenants, and the deputies, and officers of the king, helped the Jews; because the fear of Mordecai fell upon them.

4 For Mordecai was great in the king's house, and his fame went out throughout all the provinces: for this man Mordecai waxed greater and greater.

5 Thus the Jews struck all their enemies with the stroke of the sword, and slaughter, and destruction, and did what they would unto those that hated them.

6 And in Shushan the palace the Jews slew and destroyed five hundred men.

7 And Parshandatha, and Dalphon, and Aspatha,

8 And Poratha, and Adalia, and Aridatha,

9 And Parmashta, and Arisai, and Aridai, and Vajezatha,

10 The ten sons of Haman the son of Hammedatha, the enemy of the Jews, slew they; but on the spoil laid they not their hand.

11 On that day the number of those that were slain in Shushan the palace was brought before the king.

12And the king said unto Esther the queen, The Jews have slain and destroyed five hundred men in Shushan the palace, and the ten sons of Haman; what have they done in the rest of the king's provinces? now what is your petition? and it shall be granted you: or what is your request further? and it shall be done.

13 Then said Esther, If it please the king, let it be granted to the Jews which are in Shushan to do to morrow also according unto this day's decree, and let Haman's ten sons be hanged upon the gallows.

14 And the king commanded it so to be done: and the decree was given at Shushan; and they hanged Haman's ten sons.

15 For the Jews that were in Shushan gathered themselves together on the fourteenth day also of the month Adar, and slew three hundred men at Shushan; but on the prey they laid not their hand.

16 But the other Jews that were in the king's provinces gathered themselves together, and stood for their lives, and had rest from their enemies, and slew of their foes seventy and five thousand, but they laid not their hands on the prey,

17 On the thirteenth day of the month Adar; and on the fourteenth day of the same rested they, and made it a day of feasting and gladness.

18 But the Jews that were at Shushan assembled together on the thirteenth day thereof, and on the fourteenth thereof; and on the fifteenth day of the same they rested, and made it a day of feasting and gladness.

19 Therefore the Jews of the villages, that dwelt in the unwalled towns, made the fourteenth day of the month Adar a day of gladness and feasting, and a good day, and of sending portions one to another.

20 And Mordecai wrote these things, and sent letters unto all the Jews that were in all the provinces of the king Ahasuerus, both nigh and far,

21 To stablish this among them, that they should keep the fourteenth day of the month Adar, and the fifteenth day of the same, yearly,

22 As the days wherein the Jews rested from their enemies, and the month which was turned unto them from sorrow to joy, and from mourning into a good day: that they should make them days of feasting and joy, and of sending portions one to another, and gifts to the poor.

23 And the Jews undertook to do as they had begun, and as Mordecai had written unto them;

24 Because Haman the son of Hammedatha, the Agagite, the enemy of all the Jews, had devised against the Jews to destroy them, and had cast Pur, that is, the lot, to consume them, and to destroy them;

25 But when Esther came before the king, he commanded by letters that his wicked device, which he devised against the Jews, should return upon his own head, and that he and his sons should be hanged on the gallows.

26 Wherefore they called these days Purim after the name of Pur. Therefore for all the words of this letter, and of that which they had seen concerning this matter, and which had come unto them,

27 The Jews ordained, and took upon them, and upon their seed, and upon all such as joined themselves unto them, so as it should not fail, that they would keep these two days according to their writing, and according to their appointed time every year;

28 And that these days should be remembered and kept throughout every generation, every family, every province, and every city; and that these days of Purim should not fail from among the Jews, nor the memorial of them perish from their seed.

29 Then Esther the queen, the daughter of Abihail, and Mordecai the Jew, wrote with all authority, to confirm this second letter of Purim.

30 And he sent the letters unto all the Jews, to the hundred twenty and seven provinces of the kingdom of Ahasuerus, with words of peace and truth,

31 To confirm these days of Purim in their times appointed, according as Mordecai the Jew and Esther the queen had enjoined them, and as they had decreed for themselves and for their seed, the matters of the fastings and their cry.

32 And the decree of Esther confirmed these matters of Purim; and it was written in the book.

CHAPTER 10

AND the king Ahasuerus laid a tribute upon the land, and upon the isles of the sea.

2 And all the acts of his power and of his might, and the declaration of the greatness of Mordecai, whereunto the king advanced him, are they not written in the book of the chronicles of the kings of Media and Persia?

3 For Mordecai the Jew was next unto king Ahasuerus, and great among the Jews, and accepted of the multitude of his brethren, seeking the wealth of his people, and speaking peace to all his seed.

THE BOOK OF JOB.

CHAPTER 1

THERE was a man in the land of Uz, whose name was Job; and that man was perfect and upright, and one that feared God, and eschewed evil.

2 And there were born unto him seven sons and three daughters.

3 His substance also was seven thousand sheep, and three thousand camels, and five hundred yoke of oxen, and five hundred she asses, and a very great household; so that this man was the greatest of all the men of the east.

4 And his sons went and feasted in their houses, every one his day; and sent and called for their three sisters to eat and to drink with them.

5 And it was so, when the days of their feasting were gone about, that Job sent and sanctified them, and rose up early in the morning, and offered burnt offerings according to the number of them all: for Job said, It may be that my sons have sinned, and cursed God in their hearts. Thus did Job continually.

6Now there was a day when the sons of God came to present themselves before the LORD, and Satan came also among them.

7 And the LORD said unto Satan, Whence comest you ? Then Satan answered the LORD, and said, From going to and fro in the earth, and from walking up and down in it.

8 And the LORD said unto Satan, Have you considered my servant Job, that there is none like him in the earth, a perfect and an upright man, one that feareth God, and escheweth evil?

9 Then Satan answered the LORD, and said, Doth Job fear God for nought?

10 Have not you made an hedge about him, and about his house, and about all that he has on every side? you have blessed the work of his hands, and his substance is increased in the land.

11 But put forth yours hand now, and touch all that he has, and he will curse you to your face.

12 And the LORD said unto Satan, Behold, all that he has is in your power; only upon himself put not forth yours hand. So Satan went forth from the presence of the LORD.

13And there was a day when his sons and his daughters were eating and drinking wine in their eldest brother's house:

14 And there came a messenger unto Job, and said, The oxen were plowing, and the asses feeding beside them:

15 And the Sabeans fell upon them, and took them away; yea, they have slain the servants with the edge of the sword; and I only am escaped alone to tell you.

16 While he was yet speaking, there came also another, and said, The fire of God is fallen from heaven, and has burned up the sheep, and the servants, and consumed them; and I only am escaped alone to tell you.

17 While he was yet speaking, there came also another, and said, The Chaldeans made out three bands, and fell upon the camels, and have carried them away, yea, and slain the servants with the edge of the sword; and I only am escaped alone to tell you.

18 While he was yet speaking, there came also another, and said, Your sons and your daughters were eating and drinking wine in their eldest brother's house:

19 And, behold, there came a great wind from the wilderness, and struck the four corners of the house, and it fell upon the young men, and they are dead; and I only am escaped alone to tell you.

20 Then Job arose, and rent his mantle, and shaved his head, and fell down upon the ground, and worshipped,

21 And said, Naked came I out of my mother's womb, and naked shall I return thither: the LORD gave, and the LORD has taken away; blessed be the name of the LORD.

22 In all this Job sinned not, nor charged God foolishly.

CHAPTER 2

AGAIN there was a day when the sons of God came to present themselves before the LORD, and Satan came also among them to present himself before the LORD.

2 And the LORD said unto Satan, From whence comest you ? And Satan answered the LORD, and said, From going to and fro in the earth, and from walking up and down in it.

3 And the LORD said unto Satan, Have you considered my servant Job, that there is none like him in the earth, a perfect and an upright man, one that feareth God, and escheweth evil? and still he holdeth fast his integrity, although you movedst me against him, to destroy him without cause.

4 And Satan answered the LORD, and said, Skin for skin, yea, all that a man has will he give for his life.

5 But put forth yours hand now, and touch his bone and his flesh, and he will curse you to your face.

6 And the LORD said unto Satan, Behold, he is in yours hand; but save his life.

7So went Satan forth from the presence of the LORD, and struck Job with sore boils from the sole of his foot unto his crown.

8 And he took him a potsherd to scrape himself withal; and he sat down among the ashes.

9Then said his wife unto him, Dost you still retain yours integrity? curse God, and die.

10 But he said unto her, You speakest as one of the foolish women speaketh. What? shall we receive good at the hand of God, and shall we not receive evil? In all this did not Job sin with his lips.

11Now when Job's three friends heard of all this evil that was come upon him, they came every one from his own place; Eliphaz the Temanite, and Bildad the Shuhite, and Zophar the Naamathite: for they had made an appointment together to come to mourn with him and to comfort him.

12 And when they lifted up their eyes afar off, and knew him not, they lifted up their voice, and wept; and they rent every one his mantle, and sprinkled dust upon their heads toward heaven.

13 So they sat down with him upon the ground seven days and seven nights, and none spake a word unto him: for they saw that his grief was very great.

CHAPTER 3

AFTER this opened Job his mouth, and cursed his day.

2 And Job spake, and said,

3 Let the day perish wherein I was born, and the night in which it was said, There is a man child conceived.

4 Let that day be darkness; let not God regard it from above, neither let the light shine upon it.

5 Let darkness and the shadow of death stain it; let a cloud dwell upon it; let the blackness of the day terrify it.

6 As for that night, let darkness seize upon it; let it not be joined unto the days of the year, let it not come into the number of the months.

7 Lo, let that night be solitary, let no joyful voice come therein.

8 Let them curse it that curse the day, who are ready to raise up their mourning.

9 Let the stars of the twilight thereof be dark; let it look for light, but have none; neither let it see the dawning of the day:

10 Because it shut not up the doors of my mother's womb, nor hid sorrow from my eyes.

11 Why died I not from the womb? why did I not give up the ghost when I came out of the belly?

12 Why did the knees prevent me? or why the breasts that I should suck?

13 For now should I have lain still and been quiet, I should have slept: then had I been at rest,

14 With kings and counsellers of the earth, which built desolate places for themselves;

15 Or with princes that had gold, who filled their houses with silver:

16 Or as an hidden untimely birth I had not been; as infants which never saw light.

17 There the wicked cease from troubling; and there the weary be at rest.

18 There the prisoners rest together; they hear not the voice of the oppressor.

19 The small and great are there; and the servant is free from his master.

20 Wherefore is light given to him that is in misery, and life unto the bitter in soul;

21 Which long for death, but it comes not; and dig for it more than for hid treasures;

22 Which rejoice exceedingly, and are glad, when they can find the grave?

23 Why is light given to a man whose way is hid, and whom God has hedged in?

24 For my sighing comes before I eat, and my roarings are poured out like the waters.

25 For the thing which I greatly feared is come upon me, and that which I was afraid of is come unto me.

26 I was not in safety, neither had I rest, neither was I quiet; yet trouble came.

CHAPTER 4

THEN Eliphaz the Temanite answered and said,

2 If we assay to commune with you, will you be grieved? but who can withhold himself from speaking?

3 Behold, you have instructed many, and you have strengthened the weak hands.

4 Your words have upholden him that was falling, and you have strengthened the feeble knees.

5 But now it is come upon you, and you faintest; it toucheth you, and you are troubled.

6 Is not this your fear, your confidence, your hope, and the uprightness of your ways?

7 Remember, I pray you, who ever perished, being innocent? or where were the righteous cut off?

8 Even as I have seen, they that plow iniquity, and sow wickedness, reap the same.

9 By the blast of God they perish, and by the breath of his nostrils are they consumed.

10 The roaring of the lion, and the voice of the fierce lion, and the teeth of the young lions, are broken.

11 The old lion perisheth for lack of prey, and the stout lion's whelps are scattered abroad.

12 Now a thing was secretly brought to me, and my ear received a little thereof.

13 In thoughts from the visions of the night, when deep sleep falleth on men,

14 Fear came upon me, and trembling, which made all my bones to shake.

15 Then a spirit passed before my face; the hair of my flesh stood up:

16 It stood still, but I could not discern the form thereof: an image was before my eyes, there was silence, and I heard a voice, saying,

17 Shall mortal man be more just than God? shall a man be more pure than his maker?

18 Behold, he put no trust in his servants; and his angels he charged with folly:

19 How much less in them that dwell in houses of clay, whose foundation is in the dust, which are crushed before the moth?

20 They are destroyed from morning to evening: they perish for ever without any regarding it.

21 Doth not their excellency which is in them go away? they die, even without wisdom.

CHAPTER 5

CALL now, if there be any that will answer you; and to which of the saints will you turn?

2 For wrath killeth the foolish man, and envy slayeth the silly one.

3 I have seen the foolish taking root: but suddenly I cursed his habitation.

4 His children are far from safety, and they are crushed in the gate, neither is there any to deliver them.

5 Whose harvest the hungry eateth up, and taketh it even out of the thorns, and the robber swalloweth up their substance.

6 Although affliction comes not forth of the dust, neither doth trouble spring out of the ground;

7 Yet man is born unto trouble, as the sparks fly upward.

8 I would seek unto God, and unto God would I commit my cause:

9 Which doeth great things and unsearchable; marvellous things without number:

10 Who giveth rain upon the earth, and sendeth waters upon the fields:

11 To set up on high those that be low; that those which mourn may be exalted to safety.

12 He disappointeth the devices of the crafty, so that their hands cannot perform their enterprise.

13 He taketh the wise in their own craftiness: and the counsel of the froward is carried headlong.

14 They meet with darkness in the daytime, and grope in the noonday as in the night.

15 But he saveth the poor from the sword, from their mouth, and from the hand of the mighty.

16 So the poor has hope, and iniquity stoppeth her mouth.

17 Behold, happy is the man whom God correcteth: therefore despise not you the chastening of the Almighty:

18 For he maketh sore, and bindeth up: he woundeth, and his hands make whole.

19 He shall deliver you in six troubles: yea, in seven there shall no evil touch you.

20 In famine he shall redeem you from death: and in war from the power of the sword.

21 You shalt be hid from the scourge of the tongue: neither shalt you be afraid of destruction when it comes.

22 At destruction and famine you shalt laugh: neither shalt you be afraid of the beasts of the earth.

23 For you shalt be in league with the stones of the field: and the beasts of the field shall be at peace with you.

24 And you shalt know that your tabernacle shall be in peace; and you shalt visit your habitation, and shalt not sin.

25 You shalt know also that your seed shall be great, and yours offspring as the grass of the earth.

26 You shalt come to your grave in a full age, like as a shock of corn comes in in his season.

27 Lo this, we have searched it, so it is; hear it, and know you it for your good.

CHAPTER 6

BUT Job answered and said,

2 Oh that my grief were throughly weighed, and my calamity laid in the balances together!

3 For now it would be heavier than the sand of the sea: therefore my words are swallowed up.

4 For the arrows of the Almighty are within me, the poison whereof drinketh up my spirit: the terrors of God do set themselves in array against me.

5 Doth the wild ass bray when he has grass? or loweth the ox over his fodder?

6 Can that which is unsavoury be eaten without salt? or is there any taste in the white of an egg?

7 The things that my soul refused to touch are as my sorrowful meat.

8 Oh that I might have my request; and that God would grant me the thing that I long for!

9 Even that it would please God to destroy me; that he would let loose his hand, and cut me off!

10 Then should I yet have comfort; yea, I would harden myself in sorrow: let him not spare; for I have not concealed the words of the Holy One.

11 What is my strength, that I should hope? and what is my end, that I should prolong my life?

12 Is my strength the strength of stones? or is my flesh of brass?

13 Is not my help in me? and is wisdom driven quite from me?

14 To him that is afflicted pity should be shewed from his friend; but he forsaketh the fear of the Almighty.

15 My brethren have dealt deceitfully as a brook, and as the stream of brooks they pass away;

16 Which are blackish by reason of the ice, and wherein the snow is hid:

17 What time they wax warm, they vanish: when it is hot, they are consumed out of their place.

18 The paths of their way are turned aside; they go to nothing, and perish.

19 The troops of Tema looked, the companies of Sheba waited for them.

20 They were confounded because they had hoped; they came thither, and were ashamed.

21 For now you are nothing; you see my casting down, and are afraid.

22 Did I say, Bring unto me? or, Give a reward for me of your substance?

23 Or, Deliver me from the enemy's hand? or, Redeem me from the hand of the mighty?

24 Teach me, and I will hold my tongue: and cause me to understand wherein I have erred.

25 How forcible are right words! but what doth your arguing reprove?

26 Do you imagine to reprove words, and the speeches of one that is desperate, which are as wind?

27 Yea, you overwhelm the fatherless, and you dig a pit for your friend.

28 Now therefore be content, look upon me; for it is evident unto you if I lie.

29 Return, I pray you, let it not be iniquity; yea, return again, my righteousness is in it.

30 Is there iniquity in my tongue? cannot my taste discern perverse things?

CHAPTER 7

IS there not an appointed time to man upon earth? are not his days also like the days of an hireling?

2 As a servant earnestly desireth the shadow, and as an hireling looketh for the reward of his work:

3 So am I made to possess months of vanity, and wearisome nights are appointed to me.

4 When I lie down, I say, When shall I arise, and the night be gone? and I am full of tossings to and fro unto the dawning of the day.

5 My flesh is clothed with worms and clods of dust; my skin is broken, and become loathsome.

6 My days are swifter than a weaver's shuttle, and are spent without hope.

7 O remember that my life is wind: my eye shall no more see good.

8 The eye of him that has seen me shall see me no more: yours eyes are upon me, and I am not.

9 As the cloud is consumed and vanisheth away: so he that goeth down to the grave shall come up no more.

10 He shall return no more to his house, neither shall his place know him any more.

11 Therefore I will not refrain my mouth; I will speak in the anguish of my spirit; I will complain in the bitterness of my soul.

12 Am I a sea, or a whale, that you settest a watch over me?

13 When I say, My bed shall comfort me, my couch shall ease my complaint;

14 Then you scarest me with dreams, and terrifiest me through visions:

15 So that my soul chooseth strangling, and death rather than my life.

16 I loathe it; I would not live alway: let me alone; for my days are vanity.

17 What is man, that you shouldest magnify him? and that you shouldest set yours heart upon him?

18 And that you shouldest visit him every morning, and try him every moment?

19 How long will you not depart from me, nor let me alone till I swallow down my spittle?

20 I have sinned; what shall I do unto you, O you preserver of men? why have you set me as a mark against you, so that I am a burden to myself?

21 And why dost you not pardon my transgression, and take away my iniquity? for now shall I sleep in the dust; and you shalt seek me in the morning, but I shall not be.

CHAPTER 8

THEN answered Bildad the Shuhite, and said,

2 How long will you speak these things? and how long shall the words of your mouth be like a strong wind?

3 Doth God pervert judgment? or doth the Almighty pervert justice?

4 If your children have sinned against him, and he have cast them away for their transgression;

5 If you wouldest seek unto God betimes, and make your supplication to the Almighty;

6 If you wert pure and upright; surely now he would awake for you, and make the habitation of your righteousness prosperous.

7 Though your beginning was small, yet your latter end should greatly increase.

8 For inquire, I pray you, of the former age, and prepare yourself to the search of their fathers:

9 (For we are but of yesterday, and know nothing, because our days upon earth are a shadow:)

10 Shall not they teach you, and tell you, and utter words out of their heart?

11 Can the rush grow up without mire? can the flag grow without water?

12 Whilst it is yet in his greenness, and not cut down, it withereth before any other herb.

13 So are the paths of all that forget God; and the hypocrite's hope shall perish:

14 Whose hope shall be cut off, and whose trust shall be a spider's web.

15 He shall lean upon his house, but it shall not stand: he shall hold it fast, but it shall not endure.

16 He is green before the sun, and his branch shooteth forth in his garden.

17 His roots are wrapped about the heap, and seeth the place of stones.

18 If he destroy him from his place, then it shall deny him, saying, I have not seen you.

19 Behold, this is the joy of his way, and out of the earth shall others grow.

20 Behold, God will not cast away a perfect man, neither will he help the evil doers:

21 Till he fill your mouth with laughing, and your lips with rejoicing.

22 They that hate you shall be clothed with shame; and the dwelling place of the wicked shall come to nought.

CHAPTER 9

THEN Job answered and said,

2 I know it is so of a truth: but how should man be just with God?

3 If he will contend with him, he cannot answer him one of a thousand.

4 He is wise in heart, and mighty in strength: who has hardened himself against him, and has prospered?

5 Which removeth the mountains, and they know not: which overturneth them in his anger.

6 Which shaketh the earth out of her place, and the pillars thereof tremble.

7 Which commandeth the sun, and it riseth not; and sealeth up the stars.

8 Which alone spreadeth out the heavens, and treadeth upon the waves of the sea.

9 Which maketh Arcturus, Orion, and Pleiades, and the chambers of the south.

10 Which doeth great things past finding out; yea, and wonders without number.

11 Lo, he goeth by me, and I see him not: he passes on also, but I perceive him not.

12 Behold, he taketh away, who can hinder him? who will say unto him, What doest you ?

13 If God will not withdraw his anger, the proud helpers do stoop under him.

14 How much less shall I answer him, and choose out my words to reason with him?

15 Whom, though I were righteous, yet would I not answer, but I would make supplication to my judge.

16 If I had called, and he had answered me; yet would I not believe that he had hearkened unto my voice.

17 For he breaketh me with a tempest, and multiplieth my wounds without cause.

18 He will not suffer me to take my breath, but filleth me with bitterness.

19 If I speak of strength, lo, he is strong: and if of judgment, who shall set me a time to plead?

20 If I justify myself, my own mouth shall condemn me: if I say, I am perfect, it shall also prove me perverse.

21 Though I were perfect, yet would I not know my soul: I would despise my life.

22 This is one thing, therefore I said it, He destroyeth the perfect and the wicked.

23 If the scourge slay suddenly, he will laugh at the trial of the innocent.

24 The earth is given into the hand of the wicked: he covers the faces of the judges thereof; if not, where, and who is he?

25 Now my days are swifter than a post: they flee away, they see no good.

26 They are passed away as the swift ships: as the eagle that hasteth to the prey.

27 If I say, I will forget my complaint, I will leave off my heaviness, and comfort myself:

28 I am afraid of all my sorrows, I know that you will not hold me innocent.

29 If I be wicked, why then labour I in vain?

30 If I wash myself with snow water, and make my hands never so clean;

31 Yet shalt you plunge me in the ditch, and my own clothes shall abhor me.

32 For he is not a man, as I am, that I should answer him, and we should come together in judgment.

33 Neither is there any daysman betwixt us, that might lay his hand upon us both.

34 Let him take his rod away from me, and let not his fear terrify me:

35 Then would I speak, and not fear him; but it is not so with me.

CHAPTER 10

MY soul is weary of my life; I will leave my complaint upon myself; I will speak in the bitterness of my soul.

2 I will say unto God, Do not condemn me; shew me wherefore you contendest with me.

3 Is it good unto you that you shouldest oppress, that you shouldest despise the work of yours hands, and shine upon the counsel of the wicked?

4 Have you eyes of flesh? or seest you as man seeth?

5 Are your days as the days of man? are your years as man's days,

6 That you inquirest after my iniquity, and searchest after my sin?

7 You knowest that I am not wicked; and there is none that can deliver out of yours hand.

8 Yours hands have made me and fashioned me together round about; yet you dost destroy me.

9 Remember, I beseech you, that you have made me as the clay; and will you bring me into dust again?

10 Have you not poured me out as milk, and curdled me like cheese?

11 You have clothed me with skin and flesh, and have fenced me with bones and sinews.

12 You have granted me life and favour, and your visitation has preserved my spirit.

13 And these things have you hid in yours heart: I know that this is with you.

14 If I sin, then you markest me, and you will not acquit me from my iniquity.

15 If I be wicked, woe unto me; and if I be righteous, yet will I not lift up my head. I am full of confusion; therefore see you my affliction;

16 For it increaseth. You huntest me as a fierce lion: and again you shewest yourself marvellous upon me.

17 You renewest your witnesses against me, and increasest yours indignation upon me; changes and war are against me.

18 Wherefore then have you brought me forth out of the womb? Oh that I had given up the ghost, and no eye had seen me!

19 I should have been as though I had not been; I should have been carried from the womb to the grave.

20 Are not my days few? cease then, and let me alone, that I may take comfort a little,

21 Before I go whence I shall not return, even to the land of darkness and the shadow of death;

22 A land of darkness, as darkness itself; and of the shadow of death, without any order, and where the light is as darkness.

CHAPTER 11

THEN answered Zophar the Naamathite, and said,

2 Should not the multitude of words be answered? and should a man full of talk be justified?

3 Should your lies make men hold their peace? and when you mockest, shall no man make you ashamed?

4 For you have said, My doctrine is pure, and I am clean in yours eyes.

5 But oh that God would speak, and open his lips against you;

6 And that he would shew you the secrets of wisdom, that they are double to that which is! Know therefore that God exacteth of you less than yours iniquity deserveth.

7 Can you by searching find out God? can you find out the Almighty unto perfection?

8 It is as high as heaven; what can you do? deeper than hell; what can you know?

9 The measure thereof is longer than the earth, and broader than the sea.

10 If he cut off, and shut up, or gather together, then who can hinder him?

11 For he knoweth vain men: he seeth wickedness also; will he not then consider it?

12 For vain man would be wise, though man be born like a wild ass's colt.

13 If you prepare yours heart, and stretch out yours hands toward him;

14 If iniquity be in yours hand, put it far away, and let not wickedness dwell in your tabernacles.

15 For then shalt you lift up your face without spot; yea, you shalt be stedfast, and shalt not fear:

16 Because you shalt forget your misery, and remember it as waters that pass away:

17 And yours age shall be clearer than the noonday; you shalt shine forth, you shalt be as the morning.

18 And you shalt be secure, because there is hope; yea, you shalt dig about you, and you shalt take your rest in safety.

19 Also you shalt lie down, and none shall make you afraid; yea, many shall make suit unto you.

20 But the eyes of the wicked shall fail, and they shall not escape, and their hope shall be as the giving up of the ghost.

CHAPTER 12

AND Job answered and said,

2 No doubt but you are the people, and wisdom shall die with you.

3 But I have understanding as well as you; I am not inferior to you: yea, who knoweth not such things as these?

4 I am as one mocked of his neighbour, who calleth upon God, and he answereth him: the just upright man is laughed to scorn.

5 He that is ready to slip with his feet is as a lamp despised in the thought of him that is at ease.

6 The tabernacles of robbers prosper, and they that provoke God are secure; into whose hand God bringeth abundantly.

7 But ask now the beasts, and they shall teach you; and the fowls of the air, and they shall tell you:

8 Or speak to the earth, and it shall teach you: and the fishes of the sea shall declare unto you.

9 Who knoweth not in all these that the hand of the LORD has created this?

10 In whose hand is the soul of every living thing, and the breath of all mankind.

11 Doth not the ear try words? and the mouth taste his meat?

12 With the ancient is wisdom; and in length of days understanding.

13 With him is wisdom and strength, he has counsel and understanding.

14 Behold, he breaketh down, and it cannot be built again: he shutteth up a man, and there can be no opening.

15 Behold, he withholdeth the waters, and they dry up: also he sendeth them out, and they overturn the earth.

16 With him is strength and wisdom: the deceived and the deceiver are his.

17 He leadeth counsellers away spoiled, and maketh the judges fools.

18 He looseth the bond of kings, and girdeth their loins with a girdle.

19 He leadeth princes away spoiled, and overthroweth the mighty.

20 He removeth away the speech of the trusty, and taketh away the understanding of the aged.

21 He poureth contempt upon princes, and weakeneth the strength of the mighty.

22 He discovereth deep things out of darkness, and bringeth out to light the shadow of death.

23 He increaseth the nations, and destroyeth them: he enlargeth the nations, and straiteneth them again.

24 He taketh away the heart of the chief of the people of the earth, and causeth them to wander in a wilderness where there is no way.

25 They grope in the dark without light, and he maketh them to stagger like a drunken man.

CHAPTER 13

LO, my eye has seen all this, my ear has heard and understood it.

2 What you know, the same do I know also: I am not inferior unto you.

3 Surely I would speak to the Almighty, and I desire to reason with God.

4 But you are forgers of lies, you are all physicians of no value.

5 O that you would altogether hold your peace! and it should be your wisdom.

6 Hear now my reasoning, and hearken to the pleadings of my lips.

7 Will you speak wickedly for God? and talk deceitfully for him?

8 Will you accept his person? will you contend for God?

9 Is it good that he should search you out? or as one man mocketh another, do you so mock him?

10 He will surely reprove you, if you do secretly accept persons.

11 Shall not his excellency make you afraid? and his dread fall upon you?

12 Your remembrances are like unto ashes, your bodies to bodies of clay.

13 Hold your peace, let me alone, that I may speak, and let come on me what will.

14 Wherefore do I take my flesh in my teeth, and put my life in my hand?

15 Though he slay me, yet will I trust in him: but I will maintain my own ways before him.

16 He also shall be my salvation: for an hypocrite shall not come before him.

17 Hear diligently my speech, and my declaration with your ears.

18 Behold now, I have ordered my cause; I know that I shall be justified.

19 Who is he that will plead with me? for now, if I hold my tongue, I shall give up the ghost.

20 Only do not two things unto me: then will I not hide myself from you.

21 Withdraw yours hand far from me: and let not your dread make me afraid.

22 Then call you , and I will answer: or let me speak, and answer you me.

23 How many are my iniquities and sins? make me to know my transgression and my sin.

24 Wherefore hidest you your face, and holdest me for yours enemy?

25 Will you break a leaf driven to and fro? and will you pursue the dry stubble?

26 For you writest bitter things against me, and makest me to possess the iniquities of my youth.

27 You puttest my feet also in the stocks, and lookest narrowly unto all my paths; you settest a print upon the heels of my feet.

28 And he, as a rotten thing, consumeth, as a garment that is moth eaten.

CHAPTER 14

MAN that is born of a woman is of few days, and full of trouble.

2 He comes forth like a flower, and is cut down: he fleeth also as a shadow, and continueth not.

3 And dost you open yours eyes upon such an one, and bringest me into judgment with you?

4 Who can bring a clean thing out of an unclean? not one.

5 Seeing his days are determined, the number of his months are with you, you have appointed his bounds that he cannot pass;

6 Turn from him, that he may rest, till he shall accomplish, as an hireling, his day.

7 For there is hope of a tree, if it be cut down, that it will sprout again, and that the tender branch thereof will not cease.

8 Though the root thereof wax old in the earth, and the stock thereof die in the ground;

9 Yet through the scent of water it will bud, and bring forth boughs like a plant.

10 But man dieth, and wasteth away: yea, man giveth up the ghost, and where is he?

11 As the waters fail from the sea, and the flood decayeth and drieth up:

12 So man lies down, and riseth not: till the heavens be no more, they shall not awake, nor be raised out of their sleep.

13 O that you wouldest hide me in the grave, that you wouldest keep me secret, until your wrath be past, that you wouldest appoint me a set time, and remember me!

14 If a man die, shall he live again? all the days of my appointed time will I wait, till my change come.

15 You shalt call, and I will answer you: you will have a desire to the work of yours hands.

16 For now you numberest my steps: dost you not watch over my sin?

17 My transgression is sealed up in a bag, and you sewest up my iniquity.

18 And surely the mountain falling comes to nought, and the rock is removed out of his place.

19 The waters wear the stones: you washest away the things which grow out of the dust of the earth; and you destroyest the hope of man.

20 You prevailest for ever against him, and he passes: you changest his countenance, and sendest him away.

21 His sons come to honour, and he knoweth it not; and they are brought low, but he perceiveth it not of them.

22 But his flesh upon him shall have pain, and his soul within him shall mourn.

CHAPTER 15

THEN answered Eliphaz the Temanite, and said,

2 Should a wise man utter vain knowledge, and fill his belly with the east wind?

3 Should he reason with unprofitable talk? or with speeches wherewith he can do no good?

4 Yea, you castest off fear, and restrainest prayer before God.

5 For your mouth uttereth yours iniquity, and you choosest the tongue of the crafty.

6 Yours own mouth condemneth you, and not I: yea, yours own lips testify against you.

7 Are you the first man that was born? or wast you made before the hills?

8 Have you heard the secret of God? and dost you restrain wisdom to yourself?

9 What knowest you , that we know not? what understandest you , which is not in us?

10 With us are both the grayheaded and very aged men, much elder than your father.

11 Are the consolations of God small with you? is there any secret thing with you?

12 Why doth yours heart carry you away? and what do your eyes wink at,

13 That you turnest your spirit against God, and lettest such words go out of your mouth?

14 What is man, that he should be clean? and he which is born of a woman, that he should be righteous?

15 Behold, he putteth no trust in his saints; yea, the heavens are not clean in his sight.

16 How much more abominable and filthy is man, which drinketh iniquity like water?

17 I will shew you, hear me; and that which I have seen I will declare;

18 Which wise men have told from their fathers, and have not hid it:

19 Unto whom alone the earth was given, and no stranger passed among them.

20 The wicked man travaileth with pain all his days, and the number of years is hidden to the oppressor.

21 A dreadful sound is in his ears: in prosperity the destroyer shall come upon him.

22 He believeth not that he shall return out of darkness, and he is waited for of the sword.

23 He wandereth abroad for bread, saying, Where is it? he knoweth that the day of darkness is ready at his hand.

24 Trouble and anguish shall make him afraid; they shall prevail against him, as a king ready to the battle.

25 For he stretcheth out his hand against God, and strengtheneth himself against the Almighty.

26 He runneth upon him, even on his neck, upon the thick bosses of his bucklers:

27 Because he covers his face with his fatness, and maketh collops of fat on his flanks.

28 And he dwelleth in desolate cities, and in houses which no man inhabiteth, which are ready to become heaps.

29 He shall not be rich, neither shall his substance continue, neither shall he prolong the perfection thereof upon the earth.

30 He shall not depart out of darkness; the flame shall dry up his branches, and by the breath of his mouth shall he go away.

31 Let not him that is deceived trust in vanity: for vanity shall be his recompence.

32 It shall be accomplished before his time, and his branch shall not be green.

33 He shall shake off his unripe grape as the vine, and shall cast off his flower as the olive.

34 For the congregation of hypocrites shall be desolate, and fire shall consume the tabernacles of bribery.

35 They conceive mischief, and bring forth vanity, and their belly prepareth deceit.

CHAPTER 16

THEN Job answered and said,

2 I have heard many such things: miserable comforters are you all.

3 Shall vain words have an end? or what emboldeneth you that you answerest?

4 I also could speak as you do: if your soul were in my soul's stead, I could heap up words against you, and shake my head at you.

5 But I would strengthen you with my mouth, and the moving of my lips should asswage your grief.

6 Though I speak, my grief is not asswaged: and though I forbear, what am I eased?

7 But now he has made me weary: you have made desolate all my company.

8 And you have filled me with wrinkles, which is a witness against me: and my leanness rising up in me beareth witness to my face.

9 He teareth me in his wrath, who hateth me: he gnasheth upon me with his teeth; my enemy sharpeneth his eyes upon me.

10 They have gaped upon me with their mouth; they have smitten me upon the cheek reproachfully; they have gathered themselves together against me.

11 God has delivered me to the ungodly, and turned me over into the hands of the wicked.

12 I was at ease, but he has broken me asunder: he has also taken me by my neck, and shaken me to pieces, and set me up for his mark.

13 His archers compass me round about, he cleaveth my reins asunder, and doth not spare; he poureth out my gall upon the ground.

14 He breaketh me with breach upon breach, he runneth upon me like a giant.

15 I have sewed sackcloth upon my skin, and defiled my horn in the dust.

16 My face is foul with weeping, and on my eyelids is the shadow of death;

17 Not for any injustice in my hands: also my prayer is pure.

18 O earth, cover not you my blood, and let my cry have no place.

19 Also now, behold, my witness is in heaven, and my record is on high.

20 My friends scorn me: but my eye poureth out tears unto God.

21 O that one might plead for a man with God, as a man pleadeth for his neighbour!

22 When a few years are come, then I shall go the way whence I shall not return.

CHAPTER 17

MY breath is corrupt, my days are extinct, the graves are ready for me.

2 Are there not mockers with me? and doth not my eye continue in their provocation?

3 Lay down now, put me in a surety with you; who is he that will strike hands with me?

4 For you have hid their heart from understanding: therefore shalt you not exalt them.

5 He that speaketh flattery to his friends, even the eyes of his children shall fail.

6 He has made me also a byword of the people; and aforetime I was as a tabret.

7 My eye also is dim by reason of sorrow, and all my members are as a shadow.

8 Upright men shall be astonied at this, and the innocent shall stir up himself against the hypocrite.

9 The righteous also shall hold on his way, and he that has clean hands shall be stronger and stronger.

10 But as for you all, do you return, and come now: for I cannot find one wise man among you.

11 My days are past, my purposes are broken off, even the thoughts of my heart.

12 They change the night into day: the light is short because of darkness.

13 If I wait, the grave is my house: I have made my bed in the darkness.

14 I have said to corruption, You are my father: to the worm, You are my mother, and my sister.

15 And where is now my hope? as for my hope, who shall see it?

16 They shall go down to the bars of the pit, when our rest together is in the dust.

CHAPTER 18

THEN answered Bildad the Shuhite, and said,

2 How long will it be ere you make an end of words? mark, and afterwards we will speak.

3 Wherefore are we counted as beasts, and reputed vile in your sight?

4 He teareth himself in his anger: shall the earth be forsaken for you? and shall the rock be removed out of his place?

5 Yea, the light of the wicked shall be put out, and the spark of his fire shall not shine.

6 The light shall be dark in his tabernacle, and his candle shall be put out with him.

7 The steps of his strength shall be straitened, and his own counsel shall cast him down.

8 For he is cast into a net by his own feet, and he walketh upon a snare.

9 The gin shall take him by the heel, and the robber shall prevail against him.

10 The snare is laid for him in the ground, and a trap for him in the way.

11 Terrors shall make him afraid on every side, and shall drive him to his feet.

12 His strength shall be hungerbitten, and destruction shall be ready at his side.

13 It shall devour the strength of his skin: even the firstborn of death shall devour his strength.

14 His confidence shall be rooted out of his tabernacle, and it shall bring him to the king of terrors.

15 It shall dwell in his tabernacle, because it is none of his: brimstone shall be scattered upon his habitation.

16 His roots shall be dried up beneath, and above shall his branch be cut off.

17 His remembrance shall perish from the earth, and he shall have no name in the street.

18 He shall be driven from light into darkness, and chased out of the world.

19 He shall neither have son nor nephew among his people, nor any remaining in his dwellings.

20 They that come after him shall be astonied at his day, as they that went before were affrighted.

21 Surely such are the dwellings of the wicked, and this is the place of him that knoweth not God.

CHAPTER 19

THEN Job answered and said,

2 How long will you vex my soul, and break me in pieces with words?

3 These ten times have you reproached me: you are not ashamed that you make yourselves strange to me.

4 And be it indeed that I have erred, my error remaineth with myself.

5 If indeed you will magnify yourselves against me, and plead against me my reproach:

6 Know now that God has overthrown me, and has compassed me with his net.

7 Behold, I cry out of wrong, but I am not heard: I cry aloud, but there is no judgment.

8 He has fenced up my way that I cannot pass, and he has set darkness in my paths.

9 He has stripped me of my glory, and taken the crown from my head.

10 He has destroyed me on every side, and I am gone: and my hope has he removed like a tree.

11 He has also kindled his wrath against me, and he counteth me unto him as one of his enemies.

12 His troops come together, and raise up their way against me, and encamp round about my tabernacle.

13 He has put my brethren far from me, and my acquaintance are verily estranged from me.

14 My kinsfolk have failed, and my familiar friends have forgotten me.

15 They that dwell in my house, and my maids, count me for a stranger: I am an alien in their sight.

16 I called my servant, and he gave me no answer; I intreated him with my mouth.

17 My breath is strange to my wife, though I intreated for the children's sake of my own body.

18 Yea, young children despised me; I arose, and they spake against me.

19 All my inward friends abhorred me: and they whom I loved are turned against me.

20 My bone cleaveth to my skin and to my flesh, and I am escaped with the skin of my teeth.

21 Have pity upon me, have pity upon me, O you my friends; for the hand of God has touched me.

22 Why do you persecute me as God, and are not satisfied with my flesh?

23 Oh that my words were now written! oh that they were printed in a book!

24 That they were graven with an iron pen and lead in the rock for ever!

25 For I know that my redeemer liveth, and that he shall stand at the latter day upon the earth:

26 And though after my skin worms destroy this body, yet in my flesh shall I see God:

27 Whom I shall see for myself, and my eyes shall behold, and not another; though my reins be consumed within me.

28 But you should say, Why persecute we him, seeing the root of the matter is found in me?

29 Be you afraid of the sword: for wrath bringeth the punishments of the sword, that you may know there is a judgment.

CHAPTER 20

THEN answered Zophar the Naamathite, and said,

2 Therefore do my thoughts cause me to answer, and for this I make haste.

3 I have heard the check of my reproach, and the spirit of my understanding causeth me to answer.

4 Knowest you not this of old, since man was placed upon earth,

5 That the triumphing of the wicked is short, and the joy of the hypocrite but for a moment?

6 Though his excellency mount up to the heavens, and his head reach unto the clouds;

7 Yet he shall perish for ever like his own dung: they which have seen him shall say, Where is he?

8 He shall fly away as a dream, and shall not be found: yea, he shall be chased away as a vision of the night.

9 The eye also which saw him shall see him no more; neither shall his place any more behold him.

10 His children shall seek to please the poor, and his hands shall restore their goods.

11 His bones are full of the sin of his youth, which shall lie down with him in the dust.

12 Though wickedness be sweet in his mouth, though he hide it under his tongue;

13 Though he spare it, and forsake it not; but keep it still within his mouth:

14 Yet his meat in his bowels is turned, it is the gall of asps within him.

15 He has swallowed down riches, and he shall vomit them up again: God shall cast them out of his belly.

16 He shall suck the poison of asps: the viper's tongue shall slay him.

17 He shall not see the rivers, the floods, the brooks of honey and butter.

18 That which he laboured for shall he restore, and shall not swallow it down: according to his substance shall the restitution be, and he shall not rejoice therein.

19 Because he has oppressed and has forsaken the poor; because he has violently taken away an house which he builded not;

20 Surely he shall not feel quietness in his belly, he shall not save of that which he desired.

21 There shall none of his meat be left; therefore shall no man look for his goods.

22 In the fulness of his sufficiency he shall be in straits: every hand of the wicked shall come upon him.

23 When he is about to fill his belly, God shall cast the fury of his wrath upon him, and shall rain it upon him while he is eating.

24 He shall flee from the iron weapon, and the bow of steel shall strike him through.

25 It is drawn, and comes out of the body; yea, the glittering sword comes out of his gall: terrors are upon him.

26 All darkness shall be hid in his secret places: a fire not blown shall consume him; it shall go ill with him that is left in his tabernacle.

27 The heaven shall reveal his iniquity; and the earth shall rise up against him.

28 The increase of his house shall depart, and his goods shall flow away in the day of his wrath.

29 This is the portion of a wicked man from God, and the heritage appointed unto him by God.

CHAPTER 21

BUT Job answered and said,

2 Hear diligently my speech, and let this be your consolations.

3 Suffer me that I may speak; and after that I have spoken, mock on.

4 As for me, is my complaint to man? and if it were so, why should not my spirit be troubled?

5 Mark me, and be astonished, and lay your hand upon your mouth.

6 Even when I remember I am afraid, and trembling taketh hold on my flesh.

7 Wherefore do the wicked live, become old, yea, are mighty in power?

8 Their seed is established in their sight with them, and their offspring before their eyes.

9 Their houses are safe from fear, neither is the rod of God upon them.

10 Their bull gendereth, and faileth not; their cow calveth, and casteth not her calf.

11 They send forth their little ones like a flock, and their children dance.

12 They take the timbrel and harp, and rejoice at the sound of the organ.

13 They spend their days in wealth, and in a moment go down to the grave.

14 Therefore they say unto God, Depart from us; for we desire not the knowledge of your ways.

15 What is the Almighty, that we should serve him? and what profit should we have, if we pray unto him?

16 Lo, their good is not in their hand: the counsel of the wicked is far from me.

17 How oft is the candle of the wicked put out! and how oft comes their destruction upon them! God distributeth sorrows in his anger.

18 They are as stubble before the wind, and as chaff that the storm carrieth away.

19 God layeth up his iniquity for his children: he rewardeth him, and he shall know it.

20 His eyes shall see his destruction, and he shall drink of the wrath of the Almighty.

21 For what pleasure has he in his house after him, when the number of his months is cut off in the midst?

22 Shall any teach God knowledge? seeing he judgeth those that are high.

23 One dieth in his full strength, being wholly at ease and quiet.

24 His breasts are full of milk, and his bones are moistened with marrow.

25 And another dieth in the bitterness of his soul, and never eateth with pleasure.

26 They shall lie down alike in the dust, and the worms shall cover them.

27 Behold, I know your thoughts, and the devices which you wrongfully imagine against me.

28 For you say, Where is the house of the prince? and where are the dwelling places of the wicked?

29 Have you not asked them that go by the way? and do you not know their tokens,

30 That the wicked is reserved to the day of destruction? they shall be brought forth to the day of wrath.

31 Who shall declare his way to his face? and who shall repay him what he has done?

32 Yet shall he be brought to the grave, and shall remain in the tomb.

33 The clods of the valley shall be sweet unto him, and every man shall draw after him, as there are innumerable before him.

34 How then comfort you me in vain, seeing in your answers there remaineth falsehood?

CHAPTER 22

THEN Eliphaz the Temanite answered and said,

2 Can a man be profitable unto God, as he that is wise may be profitable unto himself?

3 Is it any pleasure to the Almighty, that you are righteous? or is it gain to him, that you makest your ways perfect?

4 Will he reprove you for fear of you? will he enter with you into judgment?

5 Is not your wickedness great? and yours iniquities infinite?

6 For you have taken a pledge from your brother for nought, and stripped the naked of their clothing.

7 You have not given water to the weary to drink, and you have withholden bread from the hungry.

8 But as for the mighty man, he had the earth; and the honourable man dwelt in it.

9 You have sent widows away empty, and the arms of the fatherless have been broken.

10 Therefore snares are round about you, and sudden fear troubleth you;

11 Or darkness, that you can not see; and abundance of waters cover you.

12 Is not God in the height of heaven? and behold the height of the stars, how high they are!

13 And you say, How doth God know? can he judge through the dark cloud?

14 Thick clouds are a covering to him, that he seeth not; and he walketh in the circuit of heaven.

15 Have you marked the old way which wicked men have trodden?

16 Which were cut down out of time, whose foundation was overflown with a flood:

17 Which said unto God, Depart from us: and what can the Almighty do for them?

18 Yet he filled their houses with good things: but the counsel of the wicked is far from me.

19 The righteous see it, and are glad: and the innocent laugh them to scorn.

20 Whereas our substance is not cut down, but the remnant of them the fire consumeth.

21 Acquaint now yourself with him, and be at peace: thereby good shall come unto you.

22 Receive, I pray you, the law from his mouth, and lay up his words in yours heart.

23 If you return to the Almighty, you shalt be built up, you shalt put away iniquity far from your tabernacles.

24 Then shalt you lay up gold as dust, and the gold of Ophir as the stones of the brooks.

25 Yea, the Almighty shall be your defence, and you shalt have plenty of silver.

26 For then shalt you have your delight in the Almighty, and shalt lift up your face unto God.

27 You shalt make your prayer unto him, and he shall hear you, and you shalt pay your vows.

28 You shalt also decree a thing, and it shall be established unto you: and the light shall shine upon your ways.

29 When men are cast down, then you shalt say, There is lifting up; and he shall save the humble person.

30 He shall deliver the island of the innocent: and it is delivered by the pureness of yours hands.

CHAPTER 23

THEN Job answered and said,

2 Even to day is my complaint bitter: my stroke is heavier than my groaning.

3 Oh that I knew where I might find him! that I might come even to his seat!

4 I would order my cause before him, and fill my mouth with arguments.

5 I would know the words which he would answer me, and understand what he would say unto me.

6 Will he plead against me with his great power? No; but he would put strength in me.

7 There the righteous might dispute with him; so should I be delivered for ever from my judge.

8 Behold, I go forward, but he is not there; and backward, but I cannot perceive him:

9 On the left hand, where he doth work, but I cannot behold him: he hideth himself on the right hand, that I cannot see him:

10 But he knoweth the way that I take: when he has tried me, I shall come forth as gold.

11 My foot has held his steps, his way have I kept, and not declined.

12 Neither have I gone back from the commandment of his lips; I have esteemed the words of his mouth more than my necessary food.

13 But he is in one mind, and who can turn him? and what his soul desireth, even that he doeth.

14 For he performeth the thing that is appointed for me: and many such things are with him.

15 Therefore am I troubled at his presence: when I consider, I am afraid of him.

16 For God maketh my heart soft, and the Almighty troubleth me:

17 Because I was not cut off before the darkness, neither has he covered the darkness from my face.

CHAPTER 24

WHY, seeing times are not hidden from the Almighty, do they that know him not see his days?

2 Some remove the landmarks; they violently take away flocks, and feed thereof.

3 They drive away the ass of the fatherless, they take the widow's ox for a pledge.

4 They turn the needy out of the way: the poor of the earth hide themselves together.

5 Behold, as wild asses in the desert, go they forth to their work; rising betimes for a prey: the wilderness yieldeth food for them and for their children.

6 They reap every one his corn in the field: and they gather the vintage of the wicked.

7 They cause the naked to lodge without clothing, that they have no covering in the cold.

8 They are wet with the showers of the mountains, and embrace the rock for want of a shelter.

9 They pluck the fatherless from the breast, and take a pledge of the poor.

10 They cause him to go naked without clothing, and they take away the sheaf from the hungry;

11 Which make oil within their walls, and tread their winepresses, and suffer thirst.

12 Men groan from out of the city, and the soul of the wounded crieth out: yet God layeth not folly to them.

13 They are of those that rebel against the light; they know not the ways thereof, nor abide in the paths thereof.

14 The murderer rising with the light killeth the poor and needy, and in the night is as a thief.

15 The eye also of the adulterer waiteth for the twilight, saying, No eye shall see me: and disguiseth his face.

16 In the dark they dig through houses, which they had marked for themselves in the daytime: they know not the light.

17 For the morning is to them even as the shadow of death: if one know them, they are in the terrors of the shadow of death.

18 He is swift as the waters; their portion is cursed in the earth: he beholdeth not the way of the vineyards.

19 Drought and heat consume the snow waters: so doth the grave those which have sinned.

20 The womb shall forget him; the worm shall feed sweetly on him; he shall be no more remembered; and wickedness shall be broken as a tree.

21 He evil entreateth the barren that beareth not: and doeth not good to the widow.

22 He draweth also the mighty with his power: he riseth up, and no man is sure of life.

23 Though it be given him to be in safety, whereon he resteth; yet his eyes are upon their ways.

24 They are exalted for a little while, but are gone and brought low; they are taken out of the way as all other, and cut off as the tops of the ears of corn.

25 And if it be not so now, who will make me a liar, and make my speech nothing worth?

CHAPTER 25

THEN answered Bildad the Shuhite, and said,

2 Dominion and fear are with him, he maketh peace in his high places.

3 Is there any number of his armies? and upon whom doth not his light arise?

4 How then can man be justified with God? or how can he be clean that is born of a woman?

5 Behold even to the moon, and it shineth not; yea, the stars are not pure in his sight.

6 How much less man, that is a worm? and the son of man, which is a worm?

CHAPTER 26

BUT Job answered and said,

2 How have you helped him that is without power? how savest you the arm that has no strength?

3 How have you counselled him that has no wisdom? and how have you plentifully declared the thing as it is?

4 To whom have you uttered words? and whose spirit came from you?

5 Dead things are formed from under the waters, and the inhabitants thereof.

6 Hell is naked before him, and destruction has no covering.

7 He stretcheth out the north over the empty place, and hangeth the earth upon nothing.

8 He bindeth up the waters in his thick clouds; and the cloud is not rent under them.

9 He holdeth back the face of his throne, and spreadeth his cloud upon it.

10 He has compassed the waters with bounds, until the day and night come to an end.

11 The pillars of heaven tremble and are astonished at his reproof.

12 He divideth the sea with his power, and by his understanding he smiteth through the proud.

13 By his spirit he has garnished the heavens; his hand has formed the crooked serpent.

14 Lo, these are parts of his ways: but how little a portion is heard of him? but the thunder of his power who can understand?

CHAPTER 27

MOREOVER Job continued his parable, and said,

2 As God liveth, who has taken away my judgment; and the Almighty, who has vexed my soul;

3 All the while my breath is in me, and the spirit of God is in my nostrils;

4 My lips shall not speak wickedness, nor my tongue utter deceit.

5 God forbid that I should justify you: till I die I will not remove my integrity from me.

6 My righteousness I hold fast, and will not let it go: my heart shall not reproach me so long as I live.

7 Let my enemy be as the wicked, and he that riseth up against me as the unrighteous.

8 For what is the hope of the hypocrite, though he has gained, when God taketh away his soul?

9 Will God hear his cry when trouble comes upon him?

10 Will he delight himself in the Almighty? will he always call upon God?

11 I will teach you by the hand of God: that which is with the Almighty will I not conceal.

12 Behold, all you yourselves have seen it; why then are you thus altogether vain?

13 This is the portion of a wicked man with God, and the heritage of oppressors, which they shall receive of the Almighty.

14 If his children be multiplied, it is for the sword: and his offspring shall not be satisfied with bread.

15 Those that remain of him shall be buried in death: and his widows shall not weep.

16 Though he heap up silver as the dust, and prepare raiment as the clay;

17 He may prepare it, but the just shall put it on, and the innocent shall divide the silver.

18 He buildeth his house as a moth, and as a booth that the keeper maketh.

19 The rich man shall lie down, but he shall not be gathered: he openeth his eyes, and he is not.

20 Terrors take hold on him as waters, a tempest stealeth him away in the night.

21 The east wind carrieth him away, and he departeth: and as a storm hurleth him out of his place.

22 For God shall cast upon him, and not spare: he would fain flee out of his hand.

23 Men shall clap their hands at him, and shall hiss him out of his place.

CHAPTER 28

SURELY there is a vein for the silver, and a place for gold where they fine it.

2 Iron is taken out of the earth, and brass is molten out of the stone.

3 He setteth an end to darkness, and searches out all perfection: the stones of darkness, and the shadow of death.

4 The flood breaketh out from the inhabitant; even the waters forgotten of the foot: they are dried up, they are gone away from men.

5 As for the earth, out of it comes bread: and under it is turned up as it were fire.

6 The stones of it are the place of sapphires: and it has dust of gold.

7 There is a path which no fowl knoweth, and which the vulture's eye has not seen:

8 The lion's whelps have not trodden it, nor the fierce lion passed by it.

9 He putteth forth his hand upon the rock; he overturneth the mountains by the roots.

10 He cutteth out rivers among the rocks; and his eye seeth every precious thing.

11 He bindeth the floods from overflowing; and the thing that is hid bringeth he forth to light.

12 But where shall wisdom be found? and where is the place of understanding?

13 Man knoweth not the price thereof; neither is it found in the land of the living.

14 The depth saith, It is not in me: and the sea saith, It is not with me.

15 It cannot be gotten for gold, neither shall silver be weighed for the price thereof.

16 It cannot be valued with the gold of Ophir, with the precious onyx, or the sapphire.

17 The gold and the crystal cannot equal it: and the exchange of it shall not be for jewels of fine gold.

18 No mention shall be made of coral, or of pearls: for the price of wisdom is above rubies.

19 The topaz of Ethiopia shall not equal it, neither shall it be valued with pure gold.

20 Whence then comes wisdom? and where is the place of understanding?

21 Seeing it is hid from the eyes of all living, and kept close from the fowls of the air.

22 Destruction and death say, We have heard the fame thereof with our ears.

23 God understands the way thereof, and he knoweth the place thereof.

24 For he looketh to the ends of the earth, and seeth under the whole heaven;

25 To make the weight for the winds; and he weigheth the waters by measure.

26 When he made a decree for the rain, and a way for the lightning of the thunder:

27 Then did he see it, and declare it; he prepared it, yea, and searched it out.

28 And unto man he said, Behold, the fear of the Lord, that is wisdom; and to depart from evil is understanding.

CHAPTER 29

MOREOVER Job continued his parable, and said,

2 Oh that I were as in months past, as in the days when God preserved me;

3 When his candle shined upon my head, and when by his light I walked through darkness;

4 As I was in the days of my youth, when the secret of God was upon my tabernacle;

5 When the Almighty was yet with me, when my children were about me;

6 When I washed my steps with butter, and the rock poured me out rivers of oil;

7 When I went out to the gate through the city, when I prepared my seat in the street!

8 The young men saw me, and hid themselves: and the aged arose, and stood up.

9 The princes refrained talking, and laid their hand on their mouth.

10 The nobles held their peace, and their tongue cleaved to the roof of their mouth.

11 When the ear heard me, then it blessed me; and when the eye saw me, it gave witness to me:

12 Because I delivered the poor that cried, and the fatherless, and him that had none to help him.

13 The blessing of him that was ready to perish came upon me: and I caused the widow's heart to sing for joy.

14 I put on righteousness, and it clothed me: my judgment was as a robe and a diadem.

15 I was eyes to the blind, and feet was I to the lame.

16 I was a father to the poor: and the cause which I knew not I searched out.

17 And I brake the jaws of the wicked, and plucked the spoil out of his teeth.

18 Then I said, I shall die in my nest, and I shall multiply my days as the sand.

19 My root was spread out by the waters, and the dew lay all night upon my branch.

20 My glory was fresh in me, and my bow was renewed in my hand.

21 Unto me men gave ear, and waited, and kept silence at my counsel.

22 After my words they spake not again; and my speech dropped upon them.

23 And they waited for me as for the rain; and they opened their mouth wide as for the latter rain.

24 If I laughed on them, they believed it not; and the light of my countenance they cast not down.

25 I chose out their way, and sat chief, and dwelt as a king in the army, as one that comforteth the mourners.

CHAPTER 30

BUT now they that are younger than I have me in derision, whose fathers I would have disdained to have set with the dogs of my flock.

2 Yea, whereto might the strength of their hands profit me, in whom old age was perished?

3 For want and famine they were solitary; fleeing into the wilderness in former time desolate and waste.

4 Who cut up mallows by the bushes, and juniper roots for their meat.

5 They were driven forth from among men, (they cried after them as after a thief;)

6 To dwell in the clifts of the valleys, in caves of the earth, and in the rocks.

7 Among the bushes they brayed; under the nettles they were gathered together.

8 They were children of fools, yea, children of base men: they were viler than the earth.

9 And now am I their song, yea, I am their byword.

10 They abhor me, they flee far from me, and spare not to spit in my face.

11 Because he has loosed my cord, and afflicted me, they have also let loose the bridle before me.

12 Upon my right hand rise the youth; they push away my feet, and they raise up against me the ways of their destruction.

13 They mar my path, they set forward my calamity, they have no helper.

14 They came upon me as a wide breaking in of waters: in the desolation they rolled themselves upon me.

15 Terrors are turned upon me: they pursue my soul as the wind: and my welfare passes away as a cloud.

16 And now my soul is poured out upon me; the days of affliction have taken hold upon me.

17 My bones are pierced in me in the night season: and my sinews take no rest.

18 By the great force of my disease is my garment changed: it bindeth me about as the collar of my coat.

19 He has cast me into the mire, and I am become like dust and ashes.

20 I cry unto you, and you dost not hear me: I stand up, and you regardest me not.

21 You are become cruel to me: with your strong hand you opposest yourself against me.

22 You liftest me up to the wind; you causest me to ride upon it, and dissolvest my substance.

23 For I know that you will bring me to death, and to the house appointed for all living.

24 Howbeit he will not stretch out his hand to the grave, though they cry in his destruction.

25 Did not I weep for him that was in trouble? was not my soul grieved for the poor?

26 When I looked for good, then evil came unto me: and when I waited for light, there came darkness.

27 My bowels boiled, and rested not: the days of affliction prevented me.

28 I went mourning without the sun: I stood up, and I cried in the congregation.

29 I am a brother to dragons, and a companion to owls.

30 My skin is black upon me, and my bones are burned with heat.

31 My harp also is turned to mourning, and my organ into the voice of them that weep.

CHAPTER 31

I MADE a covenant with my eyes; why then should I think upon a maid?

2 For what portion of God is there from above? and what inheritance of the Almighty from on high?

3 Is not destruction to the wicked? and a strange punishment to the workers of iniquity?

4 Doth not he see my ways, and count all my steps?

5 If I have walked with vanity, or if my foot has hasted to deceit;

6 Let me be weighed in an even balance, that God may know my integrity.

7 If my step has turned out of the way, and my heart walked after my eyes, and if any blot has cleaved to my hands;

8 Then let me sow, and let another eat; yea, let my offspring be rooted out.

9 If my heart have been deceived by a woman, or if I have laid wait at my neighbour's door;

10 Then let my wife grind unto another, and let others bow down upon her.

11 For this is an heinous crime; yea, it is an iniquity to be punished by the judges.

12 For it is a fire that consumeth to destruction, and would root out all my increase.

13 If I did despise the cause of my manservant or of my maidservant, when they contended with me;

14 What then shall I do when God riseth up? and when he visiteth, what shall I answer him?

15 Did not he that made me in the womb make him? and did not one fashion us in the womb?

16 If I have withheld the poor from their desire, or have caused the eyes of the widow to fail;

17 Or have eaten my morsel myself alone, and the fatherless has not eaten thereof;

18 (For from my youth he was brought up with me, as with a father, and I have guided her from my mother's womb;)

19 If I have seen any perish for want of clothing, or any poor without covering;

20 If his loins have not blessed me, and if he were not warmed with the fleece of my sheep;

21 If I have lifted up my hand against the fatherless, when I saw my help in the gate:

22 Then let my arm fall from my shoulder blade, and my arm be broken from the bone.

23 For destruction from God was a terror to me, and by reason of his highness I could not endure.

24 If I have made gold my hope, or have said to the fine gold, You are my confidence;

25 If I rejoiced because my wealth was great, and because my hand had gotten much;

26 If I beheld the sun when it shined, or the moon walking in brightness;

27 And my heart has been secretly enticed, or my mouth has kissed my hand:

28 This also were an iniquity to be punished by the judge: for I should have denied the God that is above.

29 If I rejoiced at the destruction of him that hated me, or lifted up myself when evil found him:

30 Neither have I suffered my mouth to sin by wishing a curse to his soul.

31 If the men of my tabernacle said not, Oh that we had of his flesh! we cannot be satisfied.

32 The stranger did not lodge in the street: but I opened my doors to the traveller.

33 If I covered my transgressions as Adam, by hiding my iniquity in my bosom:

34 Did I fear a great multitude, or did the contempt of families terrify me, that I kept silence, and went not out of the door?

35 Oh that one would hear me! behold, my desire is, that the Almighty would answer me, and that my adversary had written a book.

36 Surely I would take it upon my shoulder, and bind it as a crown to me.

37 I would declare unto him the number of my steps; as a prince would I go near unto him.

38 If my land cry against me, or that the furrows likewise thereof complain;

39 If I have eaten the fruits thereof without money, or have caused the owners thereof to lose their life:

40 Let thistles grow instead of wheat, and cockle instead of barley. The words of Job are ended.

CHAPTER 32

SO these three men ceased to answer Job, because he was righteous in his own eyes.

2 Then was kindled the wrath of Elihu the son of Barachel the Buzite, of the kindred of Ram: against Job was his wrath kindled, because he justified himself rather than God.

3 Also against his three friends was his wrath kindled, because they had found no answer, and yet had condemned Job.

4 Now Elihu had waited till Job had spoken, because they were elder than he.

5 When Elihu saw that there was no answer in the mouth of these three men, then his wrath was kindled.

6 And Elihu the son of Barachel the Buzite answered and said, I am young, and you are very old; wherefore I was afraid, and durst not shew you my opinion.

7 I said, Days should speak, and multitude of years should teach wisdom.

8 But there is a spirit in man: and the inspiration of the Almighty giveth them understanding.

9 Great men are not always wise: neither do the aged understand judgment.

10 Therefore I said, Hearken to me; I also will shew my opinion.

11 Behold, I waited for your words; I gave ear to your reasons, whilst you searched out what to say.

12 Yea, I attended unto you, and, behold, there was none of you that convinced Job, or that answered his words:

13 Lest you should say, We have found out wisdom: God thrusteth him down, not man.

14 Now he has not directed his words against me: neither will I answer him with your speeches.

15 They were amazed, they answered no more: they left off speaking.

16 When I had waited, (for they spake not, but stood still, and answered no more;)

17 I said, I will answer also my part, I also will shew my opinion.

18 For I am full of matter, the spirit within me constraineth me.

19 Behold, my belly is as wine which has no vent; it is ready to burst like new bottles.

20 I will speak, that I may be refreshed: I will open my lips and answer.

21 Let me not, I pray you, accept any man's person, neither let me give flattering titles unto man.

22 For I know not to give flattering titles; in so doing my maker would soon take me away.

CHAPTER 33

WHEREFORE, Job, I pray you, hear my speeches, and hearken to all my words.

2 Behold, now I have opened my mouth, my tongue has spoken in my mouth.

3 My words shall be of the uprightness of my heart: and my lips shall utter knowledge clearly.

4 The Spirit of God has made me, and the breath of the Almighty has given me life.

5 If you can answer me, set your words in order before me, stand up.

6 Behold, I am according to your wish in God's stead: I also am formed out of the clay.

7 Behold, my terror shall not make you afraid, neither shall my hand be heavy upon you.

8 Surely you have spoken in my hearing, and I have heard the voice of your words, saying,

9 I am clean without transgression, I am innocent; neither is there iniquity in me.

10 Behold, he findeth occasions against me, he counteth me for his enemy,

11 He putteth my feet in the stocks, he marketh all my paths.

12 Behold, in this you are not just: I will answer you, that God is greater than man.

13 Why dost you strive against him? for he giveth not account of any of his matters.

14 For God speaketh once, yea twice, yet man perceiveth it not.

15 In a dream, in a vision of the night, when deep sleep falleth upon men, in slumberings upon the bed;

16 Then he openeth the ears of men, and sealeth their instruction,

17 That he may withdraw man from his purpose, and hide pride from man.

18 He keepeth back his soul from the pit, and his life from perishing by the sword.

19 He is chastened also with pain upon his bed, and the multitude of his bones with strong pain:

20 So that his life abhorreth bread, and his soul dainty meat.

21 His flesh is consumed away, that it cannot be seen; and his bones that were not seen stick out.

22 Yea, his soul draweth near unto the grave, and his life to the destroyers.

23 If there be a messenger with him, an interpreter, one among a thousand, to shew unto man his uprightness:

24 Then he is gracious unto him, and saith, Deliver him from going down to the pit: I have found a ransom.

25 His flesh shall be fresher than a child's: he shall return to the days of his youth:

26 He shall pray unto God, and he will be favourable unto him: and he shall see his face with joy: for he will render unto man his righteousness.

27 He looketh upon men, and if any say, I have sinned, and perverted that which was right, and it profited me not;

28 He will deliver his soul from going into the pit, and his life shall see the light.

29 Lo, all these things worketh God oftentimes with man,

30 To bring back his soul from the pit, to be enlightened with the light of the living.

31 Mark well, O Job, hearken unto me: hold your peace, and I will speak.

32 If you have any thing to say, answer me: speak, for I desire to justify you.

33 If not, hearken unto me: hold your peace, and I shall teach you wisdom.

CHAPTER 34

FURTHERMORE Elihu answered and said,

2 Hear my words, O you wise men; and give ear unto me, you that have knowledge.

3 For the ear trieth words, as the mouth tasteth meat.

4 Let us choose to us judgment: let us know among ourselves what is good.

5 For Job has said, I am righteous: and God has taken away my judgment.

6 Should I lie against my right? my wound is incurable without transgression.

7 What man is like Job, who drinketh up scorning like water?

8 Which goeth in company with the workers of iniquity, and walketh with wicked men.

9 For he has said, It profiteth a man nothing that he should delight himself with God.

10 Therefore hearken unto me, you men of understanding: far be it from God, that he should do wickedness; and from the Almighty, that he should commit iniquity.

11 For the work of a man shall he render unto him, and cause every man to find according to his ways.

12 Yea, surely God will not do wickedly, neither will the Almighty pervert judgment.

13 Who has given him a charge over the earth? or who has disposed the whole world?

14 If he set his heart upon man, if he gather unto himself his spirit and his breath;

15 All flesh shall perish together, and man shall turn again unto dust.

16 If now you have understanding, hear this: hearken to the voice of my words.

17 Shall even he that hateth right govern? and will you condemn him that is most just?

18 Is it fit to say to a king, You are wicked? and to princes, You are ungodly?

19 How much less to him that accepteth not the persons of princes, nor regardeth the rich more than the poor? for they all are the work of his hands.

20 In a moment shall they die, and the people shall be troubled at midnight, and pass away: and the mighty shall be taken away without hand.

21 For his eyes are upon the ways of man, and he seeth all his goings.

22 There is no darkness, nor shadow of death, where the workers of iniquity may hide themselves.

23 For he will not lay upon man more than right; that he should enter into judgment with God.

24 He shall break in pieces mighty men without number, and set others in their stead.

25 Therefore he knoweth their works, and he overturneth them in the night, so that they are destroyed.

26 He striketh them as wicked men in the open sight of others;

27 Because they turned back from him, and would not consider any of his ways:

28 So that they cause the cry of the poor to come unto him, and he heareth the cry of the afflicted.

29 When he giveth quietness, who then can make trouble? and when he hideth his face, who then can behold him? whether it be done against a nation, or against a man only:

30 That the hypocrite reign not, lest the people be ensnared.

31 Surely it is meet to be said unto God, I have borne chastisement, I will not offend any more:

32 That which I see not teach you me: if I have done iniquity, I will do no more.

33 Should it be according to your mind? he will recompense it, whether you refuse, or whether you choose; and not I: therefore speak what you knowest.

34 Let men of understanding tell me, and let a wise man hearken unto me.

35 Job has spoken without knowledge, and his words were without wisdom.

36 My desire is that Job may be tried unto the end because of his answers for wicked men.

37 For he addeth rebellion unto his sin, he clappeth his hands among us, and multiplieth his words against God.

CHAPTER 35

ELIHU spake moreover, and said,

2 Thinkest you this to be right, that you saidst, My righteousness is more than God's?

3 For you saidst, What advantage will it be unto you? and, What profit shall I have, if I be cleansed from my sin?

4 I will answer you, and your companions with you.

5 Look unto the heavens, and see; and behold the clouds which are higher than you .

6 If you sinnest, what doest you against him? or if your transgressions be multiplied, what doest you unto him?

7 If you be righteous, what givest you him? or what receiveth he of yours hand?

8 Your wickedness may hurt a man as you are; and your righteousness may profit the son of man.

9 By reason of the multitude of oppressions they make the oppressed to cry: they cry out by reason of the arm of the mighty.

10 But none saith, Where is God my maker, who giveth songs in the night;

11 Who teacheth us more than the beasts of the earth, and maketh us wiser than the fowls of heaven?

12 There they cry, but none giveth answer, because of the pride of evil men.

13 Surely God will not hear vanity, neither will the Almighty regard it.

14 Although you say you shalt not see him, yet judgment is before him; therefore trust you in him.

15 But now, because it is not so, he has visited in his anger; yet he knoweth it not in great extremity:

16 Therefore doth Job open his mouth in vain; he multiplieth words without knowledge.

CHAPTER 36

ELIHU also proceeded, and said,

2 Suffer me a little, and I will shew you that I have yet to speak on God's behalf.

3 I will fetch my knowledge from afar, and will ascribe righteousness to my Maker.

4 For truly my words shall not be false: he that is perfect in knowledge is with you.

5 Behold, God is mighty, and despiseth not any: he is mighty in strength and wisdom.

6 He preserveth not the life of the wicked: but giveth right to the poor.

7 He withdraweth not his eyes from the righteous: but with kings are they on the throne; yea, he doth establish them for ever, and they are exalted.

8 And if they be bound in fetters, and be holden in cords of affliction;

9 Then he sheweth them their work, and their transgressions that they have exceeded.

10 He openeth also their ear to discipline, and commandeth that they return from iniquity.

11 If they obey and serve him, they shall spend their days in prosperity, and their years in pleasures.

12 But if they obey not, they shall perish by the sword, and they shall die without knowledge.

13 But the hypocrites in heart heap up wrath: they cry not when he bindeth them.

14 They die in youth, and their life is among the unclean.

15 He delivereth the poor in his affliction, and openeth their ears in oppression.

16 Even so would he have removed you out of the strait into a broad place, where there is no straitness; and that which should be set on your table should be full of fatness.

17 But you have fulfilled the judgment of the wicked: judgment and justice take hold on you.

18 Because there is wrath, beware lest he take you away with his stroke: then a great ransom cannot deliver you.

19 Will he esteem your riches? no, not gold, nor all the forces of strength.

20 Desire not the night, when people are cut off in their place.

21 Take heed, regard not iniquity: for this have you chosen rather than affliction.

22 Behold, God exalteth by his power: who teacheth like him?

23 Who has enjoined him his way? or who can say, You have created iniquity?

24 Remember that you magnify his work, which men behold.

25 Every man may see it; man may behold it afar off.

26 Behold, God is great, and we know him not, neither can the number of his years be searched out.

27 For he maketh small the drops of water: they pour down rain according to the vapour thereof:

28 Which the clouds do drop and distil upon man abundantly.

29 Also can any understand the spreadings of the clouds, or the noise of his tabernacle?

30 Behold, he spreadeth his light upon it, and covers the bottom of the sea.

31 For by them judgeth he the people; he giveth meat in abundance.

32 With clouds he covers the light; and commandeth it not to shine by the cloud that comes betwixt.

33 The noise thereof sheweth concerning it, the cattle also concerning the vapour.

CHAPTER 37

AT this also my heart trembleth, and is moved out of his place.

2 Hear attentively the noise of his voice, and the sound that goeth out of his mouth.

3 He directeth it under the whole heaven, and his lightning unto the ends of the earth.

4 After it a voice roareth: he thundereth with the voice of his excellency; and he will not stay them when his voice is heard.

5 God thundereth marvellously with his voice; great things doeth he, which we cannot comprehend.

6 For he saith to the snow, Be you on the earth; likewise to the small rain, and to the great rain of his strength.

7 He sealeth up the hand of every man; that all men may know his work.

8 Then the beasts go into dens, and remain in their places.

9 Out of the south comes the whirlwind: and cold out of the north.

10 By the breath of God frost is given: and the breadth of the waters is straitened.

11 Also by watering he wearieth the thick cloud: he scattereth his bright cloud:

12 And it is turned round about by his counsels: that they may do whatsoever he commandeth them upon the face of the world in the earth.

13 He causeth it to come, whether for correction, or for his land, or for mercy.

14 Hearken unto this, O Job: stand still, and consider the wondrous works of God.

15 Dost you know when God disposed them, and caused the light of his cloud to shine?

16 Dost you know the balancings of the clouds, the wondrous works of him which is perfect in knowledge?

17 How your garments are warm, when he quieteth the earth by the south wind?

18 Have you with him spread out the sky, which is strong, and as a molten looking glass?

19 Teach us what we shall say unto him; for we cannot order our speech by reason of darkness.

20 Shall it be told him that I speak? if a man speak, surely he shall be swallowed up.

21 And now men see not the bright light which is in the clouds: but the wind passes, and cleanseth them.

22 Fair weather comes out of the north: with God is terrible majesty.

23 Touching the Almighty, we cannot find him out: he is excellent in power, and in judgment, and in plenty of justice: he will not afflict.

24 Men do therefore fear him: he respecteth not any that are wise of heart.

CHAPTER 38

THEN the LORD answered Job out of the whirlwind, and said,

2 Who is this that darkeneth counsel by words without knowledge?

3 Gird up now your loins like a man; for I will demand of you, and answer you me.

4 Where wast you when I laid the foundations of the earth? declare, if you have understanding.

5 Who has laid the measures thereof, if you knowest? or who has stretched the line upon it?

6 Whereupon are the foundations thereof fastened? or who laid the corner stone thereof;

7 When the morning stars sang together, and all the sons of God shouted for joy?

8 Or who shut up the sea with doors, when it brake forth, as if it had issued out of the womb?

9 When I made the cloud the garment thereof, and thick darkness a swaddlingband for it,

10 And brake up for it my decreed place, and set bars and doors,

11 And said, Hitherto shalt you come, but no further: and here shall your proud waves be stayed?

12 Have you commanded the morning since your days; and caused the dayspring to know his place;

13 That it might take hold of the ends of the earth, that the wicked might be shaken out of it?

14 It is turned as clay to the seal; and they stand as a garment.

15 And from the wicked their light is withholden, and the high arm shall be broken.

16 Have you entered into the springs of the sea? or have you walked in the search of the depth?

17 Have the gates of death been opened unto you? or have you seen the doors of the shadow of death?

18 Have you perceived the breadth of the earth? declare if you knowest it all.

19 Where is the way where light dwelleth? and as for darkness, where is the place thereof,

20 That you shouldest take it to the bound thereof, and that you shouldest know the paths to the house thereof?

21 Knowest you it, because you wast then born? or because the number of your days is great?

22 Have you entered into the treasures of the snow? or have you seen the treasures of the hail,

23 Which I have reserved against the time of trouble, against the day of battle and war?

24 By what way is the light parted, which scattereth the east wind upon the earth?

25 Who has divided a watercourse for the overflowing of waters, or a way for the lightning of thunder;

26 To cause it to rain on the earth, where no man is; on the wilderness, wherein there is no man;

27 To satisfy the desolate and waste ground; and to cause the bud of the tender herb to spring forth?

28 Has the rain a father? or who has begotten the drops of dew?

29 Out of whose womb came the ice? and the hoary frost of heaven, who has gendered it?

30 The waters are hid as with a stone, and the face of the deep is frozen.

31 Can you bind the sweet influences of Pleiades, or loose the bands of Orion?

32 Can you bring forth Mazzaroth in his season? or can you guide Arcturus with his sons?

33 Knowest you the ordinances of heaven? can you set the dominion thereof in the earth?

34 Can you lift up your voice to the clouds, that abundance of waters may cover you?

35 Can you send lightnings, that they may go, and say unto you, Here we are?

36 Who has put wisdom in the inward parts? or who has given understanding to the heart?

37 Who can number the clouds in wisdom? or who can stay the bottles of heaven,

38 When the dust groweth into hardness, and the clods cleave fast together?

39 Will you hunt the prey for the lion? or fill the appetite of the young lions,

40 When they couch in their dens, and abide in the covert to lie in wait?

41 Who provideth for the raven his food? when his young ones cry unto God, they wander for lack of meat.

CHAPTER 39

KNOWEST you the time when the wild goats of the rock bring forth? or can you mark when the hinds do calve?

2 Can you number the months that they fulfil? or knowest you the time when they bring forth?

3 They bow themselves, they bring forth their young ones, they cast out their sorrows.

4 Their young ones are in good liking, they grow up with corn; they go forth, and return not unto them.

5 Who has sent out the wild ass free? or who has loosed the bands of the wild ass?

6 Whose house I have made the wilderness, and the barren land his dwellings.

7 He scorneth the multitude of the city, neither regardeth he the crying of the driver.

8 The range of the mountains is his pasture, and he searches after every green thing.

9 Will the unicorn be willing to serve you, or abide by your crib?

10 Can you bind the unicorn with his band in the furrow? or will he harrow the valleys after you?

11 Will you trust him, because his strength is great? or will you leave your labour to him?

12 Will you believe him, that he will bring home your seed, and gather it into your barn?

13 Gavest you the goodly wings unto the peacocks? or wings and feathers unto the ostrich?

14 Which leaveth her eggs in the earth, and warmeth them in dust,

15 And forgetteth that the foot may crush them, or that the wild beast may break them.

16 She is hardened against her young ones, as though they were not hers: her labour is in vain without fear;

17 Because God has deprived her of wisdom, neither has he imparted to her understanding.

18 What time she lifteth up herself on high, she scorneth the horse and his rider.

19 Have you given the horse strength? have you clothed his neck with thunder?

20 Can you make him afraid as a grasshopper? the glory of his nostrils is terrible.

21 He paweth in the valley, and rejoiceth in his strength: he goeth on to meet the armed men.

22 He mocketh at fear, and is not affrighted; neither turneth he back from the sword.

23 The quiver rattleth against him, the glittering spear and the shield.

24 He swalloweth the ground with fierceness and rage: neither believeth he that it is the sound of the trumpet.

25 He saith among the trumpets, Ha, ha; and he smelleth the battle afar off, the thunder of the captains, and the shouting.

26 Doth the hawk fly by your wisdom, and stretch her wings toward the south?

27 Doth the eagle mount up at your command, and make her nest on high?

28 She dwelleth and abideth on the rock, upon the crag of the rock, and the strong place.

29 From thence she seeketh the prey, and her eyes behold afar off.

30 Her young ones also suck up blood: and where the slain are, there is she.

CHAPTER 40

MOREOVER the LORD answered Job, and said,

2 Shall he that contendeth with the Almighty instruct him? he that reproveth God, let him answer it.

3 Then Job answered the LORD, and said,

4 Behold, I am vile; what shall I answer you? I will lay my hand upon my mouth.

5 Once have I spoken; but I will not answer: yea, twice; but I will proceed no further.

6 Then answered the LORD unto Job out of the whirlwind, and said,

7 Gird up your loins now like a man: I will demand of you, and declare you unto me.

8 Will you also disannul my judgment? will you condemn me, that you mayest be righteous?

9 Have you an arm like God? or can you thunder with a voice like him?

10 Deck yourself now with majesty and excellency; and array yourself with glory and beauty.

11 Cast abroad the rage of your wrath: and behold every one that is proud, and abase him.

12 Look on every one that is proud, and bring him low; and tread down the wicked in their place.

13 Hide them in the dust together; and bind their faces in secret.

14 Then will I also confess unto you that yours own right hand can save you.

15 Behold now behemoth, which I made with you; he eateth grass as an ox.

16 Lo now, his strength is in his loins, and his force is in the navel of his belly.

17 He moveth his tail like a cedar: the sinews of his stones are wrapped together.

18 His bones are as strong pieces of brass; his bones are like bars of iron.

19 He is the chief of the ways of God: he that made him can make his sword to approach unto him.

20 Surely the mountains bring him forth food, where all the beasts of the field play.

21 He lies under the shady trees, in the covert of the reed, and fens.

22 The shady trees cover him with their shadow; the willows of the brook compass him about.

23 Behold, he drinketh up a river, and hasteth not: he trusteth that he can draw up Jordan into his mouth.

24 He taketh it with his eyes: his nose pierceth through snares.

CHAPTER 41

CAN you draw out leviathan with an hook? or his tongue with a cord which you lettest down?

2 Can you put an hook into his nose? or bore his jaw through with a thorn?

3 Will he make many supplications unto you? will he speak soft words unto you?

4 Will he make a covenant with you? will you take him for a servant for ever?

5 Will you play with him as with a bird? or will you bind him for your maidens?

6 Shall the companions make a banquet of him? shall they part him among the merchants?

7 Can you fill his skin with barbed irons? or his head with fish spears?

8 Lay yours hand upon him, remember the battle, do no more.

9 Behold, the hope of him is in vain: shall not one be cast down even at the sight of him?

10 None is so fierce that dare stir him up: who then is able to stand before me?

11 Who has prevented me, that I should repay him? whatsoever is under the whole heaven is my.

12 I will not conceal his parts, nor his power, nor his comely proportion.

13 Who can discover the face of his garment? or who can come to him with his double bridle?

14 Who can open the doors of his face? his teeth are terrible round about.

15 His scales are his pride, shut up together as with a close seal.

16 One is so near to another, that no air can come between them.

17 They are joined one to another, they stick together, that they cannot be sundered.

18 By his neesings a light doth shine, and his eyes are like the eyelids of the morning.

19 Out of his mouth go burning lamps, and sparks of fire leap out.

20 Out of his nostrils goeth smoke, as out of a seething pot or caldron.

21 His breath kindleth coals, and a flame goeth out of his mouth.

22 In his neck remaineth strength, and sorrow is turned into joy before him.

23 The flakes of his flesh are joined together: they are firm in themselves; they cannot be moved.

24 His heart is as firm as a stone; yea, as hard as a piece of the nether millstone.

25 When he raiseth up himself, the mighty are afraid: by reason of breakings they purify themselves.

26 The sword of him that layeth at him cannot hold: the spear, the dart, nor the habergeon.

27 He esteemeth iron as straw, and brass as rotten wood.

28 The arrow cannot make him flee: slingstones are turned with him into stubble.

29 Darts are counted as stubble: he laugheth at the shaking of a spear.

30 Sharp stones are under him: he spreadeth sharp pointed things upon the mire.

31 He maketh the deep to boil like a pot: he maketh the sea like a pot of ointment.

32 He maketh a path to shine after him; one would think the deep to be hoary.

33 Upon earth there is not his like, who is made without fear.

34 He beholdeth all high things: he is a king over all the children of pride.

CHAPTER 42

THEN Job answered the LORD, and said,

2 I know that you can do every thing, and that no thought can be withholden from you.

3 Who is he that hideth counsel without knowledge? therefore have I uttered that I understood not; things too wonderful for me, which I knew not.

4 Hear, I beseech you, and I will speak: I will demand of you, and declare you unto me.

5 I have heard of you by the hearing of the ear: but now my eye seeth you.

6 Wherefore I abhor myself, and repent in dust and ashes.

7 And it was so, that after the LORD had spoken these words unto Job, the LORD said to Eliphaz the Temanite, My wrath is kindled against you, and against your two friends: for you have not spoken of me the thing that is right, as my servant Job has.

8 Therefore take unto you now seven bullocks and seven rams, and go to my servant Job, and offer up for yourselves a burnt offering; and my servant Job shall pray for you: for him will I accept: lest I deal with you after your folly, in that you have not spoken of me the thing which is right, like my servant Job.

9 So Eliphaz the Temanite and Bildad the Shuhite and Zophar the Naamathite went, and did according as the LORD commanded them: the LORD also accepted Job.

10 And the LORD turned the captivity of Job, when he prayed for his friends: also the LORD gave Job twice as much as he had before.

11 Then came there unto him all his brethren, and all his sisters, and all they that had been of his acquaintance before, and did eat bread with him in his house: and they bemoaned him, and comforted him over all the evil that the LORD had brought upon him: every man also gave him a piece of money, and every one an earring of gold.

12 So the LORD blessed the latter end of Job more than his beginning: for he had fourteen thousand sheep, and six thousand camels, and a thousand yoke of oxen, and a thousand she asses.

13 He had also seven sons and three daughters.

14 And he called the name of the first, Jemima; and the name of the second, Kezia; and the name of the third, Keren-happuch.

15 And in all the land were no women found so fair as the daughters of Job: and their father gave them inheritance among their brethren.

16 After this lived Job an hundred and forty years, and saw his sons, and his sons' sons, even four generations.

17 So Job died, being old and full of days.

THE
BOOK OF PSALMS.

PSALM 1

BLESSED is the man that walketh not in the counsel of the ungodly, nor standeth in the way of sinners, nor sitteth in the seat of the scornful.

2 But his delight is in the law of the LORD; and in his law doth he meditate day and night.

3 And he shall be like a tree planted by the rivers of water, that bringeth forth his fruit in his season; his leaf also shall not wither; and whatsoever he doeth shall prosper.

4 The ungodly are not so: but are like the chaff which the wind driveth away.

5 Therefore the ungodly shall not stand in the judgment, nor sinners in the congregation of the righteous.

6 For the LORD knoweth the way of the righteous: but the way of the ungodly shall perish.

PSALM 2

WHY do the heathen rage, and the people imagine a vain thing?

2 The kings of the earth set themselves, and the rulers take counsel together, against the LORD, and against his anointed, saying,

3 Let us break their bands asunder, and cast away their cords from us.

4 He that sitteth in the heavens shall laugh: the Lord shall have them in derision.

5 Then shall he speak unto them in his wrath, and vex them in his sore displeasure.

6 Yet have I set my king upon my holy hill of Zion.

7 I will declare the decree: the LORD has said unto me, You are my Son; this day have I begotten you.

8 Ask of me, and I shall give you the heathen for yours inheritance, and the uttermost parts of the earth for your possession.

9 You shalt break them with a rod of iron; you shalt dash them in pieces like a potter's vessel.

10 Be wise now therefore, O you kings: be instructed, you judges of the earth.

11 Serve the LORD with fear, and rejoice with trembling.

12 Kiss the Son, lest he be angry, and you perish from the way, when his wrath is kindled but a little. Blessed are all they that put their trust in him.

PSALM 3

A Psalm of David, when he fled from Absalom his son.

LORD, how are they increased that trouble me! many are they that rise up against me.

2 Many there be which say of my soul, There is no help for him in God. Selah.

3 But you, O LORD, are a shield for me; my glory, and the lifter up of my head.

4 I cried unto the LORD with my voice, and he heard me out of his holy hill. Selah.

5 I laid me down and slept; I awaked; for the LORD sustained me.

6 I will not be afraid of ten thousands of people, that have set themselves against me round about.

7 Arise, O LORD; save me, O my God: for you have smitten all my enemies upon the cheek bone; you have broken the teeth of the ungodly.

8 Salvation belongeth unto the LORD: your blessing is upon your people. Selah.

PSALM 4

To the chief Musician on Neginoth, A Psalm of David.

HEAR me when I call, O God of my righteousness: you have enlarged me when I was in distress; have mercy upon me, and hear my prayer.

2 O you sons of men, how long will you turn my glory into shame? how long will you love vanity, and seek after leasing? Selah.

3 But know that the LORD has set apart him that is godly for himself: the LORD will hear when I call unto him.

4 Stand in awe, and sin not: commune with your own heart upon your bed, and be still. Selah.

5 Offer the sacrifices of righteousness, and put your trust in the LORD.

6 There be many that say, Who will shew us any good? LORD, lift you up the light of your countenance upon us.

7 You have put gladness in my heart, more than in the time that their corn and their wine increased.

8 I will both lay me down in peace, and sleep: for you, LORD, only makest me dwell in safety.

PSALM 5

To the chief Musician upon Nehiloth, A Psalm of David.

GIVE ear to my words, O LORD, consider my meditation.

2 Hearken unto the voice of my cry, my King, and my God: for unto you will I pray.

3 My voice shalt you hear in the morning, O LORD; in the morning will I direct my prayer unto you, and will look up.

4 For you are not a God that has pleasure in wickedness: neither shall evil dwell with you.

5 The foolish shall not stand in your sight: you hatest all workers of iniquity.

6 You shalt destroy them that speak leasing: the LORD will abhor the bloody and deceitful man.

7 But as for me, I will come into your house in the multitude of your mercy: and in your fear will I worship toward your holy temple.

8 Lead me, O LORD, in your righteousness because of my enemies; make your way straight before my face.

9 For there is no faithfulness in their mouth; their inward part is very wickedness; their throat is an open sepulchre; they flatter with their tongue.

10 Destroy you them, O God; let them fall by their own counsels; cast them out in the multitude of their transgressions; for they have rebelled against you.

11 But let all those that put their trust in you rejoice: let them ever shout for joy, because you defendest them: let them also that love your name be joyful in you.

12 For you, LORD, will bless the righteous; with favour will you compass him as with a shield.

PSALM 6

To the chief Musician on Neginoth upon Sheminith, A Psalm of David.

O LORD, rebuke me not in yours anger, neither chasten me in your hot displeasure.

2 Have mercy upon me, O LORD; for I am weak: O LORD, heal me; for my bones are vexed.

3 My soul is also sore vexed: but you, O LORD, how long?

4 Return, O LORD, deliver my soul: oh save me for your mercies' sake.

5 For in death there is no remembrance of you: in the grave who shall give you thanks?

6 I am weary with my groaning; all the night make I my bed to swim; I water my couch with my tears.

7 My eye is consumed because of grief; it waxeth old because of all my enemies.

8 Depart from me, all you workers of iniquity; for the LORD has heard the voice of my weeping.

9 The LORD has heard my supplication; the LORD will receive my prayer.

10 Let all my enemies be ashamed and sore vexed: let them return and be ashamed suddenly.

PSALM 7

Shiggaion of David, which he sang unto the LORD, concerning the words of Cush the Benjamite.

O LORD my God, in you do I put my trust: save me from all them that persecute me, and deliver me:

2 Lest he tear my soul like a lion, rending it in pieces, while there is none to deliver.

3 O LORD my God, if I have done this; if there be iniquity in my hands;

4 If I have rewarded evil unto him that was at peace with me; (yea, I have delivered him that without cause is my enemy:)

5 Let the enemy persecute my soul, and take it; yea, let him tread down my life upon the earth, and lay my honour in the dust. Selah.

6 Arise, O LORD, in yours anger, lift up yourself because of the rage of my enemies: and awake for me to the judgment that you have commanded.

7 So shall the congregation of the people compass you about: for their sakes therefore return you on high.

8 The LORD shall judge the people: judge me, O LORD, according to my righteousness, and according to my integrity that is in me.

9 Oh let the wickedness of the wicked come to an end; but establish the just: for the righteous God trieth the hearts and reins.

10 My defence is of God, which saveth the upright in heart.

11 God judgeth the righteous, and God is angry with the wicked every day.

12 If he turn not, he will whet his sword; he has bent his bow, and made it ready.

13 He has also prepared for him the instruments of death; he ordaineth his arrows against the persecutors.

14 Behold, he travaileth with iniquity, and has conceived mischief, and brought forth falsehood.

15 He made a pit, and digged it, and is fallen into the ditch which he made.

16 His mischief shall return upon his own head, and his violent dealing shall come down upon his own pate.

17 I will praise the LORD according to his righteousness: and will sing praise to the name of the LORD most high.

PSALM 8

To the chief Musician upon Gittith, A Psalm of David.

O LORD our Lord, how excellent is your name in all the earth! who have set your glory above the heavens.

2 Out of the mouth of babes and sucklings have you ordained strength because of yours enemies, that you mightest still the enemy and the avenger.

3 When I consider your heavens, the work of your fingers, the moon and the stars, which you have ordained;

4 What is man, that you are mindful of him? and the son of man, that you visitest him?

5 For you have made him a little lower than the angels, and have crowned him with glory and honour.

6 You madest him to have dominion over the works of your hands; you have put all things under his feet:

7 All sheep and oxen, yea, and the beasts of the field;

8 The fowl of the air, and the fish of the sea, and whatsoever passes through the paths of the seas.

9 O LORD our Lord, how excellent is your name in all the earth!

PSALM 9

To the chief Musician upon Muth-labben, A Psalm of David.

I WILL praise you, O LORD, with my whole heart; I will shew forth all your marvellous works.

2 I will be glad and rejoice in you: I will sing praise to your name, O you most High.

3 When my enemies are turned back, they shall fall and perish at your presence.

4 For you have maintained my right and my cause; you satest in the throne judging right.

5 You have rebuked the heathen, you have destroyed the wicked, you have put out their name for ever and ever.

6 O you enemy, destructions are come to a perpetual end: and you have destroyed cities; their memorial is perished with them.

7 But the LORD shall endure for ever: he has prepared his throne for judgment.

8 And he shall judge the world in righteousness, he shall minister judgment to the people in uprightness.

9 The LORD also will be a refuge for the oppressed, a refuge in times of trouble.

10 And they that know your name will put their trust in you: for you , LORD, have not forsaken them that seek you.

11 Sing praises to the LORD, which dwelleth in Zion: declare among the people his doings.

12 When he maketh inquisition for blood, he remembereth them: he forgetteth not the cry of the humble.

13 Have mercy upon me, O LORD; consider my trouble which I suffer of them that hate me, you that liftest me up from the gates of death:

14 That I may shew forth all your praise in the gates of the daughter of Zion: I will rejoice in your salvation.

15 The heathen are sunk down in the pit that they made: in the net which they hid is their own foot taken.

16 The LORD is known by the judgment which he executeth: the wicked is snared in the work of his own hands. Higgaion. Selah.

17 The wicked shall be turned into hell, and all the nations that forget God.

18 For the needy shall not alway be forgotten: the expectation of the poor shall not perish for ever.

19 Arise, O LORD; let not man prevail: let the heathen be judged in your sight.

20 Put them in fear, O LORD: that the nations may know themselves to be but men. Selah.

PSALM 10

WHY standest you afar off, O LORD? why hidest you yourself in times of trouble?

2 The wicked in his pride doth persecute the poor: let them be taken in the devices that they have imagined.

3 For the wicked boasteth of his heart's desire, and blesseth the covetous, whom the LORD abhorreth.

4 The wicked, through the pride of his countenance, will not seek after God: God is not in all his thoughts.

5 His ways are always grievous; your judgments are far above out of his sight: as for all his enemies, he puffeth at them.

6 He has said in his heart, I shall not be moved: for I shall never be in adversity.

7 His mouth is full of cursing and deceit and fraud: under his tongue is mischief and vanity.

8 He sitteth in the lurking places of the villages: in the secret places doth he murder the innocent: his eyes are privily set against the poor.

9 He lies in wait secretly as a lion in his den: he lies in wait to catch the poor: he doth catch the poor, when he draweth him into his net.

10 He croucheth, and humbleth himself, that the poor may fall by his strong ones.

11 He has said in his heart, God has forgotten: he hideth his face; he will never see it.

12 Arise, O LORD; O God, lift up yours hand: forget not the humble.

13 Wherefore doth the wicked contemn God? he has said in his heart, You will not require it.

14 You have seen it; for you beholdest mischief and spite, to requite it with your hand: the poor committeth himself unto you; you are the helper of the fatherless.

15 Break you the arm of the wicked and the evil man: seek out his wickedness till you find none.

16 The LORD is King for ever and ever: the heathen are perished out of his land.

17 LORD, you have heard the desire of the humble: you will prepare their heart, you will cause yours ear to hear:

18 To judge the fatherless and the oppressed, that the man of the earth may no more oppress.

PSALM 11

To the chief Musician, A Psalm of David.

IN the LORD put I my trust: how say you to my soul, Flee as a bird to your mountain?

2 For, lo, the wicked bend their bow, they make ready their arrow upon the string, that they may privily shoot at the upright in heart.

3 If the foundations be destroyed, what can the righteous do?

4 The LORD is in his holy temple, the LORD's throne is in heaven: his eyes behold, his eyelids try, the children of men.

5 The LORD trieth the righteous: but the wicked and him that loveth violence his soul hateth.

6 Upon the wicked he shall rain snares, fire and brimstone, and an horrible tempest: this shall be the portion of their cup.

7 For the righteous LORD loveth righteousness; his countenance doth behold the upright.

PSALM 12

To the chief Musician upon Sheminith, A Psalm of David.

HELP, LORD; for the godly man ceaseth; for the faithful fail from among the children of men.

2 They speak vanity every one with his neighbour: with flattering lips and with a double heart do they speak.

3 The LORD shall cut off all flattering lips, and the tongue that speaketh proud things:

4 Who have said, With our tongue will we prevail; our lips are our own: who is lord over us?

5 For the oppression of the poor, for the sighing of the needy, now will I arise, saith the LORD; I will set him in safety from him that puffeth at him.

6 The words of the LORD are pure words: as silver tried in a furnace of earth, purified seven times.

7 You shalt keep them, O LORD, you shalt preserve them from this generation for ever.

8 The wicked walk on every side, when the vilest men are exalted.

PSALM 13

To the chief Musician, A Psalm of David.

HOW long will you forget me, O LORD? for ever? how long will you hide your face from me?

2 How long shall I take counsel in my soul, having sorrow in my heart daily? how long shall my enemy be exalted over me?

3 Consider and hear me, O LORD my God: lighten my eyes, lest I sleep the sleep of death;

4 Lest my enemy say, I have prevailed against him; and those that trouble me rejoice when I am moved.

5 But I have trusted in your mercy; my heart shall rejoice in your salvation.

6 I will sing unto the LORD, because he has dealt bountifully with me.

PSALM 14

To the chief Musician, A Psalm of David.

THE fool has said in his heart, There is no God. They are corrupt, they have done abominable works, there is none that doeth good.

2 The LORD looked down from heaven upon the children of men, to see if there were any that did understand, and seek God.

3 They are all gone aside, they are all together become filthy: there is none that doeth good, no, not one.

4 Have all the workers of iniquity no knowledge? who eat up my people as they eat bread, and call not upon the LORD.

5 There were they in great fear: for God is in the generation of the righteous.

6 You have shamed the counsel of the poor, because the LORD is his refuge.

7 Oh that the salvation of Israel were come out of Zion! when the LORD bringeth back the captivity of his people, Jacob shall rejoice, and Israel shall be glad.

PSALM 15

A Psalm of David.

LORD, who shall abide in your tabernacle? who shall dwell in your holy hill?

2 He that walketh uprightly, and worketh righteousness, and speaketh the truth in his heart.

3 He that backbiteth not with his tongue, nor doeth evil to his neighbour, nor taketh up a reproach against his neighbour.

4 In whose eyes a vile person is contemned; but he honoureth them that fear the LORD. He that sweareth to his own hurt, and changeth not.

5 He that putteth not out his money to usury, nor taketh reward against the innocent. He that doeth these things shall never be moved.

PSALM 16

Michtam of David.

PRESERVE me, O God: for in you do I put my trust.

2 O my soul, you have said unto the LORD, You are my Lord: my goodness extendeth not to you;

3 But to the saints that are in the earth, and to the excellent, in whom is all my delight.

4 Their sorrows shall be multiplied that hasten after another god: their drink offerings of blood will I not offer, nor take up their names into my lips.

5 The LORD is the portion of my inheritance and of my cup: you maintainest my lot.

6 The lines are fallen unto me in pleasant places; yea, I have a goodly heritage.

7 I will bless the LORD, who has given me counsel: my reins also instruct me in the night seasons.

8 I have set the LORD always before me: because he is at my right hand, I shall not be moved.

9 Therefore my heart is glad, and my glory rejoiceth: my flesh also shall rest in hope.

10 For you will not leave my soul in hell; neither will you suffer yours Holy One to see corruption.

11 You will shew me the path of life: in your presence is fulness of joy; at your right hand there are pleasures for evermore.

PSALM 17

A Prayer of David.

HEAR the right, O LORD, attend unto my cry, give ear unto my prayer, that goeth not out of feigned lips.

2 Let my sentence come forth from your presence; let yours eyes behold the things that are equal.

3 You have proved my heart; you have visited me in the night; you have tried me, and shalt find nothing; I am purposed that my mouth shall not transgress.

4 Concerning the works of men, by the word of your lips I have kept me from the paths of the destroyer.

5 Hold up my goings in your paths, that my footsteps slip not.

6 I have called upon you, for you will hear me, O God: incline yours ear unto me, and hear my speech.

7 Shew your marvellous lovingkindness, O you that savest by your right hand them which put their trust in you from those that rise up against them.

8 Keep me as the apple of the eye, hide me under the shadow of your wings,

9 From the wicked that oppress me, from my deadly enemies, who compass me about.

10 They are inclosed in their own fat: with their mouth they speak proudly.

11 They have now compassed us in our steps: they have set their eyes bowing down to the earth;

12 Like as a lion that is greedy of his prey, and as it were a young lion lurking in secret places.

13 Arise, O LORD, disappoint him, cast him down: deliver my soul from the wicked, which is your sword:

14 From men which are your hand, O LORD, from men of the world, which have their portion in this life, and whose belly you fillest with your hid treasure: they are full of children, and leave the rest of their substance to their babes.

15 As for me, I will behold your face in righteousness: I shall be satisfied, when I awake, with your likeness.

PSALM 18

To the chief Musician, A Psalm of David, the servant of the LORD, who spake unto the LORD the words of this song in the day that the LORD delivered him from the hand of all his enemies, and from the hand of Saul: And he said,

I WILL love you, O LORD, my strength.

2 The LORD is my rock, and my fortress, and my deliverer; my God, my strength, in whom I will trust; my buckler, and the horn of my salvation, and my high tower.

3 I will call upon the LORD, who is worthy to be praised: so shall I be saved from my enemies.

4 The sorrows of death compassed me, and the floods of ungodly men made me afraid.

5 The sorrows of hell compassed me about: the snares of death prevented me.

6 In my distress I called upon the LORD, and cried unto my God: he heard my voice out of his temple, and my cry came before him, even into his ears.

7 Then the earth shook and trembled; the foundations also of the hills moved and were shaken, because he was wroth.

8 There went up a smoke out of his nostrils, and fire out of his mouth devoured: coals were kindled by it.

9 He bowed the heavens also, and came down: and darkness was under his feet.

10 And he rode upon a cherub, and did fly: yea, he did fly upon the wings of the wind.

11 He made darkness his secret place; his pavilion round about him were dark waters and thick clouds of the skies.

12 At the brightness that was before him his thick clouds passed, hail stones and coals of fire.

13 The LORD also thundered in the heavens, and the Highest gave his voice; hail stones and coals of fire.

14 Yea, he sent out his arrows, and scattered them; and he shot out lightnings, and discomfited them.

15 Then the channels of waters were seen, and the foundations of the world were discovered at your rebuke, O LORD, at the blast of the breath of your nostrils.

16 He sent from above, he took me, he drew me out of many waters.

17 He delivered me from my strong enemy, and from them which hated me: for they were too strong for me.

18 They prevented me in the day of my calamity: but the LORD was my stay.

19 He brought me forth also into a large place; he delivered me, because he delighted in me.

20 The LORD rewarded me according to my righteousness; according to the cleanness of my hands has he recompensed me.

21 For I have kept the ways of the LORD, and have not wickedly departed from my God.

22 For all his judgments were before me, and I did not put away his statutes from me.

23 I was also upright before him, and I kept myself from my iniquity.

24 Therefore has the LORD recompensed me according to my righteousness, according to the cleanness of my hands in his eyesight.

25 With the merciful you will shew yourself merciful; with an upright man you will shew yourself upright;

26 With the pure you will shew yourself pure; and with the froward you will shew yourself froward.

27 For you will save the afflicted people; but will bring down high looks.

28 For you will light my candle: the LORD my God will enlighten my darkness.

29 For by you I have run through a troop; and by my God have I leaped over a wall.

30 As for God, his way is perfect: the word of the LORD is tried: he is a buckler to all those that trust in him.

31 For who is God save the LORD? or who is a rock save our God?

32 It is God that girdeth me with strength, and maketh my way perfect.

33 He maketh my feet like hinds' feet, and setteth me upon my high places.

34 He teacheth my hands to war, so that a bow of steel is broken by my arms.

35 You have also given me the shield of your salvation: and your right hand has holden me up, and your gentleness has made me great.

36 You have enlarged my steps under me, that my feet did not slip.

37 I have pursued my enemies, and overtaken them: neither did I turn again till they were consumed.

38 I have wounded them that they were not able to rise: they are fallen under my feet.

39 For you have girded me with strength unto the battle: you have subdued under me those that rose up against me.

40 You have also given me the necks of my enemies; that I might destroy them that hate me.

41 They cried, but there was none to save them: even unto the LORD, but he answered them not.

42 Then did I beat them small as the dust before the wind: I did cast them out as the dirt in the streets.

43 You have delivered me from the strivings of the people; and you have made me the head of the heathen: a people whom I have not known shall serve me.

44 As soon as they hear of me, they shall obey me: the strangers shall submit themselves unto me.

45 The strangers shall fade away, and be afraid out of their close places.

46 The LORD liveth; and blessed be my rock; and let the God of my salvation be exalted.

47 It is God that avengeth me, and subdueth the people under me.

48 He delivereth me from my enemies: yea, you liftest me up above those that rise up against me: you have delivered me from the violent man.

49 Therefore will I give thanks unto you, O LORD, among the heathen, and sing praises unto your name.

50 Great deliverance giveth he to his king; and sheweth mercy to his anointed, to David, and to his seed for evermore.

PSALM 19

To the chief Musician, A Psalm of David.

THE heavens declare the glory of God; and the firmament sheweth his handywork.

2 Day unto day uttereth speech, and night unto night sheweth knowledge.

3 There is no speech nor language, where their voice is not heard.

4 Their line is gone out through all the earth, and their words to the end of the world. In them has he set a tabernacle for the sun,

5 Which is as a bridegroom coming out of his chamber, and rejoiceth as a strong man to run a race.

6 His going forth is from the end of the heaven, and his circuit unto the ends of it: and there is nothing hid from the heat thereof.

7 The law of the LORD is perfect, converting the soul: the testimony of the LORD is sure, making wise the simple.

8 The statutes of the LORD are right, rejoicing the heart: the commandment of the LORD is pure, enlightening the eyes.

9 The fear of the LORD is clean, enduring for ever: the judgments of the LORD are true and righteous altogether.

10 More to be desired are they than gold, yea, than much fine gold: sweeter also than honey and the honeycomb.

11 Moreover by them is your servant warned: and in keeping of them there is great reward.

12 Who can understand his errors? cleanse you me from secret faults.

13 Keep back your servant also from presumptuous sins; let them not have dominion over me: then shall I be upright, and I shall be innocent from the great transgression.

14 Let the words of my mouth, and the meditation of my heart, be acceptable in your sight, O LORD, my strength, and my redeemer.

PSALM 20

To the chief Musician, A Psalm of David.

THE LORD hear you in the day of trouble; the name of the God of Jacob defend you;

2 Send you help from the sanctuary, and strengthen you out of Zion;

3 Remember all your offerings, and accept your burnt sacrifice; Selah.

4 Grant you according to yours own heart, and fulfil all your counsel.

5 We will rejoice in your salvation, and in the name of our God we will set up our banners: the LORD fulfil all your petitions.

6 Now know I that the LORD saveth his anointed; he will hear him from his holy heaven with the saving strength of his right hand.

7 Some trust in chariots, and some in horses: but we will remember the name of the LORD our God.

8 They are brought down and fallen: but we are risen, and stand upright.

9 Save, LORD: let the king hear us when we call.

PSALM 21

To the chief Musician, A Psalm of David.

THE king shall joy in your strength, O LORD; and in your salvation how greatly shall he rejoice!

2 You have given him his heart's desire, and have not withholden the request of his lips. Selah.

3 For you preventest him with the blessings of goodness: you settest a crown of pure gold on his head.

4 He asked life of you, and you gavest it him, even length of days for ever and ever.

5 His glory is great in your salvation: honour and majesty have you laid upon him.

6 For you have made him most blessed for ever: you have made him exceeding glad with your countenance.

7 For the king trusteth in the LORD, and through the mercy of the most High he shall not be moved.

8 Yours hand shall find out all yours enemies: your right hand shall find out those that hate you.

9 You shalt make them as a fiery oven in the time of yours anger: the LORD shall swallow them up in his wrath, and the fire shall devour them.

10 Their fruit shalt you destroy from the earth, and their seed from among the children of men.

11 For they intended evil against you: they imagined a mischievous device, which they are not able to perform.

12 Therefore shalt you make them turn their back, when you shalt make ready yours arrows upon your strings against the face of them.

13 Be you exalted, LORD, in yours own strength: so will we sing and praise your power.

PSALM 22

To the chief Musician upon Aijeleth Shahar, A Psalm of David.

MY God, my God, why have you forsaken me? why are you so far from helping me, and from the words of my roaring?

2 O my God, I cry in the daytime, but you hearest not; and in the night season, and am not silent.

3 But you are holy, O you that inhabitest the praises of Israel.

4 Our fathers trusted in you: they trusted, and you did deliver them.

5 They cried unto you, and were delivered: they trusted in you, and were not confounded.

6 But I am a worm, and no man; a reproach of men, and despised of the people.

7 All they that see me laugh me to scorn: they shoot out the lip, they shake the head, saying,

8 He trusted on the LORD that he would deliver him: let him deliver him, seeing he delighted in him.

9 But you are he that took me out of the womb: you did make me hope when I was upon my mother's breasts.

10 I was cast upon you from the womb: you are my God from my mother's belly.

11 Be not far from me; for trouble is near; for there is none to help.

12 Many bulls have compassed me: strong bulls of Bashan have beset me round.

13 They gaped upon me with their mouths, as a ravening and a roaring lion.

14 I am poured out like water, and all my bones are out of joint: my heart is like wax; it is melted in the midst of my bowels.

15 My strength is dried up like a potsherd; and my tongue cleaveth to my jaws; and you have brought me into the dust of death.

16 For dogs have compassed me: the assembly of the wicked have inclosed me: they pierced my hands and my feet.

17 I may tell all my bones: they look and stare upon me.

18 They part my garments among them, and cast lots upon my vesture.

19 But be not you far from me, O LORD: O my strength, haste you to help me.

20 Deliver my soul from the sword; my darling from the power of the dog.

21 Save me from the lion's mouth: for you have heard me from the horns of the unicorns.

22 I will declare your name unto my brethren: in the midst of the congregation will I praise you.

23 You that fear the LORD, praise him; all you the seed of Jacob, glorify him; and fear him, all you the seed of Israel.

24 For he has not despised nor abhorred the affliction of the afflicted; neither has he hid his face from him; but when he cried unto him, he heard.

25 My praise shall be of you in the great congregation: I will pay my vows before them that fear him.

26 The meek shall eat and be satisfied: they shall praise the LORD that seek him: your heart shall live for ever.

27 All the ends of the world shall remember and turn unto the LORD: and all the kindreds of the nations shall worship before you.

28 For the kingdom is the LORD's: and he is the governor among the nations.

29 All they that be fat upon earth shall eat and worship: all they that go down to the dust shall bow before him: and none can keep alive his own soul.

30 A seed shall serve him; it shall be accounted to the Lord for a generation.

31 They shall come, and shall declare his righteousness unto a people that shall be born, that he has done this.

PSALM 23

A Psalm of David.

THE LORD is my shepherd; I shall not want.

2 He maketh me to lie down in green pastures: he leadeth me beside the still waters.

3 He restoreth my soul: he leadeth me in the paths of righteousness for his name's sake.

4 Yea, though I walk through the valley of the shadow of death, I will fear no evil: for you are with me; your rod and your staff they comfort me.

5 You preparest a table before me in the presence of my enemies: you anointest my head with oil; my cup runneth over.

6 Surely goodness and mercy shall follow me all the days of my life: and I will dwell in the house of the LORD for ever.

PSALM 24

A Psalm of David.

THE earth is the LORD's, and the fulness thereof; the world, and they that dwell therein.

2 For he has founded it upon the seas, and established it upon the floods.

3 Who shall ascend into the hill of the LORD? or who shall stand in his holy place?

4 He that has clean hands, and a pure heart; who has not lifted up his soul unto vanity, nor sworn deceitfully.

5 He shall receive the blessing from the LORD, and righteousness from the God of his salvation.

6 This is the generation of them that seek him, that seek your face, O Jacob. Selah.

7 Lift up your heads, O you gates; and be you lift up, you everlasting doors; and the King of glory shall come in.

8 Who is this King of glory? The LORD strong and mighty, the LORD mighty in battle.

9 Lift up your heads, O you gates; even lift them up, you everlasting doors; and the King of glory shall come in.

10 Who is this King of glory? The LORD of hosts, he is the King of glory. Selah.

PSALM 25

A Psalm of David.

UNTO you, O LORD, do I lift up my soul.

2 O my God, I trust in you: let me not be ashamed, let not my enemies triumph over me.

3 Yea, let none that wait on you be ashamed: let them be ashamed which transgress without cause.

4 Shew me your ways, O LORD; teach me your paths.

5 Lead me in your truth, and teach me: for you are the God of my salvation; on you do I wait all the day.

6 Remember, O LORD, your tender mercies and your lovingkindnesses; for they have been ever of old.

7 Remember not the sins of my youth, nor my transgressions: according to your mercy remember you me for your goodness' sake, O LORD.

8 Good and upright is the LORD: therefore will he teach sinners in the way.

9 The meek will he guide in judgment: and the meek will he teach his way.

10 All the paths of the LORD are mercy and truth unto such as keep his covenant and his testimonies.

11 For your name's sake, O LORD, pardon my iniquity; for it is great.

12 What man is he that feareth the LORD? him shall he teach in the way that he shall choose.

13 His soul shall dwell at ease; and his seed shall inherit the earth.

14 The secret of the LORD is with them that fear him; and he will shew them his covenant.

15 My eyes are ever toward the LORD; for he shall pluck my feet out of the net.

16 Turn you unto me, and have mercy upon me; for I am desolate and afflicted.

17 The troubles of my heart are enlarged: O bring you me out of my distresses.

18 Look upon my affliction and my pain; and forgive all my sins.

19 Consider my enemies; for they are many; and they hate me with cruel hatred.

20 O keep my soul, and deliver me: let me not be ashamed; for I put my trust in you.

21 Let integrity and uprightness preserve me; for I wait on you.

22 Redeem Israel, O God, out of all his troubles.

PSALM 26

A Psalm of David.

JUDGE me, O LORD; for I have walked in my integrity: I have trusted also in the LORD; therefore I shall not slide.

2 Examine me, O LORD, and prove me; try my reins and my heart.

3 For your lovingkindness is before my eyes: and I have walked in your truth.

4 I have not sat with vain persons, neither will I go in with dissemblers.

5 I have hated the congregation of evil doers; and will not sit with the wicked.

6 I will wash my hands in innocency: so will I compass yours altar, O LORD:

7 That I may publish with the voice of thanksgiving, and tell of all your wondrous works.

8 LORD, I have loved the habitation of your house, and the place where yours honour dwelleth.

9 Gather not my soul with sinners, nor my life with bloody men:

10 In whose hands is mischief, and their right hand is full of bribes.

11 But as for me, I will walk in my integrity: redeem me, and be merciful unto me.

12 My foot standeth in an even place: in the congregations will I bless the LORD.

PSALM 27

A Psalm of David.

THE LORD is my light and my salvation; whom shall I fear? the LORD is the strength of my life; of whom shall I be afraid?

2 When the wicked, even my enemies and my foes, came upon me to eat up my flesh, they stumbled and fell.

3 Though an host should encamp against me, my heart shall not fear: though war should rise against me, in this will I be confident.

4 One thing have I desired of the LORD, that will I seek after; that I may dwell in the house of the LORD all the days of my life, to behold the beauty of the LORD, and to inquire in his temple.

5 For in the time of trouble he shall hide me in his pavilion: in the secret of his tabernacle shall he hide me; he shall set me up upon a rock.

6 And now shall my head be lifted up above my enemies round about me: therefore will I offer in his tabernacle sacrifices of joy; I will sing, yea, I will sing praises unto the LORD.

7 Hear, O LORD, when I cry with my voice: have mercy also upon me, and answer me.

8 When you saidst, Seek you my face; my heart said unto you, Your face, LORD, will I seek.

9 Hide not your face far from me; put not your servant away in anger: you have been my help; leave me not, neither forsake me, O God of my salvation.

10 When my father and my mother forsake me, then the LORD will take me up.

11 Teach me your way, O LORD, and lead me in a plain path, because of my enemies.

12 Deliver me not over unto the will of my enemies: for false witnesses are risen up against me, and such as breathe out cruelty.

13 I had fainted, unless I had believed to see the goodness of the LORD in the land of the living.

14 Wait on the LORD: be of good courage, and he shall strengthen yours heart: wait, I say, on the LORD.

PSALM 28

A Psalm of David.

UNTO you will I cry, O LORD my rock; be not silent to me: lest, if you be silent to me, I become like them that go down into the pit.

2 Hear the voice of my supplications, when I cry unto you, when I lift up my hands toward your holy oracle.

3 Draw me not away with the wicked, and with the workers of iniquity, which speak peace to their neighbours, but mischief is in their hearts.

4 Give them according to their deeds, and according to the wickedness of their endeavours: give them after the work of their hands; render to them their desert.

5 Because they regard not the works of the LORD, nor the operation of his hands, he shall destroy them, and not build them up.

6 Blessed be the LORD, because he has heard the voice of my supplications.

7 The LORD is my strength and my shield; my heart trusted in him, and I am helped: therefore my heart greatly rejoiceth; and with my song will I praise him.

8 The LORD is their strength, and he is the saving strength of his anointed.

9 Save your people, and bless yours inheritance: feed them also, and lift them up for ever.

PSALM 29

A Psalm of David.

GIVE unto the LORD, O you mighty, give unto the LORD glory and strength.

2 Give unto the LORD the glory due unto his name; worship the LORD in the beauty of holiness.

3 The voice of the LORD is upon the waters: the God of glory thundereth: the LORD is upon many waters.

4 The voice of the LORD is powerful; the voice of the LORD is full of majesty.

5 The voice of the LORD breaketh the cedars; yea, the LORD breaketh the cedars of Lebanon.

6 He maketh them also to skip like a calf; Lebanon and Sirion like a young unicorn.

7 The voice of the LORD divideth the flames of fire.

8 The voice of the LORD shaketh the wilderness; the LORD shaketh the wilderness of Kadesh.

9 The voice of the LORD maketh the hinds to calve, and discovereth the forests: and in his temple doth every one speak of his glory.

10 The LORD sitteth upon the flood; yea, the LORD sitteth King for ever.

11 The LORD will give strength unto his people; the LORD will bless his people with peace.

PSALM 30

A Psalm and Song at the dedication of the house of David.

I WILL extol you, O LORD; for you have lifted me up, and have not made my foes to rejoice over me.

2 O LORD my God, I cried unto you, and you have healed me.

3 O LORD, you have brought up my soul from the grave: you have kept me alive, that I should not go down to the pit.

4 Sing unto the LORD, O you saints of his, and give thanks at the remembrance of his holiness.

5 For his anger endureth but a moment; in his favour is life: weeping may endure for a night, but joy comes in the morning.

6 And in my prosperity I said, I shall never be moved.

7 LORD, by your favour you have made my mountain to stand strong: you did hide your face, and I was troubled.

8 I cried to you, O LORD; and unto the LORD I made supplication.

9 What profit is there in my blood, when I go down to the pit? Shall the dust praise you? shall it declare your truth?

10 Hear, O LORD, and have mercy upon me: LORD, be you my helper.

11 You have turned for me my mourning into dancing: you have put off my sackcloth, and girded me with gladness;

12 To the end that my glory may sing praise to you, and not be silent. O LORD my God, I will give thanks unto you for ever.

PSALM 31
To the chief Musician, A Psalm of David.

IN you, O LORD, do I put my trust; let me never be ashamed: deliver me in your righteousness.

2 Bow down yours ear to me; deliver me speedily: be you my strong rock, for an house of defence to save me.

3 For you are my rock and my fortress; therefore for your name's sake lead me, and guide me.

4 Pull me out of the net that they have laid privily for me: for you are my strength.

5 Into yours hand I commit my spirit: you have redeemed me, O LORD God of truth.

6 I have hated them that regard lying vanities: but I trust in the LORD.

7 I will be glad and rejoice in your mercy: for you have considered my trouble; you have known my soul in adversities;

8 And have not shut me up into the hand of the enemy: you have set my feet in a large room.

9 Have mercy upon me, O LORD, for I am in trouble: my eye is consumed with grief, yea, my soul and my belly.

10 For my life is spent with grief, and my years with sighing: my strength faileth because of my iniquity, and my bones are consumed.

11 I was a reproach among all my enemies, but especially among my neighbours, and a fear to my acquaintance: they that did see me without fled from me.

12 I am forgotten as a dead man out of mind: I am like a broken vessel.

13 For I have heard the slander of many: fear was on every side: while they took counsel together against me, they devised to take away my life.

14 But I trusted in you, O LORD: I said, You are my God.

15 My times are in your hand: deliver me from the hand of my enemies, and from them that persecute me.

16 Make your face to shine upon your servant: save me for your mercies' sake.

17 Let me not be ashamed, O LORD; for I have called upon you: let the wicked be ashamed, and let them be silent in the grave.

18 Let the lying lips be put to silence; which speak grievous things proudly and contemptuously against the righteous.

19 Oh how great is your goodness, which you have laid up for them that fear you; which you have created for them that trust in you before the sons of men!

20 You shalt hide them in the secret of your presence from the pride of man: you shalt keep them secretly in a pavilion from the strife of tongues.

21 Blessed be the LORD: for he has shewed me his marvellous kindness in a strong city.

22 For I said in my haste, I am cut off from before yours eyes: nevertheless you heardest the voice of my supplications when I cried unto you.

23 O love the LORD, all you his saints: for the LORD preserveth the faithful, and plentifully rewardeth the proud doer.

24 Be of good courage, and he shall strengthen your heart, all you that hope in the LORD.

PSALM 32
A Psalm of David, Maschil.

BLESSED is he whose transgression is forgiven, whose sin is covered.

2 Blessed is the man unto whom the LORD imputeth not iniquity, and in whose spirit there is no guile.

3 When I kept silence, my bones waxed old through my roaring all the day long.

4 For day and night your hand was heavy upon me: my moisture is turned into the drought of summer. Selah.

5 I acknowledged my sin unto you, and my iniquity have I not hid. I said, I will confess my transgressions unto the LORD; and you forgavest the iniquity of my sin. Selah.

6 For this shall every one that is godly pray unto you in a time when you mayest be found: surely in the floods of great waters they shall not come nigh unto him.

7 You are my hiding place; you shalt preserve me from trouble; you shalt compass me about with songs of deliverance. Selah.

8 I will instruct you and teach you in the way which you shalt go: I will guide you with my eye.

9 Be you not as the horse, or as the mule, which have no understanding: whose mouth must be held in with bit and bridle, lest they come near unto you.

10 Many sorrows shall be to the wicked: but he that trusteth in the LORD, mercy shall compass him about.

11 Be glad in the LORD, and rejoice, you righteous: and shout for joy, all you that are upright in heart.

PSALM 33
REJOICE in the LORD, O you righteous: for praise is comely for the upright.

2 Praise the LORD with harp: sing unto him with the psaltery and an instrument of ten strings.

3 Sing unto him a new song; play skilfully with a loud noise.

4 For the word of the LORD is right; and all his works are done in truth.

5 He loveth righteousness and judgment: the earth is full of the goodness of the LORD.

6 By the word of the LORD were the heavens made; and all the host of them by the breath of his mouth.

7 He gathereth the waters of the sea together as an heap: he layeth up the depth in storehouses.

8 Let all the earth fear the LORD: let all the inhabitants of the world stand in awe of him.

9 For he spake, and it was done; he commanded, and it stood fast.

10 The LORD bringeth the counsel of the heathen to nought: he maketh the devices of the people of none effect.

11 The counsel of the LORD standeth for ever, the thoughts of his heart to all generations.

12 Blessed is the nation whose God is the LORD; and the people whom he has chosen for his own inheritance.

13 The LORD looketh from heaven; he beholdeth all the sons of men.

14 From the place of his habitation he looketh upon all the inhabitants of the earth.

15 He fashioneth their hearts alike; he considereth all their works.

16 There is no king saved by the multitude of an host: a mighty man is not delivered by much strength.

17 An horse is a vain thing for safety: neither shall he deliver any by his great strength.

18 Behold, the eye of the LORD is upon them that fear him, upon them that hope in his mercy;

19 To deliver their soul from death, and to keep them alive in famine.

20 Our soul waiteth for the LORD: he is our help and our shield.

21 For our heart shall rejoice in him, because we have trusted in his holy name.

22 Let your mercy, O LORD, be upon us, according as we hope in you.

PSALM 34
A Psalm of David, when he changed his behaviour before Abimelech; who drove him away, and he departed.

I WILL bless the LORD at all times: his praise shall continually be in my mouth.

2 My soul shall make her boast in the LORD: the humble shall hear thereof, and be glad.

3 O magnify the LORD with me, and let us exalt his name together.

4 I sought the LORD, and he heard me, and delivered me from all my fears.

5 They looked unto him, and were lightened: and their faces were not ashamed.

6 This poor man cried, and the LORD heard him, and saved him out of all his troubles.

7 The angel of the LORD encampeth round about them that fear him, and delivereth them.

8 O taste and see that the LORD is good: blessed is the man that trusteth in him.

9 O fear the LORD, you his saints: for there is no want to them that fear him.

10 The young lions do lack, and suffer hunger: but they that seek the LORD shall not want any good thing.

11 Come, you children, hearken unto me: I will teach you the fear of the LORD.

12 What man is he that desireth life, and loveth many days, that he may see good?

13 Keep your tongue from evil, and your lips from speaking guile.

14 Depart from evil, and do good; seek peace, and pursue it.

15 The eyes of the LORD are upon the righteous, and his ears are open unto their cry.

16 The face of the LORD is against them that do evil, to cut off the remembrance of them from the earth.

17 The righteous cry, and the LORD heareth, and delivereth them out of all their troubles.

18 The LORD is nigh unto them that are of a broken heart; and saveth such as be of a contrite spirit.

19 Many are the afflictions of the righteous: but the LORD delivereth him out of them all.

20 He keepeth all his bones: not one of them is broken.

21 Evil shall slay the wicked: and they that hate the righteous shall be desolate.

22 The LORD redeemeth the soul of his servants: and none of them that trust in him shall be desolate.

PSALM 35
A Psalm of David.

PLEAD my cause, O LORD, with them that strive with me: fight against them that fight against me.

2 Take hold of shield and buckler, and stand up for my help.

3 Draw out also the spear, and stop the way against them that persecute me: say unto my soul, I am your salvation.

4 Let them be confounded and put to shame that seek after my soul: let them be turned back and brought to confusion that devise my hurt.

5 Let them be as chaff before the wind: and let the angel of the LORD chase them.

6 Let their way be dark and slippery: and let the angel of the LORD persecute them.

7 For without cause have they hid for me their net in a pit, which without cause they have digged for my soul.

8 Let destruction come upon him at unawares; and let his net that he has hid catch himself: into that very destruction let him fall.

9 And my soul shall be joyful in the LORD: it shall rejoice in his salvation.

10 All my bones shall say, LORD, who is like unto you, which deliverest the poor from him that is too strong for him, yea, the poor and the needy from him that spoileth him?

11 False witnesses did rise up; they laid to my charge things that I knew not.

12 They rewarded me evil for good to the spoiling of my soul.

13 But as for me, when they were sick, my clothing was sackcloth: I humbled my soul with fasting; and my prayer returned into my own bosom.

14 I behaved myself as though he had been my friend or brother: I bowed down heavily, as one that mourneth for his mother.

15 But in my adversity they rejoiced, and gathered themselves together: yea, the abjects gathered themselves together against me, and I knew it not; they did tear me, and ceased not:

16 With hypocritical mockers in feasts, they gnashed upon me with their teeth.

17 Lord, how long will you look on? rescue my soul from their destructions, my darling from the lions.

18 I will give you thanks in the great congregation: I will praise you among much people.

19 Let not them that are my enemies wrongfully rejoice over me: neither let them wink with the eye that hate me without a cause.

20 For they speak not peace: but they devise deceitful matters against them that are quiet in the land.

21 Yea, they opened their mouth wide against me, and said, Aha, aha, our eye has seen it.

22 This you have seen, O LORD: keep not silence: O Lord, be not far from me.

23 Stir up yourself, and awake to my judgment, even unto my cause, my God and my Lord.

24 Judge me, O LORD my God, according to your righteousness; and let them not rejoice over me.

25 Let them not say in their hearts, Ah, so would we have it: let them not say, We have swallowed him up.

26 Let them be ashamed and brought to confusion together that rejoice at my hurt: let them be clothed with shame and dishonour that magnify themselves against me.

27 Let them shout for joy, and be glad, that favour my righteous cause: yea, let them say continually, Let the LORD be magnified, which has pleasure in the prosperity of his servant.

28 And my tongue shall speak of your righteousness and of your praise all the day long.

PSALM 36
To the chief Musician, A Psalm of David the servant of the LORD.

THE transgression of the wicked saith within my heart, that there is no fear of God before his eyes.

2 For he flattereth himself in his own eyes, until his iniquity be found to be hateful.

3 The words of his mouth are iniquity and deceit: he has left off to be wise, and to do good.

4 He deviseth mischief upon his bed; he setteth himself in a way that is not good; he abhorreth not evil.

5 Your mercy, O LORD, is in the heavens; and your faithfulness reacheth unto the clouds.

6 Your righteousness is like the great mountains; your judgments are a great deep: O LORD, you preservest man and beast.

7 How excellent is your lovingkindness, O God! therefore the children of men put their trust under the shadow of your wings.

8 They shall be abundantly satisfied with the fatness of your house; and you shalt make them drink of the river of your pleasures.

9 For with you is the fountain of life: in your light shall we see light.

10 O continue your lovingkindness unto them that know you; and your righteousness to the upright in heart.

11 Let not the foot of pride come against me, and let not the hand of the wicked remove me.

12 There are the workers of iniquity fallen: they are cast down, and shall not be able to rise.

PSALM 37
A Psalm of David.

FRET not yourself because of evildoers, neither be you envious against the workers of iniquity.

2 For they shall soon be cut down like the grass, and wither as the green herb.

3 Trust in the LORD, and do good; so shalt you dwell in the land, and verily you shalt be fed.

4 Delight yourself also in the LORD; and he shall give you the desires of yours heart.

5 Commit your way unto the LORD; trust also in him; and he shall bring it to pass.

6 And he shall bring forth your righteousness as the light, and your judgment as the noonday.

7 Rest in the LORD, and wait patiently for him: fret not yourself because of him who prospereth in his way, because of the man who bringeth wicked devices to pass.

8 Cease from anger, and forsake wrath: fret not yourself in any wise to do evil.

9 For evildoers shall be cut off: but those that wait upon the LORD, they shall inherit the earth.

10 For yet a little while, and the wicked shall not be: yea, you shalt diligently consider his place, and it shall not be.

11 But the meek shall inherit the earth; and shall delight themselves in the abundance of peace.

12 The wicked plotteth against the just, and gnasheth upon him with his teeth.

13 The Lord shall laugh at him: for he seeth that his day is coming.

14 The wicked have drawn out the sword, and have bent their bow, to cast down the poor and needy, and to slay such as be of upright conversation.

15 Their sword shall enter into their own heart, and their bows shall be broken.

16 A little that a righteous man has is better than the riches of many wicked.

17 For the arms of the wicked shall be broken: but the LORD upholdeth the righteous.

18 The LORD knoweth the days of the upright: and their inheritance shall be for ever.

19 They shall not be ashamed in the evil time: and in the days of famine they shall be satisfied.

20 But the wicked shall perish, and the enemies of the LORD shall be as the fat of lambs: they shall consume; into smoke shall they consume away.

21 The wicked borroweth, and payeth not again: but the righteous sheweth mercy, and giveth.

22 For such as be blessed of him shall inherit the earth; and they that be cursed of him shall be cut off.

23 The steps of a good man are ordered by the LORD: and he delighteth in his way.

24 Though he fall, he shall not be utterly cast down: for the LORD upholdeth him with his hand.

25 I have been young, and now am old; yet have I not seen the righteous forsaken, nor his seed begging bread.

26 He is ever merciful, and lendeth; and his seed is blessed.

27 Depart from evil, and do good; and dwell for evermore.

28 For the LORD loveth judgment, and forsaketh not his saints; they are preserved for ever: but the seed of the wicked shall be cut off.

29 The righteous shall inherit the land, and dwell therein for ever.

30 The mouth of the righteous speaketh wisdom, and his tongue talketh of judgment.

31 The law of his God is in his heart; none of his steps shall slide.

32 The wicked watcheth the righteous, and seeketh to slay him.

33 The LORD will not leave him in his hand, nor condemn him when he is judged.

34 Wait on the LORD, and keep his way, and he shall exalt you to inherit the land: when the wicked are cut off, you shalt see it.

35 I have seen the wicked in great power, and spreading himself like a green bay tree.

36 Yet he passed away, and, lo, he was not: yea, I sought him, but he could not be found.

37 Mark the perfect man, and behold the upright: for the end of that man is peace.

38 But the transgressors shall be destroyed together: the end of the wicked shall be cut off.

39 But the salvation of the righteous is of the LORD: he is their strength in the time of trouble.

40 And the LORD shall help them, and deliver them: he shall deliver them from the wicked, and save them, because they trust in him.

PSALM 38

A Psalm of David, to bring to remembrance.

O LORD, rebuke me not in your wrath: neither chasten me in your hot displeasure.

2 For yours arrows stick fast in me, and your hand presseth me sore.

3 There is no soundness in my flesh because of yours anger; neither is there any rest in my bones because of my sin.

4 For my iniquities are gone over my head: as an heavy burden they are too heavy for me.

5 My wounds stink and are corrupt because of my foolishness.

6 I am troubled; I am bowed down greatly; I go mourning all the day long.

7 For my loins are filled with a loathsome disease: and there is no soundness in my flesh.

8 I am feeble and sore broken: I have roared by reason of the disquietness of my heart.

9 Lord, all my desire is before you; and my groaning is not hid from you.

10 My heart panteth, my strength faileth me: as for the light of my eyes, it also is gone from me.

11 My lovers and my friends stand aloof from my sore; and my kinsmen stand afar off.

12 They also that seek after my life lay snares for me: and they that seek my hurt speak mischievous things, and imagine deceits all the day long.

13 But I, as a deaf man, heard not; and I was as a dumb man that openeth not his mouth.

14 Thus I was as a man that heareth not, and in whose mouth are no reproofs.

15 For in you, O LORD, do I hope: you will hear, O Lord my God.

16 For I said, Hear me, lest otherwise they should rejoice over me: when my foot slippeth, they magnify themselves against me.

17 For I am ready to halt, and my sorrow is continually before me.

18 For I will declare my iniquity; I will be sorry for my sin.

19 But my enemies are lively, and they are strong: and they that hate me wrongfully are multiplied.

20 They also that render evil for good are my adversaries; because I follow the thing that good is.

21 Forsake me not, O LORD: O my God, be not far from me.

22 Make haste to help me, O Lord my salvation.

PSALM 39

To the chief Musician, even to Jeduthun, A Psalm of David.

I SAID, I will take heed to my ways, that I sin not with my tongue: I will keep my mouth with a bridle, while the wicked is before me.

2 I was dumb with silence, I held my peace, even from good; and my sorrow was stirred.

3 My heart was hot within me, while I was musing the fire burned: then spake I with my tongue,

4 LORD, make me to know my end, and the measure of my days, what it is; that I may know how frail I am.

5 Behold, you have made my days as an handbreadth; and my age is as nothing before you: verily every man at his best state is altogether vanity. Selah.

6 Surely every man walketh in a vain shew: surely they are disquieted in vain: he heapeth up riches, and knoweth not who shall gather them.

7 And now, Lord, what wait I for? my hope is in you.

8 Deliver me from all my transgressions: make me not the reproach of the foolish.

9 I was dumb, I opened not my mouth; because you did it.

10 Remove your stroke away from me: I am consumed by the blow of yours hand.

11 When you with rebukes dost correct man for iniquity, you makest his beauty to consume away like a moth: surely every man is vanity. Selah.

12 Hear my prayer, O LORD, and give ear unto my cry; hold not your peace at my tears: for I am a stranger with you, and a sojourner, as all my fathers were.

13 O spare me, that I may recover strength, before I go hence, and be no more.

PSALM 40

To the chief Musician, A Psalm of David.

I WAITED patiently for the LORD; and he inclined unto me, and heard my cry.

2 He brought me up also out of an horrible pit, out of the miry clay, and set my feet upon a rock, and established my goings.

3 And he has put a new song in my mouth, even praise unto our God: many shall see it, and fear, and shall trust in the LORD.

4 Blessed is that man that maketh the LORD his trust, and respecteth not the proud, nor such as turn aside to lies.

5 Many, O LORD my God, are your wonderful works which you have done, and your thoughts which are to us-ward: they cannot be reckoned up in order unto you: if I would declare and speak of them, they are more than can be numbered.

6 Sacrifice and offering you did not desire; my ears have you opened: burnt offering and sin offering have you not required.

7 Then said I, Lo, I come: in the volume of the book it is written of me,

8 I delight to do your will, O my God: yea, your law is within my heart.

9 I have preached righteousness in the great congregation: lo, I have not refrained my lips, O LORD, you knowest.

10 I have not hid your righteousness within my heart; I have declared your faithfulness and your salvation: I have not concealed your lovingkindness and your truth from the great congregation.

11 Withhold not you your tender mercies from me, O LORD: let your lovingkindness and your truth continually preserve me.

12 For innumerable evils have compassed me about: my iniquities have taken hold upon me, so that I am not able to look up; they are more than the hairs of my head: therefore my heart faileth me.

13 Be pleased, O LORD, to deliver me: O LORD, make haste to help me.

14 Let them be ashamed and confounded together that seek after my soul to destroy it; let them be driven backward and put to shame that wish me evil.

15 Let them be desolate for a reward of their shame that say unto me, Aha, aha.

16 Let all those that seek you rejoice and be glad in you: let such as love your salvation say continually, The LORD be magnified.

17 But I am poor and needy; yet the Lord thinketh upon me: you are my help and my deliverer; make no tarrying, O my God.

PSALM 41

To the chief Musician, A Psalm of David.

BLESSED is he that considereth the poor: the LORD will deliver him in time of trouble.

2 The LORD will preserve him, and keep him alive; and he shall be blessed upon the earth: and you will not deliver him unto the will of his enemies.

3 The LORD will strengthen him upon the bed of languishing: you will make all his bed in his sickness.

4 I said, LORD, be merciful unto me: heal my soul; for I have sinned against you.

5 My enemies speak evil of me, When shall he die, and his name perish?

6 And if he come to see me, he speaketh vanity: his heart gathereth iniquity to itself; when he goeth abroad, he telleth it.

7 All that hate me whisper together against me: against me do they devise my hurt.

8 An evil disease, say they, cleaveth fast unto him: and now that he lies he shall rise up no more.

9 Yea, my own familiar friend, in whom I trusted, which did eat of my bread, has lifted up his heel against me.

10 But you , O LORD, be merciful unto me, and raise me up, that I may requite them.

11 By this I know that you favourest me, because my enemy doth not triumph over me.

12 And as for me, you upholdest me in my integrity, and settest me before your face for ever.

13 Blessed be the LORD God of Israel from everlasting, and to everlasting. Amen, and Amen.

PSALM 42

To the chief Musician, Maschil, for the sons of Korah.

AS the hart panteth after the water brooks, so panteth my soul after you, O God.

2 My soul thirsteth for God, for the living God: when shall I come and appear before God?

3 My tears have been my meat day and night, while they continually say unto me, Where is your God?

4 When I remember these things, I pour out my soul in me: for I had gone with the multitude, I went with them to the house of God, with the voice of joy and praise, with a multitude that kept holyday.

5 Why are you cast down, O my soul? and why are you disquieted in me? hope you in God: for I shall yet praise him for the help of his countenance.

6 O my God, my soul is cast down within me: therefore will I remember you from the land of Jordan, and of the Hermonites, from the hill Mizar.

7 Deep calleth unto deep at the noise of your waterspouts: all your waves and your billows are gone over me.

8 Yet the LORD will command his lovingkindness in the daytime, and in the night his song shall be with me, and my prayer unto the God of my life.

9 I will say unto God my rock, Why have you forgotten me? why go I mourning because of the oppression of the enemy?

10 As with a sword in my bones, my enemies reproach me; while they say daily unto me, Where is your God?

11 Why are you cast down, O my soul? and why are you disquieted within me? hope you in God: for I shall yet praise him, who is the health of my countenance, and my God.

PSALM 43

JUDGE me, O God, and plead my cause against an ungodly nation: O deliver me from the deceitful and unjust man.

2 For you are the God of my strength: why dost you cast me off? why go I mourning because of the oppression of the enemy?

3 O send out your light and your truth: let them lead me; let them bring me unto your holy hill, and to your tabernacles.

4 Then will I go unto the altar of God, unto God my exceeding joy: yea, upon the harp will I praise you, O God my God.

5 Why are you cast down, O my soul? and why are you disquieted within me? hope in God: for I shall yet praise him, who is the health of my countenance, and my God.

PSALM 44

To the chief Musician for the sons of Korah, Maschil.

WE have heard with our ears, O God, our fathers have told us, what work you did in their days, in the times of old.

2 How you did drive out the heathen with your hand, and plantedst them; how you did afflict the people, and cast them out.

3 For they got not the land in possession by their own sword, neither did their own arm save them: but your right hand, and yours arm, and the light of your countenance, because you hadst a favour unto them.

4 You are my King, O God: command deliverances for Jacob.

5 Through you will we push down our enemies: through your name will we tread them under that rise up against us.

6 For I will not trust in my bow, neither shall my sword save me.

7 But you have saved us from our enemies, and have put them to shame that hated us.

8 In God we boast all the day long, and praise your name for ever. Selah.

9 But you have cast off, and put us to shame; and go not forth with our armies.

10 You makest us to turn back from the enemy: and they which hate us spoil for themselves.

11 You have given us like sheep appointed for meat; and have scattered us among the heathen.

12 You sellest your people for nought, and dost not increase your wealth by their price.

13 You makest us a reproach to our neighbours, a scorn and a derision to them that are round about us.

14 You makest us a byword among the heathen, a shaking of the head among the people.

15 My confusion is continually before me, and the shame of my face has covered me,

16 For the voice of him that reproacheth and blasphemeth; by reason of the enemy and avenger.

17 All this is come upon us; yet have we not forgotten you, neither have we dealt falsely in your covenant.

18 Our heart is not turned back, neither have our steps declined from your way;

19 Though you have sore broken us in the place of dragons, and covered us with the shadow of death.

20 If we have forgotten the name of our God, or stretched out our hands to a strange god;

21 Shall not God search this out? for he knoweth the secrets of the heart.

22 Yea, for your sake are we killed all the day long; we are counted as sheep for the slaughter.

23 Awake, why sleepest you, O Lord? arise, cast us not off for ever.

24 Wherefore hidest you your face, and forgettest our affliction and our oppression?

25 For our soul is bowed down to the dust: our belly cleaveth unto the earth.

26 Arise for our help, and redeem us for your mercies' sake.

PSALM 45

To the chief Musician upon Shoshannim, for the sons of Korah, Maschil, A Song of loves.

MY heart is inditing a good matter: I speak of the things which I have made touching the king: my tongue is the pen of a ready writer.

2 You are fairer than the children of men: grace is poured into your lips: therefore God has blessed you for ever.

3 Gird your sword upon your thigh, O most mighty, with your glory and your majesty.

4 And in your majesty ride prosperously because of truth and meekness and righteousness; and your right hand shall teach you terrible things.

5 Yours arrows are sharp in the heart of the king's enemies; whereby the people fall under you.

6 Your throne, O God, is for ever and ever: the sceptre of your kingdom is a right sceptre.

7 You lovest righteousness, and hatest wickedness: therefore God, your God, has anointed you with the oil of gladness above your fellows.

8 All your garments smell of myrrh, and aloes, and cassia, out of the ivory palaces, whereby they have made you glad.

9 Kings' daughters were among your honourable women: upon your right hand did stand the queen in gold of Ophir.

10 Hearken, O daughter, and consider, and incline yours ear; forget also yours own people, and your father's house;

11 So shall the king greatly desire your beauty: for he is your Lord; and worship you him.

12 And the daughter of Tyre shall be there with a gift; even the rich among the people shall intreat your favour.

13 The king's daughter is all glorious within: her clothing is of created gold.

14 She shall be brought unto the king in raiment of needlework: the virgins her companions that follow her shall be brought unto you.

15 With gladness and rejoicing shall they be brought: they shall enter into the king's palace.

16 Instead of your fathers shall be your children, whom you mayest make princes in all the earth.

17 I will make your name to be remembered in all generations: therefore shall the people praise you for ever and ever.

PSALM 46

To the chief Musician for the sons of Korah, A Song upon Alamoth.

GOD is our refuge and strength, a very present help in trouble.

2 Therefore will not we fear, though the earth be removed, and though the mountains be carried into the midst of the sea;

3 Though the waters thereof roar and be troubled, though the mountains shake with the swelling thereof. Selah.

4 There is a river, the streams whereof shall make glad the city of God, the holy place of the tabernacles of the most High.

5 God is in the midst of her; she shall not be moved: God shall help her, and that right early.

6 The heathen raged, the kingdoms were moved: he uttered his voice, the earth melted.

7 The LORD of hosts is with us; the God of Jacob is our refuge. Selah.

8 Come, behold the works of the LORD, what desolations he has made in the earth.

9 He maketh wars to cease unto the end of the earth; he breaketh the bow, and cutteth the spear in sunder; he burneth the chariot in the fire.

10 Be still, and know that I am God: I will be exalted among the heathen, I will be exalted in the earth.

11 The LORD of hosts is with us; the God of Jacob is our refuge. Selah.

PSALM 47

To the chief Musician, A Psalm for the sons of Korah.

O CLAP your hands, all you people; shout unto God with the voice of triumph.

2 For the LORD most high is terrible; he is a great King over all the earth.

3 He shall subdue the people under us, and the nations under our feet.

4 He shall choose our inheritance for us, the excellency of Jacob whom he loved. Selah.

5 God is gone up with a shout, the LORD with the sound of a trumpet.

6 Sing praises to God, sing praises: sing praises unto our King, sing praises.

7 For God is the King of all the earth: sing you praises with understanding.

8 God reigneth over the heathen: God sitteth upon the throne of his holiness.

9 The princes of the people are gathered together, even the people of the God of Abraham: for the shields of the earth belong unto God: he is greatly exalted.

PSALM 48

A Song and Psalm for the sons of Korah.

GREAT is the LORD, and greatly to be praised in the city of our God, in the mountain of his holiness.

2 Beautiful for situation, the joy of the whole earth, is mount Zion, on the sides of the north, the city of the great King.

3 God is known in her palaces for a refuge.

4 For, lo, the kings were assembled, they passed by together.

5 They saw it, and so they marvelled; they were troubled, and hasted away.

6 Fear took hold upon them there, and pain, as of a woman in travail.

7 You breakest the ships of Tarshish with an east wind.

8 As we have heard, so have we seen in the city of the LORD of hosts, in the city of our God: God will establish it for ever. Selah.

9 We have thought of your lovingkindness, O God, in the midst of your temple.

10 According to your name, O God, so is your praise unto the ends of the earth: your right hand is full of righteousness.

11 Let mount Zion rejoice, let the daughters of Judah be glad, because of your judgments.

12 Walk about Zion, and go round about her: tell the towers thereof.

13 Mark you well her bulwarks, consider her palaces; that you may tell it to the generation following.

14 For this God is our God for ever and ever: he will be our guide even unto death.

PSALM 49

To the chief Musician, A Psalm for the sons of Korah.

HEAR this, all you people; give ear, all you inhabitants of the world:

2 Both low and high, rich and poor, together.

3 My mouth shall speak of wisdom; and the meditation of my heart shall be of understanding.

4 I will incline my ear to a parable: I will open my dark saying upon the harp.

5 Wherefore should I fear in the days of evil, when the iniquity of my heels shall compass me about?

6 They that trust in their wealth, and boast themselves in the multitude of their riches;

7 None of them can by any means redeem his brother, nor give to God a ransom for him:

8 (For the redemption of their soul is precious, and it ceaseth for ever:)

9 That he should still live for ever, and not see corruption.

10 For he seeth that wise men die, likewise the fool and the brutish person perish, and leave their wealth to others.

11 Their inward thought is, that their houses shall continue for ever, and their dwelling places to all generations; they call their lands after their own names.

12 Nevertheless man being in honour abideth not: he is like the beasts that perish.

13 This their way is their folly: yet their posterity approve their sayings. Selah.

14 Like sheep they are laid in the grave; death shall feed on them; and the upright shall have dominion over them in the morning; and their beauty shall consume in the grave from their dwelling.

15 But God will redeem my soul from the power of the grave: for he shall receive me. Selah.

16 Be not you afraid when one is made rich, when the glory of his house is increased;

17 For when he dieth he shall carry nothing away: his glory shall not descend after him.

18 Though while he lived he blessed his soul: and men will praise you, when you doest well to yourself.

19 He shall go to the generation of his fathers; they shall never see light.

20 Man that is in honour, and understands not, is like the beasts that perish.

PSALM 50

A Psalm of Asaph.

THE mighty God, even the LORD, has spoken, and called the earth from the rising of the sun unto the going down thereof.

2 Out of Zion, the perfection of beauty, God has shined.

3 Our God shall come, and shall not keep silence: a fire shall devour before him, and it shall be very tempestuous round about him.

4 He shall call to the heavens from above, and to the earth, that he may judge his people.

5 Gather my saints together unto me; those that have made a covenant with me by sacrifice.

6 And the heavens shall declare his righteousness: for God is judge himself. Selah.

7 Hear, O my people, and I will speak; O Israel, and I will testify against you: I am God, even your God.

8 I will not reprove you for your sacrifices or your burnt offerings, to have been continually before me.

9 I will take no bullock out of your house, nor he goats out of your folds.

10 For every beast of the forest is my, and the cattle upon a thousand hills.

11 I know all the fowls of the mountains: and the wild beasts of the field are my.

12 If I were hungry, I would not tell you: for the world is my, and the fulness thereof.

13 Will I eat the flesh of bulls, or drink the blood of goats?

14 Offer unto God thanksgiving; and pay your vows unto the most High:

15 And call upon me in the day of trouble: I will deliver you, and you shalt glorify me.

16 But unto the wicked God saith, What have you to do to declare my statutes, or that you shouldest take my covenant in your mouth?

17 Seeing you hatest instruction, and castest my words behind you.

18 When you sawest a thief, then you consentedst with him, and have been partaker with adulterers.

19 You givest your mouth to evil, and your tongue frameth deceit.

20 You sittest and speakest against your brother; you slanderest yours own mother's son.

21 These things have you done, and I kept silence; you thoughtest that I was altogether such an one as yourself: but I will reprove you, and set them in order before yours eyes.

22 Now consider this, you that forget God, lest I tear you in pieces, and there be none to deliver.

23 Whoso offereth praise glorifieth me: and to him that ordereth his conversation aright will I shew the salvation of God.

PSALM 51

To the chief Musician, A Psalm of David, when Nathan the prophet came unto him, after he had gone in to Bath-sheba.

HAVE mercy upon me, O God, according to your lovingkindness: according unto the multitude of your tender mercies blot out my transgressions.

2 Wash me throughly from my iniquity, and cleanse me from my sin.

3 For I acknowledge my transgressions: and my sin is ever before me.

4 Against you, you only, have I sinned, and done this evil in your sight: that you mightest be justified when you speakest, and be clear when you judgest.

5 Behold, I was shapen in iniquity; and in sin did my mother conceive me.

6 Behold, you desirest truth in the inward parts: and in the hidden part you shalt make me to know wisdom.

7 Purge me with hyssop, and I shall be clean: wash me, and I shall be whiter than snow.

8 Make me to hear joy and gladness; that the bones which you have broken may rejoice.

9 Hide your face from my sins, and blot out all my iniquities.

10 Create in me a clean heart, O God; and renew a right spirit within me.

11 Cast me not away from your presence; and take not your holy spirit from me.

12 Restore unto me the joy of your salvation; and uphold me with your free spirit.

13 Then will I teach transgressors your ways; and sinners shall be converted unto you.

14 Deliver me from bloodguiltiness, O God, you God of my salvation: and my tongue shall sing aloud of your righteousness.

15 O Lord, open you my lips; and my mouth shall shew forth your praise.

16 For you desirest not sacrifice; else would I give it: you delightest not in burnt offering.

17 The sacrifices of God are a broken spirit: a broken and a contrite heart, O God, you will not despise.

18 Do good in your good pleasure unto Zion: build you the walls of Jerusalem.

19 Then shalt you be pleased with the sacrifices of righteousness, with burnt offering and whole burnt offering: then shall they offer bullocks upon yours altar.

PSALM 52

To the chief Musician, Maschil, A Psalm of David, when Doeg the Edomite came and told Saul, and said unto him, David is come to the house of Ahimelech.

WHY boastest you yourself in mischief, O mighty man? the goodness of God endureth continually.

2 Your tongue deviseth mischiefs; like a sharp rasor, working deceitfully.

3 You lovest evil more than good; and lying rather than to speak righteousness. Selah.

4 You lovest all devouring words, O you deceitful tongue.

5 God shall likewise destroy you for ever, he shall take you away, and pluck you out of your dwelling place, and root you out of the land of the living. Selah.

6 The righteous also shall see, and fear, and shall laugh at him:

7 Lo, this is the man that made not God his strength; but trusted in the abundance of his riches, and strengthened himself in his wickedness.

8 But I am like a green olive tree in the house of God: I trust in the mercy of God for ever and ever.

9 I will praise you for ever, because you have done it: and I will wait on your name; for it is good before your saints.

PSALM 53

To the chief Musician upon Mahalath, Maschil, A Psalm of David.

THE fool has said in his heart, There is no God. Corrupt are they, and have done abominable iniquity: there is none that doeth good.

2 God looked down from heaven upon the children of men, to see if there were any that did understand, that did seek God.

3 Every one of them is gone back: they are altogether become filthy; there is none that doeth good, no, not one.

4 Have the workers of iniquity no knowledge? who eat up my people as they eat bread: they have not called upon God.

5 There were they in great fear, where no fear was: for God has scattered the bones of him that encampeth against you: you have put them to shame, because God has despised them.

6 Oh that the salvation of Israel were come out of Zion! When God bringeth back the captivity of his people, Jacob shall rejoice, and Israel shall be glad.

PSALM 54

To the chief Musician on Neginoth, Maschil, A Psalm of David, when the Ziphims came and said to Saul, Doth not David hide himself with us?

SAVE me, O God, by your name, and judge me by your strength.

2 Hear my prayer, O God; give ear to the words of my mouth.

3 For strangers are risen up against me, and oppressors seek after my soul: they have not set God before them. Selah.

4 Behold, God is my helper: the Lord is with them that uphold my soul.

5 He shall reward evil unto my enemies: cut them off in your truth.

6 I will freely sacrifice unto you: I will praise your name, O LORD; for it is good.

7 For he has delivered me out of all trouble: and my eye has seen his desire upon my enemies.

PSALM 55

To the chief Musician on Neginoth, Maschil, A Psalm of David.

GIVE ear to my prayer, O God; and hide not yourself from my supplication.

2 Attend unto me, and hear me: I mourn in my complaint, and make a noise;

3 Because of the voice of the enemy, because of the oppression of the wicked: for they cast iniquity upon me, and in wrath they hate me.

4 My heart is sore pained within me: and the terrors of death are fallen upon me.

5 Fearfulness and trembling are come upon me, and horror has overwhelmed me.

6 And I said, Oh that I had wings like a dove! for then would I fly away, and be at rest.

7 Lo, then would I wander far off, and remain in the wilderness. Selah.

8 I would hasten my escape from the windy storm and tempest.

9 Destroy, O Lord, and divide their tongues: for I have seen violence and strife in the city.

10 Day and night they go about it upon the walls thereof: mischief also and sorrow are in the midst of it.

11 Wickedness is in the midst thereof: deceit and guile depart not from her streets.

12 For it was not an enemy that reproached me; then I could have borne it: neither was it he that hated me that did magnify himself against me; then I would have hid myself from him:

13 But it was you , a man my equal, my guide, and my acquaintance.

14 We took sweet counsel together, and walked unto the house of God in company.

15 Let death seize upon them, and let them go down quick into hell: for wickedness is in their dwellings, and among them.

16 As for me, I will call upon God; and the LORD shall save me.

17 Evening, and morning, and at noon, will I pray, and cry aloud: and he shall hear my voice.

18 He has delivered my soul in peace from the battle that was against me: for there were many with me.

19 God shall hear, and afflict them, even he that abideth of old. Selah. Because they have no changes, therefore they fear not God.

20 He has put forth his hands against such as be at peace with him: he has broken his covenant.

21 The words of his mouth were smoother than butter, but war was in his heart: his words were softer than oil, yet were they drawn swords.

22 Cast your burden upon the LORD, and he shall sustain you: he shall never suffer the righteous to be moved.

23 But you , O God, shalt bring them down into the pit of destruction: bloody and deceitful men shall not live out half their days; but I will trust in you.

PSALM 56

To the chief Musician upon Jonath-elem-rechokim, Michtam of David, when the Philistines took him in Gath.

BE merciful unto me, O God: for man would swallow me up; he fighting daily oppresseth me.

2 My enemies would daily swallow me up: for they be many that fight against me, O you most High.

3 What time I am afraid, I will trust in you.

4 In God I will praise his word, in God I have put my trust; I will not fear what flesh can do unto me.

5 Every day they wrest my words: all their thoughts are against me for evil.

6 They gather themselves together, they hide themselves, they mark my steps, when they wait for my soul.

7 Shall they escape by iniquity? in yours anger cast down the people, O God.

8 You tellest my wanderings: put you my tears into your bottle: are they not in your book?

9 When I cry unto you, then shall my enemies turn back: this I know; for God is for me.

10 In God will I praise his word: in the LORD will I praise his word.

11 In God have I put my trust: I will not be afraid what man can do unto me.

12 Your vows are upon me, O God: I will render praises unto you.

13 For you have delivered my soul from death: will not you deliver my feet from falling, that I may walk before God in the light of the living?

PSALM 57

To the chief Musician, Al-taschith, Michtam of David, when he fled from Saul in the cave.

BE merciful unto me, O God, be merciful unto me: for my soul trusteth in you: yea, in the shadow of your wings will I make my refuge, until these calamities be overpast.

2 I will cry unto God most high; unto God that performeth all things for me.

3 He shall send from heaven, and save me from the reproach of him that would swallow me up. Selah. God shall send forth his mercy and his truth.

4 My soul is among lions: and I lie even among them that are set on fire, even the sons of men, whose teeth are spears and arrows, and their tongue a sharp sword.

5 Be you exalted, O God, above the heavens; let your glory be above all the earth.

6 They have prepared a net for my steps; my soul is bowed down: they have digged a pit before me, into the midst whereof they are fallen themselves. Selah.

7 My heart is fixed, O God, my heart is fixed: I will sing and give praise.

8 Awake up, my glory; awake, psaltery and harp: I myself will awake early.

9 I will praise you, O Lord, among the people: I will sing unto you among the nations.

10 For your mercy is great unto the heavens, and your truth unto the clouds.

11 Be you exalted, O God, above the heavens: let your glory be above all the earth.

PSALM 58

To the chief Musician, Al-taschith, Michtam of David.

DO you indeed speak righteousness, O congregation? do you judge uprightly, O you sons of men?

2 Yea, in heart you work wickedness; you weigh the violence of your hands in the earth.

3 The wicked are estranged from the womb: they go astray as soon as they be born, speaking lies.

4 Their poison is like the poison of a serpent: they are like the deaf adder that stoppeth her ear;

5 Which will not hearken to the voice of charmers, charming never so wisely.

6 Break their teeth, O God, in their mouth: break out the great teeth of the young lions, O LORD.

7 Let them melt away as waters which run continually: when he bendeth his bow to shoot his arrows, let them be as cut in pieces.

8 As a snail which melteth, let every one of them pass away: like the untimely birth of a woman, that they may not see the sun.

9 Before your pots can feel the thorns, he shall take them away as with a whirlwind, both living, and in his wrath.

10 The righteous shall rejoice when he seeth the vengeance: he shall wash his feet in the blood of the wicked.

11 So that a man shall say, Verily there is a reward for the righteous: verily he is a God that judgeth in the earth.

PSALM 59

To the chief Musician, Al-taschith, Michtam of David; when Saul sent, and they watched the house to kill him.

DELIVER me from my enemies, O my God: defend me from them that rise up against me.

2 Deliver me from the workers of iniquity, and save me from bloody men.

3 For, lo, they lie in wait for my soul: the mighty are gathered against me; not for my transgression, nor for my sin, O LORD.

4 They run and prepare themselves without my fault: awake to help me, and behold.

5 You therefore, O LORD God of hosts, the God of Israel, awake to visit all the heathen: be not merciful to any wicked transgressors. Selah.

6 They return at evening: they make a noise like a dog, and go round about the city.

7 Behold, they belch out with their mouth: swords are in their lips: for who, say they, doth hear?

8 But you , O LORD, shalt laugh at them; you shalt have all the heathen in derision.

9 Because of his strength will I wait upon you: for God is my defence.

10 The God of my mercy shall prevent me: God shall let me see my desire upon my enemies.

11 Slay them not, lest my people forget: scatter them by your power; and bring them down, O Lord our shield.

12 For the sin of their mouth and the words of their lips let them even be taken in their pride: and for cursing and lying which they speak.

13 Consume them in wrath, consume them, that they may not be: and let them know that God ruleth in Jacob unto the ends of the earth. Selah.

14 And at evening let them return; and let them make a noise like a dog, and go round about the city.

15 Let them wander up and down for meat, and grudge if they be not satisfied.

16 But I will sing of your power; yea, I will sing aloud of your mercy in the morning: for you have been my defence and refuge in the day of my trouble.

17 Unto you, O my strength, will I sing: for God is my defence, and the God of my mercy.

PSALM 60

To the chief Musician upon Shushan-eduth, Michtam of David, to teach; when he strove with Aram-naharaim and with Aram-zobah, when Joab returned, and struck of Edom in the valley of salt twelve thousand.

O GOD, you have cast us off, you have scattered us, you have been displeased; O turn yourself to us again.

2 You have made the earth to tremble; you have broken it: heal the breaches thereof; for it shaketh.

3 You have shewed your people hard things: you have made us to drink the wine of astonishment.

4 You have given a banner to them that fear you, that it may be displayed because of the truth. Selah.

5 That your beloved may be delivered; save with your right hand, and hear me.

6 God has spoken in his holiness; I will rejoice, I will divide Shechem, and mete out the valley of Succoth.

7 Gilead is mine, and Manasseh is mine; Ephraim also is the strength of my head; Judah is my lawgiver;

8 Moab is my washpot; over Edom will I cast out my shoe: Philistia, triumph you because of me.

9 Who will bring me into the strong city? who will lead me into Edom?

10 Will not you , O God, which hadst cast us off? and you , O God, which did not go out with our armies?

11 Give us help from trouble: for vain is the help of man.

12 Through God we shall do valiantly: for he it is that shall tread down our enemies.

PSALM 61

To the chief Musician upon Neginah, A Psalm of David.

HEAR my cry, O God; attend unto my prayer.

2 From the end of the earth will I cry unto you, when my heart is overwhelmed: lead me to the rock that is higher than I.

3 For you have been a shelter for me, and a strong tower from the enemy.

4 I will abide in your tabernacle for ever: I will trust in the covert of your wings. Selah.

5 For you , O God, have heard my vows: you have given me the heritage of those that fear your name.

6 You will prolong the king's life: and his years as many generations.

7 He shall abide before God for ever: O prepare mercy and truth, which may preserve him.

8 So will I sing praise unto your name for ever, that I may daily perform my vows.

PSALM 62

To the chief Musician, to Jeduthun, A Psalm of David.

TRULY my soul waiteth upon God: from him comes my salvation.

2 He only is my rock and my salvation; he is my defence; I shall not be greatly moved.

3 How long will you imagine mischief against a man? you shall be slain all of you: as a bowing wall shall you be, and as a tottering fence.

4 They only consult to cast him down from his excellency: they delight in lies: they bless with their mouth, but they curse inwardly. Selah.

5 My soul, wait you only upon God; for my expectation is from him.

6 He only is my rock and my salvation: he is my defence; I shall not be moved.

7 In God is my salvation and my glory: the rock of my strength, and my refuge, is in God.

8 Trust in him at all times; you people, pour out your heart before him: God is a refuge for us. Selah.

9 Surely men of low degree are vanity, and men of high degree are a lie: to be laid in the balance, they are altogether lighter than vanity.

10 Trust not in oppression, and become not vain in robbery: if riches increase, set not your heart upon them.

11 God has spoken once; twice have I heard this; that power belongeth unto God.

12 Also unto you, O Lord, belongeth mercy: for you renderest to every man according to his work.

PSALM 63

A Psalm of David, when he was in the wilderness of Judah.

O GOD, you are my God; early will I seek you: my soul thirsteth for you, my flesh longeth for you in a dry and thirsty land, where no water is;

2 To see your power and your glory, so as I have seen you in the sanctuary.

3 Because your lovingkindness is better than life, my lips shall praise you.

4 Thus will I bless you while I live: I will lift up my hands in your name.

5 My soul shall be satisfied as with marrow and fatness; and my mouth shall praise you with joyful lips:

6 When I remember you upon my bed, and meditate on you in the night watches.

7 Because you have been my help, therefore in the shadow of your wings will I rejoice.

8 My soul followeth hard after you: your right hand upholdeth me.

9 But those that seek my soul, to destroy it, shall go into the lower parts of the earth.

10 They shall fall by the sword: they shall be a portion for foxes.

11 But the king shall rejoice in God; every one that sweareth by him shall glory: but the mouth of them that speak lies shall be stopped.

PSALM 64

To the chief Musician, A Psalm of David.

HEAR my voice, O God, in my prayer: preserve my life from fear of the enemy.

2 Hide me from the secret counsel of the wicked; from the insurrection of the workers of iniquity:

3 Who whet their tongue like a sword, and bend their bows to shoot their arrows, even bitter words:

4 That they may shoot in secret at the perfect: suddenly do they shoot at him, and fear not.

5 They encourage themselves in an evil matter: they commune of laying snares privily; they say, Who shall see them?

6 They search out iniquities; they accomplish a diligent search: both the inward thought of every one of them, and the heart, is deep.

7 But God shall shoot at them with an arrow; suddenly shall they be wounded.

8 So they shall make their own tongue to fall upon themselves: all that see them shall flee away.

9 And all men shall fear, and shall declare the work of God; for they shall wisely consider of his doing.

10 The righteous shall be glad in the LORD, and shall trust in him; and all the upright in heart shall glory.

PSALM 65

To the chief Musician, A Psalm and Song of David.

PRAISE waiteth for you, O God, in Sion: and unto you shall the vow be performed.

2 O you that hearest prayer, unto you shall all flesh come.

3 Iniquities prevail against me: as for our transgressions, you shalt purge them away.

4 Blessed is the man whom you choosest, and causest to approach unto you, that he may dwell in your courts: we shall be satisfied with the goodness of your house, even of your holy temple.

5 By terrible things in righteousness will you answer us, O God of our salvation; who are the confidence of all the ends of the earth, and of them that are afar off upon the sea:

6 Which by his strength setteth fast the mountains; being girded with power:

7 Which stilleth the noise of the seas, the noise of their waves, and the tumult of the people.

8 They also that dwell in the uttermost parts are afraid at your tokens: you makest the outgoings of the morning and evening to rejoice.

9 You visitest the earth, and waterest it: you greatly enrichest it with the river of God, which is full of water: you preparest them corn, when you have so provided for it.

10 You waterest the ridges thereof abundantly: you settlest the furrows thereof: you makest it soft with showers: you blessest the springing thereof.

11 You crownest the year with your goodness; and your paths drop fatness.

12 They drop upon the pastures of the wilderness: and the little hills rejoice on every side.

13 The pastures are clothed with flocks; the valleys also are covered over with corn; they shout for joy, they also sing.

PSALM 66

To the chief Musician, A Song or Psalm.

MAKE a joyful noise unto God, all you lands:

2 Sing forth the honour of his name: make his praise glorious.

3 Say unto God, How terrible are you in your works! through the greatness of your power shall yours enemies submit themselves unto you.

4 All the earth shall worship you, and shall sing unto you; they shall sing to your name. Selah.

5 Come and see the works of God: he is terrible in his doing toward the children of men.

6 He turned the sea into dry land: they went through the flood on foot: there did we rejoice in him.

7 He ruleth by his power for ever; his eyes behold the nations: let not the rebellious exalt themselves. Selah.

8 O bless our God, you people, and make the voice of his praise to be heard:

9 Which holdeth our soul in life, and suffereth not our feet to be moved.

10 For you , O God, have proved us: you have tried us, as silver is tried.

11 You broughtest us into the net; you laidst affliction upon our loins.

12 You have caused men to ride over our heads; we went through fire and through water: but you broughtest us out into a wealthy place.

13 I will go into your house with burnt offerings: I will pay you my vows,

14 Which my lips have uttered, and my mouth has spoken, when I was in trouble.

15 I will offer unto you burnt sacrifices of fatlings, with the incense of rams; I will offer bullocks with goats. Selah.

16 Come and hear, all you that fear God, and I will declare what he has done for my soul.

17 I cried unto him with my mouth, and he was extolled with my tongue.

18 If I regard iniquity in my heart, the Lord will not hear me:

19 But verily God has heard me; he has attended to the voice of my prayer.

20 Blessed be God, which has not turned away my prayer, nor his mercy from me.

PSALM 67

To the chief Musician on Neginoth, A Psalm or Song.

GOD be merciful unto us, and bless us; and cause his face to shine upon us; Selah.

2 That your way may be known upon earth, your saving health among all nations.

3 Let the people praise you, O God; let all the people praise you.

4 O let the nations be glad and sing for joy: for you shalt judge the people righteously, and govern the nations upon earth. Selah.

5 Let the people praise you, O God; let all the people praise you.

6 Then shall the earth yield her increase; and God, even our own God, shall bless us.

7 God shall bless us; and all the ends of the earth shall fear him.

PSALM 68

To the chief Musician, A Psalm or Song of David.

LET God arise, let his enemies be scattered: let them also that hate him flee before him.

2 As smoke is driven away, so drive them away: as wax melteth before the fire, so let the wicked perish at the presence of God.

3 But let the righteous be glad; let them rejoice before God: yea, let them exceedingly rejoice.

4 Sing unto God, sing praises to his name: extol him that rideth upon the heavens by his name JAH, and rejoice before him.

5 A father of the fatherless, and a judge of the widows, is God in his holy habitation.

6 God setteth the solitary in families: he bringeth out those which are bound with chains: but the rebellious dwell in a dry land.

7 O God, when you wentest forth before your people, when you did march through the wilderness; Selah:

8 The earth shook, the heavens also dropped at the presence of God: even Sinai itself was moved at the presence of God, the God of Israel.

9 You , O God, did send a plentiful rain, whereby you did confirm yours inheritance, when it was weary.

10 Your congregation has dwelt therein: you , O God, have prepared of your goodness for the poor.

11 The Lord gave the word: great was the company of those that published it.

12 Kings of armies did flee apace: and she that tarried at home divided the spoil.

13 Though you have lien among the pots, yet shall you be as the wings of a dove covered with silver, and her feathers with yellow gold.

14 When the Almighty scattered kings in it, it was white as snow in Salmon.

15 The hill of God is as the hill of Bashan; an high hill as the hill of Bashan.

16 Why leap you , you high hills? this is the hill which God desireth to dwell in; yea, the LORD will dwell in it for ever.

17 The chariots of God are twenty thousand, even thousands of angels: the Lord is among them, as in Sinai, in the holy place.

18 You have ascended on high, you have led captivity captive: you have received gifts for men; yea, for the rebellious also, that the LORD God might dwell among them.

19 Blessed be the Lord, who daily loadeth us with benefits, even the God of our salvation. Selah.

20 He that is our God is the God of salvation; and unto GOD the Lord belong the issues from death.

21 But God shall wound the head of his enemies, and the hairy scalp of such an one as goeth on still in his trespasses.

22 The Lord said, I will bring again from Bashan, I will bring my people again from the depths of the sea:

23 That your foot may be dipped in the blood of yours enemies, and the tongue of your dogs in the same.

24 They have seen your goings, O God; even the goings of my God, my King, in the sanctuary.

25 The singers went before, the players on instruments followed after; among them were the damsels playing with timbrels.

26 Bless you God in the congregations, even the Lord, from the fountain of Israel.

27 There is little Benjamin with their ruler, the princes of Judah and their council, the princes of Zebulun, and the princes of Naphtali.

28 Your God has commanded your strength: strengthen, O God, that which you have created for us.

29 Because of your temple at Jerusalem shall kings bring presents unto you.

30 Rebuke the company of spearmen, the multitude of the bulls, with the calves of the people, till every one submit himself with pieces of silver: scatter you the people that delight in war.

31 Princes shall come out of Egypt; Ethiopia shall soon stretch out her hands unto God.

32 Sing unto God, you kingdoms of the earth; O sing praises unto the Lord; Selah:

33 To him that rideth upon the heavens of heavens, which were of old; lo, he doth send out his voice, and that a mighty voice.

34 Ascribe you strength unto God: his excellency is over Israel, and his strength is in the clouds.

35 O God, you are terrible out of your holy places: the God of Israel is he that giveth strength and power unto his people. Blessed be God.

PSALM 69

To the chief Musician upon Shoshannim, A Psalm of David.

SAVE me, O God; for the waters are come in unto my soul.

2 I sink in deep mire, where there is no standing: I am come into deep waters, where the floods overflow me.

3 I am weary of my crying: my throat is dried: my eyes fail while I wait for my God.

4 They that hate me without a cause are more than the hairs of my head: they that would destroy me, being my enemies wrongfully, are mighty: then I restored that which I took not away.

5 O God, you knewest my foolishness; and my sins are not hid from you.

6 Let not them that wait on you, O Lord GOD of hosts, be ashamed for my sake: let not those that seek you be confounded for my sake, O God of Israel.

7 Because for your sake I have borne reproach; shame has covered my face.

8 I am become a stranger unto my brethren, and an alien unto my mother's children.

9 For the zeal of yours house has eaten me up; and the reproaches of them that reproached you are fallen upon me.

10 When I wept, and chastened my soul with fasting, that was to my reproach.

11 I made sackcloth also my garment; and I became a proverb to them.

12 They that sit in the gate speak against me; and I was the song of the drunkards.

13 But as for me, my prayer is unto you, O LORD, in an acceptable time: O God, in the multitude of your mercy hear me, in the truth of your salvation.

14 Deliver me out of the mire, and let me not sink: let me be delivered from them that hate me, and out of the deep waters.

15 Let not the waterflood overflow me, neither let the deep swallow me up, and let not the pit shut her mouth upon me.

16 Hear me, O LORD; for your lovingkindness is good: turn unto me according to the multitude of your tender mercies.

17 And hide not your face from your servant; for I am in trouble: hear me speedily.

18 Draw nigh unto my soul, and redeem it: deliver me because of my enemies.

19 You have known my reproach, and my shame, and my dishonour: my adversaries are all before you.

20 Reproach has broken my heart; and I am full of heaviness: and I looked for some to take pity, but there was none; and for comforters, but I found none.

21 They gave me also gall for my meat; and in my thirst they gave me vinegar to drink.

22 Let their table become a snare before them: and that which should have been for their welfare, let it become a trap.

23 Let their eyes be darkened, that they see not; and make their loins continually to shake.

24 Pour out yours indignation upon them, and let your wrathful anger take hold of them.

25 Let their habitation be desolate; and let none dwell in their tents.

26 For they persecute him whom you have smitten; and they talk to the grief of those whom you have wounded.

27 Add iniquity unto their iniquity: and let them not come into your righteousness.

28 Let them be blotted out of the book of the living, and not be written with the righteous.

29 But I am poor and sorrowful: let your salvation, O God, set me up on high.

30 I will praise the name of God with a song, and will magnify him with thanksgiving.

31 This also shall please the LORD better than an ox or bullock that has horns and hoofs.

32 The humble shall see this, and be glad: and your heart shall live that seek God.

33 For the LORD heareth the poor, and despiseth not his prisoners.

34 Let the heaven and earth praise him, the seas, and every thing that moveth therein.

35 For God will save Zion, and will build the cities of Judah: that they may dwell there, and have it in possession.

36 The seed also of his servants shall inherit it: and they that love his name shall dwell therein.

PSALM 70

To the chief Musician, A Psalm of David, to bring to remembrance.

MAKE haste, O God, to deliver me; make haste to help me, O LORD.

2 Let them be ashamed and confounded that seek after my soul: let them be turned backward, and put to confusion, that desire my hurt.

3 Let them be turned back for a reward of their shame that say, Aha, aha.

4 Let all those that seek you rejoice and be glad in you: and let such as love your salvation say continually, Let God be magnified.

5 But I am poor and needy: make haste unto me, O God: you are my help and my deliverer; O LORD, make no tarrying.

PSALM 71

IN you, O LORD, do I put my trust: let me never be put to confusion.

2 Deliver me in your righteousness, and cause me to escape: incline yours ear unto me, and save me.

3 Be you my strong habitation, whereunto I may continually resort: you have given commandment to save me; for you are my rock and my fortress.

4 Deliver me, O my God, out of the hand of the wicked, out of the hand of the unrighteous and cruel man.

5 For you are my hope, O Lord GOD: you are my trust from my youth.

6 By you have I been holden up from the womb: you are he that took me out of my mother's bowels: my praise shall be continually of you.

7 I am as a wonder unto many; but you are my strong refuge.

8 Let my mouth be filled with your praise and with your honour all the day.

9 Cast me not off in the time of old age; forsake me not when my strength faileth.

10 For my enemies speak against me; and they that lay wait for my soul take counsel together,

11 Saying, God has forsaken him: persecute and take him; for there is none to deliver him.

12 O God, be not far from me: O my God, make haste for my help.

13 Let them be confounded and consumed that are adversaries to my soul; let them be covered with reproach and dishonour that seek my hurt.

14 But I will hope continually, and will yet praise you more and more.

15 My mouth shall shew forth your righteousness and your salvation all the day; for I know not the numbers thereof.

16 I will go in the strength of the Lord GOD: I will make mention of your righteousness, even of yours only.

17 O God, you have taught me from my youth: and hitherto have I declared your wondrous works.

18 Now also when I am old and grayheaded, O God, forsake me not; until I have shewed your strength unto this generation, and your power to every one that is to come.

19 Your righteousness also, O God, is very high, who have done great things: O God, who is like unto you!

20 You , which have shewed me great and sore troubles, shalt quicken me again, and shalt bring me up again from the depths of the earth.

21 You shalt increase my greatness, and comfort me on every side.

22 I will also praise you with the psaltery, even your truth, O my God: unto you will I sing with the harp, O you Holy One of Israel.

23 My lips shall greatly rejoice when I sing unto you; and my soul, which you have redeemed.

24 My tongue also shall talk of your righteousness all the day long: for they are confounded, for they are brought unto shame, that seek my hurt.

PSALM 72

A Psalm for Solomon.

GIVE the king your judgments, O God, and your righteousness unto the king's son.

2 He shall judge your people with righteousness, and your poor with judgment.

3 The mountains shall bring peace to the people, and the little hills, by righteousness.

4 He shall judge the poor of the people, he shall save the children of the needy, and shall break in pieces the oppressor.

5 They shall fear you as long as the sun and moon endure, throughout all generations.

6 He shall come down like rain upon the mown grass: as showers that water the earth.

7 In his days shall the righteous flourish; and abundance of peace so long as the moon endureth.

8 He shall have dominion also from sea to sea, and from the river unto the ends of the earth.

9 They that dwell in the wilderness shall bow before him; and his enemies shall lick the dust.

10 The kings of Tarshish and of the isles shall bring presents: the kings of Sheba and Seba shall offer gifts.

11 Yea, all kings shall fall down before him: all nations shall serve him.

12 For he shall deliver the needy when he crieth; the poor also, and him that has no helper.

13 He shall spare the poor and needy, and shall save the souls of the needy.

14 He shall redeem their soul from deceit and violence: and precious shall their blood be in his sight.

15 And he shall live, and to him shall be given of the gold of Sheba: prayer also shall be made for him continually; and daily shall he be praised.

16 There shall be an handful of corn in the earth upon the top of the mountains; the fruit thereof shall shake like Lebanon: and they of the city shall flourish like grass of the earth.

17 His name shall endure for ever: his name shall be continued as long as the sun: and men shall be blessed in him: all nations shall call him blessed.

18 Blessed be the LORD God, the God of Israel, who only doeth wondrous things.

19 And blessed be his glorious name for ever: and let the whole earth be filled with his glory; Amen, and Amen.

20 The prayers of David the son of Jesse are ended.

PSALM 73

A Psalm of Asaph.

TRULY God is good to Israel, even to such as are of a clean heart.

2 But as for me, my feet were almost gone; my steps had well nigh slipped.

3 For I was envious at the foolish, when I saw the prosperity of the wicked.

4 For there are no bands in their death: but their strength is firm.

5 They are not in trouble as other men; neither are they plagued like other men.

6 Therefore pride compasseth them about as a chain; violence covers them as a garment.

7 Their eyes stand out with fatness: they have more than heart could wish.

8 They are corrupt, and speak wickedly concerning oppression: they speak loftily.

9 They set their mouth against the heavens, and their tongue walketh through the earth.

10 Therefore his people return hither: and waters of a full cup are wrung out to them.

11 And they say, How doth God know? and is there knowledge in the most High?

12 Behold, these are the ungodly, who prosper in the world; they increase in riches.

13 Verily I have cleansed my heart in vain, and washed my hands in innocency.

14 For all the day long have I been plagued, and chastened every morning.

15 If I say, I will speak thus; behold, I should offend against the generation of your children.

16 When I thought to know this, it was too painful for me;

17 Until I went into the sanctuary of God; then understood I their end.

18 Surely you did set them in slippery places: you castedst them down into destruction.

19 How are they brought into desolation, as in a moment! they are utterly consumed with terrors.

20 As a dream when one awaketh; so, O Lord, when you awakest, you shalt despise their image.

21 Thus my heart was grieved, and I was pricked in my reins.

22 So foolish was I, and ignorant: I was as a beast before you.

23 Nevertheless I am continually with you: you have holden me by my right hand.

24 You shalt guide me with your counsel, and afterward receive me to glory.

25 Whom have I in heaven but you? and there is none upon earth that I desire beside you.

26 My flesh and my heart faileth: but God is the strength of my heart, and my portion for ever.

27 For, lo, they that are far from you shall perish: you have destroyed all them that go a whoring from you.

28 But it is good for me to draw near to God: I have put my trust in the Lord GOD, that I may declare all your works.

PSALM 74

Maschil of Asaph.

O GOD, why have you cast us off for ever? why doth yours anger smoke against the sheep of your pasture?

2 Remember your congregation, which you have purchased of old; the rod of yours inheritance, which you have redeemed; this mount Zion, wherein you have dwelt.

3 Lift up your feet unto the perpetual desolations; even all that the enemy has done wickedly in the sanctuary.

4 Yours enemies roar in the midst of your congregations; they set up their ensigns for signs.

5 A man was famous according as he had lifted up axes upon the thick trees.

6 But now they break down the carved work thereof at once with axes and hammers.

7 They have cast fire into your sanctuary, they have defiled by casting down the dwelling place of your name to the ground.

8 They said in their hearts, Let us destroy them together: they have burned up all the synagogues of God in the land.

9 We see not our signs: there is no more any prophet: neither is there among us any that knoweth how long.

10 O God, how long shall the adversary reproach? shall the enemy blaspheme your name for ever?

11 Why withdrawest you your hand, even your right hand? pluck it out of your bosom.

12 For God is my King of old, working salvation in the midst of the earth.

13 You did divide the sea by your strength: you brakest the heads of the dragons in the waters.

14 You brakest the heads of leviathan in pieces, and gavest him to be meat to the people inhabiting the wilderness.

15 You did cleave the fountain and the flood: you driedst up mighty rivers.

16 The day is yours, the night also is yours: you have prepared the light and the sun.

17 You have set all the borders of the earth: you have made summer and winter.

18 Remember this, that the enemy has reproached, O LORD, and that the foolish people have blasphemed your name.

19 O deliver not the soul of your turtledove unto the multitude of the wicked: forget not the congregation of your poor for ever.

20 Have respect unto the covenant: for the dark places of the earth are full of the habitations of cruelty.

21 O let not the oppressed return ashamed: let the poor and needy praise your name.

22 Arise, O God, plead yours own cause: remember how the foolish man reproacheth you daily.

23 Forget not the voice of yours enemies: the tumult of those that rise up against you increaseth continually.

PSALM 75

To the chief Musician, Al-taschith, A Psalm or Song of Asaph.

UNTO you, O God, do we give thanks, unto you do we give thanks: for that your name is near your wondrous works declare.

2 When I shall receive the congregation I will judge uprightly.

3 The earth and all the inhabitants thereof are dissolved: I bear up the pillars of it. Selah.

4 I said unto the fools, Deal not foolishly: and to the wicked, Lift not up the horn:

5 Lift not up your horn on high: speak not with a stiff neck.

6 For promotion comes neither from the east, nor from the west, nor from the south.

7 But God is the judge: he putteth down one, and setteth up another.

8 For in the hand of the LORD there is a cup, and the wine is red; it is full of mixture; and he poureth out of the same: but the dregs thereof, all the wicked of the earth shall wring them out, and drink them.

9 But I will declare for ever; I will sing praises to the God of Jacob.

10 All the horns of the wicked also will I cut off; but the horns of the righteous shall be exalted.

PSALM 76

To the chief Musician on Neginoth, A Psalm or Song of Asaph.

IN Judah is God known: his name is great in Israel.

2 In Salem also is his tabernacle, and his dwelling place in Zion.

3 There brake he the arrows of the bow, the shield, and the sword, and the battle. Selah.

4 You are more glorious and excellent than the mountains of prey.

5 The stouthearted are spoiled, they have slept their sleep: and none of the men of might have found their hands.

6 At your rebuke, O God of Jacob, both the chariot and horse are cast into a dead sleep.

7 You , even you , are to be feared: and who may stand in your sight when once you are angry?

8 You did cause judgment to be heard from heaven; the earth feared, and was still,

9 When God arose to judgment, to save all the meek of the earth. Selah.

10 Surely the wrath of man shall praise you: the remainder of wrath shalt you restrain.

11 Vow, and pay unto the LORD your God: let all that be round about him bring presents unto him that ought to be feared.

12 He shall cut off the spirit of princes: he is terrible to the kings of the earth.

PSALM 77

To the chief Musician, to Jeduthun, A Psalm of Asaph.

I CRIED unto God with my voice, even unto God with my voice; and he gave ear unto me.

2 In the day of my trouble I sought the Lord: my sore ran in the night, and ceased not: my soul refused to be comforted.

3 I remembered God, and was troubled: I complained, and my spirit was overwhelmed. Selah.

4 You holdest my eyes waking: I am so troubled that I cannot speak.

5 I have considered the days of old, the years of ancient times.

6 I call to remembrance my song in the night: I commune with my own heart: and my spirit made diligent search.

7 Will the Lord cast off for ever? and will he be favourable no more?

8 Is his mercy clean gone for ever? doth his promise fail for evermore?

9 Has God forgotten to be gracious? has he in anger shut up his tender mercies? Selah.

10 And I said, This is my infirmity: but I will remember the years of the right hand of the most High.

11 I will remember the works of the LORD: surely I will remember your wonders of old.

12 I will meditate also of all your work, and talk of your doings.

13 Your way, O God, is in the sanctuary: who is so great a God as our God?

14 You are the God that doest wonders: you have declared your strength among the people.

15 You have with yours arm redeemed your people, the sons of Jacob and Joseph. Selah.

16 The waters saw you, O God, the waters saw you; they were afraid: the depths also were troubled.

17 The clouds poured out water: the skies sent out a sound: yours arrows also went abroad.

18 The voice of your thunder was in the heaven: the lightnings lightened the world: the earth trembled and shook.

19 Your way is in the sea, and your path in the great waters, and your footsteps are not known.

20 You leddest your people like a flock by the hand of Moses and Aaron.

PSALM 78

Maschil of Asaph.

GIVE ear, O my people, to my law: incline your ears to the words of my mouth.

2 I will open my mouth in a parable: I will utter dark sayings of old:

3 Which we have heard and known, and our fathers have told us.

4 We will not hide them from their children, shewing to the generation to come the praises of the LORD, and his strength, and his wonderful works that he has done.

5 For he established a testimony in Jacob, and appointed a law in Israel, which he commanded our fathers, that they should make them known to their children:

6 That the generation to come might know them, even the children which should be born; who should arise and declare them to their children:

7 That they might set their hope in God, and not forget the works of God, but keep his commandments:

8 And might not be as their fathers, a stubborn and rebellious generation; a generation that set not their heart aright, and whose spirit was not stedfast with God.

9 The children of Ephraim, being armed, and carrying bows, turned back in the day of battle.

10 They kept not the covenant of God, and refused to walk in his law;

11 And forgat his works, and his wonders that he had shewed them.

12 Marvellous things did he in the sight of their fathers, in the land of Egypt, in the field of Zoan.

13 He divided the sea, and caused them to pass through; and he made the waters to stand as an heap.

14 In the daytime also he led them with a cloud, and all the night with a light of fire.

15 He clave the rocks in the wilderness, and gave them drink as out of the great depths.

16 He brought streams also out of the rock, and caused waters to run down like rivers.

17 And they sinned yet more against him by provoking the most High in the wilderness.

18 And they tempted God in their heart by asking meat for their lust.

19 Yea, they spake against God; they said, Can God furnish a table in the wilderness?

20 Behold, he struck the rock, that the waters gushed out, and the streams overflowed; can he give bread also? can he provide flesh for his people?

21 Therefore the LORD heard this, and was wroth: so a fire was kindled against Jacob, and anger also came up against Israel;

22 Because they believed not in God, and trusted not in his salvation:

23 Though he had commanded the clouds from above, and opened the doors of heaven,

24 And had rained down manna upon them to eat, and had given them of the corn of heaven.

25 Man did eat angels' food: he sent them meat to the full.

26 He caused an east wind to blow in the heaven: and by his power he brought in the south wind.

27 He rained flesh also upon them as dust, and feathered fowls like as the sand of the sea:

28 And he let it fall in the midst of their camp, round about their habitations.

29 So they did eat, and were well filled: for he gave them their own desire;

30 They were not estranged from their lust. But while their meat was yet in their mouths,

31 The wrath of God came upon them, and slew the fattest of them, and struck down the chosen men of Israel.

32 For all this they sinned still, and believed not for his wondrous works.

33 Therefore their days did he consume in vanity, and their years in trouble.

34 When he slew them, then they sought him: and they returned and inquired early after God.

35 And they remembered that God was their rock, and the high God their redeemer.

36 Nevertheless they did flatter him with their mouth, and they lied unto him with their tongues.

37 For their heart was not right with him, neither were they stedfast in his covenant.

38 But he, being full of compassion, forgave their iniquity, and destroyed them not: yea, many a time turned he his anger away, and did not stir up all his wrath.

39 For he remembered that they were but flesh; a wind that passes away, and comes not again.

40 How oft did they provoke him in the wilderness, and grieve him in the desert!

41 Yea, they turned back and tempted God, and limited the Holy One of Israel.

42 They remembered not his hand, nor the day when he delivered them from the enemy.

43 How he had created his signs in Egypt, and his wonders in the field of Zoan:

44 And had turned their rivers into blood; and their floods, that they could not drink.

45 He sent divers sorts of flies among them, which devoured them; and frogs, which destroyed them.

46 He gave also their increase unto the caterpiller, and their labour unto the locust.

47 He destroyed their vines with hail, and their sycomore trees with frost.

48 He gave up their cattle also to the hail, and their flocks to hot thunderbolts.

49 He cast upon them the fierceness of his anger, wrath, and indignation, and trouble, by sending evil angels among them.

50 He made a way to his anger; he spared not their soul from death, but gave their life over to the pestilence;

51 And struck all the firstborn in Egypt; the chief of their strength in the tabernacles of Ham:

52 But made his own people to go forth like sheep, and guided them in the wilderness like a flock.

53 And he led them on safely, so that they feared not: but the sea overwhelmed their enemies.

54 And he brought them to the border of his sanctuary, even to this mountain, which his right hand had purchased.

55 He cast out the heathen also before them, and divided them an inheritance by line, and made the tribes of Israel to dwell in their tents.

56 Yet they tempted and provoked the most high God, and kept not his testimonies:

57 But turned back, and dealt unfaithfully like their fathers: they were turned aside like a deceitful bow.

58 For they provoked him to anger with their high places, and moved him to jealousy with their graven images.

59 When God heard this, he was wroth, and greatly abhorred Israel:

60 So that he forsook the tabernacle of Shiloh, the tent which he placed among men;

61 And delivered his strength into captivity, and his glory into the enemy's hand.

62 He gave his people over also unto the sword; and was wroth with his inheritance.

63 The fire consumed their young men; and their maidens were not given to marriage.

64 Their priests fell by the sword; and their widows made no lamentation.

65 Then the Lord awaked as one out of sleep, and like a mighty man that shouteth by reason of wine.

66 And he struck his enemies in the hinder parts: he put them to a perpetual reproach.

67 Moreover he refused the tabernacle of Joseph, and chose not the tribe of Ephraim:

68 But chose the tribe of Judah, the mount Zion which he loved.

69 And he built his sanctuary like high palaces, like the earth which he has established for ever.

70 He chose David also his servant, and took him from the sheepfolds:

71 From following the ewes great with young he brought him to feed Jacob his people, and Israel his inheritance.

72 So he fed them according to the integrity of his heart; and guided them by the skilfulness of his hands.

PSALM 79
A Psalm of Asaph.

O GOD, the heathen are come into yours inheritance; your holy temple have they defiled; they have laid Jerusalem on heaps.

2 The dead bodies of your servants have they given to be meat unto the fowls of the heaven, the flesh of your saints unto the beasts of the earth.

3 Their blood have they shed like water round about Jerusalem; and there was none to bury them.

4 We are become a reproach to our neighbours, a scorn and derision to them that are round about us.

5 How long, LORD? will you be angry for ever? shall your jealousy burn like fire?

6 Pour out your wrath upon the heathen that have not known you, and upon the kingdoms that have not called upon your name.

7 For they have devoured Jacob, and laid waste his dwelling place.

8 O remember not against us former iniquities: let your tender mercies speedily prevent us: for we are brought very low.

9 Help us, O God of our salvation, for the glory of your name: and deliver us, and purge away our sins, for your name's sake.

10 Wherefore should the heathen say, Where is their God? let him be known among the heathen in our sight by the revenging of the blood of your servants which is shed.

11 Let the sighing of the prisoner come before you; according to the greatness of your power preserve you those that are appointed to die;

12 And render unto our neighbours sevenfold into their bosom their reproach, wherewith they have reproached you, O Lord.

13 So we your people and sheep of your pasture will give you thanks for ever: we will shew forth your praise to all generations.

PSALM 80
To the chief Musician upon Shoshannim-Eduth, A Psalm of Asaph.

GIVE ear, O Shepherd of Israel, you that leadest Joseph like a flock; you that dwellest between the cherubims, shine forth.

2 Before Ephraim and Benjamin and Manasseh stir up your strength, and come and save us.

3 Turn us again, O God, and cause your face to shine; and we shall be saved.

4 O LORD God of hosts, how long will you be angry against the prayer of your people?

5 You feedest them with the bread of tears; and givest them tears to drink in great measure.

6 You makest us a strife unto our neighbours: and our enemies laugh among themselves.

7 Turn us again, O God of hosts, and cause your face to shine; and we shall be saved.

8 You have brought a vine out of Egypt: you have cast out the heathen, and planted it.

9 You preparedst room before it, and did cause it to take deep root, and it filled the land.

10 The hills were covered with the shadow of it, and the boughs thereof were like the goodly cedars.

11 She sent out her boughs unto the sea, and her branches unto the river.

12 Why have you then broken down her hedges, so that all they which pass by the way do pluck her?

13 The boar out of the wood doth waste it, and the wild beast of the field doth devour it.

14 Return, we beseech you, O God of hosts: look down from heaven, and behold, and visit this vine;

15 And the vineyard which your right hand has planted, and the branch that you madest strong for yourself.

16 It is burned with fire, it is cut down: they perish at the rebuke of your countenance.

17 Let your hand be upon the man of your right hand, upon the son of man whom you madest strong for yourself.

18 So will not we go back from you: quicken us, and we will call upon your name.

19 Turn us again, O LORD God of hosts, cause your face to shine; and we shall be saved.

PSALM 81
To the chief Musician upon Gittith, A Psalm of Asaph.

SING aloud unto God our strength: make a joyful noise unto the God of Jacob.

2 Take a psalm, and bring hither the timbrel, the pleasant harp with the psaltery.

3 Blow up the trumpet in the new moon, in the time appointed, on our solemn feast day.

4 For this was a statute for Israel, and a law of the God of Jacob.

5 This he ordained in Joseph for a testimony, when he went out through the land of Egypt: where I heard a language that I understood not.

6 I removed his shoulder from the burden: his hands were delivered from the pots.

7 You calledst in trouble, and I delivered you; I answered you in the secret place of thunder: I proved you at the waters of Meribah. Selah.

8 Hear, O my people, and I will testify unto you: O Israel, if you will hearken unto me;

9 There shall no strange god be in you; neither shalt you worship any strange god.

10 I am the LORD your God, which brought you out of the land of Egypt: open your mouth wide, and I will fill it.

11 But my people would not hearken to my voice; and Israel would none of me.

12 So I gave them up unto their own hearts' lust: and they walked in their own counsels.

13 Oh that my people had hearkened unto me, and Israel had walked in my ways!

14 I should soon have subdued their enemies, and turned my hand against their adversaries.

15 The haters of the LORD should have submitted themselves unto him: but their time should have endured for ever.

16 He should have fed them also with the finest of the wheat: and with honey out of the rock should I have satisfied you.

PSALM 82

A Psalm of Asaph.

GOD standeth in the congregation of the mighty; he judgeth among the gods.

2 How long will you judge unjustly, and accept the persons of the wicked? Selah.

3 Defend the poor and fatherless: do justice to the afflicted and needy.

4 Deliver the poor and needy: rid them out of the hand of the wicked.

5 They know not, neither will they understand; they walk on in darkness: all the foundations of the earth are out of course.

6 I have said, You are gods; and all of you are children of the most High.

7 But you shall die like men, and fall like one of the princes.

8 Arise, O God, judge the earth: for you shalt inherit all nations.

PSALM 83

A Song or Psalm of Asaph.

KEEP not you silence, O God: hold not your peace, and be not still, O God.

2 For, lo, yours enemies make a tumult: and they that hate you have lifted up the head.

3 They have taken crafty counsel against your people, and consulted against your hidden ones.

4 They have said, Come, and let us cut them off from being a nation; that the name of Israel may be no more in remembrance.

5 For they have consulted together with one consent: they are confederate against you:

6 The tabernacles of Edom, and the Ishmaelites; of Moab, and the Hagarenes;

7 Gebal, and Ammon, and Amalek; the Philistines with the inhabitants of Tyre;

8 Assur also is joined with them: they have holpen the children of Lot. Selah.

9 Do unto them as unto the Midianites; as to Sisera, as to Jabin, at the brook of Kison:

10 Which perished at En-dor: they became as dung for the earth.

11 Make their nobles like Oreb, and like Zeeb: yea, all their princes as Zebah, and as Zalmunna:

12 Who said, Let us take to ourselves the houses of God in possession.

13 O my God, make them like a wheel; as the stubble before the wind.

14 As the fire burneth a wood, and as the flame setteth the mountains on fire;

15 So persecute them with your tempest, and make them afraid with your storm.

16 Fill their faces with shame; that they may seek your name, O LORD.

17 Let them be confounded and troubled for ever; yea, let them be put to shame, and perish:

18 That men may know that you, whose name alone is JEHOVAH, are the most high over all the earth.

PSALM 84

To the chief Musician upon Gittith, A Psalm for the sons of Korah.

HOW amiable are your tabernacles, O LORD of hosts!

2 My soul longeth, yea, even fainteth for the courts of the LORD: my heart and my flesh crieth out for the living God.

3 Yea, the sparrow has found an house, and the swallow a nest for herself, where she may lay her young, even yours altars, O LORD of hosts, my King, and my God.

4 Blessed are they that dwell in your house: they will be still praising you. Selah.

5 Blessed is the man whose strength is in you; in whose heart are the ways of them.

6 Who passing through the valley of Baca make it a well; the rain also filleth the pools.

7 They go from strength to strength, every one of them in Zion appeareth before God.

8 O LORD God of hosts, hear my prayer: give ear, O God of Jacob. Selah.

9 Behold, O God our shield, and look upon the face of yours anointed.

10 For a day in your courts is better than a thousand. I had rather be a doorkeeper in the house of my God, than to dwell in the tents of wickedness.

11 For the LORD God is a sun and shield: the LORD will give grace and glory: no good thing will he withhold from them that walk uprightly.

12 O LORD of hosts, blessed is the man that trusteth in you.

PSALM 85

To the chief Musician, A Psalm for the sons of Korah.

LORD, you have been favourable unto your land: you have brought back the captivity of Jacob.

2 You have forgiven the iniquity of your people, you have covered all their sin. Selah.

3 You have taken away all your wrath: you have turned yourself from the fierceness of yours anger.

4 Turn us, O God of our salvation, and cause yours anger toward us to cease.

5 Will you be angry with us for ever? will you draw out yours anger to all generations?

6 Will you not revive us again: that your people may rejoice in you?

7 Shew us your mercy, O LORD, and grant us your salvation.

8 I will hear what God the LORD will speak: for he will speak peace unto his people, and to his saints: but let them not turn again to folly.

9 Surely his salvation is nigh them that fear him; that glory may dwell in our land.

10 Mercy and truth are met together; righteousness and peace have kissed each other.

11 Truth shall spring out of the earth; and righteousness shall look down from heaven.

12 Yea, the LORD shall give that which is good; and our land shall yield her increase.

13 Righteousness shall go before him; and shall set us in the way of his steps.

PSALM 86

A Prayer of David.

BOW down yours ear, O LORD, hear me: for I am poor and needy.

2 Preserve my soul; for I am holy: O you my God, save your servant that trusteth in you.

3 Be merciful unto me, O Lord: for I cry unto you daily.

4 Rejoice the soul of your servant: for unto you, O Lord, do I lift up my soul.

5 For you, Lord, are good, and ready to forgive; and plenteous in mercy unto all them that call upon you.

6 Give ear, O LORD, unto my prayer; and attend to the voice of my supplications.

7 In the day of my trouble I will call upon you: for you will answer me.

8 Among the gods there is none like unto you, O Lord; neither are there any works like unto your works.

9 All nations whom you have made shall come and worship before you, O Lord; and shall glorify your name.

10 For you are great, and doest wondrous things: you are God alone.

11 Teach me your way, O LORD; I will walk in your truth: unite my heart to fear your name.

12 I will praise you, O Lord my God, with all my heart: and I will glorify your name for evermore.

13 For great is your mercy toward me: and you have delivered my soul from the lowest hell.

14 O God, the proud are risen against me, and the assemblies of violent men have sought after my soul; and have not set you before them.

15 But you, O Lord, are a God full of compassion, and gracious, longsuffering, and plenteous in mercy and truth.

16 O turn unto me, and have mercy upon me; give your strength unto your servant, and save the son of yours handmaid.

17 Shew me a token for good; that they which hate me may see it, and be ashamed: because you, LORD, have holpen me, and comforted me.

PSALM 87

A Psalm or Song for the sons of Korah.

HIS foundation is in the holy mountains.

2 The LORD loveth the gates of Zion more than all the dwellings of Jacob.

3 Glorious things are spoken of you, O city of God. Selah.

4 I will make mention of Rahab and Babylon to them that know me: behold Philistia, and Tyre, with Ethiopia; this man was born there.

5 And of Zion it shall be said, This and that man was born in her: and the highest himself shall establish her.

6 The LORD shall count, when he writeth up the people, that this man was born there. Selah.

7 As well the singers as the players on instruments shall be there: all my springs are in you.

PSALM 88

A Song or Psalm for the sons of Korah, to the chief Musician upon Mahalath Leannoth, Maschil of Heman the Ezrahite.

O LORD God of my salvation, I have cried day and night before you:

2 Let my prayer come before you: incline yours ear unto my cry;

3 For my soul is full of troubles: and my life draweth nigh unto the grave.

4 I am counted with them that go down into the pit: I am as a man that has no strength:

5 Free among the dead, like the slain that lie in the grave, whom you rememberest no more: and they are cut off from your hand.

6 You have laid me in the lowest pit, in darkness, in the deeps.

7 Your wrath lies hard upon me, and you have afflicted me with all your waves. Selah.

8 You have put away my acquaintance far from me; you have made me an abomination unto them: I am shut up, and I cannot come forth.

9 My eye mourneth by reason of affliction: LORD, I have called daily upon you, I have stretched out my hands unto you.

10 Will you shew wonders to the dead? shall the dead arise and praise you? Selah.

11 Shall your lovingkindness be declared in the grave? or your faithfulness in destruction?

12 Shall your wonders be known in the dark? and your righteousness in the land of forgetfulness?

13 But unto you have I cried, O LORD; and in the morning shall my prayer prevent you.

14 LORD, why castest you off my soul? why hidest you your face from me?

15 I am afflicted and ready to die from my youth up: while I suffer your terrors I am distracted.

16 Your fierce wrath goeth over me; your terrors have cut me off.

17 They came round about me daily like water; they compassed me about together.

18 Lover and friend have you put far from me, and my acquaintance into darkness.

PSALM 89

Maschil of Ethan the Ezrahite.

I WILL sing of the mercies of the LORD for ever: with my mouth will I make known your faithfulness to all generations.

2 For I have said, Mercy shall be built up for ever: your faithfulness shalt you establish in the very heavens.

3 I have made a covenant with my chosen, I have sworn unto David my servant,

4 Your seed will I establish for ever, and build up your throne to all generations. Selah.

5 And the heavens shall praise your wonders, O LORD: your faithfulness also in the congregation of the saints.

6 For who in the heaven can be compared unto the LORD? who among the sons of the mighty can be likened unto the LORD?

7 God is greatly to be feared in the assembly of the saints, and to be had in reverence of all them that are about him.

8 O LORD God of hosts, who is a strong LORD like unto you? or to your faithfulness round about you?

9 You rulest the raging of the sea: when the waves thereof arise, you stillest them.

10 You have broken Rahab in pieces, as one that is slain; you have scattered yours enemies with your strong arm.

11 The heavens are yours, the earth also is yours: as for the world and the fulness thereof, you have founded them.

12 The north and the south you have created them: Tabor and Hermon shall rejoice in your name.

13 You have a mighty arm: strong is your hand, and high is your right hand.

14 Justice and judgment are the habitation of your throne: mercy and truth shall go before your face.

15 Blessed is the people that know the joyful sound: they shall walk, O LORD, in the light of your countenance.

16 In your name shall they rejoice all the day: and in your righteousness shall they be exalted.

17 For you are the glory of their strength: and in your favour our horn shall be exalted.

18 For the LORD is our defence; and the Holy One of Israel is our king.

19 Then you spakest in vision to your holy one, and saidst, I have laid help upon one that is mighty; I have exalted one chosen out of the people.

20 I have found David my servant; with my holy oil have I anointed him:

21 With whom my hand shall be established: my arm also shall strengthen him.

22 The enemy shall not exact upon him; nor the son of wickedness afflict him.

23 And I will beat down his foes before his face, and plague them that hate him.

24 But my faithfulness and my mercy shall be with him: and in my name shall his horn be exalted.

25 I will set his hand also in the sea, and his right hand in the rivers.

26 He shall cry unto me, You are my father, my God, and the rock of my salvation.

27 Also I will make him my firstborn, higher than the kings of the earth.

28 My mercy will I keep for him for evermore, and my covenant shall stand fast with him.

29 His seed also will I make to endure for ever, and his throne as the days of heaven.

30 If his children forsake my law, and walk not in my judgments;

31 If they break my statutes, and keep not my commandments;

32 Then will I visit their transgression with the rod, and their iniquity with stripes.

33 Nevertheless my lovingkindness will I not utterly take from him, nor suffer my faithfulness to fail.

34 My covenant will I not break, nor alter the thing that is gone out of my lips.

35 Once have I sworn by my holiness that I will not lie unto David.

36 His seed shall endure for ever, and his throne as the sun before me.

37 It shall be established for ever as the moon, and as a faithful witness in heaven. Selah.

38 But you have cast off and abhorred, you have been wroth with yours anointed.

39 You have made void the covenant of your servant: you have profaned his crown by casting it to the ground.

40 You have broken down all his hedges; you have brought his strong holds to ruin.

41 All that pass by the way spoil him: he is a reproach to his neighbours.

42 You have set up the right hand of his adversaries; you have made all his enemies to rejoice.

43 You have also turned the edge of his sword, and have not made him to stand in the battle.

44 You have made his glory to cease, and cast his throne down to the ground.

45 The days of his youth have you shortened: you have covered him with shame. Selah.

46 How long, LORD? will you hide yourself for ever? shall your wrath burn like fire?

47 Remember how short my time is: wherefore have you made all men in vain?

48 What man is he that liveth, and shall not see death? shall he deliver his soul from the hand of the grave? Selah.

49 Lord, where are your former lovingkindnesses, which you swarest unto David in your truth?

50 Remember, Lord, the reproach of your servants; how I do bear in my bosom the reproach of all the mighty people;

51 Wherewith yours enemies have reproached, O LORD; wherewith they have reproached the footsteps of yours anointed.

52 Blessed be the LORD for evermore. Amen, and Amen.

PSALM 90

A Prayer of Moses the man of God.

LORD, you have been our dwelling place in all generations.

2 Before the mountains were brought forth, or ever you hadst formed the earth and the world, even from everlasting to everlasting, you are God.

3 You turnest man to destruction; and say, Return, you children of men.

4 For a thousand years in your sight are but as yesterday when it is past, and as a watch in the night.

5 You carriest them away as with a flood; they are as a sleep: in the morning they are like grass which groweth up.

6 In the morning it flourisheth, and groweth up; in the evening it is cut down, and withereth.

7 For we are consumed by yours anger, and by your wrath are we troubled.

8 You have set our iniquities before you, our secret sins in the light of your countenance.

9 For all our days are passed away in your wrath: we spend our years as a tale that is told.

10 The days of our years are threescore years and ten; and if by reason of strength they be fourscore years, yet is their strength labour and sorrow; for it is soon cut off, and we fly away.

11 Who knoweth the power of yours anger? even according to your fear, so is your wrath.

12 So teach us to number our days, that we may apply our hearts unto wisdom.

13 Return, O LORD, how long? and let it repent you concerning your servants.

14 O satisfy us early with your mercy; that we may rejoice and be glad all our days.

15 Make us glad according to the days wherein you have afflicted us, and the years wherein we have seen evil.

16 Let your work appear unto your servants, and your glory unto their children.

17 And let the beauty of the LORD our God be upon us: and establish you the work of our hands upon us; yea, the work of our hands establish you it.

PSALM 91

HE that dwelleth in the secret place of the most High shall abide under the shadow of the Almighty.

2 I will say of the LORD, He is my refuge and my fortress: my God; in him will I trust.

3 Surely he shall deliver you from the snare of the fowler, and from the noisome pestilence.

4 He shall cover you with his feathers, and under his wings shalt you trust: his truth shall be your shield and buckler.

5 You shalt not be afraid for the terror by night; nor for the arrow that flieth by day;

6 Nor for the pestilence that walketh in darkness; nor for the destruction that wasteth at noonday.

7 A thousand shall fall at your side, and ten thousand at your right hand; but it shall not come nigh you.

8 Only with yours eyes shalt you behold and see the reward of the wicked.

9 Because you have made the LORD, which is my refuge, even the most High, your habitation;

10 There shall no evil befall you, neither shall any plague come nigh your dwelling.

11 For he shall give his angels charge over you, to keep you in all your ways.

12 They shall bear you up in their hands, lest you dash your foot against a stone.

13 You shalt tread upon the lion and adder: the young lion and the dragon shalt you trample under feet.

14 Because he has set his love upon me, therefore will I deliver him: I will set him on high, because he has known my name.

15 He shall call upon me, and I will answer him: I will be with him in trouble; I will deliver him, and honour him.

16 With long life will I satisfy him, and shew him my salvation.

PSALM 92

A Psalm or Song for the sabbath day.

IT is a good thing to give thanks unto the LORD, and to sing praises unto your name, O most High:

2 To shew forth your lovingkindness in the morning, and your faithfulness every night,

3 Upon an instrument of ten strings, and upon the psaltery; upon the harp with a solemn sound.

4 For you, LORD, have made me glad through your work: I will triumph in the works of your hands.

5 O LORD, how great are your works! and your thoughts are very deep.

6 A brutish man knoweth not; neither doth a fool understand this.

7 When the wicked spring as the grass, and when all the workers of iniquity do flourish; it is that they shall be destroyed for ever:

8 But you, LORD, are most high for evermore.

9 For, lo, yours enemies, O LORD, for, lo, yours enemies shall perish; all the workers of iniquity shall be scattered.

10 But my horn shalt you exalt like the horn of an unicorn: I shall be anointed with fresh oil.

11 My eye also shall see my desire on my enemies, and my ears shall hear my desire of the wicked that rise up against me.

12 The righteous shall flourish like the palm tree: he shall grow like a cedar in Lebanon.

13 Those that be planted in the house of the LORD shall flourish in the courts of our God.

14 They shall still bring forth fruit in old age; they shall be fat and flourishing;

15 To shew that the LORD is upright: he is my rock, and there is no unrighteousness in him.

PSALM 93

THE LORD reigneth, he is clothed with majesty; the LORD is clothed with strength, wherewith he has girded himself: the world also is stablished, that it cannot be moved.

2 Your throne is established of old: you are from everlasting.

3 The floods have lifted up, O LORD, the floods have lifted up their voice; the floods lift up their waves.

4 The LORD on high is mightier than the noise of many waters, yea, than the mighty waves of the sea.

5 Your testimonies are very sure: holiness becometh yours house, O LORD, for ever.

PSALM 94

O LORD God, to whom vengeance belongeth; O God, to whom vengeance belongeth, shew yourself.

2 Lift up yourself, you judge of the earth: render a reward to the proud.

3 LORD, how long shall the wicked, how long shall the wicked triumph?

4 How long shall they utter and speak hard things? and all the workers of iniquity boast themselves?

5 They break in pieces your people, O LORD, and afflict yours heritage.

6 They slay the widow and the stranger, and murder the fatherless.

7 Yet they say, The LORD shall not see, neither shall the God of Jacob regard it.

8 Understand, you brutish among the people: and you fools, when will you be wise?

9 He that planted the ear, shall he not hear? he that formed the eye, shall he not see?

10 He that chastiseth the heathen, shall he not correct? he that teacheth man knowledge, shall not he know?

11 The LORD knoweth the thoughts of man, that they are vanity.

12 Blessed is the man whom you chastenest, O LORD, and teachest him out of your law;

13 That you mayest give him rest from the days of adversity, until the pit be digged for the wicked.

14 For the LORD will not cast off his people, neither will he forsake his inheritance.

15 But judgment shall return unto righteousness: and all the upright in heart shall follow it.

16 Who will rise up for me against the evildoers? or who will stand up for me against the workers of iniquity?

17 Unless the LORD had been my help, my soul had almost dwelt in silence.

18 When I said, My foot slippeth; your mercy, O LORD, held me up.

19 In the multitude of my thoughts within me your comforts delight my soul.

20 Shall the throne of iniquity have fellowship with you, which frameth mischief by a law?

21 They gather themselves together against the soul of the righteous, and condemn the innocent blood.

22 But the LORD is my defence; and my God is the rock of my refuge.

23 And he shall bring upon them their own iniquity, and shall cut them off in their own wickedness; yea, the LORD our God shall cut them off.

PSALM 95

O COME, let us sing unto the LORD: let us make a joyful noise to the rock of our salvation.

2 Let us come before his presence with thanksgiving, and make a joyful noise unto him with psalms.

3 For the LORD is a great God, and a great King above all gods.

4 In his hand are the deep places of the earth: the strength of the hills is his also.

5 The sea is his, and he made it: and his hands formed the dry land.

6 O come, let us worship and bow down: let us kneel before the LORD our maker.

7 For he is our God; and we are the people of his pasture, and the sheep of his hand. To day if you will hear his voice,

8 Harden not your heart, as in the provocation, and as in the day of temptation in the wilderness:

9 When your fathers tempted me, proved me, and saw my work.

10 Forty years long was I grieved with this generation, and said, It is a people that do err in their heart, and they have not known my ways:

11 Unto whom I sware in my wrath that they should not enter into my rest.

PSALM 96

O SING unto the LORD a new song: sing unto the LORD, all the earth.

2 Sing unto the LORD, bless his name; shew forth his salvation from day to day.

3 Declare his glory among the heathen, his wonders among all people.

4 For the LORD is great, and greatly to be praised: he is to be feared above all gods.

5 For all the gods of the nations are idols: but the LORD made the heavens.

6 Honour and majesty are before him: strength and beauty are in his sanctuary.

7 Give unto the LORD, O you kindreds of the people, give unto the LORD glory and strength.

8 Give unto the LORD the glory due unto his name: bring an offering, and come into his courts.

9 O worship the LORD in the beauty of holiness: fear before him, all the earth.

10 Say among the heathen that the LORD reigneth: the world also shall be established that it shall not be moved: he shall judge the people righteously.

11 Let the heavens rejoice, and let the earth be glad; let the sea roar, and the fulness thereof.

12 Let the field be joyful, and all that is therein: then shall all the trees of the wood rejoice

13 Before the LORD: for he comes, for he comes to judge the earth: he shall judge the world with righteousness, and the people with his truth.

PSALM 97

THE LORD reigneth; let the earth rejoice; let the multitude of isles be glad thereof.

2 Clouds and darkness are round about him: righteousness and judgment are the habitation of his throne.

3 A fire goeth before him, and burneth up his enemies round about.

4 His lightnings enlightened the world: the earth saw, and trembled.

5 The hills melted like wax at the presence of the LORD, at the presence of the Lord of the whole earth.

6 The heavens declare his righteousness, and all the people see his glory.

7 Confounded be all they that serve graven images, that boast themselves of idols: worship him, all you gods.

8 Zion heard, and was glad; and the daughters of Judah rejoiced because of your judgments, O LORD.

9 For you , LORD, are high above all the earth: you are exalted far above all gods.

10 You that love the LORD, hate evil: he preserveth the souls of his saints; he delivereth them out of the hand of the wicked.

11 Light is sown for the righteous, and gladness for the upright in heart.

12 Rejoice in the LORD, you righteous; and give thanks at the remembrance of his holiness.

PSALM 98

A Psalm.

O SING unto the LORD a new song; for he has done marvellous things: his right hand, and his holy arm, has gotten him the victory.

2 The LORD has made known his salvation: his righteousness has he openly shewed in the sight of the heathen.

3 He has remembered his mercy and his truth toward the house of Israel: all the ends of the earth have seen the salvation of our God.

4 Make a joyful noise unto the LORD, all the earth: make a loud noise, and rejoice, and sing praise.

5 Sing unto the LORD with the harp; with the harp, and the voice of a psalm.

6 With trumpets and sound of cornet make a joyful noise before the LORD, the King.

7 Let the sea roar, and the fulness thereof; the world, and they that dwell therein.

8 Let the floods clap their hands: let the hills be joyful together

9 Before the LORD; for he comes to judge the earth: with righteousness shall he judge the world, and the people with equity.

PSALM 99

THE LORD reigneth; let the people tremble: he sitteth between the cherubims; let the earth be moved.

2 The LORD is great in Zion; and he is high above all the people.

3 Let them praise your great and terrible name; for it is holy.

4 The king's strength also loveth judgment; you dost establish equity, you executest judgment and righteousness in Jacob.

5 Exalt you the LORD our God, and worship at his footstool; for he is holy.

6 Moses and Aaron among his priests, and Samuel among them that call upon his name; they called upon the LORD, and he answered them.

7 He spake unto them in the cloudy pillar: they kept his testimonies, and the ordinance that he gave them.

8 You answeredst them, O LORD our God: you wast a God that forgavest them, though you tookest vengeance of their inventions.

9 Exalt the LORD our God, and worship at his holy hill; for the LORD our God is holy.

PSALM 100

A Psalm of praise.

MAKE a joyful noise unto the LORD, all you lands.

2 Serve the LORD with gladness: come before his presence with singing.

3 Know you that the LORD he is God: it is he that has made us, and not we ourselves; we are his people, and the sheep of his pasture.

4 Enter into his gates with thanksgiving, and into his courts with praise: be thankful unto him, and bless his name.

5 For the LORD is good; his mercy is everlasting; and his truth endureth to all generations.

PSALM 101

A Psalm of David.

I WILL sing of mercy and judgment: unto you, O LORD, will I sing.

2 I will behave myself wisely in a perfect way. O when will you come unto me? I will walk within my house with a perfect heart.

3 I will set no wicked thing before my eyes: I hate the work of them that turn aside; it shall not cleave to me.

4 A froward heart shall depart from me: I will not know a wicked person.

5 Whoso privily slandereth his neighbour, him will I cut off: him that has an high look and a proud heart will not I suffer.

6 My eyes shall be upon the faithful of the land, that they may dwell with me: he that walketh in a perfect way, he shall serve me.

7 He that worketh deceit shall not dwell within my house: he that telleth lies shall not tarry in my sight.

8 I will early destroy all the wicked of the land; that I may cut off all wicked doers from the city of the LORD.

PSALM 102

A Prayer of the afflicted, when he is overwhelmed, and poureth out his complaint before the LORD.

HEAR my prayer, O LORD, and let my cry come unto you.

2 Hide not your face from me in the day when I am in trouble; incline yours ear unto me: in the day when I call answer me speedily.

3 For my days are consumed like smoke, and my bones are burned as an hearth.

4 My heart is smitten, and withered like grass; so that I forget to eat my bread.

5 By reason of the voice of my groaning my bones cleave to my skin.

6 I am like a pelican of the wilderness: I am like an owl of the desert.

7 I watch, and am as a sparrow alone upon the house top.

8 My enemies reproach me all the day; and they that are mad against me are sworn against me.

9 For I have eaten ashes like bread, and mingled my drink with weeping,

10 Because of yours indignation and your wrath: for you have lifted me up, and cast me down.

11 My days are like a shadow that declineth; and I am withered like grass.

12 But you , O LORD, shalt endure for ever; and your remembrance unto all generations.

13 You shalt arise, and have mercy upon Zion: for the time to favour her, yea, the set time, is come.

14 For your servants take pleasure in her stones, and favour the dust thereof.

15 So the heathen shall fear the name of the LORD, and all the kings of the earth your glory.

16 When the LORD shall build up Zion, he shall appear in his glory.

17 He will regard the prayer of the destitute, and not despise their prayer.

18 This shall be written for the generation to come: and the people which shall be created shall praise the LORD.

19 For he has looked down from the height of his sanctuary; from heaven did the LORD behold the earth;

20 To hear the groaning of the prisoner; to loose those that are appointed to death;

21 To declare the name of the LORD in Zion, and his praise in Jerusalem;

22 When the people are gathered together, and the kingdoms, to serve the LORD.

23 He weakened my strength in the way; he shortened my days.

24 I said, O my God, take me not away in the midst of my days: your years are throughout all generations.

25 Of old have you laid the foundation of the earth: and the heavens are the work of your hands.

26 They shall perish, but you shalt endure: yea, all of them shall wax old like a garment; as a vesture shalt you change them, and they shall be changed:

27 But you are the same, and your years shall have no end.

28 The children of your servants shall continue, and their seed shall be established before you.

PSALM 103

A Psalm of David.

BLESS the LORD, O my soul: and all that is within me, bless his holy name.

2 Bless the LORD, O my soul, and forget not all his benefits:

3 Who forgiveth all yours iniquities; who healeth all your diseases;

4 Who redeemeth your life from destruction; who crowneth you with lovingkindness and tender mercies;

5 Who satisfieth your mouth with good things; so that your youth is renewed like the eagle's.

6 The LORD executeth righteousness and judgment for all that are oppressed.

7 He made known his ways unto Moses, his acts unto the children of Israel.

8 The LORD is merciful and gracious, slow to anger, and plenteous in mercy.

9 He will not always chide: neither will he keep his anger for ever.

10 He has not dealt with us after our sins; nor rewarded us according to our iniquities.

11 For as the heaven is high above the earth, so great is his mercy toward them that fear him.

12 As far as the east is from the west, so far has he removed our transgressions from us.

13 Like as a father pitieth his children, so the LORD pitieth them that fear him.

14 For he knoweth our frame; he remembereth that we are dust.

15 As for man, his days are as grass: as a flower of the field, so he flourisheth.

16 For the wind passes over it, and it is gone; and the place thereof shall know it no more.

17 But the mercy of the LORD is from everlasting to everlasting upon them that fear him, and his righteousness unto children's children;

18 To such as keep his covenant, and to those that remember his commandments to do them.

19 The LORD has prepared his throne in the heavens; and his kingdom ruleth over all.

20 Bless the LORD, you his angels, that excel in strength, that do his commandments, hearkening unto the voice of his word.

21 Bless you the LORD, all you his hosts; you ministers of his, that do his pleasure.

22 Bless the LORD, all his works in all places of his dominion: bless the LORD, O my soul.

PSALM 104

BLESS the LORD, O my soul. O LORD my God, you are very great; you are clothed with honour and majesty.

2 Who coverest yourself with light as with a garment: who stretchest out the heavens like a curtain:

3 Who layeth the beams of his chambers in the waters: who maketh the clouds his chariot: who walketh upon the wings of the wind:

4 Who maketh his angels spirits; his ministers a flaming fire:

5 Who laid the foundations of the earth, that it should not be removed for ever.

6 You coveredst it with the deep as with a garment: the waters stood above the mountains.

7 At your rebuke they fled; at the voice of your thunder they hasted away.

8 They go up by the mountains; they go down by the valleys unto the place which you have founded for them.

9 You have set a bound that they may not pass over; that they turn not again to cover the earth.

10 He sendeth the springs into the valleys, which run among the hills.

11 They give drink to every beast of the field: the wild asses quench their thirst.

12 By them shall the fowls of the heaven have their habitation, which sing among the branches.

13 He watereth the hills from his chambers: the earth is satisfied with the fruit of your works.

14 He causeth the grass to grow for the cattle, and herb for the service of man: that he may bring forth food out of the earth;

15 And wine that maketh glad the heart of man, and oil to make his face to shine, and bread which strengtheneth man's heart.

16 The trees of the LORD are full of sap; the cedars of Lebanon, which he has planted;

17 Where the birds make their nests: as for the stork, the fir trees are her house.

18 The high hills are a refuge for the wild goats; and the rocks for the conies.

19 He appointed the moon for seasons: the sun knoweth his going down.

20 You makest darkness, and it is night: wherein all the beasts of the forest do creep forth.

21 The young lions roar after their prey, and seek their meat from God.

22 The sun ariseth, they gather themselves together, and lay them down in their dens.

23 Man goeth forth unto his work and to his labour until the evening.

24 O LORD, how manifold are your works! in wisdom have you made them all: the earth is full of your riches.

25 So is this great and wide sea, wherein are things creeping innumerable, both small and great beasts.

26 There go the ships: there is that leviathan, whom you have made to play therein.

27 These wait all upon you; that you mayest give them their meat in due season.

28 That you givest them they gather: you openest yours hand, they are filled with good.

29 You hidest your face, they are troubled: you takest away their breath, they die, and return to their dust.

30 You sendest forth your spirit, they are created: and you renewest the face of the earth.

31 The glory of the LORD shall endure for ever: the LORD shall rejoice in his works.

32 He looketh on the earth, and it trembleth: he toucheth the hills, and they smoke.

33 I will sing unto the LORD as long as I live: I will sing praise to my God while I have my being.

34 My meditation of him shall be sweet: I will be glad in the LORD.

35 Let the sinners be consumed out of the earth, and let the wicked be no more. Bless you the LORD, O my soul. Praise you the LORD.

PSALM 105

O GIVE thanks unto the LORD; call upon his name: make known his deeds among the people.

2 Sing unto him, sing psalms unto him: talk you of all his wondrous works.

3 Glory you in his holy name: let the heart of them rejoice that seek the LORD.

4 Seek the LORD, and his strength: seek his face evermore.

5 Remember his marvellous works that he has done; his wonders, and the judgments of his mouth;

6 O you seed of Abraham his servant, you children of Jacob his chosen.

7 He is the LORD our God: his judgments are in all the earth.

8 He has remembered his covenant for ever, the word which he commanded to a thousand generations.

9 Which covenant he made with Abraham, and his oath unto Isaac;

10 And confirmed the same unto Jacob for a law, and to Israel for an everlasting covenant:

11 Saying, Unto you will I give the land of Canaan, the lot of your inheritance:

12 When they were but a few men in number; yea, very few, and strangers in it.

13 When they went from one nation to another, from one kingdom to another people;

14 He suffered no man to do them wrong: yea, he reproved kings for their sakes;

15 Saying, Touch not my anointed, and do my prophets no harm.

16 Moreover he called for a famine upon the land: he brake the whole staff of bread.

17 He sent a man before them, even Joseph, who was sold for a servant:

18 Whose feet they hurt with fetters: he was laid in iron:

19 Until the time that his word came: the word of the LORD tried him.

20 The king sent and loosed him; even the ruler of the people, and let him go free.

21 He made him lord of his house, and ruler of all his substance:

22 To bind his princes at his pleasure; and teach his senators wisdom.

23 Israel also came into Egypt; and Jacob sojourned in the land of Ham.

24 And he increased his people greatly; and made them stronger than their enemies.

25 He turned their heart to hate his people, to deal subtilly with his servants.

26 He sent Moses his servant; and Aaron whom he had chosen.

27 They shewed his signs among them, and wonders in the land of Ham.

28 He sent darkness, and made it dark; and they rebelled not against his word.

29 He turned their waters into blood, and slew their fish.

30 Their land brought forth frogs in abundance, in the chambers of their kings.

31 He spake, and there came divers sorts of flies, and lice in all their coasts.

32 He gave them hail for rain, and flaming fire in their land.

33 He struck their vines also and their fig trees; and brake the trees of their coasts.

34 He spake, and the locusts came, and caterpillers, and that without number,

35 And did eat up all the herbs in their land, and devoured the fruit of their ground.

36 He struck also all the firstborn in their land, the chief of all their strength.

37 He brought them forth also with silver and gold: and there was not one feeble person among their tribes.

38 Egypt was glad when they departed: for the fear of them fell upon them.

39 He spread a cloud for a covering; and fire to give light in the night.

40 The people asked, and he brought quails, and satisfied them with the bread of heaven.

41 He opened the rock, and the waters gushed out; they ran in the dry places like a river.

42 For he remembered his holy promise, and Abraham his servant.

43 And he brought forth his people with joy, and his chosen with gladness:

44 And gave them the lands of the heathen: and they inherited the labour of the people;

45 That they might observe his statutes, and keep his laws. Praise you the LORD.

PSALM 106

PRAISE you the LORD. O give thanks unto the LORD; for he is good: for his mercy endureth for ever.

2 Who can utter the mighty acts of the LORD? who can shew forth all his praise?

3 Blessed are they that keep judgment, and he that doeth righteousness at all times.

4 Remember me, O LORD, with the favour that you bearest unto your people: O visit me with your salvation;

5 That I may see the good of your chosen, that I may rejoice in the gladness of your nation, that I may glory with yours inheritance.

6 We have sinned with our fathers, we have committed iniquity, we have done wickedly.

7 Our fathers understood not your wonders in Egypt; they remembered not the multitude of your mercies; but provoked him at the sea, even at the Red sea.

8 Nevertheless he saved them for his name's sake, that he might make his mighty power to be known.

9 He rebuked the Red sea also, and it was dried up: so he led them through the depths, as through the wilderness.

10 And he saved them from the hand of him that hated them, and redeemed them from the hand of the enemy.

11 And the waters covered their enemies: there was not one of them left.

12 Then believed they his words; they sang his praise.

13 They soon forgat his works; they waited not for his counsel:

14 But lusted exceedingly in the wilderness, and tempted God in the desert.

15 And he gave them their request; but sent leanness into their soul.

16 They envied Moses also in the camp, and Aaron the saint of the LORD.

17 The earth opened and swallowed up Dathan, and covered the company of Abiram.

18 And a fire was kindled in their company; the flame burned up the wicked.

19 They made a calf in Horeb, and worshipped the molten image.

20 Thus they changed their glory into the similitude of an ox that eateth grass.

21 They forgat God their saviour, which had done great things in Egypt;

22 Wondrous works in the land of Ham, and terrible things by the Red sea.

23 Therefore he said that he would destroy them, had not Moses his chosen stood before him in the breach, to turn away his wrath, lest he should destroy them.

24 Yea, they despised the pleasant land, they believed not his word:

25 But murmured in their tents, and hearkened not unto the voice of the LORD.

26 Therefore he lifted up his hand against them, to overthrow them in the wilderness:

27 To overthrow their seed also among the nations, and to scatter them in the lands.

28 They joined themselves also unto Baal-peor, and ate the sacrifices of the dead.

29 Thus they provoked him to anger with their inventions: and the plague brake in upon them.

30 Then stood up Phinehas, and executed judgment: and so the plague was stayed.

31 And that was counted unto him for righteousness unto all generations for evermore.

32 They angered him also at the waters of strife, so that it went ill with Moses for their sakes:

33 Because they provoked his spirit, so that he spake unadvisedly with his lips.

34 They did not destroy the nations, concerning whom the LORD commanded them:

35 But were mingled among the heathen, and learned their works.

36 And they served their idols: which were a snare unto them.

37 Yea, they sacrificed their sons and their daughters unto devils,

38 And shed innocent blood, even the blood of their sons and of their daughters, whom they sacrificed unto the idols of Canaan: and the land was polluted with blood.

39 Thus were they defiled with their own works, and went a whoring with their own inventions.

40 Therefore was the wrath of the LORD kindled against his people, insomuch that he abhorred his own inheritance.

41 And he gave them into the hand of the heathen; and they that hated them ruled over them.

42 Their enemies also oppressed them, and they were brought into subjection under their hand.

43 Many times did he deliver them; but they provoked him with their counsel, and were brought low for their iniquity.

44 Nevertheless he regarded their affliction, when he heard their cry:

45 And he remembered for them his covenant, and repented according to the multitude of his mercies.

46 He made them also to be pitied of all those that carried them captives.

47 Save us, O LORD our God, and gather us from among the heathen, to give thanks unto your holy name, and to triumph in your praise.

48 Blessed be the LORD God of Israel from everlasting to everlasting: and let all the people say, Amen. Praise you the LORD.

PSALM 107

O GIVE thanks unto the LORD, for he is good: for his mercy endureth for ever.

2 Let the redeemed of the LORD say so, whom he has redeemed from the hand of the enemy;

3 And gathered them out of the lands, from the east, and from the west, from the north, and from the south.

4 They wandered in the wilderness in a solitary way; they found no city to dwell in.

5 Hungry and thirsty, their soul fainted in them.

6 Then they cried unto the LORD in their trouble, and he delivered them out of their distresses.

7 And he led them forth by the right way, that they might go to a city of habitation.

8 Oh that men would praise the LORD for his goodness, and for his wonderful works to the children of men!

9 For he satisfieth the longing soul, and filleth the hungry soul with goodness.

10 Such as sit in darkness and in the shadow of death, being bound in affliction and iron;

11 Because they rebelled against the words of God, and contemned the counsel of the most High:

12 Therefore he brought down their heart with labour; they fell down, and there was none to help.

13 Then they cried unto the LORD in their trouble, and he saved them out of their distresses.

14 He brought them out of darkness and the shadow of death, and brake their bands in sunder.

15 Oh that men would praise the LORD for his goodness, and for his wonderful works to the children of men!

16 For he has broken the gates of brass, and cut the bars of iron in sunder.

17 Fools because of their transgression, and because of their iniquities, are afflicted.

18 Their soul abhorreth all manner of meat; and they draw near unto the gates of death.

19 Then they cry unto the LORD in their trouble, and he saveth them out of their distresses.

20 He sent his word, and healed them, and delivered them from their destructions.

21 Oh that men would praise the LORD for his goodness, and for his wonderful works to the children of men!

22 And let them sacrifice the sacrifices of thanksgiving, and declare his works with rejoicing.

23 They that go down to the sea in ships, that do business in great waters;

24 These see the works of the LORD, and his wonders in the deep.

25 For he commandeth, and raiseth the stormy wind, which lifteth up the waves thereof.

26 They mount up to the heaven, they go down again to the depths: their soul is melted because of trouble.

27 They reel to and fro, and stagger like a drunken man, and are at their wits' end.

28 Then they cry unto the LORD in their trouble, and he bringeth them out of their distresses.

29 He maketh the storm a calm, so that the waves thereof are still.

30 Then are they glad because they be quiet; so he bringeth them unto their desired haven.

31 Oh that men would praise the LORD for his goodness, and for his wonderful works to the children of men!

32 Let them exalt him also in the congregation of the people, and praise him in the assembly of the elders.

33 He turneth rivers into a wilderness, and the watersprings into dry ground;

34 A fruitful land into barrenness, for the wickedness of them that dwell therein.

35 He turneth the wilderness into a standing water, and dry ground into watersprings.

36 And there he maketh the hungry to dwell, that they may prepare a city for habitation;

37 And sow the fields, and plant vineyards, which may yield fruits of increase.

38 He blesseth them also, so that they are multiplied greatly; and suffereth not their cattle to decrease.

39 Again, they are minished and brought low through oppression, affliction, and sorrow.

40 He poureth contempt upon princes, and causeth them to wander in the wilderness, where there is no way.

41 Yet setteth he the poor on high from affliction, and maketh him families like a flock.

42 The righteous shall see it, and rejoice: and all iniquity shall stop her mouth.

43 Whoso is wise, and will observe these things, even they shall understand the lovingkindness of the LORD.

PSALM 108

A Song or Psalm of David.

O GOD, my heart is fixed; I will sing and give praise, even with my glory.

2 Awake, psaltery and harp: I myself will awake early.

3 I will praise you, O LORD, among the people: and I will sing praises unto you among the nations.

4 For your mercy is great above the heavens: and your truth reacheth unto the clouds.

5 Be you exalted, O God, above the heavens: and your glory above all the earth;

6 That your beloved may be delivered: save with your right hand, and answer me.

7 God has spoken in his holiness; I will rejoice, I will divide Shechem, and mete out the valley of Succoth.

8 Gilead is my; Manasseh is my; Ephraim also is the strength of my head; Judah is my lawgiver;

9 Moab is my washpot; over Edom will I cast out my shoe; over Philistia will I triumph.

10 Who will bring me into the strong city? who will lead me into Edom?

11 Will not you , O God, who have cast us off? and will not you , O God, go forth with our hosts?

12 Give us help from trouble: for vain is the help of man.

13 Through God we shall do valiantly: for he it is that shall tread down our enemies.

PSALM 109

To the chief Musician, A Psalm of David.

HOLD not your peace, O God of my praise;

2 For the mouth of the wicked and the mouth of the deceitful are opened against me: they have spoken against me with a lying tongue.

3 They compassed me about also with words of hatred; and fought against me without a cause.

4 For my love they are my adversaries: but I give myself unto prayer.

5 And they have rewarded me evil for good, and hatred for my love.

6 Set you a wicked man over him: and let Satan stand at his right hand.

7 When he shall be judged, let him be condemned: and let his prayer become sin.

8 Let his days be few; and let another take his office.

9 Let his children be fatherless, and his wife a widow.

10 Let his children be continually vagabonds, and beg: let them seek their bread also out of their desolate places.

11 Let the extortioner catch all that he has; and let the strangers spoil his labour.

12 Let there be none to extend mercy unto him: neither let there be any to favour his fatherless children.

13 Let his posterity be cut off; and in the generation following let their name be blotted out.

14 Let the iniquity of his fathers be remembered with the LORD; and let not the sin of his mother be blotted out.

15 Let them be before the LORD continually, that he may cut off the memory of them from the earth.

16 Because that he remembered not to shew mercy, but persecuted the poor and needy man, that he might even slay the broken in heart.

17 As he loved cursing, so let it come unto him: as he delighted not in blessing, so let it be far from him.

18 As he clothed himself with cursing like as with his garment, so let it come into his bowels like water, and like oil into his bones.

19 Let it be unto him as the garment which covers him, and for a girdle wherewith he is girded continually.

20 Let this be the reward of my adversaries from the LORD, and of them that speak evil against my soul.

21 But do you for me, O GOD the Lord, for your name's sake: because your mercy is good, deliver you me.

22 For I am poor and needy, and my heart is wounded within me.

23 I am gone like the shadow when it declineth: I am tossed up and down as the locust.

24 My knees are weak through fasting; and my flesh faileth of fatness.

25 I became also a reproach unto them: when they looked upon me they shaked their heads.

26 Help me, O LORD my God: O save me according to your mercy:

27 That they may know that this is your hand; that you, LORD, have done it.

28 Let them curse, but bless you : when they arise, let them be ashamed; but let your servant rejoice.

29 Let my adversaries be clothed with shame, and let them cover themselves with their own confusion, as with a mantle.

30 I will greatly praise the LORD with my mouth; yea, I will praise him among the multitude.

31 For he shall stand at the right hand of the poor, to save him from those that condemn his soul.

PSALM 110

A Psalm of David.

THE LORD said unto my Lord, Sit you at my right hand, until I make yours enemies your footstool.

2 The LORD shall send the rod of your strength out of Zion: rule you in the midst of yours enemies.

3 Your people shall be willing in the day of your power, in the beauties of holiness from the womb of the morning: you have the dew of your youth.

4 The LORD has sworn, and will not repent, You are a priest for ever after the order of Melchizedek.

5 The Lord at your right hand shall strike through kings in the day of his wrath.

6 He shall judge among the heathen, he shall fill the places with the dead bodies; he shall wound the heads over many countries.

7 He shall drink of the brook in the way: therefore shall he lift up the head.

PSALM 111

PRAISE you the LORD. I will praise the LORD with my whole heart, in the assembly of the upright, and in the congregation.

2 The works of the LORD are great, sought out of all them that have pleasure therein.

3 His work is honourable and glorious: and his righteousness endureth for ever.

4 He has made his wonderful works to be remembered: the LORD is gracious and full of compassion.

5 He has given meat unto them that fear him: he will ever be mindful of his covenant.

6 He has shewed his people the power of his works, that he may give them the heritage of the heathen.

7 The works of his hands are verity and judgment; all his commandments are sure.

8 They stand fast for ever and ever, and are done in truth and uprightness.

9 He sent redemption unto his people: he has commanded his covenant for ever: holy and reverend is his name.

10 The fear of the LORD is the beginning of wisdom: a good understanding have all they that do his commandments: his praise endureth for ever.

PSALM 112

PRAISE you the LORD. Blessed is the man that feareth the LORD, that delighteth greatly in his commandments.

2 His seed shall be mighty upon earth: the generation of the upright shall be blessed.

3 Wealth and riches shall be in his house: and his righteousness endureth for ever.

4 Unto the upright there ariseth light in the darkness: he is gracious, and full of compassion, and righteous.

5 A good man sheweth favour, and lendeth: he will guide his affairs with discretion.

6 Surely he shall not be moved for ever: the righteous shall be in everlasting remembrance.

7 He shall not be afraid of evil tidings: his heart is fixed, trusting in the LORD.

8 His heart is established, he shall not be afraid, until he see his desire upon his enemies.

9 He has dispersed, he has given to the poor; his righteousness endureth for ever; his horn shall be exalted with honour.

10 The wicked shall see it, and be grieved; he shall gnash with his teeth, and melt away: the desire of the wicked shall perish.

PSALM 113

PRAISE you the LORD. Praise, O you servants of the LORD, praise the name of the LORD.

2 Blessed be the name of the LORD from this time forth and for evermore.

3 From the rising of the sun unto the going down of the same the LORD's name is to be praised.

4 The LORD is high above all nations, and his glory above the heavens.

5 Who is like unto the LORD our God, who dwelleth on high,

6 Who humbleth himself to behold the things that are in heaven, and in the earth!

7 He raiseth up the poor out of the dust, and lifteth the needy out of the dunghill;

8 That he may set him with princes, even with the princes of his people.

9 He maketh the barren woman to keep house, and to be a joyful mother of children. Praise you the LORD.

PSALM 114

WHEN Israel went out of Egypt, the house of Jacob from a people of strange language;

2 Judah was his sanctuary, and Israel his dominion.

3 The sea saw it, and fled: Jordan was driven back.

4 The mountains skipped like rams, and the little hills like lambs.

5 What ailed you, O you sea, that you fled? you Jordan, that you wast driven back?

6 You mountains, that you skipped like rams; and you little hills, like lambs?

7 Tremble, you earth, at the presence of the Lord, at the presence of the God of Jacob;

8 Which turned the rock into a standing water, the flint into a fountain of waters.

PSALM 115

NOT unto us, O LORD, not unto us, but unto your name give glory, for your mercy, and for your truth's sake.

2 Wherefore should the heathen say, Where is now their God?

3 But our God is in the heavens: he has done whatsoever he has pleased.

4 Their idols are silver and gold, the work of men's hands.

5 They have mouths, but they speak not: eyes have they, but they see not:

6 They have ears, but they hear not: noses have they, but they smell not:

7 They have hands, but they handle not: feet have they, but they walk not: neither speak they through their throat.

8 They that make them are like unto them; so is every one that trusteth in them.

9 O Israel, trust you in the LORD: he is their help and their shield.

10 O house of Aaron, trust in the LORD: he is their help and their shield.

11 You that fear the LORD, trust in the LORD: he is their help and their shield.

12 The LORD has been mindful of us: he will bless us; he will bless the house of Israel; he will bless the house of Aaron.

13 He will bless them that fear the LORD, both small and great.

14 The LORD shall increase you more and more, you and your children.

15 You are blessed of the LORD which made heaven and earth.

16 The heaven, even the heavens, are the LORD's: but the earth has he given to the children of men.

17 The dead praise not the LORD, neither any that go down into silence.

18 But we will bless the LORD from this time forth and for evermore. Praise the LORD.

PSALM 116

I LOVE the LORD, because he has heard my voice and my supplications.

2 Because he has inclined his ear unto me, therefore will I call upon him as long as I live.

3 The sorrows of death compassed me, and the pains of hell gat hold upon me: I found trouble and sorrow.

4 Then called I upon the name of the LORD; O LORD, I beseech you, deliver my soul.

5 Gracious is the LORD, and righteous; yea, our God is merciful.

6 The LORD preserveth the simple: I was brought low, and he helped me.

7 Return unto your rest, O my soul; for the LORD has dealt bountifully with you.

8 For you have delivered my soul from death, my eyes from tears, and my feet from falling.

9 I will walk before the LORD in the land of the living.

10 I believed, therefore have I spoken: I was greatly afflicted:

11 I said in my haste, All men are liars.

12 What shall I render unto the LORD for all his benefits toward me?

13 I will take the cup of salvation, and call upon the name of the LORD.

14 I will pay my vows unto the LORD now in the presence of all his people.

15 Precious in the sight of the LORD is the death of his saints.

16 O LORD, truly I am your servant; I am your servant, and the son of yours handmaid: you have loosed my bonds.

17 I will offer to you the sacrifice of thanksgiving, and will call upon the name of the LORD.

18 I will pay my vows unto the LORD now in the presence of all his people,

19 In the courts of the LORD's house, in the midst of you, O Jerusalem. Praise you the LORD.

PSALM 117

O PRAISE the LORD, all you nations: praise him, all you people.

2 For his merciful kindness is great toward us: and the truth of the LORD endureth for ever. Praise you the LORD.

PSALM 118

O GIVE thanks unto the LORD; for he is good: because his mercy endureth for ever.

2 Let Israel now say, that his mercy endureth for ever.

3 Let the house of Aaron now say, that his mercy endureth for ever.

4 Let them now that fear the LORD say, that his mercy endureth for ever.

5 I called upon the LORD in distress: the LORD answered me, and set me in a large place.

6 The LORD is on my side; I will not fear: what can man do unto me?

7 The LORD taketh my part with them that help me: therefore shall I see my desire upon them that hate me.

8 It is better to trust in the LORD than to put confidence in man.

9 It is better to trust in the LORD than to put confidence in princes.

10 All nations compassed me about: but in the name of the LORD will I destroy them.

11 They compassed me about; yea, they compassed me about: but in the name of the LORD I will destroy them.

12 They compassed me about like bees; they are quenched as the fire of thorns: for in the name of the LORD I will destroy them.

13 You have thrust sore at me that I might fall: but the LORD helped me.

14 The LORD is my strength and song, and is become my salvation.

15 The voice of rejoicing and salvation is in the tabernacles of the righteous: the right hand of the LORD doeth valiantly.

16 The right hand of the LORD is exalted: the right hand of the LORD doeth valiantly.

17 I shall not die, but live, and declare the works of the LORD.

18 The LORD has chastened me sore: but he has not given me over unto death.

19 Open to me the gates of righteousness: I will go into them, and I will praise the LORD:

20 This gate of the LORD, into which the righteous shall enter.

21 I will praise you: for you have heard me, and are become my salvation.

22 The stone which the builders refused is become the head stone of the corner.

23 This is the LORD's doing; it is marvellous in our eyes.

24 This is the day which the LORD has made; we will rejoice and be glad in it.

25 Save now, I beseech you, O LORD: O LORD, I beseech you, send now prosperity.

26 Blessed be he that comes in the name of the LORD: we have blessed you out of the house of the LORD.

27 God is the LORD, which has shewed us light: bind the sacrifice with cords, even unto the horns of the altar.

28 You are my God, and I will praise you: you are my God, I will exalt you.

29 O give thanks unto the LORD; for he is good: for his mercy endureth for ever.

PSALM 119

ALEPH.

BLESSED are the undefiled in the way, who walk in the law of the LORD.

2 Blessed are they that keep his testimonies, and that seek him with the whole heart.

3 They also do no iniquity: they walk in his ways.

4 You have commanded us to keep your precepts diligently.

5 O that my ways were directed to keep your statutes!

6 Then shall I not be ashamed, when I have respect unto all your commandments.

7 I will praise you with uprightness of heart, when I shall have learned your righteous judgments.

8 I will keep your statutes: O forsake me not utterly.

BETH.

9 Wherewithal shall a young man cleanse his way? by taking heed thereto according to your word.

10 With my whole heart have I sought you: O let me not wander from your commandments.

11 Your word have I hid in my heart, that I might not sin against you.

12 Blessed are you , O LORD: teach me your statutes.

13 With my lips have I declared all the judgments of your mouth.

14 I have rejoiced in the way of your testimonies, as much as in all riches.

15 I will meditate in your precepts, and have respect unto your ways.

16 I will delight myself in your statutes: I will not forget your word.

GIMEL.

17 Deal bountifully with your servant, that I may live, and keep your word.

18 Open you my eyes, that I may behold wondrous things out of your law.

19 I am a stranger in the earth: hide not your commandments from me.

20 My soul breaketh for the longing that it has unto your judgments at all times.

21 You have rebuked the proud that are cursed, which do err from your commandments.

22 Remove from me reproach and contempt; for I have kept your testimonies.

23 Princes also did sit and speak against me: but your servant did meditate in your statutes.

24 Your testimonies also are my delight and my counsellers.

DALETH.

25 My soul cleaveth unto the dust: quicken you me according to your word.

26 I have declared my ways, and you heardest me: teach me your statutes.

27 Make me to understand the way of your precepts: so shall I talk of your wondrous works.

28 My soul melteth for heaviness: strengthen you me according unto your word.

29 Remove from me the way of lying: and grant me your law graciously.

30 I have chosen the way of truth: your judgments have I laid before me.

31 I have stuck unto your testimonies: O LORD, put me not to shame.

32 I will run the way of your commandments, when you shalt enlarge my heart.

HE.

33 Teach me, O LORD, the way of your statutes; and I shall keep it unto the end.

34 Give me understanding, and I shall keep your law; yea, I shall observe it with my whole heart.

35 Make me to go in the path of your commandments; for therein do I delight.

36 Incline my heart unto your testimonies, and not to covetousness.

37 Turn away my eyes from beholding vanity; and quicken you me in your way.

38 Stablish your word unto your servant, who is devoted to your fear.

39 Turn away my reproach which I fear: for your judgments are good.

40 Behold, I have longed after your precepts: quicken me in your righteousness.

VAU.

41 Let your mercies come also unto me, O LORD, even your salvation, according to your word.

42 So shall I have wherewith to answer him that reproacheth me: for I trust in your word.

43 And take not the word of truth utterly out of my mouth; for I have hoped in your judgments.

44 So shall I keep your law continually for ever and ever.

45 And I will walk at liberty: for I seek your precepts.

46 And I will speak of your testimonies also before kings, and will not be ashamed.

47 And I will delight myself in your commandments, which I have loved.

48 My hands also will I lift up unto your commandments, which I have loved; and I will meditate in your statutes.

ZAIN.

49 Remember the word unto your servant, upon which you have caused me to hope.

50 This is my comfort in my affliction: for your word has quickened me.

51 The proud have had me greatly in derision: yet have I not declined from your law.

52 I remembered your judgments of old, O LORD; and have comforted myself.

53 Horror has taken hold upon me because of the wicked that forsake your law.

54 Your statutes have been my songs in the house of my pilgrimage.

55 I have remembered your name, O LORD, in the night, and have kept your law.

56 This I had, because I kept your precepts.

CHETH.

57 You are my portion, O LORD: I have said that I would keep your words.

58 I intreated your favour with my whole heart: be merciful unto me according to your word.

59 I thought on my ways, and turned my feet unto your testimonies.

60 I made haste, and delayed not to keep your commandments.

61 The bands of the wicked have robbed me: but I have not forgotten your law.

62 At midnight I will rise to give thanks unto you because of your righteous judgments.

63 I am a companion of all them that fear you, and of them that keep your precepts.

64 The earth, O LORD, is full of your mercy: teach me your statutes.

TETH.

65 You have dealt well with your servant, O LORD, according unto your word.

66 Teach me good judgment and knowledge: for I have believed your commandments.

67 Before I was afflicted I went astray: but now have I kept your word.

68 You are good, and doest good; teach me your statutes.

69 The proud have forged a lie against me: but I will keep your precepts with my whole heart.

70 Their heart is as fat as grease; but I delight in your law.

71 It is good for me that I have been afflicted; that I might learn your statutes.

72 The law of your mouth is better unto me than thousands of gold and silver.

JOD.

73 Your hands have made me and fashioned me: give me understanding, that I may learn your commandments.

74 They that fear you will be glad when they see me; because I have hoped in your word.

75 I know, O LORD, that your judgments are right, and that you in faithfulness have afflicted me.

76 Let, I pray you, your merciful kindness be for my comfort, according to your word unto your servant.

77 Let your tender mercies come unto me, that I may live: for your law is my delight.

78 Let the proud be ashamed; for they dealt perversely with me without a cause: but I will meditate in your precepts.

79 Let those that fear you turn unto me, and those that have known your testimonies.

80 Let my heart be sound in your statutes; that I be not ashamed.

CAPH.

81 My soul fainteth for your salvation: but I hope in your word.

82 My eyes fail for your word, saying, When will you comfort me?

83 For I am become like a bottle in the smoke; yet do I not forget your statutes.

84 How many are the days of your servant? when will you execute judgment on them that persecute me?

85 The proud have digged pits for me, which are not after your law.

86 All your commandments are faithful: they persecute me wrongfully; help you me.

87 They had almost consumed me upon earth; but I forsook not your precepts.

88 Quicken me after your lovingkindness; so shall I keep the testimony of your mouth.

LAMED.

89 For ever, O LORD, your word is settled in heaven.

90 Your faithfulness is unto all generations: you have established the earth, and it abideth.

91 They continue this day according to yours ordinances: for all are your servants.

92 Unless your law had been my delights, I should then have perished in my affliction.

93 I will never forget your precepts: for with them you have quickened me.

94 I am yours, save me; for I have sought your precepts.

95 The wicked have waited for me to destroy me: but I will consider your testimonies.

96 I have seen an end of all perfection: but your commandment is exceeding broad.

MEM.

97 O how love I your law! it is my meditation all the day.

98 You through your commandments have made me wiser than my enemies: for they are ever with me.

99 I have more understanding than all my teachers: for your testimonies are my meditation.

100 I understand more than the ancients, because I keep your precepts.

101 I have refrained my feet from every evil way, that I might keep your word.

102 I have not departed from your judgments: for you have taught me.

103 How sweet are your words unto my taste! yea, sweeter than honey to my mouth!

104 Through your precepts I get understanding: therefore I hate every false way.

NUN.

105 Your word is a lamp unto my feet, and a light unto my path.

106 I have sworn, and I will perform it, that I will keep your righteous judgments.

107 I am afflicted very much: quicken me, O LORD, according unto your word.

108 Accept, I beseech you, the freewill offerings of my mouth, O LORD, and teach me your judgments.

109 My soul is continually in my hand: yet do I not forget your law.

110 The wicked have laid a snare for me: yet I erred not from your precepts.

111 Your testimonies have I taken as an heritage for ever: for they are the rejoicing of my heart.

112 I have inclined my heart to perform your statutes alway, even unto the end.

SAMECH.

113 I hate vain thoughts: but your law do I love.

114 You are my hiding place and my shield: I hope in your word.

115 Depart from me, you evildoers: for I will keep the commandments of my God.

116 Uphold me according unto your word, that I may live: and let me not be ashamed of my hope.

117 Hold you me up, and I shall be safe: and I will have respect unto your statutes continually.

118 You have trodden down all them that err from your statutes: for their deceit is falsehood.

119 You puttest away all the wicked of the earth like dross: therefore I love your testimonies.

120 My flesh trembleth for fear of you; and I am afraid of your judgments.

AIN.

121 I have done judgment and justice: leave me not to my oppressors.

122 Be surety for your servant for good: let not the proud oppress me.

123 My eyes fail for your salvation, and for the word of your righteousness.

124 Deal with your servant according unto your mercy, and teach me your statutes.

125 I am your servant; give me understanding, that I may know your testimonies.

126 It is time for you, LORD, to work: for they have made void your law.

127 Therefore I love your commandments above gold; yea, above fine gold.

128 Therefore I esteem all your precepts concerning all things to be right; and I hate every false way.

PE.

129 Your testimonies are wonderful: therefore doth my soul keep them.

130 The entrance of your words giveth light; it giveth understanding unto the simple.

131 I opened my mouth, and panted: for I longed for your commandments.

132 Look you upon me, and be merciful unto me, as you usest to do unto those that love your name.

133 Order my steps in your word: and let not any iniquity have dominion over me.

134 Deliver me from the oppression of man: so will I keep your precepts.

135 Make your face to shine upon your servant; and teach me your statutes.

136 Rivers of waters run down my eyes, because they keep not your law.

TZADDI.

137 Righteous are you , O LORD, and upright are your judgments.

138 Your testimonies that you have commanded are righteous and very faithful.

139 My zeal has consumed me, because my enemies have forgotten your words.

140 Your word is very pure: therefore your servant loveth it.

141 I am small and despised: yet do not I forget your precepts.

142 Your righteousness is an everlasting righteousness, and your law is the truth.

143 Trouble and anguish have taken hold on me: yet your commandments are my delights.

144 The righteousness of your testimonies is everlasting: give me understanding, and I shall live.

KOPH.

145 I cried with my whole heart; hear me, O LORD: I will keep your statutes.

146 I cried unto you; save me, and I shall keep your testimonies.

147 I prevented the dawning of the morning, and cried: I hoped in your word.

148 My eyes prevent the night watches, that I might meditate in your word.

149 Hear my voice according unto your lovingkindness: O LORD, quicken me according to your judgment.

150 They draw nigh that follow after mischief: they are far from your law.

151 You are near, O LORD; and all your commandments are truth.

152 Concerning your testimonies, I have known of old that you have founded them for ever.

RESH.

153 Consider my affliction, and deliver me: for I do not forget your law.

154 Plead my cause, and deliver me: quicken me according to your word.

155 Salvation is far from the wicked: for they seek not your statutes.

156 Great are your tender mercies, O LORD: quicken me according to your judgments.

157 Many are my persecutors and my enemies; yet do I not decline from your testimonies.

158 I beheld the transgressors, and was grieved; because they kept not your word.

159 Consider how I love your precepts: quicken me, O LORD, according to your lovingkindness.

160 Your word is true from the beginning: and every one of your righteous judgments endureth for ever.

SCHIN.

161 Princes have persecuted me without a cause: but my heart standeth in awe of your word.

162 I rejoice at your word, as one that findeth great spoil.

163 I hate and abhor lying: but your law do I love.

164 Seven times a day do I praise you because of your righteous judgments.

165 Great peace have they which love your law: and nothing shall offend them.

166 LORD, I have hoped for your salvation, and done your commandments.

167 My soul has kept your testimonies; and I love them exceedingly.

168 I have kept your precepts and your testimonies: for all my ways are before you.

TAU.

169 Let my cry come near before you, O LORD: give me understanding according to your word.

170 Let my supplication come before you: deliver me according to your word.

171 My lips shall utter praise, when you have taught me your statutes.

172 My tongue shall speak of your word: for all your commandments are righteousness.

173 Let yours hand help me; for I have chosen your precepts.

174 I have longed for your salvation, O LORD; and your law is my delight.

175 Let my soul live, and it shall praise you; and let your judgments help me.

176 I have gone astray like a lost sheep; seek your servant; for I do not forget your commandments.

PSALM 120

A Song of degrees.

IN my distress I cried unto the LORD, and he heard me.

2 Deliver my soul, O LORD, from lying lips, and from a deceitful tongue.

3 What shall be given unto you? or what shall be done unto you, you false tongue?

4 Sharp arrows of the mighty, with coals of juniper.

5 Woe is me, that I sojourn in Mesech, that I dwell in the tents of Kedar!

6 My soul has long dwelt with him that hateth peace.

7 I am for peace: but when I speak, they are for war.

PSALM 121

A Song of degrees.

I WILL lift up my eyes unto the hills, from whence comes my help.

2 My help comes from the LORD, which made heaven and earth.

3 He will not suffer your foot to be moved: he that keepeth you will not slumber.

4 Behold, he that keepeth Israel shall neither slumber nor sleep.

5 The LORD is your keeper: the LORD is your shade upon your right hand.

6 The sun shall not strike you by day, nor the moon by night.

7 The LORD shall preserve you from all evil: he shall preserve your soul.

8 The LORD shall preserve your going out and your coming in from this time forth, and even for evermore.

PSALM 122

A Song of degrees of David.

I WAS glad when they said unto me, Let us go into the house of the LORD.

2 Our feet shall stand within your gates, O Jerusalem.

3 Jerusalem is builded as a city that is compact together:

4 Whither the tribes go up, the tribes of the LORD, unto the testimony of Israel, to give thanks unto the name of the LORD.

5 For there are set thrones of judgment, the thrones of the house of David.

6 Pray for the peace of Jerusalem: they shall prosper that love you.

7 Peace be within your walls, and prosperity within your palaces.

8 For my brethren and companions' sakes, I will now say, Peace be within you.

9 Because of the house of the LORD our God I will seek your good.

PSALM 123

A Song of degrees.

UNTO you lift I up my eyes, O you that dwellest in the heavens.

2 Behold, as the eyes of servants look unto the hand of their masters, and as the eyes of a maiden unto the hand of her mistress; so our eyes wait upon the LORD our God, until that he have mercy upon us.

3 Have mercy upon us, O LORD, have mercy upon us: for we are exceedingly filled with contempt.

4 Our soul is exceedingly filled with the scorning of those that are at ease, and with the contempt of the proud.

PSALM 124

A Song of degrees of David.

IF it had not been the LORD who was on our side, now may Israel say;

2 If it had not been the LORD who was on our side, when men rose up against us:

3 Then they had swallowed us up quick, when their wrath was kindled against us:

4 Then the waters had overwhelmed us, the stream had gone over our soul:

5 Then the proud waters had gone over our soul.

6 Blessed be the LORD, who has not given us as a prey to their teeth.

7 Our soul is escaped as a bird out of the snare of the fowlers: the snare is broken, and we are escaped.

8 Our help is in the name of the LORD, who made heaven and earth.

PSALM 125

A Song of degrees.

THEY that trust in the LORD shall be as mount Zion, which cannot be removed, but abideth for ever.

2 As the mountains are round about Jerusalem, so the LORD is round about his people from henceforth even for ever.

3 For the rod of the wicked shall not rest upon the lot of the righteous; lest the righteous put forth their hands unto iniquity.

4 Do good, O LORD, unto those that be good, and to them that are upright in their hearts.

5 As for such as turn aside unto their crooked ways, the LORD shall lead them forth with the workers of iniquity: but peace shall be upon Israel.

PSALM 126

A Song of degrees.

WHEN the LORD turned again the captivity of Zion, we were like them that dream.

2 Then was our mouth filled with laughter, and our tongue with singing: then said they among the heathen, The LORD has done great things for them.

3 The LORD has done great things for us; whereof we are glad.

4 Turn again our captivity, O LORD, as the streams in the south.

5 They that sow in tears shall reap in joy.

6 He that goeth forth and weepeth, bearing precious seed, shall doubtless come again with rejoicing, bringing his sheaves with him.

PSALM 127

A Song of degrees for Solomon.

EXCEPT the LORD build the house, they labour in vain that build it: except the LORD keep the city, the watchman waketh but in vain.

2 It is vain for you to rise up early, to sit up late, to eat the bread of sorrows: for so he giveth his beloved sleep.

3 Lo, children are an heritage of the LORD: and the fruit of the womb is his reward.

4 As arrows are in the hand of a mighty man; so are children of the youth.

5 Happy is the man that has his quiver full of them: they shall not be ashamed, but they shall speak with the enemies in the gate.

PSALM 128

A Song of degrees.

BLESSED is every one that feareth the LORD; that walketh in his ways.

2 For you shalt eat the labour of yours hands: happy shalt you be, and it shall be well with you.

3 Your wife shall be as a fruitful vine by the sides of yours house: your children like olive plants round about your table.

4 Behold, that thus shall the man be blessed that feareth the LORD.

5 The LORD shall bless you out of Zion: and you shalt see the good of Jerusalem all the days of your life.

6 Yea, you shalt see your children's children, and peace upon Israel.

PSALM 129

A Song of degrees.

MANY a time have they afflicted me from my youth, may Israel now say:

2 Many a time have they afflicted me from my youth: yet they have not prevailed against me.

3 The plowers plowed upon my back: they made long their furrows.

4 The LORD is righteous: he has cut asunder the cords of the wicked.

5 Let them all be confounded and turned back that hate Zion.

6 Let them be as the grass upon the housetops, which withereth afore it groweth up:

7 Wherewith the mower filleth not his hand; nor he that bindeth sheaves his bosom.

8 Neither do they which go by say, The blessing of the LORD be upon you: we bless you in the name of the LORD.

PSALM 130

A Song of degrees.

OUT of the depths have I cried unto you, O LORD.

2 Lord, hear my voice: let yours ears be attentive to the voice of my supplications.

3 If you , LORD, shouldest mark iniquities, O Lord, who shall stand?

4 But there is forgiveness with you, that you mayest be feared.

5 I wait for the LORD, my soul doth wait, and in his word do I hope.

6 My soul waiteth for the Lord more than they that watch for the morning: I say, more than they that watch for the morning.

7 Let Israel hope in the LORD: for with the LORD there is mercy, and with him is plenteous redemption.

8 And he shall redeem Israel from all his iniquities.

PSALM 131

A Song of degrees of David.

LORD, my heart is not haughty, nor my eyes lofty: neither do I exercise myself in great matters, or in things too high for me.

2 Surely I have behaved and quieted myself, as a child that is weaned of his mother: my soul is even as a weaned child.

3 Let Israel hope in the LORD from henceforth and for ever.

PSALM 132

A Song of degrees.

LORD, remember David, and all his afflictions:

2 How he sware unto the LORD, and vowed unto the mighty God of Jacob;

3 Surely I will not come into the tabernacle of my house, nor go up into my bed;

4 I will not give sleep to my eyes, or slumber to my eyelids,

5 Until I find out a place for the LORD, an habitation for the mighty God of Jacob.

6 Lo, we heard of it at Ephratah: we found it in the fields of the wood.

7 We will go into his tabernacles: we will worship at his footstool.

8 Arise, O LORD, into your rest; you , and the ark of your strength.

9 Let your priests be clothed with righteousness; and let your saints shout for joy.

10 For your servant David's sake turn not away the face of yours anointed.

11 The LORD has sworn in truth unto David; he will not turn from it; Of the fruit of your body will I set upon your throne.

12 If your children will keep my covenant and my testimony that I shall teach them, their children shall also sit upon your throne for evermore.

13 For the LORD has chosen Zion; he has desired it for his habitation.

14 This is my rest for ever: here will I dwell; for I have desired it.

15 I will abundantly bless her provision: I will satisfy her poor with bread.

16 I will also clothe her priests with salvation: and her saints shall shout aloud for joy.

17 There will I make the horn of David to bud: I have ordained a lamp for my anointed.

18 His enemies will I clothe with shame: but upon himself shall his crown flourish.

PSALM 133

A Song of degrees of David.

BEHOLD, how good and how pleasant it is for brethren to dwell together in unity!

2 It is like the precious ointment upon the head, that ran down upon the beard, even Aaron's beard: that went down to the skirts of his garments;

3 As the dew of Hermon, and as the dew that descended upon the mountains of Zion: for there the LORD commanded the blessing, even life for evermore.

PSALM 134

A Song of degrees.

BEHOLD, bless you the LORD, all you servants of the LORD, which by night stand in the house of the LORD.

2 Lift up your hands in the sanctuary, and bless the LORD.

3 The LORD that made heaven and earth bless you out of Zion.

PSALM 135

PRAISE you the LORD. Praise you the name of the LORD; praise him, O you servants of the LORD.

2 You that stand in the house of the LORD, in the courts of the house of our God,

3 Praise the LORD; for the LORD is good: sing praises unto his name; for it is pleasant.

4 For the LORD has chosen Jacob unto himself, and Israel for his peculiar treasure.

5 For I know that the LORD is great, and that our Lord is above all gods.

6 Whatsoever the LORD pleased, that did he in heaven, and in earth, in the seas, and all deep places.

7 He causeth the vapours to ascend from the ends of the earth; he maketh lightnings for the rain; he bringeth the wind out of his treasuries.

8 Who struck the firstborn of Egypt, both of man and beast.

9 Who sent tokens and wonders into the midst of you, O Egypt, upon Pharaoh, and upon all his servants.

10 Who struck great nations, and slew mighty kings;

11 Sihon king of the Amorites, and Og king of Bashan, and all the kingdoms of Canaan:

12 And gave their land for an heritage, an heritage unto Israel his people.

13 Your name, O LORD, endureth for ever; and your memorial, O LORD, throughout all generations.

14 For the LORD will judge his people, and he will repent himself concerning his servants.

15 The idols of the heathen are silver and gold, the work of men's hands.

16 They have mouths, but they speak not; eyes have they, but they see not;

17 They have ears, but they hear not; neither is there any breath in their mouths.

18 They that make them are like unto them: so is every one that trusteth in them.

19 Bless the LORD, O house of Israel: bless the LORD, O house of Aaron:

20 Bless the LORD, O house of Levi: you that fear the LORD, bless the LORD.

21 Blessed be the LORD out of Zion, which dwelleth at Jerusalem. Praise you the LORD.

PSALM 136

O GIVE thanks unto the LORD; for he is good: for his mercy endureth for ever.

2 O give thanks unto the God of gods: for his mercy endureth for ever.

3 O give thanks to the Lord of lords: for his mercy endureth for ever.

4 To him who alone doeth great wonders: for his mercy endureth for ever.

5 To him that by wisdom made the heavens: for his mercy endureth for ever.

6 To him that stretched out the earth above the waters: for his mercy endureth for ever.

7 To him that made great lights: for his mercy endureth for ever:

8 The sun to rule by day: for his mercy endureth for ever:

9 The moon and stars to rule by night: for his mercy endureth for ever.

10 To him that struck Egypt in their firstborn: for his mercy endureth for ever:

11 And brought out Israel from among them: for his mercy endureth for ever:

12 With a strong hand, and with a stretched out arm: for his mercy endureth for ever.

13 To him which divided the Red sea into parts: for his mercy endureth for ever:

14 And made Israel to pass through the midst of it: for his mercy endureth for ever:

15 But overthrew Pharaoh and his host in the Red sea: for his mercy endureth for ever.

16 To him which led his people through the wilderness: for his mercy endureth for ever.

17 To him which struck great kings: for his mercy endureth for ever:

18 And slew famous kings: for his mercy endureth for ever:

19 Sihon king of the Amorites: for his mercy endureth for ever:

20 And Og the king of Bashan: for his mercy endureth for ever:

21 And gave their land for an heritage: for his mercy endureth for ever:

22 Even an heritage unto Israel his servant: for his mercy endureth for ever.

23 Who remembered us in our low estate: for his mercy endureth for ever:

24 And has redeemed us from our enemies: for his mercy endureth for ever.

25 Who giveth food to all flesh: for his mercy endureth for ever.

26 O give thanks unto the God of heaven: for his mercy endureth for ever.

PSALM 137

BY the rivers of Babylon, there we sat down, yea, we wept, when we remembered Zion.

2 We hanged our harps upon the willows in the midst thereof.

3 For there they that carried us away captive required of us a song; and they that wasted us required of us mirth, saying, Sing us one of the songs of Zion.

4 How shall we sing the LORD's song in a strange land?

5 If I forget you, O Jerusalem, let my right hand forget her cunning.

6 If I do not remember you, let my tongue cleave to the roof of my mouth; if I prefer not Jerusalem above my chief joy.

7 Remember, O LORD, the children of Edom in the day of Jerusalem; who said, Rase it, rase it, even to the foundation thereof.

8 O daughter of Babylon, who are to be destroyed; happy shall he be, that rewardeth you as you have served us.

9 Happy shall he be, that taketh and dasheth your little ones against the stones.

PSALM 138

A Psalm of David.

I WILL praise you with my whole heart: before the gods will I sing praise unto you.

2 I will worship toward your holy temple, and praise your name for your lovingkindness and for your truth: for you have magnified your word above all your name.

3 In the day when I cried you answeredst me, and strengthenedst me with strength in my soul.

4 All the kings of the earth shall praise you, O LORD, when they hear the words of your mouth.

5 Yea, they shall sing in the ways of the LORD: for great is the glory of the LORD.

6 Though the LORD be high, yet has he respect unto the lowly: but the proud he knoweth afar off.

7 Though I walk in the midst of trouble, you will revive me: you shalt stretch forth yours hand against the wrath of my enemies, and your right hand shall save me.

8 The LORD will perfect that which concerneth me: your mercy, O LORD, endureth for ever: forsake not the works of yours own hands.

PSALM 139

To the chief Musician, A Psalm of David.

O LORD, you have searched me, and known me.

2 You knowest my downsitting and my uprising, you understandest my thought afar off.

3 You compassest my path and my lying down, and are acquainted with all my ways.

4 For there is not a word in my tongue, but, lo, O LORD, you knowest it altogether.

5 You have beset me behind and before, and laid yours hand upon me.

6 Such knowledge is too wonderful for me; it is high, I cannot attain unto it.

7 Whither shall I go from your spirit? or whither shall I flee from your presence?

8 If I ascend up into heaven, you are there: if I make my bed in hell, behold, you are there.

9 If I take the wings of the morning, and dwell in the uttermost parts of the sea;

10 Even there shall your hand lead me, and your right hand shall hold me.

11 If I say, Surely the darkness shall cover me; even the night shall be light about me.

12 Yea, the darkness hideth not from you; but the night shineth as the day: the darkness and the light are both alike to you.

13 For you have possessed my reins: you have covered me in my mother's womb.

14 I will praise you; for I am fearfully and wonderfully made: marvellous are your works; and that my soul knoweth right well.

15 My substance was not hid from you, when I was made in secret, and curiously created in the lowest parts of the earth.

16 Yours eyes did see my substance, yet being unperfect; and in your book all my members were written, which in continuance were fashioned, when as yet there was none of them.

17 How precious also are your thoughts unto me, O God! how great is the sum of them!

18 If I should count them, they are more in number than the sand: when I awake, I am still with you.

19 Surely you will slay the wicked, O God: depart from me therefore, you bloody men.

20 For they speak against you wickedly, and yours enemies take your name in vain.

21 Do not I hate them, O LORD, that hate you? and am not I grieved with those that rise up against you?

22 I hate them with perfect hatred: I count them my enemies.

23 Search me, O God, and know my heart: try me, and know my thoughts:

24 And see if there be any wicked way in me, and lead me in the way everlasting.

PSALM 140

To the chief Musician, A Psalm of David.

DELIVER me, O LORD, from the evil man: preserve me from the violent man;

2 Which imagine mischiefs in their heart; continually are they gathered together for war.

3 They have sharpened their tongues like a serpent; adders' poison is under their lips. Selah.

4 Keep me, O LORD, from the hands of the wicked; preserve me from the violent man; who have purposed to overthrow my goings.

5 The proud have hid a snare for me, and cords; they have spread a net by the wayside; they have set gins for me. Selah.

6 I said unto the LORD, You are my God: hear the voice of my supplications, O LORD.

7 O GOD the Lord, the strength of my salvation, you have covered my head in the day of battle.

8 Grant not, O LORD, the desires of the wicked: further not his wicked device; lest they exalt themselves. Selah.

9 As for the head of those that compass me about, let the mischief of their own lips cover them.

10 Let burning coals fall upon them: let them be cast into the fire; into deep pits, that they rise not up again.

11 Let not an evil speaker be established in the earth: evil shall hunt the violent man to overthrow him.

12 I know that the LORD will maintain the cause of the afflicted, and the right of the poor.

13 Surely the righteous shall give thanks unto your name: the upright shall dwell in your presence.

PSALM 141

A Psalm of David.

LORD, I cry unto you: make haste unto me; give ear unto my voice, when I cry unto you.

2 Let my prayer be set forth before you as incense; and the lifting up of my hands as the evening sacrifice.

3 Set a watch, O LORD, before my mouth; keep the door of my lips.

4 Incline not my heart to any evil thing, to practise wicked works with men that work iniquity: and let me not eat of their dainties.

5 Let the righteous strike me; it shall be a kindness: and let him reprove me; it shall be an excellent oil, which shall not break my head: for yet my prayer also shall be in their calamities.

6 When their judges are overthrown in stony places, they shall hear my words; for they are sweet.

7 Our bones are scattered at the grave's mouth, as when one cutteth and cleaveth wood upon the earth.

8 But my eyes are unto you, O GOD the Lord: in you is my trust; leave not my soul destitute.

9 Keep me from the snares which they have laid for me, and the gins of the workers of iniquity.

10 Let the wicked fall into their own nets, whilst that I withal escape.

PSALM 142

Maschil of David; A Prayer when he was in the cave.

I CRIED unto the LORD with my voice; with my voice unto the LORD did I make my supplication.

2 I poured out my complaint before him; I shewed before him my trouble.

3 When my spirit was overwhelmed within me, then you knewest my path. In the way wherein I walked have they privily laid a snare for me.

4 I looked on my right hand, and beheld, but there was no man that would know me: refuge failed me; no man cared for my soul.

5 I cried unto you, O LORD: I said, You are my refuge and my portion in the land of the living.

6 Attend unto my cry; for I am brought very low: deliver me from my persecutors; for they are stronger than I.

7 Bring my soul out of prison, that I may praise your name: the righteous shall compass me about; for you shalt deal bountifully with me.

PSALM 143

A Psalm of David.

HEAR my prayer, O LORD, give ear to my supplications: in your faithfulness answer me, and in your righteousness.

2 And enter not into judgment with your servant: for in your sight shall no man living be justified.

3 For the enemy has persecuted my soul; he has smitten my life down to the ground; he has made me to dwell in darkness, as those that have been long dead.

4 Therefore is my spirit overwhelmed within me; my heart within me is desolate.

5 I remember the days of old; I meditate on all your works; I muse on the work of your hands.

6 I stretch forth my hands unto you: my soul thirsteth after you, as a thirsty land. Selah.

7 Hear me speedily, O LORD: my spirit faileth: hide not your face from me, lest I be like unto them that go down into the pit.

8 Cause me to hear your lovingkindness in the morning; for in you do I trust: cause me to know the way wherein I should walk; for I lift up my soul unto you.

9 Deliver me, O LORD, from my enemies: I flee unto you to hide me.

10 Teach me to do your will; for you are my God: your spirit is good; lead me into the land of uprightness.

11 Quicken me, O LORD, for your name's sake: for your righteousness' sake bring my soul out of trouble.

12 And of your mercy cut off my enemies, and destroy all them that afflict my soul: for I am your servant.

PSALM 144

A Psalm of David.

BLESSED be the LORD my strength, which teacheth my hands to war, and my fingers to fight:

2 My goodness, and my fortress; my high tower, and my deliverer; my shield, and he in whom I trust; who subdueth my people under me.

3 LORD, what is man, that you takest knowledge of him! or the son of man, that you makest account of him!

4 Man is like to vanity: his days are as a shadow that passes away.

5 Bow your heavens, O LORD, and come down: touch the mountains, and they shall smoke.

6 Cast forth lightning, and scatter them: shoot out yours arrows, and destroy them.

7 Send yours hand from above; rid me, and deliver me out of great waters, from the hand of strange children;

8 Whose mouth speaketh vanity, and their right hand is a right hand of falsehood.

9 I will sing a new song unto you, O God: upon a psaltery and an instrument of ten strings will I sing praises unto you.

10 It is he that giveth salvation unto kings: who delivereth David his servant from the hurtful sword.

11 Rid me, and deliver me from the hand of strange children, whose mouth speaketh vanity, and their right hand is a right hand of falsehood:

12 That our sons may be as plants grown up in their youth; that our daughters may be as corner stones, polished after the similitude of a palace:

13 That our garners may be full, affording all manner of store: that our sheep may bring forth thousands and ten thousands in our streets:

14 That our oxen may be strong to labour; that there be no breaking in, nor going out; that there be no complaining in our streets.

15 Happy is that people, that is in such a case: yea, happy is that people, whose God is the LORD.

PSALM 145

David's Psalm of praise.

I WILL extol you, my God, O king; and I will bless your name for ever and ever.

2 Every day will I bless you; and I will praise your name for ever and ever.

3 Great is the LORD, and greatly to be praised; and his greatness is unsearchable.

4 One generation shall praise your works to another, and shall declare your mighty acts.

5 I will speak of the glorious honour of your majesty, and of your wondrous works.

6 And men shall speak of the might of your terrible acts: and I will declare your greatness.

7 They shall abundantly utter the memory of your great goodness, and shall sing of your righteousness.

8 The LORD is gracious, and full of compassion; slow to anger, and of great mercy.

9 The LORD is good to all: and his tender mercies are over all his works.

10 All your works shall praise you, O LORD; and your saints shall bless you.

11 They shall speak of the glory of your kingdom, and talk of your power;

12 To make known to the sons of men his mighty acts, and the glorious majesty of his kingdom.

13 Your kingdom is an everlasting kingdom, and your dominion endureth throughout all generations.

14 The LORD upholdeth all that fall, and raiseth up all those that be bowed down.

15 The eyes of all wait upon you; and you givest them their meat in due season.

16 You openest yours hand, and satisfiest the desire of every living thing.

17 The LORD is righteous in all his ways, and holy in all his works.

18 The LORD is nigh unto all them that call upon him, to all that call upon him in truth.

19 He will fulfil the desire of them that fear him: he also will hear their cry, and will save them.

20 The LORD preserveth all them that love him: but all the wicked will he destroy.

21 My mouth shall speak the praise of the LORD: and let all flesh bless his holy name for ever and ever.

PSALM 146

PRAISE you the LORD. Praise the LORD, O my soul.

2 While I live will I praise the LORD: I will sing praises unto my God while I have any being.

3 Put not your trust in princes, nor in the son of man, in whom there is no help.

4 His breath goeth forth, he returneth to his earth; in that very day his thoughts perish.

5 Happy is he that has the God of Jacob for his help, whose hope is in the LORD his God:

6 Which made heaven, and earth, the sea, and all that therein is: which keepeth truth for ever:

7 Which executeth judgment for the oppressed: which giveth food to the hungry. The LORD looseth the prisoners:

8 The LORD openeth the eyes of the blind: the LORD raiseth them that are bowed down: the LORD loveth the righteous:

9 The LORD preserveth the strangers; he relieveth the fatherless and widow: but the way of the wicked he turneth upside down.

10 The LORD shall reign for ever, even your God, O Zion, unto all generations. Praise you the LORD.

PSALM 147

PRAISE you the LORD: for it is good to sing praises unto our God; for it is pleasant; and praise is comely.

2 The LORD doth build up Jerusalem: he gathereth together the outcasts of Israel.

3 He healeth the broken in heart, and bindeth up their wounds.

4 He telleth the number of the stars; he calleth them all by their names.

5 Great is our Lord, and of great power: his understanding is infinite.

6 The LORD lifteth up the meek: he casteth the wicked down to the ground.

7 Sing unto the LORD with thanksgiving; sing praise upon the harp unto our God:

8 Who covers the heaven with clouds, who prepareth rain for the earth, who maketh grass to grow upon the mountains.

9 He giveth to the beast his food, and to the young ravens which cry.

10 He delighteth not in the strength of the horse: he taketh not pleasure in the legs of a man.

11 The LORD taketh pleasure in them that fear him, in those that hope in his mercy.

12 Praise the LORD, O Jerusalem; praise your God, O Zion.

13 For he has strengthened the bars of your gates; he has blessed your children within you.

14 He maketh peace in your borders, and filleth you with the finest of the wheat.

15 He sendeth forth his commandment upon earth: his word runneth very swiftly.

16 He giveth snow like wool: he scattereth the hoarfrost like ashes.

17 He casteth forth his ice like morsels: who can stand before his cold?

18 He sendeth out his word, and melteth them: he causeth his wind to blow, and the waters flow.

19 He sheweth his word unto Jacob, his statutes and his judgments unto Israel.

20 He has not dealt so with any nation: and as for his judgments, they have not known them. Praise you the LORD.

PSALM 148

PRAISE you the LORD. Praise you the LORD from the heavens: praise him in the heights.

2 Praise you him, all his angels: praise you him, all his hosts.

3 Praise you him, sun and moon: praise him, all you stars of light.

4 Praise him, you heavens of heavens, and you waters that be above the heavens.

5 Let them praise the name of the LORD: for he commanded, and they were created.

6 He has also stablished them for ever and ever: he has made a decree which shall not pass.

7 Praise the LORD from the earth, you dragons, and all deeps:

8 Fire, and hail; snow, and vapour; stormy wind fulfilling his word:

9 Mountains, and all hills; fruitful trees, and all cedars:

10 Beasts, and all cattle; creeping things, and flying fowl:

11 Kings of the earth, and all people; princes, and all judges of the earth:

12 Both young men, and maidens; old men, and children:

13 Let them praise the name of the LORD: for his name alone is excellent; his glory is above the earth and heaven.

14 He also exalteth the horn of his people, the praise of all his saints; even of the children of Israel, a people near unto him. Praise you the LORD.

PSALM 149

PRAISE you the LORD. Sing unto the LORD a new song, and his praise in the congregation of saints.

2 Let Israel rejoice in him that made him: let the children of Zion be joyful in their King.

3 Let them praise his name in the dance: let them sing praises unto him with the timbrel and harp.

4 For the LORD taketh pleasure in his people: he will beautify the meek with salvation.

5 Let the saints be joyful in glory: let them sing aloud upon their beds.

6 Let the high praises of God be in their mouth, and a twoedged sword in their hand;

7 To execute vengeance upon the heathen, and punishments upon the people;

8 To bind their kings with chains, and their nobles with fetters of iron;

9 To execute upon them the judgment written: this honour have all his saints. Praise you the LORD.

PSALM 150

PRAISE you the LORD. Praise God in his sanctuary: praise him in the firmament of his power.

2 Praise him for his mighty acts: praise him according to his excellent greatness.

3 Praise him with the sound of the trumpet: praise him with the psaltery and harp.

4 Praise him with the timbrel and dance: praise him with stringed instruments and organs.

5 Praise him upon the loud cymbals: praise him upon the high sounding cymbals.

6 Let every thing that has breath praise the LORD. Praise you the LORD.

Additional Psalm 151

I was the smallest among my brothers,
and the youngest in my father's household.
I used to take care of my father's sheep.
My hands constructed11 a musical instrument;
my fingers tuned a harp.
Who will announce this to my Lord?
The Lord himself-he is listening.
He himself sent his messenger
and took me from my father's sheep,
and anointed me with his anointing oil.
My brothers were handsome and big,
but the Lord did not approve of them.
David's Victory over Goliath
I went out to meet the foreigner;
he called down curses on me by his idols.
But I pulled out his own sword; I beheaded him and thereby removed reproach from the Israelites.

Psalm 151

Ps151.1

[2] My hands made a harp, my fingers fashioned a lyre.

[3] And who will declare it to my Lord? The Lord himself; it is he who hears.

[4] It was he who sent his messenger and took me from my father's sheep, and anointed me with his anointing oil.

[5] My brothers were handsome and tall, but the Lord was not pleased with them.

[6] I went out to meet the Philistine, and he cursed me by his idols.

[7] But I drew his own sword; I beheaded him, and removed reproach from the people of Israel.

THE PROVERBS.

CHAPTER 1

THE proverbs of Solomon the son of David, king of Israel;

2 To know wisdom and instruction; to perceive the words of understanding;

3 To receive the instruction of wisdom, justice, and judgment, and equity;

4 To give subtilty to the simple, to the young man knowledge and discretion.

5 A wise man will hear, and will increase learning; and a man of understanding shall attain unto wise counsels:

6 To understand a proverb, and the interpretation; the words of the wise, and their dark sayings.

7 The fear of the LORD is the beginning of knowledge: but fools despise wisdom and instruction.

8 My son, hear the instruction of your father, and forsake not the law of your mother:

9 For they shall be an ornament of grace unto your head, and chains about your neck.

10 My son, if sinners entice you, consent you not.

11 If they say, Come with us, let us lay wait for blood, let us lurk privily for the innocent without cause:

12 Let us swallow them up alive as the grave; and whole, as those that go down into the pit:

13 We shall find all precious substance, we shall fill our houses with spoil:

14 Cast in your lot among us; let us all have one purse:

15 My son, walk not you in the way with them; refrain your foot from their path:

16 For their feet run to evil, and make haste to shed blood.

17 Surely in vain the net is spread in the sight of any bird.

18 And they lay wait for their own blood; they lurk privily for their own lives.

19 So are the ways of every one that is greedy of gain; which taketh away the life of the owners thereof.

20 Wisdom crieth without; she uttereth her voice in the streets:

21 She crieth in the chief place of concourse, in the openings of the gates: in the city she uttereth her words, saying,

22 How long, you simple ones, will you love simplicity? and the scorners delight in their scorning, and fools hate knowledge?

23 Turn you at my reproof: behold, I will pour out my spirit unto you, I will make known my words unto you.

24 Because I have called, and you refused; I have stretched out my hand, and no man regarded;

25 But you have set at nought all my counsel, and would none of my reproof:

26 I also will laugh at your calamity; I will mock when your fear comes;

27 When your fear comes as desolation, and your destruction comes as a whirlwind; when distress and anguish comes upon you.

28 Then shall they call upon me, but I will not answer; they shall seek me early, but they shall not find me:

29 For that they hated knowledge, and did not choose the fear of the LORD:

30 They would none of my counsel: they despised all my reproof.

31 Therefore shall they eat of the fruit of their own way, and be filled with their own devices.

32 For the turning away of the simple shall slay them, and the prosperity of fools shall destroy them.

33 But whoso hearkeneth unto me shall dwell safely, and shall be quiet from fear of evil.

CHAPTER 2

MY son, if you will receive my words, and hide my commandments with you;

2 So that you incline yours ear unto wisdom, and apply yours heart to understanding;

3 Yea, if you criest after knowledge, and liftest up your voice for understanding;

4 If you seekest her as silver, and searchest for her as for hid treasures;

5 Then shalt you understand the fear of the LORD, and find the knowledge of God.

6 For the LORD giveth wisdom: out of his mouth comes knowledge and understanding.

7 He layeth up sound wisdom for the righteous: he is a buckler to them that walk uprightly.

8 He keepeth the paths of judgment, and preserveth the way of his saints.

9 Then shalt you understand righteousness, and judgment, and equity; yea, every good path.

10 When wisdom entereth into yours heart, and knowledge is pleasant unto your soul;

11 Discretion shall preserve you, understanding shall keep you:

12 To deliver you from the way of the evil man, from the man that speaketh froward things;

13 Who leave the paths of uprightness, to walk in the ways of darkness;

14 Who rejoice to do evil, and delight in the frowardness of the wicked;

15 Whose ways are crooked, and they froward in their paths:

16 To deliver you from the strange woman, even from the stranger which flattereth with her words;

17 Which forsaketh the guide of her youth, and forgetteth the covenant of her God.

18 For her house inclineth unto death, and her paths unto the dead.

19 None that go unto her return again, neither take they hold of the paths of life.

20 That you mayest walk in the way of good men, and keep the paths of the righteous.

21 For the upright shall dwell in the land, and the perfect shall remain in it.

22 But the wicked shall be cut off from the earth, and the transgressors shall be rooted out of it.

CHAPTER 3

MY son, forget not my law; but let yours heart keep my commandments:

2 For length of days, and long life, and peace, shall they add to you.

3 Let not mercy and truth forsake you: bind them about your neck; write them upon the table of yours heart:

4 So shalt you find favour and good understanding in the sight of God and man.

5 Trust in the LORD with all yours heart; and lean not unto yours own understanding.

6 In all your ways acknowledge him, and he shall direct your paths.

7 Be not wise in yours own eyes: fear the LORD, and depart from evil.

8 It shall be health to your navel, and marrow to your bones.

9 Honour the LORD with your substance, and with the firstfruits of all yours increase:

10 So shall your barns be filled with plenty, and your presses shall burst out with new wine.

11 My son, despise not the chastening of the LORD; neither be weary of his correction:

12 For whom the LORD loveth he correcteth; even as a father the son in whom he delighteth.

13 Happy is the man that findeth wisdom, and the man that getteth understanding.

14 For the merchandise of it is better than the merchandise of silver, and the gain thereof than fine gold.

15 She is more precious than rubies: and all the things you can desire are not to be compared unto her.

16 Length of days is in her right hand; and in her left hand riches and honour.

17 Her ways are ways of pleasantness, and all her paths are peace.

18 She is a tree of life to them that lay hold upon her: and happy is every one that retaineth her.

19 The LORD by wisdom has founded the earth; by understanding has he established the heavens.

20 By his knowledge the depths are broken up, and the clouds drop down the dew.

21 My son, let not them depart from yours eyes: keep sound wisdom and discretion:

22 So shall they be life unto your soul, and grace to your neck.

23 Then shalt you walk in your way safely, and your foot shall not stumble.

24 When you liest down, you shalt not be afraid: yea, you shalt lie down, and your sleep shall be sweet.

25 Be not afraid of sudden fear, neither of the desolation of the wicked, when it comes.

26 For the LORD shall be your confidence, and shall keep your foot from being taken.

27 Withhold not good from them to whom it is due, when it is in the power of yours hand to do it.

28 Say not unto your neighbour, Go, and come again, and to morrow I will give; when you have it by you.

29 Devise not evil against your neighbour, seeing he dwelleth securely by you.

30 Strive not with a man without cause, if he have done you no harm.

31 Envy you not the oppressor, and choose none of his ways.

32 For the froward is abomination to the LORD: but his secret is with the righteous.

33 The curse of the LORD is in the house of the wicked: but he blesseth the habitation of the just.

34 Surely he scorneth the scorners: but he giveth grace unto the lowly.

35 The wise shall inherit glory: but shame shall be the promotion of fools.

CHAPTER 4

HEAR, you children, the instruction of a father, and attend to know understanding.

2 For I give you good doctrine, forsake you not my law.

3 For I was my father's son, tender and only beloved in the sight of my mother.

4 He taught me also, and said unto me, Let yours heart retain my words: keep my commandments, and live.

5 Get wisdom, get understanding: forget it not; neither decline from the words of my mouth.

6 Forsake her not, and she shall preserve you: love her, and she shall keep you.

7 Wisdom is the principal thing; therefore get wisdom: and with all your getting get understanding.

8 Exalt her, and she shall promote you: she shall bring you to honour, when you dost embrace her.

9 She shall give to yours head an ornament of grace: a crown of glory shall she deliver to you.

10 Hear, O my son, and receive my sayings; and the years of your life shall be many.

11 I have taught you in the way of wisdom; I have led you in right paths.

12 When you go, your steps shall not be straitened; and when you runnest, you shalt not stumble.

13 Take fast hold of instruction; let her not go: keep her; for she is your life.

14 Enter not into the path of the wicked, and go not in the way of evil men.

15 Avoid it, pass not by it, turn from it, and pass away.

16 For they sleep not, except they have done mischief; and their sleep is taken away, unless they cause some to fall.

17 For they eat the bread of wickedness, and drink the wine of violence.

18 But the path of the just is as the shining light, that shineth more and more unto the perfect day.

19 The way of the wicked is as darkness: they know not at what they stumble.

20 My son, attend to my words; incline yours ear unto my sayings.

21 Let them not depart from yours eyes; keep them in the midst of yours heart.

22 For they are life unto those that find them, and health to all their flesh.

23 Keep your heart with all diligence; for out of it are the issues of life.

24 Put away from you a froward mouth, and perverse lips put far from you.

25 Let yours eyes look right on, and let yours eyelids look straight before you.

26 Ponder the path of your feet, and let all your ways be established.

27 Turn not to the right hand nor to the left: remove your foot from evil.

CHAPTER 5

MY son, attend unto my wisdom, and bow yours ear to my understanding:

2 That you mayest regard discretion, and that your lips may keep knowledge.

3 For the lips of a strange woman drop as an honeycomb, and her mouth is smoother than oil:

4 But her end is bitter as wormwood, sharp as a twoedged sword.

5 Her feet go down to death; her steps take hold on hell.

6 Lest you shouldest ponder the path of life, her ways are moveable, that you can not know them.

7 Hear me now therefore, O you children, and depart not from the words of my mouth.

8 Remove your way far from her, and come not nigh the door of her house:

9 Lest you give yours honour unto others, and your years unto the cruel:

10 Lest strangers be filled with your wealth; and your labours be in the house of a stranger;

11 And you mourn at the last, when your flesh and your body are consumed,

12 And say, How have I hated instruction, and my heart despised reproof;

13 And have not obeyed the voice of my teachers, nor inclined my ear to them that instructed me!

14 I was almost in all evil in the midst of the congregation and assembly.

15 Drink waters out of yours own cistern, and running waters out of yours own well.

16 Let your fountains be dispersed abroad, and rivers of waters in the streets.

17 Let them be only yours own, and not strangers' with you.

18 Let your fountain be blessed: and rejoice with the wife of your youth.

19 Let her be as the loving hind and pleasant roe; let her breasts satisfy you at all times; and be you ravished always with her love.

20 And why will you , my son, be ravished with a strange woman, and embrace the bosom of a stranger?

21 For the ways of man are before the eyes of the LORD, and he pondereth all his goings.

22 His own iniquities shall take the wicked himself, and he shall be holden with the cords of his sins.

23 He shall die without instruction; and in the greatness of his folly he shall go astray.

CHAPTER 6

MY son, if you be surety for your friend, if you have stricken your hand with a stranger,

2 You are snared with the words of your mouth, you are taken with the words of your mouth.

3 Do this now, my son, and deliver yourself, when you are come into the hand of your friend; go, humble yourself, and make sure your friend.

4 Give not sleep to yours eyes, nor slumber to yours eyelids.

5 Deliver yourself as a roe from the hand of the hunter, and as a bird from the hand of the fowler.

6 Go to the ant, you sluggard; consider her ways, and be wise:

7 Which having no guide, overseer, or ruler,

8 Provideth her meat in the summer, and gathereth her food in the harvest.

9 How long will you sleep, O sluggard? when will you arise out of your sleep?

10 Yet a little sleep, a little slumber, a little folding of the hands to sleep:

11 So shall your poverty come as one that travelleth, and your want as an armed man.

12 A naughty person, a wicked man, walketh with a froward mouth.

13 He winketh with his eyes, he speaketh with his feet, he teacheth with his fingers;

14 Frowardness is in his heart, he deviseth mischief continually; he soweth discord.

15 Therefore shall his calamity come suddenly; suddenly shall he be broken without remedy.

16 These six things doth the LORD hate: yea, seven are an abomination unto him:

17 A proud look, a lying tongue, and hands that shed innocent blood,

18 An heart that deviseth wicked imaginations, feet that be swift in running to mischief,

19 A false witness that speaketh lies, and he that soweth discord among brethren.

20 My son, keep your father's commandment, and forsake not the law of your mother:

21 Bind them continually upon yours heart, and tie them about your neck.

22 When you go, it shall lead you; when you sleepest, it shall keep you; and when you awakest, it shall talk with you.

23 For the commandment is a lamp; and the law is light; and reproofs of instruction are the way of life:

24 To keep you from the evil woman, from the flattery of the tongue of a strange woman.

25 Lust not after her beauty in yours heart; neither let her take you with her eyelids.

26 For by means of a whorish woman a man is brought to a piece of bread: and the adulteress will hunt for the precious life.

27 Can a man take fire in his bosom, and his clothes not be burned?

28 Can one go upon hot coals, and his feet not be burned?

29 So he that goeth in to his neighbour's wife; whosoever toucheth her shall not be innocent.

30 Men do not despise a thief, if he steal to satisfy his soul when he is hungry;

31 But if he be found, he shall restore sevenfold; he shall give all the substance of his house.

32 But whoso committeth adultery with a woman lacketh understanding: he that doeth it destroyeth his own soul.

33 A wound and dishonour shall he get; and his reproach shall not be wiped away.

34 For jealousy is the rage of a man: therefore he will not spare in the day of vengeance.

35 He will not regard any ransom; neither will he rest content, though you givest many gifts.

CHAPTER 7

MY son, keep my words, and lay up my commandments with you.

2 Keep my commandments, and live; and my law as the apple of yours eye.

3 Bind them upon your fingers, write them upon the table of yours heart.

4 Say unto wisdom, You are my sister; and call understanding your kinswoman:

5 That they may keep you from the strange woman, from the stranger which flattereth with her words.

6 For at the window of my house I looked through my casement,

7 And beheld among the simple ones, I discerned among the youths, a young man void of understanding,

8 Passing through the street near her corner; and he went the way to her house,

9 In the twilight, in the evening, in the black and dark night:

10 And, behold, there met him a woman with the attire of an harlot, and subtil of heart.

11 (She is loud and stubborn; her feet abide not in her house:

12 Now is she without, now in the streets, and lies in wait at every corner.)

13 So she caught him, and kissed him, and with an impudent face said unto him,

14 I have peace offerings with me; this day have I payed my vows.

15 Therefore came I forth to meet you, diligently to seek your face, and I have found you.

16 I have decked my bed with coverings of tapestry, with carved works, with fine linen of Egypt.

17 I have perfumed my bed with myrrh, aloes, and cinnamon.

18 Come, let us take our fill of love until the morning: let us solace ourselves with loves.

19 For the goodman is not at home, he is gone a long journey:

20 He has taken a bag of money with him, and will come home at the day appointed.

21 With her much fair speech she caused him to yield, with the flattering of her lips she forced him.

22 He goeth after her straightway, as an ox goeth to the slaughter, or as a fool to the correction of the stocks;

23 Till a dart strike through his liver; as a bird hasteth to the snare, and knoweth not that it is for his life.

24 Hearken unto me now therefore, O you children, and attend to the words of my mouth.

25 Let not yours heart decline to her ways, go not astray in her paths.

26 For she has cast down many wounded: yea, many strong men have been slain by her.

27 Her house is the way to hell, going down to the chambers of death.

CHAPTER 8

DOTH not wisdom cry? and understanding put forth her voice?

2 She standeth in the top of high places, by the way in the places of the paths.

3 She crieth at the gates, at the entry of the city, at the coming in at the doors.

4 Unto you, O men, I call; and my voice is to the sons of man.

5 O you simple, understand wisdom: and, you fools, be you of an understanding heart.

6 Hear; for I will speak of excellent things; and the opening of my lips shall be right things.

7 For my mouth shall speak truth; and wickedness is an abomination to my lips.

8 All the words of my mouth are in righteousness; there is nothing froward or perverse in them.

9 They are all plain to him that understands, and right to them that find knowledge.

10 Receive my instruction, and not silver; and knowledge rather than choice gold.

11 For wisdom is better than rubies; and all the things that may be desired are not to be compared to it.

12 I wisdom dwell with prudence, and find out knowledge of witty inventions.

13 The fear of the LORD is to hate evil: pride, and arrogancy, and the evil way, and the froward mouth, do I hate.

14 Counsel is my, and sound wisdom: I am understanding; I have strength.

15 By me kings reign, and princes decree justice.

16 By me princes rule, and nobles, even all the judges of the earth.

17 I love them that love me; and those that seek me early shall find me.

18 Riches and honour are with me; yea, durable riches and righteousness.

19 My fruit is better than gold, yea, than fine gold; and my revenue than choice silver.

20 I lead in the way of righteousness, in the midst of the paths of judgment:

21 That I may cause those that love me to inherit substance; and I will fill their treasures.

22 The LORD possessed me in the beginning of his way, before his works of old.

23 I was set up from everlasting, from the beginning, or ever the earth was.

24 When there were no depths, I was brought forth; when there were no fountains abounding with water.

25 Before the mountains were settled, before the hills was I brought forth:

26 While as yet he had not made the earth, nor the fields, nor the highest part of the dust of the world.

27 When he prepared the heavens, I was there: when he set a compass upon the face of the depth:

28 When he established the clouds above: when he strengthened the fountains of the deep:

29 When he gave to the sea his decree, that the waters should not pass his commandment: when he appointed the foundations of the earth:

30 Then I was by him, as one brought up with him: and I was daily his delight, rejoicing always before him;

31 Rejoicing in the habitable part of his earth; and my delights were with the sons of men.

32 Now therefore hearken unto me, O you children: for blessed are they that keep my ways.

33 Hear instruction, and be wise, and refuse it not.

34 Blessed is the man that heareth me, watching daily at my gates, waiting at the posts of my doors.

35 For whoso findeth me findeth life, and shall obtain favour of the LORD.

36 But he that sinneth against me wrongeth his own soul: all they that hate me love death.

CHAPTER 9

WISDOM has builded her house, she has hewn out her seven pillars:

2 She has killed her beasts; she has mingled her wine; she has also furnished her table.

3 She has sent forth her maidens: she crieth upon the highest places of the city,

4 Whoso is simple, let him turn in hither: as for him that wanteth understanding, she saith to him,

5 Come, eat of my bread, and drink of the wine which I have mingled.

6 Forsake the foolish, and live; and go in the way of understanding.

7 He that reproveth a scorner getteth to himself shame: and he that rebuketh a wicked man getteth himself a blot.

8 Reprove not a scorner, lest he hate you: rebuke a wise man, and he will love you.

9 Give instruction to a wise man, and he will be yet wiser: teach a just man, and he will increase in learning.

10 The fear of the LORD is the beginning of wisdom: and the knowledge of the holy is understanding.

11 For by me your days shall be multiplied, and the years of your life shall be increased.

12 If you be wise, you shalt be wise for yourself: but if you scornest, you alone shalt bear it.

13 A foolish woman is clamorous: she is simple, and knoweth nothing.

14 For she sitteth at the door of her house, on a seat in the high places of the city,

15 To call passengers who go right on their ways:

16 Whoso is simple, let him turn in hither: and as for him that wanteth understanding, she saith to him,

17 Stolen waters are sweet, and bread eaten in secret is pleasant.

18 But he knoweth not that the dead are there; and that her guests are in the depths of hell.

CHAPTER 10

THE proverbs of Solomon. A wise son maketh a glad father: but a foolish son is the heaviness of his mother.

2 Treasures of wickedness profit nothing: but righteousness delivereth from death.

3 The LORD will not suffer the soul of the righteous to famish: but he casteth away the substance of the wicked.

4 He becometh poor that dealeth with a slack hand: but the hand of the diligent maketh rich.

5 He that gathereth in summer is a wise son: but he that sleepeth in harvest is a son that causeth shame.

6 Blessings are upon the head of the just: but violence covers the mouth of the wicked.

7 The memory of the just is blessed: but the name of the wicked shall rot.

8 The wise in heart will receive commandments: but a prating fool shall fall.

9 He that walketh uprightly walketh surely: but he that perverteth his ways shall be known.

10 He that winketh with the eye causeth sorrow: but a prating fool shall fall.

11 The mouth of a righteous man is a well of life: but violence covers the mouth of the wicked.

12 Hatred stirreth up strifes: but love covers all sins.

13 In the lips of him that has understanding wisdom is found: but a rod is for the back of him that is void of understanding.

14 Wise men lay up knowledge: but the mouth of the foolish is near destruction.

15 The rich man's wealth is his strong city: the destruction of the poor is their poverty.

16 The labour of the righteous tendeth to life: the fruit of the wicked to sin.

17 He is in the way of life that keepeth instruction: but he that refuseth reproof erreth.

18 He that hideth hatred with lying lips, and he that uttereth a slander, is a fool.

19 In the multitude of words there wanteth not sin: but he that refraineth his lips is wise.

20 The tongue of the just is as choice silver: the heart of the wicked is little worth.

21 The lips of the righteous feed many: but fools die for want of wisdom.

22 The blessing of the LORD, it maketh rich, and he addeth no sorrow with it.

23 It is as sport to a fool to do mischief: but a man of understanding has wisdom.

24 The fear of the wicked, it shall come upon him: but the desire of the righteous shall be granted.

25 As the whirlwind passes, so is the wicked no more: but the righteous is an everlasting foundation.

26 As vinegar to the teeth, and as smoke to the eyes, so is the sluggard to them that send him.

27 The fear of the LORD prolongeth days: but the years of the wicked shall be shortened.

28 The hope of the righteous shall be gladness: but the expectation of the wicked shall perish.

29 The way of the LORD is strength to the upright: but destruction shall be to the workers of iniquity.

30 The righteous shall never be removed: but the wicked shall not inhabit the earth.

31 The mouth of the just bringeth forth wisdom: but the froward tongue shall be cut out.

32 The lips of the righteous know what is acceptable: but the mouth of the wicked speaketh frowardness.

CHAPTER 11

A FALSE balance is abomination to the LORD: but a just weight is his delight.

2 When pride comes, then comes shame: but with the lowly is wisdom.

3 The integrity of the upright shall guide them: but the perverseness of transgressors shall destroy them.

4 Riches profit not in the day of wrath: but righteousness delivereth from death.

5 The righteousness of the perfect shall direct his way: but the wicked shall fall by his own wickedness.

6 The righteousness of the upright shall deliver them: but transgressors shall be taken in their own naughtiness.

7 When a wicked man dieth, his expectation shall perish: and the hope of unjust men perisheth.

8 The righteous is delivered out of trouble, and the wicked comes in his stead.

9 An hypocrite with his mouth destroyeth his neighbour: but through knowledge shall the just be delivered.

10 When it goeth well with the righteous, the city rejoiceth: and when the wicked perish, there is shouting.

11 By the blessing of the upright the city is exalted: but it is overthrown by the mouth of the wicked.

12 He that is void of wisdom despiseth his neighbour: but a man of understanding holdeth his peace.

13 A talebearer revealeth secrets: but he that is of a faithful spirit concealeth the matter.

14 Where no counsel is, the people fall: but in the multitude of counsellers there is safety.

15 He that is surety for a stranger shall smart for it: and he that hateth suretiship is sure.

16 A gracious woman retaineth honour: and strong men retain riches.

17 The merciful man doeth good to his own soul: but he that is cruel troubleth his own flesh.

18 The wicked worketh a deceitful work: but to him that soweth righteousness shall be a sure reward.

19 As righteousness tendeth to life: so he that pursueth evil pursueth it to his own death.

20 They that are of a froward heart are abomination to the LORD: but such as are upright in their way are his delight.

21 Though hand join in hand, the wicked shall not be unpunished: but the seed of the righteous shall be delivered.

22 As a jewel of gold in a swine's snout, so is a fair woman which is without discretion.

23 The desire of the righteous is only good: but the expectation of the wicked is wrath.

24 There is that scattereth, and yet increaseth; and there is that withholdeth more than is meet, but it tendeth to poverty.

25 The liberal soul shall be made fat: and he that watereth shall be watered also himself.

26 He that withholdeth corn, the people shall curse him: but blessing shall be upon the head of him that selleth it.

27 He that diligently seeketh good procureth favour: but he that seeketh mischief, it shall come unto him.

28 He that trusteth in his riches shall fall: but the righteous shall flourish as a branch.

29 He that troubleth his own house shall inherit the wind: and the fool shall be servant to the wise of heart.

30 The fruit of the righteous is a tree of life; and he that winneth souls is wise.

31 Behold, the righteous shall be recompensed in the earth: much more the wicked and the sinner.

CHAPTER 12

WHOSO loveth instruction loveth knowledge: but he that hateth reproof is brutish.

2 A good man obtaineth favour of the LORD: but a man of wicked devices will he condemn.

3 A man shall not be established by wickedness: but the root of the righteous shall not be moved.

4 A virtuous woman is a crown to her husband: but she that maketh ashamed is as rottenness in his bones.

5 The thoughts of the righteous are right: but the counsels of the wicked are deceit.

6 The words of the wicked are to lie in wait for blood: but the mouth of the upright shall deliver them.

7 The wicked are overthrown, and are not: but the house of the righteous shall stand.

8 A man shall be commended according to his wisdom: but he that is of a perverse heart shall be despised.

9 He that is despised, and has a servant, is better than he that honoureth himself, and lacketh bread.

10 A righteous man regardeth the life of his beast: but the tender mercies of the wicked are cruel.

11 He that tilleth his land shall be satisfied with bread: but he that followeth vain persons is void of understanding.

12 The wicked desireth the net of evil men: but the root of the righteous yieldeth fruit.

13 The wicked is snared by the transgression of his lips: but the just shall come out of trouble.

14 A man shall be satisfied with good by the fruit of his mouth: and the recompence of a man's hands shall be rendered unto him.

15 The way of a fool is right in his own eyes: but he that hearkeneth unto counsel is wise.

16 A fool's wrath is presently known: but a prudent man covers shame.

17 He that speaketh truth sheweth forth righteousness: but a false witness deceit.

18 There is that speaketh like the piercings of a sword: but the tongue of the wise is health.

19 The lip of truth shall be established for ever: but a lying tongue is but for a moment.

20 Deceit is in the heart of them that imagine evil: but to the counsellers of peace is joy.

21 There shall no evil happen to the just: but the wicked shall be filled with mischief.

22 Lying lips are abomination to the LORD: but they that deal truly are his delight.

23 A prudent man concealeth knowledge: but the heart of fools proclaimeth foolishness.

24 The hand of the diligent shall bear rule: but the slothful shall be under tribute.

25 Heaviness in the heart of man maketh it stoop: but a good word maketh it glad.

26 The righteous is more excellent than his neighbour: but the way of the wicked seduceth them.

27 The slothful man roasteth not that which he took in hunting: but the substance of a diligent man is precious.

28 In the way of righteousness is life; and in the pathway thereof there is no death.

CHAPTER 13

A WISE son heareth his father's instruction: but a scorner heareth not rebuke.

2 A man shall eat good by the fruit of his mouth: but the soul of the transgressors shall eat violence.

3 He that keepeth his mouth keepeth his life: but he that openeth wide his lips shall have destruction.

4 The soul of the sluggard desireth, and has nothing: but the soul of the diligent shall be made fat.

5 A righteous man hateth lying: but a wicked man is loathsome, and comes to shame.

6 Righteousness keepeth him that is upright in the way: but wickedness overthroweth the sinner.

7 There is that maketh himself rich, yet has nothing: there is that maketh himself poor, yet has great riches.

8 The ransom of a man's life are his riches: but the poor heareth not rebuke.

9 The light of the righteous rejoiceth: but the lamp of the wicked shall be put out.

10 Only by pride comes contention: but with the well advised is wisdom.

11 Wealth gotten by vanity shall be diminished: but he that gathereth by labour shall increase.

12 Hope deferred maketh the heart sick: but when the desire comes, it is a tree of life.

13 Whoso despiseth the word shall be destroyed: but he that feareth the commandment shall be rewarded.

14 The law of the wise is a fountain of life, to depart from the snares of death.

15 Good understanding giveth favour: but the way of transgressors is hard.

16 Every prudent man dealeth with knowledge: but a fool layeth open his folly.

17 A wicked messenger falleth into mischief: but a faithful ambassador is health.

18 Poverty and shame shall be to him that refuseth instruction: but he that regardeth reproof shall be honoured.

19 The desire accomplished is sweet to the soul: but it is abomination to fools to depart from evil.

20 He that walketh with wise men shall be wise: but a companion of fools shall be destroyed.

21 Evil pursueth sinners: but to the righteous good shall be repayed.

22 A good man leaveth an inheritance to his children's children: and the wealth of the sinner is laid up for the just.

23 Much food is in the tillage of the poor: but there is that is destroyed for want of judgment.

24 He that spareth his rod hateth his son: but he that loveth him chasteneth him betimes.

25 The righteous eateth to the satisfying of his soul: but the belly of the wicked shall want.

CHAPTER 14

EVERY wise woman buildeth her house: but the foolish plucketh it down with her hands.

2 He that walketh in his uprightness feareth the LORD: but he that is perverse in his ways despiseth him.

3 In the mouth of the foolish is a rod of pride: but the lips of the wise shall preserve them.

4 Where no oxen are, the crib is clean: but much increase is by the strength of the ox.

5 A faithful witness will not lie: but a false witness will utter lies.

6 A scorner seeketh wisdom, and findeth it not: but knowledge is easy unto him that understands.

7 Go from the presence of a foolish man, when you perceivest not in him the lips of knowledge.

8 The wisdom of the prudent is to understand his way: but the folly of fools is deceit.

9 Fools make a mock at sin: but among the righteous there is favour.

10 The heart knoweth his own bitterness; and a stranger doth not intermeddle with his joy.

11 The house of the wicked shall be overthrown: but the tabernacle of the upright shall flourish.

12 There is a way which seemeth right unto a man, but the end thereof are the ways of death.

13 Even in laughter the heart is sorrowful; and the end of that mirth is heaviness.

14 The backslider in heart shall be filled with his own ways: and a good man shall be satisfied from himself.

15 The simple believeth every word: but the prudent man looketh well to his going.

16 A wise man feareth, and departeth from evil: but the fool rageth, and is confident.

17 He that is soon angry dealeth foolishly: and a man of wicked devices is hated.

18 The simple inherit folly: but the prudent are crowned with knowledge.

19 The evil bow before the good; and the wicked at the gates of the righteous.

20 The poor is hated even of his own neighbour: but the rich has many friends.

21 He that despiseth his neighbour sinneth: but he that has mercy on the poor, happy is he.

22 Do they not err that devise evil? but mercy and truth shall be to them that devise good.

23 In all labour is profit: but the talk of the lips tendeth only to penury.

24 The crown of the wise is their riches: but the foolishness of fools is folly.

25 A true witness delivereth souls: but a deceitful witness speaketh lies.

26 In the fear of the LORD is strong confidence: and his children shall have a place of refuge.

27 The fear of the LORD is a fountain of life, to depart from the snares of death.

28 In the multitude of people is the king's honour: but in the want of people is the destruction of the prince.

29 He that is slow to wrath is of great understanding: but he that is hasty of spirit exalteth folly.

30 A sound heart is the life of the flesh: but envy the rottenness of the bones.

31 He that oppresseth the poor reproacheth his Maker: but he that honoureth him has mercy on the poor.

32 The wicked is driven away in his wickedness: but the righteous has hope in his death.

33 Wisdom resteth in the heart of him that has understanding: but that which is in the midst of fools is made known.

34 Righteousness exalteth a nation: but sin is a reproach to any people.

35 The king's favour is toward a wise servant: but his wrath is against him that causeth shame.

CHAPTER 15

A SOFT answer turneth away wrath: but grievous words stir up anger.

2 The tongue of the wise useth knowledge aright: but the mouth of fools poureth out foolishness.

3 The eyes of the LORD are in every place, beholding the evil and the good.

4 A wholesome tongue is a tree of life: but perverseness therein is a breach in the spirit.

5 A fool despiseth his father's instruction: but he that regardeth reproof is prudent.

6 In the house of the righteous is much treasure: but in the revenues of the wicked is trouble.

7 The lips of the wise disperse knowledge: but the heart of the foolish doeth not so.

8 The sacrifice of the wicked is an abomination to the LORD: but the prayer of the upright is his delight.

9 The way of the wicked is an abomination unto the LORD: but he loveth him that followeth after righteousness.

10 Correction is grievous unto him that forsaketh the way: and he that hateth reproof shall die.

11 Hell and destruction are before the LORD: how much more then the hearts of the children of men?

12 A scorner loveth not one that reproveth him: neither will he go unto the wise.

13 A merry heart maketh a cheerful countenance: but by sorrow of the heart the spirit is broken.

14 The heart of him that has understanding seeketh knowledge: but the mouth of fools feedeth on foolishness.

15 All the days of the afflicted are evil: but he that is of a merry heart has a continual feast.

16 Better is little with the fear of the LORD than great treasure and trouble therewith.

17 Better is a dinner of herbs where love is, than a stalled ox and hatred therewith.

18 A wrathful man stirreth up strife: but he that is slow to anger appeaseth strife.

19 The way of the slothful man is as an hedge of thorns: but the way of the righteous is made plain.

20 A wise son maketh a glad father: but a foolish man despiseth his mother.

21 Folly is joy to him that is destitute of wisdom: but a man of understanding walketh uprightly.

22 Without counsel purposes are disappointed: but in the multitude of counsellers they are established.

23 A man has joy by the answer of his mouth: and a word spoken in due season, how good is it!

24 The way of life is above to the wise, that he may depart from hell beneath.

25 The LORD will destroy the house of the proud: but he will establish the border of the widow.

26 The thoughts of the wicked are an abomination to the LORD: but the words of the pure are pleasant words.

27 He that is greedy of gain troubleth his own house; but he that hateth gifts shall live.

28 The heart of the righteous studieth to answer: but the mouth of the wicked poureth out evil things.

29 The LORD is far from the wicked: but he heareth the prayer of the righteous.

30 The light of the eyes rejoiceth the heart: and a good report maketh the bones fat.

31 The ear that heareth the reproof of life abideth among the wise.

32 He that refuseth instruction despiseth his own soul: but he that heareth reproof getteth understanding.

33 The fear of the LORD is the instruction of wisdom; and before honour is humility.

CHAPTER 16

THE preparations of the heart in man, and the answer of the tongue, is from the LORD.

2 All the ways of a man are clean in his own eyes; but the LORD weigheth the spirits.

3 Commit your works unto the LORD, and your thoughts shall be established.

4 The LORD has made all things for himself: yea, even the wicked for the day of evil.

5 Every one that is proud in heart is an abomination to the LORD: though hand join in hand, he shall not be unpunished.

6 By mercy and truth iniquity is purged: and by the fear of the LORD men depart from evil.

7 When a man's ways please the LORD, he maketh even his enemies to be at peace with him.

8 Better is a little with righteousness than great revenues without right.

9 A man's heart deviseth his way: but the LORD directeth his steps.

10 A divine sentence is in the lips of the king: his mouth transgresseth not in judgment.

11 A just weight and balance are the LORD's: all the weights of the bag are his work.

12 It is an abomination to kings to commit wickedness: for the throne is established by righteousness.

13 Righteous lips are the delight of kings; and they love him that speaketh right.

14 The wrath of a king is as messengers of death: but a wise man will pacify it.

15 In the light of the king's countenance is life; and his favour is as a cloud of the latter rain.

16 How much better is it to get wisdom than gold! and to get understanding rather to be chosen than silver!

17 The highway of the upright is to depart from evil: he that keepeth his way preserveth his soul.

18 Pride goeth before destruction, and an haughty spirit before a fall.

19 Better it is to be of an humble spirit with the lowly, than to divide the spoil with the proud.

20 He that handleth a matter wisely shall find good: and whoso trusteth in the LORD, happy is he.

21 The wise in heart shall be called prudent: and the sweetness of the lips increaseth learning.

22 Understanding is a wellspring of life unto him that has it: but the instruction of fools is folly.

23 The heart of the wise teacheth his mouth, and addeth learning to his lips.

24 Pleasant words are as an honeycomb, sweet to the soul, and health to the bones.

25 There is a way that seemeth right unto a man, but the end thereof are the ways of death.

26 He that laboureth laboureth for himself; for his mouth craveth it of him.

27 An ungodly man diggeth up evil: and in his lips there is as a burning fire.

28 A froward man soweth strife: and a whisperer separateth chief friends.

29 A violent man enticeth his neighbour, and leadeth him into the way that is not good.

30 He shutteth his eyes to devise froward things: moving his lips he bringeth evil to pass.

31 The hoary head is a crown of glory, if it be found in the way of righteousness.

32 He that is slow to anger is better than the mighty; and he that ruleth his spirit than he that taketh a city.

33 The lot is cast into the lap; but the whole disposing thereof is of the LORD.

CHAPTER 17

BETTER is a dry morsel, and quietness therewith, than an house full of sacrifices with strife.

2 A wise servant shall have rule over a son that causeth shame, and shall have part of the inheritance among the brethren.

3 The fining pot is for silver, and the furnace for gold: but the LORD trieth the hearts.

4 A wicked doer giveth heed to false lips; and a liar giveth ear to a naughty tongue.

5 Whoso mocketh the poor reproacheth his Maker: and he that is glad at calamities shall not be unpunished.

6 Children's children are the crown of old men; and the glory of children are their fathers.

7 Excellent speech becometh not a fool: much less do lying lips a prince.

8 A gift is as a precious stone in the eyes of him that has it: whithersoever it turneth, it prospereth.

9 He that covers a transgression seeketh love; but he that repeateth a matter separateth very friends.

10 A reproof entereth more into a wise man than an hundred stripes into a fool.

11 An evil man seeketh only rebellion: therefore a cruel messenger shall be sent against him.

12 Let a bear robbed of her whelps meet a man, rather than a fool in his folly.

13 Whoso rewardeth evil for good, evil shall not depart from his house.

14 The beginning of strife is as when one letteth out water: therefore leave off contention, before it be meddled with.

15 He that justifieth the wicked, and he that condemneth the just, even they both are abomination to the LORD.

16 Wherefore is there a price in the hand of a fool to get wisdom, seeing he has no heart to it?

17 A friend loveth at all times, and a brother is born for adversity.

18 A man void of understanding striketh hands, and becometh surety in the presence of his friend.

19 He loveth transgression that loveth strife: and he that exalteth his gate seeketh destruction.

20 He that has a froward heart findeth no good: and he that has a perverse tongue falleth into mischief.

21 He that begetteth a fool doeth it to his sorrow: and the father of a fool has no joy.

22 A merry heart doeth good like a medicine: but a broken spirit drieth the bones.

23 A wicked man taketh a gift out of the bosom to pervert the ways of judgment.

24 Wisdom is before him that has understanding; but the eyes of a fool are in the ends of the earth.

25 A foolish son is a grief to his father, and bitterness to her that bare him.

26 Also to punish the just is not good, nor to strike princes for equity.

27 He that has knowledge spareth his words: and a man of understanding is of an excellent spirit.

28 Even a fool, when he holdeth his peace, is counted wise: and he that shutteth his lips is esteemed a man of understanding.

CHAPTER 18

THROUGH desire a man, having separated himself, seeketh and intermeddleth with all wisdom.

2 A fool has no delight in understanding, but that his heart may discover itself.

3 When the wicked comes, then comes also contempt, and with ignominy reproach.

4 The words of a man's mouth are as deep waters, and the wellspring of wisdom as a flowing brook.

5 It is not good to accept the person of the wicked, to overthrow the righteous in judgment.

6 A fool's lips enter into contention, and his mouth calleth for strokes.

7 A fool's mouth is his destruction, and his lips are the snare of his soul.

8 The words of a talebearer are as wounds, and they go down into the innermost parts of the belly.

9 He also that is slothful in his work is brother to him that is a great waster.

10 The name of the LORD is a strong tower: the righteous runneth into it, and is safe.

11 The rich man's wealth is his strong city, and as an high wall in his own conceit.

12 Before destruction the heart of man is haughty, and before honour is humility.

13 He that answereth a matter before he heareth it, it is folly and shame unto him.

14 The spirit of a man will sustain his infirmity; but a wounded spirit who can bear?

15 The heart of the prudent getteth knowledge; and the ear of the wise seeketh knowledge.

16 A man's gift maketh room for him, and bringeth him before great men.

17 He that is first in his own cause seemeth just; but his neighbour comes and searches him.

18 The lot causeth contentions to cease, and parteth between the mighty.

19 A brother offended is harder to be won than a strong city: and their contentions are like the bars of a castle.

20 A man's belly shall be satisfied with the fruit of his mouth; and with the increase of his lips shall he be filled.

21 Death and life are in the power of the tongue: and they that love it shall eat the fruit thereof.

22 Whoso findeth a wife findeth a good thing, and obtaineth favour of the LORD.

23 The poor useth intreaties; but the rich answereth roughly.

24 A man that has friends must shew himself friendly: and there is a friend that sticketh closer than a brother.

CHAPTER 19

BETTER is the poor that walketh in his integrity, than he that is perverse in his lips, and is a fool.

2 Also, that the soul be without knowledge, it is not good; and he that hasteth with his feet sinneth.

3 The foolishness of man perverteth his way: and his heart fretteth against the LORD.

4 Wealth maketh many friends; but the poor is separated from his neighbour.

5 A false witness shall not be unpunished, and he that speaketh lies shall not escape.

6 Many will intreat the favour of the prince: and every man is a friend to him that giveth gifts.

7 All the brethren of the poor do hate him: how much more do his friends go far from him? he pursueth them with words, yet they are wanting to him.

8 He that getteth wisdom loveth his own soul: he that keepeth understanding shall find good.

9 A false witness shall not be unpunished, and he that speaketh lies shall perish.

10 Delight is not seemly for a fool; much less for a servant to have rule over princes.

11 The discretion of a man deferreth his anger; and it is his glory to pass over a transgression.

12 The king's wrath is as the roaring of a lion; but his favour is as dew upon the grass.

13 A foolish son is the calamity of his father: and the contentions of a wife are a continual dropping.

14 House and riches are the inheritance of fathers: and a prudent wife is from the LORD.

15 Slothfulness casteth into a deep sleep; and an idle soul shall suffer hunger.

16 He that keepeth the commandment keepeth his own soul; but he that despiseth his ways shall die.

17 He that has pity upon the poor lendeth unto the LORD; and that which he has given will he pay him again.

18 Chasten your son while there is hope, and let not your soul spare for his crying.

19 A man of great wrath shall suffer punishment: for if you deliver him, yet you must do it again.

20 Hear counsel, and receive instruction, that you mayest be wise in your latter end.

21 There are many devices in a man's heart; nevertheless the counsel of the LORD, that shall stand.

22 The desire of a man is his kindness: and a poor man is better than a liar.

23 The fear of the LORD tendeth to life: and he that has it shall abide satisfied; he shall not be visited with evil.

24 A slothful man hideth his hand in his bosom, and will not so much as bring it to his mouth again.

25 Strike a scorner, and the simple will beware: and reprove one that has understanding, and he will understand knowledge.

26 He that wasteth his father, and chaseth away his mother, is a son that causeth shame, and bringeth reproach.

27 Cease, my son, to hear the instruction that causeth to err from the words of knowledge.

28 An ungodly witness scorneth judgment: and the mouth of the wicked devoureth iniquity.

29 Judgments are prepared for scorners, and stripes for the back of fools.

CHAPTER 20

WINE is a mocker, strong drink is raging: and whosoever is deceived thereby is not wise.

2 The fear of a king is as the roaring of a lion: whoso provoketh him to anger sinneth against his own soul.

3 It is an honour for a man to cease from strife: but every fool will be meddling.

4 The sluggard will not plow by reason of the cold; therefore shall he beg in harvest, and have nothing.

5 Counsel in the heart of man is like deep water; but a man of understanding will draw it out.

6 Most men will proclaim every one his own goodness: but a faithful man who can find?

7 The just man walketh in his integrity: his children are blessed after him.

8 A king that sitteth in the throne of judgment scattereth away all evil with his eyes.

9 Who can say, I have made my heart clean, I am pure from my sin?

10 Divers weights, and divers measures, both of them are alike abomination to the LORD.

11 Even a child is known by his doings, whether his work be pure, and whether it be right.

12 The hearing ear, and the seeing eye, the LORD has made even both of them.

13 Love not sleep, lest you come to poverty; open yours eyes, and you shalt be satisfied with bread.

14 It is naught, it is naught, saith the buyer: but when he is gone his way, then he boasteth.

15 There is gold, and a multitude of rubies: but the lips of knowledge are a precious jewel.

16 Take his garment that is surety for a stranger: and take a pledge of him for a strange woman.

17 Bread of deceit is sweet to a man; but afterwards his mouth shall be filled with gravel.

18 Every purpose is established by counsel: and with good advice make war.

19 He that goeth about as a talebearer revealeth secrets: therefore meddle not with him that flattereth with his lips.

20 Whoso curseth his father or his mother, his lamp shall be put out in obscure darkness.

21 An inheritance may be gotten hastily at the beginning; but the end thereof shall not be blessed.

22 Say not you , I will recompense evil; but wait on the LORD, and he shall save you.

23 Divers weights are an abomination unto the LORD; and a false balance is not good.

24 Man's goings are of the LORD; how can a man then understand his own way?

25 It is a snare to the man who devoureth that which is holy, and after vows to make inquiry.

26 A wise king scattereth the wicked, and bringeth the wheel over them.

27 The spirit of man is the candle of the LORD, searching all the inward parts of the belly.

28 Mercy and truth preserve the king: and his throne is upholden by mercy.

29 The glory of young men is their strength: and the beauty of old men is the gray head.

30 The blueness of a wound cleanseth away evil: so do stripes the inward parts of the belly.

CHAPTER 21

THE king's heart is in the hand of the LORD, as the rivers of water: he turneth it whithersoever he will.

2 Every way of a man is right in his own eyes: but the LORD pondereth the hearts.

3 To do justice and judgment is more acceptable to the LORD than sacrifice.

4 An high look, and a proud heart, and the plowing of the wicked, is sin.

5 The thoughts of the diligent tend only to plenteousness; but of every one that is hasty only to want.

6 The getting of treasures by a lying tongue is a vanity tossed to and fro of them that seek death.

7 The robbery of the wicked shall destroy them; because they refuse to do judgment.

8 The way of man is froward and strange: but as for the pure, his work is right.

9 It is better to dwell in a corner of the housetop, than with a brawling woman in a wide house.

10 The soul of the wicked desireth evil: his neighbour findeth no favour in his eyes.

11 When the scorner is punished, the simple is made wise: and when the wise is instructed, he receiveth knowledge.

12 The righteous man wisely considereth the house of the wicked: but God overthroweth the wicked for their wickedness.

13 Whoso stoppeth his ears at the cry of the poor, he also shall cry himself, but shall not be heard.

14 A gift in secret pacifieth anger: and a reward in the bosom strong wrath.

15 It is joy to the just to do judgment: but destruction shall be to the workers of iniquity.

16 The man that wandereth out of the way of understanding shall remain in the congregation of the dead.

17 He that loveth pleasure shall be a poor man: he that loveth wine and oil shall not be rich.

18 The wicked shall be a ransom for the righteous, and the transgressor for the upright.

19 It is better to dwell in the wilderness, than with a contentious and an angry woman.

20 There is treasure to be desired and oil in the dwelling of the wise; but a foolish man spendeth it up.

21 He that followeth after righteousness and mercy findeth life, righteousness, and honour.

22 A wise man scaleth the city of the mighty, and casteth down the strength of the confidence thereof.

23 Whoso keepeth his mouth and his tongue keepeth his soul from troubles.

24 Proud and haughty scorner is his name, who dealeth in proud wrath.

25 The desire of the slothful killeth him; for his hands refuse to labour.

26 He coveteth greedily all the day long: but the righteous giveth and spareth not.

27 The sacrifice of the wicked is abomination: how much more, when he bringeth it with a wicked mind?

28 A false witness shall perish: but the man that heareth speaketh constantly.

29 A wicked man hardeneth his face: but as for the upright, he directeth his way.

30 There is no wisdom nor understanding nor counsel against the LORD.

31 The horse is prepared against the day of battle: but safety is of the LORD.

CHAPTER 22

A GOOD name is rather to be chosen than great riches, and loving favour rather than silver and gold.

2 The rich and poor meet together: the LORD is the maker of them all.

3 A prudent man foreseeth the evil, and hideth himself: but the simple pass on, and are punished.

4 By humility and the fear of the LORD are riches, and honour, and life.

5 Thorns and snares are in the way of the froward: he that doth keep his soul shall be far from them.

6 Train up a child in the way he should go: and when he is old, he will not depart from it.

7 The rich ruleth over the poor, and the borrower is servant to the lender.

8 He that soweth iniquity shall reap vanity: and the rod of his anger shall fail.

9 He that has a bountiful eye shall be blessed; for he giveth of his bread to the poor.

10 Cast out the scorner, and contention shall go out; yea, strife and reproach shall cease.

11 He that loveth pureness of heart, for the grace of his lips the king shall be his friend.

12 The eyes of the LORD preserve knowledge, and he overthroweth the words of the transgressor.

13 The slothful man saith, There is a lion without, I shall be slain in the streets.

14 The mouth of strange women is a deep pit: he that is abhorred of the LORD shall fall therein.

15 Foolishness is bound in the heart of a child; but the rod of correction shall drive it far from him.

16 He that oppresseth the poor to increase his riches, and he that giveth to the rich, shall surely come to want.

17 Bow down yours ear, and hear the words of the wise, and apply yours heart unto my knowledge.

18 For it is a pleasant thing if you keep them within you; they shall withal be fitted in your lips.

19 That your trust may be in the LORD, I have made known to you this day, even to you.

20 Have not I written to you excellent things in counsels and knowledge,

21 That I might make you know the certainty of the words of truth; that you mightest answer the words of truth to them that send unto you?

22 Rob not the poor, because he is poor: neither oppress the afflicted in the gate:

23 For the LORD will plead their cause, and spoil the soul of those that spoiled them.

24 Make no friendship with an angry man; and with a furious man you shalt not go:

25 Lest you learn his ways, and get a snare to your soul.

26 Be not you one of them that strike hands, or of them that are sureties for debts.

27 If you have nothing to pay, why should he take away your bed from under you?

28 Remove not the ancient landmark, which your fathers have set.

29 Seest you a man diligent in his business? he shall stand before kings; he shall not stand before mean men.

CHAPTER 23

WHEN you sittest to eat with a ruler, consider diligently what is before you:

2 And put a knife to your throat, if you be a man given to appetite.

3 Be not desirous of his dainties: for they are deceitful meat.

4 Labour not to be rich: cease from yours own wisdom.

5 Will you set yours eyes upon that which is not? for riches certainly make themselves wings; they fly away as an eagle toward heaven.

6 Eat you not the bread of him that has an evil eye, neither desire you his dainty meats:

7 For as he thinketh in his heart, so is he: Eat and drink, saith he to you; but his heart is not with you.

8 The morsel which you have eaten shalt you vomit up, and lose your sweet words.

9 Speak not in the ears of a fool: for he will despise the wisdom of your words.

10 Remove not the old landmark; and enter not into the fields of the fatherless:

11 For their redeemer is mighty; he shall plead their cause with you.

12 Apply yours heart unto instruction, and yours ears to the words of knowledge.

13 Withhold not correction from the child: for if you beatest him with the rod, he shall not die.

14 You shalt beat him with the rod, and shalt deliver his soul from hell.

15 My son, if yours heart be wise, my heart shall rejoice, even my.

16 Yea, my reins shall rejoice, when your lips speak right things.

17 Let not yours heart envy sinners: but be you in the fear of the LORD all the day long.

18 For surely there is an end; and yours expectation shall not be cut off.

19 Hear you , my son, and be wise, and guide yours heart in the way.

20 Be not among winebibbers; among riotous eaters of flesh:

21 For the drunkard and the glutton shall come to poverty: and drowsiness shall clothe a man with rags.

22 Hearken unto your father that begat you, and despise not your mother when she is old.

23 Buy the truth, and sell it not; also wisdom, and instruction, and understanding.

24 The father of the righteous shall greatly rejoice: and he that begetteth a wise child shall have joy of him.

25 Your father and your mother shall be glad, and she that bare you shall rejoice.

26 My son, give me yours heart, and let yours eyes observe my ways.

27 For a whore is a deep ditch; and a strange woman is a narrow pit.

28 She also lies in wait as for a prey, and increaseth the transgressors among men.

29 Who has woe? who has sorrow? who has contentions? who has babbling? who has wounds without cause? who has redness of eyes?

30 They that tarry long at the wine; they that go to seek mixed wine.

31 Look not you upon the wine when it is red, when it giveth his colour in the cup, when it moveth itself aright.

32 At the last it biteth like a serpent, and stingeth like an adder.

33 Yours eyes shall behold strange women, and yours heart shall utter perverse things.

34 Yea, you shalt be as he that lies down in the midst of the sea, or as he that lies upon the top of a mast.

35 They have stricken me, shalt you say, and I was not sick; they have beaten me, and I felt it not: when shall I awake? I will seek it yet again.

CHAPTER 24

BE not you envious against evil men, neither desire to be with them.

2 For their heart studieth destruction, and their lips talk of mischief.

3 Through wisdom is an house builded; and by understanding it is established:

4 And by knowledge shall the chambers be filled with all precious and pleasant riches.

5 A wise man is strong; yea, a man of knowledge increaseth strength.

6 For by wise counsel you shalt make your war: and in multitude of counsellers there is safety.

7 Wisdom is too high for a fool: he openeth not his mouth in the gate.

8 He that deviseth to do evil shall be called a mischievous person.

9 The thought of foolishness is sin: and the scorner is an abomination to men.

10 If you faint in the day of adversity, your strength is small.

11 If you forbear to deliver them that are drawn unto death, and those that are ready to be slain;

12 If you say, Behold, we knew it not; doth not he that pondereth the heart consider it? and he that keepeth your soul, doth not he know it? and shall not he render to every man according to his works?

13 My son, eat you honey, because it is good; and the honeycomb, which is sweet to your taste:

14 So shall the knowledge of wisdom be unto your soul: when you have found it, then there shall be a reward, and your expectation shall not be cut off.

15 Lay not wait, O wicked man, against the dwelling of the righteous; spoil not his resting place:

16 For a just man falleth seven times, and riseth up again: but the wicked shall fall into mischief.

17 Rejoice not when yours enemy falleth, and let not yours heart be glad when he stumbleth:

18 Lest the LORD see it, and it displease him, and he turn away his wrath from him.

19 Fret not yourself because of evil men, neither be you envious at the wicked;

20 For there shall be no reward to the evil man; the candle of the wicked shall be put out.

21 My son, fear you the LORD and the king: and meddle not with them that are given to change:

22 For their calamity shall rise suddenly; and who knoweth the ruin of them both?

23 These things also belong to the wise. It is not good to have respect of persons in judgment.

24 He that saith unto the wicked, You are righteous; him shall the people curse, nations shall abhor him:

25 But to them that rebuke him shall be delight, and a good blessing shall come upon them.

26 Every man shall kiss his lips that giveth a right answer.

27 Prepare your work without, and make it fit for yourself in the field; and afterwards build yours house.

28 Be not a witness against your neighbour without cause; and deceive not with your lips.

29 Say not, I will do so to him as he has done to me: I will render to the man according to his work.

30 I went by the field of the slothful, and by the vineyard of the man void of understanding;

31 And, lo, it was all grown over with thorns, and nettles had covered the face thereof, and the stone wall thereof was broken down.

32 Then I saw, and considered it well: I looked upon it, and received instruction.

33 Yet a little sleep, a little slumber, a little folding of the hands to sleep:

34 So shall your poverty come as one that travelleth; and your want as an armed man.

CHAPTER 25

THESE are also proverbs of Solomon, which the men of Hezekiah king of Judah copied out.

2 It is the glory of God to conceal a thing: but the honour of kings is to search out a matter.

3 The heaven for height, and the earth for depth, and the heart of kings is unsearchable.

4 Take away the dross from the silver, and there shall come forth a vessel for the finer.

5 Take away the wicked from before the king, and his throne shall be established in righteousness.

6 Put not forth yourself in the presence of the king, and stand not in the place of great men:

7 For better it is that it be said unto you, Come up hither; than that you shouldest be put lower in the presence of the prince whom yours eyes have seen.

8 Go not forth hastily to strive, lest you know not what to do in the end thereof, when your neighbour has put you to shame.

9 Debate your cause with your neighbour himself; and discover not a secret to another:

10 Lest he that heareth it put you to shame, and yours infamy turn not away.

11 A word fitly spoken is like apples of gold in pictures of silver.

12 As an earring of gold, and an ornament of fine gold, so is a wise reprover upon an obedient ear.

13 As the cold of snow in the time of harvest, so is a faithful messenger to them that send him: for he refresheth the soul of his masters.

14 Whoso boasteth himself of a false gift is like clouds and wind without rain.

15 By long forbearing is a prince persuaded, and a soft tongue breaketh the bone.

16 Have you found honey? eat so much as is sufficient for you, lest you be filled therewith, and vomit it.

17 Withdraw your foot from your neighbour's house; lest he be weary of you, and so hate you.

18 A man that beareth false witness against his neighbour is a maul, and a sword, and a sharp arrow.

19 Confidence in an unfaithful man in time of trouble is like a broken tooth, and a foot out of joint.

20 As he that taketh away a garment in cold weather, and as vinegar upon nitre, so is he that singeth songs to an heavy heart.

21 If yours enemy be hungry, give him bread to eat; and if he be thirsty, give him water to drink:

22 For you shalt heap coals of fire upon his head, and the LORD shall reward you.

23 The north wind driveth away rain: so doth an angry countenance a backbiting tongue.

24 It is better to dwell in the corner of the housetop, than with a brawling woman and in a wide house.

25 As cold waters to a thirsty soul, so is good news from a far country.

26 A righteous man falling down before the wicked is as a troubled fountain, and a corrupt spring.

27 It is not good to eat much honey: so for men to search their own glory is not glory.

28 He that has no rule over his own spirit is like a city that is broken down, and without walls.

CHAPTER 26

AS snow in summer, and as rain in harvest, so honour is not seemly for a fool.

2 As the bird by wandering, as the swallow by flying, so the curse causeless shall not come.

3 A whip for the horse, a bridle for the ass, and a rod for the fool's back.

4 Answer not a fool according to his folly, lest you also be like unto him.

5 Answer a fool according to his folly, lest he be wise in his own conceit.

6 He that sendeth a message by the hand of a fool cutteth off the feet, and drinketh damage.

7 The legs of the lame are not equal: so is a parable in the mouth of fools.

8 As he that bindeth a stone in a sling, so is he that giveth honour to a fool.

9 As a thorn goeth up into the hand of a drunkard, so is a parable in the mouth of fools.

10 The great God that formed all things both rewardeth the fool, and rewardeth transgressors.

11 As a dog returneth to his vomit, so a fool returneth to his folly.

12 Seest you a man wise in his own conceit? there is more hope of a fool than of him.

13 The slothful man saith, There is a lion in the way; a lion is in the streets.

14 As the door turneth upon his hinges, so doth the slothful upon his bed.

15 The slothful hideth his hand in his bosom; it grieveth him to bring it again to his mouth.

16 The sluggard is wiser in his own conceit than seven men that can render a reason.

17 He that passes by, and meddleth with strife belonging not to him, is like one that taketh a dog by the ears.

18 As a mad man who casteth firebrands, arrows, and death,

19 So is the man that deceiveth his neighbour, and saith, Am not I in sport?

20 Where no wood is, there the fire goeth out: so where there is no talebearer, the strife ceaseth.

21 As coals are to burning coals, and wood to fire; so is a contentious man to kindle strife.

22 The words of a talebearer are as wounds, and they go down into the innermost parts of the belly.

23 Burning lips and a wicked heart are like a potsherd covered with silver dross.

24 He that hateth dissembleth with his lips, and layeth up deceit within him;

25 When he speaketh fair, believe him not: for there are seven abominations in his heart.

26 Whose hatred is covered by deceit, his wickedness shall be shewed before the whole congregation.

27 Whoso diggeth a pit shall fall therein: and he that rolleth a stone, it will return upon him.

28 A lying tongue hateth those that are afflicted by it; and a flattering mouth worketh ruin.

CHAPTER 27

BOAST not yourself of to morrow; for you knowest not what a day may bring forth.

2 Let another man praise you, and not yours own mouth; a stranger, and not yours own lips.

3 A stone is heavy, and the sand weighty; but a fool's wrath is heavier than them both.

4 Wrath is cruel, and anger is outrageous; but who is able to stand before envy?

5 Open rebuke is better than secret love.

6 Faithful are the wounds of a friend; but the kisses of an enemy are deceitful.

7 The full soul loatheth an honeycomb; but to the hungry soul every bitter thing is sweet.

8 As a bird that wandereth from her nest, so is a man that wandereth from his place.

9 Ointment and perfume rejoice the heart: so doth the sweetness of a man's friend by hearty counsel.

10 Yours own friend, and your father's friend, forsake not; neither go into your brother's house in the day of your calamity: for better is a neighbour that is near than a brother far off.

11 My son, be wise, and make my heart glad, that I may answer him that reproacheth me.

12 A prudent man foreseeth the evil, and hideth himself; but the simple pass on, and are punished.

13 Take his garment that is surety for a stranger, and take a pledge of him for a strange woman.

14 He that blesseth his friend with a loud voice, rising early in the morning, it shall be counted a curse to him.

15 A continual dropping in a very rainy day and a contentious woman are alike.

16 Whosoever hideth her hideth the wind, and the ointment of his right hand, which bewrayeth itself.

17 Iron sharpeneth iron; so a man sharpeneth the countenance of his friend.

18 Whoso keepeth the fig tree shall eat the fruit thereof: so he that waiteth on his master shall be honoured.

19 As in water face answereth to face, so the heart of man to man.

20 Hell and destruction are never full; so the eyes of man are never satisfied.

21 As the fining pot for silver, and the furnace for gold; so is a man to his praise.

22 Though you shouldest bray a fool in a mortar among wheat with a pestle, yet will not his foolishness depart from him.

23 Be you diligent to know the state of your flocks, and look well to your herds.

24 For riches are not for ever: and doth the crown endure to every generation?

25 The hay appeareth, and the tender grass sheweth itself, and herbs of the mountains are gathered.

26 The lambs are for your clothing, and the goats are the price of the field.

27 And you shalt have goats' milk enough for your food, for the food of your household, and for the maintenance for your maidens.

CHAPTER 28

THE wicked flee when no man pursueth: but the righteous are bold as a lion.

2 For the transgression of a land many are the princes thereof: but by a man of understanding and knowledge the state thereof shall be prolonged.

3 A poor man that oppresseth the poor is like a sweeping rain which leaveth no food.

4 They that forsake the law praise the wicked: but such as keep the law contend with them.

5 Evil men understand not judgment: but they that seek the LORD understand all things.

6 Better is the poor that walketh in his uprightness, than he that is perverse in his ways, though he be rich.

7 Whoso keepeth the law is a wise son: but he that is a companion of riotous men shameth his father.

8 He that by usury and unjust gain increaseth his substance, he shall gather it for him that will pity the poor.

9 He that turneth away his ear from hearing the law, even his prayer shall be abomination.

10 Whoso causeth the righteous to go astray in an evil way, he shall fall himself into his own pit: but the upright shall have good things in possession.

11 The rich man is wise in his own conceit; but the poor that has understanding searches him out.

12 When righteous men do rejoice, there is great glory: but when the wicked rise, a man is hidden.

13 He that covers his sins shall not prosper: but whoso confesseth and forsaketh them shall have mercy.

14 Happy is the man that feareth alway: but he that hardeneth his heart shall fall into mischief.

15 As a roaring lion, and a ranging bear; so is a wicked ruler over the poor people.

16 The prince that wanteth understanding is also a great oppressor: but he that hateth covetousness shall prolong his days.

17 A man that doeth violence to the blood of any person shall flee to the pit; let no man stay him.

18 Whoso walketh uprightly shall be saved: but he that is perverse in his ways shall fall at once.

19 He that tilleth his land shall have plenty of bread: but he that followeth after vain persons shall have poverty enough.

20 A faithful man shall abound with blessings: but he that maketh haste to be rich shall not be innocent.

21 To have respect of persons is not good: for for a piece of bread that man will transgress.

22 He that hasteth to be rich has an evil eye, and considereth not that poverty shall come upon him.

23 He that rebuketh a man afterwards shall find more favour than he that flattereth with the tongue.

24 Whoso robbeth his father or his mother, and saith, It is no transgression; the same is the companion of a destroyer.

25 He that is of a proud heart stirreth up strife: but he that putteth his trust in the LORD shall be made fat.

26 He that trusteth in his own heart is a fool: but whoso walketh wisely, he shall be delivered.

27 He that giveth unto the poor shall not lack: but he that hideth his eyes shall have many a curse.

28 When the wicked rise, men hide themselves: but when they perish, the righteous increase.

CHAPTER 29

HE, that being often reproved hardeneth his neck, shall suddenly be destroyed, and that without remedy.

2 When the righteous are in authority, the people rejoice: but when the wicked beareth rule, the people mourn.

3 Whoso loveth wisdom rejoiceth his father: but he that keepeth company with harlots spendeth his substance.

4 The king by judgment establisheth the land: but he that receiveth gifts overthroweth it.

5 A man that flattereth his neighbour spreadeth a net for his feet.

6 In the transgression of an evil man there is a snare: but the righteous doth sing and rejoice.

7 The righteous considereth the cause of the poor: but the wicked regardeth not to know it.

8 Scornful men bring a city into a snare: but wise men turn away wrath.

9 If a wise man contendeth with a foolish man, whether he rage or laugh, there is no rest.

10 The bloodthirsty hate the upright: but the just seek his soul.

11 A fool uttereth all his mind: but a wise man keepeth it in till afterwards.

12 If a ruler hearken to lies, all his servants are wicked.

13 The poor and the deceitful man meet together: the LORD lighteneth both their eyes.

14 The king that faithfully judgeth the poor, his throne shall be established for ever.

15 The rod and reproof give wisdom: but a child left to himself bringeth his mother to shame.

16 When the wicked are multiplied, transgression increaseth: but the righteous shall see their fall.

17 Correct your son, and he shall give you rest; yea, he shall give delight unto your soul.

18 Where there is no vision, the people perish: but he that keepeth the law, happy is he.

19 A servant will not be corrected by words: for though he understand he will not answer.

20 Seest you a man that is hasty in his words? there is more hope of a fool than of him.

21 He that delicately bringeth up his servant from a child shall have him become his son at the length.

22 An angry man stirreth up strife, and a furious man aboundeth in transgression.

23 A man's pride shall bring him low: but honour shall uphold the humble in spirit.

24 Whoso is partner with a thief hateth his own soul: he heareth cursing, and bewrayeth it not.

25 The fear of man bringeth a snare: but whoso putteth his trust in the LORD shall be safe.

26 Many seek the ruler's favour; but every man's judgment comes from the LORD.

27 An unjust man is an abomination to the just: and he that is upright in the way is abomination to the wicked.

CHAPTER 30

THE words of Agur the son of Jakeh, even the prophecy: the man spake unto Ithiel, even unto Ithiel and Ucal,

2 Surely I am more brutish than any man, and have not the understanding of a man.

3 I neither learned wisdom, nor have the knowledge of the holy.

4 Who has ascended up into heaven, or descended? who has gathered the wind in his fists? who has bound the waters in a garment? who has established all the ends of the earth? what is his name, and what is his son's name, if you can tell?

5 Every word of God is pure: he is a shield unto them that put their trust in him.

6 Add you not unto his words, lest he reprove you, and you be found a liar.

7 Two things have I required of you; deny me them not before I die:

8 Remove far from me vanity and lies: give me neither poverty nor riches; feed me with food convenient for me:

9 Lest I be full, and deny you, and say, Who is the LORD? or lest I be poor, and steal, and take the name of my God in vain.

10 Accuse not a servant unto his master, lest he curse you, and you be found guilty.

11 There is a generation that curseth their father, and doth not bless their mother.

12 There is a generation that are pure in their own eyes, and yet is not washed from their filthiness.

13 There is a generation, O how lofty are their eyes! and their eyelids are lifted up.

14 There is a generation, whose teeth are as swords, and their jaw teeth as knives, to devour the poor from off the earth, and the needy from among men.

15 The horseleach has two daughters, crying, Give, give. There are three things that are never satisfied, yea, four things say not, It is enough:

16 The grave; and the barren womb; the earth that is not filled with water; and the fire that saith not, It is enough.

17 The eye that mocketh at his father, and despiseth to obey his mother, the ravens of the valley shall pick it out, and the young eagles shall eat it.

18 There be three things which are too wonderful for me, yea, four which I know not:

19 The way of an eagle in the air; the way of a serpent upon a rock; the way of a ship in the midst of the sea; and the way of a man with a maid.

20 Such is the way of an adulterous woman; she eateth, and wipeth her mouth, and saith, I have done no wickedness.

21 For three things the earth is disquieted, and for four which it cannot bear:

22 For a servant when he reigneth; and a fool when he is filled with meat;

23 For an odious woman when she is married; and an handmaid that is heir to her mistress.

24 There be four things which are little upon the earth, but they are exceeding wise:

25 The ants are a people not strong, yet they prepare their meat in the summer;

26 The conies are but a feeble folk, yet make they their houses in the rocks;

27 The locusts have no king, yet go they forth all of them by bands;

28 The spider taketh hold with her hands, and is in kings' palaces.

29 There be three things which go well, yea, four are comely in going:

30 A lion which is strongest among beasts, and turneth not away for any;

31 A greyhound; an he goat also; and a king, against whom there is no rising up.

32 If you have done foolishly in lifting up yourself, or if you have thought evil, lay yours hand upon your mouth.

33 Surely the churning of milk bringeth forth butter, and the wringing of the nose bringeth forth blood: so the forcing of wrath bringeth forth strife.

CHAPTER 31

THE words of king Lemuel, the prophecy that his mother taught him.

2 What, my son? and what, the son of my womb? and what, the son of my vows?

3 Give not your strength unto women, nor your ways to that which destroyeth kings.

4 It is not for kings, O Lemuel, it is not for kings to drink wine; nor for princes strong drink:

5 Lest they drink, and forget the law, and pervert the judgment of any of the afflicted.

6 Give strong drink unto him that is ready to perish, and wine unto those that be of heavy hearts.

7 Let him drink, and forget his poverty, and remember his misery no more.

8 Open your mouth for the dumb in the cause of all such as are appointed to destruction.

9 Open your mouth, judge righteously, and plead the cause of the poor and needy.

10 Who can find a virtuous woman? for her price is far above rubies.

11 The heart of her husband doth safely trust in her, so that he shall have no need of spoil.

12 She will do him good and not evil all the days of her life.

13 She seeketh wool, and flax, and worketh willingly with her hands.

14 She is like the merchants' ships; she bringeth her food from afar.

15 She riseth also while it is yet night, and giveth meat to her household, and a portion to her maidens.

16 She considereth a field, and buyeth it: with the fruit of her hands she planteth a vineyard.

17 She girdeth her loins with strength, and strengtheneth her arms.

18 She perceiveth that her merchandise is good: her candle goeth not out by night.

19 She layeth her hands to the spindle, and her hands hold the distaff.

20 She stretcheth out her hand to the poor; yea, she reacheth forth her hands to the needy.

21 She is not afraid of the snow for her household: for all her household are clothed with scarlet.

22 She maketh herself coverings of tapestry; her clothing is silk and purple.

23 Her husband is known in the gates, when he sitteth among the elders of the land.

24 She maketh fine linen, and selleth it; and delivereth girdles unto the merchant.

25 Strength and honour are her clothing; and she shall rejoice in time to come.

26 She openeth her mouth with wisdom; and in her tongue is the law of kindness.

27 She looketh well to the ways of her household, and eateth not the bread of idleness.

28 Her children arise up, and call her blessed; her husband also, and he praiseth her.

29 Many daughters have done virtuously, but you excellest them all.

30 Favour is deceitful, and beauty is vain: but a woman that feareth the LORD, she shall be praised.

31 Give her of the fruit of her hands; and let her own works praise her in the gates.

ECCLESIASTES;
OR, THE PREACHER.

CHAPTER 1

THE words of the Preacher, the son of David, king in Jerusalem.

2 Vanity of vanities, saith the Preacher, vanity of vanities; all is vanity.

3 What profit has a man of all his labour which he taketh under the sun?

4 One generation passes away, and another generation comes: but the earth abideth for ever.

5 The sun also ariseth, and the sun goeth down, and hasteth to his place where he arose.

6 The wind goeth toward the south, and turneth about unto the north; it whirleth about continually, and the wind returneth again according to his circuits.

7 All the rivers run into the sea; yet the sea is not full; unto the place from whence the rivers come, thither they return again.

8 All things are full of labour; man cannot utter it: the eye is not satisfied with seeing, nor the ear filled with hearing.

9 The thing that has been, it is that which shall be; and that which is done is that which shall be done: and there is no new thing under the sun.

10 Is there any thing whereof it may be said, See, this is new? it has been already of old time, which was before us.

11 There is no remembrance of former things; neither shall there be any remembrance of things that are to come with those that shall come after.

12 I the Preacher was king over Israel in Jerusalem.

13 And I gave my heart to seek and search out by wisdom concerning all things that are done under heaven: this sore travail has God given to the sons of man to be exercised therewith.

14 I have seen all the works that are done under the sun; and, behold, all is vanity and vexation of spirit.

15 That which is crooked cannot be made straight: and that which is wanting cannot be numbered.

16 I communed with my own heart, saying, Lo, I am come to great estate, and have gotten more wisdom than all they that have been before me in Jerusalem: yea, my heart had great experience of wisdom and knowledge.

17 And I gave my heart to know wisdom, and to know madness and folly: I perceived that this also is vexation of spirit.

18 For in much wisdom is much grief: and he that increaseth knowledge increaseth sorrow.

CHAPTER 2

I SAID in my heart, Go to now, I will prove you with mirth, therefore enjoy pleasure: and, behold, this also is vanity.

2 I said of laughter, It is mad: and of mirth, What doeth it?

3 I sought in my heart to give myself unto wine, yet acquainting my heart with wisdom; and to lay hold on folly, till I might see what was that good for the sons of men, which they should do under the heaven all the days of their life.

4 I made me great works; I builded me houses; I planted me vineyards:

5 I made me gardens and orchards, and I planted trees in them of all kind of fruits:

6 I made me pools of water, to water therewith the wood that bringeth forth trees:

7 I got me servants and maidens, and had servants born in my house; also I had great possessions of great and small cattle above all that were in Jerusalem before me:

8 I gathered me also silver and gold, and the peculiar treasure of kings and of the provinces: I gat me men singers and women singers, and the delights of the sons of men, as musical instruments, and that of all sorts.

9 So I was great, and increased more than all that were before me in Jerusalem: also my wisdom remained with me.

10 And whatsoever my eyes desired I kept not from them, I withheld not my heart from any joy; for my heart rejoiced in all my labour: and this was my portion of all my labour.

11 Then I looked on all the works that my hands had created, and on the labour that I had laboured to do: and, behold, all was vanity and vexation of spirit, and there was no profit under the sun.

12 And I turned myself to behold wisdom, and madness, and folly: for what can the man do that comes after the king? even that which has been already done.

13 Then I saw that wisdom excelleth folly, as far as light excelleth darkness.

14 The wise man's eyes are in his head; but the fool walketh in darkness: and I myself perceived also that one event happeneth to them all.

15 Then said I in my heart, As it happeneth to the fool, so it happeneth even to me; and why was I then more wise? Then I said in my heart, that this also is vanity.

16 For there is no remembrance of the wise more than of the fool for ever; seeing that which now is in the days to come shall all be forgotten. And how dieth the wise man? as the fool.

17 Therefore I hated life; because the work that is created under the sun is grievous unto me: for all is vanity and vexation of spirit.

18 Yea, I hated all my labour which I had taken under the sun: because I should leave it unto the man that shall be after me.

19 And who knoweth whether he shall be a wise man or a fool? yet shall he have rule over all my labour wherein I have laboured, and wherein I have shewed myself wise under the sun. This is also vanity.

20 Therefore I went about to cause my heart to despair of all the labour which I took under the sun.

21 For there is a man whose labour is in wisdom, and in knowledge, and in equity; yet to a man that has not laboured therein shall he leave it for his portion. This also is vanity and a great evil.

22 For what has man of all his labour, and of the vexation of his heart, wherein he has laboured under the sun?

23 For all his days are sorrows, and his travail grief; yea, his heart taketh not rest in the night. This also is vanity.

24 There is nothing better for a man, than that he should eat and drink, and that he should make his soul enjoy good in his labour. This also I saw, that it was from the hand of God.

25 For who can eat, or who else can hasten hereunto, more than I?

26 For God giveth to a man that is good in his sight wisdom, and knowledge, and joy: but to the sinner he giveth travail, to gather and to heap up, that he may give to him that is good before God. This also is vanity and vexation of spirit.

CHAPTER 3

TO every thing there is a season, and a time to every purpose under the heaven:

2 A time to be born, and a time to die; a time to plant, and a time to pluck up that which is planted;

3 A time to kill, and a time to heal; a time to break down, and a time to build up;

4 A time to weep, and a time to laugh; a time to mourn, and a time to dance;

5 A time to cast away stones, and a time to gather stones together; a time to embrace, and a time to refrain from embracing;

6 A time to get, and a time to lose; a time to keep, and a time to cast away;

7 A time to rend, and a time to sew; a time to keep silence, and a time to speak;

8 A time to love, and a time to hate; a time of war, and a time of peace.

9 What profit has he that worketh in that wherein he laboureth?

10 I have seen the travail, which God has given to the sons of men to be exercised in it.

11 He has made every thing beautiful in his time: also he has set the world in their heart, so that no man can find out the work that God maketh from the beginning to the end.

12 I know that there is no good in them, but for a man to rejoice, and to do good in his life.

13 And also that every man should eat and drink, and enjoy the good of all his labour, it is the gift of God.

14 I know that, whatsoever God doeth, it shall be for ever: nothing can be put to it, nor any thing taken from it: and God doeth it, that men should fear before him.

15 That which has been is now; and that which is to be has already been; and God requireth that which is past.

16 And moreover I saw under the sun the place of judgment, that wickedness was there; and the place of righteousness, that iniquity was there.

17 I said in my heart, God shall judge the righteous and the wicked: for there is a time there for every purpose and for every work.

18 I said in my heart concerning the estate of the sons of men, that God might manifest them, and that they might see that they themselves are beasts.

19 For that which befalleth the sons of men befalleth beasts; even one thing befalleth them: as the one dieth, so dieth the other; yea, they have all one breath; so that a man has no preeminence above a beast: for all is vanity.

20 All go unto one place; all are of the dust, and all turn to dust again.

21 Who knoweth the spirit of man that goeth upward, and the spirit of the beast that goeth downward to the earth?

22 Wherefore I perceive that there is nothing better, than that a man should rejoice in his own works; for that is his portion: for who shall bring him to see what shall be after him?

CHAPTER 4

SO I returned, and considered all the oppressions that are done under the sun: and behold the tears of such as were oppressed, and they had no comforter; and on the side of their oppressors there was power; but they had no comforter.

2 Wherefore I praised the dead which are already dead more than the living which are yet alive.

3 Yea, better is he than both they, which has not yet been, who has not seen the evil work that is done under the sun.

4 Again, I considered all travail, and every right work, that for this a man is envied of his neighbour. This is also vanity and vexation of spirit.

5 The fool foldeth his hands together, and eateth his own flesh.

6 Better is an handful with quietness, than both the hands full with travail and vexation of spirit.

7 Then I returned, and I saw vanity under the sun.

8 There is one alone, and there is not a second; yea, he has neither child nor brother: yet is there no end of all his labour; neither is his eye satisfied with riches; neither saith he, For whom do I labour, and bereave my soul of good? This is also vanity, yea, it is a sore travail.

9 Two are better than one; because they have a good reward for their labour.

10 For if they fall, the one will lift up his fellow: but woe to him that is alone when he falleth; for he has not another to help him up.

11 Again, if two lie together, then they have heat: but how can one be warm alone?

12 And if one prevail against him, two shall withstand him; and a threefold cord is not quickly broken.

13 Better is a poor and a wise child than an old and foolish king, who will no more be admonished.

14 For out of prison he comes to reign; whereas also he that is born in his kingdom becometh poor.

15 I considered all the living which walk under the sun, with the second child that shall stand up in his stead.

16 There is no end of all the people, even of all that have been before them: they also that come after shall not rejoice in him. Surely this also is vanity and vexation of spirit.

CHAPTER 5

KEEP your foot when you go to the house of God, and be more ready to hear, than to give the sacrifice of fools: for they consider not that they do evil.

2 Be not rash with your mouth, and let not yours heart be hasty to utter any thing before God: for God is in heaven, and you upon earth: therefore let your words be few.

3 For a dream comes through the multitude of business; and a fool's voice is known by multitude of words.

4 When you vowest a vow unto God, defer not to pay it; for he has no pleasure in fools: pay that which you have vowed.

5 Better is it that you shouldest not vow, than that you shouldest vow and not pay.

6 Suffer not your mouth to cause your flesh to sin; neither say you before the angel, that it was an error: wherefore should God be angry at your voice, and destroy the work of yours hands?

7 For in the multitude of dreams and many words there are also divers vanities: but fear you God.

8 If you seest the oppression of the poor, and violent perverting of judgment and justice in a province, marvel not at the matter: for he that is higher than the highest regardeth; and there be higher than they.

9 Moreover the profit of the earth is for all: the king himself is served by the field.

10 He that loveth silver shall not be satisfied with silver; nor he that loveth abundance with increase: this is also vanity.

11 When goods increase, they are increased that eat them: and what good is there to the owners thereof, saving the beholding of them with their eyes?

12 The sleep of a labouring man is sweet, whether he eat little or much: but the abundance of the rich will not suffer him to sleep.

13 There is a sore evil which I have seen under the sun, namely, riches kept for the owners thereof to their hurt.

14 But those riches perish by evil travail: and he begetteth a son, and there is nothing in his hand.

15 As he came forth of his mother's womb, naked shall he return to go as he came, and shall take nothing of his labour, which he may carry away in his hand.

16 And this also is a sore evil, that in all points as he came, so shall he go: and what profit has he that has laboured for the wind?

17 All his days also he eateth in darkness, and he has much sorrow and wrath with his sickness.

18 Behold that which I have seen: it is good and comely for one to eat and to drink, and to enjoy the good of all his labour that he taketh under the sun all the days of his life, which God giveth him: for it is his portion.

19 Every man also to whom God has given riches and wealth, and has given him power to eat thereof, and to take his portion, and to rejoice in his labour; this is the gift of God.

20 For he shall not much remember the days of his life; because God answereth him in the joy of his heart.

CHAPTER 6

THERE is an evil which I have seen under the sun, and it is common among men:

2 A man to whom God has given riches, wealth, and honour, so that he wanteth nothing for his soul of all that he desireth, yet God giveth him not power to eat thereof, but a stranger eateth it: this is vanity, and it is an evil disease.

3 If a man beget an hundred children, and live many years, so that the days of his years be many, and his soul be not filled with good, and also that he have no burial; I say, that an untimely birth is better than he.

4 For he comes in with vanity, and departeth in darkness, and his name shall be covered with darkness.

5 Moreover he has not seen the sun, nor known any thing: this has more rest than the other.

6 Yea, though he live a thousand years twice told, yet has he seen no good: do not all go to one place?

7 All the labour of man is for his mouth, and yet the appetite is not filled.

8 For what has the wise more than the fool? what has the poor, that knoweth to walk before the living?

9 Better is the sight of the eyes than the wandering of the desire: this is also vanity and vexation of spirit.

10 That which has been is named already, and it is known that it is man: neither may he contend with him that is mightier than he.

11 Seeing there be many things that increase vanity, what is man the better?

12 For who knoweth what is good for man in this life, all the days of his vain life which he spendeth as a shadow? for who can tell a man what shall be after him under the sun?

CHAPTER 7

A GOOD name is better than precious ointment; and the day of death than the day of one's birth.

2 It is better to go to the house of mourning, than to go to the house of feasting: for that is the end of all men; and the living will lay it to his heart.

3 Sorrow is better than laughter: for by the sadness of the countenance the heart is made better.

4 The heart of the wise is in the house of mourning; but the heart of fools is in the house of mirth.

5 It is better to hear the rebuke of the wise, than for a man to hear the song of fools.

6 For as the crackling of thorns under a pot, so is the laughter of the fool: this also is vanity.

7 Surely oppression maketh a wise man mad; and a gift destroyeth the heart.

8 Better is the end of a thing than the beginning thereof: and the patient in spirit is better than the proud in spirit.

9 Be not hasty in your spirit to be angry: for anger resteth in the bosom of fools.

10 Say not you , What is the cause that the former days were better than these? for you dost not inquire wisely concerning this.

11 Wisdom is good with an inheritance: and by it is profit to them that see the sun.

12 For wisdom is a defence, and money is a defence: but the excellency of knowledge is, that wisdom giveth life to them that have it.

13 Consider the work of God: for who can make that straight, which he has made crooked?

14 In the day of prosperity be joyful, but in the day of adversity consider: God also has set the one over against the other, to the end that man should find nothing after him.

15 All things have I seen in the days of my vanity: there is a just man that perisheth in his righteousness, and there is a wicked man that prolongeth his life in his wickedness.

16 Be not righteous over much; neither make yourself over wise: why shouldest you destroy yourself?

17 Be not over much wicked, neither be you foolish: why shouldest you die before your time?

18 It is good that you shouldest take hold of this; yea, also from this withdraw not yours hand: for he that feareth God shall come forth of them all.

19 Wisdom strengtheneth the wise more than ten mighty men which are in the city.

20 For there is not a just man upon earth, that doeth good, and sinneth not.

21 Also take no heed unto all words that are spoken; lest you hear your servant curse you:

22 For oftentimes also yours own heart knoweth that you yourself likewise have cursed others.

23 All this have I proved by wisdom: I said, I will be wise; but it was far from me.

24 That which is far off, and exceeding deep, who can find it out?

25 I applied my heart to know, and to search, and to seek out wisdom, and the reason of things, and to know the wickedness of folly, even of foolishness and madness:

26 And I find more bitter than death the woman, whose heart is snares and nets, and her hands as bands: whoso pleases God shall escape from her; but the sinner shall be taken by her.

27 Behold, this have I found, saith the preacher, counting one by one, to find out the account:

28 Which yet my soul seeketh, but I find not: one man among a thousand have I found; but a woman among all those have I not found.

29 Lo, this only have I found, that God has made man upright; but they have sought out many inventions.

CHAPTER 8

WHO is as the wise man? and who knoweth the interpretation of a thing? a man's wisdom maketh his face to shine, and the boldness of his face shall be changed.

2 I counsel you to keep the king's commandment, and that in regard of the oath of God.

3 Be not hasty to go out of his sight: stand not in an evil thing; for he doeth whatsoever pleases him.

4 Where the word of a king is, there is power: and who may say unto him, What doest you ?

5 Whoso keepeth the commandment shall feel no evil thing: and a wise man's heart discerneth both time and judgment.

6 Because to every purpose there is time and judgment, therefore the misery of man is great upon him.

7 For he knoweth not that which shall be: for who can tell him when it shall be?

8 There is no man that has power over the spirit to retain the spirit; neither has he power in the day of death: and there is no discharge in that war; neither shall wickedness deliver those that are given to it.

9 All this have I seen, and applied my heart unto every work that is done under the sun: there is a time wherein one man ruleth over another to his own hurt.

10 And so I saw the wicked buried, who had come and gone from the place of the holy, and they were forgotten in the city where they had so done: this is also vanity.

11 Because sentence against an evil work is not executed speedily, therefore the heart of the sons of men is fully set in them to do evil.

12 Though a sinner do evil an hundred times, and his days be prolonged, yet surely I know that it shall be well with them that fear God, which fear before him:

13 But it shall not be well with the wicked, neither shall he prolong his days, which are as a shadow; because he feareth not before God.

14 There is a vanity which is done upon the earth; that there be just men, unto whom it happeneth according to the work of the wicked; again, there be wicked men, to whom it happeneth according to the work of the righteous: I said that this also is vanity.

15 Then I commended mirth, because a man has no better thing under the sun, than to eat, and to drink, and to be merry: for that shall abide with him of his labour the days of his life, which God giveth him under the sun.

16 When I applied my heart to know wisdom, and to see the business that is done upon the earth: (for also there is that neither day nor night seeth sleep with his eyes:)

17 Then I beheld all the work of God, that a man cannot find out the work that is done under the sun: because though a man labour to seek it out, yet he shall not find it; yea further; though a wise man think to know it, yet shall he not be able to find it.

CHAPTER 9

FOR all this I considered in my heart even to declare all this, that the righteous, and the wise, and their works, are in the hand of God: no man knoweth either love or hatred by all that is before them.

2 All things come alike to all: there is one event to the righteous, and to the wicked; to the good and to the clean, and to the unclean; to him that sacrificeth, and to him that sacrificeth not: as is the good, so is the sinner; and he that sweareth, as he that feareth an oath.

3 This is an evil among all things that are done under the sun, that there is one event unto all: yea, also the heart of the sons of men is full of evil, and madness is in their heart while they live, and after that they go to the dead.

4 For to him that is joined to all the living there is hope: for a living dog is better than a dead lion.

5 For the living know that they shall die: but the dead know not any thing, neither have they any more a reward; for the memory of them is forgotten.

6 Also their love, and their hatred, and their envy, is now perished; neither have they any more a portion for ever in any thing that is done under the sun.

7 Go your way, eat your bread with joy, and drink your wine with a merry heart; for God now accepteth your works.

8 Let your garments be always white; and let your head lack no ointment.

9 Live joyfully with the wife whom you lovest all the days of the life of your vanity, which he has given you under the sun, all the days of your vanity: for that is your portion in this life, and in your labour which you takest under the sun.

10 Whatsoever your hand findeth to do, do it with your might; for there is no work, nor device, nor knowledge, nor wisdom, in the grave, whither you go.

11 I returned, and saw under the sun, that the race is not to the swift, nor the battle to the strong, neither yet bread to the wise, nor yet riches to men of understanding, nor yet favour to men of skill; but time and chance happeneth to them all.

12 For man also knoweth not his time: as the fishes that are taken in an evil net, and as the birds that are caught in the snare; so are the sons of men snared in an evil time, when it falleth suddenly upon them.

13 This wisdom have I seen also under the sun, and it seemed great unto me:

14 There was a little city, and few men within it; and there came a great king against it, and besieged it, and built great bulwarks against it:

15 Now there was found in it a poor wise man, and he by his wisdom delivered the city; yet no man remembered that same poor man.

16 Then said I, Wisdom is better than strength: nevertheless the poor man's wisdom is despised, and his words are not heard.

17 The words of wise men are heard in quiet more than the cry of him that ruleth among fools.

18 Wisdom is better than weapons of war: but one sinner destroyeth much good.

CHAPTER 10

DEAD flies cause the ointment of the apothecary to send forth a stinking savour: so doth a little folly him that is in reputation for wisdom and honour.

2 A wise man's heart is at his right hand; but a fool's heart at his left.

3 Yea also, when he that is a fool walketh by the way, his wisdom faileth him, and he saith to every one that he is a fool.

4 If the spirit of the ruler rise up against you, leave not your place; for yielding pacifieth great offences.

5 There is an evil which I have seen under the sun, as an error which proceedeth from the ruler:

6 Folly is set in great dignity, and the rich sit in low place.

7 I have seen servants upon horses, and princes walking as servants upon the earth.

8 He that diggeth a pit shall fall into it; and whoso breaketh an hedge, a serpent shall bite him.

9 Whoso removeth stones shall be hurt therewith; and he that cleaveth wood shall be endangered thereby.

10 If the iron be blunt, and he do not whet the edge, then must he put to more strength: but wisdom is profitable to direct.

11 Surely the serpent will bite without enchantment; and a babbler is no better.

12 The words of a wise man's mouth are gracious; but the lips of a fool will swallow up himself.

13 The beginning of the words of his mouth is foolishness: and the end of his talk is mischievous madness.

14 A fool also is full of words: a man cannot tell what shall be; and what shall be after him, who can tell him?

15 The labour of the foolish wearieth every one of them, because he knoweth not how to go to the city.

16 Woe to you, O land, when your king is a child, and your princes eat in the morning!

17 Blessed are you , O land, when your king is the son of nobles, and your princes eat in due season, for strength, and not for drunkenness!

18 By much slothfulness the building decayeth; and through idleness of the hands the house droppeth through.

19 A feast is made for laughter, and wine maketh merry: but money answereth all things.

20 Curse not the king, no not in your thought; and curse not the rich in your bedchamber: for a bird of the air shall carry the voice, and that which has wings shall tell the matter.

CHAPTER 11

CAST your bread upon the waters: for you shalt find it after many days.

2 Give a portion to seven, and also to eight; for you knowest not what evil shall be upon the earth.

3 If the clouds be full of rain, they empty themselves upon the earth: and if the tree fall toward the south, or toward the north, in the place where the tree falleth, there it shall be.

4 He that observeth the wind shall not sow; and he that regardeth the clouds shall not reap.

5 As you knowest not what is the way of the spirit, nor how the bones do grow in the womb of her that is with child: even so you knowest not the works of God who maketh all.

6 In the morning sow your seed, and in the evening withhold not yours hand: for you knowest not whether shall prosper, either this or that, or whether they both shall be alike good.

7Truly the light is sweet, and a pleasant thing it is for the eyes to behold the sun:

8 But if a man live many years, and rejoice in them all; yet let him remember the days of darkness; for they shall be many. All that comes is vanity.

9Rejoice, O young man, in your youth; and let your heart cheer you in the days of your youth, and walk in the ways of yours heart, and in the sight of yours eyes: but know you , that for all these things God will bring you into judgment.

10 Therefore remove sorrow from your heart, and put away evil from your flesh: for childhood and youth are vanity.

CHAPTER 12

REMEMBER now your Creator in the days of your youth, while the evil days come not, nor the years draw nigh, when you shalt say, I have no pleasure in them;

2 While the sun, or the light, or the moon, or the stars, be not darkened, nor the clouds return after the rain:

3 In the day when the keepers of the house shall tremble, and the strong men shall bow themselves, and the grinders cease because they are few, and those that look out of the windows be darkened,

4 And the doors shall be shut in the streets, when the sound of the grinding is low, and he shall rise up at the voice of the bird, and all the daughters of musick shall be brought low;

5 Also when they shall be afraid of that which is high, and fears shall be in the way, and the almond tree shall flourish, and the grasshopper shall be a burden, and desire shall fail: because man goeth to his long home, and the mourners go about the streets:

6 Or ever the silver cord be loosed, or the golden bowl be broken, or the pitcher be broken at the fountain, or the wheel broken at the cistern.

7 Then shall the dust return to the earth as it was: and the spirit shall return unto God who gave it.

8Vanity of vanities, saith the preacher; all is vanity.

9 And moreover, because the preacher was wise, he still taught the people knowledge; yea, he gave good heed, and sought out, and set in order many proverbs.

10 The preacher sought to find out acceptable words: and that which was written was upright, even words of truth.

11 The words of the wise are as goads, and as nails fastened by the masters of assemblies, which are given from one shepherd.

12 And further, by these, my son, be admonished: of making many books there is no end; and much study is a weariness of the flesh.

13Let us hear the conclusion of the whole matter: Fear God, and keep his commandments: for this is the whole duty of man.

14 For God shall bring every work into judgment, with every secret thing, whether it be good, or whether it be evil.

THE
SONG OF SOLOMON.

CHAPTER 1

THE song of songs, which is Solomon's.

2 Let him kiss me with the kisses of his mouth: for your love is better than wine.

3 Because of the savour of your good ointments your name is as ointment poured forth, therefore do the virgins love you.

4 Draw me, we will run after you: the king has brought me into his chambers: we will be glad and rejoice in you, we will remember your love more than wine: the upright love you.

5 I am black, but comely, O you daughters of Jerusalem, as the tents of Kedar, as the curtains of Solomon.

6 Look not upon me, because I am black, because the sun has looked upon me: my mother's children were angry with me; they made me the keeper of the vineyards; but my own vineyard have I not kept.

7 Tell me, O you whom my soul loveth, where you feedest, where you makest your flock to rest at noon: for why should I be as one that turneth aside by the flocks of your companions?

8 If you know not, O you fairest among women, go your way forth by the footsteps of the flock, and feed your kids beside the shepherds' tents.

9 I have compared you, O my love, to a company of horses in Pharaoh's chariots.

10 Your cheeks are comely with rows of jewels, your neck with chains of gold.

11 We will make you borders of gold with studs of silver.

12 While the king sitteth at his table, my spikenard sendeth forth the smell thereof.

13 A bundle of myrrh is my wellbeloved unto me; he shall lie all night betwixt my breasts.

14 My beloved is unto me as a cluster of camphire in the vineyards of En-gedi.

15 Behold, you are fair, my love; behold, you are fair; you have doves' eyes.

16 Behold, you are fair, my beloved, yea, pleasant: also our bed is green.

17 The beams of our house are cedar, and our rafters of fir.

CHAPTER 2

I AM the rose of Sharon, and the lily of the valleys.

2 As the lily among thorns, so is my love among the daughters.

3 As the apple tree among the trees of the wood, so is my beloved among the sons. I sat down under his shadow with great delight, and his fruit was sweet to my taste.

4 He brought me to the banqueting house, and his banner over me was love.

5 Stay me with flagons, comfort me with apples: for I am sick of love.

6 His left hand is under my head, and his right hand doth embrace me.

7 I charge you, O you daughters of Jerusalem, by the roes, and by the hinds of the field, that you stir not up, nor awake my love, till he please.

8 The voice of my beloved! behold, he comes leaping upon the mountains, skipping upon the hills.

9 My beloved is like a roe or a young hart: behold, he standeth behind our wall, he looketh forth at the windows, shewing himself through the lattice.

10 My beloved spake, and said unto me, Rise up, my love, my fair one, and come away.

11 For, lo, the winter is past, the rain is over and gone;

12 The flowers appear on the earth; the time of the singing of birds is come, and the voice of the turtle is heard in our land;

13 The fig tree putteth forth her green figs, and the vines with the tender grape give a good smell. Arise, my love, my fair one, and come away.

14 O my dove, that are in the clefts of the rock, in the secret places of the stairs, let me see your countenance, let me hear your voice; for sweet is your voice, and your countenance is comely.

15 Take us the foxes, the little foxes, that spoil the vines: for our vines have tender grapes.

16 My beloved is my, and I am his: he feedeth among the lilies.

17 Until the day break, and the shadows flee away, turn, my beloved, and be you like a roe or a young hart upon the mountains of Bether.

CHAPTER 3

BY night on my bed I sought him whom my soul loveth: I sought him, but I found him not.

2 I will rise now, and go about the city in the streets, and in the broad ways I will seek him whom my soul loveth: I sought him, but I found him not.

3 The watchmen that go about the city found me: to whom I said, Saw you him whom my soul loveth?

4 It was but a little that I passed from them, but I found him whom my soul loveth: I held him, and would not let him go, until I had brought him into my mother's house, and into the chamber of her that conceived me.

5 I charge you, O you daughters of Jerusalem, by the roes, and by the hinds of the field, that you stir not up, nor awake my love, till he please.

6 Who is this that comes out of the wilderness like pillars of smoke, perfumed with myrrh and frankincense, with all powders of the merchant?

7 Behold his bed, which is Solomon's; threescore valiant men are about it, of the valiant of Israel.

8 They all hold swords, being expert in war: every man has his sword upon his thigh because of fear in the night.

9 King Solomon made himself a chariot of the wood of Lebanon.

10 He made the pillars thereof of silver, the bottom thereof of gold, the covering of it of purple, the midst thereof being paved with love, for the daughters of Jerusalem.

11 Go forth, O you daughters of Zion, and behold king Solomon with the crown wherewith his mother crowned him in the day of his espousals, and in the day of the gladness of his heart.

CHAPTER 4

BEHOLD, you are fair, my love; behold, you are fair; you have doves' eyes within your locks: your hair is as a flock of goats, that appear from mount Gilead.

2 Your teeth are like a flock of sheep that are even shorn, which came up from the washing; whereof every one bear twins, and none is barren among them.

3 Your lips are like a thread of scarlet, and your speech is comely: your temples are like a piece of a pomegranate within your locks.

4 Your neck is like the tower of David builded for an armoury, whereon there hang a thousand bucklers, all shields of mighty men.

5 Your two breasts are like two young roes that are twins, which feed among the lilies.

6 Until the day break, and the shadows flee away, I will get me to the mountain of myrrh, and to the hill of frankincense.

7 You are all fair, my love; there is no spot in you.

8 Come with me from Lebanon, my spouse, with me from Lebanon: look from the top of Amana, from the top of Shenir and Hermon, from the lions' dens, from the mountains of the leopards.

9 You have ravished my heart, my sister, my spouse; you have ravished my heart with one of yours eyes, with one chain of your neck.

10 How fair is your love, my sister, my spouse! how much better is your love than wine! and the smell of yours ointments than all spices!

11 Your lips, O my spouse, drop as the honeycomb: honey and milk are under your tongue; and the smell of your garments is like the smell of Lebanon.

12 A garden inclosed is my sister, my spouse; a spring shut up, a fountain sealed.

13 Your plants are an orchard of pomegranates, with pleasant fruits; camphire, with spikenard,

14 Spikenard and saffron; calamus and cinnamon, with all trees of frankincense; myrrh and aloes, with all the chief spices:

15 A fountain of gardens, a well of living waters, and streams from Lebanon.

16 Awake, O north wind; and come, you south; blow upon my garden, that the spices thereof may flow out. Let my beloved come into his garden, and eat his pleasant fruits.

CHAPTER 5

I AM come into my garden, my sister, my spouse: I have gathered my myrrh with my spice; I have eaten my honeycomb with my honey; I have drunk my wine with my milk: eat, O friends; drink, yea, drink abundantly, O beloved.

2 I sleep, but my heart waketh: it is the voice of my beloved that knocketh, saying, Open to me, my sister, my love, my dove, my undefiled: for my head is filled with dew, and my locks with the drops of the night.

3 I have put off my coat; how shall I put it on? I have washed my feet; how shall I defile them?

4 My beloved put in his hand by the hole of the door, and my bowels were moved for him.

5 I rose up to open to my beloved; and my hands dropped with myrrh, and my fingers with sweet smelling myrrh, upon the handles of the lock.

6 I opened to my beloved; but my beloved had withdrawn himself, and was gone: my soul failed when he spake: I sought him, but I could not find him; I called him, but he gave me no answer.

7 The watchmen that went about the city found me, they struck me, they wounded me; the keepers of the walls took away my veil from me.

8 I charge you, O daughters of Jerusalem, if you find my beloved, that you tell him, that I am sick of love.

9 What is your beloved more than another beloved, O you fairest among women? what is your beloved more than another beloved, that you dost so charge us?

10 My beloved is white and ruddy, the chiefest among ten thousand.

11 His head is as the most fine gold, his locks are bushy, and black as a raven.

12 His eyes are as the eyes of doves by the rivers of waters, washed with milk, and fitly set.

13 His cheeks are as a bed of spices, as sweet flowers: his lips like lilies, dropping sweet smelling myrrh.

14 His hands are as gold rings set with the beryl: his belly is as bright ivory overlaid with sapphires.

15 His legs are as pillars of marble, set upon sockets of fine gold: his countenance is as Lebanon, excellent as the cedars.

16 His mouth is most sweet: yea, he is altogether lovely. This is my beloved, and this is my friend, O daughters of Jerusalem.

CHAPTER 6

WHITHER is your beloved gone, O you fairest among women? whither is your beloved turned aside? that we may seek him with you.

2 My beloved is gone down into his garden, to the beds of spices, to feed in the gardens, and to gather lilies.

3 I am my beloved's, and my beloved is my: he feedeth among the lilies.

4 You are beautiful, O my love, as Tirzah, comely as Jerusalem, terrible as an army with banners.

5 Turn away yours eyes from me, for they have overcome me: your hair is as a flock of goats that appear from Gilead.

6 Your teeth are as a flock of sheep which go up from the washing, whereof every one beareth twins, and there is not one barren among them.

7 As a piece of a pomegranate are your temples within your locks.

8 There are threescore queens, and fourscore concubines, and virgins without number.

9 My dove, my undefiled is but one; she is the only one of her mother, she is the choice one of her that bare her. The daughters saw her, and blessed her; yea, the queens and the concubines, and they praised her.

10 Who is she that looketh forth as the morning, fair as the moon, clear as the sun, and terrible as an army with banners?

11 I went down into the garden of nuts to see the fruits of the valley, and to see whether the vine flourished, and the pomegranates budded.

12 Or ever I was aware, my soul made me like the chariots of Amminadib.

13 Return, return, O Shulamite; return, return, that we may look upon you. What will you see in the Shulamite? As it were the company of two armies.

CHAPTER 7

HOW beautiful are your feet with shoes, O prince's daughter! the joints of your thighs are like jewels, the work of the hands of a cunning workman.

2 Your navel is like a round goblet, which wanteth not liquor: your belly is like an heap of wheat set about with lilies.

3 Your two breasts are like two young roes that are twins.

4 Your neck is as a tower of ivory; yours eyes like the fishpools in Heshbon, by the gate of Bath-rabbim: your nose is as the tower of Lebanon which looketh toward Damascus.

5 Yours head upon you is like Carmel, and the hair of yours head like purple; the king is held in the galleries.

6 How fair and how pleasant are you, O love, for delights!

7 This your stature is like to a palm tree, and your breasts to clusters of grapes.

8 I said, I will go up to the palm tree, I will take hold of the boughs thereof: now also your breasts shall be as clusters of the vine, and the smell of your nose like apples;

9 And the roof of your mouth like the best wine for my beloved, that goeth down sweetly, causing the lips of those that are asleep to speak.

10 I am my beloved's, and his desire is toward me.

11 Come, my beloved, let us go forth into the field; let us lodge in the villages.

12 Let us get up early to the vineyards; let us see if the vine flourish, whether the tender grape appear, and the pomegranates bud forth: there will I give you my loves.

13 The mandrakes give a smell, and at our gates are all manner of pleasant fruits, new and old, which I have laid up for you, O my beloved.

CHAPTER 8

O THAT you wert as my brother, that sucked the breasts of my mother! when I should find you without, I would kiss you; yea, I should not be despised.

2 I would lead you, and bring you into my mother's house, who would instruct me: I would cause you to drink of spiced wine of the juice of my pomegranate.

3 His left hand should be under my head, and his right hand should embrace me.

4 I charge you, O daughters of Jerusalem, that you stir not up, nor awake my love, until he please.

5 Who is this that comes up from the wilderness, leaning upon her beloved? I raised you up under the apple tree: there your mother brought you forth: there she brought you forth that bare you.

6 Set me as a seal upon yours heart, as a seal upon yours arm: for love is strong as death; jealousy is cruel as the grave: the coals thereof are coals of fire, which has a most vehement flame.

7 Many waters cannot quench love, neither can the floods drown it: if a man would give all the substance of his house for love, it would utterly be contemned.

8 We have a little sister, and she has no breasts: what shall we do for our sister in the day when she shall be spoken for?

9 If she be a wall, we will build upon her a palace of silver: and if she be a door, we will inclose her with boards of cedar.

10 I am a wall, and my breasts like towers: then was I in his eyes as one that found favour.

11 Solomon had a vineyard at Baal-hamon; he let out the vineyard unto keepers; every one for the fruit thereof was to bring a thousand pieces of silver.

12 My vineyard, which is my, is before me: you, O Solomon, must have a thousand, and those that keep the fruit thereof two hundred.

13 You that dwellest in the gardens, the companions hearken to your voice: cause me to hear it.

14 Make haste, my beloved, and be you like to a roe or to a young hart upon the mountains of spices.

THE BOOK OF THE PROPHET ISAIAH.

CHAPTER 1

THE vision of Isaiah the son of Amoz, which he saw concerning Judah and Jerusalem in the days of Uzziah, Jotham, Ahaz, and Hezekiah, kings of Judah.

2 Hear, O heavens, and give ear, O earth: for the LORD has spoken, I have nourished and brought up children, and they have rebelled against me.

3 The ox knoweth his owner, and the ass his master's crib: but Israel doth not know, my people doth not consider.

4 Ah sinful nation, a people laden with iniquity, a seed of evildoers, children that are corrupters: they have forsaken the LORD, they have provoked the Holy One of Israel unto anger, they are gone away backward.

5 Why should you be stricken any more? you will revolt more and more: the whole head is sick, and the whole heart faint.

6 From the sole of the foot even unto the head there is no soundness in it; but wounds, and bruises, and putrifying sores: they have not been closed, neither bound up, neither mollified with ointment.

7 Your country is desolate, your cities are burned with fire: your land, strangers devour it in your presence, and it is desolate, as overthrown by strangers.

8 And the daughter of Zion is left as a cottage in a vineyard, as a lodge in a garden of cucumbers, as a besieged city.

9 Except the LORD of hosts had left unto us a very small remnant, we should have been as Sodom, and we should have been like unto Gomorrah.

10 Hear the word of the LORD, you rulers of Sodom; give ear unto the law of our God, you people of Gomorrah.

11 To what purpose is the multitude of your sacrifices unto me? saith the LORD: I am full of the burnt offerings of rams, and the fat of fed beasts; and I delight not in the blood of bullocks, or of lambs, or of he goats.

12 When you come to appear before me, who has required this at your hand, to tread my courts?

13 Bring no more vain oblations; incense is an abomination unto me; the new moons and sabbaths, the calling of assemblies, I cannot away with; it is iniquity, even the solemn meeting.

14 Your new moons and your appointed feasts my soul hateth: they are a trouble unto me; I am weary to bear them.

15 And when you spread forth your hands, I will hide my eyes from you: yea, when you make many prayers, I will not hear: your hands are full of blood.

16 Wash you, make you clean; put away the evil of your doings from before my eyes; cease to do evil;

17 Learn to do well; seek judgment, relieve the oppressed, judge the fatherless, plead for the widow.

18 Come now, and let us reason together, saith the LORD: though your sins be as scarlet, they shall be as white as snow; though they be red like crimson, they shall be as wool.

19 If you be willing and obedient, you shall eat the good of the land:

20 But if you refuse and rebel, you shall be devoured with the sword: for the mouth of the LORD has spoken it.

21 How is the faithful city become an harlot! it was full of judgment; righteousness lodged in it; but now murderers.

22 Your silver is become dross, your wine mixed with water:

23 Your princes are rebellious, and companions of thieves: every one loveth gifts, and followeth after rewards: they judge not the fatherless, neither doth the cause of the widow come unto them.

24 Therefore saith the Lord, the LORD of hosts, the mighty One of Israel, Ah, I will ease me of my adversaries, and avenge me of my enemies:

25 And I will turn my hand upon you, and purely purge away your dross, and take away all your tin:

26 And I will restore your judges as at the first, and your counsellers as at the beginning: afterward you shalt be called, The city of righteousness, the faithful city.

27 Zion shall be redeemed with judgment, and her converts with righteousness.

28 And the destruction of the transgressors and of the sinners shall be together, and they that forsake the LORD shall be consumed.

29 For they shall be ashamed of the oaks which you have desired, and you shall be confounded for the gardens that you have chosen.

30 For you shall be as an oak whose leaf fadeth, and as a garden that has no water.

31 And the strong shall be as tow, and the maker of it as a spark, and they shall both burn together, and none shall quench them.

CHAPTER 2

THE word that Isaiah the son of Amoz saw concerning Judah and Jerusalem.

2 And it shall come to pass in the last days, that the mountain of the LORD's house shall be established in the top of the mountains, and shall be exalted above the hills; and all nations shall flow unto it.

3 And many people shall go and say, Come you , and let us go up to the mountain of the LORD, to the house of the God of Jacob; and he will teach us of his ways, and we will walk in his paths: for out of Zion shall go forth the law, and the word of the LORD from Jerusalem.

4 And he shall judge among the nations, and shall rebuke many people: and they shall beat their swords into plowshares, and their spears into pruninghooks: nation shall not lift up sword against nation, neither shall they learn war any more.

5 O house of Jacob, come you , and let us walk in the light of the LORD.

6 Therefore you have forsaken your people the house of Jacob, because they be replenished from the east, and are soothsayers like the Philistines, and they please themselves in the children of strangers.

7 Their land also is full of silver and gold, neither is there any end of their treasures; their land is also full of horses, neither is there any end of their chariots:

8 Their land also is full of idols; they worship the work of their own hands, that which their own fingers have made:

9 And the mean man boweth down, and the great man humbleth himself: therefore forgive them not.

10 Enter into the rock, and hide you in the dust, for fear of the LORD, and for the glory of his majesty.

11 The lofty looks of man shall be humbled, and the haughtiness of men shall be bowed down, and the LORD alone shall be exalted in that day.

12 For the day of the LORD of hosts shall be upon every one that is proud and lofty, and upon every one that is lifted up; and he shall be brought low:

13 And upon all the cedars of Lebanon, that are high and lifted up, and upon all the oaks of Bashan,

14 And upon all the high mountains, and upon all the hills that are lifted up,

15 And upon every high tower, and upon every fenced wall,

16 And upon all the ships of Tarshish, and upon all pleasant pictures.

17 And the loftiness of man shall be bowed down, and the haughtiness of men shall be made low: and the LORD alone shall be exalted in that day.

18 And the idols he shall utterly abolish.

19 And they shall go into the holes of the rocks, and into the caves of the earth, for fear of the LORD, and for the glory of his majesty, when he ariseth to shake terribly the earth.

20 In that day a man shall cast his idols of silver, and his idols of gold, which they made each one for himself to worship, to the moles and to the bats;

21 To go into the clefts of the rocks, and into the tops of the ragged rocks, for fear of the LORD, and for the glory of his majesty, when he ariseth to shake terribly the earth.

22 Cease you from man, whose breath is in his nostrils: for wherein is he to be accounted of?

CHAPTER 3

FOR, behold, the Lord, the LORD of hosts, doth take away from Jerusalem and from Judah the stay and the staff, the whole stay of bread, and the whole stay of water,

2 The mighty man, and the man of war, the judge, and the prophet, and the prudent, and the ancient,

3 The captain of fifty, and the honourable man, and the counseller, and the cunning artificer, and the eloquent orator.

4 And I will give children to be their princes, and babes shall rule over them.

5 And the people shall be oppressed, every one by another, and every one by his neighbour: the child shall behave himself proudly against the ancient, and the base against the honourable.

6 When a man shall take hold of his brother of the house of his father, saying, You have clothing, be you our ruler, and let this ruin be under your hand:

7 In that day shall he swear, saying, I will not be an healer; for in my house is neither bread nor clothing: make me not a ruler of the people.

8 For Jerusalem is ruined, and Judah is fallen: because their tongue and their doings are against the LORD, to provoke the eyes of his glory.

9 The shew of their countenance doth witness against them; and they declare their sin as Sodom, they hide it not. Woe unto their soul! for they have rewarded evil unto themselves.

10 Say you to the righteous, that it shall be well with him: for they shall eat the fruit of their doings.

11 Woe unto the wicked! it shall be ill with him: for the reward of his hands shall be given him.

12 As for my people, children are their oppressors, and women rule over them. O my people, they which lead you cause you to err, and destroy the way of your paths.

13 The LORD standeth up to plead, and standeth to judge the people.

14 The LORD will enter into judgment with the ancients of his people, and the princes thereof: for you have eaten up the vineyard; the spoil of the poor is in your houses.

15 What mean you that you beat my people to pieces, and grind the faces of the poor? saith the Lord GOD of hosts.

16Moreover the LORD saith, Because the daughters of Zion are haughty, and walk with stretched forth necks and wanton eyes, walking and mincing as they go, and making a tinkling with their feet:

17 Therefore the Lord will strike with a scab the crown of the head of the daughters of Zion, and the LORD will discover their secret parts.

18 In that day the Lord will take away the bravery of their tinkling ornaments about their feet, and their cauls, and their round tires like the moon,

19 The chains, and the bracelets, and the mufflers,

20 The bonnets, and the ornaments of the legs, and the headbands, and the tablets, and the earrings,

21 The rings, and nose jewels,

22 The changeable suits of apparel, and the mantles, and the wimples, and the crisping pins,

23 The glasses, and the fine linen, and the hoods, and the vails.

24 And it shall come to pass, that instead of sweet smell there shall be stink; and instead of a girdle a rent; and instead of well set hair baldness; and instead of a stomacher a girding of sackcloth; and burning instead of beauty.

25 Your men shall fall by the sword, and your mighty in the war.

26 And her gates shall lament and mourn; and she being desolate shall sit upon the ground.

CHAPTER 4

AND in that day seven women shall take hold of one man, saying, We will eat our own bread, and wear our own apparel: only let us be called by your name, to take away our reproach.

2 In that day shall the branch of the LORD be beautiful and glorious, and the fruit of the earth shall be excellent and comely for them that are escaped of Israel.

3 And it shall come to pass, that he that is left in Zion, and he that remaineth in Jerusalem, shall be called holy, even every one that is written among the living in Jerusalem:

4 When the Lord shall have washed away the filth of the daughters of Zion, and shall have purged the blood of Jerusalem from the midst thereof by the spirit of judgment, and by the spirit of burning.

5 And the LORD will create upon every dwelling place of mount Zion, and upon her assemblies, a cloud and smoke by day, and the shining of a flaming fire by night: for upon all the glory shall be a defence.

6 And there shall be a tabernacle for a shadow in the daytime from the heat, and for a place of refuge, and for a covert from storm and from rain.

CHAPTER 5

NOW will I sing to my wellbeloved a song of my beloved touching his vineyard. My wellbeloved has a vineyard in a very fruitful hill:

2 And he fenced it, and gathered out the stones thereof, and planted it with the choicest vine, and built a tower in the midst of it, and also made a winepress therein: and he looked that it should bring forth grapes, and it brought forth wild grapes.

3 And now, O inhabitants of Jerusalem, and men of Judah, judge, I pray you, betwixt me and my vineyard.

4 What could have been done more to my vineyard, that I have not done in it? wherefore, when I looked that it should bring forth grapes, brought it forth wild grapes?

5 And now go to; I will tell you what I will do to my vineyard: I will take away the hedge thereof, and it shall be eaten up; and break down the wall thereof, and it shall be trodden down:

6 And I will lay it waste: it shall not be pruned, nor digged; but there shall come up briers and thorns: I will also command the clouds that they rain no rain upon it.

7 For the vineyard of the LORD of hosts is the house of Israel, and the men of Judah his pleasant plant: and he looked for judgment, but behold oppression; for righteousness, but behold a cry.

8Woe unto them that join house to house, that lay field to field, till there be no place, that they may be placed alone in the midst of the earth!

9 In my ears said the LORD of hosts, Of a truth many houses shall be desolate, even great and fair, without inhabitant.

10 Yea, ten acres of vineyard shall yield one bath, and the seed of an homer shall yield an ephah.

11Woe unto them that rise up early in the morning, that they may follow strong drink; that continue until night, till wine inflame them!

12 And the harp, and the viol, the tabret, and pipe, and wine, are in their feasts: but they regard not the work of the LORD, neither consider the operation of his hands.

13Therefore my people are gone into captivity, because they have no knowledge: and their honourable men are famished, and their multitude dried up with thirst.

14 Therefore hell has enlarged herself, and opened her mouth without measure: and their glory, and their multitude, and their pomp, and he that rejoiceth, shall descend into it.

15 And the mean man shall be brought down, and the mighty man shall be humbled, and the eyes of the lofty shall be humbled:

16 But the LORD of hosts shall be exalted in judgment, and God that is holy shall be sanctified in righteousness.

17 Then shall the lambs feed after their manner, and the waste places of the fat ones shall strangers eat.

18 Woe unto them that draw iniquity with cords of vanity, and sin as it were with a cart rope:

19 That say, Let him make speed, and hasten his work, that we may see it: and let the counsel of the Holy One of Israel draw nigh and come, that we may know it!

20Woe unto them that call evil good, and good evil; that put darkness for light, and light for darkness; that put bitter for sweet, and sweet for bitter!

21 Woe unto them that are wise in their own eyes, and prudent in their own sight!

22 Woe unto them that are mighty to drink wine, and men of strength to mingle strong drink:

23 Which justify the wicked for reward, and take away the righteousness of the righteous from him!

24 Therefore as the fire devoureth the stubble, and the flame consumeth the chaff, so their root shall be as rottenness, and their blossom shall go up as dust: because they have cast away the law of the LORD of hosts, and despised the word of the Holy One of Israel.

25 Therefore is the anger of the LORD kindled against his people, and he has stretched forth his hand against them, and has smitten them: and the hills did tremble, and their carcases were torn in the midst of the streets. For all this his anger is not turned away, but his hand is stretched out still.

26And he will lift up an ensign to the nations from far, and will hiss unto them from the end of the earth: and, behold, they shall come with speed swiftly:

27 None shall be weary nor stumble among them; none shall slumber nor sleep; neither shall the girdle of their loins be loosed, nor the latchet of their shoes be broken:

28 Whose arrows are sharp, and all their bows bent, their horses' hoofs shall be counted like flint, and their wheels like a whirlwind:

29 Their roaring shall be like a lion, they shall roar like young lions: yea, they shall roar, and lay hold of the prey, and shall carry it away safe, and none shall deliver it.

30 And in that day they shall roar against them like the roaring of the sea: and if one look unto the land, behold darkness and sorrow, and the light is darkened in the heavens thereof.

CHAPTER 6

IN the year that king Uzziah died I saw also the Lord sitting upon a throne, high and lifted up, and his train filled the temple.

2 Above it stood the seraphims: each one had six wings; with twain he covered his face, and with twain he covered his feet, and with twain he did fly.

3 And one cried unto another, and said, Holy, holy, holy, is the LORD of hosts: the whole earth is full of his glory.

4 And the posts of the door moved at the voice of him that cried, and the house was filled with smoke.

5Then said I, Woe is me! for I am undone; because I am a man of unclean lips, and I dwell in the midst of a people of unclean lips: for my eyes have seen the King, the LORD of hosts.

6 Then flew one of the seraphims unto me, having a live coal in his hand, which he had taken with the tongs from off the altar:

7 And he laid it upon my mouth, and said, Lo, this has touched your lips; and yours iniquity is taken away, and your sin purged.

8 Also I heard the voice of the Lord, saying, Whom shall I send, and who will go for us? Then said I, Here am I; send me.

9And he said, Go, and tell this people, Hear you indeed, but understand not; and see you indeed, but perceive not.

10 Make the heart of this people fat, and make their ears heavy, and shut their eyes; lest they see with their eyes, and hear with their ears, and understand with their heart, and convert, and be healed.

11 Then said I, Lord, how long? And he answered, Until the cities be wasted without inhabitant, and the houses without man, and the land be utterly desolate,

12 And the LORD have removed men far away, and there be a great forsaking in the midst of the land.

13But yet in it shall be a tenth, and it shall return, and shall be eaten: as a teil tree, and as an oak, whose substance is in them, when they cast their leaves: so the holy seed shall be the substance thereof.

CHAPTER 7

AND it came to pass in the days of Ahaz the son of Jotham, the son of Uzziah, king of Judah, that Rezin the king of Syria, and Pekah the son of Remaliah, king of Israel, went up toward Jerusalem to war against it, but could not prevail against it.

2 And it was told the house of David, saying, Syria is confederate with Ephraim. And his heart was moved, and the heart of his people, as the trees of the wood are moved with the wind.

3 Then said the LORD unto Isaiah, Go forth now to meet Ahaz, you , and Shear-jashub your son, at the end of the conduit of the upper pool in the highway of the fuller's field;

4 And say unto him, Take heed, and be quiet; fear not, neither be fainthearted for the two tails of these smoking firebrands, for the fierce anger of Rezin with Syria, and of the son of Remaliah.

5 Because Syria, Ephraim, and the son of Remaliah, have taken evil counsel against you, saying,

6 Let us go up against Judah, and vex it, and let us make a breach therein for us, and set a king in the midst of it, even the son of Tabeal:

7 Thus saith the Lord GOD, It shall not stand, neither shall it come to pass.

8 For the head of Syria is Damascus, and the head of Damascus is Rezin; and within threescore and five years shall Ephraim be broken, that it be not a people.

9 And the head of Ephraim is Samaria, and the head of Samaria is Remaliah's son. If you will not believe, surely you shall not be established.

10 Moreover the LORD spake again unto Ahaz, saying,

11 Ask you a sign of the LORD your God; ask it either in the depth, or in the height above.

12 But Ahaz said, I will not ask, neither will I tempt the LORD.

13 And he said, Hear you now, O house of David; Is it a small thing for you to weary men, but will you weary my God also?

14 Therefore the Lord himself shall give you a sign; Behold, a virgin shall conceive, and bear a son, and shall call his name Immanuel.

15 Butter and honey shall he eat, that he may know to refuse the evil, and choose the good.

16 For before the child shall know to refuse the evil, and choose the good, the land that you abhorrest shall be forsaken of both her kings.

17 The LORD shall bring upon you, and upon your people, and upon your father's house, days that have not come, from the day that Ephraim departed from Judah; even the king of Assyria.

18 And it shall come to pass in that day, that the LORD shall hiss for the fly that is in the uttermost part of the rivers of Egypt, and for the bee that is in the land of Assyria.

19 And they shall come, and shall rest all of them in the desolate valleys, and in the holes of the rocks, and upon all thorns, and upon all bushes.

20 In the same day shall the Lord shave with a rasor that is hired, namely, by them beyond the river, by the king of Assyria, the head, and the hair of the feet: and it shall also consume the beard.

21 And it shall come to pass in that day, that a man shall nourish a young cow, and two sheep;

22 And it shall come to pass, for the abundance of milk that they shall give he shall eat butter: for butter and honey shall every one eat that is left in the land.

23 And it shall come to pass in that day, that every place shall be, where there were a thousand vines at a thousand silverlings, it shall even be for briers and thorns.

24 With arrows and with bows shall men come thither; because all the land shall become briers and thorns.

25 And on all hills that shall be digged with the mattock, there shall not come thither the fear of briers and thorns: but it shall be for the sending forth of oxen, and for the treading of lesser cattle.

CHAPTER 8

MOREOVER the LORD said unto me, Take you a great roll, and write in it with a man's pen concerning Maher-shalal-hash-baz.

2 And I took unto me faithful witnesses to record, Uriah the priest, and Zechariah the son of Jeberechiah.

3 And I went unto the prophetess; and she conceived, and bare a son. Then said the LORD to me, Call his name Maher-shalal-hash-baz.

4 For before the child shall have knowledge to cry, My father, and my mother, the riches of Damascus and the spoil of Samaria shall be taken away before the king of Assyria.

5 The LORD spake also unto me again, saying,

6 Forasmuch as this people refuseth the waters of Shiloah that go softly, and rejoice in Rezin and Remaliah's son;

7 Now therefore, behold, the Lord bringeth up upon them the waters of the river, strong and many, even the king of Assyria, and all his glory: and he shall come up over all his channels, and go over all his banks:

8 And he shall pass through Judah; he shall overflow and go over, he shall reach even to the neck; and the stretching out of his wings shall fill the breadth of your land, O Immanuel.

9 Associate yourselves, O you people, and you shall be broken in pieces; and give ear, all you of far countries: gird yourselves, and you shall be broken in pieces; gird yourselves, and you shall be broken in pieces.

10 Take counsel together, and it shall come to nought; speak the word, and it shall not stand: for God is with us.

11 For the LORD spake thus to me with a strong hand, and instructed me that I should not walk in the way of this people, saying,

12 Say you not, A confederacy, to all them to whom this people shall say, A confederacy; neither fear you their fear, nor be afraid.

13 Sanctify the LORD of hosts himself; and let him be your fear, and let him be your dread.

14 And he shall be for a sanctuary; but for a stone of stumbling and for a rock of offence to both the houses of Israel, for a gin and for a snare to the inhabitants of Jerusalem.

15 And many among them shall stumble, and fall, and be broken, and be snared, and be taken.

16 Bind up the testimony, seal the law among my disciples.

17 And I will wait upon the LORD, that hideth his face from the house of Jacob, and I will look for him.

18 Behold, I and the children whom the LORD has given me are for signs and for wonders in Israel from the LORD of hosts, which dwelleth in mount Zion.

19 And when they shall say unto you, Seek unto them that have familiar spirits, and unto wizards that peep, and that mutter: should not a people seek unto their God? for the living to the dead?

20 To the law and to the testimony: if they speak not according to this word, it is because there is no light in them.

21 And they shall pass through it, hardly bestead and hungry: and it shall come to pass, that when they shall be hungry, they shall fret themselves, and curse their king and their God, and look upward.

22 And they shall look unto the earth; and behold trouble and darkness, dimness of anguish; and they shall be driven to darkness.

CHAPTER 9

NEVERTHELESS the dimness shall not be such as was in her vexation, when at the first he lightly afflicted the land of Zebulun and the land of Naphtali, and afterward did more grievously afflict her by the way of the sea, beyond Jordan, in Galilee of the nations.

2 The people that walked in darkness have seen a great light: they that dwell in the land of the shadow of death, upon them has the light shined.

3 You have multiplied the nation, and not increased the joy: they joy before you according to the joy in harvest, and as men rejoice when they divide the spoil.

4 For you have broken the yoke of his burden, and the staff of his shoulder, the rod of his oppressor, as in the day of Midian.

5 For every battle of the warrior is with confused noise, and garments rolled in blood; but this shall be with burning and fuel of fire.

6 For unto us a child is born, unto us a son is given: and the government shall be upon his shoulder: and his name shall be called Wonderful, Counseller, The mighty God, The everlasting Father, The Prince of Peace.

7 Of the increase of his government and peace there shall be no end, upon the throne of David, and upon his kingdom, to order it, and to establish it with judgment and with justice from henceforth even for ever. The zeal of the LORD of hosts will perform this.

8 The Lord sent a word into Jacob, and it has lighted upon Israel.

9 And all the people shall know, even Ephraim and the inhabitant of Samaria, that say in the pride and stoutness of heart,

10 The bricks are fallen down, but we will build with hewn stones: the sycomores are cut down, but we will change them into cedars.

11 Therefore the LORD shall set up the adversaries of Rezin against him, and join his enemies together;

12 The Syrians before, and the Philistines behind; and they shall devour Israel with open mouth. For all this his anger is not turned away, but his hand is stretched out still.

13 For the people turneth not unto him that smiteth them, neither do they seek the LORD of hosts.

14 Therefore the LORD will cut off from Israel head and tail, branch and rush, in one day.

15 The ancient and honourable, he is the head; and the prophet that teacheth lies, he is the tail.

16 For the leaders of this people cause them to err; and they that are led of them are destroyed.

17 Therefore the Lord shall have no joy in their young men, neither shall have mercy on their fatherless and widows: for every one is an hypocrite and an evildoer, and every mouth speaketh folly. For all this his anger is not turned away, but his hand is stretched out still.

18 For wickedness burneth as the fire: it shall devour the briers and thorns, and shall kindle in the thickets of the forest, and they shall mount up like the lifting up of smoke.

19 Through the wrath of the LORD of hosts is the land darkened, and the people shall be as the fuel of the fire: no man shall spare his brother.

20 And he shall snatch on the right hand, and be hungry; and he shall eat on the left hand, and they shall not be satisfied: they shall eat every man the flesh of his own arm:

21 Manasseh, Ephraim; and Ephraim, Manasseh: and they together shall be against Judah. For all this his anger is not turned away, but his hand is stretched out still.

CHAPTER 10

WOE unto them that decree unrighteous decrees, and that write grievousness which they have prescribed;

2 To turn aside the needy from judgment, and to take away the right from the poor of my people, that widows may be their prey, and that they may rob the fatherless!

3 And what will you do in the day of visitation, and in the desolation which shall come from far? to whom will you flee for help? and where will you leave your glory?

4 Without me they shall bow down under the prisoners, and they shall fall under the slain. For all this his anger is not turned away, but his hand is stretched out still.

5 O Assyrian, the rod of my anger, and the staff in their hand is my indignation.

6 I will send him against an hypocritical nation, and against the people of my wrath will I give him a charge, to take the spoil, and to take the prey, and to tread them down like the mire of the streets.

7 Howbeit he meaneth not so, neither doth his heart think so; but it is in his heart to destroy and cut off nations not a few.

8 For he saith, Are not my princes altogether kings?

9 Is not Calno as Carchemish? is not Hamath as Arpad? is not Samaria as Damascus?

10 As my hand has found the kingdoms of the idols, and whose graven images did excel them of Jerusalem and of Samaria;

11 Shall I not, as I have done unto Samaria and her idols, so do to Jerusalem and her idols?

12 Wherefore it shall come to pass, that when the Lord has performed his whole work upon mount Zion and on Jerusalem, I will punish the fruit of the stout heart of the king of Assyria, and the glory of his high looks.

13 For he saith, By the strength of my hand I have done it, and by my wisdom; for I am prudent: and I have removed the bounds of the people, and have robbed their treasures, and I have put down the inhabitants like a valiant man:

14 And my hand has found as a nest the riches of the people: and as one gathereth eggs that are left, have I gathered all the earth; and there was none that moved the wing, or opened the mouth, or peeped.

15 Shall the axe boast itself against him that heweth therewith? or shall the saw magnify itself against him that shaketh it? as if the rod should shake itself against them that lift it up, or as if the staff should lift up itself, as if it were no wood.

16 Therefore shall the Lord, the Lord of hosts, send among his fat ones leanness; and under his glory he shall kindle a burning like the burning of a fire.

17 And the light of Israel shall be for a fire, and his Holy One for a flame: and it shall burn and devour his thorns and his briers in one day;

18 And shall consume the glory of his forest, and of his fruitful field, both soul and body: and they shall be as when a standardbearer fainteth.

19 And the rest of the trees of his forest shall be few, that a child may write them.

20 And it shall come to pass in that day, that the remnant of Israel, and such as are escaped of the house of Jacob, shall no more again stay upon him that struck them; but shall stay upon the LORD, the Holy One of Israel, in truth.

21 The remnant shall return, even the remnant of Jacob, unto the mighty God.

22 For though your people Israel be as the sand of the sea, yet a remnant of them shall return: the consumption decreed shall overflow with righteousness.

23 For the Lord GOD of hosts shall make a consumption, even determined, in the midst of all the land.

24 Therefore thus saith the Lord GOD of hosts, O my people that dwellest in Zion, be not afraid of the Assyrian: he shall strike you with a rod, and shall lift up his staff against you, after the manner of Egypt.

25 For yet a very little while, and the indignation shall cease, and my anger in their destruction.

26 And the LORD of hosts shall stir up a scourge for him according to the slaughter of Midian at the rock of Oreb: and as his rod was upon the sea, so shall he lift it up after the manner of Egypt.

27 And it shall come to pass in that day, that his burden shall be taken away from off your shoulder, and his yoke from off your neck, and the yoke shall be destroyed because of the anointing.

28 He is come to Aiath, he is passed to Migron; at Michmash he has laid up his carriages:

29 They are gone over the passage: they have taken up their lodging at Geba; Ramah is afraid; Gibeah of Saul is fled.

30 Lift up your voice, O daughter of Gallim: cause it to be heard unto Laish, O poor Anathoth.

31 Madmenah is removed; the inhabitants of Gebim gather themselves to flee.

32 As yet shall he remain at Nob that day: he shall shake his hand against the mount of the daughter of Zion, the hill of Jerusalem.

33 Behold, the Lord, the LORD of hosts, shall lop the bough with terror: and the high ones of stature shall be hewn down, and the haughty shall be humbled.

34 And he shall cut down the thickets of the forest with iron, and Lebanon shall fall by a mighty one.

CHAPTER 11

AND there shall come forth a rod out of the stem of Jesse, and a Branch shall grow out of his roots:

2 And the spirit of the LORD shall rest upon him, the spirit of wisdom and understanding, the spirit of counsel and might, the spirit of knowledge and of the fear of the LORD;

3 And shall make him of quick understanding in the fear of the LORD: and he shall not judge after the sight of his eyes, neither reprove after the hearing of his ears:

4 But with righteousness shall he judge the poor, and reprove with equity for the meek of the earth: and he shall strike the earth with the rod of his mouth, and with the breath of his lips shall he slay the wicked.

5 And righteousness shall be the girdle of his loins, and faithfulness the girdle of his reins.

6 The wolf also shall dwell with the lamb, and the leopard shall lie down with the kid; and the calf and the young lion and the fatling together; and a little child shall lead them.

7 And the cow and the bear shall feed; their young ones shall lie down together: and the lion shall eat straw like the ox.

8 And the sucking child shall play on the hole of the asp, and the weaned child shall put his hand on the cockatrice' den.

9 They shall not hurt nor destroy in all my holy mountain: for the earth shall be full of the knowledge of the LORD, as the waters cover the sea.

10 And in that day there shall be a root of Jesse, which shall stand for an ensign of the people; to it shall the Gentiles seek: and his rest shall be glorious.

11 And it shall come to pass in that day, that the Lord shall set his hand again the second time to recover the remnant of his people, which shall be left, from Assyria, and from Egypt, and from Pathros, and from Cush, and from Elam, and from Shinar, and from Hamath, and from the islands of the sea.

12 And he shall set up an ensign for the nations, and shall assemble the outcasts of Israel, and gather together the dispersed of Judah from the four corners of the earth.

13 The envy also of Ephraim shall depart, and the adversaries of Judah shall be cut off: Ephraim shall not envy Judah, and Judah shall not vex Ephraim.

14 But they shall fly upon the shoulders of the Philistines toward the west; they shall spoil them of the east together: they shall lay their hand upon Edom and Moab; and the children of Ammon shall obey them.

15 And the LORD shall utterly destroy the tongue of the Egyptian sea; and with his mighty wind shall he shake his hand over the river, and shall strike it in the seven streams, and make men go over dryshod.

16 And there shall be an highway for the remnant of his people, which shall be left, from Assyria; like as it was to Israel in the day that he came up out of the land of Egypt.

CHAPTER 12

AND in that day you shalt say, O LORD, I will praise you: though you wast angry with me, yours anger is turned away, and you comfortedst me.

2 Behold, God is my salvation; I will trust, and not be afraid: for the LORD JEHOVAH is my strength and my song; he also is become my salvation.

3 Therefore with joy shall you draw water out of the wells of salvation.

4 And in that day shall you say, Praise the LORD, call upon his name, declare his doings among the people, make mention that his name is exalted.

5 Sing unto the LORD; for he has done excellent things: this is known in all the earth.

6 Cry out and shout, you inhabitant of Zion: for great is the Holy One of Israel in the midst of you.

CHAPTER 13

THE burden of Babylon, which Isaiah the son of Amoz did see.

2 Lift you up a banner upon the high mountain, exalt the voice unto them, shake the hand, that they may go into the gates of the nobles.

3 I have commanded my sanctified ones, I have also called my mighty ones for my anger, even them that rejoice in my highness.

4 The noise of a multitude in the mountains, like as of a great people; a tumultuous noise of the kingdoms of nations gathered together: the LORD of hosts mustereth the host of the battle.

5 They come from a far country, from the end of heaven, even the LORD, and the weapons of his indignation, to destroy the whole land.

6Howl you ; for the day of the LORD is at hand; it shall come as a destruction from the Almighty.

7 Therefore shall all hands be faint, and every man's heart shall melt:

8 And they shall be afraid: pangs and sorrows shall take hold of them; they shall be in pain as a woman that travaileth: they shall be amazed one at another; their faces shall be as flames.

9 Behold, the day of the LORD comes, cruel both with wrath and fierce anger, to lay the land desolate: and he shall destroy the sinners thereof out of it.

10 For the stars of heaven and the constellations thereof shall not give their light: the sun shall be darkened in his going forth, and the moon shall not cause her light to shine.

11 And I will punish the world for their evil, and the wicked for their iniquity; and I will cause the arrogancy of the proud to cease, and will lay low the haughtiness of the terrible.

12 I will make a man more precious than fine gold; even a man than the golden wedge of Ophir.

13 Therefore I will shake the heavens, and the earth shall remove out of her place, in the wrath of the LORD of hosts, and in the day of his fierce anger.

14 And it shall be as the chased roe, and as a sheep that no man taketh up: they shall every man turn to his own people, and flee every one into his own land.

15 Every one that is found shall be thrust through; and every one that is joined unto them shall fall by the sword.

16 Their children also shall be dashed to pieces before their eyes; their houses shall be spoiled, and their wives ravished.

17 Behold, I will stir up the Medes against them, which shall not regard silver; and as for gold, they shall not delight in it.

18 Their bows also shall dash the young men to pieces; and they shall have no pity on the fruit of the womb; their eye shall not spare children.

19And Babylon, the glory of kingdoms, the beauty of the Chaldees' excellency, shall be as when God overthrew Sodom and Gomorrah.

20 It shall never be inhabited, neither shall it be dwelt in from generation to generation: neither shall the Arabian pitch tent there; neither shall the shepherds make their fold there.

21 But wild beasts of the desert shall lie there; and their houses shall be full of doleful creatures; and owls shall dwell there, and satyrs shall dance there.

22 And the wild beasts of the islands shall cry in their desolate houses, and dragons in their pleasant palaces: and her time is near to come, and her days shall not be prolonged.

CHAPTER 14

FOR the LORD will have mercy on Jacob, and will yet choose Israel, and set them in their own land: and the strangers shall be joined with them, and they shall cleave to the house of Jacob.

2 And the people shall take them, and bring them to their place: and the house of Israel shall possess them in the land of the LORD for servants and handmaids: and they shall take them captives, whose captives they were; and they shall rule over their oppressors.

3 And it shall come to pass in the day that the LORD shall give you rest from your sorrow, and from your fear, and from the hard bondage wherein you wast made to serve,

4That you shalt take up this proverb against the king of Babylon, and say, How has the oppressor ceased! the golden city ceased!

5 The LORD has broken the staff of the wicked, and the sceptre of the rulers.

6 He who struck the people in wrath with a continual stroke, he that ruled the nations in anger, is persecuted, and none hindereth.

7 The whole earth is at rest, and is quiet: they break forth into singing.

8 Yea, the fir trees rejoice at you, and the cedars of Lebanon, saying, Since you are laid down, no feller is come up against us.

9 Hell from beneath is moved for you to meet you at your coming: it stirreth up the dead for you, even all the chief ones of the earth; it has raised up from their thrones all the kings of the nations.

10 All they shall speak and say unto you, Are you also become weak as we? are you become like unto us?

11 Your pomp is brought down to the grave, and the noise of your viols: the worm is spread under you, and the worms cover you.

12 How are you fallen from heaven, O Lucifer, son of the morning! how are you cut down to the ground, which did weaken the nations!

13 For you have said in yours heart, I will ascend into heaven, I will exalt my throne above the stars of God: I will sit also upon the mount of the congregation, in the sides of the north:

14 I will ascend above the heights of the clouds; I will be like the most High.

15 Yet you shalt be brought down to hell, to the sides of the pit.

16 They that see you shall narrowly look upon you, and consider you, saying, Is this the man that made the earth to tremble, that did shake kingdoms;

17 That made the world as a wilderness, and destroyed the cities thereof; that opened not the house of his prisoners?

18 All the kings of the nations, even all of them, lie in glory, every one in his own house.

19 But you are cast out of your grave like an abominable branch, and as the raiment of those that are slain, thrust through with a sword, that go down to the stones of the pit; as a carcase trodden under feet.

20 You shalt not be joined with them in burial, because you have destroyed your land, and slain your people: the seed of evildoers shall never be renowned.

21 Prepare slaughter for his children for the iniquity of their fathers; that they do not rise, nor possess the land, nor fill the face of the world with cities.

22 For I will rise up against them, saith the LORD of hosts, and cut off from Babylon the name, and remnant, and son, and nephew, saith the LORD.

23 I will also make it a possession for the bittern, and pools of water: and I will sweep it with the besom of destruction, saith the LORD of hosts.

24The LORD of hosts has sworn, saying, Surely as I have thought, so shall it come to pass; and as I have purposed, so shall it stand:

25 That I will break the Assyrian in my land, and upon my mountains tread him under foot: then shall his yoke depart from off them, and his burden depart from off their shoulders.

26 This is the purpose that is purposed upon the whole earth: and this is the hand that is stretched out upon all the nations.

27 For the LORD of hosts has purposed, and who shall disannul it? and his hand is stretched out, and who shall turn it back?

28 In the year that king Ahaz died was this burden.

29Rejoice not you , whole Palestina, because the rod of him that struck you is broken: for out of the serpent's root shall come forth a cockatrice, and his fruit shall be a fiery flying serpent.

30 And the firstborn of the poor shall feed, and the needy shall lie down in safety: and I will kill your root with famine, and he shall slay your remnant.

31 Howl, O gate; cry, O city; you , whole Palestina, are dissolved: for there shall come from the north a smoke, and none shall be alone in his appointed times.

32 What shall one then answer the messengers of the nation? That the LORD has founded Zion, and the poor of his people shall trust in it.

CHAPTER 15

THE burden of Moab. Because in the night Ar of Moab is laid waste, and brought to silence; because in the night Kir of Moab is laid waste, and brought to silence;

2 He is gone up to Bajith, and to Dibon, the high places, to weep: Moab shall howl over Nebo, and over Medeba: on all their heads shall be baldness, and every beard cut off.

3 In their streets they shall gird themselves with sackcloth: on the tops of their houses, and in their streets, every one shall howl, weeping abundantly.

4 And Heshbon shall cry, and Elealeh: their voice shall be heard even unto Jahaz: therefore the armed soldiers of Moab shall cry out; his life shall be grievous unto him.

5 My heart shall cry out for Moab; his fugitives shall flee unto Zoar, an heifer of three years old: for by the mounting up of Luhith with weeping shall they go it up; for in the way of Horonaim they shall raise up a cry of destruction.

6 For the waters of Nimrim shall be desolate: for the hay is withered away, the grass faileth, there is no green thing.

7 Therefore the abundance they have gotten, and that which they have laid up, shall they carry away to the brook of the willows.

8 For the cry is gone round about the borders of Moab; the howling thereof unto Eglaim, and the howling thereof unto Beer-elim.

9 For the waters of Dimon shall be full of blood: for I will bring more upon Dimon, lions upon him that escapeth of Moab, and upon the remnant of the land.

CHAPTER 16

SEND you the lamb to the ruler of the land from Sela to the wilderness, unto the mount of the daughter of Zion.

2 For it shall be, that, as a wandering bird cast out of the nest, so the daughters of Moab shall be at the fords of Arnon.

3 Take counsel, execute judgment; make your shadow as the night in the midst of the noonday; hide the outcasts; bewray not him that wandereth.

4 Let my outcasts dwell with you, Moab; be you a covert to them from the face of the spoiler: for the extortioner is at an end, the spoiler ceaseth, the oppressors are consumed out of the land.

5 And in mercy shall the throne be established: and he shall sit upon it in truth in the tabernacle of David, judging, and seeking judgment, and hasting righteousness.

6 We have heard of the pride of Moab; he is very proud: even of his haughtiness, and his pride, and his wrath: but his lies shall not be so.

7 Therefore shall Moab howl for Moab, every one shall howl: for the foundations of Kir-hareseth shall you mourn; surely they are stricken.

8 For the fields of Heshbon languish, and the vine of Sibmah: the lords of the heathen have broken down the principal plants thereof, they are come even unto Jazer, they wandered through the wilderness: her branches are stretched out, they are gone over the sea.

9 Therefore I will bewail with the weeping of Jazer the vine of Sibmah: I will water you with my tears, O Heshbon, and Elealeh: for the shouting for your summer fruits and for your harvest is fallen.

10 And gladness is taken away, and joy out of the plentiful field; and in the vineyards there shall be no singing, neither shall there be shouting: the treaders shall tread out no wine in their presses; I have made their vintage shouting to cease.

11 Wherefore my bowels shall sound like an harp for Moab, and my inward parts for Kir-haresh.

12 And it shall come to pass, when it is seen that Moab is weary on the high place, that he shall come to his sanctuary to pray; but he shall not prevail.

13 This is the word that the LORD has spoken concerning Moab since that time.

14 But now the LORD has spoken, saying, Within three years, as the years of an hireling, and the glory of Moab shall be contemned, with all that great multitude; and the remnant shall be very small and feeble.

CHAPTER 17

THE burden of Damascus. Behold, Damascus is taken away from being a city, and it shall be a ruinous heap.

2 The cities of Aroer are forsaken: they shall be for flocks, which shall lie down, and none shall make them afraid.

3 The fortress also shall cease from Ephraim, and the kingdom from Damascus, and the remnant of Syria: they shall be as the glory of the children of Israel, saith the LORD of hosts.

4 And in that day it shall come to pass, that the glory of Jacob shall be made thin, and the fatness of his flesh shall wax lean.

5 And it shall be as when the harvestman gathereth the corn, and reapeth the ears with his arm; and it shall be as he that gathereth ears in the valley of Rephaim.

6 Yet gleaning grapes shall be left in it, as the shaking of an olive tree, two or three berries in the top of the uppermost bough, four or five in the outmost fruitful branches thereof, saith the LORD God of Israel.

7 At that day shall a man look to his Maker, and his eyes shall have respect to the Holy One of Israel.

8 And he shall not look to the altars, the work of his hands, neither shall respect that which his fingers have made, either the groves, or the images.

9 In that day shall his strong cities be as a forsaken bough, and an uppermost branch, which they left because of the children of Israel: and there shall be desolation.

10 Because you have forgotten the God of your salvation, and have not been mindful of the rock of your strength, therefore shalt you plant pleasant plants, and shalt set it with strange slips:

11 In the day shalt you make your plant to grow, and in the morning shalt you make your seed to flourish: but the harvest shall be a heap in the day of grief and of desperate sorrow.

12 Woe to the multitude of many people, which make a noise like the noise of the seas; and to the rushing of nations, that make a rushing like the rushing of mighty waters!

13 The nations shall rush like the rushing of many waters: but God shall rebuke them, and they shall flee far off, and shall be chased as the chaff of the mountains before the wind, and like a rolling thing before the whirlwind.

14 And behold at eveningtide trouble; and before the morning he is not. This is the portion of them that spoil us, and the lot of them that rob us.

CHAPTER 18

WOE to the land shadowing with wings, which is beyond the rivers of Ethiopia:

2 That sendeth ambassadors by the sea, even in vessels of bulrushes upon the waters, saying, Go, you swift messengers, to a nation scattered and peeled, to a people terrible from their beginning hitherto; a nation meted out and trodden down, whose land the rivers have spoiled!

3 All you inhabitants of the world, and dwellers on the earth, see you , when he lifteth up an ensign on the mountains; and when he bloweth a trumpet, hear you .

4 For so the LORD said unto me, I will take my rest, and I will consider in my dwelling place like a clear heat upon herbs, and like a cloud of dew in the heat of harvest.

5 For afore the harvest, when the bud is perfect, and the sour grape is ripening in the flower, he shall both cut off the sprigs with pruning hooks, and take away and cut down the branches.

6 They shall be left together unto the fowls of the mountains, and to the beasts of the earth: and the fowls shall summer upon them, and all the beasts of the earth shall winter upon them.

7 In that time shall the present be brought unto the LORD of hosts of a people scattered and peeled, and from a people terrible from their beginning hitherto; a nation meted out and trodden under foot, whose land the rivers have spoiled, to the place of the name of the LORD of hosts, the mount Zion.

CHAPTER 19

THE burden of Egypt. Behold, the LORD rideth upon a swift cloud, and shall come into Egypt: and the idols of Egypt shall be moved at his presence, and the heart of Egypt shall melt in the midst of it.

2 And I will set the Egyptians against the Egyptians: and they shall fight every one against his brother, and every one against his neighbour; city against city, and kingdom against kingdom.

3 And the spirit of Egypt shall fail in the midst thereof; and I will destroy the counsel thereof: and they shall seek to the idols, and to the charmers, and to them that have familiar spirits, and to the wizards.

4 And the Egyptians will I give over into the hand of a cruel lord; and a fierce king shall rule over them, saith the Lord, the LORD of hosts.

5 And the waters shall fail from the sea, and the river shall be wasted and dried up.

6 And they shall turn the rivers far away; and the brooks of defence shall be emptied and dried up: the reeds and flags shall wither.

7 The paper reeds by the brooks, by the mouth of the brooks, and every thing sown by the brooks, shall wither, be driven away, and be no more.

8 The fishers also shall mourn, and all they that cast angle into the brooks shall lament, and they that spread nets upon the waters shall languish.

9 Moreover they that work in fine flax, and they that weave networks, shall be confounded.

10 And they shall be broken in the purposes thereof, all that make sluices and ponds for fish.

11 Surely the princes of Zoan are fools, the counsel of the wise counsellers of Pharaoh is become brutish: how say you unto Pharaoh, I am the son of the wise, the son of ancient kings?

12 Where are they? where are your wise men? and let them tell you now, and let them know what the LORD of hosts has purposed upon Egypt.

13 The princes of Zoan are become fools, the princes of Noph are deceived; they have also seduced Egypt, even they that are the stay of the tribes thereof.

14 The LORD has mingled a perverse spirit in the midst thereof: and they have caused Egypt to err in every work thereof, as a drunken man staggereth in his vomit.

15 Neither shall there be any work for Egypt, which the head or tail, branch or rush, may do.

16 In that day shall Egypt be like unto women: and it shall be afraid and fear because of the shaking of the hand of the LORD of hosts, which he shaketh over it.

17 And the land of Judah shall be a terror unto Egypt, every one that maketh mention thereof shall be afraid in himself, because of the counsel of the LORD of hosts, which he has determined against it.

18 In that day shall five cities in the land of Egypt speak the language of Canaan, and swear to the LORD of hosts; one shall be called, The city of destruction.

19 In that day shall there be an altar to the LORD in the midst of the land of Egypt, and a pillar at the border thereof to the LORD.

20 And it shall be for a sign and for a witness unto the LORD of hosts in the land of Egypt: for they shall cry unto the LORD because of the oppressors, and he shall send them a saviour, and a great one, and he shall deliver them.

21 And the LORD shall be known to Egypt, and the Egyptians shall know the LORD in that day, and shall do sacrifice and oblation; yea, they shall vow a vow unto the LORD, and perform it.

22 And the LORD shall strike Egypt: he shall strike and heal it: and they shall return even to the LORD, and he shall be intreated of them, and shall heal them.

23 In that day shall there be a highway out of Egypt to Assyria, and the Assyrian shall come into Egypt, and the Egyptian into Assyria, and the Egyptians shall serve with the Assyrians.

24 In that day shall Israel be the third with Egypt and with Assyria, even a blessing in the midst of the land:

25 Whom the LORD of hosts shall bless, saying, Blessed be Egypt my people, and Assyria the work of my hands, and Israel my inheritance.

CHAPTER 20

IN the year that Tartan came unto Ashdod, (when Sargon the king of Assyria sent him,) and fought against Ashdod, and took it;

2 At the same time spake the LORD by Isaiah the son of Amoz, saying, Go and loose the sackcloth from off your loins, and put off your shoe from your foot. And he did so, walking naked and barefoot.

3 And the LORD said, Like as my servant Isaiah has walked naked and barefoot three years for a sign and wonder upon Egypt and upon Ethiopia;

4 So shall the king of Assyria lead away the Egyptians prisoners, and the Ethiopians captives, young and old, naked and barefoot, even with their buttocks uncovered, to the shame of Egypt.

5 And they shall be afraid and ashamed of Ethiopia their expectation, and of Egypt their glory.

6 And the inhabitant of this isle shall say in that day, Behold, such is our expectation, whither we flee for help to be delivered from the king of Assyria: and how shall we escape?

CHAPTER 21

THE burden of the desert of the sea. As whirlwinds in the south pass through; so it comes from the desert, from a terrible land.

2 A grievous vision is declared unto me; the treacherous dealer dealeth treacherously, and the spoiler spoileth. Go up, O Elam: besiege, O Media; all the sighing thereof have I made to cease.

3 Therefore are my loins filled with pain: pangs have taken hold upon me, as the pangs of a woman that travaileth: I was bowed down at the hearing of it; I was dismayed at the seeing of it.

4 My heart panted, fearfulness affrighted me: the night of my pleasure has he turned into fear unto me.

5 Prepare the table, watch in the watchtower, eat, drink: arise, you princes, and anoint the shield.

6 For thus has the Lord said unto me, Go, set a watchman, let him declare what he seeth.

7 And he saw a chariot with a couple of horsemen, a chariot of asses, and a chariot of camels; and he hearkened diligently with much heed:

8 And he cried, A lion: My lord, I stand continually upon the watchtower in the daytime, and I am set in my ward whole nights:

9 And, behold, here comes a chariot of men, with a couple of horsemen. And he answered and said, Babylon is fallen, is fallen; and all the graven images of her gods he has broken unto the ground.

10 O my threshing, and the corn of my floor: that which I have heard of the LORD of hosts, the God of Israel, have I declared unto you.

11 The burden of Dumah. He calleth to me out of Seir, Watchman, what of the night? Watchman, what of the night?

12 The watchman said, The morning comes, and also the night: if you will inquire, inquire you : return, come.

13 The burden upon Arabia. In the forest in Arabia shall you lodge, O you travelling companies of Dedanim.

14 The inhabitants of the land of Tema brought water to him that was thirsty, they prevented with their bread him that fled.

15 For they fled from the swords, from the drawn sword, and from the bent bow, and from the grievousness of war.

16 For thus has the Lord said unto me, Within a year, according to the years of an hireling, and all the glory of Kedar shall fail:

17 And the residue of the number of archers, the mighty men of the children of Kedar, shall be diminished: for the LORD God of Israel has spoken it.

CHAPTER 22

THE burden of the valley of vision. What aileth you now, that you are wholly gone up to the housetops?

2 You that are full of stirs, a tumultuous city, a joyous city: your slain men are not slain with the sword, nor dead in battle.

3 All your rulers are fled together, they are bound by the archers: all that are found in you are bound together, which have fled from far.

4 Therefore said I, Look away from me; I will weep bitterly, labour not to comfort me, because of the spoiling of the daughter of my people.

5 For it is a day of trouble, and of treading down, and of perplexity by the Lord GOD of hosts in the valley of vision, breaking down the walls, and of crying to the mountains.

6 And Elam bare the quiver with chariots of men and horsemen, and Kir uncovered the shield.

7 And it shall come to pass, that your choicest valleys shall be full of chariots, and the horsemen shall set themselves in array at the gate.

8 And he discovered the covering of Judah, and you did look in that day to the armour of the house of the forest.

9 You have seen also the breaches of the city of David, that they are many: and you gathered together the waters of the lower pool.

10 And you have numbered the houses of Jerusalem, and the houses have you broken down to fortify the wall.

11 You made also a ditch between the two walls for the water of the old pool: but you have not looked unto the maker thereof, neither had respect unto him that fashioned it long ago.

12 And in that day did the Lord GOD of hosts call to weeping, and to mourning, and to baldness, and to girding with sackcloth:

13 And behold joy and gladness, slaying oxen, and killing sheep, eating flesh, and drinking wine: let us eat and drink; for to morrow we shall die.

14 And it was revealed in my ears by the LORD of hosts, Surely this iniquity shall not be purged from you till you die, saith the Lord GOD of hosts.

15 Thus saith the Lord GOD of hosts, Go, get you unto this treasurer, even unto Shebna, which is over the house, and say,

16 What have you here? and whom have you here, that you have hewed you out a sepulchre here, as he that heweth him out a sepulchre on high, and that graveth an habitation for himself in a rock?

17 Behold, the LORD will carry you away with a mighty captivity, and will surely cover you.

18 He will surely violently turn and toss you like a ball into a large country: there shalt you die, and there the chariots of your glory shall be the shame of your lord's house.

19 And I will drive you from your station, and from your state shall he pull you down.

20 And it shall come to pass in that day, that I will call my servant Eliakim the son of Hilkiah:

21 And I will clothe him with your robe, and strengthen him with your girdle, and I will commit your government into his hand: and he shall be a father to the inhabitants of Jerusalem, and to the house of Judah.

22 And the key of the house of David will I lay upon his shoulder; so he shall open, and none shall shut; and he shall shut, and none shall open.

23 And I will fasten him as a nail in a sure place; and he shall be for a glorious throne to his father's house.

24 And they shall hang upon him all the glory of his father's house, the offspring and the issue, all vessels of small quantity, from the vessels of cups, even to all the vessels of flagons.

25 In that day, saith the LORD of hosts, shall the nail that is fastened in the sure place be removed, and be cut down, and fall; and the burden that was upon it shall be cut off: for the LORD has spoken it.

CHAPTER 23

THE burden of Tyre. Howl, you ships of Tarshish; for it is laid waste, so that there is no house, no entering in: from the land of Chittim it is revealed to them.

2 Be still, you inhabitants of the isle; you whom the merchants of Zidon, that pass over the sea, have replenished.

3 And by great waters the seed of Sihor, the harvest of the river, is her revenue; and she is a mart of nations.

4 Be you ashamed, O Zidon: for the sea has spoken, even the strength of the sea, saying, I travail not, nor bring forth children, neither do I nourish up young men, nor bring up virgins.

5 As at the report concerning Egypt, so shall they be sorely pained at the report of Tyre.

6 Pass you over to Tarshish; howl, you inhabitants of the isle.

7 Is this your joyous city, whose antiquity is of ancient days? her own feet shall carry her afar off to sojourn.

8 Who has taken this counsel against Tyre, the crowning city, whose merchants are princes, whose traffickers are the honourable of the earth?

9 The LORD of hosts has purposed it, to stain the pride of all glory, and to bring into contempt all the honourable of the earth.

10 Pass through your land as a river, O daughter of Tarshish: there is no more strength.

11 He stretched out his hand over the sea, he shook the kingdoms: the LORD has given a commandment against the merchant city, to destroy the strong holds thereof.

12 And he said, You shalt no more rejoice, O you oppressed virgin, daughter of Zidon: arise, pass over to Chittim; there also shalt you have no rest.

13 Behold the land of the Chaldeans; this people was not, till the Assyrian founded it for them that dwell in the wilderness: they set up the towers thereof, they raised up the palaces thereof; and he brought it to ruin.

14 Howl, you ships of Tarshish: for your strength is laid waste.

15 And it shall come to pass in that day, that Tyre shall be forgotten seventy years, according to the days of one king: after the end of seventy years shall Tyre sing as an harlot.

16 Take an harp, go about the city, you harlot that have been forgotten; make sweet melody, sing many songs, that you mayest be remembered.

17 And it shall come to pass after the end of seventy years, that the LORD will visit Tyre, and she shall turn to her hire, and shall commit fornication with all the kingdoms of the world upon the face of the earth.

18 And her merchandise and her hire shall be holiness to the LORD: it shall not be treasured nor laid up; for her merchandise shall be for them that dwell before the LORD, to eat sufficiently, and for durable clothing.

CHAPTER 24

BEHOLD, the LORD maketh the earth empty, and maketh it waste, and turneth it upside down, and scattereth abroad the inhabitants thereof.

2 And it shall be, as with the people, so with the priest; as with the servant, so with his master; as with the maid, so with her mistress; as with the buyer, so with the seller; as with the lender, so with the borrower; as with the taker of usury, so with the giver of usury to him.

3 The land shall be utterly emptied, and utterly spoiled: for the LORD has spoken this word.

4 The earth mourneth and fadeth away, the world languisheth and fadeth away, the haughty people of the earth do languish.

5 The earth also is defiled under the inhabitants thereof; because they have transgressed the laws, changed the ordinance, broken the everlasting covenant.

6 Therefore has the curse devoured the earth, and they that dwell therein are desolate: therefore the inhabitants of the earth are burned, and few men left.

7 The new wine mourneth, the vine languisheth, all the merryhearted do sigh.

8 The mirth of tabrets ceaseth, the noise of them that rejoice endeth, the joy of the harp ceaseth.

9 They shall not drink wine with a song; strong drink shall be bitter to them that drink it.

10 The city of confusion is broken down: every house is shut up, that no man may come in.

11 There is a crying for wine in the streets; all joy is darkened, the mirth of the land is gone.

12 In the city is left desolation, and the gate is smitten with destruction.

13 When thus it shall be in the midst of the land among the people, there shall be as the shaking of an olive tree, and as the gleaning grapes when the vintage is done.

14 They shall lift up their voice, they shall sing for the majesty of the LORD, they shall cry aloud from the sea.

15 Wherefore glorify you the LORD in the fires, even the name of the LORD God of Israel in the isles of the sea.

16 From the uttermost part of the earth have we heard songs, even glory to the righteous. But I said, My leanness, my leanness, woe unto me! the treacherous dealers have dealt treacherously; yea, the treacherous dealers have dealt very treacherously.

17 Fear, and the pit, and the snare, are upon you, O inhabitant of the earth.

18 And it shall come to pass, that he who fleeth from the noise of the fear shall fall into the pit; and he that comes up out of the midst of the pit shall be taken in the snare: for the windows from on high are open, and the foundations of the earth do shake.

19 The earth is utterly broken down, the earth is clean dissolved, the earth is moved exceedingly.

20 The earth shall reel to and fro like a drunkard, and shall be removed like a cottage; and the transgression thereof shall be heavy upon it; and it shall fall, and not rise again.

21 And it shall come to pass in that day, that the LORD shall punish the host of the high ones that are on high, and the kings of the earth upon the earth.

22 And they shall be gathered together, as prisoners are gathered in the pit, and shall be shut up in the prison, and after many days shall they be visited.

23 Then the moon shall be confounded, and the sun ashamed, when the LORD of hosts shall reign in mount Zion, and in Jerusalem, and before his ancients gloriously.

CHAPTER 25

O LORD, you are my God; I will exalt you, I will praise your name; for you have done wonderful things; your counsels of old are faithfulness and truth.

2 For you have made of a city an heap; of a defenced city a ruin: a palace of strangers to be no city; it shall never be built.

3 Therefore shall the strong people glorify you, the city of the terrible nations shall fear you.

4 For you have been a strength to the poor, a strength to the needy in his distress, a refuge from the storm, a shadow from the heat, when the blast of the terrible ones is as a storm against the wall.

5 You shalt bring down the noise of strangers, as the heat in a dry place; even the heat with the shadow of a cloud: the branch of the terrible ones shall be brought low.

6 And in this mountain shall the LORD of hosts make unto all people a feast of fat things, a feast of wines on the lees, of fat things full of marrow, of wines on the lees well refined.

7 And he will destroy in this mountain the face of the covering cast over all people, and the vail that is spread over all nations.

8 He will swallow up death in victory; and the Lord GOD will wipe away tears from off all faces; and the rebuke of his people shall he take away from off all the earth: for the LORD has spoken it.

9 And it shall be said in that day, Lo, this is our God; we have waited for him, and he will save us: this is the LORD; we have waited for him, we will be glad and rejoice in his salvation.

10 For in this mountain shall the hand of the LORD rest, and Moab shall be trodden down under him, even as straw is trodden down for the dunghill.

11 And he shall spread forth his hands in the midst of them, as he that swimmeth spreadeth forth his hands to swim: and he shall bring down their pride together with the spoils of their hands.

12 And the fortress of the high fort of your walls shall he bring down, lay low, and bring to the ground, even to the dust.

CHAPTER 26

IN that day shall this song be sung in the land of Judah; We have a strong city; salvation will God appoint for walls and bulwarks.

2 Open you the gates, that the righteous nation which keepeth the truth may enter in.

3 You will keep him in perfect peace, whose mind is stayed on you: because he trusteth in you.

4 Trust you in the LORD for ever: for in the LORD JEHOVAH is everlasting strength:

5 For he bringeth down them that dwell on high; the lofty city, he layeth it low; he layeth it low, even to the ground; he bringeth it even to the dust.

6 The foot shall tread it down, even the feet of the poor, and the steps of the needy.

7 The way of the just is uprightness: you, most upright, dost weigh the path of the just.

8 Yea, in the way of your judgments, O LORD, have we waited for you; the desire of our soul is to your name, and to the remembrance of you.

9 With my soul have I desired you in the night; yea, with my spirit within me will I seek you early: for when your judgments are in the earth, the inhabitants of the world will learn righteousness.

10 Let favour be shewed to the wicked, yet will he not learn righteousness: in the land of uprightness will he deal unjustly, and will not behold the majesty of the LORD.

11 LORD, when your hand is lifted up, they will not see: but they shall see, and be ashamed for their envy at the people; yea, the fire of yours enemies shall devour them.

12 LORD, you will ordain peace for us: for you also have created all our works in us.

13 O LORD our God, other lords beside you have had dominion over us: but by you only will we make mention of your name.

14 They are dead, they shall not live; they are deceased, they shall not rise: therefore have you visited and destroyed them, and made all their memory to perish.

15 You have increased the nation, O LORD, you have increased the nation: you are glorified: you hadst removed it far unto all the ends of the earth.

16 LORD, in trouble have they visited you, they poured out a prayer when your chastening was upon them.

17 Like as a woman with child, that draweth near the time of her delivery, is in pain, and crieth out in her pangs; so have we been in your sight, O LORD.

18 We have been with child, we have been in pain, we have as it were brought forth wind; we have not created any deliverance in the earth; neither have the inhabitants of the world fallen.

19 Your dead men shall live, together with my dead body shall they arise. Awake and sing, you that dwell in dust: for your dew is as the dew of herbs, and the earth shall cast out the dead.

20 Come, my people, enter you into your chambers, and shut your doors about you: hide yourself as it were for a little moment, until the indignation be overpast.

21 For, behold, the LORD comes out of his place to punish the inhabitants of the earth for their iniquity: the earth also shall disclose her blood, and shall no more cover her slain.

CHAPTER 27

IN that day the LORD with his sore and great and strong sword shall punish leviathan the piercing serpent, even leviathan that crooked serpent; and he shall slay the dragon that is in the sea.

2 In that day sing you unto her, A vineyard of red wine.

3 I the LORD do keep it; I will water it every moment: lest any hurt it, I will keep it night and day.

4 Fury is not in me: who would set the briers and thorns against me in battle? I would go through them, I would burn them together.

5 Or let him take hold of my strength, that he may make peace with me; and he shall make peace with me.

6 He shall cause them that come of Jacob to take root: Israel shall blossom and bud, and fill the face of the world with fruit.

7 Hath he smitten him, as he struck those that struck him? or is he slain according to the slaughter of them that are slain by him?

8 In measure, when it shooteth forth, you will debate with it: he stayeth his rough wind in the day of the east wind.

9 By this therefore shall the iniquity of Jacob be purged; and this is all the fruit to take away his sin; when he maketh all the stones of the altar as chalkstones that are beaten in sunder, the groves and images shall not stand up.

10 Yet the defenced city shall be desolate, and the habitation forsaken, and left like a wilderness: there shall the calf feed, and there shall he lie down, and consume the branches thereof.

11 When the boughs thereof are withered, they shall be broken off: the women come, and set them on fire: for it is a people of no understanding: therefore he that made them will not have mercy on them, and he that formed them will shew them no favour.

12 And it shall come to pass in that day, that the LORD shall beat off from the channel of the river unto the stream of Egypt, and you shall be gathered one by one, O you children of Israel.

13 And it shall come to pass in that day, that the great trumpet shall be blown, and they shall come which were ready to perish in the land of Assyria, and the outcasts in the land of Egypt, and shall worship the LORD in the holy mount at Jerusalem.

CHAPTER 28

WOE to the crown of pride, to the drunkards of Ephraim, whose glorious beauty is a fading flower, which are on the head of the fat valleys of them that are overcome with wine!

2 Behold, the Lord has a mighty and strong one, which as a tempest of hail and a destroying storm, as a flood of mighty waters overflowing, shall cast down to the earth with the hand.

3 The crown of pride, the drunkards of Ephraim, shall be trodden under feet:

4 And the glorious beauty, which is on the head of the fat valley, shall be a fading flower, and as the hasty fruit before the summer; which when he that looketh upon it seeth, while it is yet in his hand he eateth it up.

5 In that day shall the LORD of hosts be for a crown of glory, and for a diadem of beauty, unto the residue of his people,

6 And for a spirit of judgment to him that sitteth in judgment, and for strength to them that turn the battle to the gate.

7 But they also have erred through wine, and through strong drink are out of the way; the priest and the prophet have erred through strong drink, they are swallowed up of wine, they are out of the way through strong drink; they err in vision, they stumble in judgment.

8 For all tables are full of vomit and filthiness, so that there is no place clean.

9 Whom shall he teach knowledge? and whom shall he make to understand doctrine? them that are weaned from the milk, and drawn from the breasts.

10 For precept must be upon precept, precept upon precept; line upon line, line upon line; here a little, and there a little:

11 For with stammering lips and another tongue will he speak to this people.

12 To whom he said, This is the rest wherewith you may cause the weary to rest; and this is the refreshing: yet they would not hear.

13 But the word of the LORD was unto them precept upon precept, precept upon precept; line upon line, line upon line; here a little, and there a little; that they might go, and fall backward, and be broken, and snared, and taken.

14 Wherefore hear the word of the LORD, you scornful men, that rule this people which is in Jerusalem.

15 Because you have said, We have made a covenant with death, and with hell are we at agreement; when the overflowing scourge shall pass through, it shall not come unto us: for we have made lies our refuge, and under falsehood have we hid ourselves:

16 Therefore thus saith the Lord GOD, Behold, I lay in Zion for a foundation a stone, a tried stone, a precious corner stone, a sure foundation: he that believeth shall not make haste.

17 Judgment also will I lay to the line, and righteousness to the plummet: and the hail shall sweep away the refuge of lies, and the waters shall overflow the hiding place.

18 And your covenant with death shall be disannulled, and your agreement with hell shall not stand; when the overflowing scourge shall pass through, then you shall be trodden down by it.

19 From the time that it goeth forth it shall take you: for morning by morning shall it pass over, by day and by night: and it shall be a vexation only to understand the report.

20 For the bed is shorter than that a man can stretch himself on it: and the covering narrower than that he can wrap himself in it.

21 For the LORD shall rise up as in mount Perazim, he shall be wroth as in the valley of Gibeon, that he may do his work, his strange work; and bring to pass his act, his strange act.

22 Now therefore be you not mockers, lest your bands be made strong: for I have heard from the Lord GOD of hosts a consumption, even determined upon the whole earth.

23 Give you ear, and hear my voice; hearken, and hear my speech.

24 Doth the plowman plow all day to sow? doth he open and break the clods of his ground?

25 When he has made plain the face thereof, doth he not cast abroad the fitches, and scatter the cummin, and cast in the principal wheat and the appointed barley and the rie in their place?

26 For his God doth instruct him to discretion, and doth teach him.

27 For the fitches are not threshed with a threshing instrument, neither is a cart wheel turned about upon the cummin; but the fitches are beaten out with a staff, and the cummin with a rod.

28 Bread corn is bruised; because he will not ever be threshing it, nor break it with the wheel of his cart, nor bruise it with his horsemen.

29 This also comes forth from the LORD of hosts, which is wonderful in counsel, and excellent in working.

CHAPTER 29

WOE to Ariel, to Ariel, the city where David dwelt! add you year to year; let them kill sacrifices.

2 Yet I will distress Ariel, and there shall be heaviness and sorrow: and it shall be unto me as Ariel.

3 And I will camp against you round about, and will lay siege against you with a mount, and I will raise forts against you.

4 And you shalt be brought down, and shalt speak out of the ground, and your speech shall be low out of the dust, and your voice shall be, as of one that has a familiar spirit, out of the ground, and your speech shall whisper out of the dust.

5 Moreover the multitude of your strangers shall be like small dust, and the multitude of the terrible ones shall be as chaff that passes away: yea, it shall be at an instant suddenly.

6 You shalt be visited of the LORD of hosts with thunder, and with earthquake, and great noise, with storm and tempest, and the flame of devouring fire.

7 And the multitude of all the nations that fight against Ariel, even all that fight against her and her munition, and that distress her, shall be as a dream of a night vision.

8 It shall even be as when an hungry man dreameth, and, behold, he eateth; but he awaketh, and his soul is empty: or as when a thirsty man dreameth, and, behold, he drinketh; but he awaketh, and, behold, he is faint, and his soul has appetite: so shall the multitude of all the nations be, that fight against mount Zion.

9 Stay yourselves, and wonder; cry you out, and cry: they are drunken, but not with wine; they stagger, but not with strong drink.

10 For the LORD has poured out upon you the spirit of deep sleep, and has closed your eyes: the prophets and your rulers, the seers has he covered.

11 And the vision of all is become unto you as the words of a book that is sealed, which men deliver to one that is learned, saying, Read this, I pray you: and he saith, I cannot; for it is sealed:

12 And the book is delivered to him that is not learned, saying, Read this, I pray you: and he saith, I am not learned.

13 Wherefore the Lord said, Forasmuch as this people draw near me with their mouth, and with their lips do honour me, but have removed their heart far from me, and their fear toward me is taught by the precept of men:

14 Therefore, behold, I will proceed to do a marvellous work among this people, even a marvellous work and a wonder: for the wisdom of their wise men shall perish, and the understanding of their prudent men shall be hid.

15 Woe unto them that seek deep to hide their counsel from the LORD, and their works are in the dark, and they say, Who seeth us? and who knoweth us?

16 Surely your turning of things upside down shall be esteemed as the potter's clay: for shall the work say of him that made it, He made me not? or shall the thing framed say of him that framed it, He had no understanding?

17 Is it not yet a very little while, and Lebanon shall be turned into a fruitful field, and the fruitful field shall be esteemed as a forest?

18And in that day shall the deaf hear the words of the book, and the eyes of the blind shall see out of obscurity, and out of darkness.

19 The meek also shall increase their joy in the LORD, and the poor among men shall rejoice in the Holy One of Israel.

20 For the terrible one is brought to nought, and the scorner is consumed, and all that watch for iniquity are cut off:

21 That make a man an offender for a word, and lay a snare for him that reproveth in the gate, and turn aside the just for a thing of nought.

22 Therefore thus saith the LORD, who redeemed Abraham, concerning the house of Jacob, Jacob shall not now be ashamed, neither shall his face now wax pale.

23 But when he seeth his children, the work of my hands, in the midst of him, they shall sanctify my name, and sanctify the Holy One of Jacob, and shall fear the God of Israel.

24 They also that erred in spirit shall come to understanding, and they that murmured shall learn doctrine.

CHAPTER 30

WOE to the rebellious children, saith the LORD, that take counsel, but not of me; and that cover with a covering, but not of my spirit, that they may add sin to sin:

2 That walk to go down into Egypt, and have not asked at my mouth; to strengthen themselves in the strength of Pharaoh, and to trust in the shadow of Egypt!

3 Therefore shall the strength of Pharaoh be your shame, and the trust in the shadow of Egypt your confusion.

4 For his princes were at Zoan, and his ambassadors came to Hanes.

5 They were all ashamed of a people that could not profit them, nor be an help nor profit, but a shame, and also a reproach.

6 The burden of the beasts of the south: into the land of trouble and anguish, from whence come the young and old lion, the viper and fiery flying serpent, they will carry their riches upon the shoulders of young asses, and their treasures upon the bunches of camels, to a people that shall not profit them.

7 For the Egyptians shall help in vain, and to no purpose: therefore have I cried concerning this, Their strength is to sit still.

8Now go, write it before them in a table, and note it in a book, that it may be for the time to come for ever and ever:

9 That this is a rebellious people, lying children, children that will not hear the law of the LORD:

10 Which say to the seers, See not; and to the prophets, Prophesy not unto us right things, speak unto us smooth things, prophesy deceits:

11 Get you out of the way, turn aside out of the path, cause the Holy One of Israel to cease from before us.

12 Wherefore thus saith the Holy One of Israel, Because you despise this word, and trust in oppression and perverseness, and stay thereon:

13 Therefore this iniquity shall be to you as a breach ready to fall, swelling out in a high wall, whose breaking comes suddenly at an instant.

14 And he shall break it as the breaking of the potters' vessel that is broken in pieces; he shall not spare: so that there shall not be found in the bursting of it a sherd to take fire from the hearth, or to take water withal out of the pit.

15 For thus saith the Lord GOD, the Holy One of Israel; In returning and rest shall you be saved; in quietness and in confidence shall be your strength: and you would not.

16 But you said, No; for we will flee upon horses; therefore shall you flee: and, We will ride upon the swift; therefore shall they that pursue you be swift.

17 One thousand shall flee at the rebuke of one; at the rebuke of five shall you flee: till you be left as a beacon upon the top of a mountain, and as an ensign on an hill.

18And therefore will the LORD wait, that he may be gracious unto you, and therefore will he be exalted, that he may have mercy upon you: for the LORD is a God of judgment: blessed are all they that wait for him.

19 For the people shall dwell in Zion at Jerusalem: you shalt weep no more: he will be very gracious unto you at the voice of your cry; when he shall hear it, he will answer you.

20 And though the Lord give you the bread of adversity, and the water of affliction, yet shall not your teachers be removed into a corner any more, but yours eyes shall see your teachers:

21 And yours ears shall hear a word behind you, saying, This is the way, walk you in it, when you turn to the right hand, and when you turn to the left.

22 You shall defile also the covering of your graven images of silver, and the ornament of your molten images of gold: you shalt cast them away as a menstruous cloth; you shalt say unto it, Get you hence.

23 Then shall he give the rain of your seed, that you shalt sow the ground withal; and bread of the increase of the earth, and it shall be fat and plenteous: in that day shall your cattle feed in large pastures.

24 The oxen likewise and the young asses that ear the ground shall eat clean provender, which has been winnowed with the shovel and with the fan.

25 And there shall be upon every high mountain, and upon every high hill, rivers and streams of waters in the day of the great slaughter, when the towers fall.

26 Moreover the light of the moon shall be as the light of the sun, and the light of the sun shall be sevenfold, as the light of seven days, in the day that the LORD bindeth up the breach of his people, and healeth the stroke of their wound.

27Behold, the name of the LORD comes from far, burning with his anger, and the burden thereof is heavy: his lips are full of indignation, and his tongue as a devouring fire:

28 And his breath, as an overflowing stream, shall reach to the midst of the neck, to sift the nations with the sieve of vanity: and there shall be a bridle in the jaws of the people, causing them to err.

29 You shall have a song, as in the night when a holy solemnity is kept; and gladness of heart, as when one goeth with a pipe to come into the mountain of the LORD, to the mighty One of Israel.

30 And the LORD shall cause his glorious voice to be heard, and shall shew the lighting down of his arm, with the indignation of his anger, and with the flame of a devouring fire, with scattering, and tempest, and hailstones.

31 For through the voice of the LORD shall the Assyrian be beaten down, which struck with a rod.

32 And in every place where the grounded staff shall pass, which the LORD shall lay upon him, it shall be with tabrets and harps: and in battles of shaking will he fight with it.

33 For Tophet is ordained of old; yea, for the king it is prepared; he has made it deep and large: the pile thereof is fire and much wood; the breath of the LORD, like a stream of brimstone, doth kindle it.

CHAPTER 31

WOE to them that go down to Egypt for help; and stay on horses, and trust in chariots, because they are many; and in horsemen, because they are very strong; but they look not unto the Holy One of Israel, neither seek the LORD!

2 Yet he also is wise, and will bring evil, and will not call back his words: but will arise against the house of the evildoers, and against the help of them that work iniquity.

3 Now the Egyptians are men, and not God; and their horses flesh, and not spirit. When the LORD shall stretch out his hand, both he that helpeth shall fall, and he that is holpen shall fall down, and they shall fail together.

4 For thus has the LORD spoken unto me, Like as the lion and the young lion roaring on his prey, when a multitude of shepherds is called forth against him, he will not be afraid of their voice, nor abase himself for the noise of them: so shall the LORD of hosts come down to fight for mount Zion, and for the hill thereof.

5 As birds flying, so will the LORD of hosts defend Jerusalem; defending also he will deliver it; and passing over he will preserve it.

6Turn you unto him from whom the children of Israel have deeply revolted.

7 For in that day every man shall cast away his idols of silver, and his idols of gold, which your own hands have made unto you for a sin.

8Then shall the Assyrian fall with the sword, not of a mighty man; and the sword, not of a mean man, shall devour him: but he shall flee from the sword, and his young men shall be discomfited.

9 And he shall pass over to his strong hold for fear, and his princes shall be afraid of the ensign, saith the LORD, whose fire is in Zion, and his furnace in Jerusalem.

CHAPTER 32

BEHOLD, a king shall reign in righteousness, and princes shall rule in judgment.

2 And a man shall be as an hiding place from the wind, and a covert from the tempest; as rivers of water in a dry place, as the shadow of a great rock in a weary land.

3 And the eyes of them that see shall not be dim, and the ears of them that hear shall hearken.

4 The heart also of the rash shall understand knowledge, and the tongue of the stammerers shall be ready to speak plainly.

5 The vile person shall be no more called liberal, nor the churl said to be bountiful.

6 For the vile person will speak villany, and his heart will work iniquity, to practise hypocrisy, and to utter error against the LORD, to make empty the soul of the hungry, and he will cause the drink of the thirsty to fail.

7 The instruments also of the churl are evil: he deviseth wicked devices to destroy the poor with lying words, even when the needy speaketh right.

8 But the liberal deviseth liberal things; and by liberal things shall he stand.

9Rise up, you women that are at ease; hear my voice, you careless daughters; give ear unto my speech.

10 Many days and years shall you be troubled, you careless women: for the vintage shall fail, the gathering shall not come.

11 Tremble, you women that are at ease; be troubled, you careless ones: strip you, and make you bare, and gird sackcloth upon your loins.

12 They shall lament for the teats, for the pleasant fields, for the fruitful vine.

13 Upon the land of my people shall come up thorns and briers; yea, upon all the houses of joy in the joyous city:

14 Because the palaces shall be forsaken; the multitude of the city shall be left; the forts and towers shall be for dens for ever, a joy of wild asses, a pasture of flocks;

15 Until the spirit be poured upon us from on high, and the wilderness be a fruitful field, and the fruitful field be counted for a forest.

16 Then judgment shall dwell in the wilderness, and righteousness remain in the fruitful field.

17 And the work of righteousness shall be peace; and the effect of righteousness quietness and assurance for ever.

18 And my people shall dwell in a peaceable habitation, and in sure dwellings, and in quiet resting places;

19 When it shall hail, coming down on the forest; and the city shall be low in a low place.

20 Blessed are you that sow beside all waters, that send forth thither the feet of the ox and the ass.

CHAPTER 33

WOE to you that spoilest, and you wast not spoiled; and dealest treacherously, and they dealt not treacherously with you! when you shalt cease to spoil, you shalt be spoiled; and when you shalt make an end to deal treacherously, they shall deal treacherously with you.

2 O LORD, be gracious unto us; we have waited for you: be you their arm every morning, our salvation also in the time of trouble.

3 At the noise of the tumult the people fled; at the lifting up of yourself the nations were scattered.

4 And your spoil shall be gathered like the gathering of the caterpiller: as the running to and fro of locusts shall he run upon them.

5 The LORD is exalted; for he dwelleth on high: he has filled Zion with judgment and righteousness.

6 And wisdom and knowledge shall be the stability of your times, and strength of salvation: the fear of the LORD is his treasure.

7 Behold, their valiant ones shall cry without: the ambassadors of peace shall weep bitterly.

8 The highways lie waste, the wayfaring man ceaseth: he has broken the covenant, he has despised the cities, he regardeth no man.

9 The earth mourneth and languisheth: Lebanon is ashamed and hewn down: Sharon is like a wilderness; and Bashan and Carmel shake off their fruits.

10 Now will I rise, saith the LORD; now will I be exalted; now will I lift up myself.

11 You shall conceive chaff, you shall bring forth stubble: your breath, as fire, shall devour you.

12 And the people shall be as the burnings of lime: as thorns cut up shall they be burned in the fire.

13Hear, you that are far off, what I have done; and, you that are near, acknowledge my might.

14 The sinners in Zion are afraid; fearfulness has surprised the hypocrites. Who among us shall dwell with the devouring fire? who among us shall dwell with everlasting burnings?

15 He that walketh righteously, and speaketh uprightly; he that despiseth the gain of oppressions, that shaketh his hands from holding of bribes, that stoppeth his ears from hearing of blood, and shutteth his eyes from seeing evil;

16 He shall dwell on high: his place of defence shall be the munitions of rocks: bread shall be given him; his waters shall be sure.

17 Yours eyes shall see the king in his beauty: they shall behold the land that is very far off.

18 Yours heart shall meditate terror. Where is the scribe? where is the receiver? where is he that counted the towers?

19 You shalt not see a fierce people, a people of a deeper speech than you can perceive; of a stammering tongue, that you can not understand.

20 Look upon Zion, the city of our solemnities: yours eyes shall see Jerusalem a quiet habitation, a tabernacle that shall not be taken down; not one of the stakes thereof shall ever be removed, neither shall any of the cords thereof be broken.

21 But there the glorious LORD will be unto us a place of broad rivers and streams; wherein shall go no galley with oars, neither shall gallant ship pass thereby.

22 For the LORD is our judge, the LORD is our lawgiver, the LORD is our king; he will save us.

23 Your tacklings are loosed; they could not well strengthen their mast, they could not spread the sail: then is the prey of a great spoil divided; the lame take the prey.

24 And the inhabitant shall not say, I am sick: the people that dwell therein shall be forgiven their iniquity.

CHAPTER 34

COME near, you nations, to hear; and hearken, you people: let the earth hear, and all that is therein; the world, and all things that come forth of it.

2 For the indignation of the LORD is upon all nations, and his fury upon all their armies: he has utterly destroyed them, he has delivered them to the slaughter.

3 Their slain also shall be cast out, and their stink shall come up out of their carcases, and the mountains shall be melted with their blood.

4 And all the host of heaven shall be dissolved, and the heavens shall be rolled together as a scroll: and all their host shall fall down, as the leaf falleth off from the vine, and as a falling fig from the fig tree.

5 For my sword shall be bathed in heaven: behold, it shall come down upon Idumea, and upon the people of my curse, to judgment.

6 The sword of the LORD is filled with blood, it is made fat with fatness, and with the blood of lambs and goats, with the fat of the kidneys of rams: for the LORD has a sacrifice in Bozrah, and a great slaughter in the land of Idumea.

7 And the unicorns shall come down with them, and the bullocks with the bulls; and their land shall be soaked with blood, and their dust made fat with fatness.

8 For it is the day of the LORD's vengeance, and the year of recompences for the controversy of Zion.

9 And the streams thereof shall be turned into pitch, and the dust thereof into brimstone, and the land thereof shall become burning pitch.

10 It shall not be quenched night nor day; the smoke thereof shall go up for ever: from generation to generation it shall lie waste; none shall pass through it for ever and ever.

11But the cormorant and the bittern shall possess it; the owl also and the raven shall dwell in it: and he shall stretch out upon it the line of confusion, and the stones of emptiness.

12 They shall call the nobles thereof to the kingdom, but none shall be there, and all her princes shall be nothing.

13 And thorns shall come up in her palaces, nettles and brambles in the fortresses thereof: and it shall be an habitation of dragons, and a court for owls.

14 The wild beasts of the desert shall also meet with the wild beasts of the island, and the satyr shall cry to his fellow; the screech owl also shall rest there, and find for herself a place of rest.

15 There shall the great owl make her nest, and lay, and hatch, and gather under her shadow: there shall the vultures also be gathered, every one with her mate.

16Seek you out of the book of the LORD, and read: no one of these shall fail, none shall want her mate: for my mouth it has commanded, and his spirit it has gathered them.

17 And he has cast the lot for them, and his hand has divided it unto them by line: they shall possess it for ever, from generation to generation shall they dwell therein.

CHAPTER 35

THE wilderness and the solitary place shall be glad for them; and the desert shall rejoice, and blossom as the rose.

2 It shall blossom abundantly, and rejoice even with joy and singing: the glory of Lebanon shall be given unto it, the excellency of Carmel and Sharon, they shall see the glory of the LORD, and the excellency of our God.

3Strengthen you the weak hands, and confirm the feeble knees.

4 Say to them that are of a fearful heart, Be strong, fear not: behold, your God will come with vengeance, even God with a recompence; he will come and save you.

5 Then the eyes of the blind shall be opened, and the ears of the deaf shall be unstopped.

6 Then shall the lame man leap as an hart, and the tongue of the dumb sing: for in the wilderness shall waters break out, and streams in the desert.

7 And the parched ground shall become a pool, and the thirsty land springs of water: in the habitation of dragons, where each lay, shall be grass with reeds and rushes.

8 And an highway shall be there, and a way, and it shall be called The way of holiness; the unclean shall not pass over it; but it shall be for those: the wayfaring men, though fools, shall not err therein.

9 No lion shall be there, nor any ravenous beast shall go up thereon, it shall not be found there; but the redeemed shall walk there:

10 And the ransomed of the LORD shall return, and come to Zion with songs and everlasting joy upon their heads: they shall obtain joy and gladness, and sorrow and sighing shall flee away.

CHAPTER 36

NOW it came to pass in the fourteenth year of king Hezekiah, that Sennacherib king of Assyria came up against all the defenced cities of Judah, and took them.

2 And the king of Assyria sent Rabshakeh from Lachish to Jerusalem unto king Hezekiah with a great army. And he stood by the conduit of the upper pool in the highway of the fuller's field.

3 Then came forth unto him Eliakim, Hilkiah's son, which was over the house, and Shebna the scribe, and Joah, Asaph's son, the recorder.

4And Rabshakeh said unto them, Say you now to Hezekiah, Thus saith the great king, the king of Assyria, What confidence is this wherein you trustest?

5 I say, say you , (but they are but vain words) I have counsel and strength for war: now on whom dost you trust, that you rebellest against me?

6 Lo, you trustest in the staff of this broken reed, on Egypt; whereon if a man lean, it will go into his hand, and pierce it: so is Pharaoh king of Egypt to all that trust in him.

7 But if you say to me, We trust in the LORD our God: is it not he, whose high places and whose altars Hezekiah has taken away, and said to Judah and to Jerusalem, You shall worship before this altar?

8 Now therefore give pledges, I pray you, to my master the king of Assyria, and I will give you two thousand horses, if you be able on your part to set riders upon them.

9 How then will you turn away the face of one captain of the least of my master's servants, and put your trust on Egypt for chariots and for horsemen?

10 And am I now come up without the LORD against this land to destroy it? the LORD said unto me, Go up against this land, and destroy it.

11Then said Eliakim and Shebna and Joah unto Rabshakeh, Speak, I pray you, unto your servants in the Syrian language; for we understand it: and speak not to us in the Jews' language, in the ears of the people that are on the wall.

12But Rabshakeh said, Has my master sent me to your master and to you to speak these words? has he not sent me to the men that sit upon the wall, that they may eat their own dung, and drink their own piss with you?

13 Then Rabshakeh stood, and cried with a loud voice in the Jews' language, and said, Hear you the words of the great king, the king of Assyria.

14 Thus saith the king, Let not Hezekiah deceive you: for he shall not be able to deliver you.

15 Neither let Hezekiah make you trust in the LORD, saying, The LORD will surely deliver us: this city shall not be delivered into the hand of the king of Assyria.

16 Hearken not to Hezekiah: for thus saith the king of Assyria, Make an agreement with me by a present, and come out to me: and eat you every one of his vine, and every one of his fig tree, and drink you every one the waters of his own cistern;

17 Until I come and take you away to a land like your own land, a land of corn and wine, a land of bread and vineyards.

18 Beware lest Hezekiah persuade you, saying, The LORD will deliver us. Has any of the gods of the nations delivered his land out of the hand of the king of Assyria?

19 Where are the gods of Hamath and Arphad? where are the gods of Sepharvaim? and have they delivered Samaria out of my hand?

20 Who are they among all the gods of these lands, that have delivered their land out of my hand, that the LORD should deliver Jerusalem out of my hand?

21 But they held their peace, and answered him not a word: for the king's commandment was, saying, Answer him not.

22Then came Eliakim, the son of Hilkiah, that was over the household, and Shebna the scribe, and Joah, the son of Asaph, the recorder, to Hezekiah with their clothes rent, and told him the words of Rabshakeh.

CHAPTER 37

AND it came to pass, when king Hezekiah heard it, that he rent his clothes, and covered himself with sackcloth, and went into the house of the LORD.

2 And he sent Eliakim, who was over the household, and Shebna the scribe, and the elders of the priests covered with sackcloth, unto Isaiah the prophet the son of Amoz.

3 And they said unto him, Thus saith Hezekiah, This day is a day of trouble, and of rebuke, and of blasphemy: for the children are come to the birth, and there is not strength to bring forth.

4 It may be the LORD your God will hear the words of Rabshakeh, whom the king of Assyria his master has sent to reproach the living God, and will reprove the words which the LORD your God has heard: wherefore lift up your prayer for the remnant that is left.

5 So the servants of king Hezekiah came to Isaiah.

6And Isaiah said unto them, Thus shall you say unto your master, Thus saith the LORD, Be not afraid of the words that you have heard, wherewith the servants of the king of Assyria have blasphemed me.

7 Behold, I will send a blast upon him, and he shall hear a rumour, and return to his own land; and I will cause him to fall by the sword in his own land.

8So Rabshakeh returned, and found the king of Assyria warring against Libnah: for he had heard that he was departed from Lachish.

9 And he heard say concerning Tirhakah king of Ethiopia, He is come forth to make war with you. And when he heard it, he sent messengers to Hezekiah, saying,

10 Thus shall you speak to Hezekiah king of Judah, saying, Let not your God, in whom you trustest, deceive you, saying, Jerusalem shall not be given into the hand of the king of Assyria.

11 Behold, you have heard what the kings of Assyria have done to all lands by destroying them utterly; and shalt you be delivered?

12 Have the gods of the nations delivered them which my fathers have destroyed, as Gozan, and Haran, and Rezeph, and the children of Eden which were in Telassar?

13 Where is the king of Hamath, and the king of Arphad, and the king of the city of Sepharvaim, Hena, and Ivah?

14And Hezekiah received the letter from the hand of the messengers, and read it: and Hezekiah went up unto the house of the LORD, and spread it before the LORD.

15 And Hezekiah prayed unto the LORD, saying,

16 O LORD of hosts, God of Israel, that dwellest between the cherubims, you are the God, even you alone, of all the kingdoms of the earth: you have made heaven and earth.

17 Incline yours ear, O LORD, and hear; open yours eyes, O LORD, and see: and hear all the words of Sennacherib, which has sent to reproach the living God.

18 Of a truth, LORD, the kings of Assyria have laid waste all the nations, and their countries,

19 And have cast their gods into the fire: for they were no gods, but the work of men's hands, wood and stone: therefore they have destroyed them.

20 Now therefore, O LORD our God, save us from his hand, that all the kingdoms of the earth may know that you are the LORD, even you only.

21Then Isaiah the son of Amoz sent unto Hezekiah, saying, Thus saith the LORD God of Israel, Whereas you have prayed to me against Sennacherib king of Assyria:

22 This is the word which the LORD has spoken concerning him; The virgin, the daughter of Zion, has despised you, and laughed you to scorn; the daughter of Jerusalem has shaken her head at you.

23 Whom have you reproached and blasphemed? and against whom have you exalted your voice, and lifted up yours eyes on high? even against the Holy One of Israel.

24 By your servants have you reproached the Lord, and have said, By the multitude of my chariots am I come up to the height of the mountains, to the sides of Lebanon; and I will cut down the tall cedars thereof, and the choice fir trees thereof: and I will enter into the height of his border, and the forest of his Carmel.

25 I have digged, and drunk water; and with the sole of my feet have I dried up all the rivers of the besieged places.

26 Have you not heard long ago, how I have done it; and of ancient times, that I have formed it? now have I brought it to pass, that you shouldest be to lay waste defenced cities into ruinous heaps.

27 Therefore their inhabitants were of small power, they were dismayed and confounded: they were as the grass of the field, and as the green herb, as the grass on the housetops, and as corn blasted before it be grown up.

28 But I know your abode, and your going out, and your coming in, and your rage against me.

29 Because your rage against me, and your tumult, is come up into my ears, therefore will I put my hook in your nose, and my bridle in your lips, and I will turn you back by the way by which you camest.

30 And this shall be a sign unto you, You shall eat this year such as groweth of itself; and the second year that which springeth of the same: and in the third year sow you , and reap, and plant vineyards, and eat the fruit thereof.

31 And the remnant that is escaped of the house of Judah shall again take root downward, and bear fruit upward:

32 For out of Jerusalem shall go forth a remnant, and they that escape out of mount Zion: the zeal of the LORD of hosts shall do this.

33 Therefore thus saith the LORD concerning the king of Assyria, He shall not come into this city, nor shoot an arrow there, nor come before it with shields, nor cast a bank against it.

34 By the way that he came, by the same shall he return, and shall not come into this city, saith the LORD.

35 For I will defend this city to save it for my own sake, and for my servant David's sake.

36 Then the angel of the LORD went forth, and struck in the camp of the Assyrians a hundred and fourscore and five thousand: and when they arose early in the morning, behold, they were all dead corpses.

37So Sennacherib king of Assyria departed, and went and returned, and dwelt at Nineveh.

38 And it came to pass, as he was worshipping in the house of Nisroch his god, that Adrammelech and Sharezer his sons struck him with the sword; and they escaped into the land of Armenia: and Esar-haddon his son reigned in his stead.

CHAPTER 38

IN those days was Hezekiah sick unto death. And Isaiah the prophet the son of Amoz came unto him, and said unto him, Thus saith the LORD, Set yours house in order: for you shalt die, and not live.

2 Then Hezekiah turned his face toward the wall, and prayed unto the LORD,

3 And said, Remember now, O LORD, I beseech you, how I have walked before you in truth and with a perfect heart, and have done that which is good in your sight. And Hezekiah wept sore.

4Then came the word of the LORD to Isaiah, saying,

5 Go, and say to Hezekiah, Thus saith the LORD, the God of David your father, I have heard your prayer, I have seen your tears: behold, I will add unto your days fifteen years.

6 And I will deliver you and this city out of the hand of the king of Assyria: and I will defend this city.

7 And this shall be a sign unto you from the LORD, that the LORD will do this thing that he has spoken;

8 Behold, I will bring again the shadow of the degrees, which is gone down in the sun dial of Ahaz, ten degrees backward. So the sun returned ten degrees, by which degrees it was gone down.

9The writing of Hezekiah king of Judah, when he had been sick, and was recovered of his sickness:

10 I said in the cutting off of my days, I shall go to the gates of the grave: I am deprived of the residue of my years.

11 I said, I shall not see the LORD, even the LORD, in the land of the living: I shall behold man no more with the inhabitants of the world.

12 My age is departed, and is removed from me as a shepherd's tent: I have cut off like a weaver my life: he will cut me off with pining sickness: from day even to night will you make an end of me.

13 I reckoned till morning, that, as a lion, so will he break all my bones: from day even to night will you make an end of me.

14 Like a crane or a swallow, so did I chatter: I did mourn as a dove: my eyes fail with looking upward: O LORD, I am oppressed; undertake for me.

15 What shall I say? he has both spoken unto me, and himself has done it: I shall go softly all my years in the bitterness of my soul.

16 O Lord, by these things men live, and in all these things is the life of my spirit: so will you recover me, and make me to live.

17 Behold, for peace I had great bitterness: but you have in love to my soul delivered it from the pit of corruption: for you have cast all my sins behind your back.

18 For the grave cannot praise you, death can not celebrate you: they that go down into the pit cannot hope for your truth.

19 The living, the living, he shall praise you, as I do this day: the father to the children shall make known your truth.

20 The LORD was ready to save me: therefore we will sing my songs to the stringed instruments all the days of our life in the house of the LORD.

21 For Isaiah had said, Let them take a lump of figs, and lay it for a plaister upon the boil, and he shall recover.

22 Hezekiah also had said, What is the sign that I shall go up to the house of the LORD?

CHAPTER 39

AT that time Merodach-baladan, the son of Baladan, king of Babylon, sent letters and a present to Hezekiah: for he had heard that he had been sick, and was recovered.

2 And Hezekiah was glad of them, and shewed them the house of his precious things, the silver, and the gold, and the spices, and the precious ointment, and all the house of his armour, and all that was found in his treasures: there was nothing in his house, nor in all his dominion, that Hezekiah shewed them not.

3Then came Isaiah the prophet unto king Hezekiah, and said unto him, What said these men? and from whence came they unto you? And Hezekiah said, They are come from a far country unto me, even from Babylon.

4 Then said he, What have they seen in yours house? And Hezekiah answered, All that is in my house have they seen: there is nothing among my treasures that I have not shewed them.

5 Then said Isaiah to Hezekiah, Hear the word of the LORD of hosts:

6 Behold, the days come, that all that is in yours house, and that which your fathers have laid up in store until this day, shall be carried to Babylon: nothing shall be left, saith the LORD.

7 And of your sons that shall issue from you, which you shalt beget, shall they take away; and they shall be eunuchs in the palace of the king of Babylon.

8 Then said Hezekiah to Isaiah, Good is the word of the LORD which you have spoken. He said moreover, For there shall be peace and truth in my days.

CHAPTER 40

COMFORT you , comfort you my people, saith your God.

2 Speak you comfortably to Jerusalem, and cry unto her, that her warfare is accomplished, that her iniquity is pardoned: for she has received of the LORD's hand double for all her sins.

3The voice of him that crieth in the wilderness, Prepare you the way of the LORD, make straight in the desert a highway for our God.

4 Every valley shall be exalted, and every mountain and hill shall be made low: and the crooked shall be made straight, and the rough places plain:

5 And the glory of the LORD shall be revealed, and all flesh shall see it together: for the mouth of the LORD has spoken it.

6 The voice said, Cry. And he said, What shall I cry? All flesh is grass, and all the goodliness thereof is as the flower of the field:

7 The grass withereth, the flower fadeth: because the spirit of the LORD bloweth upon it: surely the people is grass.

8 The grass withereth, the flower fadeth: but the word of our God shall stand for ever.

90 Zion, that bringest good tidings, get you up into the high mountain; O Jerusalem, that bringest good tidings, lift up your voice with strength; lift it up, be not afraid; say unto the cities of Judah, Behold your God!

10 Behold, the Lord GOD will come with strong hand, and his arm shall rule for him: behold, his reward is with him, and his work before him.

11 He shall feed his flock like a shepherd: he shall gather the lambs with his arm, and carry them in his bosom, and shall gently lead those that are with young.

12Who has measured the waters in the hollow of his hand, and meted out heaven with the span, and comprehended the dust of the earth in a measure, and weighed the mountains in scales, and the hills in a balance?

13 Who has directed the Spirit of the LORD, or being his counseller has taught him?

14 With whom took he counsel, and who instructed him, and taught him in the path of judgment, and taught him knowledge, and shewed to him the way of understanding?

15 Behold, the nations are as a drop of a bucket, and are counted as the small dust of the balance: behold, he taketh up the isles as a very little thing.

16 And Lebanon is not sufficient to burn, nor the beasts thereof sufficient for a burnt offering.

17 All nations before him are as nothing; and they are counted to him less than nothing, and vanity.

18To whom then will you liken God? or what likeness will you compare unto him?

19 The workman melteth a graven image, and the goldsmith spreadeth it over with gold, and casteth silver chains.

20 He that is so impoverished that he has no oblation chooseth a tree that will not rot; he seeketh unto him a cunning workman to prepare a graven image, that shall not be moved.

21 Have you not known? have you not heard? has it not been told you from the beginning? have you not understood from the foundations of the earth?

22 It is he that sitteth upon the circle of the earth, and the inhabitants thereof are as grasshoppers; that stretcheth out the heavens as a curtain, and spreadeth them out as a tent to dwell in:

23 That bringeth the princes to nothing; he maketh the judges of the earth as vanity.

24 Yea, they shall not be planted; yea, they shall not be sown: yea, their stock shall not take root in the earth: and he shall also blow upon them, and they shall wither, and the whirlwind shall take them away as stubble.

25 To whom then will you liken me, or shall I be equal? saith the Holy One.

26 Lift up your eyes on high, and behold who has created these things, that bringeth out their host by number: he calleth them all by names by the greatness of his might, for that he is strong in power; not one faileth.

27 Why say you , O Jacob, and speakest, O Israel, My way is hid from the LORD, and my judgment is passed over from my God?

28 Hast you not known? have you not heard, that the everlasting God, the LORD, the Creator of the ends of the earth, fainteth not, neither is weary? there is no searching of his understanding.

29 He giveth power to the faint; and to them that have no might he increaseth strength.

30 Even the youths shall faint and be weary, and the young men shall utterly fall:

31 But they that wait upon the LORD shall renew their strength; they shall mount up with wings as eagles; they shall run, and not be weary; and they shall walk, and not faint.

CHAPTER 41

KEEP silence before me, O islands; and let the people renew their strength: let them come near; then let them speak: let us come near together to judgment.

2 Who raised up the righteous man from the east, called him to his foot, gave the nations before him, and made him rule over kings? he gave them as the dust to his sword, and as driven stubble to his bow.

3 He pursued them, and passed safely; even by the way that he had not gone with his feet.

4 Who has created and done it, calling the generations from the beginning? I the LORD, the first, and with the last; I am he.

5 The isles saw it, and feared; the ends of the earth were afraid, drew near, and came.

6 They helped every one his neighbour; and every one said to his brother, Be of good courage.

7 So the carpenter encouraged the goldsmith, and he that smootheth with the hammer him that struck the anvil, saying, It is ready for the sodering: and he fastened it with nails, that it should not be moved.

8 But you , Israel, are my servant, Jacob whom I have chosen, the seed of Abraham my friend.

9 You whom I have taken from the ends of the earth, and called you from the chief men thereof, and said unto you, You are my servant; I have chosen you, and not cast you away.

10 Fear you not; for I am with you: be not dismayed; for I am your God: I will strengthen you; yea, I will help you; yea, I will uphold you with the right hand of my righteousness.

11 Behold, all they that were incensed against you shall be ashamed and confounded: they shall be as nothing; and they that strive with you shall perish.

12 You shalt seek them, and shalt not find them, even them that contended with you: they that war against you shall be as nothing, and as a thing of nought.

13 For I the LORD your God will hold your right hand, saying unto you, Fear not; I will help you.

14 Fear not, you worm Jacob, and you men of Israel; I will help you, saith the LORD, and your redeemer, the Holy One of Israel.

15 Behold, I will make you a new sharp threshing instrument having teeth: you shalt thresh the mountains, and beat them small, and shalt make the hills as chaff.

16 You shalt fan them, and the wind shall carry them away, and the whirlwind shall scatter them: and you shalt rejoice in the LORD, and shalt glory in the Holy One of Israel.

17 When the poor and needy seek water, and there is none, and their tongue faileth for thirst, I the LORD will hear them, I the God of Israel will not forsake them.

18 I will open rivers in high places, and fountains in the midst of the valleys: I will make the wilderness a pool of water, and the dry land springs of water.

19 I will plant in the wilderness the cedar, the shittah tree, and the myrtle, and the oil tree; I will set in the desert the fir tree, and the pine, and the box tree together:

20 That they may see, and know, and consider, and understand together, that the hand of the LORD has done this, and the Holy One of Israel has created it.

21 Produce your cause, saith the LORD; bring forth your strong reasons, saith the King of Jacob.

22 Let them bring them forth, and shew us what shall happen: let them shew the former things, what they be, that we may consider them, and know the latter end of them; or declare us things for to come.

23 Shew the things that are to come hereafter, that we may know that you are gods: yea, do good, or do evil, that we may be dismayed, and behold it together.

24 Behold, you are of nothing, and your work of nought: an abomination is he that chooseth you.

25 I have raised up one from the north, and he shall come: from the rising of the sun shall he call upon my name: and he shall come upon princes as upon morter, and as the potter treadeth clay.

26 Who has declared from the beginning, that we may know? and beforetime, that we may say, He is righteous? yea, there is none that sheweth, yea, there is none that declareth, yea, there is none that heareth your words.

27 The first shall say to Zion, Behold, behold them: and I will give to Jerusalem one that bringeth good tidings.

28 For I beheld, and there was no man; even among them, and there was no counseller, that, when I asked of them, could answer a word.

29 Behold, they are all vanity; their works are nothing: their molten images are wind and confusion.

CHAPTER 42

BEHOLD my servant, whom I uphold; my elect, in whom my soul delighteth; I have put my spirit upon him: he shall bring forth judgment to the Gentiles.

2 He shall not cry, nor lift up, nor cause his voice to be heard in the street.

3 A bruised reed shall he not break, and the smoking flax shall he not quench: he shall bring forth judgment unto truth.

4 He shall not fail nor be discouraged, till he have set judgment in the earth: and the isles shall wait for his law.

5 Thus saith God the LORD, he that created the heavens, and stretched them out; he that spread forth the earth, and that which comes out of it; he that giveth breath unto the people upon it, and spirit to them that walk therein:

6 I the LORD have called you in righteousness, and will hold yours hand, and will keep you, and give you for a covenant of the people, for a light of the Gentiles;

7 To open the blind eyes, to bring out the prisoners from the prison, and them that sit in darkness out of the prison house.

8 I am the LORD: that is my name: and my glory will I not give to another, neither my praise to graven images.

9 Behold, the former things are come to pass, and new things do I declare: before they spring forth I tell you of them.

10 Sing unto the LORD a new song, and his praise from the end of the earth, you that go down to the sea, and all that is therein; the isles, and the inhabitants thereof.

11 Let the wilderness and the cities thereof lift up their voice, the villages that Kedar doth inhabit: let the inhabitants of the rock sing, let them shout from the top of the mountains.

12 Let them give glory unto the LORD, and declare his praise in the islands.

13 The LORD shall go forth as a mighty man, he shall stir up jealousy like a man of war: he shall cry, yea, roar; he shall prevail against his enemies.

14 I have long time holden my peace; I have been still, and refrained myself: now will I cry like a travailing woman; I will destroy and devour at once.

15 I will make waste mountains and hills, and dry up all their herbs; and I will make the rivers islands, and I will dry up the pools.

16 And I will bring the blind by a way that they knew not; I will lead them in paths that they have not known: I will make darkness light before them, and crooked things straight. These things will I do unto them, and not forsake them.

17 They shall be turned back, they shall be greatly ashamed, that trust in graven images, that say to the molten images, You are our gods.

18 Hear, you deaf; and look, you blind, that you may see.

19 Who is blind, but my servant? or deaf, as my messenger that I sent? who is blind as he that is perfect, and blind as the LORD's servant?

20 Seeing many things, but you observest not; opening the ears, but he heareth not.

21 The LORD is well pleased for his righteousness' sake; he will magnify the law, and make it honourable.

22 But this is a people robbed and spoiled; they are all of them snared in holes, and they are hid in prison houses: they are for a prey, and none delivereth; for a spoil, and none saith, Restore.

23 Who among you will give ear to this? who will hearken and hear for the time to come?

24 Who gave Jacob for a spoil, and Israel to the robbers? did not the LORD, he against whom we have sinned? for they would not walk in his ways, neither were they obedient unto his law.

25 Therefore he has poured upon him the fury of his anger, and the strength of battle: and it has set him on fire round about, yet he knew not; and it burned him, yet he laid it not to heart.

CHAPTER 43

BUT now thus saith the LORD that created you, O Jacob, and he that formed you, O Israel, Fear not: for I have redeemed you, I have called you by your name; you are my.

2 When you passest through the waters, I will be with you; and through the rivers, they shall not overflow you: when you walkest through the fire, you shalt not be burned; neither shall the flame kindle upon you.

3 For I am the LORD your God, the Holy One of Israel, your Saviour: I gave Egypt for your ransom, Ethiopia and Seba for you.

4 Since you wast precious in my sight, you have been honourable, and I have loved you: therefore will I give men for you, and people for your life.

5 Fear not: for I am with you: I will bring your seed from the east, and gather you from the west;

6 I will say to the north, Give up; and to the south, Keep not back: bring my sons from far, and my daughters from the ends of the earth;

7 Even every one that is called by my name: for I have created him for my glory, I have formed him; yea, I have made him.

8 Bring forth the blind people that have eyes, and the deaf that have ears.

9 Let all the nations be gathered together, and let the people be assembled: who among them can declare this, and shew us former things? let them bring forth their witnesses, that they may be justified: or let them hear, and say, It is truth.

10 You are my witnesses, saith the LORD, and my servant whom I have chosen: that you may know and believe me, and understand that I am he: before me there was no God formed, neither shall there be after me.

11 I, even I, am the LORD; and beside me there is no saviour.

12 I have declared, and have saved, and I have shewed, when there was no strange god among you: therefore you are my witnesses, saith the LORD, that I am God.

13 Yea, before the day was I am he; and there is none that can deliver out of my hand: I will work, and who shall let it?

14 Thus saith the LORD, your redeemer, the Holy One of Israel; For your sake I have sent to Babylon, and have brought down all their nobles, and the Chaldeans, whose cry is in the ships.

15 I am the LORD, your Holy One, the creator of Israel, your King.

16 Thus saith the LORD, which maketh a way in the sea, and a path in the mighty waters;

17 Which bringeth forth the chariot and horse, the army and the power; they shall lie down together, they shall not rise: they are extinct, they are quenched as tow.

18 Remember you not the former things, neither consider the things of old.

19 Behold, I will do a new thing; now it shall spring forth; shall you not know it? I will even make a way in the wilderness, and rivers in the desert.

20 The beast of the field shall honour me, the dragons and the owls: because I give waters in the wilderness, and rivers in the desert, to give drink to my people, my chosen.

21 This people have I formed for myself; they shall shew forth my praise.

22 But you have not called upon me, O Jacob; but you have been weary of me, O Israel.

23 You have not brought me the small cattle of your burnt offerings; neither have you honoured me with your sacrifices. I have not caused you to serve with an offering, nor wearied you with incense.

24 You have bought me no sweet cane with money, neither have you filled me with the fat of your sacrifices: but you have made me to serve with your sins, you have wearied me with yours iniquities.

25 I, even I, am he that blotteth out your transgressions for my own sake, and will not remember your sins.

26 Put me in remembrance: let us plead together: declare you, that you mayest be justified.

27 Your first father has sinned, and your teachers have transgressed against me.

28 Therefore I have profaned the princes of the sanctuary, and have given Jacob to the curse, and Israel to reproaches.

CHAPTER 44

YET now hear, O Jacob my servant; and Israel, whom I have chosen:

2 Thus saith the LORD that made you, and formed you from the womb, which will help you; Fear not, O Jacob, my servant; and you, Jesurun, whom I have chosen.

3 For I will pour water upon him that is thirsty, and floods upon the dry ground: I will pour my spirit upon your seed, and my blessing upon yours offspring:

4 And they shall spring up as among the grass, as willows by the water courses.

5 One shall say, I am the LORD's; and another shall call himself by the name of Jacob; and another shall subscribe with his hand unto the LORD, and surname himself by the name of Israel.

6 Thus saith the LORD the King of Israel, and his redeemer the LORD of hosts; I am the first, and I am the last; and beside me there is no God.

7 And who, as I, shall call, and shall declare it, and set it in order for me, since I appointed the ancient people? and the things that are coming, and shall come, let them shew unto them.

8 Fear you not, neither be afraid: have not I told you from that time, and have declared it? you are even my witnesses. Is there a God beside me? yea, there is no God; I know not any.

9 They that make a graven image are all of them vanity; and their delectable things shall not profit; and they are their own witnesses; they see not, nor know; that they may be ashamed.

10 Who has formed a god, or molten a graven image that is profitable for nothing?

11 Behold, all his fellows shall be ashamed: and the workmen, they are of men: let them all be gathered together, let them stand up; yet they shall fear, and they shall be ashamed together.

12 The smith with the tongs both worketh in the coals, and fashioneth it with hammers, and worketh it with the strength of his arms: yea, he is hungry, and his strength faileth: he drinketh no water, and is faint.

13 The carpenter stretcheth out his rule; he marketh it out with a line; he fitteth it with planes, and he marketh it out with the compass, and maketh it after the figure of a man, according to the beauty of a man; that it may remain in the house.

14 He heweth him down cedars, and taketh the cypress and the oak, which he strengtheneth for himself among the trees of the forest: he planteth an ash, and the rain doth nourish it.

15 Then shall it be for a man to burn: for he will take thereof, and warm himself; yea, he kindleth it, and baketh bread; yea, he maketh a god, and worshippeth it; he maketh it a graven image, and falleth down thereto.

16 He burneth part thereof in the fire; with part thereof he eateth flesh; he roasteth roast, and is satisfied: yea, he warmeth himself, and saith, Aha, I am warm, I have seen the fire:

17 And the residue thereof he maketh a god, even his graven image: he falleth down unto it, and worshippeth it, and prayeth unto it, and saith, Deliver me; for you are my god.

18 They have not known nor understood: for he has shut their eyes, that they cannot see; and their hearts, that they cannot understand.

19 And none considereth in his heart, neither is there knowledge nor understanding to say, I have burned part of it in the fire; yea, also I have baked bread upon the coals thereof; I have roasted flesh, and eaten it: and shall I make the residue thereof an abomination? shall I fall down to the stock of a tree?

20 He feedeth on ashes: a deceived heart has turned him aside, that he cannot deliver his soul, nor say, Is there not a lie in my right hand?

21 Remember these, O Jacob and Israel; for you are my servant: I have formed you; you are my servant: O Israel, you shalt not be forgotten of me.

22 I have blotted out, as a thick cloud, your transgressions, and, as a cloud, your sins: return unto me; for I have redeemed you.

23 Sing, O you heavens; for the LORD has done it: shout, you lower parts of the earth: break forth into singing, you mountains, O forest, and every tree therein: for the LORD has redeemed Jacob, and glorified himself in Israel.

24 Thus saith the LORD, your redeemer, and he that formed you from the womb, I am the LORD that maketh all things; that stretcheth forth the heavens alone; that spreadeth abroad the earth by myself;

25 That frustrateth the tokens of the liars, and maketh diviners mad; that turneth wise men backward, and maketh their knowledge foolish;

26 That confirmeth the word of his servant, and performeth the counsel of his messengers; that saith to Jerusalem, You shalt be inhabited; and to the cities of Judah, You shall be built, and I will raise up the decayed places thereof:

27 That saith to the deep, Be dry, and I will dry up your rivers:

28 That saith of Cyrus, He is my shepherd, and shall perform all my pleasure: even saying to Jerusalem, You shalt be built; and to the temple, Your foundation shall be laid.

CHAPTER 45

THUS saith the LORD to his anointed, to Cyrus, whose right hand I have holden, to subdue nations before him; and I will loose the loins of kings, to open before him the two leaved gates; and the gates shall not be shut;

2 I will go before you, and make the crooked places straight: I will break in pieces the gates of brass, and cut in sunder the bars of iron:

3 And I will give you the treasures of darkness, and hidden riches of secret places, that you mayest know that I, the LORD, which call you by your name, am the God of Israel.

4 For Jacob my servant's sake, and Israel my elect, I have even called you by your name: I have surnamed you, though you have not known me.

5 I am the LORD, and there is none else, there is no God beside me: I girded you, though you have not known me:

6 That they may know from the rising of the sun, and from the west, that there is none beside me. I am the LORD, and there is none else.

7 I form the light, and create darkness: I make peace, and create evil: I the LORD do all these things.

8 Drop down, you heavens, from above, and let the skies pour down righteousness: let the earth open, and let them bring forth salvation, and let righteousness spring up together; I the LORD have created it.

9 Woe unto him that striveth with his Maker! Let the potsherd strive with the potsherds of the earth. Shall the clay say to him that fashioneth it, What makest you ? or your work, He has no hands?

10 Woe unto him that saith unto his father, What begettest you ? or to the woman, What have you brought forth?

11 Thus saith the LORD, the Holy One of Israel, and his Maker, Ask me of things to come concerning my sons, and concerning the work of my hands command you me.

12 I have made the earth, and created man upon it: I, even my hands, have stretched out the heavens, and all their host have I commanded.

13 I have raised him up in righteousness, and I will direct all his ways: he shall build my city, and he shall let go my captives, not for price nor reward, saith the LORD of hosts.

14 Thus saith the LORD, The labour of Egypt, and merchandise of Ethiopia and of the Sabeans, men of stature, shall come over unto you, and they shall be yours: they shall come after you; in chains they shall come over, and they shall fall down unto you, they shall make supplication unto you, saying, Surely God is in you; and there is none else, there is no God.

15 Verily you are a God that hidest yourself, O God of Israel, the Saviour.

16 They shall be ashamed, and also confounded, all of them: they shall go to confusion together that are makers of idols.

17 But Israel shall be saved in the LORD with an everlasting salvation: you shall not be ashamed nor confounded world without end.

18 For thus saith the LORD that created the heavens; God himself that formed the earth and made it; he has established it, he created it not in vain, he formed it to be inhabited: I am the LORD; and there is none else.

19 I have not spoken in secret, in a dark place of the earth: I said not unto the seed of Jacob, Seek you me in vain: I the LORD speak righteousness, I declare things that are right.

20 Assemble yourselves and come; draw near together, you that are escaped of the nations: they have no knowledge that set up the wood of their graven image, and pray unto a god that cannot save.

21 Tell you , and bring them near; yea, let them take counsel together: who has declared this from ancient time? who has told it from that time? have not I the LORD? and there is no God else beside me; a just God and a Saviour; there is none beside me.

22 Look unto me, and be you saved, all the ends of the earth: for I am God, and there is none else.

23 I have sworn by myself, the word is gone out of my mouth in righteousness, and shall not return, That unto me every knee shall bow, every tongue shall swear.

24 Surely, shall one say, in the LORD have I righteousness and strength: even to him shall men come; and all that are incensed against him shall be ashamed.

25 In the LORD shall all the seed of Israel be justified, and shall glory.

CHAPTER 46

BEL boweth down, Nebo stoopeth, their idols were upon the beasts, and upon the cattle: your carriages were heavy loaden; they are a burden to the weary beast.

2 They stoop, they bow down together; they could not deliver the burden, but themselves are gone into captivity.

3 Hearken unto me, O house of Jacob, and all the remnant of the house of Israel, which are borne by me from the belly, which are carried from the womb:

4 And even to your old age I am he; and even to hoar hairs will I carry you: I have made, and I will bear; even I will carry, and will deliver you.

5 To whom will you liken me, and make me equal, and compare me, that we may be like?

6 They lavish gold out of the bag, and weigh silver in the balance, and hire a goldsmith; and he maketh it a god: they fall down, yea, they worship.

7 They bear him upon the shoulder, they carry him, and set him in his place, and he standeth; from his place shall he not remove: yea, one shall cry unto him, yet can he not answer, nor save him out of his trouble.

8 Remember this, and shew yourselves men: bring it again to mind, O you transgressors.

9 Remember the former things of old: for I am God, and there is none else; I am God, and there is none like me,

10 Declaring the end from the beginning, and from ancient times the things that are not yet done, saying, My counsel shall stand, and I will do all my pleasure:

11 Calling a ravenous bird from the east, the man that executeth my counsel from a far country: yea, I have spoken it, I will also bring it to pass; I have purposed it, I will also do it.

12 Hearken unto me, you stouthearted, that are far from righteousness:

13 I bring near my righteousness; it shall not be far off, and my salvation shall not tarry: and I will place salvation in Zion for Israel my glory.

CHAPTER 47

COME down, and sit in the dust, O virgin daughter of Babylon, sit on the ground: there is no throne, O daughter of the Chaldeans: for you shalt no more be called tender and delicate.

2 Take the millstones, and grind meal: uncover your locks, make bare the leg, uncover the thigh, pass over the rivers.

3 Your nakedness shall be uncovered, yea, your shame shall be seen: I will take vengeance, and I will not meet you as a man.

4 As for our redeemer, the LORD of hosts is his name, the Holy One of Israel.

5 Sit you silent, and get you into darkness, O daughter of the Chaldeans: for you shalt no more be called, The lady of kingdoms.

6 I was wroth with my people, I have polluted my inheritance, and given them into yours hand: you did shew them no mercy; upon the ancient have you very heavily laid your yoke.

7 And you saidst, I shall be a lady for ever: so that you did not lay these things to your heart, neither did remember the latter end of it.

8 Therefore hear now this, you that are given to pleasures, that dwellest carelessly, that say in yours heart, I am, and none else beside me; I shall not sit as a widow, neither shall I know the loss of children:

9 But these two things shall come to you in a moment in one day, the loss of children, and widowhood: they shall come upon you in their perfection for the multitude of your sorceries, and for the great abundance of yours enchantments.

10 For you have trusted in your wickedness: you have said, None seeth me. Your wisdom and your knowledge, it has perverted you; and you have said in yours heart, I am, and none else beside me.

11 Therefore shall evil come upon you; you shalt not know from whence it riseth: and mischief shall fall upon you; you shalt not be able to put it off: and desolation shall come upon you suddenly, which you shalt not know.

12 Stand now with yours enchantments, and with the multitude of your sorceries, wherein you have laboured from your youth; if so be you shalt be able to profit, if so be you mayest prevail.

13 You are wearied in the multitude of your counsels. Let now the astrologers, the stargazers, the monthly prognosticators, stand up, and save you from these things that shall come upon you.

14 Behold, they shall be as stubble; the fire shall burn them; they shall not deliver themselves from the power of the flame: there shall not be a coal to warm at, nor fire to sit before it.

15 Thus shall they be unto you with whom you have laboured, even your merchants, from your youth: they shall wander every one to his quarter; none shall save you.

CHAPTER 48

HEAR you this, O house of Jacob, which are called by the name of Israel, and are come forth out of the waters of Judah, which swear by the name of the LORD, and make mention of the God of Israel, but not in truth, nor in righteousness.

2 For they call themselves of the holy city, and stay themselves upon the God of Israel; The LORD of hosts is his name.

3 I have declared the former things from the beginning; and they went forth out of my mouth, and I shewed them; I did them suddenly, and they came to pass.

4 Because I knew that you are obstinate, and your neck is an iron sinew, and your brow brass;

5 I have even from the beginning declared it to you; before it came to pass I shewed it you: lest you shouldest say, My idol has done them, and my graven image, and my molten image, has commanded them.

6 You have heard, see all this; and will not you declare it? I have shewed you new things from this time, even hidden things, and you did not know them.

7 They are created now, and not from the beginning; even before the day when you heardest them not; lest you shouldest say, Behold, I knew them.

8 Yea, you heardest not; yea, you knewest not; yea, from that time that yours ear was not opened: for I knew that you wouldest deal very treacherously, and wast called a transgressor from the womb.

9 For my name's sake will I defer my anger, and for my praise will I refrain for you, that I cut you not off.

10 Behold, I have refined you, but not with silver; I have chosen you in the furnace of affliction.

11 For my own sake, even for my own sake, will I do it: for how should my name be polluted? and I will not give my glory unto another.

12 Hearken unto me, O Jacob and Israel, my called; I am he; I am the first, I also am the last.

13 My hand also has laid the foundation of the earth, and my right hand has spanned the heavens: when I call unto them, they stand up together.

14 All you , assemble yourselves, and hear; which among them has declared these things? The LORD has loved him: he will do his pleasure on Babylon, and his arm shall be on the Chaldeans.

15 I, even I, have spoken; yea, I have called him: I have brought him, and he shall make his way prosperous.

16 Come you near unto me, hear you this; I have not spoken in secret from the beginning; from the time that it was, there am I: and now the Lord GOD, and his Spirit, has sent me.

17 Thus saith the LORD, your Redeemer, the Holy One of Israel; I am the LORD your God which teacheth you to profit, which leadeth you by the way that you shouldest go.

18 O that you hadst hearkened to my commandments! then had your peace been as a river, and your righteousness as the waves of the sea:

19 Your seed also had been as the sand, and the offspring of your bowels like the gravel thereof; his name should not have been cut off nor destroyed from before me.

20 Go you forth of Babylon, flee you from the Chaldeans, with a voice of singing declare you , tell this, utter it even to the end of the earth; say you , The LORD has redeemed his servant Jacob.

21 And they thirsted not when he led them through the deserts: he caused the waters to flow out of the rock for them: he clave the rock also, and the waters gushed out.

22 There is no peace, saith the LORD, unto the wicked.

CHAPTER 49

LISTEN, O isles, unto me; and hearken, you people, from far; The LORD has called me from the womb; from the bowels of my mother has he made mention of my name.

2 And he has made my mouth like a sharp sword; in the shadow of his hand has he hid me, and made me a polished shaft; in his quiver has he hid me;

3 And said unto me, You are my servant, O Israel, in whom I will be glorified.

4 Then I said, I have laboured in vain, I have spent my strength for nought, and in vain: yet surely my judgment is with the LORD, and my work with my God.

5 And now, saith the LORD that formed me from the womb to be his servant, to bring Jacob again to him, Though Israel be not gathered, yet shall I be glorious in the eyes of the LORD, and my God shall be my strength.

6 And he said, It is a light thing that you shouldest be my servant to raise up the tribes of Jacob, and to restore the preserved of Israel: I will also give you for a light to the Gentiles, that you mayest be my salvation unto the end of the earth.

7 Thus saith the LORD, the Redeemer of Israel, and his Holy One, to him whom man despiseth, to him whom the nation abhorreth, to a servant of rulers, Kings shall see and arise, princes also shall worship, because of the LORD that is faithful, and the Holy One of Israel, and he shall choose you.

8 Thus saith the LORD, In an acceptable time have I heard you, and in a day of salvation have I helped you: and I will preserve you, and give you for a covenant of the people, to establish the earth, to cause to inherit the desolate heritages;

9 That you mayest say to the prisoners, Go forth; to them that are in darkness, Shew yourselves. They shall feed in the ways, and their pastures shall be in all high places.

10 They shall not hunger nor thirst; neither shall the heat nor sun strike them: for he that has mercy on them shall lead them, even by the springs of water shall he guide them.

11 And I will make all my mountains a way, and my highways shall be exalted.

12 Behold, these shall come from far: and, lo, these from the north and from the west; and these from the land of Sinim.

13 Sing, O heavens; and be joyful, O earth; and break forth into singing, O mountains: for the LORD has comforted his people, and will have mercy upon his afflicted.

14 But Zion said, The LORD has forsaken me, and my Lord has forgotten me.

15 Can a woman forget her sucking child, that she should not have compassion on the son of her womb? yea, they may forget, yet will I not forget you.

16 Behold, I have graven you upon the palms of my hands; your walls are continually before me.

17 Your children shall make haste; your destroyers and they that made you waste shall go forth of you.

18 Lift up yours eyes round about, and behold: all these gather themselves together, and come to you. As I live, saith the LORD, you shalt surely clothe you with them all, as with an ornament, and bind them on you, as a bride doeth.

19 For your waste and your desolate places, and the land of your destruction, shall even now be too narrow by reason of the inhabitants, and they that swallowed you up shall be far away.

20 The children which you shalt have, after you have lost the other, shall say again in yours ears, The place is too strait for me: give place to me that I may dwell.

21 Then shalt you say in yours heart, Who has begotten me these, seeing I have lost my children, and am desolate, a captive, and removing to and fro? and who has brought up these? Behold, I was left alone; these, where had they been?

22 Thus saith the Lord GOD, Behold, I will lift up my hand to the Gentiles, and set up my standard to the people: and they shall bring your sons in their arms, and your daughters shall be carried upon their shoulders.

23 And kings shall be your nursing fathers, and their queens your nursing mothers: they shall bow down to you with their face toward the earth, and lick up the dust of your feet; and you shalt know that I am the LORD: for they shall not be ashamed that wait for me.

24 Shall the prey be taken from the mighty, or the lawful captive delivered?

25 But thus saith the LORD, Even the captives of the mighty shall be taken away, and the prey of the terrible shall be delivered: for I will contend with him that contendeth with you, and I will save your children.

26 And I will feed them that oppress you with their own flesh; and they shall be drunken with their own blood, as with sweet wine: and all flesh shall know that I the LORD am your Saviour and your Redeemer, the mighty One of Jacob.

CHAPTER 50

THUS saith the LORD, Where is the bill of your mother's divorcement, whom I have put away? or which of my creditors is it to whom I have sold you? Behold, for your iniquities have you sold yourselves, and for your transgressions is your mother put away.

2 Wherefore, when I came, was there no man? when I called, was there none to answer? Is my hand shortened at all, that it cannot redeem? or have I no power to deliver? behold, at my rebuke I dry up the sea, I make the rivers a wilderness: their fish stinketh, because there is no water, and dieth for thirst.

3 I clothe the heavens with blackness, and I make sackcloth their covering.

4 The Lord GOD has given me the tongue of the learned, that I should know how to speak a word in season to him that is weary: he wakeneth morning by morning, he wakeneth my ear to hear as the learned.

5 The Lord GOD has opened my ear, and I was not rebellious, neither turned away back.

6 I gave my back to the smiters, and my cheeks to them that plucked off the hair: I hid not my face from shame and spitting.

7 For the Lord GOD will help me; therefore shall I not be confounded: therefore have I set my face like a flint, and I know that I shall not be ashamed.

8 He is near that justifieth me; who will contend with me? let us stand together: who is my adversary? let him come near to me.

9 Behold, the Lord GOD will help me; who is he that shall condemn me? lo, they all shall wax old as a garment; the moth shall eat them up.

10 Who is among you that feareth the LORD, that obeyeth the voice of his servant, that walketh in darkness, and has no light? let him trust in the name of the LORD, and stay upon his God.

11 Behold, all you that kindle a fire, that compass yourselves about with sparks: walk in the light of your fire, and in the sparks that you have kindled. This shall you have of my hand; you shall lie down in sorrow.

CHAPTER 51

HEARKEN to me, you that follow after righteousness, you that seek the LORD: look unto the rock whence you are hewn, and to the hole of the pit whence you are digged.

2 Look unto Abraham your father, and unto Sarah that bare you: for I called him alone, and blessed him, and increased him.

3 For the LORD shall comfort Zion: he will comfort all her waste places; and he will make her wilderness like Eden, and her desert like the garden of the LORD; joy and gladness shall be found therein, thanksgiving, and the voice of melody.

4 Hearken unto me, my people; and give ear unto me, O my nation: for a law shall proceed from me, and I will make my judgment to rest for a light of the people.

5 My righteousness is near; my salvation is gone forth, and my arms shall judge the people; the isles shall wait upon me, and on my arm shall they trust.

6 Lift up your eyes to the heavens, and look upon the earth beneath: for the heavens shall vanish away like smoke, and the earth shall wax old like a garment, and they that dwell therein shall die in like manner: but my salvation shall be for ever, and my righteousness shall not be abolished.

7 Hearken unto me, you that know righteousness, the people in whose heart is my law; fear you not the reproach of men, neither be you afraid of their revilings.

8 For the moth shall eat them up like a garment, and the worm shall eat them like wool: but my righteousness shall be for ever, and my salvation from generation to generation.

9Awake, awake, put on strength, O arm of the LORD; awake, as in the ancient days, in the generations of old. Are you not it that has cut Rahab, and wounded the dragon?

10 Are you not it which has dried the sea, the waters of the great deep; that has made the depths of the sea a way for the ransomed to pass over?

11 Therefore the redeemed of the LORD shall return, and come with singing unto Zion; and everlasting joy shall be upon their head: they shall obtain gladness and joy; and sorrow and mourning shall flee away.

12 I, even I, am he that comforteth you: who are you , that you shouldest be afraid of a man that shall die, and of the son of man which shall be made as grass;

13 And forgettest the LORD your maker, that has stretched forth the heavens, and laid the foundations of the earth; and have feared continually every day because of the fury of the oppressor, as if he were ready to destroy? and where is the fury of the oppressor?

14 The captive exile hasteneth that he may be loosed, and that he should not die in the pit, nor that his bread should fail.

15 But I am the LORD your God, that divided the sea, whose waves roared: The LORD of hosts is his name.

16 And I have put my words in your mouth, and I have covered you in the shadow of my hand, that I may plant the heavens, and lay the foundations of the earth, and say unto Zion, You are my people.

17Awake, awake, stand up, O Jerusalem, which have drunk at the hand of the LORD the cup of his fury; you have drunken the dregs of the cup of trembling, and wrung them out.

18 There is none to guide her among all the sons whom she has brought forth; neither is there any that taketh her by the hand of all the sons that she has brought up.

19 These two things are come unto you; who shall be sorry for you? desolation, and destruction, and the famine, and the sword: by whom shall I comfort you?

20 Your sons have fainted, they lie at the head of all the streets, as a wild bull in a net: they are full of the fury of the LORD, the rebuke of your God.

21Therefore hear now this, you afflicted, and drunken, but not with wine:

22 Thus saith your Lord the LORD, and your God that pleadeth the cause of his people, Behold, I have taken out of yours hand the cup of trembling, even the dregs of the cup of my fury; you shalt no more drink it again:

23 But I will put it into the hand of them that afflict you; which have said to your soul, Bow down, that we may go over: and you have laid your body as the ground, and as the street, to them that went over.

CHAPTER 52

AWAKE, awake; put on your strength, O Zion; put on your beautiful garments, O Jerusalem, the holy city: for henceforth there shall no more come into you the uncircumcised and the unclean.

2 Shake yourself from the dust; arise, and sit down, O Jerusalem: loose yourself from the bands of your neck, O captive daughter of Zion.

3 For thus saith the LORD, You have sold yourselves for nought; and you shall be redeemed without money.

4 For thus saith the Lord GOD, My people went down aforetime into Egypt to sojourn there; and the Assyrian oppressed them without cause.

5 Now therefore, what have I here, saith the LORD, that my people is taken away for nought? they that rule over them make them to howl, saith the LORD; and my name continually every day is blasphemed.

6 Therefore my people shall know my name: therefore they shall know in that day that I am he that doth speak: behold, it is I.

7How beautiful upon the mountains are the feet of him that bringeth good tidings, that publisheth peace; that bringeth good tidings of good, that publisheth salvation; that saith unto Zion, Your God reigneth!

8 Your watchmen shall lift up the voice; with the voice together shall they sing: for they shall see eye to eye, when the LORD shall bring again Zion.

9Break forth into joy, sing together, you waste places of Jerusalem: for the LORD has comforted his people, he has redeemed Jerusalem.

10 The LORD has made bare his holy arm in the eyes of all the nations; and all the ends of the earth shall see the salvation of our God.

11Depart you , depart you , go you out from thence, touch no unclean thing; go you out of the midst of her; be you clean, that bear the vessels of the LORD.

12 For you shall not go out with haste, nor go by flight: for the LORD will go before you; and the God of Israel will be your rereward.

13Behold, my servant shall deal prudently, he shall be exalted and extolled, and be very high.

14 As many were astonied at you; his visage was so marred more than any man, and his form more than the sons of men:

15 So shall he sprinkle many nations; the kings shall shut their mouths at him: for that which had not been told them shall they see; and that which they had not heard shall they consider.

CHAPTER 53

WHO has believed our report? and to whom is the arm of the LORD revealed?

2 For he shall grow up before him as a tender plant, and as a root out of a dry ground: he has no form nor comeliness; and when we shall see him, there is no beauty that we should desire him.

3 He is despised and rejected of men; a man of sorrows, and acquainted with grief: and we hid as it were our faces from him; he was despised, and we esteemed him not.

4Surely he has borne our griefs, and carried our sorrows: yet we did esteem him stricken, smitten of God, and afflicted.

5 But he was wounded for our transgressions, he was bruised for our iniquities: the chastisement of our peace was upon him; and with his stripes we are healed.

6 All we like sheep have gone astray; we have turned every one to his own way; and the LORD has laid on him the iniquity of us all.

7 He was oppressed, and he was afflicted, yet he opened not his mouth: he is brought as a lamb to the slaughter, and as a sheep before her shearers is dumb, so he openeth not his mouth.

8 He was taken from prison and from judgment: and who shall declare his generation? for he was cut off out of the land of the living: for the transgression of my people was he stricken.

9 And he made his grave with the wicked, and with the rich in his death; because he had done no violence, neither was any deceit in his mouth.

10Yet it pleased the LORD to bruise him; he has put him to grief: when you shalt make his soul an offering for sin, he shall see his seed, he shall prolong his days, and the pleasure of the LORD shall prosper in his hand.

11 He shall see of the travail of his soul, and shall be satisfied: by his knowledge shall my righteous servant justify many; for he shall bear their iniquities.

12 Therefore will I divide him a portion with the great, and he shall divide the spoil with the strong; because he has poured out his soul unto death: and he was numbered with the transgressors; and he bare the sin of many, and made intercession for the transgressors.

CHAPTER 54

SING, O barren, you that did not bear; break forth into singing, and cry aloud, you that did not travail with child: for more are the children of the desolate than the children of the married wife, saith the LORD.

2 Enlarge the place of your tent, and let them stretch forth the curtains of yours habitations: spare not, lengthen your cords, and strengthen your stakes;

3 For you shalt break forth on the right hand and on the left; and your seed shall inherit the Gentiles, and make the desolate cities to be inhabited.

4 Fear not; for you shalt not be ashamed: neither be you confounded; for you shalt not be put to shame: for you shalt forget the shame of your youth, and shalt not remember the reproach of your widowhood any more.

5 For your Maker is yours husband; the LORD of hosts is his name; and your Redeemer the Holy One of Israel; The God of the whole earth shall he be called.

6 For the LORD has called you as a woman forsaken and grieved in spirit, and a wife of youth, when you wast refused, saith your God.

7 For a small moment have I forsaken you; but with great mercies will I gather you.

8 In a little wrath I hid my face from you for a moment; but with everlasting kindness will I have mercy on you, saith the LORD your Redeemer.

9 For this is as the waters of Noah unto me: for as I have sworn that the waters of Noah should no more go over the earth; so have I sworn that I would not be wroth with you, nor rebuke you.

10 For the mountains shall depart, and the hills be removed; but my kindness shall not depart from you, neither shall the covenant of my peace be removed, saith the LORD that has mercy on you.

11O you afflicted, tossed with tempest, and not comforted, behold, I will lay your stones with fair colours, and lay your foundations with sapphires.

12 And I will make your windows of agates, and your gates of carbuncles, and all your borders of pleasant stones.

13 And all your children shall be taught of the LORD; and great shall be the peace of your children.

14 In righteousness shalt you be established: you shalt be far from oppression; for you shalt not fear: and from terror; for it shall not come near you.

15 Behold, they shall surely gather together, but not by me: whosoever shall gather together against you shall fall for your sake.

16 Behold, I have created the smith that bloweth the coals in the fire, and that bringeth forth an instrument for his work; and I have created the waster to destroy.

17 No weapon that is formed against you shall prosper; and every tongue that shall rise against you in judgment you shalt condemn. This is the heritage of the servants of the LORD, and their righteousness is of me, saith the LORD.

CHAPTER 55

HO, every one that thirsteth, come you to the waters, and he that has no money; come you , buy, and eat; yea, come, buy wine and milk without money and without price.

2 Wherefore do you spend money for that which is not bread? and your labour for that which satisfieth not? hearken diligently unto me, and eat you that which is good, and let your soul delight itself in fatness.

3 Incline your ear, and come unto me: hear, and your soul shall live; and I will make an everlasting covenant with you, even the sure mercies of David.

4 Behold, I have given him for a witness to the people, a leader and commander to the people.

5 Behold, you shalt call a nation that you knowest not, and nations that knew not you shall run unto you because of the LORD your God, and for the Holy One of Israel; for he has glorified you.

6 Seek you the LORD while he may be found, call you upon him while he is near:

7 Let the wicked forsake his way, and the unrighteous man his thoughts: and let him return unto the LORD, and he will have mercy upon him; and to our God, for he will abundantly pardon.

8 For my thoughts are not your thoughts, neither are your ways my ways, saith the LORD.

9 For as the heavens are higher than the earth, so are my ways higher than your ways, and my thoughts than your thoughts.

10 For as the rain comes down, and the snow from heaven, and returneth not thither, but watereth the earth, and maketh it bring forth and bud, that it may give seed to the sower, and bread to the eater:

11 So shall my word be that goeth forth out of my mouth: it shall not return unto me void, but it shall accomplish that which I please, and it shall prosper in the thing whereto I sent it.

12 For you shall go out with joy, and be led forth with peace: the mountains and the hills shall break forth before you into singing, and all the trees of the field shall clap their hands.

13 Instead of the thorn shall come up the fir tree, and instead of the brier shall come up the myrtle tree: and it shall be to the LORD for a name, for an everlasting sign that shall not be cut off.

CHAPTER 56

THUS saith the LORD, Keep you judgment, and do justice: for my salvation is near to come, and my righteousness to be revealed.

2 Blessed is the man that doeth this, and the son of man that layeth hold on it; that keepeth the sabbath from polluting it, and keepeth his hand from doing any evil.

3 Neither let the son of the stranger, that has joined himself to the LORD, speak, saying, The LORD has utterly separated me from his people: neither let the eunuch say, Behold, I am a dry tree.

4 For thus saith the LORD unto the eunuchs that keep my sabbaths, and choose the things that please me, and take hold of my covenant;

5 Even unto them will I give in my house and within my walls a place and a name better than of sons and of daughters: I will give them an everlasting name, that shall not be cut off.

6 Also the sons of the stranger, that join themselves to the LORD, to serve him, and to love the name of the LORD, to be his servants, every one that keepeth the sabbath from polluting it, and taketh hold of my covenant;

7 Even them will I bring to my holy mountain, and make them joyful in my house of prayer: their burnt offerings and their sacrifices shall be accepted upon my altar; for my house shall be called an house of prayer for all people.

8 The Lord GOD which gathereth the outcasts of Israel saith, Yet will I gather others to him, beside those that are gathered unto him.

9 All you beasts of the field, come to devour, yea, all you beasts in the forest.

10 His watchmen are blind: they are all ignorant, they are all dumb dogs, they cannot bark; sleeping, lying down, loving to slumber.

11 Yea, they are greedy dogs which can never have enough, and they are shepherds that cannot understand: they all look to their own way, every one for his gain, from his quarter.

12 Come you , say they, I will fetch wine, and we will fill ourselves with strong drink; and to morrow shall be as this day, and much more abundant.

CHAPTER 57

THE righteous perisheth, and no man layeth it to heart: and merciful men are taken away, none considering that the righteous is taken away from the evil to come.

2 He shall enter into peace: they shall rest in their beds, each one walking in his uprightness.

3 But draw near hither, you sons of the sorceress, the seed of the adulterer and the whore.

4 Against whom do you sport yourselves? against whom make you a wide mouth, and draw out the tongue? are you not children of transgression, a seed of falsehood,

5 Enflaming yourselves with idols under every green tree, slaying the children in the valleys under the clifts of the rocks?

6 Among the smooth stones of the stream is your portion; they, they are your lot: even to them have you poured a drink offering, you have offered a meat offering. Should I receive comfort in these?

7 Upon a lofty and high mountain have you set your bed: even thither wentest you up to offer sacrifice.

8 Behind the doors also and the posts have you set up your remembrance: for you have discovered yourself to another than me, and are gone up; you have enlarged your bed, and made you a covenant with them; you lovedst their bed where you sawest it.

9 And you wentest to the king with ointment, and did increase your perfumes, and did send your messengers far off, and did debase yourself even unto hell.

10 You are wearied in the greatness of your way; yet saidst you not, There is no hope: you have found the life of yours hand; therefore you wast not grieved.

11 And of whom have you been afraid or feared, that you have lied, and have not remembered me, nor laid it to your heart? have not I held my peace even of old, and you fearest me not?

12 I will declare your righteousness, and your works; for they shall not profit you.

13 When you criest, let your companies deliver you; but the wind shall carry them all away; vanity shall take them: but he that putteth his trust in me shall possess the land, and shall inherit my holy mountain;

14 And shall say, Cast you up, cast you up, prepare the way, take up the stumblingblock out of the way of my people.

15 For thus saith the high and lofty One that inhabiteth eternity, whose name is Holy; I dwell in the high and holy place, with him also that is of a contrite and humble spirit, to revive the spirit of the humble, and to revive the heart of the contrite ones.

16 For I will not contend for ever, neither will I be always wroth: for the spirit should fail before me, and the souls which I have made.

17 For the iniquity of his covetousness was I wroth, and struck him: I hid me, and was wroth, and he went on frowardly in the way of his heart.

18 I have seen his ways, and will heal him: I will lead him also, and restore comforts unto him and to his mourners.

19 I create the fruit of the lips; Peace, peace to him that is far off, and to him that is near, saith the LORD; and I will heal him.

20 But the wicked are like the troubled sea, when it cannot rest, whose waters cast up mire and dirt.

21 There is no peace, saith my God, to the wicked.

CHAPTER 58

CRY aloud, spare not, lift up your voice like a trumpet, and shew my people their transgression, and the house of Jacob their sins.

2 Yet they seek me daily, and delight to know my ways, as a nation that did righteousness, and forsook not the ordinance of their God: they ask of me the ordinances of justice; they take delight in approaching to God.

3 Wherefore have we fasted, say they, and you seest not? wherefore have we afflicted our soul, and you takest no knowledge? Behold, in the day of your fast you find pleasure, and exact all your labours.

4 Behold, you fast for strife and debate, and to strike with the fist of wickedness: you shall not fast as you do this day, to make your voice to be heard on high.

5 Is it such a fast that I have chosen? a day for a man to afflict his soul? is it to bow down his head as a bulrush, and to spread sackcloth and ashes under him? will you call this a fast, and an acceptable day to the LORD?

6 Is not this the fast that I have chosen? to loose the bands of wickedness, to undo the heavy burdens, and to let the oppressed go free, and that you break every yoke?

7 Is it not to deal your bread to the hungry, and that you bring the poor that are cast out to your house? when you seest the naked, that you cover him; and that you hide not yourself from yours own flesh?

8 Then shall your light break forth as the morning, and yours health shall spring forth speedily: and your righteousness shall go before you; the glory of the LORD shall be your rereward.

9 Then shalt you call, and the LORD shall answer; you shalt cry, and he shall say, Here I am. If you take away from the midst of you the yoke, the putting forth of the finger, and speaking vanity;

10 And if you draw out your soul to the hungry, and satisfy the afflicted soul; then shall your light rise in obscurity, and your darkness be as the noonday:

11 And the LORD shall guide you continually, and satisfy your soul in drought, and make fat your bones: and you shalt be like a watered garden, and like a spring of water, whose waters fail not.

12 And they that shall be of you shall build the old waste places: you shalt raise up the foundations of many generations; and you shalt be called, The repairer of the breach, The restorer of paths to dwell in.

13 If you turn away your foot from the sabbath, from doing your pleasure on my holy day; and call the sabbath a delight, the holy of the LORD, honourable; and shalt honour him, not doing yours own ways, nor finding yours own pleasure, nor speaking yours own words:

14 Then shalt you delight yourself in the LORD; and I will cause you to ride upon the high places of the earth, and feed you with the heritage of Jacob your father: for the mouth of the LORD has spoken it.

CHAPTER 59

BEHOLD, the LORD's hand is not shortened, that it cannot save; neither his ear heavy, that it cannot hear:

2 But your iniquities have separated between you and your God, and your sins have hid his face from you, that he will not hear.

3 For your hands are defiled with blood, and your fingers with iniquity; your lips have spoken lies, your tongue has muttered perverseness.

4 None calleth for justice, nor any pleadeth for truth: they trust in vanity, and speak lies; they conceive mischief, and bring forth iniquity.

5 They hatch cockatrice' eggs, and weave the spider's web: he that eateth of their eggs dieth, and that which is crushed breaketh out into a viper.

6 Their webs shall not become garments, neither shall they cover themselves with their works: their works are works of iniquity, and the act of violence is in their hands.

7 Their feet run to evil, and they make haste to shed innocent blood: their thoughts are thoughts of iniquity; wasting and destruction are in their paths.

8 The way of peace they know not; and there is no judgment in their goings: they have made them crooked paths: whosoever goeth therein shall not know peace.

9 Therefore is judgment far from us, neither doth justice overtake us: we wait for light, but behold obscurity; for brightness, but we walk in darkness.

10 We grope for the wall like the blind, and we grope as if we had no eyes: we stumble at noonday as in the night; we are in desolate places as dead men.

11 We roar all like bears, and mourn sore like doves: we look for judgment, but there is none; for salvation, but it is far off from us.

12 For our transgressions are multiplied before you, and our sins testify against us: for our transgressions are with us; and as for our iniquities, we know them;

13 In transgressing and lying against the LORD, and departing away from our God, speaking oppression and revolt, conceiving and uttering from the heart words of falsehood.

14 And judgment is turned away backward, and justice standeth afar off: for truth is fallen in the street, and equity cannot enter.

15 Yea, truth faileth; and he that departeth from evil maketh himself a prey: and the LORD saw it, and it displeased him that there was no judgment.

16 And he saw that there was no man, and wondered that there was no intercessor: therefore his arm brought salvation unto him; and his righteousness, it sustained him.

17 For he put on righteousness as a breastplate, and an helmet of salvation upon his head; and he put on the garments of vengeance for clothing, and was clad with zeal as a cloke.

18 According to their deeds, accordingly he will repay, fury to his adversaries, recompence to his enemies; to the islands he will repay recompence.

19 So shall they fear the name of the LORD from the west, and his glory from the rising of the sun. When the enemy shall come in like a flood, the Spirit of the LORD shall lift up a standard against him.

20 And the Redeemer shall come to Zion, and unto them that turn from transgression in Jacob, saith the LORD.

21 As for me, this is my covenant with them, saith the LORD; My spirit that is upon you, and my words which I have put in your mouth, shall not depart out of your mouth, nor out of the mouth of your seed, nor out of the mouth of your seed's seed, saith the LORD, from henceforth and for ever.

CHAPTER 60

ARISE, shine; for your light is come, and the glory of the LORD is risen upon you.

2 For, behold, the darkness shall cover the earth, and gross darkness the people: but the LORD shall arise upon you, and his glory shall be seen upon you.

3 And the Gentiles shall come to your light, and kings to the brightness of your rising.

4 Lift up yours eyes round about, and see: all they gather themselves together, they come to you: your sons shall come from far, and your daughters shall be nursed at your side.

5 Then you shalt see, and flow together, and yours heart shall fear, and be enlarged; because the abundance of the sea shall be converted unto you, the forces of the Gentiles shall come unto you.

6 The multitude of camels shall cover you, the dromedaries of Midian and Ephah; all they from Sheba shall come: they shall bring gold and incense; and they shall shew forth the praises of the LORD.

7 All the flocks of Kedar shall be gathered together unto you, the rams of Nebaioth shall minister unto you: they shall come up with acceptance on my altar, and I will glorify the house of my glory.

8 Who are these that fly as a cloud, and as the doves to their windows?

9 Surely the isles shall wait for me, and the ships of Tarshish first, to bring your sons from far, their silver and their gold with them, unto the name of the LORD your God, and to the Holy One of Israel, because he has glorified you.

10 And the sons of strangers shall build up your walls, and their kings shall minister unto you: for in my wrath I struck you, but in my favour have I had mercy on you.

11 Therefore your gates shall be open continually; they shall not be shut day nor night; that men may bring unto you the forces of the Gentiles, and that their kings may be brought.

12 For the nation and kingdom that will not serve you shall perish; yea, those nations shall be utterly wasted.

13 The glory of Lebanon shall come unto you, the fir tree, the pine tree, and the box together, to beautify the place of my sanctuary; and I will make the place of my feet glorious.

14 The sons also of them that afflicted you shall come bending unto you; and all they that despised you shall bow themselves down at the soles of your feet; and they shall call you, The city of the LORD, The Zion of the Holy One of Israel.

15 Whereas you have been forsaken and hated, so that no man went through you, I will make you an eternal excellency, a joy of many generations.

16 You shalt also suck the milk of the Gentiles, and shalt suck the breast of kings: and you shalt know that I the LORD am your Saviour and your Redeemer, the mighty One of Jacob.

17 For brass I will bring gold, and for iron I will bring silver, and for wood brass, and for stones iron: I will also make your officers peace, and yours exactors righteousness.

18 Violence shall no more be heard in your land, wasting nor destruction within your borders; but you shalt call your walls Salvation, and your gates Praise.

19 The sun shall be no more your light by day; neither for brightness shall the moon give light unto you: but the LORD shall be unto you an everlasting light, and your God your glory.

20 Your sun shall no more go down; neither shall your moon withdraw itself: for the LORD shall be yours everlasting light, and the days of your mourning shall be ended.

21 Your people also shall be all righteous: they shall inherit the land for ever, the branch of my planting, the work of my hands, that I may be glorified.

22 A little one shall become a thousand, and a small one a strong nation: I the LORD will hasten it in his time.

CHAPTER 61

THE Spirit of the Lord GOD is upon me; because the LORD has anointed me to preach good tidings unto the meek; he has sent me to bind up the brokenhearted, to proclaim liberty to the captives, and the opening of the prison to them that are bound;

2 To proclaim the acceptable year of the LORD, and the day of vengeance of our God; to comfort all that mourn;

3 To appoint unto them that mourn in Zion, to give unto them beauty for ashes, the oil of joy for mourning, the garment of praise for the spirit of heaviness; that they might be called trees of righteousness, the planting of the LORD, that he might be glorified.

4 And they shall build the old wastes, they shall raise up the former desolations, and they shall repair the waste cities, the desolations of many generations.

5 And strangers shall stand and feed your flocks, and the sons of the alien shall be your plowmen and your vinedressers.

6 But you shall be named the Priests of the LORD: men shall call you the Ministers of our God: you shall eat the riches of the Gentiles, and in their glory shall you boast yourselves.

7 For your shame you shall have double; and for confusion they shall rejoice in their portion: therefore in their land they shall possess the double: everlasting joy shall be unto them.

8 For I the LORD love judgment, I hate robbery for burnt offering; and I will direct their work in truth, and I will make an everlasting covenant with them.

9 And their seed shall be known among the Gentiles, and their offspring among the people: all that see them shall acknowledge them, that they are the seed which the LORD has blessed.

10 I will greatly rejoice in the LORD, my soul shall be joyful in my God; for he has clothed me with the garments of salvation, he has covered me with the robe of righteousness, as a bridegroom decketh himself with ornaments, and as a bride adorneth herself with her jewels.

11 For as the earth bringeth forth her bud, and as the garden causeth the things that are sown in it to spring forth; so the Lord GOD will cause righteousness and praise to spring forth before all the nations.

CHAPTER 62

FOR Zion's sake will I not hold my peace, and for Jerusalem's sake I will not rest, until the righteousness thereof go forth as brightness, and the salvation thereof as a lamp that burneth.

2 And the Gentiles shall see your righteousness, and all kings your glory: and you shalt be called by a new name, which the mouth of the LORD shall name.

3 You shalt also be a crown of glory in the hand of the LORD, and a royal diadem in the hand of your God.

4 You shalt no more be termed Forsaken; neither shall your land any more be termed Desolate: but you shalt be called Hephzi-bah, and your land Beulah: for the LORD delighteth in you, and your land shall be married.

5 For as a young man marrieth a virgin, so shall your sons marry you: and as the bridegroom rejoiceth over the bride, so shall your God rejoice over you.

6 I have set watchmen upon your walls, O Jerusalem, which shall never hold their peace day nor night: you that make mention of the LORD, keep not silence,

7 And give him no rest, till he establish, and till he make Jerusalem a praise in the earth.

8 The LORD has sworn by his right hand, and by the arm of his strength, Surely I will no more give your corn to be meat for yours enemies; and the sons of the stranger shall not drink your wine, for the which you have laboured:

9 But they that have gathered it shall eat it, and praise the LORD; and they that have brought it together shall drink it in the courts of my holiness.

10 Go through, go through the gates; prepare you the way of the people; cast up, cast up the highway; gather out the stones; lift up a standard for the people.

11 Behold, the LORD has proclaimed unto the end of the world, Say you to the daughter of Zion, Behold, your salvation comes; behold, his reward is with him, and his work before him.

12 And they shall call them, The holy people, The redeemed of the LORD: and you shalt be called, Sought out, A city not forsaken.

CHAPTER 63

WHO is this that comes from Edom, with dyed garments from Bozrah? this that is glorious in his apparel, travelling in the greatness of his strength? I that speak in righteousness, mighty to save.

2 Wherefore are you red in yours apparel, and your garments like him that treadeth in the winefat?

3 I have trodden the winepress alone; and of the people there was none with me: for I will tread them in my anger, and trample them in my fury; and their blood shall be sprinkled upon my garments, and I will stain all my raiment.

4 For the day of vengeance is in my heart, and the year of my redeemed is come.

5 And I looked, and there was none to help; and I wondered that there was none to uphold: therefore my own arm brought salvation unto me; and my fury, it upheld me.

6 And I will tread down the people in my anger, and make them drunk in my fury, and I will bring down their strength to the earth.

7 I will mention the lovingkindnesses of the LORD, and the praises of the LORD, according to all that the LORD has bestowed on us, and the great goodness toward the house of Israel, which he has bestowed on them according to his mercies, and according to the multitude of his lovingkindnesses.

8 For he said, Surely they are my people, children that will not lie: so he was their Saviour.

9 In all their affliction he was afflicted, and the angel of his presence saved them: in his love and in his pity he redeemed them; and he bare them, and carried them all the days of old.

10 But they rebelled, and vexed his holy Spirit: therefore he was turned to be their enemy, and he fought against them.

11 Then he remembered the days of old, Moses, and his people, saying, Where is he that brought them up out of the sea with the shepherd of his flock? where is he that put his holy Spirit within him?

12 That led them by the right hand of Moses with his glorious arm, dividing the water before them, to make himself an everlasting name?

13 That led them through the deep, as an horse in the wilderness, that they should not stumble?

14 As a beast goeth down into the valley, the Spirit of the LORD caused him to rest: so did you lead your people, to make yourself a glorious name.

15 Look down from heaven, and behold from the habitation of your holiness and of your glory: where is your zeal and your strength, the sounding of your bowels and of your mercies toward me? are they restrained?

16 Doubtless you are our father, though Abraham be ignorant of us, and Israel acknowledge us not: you , O LORD, are our father, our redeemer; your name is from everlasting.

17 O LORD, why have you made us to err from your ways, and hardened our heart from your fear? Return for your servants' sake, the tribes of yours inheritance.

18 The people of your holiness have possessed it but a little while: our adversaries have trodden down your sanctuary.

19 We are yours: you never barest rule over them; they were not called by your name.

CHAPTER 64

OH that you wouldest rend the heavens, that you wouldest come down, that the mountains might flow down at your presence,

2 As when the melting fire burneth, the fire causeth the waters to boil, to make your name known to yours adversaries, that the nations may tremble at your presence!

3 When you did terrible things which we looked not for, you camest down, the mountains flowed down at your presence.

4 For since the beginning of the world men have not heard, nor perceived by the ear, neither has the eye seen, O God, beside you, what he has prepared for him that waiteth for him.

5 You meetest him that rejoiceth and worketh righteousness, those that remember you in your ways: behold, you are wroth; for we have sinned: in those is continuance, and we shall be saved.

6 But we are all as an unclean thing, and all our righteousnesses are as filthy rags; and we all do fade as a leaf; and our iniquities, like the wind, have taken us away.

7 And there is none that calleth upon your name, that stirreth up himself to take hold of you: for you have hid your face from us, and have consumed us, because of our iniquities.

8 But now, O LORD, you are our father; we are the clay, and you our potter; and we all are the work of your hand.

9 Be not wroth very sore, O LORD, neither remember iniquity for ever: behold, see, we beseech you, we are all your people.

10 Your holy cities are a wilderness, Zion is a wilderness, Jerusalem a desolation.

11 Our holy and our beautiful house, where our fathers praised you, is burned up with fire: and all our pleasant things are laid waste.

12 Will you refrain yourself for these things, O LORD? will you hold your peace, and afflict us very sore?

CHAPTER 65

I AM sought of them that asked not for me; I am found of them that sought me not: I said, Behold me, behold me, unto a nation that was not called by my name.

2 I have spread out my hands all the day unto a rebellious people, which walketh in a way that was not good, after their own thoughts;

3 A people that provoketh me to anger continually to my face; that sacrificeth in gardens, and burneth incense upon altars of brick;

4 Which remain among the graves, and lodge in the monuments, which eat swine's flesh, and broth of abominable things is in their vessels;

5 Which say, Stand by yourself, come not near to me; for I am holier than you . These are a smoke in my nose, a fire that burneth all the day.

6 Behold, it is written before me: I will not keep silence, but will recompense, even recompense into their bosom,

7 Your iniquities, and the iniquities of your fathers together, saith the LORD, which have burned incense upon the mountains, and blasphemed me upon the hills: therefore will I measure their former work into their bosom.

8 Thus saith the LORD, As the new wine is found in the cluster, and one saith, Destroy it not; for a blessing is in it: so will I do for my servants' sakes, that I may not destroy them all.

9 And I will bring forth a seed out of Jacob, and out of Judah an inheritor of my mountains: and my elect shall inherit it, and my servants shall dwell there.

10 And Sharon shall be a fold of flocks, and the valley of Achor a place for the herds to lie down in, for my people that have sought me.

11But you are they that forsake the LORD, that forget my holy mountain, that prepare a table for that troop, and that furnish the drink offering unto that number.

12 Therefore will I number you to the sword, and you shall all bow down to the slaughter: because when I called, you did not answer; when I spake, you did not hear; but did evil before my eyes, and did choose that wherein I delighted not.

13 Therefore thus saith the Lord GOD, Behold, my servants shall eat, but you shall be hungry: behold, my servants shall drink, but you shall be thirsty: behold, my servants shall rejoice, but you shall be ashamed:

14 Behold, my servants shall sing for joy of heart, but you shall cry for sorrow of heart, and shall howl for vexation of spirit.

15 And you shall leave your name for a curse unto my chosen: for the Lord GOD shall slay you, and call his servants by another name:

16 That he who blesseth himself in the earth shall bless himself in the God of truth; and he that sweareth in the earth shall swear by the God of truth; because the former troubles are forgotten, and because they are hid from my eyes.

17For, behold, I create new heavens and a new earth: and the former shall not be remembered, nor come into mind.

18 But be you glad and rejoice for ever in that which I create: for, behold, I create Jerusalem a rejoicing, and her people a joy.

19 And I will rejoice in Jerusalem, and joy in my people: and the voice of weeping shall be no more heard in her, nor the voice of crying.

20 There shall be no more thence an infant of days, nor an old man that has not filled his days: for the child shall die an hundred years old; but the sinner being an hundred years old shall be accursed.

21 And they shall build houses, and inhabit them; and they shall plant vineyards, and eat the fruit of them.

22 They shall not build, and another inhabit; they shall not plant, and another eat: for as the days of a tree are the days of my people, and my elect shall long enjoy the work of their hands.

23 They shall not labour in vain, nor bring forth for trouble; for they are the seed of the blessed of the LORD, and their offspring with them.

24 And it shall come to pass, that before they call, I will answer; and while they are yet speaking, I will hear.

25 The wolf and the lamb shall feed together, and the lion shall eat straw like the bullock: and dust shall be the serpent's meat. They shall not hurt nor destroy in all my holy mountain, saith the LORD.

CHAPTER 66

THUS saith the LORD, The heaven is my throne, and the earth is my footstool: where is the house that you build unto me? and where is the place of my rest?

2 For all those things has my hand made, and all those things have been, saith the LORD: but to this man will I look, even to him that is poor and of a contrite spirit, and trembleth at my word.

3 He that killeth an ox is as if he slew a man; he that sacrificeth a lamb, as if he cut off a dog's neck; he that offereth an oblation, as if he offered swine's blood; he that burneth incense, as if he blessed an idol. Yea, they have chosen their own ways, and their soul delighteth in their abominations.

4 I also will choose their delusions, and will bring their fears upon them; because when I called, none did answer; when I spake, they did not hear: but they did evil before my eyes, and chose that in which I delighted not.

5Hear the word of the LORD, you that tremble at his word; Your brethren that hated you, that cast you out for my name's sake, said, Let the LORD be glorified: but he shall appear to your joy, and they shall be ashamed.

6 A voice of noise from the city, a voice from the temple, a voice of the LORD that rendereth recompence to his enemies.

7 Before she travailed, she brought forth; before her pain came, she was delivered of a man child.

8 Who has heard such a thing? who has seen such things? Shall the earth be made to bring forth in one day? or shall a nation be born at once? for as soon as Zion travailed, she brought forth her children.

9 Shall I bring to the birth, and not cause to bring forth? saith the LORD: shall I cause to bring forth, and shut the womb? saith your God.

10 Rejoice you with Jerusalem, and be glad with her, all you that love her: rejoice for joy with her, all you that mourn for her:

11 That you may suck, and be satisfied with the breasts of her consolations; that you may milk out, and be delighted with the abundance of her glory.

12 For thus saith the LORD, Behold, I will extend peace to her like a river, and the glory of the Gentiles like a flowing stream: then shall you suck, you shall be borne upon her sides, and be dandled upon her knees.

13 As one whom his mother comforteth, so will I comfort you; and you shall be comforted in Jerusalem.

14 And when you see this, your heart shall rejoice, and your bones shall flourish like an herb: and the hand of the LORD shall be known toward his servants, and his indignation toward his enemies.

15 For, behold, the LORD will come with fire, and with his chariots like a whirlwind, to render his anger with fury, and his rebuke with flames of fire.

16 For by fire and by his sword will the LORD plead with all flesh: and the slain of the LORD shall be many.

17 They that sanctify themselves, and purify themselves in the gardens behind one tree in the midst, eating swine's flesh, and the abomination, and the mouse, shall be consumed together, saith the LORD.

18 For I know their works and their thoughts: it shall come, that I will gather all nations and tongues; and they shall come, and see my glory.

19 And I will set a sign among them, and I will send those that escape of them unto the nations, to Tarshish, Pul, and Lud, that draw the bow, to Tubal, and Javan, to the isles afar off, that have not heard my fame, neither have seen my glory; and they shall declare my glory among the Gentiles.

20 And they shall bring all your brethren for an offering unto the LORD out of all nations upon horses, and in chariots, and in litters, and upon mules, and upon swift beasts, to my holy mountain Jerusalem, saith the LORD, as the children of Israel bring an offering in a clean vessel into the house of the LORD.

21 And I will also take of them for priests and for Levites, saith the LORD.

22 For as the new heavens and the new earth, which I will make, shall remain before me, saith the LORD, so shall your seed and your name remain.

23 And it shall come to pass, that from one new moon to another, and from one sabbath to another, shall all flesh come to worship before me, saith the LORD.

24 And they shall go forth, and look upon the carcases of the men that have transgressed against me: for their worm shall not die, neither shall their fire be quenched; and they shall be an abhorring unto all flesh.

THE BOOK OF THE PROPHET JEREMIAH.

CHAPTER 1

THE words of Jeremiah the son of Hilkiah, of the priests that were in Anathoth in the land of Benjamin:

2 To whom the word of the LORD came in the days of Josiah the son of Amon king of Judah, in the thirteenth year of his reign.

3 It came also in the days of Jehoiakim the son of Josiah king of Judah, unto the end of the eleventh year of Zedekiah the son of Josiah king of Judah, unto the carrying away of Jerusalem captive in the fifth month.

4 Then the word of the LORD came unto me, saying,

5 Before I formed you in the belly I knew you; and before you camest forth out of the womb I sanctified you, and I ordained you a prophet unto the nations.

6 Then said I, Ah, Lord GOD! behold, I cannot speak: for I am a child.

7 But the LORD said unto me, Say not, I am a child: for you shalt go to all that I shall send you, and whatsoever I command you you shalt speak.

8 Be not afraid of their faces: for I am with you to deliver you, saith the LORD.

9 Then the LORD put forth his hand, and touched my mouth. And the LORD said unto me, Behold, I have put my words in your mouth.

10 See, I have this day set you over the nations and over the kingdoms, to root out, and to pull down, and to destroy, and to throw down, to build, and to plant.

11 Moreover the word of the LORD came unto me, saying, Jeremiah, what seest you ? And I said, I see a rod of an almond tree.

12 Then said the LORD unto me, You have well seen: for I will hasten my word to perform it.

13 And the word of the LORD came unto me the second time, saying, What seest you ? And I said, I see a seething pot; and the face thereof is toward the north.

14 Then the LORD said unto me, Out of the north an evil shall break forth upon all the inhabitants of the land.

15 For, lo, I will call all the families of the kingdoms of the north, saith the LORD; and they shall come, and they shall set every one his throne at the entering of the gates of Jerusalem, and against all the walls thereof round about, and against all the cities of Judah.

16 And I will utter my judgments against them touching all their wickedness, who have forsaken me, and have burned incense unto other gods, and worshipped the works of their own hands.

17 You therefore gird up your loins, and arise, and speak unto them all that I command you: be not dismayed at their faces, lest I confound you before them.

18 For, behold, I have made you this day a defenced city, and an iron pillar, and brasen walls against the whole land, against the kings of Judah, against the princes thereof, against the priests thereof, and against the people of the land.

19 And they shall fight against you; but they shall not prevail against you; for I am with you, saith the LORD, to deliver you.

CHAPTER 2

MOREOVER the word of the LORD came to me, saying,

2 Go and cry in the ears of Jerusalem, saying, Thus saith the LORD; I remember you, the kindness of your youth, the love of yours espousals, when you wentest after me in the wilderness, in a land that was not sown.

3 Israel was holiness unto the LORD, and the firstfruits of his increase: all that devour him shall offend; evil shall come upon them, saith the LORD.

4 Hear you the word of the LORD, O house of Jacob, and all the families of the house of Israel:

5 Thus saith the LORD, What iniquity have your fathers found in me, that they are gone far from me, and have walked after vanity, and are become vain?

6 Neither said they, Where is the LORD that brought us up out of the land of Egypt, that led us through the wilderness, through a land of deserts and of pits, through a land of drought, and of the shadow of death, through a land that no man passed through, and where no man dwelt?

7 And I brought you into a plentiful country, to eat the fruit thereof and the goodness thereof; but when you entered, you defiled my land, and made my heritage an abomination.

8 The priests said not, Where is the LORD? and they that handle the law knew me not: the pastors also transgressed against me, and the prophets prophesied by Baal, and walked after things that do not profit.

9 Wherefore I will yet plead with you, saith the LORD, and with your children's children will I plead.

10 For pass over the isles of Chittim, and see; and send unto Kedar, and consider diligently, and see if there be such a thing.

11 Has a nation changed their gods, which are yet no gods? but my people have changed their glory for that which doth not profit.

12 Be astonished, O you heavens, at this, and be horribly afraid, be you very desolate, saith the LORD.

13 For my people have committed two evils; they have forsaken me the fountain of living waters, and hewed them out cisterns, broken cisterns, that can hold no water.

14 Is Israel a servant? is he a homeborn slave? why is he spoiled?

15 The young lions roared upon him, and yelled, and they made his land waste: his cities are burned without inhabitant.

16 Also the children of Noph and Tahapanes have broken the crown of your head.

17 Have you not procured this unto yourself, in that you have forsaken the LORD your God, when he led you by the way?

18 And now what have you to do in the way of Egypt, to drink the waters of Sihor? or what have you to do in the way of Assyria, to drink the waters of the river?

19 Yours own wickedness shall correct you, and your backslidings shall reprove you: know therefore and see that it is an evil thing and bitter, that you have forsaken the LORD your God, and that my fear is not in you, saith the Lord GOD of hosts.

20 For of old time I have broken your yoke, and burst your bands; and you saidst, I will not transgress; when upon every high hill and under every green tree you wanderest, playing the harlot.

21 Yet I had planted you a noble vine, wholly a right seed: how then are you turned into the degenerate plant of a strange vine unto me?

22 For though you wash you with nitre, and take you much soap, yet yours iniquity is marked before me, saith the Lord GOD.

23 How can you say, I am not polluted, I have not gone after Baalim? see your way in the valley, know what you have done: you are a swift dromedary traversing her ways;

24 A wild ass used to the wilderness, that snuffeth up the wind at her pleasure; in her occasion who can turn her away? all they that seek her will not weary themselves; in her month they shall find her.

25 Withhold your foot from being unshod, and your throat from thirst: but you saidst, There is no hope: no; for I have loved strangers, and after them will I go.

26 As the thief is ashamed when he is found, so is the house of Israel ashamed; they, their kings, their princes, and their priests, and their prophets,

27 Saying to a stock, You are my father; and to a stone, You have brought me forth: for they have turned their back unto me, and not their face: but in the time of their trouble they will say, Arise, and save us.

28 But where are your gods that you have made you? let them arise, if they can save you in the time of your trouble: for according to the number of your cities are your gods, O Judah.

29 Wherefore will you plead with me? you all have transgressed against me, saith the LORD.

30 In vain have I smitten your children; they received no correction: your own sword has devoured your prophets, like a destroying lion.

31 O generation, see you the word of the LORD. Have I been a wilderness unto Israel? a land of darkness? wherefore say my people, We are lords; we will come no more unto you?

32 Can a maid forget her ornaments, or a bride her attire? yet my people have forgotten me days without number.

33 Why trimmest you your way to seek love? therefore have you also taught the wicked ones your ways.

34 Also in your skirts is found the blood of the souls of the poor innocents: I have not found it by secret search, but upon all these.

35 Yet you say, Because I am innocent, surely his anger shall turn from me. Behold, I will plead with you, because you say, I have not sinned.

36 Why gaddest you about so much to change your way? you also shalt be ashamed of Egypt, as you wast ashamed of Assyria.

37 Yea, you shalt go forth from him, and yours hands upon yours head: for the LORD has rejected your confidences, and you shalt not prosper in them.

CHAPTER 3

THEY say, If a man put away his wife, and she go from him, and become another man's, shall he return unto her again? shall not that land be greatly polluted? but you have played the harlot with many lovers; yet return again to me, saith the LORD.

2 Lift up yours eyes unto the high places, and see where you have not been lien with. In the ways have you sat for them, as the Arabian in the wilderness; and you have polluted the land with your whoredoms and with your wickedness.

3 Therefore the showers have been withholden, and there has been no latter rain; and you hadst a whore's forehead, you refusedst to be ashamed.

4 Will you not from this time cry unto me, My father, you are the guide of my youth?

5 Will he reserve his anger for ever? will he keep it to the end? Behold, you have spoken and done evil things as you couldest.

6 The LORD said also unto me in the days of Josiah the king, Have you seen that which backsliding Israel has done? she is gone up upon every high mountain and under every green tree, and there has played the harlot.

7 And I said after she had done all these things, Turn you unto me. But she returned not. And her treacherous sister Judah saw it.

8 And I saw, when for all the causes whereby backsliding Israel committed adultery I had put her away, and given her a bill of divorce; yet her treacherous sister Judah feared not, but went and played the harlot also.

9 And it came to pass through the lightness of her whoredom, that she defiled the land, and committed adultery with stones and with stocks.

10 And yet for all this her treacherous sister Judah has not turned unto me with her whole heart, but feignedly, saith the LORD.

11 And the LORD said unto me, The backsliding Israel has justified herself more than treacherous Judah.

12 Go and proclaim these words toward the north, and say, Return, you backsliding Israel, saith the LORD; and I will not cause my anger to fall upon you: for I am merciful, saith the LORD, and I will not keep anger for ever.

13 Only acknowledge yours iniquity, that you have transgressed against the LORD your God, and have scattered your ways to the strangers under every green tree, and you have not obeyed my voice, saith the LORD.

14 Turn, O backsliding children, saith the LORD; for I am married unto you: and I will take you one of a city, and two of a family, and I will bring you to Zion:

15 And I will give you pastors according to my heart, which shall feed you with knowledge and understanding.

16 And it shall come to pass, when you be multiplied and increased in the land, in those days, saith the LORD, they shall say no more, The ark of the covenant of the LORD: neither shall it come to mind: neither shall they remember it; neither shall they visit it; neither shall that be done any more.

17 At that time they shall call Jerusalem the throne of the LORD; and all the nations shall be gathered unto it, to the name of the LORD, to Jerusalem: neither shall they walk any more after the imagination of their evil heart.

18 In those days the house of Judah shall walk with the house of Israel, and they shall come together out of the land of the north to the land that I have given for an inheritance unto your fathers.

19 But I said, How shall I put you among the children, and give you a pleasant land, a goodly heritage of the hosts of nations? and I said, You shalt call me, My father; and shalt not turn away from me.

20 Surely as a wife treacherously departeth from her husband, so have you dealt treacherously with me, O house of Israel, saith the LORD.

21 A voice was heard upon the high places, weeping and supplications of the children of Israel: for they have perverted their way, and they have forgotten the LORD their God.

22 Return, you backsliding children, and I will heal your backslidings. Behold, we come unto you; for you are the LORD our God.

23 Truly in vain is salvation hoped for from the hills, and from the multitude of mountains: truly in the LORD our God is the salvation of Israel.

24 For shame has devoured the labour of our fathers from our youth; their flocks and their herds, their sons and their daughters.

25 We lie down in our shame, and our confusion covers us: for we have sinned against the LORD our God, we and our fathers, from our youth even unto this day, and have not obeyed the voice of the LORD our God.

CHAPTER 4

IF you will return, O Israel, saith the LORD, return unto me: and if you will put away yours abominations out of my sight, then shalt you not remove.

2 And you shalt swear, The LORD liveth, in truth, in judgment, and in righteousness; and the nations shall bless themselves in him, and in him shall they glory.

3 For thus saith the LORD to the men of Judah and Jerusalem, Break up your fallow ground, and sow not among thorns.

4 Circumcise yourselves to the LORD, and take away the foreskins of your heart, you men of Judah and inhabitants of Jerusalem: lest my fury come forth like fire, and burn that none can quench it, because of the evil of your doings.

5 Declare you in Judah, and publish in Jerusalem; and say, Blow you the trumpet in the land: cry, gather together, and say, Assemble yourselves, and let us go into the defenced cities.

6 Set up the standard toward Zion: retire, stay not: for I will bring evil from the north, and a great destruction.

7 The lion is come up from his thicket, and the destroyer of the Gentiles is on his way; he is gone forth from his place to make your land desolate; and your cities shall be laid waste, without an inhabitant.

8 For this gird you with sackcloth, lament and howl: for the fierce anger of the LORD is not turned back from us.

9 And it shall come to pass at that day, saith the LORD, that the heart of the king shall perish, and the heart of the princes; and the priests shall be astonished, and the prophets shall wonder.

10 Then said I, Ah, Lord GOD! surely you have greatly deceived this people and Jerusalem, saying, You shall have peace; whereas the sword reacheth unto the soul.

11 At that time shall it be said to this people and to Jerusalem, A dry wind of the high places in the wilderness toward the daughter of my people, not to fan, nor to cleanse,

12 Even a full wind from those places shall come unto me: now also will I give sentence against them.

13 Behold, he shall come up as clouds, and his chariots shall be as a whirlwind: his horses are swifter than eagles. Woe unto us! for we are spoiled.

14 O Jerusalem, wash yours heart from wickedness, that you mayest be saved. How long shall your vain thoughts lodge within you?

15 For a voice declareth from Dan, and publisheth affliction from mount Ephraim.

16 Make you mention to the nations; behold, publish against Jerusalem, that watchers come from a far country, and give out their voice against the cities of Judah.

17 As keepers of a field, are they against her round about; because she has been rebellious against me, saith the LORD.

18 Your way and your doings have procured these things unto you; this is your wickedness, because it is bitter, because it reacheth unto yours heart.

19 My bowels, my bowels! I am pained at my very heart; my heart maketh a noise in me; I cannot hold my peace, because you have heard, O my soul, the sound of the trumpet, the alarm of war.

20 Destruction upon destruction is cried; for the whole land is spoiled: suddenly are my tents spoiled, and my curtains in a moment.

21 How long shall I see the standard, and hear the sound of the trumpet?

22 For my people is foolish, they have not known me; they are sottish children, and they have none understanding: they are wise to do evil, but to do good they have no knowledge.

23 I beheld the earth, and, lo, it was without form, and void; and the heavens, and they had no light.

24 I beheld the mountains, and, lo, they trembled, and all the hills moved lightly.

25 I beheld, and, lo, there was no man, and all the birds of the heavens were fled.

26 I beheld, and, lo, the fruitful place was a wilderness, and all the cities thereof were broken down at the presence of the LORD, and by his fierce anger.

27 For thus has the LORD said, The whole land shall be desolate; yet will I not make a full end.

28 For this shall the earth mourn, and the heavens above be black: because I have spoken it, I have purposed it, and will not repent, neither will I turn back from it.

29 The whole city shall flee for the noise of the horsemen and bowmen; they shall go into thickets, and climb up upon the rocks: every city shall be forsaken, and not a man dwell therein.

30 And when you are spoiled, what will you do? Though you clothest yourself with crimson, though you deckest you with ornaments of gold, though you rentest your face with painting, in vain shalt you make yourself fair; your lovers will despise you, they will seek your life.

31 For I have heard a voice as of a woman in travail, and the anguish as of her that bringeth forth her first child, the voice of the daughter of Zion, that bewaileth herself, that spreadeth her hands, saying, Woe is me now! for my soul is wearied because of murderers.

CHAPTER 5

RUN you to and fro through the streets of Jerusalem, and see now, and know, and seek in the broad places thereof, if you can find a man, if there be any that executeth judgment, that seeketh the truth; and I will pardon it.

2 And though they say, The LORD liveth; surely they swear falsely.

3 O LORD, are not yours eyes upon the truth? you have stricken them, but they have not grieved; you have consumed them, but they have refused to receive correction: they have made their faces harder than a rock; they have refused to return.

4 Therefore I said, Surely these are poor; they are foolish: for they know not the way of the LORD, nor the judgment of their God.

5 I will get me unto the great men, and will speak unto them; for they have known the way of the LORD, and the judgment of their God: but these have altogether broken the yoke, and burst the bonds.

6 Wherefore a lion out of the forest shall slay them, and a wolf of the evenings shall spoil them, a leopard shall watch over their cities: every one that goeth out thence shall be torn in pieces: because their transgressions are many, and their backslidings are increased.

7How shall I pardon you for this? your children have forsaken me, and sworn by them that are no gods: when I had fed them to the full, they then committed adultery, and assembled themselves by troops in the harlots' houses.

8 They were as fed horses in the morning: every one neighed after his neighbour's wife.

9 Shall I not visit for these things? saith the LORD: and shall not my soul be avenged on such a nation as this?

10Go you up upon her walls, and destroy; but make not a full end: take away her battlements; for they are not the LORD's.

11 For the house of Israel and the house of Judah have dealt very treacherously against me, saith the LORD.

12 They have belied the LORD, and said, It is not he; neither shall evil come upon us; neither shall we see sword nor famine:

13 And the prophets shall become wind, and the word is not in them: thus shall it be done unto them.

14 Wherefore thus saith the LORD God of hosts, Because you speak this word, behold, I will make my words in your mouth fire, and this people wood, and it shall devour them.

15 Lo, I will bring a nation upon you from far, O house of Israel, saith the LORD: it is a mighty nation, it is an ancient nation, a nation whose language you knowest not, neither understandest what they say.

16 Their quiver is as an open sepulchre, they are all mighty men.

17 And they shall eat up yours harvest, and your bread, which your sons and your daughters should eat: they shall eat up your flocks and yours herds: they shall eat up your vines and your fig trees: they shall impoverish your fenced cities, wherein you trustedst, with the sword.

18 Nevertheless in those days, saith the LORD, I will not make a full end with you.

19And it shall come to pass, when you shall say, Wherefore doeth the LORD our God all these things unto us? then shalt you answer them, Like as you have forsaken me, and served strange gods in your land, so shall you serve strangers in a land that is not yours.

20 Declare this in the house of Jacob, and publish it in Judah, saying,

21 Hear now this, O foolish people, and without understanding; which have eyes, and see not; which have ears, and hear not:

22 Fear you not me? saith the LORD: will you not tremble at my presence, which have placed the sand for the bound of the sea by a perpetual decree, that it cannot pass it: and though the waves thereof toss themselves, yet can they not prevail; though they roar, yet can they not pass over it?

23 But this people has a revolting and a rebellious heart; they are revolted and gone.

24 Neither say they in their heart, Let us now fear the LORD our God, that giveth rain, both the former and the latter, in his season: he reserveth unto us the appointed weeks of the harvest.

25Your iniquities have turned away these things, and your sins have withholden good things from you.

26 For among my people are found wicked men: they lay wait, as he that setteth snares; they set a trap, they catch men.

27 As a cage is full of birds, so are their houses full of deceit: therefore they are become great, and waxen rich.

28 They are waxen fat, they shine: yea, they overpass the deeds of the wicked: they judge not the cause, the cause of the fatherless, yet they prosper; and the right of the needy do they not judge.

29 Shall I not visit for these things? saith the LORD: shall not my soul be avenged on such a nation as this?

30A wonderful and horrible thing is committed in the land;

31 The prophets prophesy falsely, and the priests bear rule by their means; and my people love to have it so: and what will you do in the end thereof?

CHAPTER 6

O YOU children of Benjamin, gather yourselves to flee out of the midst of Jerusalem, and blow the trumpet in Tekoa, and set up a sign of fire in Beth-haccerem: for evil appeareth out of the north, and great destruction.

2 I have likened the daughter of Zion to a comely and delicate woman.

3 The shepherds with their flocks shall come unto her; they shall pitch their tents against her round about; they shall feed every one in his place.

4 Prepare you war against her; arise, and let us go up at noon. Woe unto us! for the day goeth away, for the shadows of the evening are stretched out.

5 Arise, and let us go by night, and let us destroy her palaces.

6For thus has the LORD of hosts said, Hew you down trees, and cast a mount against Jerusalem: this is the city to be visited; she is wholly oppression in the midst of her.

7 As a fountain casteth out her waters, so she casteth out her wickedness: violence and spoil is heard in her; before me continually is grief and wounds.

8 Be you instructed, O Jerusalem, lest my soul depart from you; lest I make you desolate, a land not inhabited.

9Thus saith the LORD of hosts, They shall throughly glean the remnant of Israel as a vine: turn back yours hand as a grapegatherer into the baskets.

10 To whom shall I speak, and give warning, that they may hear? behold, their ear is uncircumcised, and they cannot hearken: behold, the word of the LORD is unto them a reproach; they have no delight in it.

11 Therefore I am full of the fury of the LORD; I am weary with holding in: I will pour it out upon the children abroad, and upon the assembly of young men together: for even the husband with the wife shall be taken, the aged with him that is full of days.

12 And their houses shall be turned unto others, with their fields and wives together: for I will stretch out my hand upon the inhabitants of the land, saith the LORD.

13 For from the least of them even unto the greatest of them every one is given to covetousness; and from the prophet even unto the priest every one dealeth falsely.

14 They have healed also the hurt of the daughter of my people slightly, saying, Peace, peace; when there is no peace.

15 Were they ashamed when they had committed abomination? nay, they were not at all ashamed, neither could they blush: therefore they shall fall among them that fall: at the time that I visit them they shall be cast down, saith the LORD.

16 Thus saith the LORD, Stand you in the ways, and see, and ask for the old paths, where is the good way, and walk therein, and you shall find rest for your souls. But they said, We will not walk therein.

17 Also I set watchmen over you, saying, Hearken to the sound of the trumpet. But they said, We will not hearken.

18Therefore hear, you nations, and know, O congregation, what is among them.

19 Hear, O earth: behold, I will bring evil upon this people, even the fruit of their thoughts, because they have not hearkened unto my words, nor to my law, but rejected it.

20 To what purpose comes there to me incense from Sheba, and the sweet cane from a far country? your burnt offerings are not acceptable, nor your sacrifices sweet unto me.

21 Therefore thus saith the LORD, Behold, I will lay stumblingblocks before this people, and the fathers and the sons together shall fall upon them; the neighbour and his friend shall perish.

22 Thus saith the LORD, Behold, a people comes from the north country, and a great nation shall be raised from the sides of the earth.

23 They shall lay hold on bow and spear; they are cruel, and have no mercy; their voice roareth like the sea; and they ride upon horses, set in array as men for war against you, O daughter of Zion.

24 We have heard the fame thereof: our hands wax feeble: anguish has taken hold of us, and pain, as of a woman in travail.

25 Go not forth into the field, nor walk by the way; for the sword of the enemy and fear is on every side.

26O daughter of my people, gird you with sackcloth, and wallow yourself in ashes: make you mourning, as for an only son, most bitter lamentation: for the spoiler shall suddenly come upon us.

27 I have set you for a tower and a fortress among my people, that you mayest know and try their way.

28 They are all grievous revolters, walking with slanders: they are brass and iron; they are all corrupters.

29 The bellows are burned, the lead is consumed of the fire; the founder melteth in vain: for the wicked are not plucked away.

30 Reprobate silver shall men call them, because the LORD has rejected them.

CHAPTER 7

THE word that came to Jeremiah from the LORD, saying,

2 Stand in the gate of the LORD's house, and proclaim there this word, and say, Hear the word of the LORD, all you of Judah, that enter in at these gates to worship the LORD.

3 Thus saith the LORD of hosts, the God of Israel, Amend your ways and your doings, and I will cause you to dwell in this place.

4 Trust you not in lying words, saying, The temple of the LORD, The temple of the LORD, The temple of the LORD, are these.

5 For if you throughly amend your ways and your doings; if you throughly execute judgment between a man and his neighbour;

6 If you oppress not the stranger, the fatherless, and the widow, and shed not innocent blood in this place, neither walk after other gods to your hurt:

7 Then will I cause you to dwell in this place, in the land that I gave to your fathers, for ever and ever.

8 Behold, you trust in lying words, that cannot profit.

9 Will you steal, murder, and commit adultery, and swear falsely, and burn incense unto Baal, and walk after other gods whom you know not;

10 And come and stand before me in this house, which is called by my name, and say, We are delivered to do all these abominations?

11 Is this house, which is called by my name, become a den of robbers in your eyes? Behold, even I have seen it, saith the LORD.

12 But go you now unto my place which was in Shiloh, where I set my name at the first, and see what I did to it for the wickedness of my people Israel.

13 And now, because you have done all these works, saith the LORD, and I spake unto you, rising up early and speaking, but you heard not; and I called you, but you answered not;

14 Therefore will I do unto this house, which is called by my name, wherein you trust, and unto the place which I gave to you and to your fathers, as I have done to Shiloh.

15 And I will cast you out of my sight, as I have cast out all your brethren, even the whole seed of Ephraim.

16 Therefore pray not you for this people, neither lift up cry nor prayer for them, neither make intercession to me: for I will not hear you.

17 Seest you not what they do in the cities of Judah and in the streets of Jerusalem?

18 The children gather wood, and the fathers kindle the fire, and the women knead their dough, to make cakes to the queen of heaven, and to pour out drink offerings unto other gods, that they may provoke me to anger.

19 Do they provoke me to anger? saith the LORD: do they not provoke themselves to the confusion of their own faces?

20 Therefore thus saith the Lord GOD; Behold, my anger and my fury shall be poured out upon this place, upon man, and upon beast, and upon the trees of the field, and upon the fruit of the ground; and it shall burn, and shall not be quenched.

21 Thus saith the LORD of hosts, the God of Israel; Put your burnt offerings unto your sacrifices, and eat flesh.

22 For I spake not unto your fathers, nor commanded them in the day that I brought them out of the land of Egypt, concerning burnt offerings or sacrifices:

23 But this thing commanded I them, saying, Obey my voice, and I will be your God, and you shall be my people: and walk you in all the ways that I have commanded you, that it may be well unto you.

24 But they hearkened not, nor inclined their ear, but walked in the counsels and in the imagination of their evil heart, and went backward, and not forward.

25 Since the day that your fathers came forth out of the land of Egypt unto this day I have even sent unto you all my servants the prophets, daily rising up early and sending them:

26 Yet they hearkened not unto me, nor inclined their ear, but hardened their neck: they did worse than their fathers.

27 Therefore you shalt speak all these words unto them; but they will not hearken to you: you shalt also call unto them; but they will not answer you.

28 But you shalt say unto them, This is a nation that obeyeth not the voice of the LORD their God, nor receiveth correction: truth is perished, and is cut off from their mouth.

29 Cut off yours hair, O Jerusalem, and cast it away, and take up a lamentation on high places; for the LORD has rejected and forsaken the generation of his wrath.

30 For the children of Judah have done evil in my sight, saith the LORD: they have set their abominations in the house which is called by my name, to pollute it.

31 And they have built the high places of Tophet, which is in the valley of the son of Hinnom, to burn their sons and their daughters in the fire; which I commanded them not, neither came it into my heart.

32 Therefore, behold, the days come, saith the LORD, that it shall no more be called Tophet, nor the valley of the son of Hinnom, but the valley of slaughter: for they shall bury in Tophet, till there be no place.

33 And the carcases of this people shall be meat for the fowls of the heaven, and for the beasts of the earth; and none shall fray them away.

34 Then will I cause to cease from the cities of Judah, and from the streets of Jerusalem, the voice of mirth, and the voice of gladness, the voice of the bridegroom, and the voice of the bride: for the land shall be desolate.

CHAPTER 8

AT that time, saith the LORD, they shall bring out the bones of the kings of Judah, and the bones of his princes, and the bones of the priests, and the bones of the prophets, and the bones of the inhabitants of Jerusalem, out of their graves:

2 And they shall spread them before the sun, and the moon, and all the host of heaven, whom they have loved, and whom they have served, and after whom they have walked, and whom they have sought, and whom they have worshipped: they shall not be gathered, nor be buried; they shall be for dung upon the face of the earth.

3 And death shall be chosen rather than life by all the residue of them that remain of this evil family, which remain in all the places whither I have driven them, saith the LORD of hosts.

4 Moreover you shalt say unto them, Thus saith the LORD; Shall they fall, and not arise? shall he turn away, and not return?

5 Why then is this people of Jerusalem slidden back by a perpetual backsliding? they hold fast deceit, they refuse to return.

6 I hearkened and heard, but they spake not aright: no man repented him of his wickedness, saying, What have I done? every one turned to his course, as the horse rusheth into the battle.

7 Yea, the stork in the heaven knoweth her appointed times; and the turtle and the crane and the swallow observe the time of their coming; but my people know not the judgment of the LORD.

8 How do you say, We are wise, and the law of the LORD is with us? Lo, certainly in vain made he it; the pen of the scribes is in vain.

9 The wise men are ashamed, they are dismayed and taken: lo, they have rejected the word of the LORD; and what wisdom is in them?

10 Therefore will I give their wives unto others, and their fields to them that shall inherit them: for every one from the least even unto the greatest is given to covetousness, from the prophet even unto the priest every one dealeth falsely.

11 For they have healed the hurt of the daughter of my people slightly, saying, Peace, peace; when there is no peace.

12 Were they ashamed when they had committed abomination? nay, they were not at all ashamed, neither could they blush: therefore shall they fall among them that fall: in the time of their visitation they shall be cast down, saith the LORD.

13 I will surely consume them, saith the LORD: there shall be no grapes on the vine, nor figs on the fig tree, and the leaf shall fade; and the things that I have given them shall pass away from them.

14 Why do we sit still? assemble yourselves, and let us enter into the defenced cities, and let us be silent there: for the LORD our God has put us to silence, and given us water of gall to drink, because we have sinned against the LORD.

15 We looked for peace, but no good came; and for a time of health, and behold trouble!

16 The snorting of his horses was heard from Dan: the whole land trembled at the sound of the neighing of his strong ones; for they are come, and have devoured the land, and all that is in it; the city, and those that dwell therein.

17 For, behold, I will send serpents, cockatrices, among you, which will not be charmed, and they shall bite you, saith the LORD.

18 When I would comfort myself against sorrow, my heart is faint in me.

19 Behold the voice of the cry of the daughter of my people because of them that dwell in a far country: Is not the LORD in Zion? is not her king in her? Why have they provoked me to anger with their graven images, and with strange vanities?

20 The harvest is past, the summer is ended, and we are not saved.

21 For the hurt of the daughter of my people am I hurt; I am black; astonishment has taken hold on me.

22 Is there no balm in Gilead; is there no physician there? why then is not the health of the daughter of my people recovered?

CHAPTER 9

OH that my head were waters, and my eyes a fountain of tears, that I might weep day and night for the slain of the daughter of my people!

2 Oh that I had in the wilderness a lodging place of wayfaring men; that I might leave my people, and go from them! for they be all adulterers, an assembly of treacherous men.

3 And they bend their tongues like their bow for lies: but they are not valiant for the truth upon the earth; for they proceed from evil to evil, and they know not me, saith the LORD.

4 Take you heed every one of his neighbour, and trust you not in any brother: for every brother will utterly supplant, and every neighbour will walk with slanders.

5 And they will deceive every one his neighbour, and will not speak the truth: they have taught their tongue to speak lies, and weary themselves to commit iniquity.

6 Yours habitation is in the midst of deceit; through deceit they refuse to know me, saith the LORD.

7 Therefore thus saith the LORD of hosts, Behold, I will melt them, and try them; for how shall I do for the daughter of my people?

8 Their tongue is as an arrow shot out; it speaketh deceit: one speaketh peaceably to his neighbour with his mouth, but in heart he layeth his wait.

9 Shall I not visit them for these things? saith the LORD: shall not my soul be avenged on such a nation as this?

10 For the mountains will I take up a weeping and wailing, and for the habitations of the wilderness a lamentation, because they are burned up, so that none can pass through them; neither can men hear the voice of the cattle; both the fowl of the heavens and the beast are fled; they are gone.

11 And I will make Jerusalem heaps, and a den of dragons; and I will make the cities of Judah desolate, without an inhabitant.

12 Who is the wise man, that may understand this? and who is he to whom the mouth of the LORD has spoken, that he may declare it, for what the land perisheth and is burned up like a wilderness, that none passes through?

13 And the LORD saith, Because they have forsaken my law which I set before them, and have not obeyed my voice, neither walked therein;

14 But have walked after the imagination of their own heart, and after Baalim, which their fathers taught them:

15 Therefore thus saith the LORD of hosts, the God of Israel; Behold, I will feed them, even this people, with wormwood, and give them water of gall to drink.

16 I will scatter them also among the heathen, whom neither they nor their fathers have known: and I will send a sword after them, till I have consumed them.

17 Thus saith the LORD of hosts, Consider you , and call for the mourning women, that they may come; and send for cunning women, that they may come:

18 And let them make haste, and take up a wailing for us, that our eyes may run down with tears, and our eyelids gush out with waters.

19 For a voice of wailing is heard out of Zion, How are we spoiled! we are greatly confounded, because we have forsaken the land, because our dwellings have cast us out.

20 Yet hear the word of the LORD, O you women, and let your ear receive the word of his mouth, and teach your daughters wailing, and every one her neighbour lamentation.

21 For death is come up into our windows, and is entered into our palaces, to cut off the children from without, and the young men from the streets.

22 Speak, Thus saith the LORD, Even the carcases of men shall fall as dung upon the open field, and as the handful after the harvestman, and none shall gather them.

23 Thus saith the LORD, Let not the wise man glory in his wisdom, neither let the mighty man glory in his might, let not the rich man glory in his riches:

24 But let him that glorieth glory in this, that he understands and knoweth me, that I am the LORD which exercise lovingkindness, judgment, and righteousness, in the earth: for in these things I delight, saith the LORD.

25 Behold, the days come, saith the LORD, that I will punish all them which are circumcised with the uncircumcised;

26 Egypt, and Judah, and Edom, and the children of Ammon, and Moab, and all that are in the utmost corners, that dwell in the wilderness: for all these nations are uncircumcised, and all the house of Israel are uncircumcised in the heart.

CHAPTER 10

HEAR you the word which the LORD speaketh unto you, O house of Israel:

2 Thus saith the LORD, Learn not the way of the heathen, and be not dismayed at the signs of heaven; for the heathen are dismayed at them.

3 For the customs of the people are vain: for one cutteth a tree out of the forest, the work of the hands of the workman, with the axe.

4 They deck it with silver and with gold; they fasten it with nails and with hammers, that it move not.

5 They are upright as the palm tree, but speak not: they must needs be borne, because they cannot go. Be not afraid of them; for they cannot do evil, neither also is it in them to do good.

6 Forasmuch as there is none like unto you, O LORD; you are great, and your name is great in might.

7 Who would not fear you, O King of nations? for to you doth it appertain: forasmuch as among all the wise men of the nations, and in all their kingdoms, there is none like unto you.

8 But they are altogether brutish and foolish: the stock is a doctrine of vanities.

9 Silver spread into plates is brought from Tarshish, and gold from Uphaz, the work of the workman, and of the hands of the founder: blue and purple is their clothing: they are all the work of cunning men.

10 But the LORD is the true God, he is the living God, and an everlasting king: at his wrath the earth shall tremble, and the nations shall not be able to abide his indignation.

11 Thus shall you say unto them, The gods that have not made the heavens and the earth, even they shall perish from the earth, and from under these heavens.

12 He has made the earth by his power, he has established the world by his wisdom, and has stretched out the heavens by his discretion.

13 When he uttereth his voice, there is a multitude of waters in the heavens, and he causeth the vapours to ascend from the ends of the earth; he maketh lightnings with rain, and bringeth forth the wind out of his treasures.

14 Every man is brutish in his knowledge: every founder is confounded by the graven image: for his molten image is falsehood, and there is no breath in them.

15 They are vanity, and the work of errors: in the time of their visitation they shall perish.

16 The portion of Jacob is not like them: for he is the former of all things; and Israel is the rod of his inheritance: The LORD of hosts is his name.

17 Gather up your wares out of the land, O inhabitant of the fortress.

18 For thus saith the LORD, Behold, I will sling out the inhabitants of the land at this once, and will distress them, that they may find it so.

19 Woe is me for my hurt! my wound is grievous: but I said, Truly this is a grief, and I must bear it.

20 My tabernacle is spoiled, and all my cords are broken: my children are gone forth of me, and they are not: there is none to stretch forth my tent any more, and to set up my curtains.

21 For the pastors are become brutish, and have not sought the LORD: therefore they shall not prosper, and all their flocks shall be scattered.

22 Behold, the noise of the bruit is come, and a great commotion out of the north country, to make the cities of Judah desolate, and a den of dragons.

23 O LORD, I know that the way of man is not in himself: it is not in man that walketh to direct his steps.

24 O LORD, correct me, but with judgment; not in yours anger, lest you bring me to nothing.

25 Pour out your fury upon the heathen that know you not, and upon the families that call not on your name: for they have eaten up Jacob, and devoured him, and consumed him, and have made his habitation desolate.

CHAPTER 11

THE word that came to Jeremiah from the LORD, saying,

2 Hear you the words of this covenant, and speak unto the men of Judah, and to the inhabitants of Jerusalem;

3 And say you unto them, Thus saith the LORD God of Israel; Cursed be the man that obeyeth not the words of this covenant,

4 Which I commanded your fathers in the day that I brought them forth out of the land of Egypt, from the iron furnace, saying, Obey my voice, and do them, according to all which I command you: so shall you be my people, and I will be your God:

5 That I may perform the oath which I have sworn unto your fathers, to give them a land flowing with milk and honey, as it is this day. Then answered I, and said, So be it, O LORD.

6 Then the LORD said unto me, Proclaim all these words in the cities of Judah, and in the streets of Jerusalem, saying, Hear you the words of this covenant, and do them.

7 For I earnestly protested unto your fathers in the day that I brought them up out of the land of Egypt, even unto this day, rising early and protesting, saying, Obey my voice.

8 Yet they obeyed not, nor inclined their ear, but walked every one in the imagination of their evil heart: therefore I will bring upon them all the words of this covenant, which I commanded them to do; but they did them not.

9 And the LORD said unto me, A conspiracy is found among the men of Judah, and among the inhabitants of Jerusalem.

10 They are turned back to the iniquities of their forefathers, which refused to hear my words; and they went after other gods to serve them: the house of Israel and the house of Judah have broken my covenant which I made with their fathers.

11 Therefore thus saith the LORD, Behold, I will bring evil upon them, which they shall not be able to escape; and though they shall cry unto me, I will not hearken unto them.

12 Then shall the cities of Judah and inhabitants of Jerusalem go, and cry unto the gods unto whom they offer incense: but they shall not save them at all in the time of their trouble.

13 For according to the number of your cities were your gods, O Judah; and according to the number of the streets of Jerusalem have you set up altars to that shameful thing, even altars to burn incense unto Baal.

14 Therefore pray not you for this people, neither lift up a cry or prayer for them: for I will not hear them in the time that they cry unto me for their trouble.

15 What has my beloved to do in my house, seeing she has created lewdness with many, and the holy flesh is passed from you? when you doest evil, then you rejoicest.

16 The LORD called your name, A green olive tree, fair, and of goodly fruit: with the noise of a great tumult he has kindled fire upon it, and the branches of it are broken.

17 For the LORD of hosts, that planted you, has pronounced evil against you, for the evil of the house of Israel and of the house of Judah, which they have done against themselves to provoke me to anger in offering incense unto Baal.

18 And the LORD has given me knowledge of it, and I know it: then you shewedst me their doings.

19 But I was like a lamb or an ox that is brought to the slaughter; and I knew not that they had devised devices against me, saying, Let us destroy the tree with the fruit thereof, and let us cut him off from the land of the living, that his name may be no more remembered.

20 But, O LORD of hosts, that judgest righteously, that triest the reins and the heart, let me see your vengeance on them: for unto you have I revealed my cause.

21 Therefore thus saith the LORD of the men of Anathoth, that seek your life, saying, Prophesy not in the name of the LORD, that you die not by our hand:

22 Therefore thus saith the LORD of hosts, Behold, I will punish them: the young men shall die by the sword; their sons and their daughters shall die by famine:

23 And there shall be no remnant of them: for I will bring evil upon the men of Anathoth, even the year of their visitation.

CHAPTER 12

RIGHTEOUS are you , O LORD, when I plead with you: yet let me talk with you of your judgments: Wherefore doth the way of the wicked prosper? wherefore are all they happy that deal very treacherously?

2 You have planted them, yea, they have taken root: they grow, yea, they bring forth fruit: you are near in their mouth, and far from their reins.

3 But you , O LORD, knowest me: you have seen me, and tried my heart toward you: pull them out like sheep for the slaughter, and prepare them for the day of slaughter.

4 How long shall the land mourn, and the herbs of every field wither, for the wickedness of them that dwell therein? the beasts are consumed, and the birds; because they said, He shall not see our last end.

5 If you have run with the footmen, and they have wearied you, then how can you contend with horses? and if in the land of peace, wherein you trustedst, they wearied you, then how will you do in the swelling of Jordan?

6 For even your brethren, and the house of your father, even they have dealt treacherously with you; yea, they have called a multitude after you: believe them not, though they speak fair words unto you.

7 I have forsaken my house, I have left my heritage; I have given the dearly beloved of my soul into the hand of her enemies.

8 My heritage is unto me as a lion in the forest; it crieth out against me: therefore have I hated it.

9 My heritage is unto me as a speckled bird, the birds round about are against her; come you , assemble all the beasts of the field, come to devour.

10 Many pastors have destroyed my vineyard, they have trodden my portion under foot, they have made my pleasant portion a desolate wilderness.

11 They have made it desolate, and being desolate it mourneth unto me; the whole land is made desolate, because no man layeth it to heart.

12 The spoilers are come upon all high places through the wilderness: for the sword of the LORD shall devour from the one end of the land even to the other end of the land: no flesh shall have peace.

13 They have sown wheat, but shall reap thorns: they have put themselves to pain, but shall not profit: and they shall be ashamed of your revenues because of the fierce anger of the LORD.

14 Thus saith the LORD against all my evil neighbours, that touch the inheritance which I have caused my people Israel to inherit; Behold, I will pluck them out of their land, and pluck out the house of Judah from among them.

15 And it shall come to pass, after that I have plucked them out I will return, and have compassion on them, and will bring them again, every man to his heritage, and every man to his land.

16 And it shall come to pass, if they will diligently learn the ways of my people, to swear by my name, The LORD liveth; as they taught my people to swear by Baal; then shall they be built in the midst of my people.

17 But if they will not obey, I will utterly pluck up and destroy that nation, saith the LORD.

CHAPTER 13

THUS saith the LORD unto me, Go and get you a linen girdle, and put it upon your loins, and put it not in water.

2 So I got a girdle according to the word of the LORD, and put it on my loins.

3 And the word of the LORD came unto me the second time, saying,

4 Take the girdle that you have got, which is upon your loins, and arise, go to Euphrates, and hide it there in a hole of the rock.

5 So I went, and hid it by Euphrates, as the LORD commanded me.

6 And it came to pass after many days, that the LORD said unto me, Arise, go to Euphrates, and take the girdle from thence, which I commanded you to hide there.

7 Then I went to Euphrates, and digged, and took the girdle from the place where I had hid it: and, behold, the girdle was marred, it was profitable for nothing.

8 Then the word of the LORD came unto me, saying,

9 Thus saith the LORD, After this manner will I mar the pride of Judah, and the great pride of Jerusalem.

10 This evil people, which refuse to hear my words, which walk in the imagination of their heart, and walk after other gods, to serve them, and to worship them, shall even be as this girdle, which is good for nothing.

11 For as the girdle cleaveth to the loins of a man, so have I caused to cleave unto me the whole house of Israel and the whole house of Judah, saith the LORD; that they might be unto me for a people, and for a name, and for a praise, and for a glory: but they would not hear.

12 Therefore you shalt speak unto them this word; Thus saith the LORD God of Israel, Every bottle shall be filled with wine: and they shall say unto you, Do we not certainly know that every bottle shall be filled with wine?

13 Then shalt you say unto them, Thus saith the LORD, Behold, I will fill all the inhabitants of this land, even the kings that sit upon David's throne, and the priests, and the prophets, and all the inhabitants of Jerusalem, with drunkenness.

14 And I will dash them one against another, even the fathers and the sons together, saith the LORD: I will not pity, nor spare, nor have mercy, but destroy them.

15 Hear you , and give ear; be not proud: for the LORD has spoken.

16 Give glory to the LORD your God, before he cause darkness, and before your feet stumble upon the dark mountains, and, while you look for light, he turn it into the shadow of death, and make it gross darkness.

17 But if you will not hear it, my soul shall weep in secret places for your pride; and my eye shall weep sore, and run down with tears, because the LORD's flock is carried away captive.

18 Say unto the king and to the queen, Humble yourselves, sit down: for your principalities shall come down, even the crown of your glory.

19 The cities of the south shall be shut up, and none shall open them: Judah shall be carried away captive all of it, it shall be wholly carried away captive.

20 Lift up your eyes, and behold them that come from the north: where is the flock that was given you, your beautiful flock?

21 What will you say when he shall punish you? for you have taught them to be captains, and as chief over you: shall not sorrows take you, as a woman in travail?

22 And if you say in yours heart, Wherefore come these things upon me? For the greatness of yours iniquity are your skirts discovered, and your heels made bare.

23 Can the Ethiopian change his skin, or the leopard his spots? then may you also do good, that are accustomed to do evil.

24 Therefore will I scatter them as the stubble that passes away by the wind of the wilderness.

25 This is your lot, the portion of your measures from me, saith the LORD; because you have forgotten me, and trusted in falsehood.

26 Therefore will I discover your skirts upon your face, that your shame may appear.

27 I have seen yours adulteries, and your neighings, the lewdness of your whoredom, and yours abominations on the hills in the fields. Woe unto you, O Jerusalem! will you not be made clean? when shall it once be?

CHAPTER 14

THE word of the LORD that came to Jeremiah concerning the dearth.

2 Judah mourneth, and the gates thereof languish; they are black unto the ground; and the cry of Jerusalem is gone up.

3 And their nobles have sent their little ones to the waters: they came to the pits, and found no water; they returned with their vessels empty; they were ashamed and confounded, and covered their heads.

4 Because the ground is chapt, for there was no rain in the earth, the plowmen were ashamed, they covered their heads.

5 Yea, the hind also calved in the field, and forsook it, because there was no grass.

6 And the wild asses did stand in the high places, they snuffed up the wind like dragons; their eyes did fail, because there was no grass.

70 LORD, though our iniquities testify against us, do you it for your name's sake: for our backslidings are many; we have sinned against you.

8 O the hope of Israel, the saviour thereof in time of trouble, why shouldest you be as a stranger in the land, and as a wayfaring man that turneth aside to tarry for a night?

9 Why shouldest you be as a man astonied, as a mighty man that cannot save? yet you , O LORD, are in the midst of us, and we are called by your name; leave us not.

10 Thus saith the LORD unto this people, Thus have they loved to wander, they have not refrained their feet, therefore the LORD doth not accept them; he will now remember their iniquity, and visit their sins.

11 Then said the LORD unto me, Pray not for this people for their good.

12 When they fast, I will not hear their cry; and when they offer burnt offering and an oblation, I will not accept them: but I will consume them by the sword, and by the famine, and by the pestilence.

13 Then said I, Ah, Lord GOD! behold, the prophets say unto them, You shall not see the sword, neither shall you have famine; but I will give you assured peace in this place.

14 Then the LORD said unto me, The prophets prophesy lies in my name: I sent them not, neither have I commanded them, neither spake unto them: they prophesy unto you a false vision and divination, and a thing of nought, and the deceit of their heart.

15 Therefore thus saith the LORD concerning the prophets that prophesy in my name, and I sent them not, yet they say, Sword and famine shall not be in this land; By sword and famine shall those prophets be consumed.

16 And the people to whom they prophesy shall be cast out in the streets of Jerusalem because of the famine and the sword; and they shall have none to bury them, them, their wives, nor their sons, nor their daughters: for I will pour their wickedness upon them.

17 Therefore you shalt say this word unto them; Let my eyes run down with tears night and day, and let them not cease: for the virgin daughter of my people is broken with a great breach, with a very grievous blow.

18 If I go forth into the field, then behold the slain with the sword! and if I enter into the city, then behold them that are sick with famine! yea, both the prophet and the priest go about into a land that they know not.

19 Have you utterly rejected Judah? has your soul lothed Zion? why have you smitten us, and there is no healing for us? we looked for peace, and there is no good; and for the time of healing, and behold trouble!

20 We acknowledge, O LORD, our wickedness, and the iniquity of our fathers: for we have sinned against you.

21 Do not abhor us, for your name's sake, do not disgrace the throne of your glory: remember, break not your covenant with us.

22 Are there any among the vanities of the Gentiles that can cause rain? or can the heavens give showers? are not you he, O LORD our God? therefore we will wait upon you: for you have made all these things.

CHAPTER 15

THEN said the LORD unto me, Though Moses and Samuel stood before me, yet my mind could not be toward this people: cast them out of my sight, and let them go forth.

2 And it shall come to pass, if they say unto you, Whither shall we go forth? then you shalt tell them, Thus saith the LORD; Such as are for death, to death; and such as are for the sword, to the sword; and such as are for the famine, to the famine; and such as are for the captivity, to the captivity.

3 And I will appoint over them four kinds, saith the LORD: the sword to slay, and the dogs to tear, and the fowls of the heaven, and the beasts of the earth, to devour and destroy.

4 And I will cause them to be removed into all kingdoms of the earth, because of Manasseh the son of Hezekiah king of Judah, for that which he did in Jerusalem.

5 For who shall have pity upon you, O Jerusalem? or who shall bemoan you? or who shall go aside to ask how you doest?

6 You have forsaken me, saith the LORD, you are gone backward: therefore will I stretch out my hand against you, and destroy you; I am weary with repenting.

7 And I will fan them with a fan in the gates of the land; I will bereave them of children, I will destroy my people, since they return not from their ways.

8 Their widows are increased to me above the sand of the seas: I have brought upon them against the mother of the young men a spoiler at noonday: I have caused him to fall upon it suddenly, and terrors upon the city.

9 She that has borne seven languisheth: she has given up the ghost; her sun is gone down while it was yet day: she has been ashamed and confounded: and the residue of them will I deliver to the sword before their enemies, saith the LORD.

10 Woe is me, my mother, that you have borne me a man of strife and a man of contention to the whole earth! I have neither lent on usury, nor men have lent to me on usury; yet every one of them doth curse me.

11 The LORD said, Verily it shall be well with your remnant; verily I will cause the enemy to entreat you well in the time of evil and in the time of affliction.

12 Shall iron break the northern iron and the steel?

13 Your substance and your treasures will I give to the spoil without price, and that for all your sins, even in all your borders.

14 And I will make you to pass with yours enemies into a land which you knowest not: for a fire is kindled in my anger, which shall burn upon you.

15 O LORD, you knowest: remember me, and visit me, and revenge me of my persecutors; take me not away in your longsuffering: know that for your sake I have suffered rebuke.

16 Your words were found, and I did eat them; and your word was unto me the joy and rejoicing of my heart: for I am called by your name, O LORD God of hosts.

17 I sat not in the assembly of the mockers, nor rejoiced; I sat alone because of your hand: for you have filled me with indignation.

18 Why is my pain perpetual, and my wound incurable, which refuseth to be healed? will you be altogether unto me as a liar, and as waters that fail?

19 Therefore thus saith the LORD, If you return, then will I bring you again, and you shalt stand before me: and if you take forth the precious from the vile, you shalt be as my mouth: let them return unto you; but return not you unto them.

20 And I will make you unto this people a fenced brasen wall: and they shall fight against you, but they shall not prevail against you: for I am with you to save you and to deliver you, saith the LORD.

21 And I will deliver you out of the hand of the wicked, and I will redeem you out of the hand of the terrible.

CHAPTER 16

THE word of the LORD came also unto me, saying,

2 You shalt not take you a wife, neither shalt you have sons or daughters in this place.

3 For thus saith the LORD concerning the sons and concerning the daughters that are born in this place, and concerning their mothers that bare them, and concerning their fathers that begat them in this land;

4 They shall die of grievous deaths; they shall not be lamented; neither shall they be buried; but they shall be as dung upon the face of the earth: and they shall be consumed by the sword, and by famine; and their carcases shall be meat for the fowls of heaven, and for the beasts of the earth.

5 For thus saith the LORD, Enter not into the house of mourning, neither go to lament nor bemoan them: for I have taken away my peace from this people, saith the LORD, even lovingkindness and mercies.

6 Both the great and the small shall die in this land: they shall not be buried, neither shall men lament for them, nor cut themselves, nor make themselves bald for them:

7 Neither shall men tear themselves for them in mourning, to comfort them for the dead; neither shall men give them the cup of consolation to drink for their father or for their mother.

8 You shalt not also go into the house of feasting, to sit with them to eat and to drink.

9 For thus saith the LORD of hosts, the God of Israel; Behold, I will cause to cease out of this place in your eyes, and in your days, the voice of mirth, and the voice of gladness, the voice of the bridegroom, and the voice of the bride.

10 And it shall come to pass, when you shalt shew this people all these words, and they shall say unto you, Wherefore has the LORD pronounced all this great evil against us? or what is our iniquity? or what is our sin that we have committed against the LORD our God?

11 Then shalt you say unto them, Because your fathers have forsaken me, saith the LORD, and have walked after other gods, and have served them, and have worshipped them, and have forsaken me, and have not kept my law;

12 And you have done worse than your fathers; for, behold, you walk every one after the imagination of his evil heart, that they may not hearken unto me:

13 Therefore will I cast you out of this land into a land that you know not, neither you nor your fathers; and there shall you serve other gods day and night; where I will not shew you favour.

14 Therefore, behold, the days come, saith the LORD, that it shall no more be said, The LORD liveth, that brought up the children of Israel out of the land of Egypt;

15 But, The LORD liveth, that brought up the children of Israel from the land of the north, and from all the lands whither he had driven them: and I will bring them again into their land that I gave unto their fathers.

16 Behold, I will send for many fishers, saith the LORD, and they shall fish them; and after will I send for many hunters, and they shall hunt them from every mountain, and from every hill, and out of the holes of the rocks.

17 For my eyes are upon all their ways: they are not hid from my face, neither is their iniquity hid from my eyes.

18 And first I will recompense their iniquity and their sin double; because they have defiled my land, they have filled my inheritance with the carcases of their detestable and abominable things.

19 O LORD, my strength, and my fortress, and my refuge in the day of affliction, the Gentiles shall come unto you from the ends of the earth, and shall say, Surely our fathers have inherited lies, vanity, and things wherein there is no profit.

20 Shall a man make gods unto himself, and they are no gods?

21 Therefore, behold, I will this once cause them to know, I will cause them to know my hand and my might; and they shall know that my name is The LORD.

CHAPTER 17

THE sin of Judah is written with a pen of iron, and with the point of a diamond: it is graven upon the table of their heart, and upon the horns of your altars;

2 Whilst their children remember their altars and their groves by the green trees upon the high hills.

3 O my mountain in the field, I will give your substance and all your treasures to the spoil, and your high places for sin, throughout all your borders.

4 And you , even yourself, shalt discontinue from yours heritage that I gave you; and I will cause you to serve yours enemies in the land which you knowest not: for you have kindled a fire in my anger, which shall burn for ever.

5 Thus saith the LORD; Cursed be the man that trusteth in man, and maketh flesh his arm, and whose heart departeth from the LORD.

6 For he shall be like the heath in the desert, and shall not see when good comes; but shall inhabit the parched places in the wilderness, in a salt land and not inhabited.

7 Blessed is the man that trusteth in the LORD, and whose hope the LORD is.

8 For he shall be as a tree planted by the waters, and that spreadeth out her roots by the river, and shall not see when heat comes, but her leaf shall be green; and shall not be careful in the year of drought, neither shall cease from yielding fruit.

9 The heart is deceitful above all things, and desperately wicked: who can know it?

10 I the LORD search the heart, I try the reins, even to give every man according to his ways, and according to the fruit of his doings.

11 As the partridge sitteth on eggs, and hatcheth them not; so he that getteth riches, and not by right, shall leave them in the midst of his days, and at his end shall be a fool.

12 A glorious high throne from the beginning is the place of our sanctuary.

13 O LORD, the hope of Israel, all that forsake you shall be ashamed, and they that depart from me shall be written in the earth, because they have forsaken the LORD, the fountain of living waters.

14 Heal me, O LORD, and I shall be healed; save me, and I shall be saved: for you are my praise.

15 Behold, they say unto me, Where is the word of the LORD? let it come now.

16 As for me, I have not hastened from being a pastor to follow you: neither have I desired the woeful day; you knowest: that which came out of my lips was right before you.

17 Be not a terror unto me: you are my hope in the day of evil.

18 Let them be confounded that persecute me, but let not me be confounded: let them be dismayed, but let not me be dismayed: bring upon them the day of evil, and destroy them with double destruction.

19 Thus said the LORD unto me; Go and stand in the gate of the children of the people, whereby the kings of Judah come in, and by the which they go out, and in all the gates of Jerusalem;

20 And say unto them, Hear you the word of the LORD, you kings of Judah, and all Judah, and all the inhabitants of Jerusalem, that enter in by these gates:

21 Thus saith the LORD; Take heed to yourselves, and bear no burden on the sabbath day, nor bring it in by the gates of Jerusalem;

22 Neither carry forth a burden out of your houses on the sabbath day, neither do you any work, but hallow you the sabbath day, as I commanded your fathers.

23 But they obeyed not, neither inclined their ear, but made their neck stiff, that they might not hear, nor receive instruction.

24 And it shall come to pass, if you diligently hearken unto me, saith the LORD, to bring in no burden through the gates of this city on the sabbath day, but hallow the sabbath day, to do no work therein;

25 Then shall there enter into the gates of this city kings and princes sitting upon the throne of David, riding in chariots and on horses, they, and their princes, the men of Judah, and the inhabitants of Jerusalem: and this city shall remain for ever.

26 And they shall come from the cities of Judah, and from the places about Jerusalem, and from the land of Benjamin, and from the plain, and from the mountains, and from the south, bringing burnt offerings, and sacrifices, and meat offerings, and incense, and bringing sacrifices of praise, unto the house of the LORD.

27 But if you will not hearken unto me to hallow the sabbath day, and not to bear a burden, even entering in at the gates of Jerusalem on the sabbath day; then will I kindle a fire in the gates thereof, and it shall devour the palaces of Jerusalem, and it shall not be quenched.

CHAPTER 18

THE word which came to Jeremiah from the LORD, saying,

2 Arise, and go down to the potter's house, and there I will cause you to hear my words.

3 Then I went down to the potter's house, and, behold, he created a work on the wheels.

4 And the vessel that he made of clay was marred in the hand of the potter: so he made it again another vessel, as seemed good to the potter to make it.

5 Then the word of the LORD came to me, saying,

6 O house of Israel, cannot I do with you as this potter? saith the LORD. Behold, as the clay is in the potter's hand, so are you in my hand, O house of Israel.

7 At what instant I shall speak concerning a nation, and concerning a kingdom, to pluck up, and to pull down, and to destroy it;

8 If that nation, against whom I have pronounced, turn from their evil, I will repent of the evil that I thought to do unto them.

9 And at what instant I shall speak concerning a nation, and concerning a kingdom, to build and to plant it;

10 If it do evil in my sight, that it obey not my voice, then I will repent of the good, wherewith I said I would benefit them.

11 Now therefore go to, speak to the men of Judah, and to the inhabitants of Jerusalem, saying, Thus saith the LORD; Behold, I frame evil against you, and devise a device against you: return you now every one from his evil way, and make your ways and your doings good.

12 And they said, There is no hope: but we will walk after our own devices, and we will every one do the imagination of his evil heart.

13 Therefore thus saith the LORD; Ask you now among the heathen, who has heard such things: the virgin of Israel has done a very horrible thing.

14 Will a man leave the snow of Lebanon which comes from the rock of the field? or shall the cold flowing waters that come from another place be forsaken?

15 Because my people has forgotten me, they have burned incense to vanity, and they have caused them to stumble in their ways from the ancient paths, to walk in paths, in a way not cast up;

16 To make their land desolate, and a perpetual hissing; every one that passes thereby shall be astonished, and wag his head.

17 I will scatter them as with an east wind before the enemy; I will shew them the back, and not the face, in the day of their calamity.

18 Then said they, Come, and let us devise devices against Jeremiah; for the law shall not perish from the priest, nor counsel from the wise, nor the word from the prophet. Come, and let us strike him with the tongue, and let us not give heed to any of his words.

19 Give heed to me, O LORD, and hearken to the voice of them that contend with me.

20 Shall evil be recompensed for good? for they have digged a pit for my soul. Remember that I stood before you to speak good for them, and to turn away your wrath from them.

21 Therefore deliver up their children to the famine, and pour out their blood by the force of the sword; and let their wives be bereaved of their children, and be widows; and let their men be put to death; let their young men be slain by the sword in battle.

22 Let a cry be heard from their houses, when you shalt bring a troop suddenly upon them: for they have digged a pit to take me, and hid snares for my feet.

23 Yet, LORD, you knowest all their counsel against me to slay me: forgive not their iniquity, neither blot out their sin from your sight, but let them be overthrown before you; deal thus with them in the time of yours anger.

CHAPTER 19

THUS saith the LORD, Go and get a potter's earthen bottle, and take of the ancients of the people, and of the ancients of the priests;

2 And go forth unto the valley of the son of Hinnom, which is by the entry of the east gate, and proclaim there the words that I shall tell you,

3 And say, Hear you the word of the LORD, O kings of Judah, and inhabitants of Jerusalem; Thus saith the LORD of hosts, the God of Israel; Behold, I will bring evil upon this place, the which whosoever heareth, his ears shall tingle.

4 Because they have forsaken me, and have estranged this place, and have burned incense in it unto other gods, whom neither they nor their fathers have known, nor the kings of Judah, and have filled this place with the blood of innocents;

5 They have built also the high places of Baal, to burn their sons with fire for burnt offerings unto Baal, which I commanded not, nor spake it, neither came it into my mind:

6 Therefore, behold, the days come, saith the LORD, that this place shall no more be called Tophet, nor The valley of the son of Hinnom, but The valley of slaughter.

7 And I will make void the counsel of Judah and Jerusalem in this place; and I will cause them to fall by the sword before their enemies, and by the hands of them that seek their lives: and their carcases will I give to be meat for the fowls of the heaven, and for the beasts of the earth.

8 And I will make this city desolate, and an hissing; every one that passes thereby shall be astonished and hiss because of all the plagues thereof.

9 And I will cause them to eat the flesh of their sons and the flesh of their daughters, and they shall eat every one the flesh of his friend in the siege and straitness, wherewith their enemies, and they that seek their lives, shall straiten them.

10 Then shalt you break the bottle in the sight of the men that go with you,

11 And shalt say unto them, Thus saith the LORD of hosts; Even so will I break this people and this city, as one breaketh a potter's vessel, that cannot be made whole again: and they shall bury them in Tophet, till there be no place to bury.

12 Thus will I do unto this place, saith the LORD, and to the inhabitants thereof, and even make this city as Tophet:

13 And the houses of Jerusalem, and the houses of the kings of Judah, shall be defiled as the place of Tophet, because of all the houses upon whose roofs they have burned incense unto all the host of heaven, and have poured out drink offerings unto other gods.

14 Then came Jeremiah from Tophet, whither the LORD had sent him to prophesy; and he stood in the court of the LORD's house; and said to all the people,

15 Thus saith the LORD of hosts, the God of Israel; Behold, I will bring upon this city and upon all her towns all the evil that I have pronounced against it, because they have hardened their necks, that they might not hear my words.

CHAPTER 20

NOW Pashur the son of Immer the priest, who was also chief governor in the house of the LORD, heard that Jeremiah prophesied these things.

2 Then Pashur struck Jeremiah the prophet, and put him in the stocks that were in the high gate of Benjamin, which was by the house of the LORD.

3 And it came to pass on the morrow, that Pashur brought forth Jeremiah out of the stocks. Then said Jeremiah unto him, The LORD has not called your name Pashur, but Magor-missabib.

4 For thus saith the LORD, Behold, I will make you a terror to yourself, and to all your friends: and they shall fall by the sword of their enemies, and yours eyes shall behold it: and I will give all Judah into the hand of the king of Babylon, and he shall carry them captive into Babylon, and shall slay them with the sword.

5 Moreover I will deliver all the strength of this city, and all the labours thereof, and all the precious things thereof, and all the treasures of the kings of Judah will I give into the hand of their enemies, which shall spoil them, and take them, and carry them to Babylon.

6 And you , Pashur, and all that dwell in yours house shall go into captivity: and you shalt come to Babylon, and there you shalt die, and shalt be buried there, you , and all your friends, to whom you have prophesied lies.

70 LORD, you have deceived me, and I was deceived: you are stronger than I, and have prevailed: I am in derision daily, every one mocketh me.

8 For since I spake, I cried out, I cried violence and spoil; because the word of the LORD was made a reproach unto me, and a derision, daily.

9 Then I said, I will not make mention of him, nor speak any more in his name. But his word was in my heart as a burning fire shut up in my bones, and I was weary with forbearing, and I could not stay.

10For I heard the defaming of many, fear on every side. Report, say they, and we will report it. All my familiars watched for my halting, saying, What if he will be enticed, and we shall prevail against him, and we shall take our revenge on him.

11 But the LORD is with me as a mighty terrible one: therefore my persecutors shall stumble, and they shall not prevail: they shall be greatly ashamed; for they shall not prosper: their everlasting confusion shall never be forgotten.

12 But, O LORD of hosts, that triest the righteous, and seest the reins and the heart, let me see your vengeance on them: for unto you have I opened my cause.

13 Sing unto the LORD, praise you the LORD: for he has delivered the soul of the poor from the hand of evildoers.

14Cursed be the day wherein I was born: let not the day wherein my mother bare me be blessed.

15 Cursed be the man who brought tidings to my father, saying, A man child is born unto you; making him very glad.

16 And let that man be as the cities which the LORD overthrew, and repented not: and let him hear the cry in the morning, and the shouting at noontide;

17 Because he slew me not from the womb; or that my mother might have been my grave, and her womb to be always great with me.

18 Wherefore came I forth out of the womb to see labour and sorrow, that my days should be consumed with shame?

CHAPTER 21

THE word which came unto Jeremiah from the LORD, when king Zedekiah sent unto him Pashur the son of Melchiah, and Zephaniah the son of Maaseiah the priest, saying,

2 Inquire, I pray you, of the LORD for us; for Nebuchadrezzar king of Babylon maketh war against us; if so be that the LORD will deal with us according to all his wondrous works, that he may go up from us.

3Then said Jeremiah unto them, Thus shall you say to Zedekiah:

4 Thus saith the LORD God of Israel; Behold, I will turn back the weapons of war that are in your hands, wherewith you fight against the king of Babylon, and against the Chaldeans, which besiege you without the walls, and I will assemble them into the midst of this city.

5 And I myself will fight against you with an outstretched hand and with a strong arm, even in anger, and in fury, and in great wrath.

6 And I will strike the inhabitants of this city, both man and beast: they shall die of a great pestilence.

7 And afterward, saith the LORD, I will deliver Zedekiah king of Judah, and his servants, and the people, and such as are left in this city from the pestilence, from the sword, and from the famine, into the hand of Nebuchadnezzar king of Babylon, and into the hand of their enemies, and into the hand of those that seek their life: and he shall strike them with the edge of the sword; he shall not spare them, neither have pity, nor have mercy.

8And unto this people you shalt say, Thus saith the LORD; Behold, I set before you the way of life, and the way of death.

9 He that abideth in this city shall die by the sword, and by the famine, and by the pestilence: but he that goeth out, and falleth to the Chaldeans that besiege you, he shall live, and his life shall be unto him for a prey.

10 For I have set my face against this city for evil, and not for good, saith the LORD: it shall be given into the hand of the king of Babylon, and he shall burn it with fire.

11And touching the house of the king of Judah, say, Hear you the word of the LORD;

12 O house of David, thus saith the LORD; Execute judgment in the morning, and deliver him that is spoiled out of the hand of the oppressor, lest my fury go out like fire, and burn that none can quench it, because of the evil of your doings.

13 Behold, I am against you, O inhabitant of the valley, and rock of the plain, saith the LORD; which say, Who shall come down against us? or who shall enter into our habitations?

14 But I will punish you according to the fruit of your doings, saith the LORD: and I will kindle a fire in the forest thereof, and it shall devour all things round about it.

CHAPTER 22

THUS saith the LORD; Go down to the house of the king of Judah, and speak there this word,

2 And say, Hear the word of the LORD, O king of Judah, that sittest upon the throne of David, you , and your servants, and your people that enter in by these gates:

3 Thus saith the LORD; Execute you judgment and righteousness, and deliver the spoiled out of the hand of the oppressor: and do no wrong, do no violence to the stranger, the fatherless, nor the widow, neither shed innocent blood in this place.

4 For if you do this thing indeed, then shall there enter in by the gates of this house kings sitting upon the throne of David, riding in chariots and on horses, he, and his servants, and his people.

5 But if you will not hear these words, I swear by myself, saith the LORD, that this house shall become a desolation.

6 For thus saith the LORD unto the king's house of Judah; You are Gilead unto me, and the head of Lebanon: yet surely I will make you a wilderness, and cities which are not inhabited.

7 And I will prepare destroyers against you, every one with his weapons: and they shall cut down your choice cedars, and cast them into the fire.

8 And many nations shall pass by this city, and they shall say every man to his neighbour, Wherefore has the LORD done thus unto this great city?

9 Then they shall answer, Because they have forsaken the covenant of the LORD their God, and worshipped other gods, and served them.

10 Weep you not for the dead, neither bemoan him: but weep sore for him that goeth away: for he shall return no more, nor see his native country.

11 For thus saith the LORD touching Shallum the son of Josiah king of Judah, which reigned instead of Josiah his father, which went forth out of this place; He shall not return thither any more:

12 But he shall die in the place whither they have led him captive, and shall see this land no more.

13 Woe unto him that buildeth his house by unrighteousness, and his chambers by wrong; that useth his neighbour's service without wages, and giveth him not for his work;

14 That saith, I will build me a wide house and large chambers, and cutteth him out windows; and it is cieled with cedar, and painted with vermilion.

15 Shalt you reign, because you closest yourself in cedar? did not your father eat and drink, and do judgment and justice, and then it was well with him?

16 He judged the cause of the poor and needy; then it was well with him: was not this to know me? saith the LORD.

17 But yours eyes and yours heart are not but for your covetousness, and for to shed innocent blood, and for oppression, and for violence, to do it.

18 Therefore thus saith the LORD concerning Jehoiakim the son of Josiah king of Judah; They shall not lament for him, saying, Ah my brother! or, Ah sister! they shall not lament for him, saying, Ah lord! or, Ah his glory!

19 He shall be buried with the burial of an ass, drawn and cast forth beyond the gates of Jerusalem.

20 Go up to Lebanon, and cry; and lift up your voice in Bashan, and cry from the passages: for all your lovers are destroyed.

21 I spake unto you in your prosperity; but you saidst, I will not hear. This has been your manner from your youth, that you obeyedst not my voice.

22 The wind shall eat up all your pastors, and your lovers shall go into captivity: surely then shalt you be ashamed and confounded for all your wickedness.

23 O inhabitant of Lebanon, that makest your nest in the cedars, how gracious shalt you be when pangs come upon you, the pain as of a woman in travail!

24 As I live, saith the LORD, though Coniah the son of Jehoiakim king of Judah were the signet upon my right hand, yet would I pluck you thence;

25 And I will give you into the hand of them that seek your life, and into the hand of them whose face you fearest, even into the hand of Nebuchadrezzar king of Babylon, and into the hand of the Chaldeans.

26 And I will cast you out, and your mother that bare you, into another country, where you were not born; and there shall you die.

27 But to the land whereunto they desire to return, thither shall they not return.

28 Is this man Coniah a despised broken idol? is he a vessel wherein is no pleasure? wherefore are they cast out, he and his seed, and are cast into a land which they know not?

29 O earth, earth, earth, hear the word of the LORD.

30 Thus saith the LORD, Write you this man childless, a man that shall not prosper in his days: for no man of his seed shall prosper, sitting upon the throne of David, and ruling any more in Judah.

CHAPTER 23

WOE be unto the pastors that destroy and scatter the sheep of my pasture! saith the LORD.

2 Therefore thus saith the LORD God of Israel against the pastors that feed my people; You have scattered my flock, and driven them away, and have not visited them: behold, I will visit upon you the evil of your doings, saith the LORD.

3 And I will gather the remnant of my flock out of all countries whither I have driven them, and will bring them again to their folds; and they shall be fruitful and increase.

4 And I will set up shepherds over them which shall feed them: and they shall fear no more, nor be dismayed, neither shall they be lacking, saith the LORD.

5 Behold, the days come, saith the LORD, that I will raise unto David a righteous Branch, and a King shall reign and prosper, and shall execute judgment and justice in the earth.

6 In his days Judah shall be saved, and Israel shall dwell safely: and this is his name whereby he shall be called, THE LORD OUR RIGHTEOUSNESS.

7 Therefore, behold, the days come, saith the LORD, that they shall no more say, The LORD liveth, which brought up the children of Israel out of the land of Egypt;

8 But, The LORD liveth, which brought up and which led the seed of the house of Israel out of the north country, and from all countries whither I had driven them; and they shall dwell in their own land.

9 My heart within me is broken because of the prophets; all my bones shake; I am like a drunken man, and like a man whom wine has overcome, because of the LORD, and because of the words of his holiness.

10 For the land is full of adulterers; for because of swearing the land mourneth; the pleasant places of the wilderness are dried up, and their course is evil, and their force is not right.

11 For both prophet and priest are profane; yea, in my house have I found their wickedness, saith the LORD.

12 Wherefore their way shall be unto them as slippery ways in the darkness: they shall be driven on, and fall therein: for I will bring evil upon them, even the year of their visitation, saith the LORD.

13 And I have seen folly in the prophets of Samaria; they prophesied in Baal, and caused my people Israel to err.

14 I have seen also in the prophets of Jerusalem an horrible thing: they commit adultery, and walk in lies: they strengthen also the hands of evildoers, that none doth return from his wickedness: they are all of them unto me as Sodom, and the inhabitants thereof as Gomorrah.

15 Therefore thus saith the LORD of hosts concerning the prophets; Behold, I will feed them with wormwood, and make them drink the water of gall: for from the prophets of Jerusalem is profaneness gone forth into all the land.

16 Thus saith the LORD of hosts, Hearken not unto the words of the prophets that prophesy unto you: they make you vain: they speak a vision of their own heart, and not out of the mouth of the LORD.

17 They say still unto them that despise me, The LORD has said, You shall have peace; and they say unto every one that walketh after the imagination of his own heart, No evil shall come upon you.

18 For who has stood in the counsel of the LORD, and has perceived and heard his word? who has marked his word, and heard it?

19 Behold, a whirlwind of the LORD is gone forth in fury, even a grievous whirlwind: it shall fall grievously upon the head of the wicked.

20 The anger of the LORD shall not return, until he have executed, and till he have performed the thoughts of his heart: in the latter days you shall consider it perfectly.

21 I have not sent these prophets, yet they ran: I have not spoken to them, yet they prophesied.

22 But if they had stood in my counsel, and had caused my people to hear my words, then they should have turned them from their evil way, and from the evil of their doings.

23 Am I a God at hand, saith the LORD, and not a God afar off?

24 Can any hide himself in secret places that I shall not see him? saith the LORD. Do not I fill heaven and earth? saith the LORD.

25 I have heard what the prophets said, that prophesy lies in my name, saying, I have dreamed, I have dreamed.

26 How long shall this be in the heart of the prophets that prophesy lies? yea, they are prophets of the deceit of their own heart;

27 Which think to cause my people to forget my name by their dreams which they tell every man to his neighbour, as their fathers have forgotten my name for Baal.

28 The prophet that has a dream, let him tell a dream; and he that has my word, let him speak my word faithfully. What is the chaff to the wheat? saith the LORD.

29 Is not my word like as a fire? saith the LORD; and like a hammer that breaketh the rock in pieces?

30 Therefore, behold, I am against the prophets, saith the LORD, that steal my words every one from his neighbour.

31 Behold, I am against the prophets, saith the LORD, that use their tongues, and say, He saith.

32 Behold, I am against them that prophesy false dreams, saith the LORD, and do tell them, and cause my people to err by their lies, and by their lightness; yet I sent them not, nor commanded them: therefore they shall not profit this people at all, saith the LORD.

33 And when this people, or the prophet, or a priest, shall ask you, saying, What is the burden of the LORD? you shalt then say unto them, What burden? I will even forsake you, saith the LORD.

34 And as for the prophet, and the priest, and the people, that shall say, The burden of the LORD, I will even punish that man and his house.

35 Thus shall you say every one to his neighbour, and every one to his brother, What has the LORD answered? and, What has the LORD spoken?

36 And the burden of the LORD shall you mention no more: for every man's word shall be his burden; for you have perverted the words of the living God, of the LORD of hosts our God.

37 Thus shalt you say to the prophet, What has the LORD answered you? and, What has the LORD spoken?

38 But since you say, The burden of the LORD; therefore thus saith the LORD; Because you say this word, The burden of the LORD, and I have sent unto you, saying, You shall not say, The burden of the LORD;

39 Therefore, behold, I, even I, will utterly forget you, and I will forsake you, and the city that I gave you and your fathers, and cast you out of my presence:

40 And I will bring an everlasting reproach upon you, and a perpetual shame, which shall not be forgotten.

CHAPTER 24

THE LORD shewed me, and, behold, two baskets of figs were set before the temple of the LORD, after that Nebuchadrezzar king of Babylon had carried away captive Jeconiah the son of Jehoiakim king of Judah, and the princes of Judah, with the carpenters and smiths, from Jerusalem, and had brought them to Babylon.

2 One basket had very good figs, even like the figs that are first ripe: and the other basket had very naughty figs, which could not be eaten, they were so bad.

3 Then said the LORD unto me, What seest you , Jeremiah? And I said, Figs; the good figs, very good; and the evil, very evil, that cannot be eaten, they are so evil.

4 Again the word of the LORD came unto me, saying,

5 Thus saith the LORD, the God of Israel; Like these good figs, so will I acknowledge them that are carried away captive of Judah, whom I have sent out of this place into the land of the Chaldeans for their good.

6 For I will set my eyes upon them for good, and I will bring them again to this land: and I will build them, and not pull them down; and I will plant them, and not pluck them up.

7 And I will give them an heart to know me, that I am the LORD: and they shall be my people, and I will be their God: for they shall return unto me with their whole heart.

8 And as the evil figs, which cannot be eaten, they are so evil; surely thus saith the LORD, So will I give Zedekiah the king of Judah, and his princes, and the residue of Jerusalem, that remain in this land, and them that dwell in the land of Egypt:

9 And I will deliver them to be removed into all the kingdoms of the earth for their hurt, to be a reproach and a proverb, a taunt and a curse, in all places whither I shall drive them.

10 And I will send the sword, the famine, and the pestilence, among them, till they be consumed from off the land that I gave unto them and to their fathers.

CHAPTER 25

THE word that came to Jeremiah concerning all the people of Judah in the fourth year of Jehoiakim the son of Josiah king of Judah, that was the first year of Nebuchadrezzar king of Babylon;

2 The which Jeremiah the prophet spake unto all the people of Judah, and to all the inhabitants of Jerusalem, saying,

3 From the thirteenth year of Josiah the son of Amon king of Judah, even unto this day, that is the three and twentieth year, the word of the LORD has come unto me, and I have spoken unto you, rising early and speaking; but you have not hearkened.

4 And the LORD has sent unto you all his servants the prophets, rising early and sending them; but you have not hearkened, nor inclined your ear to hear.

5 They said, Turn you again now every one from his evil way, and from the evil of your doings, and dwell in the land that the LORD has given unto you and to your fathers for ever and ever:

6 And go not after other gods to serve them, and to worship them, and provoke me not to anger with the works of your hands; and I will do you no hurt.

7 Yet you have not hearkened unto me, saith the LORD; that you might provoke me to anger with the works of your hands to your own hurt.

8 Therefore thus saith the LORD of hosts; Because you have not heard my words,

9 Behold, I will send and take all the families of the north, saith the LORD, and Nebuchadrezzar the king of Babylon, my servant, and will bring them against this land, and against the inhabitants thereof, and against all these nations round about, and will utterly destroy them, and make them an astonishment, and an hissing, and perpetual desolations.

10 Moreover I will take from them the voice of mirth, and the voice of gladness, the voice of the bridegroom, and the voice of the bride, the sound of the millstones, and the light of the candle.

11 And this whole land shall be a desolation, and an astonishment; and these nations shall serve the king of Babylon seventy years.

12 And it shall come to pass, when seventy years are accomplished, that I will punish the king of Babylon, and that nation, saith the LORD, for their iniquity, and the land of the Chaldeans, and will make it perpetual desolations.

13 And I will bring upon that land all my words which I have pronounced against it, even all that is written in this book, which Jeremiah has prophesied against all the nations.

14 For many nations and great kings shall serve themselves of them also: and I will recompense them according to their deeds, and according to the works of their own hands.

15 For thus saith the LORD God of Israel unto me; Take the wine cup of this fury at my hand, and cause all the nations, to whom I send you, to drink it.

16 And they shall drink, and be moved, and be mad, because of the sword that I will send among them.

17 Then took I the cup at the LORD's hand, and made all the nations to drink, unto whom the LORD had sent me:

18 To wit, Jerusalem, and the cities of Judah, and the kings thereof, and the princes thereof, to make them a desolation, an astonishment, an hissing, and a curse; as it is this day;

19 Pharaoh king of Egypt, and his servants, and his princes, and all his people;

20 And all the mingled people, and all the kings of the land of Uz, and all the kings of the land of the Philistines, and Ashkelon, and Azzah, and Ekron, and the remnant of Ashdod,

21 Edom, and Moab, and the children of Ammon,

22 And all the kings of Tyrus, and all the kings of Zidon, and the kings of the isles which are beyond the sea,

23 Dedan, and Tema, and Buz, and all that are in the utmost corners,

24 And all the kings of Arabia, and all the kings of the mingled people that dwell in the desert,

25 And all the kings of Zimri, and all the kings of Elam, and all the kings of the Medes,

26 And all the kings of the north, far and near, one with another, and all the kingdoms of the world, which are upon the face of the earth: and the king of Sheshach shall drink after them.

27 Therefore you shalt say unto them, Thus saith the LORD of hosts, the God of Israel; Drink you , and be drunken, and spue, and fall, and rise no more, because of the sword which I will send among you.

28 And it shall be, if they refuse to take the cup at yours hand to drink, then shalt you say unto them, Thus saith the LORD of hosts; You shall certainly drink.

29 For, lo, I begin to bring evil on the city which is called by my name, and should you be utterly unpunished? You shall not be unpunished: for I will call for a sword upon all the inhabitants of the earth, saith the LORD of hosts.

30 Therefore prophesy you against them all these words, and say unto them, The LORD shall roar from on high, and utter his voice from his holy habitation; he shall mightily roar upon his habitation; he shall give a shout, as they that tread the grapes, against all the inhabitants of the earth.

31 A noise shall come even to the ends of the earth; for the LORD has a controversy with the nations, he will plead with all flesh; he will give them that are wicked to the sword, saith the LORD.

32 Thus saith the LORD of hosts, Behold, evil shall go forth from nation to nation, and a great whirlwind shall be raised up from the coasts of the earth.

33 And the slain of the LORD shall be at that day from one end of the earth even unto the other end of the earth: they shall not be lamented, neither gathered, nor buried; they shall be dung upon the ground.

34 Howl, you shepherds, and cry; and wallow yourselves in the ashes, you principal of the flock: for the days of your slaughter and of your dispersions are accomplished; and you shall fall like a pleasant vessel.

35 And the shepherds shall have no way to flee, nor the principal of the flock to escape.

36 A voice of the cry of the shepherds, and an howling of the principal of the flock, shall be heard: for the LORD has spoiled their pasture.

37 And the peaceable habitations are cut down because of the fierce anger of the LORD.

38 He has forsaken his covert, as the lion: for their land is desolate because of the fierceness of the oppressor, and because of his fierce anger.

CHAPTER 26

IN the beginning of the reign of Jehoiakim the son of Josiah king of Judah came this word from the LORD, saying,

2 Thus saith the LORD; Stand in the court of the LORD's house, and speak unto all the cities of Judah, which come to worship in the LORD's house, all the words that I command you to speak unto them; diminish not a word:

3 If so be they will hearken, and turn every man from his evil way, that I may repent me of the evil, which I purpose to do unto them because of the evil of their doings.

4 And you shalt say unto them, Thus saith the LORD; If you will not hearken to me, to walk in my law, which I have set before you,

5 To hearken to the words of my servants the prophets, whom I sent unto you, both rising up early, and sending them, but you have not hearkened;

6 Then will I make this house like Shiloh, and will make this city a curse to all the nations of the earth.

7 So the priests and the prophets and all the people heard Jeremiah speaking these words in the house of the LORD.

8Now it came to pass, when Jeremiah had made an end of speaking all that the LORD had commanded him to speak unto all the people, that the priests and the prophets and all the people took him, saying, You shalt surely die.

9 Why have you prophesied in the name of the LORD, saying, This house shall be like Shiloh, and this city shall be desolate without an inhabitant? And all the people were gathered against Jeremiah in the house of the LORD.

10When the princes of Judah heard these things, then they came up from the king's house unto the house of the LORD, and sat down in the entry of the new gate of the LORD's house.

11 Then spake the priests and the prophets unto the princes and to all the people, saying, This man is worthy to die; for he has prophesied against this city, as you have heard with your ears.

12Then spake Jeremiah unto all the princes and to all the people, saying, The LORD sent me to prophesy against this house and against this city all the words that you have heard.

13 Therefore now amend your ways and your doings, and obey the voice of the LORD your God; and the LORD will repent him of the evil that he has pronounced against you.

14 As for me, behold, I am in your hand: do with me as seemeth good and meet unto you.

15 But know you for certain, that if you put me to death, you shall surely bring innocent blood upon yourselves, and upon this city, and upon the inhabitants thereof: for of a truth the LORD has sent me unto you to speak all these words in your ears.

16Then said the princes and all the people unto the priests and to the prophets; This man is not worthy to die: for he has spoken to us in the name of the LORD our God.

17 Then rose up certain of the elders of the land, and spake to all the assembly of the people, saying,

18 Micah the Morasthite prophesied in the days of Hezekiah king of Judah, and spake to all the people of Judah, saying, Thus saith the LORD of hosts; Zion shall be plowed like a field, and Jerusalem shall become heaps, and the mountain of the house as the high places of a forest.

19 Did Hezekiah king of Judah and all Judah put him at all to death? did he not fear the LORD, and besought the LORD, and the LORD repented him of the evil which he had pronounced against them? Thus might we procure great evil against our souls.

20 And there was also a man that prophesied in the name of the LORD, Urijah the son of Shemaiah of Kirjath-jearim, who prophesied against this city and against this land according to all the words of Jeremiah:

21 And when Jehoiakim the king, with all his mighty men, and all the princes, heard his words, the king sought to put him to death: but when Urijah heard it, he was afraid, and fled, and went into Egypt;

22 And Jehoiakim the king sent men into Egypt, namely, Elnathan the son of Achbor, and certain men with him into Egypt.

23 And they fetched forth Urijah out of Egypt, and brought him unto Jehoiakim the king; who slew him with the sword, and cast his dead body into the graves of the common people.

24 Nevertheless the hand of Ahikam the son of Shaphan was with Jeremiah, that they should not give him into the hand of the people to put him to death.

CHAPTER 27

IN the beginning of the reign of Jehoiakim the son of Josiah king of Judah came this word unto Jeremiah from the LORD, saying,

2 Thus saith the LORD to me; Make you bonds and yokes, and put them upon your neck,

3 And send them to the king of Edom, and to the king of Moab, and to the king of the Ammonites, and to the king of Tyrus, and to the king of Zidon, by the hand of the messengers which come to Jerusalem unto Zedekiah king of Judah;

4 And command them to say unto their masters, Thus saith the LORD of hosts, the God of Israel; Thus shall you say unto your masters;

5 I have made the earth, the man and the beast that are upon the ground, by my great power and by my outstretched arm, and have given it unto whom it seemed meet unto me.

6 And now have I given all these lands into the hand of Nebuchadnezzar the king of Babylon, my servant; and the beasts of the field have I given him also to serve him.

7 And all nations shall serve him, and his son, and his son's son, until the very time of his land come: and then many nations and great kings shall serve themselves of him.

8 And it shall come to pass, that the nation and kingdom which will not serve the same Nebuchadnezzar the king of Babylon, and that will not put their neck under the yoke of the king of Babylon, that nation will I punish, saith the LORD, with the sword, and with the famine, and with the pestilence, until I have consumed them by his hand.

9 Therefore hearken not you to your prophets, nor to your diviners, nor to your dreamers, nor to your enchanters, nor to your sorcerers, which speak unto you, saying, You shall not serve the king of Babylon:

10 For they prophesy a lie unto you, to remove you far from your land; and that I should drive you out, and you should perish.

11 But the nations that bring their neck under the yoke of the king of Babylon, and serve him, those will I let remain still in their own land, saith the LORD; and they shall till it, and dwell therein.

12I spake also to Zedekiah king of Judah according to all these words, saying, Bring your necks under the yoke of the king of Babylon, and serve him and his people, and live.

13 Why will you die, you and your people, by the sword, by the famine, and by the pestilence, as the LORD has spoken against the nation that will not serve the king of Babylon?

14 Therefore hearken not unto the words of the prophets that speak unto you, saying, You shall not serve the king of Babylon: for they prophesy a lie unto you.

15 For I have not sent them, saith the LORD, yet they prophesy a lie in my name; that I might drive you out, and that you might perish, you , and the prophets that prophesy unto you.

16 Also I spake to the priests and to all this people, saying, Thus saith the LORD; Hearken not to the words of your prophets that prophesy unto you, saying, Behold, the vessels of the LORD's house shall now shortly be brought again from Babylon: for they prophesy a lie unto you.

17 Hearken not unto them; serve the king of Babylon, and live: wherefore should this city be laid waste?

18 But if they be prophets, and if the word of the LORD be with them, let them now make intercession to the LORD of hosts, that the vessels which are left in the house of the LORD, and in the house of the king of Judah, and at Jerusalem, go not to Babylon.

19For thus saith the LORD of hosts concerning the pillars, and concerning the sea, and concerning the bases, and concerning the residue of the vessels that remain in this city,

20 Which Nebuchadnezzar king of Babylon took not, when he carried away captive Jeconiah the son of Jehoiakim king of Judah from Jerusalem to Babylon, and all the nobles of Judah and Jerusalem;

21 Yea, thus saith the LORD of hosts, the God of Israel, concerning the vessels that remain in the house of the LORD, and in the house of the king of Judah and of Jerusalem;

22 They shall be carried to Babylon, and there shall they be until the day that I visit them, saith the LORD; then will I bring them up, and restore them to this place.

CHAPTER 28

AND it came to pass the same year, in the beginning of the reign of Zedekiah king of Judah, in the fourth year, and in the fifth month, that Hananiah the son of Azur the prophet, which was of Gibeon, spake unto me in the house of the LORD, in the presence of the priests and of all the people, saying,

2 Thus speaketh the LORD of hosts, the God of Israel, saying, I have broken the yoke of the king of Babylon.

3 Within two full years will I bring again into this place all the vessels of the LORD's house, that Nebuchadnezzar king of Babylon took away from this place, and carried them to Babylon:

4 And I will bring again to this place Jeconiah the son of Jehoiakim king of Judah, with all the captives of Judah, that went into Babylon, saith the LORD: for I will break the yoke of the king of Babylon.

5Then the prophet Jeremiah said unto the prophet Hananiah in the presence of the priests, and in the presence of all the people that stood in the house of the LORD,

6 Even the prophet Jeremiah said, Amen: the LORD do so: the LORD perform your words which you have prophesied, to bring again the vessels of the LORD's house, and all that is carried away captive, from Babylon into this place.

7 Nevertheless hear you now this word that I speak in yours ears, and in the ears of all the people;

8 The prophets that have been before me and before you of old prophesied both against many countries, and against great kingdoms, of war, and of evil, and of pestilence.

9 The prophet which prophesieth of peace, when the word of the prophet shall come to pass, then shall the prophet be known, that the LORD has truly sent him.

10 Then Hananiah the prophet took the yoke from off the prophet Jeremiah's neck, and brake it.

11 And Hananiah spake in the presence of all the people, saying, Thus saith the LORD; Even so will I break the yoke of Nebuchadnezzar king of Babylon from the neck of all nations within the space of two full years. And the prophet Jeremiah went his way.

12 Then the word of the LORD came unto Jeremiah the prophet, after that Hananiah the prophet had broken the yoke from off the neck of the prophet Jeremiah, saying,

13 Go and tell Hananiah, saying, Thus saith the LORD; You have broken the yokes of wood; but you shalt make for them yokes of iron.

14 For thus saith the LORD of hosts, the God of Israel; I have put a yoke of iron upon the neck of all these nations, that they may serve Nebuchadnezzar king of Babylon; and they shall serve him: and I have given him the beasts of the field also.

15 Then said the prophet Jeremiah unto Hananiah the prophet, Hear now, Hananiah; The LORD has not sent you; but you makest this people to trust in a lie.

16 Therefore thus saith the LORD; Behold, I will cast you from off the face of the earth: this year you shalt die, because you have taught rebellion against the LORD.

17 So Hananiah the prophet died the same year in the seventh month.

CHAPTER 29

NOW these are the words of the letter that Jeremiah the prophet sent from Jerusalem unto the residue of the elders which were carried away captives, and to the priests, and to the prophets, and to all the people whom Nebuchadnezzar had carried away captive from Jerusalem to Babylon;

2 (After that Jeconiah the king, and the queen, and the eunuchs, the princes of Judah and Jerusalem, and the carpenters, and the smiths, were departed from Jerusalem;)

3 By the hand of Elasah the son of Shaphan, and Gemariah the son of Hilkiah, (whom Zedekiah king of Judah sent unto Babylon to Nebuchadnezzar king of Babylon) saying,

4 Thus saith the LORD of hosts, the God of Israel, unto all that are carried away captives, whom I have caused to be carried away from Jerusalem unto Babylon;

5 Build you houses, and dwell in them; and plant gardens, and eat the fruit of them;

6 Take you wives, and beget sons and daughters; and take wives for your sons, and give your daughters to husbands, that they may bear sons and daughters; that you may be increased there, and not diminished.

7 And seek the peace of the city whither I have caused you to be carried away captives, and pray unto the LORD for it: for in the peace thereof shall you have peace.

8 For thus saith the LORD of hosts, the God of Israel; Let not your prophets and your diviners, that be in the midst of you, deceive you, neither hearken to your dreams which you cause to be dreamed.

9 For they prophesy falsely unto you in my name: I have not sent them, saith the LORD.

10 For thus saith the LORD, That after seventy years be accomplished at Babylon I will visit you, and perform my good word toward you, in causing you to return to this place.

11 For I know the thoughts that I think toward you, saith the LORD, thoughts of peace, and not of evil, to give you an expected end.

12 Then shall you call upon me, and you shall go and pray unto me, and I will hearken unto you.

13 And you shall seek me, and find me, when you shall search for me with all your heart.

14 And I will be found of you, saith the LORD: and I will turn away your captivity, and I will gather you from all the nations, and from all the places whither I have driven you, saith the LORD; and I will bring you again into the place whence I caused you to be carried away captive.

15 Because you have said, The LORD has raised us up prophets in Babylon;

16 Know that thus saith the LORD of the king that sitteth upon the throne of David, and of all the people that dwelleth in this city, and of your brethren that are not gone forth with you into captivity;

17 Thus saith the LORD of hosts; Behold, I will send upon them the sword, the famine, and the pestilence, and will make them like vile figs, that cannot be eaten, they are so evil.

18 And I will persecute them with the sword, with the famine, and with the pestilence, and will deliver them to be removed to all the kingdoms of the earth, to be a curse, and an astonishment, and an hissing, and a reproach, among all the nations whither I have driven them:

19 Because they have not hearkened to my words, saith the LORD, which I sent unto them by my servants the prophets, rising up early and sending them; but you would not hear, saith the LORD.

20 Hear you therefore the word of the LORD, all you of the captivity, whom I have sent from Jerusalem to Babylon:

21 Thus saith the LORD of hosts, the God of Israel, of Ahab the son of Kolaiah, and of Zedekiah the son of Maaseiah, which prophesy a lie unto you in my name; Behold, I will deliver them into the hand of Nebuchadrezzar king of Babylon; and he shall slay them before your eyes;

22 And of them shall be taken up a curse by all the captivity of Judah which are in Babylon, saying, The LORD make you like Zedekiah and like Ahab, whom the king of Babylon roasted in the fire;

23 Because they have committed villany in Israel, and have committed adultery with their neighbours' wives, and have spoken lying words in my name, which I have not commanded them; even I know, and am a witness, saith the LORD.

24 Thus shalt you also speak to Shemaiah the Nehelamite, saying,

25 Thus speaketh the LORD of hosts, the God of Israel, saying, Because you have sent letters in your name unto all the people that are at Jerusalem, and to Zephaniah the son of Maaseiah the priest, and to all the priests, saying,

26 The LORD has made you priest in the stead of Jehoiada the priest, that you should be officers in the house of the LORD, for every man that is mad, and maketh himself a prophet, that you shouldest put him in prison, and in the stocks.

27 Now therefore why have you not reproved Jeremiah of Anathoth, which maketh himself a prophet to you?

28 For therefore he sent unto us in Babylon, saying, This captivity is long: build you houses, and dwell in them; and plant gardens, and eat the fruit of them.

29 And Zephaniah the priest read this letter in the ears of Jeremiah the prophet.

30 Then came the word of the LORD unto Jeremiah, saying,

31 Send to all them of the captivity, saying, Thus saith the LORD concerning Shemaiah the Nehelamite; Because that Shemaiah has prophesied unto you, and I sent him not, and he caused you to trust in a lie:

32 Therefore thus saith the LORD; Behold, I will punish Shemaiah the Nehelamite, and his seed: he shall not have a man to dwell among this people; neither shall he behold the good that I will do for my people, saith the LORD; because he has taught rebellion against the LORD.

CHAPTER 30

THE word that came to Jeremiah from the LORD, saying,

2 Thus speaketh the LORD God of Israel, saying, Write you all the words that I have spoken unto you in a book.

3 For, lo, the days come, saith the LORD, that I will bring again the captivity of my people Israel and Judah, saith the LORD: and I will cause them to return to the land that I gave to their fathers, and they shall possess it.

4 And these are the words that the LORD spake concerning Israel and concerning Judah.

5 For thus saith the LORD; We have heard a voice of trembling, of fear, and not of peace.

6 Ask you now, and see whether a man doth travail with child? wherefore do I see every man with his hands on his loins, as a woman in travail, and all faces are turned into paleness?

7 Alas! for that day is great, so that none is like it: it is even the time of Jacob's trouble; but he shall be saved out of it.

8 For it shall come to pass in that day, saith the LORD of hosts, that I will break his yoke from off your neck, and will burst your bonds, and strangers shall no more serve themselves of him:

9 But they shall serve the LORD their God, and David their king, whom I will raise up unto them.

10 Therefore fear you not, O my servant Jacob, saith the LORD; neither be dismayed, O Israel: for, lo, I will save you from afar, and your seed from the land of their captivity; and Jacob shall return, and shall be in rest, and be quiet, and none shall make him afraid.

11 For I am with you, saith the LORD, to save you: though I make a full end of all nations whither I have scattered you, yet will I not make a full end of you: but I will correct you in measure, and will not leave you altogether unpunished.

12 For thus saith the LORD, Your bruise is incurable, and your wound is grievous.

13 There is none to plead your cause, that you mayest be bound up: you have no healing medicines.

14 All your lovers have forgotten you; they seek you not; for I have wounded you with the wound of an enemy, with the chastisement of a cruel one, for the multitude of yours iniquity; because your sins were increased.

15 Why criest you for yours affliction? your sorrow is incurable for the multitude of yours iniquity: because your sins were increased, I have done these things unto you.

16 Therefore all they that devour you shall be devoured; and all yours adversaries, every one of them, shall go into captivity; and they that spoil you shall be a spoil, and all that prey upon you will I give for a prey.

17 For I will restore health unto you, and I will heal you of your wounds, saith the LORD; because they called you an Outcast, saying, This is Zion, whom no man seeketh after.

18 Thus saith the LORD; Behold, I will bring again the captivity of Jacob's tents, and have mercy on his dwellingplaces; and the city shall be builded upon her own heap, and the palace shall remain after the manner thereof.

19 And out of them shall proceed thanksgiving and the voice of them that make merry: and I will multiply them, and they shall not be few; I will also glorify them, and they shall not be small.

20 Their children also shall be as aforetime, and their congregation shall be established before me, and I will punish all that oppress them.

21 And their nobles shall be of themselves, and their governor shall proceed from the midst of them; and I will cause him to draw near, and he shall approach unto me: for who is this that engaged his heart to approach unto me? saith the LORD.

22 And you shall be my people, and I will be your God.

23 Behold, the whirlwind of the LORD goeth forth with fury, a continuing whirlwind: it shall fall with pain upon the head of the wicked.

24 The fierce anger of the LORD shall not return, until he have done it, and until he have performed the intents of his heart: in the latter days you shall consider it.

CHAPTER 31

AT the same time, saith the LORD, will I be the God of all the families of Israel, and they shall be my people.

2 Thus saith the LORD, The people which were left of the sword found grace in the wilderness; even Israel, when I went to cause him to rest.

3 The LORD has appeared of old unto me, saying, Yea, I have loved you with an everlasting love: therefore with lovingkindness have I drawn you.

4 Again I will build you, and you shalt be built, O virgin of Israel: you shalt again be adorned with your tabrets, and shalt go forth in the dances of them that make merry.

5 You shalt yet plant vines upon the mountains of Samaria: the planters shall plant, and shall eat them as common things.

6 For there shall be a day, that the watchmen upon the mount Ephraim shall cry, Arise you , and let us go up to Zion unto the LORD our God.

7 For thus saith the LORD; Sing with gladness for Jacob, and shout among the chief of the nations: publish you , praise you , and say, O LORD, save your people, the remnant of Israel.

8 Behold, I will bring them from the north country, and gather them from the coasts of the earth, and with them the blind and the lame, the woman with child and her that travaileth with child together: a great company shall return thither.

9 They shall come with weeping, and with supplications will I lead them: I will cause them to walk by the rivers of waters in a straight way, wherein they shall not stumble: for I am a father to Israel, and Ephraim is my firstborn.

10 Hear the word of the LORD, O you nations, and declare it in the isles afar off, and say, He that scattered Israel will gather him, and keep him, as a shepherd doth his flock.

11 For the LORD has redeemed Jacob, and ransomed him from the hand of him that was stronger than he.

12 Therefore they shall come and sing in the height of Zion, and shall flow together to the goodness of the LORD, for wheat, and for wine, and for oil, and for the young of the flock and of the herd: and their soul shall be as a watered garden; and they shall not sorrow any more at all.

13 Then shall the virgin rejoice in the dance, both young men and old together: for I will turn their mourning into joy, and will comfort them, and make them rejoice from their sorrow.

14 And I will satiate the soul of the priests with fatness, and my people shall be satisfied with my goodness, saith the LORD.

15 Thus saith the LORD; A voice was heard in Ramah, lamentation, and bitter weeping; Rahel weeping for her children refused to be comforted for her children, because they were not.

16 Thus saith the LORD; Refrain your voice from weeping, and yours eyes from tears: for your work shall be rewarded, saith the LORD; and they shall come again from the land of the enemy.

17 And there is hope in yours end, saith the LORD, that your children shall come again to their own border.

18 I have surely heard Ephraim bemoaning himself thus; You have chastised me, and I was chastised, as a bullock unaccustomed to the yoke: turn you me, and I shall be turned; for you are the LORD my God.

19 Surely after that I was turned, I repented; and after that I was instructed, I struck upon my thigh: I was ashamed, yea, even confounded, because I did bear the reproach of my youth.

20 Is Ephraim my dear son? is he a pleasant child? for since I spake against him, I do earnestly remember him still: therefore my bowels are troubled for him; I will surely have mercy upon him, saith the LORD.

21 Set you up waymarks, make you high heaps: set yours heart toward the highway, even the way which you wentest: turn again, O virgin of Israel, turn again to these your cities.

22 How long will you go about, O you backsliding daughter? for the LORD has created a new thing in the earth, A woman shall compass a man.

23 Thus saith the LORD of hosts, the God of Israel; As yet they shall use this speech in the land of Judah and in the cities thereof, when I shall bring again their captivity; The LORD bless you, O habitation of justice, and mountain of holiness.

24 And there shall dwell in Judah itself, and in all the cities thereof together, husbandmen, and they that go forth with flocks.

25 For I have satiated the weary soul, and I have replenished every sorrowful soul.

26 Upon this I awaked, and beheld; and my sleep was sweet unto me.

27 Behold, the days come, saith the LORD, that I will sow the house of Israel and the house of Judah with the seed of man, and with the seed of beast.

28 And it shall come to pass, that like as I have watched over them, to pluck up, and to break down, and to throw down, and to destroy, and to afflict; so will I watch over them, to build, and to plant, saith the LORD.

29 In those days they shall say no more, The fathers have eaten a sour grape, and the children's teeth are set on edge.

30 But every one shall die for his own iniquity: every man that eateth the sour grape, his teeth shall be set on edge.

31 Behold, the days come, saith the LORD, that I will make a new covenant with the house of Israel, and with the house of Judah:

32 Not according to the covenant that I made with their fathers in the day that I took them by the hand to bring them out of the land of Egypt; which my covenant they brake, although I was an husband unto them, saith the LORD:

33 But this shall be the covenant that I will make with the house of Israel; After those days, saith the LORD, I will put my law in their inward parts, and write it in their hearts; and will be their God, and they shall be my people.

34 And they shall teach no more every man his neighbour, and every man his brother, saying, Know the LORD: for they shall all know me, from the least of them unto the greatest of them, saith the LORD: for I will forgive their iniquity, and I will remember their sin no more.

35 Thus saith the LORD, which giveth the sun for a light by day, and the ordinances of the moon and of the stars for a light by night, which divideth the sea when the waves thereof roar; The LORD of hosts is his name:

36 If those ordinances depart from before me, saith the LORD, then the seed of Israel also shall cease from being a nation before me for ever.

37 Thus saith the LORD; If heaven above can be measured, and the foundations of the earth searched out beneath, I will also cast off all the seed of Israel for all that they have done, saith the LORD.

38 Behold, the days come, saith the LORD, that the city shall be built to the LORD from the tower of Hananeel unto the gate of the corner.

39 And the measuring line shall yet go forth over against it upon the hill Gareb, and shall compass about to Goath.

40 And the whole valley of the dead bodies, and of the ashes, and all the fields unto the brook of Kidron, unto the corner of the horse gate toward the east, shall be holy unto the LORD; it shall not be plucked up, nor thrown down any more for ever.

CHAPTER 32

THE word that came to Jeremiah from the LORD in the tenth year of Zedekiah king of Judah, which was the eighteenth year of Nebuchadrezzar.

2 For then the king of Babylon's army besieged Jerusalem: and Jeremiah the prophet was shut up in the court of the prison, which was in the king of Judah's house.

3 For Zedekiah king of Judah had shut him up, saying, Wherefore dost you prophesy, and say, Thus saith the LORD, Behold, I will give this city into the hand of the king of Babylon, and he shall take it;

4 And Zedekiah king of Judah shall not escape out of the hand of the Chaldeans, but shall surely be delivered into the hand of the king of Babylon, and shall speak with him mouth to mouth, and his eyes shall behold his eyes;

5 And he shall lead Zedekiah to Babylon, and there shall he be until I visit him, saith the LORD: though you fight with the Chaldeans, you shall not prosper?

6And Jeremiah said, The word of the LORD came unto me, saying,

7 Behold, Hanameel the son of Shallum yours uncle shall come unto you, saying, Buy you my field that is in Anathoth: for the right of redemption is yours to buy it.

8 So Hanameel my uncle's son came to me in the court of the prison according to the word of the LORD, and said unto me, Buy my field, I pray you, that is in Anathoth, which is in the country of Benjamin: for the right of inheritance is yours, and the redemption is yours; buy it for yourself. Then I knew that this was the word of the LORD.

9 And I bought the field of Hanameel my uncle's son, that was in Anathoth, and weighed him the money, even seventeen shekels of silver.

10 And I subscribed the evidence, and sealed it, and took witnesses, and weighed him the money in the balances.

11 So I took the evidence of the purchase, both that which was sealed according to the law and custom, and that which was open:

12 And I gave the evidence of the purchase unto Baruch the son of Neriah, the son of Maaseiah, in the sight of Hanameel my uncle's son, and in the presence of the witnesses that subscribed the book of the purchase, before all the Jews that sat in the court of the prison.

13And I charged Baruch before them, saying,

14 Thus saith the LORD of hosts, the God of Israel; Take these evidences, this evidence of the purchase, both which is sealed, and this evidence which is open; and put them in an earthen vessel, that they may continue many days.

15 For thus saith the LORD of hosts, the God of Israel; Houses and fields and vineyards shall be possessed again in this land.

16Now when I had delivered the evidence of the purchase unto Baruch the son of Neriah, I prayed unto the LORD, saying,

17 Ah Lord GOD! behold, you have made the heaven and the earth by your great power and stretched out arm, and there is nothing too hard for you:

18 You shewest lovingkindness unto thousands, and recompensest the iniquity of the fathers into the bosom of their children after them: the Great, the Mighty God, the LORD of hosts, is his name,

19 Great in counsel, and mighty in work: for yours eyes are open upon all the ways of the sons of men: to give every one according to his ways, and according to the fruit of his doings:

20 Which have set signs and wonders in the land of Egypt, even unto this day, and in Israel, and among other men; and have made you a name, as at this day;

21 And have brought forth your people Israel out of the land of Egypt with signs, and with wonders, and with a strong hand, and with a stretched out arm, and with great terror;

22 And have given them this land, which you did swear to their fathers to give them, a land flowing with milk and honey;

23 And they came in, and possessed it; but they obeyed not your voice, neither walked in your law; they have done nothing of all that you commandedst them to do: therefore you have caused all this evil to come upon them:

24 Behold the mounts, they are come unto the city to take it; and the city is given into the hand of the Chaldeans, that fight against it, because of the sword, and of the famine, and of the pestilence: and what you have spoken is come to pass; and, behold, you seest it.

25 And you have said unto me, O Lord GOD, Buy you the field for money, and take witnesses; for the city is given into the hand of the Chaldeans.

26Then came the word of the LORD unto Jeremiah, saying,

27 Behold, I am the LORD, the God of all flesh: is there any thing too hard for me?

28 Therefore thus saith the LORD; Behold, I will give this city into the hand of the Chaldeans, and into the hand of Nebuchadrezzar king of Babylon, and he shall take it:

29 And the Chaldeans, that fight against this city, shall come and set fire on this city, and burn it with the houses, upon whose roofs they have offered incense unto Baal, and poured out drink offerings unto other gods, to provoke me to anger.

30 For the children of Israel and the children of Judah have only done evil before me from their youth: for the children of Israel have only provoked me to anger with the work of their hands, saith the LORD.

31 For this city has been to me as a provocation of my anger and of my fury from the day that they built it even unto this day; that I should remove it from before my face,

32 Because of all the evil of the children of Israel and of the children of Judah, which they have done to provoke me to anger, they, their kings, their princes, their priests, and their prophets, and the men of Judah, and the inhabitants of Jerusalem.

33 And they have turned unto me the back, and not the face: though I taught them, rising up early and teaching them, yet they have not hearkened to receive instruction.

34 But they set their abominations in the house, which is called by my name, to defile it.

35 And they built the high places of Baal, which are in the valley of the son of Hinnom, to cause their sons and their daughters to pass through the fire unto Molech; which I commanded them not, neither came it into my mind, that they should do this abomination, to cause Judah to sin.

36And now therefore thus saith the LORD, the God of Israel, concerning this city, whereof you say, It shall be delivered into the hand of the king of Babylon by the sword, and by the famine, and by the pestilence;

37 Behold, I will gather them out of all countries, whither I have driven them in my anger, and in my fury, and in great wrath; and I will bring them again unto this place, and I will cause them to dwell safely:

38 And they shall be my people, and I will be their God:

39 And I will give them one heart, and one way, that they may fear me for ever, for the good of them, and of their children after them:

40 And I will make an everlasting covenant with them, that I will not turn away from them, to do them good; but I will put my fear in their hearts, that they shall not depart from me.

41 Yea, I will rejoice over them to do them good, and I will plant them in this land assuredly with my whole heart and with my whole soul.

42 For thus saith the LORD; Like as I have brought all this great evil upon this people, so will I bring upon them all the good that I have promised them.

43 And fields shall be bought in this land, whereof you say, It is desolate without man or beast; it is given into the hand of the Chaldeans.

44 Men shall buy fields for money, and subscribe evidences, and seal them, and take witnesses in the land of Benjamin, and in the places about Jerusalem, and in the cities of Judah, and in the cities of the mountains, and in the cities of the valley, and in the cities of the south: for I will cause their captivity to return, saith the LORD.

CHAPTER 33

MOREOVER the word of the LORD came unto Jeremiah the second time, while he was yet shut up in the court of the prison, saying,

2 Thus saith the LORD the maker thereof, the LORD that formed it, to establish it; the LORD is his name;

3 Call unto me, and I will answer you, and shew you great and mighty things, which you knowest not.

4 For thus saith the LORD, the God of Israel, concerning the houses of this city, and concerning the houses of the kings of Judah, which are thrown down by the mounts, and by the sword;

5 They come to fight with the Chaldeans, but it is to fill them with the dead bodies of men, whom I have slain in my anger and in my fury, and for all whose wickedness I have hid my face from this city.

6 Behold, I will bring it health and cure, and I will cure them, and will reveal unto them the abundance of peace and truth.

7 And I will cause the captivity of Judah and the captivity of Israel to return, and will build them, as at the first.

8 And I will cleanse them from all their iniquity, whereby they have sinned against me; and I will pardon all their iniquities, whereby they have sinned, and whereby they have transgressed against me.

9And it shall be to me a name of joy, a praise and an honour before all the nations of the earth, which shall hear all the good that I do unto them: and they shall fear and tremble for all the goodness and for all the prosperity that I procure unto it.

10 Thus saith the LORD; Again there shall be heard in this place, which you say shall be desolate without man and without beast, even in the cities of Judah, and in the streets of Jerusalem, that are desolate, without man, and without inhabitant, and without beast,

11 The voice of joy, and the voice of gladness, the voice of the bridegroom, and the voice of the bride, the voice of them that shall say, Praise the LORD of hosts: for the LORD is good; for his mercy endureth for ever: and of them that shall bring the sacrifice of praise into the house of the LORD. For I will cause to return the captivity of the land, as at the first, saith the LORD.

12 Thus saith the LORD of hosts; Again in this place, which is desolate without man and without beast, and in all the cities thereof, shall be an habitation of shepherds causing their flocks to lie down.

13 In the cities of the mountains, in the cities of the vale, and in the cities of the south, and in the land of Benjamin, and in the places about Jerusalem, and in the cities of Judah, shall the flocks pass again under the hands of him that telleth them, saith the LORD.

14 Behold, the days come, saith the LORD, that I will perform that good thing which I have promised unto the house of Israel and to the house of Judah.

15 In those days, and at that time, will I cause the Branch of righteousness to grow up unto David; and he shall execute judgment and righteousness in the land.

16 In those days shall Judah be saved, and Jerusalem shall dwell safely: and this is the name wherewith she shall be called, The LORD our righteousness.

17 For thus saith the LORD; David shall never want a man to sit upon the throne of the house of Israel;

18 Neither shall the priests the Levites want a man before me to offer burnt offerings, and to kindle meat offerings, and to do sacrifice continually.

19 And the word of the LORD came unto Jeremiah, saying,

20 Thus saith the LORD; If you can break my covenant of the day, and my covenant of the night, and that there should not be day and night in their season;

21 Then may also my covenant be broken with David my servant, that he should not have a son to reign upon his throne; and with the Levites the priests, my ministers.

22 As the host of heaven cannot be numbered, neither the sand of the sea measured: so will I multiply the seed of David my servant, and the Levites that minister unto me.

23 Moreover the word of the LORD came to Jeremiah, saying,

24 Considerest you not what this people have spoken, saying, The two families which the LORD has chosen, he has even cast them off? thus they have despised my people, that they should be no more a nation before them.

25 Thus saith the LORD; If my covenant be not with day and night, and if I have not appointed the ordinances of heaven and earth;

26 Then will I cast away the seed of Jacob, and David my servant, so that I will not take any of his seed to be rulers over the seed of Abraham, Isaac, and Jacob: for I will cause their captivity to return, and have mercy on them.

CHAPTER 34

THE word which came unto Jeremiah from the LORD, when Nebuchadnezzar king of Babylon, and all his army, and all the kingdoms of the earth of his dominion, and all the people, fought against Jerusalem, and against all the cities thereof, saying,

2 Thus saith the LORD, the God of Israel; Go and speak to Zedekiah king of Judah, and tell him, Thus saith the LORD; Behold, I will give this city into the hand of the king of Babylon, and he shall burn it with fire:

3 And you shalt not escape out of his hand, but shalt surely be taken, and delivered into his hand; and yours eyes shall behold the eyes of the king of Babylon, and he shall speak with you mouth to mouth, and you shalt go to Babylon.

4 Yet hear the word of the LORD, O Zedekiah king of Judah; Thus saith the LORD of you, You shalt not die by the sword:

5 But you shalt die in peace: and with the burnings of your fathers, the former kings which were before you, so shall they burn odours for you; and they will lament you, saying, Ah lord! for I have pronounced the word, saith the LORD.

6 Then Jeremiah the prophet spake all these words unto Zedekiah king of Judah in Jerusalem,

7 When the king of Babylon's army fought against Jerusalem, and against all the cities of Judah that were left, against Lachish, and against Azekah: for these defenced cities remained of the cities of Judah.

8 This is the word that came unto Jeremiah from the LORD, after that the king Zedekiah had made a covenant with all the people which were at Jerusalem, to proclaim liberty unto them;

9 That every man should let his manservant, and every man his maidservant, being an Hebrew or an Hebrewess, go free; that none should serve himself of them, to wit, of a Jew his brother.

10 Now when all the princes, and all the people, which had entered into the covenant, heard that every one should let his manservant, and every one his maidservant, go free, that none should serve themselves of them any more, then they obeyed, and let them go.

11 But afterward they turned, and caused the servants and the handmaids, whom they had let go free, to return, and brought them into subjection for servants and for handmaids.

12 Therefore the word of the LORD came to Jeremiah from the LORD, saying,

13 Thus saith the LORD, the God of Israel; I made a covenant with your fathers in the day that I brought them forth out of the land of Egypt, out of the house of bondmen, saying,

14 At the end of seven years let you go every man his brother an Hebrew, which has been sold unto you; and when he has served you six years, you shalt let him go free from you: but your fathers hearkened not unto me, neither inclined their ear.

15 And you were now turned, and had done right in my sight, in proclaiming liberty every man to his neighbour; and you had made a covenant before me in the house which is called by my name:

16 But you turned and polluted my name, and caused every man his servant, and every man his handmaid, whom you had set at liberty at their pleasure, to return, and brought them into subjection, to be unto you for servants and for handmaids.

17 Therefore thus saith the LORD; You have not hearkened unto me, in proclaiming liberty, every one to his brother, and every man to his neighbour: behold, I proclaim a liberty for you, saith the LORD, to the sword, to the pestilence, and to the famine; and I will make you to be removed into all the kingdoms of the earth.

18 And I will give the men that have transgressed my covenant, which have not performed the words of the covenant which they had made before me, when they cut the calf in twain, and passed between the parts thereof,

19 The princes of Judah, and the princes of Jerusalem, the eunuchs, and the priests, and all the people of the land, which passed between the parts of the calf;

20 I will even give them into the hand of their enemies, and into the hand of them that seek their life: and their dead bodies shall be for meat unto the fowls of the heaven, and to the beasts of the earth.

21 And Zedekiah king of Judah and his princes will I give into the hand of their enemies, and into the hand of them that seek their life, and into the hand of the king of Babylon's army, which are gone up from you.

22 Behold, I will command, saith the LORD, and cause them to return to this city; and they shall fight against it, and take it, and burn it with fire: and I will make the cities of Judah a desolation without an inhabitant.

CHAPTER 35

THE word which came unto Jeremiah from the LORD in the days of Jehoiakim the son of Josiah king of Judah, saying,

2 Go unto the house of the Rechabites, and speak unto them, and bring them into the house of the LORD, into one of the chambers, and give them wine to drink.

3 Then I took Jaazaniah the son of Jeremiah, the son of Habaziniah, and his brethren, and all his sons, and the whole house of the Rechabites;

4 And I brought them into the house of the LORD, into the chamber of the sons of Hanan, the son of Igdaliah, a man of God, which was by the chamber of the princes, which was above the chamber of Maaseiah the son of Shallum, the keeper of the door:

5 And I set before the sons of the house of the Rechabites pots full of wine, and cups, and I said unto them, Drink you wine.

6 But they said, We will drink no wine: for Jonadab the son of Rechab our father commanded us, saying, You shall drink no wine, neither you, nor your sons for ever:

7 Neither shall you build house, nor sow seed, nor plant vineyard, nor have any: but all your days you shall dwell in tents; that you may live many days in the land where you be strangers.

8 Thus have we obeyed the voice of Jonadab the son of Rechab our father in all that he has charged us, to drink no wine all our days, we, our wives, our sons, nor our daughters;

9 Nor to build houses for us to dwell in: neither have we vineyard, nor field, nor seed:

10 But we have dwelt in tents, and have obeyed, and done according to all that Jonadab our father commanded us.

11 But it came to pass, when Nebuchadrezzar king of Babylon came up into the land, that we said, Come, and let us go to Jerusalem for fear of the army of the Chaldeans, and for fear of the army of the Syrians: so we dwell at Jerusalem.

12 Then came the word of the LORD unto Jeremiah, saying,

13 Thus saith the LORD of hosts, the God of Israel; Go and tell the men of Judah and the inhabitants of Jerusalem, Will you not receive instruction to hearken to my words? saith the LORD.

14 The words of Jonadab the son of Rechab, that he commanded his sons not to drink wine, are performed; for unto this day they drink none, but obey their father's commandment: notwithstanding I have spoken unto you, rising early and speaking; but you hearkened not unto me.

15 I have sent also unto you all my servants the prophets, rising up early and sending them, saying, Return you now every man from his evil way, and amend your doings, and go not after other gods to serve them, and you shall dwell in the land which I have given to you and to your fathers: but you have not inclined your ear, nor hearkened unto me.

16 Because the sons of Jonadab the son of Rechab have performed the commandment of their father, which he commanded them; but this people has not hearkened unto me:

17 Therefore thus saith the LORD God of hosts, the God of Israel; Behold, I will bring upon Judah and upon all the inhabitants of Jerusalem all the evil that I have pronounced against them: because I have spoken unto them, but they have not heard; and I have called unto them, but they have not answered.

18 And Jeremiah said unto the house of the Rechabites, Thus saith the LORD of hosts, the God of Israel; Because you have obeyed the commandment of Jonadab your father, and kept all his precepts, and done according unto all that he has commanded you:

19 Therefore thus saith the LORD of hosts, the God of Israel; Jonadab the son of Rechab shall not want a man to stand before me for ever.

CHAPTER 36

AND it came to pass in the fourth year of Jehoiakim the son of Josiah king of Judah, that this word came unto Jeremiah from the LORD, saying,

2 Take you a roll of a book, and write therein all the words that I have spoken unto you against Israel, and against Judah, and against all the nations, from the day I spake unto you, from the days of Josiah, even unto this day.

3 It may be that the house of Judah will hear all the evil which I purpose to do unto them; that they may return every man from his evil way; that I may forgive their iniquity and their sin.

4 Then Jeremiah called Baruch the son of Neriah: and Baruch wrote from the mouth of Jeremiah all the words of the LORD, which he had spoken unto him, upon a roll of a book.

5 And Jeremiah commanded Baruch, saying, I am shut up; I cannot go into the house of the LORD:

6 Therefore go you , and read in the roll, which you have written from my mouth, the words of the LORD in the ears of the people in the LORD's house upon the fasting day: and also you shalt read them in the ears of all Judah that come out of their cities.

7 It may be they will present their supplication before the LORD, and will return every one from his evil way: for great is the anger and the fury that the LORD has pronounced against this people.

8 And Baruch the son of Neriah did according to all that Jeremiah the prophet commanded him, reading in the book the words of the LORD in the LORD's house.

9 And it came to pass in the fifth year of Jehoiakim the son of Josiah king of Judah, in the ninth month, that they proclaimed a fast before the LORD to all the people in Jerusalem, and to all the people that came from the cities of Judah unto Jerusalem.

10 Then read Baruch in the book the words of Jeremiah in the house of the LORD, in the chamber of Gemariah the son of Shaphan the scribe, in the higher court, at the entry of the new gate of the LORD's house, in the ears of all the people.

11 When Michaiah the son of Gemariah, the son of Shaphan, had heard out of the book all the words of the LORD,

12 Then he went down into the king's house, into the scribe's chamber: and, lo, all the princes sat there, even Elishama the scribe, and Delaiah the son of Shemaiah, and Elnathan the son of Achbor, and Gemariah the son of Shaphan, and Zedekiah the son of Hananiah, and all the princes.

13 Then Michaiah declared unto them all the words that he had heard, when Baruch read the book in the ears of the people.

14 Therefore all the princes sent Jehudi the son of Nethaniah, the son of Shelemiah, the son of Cushi, unto Baruch, saying, Take in yours hand the roll wherein you have read in the ears of the people, and come. So Baruch the son of Neriah took the roll in his hand, and came unto them.

15 And they said unto him, Sit down now, and read it in our ears. So Baruch read it in their ears.

16 Now it came to pass, when they had heard all the words, they were afraid both one and other, and said unto Baruch, We will surely tell the king of all these words.

17 And they asked Baruch, saying, Tell us now, How did you write all these words at his mouth?

18 Then Baruch answered them, He pronounced all these words unto me with his mouth, and I wrote them with ink in the book.

19 Then said the princes unto Baruch, Go, hide you, you and Jeremiah; and let no man know where you be.

20 And they went in to the king into the court, but they laid up the roll in the chamber of Elishama the scribe, and told all the words in the ears of the king.

21 So the king sent Jehudi to fetch the roll: and he took it out of Elishama the scribe's chamber. And Jehudi read it in the ears of the king, and in the ears of all the princes which stood beside the king.

22 Now the king sat in the winterhouse in the ninth month: and there was a fire on the hearth burning before him.

23 And it came to pass, that when Jehudi had read three or four leaves, he cut it with the penknife, and cast it into the fire that was on the hearth, until all the roll was consumed in the fire that was on the hearth.

24 Yet they were not afraid, nor rent their garments, neither the king, nor any of his servants that heard all these words.

25 Nevertheless Elnathan and Delaiah and Gemariah had made intercession to the king that he would not burn the roll: but he would not hear them.

26 But the king commanded Jerahmeel the son of Hammelech, and Seraiah the son of Azriel, and Shelemiah the son of Abdeel, to take Baruch the scribe and Jeremiah the prophet: but the LORD hid them.

27 Then the word of the LORD came to Jeremiah, after that the king had burned the roll, and the words which Baruch wrote at the mouth of Jeremiah, saying,

28 Take you again another roll, and write in it all the former words that were in the first roll, which Jehoiakim the king of Judah has burned.

29 And you shalt say to Jehoiakim king of Judah, Thus saith the LORD; You have burned this roll, saying, Why have you written therein, saying, The king of Babylon shall certainly come and destroy this land, and shall cause to cease from thence man and beast?

30 Therefore thus saith the LORD of Jehoiakim king of Judah; He shall have none to sit upon the throne of David: and his dead body shall be cast out in the day to the heat, and in the night to the frost.

31 And I will punish him and his seed and his servants for their iniquity; and I will bring upon them, and upon the inhabitants of Jerusalem, and upon the men of Judah, all the evil that I have pronounced against them; but they hearkened not.

32 Then took Jeremiah another roll, and gave it to Baruch the scribe, the son of Neriah; who wrote therein from the mouth of Jeremiah all the words of the book which Jehoiakim king of Judah had burned in the fire: and there were added besides unto them many like words.

CHAPTER 37

AND king Zedekiah the son of Josiah reigned instead of Coniah the son of Jehoiakim, whom Nebuchadrezzar king of Babylon made king in the land of Judah.

2 But neither he, nor his servants, nor the people of the land, did hearken unto the words of the LORD, which he spake by the prophet Jeremiah.

3 And Zedekiah the king sent Jehucal the son of Shelemiah and Zephaniah the son of Maaseiah the priest to the prophet Jeremiah, saying, Pray now unto the LORD our God for us.

4 Now Jeremiah came in and went out among the people: for they had not put him into prison.

5 Then Pharaoh's army was come forth out of Egypt: and when the Chaldeans that besieged Jerusalem heard tidings of them, they departed from Jerusalem.

6 Then came the word of the LORD unto the prophet Jeremiah, saying,

7 Thus saith the LORD, the God of Israel; Thus shall you say to the king of Judah, that sent you unto me to inquire of me; Behold, Pharaoh's army, which is come forth to help you, shall return to Egypt into their own land.

8 And the Chaldeans shall come again, and fight against this city, and take it, and burn it with fire.

9 Thus saith the LORD; Deceive not yourselves, saying, The Chaldeans shall surely depart from us: for they shall not depart.

10 For though you had smitten the whole army of the Chaldeans that fight against you, and there remained but wounded men among them, yet should they rise up every man in his tent, and burn this city with fire.

11 And it came to pass, that when the army of the Chaldeans was broken up from Jerusalem for fear of Pharaoh's army,

12 Then Jeremiah went forth out of Jerusalem to go into the land of Benjamin, to separate himself thence in the midst of the people.

13 And when he was in the gate of Benjamin, a captain of the ward was there, whose name was Irijah, the son of Shelemiah, the son of Hananiah; and he took Jeremiah the prophet, saying, You fallest away to the Chaldeans.

14 Then said Jeremiah, It is false; I fall not away to the Chaldeans. But he hearkened not to him: so Irijah took Jeremiah, and brought him to the princes.

15 Wherefore the princes were wroth with Jeremiah, and struck him, and put him in prison in the house of Jonathan the scribe: for they had made that the prison.

16 When Jeremiah was entered into the dungeon, and into the cabins, and Jeremiah had remained there many days;

17 Then Zedekiah the king sent, and took him out: and the king asked him secretly in his house, and said, Is there any word from the LORD? And Jeremiah said, There is: for, said he, you shalt be delivered into the hand of the king of Babylon.

18 Moreover Jeremiah said unto king Zedekiah, What have I offended against you, or against your servants, or against this people, that you have put me in prison?

19 Where are now your prophets which prophesied unto you, saying, The king of Babylon shall not come against you, nor against this land?

20 Therefore hear now, I pray you, O my lord the king: let my supplication, I pray you, be accepted before you; that you cause me not to return to the house of Jonathan the scribe, lest I die there.

21 Then Zedekiah the king commanded that they should commit Jeremiah into the court of the prison, and that they should give him daily a piece of bread out of the bakers' street, until all the bread in the city were spent. Thus Jeremiah remained in the court of the prison.

CHAPTER 38

THEN Shephatiah the son of Mattan, and Gedaliah the son of Pashur, and Jucal the son of Shelemiah, and Pashur the son of Malchiah, heard the words that Jeremiah had spoken unto all the people, saying,

2 Thus saith the LORD, He that remaineth in this city shall die by the sword, by the famine, and by the pestilence: but he that goeth forth to the Chaldeans shall live; for he shall have his life for a prey, and shall live.

3 Thus saith the LORD, This city shall surely be given into the hand of the king of Babylon's army, which shall take it.

4 Therefore the princes said unto the king, We beseech you, let this man be put to death: for thus he weakeneth the hands of the men of war that remain in this city, and the hands of all the people, in speaking such words unto them: for this man seeketh not the welfare of this people, but the hurt.

5 Then Zedekiah the king said, Behold, he is in your hand: for the king is not he that can do any thing against you.

6 Then took they Jeremiah, and cast him into the dungeon of Malchiah the son of Hammelech, that was in the court of the prison: and they let down Jeremiah with cords. And in the dungeon there was no water, but mire: so Jeremiah sunk in the mire.

7 Now when Ebed-melech the Ethiopian, one of the eunuchs which was in the king's house, heard that they had put Jeremiah in the dungeon; the king then sitting in the gate of Benjamin;

8 Ebed-melech went forth out of the king's house, and spake to the king, saying,

9 My lord the king, these men have done evil in all that they have done to Jeremiah the prophet, whom they have cast into the dungeon; and he is like to die for hunger in the place where he is: for there is no more bread in the city.

10 Then the king commanded Ebed-melech the Ethiopian, saying, Take from hence thirty men with you, and take up Jeremiah the prophet out of the dungeon, before he die.

11 So Ebed-melech took the men with him, and went into the house of the king under the treasury, and took thence old cast clouts and old rotten rags, and let them down by cords into the dungeon to Jeremiah.

12 And Ebed-melech the Ethiopian said unto Jeremiah, Put now these old cast clouts and rotten rags under yours armholes under the cords. And Jeremiah did so.

13 So they drew up Jeremiah with cords, and took him up out of the dungeon: and Jeremiah remained in the court of the prison.

14 Then Zedekiah the king sent, and took Jeremiah the prophet unto him into the third entry that is in the house of the LORD: and the king said unto Jeremiah, I will ask you a thing; hide nothing from me.

15 Then Jeremiah said unto Zedekiah, If I declare it unto you, will you not surely put me to death? and if I give you counsel, will you not hearken unto me?

16 So Zedekiah the king sware secretly unto Jeremiah, saying, As the LORD liveth, that made us this soul, I will not put you to death, neither will I give you into the hand of these men that seek your life.

17 Then said Jeremiah unto Zedekiah, Thus saith the LORD, the God of hosts, the God of Israel; If you will assuredly go forth unto the king of Babylon's princes, then your soul shall live, and this city shall not be burned with fire; and you shalt live, and yours house:

18 But if you will not go forth to the king of Babylon's princes, then shall this city be given into the hand of the Chaldeans, and they shall burn it with fire, and you shalt not escape out of their hand.

19 And Zedekiah the king said unto Jeremiah, I am afraid of the Jews that are fallen to the Chaldeans, lest they deliver me into their hand, and they mock me.

20 But Jeremiah said, They shall not deliver you. Obey, I beseech you, the voice of the LORD, which I speak unto you: so it shall be well unto you, and your soul shall live.

21 But if you refuse to go forth, this is the word that the LORD has shewed me:

22 And, behold, all the women that are left in the king of Judah's house shall be brought forth to the king of Babylon's princes, and those women shall say, Your friends have set you on, and have prevailed against you: your feet are sunk in the mire, and they are turned away back.

23 So they shall bring out all your wives and your children to the Chaldeans: and you shalt not escape out of their hand, but shalt be taken by the hand of the king of Babylon: and you shalt cause this city to be burned with fire.

24 Then said Zedekiah unto Jeremiah, Let no man know of these words, and you shalt not die.

25 But if the princes hear that I have talked with you, and they come unto you, and say unto you, Declare unto us now what you have said unto the king, hide it not from us, and we will not put you to death; also what the king said unto you:

26 Then you shalt say unto them, I presented my supplication before the king, that he would not cause me to return to Jonathan's house, to die there.

27 Then came all the princes unto Jeremiah, and asked him: and he told them according to all these words that the king had commanded. So they left off speaking with him; for the matter was not perceived.

28 So Jeremiah abode in the court of the prison until the day that Jerusalem was taken: and he was there when Jerusalem was taken.

CHAPTER 39

IN the ninth year of Zedekiah king of Judah, in the tenth month, came Nebuchadrezzar king of Babylon and all his army against Jerusalem, and they besieged it.

2 And in the eleventh year of Zedekiah, in the fourth month, the ninth day of the month, the city was broken up.

3 And all the princes of the king of Babylon came in, and sat in the middle gate, even Nergal-sharezer, Samgar-nebo, Sarsechim, Rab-saris, Nergal-sharezer, Rab-mag, with all the residue of the princes of the king of Babylon.

4 And it came to pass, that when Zedekiah the king of Judah saw them, and all the men of war, then they fled, and went forth out of the city by night, by the way of the king's garden, by the gate betwixt the two walls: and he went out the way of the plain.

5 But the Chaldeans' army pursued after them, and overtook Zedekiah in the plains of Jericho: and when they had taken him, they brought him up to Nebuchadnezzar king of Babylon to Riblah in the land of Hamath, where he gave judgment upon him.

6 Then the king of Babylon slew the sons of Zedekiah in Riblah before his eyes: also the king of Babylon slew all the nobles of Judah.

7 Moreover he put out Zedekiah's eyes, and bound him with chains, to carry him to Babylon.

8 And the Chaldeans burned the king's house, and the houses of the people, with fire, and brake down the walls of Jerusalem.

9 Then Nebuzar-adan the captain of the guard carried away captive into Babylon the remnant of the people that remained in the city, and those that fell away, that fell to him, with the rest of the people that remained.

10 But Nebuzar-adan the captain of the guard left of the poor of the people, which had nothing, in the land of Judah, and gave them vineyards and fields at the same time.

11 Now Nebuchadnezzar king of Babylon gave charge concerning Jeremiah to Nebuzar-adan the captain of the guard, saying,

12 Take him, and look well to him, and do him no harm; but do unto him even as he shall say unto you.

13 So Nebuzar-adan the captain of the guard sent, and Nebushasban, Rab-saris, and Nergal-sharezer, Rab-mag, and all the king of Babylon's princes;

14 Even they sent, and took Jeremiah out of the court of the prison, and committed him unto Gedaliah the son of Ahikam the son of Shaphan, that he should carry him home: so he dwelt among the people.

15 Now the word of the LORD came unto Jeremiah, while he was shut up in the court of the prison, saying,

16 Go and speak to Ebed-melech the Ethiopian, saying, Thus saith the LORD of hosts, the God of Israel; Behold, I will bring my words upon this city for evil, and not for good; and they shall be accomplished in that day before you.

17 But I will deliver you in that day, saith the LORD: and you shalt not be given into the hand of the men of whom you are afraid.

18 For I will surely deliver you, and you shalt not fall by the sword, but your life shall be for a prey unto you: because you have put your trust in me, saith the LORD.

CHAPTER 40

THE word that came to Jeremiah from the LORD, after that Nebuzar-adan the captain of the guard had let him go from Ramah, when he had taken him being bound in chains among all that were carried away captive of Jerusalem and Judah, which were carried away captive unto Babylon.

2 And the captain of the guard took Jeremiah, and said unto him, The LORD your God has pronounced this evil upon this place.

3 Now the LORD has brought it, and done according as he has said: because you have sinned against the LORD, and have not obeyed his voice, therefore this thing is come upon you.

4 And now, behold, I loose you this day from the chains which were upon yours hand. If it seem good unto you to come with me into Babylon, come; and I will look well unto you: but if it seem ill unto you to come with me into Babylon, forbear: behold, all the land is before you: whither it seemeth good and convenient for you to go, thither go.

5 Now while he was not yet gone back, he said, Go back also to Gedaliah the son of Ahikam the son of Shaphan, whom the king of Babylon has made governor over the cities of Judah, and dwell with him among the people: or go wheresoever it seemeth convenient unto you to go. So the captain of the guard gave him victuals and a reward, and let him go.

6 Then went Jeremiah unto Gedaliah the son of Ahikam to Mizpah; and dwelt with him among the people that were left in the land.

7 Now when all the captains of the forces which were in the fields, even they and their men, heard that the king of Babylon had made Gedaliah the son of Ahikam governor in the land, and had committed unto him men, and women, and children, and of the poor of the land, of them that were not carried away captive to Babylon;

8 Then they came to Gedaliah to Mizpah, even Ishmael the son of Nethaniah, and Johanan and Jonathan the sons of Kareah, and Seraiah the son of Tanhumeth, and the sons of Ephai the Netophathite, and Jezaniah the son of a Maachathite, they and their men.

9 And Gedaliah the son of Ahikam the son of Shaphan sware unto them and to their men, saying, Fear not to serve the Chaldeans: dwell in the land, and serve the king of Babylon, and it shall be well with you.

10 As for me, behold, I will dwell at Mizpah to serve the Chaldeans, which will come unto us: but you , gather you wine, and summer fruits, and oil, and put them in your vessels, and dwell in your cities that you have taken.

11 Likewise when all the Jews that were in Moab, and among the Ammonites, and in Edom, and that were in all the countries, heard that the king of Babylon had left a remnant of Judah, and that he had set over them Gedaliah the son of Ahikam the son of Shaphan;

12 Even all the Jews returned out of all places whither they were driven, and came to the land of Judah, to Gedaliah, unto Mizpah, and gathered wine and summer fruits very much.

13 Moreover Johanan the son of Kareah, and all the captains of the forces that were in the fields, came to Gedaliah to Mizpah,

14 And said unto him, Dost you certainly know that Baalis the king of the Ammonites has sent Ishmael the son of Nethaniah to slay you? But Gedaliah the son of Ahikam believed them not.

15 Then Johanan the son of Kareah spake to Gedaliah in Mizpah secretly, saying, Let me go, I pray you, and I will slay Ishmael the son of Nethaniah, and no man shall know it: wherefore should he slay you, that all the Jews which are gathered unto you should be scattered, and the remnant in Judah perish?

16 But Gedaliah the son of Ahikam said unto Johanan the son of Kareah, You shalt not do this thing: for you speakest falsely of Ishmael.

CHAPTER 41

NOW it came to pass in the seventh month, that Ishmael the son of Nethaniah the son of Elishama, of the seed royal, and the princes of the king, even ten men with him, came unto Gedaliah the son of Ahikam to Mizpah; and there they did eat bread together in Mizpah.

2 Then arose Ishmael the son of Nethaniah, and the ten men that were with him, and struck Gedaliah the son of Ahikam the son of Shaphan with the sword, and slew him, whom the king of Babylon had made governor over the land.

3 Ishmael also slew all the Jews that were with him, even with Gedaliah, at Mizpah, and the Chaldeans that were found there, and the men of war.

4 And it came to pass the second day after he had slain Gedaliah, and no man knew it,

5 That there came certain from Shechem, from Shiloh, and from Samaria, even fourscore men, having their beards shaven, and their clothes rent, and having cut themselves, with offerings and incense in their hand, to bring them to the house of the LORD.

6 And Ishmael the son of Nethaniah went forth from Mizpah to meet them, weeping all along as he went: and it came to pass, as he met them, he said unto them, Come to Gedaliah the son of Ahikam.

7 And it was so, when they came into the midst of the city, that Ishmael the son of Nethaniah slew them, and cast them into the midst of the pit, he, and the men that were with him.

8 But ten men were found among them that said unto Ishmael, Slay us not: for we have treasures in the field, of wheat, and of barley, and of oil, and of honey. So he forbare, and slew them not among their brethren.

9 Now the pit wherein Ishmael had cast all the dead bodies of the men, whom he had slain because of Gedaliah, was it which Asa the king had made for fear of Baasha king of Israel: and Ishmael the son of Nethaniah filled it with them that were slain.

10 Then Ishmael carried away captive all the residue of the people that were in Mizpah, even the king's daughters, and all the people that remained in Mizpah, whom Nebuzar-adan the captain of the guard had committed to Gedaliah the son of Ahikam: and Ishmael the son of Nethaniah carried them away captive, and departed to go over to the Ammonites.

11 But when Johanan the son of Kareah, and all the captains of the forces that were with him, heard of all the evil that Ishmael the son of Nethaniah had done,

12 Then they took all the men, and went to fight with Ishmael the son of Nethaniah, and found him by the great waters that are in Gibeon.

13 Now it came to pass, that when all the people which were with Ishmael saw Johanan the son of Kareah, and all the captains of the forces that were with him, then they were glad.

14 So all the people that Ishmael had carried away captive from Mizpah cast about and returned, and went unto Johanan the son of Kareah.

15 But Ishmael the son of Nethaniah escaped from Johanan with eight men, and went to the Ammonites.

16 Then took Johanan the son of Kareah, and all the captains of the forces that were with him, all the remnant of the people whom he had recovered from Ishmael the son of Nethaniah, from Mizpah, after that he had slain Gedaliah the son of Ahikam, even mighty men of war, and the women, and the children, and the eunuchs, whom he had brought again from Gibeon:

17 And they departed, and dwelt in the habitation of Chimham, which is by Beth-lehem, to go to enter into Egypt,

18 Because of the Chaldeans: for they were afraid of them, because Ishmael the son of Nethaniah had slain Gedaliah the son of Ahikam, whom the king of Babylon made governor in the land.

CHAPTER 42

THEN all the captains of the forces, and Johanan the son of Kareah, and Jezaniah the son of Hoshaiah, and all the people from the least even unto the greatest, came near,

2 And said unto Jeremiah the prophet, Let, we beseech you, our supplication be accepted before you, and pray for us unto the LORD your God, even for all this remnant; (for we are left but a few of many, as yours eyes do behold us:)

3 That the LORD your God may shew us the way wherein we may walk, and the thing that we may do.

4 Then Jeremiah the prophet said unto them, I have heard you; behold, I will pray unto the LORD your God according to your words; and it shall come to pass, that whatsoever thing the LORD shall answer you, I will declare it unto you; I will keep nothing back from you.

5 Then they said to Jeremiah, The LORD be a true and faithful witness between us, if we do not even according to all things for the which the LORD your God shall send you to us.

6 Whether it be good, or whether it be evil, we will obey the voice of the LORD our God, to whom we send you; that it may be well with us, when we obey the voice of the LORD our God.

7 And it came to pass after ten days, that the word of the LORD came unto Jeremiah.

8 Then called he Johanan the son of Kareah, and all the captains of the forces which were with him, and all the people from the least even to the greatest,

9 And said unto them, Thus saith the LORD, the God of Israel, unto whom you sent me to present your supplication before him;

10 If you will still abide in this land, then will I build you, and not pull you down, and I will plant you, and not pluck you up: for I repent me of the evil that I have done unto you.

11 Be not afraid of the king of Babylon, of whom you are afraid; be not afraid of him, saith the LORD: for I am with you to save you, and to deliver you from his hand.

12 And I will shew mercies unto you, that he may have mercy upon you, and cause you to return to your own land.

13 But if you say, We will not dwell in this land, neither obey the voice of the LORD your God,

14 Saying, No; but we will go into the land of Egypt, where we shall see no war, nor hear the sound of the trumpet, nor have hunger of bread; and there will we dwell:

15 And now therefore hear the word of the LORD, you remnant of Judah; Thus saith the LORD of hosts, the God of Israel; If you wholly set your faces to enter into Egypt, and go to sojourn there;

16 Then it shall come to pass, that the sword, which you feared, shall overtake you there in the land of Egypt, and the famine, whereof you were afraid, shall follow close after you there in Egypt; and there you shall die.

17 So shall it be with all the men that set their faces to go into Egypt to sojourn there; they shall die by the sword, by the famine, and by the pestilence: and none of them shall remain or escape from the evil that I will bring upon them.

18 For thus saith the LORD of hosts, the God of Israel; As my anger and my fury has been poured forth upon the inhabitants of Jerusalem; so shall my fury be poured forth upon you, when you shall enter into Egypt: and you shall be an execration, and an astonishment, and a curse, and a reproach; and you shall see this place no more.

19 The LORD has said concerning you, O you remnant of Judah; Go you not into Egypt: know certainly that I have admonished you this day.

20 For you dissembled in your hearts, when you sent me unto the LORD your God, saying, Pray for us unto the LORD our God; and according unto all that the LORD our God shall say, so declare unto us, and we will do it.

21 And now I have this day declared it to you; but you have not obeyed the voice of the LORD your God, nor any thing for the which he has sent me unto you.

22 Now therefore know certainly that you shall die by the sword, by the famine, and by the pestilence, in the place whither you desire to go and to sojourn.

CHAPTER 43

AND it came to pass, that when Jeremiah had made an end of speaking unto all the people all the words of the LORD their God, for which the LORD their God had sent him to them, even all these words,

2 Then spake Azariah the son of Hoshaiah, and Johanan the son of Kareah, and all the proud men, saying unto Jeremiah, You speakest falsely: the LORD our God has not sent you to say, Go not into Egypt to sojourn there:

3 But Baruch the son of Neriah setteth you on against us, for to deliver us into the hand of the Chaldeans, that they might put us to death, and carry us away captives into Babylon.

4 So Johanan the son of Kareah, and all the captains of the forces, and all the people, obeyed not the voice of the LORD, to dwell in the land of Judah.

5 But Johanan the son of Kareah, and all the captains of the forces, took all the remnant of Judah, that were returned from all nations, whither they had been driven, to dwell in the land of Judah;

6 Even men, and women, and children, and the king's daughters, and every person that Nebuzar-adan the captain of the guard had left with Gedaliah the son of Ahikam the son of Shaphan, and Jeremiah the prophet, and Baruch the son of Neriah.

7 So they came into the land of Egypt: for they obeyed not the voice of the LORD: thus came they even to Tahpanhes.

8 Then came the word of the LORD unto Jeremiah in Tahpanhes, saying,

9 Take great stones in yours hand, and hide them in the clay in the brickkiln, which is at the entry of Pharaoh's house in Tahpanhes, in the sight of the men of Judah;

10 And say unto them, Thus saith the LORD of hosts, the God of Israel; Behold, I will send and take Nebuchadrezzar the king of Babylon, my servant, and will set his throne upon these stones that I have hid; and he shall spread his royal pavilion over them.

11 And when he comes, he shall strike the land of Egypt, and deliver such as are for death to death; and such as are for captivity to captivity; and such as are for the sword to the sword.

12 And I will kindle a fire in the houses of the gods of Egypt; and he shall burn them, and carry them away captives: and he shall array himself with the land of Egypt, as a shepherd putteth on his garment; and he shall go forth from thence in peace.

13 He shall break also the images of Beth-shemesh, that is in the land of Egypt; and the houses of the gods of the Egyptians shall he burn with fire.

CHAPTER 44

THE word that came to Jeremiah concerning all the Jews which dwell in the land of Egypt, which dwell at Migdol, and at Tahpanhes, and at Noph, and in the country of Pathros, saying,

2 Thus saith the LORD of hosts, the God of Israel; You have seen all the evil that I have brought upon Jerusalem, and upon all the cities of Judah; and, behold, this day they are a desolation, and no man dwelleth therein,

3 Because of their wickedness which they have committed to provoke me to anger, in that they went to burn incense, and to serve other gods, whom they knew not, neither they, you, nor your fathers.

4 Howbeit I sent unto you all my servants the prophets, rising early and sending them, saying, Oh, do not this abominable thing that I hate.

5 But they hearkened not, nor inclined their ear to turn from their wickedness, to burn no incense unto other gods.

6 Wherefore my fury and my anger was poured forth, and was kindled in the cities of Judah and in the streets of Jerusalem; and they are wasted and desolate, as at this day.

7 Therefore now thus saith the LORD, the God of hosts, the God of Israel; Wherefore commit you this great evil against your souls, to cut off from you man and woman, child and suckling, out of Judah, to leave you none to remain;

8 In that you provoke me unto wrath with the works of your hands, burning incense unto other gods in the land of Egypt, whither you be gone to dwell, that you might cut yourselves off, and that you might be a curse and a reproach among all the nations of the earth?

9 Have you forgotten the wickedness of your fathers, and the wickedness of the kings of Judah, and the wickedness of their wives, and your own wickedness, and the wickedness of your wives, which they have committed in the land of Judah, and in the streets of Jerusalem?

10 They are not humbled even unto this day, neither have they feared, nor walked in my law, nor in my statutes, that I set before you and before your fathers.

11 Therefore thus saith the LORD of hosts, the God of Israel; Behold, I will set my face against you for evil, and to cut off all Judah.

12 And I will take the remnant of Judah, that have set their faces to go into the land of Egypt to sojourn there, and they shall all be consumed, and fall in the land of Egypt; they shall even be consumed by the sword and by the famine: they shall die, from the least even unto the greatest, by the sword and by the famine: and they shall be an execration, and an astonishment, and a curse, and a reproach.

13 For I will punish them that dwell in the land of Egypt, as I have punished Jerusalem, by the sword, by the famine, and by the pestilence:

14 So that none of the remnant of Judah, which are gone into the land of Egypt to sojourn there, shall escape or remain, that they should return into the land of Judah, to the which they have a desire to return to dwell there: for none shall return but such as shall escape.

15 Then all the men which knew that their wives had burned incense unto other gods, and all the women that stood by, a great multitude, even all the people that dwelt in the land of Egypt, in Pathros, answered Jeremiah, saying,

16 As for the word that you have spoken unto us in the name of the LORD, we will not hearken unto you.

17 But we will certainly do whatsoever thing goeth forth out of our own mouth, to burn incense unto the queen of heaven, and to pour out drink offerings unto her, as we have done, we, and our fathers, our kings, and our princes, in the cities of Judah, and in the streets of Jerusalem: for then had we plenty of victuals, and were well, and saw no evil.

18 But since we left off to burn incense to the queen of heaven, and to pour out drink offerings unto her, we have wanted all things, and have been consumed by the sword and by the famine.

19 And when we burned incense to the queen of heaven, and poured out drink offerings unto her, did we make her cakes to worship her, and pour out drink offerings unto her, without our men?

20 Then Jeremiah said unto all the people, to the men, and to the women, and to all the people which had given him that answer, saying,

21 The incense that you burned in the cities of Judah, and in the streets of Jerusalem, you, and your fathers, your kings, and your princes, and the people of the land, did not the LORD remember them, and came it not into his mind?

22 So that the LORD could no longer bear, because of the evil of your doings, and because of the abominations which you have committed; therefore is your land a desolation, and an astonishment, and a curse, without an inhabitant, as at this day.

23 Because you have burned incense, and because you have sinned against the LORD, and have not obeyed the voice of the LORD, nor walked in his law, nor in his statutes, nor in his testimonies; therefore this evil is happened unto you, as at this day.

24 Moreover Jeremiah said unto all the people, and to all the women, Hear the word of the LORD, all Judah that are in the land of Egypt:

25 Thus saith the LORD of hosts, the God of Israel, saying; You and your wives have both spoken with your mouths, and fulfilled with your hand, saying, We will surely perform our vows that we have vowed, to burn incense to the queen of heaven, and to pour out drink offerings unto her: you will surely accomplish your vows, and surely perform your vows.

26 Therefore hear you the word of the LORD, all Judah that dwell in the land of Egypt; Behold, I have sworn by my great name, saith the LORD, that my name shall no more be named in the mouth of any man of Judah in all the land of Egypt, saying, The Lord GOD liveth.

27 Behold, I will watch over them for evil, and not for good: and all the men of Judah that are in the land of Egypt shall be consumed by the sword and by the famine, until there be an end of them.

28 Yet a small number that escape the sword shall return out of the land of Egypt into the land of Judah, and all the remnant of Judah, that are gone into the land of Egypt to sojourn there, shall know whose words shall stand, my, or theirs.

29 And this shall be a sign unto you, saith the LORD, that I will punish you in this place, that you may know that my words shall surely stand against you for evil:

30 Thus saith the LORD; Behold, I will give Pharaoh-hophra king of Egypt into the hand of his enemies, and into the hand of them that seek his life; as I gave Zedekiah king of Judah into the hand of Nebuchadrezzar king of Babylon, his enemy, and that sought his life.

CHAPTER 45

THE word that Jeremiah the prophet spake unto Baruch the son of Neriah, when he had written these words in a book at the mouth of Jeremiah, in the fourth year of Jehoiakim the son of Josiah king of Judah, saying,

2 Thus saith the LORD, the God of Israel, unto you, O Baruch;

3 You did say, Woe is me now! for the LORD has added grief to my sorrow; I fainted in my sighing, and I find no rest.

4 Thus shalt you say unto him, The LORD saith thus; Behold, that which I have built will I break down, and that which I have planted I will pluck up, even this whole land.

5 And seekest you great things for yourself? seek them not: for, behold, I will bring evil upon all flesh, saith the LORD: but your life will I give unto you for a prey in all places whither you go.

CHAPTER 46

THE word of the LORD which came to Jeremiah the prophet against the Gentiles;

2 Against Egypt, against the army of Pharaoh-necho king of Egypt, which was by the river Euphrates in Carchemish, which Nebuchadrezzar king of Babylon struck in the fourth year of Jehoiakim the son of Josiah king of Judah.

3 Order you the buckler and shield, and draw near to battle.

4 Harness the horses; and get up, you horsemen, and stand forth with your helmets; furbish the spears, and put on the brigandines.

5 Wherefore have I seen them dismayed and turned away back? and their mighty ones are beaten down, and are fled apace, and look not back: for fear was round about, saith the LORD.

6 Let not the swift flee away, nor the mighty man escape; they shall stumble, and fall toward the north by the river Euphrates.

7 Who is this that comes up as a flood, whose waters are moved as the rivers?

8 Egypt riseth up like a flood, and his waters are moved like the rivers; and he saith, I will go up, and will cover the earth; I will destroy the city and the inhabitants thereof.

9 Come up, you horses; and rage, you chariots; and let the mighty men come forth; the Ethiopians and the Libyans, that handle the shield; and the Lydians, that handle and bend the bow.

10 For this is the day of the Lord GOD of hosts, a day of vengeance, that he may avenge him of his adversaries: and the sword shall devour, and it shall be satiate and made drunk with their blood: for the Lord GOD of hosts has a sacrifice in the north country by the river Euphrates.

11 Go up into Gilead, and take balm, O virgin, the daughter of Egypt: in vain shalt you use many medicines; for you shalt not be cured.

12 The nations have heard of your shame, and your cry has filled the land: for the mighty man has stumbled against the mighty, and they are fallen both together.

13 The word that the LORD spake to Jeremiah the prophet, how Nebuchadrezzar king of Babylon should come and strike the land of Egypt.

14 Declare you in Egypt, and publish in Migdol, and publish in Noph and in Tahpanhes: say you , Stand fast, and prepare you; for the sword shall devour round about you.

15 Why are your valiant men swept away? they stood not, because the LORD did drive them.

16 He made many to fall, yea, one fell upon another: and they said, Arise, and let us go again to our own people, and to the land of our nativity, from the oppressing sword.

17 They did cry there, Pharaoh king of Egypt is but a noise; he has passed the time appointed.

18 As I live, saith the King, whose name is the LORD of hosts, Surely as Tabor is among the mountains, and as Carmel by the sea, so shall he come.

19 O you daughter dwelling in Egypt, furnish yourself to go into captivity: for Noph shall be waste and desolate without an inhabitant.

20 Egypt is like a very fair heifer, but destruction comes; it comes out of the north.

21 Also her hired men are in the midst of her like fatted bullocks; for they also are turned back, and are fled away together: they did not stand, because the day of their calamity was come upon them, and the time of their visitation.

22 The voice thereof shall go like a serpent; for they shall march with an army, and come against her with axes, as hewers of wood.

23 They shall cut down her forest, saith the LORD, though it cannot be searched; because they are more than the grasshoppers, and are innumerable.

24 The daughter of Egypt shall be confounded; she shall be delivered into the hand of the people of the north.

25 The LORD of hosts, the God of Israel, saith; Behold, I will punish the multitude of No, and Pharaoh, and Egypt, with their gods, and their kings; even Pharaoh, and all them that trust in him:

26 And I will deliver them into the hand of those that seek their lives, and into the hand of Nebuchadrezzar king of Babylon, and into the hand of his servants: and afterward it shall be inhabited, as in the days of old, saith the LORD.

27 But fear not you , O my servant Jacob, and be not dismayed, O Israel: for, behold, I will save you from afar off, and your seed from the land of their captivity; and Jacob shall return, and be in rest and at ease, and none shall make him afraid.

28 Fear you not, O Jacob my servant, saith the LORD: for I am with you; for I will make a full end of all the nations whither I have driven you: but I will not make a full end of you, but correct you in measure; yet will I not leave you wholly unpunished.

CHAPTER 47

THE word of the LORD that came to Jeremiah the prophet against the Philistines, before that Pharaoh struck Gaza.

2 Thus saith the LORD; Behold, waters rise up out of the north, and shall be an overflowing flood, and shall overflow the land, and all that is therein; the city, and them that dwell therein: then the men shall cry, and all the inhabitants of the land shall howl.

3 At the noise of the stamping of the hoofs of his strong horses, at the rushing of his chariots, and at the rumbling of his wheels, the fathers shall not look back to their children for feebleness of hands;

4 Because of the day that comes to spoil all the Philistines, and to cut off from Tyrus and Zidon every helper that remaineth: for the LORD will spoil the Philistines, the remnant of the country of Caphtor.

5 Baldness is come upon Gaza; Ashkelon is cut off with the remnant of their valley: how long will you cut yourself?

6 O you sword of the LORD, how long will it be ere you be quiet? put up yourself into your scabbard, rest, and be still.

7 How can it be quiet, seeing the LORD has given it a charge against Ashkelon, and against the sea shore? there has he appointed it.

CHAPTER 48

AGAINST Moab thus saith the LORD of hosts, the God of Israel; Woe unto Nebo! for it is spoiled: Kiriathaim is confounded and taken: Misgab is confounded and dismayed.

2 There shall be no more praise of Moab: in Heshbon they have devised evil against it; come, and let us cut it off from being a nation. Also you shalt be cut down, O Madmen; the sword shall pursue you.

3 A voice of crying shall be from Horonaim, spoiling and great destruction.

4 Moab is destroyed; her little ones have caused a cry to be heard.

5 For in the going up of Luhith continual weeping shall go up; for in the going down of Horonaim the enemies have heard a cry of destruction.

6 Flee, save your lives, and be like the heath in the wilderness.

7 For because you have trusted in your works and in your treasures, you shalt also be taken: and Chemosh shall go forth into captivity with his priests and his princes together.

8 And the spoiler shall come upon every city, and no city shall escape: the valley also shall perish, and the plain shall be destroyed, as the LORD has spoken.

9 Give wings unto Moab, that it may flee and get away: for the cities thereof shall be desolate, without any to dwell therein.

10 Cursed be he that doeth the work of the LORD deceitfully, and cursed be he that keepeth back his sword from blood.

11 Moab has been at ease from his youth, and he has settled on his lees, and has not been emptied from vessel to vessel, neither has he gone into captivity: therefore his taste remained in him, and his scent is not changed.

12 Therefore, behold, the days come, saith the LORD, that I will send unto him wanderers, that shall cause him to wander, and shall empty his vessels, and break their bottles.

13 And Moab shall be ashamed of Chemosh, as the house of Israel was ashamed of Beth-el their confidence.

14 How say you , We are mighty and strong men for the war?

15 Moab is spoiled, and gone up out of her cities, and his chosen young men are gone down to the slaughter, saith the King, whose name is the LORD of hosts.

16 The calamity of Moab is near to come, and his affliction hasteth fast.

17 All you that are about him, bemoan him; and all you that know his name, say, How is the strong staff broken, and the beautiful rod!

18 You daughter that dost inhabit Dibon, come down from your glory, and sit in thirst; for the spoiler of Moab shall come upon you, and he shall destroy your strong holds.

19 O inhabitant of Aroer, stand by the way, and espy; ask him that fleeth, and her that escapeth, and say, What is done?

20 Moab is confounded; for it is broken down: howl and cry; tell you it in Arnon, that Moab is spoiled,

21 And judgment is come upon the plain country; upon Holon, and upon Jahazah, and upon Mephaath,

22 And upon Dibon, and upon Nebo, and upon Beth-diblathaim,

23 And upon Kiriathaim, and upon Beth-gamul, and upon Beth-meon,

24 And upon Kerioth, and upon Bozrah, and upon all the cities of the land of Moab, far or near.

25 The horn of Moab is cut off, and his arm is broken, saith the LORD.

26Make you him drunken: for he magnified himself against the LORD: Moab also shall wallow in his vomit, and he also shall be in derision.

27 For was not Israel a derision unto you? was he found among thieves? for since you spakest of him, you skippedst for joy.

28 O you that dwell in Moab, leave the cities, and dwell in the rock, and be like the dove that maketh her nest in the sides of the hole's mouth.

29 We have heard the pride of Moab, (he is exceeding proud) his loftiness, and his arrogancy, and his pride, and the haughtiness of his heart.

30 I know his wrath, saith the LORD; but it shall not be so; his lies shall not so effect it.

31 Therefore will I howl for Moab, and I will cry out for all Moab; my heart shall mourn for the men of Kir-heres.

32 O vine of Sibmah, I will weep for you with the weeping of Jazer: your plants are gone over the sea, they reach even to the sea of Jazer: the spoiler is fallen upon your summer fruits and upon your vintage.

33 And joy and gladness is taken from the plentiful field, and from the land of Moab; and I have caused wine to fail from the winepresses: none shall tread with shouting; their shouting shall be no shouting.

34 From the cry of Heshbon even unto Elealeh, and even unto Jahaz, have they uttered their voice, from Zoar even unto Horonaim, as an heifer of three years old: for the waters also of Nimrim shall be desolate.

35 Moreover I will cause to cease in Moab, saith the LORD, him that offereth in the high places, and him that burneth incense to his gods.

36 Therefore my heart shall sound for Moab like pipes, and my heart shall sound like pipes for the men of Kir-heres: because the riches that he has gotten are perished.

37 For every head shall be bald, and every beard clipped: upon all the hands shall be cuttings, and upon the loins sackcloth.

38 There shall be lamentation generally upon all the housetops of Moab, and in the streets thereof: for I have broken Moab like a vessel wherein is no pleasure, saith the LORD.

39 They shall howl, saying, How is it broken down! how has Moab turned the back with shame! so shall Moab be a derision and a dismaying to all them about him.

40 For thus saith the LORD; Behold, he shall fly as an eagle, and shall spread his wings over Moab.

41 Kerioth is taken, and the strong holds are surprised, and the mighty men's hearts in Moab at that day shall be as the heart of a woman in her pangs.

42 And Moab shall be destroyed from being a people, because he has magnified himself against the LORD.

43 Fear, and the pit, and the snare, shall be upon you, O inhabitant of Moab, saith the LORD.

44 He that fleeth from the fear shall fall into the pit; and he that getteth up out of the pit shall be taken in the snare: for I will bring upon it, even upon Moab, the year of their visitation, saith the LORD.

45 They that fled stood under the shadow of Heshbon because of the force: but a fire shall come forth out of Heshbon, and a flame from the midst of Sihon, and shall devour the corner of Moab, and the crown of the head of the tumultuous ones.

46 Woe be unto you, O Moab! the people of Chemosh perisheth: for your sons are taken captives, and your daughters captives.

47Yet will I bring again the captivity of Moab in the latter days, saith the LORD. Thus far is the judgment of Moab.

CHAPTER 49

CONCERNING the Ammonites, thus saith the LORD; Has Israel no sons? has he no heir? why then doth their king inherit Gad, and his people dwell in his cities?

2 Therefore, behold, the days come, saith the LORD, that I will cause an alarm of war to be heard in Rabbah of the Ammonites; and it shall be a desolate heap, and her daughters shall be burned with fire: then shall Israel be heir unto them that were his heirs, saith the LORD.

3 Howl, O Heshbon, for Ai is spoiled: cry, you daughters of Rabbah, gird you with sackcloth; lament, and run to and fro by the hedges; for their king shall go into captivity, and his priests and his princes together.

4 Wherefore gloriest you in the valleys, your flowing valley, O backsliding daughter? that trusted in her treasures, saying, Who shall come unto me?

5 Behold, I will bring a fear upon you, saith the Lord GOD of hosts, from all those that be about you; and you shall be driven out every man right forth; and none shall gather up him that wandereth.

6 And afterward I will bring again the captivity of the children of Ammon, saith the LORD.

7Concerning Edom, thus saith the LORD of hosts; Is wisdom no more in Teman? is counsel perished from the prudent? is their wisdom vanished?

8 Flee you , turn back, dwell deep, O inhabitants of Dedan; for I will bring the calamity of Esau upon him, the time that I will visit him.

9 If grapegatherers come to you, would they not leave some gleaning grapes? if thieves by night, they will destroy till they have enough.

10 But I have made Esau bare, I have uncovered his secret places, and he shall not be able to hide himself: his seed is spoiled, and his brethren, and his neighbours, and he is not.

11 Leave your fatherless children, I will preserve them alive; and let your widows trust in me.

12 For thus saith the LORD; Behold, they whose judgment was not to drink of the cup have assuredly drunken; and are you he that shall altogether go unpunished? you shalt not go unpunished, but you shalt surely drink of it.

13 For I have sworn by myself, saith the LORD, that Bozrah shall become a desolation, a reproach, a waste, and a curse; and all the cities thereof shall be perpetual wastes.

14 I have heard a rumour from the LORD, and an ambassador is sent unto the heathen, saying, Gather you together, and come against her, and rise up to the battle.

15 For, lo, I will make you small among the heathen, and despised among men.

16 Your terribleness has deceived you, and the pride of yours heart, O you that dwellest in the clefts of the rock, that holdest the height of the hill: though you shouldest make your nest as high as the eagle, I will bring you down from thence, saith the LORD.

17 Also Edom shall be a desolation: every one that goeth by it shall be astonished, and shall hiss at all the plagues thereof.

18 As in the overthrow of Sodom and Gomorrah and the neighbour cities thereof, saith the LORD, no man shall abide there, neither shall a son of man dwell in it.

19 Behold, he shall come up like a lion from the swelling of Jordan against the habitation of the strong: but I will suddenly make him run away from her: and who is a chosen man, that I may appoint over her? for who is like me? and who will appoint me the time? and who is that shepherd that will stand before me?

20 Therefore hear the counsel of the LORD, that he has taken against Edom; and his purposes, that he has purposed against the inhabitants of Teman: Surely the least of the flock shall draw them out: surely he shall make their habitations desolate with them.

21 The earth is moved at the noise of their fall, at the cry the noise thereof was heard in the Red sea.

22 Behold, he shall come up and fly as the eagle, and spread his wings over Bozrah: and at that day shall the heart of the mighty men of Edom be as the heart of a woman in her pangs.

23Concerning Damascus. Hamath is confounded, and Arpad: for they have heard evil tidings: they are fainthearted; there is sorrow on the sea; it cannot be quiet.

24 Damascus is waxed feeble, and turneth herself to flee, and fear has seized on her: anguish and sorrows have taken her, as a woman in travail.

25 How is the city of praise not left, the city of my joy!

26 Therefore her young men shall fall in her streets, and all the men of war shall be cut off in that day, saith the LORD of hosts.

27 And I will kindle a fire in the wall of Damascus, and it shall consume the palaces of Ben-hadad.

28Concerning Kedar, and concerning the kingdoms of Hazor, which Nebuchadrezzar king of Babylon shall strike, thus saith the LORD; Arise you , go up to Kedar, and spoil the men of the east.

29 Their tents and their flocks shall they take away: they shall take to themselves their curtains, and all their vessels, and their camels; and they shall cry unto them, Fear is on every side.

30Flee, get you far off, dwell deep, O you inhabitants of Hazor, saith the LORD; for Nebuchadrezzar king of Babylon has taken counsel against you, and has conceived a purpose against you.

31 Arise, get you up unto the wealthy nation, that dwelleth without care, saith the LORD, which have neither gates nor bars, which dwell alone.

32 And their camels shall be a booty, and the multitude of their cattle a spoil: and I will scatter into all winds them that are in the utmost corners; and I will bring their calamity from all sides thereof, saith the LORD.

33 And Hazor shall be a dwelling for dragons, and a desolation for ever: there shall no man abide there, nor any son of man dwell in it.

34The word of the LORD that came to Jeremiah the prophet against Elam in the beginning of the reign of Zedekiah king of Judah, saying,

35 Thus saith the LORD of hosts; Behold, I will break the bow of Elam, the chief of their might.

36 And upon Elam will I bring the four winds from the four quarters of heaven, and will scatter them toward all those winds; and there shall be no nation whither the outcasts of Elam shall not come.

37 For I will cause Elam to be dismayed before their enemies, and before them that seek their life: and I will bring evil upon them, even my fierce anger, saith the LORD; and I will send the sword after them, till I have consumed them:

38 And I will set my throne in Elam, and will destroy from thence the king and the princes, saith the LORD.

39But it shall come to pass in the latter days, that I will bring again the captivity of Elam, saith the LORD.

CHAPTER 50

THE word that the LORD spake against Babylon and against the land of the Chaldeans by Jeremiah the prophet.

2 Declare you among the nations, and publish, and set up a standard; publish, and conceal not: say, Babylon is taken, Bel is confounded, Merodach is broken in pieces; her idols are confounded, her images are broken in pieces.

3 For out of the north there comes up a nation against her, which shall make her land desolate, and none shall dwell therein: they shall remove, they shall depart, both man and beast.

4In those days, and in that time, saith the LORD, the children of Israel shall come, they and the children of Judah together, going and weeping: they shall go, and seek the LORD their God.

5 They shall ask the way to Zion with their faces thitherward, saying, Come, and let us join ourselves to the LORD in a perpetual covenant that shall not be forgotten.

6 My people has been lost sheep: their shepherds have caused them to go astray, they have turned them away on the mountains: they have gone from mountain to hill, they have forgotten their restingplace.

7 All that found them have devoured them: and their adversaries said, We offend not, because they have sinned against the LORD, the habitation of justice, even the LORD, the hope of their fathers.

8 Remove out of the midst of Babylon, and go forth out of the land of the Chaldeans, and be as the he goats before the flocks.

9For, lo, I will raise and cause to come up against Babylon an assembly of great nations from the north country: and they shall set themselves in array against her; from thence she shall be taken: their arrows shall be as of a mighty expert man; none shall return in vain.

10 And Chaldea shall be a spoil: all that spoil her shall be satisfied, saith the LORD.

11 Because you were glad, because you rejoiced, O you destroyers of my heritage, because you are grown fat as the heifer at grass, and bellow as bulls;

12 Your mother shall be sore confounded; she that bare you shall be ashamed: behold, the hindermost of the nations shall be a wilderness, a dry land, and a desert.

13 Because of the wrath of the LORD it shall not be inhabited, but it shall be wholly desolate: every one that goeth by Babylon shall be astonished, and hiss at all her plagues.

14 Put yourselves in array against Babylon round about: all you that bend the bow, shoot at her, spare no arrows: for she has sinned against the LORD.

15 Shout against her round about: she has given her hand: her foundations are fallen, her walls are thrown down: for it is the vengeance of the LORD: take vengeance upon her; as she has done, do unto her.

16 Cut off the sower from Babylon, and him that handleth the sickle in the time of harvest: for fear of the oppressing sword they shall turn every one to his people, and they shall flee every one to his own land.

17Israel is a scattered sheep; the lions have driven him away: first the king of Assyria has devoured him; and last this Nebuchadrezzar king of Babylon has broken his bones.

18 Therefore thus saith the LORD of hosts, the God of Israel; Behold, I will punish the king of Babylon and his land, as I have punished the king of Assyria.

19 And I will bring Israel again to his habitation, and he shall feed on Carmel and Bashan, and his soul shall be satisfied upon mount Ephraim and Gilead.

20 In those days, and in that time, saith the LORD, the iniquity of Israel shall be sought for, and there shall be none; and the sins of Judah, and they shall not be found: for I will pardon them whom I reserve.

21Go up against the land of Merathaim, even against it, and against the inhabitants of Pekod: waste and utterly destroy after them, saith the LORD, and do according to all that I have commanded you.

22 A sound of battle is in the land, and of great destruction.

23 How is the hammer of the whole earth cut asunder and broken! how is Babylon become a desolation among the nations!

24 I have laid a snare for you, and you are also taken, O Babylon, and you wast not aware: you are found, and also caught, because you have striven against the LORD.

25 The LORD has opened his armoury, and has brought forth the weapons of his indignation: for this is the work of the Lord GOD of hosts in the land of the Chaldeans.

26 Come against her from the utmost border, open her storehouses: cast her up as heaps, and destroy her utterly: let nothing of her be left.

27 Slay all her bullocks; let them go down to the slaughter: woe unto them! for their day is come, the time of their visitation.

28 The voice of them that flee and escape out of the land of Babylon, to declare in Zion the vengeance of the LORD our God, the vengeance of his temple.

29 Call together the archers against Babylon: all you that bend the bow, camp against it round about; let none thereof escape: recompense her according to her work; according to all that she has done, do unto her: for she has been proud against the LORD, against the Holy One of Israel.

30 Therefore shall her young men fall in the streets, and all her men of war shall be cut off in that day, saith the LORD.

31 Behold, I am against you, O you most proud, saith the Lord GOD of hosts: for your day is come, the time that I will visit you.

32 And the most proud shall stumble and fall, and none shall raise him up: and I will kindle a fire in his cities, and it shall devour all round about him.

33Thus saith the LORD of hosts; The children of Israel and the children of Judah were oppressed together: and all that took them captives held them fast; they refused to let them go.

34 Their Redeemer is strong; the LORD of hosts is his name: he shall throughly plead their cause, that he may give rest to the land, and disquiet the inhabitants of Babylon.

35A sword is upon the Chaldeans, saith the LORD, and upon the inhabitants of Babylon, and upon her princes, and upon her wise men.

36 A sword is upon the liars; and they shall dote: a sword is upon her mighty men; and they shall be dismayed.

37 A sword is upon their horses, and upon their chariots, and upon all the mingled people that are in the midst of her; and they shall become as women: a sword is upon her treasures; and they shall be robbed.

38 A drought is upon her waters; and they shall be dried up: for it is the land of graven images, and they are mad upon their idols.

39 Therefore the wild beasts of the desert with the wild beasts of the islands shall dwell there, and the owls shall dwell therein: and it shall be no more inhabited for ever; neither shall it be dwelt in from generation to generation.

40 As God overthrew Sodom and Gomorrah and the neighbour cities thereof, saith the LORD; so shall no man abide there, neither shall any son of man dwell therein.

41 Behold, a people shall come from the north, and a great nation, and many kings shall be raised up from the coasts of the earth.

42 They shall hold the bow and the lance: they are cruel, and will not shew mercy: their voice shall roar like the sea, and they shall ride upon horses, every one put in array, like a man to the battle, against you, O daughter of Babylon.

43 The king of Babylon has heard the report of them, and his hands waxed feeble: anguish took hold of him, and pangs as of a woman in travail.

44 Behold, he shall come up like a lion from the swelling of Jordan unto the habitation of the strong: but I will make them suddenly run away from her: and who is a chosen man, that I may appoint over her? for who is like me? and who will appoint me the time? and who is that shepherd that will stand before me?

45 Therefore hear you the counsel of the LORD, that he has taken against Babylon; and his purposes, that he has purposed against the land of the Chaldeans: Surely the least of the flock shall draw them out: surely he shall make their habitation desolate with them.

46 At the noise of the taking of Babylon the earth is moved, and the cry is heard among the nations.

CHAPTER 51

THUS saith the LORD; Behold, I will raise up against Babylon, and against them that dwell in the midst of them that rise up against me, a destroying wind;

2 And will send unto Babylon fanners, that shall fan her, and shall empty her land: for in the day of trouble they shall be against her round about.

3 Against him that bendeth let the archer bend his bow, and against him that lifteth himself up in his brigandine: and spare you not her young men; destroy you utterly all her host.

4 Thus the slain shall fall in the land of the Chaldeans, and they that are thrust through in her streets.

5 For Israel has not been forsaken, nor Judah of his God, of the LORD of hosts; though their land was filled with sin against the Holy One of Israel.

6 Flee out of the midst of Babylon, and deliver every man his soul: be not cut off in her iniquity; for this is the time of the LORD's vengeance; he will render unto her a recompence.

7 Babylon has been a golden cup in the LORD's hand, that made all the earth drunken: the nations have drunken of her wine; therefore the nations are mad.

8 Babylon is suddenly fallen and destroyed: howl for her; take balm for her pain, if so be she may be healed.

9 We would have healed Babylon, but she is not healed: forsake her, and let us go every one into his own country: for her judgment reacheth unto heaven, and is lifted up even to the skies.

10 The LORD has brought forth our righteousness: come, and let us declare in Zion the work of the LORD our God.

11 Make bright the arrows; gather the shields: the LORD has raised up the spirit of the kings of the Medes: for his device is against Babylon, to destroy it; because it is the vengeance of the LORD, the vengeance of his temple.

12 Set up the standard upon the walls of Babylon, make the watch strong, set up the watchmen, prepare the ambushes: for the LORD has both devised and done that which he spake against the inhabitants of Babylon.

13 O you that dwellest upon many waters, abundant in treasures, yours end is come, and the measure of your covetousness.

14 The LORD of hosts has sworn by himself, saying, Surely I will fill you with men, as with caterpillers; and they shall lift up a shout against you.

15 He has made the earth by his power, he has established the world by his wisdom, and has stretched out the heaven by his understanding.

16 When he uttereth his voice, there is a multitude of waters in the heavens; and he causeth the vapours to ascend from the ends of the earth: he maketh lightnings with rain, and bringeth forth the wind out of his treasures.

17 Every man is brutish by his knowledge; every founder is confounded by the graven image: for his molten image is falsehood, and there is no breath in them.

18 They are vanity, the work of errors: in the time of their visitation they shall perish.

19 The portion of Jacob is not like them; for he is the former of all things: and Israel is the rod of his inheritance: the LORD of hosts is his name.

20 You are my battle axe and weapons of war: for with you will I break in pieces the nations, and with you will I destroy kingdoms;

21 And with you will I break in pieces the horse and his rider; and with you will I break in pieces the chariot and his rider;

22 With you also will I break in pieces man and woman; and with you will I break in pieces old and young; and with you will I break in pieces the young man and the maid;

23 I will also break in pieces with you the shepherd and his flock; and with you will I break in pieces the husbandman and his yoke of oxen; and with you will I break in pieces captains and rulers.

24 And I will render unto Babylon and to all the inhabitants of Chaldea all their evil that they have done in Zion in your sight, saith the LORD.

25 Behold, I am against you, O destroying mountain, saith the LORD, which destroyest all the earth: and I will stretch out my hand upon you, and roll you down from the rocks, and will make you a burnt mountain.

26 And they shall not take of you a stone for a corner, nor a stone for foundations; but you shalt be desolate for ever, saith the LORD.

27 Set you up a standard in the land, blow the trumpet among the nations, prepare the nations against her, call together against her the kingdoms of Ararat, Minni, and Ashchenaz; appoint a captain against her; cause the horses to come up as the rough caterpillers.

28 Prepare against her the nations with the kings of the Medes, the captains thereof, and all the rulers thereof, and all the land of his dominion.

29 And the land shall tremble and sorrow: for every purpose of the LORD shall be performed against Babylon, to make the land of Babylon a desolation without an inhabitant.

30 The mighty men of Babylon have forborn to fight, they have remained in their holds: their might has failed; they became as women: they have burned her dwellingplaces; her bars are broken.

31 One post shall run to meet another, and one messenger to meet another, to shew the king of Babylon that his city is taken at one end,

32 And that the passages are stopped, and the reeds they have burned with fire, and the men of war are affrighted.

33 For thus saith the LORD of hosts, the God of Israel; The daughter of Babylon is like a threshingfloor, it is time to thresh her: yet a little while, and the time of her harvest shall come.

34 Nebuchadrezzar the king of Babylon has devoured me, he has crushed me, he has made me an empty vessel, he has swallowed me up like a dragon, he has filled his belly with my delicates, he has cast me out.

35 The violence done to me and to my flesh be upon Babylon, shall the inhabitant of Zion say; and my blood upon the inhabitants of Chaldea, shall Jerusalem say.

36 Therefore thus saith the LORD; Behold, I will plead your cause, and take vengeance for you; and I will dry up her sea, and make her springs dry.

37 And Babylon shall become heaps, a dwellingplace for dragons, an astonishment, and an hissing, without an inhabitant.

38 They shall roar together like lions: they shall yell as lions' whelps.

39 In their heat I will make their feasts, and I will make them drunken, that they may rejoice, and sleep a perpetual sleep, and not wake, saith the LORD.

40 I will bring them down like lambs to the slaughter, like rams with he goats.

41 How is Sheshach taken! and how is the praise of the whole earth surprised! how is Babylon become an astonishment among the nations!

42 The sea is come up upon Babylon: she is covered with the multitude of the waves thereof.

43 Her cities are a desolation, a dry land, and a wilderness, a land wherein no man dwelleth, neither doth any son of man pass thereby.

44 And I will punish Bel in Babylon, and I will bring forth out of his mouth that which he has swallowed up: and the nations shall not flow together any more unto him: yea, the wall of Babylon shall fall.

45 My people, go you out of the midst of her, and deliver you every man his soul from the fierce anger of the LORD.

46 And lest your heart faint, and you fear for the rumour that shall be heard in the land; a rumour shall both come one year, and after that in another year shall come a rumour, and violence in the land, ruler against ruler.

47 Therefore, behold, the days come, that I will do judgment upon the graven images of Babylon: and her whole land shall be confounded, and all her slain shall fall in the midst of her.

48 Then the heaven and the earth, and all that is therein, shall sing for Babylon: for the spoilers shall come unto her from the north, saith the LORD.

49 As Babylon has caused the slain of Israel to fall, so at Babylon shall fall the slain of all the earth.

50 You that have escaped the sword, go away, stand not still: remember the LORD afar off, and let Jerusalem come into your mind.

51 We are confounded, because we have heard reproach: shame has covered our faces: for strangers are come into the sanctuaries of the LORD's house.

52 Wherefore, behold, the days come, saith the LORD, that I will do judgment upon her graven images: and through all her land the wounded shall groan.

53 Though Babylon should mount up to heaven, and though she should fortify the height of her strength, yet from me shall spoilers come unto her, saith the LORD.

54 A sound of a cry comes from Babylon, and great destruction from the land of the Chaldeans:

55 Because the LORD has spoiled Babylon, and destroyed out of her the great voice; when her waves do roar like great waters, a noise of their voice is uttered:

56 Because the spoiler is come upon her, even upon Babylon, and her mighty men are taken, every one of their bows is broken: for the LORD God of recompences shall surely requite.

57 And I will make drunk her princes, and her wise men, her captains, and her rulers, and her mighty men: and they shall sleep a perpetual sleep, and not wake, saith the King, whose name is the LORD of hosts.

58 Thus saith the LORD of hosts; The broad walls of Babylon shall be utterly broken, and her high gates shall be burned with fire; and the people shall labour in vain, and the folk in the fire, and they shall be weary.

59 The word which Jeremiah the prophet commanded Seraiah the son of Neriah, the son of Maaseiah, when he went with Zedekiah the king of Judah into Babylon in the fourth year of his reign. And this Seraiah was a quiet prince.

60 So Jeremiah wrote in a book all the evil that should come upon Babylon, even all these words that are written against Babylon.

61 And Jeremiah said to Seraiah, When you comest to Babylon, and shalt see, and shalt read all these words;

62 Then shalt you say, O LORD, you have spoken against this place, to cut it off, that none shall remain in it, neither man nor beast, but that it shall be desolate for ever.

63 And it shall be, when you have made an end of reading this book, that you shalt bind a stone to it, and cast it into the midst of Euphrates:

64 And you shalt say, Thus shall Babylon sink, and shall not rise from the evil that I will bring upon her: and they shall be weary. Thus far are the words of Jeremiah.

CHAPTER 52

ZEDEKIAH was one and twenty years old when he began to reign, and he reigned eleven years in Jerusalem. And his mother's name was Hamutal the daughter of Jeremiah of Libnah.

2 And he did that which was evil in the eyes of the LORD, according to all that Jehoiakim had done.

3 For through the anger of the LORD it came to pass in Jerusalem and Judah, till he had cast them out from his presence, that Zedekiah rebelled against the king of Babylon.

4And it came to pass in the ninth year of his reign, in the tenth month, in the tenth day of the month, that Nebuchadrezzar king of Babylon came, he and all his army, against Jerusalem, and pitched against it, and built forts against it round about.

5 So the city was besieged unto the eleventh year of king Zedekiah.

6 And in the fourth month, in the ninth day of the month, the famine was sore in the city, so that there was no bread for the people of the land.

7 Then the city was broken up, and all the men of war fled, and went forth out of the city by night by the way of the gate between the two walls, which was by the king's garden; (now the Chaldeans were by the city round about:) and they went by the way of the plain.

8But the army of the Chaldeans pursued after the king, and overtook Zedekiah in the plains of Jericho; and all his army was scattered from him.

9 Then they took the king, and carried him up unto the king of Babylon to Riblah in the land of Hamath; where he gave judgment upon him.

10 And the king of Babylon slew the sons of Zedekiah before his eyes: he slew also all the princes of Judah in Riblah.

11 Then he put out the eyes of Zedekiah; and the king of Babylon bound him in chains, and carried him to Babylon, and put him in prison till the day of his death.

12Now in the fifth month, in the tenth day of the month, which was the nineteenth year of Nebuchadrezzar king of Babylon, came Nebuzar-adan, captain of the guard, which served the king of Babylon, into Jerusalem,

13 And burned the house of the LORD, and the king's house; and all the houses of Jerusalem, and all the houses of the great men, burned he with fire:

14 And all the army of the Chaldeans, that were with the captain of the guard, brake down all the walls of Jerusalem round about.

15 Then Nebuzar-adan the captain of the guard carried away captive certain of the poor of the people, and the residue of the people that remained in the city, and those that fell away, that fell to the king of Babylon, and the rest of the multitude.

16 But Nebuzar-adan the captain of the guard left certain of the poor of the land for vinedressers and for husbandmen.

17 Also the pillars of brass that were in the house of the LORD, and the bases, and the brasen sea that was in the house of the LORD, the Chaldeans brake, and carried all the brass of them to Babylon.

18 The caldrons also, and the shovels, and the snuffers, and the bowls, and the spoons, and all the vessels of brass wherewith they ministered, took they away.

19 And the basons, and the firepans, and the bowls, and the caldrons, and the candlesticks, and the spoons, and the cups; that which was of gold in gold, and that which was of silver in silver, took the captain of the guard away.

20 The two pillars, one sea, and twelve brasen bulls that were under the bases, which king Solomon had made in the house of the LORD: the brass of all these vessels was without weight.

21 And concerning the pillars, the height of one pillar was eighteen cubits; and a fillet of twelve cubits did compass it; and the thickness thereof was four fingers: it was hollow.

22 And a chapiter of brass was upon it; and the height of one chapiter was five cubits, with network and pomegranates upon the chapiters round about, all of brass. The second pillar also and the pomegranates were like unto these.

23 And there were ninety and six pomegranates on a side; and all the pomegranates upon the network were an hundred round about.

24And the captain of the guard took Seraiah the chief priest, and Zephaniah the second priest, and the three keepers of the door:

25 He took also out of the city an eunuch, which had the charge of the men of war; and seven men of them that were near the king's person, which were found in the city; and the principal scribe of the host, who mustered the people of the land; and threescore men of the people of the land, that were found in the midst of the city.

26 So Nebuzar-adan the captain of the guard took them, and brought them to the king of Babylon to Riblah.

27 And the king of Babylon struck them, and put them to death in Riblah in the land of Hamath. Thus Judah was carried away captive out of his own land.

28 This is the people whom Nebuchadrezzar carried away captive: in the seventh year three thousand Jews and three and twenty:

29 In the eighteenth year of Nebuchadrezzar he carried away captive from Jerusalem eight hundred thirty and two persons:

30 In the three and twentieth year of Nebuchadrezzar Nebuzar-adan the captain of the guard carried away captive of the Jews seven hundred forty and five persons: all the persons were four thousand and six hundred.

31And it came to pass in the seven and thirtieth year of the captivity of Jehoiachin king of Judah, in the twelfth month, in the five and twentieth day of the month, that Evil-merodach king of Babylon in the first year of his reign lifted up the head of Jehoiachin king of Judah, and brought him forth out of prison,

32 And spake kindly unto him, and set his throne above the throne of the kings that were with him in Babylon,

33 And changed his prison garments: and he did continually eat bread before him all the days of his life.

34 And for his diet, there was a continual diet given him of the king of Babylon, every day a portion until the day of his death, all the days of his life.

THE LAMENTATIONS OF JEREMIAH.

CHAPTER 1

HOW doth the city sit solitary, that was full of people! how is she become as a widow! she that was great among the nations, and princess among the provinces, how is she become tributary!

2 She weepeth sore in the night, and her tears are on her cheeks: among all her lovers she has none to comfort her: all her friends have dealt treacherously with her, they are become her enemies.

3 Judah is gone into captivity because of affliction, and because of great servitude: she dwelleth among the heathen, she findeth no rest: all her persecutors overtook her between the straits.

4 The ways of Zion do mourn, because none come to the solemn feasts: all her gates are desolate: her priests sigh, her virgins are afflicted, and she is in bitterness.

5 Her adversaries are the chief, her enemies prosper; for the LORD has afflicted her for the multitude of her transgressions: her children are gone into captivity before the enemy.

6 And from the daughter of Zion all her beauty is departed: her princes are become like harts that find no pasture, and they are gone without strength before the pursuer.

7 Jerusalem remembered in the days of her affliction and of her miseries all her pleasant things that she had in the days of old, when her people fell into the hand of the enemy, and none did help her: the adversaries saw her, and did mock at her sabbaths.

8 Jerusalem has grievously sinned; therefore she is removed: all that honoured her despise her, because they have seen her nakedness: yea, she sigheth, and turneth backward.

9 Her filthiness is in her skirts; she remembereth not her last end; therefore she came down wonderfully: she had no comforter. O LORD, behold my affliction: for the enemy has magnified himself.

10 The adversary has spread out his hand upon all her pleasant things: for she has seen that the heathen entered into her sanctuary, whom you did command that they should not enter into your congregation.

11 All her people sigh, they seek bread; they have given their pleasant things for meat to relieve the soul: see, O LORD, and consider; for I am become vile.

12 Is it nothing to you, all you that pass by? behold, and see if there be any sorrow like unto my sorrow, which is done unto me, wherewith the LORD has afflicted me in the day of his fierce anger.

13 From above has he sent fire into my bones, and it prevaileth against them: he has spread a net for my feet, he has turned me back: he has made me desolate and faint all the day.

14 The yoke of my transgressions is bound by his hand: they are wreathed, and come up upon my neck: he has made my strength to fall, the Lord has delivered me into their hands, from whom I am not able to rise up.

15 The Lord has trodden under foot all my mighty men in the midst of me: he has called an assembly against me to crush my young men: the Lord has trodden the virgin, the daughter of Judah, as in a winepress.

16 For these things I weep; my eye, my eye runneth down with water, because the comforter that should relieve my soul is far from me: my children are desolate, because the enemy prevailed.

17 Zion spreadeth forth her hands, and there is none to comfort her: the LORD has commanded concerning Jacob, that his adversaries should be round about him: Jerusalem is as a menstruous woman among them.

18 The LORD is righteous; for I have rebelled against his commandment: hear, I pray you, all people, and behold my sorrow: my virgins and my young men are gone into captivity.

19 I called for my lovers, but they deceived me: my priests and my elders gave up the ghost in the city, while they sought their meat to relieve their souls.

20 Behold, O LORD; for I am in distress: my bowels are troubled; my heart is turned within me; for I have grievously rebelled: abroad the sword bereaveth, at home there is as death.

21 They have heard that I sigh: there is none to comfort me: all my enemies have heard of my trouble; they are glad that you have done it: you will bring the day that you have called, and they shall be like unto me.

22 Let all their wickedness come before you; and do unto them, as you have done unto me for all my transgressions: for my sighs are many, and my heart is faint.

CHAPTER 2

HOW has the Lord covered the daughter of Zion with a cloud in his anger, and cast down from heaven unto the earth the beauty of Israel, and remembered not his footstool in the day of his anger!

2 The Lord has swallowed up all the habitations of Jacob, and has not pitied: he has thrown down in his wrath the strong holds of the daughter of Judah; he has brought them down to the ground: he has polluted the kingdom and the princes thereof.

3 He has cut off in his fierce anger all the horn of Israel: he has drawn back his right hand from before the enemy, and he burned against Jacob like a flaming fire, which devoureth round about.

4 He has bent his bow like an enemy: he stood with his right hand as an adversary, and slew all that were pleasant to the eye in the tabernacle of the daughter of Zion: he poured out his fury like fire.

5 The Lord was as an enemy: he has swallowed up Israel, he has swallowed up all her palaces: he has destroyed his strong holds, and has increased in the daughter of Judah mourning and lamentation.

6 And he has violently taken away his tabernacle, as if it were of a garden: he has destroyed his places of the assembly: the LORD has caused the solemn feasts and sabbaths to be forgotten in Zion, and has despised in the indignation of his anger the king and the priest.

7 The Lord has cast off his altar, he has abhorred his sanctuary, he has given up into the hand of the enemy the walls of her palaces; they have made a noise in the house of the LORD, as in the day of a solemn feast.

8 The LORD has purposed to destroy the wall of the daughter of Zion: he has stretched out a line, he has not withdrawn his hand from destroying: therefore he made the rampart and the wall to lament; they languished together.

9 Her gates are sunk into the ground; he has destroyed and broken her bars: her king and her princes are among the Gentiles: the law is no more; her prophets also find no vision from the LORD.

10 The elders of the daughter of Zion sit upon the ground, and keep silence: they have cast up dust upon their heads; they have girded themselves with sackcloth: the virgins of Jerusalem hang down their heads to the ground.

11 My eyes do fail with tears, my bowels are troubled, my liver is poured upon the earth, for the destruction of the daughter of my people; because the children and the sucklings swoon in the streets of the city.

12 They say to their mothers, Where is corn and wine? when they swooned as the wounded in the streets of the city, when their soul was poured out into their mothers' bosom.

13 What thing shall I take to witness for you? what thing shall I liken to you, O daughter of Jerusalem? what shall I equal to you, that I may comfort you, O virgin daughter of Zion? for your breach is great like the sea: who can heal you?

14 Your prophets have seen vain and foolish things for you: and they have not discovered yours iniquity, to turn away your captivity; but have seen for you false burdens and causes of banishment.

15 All that pass by clap their hands at you; they hiss and wag their head at the daughter of Jerusalem, saying, Is this the city that men call The perfection of beauty, The joy of the whole earth?

16 All yours enemies have opened their mouth against you: they hiss and gnash the teeth: they say, We have swallowed her up: certainly this is the day that we looked for; we have found, we have seen it.

17 The LORD has done that which he had devised; he has fulfilled his word that he had commanded in the days of old: he has thrown down, and has not pitied: and he has caused yours enemy to rejoice over you, he has set up the horn of yours adversaries.

18 Their heart cried unto the Lord, O wall of the daughter of Zion, let tears run down like a river day and night: give yourself no rest; let not the apple of yours eye cease.

19 Arise, cry out in the night: in the beginning of the watches pour out yours heart like water before the face of the Lord: lift up your hands toward him for the life of your young children, that faint for hunger in the top of every street.

20 Behold, O LORD, and consider to whom you have done this. Shall the women eat their fruit, and children of a span long? shall the priest and the prophet be slain in the sanctuary of the Lord?

21 The young and the old lie on the ground in the streets: my virgins and my young men are fallen by the sword; you have slain them in the day of yours anger; you have killed, and not pitied.

22 You have called as in a solemn day my terrors round about, so that in the day of the LORD's anger none escaped nor remained: those that I have swaddled and brought up has my enemy consumed.

CHAPTER 3

I AM the man that has seen affliction by the rod of his wrath.

2 He has led me, and brought me into darkness, but not into light.

3 Surely against me is he turned; he turneth his hand against me all the day.

4 My flesh and my skin has he made old; he has broken my bones.

5 He has builded against me, and compassed me with gall and travail.

6 He has set me in dark places, as they that be dead of old.

7 He has hedged me about, that I cannot get out: he has made my chain heavy.

8 Also when I cry and shout, he shutteth out my prayer.

9 He has inclosed my ways with hewn stone, he has made my paths crooked.

10 He was unto me as a bear lying in wait, and as a lion in secret places.

11 He has turned aside my ways, and pulled me in pieces: he has made me desolate.

12 He has bent his bow, and set me as a mark for the arrow.

13 He has caused the arrows of his quiver to enter into my reins.

14 I was a derision to all my people; and their song all the day.

15 He has filled me with bitterness, he has made me drunken with wormwood.

16 He has also broken my teeth with gravel stones, he has covered me with ashes.

17 And you have removed my soul far off from peace: I forgat prosperity.

18 And I said, My strength and my hope is perished from the LORD:

19 Remembering my affliction and my misery, the wormwood and the gall.

20 My soul has them still in remembrance, and is humbled in me.

21 This I recall to my mind, therefore have I hope.

22 It is of the LORD's mercies that we are not consumed, because his compassions fail not.

23 They are new every morning: great is your faithfulness.

24 The LORD is my portion, saith my soul; therefore will I hope in him.

25 The LORD is good unto them that wait for him, to the soul that seeketh him.

26 It is good that a man should both hope and quietly wait for the salvation of the LORD.

27 It is good for a man that he bear the yoke in his youth.

28 He sitteth alone and keepeth silence, because he has borne it upon him.

29 He putteth his mouth in the dust; if so be there may be hope.

30 He giveth his cheek to him that smiteth him: he is filled full with reproach.

31 For the Lord will not cast off for ever:

32 But though he cause grief, yet will he have compassion according to the multitude of his mercies.

33 For he doth not afflict willingly nor grieve the children of men.

34 To crush under his feet all the prisoners of the earth,

35 To turn aside the right of a man before the face of the most High,

36 To subvert a man in his cause, the Lord approveth not.

37 Who is he that saith, and it comes to pass, when the Lord commandeth it not?

38 Out of the mouth of the most High proceedeth not evil and good?

39 Wherefore doth a living man complain, a man for the punishment of his sins?

40 Let us search and try our ways, and turn again to the LORD.

41 Let us lift up our heart with our hands unto God in the heavens.

42 We have transgressed and have rebelled: you have not pardoned.

43 You have covered with anger, and persecuted us: you have slain, you have not pitied.

44 You have covered yourself with a cloud, that our prayer should not pass through.

45 You have made us as the offscouring and refuse in the midst of the people.

46 All our enemies have opened their mouths against us.

47 Fear and a snare is come upon us, desolation and destruction.

48 My eye runneth down with rivers of water for the destruction of the daughter of my people.

49 My eye trickleth down, and ceaseth not, without any intermission,

50 Till the LORD look down, and behold from heaven.

51 My eye affecteth my heart because of all the daughters of my city.

52 My enemies chased me sore, like a bird, without cause.

53 They have cut off my life in the dungeon, and cast a stone upon me.

54 Waters flowed over my head; then I said, I am cut off.

55 I called upon your name, O LORD, out of the low dungeon.

56 You have heard my voice: hide not yours ear at my breathing, at my cry.

57 You drewest near in the day that I called upon you: you saidst, Fear not.

58 O Lord, you have pleaded the causes of my soul; you have redeemed my life.

59 O LORD, you have seen my wrong: judge you my cause.

60 You have seen all their vengeance and all their imaginations against me.

61 You have heard their reproach, O LORD, and all their imaginations against me;

62 The lips of those that rose up against me, and their device against me all the day.

63 Behold their sitting down, and their rising up; I am their musick.

64 Render unto them a recompence, O LORD, according to the work of their hands.

65 Give them sorrow of heart, your curse unto them.

66 Persecute and destroy them in anger from under the heavens of the LORD.

CHAPTER 4

HOW is the gold become dim! how is the most fine gold changed! the stones of the sanctuary are poured out in the top of every street.

2 The precious sons of Zion, comparable to fine gold, how are they esteemed as earthen pitchers, the work of the hands of the potter!

3 Even the sea monsters draw out the breast, they give suck to their young ones: the daughter of my people is become cruel, like the ostriches in the wilderness.

4 The tongue of the sucking child cleaveth to the roof of his mouth for thirst: the young children ask bread, and no man breaketh it unto them.

5 They that did feed delicately are desolate in the streets: they that were brought up in scarlet embrace dunghills.

6 For the punishment of the iniquity of the daughter of my people is greater than the punishment of the sin of Sodom, that was overthrown as in a moment, and no hands stayed on her.

7 Her Nazarites were purer than snow, they were whiter than milk, they were more ruddy in body than rubies, their polishing was of sapphire:

8 Their visage is blacker than a coal; they are not known in the streets: their skin cleaveth to their bones; it is withered, it is become like a stick.

9 They that be slain with the sword are better than they that be slain with hunger: for these pine away, stricken through for want of the fruits of the field.

10 The hands of the pitiful women have sodden their own children: they were their meat in the destruction of the daughter of my people.

11 The LORD has accomplished his fury; he has poured out his fierce anger, and has kindled a fire in Zion, and it has devoured the foundations thereof.

12 The kings of the earth, and all the inhabitants of the world, would not have believed that the adversary and the enemy should have entered into the gates of Jerusalem.

13 For the sins of her prophets, and the iniquities of her priests, that have shed the blood of the just in the midst of her,

14 They have wandered as blind men in the streets, they have polluted themselves with blood, so that men could not touch their garments.

15 They cried unto them, Depart you ; it is unclean; depart, depart, touch not: when they fled away and wandered, they said among the heathen, They shall no more sojourn there.

16 The anger of the LORD has divided them; he will no more regard them: they respected not the persons of the priests, they favoured not the elders.

17 As for us, our eyes as yet failed for our vain help: in our watching we have watched for a nation that could not save us.

18 They hunt our steps, that we cannot go in our streets: our end is near, our days are fulfilled; for our end is come.

19 Our persecutors are swifter than the eagles of the heaven: they pursued us upon the mountains, they laid wait for us in the wilderness.

20 The breath of our nostrils, the anointed of the LORD, was taken in their pits, of whom we said, Under his shadow we shall live among the heathen.

21 Rejoice and be glad, O daughter of Edom, that dwellest in the land of Uz; the cup also shall pass through unto you: you shalt be drunken, and shalt make yourself naked.

22 The punishment of yours iniquity is accomplished, O daughter of Zion; he will no more carry you away into captivity: he will visit yours iniquity, O daughter of Edom; he will discover your sins.

CHAPTER 5

REMEMBER, O LORD, what is come upon us: consider, and behold our reproach.

2 Our inheritance is turned to strangers, our houses to aliens.

3 We are orphans and fatherless, our mothers are as widows.

4 We have drunken our water for money; our wood is sold unto us.

5 Our necks are under persecution: we labour, and have no rest.

6 We have given the hand to the Egyptians, and to the Assyrians, to be satisfied with bread.

7 Our fathers have sinned, and are not; and we have borne their iniquities.

8 Servants have ruled over us: there is none that doth deliver us out of their hand.

9 We gat our bread with the peril of our lives because of the sword of the wilderness.

10 Our skin was black like an oven because of the terrible famine.

11 They ravished the women in Zion, and the maids in the cities of Judah.

12 Princes are hanged up by their hand: the faces of elders were not honoured.

13 They took the young men to grind, and the children fell under the wood.

14 The elders have ceased from the gate, the young men from their musick.

15 The joy of our heart is ceased; our dance is turned into mourning.

16 The crown is fallen from our head: woe unto us, that we have sinned!

17 For this our heart is faint; for these things our eyes are dim.

18 Because of the mountain of Zion, which is desolate, the foxes walk upon it.

19 You , O LORD, remainest for ever; your throne from generation to generation.

20 Wherefore dost you forget us for ever, and forsake us so long time?

21 Turn you us unto you, O LORD, and we shall be turned; renew our days as of old.

22 But you have utterly rejected us; you are very wroth against us.

THE BOOK OF THE PROPHET EZEKIEL.

CHAPTER 1

NOW it came to pass in the thirtieth year, in the fourth month, in the fifth day of the month, as I was among the captives by the river of Chebar, that the heavens were opened, and I saw visions of God.

2 In the fifth day of the month, which was the fifth year of king Jehoiachin's captivity,

3 The word of the LORD came expressly unto Ezekiel the priest, the son of Buzi, in the land of the Chaldeans by the river Chebar; and the hand of the LORD was there upon him.

4And I looked, and, behold, a whirlwind came out of the north, a great cloud, and a fire infolding itself, and a brightness was about it, and out of the midst thereof as the colour of amber, out of the midst of the fire.

5 Also out of the midst thereof came the likeness of four living creatures. And this was their appearance; they had the likeness of a man.

6 And every one had four faces, and every one had four wings.

7 And their feet were straight feet; and the sole of their feet was like the sole of a calf's foot: and they sparkled like the colour of burnished brass.

8 And they had the hands of a man under their wings on their four sides; and they four had their faces and their wings.

9 Their wings were joined one to another; they turned not when they went; they went every one straight forward.

10 As for the likeness of their faces, they four had the face of a man, and the face of a lion, on the right side: and they four had the face of an ox on the left side; they four also had the face of an eagle.

11 Thus were their faces: and their wings were stretched upward; two wings of every one were joined one to another, and two covered their bodies.

12 And they went every one straight forward: whither the spirit was to go, they went; and they turned not when they went.

13 As for the likeness of the living creatures, their appearance was like burning coals of fire, and like the appearance of lamps: it went up and down among the living creatures; and the fire was bright, and out of the fire went forth lightning.

14 And the living creatures ran and returned as the appearance of a flash of lightning.

15Now as I beheld the living creatures, behold one wheel upon the earth by the living creatures, with his four faces.

16 The appearance of the wheels and their work was like unto the colour of a beryl: and they four had one likeness: and their appearance and their work was as it were a wheel in the middle of a wheel.

17 When they went, they went upon their four sides: and they turned not when they went.

18 As for their rings, they were so high that they were dreadful; and their rings were full of eyes round about them four.

19 And when the living creatures went, the wheels went by them: and when the living creatures were lifted up from the earth, the wheels were lifted up.

20 Whithersoever the spirit was to go, they went, thither was their spirit to go; and the wheels were lifted up over against them: for the spirit of the living creature was in the wheels.

21 When those went, these went; and when those stood, these stood; and when those were lifted up from the earth, the wheels were lifted up over against them: for the spirit of the living creature was in the wheels.

22 And the likeness of the firmament upon the heads of the living creature was as the colour of the terrible crystal, stretched forth over their heads above.

23 And under the firmament were their wings straight, the one toward the other: every one had two, which covered on this side, and every one had two, which covered on that side, their bodies.

24 And when they went, I heard the noise of their wings, like the noise of great waters, as the voice of the Almighty, the voice of speech, as the noise of an host: when they stood, they let down their wings.

25 And there was a voice from the firmament that was over their heads, when they stood, and had let down their wings.

26And above the firmament that was over their heads was the likeness of a throne, as the appearance of a sapphire stone: and upon the likeness of the throne was the likeness as the appearance of a man above upon it.

27 And I saw as the colour of amber, as the appearance of fire round about within it, from the appearance of his loins even upward, and from the appearance of his loins even downward, I saw as it were the appearance of fire, and it had brightness round about.

28 As the appearance of the bow that is in the cloud in the day of rain, so was the appearance of the brightness round about. This was the appearance of the likeness of the glory of the LORD. And when I saw it, I fell upon my face, and I heard a voice of one that spake.

CHAPTER 2

AND he said unto me, Son of man, stand upon your feet, and I will speak unto you.

2 And the spirit entered into me when he spake unto me, and set me upon my feet, that I heard him that spake unto me.

3 And he said unto me, Son of man, I send you to the children of Israel, to a rebellious nation that has rebelled against me: they and their fathers have transgressed against me, even unto this very day.

4 For they are impudent children and stiffhearted. I do send you unto them; and you shalt say unto them, Thus saith the Lord GOD.

5 And they, whether they will hear, or whether they will forbear, (for they are a rebellious house,) yet shall know that there has been a prophet among them.

6And you , son of man, be not afraid of them, neither be afraid of their words, though briers and thorns be with you, and you dost dwell among scorpions: be not afraid of their words, nor be dismayed at their looks, though they be a rebellious house.

7 And you shalt speak my words unto them, whether they will hear, or whether they will forbear: for they are most rebellious.

8 But you , son of man, hear what I say unto you; Be not you rebellious like that rebellious house: open your mouth, and eat that I give you.

9And when I looked, behold, an hand was sent unto me; and, lo, a roll of a book was therein;

10 And he spread it before me; and it was written within and without: and there was written therein lamentations, and mourning, and woe.

CHAPTER 3

MOREOVER he said unto me, Son of man, eat that you findest; eat this roll, and go speak unto the house of Israel.

2 So I opened my mouth, and he caused me to eat that roll.

3 And he said unto me, Son of man, cause your belly to eat, and fill your bowels with this roll that I give you. Then did I eat it; and it was in my mouth as honey for sweetness.

4And he said unto me, Son of man, go, get you unto the house of Israel, and speak with my words unto them.

5 For you are not sent to a people of a strange speech and of an hard language, but to the house of Israel;

6 Not to many people of a strange speech and of an hard language, whose words you can not understand. Surely, had I sent you to them, they would have hearkened unto you.

7 But the house of Israel will not hearken unto you; for they will not hearken unto me: for all the house of Israel are impudent and hardhearted.

8 Behold, I have made your face strong against their faces, and your forehead strong against their foreheads.

9 As an adamant harder than flint have I made your forehead: fear them not, neither be dismayed at their looks, though they be a rebellious house.

10 Moreover he said unto me, Son of man, all my words that I shall speak unto you receive in yours heart, and hear with yours ears.

11 And go, get you to them of the captivity, unto the children of your people, and speak unto them, and tell them, Thus saith the Lord GOD; whether they will hear, or whether they will forbear.

12 Then the spirit took me up, and I heard behind me a voice of a great rushing, saying, Blessed be the glory of the LORD from his place.

13 I heard also the noise of the wings of the living creatures that touched one another, and the noise of the wheels over against them, and a noise of a great rushing.

14 So the spirit lifted me up, and took me away, and I went in bitterness, in the heat of my spirit; but the hand of the LORD was strong upon me.

15Then I came to them of the captivity at Tel-abib, that dwelt by the river of Chebar, and I sat where they sat, and remained there astonished among them seven days.

16 And it came to pass at the end of seven days, that the word of the LORD came unto me, saying,

17 Son of man, I have made you a watchman unto the house of Israel: therefore hear the word at my mouth, and give them warning from me.

18 When I say unto the wicked, You shalt surely die; and you givest him not warning, nor speakest to warn the wicked from his wicked way, to save his life; the same wicked man shall die in his iniquity; but his blood will I require at yours hand.

19 Yet if you warn the wicked, and he turn not from his wickedness, nor from his wicked way, he shall die in his iniquity; but you have delivered your soul.

20 Again, When a righteous man doth turn from his righteousness, and commit iniquity, and I lay a stumblingblock before him, he shall die: because you have not given him warning, he shall die in his sin, and his righteousness which he has done shall not be remembered; but his blood will I require at yours hand.

21 Nevertheless if you warn the righteous man, that the righteous sin not, and he doth not sin, he shall surely live, because he is warned; also you have delivered your soul.

22 And the hand of the LORD was there upon me; and he said unto me, Arise, go forth into the plain, and I will there talk with you.

23 Then I arose, and went forth into the plain: and, behold, the glory of the LORD stood there, as the glory which I saw by the river of Chebar: and I fell on my face.

24 Then the spirit entered into me, and set me upon my feet, and spake with me, and said unto me, Go, shut yourself within yours house.

25 But you, O son of man, behold, they shall put bands upon you, and shall bind you with them, and you shalt not go out among them:

26 And I will make your tongue cleave to the roof of your mouth, that you shalt be dumb, and shalt not be to them a reprover: for they are a rebellious house.

27 But when I speak with you, I will open your mouth, and you shalt say unto them, Thus saith the Lord GOD; He that heareth, let him hear; and he that forbeareth, let him forbear: for they are a rebellious house.

CHAPTER 4

YOU also, son of man, take you a tile, and lay it before you, and pourtray upon it the city, even Jerusalem:

2 And lay siege against it, and build a fort against it, and cast a mount against it; set the camp also against it, and set battering rams against it round about.

3 Moreover take you unto you an iron pan, and set it for a wall of iron between you and the city: and set your face against it, and it shall be besieged, and you shalt lay siege against it. This shall be a sign to the house of Israel.

4 Lie you also upon your left side, and lay the iniquity of the house of Israel upon it: according to the number of the days that you shalt lie upon it you shalt bear their iniquity.

5 For I have laid upon you the years of their iniquity, according to the number of the days, three hundred and ninety days: so shalt you bear the iniquity of the house of Israel.

6 And when you have accomplished them, lie again on your right side, and you shalt bear the iniquity of the house of Judah forty days: I have appointed you each day for a year.

7 Therefore you shalt set your face toward the siege of Jerusalem, and yours arm shall be uncovered, and you shalt prophesy against it.

8 And, behold, I will lay bands upon you, and you shalt not turn you from one side to another, till you have ended the days of your siege.

9 Take you also unto you wheat, and barley, and beans, and lentiles, and millet, and fitches, and put them in one vessel, and make you bread thereof, according to the number of the days that you shalt lie upon your side, three hundred and ninety days shalt you eat thereof.

10 And your meat which you shalt eat shall be by weight, twenty shekels a day: from time to time shalt you eat it.

11 You shalt drink also water by measure, the sixth part of an hin: from time to time shalt you drink.

12 And you shalt eat it as barley cakes, and you shalt bake it with dung that comes out of man, in their sight.

13 And the LORD said, Even thus shall the children of Israel eat their defiled bread among the Gentiles, whither I will drive them.

14 Then said I, Ah Lord GOD! behold, my soul has not been polluted: for from my youth up even till now have I not eaten of that which dieth of itself, or is torn in pieces; neither came there abominable flesh into my mouth.

15 Then he said unto me, Lo, I have given you cow's dung for man's dung, and you shalt prepare your bread therewith.

16 Moreover he said unto me, Son of man, behold, I will break the staff of bread in Jerusalem: and they shall eat bread by weight, and with care; and they shall drink water by measure, and with astonishment:

17 That they may want bread and water, and be astonied one with another, and consume away for their iniquity.

CHAPTER 5

AND you, son of man, take you a sharp knife, take you a barber's rasor, and cause it to pass upon yours head and upon your beard: then take you balances to weigh, and divide the hair.

2 You shalt burn with fire a third part in the midst of the city, when the days of the siege are fulfilled: and you shalt take a third part, and strike about it with a knife: and a third part you shalt scatter in the wind; and I will draw out a sword after them.

3 You shalt also take thereof a few in number, and bind them in your skirts.

4 Then take of them again, and cast them into the midst of the fire, and burn them in the fire; for thereof shall a fire come forth into all the house of Israel.

5 Thus saith the Lord GOD; This is Jerusalem: I have set it in the midst of the nations and countries that are round about her.

6 And she has changed my judgments into wickedness more than the nations, and my statutes more than the countries that are round about her: for they have refused my judgments and my statutes, they have not walked in them.

7 Therefore thus saith the Lord GOD; Because you multiplied more than the nations that are round about you, and have not walked in my statutes, neither have kept my judgments, neither have done according to the judgments of the nations that are round about you;

8 Therefore thus saith the Lord GOD; Behold, I, even I, am against you, and will execute judgments in the midst of you in the sight of the nations.

9 And I will do in you that which I have not done, and whereunto I will not do any more the like, because of all yours abominations.

10 Therefore the fathers shall eat the sons in the midst of you, and the sons shall eat their fathers; and I will execute judgments in you, and the whole remnant of you will I scatter into all the winds.

11 Wherefore, as I live, saith the Lord GOD; Surely, because you have defiled my sanctuary with all your detestable things, and with all yours abominations, therefore will I also diminish you; neither shall my eye spare, neither will I have any pity.

12 A third part of you shall die with the pestilence, and with famine shall they be consumed in the midst of you: and a third part shall fall by the sword round about you; and I will scatter a third part into all the winds, and I will draw out a sword after them.

13 Thus shall my anger be accomplished, and I will cause my fury to rest upon them, and I will be comforted: and they shall know that I the LORD have spoken it in my zeal, when I have accomplished my fury in them.

14 Moreover I will make you waste, and a reproach among the nations that are round about you, in the sight of all that pass by.

15 So it shall be a reproach and a taunt, an instruction and an astonishment unto the nations that are round about you, when I shall execute judgments in you in anger and in fury and in furious rebukes. I the LORD have spoken it.

16 When I shall send upon them the evil arrows of famine, which shall be for their destruction, and which I will send to destroy you: and I will increase the famine upon you, and will break your staff of bread:

17 So will I send upon you famine and evil beasts, and they shall bereave you; and pestilence and blood shall pass through you; and I will bring the sword upon you. I the LORD have spoken it.

CHAPTER 6

AND the word of the LORD came unto me, saying,

2 Son of man, set your face toward the mountains of Israel, and prophesy against them,

3 And say, You mountains of Israel, hear the word of the Lord GOD; Thus saith the Lord GOD to the mountains, and to the hills, to the rivers, and to the valleys; Behold, I, even I, will bring a sword upon you, and I will destroy your high places.

4 And your altars shall be desolate, and your images shall be broken: and I will cast down your slain men before your idols.

5 And I will lay the dead carcases of the children of Israel before their idols; and I will scatter your bones round about your altars.

6 In all your dwellingplaces the cities shall be laid waste, and the high places shall be desolate; that your altars may be laid waste and made desolate, and your idols may be broken and cease, and your images may be cut down, and your works may be abolished.

7 And the slain shall fall in the midst of you, and you shall know that I am the LORD.

8 Yet will I leave a remnant, that you may have some that shall escape the sword among the nations, when you shall be scattered through the countries.

9 And they that escape of you shall remember me among the nations whither they shall be carried captives, because I am broken with their whorish heart, which has departed from me, and with their

eyes, which go a whoring after their idols: and they shall lothe themselves for the evils which they have committed in all their abominations.

10 And they shall know that I am the LORD, and that I have not said in vain that I would do this evil unto them.

11Thus saith the Lord GOD; Strike with yours hand, and stamp with your foot, and say, Alas for all the evil abominations of the house of Israel! for they shall fall by the sword, by the famine, and by the pestilence.

12 He that is far off shall die of the pestilence; and he that is near shall fall by the sword; and he that remaineth and is besieged shall die by the famine: thus will I accomplish my fury upon them.

13 Then shall you know that I am the LORD, when their slain men shall be among their idols round about their altars, upon every high hill, in all the tops of the mountains, and under every green tree, and under every thick oak, the place where they did offer sweet savour to all their idols.

14 So will I stretch out my hand upon them, and make the land desolate, yea, more desolate than the wilderness toward Diblath, in all their habitations: and they shall know that I am the LORD.

CHAPTER 7

MOREOVER the word of the LORD came unto me, saying,

2 Also, you son of man, thus saith the Lord GOD unto the land of Israel; An end, the end is come upon the four corners of the land.

3 Now is the end come upon you, and I will send my anger upon you, and will judge you according to your ways, and will recompense upon you all yours abominations.

4 And my eye shall not spare you, neither will I have pity: but I will recompense your ways upon you, and yours abominations shall be in the midst of you: and you shall know that I am the LORD.

5 Thus saith the Lord GOD; An evil, an only evil, behold, is come.

6 An end is come, the end is come: it watcheth for you; behold, it is come.

7 The morning is come unto you, O you that dwellest in the land: the time is come, the day of trouble is near, and not the sounding again of the mountains.

8 Now will I shortly pour out my fury upon you, and accomplish my anger upon you: and I will judge you according to your ways, and will recompense you for all yours abominations.

9 And my eye shall not spare, neither will I have pity: I will recompense you according to your ways and yours abominations that are in the midst of you; and you shall know that I am the LORD that smiteth.

10 Behold the day, behold, it is come: the morning is gone forth; the rod has blossomed, pride has budded.

11 Violence is risen up into a rod of wickedness: none of them shall remain, nor of their multitude, nor of any of theirs: neither shall there be wailing for them.

12 The time is come, the day draweth near: let not the buyer rejoice, nor the seller mourn: for wrath is upon all the multitude thereof.

13 For the seller shall not return to that which is sold, although they were yet alive: for the vision is touching the whole multitude thereof, which shall not return; neither shall any strengthen himself in the iniquity of his life.

14 They have blown the trumpet, even to make all ready; but none goeth to the battle: for my wrath is upon all the multitude thereof.

15 The sword is without, and the pestilence and the famine within: he that is in the field shall die with the sword; and he that is in the city, famine and pestilence shall devour him.

16But they that escape of them shall escape, and shall be on the mountains like doves of the valleys, all of them mourning, every one for his iniquity.

17 All hands shall be feeble, and all knees shall be weak as water.

18 They shall also gird themselves with sackcloth, and horror shall cover them; and shame shall be upon all faces, and baldness upon all their heads.

19 They shall cast their silver in the streets, and their gold shall be removed: their silver and their gold shall not be able to deliver them in the day of the wrath of the LORD: they shall not satisfy their souls, neither fill their bowels: because it is the stumblingblock of their iniquity.

20As for the beauty of his ornament, he set it in majesty: but they made the images of their abominations and of their detestable things therein: therefore have I set it far from them.

21 And I will give it into the hands of the strangers for a prey, and to the wicked of the earth for a spoil; and they shall pollute it.

22 My face will I turn also from them, and they shall pollute my secret place: for the robbers shall enter into it, and defile it.

23Make a chain: for the land is full of bloody crimes, and the city is full of violence.

24 Wherefore I will bring the worst of the heathen, and they shall possess their houses: I will also make the pomp of the strong to cease; and their holy places shall be defiled.

25 Destruction comes; and they shall seek peace, and there shall be none.

26 Mischief shall come upon mischief, and rumour shall be upon rumour; then shall they seek a vision of the prophet; but the law shall perish from the priest, and counsel from the ancients.

27 The king shall mourn, and the prince shall be clothed with desolation, and the hands of the people of the land shall be troubled: I will do unto them after their way, and according to their deserts will I judge them; and they shall know that I am the LORD.

CHAPTER 8

AND it came to pass in the sixth year, in the sixth month, in the fifth day of the month, as I sat in my house, and the elders of Judah sat before me, that the hand of the Lord GOD fell there upon me.

2 Then I beheld, and lo a likeness as the appearance of fire: from the appearance of his loins even downward, fire; and from his loins even upward, as the appearance of brightness, as the colour of amber.

3 And he put forth the form of an hand, and took me by a lock of my head; and the spirit lifted me up between the earth and the heaven, and brought me in the visions of God to Jerusalem, to the door of the inner gate that looketh toward the north; where was the seat of the image of jealousy, which provoketh to jealousy.

4 And, behold, the glory of the God of Israel was there, according to the vision that I saw in the plain.

5Then said he unto me, Son of man, lift up yours eyes now the way toward the north. So I lifted up my eyes the way toward the north, and behold northward at the gate of the altar this image of jealousy in the entry.

6 He said furthermore unto me, Son of man, seest you what they do? even the great abominations that the house of Israel committeth here, that I should go far off from my sanctuary? but turn you yet again, and you shalt see greater abominations.

7And he brought me to the door of the court; and when I looked, behold a hole in the wall.

8 Then said he unto me, Son of man, dig now in the wall: and when I had digged in the wall, behold a door.

9 And he said unto me, Go in, and behold the wicked abominations that they do here.

10 So I went in and saw; and behold every form of creeping things, and abominable beasts, and all the idols of the house of Israel, pourtrayed upon the wall round about.

11 And there stood before them seventy men of the ancients of the house of Israel, and in the midst of them stood Jaazaniah the son of Shaphan, with every man his censer in his hand; and a thick cloud of incense went up.

12 Then said he unto me, Son of man, have you seen what the ancients of the house of Israel do in the dark, every man in the chambers of his imagery? for they say, The LORD seeth us not; the LORD has forsaken the earth.

13He said also unto me, Turn you yet again, and you shalt see greater abominations that they do.

14 Then he brought me to the door of the gate of the LORD's house which was toward the north; and, behold, there sat women weeping for Tammuz.

15Then said he unto me, Have you seen this, O son of man? turn you yet again, and you shalt see greater abominations than these.

16 And he brought me into the inner court of the LORD's house, and, behold, at the door of the temple of the LORD, between the porch and the altar, were about five and twenty men, with their backs toward the temple of the LORD, and their faces toward the east; and they worshipped the sun toward the east.

17Then he said unto me, Have you seen this, O son of man? Is it a light thing to the house of Judah that they commit the abominations which they commit here? for they have filled the land with violence, and have returned to provoke me to anger: and, lo, they put the branch to their nose.

18 Therefore will I also deal in fury: my eye shall not spare, neither will I have pity: and though they cry in my ears with a loud voice, yet will I not hear them.

CHAPTER 9

HE cried also in my ears with a loud voice, saying, Cause them that have charge over the city to draw near, even every man with his destroying weapon in his hand.

2 And, behold, six men came from the way of the higher gate, which lies toward the north, and every man a slaughter weapon in his hand; and one man among them was clothed with linen, with a writer's inkhorn by his side: and they went in, and stood beside the brasen altar.

3 And the glory of the God of Israel was gone up from the cherub, whereupon he was, to the threshold of the house. And he called to the man clothed with linen, which had the writer's inkhorn by his side;

4 And the LORD said unto him, Go through the midst of the city, through the midst of Jerusalem, and set a mark upon the foreheads of the men that sigh and that cry for all the abominations that be done in the midst thereof.

5And to the others he said in my hearing, Go you after him through the city, and strike: let not your eye spare, neither have you pity:

6 Slay utterly old and young, both maids, and little children, and women: but come not near any man upon whom is the mark; and begin at my sanctuary. Then they began at the ancient men which were before the house.

7 And he said unto them, Defile the house, and fill the courts with the slain: go you forth. And they went forth, and slew in the city.

8And it came to pass, while they were slaying them, and I was left, that I fell upon my face, and cried, and said, Ah Lord GOD! will you destroy all the residue of Israel in your pouring out of your fury upon Jerusalem?

9 Then said he unto me, The iniquity of the house of Israel and Judah is exceeding great, and the land is full of blood, and the city full of perverseness: for they say, The LORD has forsaken the earth, and the LORD seeth not.

10 And as for me also, my eye shall not spare, neither will I have pity, but I will recompense their way upon their head.

11 And, behold, the man clothed with linen, which had the inkhorn by his side, reported the matter, saying, I have done as you have commanded me.

CHAPTER 10

THEN I looked, and, behold, in the firmament that was above the head of the cherubims there appeared over them as it were a sapphire stone, as the appearance of the likeness of a throne.

2 And he spake unto the man clothed with linen, and said, Go in between the wheels, even under the cherub, and fill yours hand with coals of fire from between the cherubims, and scatter them over the city. And he went in in my sight.

3 Now the cherubims stood on the right side of the house, when the man went in; and the cloud filled the inner court.

4 Then the glory of the LORD went up from the cherub, and stood over the threshold of the house; and the house was filled with the cloud, and the court was full of the brightness of the LORD's glory.

5 And the sound of the cherubims' wings was heard even to the outer court, as the voice of the Almighty God when he speaketh.

6 And it came to pass, that when he had commanded the man clothed with linen, saying, Take fire from between the wheels, from between the cherubims; then he went in, and stood beside the wheels.

7 And one cherub stretched forth his hand from between the cherubims unto the fire that was between the cherubims, and took thereof, and put it into the hands of him that was clothed with linen: who took it, and went out.

8And there appeared in the cherubims the form of a man's hand under their wings.

9 And when I looked, behold the four wheels by the cherubims, one wheel by one cherub, and another wheel by another cherub: and the appearance of the wheels was as the colour of a beryl stone.

10 And as for their appearances, they four had one likeness, as if a wheel had been in the midst of a wheel.

11 When they went, they went upon their four sides; they turned not as they went, but to the place whither the head looked they followed it; they turned not as they went.

12 And their whole body, and their backs, and their hands, and their wings, and the wheels, were full of eyes round about, even the wheels that they four had.

13 As for the wheels, it was cried unto them in my hearing, O wheel.

14 And every one had four faces: the first face was the face of a cherub, and the second face was the face of a man, and the third the face of a lion, and the fourth the face of an eagle.

15 And the cherubims were lifted up. This is the living creature that I saw by the river of Chebar.

16 And when the cherubims went, the wheels went by them: and when the cherubims lifted up their wings to mount up from the earth, the same wheels also turned not from beside them.

17 When they stood, these stood; and when they were lifted up, these lifted up themselves also: for the spirit of the living creature was in them.

18 Then the glory of the LORD departed from off the threshold of the house, and stood over the cherubims.

19 And the cherubims lifted up their wings, and mounted up from the earth in my sight: when they went out, the wheels also were beside them, and every one stood at the door of the east gate of the LORD's house; and the glory of the God of Israel was over them above.

20 This is the living creature that I saw under the God of Israel by the river of Chebar; and I knew that they were the cherubims.

21 Every one had four faces apiece, and every one four wings; and the likeness of the hands of a man was under their wings.

22 And the likeness of their faces was the same faces which I saw by the river of Chebar, their appearances and themselves: they went every one straight forward.

CHAPTER 11

MOREOVER the spirit lifted me up, and brought me unto the east gate of the LORD's house, which looketh eastward: and behold at the door of the gate five and twenty men; among whom I saw Jaazaniah the son of Azur, and Pelatiah the son of Benaiah, princes of the people.

2 Then said he unto me, Son of man, these are the men that devise mischief, and give wicked counsel in this city:

3 Which say, It is not near; let us build houses: this city is the caldron, and we be the flesh.

4Therefore prophesy against them, prophesy, O son of man.

5 And the Spirit of the LORD fell upon me, and said unto me, Speak; Thus saith the LORD; Thus have you said, O house of Israel: for I know the things that come into your mind, every one of them.

6 You have multiplied your slain in this city, and you have filled the streets thereof with the slain.

7 Therefore thus saith the Lord GOD; Your slain whom you have laid in the midst of it, they are the flesh, and this city is the caldron: but I will bring you forth out of the midst of it.

8 You have feared the sword; and I will bring a sword upon you, saith the Lord GOD.

9 And I will bring you out of the midst thereof, and deliver you into the hands of strangers, and will execute judgments among you.

10 You shall fall by the sword; I will judge you in the border of Israel; and you shall know that I am the LORD.

11 This city shall not be your caldron, neither shall you be the flesh in the midst thereof; but I will judge you in the border of Israel:

12 And you shall know that I am the LORD: for you have not walked in my statutes, neither executed my judgments, but have done after the manners of the heathen that are round about you.

13And it came to pass, when I prophesied, that Pelatiah the son of Benaiah died. Then fell I down upon my face, and cried with a loud voice, and said, Ah Lord GOD! will you make a full end of the remnant of Israel?

14 Again the word of the LORD came unto me, saying,

15 Son of man, your brethren, even your brethren, the men of your kindred, and all the house of Israel wholly, are they unto whom the inhabitants of Jerusalem have said, Get you far from the LORD: unto us is this land given in possession.

16 Therefore say, Thus saith the Lord GOD; Although I have cast them far off among the heathen, and although I have scattered them among the countries, yet will I be to them as a little sanctuary in the countries where they shall come.

17 Therefore say, Thus saith the Lord GOD; I will even gather you from the people, and assemble you out of the countries where you have been scattered, and I will give you the land of Israel.

18 And they shall come thither, and they shall take away all the detestable things thereof and all the abominations thereof from thence.

19 And I will give them one heart, and I will put a new spirit within you; and I will take the stony heart out of their flesh, and will give them an heart of flesh:

20 That they may walk in my statutes, and keep my ordinances, and do them: and they shall be my people, and I will be their God.

21 But as for them whose heart walketh after the heart of their detestable things and their abominations, I will recompense their way upon their own heads, saith the Lord GOD.

22Then did the cherubims lift up their wings, and the wheels beside them; and the glory of the God of Israel was over them above.

23 And the glory of the LORD went up from the midst of the city, and stood upon the mountain which is on the east side of the city.

24Afterwards the spirit took me up, and brought me in a vision by the Spirit of God into Chaldea, to them of the captivity. So the vision that I had seen went up from me.

25 Then I spake unto them of the captivity all the things that the LORD had shewed me.

CHAPTER 12

THE word of the LORD also came unto me, saying,

2 Son of man, you dwellest in the midst of a rebellious house, which have eyes to see, and see not; they have ears to hear, and hear not: for they are a rebellious house.

3 Therefore, you son of man, prepare you stuff for removing, and remove by day in their sight; and you shalt remove from your place to another place in their sight: it may be they will consider, though they be a rebellious house.

4 Then shalt you bring forth your stuff by day in their sight, as stuff for removing: and you shalt go forth at even in their sight, as they that go forth into captivity.

5 Dig you through the wall in their sight, and carry out thereby.

6 In their sight shalt you bear it upon your shoulders, and carry it forth in the twilight: you shalt cover your face, that you see not the ground: for I have set you for a sign unto the house of Israel.

7 And I did so as I was commanded: I brought forth my stuff by day, as stuff for captivity, and in the even I digged through the wall with my hand; I brought it forth in the twilight, and I bare it upon my shoulder in their sight.

8 And in the morning came the word of the LORD unto me, saying,

9 Son of man, has not the house of Israel, the rebellious house, said unto you, What doest you ?

10 Say you unto them, Thus saith the Lord GOD; This burden concerneth the prince in Jerusalem, and all the house of Israel that are among them.

11 Say, I am your sign: like as I have done, so shall it be done unto them: they shall remove and go into captivity.

12 And the prince that is among them shall bear upon his shoulder in the twilight, and shall go forth: they shall dig through the wall to carry out thereby: he shall cover his face, that he see not the ground with his eyes.

13 My net also will I spread upon him, and he shall be taken in my snare: and I will bring him to Babylon to the land of the Chaldeans; yet shall he not see it, though he shall die there.

14 And I will scatter toward every wind all that are about him to help him, and all his bands; and I will draw out the sword after them.

15 And they shall know that I am the LORD, when I shall scatter them among the nations, and disperse them in the countries.

16 But I will leave a few men of them from the sword, from the famine, and from the pestilence; that they may declare all their abominations among the heathen whither they come; and they shall know that I am the LORD.

17 Moreover the word of the LORD came to me, saying,

18 Son of man, eat your bread with quaking, and drink your water with trembling and with carefulness;

19 And say unto the people of the land, Thus saith the Lord GOD of the inhabitants of Jerusalem, and of the land of Israel; They shall eat their bread with carefulness, and drink their water with astonishment, that her land may be desolate from all that is therein, because of the violence of all them that dwell therein.

20 And the cities that are inhabited shall be laid waste, and the land shall be desolate; and you shall know that I am the LORD.

21 And the word of the LORD came unto me, saying,

22 Son of man, what is that proverb that you have in the land of Israel, saying, The days are prolonged, and every vision faileth?

23 Tell them therefore, Thus saith the Lord GOD; I will make this proverb to cease, and they shall no more use it as a proverb in Israel; but say unto them, The days are at hand, and the effect of every vision.

24 For there shall be no more any vain vision nor flattering divination within the house of Israel.

25 For I am the LORD: I will speak, and the word that I shall speak shall come to pass; it shall be no more prolonged: for in your days, O rebellious house, will I say the word, and will perform it, saith the Lord GOD.

26 Again the word of the LORD came to me, saying,

27 Son of man, behold, they of the house of Israel say, The vision that he seeth is for many days to come, and he prophesieth of the times that are far off.

28 Therefore say unto them, Thus saith the Lord GOD; There shall none of my words be prolonged any more, but the word which I have spoken shall be done, saith the Lord GOD.

CHAPTER 13

AND the word of the LORD came unto me, saying,

2 Son of man, prophesy against the prophets of Israel that prophesy, and say you unto them that prophesy out of their own hearts, Hear you the word of the LORD;

3 Thus saith the Lord GOD; Woe unto the foolish prophets, that follow their own spirit, and have seen nothing!

4 O Israel, your prophets are like the foxes in the deserts.

5 You have not gone up into the gaps, neither made up the hedge for the house of Israel to stand in the battle in the day of the LORD.

6 They have seen vanity and lying divination, saying, The LORD saith: and the LORD has not sent them: and they have made others to hope that they would confirm the word.

7 Have you not seen a vain vision, and have you not spoken a lying divination, whereas you say, The LORD saith it; albeit I have not spoken?

8 Therefore thus saith the Lord GOD; Because you have spoken vanity, and seen lies, therefore, behold, I am against you, saith the Lord GOD.

9 And my hand shall be upon the prophets that see vanity, and that divine lies: they shall not be in the assembly of my people, neither shall they be written in the writing of the house of Israel, neither shall they enter into the land of Israel; and you shall know that I am the Lord GOD.

10 Because, even because they have seduced my people, saying, Peace; and there was no peace; and one built up a wall, and, lo, others daubed it with untempered morter:

11 Say unto them which daub it with untempered morter, that it shall fall: there shall be an overflowing shower; and you , O great hailstones, shall fall; and a stormy wind shall rend it.

12 Lo, when the wall is fallen, shall it not be said unto you, Where is the daubing wherewith you have daubed it?

13 Therefore thus saith the Lord GOD; I will even rend it with a stormy wind in my fury; and there shall be an overflowing shower in my anger, and great hailstones in my fury to consume it.

14 So will I break down the wall that you have daubed with untempered morter, and bring it down to the ground, so that the foundation thereof shall be discovered, and it shall fall, and you shall be consumed in the midst thereof: and you shall know that I am the LORD.

15 Thus will I accomplish my wrath upon the wall, and upon them that have daubed it with untempered morter, and will say unto you, The wall is no more, neither they that daubed it;

16 To wit, the prophets of Israel which prophesy concerning Jerusalem, and which see visions of peace for her, and there is no peace, saith the Lord GOD.

17 Likewise, you son of man, set your face against the daughters of your people, which prophesy out of their own heart; and prophesy you against them,

18 And say, Thus saith the Lord GOD; Woe to the women that sew pillows to all armholes, and make kerchiefs upon the head of every stature to hunt souls! Will you hunt the souls of my people, and will you save the souls alive that come unto you?

19 And will you pollute me among my people for handfuls of barley and for pieces of bread, to slay the souls that should not die, and to save the souls alive that should not live, by your lying to my people that hear your lies?

20 Wherefore thus saith the Lord GOD; Behold, I am against your pillows, wherewith you there hunt the souls to make them fly, and I will tear them from your arms, and will let the souls go, even the souls that you hunt to make them fly.

21 Your kerchiefs also will I tear, and deliver my people out of your hand, and they shall be no more in your hand to be hunted; and you shall know that I am the LORD.

22 Because with lies you have made the heart of the righteous sad, whom I have not made sad; and strengthened the hands of the wicked, that he should not return from his wicked way, by promising him life:

23 Therefore you shall see no more vanity, nor divine divinations: for I will deliver my people out of your hand: and you shall know that I am the LORD.

CHAPTER 14

THEN came certain of the elders of Israel unto me, and sat before me.

2 And the word of the LORD came unto me, saying,

3 Son of man, these men have set up their idols in their heart, and put the stumblingblock of their iniquity before their face: should I be inquired of at all by them?

4 Therefore speak unto them, and say unto them, Thus saith the Lord GOD; Every man of the house of Israel that setteth up his idols in his heart, and putteth the stumblingblock of his iniquity before his face, and comes to the prophet; I the LORD will answer him that comes according to the multitude of his idols;

5 That I may take the house of Israel in their own heart, because they are all estranged from me through their idols.

6 Therefore say unto the house of Israel, Thus saith the Lord GOD; Repent, and turn yourselves from your idols; and turn away your faces from all your abominations.

7 For every one of the house of Israel, or of the stranger that sojourneth in Israel, which separateth himself from me, and setteth up his idols in his heart, and putteth the stumblingblock of his iniquity before his face, and comes to a prophet to inquire of him concerning me; I the LORD will answer him by myself:

8 And I will set my face against that man, and will make him a sign and a proverb, and I will cut him off from the midst of my people; and you shall know that I am the LORD.

9 And if the prophet be deceived when he has spoken a thing, I the LORD have deceived that prophet, and I will stretch out my hand upon him, and will destroy him from the midst of my people Israel.

10 And they shall bear the punishment of their iniquity: the punishment of the prophet shall be even as the punishment of him that seeketh unto him;

11 That the house of Israel may go no more astray from me, neither be polluted any more with all their transgressions; but that they may be my people, and I may be their God, saith the Lord GOD.

12 The word of the LORD came again to me, saying,

13 Son of man, when the land sinneth against me by trespassing grievously, then will I stretch out my hand upon it, and will break the staff of the bread thereof, and will send famine upon it, and will cut off man and beast from it:

14 Though these three men, Noah, Daniel, and Job, were in it, they should deliver but their own souls by their righteousness, saith the Lord GOD.

15 If I cause noisome beasts to pass through the land, and they spoil it, so that it be desolate, that no man may pass through because of the beasts:

16 Though these three men were in it, as I live, saith the Lord GOD, they shall deliver neither sons nor daughters; they only shall be delivered, but the land shall be desolate.

17 Or if I bring a sword upon that land, and say, Sword, go through the land; so that I cut off man and beast from it:

18 Though these three men were in it, as I live, saith the Lord GOD, they shall deliver neither sons nor daughters, but they only shall be delivered themselves.

19 Or if I send a pestilence into that land, and pour out my fury upon it in blood, to cut off from it man and beast:

20 Though Noah, Daniel, and Job, were in it, as I live, saith the Lord GOD, they shall deliver neither son nor daughter; they shall but deliver their own souls by their righteousness.

21 For thus saith the Lord GOD; How much more when I send my four sore judgments upon Jerusalem, the sword, and the famine, and the noisome beast, and the pestilence, to cut off from it man and beast?

22 Yet, behold, therein shall be left a remnant that shall be brought forth, both sons and daughters: behold, they shall come forth unto you, and you shall see their way and their doings: and you shall be comforted concerning the evil that I have brought upon Jerusalem, even concerning all that I have brought upon it.

23 And they shall comfort you, when you see their ways and their doings: and you shall know that I have not done without cause all that I have done in it, saith the Lord GOD.

CHAPTER 15

AND the word of the LORD came unto me, saying,

2 Son of man, What is the vine tree more than any tree, or than a branch which is among the trees of the forest?

3 Shall wood be taken thereof to do any work? or will men take a pin of it to hang any vessel thereon?

4 Behold, it is cast into the fire for fuel; the fire devoureth both the ends of it, and the midst of it is burned. Is it meet for any work?

5 Behold, when it was whole, it was meet for no work: how much less shall it be meet yet for any work, when the fire has devoured it, and it is burned?

6 Therefore thus saith the Lord GOD; As the vine tree among the trees of the forest, which I have given to the fire for fuel, so will I give the inhabitants of Jerusalem.

7 And I will set my face against them; they shall go out from one fire, and another fire shall devour them; and you shall know that I am the LORD, when I set my face against them.

8 And I will make the land desolate, because they have committed a trespass, saith the Lord GOD.

CHAPTER 16

AGAIN the word of the LORD came unto me, saying,

2 Son of man, cause Jerusalem to know her abominations,

3 And say, Thus saith the Lord GOD unto Jerusalem; Your birth and your nativity is of the land of Canaan; your father was an Amorite, and your mother an Hittite.

4 And as for your nativity, in the day you wast born your navel was not cut, neither wast you washed in water to supple you; you wast not salted at all, nor swaddled at all.

5 None eye pitied you, to do any of these unto you, to have compassion upon you; but you wast cast out in the open field, to the lothing of your person, in the day that you wast born.

6 And when I passed by you, and saw you polluted in yours own blood, I said unto you when you wast in your blood, Live; yea, I said unto you when you wast in your blood, Live.

7 I have caused you to multiply as the bud of the field, and you have increased and waxen great, and you are come to excellent ornaments: your breasts are fashioned, and yours hair is grown, whereas you wast naked and bare.

8 Now when I passed by you, and looked upon you, behold, your time was the time of love; and I spread my skirt over you, and covered your nakedness: yea, I sware unto you, and entered into a covenant with you, saith the Lord GOD, and you becamest my.

9 Then washed I you with water; yea, I throughly washed away your blood from you, and I anointed you with oil.

10 I clothed you also with broidered work, and shod you with badgers' skin, and I girded you about with fine linen, and I covered you with silk.

11 I decked you also with ornaments, and I put bracelets upon your hands, and a chain on your neck.

12 And I put a jewel on your forehead, and earrings in yours ears, and a beautiful crown upon yours head.

13 Thus wast you decked with gold and silver; and your raiment was of fine linen, and silk, and broidered work; you did eat fine flour, and honey, and oil: and you wast exceeding beautiful, and you did prosper into a kingdom.

14 And your renown went forth among the heathen for your beauty: for it was perfect through my comeliness, which I had put upon you, saith the Lord GOD.

15 But you did trust in yours own beauty, and playedst the harlot because of your renown, and pouredst out your fornications on every one that passed by; his it was.

16 And of your garments you did take, and deckedst your high places with divers colours, and playedst the harlot thereupon: the like things shall not come, neither shall it be so.

17 You have also taken your fair jewels of my gold and of my silver, which I had given you, and madest to yourself images of men, and did commit whoredom with them,

18 And tookest your broidered garments, and coveredst them: and you have set my oil and my incense before them.

19 My meat also which I gave you, fine flour, and oil, and honey, wherewith I fed you, you have even set it before them for a sweet savour: and thus it was, saith the Lord GOD.

20 Moreover you have taken your sons and your daughters, whom you have borne unto me, and these have you sacrificed unto them to be devoured. Is this of your whoredoms a small matter,

21 That you have slain my children, and delivered them to cause them to pass through the fire for them?

22 And in all yours abominations and your whoredoms you have not remembered the days of your youth, when you wast naked and bare, and wast polluted in your blood.

23 And it came to pass after all your wickedness, (woe, woe unto you! saith the Lord GOD;)

24 That you have also built unto you an eminent place, and have made you an high place in every street.

25 You have built your high place at every head of the way, and have made your beauty to be abhorred, and have opened your feet to every one that passed by, and multiplied your whoredoms.

26 You have also committed fornication with the Egyptians your neighbours, great of flesh; and have increased your whoredoms, to provoke me to anger.

27 Behold, therefore I have stretched out my hand over you, and have diminished yours ordinary food, and delivered you unto the will of them that hate you, the daughters of the Philistines, which are ashamed of your lewd way.

28 You have played the whore also with the Assyrians, because you wast unsatiable; yea, you have played the harlot with them, and yet couldest not be satisfied.

29 You have moreover multiplied your fornication in the land of Canaan unto Chaldea; and yet you wast not satisfied herewith.

30 How weak is yours heart, saith the Lord GOD, seeing you doest all these things, the work of an imperious whorish woman;

31 In that you buildest yours eminent place in the head of every way, and makest yours high place in every street; and have not been as an harlot, in that you scornest hire;

32 But as a wife that committeth adultery, which taketh strangers instead of her husband!

33 They give gifts to all whores: but you givest your gifts to all your lovers, and hirest them, that they may come unto you on every side for your whoredom.

34 And the contrary is in you from other women in your whoredoms, whereas none followeth you to commit whoredoms: and in that you givest a reward, and no reward is given unto you, therefore you are contrary.

35 Wherefore, O harlot, hear the word of the LORD:

36 Thus saith the Lord GOD; Because your filthiness was poured out, and your nakedness discovered through your whoredoms with your lovers, and with all the idols of your abominations, and by the blood of your children, which you did give unto them;

37 Behold, therefore I will gather all your lovers, with whom you have taken pleasure, and all them that you have loved, with all them that you have hated; I will even gather them round about against you, and will discover your nakedness unto them, that they may see all your nakedness.

38 And I will judge you, as women that break wedlock and shed blood are judged; and I will give you blood in fury and jealousy.

39 And I will also give you into their hand, and they shall throw down yours eminent place, and shall break down your high places: they shall strip you also of your clothes, and shall take your fair jewels, and leave you naked and bare.

40 They shall also bring up a company against you, and they shall stone you with stones, and thrust you through with their swords.

41 And they shall burn yours houses with fire, and execute judgments upon you in the sight of many women: and I will cause you to cease from playing the harlot, and you also shalt give no hire any more.

42 So will I make my fury toward you to rest, and my jealousy shall depart from you, and I will be quiet, and will be no more angry.

43 Because you have not remembered the days of your youth, but have fretted me in all these things; behold, therefore I also will recompense your way upon yours head, saith the Lord GOD: and you shalt not commit this lewdness above all yours abominations.

44Behold, every one that useth proverbs shall use this proverb against you, saying, As is the mother, so is her daughter.

45 You are your mother's daughter, that lotheth her husband and her children; and you are the sister of your sisters, which lothed their husbands and their children: your mother was an Hittite, and your father an Amorite.

46 And yours elder sister is Samaria, she and her daughters that dwell at your left hand: and your younger sister, that dwelleth at your right hand, is Sodom and her daughters.

47 Yet have you not walked after their ways, nor done after their abominations: but, as if that were a very little thing, you wast corrupted more than they in all your ways.

48 As I live, saith the Lord GOD, Sodom your sister has not done, she nor her daughters, as you have done, you and your daughters.

49 Behold, this was the iniquity of your sister Sodom, pride, fulness of bread, and abundance of idleness was in her and in her daughters, neither did she strengthen the hand of the poor and needy.

50 And they were haughty, and committed abomination before me: therefore I took them away as I saw good.

51 Neither has Samaria committed half of your sins; but you have multiplied yours abominations more than they, and have justified your sisters in all yours abominations which you have done.

52 You also, which have judged your sisters, bear yours own shame for your sins that you have committed more abominable than they: they are more righteous than you : yea, be you confounded also, and bear your shame, in that you have justified your sisters.

53 When I shall bring again their captivity, the captivity of Sodom and her daughters, and the captivity of Samaria and her daughters, then will I bring again the captivity of your captives in the midst of them:

54 That you mayest bear yours own shame, and mayest be confounded in all that you have done, in that you are a comfort unto them.

55 When your sisters, Sodom and her daughters, shall return to their former estate, and Samaria and her daughters shall return to their former estate, then you and your daughters shall return to your former estate.

56 For your sister Sodom was not mentioned by your mouth in the day of your pride,

57 Before your wickedness was discovered, as at the time of your reproach of the daughters of Syria, and all that are round about her, the daughters of the Philistines, which despise you round about.

58 You have borne your lewdness and yours abominations, saith the LORD.

59 For thus saith the Lord GOD; I will even deal with you as you have done, which have despised the oath in breaking the covenant.

60Nevertheless I will remember my covenant with you in the days of your youth, and I will establish unto you an everlasting covenant.

61 Then you shalt remember your ways, and be ashamed, when you shalt receive your sisters, yours elder and your younger: and I will give them unto you for daughters, but not by your covenant.

62 And I will establish my covenant with you; and you shalt know that I am the LORD:

63 That you mayest remember, and be confounded, and never open your mouth any more because of your shame, when I am pacified toward you for all that you have done, saith the Lord GOD.

CHAPTER 17

AND the word of the LORD came unto me, saying,

2 Son of man, put forth a riddle, and speak a parable unto the house of Israel;

3 And say, Thus saith the Lord GOD; A great eagle with great wings, longwinged, full of feathers, which had divers colours, came unto Lebanon, and took the highest branch of the cedar:

4 He cropped off the top of his young twigs, and carried it into a land of traffick; he set it in a city of merchants.

5 He took also of the seed of the land, and planted it in a fruitful field; he placed it by great waters, and set it as a willow tree.

6 And it grew, and became a spreading vine of low stature, whose branches turned toward him, and the roots thereof were under him: so it became a vine, and brought forth branches, and shot forth sprigs.

7 There was also another great eagle with great wings and many feathers: and, behold, this vine did bend her roots toward him, and shot forth her branches toward him, that he might water it by the furrows of her plantation.

8 It was planted in a good soil by great waters, that it might bring forth branches, and that it might bear fruit, that it might be a goodly vine.

9 Say you , Thus saith the Lord GOD; Shall it prosper? shall he not pull up the roots thereof, and cut off the fruit thereof, that it wither? it shall wither in all the leaves of her spring, even without great power or many people to pluck it up by the roots thereof.

10 Yea, behold, being planted, shall it prosper? shall it not utterly wither, when the east wind toucheth it? it shall wither in the furrows where it grew.

11Moreover the word of the LORD came unto me, saying,

12 Say now to the rebellious house, Know you not what these things mean? tell them, Behold, the king of Babylon is come to Jerusalem, and has taken the king thereof, and the princes thereof, and led them with him to Babylon;

13 And has taken of the king's seed, and made a covenant with him, and has taken an oath of him: he has also taken the mighty of the land:

14 That the kingdom might be base, that it might not lift itself up, but that by keeping of his covenant it might stand.

15 But he rebelled against him in sending his ambassadors into Egypt, that they might give him horses and much people. Shall he prosper? shall he escape that doeth such things? or shall he break the covenant, and be delivered?

16 As I live, saith the Lord GOD, surely in the place where the king dwelleth that made him king, whose oath he despised, and whose covenant he brake, even with him in the midst of Babylon he shall die.

17 Neither shall Pharaoh with his mighty army and great company make for him in the war, by casting up mounts, and building forts, to cut off many persons:

18 Seeing he despised the oath by breaking the covenant, when, lo, he had given his hand, and has done all these things, he shall not escape.

19 Therefore thus saith the Lord GOD; As I live, surely my oath that he has despised, and my covenant that he has broken, even it will I recompense upon his own head.

20 And I will spread my net upon him, and he shall be taken in my snare, and I will bring him to Babylon, and will plead with him there for his trespass that he has trespassed against me.

21 And all his fugitives with all his bands shall fall by the sword, and they that remain shall be scattered toward all winds: and you shall know that I the LORD have spoken it.

22Thus saith the Lord GOD; I will also take of the highest branch of the high cedar, and will set it; I will crop off from the top of his young twigs a tender one, and will plant it upon an high mountain and eminent:

23 In the mountain of the height of Israel will I plant it: and it shall bring forth boughs, and bear fruit, and be a goodly cedar: and under it shall dwell all fowl of every wing; in the shadow of the branches thereof shall they dwell.

24 And all the trees of the field shall know that I the LORD have brought down the high tree, have exalted the low tree, have dried up the green tree, and have made the dry tree to flourish: I the LORD have spoken and have done it.

CHAPTER 18

THE word of the LORD came unto me again, saying,

2 What mean you , that you use this proverb concerning the land of Israel, saying, The fathers have eaten sour grapes, and the children's teeth are set on edge?

3 As I live, saith the Lord GOD, you shall not have occasion any more to use this proverb in Israel.

4 Behold, all souls are my; as the soul of the father, so also the soul of the son is my: the soul that sinneth, it shall die.

5But if a man be just, and do that which is lawful and right,

6 And has not eaten upon the mountains, neither has lifted up his eyes to the idols of the house of Israel, neither has defiled his neighbour's wife, neither has come near to a menstruous woman,

7 And has not oppressed any, but has restored to the debtor his pledge, has spoiled none by violence, has given his bread to the hungry, and has covered the naked with a garment;

8 He that has not given forth upon usury, neither has taken any increase, that has withdrawn his hand from iniquity, has executed true judgment between man and man,

9 Has walked in my statutes, and has kept my judgments, to deal truly; he is just, he shall surely live, saith the Lord GOD.

10If he beget a son that is a robber, a shedder of blood, and that doeth the like to any one of these things,

11 And that doeth not any of those duties, but even has eaten upon the mountains, and defiled his neighbour's wife,

12 Has oppressed the poor and needy, has spoiled by violence, has not restored the pledge, and has lifted up his eyes to the idols, has committed abomination,

13 Has given forth upon usury, and has taken increase: shall he then live? he shall not live: he has done all these abominations; he shall surely die; his blood shall be upon him.

14Now, lo, if he beget a son, that seeth all his father's sins which he has done, and considereth, and doeth not such like,

15 That has not eaten upon the mountains, neither has lifted up his eyes to the idols of the house of Israel, has not defiled his neighbour's wife,

16 Neither has oppressed any, has not withholden the pledge, neither has spoiled by violence, but has given his bread to the hungry, and has covered the naked with a garment,

17 That has taken off his hand from the poor, that has not received usury nor increase, has executed my judgments, has walked in my statutes; he shall not die for the iniquity of his father, he shall surely live.

18 As for his father, because he cruelly oppressed, spoiled his brother by violence, and did that which is not good among his people, lo, even he shall die in his iniquity.

19Yet say you , Why? doth not the son bear the iniquity of the father? When the son has done that which is lawful and right, and has kept all my statutes, and has done them, he shall surely live.

20 The soul that sinneth, it shall die. The son shall not bear the iniquity of the father, neither shall the father bear the iniquity of the son: the righteousness of the righteous shall be upon him, and the wickedness of the wicked shall be upon him.

21 But if the wicked will turn from all his sins that he has committed, and keep all my statutes, and do that which is lawful and right, he shall surely live, he shall not die.

22 All his transgressions that he has committed, they shall not be mentioned unto him: in his righteousness that he has done he shall live.

23 Have I any pleasure at all that the wicked should die? saith the Lord GOD: and not that he should return from his ways, and live?

24But when the righteous turneth away from his righteousness, and committeth iniquity, and doeth according to all the abominations that the wicked man doeth, shall he live? All his righteousness that he has done shall not be mentioned: in his trespass that he has trespassed, and in his sin that he has sinned, in them shall he die.

25Yet you say, The way of the Lord is not equal. Hear now, O house of Israel; Is not my way equal? are not your ways unequal?

26 When a righteous man turneth away from his righteousness, and committeth iniquity, and dieth in them; for his iniquity that he has done shall he die.

27 Again, when the wicked man turneth away from his wickedness that he has committed, and doeth that which is lawful and right, he shall save his soul alive.

28 Because he considereth, and turneth away from all his transgressions that he has committed, he shall surely live, he shall not die.

29 Yet saith the house of Israel, The way of the Lord is not equal. O house of Israel, are not my ways equal? are not your ways unequal?

30 Therefore I will judge you, O house of Israel, every one according to his ways, saith the Lord GOD. Repent, and turn yourselves from all your transgressions; so iniquity shall not be your ruin.

31Cast away from you all your transgressions, whereby you have transgressed; and make you a new heart and a new spirit: for why will you die, O house of Israel?

32 For I have no pleasure in the death of him that dieth, saith the Lord GOD: wherefore turn yourselves, and live you .

CHAPTER 19

MOREOVER take you up a lamentation for the princes of Israel,

2 And say, What is your mother? A lioness: she lay down among lions, she nourished her whelps among young lions.

3 And she brought up one of her whelps: it became a young lion, and it learned to catch the prey; it devoured men.

4 The nations also heard of him; he was taken in their pit, and they brought him with chains unto the land of Egypt.

5 Now when she saw that she had waited, and her hope was lost, then she took another of her whelps, and made him a young lion.

6 And he went up and down among the lions, he became a young lion, and learned to catch the prey, and devoured men.

7 And he knew their desolate palaces, and he laid waste their cities; and the land was desolate, and the fulness thereof, by the noise of his roaring.

8 Then the nations set against him on every side from the provinces, and spread their net over him: he was taken in their pit.

9 And they put him in ward in chains, and brought him to the king of Babylon: they brought him into holds, that his voice should no more be heard upon the mountains of Israel.

10Your mother is like a vine in your blood, planted by the waters: she was fruitful and full of branches by reason of many waters.

11 And she had strong rods for the sceptres of them that bare rule, and her stature was exalted among the thick branches, and she appeared in her height with the multitude of her branches.

12 But she was plucked up in fury, she was cast down to the ground, and the east wind dried up her fruit: her strong rods were broken and withered; the fire consumed them.

13 And now she is planted in the wilderness, in a dry and thirsty ground.

14 And fire is gone out of a rod of her branches, which has devoured her fruit, so that she has no strong rod to be a sceptre to rule. This is a lamentation, and shall be for a lamentation.

CHAPTER 20

AND it came to pass in the seventh year, in the fifth month, the tenth day of the month, that certain of the elders of Israel came to inquire of the LORD, and sat before me.

2 Then came the word of the LORD unto me, saying,

3 Son of man, speak unto the elders of Israel, and say unto them, Thus saith the Lord GOD; Are you come to inquire of me? As I live, saith the Lord GOD, I will not be inquired of by you.

4 Will you judge them, son of man, will you judge them? cause them to know the abominations of their fathers:

5And say unto them, Thus saith the Lord GOD; In the day when I chose Israel, and lifted up my hand unto the seed of the house of Jacob, and made myself known unto them in the land of Egypt, when I lifted up my hand unto them, saying, I am the LORD your God;

6 In the day that I lifted up my hand unto them, to bring them forth of the land of Egypt into a land that I had espied for them, flowing with milk and honey, which is the glory of all lands:

7 Then said I unto them, Cast you away every man the abominations of his eyes, and defile not yourselves with the idols of Egypt: I am the LORD your God.

8 But they rebelled against me, and would not hearken unto me: they did not every man cast away the abominations of their eyes, neither did they forsake the idols of Egypt: then I said, I will pour out my fury upon them, to accomplish my anger against them in the midst of the land of Egypt.

9 But I created for my name's sake, that it should not be polluted before the heathen, among whom they were, in whose sight I made myself known unto them, in bringing them forth out of the land of Egypt.

10Wherefore I caused them to go forth out of the land of Egypt, and brought them into the wilderness.

11 And I gave them my statutes, and shewed them my judgments, which if a man do, he shall even live in them.

12 Moreover also I gave them my sabbaths, to be a sign between me and them, that they might know that I am the LORD that sanctify them.

13 But the house of Israel rebelled against me in the wilderness: they walked not in my statutes, and they despised my judgments, which if a man do, he shall even live in them; and my sabbaths they greatly polluted: then I said, I would pour out my fury upon them in the wilderness, to consume them.

14 But I created for my name's sake, that it should not be polluted before the heathen, in whose sight I brought them out.

15 Yet also I lifted up my hand unto them in the wilderness, that I would not bring them into the land which I had given them, flowing with milk and honey, which is the glory of all lands;

16 Because they despised my judgments, and walked not in my statutes, but polluted my sabbaths: for their heart went after their idols.

17 Nevertheless my eye spared them from destroying them, neither did I make an end of them in the wilderness.

18 But I said unto their children in the wilderness, Walk you not in the statutes of your fathers, neither observe their judgments, nor defile yourselves with their idols:

19 I am the LORD your God; walk in my statutes, and keep my judgments, and do them;

20 And hallow my sabbaths; and they shall be a sign between me and you, that you may know that I am the LORD your God.

21 Notwithstanding the children rebelled against me: they walked not in my statutes, neither kept my judgments to do them, which if a man do, he shall even live in them; they polluted my sabbaths: then I said, I would pour out my fury upon them, to accomplish my anger against them in the wilderness.

22 Nevertheless I withdrew my hand, and created for my name's sake, that it should not be polluted in the sight of the heathen, in whose sight I brought them forth.

23 I lifted up my hand unto them also in the wilderness, that I would scatter them among the heathen, and disperse them through the countries;

24 Because they had not executed my judgments, but had despised my statutes, and had polluted my sabbaths, and their eyes were after their fathers' idols.

25 Wherefore I gave them also statutes that were not good, and judgments whereby they should not live;

26 And I polluted them in their own gifts, in that they caused to pass through the fire all that openeth the womb, that I might make them desolate, to the end that they might know that I am the LORD.

27 Therefore, son of man, speak unto the house of Israel, and say unto them, Thus saith the Lord GOD; Yet in this your fathers have blasphemed me, in that they have committed a trespass against me.

28 For when I had brought them into the land, for the which I lifted up my hand to give it to them, then they saw every high hill, and all the thick trees, and they offered there their sacrifices, and there they presented the provocation of their offering: there also they made their sweet savour, and poured out there their drink offerings.

29 Then I said unto them, What is the high place whereunto you go? And the name thereof is called Bamah unto this day.

30 Wherefore say unto the house of Israel, Thus saith the Lord GOD; Are you polluted after the manner of your fathers? and commit you whoredom after their abominations?

31 For when you offer your gifts, when you make your sons to pass through the fire, you pollute yourselves with all your idols, even unto this day: and shall I be inquired of by you, O house of Israel? As I live, saith the Lord GOD, I will not be inquired of by you.

32 And that which comes into your mind shall not be at all, that you say, We will be as the heathen, as the families of the countries, to serve wood and stone.

33 As I live, saith the Lord GOD, surely with a mighty hand, and with a stretched out arm, and with fury poured out, will I rule over you:

34 And I will bring you out from the people, and will gather you out of the countries wherein you are scattered, with a mighty hand, and with a stretched out arm, and with fury poured out.

35 And I will bring you into the wilderness of the people, and there will I plead with you face to face.

36 Like as I pleaded with your fathers in the wilderness of the land of Egypt, so will I plead with you, saith the Lord GOD.

37 And I will cause you to pass under the rod, and I will bring you into the bond of the covenant:

38 And I will purge out from among you the rebels, and them that transgress against me: I will bring them forth out of the country where they sojourn, and they shall not enter into the land of Israel: and you shall know that I am the LORD.

39 As for you, O house of Israel, thus saith the Lord GOD; Go you, serve you every one his idols, and hereafter also, if you will not hearken unto me: but pollute you my holy name no more with your gifts, and with your idols.

40 For in my holy mountain, in the mountain of the height of Israel, saith the Lord GOD, there shall all the house of Israel, all of them in the land, serve me: there will I accept them, and there will I require your offerings, and the firstfruits of your oblations, with all your holy things.

41 I will accept you with your sweet savour, when I bring you out from the people, and gather you out of the countries wherein you have been scattered; and I will be sanctified in you before the heathen.

42 And you shall know that I am the LORD, when I shall bring you into the land of Israel, into the country for the which I lifted up my hand to give it to your fathers.

43 And there shall you remember your ways, and all your doings, wherein you have been defiled; and you shall lothe yourselves in your own sight for all your evils that you have committed.

44 And you shall know that I am the LORD, when I have created with you for my name's sake, not according to your wicked ways, nor according to your corrupt doings, O you house of Israel, saith the Lord GOD.

45 Moreover the word of the LORD came unto me, saying,

46 Son of man, set your face toward the south, and drop your word toward the south, and prophesy against the forest of the south field;

47 And say to the forest of the south, Hear the word of the LORD; Thus saith the Lord GOD; Behold, I will kindle a fire in you, and it shall devour every green tree in you, and every dry tree: the flaming flame shall not be quenched, and all faces from the south to the north shall be burned therein.

48 And all flesh shall see that I the LORD have kindled it: it shall not be quenched.

49 Then said I, Ah Lord GOD! they say of me, Doth he not speak parables?

CHAPTER 21

AND the word of the LORD came unto me, saying,

2 Son of man, set your face toward Jerusalem, and drop your word toward the holy places, and prophesy against the land of Israel,

3 And say to the land of Israel, Thus saith the LORD; Behold, I am against you, and will draw forth my sword out of his sheath, and will cut off from you the righteous and the wicked.

4 Seeing then that I will cut off from you the righteous and the wicked, therefore shall my sword go forth out of his sheath against all flesh from the south to the north:

5 That all flesh may know that I the LORD have drawn forth my sword out of his sheath: it shall not return any more.

6 Sigh therefore, you son of man, with the breaking of your loins; and with bitterness sigh before their eyes.

7 And it shall be, when they say unto you, Wherefore sighest you? that you shalt answer, For the tidings; because it comes: and every heart shall melt, and all hands shall be feeble, and every spirit shall faint, and all knees shall be weak as water: behold, it comes, and shall be brought to pass, saith the Lord GOD.

8 Again the word of the LORD came unto me, saying,

9 Son of man, prophesy, and say, Thus saith the LORD; Say, A sword, a sword is sharpened, and also furbished:

10 It is sharpened to make a sore slaughter; it is furbished that it may glitter: should we then make mirth? it contemneth the rod of my son, as every tree.

11 And he has given it to be furbished, that it may be handled: this sword is sharpened, and it is furbished, to give it into the hand of the slayer.

12 Cry and howl, son of man: for it shall be upon my people, it shall be upon all the princes of Israel: terrors by reason of the sword shall be upon my people: strike therefore upon your thigh.

13 Because it is a trial, and what if the sword contemn even the rod? it shall be no more, saith the Lord GOD.

14 You therefore, son of man, prophesy, and strike yours hands together, and let the sword be doubled the third time, the sword of the slain: it is the sword of the great men that are slain, which entereth into their privy chambers.

15 I have set the point of the sword against all their gates, that their heart may faint, and their ruins be multiplied: ah! it is made bright, it is wrapped up for the slaughter.

16 Go you one way or other, either on the right hand, or on the left, whithersoever your face is set.

17 I will also strike my hands together, and I will cause my fury to rest: I the LORD have said it.

18 The word of the LORD came unto me again, saying,

19 Also, you son of man, appoint you two ways, that the sword of the king of Babylon may come: both twain shall come forth out of one land: and choose you a place, choose it at the head of the way to the city.

20 Appoint a way, that the sword may come to Rabbath of the Ammonites, and to Judah in Jerusalem the defenced.

21 For the king of Babylon stood at the parting of the way, at the head of the two ways, to use divination: he made his arrows bright, he consulted with images, he looked in the liver.

22 At his right hand was the divination for Jerusalem, to appoint captains, to open the mouth in the slaughter, to lift up the voice with shouting, to appoint battering rams against the gates, to cast a mount, and to build a fort.

23 And it shall be unto them as a false divination in their sight, to them that have sworn oaths: but he will call to remembrance the iniquity, that they may be taken.

24 Therefore thus saith the Lord GOD; Because you have made your iniquity to be remembered, in that your transgressions are discovered, so that in all your doings your sins do appear; because, I say, that you are come to remembrance, you shall be taken with the hand.

25 And you, profane wicked prince of Israel, whose day is come, when iniquity shall have an end,

26 Thus saith the Lord GOD; Remove the diadem, and take off the crown: this shall not be the same: exalt him that is low, and abase him that is high.

27 I will overturn, overturn, overturn, it: and it shall be no more, until he come whose right it is; and I will give it him.

28 And you , son of man, prophesy and say, Thus saith the Lord GOD concerning the Ammonites, and concerning their reproach; even say you , The sword, the sword is drawn: for the slaughter it is furbished, to consume because of the glittering:

29 Whiles they see vanity unto you, whiles they divine a lie unto you, to bring you upon the necks of them that are slain, of the wicked, whose day is come, when their iniquity shall have an end.

30 Shall I cause it to return into his sheath? I will judge you in the place where you wast created, in the land of your nativity.

31 And I will pour out my indignation upon you, I will blow against you in the fire of my wrath, and deliver you into the hand of brutish men, and skilful to destroy.

32 You shalt be for fuel to the fire; your blood shall be in the midst of the land; you shalt be no more remembered: for I the LORD have spoken it.

CHAPTER 22

MOREOVER the word of the LORD came unto me, saying,

2 Now, you son of man, will you judge, will you judge the bloody city? yea, you shalt shew her all her abominations.

3 Then say you , Thus saith the Lord GOD, The city sheddeth blood in the midst of it, that her time may come, and maketh idols against herself to defile herself.

4 You are become guilty in your blood that you have shed; and have defiled yourself in yours idols which you have made; and you have caused your days to draw near, and are come even unto your years: therefore have I made you a reproach unto the heathen, and a mocking to all countries.

5 Those that be near, and those that be far from you, shall mock you, which are infamous and much vexed.

6 Behold, the princes of Israel, every one were in you to their power to shed blood.

7 In you have they set light by father and mother: in the midst of you have they dealt by oppression with the stranger: in you have they vexed the fatherless and the widow.

8 You have despised my holy things, and have profaned my sabbaths.

9 In you are men that carry tales to shed blood: and in you they eat upon the mountains: in the midst of you they commit lewdness.

10 In you have they discovered their fathers' nakedness: in you have they humbled her that was set apart for pollution.

11 And one has committed abomination with his neighbour's wife; and another has lewdly defiled his daughter in law; and another in you has humbled his sister, his father's daughter.

12 In you have they taken gifts to shed blood; you have taken usury and increase, and you have greedily gained of your neighbours by extortion, and have forgotten me, saith the Lord GOD.

13 Behold, therefore I have smitten my hand at your dishonest gain which you have made, and at your blood which has been in the midst of you.

14 Can yours heart endure, or can yours hands be strong, in the days that I shall deal with you? I the LORD have spoken it, and will do it.

15 And I will scatter you among the heathen, and disperse you in the countries, and will consume your filthiness out of you.

16 And you shalt take yours inheritance in yourself in the sight of the heathen, and you shalt know that I am the LORD.

17 And the word of the LORD came unto me, saying,

18 Son of man, the house of Israel is to me become dross: all they are brass, and tin, and iron, and lead, in the midst of the furnace; they are even the dross of silver.

19 Therefore thus saith the Lord GOD; Because you are all become dross, behold, therefore I will gather you into the midst of Jerusalem.

20 As they gather silver, and brass, and iron, and lead, and tin, into the midst of the furnace, to blow the fire upon it, to melt it; so will I gather you in my anger and in my fury, and I will leave you there, and melt you.

21 Yea, I will gather you, and blow upon you in the fire of my wrath, and you shall be melted in the midst thereof.

22 As silver is melted in the midst of the furnace, so shall you be melted in the midst thereof; and you shall know that I the LORD have poured out my fury upon you.

23 And the word of the LORD came unto me, saying,

24 Son of man, say unto her, You are the land that is not cleansed, nor rained upon in the day of indignation.

25 There is a conspiracy of her prophets in the midst thereof, like a roaring lion ravening the prey; they have devoured souls; they have taken the treasure and precious things; they have made her many widows in the midst thereof.

26 Her priests have violated my law, and have profaned my holy things: they have put no difference between the holy and profane, neither have they shewed difference between the unclean and the clean, and have hid their eyes from my sabbaths, and I am profaned among them.

27 Her princes in the midst thereof are like wolves ravening the prey, to shed blood, and to destroy souls, to get dishonest gain.

28 And her prophets have daubed them with untempered morter, seeing vanity, and divining lies unto them, saying, Thus saith the Lord GOD, when the LORD has not spoken.

29 The people of the land have used oppression, and exercised robbery, and have vexed the poor and needy: yea, they have oppressed the stranger wrongfully.

30 And I sought for a man among them, that should make up the hedge, and stand in the gap before me for the land, that I should not destroy it: but I found none.

31 Therefore have I poured out my indignation upon them; I have consumed them with the fire of my wrath: their own way have I recompensed upon their heads, saith the Lord GOD.

CHAPTER 23

THE word of the LORD came again unto me, saying,

2 Son of man, there were two women, the daughters of one mother:

3 And they committed whoredoms in Egypt; they committed whoredoms in their youth: there were their breasts pressed, and there they bruised the teats of their virginity.

4 And the names of them were Aholah the elder, and Aholibah her sister: and they were my, and they bare sons and daughters. Thus were their names; Samaria is Aholah, and Jerusalem Aholibah.

5 And Aholah played the harlot when she was my; and she doted on her lovers, on the Assyrians her neighbours,

6 Which were clothed with blue, captains and rulers, all of them desirable young men, horsemen riding upon horses.

7 Thus she committed her whoredoms with them, with all them that were the chosen men of Assyria, and with all on whom she doted: with all their idols she defiled herself.

8 Neither left she her whoredoms brought from Egypt: for in her youth they lay with her, and they bruised the breasts of her virginity, and poured their whoredom upon her.

9 Wherefore I have delivered her into the hand of her lovers, into the hand of the Assyrians, upon whom she doted.

10 These discovered her nakedness: they took her sons and her daughters, and slew her with the sword: and she became famous among women; for they had executed judgment upon her.

11 And when her sister Aholibah saw this, she was more corrupt in her inordinate love than she, and in her whoredoms more than her sister in her whoredoms.

12 She doted upon the Assyrians her neighbours, captains and rulers clothed most gorgeously, horsemen riding upon horses, all of them desirable young men.

13 Then I saw that she was defiled, that they took both one way,

14 And that she increased her whoredoms: for when she saw men pourtrayed upon the wall, the images of the Chaldeans pourtrayed with vermilion,

15 Girded with girdles upon their loins, exceeding in dyed attire upon their heads, all of them princes to look to, after the manner of the Babylonians of Chaldea, the land of their nativity:

16 And as soon as she saw them with her eyes, she doted upon them, and sent messengers unto them into Chaldea.

17 And the Babylonians came to her into the bed of love, and they defiled her with their whoredom, and she was polluted with them, and her mind was alienated from them.

18 So she discovered her whoredoms, and discovered her nakedness: then my mind was alienated from her, like as my mind was alienated from her sister.

19 Yet she multiplied her whoredoms, in calling to remembrance the days of her youth, wherein she had played the harlot in the land of Egypt.

20 For she doted upon their paramours, whose flesh is as the flesh of asses, and whose issue is like the issue of horses.

21 Thus you calledst to remembrance the lewdness of your youth, in bruising your teats by the Egyptians for the paps of your youth.

22 Therefore, O Aholibah, thus saith the Lord GOD; Behold, I will raise up your lovers against you, from whom your mind is alienated, and I will bring them against you on every side;

23 The Babylonians, and all the Chaldeans, Pekod, and Shoa, and Koa, and all the Assyrians with them: all of them desirable young men, captains and rulers, great lords and renowned, all of them riding upon horses.

24 And they shall come against you with chariots, wagons, and wheels, and with an assembly of people, which shall set against you buckler and shield and helmet round about: and I will set judgment before them, and they shall judge you according to their judgments.

25 And I will set my jealousy against you, and they shall deal furiously with you: they shall take away your nose and yours ears; and your remnant shall fall by the sword: they shall take your sons and your daughters; and your residue shall be devoured by the fire.

26 They shall also strip you out of your clothes, and take away your fair jewels.

27 Thus will I make your lewdness to cease from you, and your whoredom brought from the land of Egypt: so that you shalt not lift up yours eyes unto them, nor remember Egypt any more.

28 For thus saith the Lord GOD; Behold, I will deliver you into the hand of them whom you hatest, into the hand of them from whom your mind is alienated:

29 And they shall deal with you hatefully, and shall take away all your labour, and shall leave you naked and bare: and the nakedness of your whoredoms shall be discovered, both your lewdness and your whoredoms.

30 I will do these things unto you, because you have gone a whoring after the heathen, and because you are polluted with their idols.

31 You have walked in the way of your sister; therefore will I give her cup into yours hand.

32 Thus saith the Lord GOD; You shalt drink of your sister's cup deep and large: you shalt be laughed to scorn and had in derision; it containeth much.

33 You shalt be filled with drunkenness and sorrow, with the cup of astonishment and desolation, with the cup of your sister Samaria.

34 You shalt even drink it and suck it out, and you shalt break the sherds thereof, and pluck off yours own breasts: for I have spoken it, saith the Lord GOD.

35 Therefore thus saith the Lord GOD; Because you have forgotten me, and cast me behind your back, therefore bear you also your lewdness and your whoredoms.

36 The LORD said moreover unto me; Son of man, will you judge Aholah and Aholibah? yea, declare unto them their abominations;

37 That they have committed adultery, and blood is in their hands, and with their idols have they committed adultery, and have also caused their sons, whom they bare unto me, to pass for them through the fire, to devour them.

38 Moreover this they have done unto me: they have defiled my sanctuary in the same day, and have profaned my sabbaths.

39 For when they had slain their children to their idols, then they came the same day into my sanctuary to profane it; and, lo, thus have they done in the midst of my house.

40 And furthermore, that you have sent for men to come from far, unto whom a messenger was sent; and, lo, they came: for whom you did wash yourself, paintedst your eyes, and deckedst yourself with ornaments,

41 And satest upon a stately bed, and a table prepared before it, whereupon you have set my incense and my oil.

42 And a voice of a multitude being at ease was with her: and with the men of the common sort were brought Sabeans from the wilderness, which put bracelets upon their hands, and beautiful crowns upon their heads.

43 Then said I unto her that was old in adulteries, Will they now commit whoredoms with her, and she with them?

44 Yet they went in unto her, as they go in unto a woman that playeth the harlot: so went they in unto Aholah and unto Aholibah, the lewd women.

45 And the righteous men, they shall judge them after the manner of adulteresses, and after the manner of women that shed blood; because they are adulteresses, and blood is in their hands.

46 For thus saith the Lord GOD; I will bring up a company upon them, and will give them to be removed and spoiled.

47 And the company shall stone them with stones, and dispatch them with their swords; they shall slay their sons and their daughters, and burn up their houses with fire.

48 Thus will I cause lewdness to cease out of the land, that all women may be taught not to do after your lewdness.

49 And they shall recompense your lewdness upon you, and you shall bear the sins of your idols: and you shall know that I am the Lord GOD.

CHAPTER 24

AGAIN in the ninth year, in the tenth month, in the tenth day of the month, the word of the LORD came unto me, saying,

2 Son of man, write you the name of the day, even of this same day: the king of Babylon set himself against Jerusalem this same day.

3 And utter a parable unto the rebellious house, and say unto them, Thus saith the Lord GOD; Set on a pot, set it on, and also pour water into it:

4 Gather the pieces thereof into it, even every good piece, the thigh, and the shoulder; fill it with the choice bones.

5 Take the choice of the flock, and burn also the bones under it, and make it boil well, and let them seethe the bones of it therein.

6 Wherefore thus saith the Lord GOD; Woe to the bloody city, to the pot whose scum is therein, and whose scum is not gone out of it! bring it out piece by piece; let no lot fall upon it.

7 For her blood is in the midst of her; she set it upon the top of a rock; she poured it not upon the ground, to cover it with dust;

8 That it might cause fury to come up to take vengeance; I have set her blood upon the top of a rock, that it should not be covered.

9 Therefore thus saith the Lord GOD; Woe to the bloody city! I will even make the pile for fire great.

10 Heap on wood, kindle the fire, consume the flesh, and spice it well, and let the bones be burned.

11 Then set it empty upon the coals thereof, that the brass of it may be hot, and may burn, and that the filthiness of it may be molten in it, that the scum of it may be consumed.

12 She has wearied herself with lies, and her great scum went not forth out of her: her scum shall be in the fire.

13 In your filthiness is lewdness: because I have purged you, and you wast not purged, you shalt not be purged from your filthiness any more, till I have caused my fury to rest upon you.

14 I the LORD have spoken it: it shall come to pass, and I will do it; I will not go back, neither will I spare, neither will I repent; according to your ways, and according to your doings, shall they judge you, saith the Lord GOD.

15 Also the word of the LORD came unto me, saying,

16 Son of man, behold, I take away from you the desire of yours eyes with a stroke: yet neither shalt you mourn nor weep, neither shall your tears run down.

17 Forbear to cry, make no mourning for the dead, bind the tire of yours head upon you, and put on your shoes upon your feet, and cover not your lips, and eat not the bread of men.

18 So I spake unto the people in the morning: and at even my wife died; and I did in the morning as I was commanded.

19 And the people said unto me, Will you not tell us what these things are to us, that you doest so?

20 Then I answered them, The word of the LORD came unto me, saying,

21 Speak unto the house of Israel, Thus saith the Lord GOD; Behold, I will profane my sanctuary, the excellency of your strength, the desire of your eyes, and that which your soul pitieth; and your sons and your daughters whom you have left shall fall by the sword.

22 And you shall do as I have done: you shall not cover your lips, nor eat the bread of men.

23 And your tires shall be upon your heads, and your shoes upon your feet: you shall not mourn nor weep; but you shall pine away for your iniquities, and mourn one toward another.

24 Thus Ezekiel is unto you a sign: according to all that he has done shall you do: and when this comes, you shall know that I am the Lord GOD.

25 Also, you son of man, shall it not be in the day when I take from them their strength, the joy of their glory, the desire of their eyes, and that whereupon they set their minds, their sons and their daughters,

26 That he that escapeth in that day shall come unto you, to cause you to hear it with yours ears?

27 In that day shall your mouth be opened to him which is escaped, and you shalt speak, and be no more dumb: and you shalt be a sign unto them; and they shall know that I am the LORD.

CHAPTER 25

THE word of the LORD came again unto me, saying,

2 Son of man, set your face against the Ammonites, and prophesy against them;

3 And say unto the Ammonites, Hear the word of the Lord GOD; Thus saith the Lord GOD; Because you saidst, Aha, against my sanctuary, when it was profaned; and against the land of Israel, when it was desolate; and against the house of Judah, when they went into captivity;

4 Behold, therefore I will deliver you to the men of the east for a possession, and they shall set their palaces in you, and make their dwellings in you: they shall eat your fruit, and they shall drink your milk.

5 And I will make Rabbah a stable for camels, and the Ammonites a couchingplace for flocks: and you shall know that I am the LORD.

6 For thus saith the Lord GOD; Because you have clapped yours hands, and stamped with the feet, and rejoiced in heart with all your despite against the land of Israel;

7 Behold, therefore I will stretch out my hand upon you, and will deliver you for a spoil to the heathen; and I will cut you off from the people, and I will cause you to perish out of the countries: I will destroy you; and you shalt know that I am the LORD.

8 Thus saith the Lord GOD; Because that Moab and Seir do say, Behold, the house of Judah is like unto all the heathen;

9 Therefore, behold, I will open the side of Moab from the cities, from his cities which are on his frontiers, the glory of the country, Beth-jeshimoth, Baal-meon, and Kiriathaim,

10 Unto the men of the east with the Ammonites, and will give them in possession, that the Ammonites may not be remembered among the nations.

11 And I will execute judgments upon Moab; and they shall know that I am the LORD.

12 Thus saith the Lord GOD; Because that Edom has dealt against the house of Judah by taking vengeance, and has greatly offended, and revenged himself upon them;

13 Therefore thus saith the Lord GOD; I will also stretch out my hand upon Edom, and will cut off man and beast from it; and I will make it desolate from Teman; and they of Dedan shall fall by the sword.

14 And I will lay my vengeance upon Edom by the hand of my people Israel: and they shall do in Edom according to my anger and according to my fury; and they shall know my vengeance, saith the Lord GOD.

15 Thus saith the Lord GOD; Because the Philistines have dealt by revenge, and have taken vengeance with a despiteful heart, to destroy it for the old hatred;

16 Therefore thus saith the Lord GOD; Behold, I will stretch out my hand upon the Philistines, and I will cut off the Cherethims, and destroy the remnant of the sea coast.

17 And I will execute great vengeance upon them with furious rebukes; and they shall know that I am the LORD, when I shall lay my vengeance upon them.

CHAPTER 26

AND it came to pass in the eleventh year, in the first day of the month, that the word of the LORD came unto me, saying,

2 Son of man, because that Tyrus has said against Jerusalem, Aha, she is broken that was the gates of the people: she is turned unto me: I shall be replenished, now she is laid waste:

3 Therefore thus saith the Lord GOD; Behold, I am against you, O Tyrus, and will cause many nations to come up against you, as the sea causeth his waves to come up.

4 And they shall destroy the walls of Tyrus, and break down her towers: I will also scrape her dust from her, and make her like the top of a rock.

5 It shall be a place for the spreading of nets in the midst of the sea: for I have spoken it, saith the Lord GOD: and it shall become a spoil to the nations.

6 And her daughters which are in the field shall be slain by the sword; and they shall know that I am the LORD.

7 For thus saith the Lord GOD; Behold, I will bring upon Tyrus Nebuchadrezzar king of Babylon, a king of kings, from the north, with horses, and with chariots, and with horsemen, and companies, and much people.

8 He shall slay with the sword your daughters in the field: and he shall make a fort against you, and cast a mount against you, and lift up the buckler against you.

9 And he shall set engines of war against your walls, and with his axes he shall break down your towers.

10 By reason of the abundance of his horses their dust shall cover you: your walls shall shake at the noise of the horsemen, and of the wheels, and of the chariots, when he shall enter into your gates, as men enter into a city wherein is made a breach.

11 With the hoofs of his horses shall he tread down all your streets: he shall slay your people by the sword, and your strong garrisons shall go down to the ground.

12 And they shall make a spoil of your riches, and make a prey of your merchandise: and they shall break down your walls, and destroy your pleasant houses: and they shall lay your stones and your timber and your dust in the midst of the water.

13 And I will cause the noise of your songs to cease; and the sound of your harps shall be no more heard.

14 And I will make you like the top of a rock: you shalt be a place to spread nets upon; you shalt be built no more: for I the LORD have spoken it, saith the Lord GOD.

15 Thus saith the Lord GOD to Tyrus; Shall not the isles shake at the sound of your fall, when the wounded cry, when the slaughter is made in the midst of you?

16 Then all the princes of the sea shall come down from their thrones, and lay away their robes, and put off their broidered garments: they shall clothe themselves with trembling; they shall sit upon the ground, and shall tremble at every moment, and be astonished at you.

17 And they shall take up a lamentation for you, and say to you, How are you destroyed, that wast inhabited of seafaring men, the renowned city, which wast strong in the sea, she and her inhabitants, which cause their terror to be on all that haunt it!

18 Now shall the isles tremble in the day of your fall; yea, the isles that are in the sea shall be troubled at your departure.

19 For thus saith the Lord GOD; When I shall make you a desolate city, like the cities that are not inhabited; when I shall bring up the deep upon you, and great waters shall cover you;

20 When I shall bring you down with them that descend into the pit, with the people of old time, and shall set you in the low parts of the earth, in places desolate of old, with them that go down to the pit, that you be not inhabited; and I shall set glory in the land of the living;

21 I will make you a terror, and you shalt be no more: though you be sought for, yet shalt you never be found again, saith the Lord GOD.

CHAPTER 27

THE word of the LORD came again unto me, saying,

2 Now, you son of man, take up a lamentation for Tyrus;

3 And say unto Tyrus, O you that are situate at the entry of the sea, which are a merchant of the people for many isles, Thus saith the Lord GOD; O Tyrus, you have said, I am of perfect beauty.

4 Your borders are in the midst of the seas, your builders have perfected your beauty.

5 They have made all your ship boards of fir trees of Senir: they have taken cedars from Lebanon to make masts for you.

6 Of the oaks of Bashan have they made yours oars; the company of the Ashurites have made your benches of ivory, brought out of the isles of Chittim.

7 Fine linen with broidered work from Egypt was that which you spreadest forth to be your sail; blue and purple from the isles of Elishah was that which covered you.

8 The inhabitants of Zidon and Arvad were your mariners: your wise men, O Tyrus, that were in you, were your pilots.

9 The ancients of Gebal and the wise men thereof were in you your calkers: all the ships of the sea with their mariners were in you to occupy your merchandise.

10 They of Persia and of Lud and of Phut were in yours army, your men of war: they hanged the shield and helmet in you; they set forth your comeliness.

11 The men of Arvad with yours army were upon your walls round about, and the Gammadims were in your towers: they hanged their shields upon your walls round about; they have made your beauty perfect.

12 Tarshish was your merchant by reason of the multitude of all kind of riches; with silver, iron, tin, and lead, they traded in your fairs.

13 Javan, Tubal, and Meshech, they were your merchants: they traded the persons of men and vessels of brass in your market.

14 They of the house of Togarmah traded in your fairs with horses and horsemen and mules.

15 The men of Dedan were your merchants; many isles were the merchandise of yours hand: they brought you for a present horns of ivory and ebony.

16 Syria was your merchant by reason of the multitude of the wares of your making: they occupied in your fairs with emeralds, purple, and broidered work, and fine linen, and coral, and agate.

17 Judah, and the land of Israel, they were your merchants: they traded in your market wheat of Minnith, and Pannag, and honey, and oil, and balm.

18 Damascus was your merchant in the multitude of the wares of your making, for the multitude of all riches; in the wine of Helbon, and white wool.

19 Dan also and Javan going to and fro occupied in your fairs: bright iron, cassia, and calamus, were in your market.

20 Dedan was your merchant in precious clothes for chariots.

21 Arabia, and all the princes of Kedar, they occupied with you in lambs, and rams, and goats: in these were they your merchants.

22 The merchants of Sheba and Raamah, they were your merchants: they occupied in your fairs with chief of all spices, and with all precious stones, and gold.

23 Haran, and Canneh, and Eden, the merchants of Sheba, Asshur, and Chilmad, were your merchants.

24 These were your merchants in all sorts of things, in blue clothes, and broidered work, and in chests of rich apparel, bound with cords, and made of cedar, among your merchandise.

25 The ships of Tarshish did sing of you in your market: and you wast replenished, and made very glorious in the midst of the seas.

26Your rowers have brought you into great waters: the east wind has broken you in the midst of the seas.

27 Your riches, and your fairs, your merchandise, your mariners, and your pilots, your calkers, and the occupiers of your merchandise, and all your men of war, that are in you, and in all your company which is in the midst of you, shall fall into the midst of the seas in the day of your ruin.

28 The suburbs shall shake at the sound of the cry of your pilots.

29 And all that handle the oar, the mariners, and all the pilots of the sea, shall come down from their ships, they shall stand upon the land;

30 And shall cause their voice to be heard against you, and shall cry bitterly, and shall cast up dust upon their heads, they shall wallow themselves in the ashes:

31 And they shall make themselves utterly bald for you, and gird them with sackcloth, and they shall weep for you with bitterness of heart and bitter wailing.

32 And in their wailing they shall take up a lamentation for you, and lament over you, saying, What city is like Tyrus, like the destroyed in the midst of the sea?

33 When your wares went forth out of the seas, you filledst many people; you did enrich the kings of the earth with the multitude of your riches and of your merchandise.

34 In the time when you shalt be broken by the seas in the depths of the waters your merchandise and all your company in the midst of you shall fall.

35 All the inhabitants of the isles shall be astonished at you, and their kings shall be sore afraid, they shall be troubled in their countenance.

36 The merchants among the people shall hiss at you; you shalt be a terror, and never shalt be any more.

CHAPTER 28

THE word of the LORD came again unto me, saying,

2 Son of man, say unto the prince of Tyrus, Thus saith the Lord GOD; Because yours heart is lifted up, and you have said, I am a God, I sit in the seat of God, in the midst of the seas; yet you are a man, and not God, though you set yours heart as the heart of God:

3 Behold, you are wiser than Daniel; there is no secret that they can hide from you:

4 With your wisdom and with yours understanding you have gotten you riches, and have gotten gold and silver into your treasures:

5 By your great wisdom and by your traffick have you increased your riches, and yours heart is lifted up because of your riches:

6 Therefore thus saith the Lord GOD; Because you have set yours heart as the heart of God;

7 Behold, therefore I will bring strangers upon you, the terrible of the nations: and they shall draw their swords against the beauty of your wisdom, and they shall defile your brightness.

8 They shall bring you down to the pit, and you shalt die the deaths of them that are slain in the midst of the seas.

9 Will you yet say before him that slayeth you, I am God? but you shalt be a man, and no God, in the hand of him that slayeth you.

10 You shalt die the deaths of the uncircumcised by the hand of strangers: for I have spoken it, saith the Lord GOD.

11Moreover the word of the LORD came unto me, saying,

12 Son of man, take up a lamentation upon the king of Tyrus, and say unto him, Thus saith the Lord GOD; You sealest up the sum, full of wisdom, and perfect in beauty.

13 You have been in Eden the garden of God; every precious stone was your covering, the sardius, topaz, and the diamond, the beryl, the onyx, and the jasper, the sapphire, the emerald, and the carbuncle, and gold: the workmanship of your tabrets and of your pipes was prepared in you in the day that you wast created.

14 You are the anointed cherub that covers; and I have set you so: you wast upon the holy mountain of God; you have walked up and down in the midst of the stones of fire.

15 You wast perfect in your ways from the day that you wast created, till iniquity was found in you.

16 By the multitude of your merchandise they have filled the midst of you with violence, and you have sinned: therefore I will cast you as profane out of the mountain of God: and I will destroy you, O covering cherub, from the midst of the stones of fire.

17 Yours heart was lifted up because of your beauty, you have corrupted your wisdom by reason of your brightness: I will cast you to the ground, I will lay you before kings, that they may behold you.

18 You have defiled your sanctuaries by the multitude of yours iniquities, by the iniquity of your traffick; therefore will I bring forth a fire from the midst of you, it shall devour you, and I will bring you to ashes upon the earth in the sight of all them that behold you.

19 All they that know you among the people shall be astonished at you: you shalt be a terror, and never shalt you be any more.

20Again the word of the LORD came unto me, saying,

21 Son of man, set your face against Zidon, and prophesy against it,

22 And say, Thus saith the Lord GOD; Behold, I am against you, O Zidon; and I will be glorified in the midst of you: and they shall know that I am the LORD, when I shall have executed judgments in her, and shall be sanctified in her.

23 For I will send into her pestilence, and blood into her streets; and the wounded shall be judged in the midst of her by the sword upon her on every side; and they shall know that I am the LORD.

24And there shall be no more a pricking brier unto the house of Israel, nor any grieving thorn of all that are round about them, that despised them; and they shall know that I am the Lord GOD.

25 Thus saith the Lord GOD; When I shall have gathered the house of Israel from the people among whom they are scattered, and shall be sanctified in them in the sight of the heathen, then shall they dwell in their land that I have given to my servant Jacob.

26 And they shall dwell safely therein, and shall build houses, and plant vineyards; yea, they shall dwell with confidence, when I have executed judgments upon all those that despise them round about them; and they shall know that I am the LORD their God.

CHAPTER 29

IN the tenth year, in the tenth month, in the twelfth day of the month, the word of the LORD came unto me, saying,

2 Son of man, set your face against Pharaoh king of Egypt, and prophesy against him, and against all Egypt:

3 Speak, and say, Thus saith the Lord GOD; Behold, I am against you, Pharaoh king of Egypt, the great dragon that lies in the midst of his rivers, which has said, My river is my own, and I have made it for myself.

4 But I will put hooks in your jaws, and I will cause the fish of your rivers to stick unto your scales, and I will bring you up out of the midst of your rivers, and all the fish of your rivers shall stick unto your scales.

5 And I will leave you thrown into the wilderness, you and all the fish of your rivers: you shalt fall upon the open fields; you shalt not be brought together, nor gathered: I have given you for meat to the beasts of the field and to the fowls of the heaven.

6 And all the inhabitants of Egypt shall know that I am the LORD, because they have been a staff of reed to the house of Israel.

7 When they took hold of you by your hand, you did break, and rend all their shoulder: and when they leaned upon you, you brakest, and madest all their loins to be at a stand.

8Therefore thus saith the Lord GOD; Behold, I will bring a sword upon you, and cut off man and beast out of you.

9 And the land of Egypt shall be desolate and waste; and they shall know that I am the LORD: because he has said, The river is my, and I have made it.

10 Behold, therefore I am against you, and against your rivers, and I will make the land of Egypt utterly waste and desolate, from the tower of Syene even unto the border of Ethiopia.

11 No foot of man shall pass through it, nor foot of beast shall pass through it, neither shall it be inhabited forty years.

12 And I will make the land of Egypt desolate in the midst of the countries that are desolate, and her cities among the cities that are laid waste shall be desolate forty years: and I will scatter the Egyptians among the nations, and will disperse them through the countries.

13Yet thus saith the Lord GOD; At the end of forty years will I gather the Egyptians from the people whither they were scattered:

14 And I will bring again the captivity of Egypt, and will cause them to return into the land of Pathros, into the land of their habitation; and they shall be there a base kingdom.

15 It shall be the basest of the kingdoms; neither shall it exalt itself any more above the nations: for I will diminish them, that they shall no more rule over the nations.

16 And it shall be no more the confidence of the house of Israel, which bringeth their iniquity to remembrance, when they shall look after them: but they shall know that I am the Lord GOD.

17And it came to pass in the seven and twentieth year, in the first month, in the first day of the month, the word of the LORD came unto me, saying,

18 Son of man, Nebuchadrezzar king of Babylon caused his army to serve a great service against Tyrus: every head was made bald, and every shoulder was peeled: yet had he no wages, nor his army, for Tyrus, for the service that he had served against it:

19 Therefore thus saith the Lord GOD; Behold, I will give the land of Egypt unto Nebuchadrezzar king of Babylon; and he shall take her multitude, and take her spoil, and take her prey; and it shall be the wages for his army.

20 I have given him the land of Egypt for his labour wherewith he served against it, because they created for me, saith the Lord GOD.

21 In that day will I cause the horn of the house of Israel to bud forth, and I will give you the opening of the mouth in the midst of them; and they shall know that I am the LORD.

CHAPTER 30

THE word of the LORD came again unto me, saying,

2 Son of man, prophesy and say, Thus saith the Lord GOD; Howl you , Woe worth the day!

3 For the day is near, even the day of the LORD is near, a cloudy day; it shall be the time of the heathen.

4 And the sword shall come upon Egypt, and great pain shall be in Ethiopia, when the slain shall fall in Egypt, and they shall take away her multitude, and her foundations shall be broken down.

5 Ethiopia, and Libya, and Lydia, and all the mingled people, and Chub, and the men of the land that is in league, shall fall with them by the sword.

6 Thus saith the LORD; They also that uphold Egypt shall fall; and the pride of her power shall come down: from the tower of Syene shall they fall in it by the sword, saith the Lord GOD.

7 And they shall be desolate in the midst of the countries that are desolate, and her cities shall be in the midst of the cities that are wasted.

8 And they shall know that I am the LORD, when I have set a fire in Egypt, and when all her helpers shall be destroyed.

9 In that day shall messengers go forth from me in ships to make the careless Ethiopians afraid, and great pain shall come upon them, as in the day of Egypt: for, lo, it comes.

10 Thus saith the Lord GOD; I will also make the multitude of Egypt to cease by the hand of Nebuchadrezzar king of Babylon.

11 He and his people with him, the terrible of the nations, shall be brought to destroy the land: and they shall draw their swords against Egypt, and fill the land with the slain.

12 And I will make the rivers dry, and sell the land into the hand of the wicked: and I will make the land waste, and all that is therein, by the hand of strangers: I the LORD have spoken it.

13 Thus saith the Lord GOD; I will also destroy the idols, and I will cause their images to cease out of Noph; and there shall be no more a prince of the land of Egypt: and I will put a fear in the land of Egypt.

14 And I will make Pathros desolate, and will set fire in Zoan, and will execute judgments in No.

15 And I will pour my fury upon Sin, the strength of Egypt; and I will cut off the multitude of No.

16 And I will set fire in Egypt: Sin shall have great pain, and No shall be rent asunder, and Noph shall have distresses daily.

17 The young men of Aven and of Pi-beseth shall fall by the sword: and these cities shall go into captivity.

18 At Tehaphnehes also the day shall be darkened, when I shall break there the yokes of Egypt: and the pomp of her strength shall cease in her: as for her, a cloud shall cover her, and her daughters shall go into captivity.

19 Thus will I execute judgments in Egypt: and they shall know that I am the LORD.

20 And it came to pass in the eleventh year, in the first month, in the seventh day of the month, that the word of the LORD came unto me, saying,

21 Son of man, I have broken the arm of Pharaoh king of Egypt; and, lo, it shall not be bound up to be healed, to put a roller to bind it, to make it strong to hold the sword.

22 Therefore thus saith the Lord GOD; Behold, I am against Pharaoh king of Egypt, and will break his arms, the strong, and that which was broken; and I will cause the sword to fall out of his hand.

23 And I will scatter the Egyptians among the nations, and will disperse them through the countries.

24 And I will strengthen the arms of the king of Babylon, and put my sword in his hand: but I will break Pharaoh's arms, and he shall groan before him with the groanings of a deadly wounded man.

25 But I will strengthen the arms of the king of Babylon, and the arms of Pharaoh shall fall down; and they shall know that I am the LORD, when I shall put my sword into the hand of the king of Babylon, and he shall stretch it out upon the land of Egypt.

26 And I will scatter the Egyptians among the nations, and disperse them among the countries; and they shall know that I am the LORD.

CHAPTER 31

AND it came to pass in the eleventh year, in the third month, in the first day of the month, that the word of the LORD came unto me, saying,

2 Son of man, speak unto Pharaoh king of Egypt, and to his multitude; Whom are you like in your greatness?

3 Behold, the Assyrian was a cedar in Lebanon with fair branches, and with a shadowing shroud, and of an high stature; and his top was among the thick boughs.

4 The waters made him great, the deep set him up on high with her rivers running round about his plants, and sent out her little rivers unto all the trees of the field.

5 Therefore his height was exalted above all the trees of the field, and his boughs were multiplied, and his branches became long because of the multitude of waters, when he shot forth.

6 All the fowls of heaven made their nests in his boughs, and under his branches did all the beasts of the field bring forth their young, and under his shadow dwelt all great nations.

7 Thus was he fair in his greatness, in the length of his branches: for his root was by great waters.

8 The cedars in the garden of God could not hide him: the fir trees were not like his boughs, and the chesnut trees were not like his branches; nor any tree in the garden of God was like unto him in his beauty.

9 I have made him fair by the multitude of his branches: so that all the trees of Eden, that were in the garden of God, envied him.

10 Therefore thus saith the Lord GOD; Because you have lifted up yourself in height, and he has shot up his top among the thick boughs, and his heart is lifted up in his height;

11 I have therefore delivered him into the hand of the mighty one of the heathen; he shall surely deal with him: I have driven him out for his wickedness.

12 And strangers, the terrible of the nations, have cut him off, and have left him: upon the mountains and in all the valleys his branches are fallen, and his boughs are broken by all the rivers of the land; and all the people of the earth are gone down from his shadow, and have left him.

13 Upon his ruin shall all the fowls of the heaven remain, and all the beasts of the field shall be upon his branches:

14 To the end that none of all the trees by the waters exalt themselves for their height, neither shoot up their top among the thick boughs, neither their trees stand up in their height, all that drink water: for they are all delivered unto death, to the nether parts of the earth, in the midst of the children of men, with them that go down to the pit.

15 Thus saith the Lord GOD; In the day when he went down to the grave I caused a mourning: I covered the deep for him, and I restrained the floods thereof, and the great waters were stayed: and I caused Lebanon to mourn for him, and all the trees of the field fainted for him.

16 I made the nations to shake at the sound of his fall, when I cast him down to hell with them that descend into the pit: and all the trees of Eden, the choice and best of Lebanon, all that drink water, shall be comforted in the nether parts of the earth.

17 They also went down into hell with him unto them that be slain with the sword; and they that were his arm, that dwelt under his shadow in the midst of the heathen.

18 To whom are you thus like in glory and in greatness among the trees of Eden? yet shalt you be brought down with the trees of Eden unto the nether parts of the earth: you shalt lie in the midst of the uncircumcised with them that be slain by the sword. This is Pharaoh and all his multitude, saith the Lord GOD.

CHAPTER 32

AND it came to pass in the twelfth year, in the twelfth month, in the first day of the month, that the word of the LORD came unto me, saying,

2 Son of man, take up a lamentation for Pharaoh king of Egypt, and say unto him, You are like a young lion of the nations, and you are as a whale in the seas: and you camest forth with your rivers, and troubledst the waters with your feet, and fouledst their rivers.

3 Thus saith the Lord GOD; I will therefore spread out my net over you with a company of many people; and they shall bring you up in my net.

4 Then will I leave you upon the land, I will cast you forth upon the open field, and will cause all the fowls of the heaven to remain upon you, and I will fill the beasts of the whole earth with you.

5 And I will lay your flesh upon the mountains, and fill the valleys with your height.

6 I will also water with your blood the land wherein you swimmest, even to the mountains; and the rivers shall be full of you.

7 And when I shall put you out, I will cover the heaven, and make the stars thereof dark; I will cover the sun with a cloud, and the moon shall not give her light.

8 All the bright lights of heaven will I make dark over you, and set darkness upon your land, saith the Lord GOD.

9 I will also vex the hearts of many people, when I shall bring your destruction among the nations, into the countries which you have not known.

10 Yea, I will make many people amazed at you, and their kings shall be horribly afraid for you, when I shall brandish my sword before them; and they shall tremble at every moment, every man for his own life, in the day of your fall.

11 For thus saith the Lord GOD; The sword of the king of Babylon shall come upon you.

12 By the swords of the mighty will I cause your multitude to fall, the terrible of the nations, all of them: and they shall spoil the pomp of Egypt, and all the multitude thereof shall be destroyed.

13 I will destroy also all the beasts thereof from beside the great waters; neither shall the foot of man trouble them any more, nor the hoofs of beasts trouble them.

14 Then will I make their waters deep, and cause their rivers to run like oil, saith the Lord GOD.

15 When I shall make the land of Egypt desolate, and the country shall be destitute of that whereof it was full, when I shall strike all them that dwell therein, then shall they know that I am the LORD.

16 This is the lamentation wherewith they shall lament her: the daughters of the nations shall lament her: they shall lament for her, even for Egypt, and for all her multitude, saith the Lord GOD.

17 It came to pass also in the twelfth year, in the fifteenth day of the month, that the word of the LORD came unto me, saying,

18 Son of man, wail for the multitude of Egypt, and cast them down, even her, and the daughters of the famous nations, unto the nether parts of the earth, with them that go down into the pit.

19 Whom dost you pass in beauty? go down, and be you laid with the uncircumcised.

20 They shall fall in the midst of them that are slain by the sword: she is delivered to the sword: draw her and all her multitudes.

21 The strong among the mighty shall speak to him out of the midst of hell with them that help him: they are gone down, they lie uncircumcised, slain by the sword.

22 Asshur is there and all her company: his graves are about him: all of them slain, fallen by the sword:

23 Whose graves are set in the sides of the pit, and her company is round about her grave: all of them slain, fallen by the sword, which caused terror in the land of the living.

24 There is Elam and all her multitude round about her grave, all of them slain, fallen by the sword, which are gone down uncircumcised into the nether parts of the earth, which caused their terror in the land of the living; yet have they borne their shame with them that go down to the pit.

25 They have set her a bed in the midst of the slain with all her multitude: her graves are round about him: all of them uncircumcised, slain by the sword: though their terror was caused in the land of the living, yet have they borne their shame with them that go down to the pit: he is put in the midst of them that be slain.

26 There is Meshech, Tubal, and all her multitude: her graves are round about him: all of them uncircumcised, slain by the sword, though they caused their terror in the land of the living.

27 And they shall not lie with the mighty that are fallen of the uncircumcised, which are gone down to hell with their weapons of war: and they have laid their swords under their heads, but their iniquities shall be upon their bones, though they were the terror of the mighty in the land of the living.

28 Yea, you shalt be broken in the midst of the uncircumcised, and shalt lie with them that are slain with the sword.

29 There is Edom, her kings, and all her princes, which with their might are laid by them that were slain by the sword: they shall lie with the uncircumcised, and with them that go down to the pit.

30 There be the princes of the north, all of them, and all the Zidonians, which are gone down with the slain; with their terror they are ashamed of their might; and they lie uncircumcised with them that be slain by the sword, and bear their shame with them that go down to the pit.

31 Pharaoh shall see them, and shall be comforted over all his multitude, even Pharaoh and all his army slain by the sword, saith the Lord GOD.

32 For I have caused my terror in the land of the living: and he shall be laid in the midst of the uncircumcised with them that are slain with the sword, even Pharaoh and all his multitude, saith the Lord GOD.

CHAPTER 33

AGAIN the word of the LORD came unto me, saying,

2 Son of man, speak to the children of your people, and say unto them, When I bring the sword upon a land, if the people of the land take a man of their coasts, and set him for their watchman:

3 If when he seeth the sword come upon the land, he blow the trumpet, and warn the people;

4 Then whosoever heareth the sound of the trumpet, and taketh not warning; if the sword come, and take him away, his blood shall be upon his own head.

5 He heard the sound of the trumpet, and took not warning; his blood shall be upon him. But he that taketh warning shall deliver his soul.

6 But if the watchman see the sword come, and blow not the trumpet, and the people be not warned; if the sword come, and take any person from among them, he is taken away in his iniquity; but his blood will I require at the watchman's hand.

7 So you , O son of man, I have set you a watchman unto the house of Israel; therefore you shalt hear the word at my mouth, and warn them from me.

8 When I say unto the wicked, O wicked man, you shalt surely die; if you dost not speak to warn the wicked from his way, that wicked man shall die in his iniquity; but his blood will I require at yours hand.

9 Nevertheless, if you warn the wicked of his way to turn from it; if he do not turn from his way, he shall die in his iniquity; but you have delivered your soul.

10 Therefore, O you son of man, speak unto the house of Israel; Thus you speak, saying, If our transgressions and our sins be upon us, and we pine away in them, how should we then live?

11 Say unto them, As I live, saith the Lord GOD, I have no pleasure in the death of the wicked; but that the wicked turn from his way and live: turn you , turn you from your evil ways; for why will you die, O house of Israel?

12 Therefore, you son of man, say unto the children of your people, The righteousness of the righteous shall not deliver him in the day of his transgression: as for the wickedness of the wicked, he shall not fall thereby in the day that he turneth from his wickedness; neither shall the righteous be able to live for his righteousness in the day that he sinneth.

13 When I shall say to the righteous, that he shall surely live; if he trust to his own righteousness, and commit iniquity, all his righteousnesses shall not be remembered; but for his iniquity that he has committed, he shall die for it.

14 Again, when I say unto the wicked, You shalt surely die; if he turn from his sin, and do that which is lawful and right;

15 If the wicked restore the pledge, give again that he had robbed, walk in the statutes of life, without committing iniquity; he shall surely live, he shall not die.

16 None of his sins that he has committed shall be mentioned unto him: he has done that which is lawful and right; he shall surely live.

17 Yet the children of your people say, The way of the Lord is not equal: but as for them, their way is not equal.

18 When the righteous turneth from his righteousness, and committeth iniquity, he shall even die thereby.

19 But if the wicked turn from his wickedness, and do that which is lawful and right, he shall live thereby.

20 Yet you say, The way of the Lord is not equal. O you house of Israel, I will judge you every one after his ways.

21 And it came to pass in the twelfth year of our captivity, in the tenth month, in the fifth day of the month, that one that had escaped out of Jerusalem came unto me, saying, The city is smitten.

22 Now the hand of the LORD was upon me in the evening, afore he that was escaped came; and had opened my mouth, until he came to me in the morning; and my mouth was opened, and I was no more dumb.

23 Then the word of the LORD came unto me, saying,

24 Son of man, they that inhabit those wastes of the land of Israel speak, saying, Abraham was one, and he inherited the land: but we are many; the land is given us for inheritance.

25 Wherefore say unto them, Thus saith the Lord GOD; You eat with the blood, and lift up your eyes toward your idols, and shed blood: and shall you possess the land?

26 You stand upon your sword, you work abomination, and you defile every one his neighbour's wife: and shall you possess the land?

27 Say you thus unto them, Thus saith the Lord GOD; As I live, surely they that are in the wastes shall fall by the sword, and him that is in the open field will I give to the beasts to be devoured, and they that be in the forts and in the caves shall die of the pestilence.

28 For I will lay the land most desolate, and the pomp of her strength shall cease; and the mountains of Israel shall be desolate, that none shall pass through.

29 Then shall they know that I am the LORD, when I have laid the land most desolate because of all their abominations which they have committed.

30 Also, you son of man, the children of your people still are talking against you by the walls and in the doors of the houses, and speak one to another, every one to his brother, saying, Come, I pray you, and hear what is the word that comes forth from the LORD.

31 And they come unto you as the people comes, and they sit before you as my people, and they hear your words, but they will not do them: for with their mouth they shew much love, but their heart goeth after their covetousness.

32 And, lo, you are unto them as a very lovely song of one that has a pleasant voice, and can play well on an instrument: for they hear your words, but they do them not.

33 And when this comes to pass, (lo, it will come,) then shall they know that a prophet has been among them.

CHAPTER 34

AND the word of the LORD came unto me, saying,

2 Son of man, prophesy against the shepherds of Israel, prophesy, and say unto them, Thus saith the Lord GOD unto the shepherds; Woe be to the shepherds of Israel that do feed themselves! should not the shepherds feed the flocks?

3 You eat the fat, and you clothe you with the wool, you kill them that are fed: but you feed not the flock.

4 The diseased have you not strengthened, neither have you healed that which was sick, neither have you bound up that which was broken, neither have you brought again that which was driven away, neither have you sought that which was lost; but with force and with cruelty have you ruled them.

5 And they were scattered, because there is no shepherd: and they became meat to all the beasts of the field, when they were scattered.

6 My sheep wandered through all the mountains, and upon every high hill: yea, my flock was scattered upon all the face of the earth, and none did search or seek after them.

7 Therefore, you shepherds, hear the word of the LORD;

8 As I live, saith the Lord GOD, surely because my flock became a prey, and my flock became meat to every beast of the field, because there was no shepherd, neither did my shepherds search for my flock, but the shepherds fed themselves, and fed not my flock;

9 Therefore, O you shepherds, hear the word of the LORD;

10 Thus saith the Lord GOD; Behold, I am against the shepherds; and I will require my flock at their hand, and cause them to cease from feeding the flock; neither shall the shepherds feed themselves any more; for I will deliver my flock from their mouth, that they may not be meat for them.

11 For thus saith the Lord GOD; Behold, I, even I, will both search my sheep, and seek them out.

12 As a shepherd seeketh out his flock in the day that he is among his sheep that are scattered; so will I seek out my sheep, and will deliver them out of all places where they have been scattered in the cloudy and dark day.

13 And I will bring them out from the people, and gather them from the countries, and will bring them to their own land, and feed them upon the mountains of Israel by the rivers, and in all the inhabited places of the country.

14 I will feed them in a good pasture, and upon the high mountains of Israel shall their fold be: there shall they lie in a good fold, and in a fat pasture shall they feed upon the mountains of Israel.

15 I will feed my flock, and I will cause them to lie down, saith the Lord GOD.

16 I will seek that which was lost, and bring again that which was driven away, and will bind up that which was broken, and will strengthen that which was sick: but I will destroy the fat and the strong; I will feed them with judgment.

17 And as for you, O my flock, thus saith the Lord GOD; Behold, I judge between cattle and cattle, between the rams and the he goats.

18 Seemeth it a small thing unto you to have eaten up the good pasture, but you must tread down with your feet the residue of your pastures? and to have drunk of the deep waters, but you must foul the residue with your feet?

19 And as for my flock, they eat that which you have trodden with your feet; and they drink that which you have fouled with your feet.

20 Therefore thus saith the Lord GOD unto them; Behold, I, even I, will judge between the fat cattle and between the lean cattle.

21 Because you have thrust with side and with shoulder, and pushed all the diseased with your horns, till you have scattered them abroad;

22 Therefore will I save my flock, and they shall no more be a prey; and I will judge between cattle and cattle.

23 And I will set up one shepherd over them, and he shall feed them, even my servant David; he shall feed them, and he shall be their shepherd.

24 And I the LORD will be their God, and my servant David a prince among them; I the LORD have spoken it.

25 And I will make with them a covenant of peace, and will cause the evil beasts to cease out of the land: and they shall dwell safely in the wilderness, and sleep in the woods.

26 And I will make them and the places round about my hill a blessing; and I will cause the shower to come down in his season; there shall be showers of blessing.

27 And the tree of the field shall yield her fruit, and the earth shall yield her increase, and they shall be safe in their land, and shall know that I am the LORD, when I have broken the bands of their yoke, and delivered them out of the hand of those that served themselves of them.

28 And they shall no more be a prey to the heathen, neither shall the beast of the land devour them; but they shall dwell safely, and none shall make them afraid.

29 And I will raise up for them a plant of renown, and they shall be no more consumed with hunger in the land, neither bear the shame of the heathen any more.

30 Thus shall they know that I the LORD their God am with them, and that they, even the house of Israel, are my people, saith the Lord GOD.

31 And you my flock, the flock of my pasture, are men, and I am your God, saith the Lord GOD.

CHAPTER 35

MOREOVER the word of the LORD came unto me, saying,

2 Son of man, set your face against mount Seir, and prophesy against it,

3 And say unto it, Thus saith the Lord GOD; Behold, O mount Seir, I am against you, and I will stretch out my hand against you, and I will make you most desolate.

4 I will lay your cities waste, and you shalt be desolate, and you shalt know that I am the LORD.

5 Because you have had a perpetual hatred, and have shed the blood of the children of Israel by the force of the sword in the time of their calamity, in the time that their iniquity had an end:

6 Therefore, as I live, saith the Lord GOD, I will prepare you unto blood, and blood shall pursue you: sith you have not hated blood, even blood shall pursue you.

7 Thus will I make mount Seir most desolate, and cut off from it him that passes out and him that returneth.

8 And I will fill his mountains with his slain men: in your hills, and in your valleys, and in all your rivers, shall they fall that are slain with the sword.

9 I will make you perpetual desolations, and your cities shall not return: and you shall know that I am the LORD.

10 Because you have said, These two nations and these two countries shall be my, and we will possess it; whereas the LORD was there:

11 Therefore, as I live, saith the Lord GOD, I will even do according to yours anger, and according to yours envy which you have used out of your hatred against them; and I will make myself known among them, when I have judged you.

12 And you shalt know that I am the LORD, and that I have heard all your blasphemies which you have spoken against the mountains of Israel, saying, They are laid desolate, they are given us to consume.

13 Thus with your mouth you have boasted against me, and have multiplied your words against me: I have heard them.

14 Thus saith the Lord GOD; When the whole earth rejoiceth, I will make you desolate.

15 As you did rejoice at the inheritance of the house of Israel, because it was desolate, so will I do unto you: you shalt be desolate, O mount Seir, and all Idumea, even all of it: and they shall know that I am the LORD.

CHAPTER 36

ALSO, you son of man, prophesy unto the mountains of Israel, and say, You mountains of Israel, hear the word of the LORD:

2 Thus saith the Lord GOD; Because the enemy has said against you, Aha, even the ancient high places are ours in possession:

3 Therefore prophesy and say, Thus saith the Lord GOD; Because they have made you desolate, and swallowed you up on every side, that you might be a possession unto the residue of the heathen, and you are taken up in the lips of talkers, and are an infamy of the people:

4 Therefore, you mountains of Israel, hear the word of the Lord GOD; Thus saith the Lord GOD to the mountains, and to the hills, to the rivers, and to the valleys, to the desolate wastes, and to the cities that are forsaken, which became a prey and derision to the residue of the heathen that are round about;

5 Therefore thus saith the Lord GOD; Surely in the fire of my jealousy have I spoken against the residue of the heathen, and against all Idumea, which have appointed my land into their possession with the joy of all their heart, with despiteful minds, to cast it out for a prey.

6 Prophesy therefore concerning the land of Israel, and say unto the mountains, and to the hills, to the rivers, and to the valleys, Thus saith the Lord GOD; Behold, I have spoken in my jealousy and in my fury, because you have borne the shame of the heathen:

7 Therefore thus saith the Lord GOD; I have lifted up my hand, Surely the heathen that are about you, they shall bear their shame.

8 But you , O mountains of Israel, you shall shoot forth your branches, and yield your fruit to my people of Israel; for they are at hand to come.

9 For, behold, I am for you, and I will turn unto you, and you shall be tilled and sown:

10 And I will multiply men upon you, all the house of Israel, even all of it: and the cities shall be inhabited, and the wastes shall be builded:

11 And I will multiply upon you man and beast; and they shall increase and bring fruit: and I will settle you after your old estates, and will do better unto you than at your beginnings: and you shall know that I am the LORD.

12 Yea, I will cause men to walk upon you, even my people Israel; and they shall possess you, and you shalt be their inheritance, and you shalt no more henceforth bereave them of men.

13 Thus saith the Lord GOD; Because they say unto you, You land devourest up men, and have bereaved your nations;

14 Therefore you shalt devour men no more, neither bereave your nations any more, saith the Lord GOD.

15 Neither will I cause men to hear in you the shame of the heathen any more, neither shalt you bear the reproach of the people any more, neither shalt you cause your nations to fall any more, saith the Lord GOD.

16 Moreover the word of the LORD came unto me, saying,

17 Son of man, when the house of Israel dwelt in their own land, they defiled it by their own way and by their doings: their way was before me as the uncleanness of a removed woman.

18 Wherefore I poured my fury upon them for the blood that they had shed upon the land, and for their idols wherewith they had polluted it:

19 And I scattered them among the heathen, and they were dispersed through the countries: according to their way and according to their doings I judged them.

20 And when they entered unto the heathen, whither they went, they profaned my holy name, when they said to them, These are the people of the LORD, and are gone forth out of his land.

21 But I had pity for my holy name, which the house of Israel had profaned among the heathen, whither they went.

22 Therefore say unto the house of Israel, Thus saith the Lord GOD; I do not this for your sakes, O house of Israel, but for my holy name's sake, which you have profaned among the heathen, whither you went.

23 And I will sanctify my great name, which was profaned among the heathen, which you have profaned in the midst of them; and the heathen shall know that I am the LORD, saith the Lord GOD, when I shall be sanctified in you before their eyes.

24 For I will take you from among the heathen, and gather you out of all countries, and will bring you into your own land.

25 Then will I sprinkle clean water upon you, and you shall be clean: from all your filthiness, and from all your idols, will I cleanse you.

26 A new heart also will I give you, and a new spirit will I put within you: and I will take away the stony heart out of your flesh, and I will give you an heart of flesh.

27 And I will put my spirit within you, and cause you to walk in my statutes, and you shall keep my judgments, and do them.

28 And you shall dwell in the land that I gave to your fathers; and you shall be my people, and I will be your God.

29 I will also save you from all your uncleannesses: and I will call for the corn, and will increase it, and lay no famine upon you.

30 And I will multiply the fruit of the tree, and the increase of the field, that you shall receive no more reproach of famine among the heathen.

31 Then shall you remember your own evil ways, and your doings that were not good, and shall lothe yourselves in your own sight for your iniquities and for your abominations.

32 Not for your sakes do I this, saith the Lord GOD, be it known unto you: be ashamed and confounded for your own ways, O house of Israel.

33 Thus saith the Lord GOD; In the day that I shall have cleansed you from all your iniquities I will also cause you to dwell in the cities, and the wastes shall be builded.

34 And the desolate land shall be tilled, whereas it lay desolate in the sight of all that passed by.

35 And they shall say, This land that was desolate is become like the garden of Eden; and the waste and desolate and ruined cities are become fenced, and are inhabited.

36 Then the heathen that are left round about you shall know that I the LORD build the ruined places, and plant that that was desolate: I the LORD have spoken it, and I will do it.

37 Thus saith the Lord GOD; I will yet for this be inquired of by the house of Israel, to do it for them; I will increase them with men like a flock.

38 As the holy flock, as the flock of Jerusalem in her solemn feasts; so shall the waste cities be filled with flocks of men: and they shall know that I am the LORD.

CHAPTER 37

THE hand of the LORD was upon me, and carried me out in the spirit of the LORD, and set me down in the midst of the valley which was full of bones,

2 And caused me to pass by them round about: and, behold, there were very many in the open valley; and, lo, they were very dry.

3 And he said unto me, Son of man, can these bones live? And I answered, O Lord GOD, you knowest.

4 Again he said unto me, Prophesy upon these bones, and say unto them, O you dry bones, hear the word of the LORD.

5 Thus saith the Lord GOD unto these bones; Behold, I will cause breath to enter into you, and you shall live:

6 And I will lay sinews upon you, and will bring up flesh upon you, and cover you with skin, and put breath in you, and you shall live; and you shall know that I am the LORD.

7 So I prophesied as I was commanded: and as I prophesied, there was a noise, and behold a shaking, and the bones came together, bone to his bone.

8 And when I beheld, lo, the sinews and the flesh came up upon them, and the skin covered them above: but there was no breath in them.

9 Then said he unto me, Prophesy unto the wind, prophesy, son of man, and say to the wind, Thus saith the Lord GOD; Come from the four winds, O breath, and breathe upon these slain, that they may live.

10 So I prophesied as he commanded me, and the breath came into them, and they lived, and stood up upon their feet, an exceeding great army.

11 Then he said unto me, Son of man, these bones are the whole house of Israel: behold, they say, Our bones are dried, and our hope is lost: we are cut off for our parts.

12 Therefore prophesy and say unto them, Thus saith the Lord GOD; Behold, O my people, I will open your graves, and cause you to come up out of your graves, and bring you into the land of Israel.

13 And you shall know that I am the LORD, when I have opened your graves, O my people, and brought you up out of your graves,

14 And shall put my spirit in you, and you shall live, and I shall place you in your own land: then shall you know that I the LORD have spoken it, and performed it, saith the LORD.

15 The word of the LORD came again unto me, saying,

16 Moreover, you son of man, take you one stick, and write upon it, For Judah, and for the children of Israel his companions: then take another stick, and write upon it, For Joseph, the stick of Ephraim, and for all the house of Israel his companions:

17 And join them one to another into one stick; and they shall become one in yours hand.

18 And when the children of your people shall speak unto you, saying, Will you not shew us what you meanest by these?

19 Say unto them, Thus saith the Lord GOD; Behold, I will take the stick of Joseph, which is in the hand of Ephraim, and the tribes of Israel his fellows, and will put them with him, even with the stick of Judah, and make them one stick, and they shall be one in my hand.

20 And the sticks whereon you writest shall be in yours hand before their eyes.

21 And say unto them, Thus saith the Lord GOD; Behold, I will take the children of Israel from among the heathen, whither they be gone, and will gather them on every side, and bring them into their own land:

22 And I will make them one nation in the land upon the mountains of Israel; and one king shall be king to them all: and they shall be no more two nations, neither shall they be divided into two kingdoms any more at all:

23 Neither shall they defile themselves any more with their idols, nor with their detestable things, nor with any of their transgressions: but I will save them out of all their dwellingplaces, wherein they have sinned, and will cleanse them: so shall they be my people, and I will be their God.

24 And David my servant shall be king over them; and they all shall have one shepherd: they shall also walk in my judgments, and observe my statutes, and do them.

25 And they shall dwell in the land that I have given unto Jacob my servant, wherein your fathers have dwelt; and they shall dwell therein, even they, and their children, and their children's children for ever: and my servant David shall be their prince for ever.

26 Moreover I will make a covenant of peace with them; it shall be an everlasting covenant with them: and I will place them, and multiply them, and will set my sanctuary in the midst of them for evermore.

27 My tabernacle also shall be with them: yea, I will be their God, and they shall be my people.

28 And the heathen shall know that I the LORD do sanctify Israel, when my sanctuary shall be in the midst of them for evermore.

CHAPTER 38

AND the word of the LORD came unto me, saying,

2 Son of man, set your face against Gog, the land of Magog, the chief prince of Meshech and Tubal, and prophesy against him,

3 And say, Thus saith the Lord GOD; Behold, I am against you, O Gog, the chief prince of Meshech and Tubal:

4 And I will turn you back, and put hooks into your jaws, and I will bring you forth, and all yours army, horses and horsemen, all of them clothed with all sorts of armour, even a great company with bucklers and shields, all of them handling swords:

5 Persia, Ethiopia, and Libya with them; all of them with shield and helmet:

6 Gomer, and all his bands; the house of Togarmah of the north quarters, and all his bands: and many people with you.

7 Be you prepared, and prepare for yourself, you , and all your company that are assembled unto you, and be you a guard unto them.

8 After many days you shalt be visited: in the latter years you shalt come into the land that is brought back from the sword, and is gathered out of many people, against the mountains of Israel, which have been always waste: but it is brought forth out of the nations, and they shall dwell safely all of them.

9 You shalt ascend and come like a storm, you shalt be like a cloud to cover the land, you , and all your bands, and many people with you.

10 Thus saith the Lord GOD; It shall also come to pass, that at the same time shall things come into your mind, and you shalt think an evil thought:

11 And you shalt say, I will go up to the land of unwalled villages; I will go to them that are at rest, that dwell safely, all of them dwelling without walls, and having neither bars nor gates,

12 To take a spoil, and to take a prey; to turn yours hand upon the desolate places that are now inhabited, and upon the people that are gathered out of the nations, which have gotten cattle and goods, that dwell in the midst of the land.

13 Sheba, and Dedan, and the merchants of Tarshish, with all the young lions thereof, shall say unto you, Are you come to take a spoil? have you gathered your company to take a prey? to carry away silver and gold, to take away cattle and goods, to take a great spoil?

14 Therefore, son of man, prophesy and say unto Gog, Thus saith the Lord GOD; In that day when my people of Israel dwelleth safely, shalt you not know it?

15 And you shalt come from your place out of the north parts, you , and many people with you, all of them riding upon horses, a great company, and a mighty army:

16 And you shalt come up against my people of Israel, as a cloud to cover the land; it shall be in the latter days, and I will bring you against my land, that the heathen may know me, when I shall be sanctified in you, O Gog, before their eyes.

17 Thus saith the Lord GOD; Are you he of whom I have spoken in old time by my servants the prophets of Israel, which prophesied in those days many years that I would bring you against them?

18 And it shall come to pass at the same time when Gog shall come against the land of Israel, saith the Lord GOD, that my fury shall come up in my face.

19 For in my jealousy and in the fire of my wrath have I spoken, Surely in that day there shall be a great shaking in the land of Israel;

20 So that the fishes of the sea, and the fowls of the heaven, and the beasts of the field, and all creeping things that creep upon the earth, and all the men that are upon the face of the earth, shall shake at my presence, and the mountains shall be thrown down, and the steep places shall fall, and every wall shall fall to the ground.

21 And I will call for a sword against him throughout all my mountains, saith the Lord GOD: every man's sword shall be against his brother.

22 And I will plead against him with pestilence and with blood; and I will rain upon him, and upon his bands, and upon the many people that are with him, an overflowing rain, and great hailstones, fire, and brimstone.

23 Thus will I magnify myself, and sanctify myself; and I will be known in the eyes of many nations, and they shall know that I am the LORD.

CHAPTER 39

THEREFORE, you son of man, prophesy against Gog, and say, Thus saith the Lord GOD; Behold, I am against you, O Gog, the chief prince of Meshech and Tubal:

2 And I will turn you back, and leave but the sixth part of you, and will cause you to come up from the north parts, and will bring you upon the mountains of Israel:

3 And I will strike your bow out of your left hand, and will cause yours arrows to fall out of your right hand.

4 You shalt fall upon the mountains of Israel, you , and all your bands, and the people that is with you: I will give you unto the ravenous birds of every sort, and to the beasts of the field to be devoured.

5 You shalt fall upon the open field: for I have spoken it, saith the Lord GOD.

6 And I will send a fire on Magog, and among them that dwell carelessly in the isles: and they shall know that I am the LORD.

7 So will I make my holy name known in the midst of my people Israel; and I will not let them pollute my holy name any more: and the heathen shall know that I am the LORD, the Holy One in Israel.

8 Behold, it is come, and it is done, saith the Lord GOD; this is the day whereof I have spoken.

9 And they that dwell in the cities of Israel shall go forth, and shall set on fire and burn the weapons, both the shields and the bucklers, the bows and the arrows, and the handstaves, and the spears, and they shall burn them with fire seven years:

10 So that they shall take no wood out of the field, neither cut down any out of the forests; for they shall burn the weapons with fire: and they shall spoil those that spoiled them, and rob those that robbed them, saith the Lord GOD.

11 And it shall come to pass in that day, that I will give unto Gog a place there of graves in Israel, the valley of the passengers on the east of the sea: and it shall stop the noses of the passengers: and there shall they bury Gog and all his multitude: and they shall call it The valley of Hamon-gog.

12 And seven months shall the house of Israel be burying of them, that they may cleanse the land.

13 Yea, all the people of the land shall bury them; and it shall be to them a renown the day that I shall be glorified, saith the Lord GOD.

14 And they shall sever out men of continual employment, passing through the land to bury with the passengers those that remain upon the face of the earth, to cleanse it: after the end of seven months shall they search.

15 And the passengers that pass through the land, when any seeth a man's bone, then shall he set up a sign by it, till the buriers have buried it in the valley of Hamon-gog.

16 And also the name of the city shall be Hamonah. Thus shall they cleanse the land.

17 And, you son of man, thus saith the Lord GOD; Speak unto every feathered fowl, and to every beast of the field, Assemble yourselves, and come; gather yourselves on every side to my sacrifice that I do sacrifice for you, even a great sacrifice upon the mountains of Israel, that you may eat flesh, and drink blood.

18 You shall eat the flesh of the mighty, and drink the blood of the princes of the earth, of rams, of lambs, and of goats, of bullocks, all of them fatlings of Bashan.

19 And you shall eat fat till you be full, and drink blood till you be drunken, of my sacrifice which I have sacrificed for you.

20 Thus you shall be filled at my table with horses and chariots, with mighty men, and with all men of war, saith the Lord GOD.

21 And I will set my glory among the heathen, and all the heathen shall see my judgment that I have executed, and my hand that I have laid upon them.

22 So the house of Israel shall know that I am the LORD their God from that day and forward.

23 And the heathen shall know that the house of Israel went into captivity for their iniquity: because they trespassed against me, therefore hid I my face from them, and gave them into the hand of their enemies: so fell they all by the sword.

24 According to their uncleanness and according to their transgressions have I done unto them, and hid my face from them.

25 Therefore thus saith the Lord GOD; Now will I bring again the captivity of Jacob, and have mercy upon the whole house of Israel, and will be jealous for my holy name;

26 After that they have borne their shame, and all their trespasses whereby they have trespassed against me, when they dwelt safely in their land, and none made them afraid.

27 When I have brought them again from the people, and gathered them out of their enemies' lands, and am sanctified in them in the sight of many nations;

28 Then shall they know that I am the LORD their God, which caused them to be led into captivity among the heathen: but I have gathered them unto their own land, and have left none of them any more there.

29 Neither will I hide my face any more from them: for I have poured out my spirit upon the house of Israel, saith the Lord GOD.

CHAPTER 40

IN the five and twentieth year of our captivity, in the beginning of the year, in the tenth day of the month, in the fourteenth year after that the city was smitten, in the selfsame day the hand of the LORD was upon me, and brought me thither.

2 In the visions of God brought he me into the land of Israel, and set me upon a very high mountain, by which was as the frame of a city on the south.

3 And he brought me thither, and, behold, there was a man, whose appearance was like the appearance of brass, with a line of flax in his hand, and a measuring reed; and he stood in the gate.

4 And the man said unto me, Son of man, behold with yours eyes, and hear with yours ears, and set yours heart upon all that I shall shew you; for to the intent that I might shew them unto you are you brought hither: declare all that you seest to the house of Israel.

5 And behold a wall on the outside of the house round about, and in the man's hand a measuring reed of six cubits long by the cubit and an hand breadth: so he measured the breadth of the building, one reed; and the height, one reed.

6 Then came he unto the gate which looketh toward the east, and went up the stairs thereof, and measured the threshold of the gate, which was one reed broad; and the other threshold of the gate, which was one reed broad.

7 And every little chamber was one reed long, and one reed broad; and between the little chambers were five cubits; and the threshold of the gate by the porch of the gate within was one reed.

8 He measured also the porch of the gate within, one reed.

9 Then measured he the porch of the gate, eight cubits; and the posts thereof, two cubits; and the porch of the gate was inward.

10 And the little chambers of the gate eastward were three on this side, and three on that side; they three were of one measure: and the posts had one measure on this side and on that side.

11 And he measured the breadth of the entry of the gate, ten cubits; and the length of the gate, thirteen cubits.

12 The space also before the little chambers was one cubit on this side, and the space was one cubit on that side: and the little chambers were six cubits on this side, and six cubits on that side.

13 He measured then the gate from the roof of one little chamber to the roof of another: the breadth was five and twenty cubits, door against door.

14 He made also posts of threescore cubits, even unto the post of the court round about the gate.

15 And from the face of the gate of the entrance unto the face of the porch of the inner gate were fifty cubits.

16 And there were narrow windows to the little chambers, and to their posts within the gate round about, and likewise to the arches: and windows were round about inward: and upon each post were palm trees.

17 Then brought he me into the outward court, and, lo, there were chambers, and a pavement made for the court round about: thirty chambers were upon the pavement.

18 And the pavement by the side of the gates over against the length of the gates was the lower pavement.

19 Then he measured the breadth from the forefront of the lower gate unto the forefront of the inner court without, an hundred cubits eastward and northward.

20 And the gate of the outward court that looked toward the north, he measured the length thereof, and the breadth thereof.

21 And the little chambers thereof were three on this side and three on that side; and the posts thereof and the arches thereof were after the measure of the first gate: the length thereof was fifty cubits, and the breadth five and twenty cubits.

22 And their windows, and their arches, and their palm trees, were after the measure of the gate that looketh toward the east; and they went up unto it by seven steps; and the arches thereof were before them.

23 And the gate of the inner court was over against the gate toward the north, and toward the east; and he measured from gate to gate an hundred cubits.

24 After that he brought me toward the south, and behold a gate toward the south: and he measured the posts thereof and the arches thereof according to these measures.

25 And there were windows in it and in the arches thereof round about, like those windows: the length was fifty cubits, and the breadth five and twenty cubits.

26 And there were seven steps to go up to it, and the arches thereof were before them: and it had palm trees, one on this side, and another on that side, upon the posts thereof.

27 And there was a gate in the inner court toward the south: and he measured from gate to gate toward the south an hundred cubits.

28 And he brought me to the inner court by the south gate: and he measured the south gate according to these measures;

29 And the little chambers thereof, and the posts thereof, and the arches thereof, according to these measures: and there were windows in it and in the arches thereof round about: it was fifty cubits long, and five and twenty cubits broad.

30 And the arches round about were five and twenty cubits long, and five cubits broad.

31 And the arches thereof were toward the utter court; and palm trees were upon the posts thereof: and the going up to it had eight steps.

32 And he brought me into the inner court toward the east: and he measured the gate according to these measures.

33 And the little chambers thereof, and the posts thereof, and the arches thereof, were according to these measures: and there were windows therein and in the arches thereof round about: it was fifty cubits long, and five and twenty cubits broad.

34 And the arches thereof were toward the outward court; and palm trees were upon the posts thereof, on this side, and on that side: and the going up to it had eight steps.

35 And he brought me to the north gate, and measured it according to these measures;

36 The little chambers thereof, the posts thereof, and the arches thereof, and the windows to it round about: the length was fifty cubits, and the breadth five and twenty cubits.

37 And the posts thereof were toward the utter court; and palm trees were upon the posts thereof, on this side, and on that side: and the going up to it had eight steps.

38 And the chambers and the entries thereof were by the posts of the gates, where they washed the burnt offering.

39 And in the porch of the gate were two tables on this side, and two tables on that side, to slay thereon the burnt offering and the sin offering and the trespass offering.

40 And at the side without, as one goeth up to the entry of the north gate, were two tables; and on the other side, which was at the porch of the gate, were two tables.

41 Four tables were on this side, and four tables on that side, by the side of the gate; eight tables, whereupon they slew their sacrifices.

42 And the four tables were of hewn stone for the burnt offering, of a cubit and an half long, and a cubit and an half broad, and one cubit high: whereupon also they laid the instruments wherewith they slew the burnt offering and the sacrifice.

43 And within were hooks, an hand broad, fastened round about: and upon the tables was the flesh of the offering.

44 And without the inner gate were the chambers of the singers in the inner court, which was at the side of the north gate; and their prospect was toward the south: one at the side of the east gate having the prospect toward the north.

45 And he said unto me, This chamber, whose prospect is toward the south, is for the priests, the keepers of the charge of the house.

46 And the chamber whose prospect is toward the north is for the priests, the keepers of the charge of the altar: these are the sons of Zadok among the sons of Levi, which come near to the LORD to minister unto him.

47 So he measured the court, an hundred cubits long, and an hundred cubits broad, foursquare; and the altar that was before the house.

48 And he brought me to the porch of the house, and measured each post of the porch, five cubits on this side, and five cubits on that side: and the breadth of the gate was three cubits on this side, and three cubits on that side.

49 The length of the porch was twenty cubits, and the breadth eleven cubits; and he brought me by the steps whereby they went up to it: and there were pillars by the posts, one on this side, and another on that side.

CHAPTER 41

AFTERWARD he brought me to the temple, and measured the posts, six cubits broad on the one side, and six cubits broad on the other side, which was the breadth of the tabernacle.

2 And the breadth of the door was ten cubits; and the sides of the door were five cubits on the one side, and five cubits on the other side: and he measured the length thereof, forty cubits: and the breadth, twenty cubits.

3 Then went he inward, and measured the post of the door, two cubits; and the door, six cubits; and the breadth of the door, seven cubits.

4 So he measured the length thereof, twenty cubits; and the breadth, twenty cubits, before the temple: and he said unto me, This is the most holy place.

5 After he measured the wall of the house, six cubits; and the breadth of every side chamber, four cubits, round about the house on every side.

6 And the side chambers were three, one over another, and thirty in order; and they entered into the wall which was of the house for the side chambers round about, that they might have hold, but they had not hold in the wall of the house.

7 And there was an enlarging, and a winding about still upward to the side chambers: for the winding about of the house went still upward round about the house: therefore the breadth of the house was still upward, and so increased from the lowest chamber to the highest by the midst.

8 I saw also the height of the house round about: the foundations of the side chambers were a full reed of six great cubits.

9 The thickness of the wall, which was for the side chamber without, was five cubits: and that which was left was the place of the side chambers that were within.

10 And between the chambers was the wideness of twenty cubits round about the house on every side.

11 And the doors of the side chambers were toward the place that was left, one door toward the north, and another door toward the south: and the breadth of the place that was left was five cubits round about.

12 Now the building that was before the separate place at the end toward the west was seventy cubits broad; and the wall of the building was five cubits thick round about, and the length thereof ninety cubits.

13 So he measured the house, an hundred cubits long; and the separate place, and the building, with the walls thereof, an hundred cubits long;

14 Also the breadth of the face of the house, and of the separate place toward the east, an hundred cubits.

15 And he measured the length of the building over against the separate place which was behind it, and the galleries thereof on the one side and on the other side, an hundred cubits, with the inner temple, and the porches of the court;

16 The door posts, and the narrow windows, and the galleries round about on their three stories, over against the door, cieled with wood round about, and from the ground up to the windows, and the windows were covered;

17 To that above the door, even unto the inner house, and without, and by all the wall round about within and without, by measure.

18 And it was made with cherubims and palm trees, so that a palm tree was between a cherub and a cherub; and every cherub had two faces;

19 So that the face of a man was toward the palm tree on the one side, and the face of a young lion toward the palm tree on the other side: it was made through all the house round about.

20 From the ground unto above the door were cherubims and palm trees made, and on the wall of the temple.

21 The posts of the temple were squared, and the face of the sanctuary; the appearance of the one as the appearance of the other.

22 The altar of wood was three cubits high, and the length thereof two cubits; and the corners thereof, and the length thereof, and the walls thereof, were of wood: and he said unto me, This is the table that is before the LORD.

23 And the temple and the sanctuary had two doors.

24 And the doors had two leaves apiece, two turning leaves; two leaves for the one door, and two leaves for the other door.

25 And there were made on them, on the doors of the temple, cherubims and palm trees, like as were made upon the walls; and there were thick planks upon the face of the porch without.

26 And there were narrow windows and palm trees on the one side and on the other side, on the sides of the porch, and upon the side chambers of the house, and thick planks.

CHAPTER 42

THEN he brought me forth into the utter court, the way toward the north: and he brought me into the chamber that was over against the separate place, and which was before the building toward the north.

2 Before the length of an hundred cubits was the north door, and the breadth was fifty cubits.

3 Over against the twenty cubits which were for the inner court, and over against the pavement which was for the utter court, was gallery against gallery in three stories.

4 And before the chambers was a walk of ten cubits breadth inward, a way of one cubit; and their doors toward the north.

5 Now the upper chambers were shorter: for the galleries were higher than these, than the lower, and than the middlemost of the building.

6 For they were in three stories, but had not pillars as the pillars of the courts: therefore the building was straitened more than the lowest and the middlemost from the ground.

7 And the wall that was without over against the chambers, toward the utter court on the forepart of the chambers, the length thereof was fifty cubits.

8 For the length of the chambers that were in the utter court was fifty cubits: and, lo, before the temple were an hundred cubits.

9 And from under these chambers was the entry on the east side, as one goeth into them from the utter court.

10 The chambers were in the thickness of the wall of the court toward the east, over against the separate place, and over against the building.

11 And the way before them was like the appearance of the chambers which were toward the north, as long as they, and as broad as they: and all their goings out were both according to their fashions, and according to their doors.

12 And according to the doors of the chambers that were toward the south was a door in the head of the way, even the way directly before the wall toward the east, as one entereth into them.

13 Then said he unto me, The north chambers and the south chambers, which are before the separate place, they be holy chambers, where the priests that approach unto the LORD shall eat the most holy things: there shall they lay the most holy things, and the meat offering, and the sin offering, and the trespass offering; for the place is holy.

14 When the priests enter therein, then shall they not go out of the holy place into the utter court, but there they shall lay their garments wherein they minister; for they are holy; and shall put on other garments, and shall approach to those things which are for the people.

15 Now when he had made an end of measuring the inner house, he brought me forth toward the gate whose prospect is toward the east, and measured it round about.

16 He measured the east side with the measuring reed, five hundred reeds, with the measuring reed round about.

17 He measured the north side, five hundred reeds, with the measuring reed round about.

18 He measured the south side, five hundred reeds, with the measuring reed.

19 He turned about to the west side, and measured five hundred reeds with the measuring reed.

20 He measured it by the four sides: it had a wall round about, five hundred reeds long, and five hundred broad, to make a separation between the sanctuary and the profane place.

CHAPTER 43

AFTERWARD he brought me to the gate, even the gate that looketh toward the east:

2 And, behold, the glory of the God of Israel came from the way of the east: and his voice was like a noise of many waters: and the earth shined with his glory.

3 And it was according to the appearance of the vision which I saw, even according to the vision that I saw when I came to destroy the city: and the visions were like the vision that I saw by the river Chebar; and I fell upon my face.

4 And the glory of the LORD came into the house by the way of the gate whose prospect is toward the east.

5 So the spirit took me up, and brought me into the inner court; and, behold, the glory of the LORD filled the house.

6 And I heard him speaking unto me out of the house; and the man stood by me.

7 And he said unto me, Son of man, the place of my throne, and the place of the soles of my feet, where I will dwell in the midst of the children of Israel for ever, and my holy name, shall the house of Israel no more defile, neither they, nor their kings, by their whoredom, nor by the carcases of their kings in their high places.

8 In their setting of their threshold by my thresholds, and their post by my posts, and the wall between me and them, they have even defiled my holy name by their abominations that they have committed: wherefore I have consumed them in my anger.

9 Now let them put away their whoredom, and the carcases of their kings, far from me, and I will dwell in the midst of them for ever.

10 You son of man, shew the house to the house of Israel, that they may be ashamed of their iniquities: and let them measure the pattern.

11 And if they be ashamed of all that they have done, shew them the form of the house, and the fashion thereof, and the goings out thereof, and the comings in thereof, and all the forms thereof, and all the ordinances thereof, and all the forms thereof, and all the laws thereof: and write it in their sight, that they may keep the whole form thereof, and all the ordinances thereof, and do them.

12 This is the law of the house; Upon the top of the mountain the whole limit thereof round about shall be most holy. Behold, this is the law of the house.

13And these are the measures of the altar after the cubits: The cubit is a cubit and an hand breadth; even the bottom shall be a cubit, and the breadth a cubit, and the border thereof by the edge thereof round about shall be a span: and this shall be the higher place of the altar.

14 And from the bottom upon the ground even to the lower settle shall be two cubits, and the breadth one cubit; and from the lesser settle even to the greater settle shall be four cubits, and the breadth one cubit.

15 So the altar shall be four cubits; and from the altar and upward shall be four horns.

16 And the altar shall be twelve cubits long, twelve broad, square in the four squares thereof.

17 And the settle shall be fourteen cubits long and fourteen broad in the four squares thereof; and the border about it shall be half a cubit; and the bottom thereof shall be a cubit about; and his stairs shall look toward the east.

18And he said unto me, Son of man, thus saith the Lord GOD; These are the ordinances of the altar in the day when they shall make it, to offer burnt offerings thereon, and to sprinkle blood thereon.

19 And you shalt give to the priests the Levites that be of the seed of Zadok, which approach unto me, to minister unto me, saith the Lord GOD, a young bullock for a sin offering.

20 And you shalt take of the blood thereof, and put it on the four horns of it, and on the four corners of the settle, and upon the border round about: thus shalt you cleanse and purge it.

21 You shalt take the bullock also of the sin offering, and he shall burn it in the appointed place of the house, without the sanctuary.

22 And on the second day you shalt offer a kid of the goats without blemish for a sin offering; and they shall cleanse the altar, as they did cleanse it with the bullock.

23 When you have made an end of cleansing it, you shalt offer a young bullock without blemish, and a ram out of the flock without blemish.

24 And you shalt offer them before the LORD, and the priests shall cast salt upon them, and they shall offer them up for a burnt offering unto the LORD.

25 Seven days shalt you prepare every day a goat for a sin offering: they shall also prepare a young bullock, and a ram out of the flock, without blemish.

26 Seven days shall they purge the altar and purify it; and they shall consecrate themselves.

27 And when these days are expired, it shall be, that upon the eighth day, and so forward, the priests shall make your burnt offerings upon the altar, and your peace offerings; and I will accept you, saith the Lord GOD.

CHAPTER 44

THEN he brought me back the way of the gate of the outward sanctuary which looketh toward the east; and it was shut.

2 Then said the LORD unto me; This gate shall be shut, it shall not be opened, and no man shall enter in by it; because the LORD, the God of Israel, has entered in by it, therefore it shall be shut.

3 It is for the prince; the prince, he shall sit in it to eat bread before the LORD; he shall enter by the way of the porch of that gate, and shall go out by the way of the same.

4Then brought he me the way of the north gate before the house: and I looked, and, behold, the glory of the LORD filled the house of the LORD: and I fell upon my face.

5 And the LORD said unto me, Son of man, mark well, and behold with yours eyes, and hear with yours ears all that I say unto you concerning all the ordinances of the house of the LORD, and all the laws thereof; and mark well the entering in of the house, with every going forth of the sanctuary.

6 And you shalt say to the rebellious, even to the house of Israel, Thus saith the Lord GOD; O you house of Israel, let it suffice you of all your abominations,

7 In that you have brought into my sanctuary strangers, uncircumcised in heart, and uncircumcised in flesh, to be in my sanctuary, to pollute it, even my house, when you offer my bread, the fat and the blood, and they have broken my covenant because of all your abominations.

8 And you have not kept the charge of my holy things: but you have set keepers of my charge in my sanctuary for yourselves.

9Thus saith the Lord GOD; No stranger, uncircumcised in heart, nor uncircumcised in flesh, shall enter into my sanctuary, of any stranger that is among the children of Israel.

10 And the Levites that are gone away far from me, when Israel went astray, which went astray away from me after their idols; they shall even bear their iniquity.

11 Yet they shall be ministers in my sanctuary, having charge at the gates of the house, and ministering to the house: they shall slay the burnt offering and the sacrifice for the people, and they shall stand before them to minister unto them.

12 Because they ministered unto them before their idols, and caused the house of Israel to fall into iniquity; therefore have I lifted up my hand against them, saith the Lord GOD, and they shall bear their iniquity.

13 And they shall not come near unto me, to do the office of a priest unto me, nor to come near to any of my holy things, in the most holy place: but they shall bear their shame, and their abominations which they have committed.

14 But I will make them keepers of the charge of the house, for all the service thereof, and for all that shall be done therein.

15But the priests the Levites, the sons of Zadok, that kept the charge of my sanctuary when the children of Israel went astray from me, they shall come near to me to minister unto me, and they shall stand before me to offer unto me the fat and the blood, saith the Lord GOD:

16 They shall enter into my sanctuary, and they shall come near to my table, to minister unto me, and they shall keep my charge.

17And it shall come to pass, that when they enter in at the gates of the inner court, they shall be clothed with linen garments; and no wool shall come upon them, whiles they minister in the gates of the inner court, and within.

18 They shall have linen bonnets upon their heads, and shall have linen breeches upon their loins; they shall not gird themselves with any thing that causeth sweat.

19 And when they go forth into the utter court, even into the utter court to the people, they shall put off their garments wherein they ministered, and lay them in the holy chambers, and they shall put on other garments; and they shall not sanctify the people with their garments.

20 Neither shall they shave their heads, nor suffer their locks to grow long; they shall only poll their heads.

21 Neither shall any priest drink wine, when they enter into the inner court.

22 Neither shall they take for their wives a widow, nor her that is put away: but they shall take maidens of the seed of the house of Israel, or a widow that had a priest before.

23 And they shall teach my people the difference between the holy and profane, and cause them to discern between the unclean and the clean.

24 And in controversy they shall stand in judgment; and they shall judge it according to my judgments: and they shall keep my laws and my statutes in all my assemblies; and they shall hallow my sabbaths.

25 And they shall come at no dead person to defile themselves: but for father, or for mother, or for son, or for daughter, for brother, or for sister that has had no husband, they may defile themselves.

26 And after he is cleansed, they shall reckon unto him seven days.

27 And in the day that he goeth into the sanctuary, unto the inner court, to minister in the sanctuary, he shall offer his sin offering, saith the Lord GOD.

28 And it shall be unto them for an inheritance: I am their inheritance: and you shall give them no possession in Israel: I am their possession.

29 They shall eat the meat offering, and the sin offering, and the trespass offering; and every dedicated thing in Israel shall be theirs.

30 And the first of all the firstfruits of all things, and every oblation of all, of every sort of your oblations, shall be the priest's: you shall also give unto the priest the first of your dough, that he may cause the blessing to rest in yours house.

31 The priests shall not eat of any thing that is dead of itself, or torn, whether it be fowl or beast.

CHAPTER 45

MOREOVER, when you shall divide by lot the land for inheritance, you shall offer an oblation unto the LORD, an holy portion of the land: the length shall be the length of five and twenty thousand reeds, and the breadth shall be ten thousand. This shall be holy in all the borders thereof round about.

2 Of this there shall be for the sanctuary five hundred in length, with five hundred in breadth, square round about; and fifty cubits round about for the suburbs thereof.

3 And of this measure shalt you measure the length of five and twenty thousand, and the breadth of ten thousand: and in it shall be the sanctuary and the most holy place.

4 The holy portion of the land shall be for the priests the ministers of the sanctuary, which shall come near to minister unto the LORD: and it shall be a place for their houses, and an holy place for the sanctuary.

5 And the five and twenty thousand of length, and the ten thousand of breadth, shall also the Levites, the ministers of the house, have for themselves, for a possession for twenty chambers.

6And you shall appoint the possession of the city five thousand broad, and five and twenty thousand long, over against the oblation of the holy portion: it shall be for the whole house of Israel.

7And a portion shall be for the prince on the one side and on the other side of the oblation of the holy portion, and of the possession of the city, before the oblation of the holy portion, and before the possession of the city, from the west side westward, and from the east side eastward: and the length shall be over against one of the portions, from the west border unto the east border.

8 In the land shall be his possession in Israel: and my princes shall no more oppress my people; and the rest of the land shall they give to the house of Israel according to their tribes.

9Thus saith the Lord GOD; Let it suffice you, O princes of Israel: remove violence and spoil, and execute judgment and justice, take away your exactions from my people, saith the Lord GOD.

10 You shall have just balances, and a just ephah, and a just bath.

11 The ephah and the bath shall be of one measure, that the bath may contain the tenth part of an homer, and the ephah the tenth part of an homer: the measure thereof shall be after the homer.

12 And the shekel shall be twenty gerahs: twenty shekels, five and twenty shekels, fifteen shekels, shall be your maneh.

13 This is the oblation that you shall offer; the sixth part of an ephah of an homer of wheat, and you shall give the sixth part of an ephah of an homer of barley:

14 Concerning the ordinance of oil, the bath of oil, you shall offer the tenth part of a bath out of the cor, which is an homer of ten baths; for ten baths are an homer:

15 And one lamb out of the flock, out of two hundred, out of the fat pastures of Israel; for a meat offering, and for a burnt offering, and for peace offerings, to make reconciliation for them, saith the Lord GOD.

16 All the people of the land shall give this oblation for the prince in Israel.

17 And it shall be the prince's part to give burnt offerings, and meat offerings, and drink offerings, in the feasts, and in the new moons, and in the sabbaths, in all solemnities of the house of Israel: he shall prepare the sin offering, and the meat offering, and the burnt offering, and the peace offerings, to make reconciliation for the house of Israel.

18 Thus saith the Lord GOD; In the first month, in the first day of the month, you shalt take a young bullock without blemish, and cleanse the sanctuary:

19 And the priest shall take of the blood of the sin offering, and put it upon the posts of the house, and upon the four corners of the settle of the altar, and upon the posts of the gate of the inner court.

20 And so you shalt do the seventh day of the month for every one that erreth, and for him that is simple: so shall you reconcile the house.

21 In the first month, in the fourteenth day of the month, you shall have the passover, a feast of seven days; unleavened bread shall be eaten.

22 And upon that day shall the prince prepare for himself and for all the people of the land a bullock for a sin offering.

23 And seven days of the feast he shall prepare a burnt offering to the LORD, seven bullocks and seven rams without blemish daily the seven days; and a kid of the goats daily for a sin offering.

24 And he shall prepare a meat offering of an ephah for a bullock, and an ephah for a ram, and an hin of oil for an ephah.

25 In the seventh month, in the fifteenth day of the month, shall he do the like in the feast of the seven days, according to the sin offering, according to the burnt offering, and according to the meat offering, and according to the oil.

CHAPTER 46

THUS saith the Lord GOD; The gate of the inner court that looketh toward the east shall be shut the six working days; but on the sabbath it shall be opened, and in the day of the new moon it shall be opened.

2 And the prince shall enter by the way of the porch of that gate without, and shall stand by the post of the gate, and the priests shall prepare his burnt offering and his peace offerings, and he shall worship at the threshold of the gate: then he shall go forth; but the gate shall not be shut until the evening.

3 Likewise the people of the land shall worship at the door of this gate before the LORD in the sabbaths and in the new moons.

4 And the burnt offering that the prince shall offer unto the LORD in the sabbath day shall be six lambs without blemish, and a ram without blemish.

5 And the meat offering shall be an ephah for a ram, and the meat offering for the lambs as he shall be able to give, and an hin of oil to an ephah.

6 And in the day of the new moon it shall be a young bullock without blemish, and six lambs, and a ram: they shall be without blemish.

7 And he shall prepare a meat offering, an ephah for a bullock, and an ephah for a ram, and for the lambs according as his hand shall attain unto, and an hin of oil to an ephah.

8 And when the prince shall enter, he shall go in by the way of the porch of that gate, and he shall go forth by the way thereof.

9But when the people of the land shall come before the LORD in the solemn feasts, he that entereth in by the way of the north gate to worship shall go out by the way of the south gate; and he that entereth by the way of the south gate shall go forth by the way of the north gate: he shall not return by the way of the gate whereby he came in, but shall go forth over against it.

10 And the prince in the midst of them, when they go in, shall go in; and when they go forth, shall go forth.

11 And in the feasts and in the solemnities the meat offering shall be an ephah to a bullock, and an ephah to a ram, and to the lambs as he is able to give, and an hin of oil to an ephah.

12 Now when the prince shall prepare a voluntary burnt offering or peace offerings voluntarily unto the LORD, one shall then open him the gate that looketh toward the east, and he shall prepare his burnt offering and his peace offerings, as he did on the sabbath day: then he shall go forth; and after his going forth one shall shut the gate.

13 You shalt daily prepare a burnt offering unto the LORD of a lamb of the first year without blemish: you shalt prepare it every morning.

14 And you shalt prepare a meat offering for it every morning, the sixth part of an ephah, and the third part of an hin of oil, to temper with the fine flour; a meat offering continually by a perpetual ordinance unto the LORD.

15 Thus shall they prepare the lamb, and the meat offering, and the oil, every morning for a continual burnt offering.

16Thus saith the Lord GOD; If the prince give a gift unto any of his sons, the inheritance thereof shall be his sons'; it shall be their possession by inheritance.

17 But if he give a gift of his inheritance to one of his servants, then it shall be his to the year of liberty; after it shall return to the prince: but his inheritance shall be his sons' for them.

18 Moreover the prince shall not take of the people's inheritance by oppression, to thrust them out of their possession; but he shall give his sons inheritance out of his own possession: that my people be not scattered every man from his possession.

19After he brought me through the entry, which was at the side of the gate, into the holy chambers of the priests, which looked toward the north: and, behold, there was a place on the two sides westward.

20 Then said he unto me, This is the place where the priests shall boil the trespass offering and the sin offering, where they shall bake the meat offering; that they bear them not out into the utter court, to sanctify the people.

21 Then he brought me forth into the utter court, and caused me to pass by the four corners of the court; and, behold, in every corner of the court there was a court.

22 In the four corners of the court there were courts joined of forty cubits long and thirty broad: these four corners were of one measure.

23 And there was a row of building round about in them, round about them four, and it was made with boiling places under the rows round about.

24 Then said he unto me, These are the places of them that boil, where the ministers of the house shall boil the sacrifice of the people.

CHAPTER 47

AFTERWARD he brought me again unto the door of the house; and, behold, waters issued out from under the threshold of the house eastward: for the forefront of the house stood toward the east, and the waters came down from under from the right side of the house, at the south side of the altar.

2 Then brought he me out of the way of the gate northward, and led me about the way without unto the utter gate by the way that looketh eastward; and, behold, there ran out waters on the right side.

3 And when the man that had the line in his hand went forth eastward, he measured a thousand cubits, and he brought me through the waters; the waters were to the ancles.

4 Again he measured a thousand, and brought me through the waters; the waters were to the knees. Again he measured a thousand, and brought me through; the waters were to the loins.

5 Afterward he measured a thousand; and it was a river that I could not pass over: for the waters were risen, waters to swim in, a river that could not be passed over.

6And he said unto me, Son of man, have you seen this? Then he brought me, and caused me to return to the brink of the river.

7 Now when I had returned, behold, at the bank of the river were very many trees on the one side and on the other.

8 Then said he unto me, These waters issue out toward the east country, and go down into the desert, and go into the sea: which being brought forth into the sea, the waters shall be healed.

9 And it shall come to pass, that every thing that liveth, which moveth, whithersoever the rivers shall come, shall live: and there shall be a very great multitude of fish, because these waters shall come thither: for they shall be healed; and every thing shall live whither the river comes.

10 And it shall come to pass, that the fishers shall stand upon it from En-gedi even unto En-eglaim; they shall be a place to spread forth nets; their fish shall be according to their kinds, as the fish of the great sea, exceeding many.

11 But the miry places thereof and the marishes thereof shall not be healed; they shall be given to salt.

12 And by the river upon the bank thereof, on this side and on that side, shall grow all trees for meat, whose leaf shall not fade, neither shall the fruit thereof be consumed: it shall bring forth new fruit according to his months, because their waters they issued out of the sanctuary: and the fruit thereof shall be for meat, and the leaf thereof for medicine.

13 Thus saith the Lord GOD; This shall be the border, whereby you shall inherit the land according to the twelve tribes of Israel: Joseph shall have two portions.

14 And you shall inherit it, one as well as another: concerning the which I lifted up my hand to give it unto your fathers: and this land shall fall unto you for inheritance.

15 And this shall be the border of the land toward the north side, from the great sea, the way of Hethlon, as men go to Zedad;

16 Hamath, Berothah, Sibraim, which is between the border of Damascus and the border of Hamath; Hazar-hatticon, which is by the coast of Hauran.

17 And the border from the sea shall be Hazar-enan, the border of Damascus, and the north northward, and the border of Hamath. And this is the north side.

18 And the east side you shall measure from Hauran, and from Damascus, and from Gilead, and from the land of Israel by Jordan, from the border unto the east sea. And this is the east side.

19 And the south side southward, from Tamar even to the waters of strife in Kadesh, the river to the great sea. And this is the south side southward.

20 The west side also shall be the great sea from the border, till a man come over against Hamath. This is the west side.

21 So shall you divide this land unto you according to the tribes of Israel.

22 And it shall come to pass, that you shall divide it by lot for an inheritance unto you, and to the strangers that sojourn among you, which shall beget children among you: and they shall be unto you as born in the country among the children of Israel; they shall have inheritance with you among the tribes of Israel.

23 And it shall come to pass, that in what tribe the stranger sojourneth, there shall you give him his inheritance, saith the Lord GOD.

CHAPTER 48

NOW these are the names of the tribes. From the north end to the coast of the way of Hethlon, as one goeth to Hamath, Hazar-enan, the border of Damascus northward, to the coast of Hamath; for these are his sides east and west; a portion for Dan.

2 And by the border of Dan, from the east side unto the west side, a portion for Asher.

3 And by the border of Asher, from the east side even unto the west side, a portion for Naphtali.

4 And by the border of Naphtali, from the east side unto the west side, a portion for Manasseh.

5 And by the border of Manasseh, from the east side unto the west side, a portion for Ephraim.

6 And by the border of Ephraim, from the east side even unto the west side, a portion for Reuben.

7 And by the border of Reuben, from the east side unto the west side, a portion for Judah.

8 And by the border of Judah, from the east side unto the west side, shall be the offering which you shall offer of five and twenty thousand reeds in breadth, and in length as one of the other parts, from the east side unto the west side: and the sanctuary shall be in the midst of it.

9 The oblation that you shall offer unto the LORD shall be of five and twenty thousand in length, and of ten thousand in breadth.

10 And for them, even for the priests, shall be this holy oblation; toward the north five and twenty thousand in length, and toward the west ten thousand in breadth, and toward the east ten thousand in breadth, and toward the south five and twenty thousand in length: and the sanctuary of the LORD shall be in the midst thereof.

11 It shall be for the priests that are sanctified of the sons of Zadok; which have kept my charge, which went not astray when the children of Israel went astray, as the Levites went astray.

12 And this oblation of the land that is offered shall be unto them a thing most holy by the border of the Levites.

13 And over against the border of the priests the Levites shall have five and twenty thousand in length, and ten thousand in breadth: all the length shall be five and twenty thousand, and the breadth ten thousand.

14 And they shall not sell of it, neither exchange, nor alienate the firstfruits of the land: for it is holy unto the LORD.

15 And the five thousand, that are left in the breadth over against the five and twenty thousand, shall be a profane place for the city, for dwelling, and for suburbs: and the city shall be in the midst thereof.

16 And these shall be the measures thereof; the north side four thousand and five hundred, and the south side four thousand and five hundred, and on the east side four thousand and five hundred, and the west side four thousand and five hundred.

17 And the suburbs of the city shall be toward the north two hundred and fifty, and toward the south two hundred and fifty, and toward the east two hundred and fifty, and toward the west two hundred and fifty.

18 And the residue in length over against the oblation of the holy portion shall be ten thousand eastward, and ten thousand westward: and it shall be over against the oblation of the holy portion; and the increase thereof shall be for food unto them that serve the city.

19 And they that serve the city shall serve it out of all the tribes of Israel.

20 All the oblation shall be five and twenty thousand by five and twenty thousand: you shall offer the holy oblation foursquare, with the possession of the city.

21 And the residue shall be for the prince, on the one side and on the other of the holy oblation, and of the possession of the city, over against the five and twenty thousand of the oblation toward the east border, and westward over against the five and twenty thousand toward the west border, over against the portions for the prince: and it shall be the holy oblation; and the sanctuary of the house shall be in the midst thereof.

22 Moreover from the possession of the Levites, and from the possession of the city, being in the midst of that which is the prince's, between the border of Judah and the border of Benjamin, shall be for the prince.

23 As for the rest of the tribes, from the east side unto the west side, Benjamin shall have a portion.

24 And by the border of Benjamin, from the east side unto the west side, Simeon shall have a portion.

25 And by the border of Simeon, from the east side unto the west side, Issachar a portion.

26 And by the border of Issachar, from the east side unto the west side, Zebulun a portion.

27 And by the border of Zebulun, from the east side unto the west side, Gad a portion.

28 And by the border of Gad, at the south side southward, the border shall be even from Tamar unto the waters of strife in Kadesh, and to the river toward the great sea.

29 This is the land which you shall divide by lot unto the tribes of Israel for inheritance, and these are their portions, saith the Lord GOD.

30 And these are the goings out of the city on the north side, four thousand and five hundred measures.

31 And the gates of the city shall be after the names of the tribes of Israel: three gates northward; one gate of Reuben, one gate of Judah, one gate of Levi.

32 And at the east side four thousand and five hundred: and three gates; and one gate of Joseph, one gate of Benjamin, one gate of Dan.

33 And at the south side four thousand and five hundred measures: and three gates; one gate of Simeon, one gate of Issachar, one gate of Zebulun.

34 At the west side four thousand and five hundred, with their three gates; one gate of Gad, one gate of Asher, one gate of Naphtali.

35 It was round about eighteen thousand measures: and the name of the city from that day shall be, The LORD is there.

THE BOOK OF DANIEL.

CHAPTER 1

IN the third year of the reign of Jehoiakim king of Judah came Nebuchadnezzar king of Babylon unto Jerusalem, and besieged it.

2 And the Lord gave Jehoiakim king of Judah into his hand, with part of the vessels of the house of God: which he carried into the land of Shinar to the house of his god; and he brought the vessels into the treasure house of his god.

3And the king spake unto Ashpenaz the master of his eunuchs, that he should bring certain of the children of Israel, and of the king's seed, and of the princes;

4 Children in whom was no blemish, but well favoured, and skilful in all wisdom, and cunning in knowledge, and understanding science, and such as had ability in them to stand in the king's palace, and whom they might teach the learning and the tongue of the Chaldeans.

5 And the king appointed them a daily provision of the king's meat, and of the wine which he drank: so nourishing them three years, that at the end thereof they might stand before the king.

6 Now among these were of the children of Judah, Daniel, Hananiah, Mishael, and Azariah:

7 Unto whom the prince of the eunuchs gave names: for he gave unto Daniel the name of Belteshazzar; and to Hananiah, of Shadrach; and to Mishael, of Meshach; and to Azariah, of Abed-nego.

8But Daniel purposed in his heart that he would not defile himself with the portion of the king's meat, nor with the wine which he drank: therefore he requested of the prince of the eunuchs that he might not defile himself.

9 Now God had brought Daniel into favour and tender love with the prince of the eunuchs.

10 And the prince of the eunuchs said unto Daniel, I fear my lord the king, who has appointed your meat and your drink: for why should he see your faces worse liking than the children which are of your sort? then shall you make me endanger my head to the king.

11 Then said Daniel to Melzar, whom the prince of the eunuchs had set over Daniel, Hananiah, Mishael, and Azariah,

12 Prove your servants, I beseech you, ten days; and let them give us pulse to eat, and water to drink.

13 Then let our countenances be looked upon before you, and the countenance of the children that eat of the portion of the king's meat: and as you seest, deal with your servants.

14 So he consented to them in this matter, and proved them ten days.

15 And at the end of ten days their countenances appeared fairer and fatter in flesh than all the children which did eat the portion of the king's meat.

16 Thus Melzar took away the portion of their meat, and the wine that they should drink; and gave them pulse.

17As for these four children, God gave them knowledge and skill in all learning and wisdom: and Daniel had understanding in all visions and dreams.

18 Now at the end of the days that the king had said he should bring them in, then the prince of the eunuchs brought them in before Nebuchadnezzar.

19 And the king communed with them; and among them all was found none like Daniel, Hananiah, Mishael, and Azariah: therefore stood they before the king.

20 And in all matters of wisdom and understanding, that the king inquired of them, he found them ten times better than all the magicians and astrologers that were in all his realm.

21 And Daniel continued even unto the first year of king Cyrus.

CHAPTER 2

AND in the second year of the reign of Nebuchadnezzar Nebuchadnezzar dreamed dreams, wherewith his spirit was troubled, and his sleep brake from him.

2 Then the king commanded to call the magicians, and the astrologers, and the sorcerers, and the Chaldeans, for to shew the king his dreams. So they came and stood before the king.

3 And the king said unto them, I have dreamed a dream, and my spirit was troubled to know the dream.

4 Then spake the Chaldeans to the king in Syriack, O king, live for ever: tell your servants the dream, and we will shew the interpretation.

5 The king answered and said to the Chaldeans, The thing is gone from me: if you will not make known unto me the dream, with the interpretation thereof, you shall be cut in pieces, and your houses shall be made a dunghill.

6 But if you shew the dream, and the interpretation thereof, you shall receive of me gifts and rewards and great honour: therefore shew me the dream, and the interpretation thereof.

7 They answered again and said, Let the king tell his servants the dream, and we will shew the interpretation of it.

8 The king answered and said, I know of certainty that you would gain the time, because you see the thing is gone from me.

9 But if you will not make known unto me the dream, there is but one decree for you: for you have prepared lying and corrupt words to speak before me, till the time be changed: therefore tell me the dream, and I shall know that you can shew me the interpretation thereof.

10The Chaldeans answered before the king, and said, There is not a man upon the earth that can shew the king's matter: therefore there is no king, lord, nor ruler, that asked such things at any magician, or astrologer, or Chaldean.

11 And it is a rare thing that the king requireth, and there is none other that can shew it before the king, except the gods, whose dwelling is not with flesh.

12 For this cause the king was angry and very furious, and commanded to destroy all the wise men of Babylon.

13 And the decree went forth that the wise men should be slain; and they sought Daniel and his fellows to be slain.

14Then Daniel answered with counsel and wisdom to Arioch the captain of the king's guard, which was gone forth to slay the wise men of Babylon:

15 He answered and said to Arioch the king's captain, Why is the decree so hasty from the king? Then Arioch made the thing known to Daniel.

16 Then Daniel went in, and desired of the king that he would give him time, and that he would shew the king the interpretation.

17 Then Daniel went to his house, and made the thing known to Hananiah, Mishael, and Azariah, his companions:

18 That they would desire mercies of the God of heaven concerning this secret; that Daniel and his fellows should not perish with the rest of the wise men of Babylon.

19Then was the secret revealed unto Daniel in a night vision. Then Daniel blessed the God of heaven.

20 Daniel answered and said, Blessed be the name of God for ever and ever: for wisdom and might are his:

21 And he changeth the times and the seasons: he removeth kings, and setteth up kings: he giveth wisdom unto the wise, and knowledge to them that know understanding:

22 He revealeth the deep and secret things: he knoweth what is in the darkness, and the light dwelleth with him.

23 I thank you, and praise you, O you God of my fathers, who have given me wisdom and might, and have made known unto me now what we desired of you: for you have now made known unto us the king's matter.

24Therefore Daniel went in unto Arioch, whom the king had ordained to destroy the wise men of Babylon: he went and said thus unto him; Destroy not the wise men of Babylon: bring me in before the king, and I will shew unto the king the interpretation.

25 Then Arioch brought in Daniel before the king in haste, and said thus unto him, I have found a man of the captives of Judah, that will make known unto the king the interpretation.

26 The king answered and said to Daniel, whose name was Belteshazzar, Are you able to make known unto me the dream which I have seen, and the interpretation thereof?

27 Daniel answered in the presence of the king, and said, The secret which the king has demanded cannot the wise men, the astrologers, the magicians, the soothsayers, shew unto the king;

28 But there is a God in heaven that revealeth secrets, and maketh known to the king Nebuchadnezzar what shall be in the latter days. Your dream, and the visions of your head upon your bed, are these;

29 As for you, O king, your thoughts came into your mind upon your bed, what should come to pass hereafter: and he that revealeth secrets maketh known to you what shall come to pass.

30 But as for me, this secret is not revealed to me for any wisdom that I have more than any living, but for their sakes that shall make known the interpretation to the king, and that you mightest know the thoughts of your heart.

31You, O king, sawest, and behold a great image. This great image, whose brightness was excellent, stood before you; and the form thereof was terrible.

32 This image's head was of fine gold, his breast and his arms of silver, his belly and his thighs of brass,

33 His legs of iron, his feet part of iron and part of clay.

34 You sawest till that a stone was cut out without hands, which struck the image upon his feet that were of iron and clay, and brake them to pieces.

35 Then was the iron, the clay, the brass, the silver, and the gold, broken to pieces together, and became like the chaff of the summer threshingfloors; and the wind carried them away, that no place was found for them: and the stone that struck the image became a great mountain, and filled the whole earth.

36This is the dream; and we will tell the interpretation thereof before the king.

37 You , O king, are a king of kings: for the God of heaven has given you a kingdom, power, and strength, and glory.

38 And wheresoever the children of men dwell, the beasts of the field and the fowls of the heaven has he given into yours hand, and has made you ruler over them all. You are this head of gold.

39 And after you shall arise another kingdom inferior to you, and another third kingdom of brass, which shall bear rule over all the earth.

40 And the fourth kingdom shall be strong as iron: forasmuch as iron breaketh in pieces and subdueth all things: and as iron that breaketh all these, shall it break in pieces and bruise.

41 And whereas you sawest the feet and toes, part of potters' clay, and part of iron, the kingdom shall be divided; but there shall be in it of the strength of the iron, forasmuch as you sawest the iron mixed with miry clay.

42 And as the toes of the feet were part of iron, and part of clay, so the kingdom shall be partly strong, and partly broken.

43 And whereas you sawest iron mixed with miry clay, they shall mingle themselves with the seed of men: but they shall not cleave one to another, even as iron is not mixed with clay.

44 And in the days of these kings shall the God of heaven set up a kingdom, which shall never be destroyed: and the kingdom shall not be left to other people, but it shall break in pieces and consume all these kingdoms, and it shall stand for ever.

45 Forasmuch as you sawest that the stone was cut out of the mountain without hands, and that it brake in pieces the iron, the brass, the clay, the silver, and the gold; the great God has made known to the king what shall come to pass hereafter: and the dream is certain, and the interpretation thereof sure.

46Then the king Nebuchadnezzar fell upon his face, and worshipped Daniel, and commanded that they should offer an oblation and sweet odours unto him.

47 The king answered unto Daniel, and said, Of a truth it is, that your God is a God of gods, and a Lord of kings, and a revealer of secrets, seeing you couldest reveal this secret.

48 Then the king made Daniel a great man, and gave him many great gifts, and made him ruler over the whole province of Babylon, and chief of the governors over all the wise men of Babylon.

49 Then Daniel requested of the king, and he set Shadrach, Meshach, and Abed-nego, over the affairs of the province of Babylon: but Daniel sat in the gate of the king.

CHAPTER 3

NEBUCHADNEZZAR the king made an image of gold, whose height was threescore cubits, and the breadth thereof six cubits: he set it up in the plain of Dura, in the province of Babylon.

2 Then Nebuchadnezzar the king sent to gather together the princes, the governors, and the captains, the judges, the treasurers, the counsellers, the sheriffs, and all the rulers of the provinces, to come to the dedication of the image which Nebuchadnezzar the king had set up.

3 Then the princes, the governors, and captains, the judges, the treasurers, the counsellers, the sheriffs, and all the rulers of the provinces, were gathered together unto the dedication of the image that Nebuchadnezzar the king had set up; and they stood before the image that Nebuchadnezzar had set up.

4 Then an herald cried aloud, To you it is commanded, O people, nations, and languages,

5 That at what time you hear the sound of the cornet, flute, harp, sackbut, psaltery, dulcimer, and all kinds of musick, you fall down and worship the golden image that Nebuchadnezzar the king has set up:

6 And whoso falleth not down and worshippeth shall the same hour be cast into the midst of a burning fiery furnace.

7 Therefore at that time, when all the people heard the sound of the cornet, flute, harp, sackbut, psaltery, and all kinds of musick, all the people, the nations, and the languages, fell down and worshipped the golden image that Nebuchadnezzar the king had set up.

8Wherefore at that time certain Chaldeans came near, and accused the Jews.

9 They spake and said to the king Nebuchadnezzar, O king, live for ever.

10 You , O king, have made a decree, that every man that shall hear the sound of the cornet, flute, harp, sackbut, psaltery, and dulcimer, and all kinds of musick, shall fall down and worship the golden image:

11 And whoso falleth not down and worshippeth, that he should be cast into the midst of a burning fiery furnace.

12 There are certain Jews whom you have set over the affairs of the province of Babylon, Shadrach, Meshach, and Abed-nego; these men, O king, have not regarded you: they serve not your gods, nor worship the golden image which you have set up.

13Then Nebuchadnezzar in his rage and fury commanded to bring Shadrach, Meshach, and Abed-nego. Then they brought these men before the king.

14 Nebuchadnezzar spake and said unto them, Is it true, O Shadrach, Meshach, and Abed-nego, do not you serve my gods, nor worship the golden image which I have set up?

15 Now if you be ready that at what time you hear the sound of the cornet, flute, harp, sackbut, psaltery, and dulcimer, and all kinds of musick, you fall down and worship the image which I have made; well: but if you worship not, you shall be cast the same hour into the midst of a burning fiery furnace; and who is that God that shall deliver you out of my hands?

16 Shadrach, Meshach, and Abed-nego, answered and said to the king, O Nebuchadnezzar, we are not careful to answer you in this matter.

17 If it be so, our God whom we serve is able to deliver us from the burning fiery furnace, and he will deliver us out of yours hand, O king.

18 But if not, be it known unto you, O king, that we will not serve your gods, nor worship the golden image which you have set up.

19Then was Nebuchadnezzar full of fury, and the form of his visage was changed against Shadrach, Meshach, and Abed-nego: therefore he spake, and commanded that they should heat the furnace one seven times more than it was wont to be heated.

20 And he commanded the most mighty men that were in his army to bind Shadrach, Meshach, and Abed-nego, and to cast them into the burning fiery furnace.

21 Then these men were bound in their coats, their hosen, and their hats, and their other garments, and were cast into the midst of the burning fiery furnace.

22 Therefore because the king's commandment was urgent, and the furnace exceeding hot, the flame of the fire slew those men that took up Shadrach, Meshach, and Abed-nego.

23 And these three men, Shadrach, Meshach, and Abed-nego, fell down bound into the midst of the burning fiery furnace.

24 Then Nebuchadnezzar the king was astonied, and rose up in haste, and spake, and said unto his counsellers, Did not we cast three men bound into the midst of the fire? They answered and said unto the king, True, O king.

25 He answered and said, Lo, I see four men loose, walking in the midst of the fire, and they have no hurt; and the form of the fourth is like the Son of God.

26Then Nebuchadnezzar came near to the mouth of the burning fiery furnace, and spake, and said, Shadrach, Meshach, and Abed-nego, you servants of the most high God, come forth, and come hither. Then Shadrach, Meshach, and Abed-nego, came forth of the midst of the fire.

27 And the princes, governors, and captains, and the king's counsellers, being gathered together, saw these men, upon whose bodies the fire had no power, nor was an hair of their head singed, neither were their coats changed, nor the smell of fire had passed on them.

28 Then Nebuchadnezzar spake, and said, Blessed be the God of Shadrach, Meshach, and Abed-nego, who has sent his angel, and delivered his servants that trusted in him, and have changed the king's word, and yielded their bodies, that they might not serve nor worship any god, except their own God.

29 Therefore I make a decree, That every people, nation, and language, which speak any thing amiss against the God of Shadrach, Meshach, and Abed-nego, shall be cut in pieces, and their houses shall be made a dunghill: because there is no other God that can deliver after this sort.

30 Then the king promoted Shadrach, Meshach, and Abed-nego, in the province of Babylon.

CHAPTER 4

NEBUCHADNEZZAR the king, unto all people, nations, and languages, that dwell in all the earth; Peace be multiplied unto you.

2 I thought it good to shew the signs and wonders that the high God has created toward me.

3 How great are his signs! and how mighty are his wonders! his kingdom is an everlasting kingdom, and his dominion is from generation to generation.

4I Nebuchadnezzar was at rest in my house, and flourishing in my palace:

5 I saw a dream which made me afraid, and the thoughts upon my bed and the visions of my head troubled me.

6 Therefore made I a decree to bring in all the wise men of Babylon before me, that they might make known unto me the interpretation of the dream.

7 Then came in the magicians, the astrologers, the Chaldeans, and the soothsayers: and I told the dream before them; but they did not make known unto me the interpretation thereof.

8But at the last Daniel came in before me, whose name was Belteshazzar, according to the name of my god, and in whom is the spirit of the holy gods: and before him I told the dream, saying,

9 O Belteshazzar, master of the magicians, because I know that the spirit of the holy gods is in you, and no secret troubleth you, tell me the visions of my dream that I have seen, and the interpretation thereof.

10 Thus were the visions of my head in my bed; I saw, and behold a tree in the midst of the earth, and the height thereof was great.

11 The tree grew, and was strong, and the height thereof reached unto heaven, and the sight thereof to the end of all the earth:

12 The leaves thereof were fair, and the fruit thereof much, and in it was meat for all: the beasts of the field had shadow under it, and the fowls of the heaven dwelt in the boughs thereof, and all flesh was fed of it.

13 I saw in the visions of my head upon my bed, and, behold, a watcher and an holy one came down from heaven;

14 He cried aloud, and said thus, Hew down the tree, and cut off his branches, shake off his leaves, and scatter his fruit: let the beasts get away from under it, and the fowls from his branches:

15 Nevertheless leave the stump of his roots in the earth, even with a band of iron and brass, in the tender grass of the field; and let it be wet with the dew of heaven, and let his portion be with the beasts in the grass of the earth:

16 Let his heart be changed from man's, and let a beast's heart be given unto him; and let seven times pass over him.

17 This matter is by the decree of the watchers, and the demand by the word of the holy ones: to the intent that the living may know that the most High ruleth in the kingdom of men, and giveth it to whomsoever he will, and setteth up over it the basest of men.

18 This dream I king Nebuchadnezzar have seen. Now you , O Belteshazzar, declare the interpretation thereof, forasmuch as all the wise men of my kingdom are not able to make known unto me the interpretation: but you are able; for the spirit of the holy gods is in you.

19 Then Daniel, whose name was Belteshazzar, was astonied for one hour, and his thoughts troubled him. The king spake, and said, Belteshazzar, let not the dream, or the interpretation thereof, trouble you. Belteshazzar answered and said, My lord, the dream be to them that hate you, and the interpretation thereof to yours enemies.

20 The tree that you sawest, which grew, and was strong, whose height reached unto the heaven, and the sight thereof to all the earth;

21 Whose leaves were fair, and the fruit thereof much, and in it was meat for all; under which the beasts of the field dwelt, and upon whose branches the fowls of the heaven had their habitation:

22 It is you , O king, that are grown and become strong: for your greatness is grown, and reacheth unto heaven, and your dominion to the end of the earth.

23 And whereas the king saw a watcher and an holy one coming down from heaven, and saying, Hew the tree down, and destroy it; yet leave the stump of the roots thereof in the earth, even with a band of iron and brass, in the tender grass of the field; and let it be wet with the dew of heaven, and let his portion be with the beasts of the field, till seven times pass over him;

24 This is the interpretation, O king, and this is the decree of the most High, which is come upon my lord the king:

25 That they shall drive you from men, and your dwelling shall be with the beasts of the field, and they shall make you to eat grass as oxen, and they shall wet you with the dew of heaven, and seven times shall pass over you, till you know that the most High ruleth in the kingdom of men, and giveth it to whomsoever he will.

26 And whereas they commanded to leave the stump of the tree roots; your kingdom shall be sure unto you, after that you shalt have known that the heavens do rule.

27 Wherefore, O king, let my counsel be acceptable unto you, and break off your sins by righteousness, and yours iniquities by shewing mercy to the poor; if it may be a lengthening of your tranquillity.

28 All this came upon the king Nebuchadnezzar.

29 At the end of twelve months he walked in the palace of the kingdom of Babylon.

30 The king spake, and said, Is not this great Babylon, that I have built for the house of the kingdom by the might of my power, and for the honour of my majesty?

31 While the word was in the king's mouth, there fell a voice from heaven, saying, O king Nebuchadnezzar, to you it is spoken; The kingdom is departed from you.

32 And they shall drive you from men, and your dwelling shall be with the beasts of the field: they shall make you to eat grass as oxen, and seven times shall pass over you, until you know that the most High ruleth in the kingdom of men, and giveth it to whomsoever he will.

33 The same hour was the thing fulfilled upon Nebuchadnezzar: and he was driven from men, and did eat grass as oxen, and his body was wet with the dew of heaven, till his hairs were grown like eagles' feathers, and his nails like birds' claws.

34 And at the end of the days I Nebuchadnezzar lifted up my eyes unto heaven, and my understanding returned unto me, and I blessed the most High, and I praised and honoured him that liveth for ever, whose dominion is an everlasting dominion, and his kingdom is from generation to generation:

35 And all the inhabitants of the earth are reputed as nothing: and he doeth according to his will in the army of heaven, and among the inhabitants of the earth: and none can stay his hand, or say unto him, What doest you ?

36 At the same time my reason returned unto me; and for the glory of my kingdom, my honour and brightness returned unto me; and my counsellers and my lords sought unto me; and I was established in my kingdom, and excellent majesty was added unto me.

37 Now I Nebuchadnezzar praise and extol and honour the King of heaven, all whose works are truth, and his ways judgment: and those that walk in pride he is able to abase.

CHAPTER 5

BELSHAZZAR the king made a great feast to a thousand of his lords, and drank wine before the thousand.

2 Belshazzar, whiles he tasted the wine, commanded to bring the golden and silver vessels which his father Nebuchadnezzar had taken out of the temple which was in Jerusalem; that the king, and his princes, his wives, and his concubines, might drink therein.

3 Then they brought the golden vessels that were taken out of the temple of the house of God which was at Jerusalem; and the king, and his princes, his wives, and his concubines, drank in them.

4 They drank wine, and praised the gods of gold, and of silver, of brass, of iron, of wood, and of stone.

5 In the same hour came forth fingers of a man's hand, and wrote over against the candlestick upon the plaister of the wall of the king's palace: and the king saw the part of the hand that wrote.

6 Then the king's countenance was changed, and his thoughts troubled him, so that the joints of his loins were loosed, and his knees struck one against another.

7 The king cried aloud to bring in the astrologers, the Chaldeans, and the soothsayers. And the king spake, and said to the wise men of Babylon, Whosoever shall read this writing, and shew me the interpretation thereof, shall be clothed with scarlet, and have a chain of gold about his neck, and shall be the third ruler in the kingdom.

8 Then came in all the king's wise men: but they could not read the writing, nor make known to the king the interpretation thereof.

9 Then was king Belshazzar greatly troubled, and his countenance was changed in him, and his lords were astonied.

10 Now the queen, by reason of the words of the king and his lords, came into the banquet house: and the queen spake and said, O king, live for ever: let not your thoughts trouble you, nor let your countenance be changed:

11 There is a man in your kingdom, in whom is the spirit of the holy gods; and in the days of your father light and understanding and wisdom, like the wisdom of the gods, was found in him; whom the king Nebuchadnezzar your father, the king, I say, your father, made master of the magicians, astrologers, Chaldeans, and soothsayers;

12 Forasmuch as an excellent spirit, and knowledge, and understanding, interpreting of dreams, and shewing of hard sentences, and dissolving of doubts, were found in the same Daniel, whom the king named Belteshazzar: now let Daniel be called, and he will shew the interpretation.

13 Then was Daniel brought in before the king. And the king spake and said unto Daniel, Are you that Daniel, which are of the children of the captivity of Judah, whom the king my father brought out of Jewry?

14 I have even heard of you, that the spirit of the gods is in you, and that light and understanding and excellent wisdom is found in you.

15 And now the wise men, the astrologers, have been brought in before me, that they should read this writing, and make known unto me the interpretation thereof: but they could not shew the interpretation of the thing:

16 And I have heard of you, that you can make interpretations, and dissolve doubts: now if you can read the writing, and make known to me the interpretation thereof, you shalt be clothed with scarlet, and have a chain of gold about your neck, and shalt be the third ruler in the kingdom.

17 Then Daniel answered and said before the king, Let your gifts be to yourself, and give your rewards to another; yet I will read the writing unto the king, and make known to him the interpretation.

18 O you king, the most high God gave Nebuchadnezzar your father a kingdom, and majesty, and glory, and honour:

19 And for the majesty that he gave him, all people, nations, and languages, trembled and feared before him: whom he would he slew; and whom he would he kept alive; and whom he would he set up; and whom he would he put down.

20 But when his heart was lifted up, and his mind hardened in pride, he was deposed from his kingly throne, and they took his glory from him:

21 And he was driven from the sons of men; and his heart was made like the beasts, and his dwelling was with the wild asses: they fed him with grass like oxen, and his body was wet with the dew of heaven; till he knew that the most high God ruled in the kingdom of men, and that he appointeth over it whomsoever he will.

22 And you his son, O Belshazzar, have not humbled yours heart, though you knewest all this;

23 But have lifted up yourself against the Lord of heaven; and they have brought the vessels of his house before you, and you , and your lords, your wives, and your concubines, have drunk wine in them; and you have praised the gods of silver, and gold, of brass, iron, wood, and stone, which see not, nor hear, nor know: and the God in whose hand your breath is, and whose are all your ways, have you not glorified:

24 Then was the part of the hand sent from him; and this writing was written.

25 And this is the writing that was written, MENE, MENE, TEKEL, UPHARSIN.

26 This is the interpretation of the thing: MENE; God has numbered your kingdom, and finished it.

27 TEKEL; You are weighed in the balances, and are found wanting.

28 PERES; Your kingdom is divided, and given to the Medes and Persians.

29 Then commanded Belshazzar, and they clothed Daniel with scarlet, and put a chain of gold about his neck, and made a proclamation concerning him, that he should be the third ruler in the kingdom.

30 In that night was Belshazzar the king of the Chaldeans slain.

31 And Darius the Median took the kingdom, being about threescore and two years old.

CHAPTER 6

IT pleased Darius to set over the kingdom an hundred and twenty princes, which should be over the whole kingdom;

2 And over these three presidents; of whom Daniel was first: that the princes might give accounts unto them, and the king should have no damage.

3 Then this Daniel was preferred above the presidents and princes, because an excellent spirit was in him; and the king thought to set him over the whole realm.

4 Then the presidents and princes sought to find occasion against Daniel concerning the kingdom; but they could find none occasion nor fault; forasmuch as he was faithful, neither was there any error or fault found in him.

5 Then said these men, We shall not find any occasion against this Daniel, except we find it against him concerning the law of his God.

6 Then these presidents and princes assembled together to the king, and said thus unto him, King Darius, live for ever.

7 All the presidents of the kingdom, the governors, and the princes, the counsellers, and the captains, have consulted together to establish a royal statute, and to make a firm decree, that whosoever shall ask a petition of any God or man for thirty days, save of you, O king, he shall be cast into the den of lions.

8 Now, O king, establish the decree, and sign the writing, that it be not changed, according to the law of the Medes and Persians, which altereth not.

9 Wherefore king Darius signed the writing and the decree.

10 Now when Daniel knew that the writing was signed, he went into his house; and his windows being open in his chamber toward Jerusalem, he kneeled upon his knees three times a day, and prayed, and gave thanks before his God, as he did aforetime.

11 Then these men assembled, and found Daniel praying and making supplication before his God.

12 Then they came near, and spake before the king concerning the king's decree; Have you not signed a decree, that every man that shall ask a petition of any God or man within thirty days, save of you, O king, shall be cast into the den of lions? The king answered and said, The thing is true, according to the law of the Medes and Persians, which altereth not.

13 Then answered they and said before the king, That Daniel, which is of the children of the captivity of Judah, regardeth not you, O king, nor the decree that you have signed, but maketh his petition three times a day.

14 Then the king, when he heard these words, was sore displeased with himself, and set his heart on Daniel to deliver him: and he laboured till the going down of the sun to deliver him.

15 Then these men assembled unto the king, and said unto the king, Know, O king, that the law of the Medes and Persians is, That no decree nor statute which the king establisheth may be changed.

16 Then the king commanded, and they brought Daniel, and cast him into the den of lions. Now the king spake and said unto Daniel, Your God whom you servest continually, he will deliver you.

17 And a stone was brought, and laid upon the mouth of the den; and the king sealed it with his own signet, and with the signet of his lords; that the purpose might not be changed concerning Daniel.

18 Then the king went to his palace, and passed the night fasting: neither were instruments of musick brought before him: and his sleep went from him.

19 Then the king arose very early in the morning, and went in haste unto the den of lions.

20 And when he came to the den, he cried with a lamentable voice unto Daniel: and the king spake and said to Daniel, O Daniel, servant of the living God, is your God, whom you servest continually, able to deliver you from the lions?

21 Then said Daniel unto the king, O king, live for ever.

22 My God has sent his angel, and has shut the lions' mouths, that they have not hurt me: forasmuch as before him innocency was found in me; and also before you, O king, have I done no hurt.

23 Then was the king exceeding glad for him, and commanded that they should take Daniel up out of the den. So Daniel was taken up out of the den, and no manner of hurt was found upon him, because he believed in his God.

24 And the king commanded, and they brought those men which had accused Daniel, and they cast them into the den of lions, them, their children, and their wives; and the lions had the mastery of them, and brake all their bones in pieces or ever they came at the bottom of the den.

25 Then king Darius wrote unto all people, nations, and languages, that dwell in all the earth; Peace be multiplied unto you.

26 I make a decree, That in every dominion of my kingdom men tremble and fear before the God of Daniel: for he is the living God, and stedfast for ever, and his kingdom that which shall not be destroyed, and his dominion shall be even unto the end.

27 He delivereth and rescueth, and he worketh signs and wonders in heaven and in earth, who has delivered Daniel from the power of the lions.

28 So this Daniel prospered in the reign of Darius, and in the reign of Cyrus the Persian.

CHAPTER 7

IN the first year of Belshazzar king of Babylon Daniel had a dream and visions of his head upon his bed: then he wrote the dream, and told the sum of the matters.

2 Daniel spake and said, I saw in my vision by night, and, behold, the four winds of the heaven strove upon the great sea.

3 And four great beasts came up from the sea, diverse one from another.

4 The first was like a lion, and had eagle's wings: I beheld till the wings thereof were plucked, and it was lifted up from the earth, and made stand upon the feet as a man, and a man's heart was given to it.

5 And behold another beast, a second, like to a bear, and it raised up itself on one side, and it had three ribs in the mouth of it between the teeth of it: and they said thus unto it, Arise, devour much flesh.

6 After this I beheld, and lo another, like a leopard, which had upon the back of it four wings of a fowl; the beast had also four heads; and dominion was given to it.

7 After this I saw in the night visions, and behold a fourth beast, dreadful and terrible, and strong exceedingly; and it had great iron teeth: it devoured and brake in pieces, and stamped the residue with the feet of it: and it was diverse from all the beasts that were before it; and it had ten horns.

8 I considered the horns, and, behold, there came up among them another little horn, before whom there were three of the first horns plucked up by the roots: and, behold, in this horn were eyes like the eyes of man, and a mouth speaking great things.

9 I beheld till the thrones were cast down, and the Ancient of days did sit, whose garment was white as snow, and the hair of his head like the pure wool: his throne was like the fiery flame, and his wheels as burning fire.

10 A fiery stream issued and came forth from before him: thousand thousands ministered unto him, and ten thousand times ten thousand stood before him: the judgment was set, and the books were opened.

11 I beheld then because of the voice of the great words which the horn spake: I beheld even till the beast was slain, and his body destroyed, and given to the burning flame.

12 As concerning the rest of the beasts, they had their dominion taken away: yet their lives were prolonged for a season and time.

13 I saw in the night visions, and, behold, one like the Son of man came with the clouds of heaven, and came to the Ancient of days, and they brought him near before him.

14 And there was given him dominion, and glory, and a kingdom, that all people, nations, and languages, should serve him: his dominion is an everlasting dominion, which shall not pass away, and his kingdom that which shall not be destroyed.

15 I Daniel was grieved in my spirit in the midst of my body, and the visions of my head troubled me.

16 I came near unto one of them that stood by, and asked him the truth of all this. So he told me, and made me know the interpretation of the things.

17 These great beasts, which are four, are four kings, which shall arise out of the earth.

18 But the saints of the most High shall take the kingdom, and possess the kingdom for ever, even for ever and ever.

19 Then I would know the truth of the fourth beast, which was diverse from all the others, exceeding dreadful, whose teeth were of iron, and his nails of brass; which devoured, brake in pieces, and stamped the residue with his feet;

20 And of the ten horns that were in his head, and of the other which came up, and before whom three fell; even of that horn that had eyes, and a mouth that spake very great things, whose look was more stout than his fellows.

21 I beheld, and the same horn made war with the saints, and prevailed against them;

22 Until the Ancient of days came, and judgment was given to the saints of the most High; and the time came that the saints possessed the kingdom.

23 Thus he said, The fourth beast shall be the fourth kingdom upon earth, which shall be diverse from all kingdoms, and shall devour the whole earth, and shall tread it down, and break it in pieces.

24 And the ten horns out of this kingdom are ten kings that shall arise: and another shall rise after them; and he shall be diverse from the first, and he shall subdue three kings.

25 And he shall speak great words against the most High, and shall wear out the saints of the most High, and think to change times and laws: and they shall be given into his hand until a time and times and the dividing of time.

26 But the judgment shall sit, and they shall take away his dominion, to consume and to destroy it unto the end.

27 And the kingdom and dominion, and the greatness of the kingdom under the whole heaven, shall be given to the people of the saints of the most High, whose kingdom is an everlasting kingdom, and all dominions shall serve and obey him.

28 Hitherto is the end of the matter. As for me Daniel, my cogitations much troubled me, and my countenance changed in me: but I kept the matter in my heart.

CHAPTER 8

IN the third year of the reign of king Belshazzar a vision appeared unto me, even unto me Daniel, after that which appeared unto me at the first.

2 And I saw in a vision; and it came to pass, when I saw, that I was at Shushan in the palace, which is in the province of Elam; and I saw in a vision, and I was by the river of Ulai.

3 Then I lifted up my eyes, and saw, and, behold, there stood before the river a ram which had two horns: and the two horns were high; but one was higher than the other, and the higher came up last.

4 I saw the ram pushing westward, and northward, and southward; so that no beasts might stand before him, neither was there any that could deliver out of his hand; but he did according to his will, and became great.

5 And as I was considering, behold, an he goat came from the west on the face of the whole earth, and touched not the ground: and the goat had a notable horn between his eyes.

6 And he came to the ram that had two horns, which I had seen standing before the river, and ran unto him in the fury of his power.

7 And I saw him come close unto the ram, and he was moved with choler against him, and struck the ram, and brake his two horns: and there was no power in the ram to stand before him, but he cast him down to the ground, and stamped upon him: and there was none that could deliver the ram out of his hand.

8 Therefore the he goat waxed very great: and when he was strong, the great horn was broken; and for it came up four notable ones toward the four winds of heaven.

9 And out of one of them came forth a little horn, which waxed exceeding great, toward the south, and toward the east, and toward the pleasant land.

10 And it waxed great, even to the host of heaven; and it cast down some of the host and of the stars to the ground, and stamped upon them.

11 Yea, he magnified himself even to the prince of the host, and by him the daily sacrifice was taken away, and the place of his sanctuary was cast down.

12 And an host was given him against the daily sacrifice by reason of transgression, and it cast down the truth to the ground; and it practised, and prospered.

13 Then I heard one saint speaking, and another saint said unto that certain saint which spake, How long shall be the vision concerning the daily sacrifice, and the transgression of desolation, to give both the sanctuary and the host to be trodden under foot?

14 And he said unto me, Unto two thousand and three hundred days; then shall the sanctuary be cleansed.

15 And it came to pass, when I, even I Daniel, had seen the vision, and sought for the meaning, then, behold, there stood before me as the appearance of a man.

16 And I heard a man's voice between the banks of Ulai, which called, and said, Gabriel, make this man to understand the vision.

17 So he came near where I stood: and when he came, I was afraid, and fell upon my face: but he said unto me, Understand, O son of man: for at the time of the end shall be the vision.

18 Now as he was speaking with me, I was in a deep sleep on my face toward the ground: but he touched me, and set me upright.

19 And he said, Behold, I will make you know what shall be in the last end of the indignation: for at the time appointed the end shall be.

20 The ram which you sawest having two horns are the kings of Media and Persia.

21 And the rough goat is the king of Grecia: and the great horn that is between his eyes is the first king.

22 Now that being broken, whereas four stood up for it, four kingdoms shall stand up out of the nation, but not in his power.

23 And in the latter time of their kingdom, when the transgressors are come to the full, a king of fierce countenance, and understanding dark sentences, shall stand up.

24 And his power shall be mighty, but not by his own power: and he shall destroy wonderfully, and shall prosper, and practise, and shall destroy the mighty and the holy people.

25 And through his policy also he shall cause craft to prosper in his hand; and he shall magnify himself in his heart, and by peace shall destroy many: he shall also stand up against the Prince of princes; but he shall be broken without hand.

26 And the vision of the evening and the morning which was told is true: wherefore shut you up the vision; for it shall be for many days.

27 And I Daniel fainted, and was sick certain days; afterward I rose up, and did the king's business; and I was astonished at the vision, but none understood it.

CHAPTER 9

IN the first year of Darius the son of Ahasuerus, of the seed of the Medes, which was made king over the realm of the Chaldeans;

2 In the first year of his reign I Daniel understood by books the number of the years, whereof the word of the LORD came to Jeremiah the prophet, that he would accomplish seventy years in the desolations of Jerusalem.

3 And I set my face unto the Lord God, to seek by prayer and supplications, with fasting, and sackcloth, and ashes:

4 And I prayed unto the LORD my God, and made my confession, and said, O Lord, the great and dreadful God, keeping the covenant and mercy to them that love him, and to them that keep his commandments;

5 We have sinned, and have committed iniquity, and have done wickedly, and have rebelled, even by departing from your precepts and from your judgments:

6 Neither have we hearkened unto your servants the prophets, which spake in your name to our kings, our princes, and our fathers, and to all the people of the land.

7 O Lord, righteousness belongeth unto you, but unto us confusion of faces, as at this day; to the men of Judah, and to the inhabitants of Jerusalem, and unto all Israel, that are near, and that are far off, through all the countries whither you have driven them, because of their trespass that they have trespassed against you.

8 O Lord, to us belongeth confusion of face, to our kings, to our princes, and to our fathers, because we have sinned against you.

9 To the Lord our God belong mercies and forgivenesses, though we have rebelled against him;

10 Neither have we obeyed the voice of the LORD our God, to walk in his laws, which he set before us by his servants the prophets.

11 Yea, all Israel have transgressed your law, even by departing, that they might not obey your voice; therefore the curse is poured upon us, and the oath that is written in the law of Moses the servant of God, because we have sinned against him.

12 And he has confirmed his words, which he spake against us, and against our judges that judged us, by bringing upon us a great evil: for under the whole heaven has not been done as has been done upon Jerusalem.

13 As it is written in the law of Moses, all this evil is come upon us: yet made we not our prayer before the LORD our God, that we might turn from our iniquities, and understand your truth.

14 Therefore has the LORD watched upon the evil, and brought it upon us: for the LORD our God is righteous in all his works which he doeth: for we obeyed not his voice.

15 And now, O Lord our God, that have brought your people forth out of the land of Egypt with a mighty hand, and have gotten you renown, as at this day; we have sinned, we have done wickedly.

160 Lord, according to all your righteousness, I beseech you, let yours anger and your fury be turned away from your city Jerusalem, your holy mountain: because for our sins, and for the iniquities of our fathers, Jerusalem and your people are become a reproach to all that are about us.

17 Now therefore, O our God, hear the prayer of your servant, and his supplications, and cause your face to shine upon your sanctuary that is desolate, for the Lord's sake.

18 O my God, incline yours ear, and hear; open yours eyes, and behold our desolations, and the city which is called by your name: for we do not present our supplications before you for our righteousnesses, but for your great mercies.

19 O Lord, hear; O Lord, forgive; O Lord, hearken and do; defer not, for yours own sake, O my God: for your city and your people are called by your name.

20 And whiles I was speaking, and praying, and confessing my sin and the sin of my people Israel, and presenting my supplication before the LORD my God for the holy mountain of my God;

21 Yea, whiles I was speaking in prayer, even the man Gabriel, whom I had seen in the vision at the beginning, being caused to fly swiftly, touched me about the time of the evening oblation.

22 And he informed me, and talked with me, and said, O Daniel, I am now come forth to give you skill and understanding.

23 At the beginning of your supplications the commandment came forth, and I am come to shew you; for you are greatly beloved: therefore understand the matter, and consider the vision.

24 Seventy weeks are determined upon your people and upon your holy city, to finish the transgression, and to make an end of sins, and to make reconciliation for iniquity, and to bring in everlasting righteousness, and to seal up the vision and prophecy, and to anoint the most Holy.

25 Know therefore and understand, that from the going forth of the commandment to restore and to build Jerusalem unto the Messiah the Prince shall be seven weeks, and threescore and two weeks: the street shall be built again, and the wall, even in troublous times.

26 And after threescore and two weeks shall Messiah be cut off, but not for himself: and the people of the prince that shall come shall destroy the city and the sanctuary; and the end thereof shall be with a flood, and unto the end of the war desolations are determined.

27 And he shall confirm the covenant with many for one week: and in the midst of the week he shall cause the sacrifice and the oblation to cease, and for the overspreading of abominations he shall make it desolate, even until the consummation, and that determined shall be poured upon the desolate.

CHAPTER 10

IN the third year of Cyrus king of Persia a thing was revealed unto Daniel, whose name was called Belteshazzar; and the thing was true, but the time appointed was long: and he understood the thing, and had understanding of the vision.

2 In those days I Daniel was mourning three full weeks.

3 I ate no pleasant bread, neither came flesh nor wine in my mouth, neither did I anoint myself at all, till three whole weeks were fulfilled.

4 And in the four and twentieth day of the first month, as I was by the side of the great river, which is Hiddekel;

5 Then I lifted up my eyes, and looked, and behold a certain man clothed in linen, whose loins were girded with fine gold of Uphaz:

6 His body also was like the beryl, and his face as the appearance of lightning, and his eyes as lamps of fire, and his arms and his feet like in colour to polished brass, and the voice of his words like the voice of a multitude.

7 And I Daniel alone saw the vision: for the men that were with me saw not the vision; but a great quaking fell upon them, so that they fled to hide themselves.

8 Therefore I was left alone, and saw this great vision, and there remained no strength in me: for my comeliness was turned in me into corruption, and I retained no strength.

9 Yet heard I the voice of his words: and when I heard the voice of his words, then was I in a deep sleep on my face, and my face toward the ground.

10 And, behold, an hand touched me, which set me upon my knees and upon the palms of my hands.

11 And he said unto me, O Daniel, a man greatly beloved, understand the words that I speak unto you, and stand upright: for unto you am I now sent. And when he had spoken this word unto me, I stood trembling.

12 Then said he unto me, Fear not, Daniel: for from the first day that you did set yours heart to understand, and to chasten yourself before your God, your words were heard, and I am come for your words.

13 But the prince of the kingdom of Persia withstood me one and twenty days: but, lo, Michael, one of the chief princes, came to help me; and I remained there with the kings of Persia.

14 Now I am come to make you understand what shall befall your people in the latter days: for yet the vision is for many days.

15 And when he had spoken such words unto me, I set my face toward the ground, and I became dumb.

16 And, behold, one like the similitude of the sons of men touched my lips: then I opened my mouth, and spake, and said unto him that stood before me, O my lord, by the vision my sorrows are turned upon me, and I have retained no strength.

17 For how can the servant of this my lord talk with this my lord? for as for me, straightway there remained no strength in me, neither is there breath left in me.

18 Then there came again and touched me one like the appearance of a man, and he strengthened me,

19 And said, O man greatly beloved, fear not: peace be unto you, be strong, yea, be strong. And when he had spoken unto me, I was strengthened, and said, Let my lord speak; for you have strengthened me.

20 Then said he, Knowest you wherefore I come unto you? and now will I return to fight with the prince of Persia: and when I am gone forth, lo, the prince of Grecia shall come.

21 But I will shew you that which is noted in the scripture of truth: and there is none that holdeth with me in these things, but Michael your prince.

CHAPTER 11

ALSO I in the first year of Darius the Mede, even I, stood to confirm and to strengthen him.

2 And now will I shew you the truth. Behold, there shall stand up yet three kings in Persia; and the fourth shall be far richer than they all: and by his strength through his riches he shall stir up all against the realm of Grecia.

3 And a mighty king shall stand up, that shall rule with great dominion, and do according to his will.

4 And when he shall stand up, his kingdom shall be broken, and shall be divided toward the four winds of heaven; and not to his posterity, nor according to his dominion which he ruled: for his kingdom shall be plucked up, even for others beside those.

5 And the king of the south shall be strong, and one of his princes; and he shall be strong above him, and have dominion; his dominion shall be a great dominion.

6 And in the end of years they shall join themselves together; for the king's daughter of the south shall come to the king of the north to make an agreement: but she shall not retain the power of the arm; neither shall he stand, nor his arm: but she shall be given up, and they that brought her, and he that begat her, and he that strengthened her in these times.

7 But out of a branch of her roots shall one stand up in his estate, which shall come with an army, and shall enter into the fortress of the king of the north, and shall deal against them, and shall prevail:

8 And shall also carry captives into Egypt their gods, with their princes, and with their precious vessels of silver and of gold; and he shall continue more years than the king of the north.

9 So the king of the south shall come into his kingdom, and shall return into his own land.

10 But his sons shall be stirred up, and shall assemble a multitude of great forces: and one shall certainly come, and overflow, and pass through: then shall he return, and be stirred up, even to his fortress.

11 And the king of the south shall be moved with choler, and shall come forth and fight with him, even with the king of the north: and he shall set forth a great multitude; but the multitude shall be given into his hand.

12 And when he has taken away the multitude, his heart shall be lifted up; and he shall cast down many ten thousands: but he shall not be strengthened by it.

13 For the king of the north shall return, and shall set forth a multitude greater than the former, and shall certainly come after certain years with a great army and with much riches.

14 And in those times there shall many stand up against the king of the south: also the robbers of your people shall exalt themselves to establish the vision; but they shall fall.

15 So the king of the north shall come, and cast up a mount, and take the most fenced cities: and the arms of the south shall not withstand, neither his chosen people, neither shall there be any strength to withstand.

16 But he that comes against him shall do according to his own will, and none shall stand before him: and he shall stand in the glorious land, which by his hand shall be consumed.

17 He shall also set his face to enter with the strength of his whole kingdom, and upright ones with him; thus shall he do: and he shall give him the daughter of women, corrupting her: but she shall not stand on his side, neither be for him.

18 After this shall he turn his face unto the isles, and shall take many: but a prince for his own behalf shall cause the reproach offered by him to cease; without his own reproach he shall cause it to turn upon him.

19 Then he shall turn his face toward the fort of his own land: but he shall stumble and fall, and not be found.

20 Then shall stand up in his estate a raiser of taxes in the glory of the kingdom: but within few days he shall be destroyed, neither in anger, nor in battle.

21 And in his estate shall stand up a vile person, to whom they shall not give the honour of the kingdom: but he shall come in peaceably, and obtain the kingdom by flatteries.

22 And with the arms of a flood shall they be overflown from before him, and shall be broken; yea, also the prince of the covenant.

23 And after the league made with him he shall work deceitfully: for he shall come up, and shall become strong with a small people.

24 He shall enter peaceably even upon the fattest places of the province; and he shall do that which his fathers have not done, nor his fathers' fathers; he shall scatter among them the prey, and spoil, and riches: yea, and he shall forecast his devices against the strong holds, even for a time.

25 And he shall stir up his power and his courage against the king of the south with a great army; and the king of the south shall be stirred up to battle with a very great and mighty army; but he shall not stand: for they shall forecast devices against him.

26 Yea, they that feed of the portion of his meat shall destroy him, and his army shall overflow: and many shall fall down slain.

27 And both these kings' hearts shall be to do mischief, and they shall speak lies at one table; but it shall not prosper: for yet the end shall be at the time appointed.

28 Then shall he return into his land with great riches; and his heart shall be against the holy covenant; and he shall do exploits, and return to his own land.

29 At the time appointed he shall return, and come toward the south; but it shall not be as the former, or as the latter.

30 For the ships of Chittim shall come against him: therefore he shall be grieved, and return, and have indignation against the holy covenant: so shall he do; he shall even return, and have intelligence with them that forsake the holy covenant.

31 And arms shall stand on his part, and they shall pollute the sanctuary of strength, and shall take away the daily sacrifice, and they shall place the abomination that maketh desolate.

32 And such as do wickedly against the covenant shall he corrupt by flatteries: but the people that do know their God shall be strong, and do exploits.

33 And they that understand among the people shall instruct many: yet they shall fall by the sword, and by flame, by captivity, and by spoil, many days.

34 Now when they shall fall, they shall be holpen with a little help: but many shall cleave to them with flatteries.

35 And some of them of understanding shall fall, to try them, and to purge, and to make them white, even to the time of the end: because it is yet for a time appointed.

36 And the king shall do according to his will; and he shall exalt himself, and magnify himself above every god, and shall speak marvellous things against the God of gods, and shall prosper till the indignation be accomplished: for that that is determined shall be done.

37 Neither shall he regard the God of his fathers, nor the desire of women, nor regard any god: for he shall magnify himself above all.

38 But in his estate shall he honour the God of forces: and a god whom his fathers knew not shall he honour with gold, and silver, and with precious stones, and pleasant things.

39 Thus shall he do in the most strong holds with a strange god, whom he shall acknowledge and increase with glory: and he shall cause them to rule over many, and shall divide the land for gain.

40 And at the time of the end shall the king of the south push at him: and the king of the north shall come against him like a whirlwind, with chariots, and with horsemen, and with many ships; and he shall enter into the countries, and shall overflow and pass over.

41 He shall enter also into the glorious land, and many countries shall be overthrown: but these shall escape out of his hand, even Edom, and Moab, and the chief of the children of Ammon.

42 He shall stretch forth his hand also upon the countries: and the land of Egypt shall not escape.

43 But he shall have power over the treasures of gold and of silver, and over all the precious things of Egypt: and the Libyans and the Ethiopians shall be at his steps.

44 But tidings out of the east and out of the north shall trouble him: therefore he shall go forth with great fury to destroy, and utterly to make away many.

45 And he shall plant the tabernacles of his palace between the seas in the glorious holy mountain; yet he shall come to his end, and none shall help him.

CHAPTER 12

AND at that time shall Michael stand up, the great prince which standeth for the children of your people: and there shall be a time of trouble, such as never was since there was a nation even to that same time: and at that time your people shall be delivered, every one that shall be found written in the book.

2 And many of them that sleep in the dust of the earth shall awake, some to everlasting life, and some to shame and everlasting contempt.

3 And they that be wise shall shine as the brightness of the firmament; and they that turn many to righteousness as the stars for ever and ever.

4 But you , O Daniel, shut up the words, and seal the book, even to the time of the end: many shall run to and fro, and knowledge shall be increased.

5 Then I Daniel looked, and, behold, there stood other two, the one on this side of the bank of the river, and the other on that side of the bank of the river.

6 And one said to the man clothed in linen, which was upon the waters of the river, How long shall it be to the end of these wonders?

7 And I heard the man clothed in linen, which was upon the waters of the river, when he held up his right hand and his left hand unto heaven, and sware by him that liveth for ever that it shall be for a time, times, and an half; and when he shall have accomplished to scatter the power of the holy people, all these things shall be finished.

8 And I heard, but I understood not: then said I, O my Lord, what shall be the end of these things?

9 And he said, Go your way, Daniel: for the words are closed up and sealed till the time of the end.

10 Many shall be purified, and made white, and tried; but the wicked shall do wickedly: and none of the wicked shall understand; but the wise shall understand.

11 And from the time that the daily sacrifice shall be taken away, and the abomination that maketh desolate set up, there shall be a thousand two hundred and ninety days.

12 Blessed is he that waiteth, and comes to the thousand three hundred and five and thirty days.

13 But go you your way till the end be: for you shalt rest, and stand in your lot at the end of the days.

HOSEA.

CHAPTER 1

THE word of the LORD that came unto Hosea, the son of Beeri, in the days of Uzziah, Jotham, Ahaz, and Hezekiah, kings of Judah, and in the days of Jeroboam the son of Joash, king of Israel.

2 The beginning of the word of the LORD by Hosea. And the LORD said to Hosea, Go, take unto you a wife of whoredoms and children of whoredoms: for the land has committed great whoredom, departing from the LORD.

3 So he went and took Gomer the daughter of Diblaim; which conceived, and bare him a son.

4 And the LORD said unto him, Call his name Jezreel; for yet a little while, and I will avenge the blood of Jezreel upon the house of Jehu, and will cause to cease the kingdom of the house of Israel.

5 And it shall come to pass at that day, that I will break the bow of Israel in the valley of Jezreel.

6And she conceived again, and bare a daughter. And God said unto him, Call her name Lo-ruhamah: for I will no more have mercy upon the house of Israel; but I will utterly take them away.

7 But I will have mercy upon the house of Judah, and will save them by the LORD their God, and will not save them by bow, nor by sword, nor by battle, by horses, nor by horsemen.

8Now when she had weaned Lo-ruhamah, she conceived, and bare a son.

9 Then said God, Call his name Lo-ammi: for you are not my people, and I will not be your God.

10Yet the number of the children of Israel shall be as the sand of the sea, which cannot be measured nor numbered; and it shall come to pass, that in the place where it was said unto them, You are not my people, there it shall be said unto them, You are the sons of the living God.

11 Then shall the children of Judah and the children of Israel be gathered together, and appoint themselves one head, and they shall come up out of the land: for great shall be the day of Jezreel.

CHAPTER 2

SAY you unto your brethren, Ammi; and to your sisters, Ru-hamah.

2 Plead with your mother, plead: for she is not my wife, neither am I her husband: let her therefore put away her whoredoms out of her sight, and her adulteries from between her breasts;

3 Lest I strip her naked, and set her as in the day that she was born, and make her as a wilderness, and set her like a dry land, and slay her with thirst.

4 And I will not have mercy upon her children; for they be the children of whoredoms.

5 For their mother has played the harlot: she that conceived them has done shamefully: for she said, I will go after my lovers, that give me my bread and my water, my wool and my flax, my oil and my drink.

6Therefore, behold, I will hedge up your way with thorns, and make a wall, that she shall not find her paths.

7 And she shall follow after her lovers, but she shall not overtake them; and she shall seek them, but shall not find them: then shall she say, I will go and return to my first husband; for then was it better with me than now.

8 For she did not know that I gave her corn, and wine, and oil, and multiplied her silver and gold, which they prepared for Baal.

9 Therefore will I return, and take away my corn in the time thereof, and my wine in the season thereof, and will recover my wool and my flax given to cover her nakedness.

10 And now will I discover her lewdness in the sight of her lovers, and none shall deliver her out of my hand.

11 I will also cause all her mirth to cease, her feast days, her new moons, and her sabbaths, and all her solemn feasts.

12 And I will destroy her vines and her fig trees, whereof she has said, These are my rewards that my lovers have given me: and I will make them a forest, and the beasts of the field shall eat them.

13 And I will visit upon her the days of Baalim, wherein she burned incense to them, and she decked herself with her earrings and her jewels, and she went after her lovers, and forgat me, saith the LORD.

14Therefore, behold, I will allure her, and bring her into the wilderness, and speak comfortably unto her.

15 And I will give her her vineyards from thence, and the valley of Achor for a door of hope: and she shall sing there, as in the days of her youth, and as in the day when she came up out of the land of Egypt.

16 And it shall be at that day, saith the LORD, that you shalt call me Ishi; and shalt call me no more Baali.

17 For I will take away the names of Baalim out of her mouth, and they shall no more be remembered by their name.

18 And in that day will I make a covenant for them with the beasts of the field, and with the fowls of heaven, and with the creeping things of the ground: and I will break the bow and the sword and the battle out of the earth, and will make them to lie down safely.

19 And I will betroth you unto me for ever; yea, I will betroth you unto me in righteousness, and in judgment, and in lovingkindness, and in mercies.

20 I will even betroth you unto me in faithfulness: and you shalt know the LORD.

21 And it shall come to pass in that day, I will hear, saith the LORD, I will hear the heavens, and they shall hear the earth;

22 And the earth shall hear the corn, and the wine, and the oil; and they shall hear Jezreel.

23 And I will sow her unto me in the earth; and I will have mercy upon her that had not obtained mercy; and I will say to them which were not my people, You are my people; and they shall say, You are my God.

CHAPTER 3

THEN said the LORD unto me, Go yet, love a woman beloved of her friend, yet an adulteress, according to the love of the LORD toward the children of Israel, who look to other gods, and love flagons of wine.

2 So I bought her to me for fifteen pieces of silver, and for an homer of barley, and an half homer of barley:

3 And I said unto her, You shalt abide for me many days; you shalt not play the harlot, and you shalt not be for another man: so will I also be for you.

4 For the children of Israel shall abide many days without a king, and without a prince, and without a sacrifice, and without an image, and without an ephod, and without teraphim:

5 Afterward shall the children of Israel return, and seek the LORD their God, and David their king; and shall fear the LORD and his goodness in the latter days.

CHAPTER 4

HEAR the word of the LORD, you children of Israel: for the LORD has a controversy with the inhabitants of the land, because there is no truth, nor mercy, nor knowledge of God in the land.

2 By swearing, and lying, and killing, and stealing, and committing adultery, they break out, and blood toucheth blood.

3 Therefore shall the land mourn, and every one that dwelleth therein shall languish, with the beasts of the field, and with the fowls of heaven; yea, the fishes of the sea also shall be taken away.

4 Yet let no man strive, nor reprove another: for your people are as they that strive with the priest.

5 Therefore shalt you fall in the day, and the prophet also shall fall with you in the night, and I will destroy your mother.

6My people are destroyed for lack of knowledge: because you have rejected knowledge, I will also reject you, that you shalt be no priest to me: seeing you have forgotten the law of your God, I will also forget your children.

7 As they were increased, so they sinned against me: therefore will I change their glory into shame.

8 They eat up the sin of my people, and they set their heart on their iniquity.

9 And there shall be, like people, like priest: and I will punish them for their ways, and reward them their doings.

10 For they shall eat, and not have enough: they shall commit whoredom, and shall not increase: because they have left off to take heed to the LORD.

11 Whoredom and wine and new wine take away the heart.

12My people ask counsel at their stocks, and their staff declareth unto them: for the spirit of whoredoms has caused them to err, and they have gone a whoring from under their God.

13 They sacrifice upon the tops of the mountains, and burn incense upon the hills, under oaks and poplars and elms, because the shadow thereof is good: therefore your daughters shall commit whoredom, and your spouses shall commit adultery.

14 I will not punish your daughters when they commit whoredom, nor your spouses when they commit adultery: for themselves are separated with whores, and they sacrifice with harlots: therefore the people that doth not understand shall fall.

15Though you , Israel, play the harlot, yet let not Judah offend; and come not you unto Gilgal, neither go you up to Beth-aven, nor swear, The LORD liveth.

16 For Israel slideth back as a backsliding heifer: now the LORD will feed them as a lamb in a large place.

17 Ephraim is joined to idols: let him alone.

18 Their drink is sour: they have committed whoredom continually: her rulers with shame do love, Give you .

19 The wind has bound her up in her wings, and they shall be ashamed because of their sacrifices.

CHAPTER 5

HEAR you this, O priests; and hearken, you house of Israel; and give you ear, O house of the king; for judgment is toward you, because you have been a snare on Mizpah, and a net spread upon Tabor.

2 And the revolters are profound to make slaughter, though I have been a rebuker of them all.

3 I know Ephraim, and Israel is not hid from me: for now, O Ephraim, you committest whoredom, and Israel is defiled.

4 They will not frame their doings to turn unto their God: for the spirit of whoredoms is in the midst of them, and they have not known the LORD.

5 And the pride of Israel doth testify to his face: therefore shall Israel and Ephraim fall in their iniquity; Judah also shall fall with them.

6 They shall go with their flocks and with their herds to seek the LORD; but they shall not find him; he has withdrawn himself from them.

7 They have dealt treacherously against the LORD: for they have begotten strange children: now shall a month devour them with their portions.

8 Blow you the cornet in Gibeah, and the trumpet in Ramah: cry aloud at Beth-aven, after you, O Benjamin.

9 Ephraim shall be desolate in the day of rebuke: among the tribes of Israel have I made known that which shall surely be.

10 The princes of Judah were like them that remove the bound: therefore I will pour out my wrath upon them like water.

11 Ephraim is oppressed and broken in judgment, because he willingly walked after the commandment.

12 Therefore will I be unto Ephraim as a moth, and to the house of Judah as rottenness.

13 When Ephraim saw his sickness, and Judah saw his wound, then went Ephraim to the Assyrian, and sent to king Jareb: yet could he not heal you, nor cure you of your wound.

14 For I will be unto Ephraim as a lion, and as a young lion to the house of Judah: I, even I, will tear and go away; I will take away, and none shall rescue him.

15 I will go and return to my place, till they acknowledge their offence, and seek my face: in their affliction they will seek me early.

CHAPTER 6

COME, and let us return unto the LORD: for he has torn, and he will heal us; he has smitten, and he will bind us up.

2 After two days will he revive us: in the third day he will raise us up, and we shall live in his sight.

3 Then shall we know, if we follow on to know the LORD: his going forth is prepared as the morning; and he shall come unto us as the rain, as the latter and former rain unto the earth.

40 Ephraim, what shall I do unto you? O Judah, what shall I do unto you? for your goodness is as a morning cloud, and as the early dew it goeth away.

5 Therefore have I hewed them by the prophets; I have slain them by the words of my mouth: and your judgments are as the light that goeth forth.

6 For I desired mercy, and not sacrifice; and the knowledge of God more than burnt offerings.

7 But they like men have transgressed the covenant: there have they dealt treacherously against me.

8 Gilead is a city of them that work iniquity, and is polluted with blood.

9 And as troops of robbers wait for a man, so the company of priests murder in the way by consent: for they commit lewdness.

10 I have seen an horrible thing in the house of Israel: there is the whoredom of Ephraim, Israel is defiled.

11 Also, O Judah, he has set an harvest for you, when I returned the captivity of my people.

CHAPTER 7

WHEN I would have healed Israel, then the iniquity of Ephraim was discovered, and the wickedness of Samaria: for they commit falsehood; and the thief comes in, and the troop of robbers spoileth without.

2 And they consider not in their hearts that I remember all their wickedness: now their own doings have beset them about; they are before my face.

3 They make the king glad with their wickedness, and the princes with their lies.

4 They are all adulterers, as an oven heated by the baker, who ceaseth from raising after he has kneaded the dough, until it be leavened.

5 In the day of our king the princes have made him sick with bottles of wine; he stretched out his hand with scorners.

6 For they have made ready their heart like an oven, whiles they lie in wait: their baker sleepeth all the night; in the morning it burneth as a flaming fire.

7 They are all hot as an oven, and have devoured their judges; all their kings are fallen: there is none among them that calleth unto me.

8 Ephraim, he has mixed himself among the people; Ephraim is a cake not turned.

9 Strangers have devoured his strength, and he knoweth it not: yea, gray hairs are here and there upon him, yet he knoweth not.

10 And the pride of Israel testifieth to his face: and they do not return to the LORD their God, nor seek him for all this.

11 Ephraim also is like a silly dove without heart: they call to Egypt, they go to Assyria.

12 When they shall go, I will spread my net upon them; I will bring them down as the fowls of the heaven; I will chastise them, as their congregation has heard.

13 Woe unto them! for they have fled from me: destruction unto them! because they have transgressed against me: though I have redeemed them, yet they have spoken lies against me.

14 And they have not cried unto me with their heart, when they howled upon their beds: they assemble themselves for corn and wine, and they rebel against me.

15 Though I have bound and strengthened their arms, yet do they imagine mischief against me.

16 They return, but not to the most High: they are like a deceitful bow: their princes shall fall by the sword for the rage of their tongue: this shall be their derision in the land of Egypt.

CHAPTER 8

SET the trumpet to your mouth. He shall come as an eagle against the house of the LORD, because they have transgressed my covenant, and trespassed against my law.

2 Israel shall cry unto me, My God, we know you.

3 Israel has cast off the thing that is good: the enemy shall pursue him.

4 They have set up kings, but not by me: they have made princes, and I knew it not: of their silver and their gold have they made them idols, that they may be cut off.

5 Your calf, O Samaria, has cast you off; my anger is kindled against them: how long will it be ere they attain to innocency?

6 For from Israel was it also: the workman made it; therefore it is not God: but the calf of Samaria shall be broken in pieces.

7 For they have sown the wind, and they shall reap the whirlwind: it has no stalk: the bud shall yield no meal: if so be it yield, the strangers shall swallow it up.

8 Israel is swallowed up: now shall they be among the Gentiles as a vessel wherein is no pleasure.

9 For they are gone up to Assyria, a wild ass alone by himself: Ephraim has hired lovers.

10 Yea, though they have hired among the nations, now will I gather them, and they shall sorrow a little for the burden of the king of princes.

11 Because Ephraim has made many altars to sin, altars shall be unto him to sin.

12 I have written to him the great things of my law, but they were counted as a strange thing.

13 They sacrifice flesh for the sacrifices of my offerings, and eat it; but the LORD accepteth them not; now will he remember their iniquity, and visit their sins: they shall return to Egypt.

14 For Israel has forgotten his Maker, and buildeth temples; and Judah has multiplied fenced cities: but I will send a fire upon his cities, and it shall devour the palaces thereof.

CHAPTER 9

REJOICE not, O Israel, for joy, as other people: for you have gone a whoring from your God, you have loved a reward upon every cornfloor.

2 The floor and the winepress shall not feed them, and the new wine shall fail in her.

3 They shall not dwell in the LORD's land; but Ephraim shall return to Egypt, and they shall eat unclean things in Assyria.

4 They shall not offer wine offerings to the LORD, neither shall they be pleasing unto him: their sacrifices shall be unto them as the bread of mourners; all that eat thereof shall be polluted: for their bread for their soul shall not come into the house of the LORD.

5 What will you do in the solemn day, and in the day of the feast of the LORD?

6 For, lo, they are gone because of destruction: Egypt shall gather them up, Memphis shall bury them: the pleasant places for their silver, nettles shall possess them: thorns shall be in their tabernacles.

7 The days of visitation are come, the days of recompence are come; Israel shall know it: the prophet is a fool, the spiritual man is mad, for the multitude of yours iniquity, and the great hatred.

8 The watchman of Ephraim was with my God: but the prophet is a snare of a fowler in all his ways, and hatred in the house of his God.

9 They have deeply corrupted themselves, as in the days of Gibeah: therefore he will remember their iniquity, he will visit their sins.

10 I found Israel like grapes in the wilderness; I saw your fathers as the firstripe in the fig tree at her first time: but they went to Baal-peor, and separated themselves unto that shame; and their abominations were according as they loved.

11 As for Ephraim, their glory shall fly away like a bird, from the birth, and from the womb, and from the conception.

12 Though they bring up their children, yet will I bereave them, that there shall not be a man left: yea, woe also to them when I depart from them!

13 Ephraim, as I saw Tyrus, is planted in a pleasant place: but Ephraim shall bring forth his children to the murderer.

14 Give them, O LORD: what will you give? give them a miscarrying womb and dry breasts.

15 All their wickedness is in Gilgal: for there I hated them: for the wickedness of their doings I will drive them out of my house, I will love them no more: all their princes are revolters.

16 Ephraim is smitten, their root is dried up, they shall bear no fruit: yea, though they bring forth, yet will I slay even the beloved fruit of their womb.

17 My God will cast them away, because they did not hearken unto him: and they shall be wanderers among the nations.

CHAPTER 10

ISRAEL is an empty vine, he bringeth forth fruit unto himself: according to the multitude of his fruit he has increased the altars; according to the goodness of his land they have made goodly images.

2 Their heart is divided; now shall they be found faulty: he shall break down their altars, he shall spoil their images.

3 For now they shall say, We have no king, because we feared not the LORD; what then should a king do to us?

4 They have spoken words, swearing falsely in making a covenant: thus judgment springeth up as hemlock in the furrows of the field.

5 The inhabitants of Samaria shall fear because of the calves of Beth-aven: for the people thereof shall mourn over it, and the priests thereof that rejoiced on it, for the glory thereof, because it is departed from it.

6 It shall be also carried unto Assyria for a present to king Jareb: Ephraim shall receive shame, and Israel shall be ashamed of his own counsel.

7 As for Samaria, her king is cut off as the foam upon the water.

8 The high places also of Aven, the sin of Israel, shall be destroyed: the thorn and the thistle shall come up on their altars; and they shall say to the mountains, Cover us; and to the hills, Fall on us.

9 O Israel, you have sinned from the days of Gibeah: there they stood: the battle in Gibeah against the children of iniquity did not overtake them.

10 It is in my desire that I should chastise them; and the people shall be gathered against them, when they shall bind themselves in their two furrows.

11 And Ephraim is as an heifer that is taught, and loveth to tread out the corn; but I passed over upon her fair neck: I will make Ephraim to ride; Judah shall plow, and Jacob shall break his clods.

12 Sow to yourselves in righteousness, reap in mercy; break up your fallow ground: for it is time to seek the LORD, till he come and rain righteousness upon you.

13 You have plowed wickedness, you have reaped iniquity; you have eaten the fruit of lies: because you did trust in your way, in the multitude of your mighty men.

14 Therefore shall a tumult arise among your people, and all your fortresses shall be spoiled, as Shalman spoiled Beth-arbel in the day of battle: the mother was dashed in pieces upon her children.

15 So shall Beth-el do unto you because of your great wickedness: in a morning shall the king of Israel utterly be cut off.

CHAPTER 11

WHEN Israel was a child, then I loved him, and called my son out of Egypt.

2 As they called them, so they went from them: they sacrificed unto Baalim, and burned incense to graven images.

3 I taught Ephraim also to go, taking them by their arms; but they knew not that I healed them.

4 I drew them with cords of a man, with bands of love: and I was to them as they that take off the yoke on their jaws, and I laid meat unto them.

5 He shall not return into the land of Egypt, but the Assyrian shall be his king, because they refused to return.

6 And the sword shall abide on his cities, and shall consume his branches, and devour them, because of their own counsels.

7 And my people are bent to backsliding from me: though they called them to the most High, none at all would exalt him.

8 How shall I give you up, Ephraim? how shall I deliver you, Israel? how shall I make you as Admah? how shall I set you as Zeboim? my heart is turned within me, my repentings are kindled together.

9 I will not execute the fierceness of my anger, I will not return to destroy Ephraim: for I am God, and not man; the Holy One in the midst of you: and I will not enter into the city.

10 They shall walk after the LORD: he shall roar like a lion: when he shall roar, then the children shall tremble from the west.

11 They shall tremble as a bird out of Egypt, and as a dove out of the land of Assyria: and I will place them in their houses, saith the LORD.

12 Ephraim compasseth me about with lies, and the house of Israel with deceit: but Judah yet ruleth with God, and is faithful with the saints.

CHAPTER 12

EPHRAIM feedeth on wind, and followeth after the east wind: he daily increaseth lies and desolation; and they do make a covenant with the Assyrians, and oil is carried into Egypt.

2 The LORD has also a controversy with Judah, and will punish Jacob according to his ways; according to his doings will he recompense him.

3 He took his brother by the heel in the womb, and by his strength he had power with God:

4 Yea, he had power over the angel, and prevailed: he wept, and made supplication unto him: he found him in Beth-el, and there he spake with us;

5 Even the LORD God of hosts; the LORD is his memorial.

6 Therefore turn you to your God: keep mercy and judgment, and wait on your God continually.

7 He is a merchant, the balances of deceit are in his hand: he loveth to oppress.

8 And Ephraim said, Yet I am become rich, I have found me out substance: in all my labours they shall find none iniquity in me that were sin.

9 And I that am the LORD your God from the land of Egypt will yet make you to dwell in tabernacles, as in the days of the solemn feast.

10 I have also spoken by the prophets, and I have multiplied visions, and used similitudes, by the ministry of the prophets.

11 Is there iniquity in Gilead? surely they are vanity: they sacrifice bullocks in Gilgal; yea, their altars are as heaps in the furrows of the fields.

12 And Jacob fled into the country of Syria, and Israel served for a wife, and for a wife he kept sheep.

13 And by a prophet the LORD brought Israel out of Egypt, and by a prophet was he preserved.

14 Ephraim provoked him to anger most bitterly: therefore shall he leave his blood upon him, and his reproach shall his Lord return unto him.

CHAPTER 13

WHEN Ephraim spake trembling, he exalted himself in Israel; but when he offended in Baal, he died.

2 And now they sin more and more, and have made them molten images of their silver, and idols according to their own understanding, all of it the work of the craftsmen: they say of them, Let the men that sacrifice kiss the calves.

3 Therefore they shall be as the morning cloud, and as the early dew that passes away, as the chaff that is driven with the whirlwind out of the floor, and as the smoke out of the chimney.

4 Yet I am the LORD your God from the land of Egypt, and you shalt know no god but me: for there is no saviour beside me.

5 I did know you in the wilderness, in the land of great drought.

6 According to their pasture, so were they filled; they were filled, and their heart was exalted; therefore have they forgotten me.

7 Therefore I will be unto them as a lion: as a leopard by the way will I observe them:

8 I will meet them as a bear that is bereaved of her whelps, and will rend the caul of their heart, and there will I devour them like a lion: the wild beast shall tear them.

9 O Israel, you have destroyed yourself; but in me is yours help.

10 I will be your king: where is any other that may save you in all your cities? and your judges of whom you saidst, Give me a king and princes?

11 I gave you a king in my anger, and took him away in my wrath.

12 The iniquity of Ephraim is bound up; his sin is hid.

13 The sorrows of a travailing woman shall come upon him: he is an unwise son; for he should not stay long in the place of the breaking forth of children.

14 I will ransom them from the power of the grave; I will redeem them from death: O death, I will be your plagues; O grave, I will be your destruction: repentance shall be hid from my eyes.

15Though he be fruitful among his brethren, an east wind shall come, the wind of the LORD shall come up from the wilderness, and his spring shall become dry, and his fountain shall be dried up: he shall spoil the treasure of all pleasant vessels.

16 Samaria shall become desolate; for she has rebelled against her God: they shall fall by the sword: their infants shall be dashed in pieces, and their women with child shall be ripped up.

CHAPTER 14

O ISRAEL, return unto the LORD your God; for you have fallen by yours iniquity.

2 Take with you words, and turn to the LORD: say unto him, Take away all iniquity, and receive us graciously: so will we render the calves of our lips.

3 Asshur shall not save us; we will not ride upon horses: neither will we say any more to the work of our hands, You are our gods: for in you the fatherless findeth mercy.

4I will heal their backsliding, I will love them freely: for my anger is turned away from him.

5 I will be as the dew unto Israel: he shall grow as the lily, and cast forth his roots as Lebanon.

6 His branches shall spread, and his beauty shall be as the olive tree, and his smell as Lebanon.

7 They that dwell under his shadow shall return; they shall revive as the corn, and grow as the vine: the scent thereof shall be as the wine of Lebanon.

8 Ephraim shall say, What have I to do any more with idols? I have heard him, and observed him: I am like a green fir tree. From me is your fruit found.

9 Who is wise, and he shall understand these things? prudent, and he shall know them? for the ways of the LORD are right, and the just shall walk in them: but the transgressors shall fall therein.

JOEL.

CHAPTER 1

THE word of the LORD that came to Joel the son of Pethuel.

2 Hear this, you old men, and give ear, all you inhabitants of the land. Has this been in your days, or even in the days of your fathers?

3 Tell you your children of it, and let your children tell their children, and their children another generation.

4 That which the palmerworm has left has the locust eaten; and that which the locust has left has the cankerworm eaten; and that which the cankerworm has left has the caterpiller eaten.

5 Awake, you drunkards, and weep; and howl, all you drinkers of wine, because of the new wine; for it is cut off from your mouth.

6 For a nation is come up upon my land, strong, and without number, whose teeth are the teeth of a lion, and he has the cheek teeth of a great lion.

7 He has laid my vine waste, and barked my fig tree: he has made it clean bare, and cast it away; the branches thereof are made white.

8 Lament like a virgin girded with sackcloth for the husband of her youth.

9 The meat offering and the drink offering is cut off from the house of the LORD; the priests, the LORD's ministers, mourn.

10 The field is wasted, the land mourneth; for the corn is wasted: the new wine is dried up, the oil languisheth.

11 Be you ashamed, O you husbandmen; howl, O you vinedressers, for the wheat and for the barley; because the harvest of the field is perished.

12 The vine is dried up, and the fig tree languisheth; the pomegranate tree, the palm tree also, and the apple tree, even all the trees of the field, are withered: because joy is withered away from the sons of men.

13 Gird yourselves, and lament, you priests: howl, you ministers of the altar: come, lie all night in sackcloth, you ministers of my God: for the meat offering and the drink offering is withholden from the house of your God.

14 Sanctify you a fast, call a solemn assembly, gather the elders and all the inhabitants of the land into the house of the LORD your God, and cry unto the LORD,

15 Alas for the day! for the day of the LORD is at hand, and as a destruction from the Almighty shall it come.

16 Is not the meat cut off before our eyes, yea, joy and gladness from the house of our God?

17 The seed is rotten under their clods, the garners are laid desolate, the barns are broken down; for the corn is withered.

18 How do the beasts groan! the herds of cattle are perplexed, because they have no pasture; yea, the flocks of sheep are made desolate.

19 O LORD, to you will I cry: for the fire has devoured the pastures of the wilderness, and the flame has burned all the trees of the field.

20 The beasts of the field cry also unto you: for the rivers of waters are dried up, and the fire has devoured the pastures of the wilderness.

CHAPTER 2

BLOW you the trumpet in Zion, and sound an alarm in my holy mountain: let all the inhabitants of the land tremble: for the day of the LORD comes, for it is nigh at hand;

2 A day of darkness and of gloominess, a day of clouds and of thick darkness, as the morning spread upon the mountains: a great people and a strong; there has not been ever the like, neither shall be any more after it, even to the years of many generations.

3 A fire devoureth before them; and behind them a flame burneth: the land is as the garden of Eden before them, and behind them a desolate wilderness; yea, and nothing shall escape them.

4 The appearance of them is as the appearance of horses; and as horsemen, so shall they run.

5 Like the noise of chariots on the tops of mountains shall they leap, like the noise of a flame of fire that devoureth the stubble, as a strong people set in battle array.

6 Before their face the people shall be much pained: all faces shall gather blackness.

7 They shall run like mighty men; they shall climb the wall like men of war; and they shall march every one on his ways, and they shall not break their ranks:

8 Neither shall one thrust another; they shall walk every one in his path: and when they fall upon the sword, they shall not be wounded.

9 They shall run to and fro in the city; they shall run upon the wall, they shall climb up upon the houses; they shall enter in at the windows like a thief.

10 The earth shall quake before them; the heavens shall tremble: the sun and the moon shall be dark, and the stars shall withdraw their shining:

11 And the LORD shall utter his voice before his army: for his camp is very great: for he is strong that executeth his word: for the day of the LORD is great and very terrible; and who can abide it?

12 Therefore also now, saith the LORD, turn you even to me with all your heart, and with fasting, and with weeping, and with mourning:

13 And rend your heart, and not your garments, and turn unto the LORD your God: for he is gracious and merciful, slow to anger, and of great kindness, and repenteth him of the evil.

14 Who knoweth if he will return and repent, and leave a blessing behind him; even a meat offering and a drink offering unto the LORD your God?

15 Blow the trumpet in Zion, sanctify a fast, call a solemn assembly:

16 Gather the people, sanctify the congregation, assemble the elders, gather the children, and those that suck the breasts: let the bridegroom go forth of his chamber, and the bride out of her closet.

17 Let the priests, the ministers of the LORD, weep between the porch and the altar, and let them say, Spare your people, O LORD, and give not yours heritage to reproach, that the heathen should rule over them: wherefore should they say among the people, Where is their God?

18 Then will the LORD be jealous for his land, and pity his people.

19 Yea, the LORD will answer and say unto his people, Behold, I will send you corn, and wine, and oil, and you shall be satisfied therewith: and I will no more make you a reproach among the heathen:

20 But I will remove far off from you the northern army, and will drive him into a land barren and desolate, with his face toward the east sea, and his hinder part toward the utmost sea, and his stink shall come up, and his ill savour shall come up, because he has done great things.

21 Fear not, O land; be glad and rejoice: for the LORD will do great things.

22 Be not afraid, you beasts of the field: for the pastures of the wilderness do spring, for the tree beareth her fruit, the fig tree and the vine do yield their strength.

23 Be glad then, you children of Zion, and rejoice in the LORD your God: for he has given you the former rain moderately, and he will cause to come down for you the rain, the former rain, and the latter rain in the first month.

24 And the floors shall be full of wheat, and the fats shall overflow with wine and oil.

25 And I will restore to you the years that the locust has eaten, the cankerworm, and the caterpiller, and the palmerworm, my great army which I sent among you.

26 And you shall eat in plenty, and be satisfied, and praise the name of the LORD your God, that has dealt wondrously with you: and my people shall never be ashamed.

27 And you shall know that I am in the midst of Israel, and that I am the LORD your God, and none else: and my people shall never be ashamed.

28 And it shall come to pass afterward, that I will pour out my spirit upon all flesh; and your sons and your daughters shall prophesy, your old men shall dream dreams, your young men shall see visions:

29 And also upon the servants and upon the handmaids in those days will I pour out my spirit.

30 And I will shew wonders in the heavens and in the earth, blood, and fire, and pillars of smoke.

31 The sun shall be turned into darkness, and the moon into blood, before the great and the terrible day of the LORD come.

32 And it shall come to pass, that whosoever shall call on the name of the LORD shall be delivered: for in mount Zion and in Jerusalem shall be deliverance, as the LORD has said, and in the remnant whom the LORD shall call.

CHAPTER 3

FOR, behold, in those days, and in that time, when I shall bring again the captivity of Judah and Jerusalem,

2 I will also gather all nations, and will bring them down into the valley of Jehoshaphat, and will plead with them there for my people and for my heritage Israel, whom they have scattered among the nations, and parted my land.

3 And they have cast lots for my people; and have given a boy for an harlot, and sold a girl for wine, that they might drink.

4 Yea, and what have you to do with me, O Tyre, and Zidon, and all the coasts of Palestine? will you render me a recompence? and if you recompense me, swiftly and speedily will I return your recompence upon your own head;

5 Because you have taken my silver and my gold, and have carried into your temples my goodly pleasant things:

6 The children also of Judah and the children of Jerusalem have you sold unto the Grecians, that you might remove them far from their border.

7 Behold, I will raise them out of the place whither you have sold them, and will return your recompence upon your own head:

8 And I will sell your sons and your daughters into the hand of the children of Judah, and they shall sell them to the Sabeans, to a people far off: for the LORD has spoken it.

9Proclaim you this among the Gentiles; Prepare war, wake up the mighty men, let all the men of war draw near; let them come up:

10 Beat your plowshares into swords, and your pruninghooks into spears: let the weak say, I am strong.

11 Assemble yourselves, and come, all you heathen, and gather yourselves together round about: thither cause your mighty ones to come down, O LORD.

12 Let the heathen be wakened, and come up to the valley of Jehoshaphat: for there will I sit to judge all the heathen round about.

13 Put you in the sickle, for the harvest is ripe: come, get you down; for the press is full, the fats overflow; for their wickedness is great.

14 Multitudes, multitudes in the valley of decision: for the day of the LORD is near in the valley of decision.

15 The sun and the moon shall be darkened, and the stars shall withdraw their shining.

16 The LORD also shall roar out of Zion, and utter his voice from Jerusalem; and the heavens and the earth shall shake: but the LORD will be the hope of his people, and the strength of the children of Israel.

17 So shall you know that I am the LORD your God dwelling in Zion, my holy mountain: then shall Jerusalem be holy, and there shall no strangers pass through her any more.

18And it shall come to pass in that day, that the mountains shall drop down new wine, and the hills shall flow with milk, and all the rivers of Judah shall flow with waters, and a fountain shall come forth of the house of the LORD, and shall water the valley of Shittim.

19 Egypt shall be a desolation, and Edom shall be a desolate wilderness, for the violence against the children of Judah, because they have shed innocent blood in their land.

20 But Judah shall dwell for ever, and Jerusalem from generation to generation.

21 For I will cleanse their blood that I have not cleansed: for the LORD dwelleth in Zion.

AMOS.

CHAPTER 1

THE words of Amos, who was among the herdmen of Tekoa, which he saw concerning Israel in the days of Uzziah king of Judah, and in the days of Jeroboam the son of Joash king of Israel, two years before the earthquake.

2 And he said, The LORD will roar from Zion, and utter his voice from Jerusalem; and the habitations of the shepherds shall mourn, and the top of Carmel shall wither.

3 Thus saith the LORD; For three transgressions of Damascus, and for four, I will not turn away the punishment thereof; because they have threshed Gilead with threshing instruments of iron:

4 But I will send a fire into the house of Hazael, which shall devour the palaces of Ben-hadad.

5 I will break also the bar of Damascus, and cut off the inhabitant from the plain of Aven, and him that holdeth the sceptre from the house of Eden: and the people of Syria shall go into captivity unto Kir, saith the LORD.

6 Thus saith the LORD; For three transgressions of Gaza, and for four, I will not turn away the punishment thereof; because they carried away captive the whole captivity, to deliver them up to Edom:

7 But I will send a fire on the wall of Gaza, which shall devour the palaces thereof:

8 And I will cut off the inhabitant from Ashdod, and him that holdeth the sceptre from Ashkelon, and I will turn my hand against Ekron: and the remnant of the Philistines shall perish, saith the Lord GOD.

9 Thus saith the LORD; For three transgressions of Tyrus, and for four, I will not turn away the punishment thereof; because they delivered up the whole captivity to Edom, and remembered not the brotherly covenant:

10 But I will send a fire on the wall of Tyrus, which shall devour the palaces thereof.

11 Thus saith the LORD; For three transgressions of Edom, and for four, I will not turn away the punishment thereof; because he did pursue his brother with the sword, and did cast off all pity, and his anger did tear perpetually, and he kept his wrath for ever:

12 But I will send a fire upon Teman, which shall devour the palaces of Bozrah.

13 Thus saith the LORD; For three transgressions of the children of Ammon, and for four, I will not turn away the punishment thereof; because they have ripped up the women with child of Gilead, that they might enlarge their border:

14 But I will kindle a fire in the wall of Rabbah, and it shall devour the palaces thereof, with shouting in the day of battle, with a tempest in the day of the whirlwind:

15 And their king shall go into captivity, he and his princes together, saith the LORD.

CHAPTER 2

THUS saith the LORD; For three transgressions of Moab, and for four, I will not turn away the punishment thereof; because he burned the bones of the king of Edom into lime:

2 But I will send a fire upon Moab, and it shall devour the palaces of Kerioth: and Moab shall die with tumult, with shouting, and with the sound of the trumpet:

3 And I will cut off the judge from the midst thereof, and will slay all the princes thereof with him, saith the LORD.

4 Thus saith the LORD; For three transgressions of Judah, and for four, I will not turn away the punishment thereof; because they have despised the law of the LORD, and have not kept his commandments, and their lies caused them to err, after the which their fathers have walked:

5 But I will send a fire upon Judah, and it shall devour the palaces of Jerusalem.

6 Thus saith the LORD; For three transgressions of Israel, and for four, I will not turn away the punishment thereof; because they sold the righteous for silver, and the poor for a pair of shoes;

7 That pant after the dust of the earth on the head of the poor, and turn aside the way of the meek: and a man and his father will go in unto the same maid, to profane my holy name:

8 And they lay themselves down upon clothes laid to pledge by every altar, and they drink the wine of the condemned in the house of their god.

9 Yet destroyed I the Amorite before them, whose height was like the height of the cedars, and he was strong as the oaks; yet I destroyed his fruit from above, and his roots from beneath.

10 Also I brought you up from the land of Egypt, and led you forty years through the wilderness, to possess the land of the Amorite.

11 And I raised up of your sons for prophets, and of your young men for Nazarites. Is it not even thus, O you children of Israel? saith the LORD.

12 But you gave the Nazarites wine to drink; and commanded the prophets, saying, Prophesy not.

13 Behold, I am pressed under you, as a cart is pressed that is full of sheaves.

14 Therefore the flight shall perish from the swift, and the strong shall not strengthen his force, neither shall the mighty deliver himself:

15 Neither shall he stand that handleth the bow; and he that is swift of foot shall not deliver himself: neither shall he that rideth the horse deliver himself.

16 And he that is courageous among the mighty shall flee away naked in that day, saith the LORD.

CHAPTER 3

HEAR this word that the LORD has spoken against you, O children of Israel, against the whole family which I brought up from the land of Egypt, saying,

2 You only have I known of all the families of the earth: therefore I will punish you for all your iniquities.

3 Can two walk together, except they be agreed?

4 Will a lion roar in the forest, when he has no prey? will a young lion cry out of his den, if he have taken nothing?

5 Can a bird fall in a snare upon the earth, where no gin is for him? shall one take up a snare from the earth, and have taken nothing at all?

6 Shall a trumpet be blown in the city, and the people not be afraid? shall there be evil in a city, and the LORD has not done it?

7 Surely the Lord GOD will do nothing, but he revealeth his secret unto his servants the prophets.

8 The lion has roared, who will not fear? the Lord GOD has spoken, who can but prophesy?

9 Publish in the palaces at Ashdod, and in the palaces in the land of Egypt, and say, Assemble yourselves upon the mountains of Samaria, and behold the great tumults in the midst thereof, and the oppressed in the midst thereof.

10 For they know not to do right, saith the LORD, who store up violence and robbery in their palaces.

11 Therefore thus saith the Lord GOD; An adversary there shall be even round about the land; and he shall bring down your strength from you, and your palaces shall be spoiled.

12 Thus saith the LORD; As the shepherd taketh out of the mouth of the lion two legs, or a piece of an ear; so shall the children of Israel be taken out that dwell in Samaria in the corner of a bed, and in Damascus in a couch.

13 Hear you , and testify in the house of Jacob, saith the Lord GOD, the God of hosts,

14 That in the day that I shall visit the transgressions of Israel upon him I will also visit the altars of Beth-el: and the horns of the altar shall be cut off, and fall to the ground.

15 And I will strike the winter house with the summer house; and the houses of ivory shall perish, and the great houses shall have an end, saith the LORD.

CHAPTER 4

HEAR this word, you kine of Bashan, that are in the mountain of Samaria, which oppress the poor, which crush the needy, which say to their masters, Bring, and let us drink.

2 The Lord GOD has sworn by his holiness, that, lo, the days shall come upon you, that he will take you away with hooks, and your posterity with fishhooks.

3 And you shall go out at the breaches, every cow at that which is before her; and you shall cast them into the palace, saith the LORD.

4 Come to Beth-el, and transgress; at Gilgal multiply transgression; and bring your sacrifices every morning, and your tithes after three years:

5 And offer a sacrifice of thanksgiving with leaven, and proclaim and publish the free offerings: for this liketh you, O you children of Israel, saith the Lord GOD.

6 And I also have given you cleanness of teeth in all your cities, and want of bread in all your places: yet have you not returned unto me, saith the LORD.

7 And also I have withholden the rain from you, when there were yet three months to the harvest: and I caused it to rain upon one city, and caused it not to rain upon another city: one piece was rained upon, and the piece whereupon it rained not withered.

8 So two or three cities wandered unto one city, to drink water; but they were not satisfied: yet have you not returned unto me, saith the LORD.

9 I have smitten you with blasting and mildew: when your gardens and your vineyards and your fig trees and your olive trees increased, the palmerworm devoured them: yet have you not returned unto me, saith the LORD.

10 I have sent among you the pestilence after the manner of Egypt: your young men have I slain with the sword, and have taken away your horses; and I have made the stink of your camps to come up unto your nostrils: yet have you not returned unto me, saith the LORD.

11 I have overthrown some of you, as God overthrew Sodom and Gomorrah, and you were as a firebrand plucked out of the burning: yet have you not returned unto me, saith the LORD.

12 Therefore thus will I do unto you, O Israel: and because I will do this unto you, prepare to meet your God, O Israel.

13 For, lo, he that formeth the mountains, and createth the wind, and declareth unto man what is his thought, that maketh the morning darkness, and treadeth upon the high places of the earth, The LORD, The God of hosts, is his name.

CHAPTER 5

HEAR you this word which I take up against you, even a lamentation, O house of Israel.

2 The virgin of Israel is fallen; she shall no more rise: she is forsaken upon her land; there is none to raise her up.

3 For thus saith the Lord GOD; The city that went out by a thousand shall leave an hundred, and that which went forth by an hundred shall leave ten, to the house of Israel.

4 For thus saith the LORD unto the house of Israel, Seek you me, and you shall live:

5 But seek not Beth-el, nor enter into Gilgal, and pass not to Beer-sheba: for Gilgal shall surely go into captivity, and Beth-el shall come to nought.

6 Seek the LORD, and you shall live; lest he break out like fire in the house of Joseph, and devour it, and there be none to quench it in Beth-el.

7 You who turn judgment to wormwood, and leave off righteousness in the earth,

8 Seek him that maketh the seven stars and Orion, and turneth the shadow of death into the morning, and maketh the day dark with night: that calleth for the waters of the sea, and poureth them out upon the face of the earth: The LORD is his name:

9 That strengtheneth the spoiled against the strong, so that the spoiled shall come against the fortress.

10 They hate him that rebuketh in the gate, and they abhor him that speaketh uprightly.

11 Forasmuch therefore as your treading is upon the poor, and you take from him burdens of wheat: you have built houses of hewn stone, but you shall not dwell in them; you have planted pleasant vineyards, but you shall not drink wine of them.

12 For I know your manifold transgressions and your mighty sins: they afflict the just, they take a bribe, and they turn aside the poor in the gate from their right.

13 Therefore the prudent shall keep silence in that time; for it is an evil time.

14 Seek good, and not evil, that you may live: and so the LORD, the God of hosts, shall be with you, as you have spoken.

15 Hate the evil, and love the good, and establish judgment in the gate: it may be that the LORD God of hosts will be gracious unto the remnant of Joseph.

16 Therefore the LORD, the God of hosts, the Lord, saith thus; Wailing shall be in all streets; and they shall say in all the highways, Alas! alas! and they shall call the husbandman to mourning, and such as are skilful of lamentation to wailing.

17 And in all vineyards shall be wailing: for I will pass through you, saith the LORD.

18 Woe unto you that desire the day of the LORD! to what end is it for you? the day of the LORD is darkness, and not light.

19 As if a man did flee from a lion, and a bear met him; or went into the house, and leaned his hand on the wall, and a serpent bit him.

20 Shall not the day of the LORD be darkness, and not light? even very dark, and no brightness in it?

21 I hate, I despise your feast days, and I will not smell in your solemn assemblies.

22 Though you offer me burnt offerings and your meat offerings, I will not accept them: neither will I regard the peace offerings of your fat beasts.

23 Take you away from me the noise of your songs; for I will not hear the melody of your viols.

24 But let judgment run down as waters, and righteousness as a mighty stream.

25 Have you offered unto me sacrifices and offerings in the wilderness forty years, O house of Israel?

26 But you have borne the tabernacle of your Moloch and Chiun your images, the star of your god, which you made to yourselves.

27 Therefore will I cause you to go into captivity beyond Damascus, saith the LORD, whose name is The God of hosts.

CHAPTER 6

WOE to them that are at ease in Zion, and trust in the mountain of Samaria, which are named chief of the nations, to whom the house of Israel came!

2 Pass you unto Calneh, and see; and from thence go you to Hamath the great: then go down to Gath of the Philistines: be they better than these kingdoms? or their border greater than your border?

3 You that put far away the evil day, and cause the seat of violence to come near;

4 That lie upon beds of ivory, and stretch themselves upon their couches, and eat the lambs out of the flock, and the calves out of the midst of the stall;

5 That chant to the sound of the viol, and invent to themselves instruments of musick, like David;

6 That drink wine in bowls, and anoint themselves with the chief ointments: but they are not grieved for the affliction of Joseph.

7 Therefore now shall they go captive with the first that go captive, and the banquet of them that stretched themselves shall be removed.

8 The Lord GOD has sworn by himself, saith the LORD the God of hosts, I abhor the excellency of Jacob, and hate his palaces: therefore will I deliver up the city with all that is therein.

9 And it shall come to pass, if there remain ten men in one house, that they shall die.

10 And a man's uncle shall take him up, and he that burneth him, to bring out the bones out of the house, and shall say unto him that is by the sides of the house, Is there yet any with you? and he say, No. Then shall he say, Hold your tongue: for we may not make mention of the name of the LORD.

11 For, behold, the LORD commandeth, and he will strike the great house with breaches, and the little house with clefts.

12 Shall horses run upon the rock? will one plow there with oxen? for you have turned judgment into gall, and the fruit of righteousness into hemlock:

13 You which rejoice in a thing of nought, which say, Have we not taken to us horns by our own strength?

14 But, behold, I will raise up against you a nation, O house of Israel, saith the LORD the God of hosts; and they shall afflict you from the entering in of Hemath unto the river of the wilderness.

CHAPTER 7

THUS has the Lord GOD shewed unto me; and, behold, he formed grasshoppers in the beginning of the shooting up of the latter growth; and, lo, it was the latter growth after the king's mowings.

2 And it came to pass, that when they had made an end of eating the grass of the land, then I said, O Lord GOD, forgive, I beseech you: by whom shall Jacob arise? for he is small.

3 The LORD repented for this: It shall not be, saith the LORD.

4 Thus has the Lord GOD shewed unto me: and, behold, the Lord GOD called to contend by fire, and it devoured the great deep, and did eat up a part.

5 Then said I, O Lord GOD, cease, I beseech you: by whom shall Jacob arise? for he is small.

6 The LORD repented for this: This also shall not be, saith the Lord GOD.

7 Thus he shewed me: and, behold, the Lord stood upon a wall made by a plumbline, with a plumbline in his hand.

8 And the LORD said unto me, Amos, what seest you? And I said, A plumbline. Then said the Lord, Behold, I will set a plumbline in the midst of my people Israel: I will not again pass by them any more:

9 And the high places of Isaac shall be desolate, and the sanctuaries of Israel shall be laid waste; and I will rise against the house of Jeroboam with the sword.

10 Then Amaziah the priest of Beth-el sent to Jeroboam king of Israel, saying, Amos has conspired against you in the midst of the house of Israel: the land is not able to bear all his words.

11 For thus Amos saith, Jeroboam shall die by the sword, and Israel shall surely be led away captive out of their own land.

12 Also Amaziah said unto Amos, O you seer, go, flee you away into the land of Judah, and there eat bread, and prophesy there:

13 But prophesy not again any more at Beth-el: for it is the king's chapel, and it is the king's court.

14 Then answered Amos, and said to Amaziah, I was no prophet, neither was I a prophet's son; but I was an herdman, and a gatherer of sycomore fruit:

15 And the LORD took me as I followed the flock, and the LORD said unto me, Go, prophesy unto my people Israel.

16 Now therefore hear you the word of the LORD: You say, Prophesy not against Israel, and drop not your word against the house of Isaac.

17 Therefore thus saith the LORD; Your wife shall be an harlot in the city, and your sons and your daughters shall fall by the sword, and your land shall be divided by line; and you shalt die in a polluted land: and Israel shall surely go into captivity forth of his land.

CHAPTER 8

THUS has the Lord GOD shewed unto me: and behold a basket of summer fruit.

2 And he said, Amos, what seest you? And I said, A basket of summer fruit. Then said the LORD unto me, The end is come upon my people of Israel; I will not again pass by them any more.

3 And the songs of the temple shall be howlings in that day, saith the Lord GOD: there shall be many dead bodies in every place; they shall cast them forth with silence.

4 Hear this, O you that swallow up the needy, even to make the poor of the land to fail,

5 Saying, When will the new moon be gone, that we may sell corn? and the sabbath, that we may set forth wheat, making the ephah small, and the shekel great, and falsifying the balances by deceit?

6 That we may buy the poor for silver, and the needy for a pair of shoes; yea, and sell the refuse of the wheat?

7 The LORD has sworn by the excellency of Jacob, Surely I will never forget any of their works.

8 Shall not the land tremble for this, and every one mourn that dwelleth therein? and it shall rise up wholly as a flood; and it shall be cast out and drowned, as by the flood of Egypt.

9 And it shall come to pass in that day, saith the Lord GOD, that I will cause the sun to go down at noon, and I will darken the earth in the clear day:

10 And I will turn your feasts into mourning, and all your songs into lamentation; and I will bring up sackcloth upon all loins, and baldness upon every head; and I will make it as the mourning of an only son, and the end thereof as a bitter day.

11 Behold, the days come, saith the Lord GOD, that I will send a famine in the land, not a famine of bread, nor a thirst for water, but of hearing the words of the LORD:

12 And they shall wander from sea to sea, and from the north even to the east, they shall run to and fro to seek the word of the LORD, and shall not find it.

13 In that day shall the fair virgins and young men faint for thirst.

14 They that swear by the sin of Samaria, and say, Your god, O Dan, liveth; and, The manner of Beer-sheba liveth; even they shall fall, and never rise up again.

CHAPTER 9

I SAW the Lord standing upon the altar: and he said, Strike the lintel of the door, that the posts may shake: and cut them in the head, all of them; and I will slay the last of them with the sword: he that fleeth of them shall not flee away, and he that escapeth of them shall not be delivered.

2 Though they dig into hell, thence shall my hand take them; though they climb up to heaven, thence will I bring them down:

3 And though they hide themselves in the top of Carmel, I will search and take them out thence; and though they be hid from my sight in the bottom of the sea, thence will I command the serpent, and he shall bite them:

4 And though they go into captivity before their enemies, thence will I command the sword, and it shall slay them: and I will set my eyes upon them for evil, and not for good.

5 And the Lord GOD of hosts is he that toucheth the land, and it shall melt, and all that dwell therein shall mourn: and it shall rise up wholly like a flood; and shall be drowned, as by the flood of Egypt.

6 It is he that buildeth his stories in the heaven, and has founded his troop in the earth; he that calleth for the waters of the sea, and poureth them out upon the face of the earth: The LORD is his name.

7 Are you not as children of the Ethiopians unto me, O children of Israel? saith the LORD. Have not I brought up Israel out of the land of Egypt? and the Philistines from Caphtor, and the Syrians from Kir?

8 Behold, the eyes of the Lord GOD are upon the sinful kingdom, and I will destroy it from off the face of the earth; saving that I will not utterly destroy the house of Jacob, saith the LORD.

9 For, lo, I will command, and I will sift the house of Israel among all nations, like as corn is sifted in a sieve, yet shall not the least grain fall upon the earth.

10 All the sinners of my people shall die by the sword, which say, The evil shall not overtake nor prevent us.

11 In that day will I raise up the tabernacle of David that is fallen, and close up the breaches thereof; and I will raise up his ruins, and I will build it as in the days of old:

12 That they may possess the remnant of Edom, and of all the heathen, which are called by my name, saith the LORD that doeth this.

13 Behold, the days come, saith the LORD, that the plowman shall overtake the reaper, and the treader of grapes him that soweth seed; and the mountains shall drop sweet wine, and all the hills shall melt.

14 And I will bring again the captivity of my people of Israel, and they shall build the waste cities, and inhabit them; and they shall plant vineyards, and drink the wine thereof; they shall also make gardens, and eat the fruit of them.

15 And I will plant them upon their land, and they shall no more be pulled up out of their land which I have given them, saith the LORD your God.

OBADIAH.

CHAPTER 1

THE vision of Obadiah. Thus saith the Lord GOD concerning Edom; We have heard a rumour from the LORD, and an ambassador is sent among the heathen, Arise you , and let us rise up against her in battle.

2 Behold, I have made you small among the heathen: you are greatly despised.

3The pride of yours heart has deceived you, you that dwellest in the clefts of the rock, whose habitation is high; that saith in his heart, Who shall bring me down to the ground?

4 Though you exalt yourself as the eagle, and though you set your nest among the stars, thence will I bring you down, saith the LORD.

5 If thieves came to you, if robbers by night, (how are you cut off!) would they not have stolen till they had enough? if the grapegatherers came to you, would they not leave some grapes?

6 How are the things of Esau searched out! how are his hidden things sought up!

7 All the men of your confederacy have brought you even to the border: the men that were at peace with you have deceived you, and prevailed against you; they that eat your bread have laid a wound under you: there is none understanding in him.

8 Shall I not in that day, saith the LORD, even destroy the wise men out of Edom, and understanding out of the mount of Esau?

9 And your mighty men, O Teman, shall be dismayed, to the end that every one of the mount of Esau may be cut off by slaughter.

10For your violence against your brother Jacob shame shall cover you, and you shalt be cut off for ever.

11 In the day that you stoodest on the other side, in the day that the strangers carried away captive his forces, and foreigners entered into his gates, and cast lots upon Jerusalem, even you wast as one of them.

12 But you shouldest not have looked on the day of your brother in the day that he became a stranger; neither shouldest you have rejoiced over the children of Judah in the day of their destruction; neither shouldest you have spoken proudly in the day of distress.

13 You shouldest not have entered into the gate of my people in the day of their calamity; yea, you shouldest not have looked on their affliction in the day of their calamity, nor have laid hands on their substance in the day of their calamity;

14 Neither shouldest you have stood in the crossway, to cut off those of his that did escape; neither shouldest you have delivered up those of his that did remain in the day of distress.

15 For the day of the LORD is near upon all the heathen: as you have done, it shall be done unto you: your reward shall return upon yours own head.

16 For as you have drunk upon my holy mountain, so shall all the heathen drink continually, yea, they shall drink, and they shall swallow down, and they shall be as though they had not been.

17But upon mount Zion shall be deliverance, and there shall be holiness; and the house of Jacob shall possess their possessions.

18 And the house of Jacob shall be a fire, and the house of Joseph a flame, and the house of Esau for stubble, and they shall kindle in them, and devour them; and there shall not be any remaining of the house of Esau; for the LORD has spoken it.

19 And they of the south shall possess the mount of Esau; and they of the plain the Philistines: and they shall possess the fields of Ephraim, and the fields of Samaria: and Benjamin shall possess Gilead.

20 And the captivity of this host of the children of Israel shall possess that of the Canaanites, even unto Zarephath; and the captivity of Jerusalem, which is in Sepharad, shall possess the cities of the south.

21 And saviours shall come up on mount Zion to judge the mount of Esau; and the kingdom shall be the LORD's.

JONAH.

CHAPTER 1

NOW the word of the LORD came unto Jonah the son of Amittai, saying,

2 Arise, go to Nineveh, that great city, and cry against it; for their wickedness is come up before me.

3 But Jonah rose up to flee unto Tarshish from the presence of the LORD, and went down to Joppa; and he found a ship going to Tarshish: so he paid the fare thereof, and went down into it, to go with them unto Tarshish from the presence of the LORD.

4 But the LORD sent out a great wind into the sea, and there was a mighty tempest in the sea, so that the ship was like to be broken.

5 Then the mariners were afraid, and cried every man unto his god, and cast forth the wares that were in the ship into the sea, to lighten it of them. But Jonah was gone down into the sides of the ship; and he lay, and was fast asleep.

6 So the shipmaster came to him, and said unto him, What meanest you , O sleeper? arise, call upon your God, if so be that God will think upon us, that we perish not.

7 And they said every one to his fellow, Come, and let us cast lots, that we may know for whose cause this evil is upon us. So they cast lots, and the lot fell upon Jonah.

8 Then said they unto him, Tell us, we pray you, for whose cause this evil is upon us; What is yours occupation? and whence comest you ? what is your country? and of what people are you ?

9 And he said unto them, I am an Hebrew; and I fear the LORD, the God of heaven, which has made the sea and the dry land.

10 Then were the men exceedingly afraid, and said unto him, Why have you done this? For the men knew that he fled from the presence of the LORD, because he had told them.

11 Then said they unto him, What shall we do unto you, that the sea may be calm unto us? for the sea created, and was tempestuous.

12 And he said unto them, Take me up, and cast me forth into the sea; so shall the sea be calm unto you: for I know that for my sake this great tempest is upon you.

13 Nevertheless the men rowed hard to bring it to the land; but they could not: for the sea created, and was tempestuous against them.

14 Wherefore they cried unto the LORD, and said, We beseech you, O LORD, we beseech you, let us not perish for this man's life, and lay not upon us innocent blood: for you , O LORD, have done as it pleased you.

15 So they took up Jonah, and cast him forth into the sea: and the sea ceased from her raging.

16 Then the men feared the LORD exceedingly, and offered a sacrifice unto the LORD, and made vows.

17 Now the LORD had prepared a great fish to swallow up Jonah. And Jonah was in the belly of the fish three days and three nights.

CHAPTER 2

THEN Jonah prayed unto the LORD his God out of the fish's belly,

2 And said, I cried by reason of my affliction unto the LORD, and he heard me; out of the belly of hell cried I, and you heardest my voice.

3 For you hadst cast me into the deep, in the midst of the seas; and the floods compassed me about: all your billows and your waves passed over me.

4 Then I said, I am cast out of your sight; yet I will look again toward your holy temple.

5 The waters compassed me about, even to the soul: the depth closed me round about, the weeds were wrapped about my head.

6 I went down to the bottoms of the mountains; the earth with her bars was about me for ever: yet have you brought up my life from corruption, O LORD my God.

7 When my soul fainted within me I remembered the LORD: and my prayer came in unto you, into yours holy temple.

8 They that observe lying vanities forsake their own mercy.

9 But I will sacrifice unto you with the voice of thanksgiving; I will pay that that I have vowed. Salvation is of the LORD.

10 And the LORD spake unto the fish, and it vomited out Jonah upon the dry land.

CHAPTER 3

AND the word of the LORD came unto Jonah the second time, saying,

2 Arise, go unto Nineveh, that great city, and preach unto it the preaching that I bid you.

3 So Jonah arose, and went unto Nineveh, according to the word of the LORD. Now Nineveh was an exceeding great city of three days' journey.

4 And Jonah began to enter into the city a day's journey, and he cried, and said, Yet forty days, and Nineveh shall be overthrown.

5 So the people of Nineveh believed God, and proclaimed a fast, and put on sackcloth, from the greatest of them even to the least of them.

6 For word came unto the king of Nineveh, and he arose from his throne, and he laid his robe from him, and covered him with sackcloth, and sat in ashes.

7 And he caused it to be proclaimed and published through Nineveh by the decree of the king and his nobles, saying, Let neither man nor beast, herd nor flock, taste any thing: let them not feed, nor drink water:

8 But let man and beast be covered with sackcloth, and cry mightily unto God: yea, let them turn every one from his evil way, and from the violence that is in their hands.

9 Who can tell if God will turn and repent, and turn away from his fierce anger, that we perish not?

10 And God saw their works, that they turned from their evil way; and God repented of the evil, that he had said that he would do unto them; and he did it not.

CHAPTER 4

BUT it displeased Jonah exceedingly, and he was very angry.

2 And he prayed unto the LORD, and said, I pray you, O LORD, was not this my saying, when I was yet in my country? Therefore I fled before unto Tarshish: for I knew that you are a gracious God, and merciful, slow to anger, and of great kindness, and repentest you of the evil.

3 Therefore now, O LORD, take, I beseech you, my life from me; for it is better for me to die than to live.

4 Then said the LORD, Doest you well to be angry?

5 So Jonah went out of the city, and sat on the east side of the city, and there made him a booth, and sat under it in the shadow, till he might see what would become of the city.

6 And the LORD God prepared a gourd, and made it to come up over Jonah, that it might be a shadow over his head, to deliver him from his grief. So Jonah was exceeding glad of the gourd.

7 But God prepared a worm when the morning rose the next day, and it struck the gourd that it withered.

8 And it came to pass, when the sun did arise, that God prepared a vehement east wind; and the sun beat upon the head of Jonah, that he fainted, and wished in himself to die, and said, It is better for me to die than to live.

9 And God said to Jonah, Doest you well to be angry for the gourd? And he said, I do well to be angry, even unto death.

10 Then said the LORD, You have had pity on the gourd, for the which you have not laboured, neither madest it grow; which came up in a night, and perished in a night:

11 And should not I spare Nineveh, that great city, wherein are more than sixscore thousand persons that cannot discern between their right hand and their left hand; and also much cattle?

MICAH.

CHAPTER 1

THE word of the LORD that came to Micah the Morasthite in the days of Jotham, Ahaz, and Hezekiah, kings of Judah, which he saw concerning Samaria and Jerusalem.

2 Hear, all you people; hearken, O earth, and all that therein is: and let the Lord GOD be witness against you, the Lord from his holy temple.

3 For, behold, the LORD comes forth out of his place, and will come down, and tread upon the high places of the earth.

4 And the mountains shall be molten under him, and the valleys shall be cleft, as wax before the fire, and as the waters that are poured down a steep place.

5 For the transgression of Jacob is all this, and for the sins of the house of Israel. What is the transgression of Jacob? is it not Samaria? and what are the high places of Judah? are they not Jerusalem?

6 Therefore I will make Samaria as an heap of the field, and as plantings of a vineyard: and I will pour down the stones thereof into the valley, and I will discover the foundations thereof.

7 And all the graven images thereof shall be beaten to pieces, and all the hires thereof shall be burned with the fire, and all the idols thereof will I lay desolate: for she gathered it of the hire of an harlot, and they shall return to the hire of an harlot.

8 Therefore I will wail and howl, I will go stripped and naked: I will make a wailing like the dragons, and mourning as the owls.

9 For her wound is incurable; for it is come unto Judah; he is come unto the gate of my people, even to Jerusalem.

10 Declare you it not at Gath, weep you not at all: in the house of Aphrah roll yourself in the dust.

11 Pass you away, you inhabitant of Saphir, having your shame naked: the inhabitant of Zaanan came not forth in the mourning of Beth-ezel; he shall receive of you his standing.

12 For the inhabitant of Maroth waited carefully for good: but evil came down from the LORD unto the gate of Jerusalem.

13 O you inhabitant of Lachish, bind the chariot to the swift beast: she is the beginning of the sin to the daughter of Zion: for the transgressions of Israel were found in you.

14 Therefore shalt you give presents to Moresheth-gath: the houses of Achzib shall be a lie to the kings of Israel.

15 Yet will I bring an heir unto you, O inhabitant of Mareshah: he shall come unto Adullam the glory of Israel.

16 Make you bald, and poll you for your delicate children; enlarge your baldness as the eagle; for they are gone into captivity from you.

CHAPTER 2

WOE to them that devise iniquity, and work evil upon their beds! when the morning is light, they practise it, because it is in the power of their hand.

2 And they covet fields, and take them by violence; and houses, and take them away: so they oppress a man and his house, even a man and his heritage.

3 Therefore thus saith the LORD; Behold, against this family do I devise an evil, from which you shall not remove your necks; neither shall you go haughtily: for this time is evil.

4 In that day shall one take up a parable against you, and lament with a doleful lamentation, and say, We be utterly spoiled: he has changed the portion of my people: how has he removed it from me! turning away he has divided our fields.

5 Therefore you shalt have none that shall cast a cord by lot in the congregation of the LORD.

6 Prophesy you not, say they to them that prophesy: they shall not prophesy to them, that they shall not take shame.

7 O you that are named the house of Jacob, is the spirit of the LORD straitened? are these his doings? do not my words do good to him that walketh uprightly?

8 Even of late my people is risen up as an enemy: you pull off the robe with the garment from them that pass by securely as men averse from war.

9 The women of my people have you cast out from their pleasant houses; from their children have you taken away my glory for ever.

10 Arise you, and depart; for this is not your rest: because it is polluted, it shall destroy you, even with a sore destruction.

11 If a man walking in the spirit and falsehood do lie, saying, I will prophesy unto you of wine and of strong drink; he shall even be the prophet of this people.

12 I will surely assemble, O Jacob, all of you; I will surely gather the remnant of Israel; I will put them together as the sheep of Bozrah, as the flock in the midst of their fold: they shall make great noise by reason of the multitude of men.

13 The breaker is come up before them: they have broken up, and have passed through the gate, and are gone out by it: and their king shall pass before them, and the LORD on the head of them.

CHAPTER 3

AND I said, Hear, I pray you, O heads of Jacob, and you princes of the house of Israel; Is it not for you to know judgment?

2 Who hate the good, and love the evil; who pluck off their skin from off them, and their flesh from off their bones;

3 Who also eat the flesh of my people, and flay their skin from off them; and they break their bones, and chop them in pieces, as for the pot, and as flesh within the caldron.

4 Then shall they cry unto the LORD, but he will not hear them: he will even hide his face from them at that time, as they have behaved themselves ill in their doings.

5 Thus saith the LORD concerning the prophets that make my people err, that bite with their teeth, and cry, Peace; and he that putteth not into their mouths, they even prepare war against him.

6 Therefore night shall be unto you, that you shall not have a vision; and it shall be dark unto you, that you shall not divine; and the sun shall go down over the prophets, and the day shall be dark over them.

7 Then shall the seers be ashamed, and the diviners confounded: yea, they shall all cover their lips; for there is no answer of God.

8 But truly I am full of power by the spirit of the LORD, and of judgment, and of might, to declare unto Jacob his transgression, and to Israel his sin.

9 Hear this, I pray you, you heads of the house of Jacob, and princes of the house of Israel, that abhor judgment, and pervert all equity.

10 They build up Zion with blood, and Jerusalem with iniquity.

11 The heads thereof judge for reward, and the priests thereof teach for hire, and the prophets thereof divine for money: yet will they lean upon the LORD, and say, Is not the LORD among us? none evil can come upon us.

12 Therefore shall Zion for your sake be plowed as a field, and Jerusalem shall become heaps, and the mountain of the house as the high places of the forest.

CHAPTER 4

BUT in the last days it shall come to pass, that the mountain of the house of the LORD shall be established in the top of the mountains, and it shall be exalted above the hills; and people shall flow unto it.

2 And many nations shall come, and say, Come, and let us go up to the mountain of the LORD, and to the house of the God of Jacob; and he will teach us of his ways, and we will walk in his paths: for the law shall go forth of Zion, and the word of the LORD from Jerusalem.

3 And he shall judge among many people, and rebuke strong nations afar off; and they shall beat their swords into plowshares, and their spears into pruninghooks: nation shall not lift up a sword against nation, neither shall they learn war any more.

4 But they shall sit every man under his vine and under his fig tree; and none shall make them afraid: for the mouth of the LORD of hosts has spoken it.

5 For all people will walk every one in the name of his god, and we will walk in the name of the LORD our God for ever and ever.

6 In that day, saith the LORD, will I assemble her that halteth, and I will gather her that is driven out, and her that I have afflicted;

7 And I will make her that halted a remnant, and her that was cast far off a strong nation: and the LORD shall reign over them in mount Zion from henceforth, even for ever.

8 And you, O tower of the flock, the strong hold of the daughter of Zion, unto you shall it come, even the first dominion; the kingdom shall come to the daughter of Jerusalem.

9 Now why dost you cry out aloud? is there no king in you? is your counseller perished? for pangs have taken you as a woman in travail.

10 Be in pain, and labour to bring forth, O daughter of Zion, like a woman in travail: for now shalt you go forth out of the city, and you shalt dwell in the field, and you shalt go even to Babylon; there shalt you be delivered; there the LORD shall redeem you from the hand of yours enemies.

11 Now also many nations are gathered against you, that say, Let her be defiled, and let our eye look upon Zion.

12 But they know not the thoughts of the LORD, neither understand they his counsel: for he shall gather them as the sheaves into the floor.

13 Arise and thresh, O daughter of Zion: for I will make yours horn iron, and I will make your hoofs brass: and you shalt beat in pieces many people: and I will consecrate their gain unto the LORD, and their substance unto the Lord of the whole earth.

CHAPTER 5

NOW gather yourself in troops, O daughter of troops: he has laid siege against us: they shall strike the judge of Israel with a rod upon the cheek.

2 But you , Beth-lehem Ephratah, though you be little among the thousands of Judah, yet out of you shall he come forth unto me that is to be ruler in Israel; whose goings forth have been from of old, from everlasting.

3 Therefore will he give them up, until the time that she which travaileth has brought forth: then the remnant of his brethren shall return unto the children of Israel.

4And he shall stand and feed in the strength of the LORD, in the majesty of the name of the LORD his God; and they shall abide: for now shall he be great unto the ends of the earth.

5 And this man shall be the peace, when the Assyrian shall come into our land: and when he shall tread in our palaces, then shall we raise against him seven shepherds, and eight principal men.

6 And they shall waste the land of Assyria with the sword, and the land of Nimrod in the entrances thereof: thus shall he deliver us from the Assyrian, when he comes into our land, and when he treadeth within our borders.

7 And the remnant of Jacob shall be in the midst of many people as a dew from the LORD, as the showers upon the grass, that tarrieth not for man, nor waiteth for the sons of men.

8And the remnant of Jacob shall be among the Gentiles in the midst of many people as a lion among the beasts of the forest, as a young lion among the flocks of sheep: who, if he go through, both treadeth down, and teareth in pieces, and none can deliver.

9 Yours hand shall be lifted up upon yours adversaries, and all yours enemies shall be cut off.

10 And it shall come to pass in that day, saith the LORD, that I will cut off your horses out of the midst of you, and I will destroy your chariots:

11 And I will cut off the cities of your land, and throw down all your strong holds:

12 And I will cut off witchcrafts out of yours hand; and you shalt have no more soothsayers:

13 Your graven images also will I cut off, and your standing images out of the midst of you; and you shalt no more worship the work of yours hands.

14 And I will pluck up your groves out of the midst of you: so will I destroy your cities.

15 And I will execute vengeance in anger and fury upon the heathen, such as they have not heard.

CHAPTER 6

HEAR you now what the LORD saith; Arise, contend you before the mountains, and let the hills hear your voice.

2 Hear you , O mountains, the LORD's controversy, and you strong foundations of the earth: for the LORD has a controversy with his people, and he will plead with Israel.

3 O my people, what have I done unto you? and wherein have I wearied you? testify against me.

4 For I brought you up out of the land of Egypt, and redeemed you out of the house of servants; and I sent before you Moses, Aaron, and Miriam.

5 O my people, remember now what Balak king of Moab consulted, and what Balaam the son of Beor answered him from Shittim unto Gilgal; that you may know the righteousness of the LORD.

6Wherewith shall I come before the LORD, and bow myself before the high God? shall I come before him with burnt offerings, with calves of a year old?

7 Will the LORD be pleased with thousands of rams, or with ten thousands of rivers of oil? shall I give my firstborn for my transgression, the fruit of my body for the sin of my soul?

8 He has shewed you, O man, what is good; and what doth the LORD require of you, but to do justly, and to love mercy, and to walk humbly with your God?

9 The LORD's voice crieth unto the city, and the man of wisdom shall see your name: hear you the rod, and who has appointed it.

10Are there yet the treasures of wickedness in the house of the wicked, and the scant measure that is abominable?

11 Shall I count them pure with the wicked balances, and with the bag of deceitful weights?

12 For the rich men thereof are full of violence, and the inhabitants thereof have spoken lies, and their tongue is deceitful in their mouth.

13 Therefore also will I make you sick in striking you, in making you desolate because of your sins.

14 You shalt eat, but not be satisfied; and your casting down shall be in the midst of you; and you shalt take hold, but shalt not deliver; and that which you deliverest will I give up to the sword.

15 You shalt sow, but you shalt not reap; you shalt tread the olives, but you shalt not anoint you with oil; and sweet wine, but shalt not drink wine.

16For the statutes of Omri are kept, and all the works of the house of Ahab, and you walk in their counsels; that I should make you a desolation, and the inhabitants thereof an hissing: therefore you shall bear the reproach of my people.

CHAPTER 7

WOE is me! for I am as when they have gathered the summer fruits, as the grapegleanings of the vintage: there is no cluster to eat: my soul desired the firstripe fruit.

2 The good man is perished out of the earth: and there is none upright among men: they all lie in wait for blood; they hunt every man his brother with a net.

3That they may do evil with both hands earnestly, the prince asketh, and the judge asketh for a reward; and the great man, he uttereth his mischievous desire: so they wrap it up.

4 The best of them is as a brier: the most upright is sharper than a thorn hedge: the day of your watchmen and your visitation comes; now shall be their perplexity.

5Trust you not in a friend, put you not confidence in a guide: keep the doors of your mouth from her that lies in your bosom.

6 For the son dishonoureth the father, the daughter riseth up against her mother, the daughter in law against her mother in law; a man's enemies are the men of his own house.

7 Therefore I will look unto the LORD; I will wait for the God of my salvation: my God will hear me.

8Rejoice not against me, O my enemy: when I fall, I shall arise; when I sit in darkness, the LORD shall be a light unto me.

9 I will bear the indignation of the LORD, because I have sinned against him, until he plead my cause, and execute judgment for me: he will bring me forth to the light, and I shall behold his righteousness.

10 Then she that is my enemy shall see it, and shame shall cover her which said unto me, Where is the LORD your God? my eyes shall behold her: now shall she be trodden down as the mire of the streets.

11 In the day that your walls are to be built, in that day shall the decree be far removed.

12 In that day also he shall come even to you from Assyria, and from the fortified cities, and from the fortress even to the river, and from sea to sea, and from mountain to mountain.

13 Notwithstanding the land shall be desolate because of them that dwell therein, for the fruit of their doings.

14Feed your people with your rod, the flock of yours heritage, which dwell solitarily in the wood, in the midst of Carmel: let them feed in Bashan and Gilead, as in the days of old.

15 According to the days of your coming out of the land of Egypt will I shew unto him marvellous things.

16The nations shall see and be confounded at all their might: they shall lay their hand upon their mouth, their ears shall be deaf.

17 They shall lick the dust like a serpent, they shall move out of their holes like worms of the earth: they shall be afraid of the LORD our God, and shall fear because of you.

18 Who is a God like unto you, that pardoneth iniquity, and passes by the transgression of the remnant of his heritage? he retaineth not his anger for ever, because he delighteth in mercy.

19 He will turn again, he will have compassion upon us; he will subdue our iniquities; and you will cast all their sins into the depths of the sea.

20 You will perform the truth to Jacob, and the mercy to Abraham, which you have sworn unto our fathers from the days of old.

NAHUM.

CHAPTER 1

THE burden of Nineveh. The book of the vision of Nahum the Elkoshite.

2 God is jealous, and the LORD revengeth; the LORD revengeth, and is furious; the LORD will take vengeance on his adversaries, and he reserveth wrath for his enemies.

3 The LORD is slow to anger, and great in power, and will not at all acquit the wicked: the LORD has his way in the whirlwind and in the storm, and the clouds are the dust of his feet.

4 He rebuketh the sea, and maketh it dry, and drieth up all the rivers: Bashan languisheth, and Carmel, and the flower of Lebanon languisheth.

5 The mountains quake at him, and the hills melt, and the earth is burned at his presence, yea, the world, and all that dwell therein.

6 Who can stand before his indignation? and who can abide in the fierceness of his anger? his fury is poured out like fire, and the rocks are thrown down by him.

7 The LORD is good, a strong hold in the day of trouble; and he knoweth them that trust in him.

8 But with an overrunning flood he will make an utter end of the place thereof, and darkness shall pursue his enemies.

9 What do you imagine against the LORD? he will make an utter end: affliction shall not rise up the second time.

10 For while they be folden together as thorns, and while they are drunken as drunkards, they shall be devoured as stubble fully dry.

11 There is one come out of you, that imagineth evil against the LORD, a wicked counseller.

12 Thus saith the LORD; Though they be quiet, and likewise many, yet thus shall they be cut down, when he shall pass through. Though I have afflicted you, I will afflict you no more.

13 For now will I break his yoke from off you, and will burst your bonds in sunder.

14 And the LORD has given a commandment concerning you, that no more of your name be sown: out of the house of your gods will I cut off the graven image and the molten image: I will make your grave; for you are vile.

15 Behold upon the mountains the feet of him that bringeth good tidings, that publisheth peace! O Judah, keep your solemn feasts, perform your vows: for the wicked shall no more pass through you; he is utterly cut off.

CHAPTER 2

HE that dasheth in pieces is come up before your face: keep the munition, watch the way, make your loins strong, fortify your power mightily.

2 For the LORD has turned away the excellency of Jacob, as the excellency of Israel: for the emptiers have emptied them out, and marred their vine branches.

3 The shield of his mighty men is made red, the valiant men are in scarlet: the chariots shall be with flaming torches in the day of his preparation, and the fir trees shall be terribly shaken.

4 The chariots shall rage in the streets, they shall justle one against another in the broad ways: they shall seem like torches, they shall run like the lightnings.

5 He shall recount his worthies: they shall stumble in their walk; they shall make haste to the wall thereof, and the defence shall be prepared.

6 The gates of the rivers shall be opened, and the palace shall be dissolved.

7 And Huzzab shall be led away captive, she shall be brought up, and her maids shall lead her as with the voice of doves, tabering upon their breasts.

8 But Nineveh is of old like a pool of water: yet they shall flee away. Stand, stand, shall they cry; but none shall look back.

9 Take you the spoil of silver, take the spoil of gold: for there is none end of the store and glory out of all the pleasant furniture.

10 She is empty, and void, and waste: and the heart melteth, and the knees strike together, and much pain is in all loins, and the faces of them all gather blackness.

11 Where is the dwelling of the lions, and the feedingplace of the young lions, where the lion, even the old lion, walked, and the lion's whelp, and none made them afraid?

12 The lion did tear in pieces enough for his whelps, and strangled for his lionesses, and filled his holes with prey, and his dens with ravin.

13 Behold, I am against you, saith the LORD of hosts, and I will burn her chariots in the smoke, and the sword shall devour your young lions: and I will cut off your prey from the earth, and the voice of your messengers shall no more be heard.

CHAPTER 3

WOE to the bloody city! it is all full of lies and robbery; the prey departeth not;

2 The noise of a whip, and the noise of the rattling of the wheels, and of the pransing horses, and of the jumping chariots.

3 The horseman lifteth up both the bright sword and the glittering spear: and there is a multitude of slain, and a great number of carcases; and there is none end of their corpses; they stumble upon their corpses:

4 Because of the multitude of the whoredoms of the wellfavoured harlot, the mistress of witchcrafts, that selleth nations through her whoredoms, and families through her witchcrafts.

5 Behold, I am against you, saith the LORD of hosts; and I will discover your skirts upon your face, and I will shew the nations your nakedness, and the kingdoms your shame.

6 And I will cast abominable filth upon you, and make you vile, and will set you as a gazingstock.

7 And it shall come to pass, that all they that look upon you shall flee from you, and say, Nineveh is laid waste: who will bemoan her? whence shall I seek comforters for you?

8 Are you better than populous No, that was situate among the rivers, that had the waters round about it, whose rampart was the sea, and her wall was from the sea?

9 Ethiopia and Egypt were her strength, and it was infinite; Put and Lubim were your helpers.

10 Yet was she carried away, she went into captivity: her young children also were dashed in pieces at the top of all the streets: and they cast lots for her honourable men, and all her great men were bound in chains.

11 You also shalt be drunken: you shalt be hid, you also shalt seek strength because of the enemy.

12 All your strong holds shall be like fig trees with the firstripe figs: if they be shaken, they shall even fall into the mouth of the eater.

13 Behold, your people in the midst of you are women: the gates of your land shall be set wide open unto yours enemies: the fire shall devour your bars.

14 Draw you waters for the siege, fortify your strong holds: go into clay, and tread the morter, make strong the brickkiln.

15 There shall the fire devour you; the sword shall cut you off, it shall eat you up like the cankerworm: make yourself many as the cankerworm, make yourself many as the locusts.

16 You have multiplied your merchants above the stars of heaven: the cankerworm spoileth, and flieth away.

17 Your crowned are as the locusts, and your captains as the great grasshoppers, which camp in the hedges in the cold day, but when the sun ariseth they flee away, and their place is not known where they are.

18 Your shepherds slumber, O king of Assyria: your nobles shall dwell in the dust: your people is scattered upon the mountains, and no man gathereth them.

19 There is no healing of your bruise; your wound is grievous: all that hear the bruit of you shall clap the hands over you: for upon whom has not your wickedness passed continually?

HABAKKUK.

CHAPTER 1

THE burden which Habakkuk the prophet did see.

2 O LORD, how long shall I cry, and you will not hear! even cry out unto you of violence, and you will not save!

3 Why dost you shew me iniquity, and cause me to behold grievance? for spoiling and violence are before me: and there are that raise up strife and contention.

4 Therefore the law is slacked, and judgment doth never go forth: for the wicked doth compass about the righteous; therefore wrong judgment proceedeth.

5 Behold you among the heathen, and regard, and wonder marvellously: for I will work a work in your days, which you will not believe, though it be told you.

6 For, lo, I raise up the Chaldeans, that bitter and hasty nation, which shall march through the breadth of the land, to possess the dwellingplaces that are not theirs.

7 They are terrible and dreadful: their judgment and their dignity shall proceed of themselves.

8 Their horses also are swifter than the leopards, and are more fierce than the evening wolves: and their horsemen shall spread themselves, and their horsemen shall come from far; they shall fly as the eagle that hasteth to eat.

9 They shall come all for violence: their faces shall sup up as the east wind, and they shall gather the captivity as the sand.

10 And they shall scoff at the kings, and the princes shall be a scorn unto them: they shall deride every strong hold; for they shall heap dust, and take it.

11 Then shall his mind change, and he shall pass over, and offend, imputing this his power unto his god.

12 Are you not from everlasting, O LORD my God, my Holy One? we shall not die. O LORD, you have ordained them for judgment; and, O mighty God, you have established them for correction.

13 You are of purer eyes than to behold evil, and can not look on iniquity: wherefore lookest you upon them that deal treacherously, and holdest your tongue when the wicked devoureth the man that is more righteous than he?

14 And makest men as the fishes of the sea, as the creeping things, that have no ruler over them?

15 They take up all of them with the angle, they catch them in their net, and gather them in their drag: therefore they rejoice and are glad.

16 Therefore they sacrifice unto their net, and burn incense unto their drag; because by them their portion is fat, and their meat plenteous.

17 Shall they therefore empty their net, and not spare continually to slay the nations?

CHAPTER 2

I WILL stand upon my watch, and set me upon the tower, and will watch to see what he will say unto me, and what I shall answer when I am reproved.

2 And the LORD answered me, and said, Write the vision, and make it plain upon tables, that he may run that readeth it.

3 For the vision is yet for an appointed time, but at the end it shall speak, and not lie: though it tarry, wait for it; because it will surely come, it will not tarry.

4 Behold, his soul which is lifted up is not upright in him: but the just shall live by his faith.

5 Yea also, because he transgresseth by wine, he is a proud man, neither keepeth at home, who enlargeth his desire as hell, and is as death, and cannot be satisfied, but gathereth unto him all nations, and heapeth unto him all people:

6 Shall not all these take up a parable against him, and a taunting proverb against him, and say, Woe to him that increaseth that which is not his! how long? and to him that ladeth himself with thick clay!

7 Shall they not rise up suddenly that shall bite you, and awake that shall vex you, and you shalt be for booties unto them?

8 Because you have spoiled many nations, all the remnant of the people shall spoil you; because of men's blood, and for the violence of the land, of the city, and of all that dwell therein.

9 Woe to him that coveteth an evil covetousness to his house, that he may set his nest on high, that he may be delivered from the power of evil!

10 You have consulted shame to your house by cutting off many people, and have sinned against your soul.

11 For the stone shall cry out of the wall, and the beam out of the timber shall answer it.

12 Woe to him that buildeth a town with blood, and stablisheth a city by iniquity!

13 Behold, is it not of the LORD of hosts that the people shall labour in the very fire, and the people shall weary themselves for very vanity?

14 For the earth shall be filled with the knowledge of the glory of the LORD, as the waters cover the sea.

15 Woe unto him that giveth his neighbour drink, that puttest your bottle to him, and makest him drunken also, that you mayest look on their nakedness!

16 You are filled with shame for glory: drink you also, and let your foreskin be uncovered: the cup of the LORD's right hand shall be turned unto you, and shameful spewing shall be on your glory.

17 For the violence of Lebanon shall cover you, and the spoil of beasts, which made them afraid, because of men's blood, and for the violence of the land, of the city, and of all that dwell therein.

18 What profiteth the graven image that the maker thereof has graven it; the molten image, and a teacher of lies, that the maker of his work trusteth therein, to make dumb idols?

19 Woe unto him that saith to the wood, Awake; to the dumb stone, Arise, it shall teach! Behold, it is laid over with gold and silver, and there is no breath at all in the midst of it.

20 But the LORD is in his holy temple: let all the earth keep silence before him.

CHAPTER 3

A PRAYER of Habakkuk the prophet upon Shigionoth.

2 O LORD, I have heard your speech, and was afraid: O LORD, revive your work in the midst of the years, in the midst of the years make known; in wrath remember mercy.

3 God came from Teman, and the Holy One from mount Paran. Selah. His glory covered the heavens, and the earth was full of his praise.

4 And his brightness was as the light; he had horns coming out of his hand: and there was the hiding of his power.

5 Before him went the pestilence, and burning coals went forth at his feet.

6 He stood, and measured the earth: he beheld, and drove asunder the nations; and the everlasting mountains were scattered, the perpetual hills did bow: his ways are everlasting.

7 I saw the tents of Cushan in affliction: and the curtains of the land of Midian did tremble.

8 Was the LORD displeased against the rivers? was yours anger against the rivers? was your wrath against the sea, that you did ride upon yours horses and your chariots of salvation?

9 Your bow was made quite naked, according to the oaths of the tribes, even your word. Selah. You did cleave the earth with rivers.

10 The mountains saw you, and they trembled: the overflowing of the water passed by: the deep uttered his voice, and lifted up his hands on high.

11 The sun and moon stood still in their habitation: at the light of yours arrows they went, and at the shining of your glittering spear.

12 You did march through the land in indignation, you did thresh the heathen in anger.

13 You wentest forth for the salvation of your people, even for salvation with yours anointed; you woundedst the head out of the house of the wicked, by discovering the foundation unto the neck. Selah.

14 You did strike through with his staves the head of his villages: they came out as a whirlwind to scatter me: their rejoicing was as to devour the poor secretly.

15 You did walk through the sea with yours horses, through the heap of great waters.

16 When I heard, my belly trembled; my lips quivered at the voice: rottenness entered into my bones, and I trembled in myself, that I might rest in the day of trouble: when he comes up unto the people, he will invade them with his troops.

17 Although the fig tree shall not blossom, neither shall fruit be in the vines; the labour of the olive shall fail, and the fields shall yield no meat; the flock shall be cut off from the fold, and there shall be no herd in the stalls:

18 Yet I will rejoice in the LORD, I will joy in the God of my salvation.

19 The LORD God is my strength, and he will make my feet like hinds' feet, and he will make me to walk upon my high places. To the chief singer on my stringed instruments.

ZEPHANIAH.

CHAPTER 1

THE word of the LORD which came unto Zephaniah the son of Cushi, the son of Gedaliah, the son of Amariah, the son of Hizkiah, in the days of Josiah the son of Amon, king of Judah.

2 I will utterly consume all things from off the land, saith the LORD.

3 I will consume man and beast; I will consume the fowls of the heaven, and the fishes of the sea, and the stumblingblocks with the wicked; and I will cut off man from off the land, saith the LORD.

4 I will also stretch out my hand upon Judah, and upon all the inhabitants of Jerusalem; and I will cut off the remnant of Baal from this place, and the name of the Chemarims with the priests;

5 And them that worship the host of heaven upon the housetops; and them that worship and that swear by the LORD, and that swear by Malcham;

6 And them that are turned back from the LORD; and those that have not sought the LORD, nor inquired for him.

7 Hold your peace at the presence of the Lord GOD: for the day of the LORD is at hand: for the LORD has prepared a sacrifice, he has bid his guests.

8 And it shall come to pass in the day of the LORD's sacrifice, that I will punish the princes, and the king's children, and all such as are clothed with strange apparel.

9 In the same day also will I punish all those that leap on the threshold, which fill their masters' houses with violence and deceit.

10 And it shall come to pass in that day, saith the LORD, that there shall be the noise of a cry from the fish gate, and an howling from the second, and a great crashing from the hills.

11 Howl, you inhabitants of Maktesh, for all the merchant people are cut down; all they that bear silver are cut off.

12 And it shall come to pass at that time, that I will search Jerusalem with candles, and punish the men that are settled on their lees: that say in their heart, The LORD will not do good, neither will he do evil.

13 Therefore their goods shall become a booty, and their houses a desolation: they shall also build houses, but not inhabit them; and they shall plant vineyards, but not drink the wine thereof.

14 The great day of the LORD is near, it is near, and hasteth greatly, even the voice of the day of the LORD: the mighty man shall cry there bitterly.

15 That day is a day of wrath, a day of trouble and distress, a day of wasteness and desolation, a day of darkness and gloominess, a day of clouds and thick darkness,

16 A day of the trumpet and alarm against the fenced cities, and against the high towers.

17 And I will bring distress upon men, that they shall walk like blind men, because they have sinned against the LORD: and their blood shall be poured out as dust, and their flesh as the dung.

18 Neither their silver nor their gold shall be able to deliver them in the day of the LORD's wrath; but the whole land shall be devoured by the fire of his jealousy: for he shall make even a speedy riddance of all them that dwell in the land.

CHAPTER 2

GATHER yourselves together, yea, gather together, O nation not desired;

2 Before the decree bring forth, before the day pass as the chaff, before the fierce anger of the LORD come upon you, before the day of the LORD's anger come upon you.

3 Seek you the LORD, all you meek of the earth, which have created his judgment; seek righteousness, seek meekness: it may be you shall be hid in the day of the LORD's anger.

4 For Gaza shall be forsaken, and Ashkelon a desolation: they shall drive out Ashdod at the noon day, and Ekron shall be rooted up.

5 Woe unto the inhabitants of the sea coast, the nation of the Cherethites! the word of the LORD is against you; O Canaan, the land of the Philistines, I will even destroy you, that there shall be no inhabitant.

6 And the sea coast shall be dwellings and cottages for shepherds, and folds for flocks.

7 And the coast shall be for the remnant of the house of Judah; they shall feed thereupon: in the houses of Ashkelon shall they lie down in the evening: for the LORD their God shall visit them, and turn away their captivity.

8 I have heard the reproach of Moab, and the revilings of the children of Ammon, whereby they have reproached my people, and magnified themselves against their border.

9 Therefore as I live, saith the LORD of hosts, the God of Israel, Surely Moab shall be as Sodom, and the children of Ammon as Gomorrah, even the breeding of nettles, and saltpits, and a perpetual desolation: the residue of my people shall spoil them, and the remnant of my people shall possess them.

10 This shall they have for their pride, because they have reproached and magnified themselves against the people of the LORD of hosts.

11 The LORD will be terrible unto them: for he will famish all the gods of the earth; and men shall worship him, every one from his place, even all the isles of the heathen.

12 You Ethiopians also, you shall be slain by my sword.

13 And he will stretch out his hand against the north, and destroy Assyria; and will make Nineveh a desolation, and dry like a wilderness.

14 And flocks shall lie down in the midst of her, all the beasts of the nations: both the cormorant and the bittern shall lodge in the upper lintels of it; their voice shall sing in the windows; desolation shall be in the thresholds: for he shall uncover the cedar work.

15 This is the rejoicing city that dwelt carelessly, that said in her heart, I am, and there is none beside me: how is she become a desolation, a place for beasts to lie down in! every one that passes by her shall hiss, and wag his hand.

CHAPTER 3

WOE to her that is filthy and polluted, to the oppressing city!

2 She obeyed not the voice; she received not correction; she trusted not in the LORD; she drew not near to her God.

3 Her princes within her are roaring lions; her judges are evening wolves; they gnaw not the bones till the morrow.

4 Her prophets are light and treacherous persons: her priests have polluted the sanctuary, they have done violence to the law.

5 The just LORD is in the midst thereof; he will not do iniquity: every morning doth he bring his judgment to light, he faileth not; but the unjust knoweth no shame.

6 I have cut off the nations: their towers are desolate; I made their streets waste, that none passes by: their cities are destroyed, so that there is no man, that there is none inhabitant.

7 I said, Surely you will fear me, you will receive instruction; so their dwelling should not be cut off, howsoever I punished them: but they rose early, and corrupted all their doings.

8 Therefore wait you upon me, saith the LORD, until the day that I rise up to the prey: for my determination is to gather the nations, that I may assemble the kingdoms, to pour upon them my indignation, even all my fierce anger: for all the earth shall be devoured with the fire of my jealousy.

9 For then will I turn to the people a pure language, that they may all call upon the name of the LORD, to serve him with one consent.

10 From beyond the rivers of Ethiopia my suppliants, even the daughter of my dispersed, shall bring my offering.

11 In that day shalt you not be ashamed for all your doings, wherein you have transgressed against me: for then I will take away out of the midst of you them that rejoice in your pride, and you shalt no more be haughty because of my holy mountain.

12 I will also leave in the midst of you an afflicted and poor people, and they shall trust in the name of the LORD.

13 The remnant of Israel shall not do iniquity, nor speak lies; neither shall a deceitful tongue be found in their mouth: for they shall feed and lie down, and none shall make them afraid.

14 Sing, O daughter of Zion; shout, O Israel; be glad and rejoice with all the heart, O daughter of Jerusalem.

15 The LORD has taken away your judgments, he has cast out yours enemy: the king of Israel, even the LORD, is in the midst of you: you shalt not see evil any more.

16 In that day it shall be said to Jerusalem, Fear you not: and to Zion, Let not yours hands be slack.

17 The LORD your God in the midst of you is mighty; he will save, he will rejoice over you with joy; he will rest in his love, he will joy over you with singing.

18 I will gather them that are sorrowful for the solemn assembly, who are of you, to whom the reproach of it was a burden.

19 Behold, at that time I will undo all that afflict you: and I will save her that halteth, and gather her that was driven out; and I will get them praise and fame in every land where they have been put to shame.

20 At that time will I bring you again, even in the time that I gather you: for I will make you a name and a praise among all people of the earth, when I turn back your captivity before your eyes, saith the LORD.

HAGGAI.

CHAPTER 1

IN the second year of Darius the king, in the sixth month, in the first day of the month, came the word of the LORD by Haggai the prophet unto Zerubbabel the son of Shealtiel, governor of Judah, and to Joshua the son of Josedech, the high priest, saying,

2 Thus speaketh the LORD of hosts, saying, This people say, The time is not come, the time that the LORD's house should be built.

3 Then came the word of the LORD by Haggai the prophet, saying,

4 Is it time for you, O you , to dwell in your cieled houses, and this house lie waste?

5 Now therefore thus saith the LORD of hosts; Consider your ways.

6 You have sown much, and bring in little; you eat, but you have not enough; you drink, but you are not filled with drink; you clothe you, but there is none warm; and he that earneth wages earneth wages to put it into a bag with holes.

7 Thus saith the LORD of hosts; Consider your ways.

8 Go up to the mountain, and bring wood, and build the house; and I will take pleasure in it, and I will be glorified, saith the LORD.

9 You looked for much, and, lo, it came to little; and when you brought it home, I did blow upon it. Why? saith the LORD of hosts. Because of my house that is waste, and you run every man unto his own house.

10 Therefore the heaven over you is stayed from dew, and the earth is stayed from her fruit.

11 And I called for a drought upon the land, and upon the mountains, and upon the corn, and upon the new wine, and upon the oil, and upon that which the ground bringeth forth, and upon men, and upon cattle, and upon all the labour of the hands.

12 Then Zerubbabel the son of Shealtiel, and Joshua the son of Josedech, the high priest, with all the remnant of the people, obeyed the voice of the LORD their God, and the words of Haggai the prophet, as the LORD their God had sent him, and the people did fear before the LORD.

13 Then spake Haggai the LORD's messenger in the LORD's message unto the people, saying, I am with you, saith the LORD.

14 And the LORD stirred up the spirit of Zerubbabel the son of Shealtiel, governor of Judah, and the spirit of Joshua the son of Josedech, the high priest, and the spirit of all the remnant of the people; and they came and did work in the house of the LORD of hosts, their God,

15 In the four and twentieth day of the sixth month, in the second year of Darius the king.

CHAPTER 2

IN the seventh month, in the one and twentieth day of the month, came the word of the LORD by the prophet Haggai, saying,

2 Speak now to Zerubbabel the son of Shealtiel, governor of Judah, and to Joshua the son of Josedech, the high priest, and to the residue of the people, saying,

3 Who is left among you that saw this house in her first glory? and how do you see it now? is it not in your eyes in comparison of it as nothing?

4 Yet now be strong, O Zerubbabel, saith the LORD; and be strong, O Joshua, son of Josedech, the high priest; and be strong, all you people of the land, saith the LORD, and work: for I am with you, saith the LORD of hosts:

5 According to the word that I covenanted with you when you came out of Egypt, so my spirit remaineth among you: fear you not.

6 For thus saith the LORD of hosts; Yet once, it is a little while, and I will shake the heavens, and the earth, and the sea, and the dry land;

7 And I will shake all nations, and the desire of all nations shall come: and I will fill this house with glory, saith the LORD of hosts.

8 The silver is my, and the gold is my, saith the LORD of hosts.

9 The glory of this latter house shall be greater than of the former, saith the LORD of hosts: and in this place will I give peace, saith the LORD of hosts.

10 In the four and twentieth day of the ninth month, in the second year of Darius, came the word of the LORD by Haggai the prophet, saying,

11 Thus saith the LORD of hosts; Ask now the priests concerning the law, saying,

12 If one bear holy flesh in the skirt of his garment, and with his skirt do touch bread, or pottage, or wine, or oil, or any meat, shall it be holy? And the priests answered and said, No.

13 Then said Haggai, If one that is unclean by a dead body touch any of these, shall it be unclean? And the priests answered and said, It shall be unclean.

14 Then answered Haggai, and said, So is this people, and so is this nation before me, saith the LORD; and so is every work of their hands; and that which they offer there is unclean.

15 And now, I pray you, consider from this day and upward, from before a stone was laid upon a stone in the temple of the LORD:

16 Since those days were, when one came to an heap of twenty measures, there were but ten: when one came to the pressfat for to draw out fifty vessels out of the press, there were but twenty.

17 I struck you with blasting and with mildew and with hail in all the labours of your hands; yet you turned not to me, saith the LORD.

18 Consider now from this day and upward, from the four and twentieth day of the ninth month, even from the day that the foundation of the LORD's temple was laid, consider it.

19 Is the seed yet in the barn? yea, as yet the vine, and the fig tree, and the pomegranate, and the olive tree, has not brought forth: from this day will I bless you.

20 And again the word of the LORD came unto Haggai in the four and twentieth day of the month, saying,

21 Speak to Zerubbabel, governor of Judah, saying, I will shake the heavens and the earth;

22 And I will overthrow the throne of kingdoms, and I will destroy the strength of the kingdoms of the heathen; and I will overthrow the chariots, and those that ride in them; and the horses and their riders shall come down, every one by the sword of his brother.

23 In that day, saith the LORD of hosts, will I take you, O Zerubbabel, my servant, the son of Shealtiel, saith the LORD, and will make you as a signet: for I have chosen you, saith the LORD of hosts.

ZECHARIAH.

CHAPTER 1

IN the eighth month, in the second year of Darius, came the word of the LORD unto Zechariah, the son of Berechiah, the son of Iddo the prophet, saying,

2 The LORD has been sore displeased with your fathers.

3 Therefore say you unto them, Thus saith the LORD of hosts; Turn you unto me, saith the LORD of hosts, and I will turn unto you, saith the LORD of hosts.

4 Be you not as your fathers, unto whom the former prophets have cried, saying, Thus saith the LORD of hosts; Turn you now from your evil ways, and from your evil doings: but they did not hear, nor hearken unto me, saith the LORD.

5 Your fathers, where are they? and the prophets, do they live for ever?

6 But my words and my statutes, which I commanded my servants the prophets, did they not take hold of your fathers? and they returned and said, Like as the LORD of hosts thought to do unto us, according to our ways, and according to our doings, so has he dealt with us.

7 Upon the four and twentieth day of the eleventh month, which is the month Sebat, in the second year of Darius, came the word of the LORD unto Zechariah, the son of Berechiah, the son of Iddo the prophet, saying,

8 I saw by night, and behold a man riding upon a red horse, and he stood among the myrtle trees that were in the bottom; and behind him were there red horses, speckled, and white.

9 Then said I, O my lord, what are these? And the angel that talked with me said unto me, I will shew you what these be.

10 And the man that stood among the myrtle trees answered and said, These are they whom the LORD has sent to walk to and fro through the earth.

11 And they answered the angel of the LORD that stood among the myrtle trees, and said, We have walked to and fro through the earth, and, behold, all the earth sitteth still, and is at rest.

12 Then the angel of the LORD answered and said, O LORD of hosts, how long will you not have mercy on Jerusalem and on the cities of Judah, against which you have had indignation these threescore and ten years?

13 And the LORD answered the angel that talked with me with good words and comfortable words.

14 So the angel that communed with me said unto me, Cry you , saying, Thus saith the LORD of hosts; I am jealous for Jerusalem and for Zion with a great jealousy.

15 And I am very sore displeased with the heathen that are at ease: for I was but a little displeased, and they helped forward the affliction.

16 Therefore thus saith the LORD; I am returned to Jerusalem with mercies: my house shall be built in it, saith the LORD of hosts, and a line shall be stretched forth upon Jerusalem.

17 Cry yet, saying, Thus saith the LORD of hosts; My cities through prosperity shall yet be spread abroad; and the LORD shall yet comfort Zion, and shall yet choose Jerusalem.

18 Then lifted I up my eyes, and saw, and behold four horns.

19 And I said unto the angel that talked with me, What be these? And he answered me, These are the horns which have scattered Judah, Israel, and Jerusalem.

20 And the LORD shewed me four carpenters.

21 Then said I, What come these to do? And he spake, saying, These are the horns which have scattered Judah, so that no man did lift up his head: but these are come to fray them, to cast out the horns of the Gentiles, which lifted up their horn over the land of Judah to scatter it.

CHAPTER 2

I LIFTED up my eyes again, and looked, and behold a man with a measuring line in his hand.

2 Then said I, Whither go you ? And he said unto me, To measure Jerusalem, to see what is the breadth thereof, and what is the length thereof.

3 And, behold, the angel that talked with me went forth, and another angel went out to meet him,

4 And said unto him, Run, speak to this young man, saying, Jerusalem shall be inhabited as towns without walls for the multitude of men and cattle therein:

5 For I, saith the LORD, will be unto her a wall of fire round about, and will be the glory in the midst of her.

6 Ho, ho, come forth, and flee from the land of the north, saith the LORD: for I have spread you abroad as the four winds of the heaven, saith the LORD.

7 Deliver yourself, O Zion, that dwellest with the daughter of Babylon.

8 For thus saith the LORD of hosts; After the glory has he sent me unto the nations which spoiled you: for he that toucheth you toucheth the apple of his eye.

9 For, behold, I will shake my hand upon them, and they shall be a spoil to their servants: and you shall know that the LORD of hosts has sent me.

10 Sing and rejoice, O daughter of Zion: for, lo, I come, and I will dwell in the midst of you, saith the LORD.

11 And many nations shall be joined to the LORD in that day, and shall be my people: and I will dwell in the midst of you, and you shalt know that the LORD of hosts has sent me unto you.

12 And the LORD shall inherit Judah his portion in the holy land, and shall choose Jerusalem again.

13 Be silent, O all flesh, before the LORD: for he is raised up out of his holy habitation.

CHAPTER 3

AND he shewed me Joshua the high priest standing before the angel of the LORD, and Satan standing at his right hand to resist him.

2 And the LORD said unto Satan, The LORD rebuke you, O Satan; even the LORD that has chosen Jerusalem rebuke you: is not this a brand plucked out of the fire?

3 Now Joshua was clothed with filthy garments, and stood before the angel.

4 And he answered and spake unto those that stood before him, saying, Take away the filthy garments from him. And unto him he said, Behold, I have caused yours iniquity to pass from you, and I will clothe you with change of raiment.

5 And I said, Let them set a fair mitre upon his head. So they set a fair mitre upon his head, and clothed him with garments. And the angel of the LORD stood by.

6 And the angel of the LORD protested unto Joshua, saying,

7 Thus saith the LORD of hosts; If you will walk in my ways, and if you will keep my charge, then you shalt also judge my house, and shalt also keep my courts, and I will give you places to walk among these that stand by.

8 Hear now, O Joshua the high priest, you , and your fellows that sit before you: for they are men wondered at: for, behold, I will bring forth my servant the BRANCH.

9 For behold the stone that I have laid before Joshua; upon one stone shall be seven eyes: behold, I will engrave the graving thereof, saith the LORD of hosts, and I will remove the iniquity of that land in one day.

10 In that day, saith the LORD of hosts, shall you call every man his neighbour under the vine and under the fig tree.

CHAPTER 4

AND the angel that talked with me came again, and waked me, as a man that is wakened out of his sleep,

2 And said unto me, What seest you ? And I said, I have looked, and behold a candlestick all of gold, with a bowl upon the top of it, and his seven lamps thereon, and seven pipes to the seven lamps, which are upon the top thereof:

3 And two olive trees by it, one upon the right side of the bowl, and the other upon the left side thereof.

4 So I answered and spake to the angel that talked with me, saying, What are these, my lord?

5 Then the angel that talked with me answered and said unto me, Knowest you not what these be? And I said, No, my lord.

6 Then he answered and spake unto me, saying, This is the word of the LORD unto Zerubbabel, saying, Not by might, nor by power, but by my spirit, saith the LORD of hosts.

7 Who are you , O great mountain? before Zerubbabel you shalt become a plain: and he shall bring forth the headstone thereof with shoutings, crying, Grace, grace unto it.

8 Moreover the word of the LORD came unto me, saying,

9 The hands of Zerubbabel have laid the foundation of this house; his hands shall also finish it; and you shalt know that the LORD of hosts has sent me unto you.

10 For who has despised the day of small things? for they shall rejoice, and shall see the plummet in the hand of Zerubbabel with those seven; they are the eyes of the LORD, which run to and fro through the whole earth.

11 Then answered I, and said unto him, What are these two olive trees upon the right side of the candlestick and upon the left side thereof?

12 And I answered again, and said unto him, What be these two olive branches which through the two golden pipes empty the golden oil out of themselves?

13 And he answered me and said, Knowest you not what these be? And I said, No, my lord.

14 Then said he, These are the two anointed ones, that stand by the Lord of the whole earth.

CHAPTER 5

THEN I turned, and lifted up my eyes, and looked, and behold a flying roll.

2 And he said unto me, What seest you? And I answered, I see a flying roll; the length thereof is twenty cubits, and the breadth thereof ten cubits.

3 Then said he unto me, This is the curse that goeth forth over the face of the whole earth: for every one that stealeth shall be cut off as on this side according to it; and every one that sweareth shall be cut off as on that side according to it.

4 I will bring it forth, saith the LORD of hosts, and it shall enter into the house of the thief, and into the house of him that sweareth falsely by my name: and it shall remain in the midst of his house, and shall consume it with the timber thereof and the stones thereof.

5 Then the angel that talked with me went forth, and said unto me, Lift up now yours eyes, and see what is this that goeth forth.

6 And I said, What is it? And he said, This is an ephah that goeth forth. He said moreover, This is their resemblance through all the earth.

7 And, behold, there was lifted up a talent of lead: and this is a woman that sitteth in the midst of the ephah.

8 And he said, This is wickedness. And he cast it into the midst of the ephah; and he cast the weight of lead upon the mouth thereof.

9 Then lifted I up my eyes, and looked, and, behold, there came out two women, and the wind was in their wings; for they had wings like the wings of a stork: and they lifted up the ephah between the earth and the heaven.

10 Then said I to the angel that talked with me, Whither do these bear the ephah?

11 And he said unto me, To build it an house in the land of Shinar: and it shall be established, and set there upon her own base.

CHAPTER 6

AND I turned, and lifted up my eyes, and looked, and, behold, there came four chariots out from between two mountains; and the mountains were mountains of brass.

2 In the first chariot were red horses; and in the second chariot black horses;

3 And in the third chariot white horses; and in the fourth chariot grisled and bay horses.

4 Then I answered and said unto the angel that talked with me, What are these, my lord?

5 And the angel answered and said unto me, These are the four spirits of the heavens, which go forth from standing before the Lord of all the earth.

6 The black horses which are therein go forth into the north country; and the white go forth after them; and the grisled go forth toward the south country.

7 And the bay went forth, and sought to go that they might walk to and fro through the earth: and he said, Get you hence, walk to and fro through the earth. So they walked to and fro through the earth.

8 Then cried he upon me, and spake unto me, saying, Behold, these that go toward the north country have quieted my spirit in the north country.

9 And the word of the LORD came unto me, saying,

10 Take of them of the captivity, even of Heldai, of Tobijah, and of Jedaiah, which are come from Babylon, and come you the same day, and go into the house of Josiah the son of Zephaniah;

11 Then take silver and gold, and make crowns, and set them upon the head of Joshua the son of Josedech, the high priest;

12 And speak unto him, saying, Thus speaketh the LORD of hosts, saying, Behold the man whose name is The BRANCH; and he shall grow up out of his place, and he shall build the temple of the LORD:

13 Even he shall build the temple of the LORD; and he shall bear the glory, and shall sit and rule upon his throne; and he shall be a priest upon his throne: and the counsel of peace shall be between them both.

14 And the crowns shall be to Helem, and to Tobijah, and to Jedaiah, and to Hen the son of Zephaniah, for a memorial in the temple of the LORD.

15 And they that are far off shall come and build in the temple of the LORD, and you shall know that the LORD of hosts has sent me unto you. And this shall come to pass, if you will diligently obey the voice of the LORD your God.

CHAPTER 7

AND it came to pass in the fourth year of king Darius, that the word of the LORD came unto Zechariah in the fourth day of the ninth month, even in Chisleu;

2 When they had sent unto the house of God Sherezer and Regem-melech, and their men, to pray before the LORD,

3 And to speak unto the priests which were in the house of the LORD of hosts, and to the prophets, saying, Should I weep in the fifth month, separating myself, as I have done these so many years?

4 Then came the word of the LORD of hosts unto me, saying,

5 Speak unto all the people of the land, and to the priests, saying, When you fasted and mourned in the fifth and seventh month, even those seventy years, did you at all fast unto me, even to me?

6 And when you did eat, and when you did drink, did not you eat for yourselves, and drink for yourselves?

7 Should you not hear the words which the LORD has cried by the former prophets, when Jerusalem was inhabited and in prosperity, and the cities thereof round about her, when men inhabited the south and the plain?

8 And the word of the LORD came unto Zechariah, saying,

9 Thus speaketh the LORD of hosts, saying, Execute true judgment, and shew mercy and compassions every man to his brother:

10 And oppress not the widow, nor the fatherless, the stranger, nor the poor; and let none of you imagine evil against his brother in your heart.

11 But they refused to hearken, and pulled away the shoulder, and stopped their ears, that they should not hear.

12 Yea, they made their hearts as an adamant stone, lest they should hear the law, and the words which the LORD of hosts has sent in his spirit by the former prophets: therefore came a great wrath from the LORD of hosts.

13 Therefore it is come to pass, that as he cried, and they would not hear; so they cried, and I would not hear, saith the LORD of hosts:

14 But I scattered them with a whirlwind among all the nations whom they knew not. Thus the land was desolate after them, that no man passed through nor returned: for they laid the pleasant land desolate.

CHAPTER 8

AGAIN the word of the LORD of hosts came to me, saying,

2 Thus saith the LORD of hosts; I was jealous for Zion with great jealousy, and I was jealous for her with great fury.

3 Thus saith the LORD; I am returned unto Zion, and will dwell in the midst of Jerusalem: and Jerusalem shall be called a city of truth; and the mountain of the LORD of hosts the holy mountain.

4 Thus saith the LORD of hosts; There shall yet old men and old women dwell in the streets of Jerusalem, and every man with his staff in his hand for very age.

5 And the streets of the city shall be full of boys and girls playing in the streets thereof.

6 Thus saith the LORD of hosts; If it be marvellous in the eyes of the remnant of this people in these days, should it also be marvellous in my eyes? saith the LORD of hosts.

7 Thus saith the LORD of hosts; Behold, I will save my people from the east country, and from the west country;

8 And I will bring them, and they shall dwell in the midst of Jerusalem: and they shall be my people, and I will be their God, in truth and in righteousness.

9 Thus saith the LORD of hosts; Let your hands be strong, you that hear in these days these words by the mouth of the prophets, which were in the day that the foundation of the house of the LORD of hosts was laid, that the temple might be built.

10 For before these days there was no hire for man, nor any hire for beast; neither was there any peace to him that went out or came in because of the affliction: for I set all men every one against his neighbour.

11 But now I will not be unto the residue of this people as in the former days, saith the LORD of hosts.

12 For the seed shall be prosperous; the vine shall give her fruit, and the ground shall give her increase, and the heavens shall give their dew; and I will cause the remnant of this people to possess all these things.

13 And it shall come to pass, that as you were a curse among the heathen, O house of Judah, and house of Israel; so will I save you, and you shall be a blessing: fear not, but let your hands be strong.

14 For thus saith the LORD of hosts; As I thought to punish you, when your fathers provoked me to wrath, saith the LORD of hosts, and I repented not:

15 So again have I thought in these days to do well unto Jerusalem and to the house of Judah: fear you not.

16 These are the things that you shall do; Speak you every man the truth to his neighbour; execute the judgment of truth and peace in your gates:

17 And let none of you imagine evil in your hearts against his neighbour; and love no false oath: for all these are things that I hate, saith the LORD.

18 And the word of the LORD of hosts came unto me, saying,

19 Thus saith the LORD of hosts; The fast of the fourth month, and the fast of the fifth, and the fast of the seventh, and the fast of the tenth, shall be to the house of Judah joy and gladness, and cheerful feasts; therefore love the truth and peace.

20 Thus saith the LORD of hosts; It shall yet come to pass, that there shall come people, and the inhabitants of many cities:

21 And the inhabitants of one city shall go to another, saying, Let us go speedily to pray before the LORD, and to seek the LORD of hosts: I will go also.

22 Yea, many people and strong nations shall come to seek the LORD of hosts in Jerusalem, and to pray before the LORD.

23 Thus saith the LORD of hosts; In those days it shall come to pass, that ten men shall take hold out of all languages of the nations, even shall take hold of the skirt of him that is a Jew, saying, We will go with you: for we have heard that God is with you.

CHAPTER 9

THE burden of the word of the LORD in the land of Hadrach, and Damascus shall be the rest thereof: when the eyes of man, as of all the tribes of Israel, shall be toward the LORD.

2 And Hamath also shall border thereby; Tyrus, and Zidon, though it be very wise.

3 And Tyrus did build herself a strong hold, and heaped up silver as the dust, and fine gold as the mire of the streets.

4 Behold, the Lord will cast her out, and he will strike her power in the sea; and she shall be devoured with fire.

5 Ashkelon shall see it, and fear; Gaza also shall see it, and be very sorrowful, and Ekron; for her expectation shall be ashamed; and the king shall perish from Gaza, and Ashkelon shall not be inhabited.

6 And a bastard shall dwell in Ashdod, and I will cut off the pride of the Philistines.

7 And I will take away his blood out of his mouth, and his abominations from between his teeth: but he that remaineth, even he, shall be for our God, and he shall be as a governor in Judah, and Ekron as a Jebusite.

8 And I will encamp about my house because of the army, because of him that passes by, and because of him that returneth: and no oppressor shall pass through them any more: for now have I seen with my eyes.

9 Rejoice greatly, O daughter of Zion; shout, O daughter of Jerusalem: behold, your King comes unto you: he is just, and having salvation; lowly, and riding upon an ass, and upon a colt the foal of an ass.

10 And I will cut off the chariot from Ephraim, and the horse from Jerusalem, and the battle bow shall be cut off: and he shall speak peace unto the heathen: and his dominion shall be from sea even to sea, and from the river even to the ends of the earth.

11 As for you also, by the blood of your covenant I have sent forth your prisoners out of the pit wherein is no water.

12 Turn you to the strong hold, you prisoners of hope: even to day do I declare that I will render double unto you;

13 When I have bent Judah for me, filled the bow with Ephraim, and raised up your sons, O Zion, against your sons, O Greece, and made you as the sword of a mighty man.

14 And the LORD shall be seen over them, and his arrow shall go forth as the lightning: and the Lord GOD shall blow the trumpet, and shall go with whirlwinds of the south.

15 The LORD of hosts shall defend them; and they shall devour, and subdue with sling stones; and they shall drink, and make a noise as through wine; and they shall be filled like bowls, and as the corners of the altar.

16 And the LORD their God shall save them in that day as the flock of his people: for they shall be as the stones of a crown, lifted up as an ensign upon his land.

17 For how great is his goodness, and how great is his beauty! corn shall make the young men cheerful, and new wine the maids.

CHAPTER 10

ASK you of the LORD rain in the time of the latter rain; so the LORD shall make bright clouds, and give them showers of rain, to every one grass in the field.

2 For the idols have spoken vanity, and the diviners have seen a lie, and have told false dreams; they comfort in vain: therefore they went their way as a flock, they were troubled, because there was no shepherd.

3 My anger was kindled against the shepherds, and I punished the goats: for the LORD of hosts has visited his flock the house of Judah, and has made them as his goodly horse in the battle.

4 Out of him came forth the corner, out of him the nail, out of him the battle bow, out of him every oppressor together.

5 And they shall be as mighty men, which tread down their enemies in the mire of the streets in the battle: and they shall fight, because the LORD is with them, and the riders on horses shall be confounded.

6 And I will strengthen the house of Judah, and I will save the house of Joseph, and I will bring them again to place them; for I have mercy upon them: and they shall be as though I had not cast them off: for I am the LORD their God, and will hear them.

7 And they of Ephraim shall be like a mighty man, and their heart shall rejoice as through wine: yea, their children shall see it, and be glad; their heart shall rejoice in the LORD.

8 I will hiss for them, and gather them; for I have redeemed them: and they shall increase as they have increased.

9 And I will sow them among the people: and they shall remember me in far countries; and they shall live with their children, and turn again.

10 I will bring them again also out of the land of Egypt, and gather them out of Assyria; and I will bring them into the land of Gilead and Lebanon; and place shall not be found for them.

11 And he shall pass through the sea with affliction, and shall strike the waves in the sea, and all the deeps of the river shall dry up: and the pride of Assyria shall be brought down, and the sceptre of Egypt shall depart away.

12 And I will strengthen them in the LORD; and they shall walk up and down in his name, saith the LORD.

CHAPTER 11

OPEN your doors, O Lebanon, that the fire may devour your cedars.

2 Howl, fir tree; for the cedar is fallen; because the mighty are spoiled: howl, O you oaks of Bashan; for the forest of the vintage is come down.

3 There is a voice of the howling of the shepherds; for their glory is spoiled: a voice of the roaring of young lions; for the pride of Jordan is spoiled.

4 Thus saith the LORD my God; Feed the flock of the slaughter;

5 Whose possessors slay them, and hold themselves not guilty: and they that sell them say, Blessed be the LORD; for I am rich: and their own shepherds pity them not.

6 For I will no more pity the inhabitants of the land, saith the LORD: but, lo, I will deliver the men every one into his neighbour's hand, and into the hand of his king: and they shall strike the land, and out of their hand I will not deliver them.

7 And I will feed the flock of slaughter, even you, O poor of the flock. And I took unto me two staves; the one I called Beauty, and the other I called Bands; and I fed the flock.

8 Three shepherds also I cut off in one month; and my soul lothed them, and their soul also abhorred me.

9 Then said I, I will not feed you: that that dieth, let it die; and that that is to be cut off, let it be cut off; and let the rest eat every one the flesh of another.

10 And I took my staff, even Beauty, and cut it asunder, that I might break my covenant which I had made with all the people.

11 And it was broken in that day: and so the poor of the flock that waited upon me knew that it was the word of the LORD.

12 And I said unto them, If you think good, give me my price; and if not, forbear. So they weighed for my price thirty pieces of silver.

13 And the LORD said unto me, Cast it unto the potter: a goodly price that I was prised at of them. And I took the thirty pieces of silver, and cast them to the potter in the house of the LORD.

14 Then I cut asunder my other staff, even Bands, that I might break the brotherhood between Judah and Israel.

15 And the LORD said unto me, Take unto you yet the instruments of a foolish shepherd.

16 For, lo, I will raise up a shepherd in the land, which shall not visit those that be cut off, neither shall seek the young one, nor heal that that is broken, nor feed that that standeth still: but he shall eat the flesh of the fat, and tear their claws in pieces.

17 Woe to the idol shepherd that leaveth the flock! the sword shall be upon his arm, and upon his right eye: his arm shall be clean dried up, and his right eye shall be utterly darkened.

CHAPTER 12

THE burden of the word of the LORD for Israel, saith the LORD, which stretcheth forth the heavens, and layeth the foundation of the earth, and formeth the spirit of man within him.

2 Behold, I will make Jerusalem a cup of trembling unto all the people round about, when they shall be in the siege both against Judah and against Jerusalem.

3 And in that day will I make Jerusalem a burdensome stone for all people: all that burden themselves with it shall be cut in pieces, though all the people of the earth be gathered together against it.

4 In that day, saith the LORD, I will strike every horse with astonishment, and his rider with madness: and I will open my eyes upon the house of Judah, and will strike every horse of the people with blindness.

5 And the governors of Judah shall say in their heart, The inhabitants of Jerusalem shall be my strength in the LORD of hosts their God.

6 In that day will I make the governors of Judah like an hearth of fire among the wood, and like a torch of fire in a sheaf; and they shall devour all the people round about, on the right hand and on the left: and Jerusalem shall be inhabited again in her own place, even in Jerusalem.

7 The LORD also shall save the tents of Judah first, that the glory of the house of David and the glory of the inhabitants of Jerusalem do not magnify themselves against Judah.

8 In that day shall the LORD defend the inhabitants of Jerusalem; and he that is feeble among them at that day shall be as David; and the house of David shall be as God, as the angel of the LORD before them.

9 And it shall come to pass in that day, that I will seek to destroy all the nations that come against Jerusalem.

10 And I will pour upon the house of David, and upon the inhabitants of Jerusalem, the spirit of grace and of supplications: and they shall look upon me whom they have pierced, and they shall mourn for him, as one mourneth for his only son, and shall be in bitterness for him, as one that is in bitterness for his firstborn.

11 In that day shall there be a great mourning in Jerusalem, as the mourning of Hadadrimmon in the valley of Megiddon.

12 And the land shall mourn, every family apart; the family of the house of David apart, and their wives apart; the family of the house of Nathan apart, and their wives apart;

13 The family of the house of Levi apart, and their wives apart; the family of Shimei apart, and their wives apart;

14 All the families that remain, every family apart, and their wives apart.

CHAPTER 13

IN that day there shall be a fountain opened to the house of David and to the inhabitants of Jerusalem for sin and for uncleanness.

2 And it shall come to pass in that day, saith the LORD of hosts, that I will cut off the names of the idols out of the land, and they shall no more be remembered: and also I will cause the prophets and the unclean spirit to pass out of the land.

3 And it shall come to pass, that when any shall yet prophesy, then his father and his mother that begat him shall say unto him, You shalt not live; for you speakest lies in the name of the LORD: and his father and his mother that begat him shall thrust him through when he prophesieth.

4 And it shall come to pass in that day, that the prophets shall be ashamed every one of his vision, when he has prophesied; neither shall they wear a rough garment to deceive:

5 But he shall say, I am no prophet, I am an husbandman; for man taught me to keep cattle from my youth.

6 And one shall say unto him, What are these wounds in yours hands? Then he shall answer, Those with which I was wounded in the house of my friends.

7 Awake, O sword, against my shepherd, and against the man that is my fellow, saith the LORD of hosts: strike the shepherd, and the sheep shall be scattered: and I will turn my hand upon the little ones.

8 And it shall come to pass, that in all the land, saith the LORD, two parts therein shall be cut off and die; but the third shall be left therein.

9 And I will bring the third part through the fire, and will refine them as silver is refined, and will try them as gold is tried: they shall call on my name, and I will hear them: I will say, It is my people: and they shall say, The LORD is my God.

CHAPTER 14

BEHOLD, the day of the LORD comes, and your spoil shall be divided in the midst of you.

2 For I will gather all nations against Jerusalem to battle; and the city shall be taken, and the houses rifled, and the women ravished; and half of the city shall go forth into captivity, and the residue of the people shall not be cut off from the city.

3 Then shall the LORD go forth, and fight against those nations, as when he fought in the day of battle.

4 And his feet shall stand in that day upon the mount of Olives, which is before Jerusalem on the east, and the mount of Olives shall cleave in the midst thereof toward the east and toward the west, and there shall be a very great valley; and half of the mountain shall remove toward the north, and half of it toward the south.

5 And you shall flee to the valley of the mountains; for the valley of the mountains shall reach unto Azal: yea, you shall flee, like as you fled from before the earthquake in the days of Uzziah king of Judah: and the LORD my God shall come, and all the saints with you.

6 And it shall come to pass in that day, that the light shall not be clear, nor dark:

7 But it shall be one day which shall be known to the LORD, not day, nor night: but it shall come to pass, that at evening time it shall be light.

8 And it shall be in that day, that living waters shall go out from Jerusalem; half of them toward the former sea, and half of them toward the hinder sea: in summer and in winter shall it be.

9 And the LORD shall be king over all the earth: in that day shall there be one LORD, and his name one.

10 All the land shall be turned as a plain from Geba to Rimmon south of Jerusalem: and it shall be lifted up, and inhabited in her place, from Benjamin's gate unto the place of the first gate, unto the corner gate, and from the tower of Hananeel unto the king's winepresses.

11 And men shall dwell in it, and there shall be no more utter destruction; but Jerusalem shall be safely inhabited.

12 And this shall be the plague wherewith the LORD will strike all the people that have fought against Jerusalem; Their flesh shall consume away while they stand upon their feet, and their eyes shall consume away in their holes, and their tongue shall consume away in their mouth.

13 And it shall come to pass in that day, that a great tumult from the LORD shall be among them; and they shall lay hold every one on the hand of his neighbour, and his hand shall rise up against the hand of his neighbour.

14 And Judah also shall fight at Jerusalem; and the wealth of all the heathen round about shall be gathered together, gold, and silver, and apparel, in great abundance.

15 And so shall be the plague of the horse, of the mule, of the camel, and of the ass, and of all the beasts that shall be in these tents, as this plague.

16 And it shall come to pass, that every one that is left of all the nations which came against Jerusalem shall even go up from year to year to worship the King, the LORD of hosts, and to keep the feast of tabernacles.

17 And it shall be, that whoso will not come up of all the families of the earth unto Jerusalem to worship the King, the LORD of hosts, even upon them shall be no rain.

18 And if the family of Egypt go not up, and come not, that have no rain; there shall be the plague, wherewith the LORD will strike the heathen that come not up to keep the feast of tabernacles.

19 This shall be the punishment of Egypt, and the punishment of all nations that come not up to keep the feast of tabernacles.

20 In that day shall there be upon the bells of the horses, HOLINESS UNTO THE LORD; and the pots in the LORD's house shall be like the bowls before the altar.

21 Yea, every pot in Jerusalem and in Judah shall be holiness unto the LORD of hosts: and all they that sacrifice shall come and take of them, and seethe therein: and in that day there shall be no more the Canaanite in the house of the LORD of hosts.

MALACHI.

CHAPTER 1

THE burden of the word of the LORD to Israel by Malachi.

2 I have loved you, saith the LORD. Yet you say, Wherein have you loved us? Was not Esau Jacob's brother? saith the LORD: yet I loved Jacob,

3 And I hated Esau, and laid his mountains and his heritage waste for the dragons of the wilderness.

4 Whereas Edom saith, We are impoverished, but we will return and build the desolate places; thus saith the LORD of hosts, They shall build, but I will throw down; and they shall call them, The border of wickedness, and, The people against whom the LORD has indignation for ever.

5 And your eyes shall see, and you shall say, The LORD will be magnified from the border of Israel.

6 A son honoureth his father, and a servant his master: if then I be a father, where is my honour? and if I be a master, where is my fear? saith the LORD of hosts unto you, O priests, that despise my name. And you say, Wherein have we despised your name?

7 You offer polluted bread upon my altar; and you say, Wherein have we polluted you? In that you say, The table of the LORD is contemptible.

8 And if you offer the blind for sacrifice, is it not evil? and if you offer the lame and sick, is it not evil? offer it now unto your governor; will he be pleased with you, or accept your person? saith the LORD of hosts.

9 And now, I pray you, beseech God that he will be gracious unto us: this has been by your means: will he regard your persons? saith the LORD of hosts.

10 Who is there even among you that would shut the doors for nought? neither do you kindle fire on my altar for nought. I have no pleasure in you, saith the LORD of hosts, neither will I accept an offering at your hand.

11 For from the rising of the sun even unto the going down of the same my name shall be great among the Gentiles; and in every place incense shall be offered unto my name, and a pure offering: for my name shall be great among the heathen, saith the LORD of hosts.

12 But you have profaned it, in that you say, The table of the LORD is polluted; and the fruit thereof, even his meat, is contemptible.

13 You said also, Behold, what a weariness is it! and you have snuffed at it, saith the LORD of hosts; and you brought that which was torn, and the lame, and the sick; thus you brought an offering: should I accept this of your hand? saith the LORD.

14 But cursed be the deceiver, which has in his flock a male, and voweth, and sacrificeth unto the Lord a corrupt thing: for I am a great King, saith the LORD of hosts, and my name is dreadful among the heathen.

CHAPTER 2

AND now, O you priests, this commandment is for you.

2 If you will not hear, and if you will not lay it to heart, to give glory unto my name, saith the LORD of hosts, I will even send a curse upon you, and I will curse your blessings: yea, I have cursed them already, because you do not lay it to heart.

3 Behold, I will corrupt your seed, and spread dung upon your faces, even the dung of your solemn feasts; and one shall take you away with it.

4 And you shall know that I have sent this commandment unto you, that my covenant might be with Levi, saith the LORD of hosts.

5 My covenant was with him of life and peace; and I gave them to him for the fear wherewith he feared me, and was afraid before my name.

6 The law of truth was in his mouth, and iniquity was not found in his lips: he walked with me in peace and equity, and did turn many away from iniquity.

7 For the priest's lips should keep knowledge, and they should seek the law at his mouth: for he is the messenger of the LORD of hosts.

8 But you are departed out of the way; you have caused many to stumble at the law; you have corrupted the covenant of Levi, saith the LORD of hosts.

9 Therefore have I also made you contemptible and base before all the people, according as you have not kept my ways, but have been partial in the law.

10 Have we not all one father? has not one God created us? why do we deal treacherously every man against his brother, by profaning the covenant of our fathers?

11 Judah has dealt treacherously, and an abomination is committed in Israel and in Jerusalem; for Judah has profaned the holiness of the LORD which he loved, and has married the daughter of a strange god.

12 The LORD will cut off the man that doeth this, the master and the scholar, out of the tabernacles of Jacob, and him that offereth an offering unto the LORD of hosts.

13 And this have you done again, covering the altar of the LORD with tears, with weeping, and with crying out, insomuch that he regardeth not the offering any more, or receiveth it with good will at your hand.

14 Yet you say, Wherefore? Because the LORD has been witness between you and the wife of your youth, against whom you have dealt treacherously: yet is she your companion, and the wife of your covenant.

15 And did not he make one? Yet had he the residue of the spirit. And wherefore one? That he might seek a godly seed. Therefore take heed to your spirit, and let none deal treacherously against the wife of his youth.

16 For the LORD, the God of Israel, saith that he hateth putting away: for one covers violence with his garment, saith the LORD of hosts: therefore take heed to your spirit, that you deal not treacherously.

17 You have wearied the LORD with your words. Yet you say, Wherein have we wearied him? When you say, Every one that doeth evil is good in the sight of the LORD, and he delighteth in them; or, Where is the God of judgment?

CHAPTER 3

BEHOLD, I will send my messenger, and he shall prepare the way before me: and the Lord, whom you seek, shall suddenly come to his temple, even the messenger of the covenant, whom you delight in: behold, he shall come, saith the LORD of hosts.

2 But who may abide the day of his coming? and who shall stand when he appeareth? for he is like a refiner's fire, and like fullers' soap:

3 And he shall sit as a refiner and purifier of silver: and he shall purify the sons of Levi, and purge them as gold and silver, that they may offer unto the LORD an offering in righteousness.

4 Then shall the offering of Judah and Jerusalem be pleasant unto the LORD, as in the days of old, and as in former years.

5 And I will come near to you to judgment; and I will be a swift witness against the sorcerers, and against the adulterers, and against false swearers, and against those that oppress the hireling in his wages, the widow, and the fatherless, and that turn aside the stranger from his right, and fear not me, saith the LORD of hosts.

6 For I am the LORD, I change not; therefore you sons of Jacob are not consumed.

7 Even from the days of your fathers you are gone away from my ordinances, and have not kept them. Return unto me, and I will return unto you, saith the LORD of hosts. But you said, Wherein shall we return?

8 Will a man rob God? Yet you have robbed me. But you say, Wherein have we robbed you? In tithes and offerings.

9 You are cursed with a curse: for you have robbed me, even this whole nation.

10 Bring you all the tithes into the storehouse, that there may be meat in my house, and prove me now herewith, saith the LORD of hosts, if I will not open you the windows of heaven, and pour you out a blessing, that there shall not be room enough to receive it.

11 And I will rebuke the devourer for your sakes, and he shall not destroy the fruits of your ground; neither shall your vine cast her fruit before the time in the field, saith the LORD of hosts.

12 And all nations shall call you blessed: for you shall be a delightsome land, saith the LORD of hosts.

13 Your words have been stout against me, saith the LORD. Yet you say, What have we spoken so much against you?

14 You have said, It is vain to serve God: and what profit is it that we have kept his ordinance, and that we have walked mournfully before the LORD of hosts?

15 And now we call the proud happy; yea, they that work wickedness are set up; yea, they that tempt God are even delivered.

16 Then they that feared the LORD spake often one to another: and the LORD hearkened, and heard it, and a book of remembrance was written before him for them that feared the LORD, and that thought upon his name.

17 And they shall be my, saith the LORD of hosts, in that day when I make up my jewels; and I will spare them, as a man spareth his own son that serveth him.

18 Then shall you return, and discern between the righteous and the wicked, between him that serveth God and him that serveth him not.

CHAPTER 4

FOR, behold, the day comes, that shall burn as an oven; and all the proud, yea, and all that do wickedly, shall be stubble: and the day that comes shall burn them up, saith the LORD of hosts, that it shall leave them neither root nor branch.

2But unto you that fear my name shall the Sun of righteousness arise with healing in his wings; and you shall go forth, and grow up as calves of the stall.

3 And you shall tread down the wicked; for they shall be ashes under the soles of your feet in the day that I shall do this, saith the LORD of hosts.

4Remember you the law of Moses my servant, which I commanded unto him in Horeb for all Israel, with the statutes and judgments.

5Behold, I will send you Elijah the prophet before the coming of the great and dreadful day of the LORD:

6 And he shall turn the heart of the fathers to the children, and the heart of the children to their fathers, lest I come and strike the earth with a curse.

THE END OF THE PROPHETS.

THE NEW TESTAMENT OF
OUR LORD AND SAVIOUR JESUS CHRIST

TRANSLATED OUT OF THE ORIGINAL GREEK: AND WITH
THE FORMER TRANSLATIONS DILIGENTLY COMPARED
AND REVISED, BY HIS MAJESTY'S SPECIAL COMMAND

APPOINTED TO BE READ IN CHURCHES

THE GOSPEL ACCORDING TO
ST. MATTHEW.

CHAPTER 1

THE book of the generation of Jesus Christ, the son of David, the son of Abraham.

2 Abraham begat Isaac; and Isaac begat Jacob; and Jacob begat Judas and his brethren;

3 And Judas begat Phares and Zara of Thamar; and Phares begat Esrom; and Esrom begat Aram;

4 And Aram begat Aminadab; and Aminadab begat Naasson; and Naasson begat Salmon;

5 And Salmon begat Booz of Rachab; and Booz begat Obed of Ruth; and Obed begat Jesse;

6 And Jesse begat David the king; and David the king begat Solomon of her that had been the wife of Urias;

7 And Solomon begat Roboam; and Roboam begat Abia; and Abia begat Asa;

8 And Asa begat Josaphat; and Josaphat begat Joram; and Joram begat Ozias;

9 And Ozias begat Joatham; and Joatham begat Achaz; and Achaz begat Ezekias;

10 And Ezekias begat Manasses; and Manasses begat Amon; and Amon begat Josias;

11 And Josias begat Jechonias and his brethren, about the time they were carried away to Babylon:

12 And after they were brought to Babylon, Jechonias begat Salathiel; and Salathiel begat Zorobabel;

13 And Zorobabel begat Abiud; and Abiud begat Eliakim; and Eliakim begat Azor;

14 And Azor begat Sadoc; and Sadoc begat Achim; and Achim begat Eliud;

15 And Eliud begat Eleazar; and Eleazar begat Matthan; and Matthan begat Jacob;

16 And Jacob begat Joseph the husband of Mary, of whom was born Jesus, who is called Christ.

17 So all the generations from Abraham to David are fourteen generations; and from David until the carrying away into Babylon are fourteen generations; and from the carrying away into Babylon unto Christ are fourteen generations.

18 Now the birth of Jesus Christ was on this wise: When as his mother Mary was espoused to Joseph, before they came together, she was found with child of the Holy Ghost.

19 Then Joseph her husband, being a just man, and not willing to make her a publick example, was minded to put her away privily.

20 But while he thought on these things, behold, the angel of the Lord appeared unto him in a dream, saying, Joseph, you son of David, fear not to take unto you Mary your wife: for that which is conceived in her is of the Holy Ghost.

21 And she shall bring forth a son, and you shalt call his name JESUS: for he shall save his people from their sins.

22 Now all this was done, that it might be fulfilled which was spoken of the Lord by the prophet, saying,

23 Behold, a virgin shall be with child, and shall bring forth a son, and they shall call his name Emmanuel, which being interpreted is, God with us.

24 Then Joseph being raised from sleep did as the angel of the Lord had bidden him, and took unto him his wife:

25 And knew her not till she had brought forth her firstborn son: and he called his name JESUS.

CHAPTER 2

NOW when Jesus was born in Bethlehem of Judæa in the days of Herod the king, behold, there came wise men from the east to Jerusalem,

2 Saying, Where is he that is born King of the Jews? for we have seen his star in the east, and are come to worship him.

3 When Herod the king had heard these things, he was troubled, and all Jerusalem with him.

4 And when he had gathered all the chief priests and scribes of the people together, he demanded of them where Christ should be born.

5 And they said unto him, In Bethlehem of Judæa: for thus it is written by the prophet,

6 And you Bethlehem, in the land of Juda, are not the least among the princes of Juda: for out of you shall come a Governor, that shall rule my people Israel.

7 Then Herod, when he had privily called the wise men, inquired of them diligently what time the star appeared.

8 And he sent them to Bethlehem, and said, Go and search diligently for the young child; and when you have found him, bring me word again, that I may come and worship him also.

9 When they had heard the king, they departed; and, lo, the star, which they saw in the east, went before them, till it came and stood over where the young child was.

10 When they saw the star, they rejoiced with exceeding great joy.

11 And when they were come into the house, they saw the young child with Mary his mother, and fell down, and worshipped him: and when they had opened their treasures, they presented unto him gifts; gold, and frankincense, and myrrh.

12 And being warned of God in a dream that they should not return to Herod, they departed into their own country another way.

13 And when they were departed, behold, the angel of the Lord appeareth to Joseph in a dream, saying, Arise, and take the young child and his mother, and flee into Egypt, and be you there until I bring you word: for Herod will seek the young child to destroy him.

14 When he arose, he took the young child and his mother by night, and departed into Egypt:

15 And was there until the death of Herod: that it might be fulfilled which was spoken of the Lord by the prophet, saying, Out of Egypt have I called my son.

16 Then Herod, when he saw that he was mocked of the wise men, was exceeding wroth, and sent forth, and slew all the children that were in Bethlehem, and in all the coasts thereof, from two years old and under, according to the time which he had diligently inquired of the wise men.

17 Then was fulfilled that which was spoken by Jeremy the prophet, saying,

18 In Rama was there a voice heard, lamentation, and weeping, and great mourning, Rachel weeping for her children, and would not be comforted, because they are not.

19 But when Herod was dead, behold, an angel of the Lord appeareth in a dream to Joseph in Egypt,

20 Saying, Arise, and take the young child and his mother, and go into the land of Israel: for they are dead which sought the young child's life.

21 And he arose, and took the young child and his mother, and came into the land of Israel.

22 But when he heard that Archelaus did reign in Judæa in the room of his father Herod, he was afraid to go thither: notwithstanding, being warned of God in a dream, he turned aside into the parts of Galilee:

23 And he came and dwelt in a city called Nazareth: that it might be fulfilled which was spoken by the prophets, He shall be called a Nazarene.

CHAPTER 3

IN those days came John the Baptist, preaching in the wilderness of Judæa,

2 And saying, Repent you : for the kingdom of heaven is at hand.

3 For this is he that was spoken of by the prophet Esaias, saying, The voice of one crying in the wilderness, Prepare you the way of the Lord, make his paths straight.

4 And the same John had his raiment of camel's hair, and a leathern girdle about his loins; and his meat was locusts and wild honey.

5 Then went out to him Jerusalem, and all Judæa, and all the region round about Jordan,

6 And were baptized of him in Jordan, confessing their sins.

7 But when he saw many of the Pharisees and Sadducees come to his baptism, he said unto them, O generation of vipers, who has warned you to flee from the wrath to come?

8 Bring forth therefore fruits meet for repentance:

9 And think not to say within yourselves, We have Abraham to our father: for I say unto you, that God is able of these stones to raise up children unto Abraham.

10 And now also the axe is laid unto the root of the trees: therefore every tree which bringeth not forth good fruit is hewn down, and cast into the fire.

11 I indeed baptize you with water unto repentance: but he that comes after me is mightier than I, whose shoes I am not worthy to bear: he shall baptize you with the Holy Ghost, and with fire:

12 Whose fan is in his hand, and he will throughly purge his floor, and gather his wheat into the garner; but he will burn up the chaff with unquenchable fire.

13 Then comes Jesus from Galilee to Jordan unto John, to be baptized of him.

14 But John forbad him, saying, I have need to be baptized of you, and comest you to me?

15 And Jesus answering said unto him, Suffer it to be so now: for thus it becometh us to fulfil all righteousness. Then he suffered him.

16 And Jesus, when he was baptized, went up straightway out of the water: and, lo, the heavens were opened unto him, and he saw the Spirit of God descending like a dove, and lighting upon him:

17 And lo a voice from heaven, saying, This is my beloved Son, in whom I am well pleased.

CHAPTER 4

THEN was Jesus led up of the Spirit into the wilderness to be tempted of the devil.

2 And when he had fasted forty days and forty nights, he was afterward an hungred.

3 And when the tempter came to him, he said, If you be the Son of God, command that these stones be made bread.

4 But he answered and said, It is written, Man shall not live by bread alone, but by every word that proceedeth out of the mouth of God.

5 Then the devil taketh him up into the holy city, and setteth him on a pinnacle of the temple,

6 And saith unto him, If you be the Son of God, cast yourself down: for it is written, He shall give his angels charge concerning you: and in their hands they shall bear you up, lest at any time you dash your foot against a stone.

7 Jesus said unto him, It is written again, You shalt not tempt the Lord your God.

8 Again, the devil taketh him up into an exceeding high mountain, and sheweth him all the kingdoms of the world, and the glory of them;

9 And saith unto him, All these things will I give you, if you will fall down and worship me.

10 Then saith Jesus unto him, Get you hence, Satan: for it is written, You shalt worship the Lord your God, and him only shalt you serve.

11 Then the devil leaveth him, and, behold, angels came and ministered unto him.

12 Now when Jesus had heard that John was cast into prison, he departed into Galilee;

13 And leaving Nazareth, he came and dwelt in Capernaum, which is upon the sea coast, in the borders of Zabulon and Nephthalim:

14 That it might be fulfilled which was spoken by Esaias the prophet, saying,

15 The land of Zabulon, and the land of Nephthalim, by the way of the sea, beyond Jordan, Galilee of the Gentiles;

16 The people which sat in darkness saw great light; and to them which sat in the region and shadow of death light is sprung up.

17 From that time Jesus began to preach, and to say, Repent: for the kingdom of heaven is at hand.

18 And Jesus, walking by the sea of Galilee, saw two brethren, Simon called Peter, and Andrew his brother, casting a net into the sea: for they were fishers.

19 And he saith unto them, Follow me, and I will make you fishers of men.

20 And they straightway left their nets, and followed him.

21 And going on from thence, he saw other two brethren, James the son of Zebedee, and John his brother, in a ship with Zebedee their father, mending their nets; and he called them.

22 And they immediately left the ship and their father, and followed him.

23 And Jesus went about all Galilee, teaching in their synagogues, and preaching the gospel of the kingdom, and healing all manner of sickness and all manner of disease among the people.

24 And his fame went throughout all Syria: and they brought unto him all sick people that were taken with divers diseases and torments, and those which were possessed with devils, and those which were lunatick, and those that had the palsy; and he healed them.

25 And there followed him great multitudes of people from Galilee, and from Decapolis, and from Jerusalem, and from Judæa, and from beyond Jordan.

CHAPTER 5

AND seeing the multitudes, he went up into a mountain: and when he was set, his disciples came unto him:

2 And he opened his mouth, and taught them, saying,

3 Blessed are the poor in spirit: for theirs is the kingdom of heaven.

4 Blessed are they that mourn: for they shall be comforted.

5 Blessed are the meek: for they shall inherit the earth.

6 Blessed are they which do hunger and thirst after righteousness: for they shall be filled.

7 Blessed are the merciful: for they shall obtain mercy.

8 Blessed are the pure in heart: for they shall see God.

9 Blessed are the peacemakers: for they shall be called the children of God.

10 Blessed are they which are persecuted for righteousness' sake: for theirs is the kingdom of heaven.

11 Blessed are you , when men shall revile you, and persecute you, and shall say all manner of evil against you falsely, for my sake.

12 Rejoice, and be exceeding glad: for great is your reward in heaven: for so persecuted they the prophets which were before you.

13 You are the salt of the earth: but if the salt have lost his savour, wherewith shall it be salted? it is thenceforth good for nothing, but to be cast out, and to be trodden under foot of men.

14 You are the light of the world. A city that is set on an hill cannot be hid.

15 Neither do men light a candle, and put it under a bushel, but on a candlestick; and it giveth light unto all that are in the house.

16 Let your light so shine before men, that they may see your good works, and glorify your Father which is in heaven.

17 Think not that I am come to destroy the law, or the prophets: I am not come to destroy, but to fulfil.

18 For verily I say unto you, Till heaven and earth pass, one jot or one tittle shall in no wise pass from the law, till all be fulfilled.

19 Whosoever therefore shall break one of these least commandments, and shall teach men so, he shall be called the least in the kingdom of heaven: but whosoever shall do and teach them, the same shall be called great in the kingdom of heaven.

20 For I say unto you, That except your righteousness shall exceed the righteousness of the scribes and Pharisees, you shall in no case enter into the kingdom of heaven.

21 You have heard that it was said by them of old time, You shalt not kill; and whosoever shall kill shall be in danger of the judgment:

22 But I say unto you, That whosoever is angry with his brother without a cause shall be in danger of the judgment: and whosoever shall say to his brother, Raca, shall be in danger of the council: but whosoever shall say, You fool, shall be in danger of hell fire.

23 Therefore if you bring your gift to the altar, and there rememberest that your brother has ought against you;

24 Leave there your gift before the altar, and go your way; first be reconciled to your brother, and then come and offer your gift.

25 Agree with yours adversary quickly, whiles you are in the way with him; lest at any time the adversary deliver you to the judge, and the judge deliver you to the officer, and you be cast into prison.

26 Verily I say unto you, You shalt by no means come out thence, till you have paid the uttermost farthing.

27 You have heard that it was said by them of old time, You shalt not commit adultery:

28 But I say unto you, That whosoever looketh on a woman to lust after her has committed adultery with her already in his heart.

29 And if your right eye offend you, pluck it out, and cast it from you: for it is profitable for you that one of your members should perish, and not that your whole body should be cast into hell.

30 And if your right hand offend you, cut it off, and cast it from you: for it is profitable for you that one of your members should perish, and not that your whole body should be cast into hell.

31 It has been said, Whosoever shall put away his wife, let him give her a writing of divorcement:

32 But I say unto you, That whosoever shall put away his wife, saving for the cause of fornication, causeth her to commit adultery: and whosoever shall marry her that is divorced committeth adultery.

33 Again, you have heard that it has been said by them of old time, You shalt not forswear yourself, but shalt perform unto the Lord yours oaths:

34 But I say unto you, Swear not at all; neither by heaven; for it is God's throne:

35 Nor by the earth; for it is his footstool: neither by Jerusalem; for it is the city of the great King.

36 Neither shalt you swear by your head, because you can not make one hair white or black.

37 But let your communication be, Yea, yea; Nay, nay: for whatsoever is more than these comes of evil.

38 You have heard that it has been said, An eye for an eye, and a tooth for a tooth:

39 But I say unto you, That you resist not evil: but whosoever shall strike you on your right cheek, turn to him the other also.

40 And if any man will sue you at the law, and take away your coat, let him have your cloke also.

41 And whosoever shall compel you to go a mile, go with him twain.

42 Give to him that asketh you, and from him that would borrow of you turn not you away.

43 You have heard that it has been said, You shalt love your neighbour, and hate yours enemy.

44 But I say unto you, Love your enemies, bless them that curse you, do good to them that hate you, and pray for them which despitefully use you, and persecute you;

45 That you may be the children of your Father which is in heaven: for he maketh his sun to rise on the evil and on the good, and sendeth rain on the just and on the unjust.

46 For if you love them which love you, what reward have you ? do not even the publicans the same?

47 And if you salute your brethren only, what do you more than others? do not even the publicans so?

48 Be you therefore perfect, even as your Father which is in heaven is perfect.

CHAPTER 6

TAKE heed that you do not your alms before men, to be seen of them: otherwise you have no reward of your Father which is in heaven.

2 Therefore when you doest yours alms, do not sound a trumpet before you, as the hypocrites do in the synagogues and in the streets, that they may have glory of men. Verily I say unto you, They have their reward.

3 But when you doest alms, let not your left hand know what your right hand doeth:

4 That yours alms may be in secret: and your Father which seeth in secret himself shall reward you openly.

5 And when you prayest, you shalt not be as the hypocrites are: for they love to pray standing in the synagogues and in the corners of the streets, that they may be seen of men. Verily I say unto you, They have their reward.

6 But you , when you prayest, enter into your closet, and when you have shut your door, pray to your Father which is in secret; and your Father which seeth in secret shall reward you openly.

7 But when you pray, use not vain repetitions, as the heathen do: for they think that they shall be heard for their much speaking.

8 Be not you therefore like unto them: for your Father knoweth what things you have need of, before you ask him.

9 After this manner therefore pray you : Our Father which are in heaven, Hallowed be your name.

10 Your kingdom come. Your will be done in earth, as it is in heaven.

11 Give us this day our daily bread.

12 And forgive us our debts, as we forgive our debtors.

13 And lead us not into temptation, but deliver us from evil: For yours is the kingdom, and the power, and the glory, for ever. Amen.

14 For if you forgive men their trespasses, your heavenly Father will also forgive you:

15 But if you forgive not men their trespasses, neither will your Father forgive your trespasses.

16 Moreover when you fast, be not, as the hypocrites, of a sad countenance: for they disfigure their faces, that they may appear unto men to fast. Verily I say unto you, They have their reward.

17 But you , when you fastest, anoint yours head, and wash your face;

18 That you appear not unto men to fast, but unto your Father which is in secret: and your Father, which seeth in secret, shall reward you openly.

19 Lay not up for yourselves treasures upon earth, where moth and rust doth corrupt, and where thieves break through and steal:

20 But lay up for yourselves treasures in heaven, where neither moth nor rust doth corrupt, and where thieves do not break through nor steal:

21 For where your treasure is, there will your heart be also.

22 The light of the body is the eye: if therefore yours eye be single, your whole body shall be full of light.

23 But if yours eye be evil, your whole body shall be full of darkness. If therefore the light that is in you be darkness, how great is that darkness!

24 No man can serve two masters: for either he will hate the one, and love the other; or else he will hold to the one, and despise the other. You cannot serve God and mammon.

25 Therefore I say unto you, Take no thought for your life, what you shall eat, or what you shall drink; nor yet for your body, what you shall put on. Is not the life more than meat, and the body than raiment?

26 Behold the fowls of the air: for they sow not, neither do they reap, nor gather into barns; yet your heavenly Father feedeth them. Are you not much better than they?

27 Which of you by taking thought can add one cubit unto his stature?

28 And why take you thought for raiment? Consider the lilies of the field, how they grow; they toil not, neither do they spin:

29 And yet I say unto you, That even Solomon in all his glory was not arrayed like one of these.

30 Wherefore, if God so clothe the grass of the field, which to day is, and to morrow is cast into the oven, shall he not much more clothe you, O you of little faith?

31 Therefore take no thought, saying, What shall we eat? or, What shall we drink? or, Wherewithal shall we be clothed?

32 (For after all these things do the Gentiles seek:) for your heavenly Father knoweth that you have need of all these things.

33 But seek you first the kingdom of God, and his righteousness; and all these things shall be added unto you.

34 Take therefore no thought for the morrow: for the morrow shall take thought for the things of itself. Sufficient unto the day is the evil thereof.

CHAPTER 7
JUDGE not, that you be not judged.

2 For with what judgment you judge, you shall be judged: and with what measure you mete, it shall be measured to you again.

3 And why beholdest you the mote that is in your brother's eye, but considerest not the beam that is in yours own eye?

4 Or how will you say to your brother, Let me pull out the mote out of yours eye; and, behold, a beam is in yours own eye?

5 You hypocrite, first cast out the beam out of yours own eye; and then shalt you see clearly to cast out the mote out of your brother's eye.

6 Give not that which is holy unto the dogs, neither cast you your pearls before swine, lest they trample them under their feet, and turn again and rend you.

7 Ask, and it shall be given you; seek, and you shall find; knock, and it shall be opened unto you:

8 For every one that asketh receiveth; and he that seeketh findeth; and to him that knocketh it shall be opened.

9 Or what man is there of you, whom if his son ask bread, will he give him a stone?

10 Or if he ask a fish, will he give him a serpent?

11 If you then, being evil, know how to give good gifts unto your children, how much more shall your Father which is in heaven give good things to them that ask him?

12 Therefore all things whatsoever you would that men should do to you, do you even so to them: for this is the law and the prophets.

13 Enter you in at the strait gate: for wide is the gate, and broad is the way, that leadeth to destruction, and many there be which go in thereat:

14 Because strait is the gate, and narrow is the way, which leadeth unto life, and few there be that find it.

15 Beware of false prophets, which come to you in sheep's clothing, but inwardly they are ravening wolves.

16 You shall know them by their fruits. Do men gather grapes of thorns, or figs of thistles?

17 Even so every good tree bringeth forth good fruit; but a corrupt tree bringeth forth evil fruit.

18 A good tree cannot bring forth evil fruit, neither can a corrupt tree bring forth good fruit.

19 Every tree that bringeth not forth good fruit is hewn down, and cast into the fire.

20 Wherefore by their fruits you shall know them.

21 Not every one that saith unto me, Lord, Lord, shall enter into the kingdom of heaven; but he that doeth the will of my Father which is in heaven.

22 Many will say to me in that day, Lord, Lord, have we not prophesied in your name? and in your name have cast out devils? and in your name done many wonderful works?

23 And then will I profess unto them, I never knew you: depart from me, you that work iniquity.

24 Therefore whosoever heareth these sayings of my, and doeth them, I will liken him unto a wise man, which built his house upon a rock:

25 And the rain descended, and the floods came, and the winds blew, and beat upon that house; and it fell not: for it was founded upon a rock.

26 And every one that heareth these sayings of my, and doeth them not, shall be likened unto a foolish man, which built his house upon the sand:

27 And the rain descended, and the floods came, and the winds blew, and beat upon that house; and it fell: and great was the fall of it.

28 And it came to pass, when Jesus had ended these sayings, the people were astonished at his doctrine:

29 For he taught them as one having authority, and not as the scribes.

CHAPTER 8
WHEN he was come down from the mountain, great multitudes followed him.

2 And, behold, there came a leper and worshipped him, saying, Lord, if you will, you can make me clean.

3 And Jesus put forth his hand, and touched him, saying, I will; be you clean. And immediately his leprosy was cleansed.

4 And Jesus saith unto him, See you tell no man; but go your way, shew yourself to the priest, and offer the gift that Moses commanded, for a testimony unto them.

5 And when Jesus was entered into Capernaum, there came unto him a centurion, beseeching him,

6 And saying, Lord, my servant lies at home sick of the palsy, grievously tormented.

7 And Jesus saith unto him, I will come and heal him.

8 The centurion answered and said, Lord, I am not worthy that you shouldest come under my roof: but speak the word only, and my servant shall be healed.

9 For I am a man under authority, having soldiers under me: and I say to this man, Go, and he goeth; and to another, Come, and he comes; and to my servant, Do this, and he doeth it.

10 When Jesus heard it, he marvelled, and said to them that followed, Verily I say unto you, I have not found so great faith, no, not in Israel.

11 And I say unto you, That many shall come from the east and west, and shall sit down with Abraham, and Isaac, and Jacob, in the kingdom of heaven.

12 But the children of the kingdom shall be cast out into outer darkness: there shall be weeping and gnashing of teeth.

13 And Jesus said unto the centurion, Go your way; and as you have believed, so be it done unto you. And his servant was healed in the selfsame hour.

14 And when Jesus was come into Peter's house, he saw his wife's mother laid, and sick of a fever.

15 And he touched her hand, and the fever left her: and she arose, and ministered unto them.

16 When the even was come, they brought unto him many that were possessed with devils: and he cast out the spirits with his word, and healed all that were sick:

17 That it might be fulfilled which was spoken by Esaias the prophet, saying, Himself took our infirmities, and bare our sicknesses.

18 Now when Jesus saw great multitudes about him, he gave commandment to depart unto the other side.

19 And a certain scribe came, and said unto him, Master, I will follow you whithersoever you go.

20 And Jesus saith unto him, The foxes have holes, and the birds of the air have nests; but the Son of man has not where to lay his head.

21 And another of his disciples said unto him, Lord, suffer me first to go and bury my father.

22 But Jesus said unto him, Follow me; and let the dead bury their dead.

23 And when he was entered into a ship, his disciples followed him.

24 And, behold, there arose a great tempest in the sea, insomuch that the ship was covered with the waves: but he was asleep.

25 And his disciples came to him, and awoke him, saying, Lord, save us: we perish.

26 And he saith unto them, Why are you fearful, O you of little faith? Then he arose, and rebuked the winds and the sea; and there was a great calm.

27 But the men marvelled, saying, What manner of man is this, that even the winds and the sea obey him!

28 And when he was come to the other side into the country of the Gergesenes, there met him two possessed with devils, coming out of the tombs, exceeding fierce, so that no man might pass by that way.

29 And, behold, they cried out, saying, What have we to do with you, Jesus, you Son of God? are you come hither to torment us before the time?

30 And there was a good way off from them an herd of many swine feeding.

31 So the devils besought him, saying, If you cast us out, suffer us to go away into the herd of swine.

32 And he said unto them, Go. And when they were come out, they went into the herd of swine: and, behold, the whole herd of swine ran violently down a steep place into the sea, and perished in the waters.

33 And they that kept them fled, and went their ways into the city, and told every thing, and what was befallen to the possessed of the devils.

34 And, behold, the whole city came out to meet Jesus: and when they saw him, they besought him that he would depart out of their coasts.

CHAPTER 9

AND he entered into a ship, and passed over, and came into his own city.

2 And, behold, they brought to him a man sick of the palsy, lying on a bed: and Jesus seeing their faith said unto the sick of the palsy; Son, be of good cheer; your sins be forgiven you.

3 And, behold, certain of the scribes said within themselves, This man blasphemeth.

4 And Jesus knowing their thoughts said, Wherefore think you evil in your hearts?

5 For whether is easier, to say, Your sins be forgiven you; or to say, Arise, and walk?

6 But that you may know that the Son of man has power on earth to forgive sins, (then saith he to the sick of the palsy,) Arise, take up your bed, and go unto yours house.

7 And he arose, and departed to his house.

8 But when the multitudes saw it, they marvelled, and glorified God, which had given such power unto men.

9 And as Jesus passed forth from thence, he saw a man, named Matthew, sitting at the receipt of custom: and he saith unto him, Follow me. And he arose, and followed him.

10 And it came to pass, as Jesus sat at meat in the house, behold, many publicans and sinners came and sat down with him and his disciples.

11 And when the Pharisees saw it, they said unto his disciples, Why eateth your Master with publicans and sinners?

12 But when Jesus heard that, he said unto them, They that be whole need not a physician, but they that are sick.

13 But go you and learn what that meaneth, I will have mercy, and not sacrifice: for I am not come to call the righteous, but sinners to repentance.

14 Then came to him the disciples of John, saying, Why do we and the Pharisees fast oft, but your disciples fast not?

15 And Jesus said unto them, Can the children of the bridechamber mourn, as long as the bridegroom is with them? but the days will come, when the bridegroom shall be taken from them, and then shall they fast.

16 No man putteth a piece of new cloth unto an old garment, for that which is put in to fill it up taketh from the garment, and the rent is made worse.

17 Neither do men put new wine into old bottles: else the bottles break, and the wine runneth out, and the bottles perish: but they put new wine into new bottles, and both are preserved.

18 While he spake these things unto them, behold, there came a certain ruler, and worshipped him, saying, My daughter is even now dead: but come and lay your hand upon her, and she shall live.

19 And Jesus arose, and followed him, and so did his disciples.

20 And, behold, a woman, which was diseased with an issue of blood twelve years, came behind him, and touched the hem of his garment:

21 For she said within herself, If I may but touch his garment, I shall be whole.

22 But Jesus turned him about, and when he saw her, he said, Daughter, be of good comfort; your faith has made you whole. And the woman was made whole from that hour.

23 And when Jesus came into the ruler's house, and saw the minstrels and the people making a noise,

24 He said unto them, Give place: for the maid is not dead, but sleepeth. And they laughed him to scorn.

25 But when the people were put forth, he went in, and took her by the hand, and the maid arose.

26 And the fame hereof went abroad into all that land.

27 And when Jesus departed thence, two blind men followed him, crying, and saying, You Son of David, have mercy on us.

28 And when he was come into the house, the blind men came to him: and Jesus saith unto them, Believe you that I am able to do this? They said unto him, Yea, Lord.

29 Then touched he their eyes, saying, According to your faith be it unto you.

30 And their eyes were opened; and Jesus straitly charged them, saying, See that no man know it.

31 But they, when they were departed, spread abroad his fame in all that country.

32 As they went out, behold, they brought to him a dumb man possessed with a devil.

33 And when the devil was cast out, the dumb spake: and the multitudes marvelled, saying, It was never so seen in Israel.

34 But the Pharisees said, He casteth out devils through the prince of the devils.

35 And Jesus went about all the cities and villages, teaching in their synagogues, and preaching the gospel of the kingdom, and healing every sickness and every disease among the people.

36 But when he saw the multitudes, he was moved with compassion on them, because they fainted, and were scattered abroad, as sheep having no shepherd.

37 Then saith he unto his disciples, The harvest truly is plenteous, but the labourers are few;

38 Pray you therefore the Lord of the harvest, that he will send forth labourers into his harvest.

CHAPTER 10

AND when he had called unto him his twelve disciples, he gave them power against unclean spirits, to cast them out, and to heal all manner of sickness and all manner of disease.

2 Now the names of the twelve apostles are these; The first, Simon, who is called Peter, and Andrew his brother; James the son of Zebedee, and John his brother;

3 Philip, and Bartholomew; Thomas, and Matthew the publican; James the son of Alphæus, and Lebbæus, whose surname was Thaddæus;

4 Simon the Canaanite, and Judas Iscariot, who also betrayed him.

5 These twelve Jesus sent forth, and commanded them, saying, Go not into the way of the Gentiles, and into any city of the Samaritans enter you not:

6 But go rather to the lost sheep of the house of Israel.

7 And as you go, preach, saying, The kingdom of heaven is at hand.

8 Heal the sick, cleanse the lepers, raise the dead, cast out devils: freely you have received, freely give.

9 Provide neither gold, nor silver, nor brass in your purses,

10 Nor scrip for your journey, neither two coats, neither shoes, nor yet staves: for the workman is worthy of his meat.

11 And into whatsoever city or town you shall enter, inquire who in it is worthy; and there abide till you go thence.

12 And when you come into an house, salute it.

13 And if the house be worthy, let your peace come upon it: but if it be not worthy, let your peace return to you.

14 And whosoever shall not receive you, nor hear your words, when you depart out of that house or city, shake off the dust of your feet.

15 Verily I say unto you, It shall be more tolerable for the land of Sodom and Gomorrha in the day of judgment, than for that city.

16 Behold, I send you forth as sheep in the midst of wolves: be you therefore wise as serpents, and harmless as doves.

17 But beware of men: for they will deliver you up to the councils, and they will scourge you in their synagogues;

18 And you shall be brought before governors and kings for my sake, for a testimony against them and the Gentiles.

19 But when they deliver you up, take no thought how or what you shall speak: for it shall be given you in that same hour what you shall speak.

20 For it is not you that speak, but the Spirit of your Father which speaketh in you.

21 And the brother shall deliver up the brother to death, and the father the child: and the children shall rise up against their parents, and cause them to be put to death.

22 And you shall be hated of all men for my name's sake: but he that endureth to the end shall be saved.

23 But when they persecute you in this city, flee you into another: for verily I say unto you, You shall not have gone over the cities of Israel, till the Son of man be come.

24 The disciple is not above his master, nor the servant above his lord.

25 It is enough for the disciple that he be as his master, and the servant as his lord. If they have called the master of the house Beelzebub, how much more shall they call them of his household?

26 Fear them not therefore: for there is nothing covered, that shall not be revealed; and hid, that shall not be known.

27 What I tell you in darkness, that speak you in light: and what you hear in the ear, that preach you upon the housetops.

28 And fear not them which kill the body, but are not able to kill the soul: but rather fear him which is able to destroy both soul and body in hell.

29 Are not two sparrows sold for a farthing? and one of them shall not fall on the ground without your Father.

30 But the very hairs of your head are all numbered.

31 Fear you not therefore, you are of more value than many sparrows.

32 Whosoever therefore shall confess me before men, him will I confess also before my Father which is in heaven.

33 But whosoever shall deny me before men, him will I also deny before my Father which is in heaven.

34 Think not that I am come to send peace on earth: I came not to send peace, but a sword.

35 For I am come to set a man at variance against his father, and the daughter against her mother, and the daughter in law against her mother in law.

36 And a man's foes shall be they of his own household.

37 He that loveth father or mother more than me is not worthy of me: and he that loveth son or daughter more than me is not worthy of me.

38 And he that taketh not his cross, and followeth after me, is not worthy of me.

39 He that findeth his life shall lose it: and he that loseth his life for my sake shall find it.

40 He that receiveth you receiveth me, and he that receiveth me receiveth him that sent me.

41 He that receiveth a prophet in the name of a prophet shall receive a prophet's reward; and he that receiveth a righteous man in the name of a righteous man shall receive a righteous man's reward.

42 And whosoever shall give to drink unto one of these little ones a cup of cold water only in the name of a disciple, verily I say unto you, he shall in no wise lose his reward.

CHAPTER 11

AND it came to pass, when Jesus had made an end of commanding his twelve disciples, he departed thence to teach and to preach in their cities.

2 Now when John had heard in the prison the works of Christ, he sent two of his disciples,

3 And said unto him, Are you he that should come, or do we look for another?

4 Jesus answered and said unto them, Go and shew John again those things which you do hear and see:

5 The blind receive their sight, and the lame walk, the lepers are cleansed, and the deaf hear, the dead are raised up, and the poor have the gospel preached to them.

6 And blessed is he, whosoever shall not be offended in me.

7 And as they departed, Jesus began to say unto the multitudes concerning John, What went you out into the wilderness to see? A reed shaken with the wind?

8 But what went you out for to see? A man clothed in soft raiment? behold, they that wear soft clothing are in kings' houses.

9 But what went you out for to see? A prophet? yea, I say unto you, and more than a prophet.

10 For this is he, of whom it is written, Behold, I send my messenger before your face, which shall prepare your way before you.

11 Verily I say unto you, Among them that are born of women there has not risen a greater than John the Baptist: notwithstanding he that is least in the kingdom of heaven is greater than he.

12 And from the days of John the Baptist until now the kingdom of heaven suffereth violence, and the violent take it by force.

13 For all the prophets and the law prophesied until John.

14 And if you will receive it, this is Elias, which was for to come.

15 He that has ears to hear, let him hear.

16 But whereunto shall I liken this generation? It is like unto children sitting in the markets, and calling unto their fellows,

17 And saying, We have piped unto you, and you have not danced; we have mourned unto you, and you have not lamented.

18 For John came neither eating nor drinking, and they say, He has a devil.

19 The Son of man came eating and drinking, and they say, Behold a man gluttonous, and a winebibber, a friend of publicans and sinners. But wisdom is justified of her children.

20 Then began he to upbraid the cities wherein most of his mighty works were done, because they repented not:

21 Woe unto you, Chorazin! woe unto you, Bethsaida! for if the mighty works, which were done in you, had been done in Tyre and Sidon, they would have repented long ago in sackcloth and ashes.

22 But I say unto you, It shall be more tolerable for Tyre and Sidon at the day of judgment, than for you.

23 And you, Capernaum, which are exalted unto heaven, shalt be brought down to hell: for if the mighty works, which have been done in you, had been done in Sodom, it would have remained until this day.

24 But I say unto you, That it shall be more tolerable for the land of Sodom in the day of judgment, than for you.

25 At that time Jesus answered and said, I thank you, O Father, Lord of heaven and earth, because you have hid these things from the wise and prudent, and have revealed them unto babes.

26 Even so, Father: for so it seemed good in your sight.

27 All things are delivered unto me of my Father: and no man knoweth the Son, but the Father; neither knoweth any man the Father, save the Son, and he to whomsoever the Son will reveal him.

28 Come unto me, all you that labour and are heavy laden, and I will give you rest.

29 Take my yoke upon you, and learn of me; for I am meek and lowly in heart: and you shall find rest unto your souls.

30 For my yoke is easy, and my burden is light.

CHAPTER 12

AT that time Jesus went on the sabbath day through the corn; and his disciples were an hungred, and began to pluck the ears of corn, and to eat.

2 But when the Pharisees saw it, they said unto him, Behold, your disciples do that which is not lawful to do upon the sabbath day.

3 But he said unto them, Have you not read what David did, when he was an hungred, and they that were with him;

4 How he entered into the house of God, and did eat the shewbread, which was not lawful for him to eat, neither for them which were with him, but only for the priests?

5 Or have you not read in the law, how that on the sabbath days the priests in the temple profane the sabbath, and are blameless?

6 But I say unto you, That in this place is one greater than the temple.

7 But if you had known what this meaneth, I will have mercy, and not sacrifice, you would not have condemned the guiltless.

8 For the Son of man is Lord even of the sabbath day.

9 And when he was departed thence, he went into their synagogue:

10 And, behold, there was a man which had his hand withered. And they asked him, saying, Is it lawful to heal on the sabbath days? that they might accuse him.

11 And he said unto them, What man shall there be among you, that shall have one sheep, and if it fall into a pit on the sabbath day, will he not lay hold on it, and lift it out?

12 How much then is a man better than a sheep? Wherefore it is lawful to do well on the sabbath days.

13 Then saith he to the man, Stretch forth yours hand. And he stretched it forth; and it was restored whole, like as the other.

14 Then the Pharisees went out, and held a council against him, how they might destroy him.

15 But when Jesus knew it, he withdrew himself from thence: and great multitudes followed him, and he healed them all;

16 And charged them that they should not make him known:

17 That it might be fulfilled which was spoken by Esaias the prophet, saying,

18 Behold my servant, whom I have chosen; my beloved, in whom my soul is well pleased: I will put my spirit upon him, and he shall shew judgment to the Gentiles.

19 He shall not strive, nor cry; neither shall any man hear his voice in the streets.

20 A bruised reed shall he not break, and smoking flax shall he not quench, till he send forth judgment unto victory.

21 And in his name shall the Gentiles trust.

22 Then was brought unto him one possessed with a devil, blind, and dumb: and he healed him, insomuch that the blind and dumb both spake and saw.

23 And all the people were amazed, and said, Is not this the son of David?

24 But when the Pharisees heard it, they said, This fellow doth not cast out devils, but by Beelzebub the prince of the devils.

25 And Jesus knew their thoughts, and said unto them, Every kingdom divided against itself is brought to desolation; and every city or house divided against itself shall not stand:

26 And if Satan cast out Satan, he is divided against himself; how shall then his kingdom stand?

27 And if I by Beelzebub cast out devils, by whom do your children cast them out? therefore they shall be your judges.

28 But if I cast out devils by the Spirit of God, then the kingdom of God is come unto you.

29 Or else how can one enter into a strong man's house, and spoil his goods, except he first bind the strong man? and then he will spoil his house.

30 He that is not with me is against me; and he that gathereth not with me scattereth abroad.

31 Wherefore I say unto you, All manner of sin and blasphemy shall be forgiven unto men: but the blasphemy against the Holy Ghost shall not be forgiven unto men.

32 And whosoever speaketh a word against the Son of man, it shall be forgiven him: but whosoever speaketh against the Holy Ghost, it shall not be forgiven him, neither in this world, neither in the world to come.

33 Either make the tree good, and his fruit good; or else make the tree corrupt, and his fruit corrupt: for the tree is known by his fruit.

34 O generation of vipers, how can you , being evil, speak good things? for out of the abundance of the heart the mouth speaketh.

35 A good man out of the good treasure of the heart bringeth forth good things: and an evil man out of the evil treasure bringeth forth evil things.

36 But I say unto you, That every idle word that men shall speak, they shall give account thereof in the day of judgment.

37 For by your words you shalt be justified, and by your words you shalt be condemned.

38 Then certain of the scribes and of the Pharisees answered, saying, Master, we would see a sign from you.

39 But he answered and said unto them, An evil and adulterous generation seeketh after a sign; and there shall no sign be given to it, but the sign of the prophet Jonas:

40 For as Jonas was three days and three nights in the whale's belly; so shall the Son of man be three days and three nights in the heart of the earth.

41 The men of Nineveh shall rise in judgment with this generation, and shall condemn it: because they repented at the preaching of Jonas; and, behold, a greater than Jonas is here.

42 The queen of the south shall rise up in the judgment with this generation, and shall condemn it: for she came from the uttermost parts of the earth to hear the wisdom of Solomon; and, behold, a greater than Solomon is here.

43 When the unclean spirit is gone out of a man, he walketh through dry places, seeking rest, and findeth none.

44 Then he saith, I will return into my house from whence I came out; and when he is come, he findeth it empty, swept, and garnished.

45 Then goeth he, and taketh with himself seven other spirits more wicked than himself, and they enter in and dwell there: and the last state of that man is worse than the first. Even so shall it be also unto this wicked generation.

46 While he yet talked to the people, behold, his mother and his brethren stood without, desiring to speak with him.

47 Then one said unto him, Behold, your mother and your brethren stand without, desiring to speak with you.

48 But he answered and said unto him that told him, Who is my mother? and who are my brethren?

49 And he stretched forth his hand toward his disciples, and said, Behold my mother and my brethren!

50 For whosoever shall do the will of my Father which is in heaven, the same is my brother, and sister, and mother.

CHAPTER 13

THE same day went Jesus out of the house, and sat by the sea side.

2 And great multitudes were gathered together unto him, so that he went into a ship, and sat; and the whole multitude stood on the shore.

3 And he spake many things unto them in parables, saying, Behold, a sower went forth to sow;

4 And when he sowed, some seeds fell by the way side, and the fowls came and devoured them up:

5 Some fell upon stony places, where they had not much earth: and forthwith they sprung up, because they had no deepness of earth:

6 And when the sun was up, they were scorched; and because they had no root, they withered away.

7 And some fell among thorns; and the thorns sprung up, and choked them:

8 But other fell into good ground, and brought forth fruit, some an hundredfold, some sixtyfold, some thirtyfold.

9 Who has ears to hear, let him hear.

10 And the disciples came, and said unto him, Why speakest you unto them in parables?

11 He answered and said unto them, Because it is given unto you to know the mysteries of the kingdom of heaven, but to them it is not given.

12 For whosoever has, to him shall be given, and he shall have more abundance: but whosoever has not, from him shall be taken away even that he has.

13 Therefore speak I to them in parables: because they seeing see not; and hearing they hear not, neither do they understand.

14 And in them is fulfilled the prophecy of Esaias, which saith, By hearing you shall hear, and shall not understand; and seeing you shall see, and shall not perceive:

15 For this people's heart is waxed gross, and their ears are dull of hearing, and their eyes they have closed; lest at any time they should see with their eyes, and hear with their ears, and should understand with their heart, and should be converted, and I should heal them.

16 But blessed are your eyes, for they see: and your ears, for they hear.

17 For verily I say unto you, That many prophets and righteous men have desired to see those things which you see, and have not seen them; and to hear those things which you hear, and have not heard them.

18 Hear you therefore the parable of the sower.

19 When any one heareth the word of the kingdom, and understands it not, then comes the wicked one, and catcheth away that which was sown in his heart. This is he which received seed by the way side.

20 But he that received the seed into stony places, the same is he that heareth the word, and anon with joy receiveth it;

21 Yet has he not root in himself, but dureth for a while: for when tribulation or persecution ariseth because of the word, by and by he is offended.

22 He also that received seed among the thorns is he that heareth the word; and the care of this world, and the deceitfulness of riches, choke the word, and he becometh unfruitful.

23 But he that received seed into the good ground is he that heareth the word, and understands it; which also beareth fruit, and bringeth forth, some an hundredfold, some sixty, some thirty.

24 Another parable put he forth unto them, saying, The kingdom of heaven is likened unto a man which sowed good seed in his field:

25 But while men slept, his enemy came and sowed tares among the wheat, and went his way.

26 But when the blade was sprung up, and brought forth fruit, then appeared the tares also.

27 So the servants of the householder came and said unto him, Sir, did not you sow good seed in your field? from whence then has it tares?

28 He said unto them, An enemy has done this. The servants said unto him, Will you then that we go and gather them up?

29 But he said, Nay; lest while you gather up the tares, you root up also the wheat with them.

30 Let both grow together until the harvest: and in the time of harvest I will say to the reapers, Gather you together first the tares, and bind them in bundles to burn them: but gather the wheat into my barn.

31 Another parable put he forth unto them, saying, The kingdom of heaven is like to a grain of mustard seed, which a man took, and sowed in his field:

32 Which indeed is the least of all seeds: but when it is grown, it is the greatest among herbs, and becometh a tree, so that the birds of the air come and lodge in the branches thereof.

33 Another parable spake he unto them; The kingdom of heaven is like unto leaven, which a woman took, and hid in three measures of meal, till the whole was leavened.

34 All these things spake Jesus unto the multitude in parables; and without a parable spake he not unto them:

35 That it might be fulfilled which was spoken by the prophet, saying, I will open my mouth in parables; I will utter things which have been kept secret from the foundation of the world.

36 Then Jesus sent the multitude away, and went into the house: and his disciples came unto him, saying, Declare unto us the parable of the tares of the field.

37 He answered and said unto them, He that soweth the good seed is the Son of man;

38 The field is the world; the good seed are the children of the kingdom; but the tares are the children of the wicked one;

39 The enemy that sowed them is the devil; the harvest is the end of the world; and the reapers are the angels.

40 As therefore the tares are gathered and burned in the fire; so shall it be in the end of this world.

41 The Son of man shall send forth his angels, and they shall gather out of his kingdom all things that offend, and them which do iniquity;

42 And shall cast them into a furnace of fire: there shall be wailing and gnashing of teeth.

43 Then shall the righteous shine forth as the sun in the kingdom of their Father. Who has ears to hear, let him hear.

44 Again, the kingdom of heaven is like unto treasure hid in a field; the which when a man has found, he hideth, and for joy thereof goeth and selleth all that he has, and buyeth that field.

45 Again, the kingdom of heaven is like unto a merchant man, seeking goodly pearls:

46 Who, when he had found one pearl of great price, went and sold all that he had, and bought it.

47 Again, the kingdom of heaven is like unto a net, that was cast into the sea, and gathered of every kind:

48 Which, when it was full, they drew to shore, and sat down, and gathered the good into vessels, but cast the bad away.

49 So shall it be at the end of the world: the angels shall come forth, and sever the wicked from among the just,

50 And shall cast them into the furnace of fire: there shall be wailing and gnashing of teeth.

51 Jesus saith unto them, Have you understood all these things? They say unto him, Yea, Lord.

52 Then said he unto them, Therefore every scribe which is instructed unto the kingdom of heaven is like unto a man that is an householder, which bringeth forth out of his treasure things new and old.

53 And it came to pass, that when Jesus had finished these parables, he departed thence.

54 And when he was come into his own country, he taught them in their synagogue, insomuch that they were astonished, and said, Whence has this man this wisdom, and these mighty works?

55 Is not this the carpenter's son? is not his mother called Mary? and his brethren, James, and Joses, and Simon, and Judas?

56 And his sisters, are they not all with us? Whence then has this man all these things?

57 And they were offended in him. But Jesus said unto them, A prophet is not without honour, save in his own country, and in his own house.

58 And he did not many mighty works there because of their unbelief.

CHAPTER 14

AT that time Herod the tetrarch heard of the fame of Jesus,

2 And said unto his servants, This is John the Baptist; he is risen from the dead; and therefore mighty works do shew forth themselves in him.

3 For Herod had laid hold on John, and bound him, and put him in prison for Herodias' sake, his brother Philip's wife.

4 For John said unto him, It is not lawful for you to have her.

5 And when he would have put him to death, he feared the multitude, because they counted him as a prophet.

6 But when Herod's birthday was kept, the daughter of Herodias danced before them, and pleased Herod.

7 Whereupon he promised with an oath to give her whatsoever she would ask.

8 And she, being before instructed of her mother, said, Give me here John Baptist's head in a charger.

9 And the king was sorry: nevertheless for the oath's sake, and them which sat with him at meat, he commanded it to be given her.

10 And he sent, and beheaded John in the prison.

11 And his head was brought in a charger, and given to the damsel: and she brought it to her mother.

12 And his disciples came, and took up the body, and buried it, and went and told Jesus.

13 When Jesus heard of it, he departed thence by ship into a desert place apart: and when the people had heard thereof, they followed him on foot out of the cities.

14 And Jesus went forth, and saw a great multitude, and was moved with compassion toward them, and he healed their sick.

15 And when it was evening, his disciples came to him, saying, This is a desert place, and the time is now past; send the multitude away, that they may go into the villages, and buy themselves victuals.

16 But Jesus said unto them, They need not depart; give you them to eat.

17 And they say unto him, We have here but five loaves, and two fishes.

18 He said, Bring them hither to me.

19 And he commanded the multitude to sit down on the grass, and took the five loaves, and the two fishes, and looking up to heaven, he blessed, and brake, and gave the loaves to his disciples, and the disciples to the multitude.

20 And they did all eat, and were filled: and they took up of the fragments that remained twelve baskets full.

21 And they that had eaten were about five thousand men, beside women and children.

22 And straightway Jesus constrained his disciples to get into a ship, and to go before him unto the other side, while he sent the multitudes away.

23 And when he had sent the multitudes away, he went up into a mountain apart to pray: and when the evening was come, he was there alone.

24 But the ship was now in the midst of the sea, tossed with waves: for the wind was contrary.

25 And in the fourth watch of the night Jesus went unto them, walking on the sea.

26 And when the disciples saw him walking on the sea, they were troubled, saying, It is a spirit; and they cried out for fear.

27 But straightway Jesus spake unto them, saying, Be of good cheer; it is I; be not afraid.

28 And Peter answered him and said, Lord, if it be you , bid me come unto you on the water.

29 And he said, Come. And when Peter was come down out of the ship, he walked on the water, to go to Jesus.

30 But when he saw the wind boisterous, he was afraid; and beginning to sink, he cried, saying, Lord, save me.

31 And immediately Jesus stretched forth his hand, and caught him, and said unto him, O you of little faith, wherefore did you doubt?

32 And when they were come into the ship, the wind ceased.

33 Then they that were in the ship came and worshipped him, saying, Of a truth you are the Son of God.

34 And when they were gone over, they came into the land of Gennesaret.

35 And when the men of that place had knowledge of him, they sent out into all that country round about, and brought unto him all that were diseased;

36 And besought him that they might only touch the hem of his garment: and as many as touched were made perfectly whole.

CHAPTER 15

THEN came to Jesus scribes and Pharisees, which were of Jerusalem, saying,

2 Why do your disciples transgress the tradition of the elders? for they wash not their hands when they eat bread.

3 But he answered and said unto them, Why do you also transgress the commandment of God by your tradition?

4 For God commanded, saying, Honour your father and mother: and, He that curseth father or mother, let him die the death.

5 But you say, Whosoever shall say to his father or his mother, It is a gift, by whatsoever you mightest be profited by me;

6 And honour not his father or his mother, he shall be free. Thus have you made the commandment of God of none effect by your tradition.

7 You hypocrites, well did Esaias prophesy of you, saying,

8 This people draweth nigh unto me with their mouth, and honoureth me with their lips; but their heart is far from me.

9 But in vain they do worship me, teaching for doctrines the commandments of men.

10 And he called the multitude, and said unto them, Hear, and understand:

11 Not that which goeth into the mouth defileth a man; but that which comes out of the mouth, this defileth a man.

12 Then came his disciples, and said unto him, Knowest you that the Pharisees were offended, after they heard this saying?

13 But he answered and said, Every plant, which my heavenly Father has not planted, shall be rooted up.

14 Let them alone: they be blind leaders of the blind. And if the blind lead the blind, both shall fall into the ditch.

15 Then answered Peter and said unto him, Declare unto us this parable.

16 And Jesus said, Are you also yet without understanding?

17 Do not you yet understand, that whatsoever entereth in at the mouth goeth into the belly, and is cast out into the draught?

18 But those things which proceed out of the mouth come forth from the heart; and they defile the man.

19 For out of the heart proceed evil thoughts, murders, adulteries, fornications, thefts, false witness, blasphemies:

20 These are the things which defile a man: but to eat with unwashen hands defileth not a man.

21 Then Jesus went thence, and departed into the coasts of Tyre and Sidon.

22 And, behold, a woman of Canaan came out of the same coasts, and cried unto him, saying, Have mercy on me, O Lord, you Son of David; my daughter is grievously vexed with a devil.

23 But he answered her not a word. And his disciples came and besought him, saying, Send her away; for she crieth after us.

24 But he answered and said, I am not sent but unto the lost sheep of the house of Israel.

25 Then came she and worshipped him, saying, Lord, help me.

26 But he answered and said, It is not meet to take the children's bread, and to cast it to dogs.

27 And she said, Truth, Lord: yet the dogs eat of the crumbs which fall from their masters' table.

28 Then Jesus answered and said unto her, O woman, great is your faith: be it unto you even as you will. And her daughter was made whole from that very hour.

29 And Jesus departed from thence, and came nigh unto the sea of Galilee; and went up into a mountain, and sat down there.

30 And great multitudes came unto him, having with them those that were lame, blind, dumb, maimed, and many others, and cast them down at Jesus' feet; and he healed them:

31 Insomuch that the multitude wondered, when they saw the dumb to speak, the maimed to be whole, the lame to walk, and the blind to see: and they glorified the God of Israel.

32 Then Jesus called his disciples unto him, and said, I have compassion on the multitude, because they continue with me now three days, and have nothing to eat: and I will not send them away fasting, lest they faint in the way.

33 And his disciples say unto him, Whence should we have so much bread in the wilderness, as to fill so great a multitude?

34 And Jesus saith unto them, How many loaves have you ? And they said, Seven, and a few little fishes.

35 And he commanded the multitude to sit down on the ground.

36 And he took the seven loaves and the fishes, and gave thanks, and brake them, and gave to his disciples, and the disciples to the multitude.

37 And they did all eat, and were filled: and they took up of the broken meat that was left seven baskets full.

38 And they that did eat were four thousand men, beside women and children.

39 And he sent away the multitude, and took ship, and came into the coasts of Magdala.

CHAPTER 16
THE Pharisees also with the Sadducees came, and tempting desired him that he would shew them a sign from heaven.

2 He answered and said unto them, When it is evening, you say, It will be fair weather: for the sky is red.

3 And in the morning, It will be foul weather to day: for the sky is red and lowring. O you hypocrites, you can discern the face of the sky; but can you not discern the signs of the times?

4 A wicked and adulterous generation seeketh after a sign; and there shall no sign be given unto it, but the sign of the prophet Jonas. And he left them, and departed.

5 And when his disciples were come to the other side, they had forgotten to take bread.

6 Then Jesus said unto them, Take heed and beware of the leaven of the Pharisees and of the Sadducees.

7 And they reasoned among themselves, saying, It is because we have taken no bread.

8 Which when Jesus perceived, he said unto them, O you of little faith, why reason you among yourselves, because you have brought no bread?

9 Do you not yet understand, neither remember the five loaves of the five thousand, and how many baskets you took up?

10 Neither the seven loaves of the four thousand, and how many baskets you took up?

11 How is it that you do not understand that I spake it not to you concerning bread, that you should beware of the leaven of the Pharisees and of the Sadducees?

12 Then understood they how that he bade them not beware of the leaven of bread, but of the doctrine of the Pharisees and of the Sadducees.

13 When Jesus came into the coasts of Cæsarea Philippi, he asked his disciples, saying, Whom do men say that I the Son of man am?

14 And they said, Some say that you are John the Baptist: some, Elias; and others, Jeremias, or one of the prophets.

15 He saith unto them, But whom say you that I am?

16 And Simon Peter answered and said, You are the Christ, the Son of the living God.

17 And Jesus answered and said unto him, Blessed are you , Simon Bar-jona: for flesh and blood has not revealed it unto you, but my Father which is in heaven.

18 And I say also unto you, That you are Peter, and upon this rock I will build my church; and the gates of hell shall not prevail against it.

19 And I will give unto you the keys of the kingdom of heaven: and whatsoever you shalt bind on earth shall be bound in heaven: and whatsoever you shalt loose on earth shall be loosed in heaven.

20 Then charged he his disciples that they should tell no man that he was Jesus the Christ.

21 From that time forth began Jesus to shew unto his disciples, how that he must go unto Jerusalem, and suffer many things of the elders and chief priests and scribes, and be killed, and be raised again the third day.

22 Then Peter took him, and began to rebuke him, saying, Be it far from you, Lord: this shall not be unto you.

23 But he turned, and said unto Peter, Get you behind me, Satan: you are an offence unto me: for you savourest not the things that be of God, but those that be of men.

24 Then said Jesus unto his disciples, If any man will come after me, let him deny himself, and take up his cross, and follow me.

25 For whosoever will save his life shall lose it: and whosoever will lose his life for my sake shall find it.

26 For what is a man profited, if he shall gain the whole world, and lose his own soul? or what shall a man give in exchange for his soul?

27 For the Son of man shall come in the glory of his Father with his angels; and then he shall reward every man according to his works.

28 Verily I say unto you, There be some standing here, which shall not taste of death, till they see the Son of man coming in his kingdom.

CHAPTER 17
AND after six days Jesus taketh Peter, James, and John his brother, and bringeth them up into an high mountain apart,

2 And was transfigured before them: and his face did shine as the sun, and his raiment was white as the light.

3 And, behold, there appeared unto them Moses and Elias talking with him.

4 Then answered Peter, and said unto Jesus, Lord, it is good for us to be here: if you will, let us make here three tabernacles; one for you, and one for Moses, and one for Elias.

5 While he yet spake, behold, a bright cloud overshadowed them: and behold a voice out of the cloud, which said, This is my beloved Son, in whom I am well pleased; hear you him.

6 And when the disciples heard it, they fell on their face, and were sore afraid.

7 And Jesus came and touched them, and said, Arise, and be not afraid.

8 And when they had lifted up their eyes, they saw no man, save Jesus only.

9 And as they came down from the mountain, Jesus charged them, saying, Tell the vision to no man, until the Son of man be risen again from the dead.

10 And his disciples asked him, saying, Why then say the scribes that Elias must first come?

11 And Jesus answered and said unto them, Elias truly shall first come, and restore all things.

12 But I say unto you, That Elias is come already, and they knew him not, but have done unto him whatsoever they listed. Likewise shall also the Son of man suffer of them.

13 Then the disciples understood that he spake unto them of John the Baptist.

14 And when they were come to the multitude, there came to him a certain man, kneeling down to him, and saying,

15 Lord, have mercy on my son: for he is lunatick, and sore vexed: for ofttimes he falleth into the fire, and oft into the water.

16 And I brought him to your disciples, and they could not cure him.

17 Then Jesus answered and said, O faithless and perverse generation, how long shall I be with you? how long shall I suffer you? bring him hither to me.

18 And Jesus rebuked the devil; and he departed out of him: and the child was cured from that very hour.

19 Then came the disciples to Jesus apart, and said, Why could not we cast him out?

20 And Jesus said unto them, Because of your unbelief: for verily I say unto you, If you have faith as a grain of mustard seed, you shall say unto this mountain, Remove hence to yonder place; and it shall remove; and nothing shall be impossible unto you.

21 Howbeit this kind goeth not out but by prayer and fasting.

22 And while they abode in Galilee, Jesus said unto them, The Son of man shall be betrayed into the hands of men:

23 And they shall kill him, and the third day he shall be raised again. And they were exceeding sorry.

24 And when they were come to Capernaum, they that received tribute money came to Peter, and said, Doth not your master pay tribute?

25 He saith, Yes. And when he was come into the house, Jesus prevented him, saying, What thinkest you , Simon? of whom do the kings of the earth take custom or tribute? of their own children, or of strangers?

26 Peter saith unto him, Of strangers. Jesus saith unto him, Then are the children free.

27 Notwithstanding, lest we should offend them, go you to the sea, and cast an hook, and take up the fish that first comes up; and when you have opened his mouth, you shalt find a piece of money: that take, and give unto them for me and you.

CHAPTER 18

AT the same time came the disciples unto Jesus, saying, Who is the greatest in the kingdom of heaven?

2 And Jesus called a little child unto him, and set him in the midst of them,

3 And said, Verily I say unto you, Except you be converted, and become as little children, you shall not enter into the kingdom of heaven.

4 Whosoever therefore shall humble himself as this little child, the same is greatest in the kingdom of heaven.

5 And whoso shall receive one such little child in my name receiveth me.

6 But whoso shall offend one of these little ones which believe in me, it were better for him that a millstone were hanged about his neck, and that he were drowned in the depth of the sea.

7 Woe unto the world because of offences! for it must needs be that offences come; but woe to that man by whom the offence comes!

8 Wherefore if your hand or your foot offend you, cut them off, and cast them from you: it is better for you to enter into life halt or maimed, rather than having two hands or two feet to be cast into everlasting fire.

9 And if yours eye offend you, pluck it out, and cast it from you: it is better for you to enter into life with one eye, rather than having two eyes to be cast into hell fire.

10 Take heed that you despise not one of these little ones; for I say unto you, That in heaven their angels do always behold the face of my Father which is in heaven.

11 For the Son of man is come to save that which was lost.

12 How think you ? if a man have an hundred sheep, and one of them be gone astray, doth he not leave the ninety and nine, and goeth into the mountains, and seeketh that which is gone astray?

13 And if so be that he find it, verily I say unto you, he rejoiceth more of that sheep, than of the ninety and nine which went not astray.

14 Even so it is not the will of your Father which is in heaven, that one of these little ones should perish.

15 Moreover if your brother shall trespass against you, go and tell him his fault between you and him alone: if he shall hear you, you have gained your brother.

16 But if he will not hear you, then take with you one or two more, that in the mouth of two or three witnesses every word may be established.

17 And if he shall neglect to hear them, tell it unto the church: but if he neglect to hear the church, let him be unto you as an heathen man and a publican.

18 Verily I say unto you, Whatsoever you shall bind on earth shall be bound in heaven: and whatsoever you shall loose on earth shall be loosed in heaven.

19 Again I say unto you, That if two of you shall agree on earth as touching any thing that they shall ask, it shall be done for them of my Father which is in heaven.

20 For where two or three are gathered together in my name, there am I in the midst of them.

21 Then came Peter to him, and said, Lord, how oft shall my brother sin against me, and I forgive him? till seven times?

22 Jesus saith unto him, I say not unto you, Until seven times: but, Until seventy times seven.

23 Therefore is the kingdom of heaven likened unto a certain king, which would take account of his servants.

24 And when he had begun to reckon, one was brought unto him, which owed him ten thousand talents.

25 But forasmuch as he had not to pay, his lord commanded him to be sold, and his wife, and children, and all that he had, and payment to be made.

26 The servant therefore fell down, and worshipped him, saying, Lord, have patience with me, and I will pay you all.

27 Then the lord of that servant was moved with compassion, and loosed him, and forgave him the debt.

28 But the same servant went out, and found one of his fellowservants, which owed him an hundred pence: and he laid hands on him, and took him by the throat, saying, Pay me that you owest.

29 And his fellowservant fell down at his feet, and besought him, saying, Have patience with me, and I will pay you all.

30 And he would not: but went and cast him into prison, till he should pay the debt.

31 So when his fellowservants saw what was done, they were very sorry, and came and told unto their lord all that was done.

32 Then his lord, after that he had called him, said unto him, O you wicked servant, I forgave you all that debt, because you desiredst me:

33 Shouldest not you also have had compassion on your fellowservant, even as I had pity on you?

34 And his lord was wroth, and delivered him to the tormentors, till he should pay all that was due unto him.

35 So likewise shall my heavenly Father do also unto you, if you from your hearts forgive not every one his brother their trespasses.

CHAPTER 19

AND it came to pass, that when Jesus had finished these sayings, he departed from Galilee, and came into the coasts of Judæa beyond Jordan;

2 And great multitudes followed him; and he healed them there.

3 The Pharisees also came unto him, tempting him, and saying unto him, Is it lawful for a man to put away his wife for every cause?

4 And he answered and said unto them, Have you not read, that he which made them at the beginning made them male and female,

5 And said, For this cause shall a man leave father and mother, and shall cleave to his wife: and they twain shall be one flesh?

6 Wherefore they are no more twain, but one flesh. What therefore God has joined together, let not man put asunder.

7 They say unto him, Why did Moses then command to give a writing of divorcement, and to put her away?

8 He saith unto them, Moses because of the hardness of your hearts suffered you to put away your wives: but from the beginning it was not so.

9 And I say unto you, Whosoever shall put away his wife, except it be for fornication, and shall marry another, committeth adultery: and whoso marrieth her which is put away doth commit adultery.

10 His disciples say unto him, If the case of the man be so with his wife, it is not good to marry.

11 But he said unto them, All men cannot receive this saying, save they to whom it is given.

12 For there are some eunuchs, which were so born from their mother's womb: and there are some eunuchs, which were made eunuchs of men: and there be eunuchs, which have made themselves eunuchs for the kingdom of heaven's sake. He that is able to receive it, let him receive it.

13 Then were there brought unto him little children, that he should put his hands on them, and pray: and the disciples rebuked them.

14 But Jesus said, Suffer little children, and forbid them not, to come unto me: for of such is the kingdom of heaven.

15 And he laid his hands on them, and departed thence.

16 And, behold, one came and said unto him, Good Master, what good thing shall I do, that I may have eternal life?

17 And he said unto him, Why callest you me good? there is none good but one, that is, God: but if you will enter into life, keep the commandments.

18 He saith unto him, Which? Jesus said, You shalt do no murder, You shalt not commit adultery, You shalt not steal, You shalt not bear false witness,

19 Honour your father and your mother: and, You shalt love your neighbour as yourself.

20 The young man saith unto him, All these things have I kept from my youth up: what lack I yet?

21 Jesus said unto him, If you will be perfect, go and sell that you have, and give to the poor, and you shalt have treasure in heaven: and come and follow me.

22 But when the young man heard that saying, he went away sorrowful: for he had great possessions.

23 Then said Jesus unto his disciples, Verily I say unto you, That a rich man shall hardly enter into the kingdom of heaven.

24 And again I say unto you, It is easier for a camel to go through the eye of a needle, than for a rich man to enter into the kingdom of God.

25 When his disciples heard it, they were exceedingly amazed, saying, Who then can be saved?

26 But Jesus beheld them, and said unto them, With men this is impossible; but with God all things are possible.

27 Then answered Peter and said unto him, Behold, we have forsaken all, and followed you; what shall we have therefore?

28 And Jesus said unto them, Verily I say unto you, That you which have followed me, in the regeneration when the Son of man shall sit in the throne of his glory, you also shall sit upon twelve thrones, judging the twelve tribes of Israel.

29 And every one that has forsaken houses, or brethren, or sisters, or father, or mother, or wife, or children, or lands, for my name's sake, shall receive an hundredfold, and shall inherit everlasting life.

30 But many that are first shall be last; and the last shall be first.

CHAPTER 20

FOR the kingdom of heaven is like unto a man that is an householder, which went out early in the morning to hire labourers into his vineyard.

2 And when he had agreed with the labourers for a penny a day, he sent them into his vineyard.

3 And he went out about the third hour, and saw others standing idle in the marketplace,

4 And said unto them; Go you also into the vineyard, and whatsoever is right I will give you. And they went their way.

5 Again he went out about the sixth and ninth hour, and did likewise.

6 And about the eleventh hour he went out, and found others standing idle, and saith unto them, Why stand you here all the day idle?

7 They say unto him, Because no man has hired us. He saith unto them, Go you also into the vineyard; and whatsoever is right, that shall you receive.

8 So when even was come, the lord of the vineyard saith unto his steward, Call the labourers, and give them their hire, beginning from the last unto the first.

9 And when they came that were hired about the eleventh hour, they received every man a penny.

10 But when the first came, they supposed that they should have received more; and they likewise received every man a penny.

11 And when they had received it, they murmured against the goodman of the house,

12 Saying, These last have created but one hour, and you have made them equal unto us, which have borne the burden and heat of the day.

13 But he answered one of them, and said, Friend, I do you no wrong: did not you agree with me for a penny?

14 Take that yours is, and go your way: I will give unto this last, even as unto you.

15 Is it not lawful for me to do what I will with my own? Is yours eye evil, because I am good?

16 So the last shall be first, and the first last: for many be called, but few chosen.

17 And Jesus going up to Jerusalem took the twelve disciples apart in the way, and said unto them,

18 Behold, we go up to Jerusalem; and the Son of man shall be betrayed unto the chief priests and unto the scribes, and they shall condemn him to death,

19 And shall deliver him to the Gentiles to mock, and to scourge, and to crucify him: and the third day he shall rise again.

20 Then came to him the mother of Zebedee's children with her sons, worshipping him, and desiring a certain thing of him.

21 And he said unto her, What will you ? She saith unto him, Grant that these my two sons may sit, the one on your right hand, and the other on the left, in your kingdom.

22 But Jesus answered and said, You know not what you ask. Are you able to drink of the cup that I shall drink of, and to be baptized with the baptism that I am baptized with? They say unto him, We are able.

23 And he saith unto them, You shall drink indeed of my cup, and be baptized with the baptism that I am baptized with: but to sit on my right hand, and on my left, is not my to give, but it shall be given to them for whom it is prepared of my Father.

24 And when the ten heard it, they were moved with indignation against the two brethren.

25 But Jesus called them unto him, and said, You know that the princes of the Gentiles exercise dominion over them, and they that are great exercise authority upon them.

26 But it shall not be so among you: but whosoever will be great among you, let him be your minister;

27 And whosoever will be chief among you, let him be your servant:

28 Even as the Son of man came not to be ministered unto, but to minister, and to give his life a ransom for many.

29 And as they departed from Jericho, a great multitude followed him.

30 And, behold, two blind men sitting by the way side, when they heard that Jesus passed by, cried out, saying, Have mercy on us, O Lord, you Son of David.

31 And the multitude rebuked them, because they should hold their peace: but they cried the more, saying, Have mercy on us, O Lord, you Son of David.

32 And Jesus stood still, and called them, and said, What will you that I shall do unto you?

33 They say unto him, Lord, that our eyes may be opened.

34 So Jesus had compassion on them, and touched their eyes: and immediately their eyes received sight, and they followed him.

CHAPTER 21

AND when they drew nigh unto Jerusalem, and were come to Bethphage, unto the mount of Olives, then sent Jesus two disciples,

2 Saying unto them, Go into the village over against you, and straightway you shall find an ass tied, and a colt with her: loose them, and bring them unto me.

3 And if any man say ought unto you, you shall say, The Lord has need of them; and straightway he will send them.

4 All this was done, that it might be fulfilled which was spoken by the prophet, saying,

5 Tell you the daughter of Sion, Behold, your King comes unto you, meek, and sitting upon an ass, and a colt the foal of an ass.

6 And the disciples went, and did as Jesus commanded them,

7 And brought the ass, and the colt, and put on them their clothes, and they set him thereon.

8 And a very great multitude spread their garments in the way; others cut down branches from the trees, and strawed them in the way.

9 And the multitudes that went before, and that followed, cried, saying, Hosanna to the Son of David: Blessed is he that comes in the name of the Lord; Hosanna in the highest.

10 And when he was come into Jerusalem, all the city was moved, saying, Who is this?

11 And the multitude said, This is Jesus the prophet of Nazareth of Galilee.

12 And Jesus went into the temple of God, and cast out all them that sold and bought in the temple, and overthrew the tables of the moneychangers, and the seats of them that sold doves,

13 And said unto them, It is written, My house shall be called the house of prayer; but you have made it a den of thieves.

14 And the blind and the lame came to him in the temple; and he healed them.

15 And when the chief priests and scribes saw the wonderful things that he did, and the children crying in the temple, and saying, Hosanna to the Son of David; they were sore displeased,

16 And said unto him, Hearest you what these say? And Jesus saith unto them, Yea; have you never read, Out of the mouth of babes and sucklings you have perfected praise?

17 And he left them, and went out of the city into Bethany; and he lodged there.

18 Now in the morning as he returned into the city, he hungered.

19 And when he saw a fig tree in the way, he came to it, and found nothing thereon, but leaves only, and said unto it, Let no fruit grow on you henceforward for ever. And presently the fig tree withered away.

20 And when the disciples saw it, they marvelled, saying, How soon is the fig tree withered away!

21 Jesus answered and said unto them, Verily I say unto you, If you have faith, and doubt not, you shall not only do this which is done to the fig tree, but also if you shall say unto this mountain, Be you removed, and be you cast into the sea; it shall be done.

22 And all things, whatsoever you shall ask in prayer, believing, you shall receive.

23And when he was come into the temple, the chief priests and the elders of the people came unto him as he was teaching, and said, By what authority doest you these things? and who gave you this authority?

24 And Jesus answered and said unto them, I also will ask you one thing, which if you tell me, I in like wise will tell you by what authority I do these things.

25 The baptism of John, whence was it? from heaven, or of men? And they reasoned with themselves, saying, If we shall say, From heaven; he will say unto us, Why did you not then believe him?

26 But if we shall say, Of men; we fear the people; for all hold John as a prophet.

27 And they answered Jesus, and said, We cannot tell. And he said unto them, Neither tell I you by what authority I do these things.

28But what think you ? A certain man had two sons; and he came to the first, and said, Son, go work to day in my vineyard.

29 He answered and said, I will not: but afterward he repented, and went.

30 And he came to the second, and said likewise. And he answered and said, I go, sir: and went not.

31 Whether of them twain did the will of his father? They say unto him, The first. Jesus saith unto them, Verily I say unto you, That the publicans and the harlots go into the kingdom of God before you.

32 For John came unto you in the way of righteousness, and you believed him not: but the publicans and the harlots believed him: and you , when you had seen it, repented not afterward, that you might believe him.

33Hear another parable: There was a certain householder, which planted a vineyard, and hedged it round about, and digged a winepress in it, and built a tower, and let it out to husbandmen, and went into a far country:

34 And when the time of the fruit drew near, he sent his servants to the husbandmen, that they might receive the fruits of it.

35 And the husbandmen took his servants, and beat one, and killed another, and stoned another.

36 Again, he sent other servants more than the first: and they did unto them likewise.

37 But last of all he sent unto them his son, saying, They will reverence my son.

38 But when the husbandmen saw the son, they said among themselves, This is the heir; come, let us kill him, and let us seize on his inheritance.

39 And they caught him, and cast him out of the vineyard, and slew him.

40 When the lord therefore of the vineyard comes, what will he do unto those husbandmen?

41 They say unto him, He will miserably destroy those wicked men, and will let out his vineyard unto other husbandmen, which shall render him the fruits in their seasons.

42 Jesus saith unto them, Did you never read in the scriptures, The stone which the builders rejected, the same is become the head of the corner: this is the Lord's doing, and it is marvellous in our eyes?

43 Therefore say I unto you, The kingdom of God shall be taken from you, and given to a nation bringing forth the fruits thereof.

44 And whosoever shall fall on this stone shall be broken: but on whomsoever it shall fall, it will grind him to powder.

45 And when the chief priests and Pharisees had heard his parables, they perceived that he spake of them.

46 But when they sought to lay hands on him, they feared the multitude, because they took him for a prophet.

CHAPTER 22

AND Jesus answered and spake unto them again by parables, and said,

2 The kingdom of heaven is like unto a certain king, which made a marriage for his son,

3 And sent forth his servants to call them that were bidden to the wedding: and they would not come.

4 Again, he sent forth other servants, saying, Tell them which are bidden, Behold, I have prepared my dinner: my oxen and my fatlings are killed, and all things are ready: come unto the marriage.

5 But they made light of it, and went their ways, one to his farm, another to his merchandise:

6 And the remnant took his servants, and entreated them spitefully, and slew them.

7 But when the king heard thereof, he was wroth: and he sent forth his armies, and destroyed those murderers, and burned up their city.

8 Then saith he to his servants, The wedding is ready, but they which were bidden were not worthy.

9 Go you therefore into the highways, and as many as you shall find, bid to the marriage.

10 So those servants went out into the highways, and gathered together all as many as they found, both bad and good: and the wedding was furnished with guests.

11And when the king came in to see the guests, he saw there a man which had not on a wedding garment:

12 And he saith unto him, Friend, how camest you in hither not having a wedding garment? And he was speechless.

13 Then said the king to the servants, Bind him hand and foot, and take him away, and cast him into outer darkness; there shall be weeping and gnashing of teeth.

14 For many are called, but few are chosen.

15Then went the Pharisees, and took counsel how they might entangle him in his talk.

16 And they sent out unto him their disciples with the Herodians, saying, Master, we know that you are true, and teachest the way of God in truth, neither carest you for any man: for you regardest not the person of men.

17 Tell us therefore, What thinkest you ? Is it lawful to give tribute unto Cæsar, or not?

18 But Jesus perceived their wickedness, and said, Why tempt you me, you hypocrites?

19 Shew me the tribute money. And they brought unto him a penny.

20 And he saith unto them, Whose is this image and superscription?

21 They say unto him, Cæsar's. Then saith he unto them, Render therefore unto Cæsar the things which are Cæsar's; and unto God the things that are God's.

22 When they had heard these words, they marvelled, and left him, and went their way.

23The same day came to him the Sadducees, which say that there is no resurrection, and asked him,

24 Saying, Master, Moses said, If a man die, having no children, his brother shall marry his wife, and raise up seed unto his brother.

25 Now there were with us seven brethren: and the first, when he had married a wife, deceased, and, having no issue, left his wife unto his brother:

26 Likewise the second also, and the third, unto the seventh.

27 And last of all the woman died also.

28 Therefore in the resurrection whose wife shall she be of the seven? for they all had her.

29 Jesus answered and said unto them, You do err, not knowing the scriptures, nor the power of God.

30 For in the resurrection they neither marry, nor are given in marriage, but are as the angels of God in heaven.

31 But as touching the resurrection of the dead, have you not read that which was spoken unto you by God, saying,

32 I am the God of Abraham, and the God of Isaac, and the God of Jacob? God is not the God of the dead, but of the living.

33 And when the multitude heard this, they were astonished at his doctrine.

34But when the Pharisees had heard that he had put the Sadducees to silence, they were gathered together.

35 Then one of them, which was a lawyer, asked him a question, tempting him, and saying,

36 Master, which is the great commandment in the law?

37 Jesus said unto him, You shalt love the Lord your God with all your heart, and with all your soul, and with all your mind.

38 This is the first and great commandment.

39 And the second is like unto it, You shalt love your neighbour as yourself.

40 On these two commandments hang all the law and the prophets.

41While the Pharisees were gathered together, Jesus asked them,

42 Saying, What think you of Christ? whose son is he? They say unto him, The Son of David.

43 He saith unto them, How then doth David in spirit call him Lord, saying,

44 The LORD said unto my Lord, Sit you on my right hand, till I make yours enemies your footstool?

45 If David then call him Lord, how is he his son?

46 And no man was able to answer him a word, neither durst any man from that day forth ask him any more questions.

CHAPTER 23

THEN spake Jesus to the multitude, and to his disciples,

2 Saying, The scribes and the Pharisees sit in Moses' seat:

3 All therefore whatsoever they bid you observe, that observe and do; but do not you after their works: for they say, and do not.

4 For they bind heavy burdens and grievous to be borne, and lay them on men's shoulders; but they themselves will not move them with one of their fingers.

5 But all their works they do for to be seen of men: they make broad their phylacteries, and enlarge the borders of their garments,

6 And love the uppermost rooms at feasts, and the chief seats in the synagogues,

7 And greetings in the markets, and to be called of men, Rabbi, Rabbi.

8 But be not you called Rabbi: for one is your Master, even Christ; and all you are brethren.

9 And call no man your father upon the earth: for one is your Father, which is in heaven.

10 Neither be you called masters: for one is your Master, even Christ.

11 But he that is greatest among you shall be your servant.

12 And whosoever shall exalt himself shall be abased; and he that shall humble himself shall be exalted.

13 But woe unto you, scribes and Pharisees, hypocrites! for you shut up the kingdom of heaven against men: for you neither go in yourselves, neither suffer you them that are entering to go in.

14 Woe unto you, scribes and Pharisees, hypocrites! for you devour widows' houses, and for a pretence make long prayer: therefore you shall receive the greater damnation.

15 Woe unto you, scribes and Pharisees, hypocrites! for you compass sea and land to make one proselyte, and when he is made, you make him twofold more the child of hell than yourselves.

16 Woe unto you, you blind guides, which say, Whosoever shall swear by the temple, it is nothing; but whosoever shall swear by the gold of the temple, he is a debtor!

17 You fools and blind: for whether is greater, the gold, or the temple that sanctifieth the gold?

18 And, Whosoever shall swear by the altar, it is nothing; but whosoever sweareth by the gift that is upon it, he is guilty.

19 You fools and blind: for whether is greater, the gift, or the altar that sanctifieth the gift?

20 Whoso therefore shall swear by the altar, sweareth by it, and by all things thereon.

21 And whoso shall swear by the temple, sweareth by it, and by him that dwelleth therein.

22 And he that shall swear by heaven, sweareth by the throne of God, and by him that sitteth thereon.

23 Woe unto you, scribes and Pharisees, hypocrites! for you pay tithe of mint and anise and cummin, and have omitted the weightier matters of the law, judgment, mercy, and faith: these ought you to have done, and not to leave the other undone.

24 You blind guides, which strain at a gnat, and swallow a camel.

25 Woe unto you, scribes and Pharisees, hypocrites! for you make clean the outside of the cup and of the platter, but within they are full of extortion and excess.

26 You blind Pharisee, cleanse first that which is within the cup and platter, that the outside of them may be clean also.

27 Woe unto you, scribes and Pharisees, hypocrites! for you are like unto whited sepulchres, which indeed appear beautiful outward, but are within full of dead men's bones, and of all uncleanness.

28 Even so you also outwardly appear righteous unto men, but within you are full of hypocrisy and iniquity.

29 Woe unto you, scribes and Pharisees, hypocrites! because you build the tombs of the prophets, and garnish the sepulchres of the righteous,

30 And say, If we had been in the days of our fathers, we would not have been partakers with them in the blood of the prophets.

31 Wherefore you be witnesses unto yourselves, that you are the children of them which killed the prophets.

32 Fill you up then the measure of your fathers.

33 You serpents, you generation of vipers, how can you escape the damnation of hell?

34 Wherefore, behold, I send unto you prophets, and wise men, and scribes: and some of them you shall kill and crucify; and some of them shall you scourge in your synagogues, and persecute them from city to city:

35 That upon you may come all the righteous blood shed upon the earth, from the blood of righteous Abel unto the blood of Zacharias son of Barachias, whom you slew between the temple and the altar.

36 Verily I say unto you, All these things shall come upon this generation.

37 O Jerusalem, Jerusalem, you that killest the prophets, and stonest them which are sent unto you, how often would I have gathered your children together, even as a hen gathereth her chickens under her wings, and you would not!

38 Behold, your house is left unto you desolate.

39 For I say unto you, You shall not see me henceforth, till you shall say, Blessed is he that comes in the name of the Lord.

CHAPTER 24

AND Jesus went out, and departed from the temple: and his disciples came to him for to shew him the buildings of the temple.

2 And Jesus said unto them, See you not all these things? verily I say unto you, There shall not be left here one stone upon another, that shall not be thrown down.

3 And as he sat upon the mount of Olives, the disciples came unto him privately, saying, Tell us, when shall these things be? and what shall be the sign of your coming, and of the end of the world?

4 And Jesus answered and said unto them, Take heed that no man deceive you.

5 For many shall come in my name, saying, I am Christ; and shall deceive many.

6 And you shall hear of wars and rumours of wars: see that you be not troubled: for all these things must come to pass, but the end is not yet.

7 For nation shall rise against nation, and kingdom against kingdom: and there shall be famines, and pestilences, and earthquakes, in divers places.

8 All these are the beginning of sorrows.

9 Then shall they deliver you up to be afflicted, and shall kill you: and you shall be hated of all nations for my name's sake.

10 And then shall many be offended, and shall betray one another, and shall hate one another.

11 And many false prophets shall rise, and shall deceive many.

12 And because iniquity shall abound, the love of many shall wax cold.

13 But he that shall endure unto the end, the same shall be saved.

14 And this gospel of the kingdom shall be preached in all the world for a witness unto all nations; and then shall the end come.

15 When you therefore shall see the abomination of desolation, spoken of by Daniel the prophet, stand in the holy place, (whoso readeth, let him understand:)

16 Then let them which be in Judæa flee into the mountains:

17 Let him which is on the housetop not come down to take any thing out of his house:

18 Neither let him which is in the field return back to take his clothes.

19 And woe unto them that are with child, and to them that give suck in those days!

20 But pray you that your flight be not in the winter, neither on the sabbath day:

21 For then shall be great tribulation, such as was not since the beginning of the world to this time, no, nor ever shall be.

22 And except those days should be shortened, there should no flesh be saved: but for the elect's sake those days shall be shortened.

23 Then if any man shall say unto you, Lo, here is Christ, or there; believe it not.

24 For there shall arise false Christs, and false prophets, and shall shew great signs and wonders; insomuch that, if it were possible, they shall deceive the very elect.

25 Behold, I have told you before.

26 Wherefore if they shall say unto you, Behold, he is in the desert; go not forth: behold, he is in the secret chambers; believe it not.

27 For as the lightning comes out of the east, and shineth even unto the west; so shall also the coming of the Son of man be.

28 For wheresoever the carcase is, there will the eagles be gathered together.

29 Immediately after the tribulation of those days shall the sun be darkened, and the moon shall not give her light, and the stars shall fall from heaven, and the powers of the heavens shall be shaken:

30 And then shall appear the sign of the Son of man in heaven: and then shall all the tribes of the earth mourn, and they shall see the Son of man coming in the clouds of heaven with power and great glory.

31 And he shall send his angels with a great sound of a trumpet, and they shall gather together his elect from the four winds, from one end of heaven to the other.

32 Now learn a parable of the fig tree; When his branch is yet tender, and putteth forth leaves, you know that summer is nigh:

33 So likewise you, when you shall see all these things, know that it is near, even at the doors.

34 Verily I say unto you, This generation shall not pass, till all these things be fulfilled.

35 Heaven and earth shall pass away, but my words shall not pass away.

36 But of that day and hour knoweth no man, no, not the angels of heaven, but my Father only.

37 But as the days of Noe were, so shall also the coming of the Son of man be.

38 For as in the days that were before the flood they were eating and drinking, marrying and giving in marriage, until the day that Noe entered into the ark,

39 And knew not until the flood came, and took them all away; so shall also the coming of the Son of man be.

40 Then shall two be in the field; the one shall be taken, and the other left.

41 Two women shall be grinding at the mill; the one shall be taken, and the other left.

42 Watch therefore: for you know not what hour your Lord doth come.

43 But know this, that if the goodman of the house had known in what watch the thief would come, he would have watched, and would not have suffered his house to be broken up.

44 Therefore be you also ready: for in such an hour as you think not the Son of man comes.

45 Who then is a faithful and wise servant, whom his lord has made ruler over his household, to give them meat in due season?

46 Blessed is that servant, whom his lord when he comes shall find so doing.

47 Verily I say unto you, That he shall make him ruler over all his goods.

48 But and if that evil servant shall say in his heart, My lord delayeth his coming;

49 And shall begin to strike his fellowservants, and to eat and drink with the drunken;

50 The lord of that servant shall come in a day when he looketh not for him, and in an hour that he is not aware of,

51 And shall cut him asunder, and appoint him his portion with the hypocrites: there shall be weeping and gnashing of teeth.

CHAPTER 25

THEN shall the kingdom of heaven be likened unto ten virgins, which took their lamps, and went forth to meet the bridegroom.

2 And five of them were wise, and five were foolish.

3 They that were foolish took their lamps, and took no oil with them:

4 But the wise took oil in their vessels with their lamps.

5 While the bridegroom tarried, they all slumbered and slept.

6 And at midnight there was a cry made, Behold, the bridegroom comes; go you out to meet him.

7 Then all those virgins arose, and trimmed their lamps.

8 And the foolish said unto the wise, Give us of your oil; for our lamps are gone out.

9 But the wise answered, saying, Not so; lest there be not enough for us and you: but go you rather to them that sell, and buy for yourselves.

10 And while they went to buy, the bridegroom came; and they that were ready went in with him to the marriage: and the door was shut.

11 Afterward came also the other virgins, saying, Lord, Lord, open to us.

12 But he answered and said, Verily I say unto you, I know you not.

13 Watch therefore, for you know neither the day nor the hour wherein the Son of man comes.

14 For the kingdom of heaven is as a man travelling into a far country, who called his own servants, and delivered unto them his goods.

15 And unto one he gave five talents, to another two, and to another one; to every man according to his several ability; and straightway took his journey.

16 Then he that had received the five talents went and traded with the same, and made them other five talents.

17 And likewise he that had received two, he also gained other two.

18 But he that had received one went and digged in the earth, and hid his lord's money.

19 After a long time the lord of those servants comes, and reckoneth with them.

20 And so he that had received five talents came and brought other five talents, saying, Lord, you deliveredst unto me five talents: behold, I have gained beside them five talents more.

21 His lord said unto him, Well done, you good and faithful servant: you have been faithful over a few things, I will make you ruler over many things: enter you into the joy of your lord.

22 He also that had received two talents came and said, Lord, you deliveredst unto me two talents: behold, I have gained two other talents beside them.

23 His lord said unto him, Well done, good and faithful servant; you have been faithful over a few things, I will make you ruler over many things: enter you into the joy of your lord.

24 Then he which had received the one talent came and said, Lord, I knew you that you are an hard man, reaping where you have not sown, and gathering where you have not strawed:

25 And I was afraid, and went and hid your talent in the earth: lo, there you have that is yours.

26 His lord answered and said unto him, You wicked and slothful servant, you knewest that I reap where I sowed not, and gather where I have not strawed:

27 You oughtest therefore to have put my money to the exchangers, and then at my coming I should have received my own with usury.

28 Take therefore the talent from him, and give it unto him which has ten talents.

29 For unto every one that has shall be given, and he shall have abundance: but from him that has not shall be taken away even that which he has.

30 And cast you the unprofitable servant into outer darkness: there shall be weeping and gnashing of teeth.

31 When the Son of man shall come in his glory, and all the holy angels with him, then shall he sit upon the throne of his glory:

32 And before him shall be gathered all nations: and he shall separate them one from another, as a shepherd divideth his sheep from the goats:

33 And he shall set the sheep on his right hand, but the goats on the left.

34 Then shall the King say unto them on his right hand, Come, you blessed of my Father, inherit the kingdom prepared for you from the foundation of the world:

35 For I was an hungred, and you gave me meat: I was thirsty, and you gave me drink: I was a stranger, and you took me in:

36 Naked, and you clothed me: I was sick, and you visited me: I was in prison, and you came unto me.

37 Then shall the righteous answer him, saying, Lord, when saw we you an hungred, and fed you? or thirsty, and gave you drink?

38 When saw we you a stranger, and took you in? or naked, and clothed you?

39 Or when saw we you sick, or in prison, and came unto you?

40 And the King shall answer and say unto them, Verily I say unto you, Inasmuch as you have done it unto one of the least of these my brethren, you have done it unto me.

41 Then shall he say also unto them on the left hand, Depart from me, you cursed, into everlasting fire, prepared for the devil and his angels:

42 For I was an hungred, and you gave me no meat: I was thirsty, and you gave me no drink:

43 I was a stranger, and you took me not in: naked, and you clothed me not: sick, and in prison, and you visited me not.

44 Then shall they also answer him, saying, Lord, when saw we you an hungred, or athirst, or a stranger, or naked, or sick, or in prison, and did not minister unto you?

45 Then shall he answer them, saying, Verily I say unto you, Inasmuch as you did it not to one of the least of these, you did it not to me.

46 And these shall go away into everlasting punishment: but the righteous into life eternal.

CHAPTER 26

AND it came to pass, when Jesus had finished all these sayings, he said unto his disciples,

2 You know that after two days is the feast of the passover, and the Son of man is betrayed to be crucified.

3 Then assembled together the chief priests, and the scribes, and the elders of the people, unto the palace of the high priest, who was called Caiaphas,

4 And consulted that they might take Jesus by subtilty, and kill him.

5 But they said, Not on the feast day, lest there be an uproar among the people.

6 Now when Jesus was in Bethany, in the house of Simon the leper,

7 There came unto him a woman having an alabaster box of very precious ointment, and poured it on his head, as he sat at meat.

8 But when his disciples saw it, they had indignation, saying, To what purpose is this waste?

9 For this ointment might have been sold for much, and given to the poor.

10 When Jesus understood it, he said unto them, Why trouble you the woman? for she has created a good work upon me.

11 For you have the poor always with you; but me you have not always.

12 For in that she has poured this ointment on my body, she did it for my burial.

13 Verily I say unto you, Wheresoever this gospel shall be preached in the whole world, there shall also this, that this woman has done, be told for a memorial of her.

14 Then one of the twelve, called Judas Iscariot, went unto the chief priests,

15 And said unto them, What will you give me, and I will deliver him unto you? And they covenanted with him for thirty pieces of silver.

16 And from that time he sought opportunity to betray him.

17 Now the first day of the feast of unleavened bread the disciples came to Jesus, saying unto him, Where will you that we prepare for you to eat the passover?

18 And he said, Go into the city to such a man, and say unto him, The Master saith, My time is at hand; I will keep the passover at your house with my disciples.

19 And the disciples did as Jesus had appointed them; and they made ready the passover.

20 Now when the even was come, he sat down with the twelve.

21 And as they did eat, he said, Verily I say unto you, that one of you shall betray me.

22 And they were exceeding sorrowful, and began every one of them to say unto him, Lord, is it I?

23 And he answered and said, He that dippeth his hand with me in the dish, the same shall betray me.

24 The Son of man goeth as it is written of him: but woe unto that man by whom the Son of man is betrayed! it had been good for that man if he had not been born.

25 Then Judas, which betrayed him, answered and said, Master, is it I? He said unto him, You have said.

26And as they were eating, Jesus took bread, and blessed it, and brake it, and gave it to the disciples, and said, Take, eat; this is my body.

27 And he took the cup, and gave thanks, and gave it to them, saying, Drink you all of it;

28 For this is my blood of the new testament, which is shed for many for the remission of sins.

29 But I say unto you, I will not drink henceforth of this fruit of the vine, until that day when I drink it new with you in my Father's kingdom.

30 And when they had sung an hymn, they went out into the mount of Olives.

31 Then saith Jesus unto them, All you shall be offended because of me this night: for it is written, I will strike the shepherd, and the sheep of the flock shall be scattered abroad.

32 But after I am risen again, I will go before you into Galilee.

33 Peter answered and said unto him, Though all men shall be offended because of you, yet will I never be offended.

34 Jesus said unto him, Verily I say unto you, That this night, before the cock crow, you shalt deny me thrice.

35 Peter said unto him, Though I should die with you, yet will I not deny you. Likewise also said all the disciples.

36Then comes Jesus with them unto a place called Gethsemane, and saith unto the disciples, Sit you here, while I go and pray yonder.

37 And he took with him Peter and the two sons of Zebedee, and began to be sorrowful and very heavy.

38 Then saith he unto them, My soul is exceeding sorrowful, even unto death: tarry you here, and watch with me.

39 And he went a little further, and fell on his face, and prayed, saying, O my Father, if it be possible, let this cup pass from me: nevertheless not as I will, but as you will.

40 And he comes unto the disciples, and findeth them asleep, and saith unto Peter, What, could you not watch with me one hour?

41 Watch and pray, that you enter not into temptation: the spirit indeed is willing, but the flesh is weak.

42 He went away again the second time, and prayed, saying, O my Father, if this cup may not pass away from me, except I drink it, your will be done.

43 And he came and found them asleep again: for their eyes were heavy.

44 And he left them, and went away again, and prayed the third time, saying the same words.

45 Then comes he to his disciples, and saith unto them, Sleep on now, and take your rest: behold, the hour is at hand, and the Son of man is betrayed into the hands of sinners.

46 Rise, let us be going: behold, he is at hand that doth betray me.

47And while he yet spake, lo, Judas, one of the twelve, came, and with him a great multitude with swords and staves, from the chief priests and elders of the people.

48 Now he that betrayed him gave them a sign, saying, Whomsoever I shall kiss, that same is he: hold him fast.

49 And forthwith he came to Jesus, and said, Hail, master; and kissed him.

50 And Jesus said unto him, Friend, wherefore are you come? Then came they, and laid hands on Jesus, and took him.

51 And, behold, one of them which were with Jesus stretched out his hand, and drew his sword, and struck a servant of the high priest's, and struck off his ear.

52 Then said Jesus unto him, Put up again your sword into his place: for all they that take the sword shall perish with the sword.

53 Thinkest you that I cannot now pray to my Father, and he shall presently give me more than twelve legions of angels?

54 But how then shall the scriptures be fulfilled, that thus it must be?

55 In that same hour said Jesus to the multitudes, Are you come out as against a thief with swords and staves for to take me? I sat daily with you teaching in the temple, and you laid no hold on me.

56 But all this was done, that the scriptures of the prophets might be fulfilled. Then all the disciples forsook him, and fled.

57And they that had laid hold on Jesus led him away to Caiaphas the high priest, where the scribes and the elders were assembled.

58 But Peter followed him afar off unto the high priest's palace, and went in, and sat with the servants, to see the end.

59 Now the chief priests, and elders, and all the council, sought false witness against Jesus, to put him to death;

60 But found none: yea, though many false witnesses came, yet found they none. At the last came two false witnesses,

61 And said, This fellow said, I am able to destroy the temple of God, and to build it in three days.

62 And the high priest arose, and said unto him, Answerest you nothing? what is it which these witness against you?

63 But Jesus held his peace. And the high priest answered and said unto him, I adjure you by the living God, that you tell us whether you be the Christ, the Son of God.

64 Jesus saith unto him, You have said: nevertheless I say unto you, Hereafter shall you see the Son of man sitting on the right hand of power, and coming in the clouds of heaven.

65 Then the high priest rent his clothes, saying, He has spoken blasphemy; what further need have we of witnesses? behold, now you have heard his blasphemy.

66 What think you ? They answered and said, He is guilty of death.

67 Then did they spit in his face, and buffeted him; and others struck him with the palms of their hands,

68 Saying, Prophesy unto us, you Christ, Who is he that struck you?

69Now Peter sat without in the palace: and a damsel came unto him, saying, You also wast with Jesus of Galilee.

70 But he denied before them all, saying, I know not what you say.

71 And when he was gone out into the porch, another maid saw him, and said unto them that were there, This fellow was also with Jesus of Nazareth.

72 And again he denied with an oath, I do not know the man.

73 And after a while came unto him they that stood by, and said to Peter, Surely you also are one of them; for your speech bewrayeth you.

74 Then began he to curse and to swear, saying, I know not the man. And immediately the cock crew.

75 And Peter remembered the word of Jesus, which said unto him, Before the cock crow, you shalt deny me thrice. And he went out, and wept bitterly.

CHAPTER 27

WHEN the morning was come, all the chief priests and elders of the people took counsel against Jesus to put him to death:

2 And when they had bound him, they led him away, and delivered him to Pontius Pilate the governor.

3Then Judas, which had betrayed him, when he saw that he was condemned, repented himself, and brought again the thirty pieces of silver to the chief priests and elders,

4 Saying, I have sinned in that I have betrayed the innocent blood. And they said, What is that to us? see you to that.

5 And he cast down the pieces of silver in the temple, and departed, and went and hanged himself.

6 And the chief priests took the silver pieces, and said, It is not lawful for to put them into the treasury, because it is the price of blood.

7 And they took counsel, and bought with them the potter's field, to bury strangers in.

8 Wherefore that field was called, The field of blood, unto this day.

9 Then was fulfilled that which was spoken by Jeremy the prophet, saying, And they took the thirty pieces of silver, the price of him that was valued, whom they of the children of Israel did value;

10 And gave them for the potter's field, as the Lord appointed me.

11 And Jesus stood before the governor: and the governor asked him, saying, Are you the King of the Jews? And Jesus said unto him, You say.

12 And when he was accused of the chief priests and elders, he answered nothing.

13 Then said Pilate unto him, Hearest you not how many things they witness against you?

14 And he answered him to never a word; insomuch that the governor marvelled greatly.

15 Now at that feast the governor was wont to release unto the people a prisoner, whom they would.

16 And they had then a notable prisoner, called Barabbas.

17 Therefore when they were gathered together, Pilate said unto them, Whom will you that I release unto you? Barabbas, or Jesus which is called Christ?

18 For he knew that for envy they had delivered him.

19When he was set down on the judgment seat, his wife sent unto him, saying, Have you nothing to do with that just man: for I have suffered many things this day in a dream because of him.

20 But the chief priests and elders persuaded the multitude that they should ask Barabbas, and destroy Jesus.

21 The governor answered and said unto them, Whether of the twain will you that I release unto you? They said, Barabbas.

22 Pilate saith unto them, What shall I do then with Jesus which is called Christ? They all say unto him, Let him be crucified.

23 And the governor said, Why, what evil has he done? But they cried out the more, saying, Let him be crucified.

24When Pilate saw that he could prevail nothing, but that rather a tumult was made, he took water, and washed his hands before the multitude, saying, I am innocent of the blood of this just person: see you to it.

25 Then answered all the people, and said, His blood be on us, and on our children.

26Then released he Barabbas unto them: and when he had scourged Jesus, he delivered him to be crucified.

27 Then the soldiers of the governor took Jesus into the common hall, and gathered unto him the whole band of soldiers.

28 And they stripped him, and put on him a scarlet robe.

29And when they had platted a crown of thorns, they put it upon his head, and a reed in his right hand: and they bowed the knee before him, and mocked him, saying, Hail, King of the Jews!

30 And they spit upon him, and took the reed, and struck him on the head.

31 And after that they had mocked him, they took the robe off from him, and put his own raiment on him, and led him away to crucify him.

32 And as they came out, they found a man of Cyrene, Simon by name: him they compelled to bear his cross.

33 And when they were come unto a place called Golgotha, that is to say, a place of a skull,

34They gave him vinegar to drink mingled with gall: and when he had tasted thereof, he would not drink.

35 And they crucified him, and parted his garments, casting lots: that it might be fulfilled which was spoken by the prophet, They parted my garments among them, and upon my vesture did they cast lots.

36 And sitting down they watched him there;

37 And set up over his head his accusation written, THIS IS JESUS THE KING OF THE JEWS.

38 Then were there two thieves crucified with him, one on the right hand, and another on the left.

39And they that passed by reviled him, wagging their heads,

40 And saying, You that destroyest the temple, and buildest it in three days, save yourself. If you be the Son of God, come down from the cross.

41 Likewise also the chief priests mocking him, with the scribes and elders, said,

42 He saved others; himself he cannot save. If he be the King of Israel, let him now come down from the cross, and we will believe him.

43 He trusted in God; let him deliver him now, if he will have him: for he said, I am the Son of God.

44 The thieves also, which were crucified with him, cast the same in his teeth.

45 Now from the sixth hour there was darkness over all the land unto the ninth hour.

46 And about the ninth hour Jesus cried with a loud voice, saying, Eli, Eli, lama sabachthani? that is to say, My God, my God, why have you forsaken me?

47 Some of them that stood there, when they heard that, said, This man calleth for Elias.

48 And straightway one of them ran, and took a sponge, and filled it with vinegar, and put it on a reed, and gave him to drink.

49 The rest said, Let be, let us see whether Elias will come to save him.

50Jesus, when he had cried again with a loud voice, yielded up the ghost.

51 And, behold, the veil of the temple was rent in twain from the top to the bottom; and the earth did quake, and the rocks rent;

52 And the graves were opened; and many bodies of the saints which slept arose,

53 And came out of the graves after his resurrection, and went into the holy city, and appeared unto many.

54 Now when the centurion, and they that were with him, watching Jesus, saw the earthquake, and those things that were done, they feared greatly, saying, Truly this was the Son of God.

55 And many women were there beholding afar off, which followed Jesus from Galilee, ministering unto him:

56 Among which was Mary Magdalene, and Mary the mother of James and Joses, and the mother of Zebedee's children.

57 When the even was come, there came a rich man of Arimathæa, named Joseph, who also himself was Jesus' disciple:

58 He went to Pilate, and begged the body of Jesus. Then Pilate commanded the body to be delivered.

59 And when Joseph had taken the body, he wrapped it in a clean linen cloth,

60 And laid it in his own new tomb, which he had hewn out in the rock: and he rolled a great stone to the door of the sepulchre, and departed.

61 And there was Mary Magdalene, and the other Mary, sitting over against the sepulchre.

62Now the next day, that followed the day of the preparation, the chief priests and Pharisees came together unto Pilate,

63 Saying, Sir, we remember that that deceiver said, while he was yet alive, After three days I will rise again.

64 Command therefore that the sepulchre be made sure until the third day, lest his disciples come by night, and steal him away, and say unto the people, He is risen from the dead: so the last error shall be worse than the first.

65 Pilate said unto them, You have a watch: go your way, make it as sure as you can.

66 So they went, and made the sepulchre sure, sealing the stone, and setting a watch.

CHAPTER 28

IN the end of the sabbath, as it began to dawn toward the first day of the week, came Mary Magdalene and the other Mary to see the sepulchre.

2 And, behold, there was a great earthquake: for the angel of the Lord descended from heaven, and came and rolled back the stone from the door, and sat upon it.

3 His countenance was like lightning, and his raiment white as snow:

4 And for fear of him the keepers did shake, and became as dead men.

5 And the angel answered and said unto the women, Fear not you : for I know that you seek Jesus, which was crucified.

6 He is not here: for he is risen, as he said. Come, see the place where the Lord lay.

7 And go quickly, and tell his disciples that he is risen from the dead; and, behold, he goeth before you into Galilee; there shall you see him: lo, I have told you.

8 And they departed quickly from the sepulchre with fear and great joy; and did run to bring his disciples word.

9And as they went to tell his disciples, behold, Jesus met them, saying, All hail. And they came and held him by the feet, and worshipped him.

10 Then said Jesus unto them, Be not afraid: go tell my brethren that they go into Galilee, and there shall they see me.

11Now when they were going, behold, some of the watch came into the city, and shewed unto the chief priests all the things that were done.

12 And when they were assembled with the elders, and had taken counsel, they gave large money unto the soldiers,

13 Saying, Say you , His disciples came by night, and stole him away while we slept.

14 And if this come to the governor's ears, we will persuade him, and secure you.

15 So they took the money, and did as they were taught: and this saying is commonly reported among the Jews until this day.

16Then the eleven disciples went away into Galilee, into a mountain where Jesus had appointed them.

17 And when they saw him, they worshipped him: but some doubted.

18 And Jesus came and spake unto them, saying, All power is given unto me in heaven and in earth.

19Go you therefore, and teach all nations, baptizing them in the name of the Father, and of the Son, and of the Holy Ghost:

20 Teaching them to observe all things whatsoever I have commanded you: and, lo, I am with you alway, even unto the end of the world. Amen.

THE GOSPEL ACCORDING TO ST. MARK.

CHAPTER 1

THE beginning of the gospel of Jesus Christ, the Son of God;

2 As it is written in the prophets, Behold, I send my messenger before your face, which shall prepare your way before you.

3 The voice of one crying in the wilderness, Prepare you the way of the Lord, make his paths straight.

4 John did baptize in the wilderness, and preach the baptism of repentance for the remission of sins.

5 And there went out unto him all the land of Judæa, and they of Jerusalem, and were all baptized of him in the river of Jordan, confessing their sins.

6 And John was clothed with camel's hair, and with a girdle of a skin about his loins; and he did eat locusts and wild honey;

7 And preached, saying, There comes one mightier than I after me, the latchet of whose shoes I am not worthy to stoop down and unloose.

8 I indeed have baptized you with water: but he shall baptize you with the Holy Ghost.

9 And it came to pass in those days, that Jesus came from Nazareth of Galilee, and was baptized of John in Jordan.

10 And straightway coming up out of the water, he saw the heavens opened, and the Spirit like a dove descending upon him:

11 And there came a voice from heaven, saying, You are my beloved Son, in whom I am well pleased.

12 And immediately the Spirit driveth him into the wilderness.

13 And he was there in the wilderness forty days, tempted of Satan; and was with the wild beasts; and the angels ministered unto him.

14 Now after that John was put in prison, Jesus came into Galilee, preaching the gospel of the kingdom of God,

15 And saying, The time is fulfilled, and the kingdom of God is at hand: repent you , and believe the gospel.

16 Now as he walked by the sea of Galilee, he saw Simon and Andrew his brother casting a net into the sea: for they were fishers.

17 And Jesus said unto them, Come you after me, and I will make you to become fishers of men.

18 And straightway they forsook their nets, and followed him.

19 And when he had gone a little further thence, he saw James the son of Zebedee, and John his brother, who also were in the ship mending their nets.

20 And straightway he called them: and they left their father Zebedee in the ship with the hired servants, and went after him.

21 And they went into Capernaum; and straightway on the sabbath day he entered into the synagogue, and taught.

22 And they were astonished at his doctrine: for he taught them as one that had authority, and not as the scribes.

23 And there was in their synagogue a man with an unclean spirit; and he cried out,

24 Saying, Let us alone; what have we to do with you, you Jesus of Nazareth? are you come to destroy us? I know you who you are, the Holy One of God.

25 And Jesus rebuked him, saying, Hold your peace, and come out of him.

26 And when the unclean spirit had torn him, and cried with a loud voice, he came out of him.

27 And they were all amazed, insomuch that they questioned among themselves, saying, What thing is this? what new doctrine is this? for with authority commandeth he even the unclean spirits, and they do obey him.

28 And immediately his fame spread abroad throughout all the region round about Galilee.

29 And forthwith, when they were come out of the synagogue, they entered into the house of Simon and Andrew, with James and John.

30 But Simon's wife's mother lay sick of a fever, and anon they tell him of her.

31 And he came and took her by the hand, and lifted her up; and immediately the fever left her, and she ministered unto them.

32 And at even, when the sun did set, they brought unto him all that were diseased, and them that were possessed with devils.

33 And all the city was gathered together at the door.

34 And he healed many that were sick of divers diseases, and cast out many devils; and suffered not the devils to speak, because they knew him.

35 And in the morning, rising up a great while before day, he went out, and departed into a solitary place, and there prayed.

36 And Simon and they that were with him followed after him.

37 And when they had found him, they said unto him, All men seek for you.

38 And he said unto them, Let us go into the next towns, that I may preach there also: for therefore came I forth.

39 And he preached in their synagogues throughout all Galilee, and cast out devils.

40 And there came a leper to him, beseeching him, and kneeling down to him, and saying unto him, If you will, you can make me clean.

41 And Jesus, moved with compassion, put forth his hand, and touched him, and saith unto him, I will; be you clean.

42 And as soon as he had spoken, immediately the leprosy departed from him, and he was cleansed.

43 And he straitly charged him, and forthwith sent him away;

44 And saith unto him, See you say nothing to any man: but go your way, shew yourself to the priest, and offer for your cleansing those things which Moses commanded, for a testimony unto them.

45 But he went out, and began to publish it much, and to blaze abroad the matter, insomuch that Jesus could no more openly enter into the city, but was without in desert places: and they came to him from every quarter.

CHAPTER 2

AND again he entered into Capernaum, after some days; and it was noised that he was in the house.

2 And straightway many were gathered together, insomuch that there was no room to receive them, no, not so much as about the door: and he preached the word unto them.

3 And they come unto him, bringing one sick of the palsy, which was borne of four.

4 And when they could not come nigh unto him for the press, they uncovered the roof where he was: and when they had broken it up, they let down the bed wherein the sick of the palsy lay.

5 When Jesus saw their faith, he said unto the sick of the palsy, Son, your sins be forgiven you.

6 But there were certain of the scribes sitting there, and reasoning in their hearts,

7 Why doth this man thus speak blasphemies? who can forgive sins but God only?

8 And immediately when Jesus perceived in his spirit that they so reasoned within themselves, he said unto them, Why reason you these things in your hearts?

9 Whether is it easier to say to the sick of the palsy, Your sins be forgiven you; or to say, Arise, and take up your bed, and walk?

10 But that you may know that the Son of man has power on earth to forgive sins, (he saith to the sick of the palsy,)

11 I say unto you, Arise, and take up your bed, and go your way into yours house.

12 And immediately he arose, took up the bed, and went forth before them all; insomuch that they were all amazed, and glorified God, saying, We never saw it on this fashion.

13 And he went forth again by the sea side; and all the multitude resorted unto him, and he taught them.

14 And as he passed by, he saw Levi the son of Alphæus sitting at the receipt of custom, and said unto him, Follow me. And he arose and followed him.

15 And it came to pass, that, as Jesus sat at meat in his house, many publicans and sinners sat also together with Jesus and his disciples: for there were many, and they followed him.

16 And when the scribes and Pharisees saw him eat with publicans and sinners, they said unto his disciples, How is it that he eateth and drinketh with publicans and sinners?

17 When Jesus heard it, he saith unto them, They that are whole have no need of the physician, but they that are sick: I came not to call the righteous, but sinners to repentance.

18 And the disciples of John and of the Pharisees used to fast: and they come and say unto him, Why do the disciples of John and of the Pharisees fast, but your disciples fast not?

19 And Jesus said unto them, Can the children of the bridechamber fast, while the bridegroom is with them? as long as they have the bridegroom with them, they cannot fast.

20 But the days will come, when the bridegroom shall be taken away from them, and then shall they fast in those days.

21 No man also seweth a piece of new cloth on an old garment: else the new piece that filled it up taketh away from the old, and the rent is made worse.

22 And no man putteth new wine into old bottles: else the new wine doth burst the bottles, and the wine is spilled, and the bottles will be marred: but new wine must be put into new bottles.

23 And it came to pass, that he went through the corn fields on the sabbath day; and his disciples began, as they went, to pluck the ears of corn.

24 And the Pharisees said unto him, Behold, why do they on the sabbath day that which is not lawful?

25 And he said unto them, Have you never read what David did, when he had need, and was an hungred, he, and they that were with him?

26 How he went into the house of God in the days of Abiathar the high priest, and did eat the shewbread, which is not lawful to eat but for the priests, and gave also to them which were with him?

27 And he said unto them, The sabbath was made for man, and not man for the sabbath:

28 Therefore the Son of man is Lord also of the sabbath.

CHAPTER 3

AND he entered again into the synagogue; and there was a man there which had a withered hand.

2 And they watched him, whether he would heal him on the sabbath day; that they might accuse him.

3 And he saith unto the man which had the withered hand, Stand forth.

4 And he saith unto them, Is it lawful to do good on the sabbath days, or to do evil? to save life, or to kill? But they held their peace.

5 And when he had looked round about on them with anger, being grieved for the hardness of their hearts, he saith unto the man, Stretch forth yours hand. And he stretched it out: and his hand was restored whole as the other.

6 And the Pharisees went forth, and straightway took counsel with the Herodians against him, how they might destroy him.

7 But Jesus withdrew himself with his disciples to the sea: and a great multitude from Galilee followed him, and from Judæa,

8 And from Jerusalem, and from Idumæa, and from beyond Jordan; and they about Tyre and Sidon, a great multitude, when they had heard what great things he did, came unto him.

9 And he spake to his disciples, that a small ship should wait on him because of the multitude, lest they should throng him.

10 For he had healed many; insomuch that they pressed upon him for to touch him, as many as had plagues.

11 And unclean spirits, when they saw him, fell down before him, and cried, saying, You are the Son of God.

12 And he straitly charged them that they should not make him known.

13 And he goeth up into a mountain, and calleth unto him whom he would: and they came unto him.

14 And he ordained twelve, that they should be with him, and that he might send them forth to preach,

15 And to have power to heal sicknesses, and to cast out devils:

16 And Simon he surnamed Peter;

17 And James the son of Zebedee, and John the brother of James; and he surnamed them Boanerges, which is, The sons of thunder:

18 And Andrew, and Philip, and Bartholomew, and Matthew, and Thomas, and James the son of Alphæus, and Thaddæus, and Simon the Canaanite,

19 And Judas Iscariot, which also betrayed him: and they went into an house.

20 And the multitude comes together again, so that they could not so much as eat bread.

21 And when his friends heard of it, they went out to lay hold on him: for they said, He is beside himself.

22And the scribes which came down from Jerusalem said, He has Beelzebub, and by the prince of the devils casteth he out devils.

23 And he called them unto him, and said unto them in parables, How can Satan cast out Satan?

24 And if a kingdom be divided against itself, that kingdom cannot stand.

25 And if a house be divided against itself, that house cannot stand.

26 And if Satan rise up against himself, and be divided, he cannot stand, but has an end.

27 No man can enter into a strong man's house, and spoil his goods, except he will first bind the strong man; and then he will spoil his house.

28 Verily I say unto you, All sins shall be forgiven unto the sons of men, and blasphemies wherewith soever they shall blaspheme:

29 But he that shall blaspheme against the Holy Ghost has never forgiveness, but is in danger of eternal damnation:

30 Because they said, He has an unclean spirit.

31There came then his brethren and his mother, and, standing without, sent unto him, calling him.

32 And the multitude sat about him, and they said unto him, Behold, your mother and your brethren without seek for you.

33 And he answered them, saying, Who is my mother, or my brethren?

34 And he looked round about on them which sat about him, and said, Behold my mother and my brethren!

35 For whosoever shall do the will of God, the same is my brother, and my sister, and mother.

CHAPTER 4

AND he began again to teach by the sea side: and there was gathered unto him a great multitude, so that he entered into a ship, and sat in the sea; and the whole multitude was by the sea on the land.

2 And he taught them many things by parables, and said unto them in his doctrine,

3 Hearken; Behold, there went out a sower to sow:

4 And it came to pass, as he sowed, some fell by the way side, and the fowls of the air came and devoured it up.

5 And some fell on stony ground, where it had not much earth; and immediately it sprang up, because it had no depth of earth:

6 But when the sun was up, it was scorched; and because it had no root, it withered away.

7 And some fell among thorns, and the thorns grew up, and choked it, and it yielded no fruit.

8 And other fell on good ground, and did yield fruit that sprang up and increased; and brought forth, some thirty, and some sixty, and some an hundred.

9 And he said unto them, He that has ears to hear, let him hear.

10 And when he was alone, they that were about him with the twelve asked of him the parable.

11 And he said unto them, Unto you it is given to know the mystery of the kingdom of God: but unto them that are without, all these things are done in parables:

12 That seeing they may see, and not perceive; and hearing they may hear, and not understand; lest at any time they should be converted, and their sins should be forgiven them.

13 And he said unto them, Know you not this parable? and how then will you know all parables?

14The sower soweth the word.

15 And these are they by the way side, where the word is sown; but when they have heard, Satan comes immediately, and taketh away the word that was sown in their hearts.

16 And these are they likewise which are sown on stony ground; who, when they have heard the word, immediately receive it with gladness;

17 And have no root in themselves, and so endure but for a time: afterward, when affliction or persecution ariseth for the word's sake, immediately they are offended.

18 And these are they which are sown among thorns; such as hear the word,

19 And the cares of this world, and the deceitfulness of riches, and the lusts of other things entering in, choke the word, and it becometh unfruitful.

20 And these are they which are sown on good ground; such as hear the word, and receive it, and bring forth fruit, some thirtyfold, some sixty, and some an hundred.

21And he said unto them, Is a candle brought to be put under a bushel, or under a bed? and not to be set on a candlestick?

22 For there is nothing hid, which shall not be manifested; neither was any thing kept secret, but that it should come abroad.

23 If any man have ears to hear, let him hear.

24 And he said unto them, Take heed what you hear: with what measure you mete, it shall be measured to you: and unto you that hear shall more be given.

25 For he that has, to him shall be given: and he that has not, from him shall be taken even that which he has.

26And he said, So is the kingdom of God, as if a man should cast seed into the ground;

27 And should sleep, and rise night and day, and the seed should spring and grow up, he knoweth not how.

28 For the earth bringeth forth fruit of herself; first the blade, then the ear, after that the full corn in the ear.

29 But when the fruit is brought forth, immediately he putteth in the sickle, because the harvest is come.

30And he said, Whereunto shall we liken the kingdom of God? or with what comparison shall we compare it?

31 It is like a grain of mustard seed, which, when it is sown in the earth, is less than all the seeds that be in the earth:

32 But when it is sown, it groweth up, and becometh greater than all herbs, and shooteth out great branches; so that the fowls of the air may lodge under the shadow of it.

33 And with many such parables spake he the word unto them, as they were able to hear it.

34 But without a parable spake he not unto them: and when they were alone, he expounded all things to his disciples.

35 And the same day, when the even was come, he saith unto them, Let us pass over unto the other side.

36 And when they had sent away the multitude, they took him even as he was in the ship. And there were also with him other little ships.

37 And there arose a great storm of wind, and the waves beat into the ship, so that it was now full.

38 And he was in the hinder part of the ship, asleep on a pillow: and they awake him, and say unto him, Master, carest you not that we perish?

39 And he arose, and rebuked the wind, and said unto the sea, Peace, be still. And the wind ceased, and there was a great calm.

40 And he said unto them, Why are you so fearful? how is it that you have no faith?

41 And they feared exceedingly, and said one to another, What manner of man is this, that even the wind and the sea obey him?

CHAPTER 5

AND they came over unto the other side of the sea, into the country of the Gadarenes.

2 And when he was come out of the ship, immediately there met him out of the tombs a man with an unclean spirit,

3 Who had his dwelling among the tombs; and no man could bind him, no, not with chains:

4 Because that he had been often bound with fetters and chains, and the chains had been plucked asunder by him, and the fetters broken in pieces: neither could any man tame him.

5 And always, night and day, he was in the mountains, and in the tombs, crying, and cutting himself with stones.

6 But when he saw Jesus afar off, he ran and worshipped him,

7 And cried with a loud voice, and said, What have I to do with you, Jesus, you Son of the most high God? I adjure you by God, that you torment me not.

8 For he said unto him, Come out of the man, you unclean spirit.

9 And he asked him, What is your name? And he answered, saying, My name is Legion: for we are many.

10 And he besought him much that he would not send them away out of the country.

11 Now there was there nigh unto the mountains a great herd of swine feeding.

12 And all the devils besought him, saying, Send us into the swine, that we may enter into them.

13 And forthwith Jesus gave them leave. And the unclean spirits went out, and entered into the swine: and the herd ran violently down a steep place into the sea, (they were about two thousand;) and were choked in the sea.

14 And they that fed the swine fled, and told it in the city, and in the country. And they went out to see what it was that was done.

15 And they come to Jesus, and see him that was possessed with the devil, and had the legion, sitting, and clothed, and in his right mind: and they were afraid.

16 And they that saw it told them how it befell to him that was possessed with the devil, and also concerning the swine.

17 And they began to pray him to depart out of their coasts.

18 And when he was come into the ship, he that had been possessed with the devil prayed him that he might be with him.

19 Howbeit Jesus suffered him not, but saith unto him, Go home to your friends, and tell them how great things the Lord has done for you, and has had compassion on you.

20 And he departed, and began to publish in Decapolis how great things Jesus had done for him: and all men did marvel.

21 And when Jesus was passed over again by ship unto the other side, much people gathered unto him: and he was nigh unto the sea.

22 And, behold, there comes one of the rulers of the synagogue, Jairus by name; and when he saw him, he fell at his feet,

23 And besought him greatly, saying, My little daughter lies at the point of death: I pray you, come and lay your hands on her, that she may be healed; and she shall live.

24 And Jesus went with him; and much people followed him, and thronged him.

25 And a certain woman, which had an issue of blood twelve years,

26 And had suffered many things of many physicians, and had spent all that she had, and was nothing bettered, but rather grew worse,

27 When she had heard of Jesus, came in the press behind, and touched his garment.

28 For she said, If I may touch but his clothes, I shall be whole.

29 And straightway the fountain of her blood was dried up; and she felt in her body that she was healed of that plague.

30 And Jesus, immediately knowing in himself that virtue had gone out of him, turned him about in the press, and said, Who touched my clothes?

31 And his disciples said unto him, You seest the multitude thronging you, and say you, Who touched me?

32 And he looked round about to see her that had done this thing.

33 But the woman fearing and trembling, knowing what was done in her, came and fell down before him, and told him all the truth.

34 And he said unto her, Daughter, your faith has made you whole; go in peace, and be whole of your plague.

35 While he yet spake, there came from the ruler of the synagogue's house certain which said, Your daughter is dead: why troublest you the Master any further?

36 As soon as Jesus heard the word that was spoken, he saith unto the ruler of the synagogue, Be not afraid, only believe.

37 And he suffered no man to follow him, save Peter, and James, and John the brother of James.

38 And he comes to the house of the ruler of the synagogue, and seeth the tumult, and them that wept and wailed greatly.

39 And when he was come in, he saith unto them, Why make you this ado, and weep? the damsel is not dead, but sleepeth.

40 And they laughed him to scorn. But when he had put them all out, he taketh the father and the mother of the damsel, and them that were with him, and entereth in where the damsel was lying.

41 And he took the damsel by the hand, and said unto her, Talitha cumi; which is, being interpreted, Damsel, I say unto you, arise.

42 And straightway the damsel arose, and walked; for she was of the age of twelve years. And they were astonished with a great astonishment.

43 And he charged them straitly that no man should know it; and commanded that something should be given her to eat.

CHAPTER 6

AND he went out from thence, and came into his own country; and his disciples follow him.

2 And when the sabbath day was come, he began to teach in the synagogue: and many hearing him were astonished, saying, From whence has this man these things? and what wisdom is this which is given unto him, that even such mighty works are created by his hands?

3 Is not this the carpenter, the son of Mary, the brother of James, and Joses, and of Juda, and Simon? and are not his sisters here with us? And they were offended at him.

4 But Jesus said unto them, A prophet is not without honour, but in his own country, and among his own kin, and in his own house.

5 And he could there do no mighty work, save that he laid his hands upon a few sick folk, and healed them.

6 And he marvelled because of their unbelief. And he went round about the villages, teaching.

7 And he called unto him the twelve, and began to send them forth by two and two; and gave them power over unclean spirits;

8 And commanded them that they should take nothing for their journey, save a staff only; no scrip, no bread, no money in their purse:

9 But be shod with sandals; and not put on two coats.

10 And he said unto them, In what place soever you enter into an house, there abide till you depart from that place.

11 And whosoever shall not receive you, nor hear you, when you depart thence, shake off the dust under your feet for a testimony against them. Verily I say unto you, It shall be more tolerable for Sodom and Gomorrha in the day of judgment, than for that city.

12 And they went out, and preached that men should repent.

13 And they cast out many devils, and anointed with oil many that were sick, and healed them.

14 And king Herod heard of him; (for his name was spread abroad:) and he said, That John the Baptist was risen from the dead, and therefore mighty works do shew forth themselves in him.

15 Others said, That it is Elias. And others said, That it is a prophet, or as one of the prophets.

16 But when Herod heard thereof, he said, It is John, whom I beheaded: he is risen from the dead.

17 For Herod himself had sent forth and laid hold upon John, and bound him in prison for Herodias' sake, his brother Philip's wife: for he had married her.

18 For John had said unto Herod, It is not lawful for you to have your brother's wife.

19 Therefore Herodias had a quarrel against him, and would have killed him; but she could not:

20 For Herod feared John, knowing that he was a just man and an holy, and observed him; and when he heard him, he did many things, and heard him gladly.

21 And when a convenient day was come, that Herod on his birthday made a supper to his lords, high captains, and chief estates of Galilee;

22 And when the daughter of the said Herodias came in, and danced, and pleased Herod and them that sat with him, the king said unto the damsel, Ask of me whatsoever you will, and I will give it you.

23 And he sware unto her, Whatsoever you shalt ask of me, I will give it you, unto the half of my kingdom.

24 And she went forth, and said unto her mother, What shall I ask? And she said, The head of John the Baptist.

25 And she came in straightway with haste unto the king, and asked, saying, I will that you give me by and by in a charger the head of John the Baptist.

26 And the king was exceeding sorry; yet for his oath's sake, and for their sakes which sat with him, he would not reject her.

27 And immediately the king sent an executioner, and commanded his head to be brought: and he went and beheaded him in the prison,

28 And brought his head in a charger, and gave it to the damsel: and the damsel gave it to her mother.

29 And when his disciples heard of it, they came and took up his corpse, and laid it in a tomb.

30 And the apostles gathered themselves together unto Jesus, and told him all things, both what they had done, and what they had taught.

31 And he said unto them, Come you yourselves apart into a desert place, and rest a while: for there were many coming and going, and they had no leisure so much as to eat.

32 And they departed into a desert place by ship privately.

33 And the people saw them departing, and many knew him, and ran afoot thither out of all cities, and outwent them, and came together unto him.

34 And Jesus, when he came out, saw much people, and was moved with compassion toward them, because they were as sheep not having a shepherd: and he began to teach them many things.

35 And when the day was now far spent, his disciples came unto him, and said, This is a desert place, and now the time is far passed:

36 Send them away, that they may go into the country round about, and into the villages, and buy themselves bread: for they have nothing to eat.

37 He answered and said unto them, Give you them to eat. And they say unto him, Shall we go and buy two hundred pennyworth of bread, and give them to eat?

38 He saith unto them, How many loaves have you? go and see. And when they knew, they say, Five, and two fishes.

39 And he commanded them to make all sit down by companies upon the green grass.

40 And they sat down in ranks, by hundreds, and by fifties.

41 And when he had taken the five loaves and the two fishes, he looked up to heaven, and blessed, and brake the loaves, and gave them to his disciples to set before them; and the two fishes divided he among them all.

42 And they did all eat, and were filled.

43 And they took up twelve baskets full of the fragments, and of the fishes.

44 And they that did eat of the loaves were about five thousand men.

45 And straightway he constrained his disciples to get into the ship, and to go to the other side before unto Bethsaida, while he sent away the people.

46 And when he had sent them away, he departed into a mountain to pray.

47 And when even was come, the ship was in the midst of the sea, and he alone on the land.

48 And he saw them toiling in rowing; for the wind was contrary unto them: and about the fourth watch of the night he comes unto them, walking upon the sea, and would have passed by them.

49 But when they saw him walking upon the sea, they supposed it had been a spirit, and cried out:

50 For they all saw him, and were troubled. And immediately he talked with them, and saith unto them, Be of good cheer: it is I; be not afraid.

51 And he went up unto them into the ship; and the wind ceased: and they were sore amazed in themselves beyond measure, and wondered.

52 For they considered not the miracle of the loaves: for their heart was hardened.

53 And when they had passed over, they came into the land of Gennesaret, and drew to the shore.

54 And when they were come out of the ship, straightway they knew him,

55 And ran through that whole region round about, and began to carry about in beds those that were sick, where they heard he was.

56 And whithersoever he entered, into villages, or cities, or country, they laid the sick in the streets, and besought him that they might touch if it were but the border of his garment: and as many as touched him were made whole.

CHAPTER 7

THEN came together unto him the Pharisees, and certain of the scribes, which came from Jerusalem.

2 And when they saw some of his disciples eat bread with defiled, that is to say, with unwashen, hands, they found fault.

3 For the Pharisees, and all the Jews, except they wash their hands oft, eat not, holding the tradition of the elders.

4 And when they come from the market, except they wash, they eat not. And many other things there be, which they have received to hold, as the washing of cups, and pots, brasen vessels, and of tables.

5 Then the Pharisees and scribes asked him, Why walk not your disciples according to the tradition of the elders, but eat bread with unwashen hands?

6 He answered and said unto them, Well has Esaias prophesied of you hypocrites, as it is written, This people honoureth me with their lips, but their heart is far from me.

7 Howbeit in vain do they worship me, teaching for doctrines the commandments of men.

8 For laying aside the commandment of God, you hold the tradition of men, as the washing of pots and cups: and many other such like things you do.

9 And he said unto them, Full well you reject the commandment of God, that you may keep your own tradition.

10 For Moses said, Honour your father and your mother; and, Whoso curseth father or mother, let him die the death:

11 But you say, If a man shall say to his father or mother, It is Corban, that is to say, a gift, by whatsoever you mightest be profited by me; he shall be free.

12 And you suffer him no more to do ought for his father or his mother;

13 Making the word of God of none effect through your tradition, which you have delivered: and many such like things do you.

14 And when he had called all the people unto him, he said unto them, Hearken unto me every one of you, and understand:

15 There is nothing from without a man, that entering into him can defile him: but the things which come out of him, those are they that defile the man.

16 If any man have ears to hear, let him hear.

17 And when he was entered into the house from the people, his disciples asked him concerning the parable.

18 And he saith unto them, Are you so without understanding also? Do you not perceive, that whatsoever thing from without entereth into the man, it cannot defile him;

19 Because it entereth not into his heart, but into the belly, and goeth out into the draught, purging all meats?

20 And he said, That which comes out of the man, that defileth the man.

21 For from within, out of the heart of men, proceed evil thoughts, adulteries, fornications, murders,

22 Thefts, covetousness, wickedness, deceit, lasciviousness, an evil eye, blasphemy, pride, foolishness:

23 All these evil things come from within, and defile the man.

24 And from thence he arose, and went into the borders of Tyre and Sidon, and entered into an house, and would have no man know it: but he could not be hid.

25 For a certain woman, whose young daughter had an unclean spirit, heard of him, and came and fell at his feet:

26 The woman was a Greek, a Syrophenician by nation; and she besought him that he would cast forth the devil out of her daughter.

27 But Jesus said unto her, Let the children first be filled: for it is not meet to take the children's bread, and to cast it unto the dogs.

28 And she answered and said unto him, Yes, Lord: yet the dogs under the table eat of the children's crumbs.

29 And he said unto her, For this saying go your way; the devil is gone out of your daughter.

30 And when she was come to her house, she found the devil gone out, and her daughter laid upon the bed.

31 And again, departing from the coasts of Tyre and Sidon, he came unto the sea of Galilee, through the midst of the coasts of Decapolis.

32 And they bring unto him one that was deaf, and had an impediment in his speech; and they beseech him to put his hand upon him.

33 And he took him aside from the multitude, and put his fingers into his ears, and he spit, and touched his tongue;

34 And looking up to heaven, he sighed, and saith unto him, Ephphatha, that is, Be opened.

35 And straightway his ears were opened, and the string of his tongue was loosed, and he spake plain.

36 And he charged them that they should tell no man: but the more he charged them, so much the more a great deal they published it;

37 And were beyond measure astonished, saying, He has done all things well: he maketh both the deaf to hear, and the dumb to speak.

CHAPTER 8

IN those days the multitude being very great, and having nothing to eat, Jesus called his disciples unto him, and saith unto them,

2 I have compassion on the multitude, because they have now been with me three days, and have nothing to eat:

3 And if I send them away fasting to their own houses, they will faint by the way: for divers of them came from far.

4 And his disciples answered him, From whence can a man satisfy these men with bread here in the wilderness?

5 And he asked them, How many loaves have you ? And they said, Seven.

6 And he commanded the people to sit down on the ground: and he took the seven loaves, and gave thanks, and brake, and gave to his disciples to set before them; and they did set them before the people.

7 And they had a few small fishes: and he blessed, and commanded to set them also before them.

8 So they did eat, and were filled: and they took up of the broken meat that was left seven baskets.

9 And they that had eaten were about four thousand: and he sent them away.

10And straightway he entered into a ship with his disciples, and came into the parts of Dalmanutha.

11 And the Pharisees came forth, and began to question with him, seeking of him a sign from heaven, tempting him.

12 And he sighed deeply in his spirit, and saith, Why doth this generation seek after a sign? verily I say unto you, There shall no sign be given unto this generation.

13 And he left them, and entering into the ship again departed to the other side.

14Now the disciples had forgotten to take bread, neither had they in the ship with them more than one loaf.

15 And he charged them, saying, Take heed, beware of the leaven of the Pharisees, and of the leaven of Herod.

16 And they reasoned among themselves, saying, It is because we have no bread.

17 And when Jesus knew it, he saith unto them, Why reason you , because you have no bread? perceive you not yet, neither understand? have you your heart yet hardened?

18 Having eyes, see you not? and having ears, hear you not? and do you not remember?

19 When I brake the five loaves among five thousand, how many baskets full of fragments took you up? They say unto him, Twelve.

20 And when the seven among four thousand, how many baskets full of fragments took you up? And they said, Seven.

21 And he said unto them, How is it that you do not understand?

22And he comes to Bethsaida; and they bring a blind man unto him, and besought him to touch him.

23 And he took the blind man by the hand, and led him out of the town; and when he had spit on his eyes, and put his hands upon him, he asked him if he saw ought.

24 And he looked up, and said, I see men as trees, walking.

25 After that he put his hands again upon his eyes, and made him look up: and he was restored, and saw every man clearly.

26 And he sent him away to his house, saying, Neither go into the town, nor tell it to any in the town.

27And Jesus went out, and his disciples, into the towns of Cæsarea Philippi: and by the way he asked his disciples, saying unto them, Whom do men say that I am?

28 And they answered, John the Baptist: but some say, Elias; and others, One of the prophets.

29 And he saith unto them, But whom say you that I am? And Peter answereth and saith unto him, You are the Christ.

30 And he charged them that they should tell no man of him.

31 And he began to teach them, that the Son of man must suffer many things, and be rejected of the elders, and of the chief priests, and scribes, and be killed, and after three days rise again.

32 And he spake that saying openly. And Peter took him, and began to rebuke him.

33 But when he had turned about and looked on his disciples, he rebuked Peter, saying, Get you behind me, Satan: for you savourest not the things that be of God, but the things that be of men.

34And when he had called the people unto him with his disciples also, he said unto them, Whosoever will come after me, let him deny himself, and take up his cross, and follow me.

35 For whosoever will save his life shall lose it; but whosoever shall lose his life for my sake and the gospel's, the same shall save it.

36 For what shall it profit a man, if he shall gain the whole world, and lose his own soul?

37 Or what shall a man give in exchange for his soul?

38 Whosoever therefore shall be ashamed of me and of my words in this adulterous and sinful generation; of him also shall the Son of man be ashamed, when he comes in the glory of his Father with the holy angels.

CHAPTER 9

AND he said unto them, Verily I say unto you, That there be some of them that stand here, which shall not taste of death, till they have seen the kingdom of God come with power.

2And after six days Jesus taketh with him Peter, and James, and John, and leadeth them up into an high mountain apart by themselves: and he was transfigured before them.

3 And his raiment became shining, exceeding white as snow; so as no fuller on earth can white them.

4 And there appeared unto them Elias with Moses: and they were talking with Jesus.

5 And Peter answered and said to Jesus, Master, it is good for us to be here: and let us make three tabernacles; one for you, and one for Moses, and one for Elias.

6 For he wist not what to say; for they were sore afraid.

7 And there was a cloud that overshadowed them: and a voice came out of the cloud, saying, This is my beloved Son: hear him.

8 And suddenly, when they had looked round about, they saw no man any more, save Jesus only with themselves.

9 And as they came down from the mountain, he charged them that they should tell no man what things they had seen, till the Son of man were risen from the dead.

10 And they kept that saying with themselves, questioning one with another what the rising from the dead should mean.

11And they asked him, saying, Why say the scribes that Elias must first come?

12 And he answered and told them, Elias verily comes first, and restoreth all things; and how it is written of the Son of man, that he must suffer many things, and be set at nought.

13 But I say unto you, That Elias is indeed come, and they have done unto him whatsoever they listed, as it is written of him.

14And when he came to his disciples, he saw a great multitude about them, and the scribes questioning with them.

15 And straightway all the people, when they beheld him, were greatly amazed, and running to him saluted him.

16 And he asked the scribes, What question you with them?

17 And one of the multitude answered and said, Master, I have brought unto you my son, which has a dumb spirit;

18 And wheresoever he taketh him, he teareth him: and he foameth, and gnasheth with his teeth, and pineth away: and I spake to your disciples that they should cast him out; and they could not.

19 He answereth him, and saith, O faithless generation, how long shall I be with you? how long shall I suffer you? bring him unto me.

20 And they brought him unto him: and when he saw him, straightway the spirit tare him; and he fell on the ground, and wallowed foaming.

21 And he asked his father, How long is it ago since this came unto him? And he said, Of a child.

22 And ofttimes it has cast him into the fire, and into the waters, to destroy him: but if you can do any thing, have compassion on us, and help us.

23 Jesus said unto him, If you can believe, all things are possible to him that believeth.

24 And straightway the father of the child cried out, and said with tears, Lord, I believe; help you my unbelief.

25 When Jesus saw that the people came running together, he rebuked the foul spirit, saying unto him, You dumb and deaf spirit, I charge you, come out of him, and enter no more into him.

26 And the spirit cried, and rent him sore, and came out of him: and he was as one dead; insomuch that many said, He is dead.

27 But Jesus took him by the hand, and lifted him up; and he arose.

28 And when he was come into the house, his disciples asked him privately, Why could not we cast him out?

29 And he said unto them, This kind can come forth by nothing, but by prayer and fasting.

30And they departed thence, and passed through Galilee; and he would not that any man should know it.

31 For he taught his disciples, and said unto them, The Son of man is delivered into the hands of men, and they shall kill him; and after that he is killed, he shall rise the third day.

32 But they understood not that saying, and were afraid to ask him.

33And he came to Capernaum: and being in the house he asked them, What was it that you disputed among yourselves by the way?

34 But they held their peace: for by the way they had disputed among themselves, who should be the greatest.

35 And he sat down, and called the twelve, and saith unto them, If any man desire to be first, the same shall be last of all, and servant of all.

36 And he took a child, and set him in the midst of them: and when he had taken him in his arms, he said unto them,

37 Whosoever shall receive one of such children in my name, receiveth me: and whosoever shall receive me, receiveth not me, but him that sent me.

38 And John answered him, saying, Master, we saw one casting out devils in your name, and he followeth not us: and we forbad him, because he followeth not us.

39 But Jesus said, Forbid him not: for there is no man which shall do a miracle in my name, that can lightly speak evil of me.

40 For he that is not against us is on our part.

41 For whosoever shall give you a cup of water to drink in my name, because you belong to Christ, verily I say unto you, he shall not lose his reward.

42 And whosoever shall offend one of these little ones that believe in me, it is better for him that a millstone were hanged about his neck, and he were cast into the sea.

43 And if your hand offend you, cut it off: it is better for you to enter into life maimed, than having two hands to go into hell, into the fire that never shall be quenched:

44 Where their worm dieth not, and the fire is not quenched.

45 And if your foot offend you, cut it off: it is better for you to enter halt into life, than having two feet to be cast into hell, into the fire that never shall be quenched:

46 Where their worm dieth not, and the fire is not quenched.

47 And if yours eye offend you, pluck it out: it is better for you to enter into the kingdom of God with one eye, than having two eyes to be cast into hell fire:

48 Where their worm dieth not, and the fire is not quenched.

49 For every one shall be salted with fire, and every sacrifice shall be salted with salt.

50 Salt is good: but if the salt have lost his saltness, wherewith will you season it? Have salt in yourselves, and have peace one with another.

CHAPTER 10

AND he arose from thence, and comes into the coasts of Judæa by the farther side of Jordan: and the people resort unto him again; and, as he was wont, he taught them again.

2 And the Pharisees came to him, and asked him, Is it lawful for a man to put away his wife? tempting him.

3 And he answered and said unto them, What did Moses command you?

4 And they said, Moses suffered to write a bill of divorcement, and to put her away.

5 And Jesus answered and said unto them, For the hardness of your heart he wrote you this precept.

6 But from the beginning of the creation God made them male and female.

7 For this cause shall a man leave his father and mother, and cleave to his wife;

8 And they twain shall be one flesh: so then they are no more twain, but one flesh.

9 What therefore God has joined together, let not man put asunder.

10 And in the house his disciples asked him again of the same matter.

11 And he saith unto them, Whosoever shall put away his wife, and marry another, committeth adultery against her.

12 And if a woman shall put away her husband, and be married to another, she committeth adultery.

13 And they brought young children to him, that he should touch them: and his disciples rebuked those that brought them.

14 But when Jesus saw it, he was much displeased, and said unto them, Suffer the little children to come unto me, and forbid them not: for of such is the kingdom of God.

15 Verily I say unto you, Whosoever shall not receive the kingdom of God as a little child, he shall not enter therein.

16 And he took them up in his arms, put his hands upon them, and blessed them.

17 And when he was gone forth into the way, there came one running, and kneeled to him, and asked him, Good Master, what shall I do that I may inherit eternal life?

18 And Jesus said unto him, Why callest you me good? there is none good but one, that is, God.

19 You knowest the commandments, Do not commit adultery, Do not kill, Do not steal, Do not bear false witness, Defraud not, Honour your father and mother.

20 And he answered and said unto him, Master, all these have I observed from my youth.

21 Then Jesus beholding him loved him, and said unto him, One thing you lackest: go your way, sell whatsoever you have, and give to the poor, and you shalt have treasure in heaven: and come, take up the cross, and follow me.

22 And he was sad at that saying, and went away grieved: for he had great possessions.

23 And Jesus looked round about, and saith unto his disciples, How hardly shall they that have riches enter into the kingdom of God!

24 And the disciples were astonished at his words. But Jesus answereth again, and saith unto them, Children, how hard is it for them that trust in riches to enter into the kingdom of God!

25 It is easier for a camel to go through the eye of a needle, than for a rich man to enter into the kingdom of God.

26 And they were astonished out of measure, saying among themselves, Who then can be saved?

27 And Jesus looking upon them saith, With men it is impossible, but not with God: for with God all things are possible.

28 Then Peter began to say unto him, Lo, we have left all, and have followed you.

29 And Jesus answered and said, Verily I say unto you, There is no man that has left house, or brethren, or sisters, or father, or mother, or wife, or children, or lands, for my sake, and the gospel's,

30 But he shall receive an hundredfold now in this time, houses, and brethren, and sisters, and mothers, and children, and lands, with persecutions; and in the world to come eternal life.

31 But many that are first shall be last; and the last first.

32 And they were in the way going up to Jerusalem; and Jesus went before them: and they were amazed; and as they followed, they were afraid. And he took again the twelve, and began to tell them what things should happen unto him,

33 Saying, Behold, we go up to Jerusalem; and the Son of man shall be delivered unto the chief priests, and unto the scribes; and they shall condemn him to death, and shall deliver him to the Gentiles:

34 And they shall mock him, and shall scourge him, and shall spit upon him, and shall kill him: and the third day he shall rise again.

35 And James and John, the sons of Zebedee, come unto him, saying, Master, we would that you shouldest do for us whatsoever we shall desire.

36 And he said unto them, What would you that I should do for you?

37 They said unto him, Grant unto us that we may sit, one on your right hand, and the other on your left hand, in your glory.

38 But Jesus said unto them, You know not what you ask: can you drink of the cup that I drink of? and be baptized with the baptism that I am baptized with?

39 And they said unto him, We can. And Jesus said unto them, You shall indeed drink of the cup that I drink of; and with the baptism that I am baptized withal shall you be baptized:

40 But to sit on my right hand and on my left hand is not my to give; but it shall be given to them for whom it is prepared.

41 And when the ten heard it, they began to be much displeased with James and John.

42 But Jesus called them to him, and saith unto them, You know that they which are accounted to rule over the Gentiles exercise lordship over them; and their great ones exercise authority upon them.

43 But so shall it not be among you: but whosoever will be great among you, shall be your minister:

44 And whosoever of you will be the chiefest, shall be servant of all.

45 For even the Son of man came not to be ministered unto, but to minister, and to give his life a ransom for many.

46 And they came to Jericho: and as he went out of Jericho with his disciples and a great number of people, blind Bartimæus, the son of Timæus, sat by the highway side begging.

47 And when he heard that it was Jesus of Nazareth, he began to cry out, and say, Jesus, you Son of David, have mercy on me.

48 And many charged him that he should hold his peace: but he cried the more a great deal, You Son of David, have mercy on me.

49 And Jesus stood still, and commanded him to be called. And they call the blind man, saying unto him, Be of good comfort, rise; he calleth you.

50 And he, casting away his garment, rose, and came to Jesus.

51 And Jesus answered and said unto him, What will you that I should do unto you? The blind man said unto him, Lord, that I might receive my sight.

52 And Jesus said unto him, Go your way; your faith has made you whole. And immediately he received his sight, and followed Jesus in the way.

CHAPTER 11

AND when they came nigh to Jerusalem, unto Bethphage and Bethany, at the mount of Olives, he sendeth forth two of his disciples,

2 And saith unto them, Go your way into the village over against you: and as soon as you be entered into it, you shall find a colt tied, whereon never man sat; loose him, and bring him.

3 And if any man say unto you, Why do you this? say you that the Lord has need of him; and straightway he will send him hither.

4 And they went their way, and found the colt tied by the door without in a place where two ways met; and they loose him.

5 And certain of them that stood there said unto them, What do you , loosing the colt?

6 And they said unto them even as Jesus had commanded: and they let them go.

7 And they brought the colt to Jesus, and cast their garments on him; and he sat upon him.

8 And many spread their garments in the way: and others cut down branches off the trees, and strawed them in the way.

9 And they that went before, and they that followed, cried, saying, Hosanna; Blessed is he that comes in the name of the Lord:

10 Blessed be the kingdom of our father David, that comes in the name of the Lord: Hosanna in the highest.

11 And Jesus entered into Jerusalem, and into the temple: and when he had looked round about upon all things, and now the eventide was come, he went out unto Bethany with the twelve.

12 And on the morrow, when they were come from Bethany, he was hungry:

13 And seeing a fig tree afar off having leaves, he came, if haply he might find any thing thereon: and when he came to it, he found nothing but leaves; for the time of figs was not yet.

14 And Jesus answered and said unto it, No man eat fruit of you hereafter for ever. And his disciples heard it.

15 And they come to Jerusalem: and Jesus went into the temple, and began to cast out them that sold and bought in the temple, and overthrew the tables of the moneychangers, and the seats of them that sold doves;

16 And would not suffer that any man should carry any vessel through the temple.

17 And he taught, saying unto them, Is it not written, My house shall be called of all nations the house of prayer? but you have made it a den of thieves.

18 And the scribes and chief priests heard it, and sought how they might destroy him: for they feared him, because all the people was astonished at his doctrine.

19 And when even was come, he went out of the city.

20 And in the morning, as they passed by, they saw the fig tree dried up from the roots.

21 And Peter calling to remembrance saith unto him, Master, behold, the fig tree which you cursedst is withered away.

22 And Jesus answering saith unto them, Have faith in God.

23 For verily I say unto you, That whosoever shall say unto this mountain, Be you removed, and be you cast into the sea; and shall not doubt in his heart, but shall believe that those things which he saith shall come to pass; he shall have whatsoever he saith.

24 Therefore I say unto you, What things soever you desire, when you pray, believe that you receive them, and you shall have them.

25 And when you stand praying, forgive, if you have ought against any: that your Father also which is in heaven may forgive you your trespasses.

26 But if you do not forgive, neither will your Father which is in heaven forgive your trespasses.

27 And they come again to Jerusalem: and as he was walking in the temple, there come to him the chief priests, and the scribes, and the elders,

28 And say unto him, By what authority doest you these things? and who gave you this authority to do these things?

29 And Jesus answered and said unto them, I will also ask of you one question, and answer me, and I will tell you by what authority I do these things.

30 The baptism of John, was it from heaven, or of men? answer me.

31 And they reasoned with themselves, saying, If we shall say, From heaven; he will say, Why then did you not believe him?

32 But if we shall say, Of men; they feared the people: for all men counted John, that he was a prophet indeed.

33 And they answered and said unto Jesus, We cannot tell. And Jesus answering saith unto them, Neither do I tell you by what authority I do these things.

CHAPTER 12

AND he began to speak unto them by parables. A certain man planted a vineyard, and set an hedge about it, and digged a place for the winefat, and built a tower, and let it out to husbandmen, and went into a far country.

2 And at the season he sent to the husbandmen a servant, that he might receive from the husbandmen of the fruit of the vineyard.

3 And they caught him, and beat him, and sent him away empty.

4 And again he sent unto them another servant; and at him they cast stones, and wounded him in the head, and sent him away shamefully handled.

5 And again he sent another; and him they killed, and many others; beating some, and killing some.

6 Having yet therefore one son, his wellbeloved, he sent him also last unto them, saying, They will reverence my son.

7 But those husbandmen said among themselves, This is the heir; come, let us kill him, and the inheritance shall be ours.

8 And they took him, and killed him, and cast him out of the vineyard.

9 What shall therefore the lord of the vineyard do? he will come and destroy the husbandmen, and will give the vineyard unto others.

10 And have you not read this scripture; The stone which the builders rejected is become the head of the corner:

11 This was the Lord's doing, and it is marvellous in our eyes?

12 And they sought to lay hold on him, but feared the people: for they knew that he had spoken the parable against them: and they left him, and went their way.

13 And they send unto him certain of the Pharisees and of the Herodians, to catch him in his words.

14 And when they were come, they say unto him, Master, we know that you are true, and carest for no man: for you regardest not the person of men, but teachest the way of God in truth: Is it lawful to give tribute to Cæsar, or not?

15 Shall we give, or shall we not give? But he, knowing their hypocrisy, said unto them, Why tempt you me? bring me a penny, that I may see it.

16 And they brought it. And he saith unto them, Whose is this image and superscription? And they said unto him, Cæsar's.

17 And Jesus answering said unto them, Render to Cæsar the things that are Cæsar's, and to God the things that are God's. And they marvelled at him.

18 Then come unto him the Sadducees, which say there is no resurrection; and they asked him, saying,

19 Master, Moses wrote unto us, If a man's brother die, and leave his wife behind him, and leave no children, that his brother should take his wife, and raise up seed unto his brother.

20 Now there were seven brethren: and the first took a wife, and dying left no seed.

21 And the second took her, and died, neither left he any seed: and the third likewise.

22 And the seven had her, and left no seed: last of all the woman died also.

23 In the resurrection therefore, when they shall rise, whose wife shall she be of them? for the seven had her to wife.

24 And Jesus answering said unto them, Do you not therefore err, because you know not the scriptures, neither the power of God?

25 For when they shall rise from the dead, they neither marry, nor are given in marriage; but are as the angels which are in heaven.

26 And as touching the dead, that they rise: have you not read in the book of Moses, how in the bush God spake unto him, saying, I am the God of Abraham, and the God of Isaac, and the God of Jacob?

27 He is not the God of the dead, but the God of the living: you therefore do greatly err.

28 And one of the scribes came, and having heard them reasoning together, and perceiving that he had answered them well, asked him, Which is the first commandment of all?

29 And Jesus answered him, The first of all the commandments is, Hear, O Israel; The Lord our God is one Lord:

30 And you shalt love the Lord your God with all your heart, and with all your soul, and with all your mind, and with all your strength: this is the first commandment.

31 And the second is like, namely this, You shalt love your neighbour as yourself. There is none other commandment greater than these.

32 And the scribe said unto him, Well, Master, you have said the truth: for there is one God; and there is none other but he:

33 And to love him with all the heart, and with all the understanding, and with all the soul, and with all the strength, and to love his neighbour as himself, is more than all whole burnt offerings and sacrifices.

34 And when Jesus saw that he answered discreetly, he said unto him, You are not far from the kingdom of God. And no man after that durst ask him any question.

35 And Jesus answered and said, while he taught in the temple, How say the scribes that Christ is the Son of David?

36 For David himself said by the Holy Ghost, The LORD said to my Lord, Sit you on my right hand, till I make yours enemies your footstool.

37 David therefore himself calleth him Lord; and whence is he then his son? And the common people heard him gladly.

38And he said unto them in his doctrine, Beware of the scribes, which love to go in long clothing, and love salutations in the marketplaces,

39 And the chief seats in the synagogues, and the uppermost rooms at feasts:

40 Which devour widows' houses, and for a pretence make long prayers: these shall receive greater damnation.

41And Jesus sat over against the treasury, and beheld how the people cast money into the treasury: and many that were rich cast in much.

42 And there came a certain poor widow, and she threw in two mites, which make a farthing.

43 And he called unto him his disciples, and saith unto them, Verily I say unto you, That this poor widow has cast more in, than all they which have cast into the treasury:

44 For all they did cast in of their abundance; but she of her want did cast in all that she had, even all her living.

CHAPTER 13

AND as he went out of the temple, one of his disciples saith unto him, Master, see what manner of stones and what buildings are here!

2 And Jesus answering said unto him, Seest you these great buildings? there shall not be left one stone upon another, that shall not be thrown down.

3 And as he sat upon the mount of Olives over against the temple, Peter and James and John and Andrew asked him privately,

4 Tell us, when shall these things be? and what shall be the sign when all these things shall be fulfilled?

5 And Jesus answering them began to say, Take heed lest any man deceive you:

6 For many shall come in my name, saying, I am Christ; and shall deceive many.

7 And when you shall hear of wars and rumours of wars, be you not troubled: for such things must needs be; but the end shall not be yet.

8 For nation shall rise against nation, and kingdom against kingdom: and there shall be earthquakes in divers places, and there shall be famines and troubles: these are the beginnings of sorrows.

9But take heed to yourselves: for they shall deliver you up to councils; and in the synagogues you shall be beaten: and you shall be brought before rulers and kings for my sake, for a testimony against them.

10 And the gospel must first be published among all nations.

11 But when they shall lead you, and deliver you up, take no thought beforehand what you shall speak, neither do you premeditate: but whatsoever shall be given you in that hour, that speak you : for it is not you that speak, but the Holy Ghost.

12 Now the brother shall betray the brother to death, and the father the son; and children shall rise up against their parents, and shall cause them to be put to death.

13 And you shall be hated of all men for my name's sake: but he that shall endure unto the end, the same shall be saved.

14But when you shall see the abomination of desolation, spoken of by Daniel the prophet, standing where it ought not, (let him that readeth understand,) then let them that be in Judæa flee to the mountains:

15 And let him that is on the housetop not go down into the house, neither enter therein, to take any thing out of his house:

16 And let him that is in the field not turn back again for to take up his garment.

17 But woe to them that are with child, and to them that give suck in those days!

18 And pray you that your flight be not in the winter.

19 For in those days shall be affliction, such as was not from the beginning of the creation which God created unto this time, neither shall be.

20 And except that the Lord had shortened those days, no flesh should be saved: but for the elect's sake, whom he has chosen, he has shortened the days.

21 And then if any man shall say to you, Lo, here is Christ; or, lo, he is there; believe him not:

22 For false Christs and false prophets shall rise, and shall shew signs and wonders, to seduce, if it were possible, even the elect.

23 But take you heed: behold, I have foretold you all things.

24But in those days, after that tribulation, the sun shall be darkened, and the moon shall not give her light,

25 And the stars of heaven shall fall, and the powers that are in heaven shall be shaken.

26 And then shall they see the Son of man coming in the clouds with great power and glory.

27 And then shall he send his angels, and shall gather together his elect from the four winds, from the uttermost part of the earth to the uttermost part of heaven.

28 Now learn a parable of the fig tree; When her branch is yet tender, and putteth forth leaves, you know that summer is near:

29 So you in like manner, when you shall see these things come to pass, know that it is nigh, even at the doors.

30 Verily I say unto you, that this generation shall not pass, till all these things be done.

31 Heaven and earth shall pass away: but my words shall not pass away.

32But of that day and that hour knoweth no man, no, not the angels which are in heaven, neither the Son, but the Father.

33 Take you heed, watch and pray: for you know not when the time is.

34 For the Son of man is as a man taking a far journey, who left his house, and gave authority to his servants, and to every man his work, and commanded the porter to watch.

35 Watch you therefore: for you know not when the master of the house comes, at even, or at midnight, or at the cockcrowing, or in the morning:

36 Lest coming suddenly he find you sleeping.

37 And what I say unto you I say unto all, Watch.

CHAPTER 14

AFTER two days was the feast of the passover, and of unleavened bread: and the chief priests and the scribes sought how they might take him by craft, and put him to death.

2 But they said, Not on the feast day, lest there be an uproar of the people.

3And being in Bethany in the house of Simon the leper, as he sat at meat, there came a woman having an alabaster box of ointment of spikenard very precious; and she brake the box, and poured it on his head.

4 And there were some that had indignation within themselves, and said, Why was this waste of the ointment made?

5 For it might have been sold for more than three hundred pence, and have been given to the poor. And they murmured against her.

6 And Jesus said, Let her alone; why trouble you her? she has created a good work on me.

7 For you have the poor with you always, and whensoever you will you may do them good: but me you have not always.

8 She has done what she could: she is come aforehand to anoint my body to the burying.

9 Verily I say unto you, Wheresoever this gospel shall be preached throughout the whole world, this also that she has done shall be spoken of for a memorial of her.

10And Judas Iscariot, one of the twelve, went unto the chief priests, to betray him unto them.

11 And when they heard it, they were glad, and promised to give him money. And he sought how he might conveniently betray him.

12And the first day of unleavened bread, when they killed the passover, his disciples said unto him, Where will you that we go and prepare that you mayest eat the passover?

13 And he sendeth forth two of his disciples, and saith unto them, Go you into the city, and there shall meet you a man bearing a pitcher of water: follow him.

14 And wheresoever he shall go in, say you to the goodman of the house, The Master saith, Where is the guestchamber, where I shall eat the passover with my disciples?

15 And he will shew you a large upper room furnished and prepared: there make ready for us.

16 And his disciples went forth, and came into the city, and found as he had said unto them: and they made ready the passover.

17 And in the evening he comes with the twelve.

18 And as they sat and did eat, Jesus said, Verily I say unto you, One of you which eateth with me shall betray me.

19 And they began to be sorrowful, and to say unto him one by one, Is it I? and another said, Is it I?

20 And he answered and said unto them, It is one of the twelve, that dippeth with me in the dish.

21 The Son of man indeed goeth, as it is written of him: but woe to that man by whom the Son of man is betrayed! good were it for that man if he had never been born.

22And as they did eat, Jesus took bread, and blessed, and brake it, and gave to them, and said, Take, eat: this is my body.

23 And he took the cup, and when he had given thanks, he gave it to them: and they all drank of it.

24 And he said unto them, This is my blood of the new testament, which is shed for many.

25 Verily I say unto you, I will drink no more of the fruit of the vine, until that day that I drink it new in the kingdom of God.

26And when they had sung an hymn, they went out into the mount of Olives.

27 And Jesus saith unto them, All you shall be offended because of me this night: for it is written, I will strike the shepherd, and the sheep shall be scattered.

28 But after that I am risen, I will go before you into Galilee.

29 But Peter said unto him, Although all shall be offended, yet will not I.

30 And Jesus saith unto him, Verily I say unto you, That this day, even in this night, before the cock crow twice, you shalt deny me thrice.

31 But he spake the more vehemently, If I should die with you, I will not deny you in any wise. Likewise also said they all.

32 And they came to a place which was named Gethsemane: and he saith to his disciples, Sit you here, while I shall pray.

33 And he taketh with him Peter and James and John, and began to be sore amazed, and to be very heavy;

34 And saith unto them, My soul is exceeding sorrowful unto death: tarry you here, and watch.

35 And he went forward a little, and fell on the ground, and prayed that, if it were possible, the hour might pass from him.

36 And he said, Abba, Father, all things are possible unto you; take away this cup from me: nevertheless not what I will, but what you will.

37 And he comes, and findeth them sleeping, and saith unto Peter, Simon, sleepest you ? couldest not you watch one hour?

38 Watch you and pray, lest you enter into temptation. The spirit truly is ready, but the flesh is weak.

39 And again he went away, and prayed, and spake the same words.

40 And when he returned, he found them asleep again, (for their eyes were heavy,) neither wist they what to answer him.

41 And he comes the third time, and saith unto them, Sleep on now, and take your rest: it is enough, the hour is come; behold, the Son of man is betrayed into the hands of sinners.

42 Rise up, let us go; lo, he that betrayeth me is at hand.

43 And immediately, while he yet spake, comes Judas, one of the twelve, and with him a great multitude with swords and staves, from the chief priests and the scribes and the elders.

44 And he that betrayed him had given them a token, saying, Whomsoever I shall kiss, that same is he; take him, and lead him away safely.

45 And as soon as he was come, he goeth straightway to him, and saith, Master, master; and kissed him.

46 And they laid their hands on him, and took him.

47 And one of them that stood by drew a sword, and struck a servant of the high priest, and cut off his ear.

48 And Jesus answered and said unto them, Are you come out, as against a thief, with swords and with staves to take me?

49 I was daily with you in the temple teaching, and you took me not: but the scriptures must be fulfilled.

50 And they all forsook him, and fled.

51 And there followed him a certain young man, having a linen cloth cast about his naked body; and the young men laid hold on him:

52 And he left the linen cloth, and fled from them naked.

53 And they led Jesus away to the high priest: and with him were assembled all the chief priests and the elders and the scribes.

54 And Peter followed him afar off, even into the palace of the high priest: and he sat with the servants, and warmed himself at the fire.

55 And the chief priests and all the council sought for witness against Jesus to put him to death; and found none.

56 For many bare false witness against him, but their witness agreed not together.

57 And there arose certain, and bare false witness against him, saying,

58 We heard him say, I will destroy this temple that is made with hands, and within three days I will build another made without hands.

59 But neither so did their witness agree together.

60 And the high priest stood up in the midst, and asked Jesus, saying, Answerest you nothing? what is it which these witness against you?

61 But he held his peace, and answered nothing. Again the high priest asked him, and said unto him, Are you the Christ, the Son of the Blessed?

62 And Jesus said, I am: and you shall see the Son of man sitting on the right hand of power, and coming in the clouds of heaven.

63 Then the high priest rent his clothes, and saith, What need we any further witnesses?

64 You have heard the blasphemy: what think you ? And they all condemned him to be guilty of death.

65 And some began to spit on him, and to cover his face, and to buffet him, and to say unto him, Prophesy: and the servants did strike him with the palms of their hands.

66 And as Peter was beneath in the palace, there comes one of the maids of the high priest:

67 And when she saw Peter warming himself, she looked upon him, and said, And you also wast with Jesus of Nazareth.

68 But he denied, saying, I know not, neither understand I what you say. And he went out into the porch; and the cock crew.

69 And a maid saw him again, and began to say to them that stood by, This is one of them.

70 And he denied it again. And a little after, they that stood by said again to Peter, Surely you are one of them: for you are a Galilæan, and your speech agreeth thereto.

71 But he began to curse and to swear, saying, I know not this man of whom you speak.

72 And the second time the cock crew. And Peter called to mind the word that Jesus said unto him, Before the cock crow twice, you shalt deny me thrice. And when he thought thereon, he wept.

CHAPTER 15

AND straightway in the morning the chief priests held a consultation with the elders and scribes and the whole council, and bound Jesus, and carried him away, and delivered him to Pilate.

2 And Pilate asked him, Are you the King of the Jews? And he answering said unto him, You say it.

3 And the chief priests accused him of many things: but he answered nothing.

4 And Pilate asked him again, saying, Answerest you nothing? behold how many things they witness against you.

5 But Jesus yet answered nothing; so that Pilate marvelled.

6 Now at that feast he released unto them one prisoner, whomsoever they desired.

7 And there was one named Barabbas, which lay bound with them that had made insurrection with him, who had committed murder in the insurrection.

8 And the multitude crying aloud began to desire him to do as he had ever done unto them.

9 But Pilate answered them, saying, Will you that I release unto you the King of the Jews?

10 For he knew that the chief priests had delivered him for envy.

11 But the chief priests moved the people, that he should rather release Barabbas unto them.

12 And Pilate answered and said again unto them, What will you then that I shall do unto him whom you call the King of the Jews?

13 And they cried out again, Crucify him.

14 Then Pilate said unto them, Why, what evil has he done? And they cried out the more exceedingly, Crucify him.

15 And so Pilate, willing to content the people, released Barabbas unto them, and delivered Jesus, when he had scourged him, to be crucified.

16 And the soldiers led him away into the hall, called Prætorium; and they call together the whole band.

17 And they clothed him with purple, and platted a crown of thorns, and put it about his head,

18 And began to salute him, Hail, King of the Jews!

19 And they struck him on the head with a reed, and did spit upon him, and bowing their knees worshipped him.

20 And when they had mocked him, they took off the purple from him, and put his own clothes on him, and led him out to crucify him.

21 And they compel one Simon a Cyrenian, who passed by, coming out of the country, the father of Alexander and Rufus, to bear his cross.

22 And they bring him unto the place Golgotha, which is, being interpreted, The place of a skull.

23 And they gave him to drink wine mingled with myrrh: but he received it not.

24 And when they had crucified him, they parted his garments, casting lots upon them, what every man should take.

25 And it was the third hour, and they crucified him.

26 And the superscription of his accusation was written over, THE KING OF THE JEWS.

27 And with him they crucify two thieves; the one on his right hand, and the other on his left.

28 And the scripture was fulfilled, which saith, And he was numbered with the transgressors.

29 And they that passed by railed on him, wagging their heads, and saying, Ah, you that destroyest the temple, and buildest it in three days,

30 Save yourself, and come down from the cross.

31 Likewise also the chief priests mocking said among themselves with the scribes, He saved others; himself he cannot save.

32 Let Christ the King of Israel descend now from the cross, that we may see and believe. And they that were crucified with him reviled him.

33 And when the sixth hour was come, there was darkness over the whole land until the ninth hour.

34 And at the ninth hour Jesus cried with a loud voice, saying, Eloi, Eloi, lama sabachthani? which is, being interpreted, My God, my God, why have you forsaken me?

35 And some of them that stood by, when they heard it, said, Behold, he calleth Elias.

36 And one ran and filled a spunge full of vinegar, and put it on a reed, and gave him to drink, saying, Let alone; let us see whether Elias will come to take him down.

37 And Jesus cried with a loud voice, and gave up the ghost.

38 And the veil of the temple was rent in twain from the top to the bottom.

39And when the centurion, which stood over against him, saw that he so cried out, and gave up the ghost, he said, Truly this man was the Son of God.

40 There were also women looking on afar off: among whom was Mary Magdalene, and Mary the mother of James the less and of Joses, and Salome;

41 (Who also, when he was in Galilee, followed him, and ministered unto him;) and many other women which came up with him unto Jerusalem.

42And now when the even was come, because it was the preparation, that is, the day before the sabbath,

43 Joseph of Arimathæa, an honourable counseller, which also waited for the kingdom of God, came, and went in boldly unto Pilate, and craved the body of Jesus.

44 And Pilate marvelled if he were already dead: and calling unto him the centurion, he asked him whether he had been any while dead.

45 And when he knew it of the centurion, he gave the body to Joseph.

46 And he bought fine linen, and took him down, and wrapped him in the linen, and laid him in a sepulchre which was hewn out of a rock, and rolled a stone unto the door of the sepulchre.

47 And Mary Magdalene and Mary the mother of Joses beheld where he was laid.

CHAPTER 16

AND when the sabbath was past, Mary Magdalene, and Mary the mother of James, and Salome, had bought sweet spices, that they might come and anoint him.

2 And very early in the morning the first day of the week, they came unto the sepulchre at the rising of the sun.

3 And they said among themselves, Who shall roll us away the stone from the door of the sepulchre?

4 And when they looked, they saw that the stone was rolled away: for it was very great.

5 And entering into the sepulchre, they saw a young man sitting on the right side, clothed in a long white garment; and they were affrighted.

6 And he saith unto them, Be not affrighted: You seek Jesus of Nazareth, which was crucified: he is risen; he is not here: behold the place where they laid him.

7 But go your way, tell his disciples and Peter that he goeth before you into Galilee: there shall you see him, as he said unto you.

8 And they went out quickly, and fled from the sepulchre; for they trembled and were amazed: neither said they any thing to any man; for they were afraid.

9Now when Jesus was risen early the first day of the week, he appeared first to Mary Magdalene, out of whom he had cast seven devils.

10 And she went and told them that had been with him, as they mourned and wept.

11 And they, when they had heard that he was alive, and had been seen of her, believed not.

12After that he appeared in another form unto two of them, as they walked, and went into the country.

13 And they went and told it unto the residue: neither believed they them.

14Afterward he appeared unto the eleven as they sat at meat, and upbraided them with their unbelief and hardness of heart, because they believed not them which had seen him after he was risen.

15 And he said unto them, Go you into all the world, and preach the gospel to every creature.

16 He that believeth and is baptized shall be saved; but he that believeth not shall be damned.

17 And these signs shall follow them that believe; In my name shall they cast out devils; they shall speak with new tongues;

18 They shall take up serpents; and if they drink any deadly thing, it shall not hurt them; they shall lay hands on the sick, and they shall recover.

19So then after the Lord had spoken unto them, he was received up into heaven, and sat on the right hand of God.

20 And they went forth, and preached every where, the Lord working with them, and confirming the word with signs following. Amen.

THE GOSPEL ACCORDING TO ST. LUKE.

CHAPTER 1

FORASMUCH as many have taken in hand to set forth in order a declaration of those things which are most surely believed among us,

2 Even as they delivered them unto us, which from the beginning were eyewitnesses, and ministers of the word;

3 It seemed good to me also, having had perfect understanding of all things from the very first, to write unto you in order, most excellent Theophilus,

4 That you mightest know the certainty of those things, wherein you have been instructed.

5 THERE was in the days of Herod, the king of Judæa, a certain priest named Zacharias, of the course of Abia: and his wife was of the daughters of Aaron, and her name was Elisabeth.

6 And they were both righteous before God, walking in all the commandments and ordinances of the Lord blameless.

7 And they had no child, because that Elisabeth was barren, and they both were now well stricken in years.

8 And it came to pass, that while he executed the priest's office before God in the order of his course,

9 According to the custom of the priest's office, his lot was to burn incense when he went into the temple of the Lord.

10 And the whole multitude of the people were praying without at the time of incense.

11 And there appeared unto him an angel of the Lord standing on the right side of the altar of incense.

12 And when Zacharias saw him, he was troubled, and fear fell upon him.

13 But the angel said unto him, Fear not, Zacharias: for your prayer is heard; and your wife Elisabeth shall bear you a son, and you shalt call his name John.

14 And you shalt have joy and gladness; and many shall rejoice at his birth.

15 For he shall be great in the sight of the Lord, and shall drink neither wine nor strong drink; and he shall be filled with the Holy Ghost, even from his mother's womb.

16 And many of the children of Israel shall he turn to the Lord their God.

17 And he shall go before him in the spirit and power of Elias, to turn the hearts of the fathers to the children, and the disobedient to the wisdom of the just; to make ready a people prepared for the Lord.

18 And Zacharias said unto the angel, Whereby shall I know this? for I am an old man, and my wife well stricken in years.

19 And the angel answering said unto him, I am Gabriel, that stand in the presence of God; and am sent to speak unto you, and to shew you these glad tidings.

20 And, behold, you shalt be dumb, and not able to speak, until the day that these things shall be performed, because you believest not my words, which shall be fulfilled in their season.

21 And the people waited for Zacharias, and marvelled that he tarried so long in the temple.

22 And when he came out, he could not speak unto them: and they perceived that he had seen a vision in the temple: for he beckoned unto them, and remained speechless.

23 And it came to pass, that, as soon as the days of his ministration were accomplished, he departed to his own house.

24 And after those days his wife Elisabeth conceived, and hid herself five months, saying,

25 Thus has the Lord dealt with me in the days wherein he looked on me, to take away my reproach among men.

26 And in the sixth month the angel Gabriel was sent from God unto a city of Galilee, named Nazareth,

27 To a virgin espoused to a man whose name was Joseph, of the house of David; and the virgin's name was Mary.

28 And the angel came in unto her, and said, Hail, you that are highly favoured, the Lord is with you: blessed are you among women.

29 And when she saw him, she was troubled at his saying, and cast in her mind what manner of salutation this should be.

30 And the angel said unto her, Fear not, Mary: for you have found favour with God.

31 And, behold, you shalt conceive in your womb, and bring forth a son, and shalt call his name JESUS.

32 He shall be great, and shall be called the Son of the Highest: and the Lord God shall give unto him the throne of his father David:

33 And he shall reign over the house of Jacob for ever; and of his kingdom there shall be no end.

34 Then said Mary unto the angel, How shall this be, seeing I know not a man?

35 And the angel answered and said unto her, The Holy Ghost shall come upon you, and the power of the Highest shall overshadow you: therefore also that holy thing which shall be born of you shall be called the Son of God.

36 And, behold, your cousin Elisabeth, she has also conceived a son in her old age: and this is the sixth month with her, who was called barren.

37 For with God nothing shall be impossible.

38 And Mary said, Behold the handmaid of the Lord; be it unto me according to your word. And the angel departed from her.

39 And Mary arose in those days, and went into the hill country with haste, into a city of Juda;

40 And entered into the house of Zacharias, and saluted Elisabeth.

41 And it came to pass, that, when Elisabeth heard the salutation of Mary, the babe leaped in her womb; and Elisabeth was filled with the Holy Ghost:

42 And she spake out with a loud voice, and said, Blessed are you among women, and blessed is the fruit of your womb.

43 And whence is this to me, that the mother of my Lord should come to me?

44 For, lo, as soon as the voice of your salutation sounded in my ears, the babe leaped in my womb for joy.

45 And blessed is she that believed: for there shall be a performance of those things which were told her from the Lord.

46 And Mary said, My soul doth magnify the Lord,

47 And my spirit has rejoiced in God my Saviour.

48 For he has regarded the low estate of his handmaiden: for, behold, from henceforth all generations shall call me blessed.

49 For he that is mighty has done to me great things; and holy is his name.

50 And his mercy is on them that fear him from generation to generation.

51 He has shewed strength with his arm; he has scattered the proud in the imagination of their hearts.

52 He has put down the mighty from their seats, and exalted them of low degree.

53 He has filled the hungry with good things; and the rich he has sent empty away.

54 He has holpen his servant Israel, in remembrance of his mercy;

55 As he spake to our fathers, to Abraham, and to his seed for ever.

56 And Mary abode with her about three months, and returned to her own house.

57 Now Elisabeth's full time came that she should be delivered; and she brought forth a son.

58 And her neighbours and her cousins heard how the Lord had shewed great mercy upon her; and they rejoiced with her.

59 And it came to pass, that on the eighth day they came to circumcise the child; and they called him Zacharias, after the name of his father.

60 And his mother answered and said, Not so; but he shall be called John.

61 And they said unto her, There is none of your kindred that is called by this name.

62 And they made signs to his father, how he would have him called.

63 And he asked for a writing table, and wrote, saying, His name is John. And they marvelled all.

64 And his mouth was opened immediately, and his tongue loosed, and he spake, and praised God.

65 And fear came on all that dwelt round about them: and all these sayings were noised abroad throughout all the hill country of Judæa.

66 And all they that heard them laid them up in their hearts, saying, What manner of child shall this be! And the hand of the Lord was with him.

67 And his father Zacharias was filled with the Holy Ghost, and prophesied, saying,

68 Blessed be the Lord God of Israel; for he has visited and redeemed his people,

69 And has raised up an horn of salvation for us in the house of his servant David;

70 As he spake by the mouth of his holy prophets, which have been since the world began:

71 That we should be saved from our enemies, and from the hand of all that hate us;

72 To perform the mercy promised to our fathers, and to remember his holy covenant;

73 The oath which he sware to our father Abraham,

74 That he would grant unto us, that we being delivered out of the hand of our enemies might serve him without fear,

75 In holiness and righteousness before him, all the days of our life.

76 And you , child, shalt be called the prophet of the Highest: for you shalt go before the face of the Lord to prepare his ways;

77 To give knowledge of salvation unto his people by the remission of their sins,

78 Through the tender mercy of our God; whereby the dayspring from on high has visited us,

79 To give light to them that sit in darkness and in the shadow of death, to guide our feet into the way of peace.

80 And the child grew, and waxed strong in spirit, and was in the deserts till the day of his shewing unto Israel.

CHAPTER 2

AND it came to pass in those days, that there went out a decree from Cæsar Augustus, that all the world should be taxed.

2 (And this taxing was first made when Cyrenius was governor of Syria.)

3 And all went to be taxed, every one into his own city.

4 And Joseph also went up from Galilee, out of the city of Nazareth, into Judæa, unto the city of David, which is called Bethlehem; (because he was of the house and lineage of David:)

5 To be taxed with Mary his espoused wife, being great with child.

6 And so it was, that, while they were there, the days were accomplished that she should be delivered.

7 And she brought forth her firstborn son, and wrapped him in swaddling clothes, and laid him in a manger; because there was no room for them in the inn.

8 And there were in the same country shepherds abiding in the field, keeping watch over their flock by night.

9 And, lo, the angel of the Lord came upon them, and the glory of the Lord shone round about them: and they were sore afraid.

10 And the angel said unto them, Fear not: for, behold, I bring you good tidings of great joy, which shall be to all people.

11 For unto you is born this day in the city of David a Saviour, which is Christ the Lord.

12 And this shall be a sign unto you; You shall find the babe wrapped in swaddling clothes, lying in a manger.

13 And suddenly there was with the angel a multitude of the heavenly host praising God, and saying,

14 Glory to God in the highest, and on earth peace, good will toward men.

15 And it came to pass, as the angels were gone away from them into heaven, the shepherds said one to another, Let us now go even unto Bethlehem, and see this thing which is come to pass, which the Lord has made known unto us.

16 And they came with haste, and found Mary, and Joseph, and the babe lying in a manger.

17 And when they had seen it, they made known abroad the saying which was told them concerning this child.

18 And all they that heard it wondered at those things which were told them by the shepherds.

19 But Mary kept all these things, and pondered them in her heart.

20 And the shepherds returned, glorifying and praising God for all the things that they had heard and seen, as it was told unto them.

21 And when eight days were accomplished for the circumcising of the child, his name was called JESUS, which was so named of the angel before he was conceived in the womb.

22 And when the days of her purification according to the law of Moses were accomplished, they brought him to Jerusalem, to present him to the Lord;

23 (As it is written in the law of the Lord, Every male that openeth the womb shall be called holy to the Lord;)

24 And to offer a sacrifice according to that which is said in the law of the Lord, A pair of turtledoves, or two young pigeons.

25 And, behold, there was a man in Jerusalem, whose name was Simeon; and the same man was just and devout, waiting for the consolation of Israel: and the Holy Ghost was upon him.

26 And it was revealed unto him by the Holy Ghost, that he should not see death, before he had seen the Lord's Christ.

27 And he came by the Spirit into the temple: and when the parents brought in the child Jesus, to do for him after the custom of the law,

28 Then took he him up in his arms, and blessed God, and said,

29 Lord, now lettest you your servant depart in peace, according to your word:

30 For my eyes have seen your salvation,

31 Which you have prepared before the face of all people;

32 A light to lighten the Gentiles, and the glory of your people Israel.

33 And Joseph and his mother marvelled at those things which were spoken of him.

34 And Simeon blessed them, and said unto Mary his mother, Behold, this child is set for the fall and rising again of many in Israel; and for a sign which shall be spoken against;

35 (Yea, a sword shall pierce through your own soul also,) that the thoughts of many hearts may be revealed.

36 And there was one Anna, a prophetess, the daughter of Phanuel, of the tribe of Aser: she was of a great age, and had lived with an husband seven years from her virginity;

37 And she was a widow of about fourscore and four years, which departed not from the temple, but served God with fastings and prayers night and day.

38 And she coming in that instant gave thanks likewise unto the Lord, and spake of him to all them that looked for redemption in Jerusalem.

39 And when they had performed all things according to the law of the Lord, they returned into Galilee, to their own city Nazareth.

40 And the child grew, and waxed strong in spirit, filled with wisdom: and the grace of God was upon him.

41 Now his parents went to Jerusalem every year at the feast of the passover.

42 And when he was twelve years old, they went up to Jerusalem after the custom of the feast.

43 And when they had fulfilled the days, as they returned, the child Jesus tarried behind in Jerusalem; and Joseph and his mother knew not of it.

44 But they, supposing him to have been in the company, went a day's journey; and they sought him among their kinsfolk and acquaintance.

45 And when they found him not, they turned back again to Jerusalem, seeking him.

46 And it came to pass, that after three days they found him in the temple, sitting in the midst of the doctors, both hearing them, and asking them questions.

47 And all that heard him were astonished at his understanding and answers.

48 And when they saw him, they were amazed: and his mother said unto him, Son, why have you thus dealt with us? behold, your father and I have sought you sorrowing.

49 And he said unto them, How is it that you sought me? wist you not that I must be about my Father's business?

50 And they understood not the saying which he spake unto them.

51 And he went down with them, and came to Nazareth, and was subject unto them: but his mother kept all these sayings in her heart.

52 And Jesus increased in wisdom and stature, and in favour with God and man.

CHAPTER 3

NOW in the fifteenth year of the reign of Tiberius Cæsar, Pontius Pilate being governor of Judæa, and Herod being tetrarch of Galilee, and his brother Philip tetrarch of Ituræa and of the region of Trachonitis, and Lysanias the tetrarch of Abilene,

2 Annas and Caiaphas being the high priests, the word of God came unto John the son of Zacharias in the wilderness.

3 And he came into all the country about Jordan, preaching the baptism of repentance for the remission of sins;

4 As it is written in the book of the words of Esaias the prophet, saying, The voice of one crying in the wilderness, Prepare you the way of the Lord, make his paths straight.

5 Every valley shall be filled, and every mountain and hill shall be brought low; and the crooked shall be made straight, and the rough ways shall be made smooth;

6 And all flesh shall see the salvation of God.

7 Then said he to the multitude that came forth to be baptized of him, O generation of vipers, who has warned you to flee from the wrath to come?

8 Bring forth therefore fruits worthy of repentance, and begin not to say within yourselves, We have Abraham to our father: for I say unto you, That God is able of these stones to raise up children unto Abraham.

9 And now also the axe is laid unto the root of the trees: every tree therefore which bringeth not forth good fruit is hewn down, and cast into the fire.

10 And the people asked him, saying, What shall we do then?

11 He answereth and saith unto them, He that has two coats, let him impart to him that has none; and he that has meat, let him do likewise.

12 Then came also publicans to be baptized, and said unto him, Master, what shall we do?

13 And he said unto them, Exact no more than that which is appointed you.

14 And the soldiers likewise demanded of him, saying, And what shall we do? And he said unto them, Do violence to no man, neither accuse any falsely; and be content with your wages.

15 And as the people were in expectation, and all men mused in their hearts of John, whether he were the Christ, or not;

16 John answered, saying unto them all, I indeed baptize you with water; but one mightier than I comes, the latchet of whose shoes I am not worthy to unloose: he shall baptize you with the Holy Ghost and with fire:

17 Whose fan is in his hand, and he will throughly purge his floor, and will gather the wheat into his garner; but the chaff he will burn with fire unquenchable.

18 And many other things in his exhortation preached he unto the people.

19 But Herod the tetrarch, being reproved by him for Herodias his brother Philip's wife, and for all the evils which Herod had done,

20 Added yet this above all, that he shut up John in prison.

21 Now when all the people were baptized, it came to pass, that Jesus also being baptized, and praying, the heaven was opened,

22 And the Holy Ghost descended in a bodily shape like a dove upon him, and a voice came from heaven, which said, You are my beloved Son; in you I am well pleased.

23 And Jesus himself began to be about thirty years of age, being (as was supposed) the son of Joseph, which was the son of Heli,

24 Which was the son of Matthat, which was the son of Levi, which was the son of Melchi, which was the son of Janna, which was the son of Joseph,

25 Which was the son of Mattathias, which was the son of Amos, which was the son of Naum, which was the son of Esli, which was the son of Nagge,

26 Which was the son of Maath, which was the son of Mattathias, which was the son of Semei, which was the son of Joseph, which was the son of Juda,

27 Which was the son of Joanna, which was the son of Rhesa, which was the son of Zorobabel, which was the son of Salathiel, which was the son of Neri,

28 Which was the son of Melchi, which was the son of Addi, which was the son of Cosam, which was the son of Elmodam, which was the son of Er,

29 Which was the son of Jose, which was the son of Eliezer, which was the son of Jorim, which was the son of Matthat, which was the son of Levi,

30 Which was the son of Simeon, which was the son of Juda, which was the son of Joseph, which was the son of Jonan, which was the son of Eliakim,

31 Which was the son of Melea, which was the son of Menan, which was the son of Mattatha, which was the son of Nathan, which was the son of David,

32 Which was the son of Jesse, which was the son of Obed, which was the son of Booz, which was the son of Salmon, which was the son of Naasson,

33 Which was the son of Aminadab, which was the son of Aram, which was the son of Esrom, which was the son of Phares, which was the son of Juda,

34 Which was the son of Jacob, which was the son of Isaac, which was the son of Abraham, which was the son of Thara, which was the son of Nachor,

35 Which was the son of Saruch, which was the son of Ragau, which was the son of Phalec, which was the son of Heber, which was the son of Sala,

36 Which was the son of Cainan, which was the son of Arphaxad, which was the son of Sem, which was the son of Noe, which was the son of Lamech,

37 Which was the son of Mathusala, which was the son of Enoch, which was the son of Jared, which was the son of Maleleel, which was the son of Cainan,

38 Which was the son of Enos, which was the son of Seth, which was the son of Adam, which was the son of God.

CHAPTER 4

AND Jesus being full of the Holy Ghost returned from Jordan, and was led by the Spirit into the wilderness,

2 Being forty days tempted of the devil. And in those days he did eat nothing: and when they were ended, he afterward hungered.

3 And the devil said unto him, If you be the Son of God, command this stone that it be made bread.

4 And Jesus answered him, saying, It is written, That man shall not live by bread alone, but by every word of God.

5 And the devil, taking him up into an high mountain, shewed unto him all the kingdoms of the world in a moment of time.

6 And the devil said unto him, All this power will I give you, and the glory of them: for that is delivered unto me; and to whomsoever I will I give it.

7 If you therefore will worship me, all shall be yours.

8 And Jesus answered and said unto him, Get you behind me, Satan: for it is written, You shalt worship the Lord your God, and him only shalt you serve.

9 And he brought him to Jerusalem, and set him on a pinnacle of the temple, and said unto him, If you be the Son of God, cast yourself down from hence:

10 For it is written, He shall give his angels charge over you, to keep you:

11 And in their hands they shall bear you up, lest at any time you dash your foot against a stone.

12 And Jesus answering said unto him, It is said, You shalt not tempt the Lord your God.

13 And when the devil had ended all the temptation, he departed from him for a season.

14 And Jesus returned in the power of the Spirit into Galilee: and there went out a fame of him through all the region round about.

15 And he taught in their synagogues, being glorified of all.

16 And he came to Nazareth, where he had been brought up: and, as his custom was, he went into the synagogue on the sabbath day, and stood up for to read.

17 And there was delivered unto him the book of the prophet Esaias. And when he had opened the book, he found the place where it was written,

18 The Spirit of the Lord is upon me, because he has anointed me to preach the gospel to the poor; he has sent me to heal the brokenhearted, to preach deliverance to the captives, and recovering of sight to the blind, to set at liberty them that are bruised,

19 To preach the acceptable year of the Lord.

20 And he closed the book, and he gave it again to the minister, and sat down. And the eyes of all them that were in the synagogue were fastened on him.

21 And he began to say unto them, This day is this scripture fulfilled in your ears.

22 And all bare him witness, and wondered at the gracious words which proceeded out of his mouth. And they said, Is not this Joseph's son?

23 And he said unto them, You will surely say unto me this proverb, Physician, heal yourself: whatsoever we have heard done in Capernaum, do also here in your country.

24 And he said, Verily I say unto you, No prophet is accepted in his own country.

25 But I tell you of a truth, many widows were in Israel in the days of Elias, when the heaven was shut up three years and six months, when great famine was throughout all the land;

26 But unto none of them was Elias sent, save unto Sarepta, a city of Sidon, unto a woman that was a widow.

27 And many lepers were in Israel in the time of Eliseus the prophet; and none of them was cleansed, saving Naaman the Syrian.

28 And all they in the synagogue, when they heard these things, were filled with wrath,

29 And rose up, and thrust him out of the city, and led him unto the brow of the hill whereon their city was built, that they might cast him down headlong.

30 But he passing through the midst of them went his way,

31 And came down to Capernaum, a city of Galilee, and taught them on the sabbath days.

32 And they were astonished at his doctrine: for his word was with power.

33 And in the synagogue there was a man, which had a spirit of an unclean devil, and cried out with a loud voice,

34 Saying, Let us alone; what have we to do with you, you Jesus of Nazareth? are you come to destroy us? I know you who you are; the Holy One of God.

35 And Jesus rebuked him, saying, Hold your peace, and come out of him. And when the devil had thrown him in the midst, he came out of him, and hurt him not.

36 And they were all amazed, and spake among themselves, saying, What a word is this! for with authority and power he commandeth the unclean spirits, and they come out.

37 And the fame of him went out into every place of the country round about.

38 And he arose out of the synagogue, and entered into Simon's house. And Simon's wife's mother was taken with a great fever; and they besought him for her.

39 And he stood over her, and rebuked the fever; and it left her: and immediately she arose and ministered unto them.

40 Now when the sun was setting, all they that had any sick with divers diseases brought them unto him; and he laid his hands on every one of them, and healed them.

41 And devils also came out of many, crying out, and saying, You are Christ the Son of God. And he rebuking them suffered them not to speak: for they knew that he was Christ.

42 And when it was day, he departed and went into a desert place: and the people sought him, and came unto him, and stayed him, that he should not depart from them.

43 And he said unto them, I must preach the kingdom of God to other cities also: for therefore am I sent.

44 And he preached in the synagogues of Galilee.

CHAPTER 5

AND it came to pass, that, as the people pressed upon him to hear the word of God, he stood by the lake of Gennesaret,

2 And saw two ships standing by the lake: but the fishermen were gone out of them, and were washing their nets.

3 And he entered into one of the ships, which was Simon's, and prayed him that he would thrust out a little from the land. And he sat down, and taught the people out of the ship.

4 Now when he had left speaking, he said unto Simon, Launch out into the deep, and let down your nets for a draught.

5 And Simon answering said unto him, Master, we have toiled all the night, and have taken nothing: nevertheless at your word I will let down the net.

6 And when they had this done, they inclosed a great multitude of fishes: and their net brake.

7 And they beckoned unto their partners, which were in the other ship, that they should come and help them. And they came, and filled both the ships, so that they began to sink.

8 When Simon Peter saw it, he fell down at Jesus' knees, saying, Depart from me; for I am a sinful man, O Lord.

9 For he was astonished, and all that were with him, at the draught of the fishes which they had taken:

10 And so was also James, and John, the sons of Zebedee, which were partners with Simon. And Jesus said unto Simon, Fear not; from henceforth you shalt catch men.

11 And when they had brought their ships to land, they forsook all, and followed him.

12 And it came to pass, when he was in a certain city, behold a man full of leprosy: who seeing Jesus fell on his face, and besought him, saying, Lord, if you will, you can make me clean.

13 And he put forth his hand, and touched him, saying, I will: be you clean. And immediately the leprosy departed from him.

14 And he charged him to tell no man: but go, and shew yourself to the priest, and offer for your cleansing, according as Moses commanded, for a testimony unto them.

15 But so much the more went there a fame abroad of him: and great multitudes came together to hear, and to be healed by him of their infirmities.

16 And he withdrew himself into the wilderness, and prayed.

17 And it came to pass on a certain day, as he was teaching, that there were Pharisees and doctors of the law sitting by, which were come out of every town of Galilee, and Judæa, and Jerusalem: and the power of the Lord was present to heal them.

18 And, behold, men brought in a bed a man which was taken with a palsy: and they sought means to bring him in, and to lay him before him.

19 And when they could not find by what way they might bring him in because of the multitude, they went upon the housetop, and let him down through the tiling with his couch into the midst before Jesus.

20 And when he saw their faith, he said unto him, Man, your sins are forgiven you.

21 And the scribes and the Pharisees began to reason, saying, Who is this which speaketh blasphemies? Who can forgive sins, but God alone?

22 But when Jesus perceived their thoughts, he answering said unto them, What reason you in your hearts?

23 Whether is easier, to say, Your sins be forgiven you; or to say, Rise up and walk?

24 But that you may know that the Son of man has power upon earth to forgive sins, (he said unto the sick of the palsy,) I say unto you, Arise, and take up your couch, and go into yours house.

25 And immediately he rose up before them, and took up that whereon he lay, and departed to his own house, glorifying God.

26 And they were all amazed, and they glorified God, and were filled with fear, saying, We have seen strange things to day.

27 And after these things he went forth, and saw a publican, named Levi, sitting at the receipt of custom: and he said unto him, Follow me.

28 And he left all, rose up, and followed him.

29 And Levi made him a great feast in his own house: and there was a great company of publicans and of others that sat down with them.

30 But their scribes and Pharisees murmured against his disciples, saying, Why do you eat and drink with publicans and sinners?

31 And Jesus answering said unto them, They that are whole need not a physician; but they that are sick.

32 I came not to call the righteous, but sinners to repentance.

33 And they said unto him, Why do the disciples of John fast often, and make prayers, and likewise the disciples of the Pharisees; but yours eat and drink?

34 And he said unto them, Can you make the children of the bridechamber fast, while the bridegroom is with them?

35 But the days will come, when the bridegroom shall be taken away from them, and then shall they fast in those days.

36 And he spake also a parable unto them; No man putteth a piece of a new garment upon an old; if otherwise, then both the new maketh a rent, and the piece that was taken out of the new agreeth not with the old.

37 And no man putteth new wine into old bottles; else the new wine will burst the bottles, and be spilled, and the bottles shall perish.

38 But new wine must be put into new bottles; and both are preserved.

39 No man also having drunk old wine straightway desireth new: for he saith, The old is better.

CHAPTER 6

AND it came to pass on the second sabbath after the first, that he went through the corn fields; and his disciples plucked the ears of corn, and did eat, rubbing them in their hands.

2 And certain of the Pharisees said unto them, Why do you that which is not lawful to do on the sabbath days?

3 And Jesus answering them said, Have you not read so much as this, what David did, when himself was an hungred, and they which were with him;

4 How he went into the house of God, and did take and eat the shewbread, and gave also to them that were with him; which it is not lawful to eat but for the priests alone?

5 And he said unto them, That the Son of man is Lord also of the sabbath.

6 And it came to pass also on another sabbath, that he entered into the synagogue and taught: and there was a man whose right hand was withered.

7 And the scribes and Pharisees watched him, whether he would heal on the sabbath day; that they might find an accusation against him.

8 But he knew their thoughts, and said to the man which had the withered hand, Rise up, and stand forth in the midst. And he arose and stood forth.

9 Then said Jesus unto them, I will ask you one thing; Is it lawful on the sabbath days to do good, or to do evil? to save life, or to destroy it?

10 And looking round about upon them all, he said unto the man, Stretch forth your hand. And he did so: and his hand was restored whole as the other.

11 And they were filled with madness; and communed one with another what they might do to Jesus.

12 And it came to pass in those days, that he went out into a mountain to pray, and continued all night in prayer to God.

13 And when it was day, he called unto him his disciples: and of them he chose twelve, whom also he named apostles;

14 Simon, (whom he also named Peter,) and Andrew his brother, James and John, Philip and Bartholomew,

15 Matthew and Thomas, James the son of Alphæus, and Simon called Zelotes,

16 And Judas the brother of James, and Judas Iscariot, which also was the traitor.

17 And he came down with them, and stood in the plain, and the company of his disciples, and a great multitude of people out of all Judæa and Jerusalem, and from the sea coast of Tyre and Sidon, which came to hear him, and to be healed of their diseases;

18 And they that were vexed with unclean spirits: and they were healed.

19 And the whole multitude sought to touch him: for there went virtue out of him, and healed them all.

20 And he lifted up his eyes on his disciples, and said, Blessed be you poor: for yours is the kingdom of God.

21 Blessed are you that hunger now: for you shall be filled. Blessed are you that weep now: for you shall laugh.

22 Blessed are you, when men shall hate you, and when they shall separate you from their company, and shall reproach you, and cast out your name as evil, for the Son of man's sake.

23 Rejoice you in that day, and leap for joy: for, behold, your reward is great in heaven: for in the like manner did their fathers unto the prophets.

24 But woe unto you that are rich! for you have received your consolation.

25 Woe unto you that are full! for you shall hunger. Woe unto you that laugh now! for you shall mourn and weep.

26 Woe unto you, when all men shall speak well of you! for so did their fathers to the false prophets.

27 But I say unto you which hear, Love your enemies, do good to them which hate you,

28 Bless them that curse you, and pray for them which despitefully use you.

29 And unto him that smiteth you on the one cheek offer also the other; and him that taketh away your cloke forbid not to take your coat also.

30 Give to every man that asketh of you; and of him that taketh away your goods ask them not again.

31 And as you would that men should do to you, do you also to them likewise.

32 For if you love them which love you, what thank have you? for sinners also love those that love them.

33 And if you do good to them which do good to you, what thank have you? for sinners also do even the same.

34 And if you lend to them of whom you hope to receive, what thank have you ? for sinners also lend to sinners, to receive as much again.

35 But love you your enemies, and do good, and lend, hoping for nothing again; and your reward shall be great, and you shall be the children of the Highest: for he is kind unto the unthankful and to the evil.

36 Be you therefore merciful, as your Father also is merciful.

37 Judge not, and you shall not be judged: condemn not, and you shall not be condemned: forgive, and you shall be forgiven:

38 Give, and it shall be given unto you; good measure, pressed down, and shaken together, and running over, shall men give into your bosom. For with the same measure that you mete withal it shall be measured to you again.

39 And he spake a parable unto them, Can the blind lead the blind? shall they not both fall into the ditch?

40 The disciple is not above his master: but every one that is perfect shall be as his master.

41 And why beholdest you the mote that is in your brother's eye, but perceivest not the beam that is in yours own eye?

42 Either how can you say to your brother, Brother, let me pull out the mote that is in yours eye, when you yourself beholdest not the beam that is in yours own eye? You hypocrite, cast out first the beam out of yours own eye, and then shalt you see clearly to pull out the mote that is in your brother's eye.

43 For a good tree bringeth not forth corrupt fruit; neither doth a corrupt tree bring forth good fruit.

44 For every tree is known by his own fruit. For of thorns men do not gather figs, nor of a bramble bush gather they grapes.

45 A good man out of the good treasure of his heart bringeth forth that which is good; and an evil man out of the evil treasure of his heart bringeth forth that which is evil: for of the abundance of the heart his mouth speaketh.

46And why call you me, Lord, Lord, and do not the things which I say?

47 Whosoever comes to me, and heareth my sayings, and doeth them, I will shew you to whom he is like:

48 He is like a man which built an house, and digged deep, and laid the foundation on a rock: and when the flood arose, the stream beat vehemently upon that house, and could not shake it: for it was founded upon a rock.

49 But he that heareth, and doeth not, is like a man that without a foundation built an house upon the earth; against which the stream did beat vehemently, and immediately it fell; and the ruin of that house was great.

CHAPTER 7

NOW when he had ended all his sayings in the audience of the people, he entered into Capernaum.

2 And a certain centurion's servant, who was dear unto him, was sick, and ready to die.

3 And when he heard of Jesus, he sent unto him the elders of the Jews, beseeching him that he would come and heal his servant.

4 And when they came to Jesus, they besought him instantly, saying, That he was worthy for whom he should do this:

5 For he loveth our nation, and he has built us a synagogue.

6 Then Jesus went with them. And when he was now not far from the house, the centurion sent friends to him, saying unto him, Lord, trouble not yourself: for I am not worthy that you shouldest enter under my roof:

7 Wherefore neither thought I myself worthy to come unto you: but say in a word, and my servant shall be healed.

8 For I also am a man set under authority, having under me soldiers, and I say unto one, Go, and he goeth; and to another, Come, and he comes; and to my servant, Do this, and he doeth it.

9 When Jesus heard these things, he marvelled at him, and turned him about, and said unto the people that followed him, I say unto you, I have not found so great faith, no, not in Israel.

10 And they that were sent, returning to the house, found the servant whole that had been sick.

11And it came to pass the day after, that he went into a city called Nain; and many of his disciples went with him, and much people.

12 Now when he came nigh to the gate of the city, behold, there was a dead man carried out, the only son of his mother, and she was a widow: and much people of the city was with her.

13 And when the Lord saw her, he had compassion on her, and said unto her, Weep not.

14 And he came and touched the bier: and they that bare him stood still. And he said, Young man, I say unto you, Arise.

15 And he that was dead sat up, and began to speak. And he delivered him to his mother.

16 And there came a fear on all: and they glorified God, saying, That a great prophet is risen up among us; and, That God has visited his people.

17 And this rumour of him went forth throughout all Judæa, and throughout all the region round about.

18 And the disciples of John shewed him of all these things.

19And John calling unto him two of his disciples sent them to Jesus, saying, Are you he that should come? or look we for another?

20 When the men were come unto him, they said, John Baptist has sent us unto you, saying, Are you he that should come? or look we for another?

21 And in that same hour he cured many of their infirmities and plagues, and of evil spirits; and unto many that were blind he gave sight.

22 Then Jesus answering said unto them, Go your way, and tell John what things you have seen and heard; how that the blind see, the lame walk, the lepers are cleansed, the deaf hear, the dead are raised, to the poor the gospel is preached.

23 And blessed is he, whosoever shall not be offended in me.

24And when the messengers of John were departed, he began to speak unto the people concerning John, What went you out into the wilderness for to see? A reed shaken with the wind?

25 But what went you out for to see? A man clothed in soft raiment? Behold, they which are gorgeously apparelled, and live delicately, are in kings' courts.

26 But what went you out for to see? A prophet? Yea, I say unto you, and much more than a prophet.

27 This is he, of whom it is written, Behold, I send my messenger before your face, which shall prepare your way before you.

28 For I say unto you, Among those that are born of women there is not a greater prophet than John the Baptist: but he that is least in the kingdom of God is greater than he.

29 And all the people that heard him, and the publicans, justified God, being baptized with the baptism of John.

30 But the Pharisees and lawyers rejected the counsel of God against themselves, being not baptized of him.

31And the Lord said, Whereunto then shall I liken the men of this generation? and to what are they like?

32 They are like unto children sitting in the marketplace, and calling one to another, and saying, We have piped unto you, and you have not danced; we have mourned to you, and you have not wept.

33 For John the Baptist came neither eating bread nor drinking wine; and you say, He has a devil.

34 The Son of man is come eating and drinking; and you say, Behold a gluttonous man, and a winebibber, a friend of publicans and sinners!

35 But wisdom is justified of all her children.

36And one of the Pharisees desired him that he would eat with him. And he went into the Pharisee's house, and sat down to meat.

37 And, behold, a woman in the city, which was a sinner, when she knew that Jesus sat at meat in the Pharisee's house, brought an alabaster box of ointment,

38 And stood at his feet behind him weeping, and began to wash his feet with tears, and did wipe them with the hairs of her head, and kissed his feet, and anointed them with the ointment.

39 Now when the Pharisee which had bidden him saw it, he spake within himself, saying, This man, if he were a prophet, would have known who and what manner of woman this is that toucheth him: for she is a sinner.

40 And Jesus answering said unto him, Simon, I have somewhat to say unto you. And he saith, Master, say on.

41 There was a certain creditor which had two debtors: the one owed five hundred pence, and the other fifty.

42 And when they had nothing to pay, he frankly forgave them both. Tell me therefore, which of them will love him most?

43 Simon answered and said, I suppose that he, to whom he forgave most. And he said unto him, You have rightly judged.

44 And he turned to the woman, and said unto Simon, Seest you this woman? I entered into yours house, you gavest me no water for my feet: but she has washed my feet with tears, and wiped them with the hairs of her head.

45 You gavest me no kiss: but this woman since the time I came in has not ceased to kiss my feet.

46 My head with oil you did not anoint: but this woman has anointed my feet with ointment.

47 Wherefore I say unto you, Her sins, which are many, are forgiven; for she loved much: but to whom little is forgiven, the same loveth little.

48 And he said unto her, Your sins are forgiven.

49 And they that sat at meat with him began to say within themselves, Who is this that forgiveth sins also?

50 And he said to the woman, Your faith has saved you; go in peace.

CHAPTER 8

AND it came to pass afterward, that he went throughout every city and village, preaching and shewing the glad tidings of the kingdom of God: and the twelve were with him,

2 And certain women, which had been healed of evil spirits and infirmities, Mary called Magdalene, out of whom went seven devils,

3 And Joanna the wife of Chuza Herod's steward, and Susanna, and many others, which ministered unto him of their substance.

4And when much people were gathered together, and were come to him out of every city, he spake by a parable:

5 A sower went out to sow his seed: and as he sowed, some fell by the way side; and it was trodden down, and the fowls of the air devoured it.

6 And some fell upon a rock; and as soon as it was sprung up, it withered away, because it lacked moisture.

7 And some fell among thorns; and the thorns sprang up with it, and choked it.

8 And other fell on good ground, and sprang up, and bare fruit an hundredfold. And when he had said these things, he cried, He that has ears to hear, let him hear.

9 And his disciples asked him, saying, What might this parable be?

10 And he said, Unto you it is given to know the mysteries of the kingdom of God: but to others in parables; that seeing they might not see, and hearing they might not understand.

11 Now the parable is this: The seed is the word of God.

12 Those by the way side are they that hear; then comes the devil, and taketh away the word out of their hearts, lest they should believe and be saved.

13 They on the rock are they, which, when they hear, receive the word with joy; and these have no root, which for a while believe, and in time of temptation fall away.

14 And that which fell among thorns are they, which, when they have heard, go forth, and are choked with cares and riches and pleasures of this life, and bring no fruit to perfection.

15 But that on the good ground are they, which in an honest and good heart, having heard the word, keep it, and bring forth fruit with patience.

16No man, when he has lighted a candle, covers it with a vessel, or putteth it under a bed; but setteth it on a candlestick, that they which enter in may see the light.

17 For nothing is secret, that shall not be made manifest; neither any thing hid, that shall not be known and come abroad.

18 Take heed therefore how you hear: for whosoever has, to him shall be given; and whosoever has not, from him shall be taken even that which he seemeth to have.

19Then came to him his mother and his brethren, and could not come at him for the press.

20 And it was told him by certain which said, Your mother and your brethren stand without, desiring to see you.

21 And he answered and said unto them, My mother and my brethren are these which hear the word of God, and do it.

22Now it came to pass on a certain day, that he went into a ship with his disciples: and he said unto them, Let us go over unto the other side of the lake. And they launched forth.

23 But as they sailed he fell asleep: and there came down a storm of wind on the lake; and they were filled with water, and were in jeopardy.

24 And they came to him, and awoke him, saying, Master, master, we perish. Then he arose, and rebuked the wind and the raging of the water: and they ceased, and there was a calm.

25 And he said unto them, Where is your faith? And they being afraid wondered, saying one to another, What manner of man is this! for he commandeth even the winds and water, and they obey him.

26And they arrived at the country of the Gadarenes, which is over against Galilee.

27 And when he went forth to land, there met him out of the city a certain man, which had devils long time, and ware no clothes, neither abode in any house, but in the tombs.

28 When he saw Jesus, he cried out, and fell down before him, and with a loud voice said, What have I to do with you, Jesus, you Son of God most high? I beseech you, torment me not.

29 (For he had commanded the unclean spirit to come out of the man. For oftentimes it had caught him: and he was kept bound with chains and in fetters; and he brake the bands, and was driven of the devil into the wilderness.)

30 And Jesus asked him, saying, What is your name? And he said, Legion: because many devils were entered into him.

31 And they besought him that he would not command them to go out into the deep.

32 And there was there an herd of many swine feeding on the mountain: and they besought him that he would suffer them to enter into them. And he suffered them.

33 Then went the devils out of the man, and entered into the swine: and the herd ran violently down a steep place into the lake, and were choked.

34 When they that fed them saw what was done, they fled, and went and told it in the city and in the country.

35 Then they went out to see what was done; and came to Jesus, and found the man, out of whom the devils were departed, sitting at the feet of Jesus, clothed, and in his right mind: and they were afraid.

36 They also which saw it told them by what means he that was possessed of the devils was healed.

37Then the whole multitude of the country of the Gadarenes round about besought him to depart from them; for they were taken with great fear: and he went up into the ship, and returned back again.

38 Now the man out of whom the devils were departed besought him that he might be with him: but Jesus sent him away, saying,

39 Return to yours own house, and shew how great things God has done unto you. And he went his way, and published throughout the whole city how great things Jesus had done unto him.

40 And it came to pass, that, when Jesus was returned, the people gladly received him: for they were all waiting for him.

41And, behold, there came a man named Jairus, and he was a ruler of the synagogue: and he fell down at Jesus' feet, and besought him that he would come into his house:

42 For he had one only daughter, about twelve years of age, and she lay a dying. But as he went the people thronged him.

43And a woman having an issue of blood twelve years, which had spent all her living upon physicians, neither could be healed of any,

44 Came behind him, and touched the border of his garment: and immediately her issue of blood stanched.

45 And Jesus said, Who touched me? When all denied, Peter and they that were with him said, Master, the multitude throng you and press you, and say you, Who touched me?

46 And Jesus said, Somebody has touched me: for I perceive that virtue is gone out of me.

47 And when the woman saw that she was not hid, she came trembling, and falling down before him, she declared unto him before all the people for what cause she had touched him, and how she was healed immediately.

48 And he said unto her, Daughter, be of good comfort: your faith has made you whole; go in peace.

49While he yet spake, there comes one from the ruler of the synagogue's house, saying to him, Your daughter is dead; trouble not the Master.

50 But when Jesus heard it, he answered him, saying, Fear not: believe only, and she shall be made whole.

51 And when he came into the house, he suffered no man to go in, save Peter, and James, and John, and the father and the mother of the maiden.

52 And all wept, and bewailed her: but he said, Weep not; she is not dead, but sleepeth.

53 And they laughed him to scorn, knowing that she was dead.

54 And he put them all out, and took her by the hand, and called, saying, Maid, arise.

55 And her spirit came again, and she arose straightway: and he commanded to give her meat.

56 And her parents were astonished: but he charged them that they should tell no man what was done.

CHAPTER 9

THEN he called his twelve disciples together, and gave them power and authority over all devils, and to cure diseases.

2 And he sent them to preach the kingdom of God, and to heal the sick.

3 And he said unto them, Take nothing for your journey, neither staves, nor scrip, neither bread, neither money; neither have two coats apiece.

4 And whatsoever house you enter into, there abide, and thence depart.

5 And whosoever will not receive you, when you go out of that city, shake off the very dust from your feet for a testimony against them.

6 And they departed, and went through the towns, preaching the gospel, and healing every where.

7Now Herod the tetrarch heard of all that was done by him: and he was perplexed, because that it was said of some, that John was risen from the dead;

8 And of some, that Elias had appeared; and of others, that one of the old prophets was risen again.

9 And Herod said, John have I beheaded: but who is this, of whom I hear such things? And he desired to see him.

10 And the apostles, when they were returned, told him all that they had done. And he took them, and went aside privately into a desert place belonging to the city called Bethsaida.

11 And the people, when they knew it, followed him: and he received them, and spake unto them of the kingdom of God, and healed them that had need of healing.

12 And when the day began to wear away, then came the twelve, and said unto him, Send the multitude away, that they may go into the towns and country round about, and lodge, and get victuals: for we are here in a desert place.

13 But he said unto them, Give you them to eat. And they said, We have no more but five loaves and two fishes; except we should go and buy meat for all this people.

14 For they were about five thousand men. And he said to his disciples, Make them sit down by fifties in a company.

15 And they did so, and made them all sit down.

16 Then he took the five loaves and the two fishes, and looking up to heaven, he blessed them, and brake, and gave to the disciples to set before the multitude.

17 And they did eat, and were all filled: and there was taken up of fragments that remained to them twelve baskets.

18 And it came to pass, as he was alone praying, his disciples were with him: and he asked them, saying, Whom say the people that I am?

19 They answering said, John the Baptist; but some say, Elias; and others say, that one of the old prophets is risen again.

20 He said unto them, But whom say you that I am? Peter answering said, The Christ of God.

21 And he straitly charged them, and commanded them to tell no man that thing;

22 Saying, The Son of man must suffer many things, and be rejected of the elders and chief priests and scribes, and be slain, and be raised the third day.

23 And he said to them all, If any man will come after me, let him deny himself, and take up his cross daily, and follow me.

24 For whosoever will save his life shall lose it: but whosoever will lose his life for my sake, the same shall save it.

25 For what is a man advantaged, if he gain the whole world, and lose himself, or be cast away?

26 For whosoever shall be ashamed of me and of my words, of him shall the Son of man be ashamed, when he shall come in his own glory, and in his Father's, and of the holy angels.

27 But I tell you of a truth, there be some standing here, which shall not taste of death, till they see the kingdom of God.

28 And it came to pass about an eight days after these sayings, he took Peter and John and James, and went up into a mountain to pray.

29 And as he prayed, the fashion of his countenance was altered, and his raiment was white and glistering.

30 And, behold, there talked with him two men, which were Moses and Elias:

31 Who appeared in glory, and spake of his decease which he should accomplish at Jerusalem.

32 But Peter and they that were with him were heavy with sleep: and when they were awake, they saw his glory, and the two men that stood with him.

33 And it came to pass, as they departed from him, Peter said unto Jesus, Master, it is good for us to be here: and let us make three tabernacles; one for you, and one for Moses, and one for Elias: not knowing what he said.

34 While he thus spake, there came a cloud, and overshadowed them: and they feared as they entered into the cloud.

35 And there came a voice out of the cloud, saying, This is my beloved Son: hear him.

36 And when the voice was past, Jesus was found alone. And they kept it close, and told no man in those days any of those things which they had seen.

37 And it came to pass, that on the next day, when they were come down from the hill, much people met him.

38 And, behold, a man of the company cried out, saying, Master, I beseech you, look upon my son: for he is my only child.

39 And, lo, a spirit taketh him, and he suddenly crieth out; and it teareth him that he foameth again, and bruising him hardly departeth from him.

40 And I besought your disciples to cast him out; and they could not.

41 And Jesus answering said, O faithless and perverse generation, how long shall I be with you, and suffer you? Bring your son hither.

42 And as he was yet a coming, the devil threw him down, and tare him. And Jesus rebuked the unclean spirit, and healed the child, and delivered him again to his father.

43 And they were all amazed at the mighty power of God. But while they wondered every one at all things which Jesus did, he said unto his disciples,

44 Let these sayings sink down into your ears: for the Son of man shall be delivered into the hands of men.

45 But they understood not this saying, and it was hid from them, that they perceived it not: and they feared to ask him of that saying.

46 Then there arose a reasoning among them, which of them should be greatest.

47 And Jesus, perceiving the thought of their heart, took a child, and set him by him,

48 And said unto them, Whosoever shall receive this child in my name receiveth me: and whosoever shall receive me receiveth him that sent me: for he that is least among you all, the same shall be great.

49 And John answered and said, Master, we saw one casting out devils in your name; and we forbad him, because he followeth not with us.

50 And Jesus said unto him, Forbid him not: for he that is not against us is for us.

51 And it came to pass, when the time was come that he should be received up, he stedfastly set his face to go to Jerusalem,

52 And sent messengers before his face: and they went, and entered into a village of the Samaritans, to make ready for him.

53 And they did not receive him, because his face was as though he would go to Jerusalem.

54 And when his disciples James and John saw this, they said, Lord, will you that we command fire to come down from heaven, and consume them, even as Elias did?

55 But he turned, and rebuked them, and said, You know not what manner of spirit you are of.

56 For the Son of man is not come to destroy men's lives, but to save them. And they went to another village.

57 And it came to pass, that, as they went in the way, a certain man said unto him, Lord, I will follow you whithersoever you go.

58 And Jesus said unto him, Foxes have holes, and birds of the air have nests; but the Son of man has not where to lay his head.

59 And he said unto another, Follow me. But he said, Lord, suffer me first to go and bury my father.

60 Jesus said unto him, Let the dead bury their dead: but go you and preach the kingdom of God.

61 And another also said, Lord, I will follow you; but let me first go bid them farewell, which are at home at my house.

62 And Jesus said unto him, No man, having put his hand to the plough, and looking back, is fit for the kingdom of God.

CHAPTER 10

AFTER these things the Lord appointed other seventy also, and sent them two and two before his face into every city and place, whither he himself would come.

2 Therefore said he unto them, The harvest truly is great, but the labourers are few: pray you therefore the Lord of the harvest, that he would send forth labourers into his harvest.

3 Go your ways: behold, I send you forth as lambs among wolves.

4 Carry neither purse, nor scrip, nor shoes: and salute no man by the way.

5 And into whatsoever house you enter, first say, Peace be to this house.

6 And if the son of peace be there, your peace shall rest upon it: if not, it shall turn to you again.

7 And in the same house remain, eating and drinking such things as they give: for the labourer is worthy of his hire. Go not from house to house.

8 And into whatsoever city you enter, and they receive you, eat such things as are set before you:

9 And heal the sick that are therein, and say unto them, The kingdom of God is come nigh unto you.

10 But into whatsoever city you enter, and they receive you not, go your ways out into the streets of the same, and say,

11 Even the very dust of your city, which cleaveth on us, we do wipe off against you: notwithstanding be you sure of this, that the kingdom of God is come nigh unto you.

12 But I say unto you, that it shall be more tolerable in that day for Sodom, than for that city.

13 Woe unto you, Chorazin! woe unto you, Bethsaida! for if the mighty works had been done in Tyre and Sidon, which have been done in you, they had a great while ago repented, sitting in sackcloth and ashes.

14 But it shall be more tolerable for Tyre and Sidon at the judgment, than for you.

15 And you, Capernaum, which are exalted to heaven, shalt be thrust down to hell.

16 He that heareth you heareth me; and he that despiseth you despiseth me; and he that despiseth me despiseth him that sent me.

17 And the seventy returned again with joy, saying, Lord, even the devils are subject unto us through your name.

18 And he said unto them, I beheld Satan as lightning fall from heaven.

19 Behold, I give unto you power to tread on serpents and scorpions, and over all the power of the enemy: and nothing shall by any means hurt you.

20 Notwithstanding in this rejoice not, that the spirits are subject unto you; but rather rejoice, because your names are written in heaven.

21 In that hour Jesus rejoiced in spirit, and said, I thank you, O Father, Lord of heaven and earth, that you have hid these things from the wise and prudent, and have revealed them unto babes: even so, Father; for so it seemed good in your sight.

22 All things are delivered to me of my Father: and no man knoweth who the Son is, but the Father; and who the Father is, but the Son, and he to whom the Son will reveal him.

23 And he turned him unto his disciples, and said privately, Blessed are the eyes which see the things that you see:

24 For I tell you, that many prophets and kings have desired to see those things which you see, and have not seen them; and to hear those things which you hear, and have not heard them.

25 And, behold, a certain lawyer stood up, and tempted him, saying, Master, what shall I do to inherit eternal life?

26 He said unto him, What is written in the law? how readest you?

27 And he answering said, You shalt love the Lord your God with all your heart, and with all your soul, and with all your strength, and with all your mind; and your neighbour as yourself.

28 And he said unto him, You have answered right: this do, and you shalt live.

29 But he, willing to justify himself, said unto Jesus, And who is my neighbour?

30 And Jesus answering said, A certain man went down from Jerusalem to Jericho, and fell among thieves, which stripped him of his raiment, and wounded him, and departed, leaving him half dead.

31 And by chance there came down a certain priest that way: and when he saw him, he passed by on the other side.

32 And likewise a Levite, when he was at the place, came and looked on him, and passed by on the other side.

33 But a certain Samaritan, as he journeyed, came where he was: and when he saw him, he had compassion on him,

34 And went to him, and bound up his wounds, pouring in oil and wine, and set him on his own beast, and brought him to an inn, and took care of him.

35 And on the morrow when he departed, he took out two pence, and gave them to the host, and said unto him, Take care of him; and whatsoever you spendest more, when I come again, I will repay you.

36 Which now of these three, thinkest you, was neighbour unto him that fell among the thieves?

37 And he said, He that shewed mercy on him. Then said Jesus unto him, Go, and do you likewise.

38 Now it came to pass, as they went, that he entered into a certain village: and a certain woman named Martha received him into her house.

39 And she had a sister called Mary, which also sat at Jesus' feet, and heard his word.

40 But Martha was cumbered about much serving, and came to him, and said, Lord, dost you not care that my sister has left me to serve alone? bid her therefore that she help me.

41 And Jesus answered and said unto her, Martha, Martha, you are careful and troubled about many things:

42 But one thing is needful: and Mary has chosen that good part, which shall not be taken away from her.

CHAPTER 11

AND it came to pass, that, as he was praying in a certain place, when he ceased, one of his disciples said unto him, Lord, teach us to pray, as John also taught his disciples.

2 And he said unto them, When you pray, say, Our Father which are in heaven, Hallowed be your name. Your kingdom come. Your will be done, as in heaven, so in earth.

3 Give us day by day our daily bread.

4 And forgive us our sins; for we also forgive every one that is indebted to us. And lead us not into temptation; but deliver us from evil.

5 And he said unto them, Which of you shall have a friend, and shall go unto him at midnight, and say unto him, Friend, lend me three loaves;

6 For a friend of my in his journey is come to me, and I have nothing to set before him?

7 And he from within shall answer and say, Trouble me not: the door is now shut, and my children are with me in bed; I cannot rise and give you.

8 I say unto you, Though he will not rise and give him, because he is his friend, yet because of his importunity he will rise and give him as many as he needeth.

9 And I say unto you, Ask, and it shall be given you; seek, and you shall find; knock, and it shall be opened unto you.

10 For every one that asketh receiveth; and he that seeketh findeth; and to him that knocketh it shall be opened.

11 If a son shall ask bread of any of you that is a father, will he give him a stone? or if he ask a fish, will he for a fish give him a serpent?

12 Or if he shall ask an egg, will he offer him a scorpion?

13 If you then, being evil, know how to give good gifts unto your children: how much more shall your heavenly Father give the Holy Spirit to them that ask him?

14 And he was casting out a devil, and it was dumb. And it came to pass, when the devil was gone out, the dumb spake; and the people wondered.

15 But some of them said, He casteth out devils through Beelzebub the chief of the devils.

16 And others, tempting him, sought of him a sign from heaven.

17 But he, knowing their thoughts, said unto them, Every kingdom divided against itself is brought to desolation; and a house divided against a house falleth.

18 If Satan also be divided against himself, how shall his kingdom stand? because you say that I cast out devils through Beelzebub.

19 And if I by Beelzebub cast out devils, by whom do your sons cast them out? therefore shall they be your judges.

20 But if I with the finger of God cast out devils, no doubt the kingdom of God is come upon you.

21 When a strong man armed keepeth his palace, his goods are in peace:

22 But when a stronger than he shall come upon him, and overcome him, he taketh from him all his armour wherein he trusted, and divideth his spoils.

23 He that is not with me is against me: and he that gathereth not with me scattereth.

24 When the unclean spirit is gone out of a man, he walketh through dry places, seeking rest; and finding none, he saith, I will return unto my house whence I came out.

25 And when he comes, he findeth it swept and garnished.

26 Then goeth he, and taketh to him seven other spirits more wicked than himself; and they enter in, and dwell there: and the last state of that man is worse than the first.

27 And it came to pass, as he spake these things, a certain woman of the company lifted up her voice, and said unto him, Blessed is the womb that bare you, and the paps which you have sucked.

28 But he said, Yea rather, blessed are they that hear the word of God, and keep it.

29 And when the people were gathered thick together, he began to say, This is an evil generation: they seek a sign; and there shall no sign be given it, but the sign of Jonas the prophet.

30 For as Jonas was a sign unto the Ninevites, so shall also the Son of man be to this generation.

31 The queen of the south shall rise up in the judgment with the men of this generation, and condemn them: for she came from the utmost parts of the earth to hear the wisdom of Solomon; and, behold, a greater than Solomon is here.

32 The men of Nineve shall rise up in the judgment with this generation, and shall condemn it: for they repented at the preaching of Jonas; and, behold, a greater than Jonas is here.

33 No man, when he has lighted a candle, putteth it in a secret place, neither under a bushel, but on a candlestick, that they which come in may see the light.

34 The light of the body is the eye: therefore when yours eye is single, your whole body also is full of light; but when yours eye is evil, your body also is full of darkness.

35 Take heed therefore that the light which is in you be not darkness.

36 If your whole body therefore be full of light, having no part dark, the whole shall be full of light, as when the bright shining of a candle doth give you light.

37 And as he spake, a certain Pharisee besought him to dine with him: and he went in, and sat down to meat.

38 And when the Pharisee saw it, he marvelled that he had not first washed before dinner.

39 And the Lord said unto him, Now do you Pharisees make clean the outside of the cup and the platter; but your inward part is full of ravening and wickedness.

40 You fools, did not he that made that which is without make that which is within also?

41 But rather give alms of such things as you have; and, behold, all things are clean unto you.

42 But woe unto you, Pharisees! for you tithe mint and rue and all manner of herbs, and pass over judgment and the love of God: these ought you to have done, and not to leave the other undone.

43 Woe unto you, Pharisees! for you love the uppermost seats in the synagogues, and greetings in the markets.

44 Woe unto you, scribes and Pharisees, hypocrites! for you are as graves which appear not, and the men that walk over them are not aware of them.

45 Then answered one of the lawyers, and said unto him, Master, thus saying you reproachest us also.

46 And he said, Woe unto you also, you lawyers! for you lade men with burdens grievous to be borne, and you yourselves touch not the burdens with one of your fingers.

47 Woe unto you! for you build the sepulchres of the prophets, and your fathers killed them.

48 Truly you bear witness that you allow the deeds of your fathers: for they indeed killed them, and you build their sepulchres.

49 Therefore also said the wisdom of God, I will send them prophets and apostles, and some of them they shall slay and persecute:

50 That the blood of all the prophets, which was shed from the foundation of the world, may be required of this generation;

51 From the blood of Abel unto the blood of Zacharias, which perished between the altar and the temple: verily I say unto you, It shall be required of this generation.

52 Woe unto you, lawyers! for you have taken away the key of knowledge: you entered not in yourselves, and them that were entering in you hindered.

53 And as he said these things unto them, the scribes and the Pharisees began to urge him vehemently, and to provoke him to speak of many things:

54 Laying wait for him, and seeking to catch something out of his mouth, that they might accuse him.

CHAPTER 12

IN the mean time, when there were gathered together an innumerable multitude of people, insomuch that they trode one upon another, he began to say unto his disciples first of all, Beware you of the leaven of the Pharisees, which is hypocrisy.

2 For there is nothing covered, that shall not be revealed; neither hid, that shall not be known.

3 Therefore whatsoever you have spoken in darkness shall be heard in the light; and that which you have spoken in the ear in closets shall be proclaimed upon the housetops.

4 And I say unto you my friends, Be not afraid of them that kill the body, and after that have no more that they can do.

5 But I will forewarn you whom you shall fear: Fear him, which after he has killed has power to cast into hell; yea, I say unto you, Fear him.

6 Are not five sparrows sold for two farthings, and not one of them is forgotten before God?

7 But even the very hairs of your head are all numbered. Fear not therefore: you are of more value than many sparrows.

8 Also I say unto you, Whosoever shall confess me before men, him shall the Son of man also confess before the angels of God:

9 But he that denieth me before men shall be denied before the angels of God.

10 And whosoever shall speak a word against the Son of man, it shall be forgiven him: but unto him that blasphemeth against the Holy Ghost it shall not be forgiven.

11 And when they bring you unto the synagogues, and unto magistrates, and powers, take you no thought how or what thing you shall answer, or what you shall say:

12 For the Holy Ghost shall teach you in the same hour what you ought to say.

13 And one of the company said unto him, Master, speak to my brother, that he divide the inheritance with me.

14 And he said unto him, Man, who made me a judge or a divider over you?

15 And he said unto them, Take heed, and beware of covetousness: for a man's life consisteth not in the abundance of the things which he possesseth.

16 And he spake a parable unto them, saying, The ground of a certain rich man brought forth plentifully:

17 And he thought within himself, saying, What shall I do, because I have no room where to bestow my fruits?

18 And he said, This will I do: I will pull down my barns, and build greater; and there will I bestow all my fruits and my goods.

19 And I will say to my soul, Soul, you have much goods laid up for many years; take yours ease, eat, drink, and be merry.

20 But God said unto him, You fool, this night your soul shall be required of you: then whose shall those things be, which you have provided?

21 So is he that layeth up treasure for himself, and is not rich toward God.

22 And he said unto his disciples, Therefore I say unto you, Take no thought for your life, what you shall eat; neither for the body, what you shall put on.

23 The life is more than meat, and the body is more than raiment.

24 Consider the ravens: for they neither sow nor reap; which neither have storehouse nor barn; and God feedeth them: how much more are you better than the fowls?

25 And which of you with taking thought can add to his stature one cubit?

26 If you then be not able to do that thing which is least, why take you thought for the rest?

27 Consider the lilies how they grow: they toil not, they spin not; and yet I say unto you, that Solomon in all his glory was not arrayed like one of these.

28 If then God so clothe the grass, which is to day in the field, and to morrow is cast into the oven; how much more will he clothe you, O you of little faith?

29 And seek not you what you shall eat, or what you shall drink, neither be you of doubtful mind.

30 For all these things do the nations of the world seek after: and your Father knoweth that you have need of these things.

31 But rather seek you the kingdom of God; and all these things shall be added unto you.

32 Fear not, little flock; for it is your Father's good pleasure to give you the kingdom.

33 Sell that you have, and give alms; provide yourselves bags which wax not old, a treasure in the heavens that faileth not, where no thief approacheth, neither moth corrupteth.

34 For where your treasure is, there will your heart be also.

35 Let your loins be girded about, and your lights burning;

36 And you yourselves like unto men that wait for their lord, when he will return from the wedding; that when he comes and knocketh, they may open unto him immediately.

37 Blessed are those servants, whom the lord when he comes shall find watching: verily I say unto you, that he shall gird himself, and make them to sit down to meat, and will come forth and serve them.

38 And if he shall come in the second watch, or come in the third watch, and find them so, blessed are those servants.

39 And this know, that if the goodman of the house had known what hour the thief would come, he would have watched, and not have suffered his house to be broken through.

40 Be you therefore ready also: for the Son of man comes at an hour when you think not.

41 Then Peter said unto him, Lord, speakest you this parable unto us, or even to all?

42 And the Lord said, Who then is that faithful and wise steward, whom his lord shall make ruler over his household, to give them their portion of meat in due season?

43 Blessed is that servant, whom his lord when he comes shall find so doing.

44 Of a truth I say unto you, that he will make him ruler over all that he has.

45 But and if that servant say in his heart, My lord delayeth his coming; and shall begin to beat the menservants and maidens, and to eat and drink, and to be drunken;

46 The lord of that servant will come in a day when he looketh not for him, and at an hour when he is not aware, and will cut him in sunder, and will appoint him his portion with the unbelievers.

47 And that servant, which knew his lord's will, and prepared not himself, neither did according to his will, shall be beaten with many stripes.

48 But he that knew not, and did commit things worthy of stripes, shall be beaten with few stripes. For unto whomsoever much is given, of him shall be much required: and to whom men have committed much, of him they will ask the more.

49 I am come to send fire on the earth; and what will I, if it be already kindled?

50 But I have a baptism to be baptized with; and how am I straitened till it be accomplished!

51 Suppose you that I am come to give peace on earth? I tell you, Nay; but rather division:

52 For from henceforth there shall be five in one house divided, three against two, and two against three.

53 The father shall be divided against the son, and the son against the father; the mother against the daughter, and the daughter against the mother; the mother in law against her daughter in law, and the daughter in law against her mother in law.

54 And he said also to the people, When you see a cloud rise out of the west, straightway you say, There comes a shower; and so it is.

55 And when you see the south wind blow, you say, There will be heat; and it comes to pass.

56 You hypocrites, you can discern the face of the sky and of the earth; but how is it that you do not discern this time?

57 Yea, and why even of yourselves judge you not what is right?

58 When you go with yours adversary to the magistrate, as you are in the way, give diligence that you mayest be delivered from him; lest he hale you to the judge, and the judge deliver you to the officer, and the officer cast you into prison.

59 I tell you, you shalt not depart thence, till you have paid the very last mite.

CHAPTER 13

THERE were present at that season some that told him of the Galilæans, whose blood Pilate had mingled with their sacrifices.

2 And Jesus answering said unto them, Suppose you that these Galilæans were sinners above all the Galilæans, because they suffered such things?

3 I tell you, Nay: but, except you repent, you shall all likewise perish.

4 Or those eighteen, upon whom the tower in Siloam fell, and slew them, think you that they were sinners above all men that dwelt in Jerusalem?

5 I tell you, Nay: but, except you repent, you shall all likewise perish.

6 He spake also this parable; A certain man had a fig tree planted in his vineyard; and he came and sought fruit thereon, and found none.

7 Then said he unto the dresser of his vineyard, Behold, these three years I come seeking fruit on this fig tree, and find none: cut it down; why cumbereth it the ground?

8 And he answering said unto him, Lord, let it alone this year also, till I shall dig about it, and dung it:

9 And if it bear fruit, well: and if not, then after that you shalt cut it down.

10 And he was teaching in one of the synagogues on the sabbath.

11 And, behold, there was a woman which had a spirit of infirmity eighteen years, and was bowed together, and could in no wise lift up herself.

12 And when Jesus saw her, he called her to him, and said unto her, Woman, you are loosed from yours infirmity.

13 And he laid his hands on her: and immediately she was made straight, and glorified God.

14 And the ruler of the synagogue answered with indignation, because that Jesus had healed on the sabbath day, and said unto the people, There are six days in which men ought to work: in them therefore come and be healed, and not on the sabbath day.

15 The Lord then answered him, and said, You hypocrite, doth not each one of you on the sabbath loose his ox or his ass from the stall, and lead him away to watering?

16 And ought not this woman, being a daughter of Abraham, whom Satan has bound, lo, these eighteen years, be loosed from this bond on the sabbath day?

17 And when he had said these things, all his adversaries were ashamed: and all the people rejoiced for all the glorious things that were done by him.

18 Then said he, Unto what is the kingdom of God like? and whereunto shall I resemble it?

19 It is like a grain of mustard seed, which a man took, and cast into his garden; and it grew, and waxed a great tree; and the fowls of the air lodged in the branches of it.

20 And again he said, Whereunto shall I liken the kingdom of God?

21 It is like leaven, which a woman took and hid in three measures of meal, till the whole was leavened.

22 And he went through the cities and villages, teaching, and journeying toward Jerusalem.

23 Then said one unto him, Lord, are there few that be saved? And he said unto them,

24 Strive to enter in at the strait gate: for many, I say unto you, will seek to enter in, and shall not be able.

25 When once the master of the house is risen up, and has shut to the door, and you begin to stand without, and to knock at the door, saying, Lord, Lord, open unto us; and he shall answer and say unto you, I know you not whence you are:

26 Then shall you begin to say, We have eaten and drunk in your presence, and you have taught in our streets.

27 But he shall say, I tell you, I know you not whence you are; depart from me, all you workers of iniquity.

28 There shall be weeping and gnashing of teeth, when you shall see Abraham, and Isaac, and Jacob, and all the prophets, in the kingdom of God, and you yourselves thrust out.

29 And they shall come from the east, and from the west, and from the north, and from the south, and shall sit down in the kingdom of God.

30 And, behold, there are last which shall be first, and there are first which shall be last.

31 The same day there came certain of the Pharisees, saying unto him, Get you out, and depart hence: for Herod will kill you.

32 And he said unto them, Go you , and tell that fox, Behold, I cast out devils, and I do cures to day and to morrow, and the third day I shall be perfected.

33 Nevertheless I must walk to day, and to morrow, and the day following: for it cannot be that a prophet perish out of Jerusalem.

34 O Jerusalem, Jerusalem, which killest the prophets, and stonest them that are sent unto you; how often would I have gathered your children together, as a hen doth gather her brood under her wings, and you would not!

35 Behold, your house is left unto you desolate: and verily I say unto you, You shall not see me, until the time come when you shall say, Blessed is he that comes in the name of the Lord.

CHAPTER 14

AND it came to pass, as he went into the house of one of the chief Pharisees to eat bread on the sabbath day, that they watched him.

2 And, behold, there was a certain man before him which had the dropsy.

3 And Jesus answering spake unto the lawyers and Pharisees, saying, Is it lawful to heal on the sabbath day?

4 And they held their peace. And he took him, and healed him, and let him go;

5 And answered them, saying, Which of you shall have an ass or an ox fallen into a pit, and will not straightway pull him out on the sabbath day?

6 And they could not answer him again to these things.

7 And he put forth a parable to those which were bidden, when he marked how they chose out the chief rooms; saying unto them,

8 When you are bidden of any man to a wedding, sit not down in the highest room; lest a more honourable man than you be bidden of him;

9 And he that bade you and him come and say to you, Give this man place; and you begin with shame to take the lowest room.

10 But when you are bidden, go and sit down in the lowest room; that when he that bade you comes, he may say unto you, Friend, go up higher: then shalt you have worship in the presence of them that sit at meat with you.

11 For whosoever exalteth himself shall be abased; and he that humbleth himself shall be exalted.

12 Then said he also to him that bade him, When you makest a dinner or a supper, call not your friends, nor your brethren, neither your kinsmen, nor your rich neighbours; lest they also bid you again, and a recompence be made you.

13 But when you makest a feast, call the poor, the maimed, the lame, the blind:

14 And you shalt be blessed; for they cannot recompense you: for you shalt be recompensed at the resurrection of the just.

15 And when one of them that sat at meat with him heard these things, he said unto him, Blessed is he that shall eat bread in the kingdom of God.

16 Then said he unto him, A certain man made a great supper, and bade many:

17 And sent his servant at supper time to say to them that were bidden, Come; for all things are now ready.

18 And they all with one consent began to make excuse. The first said unto him, I have bought a piece of ground, and I must needs go and see it: I pray you have me excused.

19 And another said, I have bought five yoke of oxen, and I go to prove them: I pray you have me excused.

20 And another said, I have married a wife, and therefore I cannot come.

21 So that servant came, and shewed his lord these things. Then the master of the house being angry said to his servant, Go out quickly into the streets and lanes of the city, and bring in hither the poor, and the maimed, and the halt, and the blind.

22 And the servant said, Lord, it is done as you have commanded, and yet there is room.

23 And the lord said unto the servant, Go out into the highways and hedges, and compel them to come in, that my house may be filled.

24 For I say unto you, That none of those men which were bidden shall taste of my supper.

25 And there went great multitudes with him: and he turned, and said unto them,

26 If any man come to me, and hate not his father, and mother, and wife, and children, and brethren, and sisters, yea, and his own life also, he cannot be my disciple.

27 And whosoever doth not bear his cross, and come after me, cannot be my disciple.

28 For which of you, intending to build a tower, sitteth not down first, and counteth the cost, whether he have sufficient to finish it?

29 Lest haply, after he has laid the foundation, and is not able to finish it, all that behold it begin to mock him,

30 Saying, This man began to build, and was not able to finish.

31 Or what king, going to make war against another king, sitteth not down first, and consulteth whether he be able with ten thousand to meet him that comes against him with twenty thousand?

32 Or else, while the other is yet a great way off, he sendeth an ambassage, and desireth conditions of peace.

33 So likewise, whosoever he be of you that forsaketh not all that he has, he cannot be my disciple.

34 Salt is good: but if the salt have lost his savour, wherewith shall it be seasoned?

35 It is neither fit for the land, nor yet for the dunghill; but men cast it out. He that has ears to hear, let him hear.

CHAPTER 15

THEN drew near unto him all the publicans and sinners for to hear him.

2 And the Pharisees and scribes murmured, saying, This man receiveth sinners, and eateth with them.

3 And he spake this parable unto them, saying,

4 What man of you, having an hundred sheep, if he lose one of them, doth not leave the ninety and nine in the wilderness, and go after that which is lost, until he find it?

5 And when he has found it, he layeth it on his shoulders, rejoicing.

6 And when he comes home, he calleth together his friends and neighbours, saying unto them, Rejoice with me; for I have found my sheep which was lost.

7 I say unto you, that likewise joy shall be in heaven over one sinner that repenteth, more than over ninety and nine just persons, which need no repentance.

8 Either what woman having ten pieces of silver, if she lose one piece, doth not light a candle, and sweep the house, and seek diligently till she find it?

9 And when she has found it, she calleth her friends and her neighbours together, saying, Rejoice with me; for I have found the piece which I had lost.

10 Likewise, I say unto you, there is joy in the presence of the angels of God over one sinner that repenteth.

11 And he said, A certain man had two sons:

12 And the younger of them said to his father, Father, give me the portion of goods that falleth to me. And he divided unto them his living.

13 And not many days after the younger son gathered all together, and took his journey into a far country, and there wasted his substance with riotous living.

14 And when he had spent all, there arose a mighty famine in that land; and he began to be in want.

15 And he went and joined himself to a citizen of that country; and he sent him into his fields to feed swine.

16 And he would fain have filled his belly with the husks that the swine did eat: and no man gave unto him.

17 And when he came to himself, he said, How many hired servants of my father's have bread enough and to spare, and I perish with hunger!

18 I will arise and go to my father, and will say unto him, Father, I have sinned against heaven, and before you,

19 And am no more worthy to be called your son: make me as one of your hired servants.

20 And he arose, and came to his father. But when he was yet a great way off, his father saw him, and had compassion, and ran, and fell on his neck, and kissed him.

21 And the son said unto him, Father, I have sinned against heaven, and in your sight, and am no more worthy to be called your son.

22 But the father said to his servants, Bring forth the best robe, and put it on him; and put a ring on his hand, and shoes on his feet:

23 And bring hither the fatted calf, and kill it; and let us eat, and be merry:

24 For this my son was dead, and is alive again; he was lost, and is found. And they began to be merry.

25 Now his elder son was in the field: and as he came and drew nigh to the house, he heard musick and dancing.

26 And he called one of the servants, and asked what these things meant.

27 And he said unto him, Your brother is come; and your father has killed the fatted calf, because he has received him safe and sound.

28 And he was angry, and would not go in: therefore came his father out, and intreated him.

29 And he answering said to his father, Lo, these many years do I serve you, neither transgressed I at any time your commandment: and yet you never gavest me a kid, that I might make merry with my friends:

30 But as soon as this your son was come, which has devoured your living with harlots, you have killed for him the fatted calf.

31 And he said unto him, Son, you are ever with me, and all that I have is yours.

32 It was meet that we should make merry, and be glad: for this your brother was dead, and is alive again; and was lost, and is found.

CHAPTER 16

AND he said also unto his disciples, There was a certain rich man, which had a steward; and the same was accused unto him that he had wasted his goods.

2 And he called him, and said unto him, How is it that I hear this of you? give an account of your stewardship; for you mayest be no longer steward.

3 Then the steward said within himself, What shall I do? for my lord taketh away from me the stewardship: I cannot dig; to beg I am ashamed.

4 I am resolved what to do, that, when I am put out of the stewardship, they may receive me into their houses.

5 So he called every one of his lord's debtors unto him, and said unto the first, How much owest you unto my lord?

6 And he said, An hundred measures of oil. And he said unto him, Take your bill, and sit down quickly, and write fifty.

7 Then said he to another, And how much owest you? And he said, An hundred measures of wheat. And he said unto him, Take your bill, and write fourscore.

8 And the lord commended the unjust steward, because he had done wisely: for the children of this world are in their generation wiser than the children of light.

9 And I say unto you, Make to yourselves friends of the mammon of unrighteousness; that, when you fail, they may receive you into everlasting habitations.

10 He that is faithful in that which is least is faithful also in much: and he that is unjust in the least is unjust also in much.

11 If therefore you have not been faithful in the unrighteous mammon, who will commit to your trust the true riches?

12 And if you have not been faithful in that which is another man's, who shall give you that which is your own?

13 No servant can serve two masters: for either he will hate the one, and love the other; or else he will hold to the one, and despise the other. You cannot serve God and mammon.

14 And the Pharisees also, who were covetous, heard all these things: and they derided him.

15 And he said unto them, You are they which justify yourselves before men; but God knoweth your hearts: for that which is highly esteemed among men is abomination in the sight of God.

16 The law and the prophets were until John: since that time the kingdom of God is preached, and every man presseth into it.

17 And it is easier for heaven and earth to pass, than one tittle of the law to fail.

18 Whosoever putteth away his wife, and marrieth another, committeth adultery: and whosoever marrieth her that is put away from her husband committeth adultery.

19 There was a certain rich man, which was clothed in purple and fine linen, and fared sumptuously every day:

20 And there was a certain beggar named Lazarus, which was laid at his gate, full of sores,

21 And desiring to be fed with the crumbs which fell from the rich man's table: moreover the dogs came and licked his sores.

22 And it came to pass, that the beggar died, and was carried by the angels into Abraham's bosom: the rich man also died, and was buried;

23 And in hell he lift up his eyes, being in torments, and seeth Abraham afar off, and Lazarus in his bosom.

24 And he cried and said, Father Abraham, have mercy on me, and send Lazarus, that he may dip the tip of his finger in water, and cool my tongue; for I am tormented in this flame.

25 But Abraham said, Son, remember that you in your lifetime receivedst your good things, and likewise Lazarus evil things: but now he is comforted, and you are tormented.

26 And beside all this, between us and you there is a great gulf fixed: so that they which would pass from hence to you cannot; neither can they pass to us, that would come from thence.

27 Then he said, I pray you therefore, father, that you wouldest send him to my father's house:

28 For I have five brethren; that he may testify unto them, lest they also come into this place of torment.

29 Abraham saith unto him, They have Moses and the prophets; let them hear them.

30 And he said, Nay, father Abraham: but if one went unto them from the dead, they will repent.

31 And he said unto him, If they hear not Moses and the prophets, neither will they be persuaded, though one rose from the dead.

CHAPTER 17

THEN said he unto the disciples, It is impossible but that offences will come: but woe unto him, through whom they come!

2 It were better for him that a millstone were hanged about his neck, and he cast into the sea, than that he should offend one of these little ones.

3 Take heed to yourselves: If your brother trespass against you, rebuke him; and if he repent, forgive him.

4 And if he trespass against you seven times in a day, and seven times in a day turn again to you, saying, I repent; you shalt forgive him.

5 And the apostles said unto the Lord, Increase our faith.

6 And the Lord said, If you had faith as a grain of mustard seed, you might say unto this sycamine tree, Be you plucked up by the root, and be you planted in the sea; and it should obey you.

7 But which of you, having a servant plowing or feeding cattle, will say unto him by and by, when he is come from the field, Go and sit down to meat?

8 And will not rather say unto him, Make ready wherewith I may sup, and gird yourself, and serve me, till I have eaten and drunken; and afterward you shalt eat and drink?

9 Doth he thank that servant because he did the things that were commanded him? I trow not.

10 So likewise you , when you shall have done all those things which are commanded you, say, We are unprofitable servants: we have done that which was our duty to do.

11And it came to pass, as he went to Jerusalem, that he passed through the midst of Samaria and Galilee.

12 And as he entered into a certain village, there met him ten men that were lepers, which stood afar off:

13 And they lifted up their voices, and said, Jesus, Master, have mercy on us.

14 And when he saw them, he said unto them, Go shew yourselves unto the priests. And it came to pass, that, as they went, they were cleansed.

15 And one of them, when he saw that he was healed, turned back, and with a loud voice glorified God,

16 And fell down on his face at his feet, giving him thanks: and he was a Samaritan.

17 And Jesus answering said, Were there not ten cleansed? but where are the nine?

18 There are not found that returned to give glory to God, save this stranger.

19 And he said unto him, Arise, go your way: your faith has made you whole.

20And when he was demanded of the Pharisees, when the kingdom of God should come, he answered them and said, The kingdom of God comes not with observation:

21 Neither shall they say, Lo here! or, lo there! for, behold, the kingdom of God is within you.

22 And he said unto the disciples, The days will come, when you shall desire to see one of the days of the Son of man, and you shall not see it.

23 And they shall say to you, See here; or, see there: go not after them, nor follow them.

24 For as the lightning, that lighteneth out of the one part under heaven, shineth unto the other part under heaven; so shall also the Son of man be in his day.

25 But first must he suffer many things, and be rejected of this generation.

26 And as it was in the days of Noe, so shall it be also in the days of the Son of man.

27 They did eat, they drank, they married wives, they were given in marriage, until the day that Noe entered into the ark, and the flood came, and destroyed them all.

28 Likewise also as it was in the days of Lot; they did eat, they drank, they bought, they sold, they planted, they builded;

29 But the same day that Lot went out of Sodom it rained fire and brimstone from heaven, and destroyed them all.

30 Even thus shall it be in the day when the Son of man is revealed.

31 In that day, he which shall be upon the housetop, and his stuff in the house, let him not come down to take it away: and he that is in the field, let him likewise not return back.

32 Remember Lot's wife.

33 Whosoever shall seek to save his life shall lose it; and whosoever shall lose his life shall preserve it.

34 I tell you, in that night there shall be two men in one bed; the one shall be taken, and the other shall be left.

35 Two women shall be grinding together; the one shall be taken, and the other left.

36 Two men shall be in the field; the one shall be taken, and the other left.

37 And they answered and said unto him, Where, Lord? And he said unto them, Wheresoever the body is, thither will the eagles be gathered together.

CHAPTER 18

AND he spake a parable unto them to this end, that men ought always to pray, and not to faint;

2 Saying, There was in a city a judge, which feared not God, neither regarded man:

3 And there was a widow in that city; and she came unto him, saying, Avenge me of my adversary.

4 And he would not for a while: but afterward he said within himself, Though I fear not God, nor regard man;

5 Yet because this widow troubleth me, I will avenge her, lest by her continual coming she weary me.

6 And the Lord said, Hear what the unjust judge saith.

7 And shall not God avenge his own elect, which cry day and night unto him, though he bear long with them?

8 I tell you that he will avenge them speedily. Nevertheless when the Son of man comes, shall he find faith on the earth?

9 And he spake this parable unto certain which trusted in themselves that they were righteous, and despised others:

10 Two men went up into the temple to pray; the one a Pharisee, and the other a publican.

11 The Pharisee stood and prayed thus with himself, God, I thank you, that I am not as other men are, extortioners, unjust, adulterers, or even as this publican.

12 I fast twice in the week, I give tithes of all that I possess.

13 And the publican, standing afar off, would not lift up so much as his eyes unto heaven, but struck upon his breast, saying, God be merciful to me a sinner.

14 I tell you, this man went down to his house justified rather than the other: for every one that exalteth himself shall be abased; and he that humbleth himself shall be exalted.

15 And they brought unto him also infants, that he would touch them: but when his disciples saw it, they rebuked them.

16 But Jesus called them unto him, and said, Suffer little children to come unto me, and forbid them not: for of such is the kingdom of God.

17 Verily I say unto you, Whosoever shall not receive the kingdom of God as a little child shall in no wise enter therein.

18 And a certain ruler asked him, saying, Good Master, what shall I do to inherit eternal life?

19 And Jesus said unto him, Why callest you me good? none is good, save one, that is, God.

20 You knowest the commandments, Do not commit adultery, Do not kill, Do not steal, Do not bear false witness, Honour your father and your mother.

21 And he said, All these have I kept from my youth up.

22 Now when Jesus heard these things, he said unto him, Yet lackest you one thing: sell all that you have, and distribute unto the poor, and you shalt have treasure in heaven: and come, follow me.

23 And when he heard this, he was very sorrowful: for he was very rich.

24 And when Jesus saw that he was very sorrowful, he said, How hardly shall they that have riches enter into the kingdom of God!

25 For it is easier for a camel to go through a needle's eye, than for a rich man to enter into the kingdom of God.

26 And they that heard it said, Who then can be saved?

27 And he said, The things which are impossible with men are possible with God.

28 Then Peter said, Lo, we have left all, and followed you.

29 And he said unto them, Verily I say unto you, There is no man that has left house, or parents, or brethren, or wife, or children, for the kingdom of God's sake,

30 Who shall not receive manifold more in this present time, and in the world to come life everlasting.

31Then he took unto him the twelve, and said unto them, Behold, we go up to Jerusalem, and all things that are written by the prophets concerning the Son of man shall be accomplished.

32 For he shall be delivered unto the Gentiles, and shall be mocked, and spitefully entreated, and spitted on:

33 And they shall scourge him, and put him to death: and the third day he shall rise again.

34 And they understood none of these things: and this saying was hid from them, neither knew they the things which were spoken.

35And it came to pass, that as he was come nigh unto Jericho, a certain blind man sat by the way side begging:

36 And hearing the multitude pass by, he asked what it meant.

37 And they told him, that Jesus of Nazareth passes by.

38 And he cried, saying, Jesus, you Son of David, have mercy on me.

39 And they which went before rebuked him, that he should hold his peace: but he cried so much the more, You Son of David, have mercy on me.

40 And Jesus stood, and commanded him to be brought unto him: and when he was come near, he asked him,

41 Saying, What will you that I shall do unto you? And he said, Lord, that I may receive my sight.

42 And Jesus said unto him, Receive your sight: your faith has saved you.

43 And immediately he received his sight, and followed him, glorifying God: and all the people, when they saw it, gave praise unto God.

CHAPTER 19

AND Jesus entered and passed through Jericho.

2 And, behold, there was a man named Zacchæus, which was the chief among the publicans, and he was rich.

3 And he sought to see Jesus who he was; and could not for the press, because he was little of stature.

4 And he ran before, and climbed up into a sycomore tree to see him: for he was to pass that way.

5 And when Jesus came to the place, he looked up, and saw him, and said unto him, Zacchæus, make haste, and come down; for to day I must abide at your house.

6 And he made haste, and came down, and received him joyfully.

7 And when they saw it, they all murmured, saying, That he was gone to be guest with a man that is a sinner.

8 And Zacchæus stood, and said unto the Lord; Behold, Lord, the half of my goods I give to the poor; and if I have taken any thing from any man by false accusation, I restore him fourfold.

9 And Jesus said unto him, This day is salvation come to this house, forsomuch as he also is a son of Abraham.

10 For the Son of man is come to seek and to save that which was lost.

11 And as they heard these things, he added and spake a parable, because he was nigh to Jerusalem, and because they thought that the kingdom of God should immediately appear.

12 He said therefore, A certain nobleman went into a far country to receive for himself a kingdom, and to return.

13 And he called his ten servants, and delivered them ten pounds, and said unto them, Occupy till I come.

14 But his citizens hated him, and sent a message after him, saying, We will not have this man to reign over us.

15 And it came to pass, that when he was returned, having received the kingdom, then he commanded these servants to be called unto him, to whom he had given the money, that he might know how much every man had gained by trading.

16 Then came the first, saying, Lord, your pound has gained ten pounds.

17 And he said unto him, Well, you good servant: because you have been faithful in a very little, have you authority over ten cities.

18 And the second came, saying, Lord, your pound has gained five pounds.

19 And he said likewise to him, Be you also over five cities.

20 And another came, saying, Lord, behold, here is your pound, which I have kept laid up in a napkin:

21 For I feared you, because you are an austere man: you takest up that you layedst not down, and reapest that you did not sow.

22 And he saith unto him, Out of yours own mouth will I judge you, you wicked servant. You knewest that I was an austere man, taking up that I laid not down, and reaping that I did not sow:

23 Wherefore then gavest not you my money into the bank, that at my coming I might have required my own with usury?

24 And he said unto them that stood by, Take from him the pound, and give it to him that has ten pounds.

25 (And they said unto him, Lord, he has ten pounds.)

26 For I say unto you, That unto every one which has shall be given; and from him that has not, even that he has shall be taken away from him.

27 But those my enemies, which would not that I should reign over them, bring hither, and slay them before me.

28 And when he had thus spoken, he went before, ascending up to Jerusalem.

29 And it came to pass, when he was come nigh to Bethphage and Bethany, at the mount called the mount of Olives, he sent two of his disciples,

30 Saying, Go you into the village over against you; in the which at your entering you shall find a colt tied, whereon yet never man sat: loose him, and bring him hither.

31 And if any man ask you, Why do you loose him? thus shall you say unto him, Because the Lord has need of him.

32 And they that were sent went their way, and found even as he had said unto them.

33 And as they were loosing the colt, the owners thereof said unto them, Why loose you the colt?

34 And they said, The Lord has need of him.

35 And they brought him to Jesus: and they cast their garments upon the colt, and they set Jesus thereon.

36 And as he went, they spread their clothes in the way.

37 And when he was come nigh, even now at the descent of the mount of Olives, the whole multitude of the disciples began to rejoice and praise God with a loud voice for all the mighty works that they had seen;

38 Saying, Blessed be the King that comes in the name of the Lord: peace in heaven, and glory in the highest.

39 And some of the Pharisees from among the multitude said unto him, Master, rebuke your disciples.

40 And he answered and said unto them, I tell you that, if these should hold their peace, the stones would immediately cry out.

41 And when he was come near, he beheld the city, and wept over it,

42 Saying, If you hadst known, even you , at least in this your day, the things which belong unto your peace! but now they are hid from yours eyes.

43 For the days shall come upon you, that yours enemies shall cast a trench about you, and compass you round, and keep you in on every side,

44 And shall lay you even with the ground, and your children within you; and they shall not leave in you one stone upon another; because you knewest not the time of your visitation.

45 And he went into the temple, and began to cast out them that sold therein, and them that bought;

46 Saying unto them, It is written, My house is the house of prayer: but you have made it a den of thieves.

47 And he taught daily in the temple. But the chief priests and the scribes and the chief of the people sought to destroy him,

48 And could not find what they might do: for all the people were very attentive to hear him.

CHAPTER 20

AND it came to pass, that on one of those days, as he taught the people in the temple, and preached the gospel, the chief priests and the scribes came upon him with the elders,

2 And spake unto him, saying, Tell us, by what authority doest you these things? or who is he that gave you this authority?

3 And he answered and said unto them, I will also ask you one thing; and answer me:

4 The baptism of John, was it from heaven, or of men?

5 And they reasoned with themselves, saying, If we shall say, From heaven; he will say, Why then believed you him not?

6 But and if we say, Of men; all the people will stone us: for they be persuaded that John was a prophet.

7 And they answered, that they could not tell whence it was.

8 And Jesus said unto them, Neither tell I you by what authority I do these things.

9 Then began he to speak to the people this parable; A certain man planted a vineyard, and let it forth to husbandmen, and went into a far country for a long time.

10 And at the season he sent a servant to the husbandmen, that they should give him of the fruit of the vineyard: but the husbandmen beat him, and sent him away empty.

11 And again he sent another servant: and they beat him also, and entreated him shamefully, and sent him away empty.

12 And again he sent a third: and they wounded him also, and cast him out.

13 Then said the lord of the vineyard, What shall I do? I will send my beloved son: it may be they will reverence him when they see him.

14 But when the husbandmen saw him, they reasoned among themselves, saying, This is the heir: come, let us kill him, that the inheritance may be ours.

15 So they cast him out of the vineyard, and killed him. What therefore shall the lord of the vineyard do unto them?

16 He shall come and destroy these husbandmen, and shall give the vineyard to others. And when they heard it, they said, God forbid.

17 And he beheld them, and said, What is this then that is written, The stone which the builders rejected, the same is become the head of the corner?

18 Whosoever shall fall upon that stone shall be broken; but on whomsoever it shall fall, it will grind him to powder.

19 And the chief priests and the scribes the same hour sought to lay hands on him; and they feared the people: for they perceived that he had spoken this parable against them.

20 And they watched him, and sent forth spies, which should feign themselves just men, that they might take hold of his words, that so they might deliver him unto the power and authority of the governor.

21 And they asked him, saying, Master, we know that you say and teachest rightly, neither acceptest you the person of any, but teachest the way of God truly:

22 Is it lawful for us to give tribute unto Cæsar, or no?

23 But he perceived their craftiness, and said unto them, Why tempt you me?

24 Shew me a penny. Whose image and superscription has it? They answered and said, Cæsar's.

25 And he said unto them, Render therefore unto Cæsar the things which be Cæsar's, and unto God the things which be God's.

26 And they could not take hold of his words before the people: and they marvelled at his answer, and held their peace.

27 Then came to him certain of the Sadducees, which deny that there is any resurrection; and they asked him,

28 Saying, Master, Moses wrote unto us, If any man's brother die, having a wife, and he die without children, that his brother should take his wife, and raise up seed unto his brother.

29 There were therefore seven brethren: and the first took a wife, and died without children.

30 And the second took her to wife, and he died childless.

31 And the third took her; and in like manner the seven also: and they left no children, and died.

32 Last of all the woman died also.

33 Therefore in the resurrection whose wife of them is she? for seven had her to wife.

34 And Jesus answering said unto them, The children of this world marry, and are given in marriage:

35 But they which shall be accounted worthy to obtain that world, and the resurrection from the dead, neither marry, nor are given in marriage:

36 Neither can they die any more: for they are equal unto the angels; and are the children of God, being the children of the resurrection.

37 Now that the dead are raised, even Moses shewed at the bush, when he calleth the Lord the God of Abraham, and the God of Isaac, and the God of Jacob.

38 For he is not a God of the dead, but of the living: for all live unto him.

39 Then certain of the scribes answering said, Master, you have well said.

40 And after that they durst not ask him any question at all.

41 And he said unto them, How say they that Christ is David's son?

42 And David himself saith in the book of Psalms, The LORD said unto my Lord, Sit you on my right hand,

43 Till I make yours enemies your footstool.

44 David therefore calleth him Lord, how is he then his son?

45 Then in the audience of all the people he said unto his disciples,

46 Beware of the scribes, which desire to walk in long robes, and love greetings in the markets, and the highest seats in the synagogues, and the chief rooms at feasts;

47 Which devour widows' houses, and for a shew make long prayers: the same shall receive greater damnation.

CHAPTER 21

AND he looked up, and saw the rich men casting their gifts into the treasury.

2 And he saw also a certain poor widow casting in thither two mites.

3 And he said, Of a truth I say unto you, that this poor widow has cast in more than they all:

4 For all these have of their abundance cast in unto the offerings of God: but she of her penury has cast in all the living that she had.

5 And as some spake of the temple, how it was adorned with goodly stones and gifts, he said,

6 As for these things which you behold, the days will come, in the which there shall not be left one stone upon another, that shall not be thrown down.

7 And they asked him, saying, Master, but when shall these things be? and what sign will there be when these things shall come to pass?

8 And he said, Take heed that you be not deceived: for many shall come in my name, saying, I am Christ; and the time draweth near: go you not therefore after them.

9 But when you shall hear of wars and commotions, be not terrified: for these things must first come to pass; but the end is not by and by.

10 Then said he unto them, Nation shall rise against nation, and kingdom against kingdom:

11 And great earthquakes shall be in divers places, and famines, and pestilences; and fearful sights and great signs shall there be from heaven.

12 But before all these, they shall lay their hands on you, and persecute you, delivering you up to the synagogues, and into prisons, being brought before kings and rulers for my name's sake.

13 And it shall turn to you for a testimony.

14 Settle it therefore in your hearts, not to meditate before what you shall answer:

15 For I will give you a mouth and wisdom, which all your adversaries shall not be able to gainsay nor resist.

16 And you shall be betrayed both by parents, and brethren, and kinsfolks, and friends; and some of you shall they cause to be put to death.

17 And you shall be hated of all men for my name's sake.

18 But there shall not an hair of your head perish.

19 In your patience possess you your souls.

20 And when you shall see Jerusalem compassed with armies, then know that the desolation thereof is nigh.

21 Then let them which are in Judæa flee to the mountains; and let them which are in the midst of it depart out; and let not them that are in the countries enter thereinto.

22 For these be the days of vengeance, that all things which are written may be fulfilled.

23 But woe unto them that are with child, and to them that give suck, in those days! for there shall be great distress in the land, and wrath upon this people.

24 And they shall fall by the edge of the sword, and shall be led away captive into all nations: and Jerusalem shall be trodden down of the Gentiles, until the times of the Gentiles be fulfilled.

25 And there shall be signs in the sun, and in the moon, and in the stars; and upon the earth distress of nations, with perplexity; the sea and the waves roaring;

26 Men's hearts failing them for fear, and for looking after those things which are coming on the earth: for the powers of heaven shall be shaken.

27 And then shall they see the Son of man coming in a cloud with power and great glory.

28 And when these things begin to come to pass, then look up, and lift up your heads; for your redemption draweth nigh.

29 And he spake to them a parable; Behold the fig tree, and all the trees;

30 When they now shoot forth, you see and know of your own selves that summer is now nigh at hand.

31 So likewise you , when you see these things come to pass, know you that the kingdom of God is nigh at hand.

32 Verily I say unto you, This generation shall not pass away, till all be fulfilled.

33 Heaven and earth shall pass away: but my words shall not pass away.

34 And take heed to yourselves, lest at any time your hearts be overcharged with surfeiting, and drunkenness, and cares of this life, and so that day come upon you unawares.

35 For as a snare shall it come on all them that dwell on the face of the whole earth.

36 Watch you therefore, and pray always, that you may be accounted worthy to escape all these things that shall come to pass, and to stand before the Son of man.

37 And in the day time he was teaching in the temple; and at night he went out, and abode in the mount that is called the mount of Olives.

38 And all the people came early in the morning to him in the temple, for to hear him.

CHAPTER 22

NOW the feast of unleavened bread drew nigh, which is called the Passover.

2 And the chief priests and scribes sought how they might kill him; for they feared the people.

3 Then entered Satan into Judas surnamed Iscariot, being of the number of the twelve.

4 And he went his way, and communed with the chief priests and captains, how he might betray him unto them.

5 And they were glad, and covenanted to give him money.

6 And he promised, and sought opportunity to betray him unto them in the absence of the multitude.

7 Then came the day of unleavened bread, when the passover must be killed.

8 And he sent Peter and John, saying, Go and prepare us the passover, that we may eat.

9 And they said unto him, Where will you that we prepare?

10 And he said unto them, Behold, when you are entered into the city, there shall a man meet you, bearing a pitcher of water; follow him into the house where he entereth in.

11 And you shall say unto the goodman of the house, The Master saith unto you, Where is the guestchamber, where I shall eat the passover with my disciples?

12 And he shall shew you a large upper room furnished: there make ready.

13 And they went, and found as he had said unto them: and they made ready the passover.

14 And when the hour was come, he sat down, and the twelve apostles with him.

15 And he said unto them, With desire I have desired to eat this passover with you before I suffer:

16 For I say unto you, I will not any more eat thereof, until it be fulfilled in the kingdom of God.

17 And he took the cup, and gave thanks, and said, Take this, and divide it among yourselves:

18 For I say unto you, I will not drink of the fruit of the vine, until the kingdom of God shall come.

19 And he took bread, and gave thanks, and brake it, and gave unto them, saying, This is my body which is given for you: this do in remembrance of me.

20 Likewise also the cup after supper, saying, This cup is the new testament in my blood, which is shed for you.

21 But, behold, the hand of him that betrayeth me is with me on the table.

22 And truly the Son of man goeth, as it was determined: but woe unto that man by whom he is betrayed!

23 And they began to inquire among themselves, which of them it was that should do this thing.

24 And there was also a strife among them, which of them should be accounted the greatest.

25 And he said unto them, The kings of the Gentiles exercise lordship over them; and they that exercise authority upon them are called benefactors.

26 But you shall not be so: but he that is greatest among you, let him be as the younger; and he that is chief, as he that doth serve.

27 For whether is greater, he that sitteth at meat, or he that serveth? is not he that sitteth at meat? but I am among you as he that serveth.

28 You are they which have continued with me in my temptations.

29 And I appoint unto you a kingdom, as my Father has appointed unto me;

30 That you may eat and drink at my table in my kingdom, and sit on thrones judging the twelve tribes of Israel.

31And the Lord said, Simon, Simon, behold, Satan has desired to have you, that he may sift you as wheat:

32 But I have prayed for you, that your faith fail not: and when you are converted, strengthen your brethren.

33 And he said unto him, Lord, I am ready to go with you, both into prison, and to death.

34 And he said, I tell you, Peter, the cock shall not crow this day, before that you shalt thrice deny that you knowest me.

35 And he said unto them, When I sent you without purse, and scrip, and shoes, lacked you any thing? And they said, Nothing.

36 Then said he unto them, But now, he that has a purse, let him take it, and likewise his scrip: and he that has no sword, let him sell his garment, and buy one.

37 For I say unto you, that this that is written must yet be accomplished in me, And he was reckoned among the transgressors: for the things concerning me have an end.

38 And they said, Lord, behold, here are two swords. And he said unto them, It is enough.

39And he came out, and went, as he was wont, to the mount of Olives; and his disciples also followed him.

40 And when he was at the place, he said unto them, Pray that you enter not into temptation.

41 And he was withdrawn from them about a stone's cast, and kneeled down, and prayed,

42 Saying, Father, if you be willing, remove this cup from me: nevertheless not my will, but yours, be done.

43 And there appeared an angel unto him from heaven, strengthening him.

44 And being in an agony he prayed more earnestly: and his sweat was as it were great drops of blood falling down to the ground.

45 And when he rose up from prayer, and was come to his disciples, he found them sleeping for sorrow,

46 And said unto them, Why sleep you ? rise and pray, lest you enter into temptation.

47And while he yet spake, behold a multitude, and he that was called Judas, one of the twelve, went before them, and drew near unto Jesus to kiss him.

48 But Jesus said unto him, Judas, betrayest you the Son of man with a kiss?

49 When they which were about him saw what would follow, they said unto him, Lord, shall we strike with the sword?

50And one of them struck the servant of the high priest, and cut off his right ear.

51 And Jesus answered and said, Suffer you thus far. And he touched his ear, and healed him.

52 Then Jesus said unto the chief priests, and captains of the temple, and the elders, which were come to him, Be you come out, as against a thief, with swords and staves?

53 When I was daily with you in the temple, you stretched forth no hands against me: but this is your hour, and the power of darkness.

54Then took they him, and led him, and brought him into the high priest's house. And Peter followed afar off.

55 And when they had kindled a fire in the midst of the hall, and were set down together, Peter sat down among them.

56 But a certain maid beheld him as he sat by the fire, and earnestly looked upon him, and said, This man was also with him.

57 And he denied him, saying, Woman, I know him not.

58 And after a little while another saw him, and said, You are also of them. And Peter said, Man, I am not.

59 And about the space of one hour after another confidently affirmed, saying, Of a truth this fellow also was with him: for he is a Galilæan.

60 And Peter said, Man, I know not what you say. And immediately, while he yet spake, the cock crew.

61 And the Lord turned, and looked upon Peter. And Peter remembered the word of the Lord, how he had said unto him, Before the cock crow, you shalt deny me thrice.

62 And Peter went out, and wept bitterly.

63And the men that held Jesus mocked him, and struck him.

64 And when they had blindfolded him, they struck him on the face, and asked him, saying, Prophesy, who is it that struck you?

65 And many other things blasphemously spake they against him.

66And as soon as it was day, the elders of the people and the chief priests and the scribes came together, and led him into their council, saying,

67 Are you the Christ? tell us. And he said unto them, If I tell you, you will not believe:

68 And if I also ask you, you will not answer me, nor let me go.

69 Hereafter shall the Son of man sit on the right hand of the power of God.

70 Then said they all, Are you then the Son of God? And he said unto them, You say that I am.

71 And they said, What need we any further witness? for we ourselves have heard of his own mouth.

CHAPTER 23

AND the whole multitude of them arose, and led him unto Pilate.

2 And they began to accuse him, saying, We found this fellow perverting the nation, and forbidding to give tribute to Cæsar, saying that he himself is Christ a King.

3 And Pilate asked him, saying, Are you the King of the Jews? And he answered him and said, You say it.

4 Then said Pilate to the chief priests and to the people, I find no fault in this man.

5 And they were the more fierce, saying, He stirreth up the people, teaching throughout all Jewry, beginning from Galilee to this place.

6 When Pilate heard of Galilee, he asked whether the man were a Galilæan.

7 And as soon as he knew that he belonged unto Herod's jurisdiction, he sent him to Herod, who himself also was at Jerusalem at that time.

8And when Herod saw Jesus, he was exceeding glad: for he was desirous to see him of a long season, because he had heard many things of him; and he hoped to have seen some miracle done by him.

9 Then he questioned with him in many words; but he answered him nothing.

10 And the chief priests and scribes stood and vehemently accused him.

11 And Herod with his men of war set him at nought, and mocked him, and arrayed him in a gorgeous robe, and sent him again to Pilate.

12And the same day Pilate and Herod were made friends together: for before they were at enmity between themselves.

13And Pilate, when he had called together the chief priests and the rulers and the people,

14 Said unto them, You have brought this man unto me, as one that perverteth the people: and, behold, I, having examined him before you, have found no fault in this man touching those things whereof you accuse him:

15 No, nor yet Herod: for I sent you to him; and, lo, nothing worthy of death is done unto him.

16 I will therefore chastise him, and release him.

17 (For of necessity he must release one unto them at the feast.)

18 And they cried out all at once, saying, Away with this man, and release unto us Barabbas:

19 (Who for a certain sedition made in the city, and for murder, was cast into prison.)

20 Pilate therefore, willing to release Jesus, spake again to them.

21 But they cried, saying, Crucify him, crucify him.

22 And he said unto them the third time, Why, what evil has he done? I have found no cause of death in him: I will therefore chastise him, and let him go.

23 And they were instant with loud voices, requiring that he might be crucified. And the voices of them and of the chief priests prevailed.

24 And Pilate gave sentence that it should be as they required.

25 And he released unto them him that for sedition and murder was cast into prison, whom they had desired; but he delivered Jesus to their will.

26 And as they led him away, they laid hold upon one Simon, a Cyrenian, coming out of the country, and on him they laid the cross, that he might bear it after Jesus.

27And there followed him a great company of people, and of women, which also bewailed and lamented him.

28 But Jesus turning unto them said, Daughters of Jerusalem, weep not for me, but weep for yourselves, and for your children.

29 For, behold, the days are coming, in the which they shall say, Blessed are the barren, and the wombs that never bare, and the paps which never gave suck.

30 Then shall they begin to say to the mountains, Fall on us; and to the hills, Cover us.

31 For if they do these things in a green tree, what shall be done in the dry?

32 And there were also two other, malefactors, led with him to be put to death.

33 And when they were come to the place, which is called Calvary, there they crucified him, and the malefactors, one on the right hand, and the other on the left.

34 Then said Jesus, Father, forgive them; for they know not what they do. And they parted his raiment, and cast lots.

35 And the people stood beholding. And the rulers also with them derided him, saying, He saved others; let him save himself, if he be Christ, the chosen of God.

36 And the soldiers also mocked him, coming to him, and offering him vinegar,

37 And saying, If you be the king of the Jews, save yourself.

38 And a superscription also was written over him in letters of Greek, and Latin, and Hebrew, THIS IS THE KING OF THE JEWS.

39 And one of the malefactors which were hanged railed on him, saying, If you be Christ, save yourself and us.

40 But the other answering rebuked him, saying, Dost not you fear God, seeing you are in the same condemnation?

41 And we indeed justly; for we receive the due reward of our deeds: but this man has done nothing amiss.

42 And he said unto Jesus, Lord, remember me when you comest into your kingdom.

43 And Jesus said unto him, Verily I say unto you, To day shalt you be with me in paradise.

44 And it was about the sixth hour, and there was a darkness over all the earth until the ninth hour.

45 And the sun was darkened, and the veil of the temple was rent in the midst.

46 And when Jesus had cried with a loud voice, he said, Father, into your hands I commend my spirit: and having said thus, he gave up the ghost.

47 Now when the centurion saw what was done, he glorified God, saying, Certainly this was a righteous man.

48 And all the people that came together to that sight, beholding the things which were done, struck their breasts, and returned.

49 And all his acquaintance, and the women that followed him from Galilee, stood afar off, beholding these things.

50 And, behold, there was a man named Joseph, a counseller; and he was a good man, and a just:

51 (The same had not consented to the counsel and deed of them;) he was of Arimathæa, a city of the Jews: who also himself waited for the kingdom of God.

52 This man went unto Pilate, and begged the body of Jesus.

53 And he took it down, and wrapped it in linen, and laid it in a sepulchre that was hewn in stone, wherein never man before was laid.

54 And that day was the preparation, and the sabbath drew on.

55 And the women also, which came with him from Galilee, followed after, and beheld the sepulchre, and how his body was laid.

56 And they returned, and prepared spices and ointments; and rested the sabbath day according to the commandment.

CHAPTER 24

NOW upon the first day of the week, very early in the morning, they came unto the sepulchre, bringing the spices which they had prepared, and certain others with them.

2 And they found the stone rolled away from the sepulchre.

3 And they entered in, and found not the body of the Lord Jesus.

4 And it came to pass, as they were much perplexed thereabout, behold, two men stood by them in shining garments:

5 And as they were afraid, and bowed down their faces to the earth, they said unto them, Why seek you the living among the dead?

6 He is not here, but is risen: remember how he spake unto you when he was yet in Galilee,

7 Saying, The Son of man must be delivered into the hands of sinful men, and be crucified, and the third day rise again.

8 And they remembered his words,

9 And returned from the sepulchre, and told all these things unto the eleven, and to all the rest.

10 It was Mary Magdalene, and Joanna, and Mary the mother of James, and other women that were with them, which told these things unto the apostles.

11 And their words seemed to them as idle tales, and they believed them not.

12 Then arose Peter, and ran unto the sepulchre; and stooping down, he beheld the linen clothes laid by themselves, and departed, wondering in himself at that which was come to pass.

13 And, behold, two of them went that same day to a village called Emmaus, which was from Jerusalem about threescore furlongs.

14 And they talked together of all these things which had happened.

15 And it came to pass, that, while they communed together and reasoned, Jesus himself drew near, and went with them.

16 But their eyes were holden that they should not know him.

17 And he said unto them, What manner of communications are these that you have one to another, as you walk, and are sad?

18 And the one of them, whose name was Cleopas, answering said unto him, Are you only a stranger in Jerusalem, and have not known the things which are come to pass there in these days?

19 And he said unto them, What things? And they said unto him, Concerning Jesus of Nazareth, which was a prophet mighty in deed and word before God and all the people:

20 And how the chief priests and our rulers delivered him to be condemned to death, and have crucified him.

21 But we trusted that it had been he which should have redeemed Israel: and beside all this, to day is the third day since these things were done.

22 Yea, and certain women also of our company made us astonished, which were early at the sepulchre;

23 And when they found not his body, they came, saying, that they had also seen a vision of angels, which said that he was alive.

24 And certain of them which were with us went to the sepulchre, and found it even so as the women had said: but him they saw not.

25 Then he said unto them, O fools, and slow of heart to believe all that the prophets have spoken:

26 Ought not Christ to have suffered these things, and to enter into his glory?

27 And beginning at Moses and all the prophets, he expounded unto them in all the scriptures the things concerning himself.

28 And they drew nigh unto the village, whither they went: and he made as though he would have gone further.

29 But they constrained him, saying, Abide with us: for it is toward evening, and the day is far spent. And he went in to tarry with them.

30 And it came to pass, as he sat at meat with them, he took bread, and blessed it, and brake, and gave to them.

31 And their eyes were opened, and they knew him; and he vanished out of their sight.

32 And they said one to another, Did not our heart burn within us, while he talked with us by the way, and while he opened to us the scriptures?

33 And they rose up the same hour, and returned to Jerusalem, and found the eleven gathered together, and them that were with them,

34 Saying, The Lord is risen indeed, and has appeared to Simon.

35 And they told what things were done in the way, and how he was known of them in breaking of bread.

36 And as they thus spake, Jesus himself stood in the midst of them, and saith unto them, Peace be unto you.

37 But they were terrified and affrighted, and supposed that they had seen a spirit.

38 And he said unto them, Why are you troubled? and why do thoughts arise in your hearts?

39 Behold my hands and my feet, that it is I myself: handle me, and see; for a spirit has not flesh and bones, as you see me have.

40 And when he had thus spoken, he shewed them his hands and his feet.

41 And while they yet believed not for joy, and wondered, he said unto them, Have you here any meat?

42 And they gave him a piece of a broiled fish, and of an honeycomb.

43 And he took it, and did eat before them.

44 And he said unto them, These are the words which I spake unto you, while I was yet with you, that all things must be fulfilled, which were written in the law of Moses, and in the prophets, and in the psalms, concerning me.

45 Then opened he their understanding, that they might understand the scriptures,

46 And said unto them, Thus it is written, and thus it behoved Christ to suffer, and to rise from the dead the third day:

47 And that repentance and remission of sins should be preached in his name among all nations, beginning at Jerusalem.

48 And you are witnesses of these things.

49 And, behold, I send the promise of my Father upon you: but tarry you in the city of Jerusalem, until you be endued with power from on high.

50 And he led them out as far as to Bethany, and he lifted up his hands, and blessed them.

51 And it came to pass, while he blessed them, he was parted from them, and carried up into heaven.

52 And they worshipped him, and returned to Jerusalem with great joy:

53 And were continually in the temple, praising and blessing God. Amen.

THE GOSPEL ACCORDING TO ST. JOHN.

CHAPTER 1

IN the beginning was the Word, and the Word was with God, and the Word was God.

2 The same was in the beginning with God.

3 All things were made by him; and without him was not any thing made that was made.

4 In him was life; and the life was the light of men.

5 And the light shineth in darkness; and the darkness comprehended it not.

6 There was a man sent from God, whose name was John.

7 The same came for a witness, to bear witness of the Light, that all men through him might believe.

8 He was not that Light, but was sent to bear witness of that Light.

9 That was the true Light, which lighteth every man that comes into the world.

10 He was in the world, and the world was made by him, and the world knew him not.

11 He came unto his own, and his own received him not.

12 But as many as received him, to them gave he power to become the sons of God, even to them that believe on his name:

13 Which were born, not of blood, nor of the will of the flesh, nor of the will of man, but of God.

14 And the Word was made flesh, and dwelt among us, (and we beheld his glory, the glory as of the only begotten of the Father,) full of grace and truth.

15 John bare witness of him, and cried, saying, This was he of whom I spake, He that comes after me is preferred before me: for he was before me.

16 And of his fulness have all we received, and grace for grace.

17 For the law was given by Moses, but grace and truth came by Jesus Christ.

18 No man has seen God at any time; the only begotten Son, which is in the bosom of the Father, he has declared him.

19 And this is the record of John, when the Jews sent priests and Levites from Jerusalem to ask him, Who are you ?

20 And he confessed, and denied not; but confessed, I am not the Christ.

21 And they asked him, What then? Are you Elias? And he saith, I am not. Are you that prophet? And he answered, No.

22 Then said they unto him, Who are you ? that we may give an answer to them that sent us. What say you of yourself?

23 He said, I am the voice of one crying in the wilderness, Make straight the way of the Lord, as said the prophet Esaias.

24 And they which were sent were of the Pharisees.

25 And they asked him, and said unto him, Why baptizest you then, if you be not that Christ, nor Elias, neither that prophet?

26 John answered them, saying, I baptize with water: but there standeth one among you, whom you know not;

27 He it is, who coming after me is preferred before me, whose shoe's latchet I am not worthy to unloose.

28 These things were done in Bethabara beyond Jordan, where John was baptizing.

29 The next day John seeth Jesus coming unto him, and saith, Behold the Lamb of God, which taketh away the sin of the world.

30 This is he of whom I said, After me comes a man which is preferred before me: for he was before me.

31 And I knew him not: but that he should be made manifest to Israel, therefore am I come baptizing with water.

32 And John bare record, saying, I saw the Spirit descending from heaven like a dove, and it abode upon him.

33 And I knew him not: but he that sent me to baptize with water, the same said unto me, Upon whom you shalt see the Spirit descending, and remaining on him, the same is he which baptizeth with the Holy Ghost.

34 And I saw, and bare record that this is the Son of God.

35 Again the next day after John stood, and two of his disciples;

36 And looking upon Jesus as he walked, he saith, Behold the Lamb of God!

37 And the two disciples heard him speak, and they followed Jesus.

38 Then Jesus turned, and saw them following, and saith unto them, What seek you ? They said unto him, Rabbi, (which is to say, being interpreted, Master,) where dwellest you ?

39 He saith unto them, Come and see. They came and saw where he dwelt, and abode with him that day: for it was about the tenth hour.

40 One of the two which heard John speak, and followed him, was Andrew, Simon Peter's brother.

41 He first findeth his own brother Simon, and saith unto him, We have found the Messias, which is, being interpreted, the Christ.

42 And he brought him to Jesus. And when Jesus beheld him, he said, You are Simon the son of Jona: you shalt be called Cephas, which is by interpretation, A stone.

43 The day following Jesus would go forth into Galilee, and findeth Philip, and saith unto him, Follow me.

44 Now Philip was of Bethsaida, the city of Andrew and Peter.

45 Philip findeth Nathanael, and saith unto him, We have found him, of whom Moses in the law, and the prophets, did write, Jesus of Nazareth, the son of Joseph.

46 And Nathanael said unto him, Can there any good thing come out of Nazareth? Philip saith unto him, Come and see.

47 Jesus saw Nathanael coming to him, and saith of him, Behold an Israelite indeed, in whom is no guile!

48 Nathanael saith unto him, Whence knowest you me? Jesus answered and said unto him, Before that Philip called you, when you wast under the fig tree, I saw you.

49 Nathanael answered and saith unto him, Rabbi, you are the Son of God; you are the King of Israel.

50 Jesus answered and said unto him, Because I said unto you, I saw you under the fig tree, believest you ? you shalt see greater things than these.

51 And he saith unto him, Verily, verily, I say unto you, Hereafter you shall see heaven open, and the angels of God ascending and descending upon the Son of man.

CHAPTER 2

AND the third day there was a marriage in Cana of Galilee; and the mother of Jesus was there:

2 And both Jesus was called, and his disciples, to the marriage.

3 And when they wanted wine, the mother of Jesus saith unto him, They have no wine.

4 Jesus saith unto her, Woman, what have I to do with you? my hour is not yet come.

5 His mother saith unto the servants, Whatsoever he saith unto you, do it.

6 And there were set there six waterpots of stone, after the manner of the purifying of the Jews, containing two or three firkins apiece.

7 Jesus saith unto them, Fill the waterpots with water. And they filled them up to the brim.

8 And he saith unto them, Draw out now, and bear unto the governor of the feast. And they bare it.

9 When the ruler of the feast had tasted the water that was made wine, and knew not whence it was: (but the servants which drew the water knew;) the governor of the feast called the bridegroom,

10 And saith unto him, Every man at the beginning doth set forth good wine; and when men have well drunk, then that which is worse: but you have kept the good wine until now.

11 This beginning of miracles did Jesus in Cana of Galilee, and manifested forth his glory; and his disciples believed on him.

12 After this he went down to Capernaum, he, and his mother, and his brethren, and his disciples: and they continued there not many days.

13 And the Jews' passover was at hand, and Jesus went up to Jerusalem,

14 And found in the temple those that sold oxen and sheep and doves, and the changers of money sitting:

15 And when he had made a scourge of small cords, he drove them all out of the temple, and the sheep, and the oxen; and poured out the changers' money, and overthrew the tables;

16 And said unto them that sold doves, Take these things hence; make not my Father's house an house of merchandise.

17 And his disciples remembered that it was written, The zeal of yours house has eaten me up.

18 Then answered the Jews and said unto him, What sign shewest you unto us, seeing that you doest these things?

19 Jesus answered and said unto them, Destroy this temple, and in three days I will raise it up.

20 Then said the Jews, Forty and six years was this temple in building, and will you rear it up in three days?

21 But he spake of the temple of his body.

22 When therefore he was risen from the dead, his disciples remembered that he had said this unto them; and they believed the scripture, and the word which Jesus had said.

23 Now when he was in Jerusalem at the passover, in the feast day, many believed in his name, when they saw the miracles which he did.

24 But Jesus did not commit himself unto them, because he knew all men,

25 And needed not that any should testify of man: for he knew what was in man.

CHAPTER 3

THERE was a man of the Pharisees, named Nicodemus, a ruler of the Jews:

2 The same came to Jesus by night, and said unto him, Rabbi, we know that you are a teacher come from God: for no man can do these miracles that you doest, except God be with him.

3 Jesus answered and said unto him, Verily, verily, I say unto you, Except a man be born again, he cannot see the kingdom of God.

4 Nicodemus saith unto him, How can a man be born when he is old? can he enter the second time into his mother's womb, and be born?

5 Jesus answered, Verily, verily, I say unto you, Except a man be born of water and of the Spirit, he cannot enter into the kingdom of God.

6 That which is born of the flesh is flesh; and that which is born of the Spirit is spirit.

7 Marvel not that I said unto you, You must be born again.

8 The wind bloweth where it listeth, and you hearest the sound thereof, but can not tell whence it comes, and whither it goeth: so is every one that is born of the Spirit.

9 Nicodemus answered and said unto him, How can these things be?

10 Jesus answered and said unto him, Are you a master of Israel, and knowest not these things?

11 Verily, verily, I say unto you, We speak that we do know, and testify that we have seen; and you receive not our witness.

12 If I have told you earthly things, and you believe not, how shall you believe, if I tell you of heavenly things?

13 And no man has ascended up to heaven, but he that came down from heaven, even the Son of man which is in heaven.

14 And as Moses lifted up the serpent in the wilderness, even so must the Son of man be lifted up:

15 That whosoever believeth in him should not perish, but have eternal life.

16 For God so loved the world, that he gave his only begotten Son, that whosoever believeth in him should not perish, but have everlasting life.

17 For God sent not his Son into the world to condemn the world; but that the world through him might be saved.

18 He that believeth on him is not condemned: but he that believeth not is condemned already, because he has not believed in the name of the only begotten Son of God.

19 And this is the condemnation, that light is come into the world, and men loved darkness rather than light, because their deeds were evil.

20 For every one that doeth evil hateth the light, neither comes to the light, lest his deeds should be reproved.

21 But he that doeth truth comes to the light, that his deeds may be made manifest, that they are created in God.

22 After these things came Jesus and his disciples into the land of Judæa; and there he tarried with them, and baptized.

23 And John also was baptizing in Ænon near to Salim, because there was much water there: and they came, and were baptized.

24 For John was not yet cast into prison.

25 Then there arose a question between some of John's disciples and the Jews about purifying.

26 And they came unto John, and said unto him, Rabbi, he that was with you beyond Jordan, to whom you barest witness, behold, the same baptizeth, and all men come to him.

27 John answered and said, A man can receive nothing, except it be given him from heaven.

28 You yourselves bear me witness, that I said, I am not the Christ, but that I am sent before him.

29 He that has the bride is the bridegroom: but the friend of the bridegroom, which standeth and heareth him, rejoiceth greatly because of the bridegroom's voice: this my joy therefore is fulfilled.

30 He must increase, but I must decrease.

31 He that comes from above is above all: he that is of the earth is earthly, and speaketh of the earth: he that comes from heaven is above all.

32 And what he has seen and heard, that he testifieth; and no man receiveth his testimony.

33 He that has received his testimony has set to his seal that God is true.

34 For he whom God has sent speaketh the words of God: for God giveth not the Spirit by measure unto him.

35 The Father loveth the Son, and has given all things into his hand.

36 He that believeth on the Son has everlasting life: and he that believeth not the Son shall not see life; but the wrath of God abideth on him.

CHAPTER 4

WHEN therefore the Lord knew how the Pharisees had heard that Jesus made and baptized more disciples than John,

2 (Though Jesus himself baptized not, but his disciples,)

3 He left Judæa, and departed again into Galilee.

4 And he must needs go through Samaria.

5 Then comes he to a city of Samaria, which is called Sychar, near to the parcel of ground that Jacob gave to his son Joseph.

6 Now Jacob's well was there. Jesus therefore, being wearied with his journey, sat thus on the well: and it was about the sixth hour.

7 There comes a woman of Samaria to draw water: Jesus saith unto her, Give me to drink.

8 (For his disciples were gone away unto the city to buy meat.)

9 Then saith the woman of Samaria unto him, How is it that you, being a Jew, askest drink of me, which am a woman of Samaria? for the Jews have no dealings with the Samaritans.

10 Jesus answered and said unto her, If you knewest the gift of God, and who it is that saith to you, Give me to drink; you wouldest have asked of him, and he would have given you living water.

11 The woman saith unto him, Sir, you have nothing to draw with, and the well is deep: from whence then have you that living water?

12 Are you greater than our father Jacob, which gave us the well, and drank thereof himself, and his children, and his cattle?

13 Jesus answered and said unto her, Whosoever drinketh of this water shall thirst again:

14 But whosoever drinketh of the water that I shall give him shall never thirst; but the water that I shall give him shall be in him a well of water springing up into everlasting life.

15 The woman saith unto him, Sir, give me this water, that I thirst not, neither come hither to draw.

16 Jesus saith unto her, Go, call your husband, and come hither.

17 The woman answered and said, I have no husband. Jesus said unto her, You have well said, I have no husband:

18 For you have had five husbands; and he whom you now have is not your husband: in that saidst you truly.

19 The woman saith unto him, Sir, I perceive that you are a prophet.

20 Our fathers worshipped in this mountain; and you say, that in Jerusalem is the place where men ought to worship.

21 Jesus saith unto her, Woman, believe me, the hour comes, when you shall neither in this mountain, nor yet at Jerusalem, worship the Father.

22 You worship you know not what: we know what we worship: for salvation is of the Jews.

23 But the hour comes, and now is, when the true worshippers shall worship the Father in spirit and in truth: for the Father seeketh such to worship him.

24 God is a Spirit: and they that worship him must worship him in spirit and in truth.

25 The woman saith unto him, I know that Messias comes, which is called Christ: when he is come, he will tell us all things.

26 Jesus saith unto her, I that speak unto you am he.

27 And upon this came his disciples, and marvelled that he talked with the woman: yet no man said, What seekest you? or, Why talkest you with her?

28 The woman then left her waterpot, and went her way into the city, and saith to the men,

29 Come, see a man, which told me all things that ever I did: is not this the Christ?

30 Then they went out of the city, and came unto him.

31 In the mean while his disciples prayed him, saying, Master, eat.

32 But he said unto them, I have meat to eat that you know not of.

33 Therefore said the disciples one to another, Has any man brought him ought to eat?

34 Jesus saith unto them, My meat is to do the will of him that sent me, and to finish his work.

35 Say not you, There are yet four months, and then comes harvest? behold, I say unto you, Lift up your eyes, and look on the fields; for they are white already to harvest.

36 And he that reapeth receiveth wages, and gathereth fruit unto life eternal: that both he that soweth and he that reapeth may rejoice together.

37 And herein is that saying true, One soweth, and another reapeth.

38 I sent you to reap that whereon you bestowed no labour: other men laboured, and you are entered into their labours.

39 And many of the Samaritans of that city believed on him for the saying of the woman, which testified, He told me all that ever I did.

40 So when the Samaritans were come unto him, they besought him that he would tarry with them: and he abode there two days.

41 And many more believed because of his own word;

42 And said unto the woman, Now we believe, not because of your saying: for we have heard him ourselves, and know that this is indeed the Christ, the Saviour of the world.

43 Now after two days he departed thence, and went into Galilee.

44 For Jesus himself testified, that a prophet has no honour in his own country.

45 Then when he was come into Galilee, the Galilæans received him, having seen all the things that he did at Jerusalem at the feast: for they also went unto the feast.

46 So Jesus came again into Cana of Galilee, where he made the water wine. And there was a certain nobleman, whose son was sick at Capernaum.

47 When he heard that Jesus was come out of Judæa into Galilee, he went unto him, and besought him that he would come down, and heal his son: for he was at the point of death.

48 Then said Jesus unto him, Except you see signs and wonders, you will not believe.

49 The nobleman saith unto him, Sir, come down ere my child die.

50 Jesus saith unto him, Go your way; your son liveth. And the man believed the word that Jesus had spoken unto him, and he went his way.

51 And as he was now going down, his servants met him, and told him, saying, Your son liveth.

52 Then inquired he of them the hour when he began to amend. And they said unto him, Yesterday at the seventh hour the fever left him.

53 So the father knew that it was at the same hour, in the which Jesus said unto him, Your son liveth: and himself believed, and his whole house.

54 This is again the second miracle that Jesus did, when he was come out of Judæa into Galilee.

CHAPTER 5

AFTER this there was a feast of the Jews; and Jesus went up to Jerusalem.

2 Now there is at Jerusalem by the sheep market a pool, which is called in the Hebrew tongue Bethesda, having five porches.

3 In these lay a great multitude of impotent folk, of blind, halt, withered, waiting for the moving of the water.

4 For an angel went down at a certain season into the pool, and troubled the water: whosoever then first after the troubling of the water stepped in was made whole of whatsoever disease he had.

5 And a certain man was there, which had an infirmity thirty and eight years.

6 When Jesus saw him lie, and knew that he had been now a long time in that case, he saith unto him, Will you be made whole?

7 The impotent man answered him, Sir, I have no man, when the water is troubled, to put me into the pool: but while I am coming, another steppeth down before me.

8 Jesus saith unto him, Rise, take up your bed, and walk.

9 And immediately the man was made whole, and took up his bed, and walked: and on the same day was the sabbath.

10 The Jews therefore said unto him that was cured, It is the sabbath day: it is not lawful for you to carry your bed.

11 He answered them, He that made me whole, the same said unto me, Take up your bed, and walk.

12 Then asked they him, What man is that which said unto you, Take up your bed, and walk?

13 And he that was healed wist not who it was: for Jesus had conveyed himself away, a multitude being in that place.

14 Afterward Jesus findeth him in the temple, and said unto him, Behold, you are made whole: sin no more, lest a worse thing come unto you.

15 The man departed, and told the Jews that it was Jesus, which had made him whole.

16 And therefore did the Jews persecute Jesus, and sought to slay him, because he had done these things on the sabbath day.

17 But Jesus answered them, My Father worketh hitherto, and I work.

18 Therefore the Jews sought the more to kill him, because he not only had broken the sabbath, but said also that God was his Father, making himself equal with God.

19 Then answered Jesus and said unto them, Verily, verily, I say unto you, The Son can do nothing of himself, but what he seeth the Father do: for what things soever he doeth, these also doeth the Son likewise.

20 For the Father loveth the Son, and sheweth him all things that himself doeth: and he will shew him greater works than these, that you may marvel.

21 For as the Father raiseth up the dead, and quickeneth them; even so the Son quickeneth whom he will.

22 For the Father judgeth no man, but has committed all judgment unto the Son:

23 That all men should honour the Son, even as they honour the Father. He that honoureth not the Son honoureth not the Father which has sent him.

24 Verily, verily, I say unto you, He that heareth my word, and believeth on him that sent me, has everlasting life, and shall not come into condemnation; but is passed from death unto life.

25 Verily, verily, I say unto you, The hour is coming, and now is, when the dead shall hear the voice of the Son of God: and they that hear shall live.

26 For as the Father has life in himself; so has he given to the Son to have life in himself;

27 And has given him authority to execute judgment also, because he is the Son of man.

28 Marvel not at this: for the hour is coming, in the which all that are in the graves shall hear his voice,

29 And shall come forth; they that have done good, unto the resurrection of life; and they that have done evil, unto the resurrection of damnation.

30 I can of my own self do nothing: as I hear, I judge: and my judgment is just; because I seek not my own will, but the will of the Father which has sent me.

31 If I bear witness of myself, my witness is not true.

32 There is another that beareth witness of me; and I know that the witness which he witnesseth of me is true.

33 You sent unto John, and he bare witness unto the truth.

34 But I receive not testimony from man: but these things I say, that you might be saved.

35 He was a burning and a shining light: and you were willing for a season to rejoice in his light.

36 But I have greater witness than that of John: for the works which the Father has given me to finish, the same works that I do, bear witness of me, that the Father has sent me.

37 And the Father himself, which has sent me, has borne witness of me. You have neither heard his voice at any time, nor seen his shape.

38 And you have not his word abiding in you: for whom he has sent, him you believe not.

39 Search the scriptures; for in them you think you have eternal life: and they are they which testify of me.

40 And you will not come to me, that you might have life.

41 I receive not honour from men.

42 But I know you, that you have not the love of God in you.

43 I am come in my Father's name, and you receive me not: if another shall come in his own name, him you will receive.

44 How can you believe, which receive honour one of another, and seek not the honour that comes from God only?

45 Do not think that I will accuse you to the Father: there is one that accuseth you, even Moses, in whom you trust.

46 For had you believed Moses, you would have believed me: for he wrote of me.

47 But if you believe not his writings, how shall you believe my words?

CHAPTER 6

AFTER these things Jesus went over the sea of Galilee, which is the sea of Tiberias.

2 And a great multitude followed him, because they saw his miracles which he did on them that were diseased.

3 And Jesus went up into a mountain, and there he sat with his disciples.

4 And the passover, a feast of the Jews, was nigh.

5 When Jesus then lifted up his eyes, and saw a great company come unto him, he saith unto Philip, Whence shall we buy bread, that these may eat?

6 And this he said to prove him: for he himself knew what he would do.

7 Philip answered him, Two hundred pennyworth of bread is not sufficient for them, that every one of them may take a little.

8 One of his disciples, Andrew, Simon Peter's brother, saith unto him,

9 There is a lad here, which has five barley loaves, and two small fishes: but what are they among so many?

10 And Jesus said, Make the men sit down. Now there was much grass in the place. So the men sat down, in number about five thousand.

11 And Jesus took the loaves; and when he had given thanks, he distributed to the disciples, and the disciples to them that were set down; and likewise of the fishes as much as they would.

12 When they were filled, he said unto his disciples, Gather up the fragments that remain, that nothing be lost.

13 Therefore they gathered them together, and filled twelve baskets with the fragments of the five barley loaves, which remained over and above unto them that had eaten.

14 Then those men, when they had seen the miracle that Jesus did, said, This is of a truth that prophet that should come into the world.

15When Jesus therefore perceived that they would come and take him by force, to make him a king, he departed again into a mountain himself alone.

16 And when even was now come, his disciples went down unto the sea,

17 And entered into a ship, and went over the sea toward Capernaum. And it was now dark, and Jesus was not come to them.

18 And the sea arose by reason of a great wind that blew.

19 So when they had rowed about five and twenty or thirty furlongs, they see Jesus walking on the sea, and drawing nigh unto the ship: and they were afraid.

20 But he saith unto them, It is I; be not afraid.

21 Then they willingly received him into the ship: and immediately the ship was at the land whither they went.

22The day following, when the people which stood on the other side of the sea saw that there was none other boat there, save that one whereinto his disciples were entered, and that Jesus went not with his disciples into the boat, but that his disciples were gone away alone;

23 (Howbeit there came other boats from Tiberias nigh unto the place where they did eat bread, after that the Lord had given thanks:)

24 When the people therefore saw that Jesus was not there, neither his disciples, they also took shipping, and came to Capernaum, seeking for Jesus.

25 And when they had found him on the other side of the sea, they said unto him, Rabbi, when camest you hither?

26 Jesus answered them and said, Verily, verily, I say unto you, You seek me, not because you saw the miracles, but because you did eat of the loaves, and were filled.

27 Labour not for the meat which perisheth, but for that meat which endureth unto everlasting life, which the Son of man shall give unto you: for him has God the Father sealed.

28 Then said they unto him, What shall we do, that we might work the works of God?

29 Jesus answered and said unto them, This is the work of God, that you believe on him whom he has sent.

30 They said therefore unto him, What sign shewest you then, that we may see, and believe you? what dost you work?

31 Our fathers did eat manna in the desert; as it is written, He gave them bread from heaven to eat.

32 Then Jesus said unto them, Verily, verily, I say unto you, Moses gave you not that bread from heaven; but my Father giveth you the true bread from heaven.

33 For the bread of God is he which comes down from heaven, and giveth life unto the world.

34 Then said they unto him, Lord, evermore give us this bread.

35 And Jesus said unto them, I am the bread of life: he that comes to me shall never hunger; and he that believeth on me shall never thirst.

36 But I said unto you, That you also have seen me, and believe not.

37 All that the Father giveth me shall come to me; and him that comes to me I will in no wise cast out.

38 For I came down from heaven, not to do my own will, but the will of him that sent me.

39 And this is the Father's will which has sent me, that of all which he has given me I should lose nothing, but should raise it up again at the last day.

40 And this is the will of him that sent me, that every one which seeth the Son, and believeth on him, may have everlasting life: and I will raise him up at the last day.

41 The Jews then murmured at him, because he said, I am the bread which came down from heaven.

42 And they said, Is not this Jesus, the son of Joseph, whose father and mother we know? how is it then that he saith, I came down from heaven?

43 Jesus therefore answered and said unto them, Murmur not among yourselves.

44 No man can come to me, except the Father which has sent me draw him: and I will raise him up at the last day.

45 It is written in the prophets, And they shall be all taught of God. Every man therefore that has heard, and has learned of the Father, comes unto me.

46 Not that any man has seen the Father, save he which is of God, he has seen the Father.

47 Verily, verily, I say unto you, He that believeth on me has everlasting life.

48 I am that bread of life.

49 Your fathers did eat manna in the wilderness, and are dead.

50 This is the bread which comes down from heaven, that a man may eat thereof, and not die.

51 I am the living bread which came down from heaven: if any man eat of this bread, he shall live for ever: and the bread that I will give is my flesh, which I will give for the life of the world.

52 The Jews therefore strove among themselves, saying, How can this man give us his flesh to eat?

53 Then Jesus said unto them, Verily, verily, I say unto you, Except you eat the flesh of the Son of man, and drink his blood, you have no life in you.

54 Whoso eateth my flesh, and drinketh my blood, has eternal life; and I will raise him up at the last day.

55 For my flesh is meat indeed, and my blood is drink indeed.

56 He that eateth my flesh, and drinketh my blood, dwelleth in me, and I in him.

57 As the living Father has sent me, and I live by the Father: so he that eateth me, even he shall live by me.

58 This is that bread which came down from heaven: not as your fathers did eat manna, and are dead: he that eateth of this bread shall live for ever.

59 These things said he in the synagogue, as he taught in Capernaum.

60 Many therefore of his disciples, when they had heard this, said, This is an hard saying; who can hear it?

61 When Jesus knew in himself that his disciples murmured at it, he said unto them, Doth this offend you?

62 What and if you shall see the Son of man ascend up where he was before?

63 It is the spirit that quickeneth; the flesh profiteth nothing: the words that I speak unto you, they are spirit, and they are life.

64 But there are some of you that believe not. For Jesus knew from the beginning who they were that believed not, and who should betray him.

65 And he said, Therefore said I unto you, that no man can come unto me, except it were given unto him of my Father.

66From that time many of his disciples went back, and walked no more with him.

67 Then said Jesus unto the twelve, Will you also go away?

68 Then Simon Peter answered him, Lord, to whom shall we go? you have the words of eternal life.

69 And we believe and are sure that you are that Christ, the Son of the living God.

70 Jesus answered them, Have not I chosen you twelve, and one of you is a devil?

71 He spake of Judas Iscariot the son of Simon: for he it was that should betray him, being one of the twelve.

CHAPTER 7

AFTER these things Jesus walked in Galilee: for he would not walk in Jewry, because the Jews sought to kill him.

2 Now the Jews' feast of tabernacles was at hand.

3 His brethren therefore said unto him, Depart hence, and go into Judæa, that your disciples also may see the works that you doest.

4 For there is no man that doeth any thing in secret, and he himself seeketh to be known openly. If you do these things, shew yourself to the world.

5 For neither did his brethren believe in him.

6 Then Jesus said unto them, My time is not yet come: but your time is alway ready.

7 The world cannot hate you; but me it hateth, because I testify of it, that the works thereof are evil.

8 Go you up unto this feast: I go not up yet unto this feast; for my time is not yet full come.

9 When he had said these words unto them, he abode still in Galilee.

10But when his brethren were gone up, then went he also up unto the feast, not openly, but as it were in secret.

11 Then the Jews sought him at the feast, and said, Where is he?

12 And there was much murmuring among the people concerning him: for some said, He is a good man: others said, Nay; but he deceiveth the people.

13 Howbeit no man spake openly of him for fear of the Jews.

14Now about the midst of the feast Jesus went up into the temple, and taught.

15 And the Jews marvelled, saying, How knoweth this man letters, having never learned?

16 Jesus answered them, and said, My doctrine is not my, but his that sent me.

17 If any man will do his will, he shall know of the doctrine, whether it be of God, or whether I speak of myself.

18 He that speaketh of himself seeketh his own glory: but he that seeketh his glory that sent him, the same is true, and no unrighteousness is in him.

19 Did not Moses give you the law, and yet none of you keepeth the law? Why go you about to kill me?

20 The people answered and said, You have a devil: who goeth about to kill you?

21 Jesus answered and said unto them, I have done one work, and you all marvel.

22 Moses therefore gave unto you circumcision; (not because it is of Moses, but of the fathers;) and you on the sabbath day circumcise a man.

23 If a man on the sabbath day receive circumcision, that the law of Moses should not be broken; are you angry at me, because I have made a man every whit whole on the sabbath day?

24 Judge not according to the appearance, but judge righteous judgment.

25 Then said some of them of Jerusalem, Is not this he, whom they seek to kill?

26 But, lo, he speaketh boldly, and they say nothing unto him. Do the rulers know indeed that this is the very Christ?

27 Howbeit we know this man whence he is: but when Christ comes, no man knoweth whence he is.

28 Then cried Jesus in the temple as he taught, saying, You both know me, and you know whence I am: and I am not come of myself, but he that sent me is true, whom you know not.

29 But I know him: for I am from him, and he has sent me.

30 Then they sought to take him: but no man laid hands on him, because his hour was not yet come.

31 And many of the people believed on him, and said, When Christ comes, will he do more miracles than these which this man has done?

32 The Pharisees heard that the people murmured such things concerning him; and the Pharisees and the chief priests sent officers to take him.

33 Then said Jesus unto them, Yet a little while am I with you, and then I go unto him that sent me.

34 You shall seek me, and shall not find me: and where I am, thither you cannot come.

35 Then said the Jews among themselves, Whither will he go, that we shall not find him? will he go unto the dispersed among the Gentiles, and teach the Gentiles?

36 What manner of saying is this that he said, You shall seek me, and shall not find me: and where I am, thither you cannot come?

37 In the last day, that great day of the feast, Jesus stood and cried, saying, If any man thirst, let him come unto me, and drink.

38 He that believeth on me, as the scripture has said, out of his belly shall flow rivers of living water.

39 (But this spake he of the Spirit, which they that believe on him should receive: for the Holy Ghost was not yet given; because that Jesus was not yet glorified.)

40 Many of the people therefore, when they heard this saying, said, Of a truth this is the Prophet.

41 Others said, This is the Christ. But some said, Shall Christ come out of Galilee?

42 Has not the scripture said, That Christ comes of the seed of David, and out of the town of Bethlehem, where David was?

43 So there was a division among the people because of him.

44 And some of them would have taken him; but no man laid hands on him.

45 Then came the officers to the chief priests and Pharisees; and they said unto them, Why have you not brought him?

46 The officers answered, Never man spake like this man.

47 Then answered them the Pharisees, Are you also deceived?

48 Have any of the rulers or of the Pharisees believed on him?

49 But this people who knoweth not the law are cursed.

50 Nicodemus saith unto them, (he that came to Jesus by night, being one of them,)

51 Doth our law judge any man, before it hear him, and know what he doeth?

52 They answered and said unto him, Are you also of Galilee? Search, and look: for out of Galilee ariseth no prophet.

53 And every man went unto his own house.

CHAPTER 8

JESUS went unto the mount of Olives.

2 And early in the morning he came again into the temple, and all the people came unto him; and he sat down, and taught them.

3 And the scribes and Pharisees brought unto him a woman taken in adultery; and when they had set her in the midst,

4 They say unto him, Master, this woman was taken in adultery, in the very act.

5 Now Moses in the law commanded us, that such should be stoned: but what say you?

6 This they said, tempting him, that they might have to accuse him. But Jesus stooped down, and with his finger wrote on the ground, as though he heard them not.

7 So when they continued asking him, he lifted up himself, and said unto them, He that is without sin among you, let him first cast a stone at her.

8 And again he stooped down, and wrote on the ground.

9 And they which heard it, being convicted by their own conscience, went out one by one, beginning at the eldest, even unto the last: and Jesus was left alone, and the woman standing in the midst.

10 When Jesus had lifted up himself, and saw none but the woman, he said unto her, Woman, where are those yours accusers? has no man condemned you?

11 She said, No man, Lord. And Jesus said unto her, Neither do I condemn you: go, and sin no more.

12 Then spake Jesus again unto them, saying, I am the light of the world: he that followeth me shall not walk in darkness, but shall have the light of life.

13 The Pharisees therefore said unto him, You bearest record of yourself; your record is not true.

14 Jesus answered and said unto them, Though I bear record of myself, yet my record is true: for I know whence I came, and whither I go; but you cannot tell whence I come, and whither I go.

15 You judge after the flesh; I judge no man.

16 And yet if I judge, my judgment is true: for I am not alone, but I and the Father that sent me.

17 It is also written in your law, that the testimony of two men is true.

18 I am one that bear witness of myself, and the Father that sent me beareth witness of me.

19 Then said they unto him, Where is your Father? Jesus answered, You neither know me, nor my Father: if you had known me, you should have known my Father also.

20 These words spake Jesus in the treasury, as he taught in the temple: and no man laid hands on him; for his hour was not yet come.

21 Then said Jesus again unto them, I go my way, and you shall seek me, and shall die in your sins: whither I go, you cannot come.

22 Then said the Jews, Will he kill himself? because he saith, Whither I go, you cannot come.

23 And he said unto them, You are from beneath; I am from above: you are of this world; I am not of this world.

24 I said therefore unto you, that you shall die in your sins: for if you believe not that I am he, you shall die in your sins.

25 Then said they unto him, Who are you? And Jesus saith unto them, Even the same that I said unto you from the beginning.

26 I have many things to say and to judge of you: but he that sent me is true; and I speak to the world those things which I have heard of him.

27 They understood not that he spake to them of the Father.

28 Then said Jesus unto them, When you have lifted up the Son of man, then shall you know that I am he, and that I do nothing of myself; but as my Father has taught me, I speak these things.

29 And he that sent me is with me: the Father has not left me alone; for I do always those things that please him.

30 As he spake these words, many believed on him.

31 Then said Jesus to those Jews which believed on him, If you continue in my word, then are you my disciples indeed;

32 And you shall know the truth, and the truth shall make you free.

33 They answered him, We be Abraham's seed, and were never in bondage to any man: how say you, You shall be made free?

34 Jesus answered them, Verily, verily, I say unto you, Whosoever committeth sin is the servant of sin.

35 And the servant abideth not in the house for ever: but the Son abideth ever.

36 If the Son therefore shall make you free, you shall be free indeed.

37 I know that you are Abraham's seed; but you seek to kill me, because my word has no place in you.

38 I speak that which I have seen with my Father: and you do that which you have seen with your father.

39 They answered and said unto him, Abraham is our father. Jesus saith unto them, If you were Abraham's children, you would do the works of Abraham.

40 But now you seek to kill me, a man that has told you the truth, which I have heard of God: this did not Abraham.

41 You do the deeds of your father. Then said they to him, We be not born of fornication; we have one Father, even God.

42 Jesus said unto them, If God were your Father, you would love me: for I proceeded forth and came from God; neither came I of myself, but he sent me.

43 Why do you not understand my speech? even because you cannot hear my word.

44 You are of your father the devil, and the lusts of your father you will do. He was a murderer from the beginning, and abode not in the truth, because there is no truth in him. When he speaketh a lie, he speaketh of his own: for he is a liar, and the father of it.

45 And because I tell you the truth, you believe me not.

46 Which of you convinceth me of sin? And if I say the truth, why do you not believe me?

47 He that is of God heareth God's words: you therefore hear them not, because you are not of God.

48 Then answered the Jews, and said unto him, Say we not well that you are a Samaritan, and have a devil?

49 Jesus answered, I have not a devil; but I honour my Father, and you do dishonour me.

50 And I seek not my own glory: there is one that seeketh and judgeth.

51 Verily, verily, I say unto you, If a man keep my saying, he shall never see death.

52 Then said the Jews unto him, Now we know that you have a devil. Abraham is dead, and the prophets; and you say, If a man keep my saying, he shall never taste of death.

53 Are you greater than our father Abraham, which is dead? and the prophets are dead: whom makest you yourself?

54 Jesus answered, If I honour myself, my honour is nothing: it is my Father that honoureth me; of whom you say, that he is your God:

55 Yet you have not known him; but I know him: and if I should say, I know him not, I shall be a liar like unto you: but I know him, and keep his saying.

56 Your father Abraham rejoiced to see my day: and he saw it, and was glad.

57 Then said the Jews unto him, You are not yet fifty years old, and have you seen Abraham?

58 Jesus said unto them, Verily, verily, I say unto you, Before Abraham was, I am.

59 Then took they up stones to cast at him: but Jesus hid himself, and went out of the temple, going through the midst of them, and so passed by.

CHAPTER 9

AND as Jesus passed by, he saw a man which was blind from his birth.

2 And his disciples asked him, saying, Master, who did sin, this man, or his parents, that he was born blind?

3 Jesus answered, Neither has this man sinned, nor his parents: but that the works of God should be made manifest in him.

4 I must work the works of him that sent me, while it is day: the night comes, when no man can work.

5 As long as I am in the world, I am the light of the world.

6 When he had thus spoken, he spat on the ground, and made clay of the spittle, and he anointed the eyes of the blind man with the clay,

7 And said unto him, Go, wash in the pool of Siloam, (which is by interpretation, Sent.) He went his way therefore, and washed, and came seeing.

8 The neighbours therefore, and they which before had seen him that he was blind, said, Is not this he that sat and begged?

9 Some said, This is he: others said, He is like him: but he said, I am he.

10 Therefore said they unto him, How were yours eyes opened?

11 He answered and said, A man that is called Jesus made clay, and anointed my eyes, and said unto me, Go to the pool of Siloam, and wash: and I went and washed, and I received sight.

12 Then said they unto him, Where is he? He said, I know not.

13 They brought to the Pharisees him that aforetime was blind.

14 And it was the sabbath day when Jesus made the clay, and opened his eyes.

15 Then again the Pharisees also asked him how he had received his sight. He said unto them, He put clay upon my eyes, and I washed, and do see.

16 Therefore said some of the Pharisees, This man is not of God, because he keepeth not the sabbath day. Others said, How can a man that is a sinner do such miracles? And there was a division among them.

17 They say unto the blind man again, What say you of him, that he has opened yours eyes? He said, He is a prophet.

18 But the Jews did not believe concerning him, that he had been blind, and received his sight, until they called the parents of him that had received his sight.

19 And they asked them, saying, Is this your son, who you say was born blind? how then doth he now see?

20 His parents answered them and said, We know that this is our son, and that he was born blind:

21 But by what means he now seeth, we know not; or who has opened his eyes, we know not: he is of age; ask him: he shall speak for himself.

22 These words spake his parents, because they feared the Jews: for the Jews had agreed already, that if any man did confess that he was Christ, he should be put out of the synagogue.

23 Therefore said his parents, He is of age; ask him.

24 Then again called they the man that was blind, and said unto him, Give God the praise: we know that this man is a sinner.

25 He answered and said, Whether he be a sinner or no, I know not: one thing I know, that, whereas I was blind, now I see.

26 Then said they to him again, What did he to you? how opened yours eyes?

27 He answered them, I have told you already, and you did not hear: wherefore would you hear it again? will you also be his disciples?

28 Then they reviled him, and said, You are his disciple; but we are Moses' disciples.

29 We know that God spake unto Moses: as for this fellow, we know not from whence he is.

30 The man answered and said unto them, Why herein is a marvellous thing, that you know not from whence he is, and yet he has opened my eyes.

31 Now we know that God heareth not sinners: but if any man be a worshipper of God, and doeth his will, him he heareth.

32 Since the world began was it not heard that any man opened the eyes of one that was born blind.

33 If this man were not of God, he could do nothing.

34 They answered and said unto him, You wast altogether born in sins, and dost you teach us? And they cast him out.

35 Jesus heard that they had cast him out; and when he had found him, he said unto him, Dost you believe on the Son of God?

36 He answered and said, Who is he, Lord, that I might believe on him?

37 And Jesus said unto him, You have both seen him, and it is he that talketh with you.

38 And he said, Lord, I believe. And he worshipped him.

39 And Jesus said, For judgment I am come into this world, that they which see not might see; and that they which see might be made blind.

40 And some of the Pharisees which were with him heard these words, and said unto him, Are we blind also?

41 Jesus said unto them, If you were blind, you should have no sin: but now you say, We see; therefore your sin remaineth.

CHAPTER 10

VERILY, verily, I say unto you, He that entereth not by the door into the sheepfold, but climbeth up some other way, the same is a thief and a robber.

2 But he that entereth in by the door is the shepherd of the sheep.

3 To him the porter openeth; and the sheep hear his voice: and he calleth his own sheep by name, and leadeth them out.

4 And when he putteth forth his own sheep, he goeth before them, and the sheep follow him: for they know his voice.

5 And a stranger will they not follow, but will flee from him: for they know not the voice of strangers.

6 This parable spake Jesus unto them: but they understood not what things they were which he spake unto them.

7 Then said Jesus unto them again, Verily, verily, I say unto you, I am the door of the sheep.

8 All that ever came before me are thieves and robbers: but the sheep did not hear them.

9 I am the door: by me if any man enter in, he shall be saved, and shall go in and out, and find pasture.

10 The thief comes not, but for to steal, and to kill, and to destroy: I am come that they might have life, and that they might have it more abundantly.

11 I am the good shepherd: the good shepherd giveth his life for the sheep.

12 But he that is an hireling, and not the shepherd, whose own the sheep are not, seeth the wolf coming, and leaveth the sheep, and fleeth: and the wolf catcheth them, and scattereth the sheep.

13 The hireling fleeth, because he is an hireling, and careth not for the sheep.

14 I am the good shepherd, and know my sheep, and am known of my.

15 As the Father knoweth me, even so know I the Father: and I lay down my life for the sheep.

16 And other sheep I have, which are not of this fold: them also I must bring, and they shall hear my voice; and there shall be one fold, and one shepherd.

17 Therefore doth my Father love me, because I lay down my life, that I might take it again.

18 No man taketh it from me, but I lay it down of myself. I have power to lay it down, and I have power to take it again. This commandment have I received of my Father.

19 There was a division therefore again among the Jews for these sayings.

20 And many of them said, He has a devil, and is mad; why hear you him?

21 Others said, These are not the words of him that has a devil. Can a devil open the eyes of the blind?

22 And it was at Jerusalem the feast of the dedication, and it was winter.

23 And Jesus walked in the temple in Solomon's porch.

24 Then came the Jews round about him, and said unto him, How long dost you make us to doubt? If you be the Christ, tell us plainly.

25 Jesus answered them, I told you, and you believed not: the works that I do in my Father's name, they bear witness of me.

26 But you believe not, because you are not of my sheep, as I said unto you.

27 My sheep hear my voice, and I know them, and they follow me:

28 And I give unto them eternal life; and they shall never perish, neither shall any man pluck them out of my hand.

29 My Father, which gave them me, is greater than all; and no man is able to pluck them out of my Father's hand.

30 I and my Father are one.

31 Then the Jews took up stones again to stone him.

32 Jesus answered them, Many good works have I shewed you from my Father; for which of those works do you stone me?

33 The Jews answered him, saying, For a good work we stone you not; but for blasphemy; and because that you , being a man, makest yourself God.

34 Jesus answered them, Is it not written in your law, I said, You are gods?

35 If he called them gods, unto whom the word of God came, and the scripture cannot be broken;

36 Say you of him, whom the Father has sanctified, and sent into the world, You blasphemest; because I said, I am the Son of God?

37 If I do not the works of my Father, believe me not.

38 But if I do, though you believe not me, believe the works: that you may know, and believe, that the Father is in me, and I in him.

39 Therefore they sought again to take him: but he escaped out of their hand,

40 And went away again beyond Jordan into the place where John at first baptized; and there he abode.

41 And many resorted unto him, and said, John did no miracle: but all things that John spake of this man were true.

42 And many believed on him there.

CHAPTER 11

NOW a certain man was sick, named Lazarus, of Bethany, the town of Mary and her sister Martha.

2 (It was that Mary which anointed the Lord with ointment, and wiped his feet with her hair, whose brother Lazarus was sick.)

3 Therefore his sisters sent unto him, saying, Lord, behold, he whom you lovest is sick.

4 When Jesus heard that, he said, This sickness is not unto death, but for the glory of God, that the Son of God might be glorified thereby.

5 Now Jesus loved Martha, and her sister, and Lazarus.

6 When he had heard therefore that he was sick, he abode two days still in the same place where he was.

7 Then after that saith he to his disciples, Let us go into Judæa again.

8 His disciples say unto him, Master, the Jews of late sought to stone you; and go you thither again?

9 Jesus answered, Are there not twelve hours in the day? If any man walk in the day, he stumbleth not, because he seeth the light of this world.

10 But if a man walk in the night, he stumbleth, because there is no light in him.

11 These things said he: and after that he saith unto them, Our friend Lazarus sleepeth; but I go, that I may awake him out of sleep.

12 Then said his disciples, Lord, if he sleep, he shall do well.

13 Howbeit Jesus spake of his death: but they thought that he had spoken of taking of rest in sleep.

14 Then said Jesus unto them plainly, Lazarus is dead.

15 And I am glad for your sakes that I was not there, to the intent you may believe; nevertheless let us go unto him.

16 Then said Thomas, which is called Didymus, unto his fellowdisciples, Let us also go, that we may die with him.

17 Then when Jesus came, he found that he had lain in the grave four days already.

18 Now Bethany was nigh unto Jerusalem, about fifteen furlongs off:

19 And many of the Jews came to Martha and Mary, to comfort them concerning their brother.

20 Then Martha, as soon as she heard that Jesus was coming, went and met him: but Mary sat still in the house.

21 Then said Martha unto Jesus, Lord, if you hadst been here, my brother had not died.

22 But I know, that even now, whatsoever you will ask of God, God will give it you.

23 Jesus saith unto her, Your brother shall rise again.

24 Martha saith unto him, I know that he shall rise again in the resurrection at the last day.

25 Jesus said unto her, I am the resurrection, and the life: he that believeth in me, though he were dead, yet shall he live:

26 And whosoever liveth and believeth in me shall never die. Believest you this?

27 She saith unto him, Yea, Lord: I believe that you are the Christ, the Son of God, which should come into the world.

28 And when she had so said, she went her way, and called Mary her sister secretly, saying, The Master is come, and calleth for you.

29 As soon as she heard that, she arose quickly, and came unto him.

30 Now Jesus was not yet come into the town, but was in that place where Martha met him.

31 The Jews then which were with her in the house, and comforted her, when they saw Mary, that she rose up hastily and went out, followed her, saying, She goeth unto the grave to weep there.

32 Then when Mary was come where Jesus was, and saw him, she fell down at his feet, saying unto him, Lord, if you hadst been here, my brother had not died.

33 When Jesus therefore saw her weeping, and the Jews also weeping which came with her, he groaned in the spirit, and was troubled,

34 And said, Where have you laid him? They said unto him, Lord, come and see.

35 Jesus wept.

36 Then said the Jews, Behold how he loved him!

37 And some of them said, Could not this man, which opened the eyes of the blind, have caused that even this man should not have died?

38 Jesus therefore again groaning in himself comes to the grave. It was a cave, and a stone lay upon it.

39 Jesus said, Take you away the stone. Martha, the sister of him that was dead, saith unto him, Lord, by this time he stinketh: for he has been dead four days.

40 Jesus saith unto her, Said I not unto you, that, if you wouldest believe, you shouldest see the glory of God?

41 Then they took away the stone from the place where the dead was laid. And Jesus lifted up his eyes, and said, Father, I thank you that you have heard me.

42 And I knew that you hearest me always: but because of the people which stand by I said it, that they may believe that you have sent me.

43 And when he thus had spoken, he cried with a loud voice, Lazarus, come forth.

44 And he that was dead came forth, bound hand and foot with graveclothes: and his face was bound about with a napkin. Jesus saith unto them, Loose him, and let him go.

45 Then many of the Jews which came to Mary, and had seen the things which Jesus did, believed on him.

46 But some of them went their ways to the Pharisees, and told them what things Jesus had done.

47 Then gathered the chief priests and the Pharisees a council, and said, What do we? for this man doeth many miracles.

48 If we let him thus alone, all men will believe on him: and the Romans shall come and take away both our place and nation.

49 And one of them, named Caiaphas, being the high priest that same year, said unto them, You know nothing at all,

50 Nor consider that it is expedient for us, that one man should die for the people, and that the whole nation perish not.

51 And this spake he not of himself: but being high priest that year, he prophesied that Jesus should die for that nation;

52 And not for that nation only, but that also he should gather together in one the children of God that were scattered abroad.

53 Then from that day forth they took counsel together for to put him to death.

54 Jesus therefore walked no more openly among the Jews; but went thence unto a country near to the wilderness, into a city called Ephraim, and there continued with his disciples.

55 And the Jews' passover was nigh at hand: and many went out of the country up to Jerusalem before the passover, to purify themselves.

56 Then sought they for Jesus, and spake among themselves, as they stood in the temple, What think you , that he will not come to the feast?

57 Now both the chief priests and the Pharisees had given a commandment, that, if any man knew where he were, he should shew it, that they might take him.

CHAPTER 12

THEN Jesus six days before the passover came to Bethany, where Lazarus was which had been dead, whom he raised from the dead.

2 There they made him a supper; and Martha served: but Lazarus was one of them that sat at the table with him.

3 Then took Mary a pound of ointment of spikenard, very costly, and anointed the feet of Jesus, and wiped his feet with her hair: and the house was filled with the odour of the ointment.

4 Then saith one of his disciples, Judas Iscariot, Simon's son, which should betray him,

5 Why was not this ointment sold for three hundred pence, and given to the poor?

6 This he said, not that he cared for the poor; but because he was a thief, and had the bag, and bare what was put therein.

7 Then said Jesus, Let her alone: against the day of my burying has she kept this.

8 For the poor always you have with you; but me you have not always.

9 Much people of the Jews therefore knew that he was there: and they came not for Jesus' sake only, but that they might see Lazarus also, whom he had raised from the dead.

10But the chief priests consulted that they might put Lazarus also to death;

11 Because that by reason of him many of the Jews went away, and believed on Jesus.

12On the next day much people that were come to the feast, when they heard that Jesus was coming to Jerusalem,

13 Took branches of palm trees, and went forth to meet him, and cried, Hosanna: Blessed is the King of Israel that comes in the name of the Lord.

14 And Jesus, when he had found a young ass, sat thereon; as it is written,

15 Fear not, daughter of Sion: behold, your King comes, sitting on an ass's colt.

16 These things understood not his disciples at the first: but when Jesus was glorified, then remembered they that these things were written of him, and that they had done these things unto him.

17 The people therefore that was with him when he called Lazarus out of his grave, and raised him from the dead, bare record.

18 For this cause the people also met him, for that they heard that he had done this miracle.

19 The Pharisees therefore said among themselves, Perceive you how you prevail nothing? behold, the world is gone after him.

20And there were certain Greeks among them that came up to worship at the feast:

21 The same came therefore to Philip, which was of Bethsaida of Galilee, and desired him, saying, Sir, we would see Jesus.

22 Philip comes and telleth Andrew: and again Andrew and Philip tell Jesus.

23And Jesus answered them, saying, The hour is come, that the Son of man should be glorified.

24 Verily, verily, I say unto you, Except a corn of wheat fall into the ground and die, it abideth alone: but if it die, it bringeth forth much fruit.

25 He that loveth his life shall lose it; and he that hateth his life in this world shall keep it unto life eternal.

26 If any man serve me, let him follow me; and where I am, there shall also my servant be: if any man serve me, him will my Father honour.

27 Now is my soul troubled; and what shall I say? Father, save me from this hour: but for this cause came I unto this hour.

28 Father, glorify your name. Then came there a voice from heaven, saying, I have both glorified it, and will glorify it again.

29 The people therefore, that stood by, and heard it, said that it thundered: others said, An angel spake to him.

30 Jesus answered and said, This voice came not because of me, but for your sakes.

31 Now is the judgment of this world: now shall the prince of this world be cast out.

32 And I, if I be lifted up from the earth, will draw all men unto me.

33 This he said, signifying what death he should die.

34 The people answered him, We have heard out of the law that Christ abideth for ever: and how say you , The Son of man must be lifted up? who is this Son of man?

35 Then Jesus said unto them, Yet a little while is the light with you. Walk while you have the light, lest darkness come upon you: for he that walketh in darkness knoweth not whither he goeth.

36 While you have light, believe in the light, that you may be the children of light. These things spake Jesus, and departed, and did hide himself from them.

37But though he had done so many miracles before them, yet they believed not on him:

38 That the saying of Esaias the prophet might be fulfilled, which he spake, Lord, who has believed our report? and to whom has the arm of the Lord been revealed?

39 Therefore they could not believe, because that Esaias said again,

40 He has blinded their eyes, and hardened their heart; that they should not see with their eyes, nor understand with their heart, and be converted, and I should heal them.

41 These things said Esaias, when he saw his glory, and spake of him.

42Nevertheless among the chief rulers also many believed on him; but because of the Pharisees they did not confess him, lest they should be put out of the synagogue:

43 For they loved the praise of men more than the praise of God.

44Jesus cried and said, He that believeth on me, believeth not on me, but on him that sent me.

45 And he that seeth me seeth him that sent me.

46 I am come a light into the world, that whosoever believeth on me should not abide in darkness.

47 And if any man hear my words, and believe not, I judge him not: for I came not to judge the world, but to save the world.

48 He that rejecteth me, and receiveth not my words, has one that judgeth him: the word that I have spoken, the same shall judge him in the last day.

49 For I have not spoken of myself; but the Father which sent me, he gave me a commandment, what I should say, and what I should speak.

50 And I know that his commandment is life everlasting: whatsoever I speak therefore, even as the Father said unto me, so I speak.

CHAPTER 13

NOW before the feast of the passover, when Jesus knew that his hour was come that he should depart out of this world unto the Father, having loved his own which were in the world, he loved them unto the end.

2 And supper being ended, the devil having now put into the heart of Judas Iscariot, Simon's son, to betray him;

3 Jesus knowing that the Father had given all things into his hands, and that he was come from God, and went to God;

4 He riseth from supper, and laid aside his garments; and took a towel, and girded himself.

5 After that he poureth water into a bason, and began to wash the disciples' feet, and to wipe them with the towel wherewith he was girded.

6 Then comes he to Simon Peter: and Peter saith unto him, Lord, dost you wash my feet?

7 Jesus answered and said unto him, What I do you knowest not now; but you shalt know hereafter.

8 Peter saith unto him, You shalt never wash my feet. Jesus answered him, If I wash you not, you have no part with me.

9 Simon Peter saith unto him, Lord, not my feet only, but also my hands and my head.

10 Jesus saith to him, He that is washed needeth not save to wash his feet, but is clean every whit: and you are clean, but not all.

11 For he knew who should betray him; therefore said he, You are not all clean.

12 So after he had washed their feet, and had taken his garments, and was set down again, he said unto them, Know you what I have done to you?

13 You call me Master and Lord: and you say well; for so I am.

14 If I then, your Lord and Master, have washed your feet; you also ought to wash one another's feet.

15 For I have given you an example, that you should do as I have done to you.

16 Verily, verily, I say unto you, The servant is not greater than his lord; neither he that is sent greater than he that sent him.

17 If you know these things, happy are you if you do them.

18I speak not of you all: I know whom I have chosen: but that the scripture may be fulfilled, He that eateth bread with me has lifted up his heel against me.

19 Now I tell you before it come, that, when it is come to pass, you may believe that I am he.

20 Verily, verily, I say unto you, He that receiveth whomsoever I send receiveth me; and he that receiveth me receiveth him that sent me.

21 When Jesus had thus said, he was troubled in spirit, and testified, and said, Verily, verily, I say unto you, that one of you shall betray me.

22 Then the disciples looked one on another, doubting of whom he spake.

23 Now there was leaning on Jesus' bosom one of his disciples, whom Jesus loved.

24 Simon Peter therefore beckoned to him, that he should ask who it should be of whom he spake.

25 He then lying on Jesus' breast saith unto him, Lord, who is it?

26 Jesus answered, He it is, to whom I shall give a sop, when I have dipped it. And when he had dipped the sop, he gave it to Judas Iscariot, the son of Simon.

27 And after the sop Satan entered into him. Then said Jesus unto him, That you doest, do quickly.

28 Now no man at the table knew for what intent he spake this unto him.

29 For some of them thought, because Judas had the bag, that Jesus had said unto him, Buy those things that we have need of against the feast; or, that he should give something to the poor.

30 He then having received the sop went immediately out: and it was night.

31Therefore, when he was gone out, Jesus said, Now is the Son of man glorified, and God is glorified in him.

32 If God be glorified in him, God shall also glorify him in himself, and shall straightway glorify him.

33 Little children, yet a little while I am with you. You shall seek me: and as I said unto the Jews, Whither I go, you cannot come; so now I say to you.

34 A new commandment I give unto you, That you love one another; as I have loved you, that you also love one another.

35 By this shall all men know that you are my disciples, if you have love one to another.

36Simon Peter said unto him, Lord, whither go you ? Jesus answered him, Whither I go, you can not follow me now; but you shalt follow me afterwards.

37 Peter said unto him, Lord, why cannot I follow you now? I will lay down my life for your sake.

38 Jesus answered him, Will you lay down your life for my sake? Verily, verily, I say unto you, The cock shall not crow, till you have denied me thrice.

CHAPTER 14

LET not your heart be troubled: you believe in God, believe also in me.

2 In my Father's house are many mansions: if it were not so, I would have told you. I go to prepare a place for you.

3 And if I go and prepare a place for you, I will come again, and receive you unto myself; that where I am, there you may be also.

4 And whither I go you know, and the way you know.

5 Thomas saith unto him, Lord, we know not whither you go; and how can we know the way?

6 Jesus saith unto him, I am the way, the truth, and the life: no man comes unto the Father, but by me.

7 If you had known me, you should have known my Father also: and from henceforth you know him, and have seen him.

8 Philip saith unto him, Lord, shew us the Father, and it sufficeth us.

9 Jesus saith unto him, Have I been so long time with you, and yet have you not known me, Philip? he that has seen me has seen the Father; and how say you then, Shew us the Father?

10 Believest you not that I am in the Father, and the Father in me? the words that I speak unto you I speak not of myself: but the Father that dwelleth in me, he doeth the works.

11 Believe me that I am in the Father, and the Father in me: or else believe me for the very works' sake.

12 Verily, verily, I say unto you, He that believeth on me, the works that I do shall he do also; and greater works than these shall he do; because I go unto my Father.

13 And whatsoever you shall ask in my name, that will I do, that the Father may be glorified in the Son.

14 If you shall ask any thing in my name, I will do it.

15If you love me, keep my commandments.

16 And I will pray the Father, and he shall give you another Comforter, that he may abide with you for ever;

17 Even the Spirit of truth; whom the world cannot receive, because it seeth him not, neither knoweth him: but you know him; for he dwelleth with you, and shall be in you.

18 I will not leave you comfortless: I will come to you.

19 Yet a little while, and the world seeth me no more; but you see me: because I live, you shall live also.

20 At that day you shall know that I am in my Father, and you in me, and I in you.

21 He that has my commandments, and keepeth them, he it is that loveth me: and he that loveth me shall be loved of my Father, and I will love him, and will manifest myself to him.

22 Judas saith unto him, not Iscariot, Lord, how is it that you will manifest yourself unto us, and not unto the world?

23 Jesus answered and said unto him, If a man love me, he will keep my words: and my Father will love him, and we will come unto him, and make our abode with him.

24 He that loveth me not keepeth not my sayings: and the word which you hear is not my, but the Father's which sent me.

25 These things have I spoken unto you, being yet present with you.

26 But the Comforter, which is the Holy Ghost, whom the Father will send in my name, he shall teach you all things, and bring all things to your remembrance, whatsoever I have said unto you.

27 Peace I leave with you, my peace I give unto you: not as the world giveth, give I unto you. Let not your heart be troubled, neither let it be afraid.

28 You have heard how I said unto you, I go away, and come again unto you. If you loved me, you would rejoice, because I said, I go unto the Father: for my Father is greater than I.

29 And now I have told you before it come to pass, that, when it is come to pass, you might believe.

30 Hereafter I will not talk much with you: for the prince of this world comes, and has nothing in me.

31 But that the world may know that I love the Father; and as the Father gave me commandment, even so I do. Arise, let us go hence.

CHAPTER 15

I AM the true vine, and my Father is the husbandman.

2 Every branch in me that beareth not fruit he taketh away: and every branch that beareth fruit, he purgeth it, that it may bring forth more fruit.

3 Now you are clean through the word which I have spoken unto you.

4 Abide in me, and I in you. As the branch cannot bear fruit of itself, except it abide in the vine; no more can you , except you abide in me.

5 I am the vine, you are the branches: He that abideth in me, and I in him, the same bringeth forth much fruit: for without me you can do nothing.

6 If a man abide not in me, he is cast forth as a branch, and is withered; and men gather them, and cast them into the fire, and they are burned.

7 If you abide in me, and my words abide in you, you shall ask what you will, and it shall be done unto you.

8 Herein is my Father glorified, that you bear much fruit; so shall you be my disciples.

9 As the Father has loved me, so have I loved you: continue you in my love.

10 If you keep my commandments, you shall abide in my love; even as I have kept my Father's commandments, and abide in his love.

11 These things have I spoken unto you, that my joy might remain in you, and that your joy might be full.

12 This is my commandment, That you love one another, as I have loved you.

13 Greater love has no man than this, that a man lay down his life for his friends.

14 You are my friends, if you do whatsoever I command you.

15 Henceforth I call you not servants; for the servant knoweth not what his lord doeth: but I have called you friends; for all things that I have heard of my Father I have made known unto you.

16 You have not chosen me, but I have chosen you, and ordained you, that you should go and bring forth fruit, and that your fruit should remain: that whatsoever you shall ask of the Father in my name, he may give it you.

17 These things I command you, that you love one another.

18 If the world hate you, you know that it hated me before it hated you.

19 If you were of the world, the world would love his own: but because you are not of the world, but I have chosen you out of the world, therefore the world hateth you.

20 Remember the word that I said unto you, The servant is not greater than his lord. If they have persecuted me, they will also persecute you; if they have kept my saying, they will keep yours also.

21 But all these things will they do unto you for my name's sake, because they know not him that sent me.

22 If I had not come and spoken unto them, they had not had sin: but now they have no cloke for their sin.

23 He that hateth me hateth my Father also.

24 If I had not done among them the works which none other man did, they had not had sin: but now have they both seen and hated both me and my Father.

25 But this comes to pass, that the word might be fulfilled that is written in their law, They hated me without a cause.

26 But when the Comforter is come, whom I will send unto you from the Father, even the Spirit of truth, which proceedeth from the Father, he shall testify of me:

27 And you also shall bear witness, because you have been with me from the beginning.

CHAPTER 16

THESE things have I spoken unto you, that you should not be offended.

2 They shall put you out of the synagogues: yea, the time comes, that whosoever killeth you will think that he doeth God service.

3 And these things will they do unto you, because they have not known the Father, nor me.

4 But these things have I told you, that when the time shall come, you may remember that I told you of them. And these things I said not unto you at the beginning, because I was with you.

5 But now I go my way to him that sent me; and none of you asketh me, Whither go you ?

6 But because I have said these things unto you, sorrow has filled your heart.

7 Nevertheless I tell you the truth; It is expedient for you that I go away: for if I go not away, the Comforter will not come unto you; but if I depart, I will send him unto you.

8 And when he is come, he will reprove the world of sin, and of righteousness, and of judgment:

9 Of sin, because they believe not on me;

10 Of righteousness, because I go to my Father, and you see me no more;

11 Of judgment, because the prince of this world is judged.

12 I have yet many things to say unto you, but you cannot bear them now.

13 Howbeit when he, the Spirit of truth, is come, he will guide you into all truth: for he shall not speak of himself; but whatsoever he shall hear, that shall he speak: and he will shew you things to come.

14 He shall glorify me: for he shall receive of my, and shall shew it unto you.

15 All things that the Father has are my: therefore said I, that he shall take of my, and shall shew it unto you.

16 A little while, and you shall not see me: and again, a little while, and you shall see me, because I go to the Father.

17 Then said some of his disciples among themselves, What is this that he saith unto us, A little while, and you shall not see me: and again, a little while, and you shall see me: and, Because I go to the Father?

18 They said therefore, What is this that he saith, A little while? we cannot tell what he saith.

19 Now Jesus knew that they were desirous to ask him, and said unto them, Do you inquire among yourselves of that I said, A little while, and you shall not see me: and again, a little while, and you shall see me?

20 Verily, verily, I say unto you, That you shall weep and lament, but the world shall rejoice: and you shall be sorrowful, but your sorrow shall be turned into joy.

21 A woman when she is in travail has sorrow, because her hour is come: but as soon as she is delivered of the child, she remembereth no more the anguish, for joy that a man is born into the world.

22 And you now therefore have sorrow: but I will see you again, and your heart shall rejoice, and your joy no man taketh from you.

23 And in that day you shall ask me nothing. Verily, verily, I say unto you, Whatsoever you shall ask the Father in my name, he will give it you.

24 Hitherto have you asked nothing in my name: ask, and you shall receive, that your joy may be full.

25 These things have I spoken unto you in proverbs: but the time comes, when I shall no more speak unto you in proverbs, but I shall shew you plainly of the Father.

26 At that day you shall ask in my name: and I say not unto you, that I will pray the Father for you:

27 For the Father himself loveth you, because you have loved me, and have believed that I came out from God.

28 I came forth from the Father, and am come into the world: again, I leave the world, and go to the Father.

29 His disciples said unto him, Lo, now speakest you plainly, and speakest no proverb.

30 Now are we sure that you knowest all things, and needest not that any man should ask you: by this we believe that you camest forth from God.

31 Jesus answered them, Do you now believe?

32 Behold, the hour comes, yea, is now come, that you shall be scattered, every man to his own, and shall leave me alone: and yet I am not alone, because the Father is with me.

33 These things I have spoken unto you, that in me you might have peace. In the world you shall have tribulation: but be of good cheer; I have overcome the world.

CHAPTER 17

THESE words spake Jesus, and lifted up his eyes to heaven, and said, Father, the hour is come; glorify your Son, that your Son also may glorify you:

2 As you have given him power over all flesh, that he should give eternal life to as many as you have given him.

3 And this is life eternal, that they might know you the only true God, and Jesus Christ, whom you have sent.

4 I have glorified you on the earth: I have finished the work which you gavest me to do.

5 And now, O Father, glorify you me with yours own self with the glory which I had with you before the world was.

6 I have manifested your name unto the men which you gavest me out of the world: yours they were, and you gavest them me; and they have kept your word.

7 Now they have known that all things whatsoever you have given me are of you.

8 For I have given unto them the words which you gavest me; and they have received them, and have known surely that I came out from you, and they have believed that you did send me.

9 I pray for them: I pray not for the world, but for them which you have given me; for they are yours.

10 And all my are yours, and yours are my; and I am glorified in them.

11 And now I am no more in the world, but these are in the world, and I come to you. Holy Father, keep through yours own name those whom you have given me, that they may be one, as we are.

12 While I was with them in the world, I kept them in your name: those that you gavest me I have kept, and none of them is lost, but the son of perdition; that the scripture might be fulfilled.

13 And now come I to you; and these things I speak in the world, that they might have my joy fulfilled in themselves.

14 I have given them your word; and the world has hated them, because they are not of the world, even as I am not of the world.

15 I pray not that you shouldest take them out of the world, but that you shouldest keep them from the evil.

16 They are not of the world, even as I am not of the world.

17 Sanctify them through your truth: your word is truth.

18 As you have sent me into the world, even so have I also sent them into the world.

19 And for their sakes I sanctify myself, that they also might be sanctified through the truth.

20 Neither pray I for these alone, but for them also which shall believe on me through their word;

21 That they all may be one; as you , Father, are in me, and I in you, that they also may be one in us: that the world may believe that you have sent me.

22 And the glory which you gavest me I have given them; that they may be one, even as we are one:

23 I in them, and you in me, that they may be made perfect in one; and that the world may know that you have sent me, and have loved them, as you have loved me.

24 Father, I will that they also, whom you have given me, be with me where I am; that they may behold my glory, which you have given me: for you lovedst me before the foundation of the world.

25 O righteous Father, the world has not known you: but I have known you, and these have known that you have sent me.

26 And I have declared unto them your name, and will declare it: that the love wherewith you have loved me may be in them, and I in them.

CHAPTER 18

WHEN Jesus had spoken these words, he went forth with his disciples over the brook Cedron, where was a garden, into the which he entered, and his disciples.

2 And Judas also, which betrayed him, knew the place: for Jesus ofttimes resorted thither with his disciples.

3 Judas then, having received a band of men and officers from the chief priests and Pharisees, comes thither with lanterns and torches and weapons.

4 Jesus therefore, knowing all things that should come upon him, went forth, and said unto them, Whom seek you ?

5 They answered him, Jesus of Nazareth. Jesus saith unto them, I am he. And Judas also, which betrayed him, stood with them.

6 As soon then as he had said unto them, I am he, they went backward, and fell to the ground.

7 Then asked he them again, Whom seek you ? And they said, Jesus of Nazareth.

8 Jesus answered, I have told you that I am he: if therefore you seek me, let these go their way:

9 That the saying might be fulfilled, which he spake, Of them which you gavest me have I lost none.

10 Then Simon Peter having a sword drew it, and struck the high priest's servant, and cut off his right ear. The servant's name was Malchus.

11 Then said Jesus unto Peter, Put up your sword into the sheath: the cup which my Father has given me, shall I not drink it?

12 Then the band and the captain and officers of the Jews took Jesus, and bound him,

13 And led him away to Annas first; for he was father in law to Caiaphas, which was the high priest that same year.

14 Now Caiaphas was he, which gave counsel to the Jews, that it was expedient that one man should die for the people.

15 And Simon Peter followed Jesus, and so did another disciple: that disciple was known unto the high priest, and went in with Jesus into the palace of the high priest.

16 But Peter stood at the door without. Then went out that other disciple, which was known unto the high priest, and spake unto her that kept the door, and brought in Peter.

17 Then saith the damsel that kept the door unto Peter, Are not you also one of this man's disciples? He saith, I am not.

18 And the servants and officers stood there, who had made a fire of coals; for it was cold: and they warmed themselves: and Peter stood with them, and warmed himself.

19 The high priest then asked Jesus of his disciples, and of his doctrine.

20 Jesus answered him, I spake openly to the world; I ever taught in the synagogue, and in the temple, whither the Jews always resort; and in secret have I said nothing.

21 Why askest you me? ask them which heard me, what I have said unto them: behold, they know what I said.

22 And when he had thus spoken, one of the officers which stood by struck Jesus with the palm of his hand, saying, Answerest you the high priest so?

23 Jesus answered him, If I have spoken evil, bear witness of the evil: but if well, why smitest you me?

24 Now Annas had sent him bound unto Caiaphas the high priest.

25 And Simon Peter stood and warmed himself. They said therefore unto him, Are not you also one of his disciples? He denied it, and said, I am not.

26 One of the servants of the high priest, being his kinsman whose ear Peter cut off, saith, Did not I see you in the garden with him?

27 Peter then denied again: and immediately the cock crew.

28 Then led they Jesus from Caiaphas unto the hall of judgment: and it was early; and they themselves went not into the judgment hall, lest they should be defiled; but that they might eat the passover.

29 Pilate then went out unto them, and said, What accusation bring you against this man?

30 They answered and said unto him, If he were not a malefactor, we would not have delivered him up unto you.

31 Then said Pilate unto them, Take you him, and judge him according to your law. The Jews therefore said unto him, It is not lawful for us to put any man to death:

32 That the saying of Jesus might be fulfilled, which he spake, signifying what death he should die.

33 Then Pilate entered into the judgment hall again, and called Jesus, and said unto him, Are you the King of the Jews?

34 Jesus answered him, Say you this thing of yourself, or did others tell it you of me?

35 Pilate answered, Am I a Jew? Yours own nation and the chief priests have delivered you unto me: what have you done?

36 Jesus answered, My kingdom is not of this world: if my kingdom were of this world, then would my servants fight, that I should not be delivered to the Jews: but now is my kingdom not from hence.

37 Pilate therefore said unto him, Are you a king then? Jesus answered, You say that I am a king. To this end was I born, and for this cause came I into the world, that I should bear witness unto the truth. Every one that is of the truth heareth my voice.

38 Pilate saith unto him, What is truth? And when he had said this, he went out again unto the Jews, and saith unto them, I find in him no fault at all.

39 But you have a custom, that I should release unto you one at the passover: will you therefore that I release unto you the King of the Jews?

40 Then cried they all again, saying, Not this man, but Barabbas. Now Barabbas was a robber.

CHAPTER 19

THEN Pilate therefore took Jesus, and scourged him.

2 And the soldiers platted a crown of thorns, and put it on his head, and they put on him a purple robe,

3 And said, Hail, King of the Jews! and they struck him with their hands.

4 Pilate therefore went forth again, and saith unto them, Behold, I bring him forth to you, that you may know that I find no fault in him.

5 Then came Jesus forth, wearing the crown of thorns, and the purple robe. And Pilate saith unto them, Behold the man!

6 When the chief priests therefore and officers saw him, they cried out, saying, Crucify him, crucify him. Pilate saith unto them, Take you him, and crucify him: for I find no fault in him.

7 The Jews answered him, We have a law, and by our law he ought to die, because he made himself the Son of God.

8 When Pilate therefore heard that saying, he was the more afraid;

9 And went again into the judgment hall, and saith unto Jesus, Whence are you? But Jesus gave him no answer.

10 Then saith Pilate unto him, Speakest you not unto me? knowest you not that I have power to crucify you, and have power to release you?

11 Jesus answered, You couldest have no power at all against me, except it were given you from above: therefore he that delivered me unto you has the greater sin.

12 And from thenceforth Pilate sought to release him: but the Jews cried out, saying, If you let this man go, you are not Cæsar's friend: whosoever maketh himself a king speaketh against Cæsar.

13 When Pilate therefore heard that saying, he brought Jesus forth, and sat down in the judgment seat in a place that is called the Pavement, but in the Hebrew, Gabbatha.

14 And it was the preparation of the passover, and about the sixth hour: and he saith unto the Jews, Behold your King!

15 But they cried out, Away with him, away with him, crucify him. Pilate saith unto them, Shall I crucify your King? The chief priests answered, We have no king but Cæsar.

16 Then delivered he him therefore unto them to be crucified. And they took Jesus, and led him away.

17 And he bearing his cross went forth into a place called the place of a skull, which is called in the Hebrew Golgotha:

18 Where they crucified him, and two other with him, on either side one, and Jesus in the midst.

19 And Pilate wrote a title, and put it on the cross. And the writing was, JESUS OF NAZARETH THE KING OF THE JEWS.

20 This title then read many of the Jews: for the place where Jesus was crucified was nigh to the city: and it was written in Hebrew, and Greek, and Latin.

21 Then said the chief priests of the Jews to Pilate, Write not, The King of the Jews; but that he said, I am King of the Jews.

22 Pilate answered, What I have written I have written.

23 Then the soldiers, when they had crucified Jesus, took his garments, and made four parts, to every soldier a part; and also his coat: now the coat was without seam, woven from the top throughout.

24 They said therefore among themselves, Let us not rend it, but cast lots for it, whose it shall be: that the scripture might be fulfilled, which saith, They parted my raiment among them, and for my vesture they did cast lots. These things therefore the soldiers did.

25 Now there stood by the cross of Jesus his mother, and his mother's sister, Mary the wife of Cleophas, and Mary Magdalene.

26 When Jesus therefore saw his mother, and the disciple standing by, whom he loved, he saith unto his mother, Woman, behold your son!

27 Then saith he to the disciple, Behold your mother! And from that hour that disciple took her unto his own home.

28 After this, Jesus knowing that all things were now accomplished, that the scripture might be fulfilled, saith, I thirst.

29 Now there was set a vessel full of vinegar: and they filled a spunge with vinegar, and put it upon hyssop, and put it to his mouth.

30 When Jesus therefore had received the vinegar, he said, It is finished: and he bowed his head, and gave up the ghost.

31 The Jews therefore, because it was the preparation, that the bodies should not remain upon the cross on the sabbath day, (for that sabbath day was an high day,) besought Pilate that their legs might be broken, and that they might be taken away.

32 Then came the soldiers, and brake the legs of the first, and of the other which was crucified with him.

33 But when they came to Jesus, and saw that he was dead already, they brake not his legs:

34 But one of the soldiers with a spear pierced his side, and forthwith came there out blood and water.

35 And he that saw it bare record, and his record is true: and he knoweth that he saith true, that you might believe.

36 For these things were done, that the scripture should be fulfilled, A bone of him shall not be broken.

37 And again another scripture saith, They shall look on him whom they pierced.

38 And after this Joseph of Arimathæa, being a disciple of Jesus, but secretly for fear of the Jews, besought Pilate that he might take away the body of Jesus: and Pilate gave him leave. He came therefore, and took the body of Jesus.

39 And there came also Nicodemus, which at the first came to Jesus by night, and brought a mixture of myrrh and aloes, about an hundred pound weight.

40 Then took they the body of Jesus, and wound it in linen clothes with the spices, as the manner of the Jews is to bury.

41 Now in the place where he was crucified there was a garden; and in the garden a new sepulchre, wherein was never man yet laid.

42 There laid they Jesus therefore because of the Jews' preparation day; for the sepulchre was nigh at hand.

CHAPTER 20

THE first day of the week comes Mary Magdalene early, when it was yet dark, unto the sepulchre, and seeth the stone taken away from the sepulchre.

2 Then she runneth, and comes to Simon Peter, and to the other disciple, whom Jesus loved, and saith unto them, They have taken away the Lord out of the sepulchre, and we know not where they have laid him.

3 Peter therefore went forth, and that other disciple, and came to the sepulchre.

4 So they ran both together: and the other disciple did outrun Peter, and came first to the sepulchre.

5 And he stooping down, and looking in, saw the linen clothes lying; yet went he not in.

6 Then comes Simon Peter following him, and went into the sepulchre, and seeth the linen clothes lie,

7 And the napkin, that was about his head, not lying with the linen clothes, but wrapped together in a place by itself.

8 Then went in also that other disciple, which came first to the sepulchre, and he saw, and believed.

9 For as yet they knew not the scripture, that he must rise again from the dead.

10 Then the disciples went away again unto their own home.

11 But Mary stood without at the sepulchre weeping: and as she wept, she stooped down, and looked into the sepulchre,

12 And seeth two angels in white sitting, the one at the head, and the other at the feet, where the body of Jesus had lain.

13 And they say unto her, Woman, why weepest you ? She saith unto them, Because they have taken away my Lord, and I know not where they have laid him.

14 And when she had thus said, she turned herself back, and saw Jesus standing, and knew not that it was Jesus.

15 Jesus saith unto her, Woman, why weepest you ? whom seekest you ? She, supposing him to be the gardener, saith unto him, Sir, if you have borne him hence, tell me where you have laid him, and I will take him away.

16 Jesus saith unto her, Mary. She turned herself, and saith unto him, Rabboni; which is to say, Master.

17 Jesus saith unto her, Touch me not; for I am not yet ascended to my Father: but go to my brethren, and say unto them, I ascend unto my Father, and your Father; and to my God, and your God.

18 Mary Magdalene came and told the disciples that she had seen the Lord, and that he had spoken these things unto her.

19 Then the same day at evening, being the first day of the week, when the doors were shut where the disciples were assembled for fear of the Jews, came Jesus and stood in the midst, and saith unto them, Peace be unto you.

20 And when he had so said, he shewed unto them his hands and his side. Then were the disciples glad, when they saw the Lord.

21 Then said Jesus to them again, Peace be unto you: as my Father has sent me, even so send I you.

22 And when he had said this, he breathed on them, and saith unto them, Receive you the Holy Ghost:

23 Whose soever sins you remit, they are remitted unto them; and whose soever sins you retain, they are retained.

24 But Thomas, one of the twelve, called Didymus, was not with them when Jesus came.

25 The other disciples therefore said unto him, We have seen the Lord. But he said unto them, Except I shall see in his hands the print of the nails, and put my finger into the print of the nails, and thrust my hand into his side, I will not believe.

26 And after eight days again his disciples were within, and Thomas with them: then came Jesus, the doors being shut, and stood in the midst, and said, Peace be unto you.

27 Then saith he to Thomas, Reach hither your finger, and behold my hands; and reach hither your hand, and thrust it into my side: and be not faithless, but believing.

28 And Thomas answered and said unto him, My Lord and my God.

29 Jesus saith unto him, Thomas, because you have seen me, you have believed: blessed are they that have not seen, and yet have believed.

30 And many other signs truly did Jesus in the presence of his disciples, which are not written in this book:

31 But these are written, that you might believe that Jesus is the Christ, the Son of God; and that believing you might have life through his name.

CHAPTER 21

AFTER these things Jesus shewed himself again to the disciples at the sea of Tiberias; and on this wise shewed he himself.

2 There were together Simon Peter, and Thomas called Didymus, and Nathanael of Cana in Galilee, and the sons of Zebedee, and two other of his disciples.

3 Simon Peter saith unto them, I go a fishing. They say unto him, We also go with you. They went forth, and entered into a ship immediately; and that night they caught nothing.

4 But when the morning was now come, Jesus stood on the shore: but the disciples knew not that it was Jesus.

5 Then Jesus saith unto them, Children, have you any meat? They answered him, No.

6 And he said unto them, Cast the net on the right side of the ship, and you shall find. They cast therefore, and now they were not able to draw it for the multitude of fishes.

7 Therefore that disciple whom Jesus loved saith unto Peter, It is the Lord. Now when Simon Peter heard that it was the Lord, he girt his fisher's coat unto him, (for he was naked,) and did cast himself into the sea.

8 And the other disciples came in a little ship; (for they were not far from land, but as it were two hundred cubits,) dragging the net with fishes.

9 As soon then as they were come to land, they saw a fire of coals there, and fish laid thereon, and bread.

10 Jesus saith unto them, Bring of the fish which you have now caught.

11 Simon Peter went up, and drew the net to land full of great fishes, an hundred and fifty and three: and for all there were so many, yet was not the net broken.

12 Jesus saith unto them, Come and dine. And none of the disciples durst ask him, Who are you ? knowing that it was the Lord.

13 Jesus then comes, and taketh bread, and giveth them, and fish likewise.

14 This is now the third time that Jesus shewed himself to his disciples, after that he was risen from the dead.

15 So when they had dined, Jesus saith to Simon Peter, Simon, son of Jonas, lovest you me more than these? He saith unto him, Yea, Lord; you knowest that I love you. He saith unto him, Feed my lambs.

16 He saith to him again the second time, Simon, son of Jonas, lovest you me? He saith unto him, Yea, Lord; you knowest that I love you. He saith unto him, Feed my sheep.

17 He saith unto him the third time, Simon, son of Jonas, lovest you me? Peter was grieved because he said unto him the third time, Lovest you me? And he said unto him, Lord, you knowest all things; you knowest that I love you. Jesus saith unto him, Feed my sheep.

18 Verily, verily, I say unto you, When you wast young, you girdedst yourself, and walkedst whither you wouldest: but when you shalt be old, you shalt stretch forth your hands, and another shall gird you, and carry you whither you wouldest not.

19 This spake he, signifying by what death he should glorify God. And when he had spoken this, he saith unto him, Follow me.

20 Then Peter, turning about, seeth the disciple whom Jesus loved following; which also leaned on his breast at supper, and said, Lord, which is he that betrayeth you?

21 Peter seeing him saith to Jesus, Lord, and what shall this man do?

22 Jesus saith unto him, If I will that he tarry till I come, what is that to you? follow you me.

23 Then went this saying abroad among the brethren, that that disciple should not die: yet Jesus said not unto him, He shall not die; but, If I will that he tarry till I come, what is that to you?

24 This is the disciple which testifieth of these things, and wrote these things: and we know that his testimony is true.

25 And there are also many other things which Jesus did, the which, if they should be written every one, I suppose that even the world itself could not contain the books that should be written. Amen.

THE
ACTS OF THE APOSTLES.

CHAPTER 1

THE former treatise have I made, O Theophilus, of all that Jesus began both to do and teach,

2 Until the day in which he was taken up, after that he through the Holy Ghost had given commandments unto the apostles whom he had chosen:

3 To whom also he shewed himself alive after his passion by many infallible proofs, being seen of them forty days, and speaking of the things pertaining to the kingdom of God:

4 And, being assembled together with them, commanded them that they should not depart from Jerusalem, but wait for the promise of the Father, which, saith he, you have heard of me.

5 For John truly baptized with water; but you shall be baptized with the Holy Ghost not many days hence.

6 When they therefore were come together, they asked of him, saying, Lord, will you at this time restore again the kingdom to Israel?

7 And he said unto them, It is not for you to know the times or the seasons, which the Father has put in his own power.

8 But you shall receive power, after that the Holy Ghost is come upon you: and you shall be witnesses unto me both in Jerusalem, and in all Judæa, and in Samaria, and unto the uttermost part of the earth.

9 And when he had spoken these things, while they beheld, he was taken up; and a cloud received him out of their sight.

10 And while they looked stedfastly toward heaven as he went up, behold, two men stood by them in white apparel;

11 Which also said, You men of Galilee, why stand you gazing up into heaven? this same Jesus, which is taken up from you into heaven, shall so come in like manner as you have seen him go into heaven.

12 Then returned they unto Jerusalem from the mount called Olivet, which is from Jerusalem a sabbath day's journey.

13 And when they were come in, they went up into an upper room, where abode both Peter, and James, and John, and Andrew, Philip, and Thomas, Bartholomew, and Matthew, James the son of Alphæus, and Simon Zelotes, and Judas the brother of James.

14 These all continued with one accord in prayer and supplication, with the women, and Mary the mother of Jesus, and with his brethren.

15 And in those days Peter stood up in the midst of the disciples, and said, (the number of names together were about an hundred and twenty,)

16 Men and brethren, this scripture must needs have been fulfilled, which the Holy Ghost by the mouth of David spake before concerning Judas, which was guide to them that took Jesus.

17 For he was numbered with us, and had obtained part of this ministry.

18 Now this man purchased a field with the reward of iniquity; and falling headlong, he burst asunder in the midst, and all his bowels gushed out.

19 And it was known unto all the dwellers at Jerusalem; insomuch as that field is called in their proper tongue, Aceldama, that is to say, The field of blood.

20 For it is written in the book of Psalms, Let his habitation be desolate, and let no man dwell therein: and his bishoprick let another take.

21 Wherefore of these men which have companied with us all the time that the Lord Jesus went in and out among us,

22 Beginning from the baptism of John, unto that same day that he was taken up from us, must one be ordained to be a witness with us of his resurrection.

23 And they appointed two, Joseph called Barsabas, who was surnamed Justus, and Matthias.

24 And they prayed, and said, You , Lord, which knowest the hearts of all men, shew whether of these two you have chosen,

25 That he may take part of this ministry and apostleship, from which Judas by transgression fell, that he might go to his own place.

26 And they gave forth their lots; and the lot fell upon Matthias; and he was numbered with the eleven apostles.

CHAPTER 2

AND when the day of Pentecost was fully come, they were all with one accord in one place.

2 And suddenly there came a sound from heaven as of a rushing mighty wind, and it filled all the house where they were sitting.

3 And there appeared unto them cloven tongues like as of fire, and it sat upon each of them.

4 And they were all filled with the Holy Ghost, and began to speak with other tongues, as the Spirit gave them utterance.

5 And there were dwelling at Jerusalem Jews, devout men, out of every nation under heaven.

6 Now when this was noised abroad, the multitude came together, and were confounded, because that every man heard them speak in his own language.

7 And they were all amazed and marvelled, saying one to another, Behold, are not all these which speak Galilæans?

8 And how hear we every man in our own tongue, wherein we were born?

9 Parthians, and Medes, and Elamites, and the dwellers in Mesopotamia, and in Judæa, and Cappadocia, in Pontus, and Asia,

10 Phrygia, and Pamphylia, in Egypt, and in the parts of Libya about Cyrene, and strangers of Rome, Jews and proselytes,

11 Cretes and Arabians, we do hear them speak in our tongues the wonderful works of God.

12 And they were all amazed, and were in doubt, saying one to another, What meaneth this?

13 Others mocking said, These men are full of new wine.

14 But Peter, standing up with the eleven, lifted up his voice, and said unto them, You men of Judæa, and all you that dwell at Jerusalem, be this known unto you, and hearken to my words:

15 For these are not drunken, as you suppose, seeing it is but the third hour of the day.

16 But this is that which was spoken by the prophet Joel;

17 And it shall come to pass in the last days, saith God, I will pour out of my Spirit upon all flesh: and your sons and your daughters shall prophesy, and your young men shall see visions, and your old men shall dream dreams:

18 And on my servants and on my handmaidens I will pour out in those days of my Spirit; and they shall prophesy:

19 And I will shew wonders in heaven above, and signs in the earth beneath; blood, and fire, and vapour of smoke:

20 The sun shall be turned into darkness, and the moon into blood, before that great and notable day of the Lord come:

21 And it shall come to pass, that whosoever shall call on the name of the Lord shall be saved.

22 You men of Israel, hear these words; Jesus of Nazareth, a man approved of God among you by miracles and wonders and signs, which God did by him in the midst of you, as you yourselves also know:

23 Him, being delivered by the determinate counsel and foreknowledge of God, you have taken, and by wicked hands have crucified and slain:

24 Whom God has raised up, having loosed the pains of death: because it was not possible that he should be holden of it.

25 For David speaketh concerning him, I foresaw the Lord always before my face, for he is on my right hand, that I should not be moved:

26 Therefore did my heart rejoice, and my tongue was glad; moreover also my flesh shall rest in hope:

27 Because you will not leave my soul in hell, neither will you suffer yours Holy One to see corruption.

28 You have made known to me the ways of life; you shalt make me full of joy with your countenance.

29 Men and brethren, let me freely speak unto you of the patriarch David, that he is both dead and buried, and his sepulchre is with us unto this day.

30 Therefore being a prophet, and knowing that God had sworn with an oath to him, that of the fruit of his loins, according to the flesh, he would raise up Christ to sit on his throne;

31 He seeing this before spake of the resurrection of Christ, that his soul was not left in hell, neither his flesh did see corruption.

32 This Jesus has God raised up, whereof we all are witnesses.

33 Therefore being by the right hand of God exalted, and having received of the Father the promise of the Holy Ghost, he has shed forth this, which you now see and hear.

34 For David is not ascended into the heavens: but he saith himself, The LORD said unto my Lord, Sit you on my right hand,

35 Until I make your foes your footstool.

36 Therefore let all the house of Israel know assuredly, that God has made that same Jesus, whom you have crucified, both Lord and Christ.

37 Now when they heard this, they were pricked in their heart, and said unto Peter and to the rest of the apostles, Men and brethren, what shall we do?

38 Then Peter said unto them, Repent, and be baptized every one of you in the name of Jesus Christ for the remission of sins, and you shall receive the gift of the Holy Ghost.

39 For the promise is unto you, and to your children, and to all that are afar off, even as many as the Lord our God shall call.

40 And with many other words did he testify and exhort, saying, Save yourselves from this untoward generation.

41 Then they that gladly received his word were baptized: and the same day there were added unto them about three thousand souls.

42 And they continued stedfastly in the apostles' doctrine and fellowship, and in breaking of bread, and in prayers.

43 And fear came upon every soul: and many wonders and signs were done by the apostles.

44 And all that believed were together, and had all things common;

45 And sold their possessions and goods, and parted them to all men, as every man had need.

46 And they, continuing daily with one accord in the temple, and breaking bread from house to house, did eat their meat with gladness and singleness of heart,

47 Praising God, and having favour with all the people. And the Lord added to the church daily such as should be saved.

CHAPTER 3

NOW Peter and John went up together into the temple at the hour of prayer, being the ninth hour.

2 And a certain man lame from his mother's womb was carried, whom they laid daily at the gate of the temple which is called Beautiful, to ask alms of them that entered into the temple;

3 Who seeing Peter and John about to go into the temple asked an alms.

4 And Peter, fastening his eyes upon him with John, said, Look on us.

5 And he gave heed unto them, expecting to receive something of them.

6 Then Peter said, Silver and gold have I none; but such as I have give I you: In the name of Jesus Christ of Nazareth rise up and walk.

7 And he took him by the right hand, and lifted him up: and immediately his feet and ancle bones received strength.

8 And he leaping up stood, and walked, and entered with them into the temple, walking, and leaping, and praising God.

9 And all the people saw him walking and praising God:

10 And they knew that it was he which sat for alms at the Beautiful gate of the temple: and they were filled with wonder and amazement at that which had happened unto him.

11 And as the lame man which was healed held Peter and John, all the people ran together unto them in the porch that is called Solomon's, greatly wondering.

12 And when Peter saw it, he answered unto the people, You men of Israel, why marvel you at this? or why look you so earnestly on us, as though by our own power or holiness we had made this man to walk?

13 The God of Abraham, and of Isaac, and of Jacob, the God of our fathers, has glorified his Son Jesus; whom you delivered up, and denied him in the presence of Pilate, when he was determined to let him go.

14 But you denied the Holy One and the Just, and desired a murderer to be granted unto you;

15 And killed the Prince of life, whom God has raised from the dead; whereof we are witnesses.

16 And his name through faith in his name has made this man strong, whom you see and know: yea, the faith which is by him has given him this perfect soundness in the presence of you all.

17 And now, brethren, I wot that through ignorance you did it, as did also your rulers.

18 But those things, which God before had shewed by the mouth of all his prophets, that Christ should suffer, he has so fulfilled.

19 Repent you therefore, and be converted, that your sins may be blotted out, when the times of refreshing shall come from the presence of the Lord;

20 And he shall send Jesus Christ, which before was preached unto you:

21 Whom the heaven must receive until the times of restitution of all things, which God has spoken by the mouth of all his holy prophets since the world began.

22 For Moses truly said unto the fathers, A prophet shall the Lord your God raise up unto you of your brethren, like unto me; him shall you hear in all things whatsoever he shall say unto you.

23 And it shall come to pass, that every soul, which will not hear that prophet, shall be destroyed from among the people.

24 Yea, and all the prophets from Samuel and those that follow after, as many as have spoken, have likewise foretold of these days.

25 You are the children of the prophets, and of the covenant which God made with our fathers, saying unto Abraham, And in your seed shall all the kindreds of the earth be blessed.

26 Unto you first God, having raised up his Son Jesus, sent him to bless you, in turning away every one of you from his iniquities.

CHAPTER 4

AND as they spake unto the people, the priests, and the captain of the temple, and the Sadducees, came upon them,

2 Being grieved that they taught the people, and preached through Jesus the resurrection from the dead.

3 And they laid hands on them, and put them in hold unto the next day: for it was now eventide.

4 Howbeit many of them which heard the word believed; and the number of the men was about five thousand.

5 And it came to pass on the morrow, that their rulers, and elders, and scribes,

6 And Annas the high priest, and Caiaphas, and John, and Alexander, and as many as were of the kindred of the high priest, were gathered together at Jerusalem.

7 And when they had set them in the midst, they asked, By what power, or by what name, have you done this?

8 Then Peter, filled with the Holy Ghost, said unto them, You rulers of the people, and elders of Israel,

9 If we this day be examined of the good deed done to the impotent man, by what means he is made whole;

10 Be it known unto you all, and to all the people of Israel, that by the name of Jesus Christ of Nazareth, whom you crucified, whom God raised from the dead, even by him doth this man stand here before you whole.

11 This is the stone which was set at nought of you builders, which is become the head of the corner.

12 Neither is there salvation in any other: for there is none other name under heaven given among men, whereby we must be saved.

13 Now when they saw the boldness of Peter and John, and perceived that they were unlearned and ignorant men, they marvelled; and they took knowledge of them, that they had been with Jesus.

14 And beholding the man which was healed standing with them, they could say nothing against it.

15 But when they had commanded them to go aside out of the council, they conferred among themselves,

16 Saying, What shall we do to these men? for that indeed a notable miracle has been done by them is manifest to all them that dwell in Jerusalem; and we cannot deny it.

17 But that it spread no further among the people, let us straitly threaten them, that they speak henceforth to no man in this name.

18 And they called them, and commanded them not to speak at all nor teach in the name of Jesus.

19 But Peter and John answered and said unto them, Whether it be right in the sight of God to hearken unto you more than unto God, judge you .

20 For we cannot but speak the things which we have seen and heard.

21 So when they had further threatened them, they let them go, finding nothing how they might punish them, because of the people: for all men glorified God for that which was done.

22 For the man was above forty years old, on whom this miracle of healing was shewed.

23 And being let go, they went to their own company, and reported all that the chief priests and elders had said unto them.

24 And when they heard that, they lifted up their voice to God with one accord, and said, Lord, you are God, which have made heaven, and earth, and the sea, and all that in them is:

25 Who by the mouth of your servant David have said, Why did the heathen rage, and the people imagine vain things?

26 The kings of the earth stood up, and the rulers were gathered together against the Lord, and against his Christ.

27 For of a truth against your holy child Jesus, whom you have anointed, both Herod, and Pontius Pilate, with the Gentiles, and the people of Israel, were gathered together,

28 For to do whatsoever your hand and your counsel determined before to be done.

29 And now, Lord, behold their threatenings: and grant unto your servants, that with all boldness they may speak your word,

30 By stretching forth yours hand to heal; and that signs and wonders may be done by the name of your holy child Jesus.

31 And when they had prayed, the place was shaken where they were assembled together; and they were all filled with the Holy Ghost, and they spake the word of God with boldness.

32 And the multitude of them that believed were of one heart and of one soul: neither said any of them that ought of the things which he possessed was his own; but they had all things common.

33 And with great power gave the apostles witness of the resurrection of the Lord Jesus: and great grace was upon them all.

34 Neither was there any among them that lacked: for as many as were possessors of lands or houses sold them, and brought the prices of the things that were sold,

35 And laid them down at the apostles' feet: and distribution was made unto every man according as he had need.

36 And Joses, who by the apostles was surnamed Barnabas, (which is, being interpreted, The son of consolation,) a Levite, and of the country of Cyprus,

37 Having land, sold it, and brought the money, and laid it at the apostles' feet.

CHAPTER 5

BUT a certain man named Ananias, with Sapphira his wife, sold a possession,

2 And kept back part of the price, his wife also being privy to it, and brought a certain part, and laid it at the apostles' feet.

3 But Peter said, Ananias, why has Satan filled yours heart to lie to the Holy Ghost, and to keep back part of the price of the land?

4 Whiles it remained, was it not yours own? and after it was sold, was it not in yours own power? why have you conceived this thing in yours heart? you have not lied unto men, but unto God.

5 And Ananias hearing these words fell down, and gave up the ghost: and great fear came on all them that heard these things.

6 And the young men arose, wound him up, and carried him out, and buried him.

7 And it was about the space of three hours after, when his wife, not knowing what was done, came in.

8 And Peter answered unto her, Tell me whether you sold the land for so much? And she said, Yea, for so much.

9 Then Peter said unto her, How is it that you have agreed together to tempt the Spirit of the Lord? behold, the feet of them which have buried your husband are at the door, and shall carry you out.

10 Then fell she down straightway at his feet, and yielded up the ghost: and the young men came in, and found her dead, and, carrying her forth, buried her by her husband.

11 And great fear came upon all the church, and upon as many as heard these things.

12And by the hands of the apostles were many signs and wonders created among the people; (and they were all with one accord in Solomon's porch.

13 And of the rest durst no man join himself to them: but the people magnified them.

14 And believers were the more added to the Lord, multitudes both of men and women.)

15 Insomuch that they brought forth the sick into the streets, and laid them on beds and couches, that at the least the shadow of Peter passing by might overshadow some of them.

16 There came also a multitude out of the cities round about unto Jerusalem, bringing sick folks, and them which were vexed with unclean spirits: and they were healed every one.

17Then the high priest rose up, and all they that were with him, (which is the sect of the Sadducees,) and were filled with indignation,

18 And laid their hands on the apostles, and put them in the common prison.

19 But the angel of the Lord by night opened the prison doors, and brought them forth, and said,

20 Go, stand and speak in the temple to the people all the words of this life.

21 And when they heard that, they entered into the temple early in the morning, and taught. But the high priest came, and they that were with him, and called the council together, and all the senate of the children of Israel, and sent to the prison to have them brought.

22 But when the officers came, and found them not in the prison, they returned, and told,

23 Saying, The prison truly found we shut with all safety, and the keepers standing without before the doors: but when we had opened, we found no man within.

24 Now when the high priest and the captain of the temple and the chief priests heard these things, they doubted of them whereunto this would grow.

25 Then came one and told them, saying, Behold, the men whom you put in prison are standing in the temple, and teaching the people.

26 Then went the captain with the officers, and brought them without violence: for they feared the people, lest they should have been stoned.

27 And when they had brought them, they set them before the council: and the high priest asked them,

28 Saying, Did not we straitly command you that you should not teach in this name? and, behold, you have filled Jerusalem with your doctrine, and intend to bring this man's blood upon us.

29Then Peter and the other apostles answered and said, We ought to obey God rather than men.

30 The God of our fathers raised up Jesus, whom you slew and hanged on a tree.

31 Him has God exalted with his right hand to be a Prince and a Saviour, for to give repentance to Israel, and forgiveness of sins.

32 And we are his witnesses of these things; and so is also the Holy Ghost, whom God has given to them that obey him.

33When they heard that, they were cut to the heart, and took counsel to slay them.

34 Then stood there up one in the council, a Pharisee, named Gamaliel, a doctor of the law, had in reputation among all the people, and commanded to put the apostles forth a little space;

35 And said unto them, You men of Israel, take heed to yourselves what you intend to do as touching these men.

36 For before these days rose up Theudas, boasting himself to be somebody; to whom a number of men, about four hundred, joined themselves: who was slain; and all, as many as obeyed him, were scattered, and brought to nought.

37 After this man rose up Judas of Galilee in the days of the taxing, and drew away much people after him: he also perished; and all, even as many as obeyed him, were dispersed.

38 And now I say unto you, Refrain from these men, and let them alone: for if this counsel or this work be of men, it will come to nought:

39 But if it be of God, you cannot overthrow it; lest haply you be found even to fight against God.

40 And to him they agreed: and when they had called the apostles, and beaten them, they commanded that they should not speak in the name of Jesus, and let them go.

41And they departed from the presence of the council, rejoicing that they were counted worthy to suffer shame for his name.

42 And daily in the temple, and in every house, they ceased not to teach and preach Jesus Christ.

CHAPTER 6

AND in those days, when the number of the disciples was multiplied, there arose a murmuring of the Grecians against the Hebrews, because their widows were neglected in the daily ministration.

2 Then the twelve called the multitude of the disciples unto them, and said, It is not reason that we should leave the word of God, and serve tables.

3 Wherefore, brethren, look you out among you seven men of honest report, full of the Holy Ghost and wisdom, whom we may appoint over this business.

4 But we will give ourselves continually to prayer, and to the ministry of the word.

5And the saying pleased the whole multitude: and they chose Stephen, a man full of faith and of the Holy Ghost, and Philip, and Prochorus, and Nicanor, and Timon, and Parmenas, and Nicolas a proselyte of Antioch:

6 Whom they set before the apostles: and when they had prayed, they laid their hands on them.

7 And the word of God increased; and the number of the disciples multiplied in Jerusalem greatly; and a great company of the priests were obedient to the faith.

8 And Stephen, full of faith and power, did great wonders and miracles among the people.

9Then there arose certain of the synagogue, which is called the synagogue of the Libertines, and Cyrenians, and Alexandrians, and of them of Cilicia and of Asia, disputing with Stephen.

10 And they were not able to resist the wisdom and the spirit by which he spake.

11 Then they suborned men, which said, We have heard him speak blasphemous words against Moses, and against God.

12 And they stirred up the people, and the elders, and the scribes, and came upon him, and caught him, and brought him to the council,

13 And set up false witnesses, which said, This man ceaseth not to speak blasphemous words against this holy place, and the law:

14 For we have heard him say, that this Jesus of Nazareth shall destroy this place, and shall change the customs which Moses delivered us.

15 And all that sat in the council, looking stedfastly on him, saw his face as it had been the face of an angel.

CHAPTER 7

THEN said the high priest, Are these things so?

2 And he said, Men, brethren, and fathers, hearken; The God of glory appeared unto our father Abraham, when he was in Mesopotamia, before he dwelt in Charran,

3 And said unto him, Get you out of your country, and from your kindred, and come into the land which I shall shew you.

4 Then came he out of the land of the Chaldæans, and dwelt in Charran: and from thence, when his father was dead, he removed him into this land, wherein you now dwell.

5 And he gave him none inheritance in it, no, not so much as to set his foot on: yet he promised that he would give it to him for a possession, and to his seed after him, when as yet he had no child.

6 And God spake on this wise, That his seed should sojourn in a strange land; and that they should bring them into bondage, and entreat them evil four hundred years.

7 And the nation to whom they shall be in bondage will I judge, said God: and after that shall they come forth, and serve me in this place.

8 And he gave him the covenant of circumcision: and so Abraham begat Isaac, and circumcised him the eighth day; and Isaac begat Jacob; and Jacob begat the twelve patriarchs.

9 And the patriarchs, moved with envy, sold Joseph into Egypt: but God was with him,

10 And delivered him out of all his afflictions, and gave him favour and wisdom in the sight of Pharaoh king of Egypt; and he made him governor over Egypt and all his house.

11 Now there came a dearth over all the land of Egypt and Chanaan, and great affliction: and our fathers found no sustenance.

12 But when Jacob heard that there was corn in Egypt, he sent out our fathers first.

13 And at the second time Joseph was made known to his brethren; and Joseph's kindred was made known unto Pharaoh.

14 Then sent Joseph, and called his father Jacob to him, and all his kindred, threescore and fifteen souls.

15 So Jacob went down into Egypt, and died, he, and our fathers,

16 And were carried over into Sychem, and laid in the sepulchre that Abraham bought for a sum of money of the sons of Emmor the father of Sychem.

17 But when the time of the promise drew nigh, which God had sworn to Abraham, the people grew and multiplied in Egypt,

18 Till another king arose, which knew not Joseph.

19 The same dealt subtilly with our kindred, and evil entreated our fathers, so that they cast out their young children, to the end they might not live.

20 In which time Moses was born, and was exceeding fair, and nourished up in his father's house three months:

21 And when he was cast out, Pharaoh's daughter took him up, and nourished him for her own son.

22 And Moses was learned in all the wisdom of the Egyptians, and was mighty in words and in deeds.

23 And when he was full forty years old, it came into his heart to visit his brethren the children of Israel.

24 And seeing one of them suffer wrong, he defended him, and avenged him that was oppressed, and struck the Egyptian:

25 For he supposed his brethren would have understood how that God by his hand would deliver them: but they understood not.

26 And the next day he shewed himself unto them as they strove, and would have set them at one again, saying, Sirs, you are brethren; why do you wrong one to another?

27 But he that did his neighbour wrong thrust him away, saying, Who made you a ruler and a judge over us?

28 Will you kill me, as you diddest the Egyptian yesterday?

29 Then fled Moses at this saying, and was a stranger in the land of Madian, where he begat two sons.

30 And when forty years were expired, there appeared to him in the wilderness of mount Sina an angel of the Lord in a flame of fire in a bush.

31 When Moses saw it, he wondered at the sight: and as he drew near to behold it, the voice of the Lord came unto him,

32 Saying, I am the God of your fathers, the God of Abraham, and the God of Isaac, and the God of Jacob. Then Moses trembled, and durst not behold.

33 Then said the Lord to him, Put off your shoes from your feet: for the place where you standest is holy ground.

34 I have seen, I have seen the affliction of my people which is in Egypt, and I have heard their groaning, and am come down to deliver them. And now come, I will send you into Egypt.

35 This Moses whom they refused, saying, Who made you a ruler and a judge? the same did God send to be a ruler and a deliverer by the hand of the angel which appeared to him in the bush.

36 He brought them out, after that he had shewed wonders and signs in the land of Egypt, and in the Red sea, and in the wilderness forty years.

37 This is that Moses, which said unto the children of Israel, A prophet shall the Lord your God raise up unto you of your brethren, like unto me; him shall you hear.

38 This is he, that was in the church in the wilderness with the angel which spake to him in the mount Sina, and with our fathers: who received the lively oracles to give unto us:

39 To whom our fathers would not obey, but thrust him from them, and in their hearts turned back again into Egypt,

40 Saying unto Aaron, Make us gods to go before us: for as for this Moses, which brought us out of the land of Egypt, we wot not what is become of him.

41 And they made a calf in those days, and offered sacrifice unto the idol, and rejoiced in the works of their own hands.

42 Then God turned, and gave them up to worship the host of heaven; as it is written in the book of the prophets, O you house of Israel, have you offered to me slain beasts and sacrifices by the space of forty years in the wilderness?

43 Yea, you took up the tabernacle of Moloch, and the star of your god Remphan, figures which you made to worship them: and I will carry you away beyond Babylon.

44 Our fathers had the tabernacle of witness in the wilderness, as he had appointed, speaking unto Moses, that he should make it according to the fashion that he had seen.

45 Which also our fathers that came after brought in with Jesus into the possession of the Gentiles, whom God drave out before the face of our fathers, unto the days of David;

46 Who found favour before God, and desired to find a tabernacle for the God of Jacob.

47 But Solomon built him an house.

48 Howbeit the most High dwelleth not in temples made with hands; as saith the prophet,

49 Heaven is my throne, and earth is my footstool: what house will you build me? saith the Lord: or what is the place of my rest?

50 Has not my hand made all these things?

51 You stiffnecked and uncircumcised in heart and ears, you do always resist the Holy Ghost: as your fathers did, so do you .

52 Which of the prophets have not your fathers persecuted? and they have slain them which shewed before of the coming of the Just One; of whom you have been now the betrayers and murderers:

53 Who have received the law by the disposition of angels, and have not kept it.

54 When they heard these things, they were cut to the heart, and they gnashed on him with their teeth.

55 But he, being full of the Holy Ghost, looked up stedfastly into heaven, and saw the glory of God, and Jesus standing on the right hand of God,

56 And said, Behold, I see the heavens opened, and the Son of man standing on the right hand of God.

57 Then they cried out with a loud voice, and stopped their ears, and ran upon him with one accord,

58 And cast him out of the city, and stoned him: and the witnesses laid down their clothes at a young man's feet, whose name was Saul.

59 And they stoned Stephen, calling upon God, and saying, Lord Jesus, receive my spirit.

60 And he kneeled down, and cried with a loud voice, Lord, lay not this sin to their charge. And when he had said this, he fell asleep.

CHAPTER 8

AND Saul was consenting unto his death. And at that time there was a great persecution against the church which was at Jerusalem; and they were all scattered abroad throughout the regions of Judæa and Samaria, except the apostles.

2 And devout men carried Stephen to his burial, and made great lamentation over him.

3 As for Saul, he made havock of the church, entering into every house, and haling men and women committed them to prison.

4 Therefore they that were scattered abroad went every where preaching the word.

5 Then Philip went down to the city of Samaria, and preached Christ unto them.

6 And the people with one accord gave heed unto those things which Philip spake, hearing and seeing the miracles which he did.

7 For unclean spirits, crying with loud voice, came out of many that were possessed with them: and many taken with palsies, and that were lame, were healed.

8 And there was great joy in that city.

9 But there was a certain man, called Simon, which beforetime in the same city used sorcery, and bewitched the people of Samaria, giving out that himself was some great one:

10 To whom they all gave heed, from the least to the greatest, saying, This man is the great power of God.

11 And to him they had regard, because that of long time he had bewitched them with sorceries.

12 But when they believed Philip preaching the things concerning the kingdom of God, and the name of Jesus Christ, they were baptized, both men and women.

13 Then Simon himself believed also: and when he was baptized, he continued with Philip, and wondered, beholding the miracles and signs which were done.

14 Now when the apostles which were at Jerusalem heard that Samaria had received the word of God, they sent unto them Peter and John:

15 Who, when they were come down, prayed for them, that they might receive the Holy Ghost:

16 (For as yet he was fallen upon none of them: only they were baptized in the name of the Lord Jesus.)

17 Then laid they their hands on them, and they received the Holy Ghost.

18 And when Simon saw that through laying on of the apostles' hands the Holy Ghost was given, he offered them money,

19 Saying, Give me also this power, that on whomsoever I lay hands, he may receive the Holy Ghost.

20 But Peter said unto him, Your money perish with you, because you have thought that the gift of God may be purchased with money.

21 You have neither part nor lot in this matter: for your heart is not right in the sight of God.

22 Repent therefore of this your wickedness, and pray God, if perhaps the thought of yours heart may be forgiven you.

23 For I perceive that you are in the gall of bitterness, and in the bond of iniquity.

24 Then answered Simon, and said, Pray you to the Lord for me, that none of these things which you have spoken come upon me.

25 And they, when they had testified and preached the word of the Lord, returned to Jerusalem, and preached the gospel in many villages of the Samaritans.

26 And the angel of the Lord spake unto Philip, saying, Arise, and go toward the south unto the way that goeth down from Jerusalem unto Gaza, which is desert.

27 And he arose and went: and, behold, a man of Ethiopia, an eunuch of great authority under Candace queen of the Ethiopians, who had the charge of all her treasure, and had come to Jerusalem for to worship,

28 Was returning, and sitting in his chariot read Esaias the prophet.

29 Then the Spirit said unto Philip, Go near, and join yourself to this chariot.

30 And Philip ran thither to him, and heard him read the prophet Esaias, and said, Understandest you what you readest?

31 And he said, How can I, except some man should guide me? And he desired Philip that he would come up and sit with him.

32 The place of the scripture which he read was this, He was led as a sheep to the slaughter; and like a lamb dumb before his shearer, so opened he not his mouth:

33 In his humiliation his judgment was taken away: and who shall declare his generation? for his life is taken from the earth.

34 And the eunuch answered Philip, and said, I pray you, of whom speaketh the prophet this? of himself, or of some other man?

35 Then Philip opened his mouth, and began at the same scripture, and preached unto him Jesus.

36 And as they went on their way, they came unto a certain water: and the eunuch said, See, here is water; what doth hinder me to be baptized?

37 And Philip said, If you believest with all yours heart, you mayest. And he answered and said, I believe that Jesus Christ is the Son of God.

38 And he commanded the chariot to stand still: and they went down both into the water, both Philip and the eunuch; and he baptized him.

39 And when they were come up out of the water, the Spirit of the Lord caught away Philip, that the eunuch saw him no more: and he went on his way rejoicing.

40 But Philip was found at Azotus: and passing through he preached in all the cities, till he came to Cæsarea.

CHAPTER 9

AND Saul, yet breathing out threatenings and slaughter against the disciples of the Lord, went unto the high priest,

2 And desired of him letters to Damascus to the synagogues, that if he found any of this way, whether they were men or women, he might bring them bound unto Jerusalem.

3 And as he journeyed, he came near Damascus: and suddenly there shined round about him a light from heaven:

4 And he fell to the earth, and heard a voice saying unto him, Saul, Saul, why persecutest you me?

5 And he said, Who are you , Lord? And the Lord said, I am Jesus whom you persecutest: it is hard for you to kick against the pricks.

6 And he trembling and astonished said, Lord, what will you have me to do? And the Lord said unto him, Arise, and go into the city, and it shall be told you what you must do.

7 And the men which journeyed with him stood speechless, hearing a voice, but seeing no man.

8 And Saul arose from the earth; and when his eyes were opened, he saw no man: but they led him by the hand, and brought him into Damascus.

9 And he was three days without sight, and neither did eat nor drink.

10 And there was a certain disciple at Damascus, named Ananias; and to him said the Lord in a vision, Ananias. And he said, Behold, I am here, Lord.

11 And the Lord said unto him, Arise, and go into the street which is called Straight, and inquire in the house of Judas for one called Saul, of Tarsus: for, behold, he prayeth,

12 And has seen in a vision a man named Ananias coming in, and putting his hand on him, that he might receive his sight.

13 Then Ananias answered, Lord, I have heard by many of this man, how much evil he has done to your saints at Jerusalem:

14 And here he has authority from the chief priests to bind all that call on your name.

15 But the Lord said unto him, Go your way: for he is a chosen vessel unto me, to bear my name before the Gentiles, and kings, and the children of Israel:

16 For I will shew him how great things he must suffer for my name's sake.

17 And Ananias went his way, and entered into the house; and putting his hands on him said, Brother Saul, the Lord, even Jesus, that appeared unto you in the way as you camest, has sent me, that you mightest receive your sight, and be filled with the Holy Ghost.

18 And immediately there fell from his eyes as it had been scales: and he received sight forthwith, and arose, and was baptized.

19 And when he had received meat, he was strengthened. Then was Saul certain days with the disciples which were at Damascus.

20 And straightway he preached Christ in the synagogues, that he is the Son of God.

21 But all that heard him were amazed, and said; Is not this he that destroyed them which called on this name in Jerusalem, and came hither for that intent, that he might bring them bound unto the chief priests?

22 But Saul increased the more in strength, and confounded the Jews which dwelt at Damascus, proving that this is very Christ.

23 And after that many days were fulfilled, the Jews took counsel to kill him:

24 But their laying await was known of Saul. And they watched the gates day and night to kill him.

25 Then the disciples took him by night, and let him down by the wall in a basket.

26 And when Saul was come to Jerusalem, he assayed to join himself to the disciples: but they were all afraid of him, and believed not that he was a disciple.

27 But Barnabas took him, and brought him to the apostles, and declared unto them how he had seen the Lord in the way, and that he had spoken to him, and how he had preached boldly at Damascus in the name of Jesus.

28 And he was with them coming in and going out at Jerusalem.

29 And he spake boldly in the name of the Lord Jesus, and disputed against the Grecians: but they went about to slay him.

30 Which when the brethren knew, they brought him down to Cæsarea, and sent him forth to Tarsus.

31 Then had the churches rest throughout all Judæa and Galilee and Samaria, and were edified; and walking in the fear of the Lord, and in the comfort of the Holy Ghost, were multiplied.

32 And it came to pass, as Peter passed throughout all quarters, he came down also to the saints which dwelt at Lydda.

33 And there he found a certain man named Æneas, which had kept his bed eight years, and was sick of the palsy.

34 And Peter said unto him, Æneas, Jesus Christ maketh you whole: arise, and make your bed. And he arose immediately.

35 And all that dwelt at Lydda and Saron saw him, and turned to the Lord.

36 Now there was at Joppa a certain disciple named Tabitha, which by interpretation is called Dorcas: this woman was full of good works and almsdeeds which she did.

37 And it came to pass in those days, that she was sick, and died: whom when they had washed, they laid her in an upper chamber.

38 And forasmuch as Lydda was nigh to Joppa, and the disciples had heard that Peter was there, they sent unto him two men, desiring him that he would not delay to come to them.

39 Then Peter arose and went with them. When he was come, they brought him into the upper chamber: and all the widows stood by him weeping, and shewing the coats and garments which Dorcas made, while she was with them.

40 But Peter put them all forth, and kneeled down, and prayed; and turning him to the body said, Tabitha, arise. And she opened her eyes: and when she saw Peter, she sat up.

41 And he gave her his hand, and lifted her up, and when he had called the saints and widows, presented her alive.

42 And it was known throughout all Joppa; and many believed in the Lord.

43 And it came to pass, that he tarried many days in Joppa with one Simon a tanner.

CHAPTER 10

THERE was a certain man in Cæsarea called Cornelius, a centurion of the band called the Italian band,

2 A devout man, and one that feared God with all his house, which gave much alms to the people, and prayed to God alway.

3 He saw in a vision evidently about the ninth hour of the day an angel of God coming in to him, and saying unto him, Cornelius.

4 And when he looked on him, he was afraid, and said, What is it, Lord? And he said unto him, Your prayers and yours alms are come up for a memorial before God.

5 And now send men to Joppa, and call for one Simon, whose surname is Peter:

6 He lodgeth with one Simon a tanner, whose house is by the sea side: he shall tell you what you oughtest to do.

7 And when the angel which spake unto Cornelius was departed, he called two of his household servants, and a devout soldier of them that waited on him continually;

8 And when he had declared all these things unto them, he sent them to Joppa.

9 On the morrow, as they went on their journey, and drew nigh unto the city, Peter went up upon the housetop to pray about the sixth hour:

10 And he became very hungry, and would have eaten: but while they made ready, he fell into a trance,

11 And saw heaven opened, and a certain vessel descending unto him, as it had been a great sheet knit at the four corners, and let down to the earth:

12 Wherein were all manner of fourfooted beasts of the earth, and wild beasts, and creeping things, and fowls of the air.

13 And there came a voice to him, Rise, Peter; kill, and eat.

14 But Peter said, Not so, Lord; for I have never eaten any thing that is common or unclean.

15 And the voice spake unto him again the second time, What God has cleansed, that call not you common.

16 This was done thrice: and the vessel was received up again into heaven.

17 Now while Peter doubted in himself what this vision which he had seen should mean, behold, the men which were sent from Cornelius had made inquiry for Simon's house, and stood before the gate,

18 And called, and asked whether Simon, which was surnamed Peter, were lodged there.

19 While Peter thought on the vision, the Spirit said unto him, Behold, three men seek you.

20 Arise therefore, and get you down, and go with them, doubting nothing: for I have sent them.

21 Then Peter went down to the men which were sent unto him from Cornelius; and said, Behold, I am he whom you seek: what is the cause wherefore you are come?

22 And they said, Cornelius the centurion, a just man, and one that feareth God, and of good report among all the nation of the Jews, was warned from God by an holy angel to send for you into his house, and to hear words of you.

23 Then called he them in, and lodged them. And on the morrow Peter went away with them, and certain brethren from Joppa accompanied him.

24 And the morrow after they entered into Cæsarea. And Cornelius waited for them, and had called together his kinsmen and near friends.

25 And as Peter was coming in, Cornelius met him, and fell down at his feet, and worshipped him.

26 But Peter took him up, saying, Stand up; I myself also am a man.

27 And as he talked with him, he went in, and found many that were come together.

28 And he said unto them, You know how that it is an unlawful thing for a man that is a Jew to keep company, or come unto one of another nation; but God has shewed me that I should not call any man common or unclean.

29 Therefore came I unto you without gainsaying, as soon as I was sent for: I ask therefore for what intent you have sent for me?

30 And Cornelius said, Four days ago I was fasting until this hour; and at the ninth hour I prayed in my house, and, behold, a man stood before me in bright clothing,

31 And said, Cornelius, your prayer is heard, and yours alms are had in remembrance in the sight of God.

32 Send therefore to Joppa, and call hither Simon, whose surname is Peter; he is lodged in the house of one Simon a tanner by the sea side: who, when he comes, shall speak unto you.

33 Immediately therefore I sent to you; and you have well done that you are come. Now therefore are we all here present before God, to hear all things that are commanded you of God.

34 Then Peter opened his mouth, and said, Of a truth I perceive that God is no respecter of persons:

35 But in every nation he that feareth him, and worketh righteousness, is accepted with him.

36 The word which God sent unto the children of Israel, preaching peace by Jesus Christ: (he is Lord of all:)

37 That word, I say, you know, which was published throughout all Judæa, and began from Galilee, after the baptism which John preached;

38 How God anointed Jesus of Nazareth with the Holy Ghost and with power: who went about doing good, and healing all that were oppressed of the devil; for God was with him.

39 And we are witnesses of all things which he did both in the land of the Jews, and in Jerusalem; whom they slew and hanged on a tree:

40 Him God raised up the third day, and shewed him openly;

41 Not to all the people, but unto witnesses chosen before of God, even to us, who did eat and drink with him after he rose from the dead.

42 And he commanded us to preach unto the people, and to testify that it is he which was ordained of God to be the Judge of quick and dead.

43 To him give all the prophets witness, that through his name whosoever believeth in him shall receive remission of sins.

44 While Peter yet spake these words, the Holy Ghost fell on all them which heard the word.

45 And they of the circumcision which believed were astonished, as many as came with Peter, because that on the Gentiles also was poured out the gift of the Holy Ghost.

46 For they heard them speak with tongues, and magnify God. Then answered Peter,

47 Can any man forbid water, that these should not be baptized, which have received the Holy Ghost as well as we?

48 And he commanded them to be baptized in the name of the Lord. Then prayed they him to tarry certain days.

CHAPTER 11

AND the apostles and brethren that were in Judæa heard that the Gentiles had also received the word of God.

2 And when Peter was come up to Jerusalem, they that were of the circumcision contended with him,

3 Saying, You wentest in to men uncircumcised, and did eat with them.

4 But Peter rehearsed the matter from the beginning, and expounded it by order unto them, saying,

5 I was in the city of Joppa praying: and in a trance I saw a vision, A certain vessel descend, as it had been a great sheet, let down from heaven by four corners; and it came even to me:

6 Upon the which when I had fastened my eyes, I considered, and saw fourfooted beasts of the earth, and wild beasts, and creeping things, and fowls of the air.

7 And I heard a voice saying unto me, Arise, Peter; slay and eat.

8 But I said, Not so, Lord: for nothing common or unclean has at any time entered into my mouth.

9 But the voice answered me again from heaven, What God has cleansed, that call not you common.

10 And this was done three times: and all were drawn up again into heaven.

11 And, behold, immediately there were three men already come unto the house where I was, sent from Cæsarea unto me.

12 And the spirit bade me go with them, nothing doubting. Moreover these six brethren accompanied me, and we entered into the man's house:

13 And he shewed us how he had seen an angel in his house, which stood and said unto him, Send men to Joppa, and call for Simon, whose surname is Peter;

14 Who shall tell you words, whereby you and all your house shall be saved.

15 And as I began to speak, the Holy Ghost fell on them, as on us at the beginning.

16 Then remembered I the word of the Lord, how that he said, John indeed baptized with water; but you shall be baptized with the Holy Ghost.

17 Forasmuch then as God gave them the like gift as he did unto us, who believed on the Lord Jesus Christ; what was I, that I could withstand God?

18 When they heard these things, they held their peace, and glorified God, saying, Then has God also to the Gentiles granted repentance unto life.

19 Now they which were scattered abroad upon the persecution that arose about Stephen travelled as far as Phenice, and Cyprus, and Antioch, preaching the word to none but unto the Jews only.

20 And some of them were men of Cyprus and Cyrene, which, when they were come to Antioch, spake unto the Grecians, preaching the Lord Jesus.

21 And the hand of the Lord was with them: and a great number believed, and turned unto the Lord.

22 Then tidings of these things came unto the ears of the church which was in Jerusalem: and they sent forth Barnabas, that he should go as far as Antioch.

23 Who, when he came, and had seen the grace of God, was glad, and exhorted them all, that with purpose of heart they would cleave unto the Lord.

24 For he was a good man, and full of the Holy Ghost and of faith: and much people was added unto the Lord.

25 Then departed Barnabas to Tarsus, for to seek Saul:

26 And when he had found him, he brought him unto Antioch. And it came to pass, that a whole year they assembled themselves with the church, and taught much people. And the disciples were called Christians first in Antioch.

27And in these days came prophets from Jerusalem unto Antioch.

28 And there stood up one of them named Agabus, and signified by the spirit that there should be great dearth throughout all the world: which came to pass in the days of Claudius Cæsar.

29 Then the disciples, every man according to his ability, determined to send relief unto the brethren which dwelt in Judæa:

30 Which also they did, and sent it to the elders by the hands of Barnabas and Saul.

CHAPTER 12

NOW about that time Herod the king stretched forth his hands to vex certain of the church.

2 And he killed James the brother of John with the sword.

3 And because he saw it pleased the Jews, he proceeded further to take Peter also. (Then were the days of unleavened bread.)

4 And when he had apprehended him, he put him in prison, and delivered him to four quaternions of soldiers to keep him; intending after Easter to bring him forth to the people.

5 Peter therefore was kept in prison: but prayer was made without ceasing of the church unto God for him.

6 And when Herod would have brought him forth, the same night Peter was sleeping between two soldiers, bound with two chains: and the keepers before the door kept the prison.

7 And, behold, the angel of the Lord came upon him, and a light shined in the prison: and he struck Peter on the side, and raised him up, saying, Arise up quickly. And his chains fell off from his hands.

8 And the angel said unto him, Gird yourself, and bind on your sandals. And so he did. And he saith unto him, Cast your garment about you, and follow me.

9 And he went out, and followed him; and wist not that it was true which was done by the angel; but thought he saw a vision.

10 When they were past the first and the second ward, they came unto the iron gate that leadeth unto the city; which opened to them of his own accord: and they went out, and passed on through one street; and forthwith the angel departed from him.

11 And when Peter was come to himself, he said, Now I know of a surety, that the Lord has sent his angel, and has delivered me out of the hand of Herod, and from all the expectation of the people of the Jews.

12 And when he had considered the thing, he came to the house of Mary the mother of John, whose surname was Mark; where many were gathered together praying.

13 And as Peter knocked at the door of the gate, a damsel came to hearken, named Rhoda.

14 And when she knew Peter's voice, she opened not the gate for gladness, but ran in, and told how Peter stood before the gate.

15 And they said unto her, You are mad. But she constantly affirmed that it was even so. Then said they, It is his angel.

16 But Peter continued knocking: and when they had opened the door, and saw him, they were astonished.

17 But he, beckoning unto them with the hand to hold their peace, declared unto them how the Lord had brought him out of the prison. And he said, Go shew these things unto James, and to the brethren. And he departed, and went into another place.

18 Now as soon as it was day, there was no small stir among the soldiers, what was become of Peter.

19 And when Herod had sought for him, and found him not, he examined the keepers, and commanded that they should be put to death. And he went down from Judæa to Cæsarea, and there abode.

20And Herod was highly displeased with them of Tyre and Sidon: but they came with one accord to him, and, having made Blastus the king's chamberlain their friend, desired peace; because their country was nourished by the king's country.

21 And upon a set day Herod, arrayed in royal apparel, sat upon his throne, and made an oration unto them.

22 And the people gave a shout, saying, It is the voice of a god, and not of a man.

23 And immediately the angel of the Lord struck him, because he gave not God the glory: and he was eaten of worms, and gave up the ghost.

24But the word of God grew and multiplied.

25 And Barnabas and Saul returned from Jerusalem, when they had fulfilled their ministry, and took with them John, whose surname was Mark.

CHAPTER 13

NOW there were in the church that was at Antioch certain prophets and teachers; as Barnabas, and Simeon that was called Niger, and Lucius of Cyrene, and Manaen, which had been brought up with Herod the tetrarch, and Saul.

2 As they ministered to the Lord, and fasted, the Holy Ghost said, Separate me Barnabas and Saul for the work whereunto I have called them.

3 And when they had fasted and prayed, and laid their hands on them, they sent them away.

4So they, being sent forth by the Holy Ghost, departed unto Seleucia; and from thence they sailed to Cyprus.

5 And when they were at Salamis, they preached the word of God in the synagogues of the Jews: and they had also John to their minister.

6 And when they had gone through the isle unto Paphos, they found a certain sorcerer, a false prophet, a Jew, whose name was Bar-jesus:

7 Which was with the deputy of the country, Sergius Paulus, a prudent man; who called for Barnabas and Saul, and desired to hear the word of God.

8 But Elymas the sorcerer (for so is his name by interpretation) withstood them, seeking to turn away the deputy from the faith.

9 Then Saul, (who also is called Paul,) filled with the Holy Ghost, set his eyes on him,

10 And said, O full of all subtilty and all mischief, you child of the devil, you enemy of all righteousness, will you not cease to pervert the right ways of the Lord?

11 And now, behold, the hand of the Lord is upon you, and you shalt be blind, not seeing the sun for a season. And immediately there fell on him a mist and a darkness; and he went about seeking some to lead him by the hand.

12 Then the deputy, when he saw what was done, believed, being astonished at the doctrine of the Lord.

13 Now when Paul and his company loosed from Paphos, they came to Perga in Pamphylia: and John departing from them returned to Jerusalem.

14But when they departed from Perga, they came to Antioch in Pisidia, and went into the synagogue on the sabbath day, and sat down.

15 And after the reading of the law and the prophets the rulers of the synagogue sent unto them, saying, You men and brethren, if you have any word of exhortation for the people, say on.

16 Then Paul stood up, and beckoning with his hand said, Men of Israel, and you that fear God, give audience.

17 The God of this people of Israel chose our fathers, and exalted the people when they dwelt as strangers in the land of Egypt, and with an high arm brought he them out of it.

18 And about the time of forty years suffered he their manners in the wilderness.

19 And when he had destroyed seven nations in the land of Chanaan, he divided their land to them by lot.

20 And after that he gave unto them judges about the space of four hundred and fifty years, until Samuel the prophet.

21 And afterward they desired a king: and God gave unto them Saul the son of Cis, a man of the tribe of Benjamin, by the space of forty years.

22 And when he had removed him, he raised up unto them David to be their king; to whom also he gave testimony, and said, I have found David the son of Jesse, a man after my own heart, which shall fulfil all my will.

23 Of this man's seed has God according to his promise raised unto Israel a Saviour, Jesus:

24 When John had first preached before his coming the baptism of repentance to all the people of Israel.

25 And as John fulfilled his course, he said, Whom think you that I am? I am not he. But, behold, there comes one after me, whose shoes of his feet I am not worthy to loose.

26 Men and brethren, children of the stock of Abraham, and whosoever among you feareth God, to you is the word of this salvation sent.

27 For they that dwell at Jerusalem, and their rulers, because they knew him not, nor yet the voices of the prophets which are read every sabbath day, they have fulfilled them in condemning him.

28 And though they found no cause of death in him, yet desired they Pilate that he should be slain.

29 And when they had fulfilled all that was written of him, they took him down from the tree, and laid him in a sepulchre.

30 But God raised him from the dead:

31 And he was seen many days of them which came up with him from Galilee to Jerusalem, who are his witnesses unto the people.

32 And we declare unto you glad tidings, how that the promise which was made unto the fathers,

33 God has fulfilled the same unto us their children, in that he has raised up Jesus again; as it is also written in the second psalm, You are my Son, this day have I begotten you.

34 And as concerning that he raised him up from the dead, now no more to return to corruption, he said on this wise, I will give you the sure mercies of David.

35 Wherefore he saith also in another psalm, You shalt not suffer yours Holy One to see corruption.

36 For David, after he had served his own generation by the will of God, fell on sleep, and was laid unto his fathers, and saw corruption:

37 But he, whom God raised again, saw no corruption.

38 Be it known unto you therefore, men and brethren, that through this man is preached unto you the forgiveness of sins:

39 And by him all that believe are justified from all things, from which you could not be justified by the law of Moses.

40 Beware therefore, lest that come upon you, which is spoken of in the prophets;

41 Behold, you despisers, and wonder, and perish: for I work a work in your days, a work which you shall in no wise believe, though a man declare it unto you.

42 And when the Jews were gone out of the synagogue, the Gentiles besought that these words might be preached to them the next sabbath.

43 Now when the congregation was broken up, many of the Jews and religious proselytes followed Paul and Barnabas: who, speaking to them, persuaded them to continue in the grace of God.

44 And the next sabbath day came almost the whole city together to hear the word of God.

45 But when the Jews saw the multitudes, they were filled with envy, and spake against those things which were spoken by Paul, contradicting and blaspheming.

46 Then Paul and Barnabas waxed bold, and said, It was necessary that the word of God should first have been spoken to you: but seeing you put it from you, and judge yourselves unworthy of everlasting life, lo, we turn to the Gentiles.

47 For so has the Lord commanded us, saying, I have set you to be a light of the Gentiles, that you shouldest be for salvation unto the ends of the earth.

48 And when the Gentiles heard this, they were glad, and glorified the word of the Lord: and as many as were ordained to eternal life believed.

49 And the word of the Lord was published throughout all the region.

50 But the Jews stirred up the devout and honourable women, and the chief men of the city, and raised persecution against Paul and Barnabas, and expelled them out of their coasts.

51 But they shook off the dust of their feet against them, and came unto Iconium.

52 And the disciples were filled with joy, and with the Holy Ghost.

CHAPTER 14

AND it came to pass in Iconium, that they went both together into the synagogue of the Jews, and so spake, that a great multitude both of the Jews and also of the Greeks believed.

2 But the unbelieving Jews stirred up the Gentiles, and made their minds evil affected against the brethren.

3 Long time therefore abode they speaking boldly in the Lord, which gave testimony unto the word of his grace, and granted signs and wonders to be done by their hands.

4 But the multitude of the city was divided: and part held with the Jews, and part with the apostles.

5 And when there was an assault made both of the Gentiles, and also of the Jews with their rulers, to use them despitefully, and to stone them,

6 They were ware of it, and fled unto Lystra and Derbe, cities of Lycaonia, and unto the region that lies round about:

7 And there they preached the gospel.

8 And there sat a certain man at Lystra, impotent in his feet, being a cripple from his mother's womb, who never had walked:

9 The same heard Paul speak: who stedfastly beholding him, and perceiving that he had faith to be healed,

10 Said with a loud voice, Stand upright on your feet. And he leaped and walked.

11 And when the people saw what Paul had done, they lifted up their voices, saying in the speech of Lycaonia, The gods are come down to us in the likeness of men.

12 And they called Barnabas, Jupiter; and Paul, Mercurius, because he was the chief speaker.

13 Then the priest of Jupiter, which was before their city, brought oxen and garlands unto the gates, and would have done sacrifice with the people.

14 Which when the apostles, Barnabas and Paul, heard of, they rent their clothes, and ran in among the people, crying out,

15 And saying, Sirs, why do you these things? We also are men of like passions with you, and preach unto you that you should turn from these vanities unto the living God, which made heaven, and earth, and the sea, and all things that are therein:

16 Who in times past suffered all nations to walk in their own ways.

17 Nevertheless he left not himself without witness, in that he did good, and gave us rain from heaven, and fruitful seasons, filling our hearts with food and gladness.

18 And with these sayings scarce restrained they the people, that they had not done sacrifice unto them.

19 And there came thither certain Jews from Antioch and Iconium, who persuaded the people, and, having stoned Paul, drew him out of the city, supposing he had been dead.

20 Howbeit, as the disciples stood round about him, he rose up, and came into the city: and the next day he departed with Barnabas to Derbe.

21 And when they had preached the gospel to that city, and had taught many, they returned again to Lystra, and to Iconium, and Antioch,

22 Confirming the souls of the disciples, and exhorting them to continue in the faith, and that we must through much tribulation enter into the kingdom of God.

23 And when they had ordained them elders in every church, and had prayed with fasting, they commended them to the Lord, on whom they believed.

24 And after they had passed throughout Pisidia, they came to Pamphylia.

25 And when they had preached the word in Perga, they went down into Attalia:

26 And thence sailed to Antioch, from whence they had been recommended to the grace of God for the work which they fulfilled.

27 And when they were come, and had gathered the church together, they rehearsed all that God had done with them, and how he had opened the door of faith unto the Gentiles.

28 And there they abode long time with the disciples.

CHAPTER 15

AND certain men which came down from Judæa taught the brethren, and said, Except you be circumcised after the manner of Moses, you cannot be saved.

2 When therefore Paul and Barnabas had no small dissension and disputation with them, they determined that Paul and Barnabas, and certain other of them, should go up to Jerusalem unto the apostles and elders about this question.

3 And being brought on their way by the church, they passed through Phenice and Samaria, declaring the conversion of the Gentiles: and they caused great joy unto all the brethren.

4 And when they were come to Jerusalem, they were received of the church, and of the apostles and elders, and they declared all things that God had done with them.

5 But there rose up certain of the sect of the Pharisees which believed, saying, That it was needful to circumcise them, and to command them to keep the law of Moses.

6 And the apostles and elders came together for to consider of this matter.

7 And when there had been much disputing, Peter rose up, and said unto them, Men and brethren, you know how that a good while ago God made choice among us, that the Gentiles by my mouth should hear the word of the gospel, and believe.

8 And God, which knoweth the hearts, bare them witness, giving them the Holy Ghost, even as he did unto us;

9 And put no difference between us and them, purifying their hearts by faith.

10 Now therefore why tempt you God, to put a yoke upon the neck of the disciples, which neither our fathers nor we were able to bear?

11 But we believe that through the grace of the Lord Jesus Christ we shall be saved, even as they.

12 Then all the multitude kept silence, and gave audience to Barnabas and Paul, declaring what miracles and wonders God had created among the Gentiles by them.

13 And after they had held their peace, James answered, saying, Men and brethren, hearken unto me:

14 Simeon has declared how God at the first did visit the Gentiles, to take out of them a people for his name.

15 And to this agree the words of the prophets; as it is written,

16 After this I will return, and will build again the tabernacle of David, which is fallen down; and I will build again the ruins thereof, and I will set it up:

17 That the residue of men might seek after the Lord, and all the Gentiles, upon whom my name is called, saith the Lord, who doeth all these things.

18 Known unto God are all his works from the beginning of the world.

19 Wherefore my sentence is, that we trouble not them, which from among the Gentiles are turned to God:

20 But that we write unto them, that they abstain from pollutions of idols, and from fornication, and from things strangled, and from blood.

21 For Moses of old time has in every city them that preach him, being read in the synagogues every sabbath day.

22 Then pleased it the apostles and elders, with the whole church, to send chosen men of their own company to Antioch with Paul and Barnabas; namely, Judas surnamed Barsabas, and Silas, chief men among the brethren:

23 And they wrote letters by them after this manner; The apostles and elders and brethren send greeting unto the brethren which are of the Gentiles in Antioch and Syria and Cilicia:

24 Forasmuch as we have heard, that certain which went out from us have troubled you with words, subverting your souls, saying, You must be circumcised, and keep the law: to whom we gave no such commandment:

25 It seemed good unto us, being assembled with one accord, to send chosen men unto you with our beloved Barnabas and Paul,

26 Men that have hazarded their lives for the name of our Lord Jesus Christ.

27 We have sent therefore Judas and Silas, who shall also tell you the same things by mouth.

28 For it seemed good to the Holy Ghost, and to us, to lay upon you no greater burden than these necessary things;

29 That you abstain from meats offered to idols, and from blood, and from things strangled, and from fornication: from which if you keep yourselves, you shall do well. Fare you well.

30 So when they were dismissed, they came to Antioch: and when they had gathered the multitude together, they delivered the epistle:

31 Which when they had read, they rejoiced for the consolation.

32 And Judas and Silas, being prophets also themselves, exhorted the brethren with many words, and confirmed them.

33 And after they had tarried there a space, they were let go in peace from the brethren unto the apostles.

34 Notwithstanding it pleased Silas to abide there still.

35 Paul also and Barnabas continued in Antioch, teaching and preaching the word of the Lord, with many others also.

36 And some days after Paul said unto Barnabas, Let us go again and visit our brethren in every city where we have preached the word of the Lord, and see how they do.

37 And Barnabas determined to take with them John, whose surname was Mark.

38 But Paul thought not good to take him with them, who departed from them from Pamphylia, and went not with them to the work.

39 And the contention was so sharp between them, that they departed asunder one from the other: and so Barnabas took Mark, and sailed unto Cyprus;

40 And Paul chose Silas, and departed, being recommended by the brethren unto the grace of God.

41 And he went through Syria and Cilicia, confirming the churches.

CHAPTER 16

THEN came he to Derbe and Lystra: and, behold, a certain disciple was there, named Timotheus, the son of a certain woman, which was a Jewess, and believed; but his father was a Greek:

2 Which was well reported of by the brethren that were at Lystra and Iconium.

3 Him would Paul have to go forth with him; and took and circumcised him because of the Jews which were in those quarters: for they knew all that his father was a Greek.

4 And as they went through the cities, they delivered them the decrees for to keep, that were ordained of the apostles and elders which were at Jerusalem.

5 And so were the churches established in the faith, and increased in number daily.

6 Now when they had gone throughout Phrygia and the region of Galatia, and were forbidden of the Holy Ghost to preach the word in Asia,

7 After they were come to Mysia, they assayed to go into Bithynia: but the Spirit suffered them not.

8 And they passing by Mysia came down to Troas.

9 And a vision appeared to Paul in the night; There stood a man of Macedonia, and prayed him, saying, Come over into Macedonia, and help us.

10 And after he had seen the vision, immediately we endeavoured to go into Macedonia, assuredly gathering that the Lord had called us for to preach the gospel unto them.

11 Therefore loosing from Troas, we came with a straight course to Samothracia, and the next day to Neapolis;

12 And from thence to Philippi, which is the chief city of that part of Macedonia, and a colony: and we were in that city abiding certain days.

13 And on the sabbath we went out of the city by a river side, where prayer was wont to be made; and we sat down, and spake unto the women which resorted thither.

14 And a certain woman named Lydia, a seller of purple, of the city of Thyatira, which worshipped God, heard us: whose heart the Lord opened, that she attended unto the things which were spoken of Paul.

15 And when she was baptized, and her household, she besought us, saying, If you have judged me to be faithful to the Lord, come into my house, and abide there. And she constrained us.

16 And it came to pass, as we went to prayer, a certain damsel possessed with a spirit of divination met us, which brought her masters much gain by soothsaying:

17 The same followed Paul and us, and cried, saying, These men are the servants of the most high God, which shew unto us the way of salvation.

18 And this did she many days. But Paul, being grieved, turned and said to the spirit, I command you in the name of Jesus Christ to come out of her. And he came out the same hour.

19 And when her masters saw that the hope of their gains was gone, they caught Paul and Silas, and drew them into the marketplace unto the rulers,

20 And brought them to the magistrates, saying, These men, being Jews, do exceedingly trouble our city,

21 And teach customs, which are not lawful for us to receive, neither to observe, being Romans.

22 And the multitude rose up together against them: and the magistrates rent off their clothes, and commanded to beat them.

23 And when they had laid many stripes upon them, they cast them into prison, charging the jailor to keep them safely:

24 Who, having received such a charge, thrust them into the inner prison, and made their feet fast in the stocks.

25 And at midnight Paul and Silas prayed, and sang praises unto God: and the prisoners heard them.

26 And suddenly there was a great earthquake, so that the foundations of the prison were shaken: and immediately all the doors were opened, and every one's bands were loosed.

27 And the keeper of the prison awaking out of his sleep, and seeing the prison doors open, he drew out his sword, and would have killed himself, supposing that the prisoners had been fled.

28 But Paul cried with a loud voice, saying, Do yourself no harm: for we are all here.

29 Then he called for a light, and sprang in, and came trembling, and fell down before Paul and Silas,

30 And brought them out, and said, Sirs, what must I do to be saved?

31 And they said, Believe on the Lord Jesus Christ, and you shalt be saved, and your house.

32 And they spake unto him the word of the Lord, and to all that were in his house.

33 And he took them the same hour of the night, and washed their stripes; and was baptized, he and all his, straightway.

34 And when he had brought them into his house, he set meat before them, and rejoiced, believing in God with all his house.

35 And when it was day, the magistrates sent the serjeants, saying, Let those men go.

36 And the keeper of the prison told this saying to Paul, The magistrates have sent to let you go: now therefore depart, and go in peace.

37 But Paul said unto them, They have beaten us openly uncondemned, being Romans, and have cast us into prison; and now do they thrust us out privily? nay verily; but let them come themselves and fetch us out.

38 And the serjeants told these words unto the magistrates: and they feared, when they heard that they were Romans.

39 And they came and besought them, and brought them out, and desired them to depart out of the city.

40 And they went out of the prison, and entered into the house of Lydia: and when they had seen the brethren, they comforted them, and departed.

CHAPTER 17

NOW when they had passed through Amphipolis and Apollonia, they came to Thessalonica, where was a synagogue of the Jews:

2 And Paul, as his manner was, went in unto them, and three sabbath days reasoned with them out of the scriptures,

3 Opening and alleging, that Christ must needs have suffered, and risen again from the dead; and that this Jesus, whom I preach unto you, is Christ.

4 And some of them believed, and consorted with Paul and Silas; and of the devout Greeks a great multitude, and of the chief women not a few.

5 But the Jews which believed not, moved with envy, took unto them certain lewd fellows of the baser sort, and gathered a company, and set all the city on an uproar, and assaulted the house of Jason, and sought to bring them out to the people.

6 And when they found them not, they drew Jason and certain brethren unto the rulers of the city, crying, These that have turned the world upside down are come hither also;

7 Whom Jason has received: and these all do contrary to the decrees of Cæsar, saying that there is another king, one Jesus.

8 And they troubled the people and the rulers of the city, when they heard these things.

9 And when they had taken security of Jason, and of the other, they let them go.

10And the brethren immediately sent away Paul and Silas by night unto Berea: who coming thither went into the synagogue of the Jews.

11 These were more noble than those in Thessalonica, in that they received the word with all readiness of mind, and searched the scriptures daily, whether those things were so.

12 Therefore many of them believed; also of honourable women which were Greeks, and of men, not a few.

13 But when the Jews of Thessalonica had knowledge that the word of God was preached of Paul at Berea, they came thither also, and stirred up the people.

14 And then immediately the brethren sent away Paul to go as it were to the sea: but Silas and Timotheus abode there still.

15 And they that conducted Paul brought him unto Athens: and receiving a commandment unto Silas and Timotheus for to come to him with all speed, they departed.

16Now while Paul waited for them at Athens, his spirit was stirred in him, when he saw the city wholly given to idolatry.

17 Therefore disputed he in the synagogue with the Jews, and with the devout persons, and in the market daily with them that met with him.

18 Then certain philosophers of the Epicureans, and of the Stoicks, encountered him. And some said, What will this babbler say? other some, He seemeth to be a setter forth of strange gods: because he preached unto them Jesus, and the resurrection.

19 And they took him, and brought him unto Areopagus, saying, May we know what this new doctrine, whereof you speakest, is?

20 For you bringest certain strange things to our ears: we would know therefore what these things mean.

21 (For all the Athenians and strangers which were there spent their time in nothing else, but either to tell, or to hear some new thing.)

22Then Paul stood in the midst of Mars' hill, and said, You men of Athens, I perceive that in all things you are too superstitious.

23 For as I passed by, and beheld your devotions, I found an altar with this inscription, TO THE UNKNOWN GOD. Whom therefore you ignorantly worship, him declare I unto you.

24 God that made the world and all things therein, seeing that he is Lord of heaven and earth, dwelleth not in temples made with hands;

25 Neither is worshipped with men's hands, as though he needed any thing, seeing he giveth to all life, and breath, and all things;

26 And has made of one blood all nations of men for to dwell on all the face of the earth, and has determined the times before appointed, and the bounds of their habitation;

27 That they should seek the Lord, if haply they might feel after him, and find him, though he be not far from every one of us:

28 For in him we live, and move, and have our being; as certain also of your own poets have said, For we are also his offspring.

29 Forasmuch then as we are the offspring of God, we ought not to think that the Godhead is like unto gold, or silver, or stone, graven by are and man's device.

30 And the times of this ignorance God winked at; but now commandeth all men every where to repent:

31 Because he has appointed a day, in the which he will judge the world in righteousness by that man whom he has ordained; whereof he has given assurance unto all men, in that he has raised him from the dead.

32And when they heard of the resurrection of the dead, some mocked: and others said, We will hear you again of this matter.

33 So Paul departed from among them.

34 Howbeit certain men clave unto him, and believed: among the which was Dionysius the Areopagite, and a woman named Damaris, and others with them.

CHAPTER 18

AFTER these things Paul departed from Athens, and came to Corinth;

2 And found a certain Jew named Aquila, born in Pontus, lately come from Italy, with his wife Priscilla; (because that Claudius had commanded all Jews to depart from Rome:) and came unto them.

3 And because he was of the same craft, he abode with them, and created: for by their occupation they were tentmakers.

4 And he reasoned in the synagogue every sabbath, and persuaded the Jews and the Greeks.

5 And when Silas and Timotheus were come from Macedonia, Paul was pressed in the spirit, and testified to the Jews that Jesus was Christ.

6 And when they opposed themselves, and blasphemed, he shook his raiment, and said unto them, Your blood be upon your own heads; I am clean: from henceforth I will go unto the Gentiles.

7And he departed thence, and entered into a certain man's house, named Justus, one that worshipped God, whose house joined hard to the synagogue.

8 And Crispus, the chief ruler of the synagogue, believed on the Lord with all his house; and many of the Corinthians hearing believed, and were baptized.

9 Then spake the Lord to Paul in the night by a vision, Be not afraid, but speak, and hold not your peace:

10 For I am with you, and no man shall set on you to hurt you: for I have much people in this city.

11 And he continued there a year and six months, teaching the word of God among them.

12And when Gallio was the deputy of Achaia, the Jews made insurrection with one accord against Paul, and brought him to the judgment seat,

13 Saying, This fellow persuadeth men to worship God contrary to the law.

14 And when Paul was now about to open his mouth, Gallio said unto the Jews, If it were a matter of wrong or wicked lewdness, O you Jews, reason would that I should bear with you:

15 But if it be a question of words and names, and of your law, look you to it; for I will be no judge of such matters.

16 And he drave them from the judgment seat.

17 Then all the Greeks took Sosthenes, the chief ruler of the synagogue, and beat him before the judgment seat. And Gallio cared for none of those things.

18And Paul after this tarried there yet a good while, and then took his leave of the brethren, and sailed thence into Syria, and with him Priscilla and Aquila; having shorn his head in Cenchrea: for he had a vow.

19 And he came to Ephesus, and left them there: but he himself entered into the synagogue, and reasoned with the Jews.

20 When they desired him to tarry longer time with them, he consented not;

21 But bade them farewell, saying, I must by all means keep this feast that comes in Jerusalem: but I will return again unto you, if God will. And he sailed from Ephesus.

22 And when he had landed at Cæsarea, and gone up, and saluted the church, he went down to Antioch.

23 And after he had spent some time there, he departed, and went over all the country of Galatia and Phrygia in order, strengthening all the disciples.

24And a certain Jew named Apollos, born at Alexandria, an eloquent man, and mighty in the scriptures, came to Ephesus.

25 This man was instructed in the way of the Lord; and being fervent in the spirit, he spake and taught diligently the things of the Lord, knowing only the baptism of John.

26 And he began to speak boldly in the synagogue: whom when Aquila and Priscilla had heard, they took him unto them, and expounded unto him the way of God more perfectly.

27 And when he was disposed to pass into Achaia, the brethren wrote, exhorting the disciples to receive him: who, when he was come, helped them much which had believed through grace:

28 For he mightily convinced the Jews, and that publickly, shewing by the scriptures that Jesus was Christ.

CHAPTER 19

AND it came to pass, that, while Apollos was at Corinth, Paul having passed through the upper coasts came to Ephesus: and finding certain disciples,

2 He said unto them, Have you received the Holy Ghost since you believed? And they said unto him, We have not so much as heard whether there be any Holy Ghost.

3 And he said unto them, Unto what then were you baptized? And they said, Unto John's baptism.

4 Then said Paul, John verily baptized with the baptism of repentance, saying unto the people, that they should believe on him which should come after him, that is, on Christ Jesus.

5 When they heard this, they were baptized in the name of the Lord Jesus.

6 And when Paul had laid his hands upon them, the Holy Ghost came on them; and they spake with tongues, and prophesied.

7 And all the men were about twelve.

8 And he went into the synagogue, and spake boldly for the space of three months, disputing and persuading the things concerning the kingdom of God.

9 But when divers were hardened, and believed not, but spake evil of that way before the multitude, he departed from them, and separated the disciples, disputing daily in the school of one Tyrannus.

10 And this continued by the space of two years; so that all they which dwelt in Asia heard the word of the Lord Jesus, both Jews and Greeks.

11 And God created special miracles by the hands of Paul:

12 So that from his body were brought unto the sick handkerchiefs or aprons, and the diseases departed from them, and the evil spirits went out of them.

13 Then certain of the vagabond Jews, exorcists, took upon them to call over them which had evil spirits the name of the Lord Jesus, saying, We adjure you by Jesus whom Paul preacheth.

14 And there were seven sons of one Sceva, a Jew, and chief of the priests, which did so.

15 And the evil spirit answered and said, Jesus I know, and Paul I know; but who are you ?

16 And the man in whom the evil spirit was leaped on them, and overcame them, and prevailed against them, so that they fled out of that house naked and wounded.

17 And this was known to all the Jews and Greeks also dwelling at Ephesus; and fear fell on them all, and the name of the Lord Jesus was magnified.

18 And many that believed came, and confessed, and shewed their deeds.

19 Many of them also which used curious arts brought their books together, and burned them before all men: and they counted the price of them, and found it fifty thousand pieces of silver.

20 So mightily grew the word of God and prevailed.

21 After these things were ended, Paul purposed in the spirit, when he had passed through Macedonia and Achaia, to go to Jerusalem, saying, After I have been there, I must also see Rome.

22 So he sent into Macedonia two of them that ministered unto him, Timotheus and Erastus; but he himself stayed in Asia for a season.

23 And the same time there arose no small stir about that way.

24 For a certain man named Demetrius, a silversmith, which made silver shrines for Diana, brought no small gain unto the craftsmen;

25 Whom he called together with the workmen of like occupation, and said, Sirs, you know that by this craft we have our wealth.

26 Moreover you see and hear, that not alone at Ephesus, but almost throughout all Asia, this Paul has persuaded and turned away much people, saying that they be no gods, which are made with hands:

27 So that not only this our craft is in danger to be set at nought; but also that the temple of the great goddess Diana should be despised, and her magnificence should be destroyed, whom all Asia and the world worshippeth.

28 And when they heard these sayings, they were full of wrath, and cried out, saying, Great is Diana of the Ephesians.

29 And the whole city was filled with confusion: and having caught Gaius and Aristarchus, men of Macedonia, Paul's companions in travel, they rushed with one accord into the theatre.

30 And when Paul would have entered in unto the people, the disciples suffered him not.

31 And certain of the chief of Asia, which were his friends, sent unto him, desiring him that he would not adventure himself into the theatre.

32 Some therefore cried one thing, and some another: for the assembly was confused; and the more part knew not wherefore they were come together.

33 And they drew Alexander out of the multitude, the Jews putting him forward. And Alexander beckoned with the hand, and would have made his defence unto the people.

34 But when they knew that he was a Jew, all with one voice about the space of two hours cried out, Great is Diana of the Ephesians.

35 And when the townclerk had appeased the people, he said, You men of Ephesus, what man is there that knoweth not how that the city of the Ephesians is a worshipper of the great goddess Diana, and of the image which fell down from Jupiter?

36 Seeing then that these things cannot be spoken against, you ought to be quiet, and to do nothing rashly.

37 For you have brought hither these men, which are neither robbers of churches, nor yet blasphemers of your goddess.

38 Wherefore if Demetrius, and the craftsmen which are with him, have a matter against any man, the law is open, and there are deputies: let them implead one another.

39 But if you inquire any thing concerning other matters, it shall be determined in a lawful assembly.

40 For we are in danger to be called in question for this day's uproar, there being no cause whereby we may give an account of this concourse.

41 And when he had thus spoken, he dismissed the assembly.

CHAPTER 20

AND after the uproar was ceased, Paul called unto him the disciples, and embraced them, and departed for to go into Macedonia.

2 And when he had gone over those parts, and had given them much exhortation, he came into Greece,

3 And there abode three months. And when the Jews laid wait for him, as he was about to sail into Syria, he purposed to return through Macedonia.

4 And there accompanied him into Asia Sopater of Berea; and of the Thessalonians, Aristarchus and Secundus; and Gaius of Derbe, and Timotheus; and of Asia, Tychicus and Trophimus.

5 These going before tarried for us at Troas.

6 And we sailed away from Philippi after the days of unleavened bread, and came unto them to Troas in five days; where we abode seven days.

7 And upon the first day of the week, when the disciples came together to break bread, Paul preached unto them, ready to depart on the morrow; and continued his speech until midnight.

8 And there were many lights in the upper chamber, where they were gathered together.

9 And there sat in a window a certain young man named Eutychus, being fallen into a deep sleep: and as Paul was long preaching, he sunk down with sleep, and fell down from the third loft, and was taken up dead.

10 And Paul went down, and fell on him, and embracing him said, Trouble not yourselves; for his life is in him.

11 When he therefore was come up again, and had broken bread, and eaten, and talked a long while, even till break of day, so he departed.

12 And they brought the young man alive, and were not a little comforted.

13 And we went before to ship, and sailed unto Assos, there intending to take in Paul: for so had he appointed, minding himself to go afoot.

14 And when he met with us at Assos, we took him in, and came to Mitylene.

15 And we sailed thence, and came the next day over against Chios; and the next day we arrived at Samos, and tarried at Trogyllium; and the next day we came to Miletus.

16 For Paul had determined to sail by Ephesus, because he would not spend the time in Asia: for he hasted, if it were possible for him, to be at Jerusalem the day of Pentecost.

17 And from Miletus he sent to Ephesus, and called the elders of the church.

18 And when they were come to him, he said unto them, You know, from the first day that I came into Asia, after what manner I have been with you at all seasons,

19 Serving the Lord with all humility of mind, and with many tears, and temptations, which befell me by the lying in wait of the Jews:

20 And how I kept back nothing that was profitable unto you, but have shewed you, and have taught you publickly, and from house to house,

21 Testifying both to the Jews, and also to the Greeks, repentance toward God, and faith toward our Lord Jesus Christ.

22 And now, behold, I go bound in the spirit unto Jerusalem, not knowing the things that shall befall me there:

23 Save that the Holy Ghost witnesseth in every city, saying that bonds and afflictions abide me.

24 But none of these things move me, neither count I my life dear unto myself, so that I might finish my course with joy, and the ministry, which I have received of the Lord Jesus, to testify the gospel of the grace of God.

25 And now, behold, I know that you all, among whom I have gone preaching the kingdom of God, shall see my face no more.

26 Wherefore I take you to record this day, that I am pure from the blood of all men.

27 For I have not shunned to declare unto you all the counsel of God.

28 Take heed therefore unto yourselves, and to all the flock, over the which the Holy Ghost has made you overseers, to feed the church of God, which he has purchased with his own blood.

29 For I know this, that after my departing shall grievous wolves enter in among you, not sparing the flock.

30 Also of your own selves shall men arise, speaking perverse things, to draw away disciples after them.

31 Therefore watch, and remember, that by the space of three years I ceased not to warn every one night and day with tears.

32 And now, brethren, I commend you to God, and to the word of his grace, which is able to build you up, and to give you an inheritance among all them which are sanctified.

33 I have coveted no man's silver, or gold, or apparel.

34 Yea, you yourselves know, that these hands have ministered unto my necessities, and to them that were with me.

35 I have shewed you all things, how that so labouring you ought to support the weak, and to remember the words of the Lord Jesus, how he said, It is more blessed to give than to receive.

36 And when he had thus spoken, he kneeled down, and prayed with them all.

37 And they all wept sore, and fell on Paul's neck, and kissed him,

38 Sorrowing most of all for the words which he spake, that they should see his face no more. And they accompanied him unto the ship.

CHAPTER 21

AND it came to pass, that after we were gotten from them, and had launched, we came with a straight course unto Coos, and the day following unto Rhodes, and from thence unto Patara:

2 And finding a ship sailing over unto Phenicia, we went aboard, and set forth.

3 Now when we had discovered Cyprus, we left it on the left hand, and sailed into Syria, and landed at Tyre: for there the ship was to unlade her burden.

4 And finding disciples, we tarried there seven days: who said to Paul through the Spirit, that he should not go up to Jerusalem.

5 And when we had accomplished those days, we departed and went our way; and they all brought us on our way, with wives and children, till we were out of the city: and we kneeled down on the shore, and prayed.

6 And when we had taken our leave one of another, we took ship; and they returned home again.

7 And when we had finished our course from Tyre, we came to Ptolemais, and saluted the brethren, and abode with them one day.

8 And the next day we that were of Paul's company departed, and came unto Cæsarea: and we entered into the house of Philip the evangelist, which was one of the seven; and abode with him.

9 And the same man had four daughters, virgins, which did prophesy.

10 And as we tarried there many days, there came down from Judæa a certain prophet, named Agabus.

11 And when he was come unto us, he took Paul's girdle, and bound his own hands and feet, and said, Thus saith the Holy Ghost, So shall the Jews at Jerusalem bind the man that owneth this girdle, and shall deliver him into the hands of the Gentiles.

12 And when we heard these things, both we, and they of that place, besought him not to go up to Jerusalem.

13 Then Paul answered, What mean you to weep and to break my heart? for I am ready not to be bound only, but also to die at Jerusalem for the name of the Lord Jesus.

14 And when he would not be persuaded, we ceased, saying, The will of the Lord be done.

15 And after those days we took up our carriages, and went up to Jerusalem.

16 There went with us also certain of the disciples of Cæsarea, and brought with them one Mnason of Cyprus, an old disciple, with whom we should lodge.

17 And when we were come to Jerusalem, the brethren received us gladly.

18 And the day following Paul went in with us unto James; and all the elders were present.

19 And when he had saluted them, he declared particularly what things God had created among the Gentiles by his ministry.

20 And when they heard it, they glorified the Lord, and said unto him, You seest, brother, how many thousands of Jews there are which believe; and they are all zealous of the law:

21 And they are informed of you, that you teachest all the Jews which are among the Gentiles to forsake Moses, saying that they ought not to circumcise their children, neither to walk after the customs.

22 What is it therefore? the multitude must needs come together: for they will hear that you are come.

23 Do therefore this that we say to you: We have four men which have a vow on them;

24 Them take, and purify yourself with them, and be at charges with them, that they may shave their heads: and all may know that those things, whereof they were informed concerning you, are nothing; but that you yourself also walkest orderly, and keepest the law.

25 As touching the Gentiles which believe, we have written and concluded that they observe no such thing, save only that they keep themselves from things offered to idols, and from blood, and from strangled, and from fornication.

26 Then Paul took the men, and the next day purifying himself with them entered into the temple, to signify the accomplishment of the days of purification, until that an offering should be offered for every one of them.

27 And when the seven days were almost ended, the Jews which were of Asia, when they saw him in the temple, stirred up all the people, and laid hands on him,

28 Crying out, Men of Israel, help: This is the man, that teacheth all men every where against the people, and the law, and this place: and further brought Greeks also into the temple, and has polluted this holy place.

29 (For they had seen before with him in the city Trophimus an Ephesian, whom they supposed that Paul had brought into the temple.)

30 And all the city was moved, and the people ran together: and they took Paul, and drew him out of the temple: and forthwith the doors were shut.

31 And as they went about to kill him, tidings came unto the chief captain of the band, that all Jerusalem was in an uproar.

32 Who immediately took soldiers and centurions, and ran down unto them: and when they saw the chief captain and the soldiers, they left beating of Paul.

33 Then the chief captain came near, and took him, and commanded him to be bound with two chains; and demanded who he was, and what he had done.

34 And some cried one thing, some another, among the multitude: and when he could not know the certainty for the tumult, he commanded him to be carried into the castle.

35 And when he came upon the stairs, so it was, that he was borne of the soldiers for the violence of the people.

36 For the multitude of the people followed after, crying, Away with him.

37 And as Paul was to be led into the castle, he said unto the chief captain, May I speak unto you? Who said, Can you speak Greek?

38 Are not you that Egyptian, which before these days madest an uproar, and leddest out into the wilderness four thousand men that were murderers?

39 But Paul said, I am a man which am a Jew of Tarsus, a city in Cilicia, a citizen of no mean city: and, I beseech you, suffer me to speak unto the people.

40 And when he had given him licence, Paul stood on the stairs, and beckoned with the hand unto the people. And when there was made a great silence, he spake unto them in the Hebrew tongue, saying,

CHAPTER 22

MEN, brethren, and fathers, hear you my defence which I make now unto you.

2 (And when they heard that he spake in the Hebrew tongue to them, they kept the more silence: and he saith,)

3 I am verily a man which am a Jew, born in Tarsus, a city in Cilicia, yet brought up in this city at the feet of Gamaliel, and taught according to the perfect manner of the law of the fathers, and was zealous toward God, as you all are this day.

4 And I persecuted this way unto the death, binding and delivering into prisons both men and women.

5 As also the high priest doth bear me witness, and all the estate of the elders: from whom also I received letters unto the brethren, and went to Damascus, to bring them which were there bound unto Jerusalem, for to be punished.

6 And it came to pass, that, as I made my journey, and was come nigh unto Damascus about noon, suddenly there shone from heaven a great light round about me.

7 And I fell unto the ground, and heard a voice saying unto me, Saul, Saul, why persecutest you me?

8 And I answered, Who are you, Lord? And he said unto me, I am Jesus of Nazareth, whom you persecutest.

9 And they that were with me saw indeed the light, and were afraid; but they heard not the voice of him that spake to me.

10 And I said, What shall I do, Lord? And the Lord said unto me, Arise, and go into Damascus; and there it shall be told you of all things which are appointed for you to do.

11 And when I could not see for the glory of that light, being led by the hand of them that were with me, I came into Damascus.

12 And one Ananias, a devout man according to the law, having a good report of all the Jews which dwelt there,

13 Came unto me, and stood, and said unto me, Brother Saul, receive your sight. And the same hour I looked up upon him.

14 And he said, The God of our fathers has chosen you, that you shouldest know his will, and see that Just One, and shouldest hear the voice of his mouth.

15 For you shalt be his witness unto all men of what you have seen and heard.

16 And now why tarriest you? arise, and be baptized, and wash away your sins, calling on the name of the Lord.

17 And it came to pass, that, when I was come again to Jerusalem, even while I prayed in the temple, I was in a trance;

18 And saw him saying unto me, Make haste, and get you quickly out of Jerusalem: for they will not receive your testimony concerning me.

19 And I said, Lord, they know that I imprisoned and beat in every synagogue them that believed on you:

20 And when the blood of your martyr Stephen was shed, I also was standing by, and consenting unto his death, and kept the raiment of them that slew him.

21 And he said unto me, Depart: for I will send you far hence unto the Gentiles.

22 And they gave him audience unto this word, and then lifted up their voices, and said, Away with such a fellow from the earth: for it is not fit that he should live.

23 And as they cried out, and cast off their clothes, and threw dust into the air,

24 The chief captain commanded him to be brought into the castle, and bade that he should be examined by scourging; that he might know wherefore they cried so against him.

25 And as they bound him with thongs, Paul said unto the centurion that stood by, Is it lawful for you to scourge a man that is a Roman, and uncondemned?

26 When the centurion heard that, he went and told the chief captain, saying, Take heed what you doest: for this man is a Roman.

27 Then the chief captain came, and said unto him, Tell me, are you a Roman? He said, Yea.

28 And the chief captain answered, With a great sum obtained I this freedom. And Paul said, But I was free born.

29 Then straightway they departed from him which should have examined him: and the chief captain also was afraid, after he knew that he was a Roman, and because he had bound him.

30 On the morrow, because he would have known the certainty wherefore he was accused of the Jews, he loosed him from his bands, and commanded the chief priests and all their council to appear, and brought Paul down, and set him before them.

CHAPTER 23

AND Paul, earnestly beholding the council, said, Men and brethren, I have lived in all good conscience before God until this day.

2 And the high priest Ananias commanded them that stood by him to strike him on the mouth.

3 Then said Paul unto him, God shall strike you, you whited wall: for sittest you to judge me after the law, and commandest me to be smitten contrary to the law?

4 And they that stood by said, Revilest you God's high priest?

5 Then said Paul, I wist not, brethren, that he was the high priest: for it is written, You shalt not speak evil of the ruler of your people.

6 But when Paul perceived that the one part were Sadducees, and the other Pharisees, he cried out in the council, Men and brethren, I am a Pharisee, the son of a Pharisee: of the hope and resurrection of the dead I am called in question.

7 And when he had so said, there arose a dissension between the Pharisees and the Sadducees: and the multitude was divided.

8 For the Sadducees say that there is no resurrection, neither angel, nor spirit: but the Pharisees confess both.

9 And there arose a great cry: and the scribes that were of the Pharisees' part arose, and strove, saying, We find no evil in this man: but if a spirit or an angel has spoken to him, let us not fight against God.

10 And when there arose a great dissension, the chief captain, fearing lest Paul should have been pulled in pieces of them, commanded the soldiers to go down, and to take him by force from among them, and to bring him into the castle.

11 And the night following the Lord stood by him, and said, Be of good cheer, Paul: for as you have testified of me in Jerusalem, so must you bear witness also at Rome.

12 And when it was day, certain of the Jews banded together, and bound themselves under a curse, saying that they would neither eat nor drink till they had killed Paul.

13 And they were more than forty which had made this conspiracy.

14 And they came to the chief priests and elders, and said, We have bound ourselves under a great curse, that we will eat nothing until we have slain Paul.

15 Now therefore you with the council signify to the chief captain that he bring him down unto you to morrow, as though you would inquire something more perfectly concerning him: and we, or ever he come near, are ready to kill him.

16 And when Paul's sister's son heard of their lying in wait, he went and entered into the castle, and told Paul.

17 Then Paul called one of the centurions unto him, and said, Bring this young man unto the chief captain: for he has a certain thing to tell him.

18 So he took him, and brought him to the chief captain, and said, Paul the prisoner called me unto him, and prayed me to bring this young man unto you, who has something to say unto you.

19 Then the chief captain took him by the hand, and went with him aside privately, and asked him, What is that you have to tell me?

20 And he said, The Jews have agreed to desire you that you wouldest bring down Paul to morrow into the council, as though they would inquire somewhat of him more perfectly.

21 But do not you yield unto them: for there lie in wait for him of them more than forty men, which have bound themselves with an oath, that they will neither eat nor drink till they have killed him: and now are they ready, looking for a promise from you.

22 So the chief captain then let the young man depart, and charged him, See you tell no man that you have shewed these things to me.

23 And he called unto him two centurions, saying, Make ready two hundred soldiers to go to Cæsarea, and horsemen threescore and ten, and spearmen two hundred, at the third hour of the night;

24 And provide them beasts, that they may set Paul on, and bring him safe unto Felix the governor.

25 And he wrote a letter after this manner:

26 Claudius Lysias unto the most excellent governor Felix sendeth greeting.

27 This man was taken of the Jews, and should have been killed of them: then came I with an army, and rescued him, having understood that he was a Roman.

28 And when I would have known the cause wherefore they accused him, I brought him forth into their council:

29 Whom I perceived to be accused of questions of their law, but to have nothing laid to his charge worthy of death or of bonds.

30 And when it was told me how that the Jews laid wait for the man, I sent straightway to you, and gave commandment to his accusers also to say before you what they had against him. Farewell.

31 Then the soldiers, as it was commanded them, took Paul, and brought him by night to Antipatris.

32 On the morrow they left the horsemen to go with him, and returned to the castle:

33 Who, when they came to Cæsarea, and delivered the epistle to the governor, presented Paul also before him.

34 And when the governor had read the letter, he asked of what province he was. And when he understood that he was of Cilicia;

35 I will hear you, said he, when yours accusers are also come. And he commanded him to be kept in Herod's judgment hall.

CHAPTER 24

AND after five days Ananias the high priest descended with the elders, and with a certain orator named Tertullus, who informed the governor against Paul.

2 And when he was called forth, Tertullus began to accuse him, saying, Seeing that by you we enjoy great quietness, and that very worthy deeds are done unto this nation by your providence,

3 We accept it always, and in all places, most noble Felix, with all thankfulness.

4 Notwithstanding, that I be not further tedious unto you, I pray you that you wouldest hear us of your clemency a few words.

5 For we have found this man a pestilent fellow, and a mover of sedition among all the Jews throughout the world, and a ringleader of the sect of the Nazarenes:

6 Who also has gone about to profane the temple: whom we took, and would have judged according to our law.

7 But the chief captain Lysias came upon us, and with great violence took him away out of our hands,

8 Commanding his accusers to come unto you: by examining of whom yourself mayest take knowledge of all these things, whereof we accuse him.

9 And the Jews also assented, saying that these things were so.

10 Then Paul, after that the governor had beckoned unto him to speak, answered, Forasmuch as I know that you have been of many years a judge unto this nation, I do the more cheerfully answer for myself:

11 Because that you mayest understand, that there are yet but twelve days since I went up to Jerusalem for to worship.

12 And they neither found me in the temple disputing with any man, neither raising up the people, neither in the synagogues, nor in the city:

13 Neither can they prove the things whereof they now accuse me.

14 But this I confess unto you, that after the way which they call heresy, so worship I the God of my fathers, believing all things which are written in the law and in the prophets:

15 And have hope toward God, which they themselves also allow, that there shall be a resurrection of the dead, both of the just and unjust.

16 And herein do I exercise myself, to have always a conscience void of offence toward God, and toward men.

17 Now after many years I came to bring alms to my nation, and offerings.

18 Whereupon certain Jews from Asia found me purified in the temple, neither with multitude, nor with tumult.

19 Who ought to have been here before you, and object, if they had ought against me.

20 Or else let these same here say, if they have found any evil doing in me, while I stood before the council,

21 Except it be for this one voice, that I cried standing among them, Touching the resurrection of the dead I am called in question by you this day.

22 And when Felix heard these things, having more perfect knowledge of that way, he deferred them, and said, When Lysias the chief captain shall come down, I will know the uttermost of your matter.

23 And he commanded a centurion to keep Paul, and to let him have liberty, and that he should forbid none of his acquaintance to minister or come unto him.

24 And after certain days, when Felix came with his wife Drusilla, which was a Jewess, he sent for Paul, and heard him concerning the faith in Christ.

25 And as he reasoned of righteousness, temperance, and judgment to come, Felix trembled, and answered, Go your way for this time; when I have a convenient season, I will call for you.

26 He hoped also that money should have been given him of Paul, that he might loose him: wherefore he sent for him the oftener, and communed with him.

27 But after two years Porcius Festus came into Felix' room: and Felix, willing to shew the Jews a pleasure, left Paul bound.

CHAPTER 25

NOW when Festus was come into the province, after three days he ascended from Cæsarea to Jerusalem.

2 Then the high priest and the chief of the Jews informed him against Paul, and besought him,

3 And desired favour against him, that he would send for him to Jerusalem, laying wait in the way to kill him.

4 But Festus answered, that Paul should be kept at Cæsarea, and that he himself would depart shortly thither.

5 Let them therefore, said he, which among you are able, go down with me, and accuse this man, if there be any wickedness in him.

6 And when he had tarried among them more than ten days, he went down unto Cæsarea; and the next day sitting on the judgment seat commanded Paul to be brought.

7 And when he was come, the Jews which came down from Jerusalem stood round about, and laid many and grievous complaints against Paul, which they could not prove.

8 While he answered for himself, Neither against the law of the Jews, neither against the temple, nor yet against Cæsar, have I offended any thing at all.

9 But Festus, willing to do the Jews a pleasure, answered Paul, and said, Will you go up to Jerusalem, and there be judged of these things before me?

10 Then said Paul, I stand at Cæsar's judgment seat, where I ought to be judged: to the Jews have I done no wrong, as you very well knowest.

11 For if I be an offender, or have committed any thing worthy of death, I refuse not to die: but if there be none of these things whereof these accuse me, no man may deliver me unto them. I appeal unto Cæsar.

12 Then Festus, when he had conferred with the council, answered, Have you appealed unto Cæsar? unto Cæsar shalt you go.

13 And after certain days king Agrippa and Bernice came unto Cæsarea to salute Festus.

14 And when they had been there many days, Festus declared Paul's cause unto the king, saying, There is a certain man left in bonds by Felix:

15 About whom, when I was at Jerusalem, the chief priests and the elders of the Jews informed me, desiring to have judgment against him.

16 To whom I answered, It is not the manner of the Romans to deliver any man to die, before that he which is accused have the accusers face to face, and have licence to answer for himself concerning the crime laid against him.

17 Therefore, when they were come hither, without any delay on the morrow I sat on the judgment seat, and commanded the man to be brought forth.

18 Against whom when the accusers stood up, they brought none accusation of such things as I supposed:

19 But had certain questions against him of their own superstition, and of one Jesus, which was dead, whom Paul affirmed to be alive.

20 And because I doubted of such manner of questions, I asked him whether he would go to Jerusalem, and there be judged of these matters.

21 But when Paul had appealed to be reserved unto the hearing of Augustus, I commanded him to be kept till I might send him to Cæsar.

22 Then Agrippa said unto Festus, I would also hear the man myself. To morrow, said he, you shalt hear him.

23 And on the morrow, when Agrippa was come, and Bernice, with great pomp, and was entered into the place of hearing, with the chief captains, and principal men of the city, at Festus' commandment Paul was brought forth.

24 And Festus said, King Agrippa, and all men which are here present with us, you see this man, about whom all the multitude of the Jews have dealt with me, both at Jerusalem, and also here, crying that he ought not to live any longer.

25 But when I found that he had committed nothing worthy of death, and that he himself has appealed to Augustus, I have determined to send him.

26 Of whom I have no certain thing to write unto my lord. Wherefore I have brought him forth before you, and specially before you, O king Agrippa, that, after examination had, I might have somewhat to write.

27 For it seemeth to me unreasonable to send a prisoner, and not withal to signify the crimes laid against him.

CHAPTER 26

THEN Agrippa said unto Paul, You are permitted to speak for yourself. Then Paul stretched forth the hand, and answered for himself:

2 I think myself happy, king Agrippa, because I shall answer for myself this day before you touching all the things whereof I am accused of the Jews:

3 Especially because I know you to be expert in all customs and questions which are among the Jews: wherefore I beseech you to hear me patiently.

4 My manner of life from my youth, which was at the first among my own nation at Jerusalem, know all the Jews;

5 Which knew me from the beginning, if they would testify, that after the most straitest sect of our religion I lived a Pharisee.

6 And now I stand and am judged for the hope of the promise made of God unto our fathers:

7 Unto which promise our twelve tribes, instantly serving God day and night, hope to come. For which hope's sake, king Agrippa, I am accused of the Jews.

8 Why should it be thought a thing incredible with you, that God should raise the dead?

9 I verily thought with myself, that I ought to do many things contrary to the name of Jesus of Nazareth.

10 Which thing I also did in Jerusalem: and many of the saints did I shut up in prison, having received authority from the chief priests; and when they were put to death, I gave my voice against them.

11 And I punished them oft in every synagogue, and compelled them to blaspheme; and being exceedingly mad against them, I persecuted them even unto strange cities.

12 Whereupon as I went to Damascus with authority and commission from the chief priests,

13 At midday, O king, I saw in the way a light from heaven, above the brightness of the sun, shining round about me and them which journeyed with me.

14 And when we were all fallen to the earth, I heard a voice speaking unto me, and saying in the Hebrew tongue, Saul, Saul, why persecutest you me? it is hard for you to kick against the pricks.

15 And I said, Who are you, Lord? And he said, I am Jesus whom you persecutest.

16 But rise, and stand upon your feet: for I have appeared unto you for this purpose, to make you a minister and a witness both of these things which you have seen, and of those things in the which I will appear unto you;

17 Delivering you from the people, and from the Gentiles, unto whom now I send you,

18 To open their eyes, and to turn them from darkness to light, and from the power of Satan unto God, that they may receive forgiveness of sins, and inheritance among them which are sanctified by faith that is in me.

19 Whereupon, O king Agrippa, I was not disobedient unto the heavenly vision:

20 But shewed first unto them of Damascus, and at Jerusalem, and throughout all the coasts of Judæa, and then to the Gentiles, that they should repent and turn to God, and do works meet for repentance.

21 For these causes the Jews caught me in the temple, and went about to kill me.

22 Having therefore obtained help of God, I continue unto this day, witnessing both to small and great, saying none other things than those which the prophets and Moses did say should come:

23 That Christ should suffer, and that he should be the first that should rise from the dead, and should shew light unto the people, and to the Gentiles.

24 And as he thus spake for himself, Festus said with a loud voice, Paul, you are beside yourself; much learning doth make you mad.

25 But he said, I am not mad, most noble Festus; but speak forth the words of truth and soberness.

26 For the king knoweth of these things, before whom also I speak freely: for I am persuaded that none of these things are hidden from him; for this thing was not done in a corner.

27 King Agrippa, believest you the prophets? I know that you believest.

28 Then Agrippa said unto Paul, Almost you persuadest me to be a Christian.

29 And Paul said, I would to God, that not only you , but also all that hear me this day, were both almost, and altogether such as I am, except these bonds.

30 And when he had thus spoken, the king rose up, and the governor, and Bernice, and they that sat with them:

31 And when they were gone aside, they talked between themselves, saying, This man doeth nothing worthy of death or of bonds.

32 Then said Agrippa unto Festus, This man might have been set at liberty, if he had not appealed unto Cæsar.

CHAPTER 27

AND when it was determined that we should sail into Italy, they delivered Paul and certain other prisoners unto one named Julius, a centurion of Augustus' band.

2 And entering into a ship of Adramyttium, we launched, meaning to sail by the coasts of Asia; one Aristarchus, a Macedonian of Thessalonica, being with us.

3 And the next day we touched at Sidon. And Julius courteously entreated Paul, and gave him liberty to go unto his friends to refresh himself.

4 And when we had launched from thence, we sailed under Cyprus, because the winds were contrary.

5 And when we had sailed over the sea of Cilicia and Pamphylia, we came to Myra, a city of Lycia.

6 And there the centurion found a ship of Alexandria sailing into Italy; and he put us therein.

7 And when we had sailed slowly many days, and scarce were come over against Cnidus, the wind not suffering us, we sailed under Crete, over against Salmone;

8 And, hardly passing it, came unto a place which is called The fair havens; nigh whereunto was the city of Lasea.

9 Now when much time was spent, and when sailing was now dangerous, because the fast was now already past, Paul admonished them,

10 And said unto them, Sirs, I perceive that this voyage will be with hurt and much damage, not only of the lading and ship, but also of our lives.

11 Nevertheless the centurion believed the master and the owner of the ship, more than those things which were spoken by Paul.

12 And because the haven was not commodious to winter in, the more part advised to depart thence also, if by any means they might attain to Phenice, and there to winter; which is an haven of Crete, and lies toward the south west and north west.

13 And when the south wind blew softly, supposing that they had obtained their purpose, loosing thence, they sailed close by Crete.

14 But not long after there arose against it a tempestuous wind, called Euroclydon.

15 And when the ship was caught, and could not bear up into the wind, we let her drive.

16 And running under a certain island which is called Clauda, we had much work to come by the boat:

17 Which when they had taken up, they used helps, undergirding the ship; and, fearing lest they should fall into the quicksands, strake sail, and so were driven.

18 And we being exceedingly tossed with a tempest, the next day they lightened the ship;

19 And the third day we cast out with our own hands the tackling of the ship.

20 And when neither sun nor stars in many days appeared, and no small tempest lay on us, all hope that we should be saved was then taken away.

21 But after long abstinence Paul stood forth in the midst of them, and said, Sirs, you should have hearkened unto me, and not have loosed from Crete, and to have gained this harm and loss.

22 And now I exhort you to be of good cheer: for there shall be no loss of any man's life among you, but of the ship.

23 For there stood by me this night the angel of God, whose I am, and whom I serve,

24 Saying, Fear not, Paul; you must be brought before Cæsar: and, lo, God has given you all them that sail with you.

25 Wherefore, sirs, be of good cheer: for I believe God, that it shall be even as it was told me.

26 Howbeit we must be cast upon a certain island.

27 But when the fourteenth night was come, as we were driven up and down in Adria, about midnight the shipmen deemed that they drew near to some country;

28 And sounded, and found it twenty fathoms: and when they had gone a little further, they sounded again, and found it fifteen fathoms.

29 Then fearing lest we should have fallen upon rocks, they cast four anchors out of the stern, and wished for the day.

30 And as the shipmen were about to flee out of the ship, when they had let down the boat into the sea, under colour as though they would have cast anchors out of the foreship,

31 Paul said to the centurion and to the soldiers, Except these abide in the ship, you cannot be saved.

32 Then the soldiers cut off the ropes of the boat, and let her fall off.

33 And while the day was coming on, Paul besought them all to take meat, saying, This day is the fourteenth day that you have tarried and continued fasting, having taken nothing.

34 Wherefore I pray you to take some meat: for this is for your health: for there shall not an hair fall from the head of any of you.

35 And when he had thus spoken, he took bread, and gave thanks to God in presence of them all: and when he had broken it, he began to eat.

36 Then were they all of good cheer, and they also took some meat.

37 And we were in all in the ship two hundred threescore and sixteen souls.

38 And when they had eaten enough, they lightened the ship, and cast out the wheat into the sea.

39 And when it was day, they knew not the land: but they discovered a certain creek with a shore, into the which they were minded, if it were possible, to thrust in the ship.

40 And when they had taken up the anchors, they committed themselves unto the sea, and loosed the rudder bands, and hoised up the mainsail to the wind, and made toward shore.

41 And falling into a place where two seas met, they ran the ship aground; and the forepart stuck fast, and remained unmoveable, but the hinder part was broken with the violence of the waves.

42 And the soldiers' counsel was to kill the prisoners, lest any of them should swim out, and escape.

43 But the centurion, willing to save Paul, kept them from their purpose; and commanded that they which could swim should cast themselves first into the sea, and get to land:

44 And the rest, some on boards, and some on broken pieces of the ship. And so it came to pass, that they escaped all safe to land.

CHAPTER 28

AND when they were escaped, then they knew that the island was called Melita.

2 And the barbarous people shewed us no little kindness: for they kindled a fire, and received us every one, because of the present rain, and because of the cold.

3 And when Paul had gathered a bundle of sticks, and laid them on the fire, there came a viper out of the heat, and fastened on his hand.

4 And when the barbarians saw the venomous beast hang on his hand, they said among themselves, No doubt this man is a murderer, whom, though he has escaped the sea, yet vengeance suffereth not to live.

5 And he shook off the beast into the fire, and felt no harm.

6 Howbeit they looked when he should have swollen, or fallen down dead suddenly: but after they had looked a great while, and saw no harm come to him, they changed their minds, and said that he was a god.

7 In the same quarters were possessions of the chief man of the island, whose name was Publius; who received us, and lodged us three days courteously.

8 And it came to pass, that the father of Publius lay sick of a fever and of a bloody flux: to whom Paul entered in, and prayed, and laid his hands on him, and healed him.

9 So when this was done, others also, which had diseases in the island, came, and were healed:

10 Who also honoured us with many honours; and when we departed, they laded us with such things as were necessary.

11 And after three months we departed in a ship of Alexandria, which had wintered in the isle, whose sign was Castor and Pollux.

12 And landing at Syracuse, we tarried there three days.

13 And from thence we fetched a compass, and came to Rhegium: and after one day the south wind blew, and we came the next day to Puteoli:

14 Where we found brethren, and were desired to tarry with them seven days: and so we went toward Rome.

15 And from thence, when the brethren heard of us, they came to meet us as far as Appii forum, and The three taverns: whom when Paul saw, he thanked God, and took courage.

16 And when we came to Rome, the centurion delivered the prisoners to the captain of the guard: but Paul was suffered to dwell by himself with a soldier that kept him.

17 And it came to pass, that after three days Paul called the chief of the Jews together: and when they were come together, he said unto them, Men and brethren, though I have committed nothing against the people, or customs of our fathers, yet was I delivered prisoner from Jerusalem into the hands of the Romans.

18 Who, when they had examined me, would have let me go, because there was no cause of death in me.

19 But when the Jews spake against it, I was constrained to appeal unto Cæsar; not that I had ought to accuse my nation of.

20 For this cause therefore have I called for you, to see you, and to speak with you: because that for the hope of Israel I am bound with this chain.

21 And they said unto him, We neither received letters out of Judæa concerning you, neither any of the brethren that came shewed or spake any harm of you.

22 But we desire to hear of you what you thinkest: for as concerning this sect, we know that every where it is spoken against.

23 And when they had appointed him a day, there came many to him into his lodging; to whom he expounded and testified the kingdom of God, persuading them concerning Jesus, both out of the law of Moses, and out of the prophets, from morning till evening.

24 And some believed the things which were spoken, and some believed not.

25 And when they agreed not among themselves, they departed, after that Paul had spoken one word, Well spake the Holy Ghost by Esaias the prophet unto our fathers,

26 Saying, Go unto this people, and say, Hearing you shall hear, and shall not understand; and seeing you shall see, and not perceive:

27 For the heart of this people is waxed gross, and their ears are dull of hearing, and their eyes have they closed; lest they should see with their eyes, and hear with their ears, and understand with their heart, and should be converted, and I should heal them.

28 Be it known therefore unto you, that the salvation of God is sent unto the Gentiles, and that they will hear it.

29 And when he had said these words, the Jews departed, and had great reasoning among themselves.

30 And Paul dwelt two whole years in his own hired house, and received all that came in unto him,

31 Preaching the kingdom of God, and teaching those things which concern the Lord Jesus Christ, with all confidence, no man forbidding him.

Acts 29 is only found in one manuscript and is not considered canon.

ACTS Chapter 29

Verse 1. Paul, full of the blessing of Christ, and overflowing in the Spirit, left Rome, having decided to go into Spain, becuase he had wanted to travel there for a long time, and he thought also to go from there to Britain.

Verse 2. Because he had heard in Phoenicia that some of the children of Israel, around the time of the Assyrian captivity,had escaped by sea to "the Islands far away" as proclaimed by the Prophet, and called by the Romans, Britain.

Verse 3. Since the Lord commanded the gospel to be preached far and wide to the Gentiles, and to the lost sheep of the House of Israel.

Verse 4. And no man hindered Paul because he testified boldly of
Jesus before the governents and among the people; and be took with
him certain of the brethren which lived with him at Rome, and
they boarded a ship at Ostium, and having fair winds were
brought safely into an safety (harbour) of Spain.

Verse 5. And many people gathered from the towns and villages, and the hill country; for they had heard of the conversion of the Apostles, and the many miracles he had performed.

Verse 6. And Paul preached with might in Spain, and great many people believed and were converted, for they knew he was an apostle sent from God.

Verse 7. And finding a ship in Armorica sailing to Britain they departed from Spain. Paul and his company passed along the South coast and reached a port called Raphinus.

Verse 8. Now when word spread wide that the Apostle had landed on their coast, large numbers of the inhabitants met him, and they treated Paul courteously and he entered in at the east gate of their city, and was housed in the house of a Hebrew and one of his own nation.

Verse 9. And the next day he came and stood upon Mount Lud;(Now the site of St. Paul's Cathedral.) and the people amassed at the gate, and assembled in the main street, and he preached Christ unto them, and they believed the word and the testimony of Jesus.

Verse 10. And at sunset the Holy Ghost fell upon Paul, and he prophesied, saying, "BEHOLD IN THE LAST DAYS THE GOD OF PEACE
SHALL LIVE IN THE CITIES, AND THE INHABITANTS OF THEM SHALL BE COUNTED: AND IN THE SEVENTH CENSUS OF THE PEOPLE, THEIR EYES SHALL BE OPENED, AND THE GLORY OF THEIR INHERITANCE WILL SHINE OUT BEFORE THEM. NATIONS SHALL COME UP TO WORSHIP ON THE MOUNT THAT TESTIFIES OF THE PATIENCE AND LONG SUFFERING OF A SERVANT OF THE LORD."

Verse 11. And in the last days new announcements of the Gospel shall come forth out of Jerusalem, and the hearts of the people shall be filled with joy, and they shall look and spring of water shall be opened, and there shall be no more disease.

Verse 12. In those days there shall be wars and rumours of wars; and a king shall rise up, and his sword shall be for the healing of the nations, and peace he makes shall last, and the glory of his kingdom will be a wonder among princes.

Verse 13. And it came to pass that certain of the Druids came to Paul privately and showed by their rites and ceremonies (to prove) they were descended from the Jews which escaped from bondage in the land of Egypt, and the apostle believed these things, and he gave them the kiss of peace.

Verse 14. And Paul lived in his housing for three months proving the faith and preaching Christ continually.

Verse 15. And after these things Paul and his brethren left Raphinus, and sailed to Atium in Gaul.

Verse 16. And Paul preached in the Roman garrisons and among the people, encouraging all men to repent and confess their sins.

Verse 17. And there came to him certain of the Belgae to ask him about the new doctrine, and of the man Jesus; and Paul opened his heart unto them, and told them all things that had happened to him, how Christ
Jesus came into the world to save sinners; and they departed wondering among themselves about the things they had heard.

Verse 18. And after he preached and toiled muched Paul and his fellow workers went to Helvetia, and came to Mount Pontius Pilate, where he who condemned the Lord Jesus threw himself down headlong, and so miserably perished.

Verse 19. And immediately a torrent gushed from the mountain and washed his body (which had been) broken in pieces, into a lake.

Verse 20. And Paul stretched forth his hands upon the water, and prayed unto the Lord, saying, O Lord God, give a sign unto all nations that here Pontius Pilate, which condemned your only-begotten Son, plunged down headlong in to the pit.

Verse 21. And while Paul was still speaking, they looked there came a great earthquake, and the face of the waters was changed, and the lake took the form like unto the Son of Man hanging in an agony upon the Cross.

Verse 22. And a voice came out of heaven saying, Even Pilate has escaped the wrath to come, (See second death, Rev.21:8) for he washed his hands before the multitude at the shedding of the Lord Jesus' blood.

Verse 23. Because of this, when Paul and those with him saw the earthquake and heard the voice of the angel they glorified God and their spirits were greatly strenghtned.

Verse 24. And they journeyed and came to Mount Julius where two pillars stood, one on the right hand and one on the left hand, erected by Caesar Augustus.

Verse 25. And Paul was filled with the Holy Ghost and stood up between the two pillars, saying, Men and brethren, these stones which you see this day shall testify of my journey here and truly I say they shall remain until the outpouring of the spirit upon all nations, and the way will not be hindered throughout all generations.

Verse 26. And they went forth and came to Illyricum, intending to go by Macedonia into Asia, and grace was found in all the churches; and they prospered and had peace. Amen.

THE EPISTLE OF PAUL THE APOSTLE TO THE ROMANS.

CHAPTER 1

PAUL, a servant of Jesus Christ, called to be an apostle, separated unto the gospel of God,

2 (Which he had promised afore by his prophets in the holy scriptures,)

3 Concerning his Son Jesus Christ our Lord, which was made of the seed of David according to the flesh;

4 And declared to be the Son of God with power, according to the spirit of holiness, by the resurrection from the dead:

5 By whom we have received grace and apostleship, for obedience to the faith among all nations, for his name:

6 Among whom are you also the called of Jesus Christ:

7 To all that be in Rome, beloved of God, called to be saints: Grace to you and peace from God our Father, and the Lord Jesus Christ.

8 First, I thank my God through Jesus Christ for you all, that your faith is spoken of throughout the whole world.

9 For God is my witness, whom I serve with my spirit in the gospel of his Son, that without ceasing I make mention of you always in my prayers;

10 Making request, if by any means now at length I might have a prosperous journey by the will of God to come unto you.

11 For I long to see you, that I may impart unto you some spiritual gift, to the end you may be established;

12 That is, that I may be comforted together with you by the mutual faith both of you and me.

13 Now I would not have you ignorant, brethren, that oftentimes I purposed to come unto you, (but was let hitherto,) that I might have some fruit among you also, even as among other Gentiles.

14 I am debtor both to the Greeks, and to the Barbarians; both to the wise, and to the unwise.

15 So, as much as in me is, I am ready to preach the gospel to you that are at Rome also.

16 For I am not ashamed of the gospel of Christ: for it is the power of God unto salvation to every one that believeth; to the Jew first, and also to the Greek.

17 For therein is the righteousness of God revealed from faith to faith: as it is written, The just shall live by faith.

18 For the wrath of God is revealed from heaven against all ungodliness and unrighteousness of men, who hold the truth in unrighteousness;

19 Because that which may be known of God is manifest in them; for God has shewed it unto them.

20 For the invisible things of him from the creation of the world are clearly seen, being understood by the things that are made, even his eternal power and Godhead; so that they are without excuse:

21 Because that, when they knew God, they glorified him not as God, neither were thankful; but became vain in their imaginations, and their foolish heart was darkened.

22 Professing themselves to be wise, they became fools,

23 And changed the glory of the uncorruptible God into an image made like to corruptible man, and to birds, and fourfooted beasts, and creeping things.

24 Wherefore God also gave them up to uncleanness through the lusts of their own hearts, to dishonour their own bodies between themselves:

25 Who changed the truth of God into a lie, and worshipped and served the creature more than the Creator, who is blessed for ever. Amen.

26 For this cause God gave them up unto vile affections: for even their women did change the natural use into that which is against nature:

27 And likewise also the men, leaving the natural use of the woman, burned in their lust one toward another; men with men working that which is unseemly, and receiving in themselves that recompence of their error which was meet.

28 And even as they did not like to retain God in their knowledge, God gave them over to a reprobate mind, to do those things which are not convenient;

29 Being filled with all unrighteousness, fornication, wickedness, covetousness, maliciousness; full of envy, murder, debate, deceit, malignity; whisperers,

30 Backbiters, haters of God, despiteful, proud, boasters, inventors of evil things, disobedient to parents,

31 Without understanding, covenantbreakers, without natural affection, implacable, unmerciful:

32 Who knowing the judgment of God, that they which commit such things are worthy of death, not only do the same, but have pleasure in them that do them.

CHAPTER 2

THEREFORE you are inexcusable, O man, whosoever you are that judgest: for wherein you judgest another, you condemnest yourself; for you that judgest doest the same things.

2 But we are sure that the judgment of God is according to truth against them which commit such things.

3 And thinkest you this, O man, that judgest them which do such things, and doest the same, that you shalt escape the judgment of God?

4 Or despisest you the riches of his goodness and forbearance and longsuffering; not knowing that the goodness of God leadeth you to repentance?

5 But after your hardness and impenitent heart treasurest up unto yourself wrath against the day of wrath and revelation of the righteous judgment of God;

6 Who will render to every man according to his deeds:

7 To them who by patient continuance in well doing seek for glory and honour and immortality, eternal life:

8 But unto them that are contentious, and do not obey the truth, but obey unrighteousness, indignation and wrath,

9 Tribulation and anguish, upon every soul of man that doeth evil, of the Jew first, and also of the Gentile;

10 But glory, honour, and peace, to every man that worketh good, to the Jew first, and also to the Gentile:

11 For there is no respect of persons with God.

12 For as many as have sinned without law shall also perish without law: and as many as have sinned in the law shall be judged by the law;

13 (For not the hearers of the law are just before God, but the doers of the law shall be justified.

14 For when the Gentiles, which have not the law, do by nature the things contained in the law, these, having not the law, are a law unto themselves:

15 Which shew the work of the law written in their hearts, their conscience also bearing witness, and their thoughts the mean while accusing or else excusing one another;)

16 In the day when God shall judge the secrets of men by Jesus Christ according to my gospel.

17 Behold, you are called a Jew, and restest in the law, and makest your boast of God,

18 And knowest his will, and approvest the things that are more excellent, being instructed out of the law;

19 And are confident that you yourself are a guide of the blind, a light of them which are in darkness,

20 An instructor of the foolish, a teacher of babes, which have the form of knowledge and of the truth in the law.

21 You therefore which teachest another, teachest you not yourself? you that preachest a man should not steal, dost you steal?

22 You that say a man should not commit adultery, dost you commit adultery? you that abhorrest idols, dost you commit sacrilege?

23 You that makest your boast of the law, through breaking the law dishonourest you God?

24 For the name of God is blasphemed among the Gentiles through you, as it is written.

25 For circumcision verily profiteth, if you keep the law: but if you be a breaker of the law, your circumcision is made uncircumcision.

26 Therefore if the uncircumcision keep the righteousness of the law, shall not his uncircumcision be counted for circumcision?

27 And shall not uncircumcision which is by nature, if it fulfil the law, judge you, who by the letter and circumcision dost transgress the law?

28 For he is not a Jew, which is one outwardly; neither is that circumcision, which is outward in the flesh:

29 But he is a Jew, which is one inwardly; and circumcision is that of the heart, in the spirit, and not in the letter; whose praise is not of men, but of God.

CHAPTER 3

WHAT advantage then has the Jew? or what profit is there of circumcision?

2 Much every way: chiefly, because that unto them were committed the oracles of God.

3 For what if some did not believe? shall their unbelief make the faith of God without effect?

4 God forbid: yea, let God be true, but every man a liar; as it is written, That you mightest be justified in your sayings, and mightest overcome when you are judged.

5 But if our unrighteousness commend the righteousness of God, what shall we say? Is God unrighteous who taketh vengeance? (I speak as a man)

6 God forbid: for then how shall God judge the world?

7 For if the truth of God has more abounded through my lie unto his glory; why yet am I also judged as a sinner?

8 And not rather, (as we be slanderously reported, and as some affirm that we say,) Let us do evil, that good may come? whose damnation is just.

9 What then? are we better than they? No, in no wise: for we have before proved both Jews and Gentiles, that they are all under sin;

10 As it is written, There is none righteous, no, not one:

11 There is none that understands, there is none that seeketh after God.

12 They are all gone out of the way, they are together become unprofitable; there is none that doeth good, no, not one.

13 Their throat is an open sepulchre; with their tongues they have used deceit; the poison of asps is under their lips:

14 Whose mouth is full of cursing and bitterness:

15 Their feet are swift to shed blood:

16 Destruction and misery are in their ways:

17 And the way of peace have they not known:

18 There is no fear of God before their eyes.

19 Now we know that what things soever the law saith, it saith to them who are under the law: that every mouth may be stopped, and all the world may become guilty before God.

20 Therefore by the deeds of the law there shall no flesh be justified in his sight: for by the law is the knowledge of sin.

21 But now the righteousness of God without the law is manifested, being witnessed by the law and the prophets;

22 Even the righteousness of God which is by faith of Jesus Christ unto all and upon all them that believe: for there is no difference:

23 For all have sinned, and come short of the glory of God;

24 Being justified freely by his grace through the redemption that is in Christ Jesus:

25 Whom God has set forth to be a propitiation through faith in his blood, to declare his righteousness for the remission of sins that are past, through the forbearance of God;

26 To declare, I say, at this time his righteousness: that he might be just, and the justifier of him which believeth in Jesus.

27 Where is boasting then? It is excluded. By what law? of works? Nay: but by the law of faith.

28 Therefore we conclude that a man is justified by faith without the deeds of the law.

29 Is he the God of the Jews only? is he not also of the Gentiles? Yes, of the Gentiles also:

30 Seeing it is one God, which shall justify the circumcision by faith, and uncircumcision through faith.

31 Do we then make void the law through faith? God forbid: yea, we establish the law.

CHAPTER 4

WHAT shall we say then that Abraham our father, as pertaining to the flesh, has found?

2 For if Abraham were justified by works, he has whereof to glory; but not before God.

3 For what saith the scripture? Abraham believed God, and it was counted unto him for righteousness.

4 Now to him that worketh is the reward not reckoned of grace, but of debt.

5 But to him that worketh not, but believeth on him that justifieth the ungodly, his faith is counted for righteousness.

6 Even as David also describeth the blessedness of the man, unto whom God imputeth righteousness without works,

7 Saying, Blessed are they whose iniquities are forgiven, and whose sins are covered.

8 Blessed is the man to whom the Lord will not impute sin.

9 Comes this blessedness then upon the circumcision only, or upon the uncircumcision also? for we say that faith was reckoned to Abraham for righteousness.

10 How was it then reckoned? when he was in circumcision, or in uncircumcision? Not in circumcision, but in uncircumcision.

11 And he received the sign of circumcision, a seal of the righteousness of the faith which he had yet being uncircumcised: that he might be the father of all them that believe, though they be not circumcised; that righteousness might be imputed unto them also:

12 And the father of circumcision to them who are not of the circumcision only, but who also walk in the steps of that faith of our father Abraham, which he had being yet uncircumcised.

13 For the promise, that he should be the heir of the world, was not to Abraham, or to his seed, through the law, but through the righteousness of faith.

14 For if they which are of the law be heirs, faith is made void, and the promise made of none effect:

15 Because the law worketh wrath: for where no law is, there is no transgression.

16 Therefore it is of faith, that it might be by grace; to the end the promise might be sure to all the seed; not to that only which is of the law, but to that also which is of the faith of Abraham; who is the father of us all,

17 (As it is written, I have made you a father of many nations,) before him whom he believed, even God, who quickeneth the dead, and calleth those things which be not as though they were.

18 Who against hope believed in hope, that he might become the father of many nations; according to that which was spoken, So shall your seed be.

19 And being not weak in faith, he considered not his own body now dead, when he was about an hundred years old, neither yet the deadness of Sara's womb:

20 He staggered not at the promise of God through unbelief; but was strong in faith, giving glory to God;

21 And being fully persuaded that, what he had promised, he was able also to perform.

22 And therefore it was imputed to him for righteousness.

23 Now it was not written for his sake alone, that it was imputed to him;

24 But for us also, to whom it shall be imputed, if we believe on him that raised up Jesus our Lord from the dead;

25 Who was delivered for our offences, and was raised again for our justification.

CHAPTER 5

THEREFORE being justified by faith, we have peace with God through our Lord Jesus Christ:

2 By whom also we have access by faith into this grace wherein we stand, and rejoice in hope of the glory of God.

3 And not only so, but we glory in tribulations also: knowing that tribulation worketh patience;

4 And patience, experience; and experience, hope:

5 And hope maketh not ashamed; because the love of God is shed abroad in our hearts by the Holy Ghost which is given unto us.

6 For when we were yet without strength, in due time Christ died for the ungodly.

7 For scarcely for a righteous man will one die: yet what if for a good man some would even dare to die.

8 But God commendeth his love toward us, in that, while we were yet sinners, Christ died for us.

9 Much more then, being now justified by his blood, we shall be saved from wrath through him.

10 For if, when we were enemies, we were reconciled to God by the death of his Son, much more, being reconciled, we shall be saved by his life.

11 And not only so, but we also joy in God through our Lord Jesus Christ, by whom we have now received the atonement.

12 Wherefore, as by one man sin entered into the world, and death by sin; and so death passed upon all men, for that all have sinned:

13 (For until the law sin was in the world: but sin is not imputed when there is no law.

14 Nevertheless death reigned from Adam to Moses, even over them that had not sinned after the similitude of Adam's transgression, who is the figure of him that was to come.

15 But not as the offence, so also is the free gift. For if through the offence of one many be dead, much more the grace of God, and the gift by grace, which is by one man, Jesus Christ, has abounded unto many.

16 And not as it was by one that sinned, so is the gift: for the judgment was by one to condemnation, but the free gift is of many offences unto justification.

17 For if by one man's offence death reigned by one; much more they which receive abundance of grace and of the gift of righteousness shall reign in life by one, Jesus Christ.)

18 Therefore as by the offence of one judgment came upon all men to condemnation; even so by the righteousness of one the free gift came upon all men unto justification of life.

19 For as by one man's disobedience many were made sinners, so by the obedience of one shall many be made righteous.

20 Moreover the law entered, that the offence might abound. But where sin abounded, grace did much more abound:

21 That as sin has reigned unto death, even so might grace reign through righteousness unto eternal life by Jesus Christ our Lord.

CHAPTER 6

WHAT shall we say then? Shall we continue in sin, that grace may abound?

2 God forbid. How shall we, that are dead to sin, live any longer therein?

3 Know you not, that so many of us as were baptized into Jesus Christ were baptized into his death?

4 Therefore we are buried with him by baptism into death: that like as Christ was raised up from the dead by the glory of the Father, even so we also should walk in newness of life.

5 For if we have been planted together in the likeness of his death, we shall be also in the likeness of his resurrection:

6 Knowing this, that our old man is crucified with him, that the body of sin might be destroyed, that henceforth we should not serve sin.

7 For he that is dead is freed from sin.

8 Now if we be dead with Christ, we believe that we shall also live with him:

9 Knowing that Christ being raised from the dead dieth no more; death has no more dominion over him.

10 For in that he died, he died unto sin once: but in that he liveth, he liveth unto God.

11 Likewise reckon you also yourselves to be dead indeed unto sin, but alive unto God through Jesus Christ our Lord.

12 Let not sin therefore reign in your mortal body, that you should obey it in the lusts thereof.

13 Neither yield you your members as instruments of unrighteousness unto sin: but yield yourselves unto God, as those that are alive from the dead, and your members as instruments of righteousness unto God.

14 For sin shall not have dominion over you: for you are not under the law, but under grace.

15 What then? shall we sin, because we are not under the law, but under grace? God forbid.

16 Know you not, that to whom you yield yourselves servants to obey, his servants you are to whom you obey; whether of sin unto death, or of obedience unto righteousness?

17 But God be thanked, that you were the servants of sin, but you have obeyed from the heart that form of doctrine which was delivered you.

18 Being then made free from sin, you became the servants of righteousness.

19 I speak after the manner of men because of the infirmity of your flesh: for as you have yielded your members servants to uncleanness and to iniquity unto iniquity; even so now yield your members servants to righteousness unto holiness.

20 For when you were the servants of sin, you were free from righteousness.

21 What fruit had you then in those things whereof you are now ashamed? for the end of those things is death.

22 But now being made free from sin, and become servants to God, you have your fruit unto holiness, and the end everlasting life.

23 For the wages of sin is death; but the gift of God is eternal life through Jesus Christ our Lord.

CHAPTER 7

KNOW you not, brethren, (for I speak to them that know the law,) how that the law has dominion over a man as long as he liveth?

2 For the woman which has an husband is bound by the law to her husband so long as he liveth; but if the husband be dead, she is loosed from the law of her husband.

3 So then if, while her husband liveth, she be married to another man, she shall be called an adulteress: but if her husband be dead, she is free from that law; so that she is no adulteress, though she be married to another man.

4 Wherefore, my brethren, you also are become dead to the law by the body of Christ; that you should be married to another, even to him who is raised from the dead, that we should bring forth fruit unto God.

5 For when we were in the flesh, the motions of sins, which were by the law, did work in our members to bring forth fruit unto death.

6 But now we are delivered from the law, that being dead wherein we were held; that we should serve in newness of spirit, and not in the oldness of the letter.

7 What shall we say then? Is the law sin? God forbid. Nay, I had not known sin, but by the law: for I had not known lust, except the law had said, You shalt not covet.

8 But sin, taking occasion by the commandment, created in me all manner of concupiscence. For without the law sin was dead.

9 For I was alive without the law once: but when the commandment came, sin revived, and I died.

10 And the commandment, which was ordained to life, I found to be unto death.

11 For sin, taking occasion by the commandment, deceived me, and by it slew me.

12 Wherefore the law is holy, and the commandment holy, and just, and good.

13 Was then that which is good made death unto me? God forbid. But sin, that it might appear sin, working death in me by that which is good; that sin by the commandment might become exceeding sinful.

14 For we know that the law is spiritual: but I am carnal, sold under sin.

15 For that which I do I allow not: for what I would, that do I not; but what I hate, that do I.

16 If then I do that which I would not, I consent unto the law that it is good.

17 Now then it is no more I that do it, but sin that dwelleth in me.

18 For I know that in me (that is, in my flesh,) dwelleth no good thing: for to will is present with me; but how to perform that which is good I find not.

19 For the good that I would I do not: but the evil which I would not, that I do.

20 Now if I do that I would not, it is no more I that do it, but sin that dwelleth in me.

21 I find then a law, that, when I would do good, evil is present with me.

22 For I delight in the law of God after the inward man:

23 But I see another law in my members, warring against the law of my mind, and bringing me into captivity to the law of sin which is in my members.

24 O wretched man that I am! who shall deliver me from the body of this death?

25 I thank God through Jesus Christ our Lord. So then with the mind I myself serve the law of God; but with the flesh the law of sin.

CHAPTER 8

THERE is therefore now no condemnation to them which are in Christ Jesus, who walk not after the flesh, but after the Spirit.

2 For the law of the Spirit of life in Christ Jesus has made me free from the law of sin and death.

3 For what the law could not do, in that it was weak through the flesh, God sending his own Son in the likeness of sinful flesh, and for sin, condemned sin in the flesh:

4 That the righteousness of the law might be fulfilled in us, who walk not after the flesh, but after the Spirit.

5 For they that are after the flesh do mind the things of the flesh; but they that are after the Spirit the things of the Spirit.

6 For to be carnally minded is death; but to be spiritually minded is life and peace.

7 Because the carnal mind is enmity against God: for it is not subject to the law of God, neither indeed can be.

8 So then they that are in the flesh cannot please God.

9 But you are not in the flesh, but in the Spirit, if so be that the Spirit of God dwell in you. Now if any man have not the Spirit of Christ, he is none of his.

10 And if Christ be in you, the body is dead because of sin; but the Spirit is life because of righteousness.

11 But if the Spirit of him that raised up Jesus from the dead dwell in you, he that raised up Christ from the dead shall also quicken your mortal bodies by his Spirit that dwelleth in you.

12 Therefore, brethren, we are debtors, not to the flesh, to live after the flesh.

13 For if you live after the flesh, you shall die: but if you through the Spirit do mortify the deeds of the body, you shall live.

14 For as many as are led by the Spirit of God, they are the sons of God.

15 For you have not received the spirit of bondage again to fear; but you have received the Spirit of adoption, whereby we cry, Abba, Father.

16 The Spirit itself beareth witness with our spirit, that we are the children of God:

17 And if children, then heirs; heirs of God, and joint-heirs with Christ; if so be that we suffer with him, that we may be also glorified together.

18 For I reckon that the sufferings of this present time are not worthy to be compared with the glory which shall be revealed in us.

19 For the earnest expectation of the creature waiteth for the manifestation of the sons of God.

20 For the creature was made subject to vanity, not willingly, but by reason of him who has subjected the same in hope,

21 Because the creature itself also shall be delivered from the bondage of corruption into the glorious liberty of the children of God.

22 For we know that the whole creation groaneth and travaileth in pain together until now.

23 And not only they, but ourselves also, which have the firstfruits of the Spirit, even we ourselves groan within ourselves, waiting for the adoption, to wit, the redemption of our body.

24 For we are saved by hope: but hope that is seen is not hope: for what a man seeth, why doth he yet hope for?

25 But if we hope for that we see not, then do we with patience wait for it.

26 Likewise the Spirit also helpeth our infirmities: for we know not what we should pray for as we ought: but the Spirit itself maketh intercession for us with groanings which cannot be uttered.

27 And he that searches the hearts knoweth what is the mind of the Spirit, because he maketh intercession for the saints according to the will of God.

28 And we know that all things work together for good to them that love God, to them who are the called according to his purpose.

29 For whom he did foreknow, he also did predestinate to be conformed to the image of his Son, that he might be the firstborn among many brethren.

30 Moreover whom he did predestinate, them he also called: and whom he called, them he also justified: and whom he justified, them he also glorified.

31 What shall we then say to these things? If God be for us, who can be against us?

32 He that spared not his own Son, but delivered him up for us all, how shall he not with him also freely give us all things?

33 Who shall lay any thing to the charge of God's elect? It is God that justifieth.

34 Who is he that condemneth? It is Christ that died, yea rather, that is risen again, who is even at the right hand of God, who also maketh intercession for us.

35 Who shall separate us from the love of Christ? shall tribulation, or distress, or persecution, or famine, or nakedness, or peril, or sword?

36 As it is written, For your sake we are killed all the day long; we are accounted as sheep for the slaughter.

37 Nay, in all these things we are more than conquerors through him that loved us.

38 For I am persuaded, that neither death, nor life, nor angels, nor principalities, nor powers, nor things present, nor things to come,

39 Nor height, nor depth, nor any other creature, shall be able to separate us from the love of God, which is in Christ Jesus our Lord.

CHAPTER 9

I SAY the truth in Christ, I lie not, my conscience also bearing me witness in the Holy Ghost,

2 That I have great heaviness and continual sorrow in my heart.

3 For I could wish that myself were accursed from Christ for my brethren, my kinsmen according to the flesh:

4 Who are Israelites; to whom pertaineth the adoption, and the glory, and the covenants, and the giving of the law, and the service of God, and the promises;

5 Whose are the fathers, and of whom as concerning the flesh Christ came, who is over all, God blessed for ever. Amen.

6 Not as though the word of God has taken none effect. For they are not all Israel, which are of Israel:

7 Neither, because they are the seed of Abraham, are they all children: but, In Isaac shall your seed be called.

8 That is, They which are the children of the flesh, these are not the children of God: but the children of the promise are counted for the seed.

9 For this is the word of promise, At this time will I come, and Sara shall have a son.

10 And not only this; but when Rebecca also had conceived by one, even by our father Isaac;

11 (For the children being not yet born, neither having done any good or evil, that the purpose of God according to election might stand, not of works, but of him that calleth;)

12 It was said unto her, The elder shall serve the younger.

13 As it is written, Jacob have I loved, but Esau have I hated.

14 What shall we say then? Is there unrighteousness with God? God forbid.

15 For he saith to Moses, I will have mercy on whom I will have mercy, and I will have compassion on whom I will have compassion.

16 So then it is not of him that willeth, nor of him that runneth, but of God that sheweth mercy.

17 For the scripture saith unto Pharaoh, Even for this same purpose have I raised you up, that I might shew my power in you, and that my name might be declared throughout all the earth.

18 Therefore has he mercy on whom he will have mercy, and whom he will he hardeneth.

19 You will say then unto me, Why doth he yet find fault? For who has resisted his will?

20 Nay but, O man, who are you that repliest against God? Shall the thing formed say to him that formed it, Why have you made me thus?

21 Has not the potter power over the clay, of the same lump to make one vessel unto honour, and another unto dishonour?

22 What if God, willing to shew his wrath, and to make his power known, endured with much longsuffering the vessels of wrath fitted to destruction:

23 And that he might make known the riches of his glory on the vessels of mercy, which he had afore prepared unto glory,

24 Even us, whom he has called, not of the Jews only, but also of the Gentiles?

25 As he saith also in Osee, I will call them my people, which were not my people; and her beloved, which was not beloved.

26 And it shall come to pass, that in the place where it was said unto them, You are not my people; there shall they be called the children of the living God.

27 Esaias also crieth concerning Israel, Though the number of the children of Israel be as the sand of the sea, a remnant shall be saved:

28 For he will finish the work, and cut it short in righteousness: because a short work will the Lord make upon the earth.

29 And as Esaias said before, Except the Lord of Sabaoth had left us a seed, we had been as Sodoma, and been made like unto Gomorrha.

30 What shall we say then? That the Gentiles, which followed not after righteousness, have attained to righteousness, even the righteousness which is of faith.

31 But Israel, which followed after the law of righteousness, has not attained to the law of righteousness.

32 Wherefore? Because they sought it not by faith, but as it were by the works of the law. For they stumbled at that stumblingstone;

33 As it is written, Behold, I lay in Sion a stumblingstone and rock of offence: and whosoever believeth on him shall not be ashamed.

CHAPTER 10

BRETHREN, my heart's desire and prayer to God for Israel is, that they might be saved.

2 For I bear them record that they have a zeal of God, but not according to knowledge.

3 For they being ignorant of God's righteousness, and going about to establish their own righteousness, have not submitted themselves unto the righteousness of God.

4 For Christ is the end of the law for righteousness to every one that believeth.

5 For Moses describeth the righteousness which is of the law, That the man which doeth those things shall live by them.

6 But the righteousness which is of faith speaketh on this wise, Say not in yours heart, Who shall ascend into heaven? (that is, to bring Christ down from above:)

7 Or, Who shall descend into the deep? (that is, to bring up Christ again from the dead.)

8 But what saith it? The word is nigh you, even in your mouth, and in your heart: that is, the word of faith, which we preach;

9 That if you shalt confess with your mouth the Lord Jesus, and shalt believe in yours heart that God has raised him from the dead, you shalt be saved.

10 For with the heart man believeth unto righteousness; and with the mouth confession is made unto salvation.

11 For the scripture saith, Whosoever believeth on him shall not be ashamed.

12 For there is no difference between the Jew and the Greek: for the same Lord over all is rich unto all that call upon him.

13 For whosoever shall call upon the name of the Lord shall be saved.

14 How then shall they call on him in whom they have not believed? and how shall they believe in him of whom they have not heard? and how shall they hear without a preacher?

15 And how shall they preach, except they be sent? as it is written, How beautiful are the feet of them that preach the gospel of peace, and bring glad tidings of good things!

16 But they have not all obeyed the gospel. For Esaias saith, Lord, who has believed our report?

17 So then faith comes by hearing, and hearing by the word of God.

18 But I say, Have they not heard? Yes verily, their sound went into all the earth, and their words unto the ends of the world.

19 But I say, Did not Israel know? First Moses saith, I will provoke you to jealousy by them that are no people, and by a foolish nation I will anger you.

20 But Esaias is very bold, and saith, I was found of them that sought me not; I was made manifest unto them that asked not after me.

21 But to Israel he saith, All day long I have stretched forth my hands unto a disobedient and gainsaying people.

CHAPTER 11

I SAY then, Has God cast away his people? God forbid. For I also am an Israelite, of the seed of Abraham, of the tribe of Benjamin.

2 God has not cast away his people which he foreknew. Wot you not what the scripture saith of Elias? how he maketh intercession to God against Israel, saying,

3 Lord, they have killed your prophets, and digged down yours altars; and I am left alone, and they seek my life.

4 But what saith the answer of God unto him? I have reserved to myself seven thousand men, who have not bowed the knee to the image of Baal.

5 Even so then at this present time also there is a remnant according to the election of grace.

6 And if by grace, then is it no more of works: otherwise grace is no more grace. But if it be of works, then is it no more grace: otherwise work is no more work.

7 What then? Israel has not obtained that which he seeketh for; but the election has obtained it, and the rest were blinded

8 (According as it is written, God has given them the spirit of slumber, eyes that they should not see, and ears that they should not hear;) unto this day.

9 And David saith, Let their table be made a snare, and a trap, and a stumblingblock, and a recompence unto them:

10 Let their eyes be darkened, that they may not see, and bow down their back alway.

11 I say then, Have they stumbled that they should fall? God forbid: but rather through their fall salvation is come unto the Gentiles, for to provoke them to jealousy.

12 Now if the fall of them be the riches of the world, and the diminishing of them the riches of the Gentiles; how much more their fulness?

13 For I speak to you Gentiles, inasmuch as I am the apostle of the Gentiles, I magnify my office:

14 If by any means I may provoke to emulation them which are my flesh, and might save some of them.

15 For if the casting away of them be the reconciling of the world, what shall the receiving of them be, but life from the dead?

16 For if the firstfruit be holy, the lump is also holy: and if the root be holy, so are the branches.

17 And if some of the branches be broken off, and you , being a wild olive tree, wert graffed in among them, and with them partakest of the root and fatness of the olive tree;

18 Boast not against the branches. But if you boast, you bearest not the root, but the root you.

19 You will say then, The branches were broken off, that I might be graffed in.

20 Well; because of unbelief they were broken off, and you standest by faith. Be not highminded, but fear:

21 For if God spared not the natural branches, take heed lest he also spare not you.

22 Behold therefore the goodness and severity of God: on them which fell, severity; but toward you, goodness, if you continue in his goodness: otherwise you also shalt be cut off.

23 And they also, if they abide not still in unbelief, shall be graffed in: for God is able to graff them in again.

24 For if you wert cut out of the olive tree which is wild by nature, and wert graffed contrary to nature into a good olive tree: how much more shall these, which be the natural branches, be graffed into their own olive tree?

25 For I would not, brethren, that you should be ignorant of this mystery, lest you should be wise in your own conceits; that blindness in part is happened to Israel, until the fulness of the Gentiles be come in.

26 And so all Israel shall be saved: as it is written, There shall come out of Sion the Deliverer, and shall turn away ungodliness from Jacob:

27 For this is my covenant unto them, when I shall take away their sins.

28 As concerning the gospel, they are enemies for your sakes: but as touching the election, they are beloved for the fathers' sakes.

29 For the gifts and calling of God are without repentance.

30 For as you in times past have not believed God, yet have now obtained mercy through their unbelief:

31 Even so have these also now not believed, that through your mercy they also may obtain mercy.

32 For God has concluded them all in unbelief, that he might have mercy upon all.

33 O the depth of the riches both of the wisdom and knowledge of God! how unsearchable are his judgments, and his ways past finding out!

34 For who has known the mind of the Lord? or who has been his counseller?

35 Or who has first given to him, and it shall be recompensed unto him again?

36 For of him, and through him, and to him, are all things: to whom be glory for ever. Amen.

CHAPTER 12

I BESEECH you therefore, brethren, by the mercies of God, that you present your bodies a living sacrifice, holy, acceptable unto God, which is your reasonable service.

2 And be not conformed to this world: but be you transformed by the renewing of your mind, that you may prove what is that good, and acceptable, and perfect, will of God.

3 For I say, through the grace given unto me, to every man that is among you, not to think of himself more highly than he ought to think; but to think soberly, according as God has dealt to every man the measure of faith.

4 For as we have many members in one body, and all members have not the same office:

5 So we, being many, are one body in Christ, and every one members one of another.

6 Having then gifts differing according to the grace that is given to us, whether prophecy, let us prophesy according to the proportion of faith;

7 Or ministry, let us wait on our ministering: or he that teacheth, on teaching;

8 Or he that exhorteth, on exhortation: he that giveth, let him do it with simplicity; he that ruleth, with diligence; he that sheweth mercy, with cheerfulness.

9 Let love be without dissimulation. Abhor that which is evil; cleave to that which is good.

10 Be kindly affectioned one to another with brotherly love; in honour preferring one another;

11 Not slothful in business; fervent in spirit; serving the Lord;

12 Rejoicing in hope; patient in tribulation; continuing instant in prayer;

13 Distributing to the necessity of saints; given to hospitality.

14 Bless them which persecute you: bless, and curse not.

15 Rejoice with them that do rejoice, and weep with them that weep.

16 Be of the same mind one toward another. Mind not high things, but condescend to men of low estate. Be not wise in your own conceits.

17 Recompense to no man evil for evil. Provide things honest in the sight of all men.

18 If it be possible, as much as lies in you, live peaceably with all men.

19 Dearly beloved, avenge not yourselves, but rather give place unto wrath: for it is written, Vengeance is my; I will repay, saith the Lord.

20 Therefore if yours enemy hunger, feed him; if he thirst, give him drink: for in so doing you shalt heap coals of fire on his head.

21 Be not overcome of evil, but overcome evil with good.

CHAPTER 13

LET every soul be subject unto the higher powers. For there is no power but of God: the powers that be are ordained of God.

2 Whosoever therefore resisteth the power, resisteth the ordinance of God: and they that resist shall receive to themselves damnation.

3 For rulers are not a terror to good works, but to the evil. Will you then not be afraid of the power? do that which is good, and you shalt have praise of the same:

4 For he is the minister of God to you for good. But if you do that which is evil, be afraid; for he beareth not the sword in vain: for he is the minister of God, a revenger to execute wrath upon him that doeth evil.

5 Wherefore you must needs be subject, not only for wrath, but also for conscience sake.

6 For for this cause pay you tribute also: for they are God's ministers, attending continually upon this very thing.

7 Render therefore to all their dues: tribute to whom tribute is due; custom to whom custom; fear to whom fear; honour to whom honour.

8 Owe no man any thing, but to love one another: for he that loveth another has fulfilled the law.

9 For this, You shalt not commit adultery, You shalt not kill, You shalt not steal, You shalt not bear false witness, You shalt not covet; and if there be any other commandment, it is briefly comprehended in this saying, namely, You shalt love your neighbour as yourself.

10 Love worketh no ill to his neighbour: therefore love is the fulfilling of the law.

11 And that, knowing the time, that now it is high time to awake out of sleep: for now is our salvation nearer than when we believed.

12 The night is far spent, the day is at hand: let us therefore cast off the works of darkness, and let us put on the armour of light.

13 Let us walk honestly, as in the day; not in rioting and drunkenness, not in chambering and wantonness, not in strife and envying.

14 But put you on the Lord Jesus Christ, and make not provision for the flesh, to fulfil the lusts thereof.

CHAPTER 14

HIM that is weak in the faith receive you , but not to doubtful disputations.

2 For one believeth that he may eat all things: another, who is weak, eateth herbs.

3 Let not him that eateth despise him that eateth not; and let not him which eateth not judge him that eateth: for God has received him.

4 Who are you that judgest another man's servant? to his own master he standeth or falleth. Yea, he shall be holden up: for God is able to make him stand.

5 One man esteemeth one day above another: another esteemeth every day alike. Let every man be fully persuaded in his own mind.

6 He that regardeth the day, regardeth it unto the Lord; and he that regardeth not the day, to the Lord he doth not regard it. He that eateth, eateth to the Lord, for he giveth God thanks; and he that eateth not, to the Lord he eateth not, and giveth God thanks.

7 For none of us liveth to himself, and no man dieth to himself.

8 For whether we live, we live unto the Lord; and whether we die, we die unto the Lord: whether we live therefore, or die, we are the Lord's.

9 For to this end Christ both died, and rose, and revived, that he might be Lord both of the dead and living.

10 But why dost you judge your brother? or why dost you set at nought your brother? for we shall all stand before the judgment seat of Christ.

11 For it is written, As I live, saith the Lord, every knee shall bow to me, and every tongue shall confess to God.

12 So then every one of us shall give account of himself to God.

13 Let us not therefore judge one another any more: but judge this rather, that no man put a stumblingblock or an occasion to fall in his brother's way.

14 I know, and am persuaded by the Lord Jesus, that there is nothing unclean of itself: but to him that esteemeth any thing to be unclean, to him it is unclean.

15 But if your brother be grieved with your meat, now walkest you not charitably. Destroy not him with your meat, for whom Christ died.

16 Let not then your good be evil spoken of:

17 For the kingdom of God is not meat and drink; but righteousness, and peace, and joy in the Holy Ghost.

18 For he that in these things serveth Christ is acceptable to God, and approved of men.

19 Let us therefore follow after the things which make for peace, and things wherewith one may edify another.

20 For meat destroy not the work of God. All things indeed are pure; but it is evil for that man who eateth with offence.

21 It is good neither to eat flesh, nor to drink wine, nor any thing whereby your brother stumbleth, or is offended, or is made weak.

22 Have you faith? have it to yourself before God. Happy is he that condemneth not himself in that thing which he alloweth.

23 And he that doubteth is damned if he eat, because he eateth not of faith: for whatsoever is not of faith is sin.

CHAPTER 15

WE then that are strong ought to bear the infirmities of the weak, and not to please ourselves.

2 Let every one of us please his neighbour for his good to edification.

3 For even Christ pleased not himself; but, as it is written, The reproaches of them that reproached you fell on me.

4 For whatsoever things were written aforetime were written for our learning, that we through patience and comfort of the scriptures might have hope.

5 Now the God of patience and consolation grant you to be likeminded one toward another according to Christ Jesus:

6 That you may with one mind and one mouth glorify God, even the Father of our Lord Jesus Christ.

7 Wherefore receive you one another, as Christ also received us to the glory of God.

8 Now I say that Jesus Christ was a minister of the circumcision for the truth of God, to confirm the promises made unto the fathers:

9 And that the Gentiles might glorify God for his mercy; as it is written, For this cause I will confess to you among the Gentiles, and sing unto your name.

10 And again he saith, Rejoice, you Gentiles, with his people.

11 And again, Praise the Lord, all you Gentiles; and laud him, all you people.

12 And again, Esaias saith, There shall be a root of Jesse, and he that shall rise to reign over the Gentiles; in him shall the Gentiles trust.

13 Now the God of hope fill you with all joy and peace in believing, that you may abound in hope, through the power of the Holy Ghost.

14 And I myself also am persuaded of you, my brethren, that you also are full of goodness, filled with all knowledge, able also to admonish one another.

15 Nevertheless, brethren, I have written the more boldly unto you in some sort, as putting you in mind, because of the grace that is given to me of God,

16 That I should be the minister of Jesus Christ to the Gentiles, ministering the gospel of God, that the offering up of the Gentiles might be acceptable, being sanctified by the Holy Ghost.

17 I have therefore whereof I may glory through Jesus Christ in those things which pertain to God.

18 For I will not dare to speak of any of those things which Christ has not created by me, to make the Gentiles obedient, by word and deed,

19 Through mighty signs and wonders, by the power of the Spirit of God; so that from Jerusalem, and round about unto Illyricum, I have fully preached the gospel of Christ.

20 Yea, so have I strived to preach the gospel, not where Christ was named, lest I should build upon another man's foundation:

21 But as it is written, To whom he was not spoken of, they shall see: and they that have not heard shall understand.

22 For which cause also I have been much hindered from coming to you.

23 But now having no more place in these parts, and having a great desire these many years to come unto you;

24 Whensoever I take my journey into Spain, I will come to you: for I trust to see you in my journey, and to be brought on my way thitherward by you, if first I be somewhat filled with your company.

25 But now I go unto Jerusalem to minister unto the saints.

26 For it has pleased them of Macedonia and Achaia to make a certain contribution for the poor saints which are at Jerusalem.

27 It has pleased them verily; and their debtors they are. For if the Gentiles have been made partakers of their spiritual things, their duty is also to minister unto them in carnal things.

28 When therefore I have performed this, and have sealed to them this fruit, I will come by you into Spain.

29 And I am sure that, when I come unto you, I shall come in the fulness of the blessing of the gospel of Christ.

30 Now I beseech you, brethren, for the Lord Jesus Christ's sake, and for the love of the Spirit, that you strive together with me in your prayers to God for me;

31 That I may be delivered from them that do not believe in Judæa; and that my service which I have for Jerusalem may be accepted of the saints;

32 That I may come unto you with joy by the will of God, and may with you be refreshed.

33 Now the God of peace be with you all. Amen.

CHAPTER 16

I COMMEND unto you Phebe our sister, which is a servant of the church which is at Cenchrea:

2 That you receive her in the Lord, as becometh saints, and that you assist her in whatsoever business she has need of you: for she has been a succourer of many, and of myself also.

3 Greet Priscilla and Aquila my helpers in Christ Jesus:

4 Who have for my life laid down their own necks: unto whom not only I give thanks, but also all the churches of the Gentiles.

5 Likewise greet the church that is in their house. Salute my wellbeloved Epænetus, who is the firstfruits of Achaia unto Christ.

6 Greet Mary, who bestowed much labour on us.

7 Salute Andronicus and Junia, my kinsmen, and my fellowprisoners, who are of note among the apostles, who also were in Christ before me.

8 Greet Amplias my beloved in the Lord.

9 Salute Urbane, our helper in Christ, and Stachys my beloved.

10 Salute Apelles approved in Christ. Salute them which are of Aristobulus' household.

11 Salute Herodion my kinsman. Greet them that be of the household of Narcissus, which are in the Lord.

12 Salute Tryphena and Tryphosa, who labour in the Lord. Salute the beloved Persis, which laboured much in the Lord.

13 Salute Rufus chosen in the Lord, and his mother and my.

14 Salute Asyncritus, Phlegon, Hermas, Patrobas, Hermes, and the brethren which are with them.

15 Salute Philologus, and Julia, Nereus, and his sister, and Olympas, and all the saints which are with them.

16 Salute one another with an holy kiss. The churches of Christ salute you.

17 Now I beseech you, brethren, mark them which cause divisions and offences contrary to the doctrine which you have learned; and avoid them.

18 For they that are such serve not our Lord Jesus Christ, but their own belly; and by good words and fair speeches deceive the hearts of the simple.

19 For your obedience is come abroad unto all men. I am glad therefore on your behalf: but yet I would have you wise unto that which is good, and simple concerning evil.

20 And the God of peace shall bruise Satan under your feet shortly. The grace of our Lord Jesus Christ be with you. Amen.

21 Timotheus my workfellow, and Lucius, and Jason, and Sosipater, my kinsmen, salute you.

22 I Tertius, who wrote this epistle, salute you in the Lord.

23 Gaius my host, and of the whole church, saluteth you. Erastus the chamberlain of the city saluteth you, and Quartus a brother.

24 The grace of our Lord Jesus Christ be with you all. Amen.

25 Now to him that is of power to stablish you according to my gospel, and the preaching of Jesus Christ, according to the revelation of the mystery, which was kept secret since the world began,

26 But now is made manifest, and by the scriptures of the prophets, according to the commandment of the everlasting God, made known to all nations for the obedience of faith:

27 To God only wise, be glory through Jesus Christ for ever. Amen.

Written to the Romans from Corinthus, and sent by Phebe servant of the church at Cenchrea.

THE
FIRST EPISTLE OF PAUL THE APOSTLE
TO THE
CORINTHIANS.

CHAPTER 1

PAUL, called to be an apostle of Jesus Christ through the will of God, and Sosthenes our brother,

2 Unto the church of God which is at Corinth, to them that are sanctified in Christ Jesus, called to be saints, with all that in every place call upon the name of Jesus Christ our Lord, both theirs and ours:

3 Grace be unto you, and peace, from God our Father, and from the Lord Jesus Christ.

4 I thank my God always on your behalf, for the grace of God which is given you by Jesus Christ;

5 That in every thing you are enriched by him, in all utterance, and in all knowledge;

6 Even as the testimony of Christ was confirmed in you:

7 So that you come behind in no gift; waiting for the coming of our Lord Jesus Christ:

8 Who shall also confirm you unto the end, that you may be blameless in the day of our Lord Jesus Christ.

9 God is faithful, by whom you were called unto the fellowship of his Son Jesus Christ our Lord.

10 Now I beseech you, brethren, by the name of our Lord Jesus Christ, that you all speak the same thing, and that there be no divisions among you; but that you be perfectly joined together in the same mind and in the same judgment.

11 For it has been declared unto me of you, my brethren, by them which are of the house of Chloe, that there are contentions among you.

12 Now this I say, that every one of you saith, I am of Paul; and I of Apollos; and I of Cephas; and I of Christ.

13 Is Christ divided? was Paul crucified for you? or were you baptized in the name of Paul?

14 I thank God that I baptized none of you, but Crispus and Gaius;

15 Lest any should say that I had baptized in my own name.

16 And I baptized also the household of Stephanas: besides, I know not whether I baptized any other.

17 For Christ sent me not to baptize, but to preach the gospel: not with wisdom of words, lest the cross of Christ should be made of none effect.

18 For the preaching of the cross is to them that perish foolishness; but unto us which are saved it is the power of God.

19 For it is written, I will destroy the wisdom of the wise, and will bring to nothing the understanding of the prudent.

20 Where is the wise? where is the scribe? where is the disputer of this world? has not God made foolish the wisdom of this world?

21 For after that in the wisdom of God the world by wisdom knew not God, it pleased God by the foolishness of preaching to save them that believe.

22 For the Jews require a sign, and the Greeks seek after wisdom:

23 But we preach Christ crucified, unto the Jews a stumblingblock, and unto the Greeks foolishness;

24 But unto them which are called, both Jews and Greeks, Christ the power of God, and the wisdom of God.

25 Because the foolishness of God is wiser than men; and the weakness of God is stronger than men.

26 For you see your calling, brethren, how that not many wise men after the flesh, not many mighty, not many noble, are called:

27 But God has chosen the foolish things of the world to confound the wise; and God has chosen the weak things of the world to confound the things which are mighty;

28 And base things of the world, and things which are despised, has God chosen, yea, and things which are not, to bring to nought things that are:

29 That no flesh should glory in his presence.

30 But of him are you in Christ Jesus, who of God is made unto us wisdom, and righteousness, and sanctification, and redemption:

31 That, according as it is written, He that glorieth, let him glory in the Lord.

CHAPTER 2

AND I, brethren, when I came to you, came not with excellency of speech or of wisdom, declaring unto you the testimony of God.

2 For I determined not to know any thing among you, save Jesus Christ, and him crucified.

3 And I was with you in weakness, and in fear, and in much trembling.

4 And my speech and my preaching was not with enticing words of man's wisdom, but in demonstration of the Spirit and of power:

5 That your faith should not stand in the wisdom of men, but in the power of God.

6 Howbeit we speak wisdom among them that are perfect: yet not the wisdom of this world, nor of the princes of this world, that come to nought:

7 But we speak the wisdom of God in a mystery, even the hidden wisdom, which God ordained before the world unto our glory:

8 Which none of the princes of this world knew: for had they known it, they would not have crucified the Lord of glory.

9 But as it is written, Eye has not seen, nor ear heard, neither have entered into the heart of man, the things which God has prepared for them that love him.

10 But God has revealed them unto us by his Spirit: for the Spirit searches all things, yea, the deep things of God.

11 For what man knoweth the things of a man, save the spirit of man which is in him? even so the things of God knoweth no man, but the Spirit of God.

12 Now we have received, not the spirit of the world, but the spirit which is of God; that we might know the things that are freely given to us of God.

13 Which things also we speak, not in the words which man's wisdom teacheth, but which the Holy Ghost teacheth; comparing spiritual things with spiritual.

14 But the natural man receiveth not the things of the Spirit of God: for they are foolishness unto him: neither can he know them, because they are spiritually discerned.

15 But he that is spiritual judgeth all things, yet he himself is judged of no man.

16 For who has known the mind of the Lord, that he may instruct him? But we have the mind of Christ.

CHAPTER 3

AND I, brethren, could not speak unto you as unto spiritual, but as unto carnal, even as unto babes in Christ.

2 I have fed you with milk, and not with meat: for hitherto you were not able to bear it, neither yet now are you able.

3 For you are yet carnal: for whereas there is among you envying, and strife, and divisions, are you not carnal, and walk as men?

4 For while one saith, I am of Paul; and another, I am of Apollos; are you not carnal?

5 Who then is Paul, and who is Apollos, but ministers by whom you believed, even as the Lord gave to every man?

6 I have planted, Apollos watered; but God gave the increase.

7 So then neither is he that planteth any thing, neither he that watereth; but God that giveth the increase.

8 Now he that planteth and he that watereth are one: and every man shall receive his own reward according to his own labour.

9 For we are labourers together with God: you are God's husbandry, you are God's building.

10 According to the grace of God which is given unto me, as a wise masterbuilder, I have laid the foundation, and another buildeth thereon. But let every man take heed how he buildeth thereupon.

11 For other foundation can no man lay than that is laid, which is Jesus Christ.

12 Now if any man build upon this foundation gold, silver, precious stones, wood, hay, stubble;

13 Every man's work shall be made manifest: for the day shall declare it, because it shall be revealed by fire; and the fire shall try every man's work of what sort it is.

14 If any man's work abide which he has built thereupon, he shall receive a reward.

15 If any man's work shall be burned, he shall suffer loss: but he himself shall be saved; yet so as by fire.

16 Know you not that you are the temple of God, and that the Spirit of God dwelleth in you?

17 If any man defile the temple of God, him shall God destroy; for the temple of God is holy, which temple you are.

18 Let no man deceive himself. If any man among you seemeth to be wise in this world, let him become a fool, that he may be wise.

19 For the wisdom of this world is foolishness with God. For it is written, He taketh the wise in their own craftiness.

20 And again, The Lord knoweth the thoughts of the wise, that they are vain.

21 Therefore let no man glory in men. For all things are yours;

22 Whether Paul, or Apollos, or Cephas, or the world, or life, or death, or things present, or things to come; all are yours;

23 And you are Christ's; and Christ is God's.

CHAPTER 4

LET a man so account of us, as of the ministers of Christ, and stewards of the mysteries of God.

2 Moreover it is required in stewards, that a man be found faithful.

3 But with me it is a very small thing that I should be judged of you, or of man's judgment: yea, I judge not my own self.

4 For I know nothing by myself; yet am I not hereby justified: but he that judgeth me is the Lord.

5 Therefore judge nothing before the time, until the Lord come, who both will bring to light the hidden things of darkness, and will make manifest the counsels of the hearts: and then shall every man have praise of God.

6 And these things, brethren, I have in a figure transferred to myself and to Apollos for your sakes; that you might learn in us not to think of men above that which is written, that no one of you be puffed up for one against another.

7 For who maketh you to differ from another? and what have you that you did not receive? now if you did receive it, why dost you glory, as if you hadst not received it?

8 Now you are full, now you are rich, you have reigned as kings without us: and I would to God you did reign, that we also might reign with you.

9 For I think that God has set forth us the apostles last, as it were appointed to death: for we are made a spectacle unto the world, and to angels, and to men.

10 We are fools for Christ's sake, but you are wise in Christ; we are weak, but you are strong; you are honourable, but we are despised.

11 Even unto this present hour we both hunger, and thirst, and are naked, and are buffeted, and have no certain dwellingplace;

12 And labour, working with our own hands: being reviled, we bless; being persecuted, we suffer it:

13 Being defamed, we intreat: we are made as the filth of the world, and are the offscouring of all things unto this day.

14 I write not these things to shame you, but as my beloved sons I warn you.

15 For though you have ten thousand instructors in Christ, yet have you not many fathers: for in Christ Jesus I have begotten you through the gospel.

16 Wherefore I beseech you, be you followers of me.

17 For this cause have I sent unto you Timotheus, who is my beloved son, and faithful in the Lord, who shall bring you into remembrance of my ways which be in Christ, as I teach every where in every church.

18 Now some are puffed up, as though I would not come to you.

19 But I will come to you shortly, if the Lord will, and will know, not the speech of them which are puffed up, but the power.

20 For the kingdom of God is not in word, but in power.

21 What will you? shall I come unto you with a rod, or in love, and in the spirit of meekness?

CHAPTER 5

IT is reported commonly that there is fornication among you, and such fornication as is not so much as named among the Gentiles, that one should have his father's wife.

2 And you are puffed up, and have not rather mourned, that he that has done this deed might be taken away from among you.

3 For I verily, as absent in body, but present in spirit, have judged already, as though I were present, concerning him that has so done this deed,

4 In the name of our Lord Jesus Christ, when you are gathered together, and my spirit, with the power of our Lord Jesus Christ,

5 To deliver such an one unto Satan for the destruction of the flesh, that the spirit may be saved in the day of the Lord Jesus.

6 Your glorying is not good. Know you not that a little leaven leaveneth the whole lump?

7 Purge out therefore the old leaven, that you may be a new lump, as you are unleavened. For even Christ our passover is sacrificed for us:

8 Therefore let us keep the feast, not with old leaven, neither with the leaven of malice and wickedness; but with the unleavened bread of sincerity and truth.

9 I wrote unto you in an epistle not to company with fornicators:

10 Yet not altogether with the fornicators of this world, or with the covetous, or extortioners, or with idolaters; for then must you needs go out of the world.

11 But now I have written unto you not to keep company, if any man that is called a brother be a fornicator, or covetous, or an idolater, or a railer, or a drunkard, or an extortioner; with such an one no not to eat.

12 For what have I to do to judge them also that are without? do not you judge them that are within?

13 But them that are without God judgeth. Therefore put away from among yourselves that wicked person.

CHAPTER 6

DARE any of you, having a matter against another, go to law before the unjust, and not before the saints?

2 Do you not know that the saints shall judge the world? and if the world shall be judged by you, are you unworthy to judge the smallest matters?

3 Know you not that we shall judge angels? how much more things that pertain to this life?

4 If then you have judgments of things pertaining to this life, set them to judge who are least esteemed in the church.

5 I speak to your shame. Is it so, that there is not a wise man among you? no, not one that shall be able to judge between his brethren?

6 But brother goeth to law with brother, and that before the unbelievers.

7 Now therefore there is utterly a fault among you, because you go to law one with another. Why do you not rather take wrong? why do you not rather suffer yourselves to be defrauded?

8 Nay, you do wrong, and defraud, and that your brethren.

9 Know you not that the unrighteous shall not inherit the kingdom of God? Be not deceived: neither fornicators, nor idolaters, nor adulterers, nor effeminate, nor abusers of themselves with mankind,

10 Nor thieves, nor covetous, nor drunkards, nor revilers, nor extortioners, shall inherit the kingdom of God.

11 And such were some of you: but you are washed, but you are sanctified, but you are justified in the name of the Lord Jesus, and by the Spirit of our God.

12 All things are lawful unto me, but all things are not expedient: all things are lawful for me, but I will not be brought under the power of any.

13 Meats for the belly, and the belly for meats: but God shall destroy both it and them. Now the body is not for fornication, but for the Lord; and the Lord for the body.

14 And God has both raised up the Lord, and will also raise us up by his own power.

15 Know you not that your bodies are the members of Christ? shall I then take the members of Christ, and make them the members of an harlot? God forbid.

16 What? know you not that he which is joined to an harlot is one body? for two, saith he, shall be one flesh.

17 But he that is joined unto the Lord is one spirit.

18 Flee fornication. Every sin that a man doeth is without the body; but he that committeth fornication sinneth against his own body.

19 What? know you not that your body is the temple of the Holy Ghost which is in you, which you have of God, and you are not your own?

20 For you are bought with a price: therefore glorify God in your body, and in your spirit, which are God's.

CHAPTER 7

NOW concerning the things whereof you wrote unto me: It is good for a man not to touch a woman.

2 Nevertheless, to avoid fornication, let every man have his own wife, and let every woman have her own husband.

3 Let the husband render unto the wife due benevolence: and likewise also the wife unto the husband.

4 The wife has not power of her own body, but the husband: and likewise also the husband has not power of his own body, but the wife.

5 Defraud you not one the other, except it be with consent for a time, that you may give yourselves to fasting and prayer; and come together again, that Satan tempt you not for your incontinency.

6 But I speak this by permission, and not of commandment.

7 For I would that all men were even as I myself. But every man has his proper gift of God, one after this manner, and another after that.

8 I say therefore to the unmarried and widows, It is good for them if they abide even as I.

9 But if they cannot contain, let them marry: for it is better to marry than to burn.

10 And unto the married I command, yet not I, but the Lord, Let not the wife depart from her husband:

11 But and if she depart, let her remain unmarried, or be reconciled to her husband: and let not the husband put away his wife.

12 But to the rest speak I, not the Lord: If any brother has a wife that believeth not, and she be pleased to dwell with him, let him not put her away.

13 And the woman which has an husband that believeth not, and if he be pleased to dwell with her, let her not leave him.

14 For the unbelieving husband is sanctified by the wife, and the unbelieving wife is sanctified by the husband: else were your children unclean; but now are they holy.

15 But if the unbelieving depart, let him depart. A brother or a sister is not under bondage in such cases: but God has called us to peace.

16 For what knowest you, O wife, whether you shalt save your husband? or how knowest you, O man, whether you shalt save your wife?

17 But as God has distributed to every man, as the Lord has called every one, so let him walk. And so ordain I in all churches.

18 Is any man called being circumcised? let him not become uncircumcised. Is any called in uncircumcision? let him not be circumcised.

19 Circumcision is nothing, and uncircumcision is nothing, but the keeping of the commandments of God.

20 Let every man abide in the same calling wherein he was called.

21 Are you called being a servant? care not for it: but if you mayest be made free, use it rather.

22 For he that is called in the Lord, being a servant, is the Lord's freeman: likewise also he that is called, being free, is Christ's servant.

23 You are bought with a price; be not you the servants of men.

24 Brethren, let every man, wherein he is called, therein abide with God.

25 Now concerning virgins I have no commandment of the Lord: yet I give my judgment, as one that has obtained mercy of the Lord to be faithful.

26 I suppose therefore that this is good for the present distress, I say, that it is good for a man so to be.

27 Are you bound unto a wife? seek not to be loosed. Are you loosed from a wife? seek not a wife.

28 But and if you marry, you have not sinned; and if a virgin marry, she has not sinned. Nevertheless such shall have trouble in the flesh: but I spare you.

29 But this I say, brethren, the time is short: it remaineth, that both they that have wives be as though they had none;

30 And they that weep, as though they wept not; and they that rejoice, as though they rejoiced not; and they that buy, as though they possessed not;

31 And they that use this world, as not abusing it: for the fashion of this world passes away.

32 But I would have you without carefulness. He that is unmarried careth for the things that belong to the Lord, how he may please the Lord:

33 But he that is married careth for the things that are of the world, how he may please his wife.

34 There is difference also between a wife and a virgin. The unmarried woman careth for the things of the Lord, that she may be holy both in body and in spirit: but she that is married careth for the things of the world, how she may please her husband.

35 And this I speak for your own profit; not that I may cast a snare upon you, but for that which is comely, and that you may attend upon the Lord without distraction.

36 But if any man think that he behaveth himself uncomely toward his virgin, if she pass the flower of her age, and need so require, let him do what he will, he sinneth not: let them marry.

37 Nevertheless he that standeth stedfast in his heart, having no necessity, but has power over his own will, and has so decreed in his heart that he will keep his virgin, doeth well.

38 So then he that giveth her in marriage doeth well; but he that giveth her not in marriage doeth better.

39 The wife is bound by the law as long as her husband liveth; but if her husband be dead, she is at liberty to be married to whom she will; only in the Lord.

40 But she is happier if she so abide, after my judgment: and I think also that I have the Spirit of God.

CHAPTER 8

NOW as touching things offered unto idols, we know that we all have knowledge. Knowledge puffeth up, but charity edifieth.

2 And if any man think that he knoweth any thing, he knoweth nothing yet as he ought to know.

3 But if any man love God, the same is known of him.

4 As concerning therefore the eating of those things that are offered in sacrifice unto idols, we know that an idol is nothing in the world, and that there is none other God but one.

5 For though there be that are called gods, whether in heaven or in earth, (as there be gods many, and lords many,)

6 But to us there is but one God, the Father, of whom are all things, and we in him; and one Lord Jesus Christ, by whom are all things, and we by him.

7 Howbeit there is not in every man that knowledge: for some with conscience of the idol unto this hour eat it as a thing offered unto an idol; and their conscience being weak is defiled.

8 But meat commendeth us not to God: for neither, if we eat, are we the better; neither, if we eat not, are we the worse.

9 But take heed lest by any means this liberty of yours become a stumblingblock to them that are weak.

10 For if any man see you which have knowledge sit at meat in the idol's temple, shall not the conscience of him which is weak be emboldened to eat those things which are offered to idols;

11 And through your knowledge shall the weak brother perish, for whom Christ died?

12 But when you sin so against the brethren, and wound their weak conscience, you sin against Christ.

13 Wherefore, if meat make my brother to offend, I will eat no flesh while the world standeth, lest I make my brother to offend.

CHAPTER 9

AM I not an apostle? am I not free? have I not seen Jesus Christ our Lord? are not you my work in the Lord?

2 If I be not an apostle unto others, yet doubtless I am to you: for the seal of my apostleship are you in the Lord.

3 My answer to them that do examine me is this,

4 Have we not power to eat and to drink?

5 Have we not power to lead about a sister, a wife, as well as other apostles, and as the brethren of the Lord, and Cephas?

6 Or I only and Barnabas, have not we power to forbear working?

7 Who goeth a warfare any time at his own charges? who planteth a vineyard, and eateth not of the fruit thereof? or who feedeth a flock, and eateth not of the milk of the flock?

8 Say I these things as a man? or saith not the law the same also?

9 For it is written in the law of Moses, You shalt not muzzle the mouth of the ox that treadeth out the corn. Doth God take care for oxen?

10 Or saith he it altogether for our sakes? For our sakes, no doubt, this is written: that he that ploweth should plow in hope; and that he that thresheth in hope should be partaker of his hope.

11 If we have sown unto you spiritual things, is it a great thing if we shall reap your carnal things?

12 If others be partakers of this power over you, are not we rather? Nevertheless we have not used this power; but suffer all things, lest we should hinder the gospel of Christ.

13 Do you not know that they which minister about holy things live of the things of the temple? and they which wait at the altar are partakers with the altar?

14 Even so has the Lord ordained that they which preach the gospel should live of the gospel.

15 But I have used none of these things: neither have I written these things, that it should be so done unto me: for it were better for me to die, than that any man should make my glorying void.

16 For though I preach the gospel, I have nothing to glory of: for necessity is laid upon me; yea, woe is unto me, if I preach not the gospel!

17 For if I do this thing willingly, I have a reward: but if against my will, a dispensation of the gospel is committed unto me.

18 What is my reward then? Verily that, when I preach the gospel, I may make the gospel of Christ without charge, that I abuse not my power in the gospel.

19 For though I be free from all men, yet have I made myself servant unto all, that I might gain the more.

20 And unto the Jews I became as a Jew, that I might gain the Jews; to them that are under the law, as under the law, that I might gain them that are under the law;

21 To them that are without law, as without law, (being not without law to God, but under the law to Christ,) that I might gain them that are without law.

22 To the weak became I as weak, that I might gain the weak: I am made all things to all men, that I might by all means save some.

23 And this I do for the gospel's sake, that I might be partaker thereof with you.

24 Know you not that they which run in a race run all, but one receiveth the prize? So run, that you may obtain.

25 And every man that striveth for the mastery is temperate in all things. Now they do it to obtain a corruptible crown; but we an incorruptible.

26 I therefore so run, not as uncertainly; so fight I, not as one that beateth the air:

27 But I keep under my body, and bring it into subjection: lest that by any means, when I have preached to others, I myself should be a castaway.

CHAPTER 10

MOREOVER, brethren, I would not that you should be ignorant, how that all our fathers were under the cloud, and all passed through the sea;

2 And were all baptized unto Moses in the cloud and in the sea;

3 And did all eat the same spiritual meat;

4 And did all drink the same spiritual drink: for they drank of that spiritual Rock that followed them: and that Rock was Christ.

5 But with many of them God was not well pleased: for they were overthrown in the wilderness.

6 Now these things were our examples, to the intent we should not lust after evil things, as they also lusted.

7 Neither be you idolaters, as were some of them; as it is written, The people sat down to eat and drink, and rose up to play.

8 Neither let us commit fornication, as some of them committed, and fell in one day three and twenty thousand.

9 Neither let us tempt Christ, as some of them also tempted, and were destroyed of serpents.

10 Neither murmur you , as some of them also murmured, and were destroyed of the destroyer.

11 Now all these things happened unto them for ensamples: and they are written for our admonition, upon whom the ends of the world are come.

12 Wherefore let him that thinketh he standeth take heed lest he fall.

13 There has no temptation taken you but such as is common to man: but God is faithful, who will not suffer you to be tempted above that you are able; but will with the temptation also make a way to escape, that you may be able to bear it.

14 Wherefore, my dearly beloved, flee from idolatry.

15 I speak as to wise men; judge you what I say.

16 The cup of blessing which we bless, is it not the communion of the blood of Christ? The bread which we break, is it not the communion of the body of Christ?

17 For we being many are one bread, and one body: for we are all partakers of that one bread.

18 Behold Israel after the flesh: are not they which eat of the sacrifices partakers of the altar?

19 What say I then? that the idol is any thing, or that which is offered in sacrifice to idols is any thing?

20 But I say, that the things which the Gentiles sacrifice, they sacrifice to devils, and not to God: and I would not that you should have fellowship with devils.

21 You cannot drink the cup of the Lord, and the cup of devils: you cannot be partakers of the Lord's table, and of the table of devils.

22 Do we provoke the Lord to jealousy? are we stronger than he?

23 All things are lawful for me, but all things are not expedient: all things are lawful for me, but all things edify not.

24 Let no man seek his own, but every man another's wealth.

25 Whatsoever is sold in the shambles, that eat, asking no question for conscience sake:

26 For the earth is the Lord's, and the fulness thereof.

27 If any of them that believe not bid you to a feast, and you be disposed to go; whatsoever is set before you, eat, asking no question for conscience sake.

28 But if any man say unto you, This is offered in sacrifice unto idols, eat not for his sake that shewed it, and for conscience sake: for the earth is the Lord's, and the fulness thereof:

29 Conscience, I say, not yours own, but of the other: for why is my liberty judged of another man's conscience?

30 For if I by grace be a partaker, why am I evil spoken of for that for which I give thanks?

31 Whether therefore you eat, or drink, or whatsoever you do, do all to the glory of God.

32 Give none offence, neither to the Jews, nor to the Gentiles, nor to the church of God:

33 Even as I please all men in all things, not seeking my own profit, but the profit of many, that they may be saved.

CHAPTER 11

BE you followers of me, even as I also am of Christ.

2 Now I praise you, brethren, that you remember me in all things, and keep the ordinances, as I delivered them to you.

3 But I would have you know, that the head of every man is Christ; and the head of the woman is the man; and the head of Christ is God.

4 Every man praying or prophesying, having his head covered, dishonoureth his head.

5 But every woman that prayeth or prophesieth with her head uncovered dishonoureth her head: for that is even all one as if she were shaven.

6 For if the woman be not covered, let her also be shorn: but if it be a shame for a woman to be shorn or shaven, let her be covered.

7 For a man indeed ought not to cover his head, forasmuch as he is the image and glory of God: but the woman is the glory of the man.

8 For the man is not of the woman; but the woman of the man.

9 Neither was the man created for the woman; but the woman for the man.

10 For this cause ought the woman to have power on her head because of the angels.

11 Nevertheless neither is the man without the woman, neither the woman without the man, in the Lord.

12 For as the woman is of the man, even so is the man also by the woman; but all things of God.

13 Judge in yourselves: is it comely that a woman pray unto God uncovered?

14 Doth not even nature itself teach you, that, if a man have long hair, it is a shame unto him?

15 But if a woman have long hair, it is a glory to her: for her hair is given her for a covering.

16 But if any man seem to be contentious, we have no such custom, neither the churches of God.

17 Now in this that I declare unto you I praise you not, that you come together not for the better, but for the worse.

18 For first of all, when you come together in the church, I hear that there be divisions among you; and I partly believe it.

19 For there must be also heresies among you, that they which are approved may be made manifest among you.

20 When you come together therefore into one place, this is not to eat the Lord's supper.

21 For in eating every one taketh before other his own supper: and one is hungry, and another is drunken.

22 What? have you not houses to eat and to drink in? or despise you the church of God, and shame them that have not? What shall I say to you? shall I praise you in this? I praise you not.

23 For I have received of the Lord that which also I delivered unto you, That the Lord Jesus the same night in which he was betrayed took bread:

24 And when he had given thanks, he brake it, and said, Take, eat: this is my body, which is broken for you: this do in remembrance of me.

25 After the same manner also he took the cup, when he had supped, saying, This cup is the new testament in my blood: this do you , as oft as you drink it, in remembrance of me.

26 For as often as you eat this bread, and drink this cup, you do shew the Lord's death till he come.

27 Wherefore whosoever shall eat this bread, and drink this cup of the Lord, unworthily, shall be guilty of the body and blood of the Lord.

28 But let a man examine himself, and so let him eat of that bread, and drink of that cup.

29 For he that eateth and drinketh unworthily, eateth and drinketh damnation to himself, not discerning the Lord's body.

30 For this cause many are weak and sickly among you, and many sleep.

31 For if we would judge ourselves, we should not be judged.

32 But when we are judged, we are chastened of the Lord, that we should not be condemned with the world.

33 Wherefore, my brethren, when you come together to eat, tarry one for another.

34 And if any man hunger, let him eat at home; that you come not together unto condemnation. And the rest will I set in order when I come.

CHAPTER 12

NOW concerning spiritual gifts, brethren, I would not have you ignorant.

2 You know that you were Gentiles, carried away unto these dumb idols, even as you were led.

3 Wherefore I give you to understand, that no man speaking by the Spirit of God calleth Jesus accursed: and that no man can say that Jesus is the Lord, but by the Holy Ghost.

4 Now there are diversities of gifts, but the same Spirit.

5 And there are differences of administrations, but the same Lord.

6 And there are diversities of operations, but it is the same God which worketh all in all.

7 But the manifestation of the Spirit is given to every man to profit withal.

8 For to one is given by the Spirit the word of wisdom; to another the word of knowledge by the same Spirit;

9 To another faith by the same Spirit; to another the gifts of healing by the same Spirit;

10 To another the working of miracles; to another prophecy; to another discerning of spirits; to another divers kinds of tongues; to another the interpretation of tongues:

11 But all these worketh that one and the selfsame Spirit, dividing to every man severally as he will.

12 For as the body is one, and has many members, and all the members of that one body, being many, are one body: so also is Christ.

13 For by one Spirit are we all baptized into one body, whether we be Jews or Gentiles, whether we be bond or free; and have been all made to drink into one Spirit.

14 For the body is not one member, but many.

15 If the foot shall say, Because I am not the hand, I am not of the body; is it therefore not of the body?

16 And if the ear shall say, Because I am not the eye, I am not of the body; is it therefore not of the body?

17 If the whole body were an eye, where were the hearing? If the whole were hearing, where were the smelling?

18 But now has God set the members every one of them in the body, as it has pleased him.

19 And if they were all one member, where were the body?

20 But now are they many members, yet but one body.

21 And the eye cannot say unto the hand, I have no need of you: nor again the head to the feet, I have no need of you.

22 Nay, much more those members of the body, which seem to be more feeble, are necessary:

23 And those members of the body, which we think to be less honourable, upon these we bestow more abundant honour; and our uncomely parts have more abundant comeliness.

24 For our comely parts have no need: but God has tempered the body together, having given more abundant honour to that part which lacked:

25 That there should be no schism in the body; but that the members should have the same care one for another.

26 And whether one member suffer, all the members suffer with it; or one member be honoured, all the members rejoice with it.

27 Now you are the body of Christ, and members in particular.

28 And God has set some in the church, first apostles, secondarily prophets, thirdly teachers, after that miracles, then gifts of healings, helps, governments, diversities of tongues.

29 Are all apostles? are all prophets? are all teachers? are all workers of miracles?

30 Have all the gifts of healing? do all speak with tongues? do all interpret?

31 But covet earnestly the best gifts: and yet shew I unto you a more excellent way.

CHAPTER 13

THOUGH I speak with the tongues of men and of angels, and have not charity, I am become as sounding brass, or a tinkling cymbal.

2 And though I have the gift of prophecy, and understand all mysteries, and all knowledge; and though I have all faith, so that I could remove mountains, and have not charity, I am nothing.

3 And though I bestow all my goods to feed the poor, and though I give my body to be burned, and have not charity, it profiteth me nothing.

4 Charity suffereth long, and is kind; charity envieth not; charity vaunteth not itself, is not puffed up,

5 Doth not behave itself unseemly, seeketh not her own, is not easily provoked, thinketh no evil;

6 Rejoiceth not in iniquity, but rejoiceth in the truth;

7 Beareth all things, believeth all things, hopeth all things, endureth all things.

8 Charity never faileth: but whether there be prophecies, they shall fail; whether there be tongues, they shall cease; whether there be knowledge, it shall vanish away.

9 For we know in part, and we prophesy in part.

10 But when that which is perfect is come, then that which is in part shall be done away.

11 When I was a child, I spake as a child, I understood as a child, I thought as a child: but when I became a man, I put away childish things.

12 For now we see through a glass, darkly; but then face to face: now I know in part; but then shall I know even as also I am known.

13 And now abideth faith, hope, charity, these three; but the greatest of these is charity.

CHAPTER 14

FOLLOW after charity, and desire spiritual gifts, but rather that you may prophesy.

2 For he that speaketh in an unknown tongue speaketh not unto men, but unto God: for no man understands him; howbeit in the spirit he speaketh mysteries.

3 But he that prophesieth speaketh unto men to edification, and exhortation, and comfort.

4 He that speaketh in an unknown tongue edifieth himself; but he that prophesieth edifieth the church.

5 I would that you all spake with tongues, but rather that you prophesied: for greater is he that prophesieth than he that speaketh with tongues, except he interpret, that the church may receive edifying.

6 Now, brethren, if I come unto you speaking with tongues, what shall I profit you, except I shall speak to you either by revelation, or by knowledge, or by prophesying, or by doctrine?

7 And even things without life giving sound, whether pipe or harp, except they give a distinction in the sounds, how shall it be known what is piped or harped?

8 For if the trumpet give an uncertain sound, who shall prepare himself to the battle?

9 So likewise you, except you utter by the tongue words easy to be understood, how shall it be known what is spoken? for you shall speak into the air.

10 There are, it may be, so many kinds of voices in the world, and none of them is without signification.

11 Therefore if I know not the meaning of the voice, I shall be unto him that speaketh a barbarian, and he that speaketh shall be a barbarian unto me.

12 Even so you, forasmuch as you are zealous of spiritual gifts, seek that you may excel to the edifying of the church.

13 Wherefore let him that speaketh in an unknown tongue pray that he may interpret.

14 For if I pray in an unknown tongue, my spirit prayeth, but my understanding is unfruitful.

15 What is it then? I will pray with the spirit, and I will pray with the understanding also: I will sing with the spirit, and I will sing with the understanding also.

16 Else when you shalt bless with the spirit, how shall he that occupieth the room of the unlearned say Amen at your giving of thanks, seeing he understands not what you say?

17 For you verily givest thanks well, but the other is not edified.

18 I thank my God, I speak with tongues more than you all:

19 Yet in the church I had rather speak five words with my understanding, that by my voice I might teach others also, than ten thousand words in an unknown tongue.

20 Brethren, be not children in understanding: howbeit in malice be you children, but in understanding be men.

21 In the law it is written, With men of other tongues and other lips will I speak unto this people; and yet for all that will they not hear me, saith the Lord.

22 Wherefore tongues are for a sign, not to them that believe, but to them that believe not: but prophesying serveth not for them that believe not, but for them which believe.

23 If therefore the whole church be come together into one place, and all speak with tongues, and there come in those that are unlearned, or unbelievers, will they not say that you are mad?

24 But if all prophesy, and there come in one that believeth not, or one unlearned, he is convinced of all, he is judged of all:

25 And thus are the secrets of his heart made manifest; and so falling down on his face he will worship God, and report that God is in you of a truth.

26 How is it then, brethren? when you come together, every one of you has a psalm, has a doctrine, has a tongue, has a revelation, has an interpretation. Let all things be done unto edifying.

27 If any man speak in an unknown tongue, let it be by two, or at the most by three, and that by course; and let one interpret.

28 But if there be no interpreter, let him keep silence in the church; and let him speak to himself, and to God.

29 Let the prophets speak two or three, and let the other judge.

30 If any thing be revealed to another that sitteth by, let the first hold his peace.

31 For you may all prophesy one by one, that all may learn, and all may be comforted.

32 And the spirits of the prophets are subject to the prophets.

33 For God is not the author of confusion, but of peace, as in all churches of the saints.

34 Let your women keep silence in the churches: for it is not permitted unto them to speak; but they are commanded to be under obedience, as also saith the law.

35 And if they will learn any thing, let them ask their husbands at home: for it is a shame for women to speak in the church.

36 What? came the word of God out from you? or came it unto you only?

37 If any man think himself to be a prophet, or spiritual, let him acknowledge that the things that I write unto you are the commandments of the Lord.

38 But if any man be ignorant, let him be ignorant.

39 Wherefore, brethren, covet to prophesy, and forbid not to speak with tongues.

40 Let all things be done decently and in order.

CHAPTER 15

MOREOVER, brethren, I declare unto you the gospel which I preached unto you, which also you have received, and wherein you stand;

2 By which also you are saved, if you keep in memory what I preached unto you, unless you have believed in vain.

3 For I delivered unto you first of all that which I also received, how that Christ died for our sins according to the scriptures;

4 And that he was buried, and that he rose again the third day according to the scriptures:

5 And that he was seen of Cephas, then of the twelve:

6 After that, he was seen of above five hundred brethren at once; of whom the greater part remain unto this present, but some are fallen asleep.

7 After that, he was seen of James; then of all the apostles.

8 And last of all he was seen of me also, as of one born out of due time.

9 For I am the least of the apostles, that am not meet to be called an apostle, because I persecuted the church of God.

10 But by the grace of God I am what I am: and his grace which was bestowed upon me was not in vain; but I laboured more abundantly than they all: yet not I, but the grace of God which was with me.

11 Therefore whether it were I or they, so we preach, and so you believed.

12 Now if Christ be preached that he rose from the dead, how say some among you that there is no resurrection of the dead?

13 But if there be no resurrection of the dead, then is Christ not risen:

14 And if Christ be not risen, then is our preaching vain, and your faith is also vain.

15 Yea, and we are found false witnesses of God; because we have testified of God that he raised up Christ: whom he raised not up, if so be that the dead rise not.

16 For if the dead rise not, then is not Christ raised:

17 And if Christ be not raised, your faith is vain; you are yet in your sins.

18 Then they also which are fallen asleep in Christ are perished.

19 If in this life only we have hope in Christ, we are of all men most miserable.

20 But now is Christ risen from the dead, and become the firstfruits of them that slept.

21 For since by man came death, by man came also the resurrection of the dead.

22 For as in Adam all die, even so in Christ shall all be made alive.

23 But every man in his own order: Christ the firstfruits; afterward they that are Christ's at his coming.

24 Then comes the end, when he shall have delivered up the kingdom to God, even the Father; when he shall have put down all rule and all authority and power.

25 For he must reign, till he has put all enemies under his feet.

26 The last enemy that shall be destroyed is death.

27 For he has put all things under his feet. But when he saith, all things are put under him, it is manifest that he is excepted, which did put all things under him.

28 And when all things shall be subdued unto him, then shall the Son also himself be subject unto him that put all things under him, that God may be all in all.

29 Else what shall they do which are baptized for the dead, if the dead rise not at all? why are they then baptized for the dead?

30 And why stand we in jeopardy every hour?

31 I protest by your rejoicing which I have in Christ Jesus our Lord, I die daily.

32 If after the manner of men I have fought with beasts at Ephesus, what advantageth it me, if the dead rise not? let us eat and drink; for to morrow we die.

33 Be not deceived: evil communications corrupt good manners.

34 Awake to righteousness, and sin not; for some have not the knowledge of God: I speak this to your shame.

35 But some man will say, How are the dead raised up? and with what body do they come?

36 You fool, that which you sowest is not quickened, except it die:

37 And that which you sowest, you sowest not that body that shall be, but bare grain, it may chance of wheat, or of some other grain:

38 But God giveth it a body as it has pleased him, and to every seed his own body.

39 All flesh is not the same flesh: but there is one kind of flesh of men, another flesh of beasts, another of fishes, and another of birds.

40 There are also celestial bodies, and bodies terrestrial: but the glory of the celestial is one, and the glory of the terrestrial is another.

41 There is one glory of the sun, and another glory of the moon, and another glory of the stars: for one star differeth from another star in glory.

42 So also is the resurrection of the dead. It is sown in corruption; it is raised in incorruption:

43 It is sown in dishonour; it is raised in glory: it is sown in weakness; it is raised in power:

44 It is sown a natural body; it is raised a spiritual body. There is a natural body, and there is a spiritual body.

45 And so it is written, The first man Adam was made a living soul; the last Adam was made a quickening spirit.

46 Howbeit that was not first which is spiritual, but that which is natural; and afterward that which is spiritual.

47 The first man is of the earth, earthy: the second man is the Lord from heaven.

48 As is the earthy, such are they also that are earthy: and as is the heavenly, such are they also that are heavenly.

49 And as we have borne the image of the earthy, we shall also bear the image of the heavenly.

50 Now this I say, brethren, that flesh and blood cannot inherit the kingdom of God; neither doth corruption inherit incorruption.

51 Behold, I shew you a mystery; We shall not all sleep, but we shall all be changed,

52 In a moment, in the twinkling of an eye, at the last trump: for the trumpet shall sound, and the dead shall be raised incorruptible, and we shall be changed.

53 For this corruptible must put on incorruption, and this mortal must put on immortality.

54 So when this corruptible shall have put on incorruption, and this mortal shall have put on immortality, then shall be brought to pass the saying that is written, Death is swallowed up in victory.

55 O death, where is your sting? O grave, where is your victory?

56 The sting of death is sin; and the strength of sin is the law.

57 But thanks be to God, which giveth us the victory through our Lord Jesus Christ.

58 Therefore, my beloved brethren, be you stedfast, unmoveable, always abounding in the work of the Lord, forasmuch as you know that your labour is not in vain in the Lord.

CHAPTER 16

NOW concerning the collection for the saints, as I have given order to the churches of Galatia, even so do you .

2 Upon the first day of the week let every one of you lay by him in store, as God has prospered him, that there be no gatherings when I come.

3 And when I come, whomsoever you shall approve by your letters, them will I send to bring your liberality unto Jerusalem.

4 And if it be meet that I go also, they shall go with me.

5 Now I will come unto you, when I shall pass through Macedonia: for I do pass through Macedonia.

6 And it may be that I will abide, yea, and winter with you, that you may bring me on my journey whithersoever I go.

7 For I will not see you now by the way; but I trust to tarry a while with you, if the Lord permit.

8 But I will tarry at Ephesus until Pentecost.

9 For a great door and effectual is opened unto me, and there are many adversaries.

10 Now if Timotheus come, see that he may be with you without fear: for he worketh the work of the Lord, as I also do.

11 Let no man therefore despise him: but conduct him forth in peace, that he may come unto me: for I look for him with the brethren.

12 As touching our brother Apollos, I greatly desired him to come unto you with the brethren: but his will was not at all to come at this time; but he will come when he shall have convenient time.

13 Watch you , stand fast in the faith, quit you like men, be strong.

14 Let all your things be done with charity.

15 I beseech you, brethren, (you know the house of Stephanas, that it is the firstfruits of Achaia, and that they have addicted themselves to the ministry of the saints,)

16 That you submit yourselves unto such, and to every one that helpeth with us, and laboureth.

17 I am glad of the coming of Stephanas and Fortunatus and Achaicus: for that which was lacking on your part they have supplied.

18 For they have refreshed my spirit and yours: therefore acknowledge you them that are such.

19 The churches of Asia salute you. Aquila and Priscilla salute you much in the Lord, with the church that is in their house.

20 All the brethren greet you. Greet you one another with an holy kiss.

21 The salutation of me Paul with my own hand.

22 If any man love not the Lord Jesus Christ, let him be Anathema Maran-atha.

23 The grace of our Lord Jesus Christ be with you.

24 My love be with you all in Christ Jesus. Amen.

The first epistle to the Corinthians was written from Philippi by Stephanas, and Fortunatus, and Achaicus, and Timotheus.

THE
SECOND EPISTLE OF PAUL THE APOSTLE TO THE CORINTHIANS.

CHAPTER 1

PAUL, an apostle of Jesus Christ by the will of God, and Timothy our brother, unto the church of God which is at Corinth, with all the saints which are in all Achaia:

2 Grace be to you and peace from God our Father, and from the Lord Jesus Christ.

3 Blessed be God, even the Father of our Lord Jesus Christ, the Father of mercies, and the God of all comfort;

4 Who comforteth us in all our tribulation, that we may be able to comfort them which are in any trouble, by the comfort wherewith we ourselves are comforted of God.

5 For as the sufferings of Christ abound in us, so our consolation also aboundeth by Christ.

6 And whether we be afflicted, it is for your consolation and salvation, which is effectual in the enduring of the same sufferings which we also suffer: or whether we be comforted, it is for your consolation and salvation.

7 And our hope of you is stedfast, knowing, that as you are partakers of the sufferings, so shall you be also of the consolation.

8 For we would not, brethren, have you ignorant of our trouble which came to us in Asia, that we were pressed out of measure, above strength, insomuch that we despaired even of life:

9 But we had the sentence of death in ourselves, that we should not trust in ourselves, but in God which raiseth the dead:

10 Who delivered us from so great a death, and doth deliver: in whom we trust that he will yet deliver us;

11 You also helping together by prayer for us, that for the gift bestowed upon us by the means of many persons thanks may be given by many on our behalf.

12 For our rejoicing is this, the testimony of our conscience, that in simplicity and godly sincerity, not with fleshly wisdom, but by the grace of God, we have had our conversation in the world, and more abundantly to you-ward.

13 For we write none other things unto you, than what you read or acknowledge; and I trust you shall acknowledge even to the end;

14 As also you have acknowledged us in part, that we are your rejoicing, even as you also are ours in the day of the Lord Jesus.

15 And in this confidence I was minded to come unto you before, that you might have a second benefit;

16 And to pass by you into Macedonia, and to come again out of Macedonia unto you, and of you to be brought on my way toward Judæa.

17 When I therefore was thus minded, did I use lightness? or the things that I purpose, do I purpose according to the flesh, that with me there should be yea yea, and nay nay?

18 But as God is true, our word toward you was not yea and nay.

19 For the Son of God, Jesus Christ, who was preached among you by us, even by me and Silvanus and Timotheus, was not yea and nay, but in him was yea.

20 For all the promises of God in him are yea, and in him Amen, unto the glory of God by us.

21 Now he which stablisheth us with you in Christ, and has anointed us, is God;

22 Who has also sealed us, and given the earnest of the Spirit in our hearts.

23 Moreover I call God for a record upon my soul, that to spare you I came not as yet unto Corinth.

24 Not for that we have dominion over your faith, but are helpers of your joy: for by faith you stand.

CHAPTER 2

BUT I determined this with myself, that I would not come again to you in heaviness.

2 For if I make you sorry, who is he then that maketh me glad, but the same which is made sorry by me?

3 And I wrote this same unto you, lest, when I came, I should have sorrow from them of whom I ought to rejoice; having confidence in you all, that my joy is the joy of you all.

4 For out of much affliction and anguish of heart I wrote unto you with many tears; not that you should be grieved, but that you might know the love which I have more abundantly unto you.

5 But if any have caused grief, he has not grieved me, but in part: that I may not overcharge you all.

6 Sufficient to such a man is this punishment, which was inflicted of many.

7 So that contrariwise you ought rather to forgive him, and comfort him, lest perhaps such a one should be swallowed up with overmuch sorrow.

8 Wherefore I beseech you that you would confirm your love toward him.

9 For to this end also did I write, that I might know the proof of you, whether you be obedient in all things.

10 To whom you forgive any thing, I forgive also: for if I forgave any thing, to whom I forgave it, for your sakes forgave I it in the person of Christ;

11 Lest Satan should get an advantage of us: for we are not ignorant of his devices.

12 Furthermore, when I came to Troas to preach Christ's gospel, and a door was opened unto me of the Lord,

13 I had no rest in my spirit, because I found not Titus my brother: but taking my leave of them, I went from thence into Macedonia.

14 Now thanks be unto God, which always causeth us to triumph in Christ, and maketh manifest the savour of his knowledge by us in every place.

15 For we are unto God a sweet savour of Christ, in them that are saved, and in them that perish:

16 To the one we are the savour of death unto death; and to the other the savour of life unto life. And who is sufficient for these things?

17 For we are not as many, which corrupt the word of God: but as of sincerity, but as of God, in the sight of God speak we in Christ.

CHAPTER 3

DO we begin again to commend ourselves? or need we, as some others, epistles of commendation to you, or letters of commendation from you?

2 You are our epistle written in our hearts, known and read of all men:

3 Forasmuch as you are manifestly declared to be the epistle of Christ ministered by us, written not with ink, but with the Spirit of the living God; not in tables of stone, but in fleshy tables of the heart.

4 And such trust have we through Christ to God-ward:

5 Not that we are sufficient of ourselves to think any thing as of ourselves; but our sufficiency is of God;

6 Who also has made us able ministers of the new testament; not of the letter, but of the spirit: for the letter killeth, but the spirit giveth life.

7 But if the ministration of death, written and engraven in stones, was glorious, so that the children of Israel could not stedfastly behold the face of Moses for the glory of his countenance; which glory was to be done away:

8 How shall not the ministration of the spirit be rather glorious?

9 For if the ministration of condemnation be glory, much more doth the ministration of righteousness exceed in glory.

10 For even that which was made glorious had no glory in this respect, by reason of the glory that excelleth.

11 For if that which is done away was glorious, much more that which remaineth is glorious.

12 Seeing then that we have such hope, we use great plainness of speech:

13 And not as Moses, which put a vail over his face, that the children of Israel could not stedfastly look to the end of that which is abolished:

14 But their minds were blinded: for until this day remaineth the same vail untaken away in the reading of the old testament; which vail is done away in Christ.

15 But even unto this day, when Moses is read, the vail is upon their heart.

16 Nevertheless when it shall turn to the Lord, the vail shall be taken away.

17 Now the Lord is that Spirit: and where the Spirit of the Lord is, there is liberty.

18 But we all, with open face beholding as in a glass the glory of the Lord, are changed into the same image from glory to glory, even as by the Spirit of the Lord.

CHAPTER 4

THEREFORE seeing we have this ministry, as we have received mercy, we faint not;

2 But have renounced the hidden things of dishonesty, not walking in craftiness, nor handling the word of God deceitfully; but by manifestation of the truth commending ourselves to every man's conscience in the sight of God.

3 But if our gospel be hid, it is hid to them that are lost:

4 In whom the god of this world has blinded the minds of them which believe not, lest the light of the glorious gospel of Christ, who is the image of God, should shine unto them.

5 For we preach not ourselves, but Christ Jesus the Lord; and ourselves your servants for Jesus' sake.

6 For God, who commanded the light to shine out of darkness, has shined in our hearts, to give the light of the knowledge of the glory of God in the face of Jesus Christ.

7 But we have this treasure in earthen vessels, that the excellency of the power may be of God, and not of us.

8 We are troubled on every side, yet not distressed; we are perplexed, but not in despair;

9 Persecuted, but not forsaken; cast down, but not destroyed;

10 Always bearing about in the body the dying of the Lord Jesus, that the life also of Jesus might be made manifest in our body.

11 For we which live are alway delivered unto death for Jesus' sake, that the life also of Jesus might be made manifest in our mortal flesh.

12 So then death worketh in us, but life in you.

13 We having the same spirit of faith, according as it is written, I believed, and therefore have I spoken; we also believe, and therefore speak;

14 Knowing that he which raised up the Lord Jesus shall raise up us also by Jesus, and shall present us with you.

15 For all things are for your sakes, that the abundant grace might through the thanksgiving of many redound to the glory of God.

16 For which cause we faint not; but though our outward man perish, yet the inward man is renewed day by day.

17 For our light affliction, which is but for a moment, worketh for us a far more exceeding and eternal weight of glory;

18 While we look not at the things which are seen, but at the things which are not seen: for the things which are seen are temporal; but the things which are not seen are eternal.

CHAPTER 5

FOR we know that if our earthly house of this tabernacle were dissolved, we have a building of God, an house not made with hands, eternal in the heavens.

2 For in this we groan, earnestly desiring to be clothed upon with our house which is from heaven:

3 If so be that being clothed we shall not be found naked.

4 For we that are in this tabernacle do groan, being burdened: not for that we would be unclothed, but clothed upon, that mortality might be swallowed up of life.

5 Now he that has created us for the selfsame thing is God, who also has given unto us the earnest of the Spirit.

6 Therefore we are always confident, knowing that, whilst we are at home in the body, we are absent from the Lord:

7 (For we walk by faith, not by sight:)

8 We are confident, I say, and willing rather to be absent from the body, and to be present with the Lord.

9 Wherefore we labour, that, whether present or absent, we may be accepted of him.

10 For we must all appear before the judgment seat of Christ; that every one may receive the things done in his body, according to that he has done, whether it be good or bad.

11 Knowing therefore the terror of the Lord, we persuade men; but we are made manifest unto God; and I trust also are made manifest in your consciences.

12 For we commend not ourselves again unto you, but give you occasion to glory on our behalf, that you may have somewhat to answer them which glory in appearance, and not in heart.

13 For whether we be beside ourselves, it is to God: or whether we be sober, it is for your cause.

14 For the love of Christ constraineth us; because we thus judge, that if one died for all, then were all dead:

15 And that he died for all, that they which live should not henceforth live unto themselves, but unto him which died for them, and rose again.

16 Wherefore henceforth know we no man after the flesh: yea, though we have known Christ after the flesh, yet now henceforth know we him no more.

17 Therefore if any man be in Christ, he is a new creature: old things are passed away; behold, all things are become new.

18 And all things are of God, who has reconciled us to himself by Jesus Christ, and has given to us the ministry of reconciliation;

19 To wit, that God was in Christ, reconciling the world unto himself, not imputing their trespasses unto them; and has committed unto us the word of reconciliation.

20 Now then we are ambassadors for Christ, as though God did beseech you by us: we pray you in Christ's stead, be you reconciled to God.

21 For he has made him to be sin for us, who knew no sin; that we might be made the righteousness of God in him.

CHAPTER 6

WE then, as workers together with him, beseech you also that you receive not the grace of God in vain.

2 (For he saith, I have heard you in a time accepted, and in the day of salvation have I succoured you: behold, now is the accepted time; behold, now is the day of salvation.)

3 Giving no offence in any thing, that the ministry be not blamed:

4 But in all things approving ourselves as the ministers of God, in much patience, in afflictions, in necessities, in distresses,

5 In stripes, in imprisonments, in tumults, in labours, in watchings, in fastings;

6 By pureness, by knowledge, by longsuffering, by kindness, by the Holy Ghost, by love unfeigned,

7 By the word of truth, by the power of God, by the armour of righteousness on the right hand and on the left,

8 By honour and dishonour, by evil report and good report: as deceivers, and yet true;

9 As unknown, and yet well known; as dying, and, behold, we live; as chastened, and not killed;

10 As sorrowful, yet alway rejoicing; as poor, yet making many rich; as having nothing, and yet possessing all things.

11 O you Corinthians, our mouth is open unto you, our heart is enlarged.

12 You are not straitened in us, but you are straitened in your own bowels.

13 Now for a recompence in the same, (I speak as unto my children,) be you also enlarged.

14 Be you not unequally yoked together with unbelievers: for what fellowship has righteousness with unrighteousness? and what communion has light with darkness?

15 And what concord has Christ with Belial? or what part has he that believeth with an infidel?

16 And what agreement has the temple of God with idols? for you are the temple of the living God; as God has said, I will dwell in them, and walk in them; and I will be their God, and they shall be my people.

17 Wherefore come out from among them, and be you separate, saith the Lord, and touch not the unclean thing; and I will receive you,

18 And will be a Father unto you, and you shall be my sons and daughters, saith the Lord Almighty.

CHAPTER 7

HAVING therefore these promises, dearly beloved, let us cleanse ourselves from all filthiness of the flesh and spirit, perfecting holiness in the fear of God.

2 Receive us; we have wronged no man, we have corrupted no man, we have defrauded no man.

3 I speak not this to condemn you: for I have said before, that you are in our hearts to die and live with you.

4 Great is my boldness of speech toward you, great is my glorying of you: I am filled with comfort, I am exceeding joyful in all our tribulation.

5 For, when we were come into Macedonia, our flesh had no rest, but we were troubled on every side; without were fightings, within were fears.

6 Nevertheless God, that comforteth those that are cast down, comforted us by the coming of Titus;

7 And not by his coming only, but by the consolation wherewith he was comforted in you, when he told us your earnest desire, your mourning, your fervent mind toward me; so that I rejoiced the more.

8 For though I made you sorry with a letter, I do not repent, though I did repent: for I perceive that the same epistle has made you sorry, though it were but for a season.

9 Now I rejoice, not that you were made sorry, but that you sorrowed to repentance: for you were made sorry after a godly manner, that you might receive damage by us in nothing.

10 For godly sorrow worketh repentance to salvation not to be repented of: but the sorrow of the world worketh death.

11 For behold this selfsame thing, that you sorrowed after a godly sort, what carefulness it created in you, yea, what clearing of yourselves, yea, what indignation, yea, what fear, yea, what vehement desire, yea, what zeal, yea, what revenge! In all things you have approved yourselves to be clear in this matter.

12 Wherefore, though I wrote unto you, I did it not for his cause that had done the wrong, nor for his cause that suffered wrong, but that our care for you in the sight of God might appear unto you.

13 Therefore we were comforted in your comfort: yea, and exceedingly the more joyed we for the joy of Titus, because his spirit was refreshed by you all.

14 For if I have boasted any thing to him of you, I am not ashamed; but as we spake all things to you in truth, even so our boasting, which I made before Titus, is found a truth.

15 And his inward affection is more abundant toward you, whilst he remembereth the obedience of you all, how with fear and trembling you received him.

16 I rejoice therefore that I have confidence in you in all things.

CHAPTER 8

MOREOVER, brethren, we do you to wit of the grace of God bestowed on the churches of Macedonia;

2 How that in a great trial of affliction the abundance of their joy and their deep poverty abounded unto the riches of their liberality.

3 For to their power, I bear record, yea, and beyond their power they were willing of themselves;

4 Praying us with much intreaty that we would receive the gift, and take upon us the fellowship of the ministering to the saints.

5 And this they did, not as we hoped, but first gave their own selves to the Lord, and unto us by the will of God.

6 Insomuch that we desired Titus, that as he had begun, so he would also finish in you the same grace also.

7 Therefore, as you abound in every thing, in faith, and utterance, and knowledge, and in all diligence, and in your love to us, see that you abound in this grace also.

8 I speak not by commandment, but by occasion of the forwardness of others, and to prove the sincerity of your love.

9 For you know the grace of our Lord Jesus Christ, that, though he was rich, yet for your sakes he became poor, that you through his poverty might be rich.

10 And herein I give my advice: for this is expedient for you, who have begun before, not only to do, but also to be forward a year ago.

11 Now therefore perform the doing of it; that as there was a readiness to will, so there may be a performance also out of that which you have.

12 For if there be first a willing mind, it is accepted according to that a man has, and not according to that he has not.

13 For I mean not that other men be eased, and you burdened:

14 But by an equality, that now at this time your abundance may be a supply for their want, that their abundance also may be a supply for your want: that there may be equality:

15 As it is written, He that had gathered much had nothing over; and he that had gathered little had no lack.

16 But thanks be to God, which put the same earnest care into the heart of Titus for you.

17 For indeed he accepted the exhortation; but being more forward, of his own accord he went unto you.

18 And we have sent with him the brother, whose praise is in the gospel throughout all the churches;

19 And not that only, but who was also chosen of the churches to travel with us with this grace, which is administered by us to the glory of the same Lord, and declaration of your ready mind:

20 Avoiding this, that no man should blame us in this abundance which is administered by us:

21 Providing for honest things, not only in the sight of the Lord, but also in the sight of men.

22 And we have sent with them our brother, whom we have oftentimes proved diligent in many things, but now much more diligent, upon the great confidence which I have in you.

23 Whether any do inquire of Titus, he is my partner and fellowhelper concerning you: or our brethren be inquired of, they are the messengers of the churches, and the glory of Christ.

24 Wherefore shew you to them, and before the churches, the proof of your love, and of our boasting on your behalf.

CHAPTER 9

FOR as touching the ministering to the saints, it is superfluous for me to write to you:

2 For I know the forwardness of your mind, for which I boast of you to them of Macedonia, that Achaia was ready a year ago; and your zeal has provoked very many.

3 Yet have I sent the brethren, lest our boasting of you should be in vain in this behalf; that, as I said, you may be ready:

4 Lest haply if they of Macedonia come with me, and find you unprepared, we (that we say not, you) should be ashamed in this same confident boasting.

5 Therefore I thought it necessary to exhort the brethren, that they would go before unto you, and make up beforehand your bounty, whereof you had notice before, that the same might be ready, as a matter of bounty, and not as of covetousness.

6 But this I say, He which soweth sparingly shall reap also sparingly; and he which soweth bountifully shall reap also bountifully.

7 Every man according as he purposeth in his heart, so let him give; not grudgingly, or of necessity: for God loveth a cheerful giver.

8 And God is able to make all grace abound toward you; that you , always having all sufficiency in all things, may abound to every good work:

9 (As it is written, He has dispersed abroad; he has given to the poor: his righteousness remaineth for ever.

10 Now he that ministereth seed to the sower both minister bread for your food, and multiply your seed sown, and increase the fruits of your righteousness;)

11 Being enriched in every thing to all bountifulness, which causeth through us thanksgiving to God.

12 For the administration of this service not only supplieth the want of the saints, but is abundant also by many thanksgivings unto God;

13 Whiles by the experiment of this ministration they glorify God for your professed subjection unto the gospel of Christ, and for your liberal distribution unto them, and unto all men;

14 And by their prayer for you, which long after you for the exceeding grace of God in you.

15 Thanks be unto God for his unspeakable gift.

CHAPTER 10

NOW I Paul myself beseech you by the meekness and gentleness of Christ, who in presence am base among you, but being absent am bold toward you:

2 But I beseech you, that I may not be bold when I am present with that confidence, wherewith I think to be bold against some, which think of us as if we walked according to the flesh.

3 For though we walk in the flesh, we do not war after the flesh:

4 (For the weapons of our warfare are not carnal, but mighty through God to the pulling down of strong holds;)

5 Casting down imaginations, and every high thing that exalteth itself against the knowledge of God, and bringing into captivity every thought to the obedience of Christ;

6 And having in a readiness to revenge all disobedience, when your obedience is fulfilled.

7 Do you look on things after the outward appearance? If any man trust to himself that he is Christ's, let him of himself think this again, that, as he is Christ's, even so are we Christ's.

8 For though I should boast somewhat more of our authority, which the Lord has given us for edification, and not for your destruction, I should not be ashamed:

9 That I may not seem as if I would terrify you by letters.

10 For his letters, say they, are weighty and powerful; but his bodily presence is weak, and his speech contemptible.

11 Let such an one think this, that, such as we are in word by letters when we are absent, such will we be also in deed when we are present.

12 For we dare not make ourselves of the number, or compare ourselves with some that commend themselves: but they measuring themselves by themselves, and comparing themselves among themselves, are not wise.

13 But we will not boast of things without our measure, but according to the measure of the rule which God has distributed to us, a measure to reach even unto you.

14 For we stretch not ourselves beyond our measure, as though we reached not unto you: for we are come as far as to you also in preaching the gospel of Christ:

15 Not boasting of things without our measure, that is, of other men's labours; but having hope, when your faith is increased, that we shall be enlarged by you according to our rule abundantly,

16 To preach the gospel in the regions beyond you, and not to boast in another man's line of things made ready to our hand.

17 But he that glorieth, let him glory in the Lord.

18 For not he that commendeth himself is approved, but whom the Lord commendeth.

CHAPTER 11

WOULD to God you could bear with me a little in my folly: and indeed bear with me.

2 For I am jealous over you with godly jealousy: for I have espoused you to one husband, that I may present you as a chaste virgin to Christ.

3 But I fear, lest by any means, as the serpent beguiled Eve through his subtilty, so your minds should be corrupted from the simplicity that is in Christ.

4 For if he that comes preacheth another Jesus, whom we have not preached, or if you receive another spirit, which you have not received, or another gospel, which you have not accepted, you might well bear with him.

5 For I suppose I was not a whit behind the very chiefest apostles.

6 But though I be rude in speech, yet not in knowledge; but we have been throughly made manifest among you in all things.

7 Have I committed an offence in abasing myself that you might be exalted, because I have preached to you the gospel of God freely?

8 I robbed other churches, taking wages of them, to do you service.

9 And when I was present with you, and wanted, I was chargeable to no man: for that which was lacking to me the brethren which came from Macedonia supplied: and in all things I have kept myself from being burdensome unto you, and so will I keep myself.

10 As the truth of Christ is in me, no man shall stop me of this boasting in the regions of Achaia.

11 Wherefore? because I love you not? God knoweth.

12 But what I do, that I will do, that I may cut off occasion from them which desire occasion; that wherein they glory, they may be found even as we.

13 For such are false apostles, deceitful workers, transforming themselves into the apostles of Christ.

14 And no marvel; for Satan himself is transformed into an angel of light.

15 Therefore it is no great thing if his ministers also be transformed as the ministers of righteousness; whose end shall be according to their works.

16 I say again, Let no man think me a fool; if otherwise, yet as a fool receive me, that I may boast myself a little.

17 That which I speak, I speak it not after the Lord, but as it were foolishly, in this confidence of boasting.

18 Seeing that many glory after the flesh, I will glory also.

19 For you suffer fools gladly, seeing you yourselves are wise.

20 For you suffer, if a man bring you into bondage, if a man devour you, if a man take of you, if a man exalt himself, if a man strike you on the face.

21 I speak as concerning reproach, as though we had been weak. Howbeit wheresoever any is bold, (I speak foolishly,) I am bold also.

22 Are they Hebrews? so am I. Are they Israelites? so am I. Are they the seed of Abraham? so am I.

23 Are they ministers of Christ? (I speak as a fool) I am more; in labours more abundant, in stripes above measure, in prisons more frequent, in deaths oft.

24 Of the Jews five times received I forty stripes save one.

25 Thrice was I beaten with rods, once was I stoned, thrice I suffered shipwreck, a night and a day I have been in the deep;

26 In journeyings often, in perils of waters, in perils of robbers, in perils by my own countrymen, in perils by the heathen, in perils in the city, in perils in the wilderness, in perils in the sea, in perils among false brethren;

27 In weariness and painfulness, in watchings often, in hunger and thirst, in fastings often, in cold and nakedness.

28 Beside those things that are without, that which comes upon me daily, the care of all the churches.

29 Who is weak, and I am not weak? who is offended, and I burn not?

30 If I must needs glory, I will glory of the things which concern my infirmities.

31 The God and Father of our Lord Jesus Christ, which is blessed for evermore, knoweth that I lie not.

32 In Damascus the governor under Aretas the king kept the city of the Damascenes with a garrison, desirous to apprehend me:

33 And through a window in a basket was I let down by the wall, and escaped his hands.

CHAPTER 12

IT is not expedient for me doubtless to glory. I will come to visions and revelations of the Lord.

2 I knew a man in Christ above fourteen years ago, (whether in the body, I cannot tell; or whether out of the body, I cannot tell: God knoweth;) such an one caught up to the third heaven.

3 And I knew such a man, (whether in the body, or out of the body, I cannot tell: God knoweth;)

4 How that he was caught up into paradise, and heard unspeakable words, which it is not lawful for a man to utter.

5 Of such an one will I glory: yet of myself I will not glory, but in my infirmities.

6 For though I would desire to glory, I shall not be a fool; for I will say the truth: but now I forbear, lest any man should think of me above that which he seeth me to be, or that he heareth of me.

7 And lest I should be exalted above measure through the abundance of the revelations, there was given to me a thorn in the flesh, the messenger of Satan to buffet me, lest I should be exalted above measure.

8 For this thing I besought the Lord thrice, that it might depart from me.

9 And he said unto me, My grace is sufficient for you: for my strength is made perfect in weakness. Most gladly therefore will I rather glory in my infirmities, that the power of Christ may rest upon me.

10 Therefore I take pleasure in infirmities, in reproaches, in necessities, in persecutions, in distresses for Christ's sake: for when I am weak, then am I strong.

11 I am become a fool in glorying; you have compelled me: for I ought to have been commended of you: for in nothing am I behind the very chiefest apostles, though I be nothing.

12 Truly the signs of an apostle were created among you in all patience, in signs, and wonders, and mighty deeds.

13 For what is it wherein you were inferior to other churches, except it be that I myself was not burdensome to you? forgive me this wrong.

14 Behold, the third time I am ready to come to you; and I will not be burdensome to you: for I seek not yours, but you: for the children ought not to lay up for the parents, but the parents for the children.

15 And I will very gladly spend and be spent for you; though the more abundantly I love you, the less I be loved.

16 But be it so, I did not burden you: nevertheless, being crafty, I caught you with guile.

17 Did I make a gain of you by any of them whom I sent unto you?

18 I desired Titus, and with him I sent a brother. Did Titus make a gain of you? walked we not in the same spirit? walked we not in the same steps?

19 Again, think you that we excuse ourselves unto you? we speak before God in Christ: but we do all things, dearly beloved, for your edifying.

20 For I fear, lest, when I come, I shall not find you such as I would, and that I shall be found unto you such as you would not: lest there be debates, envyings, wraths, strifes, backbitings, whisperings, swellings, tumults:

21 And lest, when I come again, my God will humble me among you, and that I shall bewail many which have sinned already, and have not repented of the uncleanness and fornication and lasciviousness which they have committed.

CHAPTER 13

THIS is the third time I am coming to you. In the mouth of two or three witnesses shall every word be established.

2 I told you before, and foretell you, as if I were present, the second time; and being absent now I write to them which heretofore have sinned, and to all other, that, if I come again, I will not spare:

3 Since you seek a proof of Christ speaking in me, which to you-ward is not weak, but is mighty in you.

4 For though he was crucified through weakness, yet he liveth by the power of God. For we also are weak in him, but we shall live with him by the power of God toward you.

5 Examine yourselves, whether you be in the faith; prove your own selves. Know you not your own selves, how that Jesus Christ is in you, except you be reprobates?

6 But I trust that you shall know that we are not reprobates.

7 Now I pray to God that you do no evil; not that we should appear approved, but that you should do that which is honest, though we be as reprobates.

8 For we can do nothing against the truth, but for the truth.

9 For we are glad, when we are weak, and you are strong: and this also we wish, even your perfection.

10 Therefore I write these things being absent, lest being present I should use sharpness, according to the power which the Lord has given me to edification, and not to destruction.

11 Finally, brethren, farewell. Be perfect, be of good comfort, be of one mind, live in peace; and the God of love and peace shall be with you.

12 Greet one another with an holy kiss.

13 All the saints salute you.

14 The grace of the Lord Jesus Christ, and the love of God, and the communion of the Holy Ghost, be with you all. Amen.

The second epistle to the Corinthians was written from Philippi, a city of Macedonia, by Titus and Lucas.

THE EPISTLE OF PAUL THE APOSTLE TO THE GALATIANS.

CHAPTER 1

PAUL, an apostle, (not of men, neither by man, but by Jesus Christ, and God the Father, who raised him from the dead;)

2 And all the brethren which are with me, unto the churches of Galatia:

3 Grace be to you and peace from God the Father, and from our Lord Jesus Christ,

4 Who gave himself for our sins, that he might deliver us from this present evil world, according to the will of God and our Father:

5 To whom be glory for ever and ever. Amen.

6 I marvel that you are so soon removed from him that called you into the grace of Christ unto another gospel:

7 Which is not another; but there be some that trouble you, and would pervert the gospel of Christ.

8 But though we, or an angel from heaven, preach any other gospel unto you than that which we have preached unto you, let him be accursed.

9 As we said before, so say I now again, If any man preach any other gospel unto you than that you have received, let him be accursed.

10 For do I now persuade men, or God? or do I seek to please men? for if I yet pleased men, I should not be the servant of Christ.

11 But I certify you, brethren, that the gospel which was preached of me is not after man.

12 For I neither received it of man, neither was I taught it, but by the revelation of Jesus Christ.

13 For you have heard of my conversation in time past in the Jews' religion, how that beyond measure I persecuted the church of God, and wasted it:

14 And profited in the Jews' religion above many my equals in my own nation, being more exceedingly zealous of the traditions of my fathers.

15 But when it pleased God, who separated me from my mother's womb, and called me by his grace,

16 To reveal his Son in me, that I might preach him among the heathen; immediately I conferred not with flesh and blood:

17 Neither went I up to Jerusalem to them which were apostles before me; but I went into Arabia, and returned again unto Damascus.

18 Then after three years I went up to Jerusalem to see Peter, and abode with him fifteen days.

19 But other of the apostles saw I none, save James the Lord's brother.

20 Now the things which I write unto you, behold, before God, I lie not.

21 Afterwards I came into the regions of Syria and Cilicia;

22 And was unknown by face unto the churches of Judæa which were in Christ:

23 But they had heard only, That he which persecuted us in times past now preacheth the faith which once he destroyed.

24 And they glorified God in me.

CHAPTER 2

THEN fourteen years after I went up again to Jerusalem with Barnabas, and took Titus with me also.

2 And I went up by revelation, and communicated unto them that gospel which I preach among the Gentiles, but privately to them which were of reputation, lest by any means I should run, or had run, in vain.

3 But neither Titus, who was with me, being a Greek, was compelled to be circumcised:

4 And that because of false brethren unawares brought in, who came in privily to spy out our liberty which we have in Christ Jesus, that they might bring us into bondage:

5 To whom we gave place by subjection, no, not for an hour; that the truth of the gospel might continue with you.

6 But of these who seemed to be somewhat, (whatsoever they were, it maketh no matter to me: God accepteth no man's person:) for they who seemed to be somewhat in conference added nothing to me:

7 But contrariwise, when they saw that the gospel of the uncircumcision was committed unto me, as the gospel of the circumcision was unto Peter;

8 (For he that created effectually in Peter to the apostleship of the circumcision, the same was mighty in me toward the Gentiles:)

9 And when James, Cephas, and John, who seemed to be pillars, perceived the grace that was given unto me, they gave to me and Barnabas the right hands of fellowship; that we should go unto the heathen, and they unto the circumcision.

10 Only they would that we should remember the poor; the same which I also was forward to do.

11 But when Peter was come to Antioch, I withstood him to the face, because he was to be blamed.

12 For before that certain came from James, he did eat with the Gentiles: but when they were come, he withdrew and separated himself, fearing them which were of the circumcision.

13 And the other Jews dissembled likewise with him; insomuch that Barnabas also was carried away with their dissimulation.

14 But when I saw that they walked not uprightly according to the truth of the gospel, I said unto Peter before them all, If you , being a Jew, livest after the manner of Gentiles, and not as do the Jews, why compellest you the Gentiles to live as do the Jews?

15 We who are Jews by nature, and not sinners of the Gentiles,

16 Knowing that a man is not justified by the works of the law, but by the faith of Jesus Christ, even we have believed in Jesus Christ, that we might be justified by the faith of Christ, and not by the works of the law: for by the works of the law shall no flesh be justified.

17 But if, while we seek to be justified by Christ, we ourselves also are found sinners, is therefore Christ the minister of sin? God forbid.

18 For if I build again the things which I destroyed, I make myself a transgressor.

19 For I through the law am dead to the law, that I might live unto God.

20 I am crucified with Christ: nevertheless I live; yet not I, but Christ liveth in me: and the life which I now live in the flesh I live by the faith of the Son of God, who loved me, and gave himself for me.

21 I do not frustrate the grace of God: for if righteousness come by the law, then Christ is dead in vain.

CHAPTER 3

O FOOLISH Galatians, who has bewitched you, that you should not obey the truth, before whose eyes Jesus Christ has been evidently set forth, crucified among you?

2 This only would I learn of you, Received you the Spirit by the works of the law, or by the hearing of faith?

3 Are you so foolish? having begun in the Spirit, are you now made perfect by the flesh?

4 Have you suffered so many things in vain? if it be yet in vain.

5 He therefore that ministereth to you the Spirit, and worketh miracles among you, doeth he it by the works of the law, or by the hearing of faith?

6 Even as Abraham believed God, and it was accounted to him for righteousness.

7 Know you therefore that they which are of faith, the same are the children of Abraham.

8 And the scripture, foreseeing that God would justify the heathen through faith, preached before the gospel unto Abraham, saying, In you shall all nations be blessed.

9 So then they which be of faith are blessed with faithful Abraham.

10 For as many as are of the works of the law are under the curse: for it is written, Cursed is every one that continueth not in all things which are written in the book of the law to do them.

11 But that no man is justified by the law in the sight of God, it is evident: for, The just shall live by faith.

12 And the law is not of faith: but, The man that doeth them shall live in them.

13 Christ has redeemed us from the curse of the law, being made a curse for us: for it is written, Cursed is every one that hangeth on a tree:

14 That the blessing of Abraham might come on the Gentiles through Jesus Christ; that we might receive the promise of the Spirit through faith.

15 Brethren, I speak after the manner of men; Though it be but a man's covenant, yet if it be confirmed, no man disannulleth, or addeth thereto.

16 Now to Abraham and his seed were the promises made. He saith not, And to seeds, as of many; but as of one, And to your seed, which is Christ.

17 And this I say, that the covenant, that was confirmed before of God in Christ, the law, which was four hundred and thirty years after, cannot disannul, that it should make the promise of none effect.

18 For if the inheritance be of the law, it is no more of promise: but God gave it to Abraham by promise.

19 Wherefore then serveth the law? It was added because of transgressions, till the seed should come to whom the promise was made; and it was ordained by angels in the hand of a mediator.

20 Now a mediator is not a mediator of one, but God is one.

21 Is the law then against the promises of God? God forbid: for if there had been a law given which could have given life, verily righteousness should have been by the law.

22 But the scripture has concluded all under sin, that the promise by faith of Jesus Christ might be given to them that believe.

23 But before faith came, we were kept under the law, shut up unto the faith which should afterwards be revealed.

24 Wherefore the law was our schoolmaster to bring us unto Christ, that we might be justified by faith.

25 But after that faith is come, we are no longer under a schoolmaster.

26 For you are all the children of God by faith in Christ Jesus.

27 For as many of you as have been baptized into Christ have put on Christ.

28 There is neither Jew nor Greek, there is neither bond nor free, there is neither male nor female: for you are all one in Christ Jesus.

29 And if you be Christ's, then are you Abraham's seed, and heirs according to the promise.

CHAPTER 4

NOW I say, That the heir, as long as he is a child, differeth nothing from a servant, though he be lord of all;

2 But is under tutors and governors until the time appointed of the father.

3 Even so we, when we were children, were in bondage under the elements of the world:

4 But when the fulness of the time was come, God sent forth his Son, made of a woman, made under the law,

5 To redeem them that were under the law, that we might receive the adoption of sons.

6 And because you are sons, God has sent forth the Spirit of his Son into your hearts, crying, Abba, Father.

7 Wherefore you are no more a servant, but a son; and if a son, then an heir of God through Christ.

8 Howbeit then, when you knew not God, you did service unto them which by nature are no gods.

9 But now, after that you have known God, or rather are known of God, how turn you again to the weak and beggarly elements, whereunto you desire again to be in bondage?

10 You observe days, and months, and times, and years.

11 I am afraid of you, lest I have bestowed upon you labour in vain.

12 Brethren, I beseech you, be as I am; for I am as you are: you have not injured me at all.

13 You know how through infirmity of the flesh I preached the gospel unto you at the first.

14 And my temptation which was in my flesh you despised not, nor rejected; but received me as an angel of God, even as Christ Jesus.

15 Where is then the blessedness you spake of? for I bear you record, that, if it had been possible, you would have plucked out your own eyes, and have given them to me.

16 Am I therefore become your enemy, because I tell you the truth?

17 They zealously affect you, but not well; yea, they would exclude you, that you might affect them.

18 But it is good to be zealously affected always in a good thing, and not only when I am present with you.

19 My little children, of whom I travail in birth again until Christ be formed in you,

20 I desire to be present with you now, and to change my voice; for I stand in doubt of you.

21 Tell me, you that desire to be under the law, do you not hear the law?

22 For it is written, that Abraham had two sons, the one by a bondmaid, the other by a freewoman.

23 But he who was of the bondwoman was born after the flesh; but he of the freewoman was by promise.

24 Which things are an allegory: for these are the two covenants; the one from the mount Sinai, which gendereth to bondage, which is Agar.

25 For this Agar is mount Sinai in Arabia, and answereth to Jerusalem which now is, and is in bondage with her children.

26 But Jerusalem which is above is free, which is the mother of us all.

27 For it is written, Rejoice, you barren that bearest not; break forth and cry, you that travailest not: for the desolate has many more children than she which has an husband.

28 Now we, brethren, as Isaac was, are the children of promise.

29 But as then he that was born after the flesh persecuted him that was born after the Spirit, even so it is now.

30 Nevertheless what saith the scripture? Cast out the bondwoman and her son: for the son of the bondwoman shall not be heir with the son of the freewoman.

31 So then, brethren, we are not children of the bondwoman, but of the free.

CHAPTER 5

STAND fast therefore in the liberty wherewith Christ has made us free, and be not entangled again with the yoke of bondage.

2 Behold, I Paul say unto you, that if you be circumcised, Christ shall profit you nothing.

3 For I testify again to every man that is circumcised, that he is a debtor to do the whole law.

4 Christ is become of no effect unto you, whosoever of you are justified by the law; you are fallen from grace.

5 For we through the Spirit wait for the hope of righteousness by faith.

6 For in Jesus Christ neither circumcision availeth any thing, nor uncircumcision; but faith which worketh by love.

7 You did run well; who did hinder you that you should not obey the truth?

8 This persuasion comes not of him that calleth you.

9 A little leaven leaveneth the whole lump.

10 I have confidence in you through the Lord, that you will be none otherwise minded: but he that troubleth you shall bear his judgment, whosoever he be.

11 And I, brethren, if I yet preach circumcision, why do I yet suffer persecution? then is the offence of the cross ceased.

12 I would they were even cut off which trouble you.

13 For, brethren, you have been called unto liberty; only use not liberty for an occasion to the flesh, but by love serve one another.

14 For all the law is fulfilled in one word, even in this; You shalt love your neighbour as yourself.

15 But if you bite and devour one another, take heed that you be not consumed one of another.

16 This I say then, Walk in the Spirit, and you shall not fulfil the lust of the flesh.

17 For the flesh lusteth against the Spirit, and the Spirit against the flesh: and these are contrary the one to the other: so that you cannot do the things that you would.

18 But if you be led of the Spirit, you are not under the law.

19 Now the works of the flesh are manifest, which are these; Adultery, fornication, uncleanness, lasciviousness,

20 Idolatry, witchcraft, hatred, variance, emulations, wrath, strife, seditions, heresies,

21 Envyings, murders, drunkenness, revellings, and such like: of the which I tell you before, as I have also told you in time past, that they which do such things shall not inherit the kingdom of God.

22 But the fruit of the Spirit is love, joy, peace, longsuffering, gentleness, goodness, faith,

23 Meekness, temperance: against such there is no law.

24 And they that are Christ's have crucified the flesh with the affections and lusts.

25 If we live in the Spirit, let us also walk in the Spirit.

26 Let us not be desirous of vain glory, provoking one another, envying one another.

CHAPTER 6

BRETHREN, if a man be overtaken in a fault, you which are spiritual, restore such an one in the spirit of meekness; considering yourself, lest you also be tempted.

2 Bear you one another's burdens, and so fulfil the law of Christ.

3 For if a man think himself to be something, when he is nothing, he deceiveth himself.

4 But let every man prove his own work, and then shall he have rejoicing in himself alone, and not in another.

5 For every man shall bear his own burden.

6 Let him that is taught in the word communicate unto him that teacheth in all good things.

7 Be not deceived; God is not mocked: for whatsoever a man soweth, that shall he also reap.

8 For he that soweth to his flesh shall of the flesh reap corruption; but he that soweth to the Spirit shall of the Spirit reap life everlasting.

9 And let us not be weary in well doing: for in due season we shall reap, if we faint not.

10 As we have therefore opportunity, let us do good unto all men, especially unto them who are of the household of faith.

11 You see how large a letter I have written unto you with my own hand.

12 As many as desire to make a fair shew in the flesh, they constrain you to be circumcised; only lest they should suffer persecution for the cross of Christ.

13 For neither they themselves who are circumcised keep the law; but desire to have you circumcised, that they may glory in your flesh.

14 But God forbid that I should glory, save in the cross of our Lord Jesus Christ, by whom the world is crucified unto me, and I unto the world.

15 For in Christ Jesus neither circumcision availeth any thing, nor uncircumcision, but a new creature.

16 And as many as walk according to this rule, peace be on them, and mercy, and upon the Israel of God.

17 From henceforth let no man trouble me: for I bear in my body the marks of the Lord Jesus.

18 Brethren, the grace of our Lord Jesus Christ be with your spirit. Amen.

Unto the Galatians written from Rome.

THE EPISTLE OF PAUL THE APOSTLE TO THE EPHESIANS.

CHAPTER 1

PAUL, an apostle of Jesus Christ by the will of God, to the saints which are at Ephesus, and to the faithful in Christ Jesus:

2 Grace be to you, and peace, from God our Father, and from the Lord Jesus Christ.

3 Blessed be the God and Father of our Lord Jesus Christ, who has blessed us with all spiritual blessings in heavenly places in Christ:

4 According as he has chosen us in him before the foundation of the world, that we should be holy and without blame before him in love:

5 Having predestinated us unto the adoption of children by Jesus Christ to himself, according to the good pleasure of his will,

6 To the praise of the glory of his grace, wherein he has made us accepted in the beloved.

7 In whom we have redemption through his blood, the forgiveness of sins, according to the riches of his grace;

8 Wherein he has abounded toward us in all wisdom and prudence;

9 Having made known unto us the mystery of his will, according to his good pleasure which he has purposed in himself:

10 That in the dispensation of the fulness of times he might gather together in one all things in Christ, both which are in heaven, and which are on earth; even in him:

11 In whom also we have obtained an inheritance, being predestinated according to the purpose of him who worketh all things after the counsel of his own will:

12 That we should be to the praise of his glory, who first trusted in Christ.

13 In whom you also trusted, after that you heard the word of truth, the gospel of your salvation: in whom also after that you believed, you were sealed with that holy Spirit of promise,

14 Which is the earnest of our inheritance until the redemption of the purchased possession, unto the praise of his glory.

15 Wherefore I also, after I heard of your faith in the Lord Jesus, and love unto all the saints,

16 Cease not to give thanks for you, making mention of you in my prayers;

17 That the God of our Lord Jesus Christ, the Father of glory, may give unto you the spirit of wisdom and revelation in the knowledge of him:

18 The eyes of your understanding being enlightened; that you may know what is the hope of his calling, and what the riches of the glory of his inheritance in the saints,

19 And what is the exceeding greatness of his power to us-ward who believe, according to the working of his mighty power,

20 Which he created in Christ, when he raised him from the dead, and set him at his own right hand in the heavenly places,

21 Far above all principality, and power, and might, and dominion, and every name that is named, not only in this world, but also in that which is to come:

22 And has put all things under his feet, and gave him to be the head over all things to the church,

23 Which is his body, the fulness of him that filleth all in all.

CHAPTER 2

AND you has he quickened, who were dead in trespasses and sins;

2 Wherein in time past you walked according to the course of this world, according to the prince of the power of the air, the spirit that now worketh in the children of disobedience:

3 Among whom also we all had our conversation in times past in the lusts of our flesh, fulfilling the desires of the flesh and of the mind; and were by nature the children of wrath, even as others.

4 But God, who is rich in mercy, for his great love wherewith he loved us,

5 Even when we were dead in sins, has quickened us together with Christ, (by grace you are saved;)

6 And has raised us up together, and made us sit together in heavenly places in Christ Jesus:

7 That in the ages to come he might shew the exceeding riches of his grace in his kindness toward us through Christ Jesus.

8 For by grace are you saved through faith; and that not of yourselves: it is the gift of God:

9 Not of works, lest any man should boast.

10 For we are his workmanship, created in Christ Jesus unto good works, which God has before ordained that we should walk in them.

11 Wherefore remember, that you being in time past Gentiles in the flesh, who are called Uncircumcision by that which is called the Circumcision in the flesh made by hands;

12 That at that time you were without Christ, being aliens from the commonwealth of Israel, and strangers from the covenants of promise, having no hope, and without God in the world:

13 But now in Christ Jesus you who sometimes were far off are made nigh by the blood of Christ.

14 For he is our peace, who has made both one, and has broken down the middle wall of partition between us;

15 Having abolished in his flesh the enmity, even the law of commandments contained in ordinances; for to make in himself of twain one new man, so making peace;

16 And that he might reconcile both unto God in one body by the cross, having slain the enmity thereby:

17 And came and preached peace to you which were afar off, and to them that were nigh.

18 For through him we both have access by one Spirit unto the Father.

19 Now therefore you are no more strangers and foreigners, but fellowcitizens with the saints, and of the household of God;

20 And are built upon the foundation of the apostles and prophets, Jesus Christ himself being the chief corner stone;

21 In whom all the building fitly framed together groweth unto an holy temple in the Lord:

22 In whom you also are builded together for an habitation of God through the Spirit.

CHAPTER 3

FOR this cause I Paul, the prisoner of Jesus Christ for you Gentiles,

2 If you have heard of the dispensation of the grace of God which is given me to you-ward:

3 How that by revelation he made known unto me the mystery; (as I wrote afore in few words,

4 Whereby, when you read, you may understand my knowledge in the mystery of Christ)

5 Which in other ages was not made known unto the sons of men, as it is now revealed unto his holy apostles and prophets by the Spirit;

6 That the Gentiles should be fellowheirs, and of the same body, and partakers of his promise in Christ by the gospel:

7 Whereof I was made a minister, according to the gift of the grace of God given unto me by the effectual working of his power.

8 Unto me, who am less than the least of all saints, is this grace given, that I should preach among the Gentiles the unsearchable riches of Christ;

9 And to make all men see what is the fellowship of the mystery, which from the beginning of the world has been hid in God, who created all things by Jesus Christ:

10 To the intent that now unto the principalities and powers in heavenly places might be known by the church the manifold wisdom of God,

11 According to the eternal purpose which he purposed in Christ Jesus our Lord:

12 In whom we have boldness and access with confidence by the faith of him.

13 Wherefore I desire that you faint not at my tribulations for you, which is your glory.

14 For this cause I bow my knees unto the Father of our Lord Jesus Christ,

15 Of whom the whole family in heaven and earth is named,

16 That he would grant you, according to the riches of his glory, to be strengthened with might by his Spirit in the inner man;

17 That Christ may dwell in your hearts by faith; that you , being rooted and grounded in love,

18 May be able to comprehend with all saints what is the breadth, and length, and depth, and height;

19 And to know the love of Christ, which passes knowledge, that you might be filled with all the fulness of God.

20 Now unto him that is able to do exceeding abundantly above all that we ask or think, according to the power that worketh in us,

21 Unto him be glory in the church by Christ Jesus throughout all ages, world without end. Amen.

CHAPTER 4

I THEREFORE, the prisoner of the Lord, beseech you that you walk worthy of the vocation wherewith you are called,

2 With all lowliness and meekness, with longsuffering, forbearing one another in love;

3 Endeavouring to keep the unity of the Spirit in the bond of peace.

4 There is one body, and one Spirit, even as you are called in one hope of your calling;

5 One Lord, one faith, one baptism,

6 One God and Father of all, who is above all, and through all, and in you all.

7 But unto every one of us is given grace according to the measure of the gift of Christ.

8 Wherefore he saith, When he ascended up on high, he led captivity captive, and gave gifts unto men.

9 (Now that he ascended, what is it but that he also descended first into the lower parts of the earth?

10 He that descended is the same also that ascended up far above all heavens, that he might fill all things.)

11 And he gave some, apostles; and some, prophets; and some, evangelists; and some, pastors and teachers;

12 For the perfecting of the saints, for the work of the ministry, for the edifying of the body of Christ:

13 Till we all come in the unity of the faith, and of the knowledge of the Son of God, unto a perfect man, unto the measure of the stature of the fulness of Christ:

14 That we henceforth be no more children, tossed to and fro, and carried about with every wind of doctrine, by the sleight of men, and cunning craftiness, whereby they lie in wait to deceive;

15 But speaking the truth in love, may grow up into him in all things, which is the head, even Christ:

16 From whom the whole body fitly joined together and compacted by that which every joint supplieth, according to the effectual working in the measure of every part, maketh increase of the body unto the edifying of itself in love.

17 This I say therefore, and testify in the Lord, that you henceforth walk not as other Gentiles walk, in the vanity of their mind,

18 Having the understanding darkened, being alienated from the life of God through the ignorance that is in them, because of the blindness of their heart:

19 Who being past feeling have given themselves over unto lasciviousness, to work all uncleanness with greediness.

20 But you have not so learned Christ;

21 If so be that you have heard him, and have been taught by him, as the truth is in Jesus:

22 That you put off concerning the former conversation the old man, which is corrupt according to the deceitful lusts;

23 And be renewed in the spirit of your mind;

24 And that you put on the new man, which after God is created in righteousness and true holiness.

25 Wherefore putting away lying, speak every man truth with his neighbour: for we are members one of another.

26 Be you angry, and sin not: let not the sun go down upon your wrath:

27 Neither give place to the devil.

28 Let him that stole steal no more: but rather let him labour, working with his hands the thing which is good, that he may have to give to him that needeth.

29 Let no corrupt communication proceed out of your mouth, but that which is good to the use of edifying, that it may minister grace unto the hearers.

30 And grieve not the holy Spirit of God, whereby you are sealed unto the day of redemption.

31 Let all bitterness, and wrath, and anger, and clamour, and evil speaking, be put away from you, with all malice:

32 And be you kind one to another, tenderhearted, forgiving one another, even as God for Christ's sake has forgiven you.

CHAPTER 5

BE you therefore followers of God, as dear children;

2 And walk in love, as Christ also has loved us, and has given himself for us an offering and a sacrifice to God for a sweetsmelling savour.

3 But fornication, and all uncleanness, or covetousness, let it not be once named among you, as becometh saints;

4 Neither filthiness, nor foolish talking, nor jesting, which are not convenient: but rather giving of thanks.

5 For this you know, that no whoremonger, nor unclean person, nor covetous man, who is an idolater, has any inheritance in the kingdom of Christ and of God.

6 Let no man deceive you with vain words: for because of these things comes the wrath of God upon the children of disobedience.

7 Be not you therefore partakers with them.

8 For you were sometimes darkness, but now are you light in the Lord: walk as children of light:

9 (For the fruit of the Spirit is in all goodness and righteousness and truth;)

10 Proving what is acceptable unto the Lord.

11 And have no fellowship with the unfruitful works of darkness, but rather reprove them.

12 For it is a shame even to speak of those things which are done of them in secret.

13 But all things that are reproved are made manifest by the light: for whatsoever doth make manifest is light.

14 Wherefore he saith, Awake you that sleepest, and arise from the dead, and Christ shall give you light.

15 See then that you walk circumspectly, not as fools, but as wise,

16 Redeeming the time, because the days are evil.

17 Wherefore be you not unwise, but understanding what the will of the Lord is.

18 And be not drunk with wine, wherein is excess; but be filled with the Spirit;

19 Speaking to yourselves in psalms and hymns and spiritual songs, singing and making melody in your heart to the Lord;

20 Giving thanks always for all things unto God and the Father in the name of our Lord Jesus Christ;

21 Submitting yourselves one to another in the fear of God.

22 Wives, submit yourselves unto your own husbands, as unto the Lord.

23 For the husband is the head of the wife, even as Christ is the head of the church: and he is the saviour of the body.

24 Therefore as the church is subject unto Christ, so let the wives be to their own husbands in every thing.

25 Husbands, love your wives, even as Christ also loved the church, and gave himself for it;

26 That he might sanctify and cleanse it with the washing of water by the word,

27 That he might present it to himself a glorious church, not having spot, or wrinkle, or any such thing; but that it should be holy and without blemish.

28 So ought men to love their wives as their own bodies. He that loveth his wife loveth himself.

29 For no man ever yet hated his own flesh; but nourisheth and cherisheth it, even as the Lord the church:

30 For we are members of his body, of his flesh, and of his bones.

31 For this cause shall a man leave his father and mother, and shall be joined unto his wife, and they two shall be one flesh.

32 This is a great mystery: but I speak concerning Christ and the church.

33 Nevertheless let every one of you in particular so love his wife even as himself; and the wife see that she reverence her husband.

CHAPTER 6

CHILDREN, obey your parents in the Lord: for this is right.

2 Honour your father and mother; (which is the first commandment with promise;)

3 That it may be well with you, and you mayest live long on the earth.

4 And, you fathers, provoke not your children to wrath: but bring them up in the nurture and admonition of the Lord.

5 Servants, be obedient to them that are your masters according to the flesh, with fear and trembling, in singleness of your heart, as unto Christ;

6 Not with eyeservice, as menpleasers; but as the servants of Christ, doing the will of God from the heart;

7 With good will doing service, as to the Lord, and not to men:

8 Knowing that whatsoever good thing any man doeth, the same shall he receive of the Lord, whether he be bond or free.

9 And, you masters, do the same things unto them, forbearing threatening: knowing that your Master also is in heaven; neither is there respect of persons with him.

10 Finally, my brethren, be strong in the Lord, and in the power of his might.

11 Put on the whole armour of God, that you may be able to stand against the wiles of the devil.

12 For we wrestle not against flesh and blood, but against principalities, against powers, against the rulers of the darkness of this world, against spiritual wickedness in high places.

13 Wherefore take unto you the whole armour of God, that you may be able to withstand in the evil day, and having done all, to stand.

14 Stand therefore, having your loins girt about with truth, and having on the breastplate of righteousness;

15 And your feet shod with the preparation of the gospel of peace;

16 Above all, taking the shield of faith, wherewith you shall be able to quench all the fiery darts of the wicked.

17 And take the helmet of salvation, and the sword of the Spirit, which is the word of God:

18 Praying always with all prayer and supplication in the Spirit, and watching thereunto with all perseverance and supplication for all saints;

19 And for me, that utterance may be given unto me, that I may open my mouth boldly, to make known the mystery of the gospel,

20 For which I am an ambassador in bonds: that therein I may speak boldly, as I ought to speak.

21 But that you also may know my affairs, and how I do, Tychicus, a beloved brother and faithful minister in the Lord, shall make known to you all things:

22 Whom I have sent unto you for the same purpose, that you might know our affairs, and that he might comfort your hearts.

23 Peace be to the brethren, and love with faith, from God the Father and the Lord Jesus Christ.

24 Grace be with all them that love our Lord Jesus Christ in sincerity. Amen.

Written from Rome unto the Ephesians by Tychicus.

THE EPISTLE OF PAUL THE APOSTLE
TO THE
PHILIPPIANS.

CHAPTER 1

PAUL and Timotheus, the servants of Jesus Christ, to all the saints in Christ Jesus which are at Philippi, with the bishops and deacons:

2 Grace be unto you, and peace, from God our Father, and from the Lord Jesus Christ.

3 I thank my God upon every remembrance of you,

4 Always in every prayer of my for you all making request with joy,

5 For your fellowship in the gospel from the first day until now;

6 Being confident of this very thing, that he which has begun a good work in you will perform it until the day of Jesus Christ:

7 Even as it is meet for me to think this of you all, because I have you in my heart; inasmuch as both in my bonds, and in the defence and confirmation of the gospel, you all are partakers of my grace.

8 For God is my record, how greatly I long after you all in the bowels of Jesus Christ.

9 And this I pray, that your love may abound yet more and more in knowledge and in all judgment;

10 That you may approve things that are excellent; that you may be sincere and without offence till the day of Christ;

11 Being filled with the fruits of righteousness, which are by Jesus Christ, unto the glory and praise of God.

12 But I would you should understand, brethren, that the things which happened unto me have fallen out rather unto the furtherance of the gospel;

13 So that my bonds in Christ are manifest in all the palace, and in all other places;

14 And many of the brethren in the Lord, waxing confident by my bonds, are much more bold to speak the word without fear.

15 Some indeed preach Christ even of envy and strife; and some also of good will:

16 The one preach Christ of contention, not sincerely, supposing to add affliction to my bonds:

17 But the other of love, knowing that I am set for the defence of the gospel.

18 What then? notwithstanding, every way, whether in pretence, or in truth, Christ is preached; and I therein do rejoice, yea, and will rejoice.

19 For I know that this shall turn to my salvation through your prayer, and the supply of the Spirit of Jesus Christ,

20 According to my earnest expectation and my hope, that in nothing I shall be ashamed, but that with all boldness, as always, so now also Christ shall be magnified in my body, whether it be by life, or by death.

21 For to me to live is Christ, and to die is gain.

22 But if I live in the flesh, this is the fruit of my labour: yet what I shall choose I wot not.

23 For I am in a strait betwixt two, having a desire to depart, and to be with Christ; which is far better:

24 Nevertheless to abide in the flesh is more needful for you.

25 And having this confidence, I know that I shall abide and continue with you all for your furtherance and joy of faith;

26 That your rejoicing may be more abundant in Jesus Christ for me by my coming to you again.

27 Only let your conversation be as it becometh the gospel of Christ: that whether I come and see you, or else be absent, I may hear of your affairs, that you stand fast in one spirit, with one mind striving together for the faith of the gospel;

28 And in nothing terrified by your adversaries: which is to them an evident token of perdition, but to you of salvation, and that of God.

29 For unto you it is given in the behalf of Christ, not only to believe on him, but also to suffer for his sake;

30 Having the same conflict which you saw in me, and now hear to be in me.

CHAPTER 2

IF there be therefore any consolation in Christ, if any comfort of love, if any fellowship of the Spirit, if any bowels and mercies,

2 Fulfil you my joy, that you be likeminded, having the same love, being of one accord, of one mind.

3 Let nothing be done through strife or vainglory; but in lowliness of mind let each esteem other better than themselves.

4 Look not every man on his own things, but every man also on the things of others.

5 Let this mind be in you, which was also in Christ Jesus:

6 Who, being in the form of God, thought it not robbery to be equal with God:

7 But made himself of no reputation, and took upon him the form of a servant, and was made in the likeness of men:

8 And being found in fashion as a man, he humbled himself, and became obedient unto death, even the death of the cross.

9 Wherefore God also has highly exalted him, and given him a name which is above every name:

10 That at the name of Jesus every knee should bow, of things in heaven, and things in earth, and things under the earth;

11 And that every tongue should confess that Jesus Christ is Lord, to the glory of God the Father.

12 Wherefore, my beloved, as you have always obeyed, not as in my presence only, but now much more in my absence, work out your own salvation with fear and trembling.

13 For it is God which worketh in you both to will and to do of his good pleasure.

14 Do all things without murmurings and disputings:

15 That you may be blameless and harmless, the sons of God, without rebuke, in the midst of a crooked and perverse nation, among whom you shine as lights in the world;

16 Holding forth the word of life; that I may rejoice in the day of Christ, that I have not run in vain, neither laboured in vain.

17 Yea, and if I be offered upon the sacrifice and service of your faith, I joy, and rejoice with you all.

18 For the same cause also do you joy, and rejoice with me.

19 But I trust in the Lord Jesus to send Timotheus shortly unto you, that I also may be of good comfort, when I know your state.

20 For I have no man likeminded, who will naturally care for your state.

21 For all seek their own, not the things which are Jesus Christ's.

22 But you know the proof of him, that, as a son with the father, he has served with me in the gospel.

23 Him therefore I hope to send presently, so soon as I shall see how it will go with me.

24 But I trust in the Lord that I also myself shall come shortly.

25 Yet I supposed it necessary to send to you Epaphroditus, my brother, and companion in labour, and fellowsoldier, but your messenger, and he that ministered to my wants.

26 For he longed after you all, and was full of heaviness, because that you had heard that he had been sick.

27 For indeed he was sick nigh unto death: but God had mercy on him; and not on him only, but on me also, lest I should have sorrow upon sorrow.

28 I sent him therefore the more carefully, that, when you see him again, you may rejoice, and that I may be the less sorrowful.

29 Receive him therefore in the Lord with all gladness; and hold such in reputation:

30 Because for the work of Christ he was nigh unto death, not regarding his life, to supply your lack of service toward me.

CHAPTER 3

FINALLY, my brethren, rejoice in the Lord. To write the same things to you, to me indeed is not grievous, but for you it is safe.

2 Beware of dogs, beware of evil workers, beware of the concision.

3 For we are the circumcision, which worship God in the spirit, and rejoice in Christ Jesus, and have no confidence in the flesh.

4 Though I might also have confidence in the flesh. If any other man thinketh that he has whereof he might trust in the flesh, I more:

5 Circumcised the eighth day, of the stock of Israel, of the tribe of Benjamin, an Hebrew of the Hebrews; as touching the law, a Pharisee;

6 Concerning zeal, persecuting the church; touching the righteousness which is in the law, blameless.

7 But what things were gain to me, those I counted loss for Christ.

8 Yea doubtless, and I count all things but loss for the excellency of the knowledge of Christ Jesus my Lord: for whom I have suffered the loss of all things, and do count them but dung, that I may win Christ,

9 And be found in him, not having my own righteousness, which is of the law, but that which is through the faith of Christ, the righteousness which is of God by faith:

10 That I may know him, and the power of his resurrection, and the fellowship of his sufferings, being made conformable unto his death;

11 If by any means I might attain unto the resurrection of the dead.

12 Not as though I had already attained, either were already perfect: but I follow after, if that I may apprehend that for which also I am apprehended of Christ Jesus.

13 Brethren, I count not myself to have apprehended: but this one thing I do, forgetting those things which are behind, and reaching forth unto those things which are before,

14 I press toward the mark for the prize of the high calling of God in Christ Jesus.

15 Let us therefore, as many as be perfect, be thus minded: and if in any thing you be otherwise minded, God shall reveal even this unto you.

16 Nevertheless, whereto we have already attained, let us walk by the same rule, let us mind the same thing.

17 Brethren, be followers together of me, and mark them which walk so as you have us for an ensample.

18 (For many walk, of whom I have told you often, and now tell you even weeping, that they are the enemies of the cross of Christ:

19 Whose end is destruction, whose God is their belly, and whose glory is in their shame, who mind earthly things.)

20 For our conversation is in heaven; from whence also we look for the Saviour, the Lord Jesus Christ:

21 Who shall change our vile body, that it may be fashioned like unto his glorious body, according to the working whereby he is able even to subdue all things unto himself.

CHAPTER 4

THEREFORE, my brethren dearly beloved and longed for, my joy and crown, so stand fast in the Lord, my dearly beloved.

2 I beseech Euodias, and beseech Syntyche, that they be of the same mind in the Lord.

3 And I intreat you also, true yokefellow, help those women which laboured with me in the gospel, with Clement also, and with other my fellowlabourers, whose names are in the book of life.

4 Rejoice in the Lord alway: and again I say, Rejoice.

5 Let your moderation be known unto all men. The Lord is at hand.

6 Be careful for nothing; but in every thing by prayer and supplication with thanksgiving let your requests be made known unto God.

7 And the peace of God, which passes all understanding, shall keep your hearts and minds through Christ Jesus.

8 Finally, brethren, whatsoever things are true, whatsoever things are honest, whatsoever things are just, whatsoever things are pure, whatsoever things are lovely, whatsoever things are of good report; if there be any virtue, and if there be any praise, think on these things.

9 Those things, which you have both learned, and received, and heard, and seen in me, do: and the God of peace shall be with you.

10 But I rejoiced in the Lord greatly, that now at the last your care of me has flourished again; wherein you were also careful, but you lacked opportunity.

11 Not that I speak in respect of want: for I have learned, in whatsoever state I am, therewith to be content.

12 I know both how to be abased, and I know how to abound: every where and in all things I am instructed both to be full and to be hungry, both to abound and to suffer need.

13 I can do all things through Christ which strengtheneth me.

14 Notwithstanding you have well done, that you did communicate with my affliction.

15 Now you Philippians know also, that in the beginning of the gospel, when I departed from Macedonia, no church communicated with me as concerning giving and receiving, but you only.

16 For even in Thessalonica you sent once and again unto my necessity.

17 Not because I desire a gift: but I desire fruit that may abound to your account.

18 But I have all, and abound: I am full, having received of Epaphroditus the things which were sent from you, an odour of a sweet smell, a sacrifice acceptable, wellpleasing to God.

19 But my God shall supply all your need according to his riches in glory by Christ Jesus.

20 Now unto God and our Father be glory for ever and ever. Amen.

21 Salute every saint in Christ Jesus. The brethren which are with me greet you.

22 All the saints salute you, chiefly they that are of Cæsar's household.

23 The grace of our Lord Jesus Christ be with you all. Amen.

It was written to the Philippians from Rome by Epaphroditus.

THE EPISTLE OF PAUL THE APOSTLE TO THE COLOSSIANS.

CHAPTER 1

PAUL, an apostle of Jesus Christ by the will of God, and Timotheus our brother,

2 To the saints and faithful brethren in Christ which are at Colosse: Grace be unto you, and peace, from God our Father and the Lord Jesus Christ.

3 We give thanks to God and the Father of our Lord Jesus Christ, praying always for you,

4 Since we heard of your faith in Christ Jesus, and of the love which you have to all the saints,

5 For the hope which is laid up for you in heaven, whereof you heard before in the word of the truth of the gospel;

6 Which is come unto you, as it is in all the world; and bringeth forth fruit, as it doth also in you, since the day you heard of it, and knew the grace of God in truth:

7 As you also learned of Epaphras our dear fellowservant, who is for you a faithful minister of Christ;

8 Who also declared unto us your love in the Spirit.

9 For this cause we also, since the day we heard it, do not cease to pray for you, and to desire that you might be filled with the knowledge of his will in all wisdom and spiritual understanding;

10 That you might walk worthy of the Lord unto all pleasing, being fruitful in every good work, and increasing in the knowledge of God;

11 Strengthened with all might, according to his glorious power, unto all patience and longsuffering with joyfulness;

12 Giving thanks unto the Father, which has made us meet to be partakers of the inheritance of the saints in light:

13 Who has delivered us from the power of darkness, and has translated us into the kingdom of his dear Son:

14 In whom we have redemption through his blood, even the forgiveness of sins:

15 Who is the image of the invisible God, the firstborn of every creature:

16 For by him were all things created, that are in heaven, and that are in earth, visible and invisible, whether they be thrones, or dominions, or principalities, or powers: all things were created by him, and for him:

17 And he is before all things, and by him all things consist.

18 And he is the head of the body, the church: who is the beginning, the firstborn from the dead; that in all things he might have the preeminence.

19 For it pleased the Father that in him should all fulness dwell;

20 And, having made peace through the blood of his cross, by him to reconcile all things unto himself; by him, I say, whether they be things in earth, or things in heaven.

21 And you, that were sometime alienated and enemies in your mind by wicked works, yet now has he reconciled

22 In the body of his flesh through death, to present you holy and unblameable and unreproveable in his sight:

23 If you continue in the faith grounded and settled, and be not moved away from the hope of the gospel, which you have heard, and which was preached to every creature which is under heaven; whereof I Paul am made a minister;

24 Who now rejoice in my sufferings for you, and fill up that which is behind of the afflictions of Christ in my flesh for his body's sake, which is the church:

25 Whereof I am made a minister, according to the dispensation of God which is given to me for you, to fulfil the word of God;

26 Even the mystery which has been hid from ages and from generations, but now is made manifest to his saints:

27 To whom God would make known what is the riches of the glory of this mystery among the Gentiles; which is Christ in you, the hope of glory:

28 Whom we preach, warning every man, and teaching every man in all wisdom; that we may present every man perfect in Christ Jesus:

29 Whereunto I also labour, striving according to his working, which worketh in me mightily.

CHAPTER 2

FOR I would that you knew what great conflict I have for you, and for them at Laodicea, and for as many as have not seen my face in the flesh;

2 That their hearts might be comforted, being knit together in love, and unto all riches of the full assurance of understanding, to the acknowledgement of the mystery of God, and of the Father, and of Christ;

3 In whom are hid all the treasures of wisdom and knowledge.

4 And this I say, lest any man should beguile you with enticing words.

5 For though I be absent in the flesh, yet am I with you in the spirit, joying and beholding your order, and the stedfastness of your faith in Christ.

6 As you have therefore received Christ Jesus the Lord, so walk you in him:

7 Rooted and built up in him, and stablished in the faith, as you have been taught, abounding therein with thanksgiving.

8 Beware lest any man spoil you through philosophy and vain deceit, after the tradition of men, after the rudiments of the world, and not after Christ.

9 For in him dwelleth all the fulness of the Godhead bodily.

10 And you are complete in him, which is the head of all principality and power:

11 In whom also you are circumcised with the circumcision made without hands, in putting off the body of the sins of the flesh by the circumcision of Christ:

12 Buried with him in baptism, wherein also you are risen with him through the faith of the operation of God, who has raised him from the dead.

13 And you, being dead in your sins and the uncircumcision of your flesh, has he quickened together with him, having forgiven you all trespasses;

14 Blotting out the handwriting of ordinances that was against us, which was contrary to us, and took it out of the way, nailing it to his cross;

15 And having spoiled principalities and powers, he made a shew of them openly, triumphing over them in it.

16 Let no man therefore judge you in meat, or in drink, or in respect of an holyday, or of the new moon, or of the sabbath days:

17 Which are a shadow of things to come; but the body is of Christ.

18 Let no man beguile you of your reward in a voluntary humility and worshipping of angels, intruding into those things which he has not seen, vainly puffed up by his fleshly mind,

19 And not holding the Head, from which all the body by joints and bands having nourishment ministered, and knit together, increaseth with the increase of God.

20 Wherefore if you be dead with Christ from the rudiments of the world, why, as though living in the world, are you subject to ordinances,

21 (Touch not; taste not; handle not;

22 Which all are to perish with the using;) after the commandments and doctrines of men?

23 Which things have indeed a shew of wisdom in will worship, and humility, and neglecting of the body; not in any honour to the satisfying of the flesh.

CHAPTER 3

IF you then be risen with Christ, seek those things which are above, where Christ sitteth on the right hand of God.

2 Set your affection on things above, not on things on the earth.

3 For you are dead, and your life is hid with Christ in God.

4 When Christ, who is our life, shall appear, then shall you also appear with him in glory.

5 Mortify therefore your members which are upon the earth; fornication, uncleanness, inordinate affection, evil concupiscence, and covetousness, which is idolatry:

6 For which things' sake the wrath of God comes on the children of disobedience:

7 In the which you also walked some time, when you lived in them.

8 But now you also put off all these; anger, wrath, malice, blasphemy, filthy communication out of your mouth.

9 Lie not one to another, seeing that you have put off the old man with his deeds;

10 And have put on the new man, which is renewed in knowledge after the image of him that created him:

11 Where there is neither Greek nor Jew, circumcision nor uncircumcision, Barbarian, Scythian, bond nor free: but Christ is all, and in all.

12 Put on therefore, as the elect of God, holy and beloved, bowels of mercies, kindness, humbleness of mind, meekness, longsuffering;

13 Forbearing one another, and forgiving one another, if any man have a quarrel against any: even as Christ forgave you, so also do you .

14 And above all these things put on charity, which is the bond of perfectness.

15 And let the peace of God rule in your hearts, to the which also you are called in one body; and be you thankful.

16 Let the word of Christ dwell in you richly in all wisdom; teaching and admonishing one another in psalms and hymns and spiritual songs, singing with grace in your hearts to the Lord.

17 And whatsoever you do in word or deed, do all in the name of the Lord Jesus, giving thanks to God and the Father by him.

18 Wives, submit yourselves unto your own husbands, as it is fit in the Lord.

19 Husbands, love your wives, and be not bitter against them.

20 Children, obey your parents in all things: for this is well pleasing unto the Lord.

21 Fathers, provoke not your children to anger, lest they be discouraged.

22 Servants, obey in all things your masters according to the flesh; not with eyeservice, as menpleasers; but in singleness of heart, fearing God:

23 And whatsoever you do, do it heartily, as to the Lord, and not unto men;

24 Knowing that of the Lord you shall receive the reward of the inheritance: for you serve the Lord Christ.

25 But he that doeth wrong shall receive for the wrong which he has done: and there is no respect of persons.

CHAPTER 4

MASTERS, give unto your servants that which is just and equal; knowing that you also have a Master in heaven.

2 Continue in prayer, and watch in the same with thanksgiving;

3 Withal praying also for us, that God would open unto us a door of utterance, to speak the mystery of Christ, for which I am also in bonds:

4 That I may make it manifest, as I ought to speak.

5 Walk in wisdom toward them that are without, redeeming the time.

6 Let your speech be alway with grace, seasoned with salt, that you may know how you ought to answer every man.

7 All my state shall Tychicus declare unto you, who is a beloved brother, and a faithful minister and fellowservant in the Lord:

8 Whom I have sent unto you for the same purpose, that he might know your estate, and comfort your hearts;

9 With Onesimus, a faithful and beloved brother, who is one of you. They shall make known unto you all things which are done here.

10 Aristarchus my fellowprisoner saluteth you, and Marcus, sister's son to Barnabas, (touching whom you received commandments: if he come unto you, receive him;)

11 And Jesus, which is called Justus, who are of the circumcision. These only are my fellowworkers unto the kingdom of God, which have been a comfort unto me.

12 Epaphras, who is one of you, a servant of Christ, saluteth you, always labouring fervently for you in prayers, that you may stand perfect and complete in all the will of God.

13 For I bear him record, that he has a great zeal for you, and them that are in Laodicea, and them in Hierapolis.

14 Luke, the beloved physician, and Demas, greet you.

15 Salute the brethren which are in Laodicea, and Nymphas, and the church which is in his house.

16 And when this epistle is read among you, cause that it be read also in the church of the Laodiceans; and that you likewise read the epistle from Laodicea.

17 And say to Archippus, Take heed to the ministry which you have received in the Lord, that you fulfil it.

18 The salutation by the hand of me Paul. Remember my bonds. Grace be with you. Amen.

Written from Rome to the Colossians by Tychicus and Onesimus.

THE
FIRST EPISTLE OF PAUL THE APOSTLE
TO THE
THESSALONIANS.

CHAPTER 1

PAUL, and Silvanus, and Timotheus, unto the church of the Thessalonians which is in God the Father and in the Lord Jesus Christ: Grace be unto you, and peace, from God our Father, and the Lord Jesus Christ.

2 We give thanks to God always for you all, making mention of you in our prayers;

3 Remembering without ceasing your work of faith, and labour of love, and patience of hope in our Lord Jesus Christ, in the sight of God and our Father;

4 Knowing, brethren beloved, your election of God.

5 For our gospel came not unto you in word only, but also in power, and in the Holy Ghost, and in much assurance; as you know what manner of men we were among you for your sake.

6 And you became followers of us, and of the Lord, having received the word in much affliction, with joy of the Holy Ghost:

7 So that you were ensamples to all that believe in Macedonia and Achaia.

8 For from you sounded out the word of the Lord not only in Macedonia and Achaia, but also in every place your faith to God-ward is spread abroad; so that we need not to speak any thing.

9 For they themselves shew of us what manner of entering in we had unto you, and how you turned to God from idols to serve the living and true God;

10 And to wait for his Son from heaven, whom he raised from the dead, even Jesus, which delivered us from the wrath to come.

CHAPTER 2

FOR yourselves, brethren, know our entrance in unto you, that it was not in vain:

2 But even after that we had suffered before, and were shamefully entreated, as you know, at Philippi, we were bold in our God to speak unto you the gospel of God with much contention.

3 For our exhortation was not of deceit, nor of uncleanness, nor in guile:

4 But as we were allowed of God to be put in trust with the gospel, even so we speak; not as pleasing men, but God, which trieth our hearts.

5 For neither at any time used we flattering words, as you know, nor a cloke of covetousness; God is witness:

6 Nor of men sought we glory, neither of you, nor yet of others, when we might have been burdensome, as the apostles of Christ.

7 But we were gentle among you, even as a nurse cherisheth her children:

8 So being affectionately desirous of you, we were willing to have imparted unto you, not the gospel of God only, but also our own souls, because you were dear unto us.

9 For you remember, brethren, our labour and travail: for labouring night and day, because we would not be chargeable unto any of you, we preached unto you the gospel of God.

10 You are witnesses, and God also, how holily and justly and unblameably we behaved ourselves among you that believe:

11 As you know how we exhorted and comforted and charged every one of you, as a father doth his children,

12 That you would walk worthy of God, who has called you unto his kingdom and glory.

13 For this cause also thank we God without ceasing, because, when you received the word of God which you heard of us, you received it not as the word of men, but as it is in truth, the word of God, which effectually worketh also in you that believe.

14 For you, brethren, became followers of the churches of God which in Judæa are in Christ Jesus: for you also have suffered like things of your own countrymen, even as they have of the Jews:

15 Who both killed the Lord Jesus, and their own prophets, and have persecuted us; and they please not God, and are contrary to all men:

16 Forbidding us to speak to the Gentiles that they might be saved, to fill up their sins alway: for the wrath is come upon them to the uttermost.

17 But we, brethren, being taken from you for a short time in presence, not in heart, endeavoured the more abundantly to see your face with great desire.

18 Wherefore we would have come unto you, even I Paul, once and again; but Satan hindered us.

19 For what is our hope, or joy, or crown of rejoicing? Are not even you in the presence of our Lord Jesus Christ at his coming?

20 For you are our glory and joy.

CHAPTER 3

WHEREFORE when we could no longer forbear, we thought it good to be left at Athens alone;

2 And sent Timotheus, our brother, and minister of God, and our fellowlabourer in the gospel of Christ, to establish you, and to comfort you concerning your faith:

3 That no man should be moved by these afflictions: for yourselves know that we are appointed thereunto.

4 For verily, when we were with you, we told you before that we should suffer tribulation; even as it came to pass, and you know.

5 For this cause, when I could no longer forbear, I sent to know your faith, lest by some means the tempter have tempted you, and our labour be in vain.

6 But now when Timotheus came from you unto us, and brought us good tidings of your faith and charity, and that you have good remembrance of us always, desiring greatly to see us, as we also to see you:

7 Therefore, brethren, we were comforted over you in all our affliction and distress by your faith:

8 For now we live, if you stand fast in the Lord.

9 For what thanks can we render to God again for you, for all the joy wherewith we joy for your sakes before our God;

10 Night and day praying exceedingly that we might see your face, and might perfect that which is lacking in your faith?

11 Now God himself and our Father, and our Lord Jesus Christ, direct our way unto you.

12 And the Lord make you to increase and abound in love one toward another, and toward all men, even as we do toward you:

13 To the end he may stablish your hearts unblameable in holiness before God, even our Father, at the coming of our Lord Jesus Christ with all his saints.

CHAPTER 4

FURTHERMORE then we beseech you, brethren, and exhort you by the Lord Jesus, that as you have received of us how you ought to walk and to please God, so you would abound more and more.

2 For you know what commandments we gave you by the Lord Jesus.

3 For this is the will of God, even your sanctification, that you should abstain from fornication:

4 That every one of you should know how to possess his vessel in sanctification and honour;

5 Not in the lust of concupiscence, even as the Gentiles which know not God:

6 That no man go beyond and defraud his brother in any matter: because that the Lord is the avenger of all such, as we also have forewarned you and testified.

7 For God has not called us unto uncleanness, but unto holiness.

8 He therefore that despiseth, despiseth not man, but God, who has also given unto us his holy Spirit.

9 But as touching brotherly love you need not that I write unto you: for you yourselves are taught of God to love one another.

10 And indeed you do it toward all the brethren which are in all Macedonia: but we beseech you, brethren, that you increase more and more;

11 And that you study to be quiet, and to do your own business, and to work with your own hands, as we commanded you;

12 That you may walk honestly toward them that are without, and that you may have lack of nothing.

13 But I would not have you to be ignorant, brethren, concerning them which are asleep, that you sorrow not, even as others which have no hope.

14 For if we believe that Jesus died and rose again, even so them also which sleep in Jesus will God bring with him.

15 For this we say unto you by the word of the Lord, that we which are alive and remain unto the coming of the Lord shall not prevent them which are asleep.

16 For the Lord himself shall descend from heaven with a shout, with the voice of the archangel, and with the trump of God: and the dead in Christ shall rise first:

17 Then we which are alive and remain shall be caught up together with them in the clouds, to meet the Lord in the air: and so shall we ever be with the Lord.

18 Wherefore comfort one another with these words.

CHAPTER 5

BUT of the times and the seasons, brethren, you have no need that I write unto you.

2 For yourselves know perfectly that the day of the Lord so comes as a thief in the night.

3 For when they shall say, Peace and safety; then sudden destruction comes upon them, as travail upon a woman with child; and they shall not escape.

4 But you , brethren, are not in darkness, that that day should overtake you as a thief.

5 You are all the children of light, and the children of the day: we are not of the night, nor of darkness.

6 Therefore let us not sleep, as do others; but let us watch and be sober.

7 For they that sleep sleep in the night; and they that be drunken are drunken in the night.

8 But let us, who are of the day, be sober, putting on the breastplate of faith and love; and for an helmet, the hope of salvation.

9 For God has not appointed us to wrath, but to obtain salvation by our Lord Jesus Christ,

10 Who died for us, that, whether we wake or sleep, we should live together with him.

11 Wherefore comfort yourselves together, and edify one another, even as also you do.

12 And we beseech you, brethren, to know them which labour among you, and are over you in the Lord, and admonish you;

13 And to esteem them very highly in love for their work's sake. And be at peace among yourselves.

14 Now we exhort you, brethren, warn them that are unruly, comfort the feebleminded, support the weak, be patient toward all men.

15 See that none render evil for evil unto any man; but ever follow that which is good, both among yourselves, and to all men.

16 Rejoice evermore.

17 Pray without ceasing.

18 In every thing give thanks: for this is the will of God in Christ Jesus concerning you.

19 Quench not the Spirit.

20 Despise not prophesyings.

21 Prove all things; hold fast that which is good.

22 Abstain from all appearance of evil.

23 And the very God of peace sanctify you wholly; and I pray God your whole spirit and soul and body be preserved blameless unto the coming of our Lord Jesus Christ.

24 Faithful is he that calleth you, who also will do it.

25 Brethren, pray for us.

26 Greet all the brethren with an holy kiss.

27 I charge you by the Lord that this epistle be read unto all the holy brethren.

28 The grace of our Lord Jesus Christ be with you. Amen.

The first epistle unto the Thessalonians was written from Athens.

THE
SECOND EPISTLE OF PAUL THE APOSTLE
TO THE
THESSALONIANS.

CHAPTER 1

PAUL, and Silvanus, and Timotheus, unto the church of the Thessalonians in God our Father and the Lord Jesus Christ:

2 Grace unto you, and peace, from God our Father and the Lord Jesus Christ.

3 We are bound to thank God always for you, brethren, as it is meet, because that your faith groweth exceedingly, and the charity of every one of you all toward each other aboundeth;

4 So that we ourselves glory in you in the churches of God for your patience and faith in all your persecutions and tribulations that you endure:

5 Which is a manifest token of the righteous judgment of God, that you may be counted worthy of the kingdom of God, for which you also suffer:

6 Seeing it is a righteous thing with God to recompense tribulation to them that trouble you;

7 And to you who are troubled rest with us, when the Lord Jesus shall be revealed from heaven with his mighty angels,

8 In flaming fire taking vengeance on them that know not God, and that obey not the gospel of our Lord Jesus Christ:

9 Who shall be punished with everlasting destruction from the presence of the Lord, and from the glory of his power;

10 When he shall come to be glorified in his saints, and to be admired in all them that believe (because our testimony among you was believed) in that day.

11 Wherefore also we pray always for you, that our God would count you worthy of this calling, and fulfil all the good pleasure of his goodness, and the work of faith with power:

12 That the name of our Lord Jesus Christ may be glorified in you, and you in him, according to the grace of our God and the Lord Jesus Christ.

CHAPTER 2

NOW we beseech you, brethren, by the coming of our Lord Jesus Christ, and by our gathering together unto him,

2 That you be not soon shaken in mind, or be troubled, neither by spirit, nor by word, nor by letter as from us, as that the day of Christ is at hand.

3 Let no man deceive you by any means: for that day shall not come, except there come a falling away first, and that man of sin be revealed, the son of perdition;

4 Who opposeth and exalteth himself above all that is called God, or that is worshipped; so that he as God sitteth in the temple of God, shewing himself that he is God.

5 Remember you not, that, when I was yet with you, I told you these things?

6 And now you know what withholdeth that he might be revealed in his time.

7 For the mystery of iniquity doth already work: only he who now letteth will let, until he be taken out of the way.

8 And then shall that Wicked be revealed, whom the Lord shall consume with the spirit of his mouth, and shall destroy with the brightness of his coming:

9 Even him, whose coming is after the working of Satan with all power and signs and lying wonders,

10 And with all deceivableness of unrighteousness in them that perish; because they received not the love of the truth, that they might be saved.

11 And for this cause God shall send them strong delusion, that they should believe a lie:

12 That they all might be damned who believed not the truth, but had pleasure in unrighteousness.

13 But we are bound to give thanks alway to God for you, brethren beloved of the Lord, because God has from the beginning chosen you to salvation through sanctification of the Spirit and belief of the truth:

14 Whereunto he called you by our gospel, to the obtaining of the glory of our Lord Jesus Christ.

15 Therefore, brethren, stand fast, and hold the traditions which you have been taught, whether by word, or our epistle.

16 Now our Lord Jesus Christ himself, and God, even our Father, which has loved us, and has given us everlasting consolation and good hope through grace,

17 Comfort your hearts, and stablish you in every good word and work.

CHAPTER 3

FINALLY, brethren, pray for us, that the word of the Lord may have free course, and be glorified, even as it is with you:

2 And that we may be delivered from unreasonable and wicked men: for all men have not faith.

3 But the Lord is faithful, who shall stablish you, and keep you from evil.

4 And we have confidence in the Lord touching you, that you both do and will do the things which we command you.

5 And the Lord direct your hearts into the love of God, and into the patient waiting for Christ.

6 Now we command you, brethren, in the name of our Lord Jesus Christ, that you withdraw yourselves from every brother that walketh disorderly, and not after the tradition which he received of us.

7 For yourselves know how you ought to follow us: for we behaved not ourselves disorderly among you;

8 Neither did we eat any man's bread for nought; but created with labour and travail night and day, that we might not be chargeable to any of you:

9 Not because we have not power, but to make ourselves an ensample unto you to follow us.

10 For even when we were with you, this we commanded you, that if any would not work, neither should he eat.

11 For we hear that there are some which walk among you disorderly, working not at all, but are busybodies.

12 Now them that are such we command and exhort by our Lord Jesus Christ, that with quietness they work, and eat their own bread.

13 But you , brethren, be not weary in well doing.

14 And if any man obey not our word by this epistle, note that man, and have no company with him, that he may be ashamed.

15 Yet count him not as an enemy, but admonish him as a brother.

16 Now the Lord of peace himself give you peace always by all means. The Lord be with you all.

17 The salutation of Paul with my own hand, which is the token in every epistle: so I write.

18 The grace of our Lord Jesus Christ be with you all. Amen.

The second epistle to the Thessalonians was written from Athens.

THE FIRST
EPISTLE OF PAUL THE APOSTLE TO TIMOTHY.

CHAPTER 1

PAUL, an apostle of Jesus Christ by the commandment of God our Saviour, and Lord Jesus Christ, which is our hope;

2 Unto Timothy, my own son in the faith: Grace, mercy, and peace, from God our Father and Jesus Christ our Lord.

3 As I besought you to abide still at Ephesus, when I went into Macedonia, that you mightest charge some that they teach no other doctrine,

4 Neither give heed to fables and endless genealogies, which minister questions, rather than godly edifying which is in faith: so do.

5 Now the end of the commandment is charity out of a pure heart, and of a good conscience, and of faith unfeigned:

6 From which some having swerved have turned aside unto vain jangling;

7 Desiring to be teachers of the law; understanding neither what they say, nor whereof they affirm.

8 But we know that the law is good, if a man use it lawfully;

9 Knowing this, that the law is not made for a righteous man, but for the lawless and disobedient, for the ungodly and for sinners, for unholy and profane, for murderers of fathers and murderers of mothers, for manslayers,

10 For whoremongers, for them that defile themselves with mankind, for menstealers, for liars, for perjured persons, and if there be any other thing that is contrary to sound doctrine;

11 According to the glorious gospel of the blessed God, which was committed to my trust.

12 And I thank Christ Jesus our Lord, who has enabled me, for that he counted me faithful, putting me into the ministry;

13 Who was before a blasphemer, and a persecutor, and injurious: but I obtained mercy, because I did it ignorantly in unbelief.

14 And the grace of our Lord was exceeding abundant with faith and love which is in Christ Jesus.

15 This is a faithful saying, and worthy of all acceptation, that Christ Jesus came into the world to save sinners; of whom I am chief.

16 Howbeit for this cause I obtained mercy, that in me first Jesus Christ might shew forth all longsuffering, for a pattern to them which should hereafter believe on him to life everlasting.

17 Now unto the King eternal, immortal, invisible, the only wise God, be honour and glory for ever and ever. Amen.

18 This charge I commit unto you, son Timothy, according to the prophecies which went before on you, that you by them mightest war a good warfare;

19 Holding faith, and a good conscience; which some having put away concerning faith have made shipwreck:

20 Of whom is Hymenæus and Alexander; whom I have delivered unto Satan, that they may learn not to blaspheme.

CHAPTER 2

I EXHORT therefore, that, first of all, supplications, prayers, intercessions, and giving of thanks, be made for all men;

2 For kings, and for all that are in authority; that we may lead a quiet and peaceable life in all godliness and honesty.

3 For this is good and acceptable in the sight of God our Saviour;

4 Who will have all men to be saved, and to come unto the knowledge of the truth.

5 For there is one God, and one mediator between God and men, the man Christ Jesus;

6 Who gave himself a ransom for all, to be testified in due time.

7 Whereunto I am ordained a preacher, and an apostle, (I speak the truth in Christ, and lie not;) a teacher of the Gentiles in faith and verity.

8 I will therefore that men pray every where, lifting up holy hands, without wrath and doubting.

9 In like manner also, that women adorn themselves in modest apparel, with shamefacedness and sobriety; not with broided hair, or gold, or pearls, or costly array;

10 But (which becometh women professing godliness) with good works.

11 Let the woman learn in silence with all subjection.

12 But I suffer not a woman to teach, nor to usurp authority over the man, but to be in silence.

13 For Adam was first formed, then Eve.

14 And Adam was not deceived, but the woman being deceived was in the transgression.

15 Notwithstanding she shall be saved in childbearing, if they continue in faith and charity and holiness with sobriety.

CHAPTER 3

THIS is a true saying, If a man desire the office of a bishop, he desireth a good work.

2 A bishop then must be blameless, the husband of one wife, vigilant, sober, of good behaviour, given to hospitality, apt to teach;

3 Not given to wine, no striker, not greedy of filthy lucre; but patient, not a brawler, not covetous;

4 One that ruleth well his own house, having his children in subjection with all gravity;

5 (For if a man know not how to rule his own house, how shall he take care of the church of God?)

6 Not a novice, lest being lifted up with pride he fall into the condemnation of the devil.

7 Moreover he must have a good report of them which are without; lest he fall into reproach and the snare of the devil.

8 Likewise must the deacons be grave, not doubletongued, not given to much wine, not greedy of filthy lucre;

9 Holding the mystery of the faith in a pure conscience.

10 And let these also first be proved; then let them use the office of a deacon, being found blameless.

11 Even so must their wives be grave, not slanderers, sober, faithful in all things.

12 Let the deacons be the husbands of one wife, ruling their children and their own houses well.

13 For they that have used the office of a deacon well purchase to themselves a good degree, and great boldness in the faith which is in Christ Jesus.

14 These things write I unto you, hoping to come unto you shortly:

15 But if I tarry long, that you mayest know how you oughtest to behave yourself in the house of God, which is the church of the living God, the pillar and ground of the truth.

16 And without controversy great is the mystery of godliness: God was manifest in the flesh, justified in the Spirit, seen of angels, preached unto the Gentiles, believed on in the world, received up into glory.

CHAPTER 4

NOW the Spirit speaketh expressly, that in the latter times some shall depart from the faith, giving heed to seducing spirits, and doctrines of devils;

2 Speaking lies in hypocrisy; having their conscience seared with a hot iron;

3 Forbidding to marry, and commanding to abstain from meats, which God has created to be received with thanksgiving of them which believe and know the truth.

4 For every creature of God is good, and nothing to be refused, if it be received with thanksgiving:

5 For it is sanctified by the word of God and prayer.

6 If you put the brethren in remembrance of these things, you shalt be a good minister of Jesus Christ, nourished up in the words of faith and of good doctrine, whereunto you have attained.

7 But refuse profane and old wives' fables, and exercise yourself rather unto godliness.

8 For bodily exercise profiteth little: but godliness is profitable unto all things, having promise of the life that now is, and of that which is to come.

9 This is a faithful saying and worthy of all acceptation.

10 For therefore we both labour and suffer reproach, because we trust in the living God, who is the Saviour of all men, specially of those that believe.

11 These things command and teach.

12 Let no man despise your youth; but be you an example of the believers, in word, in conversation, in charity, in spirit, in faith, in purity.

13 Till I come, give attendance to reading, to exhortation, to doctrine.

14 Neglect not the gift that is in you, which was given you by prophecy, with the laying on of the hands of the presbytery.

15 Meditate upon these things; give yourself wholly to them; that your profiting may appear to all.

16 Take heed unto yourself, and unto the doctrine; continue in them: for in doing this you shalt both save yourself, and them that hear you.

CHAPTER 5

REBUKE not an elder, but intreat him as a father; and the younger men as brethren;

2 The elder women as mothers; the younger as sisters, with all purity.

3 Honour widows that are widows indeed.

4 But if any widow have children or nephews, let them learn first to shew piety at home, and to requite their parents: for that is good and acceptable before God.

5 Now she that is a widow indeed, and desolate, trusteth in God, and continueth in supplications and prayers night and day.

6 But she that liveth in pleasure is dead while she liveth.

7 And these things give in charge, that they may be blameless.

8 But if any provide not for his own, and specially for those of his own house, he has denied the faith, and is worse than an infidel.

9 Let not a widow be taken into the number under threescore years old, having been the wife of one man,

10 Well reported of for good works; if she have brought up children, if she have lodged strangers, if she have washed the saints' feet, if she have relieved the afflicted, if she have diligently followed every good work.

11 But the younger widows refuse: for when they have begun to wax wanton against Christ, they will marry;

12 Having damnation, because they have cast off their first faith.

13 And withal they learn to be idle, wandering about from house to house; and not only idle, but tattlers also and busybodies, speaking things which they ought not.

14 I will therefore that the younger women marry, bear children, guide the house, give none occasion to the adversary to speak reproachfully.

15 For some are already turned aside after Satan.

16 If any man or woman that believeth have widows, let them relieve them, and let not the church be charged; that it may relieve them that are widows indeed.

17 Let the elders that rule well be counted worthy of double honour, especially they who labour in the word and doctrine.

18 For the scripture saith, You shalt not muzzle the ox that treadeth out the corn. And, The labourer is worthy of his reward.

19 Against an elder receive not an accusation, but before two or three witnesses.

20 Them that sin rebuke before all, that others also may fear.

21 I charge you before God, and the Lord Jesus Christ, and the elect angels, that you observe these things without preferring one before another, doing nothing by partiality.

22 Lay hands suddenly on no man, neither be partaker of other men's sins: keep yourself pure.

23 Drink no longer water, but use a little wine for your stomach's sake and yours often infirmities.

24 Some men's sins are open beforehand, going before to judgment; and some men they follow after.

25 Likewise also the good works of some are manifest beforehand; and they that are otherwise cannot be hid.

CHAPTER 6

LET as many servants as are under the yoke count their own masters worthy of all honour, that the name of God and his doctrine be not blasphemed.

2 And they that have believing masters, let them not despise them, because they are brethren; but rather do them service, because they are faithful and beloved, partakers of the benefit. These things teach and exhort.

3 If any man teach otherwise, and consent not to wholesome words, even the words of our Lord Jesus Christ, and to the doctrine which is according to godliness;

4 He is proud, knowing nothing, but doting about questions and strifes of words, whereof comes envy, strife, railings, evil surmisings,

5 Perverse disputings of men of corrupt minds, and destitute of the truth, supposing that gain is godliness: from such withdraw yourself.

6 But godliness with contentment is great gain.

7 For we brought nothing into this world, and it is certain we can carry nothing out.

8 And having food and raiment let us be therewith content.

9 But they that will be rich fall into temptation and a snare, and into many foolish and hurtful lusts, which drown men in destruction and perdition.

10 For the love of money is the root of all evil: which while some coveted after, they have erred from the faith, and pierced themselves through with many sorrows.

11 But you , O man of God, flee these things; and follow after righteousness, godliness, faith, love, patience, meekness.

12 Fight the good fight of faith, lay hold on eternal life, whereunto you are also called, and have professed a good profession before many witnesses.

13 I give you charge in the sight of God, who quickeneth all things, and before Christ Jesus, who before Pontius Pilate witnessed a good confession;

14 That you keep this commandment without spot, unrebukeable, until the appearing of our Lord Jesus Christ:

15 Which in his times he shall shew, who is the blessed and only Potentate, the King of kings, and Lord of lords;

16 Who only has immortality, dwelling in the light which no man can approach unto; whom no man has seen, nor can see: to whom be honour and power everlasting. Amen.

17 Charge them that are rich in this world, that they be not highminded, nor trust in uncertain riches, but in the living God, who giveth us richly all things to enjoy;

18 That they do good, that they be rich in good works, ready to distribute, willing to communicate;

19 Laying up in store for themselves a good foundation against the time to come, that they may lay hold on eternal life.

20 O Timothy, keep that which is committed to your trust, avoiding profane and vain babblings, and oppositions of science falsely so called:

21 Which some professing have erred concerning the faith. Grace be with you. Amen.

The first to Timothy was written from Laodicea, which is the chiefest city of Phrygia Pacatiana.

THE SECOND
EPISTLE OF PAUL THE APOSTLE TO TIMOTHY.

CHAPTER 1

PAUL, an apostle of Jesus Christ by the will of God, according to the promise of life which is in Christ Jesus,

2 To Timothy, my dearly beloved son: Grace, mercy, and peace, from God the Father and Christ Jesus our Lord.

3 I thank God, whom I serve from my forefathers with pure conscience, that without ceasing I have remembrance of you in my prayers night and day;

4 Greatly desiring to see you, being mindful of your tears, that I may be filled with joy;

5 When I call to remembrance the unfeigned faith that is in you, which dwelt first in your grandmother Lois, and your mother Eunice; and I am persuaded that in you also.

6 Wherefore I put you in remembrance that you stir up the gift of God, which is in you by the putting on of my hands.

7 For God has not given us the spirit of fear; but of power, and of love, and of a sound mind.

8 Be not you therefore ashamed of the testimony of our Lord, nor of me his prisoner: but be you partaker of the afflictions of the gospel according to the power of God;

9 Who has saved us, and called us with an holy calling, not according to our works, but according to his own purpose and grace, which was given us in Christ Jesus before the world began,

10 But is now made manifest by the appearing of our Saviour Jesus Christ, who has abolished death, and has brought life and immortality to light through the gospel:

11 Whereunto I am appointed a preacher, and an apostle, and a teacher of the Gentiles.

12 For the which cause I also suffer these things: nevertheless I am not ashamed: for I know whom I have believed, and am persuaded that he is able to keep that which I have committed unto him against that day.

13 Hold fast the form of sound words, which you have heard of me, in faith and love which is in Christ Jesus.

14 That good thing which was committed unto you keep by the Holy Ghost which dwelleth in us.

15 This you knowest, that all they which are in Asia be turned away from me; of whom are Phygellus and Hermogenes.

16 The Lord give mercy unto the house of Onesiphorus; for he oft refreshed me, and was not ashamed of my chain:

17 But, when he was in Rome, he sought me out very diligently, and found me.

18 The Lord grant unto him that he may find mercy of the Lord in that day: and in how many things he ministered unto me at Ephesus, you knowest very well.

CHAPTER 2

YOU therefore, my son, be strong in the grace that is in Christ Jesus.

2 And the things that you have heard of me among many witnesses, the same commit you to faithful men, who shall be able to teach others also.

3 You therefore endure hardness, as a good soldier of Jesus Christ.

4 No man that warreth entangleth himself with the affairs of this life; that he may please him who has chosen him to be a soldier.

5 And if a man also strive for masteries, yet is he not crowned, except he strive lawfully.

6 The husbandman that laboureth must be first partaker of the fruits.

7 Consider what I say; and the Lord give you understanding in all things.

8 Remember that Jesus Christ of the seed of David was raised from the dead according to my gospel:

9 Wherein I suffer trouble, as an evil doer, even unto bonds; but the word of God is not bound.

10 Therefore I endure all things for the elect's sakes, that they may also obtain the salvation which is in Christ Jesus with eternal glory.

11 It is a faithful saying: For if we be dead with him, we shall also live with him:

12 If we suffer, we shall also reign with him: if we deny him, he also will deny us:

13 If we believe not, yet he abideth faithful: he cannot deny himself.

14 Of these things put them in remembrance, charging them before the Lord that they strive not about words to no profit, but to the subverting of the hearers.

15 Study to shew yourself approved unto God, a workman that needeth not to be ashamed, rightly dividing the word of truth.

16 But shun profane and vain babblings: for they will increase unto more ungodliness.

17 And their word will eat as doth a canker: of whom is Hymenæus and Philetus;

18 Who concerning the truth have erred, saying that the resurrection is past already; and overthrow the faith of some.

19 Nevertheless the foundation of God standeth sure, having this seal, The Lord knoweth them that are his. And, Let every one that nameth the name of Christ depart from iniquity.

20 But in a great house there are not only vessels of gold and of silver, but also of wood and of earth; and some to honour, and some to dishonour.

21 If a man therefore purge himself from these, he shall be a vessel unto honour, sanctified, and meet for the master's use, and prepared unto every good work.

22 Flee also youthful lusts: but follow righteousness, faith, charity, peace, with them that call on the Lord out of a pure heart.

23 But foolish and unlearned questions avoid, knowing that they do gender strifes.

24 And the servant of the Lord must not strive; but be gentle unto all men, apt to teach, patient,

25 In meekness instructing those that oppose themselves; if God what if will give them repentance to the acknowledging of the truth;

26 And that they may recover themselves out of the snare of the devil, who are taken captive by him at his will.

CHAPTER 3

THIS know also, that in the last days perilous times shall come.

2 For men shall be lovers of their own selves, covetous, boasters, proud, blasphemers, disobedient to parents, unthankful, unholy,

3 Without natural affection, trucebreakers, false accusers, incontinent, fierce, despisers of those that are good,

4 Traitors, heady, highminded, lovers of pleasures more than lovers of God;

5 Having a form of godliness, but denying the power thereof: from such turn away.

6 For of this sort are they which creep into houses, and lead captive silly women laden with sins, led away with divers lusts,

7 Ever learning, and never able to come to the knowledge of the truth.

8 Now as Jannes and Jambres withstood Moses, so do these also resist the truth: men of corrupt minds, reprobate concerning the faith.

9 But they shall proceed no further: for their folly shall be manifest unto all men, as theirs also was.

10 But you have fully known my doctrine, manner of life, purpose, faith, longsuffering, charity, patience,

11 Persecutions, afflictions, which came unto me at Antioch, at Iconium, at Lystra; what persecutions I endured: but out of them all the Lord delivered me.

12 Yea, and all that will live godly in Christ Jesus shall suffer persecution.

13 But evil men and seducers shall wax worse and worse, deceiving, and being deceived.

14 But continue you in the things which you have learned and have been assured of, knowing of whom you have learned them;

15 And that from a child you have known the holy scriptures, which are able to make you wise unto salvation through faith which is in Christ Jesus.

16 All scripture is given by inspiration of God, and is profitable for doctrine, for reproof, for correction, for instruction in righteousness:

17 That the man of God may be perfect, throughly furnished unto all good works.

CHAPTER 4

I CHARGE you therefore before God, and the Lord Jesus Christ, who shall judge the quick and the dead at his appearing and his kingdom;

2 Preach the word; be instant in season, out of season; reprove, rebuke, exhort with all longsuffering and doctrine.

3 For the time will come when they will not endure sound doctrine; but after their own lusts shall they heap to themselves teachers, having itching ears;

4 And they shall turn away their ears from the truth, and shall be turned unto fables.

5 But watch you in all things, endure afflictions, do the work of an evangelist, make full proof of your ministry.

6 For I am now ready to be offered, and the time of my departure is at hand.

7 I have fought a good fight, I have finished my course, I have kept the faith:

8 Henceforth there is laid up for me a crown of righteousness, which the Lord, the righteous judge, shall give me at that day: and not to me only, but unto all them also that love his appearing.

9 Do your diligence to come shortly unto me:

10 For Demas has forsaken me, having loved this present world, and is departed unto Thessalonica; Crescens to Galatia, Titus unto Dalmatia.

11 Only Luke is with me. Take Mark, and bring him with you: for he is profitable to me for the ministry.

12 And Tychicus have I sent to Ephesus.

13 The cloke that I left at Troas with Carpus, when you comest, bring with you, and the books, but especially the parchments.

14 Alexander the coppersmith did me much evil: the Lord reward him according to his works:

15 Of whom be you ware also; for he has greatly withstood our words.

16 At my first answer no man stood with me, but all men forsook me: I pray God that it may not be laid to their charge.

17 Notwithstanding the Lord stood with me, and strengthened me; that by me the preaching might be fully known, and that all the Gentiles might hear: and I was delivered out of the mouth of the lion.

18 And the Lord shall deliver me from every evil work, and will preserve me unto his heavenly kingdom: to whom be glory for ever and ever. Amen.

19 Salute Prisca and Aquila, and the household of Onesiphorus.

20 Erastus abode at Corinth: but Trophimus have I left at Miletum sick.

21 Do your diligence to come before winter. Eubulus greeteth you, and Pudens, and Linus, and Claudia, and all the brethren.

22 The Lord Jesus Christ be with your spirit. Grace be with you. Amen.

The second epistle unto Timotheus, ordained the first bishop of the church of the Ephesians, was written from Rome, when Paul was brought before Nero the second time.

THE EPISTLE OF PAUL TO TITUS.

CHAPTER 1

PAUL, a servant of God, and an apostle of Jesus Christ, according to the faith of God's elect, and the acknowledging of the truth which is after godliness;

2 In hope of eternal life, which God, that cannot lie, promised before the world began;

3 But has in due times manifested his word through preaching, which is committed unto me according to the commandment of God our Saviour;

4 To Titus, my own son after the common faith: Grace, mercy, and peace, from God the Father and the Lord Jesus Christ our Saviour.

5 For this cause left I you in Crete, that you shouldest set in order the things that are wanting, and ordain elders in every city, as I had appointed you:

6 If any be blameless, the husband of one wife, having faithful children not accused of riot or unruly.

7 For a bishop must be blameless, as the steward of God; not selfwilled, not soon angry, not given to wine, no striker, not given to filthy lucre;

8 But a lover of hospitality, a lover of good men, sober, just, holy, temperate;

9 Holding fast the faithful word as he has been taught, that he may be able by sound doctrine both to exhort and to convince the gainsayers.

10 For there are many unruly and vain talkers and deceivers, specially they of the circumcision:

11 Whose mouths must be stopped, who subvert whole houses, teaching things which they ought not, for filthy lucre's sake.

12 One of themselves, even a prophet of their own, said, The Cretians are alway liars, evil beasts, slow bellies.

13 This witness is true. Wherefore rebuke them sharply, that they may be sound in the faith;

14 Not giving heed to Jewish fables, and commandments of men, that turn from the truth.

15 Unto the pure all things are pure: but unto them that are defiled and unbelieving is nothing pure; but even their mind and conscience is defiled.

16 They profess that they know God; but in works they deny him, being abominable, and disobedient, and unto every good work reprobate.

CHAPTER 2

BUT speak you the things which become sound doctrine:

2 That the aged men be sober, grave, temperate, sound in faith, in charity, in patience.

3 The aged women likewise, that they be in behaviour as becometh holiness, not false accusers, not given to much wine, teachers of good things;

4 That they may teach the young women to be sober, to love their husbands, to love their children,

5 To be discreet, chaste, keepers at home, good, obedient to their own husbands, that the word of God be not blasphemed.

6 Young men likewise exhort to be sober minded.

7 In all things shewing yourself a pattern of good works: in doctrine shewing uncorruptness, gravity, sincerity,

8 Sound speech, that cannot be condemned; that he that is of the contrary part may be ashamed, having no evil thing to say of you.

9 Exhort servants to be obedient unto their own masters, and to please them well in all things; not answering again;

10 Not purloining, but shewing all good fidelity; that they may adorn the doctrine of God our Saviour in all things.

11 For the grace of God that bringeth salvation has appeared to all men,

12 Teaching us that, denying ungodliness and worldly lusts, we should live soberly, righteously, and godly, in this present world;

13 Looking for that blessed hope, and the glorious appearing of the great God and our Saviour Jesus Christ;

14 Who gave himself for us, that he might redeem us from all iniquity, and purify unto himself a peculiar people, zealous of good works.

15 These things speak, and exhort, and rebuke with all authority. Let no man despise you.

CHAPTER 3

PUT them in mind to be subject to principalities and powers, to obey magistrates, to be ready to every good work,

2 To speak evil of no man, to be no brawlers, but gentle, shewing all meekness unto all men.

3 For we ourselves also were sometimes foolish, disobedient, deceived, serving divers lusts and pleasures, living in malice and envy, hateful, and hating one another.

4 But after that the kindness and love of God our Saviour toward man appeared,

5 Not by works of righteousness which we have done, but according to his mercy he saved us, by the washing of regeneration, and renewing of the Holy Ghost;

6 Which he shed on us abundantly through Jesus Christ our Saviour;

7 That being justified by his grace, we should be made heirs according to the hope of eternal life.

8 This is a faithful saying, and these things I will that you affirm constantly, that they which have believed in God might be careful to maintain good works. These things are good and profitable unto men.

9 But avoid foolish questions, and genealogies, and contentions, and strivings about the law; for they are unprofitable and vain.

10 A man that is an heretick after the first and second admonition reject;

11 Knowing that he that is such is subverted, and sinneth, being condemned of himself.

12 When I shall send Artemas unto you, or Tychicus, be diligent to come unto me to Nicopolis: for I have determined there to winter.

13 Bring Zenas the lawyer and Apollos on their journey diligently, that nothing be wanting unto them.

14 And let ours also learn to maintain good works for necessary uses, that they be not unfruitful.

15 All that are with me salute you. Greet them that love us in the faith. Grace be with you all. Amen.

It was written to Titus, ordained the first bishop of the church of the Cretians, from Nicopolis of Macedonia.

THE EPISTLE OF PAUL TO PHILEMON.

CHAPTER 1

PAUL, a prisoner of Jesus Christ, and Timothy our brother, unto Philemon our dearly beloved, and fellowlabourer,

2 And to our beloved Apphia, and Archippus our fellowsoldier, and to the church in your house:

3 Grace to you, and peace, from God our Father and the Lord Jesus Christ.

4 I thank my God, making mention of you always in my prayers,

5 Hearing of your love and faith, which you have toward the Lord Jesus, and toward all saints;

6 That the communication of your faith may become effectual by the acknowledging of every good thing which is in you in Christ Jesus.

7 For we have great joy and consolation in your love, because the bowels of the saints are refreshed by you, brother.

8 Wherefore, though I might be much bold in Christ to enjoin you that which is convenient,

9 Yet for love's sake I rather beseech you, being such an one as Paul the aged, and now also a prisoner of Jesus Christ.

10 I beseech you for my son Onesimus, whom I have begotten in my bonds:

11 Which in time past was to you unprofitable, but now profitable to you and to me:

12 Whom I have sent again: you therefore receive him, that is, my own bowels:

13 Whom I would have retained with me, that in your stead he might have ministered unto me in the bonds of the gospel:

14 But without your mind would I do nothing; that your benefit should not be as it were of necessity, but willingly.

15 For perhaps he therefore departed for a season, that you shouldest receive him for ever;

16 Not now as a servant, but above a servant, a brother beloved, specially to me, but how much more unto you, both in the flesh, and in the Lord?

17 If you count me therefore a partner, receive him as myself.

18 If he has wronged you, or oweth you ought, put that on my account;

19 I Paul have written it with my own hand, I will repay it: albeit I do not say to you how you owest unto me even yours own self besides.

20 Yea, brother, let me have joy of you in the Lord: refresh my bowels in the Lord.

21 Having confidence in your obedience I wrote unto you, knowing that you will also do more than I say.

22 But withal prepare me also a lodging: for I trust that through your prayers I shall be given unto you.

23 There salute you Epaphras, my fellowprisoner in Christ Jesus;

24 Marcus, Aristarchus, Demas, Lucas, my fellowlabourers.

25 The grace of our Lord Jesus Christ be with your spirit. Amen.

Written from Rome to Philemon, by Onesimus a servant.

THE EPISTLE OF PAUL THE APOSTLE
TO THE
HEBREWS.

CHAPTER 1

GOD, who at sundry times and in divers manners spake in time past unto the fathers by the prophets,

2 Has in these last days spoken unto us by his Son, whom he has appointed heir of all things, by whom also he made the worlds;

3 Who being the brightness of his glory, and the express image of his person, and upholding all things by the word of his power, when he had by himself purged our sins, sat down on the right hand of the Majesty on high;

4 Being made so much better than the angels, as he has by inheritance obtained a more excellent name than they.

5 For unto which of the angels said he at any time, You are my Son, this day have I begotten you? And again, I will be to him a Father, and he shall be to me a Son?

6 And again, when he bringeth in the firstbegotten into the world, he saith, And let all the angels of God worship him.

7 And of the angels he saith, Who maketh his angels spirits, and his ministers a flame of fire.

8 But unto the Son he saith, Your throne, O God, is for ever and ever: a sceptre of righteousness is the sceptre of your kingdom.

9 You have loved righteousness, and hated iniquity; therefore God, even your God, has anointed you with the oil of gladness above your fellows.

10 And, You , Lord, in the beginning have laid the foundation of the earth; and the heavens are the works of yours hands:

11 They shall perish; but you remainest; and they all shall wax old as doth a garment;

12 And as a vesture shalt you fold them up, and they shall be changed: but you are the same, and your years shall not fail.

13 But to which of the angels said he at any time, Sit on my right hand, until I make yours enemies your footstool?

14 Are they not all ministering spirits, sent forth to minister for them who shall be heirs of salvation?

CHAPTER 2

THEREFORE we ought to give the more earnest heed to the things which we have heard, lest at any time we should let them slip.

2 For if the word spoken by angels was stedfast, and every transgression and disobedience received a just recompence of reward;

3 How shall we escape, if we neglect so great salvation; which at the first began to be spoken by the Lord, and was confirmed unto us by them that heard him;

4 God also bearing them witness, both with signs and wonders, and with divers miracles, and gifts of the Holy Ghost, according to his own will?

5 For unto the angels has he not put in subjection the world to come, whereof we speak.

6 But one in a certain place testified, saying, What is man, that you are mindful of him? or the son of man, that you visitest him?

7 You madest him a little lower than the angels; you crownedst him with glory and honour, and did set him over the works of your hands:

8 You have put all things in subjection under his feet. For in that he put all in subjection under him, he left nothing that is not put under him. But now we see not yet all things put under him.

9 But we see Jesus, who was made a little lower than the angels for the suffering of death, crowned with glory and honour; that he by the grace of God should taste death for every man.

10 For it became him, for whom are all things, and by whom are all things, in bringing many sons unto glory, to make the captain of their salvation perfect through sufferings.

11 For both he that sanctifieth and they who are sanctified are all of one: for which cause he is not ashamed to call them brethren,

12 Saying, I will declare your name unto my brethren, in the midst of the church will I sing praise unto you.

13 And again, I will put my trust in him. And again, Behold I and the children which God has given me.

14 Forasmuch then as the children are partakers of flesh and blood, he also himself likewise took part of the same; that through death he might destroy him that had the power of death, that is, the devil;

15 And deliver them who through fear of death were all their lifetime subject to bondage.

16 For verily he took not on him the nature of angels; but he took on him the seed of Abraham.

17 Wherefore in all things it behoved him to be made like unto his brethren, that he might be a merciful and faithful high priest in things pertaining to God, to make reconciliation for the sins of the people.

18 For in that he himself has suffered being tempted, he is able to succour them that are tempted.

CHAPTER 3

WHEREFORE, holy brethren, partakers of the heavenly calling, consider the Apostle and High Priest of our profession, Christ Jesus;

2 Who was faithful to him that appointed him, as also Moses was faithful in all his house.

3 For this man was counted worthy of more glory than Moses, inasmuch as he who has builded the house has more honour than the house.

4 For every house is builded by some man; but he that built all things is God.

5 And Moses verily was faithful in all his house, as a servant, for a testimony of those things which were to be spoken after;

6 But Christ as a son over his own house; whose house are we, if we hold fast the confidence and the rejoicing of the hope firm unto the end.

7 Wherefore (as the Holy Ghost saith, To day if you will hear his voice,

8 Harden not your hearts, as in the provocation, in the day of temptation in the wilderness:

9 When your fathers tempted me, proved me, and saw my works forty years.

10 Wherefore I was grieved with that generation, and said, They do alway err in their heart; and they have not known my ways.

11 So I sware in my wrath, They shall not enter into my rest.)

12 Take heed, brethren, lest there be in any of you an evil heart of unbelief, in departing from the living God.

13 But exhort one another daily, while it is called To day; lest any of you be hardened through the deceitfulness of sin.

14 For we are made partakers of Christ, if we hold the beginning of our confidence stedfast unto the end;

15 While it is said, To day if you will hear his voice, harden not your hearts, as in the provocation.

16 For some, when they had heard, did provoke: howbeit not all that came out of Egypt by Moses.

17 But with whom was he grieved forty years? was it not with them that had sinned, whose carcases fell in the wilderness?

18 And to whom sware he that they should not enter into his rest, but to them that believed not?

19 So we see that they could not enter in because of unbelief.

CHAPTER 4

LET us therefore fear, lest, a promise being left us of entering into his rest, any of you should seem to come short of it.

2 For unto us was the gospel preached, as well as unto them: but the word preached did not profit them, not being mixed with faith in them that heard it.

3 For we which have believed do enter into rest, as he said, As I have sworn in my wrath, if they shall enter into my rest: although the works were finished from the foundation of the world.

4 For he spake in a certain place of the seventh day on this wise, And God did rest the seventh day from all his works.

5 And in this place again, If they shall enter into my rest.

6 Seeing therefore it remaineth that some must enter therein, and they to whom it was first preached entered not in because of unbelief:

7 Again, he limiteth a certain day, saying in David, To day, after so long a time; as it is said, To day if you will hear his voice, harden not your hearts.

8 For if Jesus had given them rest, then would he not afterward have spoken of another day.

9 There remaineth therefore a rest to the people of God.

10 For he that is entered into his rest, he also has ceased from his own works, as God did from his.

11 Let us labour therefore to enter into that rest, lest any man fall after the same example of unbelief.

12 For the word of God is quick, and powerful, and sharper than any twoedged sword, piercing even to the dividing asunder of soul and spirit, and of the joints and marrow, and is a discerner of the thoughts and intents of the heart.

13 Neither is there any creature that is not manifest in his sight: but all things are naked and opened unto the eyes of him with whom we have to do.

14 Seeing then that we have a great high priest, that is passed into the heavens, Jesus the Son of God, let us hold fast our profession.

15 For we have not an high priest which cannot be touched with the feeling of our infirmities; but was in all points tempted like as we are, yet without sin.

16 Let us therefore come boldly unto the throne of grace, that we may obtain mercy, and find grace to help in time of need.

CHAPTER 5

FOR every high priest taken from among men is ordained for men in things pertaining to God, that he may offer both gifts and sacrifices for sins:

2 Who can have compassion on the ignorant, and on them that are out of the way; for that he himself also is compassed with infirmity.

3 And by reason hereof he ought, as for the people, so also for himself, to offer for sins.

4 And no man taketh this honour unto himself, but he that is called of God, as was Aaron.

5 So also Christ glorified not himself to be made an high priest; but he that said unto him, You are my Son, to day have I begotten you.

6 As he saith also in another place, You are a priest for ever after the order of Melchisedec.

7 Who in the days of his flesh, when he had offered up prayers and supplications with strong crying and tears unto him that was able to save him from death, and was heard in that he feared;

8 Though he were a Son, yet learned he obedience by the things which he suffered;

9 And being made perfect, he became the author of eternal salvation unto all them that obey him;

10 Called of God an high priest after the order of Melchisedec.

11 Of whom we have many things to say, and hard to be uttered, seeing you are dull of hearing.

12 For when for the time you ought to be teachers, you have need that one teach you again which be the first principles of the oracles of God; and are become such as have need of milk, and not of strong meat.

13 For every one that useth milk is unskilful in the word of righteousness: for he is a babe.

14 But strong meat belongeth to them that are of full age, even those who by reason of use have their senses exercised to discern both good and evil.

CHAPTER 6

THEREFORE leaving the principles of the doctrine of Christ, let us go on unto perfection; not laying again the foundation of repentance from dead works, and of faith toward God,

2 Of the doctrine of baptisms, and of laying on of hands, and of resurrection of the dead, and of eternal judgment.

3 And this will we do, if God permit.

4 For it is impossible for those who were once enlightened, and have tasted of the heavenly gift, and were made partakers of the Holy Ghost,

5 And have tasted the good word of God, and the powers of the world to come,

6 If they shall fall away, to renew them again unto repentance; seeing they crucify to themselves the Son of God afresh, and put him to an open shame.

7 For the earth which drinketh in the rain that comes oft upon it, and bringeth forth herbs meet for them by whom it is dressed, receiveth blessing from God:

8 But that which beareth thorns and briers is rejected, and is nigh unto cursing; whose end is to be burned.

9 But, beloved, we are persuaded better things of you, and things that accompany salvation, though we thus speak.

10 For God is not unrighteous to forget your work and labour of love, which you have shewed toward his name, in that you have ministered to the saints, and do minister.

11 And we desire that every one of you do shew the same diligence to the full assurance of hope unto the end:

12 That you be not slothful, but followers of them who through faith and patience inherit the promises.

13 For when God made promise to Abraham, because he could swear by no greater, he sware by himself,

14 Saying, Surely blessing I will bless you, and multiplying I will multiply you.

15 And so, after he had patiently endured, he obtained the promise.

16 For men verily swear by the greater: and an oath for confirmation is to them an end of all strife.

17 Wherein God, willing more abundantly to shew unto the heirs of promise the immutability of his counsel, confirmed it by an oath:

18 That by two immutable things, in which it was impossible for God to lie, we might have a strong consolation, who have fled for refuge to lay hold upon the hope set before us:

19 Which hope we have as an anchor of the soul, both sure and stedfast, and which entereth into that within the veil;

20 Whither the forerunner is for us entered, even Jesus, made an high priest for ever after the order of Melchisedec.

CHAPTER 7

FOR this Melchisedec, king of Salem, priest of the most high God, who met Abraham returning from the slaughter of the kings, and blessed him;

2 To whom also Abraham gave a tenth part of all; first being by interpretation King of righteousness, and after that also King of Salem, which is, King of peace;

3 Without father, without mother, without descent, having neither beginning of days, nor end of life; but made like unto the Son of God; abideth a priest continually.

4 Now consider how great this man was, unto whom even the patriarch Abraham gave the tenth of the spoils.

5 And verily they that are of the sons of Levi, who receive the office of the priesthood, have a commandment to take tithes of the people according to the law, that is, of their brethren, though they come out of the loins of Abraham:

6 But he whose descent is not counted from them received tithes of Abraham, and blessed him that had the promises.

7 And without all contradiction the less is blessed of the better.

8 And here men that die receive tithes; but there he receiveth them, of whom it is witnessed that he liveth.

9 And as I may so say, Levi also, who receiveth tithes, payed tithes in Abraham.

10 For he was yet in the loins of his father, when Melchisedec met him.

11 If therefore perfection were by the Levitical priesthood, (for under it the people received the law,) what further need was there that another priest should rise after the order of Melchisedec, and not be called after the order of Aaron?

12 For the priesthood being changed, there is made of necessity a change also of the law.

13 For he of whom these things are spoken pertaineth to another tribe, of which no man gave attendance at the altar.

14 For it is evident that our Lord sprang out of Juda; of which tribe Moses spake nothing concerning priesthood.

15 And it is yet far more evident: for that after the similitude of Melchisedec there ariseth another priest,

16 Who is made, not after the law of a carnal commandment, but after the power of an endless life.

17 For he testifieth, You are a priest for ever after the order of Melchisedec.

18 For there is verily a disannulling of the commandment going before for the weakness and unprofitableness thereof.

19 For the law made nothing perfect, but the bringing in of a better hope did; by the which we draw nigh unto God.

20 And inasmuch as not without an oath he was made priest:

21 (For those priests were made without an oath; but this with an oath by him that said unto him, The Lord sware and will not repent, You are a priest for ever after the order of Melchisedec:)

22 By so much was Jesus made a surety of a better testament.

23 And they truly were many priests, because they were not suffered to continue by reason of death:

24 But this man, because he continueth ever, has an unchangeable priesthood.

25 Wherefore he is able also to save them to the uttermost that come unto God by him, seeing he ever liveth to make intercession for them.

26 For such an high priest became us, who is holy, harmless, undefiled, separate from sinners, and made higher than the heavens;

27 Who needeth not daily, as those high priests, to offer up sacrifice, first for his own sins, and then for the people's: for this he did once, when he offered up himself.

28 For the law maketh men high priests which have infirmity; but the word of the oath, which was since the law, maketh the Son, who is consecrated for evermore.

CHAPTER 8

NOW of the things which we have spoken this is the sum: We have such an high priest, who is set on the right hand of the throne of the Majesty in the heavens;

2 A minister of the sanctuary, and of the true tabernacle, which the Lord pitched, and not man.

3 For every high priest is ordained to offer gifts and sacrifices: wherefore it is of necessity that this man have somewhat also to offer.

4 For if he were on earth, he should not be a priest, seeing that there are priests that offer gifts according to the law:

5 Who serve unto the example and shadow of heavenly things, as Moses was admonished of God when he was about to make the tabernacle: for, See, saith he, that you make all things according to the pattern shewed to you in the mount.

6 But now has he obtained a more excellent ministry, by how much also he is the mediator of a better covenant, which was established upon better promises.

7 For if that first covenant had been faultless, then should no place have been sought for the second.

8 For finding fault with them, he saith, Behold, the days come, saith the Lord, when I will make a new covenant with the house of Israel and with the house of Judah:

9 Not according to the covenant that I made with their fathers in the day when I took them by the hand to lead them out of the land of Egypt; because they continued not in my covenant, and I regarded them not, saith the Lord.

10 For this is the covenant that I will make with the house of Israel after those days, saith the Lord; I will put my laws into their mind, and write them in their hearts: and I will be to them a God, and they shall be to me a people:

11 And they shall not teach every man his neighbour, and every man his brother, saying, Know the Lord: for all shall know me, from the least to the greatest.

12 For I will be merciful to their unrighteousness, and their sins and their iniquities will I remember no more.

13 In that he saith, A new covenant, he has made the first old. Now that which decayeth and waxeth old is ready to vanish away.

CHAPTER 9

THEN verily the first covenant had also ordinances of divine service, and a worldly sanctuary.

2 For there was a tabernacle made; the first, wherein was the candlestick, and the table, and the shewbread; which is called the sanctuary.

3 And after the second veil, the tabernacle which is called the Holiest of all;

4 Which had the golden censer, and the ark of the covenant overlaid round about with gold, wherein was the golden pot that had manna, and Aaron's rod that budded, and the tables of the covenant;

5 And over it the cherubims of glory shadowing the mercyseat; of which we cannot now speak particularly.

6 Now when these things were thus ordained, the priests went always into the first tabernacle, accomplishing the service of God.

7 But into the second went the high priest alone once every year, not without blood, which he offered for himself, and for the errors of the people:

8 The Holy Ghost this signifying, that the way into the holiest of all was not yet made manifest, while as the first tabernacle was yet standing:

9 Which was a figure for the time then present, in which were offered both gifts and sacrifices, that could not make him that did the service perfect, as pertaining to the conscience;

10 Which stood only in meats and drinks, and divers washings, and carnal ordinances, imposed on them until the time of reformation.

11 But Christ being come an high priest of good things to come, by a greater and more perfect tabernacle, not made with hands, that is to say, not of this building;

12 Neither by the blood of goats and calves, but by his own blood he entered in once into the holy place, having obtained eternal redemption for us.

13 For if the blood of bulls and of goats, and the ashes of an heifer sprinkling the unclean, sanctifieth to the purifying of the flesh:

14 How much more shall the blood of Christ, who through the eternal Spirit offered himself without spot to God, purge your conscience from dead works to serve the living God?

15 And for this cause he is the mediator of the new testament, that by means of death, for the redemption of the transgressions that were under the first testament, they which are called might receive the promise of eternal inheritance.

16 For where a testament is, there must also of necessity be the death of the testator.

17 For a testament is of force after men are dead: otherwise it is of no strength at all while the testator liveth.

18 Whereupon neither the first testament was dedicated without blood.

19 For when Moses had spoken every precept to all the people according to the law, he took the blood of calves and of goats, with water, and scarlet wool, and hyssop, and sprinkled both the book, and all the people,

20 Saying, This is the blood of the testament which God has enjoined unto you.

21 Moreover he sprinkled with blood both the tabernacle, and all the vessels of the ministry.

22 And almost all things are by the law purged with blood; and without shedding of blood is no remission.

23 It was therefore necessary that the patterns of things in the heavens should be purified with these; but the heavenly things themselves with better sacrifices than these.

24 For Christ is not entered into the holy places made with hands, which are the figures of the true; but into heaven itself, now to appear in the presence of God for us:

25 Nor yet that he should offer himself often, as the high priest entereth into the holy place every year with blood of others;

26 For then must he often have suffered since the foundation of the world: but now once in the end of the world has he appeared to put away sin by the sacrifice of himself.

27 And as it is appointed unto men once to die, but after this the judgment:

28 So Christ was once offered to bear the sins of many; and unto them that look for him shall he appear the second time without sin unto salvation.

CHAPTER 10

FOR the law having a shadow of good things to come, and not the very image of the things, can never with those sacrifices which they offered year by year continually make the comers thereunto perfect.

2 For then would they not have ceased to be offered? because that the worshippers once purged should have had no more conscience of sins.

3 But in those sacrifices there is a remembrance again made of sins every year.

4 For it is not possible that the blood of bulls and of goats should take away sins.

5 Wherefore when he comes into the world, he saith, Sacrifice and offering you wouldest not, but a body have you prepared me:

6 In burnt offerings and sacrifices for sin you have had no pleasure.

7 Then said I, Lo, I come (in the volume of the book it is written of me,) to do your will, O God.

8 Above when he said, Sacrifice and offering and burnt offerings and offering for sin you wouldest not, neither hadst pleasure therein; which are offered by the law;

9 Then said he, Lo, I come to do your will, O God. He taketh away the first, that he may establish the second.

10 By the which will we are sanctified through the offering of the body of Jesus Christ once for all.

11 And every priest standeth daily ministering and offering oftentimes the same sacrifices, which can never take away sins:

12 But this man, after he had offered one sacrifice for sins for ever, sat down on the right hand of God;

13 From henceforth expecting till his enemies be made his footstool.

14 For by one offering he has perfected for ever them that are sanctified.

15 Whereof the Holy Ghost also is a witness to us: for after that he had said before,

16 This is the covenant that I will make with them after those days, saith the Lord, I will put my laws into their hearts, and in their minds will I write them;

17 And their sins and iniquities will I remember no more.

18 Now where remission of these is, there is no more offering for sin.

19 Having therefore, brethren, boldness to enter into the holiest by the blood of Jesus,

20 By a new and living way, which he has consecrated for us, through the veil, that is to say, his flesh;

21 And having an high priest over the house of God;

22 Let us draw near with a true heart in full assurance of faith, having our hearts sprinkled from an evil conscience, and our bodies washed with pure water.

23 Let us hold fast the profession of our faith without wavering; (for he is faithful that promised;)

24 And let us consider one another to provoke unto love and to good works:

25 Not forsaking the assembling of ourselves together, as the manner of some is; but exhorting one another: and so much the more, as you see the day approaching.

26 For if we sin wilfully after that we have received the knowledge of the truth, there remaineth no more sacrifice for sins,

27 But a certain fearful looking for of judgment and fiery indignation, which shall devour the adversaries.

28 He that despised Moses' law died without mercy under two or three witnesses:

29 Of how much sorer punishment, suppose you , shall he be thought worthy, who has trodden under foot the Son of God, and has counted the blood of the covenant, wherewith he was sanctified, an unholy thing, and has done despite unto the Spirit of grace?

30 For we know him that has said, Vengeance belongeth unto me, I will recompense, saith the Lord. And again, The Lord shall judge his people.

31 It is a fearful thing to fall into the hands of the living God.

32 But call to remembrance the former days, in which, after you were illuminated, you endured a great fight of afflictions;

33 Partly, whilst you were made a gazingstock both by reproaches and afflictions; and partly, whilst you became companions of them that were so used.

34 For you had compassion of me in my bonds, and took joyfully the spoiling of your goods, knowing in yourselves that you have in heaven a better and an enduring substance.

35 Cast not away therefore your confidence, which has great recompence of reward.

36 For you have need of patience, that, after you have done the will of God, you might receive the promise.

37 For yet a little while, and he that shall come will come, and will not tarry.

38 Now the just shall live by faith: but if any man draw back, my soul shall have no pleasure in him.

39 But we are not of them who draw back unto perdition; but of them that believe to the saving of the soul.

CHAPTER 11

NOW faith is the substance of things hoped for, the evidence of things not seen.

2 For by it the elders obtained a good report.

3 Through faith we understand that the worlds were framed by the word of God, so that things which are seen were not made of things which do appear.

4 By faith Abel offered unto God a more excellent sacrifice than Cain, by which he obtained witness that he was righteous, God testifying of his gifts: and by it he being dead yet speaketh.

5 By faith Enoch was translated that he should not see death; and was not found, because God had translated him: for before his translation he had this testimony, that he pleased God.

6 But without faith it is impossible to please him: for he that comes to God must believe that he is, and that he is a rewarder of them that diligently seek him.

7 By faith Noah, being warned of God of things not seen as yet, moved with fear, prepared an ark to the saving of his house; by the which he condemned the world, and became heir of the righteousness which is by faith.

8 By faith Abraham, when he was called to go out into a place which he should after receive for an inheritance, obeyed; and he went out, not knowing whither he went.

9 By faith he sojourned in the land of promise, as in a strange country, dwelling in tabernacles with Isaac and Jacob, the heirs with him of the same promise:

10 For he looked for a city which has foundations, whose builder and maker is God.

11 Through faith also Sara herself received strength to conceive seed, and was delivered of a child when she was past age, because she judged him faithful who had promised.

12 Therefore sprang there even of one, and him as good as dead, so many as the stars of the sky in multitude, and as the sand which is by the sea shore innumerable.

13 These all died in faith, not having received the promises, but having seen them afar off, and were persuaded of them, and embraced them, and confessed that they were strangers and pilgrims on the earth.

14 For they that say such things declare plainly that they seek a country.

15 And truly, if they had been mindful of that country from whence they came out, they might have had opportunity to have returned.

16 But now they desire a better country, that is, an heavenly: wherefore God is not ashamed to be called their God: for he has prepared for them a city.

17 By faith Abraham, when he was tried, offered up Isaac: and he that had received the promises offered up his only begotten son,

18 Of whom it was said, That in Isaac shall your seed be called:

19 Accounting that God was able to raise him up, even from the dead; from whence also he received him in a figure.

20 By faith Isaac blessed Jacob and Esau concerning things to come.

21 By faith Jacob, when he was a dying, blessed both the sons of Joseph; and worshipped, leaning upon the top of his staff.

22 By faith Joseph, when he died, made mention of the departing of the children of Israel; and gave commandment concerning his bones.

23 By faith Moses, when he was born, was hid three months of his parents, because they saw he was a proper child; and they were not afraid of the king's commandment.

24 By faith Moses, when he was come to years, refused to be called the son of Pharaoh's daughter;

25 Choosing rather to suffer affliction with the people of God, than to enjoy the pleasures of sin for a season;

26 Esteeming the reproach of Christ greater riches than the treasures in Egypt: for he had respect unto the recompence of the reward.

27 By faith he forsook Egypt, not fearing the wrath of the king: for he endured, as seeing him who is invisible.

28 Through faith he kept the passover, and the sprinkling of blood, lest he that destroyed the firstborn should touch them.

29 By faith they passed through the Red sea as by dry land: which the Egyptians assaying to do were drowned.

30 By faith the walls of Jericho fell down, after they were compassed about seven days.

31 By faith the harlot Rahab perished not with them that believed not, when she had received the spies with peace.

32 And what shall I more say? for the time would fail me to tell of Gedeon, and of Barak, and of Samson, and of Jephthae; of David also, and Samuel, and of the prophets:

33 Who through faith subdued kingdoms, created righteousness, obtained promises, stopped the mouths of lions,

34 Quenched the violence of fire, escaped the edge of the sword, out of weakness were made strong, waxed valiant in fight, turned to flight the armies of the aliens.

35 Women received their dead raised to life again: and others were tortured, not accepting deliverance; that they might obtain a better resurrection:

36 And others had trial of cruel mockings and scourgings, yea, moreover of bonds and imprisonment:

37 They were stoned, they were sawn asunder, were tempted, were slain with the sword: they wandered about in sheepskins and goatskins; being destitute, afflicted, tormented;

38 (Of whom the world was not worthy:) they wandered in deserts, and in mountains, and in dens and caves of the earth.

39 And these all, having obtained a good report through faith, received not the promise:

40 God having provided some better thing for us, that they without us should not be made perfect.

CHAPTER 12

WHEREFORE seeing we also are compassed about with so great a cloud of witnesses, let us lay aside every weight, and the sin which doth so easily beset us, and let us run with patience the race that is set before us,

2 Looking unto Jesus the author and finisher of our faith; who for the joy that was set before him endured the cross, despising the shame, and is set down at the right hand of the throne of God.

3 For consider him that endured such contradiction of sinners against himself, lest you be wearied and faint in your minds.

4 You have not yet resisted unto blood, striving against sin.

5 And you have forgotten the exhortation which speaketh unto you as unto children, My son, despise not you the chastening of the Lord, nor faint when you are rebuked of him:

6 For whom the Lord loveth he chasteneth, and scourgeth every son whom he receiveth.

7 If you endure chastening, God dealeth with you as with sons; for what son is he whom the father chasteneth not?

8 But if you be without chastisement, whereof all are partakers, then are you bastards, and not sons.

9 Furthermore we have had fathers of our flesh which corrected us, and we gave them reverence: shall we not much rather be in subjection unto the Father of spirits, and live?

10 For they verily for a few days chastened us after their own pleasure; but he for our profit, that we might be partakers of his holiness.

11 Now no chastening for the present seemeth to be joyous, but grievous: nevertheless afterward it yieldeth the peaceable fruit of righteousness unto them which are exercised thereby.

12 Wherefore lift up the hands which hang down, and the feeble knees;

13 And make straight paths for your feet, lest that which is lame be turned out of the way; but let it rather be healed.

14 Follow peace with all men, and holiness, without which no man shall see the Lord:

15 Looking diligently lest any man fail of the grace of God; lest any root of bitterness springing up trouble you, and thereby many be defiled;

16 Lest there be any fornicator, or profane person, as Esau, who for one morsel of meat sold his birthright.

17 For you know how that afterward, when he would have inherited the blessing, he was rejected: for he found no place of repentance, though he sought it carefully with tears.

18 For you are not come unto the mount that might be touched, and that burned with fire, nor unto blackness, and darkness, and tempest,

19 And the sound of a trumpet, and the voice of words; which voice they that heard intreated that the word should not be spoken to them any more:

20 (For they could not endure that which was commanded, And if so much as a beast touch the mountain, it shall be stoned, or thrust through with a dart:

21 And so terrible was the sight, that Moses said, I exceedingly fear and quake:)

22 But you are come unto mount Sion, and unto the city of the living God, the heavenly Jerusalem, and to an innumerable company of angels,

23 To the general assembly and church of the firstborn, which are written in heaven, and to God the Judge of all, and to the spirits of just men made perfect,

24 And to Jesus the mediator of the new covenant, and to the blood of sprinkling, that speaketh better things than that of Abel.

25 See that you refuse not him that speaketh. For if they escaped not who refused him that spake on earth, much more shall not we escape, if we turn away from him that speaketh from heaven:

26 Whose voice then shook the earth: but now he has promised, saying, Yet once more I shake not the earth only, but also heaven.

27 And this word, Yet once more, signifieth the removing of those things that are shaken, as of things that are made, that those things which cannot be shaken may remain.

28 Wherefore we receiving a kingdom which cannot be moved, let us have grace, whereby we may serve God acceptably with reverence and godly fear:

29 For our God is a consuming fire.

CHAPTER 13

LET brotherly love continue.

2 Be not forgetful to entertain strangers: for thereby some have entertained angels unawares.

3 Remember them that are in bonds, as bound with them; and them which suffer adversity, as being yourselves also in the body.

4 Marriage is honourable in all, and the bed undefiled: but whoremongers and adulterers God will judge.

5 Let your conversation be without covetousness; and be content with such things as you have: for he has said, I will never leave you, nor forsake you.

6 So that we may boldly say, The Lord is my helper, and I will not fear what man shall do unto me.

7 Remember them which have the rule over you, who have spoken unto you the word of God: whose faith follow, considering the end of their conversation.

8 Jesus Christ the same yesterday, and to day, and for ever.

9 Be not carried about with divers and strange doctrines. For it is a good thing that the heart be established with grace; not with meats, which have not profited them that have been occupied therein.

10 We have an altar, whereof they have no right to eat which serve the tabernacle.

11 For the bodies of those beasts, whose blood is brought into the sanctuary by the high priest for sin, are burned without the camp.

12 Wherefore Jesus also, that he might sanctify the people with his own blood, suffered without the gate.

13 Let us go forth therefore unto him without the camp, bearing his reproach.

14 For here have we no continuing city, but we seek one to come.

15 By him therefore let us offer the sacrifice of praise to God continually, that is, the fruit of our lips giving thanks to his name.

16 But to do good and to communicate forget not: for with such sacrifices God is well pleased.

17 Obey them that have the rule over you, and submit yourselves: for they watch for your souls, as they that must give account, that they may do it with joy, and not with grief: for that is unprofitable for you.

18 Pray for us: for we trust we have a good conscience, in all things willing to live honestly.

19 But I beseech you the rather to do this, that I may be restored to you the sooner.

20 Now the God of peace, that brought again from the dead our Lord Jesus, that great shepherd of the sheep, through the blood of the everlasting covenant,

21 Make you perfect in every good work to do his will, working in you that which is wellpleasing in his sight, through Jesus Christ; to whom be glory for ever and ever. Amen.

22 And I beseech you, brethren, suffer the word of exhortation: for I have written a letter unto you in few words.

23 Know you that our brother Timothy is set at liberty; with whom, if he come shortly, I will see you.

24 Salute all them that have the rule over you, and all the saints. They of Italy salute you.

25 Grace be with you all. Amen.

Written to the Hebrews from Italy by Timothy.

THE GENERAL EPISTLE OF
JAMES.

CHAPTER 1

JAMES, a servant of God and of the Lord Jesus Christ, to the twelve tribes which are scattered abroad, greeting.

2 My brethren, count it all joy when you fall into divers temptations;

3 Knowing this, that the trying of your faith worketh patience.

4 But let patience have her perfect work, that you may be perfect and entire, wanting nothing.

5 If any of you lack wisdom, let him ask of God, that giveth to all men liberally, and upbraideth not; and it shall be given him.

6 But let him ask in faith, nothing wavering. For he that wavereth is like a wave of the sea driven with the wind and tossed.

7 For let not that man think that he shall receive any thing of the Lord.

8 A double minded man is unstable in all his ways.

9 Let the brother of low degree rejoice in that he is exalted:

10 But the rich, in that he is made low: because as the flower of the grass he shall pass away.

11 For the sun is no sooner risen with a burning heat, but it withereth the grass, and the flower thereof falleth, and the grace of the fashion of it perisheth: so also shall the rich man fade away in his ways.

12 Blessed is the man that endureth temptation: for when he is tried, he shall receive the crown of life, which the Lord has promised to them that love him.

13 Let no man say when he is tempted, I am tempted of God: for God cannot be tempted with evil, neither tempteth he any man:

14 But every man is tempted, when he is drawn away of his own lust, and enticed.

15 Then when lust has conceived, it bringeth forth sin: and sin, when it is finished, bringeth forth death.

16 Do not err, my beloved brethren.

17 Every good gift and every perfect gift is from above, and comes down from the Father of lights, with whom is no variableness, neither shadow of turning.

18 Of his own will begat he us with the word of truth, that we should be a kind of firstfruits of his creatures.

19 Wherefore, my beloved brethren, let every man be swift to hear, slow to speak, slow to wrath:

20 For the wrath of man worketh not the righteousness of God.

21 Wherefore lay apart all filthiness and superfluity of naughtiness, and receive with meekness the engrafted word, which is able to save your souls.

22 But be you doers of the word, and not hearers only, deceiving your own selves.

23 For if any be a hearer of the word, and not a doer, he is like unto a man beholding his natural face in a glass:

24 For he beholdeth himself, and goeth his way, and straightway forgetteth what manner of man he was.

25 But whoso looketh into the perfect law of liberty, and continueth therein, he being not a forgetful hearer, but a doer of the work, this man shall be blessed in his deed.

26 If any man among you seem to be religious, and bridleth not his tongue, but deceiveth his own heart, this man's religion is vain.

27 Pure religion and undefiled before God and the Father is this, To visit the fatherless and widows in their affliction, and to keep himself unspotted from the world.

CHAPTER 2

MY brethren, have not the faith of our Lord Jesus Christ, the Lord of glory, with respect of persons.

2 For if there come unto your assembly a man with a gold ring, in goodly apparel, and there come in also a poor man in vile raiment;

3 And you have respect to him that weareth the gay clothing, and say unto him, Sit you here in a good place; and say to the poor, Stand you there, or sit here under my footstool:

4 Are you not then partial in yourselves, and are become judges of evil thoughts?

5 Hearken, my beloved brethren, Has not God chosen the poor of this world rich in faith, and heirs of the kingdom which he has promised to them that love him?

6 But you have despised the poor. Do not rich men oppress you, and draw you before the judgment seats?

7 Do not they blaspheme that worthy name by the which you are called?

8 If you fulfil the royal law according to the scripture, You shalt love your neighbour as yourself, you do well:

9 But if you have respect to persons, you commit sin, and are convinced of the law as transgressors.

10 For whosoever shall keep the whole law, and yet offend in one point, he is guilty of all.

11 For he that said, Do not commit adultery, said also, Do not kill. Now if you commit no adultery, yet if you kill, you are become a transgressor of the law.

12 So speak you , and so do, as they that shall be judged by the law of liberty.

13 For he shall have judgment without mercy, that has shewed no mercy; and mercy rejoiceth against judgment.

14 What doth it profit, my brethren, though a man say he has faith, and have not works? can faith save him?

15 If a brother or sister be naked, and destitute of daily food,

16 And one of you say unto them, Depart in peace, be you warmed and filled; notwithstanding you give them not those things which are needful to the body; what doth it profit?

17 Even so faith, if it has not works, is dead, being alone.

18 Yea, a man may say, You have faith, and I have works: shew me your faith without your works, and I will shew you my faith by my works.

19 You believest that there is one God; you doest well: the devils also believe, and tremble.

20 But will you know, O vain man, that faith without works is dead?

21 Was not Abraham our father justified by works, when he had offered Isaac his son upon the altar?

22 Seest you how faith created with his works, and by works was faith made perfect?

23 And the scripture was fulfilled which saith, Abraham believed God, and it was imputed unto him for righteousness: and he was called the Friend of God.

24 You see then how that by works a man is justified, and not by faith only.

25 Likewise also was not Rahab the harlot justified by works, when she had received the messengers, and had sent them out another way?

26 For as the body without the spirit is dead, so faith without works is dead also.

CHAPTER 3

MY brethren, be not many masters, knowing that we shall receive the greater condemnation.

2 For in many things we offend all. If any man offend not in word, the same is a perfect man, and able also to bridle the whole body.

3 Behold, we put bits in the horses' mouths, that they may obey us; and we turn about their whole body.

4 Behold also the ships, which though they be so great, and are driven of fierce winds, yet are they turned about with a very small helm, whithersoever the governor listeth.

5 Even so the tongue is a little member, and boasteth great things. Behold, how great a matter a little fire kindleth!

6 And the tongue is a fire, a world of iniquity: so is the tongue among our members, that it defileth the whole body, and setteth on fire the course of nature; and it is set on fire of hell.

7 For every kind of beasts, and of birds, and of serpents, and of things in the sea, is tamed, and has been tamed of mankind:

8 But the tongue can no man tame; it is an unruly evil, full of deadly poison.

9 Therewith bless we God, even the Father; and therewith curse we men, which are made after the similitude of God.

10 Out of the same mouth proceedeth blessing and cursing. My brethren, these things ought not so to be.

11 Doth a fountain send forth at the same place sweet water and bitter?

12 Can the fig tree, my brethren, bear olive berries? either a vine, figs? so can no fountain both yield salt water and fresh.

13 Who is a wise man and endued with knowledge among you? let him shew out of a good conversation his works with meekness of wisdom.

14 But if you have bitter envying and strife in your hearts, glory not, and lie not against the truth.

15 This wisdom descendeth not from above, but is earthly, sensual, devilish.

16 For where envying and strife is, there is confusion and every evil work.

17 But the wisdom that is from above is first pure, then peaceable, gentle, and easy to be intreated, full of mercy and good fruits, without partiality, and without hypocrisy.

18 And the fruit of righteousness is sown in peace of them that make peace.

CHAPTER 4

FROM whence come wars and fightings among you? come they not hence, even of your lusts that war in your members?

2 You lust, and have not: you kill, and desire to have, and cannot obtain: you fight and war, yet you have not, because you ask not.

3 You ask, and receive not, because you ask amiss, that you may consume it upon your lusts.

4 You adulterers and adulteresses, know you not that the friendship of the world is enmity with God? whosoever therefore will be a friend of the world is the enemy of God.

5 Do you think that the scripture saith in vain, The spirit that dwelleth in us lusteth to envy?

6 But he giveth more grace. Wherefore he saith, God resisteth the proud, but giveth grace unto the humble.

7 Submit yourselves therefore to God. Resist the devil, and he will flee from you.

8 Draw nigh to God, and he will draw nigh to you. Cleanse your hands, you sinners; and purify your hearts, you double minded.

9 Be afflicted, and mourn, and weep: let your laughter be turned to mourning, and your joy to heaviness.

10 Humble yourselves in the sight of the Lord, and he shall lift you up.

11 Speak not evil one of another, brethren. He that speaketh evil of his brother, and judgeth his brother, speaketh evil of the law, and judgeth the law: but if you judge the law, you are not a doer of the law, but a judge.

12 There is one lawgiver, who is able to save and to destroy: who are you that judgest another?

13 Go to now, you that say, To day or to morrow we will go into such a city, and continue there a year, and buy and sell, and get gain:

14 Whereas you know not what shall be on the morrow. For what is your life? It is even a vapour, that appeareth for a little time, and then vanisheth away.

15 For that you ought to say, If the Lord will, we shall live, and do this, or that.

16 But now you rejoice in your boastings: all such rejoicing is evil.

17 Therefore to him that knoweth to do good, and doeth it not, to him it is sin.

CHAPTER 5

GO to now, you rich men, weep and howl for your miseries that shall come upon you.

2 Your riches are corrupted, and your garments are motheaten.

3 Your gold and silver is cankered; and the rust of them shall be a witness against you, and shall eat your flesh as it were fire. You have heaped treasure together for the last days.

4 Behold, the hire of the labourers who have reaped down your fields, which is of you kept back by fraud, crieth: and the cries of them which have reaped are entered into the ears of the Lord of sabaoth.

5 You have lived in pleasure on the earth, and been wanton; you have nourished your hearts, as in a day of slaughter.

6 You have condemned and killed the just; and he doth not resist you.

7 Be patient therefore, brethren, unto the coming of the Lord. Behold, the husbandman waiteth for the precious fruit of the earth, and has long patience for it, until he receive the early and latter rain.

8 Be you also patient; stablish your hearts: for the coming of the Lord draweth nigh.

9 Grudge not one against another, brethren, lest you be condemned: behold, the judge standeth before the door.

10 Take, my brethren, the prophets, who have spoken in the name of the Lord, for an example of suffering affliction, and of patience.

11 Behold, we count them happy which endure. You have heard of the patience of Job, and have seen the end of the Lord; that the Lord is very pitiful, and of tender mercy.

12 But above all things, my brethren, swear not, neither by heaven, neither by the earth, neither by any other oath: but let your yea be yea; and your nay, nay; lest you fall into condemnation.

13 Is any among you afflicted? let him pray. Is any merry? let him sing psalms.

14 Is any sick among you? let him call for the elders of the church; and let them pray over him, anointing him with oil in the name of the Lord:

15 And the prayer of faith shall save the sick, and the Lord shall raise him up; and if he have committed sins, they shall be forgiven him.

16 Confess your faults one to another, and pray one for another, that you may be healed. The effectual fervent prayer of a righteous man availeth much.

17 Elias was a man subject to like passions as we are, and he prayed earnestly that it might not rain: and it rained not on the earth by the space of three years and six months.

18 And he prayed again, and the heaven gave rain, and the earth brought forth her fruit.

19 Brethren, if any of you do err from the truth, and one convert him;

20 Let him know, that he which converteth the sinner from the error of his way shall save a soul from death, and shall hide a multitude of sins.

THE FIRST EPISTLE GENERAL OF PETER.

CHAPTER 1

PETER, an apostle of Jesus Christ, to the strangers scattered throughout Pontus, Galatia, Cappadocia, Asia, and Bithynia,

2 Elect according to the foreknowledge of God the Father, through sanctification of the Spirit, unto obedience and sprinkling of the blood of Jesus Christ: Grace unto you, and peace, be multiplied.

3 Blessed be the God and Father of our Lord Jesus Christ, which according to his abundant mercy has begotten us again unto a lively hope by the resurrection of Jesus Christ from the dead,

4 To an inheritance incorruptible, and undefiled, and that fadeth not away, reserved in heaven for you,

5 Who are kept by the power of God through faith unto salvation ready to be revealed in the last time.

6 Wherein you greatly rejoice, though now for a season, if need be, you are in heaviness through manifold temptations:

7 That the trial of your faith, being much more precious than of gold that perisheth, though it be tried with fire, might be found unto praise and honour and glory at the appearing of Jesus Christ:

8 Whom having not seen, you love; in whom, though now you see him not, yet believing, you rejoice with joy unspeakable and full of glory:

9 Receiving the end of your faith, even the salvation of your souls.

10 Of which salvation the prophets have inquired and searched diligently, who prophesied of the grace that should come unto you:

11 Searching what, or what manner of time the Spirit of Christ which was in them did signify, when it testified beforehand the sufferings of Christ, and the glory that should follow.

12 Unto whom it was revealed, that not unto themselves, but unto us they did minister the things, which are now reported unto you by them that have preached the gospel unto you with the Holy Ghost sent down from heaven; which things the angels desire to look into.

13 Wherefore gird up the loins of your mind, be sober, and hope to the end for the grace that is to be brought unto you at the revelation of Jesus Christ;

14 As obedient children, not fashioning yourselves according to the former lusts in your ignorance:

15 But as he which has called you is holy, so be you holy in all manner of conversation;

16 Because it is written, Be you holy; for I am holy.

17 And if you call on the Father, who without respect of persons judgeth according to every man's work, pass the time of your sojourning here in fear:

18 Forasmuch as you know that you were not redeemed with corruptible things, as silver and gold, from your vain conversation received by tradition from your fathers;

19 But with the precious blood of Christ, as of a lamb without blemish and without spot:

20 Who verily was foreordained before the foundation of the world, but was manifest in these last times for you,

21 Who by him do believe in God, that raised him up from the dead, and gave him glory; that your faith and hope might be in God.

22 Seeing you have purified your souls in obeying the truth through the Spirit unto unfeigned love of the brethren, see that you love one another with a pure heart fervently:

23 Being born again, not of corruptible seed, but of incorruptible, by the word of God, which liveth and abideth for ever.

24 For all flesh is as grass, and all the glory of man as the flower of grass. The grass withereth, and the flower thereof falleth away:

25 But the word of the Lord endureth for ever. And this is the word which by the gospel is preached unto you.

CHAPTER 2

WHEREFORE laying aside all malice, and all guile, and hypocrisies, and envies, and all evil speakings,

2 As newborn babes, desire the sincere milk of the word, that you may grow thereby:

3 If so be you have tasted that the Lord is gracious.

4 To whom coming, as unto a living stone, disallowed indeed of men, but chosen of God, and precious,

5 You also, as lively stones, are built up a spiritual house, an holy priesthood, to offer up spiritual sacrifices, acceptable to God by Jesus Christ.

6 Wherefore also it is contained in the scripture, Behold, I lay in Sion a chief corner stone, elect, precious: and he that believeth on him shall not be confounded.

7 Unto you therefore which believe he is precious: but unto them which be disobedient, the stone which the builders disallowed, the same is made the head of the corner,

8 And a stone of stumbling, and a rock of offence, even to them which stumble at the word, being disobedient: whereunto also they were appointed.

9 But you are a chosen generation, a royal priesthood, an holy nation, a peculiar people; that you should shew forth the praises of him who has called you out of darkness into his marvellous light:

10 Which in time past were not a people, but are now the people of God: which had not obtained mercy, but now have obtained mercy.

11 Dearly beloved, I beseech you as strangers and pilgrims, abstain from fleshly lusts, which war against the soul;

12 Having your conversation honest among the Gentiles: that, whereas they speak against you as evildoers, they may by your good works, which they shall behold, glorify God in the day of visitation.

13 Submit yourselves to every ordinance of man for the Lord's sake: whether it be to the king, as supreme;

14 Or unto governors, as unto them that are sent by him for the punishment of evildoers, and for the praise of them that do well.

15 For so is the will of God, that with well doing you may put to silence the ignorance of foolish men:

16 As free, and not using your liberty for a cloke of maliciousness, but as the servants of God.

17 Honour all men. Love the brotherhood. Fear God. Honour the king.

18 Servants, be subject to your masters with all fear; not only to the good and gentle, but also to the froward.

19 For this is thankworthy, if a man for conscience toward God endure grief, suffering wrongfully.

20 For what glory is it, if, when you be buffeted for your faults, you shall take it patiently? but if, when you do well, and suffer for it, you take it patiently, this is acceptable with God.

21 For even hereunto were you called: because Christ also suffered for us, leaving us an example, that you should follow his steps:

22 Who did no sin, neither was guile found in his mouth:

23 Who, when he was reviled, reviled not again; when he suffered, he threatened not; but committed himself to him that judgeth righteously:

24 Who his own self bare our sins in his own body on the tree, that we, being dead to sins, should live unto righteousness: by whose stripes you were healed.

25 For you were as sheep going astray; but are now returned unto the Shepherd and Bishop of your souls.

CHAPTER 3

LIKEWISE, you wives, be in subjection to your own husbands; that, if any obey not the word, they also may without the word be won by the conversation of the wives;

2 While they behold your chaste conversation coupled with fear.

3 Whose adorning let it not be that outward adorning of plaiting the hair, and of wearing of gold, or of putting on of apparel;

4 But let it be the hidden man of the heart, in that which is not corruptible, even the ornament of a meek and quiet spirit, which is in the sight of God of great price.

5 For after this manner in the old time the holy women also, who trusted in God, adorned themselves, being in subjection unto their own husbands:

6 Even as Sara obeyed Abraham, calling him lord: whose daughters you are, as long as you do well, and are not afraid with any amazement.

7 Likewise, you husbands, dwell with them according to knowledge, giving honour unto the wife, as unto the weaker vessel, and as being heirs together of the grace of life; that your prayers be not hindered.

8 Finally, be you all of one mind, having compassion one of another, love as brethren, be pitiful, be courteous:

9 Not rendering evil for evil, or railing for railing: but contrariwise blessing; knowing that you are thereunto called, that you should inherit a blessing.

10 For he that will love life, and see good days, let him refrain his tongue from evil, and his lips that they speak no guile:

11 Let him eschew evil, and do good; let him seek peace, and ensue it.

12 For the eyes of the Lord are over the righteous, and his ears are open unto their prayers: but the face of the Lord is against them that do evil.

13 And who is he that will harm you, if you be followers of that which is good?

14 But and if you suffer for righteousness' sake, happy are you : and be not afraid of their terror, neither be troubled;

15 But sanctify the Lord God in your hearts: and be ready always to give an answer to every man that asketh you a reason of the hope that is in you with meekness and fear:

16 Having a good conscience; that, whereas they speak evil of you, as of evildoers, they may be ashamed that falsely accuse your good conversation in Christ.

17 For it is better, if the will of God be so, that you suffer for well doing, than for evil doing.

18 For Christ also has once suffered for sins, the just for the unjust, that he might bring us to God, being put to death in the flesh, but quickened by the Spirit:

19 By which also he went and preached unto the spirits in prison;

20 Which sometime were disobedient, when once the longsuffering of God waited in the days of Noah, while the ark was a preparing, wherein few, that is, eight souls were saved by water.

21 The like figure whereunto even baptism doth also now save us (not the putting away of the filth of the flesh, but the answer of a good conscience toward God,) by the resurrection of Jesus Christ:

22 Who is gone into heaven, and is on the right hand of God; angels and authorities and powers being made subject unto him.

CHAPTER 4

FORASMUCH then as Christ has suffered for us in the flesh, arm yourselves likewise with the same mind: for he that has suffered in the flesh has ceased from sin;

2 That he no longer should live the rest of his time in the flesh to the lusts of men, but to the will of God.

3 For the time past of our life may suffice us to have created the will of the Gentiles, when we walked in lasciviousness, lusts, excess of wine, revellings, banquetings, and abominable idolatries:

4 Wherein they think it strange that you run not with them to the same excess of riot, speaking evil of you:

5 Who shall give account to him that is ready to judge the quick and the dead.

6 For for this cause was the gospel preached also to them that are dead, that they might be judged according to men in the flesh, but live according to God in the spirit.

7 But the end of all things is at hand: be you therefore sober, and watch unto prayer.

8 And above all things have fervent charity among yourselves: for charity shall cover the multitude of sins.

9 Use hospitality one to another without grudging.

10 As every man has received the gift, even so minister the same one to another, as good stewards of the manifold grace of God.

11 If any man speak, let him speak as the oracles of God; if any man minister, let him do it as of the ability which God giveth: that God in all things may be glorified through Jesus Christ, to whom be praise and dominion for ever and ever. Amen.

12 Beloved, think it not strange concerning the fiery trial which is to try you, as though some strange thing happened unto you:

13 But rejoice, inasmuch as you are partakers of Christ's sufferings; that, when his glory shall be revealed, you may be glad also with exceeding joy.

14 If you be reproached for the name of Christ, happy are you ; for the spirit of glory and of God resteth upon you: on their part he is evil spoken of, but on your part he is glorified.

15 But let none of you suffer as a murderer, or as a thief, or as an evildoer, or as a busybody in other men's matters.

16 Yet if any man suffer as a Christian, let him not be ashamed; but let him glorify God on this behalf.

17 For the time is come that judgment must begin at the house of God: and if it first begin at us, what shall the end be of them that obey not the gospel of God?

18 And if the righteous scarcely be saved, where shall the ungodly and the sinner appear?

19 Wherefore let them that suffer according to the will of God commit the keeping of their souls to him in well doing, as unto a faithful Creator.

CHAPTER 5

THE elders which are among you I exhort, who am also an elder, and a witness of the sufferings of Christ, and also a partaker of the glory that shall be revealed:

2 Feed the flock of God which is among you, taking the oversight thereof, not by constraint, but willingly; not for filthy lucre, but of a ready mind;

3 Neither as being lords over God's heritage, but being ensamples to the flock.

4 And when the chief Shepherd shall appear, you shall receive a crown of glory that fadeth not away.

5 Likewise, you younger, submit yourselves unto the elder. Yea, all of you be subject one to another, and be clothed with humility: for God resisteth the proud, and giveth grace to the humble.

6 Humble yourselves therefore under the mighty hand of God, that he may exalt you in due time:

7 Casting all your care upon him; for he careth for you.

8 Be sober, be vigilant; because your adversary the devil, as a roaring lion, walketh about, seeking whom he may devour:

9 Whom resist stedfast in the faith, knowing that the same afflictions are accomplished in your brethren that are in the world.

10 But the God of all grace, who has called us unto his eternal glory by Christ Jesus, after that you have suffered a while, make you perfect, stablish, strengthen, settle you.

11 To him be glory and dominion for ever and ever. Amen.

12 By Silvanus, a faithful brother unto you, as I suppose, I have written briefly, exhorting, and testifying that this is the true grace of God wherein you stand.

13 The church that is at Babylon, elected together with you, saluteth you; and so doth Marcus my son.

14 Greet you one another with a kiss of charity. Peace be with you all that are in Christ Jesus. Amen.

THE SECOND EPISTLE GENERAL OF PETER.

CHAPTER 1

SIMON Peter, a servant and an apostle of Jesus Christ, to them that have obtained like precious faith with us through the righteousness of God and our Saviour Jesus Christ:

2 Grace and peace be multiplied unto you through the knowledge of God, and of Jesus our Lord,

3 According as his divine power has given unto us all things that pertain unto life and godliness, through the knowledge of him that has called us to glory and virtue:

4 Whereby are given unto us exceeding great and precious promises: that by these you might be partakers of the divine nature, having escaped the corruption that is in the world through lust.

5 And beside this, giving all diligence, add to your faith virtue; and to virtue knowledge;

6 And to knowledge temperance; and to temperance patience; and to patience godliness;

7 And to godliness brotherly kindness; and to brotherly kindness charity.

8 For if these things be in you, and abound, they make you that you shall neither be barren nor unfruitful in the knowledge of our Lord Jesus Christ.

9 But he that lacketh these things is blind, and cannot see afar off, and has forgotten that he was purged from his old sins.

10 Wherefore the rather, brethren, give diligence to make your calling and election sure: for if you do these things, you shall never fall:

11 For so an entrance shall be ministered unto you abundantly into the everlasting kingdom of our Lord and Saviour Jesus Christ.

12 Wherefore I will not be negligent to put you always in remembrance of these things, though you know them, and be established in the present truth.

13 Yea, I think it meet, as long as I am in this tabernacle, to stir you up by putting you in remembrance;

14 Knowing that shortly I must put off this my tabernacle, even as our Lord Jesus Christ has shewed me.

15 Moreover I will endeavour that you may be able after my decease to have these things always in remembrance.

16 For we have not followed cunningly devised fables, when we made known unto you the power and coming of our Lord Jesus Christ, but were eyewitnesses of his majesty.

17 For he received from God the Father honour and glory, when there came such a voice to him from the excellent glory, This is my beloved Son, in whom I am well pleased.

18 And this voice which came from heaven we heard, when we were with him in the holy mount.

19 We have also a more sure word of prophecy; whereunto you do well that you take heed, as unto a light that shineth in a dark place, until the day dawn, and the day star arise in your hearts:

20 Knowing this first, that no prophecy of the scripture is of any private interpretation.

21 For the prophecy came not in old time by the will of man: but holy men of God spake as they were moved by the Holy Ghost.

CHAPTER 2

BUT there were false prophets also among the people, even as there shall be false teachers among you, who privily shall bring in damnable heresies, even denying the Lord that bought them, and bring upon themselves swift destruction.

2 And many shall follow their pernicious ways; by reason of whom the way of truth shall be evil spoken of.

3 And through covetousness shall they with feigned words make merchandise of you: whose judgment now of a long time lingereth not, and their damnation slumbereth not.

4 For if God spared not the angels that sinned, but cast them down to hell, and delivered them into chains of darkness, to be reserved unto judgment;

5 And spared not the old world, but saved Noah the eighth person, a preacher of righteousness, bringing in the flood upon the world of the ungodly;

6 And turning the cities of Sodom and Gomorrha into ashes condemned them with an overthrow, making them an ensample unto those that after should live ungodly;

7 And delivered just Lot, vexed with the filthy conversation of the wicked:

8 (For that righteous man dwelling among them, in seeing and hearing, vexed his righteous soul from day to day with their unlawful deeds;)

9 The Lord knoweth how to deliver the godly out of temptations, and to reserve the unjust unto the day of judgment to be punished:

10 But chiefly them that walk after the flesh in the lust of uncleanness, and despise government. Presumptuous are they, selfwilled, they are not afraid to speak evil of dignities.

11 Whereas angels, which are greater in power and might, bring not railing accusation against them before the Lord.

12 But these, as natural brute beasts, made to be taken and destroyed, speak evil of the things that they understand not; and shall utterly perish in their own corruption;

13 And shall receive the reward of unrighteousness, as they that count it pleasure to riot in the day time. Spots they are and blemishes, sporting themselves with their own deceivings while they feast with you;

14 Having eyes full of adultery, and that cannot cease from sin; beguiling unstable souls: an heart they have exercised with covetous practices; cursed children:

15 Which have forsaken the right way, and are gone astray, following the way of Balaam the son of Bosor, who loved the wages of unrighteousness;

16 But was rebuked for his iniquity: the dumb ass speaking with man's voice forbad the madness of the prophet.

17 These are wells without water, clouds that are carried with a tempest; to whom the mist of darkness is reserved for ever.

18 For when they speak great swelling words of vanity, they allure through the lusts of the flesh, through much wantonness, those that were clean escaped from them who live in error.

19 While they promise them liberty, they themselves are the servants of corruption: for of whom a man is overcome, of the same is he brought in bondage.

20 For if after they have escaped the pollutions of the world through the knowledge of the Lord and Saviour Jesus Christ, they are again entangled therein, and overcome, the latter end is worse with them than the beginning.

21 For it had been better for them not to have known the way of righteousness, than, after they have known it, to turn from the holy commandment delivered unto them.

22 But it is happened unto them according to the true proverb, The dog is turned to his own vomit again; and the sow that was washed to her wallowing in the mire.

CHAPTER 3

THIS second epistle, beloved, I now write unto you; in both which I stir up your pure minds by way of remembrance:

2 That you may be mindful of the words which were spoken before by the holy prophets, and of the commandment of us the apostles of the Lord and Saviour:

3 Knowing this first, that there shall come in the last days scoffers, walking after their own lusts,

4 And saying, Where is the promise of his coming? for since the fathers fell asleep, all things continue as they were from the beginning of the creation.

5 For this they willingly are ignorant of, that by the word of God the heavens were of old, and the earth standing out of the water and in the water:

6 Whereby the world that then was, being overflowed with water, perished:

7 But the heavens and the earth, which are now, by the same word are kept in store, reserved unto fire against the day of judgment and perdition of ungodly men.

8 But, beloved, be not ignorant of this one thing, that one day is with the Lord as a thousand years, and a thousand years as one day.

9 The Lord is not slack concerning his promise, as some men count slackness; but is longsuffering to us-ward, not willing that any should perish, but that all should come to repentance.

10 But the day of the Lord will come as a thief in the night; in the which the heavens shall pass away with a great noise, and the elements shall melt with fervent heat, the earth also and the works that are therein shall be burned up.

11 Seeing then that all these things shall be dissolved, what manner of persons ought you to be in all holy conversation and godliness,

12 Looking for and hasting unto the coming of the day of God, wherein the heavens being on fire shall be dissolved, and the elements shall melt with fervent heat?

13 Nevertheless we, according to his promise, look for new heavens and a new earth, wherein dwelleth righteousness.

14 Wherefore, beloved, seeing that you look for such things, be diligent that you may be found of him in peace, without spot, and blameless.

15 And account that the longsuffering of our Lord is salvation; even as our beloved brother Paul also according to the wisdom given unto him has written unto you;

16 As also in all his epistles, speaking in them of these things; in which are some things hard to be understood, which they that are unlearned and unstable wrest, as they do also the other scriptures, unto their own destruction.

17 You therefore, beloved, seeing you know these things before, beware lest you also, being led away with the error of the wicked, fall from your own stedfastness.

18 But grow in grace, and in the knowledge of our Lord and Saviour Jesus Christ. To him be glory both now and for ever. Amen.

THE FIRST EPISTLE GENERAL OF JOHN.

CHAPTER 1

THAT which was from the beginning, which we have heard, which we have seen with our eyes, which we have looked upon, and our hands have handled, of the Word of life;

2 (For the life was manifested, and we have seen it, and bear witness, and shew unto you that eternal life, which was with the Father, and was manifested unto us;)

3 That which we have seen and heard declare we unto you, that you also may have fellowship with us: and truly our fellowship is with the Father, and with his Son Jesus Christ.

4 And these things write we unto you, that your joy may be full.

5 This then is the message which we have heard of him, and declare unto you, that God is light, and in him is no darkness at all.

6 If we say that we have fellowship with him, and walk in darkness, we lie, and do not the truth:

7 But if we walk in the light, as he is in the light, we have fellowship one with another, and the blood of Jesus Christ his Son cleanseth us from all sin.

8 If we say that we have no sin, we deceive ourselves, and the truth is not in us.

9 If we confess our sins, he is faithful and just to forgive us our sins, and to cleanse us from all unrighteousness.

10 If we say that we have not sinned, we make him a liar, and his word is not in us.

CHAPTER 2

MY little children, these things write I unto you, that you sin not. And if any man sin, we have an advocate with the Father, Jesus Christ the righteous:

2 And he is the propitiation for our sins: and not for ours only, but also for the sins of the whole world.

3 And hereby we do know that we know him, if we keep his commandments.

4 He that saith, I know him, and keepeth not his commandments, is a liar, and the truth is not in him.

5 But whoso keepeth his word, in him verily is the love of God perfected: hereby know we that we are in him.

6 He that saith he abideth in him ought himself also so to walk, even as he walked.

7 Brethren, I write no new commandment unto you, but an old commandment which you had from the beginning. The old commandment is the word which you have heard from the beginning.

8 Again, a new commandment I write unto you, which thing is true in him and in you: because the darkness is past, and the true light now shineth.

9 He that saith he is in the light, and hateth his brother, is in darkness even until now.

10 He that loveth his brother abideth in the light, and there is none occasion of stumbling in him.

11 But he that hateth his brother is in darkness, and walketh in darkness, and knoweth not whither he goeth, because that darkness has blinded his eyes.

12 I write unto you, little children, because your sins are forgiven you for his name's sake.

13 I write unto you, fathers, because you have known him that is from the beginning. I write unto you, young men, because you have overcome the wicked one. I write unto you, little children, because you have known the Father.

14 I have written unto you, fathers, because you have known him that is from the beginning. I have written unto you, young men, because you are strong, and the word of God abideth in you, and you have overcome the wicked one.

15 Love not the world, neither the things that are in the world. If any man love the world, the love of the Father is not in him.

16 For all that is in the world, the lust of the flesh, and the lust of the eyes, and the pride of life, is not of the Father, but is of the world.

17 And the world passes away, and the lust thereof: but he that doeth the will of God abideth for ever.

18 Little children, it is the last time: and as you have heard that antichrist shall come, even now are there many antichrists; whereby we know that it is the last time.

19 They went out from us, but they were not of us; for if they had been of us, they would no doubt have continued with us: but they went out, that they might be made manifest that they were not all of us.

20 But you have an unction from the Holy One, and you know all things.

21 I have not written unto you because you know not the truth, but because you know it, and that no lie is of the truth.

22 Who is a liar but he that denieth that Jesus is the Christ? He is antichrist, that denieth the Father and the Son.

23 Whosoever denieth the Son, the same has not the Father: [but] he that acknowledgeth the Son has the Father also.

24 Let that therefore abide in you, which you have heard from the beginning. If that which you have heard from the beginning shall remain in you, you also shall continue in the Son, and in the Father.

25 And this is the promise that he has promised us, even eternal life.

26 These things have I written unto you concerning them that seduce you.

27 But the anointing which you have received of him abideth in you, and you need not that any man teach you: but as the same anointing teacheth you of all things, and is truth, and is no lie, and even as it has taught you, you shall abide in him.

28 And now, little children, abide in him; that, when he shall appear, we may have confidence, and not be ashamed before him at his coming.

29 If you know that he is righteous, you know that every one that doeth righteousness is born of him.

CHAPTER 3

BEHOLD, what manner of love the Father has bestowed upon us, that we should be called the sons of God: therefore the world knoweth us not, because it knew him not.

2 Beloved, now are we the sons of God, and it doth not yet appear what we shall be: but we know that, when he shall appear, we shall be like him; for we shall see him as he is.

3 And every man that has this hope in him purifieth himself, even as he is pure.

4 Whosoever committeth sin transgresseth also the law: for sin is the transgression of the law.

5 And you know that he was manifested to take away our sins; and in him is no sin.

6 Whosoever abideth in him sinneth not: whosoever sinneth has not seen him, neither known him.

7 Little children, let no man deceive you: he that doeth righteousness is righteous, even as he is righteous.

8 He that committeth sin is of the devil; for the devil sinneth from the beginning. For this purpose the Son of God was manifested, that he might destroy the works of the devil.

9 Whosoever is born of God doth not commit sin; for his seed remaineth in him: and he cannot sin, because he is born of God.

10 In this the children of God are manifest, and the children of the devil: whosoever doeth not righteousness is not of God, neither he that loveth not his brother.

11 For this is the message that you heard from the beginning, that we should love one another.

12 Not as Cain, who was of that wicked one, and slew his brother. And wherefore slew he him? Because his own works were evil, and his brother's righteous.

13 Marvel not, my brethren, if the world hate you.

14 We know that we have passed from death unto life, because we love the brethren. He that loveth not his brother abideth in death.

15 Whosoever hateth his brother is a murderer: and you know that no murderer has eternal life abiding in him.

16 Hereby perceive we the love of God, because he laid down his life for us: and we ought to lay down our lives for the brethren.

17 But whoso has this world's good, and seeth his brother have need, and shutteth up his bowels of compassion from him, how dwelleth the love of God in him?

18 My little children, let us not love in word, neither in tongue; but in deed and in truth.

19 And hereby we know that we are of the truth, and shall assure our hearts before him.

20 For if our heart condemn us, God is greater than our heart, and knoweth all things.

21 Beloved, if our heart condemn us not, then have we confidence toward God.

22 And whatsoever we ask, we receive of him, because we keep his commandments, and do those things that are pleasing in his sight.

23 And this is his commandment, That we should believe on the name of his Son Jesus Christ, and love one another, as he gave us commandment.

24 And he that keepeth his commandments dwelleth in him, and he in him. And hereby we know that he abideth in us, by the Spirit which he has given us.

CHAPTER 4

BELOVED, believe not every spirit, but try the spirits whether they are of God: because many false prophets are gone out into the world.

2 Hereby know you the Spirit of God: Every spirit that confesseth that Jesus Christ is come in the flesh is of God:

3 And every spirit that confesseth not that Jesus Christ is come in the flesh is not of God: and this is that spirit of antichrist, whereof you have heard that it should come; and even now already is it in the world.

4 You are of God, little children, and have overcome them: because greater is he that is in you, than he that is in the world.

5 They are of the world: therefore speak they of the world, and the world heareth them.

6 We are of God: he that knoweth God heareth us; he that is not of God heareth not us. Hereby know we the spirit of truth, and the spirit of error.

7 Beloved, let us love one another: for love is of God; and every one that loveth is born of God, and knoweth God.

8 He that loveth not knoweth not God; for God is love.

9 In this was manifested the love of God toward us, because that God sent his only begotten Son into the world, that we might live through him.

10 Herein is love, not that we loved God, but that he loved us, and sent his Son to be the propitiation for our sins.

11 Beloved, if God so loved us, we ought also to love one another.

12 No man has seen God at any time. If we love one another, God dwelleth in us, and his love is perfected in us.

13 Hereby know we that we dwell in him, and he in us, because he has given us of his Spirit.

14 And we have seen and do testify that the Father sent the Son to be the Saviour of the world.

15 Whosoever shall confess that Jesus is the Son of God, God dwelleth in him, and he in God.

16 And we have known and believed the love that God has to us. God is love; and he that dwelleth in love dwelleth in God, and God in him.

17 Herein is our love made perfect, that we may have boldness in the day of judgment: because as he is, so are we in this world.

18 There is no fear in love; but perfect love casteth out fear: because fear has torment. He that feareth is not made perfect in love.

19 We love him, because he first loved us.

20 If a man say, I love God, and hateth his brother, he is a liar: for he that loveth not his brother whom he has seen, how can he love God whom he has not seen?

21 And this commandment have we from him, That he who loveth God love his brother also.

CHAPTER 5

WHOSOEVER believeth that Jesus is the Christ is born of God: and every one that loveth him that begat loveth him also that is begotten of him.

2 By this we know that we love the children of God, when we love God, and keep his commandments.

3 For this is the love of God, that we keep his commandments: and his commandments are not grievous.

4 For whatsoever is born of God overcometh the world: and this is the victory that overcometh the world, even our faith.

5 Who is he that overcometh the world, but he that believeth that Jesus is the Son of God?

6 This is he that came by water and blood, even Jesus Christ; not by water only, but by water and blood. And it is the Spirit that beareth witness, because the Spirit is truth.

7 For there are three that bear record in heaven, the Father, the Word, and the Holy Ghost: and these three are one.

8 And there are three that bear witness in earth, the spirit, and the water, and the blood: and these three agree in one.

9 If we receive the witness of men, the witness of God is greater: for this is the witness of God which he has testified of his Son.

10 He that believeth on the Son of God has the witness in himself: he that believeth not God has made him a liar; because he believeth not the record that God gave of his Son.

11 And this is the record, that God has given to us eternal life, and this life is in his Son.

12 He that has the Son has life; and he that has not the Son of God has not life.

13 These things have I written unto you that believe on the name of the Son of God; that you may know that you have eternal life, and that you may believe on the name of the Son of God.

14 And this is the confidence that we have in him, that, if we ask any thing according to his will, he heareth us:

15 And if we know that he hear us, whatsoever we ask, we know that we have the petitions that we desired of him.

16 If any man see his brother sin a sin which is not unto death, he shall ask, and he shall give him life for them that sin not unto death. There is a sin unto death: I do not say that he shall pray for it.

17 All unrighteousness is sin: and there is a sin not unto death.

18 We know that whosoever is born of God sinneth not; but he that is begotten of God keepeth himself, and that wicked one toucheth him not.

19 And we know that we are of God, and the whole world lies in wickedness.

20 And we know that the Son of God is come, and has given us an understanding, that we may know him that is true, and we are in him that is true, even in his Son Jesus Christ. This is the true God, and eternal life.

21 Little children, keep yourselves from idols. Amen.

THE SECOND EPISTLE OF JOHN.

CHAPTER 1

THE elder unto the elect lady and her children, whom I love in the truth; and not I only, but also all they that have known the truth;

2 For the truth's sake, which dwelleth in us, and shall be with us for ever.

3 Grace be with you, mercy, and peace, from God the Father, and from the Lord Jesus Christ, the Son of the Father, in truth and love.

4 I rejoiced greatly that I found of your children walking in truth, as we have received a commandment from the Father.

5 And now I beseech you, lady, not as though I wrote a new commandment unto you, but that which we had from the beginning, that we love one another.

6 And this is love, that we walk after his commandments. This is the commandment, That, as you have heard from the beginning, you should walk in it.

7 For many deceivers are entered into the world, who confess not that Jesus Christ is come in the flesh. This is a deceiver and an antichrist.

8 Look to yourselves, that we lose not those things which we have created, but that we receive a full reward.

9 Whosoever transgresseth, and abideth not in the doctrine of Christ, has not God. He that abideth in the doctrine of Christ, he has both the Father and the Son.

10 If there come any unto you, and bring not this doctrine, receive him not into your house, neither bid him God speed:

11 For he that biddeth him God speed is partaker of his evil deeds.

12 Having many things to write unto you, I would not write with paper and ink: but I trust to come unto you, and speak face to face, that our joy may be full.

13 The children of your elect sister greet you. Amen.

THE THIRD EPISTLE OF JOHN.

CHAPTER 1

THE elder unto the wellbeloved Gaius, whom I love in the truth.

2 Beloved, I wish above all things that you mayest prosper and be in health, even as your soul prospereth.

3 For I rejoiced greatly, when the brethren came and testified of the truth that is in you, even as you walkest in the truth.

4 I have no greater joy than to hear that my children walk in truth.

5 Beloved, you doest faithfully whatsoever you doest to the brethren, and to strangers;

6 Which have borne witness of your charity before the church: whom if you bring forward on their journey after a godly sort, you shalt do well:

7 Because that for his name's sake they went forth, taking nothing of the Gentiles.

8 We therefore ought to receive such, that we might be fellowhelpers to the truth.

9 I wrote unto the church: but Diotrephes, who loveth to have the preeminence among them, receiveth us not.

10 Wherefore, if I come, I will remember his deeds which he doeth, prating against us with malicious words: and not content therewith, neither doth he himself receive the brethren, and forbiddeth them that would, and casteth them out of the church.

11 Beloved, follow not that which is evil, but that which is good. He that doeth good is of God: but he that doeth evil has not seen God.

12 Demetrius has good report of all men, and of the truth itself: yea, and we also bear record; and you know that our record is true.

13 I had many things to write, but I will not with ink and pen write unto you:

14 But I trust I shall shortly see you, and we shall speak face to face. Peace be to you. Our friends salute you. Greet the friends by name.

THE GENERAL EPISTLE OF JUDE.

CHAPTER 1

JUDE, the servant of Jesus Christ, and brother of James, to them that are sanctified by God the Father, and preserved in Jesus Christ, and called:

2 Mercy unto you, and peace, and love, be multiplied.

3 Beloved, when I gave all diligence to write unto you of the common salvation, it was needful for me to write unto you, and exhort you that you should earnestly contend for the faith which was once delivered unto the saints.

4 For there are certain men crept in unawares, who were before of old ordained to this condemnation, ungodly men, turning the grace of our God into lasciviousness, and denying the only Lord God, and our Lord Jesus Christ.

5 I will therefore put you in remembrance, though you once knew this, how that the Lord, having saved the people out of the land of Egypt, afterward destroyed them that believed not.

6 And the angels which kept not their first estate, but left their own habitation, he has reserved in everlasting chains under darkness unto the judgment of the great day.

7 Even as Sodom and Gomorrha, and the cities about them in like manner, giving themselves over to fornication, and going after strange flesh, are set forth for an example, suffering the vengeance of eternal fire.

8 Likewise also these filthy dreamers defile the flesh, despise dominion, and speak evil of dignities.

9 Yet Michael the archangel, when contending with the devil he disputed about the body of Moses, durst not bring against him a railing accusation, but said, The Lord rebuke you.

10 But these speak evil of those things which they know not: but what they know naturally, as brute beasts, in those things they corrupt themselves.

11 Woe unto them! for they have gone in the way of Cain, and ran greedily after the error of Balaam for reward, and perished in the gainsaying of Core.

12 These are spots in your feasts of charity, when they feast with you, feeding themselves without fear: clouds they are without water, carried about of winds; trees whose fruit withereth, without fruit, twice dead, plucked up by the roots;

13 Raging waves of the sea, foaming out their own shame; wandering stars, to whom is reserved the blackness of darkness for ever.

14 And Enoch also, the seventh from Adam, prophesied of these, saying, Behold, the Lord comes with ten thousands of his saints,

15 To execute judgment upon all, and to convince all that are ungodly among them of all their ungodly deeds which they have ungodly committed, and of all their hard speeches which ungodly sinners have spoken against him.

16 These are murmurers, complainers, walking after their own lusts; and their mouth speaketh great swelling words, having men's persons in admiration because of advantage.

17 But, beloved, remember you the words which were spoken before of the apostles of our Lord Jesus Christ;

18 How that they told you there should be mockers in the last time, who should walk after their own ungodly lusts.

19 These be they who separate themselves, sensual, having not the Spirit.

20 But you , beloved, building up yourselves on your most holy faith, praying in the Holy Ghost,

21 Keep yourselves in the love of God, looking for the mercy of our Lord Jesus Christ unto eternal life.

22 And of some have compassion, making a difference:

23 And others save with fear, pulling them out of the fire; hating even the garment spotted by the flesh.

24 Now unto him that is able to keep you from falling, and to present you faultless before the presence of his glory with exceeding joy,

25 To the only wise God our Saviour, be glory and majesty, dominion and power, both now and ever. Amen.

THE REVELATION
OF
ST. JOHN THE DIVINE.

CHAPTER 1

THE Revelation of Jesus Christ, which God gave unto him, to shew unto his servants things which must shortly come to pass; and he sent and signified it by his angel unto his servant John:

2 Who bare record of the word of God, and of the testimony of Jesus Christ, and of all things that he saw.

3 Blessed is he that readeth, and they that hear the words of this prophecy, and keep those things which are written therein: for the time is at hand.

4 JOHN to the seven churches which are in Asia: Grace be unto you, and peace, from him which is, and which was, and which is to come; and from the seven Spirits which are before his throne;

5 And from Jesus Christ, who is the faithful witness, and the first begotten of the dead, and the prince of the kings of the earth. Unto him that loved us, and washed us from our sins in his own blood,

6 And has made us kings and priests unto God and his Father; to him be glory and dominion for ever and ever. Amen.

7 Behold, he comes with clouds; and every eye shall see him, and they also which pierced him: and all kindreds of the earth shall wail because of him. Even so, Amen.

8 I am Alpha and Omega, the beginning and the ending, saith the Lord, which is, and which was, and which is to come, the Almighty.

9 I John, who also am your brother, and companion in tribulation, and in the kingdom and patience of Jesus Christ, was in the isle that is called Patmos, for the word of God, and for the testimony of Jesus Christ.

10 I was in the Spirit on the Lord's day, and heard behind me a great voice, as of a trumpet,

11 Saying, I am Alpha and Omega, the first and the last: and, What you seest, write in a book, and send it unto the seven churches which are in Asia; unto Ephesus, and unto Smyrna, and unto Pergamos, and unto Thyatira, and unto Sardis, and unto Philadelphia, and unto Laodicea.

12 And I turned to see the voice that spake with me. And being turned, I saw seven golden candlesticks;

13 And in the midst of the seven candlesticks one like unto the Son of man, clothed with a garment down to the foot, and girt about the paps with a golden girdle.

14 His head and his hairs were white like wool, as white as snow; and his eyes were as a flame of fire;

15 And his feet like unto fine brass, as if they burned in a furnace; and his voice as the sound of many waters.

16 And he had in his right hand seven stars: and out of his mouth went a sharp twoedged sword: and his countenance was as the sun shineth in his strength.

17 And when I saw him, I fell at his feet as dead. And he laid his right hand upon me, saying unto me, Fear not; I am the first and the last:

18 I am he that liveth, and was dead; and, behold, I am alive for evermore, Amen; and have the keys of hell and of death.

19 Write the things which you have seen, and the things which are, and the things which shall be hereafter;

20 The mystery of the seven stars which you sawest in my right hand, and the seven golden candlesticks. The seven stars are the angels of the seven churches: and the seven candlesticks which you sawest are the seven churches.

CHAPTER 2

UNTO the angel of the church of Ephesus write; These things saith he that holdeth the seven stars in his right hand, who walketh in the midst of the seven golden candlesticks;

2 I know your works, and your labour, and your patience, and how you can not bear them which are evil: and you have tried them which say they are apostles, and are not, and have found them liars:

3 And have borne, and have patience, and for my name's sake have laboured, and have not fainted.

4 Nevertheless I have somewhat against you, because you have left your first love.

5 Remember therefore from whence you are fallen, and repent, and do the first works; or else I will come unto you quickly, and will remove your candlestick out of his place, except you repent.

6 But this you have, that you hatest the deeds of the Nicolaitans, which I also hate.

7 He that has an ear, let him hear what the Spirit saith unto the churches; To him that overcometh will I give to eat of the tree of life, which is in the midst of the paradise of God.

8 And unto the angel of the church in Smyrna write; These things saith the first and the last, which was dead, and is alive;

9 I know your works, and tribulation, and poverty, (but you are rich) and I know the blasphemy of them which say they are Jews, and are not, but are the synagogue of Satan.

10 Fear none of those things which you shalt suffer: behold, the devil shall cast some of you into prison, that you may be tried; and you shall have tribulation ten days: be you faithful unto death, and I will give you a crown of life.

11 He that has an ear, let him hear what the Spirit saith unto the churches; He that overcometh shall not be hurt of the second death.

12 And to the angel of the church in Pergamos write; These things saith he which has the sharp sword with two edges;

13 I know your works, and where you dwellest, even where Satan's seat is: and you holdest fast my name, and have not denied my faith, even in those days wherein Antipas was my faithful martyr, who was slain among you, where Satan dwelleth.

14 But I have a few things against you, because you have there them that hold the doctrine of Balaam, who taught Balac to cast a stumblingblock before the children of Israel, to eat things sacrificed unto idols, and to commit fornication.

15 So have you also them that hold the doctrine of the Nicolaitans, which thing I hate.

16 Repent; or else I will come unto you quickly, and will fight against them with the sword of my mouth.

17 He that has an ear, let him hear what the Spirit saith unto the churches; To him that overcometh will I give to eat of the hidden manna, and will give him a white stone, and in the stone a new name written, which no man knoweth saving he that receiveth it.

18 And unto the angel of the church in Thyatira write; These things saith the Son of God, who has his eyes like unto a flame of fire, and his feet are like fine brass;

19 I know your works, and charity, and service, and faith, and your patience, and your works; and the last to be more than the first.

20 Notwithstanding I have a few things against you, because you sufferest that woman Jezebel, which calleth herself a prophetess, to teach and to seduce my servants to commit fornication, and to eat things sacrificed unto idols.

21 And I gave her space to repent of her fornication; and she repented not.

22 Behold, I will cast her into a bed, and them that commit adultery with her into great tribulation, except they repent of their deeds.

23 And I will kill her children with death; and all the churches shall know that I am he which searches the reins and hearts: and I will give unto every one of you according to your works.

24 But unto you I say, and unto the rest in Thyatira, as many as have not this doctrine, and which have not known the depths of Satan, as they speak; I will put upon you none other burden.

25 But that which you have already hold fast till I come.

26 And he that overcometh, and keepeth my works unto the end, to him will I give power over the nations:

27 And he shall rule them with a rod of iron; as the vessels of a potter shall they be broken to shivers: even as I received of my Father.

28 And I will give him the morning star.

29 He that has an ear, let him hear what the Spirit saith unto the churches.

CHAPTER 3

AND unto the angel of the church in Sardis write; These things saith he that has the seven Spirits of God, and the seven stars; I know your works, that you have a name that you livest, and are dead.

2 Be watchful, and strengthen the things which remain, that are ready to die: for I have not found your works perfect before God.

3 Remember therefore how you have received and heard, and hold fast, and repent. If therefore you shalt not watch, I will come on you as a thief, and you shalt not know what hour I will come upon you.

4 You have a few names even in Sardis which have not defiled their garments; and they shall walk with me in white: for they are worthy.

5 He that overcometh, the same shall be clothed in white raiment; and I will not blot out his name out of the book of life, but I will confess his name before my Father, and before his angels.

6 He that has an ear, let him hear what the Spirit saith unto the churches.

7 And to the angel of the church in Philadelphia write; These things saith he that is holy, he that is true, he that has the key of David, he that openeth, and no man shutteth; and shutteth, and no man openeth;

8 I know your works: behold, I have set before you an open door, and no man can shut it: for you have a little strength, and have kept my word, and have not denied my name.

9 Behold, I will make them of the synagogue of Satan, which say they are Jews, and are not, but do lie; behold, I will make them to come and worship before your feet, and to know that I have loved you.

10 Because you have kept the word of my patience, I also will keep you from the hour of temptation, which shall come upon all the world, to try them that dwell upon the earth.

11 Behold, I come quickly: hold that fast which you have, that no man take your crown.

12 Him that overcometh will I make a pillar in the temple of my God, and he shall go no more out: and I will write upon him the name of my God, and the name of the city of my God, which is new Jerusalem, which comes down out of heaven from my God: and I will write upon him my new name.

13 He that has an ear, let him hear what the Spirit saith unto the churches.

14 And unto the angel of the church of the Laodiceans write; These things saith the Amen, the faithful and true witness, the beginning of the creation of God;

15 I know your works, that you are neither cold nor hot: I would you wert cold or hot.

16 So then because you are lukewarm, and neither cold nor hot, I will spue you out of my mouth.

17 Because you say, I am rich, and increased with goods, and have need of nothing; and knowest not that you are wretched, and miserable, and poor, and blind, and naked:

18 I counsel you to buy of me gold tried in the fire, that you mayest be rich; and white raiment, that you mayest be clothed, and that the shame of your nakedness do not appear; and anoint yours eyes with eyesalve, that you mayest see.

19 As many as I love, I rebuke and chasten: be zealous therefore, and repent.

20 Behold, I stand at the door, and knock: if any man hear my voice, and open the door, I will come in to him, and will sup with him, and he with me.

21 To him that overcometh will I grant to sit with me in my throne, even as I also overcame, and am set down with my Father in his throne.

22 He that has an ear, let him hear what the Spirit saith unto the churches.

CHAPTER 4

AFTER this I looked, and, behold, a door was opened in heaven: and the first voice which I heard was as it were of a trumpet talking with me; which said, Come up hither, and I will shew you things which must be hereafter.

2 And immediately I was in the spirit: and, behold, a throne was set in heaven, and one sat on the throne.

3 And he that sat was to look upon like a jasper and a sardine stone: and there was a rainbow round about the throne, in sight like unto an emerald.

4 And round about the throne were four and twenty seats: and upon the seats I saw four and twenty elders sitting, clothed in white raiment; and they had on their heads crowns of gold.

5 And out of the throne proceeded lightnings and thunderings and voices: and there were seven lamps of fire burning before the throne, which are the seven Spirits of God.

6 And before the throne there was a sea of glass like unto crystal: and in the midst of the throne, and round about the throne, were four beasts full of eyes before and behind.

7 And the first beast was like a lion, and the second beast like a calf, and the third beast had a face as a man, and the fourth beast was like a flying eagle.

8 And the four beasts had each of them six wings about him; and they were full of eyes within: and they rest not day and night, saying, Holy, holy, holy, Lord God Almighty, which was, and is, and is to come.

9 And when those beasts give glory and honour and thanks to him that sat on the throne, who liveth for ever and ever,

10 The four and twenty elders fall down before him that sat on the throne, and worship him that liveth for ever and ever, and cast their crowns before the throne, saying,

11 You are worthy, O Lord, to receive glory and honour and power: for you have created all things, and for your pleasure they are and were created.

CHAPTER 5

AND I saw in the right hand of him that sat on the throne a book written within and on the backside, sealed with seven seals.

2 And I saw a strong angel proclaiming with a loud voice, Who is worthy to open the book, and to loose the seals thereof?

3 And no man in heaven, nor in earth, neither under the earth, was able to open the book, neither to look thereon.

4 And I wept much, because no man was found worthy to open and to read the book, neither to look thereon.

5 And one of the elders saith unto me, Weep not: behold, the Lion of the tribe of Juda, the Root of David, has prevailed to open the book, and to loose the seven seals thereof.

6 And I beheld, and, lo, in the midst of the throne and of the four beasts, and in the midst of the elders, stood a Lamb as it had been slain, having seven horns and seven eyes, which are the seven Spirits of God sent forth into all the earth.

7 And he came and took the book out of the right hand of him that sat upon the throne.

8 And when he had taken the book, the four beasts and four and twenty elders fell down before the Lamb, having every one of them harps, and golden vials full of odours, which are the prayers of saints.

9 And they sung a new song, saying, You are worthy to take the book, and to open the seals thereof: for you wast slain, and have redeemed us to God by your blood out of every kindred, and tongue, and people, and nation;

10 And have made us unto our God kings and priests: and we shall reign on the earth.

11 And I beheld, and I heard the voice of many angels round about the throne and the beasts and the elders: and the number of them was ten thousand times ten thousand, and thousands of thousands;

12 Saying with a loud voice, Worthy is the Lamb that was slain to receive power, and riches, and wisdom, and strength, and honour, and glory, and blessing.

13 And every creature which is in heaven, and on the earth, and under the earth, and such as are in the sea, and all that are in them, heard I saying, Blessing, and honour, and glory, and power, be unto him that sitteth upon the throne, and unto the Lamb for ever and ever.

14 And the four beasts said, Amen. And the four and twenty elders fell down and worshipped him that liveth for ever and ever.

CHAPTER 6

AND I saw when the Lamb opened one of the seals, and I heard, as it were the noise of thunder, one of the four beasts saying, Come and see.

2 And I saw, and behold a white horse: and he that sat on him had a bow; and a crown was given unto him: and he went forth conquering, and to conquer.

3 And when he had opened the second seal, I heard the second beast say, Come and see.

4 And there went out another horse that was red: and power was given to him that sat thereon to take peace from the earth, and that they should kill one another: and there was given unto him a great sword.

5 And when he had opened the third seal, I heard the third beast say, Come and see. And I beheld, and lo a black horse; and he that sat on him had a pair of balances in his hand.

6 And I heard a voice in the midst of the four beasts say, A measure of wheat for a penny, and three measures of barley for a penny; and see you hurt not the oil and the wine.

7 And when he had opened the fourth seal, I heard the voice of the fourth beast say, Come and see.

8 And I looked, and behold a pale horse: and his name that sat on him was Death, and Hell followed with him. And power was given unto them over the fourth part of the earth, to kill with sword, and with hunger, and with death, and with the beasts of the earth.

9 And when he had opened the fifth seal, I saw under the altar the souls of them that were slain for the word of God, and for the testimony which they held:

10 And they cried with a loud voice, saying, How long, O Lord, holy and true, dost you not judge and avenge our blood on them that dwell on the earth?

11 And white robes were given unto every one of them; and it was said unto them, that they should rest yet for a little season, until their fellowservants also and their brethren, that should be killed as they were, should be fulfilled.

12 And I beheld when he had opened the sixth seal, and, lo, there was a great earthquake; and the sun became black as sackcloth of hair, and the moon became as blood;

13 And the stars of heaven fell unto the earth, even as a fig tree casteth her untimely figs, when she is shaken of a mighty wind.

14 And the heaven departed as a scroll when it is rolled together; and every mountain and island were moved out of their places.

15 And the kings of the earth, and the great men, and the rich men, and the chief captains, and the mighty men, and every bondman, and every free man, hid themselves in the dens and in the rocks of the mountains;

16 And said to the mountains and rocks, Fall on us, and hide us from the face of him that sitteth on the throne, and from the wrath of the Lamb:

17 For the great day of his wrath is come; and who shall be able to stand?

CHAPTER 7

AND after these things I saw four angels standing on the four corners of the earth, holding the four winds of the earth, that the wind should not blow on the earth, nor on the sea, nor on any tree.

2 And I saw another angel ascending from the east, having the seal of the living God: and he cried with a loud voice to the four angels, to whom it was given to hurt the earth and the sea,

3 Saying, Hurt not the earth, neither the sea, nor the trees, till we have sealed the servants of our God in their foreheads.

4 And I heard the number of them which were sealed: and there were sealed an hundred and forty and four thousand of all the tribes of the children of Israel.

5 Of the tribe of Juda were sealed twelve thousand. Of the tribe of Reuben were sealed twelve thousand. Of the tribe of Gad were sealed twelve thousand.

6 Of the tribe of Aser were sealed twelve thousand. Of the tribe of Nepthalim were sealed twelve thousand. Of the tribe of Manasses were sealed twelve thousand.

7 Of the tribe of Simeon were sealed twelve thousand. Of the tribe of Levi were sealed twelve thousand. Of the tribe of Issachar were sealed twelve thousand.

8 Of the tribe of Zabulon were sealed twelve thousand. Of the tribe of Joseph were sealed twelve thousand. Of the tribe of Benjamin were sealed twelve thousand.

9 After this I beheld, and, lo, a great multitude, which no man could number, of all nations, and kindreds, and people, and tongues, stood before the throne, and before the Lamb, clothed with white robes, and palms in their hands;

10 And cried with a loud voice, saying, Salvation to our God which sitteth upon the throne, and unto the Lamb.

11 And all the angels stood round about the throne, and about the elders and the four beasts, and fell before the throne on their faces, and worshipped God,

12 Saying, Amen: Blessing, and glory, and wisdom, and thanksgiving, and honour, and power, and might, be unto our God for ever and ever. Amen.

13 And one of the elders answered, saying unto me, What are these which are arrayed in white robes? and whence came they?

14 And I said unto him, Sir, you knowest. And he said to me, These are they which came out of great tribulation, and have washed their robes, and made them white in the blood of the Lamb.

15 Therefore are they before the throne of God, and serve him day and night in his temple: and he that sitteth on the throne shall dwell among them.

16 They shall hunger no more, neither thirst any more; neither shall the sun light on them, nor any heat.

17 For the Lamb which is in the midst of the throne shall feed them, and shall lead them unto living fountains of waters: and God shall wipe away all tears from their eyes.

CHAPTER 8

AND when he had opened the seventh seal, there was silence in heaven about the space of half an hour.

2 And I saw the seven angels which stood before God; and to them were given seven trumpets.

3 And another angel came and stood at the altar, having a golden censer; and there was given unto him much incense, that he should offer it with the prayers of all saints upon the golden altar which was before the throne.

4 And the smoke of the incense, which came with the prayers of the saints, ascended up before God out of the angel's hand.

5 And the angel took the censer, and filled it with fire of the altar, and cast it into the earth: and there were voices, and thunderings, and lightnings, and an earthquake.

6 And the seven angels which had the seven trumpets prepared themselves to sound.

7 The first angel sounded, and there followed hail and fire mingled with blood, and they were cast upon the earth: and the third part of trees was burnt up, and all green grass was burnt up.

8 And the second angel sounded, and as it were a great mountain burning with fire was cast into the sea: and the third part of the sea became blood;

9 And the third part of the creatures which were in the sea, and had life, died; and the third part of the ships were destroyed.

10 And the third angel sounded, and there fell a great star from heaven, burning as it were a lamp, and it fell upon the third part of the rivers, and upon the fountains of waters;

11 And the name of the star is called Wormwood: and the third part of the waters became wormwood; and many men died of the waters, because they were made bitter.

12 And the fourth angel sounded, and the third part of the sun was smitten, and the third part of the moon, and the third part of the stars; so as the third part of them was darkened, and the day shone not for a third part of it, and the night likewise.

13 And I beheld, and heard an angel flying through the midst of heaven, saying with a loud voice, Woe, woe, woe, to the inhabiters of the earth by reason of the other voices of the trumpet of the three angels, which are yet to sound!

CHAPTER 9

AND the fifth angel sounded, and I saw a star fall from heaven unto the earth: and to him was given the key of the bottomless pit.

2 And he opened the bottomless pit; and there arose a smoke out of the pit, as the smoke of a great furnace; and the sun and the air were darkened by reason of the smoke of the pit.

3 And there came out of the smoke locusts upon the earth: and unto them was given power, as the scorpions of the earth have power.

4 And it was commanded them that they should not hurt the grass of the earth, neither any green thing, neither any tree; but only those men which have not the seal of God in their foreheads.

5 And to them it was given that they should not kill them, but that they should be tormented five months: and their torment was as the torment of a scorpion, when he striketh a man.

6 And in those days shall men seek death, and shall not find it; and shall desire to die, and death shall flee from them.

7 And the shapes of the locusts were like unto horses prepared unto battle; and on their heads were as it were crowns like gold, and their faces were as the faces of men.

8 And they had hair as the hair of women, and their teeth were as the teeth of lions.

9 And they had breastplates, as it were breastplates of iron; and the sound of their wings was as the sound of chariots of many horses running to battle.

10 And they had tails like unto scorpions, and there were stings in their tails: and their power was to hurt men five months.

11 And they had a king over them, which is the angel of the bottomless pit, whose name in the Hebrew tongue is Abaddon, but in the Greek tongue has his name Apollyon.

12 One woe is past; and, behold, there come two woes more hereafter.

13 And the sixth angel sounded, and I heard a voice from the four horns of the golden altar which is before God,

14 Saying to the sixth angel which had the trumpet, Loose the four angels which are bound in the great river Euphrates.

15 And the four angels were loosed, which were prepared for an hour, and a day, and a month, and a year, for to slay the third part of men.

16 And the number of the army of the horsemen were two hundred thousand thousand: and I heard the number of them.

17 And thus I saw the horses in the vision, and them that sat on them, having breastplates of fire, and of jacinth, and brimstone: and the heads of the horses were as the heads of lions; and out of their mouths issued fire and smoke and brimstone.

18 By these three was the third part of men killed, by the fire, and by the smoke, and by the brimstone, which issued out of their mouths.

19 For their power is in their mouth, and in their tails: for their tails were like unto serpents, and had heads, and with them they do hurt.

20 And the rest of the men which were not killed by these plagues yet repented not of the works of their hands, that they should not worship devils, and idols of gold, and silver, and brass, and stone, and of wood: which neither can see, nor hear, nor walk:

21 Neither repented they of their murders, nor of their sorceries, nor of their fornication, nor of their thefts.

CHAPTER 10

AND I saw another mighty angel come down from heaven, clothed with a cloud: and a rainbow was upon his head, and his face was as it were the sun, and his feet as pillars of fire:

2 And he had in his hand a little book open: and he set his right foot upon the sea, and his left foot on the earth,

3 And cried with a loud voice, as when a lion roareth: and when he had cried, seven thunders uttered their voices.

4 And when the seven thunders had uttered their voices, I was about to write: and I heard a voice from heaven saying unto me, Seal up those things which the seven thunders uttered, and write them not.

5 And the angel which I saw stand upon the sea and upon the earth lifted up his hand to heaven,

6 And sware by him that liveth for ever and ever, who created heaven, and the things that therein are, and the earth, and the things that therein are, and the sea, and the things which are therein, that there should be time no longer:

7 But in the days of the voice of the seventh angel, when he shall begin to sound, the mystery of God should be finished, as he has declared to his servants the prophets.

8 And the voice which I heard from heaven spake unto me again, and said, Go and take the little book which is open in the hand of the angel which standeth upon the sea and upon the earth.

9 And I went unto the angel, and said unto him, Give me the little book. And he said unto me, Take it, and eat it up; and it shall make your belly bitter, but it shall be in your mouth sweet as honey.

10 And I took the little book out of the angel's hand, and ate it up; and it was in my mouth sweet as honey: and as soon as I had eaten it, my belly was bitter.

11 And he said unto me, You must prophesy again before many peoples, and nations, and tongues, and kings.

CHAPTER 11

AND there was given me a reed like unto a rod: and the angel stood, saying, Rise, and measure the temple of God, and the altar, and them that worship therein.

2 But the court which is without the temple leave out, and measure it not; for it is given unto the Gentiles: and the holy city shall they tread under foot forty and two months.

3 And I will give power unto my two witnesses, and they shall prophesy a thousand two hundred and threescore days, clothed in sackcloth.

4 These are the two olive trees, and the two candlesticks standing before the God of the earth.

5 And if any man will hurt them, fire proceedeth out of their mouth, and devoureth their enemies: and if any man will hurt them, he must in this manner be killed.

6 These have power to shut heaven, that it rain not in the days of their prophecy: and have power over waters to turn them to blood, and to strike the earth with all plagues, as often as they will.

7 And when they shall have finished their testimony, the beast that ascendeth out of the bottomless pit shall make war against them, and shall overcome them, and kill them.

8 And their dead bodies shall lie in the street of the great city, which spiritually is called Sodom and Egypt, where also our Lord was crucified.

9 And they of the people and kindreds and tongues and nations shall see their dead bodies three days and an half, and shall not suffer their dead bodies to be put in graves.

10 And they that dwell upon the earth shall rejoice over them, and make merry, and shall send gifts one to another; because these two prophets tormented them that dwelt on the earth.

11 And after three days and an half the Spirit of life from God entered into them, and they stood upon their feet; and great fear fell upon them which saw them.

12 And they heard a great voice from heaven saying unto them, Come up hither. And they ascended up to heaven in a cloud; and their enemies beheld them.

13 And the same hour was there a great earthquake, and the tenth part of the city fell, and in the earthquake were slain of men seven thousand: and the remnant were affrighted, and gave glory to the God of heaven.

14 The second woe is past; and, behold, the third woe comes quickly.

15 And the seventh angel sounded; and there were great voices in heaven, saying, The kingdoms of this world are become the kingdoms of our Lord, and of his Christ; and he shall reign for ever and ever.

16 And the four and twenty elders, which sat before God on their seats, fell upon their faces, and worshipped God,

17 Saying, We give you thanks, O Lord God Almighty, which are, and wast, and are to come; because you have taken to you your great power, and have reigned.

18 And the nations were angry, and your wrath is come, and the time of the dead, that they should be judged, and that you shouldest give reward unto your servants the prophets, and to the saints, and them that fear your name, small and great; and shouldest destroy them which destroy the earth.

19 And the temple of God was opened in heaven, and there was seen in his temple the ark of his testament: and there were lightnings, and voices, and thunderings, and an earthquake, and great hail.

CHAPTER 12

AND there appeared a great wonder in heaven; a woman clothed with the sun, and the moon under her feet, and upon her head a crown of twelve stars:

2 And she being with child cried, travailing in birth, and pained to be delivered.

3 And there appeared another wonder in heaven; and behold a great red dragon, having seven heads and ten horns, and seven crowns upon his heads.

4 And his tail drew the third part of the stars of heaven, and did cast them to the earth: and the dragon stood before the woman which was ready to be delivered, for to devour her child as soon as it was born.

5 And she brought forth a man child, who was to rule all nations with a rod of iron: and her child was caught up unto God, and to his throne.

6 And the woman fled into the wilderness, where she has a place prepared of God, that they should feed her there a thousand two hundred and threescore days.

7 And there was war in heaven: Michael and his angels fought against the dragon; and the dragon fought and his angels,

8 And prevailed not; neither was their place found any more in heaven.

9 And the great dragon was cast out, that old serpent, called the Devil, and Satan, which deceiveth the whole world: he was cast out into the earth, and his angels were cast out with him.

10 And I heard a loud voice saying in heaven, Now is come salvation, and strength, and the kingdom of our God, and the power of his Christ: for the accuser of our brethren is cast down, which accused them before our God day and night.

11 And they overcame him by the blood of the Lamb, and by the word of their testimony; and they loved not their lives unto the death.

12 Therefore rejoice, you heavens, and you that dwell in them. Woe to the inhabiters of the earth and of the sea! for the devil is come down unto you, having great wrath, because he knoweth that he has but a short time.

13 And when the dragon saw that he was cast unto the earth, he persecuted the woman which brought forth the man child.

14 And to the woman were given two wings of a great eagle, that she might fly into the wilderness, into her place, where she is nourished for a time, and times, and half a time, from the face of the serpent.

15 And the serpent cast out of his mouth water as a flood after the woman, that he might cause her to be carried away of the flood.

16 And the earth helped the woman, and the earth opened her mouth, and swallowed up the flood which the dragon cast out of his mouth.

17 And the dragon was wroth with the woman, and went to make war with the remnant of her seed, which keep the commandments of God, and have the testimony of Jesus Christ.

CHAPTER 13

AND I stood upon the sand of the sea, and saw a beast rise up out of the sea, having seven heads and ten horns, and upon his horns ten crowns, and upon his heads the name of blasphemy.

2 And the beast which I saw was like unto a leopard, and his feet were as the feet of a bear, and his mouth as the mouth of a lion: and the dragon gave him his power, and his seat, and great authority.

3 And I saw one of his heads as it were wounded to death; and his deadly wound was healed: and all the world wondered after the beast.

4 And they worshipped the dragon which gave power unto the beast: and they worshipped the beast, saying, Who is like unto the beast? who is able to make war with him?

5 And there was given unto him a mouth speaking great things and blasphemies; and power was given unto him to continue forty and two months.

6 And he opened his mouth in blasphemy against God, to blaspheme his name, and his tabernacle, and them that dwell in heaven.

7 And it was given unto him to make war with the saints, and to overcome them: and power was given him over all kindreds, and tongues, and nations.

8 And all that dwell upon the earth shall worship him, whose names are not written in the book of life of the Lamb slain from the foundation of the world.

9 If any man have an ear, let him hear.

10 He that leadeth into captivity shall go into captivity: he that killeth with the sword must be killed with the sword. Here is the patience and the faith of the saints.

11 And I beheld another beast coming up out of the earth; and he had two horns like a lamb, and he spake as a dragon.

12 And he exerciseth all the power of the first beast before him, and causeth the earth and them which dwell therein to worship the first beast, whose deadly wound was healed.

13 And he doeth great wonders, so that he maketh fire come down from heaven on the earth in the sight of men,

14 And deceiveth them that dwell on the earth by the means of those miracles which he had power to do in the sight of the beast; saying to them that dwell on the earth, that they should make an image to the beast, which had the wound by a sword, and did live.

15 And he had power to give life unto the image of the beast, that the image of the beast should both speak, and cause that as many as would not worship the image of the beast should be killed.

16 And he causeth all, both small and great, rich and poor, free and bond, to receive a mark in their right hand, or in their foreheads:

17 And that no man might buy or sell, save he that had the mark, or the name of the beast, or the number of his name.

18 Here is wisdom. Let him that has understanding count the number of the beast: for it is the number of a man; and his number is Six hundred threescore and six.

CHAPTER 14

AND I looked, and, lo, a Lamb stood on the mount Sion, and with him an hundred forty and four thousand, having his Father's name written in their foreheads.

2 And I heard a voice from heaven, as the voice of many waters, and as the voice of a great thunder: and I heard the voice of harpers harping with their harps:

3 And they sung as it were a new song before the throne, and before the four beasts, and the elders: and no man could learn that song but the hundred and forty and four thousand, which were redeemed from the earth.

4 These are they which were not defiled with women; for they are virgins. These are they which follow the Lamb whithersoever he goeth. These were redeemed from among men, being the firstfruits unto God and to the Lamb.

5 And in their mouth was found no guile: for they are without fault before the throne of God.

6 And I saw another angel fly in the midst of heaven, having the everlasting gospel to preach unto them that dwell on the earth, and to every nation, and kindred, and tongue, and people,

7 Saying with a loud voice, Fear God, and give glory to him; for the hour of his judgment is come: and worship him that made heaven, and earth, and the sea, and the fountains of waters.

8 And there followed another angel, saying, Babylon is fallen, is fallen, that great city, because she made all nations drink of the wine of the wrath of her fornication.

9 And the third angel followed them, saying with a loud voice, If any man worship the beast and his image, and receive his mark in his forehead, or in his hand,

10 The same shall drink of the wine of the wrath of God, which is poured out without mixture into the cup of his indignation; and he shall be tormented with fire and brimstone in the presence of the holy angels, and in the presence of the Lamb:

11 And the smoke of their torment ascendeth up for ever and ever: and they have no rest day nor night, who worship the beast and his image, and whosoever receiveth the mark of his name.

12 Here is the patience of the saints: here are they that keep the commandments of God, and the faith of Jesus.

13 And I heard a voice from heaven saying unto me, Write, Blessed are the dead which die in the Lord from henceforth: Yea, saith the Spirit, that they may rest from their labours; and their works do follow them.

14 And I looked, and behold a white cloud, and upon the cloud one sat like unto the Son of man, having on his head a golden crown, and in his hand a sharp sickle.

15 And another angel came out of the temple, crying with a loud voice to him that sat on the cloud, Thrust in your sickle, and reap: for the time is come for you to reap; for the harvest of the earth is ripe.

16 And he that sat on the cloud thrust in his sickle on the earth; and the earth was reaped.

17 And another angel came out of the temple which is in heaven, he also having a sharp sickle.

18 And another angel came out from the altar, which had power over fire; and cried with a loud cry to him that had the sharp sickle, saying, Thrust in your sharp sickle, and gather the clusters of the vine of the earth; for her grapes are fully ripe.

19 And the angel thrust in his sickle into the earth, and gathered the vine of the earth, and cast it into the great winepress of the wrath of God.

20 And the winepress was trodden without the city, and blood came out of the winepress, even unto the horse bridles, by the space of a thousand and six hundred furlongs.

CHAPTER 15

AND I saw another sign in heaven, great and marvellous, seven angels having the seven last plagues; for in them is filled up the wrath of God.

2 And I saw as it were a sea of glass mingled with fire: and them that had gotten the victory over the beast, and over his image, and over his mark, and over the number of his name, stand on the sea of glass, having the harps of God.

3 And they sing the song of Moses the servant of God, and the song of the Lamb, saying, Great and marvellous are your works, Lord God Almighty; just and true are your ways, you King of saints.

4 Who shall not fear you, O Lord, and glorify your name? for you only are holy: for all nations shall come and worship before you; for your judgments are made manifest.

5 And after that I looked, and, behold, the temple of the tabernacle of the testimony in heaven was opened:

6 And the seven angels came out of the temple, having the seven plagues, clothed in pure and white linen, and having their breasts girded with golden girdles.

7 And one of the four beasts gave unto the seven angels seven golden vials full of the wrath of God, who liveth for ever and ever.

8 And the temple was filled with smoke from the glory of God, and from his power; and no man was able to enter into the temple, till the seven plagues of the seven angels were fulfilled.

CHAPTER 16

AND I heard a great voice out of the temple saying to the seven angels, Go your ways, and pour out the vials of the wrath of God upon the earth.

2 And the first went, and poured out his vial upon the earth; and there fell a noisome and grievous sore upon the men which had the mark of the beast, and upon them which worshipped his image.

3 And the second angel poured out his vial upon the sea; and it became as the blood of a dead man: and every living soul died in the sea.

4 And the third angel poured out his vial upon the rivers and fountains of waters; and they became blood.

5 And I heard the angel of the waters say, You are righteous, O Lord, which are, and wast, and shalt be, because you have judged thus.

6 For they have shed the blood of saints and prophets, and you have given them blood to drink; for they are worthy.

7 And I heard another out of the altar say, Even so, Lord God Almighty, true and righteous are your judgments.

8 And the fourth angel poured out his vial upon the sun; and power was given unto him to scorch men with fire.

9 And men were scorched with great heat, and blasphemed the name of God, which has power over these plagues: and they repented not to give him glory.

10 And the fifth angel poured out his vial upon the seat of the beast; and his kingdom was full of darkness; and they gnawed their tongues for pain,

11 And blasphemed the God of heaven because of their pains and their sores, and repented not of their deeds.

12 And the sixth angel poured out his vial upon the great river Euphrates; and the water thereof was dried up, that the way of the kings of the east might be prepared.

13 And I saw three unclean spirits like frogs come out of the mouth of the dragon, and out of the mouth of the beast, and out of the mouth of the false prophet.

14 For they are the spirits of devils, working miracles, which go forth unto the kings of the earth and of the whole world, to gather them to the battle of that great day of God Almighty.

15 Behold, I come as a thief. Blessed is he that watcheth, and keepeth his garments, lest he walk naked, and they see his shame.

16 And he gathered them together into a place called in the Hebrew tongue Armageddon.

17 And the seventh angel poured out his vial into the air; and there came a great voice out of the temple of heaven, from the throne, saying, It is done.

18 And there were voices, and thunders, and lightnings; and there was a great earthquake, such as was not since men were upon the earth, so mighty an earthquake, and so great.

19 And the great city was divided into three parts, and the cities of the nations fell: and great Babylon came in remembrance before God, to give unto her the cup of the wine of the fierceness of his wrath.

20 And every island fled away, and the mountains were not found.

21 And there fell upon men a great hail out of heaven, every stone about the weight of a talent: and men blasphemed God because of the plague of the hail; for the plague thereof was exceeding great.

CHAPTER 17

AND there came one of the seven angels which had the seven vials, and talked with me, saying unto me, Come hither; I will shew unto you the judgment of the great whore that sitteth upon many waters:

2 With whom the kings of the earth have committed fornication, and the inhabitants of the earth have been made drunk with the wine of her fornication.

3 So he carried me away in the spirit into the wilderness: and I saw a woman sit upon a scarlet coloured beast, full of names of blasphemy, having seven heads and ten horns.

4 And the woman was arrayed in purple and scarlet colour, and decked with gold and precious stones and pearls, having a golden cup in her hand full of abominations and filthiness of her fornication:

5 And upon her forehead was a name written, MYSTERY, BABYLON THE GREAT, THE MOTHER OF HARLOTS AND ABOMINATIONS OF THE EARTH.

6 And I saw the woman drunken with the blood of the saints, and with the blood of the martyrs of Jesus: and when I saw her, I wondered with great admiration.

7 And the angel said unto me, Wherefore did you marvel? I will tell you the mystery of the woman, and of the beast that carrieth her, which has the seven heads and ten horns.

8 The beast that you sawest was, and is not; and shall ascend out of the bottomless pit, and go into perdition: and they that dwell on the earth shall wonder, whose names were not written in the book of life from the foundation of the world, when they behold the beast that was, and is not, and yet is.

9 And here is the mind which has wisdom. The seven heads are seven mountains, on which the woman sitteth.

10 And there are seven kings: five are fallen, and one is, and the other is not yet come; and when he comes, he must continue a short space.

11 And the beast that was, and is not, even he is the eighth, and is of the seven, and goeth into perdition.

12 And the ten horns which you sawest are ten kings, which have received no kingdom as yet; but receive power as kings one hour with the beast.

13 These have one mind, and shall give their power and strength unto the beast.

14 These shall make war with the Lamb, and the Lamb shall overcome them: for he is Lord of lords, and King of kings: and they that are with him are called, and chosen, and faithful.

15 And he saith unto me, The waters which you sawest, where the whore sitteth, are peoples, and multitudes, and nations, and tongues.

16 And the ten horns which you sawest upon the beast, these shall hate the whore, and shall make her desolate and naked, and shall eat her flesh, and burn her with fire.

17 For God has put in their hearts to fulfil his will, and to agree, and give their kingdom unto the beast, until the words of God shall be fulfilled.

18 And the woman which you sawest is that great city, which reigneth over the kings of the earth.

CHAPTER 18

AND after these things I saw another angel come down from heaven, having great power; and the earth was lightened with his glory.

2 And he cried mightily with a strong voice, saying, Babylon the great is fallen, is fallen, and is become the habitation of devils, and the hold of every foul spirit, and a cage of every unclean and hateful bird.

3 For all nations have drunk of the wine of the wrath of her fornication, and the kings of the earth have committed fornication with her, and the merchants of the earth are waxed rich through the abundance of her delicacies.

4 And I heard another voice from heaven, saying, Come out of her, my people, that you be not partakers of her sins, and that you receive not of her plagues.

5 For her sins have reached unto heaven, and God has remembered her iniquities.

6 Reward her even as she rewarded you, and double unto her double according to her works: in the cup which she has filled fill to her double.

7 How much she has glorified herself, and lived deliciously, so much torment and sorrow give her: for she saith in her heart, I sit a queen, and am no widow, and shall see no sorrow.

8 Therefore shall her plagues come in one day, death, and mourning, and famine; and she shall be utterly burned with fire: for strong is the Lord God who judgeth her.

9 And the kings of the earth, who have committed fornication and lived deliciously with her, shall bewail her, and lament for her, when they shall see the smoke of her burning,

10 Standing afar off for the fear of her torment, saying, Alas, alas, that great city Babylon, that mighty city! for in one hour is your judgment come.

11 And the merchants of the earth shall weep and mourn over her; for no man buyeth their merchandise any more:

12 The merchandise of gold, and silver, and precious stones, and of pearls, and fine linen, and purple, and silk, and scarlet, and all thyine wood, and all manner vessels of ivory, and all manner vessels of most precious wood, and of brass, and iron, and marble,

13 And cinnamon, and odours, and ointments, and frankincense, and wine, and oil, and fine flour, and wheat, and beasts, and sheep, and horses, and chariots, and slaves, and souls of men.

14 And the fruits that your soul lusted after are departed from you, and all things which were dainty and goodly are departed from you, and you shalt find them no more at all.

15 The merchants of these things, which were made rich by her, shall stand afar off for the fear of her torment, weeping and wailing,

16 And saying, Alas, alas, that great city, that was clothed in fine linen, and purple, and scarlet, and decked with gold, and precious stones, and pearls!

17 For in one hour so great riches is come to nought. And every shipmaster, and all the company in ships, and sailors, and as many as trade by sea, stood afar off,

18 And cried when they saw the smoke of her burning, saying, What city is like unto this great city!

19 And they cast dust on their heads, and cried, weeping and wailing, saying, Alas, alas, that great city, wherein were made rich all that had ships in the sea by reason of her costliness! for in one hour is she made desolate.

20 Rejoice over her, you heaven, and you holy apostles and prophets; for God has avenged you on her.

21 And a mighty angel took up a stone like a great millstone, and cast it into the sea, saying, Thus with violence shall that great city Babylon be thrown down, and shall be found no more at all.

22 And the voice of harpers, and musicians, and of pipers, and trumpeters, shall be heard no more at all in you; and no craftsman, of whatsoever craft he be, shall be found any more in you; and the sound of a millstone shall be heard no more at all in you;

23 And the light of a candle shall shine no more at all in you; and the voice of the bridegroom and of the bride shall be heard no more at all in you: for your merchants were the great men of the earth; for by your sorceries were all nations deceived.

24 And in her was found the blood of prophets, and of saints, and of all that were slain upon the earth.

CHAPTER 19

AND after these things I heard a great voice of much people in heaven, saying, Alleluia; Salvation, and glory, and honour, and power, unto the Lord our God:

2 For true and righteous are his judgments: for he has judged the great whore, which did corrupt the earth with her fornication, and has avenged the blood of his servants at her hand.

3 And again they said, Alleluia. And her smoke rose up for ever and ever.

4 And the four and twenty elders and the four beasts fell down and worshipped God that sat on the throne, saying, Amen; Alleluia.

5 And a voice came out of the throne, saying, Praise our God, all you his servants, and you that fear him, both small and great.

6 And I heard as it were the voice of a great multitude, and as the voice of many waters, and as the voice of mighty thunderings, saying, Alleluia: for the Lord God omnipotent reigneth.

7 Let us be glad and rejoice, and give honour to him: for the marriage of the Lamb is come, and his wife has made herself ready.

8 And to her was granted that she should be arrayed in fine linen, clean and white: for the fine linen is the righteousness of saints.

9 And he saith unto me, Write, Blessed are they which are called unto the marriage supper of the Lamb. And he saith unto me, These are the true sayings of God.

10 And I fell at his feet to worship him. And he said unto me, See you do it not: I am your fellowservant, and of your brethren that have the testimony of Jesus: worship God: for the testimony of Jesus is the spirit of prophecy.

11 And I saw heaven opened, and behold a white horse; and he that sat upon him was called Faithful and True, and in righteousness he doth judge and make war.

12 His eyes were as a flame of fire, and on his head were many crowns; and he had a name written, that no man knew, but he himself.

13 And he was clothed with a vesture dipped in blood: and his name is called The Word of God.

14 And the armies which were in heaven followed him upon white horses, clothed in fine linen, white and clean.

15 And out of his mouth goeth a sharp sword, that with it he should strike the nations: and he shall rule them with a rod of iron: and he treadeth the winepress of the fierceness and wrath of Almighty God.

16 And he has on his vesture and on his thigh a name written, KING OF KINGS, AND LORD OF LORDS.

17 And I saw an angel standing in the sun; and he cried with a loud voice, saying to all the fowls that fly in the midst of heaven, Come and gather yourselves together unto the supper of the great God;

18 That you may eat the flesh of kings, and the flesh of captains, and the flesh of mighty men, and the flesh of horses, and of them that sit on them, and the flesh of all men, both free and bond, both small and great.

19 And I saw the beast, and the kings of the earth, and their armies, gathered together to make war against him that sat on the horse, and against his army.

20 And the beast was taken, and with him the false prophet that created miracles before him, with which he deceived them that had received the mark of the beast, and them that worshipped his image. These both were cast alive into a lake of fire burning with brimstone.

21 And the remnant were slain with the sword of him that sat upon the horse, which sword proceeded out of his mouth: and all the fowls were filled with their flesh.

CHAPTER 20

AND I saw an angel come down from heaven, having the key of the bottomless pit and a great chain in his hand.

2 And he laid hold on the dragon, that old serpent, which is the Devil, and Satan, and bound him a thousand years,

3 And cast him into the bottomless pit, and shut him up, and set a seal upon him, that he should deceive the nations no more, till the thousand years should be fulfilled: and after that he must be loosed a little season.

4 And I saw thrones, and they sat upon them, and judgment was given unto them: and I saw the souls of them that were beheaded for the witness of Jesus, and for the word of God, and which had not worshipped the beast, neither his image, neither had received his mark upon their foreheads, or in their hands; and they lived and reigned with Christ a thousand years.

5 But the rest of the dead lived not again until the thousand years were finished. This is the first resurrection.

6 Blessed and holy is he that has part in the first resurrection: on such the second death has no power, but they shall be priests of God and of Christ, and shall reign with him a thousand years.

7 And when the thousand years are expired, Satan shall be loosed out of his prison,

8 And shall go out to deceive the nations which are in the four quarters of the earth, Gog and Magog, to gather them together to battle: the number of whom is as the sand of the sea.

9 And they went up on the breadth of the earth, and compassed the camp of the saints about, and the beloved city: and fire came down from God out of heaven, and devoured them.

10 And the devil that deceived them was cast into the lake of fire and brimstone, where the beast and the false prophet are, and shall be tormented day and night for ever and ever.

11 And I saw a great white throne, and him that sat on it, from whose face the earth and the heaven fled away; and there was found no place for them.

12 And I saw the dead, small and great, stand before God; and the books were opened: and another book was opened, which is the book of life: and the dead were judged out of those things which were written in the books, according to their works.

13 And the sea gave up the dead which were in it; and death and hell delivered up the dead which were in them: and they were judged every man according to their works.

14 And death and hell were cast into the lake of fire. This is the second death.

15 And whosoever was not found written in the book of life was cast into the lake of fire.

CHAPTER 21

AND I saw a new heaven and a new earth: for the first heaven and the first earth were passed away; and there was no more sea.

2 And I John saw the holy city, new Jerusalem, coming down from God out of heaven, prepared as a bride adorned for her husband.

3 And I heard a great voice out of heaven saying, Behold, the tabernacle of God is with men, and he will dwell with them, and they shall be his people, and God himself shall be with them, and be their God.

4 And God shall wipe away all tears from their eyes; and there shall be no more death, neither sorrow, nor crying, neither shall there be any more pain: for the former things are passed away.

5 And he that sat upon the throne said, Behold, I make all things new. And he said unto me, Write: for these words are true and faithful.

6 And he said unto me, It is done. I am Alpha and Omega, the beginning and the end. I will give unto him that is athirst of the fountain of the water of life freely.

7 He that overcometh shall inherit all things; and I will be his God, and he shall be my son.

8 But the fearful, and unbelieving, and the abominable, and murderers, and whoremongers, and sorcerers, and idolaters, and all liars, shall have their part in the lake which burneth with fire and brimstone: which is the second death.

9 And there came unto me one of the seven angels which had the seven vials full of the seven last plagues, and talked with me, saying, Come hither, I will shew you the bride, the Lamb's wife.

10 And he carried me away in the spirit to a great and high mountain, and shewed me that great city, the holy Jerusalem, descending out of heaven from God,

11 Having the glory of God: and her light was like unto a stone most precious, even like a jasper stone, clear as crystal;

12 And had a wall great and high, and had twelve gates, and at the gates twelve angels, and names written thereon, which are the names of the twelve tribes of the children of Israel:

13 On the east three gates; on the north three gates; on the south three gates; and on the west three gates.

14 And the wall of the city had twelve foundations, and in them the names of the twelve apostles of the Lamb.

15 And he that talked with me had a golden reed to measure the city, and the gates thereof, and the wall thereof.

16 And the city lies foursquare, and the length is as large as the breadth: and he measured the city with the reed, twelve thousand furlongs. The length and the breadth and the height of it are equal.

17 And he measured the wall thereof, an hundred and forty four cubits, according to the measure of a man, that is, of the angel.

18 And the building of the wall of it was of jasper: and the city was pure gold, like unto clear glass.

19 And the foundations of the wall of the city were garnished with all manner of precious stones. The first foundation was jasper; the second, sapphire; the third, a chalcedony; the fourth, an emerald;

20 The fifth, sardonyx; the sixth, sardius; the seventh, chrysolite; the eighth, beryl; the ninth, a topaz; the tenth, a chrysoprasus; the eleventh, a jacinth; the twelfth, an amethyst.

21 And the twelve gates were twelve pearls; every several gate was of one pearl: and the street of the city was pure gold, as it were transparent glass.

22 And I saw no temple therein: for the Lord God Almighty and the Lamb are the temple of it.

23 And the city had no need of the sun, neither of the moon, to shine in it: for the glory of God did lighten it, and the Lamb is the light thereof.

24 And the nations of them which are saved shall walk in the light of it: and the kings of the earth do bring their glory and honour into it.

25 And the gates of it shall not be shut at all by day: for there shall be no night there.

26 And they shall bring the glory and honour of the nations into it.

27 And there shall in no wise enter into it any thing that defileth, neither whatsoever worketh abomination, or maketh a lie: but they which are written in the Lamb's book of life.

CHAPTER 22

AND he shewed me a pure river of water of life, clear as crystal, proceeding out of the throne of God and of the Lamb.

2 In the midst of the street of it, and on either side of the river, was there the tree of life, which bare twelve manner of fruits, and yielded her fruit every month: and the leaves of the tree were for the healing of the nations.

3 And there shall be no more curse: but the throne of God and of the Lamb shall be in it; and his servants shall serve him:

4 And they shall see his face; and his name shall be in their foreheads.

5 And there shall be no night there; and they need no candle, neither light of the sun; for the Lord God giveth them light: and they shall reign for ever and ever.

6 And he said unto me, These sayings are faithful and true: and the Lord God of the holy prophets sent his angel to shew unto his servants the things which must shortly be done.

7 Behold, I come quickly: blessed is he that keepeth the sayings of the prophecy of this book.

8 And I John saw these things, and heard them. And when I had heard and seen, I fell down to worship before the feet of the angel which shewed me these things.

9 Then saith he unto me, See you do it not: for I am your fellowservant, and of your brethren the prophets, and of them which keep the sayings of this book: worship God.

10 And he saith unto me, Seal not the sayings of the prophecy of this book: for the time is at hand.

11 He that is unjust, let him be unjust still: and he which is filthy, let him be filthy still: and he that is righteous, let him be righteous still: and he that is holy, let him be holy still.

12 And, behold, I come quickly; and my reward is with me, to give every man according as his work shall be.

13 I am Alpha and Omega, the beginning and the end, the first and the last.

14 Blessed are they that do his commandments, that they may have right to the tree of life, and may enter in through the gates into the city.

15 For without are dogs, and sorcerers, and whoremongers, and murderers, and idolaters, and whosoever loveth and maketh a lie.

16 I Jesus have sent my angel to testify unto you these things in the churches. I am the root and the offspring of David, and the bright and morning star.

17 And the Spirit and the bride say, Come. And let him that heareth say, Come. And let him that is athirst come. And whosoever will, let him take the water of life freely.

18 For I testify unto every man that heareth the words of the prophecy of this book, If any man shall add unto these things, God shall add unto him the plagues that are written in this book:

19 And if any man shall take away from the words of the book of this prophecy, God shall take away his part out of the book of life, and out of the holy city, and from the things which are written in this book.

20 He which testifieth these things saith, Surely I come quickly. Amen. Even so, come, Lord Jesus.

21 The grace of our Lord Jesus Christ be with you all. Amen.

1 Paul, an apostle not of men nor by man, but by Jesus Christ, unto the brethren that are at Laodicea.

2 Grace be unto you and peace from God the Father and the Lord Jesus Christ.

3 I give thanks unto Christ in all my prayers, that ye continue in him and persevere in his works, looking for the promise at the day of judgement.

4 Neither do the vain talkings of some overset you, which creep in, that they may turn you away from the truth of the Gospel which is preached by me.

5 And now shall God cause that they that are of me shall continue ministering unto the increase of the truth of the Gospel and accomplishing goodness, and the work of salvation, even eternal life.

5 And now are my bonds seen of all men, which I suffer in Christ, wherein I rejoice and am glad.

7 And unto me this is for everlasting salvation, which also is brought about by your prayers, and the ministry of the Holy Ghost, whether by life or by death.

8 For verily to me life is in Christ, and to die is joy.

9 And unto him (or And also) shall he work his mercy in you that ye may have the same love, and be of one mind.

10 Therefore, dearly beloved, as ye have heard in my presence so hold fast and work in the fear of God, and it shall be unto you for life eternal.

11 For it is God that worketh in you.

12 And do ye without afterthought whatsoever ye do.

13 And for the rest, dearly beloved, rejoice in Christ, and beware of them that are filthy in lucre.

14 Let all your petitions be made openly before God, and be ye steadfast in the mind of Christ.

15 And what things are sound and true and sober and just and to be loved, do ye.

16 And what ye have heard and received, keep fast in your heart.

17 And peace shall be unto you.

18 The saints salute you.

19 The grace of the Lord Jesus be with your spirit.

20 And cause this epistle to be read unto them of Colossae, and the epistle of the Colossians to be read unto you.

THE ACTS OF PAUL AND THECLA

CHAPTER I

1:1 When Paul went up to Iconium, after his flight from Antioch, Demas and Hermogenes became his companions, who were then full of hypocrisy.

1:2 But Paul looking only at the goodness of God, did them no harm, but loved them greatly.

1:3 Accordingly he endeavoured to make agreeable to them all the oracles and doctrines of Christ, and the design of the Gospel of God's well-beloved Son, instructing them in the knowledge of Christ, as it was revealed to him.

1:4 And a certain man named Onesiphorus, hearing that Paul was come to Iconium, went out speedily to meet him, together with his wife Lectra, and his sons Simmia and Xeno, to invite him to their house.

1:5 For Titus had given them a description of Paul's personage, they as yet not knowing him in person, but only being acquainted with his character.

1:6 They went in the king's highway to Lystra, and stood there waiting for him, comparing all who passed by, with that description which Titus had given them.

1:7 At length they saw a man coming (namely Paul), of a low stature, bald (or shaved) on the head, crooked thighs, handsome legs, hollow-eyed; had a crooked nose; full of grace; for sometimes he appeared as a man, sometimes he had the countenance of an angel. And Paul saw Onesiphorus, and was glad.

1:8 And Onesiphorus said: Hail, thou servant of the blessed God. Paul replied, The grace of God be with thee and thy family.

1:9 But Demas and Hermogenes were moved with envy, and, under a show of great religion, Demas said, And are not we also servants of the blessed God? Why didst thou not salute us?

1:10 Onesiphorus replied, Because I have not perceived in you the fruits of righteousness; nevertheless, if ye are of that sort, ye shall be welcome to my house also.

1:11 Then Paul went into the house of Onesiphorus, and here was great joy among the family on that account: and they employed themselves in prayer, breaking of bread, and hearing Paul preach the word of God concerning the temperance and the resurrection, in the following manner:

1:12 Blessed are the pure in heart; for they shall see God.

1:13 Blessed are they who keep their flesh undefiled (or pure); for they shall be the temple of God.

1:14 Blessed are the temperate (or chaste); for God will reveal himself to them.

1:15 Blessed are they who abandon their secular enjoyments; for they shall be accepted of God.

1:16 Blessed are they who have wives, as though they had them not; for they shall be made angels of God.

1:17 Blessed are they who tremble at the word of God; for they shall be comforted.

1:18 Blessed are they who keep their baptism pure; for they shall find peace with the Father, Son, and Holy Ghost.

1:19 Blessed are they who pursue the wisdom (or doctrine) of Jesus Christ; for they shall be called the sons of the Most High.

1:20 Blessed are they who observe the instructions of Jesus Christ; for they shall dwell in eternal light.

1:21 Blessed are they, who for the love of Christ abandon the glories of the world; for they shall judge angels, and be placed at the right hand of Christ, and shall not suffer the bitterness of the last judgment.

1:22 Blessed are the bodies and souls of virgins; for they are acceptable to God, and shall not lose the reward of their virginity; for the word of their (heavenly) Father shall prove effectual to their salvation in the day of his Son, and they shall enjoy rest for evermore.

CHAPTER II

2:1 While Paul was preaching this sermon in the church which was in the house of Onesiphorus, a certain virgin, named Thecla (whose mother's name was Theoclia, and who was betrothed to a man named Thamyris) sat at a certain window in her house.

2:2 From whence, by the advantage of a window in the house where Paul was, she both night and day heard Paul's sermons concerning God, concerning charity, concerning faith in Christ, and concerning prayer;

2:3 Nor would she depart from the window, till with exceeding joy she was subdued to the doctrines of faith.

2:4 At length, when she saw many women and virgins going in to Paul, she earnestly desired that she might be thought worthy to appear in his presence, and hear the word of Christ; for she had not yet seen Paul's person, but only heard his sermons, and that alone.

2:5 But when she would not be prevailed upon to depart from the window, her mother sent to Thamyris,

who came with the greatest pleasure, as hoping now to marry her. Accordingly he said to Theoclia, Where is my Thecla?

2:6 Theoclia replied, Thamyris, I have something very strange to tell you; for Thecla, for the space of three days, will not move from the window not so much as to eat or drink, but is so intent on hearing the artful and delusive discourses of a certain foreigner, that I perfectly admire, Thamyris, that a young woman of her known modesty, will suffer herself to be so prevailed upon.

2:7 For that man has disturbed the whole city of Iconium, and even your Thecla, among others. All the women and young men flock to him to receive his doctrine; who, besides all the rest, tells them that there is but one God, who alone is to be worshipped, and that we ought to live in chastity.

2:8 Notwithstanding this, my daughter Thecla, like a spider's web fastened to the window, is captivated by the discourses of Paul, and attends upon them with prodigious eagerness, and vast delight; and thus, by attending on what he says, the young woman is seduced. Now then do you go, and speak to her, for she is betrothed to you.

2:9 Accordingly Thamyris went, and having saluted her, and taking care not to surprise her, he said, Thecla, my spouse, why sittest thou in this melancholy posture? What strange impressions are made upon thee? Turn to Thamyris, and blush.

2:10 Her mother also spake to her after the same manner, and said, Child, why dost thou sit so melancholy, and, like one astonished, makest no reply?

2:11 Then they wept exceedingly: Thamyris, that he had lost his spouse; Theoclia, that she had lost her daughter; and the maids, that they had lost their mistress; and there was an universal mourning in the family.

2:12 But all these things made no impression upon Thecla, so as to incline her so much as to turn to them, and take notice of them; for she still regarded the discourses of Paul.

2:13 Then Thamyris ran forth into the street to observe who they were who went into Paul, and came out from him; and he saw two men engaged in a very warm dispute, and said to them;

2:14 Sirs, what business have you here? and who is that man within, belonging to you, who deludes the minds of men, both young men and virgins, persuading them, that they ought not to marry, but continue as they are?

2:15 I promise to give you a considerable sum, if you will give me a just account of him; for I am the chief person of this city.

2:16 Demas and Hermogenes replied, We cannot so exactly tell who he is; but this we know, that he deprives young men of their (intended) wives, and virgins of their (intended) husbands, by teaching, There can be no future resurrection, unless ye continue in chastity, and do not defile your flesh.

CHAPTER III

3:1 Then said Thamyris, Come along with me to my house, and refresh yourselves. So they went to a very splendid entertainment, where there was wine in abundance, and very rich provision.

3:2 They were brought to a table richly spread, and made to drink plentifully by Thamyris, on account of the love he had for Thecla, and his desire to marry her.

3:3 Then Thamyris said, I desire ye would inform me what the doctrines of this Paul are, that I may understand them; for I am under no small concern about Thecla, seeing she so delights in that stranger's discourses, that I am in danger of losing my intended wife.

3:4 Then Demas and Hermogenes answered both together, and said, Let him be brought before the governor Castillius, as one who endeavours to persuade the people into the new religion of the Christians, and he, according to the order of Caesar, will put him to death, by which means you will obtain your wife;

3:5 While we at the same time will teach her, that the resurrection which he speaks of is already come, and consists in our having children; and that we then arose again, when we came to the knowledge of God.

3:6 Thamyris having this account from them, was filled with hot resentment:

3:7 And rising early in the morning he went to the house of Onesiphorus, attended by the magistrates, the jailer, and a great multitude of people with staves, and said to Paul;

3:8 Thou hast perverted the city of Iconium, and among the rest, Thecla, who is betrothed to me, so that now she will not marry me. Thou shalt therefore go with us to the governor Castillius.

3:9 And all the multitude cried out, Away with this imposter (magician), for he has perverted the minds of our wives, and all the people hearken to him.

CHAPTER IV

4:1 Then Thamyris standing before the governor's judgment-seat, spake with a loud voice in the following manner.

4:2 O governor, I know not whence this man cometh; but he is one who teaches that matrimony is unlawful. Command him therefore to declare before you for what reason he publishes such doctrines.

4:3 While he was saying thus, Demas and Hermogenes (whispered to Thamyris, and) said; Say that he is a Christian, and he will presently be put to death.

4:4 But the governor was more deliberate, and calling to Paul, he said, Who art thou? What dost thou teach? They seem to lay gross crimes to thy charge.

4:5 Paul then spake with a loud voice, saying, As I am now called to give an account, O governor, of my doctrines, I desire your audience.

4:6 That God, who is a God of vengeance, and who stands in need of nothing but the salvation of his creatures, has sent me to reclaim them from their wickedness and corruptions, from all (sinful) pleasures, and from death; and to persuade them to sin no more.

4:7 On this account, God sent his Son Jesus Christ, whom I preach, and in whom I instruct men to place their hopes as that person who only had such compassion on the deluded world, that it might not, O governor, be condemned, but have faith, the fear of God, the knowledge of religion, and the love of truth.

4:8 So that if I only teach those things which I have received by revelation from God, where is my crime?

4:9 When the governor heard this, he ordered Paul to be bound, and to be put in prison, till he should be more at leisure to hear him more fully.

4:10 But in the night, THecla taking off her earrings, gave them to the turnkey of the prison, who then opened the doors to her, and let her in;

4:11 And when she made a present of a silver looking-glass to the jailer, was allowed to go into the room where Paul was; then she sat down at his feet, and heard from him the great things of God.

4:12 And as she perceived Paul not to be afraid of suffering, but that by divine assistance he behaved himself with courage, her faith so far increased that she kissed his chains.

CHAPTER V

5:1 At length Thecla was missed, and sought for by the family and by Thamyris in every street, as though she had been lost, but one of the porter's fellow-servants told them, that she had gone out in the night-time.

5:2 Then they examined the porter, and he told them, that she was gone to the prison to the strange man.

5:3 They went therefore according to his direction, and there found her; and when they came out, they got a mob together, and went and told the governor all that happened.

5:4 Upon which he ordered Paul to be brought before his judgement seat.

5:5 Thecla in the mean time lay wallowing on the ground in the prison, in that same place where Paul had sat to teach her; upon which the governor also ordered her to be brought before his judgement-seat; which summons she received with joy, and went.

5:6 When Paul was brought thither, the mob with more vehemence cried out, He is a magician, let him die.

5:7 Nevertheless the governor attended with pleasure upon Paul's discourses of the holy works of Christ; and, after a council called, he summoned Thecla, and said to her, Why do you not, according to the law of the Iconians, marry Thamyris?

5:8 She stood still, with her eyes fixed upon Paul; and finding she made no reply, Theoclia, her mother, cried out, saying, Let the unjust creature be burnt; let her be burnt in the midst of the theatre, for refusing Thamyris, that all women may learn from her to avoid such practices.

5:9 Then the governor was exceedingly concerned, and ordered Paul to be whipt out of the city, and Thecla to be burnt.

5:10 So the governor arose, and went immediately into the theatre; and all the people went forth to see the dismal sight.

5:11 But Thecla, just as a lamb in the wilderness looks every way to see his shepherd, looked around for Paul;

5:12 And as she was looking upon the multitude, she saw the Lord Jesus in the likeness of Paul, and said to herself, Paul is come to see me in my distressed circumstances. And she fixed her eyes upon him; but he instantly ascended up to heaven, while she looked on him.

5:13 The the young men and women brought wood and straw for the burning of Thecla; who, being brought naked to the stake, extorted tears from the governor, with surprise beholding the greatness of her beauty.

5:14 And when they had placed the wood in order, the people commanded her to go upon it; which she

did, first making the sign of the cross.

5:15 Then the people set fire to the pile; though the flame was exceeding large, it did not touch her, for God took compassion on her, and caused a great eruption from the earth beneath, and a cloud from above to pour down great quantities of rain and hail;

5:16 Insomuch that by the rupture of the earth, very many were in great danger, and some were killed, the fire was extinguished, and Thecla was preserved.

CHAPTER VI

6:1 In the mean time Paul, together with Onesiphorus, his wife and children, was keeping a fast in a certain cave, which was in the road from Iconium to Daphne.

6:2 And when they had fasted for several days, the children said to Paul, Father, we are hungry, and have not wherewithal to buy bread ; for Onesiphorus had left all his substance to follow Paul with his family.

6:3 Then Paul, taking off his coat, said to the boy, Go, child, and buy bread, and bring it hither.

6:4 But while the boy was buying the bread, he saw his neighbour Thecla and was surprised, and said to her, Thecla, where are you going?

6:5 She replied, I am in pursuit of Paul, having been delivered from the flames.

6:6 The boy then said, I will bring you to him, for he is under great concern on your account, and has been in prayer and fasting these six days.

6:7 When Thecla came to the cave, she found Paul upon his knees praying and saying, O holy Father, O Lord Jesus Christ, grant that the fire may not touch Thecla; but be her helper, for she is thy servant.

6:8 Thecla then standing behind him, cried out in the following words: O sovereign Lord, Creator of heaven and earth, the Father of thy beloved and holy Son, I praise thee that thou hast preserved me from the fire, to see Paul again.

6:9 Paul then arose, and when he saw her, said, O God, who searchest the heart, Father of my Lord Jesus Christ, I praise thee that thou has answered my prayer.

6:10 And there prevailed among them in the cave an entire affection to each other; Paul, Onesiphorus and all that were with them being filled with joy.

6:11 They had five loaves, some herbs and water, and they solaced each other in reflections upon the holy works of Christ.

6:12 Then said Thecla to Paul, If you be pleased with it, I will follow you withersoever you go.

6:13 He replied to her, Persons are now much given to fornication, and you being handsome, I am afraid lest you should meet with greater temptation than the former, and should not withstand, but be overcome by it.

6:14 Thecla replied, Grant me only the seal of Christ, and no temptation shall affect me.

6:15 Paul answered, Thecla, wait with patience, and you shall receive the gift of Christ.

CHAPTER VII

7:1 Then Paul sent back Onesiphorus and his family to their own home, and taking Thecla along with him, went for Antioch;

7:2 And as soon as they came into the city, a certain Syrian, named Alexander, a magistrate, in the city, who had done many considerable services for the city during his magistracy, saw Thecla and fell in love with her, and endeavoured by many rich presents to engage Paul in his interest.

7:3 But Paul told him, I know not the woman of whom you speak, nor does she belong to me.

7:4 But he being a person of great power in Antioch, seized her in the street and kissed her; which Thecla would not bear, but looking about for Paul, cried out in a distressed loud tone, Force me not, who am a stranger; force me not, who am a servant of God; I am one of the principal persons of Iconium, and was obliged to leave that city because I would not be married to Thamyris.

7:5 Then she laid hold on Alexander, tore his coat, and took his crown off his head, and made him appear ridiculous before all the people.

7:6 But Alexander, partly as he loved her, and partly being ashamed of what had been done, led her to the governor, and upon her confession of what she had done, he condemned her to be thrown among the beasts.

CHAPTER VIII

8:1 Which when the people saw, they said: The judgments passed in this city are unjust. But Thecla desired the favour of the governor, that her chastity might not be attacked, but preserved till she should be cast to the beasts.

8:2 The governor then inquired, Who would entertain her; upon which a certain very rich widow, named Trifina, whose daughter was lately dead, desired that she might have the keeping of her; and she began to treat her in her house as her own daughter.

8:3 At length a day came, when the beasts were to be brought forth to be seen; and Thecla was brought to the amphitheatre, and put into a den in which was an exceeding fierce she-lion, in the presence of a multitude of spectators.

8:4 Trifina, without any surprise, accompanied Thecla, and the she-lion licked the feet of Thecla. The title written which denotes her crime was: Sacrilege. Then the woman cried out, O God, the judgments of this city are unrighteous.

8:5 After the beasts had been shewn, Trifina took Thecla home with her, and they went to bed; and behold, the daughter of Trifina, who was dead, appeared to her mother, and said; Mother, let the young woman, Thecla, be reputed by you as your daughter in my stead; and desire her that she should pray for me, that I may be translated to a state of happiness.

8:6 Upon which Trifina, with a mournful air, said, My daughter Falconilla has appeared to me, and ordered me to receive you in her room; wherefore I desire, Thecla, that you would pray for my daughter, that she may be translated into a state of happiness, and to life eternal.

8:7 When Thecla heard this, she immediately prayed to the Lord, and said: O Lord God of heaven and earth, Jesus Christ, thou Son of the Most High, grant that her daughter Falconilla may live forever. Trifina hearing this groaned again, and said: O unrighteous judgments! O unreasonable wickedness! that such a creature should (again) be cast to the beasts!

8:8 On the morrow, at break of day, Alexander came to Trifina's house, and said: The governor and the people are waiting; bring the criminal forth.

8:9 But Trifina ran in so violently upon him, that he was affrighted, and ran away. Trifina was one of the royal family; and she thus expressed her sorrow, and said: Alas! I have trouble in my house on two accounts, and there is no one who will relieve me, either under the loss of my daughter, or my being able to save Thecla. But now, O Lord God, be thou the helper of Thecla thy servant.

8:10 While she was thus engaged, the governor sent one of his own officers to bring Thecla. Trifina took her by the hand, and, going with her, said: I went with Falconilla to her grave, and now must go with Thecla to the beasts.

8:11 When Thecla heard this, she weeping prayed, and said: O Lord God, whom I have made my confidence and refuge, reward Trifina for her compassion to me, and preserving my chastity.

8:12 Upon this there was a great noise in the amphitheatre; the beasts roared, and the people cried out, Bring in the criminal.

8:13 But the woman cried out, and said: Let the whole city suffer for such crimes; and order all of us, O governor, to the same punishment. O unjust judgment! O cruel sight!

8:14 Others said, Let the whole city be destroyed for this vile action. Kill us all, O governor. O cruel sight! O unrighteous judgment.

CHAPTER IX

9:1 Then Thecla was taken out of the hand of Trifina, stripped naked, had a girdle put on, and thrown into the place appointed for fighting with the beasts: and the lions and the bears were let loose upon her.

9:2 But a she-lion, which was of all the most fierce, ran to Thecla, and fell down at her feet. Upon which the multitude of women shouted aloud.

9:3 Then a she-bear ran fiercely towards her; but the she-lion met the bear, and tore it to pieces.

9:4 Again, a he-lion, who had been wont to devour men, and which belonged to Alexander, ran towards her; but the she-lion encountered the he-lion, and they killed each other.

9:5 Then the women were under a greater concern, because the she-lion, which had helped Thecla, was dead.

9:6 Afterwards they brought out many other wild beasts; but Thecla stood with her hands stretched towards heaven, and prayed; and when she had done praying, she turned about, and saw a pit of water, and said, Now it is a proper time for me to be baptized.

9:7 Accordingly she threw herself into the water, and said, In thy name, O my Lord Jesus Christ, I am this last day baptized. The women and the people seeing this, cried out, and said, Do not throw yourself into the water. And the governor himself cried out, to think that the fish (sea-calves) were like to devour so much beauty.

9:8 Notwithstanding all this, Thecla threw herself into the water, in the name of our Lord Jesus Christ.

9:9 But the fish (sea-calves,) when they saw the lighting and fire, were killed, and swam dead upon the surface of the water, and a cloud of fire surrounded Thecla, so that as the beasts could not come near her, so the people could not see her nakedness.

9:10 Yet they turned other wild beasts upon her; upon which they made a very mournful outcry; and some of them scattered spikenard, others cassia, other amomus [a sort of spikenard, or the herb of Jerusalem, or ladies-rose], others ointment; so that the quantity of ointment was large, in proportion to the number of people; and upon this all the beasts lay as though they had been fast asleep, and did not touch Thecla.

9:11 Whereupon Alexander said to the Governor, I have some very terrible bulls; let us bind her to them. To which the governor, with concern, replied, You may do what you think fit.

9:12 Then they put a cord round Thecla's waist, which bound also her feet, and with it tied her to the bulls, to whose privy-parts they applied red-hot irons, that so they being the more tormented, might more violently drag Thecla about, till they had killed her.

9:13 The bulls accordingly tore about, making a most hideous noise, but the flame which was about Thecla, burnt off the cords which were fastened to the members of the bulls, and she stood in the middle of the stage, as unconcerned as if she had not been bound.

9:14 But in the mean time Trifina, who sat upon one of the benches, fainted away and died; upon which the whole city was under a very great concern.

9:15 And Alexander himself was afraid, and desired the governor, saying: I entreat you, take compassion on me and the city, and release this woman, who has fought with the beasts; lest, both you and I, and the whole city be destroyed:

9:16 For if Caesar should have any account of what has passed now, he will certainly immediately destroy the city, because Trifina, a person of royal extract, and a relation of his, is dead upon her seat.

9:17 Upon this the governor called Thecla from among the beasts to him, and said to her, Who art thou? and what are thy circumstances, that not one of the beasts will touch thee?

9:18 Thecla replied to him; I am a servant of the living God; and as to my state, I am a believer on Jesus Christ his Son, in whom God is well pleased; and for that reason none of the beasts could touch me.

9:19 He alone is the way to eternal salvation, and the foundation of eternal life. He is a refuge to those who are in distress; a support to the afflicted, hope and defence to those who are hopeless; and, in a word, all those who do not believe on him, shall not live, but suffer eternal death.

9:20 When the governor heard these things, he ordered her clothes to be brought, and said to her put on your clothes.

9:21 Thecla replied: May that God who clothed me when I was naked among the beasts, in the day of judgment clothe your soul with the robe of salvation. Then she took her clothes, and put them on; and the governor immediately published an order in these words; I release to you Thecla the servant of God.

9:22 Upon which the women cried out together with a loud voice, and with one accord gave praise unto God, and said: There is but one God, who is the God of Thecla; the one God who hath delivered Thecla.

9:23 So loud were their voices that the whole city seemed to be shaken; and Trifina herself heard the glad tidings, and arose again, and ran with the multitude to meet Thecla; and embracing her, said: Now I believe there shall be a resurrection of the dead; now I am persuaded that my daughter is alive. Come therefore home with me, my daughter Thecla, and I will make over all that I have to you.

9:24 So Thecla went with Trifina, and was entertained there a few days, teaching her the word of the Lord, whereby many young women were converted; and there was great joy in the family of Trifina.

9:25 But Thecla longed to see Paul, and inquired and sent everywhere to find him; and when at length she was informed that he was at Myra, in Lycia, she took with her many young men and women; and putting on a girdle, and dressing herself in the habit of a man, she went to him in Myra in Lycia, and there found Paul preaching the word of God; and she stood by him among the throng.

CHAPTER X

10:1 But it was no small surprise to Paul when he saw her and the people with her; for he imagined some fresh trial was coming upon them;

10:2 Which when Thecla perceived, she said to him: I have been baptized, O Paul; for he who assists you in preaching has assisted me to baptize.

10:3 Then Paul took her, and led her to the house of Hermes; and Thecla related to Paul all that had befallen her in Antioch, insomuch that Paul exceedingly wondered, and all who heard were confirmed in the faith, and prayed for Trifina's happiness.

10:4 Then Thecla arose, and said to Paul, I am going to Iconium. Paul replied to her: Go, and teach the word of the Lord.

10:5 But Trifina had sent large sums of money to Paul, and also clothing by the hands of Thecla, for the relief of the poor.

10:6 So Thecla went to Iconium. And when she came to the house of Onesiphorus, she fell down upon the floor where Paul had sat and preached, and mixing her tears with her prayers, she praised and glorified God in the follwing words:

10:7 O Lord the God of this house, in which I was first enlightened by thee; O Jesus, son of the living God, who wast my helper before the governor, my helper in the fire, and my helper among the beasts; thou alone art God forever and ever. Amen.

10:8 Thecla now (on her return) found Thamyris dead, but her mother living. So calling her mother, she said to her: Theoclia, my mother, is it possible for you to be brought to a belief, that there is but one Lord God, who dwells in the heavens? If yo desire great riches, God will give them to you by me; if you want your daughter again, here I am.

10:9 These and many other things she represented to her mother, [endeavouring] to persuade her [to her opinion]. But her mother Theoclia gave no credit to the things which were said by the martyr Thecla.

10:10 So that Thecla perceiving she discoursed to no purpose, signing her whole body with the sign [of the cross], left the house and went to Daphine; and when she came there, she went to the cave, where she had found Paul with Onesiphorus, and fell down on the ground; and wept before God.

10:11 When she departed thence, she went to Seleucia, and enlightened many in the knowledge of Christ.

10:12 And a bright cloud conducted her in her journey.

10:13 And after she had arrived at Seleucia she went to a place out of the city, about the distance of a furlong, being afraid of the inhabitants, because they were worshippers of idols.

10:14 And she was led [by the cloud] into a mountain called Calamon, or Rodeon. There she abode many years, and underwent a great many grievous temptations of the devil, which she bore in a becoming manner, by the assistance which she had from Christ.

10:15 At length, certain gentlewomen hearing of the virgin Thecla, went to her, and were instructed by her in the oracles of God, and many of them abandoned this world, and led a monastic life with her.

10:16 Hereby a good report was spread everywhere of Thecla, and she wrought several [miraculous] cures, so that all the city and adjacent countries brought their sick to that mountain, and before they came as far as the door of the cave, they were instantly cured of whatsoever distemper they had.

10:17 The unclean spirits were cast out, making a noise; all received their sick made whole, and glorified God, who had bestowed such power on the virgin Thecla;

10:18 Insomuch that the physicians of Seleucia were now of no more account, and lost all the profit of their trade, because no one regarded them; upon which they were filled with envy, and began to contrive what methods to take with this servant of Christ.

CHAPTER XI

11:1 The devil then suggested bad advice to their minds; and being on a certain day met together to consult, they reasoned among each other thus: The virgin is a priestess of the great goddess Diana, and whatsoever she requests from her, is granted, because she is a virgin, and so is beloved by all the gods.

11:2 Now then let us procure some rakish fellows, and after we have made them sufficiently drunk, and given them a good sum of money, let us order them to go and debauch this virgin, promising them, if they do it, a larger reward.

11:3 (For they thus concluded among themselves, that if they be able to debauch her, the gods will no more regard her, nor Diana cure the sick for her.)

11:4 They proceeded according to this resolution, and the fellows went to the mountain, and as fierce as lions to the cave, knocking at the door.

11:5 The holy martyr Thecla, relying upon the God in whom she believed, opened the door, although she was before apprized of their design, and said to them, Young men, what is your business?

11:6 They replied, Is there any one within, whose name is Thecla? She answered, What would you have with her? They said, We have a mind to lie with her.

11:7 The blessed Thecla answered: Though I am a mean old woman, I am the servant of my Lord Jesus Christ; and though you have a vile design against me, ye shall not be able to accomplish it. They replied: It is impossible but we must be able to do with you what we have a mind.

11:8 And while they were saying this, they laid hold on her by main force, and would have ravished her. Then she with the (greatest) mildness said to them: Young men have patience, and see the glory of the Lord.

11:9 And while they held her, she looked up to heaven and said; O God most reverend to whom none can be likened; who makest thyself glorious over thine enemies; who didst deliver me from the fire, and didst not give me up to Thamyris, didst not give me up to Alexander; who deliveredst me from the wild beasts; who didst preserve me in the deep waters; who hast everywhere been my helper, and hast glorified thy name in me;

11:10 Now also deliver me from the hands of these wicked and unreasonable men, nor suffer them to debauch my chastity which I have hitherto preserved for thy honour; for I love thee and long for thee,

and worship thee, O Father, Son, and Holy Ghost, for evermore. Amen.

11:11 Then came a voice from heaven, saying, Fear not, Thecla, my faithful servant, for I am with thee. Look and see the place which is opened for thee: there thy eternal abode shall be; there thou shalt receive the beatific vision.

11:12 The blessed Thecla observing, saw the rock opened to as large a degree as that a man might enter in; she did as she was commanded, bravely fled from the vile crew, and went into the rock, which instantly so closed, that there was not any crack visible where it had opened.

11:13 The men stood perfectly astonished at so prodigious a miracle, and had no power to detain the servant of God; but only, catching hold of her veil, or hood, they tore off a piece of it;

11:14 And even that was by the permission of God, for the confirmation of their faith who should come to see this venerable place, and to convey blessings to those in succeeding ages, who should believe on our Lord Jesus Christ from a pure heart.

11:15 Thus suffered that first martyr and apostle of God, and virgin, Thecla; who came from Iconium at eighteen years of age; afterwards, partly in journeys and travels, and partly in a monastic life in the cave, she lived seventy-two years; so that she was ninety years old when the Lord translated her.

11:16 Thus ends her life.

11:17 The day which is kept sacred to her memory, is the twenty-fourth of September, to the glory of the Father, and the Son, and the Holy Ghost, now and for evermore. Amen.

Third Corinthians

From Corinth to Paul

To Stephanus and the presbyters who are with him, who are Daphnus, Eubulus, Theophilus and Xenon, from Paul, their brother in the Lord, greeting. Two men have come to Corinth, Simon and Cleobius, who pervert the faith of many through pernicious words we want you to respond to. We have never heard such things from you or the other apostles. What ever you and the other apostles teach we will believe. The Lord has shown mercy to us, since you are still alive we wish to hear from you again. Please do write or come to us. We believe, what has been revealed to Theonoe, that the Lord delivered you out of the hand of the lawless one. What they teach is as follows: 1. We must not appeal to the prophets. 2. God is not almighty. 3. There is no resurrection of the flesh. 4. Creation is not the work of God. 5. The Lord did not come in the flesh. 6. The Lord was not born of Mary. 7. The world is not of God but belongs to the Angels. So brother, hurry and come here, so that the church here in Corinth may remain pure, and the foolishness of these men may be made known to all. Farewell in the Lord.

From Paul to Corinth

Paul, the prisoner of Jesus Christ, to the brothers in Corinth, greeting! Since I am in prison, I am not surprised that the teachings of the evil one are quickly gaining ground. My Lord Jesus Christ will quickly come, since he is rejected by those who falsify His words. I delivered to you from the beginning what I received from the apostles who were before me, who were at all times together with the Lord Jesus Christ. Our Lord Jesus Christ was born of Mary of the seed of David. The Holy Spirit was sent from Heaven by the Father into her, that he might come into this world to redeem all flesh through his own flesh, and that he might raise up from the dead we who are fleshly, just as He has shown Himself as our example. Since man was molded by his Father, man was sought for when he was lost, that he might be quickened by adoption into sonship. The almighty God, who made heaven and earth, first sent the prophets to the Jews, that they might turn from their sins; for he had determined how to save the house of Israel, therefore he sent a portion of the spirit of Christ into the prophets, who at many times proclaimed the faultless worship of God. But since the prince who was unrighteous wished to be God, he laid hands on them and killed them, and so all the flesh of men were bound to passions. But God, the almighty, who is righteous and would not repudiate his own creation, sent the Holy Spirit to Mary the Galilean, who believed with all her heart, and she received the Holy Spirit into her womb that Jesus might enter the world, in order that the evil one might be conquered by the same flesh which he held sway, and be convinced that he was not God. For by his own body Jesus Christ saved all flesh and brought it to eternal life through faith, that he might present a temple of righteousness in his own body, through whom we are redeemed. These are not children of righteousness but of wrath, who reject the providence of God, saying that heaven and earth and all that is in them are not the works of the Father. They are themselves therefore children of wrath, for they have the accursed faith of the serpent. From them turn away, and flee from there teaching! For you are not sons of disobedience but of the church most dearly beloved. This is why the time of the resurrection is proclaimed. As for those who tell you there is no resurrection of the flesh, for them there is no resurrection, who do not believe in Him who has risen. You men of Corinth must understand that they don't know about the sowing of wheat or other seeds. That they are cast naked to the ground and when they have perished below and are raised again by the will of God in a body and clothed. The body is not only raised up, but abundantly blessed. And consider not only the seeds, but nobler bodies. You know how Jonah the son of Amathios, when he would not preach in Nineveh but fled, was swallowed by a whale and after three days and three nights God heard Jonah's prayer out of the deepest hell, and no part of him was corrupted, not even an eyelid. How much more, you of so little faith, will he raise up you who have believed in Christ Jesus, as he himself rose up? And if, when a corpse was thrown by the children of Israel on the bones of the prophet Elisha, the man's body rose up, so you also who have been cast upon the body and bones and spirit of the Lord will rise up on that day with your flesh whole. But if you receive anything else, do not cause me trouble; for I have these fetters on my hands that I may gain Christ, and his marks on my body that I may attain to the resurrection form the dead. And whoever abides by the rule which he received by the prophets and the holy Gospel, he shall receive a reward and when he has risen form the dead shall obtain eternal life. But to him that turns aside form them - there is fire with him and those who go before him in the way, since they are men without God, a generation of vipers; from these turn away in the power of the Lord May peace, grace and love be with you. Amen.

Introduction:

A Brief History of the Apocrypha

The official editions of the King James contained the books of the Apocrypha until 1796. Most printers did not clear inventories and change to the sixty-six book version we know today until the mid 1800's. Thus, most Bibles printed before 1840 still had the Apocrypha, or at least most of the Apocrypha. As it turns out, various religions have differing versions of the Bible, made up of divergent lists of books. The Protestant church has its sixty-six books, the Catholics have kept most of the Apocrypha. The Eastern Orthodox Church claims three more books than the Catholics, and the Ethiopic Church has a total of eighty-one books in its Bible.

The Etymologically of the word "apocrypha" means "things that are hidden," but why they were hidden is not clear. Some have suggested that the books were "hidden" from common use because they contained esoteric knowledge, too profound to be communicated to any except the initiated (compare 2 Esd 14.45-46). Others have suggested that such books were hidden due to their spurious or heretical teaching.

According to traditional usage "Apocrypha" has been the designation applied to the fifteen books, or portions of books, listed below. (in many earlier editions of the Apocrypha, the Letter of Jeremiah is incorporated as the final chapter of the Book of Baruch; hence in these editions there are fourteen books.)

Tobit, Judith, The Additions to the Book of Esther (contained in the Greek version of Esther), The Wisdom of Solomon, Ecclesiasticus, The Wisdom of Jesus son of Sirach, Baruch, The Letter of Jeremiah, The Prayer of Azariah, The Song of the Three Jews ,"Susanna, Bel, and the Dragon", 1 Maccabees, 2 Maccabees, 1 Esdras, The Prayer of Manasseh, and 2 Esdras.

In addition, the present expanded edition includes the following three texts that are of special interest to Eastern Orthodox readers are 3 Maccabees, 4 Maccabees, and Psalm 151.

None of these books are included in the Hebrew canon of Holy Scripture. All of them, however, with the exception of 2 Esdras, are present in copies of the Greek version of the Old Testament known as the Septuagint. The Old Latin translations of the Old Testament, made from the Septuagint, also include them, along with 2 Esdras. The Eastern Orthodox Churches chose to include 1 Esdras, Psalm 151, the Prayer of Manasseh, and 3 Maccabees, and 4 Maccabees, which is placed in an appendix as a historical work.

At the end of the fourth century, Pope Damasus commissioned Jerome to prepare a standard Latin version of the Scriptures called the Latin Vulgate. Jerome wrote a note or preface, designating a separate category for the apocryphal books. However, copyists failed the include Jerome's prefaces. Thus, during the medieval period the Western Church generally regarded these books as part of the holy Scriptures.

In 1546 the Council of Trent decreed that the canon of the Old Testament includes the Apocrypha with the exception of the Prayer of Manasseh and 1 and 2 Esdras. Later, the church completed the decision by writing in its Roman Catholic Catechism, "Deuterocanonical does not mean Apocryphal, but simply 'later added to the canon."

But wait, there's more.

he narrow canon of the Ethiopic church contains the following Old Testament books:

Genesis
Exodus
Leviticus
Numbers
Deuteronomy
Enoch
Jubilees
Joshua
Judges
Ruth
1 Samuel
2 Samuel
1 Kings
2 Kings
1 Chronicles
2 Chronicles
Ezra
Nehemiah
3rd Ezra
4rth Ezra
Tobit
Judith
Esther (includes additions to Esther)
1 Macabees
2 Macabees
3 Macabees
Job
Psalms (+ Psalm 151)
Proverbs (Proverbs 1-24)
Täagsas (Proverbs 25-31)
Wisdom of Solomon
Ecclesiastes
Song of Solomon
Sirach (Ecclesiasticus)
Isaiah
Jeremiah
Baruch (includes Letter of Jeremiah)
Lamentations
Ezekiel
Daniel
Hosea
Amos
Micah
Joel
Obadiah
Jonah
Nahum
Habakkuk
Zephaniah
Haggai
Zecariah
Malachi

The Ethiopic Church also adds Clements and the Shepherd of Hermas to its New Testament canon. As stated before, the largest canon belongs to the Ethiopic Church, which is a part of a set of Eastern Orthodox churches. "The position of Eastern Orthodox Churches tend to have a more flexible canon of the Old Testament, and at times the list is not at all clear. For example, the Ethiopic Church has what is called a Narrow and Broad Canon.

The Broader Canon gives 46 as the total for the books of the Old Testament, made up as follows: - Octateuch (8), Judith (1), Samuel and Kings (4), Chronicles (2), 1 Esdras and the Ezra Apocalypse (2), Esther (1), Tobit (1), Maccabees (2), Job (1), Psalms (1), books of Solomon (5), Prophets (16),

Ecclesiasticus (1), Pseudo-Josephus (1); Jubilees and Enoch are to be included in the number (by counting Samuel and Kings as only 2 books).

The New Testament has 35 books consisting of the Gospels (4), Acts (1), the Catholic epistles (7), the Pauline epistles (14), Revelation (1), Sinodos (4 sections), the Book of the Covenant (2 sections), Clement (1), Didascalia (1).

The Narrower Canon is made up of the Prayers of the Church and the list of the books actually printed in the large Geez and Amharic diglot, and Amharic Bibles, issued by the Emperor's command. In this, the universally accepted 39 Old Testament books are counted as 40 by the separation of Messale (Prov. 1-24) and Tägsas (Prov. 25-31), and then 14 further books are listed as equally fully canonical, namely Enoch, Jubilees, Wisdom, 1 Esdras, Ezra Apocalypse, Judith, Tobit, Ecclesiasticus, Baruch, 'the rest of Jeremiah', book of Susanna, 'the remainder of Daniel', 1 and 2 Maccabees. This brings the Old Testament total to 54, which together with the universally accepted 27 Old Testament books makes a total of 81.

The position of the Russian Orthodox Church as regards the Apocrypha appears to have changed during the centuries. The Holy Synod ruling from St. Petersburg were in sympathy with the position of the Reformers and decided to exclude the Apocrypha and since similar influences were emanating from the universities of Kiev, Moscow, Petersburg, and Kazan, the Russian Church became united in its rejection of the Apocrypha.

A full explanation of how the church of today got from the hundreds of books examined for canon to the eighty-one books of Ethiopia and finally to the mere sixty-six books of the Protestant Bible, is a matter of wide ranging discussion and varied opinions, to be taken up at another time. For now, let us simply acknowledge that the Bible many hold to with such passion and steadfastness is not the same book throughout Christendom. For now, we will simply enjoy the texts themselves.

The source of the books printed herein are in Public Domain with the exception of Enoch and Jubilees, which are my own renderings. Clements and Hermas use the J.B. Lightfoot translations as their source, but some of the archaic pronouns have been replaced. However, the "Elizabethan" sentence structure was left in place to keep the regal feel of those writings while modern pronouns assist in ease of reading.

[1] Josiah kept the passover to his Lord in Jerusalem; he killed the passover lamb on the fourteenth day of the first month,

[2] having placed the priests according to their divisions, arrayed in their garments, in the temple of the Lord.

[3] And he told the Levites, the temple servants of Israel, that they should sanctify themselves to the Lord and put the holy ark of the Lord in the house which Solomon the king, the son of David, had built;

[4] and he said, "You need no longer carry it upon your shoulders. Now worship the Lord your God and serve his people Israel; and prepare yourselves by your families and kindred,

[5] in accordance with the directions of David king of Israel and the magnificence of Solomon his son. Stand in order in the temple according to the groupings of the fathers' houses of you Levites, who minister before your brethren the people of Israel,

[6] and kill the passover lamb and prepare the sacrifices for your brethren, and keep the passover according to the commandment of the Lord which was given to Moses."

[7] And Josiah gave to the people who were present thirty thousand lambs and kids, and three thousand calves; these were given from the king's possessions, as he promised, to the people and the priests and Levites.

[8] And Hilkiah, Zechariah, and Jehiel, the chief officers of the temple, gave to the priests for the passover two thousand six hundred sheep and three hundred calves. [9] And Jeconiah and Shemaiah and Nethanel his brother, and Hashabiah and Ochiel and Joram, captains over thousands, gave the Levites for the passover five thousand sheep and seven hundred calves. [10] And this is what took place. The priests and the Levites, properly arrayed and having the unleavened bread, stood according to kindred

[11] and the grouping of the fathers' houses, before the people, to make the offering to the Lord as it is written in the book of Moses; this they did in the morning. [12] They roasted the passover lamb with fire, as required; and they boiled the sacrifices in brass pots and caldrons, with a pleasing odor, [13] and carried them to all the people. Afterward they prepared the passover for themselves and for their brethren the priests, the sons of Aaron, [14] because the priests were offering the fat until night; so the Levites prepared it for themselves and for their brethren the priests, the sons of Aaron. [15] And the temple singers, the sons of Asaph, were in their place according to the arrangement made by David, and also Asaph, Zechariah, and Eddinus, who represented the king. [16] The gatekeepers were at each gate; no one needed to depart from his duties, for their brethren the Levites prepared the passover for them. [17] So the things that had to do with the sacrifices to the Lord were accomplished that day: the passover was kept

[18] and the sacrifices were offered on the altar of the Lord, according to the command of King Josiah. [19] And the people of Israel who were present at that time kept the passover and the feast of unleavened bread seven days. [20] No passover like it had been kept in Israel since the times of Samuel the prophet; [21] none of the kings of Israel had kept such a passover as was kept by Josiah and the priests and Levites and the men of Judah and all of Israel who were dwelling in Jerusalem. [22] In the eighteenth year of the reign of Josiah this passover was kept. [23] And the deeds of Josiah were upright in the sight of the Lord, for his heart was full of godliness. [24] The events of his reign have been recorded in the past, concerning those who sinned and acted wickedly toward the Lord beyond any other people or kingdom, and how they grieved the Lord deeply, so that the words of the Lord rose up against Israel. [25] After all these acts of Josiah, it happened that Pharaoh, king of Egypt, went to make war at Carchemish on the Euphrates, and Josiah went out against him.

[26] And the king of Egypt sent word to him saying, "What have we to do with each other, king of Judea? [27] I was not sent against you by the Lord God, for my war is at the Euphrates. And now the Lord is with me! The Lord is with me, urging me on! Stand aside, and do not oppose the Lord." [28] But Josiah did not turn back to his chariot, but tried to fight with him, and did not heed the words of Jeremiah the prophet from the mouth of the Lord.

[29] He joined battle with him in the plain of Megiddo, and the commanders came down against King Josiah. [30] And the king said to his servants, "Take me away from the battle, for I am very weak." And immediately his servants took him out of the line of battle. [31] And he got into his second chariot; and after he was brought back to Jerusalem he died, and was buried in the tomb of his fathers. [32] And in all Judea they mourned for Josiah. Jeremiah the prophet lamented for Josiah, and the principal men, with the women, have made lamentation for him to this day; it was ordained that this should always be done throughout the whole nation of Israel. [33] These things are written in the book of the histories of the kings of Judea; and every one of the acts of Josiah, and his splendor, and his understanding of the law of the Lord, and the things that he had done before and these that are now told, are recorded in the book of the kings of Israel and Judah. [34] And the men of the nation took

Jeconiah the son of Josiah, who was twenty-three years old, and made him king in succession to Josiah his father.

[35] And he reigned three months in Judah and Jerusalem. Then the king of Egypt deposed him from reigning in Jerusalem, [36] and fined the nation a hundred talents of silver and a talent of gold. [37] And the king of Egypt made Jehoiakim his brother king of Judea and Jerusalem. [38] Jehoiakim put the nobles in prison, and seized his brother Zarius and brought him up out of Egypt. [39] Jehoiakim was twenty-five years old when he began to reign in Judea and Jerusalem, and he did what was evil in the sight of the Lord.

[40] And Nebuchadnezzar king of Babylon came up against him, and bound him with a chain of brass and took him away to Babylon. [41] Nebuchadnezzar also took some holy vessels of the Lord, and carried them away, and stored them in his temple in Babylon. [42] But the things that are reported about Jehoiakim and his uncleanness and impiety are written in the chronicles of the kings. [43] Jehoiachin his son became king in his stead; when he was made king he was eighteen years old,

[44] and he reigned three months and ten days in Jerusalem. He did what was evil in the sight of the Lord. [45] So after a year Nebuchadnezzar sent and removed him to Babylon, with the holy vessels of the Lord, [46] and made Zedekiah king of Judea and Jerusalem.

Zedekiah was twenty-one years old, and he reigned eleven years.

[47] He also did what was evil in the sight of the Lord, and did not heed the words that were spoken by Jeremiah the prophet from the mouth of the Lord. [48] And though King Nebuchadnezzar had made him swear by the name of the Lord, he broke his oath and rebelled; and he stiffened his neck and hardened his heart and transgressed the laws of the Lord, the God of Israel. [49] Even the leaders of the people and of the priests committed many acts of sacrilege and lawlessness beyond all the unclean deeds of all the nations, and polluted the temple of the Lord which had been hallowed in Jerusalem.

[50] So the God of their fathers sent by his messenger to call them back, because he would have spared them and his dwelling place. [51] But they mocked his messengers, and whenever the Lord spoke, they scoffed at his prophets, [52] until in his anger against his people because of their ungodly acts he gave command to bring against them the kings of the Chaldeans. [53] These slew their young men with the sword around their holy temple, and did not spare young man or virgin, old man or child, for he gave them all into their hands. [54] And all the holy vessels of the Lord, great and small, and the treasure chests of the Lord, and the royal stores, they took and carried away to Babylon. [55] And they burned the house of the Lord and broke down the walls of Jerusalem and burned their towers with fire, [56] and utterly destroyed all its glorious things. The survivors he led away to Babylon with the sword, [57] and they were servants to him and to his sons until the Persians began to reign, in fulfillment of the word of the Lord by the mouth of Jeremiah: [58] "Until the land has enjoyed its sabbaths, it shall keep sabbath all the time of its desolation until the completion of seventy years."

2

[1] In the first year of Cyrus as king of the Persians, that the word of the Lord by the mouth of Jeremiah might be accomplished,

[2] the Lord stirred up the spirit of Cyrus king of the Persians, and he made a proclamation throughout all his kingdom and also put it in writing: [3] "Thus says Cyrus king of the Persians: The Lord of Israel, the Lord Most High, has made me king of the world,

[4] and he has commanded me to build him a house at Jerusalem, which is in Judea. [5] If any one of you, therefore, is of his people, may his Lord be with him, and let him go up to Jerusalem, which is in Judea, and build the house of the Lord of Israel -- he is the Lord who dwells in Jerusalem, [6] and let each man, wherever he may live, be helped by the men of his place with gold and silver, [7] with gifts and with horses and cattle, besides the other things added as votive offerings for the temple of the Lord which is in Jerusalem." [8] Then arose the heads of families of the tribes of Judah and Benjamin, and the priests and the Levites, and all whose spirit the Lord had stirred to go up to build the house in Jerusalem for the Lord;

[9] and their neighbors helped them with everything, with silver and gold, with horses and cattle, and with a very great number of votive offerings from many whose hearts were stirred. [10] Cyrus the king also brought out the holy vessels of the Lord which Nebuchadnezzar had carried away from Jerusalem and stored in his temple of idols.

[11] When Cyrus king of the Perians brought these out, he gave them to Mithridates his treasurer, [12] and by him they were given to Sheshbazzar the governor of Judea. [13] The number of these was: a thousand gold cups, a thousand silver cups, twenty-nine silver censers, thirty gold bowls, two thousand four hundred and ten silver bowls, and a thousand other vessels. [14] All the vessels were handed over, gold and silver, five thousand four hundred and sixty-nine, [15] and they were carried back by Sheshbazzar with the returning exiles from Babylon to Jerusalem. [16] But in the time of Artaxerxes king of the Persians, Bishlam, Mithridates, Tabeel, Rehum, Beltethmus, Shimshai the scribe, and the

rest of their associates, living in Samaria and other places, wrote him the following letter, against those who were living in Judea and Jerusalem:

[17] "To King Artaxerxes our lord, Your servants Rehum the recorder and Shimshai the scribe and the other judges of their council in Coelesyria and Phoenicia:

[18] Now be it known to our lord the king that the Jews who came up from you to us have gone to Jerusalem and are building that rebellious and wicked city, repairing its market places and walls and laying the foundations for a temple. [19] Now if this city is built and the walls finished, they will not only refuse to pay tribute but will even resist kings. [20] And since the building of the temple is now going on, we think it best not to neglect such a matter, [21] but to speak to our lord the king, in order that, if it seems good to you, search may be made in the records of your fathers. [22] You will find in the chronicles what has been written about them, and will learn that this city was rebellious, troubling both kings and other cities, [23] and that the Jews were rebels and kept setting up blockades in it from of old. That is why this city was laid waste. [24] Therefore we now make known to you, O lord and king, that if this city is built and its walls finished, you will no longer have access to Coelesyria and Phoenicia." [25] Then the king, in reply to Rehum the recorder and Beltethmus and Shimshai the scribe and the others associated with them and living in Samaria and Syria and Phoenicia, wrote as follows:

[26] "I have read the letter which you sent me. So I ordered search to be made, and it has been found that this city from of old has fought against kings, [27] and that the men in it were given to rebellion and war, and that mighty and cruel kings ruled in Jerusalem and exacted tribute from Coelesyria and Phoenicia. [28] Therefore I have now issued orders to prevent these men from building the city and to take care that nothing more be done [29] and that such wicked proceedings go no further to the annoyance of kings." [30] Then, when the letter from King Artaxerxes was read, Rehum and Shimshai the scribe and their associates went in haste to Jerusalem, with horsemen and a multitude in battle array, and began to hinder the builders. And the building of the temple in Jerusalem ceased until the second year of the reign of Darius king of the Persians.

3

[1] Now King Darius gave a great banquet for all that were under him and all that were born in his house and all the nobles of Media and Persia [2] and all the satraps and generals and governors that were under him in the hundred and twenty-seven satrapies from India to Ethiopia. [3] They ate and drank, and when they were satisfied they departed; and Darius the king went to his bedroom, and went to sleep, and then awoke. [4] Then the three young men of the bodyguard, who kept guard over the person of the king, said to one another, [5] "Let each of us state what one thing is strongest; and to him whose statement seems wisest, Darius the king will give rich gifts and great honors of victory. [6] He shall be clothed in purple, and drink from gold cups, and sleep on a gold bed, and have a chariot with gold bridles, and a turban of fine linen, and a necklace about his neck; [7] and because of his wisdom he shall sit next to Darius and shall be called kinsman of Darius." [8] Then each wrote his own statement, and they sealed them and put them under the pillow of Darius the king, [9] and said, "When the king wakes, they will give him the writing; and to the one whose statement the king and the three nobles of Persia judge to be wisest the victory shall be given according to what is written." [10] The first wrote, "Wine is strongest." [11] The second wrote, "The king is strongest." [12] The third wrote, "Women are strongest, but truth is victor over all things." [13] When the king awoke, they took the writing and gave it to him, and he read it.

[14] Then he sent and summoned all the nobles of Persia and Media and the satraps and generals and governors and prefects, [15] and he took his seat in the council chamber, and the writing was read in their presence. [16] And he said, "Call the young men, and they shall explain their statements." So they were summoned, and came in. [17] And they said to them, "Explain to us what you have written." Then the first, who had spoken of the strength of wine, began and said:

[18] "Gentlemen, how is wine the strongest? It leads astray the minds of all who drink it. [19] It makes equal the mind of the king and the orphan, of the slave and the free, of the poor and the rich. [20] It turns every thought to feasting and mirth, and forgets all sorrow and debt. [21] It makes all hearts feel rich, forgets kings and satraps, and makes every one talk in millions. [22] When men drink they forget to be friendly with friends and brothers, and before long they draw their swords. [23] And when they recover from the wine, they do not remember what they have done. [24] Gentlemen, is not wine the strongest, since it forces men to do these things?" When he had said this, he stopped speaking.

4

[1] Then the second, who had spoken of the strength of the king, began to speak: [2] "Gentlemen, are not men strongest, who rule over land and sea and all that is in them? [3] But the king is stronger; he is their lord and master, and whatever he says to them they obey. [4] If he tells them to make war on one another, they do it; and if he sends them out against the enemy, they go, and conquer mountains, walls, and towers. [5] They kill and are killed, and do not disobey the king's command; if they win the victory, they bring everything to the king -- whatever spoil they take and everything else. [6] Likewise those who do not serve in the army or make war but till the soil, whenever they sow, reap the harvest and bring some to the king; and they compel one another to pay taxes to the king. [7] And yet he is only one man! If he tells them to kill, they kill; if he tells them to release, they release; [8] if he tells them to attack, they attack; if he tells them to lay waste, they lay waste; if he tells them to build, they build; [9] if he tells them to cut down, they cut down; if he tells them to plant, they plant. [10] All his people and his armies obey him. Moreover, he reclines, he eats and drinks and sleeps, [11] but they keep watch around him and no one may go away to attend to his own affairs, nor do they disobey him. [12] Gentlemen, why is not the king the strongest, since he is to be obeyed in this fashion?" And he stopped speaking. [13] Then the third, that is Zerubbabel, who had spoken of women and truth, began to speak:

[14] Gentlemen, is not the king great, and are not men many, and is not wine strong? Who then is their master, or who is their lord? Is it not women? [15] Women gave birth to the king and to every people that rules over sea and land. [16] From women they came; and women brought up the very men who plant the vineyards from which comes wine. [17] Women make men's clothes; they bring men glory; men cannot exist without women. [18] If men gather gold and silver or any other beautiful thing, and then see a woman lovely in appearance and beauty, [19] they let all those things go, and gape at her, and with open mouths stare at her, and all prefer her to gold or silver or any other beautiful thing. [20] A man leaves his own father, who brought him up, and his own country, and cleaves to his wife. [21] With his wife he ends his days, with no thought of his father or his mother or his country. [22] Hence you must realize that women rule over you!

"Do you not labor and toil, and bring everything and give it to women?

[23] A man takes his sword, and goes out to travel and rob and steal and to sail the sea and rivers; [24] he faces lions, and he walks in darkness, and when he steals and robs and plunders, he brings it back to the woman he loves. [25] A man loves his wife more than his father or his mother. [26] Many men have lost their minds because of women, and have become slaves because of them. [27] Many have perished, or stumbled, or sinned, because of women. [28] And now do you not believe me?

"Is not the king great in his power? Do not all lands fear to touch him?

[29] Yet I have seen him with Apame, the king's concubine, the daughter of the illustrious Bartacus; she would sit at the king's right hand [30] and take the crown from the king's head and put it on her own, and slap the king with her left hand. [31] At this the king would gaze at her with mouth agape. If she smiles at him, he laughs; if she loses her temper with him, he flatters her, that she may be reconciled to him. [32] Gentlemen, why are not women strong, since they do such things?" [33] Then the king and the nobles looked at one another; and he began to speak about truth:

[34] "Gentlemen, are not women strong? The earth is vast, and heaven is high, and the sun is swift in its course, for it makes the circuit of the heavens and returns to its place in one day. [35] Is he not great who does these things? But truth is great, and stronger than all things. [36] The whole earth calls upon truth, and heaven blesses her. All God's works quake and tremble, and with him there is nothing unrighteous. [37] Wine is unrighteous, the king is unrighteous, women are unrighteous, all the sons of men are unrighteous, all their works are unrighteous, and all such things. There is no truth in them and in their unrighteousness they will perish. [38] But truth endures and is strong for ever, and lives and prevails for ever and ever. [39] With her there is no partiality or preference, but she does what is righteous instead of anything that is unrighteous or wicked. All men approve her deeds, [40] and there is nothing unrighteous in her judgment. To her belongs the strength and the kingship and the power and the majesty of all the ages. Blessed be the God of truth!" [41] He ceased speaking; then all the people shouted, and said, "Great is truth, and strongest of all!" [42] Then the king said to him, "Ask what you wish, even beyond what is written, and we will give it to you, for you have been found to be the wisest. And you shall sit next to me, and be called my kinsman."

[43] Then he said to the king, "Remember the vow which you made to build Jerusalem, in the day when you became king, [44] and to send back all the vessels that were taken from Jerusalem, which Cyrus set apart when he began to destroy Babylon, and vowed to send them back there. [45] You also vowed to build the temple, which the Edomites burned when Judea was laid waste by the Chaldeans. [46] And now, O lord the king, this is what I ask and request of you, and this befits your greatness. I pray

therefore that you fulfil the vow whose fulfilment you vowed to the King of heaven with your own lips."

[47] Then Darius the king rose, and kissed him, and wrote letters for him to all the treasurers and governors and generals and satraps, that they should give escort to him and all who were going up with him to build Jerusalem.

[48] And he wrote letters to all the governors in Coelesyria and Phoenicia and to those in Lebanon, to bring cedar timber from Lebanon to Jerusalem, and to help him build the city. [49] And he wrote for all the Jews who were going up from his kingdom to Judea, in the interest of their freedom, that no officer or satrap or governor or treasurer should forcibly enter their doors; [50] that all the country which they would occupy should be theirs without tribute; that the Idumeans should give up the villages of the Jews which they held; [51] that twenty talents a year should be given for the building of the temple until it was completed, [52] and an additional ten talents a year for burnt offerings to be offered on the altar every day, in accordance with the commandment to make seventeen offerings; [53] and that all who came from Babylonia to build the city should have their freedom, they and their children and all the priests who came. [54] He wrote also concerning their support and the priests' garments in which they were to minister. [55] He wrote that the support for the Levites should be provided until the day when the temple should be finished and Jerusalem built. [56] He wrote that land and wages should be provided for all who guarded the city. [57] And he sent back from Babylon all the vessels which Cyrus had set apart; everything that Cyrus had ordered to be done, he also commanded to be done and to be sent to Jerusalem. [58] When the young man went out, he lifted up his face to heaven toward Jerusalem, and praised the King of heaven, saying,

[59] "From thee is the victory; from thee is wisdom, and your is the glory. I am thy servant. [60] Blessed art thou, who hast given me wisdom; I give thee thanks, O Lord of our fathers." [61] So he took the letters, and went to Babylon and told this to all his brethren.

[62] And they praised the God of their fathers, because he had given them release and permission [63] to go up and build Jerusalem and the temple which is called by his name; and they feasted, with music and rejoicing, for seven days.

5

[1] After this the heads of fathers' houses were chosen to go up, according to their tribes, with their wives and sons and daughters, and their menservants and maidservants, and their cattle.

[2] And Darius sent with them a thousand horsemen to take them back to Jerusalem in safety, with the music of drums and flutes; [3] and all their brethren were making merry. And he made them go up with them. [4] These are the names of the men who went up, according to their fathers' houses in the tribes, over their groups:

[5] the priests, the sons of Phinehas, son of Aaron; Jeshua the son of Jozadak, son of Seraiah, and Joakim the son of Zerubbabel, son of Shealtiel, of the house of David, of the lineage of Phares, of the tribe of Judah, [6] who spoke wise words before Darius the king of the Persians, in the second year of his reign, in the month of Nisan, the first month. [7] These are the men of Judea who came up out of their sojourn in captivity, whom Nebuchadnezzar king of Babylon had carried away to Babylon [8] and who returned to Jerusalem and the rest of Judea, each to his own town. They came with Zerubbabel and Jeshua, Nehemiah, Seraiah, Resaiah, Bigvai, Mordecai, Bilshan, Mispar, Reeliah, Rehum, and Baanah, their leaders. [9] The number of the men of the nation and their leaders: the sons of Parosh, two thousand one hundred and seventy-two. The sons of Shephatiah, four hundred and seventy-two.

[10] The sons of Arah, seven hundred and fifty-six. [11] The sons of Pahathmoab, of the sons of Jeshua and Joab, two thousand eight hundred and twelve. [12] The sons of Elam, one thousand two hundred and fifty-four. The sons of Zattu, nine hundred and forty-five. The sons of Chorbe, seven hundred and five. The sons of Bani, six hundred and forty-eight. [13] The sons of Bebai, six hundred and twenty-three. The sons of Azgad, one thousand three hundred and twenty-two. [14] The sons of Adonikam, six hundred and sixty-seven. The sons of Bigvai, two thousand and sixty-six. The sons of Adin, four hundred and fifty-four. [15] The sons of Ater, namely of Hezekiah, ninety-two. The sons of Kilan and Azetas, sixty-seven. The sons of Azaru, four hundred and thirty-two. [16] The sons of Annias, one hundred and one. The sons of Arom. The sons of Bezai, three hundred and twenty-three. The sons of Jorah, one hundred and twelve. [17] The sons of Baiterus, three thousand and five. The sons of Bethlehem, one hundred and twenty-three. [18] The men of Netophah, fifty-five. The men of Anathoth, one hundred and fifty-eight. The men of Bethasmoth, forty-two. [19] The men of Kiriatharim, twenty-five. The men of Chephirah and Beeroth, seven hundred and forty-three. [20] The Chadiasans and Ammidians, four hundred and twenty-two. The men of Ramah and Geba, six hundred and twenty-one. [21] The men of Michmas, one hundred and twenty-two. The men of Bethel, fifty-two. The sons of Magbish, one hundred and fifty-six. [22] The sons of the other Elam and Ono, seven hundred and twenty-five. The sons of Jericho, three hundred and forty-five. [23] The sons of Senaah, three thousand

three hundred and thirty. [24] The priests: the sons of Jedaiah the son of Jeshua, of the sons of Anasib, nine hundred and seventy-two. The sons of Immer, one thousand and fifty-two.

[25] The sons of Pashhur, one thousand two hundred and forty-seven. The sons of Harim, one thousand and seventeen. [26] The Levites: the sons of Jeshua and Kadmiel and Bannas and Sudias, seventy-four. [27] The temple singers: the sons of Asaph, one hundred and twenty-eight. [28] The gatekeepers: the sons of Shallum, the sons of Ater, the sons of Talmon, the sons of Akkub, the sons of Hatita, the sons of Shobai, in all one hundred and thirty-nine. [29] The temple servants: the sons of Ziha, the sons of Hasupha, the sons of Tabbaoth, the sons of Keros, the sons of Siaha, the sons of Padon, the sons of Lebanah, the sons of Hagabah,

[30] the sons of Akkub, the sons of Uthai, the sons of Ketab, the sons of Hagab, the sons of Shamlai, the sons of Hana, the sons of Cathua, the sons of Gahar, [31] The sons of Reaiah, the sons of Rezin, the sons of Nekoda, the sons of Chezib, the sons of Gazzam, the sons of Uzza, the sons of Paseah, the sons of Hasrah, the sons of Besai, the sons of Asnah, the sons of the Meunites, the sons of Nephisim, the sons of Bakbuk, the sons of Hakupha, the sons of Asur, the sons of Pharakim, the sons of Bazluth, [32] the sons of Mehida, the sons of Cutha, the sons of Charea, the sons of Barkos, the sons of Sisera, the sons of Temah, the sons of Neziah, the sons of Hatipha. [33] The sons of Solomon's servants: the sons of Hassophereth, the sons of Peruda, the sons of Jaalah, the sons of Lozon, the sons of Giddel, the sons of Shephatiah,

[34] the sons of Hattil, the sons of Pochereth-hazzebaim, the sons of Sarothie, the sons of Masiah, the sons of Gas, the sons of Addus, the sons of Subas, the sons of Apherra, the sons of Barodis, the sons of Shaphat, the sons of Ami. [35] All the temple servants and the sons of Solomon's servants were three hundred and seventy-two.

[36] The following are those who came up from Telmelah and Telharsha, under the leadership of Cherub, Addan, and Immer,

[37] though they could not prove by their fathers' houses or lineage that they belonged to Israel: the sons of Delaiah the son of Tobiah, the sons of Nekoda, six hundred and fifty-two. [38] Of the priests the following had assumed the priesthood but were not found registered: the sons of Habaiah, the sons of Hakkoz, the sons of Jaddus who had married Agia, one of the daughters of Barzillai, and was called by his name.

[39] And when the genealogy of these men was sought in the register and was not found, they were excluded from serving as priests. [40] And Nehemiah and Attharias told them not to share in the holy things until a high priest should appear wearing Urim and Thummim. [41] All those of Israel, twelve or more years of age, besides menservants and maidservants, were forty-two thousand three hundred and sixty;

[42] their menservants and maidservants were seven thousand three hundred and thirty-seven; there were two hundred and forty-five musicians and singers. [43] There were four hundred and thirty-five camels, and seven thousand and thirty-six horses, two hundred and forty-five mules, and five thousand five hundred and twenty-five asses. [44] Some of the heads of families, when they came to the temple of God which is in Jerusalem, vowed that they would erect the house on its site, to the best of their ability,

[45] and that they would give to the sacred treasury for the work a thousand minas of gold, five thousand minas of silver, and one hundred priests' garments. [46] The priests, the Levites, and some of the people settled in Jerusalem and its vicinity; and the temple singers, the gatekeepers, and all Israel in their towns.

[47] When the seventh month came, and the sons of Israel were each in his own home, they gathered as one man in the square before the first gate toward the east.

[48] Then Jeshua the son of Jozadak, with his fellow priests, and Zerubbabel the son of Shealtiel, with his kinsmen, took their places and prepared the altar of the God of Israel, [49] to offer burnt offerings upon it, in accordance with the directions in the book of Moses the man of God. [50] And some joined them from the other peoples of the land. And they erected the altar in its place, for all the peoples of the land were hostile to them and were stronger than they; and they offered sacrifices at the proper times and burnt offerings to the Lord morning and evening. [51] They kept the feast of booths, as it is commanded in the law, and offered the proper sacrifices every day, [52] and thereafter the continual offerings and sacrifices on sabbaths and at new moons and at all the consecrated feasts. [53] And all who had made any vow to God began to offer sacrifices to God, from the new moon of the seventh month, though the temple of God was not yet built. [54] And they gave money to the masons and the carpenters, and food and drink [55] and carts to the Sidonians and the Tyrians, to bring cedar logs from Lebanon and convey them in rafts to the harbor of Joppa, according to the decree which they had in writing from Cyrus king of the Persians. [56] In the second year after their coming to the temple of God in Jerusalem, in the second month, Zerubbabel the son of Shealtiel and Jeshua the son of Jozadak made a beginning, together with their brethren and the Levitical priests and all who had come to

Jerusalem from the captivity;

[57] and they laid the foundation of the temple of God on the new moon of the second month in the second year after they came to Judea and Jerusalem. [58] And they appointed the Levites who were twenty or more years of age to have charge of the work of the Lord. And Jeshua arose, and his sons and brethren and Kadmiel his brother and the sons of Jeshua Emadabun and the sons of Joda son of Iliadun, with their sons and brethren, all the Levites, as one man pressing forward the work on the house of God.

So the builders built the temple of the Lord.

[59] And the priests stood arrayed in their garments, with musical instruments and trumpets, and the Levites, the sons of Asaph, with cymbals, [60] praising the Lord and blessing him, according to the directions of David king of Israel; [61] and they sang hymns, giving thanks to the Lord, because his goodness and his glory are for ever upon all Israel. [62] And all the people sounded trumpets and shouted with a great shout, praising the Lord for the erection of the house of the Lord. [63] Some of the Levitical priests and heads of fathers' houses, old men who had seen the former house, came to the building of this one with outcries and loud weeping, [64] while many came with trumpets and a joyful noise, [65] so that the people could not hear the trumpets because of the weeping of the people. For the multitude sounded the trumpets loudly, so that the sound was heard afar;

[66] and when the enemies of the tribe of Judah and Benjamin heard it, they came to find out what the sound of the trumpets meant. [67] And they learned that those who had returned from captivity were building the temple for the Lord God of Israel. [68] So they approached Zerubbabel and Jeshua and the heads of the fathers' houses and said to them, "We will build with you. [69] For we obey your Lord just as you do and we have been sacrificing to him ever since the days of Esarhaddon king of the Assyrians, who brought us here." [70] But Zerubbabel and Jeshua and the heads of the fathers' houses in Israel said to them, "You have nothing to do with us in building the house for the Lord our God, [71] for we alone will build it for the Lord of Israel, as Cyrus the king of the Persians has commanded us." [72] But the peoples of the land pressed hard upon those in Judea, cut off their supplies, and hindered their building; [73] and by plots and demagoguery and uprisings they prevented the completion of the building as long as King Cyrus lived. And they were kept from building for two years, until the reign of Darius.

6

[1] Now in the second year of the reign of Darius, the prophets Haggai and Zechariah the son of Iddo prophesied to the Jews who were in Judea and Jerusalem, they prophesied to them in the name of the Lord God of Israel.

[2] Then Zerubbabel the son of Shealtiel and Jeshua the son of Jozadak arose and began to build the house of the Lord which is in Jerusalem, with the help of the prophets of the Lord who were with them. [3] At the same time Sisinnes the governor of Syria and Phoenicia and Sathrabuzanes and their associates came to them and said, [4] "By whose order are you building this house and this roof and finishing all the other things? And who are the builders that are finishing these things?" [5] Yet the elders of the Jews were dealt with kindly, for the providence of the Lord was over the captives; [6] and they were not prevented from building until word could be sent to Darius concerning them and a report made. [7] A copy of the letter which Sisinnes the governor of Syria and Phoenicia, and Sathrabuzanes, and their associates the local rulers in Syria and Phoenicia, wrote and sent to Darius:

[8] "To King Darius, greeting. Let it be fully known to our lord the king that, when we went to the country of Judea and entered the city of Jerusalem, we found the elders of the Jews, who had been in captivity,

[9] building in the city of Jerusalem a great new house for the Lord, of hewn stone, with costly timber laid in the walls. [10] These operations are going on rapidly, and the work is prospering in their hands and being completed with all splendor and care. [11] Then we asked these elders, `At whose command are you building this house and laying the foundations of this structure?' [12] And in order that we might inform you in writing who the leaders are, we questioned them and asked them for a list of the names of those who are at their head. [13] They answered us, `We are the servants of the Lord who created the heaven and the earth. [14] And the house was built many years ago by a king of Israel who was great and strong, and it was finished. [15] But when our fathers sinned against the Lord of Israel who is in heaven, and provoked him, he gave them over into the hands of Nebuchadnezzar king of Babylon, king of the Chaldeans; [16] and they pulled down the house, and burned it, and carried the people away captive to Babylon. [17] But in the first year that Cyrus reigned over the country of Babylonia, King Cyrus wrote that this house should be rebuilt. [18] And the holy vessels of gold and of silver, which Nebuchadnezzar had taken out of the house in Jerusalem and stored in his own temple, these Cyrus the king took out again from the temple in Babylon, and they were delivered to Zerubbabel

and Sheshbazzar the governor [19] with the command that he should take all these vessels back and put them in the temple at Jerusalem, and that this temple of the Lord should be rebuilt on its site. [20] Then this Sheshbazzar, after coming here, laid the foundations of the house of the Lord which is in Jerusalem, and although it has been in process of construction from that time until now, it has not yet reached completion.' [21] Now therefore, if it seems wise, O king, let search be made in the royal archives of our lord the king that are in Babylon; [22] and if it is found that the building of the house of the Lord in Jerusalem was done with the consent of King Cyrus, and if it is approved by our lord the king, let him send us directions concerning these things." [23] Then Darius commanded that search be made in the royal archives that were deposited in Babylon. And in Ecbatana, the fortress which is in the country of Media, a scroll was found in which this was recorded:

[24] "In the first year of the reign of Cyrus, King Cyrus ordered the building of the house of the Lord in Jerusalem, where they sacrifice with perpetual fire; [25] its height to be sixty cubits and its breadth sixty cubits, with three courses of hewn stone and one course of new native timber; the cost to be paid from the treasury of Cyrus the king; [26] and that the holy vessels of the house of the Lord, both of gold and of silver, which Nebuchadnezzar took out of the house in Jerusalem and carried away to Babylon, should be restored to the house in Jerusalem, to be placed where they had been." [27] So Darius commanded Sisinnes the governor of Syria and Phoenicia, and Sathrabuzanes, and their associates, and those who were appointed as local rulers in Syria and Phoenicia, to keep away from the place, and to permit Zerubbabel, the servant of the Lord and governor of Judea, and the elders of the Jews to build this house of the Lord on its site.

[28] "And I command that it be built completely, and that full effort be made to help the men who have returned from the captivity of Judea, until the house of the Lord is finished; [29] and that out of the tribute of Coelesyria and Phoenicia a portion be scrupulously given to these men, that is, to Zerubbabel the governor, for sacrifices to the Lord, for bulls and rams and lambs, [30] and likewise wheat and salt and wine and oil, regularly every year, without quibbling, for daily use as the priests in Jerusalem may indicate, [31] in order that libations may be made to the Most High God for the king and his children, and prayers be offered for their life." [32] And he commanded that if any should transgress or nullify any of the things herein written, a beam should be taken out of his house and he should be hanged upon it, and his property should be forfeited to the king.

[33] "Therefore may the Lord, whose name is there called upon, destroy every king and nation that shall stretch out their hands to hinder or damage that house of the Lord in Jerusalem.

[34] "I, King Darius, have decreed that it be done with all diligence as here prescribed."

7

[1] Then Sisinnes the governor of Coelesyria and Phoenicia, and Sathrabuzanes, and their associates, following the orders of King Darius,

[2] supervised the holy work with very great care, assisting the elders of the Jews and the chief officers of the temple. [3] And the holy work prospered, while the prophets Haggai and Zechariah prophesied; [4] and they completed it by the command of the Lord God of Israel. So with the consent of Cyrus and Darius and Artaxerxes, kings of the Persians, [5] the holy house was finished by the twenty-third day of the month of Adar, in the sixth year of King Darius. [6] And the people of Israel, the priests, the Levites, and the rest of those from the captivity who joined them, did according to what was written in the book of Moses. [7] They offered at the dedication of the temple of the Lord one hundred bulls, two hundred rams, four hundred lambs, [8] and twelve he-goats for the sin of all Israel, according to the number of the twelve leaders of the tribes of Israel; [9] and the priests and the Levites stood arrayed in their garments, according to kindred, for the services of the Lord God of Israel in accordance with the book of Moses; and the gatekeepers were at each gate. [10] The people of Israel who came from the captivity kept the passover on the fourteenth day of the first month, after the priests and the Levites were purified together.

[11] Not all of the returned captives were purified, but the Levites were all purified together, [12] they sacrificed the passover lamb for all the returned captives and for their brethren the priests and for themselves. [13] And the people of Israel who came from the captivity ate it, all those who had separated themselves from the abominations of the peoples of the land and sought the Lord. [14] And they kept the feast of unleavened bread seven days, rejoicing before the Lord, [15] Because he had changed the will of the king of the Assyrians concerning them, to strengthen their hands for the service of the Lord God of Israel.

8

[1] After these things, when Artaxerxes the king of the Persians was reigning, Ezra came, the son of Seraiah, son of Azariah, son of Hilkiah, son of Shallum,
[2] son of Zadok, son of Ahitub, son of Amariah, son of Uzzi, son of Bukki, son of Abishua, son of Phineas, son of Eleazar, son of Aaron the chief priest. [3] This Ezra came up from Babylon as a scribe skilled in the law of Moses, which was given by the God of Israel; [4] and the king showed him honor, for he found favor before the king in all his requests. [5] There came up with him to Jerusalem some of the people of Israel and some of the priests and Levites and temple singers and gatekeepers and temple servants, [6] in the seventh year of the reign of Artaxerxes, in the fifth month (this was the king's seventh year); for they left Babylon on the new moon of the first month and arrived in Jerusalem on the new moon of the fifth month, by the prosperous journey which the Lord gave them. [7] For Ezra possessed great knowledge, so that he omitted nothing from the law of the Lord or the commandments, but taught all Israel all the ordinances and judgments. [8] The following is a copy of the written commission from Artaxerxes the king which was delivered to Ezra the priest and reader of the law of the Lord:
[9] "King Artaxerxes to Ezra the priest and reader of the law of the Lord, greeting.
[10] In accordance with my gracious decision, I have given orders that those of the Jewish nation and of the priests and Levites and others in our realm, who freely choose to do so, may go with you to Jerusalem. [11] Let as many as are so disposed, therefore, depart with you as I and the seven friends who are my counselors have decided, [12] in order to look into matters in Judea and Jerusalem, in accordance with what is in the law of the Lord, [13] and to carry to Jerusalem the gifts for the Lord of Israel which I and my friends have vowed, and to collect for the Lord in Jerusalem all the gold and silver that may be found in the country of Babylonia, [14] together with what is given by the nation for the temple of their Lord which is in Jerusalem, both gold and silver for bulls and rams and lambs and what goes with them, [15] so as to offer sacrifices upon the altar of their Lord which is in Jerusalem. [16] And whatever you and your brethren are minded to do with the gold and silver, perform it in accordance with the will of your God; [17] and deliver the holy vessels of the Lord which are given you for the use of the temple of your God which is in Jerusalem. [18] And whatever else occurs to you as necessary for the temple of your God, you may provide out of the royal treasury. [19] "And I, Artaxerxes the king, have commanded the treasurers of Syria and Phoenicia that whatever Ezra the priest and reader of the law of the Most High God sends for, they shall take care to give him, [20] up to a hundred talents of silver, and likewise up to a hundred cors of wheat, a hundred baths of wine, and salt in abundance. [21] Let all things prescribed in the law of God be scrupulously fulfilled for the Most High God, so that wrath may not come upon the kingdom of the king and his sons. [22] You are also informed that no tribute or any other tax is to be laid on any of the priests or Levites or temple singers or gatekeepers or temple servants or persons employed in this temple, and that no one has authority to impose any tax upon them. [23] "And you, Ezra, according to the wisdom of God, appoint judges and justices to judge all those who know the law of your God, throughout all Syria and Phoenicia; and those who do not know it you shall teach.
[24] And all who transgress the law of your God or the law of the kingdom shall be strictly punished, whether by death or some other punishment, either fine or imprisonment." [25] Blessed be the Lord alone, who put this into the heart of the king, to glorify his house which is in Jerusalem,
[26] and who honored me in the sight of the king and his counselors and all his friends and nobles.
[27] I was encouraged by the help of the Lord my God, and I gathered men from Israel to go up with me. [28] These are the principal men, according to their fathers' houses and their groups, who went up with me from Babylon, in the reign of Artaxerxes the king:
[29] Of the sons of Phineas, Gershom. Of the sons of Ithamar, Gamael. Of the sons of David, Hattush the son of Shecaniah. [30] Of the sons of Parosh, Zechariah, and with him a hundred and fifty men enrolled. [31] Of the sons of Pahathmoab, Eliehoenai the son of Zerahiah, and with him two hundred men. [32] Of the sons of Zattu, Shecaniah the son of Jahaziel, and with him three hundred men. Of the sons of Adin, Obed the son of Jonathan, and with him two hundred and fifty men. [33] Of the sons of Elam, Jeshaiah the son of Gotholiah, and with him seventy men. [34] Of the sons of Shephatiah, Zeraiah the son of Michael, and with him seventy men, [35] Of the sons of Joab, Obadiah the son of Jehiel, and with him two hundred and twelve men. [36] Of the sons of Bani, Shelomith the son of Josiphiah, and with him a hundred and sixty men. [37] Of the sons of Bebai, Zechariah the son of Bebai, and with him twenty-eight men. [38] Of the sons of Azgad, Johanan the son of Hakkatan, and with him a hundred and ten men. [39] Of the sons of Adonikam, the last ones, their names being Eliphelet, Jeuel, and Shemaiah, and with them seventy men. [40] Of the sons of Bigvai, Uthai the son of Istalcurus, and with him seventy men. [41] I assembled them at the river called Theras, and we encamped there three days, and I inspected them.
[42] When I found there none of the sons of the priests or of the Levites, [43] I sent word to Eliezar, Iduel, Maasmas, [44] Elnathan, Shemaiah, Jarib, Nathan, Elnathan, Zechariah, and Meshullam, who were leaders and men of understanding; [45] and I told them to go to Iddo, who was the leading man at the place of the treasury, [46] and ordered them to tell Iddo and his brethren and the treasurers at that place to send us men to serve as priests in the house of our Lord. [47] And by the mighty hand of our Lord they brought us competent men of the sons of Mahli the son of Levi, son of Israel, namely Sherebiah with his sons and kinsmen, eighteen; [48] also Hashabiah and Annunus and Jeshaiah his brother, of the sons of Hananiah, and their sons, twenty men; [49] and of the temple servants, whom David and the leaders had given for the service of the Levites, two hundred and twenty temple servants; the list of all their names was reported. [50] There I proclaimed a fast for the young men before our Lord, to seek from him a prosperous journey for ourselves and for our children and the cattle that were with us.
[51] For I was ashamed to ask the king for foot soldiers and horsemen and an escort to keep us safe from our adversaries; [52] for we had said to the king, "The power of our Lord will be with those who seek him, and will support them in every way." [53] And again we prayed to our Lord about these things, and we found him very merciful. [54] Then I set apart twelve of the leaders of the priests, Sherebiah and Hashabiah, and ten of their kinsmen with them;
[55] and I weighed out to them the silver and the gold and the holy vessels of the house of our Lord, which the king himself and his counselors and the nobles and all Israel had given. [56] I weighed and gave to them six hundred and fifty talents of silver, and silver vessels worth a hundred talents, and a hundred talents of gold, [57] and twenty golden bowls, and twelve bronze vessels of fine bronze that glittered like gold. [58] And I said to them, "You are holy to the Lord, and the vessels are holy, and the silver and the gold are vowed to the Lord, the Lord of our fathers. [59] Be watchful and on guard until you deliver them to the leaders of the priests and the Levites, and to the heads of the fathers' houses of Israel, in Jerusalem, in the chambers of the house of our Lord." [60] So the priests and the Levites who took the silver and the gold and the vessels which had been in Jerusalem carried them to the temple of the Lord. [61] We departed from the river Theras on the twelfth day of the first month; and we arrived in Jerusalem by the mighty hand of our Lord which was upon us; he delivered us from every enemy on the way, and so we came to Jerusalem.
[62] When we had been there three days, the silver and the gold were weighed and delivered in the house of our Lord to Meremoth the priest, son of Uriah; [63] and with him was Eleazar the son of Phinehas, and with them were Jozabad the son of Jeshua and Moeth the son of Binnui, the Levites. [64] The whole was counted and weighed, and the weight of everything was recorded at that very time. [65] And those who had come back from captivity offered sacrifices to the Lord, the God of Israel, twelve bulls for all Israel, ninety-six rams, [66] seventy-two lambs, and as a thank offering twelve he-goats -- all as a sacrifice to the Lord. [67] And they delivered the king's orders to the royal stewards and to the governors of Coelesyria and Phoenicia; and these officials honored the people and the temple of the Lord. [68] After these things had been done, the principal men came to me and said,
[69] "The people of Israel and the leaders and the priests and the Levites have not put away from themselves the alien peoples of the land and their pollutions, the Canaanites, the Hittites, the Perizzites, the Jebusites, the Moabites, the Egyptians, and the Edomites. [70] For they and their sons have married the daughters of these people, and the holy race has been mixed with the alien peoples of the land; and from the beginning of this matter the leaders and the nobles have been sharing in this iniquity." [71] As soon as I heard these things I rent my garments and my holy mantle, and pulled out hair from my head and beard, and sat down in anxiety and grief.
[72] And all who were ever moved at the word of the Lord of Israel gathered round me, as I mourned over this iniquity, and I sat grief-stricken until the evening sacrifice. [73] Then I rose from my fast, with my garments and my holy mantle rent, and kneeling down and stretching forth my hands to the Lord [74] I said, "O Lord, I am ashamed and confounded before thy face.
[75] For our sins have risen higher than our heads, and our mistakes have mounted up to heaven [76] from the times of our fathers, and we are in great sin to this day. [77] And because of our sins and the sins of our fathers we with our brethren and our kings and our priests were given over to the kings of the earth, to the sword and captivity and plundering, in shame until this day. [78] And now in some measure mercy has come to us from thee, O Lord, to leave to us a root and a name in thy holy place, [79] and to uncover a light for us in the house of the Lord our God, and to give us food in the time of our servitude. [80] Even in our bondage we were not forsaken by our Lord, but he brought us into favor with the kings of the Persians, so that they have given us food [81] and glorified the temple of our Lord, and raised Zion from desolation, to give us a stronghold in Judea and Jerusalem. [82] "And now, O Lord, what shall we say, when we have these things? For we have transgressed thy commandments, which thou didst give by thy servants the prophets, saying,
[83] `The land which you are entering to take possession of it is a land polluted with the pollution of the aliens of the land, and they have filled it with their uncleanness. [84] Therefore do not give your daughters in marriage to their sons, and do not take their daughters for your sons; [85] and do not

seek ever to have peace with them, in order that you may be strong and eat the good things of the land and leave it for an inheritance to your children for ever.' [86] And all that has happened to us has come about because of our evil deeds and our great sins. For thou, O Lord, didst lift the burden of our sins [87] and give us such a root as this; but we turned back again to transgress thy law by mixing with the uncleanness of the peoples of the land. [88] Wast thou not angry enough with us to destroy us without leaving a root or seed or name? [89] O Lord of Israel, thou art true; for we are left as a root to this day. [90] Behold, we are now before thee in our iniquities; for we can no longer stand in thy presence because of these things." [91] While Ezra was praying and making his confession, weeping and lying upon the ground before the temple, there gathered about him a very great throng from Jerusalem, men and women and youths; for there was great weeping among the multitude.

[92] Then Shecaniah the son of Jehiel, one of the men of Israel, called out, and said to Ezra, "We have sinned against the Lord, and have married foreign women from the peoples of the land; but even now there is hope for Israel. [93] Let us take an oath to the Lord about this, that we will put away all our foreign wives, with their children, [94] as seems good to you and to all who obey the law of the Lord. [95] Arise and take action, for it is your task, and we are with you to take strong measures." [96] Then Ezra arose and had the leaders of the priests and Levites of all Israel take oath that they would do this. And they took the oath.

9

[1] Then Ezra rose and went from the court of the temple to the chamber of Jehohanan the son of Eliashib,

[2] and spent the night there; and he did not eat bread or drink water, for he was mourning over the great iniquities of the multitude. [3] And a proclamation was made throughout Judea and Jerusalem to all who had returned from the captivity that they should assemble at Jerusalem, [4] and that if any did not meet there within two or three days, in accordance with the decision of the ruling elders, their cattle should be seized for sacrifice and the men themselves expelled from the multitude of those who had returned from the captivity. [5] Then the men of the tribe of Judah and Benjamin assembled at Jerusalem within three days; this was the ninth month, on the twentieth day of the month.

[6] And all the multitude sat in the open square before the temple, shivering because of the bad weather that prevailed. [7] Then Ezra rose and said to them, "You have broken the law and married foreign women, and so have increased the sin of Israel. [8] Now then make confession and give glory to the Lord the God of our fathers, [9] and do his will; separate yourselves from the peoples of the land and from your foreign wives." [10] Then all the multitude shouted and said with a loud voice, "We will do as you have said. [11] But the multitude is great and it is winter, and we are not able to stand in the open air. This is not a work we can do in one day or two, for we have sinned too much in these things. [12] so let the leaders of the multitude stay, and let all those in our settlements who have foreign wives come at the time appointed, [13] with the elders and judges of each place, until we are freed from the wrath of the Lord over this matter." [14] Jonathan the son of Asahel and Jahzeiah the son of Tikvah undertook the matter on these terms, and Meshullam and Levi and Shabbethai served with them as judges. [15] And those who had returned from the captivity acted in accordance with all this. [16] Ezra the priest chose for himself the leading men of their fathers' houses, all of them by name; and on the new moon of the tenth month they began their sessions to investigate the matter.

[17] And the cases of the men who had foreign wives were brought to an end by the new moon of the first month. [18] Of the priests those who were brought in and found to have foreign wives were:

[19] of the sons of Jeshua the son of Jozadak and his brethren, Maaseiah, Eliezar, Jarib, and Jodan. [20] They pledged themselves to put away their wives, and to give rams in expiation of their error. [21] Of the sons of Immer: Hanani and Zebadiah and Maaseiah and Shemaiah and Jehiel and Azariah. [22] Of the sons of Pashhur: Elioenai, Maaseiah, Ishmael, and Nathanael, and Gedaliah, and Elasah. [23] And of the Levites: Jozabad and Shimei and Kelaiah, who was Kelita, and Pethahiah and Judah and Jonah.

[24] Of the temple singers: Eliashib and Zaccur. [25] Of the gatekeepers: Shallum and Telem. [26] Of Israel: of the sons of Parosh: Ramiah, Izziah, Malchijah, Mijamin, and Eleazar, and Asibias, and Benaiah. [27] Of the sons of Elam: Mattaniah and Zechariah, Jehiel and Abdi, and Jeremoth and Elijah. [28] Of the sons of Zattu: Elioenai, Eliashib, Othoniah, Jeremoth, and Zabad and Zerdaiah. [29] Of the sons of Bebai: Jehohanan and Hananiah and Zabbai and Emathis. [30] Of the sons of Bani: Meshullam, Malluch, Adaiah, Jashub, and Sheal and Jeremoth. [31] Of the sons of Addi: Naathus and Moossias, Laccunus and Naidus, and Bescaspasmys and Sesthel, and Belnuus and Manasseas. [32] Of the sons of Annan, Elionas and Asaias and Melchias and Sabbaias and Simon Chosamaeus. [33] Of the sons of Hashum: Mattenai and Mattattah and Zabad and Eliphelet and Manasseh and Shimei. [34] Of the sons of Bani: Jeremai, Maadai, Amram, Joel, Mamdai and Bedeiah and Vaniah, Carabasion and Eliashib and Machnadebai, Eliasis, Binnui, Elialis, Shimei, Shelemiah, Nethaniah. Of the sons of Ezora: Shashai,

Azarel, Azael, Shemaiah, Amariah, Joseph. [35] Of the sons of Nebo: Mattithiah, Zabad, Iddo, Joel, Benaiah. [36] All these had married foreign women, and they put them away with their children. [37] The priests and the Levites and the men of Israel settled in Jerusalem and in the country. On the new moon of the seventh month, when the sons of Israel were in their settlements, [38] the whole multitude gathered with one accord into the open square before the east gate of the temple; [39] and they told Ezra the chief priest and reader to bring the law of Moses which had been given by the Lord God of Israel. [40] So Ezra the chief priest brought the law, for all the multitude, men and women, and all the priests to hear the law, on the new moon of the seventh month. [41] And he read aloud in the open square before the gate of the temple from early morning until midday, in the presence of both men and women; and all the multitude gave attention to the law. [42] Ezra the priest and reader of the law stood on the wooden platform which had been prepared; [43] and beside him stood Mattathiah, Shema, Anaiah, Azariah, Uriah, Hezekiah, and Baalsamus on his right hand, [44] and on his left Pedaiah, Mishael, Malchijah, Lothasubus, Nabariah, and Zechariah. [45] Then Ezra took up the book of the law in the sight of the multitude, for he had the place of honor in the presence of all.

[46] And when he opened the law, they all stood erect. And Ezra blessed the Lord God Most High, the God of hosts, the Almighty; [47] and all the multitude answered, "Amen." And they lifted up their hands, and fell to the ground and worshiped the Lord. [48] Jeshua and Anniuth and Sherebiah, Jamin, Akkub, Shabbethai, Hodiah, Maaseiah and Kelita, Azariah and Jozabad, Hanan, Pelaiah, the Levites, taught the law of the Lord, at the same time explaining what was read. [49] Then Attharates said to Ezra the chief priest and reader, and to the Levites who were teaching the multitude, and to all, [50] "This day is holy to the Lord" -- now they were all weeping as they heard the law -- [51] "so go your way, eat the fat and drink the sweet, and send portions to those who have none; [52] for the day is holy to the Lord; and do not be sorrowful, for the Lord will exalt you." [53] And the Levites commanded all the people, saying, "This day is holy; do not be sorrowful." [54] Then they all went their way, to eat and drink and enjoy themselves, and to give portions to those who had none, and to make great rejoicing; [55] because they were inspired by the words which they had been taught. And they came together.

2 Esdras

4Ezra.1

[1] The second book of the prophet Ezra the son of Seraiah, son of Azariah, son of Hilkiah, son of Shallum, son of Zadok, son of Ahitub,

[2] son of Ahijah, son of Phinehas, son of Eli, son of Amariah, son of Azariah, son of Meraioth, son of Arna, son of Uzzi, son of Borith, son of Abishua, son of Phinehas, son of Eleazar,

[3] son of Aaron, of the tribe of Levi, who was a captive in the country of the Medes in the reign of Artaxerxes, king of the Persians.

[4] The word of the Lord came to me, saying,

[5] "Go and declare to my people their evil deeds, and to their children the iniquities which they have committed against me, so that they may tell their children's children [6] that the sins of their parents have increased in them, for they have forgotten me and have offered sacrifices to strange gods. [7] Was it not I who brought them out of the land of Egypt, out of the house of bondage? But they have angered me and despised my counsels. [8] Pull out the hair of your head and hurl all evils upon them, for they have not obeyed my law -- they are a rebellious people. [9] How long shall I endure them, on whom I have bestowed such great benefits? [10] For their sake I have overthrown many kings; I struck down Pharaoh with his servants, and all his army. [11] I have destroyed all nations before them, and scattered in the east the people of two provinces, Tyre and Sidon; I have slain all their enemies. [12] "But speak to them and say, Thus says the Lord:

[13] Surely it was I who brought you through the sea, and made safe highways for you where there was no road; I gave you Moses as leader and Aaron as priest; [14] I provided light for you from a pillar of fire, and did great wonders among you. Yet you have forgotten me, says the Lord. [15] "Thus says the Lord Almighty: The quails were a sign to you; I gave you camps for your protection, and in them you complained.

[16] You have not exulted in my name at the destruction of your enemies, but to this day you still complain. [17] Where are the benefits which I bestowed on you? When you were hungry and thirsty in the wilderness, did you not cry out to me, [18] saying, `Why hast thou led us into this wilderness to kill us? It would have been better for us to serve the Egyptians than to die in this wilderness.' [19] I pitied your groanings and gave you manna for food; you ate the bread of angels. [20] When you were thirsty, did I not cleave the rock so that waters flowed in abundance? Because of the heat I covered you with the leaves of trees. [21] I divided fertile lands among you; I drove out the Canaanites, the Perizzites, and the Philistines before you. What more can I do for you? says the Lord. [22] Thus says the Lord Almighty: When you were in the wilderness, at the bitter stream, thirsty and blaspheming my name, [23] I did not send fire upon you for your blasphemies, but threw a tree into the water and made the stream sweet. [24] "What shall I do to you, O Jacob? You would not obey me, O Judah. I will turn to other nations and will give them my name, that they may keep my statutes.

[25] Because you have forsaken me, I also will forsake you. When you beg mercy of me, I will show you no mercy. [26] When you call upon me, I will not listen to you; for you have defiled your hands with blood, and your feet are swift to commit murder. [27] It is not as though you had forsaken me; you have forsaken yourselves, says the Lord. [28] "Thus says the Lord Almighty: Have I not entreated you as a father entreats his sons or a mother her daughters or a nurse her children,

[29] that you should be my people and I should be your God, and that you should be my sons and I should be your father? [30] I gathered you as a hen gathers her brood under her wings. But now, what shall I do to you? I will cast you out from my presence. [31] When you offer oblations to me, I will turn my face from you; for I have rejected your feast days, and new moons, and circumcisions of the flesh.

[32] I sent to you my servants the prophets, but you have taken and slain them and torn their bodies in pieces; their blood I will require of you, says the Lord. [33] "Thus says the Lord Almighty: Your house is desolate; I will drive you out as the wind drives straw;

[34] and your sons will have no children, because with you they have neglected my commandment and have done what is evil in my sight. [35] I will give your houses to a people that will come, who without having heard me will believe. Those to whom I have shown no signs will do what I have commanded.

[36] They have seen no prophets, yet will recall their former state. [37] I call to witness the gratitude of the people that is to come, whose children rejoice with gladness; though they do not see me with bodily eyes, yet with the spirit they will believe the things I have said. [38] "And now, father, look with pride and see the people coming from the east;

[39] to them I will give as leaders Abraham, Isaac, and Jacob and Hosea and Amos and Micah and Joel and Obadiah and Jonah [40] and Nahum and Habakkuk, Zephaniah, Haggai, Zechariah and Malachi,

who is also called the messenger of the Lord.

2

[1] "Thus says the Lord: I brought this people out of bondage, and I gave them commandments through my servants the prophets; but they would not listen to them, and made my counsels void.

[2] The mother who bore them says to them, `Go, my children, because I am a widow and forsaken.

[3] I brought you up with gladness; but with mourning and sorrow I have lost you, because you have sinned before the Lord God and have done what is evil in my sight. [4] But now what can I do for you? For I am a widow and forsaken. Go, my children, and ask for mercy from the Lord.' [5] I call upon you, father, as a witness in addition to the mother of the children, because they would not keep my covenant,

[6] that you may bring confusion upon them and bring their mother to ruin, so that they may have no offspring. [7] Let them be scattered among the nations, let their names be blotted out from the earth, because they have despised my covenant. [8] "Woe to you, Assyria, who conceal the unrighteous in your midst! O wicked nation, remember what I did to Sodom and Gomorrah,

[9] whose land lies in lumps of pitch and heaps of ashes. So will I do to those who have not listened to me, says the Lord Almighty." [10] Thus says the Lord to Ezra: "Tell my people that I will give them the kingdom of Jerusalem, which I was going to give to Israel.

[11] Moreover, I will take back to myself their glory, and will give to these others the everlasting habitations, which I had prepared for Israel. [12] The tree of life shall give them fragrant perfume, and they shall neither toil nor become weary. [13] Ask and you will receive; pray that your days may be few, that they may be shortened. The kingdom is already prepared for you; watch! [14] Call, O call heaven and earth to witness, for I left out evil and created good, because I live, says the Lord. [15] "Mother, embrace your sons; bring them up with gladness, as does the dove; establish their feet, because I have chosen you, says the Lord.

[16] And I will raise up the dead from their places, and will bring them out from their tombs, because I recognize my name in them. [17] Do not fear, mother of sons, for I have chosen you, says the Lord. [18] I will send you help, my servants Isaiah and Jeremiah. According to their counsel I have consecrated and prepared for you twelve trees loaded with various fruits, [19] and the same number of springs flowing with milk and honey, and seven mighty mountains on which roses and lilies grow; by these I will fill your children with joy. [20] Guard the rights of the widow, secure justice for the fatherless, give to the needy, defend the orphan, clothe the naked, [21] care for the injured and the weak, do not ridicule a lame man, protect the maimed, and let the blind man have a vision of my splendor. [22] Protect the old and the young within your walls; [23] When you find any who are dead, commit them to the grave and mark it, and I will give you the first place in my resurrection. [24] Pause and be quiet, my people, because your rest will come. [25] Good nurse, nourish your sons, and strengthen their feet. [26] Not one of the servants whom I have given you will perish, for I will require them from among your number. [27] Do not be anxious, for when the day of tribulation and anguish comes, others shall weep and be sorrowful, but you shall rejoice and have abundance. [28] The nations shall envy you but they shall not be able to do anything against you, says the Lord. [29] My hands will cover you, that your sons may not see Gehenna. [30] Rejoice, O mother, with your sons, because I will deliver you, says the Lord. [31] Remember your sons that sleep, because I will bring them out of the hiding places of the earth, and will show mercy to them; for I am merciful, says the Lord Almighty. [32] Embrace your children until I come, and proclaim mercy to them; because my springs run over, and my grace will not fail." [33] I, Ezra, received a command from the Lord on Mount Horeb to go to Israel. When I came to them they rejected me and refused the Lord's commandment.

[34] Therefore I say to you, O nations that hear and understand, "Await your shepherd; he will give you everlasting rest, because he who will come at the end of the age is close at hand. [35] Be ready for the rewards of the kingdom, because the eternal light will shine upon you for evermore. [36] Flee from the shadow of this age, receive the joy of your glory; I publicly call on my Savior to witness. [37] Receive what the Lord has entrusted to you and be joyful, giving thanks to him who has called you to heavenly kingdoms. [38] Rise and stand, and see at the feast of the Lord the number of those who have been sealed. [39] Those who have departed from the shadow of this age have received glorious garments from the Lord. [40] Take again your full number, O Zion, and conclude the list of your people who are clothed in white, who have fulfilled the law of the Lord. [41] The number of your children, whom you desired, is full; beseech the Lord's power that your people, who have been called from the beginning, may be made holy." [42] I, Ezra, saw on Mount Zion a great multitude, which I could not number, and they all were praising the Lord with songs.

[43] In their midst was a young man of great stature, taller than any of the others, and on the head of each of them he placed a crown, but he was more exalted than they. And I was held spellbound. [44] Then I asked an angel, "Who are these, my lord?" [45] He answered and said to me, "These are they who have put off mortal clothing and have put on the immortal, and they have confessed the name of

God; now they are being crowned, and receive palms." [46] Then I said to the angel, "Who is that young man who places crowns on them and puts palms in their hands?" [47] He answered and said to me, "He is the Son of God, whom they confessed in the world." So I began to praise those who had stood valiantly for the name of the Lord. [48] Then the angel said to me, "Go, tell my people how great and many are the wonders of the Lord God which you have seen."

3

[1] In the thirtieth year after the destruction of our city, I Salathiel, who am also called Ezra, was in Babylon. I was troubled as I lay on my bed, and my thoughts welled up in my heart,
[2] because I saw the desolation of Zion and the wealth of those who lived in Babylon. [3] My spirit was greatly agitated, and I began to speak anxious words to the Most High, and said, [4] "O sovereign Lord, didst thou not speak at the beginning when thou didst form the earth -- and that without help -- and didst command the dust [5] and it gave thee Adam, a lifeless body? Yet he was the workmanship of thy hands, and thou didst breathe into him the breath of life, and he was made alive in thy presence. [6] And thou didst lead him into the garden which thy right hand had planted before the earth appeared.
[7] And thou didst lay upon him one commandment of your; but he transgressed it, and immediately thou didst appoint death for him and for his descendants. From him there sprang nations and tribes, peoples and clans without number. [8] And every nation walked after its own will and did ungodly things before thee and scorned thee, and thou didst not hinder them. [9] But again, in its time thou didst bring the flood upon the inhabitants of the world and destroy them. [10] And the same fate befell them: as death came upon Adam, so the flood upon them. [11] But thou didst leave one of them, Noah with his household, and all the righteous who have descended from him. [12] "When those who dwelt on earth began to multiply, they produced children and peoples and many nations, and again they began to be more ungodly than were their ancestors.
[13] And when they were committing iniquity before thee, thou didst choose for thyself one of them, whose name was Abraham; [14] and thou didst love him, and to him only didst thou reveal the end of the times, secretly by night. [15] Thou didst make with him an everlasting covenant, and promise him that thou wouldst never forsake his descendants; and thou gavest to him Isaac, and to Isaac thou gavest Jacob and Esau. [16] And thou didst set apart Jacob for thyself, but Esau thou didst reject; and Jacob became a great multitude. [17] And when thou didst lead his descendants out of Egypt, thou didst bring them to Mount Sinai. [18] Thou didst bend down the heavens and shake the earth, and move the world, and make the depths to tremble, and trouble the times. [19] And thy glory passed through the four gates of fire and earthquake and wind and ice, to give the law to the descendants of Jacob, and thy commandment to the posterity of Israel. [20] "Yet thou didst not take away from them their evil heart, so that thy law might bring forth fruit in them.
[21] For the first Adam, burdened with an evil heart, transgressed and was overcome, as were also all who were descended from him. [22] Thus the disease became permanent; the law was in the people's heart along with the evil root, but what was good departed, and the evil remained. [23] So the times passed and the years were completed, and thou didst raise up for thyself a servant, named David. [24] And thou didst command him to build a city for thy name, and in it to offer thee oblations from what is your. [25] This was done for many years; but the inhabitants of the city transgressed, [26] in everything doing as Adam and all his descendants had done, for they also had the evil heart. [27] So thou didst deliver the city into the hands of thy enemies. [28] "Then I said in my heart, Are the deeds of those who inhabit Babylon any better? Is that why she has gained dominion over Zion?
[29] For when I came here I saw ungodly deeds without number, and my soul has seen many sinners during these thirty years. And my heart failed me, [30] for I have seen how thou do endure those who sin, and hast spared those who act wickedly, and hast destroyed thy people, and hast preserved thy enemies, [31] and hast not shown to any one how thy way may be comprehended. Are the deeds of Babylon better than those of Zion? [32] Or has another nation known thee besides Israel? Or what tribes have so believed thy covenants as these tribes of Jacob? [33] Yet their reward has not appeared and their labor has borne no fruit. For I have traveled widely among the nations and have seen that they abound in wealth, though they are unmindful of thy commandments. [34] Now therefore weigh in a balance our iniquities and those of the inhabitants of the world; and so it will be found which way the turn of the scale will incline. [35] When have the inhabitants of the earth not sinned in thy sight? Or what nation has kept thy commandments so well? [36] Thou mayest indeed find individual men who have kept thy commandments, but nations thou wilt not find."

4

[1] Then the angel that had been sent to me, whose name was Uriel, answered
[2] and said to me, "Your understanding has utterly failed regarding this world, and do you think you

can comprehend the way of the Most High?" [3] Then I said, "Yes, my lord." And he replied to me, "I have been sent to show you three ways, and to put before you three problems. [4] If you can solve one of them for me, I also will show you the way you desire to see, and will teach you why the heart is evil."
[5] I said, "Speak on, my lord." And he said to me, "Go, weigh for me the weight of fire, or measure for me a measure of wind, or call back for me the day that is past."
[6] I answered and said, "Who of those that have been born can do this, that you ask me concerning these things?"
[7] And he said to me, "If I had asked you, `How many dwellings are in the heart of the sea, or how many streams are at the source of the deep, or how many streams are above the firmament, or which are the exits of hell, or which are the entrances of paradise?'
[8] Perhaps you would have said to me, `I never went down into the deep, nor as yet into hell, neither did I ever ascend into heaven.' [9] But now I have asked you only about fire and wind and the day, things through which you have passed and without which you cannot exist, and you have given me no answer about them!" [10] And he said to me, "You cannot understand the things with which you have grown up; [11] how then can your mind comprehend the way of the Most High? And how can one who is already worn out by the corrupt world understand incorruption?" When I heard this, I fell on my face
[12] and said to him, "It would be better for us not to be here than to come here and live in ungodliness, and to suffer and not understand why." [13] He answered me and said, "I went into a forest of trees of the plain, and they made a plan
[14] and said, `Come, let us go and make war against the sea, that it may recede before us, and that we may make for ourselves more forests.' [15] And in like manner the waves of the sea also made a plan and said, `Come, let us go up and subdue the forest of the plain so that there also we may gain more territory for ourselves.' [16] But the plan of the forest was in vain, for the fire came and consumed it; [17] likewise also the plan of the waves of the sea, for the sand stood firm and stopped them. [18] If now you were a judge between them, which would you undertake to justify, and which to condemn?"
[19] I answered and said, "Each has made a foolish plan, for the land is assigned to the forest, and to the sea is assigned a place to carry its waves."
[20] He answered me and said, "You have judged rightly, but why have you not judged so in your own case?
[21] For as the land is assigned to the forest and the sea to its waves, so also those who dwell upon earth can understand only what is on the earth, and he who is above the heavens can understand what is above the height of the heavens." [22] Then I answered and said, "I beseech you, my lord, why have I been endowed with the power of understanding?
[23] For I did not wish to inquire about the ways above, but about those things which we daily experience: why Israel has been given over to the Gentiles as a reproach; why the people whom you loved has been given over to godless tribes, and the law of our fathers has been made of no effect and the written covenants no longer exist; [24] and why we pass from the world like locusts, and our life is like a mist, and we are not worthy to obtain mercy. [25] But what will he do for his name, by which we are called? It is about these things that I have asked." [26] He answered me and said, "If you are alive, you will see, and if you live long, you will often marvel, because the age is hastening swiftly to its end. [27] For it will not be able to bring the things that have been promised to the righteous in their appointed times, because this age is full of sadness and infirmities. [28] For the evil about which you ask me has been sown, but the harvest of it has not yet come. [29] If therefore that which has been sown is not reaped, and if the place where the evil has been sown does not pass away, the field where the good has been sown will not come. [30] For a grain of evil seed was sown in Adam's heart from the beginning, and how much ungodliness it has produced until now, and will produce until the time of threshing comes! [31] Consider now for yourself how much fruit of ungodliness a grain of evil seed has produced. [32] When heads of grain without number are sown, how great a threshing floor they will fill!" [33] Then I answered and said, "How long and when will these things be? Why are our years few and evil?"
[34] He answered me and said, "You do not hasten faster than the Most High, for your haste is for yourself, but the Highest hastens on behalf of many. [35] Did not the souls of the righteous in their chambers ask about these matters, saying, `How long are we to remain here? And when will come the harvest of our reward? [36] And Jeremiel the archangel answered them and said, `When the number of those like yourselves is completed; for he has weighed the age in the balance, [37] and measured the times by measure, and numbered the times by number; and he will not move or arouse them until that measure is fulfilled.'" [38] Then I answered and said, "O sovereign Lord, but all of us also are full of ungodliness.
[39] And it is perhaps on account of us that the time of threshing is delayed for the righteous -- on account of the sins of those who dwell on earth." [40] He answered me and said, "Go and ask a woman who is with child if, when her nine months have been completed, her womb can keep the child

within her any longer."

[41] And I said, "No, lord, it cannot."

And he said to me, "In Hades the chambers of the souls are like the womb.

[42] For just as a woman who is in travail makes haste to escape the pangs of birth, so also do these places hasten to give back those things that were committed to them from the beginning. [43] Then the things that you desire to see will be disclosed to you." [44] I answered and said, "If I have found favor in your sight, and if it is possible, and if I am worthy,

[45] show me this also: whether more time is to come than has passed, or whether for us the greater part has gone by. [46] For I know what has gone by, but I do not know what is to come." [47] And he said to me, "Stand at my right side, and I will show you the interpretation of a parable."

[48] So I stood and looked, and behold, a flaming furnace passed by before me, and when the flame had gone by I looked, and behold, the smoke remained.

[49] And after this a cloud full of water passed before me and poured down a heavy and violent rain, and when the rainstorm had passed, drops remained in the cloud. [50] And he said to me, "Consider it for yourself; for as the rain is more than the drops, and the fire is greater than the smoke, so the quantity that passed was far greater; but drops and smoke remained."

[51] Then I prayed and said, "Do you think that I shall live until those days? Or who will be alive in those days?"

[52] He answered me and said, "Concerning the signs about which you ask me, I can tell you in part; but I was not sent to tell you concerning your life, for I do not know.

5

[1] "Now concerning the signs: behold, the days are coming when those who dwell on earth shall be seized with great terror, and the way of truth shall be hidden, and the land shall be barren of faith. [2] And unrighteousness shall be increased beyond what you yourself see, and beyond what you heard of formerly. [3] And the land which you now see ruling shall be waste and untrodden, and men shall see it desolate. [4] But if the Most High grants that you live, you shall see it thrown into confusion after the third period; and the sun shall suddenly shine forth at night,and the moon during the day. [5] Blood shall drip from wood,and the stone shall utter its voice;the peoples shall be troubled, and the stars shall fall. [6] And one shall reign whom those who dwell on earth do not expect, and the birds shall fly away together; [7] and the sea of Sodom shall cast up fish; and one whom the many do not know shall make his voice heard by night, and all shall hear his voice. [8] There shall be chaos also in many places, and fire shall often break out, and the wild beasts shall roam beyond their haunts, and menstruous women shall bring forth monsters. [9] And salt waters shall be found in the sweet, and all friends shall conquer one another; then shall reason hide itself, and wisdom shall withdraw into its chamber, [10] and it shall be sought by many but shall not be found, and unrighteousness and unrestraint shall increase on earth.

[11] And one country shall ask its neighbor, `Has righteousness, or any one who does right, passed through you?' And it will answer, `No.' [12] And at that time men shall hope but not obtain; they shall labor but their ways shall not prosper. [13] These are the signs which I am permitted to tell you, and if you pray again, and weep as you do now, and fast for seven days, you shall hear yet greater things than these." [14] Then I awoke, and my body shuddered violently, and my soul was so troubled that it fainted.

[15] But the angel who had come and talked with me held me and strengthened me and set me on my feet. [16] Now on the second night Phaltiel, a chief of the people, came to me and said, "Where have you been? And why is your face sad?

[17] Or do you not know that Israel has been entrusted to you in the land of their exile? [18] Rise therefore and eat some bread, so that you may not forsake us, like a shepherd who leaves his flock in the power of cruel wolves." [19] Then I said to him, "Depart from me and do not come near me for seven days, and then you may come to me." He heard what I said and left me.

[20] So I fasted seven days, mourning and weeping, as Uriel the angel had commanded me. [21] And after seven days the thoughts of my heart were very grievous to me again.

[22] Then my soul recovered the spirit of understanding, and I began once more to speak words in the presence of the Most High. [23] And I said, "O sovereign Lord, from every forest of the earth and from all its trees thou hast chosen one vine, [24] and from all the lands of the world thou hast chosen for thyself one region, and from all the flowers of the world thou hast chosen for thyself one lily, [25] and from all the depths of the sea thou hast filled for thyself one river, and from all the cities that have been built thou hast consecrated Zion for thyself, [26] and from all the birds that have been created thou hast named for thyself one dove, and from all the flocks that have been made thou hast provided for thyself one sheep, [27] and from all the multitude of peoples thou hast gotten for thyself one people; and to this people, whom thou hast loved, thou hast given the law which is approved by all. [28] And now, O Lord, why hast thou given over the one to the many, and dishonored the one root beyond the

others, and scattered your only one among the many? [29] And those who opposed thy promises have trodden down those who believed thy covenants. [30] If thou do really hate thy people, they should be punished at thy own hands." [31] When I had spoken these words, the angel who had come to me on a previous night was sent to me,

[32] and he said to me, "Listen to me, and I will instruct you; pay attention to me, and I will tell you more." [33] And I said, "Speak, my lord." And he said to me, "Are you greatly disturbed in mind over Israel? Or do you love him more than his Maker does?"

[34] And I said, "No, my lord, but because of my grief I have spoken; for every hour I suffer agonies of heart, while I strive to understand the way of the Most High and to search out part of his judgment."

[35] And he said to me, "You cannot." And I said, "Why not, my lord? Why then was I born? Or why did not my mother's womb become my grave, that I might not see the travail of Jacob and the exhaustion of the people of Israel?"

[36] He said to me, "Count up for me those who have not yet come, and gather for me the scattered raindrops, and make the withered flowers bloom again for me;

[37] open for me the closed chambers, and bring forth for me the winds shut up in them, or show me the picture of a voice; and then I will explain to you the travail that you ask to understand." [38] And I said, "O sovereign Lord, who is able to know these things except he whose dwelling is not with men? [39] As for me, I am without wisdom, and how can I speak concerning the things which thou hast asked me?" [40] He said to me, "Just as you cannot do one of the things that were mentioned, so you cannot discover my judgment, or the goal of the love that I have promised my people."

[41] And I said, "Yet behold, O Lord, thou do have charge of those who are alive at the end, but what will those do who were before us, or we, or those who come after us?"

[42] He said to me, "I shall liken my judgment to a circle; just as for those who are last there is no slowness, so for those who are first there is no haste."

[43] Then I answered and said, "Couldst thou not have created at one time those who have been and those who are and those who will be, that thou mightest show thy judgment the sooner?"

[44] He replied to me and said, "The creation cannot make more haste than the Creator, neither can the world hold at one time those who have been created in it."

[45] And I said, "How hast thou said to thy servant that thou wilt certainly give life at one time to thy creation? If therefore all creatures will live at one time and the creation will sustain them, it might even now be able to support all of them present at one time."

[46] He said to me, "Ask a woman's womb, and say to it, `If you bear ten children, why one after another?' Request it therefore to produce ten at one time."

[47] I said, "Of course it cannot, but only each in its own time."

[48] He said to me, "Even so have I given the womb of the earth to those who from time to time are sown in it.

[49] For as an infant does not bring forth, and a woman who has become old does not bring forth any longer, so have I organized the world which I created." [50] Then I inquired and said, "Since thou hast now given me the opportunity, let me speak before thee. Is our mother, of whom thou hast told me, still young? Or is she now approaching old age?"

[51] He replied to me, "Ask a woman who bears children, and she will tell you.

[52] Say to her, `Why are those whom you have borne recently not like those whom you bore before, but smaller in stature?' [53] And she herself will answer you, `Those born in the strength of youth are different from those born during the time of old age, when the womb is failing.' [54] Therefore you also should consider that you and your contemporaries are smaller in stature than those who were before you, [55] and those who come after you will be smaller than you, as born of a creation which already is aging and passing the strength of youth." [56] And I said, "O Lord, I beseech thee, if I have found favor in thy sight, show thy servant through whom thou do visit thy creation."

6

[1] And he said to me, "At the beginning of the circle of the earth, before the portals of the world were in place, and before the assembled winds blew,

[2] and before the rumblings of thunder sounded, and before the flashes of lightning shone, and before the foundations of paradise were laid, [3] and before the beautiful flowers were seen, and before the powers of movement were established, and before the innumerable hosts of angels were gathered together, [4] and before the heights of the air were lifted up, and before the measures of the firmaments were named, and before the footstool of Zion was established, [5] and before the present years were reckoned; and before the imaginations of those who now sin were estranged, and before those who stored up treasures of faith were sealed -- [6] then I planned these things, and they were made through me and not through another, just as the end shall come through me and not through another." [7] And I answered and said, "What will be the dividing of the times? Or when will be the

end of the first age and the beginning of the age that follows?"

[8] He said to me, "From Abraham to Isaac, because from him were born Jacob and Esau, for Jacob's hand held Esau's heel from the beginning.

[9] For Esau is the end of this age, and Jacob is the beginning of the age that follows. [10] For the beginning of a man is his hand, and the end of a man is his heel; between the heel and the hand seek for nothing else, Ezra!" [11] I answered and said, "O sovereign Lord, if I have found favor in thy sight, [12] show thy servant the end of thy signs which thou didst show me in part on a previous night." [13] He answered and said to me, "Rise to your feet and you will hear a full, resounding voice.

[14] And if the place where you are standing is greatly shaken [15] while the voice is speaking, do not be terrified; because the word concerns the end, and the foundations of the earth will understand [16] that the speech concerns them. They will tremble and be shaken, for they know that their end must be changed." [17] When I heard this, I rose to my feet and listened, and behold, a voice was speaking, and its sound was like the sound of many waters.

[18] And it said, "Behold, the days are coming, and it shall be that when I draw near to visit the inhabitants of the earth, [19] and when I require from the doers of iniquity the penalty of their iniquity, and when the humiliation of Zion is complete, [20] and when the seal is placed upon the age which is about to pass away, then I will show these signs: the books shall be opened before the firmament, and all shall see it together. [21] Infants a year old shall speak with their voices, and women with child shall give birth to premature children at three and four months, and these shall live and dance. [22] Sown places shall suddenly appear unsown, and full storehouses shall suddenly be found to be empty; [23] and the trumpet shall sound aloud, and when all hear it, they shall suddenly be terrified. [24] At that time friends shall make war on friends like enemies, and the earth and those who inhabit it shall be terrified, and the springs of the fountains shall stand still, so that for three hours they shall not flow.

[25] "And it shall be that whoever remains after all that I have foretold to you shall himself be saved and shall see my salvation and the end of my world.

[26] And they shall see the men who were taken up, who from their birth have not tasted death; and the heart of the earth's inhabitants shall be changed and converted to a different spirit. [27] For evil shall be blotted out, and deceit shall be quenched; [28] faithfulness shall flourish, and corruption shall be overcome, and the truth, which has been so long without fruit, shall be revealed." [29] While he spoke to me, behold, little by little the place where I was standing began to rock to and fro.

[30] And he said to me, "I have come to show you these things this night. [31] If therefore you will pray again and fast again for seven days, I will again declare to you greater things than these, [32] because your voice has surely been heard before the Most High; for the Mighty One has seen your uprightness and has also observed the purity which you have maintained from your youth. [33] Therefore he sent me to show you all these things, and to say to you: `Believe and do not be afraid! [34] Do not be quick to think vain thoughts concerning the former times, lest you be hasty concerning the last times.'" [35] Now after this I wept again and fasted seven days as before, in order to complete the three weeks as I had been told.

[36] And on the eighth night my heart was troubled within me again, and I began to speak in the presence of the Most High. [37] For my spirit was greatly aroused, and my soul was in distress. [38] I said, "O Lord, thou didst speak at the beginning of creation, and didst say on the first day, `Let heaven and earth be made,' and thy word accomplished the work.

[39] And then the Spirit was hovering, and darkness and silence embraced everything; the sound of man's voice was not yet there. [40] Then thou didst command that a ray of light be brought forth from thy treasuries, so that thy works might then appear. [41] "Again, on the second day, thou didst create the spirit of the firmament, and didst command him to divide and separate the waters, that one part might move upward and the other part remain beneath.

[42] "On the third day thou didst command the waters to be gathered together in the seventh part of the earth; six parts thou didst dry up and keep so that some of them might be planted and cultivated and be of service before thee.

[43] For thy word went forth, and at once the work was done. [44] For immediately fruit came forth in endless abundance and of varied appeal to the taste; and flowers of inimitable color; and odors of inexpressible fragrance. These were made on the third day. [45] "On the fourth day thou didst command the brightness of the sun, the light of the moon, and the arrangement of the stars to come into being;

[46] and thou didst command them to serve man, who was about to be formed. [47] "On the fifth day thou didst command the seventh part, where the water had been gathered together, to bring forth living creatures, birds, and fishes; and so it was done.

[48] The dumb and lifeless water produced living creatures, as it was commanded, that therefore the nations might declare thy wondrous works. [49] "Then thou didst keep in existence two living creatures; the name of one thou didst call Behemoth and the name of the other Leviathan.

[50] And thou didst separate one from the other, for the seventh part where the water had been gathered together could not hold them both. [51] And thou didst give Behemoth one of the parts which had been dried up on the third day, to live in it, where there are a thousand mountains; [52] but to Leviathan thou didst give the seventh part, the watery part; and thou hast kept them to be eaten by whom thou wilt, and when thou wilt. [53] "On the sixth day thou didst command the earth to bring forth before thee cattle, beasts, and creeping things;

[54] and over these thou didst place Adam, as ruler over all the works which thou hadst made; and from him we have all come, the people whom thou hast chosen. [55] "All this I have spoken before thee, O Lord, because thou hast said that it was for us that thou didst create this world.

[56] As for the other nations which have descended from Adam, thou hast said that they are nothing, and that they are like spittle, and thou hast compared their abundance to a drop from a bucket. [57] And now, O Lord, behold, these nations, which are reputed as nothing, domineer over us and devour us. [58] But we thy people, whom thou hast called thy first-born, only begotten, zealous for thee, and most dear, have been given into their hands. [59] If the world has indeed been created for us, why do we not possess our world as an inheritance? How long will this be so?"

7

[1] When I had finished speaking these words, the angel who had been sent to me on the former nights was sent to me again,

[2] and he said to me, "Rise, Ezra, and listen to the words that I have come to speak to you." [3] I said, "Speak, my lord." And he said to me, "There is a sea set in a wide expanse so that it is broad and vast,

[4] but it has an entrance set in a narrow place, so that it is like a river. [5] If any one, then, wishes to reach the sea, to look at it or to navigate it, how can he come to the broad part unless he passes through the narrow part? [6] Another example: There is a city built and set on a plain, and it is full of all good things; [7] but the entrance to it is narrow and set in a precipitous place, so that there is fire on the right hand and deep water on the left; [8] and there is only one path lying between them, that is, between the fire and the water, so that only one man can walk upon that path. [9] If now that city is given to a man for an inheritance, how will the heir receive his inheritance unless he passes through the danger set before him?" [10] I said, "He cannot, lord." And he said to me, "So also is Israel's portion. [11] For I made the world for their sake, and when Adam transgressed my statutes, what had been made was judged. [12] And so the entrances of this world were made narrow and sorrowful and toilsome; they are few and evil, full of dangers and involved in great hardships. [13] But the entrances of the greater world are broad and safe, and really yield the fruit of immortality. [14] Therefore unless the living pass through the difficult and vain experiences, they can never receive those things that have been reserved for them. [15] But now why are you disturbed, seeing that you are to perish? And why are you moved, seeing that you are mortal? [16] And why have you not considered in your mind what is to come, rather than what is now present?" [17] Then I answered and said, "O sovereign Lord, behold, thou hast ordained in thy law that the righteous shall inherit these things, but that the ungodly shall perish.

[18] The righteous therefore can endure difficult circumstances while hoping for easier ones; but those who have done wickedly have suffered the difficult circumstances and will not see the easier ones."

[19] And he said to me, "You are not a better judge than God, or wiser than the Most High!

[20] Let many perish who are now living, rather than that the law of God which is set before them be disregarded! [21] For God strictly commanded those who came into the world, when they came, what they should do to live, and what they should observe to avoid punishment. [22] Nevertheless they were not obedient, and spoke against him; they devised for themselves vain thoughts, [23] and proposed to themselves wicked frauds; they even declared that the Most High does not exist, and they ignored his ways! [24] They scorned his law, and denied his covenants; they have been unfaithful to his statutes, and have not performed his works. [25] "Therefore, Ezra, empty things are for the empty, and full things are for the full.

[26] For behold, the time will come, when the signs which I have foretold to you will come to pass, that the city which now is not seen shall appear, and the land which now is hidden shall be disclosed. [27] And every one who has been delivered from the evils that I have foretold shall see my wonders. [28] For my son the Messiah shall be revealed with those who are with him, and those who remain shall rejoice four hundred years. [29] And after these years my son the Messiah shall die, and all who draw human breath. [30] And the world shall be turned back to primeval silence for seven days, as it was at the first beginnings; so that no one shall be left. [31] And after seven days the world, which is not yet awake, shall be roused, and that which is corruptible shall perish. [32] And the earth shall give up those who are asleep in it, and the dust those who dwell silently in it; and the chambers shall give up the souls which have been committed to them. [33] And the Most High shall be revealed upon the seat of

judgment, and compassion shall pass away, and patience shall be withdrawn; [34] but only judgment shall remain, truth shall stand, and faithfulness shall grow strong. [35] And recompense shall follow, and the reward shall be manifested; righteous deeds shall awake, and unrighteous deeds shall not sleep. [36] Then the pit of torment shall appear, and opposite it shall be the place of rest; and the furnace of hell shall be disclosed, and opposite it the paradise of delight. [37] Then the Most High will say to the nations that have been raised from the dead, `Look now, and understand whom you have denied, whom you have not served, whose commandments you have despised! [38] Look on this side and on that; here are delight and rest, and there are fire and torments!' Thus he will speak to them on the day of judgment -- [39] a day that has no sun or moon or stars, [40] or cloud or thunder or lightning or wind or water or air, or darkness or evening or morning, [41] or summer or spring or heat or winter or frost or cold or hail or rain or dew, [42] or noon or night, or dawn or shining or brightness or light, but only the splendor of the glory of the Most High, by which all shall see what has been determined for them. [43] For it will last for about a week of years. [44] This is my judgment and its prescribed order; and to you alone have I shown these things." [45] I answered and said, "O sovereign Lord, I said then and I say now: Blessed are those who are alive and keep thy commandments!

[46] But what of those for whom I prayed? For who among the living is there that has not sinned, or who among men that has not transgressed thy covenant? [47] And now I see that the world to come will bring delight to few, but torments to many. [48] For an evil heart has grown up in us, which has alienated us from God, and has brought us into corruption and the ways of death, and has shown us the paths of perdition and removed us far from life -- and that not just a few of us but almost all who have been created!" [49] He answered me and said, "Listen to me, Ezra, and I will instruct you, and will admonish you yet again.

[50] For this reason the Most High has made not one world but two. [51] For whereas you have said that the righteous are not many but few, while the ungodly abound, hear the explanation for this. [52] "If you have just a few precious stones, will you add to them lead and clay?"

[53] I said, "Lord, how could that be?"

[54] And he said to me, "Not only that, but ask the earth and she will tell you; defer to her, and she will declare it to you.

[55] Say to her, `You produce gold and silver and brass, and also iron and lead and clay; [56] but silver is more abundant than gold, and brass than silver, and iron than brass, and lead than iron, and clay than lead.' [57] Judge therefore which things are precious and desirable, those that are abundant or those that are rare?" [58] I said, "O sovereign Lord, what is plentiful is of less worth, for what is more rare is more precious."

[59] He answered me and said, "Weigh within yourself what you have thought, for he who has what is hard to get rejoices more than he who has what is plentiful.

[60] So also will be the judgment which I have promised; for I will rejoice over the few who shall be saved, because it is they who have made my glory to prevail now, and through them my name has now been honored. [61] And I will not grieve over the multitude of those who perish; for it is they who are now like a mist, and are similar to a flame and smoke -- they are set on fire and burn hotly, and are extinguished." [62] I replied and said, "O earth, what have you brought forth, if the mind is made out of the dust like the other created things!

[63] For it would have been better if the dust itself had not been born, so that the mind might not have been made from it. [64] But now the mind grows with us, and therefore we are tormented, because we perish and know it. [65] Let the human race lament, but let the beasts of the field be glad; let all who have been born lament, but let the four-footed beasts and the flocks rejoice! [66] For it is much better with them than with us; for they do not look for a judgment, nor do they know of any torment or salvation promised to them after death. [67] For what does it profit us that we shall be preserved alive but cruelly tormented? [68] For all who have been born are involved in iniquities, and are full of sins and burdened with transgressions. [69] And if we were not to come into judgment after death, perhaps it would have been better for us." [70] He answered me and said, "When the Most High made the world and Adam and all who have come from him, he first prepared the judgment and the things that pertain to the judgment.

[71] And now understand from your own words, for you have said that the mind grows with us. [72] For this reason, therefore, those who dwell on earth shall be tormented, because though they had understanding they committed iniquity, and though they received the commandments they did not keep them, and though they obtained the law they dealt unfaithfully with what they received. [73] What, then, will they have to say in the judgment, or how will they answer in the last times? [74] For how long the time is that the Most High has been patient with those who inhabit the world, and not for their sake, but because of the times which he has foreordained!" [75] I answered and said, "If I have found favor in thy sight, O Lord, show this also to thy servant: whether after death, as soon as every one of us yields up his soul, we shall be kept in rest until those times come when thou wilt renew the creation, or

whether we shall be tormented at once?"

[76] He answered me and said, "I will show you that also, but do not be associated with those who have shown scorn, nor number yourself among those who are tormented.

[77] For you have a treasure of works laid up with the Most High; but it will not be shown to you until the last times. [78] Now, concerning death, the teaching is: When the decisive decree has gone forth from the Most High that a man shall die, as the spirit leaves the body to return again to him who gave it, first of all it adores the glory of the Most High. [79] And if it is one of those who have shown scorn and have not kept the way of the Most High, and who have despised his law, and who have hated those who fear God -- [80] such spirits shall not enter into habitations, but shall immediately wander about in torments, ever grieving and sad, in seven ways. [81] The first way, because they have scorned the law of the Most High. [82] The second way, because they cannot now make a good repentance that they may live. [83] The third way, they shall see the reward laid up for those who have trusted the covenants of the Most High. [84] The fourth way, they shall consider the torment laid up for themselves in the last days. [85] The fifth way, they shall see how the habitations of the others are guarded by angels in profound quiet. [86] The sixth way, they shall see how some of them will pass over into torments. [87] The seventh way, which is worse than all the ways that have been mentioned, because they shall utterly waste away in confusion and be consumed with shame, and shall wither with fear at seeing the glory of the Most High before whom they sinned while they were alive, and before whom they are to be judged in the last times. [88] "Now this is the order of those who have kept the ways of the Most High, when they shall be separated from their mortal body.

[89] During the time that they lived in it, they laboriously served the Most High, and withstood danger every hour, that they might keep the law of the Lawgiver perfectly. [90] Therefore this is the teaching concerning them: [91] First of all, they shall see with great joy the glory of him who receives them, for they shall have rest in seven orders. [92] The first order, because they have striven with great effort to overcome the evil thought which was formed with them, that it might not lead them astray from life into death. [93] The second order, because they see the perplexity in which the souls of the ungodly wander, and the punishment that awaits them. [94] The third order, they see the witness which he who formed them bears concerning them, that while they were alive they kept the law which was given them in trust. [95] The fourth order, they understand the rest which they now enjoy, being gathered into their chambers and guarded by angels in profound quiet, and the glory which awaits them in the last days. [96] The fifth order, they rejoice that they have now escaped what is corruptible, and shall inherit what is to come; and besides they see the straits and toil from which they have been delivered, and the spacious liberty which they are to receive and enjoy in immortality. [97] The sixth order, when it is shown to them how their face is to shine like the sun, and how they are to be made like the light of the stars, being incorruptible from then on. [98] The seventh order, which is greater than all that have been mentioned, because they shall rejoice with boldness, and shall be confident without confusion, and shall be glad without fear, for they hasten to behold the face of him whom they served in life and from whom they are to receive their reward when glorified. [99] This is the order of the souls of the righteous, as henceforth is announced; and the aforesaid are the ways of torment which those who would not give heed shall suffer hereafter." [100] I answered and said, "Will time therefore be given to the souls, after they have been separated from the bodies, to see what you have described to me?"

[101] He said to me, "They shall have freedom for seven days, so that during these seven days they may see the things of which you have been told, and afterwards they shall be gathered in their habitations."

[102] I answered and said, "If I have found favor in thy sight, show further to me, thy servant, whether on the day of judgment the righteous will be able to intercede for the ungodly or to entreat the Most High for them,

[103] fathers for sons or sons for parents, brothers for brothers, relatives for their kinsmen, or friends for those who are most dear." [104] He answered me and said, "Since you have found favor in my sight, I will show you this also. The day of judgment is decisive and displays to all the seal of truth. Just as now a father does not send his son, or a son his father, or a master his servant, or a friend his dearest friend, to be ill or sleep or eat or be healed in his stead,

[105] so no one shall ever pray for another on that day, neither shall any one lay a burden on another; for then every one shall bear his own righteousness and unrighteousness." [36(106)] I answered and said, "How then do we find that first Abraham prayed for the people of Sodom, and Moses for our fathers who sinned in the desert,

[37(107)] and Joshua after him for Israel in the days of Achan, [38(108)] and Samuel in the days of Saul, and David for the plague, and Solomon for those in the sanctuary, [39(109)] and Elijah for those who received the rain, and for the one who was dead, that he might live, [40(110)] and Hezekiah for the people in the days of Sennacherib, and many others prayed for many? [41(111)] If therefore the righteous have prayed for the ungodly now, when corruption has increased and unrighteousness has multiplied, why will it not be so then as well?" [42(112)] He answered me and said, "This present world is not the end; the full glory does not abide in it; therefore those who were strong prayed for the weak.

[43(113)] But the day of judgment will be the end of this age and the beginning of the immortal age to come, in which corruption has passed away, [44(114)] sinful indulgence has come to an end, unbelief has been cut off, and righteousness has increased and truth has appeared. [45(115)] Therefore no one will then be able to have mercy on him who has been condemned in the judgment, or to harm him who is victorious." [46(116)] I answered and said, "This is my first and last word, that it would have been better if the earth had not produced Adam, or else, when it had produced him, had restrained him from sinning.

[47(117)] For what good is it to all that they live in sorrow now and expect punishment after death? [48(118)] O Adam, what have you done? For though it was you who sinned, the fall was not yours alone, but ours also who are your descendants. [49(119)] For what good is it to us, if an eternal age has been promised to us, but we have done deeds that bring death? [50(120)] And what good is it that an everlasting hope has been promised to us, but we have miserably failed? [51(121)] Or that safe and healthful habitations have been reserved for us, but we have lived wickedly? [52(122)] Or that the glory of the Most High will defend those who have led a pure life, but we have walked in the most wicked ways? [53(123)] Or that a paradise shall be revealed, whose fruit remains unspoiled and in which are abundance and healing, but we shall not enter it, [54(124)] because we have lived in unseemly places? [55(125)] Or that the faces of those who practiced self-control shall shine more than the stars, but our faces shall be blacker than darkness? [56(126)] For while we lived and committed iniquity we did not consider what we should suffer after death." [57(127)] He answered and said, "This is the meaning of the contest which every man who is born on earth shall wage, [58(128)] that if he is defeated he shall suffer what you have said, but if he is victorious he shall receive what I have said. [59(129)] For this is the way of which Moses, while he was alive, spoke to the people, saying, `Choose for yourself life, that you may live!' [60(130)] But they did not believe him, or the prophets after him, or even myself who have spoken to them. [61(131)] Therefore there shall not be grief at their destruction, so much as joy over those to whom salvation is assured."

[62(132)] I answered and said, "I know, O Lord, that the Most High is now called merciful, because he has mercy on those who have not yet come into the world; [63(133)] and gracious, because he is gracious to those who turn in repentance to his law; [64(134)] and patient, because he shows patience toward those who have sinned, since they are his own works; [65(135)] and bountiful, because he would rather give than take away; [66(136)] and abundant in compassion, because he makes his compassions abound more and more to those now living and to those who are gone and to those yet to come, [67(137)] for if he did not make them abound, the world with those who inhabit it would not have life; [68(138)] and he is called giver, because if he did not give out of his goodness so that those who have committed iniquities might be relieved of them, not one ten-thousandth of mankind could have life; [69(139)] and judge, because if he did not pardon those who were created by his word and blot out the multitude of their sins, [70(140)] there would probably be left only very few of the innumerable multitude."

8

[1] He answered me and said, "The Most High made this world for the sake of many, but the world to come for the sake of few.
[2] But I tell you a parable, Ezra. Just as, when you ask the earth, it will tell you that it provides very much clay from which earthenware is made, but only a little dust from which gold comes; so is the course of the present world.
[3] Many have been created, but few shall be saved."
[4] I answered and said, "Then drink your fill of understanding, O my soul, and drink wisdom, O my heart!
[5] For not of your own will did you come into the world, and against your will you depart, for you have been given only a short time to live.
[6] O Lord who are over us, grant to thy servant that we may pray before thee, and give us seed for our heart and cultivation of our understanding so that fruit may be produced, by which every mortal who bears the likeness of a human being may be able to live.
[7] For thou alone do exist, and we are a work of thy hands, as thou hast declared.
[8] And because thou do give life to the body which is now fashioned in the womb, and do furnish it with members, what thou hast created is preserved in fire and water, and for nine months the womb which thou has formed endures thy creation which has been created in it.
[9] But that which keeps and that which is kept shall both be kept by thy keeping. And when the womb gives up again what has been created in it,

[10] thou hast commanded that from the members themselves (that is, from the breasts) milk should be supplied which is the fruit of the breasts,
[11] so that what has been fashioned may be nourished for a time; and afterwards thou wilt guide him in thy mercy.
[12] Thou hast brought him up in thy righteousness, and instructed him in thy law, and reproved him in thy wisdom.
[13] Thou wilt take away his life, for he is thy creation; and thou wilt make him live, for he is thy work.
[14] If then thou wilt suddenly and quickly destroy him who with so great labor was fashioned by thy command, to what purpose was he made?
[15] And now I will speak out: About all mankind thou knowest best; but I will speak about thy people, for whom I am grieved,
[16] and about thy inheritance, for whom I lament, and about Israel, for whom I am sad, and about the seed of Jacob, for whom I am troubled.
[17] Therefore I will pray before thee for myself and for them, for I see the failings of us who dwell in the land,
[18] and I have heard of the swiftness of the judgment that is to come.
[19] Therefore hear my voice, and understand my words, and I will speak before thee." The beginning of the words of Ezra's prayer, before he was taken up. He said:
[20] "O Lord who inhabitest eternity, whose eyes are exalted and whose upper chambers are in the air,
[21] whose throne is beyond measure and whose glory is beyond comprehension, before whom the hosts of angels stand trembling
[22] and at whose command they are changed to wind and fire, whose word is sure and whose utterances are certain, whose ordinance is strong and whose command is terrible,
[23] whose look dries up the depths and whose indignation makes the mountains melt away, and whose truth is established for ever --
[24] hear, O Lord, the prayer of thy servant, and give ear to the petition of thy creature; attend to my words.
[25] For as long as I live I will speak, and as long as I have understanding I will answer.
[26] O look not upon the sins of thy people, but at those who have served thee in truth.
[27] Regard not the endeavors of those who act wickedly, but the endeavors of those who have kept thy covenants amid afflictions.
[28] Think not on those who have lived wickedly in thy sight; but remember those who have willingly acknowledged that thou art to be feared.
[29] Let it not be thy will to destroy those who have had the ways of cattle; but regard those who have gloriously taught thy law.
[30] Be not angry with those who are deemed worse than beasts; but love those who have always put their trust in thy glory.
[31] For we and our fathers have passed our lives in ways that bring death, but thou, because of us sinners, are called merciful.
[32] For if thou hast desired to have pity on us, who have no works of righteousness, then thou wilt be called merciful.
[33] For the righteous, who have many works laid up with thee, shall receive their reward in consequence of their own deeds.
[34] But what is man, that thou art angry with him; or what is a corruptible race, that thou art so bitter against it?
[35] For in truth there is no one among those who have been born who has not acted wickedly, and among those who have existed there is no one who has not transgressed.
[36] For in this, O Lord, thy righteousness and goodness will be declared, when thou art merciful to those who have no store of good works."
[37] He answered me and said, "Some things you have spoken rightly, and it will come to pass according to your words.
[38] For indeed I will not concern myself about the fashioning of those who have sinned, or about their death, their judgment, or their destruction;
[39] but I will rejoice over the creation of the righteous, over their pilgrimage also, and their salvation, and their receiving their reward.
[40] As I have spoken, therefore, so it shall be.
[41] "For just as the farmer sows many seeds upon the ground and plants a multitude of seedlings, and yet not all that have been sown will come up in due season, and not all that were planted will take root; so also those who have been sown in the world will not all be saved."
[42] I answered and said, "If I have found favor before thee, let me speak.
[43] For if the farmer's seed does not come up, because it has not received thy rain in due season, or if

it has been ruined by too much rain, it perishes.

[44] But man, who has been formed by thy hands and is called thy own image because he is made like thee, and for whose sake thou hast formed all things -- hast thou also made him like the farmer's seed?

[45] No, O Lord who art over us! But spare thy people and have mercy on thy inheritance, for thou hast mercy on thy own creation."

[46] He answered me and said, "Things that are present are for those who live now, and things that are future are for those who will live hereafter.

[47] For you come far short of being able to love my creation more than I love it. But you have often compared yourself to the unrighteous. Never do so!

[48] But even in this respect you will be praiseworthy before the Most High,

[49] because you have humbled yourself, as is becoming for you, and have not deemed yourself to be among the righteous in order to receive the greatest glory.

[50] For many miseries will affect those who inhabit the world in the last times, because they have walked in great pride.

[51] But think of your own case, and inquire concerning the glory of those who are like yourself,

[52] because it is for you that paradise is opened, the tree of life is planted, the age to come is prepared, plenty is provided, a city is built, rest is appointed, goodness is established and wisdom perfected beforehand.

[53] The root of evil is sealed up from you, illness is banished from you, and death is hidden; hell has fled and corruption has been forgotten;

[54] sorrows have passed away, and in the end the treasure of immortality is made manifest.

[55] Therefore do not ask any more questions about the multitude of those who perish.

[56] For they also received freedom , but they despised the Most High, and were contemptuous of his law, and forsook his ways.

[57] Moreover they have even trampled upon his righteous ones,

[58] and said in their hearts that there is not God -- though knowing full well that they must die.

[59] For just as the things which I have predicted await you, so the thirst and torment which are prepared await them. For the Most High did not intend that men should be destroyed;

[60] but they themselves who were created have defiled the name of him who made them, and have been ungrateful to him who prepared life for them.

[61] Therefore my judgment is now drawing near;

[62] I have not shown this to all men, but only to you and a few like you." Then I answered and said,

[63] "Behold, O Lord, thou hast now shown me a multitude of the signs which thou wilt do in the last times, but thou hast not shown me when thou wilt do them."

9

[1] He answered me and said, "Measure carefully in your mind, and when you see that a certain part of the predicted signs are past,

[2] then you will know that it is the very time when the Most High is about to visit the world which he has made.

[3] So when there shall appear in the world earthquakes, tumult of peoples, intrigues of nations, wavering of leaders, confusion of princes,

[4] then you will know that it was of these that the Most High spoke from the days that were of old, from the beginning.

[5] For just as with everything that has occurred in the world, the beginning is evident, and the end manifest;

[6] so also are the times of the Most High: the beginnings are manifest in wonders and mighty works, and the end in requital and in signs.

[7] And it shall be that every one who will be saved and will be able to escape on account of his works, or on account of the faith by which he has believed,

[8] will survive the dangers that have been predicted, and will see my salvation in my land and within my borders, which I have sanctified for myself from the beginning.

[9] Then those who have now abused my ways shall be amazed, and those who have rejected them with contempt shall dwell in torments.

[10] For as many as did not acknowledge me in their lifetime, although they received my benefits,

[11] and as many as scorned my law while they still had freedom, and did not understand but despised it while an opportunity of repentance was still open to them,

[12] these must in torment acknowledge it after death.

[13] Therefore, do not continue to be curious as to how the ungodly will be punished; but inquire how the righteous will be saved, those to whom the age belongs and for whose sake the age was made."

[14] I answered and said,

[15] "I said before, and I say now, and will say it again: there are more who perish than those who will be saved,

[16] as a wave is greater than a drop of water."

[17] He answered me and said, "As is the field, so is the seed; and as are the flowers, so are the colors; and as is the work, so is the product; and as is the farmer, so is the threshing floor.

[18] For there was a time in this age when I was preparing for those who now exist, before the world was made for them to dwell in, and no one opposed me then, for no one existed;

[19] but now those who have been created in this world which is supplied both with an unfailing table and an inexhaustible pasture, have become corrupt in their ways.

[20] So I considered my world, and behold, it was lost, and my earth, and behold, it was in peril because of the devices of those who had come into it.

[21] And I saw and spared some with great difficulty, and saved for myself one grape out of a cluster, and one plant out of a great forest.

[22] So let the multitude perish which has been born in vain, but let my grape and my plant be saved, because with much labor I have perfected them.

[23] But if you will let seven days more pass -- do not fast during them, however;

[24] but go into a field of flowers where no house has been built, and eat only of the flowers of the field, and taste no meat and drink no wine, but eat only flowers,

[25] and pray to the Most High continually -- then I will come and talk with you."

[26] So I went, as he directed me, into the field which is called Ardat; and there I sat among the flowers and ate of the plants of the field, and the nourishment they afforded satisfied me.

[27] And after seven days, as I lay on the grass, my heart was troubled again as it was before.

[28] And my mouth was opened, and I began to speak before the Most High, and said,

[29] "O Lord, thou didst show thyself among us, to our fathers in the wilderness when they came out from Egypt and when they came into the untrodden and unfruitful wilderness;

[30] and thou didst say, `Hear me, O Israel, and give heed to my words, O descendants of Jacob.

[31] For behold, I sow my law in you, and it shall bring forth fruit in you and you shall be glorified through it for ever.'

[32] But though our fathers received the law, they did not keep it, and did not observe the statutes; yet the fruit of the law did not perish -- for it could not, because it was your.

[33] Yet those who received it perished, because they did not keep what had been sown in them.

[34] And behold, it is the rule that, when the ground has received seed, or the sea a ship, or any dish food or drink, and when it happens that what was sown or what was launched or what was put in is destroyed,

[35] they are destroyed, but the things that held them remain; yet with us it has not been so.

[36] For we who have received the law and sinned will perish, as well as our heart which received it;

[37] the law, however, does not perish but remains in its glory."

[38] When I said these things in my heart, I lifted up my eyes and saw a woman on my right, and behold, she was mourning and weeping with a loud voice, and was deeply grieved at heart, and her clothes were rent, and there were ashes on her head.

[39] Then I dismissed the thoughts with which I had been engaged, and turned to her

[40] and said to her, "Why are you weeping, and why are you grieved at heart?"

[41] And she said to me, "Let me alone, my lord, that I may weep for myself and continue to mourn, for I am greatly embittered in spirit and deeply afflicted."

[42] And I said to her, "What has happened to you? Tell me."

[43] And she said to me, "Your servant was barren and had no child, though I lived with my husband thirty years.

[44] And every hour and every day during those thirty years I besought the Most High, night and day.

[45] And after thirty years God heard your handmaid, and looked upon my low estate, and considered my distress, and gave me a son. And I rejoiced greatly over him, I and my husband and all my neighbors; and we gave great glory to the Mighty One.

[46] And I brought him up with much care.

[47] So when he grew up and I came to take a wife for him, I set a day for the marriage feast.

10

[1] "But it happened that when my son entered his wedding chamber, he fell down and died.

[2] Then we all put out the lamps, and all my neighbors attempted to console me; and I remained quiet until evening of the second day.

[3] But when they all had stopped consoling me, that I might be quiet, I got up in the night and fled, and came to this field, as you see.

[4] And now I intend not to return to the city, but to stay here, and I will neither eat nor drink, but without ceasing mourn and fast until I die."

[5] Then I broke off the reflections with which I was still engaged, and answered her in anger and said,

[6] "You most foolish of women, do you not see our mourning, and what has happened to us?

[7] For Zion, the mother of us all, is in deep grief and great affliction.

[8] It is most appropriate to mourn now, because we are all mourning, and to be sorrowful, because we are all sorrowing; you are sorrowing for one son, but we, the whole world, for our mother.

[9] Now ask the earth, and she will tell you that it is she who ought to mourn over so many who have come into being upon her.

[10] And from the beginning all have been born of her, and others will come; and behold, almost all go to perdition, and a multitude of them are destined for destruction.

[11] Who then ought to mourn the more, she who lost so great a multitude, or you who are grieving for one?

[12] But if you say to me, `My lamentation is not like the earth's, for I have lost the fruit of my womb, which I brought forth in pain and bore in sorrow;

[13] but it is with the earth according to the way of the earth -- the multitude that is now in it goes as it came';

[14] then I say to you, `As you brought forth in sorrow, so the earth also has from the beginning given her fruit, that is, man, to him who made her.'

[15] Now, therefore, keep your sorrow to yourself, and bear bravely the troubles that have come upon you.

[16] For if you acknowledge the decree of God to be just, you will receive your son back in due time, and will be praised among women.

[17] Therefore go into the city to your husband."

[18] She said to me, "I will not do so; I will not go into the city, but I will die here."

[19] So I spoke again to her, and said,

[20] "Do not say that, but let yourself be persuaded because of the troubles of Zion, and be consoled because of the sorrow of Jerusalem.

[21] For you see that our sanctuary has been laid waste, our altar thrown down, our temple destroyed;

[22] our harp has been laid low, our song has been silenced, and our rejoicing has been ended; the light of our lampstand has been put out, the ark of our covenant has been plundered, our holy things have been polluted, and the name by which we are called has been profaned; our free men have suffered abuse, our priests have been burned to death, our Levites have gone into captivity, our virgins have been defiled, and our wives have been ravished; our righteous men have been carried off, our little ones have been cast out, our young men have been enslaved and our strong men made powerless.

[23] And, what is more than all, the seal of Zion -- for she has now lost the seal of her glory, and has been given over into the hands of those that hate us.

[24] Therefore shake off your great sadness and lay aside your many sorrows, so that the Mighty One may be merciful to you again, and the Most High may give you rest, a relief from your troubles."

[25] While I was talking to her, behold, her face suddenly shone exceedingly, and her countenance flashed like lightning, so that I was too frightened to approach her, and my heart was terrified. While I was wondering what this meant,

[26] behold, she suddenly uttered a loud and fearful cry, so that the earth shook at the sound.

[27] And I looked, and behold, the woman was no longer visible to me, but there was an established city, and a place of huge foundations showed itself. Then I was afraid, and cried with a loud voice and said,

[28] "Where is the angel Uriel, who came to me at first? For it was he who brought me into this overpowering bewilderment; my end has become corruption, and my prayer a reproach."

[29] As I was speaking these words, behold, the angel who had come to me at first came to me, and he looked upon me;

[30] and behold, I lay there like a corpse and I was deprived of my understanding. Then he grasped my right hand and strengthened me and set me on my feet, and said to me,

[31] "What is the matter with you? And why are you troubled? And why are your understanding and the thoughts of your mind troubled?"

[32] I said, "Because you have forsaken me! I did as you directed, and went out into the field, and behold, I saw, and still see, what I am unable to explain."

[33] He said to me, "Stand up like a man, and I will instruct you."

[34] I said, "Speak, my lord; only do not forsake me, lest I die before my time.

[35] For I have seen what I did not know, and I have heard what I do not understand.

[36] Or is my mind deceived, and my soul dreaming?

[37] Now therefore I entreat you to give your servant an explanation of this bewildering vision."

[38] He answered me and said, "Listen to me and I will inform you, and tell you about the things which you fear, for the Most High has revealed many secrets to you.

[39] For he has seen your righteous conduct, that you have sorrowed continually for your people, and

mourned greatly over Zion.

[40] This therefore is the meaning of the vision.

[41] The woman who appeared to you a little while ago, whom you saw mourning and began to console --

[42] but you do not now see the form of a woman, but an established city has appeared to you --

[43] and as for her telling you about the misfortune of her son, this is the interpretation:

[44] This woman whom you saw, whom you now behold as an established city, is Zion.

[45] And as for her telling you that she was barren for thirty years, it is because there were three thousand years in the world before any offering was offered in it.

[46] And after three thousand years Solomon built the city, and offered offerings; then it was that the barren woman bore a son.

[47] And as for her telling you that she brought him up with much care, that was the period of residence in Jerusalem.

[48] And as for her saying to you , `When my son entered his wedding chamber he died,' and that misfortune had overtaken her, that was the destruction which befell Jerusalem.

[49] And behold, you saw her likeness, how she mourned for her son, and you began to console her for what had happened.

[50] For now the Most High, seeing that you are sincerely grieved and profoundly distressed for her, has shown you the brilliance of her glory, and the loveliness of her beauty.

[51] Therefore I told you to remain in the field where no house had been built,

[52] for I knew that the Most High would reveal these things to you.

[53] Therefore I told you to go into the field where there was no foundation of any building,

[54] for no work of man's building could endure in a place where the city of the Most High was to be revealed.

[55] "Therefore do not be afraid, and do not let your heart be terrified; but go in and see the splendor and vastness of the building, as far as it is possible for your eyes to see it,

[56] and afterward you will hear as much as your ears can hear.

[57] For you are more blessed than many, and you have been called before the Most High, as but few have been.

[58] But tomorrow night you shall remain here,

[59] and the Most High will show you in those dream visions what the Most High will do to those who dwell on earth in the last days." So I slept that night and the following one, as he had commanded me.
11
[1] On the second night I had a dream, and behold, there came up from the sea an eagle that had twelve feathered wings and three heads.

[2] And I looked, and behold, he spread his wings over all the earth, and all the winds of heaven blew upon him, and the clouds were gathered about him.

[3] And I looked, and out of his wings there grew opposing wings; but they became little, puny wings.

[4] But his heads were at rest; the middle head was larger than the other heads, but it also was at rest with them.

[5] And I looked, and behold, the eagle flew with his wings, to reign over the earth and over those who dwell in it.

[6] And I saw how all things under heaven were subjected to him, and no one spoke against him, not even one creature that was on the earth.

[7] And I looked, and behold, the eagle rose upon his talons, and uttered a cry to his wings, saying,

[8] "Do not all watch at the same time; let each sleep in his own place, and watch in his turn;

[9] but let the heads be reserved for the last."

[10] And I looked, and behold, the voice did not come from his heads, but from the midst of his body.

[11] And I counted his opposing wings, and behold, there were eight of them.

[12] And I looked, and behold, on the right side one wing arose, and it reigned over all the earth.

[13] And while it was reigning it came to its end and disappeared, so that its place was not seen. Then the next wing arose and reigned, and it continued to reign a long time.

[14] And while it was reigning its end came also, so that it disappeared like the first.

[15] And behold, a voice sounded, saying to it.

[16] "Hear me, you who have ruled the earth all this time; I announce this to you before you disappear.

[17] After you no one shall rule as long as you, or even half as long."

[18] Then the third wing raised itself up, and held the rule like the former ones, and it also disappeared.

[19] And so it went with all the wings; they wielded power one after another and then were never seen again.

[20] And I looked, and behold, in due course the wings that followed also rose up on the right side, in order to rule. There were some of them that ruled, yet disappeared suddenly;

546

[21] and others of them rose up, but did not hold the rule.

[22] And after this I looked, and behold, the twelve wings and the two little wings disappeared;

[23] and nothing remained on the eagle's body except the three heads that were at rest and six little wings.

[24] And I looked, and behold, two little wings separated from the six and remained under the head that was on the right side; but four remained in their place.

[25] And I looked, and behold, these little wings planned to set themselves up and hold the rule.

[26] And I looked, and behold, one was set up, but suddenly disappeared;

[27] a second also, and this disappeared more quickly than the first.

[28] And I looked, and behold, the two that remained were planning between themselves to reign together;

[29] and while they were planning, behold, one of the heads that were at rest (the one which was in the middle) awoke; for it was greater than the other two heads.

[30] And I saw how it allied the two heads with itself,

[31] and behold, the head turned with those that were with it, and it devoured the two little wings which were planning to reign.

[32] Moreover this head gained control of the whole earth, and with much oppression dominated its inhabitants; and it had greater power over the world than all the wings that had gone before.

[33] And after this I looked, and behold, the middle head also suddenly disappeared, just as the wings had done.

[34] But the two heads remained, which also ruled over the earth and its inhabitants.

[35] And I looked, and behold, the head on the right side devoured the one on the left.

[36] Then I heard a voice saying to me, "Look before you and consider what you see."

[37] And I looked, and behold, a creature like a lion was aroused out of the forest, roaring; and I heard how he uttered a man's voice to the eagle, and spoke, saying,

[38] "Listen and I will speak to you. The Most High says to you,

[39] `Are you not the one that remains of the four beasts which I had made to reign in my world, so that the end of my times might come through them?

[40] You, the fourth that has come, have conquered all the beasts that have gone before; and you have held sway over the world with much terror, and over all the earth with grievous oppression; and for so long you have dwelt on the earth with deceit.

[41] And you have judged the earth, but not with truth;

[42] for you have afflicted the meek and injured the peaceable; you have hated those who tell the truth, and have loved liars; you have destroyed the dwellings of those who brought forth fruit, and have laid low the walls of those who did you no harm.

[43] And so your insolence has come up before the Most High, and your pride to the Mighty One.

[44] And the Most High has looked upon his times, and behold, they are ended, and his ages are completed!

[45] Therefore you will surely disappear, you eagle, and your terrifying wings, and your most evil little wings, and your malicious heads, and your most evil talons, and your whole worthless body,

[46] so that the whole earth, freed from your violence, may be refreshed and relieved, and may hope for the judgment and mercy of him who made it.'"

12

[1] While the lion was saying these words to the eagle, I looked,

[2] and behold, the remaining head disappeared. And the two wings that had gone over to it arose and set themselves up to reign, and their reign was brief and full of tumult.

[3] And I looked, and behold, they also disappeared, and the whole body of the eagle was burned, and the earth was exceedingly terrified. Then I awoke in great perplexity of mind and great fear, and I said to my spirit,

[4] "Behold, you have brought this upon me, because you search out the ways of the Most High.

[5] Behold, I am still weary in mind and very weak in my spirit, and not even a little strength is left in me, because of the great fear with which I have been terrified this night.

[6] Therefore I will now beseech the Most High that he may strengthen me to the end."

[7] And I said, "O sovereign Lord, if I have found favor in thy sight, and if I have been accounted righteous before thee beyond many others, and if my prayer has indeed come up before thy face,

[8] strengthen me and show me, thy servant, the interpretation and meaning of this terrifying vision, that thou mayest fully comfort my soul.

[9] For thou hast judged me worthy to be shown the end of the times and the last events of the times."

[10] He said to me, "This is the interpretation of this vision which you have seen:

[11] The eagle which you saw coming up from the sea is the fourth kingdom which appeared in a vision to your brother Daniel.

[12] But it was not explained to him as I now explain or have explained it to you.

[13] Behold, the days are coming when a kingdom shall arise on earth, and it shall be more terrifying than all the kingdoms that have been before it.

[14] And twelve kings shall reign in it, one after another.

[15] But the second that is to reign shall hold sway for a longer time than any other of the twelve.

[16] This is the interpretation of the twelve wings which you saw.

[17] As for your hearing a voice that spoke, coming not from the eagle's heads but from the midst of his body, this is the interpretation:

[18] In the midst of the time of that kingdom great struggles shall arise, and it shall be in danger of falling; nevertheless it shall not fall then, but shall regain its former power.

[19] As for your seeing eight little wings clinging to his wings, this is the interpretation:

[20] Eight kings shall arise in it, whose times shall be short and their years swift;

[21] and two of them shall perish when the middle of its time draws near; and four shall be kept for the time when its end approaches; but two shall be kept until the end.

[22] As for your seeing three heads at rest, this is the interpretation:

[23] In its last days the Most High will raise up three kings, and they shall renew many things in it, and shall rule the earth

[24] and its inhabitants more oppressively than all who were before them; therefore they are called the heads of the eagle.

[25] For it is they who shall sum up his wickedness and perform his last actions.

[26] As for your seeing that the large head disappeared, one of the kings shall die in his bed, but in agonies.

[27] But as for the two who remained, the sword shall devour them.

[28] For the sword of one shall devour him who was with him; but he also shall fall by the sword in the last days.

[29] As for your seeing two little wings passing over to the head which was on the right side,

[30] this is the interpretation: It is these whom the Most High has kept for the eagle's end; this was the reign which was brief and full of tumult, as you have seen.

[31] "And as for the lion whom you saw rousing up out of the forest and roaring and speaking to the eagle and reproving him for his unrighteousness, and as for all his words that you have heard,

[32] this is the Messiah whom the Most High has kept until the end of days, who will arise from the posterity of David, and will come and speak to them; he will denounce them for their ungodliness and for their wickedness, and will cast up before them their contemptuous dealings.

[33] For first he will set them living before his judgment seat, and when he has reproved them, then he will destroy them.

[34] But he will deliver in mercy the remnant of my people, those who have been saved throughout my borders, and he will make them joyful until the end comes, the day of judgment, of which I spoke to you at the beginning.

[35] This is the dream that you saw, and this is its interpretation.

[36] And you alone were worthy to learn this secret of the Most High.

[37] Therefore write all these things that you have seen in a book, and put it in a hidden place;

[38] and you shall teach them to the wise among your people, whose hearts you know are able to comprehend and keep these secrets.

[39] But wait here seven days more, so that you may be shown whatever it pleases the Most High to show you." Then he left me.

[40] When all the people heard that the seven days were past and I had not returned to the city, they all gathered together, from the least to the greatest, and came to me and spoke to me, saying,

[41] "How have we offended you, and what harm have we done you, that you have forsaken us and sit in this place?

[42] For of all the prophets you alone are left to us, like a cluster of grapes from the vintage, and like a lamp in a dark place, and like a haven for a ship saved from a storm.

[43] Are not the evils which have befallen us sufficient?

[44] Therefore if you forsake us, how much better it would have been for us if we also had been consumed in the burning of Zion!

[45] For we are no better than those who died there." And they wept with a loud voice. Then I answered them and said,

[46] "Take courage, O Israel; and do not be sorrowful, O house of Jacob;

[47] for the Most High has you in remembrance, and the Mighty One has not forgotten you in your struggle.

[48] As for me, I have neither forsaken you nor withdrawn from you; but I have come to this place to pray on account of the desolation of Zion, and to seek mercy on account of the humiliation of our

sanctuary.

[49] Now go, every one of you to his house, and after these days I will come to you."

[50] So the people went into the city, as I told them to do.

[51] But I sat in the field seven days, as the angel had commanded me; and I ate only of the flowers of the field, and my food was of plants during those days.

13

[1] After seven days I dreamed a dream in the night;

[2] and behold, a wind arose from the sea and stirred up all its waves.

[3] And I looked, and behold, this wind made something like the figure of a man come up out of the heart of the sea. And I looked, and behold, that man flew with the clouds of heaven; and wherever he turned his face to look, everything under his gaze trembled,

[4] and whenever his voice issued from his mouth, all who heard his voice melted as wax melts when it feels the fire.

[5] After this I looked, and behold, an innumerable multitude of men were gathered together from the four winds of heaven to make war against the man who came up out of the sea.

[6] And I looked, and behold, he carved out for himself a great mountain, and flew up upon it. < br>[7] And I tried to see the region or place from which the mountain was carved, but I could not.

[8] After this I looked, and behold, all who had gathered together against him, to wage war with him, were much afraid, yet dared to fight.

[9] And behold, when he saw the onrush of the approaching multitude, he neither lifted his hand nor held a spear or any weapon of war;

[10] but I saw only how he sent forth from his mouth as it were a stream of fire, and from his lips a flaming breath, and from his tongue he shot forth a storm of sparks.

[11] All these were mingled together, the stream of fire and the flaming breath and the great storm, and fell on the onrushing multitude which was prepared to fight, and burned them all up, so that suddenly nothing was seen of the innumerable multitude but only the dust of ashes and the smell of smoke. When I saw it, I was amazed.

[12] After this I saw the same man come down from the mountain and call to him another multitude which was peaceable.

[13] Then many people came to him, some of whom were joyful and some sorrowful; some of them were bound, and some were bringing others as offerings. Then in great fear I awoke; and I besought the Most High, and said,

[14] "From the beginning thou hast shown thy servant these wonders, and hast deemed me worthy to have my prayer heard by thee;

[15] now show me also the interpretation of this dream.

[16] For as I consider it in my mind, alas for those who will be left in those days! And still more, alas for those who are not left!

[17] For those who are not left will be sad,

[18] because they understand what is reserved for the last days, but cannot attain it.

[19] But alas for those also who are left, and for that very reason! For they shall see great dangers and much distress, as these dreams show.

[20] Yet it is better to come into these things, though incurring peril, than to pass from the world like a cloud, and not to see what shall happen in the last days." He answered me and said,

[21] "I will tell you the interpretation of the vision, and I will also explain to you the things which you have mentioned.

[22] As for what you said about those who are left, this is the interpretation:

[23] He who brings the peril at that time will himself protect those who fall into peril, who have works and have faith in the Almighty.

[24] Understand therefore that those who are left are more blessed than those who have died.

[25] This is the interpretation of the vision: As for your seeing a man come up from the heart of the sea,

[26] this is he whom the Most High has been keeping for many ages, who will himself deliver his creation; and he will direct those who are left.

[27] And as for your seeing wind and fire and a storm coming out of his mouth,

[28] and as for his not holding a spear or weapon of war, yet destroying the onrushing multitude which came to conquer him, this is the interpretation:

[29] Behold, the days are coming when the Most High will deliver those who are on the earth.

[30] And bewilderment of mind shall come over those who dwell on the earth.

[31] And they shall plan to make war against one another, city against city, place against place, people against people, and kingdom against kingdom.

[32] And when these things come to pass and the signs occur which I showed you before, then my Son will be revealed, whom you saw as a man coming up from the sea.

[33] And when all the nations hear his voice, every man shall leave his own land and the warfare that they have against one another;

[34] and an innumerable multitude shall be gathered together, as you saw, desiring to come and conquer him.

[35] But he shall stand on the top of Mount Zion.

[36] And Zion will come and be made manifest to all people, prepared and built, as you saw the mountain carved out without hands.

[37] And he, my Son, will reprove the assembled nations for their ungodliness (this was symbolized by the storm),

[38] and will reproach them to their face with their evil thoughts and the torments with which they are to be tortured (which were symbolized by the flames), and will destroy them without effort by the law (which was symbolized by the fire).

[39] And as for your seeing him gather to himself another multitude that was peaceable,

[40] these are the ten tribes which were led away from their own land into captivity in the days of King Hoshea, whom Shalmaneser the king of the Assyrians led captive; he took them across the river, and they were taken into another land.

[41] But they formed this plan for themselves, that they would leave the multitude of the nations and go to a more distant region, where mankind had never lived,

[42] that there at least they might keep their statutes which they had not kept in their own land.

[43] And they went in by the narrow passages of the Euphrates river.

[44] For at that time the Most High performed signs for them, and stopped the channels of the river until they had passed over.

[45] Through that region there was a long way to go, a journey of a year and a half; and that country is called Arzareth.

[46] "Then they dwelt there until the last times; and now, when they are about to come again,

[47] the Most High will stop the channels of the river again, so that they may be able to pass over. Therefore you saw the multitude gathered together in peace.

[48] But those who are left of your people, who are found within my holy borders, shall be saved.

[49] Therefore when he destroys the multitude of the nations that are gathered together, he will defend the people who remain.

[50] And then he will show them very many wonders."

[51] I said, "O sovereign Lord, explain this to me: Why did I see the man coming up from the heart of the sea?"

[52] He said to me, "Just as no one can explore or know what is in the depths of the sea, so no one on earth can see my Son or those who are with him, except in the time of his day.

[53] This is the interpretation of the dream which you saw. And you alone have been enlightened about this,

[54] because you have forsaken your own ways and have applied yourself to mine, and have searched out my law;

[55] for you have devoted your life to wisdom, and called understanding your mother.

[56] Therefore I have shown you this, for there is a reward laid up with the Most High. And after three more days I will tell you other things, and explain weighty and wondrous matters to you."

[57] Then I arose and walked in the field, giving great glory and praise to the Most High because of his wonders, which he did from time to time,

[58] and because he governs the times and whatever things come to pass in their seasons. And I stayed there three days.

14

[1] On the third day, while I was sitting under an oak, behold, a voice came out of a bush opposite me and said, "Ezra, Ezra."

[2] And I said, "Here I am, Lord," and I rose to my feet.

[3] Then he said to me, "I revealed myself in a bush and spoke to Moses, when my people were in bondage in Egypt;

[4] and I sent him and led my people out of Egypt; and I led him up on Mount Sinai, where I kept him with me many days;

[5] and I told him many wondrous things, and showed him the secrets of the times and declared to him the end of the times. Then I commanded him, saying,

[6] `These words you shall publish openly, and these you shall keep secret.'

[7] And now I say to you;

[8] Lay up in your heart the signs that I have shown you, the dreams that you have seen, and the interpretations that you have heard;

[9] for you shall be taken up from among men, and henceforth you shall live with my Son and with those

who are like you, until the times are ended.

[10] For the age has lost its youth, and the times begin to grow old.

[11] For the age is divided into twelve parts, and nine of its parts have already passed,

[12] as well as half of the tenth part; so two of its parts remain, besides half of the tenth part.

[13] Now therefore, set your house in order, and reprove your people; comfort the lowly among them, and instruct those that are wise. And now renounce the life that is corruptible,

[14] and put away from you mortal thoughts; cast away from you the burdens of man, and divest yourself now of your weak nature,

[15] and lay to one side the thoughts that are most grievous to you, and hasten to escape from these times.

[16] For evils worse than those which you have now seen happen shall be done hereafter.

[17] For the weaker the world becomes through old age, the more shall evils be multiplied among its inhabitants.

[18] For truth shall go farther away, and falsehood shall come near. For the eagle which you saw in the vision is already hastening to come."

[19] Then I answered and said, "Let me speak in thy presence, Lord.

[20] For behold, I will go, as thou hast commanded me, and I will reprove the people who are now living; but who will warn those who will be born hereafter? For the world lies in darkness, and its inhabitants are without light.

[21] For thy law has been burned, and so no one knows the things which have been done or will be done by thee.

[22] If then I have found favor before thee, send the Holy Spirit into me, and I will write everything that has happened in the world from the beginning, the things which were written in thy law, that men may be able to find the path, and that those who wish to live in the last days may live."

[23] He answered me and said, "Go and gather the people, and tell them not to seek you for forty days.

[24] But prepare for yourself many writing tablets, and take with you Sarea, Dabria, Selemia, Ethanus, and Asiel -- these five, because they are trained to write rapidly;

[25] and you shall come here, and I will light in your heart the lamp of understanding, which shall not be put out until what you are about to write is finished.

[26] And when you have finished, some things you shall make public, and some you shall deliver in secret to the wise; tomorrow at this hour you shall begin to write."

[27] Then I went as he commanded me, and I gathered all the people together, and said,

[28] "Hear these words, O Israel

[29] At first our fathers dwelt as aliens in Egypt, and they were delivered from there,

[30] and received the law of life, which they did not keep, which you also have transgressed after them.

[31] Then land was given to you for a possession in the land of Zion; but you and your fathers committed iniquity and did not keep the ways which the Most High commanded you.

[32] And because he is a righteous judge, in due time he took from you what he had given.

[33] And now you are here, and your brethren are farther in the interior.

[34] If you, then, will rule over your minds and discipline your hearts, you shall be kept alive, and after death you shall obtain mercy.

[35] For after death the judgment will come, when we shall live again; and then the names of the righteous will become manifest, and the deeds of the ungodly will be disclosed.

[36] But let no one come to me now, and let no one seek me for forty days."

[37] So I took the five men, as he commanded me, and we proceeded to the field, and remained there.

[38] And on the next day, behold, a voice called me, saying, "Ezra, open your mouth and drink what I give you to drink."

[39] Then I opened my mouth, and behold, a full cup was offered to me; it was full of something like water, but its color was like fire.

[40] And I took it and drank; and when I had drunk it, my heart poured forth understanding, and wisdom increased in my breast, for my spirit retained its memory;

[41] and my mouth was opened, and was no longer closed.

[42] And the Most High gave understanding to the five men, and by turns they wrote what was dictated, in characters which they did not know. They sat forty days, and wrote during the daytime, and ate their bread at night.

[43] As for me, I spoke in the daytime and was not silent at night.

[44] So during the forty days ninety-four books were written.

[45] And when the forty days were ended, the Most High spoke to me, saying, "Make public the twenty-four books that you wrote first and let the worthy and the unworthy read them;

[46] but keep the seventy that were written last, in order to give them to the wise among your people.

[47] For in them is the spring of understanding, the fountain of wisdom, and the river of knowledge."

[48] And I did so.

15

[1] The Lord says, "Behold, speak in the ears of my people the words of the prophecy which I will put in your mouth,

[2] and cause them to be written on paper; for they are trustworthy and true.

[3] Do not fear the plots against you, and do not be troubled by the unbelief of those who oppose you.

[4] For every unbeliever shall die in his unbelief."

[5] "Behold," says the Lord, "I bring evils upon the world, the sword and famine and death and destruction.

[6] For iniquity has spread throughout every land, and their harmful deeds have reached their limit.

[7] Therefore," says the Lord,

[8] "I will be silent no longer concerning their ungodly deeds which they impiously commit, neither will I tolerate their wicked practices. Behold, innocent and righteous blood cries out to me, and the souls of the righteous cry out continually.

[9] I will surely avenge them," says the Lord, "and will receive to myself all the innocent blood from among them.

[10] Behold, my people is led like a flock to the slaughter; I will not allow them to live any longer in the land of Egypt,

[11] but I will bring them out with a mighty hand and with an uplifted arm, and will smite Egypt with plagues, as before, and will destroy all its land."

[12] Let Egypt mourn, and its foundations, for the plague of chastisement and punishment that the Lord will bring upon it.

[13] Let the farmers that till the ground mourn, because their seed shall fail and their trees shall be ruined by blight and hail and by a terrible tempest.

[14] Alas for the world and for those who live in it!

[15] For the sword and misery draw near them, and nation shall rise up to fight against nation, with swords in their hands.

[16] For there shall be unrest among men; growing strong against one another, they shall in their might have no respect for their king or the chief of their leaders.

[17] For a man will desire to go into a city, and shall not be able.

[18] For because of their pride the cities shall be in confusion, the houses shall be destroyed, and people shall be afraid.

[19] A man shall have no pity upon his neighbors, but shall make an assault upon their houses with the sword, and plunder their goods, because of hunger for bread and because of great tribulation.

[20] "Behold," says God, "I call together all the kings of the earth to fear me, from the rising sun and from the south, from the east and from Lebanon; to turn and repay what they have given them.

[21] Just as they have done to my elect until this day, so I will do, and will repay into their bosom." Thus says the Lord God:

[22] "My right hand will not spare the sinners, and my sword will not cease from those who shed innocent blood on earth."

[23] And a fire will go forth from his wrath, and will consume the foundations of the earth, and the sinners, like straw that is kindled.

[24] "Woe to those who sin and do not observe my commandments," says the Lord;

[25] "I will not spare them. Depart, you faithless children! Do not pollute my sanctuary."

[26] For the Lord knows all who transgress against him; therefore he will hand them over to death and slaughter.

[27] For now calamities have come upon the whole earth, and you shall remain in them; for God will not deliver you, because you have sinned against him.

[28] Behold, a terrifying sight, appearing from the east!

[29] The nations of the dragons of Arabia shall come out with many chariots, and from the day that they set out, their hissing shall spread over the earth, so that all who hear them fear and tremble.

[30] Also the Carmonians, raging in wrath, shall go forth like wild boars of the forest, and with great power they shall come, and engage them in battle, and shall devastate a portion of the land of the Assyrians with their teeth.

[31] And then the dragons, remembering their origin, shall become still stronger; and if they combine in great power and turn to pursue them,

[32] then these shall be disorganized and silenced by their power, and shall turn and flee.

[33] And from the land of the Assyrians an enemy in ambush shall beset them and destroy one of them, and fear and trembling shall come upon their army, and indecision upon their kings.

[34] Behold, clouds from the east, and from the north to the south; and their appearance is very threatening, full of wrath and storm.

[35] They shall dash against one another and shall pour out a heavy tempest upon the earth, and their own tempest; and there shall be blood from the sword as high as a horse's belly

[36] and a man's thigh and a camel's hock.

[37] And there shall be fear and great trembling upon the earth; and those who see that wrath shall be horror-stricken, and they shall be seized with trembling.

[38] And, after that, heavy storm clouds shall be stirred up from the south, and from the north, and another part from the west.

[39] And the winds from the east shall prevail over the cloud that was raised in wrath, and shall dispel it; and the tempest that was to cause destruction by the east wind shall be driven violently toward the south and west.

[40] And great and mighty clouds, full of wrath and tempest, shall rise, to destroy all the earth and its inhabitants, and shall pour out upon every high and lofty place a terrible tempest,

[41] fire and hail and flying swords and floods of water, that all the fields and all the streams may be filled with the abundance of those waters.

[42] And they shall destroy cities and walls, mountains and hills, trees of the forests, and grass of the meadows, and their grain.

[43] And they shall go on steadily to Babylon, and shall destroy her.

[44] They shall come to her and surround her; they shall pour out the tempest and all its wrath upon her; then the dust and smoke shall go up to heaven, and all who are about her shall wail over her.

[45] And those who survive shall serve those who have destroyed her.

[46] And you, Asia, who share in the glamour of Babylon and the glory of her person --

[47] woe to you, miserable wretch! For you have made yourself like her; you have decked out your daughters in harlotry to please and glory in your lovers, who have always lusted after you.

[48] You have imitated that hateful harlot in all her deeds and devices; therefore God says,

[49] "I will send evils upon you, widowhood, poverty, famine, sword, and pestilence, to lay waste your houses and bring you to destruction and death.

[50] And the glory of your power shall wither like a flower, when the heat rises that is sent upon you.

[51] You shall be weakened like a wretched woman who is beaten and wounded, so that you cannot receive your mighty lovers.

[52] Would I have dealt with you so violently," says the Lord,

[53] "If you had not always killed my chosen people, exulting and clapping your hands and talking about their death when you were drunk?

[54] Trick out the beauty of your face!

[55] The reward of a harlot is in your bosom, therefore you shall receive your recompense.

[56] As you will do to my chosen people," says the Lord, "so God will do to you, and will hand you over to adversities.

[57] Your children shall die of hunger, and you shall fall by the sword, and your cities shall be wiped out, and all your people who are in the open country shall fall by the sword.

[58] And those who are in the mountains and highlands shall perish of hunger, and they shall eat their own flesh in hunger for bread and drink their own blood in thirst for water.

[59] Unhappy above all others, you shall come and suffer fresh afflictions.

[60] And as they pass they shall wreck the hateful city, and shall destroy a part of your land and abolish a portion of your glory, as they return from devastated Babylon.

[61] And you shall be broken down by them like stubble, and they shall be like fire to you.

[62] And they shall devour you and your cities, your land and your mountains; they shall burn with fire all your forests and your fruitful trees.

[63] They shall carry your children away captive, and shall plunder your wealth, and abolish the glory of your countenance."

16

[1] Woe to you, Babylon and Asia! Woe to you, Egypt and Syria!

[2] Gird yourselves with sackcloth and haircloth, and wail for your children, and lament for them; for your destruction is at hand.

[3] The sword has been sent upon you, and who is there to turn it back?

[4] A fire has been sent upon you, and who is there to quench it?

[5] Calamities have been sent upon you, and who is there to drive them away?

[6] Can one drive off a hungry lion in the forest, or quench a fire in the stubble, when once it has begun to burn?

[7] Can one turn back an arrow shot by a strong archer?

[8] The Lord God sends calamities, and who will drive them away?

[9] Fire will go forth from his wrath, and who is there to quench it?

[10] He will flash lightning, and who will not be afraid? He will thunder, and who will not be terrified?

[11] The Lord will threaten, and who will not be utterly shattered at his presence?

[12] The earth and its foundations quake, the sea is churned up from the depths, and its waves and the fish also shall be troubled at the presence of the Lord and before the glory of his power.

[13] For his right hand that bends the bow is strong, and his arrows that he shoots are sharp and will not miss when they begin to be shot to the ends of the world.

[14] Behold, calamities are sent forth and shall not return until they come over the earth.

[15] The fire is kindled, and shall not be put out until it consumes the foundations of the earth.

[16] Just as an arrow shot by a mighty archer does not return, so the calamities that are sent upon the earth shall not return.

[17] Alas for me! Alas for me! Who will deliver me in those days?

[18] The beginning of sorrows, when there shall be much lamentation; the beginning of famine, when many shall perish; the beginning of wars, when the powers shall be terrified; the beginning of calamities, when all shall tremble. What shall they do in these circumstances, when the calamities come?

[19] Behold, famine and plague, tribulation and anguish are sent as scourges for the correction of men.

[20] Yet for all this they will not turn from their iniquities, nor be always mindful of the scourges.

[21] Behold, provision will be so cheap upon earth that men will imagine that peace is assured for them, and then the calamities shall spring up on the earth -- the sword, famine, and great confusion.

[22] For many of those who live on the earth shall perish by famine; and those who survive the famine shall die by the sword.

[23] And the dead shall be cast out like dung, and there shall be no one to console them; for the earth shall be left desolate, and its cities shall be demolished.

[24] No one shall be left to cultivate the earth or to sow it.

[25] The trees shall bear fruit, and who will gather it?

[26] The grapes shall ripen, and who will tread them? For in all places there shall be great solitude;

[27] one man will long to see another, or even to hear his voice.

[28] For out of a city, ten shall be left; and out of the field, two who have hidden themselves in thick groves and clefts in the rocks.

[29] As in an olive orchard three or four olives may be left on every tree,

[30] or as when a vineyard is gathered some clusters may be left by those who search carefully through the vineyard,

[31] so in those days three or four shall be left by those who search their houses with the sword.

[32] And the earth shall be left desolate, and its fields shall be for briers, and its roads and all its paths shall bring forth thorns, because no sheep will go along them.

[33] Virgins shall mourn because they have no bridegrooms; women shall mourn because they have no husbands; their daughters shall mourn, because they have no helpers.

[34] Their bridegrooms shall be killed in war, and their husbands shall perish of famine.

[35] Listen now to these things, and understand them, O servants of the Lord.

[36] Behold the word of the Lord, receive it; do not disbelieve what the Lord says.

[37] Behold, the calamities draw near, and are not delayed.

[38] Just as a woman with child, in the ninth month, when the time of her delivery draws near, has great pains about her womb for two or three hours beforehand, and when the child comes forth from the womb, there will not be a moment's delay,

[39] so the calamities will not delay in coming forth upon the earth, and the world will groan, and pains will seize it on every side.

[40] "Hear my words, O my people; prepare for battle, and in the midst of the calamities be like strangers on the earth.

[41] Let him that sells be like one who will flee; let him that buys be like one who will lose;

[42] let him that does business be like one who will not make a profit; and let him that builds a house be like one who will not live in it;

[43] let him that sows be like one who will not reap; so also him that prunes the vines, like one who will not gather the grapes;

[44] them that marry, like those who will have no children; and them that do not marry, like those who are widowed.

[45] Because those who labor, labor in vain;

[46] for strangers shall gather their fruits, and plunder their goods, and overthrow their houses, and take their children captive; for in captivity and famine they will beget their children.

[47] Those who conduct business, do it only to be plundered; the more they adorn their cities, their houses and possessions, and their persons,

[48] the more angry I will be with them for their sins," says the Lord.

[49] Just as a respectable and virtuous woman abhors a harlot,

[50] so righteousness shall abhor iniquity, when she decks herself out, and shall accuse her to her face, when he comes who will defend him who searches out every sin on earth.

[51] Therefore do not be like her or her works.

[52] For behold, just a little while, and iniquity will be removed from the earth, and righteousness will reign over us.

[53] Let no sinner say that he has not sinned; for God will burn coals of fire on the head of him who says, "I have not sinned before God and his glory."

[54] Behold, the Lord knows all the works of men, their imaginations and their thoughts and their hearts.

[55] He said, "Let the earth be made," and it was made; "Let the heaven be made," and it was made.

[56] At his word the stars were fixed, and he knows the number of the stars.

[57] It is he who searches the deep and its treasures, who has measured the sea and its contents;

[58] who has enclosed the sea in the midst of the waters, and by his word has suspended the earth over the water;

[59] who has spread out the heaven like an arch, and founded it upon the waters;

[60] who has put springs of water in the desert, and pools on the tops of the mountains, to send rivers from the heights to water the earth;

[61] who formed man, and put a heart in the midst of his body, and gave him breath and life and understanding

[62] and the spirit of Almighty God; who made all things and searches out hidden things in hidden places.

[63] Surely he knows your imaginations and what you think in your hearts! Woe to those who sin and want to hide their sins!

[64] Because the Lord will strictly examine all their works, and will make a public spectacle of all of you.

[65] And when your sins come out before men, you shall be put to shame; and your own iniquities shall stand as your accusers in that day.

[66] What will you do? Or how will you hide your sins before God and his angels?

[67] Behold, God is the judge, fear him! Cease from your sins, and forget your iniquities, never to commit them again; so God will lead you forth and deliver you from all tribulation.

[68] For behold, the burning wrath of a great multitude is kindled over you, and they shall carry off some of you and shall feed you what was sacrificed to idols.

[69] And those who consent to eat shall be held in derision and contempt, and be trodden under foot.

[70] For in many places and in neighboring cities there shall be a great insurrection against those who fear the Lord.

[71] They shall be like mad men, sparing no one, but plundering and destroying those who continue to fear the Lord.

[72] For they shall destroy and plunder their goods, and drive them out of their houses.

[73] Then the tested quality of my elect shall be manifest, as gold that is tested by fire.

[74] "Hear, my elect," says the Lord. "Behold, the days of tribulation are at hand, and I will deliver you from them.

[75] Do not fear or doubt, for God is your guide.

[76] You who keep my commandments and precepts," says the Lord God, "do not let your sins pull you down, or your iniquities prevail over you."

[77] Woe to those who are choked by their sins and overwhelmed by their iniquities, as a field is choked with underbrush and its path overwhelmed with thorns, so that no one can pass through!

[78] It is shut off and given up to be consumed by fire.

1 Maccabees

1Mac.1

[1] After Alexander son of Philip, the Macedonian, who came from the land of Kittim, had defeated Darius, king of the Persians and the Medes, he succeeded him as king. (He had previously become king of Greece.)

[2] He fought many battles, conquered strongholds, and put to death the kings of the earth.

[3] He advanced to the ends of the earth, and plundered many nations. When the earth became quiet before him, he was exalted, and his heart was lifted up.

[4] He gathered a very strong army and ruled over countries, nations, and princes, and they became tributary to him.

[5] After this he fell sick and perceived that he was dying.

[6] So he summoned his most honored officers, who had been brought up with him from youth, and divided his kingdom among them while he was still alive.

[7] And after Alexander had reigned twelve years, he died.

[8] Then his officers began to rule, each in his own place.

[9] They all put on crowns after his death, and so did their sons after them for many years; and they caused many evils on the earth.

[10] From them came forth a sinful root, Antiochus Epiphanes, son of Antiochus the king; he had been a hostage in Rome. He began to reign in the one hundred and thirty-seventh year of the kingdom of the Greeks.

[11] In those days lawless men came forth from Israel, and misled many, saying, "Let us go and make a covenant with the Gentiles round about us, for since we separated from them many evils have come upon us."

[12] This proposal pleased them,

[13] and some of the people eagerly went to the king. He authorized them to observe the ordinances of the Gentiles.

[14] So they built a gymnasium in Jerusalem, according to Gentile custom,

[15] and removed the marks of circumcision, and abandoned the holy covenant. They joined with the Gentiles and sold themselves to do evil.

[16] When Antiochus saw that his kingdom was established, he determined to become king of the land of Egypt, that he might reign over both kingdoms.

[17] So he invaded Egypt with a strong force, with chariots and elephants and cavalry and with a large fleet.

[18] He engaged Ptolemy king of Egypt in battle, and Ptolemy turned and fled before him, and many were wounded and fell.

[19] And they captured the fortified cities in the land of Egypt, and he plundered the land of Egypt.

[20] After subduing Egypt, Antiochus returned in the one hundred and forty-third year. He went up against Israel and came to Jerusalem with a strong force.

[21] He arrogantly entered the sanctuary and took the golden altar, the lampstand for the light, and all its utensils.

[22] He took also the table for the bread of the Presence, the cups for drink offerings, the bowls, the golden censers, the curtain, the crowns, and the gold decoration on the front of the temple; he stripped it all off.

[23] He took the silver and the gold, and the costly vessels; he took also the hidden treasures which he found.

[24] Taking them all, he departed to his own land. He committed deeds of murder, and spoke with great arrogance.

[25] Israel mourned deeply in every community,

[26] rulers and elders groaned, maidens and young men became faint, the beauty of women faded.

[27] Every bridegroom took up the lament; she who sat in the bridal chamber was mourning.

[28] Even the land shook for its inhabitants, and all the house of Jacob was clothed with shame.

[29] Two years later the king sent to the cities of Judah a chief collector of tribute, and he came to Jerusalem with a large force.

[30] Deceitfully he spoke peaceable words to them, and they believed him; but he suddenly fell upon the city, dealt it a severe blow, and destroyed many people of Israel.

[31] He plundered the city, burned it with fire, and tore down its houses and its surrounding walls.

[32] And they took captive the women and children, and seized the cattle.

[33] Then they fortified the city of David with a great strong wall and strong towers, and it became their citadel.

[34] And they stationed there a sinful people, lawless men. These strengthened their position;

[35] they stored up arms and food, and collecting the spoils of Jerusalem they stored them there, and became a great snare.

[36] It became an ambush against the sanctuary, an evil adversary of Israel continually.

[37] On every side of the sanctuary they shed innocent blood; they even defiled the sanctuary.

[38] Because of them the residents of Jerusalem fled; she became a dwelling of strangers; she became strange to her offspring, and her children forsook her.

[39] Her sanctuary became desolate as a desert; her feasts were turned into mourning, her sabbaths into a reproach,

her honor into contempt.

[40] Her dishonor now grew as great as her glory; her exaltation was turned into mourning.

[41] Then the king wrote to his whole kingdom that all should be one people,

[42] and that each should give up his customs.

[43] All the Gentiles accepted the command of the king. Many even from Israel gladly adopted his religion; they sacrificed to idols and profaned the sabbath.

[44] And the king sent letters by messengers to Jerusalem and the cities of Judah; he directed them to follow customs strange to the land,

[45] to forbid burnt offerings and sacrifices and drink offerings in the sanctuary, to profane sabbaths and feasts,

[46] to defile the sanctuary and the priests,

[47] to build altars and sacred precincts and shrines for idols, to sacrifice swine and unclean animals,

[48] and to leave their sons uncircumcised. They were to make themselves abominable by everything unclean and profane,

[49] so that they should forget the law and change all the ordinances.

[50] "And whoever does not obey the command of the king shall die."

[51] In such words he wrote to his whole kingdom. And he appointed inspectors over all the people and commanded the cities of Judah to offer sacrifice, city by city.

[52] Many of the people, every one who forsook the law, joined them, and they did evil in the land;

[53] they drove Israel into hiding in every place of refuge they had.

[54] Now on the fifteenth day of Chislev, in the one hundred and forty-fifth year, they erected a desolating sacrilege upon the altar of burnt offering. They also built altars in the surrounding cities of Judah,

[55] and burned incense at the doors of the houses and in the streets.

[56] The books of the law which they found they tore to pieces and burned with fire.

[57] Where the book of the covenant was found in the possession of any one, or if any one adhered to the law, the decree of the king condemned him to death.

[58] They kept using violence against Israel, against those found month after month in the cities.

[59] And on the twenty-fifth day of the month they offered sacrifice on the altar which was upon the altar of burnt offering.

[60] According to the decree, they put to death the women who had their children circumcised,

[61] and their families and those who circumcised them; and they hung the infants from their mothers' necks.

[62] But many in Israel stood firm and were resolved in their hearts not to eat unclean food.

[63] They chose to die rather than to be defiled by food or to profane the holy covenant; and they did die.

[64] And very great wrath came upon Israel.

1Mac.2

[1] In those days Mattathias the son of John, son of Simeon, a priest of the sons of Joarib, moved from Jerusalem and settled in Modein.

[2] He had five sons, John surnamed Gaddi,

[3] Simon called Thassi,

[4] Judas called Maccabeus,

[5] Eleazar called Avaran, and Jonathan called Apphus.

[6] He saw the blasphemies being committed in Judah and Jerusalem,

[7] and said, "Alas! Why was I born to see this, the ruin of my people, the ruin of the holy city, and to dwell there when it was given over to the enemy, the sanctuary given over to aliens?

[8] Her temple has become like a man without honor;

[9] her glorious vessels have been carried into captivity. Her babes have been killed in her streets, her youths by the sword of the foe.

[10] What nation has not inherited her palaces and has not seized her spoils?

[11] All her adornment has been taken away; no longer free, she has become a slave.

[12] And behold, our holy place, our beauty, and our glory have been laid waste; the Gentiles have profaned it.

[13] Why should we live any longer?"

[14] And Mattathias and his sons rent their clothes, put on sackcloth, and mourned greatly.

[15] Then the king's officers who were enforcing the apostasy came to the city of Modein to make them offer sacrifice.

[16] Many from Israel came to them; and Mattathias and his sons were assembled.

[17] Then the king's officers spoke to Mattathias as follows: "You are a leader, honored and great in this city, and supported by sons and brothers.

[18] Now be the first to come and do what the king commands, as all the Gentiles and the men of Judah and those that are left in Jerusalem have done. Then you and your sons will be numbered among the friends of the king, and you and your sons will be honored with silver and gold and many gifts."

[19] But Mattathias answered and said in a loud voice: "Even if all the nations that live under the rule of the king obey him, and have chosen to do his commandments, departing each one from the religion of his fathers,

[20] yet I and my sons and my brothers will live by the covenant of our fathers.

[21] Far be it from us to desert the law and the ordinances.

[22] We will not obey the king's words by turning aside from our religion to the right hand or to the left."

[23] When he had finished speaking these words, a Jew came forward in the sight of all to offer sacrifice upon the altar in Modein, according to the king's command.

[24] When Mattathias saw it, be burned with zeal and his heart was stirred. He gave vent to righteous anger; he ran and killed him upon the altar.

[25] At the same time he killed the king's officer who was forcing them to sacrifice, and he tore down the altar.

[26] Thus he burned with zeal for the law, as Phinehas did against Zimri the son of Salu.

[27] Then Mattathias cried out in the city with a loud voice, saying: "Let every one who is zealous for the law and supports the covenant come out with me!"

[28] And he and his sons fled to the hills and left all that they had in the city.

[29] Then many who were seeking righteousness and justice went down to the wilderness to dwell there,

[30] they, their sons, their wives, and their cattle, because evils pressed heavily upon them.

[31] And it was reported to the king's officers, and to the troops in Jerusalem the city of David, that men who had rejected the king's command had gone down to the hiding places in the wilderness.

[32] Many pursued them, and overtook them; they encamped opposite them and prepared for battle against them on the sabbath day.

[33] And they said to them, "Enough of this! Come out and do what the king commands, and you will live."

[34] But they said, "We will not come out, nor will we do what the king commands and so profane the sabbath day."

[35] Then the enemy hastened to attack them.

[36] But they did not answer them or hurl a stone at them or block up their hiding places,

[37] for they said, "Let us all die in our innocence; heaven and earth testify for us that you are killing us unjustly."

[38] So they attacked them on the sabbath, and they died, with their wives and children and cattle, to the number of a thousand persons.

[39] When Mattathias and his friends learned of it, they mourned for them deeply.

[40] And each said to his neighbor: "If we all do as our brethren have done and refuse to fight with the Gentiles for our lives and for our ordinances, they will quickly destroy us from the earth."

[41] So they made this decision that day: "Let us fight against every man who comes to attack us on the sabbath day; let us not all die as our brethren died in their hiding places."

[42] Then there united with them a company of Hasideans, mighty warriors of Israel, every one who offered himself willingly for the law.

[43] And all who became fugitives to escape their troubles joined them and reinforced them.

[44] They organized an army, and struck down sinners in their anger and lawless men in their wrath; the survivors fled to the Gentiles for safety.

[45] And Mattathias and his friends went about and tore down the altars;

[46] they forcibly circumcised all the uncircumcised boys that they found within the borders of Israel.

[47] They hunted down the arrogant men, and the work prospered in their hands.

[48] They rescued the law out of the hands of the Gentiles and kings, and they never let the sinner gain the upper hand.

[49] Now the days drew near for Mattathias to die, and he said to his sons: "Arrogance and reproach have now become strong; it is a time of ruin and furious anger.

[50] Now, my children, show zeal for the law, and give your lives for the covenant of our fathers.

[51] "Remember the deeds of the fathers, which they did in their generations; and receive great honor and an everlasting name.

[52] Was not Abraham found faithful when tested, and it was reckoned to him as righteousness?

[53] Joseph in the time of his distress kept the commandment, and became lord of Egypt.

[54] Phinehas our father, because he was deeply zealous, received the covenant of everlasting priesthood.

[55] Joshua, because he fulfilled the command, became a judge in Israel.

[56] Caleb, because he testified in the assembly, received an inheritance in the land.

[57] David, because he was merciful, inherited the throne of the kingdom for ever.

[58] Elijah because of great zeal for the law was taken up into heaven.

[59] Hannaniah, Azariah, and Mishael believed and were saved from the flame.

[60] Daniel because of his innocence was delivered from the mouth of the lions.

[61] "And so observe, from generation to generation, that none who put their trust in him will lack strength.

[62] Do not fear the words of a sinner, for his splendor will turn into dung and worms.

[63] Today he will be exalted, but tomorrow he will not be found, because he has returned to the dust, and his plans will perish.

[64] My children, be courageous and grow strong in the law, for by it you will gain honor.

[65] "Now behold, I know that Simeon your brother is wise in counsel; always listen to him; he shall be your father.

[66] Judas Maccabeus has been a mighty warrior from his youth; he shall command the army for you and fight the battle against the peoples.

[67] You shall rally about you all who observe the law, and avenge the wrong done to your people.

[68] Pay back the Gentiles in full, and heed what the law commands."

[69] Then he blessed them, and was gathered to his fathers.

[70] He died in the one hundred and forty-sixth year and was buried in the tomb of his fathers at Modein. And all Israel mourned for him with great lamentation.

1Mac.3

[1] Then Judas his son, who was called Maccabeus, took command in his place.

[2] All his brothers and all who had joined his father helped him; they gladly fought for Israel.

[3] He extended the glory of his people. Like a giant he put on his breastplate; he girded on his armor of war and waged battles, protecting the host by his sword.

[4] He was like a lion in his deeds, like a lion's cub roaring for prey.

[5] He searched out and pursued the lawless; he burned those who troubled his people.

[6] Lawless men shrank back for fear of him; all the evildoers were confounded; and deliverance prospered by his hand.

[7] He embittered many kings, but he made Jacob glad by his deeds, and his memory is blessed for ever.

[8] He went through the cities of Judah; he destroyed the ungodly out of the land; thus he turned away wrath from Israel.

[9] He was renowned to the ends of the earth; he gathered in those who were perishing.

[10] But Apollonius gathered together Gentiles and a large force from Samaria to fight against Israel.

[11] When Judas learned of it, he went out to meet him, and he defeated and killed him. Many were wounded and fell, and the rest fled.

[12] Then they seized their spoils; and Judas took the sword of Apollonius, and used it in battle the rest of his life.

[13] Now when Seron, the commander of the Syrian army, heard that Judas had gathered a large company, including a body of faithful men who stayed with him and went out to battle,

[14] he said, "I will make a name for myself and win honor in the kingdom. I will make war on Judas and his companions, who scorn the king's command."

[15] And again a strong army of ungodly men went up with him to help him, to take vengeance on the sons of Israel.

[16] When he approached the ascent of Beth-horon, Judas went out to meet him with a small company.

[17] But when they saw the army coming to meet them, they said to Judas, "How can we, few as we are, fight against so great and strong a multitude? And we are faint, for we have eaten nothing today."

[18] Judas replied, "It is easy for many to be hemmed in by few, for in the sight of Heaven there is no

difference between saving by many or by few.

[19] It is not on the size of the army that victory in battle depends, but strength comes from Heaven.

[20] They come against us in great pride and lawlessness to destroy us and our wives and our children, and to despoil us;

[21] but we fight for our lives and our laws.

[22] He himself will crush them before us; as for you, do not be afraid of them."

[23] When he finished speaking, he rushed suddenly against Seron and his army, and they were crushed before him.

[24] They pursued them down the descent of Beth-horon to the plain; eight hundred of them fell, and the rest fled into the land of the Philistines.

[25] Then Judas and his brothers began to be feared, and terror fell upon the Gentiles round about them.

[26] His fame reached the king, and the Gentiles talked of the battles of Judas.

[27] When king Antiochus heard these reports, he was greatly angered; and he sent and gathered all the forces of his kingdom, a very strong army.

[28] And he opened his coffers and gave a year's pay to his forces, and ordered them to be ready for any need.

[29] Then he saw that the money in the treasury was exhausted, and that the revenues from the country were small because of the dissension and disaster which he had caused in the land by abolishing the laws that had existed from the earliest days.

[30] He feared that he might not have such funds as he had before for his expenses and for the gifts which he used to give more lavishly than preceding kings.

[31] He was greatly perplexed in mind, and determined to go to Persia and collect the revenues from those regions and raise a large fund.

[32] He left Lysias, a distinguished man of royal lineage, in charge of the king's affairs from the river Euphrates to the borders of Egypt.

[33] Lysias was also to take care of Antiochus his son until he returned.

[34] And he turned over to Lysias half of his troops and the elephants, and gave him orders about all that he wanted done. As for the residents of Judea and Jerusalem,

[35] Lysias was to send a force against them to wipe out and destroy the strength of Israel and the remnant of Jerusalem; he was to banish the memory of them from the place,

[36] settle aliens in all their territory, and distribute their land.

[37] Then the king took the remaining half of his troops and departed from Antioch his capital in the one hundred and forty-seventh year. He crossed the Euphrates river and went through the upper provinces.

[38] Lysias chose Ptolemy the son of Dorymenes, and Nicanor and Gorgias, mighty men among the friends of the king,

[39] and sent with them forty thousand infantry and seven thousand cavalry to go into the land of Judah and destroy it, as the king had commanded.

[40] so they departed with their entire force, and when they arrived they encamped near Emmaus in the plain.

[41] When the traders of the region heard what was said to them, they took silver and gold in immense amounts, and fetters, and went to the camp to get the sons of Israel for slaves. And forces from Syria and the land of the Philistines joined with them.

[42] Now Judas and his brothers saw that misfortunes had increased and that the forces were encamped in their territory. They also learned what the king had commanded to do to the people to cause their final destruction.

[43] But they said to one another, "Let us repair the destruction of our people, and fight for our people and the sanctuary."

[44] And the congregation assembled to be ready for battle, and to pray and ask for mercy and compassion.

[45] Jerusalem was uninhabited like a wilderness; not one of her children went in or out.The sanctuary was trampled own,

and the sons of aliens held the citadel; it was a lodging place for the Gentiles. Joy was taken from Jacob; the flute and the harp ceased to play.

[46] So they assembled and went to Mizpah, opposite Jerusalem, because Israel formerly had a place of prayer in Mizpah.

[47] They fasted that day, put on sackcloth and sprinkled ashes on their heads, and rent their clothes.

[48] And they opened the book of the law to inquire into those matters about which the Gentiles were consulting the images of their idols.

[49] They also brought the garments of the priesthood and the first fruits and the tithes, and they

stirred up the Nazirites who had completed their days;

[50] and they cried aloud to Heaven, saying, "What shall we do with these? Where shall we take them?

[51] Your sanctuary is trampled down and profaned, and thy priests mourn in humiliation.

[52] And behold, the Gentiles are assembled against us to destroy us; thou knowest what they plot against us.

[53] How will we be able to withstand them, if thou do not help us?"

[54] Then they sounded the trumpets and gave a loud shout.

[55] After this Judas appointed leaders of the people, in charge of thousands and hundreds and fifties and tens.

[56] And he said to those who were building houses, or were betrothed, or were planting vineyards, or were fainthearted, that each should return to his home, according to the law.

[57] Then the army marched out and encamped to the south of Emmaus.

[58] And Judas said, "Gird yourselves and be valiant. Be ready early in the morning to fight with these Gentiles who have assembled against us to destroy us and our sanctuary.

[59] It is better for us to die in battle than to see the misfortunes of our nation and of the sanctuary.

[60] But as his will in heaven may be, so he will do."

1Mac.4

[1] Now Gorgias took five thousand infantry and a thousand picked cavalry, and this division moved out by night

[2] to fall upon the camp of the Jews and attack them suddenly. Men from the citadel were his guides.

[3] But Judas heard of it, and he and his mighty men moved out to attack the king's force in Emmaus

[4] while the division was still absent from the camp.

[5] When Gorgias entered the camp of Judas by night, he found no one there, so he looked for them in the hills, because he said, "These men are fleeing from us."

[6] At daybreak Judas appeared in the plain with three thousand men, but they did not have armor and swords such as they desired.

[7] And they saw the camp of the Gentiles, strong and fortified, with cavalry round about it; and these men were trained in war.

[8] But Judas said to the men who were with him, "Do not fear their numbers or be afraid when they charge.

[9] Remember how our fathers were saved at the Red Sea, when Pharaoh with his forces pursued them.

[10] And now let us cry to Heaven, to see whether he will favor us and remember his covenant with our fathers and crush this army before us today.

[11] Then all the Gentiles will know that there is one who redeems and saves Israel."

[12] When the foreigners looked up and saw them coming against them,

[13] they went forth from their camp to battle. Then the men with Judas blew their trumpets

[14] and engaged in battle. The Gentiles were crushed and fled into the plain,

[15] and all those in the rear fell by the sword. They pursued them to Gazara, and to the plains of Idumea, and to Azotus and Jamnia; and three thousand of them fell.

[16] Then Judas and his force turned back from pursuing them,

[17] and he said to the people, "Do not be greedy for plunder, for there is a battle before us;

[18] Gorgias and his force are near us in the hills. But stand now against our enemies and fight them, and afterward seize the plunder boldly."

[19] Just as Judas was finishing this speech, a detachment appeared, coming out of the hills.

[20] They saw that their army had been put to flight, and that the Jews were burning the camp, for the smoke that was seen showed what had happened.

[21] When they perceived this they were greatly frightened, and when they also saw the army of Judas drawn up in the plain for battle,

[22] they all fled into the land of the Philistines.

[23] Then Judas returned to plunder the camp, and they seized much gold and silver, and cloth dyed blue and sea purple, and great riches.

[24] On their return they sang hymns and praises to Heaven, for he is good, for his mercy endures for ever.

[25] Thus Israel had a great deliverance that day.

[26] Those of the foreigners who escaped went and reported to Lysias all that had happened.

[27] When he heard it, he was perplexed and discouraged, for things had not happened to Israel as he had intended, nor had they turned out as the king had commanded him.

[28] But the next year he mustered sixty thousand picked infantrymen and five thousand cavalry to subdue them.

[29] They came into Idumea and encamped at Beth-zur, and Judas met them with ten thousand men.

[30] When he saw that the army was strong, he prayed, saying, "Blessed art thou, O Savior of Israel,

who didst crush the attack of the mighty warrior by the hand of thy servant David, and didst give the camp of the Philistines into the hands of Jonathan, the son of Saul, and of the man who carried his armor.

[31] So do thou hem in this army by the hand of thy people Israel, and let them be ashamed of their troops and their cavalry.

[32] Fill them with cowardice; melt the boldness of their strength; let them tremble in their destruction.

[33] Strike them down with the sword of those who love thee, and let all who know thy name praise thee with hymns."

[34] Then both sides attacked, and there fell of the army of Lysias five thousand men; they fell in action.

[35] And when Lysias saw the rout of his troops and observed the boldness which inspired those of Judas, and how ready they were either to live or to die nobly, he departed to Antioch and enlisted mercenaries, to invade Judea again with an even larger army.

[36] Then said Judas and his brothers, "Behold, our enemies are crushed; let us go up to cleanse the sanctuary and dedicate it."

[37] So all the army assembled and they went up to Mount Zion.

[38] And they saw the sanctuary desolate, the altar profaned, and the gates burned. In the courts they saw bushes sprung up as in a thicket, or as on one of the mountains. They saw also the chambers of the priests in ruins.

[39] Then they rent their clothes, and mourned with great lamentation, and sprinkled themselves with ashes.

[40] They fell face down on the ground, and sounded the signal on the trumpets, and cried out to Heaven.

[41] Then Judas detailed men to fight against those in the citadel until he had cleansed the sanctuary.

[42] He chose blameless priests devoted to the law,

[43] and they cleansed the sanctuary and removed the defiled stones to an unclean place.

[44] They deliberated what to do about the altar of burnt offering, which had been profaned.

[45] And they thought it best to tear it down, lest it bring reproach upon them, for the Gentiles had defiled it. So they tore down the altar,

[46] and stored the stones in a convenient place on the temple hill until there should come a prophet to tell what to do with them.

[47] Then they took unhewn stones, as the law directs, and built a new altar like the former one.

[48] They also rebuilt the sanctuary and the interior of the temple, and consecrated the courts.

[49] They made new holy vessels, and brought the lampstand, the altar of incense, and the table into the temple.

[50] Then they burned incense on the altar and lighted the lamps on the lampstand, and these gave light in the temple.

[51] They placed the bread on the table and hung up the curtains. Thus they finished all the work they had undertaken.

[52] Early in the morning on the twenty-fifth day of the ninth month, which is the month of Chislev, in the one hundred and forty-eighth year,

[53] they rose and offered sacrifice, as the law directs, on the new altar of burnt offering which they had built.

[54] At the very season and on the very day that the Gentiles had profaned it, it was dedicated with songs and harps and lutes and cymbals.

[55] All the people fell on their faces and worshiped and blessed Heaven, who had prospered them.

[56] So they celebrated the dedication of the altar for eight days, and offered burnt offerings with gladness; they offered a sacrifice of deliverance and praise.

[57] They decorated the front of the temple with golden crowns and small shields; they restored the gates and the chambers for the priests, and furnished them with doors.

[58] There was very great gladness among the people, and the reproach of the Gentiles was removed.

[59] Then Judas and his brothers and all the assembly of Israel determined that every year at that season the days of dedication of the altar should be observed with gladness and joy for eight days, beginning with the twenty-fifth day of the month of Chislev.

[60] At that time they fortified Mount Zion with high walls and strong towers round about, to keep the Gentiles from coming and trampling them down as they had done before.

[61] And he stationed a garrison there to hold it. He also fortified Beth-zur, so that the people might have a stronghold that faced Idumea.

1Mac.5

[1] When the Gentiles round about heard that the altar had been built and the sanctuary dedicated as it was before, they became very angry,

[2] and they determined to destroy the descendants of Jacob who lived among them. So they began to kill and destroy among the people.

[3] But Judas made war on the sons of Esau in Idumea, at Akrabattene, because they kept lying in wait for Israel. He dealt them a heavy blow and humbled them and despoiled them.

[4] He also remembered the wickedness of the sons of Baean, who were a trap and a snare to the people and ambushed them on the highways.

[5] They were shut up by him in their towers; and he encamped against them, vowed their complete destruction, and burned with fire their towers and all who were in them.

[6] Then he crossed over to attack the Ammonites, where he found a strong band and many people with Timothy as their leader.

[7] He engaged in many battles with them and they were crushed before him; he struck them down.

[8] He also took Jazer and its villages; then he returned to Judea.

[9] Now the Gentiles in Gilead gathered together against the Israelites who lived in their territory, and planned to destroy them. But they fled to the stronghold of Dathema,

[10] and sent to Judas and his brothers a letter which said, "The Gentiles around us have gathered together against us to destroy us.

[11] They are preparing to come and capture the stronghold to which we have fled, and Timothy is leading their forces.

[12] Now then come and rescue us from their hands, for many of us have fallen,

[13] and all our brethren who were in the land of Tob have been killed; the enemy have captured their wives and children and goods, and have destroyed about a thousand men there."

[14] While the letter was still being read, behold, other messengers, with their garments rent, came from Galilee and made a similar report;

[15] they said that against them had gathered together men of Ptolemais and Tyre and Sidon, and all Galilee of the Gentiles, "to annihilate us."

[16] When Judas and the people heard these messages, a great assembly was called to determine what they should do for their brethren who were in distress and were being attacked by enemies.

[17] Then Judas said to Simon his brother, "Choose your men and go and rescue your brethren in Galilee; I and Jonathan my brother will go to Gilead."

[18] But he left Joseph, the son of Zechariah, and Azariah, a leader of the people, with the rest of the forces, in Judea to guard it;

[19] and he gave them this command, "Take charge of this people, but do not engage in battle with the Gentiles until we return."

[20] Then three thousand men were assigned to Simon to go to Galilee, and eight thousand to Judas for Gilead.

[21] so Simon went to Galilee and fought many battles against the Gentiles, and the Gentiles were crushed before him.

[22] He pursued them to the gate of Ptolemais, and as many as three thousand of the Gentiles fell, and he despoiled them.

[23] Then he took the Jews of Galilee and Arbatta, with their wives and children, and all they possessed, and led them to Judea with great rejoicing.

[24] Judas Maccabeus and Jonathan his brother crossed the Jordan and went three days' journey into the wilderness.

[25] They encountered the Nabateans, who met them peaceably and told them all that had happened to their brethren in Gilead:

[26] "Many of them have been shut up in Bozrah and Bosor, in Alema and Chaspho, Maked and Carnaim" -- all these cities were strong and large--

[27] "and some have been shut up in the other cities of Gilead; the enemy are getting ready to attack the strongholds tomorrow and take and destroy all these men in one day."

[28] Then Judas and his army quickly turned back by the wilderness road to Bozrah; and he took the city, and killed every male by the edge of the sword; then he seized all its spoils and burned it with fire.

[29] He departed from there at night, and they went all the way to the stronghold of Dathema.

[30] At dawn they looked up, and behold, a large company, that could not be counted, carrying ladders and engines of war to capture the stronghold, and attacking the Jews within.

[31] So Judas saw that the battle had begun and that the cry of the city went up to Heaven with trumpets and loud shouts,

[32] and he said to the men of his forces, "Fight today for your brethren!"

[33] Then he came up behind them in three companies, who sounded their trumpets and cried aloud in prayer.

[34] And when the army of Timothy realized that it was Maccabeus, they fled before him, and he dealt them a heavy blow. As many as eight thousand of them fell that day.

[35] Next he turned aside to Alema, and fought against it and took it; and he killed every male in it,

plundered it, and burned it with fire.

[36] From there he marched on and took Chaspho, Maked, and Bosor, and the other cities of Gilead.

[37] After these things Timothy gathered another army and encamped opposite Raphon, on the other side of the stream.

[38] Judas sent men to spy out the camp, and they reported to him, "All the Gentiles around us have gathered to him; it is a very large force.

[39] They also have hired Arabs to help them, and they are encamped across the stream, ready to come and fight against you." And Judas went to meet them.

[40] Now as Judas and his army drew near to the stream of water, Timothy said to the officers of his forces, "If he crosses over to us first, we will not be able to resist him, for he will surely defeat us.

[41] But if he shows fear and camps on the other side of the river, we will cross over to him and defeat him."

[42] When Judas approached the stream of water, he stationed the scribes of the people at the stream and gave them this command, "Permit no man to encamp, but make them all enter the battle."

[43] Then he crossed over against them first, and the whole army followed him. All the Gentiles were defeated before him, and they threw away their arms and fled into the sacred precincts at Carnaim.

[44] But he took the city and burned the sacred precincts with fire, together with all who were in them. Thus Carnaim was conquered; they could stand before Judas no longer.

[45] Then Judas gathered together all the Israelites in Gilead, the small and the great, with their wives and children and goods, a very large company, to go to the land of Judah.

[46] So they came to Ephron. This was a large and very strong city on the road, and they could not go round it to the right or to the left; they had to go through it.

[47] But the men of the city shut them out and blocked up the gates with stones.

[48] And Judas sent them this friendly message, "Let us pass through your land to get to our land. No one will do you harm; we will simply pass by on foot." But they refused to open to him.

[49] Then Judas ordered proclamation to be made to the army that each should encamp where he was.

[50] So the men of the forces encamped, and he fought against the city all that day and all the night, and the city was delivered into his hands.

[51] He destroyed every male by the edge of the sword, and razed and plundered the city. Then he passed through the city over the slain.

[52] And they crossed the Jordan into the large plain before Beth-shan.

[53] And Judas kept rallying the laggards and encouraging the people all the way till he came to the land of Judah.

[54] So they went up to Mount Zion with gladness and joy, and offered burnt offerings, because not one of them had fallen before they returned in safety.

[55] Now while Judas and Jonathan were in Gilead and Simon his brother was in Galilee before Ptolemais,

[56] Joseph, the son of Zechariah, and Azariah, the commanders of the forces, heard of their brave deeds and of the heroic war they had fought.

[57] So they said, "Let us also make a name for ourselves; let us go and make war on the Gentiles around us."

[58] And they issued orders to the men of the forces that were with them, and they marched against Jamnia.

[59] And Gorgias and his men came out of the city to meet them in battle.

[60] Then Joseph and Azariah were routed, and were pursued to the borders of Judea; as many as two thousand of the people of Israel fell that day.

[61] Thus the people suffered a great rout because, thinking to do a brave deed, they did not listen to Judas and his brothers.

[62] But they did not belong to the family of those men through whom deliverance was given to Israel.

[63] The man Judas and his brothers were greatly honored in all Israel and among all the Gentiles, wherever their name was heard.

[64] Men gathered to them and praised them.

[65] Then Judas and his brothers went forth and fought the sons of Esau in the land to the south. He struck Hebron and its villages and tore down its strongholds and burned its towers round about.

[66] Then he marched off to go into the land of the Philistines, and passed through Marisa.

[67] On that day some priests, who wished to do a brave deed, fell in battle, for they went out to battle unwisely.

[68] But Judas turned aside to Azotus in the land of the Philistines; he tore down their altars, and the graven images of their gods he burned with fire; he plundered the cities and returned to the land of Judah.

1Mac.6

[1] King Antiochus was going through the upper provinces when he heard that Elymais in Persia was a city famed for its wealth in silver and gold.

[2] Its temple was very rich, containing golden shields, breastplates, and weapons left there by Alexander, the son of Philip, the Macedonian king who first reigned over the Greeks.

[3] So he came and tried to take the city and plunder it, but he could not, because his plan became known to the men of the city

[4] and they withstood him in battle. So he fled and in great grief departed from there to return to Babylon.

[5] Then some one came to him in Persia and reported that the armies which had gone into the land of Judah had been routed;

[6] that Lysias had gone first with a strong force, but had turned and fled before the Jews; that the Jews had grown strong from the arms, supplies, and abundant spoils which they had taken from the armies they had cut down;

[7] that they had torn down the abomination which he had erected upon the altar in Jerusalem; and that they had surrounded the sanctuary with high walls as before, and also Beth-zur, his city.

[8] When the king heard this news, he was astounded and badly shaken. He took to his bed and became sick from grief, because things had not turned out for him as he had planned.

[9] He lay there for many days, because deep grief continually gripped him, and he concluded that he was dying.

[10] So he called all his friends and said to them, "Sleep departs from my eyes and I am downhearted with worry.

[11] I said to myself, `To what distress I have come! And into what a great flood I now am plunged! For I was kind and beloved in my power.'

[12] But now I remember the evils I did in Jerusalem. I seized all her vessels of silver and gold; and I sent to destroy the inhabitants of Judah without good reason.

[13] I know that it is because of this that these evils have come upon me; and behold, I am perishing of deep grief in a strange land."

[14] Then he called for Philip, one of his friends, and made him ruler over all his kingdom.

[15] He gave him the crown and his robe and the signet, that he might guide Antiochus his son and bring him up to be king.

[16] Thus Antiochus the king died there in the one hundred and forty-ninth year.

[17] And when Lysias learned that the king was dead, he set up Antiochus the king's son to reign. Lysias had brought him up as a boy, and he named him Eupator.

[18] Now the men in the citadel kept hemming Israel in around the sanctuary. They were trying in every way to harm them and strengthen the Gentiles.

[19] So Judas decided to destroy them, and assembled all the people to besiege them.

[20] They gathered together and besieged the citadel in the one hundred and fiftieth year; and he built siege towers and other engines of war.

[21] But some of the garrison escaped from the siege and some of the ungodly Israelites joined them.

[22] They went to the king and said, "How long will you fail to do justice and to avenge our brethren?

[23] We were happy to serve your father, to live by what he said and to follow his commands.

[24] For this reason the sons of our people besieged the citadel and became hostile to us; moreover, they have put to death as many of us as they have caught, and they have seized our inheritances.

[25] And not against us alone have they stretched out their hands, but also against all the lands on their borders.

[26] And behold, today they have encamped against the citadel in Jerusalem to take it; they have fortified both the sanctuary and Beth-zur;

[27] and unless you quickly prevent them, they will do still greater things, and you will not be able to stop them."

[28] The king was enraged when he heard this. He assembled all his friends, the commanders of his forces and those in authority.

[29] And mercenary forces came to him from other kingdoms and from islands of the seas.

[30] The number of his forces was a hundred thousand foot soldiers, twenty thousand horsemen, and thirty-two elephants accustomed to war.

[31] They came through Idumea and encamped against Beth-zur, and for many days they fought and built engines of war; but the Jews sallied out and burned these with fire, and fought manfully.

[32] Then Judas marched away from the citadel and encamped at Beth-zechariah, opposite the camp of the king.

[33] Early in the morning the king rose and took his army by a forced march along the road to Beth-zechariah, and his troops made ready for battle and sounded their trumpets.

[34] They showed the elephants the juice of grapes and mulberries, to arouse them for battle.

[35] And they distributed the beasts among the phalanxes; with each elephant they stationed a thousand men armed with coats of mail, and with brass helmets on their heads; and five hundred picked horsemen were assigned to each beast.

[36] These took their position beforehand wherever the beast was; wherever it went they went with it, and they never left it.

[37] And upon the elephants were wooden towers, strong and covered; they were fastened upon each beast by special harness, and upon each were four armed men who fought from there, and also its Indian driver.

[38] The rest of the horsemen were stationed on either side, on the two flanks of the army, to harass the enemy while being themselves protected by the phalanxes.

[39] When the sun shone upon the shields of gold and brass, the hills were ablaze with them and gleamed like flaming torches.

[40] Now a part of the king's army was spread out on the high hills, and some troops were on the plain, and they advanced steadily and in good order.

[41] All who heard the noise made by their multitude, by the marching of the multitude and the clanking of their arms, trembled, for the army was very large and strong.

[42] But Judas and his army advanced to the battle, and six hundred men of the king's army fell.

[43] And Eleazar, called Avaran, saw that one of the beasts was equipped with royal armor. It was taller than all the others, and he supposed that the king was upon it.

[44] So he gave his life to save his people and to win for himself an everlasting name.

[45] He courageously ran into the midst of the phalanx to reach it; he killed men right and left, and they parted before him on both sides.

[46] He got under the elephant, stabbed it from beneath, and killed it; but it fell to the ground upon him and he died.

[47] And when the Jews saw the royal might and the fierce attack of the forces, they turned away in flight.

[48] The soldiers of the king's army went up to Jerusalem against them, and the king encamped in Judea and at Mount Zion.

[49] He made peace with the men of Beth-zur, and they evacuated the city, because they had no provisions there to withstand a siege, since it was a sabbatical year for the land.

[50] So the king took Beth-zur and stationed a guard there to hold it.

[51] Then he encamped before the sanctuary for many days. He set up siege towers, engines of war to throw fire and stones, machines to shoot arrows, and catapults.

[52] The Jews also made engines of war to match theirs, and fought for many days.

[53] But they had no food in storage, because it was the seventh year; those who found safety in Judea from the Gentiles had consumed the last of the stores.

[54] Few men were left in the sanctuary, because famine had prevailed over the rest and they had been scattered, each to his own place.

[55] Then Lysias heard that Philip, whom King Antiochus while still living had appointed to bring up Antiochus his son to be king,

[56] had returned from Persia and Media with the forces that had gone with the king, and that he was trying to seize control of the government.

[57] So he quickly gave orders to depart, and said to the king, to the commanders of the forces, and to the men, "We daily grow weaker, our food supply is scant, the place against which we are fighting is strong, and the affairs of the kingdom press urgently upon us.

[58] Now then let us come to terms with these men, and make peace with them and with all their nation,

[59] and agree to let them live by their laws as they did before; for it was on account of their laws which we abolished that they became angry and did all these things."

[60] The speech pleased the king and the commanders, and he sent to the Jews an offer of peace, and they accepted it.

[61] So the king and the commanders gave them their oath. On these conditions the Jews evacuated the stronghold.

[62] But when the king entered Mount Zion and saw what a strong fortress the place was, he broke the oath he had sworn and gave orders to tear down the wall all around.

[63] Then he departed with haste and returned to Antioch. He found Philip in control of the city, but he fought against him, and took the city by force.

1Mac.7

[1] In the one hundred and fifty-first year Demetrius the son of Seleucus set forth from Rome, sailed with a few men to a city by the sea, and there began to reign.

[2] As he was entering the royal palace of his fathers, the army seized Antiochus and Lysias to bring them to him.

[3] But when this act became known to him, he said, "Do not let me see their faces!"

[4] So the army killed them, and Demetrius took his seat upon the throne of his kingdom.

[5] Then there came to him all the lawless and ungodly men of Israel; they were led by Alcimus, who wanted to be high priest.

[6] And they brought to the king this accusation against the people: "Judas and his brothers have destroyed all your friends, and have driven us out of our land.

[7] Now then send a man whom you trust; let him go and see all the ruin which Judas has brought upon us and upon the land of the king, and let him punish them and all who help them."

[8] So the king chose Bacchides, one of the king's friends, governor of the province Beyond the River; he was a great man in the kingdom and was faithful to the king.

[9] And he sent him, and with him the ungodly Alcimus, whom he made high priest; and he commanded him to take vengeance on the sons of Israel.

[10] So they marched away and came with a large force into the land of Judah; and he sent messengers to Judas and his brothers with peaceable but treacherous words.

[11] But they paid no attention to their words, for they saw that they had come with a large force.

[12] Then a group of scribes appeared in a body before Alcimus and Bacchides to ask for just terms.

[13] The Hasideans were first among the sons of Israel to seek peace from them,

[14] for they said, "A priest of the line of Aaron has come with the army, and he will not harm us."

[15] And he spoke peaceable words to them and swore this oath to them, "We will not seek to injure you or your friends."

[16] So they trusted him; but he seized sixty of them and killed them in one day, in accordance with the word which was written,

[17] "The flesh of thy saints and their blood they poured out round about Jerusalem, and there was none to bury them."

[18] Then the fear and dread of them fell upon all the people, for they said, "There is no truth or justice in them, for they have violated the agreement and the oath which they swore."

[19] Then Bacchides departed from Jerusalem and encamped in Beth-zaith. And he sent and seized many of the men who had deserted to him, and some of the people, and killed them and threw them into a great pit.

[20] He placed Alcimus in charge of the country and left with him a force to help him; then Bacchides went back to the king.

[21] Alcimus strove for the high priesthood,

[22] and all who were troubling their people joined him. They gained control of the land of Judah and did great damage in Israel.

[23] And Judas saw all the evil that Alcimus and those with him had done among the sons of Israel; it was more than the Gentiles had done.

[24] So Judas went out into all the surrounding parts of Judea, and took vengeance on the men who had deserted, and he prevented those in the city from going out into the country.

[25] When Alcimus saw that Judas and those with him had grown strong, and realized that he could not withstand them, he returned to the king and brought wicked charges against them.

[26] Then the king sent Nicanor, one of his honored princes, who hated and detested Israel, and he commanded him to destroy the people.

[27] So Nicanor came to Jerusalem with a large force, and treacherously sent to Judas and his brothers this peaceable message,

[28] "Let there be no fighting between me and you; I shall come with a few men to see you face to face in peace."

[29] So he came to Judas, and they greeted one another peaceably. But the enemy were ready to seize Judas.

[30] It became known to Judas that Nicanor had come to him with treacherous intent, and he was afraid of him and would not meet him again.

[31] When Nicanor learned that his plan had been disclosed, he went out to meet Judas in battle near Caphar-salama.

[32] About five hundred men of the army of Nicanor fell, and the rest fled into the city of David.

[33] After these events Nicanor went up to Mount Zion. Some of the priests came out of the sanctuary, and some of the elders of the people, to greet him peaceably and to show him the burnt offering that was being offered for the king.

[34] But he mocked them and derided them and defiled them and spoke arrogantly,

[35] and in anger he swore this oath, "Unless Judas and his army are delivered into my hands this time, then if I return safely I will burn up this house." And he went out in great anger.

[36] Then the priests went in and stood before the altar and the temple, and they wept and said,

[37] "Thou didst choose this house to be called by thy name, and to be for thy people a house of prayer and supplication.

[38] Take vengeance on this man and on his army, and let them fall by the sword; remember their blasphemies, and let them live no longer."

[39] Now Nicanor went out from Jerusalem and encamped in Beth-horon, and the Syrian army joined him.

[40] And Judas encamped in Adasa with three thousand men. Then Judas prayed and said,

[41] "When the messengers from the king spoke blasphemy, thy angel went forth and struck down one hundred and eighty-five thousand of the Assyrians.

[42] So also crush this army before us today; let the rest learn that Nicanor has spoken wickedly against the sanctuary, and judge him according to this wickedness."

[43] So the armies met in battle on the thirteenth day of the month of Adar. The army of Nicanor was crushed, and he himself was the first to fall in the battle.

[44] When his army saw that Nicanor had fallen, they threw down their arms and fled.

[45] The Jews pursued them a day's journey, from Adasa as far as Gazara, and as they followed kept sounding the battle call on the trumpets.

[46] And men came out of all the villages of Judea round about, and they out-flanked the enemy and drove them back to their pursuers, so that they all fell by the sword; not even one of them was left.

[47] Then the Jews seized the spoils and the plunder, and they cut off Nicanor's head and the right hand which he so arrogantly stretched out, and brought them and displayed them just outside Jerusalem.

[48] The people rejoiced greatly and celebrated that day as a day of great gladness.

[49] And they decreed that this day should be celebrated each year on the thirteenth day of Adar.

[50] So the land of Judah had rest for a few days.

1Mac.8

[1] Now Judas heard of the fame of the Romans, that they were very strong and were well-disposed toward all who made an alliance with them, that they pledged friendship to those who came to them,

[2] and that they were very strong. Men told him of their wars and of the brave deeds which they were doing among the Gauls, how they had defeated them and forced them to pay tribute,

[3] and what they had done in the land of Spain to get control of the silver and gold mines there,

[4] and how they had gained control of the whole region by their planning and patience, even though the place was far distant from them. They also subdued the kings who came against them from the ends of the earth, until they crushed them and inflicted great disaster upon them; the rest paid them tribute every year.

[5] Philip, and Perseus king of the Macedonians, and the others who rose up against them, they crushed in battle and conquered.

[6] They also defeated Antiochus the Great, king of Asia, who went to fight against them with a hundred and twenty elephants and with cavalry and chariots and a very large army. He was crushed by them;

[7] they took him alive and decreed that he and those who should reign after him should pay a heavy tribute and give hostages and surrender some of their best provinces,

[8] the country of India and Media and Lydia. These they took from him and gave to Eumenes the king.

[9] The Greeks planned to come and destroy them,

[10] but this became known to them, and they sent a general against the Greeks and attacked them. Many of them were wounded and fell, and the Romans took captive their wives and children; they plundered them, conquered the land, tore down their strongholds, and enslaved them to this day.

[11] The remaining kingdoms and islands, as many as ever opposed them, they destroyed and enslaved;

[12] but with their friends and those who rely on them they have kept friendship. They have subdued kings far and near, and as many as have heard of their fame have feared them.

[13] Those whom they wish to help and to make kings, they make kings, and those whom they wish they depose; and they have been greatly exalted.

[14] Yet for all this not one of them has put on a crown or worn purple as a mark of pride,

[15] but they have built for themselves a senate chamber, and every day three hundred and twenty senators constantly deliberate concerning the people, to govern them well.

[16] They trust one man each year to rule over them and to control all their land; they all heed the one man, and there is no envy or jealousy among them.

[17] So Judas chose Eupolemus the son of John, son of Accos, and Jason the son of Eleazar, and sent them to Rome to establish friendship and alliance,

[18] and to free themselves from the yoke; for they saw that the kingdom of the Greeks was completely enslaving Israel.

[19] They went to Rome, a very long journey; and they entered the senate chamber and spoke as follows:

[20] "Judas, who is also called Maccabeus, and his brothers and the people of the Jews have sent us to you to establish alliance and peace with you, that we may be enrolled as your allies and friends."

[21] The proposal pleased them,

[22] and this is a copy of the letter which they wrote in reply, on bronze tablets, and sent to Jerusalem to remain with them there as a memorial of peace and alliance:

[23] "May all go well with the Romans and with the nation of the Jews at sea and on land for ever, and may sword and enemy be far from them.

[24] If war comes first to Rome or to any of their allies in all their dominion,

[25] the nation of the Jews shall act as their allies wholeheartedly, as the occasion may indicate to them.

[26] And to the enemy who makes war they shall not give or supply grain, arms, money, or ships, as Rome has decided; and they shall keep their obligations without receiving any return.

[27] In the same way, if war comes first to the nation of the Jews, the Romans shall willingly act as their allies, as the occasion may indicate to them.

[28] And to the enemy allies shall be given no grain, arms, money, or ships, as Rome has decided; and they shall keep these obligations and do so without deceit.

[29] Thus on these terms the Romans make a treaty with the Jewish people.

[30] If after these terms are in effect both parties shall determine to add or delete anything, they shall do so at their discretion, and any addition or deletion that they may make shall be valid.

[31] "And concerning the wrongs which King Demetrius is doing to them we have written to him as follows, `Why have you made your yoke heavy upon our friends and allies the Jews?

[32] If now they appeal again for help against you, we will defend their rights and fight you on sea and on land.'"

1Mac.9

[1] When Demetrius heard that Nicanor and his army had fallen in battle, he sent Bacchides and Alcimus into the land of Judah a second time, and with them the right wing of the army.

[2] They went by the road which leads to Gilgal and encamped against Mesaloth in Arbela, and they took it and killed many people.

[3] In the first month of the one hundred and fifty-second year they encamped against Jerusalem;

[4] then they marched off and went to Berea with twenty thousand foot soldiers and two thousand cavalry.

[5] Now Judas was encamped in Elasa, and with him were three thousand picked men.

[6] When they saw the huge number of the enemy forces, they were greatly frightened, and many slipped away from the camp, until no more than eight hundred of them were left.

[7] When Judas saw that his army had slipped away and the battle was imminent, he was crushed in spirit, for he had no time to assemble them.

[8] He became faint, but he said to those who were left, "Let us rise and go up against our enemies. We may be able to fight them."

[9] But they tried to dissuade him, saying, "We are not able. Let us rather save our own lives now, and let us come back with our brethren and fight them; we are too few."

[10] But Judas said, "Far be it from us to do such a thing as to flee from them. If our time has come, let us die bravely for our brethren, and leave no cause to question our honor."

[11] Then the army of Bacchides marched out from the camp and took its stand for the encounter. The cavalry was divided into two companies, and the slingers and the archers went ahead of the army, as did all the chief warriors.

[12] Bacchides was on the right wing. Flanked by the two companies, the phalanx advanced to the sound of the trumpets; and the men with Judas also blew their trumpets.

[13] The earth was shaken by the noise of the armies, and the battle raged from morning till evening.

[14] Judas saw that Bacchides and the strength of his army were on the right; then all the stouthearted men went with him,

[15] and they crushed the right wing, and he pursued them as far as Mount Azotus.

[16] When those on the left wing saw that the right wing was crushed, they turned and followed close behind Judas and his men.

[17] The battle became desperate, and many on both sides were wounded and fell.

[18] Judas also fell, and the rest fled.

[19] Then Jonathan and Simon took Judas their brother and buried him in the tomb of their fathers at Modein,

[20] and wept for him. And all Israel made great lamentation for him; they mourned many days and said,

[21] "How is the mighty fallen, the savior of Israel!"

[22] Now the rest of the acts of Judas, and his wars and the brave deeds that he did, and his greatness, have not been recorded, for they were very many.

[23] After the death of Judas, the lawless emerged in all parts of Israel; all the doers of injustice appeared.

[24] In those days a very great famine occurred, and the country deserted with them to the enemy.

[25] And Bacchides chose the ungodly and put them in charge of the country.

[26] They sought and searched for the friends of Judas, and brought them to Bacchides, and he took vengeance on them and made sport of them.

[27] Thus there was great distress in Israel, such as had not been since the time that prophets ceased to appear among them.

[28] Then all the friends of Judas assembled and said to Jonathan,

[29] "Since the death of your brother Judas there has been no one like him to go against our enemies and Bacchides, and to deal with those of our nation who hate us.

[30] So now we have chosen you today to take his place as our ruler and leader, to fight our battle."

[31] And Jonathan at that time accepted the leadership and took the place of Judas his brother.

[32] When Bacchides learned of this, he tried to kill him.

[33] But Jonathan and Simon his brother and all who were with him heard of it, and they fled into the wilderness of Tekoa and camped by the water of the pool of Asphar.

[34] Bacchides found this out on the sabbath day, and he with all his army crossed the Jordan.

[35] And Jonathan sent his brother as leader of the multitude and begged the Nabateans, who were his friends, for permission to store with them the great amount of baggage which they had.

[36] But the sons of Jambri from Medeba came out and seized John and all that he had, and departed with it.

[37] After these things it was reported to Jonathan and Simon his brother, "The sons of Jambri are celebrating a great wedding, and are conducting the bride, a daughter of one of the great nobles of Canaan, from Nadabath with a large escort."

[38] And they remembered the blood of John their brother, and went up and hid under cover of the mountain.

[39] They raised their eyes and looked, and saw a tumultuous procession with much baggage; and the bridegroom came out with his friends and his brothers to meet them with tambourines and musicians and many weapons.

[40] Then they rushed upon them from the ambush and began killing them. Many were wounded and fell, and the rest fled to the mountain; and they took all their goods.

[41] Thus the wedding was turned into mourning and the voice of their musicians into a funeral dirge.

[42] And when they had fully avenged the blood of their brother, they returned to the marshes of the Jordan.

[43] When Bacchides heard of this, he came with a large force on the sabbath day to the banks of the Jordan.

[44] And Jonathan said to those with him, "Let us rise up now and fight for our lives, for today things are not as they were before.

[45] For look! the battle is in front of us and behind us; the water of the Jordan is on this side and on that, with marsh and thicket; there is no place to turn.

[46] Cry out now to Heaven that you may be delivered from the hands of our enemies."

[47] So the battle began, and Jonathan stretched out his hand to strike Bacchides, but he eluded him and went to the rear.

[48] Then Jonathan and the men with him leaped into the Jordan and swam across to the other side, and the enemy did not cross the Jordan to attack them.

[49] And about one thousand of Bacchides' men fell that day.

[50] Bacchides then returned to Jerusalem and built strong cities in Judea: the fortress in Jericho, and Emmaus, and Beth-horon, and Bethel, and Timnath, and Pharathon, and Tephon, with high walls and gates and bars.

[51] And he placed garrisons in them to harass Israel.

[52] He also fortified the city of Beth-zur, and Gazara, and the citadel, and in them he put troops and stores of food.

[53] And he took the sons of the leading men of the land as hostages and put them under guard in the citadel at Jerusalem.

[54] In the one hundred and fifty-third year, in the second month, Alcimus gave orders to tear down the wall of the inner court of the sanctuary. He tore down the work of the prophets!

[55] But he only began to tear it down, for at that time Alcimus was stricken and his work was hindered; his mouth was stopped and he was paralyzed, so that he could no longer say a word or give commands concerning his house.

[56] And Alcimus died at that time in great agony.

[57] When Bacchides saw that Alcimus was dead, he returned to the king, and the land of Judah had rest for two years.

[58] Then all the lawless plotted and said, "See! Jonathan and his men are living in quiet and confidence. So now let us bring Bacchides back, and he will capture them all in one night."

[59] And they went and consulted with him.

[60] He started to come with a large force, and secretly sent letters to all his allies in Judea, telling them to seize Jonathan and his men; but they were unable to do it, because their plan became known.

[61] And Jonathan's men seized about fifty of the men of the country who were leaders in this treachery, and killed them.

[62] Then Jonathan with his men, and Simon, withdrew to Bethbasi in the wilderness; he rebuilt the parts of it that had been demolished, and they fortified it.

[63] When Bacchides learned of this, he assembled all his forces, and sent orders to the men of Judea.

[64] Then he came and encamped against Bethbasi; he fought against it for many days and made machines of war.

[65] But Jonathan left Simon his brother in the city, while he went out into the country; and he went with only a few men.

[66] He struck down Odomera and his brothers and the sons of Phasiron in their tents.

[67] Then he began to attack and went into battle with his forces; and Simon and his men sallied out from the city and set fire to the machines of war.

[68] They fought with Bacchides, and he was crushed by them. They distressed him greatly, for his plan and his expedition had been in vain.

[69] So he was greatly enraged at the lawless men who had counseled him to come into the country, and he killed many of them. Then he decided to depart to his own land.

[70] When Jonathan learned of this, he sent ambassadors to him to make peace with him and obtain release of the captives.

[71] He agreed, and did as he said; and he swore to Jonathan that he would not try to harm him as long as he lived.

[72] He restored to him the captives whom he had formerly taken from the land of Judah; then he turned and departed to his own land, and came no more into their territory.

[73] Thus the sword ceased from Israel. And Jonathan dwelt in Michmash. And Jonathan began to judge the people, and he destroyed the ungodly out of Israel.

1Mac.10

[1] In the one hundred and sixtieth year Alexander Epiphanes, the son of Antiochus, landed and occupied Ptolemais. They welcomed him, and there he began to reign.

[2] When Demetrius the king heard of it, he assembled a very large army and marched out to meet him in battle.

[3] And Demetrius sent Jonathan a letter in peaceable words to honor him;

[4] for he said, "Let us act first to make peace with him before he makes peace with Alexander against us,

[5] for he will remember all the wrongs which we did to him and to his brothers and his nation."

[6] So Demetrius gave him authority to recruit troops, to equip them with arms, and to become his ally; and he commanded that the hostages in the citadel should be released to him.

[7] Then Jonathan came to Jerusalem and read the letter in the hearing of all the people and of the men in the citadel.

[8] They were greatly alarmed when they heard that the king had given him authority to recruit troops.

[9] But the men in the citadel released the hostages to Jonathan, and he returned them to their parents.

[10] And Jonathan dwelt in Jerusalem and began to rebuild and restore the city.

[11] He directed those who were doing the work to build the walls and encircle Mount Zion with squared stones, for better fortification; and they did so.

[12] Then the foreigners who were in the strongholds that Bacchides had built fled;

[13] each left his place and departed to his own land.

[14] Only in Beth-zur did some remain who had forsaken the law and the commandments, for it served as a place of refuge.

[15] Now Alexander the king heard of all the promises which Demetrius had sent to Jonathan, and men told him of the battles that Jonathan and his brothers had fought, of the brave deeds that they had done, and of the troubles that they had endured.

[16] So he said, "Shall we find another such man? Come now, we will make him our friend and ally."

[17] And he wrote a letter and sent it to him, in the following words:

[18] "King Alexander to his brother Jonathan, greeting.

[19] We have heard about you, that you are a mighty warrior and worthy to be our friend.

[20] And so we have appointed you today to be the high priest of your nation; you are to be called the king's friend" (and he sent him a purple robe and a golden crown) "and you are to take our side and

keep friendship with us."

[21] So Jonathan put on the holy garments in the seventh month of the one hundred and sixtieth year, at the feast of tabernacles, and he recruited troops and equipped them with arms in abundance.

[22] When Demetrius heard of these things he was grieved and said,

[23] "What is this that we have done? Alexander has gotten ahead of us in forming a friendship with the Jews to strengthen himself.

[24] I also will write them words of encouragement and promise them honor and gifts, that I may have their help."

[25] So he sent a message to them in the following words: "King Demetrius to the nation of the Jews, greeting.

[26] Since you have kept your agreement with us and have continued your friendship with us, and have not sided with our enemies, we have heard of it and rejoiced.

[27] And now continue still to keep faith with us, and we will repay you with good for what you do for us.

[28] We will grant you many immunities and give you gifts.

[29] "And now I free you and exempt all the Jews from payment of tribute and salt tax and crown levies,

[30] and instead of collecting the third of the grain and the half of the fruit of the trees that I should receive, I release them from this day and henceforth. I will not collect them from the land of Judah or from the three districts added to it from Samaria and Galilee, from this day and for all time.

[31] And let Jerusalem and her environs, her tithes and her revenues, be holy and free from tax.

[32] I release also my control of the citadel in Jerusalem and give it to the high priest, that he may station in it men of his own choice to guard it.

[33] And every one of the Jews taken as a captive from the land of Judah into any part of my kingdom, I set free without payment; and let all officials cancel also the taxes on their cattle.

[34] "And all the feasts and sabbaths and new moons and appointed days, and the three days before a feast and the three after a feast -- let them all be days of immunity and release for all the Jews who are in my kingdom.

[35] No one shall have authority to exact anything from them or annoy any of them about any matter.

[36] "Let Jews be enrolled in the king's forces to the number of thirty thousand men, and let the maintenance be given them that is due to all the forces of the king.

[37] Let some of them be stationed in the great strongholds of the king, and let some of them be put in positions of trust in the kingdom. Let their officers and leaders be of their own number, and let them live by their own laws, just as the king has commanded in the land of Judah.

[38] "As for the three districts that have been added to Judea from the country of Samaria, let them be so annexed to Judea that they are considered to be under one ruler and obey no other authority but the high priest.

[39] Ptolemais and the land adjoining it I have given as a gift to the sanctuary in Jerusalem, to meet the necessary expenses of the sanctuary.

[40] I also grant fifteen thousand shekels of silver yearly out of the king's revenues from appropriate places.

[41] And all the additional funds which the government officials have not paid as they did in the first years, they shall give from now on for the service of the temple.

[42] Moreover, the five thousand shekels of silver which my officials have received every year from the income of the services of the temple, this too is canceled, because it belongs to the priests who minister there.

[43] And whoever takes refuge at the temple in Jerusalem, or in any of its precincts, because he owes money to the king or has any debt, let him be released and receive back all his property in my kingdom.

[44] "Let the cost of rebuilding and restoring the structures of the sanctuary be paid from the revenues of the king.

[45] And let the cost of rebuilding the walls of Jerusalem and fortifying it round about, and the cost of rebuilding the walls in Judea, also be paid from the revenues of the king."

[46] When Jonathan and the people heard these words, they did not believe or accept them, because they remembered the great wrongs which Demetrius had done in Israel and how he had greatly oppressed them.

[47] They favored Alexander, because he had been the first to speak peaceable words to them, and they remained his allies all his days.

[48] Now Alexander the king assembled large forces and encamped opposite Demetrius.

[49] The two kings met in battle, and the army of Demetrius fled, and Alexander pursued him and defeated them.

[50] He pressed the battle strongly until the sun set, and Demetrius fell on that day.

[51] Then Alexander sent ambassadors to Ptolemy king of Egypt with the following message:

[52] "Since I have returned to my kingdom and have taken my seat on the throne of my fathers, and established my rule -- for I crushed Demetrius and gained control of our country;

[53] I met him in battle, and he and his army were crushed by us, and we have taken our seat on the throne of his kingdom --

[54] now therefore let us establish friendship with one another; give me now your daughter as my wife, and I will become your son-in-law, and will make gifts to you and to her in keeping with your position."

[55] Ptolemy the king replied and said, "Happy was the day on which you returned to the land of your fathers and took your seat on the throne of their kingdom.

[56] And now I will do for you as you wrote, but meet me at Ptolemais, so that we may see one another, and I will become your father-in-law, as you have said."

[57] So Ptolemy set out from Egypt, he and Cleopatra his daughter, and came to Ptolemais in the one hundred and sixty-second year.

[58] Alexander the king met him, and Ptolemy gave him Cleopatra his daughter in marriage, and celebrated her wedding at Ptolemais with great pomp, as kings do.

[59] Then Alexander the king wrote to Jonathan to come to meet him.

[60] So he went with pomp to Ptolemais and met the two kings; he gave them and their friends silver and gold and many gifts, and found favor with them.

[61] A group of pestilent men from Israel, lawless men, gathered together against him to accuse him; but the king paid no attention to them.

[62] The king gave orders to take off Jonathan's garments and to clothe him in purple, and they did so.

[63] The king also seated him at his side; and he said to his officers, "Go forth with him into the middle of the city and proclaim that no one is to bring charges against him about any matter, and let no one annoy him for any reason."

[64] And when his accusers saw the honor that was paid him, in accordance with the proclamation, and saw him clothed in purple, they all fled.

[65] Thus the king honored him and enrolled him among his chief friends, and made him general and governor of the province.

[66] And Jonathan returned to Jerusalem in peace and gladness.

[67] In the one hundred and sixty-fifth year Demetrius the son of Demetrius came from Crete to the land of his fathers.

[68] When Alexander the king heard of it, he was greatly grieved and returned to Antioch.

[69] And Demetrius appointed Apollonius the governor of Coelesyria, and he assembled a large force and encamped against Jamnia. Then he sent the following message to Jonathan the high priest:

[70] "You are the only one to rise up against us, and I have become a laughingstock and reproach because of you. Why do you assume authority against us in the hill country?

[71] If you now have confidence in your forces, come down to the plain to meet us, and let us match strength with each other there, for I have with me the power of the cities.

[72] Ask and learn who I am and who the others are that are helping us. Men will tell you that you cannot stand before us, for your fathers were twice put to flight in their own land.

[73] And now you will not be able to withstand my cavalry and such an army in the plain, where there is no stone or pebble, or place to flee."

[74] When Jonathan heard the words of Apollonius, his spirit was aroused. He chose ten thousand men and set out from Jerusalem, and Simon his brother met him to help him.

[75] He encamped before Joppa, but the men of the city closed its gates, for Apollonius had a garrison in Joppa.

[76] So they fought against it, and the men of the city became afraid and opened the gates, and Jonathan gained possession of Joppa.

[77] When Apollonius heard of it, he mustered three thousand cavalry and a large army, and went to Azotus as though he were going farther. At the same time he advanced into the plain, for he had a large troop of cavalry and put confidence in it.

[78] Jonathan pursued him to Azotus, and the armies engaged in battle.

[79] Now Apollonius had secretly left a thousand cavalry behind them.

[80] Jonathan learned that there was an ambush behind him, for they surrounded his army and shot arrows at his men from early morning till late afternoon.

[81] But his men stood fast, as Jonathan commanded, and the enemy's horses grew tired.

[82] Then Simon brought forward his force and engaged the phalanx in battle (for the cavalry was exhausted); they were overwhelmed by him and fled,

[83] and the cavalry was dispersed in the plain. They fled to Azotus and entered Beth-dagon, the temple of their idol, for safety.

[84] But Jonathan burned Azotus and the surrounding towns and plundered them; and the temple of

Dagon, and those who had taken refuge in it he burned with fire.

[85] The number of those who fell by the sword, with those burned alive, came to eight thousand men.

[86] Then Jonathan departed from there and encamped against Askalon, and the men of the city came out to meet him with great pomp.

[87] And Jonathan and those with him returned to Jerusalem with much booty.

[88] When Alexander the king heard of these things, he honored Jonathan still more;

[89] and he sent to him a golden buckle, such as it is the custom to give to the kinsmen of kings. He also gave him Ekron and all its environs as his possession.

1Mac.11

[1] Then the king of Egypt gathered great forces, like the sand by the seashore, and many ships; and he tried to get possession of Alexander's kingdom by trickery and add it to his own kingdom.

[2] He set out for Syria with peaceable words, and the people of the cities opened their gates to him and went to meet him, for Alexander the king had commanded them to meet him, since he was Alexander's father-in-law.

[3] But when Ptolemy entered the cities he stationed forces as a garrison in each city.

[4] When he approached Azotus, they showed him the temple of Dagon burned down, and Azotus and its suburbs destroyed, and the corpses lying about, and the charred bodies of those whom Jonathan had burned in the war, for they had piled them in heaps along his route.

[5] They also told the king what Jonathan had done, to throw blame on him; but the king kept silent.

[6] Jonathan met the king at Joppa with pomp, and they greeted one another and spent the night there.

[7] And Jonathan went with the king as far as the river called Eleutherus; then he returned to Jerusalem.

[8] So King Ptolemy gained control of the coastal cities as far as Seleucia by the sea, and he kept devising evil designs against Alexander.

[9] He sent envoys to Demetrius the king, saying, "Come, let us make a covenant with each other, and I will give you in marriage my daughter who was Alexander's wife, and you shall reign over your father's kingdom.

[10] For I now regret that I gave him my daughter, for he has tried to kill me."

[11] He threw blame on Alexander because he coveted his kingdom.

[12] So he took his daughter away from him and gave her to Demetrius. He was estranged from Alexander, and their enmity became manifest.

[13] Then Ptolemy entered Antioch and put on the crown of Asia. Thus he put two crowns upon his head, the crown of Egypt and that of Asia.

[14] Now Alexander the king was in Cilicia at that time, because the people of that region were in revolt.

[15] And Alexander heard of it and came against him in battle. Ptolemy marched out and met him with a strong force, and put him to flight.

[16] So Alexander fled into Arabia to find protection there, and King Ptolemy was exalted.

[17] And Zabdiel the Arab cut off the head of Alexander and sent it to Ptolemy.

[18] But King Ptolemy died three days later, and his troops in the strongholds were killed by the inhabitants of the strongholds.

[19] So Demetrius became king in the one hundred and sixty-seventh year.

[20] In those days Jonathan assembled the men of Judea to attack the citadel in Jerusalem, and he built many engines of war to use against it.

[21] But certain lawless men who hated their nation went to the king and reported to him that Jonathan was besieging the citadel.

[22] When he heard this he was angry, and as soon as he heard it he set out and came to Ptolemais; and he wrote Jonathan not to continue the siege, but to meet him for a conference at Ptolemais as quickly as possible.

[23] When Jonathan heard this, he gave orders to continue the siege; and he chose some of the elders of Israel and some of the priests, and put himself in danger,

[24] for he went to the king at Ptolemais, taking silver and gold and clothing and numerous other gifts. And he won his favor.

[25] Although certain lawless men of his nation kept making complaints against him,

[26] the king treated him as his predecessors had treated him; he exalted him in the presence of all his friends.

[27] He confirmed him in the high priesthood and in as many other honors as he had formerly had, and made him to be regarded as one of his chief friends.

[28] Then Jonathan asked the king to free Judea and the three districts of Samaria from tribute, and promised him three hundred talents.

[29] The king consented, and wrote a letter to Jonathan about all these things; its contents were as follows:

[30] "King Demetrius to Jonathan his brother and to the nation of the Jews, greeting.

[31] This copy of the letter which we wrote concerning you to Lasthenes our kinsman we have written to you also, so that you may know what it says.

[32] `King Demetrius to Lasthenes his father, greeting.

[33] To the nation of the Jews, who are our friends and fulfil their obligations to us, we have determined to do good, because of the good will they show toward us.

[34] We have confirmed as their possession both the territory of Judea and the three districts of Aphairema and Lydda and Rathamin; the latter, with all the region bordering them, were added to Judea from Samaria. To all those who offer sacrifice in Jerusalem, we have granted release from the royal taxes which the king formerly received from them each year, from the crops of the land and the fruit of the trees.

[35] And the other payments henceforth due to us of the tithes, and the taxes due to us, and the salt pits and the crown taxes due to us -- from all these we shall grant them release.

[36] And not one of these grants shall be canceled from this time forth for ever.

[37] Now therefore take care to make a copy of this, and let it be given to Jonathan and put up in a conspicuous place on the holy mountain.'"

[38] Now when Demetrius the king saw that the land was quiet before him and that there was no opposition to him, he dismissed all his troops, each man to his own place, except the foreign troops which he had recruited from the islands of the nations. So all the troops who had served his fathers hated him.

[39] Now Trypho had formerly been one of Alexander's supporters. He saw that all the troops were murmuring against Demetrius. So he went to Imalkue the Arab, who was bringing up Antiochus, the young son of Alexander,

[40] and insistently urged him to hand Antiochus over to him, to become king in place of his father. He also reported to Imalkue what Demetrius had done and told of the hatred which the troops of Demetrius had for him; and he stayed there many days.

[41] Now Jonathan sent to Demetrius the king the request that he remove the troops of the citadel from Jerusalem, and the troops in the strongholds; for they kept fighting against Israel.

[42] And Demetrius sent this message to Jonathan, "Not only will I do these things for you and your nation, but I will confer great honor on you and your nation, if I find an opportunity.

[43] Now then you will do well to send me men who will help me, for all my troops have revolted."

[44] So Jonathan sent three thousand stalwart men to him at Antioch, and when they came to the king, the king rejoiced at their arrival.

[45] Then the men of the city assembled within the city, to the number of a hundred and twenty thousand, and they wanted to kill the king.

[46] But the king fled into the palace. Then the men of the city seized the main streets of the city and began to fight.

[47] So the king called the Jews to his aid, and they all rallied about him and then spread out through the city; and they killed on that day as many as a hundred thousand men.

[48] They set fire to the city and seized much spoil on that day, and they saved the king.

[49] When the men of the city saw that the Jews had gained control of the city as they pleased, their courage failed and they cried out to the king with this entreaty,

[50] "Grant us peace, and make the Jews stop fighting against us and our city."

[51] And they threw down their arms and made peace. So the Jews gained glory in the eyes of the king and of all the people in his kingdom, and they returned to Jerusalem with much spoil.

[52] So Demetrius the king sat on the throne of his kingdom, and the land was quiet before him.

[53] But he broke his word about all that he had promised; and he became estranged from Jonathan and did not repay the favors which Jonathan had done him, but oppressed him greatly.

[54] After this Trypho returned, and with him the young boy Antiochus who began to reign and put on the crown.

[55] All the troops that Demetrius had cast off gathered around him, and they fought against Demetrius, and he fled and was routed.

[56] And Trypho captured the elephants and gained control of Antioch.

[57] Then the young Antiochus wrote to Jonathan, saying, "I confirm you in the high priesthood and set you over the four districts and make you one of the friends of the king."

[58] And he sent him gold plate and a table service, and granted him the right to drink from gold cups and dress in purple and wear a gold buckle.

[59] Simon his brother he made governor from the Ladder of Tyre to the borders of Egypt.

[60] Then Jonathan set forth and traveled beyond the river and among the cities, and all the army of Syria gathered to him as allies. When he came to Askalon, the people of the city met him and paid him

honor.

[61] From there he departed to Gaza, but the men of Gaza shut him out. So he besieged it and burned its suburbs with fire and plundered them.

[62] Then the people of Gaza pleaded with Jonathan, and he made peace with them, and took the sons of their rulers as hostages and sent them to Jerusalem. And he passed through the country as far as Damascus.

[63] Then Jonathan heard that the officers of Demetrius had come to Kadesh in Galilee with a large army, intending to remove him from office.

[64] He went to meet them, but left his brother Simon in the country.

[65] Simon encamped before Beth-zur and fought against it for many days and hemmed it in.

[66] Then they asked him to grant them terms of peace, and he did so. He removed them from there, took possession of the city, and set a garrison over it.

[67] Jonathan and his army encamped by the waters of Gennesaret. Early in the morning they marched to the plain of Hazor,

[68] and behold, the army of the foreigners met him in the plain; they had set an ambush against him in the mountains, but they themselves met him face to face.

[69] Then the men in ambush emerged from their places and joined battle.

[70] All the men with Jonathan fled; not one of them was left except Mattathias the son of Absalom and Judas the son of Chalphi, commanders of the forces of the army.

[71] Jonathan rent his garments and put dust on his head, and prayed.

[72] Then he turned back to the battle against the enemy and routed them, and they fled.

[73] When his men who were fleeing saw this, they returned to him and joined him in the pursuit as far as Kadesh, to their camp, and there they encamped.

[74] As many as three thousand of the foreigners fell that day. And Jonathan returned to Jerusalem.

1Mac.12

[1] Now when Jonathan saw that the time was favorable for him, he chose men and sent them to Rome to confirm and renew the friendship with them.

[2] He also sent letters to the same effect to the Spartans and to other places.

[3] So they went to Rome and entered the senate chamber and said, "Jonathan the high priest and the Jewish nation have sent us to renew the former friendship and alliance with them."

[4] And the Romans gave them letters to the people in every place, asking them to provide for the envoys safe conduct to the land of Judah.

[5] This is a copy of the letter which Jonathan wrote to the Spartans:

[6] "Jonathan the high priest, the senate of the nation, the priests, and the rest of the Jewish people to their brethren the Spartans, greeting.

[7] Already in time past a letter was sent to Onias the high priest from Arius, who was king among you, stating that you are our brethren, as the appended copy shows.

[8] Onias welcomed the envoy with honor, and received the letter, which contained a clear declaration of alliance and friendship.

[9] Therefore, though we have no need of these things, since we have as encouragement the holy books which are in our hands,

[10] we have undertaken to send to renew our brotherhood and friendship with you, so that we may not become estranged from you, for considerable time has passed since you sent your letter to us.

[11] We therefore remember you constantly on every occasion, both in our feasts and on other appropriate days, at the sacrifices which we offer and in our prayers, as it is right and proper to remember brethren.

[12] And we rejoice in your glory.

[13] But as for ourselves, many afflictions and many wars have encircled us; the kings round about us have waged war against us.

[14] We were unwilling to annoy you and our other allies and friends with these wars,

[15] for we have the help which comes from Heaven for our aid; and we were delivered from our enemies and our enemies were humbled.

[16] We therefore have chosen Numenius the son of Antiochus and Antipater the son of Jason, and have sent them to Rome to renew our former friendship and alliance with them.

[17] We have commanded them to go also to you and greet you and deliver to you this letter from us concerning the renewal of our brotherhood.

[18] And now please send us a reply to this."

[19] This is a copy of the letter which they sent to Onias:

[20] "Arius, king of the Spartans, to Onias the high priest, greeting.

[21] It has been found in writing concerning the Spartans and the Jews that they are brethren and are of the family of Abraham.

[22] And now that we have learned this, please write us concerning your welfare;

[23] we on our part write to you that your cattle and your property belong to us, and ours belong to you. We therefore command that our envoys report to you accordingly."

[24] Now Jonathan heard that the commanders of Demetrius had returned, with a larger force than before, to wage war against him.

[25] So he marched away from Jerusalem and met them in the region of Hamath, for he gave them no opportunity to invade his own country.

[26] He sent spies to their camp, and they returned and reported to him that the enemy were being drawn up in formation to fall upon the Jews by night.

[27] So when the sun set, Jonathan commanded his men to be alert and to keep their arms at hand so as to be ready all night for battle, and he stationed outposts around the camp.

[28] When the enemy heard that Jonathan and his men were prepared for battle, they were afraid and were terrified at heart; so they kindled fires in their camp and withdrew.

[29] But Jonathan and his men did not know it until morning, for they saw the fires burning.

[30] Then Jonathan pursued them, but he did not overtake them, for they had crossed the Eleutherus river.

[31] So Jonathan turned aside against the Arabs who are called Zabadeans, and he crushed them and plundered them.

[32] Then he broke camp and went to Damascus, and marched through all that region.

[33] Simon also went forth and marched through the country as far as Askalon and the neighboring strongholds. He turned aside to Joppa and took it by surprise,

[34] for he had heard that they were ready to hand over the stronghold to the men whom Demetrius had sent. And he stationed a garrison there to guard it.

[35] When Jonathan returned he convened the elders of the people and planned with them to build strongholds in Judea,

[36] to build the walls of Jerusalem still higher, and to erect a high barrier between the citadel and the city to separate it from the city, in order to isolate it so that its garrison could neither buy nor sell.

[37] So they gathered together to build up the city; part of the wall on the valley to the east had fallen, and he repaired the section called Chaphenatha.

[38] And Simon built Adida in the Shephelah; he fortified it and installed gates with bolts.

[39] Then Trypho attempted to become king in Asia and put on the crown, and to raise his hand against Antiochus the king.

[40] He feared that Jonathan might not permit him to do so, but might make war on him, so he kept seeking to seize and kill him, and he marched forth and came to Beth-shan.

[41] Jonathan went out to meet him with forty thousand picked fighting men, and he came to Beth-shan.

[42] When Trypho saw that he had come with a large army, he was afraid to raise his hand against him.

[43] So he received him with honor and commended him to all his friends, and he gave him gifts and commanded his friends and his troops to obey him as they would himself.

[44] Then he said to Jonathan, "Why have you wearied all these people when we are not at war?

[45] Dismiss them now to their homes and choose for yourself a few men to stay with you, and come with me to Ptolemais. I will hand it over to you as well as the other strongholds and the remaining troops and all the officials, and will turn round and go home. For that is why I am here."

[46] Jonathan trusted him and did as he said; he sent away the troops, and they returned to the land of Judah.

[47] He kept with himself three thousand men, two thousand of whom he left in Galilee, while a thousand accompanied him.

[48] But when Jonathan entered Ptolemais, the men of Ptolemais closed the gates and seized him, and all who had entered with him they killed with the sword.

[49] Then Trypho sent troops and cavalry into Galilee and the Great Plain to destroy all Jonathan's soldiers.

[50] But they realized that Jonathan had been seized and had perished along with his men, and they encouraged one another and kept marching in close formation, ready for battle.

[51] When their pursuers saw that they would fight for their lives, they turned back.

[52] So they all reached the land of Judah safely, and they mourned for Jonathan and his companions and were in great fear; and all Israel mourned deeply.

[53] And all the nations round about them tried to destroy them, for they said, "They have no leader or helper. Now therefore let us make war on them and blot out the memory of them from among men."

1Mac.13

[1] Simon heard that Trypho had assembled a large army to invade the land of Judah and destroy it,

[2] and he saw that the people were trembling and fearful. So he went up to Jerusalem, and gathering the people together

[3] he encouraged them, saying to them, "You yourselves know what great things I and my brothers and the house of my father have done for the laws and the sanctuary; you know also the wars and the difficulties which we have seen.

[4] By reason of this all my brothers have perished for the sake of Israel, and I alone am left.

[5] And now, far be it from me to spare my life in any time of distress, for I am not better than my brothers.

[6] But I will avenge my nation and the sanctuary and your wives and children, for all the nations have gathered together out of hatred to destroy us."

[7] The spirit of the people was rekindled when they heard these words,

[8] and they answered in a loud voice, "You are our leader in place of Judas and Jonathan your brother.

[9] Fight our battles, and all that you say to us we will do."

[10] So he assembled all the warriors and hastened to complete the walls of Jerusalem, and he fortified it on every side.

[11] He sent Jonathan the son of Absalom to Joppa, and with him a considerable army; he drove out its occupants and remained there.

[12] Then Trypho departed from Ptolemais with a large army to invade the land of Judah, and Jonathan was with him under guard.

[13] And Simon encamped in Adida, facing the plain.

[14] Trypho learned that Simon had risen up in place of Jonathan his brother, and that he was about to join battle with him, so he sent envoys to him and said,

[15] "It is for the money that Jonathan your brother owed the royal treasury, in connection with the offices he held, that we are detaining him.

[16] Send now a hundred talents of silver and two of his sons as hostages, so that when released he will not revolt against us, and we will release him."

[17] Simon knew that they were speaking deceitfully to him, but he sent to get the money and the sons, lest he arouse great hostility among the people, who might say,

[18] "Because Simon did not send him the money and the sons, he perished."

[19] So he sent the sons and the hundred talents, but Trypho broke his word and did not release Jonathan.

[20] After this Trypho came to invade the country and destroy it, and he circled around by the way to Adora. But Simon and his army kept marching along opposite him to every place he went.

[21] Now the men in the citadel kept sending envoys to Trypho urging him to come to them by way of the wilderness and to send them food.

[22] So Trypho got all his cavalry ready to go, but that night a very heavy snow fell, and he did not go because of the snow. He marched off and went into the land of Gilead.

[23] When he approached Baskama, he killed Jonathan, and he was buried there.

[24] Then Trypho turned back and departed to his own land.

[25] And Simon sent and took the bones of Jonathan his brother, and buried him in Modein, the city of his fathers.

[26] All Israel bewailed him with great lamentation, and mourned for him many days.

[27] And Simon built a monument over the tomb of his father and his brothers; he made it high that it might be seen, with polished stone at the front and back.

[28] He also erected seven pyramids, opposite one another, for his father and mother and four brothers.

[29] And for the pyramids he devised an elaborate setting, erecting about them great columns, and upon the columns he put suits of armor for a permanent memorial, and beside the suits of armor carved ships, so that they could be seen by all who sail the sea.

[30] This is the tomb which he built in Modein; it remains to this day.

[31] Trypho dealt treacherously with the young king Antiochus; he killed him

[32] and became king in his place, putting on the crown of Asia; and he brought great calamity upon the land.

[33] But Simon built up the strongholds of Judea and walled them all around, with high towers and great walls and gates and bolts, and he stored food in the strongholds.

[34] Simon also chose men and sent them to Demetrius the king with a request to grant relief to the country, for all that Trypho did was to plunder.

[35] Demetrius the king sent him a favorable reply to this request, and wrote him a letter as follows,

[36] "King Demetrius to Simon, the high priest and friend of kings, and to the elders and nation of the Jews, greeting.

[37] We have received the gold crown and the palm branch which you sent, and we are ready to make a general peace with you and to write to our officials to grant you release from tribute.

[38] All the grants that we have made to you remain valid, and let the strongholds that you have built be your possession.

[39] We pardon any errors and offenses committed to this day, and cancel the crown tax which you owe; and whatever other tax has been collected in Jerusalem shall be collected no longer.

[40] And if any of you are qualified to be enrolled in our bodyguard, let them be enrolled, and let there be peace between us."

[41] In the one hundred and seventieth year the yoke of the Gentiles was removed from Israel,

[42] and the people began to write in their documents and contracts, "In the first year of Simon the great high priest and commander and leader of the Jews."

[43] In those days Simon encamped against Gazara and surrounded it with troops. He made a siege engine, brought it up to the city, and battered and captured one tower.

[44] The men in the siege engine leaped out into the city, and a great tumult arose in the city.

[45] The men in the city, with their wives and children, went up on the wall with their clothes rent, and they cried out with a loud voice, asking Simon to make peace with them;

[46] they said, "Do not treat us according to our wicked acts but according to your mercy."

[47] So Simon reached an agreement with them and stopped fighting against them. But he expelled them from the city and cleansed the houses in which the idols were, and then entered it with hymns and praise.

[48] He cast out of it all uncleanness, and settled in it men who observed the law. He also strengthened its fortifications and built in it a house for himself.

[49] The men in the citadel at Jerusalem were prevented from going out to the country and back to buy and sell. So they were very hungry, and many of them perished from famine.

[50] Then they cried to Simon to make peace with them, and he did so. But he expelled them from there and cleansed the citadel from its pollutions.

[51] On the twenty-third day of the second month, in the one hundred and seventy-first year, the Jews entered it with praise and palm branches, and with harps and cymbals and stringed instruments, and with hymns and songs, because a great enemy had been crushed and removed from Israel.

[52] And Simon decreed that every year they should celebrate this day with rejoicing. He strengthened the fortifications of the temple hill alongside the citadel, and he and his men dwelt there.

[53] And Simon saw that John his son had reached manhood, so he made him commander of all the forces, and he dwelt in Gazara.

1Mac.14

[1] In the one hundred and seventy-second year Demetrius the king assembled his forces and marched into Media to secure help, so that he could make war against Trypho.

[2] When Arsaces the king of Persia and Media heard that Demetrius had invaded his territory, he sent one of his commanders to take him alive.

[3] And he went and defeated the army of Demetrius, and seized him and took him to Arsaces, who put him under guard.

[4] The land had rest all the days of Simon. He sought the good of his nation; his rule was pleasing to them, as was the honor shown him, all his days.

[5] To crown all his honors he took Joppa for a harbor, and opened a way to the isles of the sea.

[6] He extended the borders of his nation, and gained full control of the country.

[7] He gathered a host of captives; he ruled over Gazara and Beth-zur and the citadel, and he removed its uncleanness from it; and there was none to oppose him.

[8] They tilled their land in peace; the ground gave its increase, and the trees of the plains their fruit.

[9] Old men sat in the streets; they all talked together of good things; and the youths donned the glories and garments of war.

[10] He supplied the cities with food, and furnished them with the means of defense, till his renown spread to the ends of the earth.

[11] He established peace in the land, and Israel rejoiced with great joy.

[12] Each man sat under his vine and his fig tree, and there was none to make them afraid.

[13] No one was left in the land to fight them, and the kings were crushed in those days.

[14] He strengthened all the humble of his people; he sought out the law, and did away with every lawless and wicked man.

[15] He made the sanctuary glorious, and added to the vessels of the sanctuary.

[16] It was heard in Rome, and as far away as Sparta, that Jonathan had died, and they were deeply grieved.

[17] When they heard that Simon his brother had become high priest in his place, and that he was ruling over the country and the cities in it,

[18] they wrote to him on bronze tablets to renew with him the friendship and alliance which they had established with Judas and Jonathan his brothers.

[19] And these were read before the assembly in Jerusalem.

[20] This is a copy of the letter which the Spartans sent: "The rulers and the city of the Spartans to Simon the high priest and to the elders and the priests and the rest of the Jewish people, our brethren, greeting.

[21] The envoys who were sent to our people have told us about your glory and honor, and we rejoiced at their coming.

[22] And what they said we have recorded in our public decrees, as follows, `Numenius the son of Antiochus and Antipater the son of Jason, envoys of the Jews, have come to us to renew their friendship with us.

[23] It has pleased our people to receive these men with honor and to put a copy of their words in the public archives, so that the people of the Spartans may have a record of them. And they have sent a copy of this to Simon the high priest.'"

[24] After this Simon sent Numenius to Rome with a large gold shield weighing a thousand minas, to confirm the alliance with the Romans.

[25] When the people heard these things they said, "How shall we thank Simon and his sons?

[26] For he and his brothers and the house of his father have stood firm; they have fought and repulsed Israel's enemies and established its freedom."

[27] So they made a record on bronze tablets and put it upon pillars on Mount Zion. This is a copy of what they wrote: "On the eighteenth day of Elul, in the one hundred and seventy-second year, which is the third year of Simon the great high priest,

[28] in Asaramel, in the great assembly of the priests and the people and the rulers of the nation and the elders of the country, the following was proclaimed to us:

[29] "Since wars often occurred in the country, Simon the son of Mattathias, a priest of the sons of Joarib, and his brothers, exposed themselves to danger and resisted the enemies of their nation, in order that their sanctuary and the law might be perserved; and they brought great glory to their nation.

[30] Jonathan rallied the nation, and became their high priest, and was gathered to his people.

[31] And when their enemies decided to invade their country and lay hands on their sanctuary,

[32] then Simon rose up and fought for his nation. He spent great sums of his own money; he armed the men of his nation's forces and paid them wages.

[33] He fortified the cities of Judea, and Beth-zur on the borders of Judea, where formerly the arms of the enemy had been stored, and he placed there a garrison of Jews.

[34] He also fortified Joppa, which is by the sea, and Gazara, which is on the borders of Azotus, where the enemy formerly dwelt. He settled Jews there, and provided in those cities whatever was necessary for their restoration.

[35] "The people saw Simon's faithfulness and the glory which he had resolved to win for his nation, and they made him their leader and high priest, because he had done all these things and because of the justice and loyalty which he had maintained toward his nation. He sought in every way to exalt his people.

[36] And in his days things prospered in his hands, so that the Gentiles were put out of the country, as were also the men in the city of David in Jerusalem, who had built themselves a citadel from which they used to sally forth and defile the environs of the sanctuary and do great damage to its purity.

[37] He settled Jews in it, and fortified it for the safety of the country and of the city, and built the walls of Jerusalem higher.

[38] "In view of these things King Demetrius confirmed him in the high priesthood,

[39] and he made him one of the king's friends and paid him high honors.

[40] For he had heard that the Jews were addressed by the Romans as friends and allies and brethren, and that the Romans had received the envoys of Simon with honor.

[41] "And the Jews and their priests decided that Simon should be their leader and high priest for ever, until a trustworthy prophet should arise,

[42] and that he should be governor over them and that he should take charge of the sanctuary and appoint men over its tasks and over the country and the weapons and the strongholds, and that he should take charge of the sanctuary,

[43] and that he should be obeyed by all, and that all contracts in the country should be written in his name, and that he should be clothed in purple and wear gold.

[44] "And none of the people or priests shall be permitted to nullify any of these decisions or to oppose what he says, or to convene an assembly in the country without his permission, or to be clothed in purple or put on a gold buckle.

[45] Whoever acts contrary to these decisions or nullifies any of them shall be liable to punishment."

[46] And all the people agreed to grant Simon the right to act in accord with these decisions.

[47] So Simon accepted and agreed to be high priest, to be commander and ethnarch of the Jews and priests, and to be protector of them all.

[48] And they gave orders to inscribe this decree upon bronze tablets, to put them up in a conspicuous place in the precincts of the sanctuary,

[49] and to deposit copies of them in the treasury, so that Simon and his sons might have them.

1Mac.15

[1] Antiochus, the son of Demetrius the king, sent a letter from the islands of the sea to Simon, the priest and ethnarch of the Jews, and to all the nation;

[2] its contents were as follows: "King Antiochus to Simon the high priest and ethnarch and to the nation of the Jews, greeting.

[3] Whereas certain pestilent men have gained control of the kingdom of our fathers, and I intend to lay claim to the kingdom so that I may restore it as it formerly was, and have recruited a host of mercenary troops and have equipped warships,

[4] and intend to make a landing in the country so that I may proceed against those who have destroyed our country and those who have devastated many cities in my kingdom,

[5] now therefore I confirm to you all the tax remissions that the kings before me have granted you, and release from all the other payments from which they have released you.

[6] I permit you to mint your own coinage as money for your country,

[7] and I grant freedom to Jerusalem and the sanctuary. All the weapons which you have prepared and the strongholds which you have built and now hold shall remain yours.

[8] Every debt you owe to the royal treasury and any such future debts shall be canceled for you from henceforth and for all time.

[9] When we gain control of our kingdom, we will bestow great honor upon you and your nation and the temple, so that your glory will become manifest in all the earth."

[10] In the one hundred and seventy-fourth year Antiochus set out and invaded the land of his fathers. All the troops rallied to him, so that there were few with Trypho.

[11] Antiochus pursued him, and he came in his flight to Dor, which is by the sea;

[12] for he knew that troubles had converged upon him, and his troops had deserted him.

[13] So Antiochus encamped against Dor, and with him were a hundred and twenty thousand warriors and eight thousand cavalry.

[14] He surrounded the city, and the ships joined battle from the sea; he pressed the city hard from land and sea, and permitted no one to leave or enter it.

[15] Then Numenius and his companions arrived from Rome, with letters to the kings and countries, in which the following was written:

[16] "Lucius, consul of the Romans, to King Ptolemy, greeting.

[17] The envoys of the Jews have come to us as our friends and allies to renew our ancient friendship and alliance. They had been sent by Simon the high priest and by the people of the Jews,

[18] and have brought a gold shield weighing a thousand minas.

[19] We therefore have decided to write to the kings and countries that they should not seek their harm or make war against them and their cities and their country, or make alliance with those who war against them.

[20] And it has seemed good to us to accept the shield from them.

[21] Therefore if any pestilent men have fled to you from their country, hand them over to Simon the high priest, that he may punish them according to their law."

[22] The consul wrote the same thing to Demetrius the king and to Attalus and Ariarathes and Arsaces,

[23] and to all the countries, and to Sampsames, and to the Spartans, and to Delos, and to Myndos, and to Sicyon, and to Caria, and to Samos, and to Pamphylia, and to Lycia, and to Halicarnassus, and to Rhodes, and to Phaselis, and to Cos, and to Side, and to Aradus and Gortyna and Cnidus and Cyprus and Cyrene.

[24] They also sent a copy of these things to Simon the high priest.

[25] Antiochus the king besieged Dor anew, continually throwing his forces against it and making engines of war; and he shut Trypho up and kept him from going out or in.

[26] And Simon sent to Antiochus two thousand picked men, to fight for him, and silver and gold and much military equipment.

[27] But he refused to receive them, and he broke all the agreements he formerly had made with Simon, and became estranged from him.

[28] He sent to him Athenobius, one of his friends, to confer with him, saying, "You hold control of Joppa and Gazara and the citadel in Jerusalem; they are cities of my kingdom.

[29] You have devastated their territory, you have done great damage in the land, and you have taken possession of many places in my kingdom.

[30] Now then, hand over the cities which you have seized and the tribute money of the places which you have conquered outside the borders of Judea;

[31] or else give me for them five hundred talents of silver, and for the destruction that you have caused

and the tribute money of the cities, five hundred talents more. Otherwise we will come and conquer you."

[32] So Athenobius the friend of the king came to Jerusalem, and when he saw the splendor of Simon, and the sideboard with its gold and silver plate, and his great magnificence, he was amazed. He reported to him the words of the king,

[33] but Simon gave him this reply: "We have neither taken foreign land nor seized foreign property, but only the inheritance of our fathers, which at one time had been unjustly taken by our enemies.

[34] Now that we have the opportunity, we are firmly holding the inheritance of our fathers.

[35] As for Joppa and Gazara, which you demand, they were causing great damage among the people and to our land; for them we will give you a hundred talents." Athenobius did not answer him a word,

[36] but returned in wrath to the king and reported to him these words and the splendor of Simon and all that he had seen. And the king was greatly angered.

[37] Now Trypho embarked on a ship and escaped to Orthosia.

[38] Then the king made Cendebeus commander-in-chief of the coastal country, and gave him troops of infantry and cavalry.

[39] He commanded him to encamp against Judea, and commanded him to build up Kedron and fortify its gates, and to make war on the people; but the king pursued Trypho.

[40] So Cendebeus came to Jamnia and began to provoke the people and invade Judea and take the people captive and kill them.

[41] He built up Kedron and stationed there horsemen and troops, so that they might go out and make raids along the highways of Judea, as the king had ordered him.

1Mac.16

[1] John went up from Gazara and reported to Simon his father what Cendebeus had done.

[2] And Simon called in his two older sons Judas and John, and said to them: "I and my brothers and the house of my father have fought the wars of Israel from our youth until this day, and things have prospered in our hands so that we have delivered Israel many times.

[3] But now I have grown old, and you by His mercy are mature in years. Take my place and my brother's, and go out and fight for our nation, and may the help which comes from Heaven be with you."

[4] So John chose out of the country twenty thousand warriors and horsemen, and they marched against Cendebeus and camped for the night in Modein.

[5] Early in the morning they arose and marched into the plain, and behold, a large force of infantry and horsemen was coming to meet them; and a stream lay between them.

[6] Then he and his army lined up against them. And he saw that the soldiers were afraid to cross the stream, so he crossed over first; and when his men saw him, they crossed over after him.

[7] Then he divided the army and placed the horsemen in the midst of the infantry, for the cavalry of the enemy were very numerous.

[8] And they sounded the trumpets, and Cendebeus and his army were put to flight, and many of them were wounded and fell; the rest fled into the stronghold.

[9] At that time Judas the brother of John was wounded, but John pursued them until Cendebeus reached Kedron, which he had built.

[10] They also fled into the towers that were in the fields of Azotus, and John burned it with fire, and about two thousand of them fell. And he returned to Judea safely.

[11] Now Ptolemy the son of Abubus had been appointed governor over the plain of Jericho, and he had much silver and gold,

[12] for he was son-in-law of the high priest.

[13] His heart was lifted up; he determined to get control of the country, and made treacherous plans against Simon and his sons, to do away with them.

[14] Now Simon was visiting the cities of the country and attending to their needs, and he went down to Jericho with Mattathias and Judas his sons, in the one hundred and seventy-seventh year, in the eleventh month, which is the month of Shebat.

[15] The son of Abubus received them treacherously in the little stronghold called Dok, which he had built; he gave them a great banquet, and hid men there.

[16] When Simon and his sons were drunk, Ptolemy and his men rose up, took their weapons, and rushed in against Simon in the banquet hall, and they killed him and his two sons and some of his servants.

[17] So he committed an act of great treachery and returned evil for good.

[18] Then Ptolemy wrote a report about these things and sent it to the king, asking him to send troops to aid him and to turn over to him the cities and the country.

[19] He sent other men to Gazara to do away with John; he sent letters to the captains asking them to come to him so that he might give them silver and gold and gifts;

[20] and he sent other men to take possession of Jerusalem and the temple hill.

[21] But some one ran ahead and reported to John at Gazara that his father and brothers had perished, and that "he has sent men to kill you also."

[22] When he heard this, he was greatly shocked; and he seized the men who came to destroy him and killed them, for he had found out that they were seeking to destroy him.

[23] The rest of the acts of John and his wars and the brave deeds which he did, and the building of the walls which he built, and his achievements,

[24] behold, they are written in the chronicles of his high priesthood, from the time that he became high priest after his father.

2 Maccabees

2Mac.1

[1] The Jewish brethren in Jerusalem and those in the land of Judea, To their Jewish brethren in Egypt, Greeting, and good peace.

[2] May God do good to you, and may he remember his covenant with Abraham and Isaac and Jacob, his faithful servants.

[3] May he give you all a heart to worship him and to do his will with a strong heart and a willing spirit.

[4] May he open your heart to his law and his commandments, and may he bring peace.

[5] May he hear your prayers and be reconciled to you, and may he not forsake you in time of evil.

[6] We are now praying for you here.

[7] In the reign of Demetrius, in the one hundred and sixty-ninth year, we Jews wrote to you, in the critical distress which came upon us in those years after Jason and his company revolted from the holy land and the kingdom

[8] and burned the gate and shed innocent blood. We besought the Lord and we were heard, and we offered sacrifice and cereal offering, and we lighted the lamps and we set out the loaves.

[9] And now see that you keep the feast of booths in the month of Chislev, in the one hundred and eighty-eighth year.

[10] Those in Jerusalem and those in Judea and the senate and Judas, To Aristobulus, who is of the family of the anointed priests, teacher of Ptolemy the king, and to the Jews in Egypt, Greeting, and good health.

[11] Having been saved by God out of grave dangers we thank him greatly for taking our side against the king.

[12] For he drove out those who fought against the holy city.

[13] For when the leader reached Persia with a force that seemed irresistible, they were cut to pieces in the temple of Nanea by a deception employed by the priests of Nanea.

[14] For under pretext of intending to marry her, Antiochus came to the place together with his friends, to secure most of its treasures as a dowry.

[15] When the priests of the temple of Nanea had set out the treasures and Antiochus had come with a few men inside the wall of the sacred precinct, they closed the temple as soon as he entered it.

[16] Opening the secret door in the ceiling, they threw stones and struck down the leader and his men, and dismembered them and cut off their heads and threw them to the people outside.

[17] Blessed in every way be our God, who has brought judgment upon those who have behaved impiously.

[18] Since on the twenty-fifth day of Chislev we shall celebrate the purification of the temple, we thought it necessary to notify you, in order that you also may celebrate the feast of booths and the feast of the fire given when Nehemiah, who built the temple and the altar, offered sacrifices.

[19] For when our fathers were being led captive to Persia, the pious priests of that time took some of the fire of the altar and secretly hid it in the hollow of a dry cistern, where they took such precautions that the place was unknown to any one.

[20] But after many years had passed, when it pleased God, Nehemiah, having been commissioned by the king of Persia, sent the descendants of the priests who had hidden the fire to get it. And when they reported to us that they had not found fire but thick liquid, he ordered them to dip it out and bring it.

[21] And when the materials for the sacrifices were presented, Nehemiah ordered the priests to sprinkle the liquid on the wood and what was laid upon it.

[22] When this was done and some time had passed and the sun, which had been clouded over, shone out, a great fire blazed up, so that all marveled.

[23] And while the sacrifice was being consumed, the priests offered prayer -- the priests and every one. Jonathan led, and the rest responded, as did Nehemiah.

[24] The prayer was to this effect: "O Lord, Lord God, Creator of all things, who art awe-inspiring and strong and just and merciful, who alone art King and art kind, [25] who alone art bountiful, who alone art just and almighty and eternal, who do rescue Israel from every evil, who didst choose the fathers and consecrate them, [26] accept this sacrifice on behalf of all thy people Israel and preserve thy portion and make it holy. [27] Gather together our scattered people, set free those who are slaves among the Gentiles, look upon those who are rejected and despised, and let the Gentiles know that thou art our God. [28] Afflict those who oppress and are insolent with pride. [29] Plant thy people in thy holy place, as Moses said." [30] Then the priests sang the hymns. [31] And when the materials of the sacrifice were consumed, Nehemiah ordered that the liquid that was left should be poured upon large stones. [32] When this was done, a flame blazed up; but when the light from the altar shone back, it went out. [33] When this matter became known, and it was reported to the king of the Persians that, in the place where the exiled priests had hidden the fire, the liquid had appeared with which Nehemiah and his associates had burned the materials of the sacrifice, [34] the king investigated the matter, and enclosed the place and made it sacred. [35] And with those persons whom the king favored he exchanged many excellent gifts. [36] Nehemiah and his associates called this "nephthar," which means purification, but by most people it is called naphtha.

2Mac.2

[1] One finds in the records that Jeremiah the prophet ordered those who were being deported to take some of the fire, as has been told,

[2] and that the prophet after giving them the law instructed those who were being deported not to forget the commandments of the Lord, nor to be led astray in their thoughts upon seeing the gold and silver statues and their adornment.

[3] And with other similar words he exhorted them that the law should not depart from their hearts.

[4] It was also in the writing that the prophet, having received an oracle, ordered that the tent and the ark should follow with him, and that he went out to the mountain where Moses had gone up and had seen the inheritance of God.

[5] And Jeremiah came and found a cave, and he brought there the tent and the ark and the altar of incense, and he sealed up the entrance.

[6] Some of those who followed him came up to mark the way, but could not find it.

[7] When Jeremiah learned of it, he rebuked them and declared: "The place shall be unknown until God gathers his people together again and shows his mercy.

[8] And then the Lord will disclose these things, and the glory of the Lord and the cloud will appear, as they were shown in the case of Moses, and as Solomon asked that the place should be specially consecrated."

[9] It was also made clear that being possessed of wisdom Solomon offered sacrifice for the dedication and completion of the temple.

[10] Just as Moses prayed to the Lord, and fire came down from heaven and devoured the sacrifices, so also Solomon prayed, and the fire came down and consumed the whole burnt offerings.

[11] And Moses said, "They were consumed because the sin offering had not been eaten."

[12] Likewise Solomon also kept the eight days.

[13] The same things are reported in the records and in the memoirs of Nehemiah, and also that he founded a library and collected the books about the kings and prophets, and the writings of David, and letters of kings about votive offerings.

[14] In the same way Judas also collected all the books that had been lost on account of the war which had come upon us, and they are in our possession.

[15] So if you have need of them, send people to get them for you.

[16] Since, therefore, we are about to celebrate the purification, we write to you. Will you therefore please keep the days?

[17] It is God who has saved all his people, and has returned the inheritance to all, and the kingship and priesthood and consecration,

[18] as he promised through the law. For we have hope in God that he will soon have mercy upon us and will gather us from everywhere under heaven into his holy place, for he has rescued us from great evils and has purified the place.

[19] The story of Judas Maccabeus and his brothers, and the purification of the great temple, and the dedication of the altar,

[20] and further the wars against Antiochus Epiphanes and his son Eupator,

[21] and the appearances which came from heaven to those who strove zealously on behalf of Judaism, so that though few in number they seized the whole land and pursued the barbarian hordes,

[22] and recovered the temple famous throughout the world and freed the city and restored the laws that were about to be abolished, while the Lord with great kindness became gracious to them --

[23] all this, which has been set forth by Jason of Cyrene in five volumes, we shall attempt to condense into a single book.

[24] For considering the flood of numbers involved and the difficulty there is for those who wish to enter upon the narratives of history because of the mass of material,

[25] we have aimed to please those who wish to read, to make it easy for those who are inclined to memorize, and to profit all readers.

[26] For us who have undertaken the toil of abbreviating, it is no light matter but calls for sweat and loss of sleep,

[27] just as it is not easy for one who prepares a banquet and seeks the benefit of others. However, to secure the gratitude of many we will gladly endure the uncomfortable toil,

[28] leaving the responsibility for exact details to the compiler, while devoting our effort to arriving at the outlines of the condensation.

[29] For as the master builder of a new house must be concerned with the whole construction, while the one who undertakes its painting and decoration has to consider only what is suitable for its adornment, such in my judgment is the case with us.

[30] It is the duty of the original historian to occupy the ground and to discuss matters from every side and to take trouble with details,

[31] but the one who recasts the narrative should be allowed to strive for brevity of expression and to forego exhaustive treatment.

[32] At this point therefore let us begin our narrative, adding only so much to what has already been said; for it is foolish to lengthen the preface while cutting short the history itself.

2Mac.3

[1] While the holy city was inhabited in unbroken peace and the laws were very well observed because of the piety of the high priest Onias and his hatred of wickedness,

[2] it came about that the kings themselves honored the place and glorified the temple with the finest presents,

[3] so that even Seleucus, the king of Asia, defrayed from his own revenues all the expenses connected with the service of the sacrifices.

[4] But a man named Simon, of the tribe of Benjamin, who had been made captain of the temple, had a disagreement with the high priest about the administration of the city market;

[5] and when he could not prevail over Onias he went to Apollonius of Tarsus, who at that time was governor of Coelesyria and Phoenicia.

[6] He reported to him that the treasury in Jerusalem was full of untold sums of money, so that the amount of the funds could not be reckoned, and that they did not belong to the account of the sacrifices, but that it was possible for them to fall under the control of the king.

[7] When Apollonius met the king, he told him of the money about which he had been informed. The king chose Heliodorus, who was in charge of his affairs, and sent him with commands to effect the removal of the aforesaid money.

[8] Heliodorus at once set out on his journey, ostensibly to make a tour of inspection of the cities of Coelesyria and Phoenicia, but in fact to carry out the king's purpose.

[9] When he had arrived at Jerusalem and had been kindly welcomed by the high priest of the city, he told about the disclosure that had been made and stated why he had come, and he inquired whether this really was the situation.

[10] The high priest explained that there were some deposits belonging to widows and orphans,

[11] and also some money of Hyrcanus, son of Tobias, a man of very prominent position, and that it totaled in all four hundred talents of silver and two hundred of gold. To such an extent the impious Simon had misrepresented the facts.

[12] And he said that it was utterly impossible that wrong should be done to those people who had trusted in the holiness of the place and in the sanctity and inviolability of the temple which is honored throughout the whole world.

[13] But Heliodorus, because of the king's commands which he had, said that this money must in any case be confiscated for the king's treasury.

[14] So he set a day and went in to direct the inspection of these funds. There was no little distress throughout the whole city.

[15] The priests prostrated themselves before the altar in their priestly garments and called toward heaven upon him who had given the law about deposits, that he should keep them safe for those who had deposited them.

[16] To see the appearance of the high priest was to be wounded at heart, for his face and the change in his color disclosed the anguish of his soul.

[17] For terror and bodily trembling had come over the man, which plainly showed to those who looked at him the pain lodged in his heart.

[18] People also hurried out of their houses in crowds to make a general supplication because the holy place was about to be brought into contempt.

[19] Women, girded with sackcloth under their breasts, thronged the streets. Some of the maidens who were kept indoors ran together to the gates, and some to the walls, while others peered out of the windows.

[20] And holding up their hands to heaven, they all made entreaty.

[21] There was something pitiable in the prostration of the whole populace and the anxiety of the high priest in his great anguish.

[22] While they were calling upon the Almighty Lord that he would keep what had been entrusted safe and secure for those who had entrusted it,

[23] Heliodorus went on with what had been decided.

[24] But when he arrived at the treasury with his bodyguard, then and there the Sovereign of spirits and of all authority caused so great a manifestation that all who had been so bold as to accompany him were astounded by the power of God, and became faint with terror.

[25] For there appeared to them a magnificently caparisoned horse, with a rider of frightening mien, and it rushed furiously at Heliodorus and struck at him with its front hoofs. Its rider was seen to have armor and weapons of gold.

[26] Two young men also appeared to him, remarkably strong, gloriously beautiful and splendidly dressed, who stood on each side of him and scourged him continuously, inflicting many blows on him.

[27] When he suddenly fell to the ground and deep darkness came over him, his men took him up and put him on a stretcher

[28] and carried him away, this man who had just entered the aforesaid treasury with a great retinue and all his bodyguard but was now unable to help himself; and they recognized clearly the sovereign power of God.

[29] While he lay prostrate, speechless because of the divine intervention and deprived of any hope of recovery,

[30] they praised the Lord who had acted marvelously for his own place. And the temple, which a little while before was full of fear and disturbance, was filled with joy and gladness, now that the Almighty Lord had appeared.

[31] Quickly some of Heliodorus' friends asked Onias to call upon the Most High and to grant life to one who was lying quite at his last breath.

[32] And the high priest, fearing that the king might get the notion that some foul play had been perpetrated by the Jews with regard to Heliodorus, offered sacrifice for the man's recovery.

[33] While the high priest was making the offering of atonement, the same young men appeared again to Heliodorus dressed in the same clothing, and they stood and said, "Be very grateful to Onias the high priest, since for his sake the Lord has granted you your life.

[34] And see that you, who have been scourged by heaven, report to all men the majestic power of God." Having said this they vanished.

[35] Then Heliodorus offered sacrifice to the Lord and made very great vows to the Savior of his life, and having bidden Onias farewell, he marched off with his forces to the king.

[36] And he bore testimony to all men of the deeds of the supreme God, which he had seen with his own eyes.

[37] When the king asked Heliodorus what sort of person would be suitable to send on another mission to Jerusalem, he replied,

[38] "If you have any enemy or plotter against your government, send him there, for you will get him back thoroughly scourged, if he escapes at all, for there certainly is about the place some power of God.

[39] For he who has his dwelling in heaven watches over that place himself and brings it aid, and he strikes and destroys those who come to do it injury."

[40] This was the outcome of the episode of Heliodorus and the protection of the treasury.

2Mac.4

[1] The previously mentioned Simon, who had informed about the money against his own country, slandered Onias, saying that it was he who had incited Heliodorus and had been the real cause of the misfortune.

[2] He dared to designate as a plotter against the government the man who was the benefactor of the city, the protector of his fellow countrymen, and a zealot for the laws.

[3] When his hatred progressed to such a degree that even murders were committed by one of Simon's approved agents,

[4] Onias recognized that the rivalry was serious and that Apollonius, the son of Menestheus and governor of Coelesyria and Phoenicia, was intensifying the malice of Simon.

[5] So he betook himself to the king, not accusing his fellow citizens but having in view the welfare, both public and private, of all the people.

[6] For he saw that without the king's attention public affairs could not again reach a peaceful settlement, and that Simon would not stop his folly.

[7] When Seleucus died and Antiochus who was called Epiphanes succeeded to the kingdom, Jason the brother of Onias obtained the high priesthood by corruption,

[8] promising the king at an interview three hundred and sixty talents of silver and, from another source of revenue, eighty talents.

[9] In addition to this he promised to pay one hundred and fifty more if permission were given to establish by his authority a gymnasium and a body of youth for it, and to enrol the men of Jerusalem as citizens of Antioch.

[10] When the king assented and Jason came to office, he at once shifted his countrymen over to the Greek way of life.

[11] He set aside the existing royal concessions to the Jews, secured through John the father of Eupolemus, who went on the mission to establish friendship and alliance with the Romans; and he destroyed the lawful ways of living and introduced new customs contrary to the law.

[12] For with alacrity he founded a gymnasium right under the citadel, and he induced the noblest of the young men to wear the Greek hat.

[13] There was such an extreme of Hellenization and increase in the adoption of foreign ways because of the surpassing wickedness of Jason, who was ungodly and no high priest,

[14] that the priests were no longer intent upon their service at the altar. Despising the sanctuary and neglecting the sacrifices, they hastened to take part in the unlawful proceedings in the wrestling arena after the call to the discus,

[15] disdaining the honors prized by their fathers and putting the highest value upon Greek forms of prestige.

[16] For this reason heavy disaster overtook them, and those whose ways of living they admired and wished to imitate completely became their enemies and punished them.

[17] For it is no light thing to show irreverence to the divine laws -- a fact which later events will make clear.

[18] When the quadrennial games were being held at Tyre and the king was present,

[19] the vile Jason sent envoys, chosen as being Antiochian citizens from Jerusalem, to carry three hundred silver drachmas for the sacrifice to Hercules. Those who carried the money, however, thought best not to use it for sacrifice, because that was inappropriate, but to expend it for another purpose.

[20] So this money was intended by the sender for the sacrifice to Hercules, but by the decision of its carriers it was applied to the construction of triremes.

[21] When Apollonius the son of Menestheus was sent to Egypt for the coronation of Philometor as king, Antiochus learned that Philometor had become hostile to his government, and he took measures for his own security. Therefore upon arriving at Joppa he proceeded to Jerusalem.

[22] He was welcomed magnificently by Jason and the city, and ushered in with a blaze of torches and with shouts. Then he marched into Phoenicia.

[23] After a period of three years Jason sent Menelaus, the brother of the previously mentioned Simon, to carry the money to the king and to complete the records of essential business.

[24] But he, when presented to the king, extolled him with an air of authority, and secured the high priesthood for himself, outbidding Jason by three hundred talents of silver.

[25] After receiving the king's orders he returned, possessing no qualification for the high priesthood, but having the hot temper of a cruel tyrant and the rage of a savage wild beast.

[26] So Jason, who after supplanting his own brother was supplanted by another man, was driven as a fugitive into the land of Ammon.

[27] And Menelaus held the office, but he did not pay regularly any of the money promised to the king.

[28] When Sostratus the captain of the citadel kept requesting payment, for the collection of the revenue was his responsibility, the two of them were summoned by the king on account of this issue.

[29] Menelaus left his own brother Lysimachus as deputy in the high priesthood, while Sostratus left Crates, the commander of the Cyprian troops.

[30] While such was the state of affairs, it happened that the people of Tarsus and of Mallus revolted because their cities had been given as a present to Antiochis, the king's concubine.

[31] So the king went hastily to settle the trouble, leaving Andronicus, a man of high rank, to act as his deputy.

[32] But Menelaus, thinking he had obtained a suitable opportunity, stole some of the gold vessels of the temple and gave them to Andronicus; other vessels, as it happened, he had sold to Tyre and the neighboring cities.

[33] When Onias became fully aware of these acts he publicly exposed them, having first withdrawn to a place of sanctuary at Daphne near Antioch.

[34] Therefore Menelaus, taking Andronicus aside, urged him to kill Onias. Andronicus came to Onias, and resorting to treachery offered him sworn pledges and gave him his right hand, and in spite of his suspicion persuaded Onias to come out from the place of sanctuary; then, with no regard for justice, he immediately put him out of the way.

[35] For this reason not only Jews, but many also of other nations, were grieved and displeased at the unjust murder of the man.

[36] When the king returned from the region of Cilicia, the Jews in the city appealed to him with regard

to the unreasonable murder of Onias, and the Greeks shared their hatred of the crime.

[37] Therefore Antiochus was grieved at heart and filled with pity, and wept because of the moderation and good conduct of the deceased;

[38] and inflamed with anger, he immediately stripped off the purple robe from Andronicus, tore off his garments, and led him about the whole city to that very place where he had committed the outrage against Onias, and there he dispatched the bloodthirsty fellow. The Lord thus repaid him with the punishment he deserved.

[39] When many acts of sacrilege had been committed in the city by Lysimachus with the connivance of Menelaus, and when report of them had spread abroad, the populace gathered against Lysimachus, because many of the gold vessels had already been stolen.

[40] And since the crowds were becoming aroused and filled with anger, Lysimachus armed about three thousand men and launched an unjust attack, under the leadership of a certain Auranus, a man advanced in years and no less advanced in folly.

[41] But when the Jews became aware of Lysimachus' attack, some picked up stones, some blocks of wood, and others took handfuls of the ashes that were lying about, and threw them in wild confusion at Lysimachus and his men.

[42] As a result, they wounded many of them, and killed some, and put them all to flight; and the temple robber himself they killed close by the treasury.

[43] Charges were brought against Menelaus about this incident.

[44] When the king came to Tyre, three men sent by the senate presented the case before him.

[45] But Menelaus, already as good as beaten, promised a substantial bribe to Ptolemy son of Dorymenes to win over the king.

[46] Therefore Ptolemy, taking the king aside into a colonnade as if for refreshment, induced the king to change his mind.

[47] Menelaus, the cause of all the evil, he acquitted of the charges against him, while he sentenced to death those unfortunate men, who would have been freed uncondemned if they had pleaded even before Scythians.

[48] And so those who had spoken for the city and the villages and the holy vessels quickly suffered the unjust penalty.

[49] Therefore even the Tyrians, showing their hatred of the crime, provided magnificently for their funeral.

[50] But Menelaus, because of the cupidity of those in power, remained in office, growing in wickedness, having become the chief plotter against his fellow citizens.

2Mac.5

[1] About this time Antiochus made his second invasion of Egypt.

[2] And it happened that over all the city, for almost forty days, there appeared golden-clad horsemen charging through the air, in companies fully armed with lances and drawn swords --

[3] troops of horsemen drawn up, attacks and counterattacks made on this side and on that, brandishing of shields, massing of spears, hurling of missiles, the flash of golden trappings, and armor of all sorts.

[4] Therefore all men prayed that the apparition might prove to have been a good omen.

[5] When a false rumor arose that Antiochus was dead, Jason took no less than a thousand men and suddenly made an assault upon the city. When the troops upon the wall had been forced back and at last the city was being taken, Menelaus took refuge in the citadel.

[6] But Jason kept relentlessly slaughtering his fellow citizens, not realizing that success at the cost of one's kindred is the greatest misfortune, but imagining that he was setting up trophies of victory over enemies and not over fellow countrymen.

[7] He did not gain control of the government, however; and in the end got only disgrace from his conspiracy, and fled again into the country of the Ammonites.

[8] Finally he met a miserable end. Accused before Aretas the ruler of the Arabs, fleeing from city to city, pursued by all men, hated as a rebel against the laws, and abhorred as the executioner of his country and his fellow citizens, he was cast ashore in Egypt;

[9] and he who had driven many from their own country into exile died in exile, having embarked to go to the Lacedaemonians in hope of finding protection because of their kinship.

[10] He who had cast out many to lie unburied had no one to mourn for him; he had no funeral of any sort and no place in the tomb of his fathers.

[11] When news of what had happened reached the king, he took it to mean that Judea was in revolt. So, raging inwardly, he left Egypt and took the city by storm.

[12] And he commanded his soldiers to cut down relentlessly every one they met and to slay those who went into the houses.

[13] Then there was killing of young and old, destruction of boys, women, and children, and slaughter

of virgins and infants.

[14] Within the total of three days eighty thousand were destroyed, forty thousand in hand-to-hand fighting; and as many were sold into slavery as were slain.

[15] Not content with this, Antiochus dared to enter the most holy temple in all the world, guided by Menelaus, who had become a traitor both to the laws and to his country.

[16] He took the holy vessels with his polluted hands, and swept away with profane hands the votive offerings which other kings had made to enhance the glory and honor of the place.

[17] Antiochus was elated in spirit, and did not perceive that the Lord was angered for a little while because of the sins of those who dwelt in the city, and that therefore he was disregarding the holy place.

[18] But if it had not happened that they were involved in many sins, this man would have been scourged and turned back from his rash act as soon as he came forward, just as Heliodorus was, whom Seleucus the king sent to inspect the treasury.

[19] But the Lord did not choose the nation for the sake of the holy place, but the place for the sake of the nation.

[20] Therefore the place itself shared in the misfortunes that befell the nation and afterward participated in its benefits; and what was forsaken in the wrath of the Almighty was restored again in all its glory when the great Lord became reconciled.

[21] So Antiochus carried off eighteen hundred talents from the temple, and hurried away to Antioch, thinking in his arrogance that he could sail on the land and walk on the sea, because his mind was elated.

[22] And he left governors to afflict the people: at Jerusalem, Philip, by birth a Phrygian and in character more barbarous than the man who appointed him;

[23] and at Gerizim, Andronicus; and besides these Menelaus, who lorded it over his fellow citizens worse than the others did. In his malice toward the Jewish citizens,

[24] Antiochus sent Apollonius, the captain of the Mysians, with an army of twenty-two thousand, and commanded him to slay all the grown men and to sell the women and boys as slaves.

[25] When this man arrived in Jerusalem, he pretended to be peaceably disposed and waited until the holy sabbath day; then, finding the Jews not at work, he ordered his men to parade under arms.

[26] He put to the sword all those who came out to see them, then rushed into the city with his armed men and killed great numbers of people.

[27] But Judas Maccabeus, with about nine others, got away to the wilderness, and kept himself and his companions alive in the mountains as wild animals do; they continued to live on what grew wild, so that they might not share in the defilement.

2Mac.6

[1] Not long after this, the king sent an Athenian senator to compel the Jews to forsake the laws of their fathers and cease to live by the laws of God,

[2] and also to pollute the temple in Jerusalem and call it the temple of Olympian Zeus, and to call the one in Gerizim the temple of Zeus the Friend of Strangers, as did the people who dwelt in that place.

[3] Harsh and utterly grievous was the onslaught of evil.

[4] For the temple was filled with debauchery and reveling by the Gentiles, who dallied with harlots and had intercourse with women within the sacred precincts, and besides brought in things for sacrifice that were unfit.

[5] The altar was covered with abominable offerings which were forbidden by the laws.

[6] A man could neither keep the sabbath, nor observe the feasts of his fathers, nor so much as confess himself to be a Jew.

[7] On the monthly celebration of the king's birthday, the Jews were taken, under bitter constraint, to partake of the sacrifices; and when the feast of Dionysus came, they were compelled to walk in the procession in honor of Dionysus, wearing wreaths of ivy.

[8] At the suggestion of Ptolemy a decree was issued to the neighboring Greek cities, that they should adopt the same policy toward the Jews and make them partake of the sacrifices,

[9] and should slay those who did not choose to change over to Greek customs. One could see, therefore, the misery that had come upon them.

[10] For example, two women were brought in for having circumcised their children. These women they publicly paraded about the city, with their babies hung at their breasts, then hurled them down headlong from the wall.

[11] Others who had assembled in the caves near by, to observe the seventh day secretly, were betrayed to Philip and were all burned together, because their piety kept them from defending themselves, in view of their regard for that most holy day.

[12] Now I urge those who read this book not to be depressed by such calamities, but to recognize that these punishments were designed not to destroy but to discipline our people.

[13] In fact, not to let the impious alone for long, but to punish them immediately, is a sign of great kindness.

[14] For in the case of the other nations the Lord waits patiently to punish them until they have reached the full measure of their sins; but he does not deal in this way with us,

[15] in order that he may not take vengeance on us afterward when our sins have reached their height.

[16] Therefore he never withdraws his mercy from us. Though he disciplines us with calamities, he does not forsake his own people.

[17] Let what we have said serve as a reminder; we must go on briefly with the story.

[18] Eleazar, one of the scribes in high position, a man now advanced in age and of noble presence, was being forced to open his mouth to eat swine's flesh.

[19] But he, welcoming death with honor rather than life with pollution, went up to the the rack of his own accord, spitting out the flesh,

[20] as men ought to go who have the courage to refuse things that it is not right to taste, even for the natural love of life.

[21] Those who were in charge of that unlawful sacrifice took the man aside, because of their long acquaintance with him, and privately urged him to bring meat of his own providing, proper for him to use, and pretend that he was eating the flesh of the sacrificial meal which had been commanded by the king,

[22] so that by doing this he might be saved from death, and be treated kindly on account of his old friendship with them.

[23] But making a high resolve, worthy of his years and the dignity of his old age and the gray hairs which he had reached with distinction and his excellent life even from childhood, and moreover according to the holy God-given law, he declared himself quickly, telling them to send him to Hades.

[24] "Such pretense is not worthy of our time of life," he said, "lest many of the young should suppose that Eleazar in his ninetieth year has gone over to an alien religion,

[25] and through my pretense, for the sake of living a brief moment longer, they should be led astray because of me, while I defile and disgrace my old age.

[26] For even if for the present I should avoid the punishment of men, yet whether I live or die I shall not escape the hands of the Almighty.

[27] Therefore, by manfully giving up my life now, I will show myself worthy of my old age

[28] and leave to the young a noble example of how to die a good death willingly and nobly for the revered and holy laws." When he had said this, he went at once to the rack.

[29] And those who a little before had acted toward him with good will now changed to ill will, because the words he had uttered were in their opinion sheer madness.

[30] When he was about to die under the blows, he groaned aloud and said: "It is clear to the Lord in his holy knowledge that, though I might have been saved from death, I am enduring terrible sufferings in my body under this beating, but in my soul I am glad to suffer these things because I fear him."

[31] So in this way he died, leaving in his death an example of nobility and a memorial of courage, not only to the young but to the great body of his nation.

2Mac.7

[1] It happened also that seven brothers and their mother were arrested and were being compelled by the king, under torture with whips and cords, to partake of unlawful swine's flesh.

[2] One of them, acting as their spokesman, said, "What do you intend to ask and learn from us? For we are ready to die rather than transgress the laws of our fathers."

[3] The king fell into a rage, and gave orders that pans and caldrons be heated.

[4] These were heated immediately, and he commanded that the tongue of their spokesman be cut out and that they scalp him and cut off his hands and feet, while the rest of the brothers and the mother looked on.

[5] When he was utterly helpless, the king ordered them to take him to the fire, still breathing, and to fry him in a pan. The smoke from the pan spread widely, but the brothers and their mother encouraged one another to die nobly, saying,

[6] "The Lord God is watching over us and in truth has compassion on us, as Moses declared in his song which bore witness against the people to their faces, when he said, `And he will have compassion on his servants.'"

[7] After the first brother had died in this way, they brought forward the second for their sport. They tore off the skin of his head with the hair, and asked him, "Will you eat rather than have your body punished limb by limb?"

[8] He replied in the language of his fathers, and said to them, "No." Therefore he in turn underwent tortures as the first brother had done.

[9] And when he was at his last breath, he said, "You accursed wretch, you dismiss us from this present life, but the King of the universe will raise us up to an everlasting renewal of life, because we have died for his laws."

[10] After him, the third was the victim of their sport. When it was demanded, he quickly put out his tongue and courageously stretched forth his hands,

[11] and said nobly, "I got these from Heaven, and because of his laws I disdain them, and from him I hope to get them back again."

[12] As a result the king himself and those with him were astonished at the young man's spirit, for he regarded his sufferings as nothing.

[13] When he too had died, they maltreated and tortured the fourth in the same way.

[14] And when he was near death, he said, "One cannot but choose to die at the hands of men and to cherish the hope that God gives of being raised again by him. But for you there will be no resurrection to life!"

[15] Next they brought forward the fifth and maltreated him.

[16] But he looked at the king, and said, "Because you have authority among men, mortal though you are, you do what you please. But do not think that God has forsaken our people.

[17] Keep on, and see how his mighty power will torture you and your descendants!"

[18] After him they brought forward the sixth. And when he was about to die, he said, "Do not deceive yourself in vain. For we are suffering these things on our own account, because of our sins against our own God. Therefore astounding things have happened.

[19] But do not think that you will go unpunished for having tried to fight against God!"

[20] The mother was especially admirable and worthy of honorable memory. Though she saw her seven sons perish within a single day, she bore it with good courage because of her hope in the Lord.

[21] She encouraged each of them in the language of their fathers. Filled with a noble spirit, she fired her woman's reasoning with a man's courage, and said to them,

[22] "I do not know how you came into being in my womb. It was not I who gave you life and breath, nor I who set in order the elements within each of you.

[23] Therefore the Creator of the world, who shaped the beginning of man and devised the origin of all things, will in his mercy give life and breath back to you again, since you now forget yourselves for the sake of his laws."

[24] Antiochus felt that he was being treated with contempt, and he was suspicious of her reproachful tone. The youngest brother being still alive, Antiochus not only appealed to him in words, but promised with oaths that he would make him rich and enviable if he would turn from the ways of his fathers, and that he would take him for his friend and entrust him with public affairs.

[25] Since the young man would not listen to him at all, the king called the mother to him and urged her to advise the youth to save himself.

[26] After much urging on his part, she undertook to persuade her son.

[27] But, leaning close to him, she spoke in their native tongue as follows, deriding the cruel tyrant: "My son, have pity on me. I carried you nine months in my womb, and nursed you for three years, and have reared you and brought you up to this point in your life, and have taken care of you.

[28] I beseech you, my child, to look at the heaven and the earth and see everything that is in them, and recognize that God did not make them out of things that existed. Thus also mankind comes into being.

[29] Do not fear this butcher, but prove worthy of your brothers. Accept death, so that in God's mercy I may get you back again with your brothers."

[30] While she was still speaking, the young man said, "What are you waiting for? I will not obey the king's command, but I obey the command of the law that was given to our fathers through Moses.

[31] But you, who have contrived all sorts of evil against the Hebrews, will certainly not escape the hands of God.

[32] For we are suffering because of our own sins.

[33] And if our living Lord is angry for a little while, to rebuke and discipline us, he will again be reconciled with his own servants.

[34] But you, unholy wretch, you most defiled of all men, do not be elated in vain and puffed up by uncertain hopes, when you raise your hand against the children of heaven.

[35] You have not yet escaped the judgment of the almighty, all-seeing God.

[36] For our brothers after enduring a brief suffering have drunk of everflowing life under God's covenant; but you, by the judgment of God, will receive just punishment for your arrogance.

[37] I, like my brothers, give up body and life for the laws of our fathers, appealing to God to show mercy soon to our nation and by afflictions and plagues to make you confess that he alone is God,

[38] and through me and my brothers to bring to an end the wrath of the Almighty which has justly fallen on our whole nation."

[39] The king fell into a rage, and handled him worse than the others, being exasperated at his scorn.

[40] So he died in his integrity, putting his whole trust in the Lord.

[41] Last of all, the mother died, after her sons.

[42] Let this be enough, then, about the eating of sacrifices and the extreme tortures.

2Mac.8

[1] But Judas, who was also called Maccabeus, and his companions secretly entered the villages and summoned their kinsmen and enlisted those who had continued in the Jewish faith, and so they gathered about six thousand men.

[2] They besought the Lord to look upon the people who were oppressed by all, and to have pity on the temple which had been profaned by ungodly men,

[3] and to have mercy on the city which was being destroyed and about to be leveled to the ground, and to hearken to the blood that cried out to him,

[4] and to remember also the lawless destruction of the innocent babies and the blasphemies committed against his name, and to show his hatred of evil.

[5] As soon as Maccabeus got his army organized, the Gentiles could not withstand him, for the wrath of the Lord had turned to mercy.

[6] Coming without warning, he would set fire to towns and villages. He captured strategic positions and put to flight not a few of the enemy.

[7] He found the nights most advantageous for such attacks. And talk of his valor spread everywhere.

[8] When Philip saw that the man was gaining ground little by little, and that he was pushing ahead with more frequent successes, he wrote to Ptolemy, the governor of Coelesyria and Phoenicia, for aid to the king's government.

[9] And Ptolemy promptly appointed Nicanor the son of Patroclus, one of the king's chief friends, and sent him, in command of no fewer than twenty thousand Gentiles of all nations, to wipe out the whole race of Judea. He associated with him Gorgias, a general and a man of experience in military service.

[10] Nicanor determined to make up for the king the tribute due to the Romans, two thousand talents, by selling the captured Jews into slavery.

[11] And he immediately sent to the cities on the seacoast, inviting them to buy Jewish slaves and promising to hand over ninety slaves for a talent, not expecting the judgment from the Almighty that was about to overtake him.

[12] Word came to Judas concerning Nicanor's invasion; and when he told his companions of the arrival of the army,

[13] those who were cowardly and distrustful of God's justice ran off and got away.

[14] Others sold all their remaining property, and at the same time besought the Lord to rescue those who had been sold by the ungodly Nicanor before he ever met them,

[15] if not for their own sake, yet for the sake of the covenants made with their fathers, and because he had called them by his holy and glorious name.

[16] But Maccabeus gathered his men together, to the number six thousand, and exhorted them not to be frightened by the enemy and not to fear the great multitude of Gentiles who were wickedly coming against them, but to fight nobly,

[17] keeping before their eyes the lawless outrage which the Gentiles had committed against the holy place, and the torture of the derided city, and besides, the overthrow of their ancestral way of life.

[18] "For they trust to arms and acts of daring," he said, "but we trust in the Almighty God, who is able with a single nod to strike down those who are coming against us and even the whole world."

[19] Moreover, he told them of the times when help came to their ancestors; both the time of Sennacherib, when one hundred and eighty-five thousand perished,

[20] and the time of the battle with the Galatians that took place in Babylonia, when eight thousand in all went into the affair, with four thousand Macedonians; and when the Macedonians were hard pressed, the eight thousand, by the help that came to them from heaven, destroyed one hundred and twenty thousand and took much booty.

[21] With these words he filled them with good courage and made them ready to die for their laws and their country; then he divided his army into four parts.

[22] He appointed his brothers also, Simon and Joseph and Jonathan, each to command a division, putting fifteen hundred men under each.

[23] Besides, he appointed Eleazar to read aloud from the holy book, and gave the watchword, "God's help"; then, leading the first division himself, he joined battle with Nicanor.

[24] With the Almighty as their ally, they slew more than nine thousand of the enemy, and wounded and disabled most of Nicanor's army, and forced them all to flee.

[25] They captured the money of those who had come to buy them as slaves. After pursuing them for some distance, they were obliged to return because the hour was late.

[26] For it was the day before the sabbath, and for that reason they did not continue their pursuit.

[27] And when they had collected the arms of the enemy and stripped them of their spoils, they kept the sabbath, giving great praise and thanks to the Lord, who had preserved them for that day and allotted it to them as the beginning of mercy.

[28] After the sabbath they gave some of the spoils to those who had been tortured and to the widows

and orphans, and distributed the rest among themselves and their children.

[29] When they had done this, they made common supplication and besought the merciful Lord to be wholly reconciled with his servants.

[30] In encounters with the forces of Timothy and Bacchides they killed more than twenty thousand of them and got possession of some exceedingly high strongholds, and they divided very much plunder, giving to those who had been tortured and to the orphans and widows, and also to the aged, shares equal to their own.

[31] Collecting the arms of the enemy, they stored them all carefully in strategic places, and carried the rest of the spoils to Jerusalem.

[32] They killed the commander of Timothy's forces, a most unholy man, and one who had greatly troubled the Jews.

[33] While they were celebrating the victory in the city of their fathers, they burned those who had set fire to the sacred gates, Callisthenes and some others, who had fled into one little house; so these received the proper recompense for their impiety.

[34] The thrice-accursed Nicanor, who had brought the thousand merchants to buy the Jews,

[35] having been humbled with the help of the Lord by opponents whom he regarded as of the least account, took off his splendid uniform and made his way alone like a runaway slave across the country till he reached Antioch, having succeeded chiefly in the destruction of his own army!

[36] Thus he who had undertaken to secure tribute for the Romans by the capture of the people of Jerusalem proclaimed that the Jews had a Defender, and that therefore the Jews were invulnerable, because they followed the laws ordained by him.

2Mac.9

[1] About that time, as it happened, Antiochus had retreated in disorder from the region of Persia.

[2] For he had entered the city called Persepolis, and attempted to rob the temples and control the city. Therefore the people rushed to the rescue with arms, and Antiochus and his men were defeated, with the result that Antiochus was put to flight by the inhabitants and beat a shameful retreat.

[3] While he was in Ecbatana, news came to him of what had happened to Nicanor and the forces of Timothy.

[4] Transported with rage, he conceived the idea of turning upon the Jews the injury done by those who had put him to flight; so he ordered his charioteer to drive without stopping until he completed the journey. But the judgment of heaven rode with him! For in his arrogance he said, "When I get there I will make Jerusalem a cemetery of Jews."

[5] But the all-seeing Lord, the God of Israel, struck him an incurable and unseen blow. As soon as he ceased speaking he was seized with a pain in his bowels for which there was no relief and with sharp internal tortures --

[6] and that very justly, for he had tortured the bowels of others with many and strange inflictions.

[7] Yet he did not in any way stop his insolence, but was even more filled with arrogance, breathing fire in his rage against the Jews, and giving orders to hasten the journey. And so it came about that he fell out of his chariot as it was rushing along, and the fall was so hard as to torture every limb of his body.

[8] Thus he who had just been thinking that he could command the waves of the sea, in his superhuman arrogance, and imagining that he could weigh the high mountains in a balance, was brought down to earth and carried in a litter, making the power of God manifest to all.

[9] And so the ungodly man's body swarmed with worms, and while he was still living in anguish and pain, his flesh rotted away, and because of his stench the whole army felt revulsion at his decay.

[10] Because of his intolerable stench no one was able to carry the man who a little while before had thought that he could touch the stars of heaven.

[11] Then it was that, broken in spirit, he began to lose much of his arrogance and to come to his senses under the scourge of God, for he was tortured with pain every moment.

[12] And when he could not endure his own stench, he uttered these words: "It is right to be subject to God, and no mortal should think that he is equal to God."

[13] Then the abominable fellow made a vow to the Lord, who would no longer have mercy on him, stating

[14] that the holy city, which he was hastening to level to the ground and to make a cemetery, he was now declaring to be free;

[15] and the Jews, whom he had not considered worth burying but had planned to throw out with their children to the beasts, for the birds to pick, he would make, all of them, equal to citizens of Athens;

[16] and the holy sanctuary, which he had formerly plundered, he would adorn with the finest offerings; and the holy vessels he would give back, all of them, many times over; and the expenses incurred for the sacrifices he would provide from his own revenues;

[17] and in addition to all this he also would become a Jew and would visit every inhabited place to proclaim the power of God.

[18] But when his sufferings did not in any way abate, for the judgment of God had justly come upon him, he gave up all hope for himself and wrote to the Jews the following letter, in the form of a supplication. This was its content:

[19] "To his worthy Jewish citizens, Antiochus their king and general sends hearty greetings and good wishes for their health and prosperity.

[20] If you and your children are well and your affairs are as you wish, I am glad. As my hope is in heaven,

[21] I remember with affection your esteem and good will. On my way back from the region of Persia I suffered an annoying illness, and I have deemed it necessary to take thought for the general security of all.

[22] I do not despair of my condition, for I have good hope of recovering from my illness,

[23] but I observed that my father, on the occasions when he made expeditions into the upper country, appointed his successor,

[24] so that, if anything unexpected happened or any unwelcome news came, the people throughout the realm would not be troubled, for they would know to whom the government was left.

[25] Moreover, I understand how the princes along the borders and the neighbors to my kingdom keep watching for opportunities and waiting to see what will happen. So I have appointed my son Antiochus to be king, whom I have often entrusted and commended to most of you when I hastened off to the upper provinces; and I have written to him what is written here.

[26] I therefore urge and beseech you to remember the public and private services rendered to you and to maintain your present good will, each of you, toward me and my son.

[27] For I am sure that he will follow my policy and will treat you with moderation and kindness."

[28] So the murderer and blasphemer, having endured the more intense suffering, such as he had inflicted on others, came to the end of his life by a most pitiable fate, among the mountains in a strange land.

[29] And Philip, one of his courtiers, took his body home; then, fearing the son of Antiochus, he betook himself to Ptolemy Philometor in Egypt.

2Mac.10

[1] Now Maccabeus and his followers, the Lord leading them on, recovered the temple and the city;

[2] and they tore down the altars which had been built in the public square by the foreigners, and also destroyed the sacred precincts.

[3] They purified the sanctuary, and made another altar of sacrifice; then, striking fire out of flint, they offered sacrifices, after a lapse of two years, and they burned incense and lighted lamps and set out the bread of the Presence.

[4] And when they had done this, they fell prostrate and besought the Lord that they might never again fall into such misfortunes, but that, if they should ever sin, they might be disciplined by him with forbearance and not be handed over to blasphemous and barbarous nations.

[5] It happened that on the same day on which the sanctuary had been profaned by the foreigners, the purification of the sanctuary took place, that is, on the twenty-fifth day of the same month, which was Chislev.

[6] And they celebrated it for eight days with rejoicing, in the manner of the feast of booths, remembering how not long before, during the feast of booths, they had been wandering in the mountains and caves like wild animals.

[7] Therefore bearing ivy-wreathed wands and beautiful branches and also fronds of palm, they offered hymns of thanksgiving to him who had given success to the purifying of his own holy place.

[8] They decreed by public ordinance and vote that the whole nation of the Jews should observe these days every year.

[9] Such then was the end of Antiochus, who was called Epiphanes.

[10] Now we will tell what took place under Antiochus Eupator, who was the son of that ungodly man, and will give a brief summary of the principal calamities of the wars.

[11] This man, when he succeeded to the kingdom, appointed one Lysias to have charge of the government and to be chief governor of Coelesyria and Phoenicia.

[12] Ptolemy, who was called Macron, took the lead in showing justice to the Jews because of the wrong that had been done to them, and attempted to maintain peaceful relations with them.

[13] As a result he was accused before Eupator by the king's friends. He heard himself called a traitor at every turn, because he had abandoned Cyprus, which Philometor had entrusted to him, and had gone over to Antiochus Epiphanes. Unable to command the respect due his office, he took poison and ended his life.

[14] When Gorgias became governor of the region, he maintained a force of mercenaries, and at every turn kept on warring against the Jews.

[15] Besides this, the Idumeans, who had control of important strongholds, were harassing the Jews;

they received those who were banished from Jerusalem, and endeavored to keep up the war.

[16] But Maccabeus and his men, after making solemn supplication and beseeching God to fight on their side, rushed to the strongholds of the Idumeans.

[17] Attacking them vigorously, they gained possession of the places, and beat off all who fought upon the wall, and slew those whom they encountered, killing no fewer than twenty thousand.

[18] When no less than nine thousand took refuge in two very strong towers well equipped to withstand a siege,

[19] Maccabeus left Simon and Joseph, and also Zacchaeus and his men, a force sufficient to besiege them; and he himself set off for places where he was more urgently needed.

[20] But the men with Simon, who were money-hungry, were bribed by some of those who were in the towers, and on receiving seventy thousand drachmas let some of them slip away.

[21] When word of what had happened came to Maccabeus, he gathered the leaders of the people, and accused these men of having sold their brethren for money by setting their enemies free to fight against them.

[22] Then he slew these men who had turned traitor, and immediately captured the two towers.

[23] Having success at arms in everything he undertook, he destroyed more than twenty thousand in the two strongholds.

[24] Now Timothy, who had been defeated by the Jews before, gathered a tremendous force of mercenaries and collected the cavalry from Asia in no small number. He came on, intending to take Judea by storm.

[25] As he drew near, Maccabeus and his men sprinkled dust upon their heads and girded their loins with sackcloth, in supplication to God.

[26] Falling upon the steps before the altar, they besought him to be gracious to them and to be an enemy to their enemies and an adversary to their adversaries, as the law declares.

[27] And rising from their prayer they took up their arms and advanced a considerable distance from the city; and when they came near to the enemy they halted.

[28] Just as dawn was breaking, the two armies joined battle, the one having as pledge of success and victory not only their valor but their reliance upon the Lord, while the other made rage their leader in the fight.

[29] When the battle became fierce, there appeared to the enemy from heaven five resplendent men on horses with golden bridles, and they were leading the Jews.

[30] Surrounding Maccabeus and protecting him with their own armor and weapons, they kept him from being wounded. And they showered arrows and thunderbolts upon the enemy, so that, confused and blinded, they were thrown into disorder and cut to pieces.

[31] Twenty thousand five hundred were slaughtered, besides six hundred horsemen.

[32] Timothy himself fled to a stronghold called Gazara, especially well garrisoned, where Chaereas was commander.

[33] Then Maccabeus and his men were glad, and they besieged the fort for four days.

[34] The men within, relying on the strength of the place, blasphemed terribly and hurled out wicked words.

[35] But at dawn of the fifth day, twenty young men in the army of Maccabeus, fired with anger because of the blasphemies, bravely stormed the wall and with savage fury cut down every one they met.

[36] Others who came up in the same way wheeled around against the defenders and set fire to the towers; they kindled fires and burned the blasphemers alive. Others broke open the gates and let in the rest of the force, and they occupied the city.

[37] They killed Timothy, who was hidden in a cistern, and his brother Chaereas, and Apollophanes.

[38] When they had accomplished these things, with hymns and thanksgivings they blessed the Lord who shows great kindness to Israel and gives them the victory.

2Mac.11

[1] Very soon after this, Lysias, the king's guardian and kinsman, who was in charge of the government, being vexed at what had happened,

[2] gathered about eighty thousand men and all his cavalry and came against the Jews. He intended to make the city a home for Greeks,

[3] and to levy tribute on the temple as he did on the sacred places of the other nations, and to put up the high priesthood for sale every year.

[4] He took no account whatever of the power of God, but was elated with his ten thousands of infantry, and his thousands of cavalry, and his eighty elephants.

[5] Invading Judea, he approached Beth-zur, which was a fortified place about five leagues from Jerusalem, and pressed it hard.

[6] When Maccabeus and his men got word that Lysias was besieging the strongholds, they and all the people, with lamentations and tears, besought the Lord to send a good angel to save Israel.

[7] Maccabeus himself was the first to take up arms, and he urged the others to risk their lives with him to aid their brethren. Then they eagerly rushed off together.

[8] And there, while they were still near Jerusalem, a horseman appeared at their head, clothed in white and brandishing weapons of gold.

[9] And they all together praised the merciful God, and were strengthened in heart, ready to assail not only men but the wildest beasts or walls of iron.

[10] They advanced in battle order, having their heavenly ally, for the Lord had mercy on them.

[11] They hurled themselves like lions against the enemy, and slew eleven thousand of them and sixteen hundred horsemen, and forced all the rest to flee.

[12] Most of them got away stripped and wounded, and Lysias himself escaped by disgraceful flight.

[13] And as he was not without intelligence, he pondered over the defeat which had befallen him, and realized that the Hebrews were invincible because the mighty God fought on their side. So he sent to them

[14] and persuaded them to settle everything on just terms, promising that he would persuade the king, constraining him to be their friend.

[15] Maccabeus, having regard for the common good, agreed to all that Lysias urged. For the king granted every request in behalf of the Jews which Maccabeus delivered to Lysias in writing.

[16] The letter written to the Jews by Lysias was to this effect: "Lysias to the people of the Jews, greeting.

[17] John and Absalom, who were sent by you, have delivered your signed communication and have asked about the matters indicated therein.

[18] I have informed the king of everything that needed to be brought before him, and he has agreed to what was possible.

[19] If you will maintain your good will toward the government, I will endeavor for the future to help promote your welfare.

[20] And concerning these matters and their details, I have ordered these men and my representatives to confer with you.

[21] Farewell. The one hundred and forty-eighth year, Dioscorinthius twenty-fourth."

[22] The king's letter ran thus: "King Antiochus to his brother Lysias, greeting.

[23] Now that our father has gone on to the gods, we desire that the subjects of the kingdom be undisturbed in caring for their own affairs.

[24] We have heard that the Jews do not consent to our father's change to Greek customs but prefer their own way of living and ask that their own customs be allowed them.

[25] Accordingly, since we choose that this nation also be free from disturbance, our decision is that their temple be restored to them and that they live according to the customs of their ancestors.

[26] You will do well, therefore, to send word to them and give them pledges of friendship, so that they may know our policy and be of good cheer and go on happily in the conduct of their own affairs."

[27] To the nation the king's letter was as follows: "King Antiochus to the senate of the Jews and to the other Jews, greeting.

[28] If you are well, it is as we desire. We also are in good health.

[29] Menelaus has informed us that you wish to return home and look after your own affairs.

[30] Therefore those who go home by the thirtieth day of Xanthicus will have our pledge of friendship and full permission

[31] for the Jews to enjoy their own food and laws, just as formerly, and none of them shall be molested in any way for what he may have done in ignorance.

[32] And I have also sent Menelaus to encourage you.

[33] Farewell. The one hundred and forty-eighth year, Xanthicus fifteenth."

[34] The Romans also sent them a letter, which read thus: "Quintus Memmius and Titus Manius, envoys of the Romans, to the people of the Jews, greeting.

[35] With regard to what Lysias the kinsman of the king has granted you, we also give consent.

[36] But as to the matters which he decided are to be referred to the king, as soon as you have considered them, send some one promptly, so that we may make proposals appropriate for you. For we are on our way to Antioch.

[37] Therefore make haste and send some men, so that we may have your judgment.

[38] Farewell. The one hundred and forty-eighth year, Xanthicus fifteenth."

2Mac.12

[1] When this agreement had been reached, Lysias returned to the king, and the Jews went about their farming.

[2] But some of the governors in various places, Timothy and Apollonius the son of Gennaeus, as well as Hieronymus and Demophon, and in addition to these Nicanor the governor of Cyprus, would not let them live quietly and in peace.

[3] And some men of Joppa did so ungodly a deed as this: they invited the Jews who lived among them to embark, with their wives and children, on boats which they had provided, as though there were no ill will to the Jews;

[4] and this was done by public vote of the city. And when they accepted, because they wished to live peaceably and suspected nothing, the men of Joppa took them out to sea and drowned them, not less than two hundred.

[5] When Judas heard of the cruelty visited on his countrymen, he gave orders to his men

[6] and, calling upon God the righteous Judge, attacked the murderers of his brethren. He set fire to the harbor by night, and burned the boats, and massacred those who had taken refuge there.

[7] Then, because the city's gates were closed, he withdrew, intending to come again and root out the whole community of Joppa.

[8] But learning that the men in Jamnia meant in the same way to wipe out the Jews who were living among them,

[9] he attacked the people of Jamnia by night and set fire to the harbor and the fleet, so that the glow of the light was seen in Jerusalem, thirty miles distant.

[10] When they had gone more than a mile from there, on their march against Timothy, not less than five thousand Arabs with five hundred horsemen attacked them.

[11] After a hard fight Judas and his men won the victory, by the help of God. The defeated nomads besought Judas to grant them pledges of friendship, promising to give him cattle and to help his people in all other ways.

[12] Judas, thinking that they might really be useful in many ways, agreed to make peace with them; and after receiving his pledges they departed to their tents.

[13] He also attacked a certain city which was strongly fortified with earthworks and walls, and inhabited by all sorts of Gentiles. Its name was Caspin.

[14] And those who were within, relying on the strength of the walls and on their supply of provisions, behaved most insolently toward Judas and his men, railing at them and even blaspheming and saying unholy things.

[15] But Judas and his men, calling upon the great Sovereign of the world, who without battering-rams or engines of war overthrew Jericho in the days of Joshua, rushed furiously upon the walls.

[16] They took the city by the will of God, and slaughtered untold numbers, so that the adjoining lake, a quarter of a mile wide, appeared to be running over with blood.

[17] When they had gone ninety-five miles from there, they came to Charax, to the Jews who are called Toubiani.

[18] They did not find Timothy in that region, for he had by then departed from the region without accomplishing anything, though in one place he had left a very strong garrison.

[19] Dositheus and Sosipater, who were captains under Maccabeus, marched out and destroyed those whom Timothy had left in the stronghold, more than ten thousand men.

[20] But Maccabeus arranged his army in divisions, set men in command of the divisions, and hastened after Timothy, who had with him a hundred and twenty thousand infantry and two thousand five hundred cavalry.

[21] When Timothy learned of the approach of Judas, he sent off the women and the children and also the baggage to a place called Carnaim; for that place was hard to besiege and difficult of access because of the narrowness of all the approaches.

[22] But when Judas' first division appeared, terror and fear came over the enemy at the manifestation to them of him who sees all things; and they rushed off in flight and were swept on, this way and that, so that often they were injured by their own men and pierced by the points of their swords.

[23] And Judas pressed the pursuit with the utmost vigor, putting the sinners to the sword, and destroyed as many as thirty thousand men.

[24] Timothy himself fell into the hands of Dositheus and Sosipater and their men. With great guile he besought them to let him go in safety, because he held the parents of most of them and the brothers of some and no consideration would be shown them.

[25] And when with many words he had confirmed his solemn promise to restore them unharmed, they let him go, for the sake of saving their brethren.

[26] Then Judas marched against Carnaim and the temple of Atargatis, and slaughtered twenty-five thousand people.

[27] After the rout and destruction of these, he marched also against Ephron, a fortified city where Lysias dwelt with multitudes of people of all nationalities. Stalwart young men took their stand before the walls and made a vigorous defense; and great stores of war engines and missiles were there.

[28] But the Jews called upon the Sovereign who with power shatters the might of his enemies, and they got the city into their hands, and killed as many as twenty-five thousand of those who were within it.

[29] Setting out from there, they hastened to Scythopolis, which is seventy-five miles from Jerusalem.

[30] But when the Jews who dwelt there bore witness to the good will which the people of Scythopolis had shown them and their kind treatment of them in times of misfortune,

[31] they thanked them and exhorted them to be well disposed to their race in the future also. Then they went up to Jerusalem, as the feast of weeks was close at hand.

[32] After the feast called Pentecost, they hastened against Gorgias, the governor of Idumea.

[33] And he came out with three thousand infantry and four hundred cavalry.

[34] When they joined battle, it happened that a few of the Jews fell.

[35] But a certain Dositheus, one of Bacenor's men, who was on horseback and was a strong man, caught hold of Gorgias, and grasping his cloak was dragging him off by main strength, wishing to take the accursed man alive, when one of the Thracian horsemen bore down upon him and cut off his arm; so Gorgias escaped and reached Marisa.

[36] As Esdris and his men had been fighting for a long time and were weary, Judas called upon the Lord to show himself their ally and leader in the battle.

[37] In the language of their fathers he raised the battle cry, with hymns; then he charged against Gorgias' men when they were not expecting it, and put them to flight.

[38] Then Judas assembled his army and went to the city of Adullam. As the seventh day was coming on, they purified themselves according to the custom, and they kept the sabbath there.

[39] On the next day, as by that time it had become necessary, Judas and his men went to take up the bodies of the fallen and to bring them back to lie with their kinsmen in the sepulchres of their fathers.

[40] Then under the tunic of every one of the dead they found sacred tokens of the idols of Jamnia, which the law forbids the Jews to wear. And it became clear to all that this was why these men had fallen.

[41] So they all blessed the ways of the Lord, the righteous Judge, who reveals the things that are hidden;

[42] and they turned to prayer, beseeching that the sin which had been committed might be wholly blotted out. And the noble Judas exhorted the people to keep themselves free from sin, for they had seen with their own eyes what had happened because of the sin of those who had fallen.

[43] He also took up a collection, man by man, to the amount of two thousand drachmas of silver, and sent it to Jerusalem to provide for a sin offering. In doing this he acted very well and honorably, taking account of the resurrection.

[44] For if he were not expecting that those who had fallen would rise again, it would have been superfluous and foolish to pray for the dead.

[45] But if he was looking to the splendid reward that is laid up for those who fall asleep in godliness, it was a holy and pious thought. Therefore he made atonement for the dead, that they might be delivered from their sin.

2Mac.13

[1] In the one hundred and forty-ninth year word came to Judas and his men that Antiochus Eupator was coming with a great army against Judea,

[2] and with him Lysias, his guardian, who had charge of the government. Each of them had a Greek force of one hundred and ten thousand infantry, five thousand three hundred cavalry, twenty-two elephants, and three hundred chariots armed with scythes.

[3] Menelaus also joined them and with utter hypocrisy urged Antiochus on, not for the sake of his country's welfare, but because he thought that he would be established in office.

[4] But the King of kings aroused the anger of Antiochus against the scoundrel; and when Lysias informed him that this man was to blame for all the trouble, he ordered them to take him to Beroea and to put him to death by the method which is the custom in that place.

[5] For there is a tower in that place, fifty cubits high, full of ashes, and it has a rim running around it which on all sides inclines precipitously into the ashes.

[6] There they all push to destruction any man guilty of sacrilege or notorious for other crimes.

[7] By such a fate it came about that Menelaus the lawbreaker died, without even burial in the earth.

[8] And this was eminently just; because he had committed many sins against the altar whose fire and ashes were holy, he met his death in ashes.

[9] The king with barbarous arrogance was coming to show the Jews things far worse than those that had been done in his father's time.

[10] But when Judas heard of this, he ordered the people to call upon the Lord day and night, now if ever to help those who were on the point of being deprived of the law and their country and the holy temple,

[11] and not to let the people who had just begun to revive fall into the hands of the blasphemous Gentiles.

[12] When they had all joined in the same petition and had besought the merciful Lord with weeping

and fasting and lying prostrate for three days without ceasing, Judas exhorted them and ordered them to stand ready.

[13] After consulting privately with the elders, he determined to march out and decide the matter by the help of God before the king's army could enter Judea and get possession of the city.

[14] So, committing the decision to the Creator of the world and exhorting his men to fight nobly to the death for the laws, temple, city, country, and commonwealth, he pitched his camp near Modein.

[15] He gave his men the watchword, "God's victory," and with a picked force of the bravest young men, he attacked the king's pavilion at night and slew as many as two thousand men in the camp. He stabbed the leading elephant and its rider.

[16] In the end they filled the camp with terror and confusion and withdrew in triumph.

[17] This happened, just as day was dawning, because the Lord's help protected him.

[18] The king, having had a taste of the daring of the Jews, tried strategy in attacking their positions.

[19] He advanced against Beth-zur, a strong fortress of the Jews, was turned back, attacked again, and was defeated.

[20] Judas sent in to the garrison whatever was necessary.

[21] But Rhodocus, a man from the ranks of the Jews, gave secret information to the enemy; he was sought for, caught, and put in prison.

[22] The king negotiated a second time with the people in Beth-zur, gave pledges, received theirs, withdrew, attacked Judas and his men, was defeated;

[23] he got word that Philip, who had been left in charge of the government, had revolted in Antioch; he was dismayed, called in the Jews, yielded and swore to observe all their rights, settled with them and offered sacrifice, honored the sanctuary and showed generosity to the holy place.

[24] He received Maccabeus, left Hegemonides as governor from Ptolemais to Gerar,

[25] and went to Ptolemais. The people of Ptolemais were indignant over the treaty; in fact they were so angry that they wanted to annul its terms.

[26] Lysias took the public platform, made the best possible defense, convinced them, appeased them, gained their good will, and set out for Antioch. This is how the king's attack and withdrawal turned out.

2Mac.14

[1] Three years later, word came to Judas and his men that Demetrius, the son of Seleucus, had sailed into the harbor of Tripolis with a strong army and a fleet,

[2] and had taken possession of the country, having made away with Antiochus and his guardian Lysias.

[3] Now a certain Alcimus, who had formerly been high priest but had wilfully defiled himself in the times of separation, realized that there was no way for him to be safe or to have access again to the holy altar,

[4] and went to King Demetrius in about the one hundred and fifty-first year, presenting to him a crown of gold and a palm, and besides these some of the customary olive branches from the temple. During that day he kept quiet.

[5] But he found an opportunity that furthered his mad purpose when he was invited by Demetrius to a meeting of the council and was asked about the disposition and intentions of the Jews. He answered:

[6] "Those of the Jews who are called Hasideans, whose leader is Judas Maccabeus, are keeping up war and stirring up sedition, and will not let the kingdom attain tranquillity.

[7] Therefore I have laid aside my ancestral glory -- I mean the high priesthood -- and have now come here,

[8] first because I am genuinely concerned for the interests of the king, and second because I have regard also for my fellow citizens. For through the folly of those whom I have mentioned our whole nation is now in no small misfortune.

[9] Since you are acquainted, O king, with the details of this matter, deign to take thought for our country and our hard-pressed nation with the gracious kindness which you show to all.

[10] For as long as Judas lives, it is impossible for the government to find peace."

[11] When he had said this, the rest of the king's friends, who were hostile to Judas, quickly inflamed Demetrius still more.

[12] And he immediately chose Nicanor, who had been in command of the elephants, appointed him governor of Judea, and sent him off

[13] with orders to kill Judas and scatter his men, and to set up Alcimus as high priest of the greatest temple.

[14] And the Gentiles throughout Judea, who had fled before Judas, flocked to join Nicanor, thinking that the misfortunes and calamities of the Jews would mean prosperity for themselves.

[15] When the Jews heard of Nicanor's coming and the gathering of the Gentiles, they sprinkled dust upon their heads and prayed to him who established his own people for ever and always upholds his own heritage by manifesting himself.

[16] At the command of the leader, they set out from there immediately and engaged them in battle at a village called Dessau.

[17] Simon, the brother of Judas, had encountered Nicanor, but had been temporarily checked because of the sudden consternation created by the enemy.

[18] Nevertheless Nicanor, hearing of the valor of Judas and his men and their courage in battle for their country, shrank from deciding the issue by bloodshed.

[19] Therefore he sent Posidonius and Theodotus and Mattathias to give and receive pledges of friendship.

[20] When the terms had been fully considered, and the leader had informed the people, and it had appeared that they were of one mind, they agreed to the covenant.

[21] And the leaders set a day on which to meet by themselves. A chariot came forward from each army; seats of honor were set in place;

[22] Judas posted armed men in readiness at key places to prevent sudden treachery on the part of the enemy; they held the proper conference.

[23] Nicanor stayed on in Jerusalem and did nothing out of the way, but dismissed the flocks of people that had gathered.

[24] And he kept Judas always in his presence; he was warmly attached to the man.

[25] And he urged him to marry and have children; so he married, settled down, and shared the common life.

[26] But when Alcimus noticed their good will for one another, he took the covenant that had been made and went to Demetrius. He told him that Nicanor was disloyal to the government, for he had appointed that conspirator against the kingdom, Judas, to be his successor.

[27] The king became excited and, provoked by the false accusations of that depraved man, wrote to Nicanor, stating that he was displeased with the covenant and commanding him to send Maccabeus to Antioch as a prisoner without delay.

[28] When this message came to Nicanor, he was troubled and grieved that he had to annul their agreement when the man had done no wrong.

[29] Since it was not possible to oppose the king, he watched for an opportunity to accomplish this by a stratagem.

[30] But Maccabeus, noticing that Nicanor was more austere in his dealings with him and was meeting him more rudely than had been his custom, concluded that this austerity did not spring from the best motives. So he gathered not a few of his men, and went into hiding from Nicanor.

[31] When the latter became aware that he had been cleverly outwitted by the man, he went to the great and holy temple while the priests were offering the customary sacrifices, and commanded them to hand the man over.

[32] And when they declared on oath that they did not know where the man was whom he sought,

[33] he stretched out his right hand toward the sanctuary, and swore this oath: "If you do not hand Judas over to me as a prisoner, I will level this precinct of God to the ground and tear down the altar, and I will build here a splendid temple to Dionysus."

[34] Having said this, he went away. Then the priests stretched forth their hands toward heaven and called upon the constant Defender of our nation, in these words:

[35] "O Lord of all, who hast need of nothing, thou wast pleased that there be a temple for thy habitation among us;

[36] so now, O holy One, Lord of all holiness, keep undefiled for ever this house that has been so recently purified."

[37] A certain Razis, one of the elders of Jerusalem, was denounced to Nicanor as a man who loved his fellow citizens and was very well thought of and for his good will was called father of the Jews.

[38] For in former times, when there was no mingling with the Gentiles, he had been accused of Judaism, and for Judaism he had with all zeal risked body and life.

[39] Nicanor, wishing to exhibit the enmity which he had for the Jews, sent more than five hundred soldiers to arrest him;

[40] for he thought that by arresting him he would do them an injury.

[41] When the troops were about to capture the tower and were forcing the door of the courtyard, they ordered that fire be brought and the doors burned. Being surrounded, Razis fell upon his own sword,

[42] preferring to die nobly rather than to fall into the hands of sinners and suffer outrages unworthy of his noble birth.

[43] But in the heat of the struggle he did not hit exactly, and the crowd was now rushing in through the doors. He bravely ran up on the wall, and manfully threw himself down into the crowd.

[44] But as they quickly drew back, a space opened and he fell in the middle of the empty space.

[45] Still alive and aflame with anger, he rose, and though his blood gushed forth and his wounds were severe he ran through the crowd; and standing upon a steep rock,

[46] with his blood now completely drained from him, he tore out his entrails, took them with both

hands and hurled them at the crowd, calling upon the Lord of life and spirit to give them back to him again. This was the manner of his death.

2Mac.15

[1] When Nicanor heard that Judas and his men were in the region of Samaria, he made plans to attack them with complete safety on the day of rest.

[2] And when the Jews who were compelled to follow him said, "Do not destroy so savagely and barbarously, but show respect for the day which he who sees all things has honored and hallowed above other days,"

[3] the thrice-accursed wretch asked if there were a sovereign in heaven who had commanded the keeping of the sabbath day.

[4] And when they declared, "It is the living Lord himself, the Sovereign in heaven, who ordered us to observe the seventh day,"

[5] he replied, "And I am a sovereign also, on earth, and I command you to take up arms and finish the king's business." Nevertheless, he did not succeed in carrying out his abominable design.

[6] This Nicanor in his utter boastfulness and arrogance had determined to erect a public monument of victory over Judas and his men.

[7] But Maccabeus did not cease to trust with all confidence that he would get help from the Lord.

[8] And he exhorted his men not to fear the attack of the Gentiles, but to keep in mind the former times when help had come to them from heaven, and now to look for the victory which the Almighty would give them.

[9] Encouraging them from the law and the prophets, and reminding them also of the struggles they had won, he made them the more eager.

[10] And when he had aroused their courage, he gave his orders, at the same time pointing out the perfidy of the Gentiles and their violation of oaths.

[11] He armed each of them not so much with confidence in shields and spears as with the inspiration of brave words, and he cheered them all by relating a dream, a sort of vision, which was worthy of belief.

[12] What he saw was this: Onias, who had been high priest, a noble and good man, of modest bearing and gentle manner, one who spoke fittingly and had been trained from childhood in all that belongs to excellence, was praying with outstretched hands for the whole body of the Jews.

[13] Then likewise a man appeared, distinguished by his gray hair and dignity, and of marvelous majesty and authority.

[14] And Onias spoke, saying, "This is a man who loves the brethren and prays much for the people and the holy city, Jeremiah, the prophet of God."

[15] Jeremiah stretched out his right hand and gave to Judas a golden sword, and as he gave it he addressed him thus:

[16] "Take this holy sword, a gift from God, with which you will strike down your adversaries."

[17] Encouraged by the words of Judas, so noble and so effective in arousing valor and awaking manliness in the souls of the young, they determined not to carry on a campaign but to attack bravely, and to decide the matter, by fighting hand to hand with all courage, because the city and the sanctuary and the temple were in danger.

[18] Their concern for wives and children, and also for brethren and relatives, lay upon them less heavily; their greatest and first fear was for the consecrated sanctuary.

[19] And those who had to remain in the city were in no little distress, being anxious over the encounter in the open country.

[20] When all were now looking forward to the coming decision, and the enemy was already close at hand with their army drawn up for battle, the elephants strategically stationed and the cavalry deployed on the flanks,

[21] Maccabeus, perceiving the hosts that were before him and the varied supply of arms and the savagery of the elephants, stretched out his hands toward heaven and called upon the Lord who works wonders; for he knew that it is not by arms, but as the Lord decides, that he gains the victory for those who deserve it.

[22] And he called upon him in these words: "O Lord, thou didst send thy angel in the time of Hezekiah king of Judea, and he slew fully a hundred and eighty-five thousand in the camp of Sennacherib.

[23] So now, O Sovereign of the heavens, send a good angel to carry terror and trembling before us.

[24] By the might of thy arm may these blasphemers who come against thy holy people be struck down." With these words he ended his prayer.

[25] Nicanor and his men advanced with trumpets and battle songs;

[26] and Judas and his men met the enemy in battle with invocation to God and prayers.

[27] So, fighting with their hands and praying to God in their hearts, they laid low no less than thirty-five thousand men, and were greatly gladdened by God's manifestation.

[28] When the action was over and they were returning with joy, they recognized Nicanor, lying dead, in full armor.

[29] Then there was shouting and tumult, and they blessed the Sovereign Lord in the language of their fathers.

[30] And the man who was ever in body and soul the defender of his fellow citizens, the man who maintained his youthful good will toward his countrymen, ordered them to cut off Nicanor's head and arm and carry them to Jerusalem.

[31] And when he arrived there and had called his countrymen together and stationed the priests before the altar, he sent for those who were in the citadel.

[32] He showed them the vile Nicanor's head and that profane man's arm, which had been boastfully stretched out against the holy house of the Almighty;

[33] and he cut out the tongue of the ungodly Nicanor and said that he would give it piecemeal to the birds and hang up these rewards of his folly opposite the sanctuary.

[34] And they all, looking to heaven, blessed the Lord who had manifested himself, saying, "Blessed is he who has kept his own place undefiled."

[35] And he hung Nicanor's head from the citadel, a clear and conspicuous sign to every one of the help of the Lord.

[36] And they all decreed by public vote never to let this day go unobserved, but to celebrate the thirteenth day of the twelfth month -- which is called Adar in the Syrian language -- the day before Mordecai's day.

[37] This, then, is how matters turned out with Nicanor. And from that time the city has been in the possession of the Hebrews. So I too will here end my story.

[38] If it is well told and to the point, that is what I myself desired; if it is poorly done and mediocre, that was the best I could do.

[39] For just as it is harmful to drink wine alone, or, again, to drink water alone, while wine mixed with water is sweet and delicious and enhances one's enjoyment, so also the style of the story delights the ears of those who read the work. And here will be the end.

3 Maccabees

3Mac.1

[1] When Philopator learned from those who returned that the regions which he had controlled had been seized by Antiochus, he gave orders to all his forces, both infantry and cavalry, took with him his sister Arsinoe, and marched out to the region near Raphia, where Antiochus's supporters were encamped.

[2] But a certain Theodotus, determined to carry out the plot he had devised, took with him the best of the Ptolemaic arms that had been previously issued to him, and crossed over by night to the tent of Ptolemy, intending single-handed to kill him and thereby end the war.

[3] But Dositheus, known as the son of Drimylus, a Jew by birth who later changed his religion and apostatized from the ancestral traditions, had led the king away and arranged that a certain insignificant man should sleep in the tent; and so it turned out that this man incurred the vengeance meant for the king.

[4] When a bitter fight resulted, and matters were turning out rather in favor of Antiochus, Arsinoe went to the troops with wailing and tears, her locks all disheveled, and exhorted them to defend themselves and their children and wives bravely, promising to give them each two minas of gold if they won the battle.

[5] And so it came about that the enemy was routed in the action, and many captives also were taken.

[6] Now that he had foiled the plot, Ptolemy decided to visit the neighboring cities and encourage them.

[7] By doing this, and by endowing their sacred enclosures with gifts, he strengthened the morale of his subjects.

[8] Since the Jews had sent some of their council and elders to greet him, to bring him gifts of welcome, and to congratulate him on what had happened, he was all the more eager to visit them as soon as possible.

[9] After he had arrived in Jerusalem, he offered sacrifice to the supreme God and made thank-offerings and did what was fitting for the holy place. Then, upon entering the place and being impressed by its excellence and its beauty,

[10] he marveled at the good order of the temple, and conceived a desire to enter the holy of holies.

[11] When they said that this was not permitted, because not even members of their own nation were allowed to enter, nor even all of the priests, but only the high priest who was pre-eminent over all, and he only once a year, the king was by no means persuaded.

[12] Even after the law had been read to him, he did not cease to maintain that he ought to enter, saying, "Even if those men are deprived of this honor, I ought not to be."

[13] And he inquired why, when he entered every other temple, no one there had stopped him.

[14] And someone heedlessly said that it was wrong to take this as a sign in itself.

[15] "But since this has happened," the king said, "why should not I at least enter, whether they wish it or not?"

[16] Then the priests in all their vestments prostrated themselves and entreated the supreme God to aid in the present situation and to avert the violence of this evil design, and they filled the temple with cries and tears;

[17] and those who remained behind in the city were agitated and hurried out, supposing that something mysterious was occurring.

[18] The virgins who had been enclosed in their chambers rushed out with their mothers, sprinkled their hair with dust, and filled the streets with groans and lamentations.

[19] Those women who had recently been arrayed for marriage abandoned the bridal chambers prepared for wedded union, and, neglecting proper modesty, in a disorderly rush flocked together in the city.

[20] Mothers and nurses abandoned even newborn children here and there, some in houses and some in the streets, and without a backward look they crowded together at the most high temple.

[21] Various were the supplications of those gathered there because of what the king was profanely plotting.

[22] In addition, the bolder of the citizens would not tolerate the completion of his plans or the fulfillment of his intended purpose.

[23] They shouted to their fellows to take arms and die courageously for the ancestral law, and created a considerable disturbance in the holy place; and being barely restrained by the old men and the elders, they resorted to the same posture of supplication as the others.

[24] Meanwhile the crowd, as before, was engaged in prayer,

[25] while the elders near the king tried in various ways to change his arrogant mind from the plan that he had conceived.

[26] But he, in his arrogance, took heed of nothing, and began now to approach, determined to bring the aforesaid plan to a conclusion.

[27] When those who were around him observed this, they turned, together with our people, to call upon him who has all power to defend them in the present trouble and not to overlook this unlawful and haughty deed.

[28] The continuous, vehement, and concerted cry of the crowds resulted in an immense uproar;

[29] for it seemed that not only the men but also the walls and the whole earth around echoed, because indeed all at that time preferred death to the profanation of the place.

3Mac.2

[1] Then the high priest Simon, facing the sanctuary, bending his knees and extending his hands with calm dignity, prayed as follows:

[2] "Lord, Lord, king of the heavens, and sovereign of all creation, holy among the holy ones, the only ruler, almighty, give attention to us who are suffering grievously from an impious and profane man, puffed up in his audacity and power.

[3] For you, the creator of all things and the governor of all, are a just Ruler, and you judge those who have done anything in insolence and arrogance.

[4] You destroyed those who in the past committed injustice, among whom were even giants who trusted in their strength and boldness, whom you destroyed by bringing upon them a boundless flood.

[5] You consumed with fire and sulphur the men of Sodom who acted arrogantly, who were notorious for their vices; and you made them an example to those who should come afterward.

[6] You made known your mighty power by inflicting many and varied punishments on the audacious Pharaoh who had enslaved your holy people Israel.

[7] And when he pursued them with chariots and a mass of troops, you overwhelmed him in the depths of the sea, but carried through safely those who had put their confidence in you, the Ruler over the whole creation.

[8] And when they had seen works of your hands, they praised you, the Almighty.

[9] You, O King, when you had created the boundless and immeasurable earth, chose this city and sanctified this place for your name, though you have no need of anything; and when you had glorified it by your magnificent manifestation, you made it a firm foundation for the glory of your great and honored name.

[10] And because you love the house of Israel, you promised that if we should have reverses, and tribulation overtake us, you would listen to our petition when we come to this place and pray.

[11] And indeed you are faithful and true.

[12] And because oftentimes when our fathers were oppressed you helped them in their humiliation, and rescued them from great evils,

[13] see now, O holy King, that because of our many and great sins we are crushed with suffering, subjected to our enemies, and overtaken by helplessness.

[14] In our downfall this audacious and profane man undertakes to violate the holy place on earth dedicated to your glorious name.

[15] For your dwelling, the heaven of heavens, is unapproachable by man.

[16] But because you graciously bestowed your glory upon your people Israel, you sanctified this place.

[17] Do not punish us for the defilement committed by these men, or call us to account for this profanation, lest the transgressors boast in their wrath or exult in the arrogance of their tongue, saying,

[18] `We have trampled down the house of the sanctuary as offensive houses are trampled down.'

[19] Wipe away our sins and disperse our errors, and reveal your mercy at this hour.

[20] Speedily let your mercies overtake us, and put praises in the mouth of those who are downcast and broken in spirit, and give us peace."

[21] Thereupon God, who oversees all things, the first Father of all, holy among the holy ones, having heard the lawful supplication, scourged him who had exalted himself in insolence and audacity.

[22] He shook him on this side and that as a reed is shaken by the wind, so that he lay helpless on the ground and, besides being paralyzed in his limbs, was unable even to speak, since he was smitten by a righteous judgment.

[23] Then both friends and bodyguards, seeing the severe punishment that had overtaken him, and fearing lest he should lose his life, quickly dragged him out, panic-stricken in their exceedingly great fear.

[24] After a while he recovered, and though he had been punished, he by no means repented, but went away uttering bitter threats.

[25] When he arrived in Egypt, he increased in his deeds of malice, abetted by the previously mentioned drinking companions and comrades, who were strangers to everything just.

[26] He was not content with his uncounted licentious deeds, but he also continued with such audacity that he framed evil reports in the various localities; and many of his friends, intently observing the king's purpose, themselves also followed his will.

[27] He proposed to inflict public disgrace upon the Jewish community, and he set up a stone on the tower in the courtyard with this inscription:

[28] "None of those who do not sacrifice shall enter their sanctuaries, and all Jews shall be subjected to a registration involving poll tax and to the status of slaves. Those who object to this are to be taken by force and put to death;

[29] those who are registered are also to be branded on their bodies by fire with the ivy-leaf symbol of Dionysus, and they shall also be reduced to their former limited status."

[30] In order that he might not appear to be an enemy to all, he inscribed below: "But if any of them prefer to join those who have been initiated into the mysteries, they shall have equal citizenship with the Alexandrians."

[31] Now some, however, with an obvious abhorrence of the price to be exacted for maintaining the religion of their city, readily gave themselves up, since they expected to enhance their reputation by their future association with the king.

[32] But the majority acted firmly with a courageous spirit and did not depart from their religion; and by paying money in exchange for life they confidently attempted to save themselves from the registration.

[33] They remained resolutely hopeful of obtaining help, and they abhorred those who separated themselves from them, considering them to be enemies of the Jewish nation, and depriving them of common fellowship and mutual help.

3Mac.3

[1] When the impious king comprehended this situation, he became so infuriated that not only was he enraged against those Jews who lived in Alexandria, but was still more bitterly hostile toward those in the countryside; and he ordered that all should promptly be gathered into one place, and put to death by the most cruel means.

[2] While these matters were being arranged, a hostile rumor was circulated against the Jewish nation by men who conspired to do them ill, a pretext being given by a report that they hindered others from the observance of their customs.

[3] The Jews, however, continued to maintain good will and unswerving loyalty toward the dynasty;

[4] but because they worshiped God and conducted themselves by his law, they kept their separateness with respect to foods. For this reason they appeared hateful to some;

[5] but since they adorned their style of life with the good deeds of upright people, they were established in good repute among all men.

[6] Nevertheless those of other races paid no heed to their good service to their nation, which was common talk among all;

[7] instead they gossiped about the differences in worship and foods, alleging that these people were loyal neither to the king nor to his authorities, but were hostile and greatly opposed to his government. So they attached no ordinary reproach to them.

[8] The Greeks in the city, though wronged in no way, when they saw an unexpected tumult around these people and the crowds that suddenly were forming, were not strong enough to help them, for they lived under tyranny. They did try to console them, being grieved at the situation, and expected that matters would change;

[9] for such a great community ought not be left to its fate when it had committed no offense.

[10] And already some of their neighbors and friends and business associates had taken some of them aside privately and were pledging to protect them and to exert more earnest efforts for their assistance.

[11] Then the king, boastful of his present good fortune, and not considering the might of the supreme God, but assuming that he would persevere constantly in his same purpose, wrote this letter against them:

[12] "King Ptolemy Philopator to his generals and soldiers in Egypt and all its districts, greetings and good health.

[13] I myself and our government are faring well.

[14] When our expedition took place in Asia, as you yourselves know, it was brought to conclusion, according to plan, by the gods' deliberate alliance with us in battle,

[15] and we considered that we should not rule the nations inhabiting Coele-Syria and Phoenicia by the power of the spear but should cherish them with clemency and great benevolence, gladly treating them well.

[16] And when we had granted very great revenues to the temples in the cities, we came on to Jerusalem also, and went up to honor the temple of those wicked people, who never cease from their folly.

[17] They accepted our presence by word, but insincerely by deed, because when we proposed to enter their inner temple and honor it with magnificent and most beautiful offerings,

[18] they were carried away by their traditional conceit, and excluded us from entering; but they were spared the exercise of our power because of the benevolence which we have toward all.

[19] By maintaining their manifest ill-will toward us, they become the only people among all nations who hold their heads high in defiance of kings and their own benefactors, and are unwilling to regard any action as sincere.

[20] "But we, when we arrived in Egypt victorious, accommodated ourselves to their folly and did as was proper, since we treat all nations with benevolence.

[21] Among other things, we made known to all our amnesty toward their compatriots here, both because of their alliance with us and the myriad affairs liberally entrusted to them from the beginning; and we ventured to make a change, by deciding both to deem them worthy of Alexandrian citizenship and to make them participants in our regular religious rites.

[22] But in their innate malice they took this in a contrary spirit, and disdained what is good. Since they incline constantly to evil,

[23] they not only spurn the priceless citizenship, but also both by speech and by silence they abominate those few among them who are sincerely disposed toward us; in every situation, in accordance with their infamous way of life, they secretly suspect that we may soon alter our policy.

[24] Therefore, fully convinced by these indications that they are ill-disposed toward us in every way, we have taken precautions lest, if a sudden disorder should later arise against us, we should have these impious people behind our backs as traitors and barbarous enemies.

[25] Therefore we have given orders that, as soon as this letter shall arrive, you are to send to us those who live among you, together with their wives and children, with insulting and harsh treatment, and bound securely with iron fetters, to suffer the sure and shameful death that befits enemies.

[26] For when these all have been punished, we are sure that for the remaining time the government will be established for ourselves in good order and in the best state.

[27] But whoever shelters any of the Jews, old people or children or even infants, will be tortured to death with the most hateful torments, together with his family.

[28] Any one willing to give information will receive the property of the one who incurs the punishment, and also two thousand drachmas from the royal treasury, and will be awarded his freedom.

[29] Every place detected sheltering a Jew is to be made unapproachable and burned with fire, and shall become useless for all time to any mortal creature."

[30] The letter was written in the above form.

3Mac.4

[1] In every place, then, where this decree arrived, a feast at public expense was arranged for the Gentiles with shouts and gladness, for the inveterate enmity which had long ago been in their minds was now made evident and outspoken.

[2] But among the Jews there was incessant mourning, lamentation, and tearful cries; everywhere their hearts were burning, and they groaned because of the unexpected destruction that had suddenly been decreed for them.

[3] What district or city, or what habitable place at all, or what streets were not filled with mourning and wailing for them?

[4] For with such a harsh and ruthless spirit were they being sent off, all together, by the generals in the several cities, that at the sight of their unusual punishments, even some of their enemies, perceiving the common object of pity before their eyes, reflected upon the uncertainty of life and shed tears at the most miserable expulsion of these people.

[5] For a multitude of gray-headed old men, sluggish and bent with age, was being led away, forced to march at a swift pace by the violence with which they were driven in such a shameful manner.

[6] And young women who had just entered the bridal chamber to share married life exchanged joy for wailing, their myrrh-perfumed hair sprinkled with ashes, and were carried away unveiled, all together raising a lament instead of a wedding song, as they were torn by the harsh treatment of the heathen.

[7] In bonds and in public view they were violently dragged along as far as the place of embarkation.

[8] Their husbands, in the prime of youth, their necks encircled with ropes instead of garlands, spent the remaining days of their marriage festival in lamentations instead of good cheer and youthful revelry, seeing death immediately before them.

[9] They were brought on board like wild animals, driven under the constraint of iron bonds; some were fastened by the neck to the benches of the boats, others had their feet secured by unbreakable fetters,

[10] and in addition they were confined under a solid deck, so that with their eyes in total darkness, they should undergo treatment befitting traitors during the whole voyage.

[11] When these men had been brought to the place called Schedia, and the voyage was concluded as the king had decreed, he commanded that they should be enclosed in the hippodrome which had been built with a monstrous perimeter wall in front of the city, and which was well suited to make them an obvious spectacle to all coming back into the city and to those from the city going out into the country, so that they could neither communicate with the king's forces nor in any way claim to be inside the circuit of the city.

[12] And when this had happened, the king, hearing that the Jews' compatriots from the city frequently went out in secret to lament bitterly the ignoble misfortune of their brothers,

[13] ordered in his rage that these men be dealt with in precisely the same fashion as the others, not omitting any detail of their punishment.

[14] The entire race was to be registered individually, not for the hard labor that has been briefly mentioned before, but to be tortured with the outrages that he had ordered, and at the end to be destroyed in the space of a single day.

[15] The registration of these people was therefore conducted with bitter haste and zealous intentness from the rising of the sun till its setting, and though uncompleted it stopped after forty days.

[16] The king was greatly and continually filled with joy, organizing feasts in honor of all his idols, with a mind alienated from truth and with a profane mouth, praising speechless things that are not able even to communicate or to come to one's help, and uttering improper words against the supreme God.

[17] But after the previously mentioned interval of time the scribes declared to the king that they were no longer able to take the census of the Jews because of their innumerable multitude,

[18] although most of them were still in the country, some still residing in their homes, and some at the place; the task was impossible for all the generals in Egypt.

[19] After he had threatened them severely, charging that they had been bribed to contrive a means of escape, he was clearly convinced about the matter

[20] when they said and proved that both the paper and the pens they used for writing had already given out.

[21] But this was an act of the invincible providence of him who was aiding the Jews from heaven.

3Mac.5

[1] Then the king, completely inflexible, was filled with overpowering anger and wrath; so he summoned Hermon, keeper of the elephants,

[2] and ordered him on the following day to drug all the elephants -- five hundred in number -- with large handfuls of frankincense and plenty of unmixed wine, and to drive them in, maddened by the lavish abundance of liquor, so that the Jews might meet their doom.

[3] When he had given these orders he returned to his feasting, together with those of his friends and of the army who were especially hostile toward the Jews.

[4] And Hermon, keeper of the elephants, proceeded faithfully to carry out the orders.

[5] The servants in charge of the Jews went out in the evening and bound the hands of the wretched people and arranged for their continued custody through the night, convinced that the whole nation would experience its final destruction.

[6] For to the Gentiles it appeared that the Jews were left without any aid,

[7] because in their bonds they were forcibly confined on every side. But with tears and a voice hard to silence they all called upon the Almighty Lord and Ruler of all power, their merciful God and Father, praying

[8] that he avert with vengeance the evil plot against them and in a glorious manifestation rescue them from the fate now prepared for them.

[9] So their entreaty ascended fervently to heaven.

[10] Hermon, however, when he had drugged the pitiless elephants until they had been filled with a great abundance of wine and satiated with frankincense, presented himself at the courtyard early in the morning to report to the king about these preparations.

[11] But the Lord sent upon the king a portion of sleep, that beneficence which from the beginning, night and day, is bestowed by him who grants it to whomever he wishes.

[12] And by the action of the Lord he was overcome by so pleasant and deep a sleep that he quite failed in his lawless purpose and was completely frustrated in his inflexible plan.

[13] Then the Jews, since they had escaped the appointed hour, praised their holy God and again begged him who is easily reconciled to show the might of his all-powerful hand to the arrogant Gentiles.

[14] But now, since it was nearly the middle of the tenth hour, the person who was in charge of the invitations, seeing that the guests were assembled, approached the king and nudged him.

[15] And when he had with difficulty roused him, he pointed out that the hour of the banquet was already slipping by, and he gave him an account of the situation.

[16] The king, after considering this, returned to his drinking, and ordered those present for the banquet to recline opposite him.

[17] When this was done he urged them to give themselves over to revelry and to make the present portion of the banquet joyful by celebrating all the more.

[18] After the party had been going on for some time, the king summoned Hermon and with sharp threats demanded to know why the Jews had been allowed to remain alive through the present day.

[19] But when he, with the corroboration of his friends, pointed out that while it was still night he had carried out completely the order given him,

[20] the king, possessed by a savagery worse than that of Phalaris, said that the Jews were benefited by today's sleep, "but," he added, "tomorrow without delay prepare the elephants in the same way for the destruction of the lawless Jews!"

[21] When the king had spoken, all those present readily and joyfully with one accord gave their approval, and each departed to his own home.

[22] But they did not so much employ the duration of the night in sleep as in devising all sorts of insults for those they thought to be doomed.

[23] Then, as soon as the cock had crowed in the early morning, Hermon, having equipped the beasts, began to move them along in the great colonnade.

[24] The crowds of the city had been assembled for this most pitiful spectacle and they were eagerly waiting for daybreak.

[25] But the Jews, at their last gasp, since the time had run out, stretched their hands toward heaven and with most tearful supplication and mournful dirges implored the supreme God to help them again at once.

[26] The rays of the sun were not yet shed abroad, and while the king was receiving his friends, Hermon arrived and invited him to come out, indicating that what the king desired was ready for action.

[27] But he, upon receiving the report and being struck by the unusual invitation to come out -- since he had been completely overcome by incomprehension -- inquired what the matter was for which this had been so zealously completed for him.

[28] This was the act of God who rules over all things, for he had implanted in the king's mind a forgetfulness of the things he had previously devised.

[29] Then Hermon and all the king's friends pointed out that the beasts and the armed forces were ready, "O king, according to your eager purpose."

[30] But at these words he was filled with an overpowering wrath, because by the providence of God his whole mind had been deranged in regard to these matters; and with a threatening look he said,

[31] "Were your parents or children present, I would have prepared them to be a rich feast for the savage beasts instead of the Jews, who give me no ground for complaint and have exhibited to an extraordinary degree a full and firm loyalty to my ancestors.

[32] In fact you would have been deprived of life instead of these, were it not for an affection arising from our nurture in common and your usefulness."

[33] So Hermon suffered an unexpected and dangerous threat, and his eyes wavered and his face fell.

[34] The king's friends one by one sullenly slipped away and dismissed the assembled people, each to his own occupation.

[35] Then the Jews, upon hearing what the king had said, praised the manifest Lord God, King of kings, since this also was his aid which they had received.

[36] The king, however, reconvened the party in the same manner and urged the guests to return to their celebrating.

[37] After summoning Hermon he said in a threatening tone, "How many times, you poor wretch, must I give you orders about these things?

[38] Equip the elephants now once more for the destruction of the Jews tomorrow!"

[39] But the officials who were at table with him, wondering at his instability of mind, remonstrated as follows:

[40] "O king, how long will you try us, as though we are idiots, ordering now for a third time that they be destroyed, and again revoking your decree in the matter?

[41] As a result the city is in a tumult because of its expectation; it is crowded with masses of people, and also in constant danger of being plundered."

[42] Upon this the king, a Phalaris in everything and filled with madness, took no account of the changes of mind which had come about within him for the protection of the Jews, and he firmly swore an irrevocable oath that he would send them to death without delay, mangled by the knees and feet of the beasts,

[43] and would also march against Judea and rapidly level it to the ground with fire and spear, and by burning to the ground the temple inaccessible to him would quickly render it forever empty of those who offered sacrifices there.

[44] Then the friends and officers departed with great joy, and they confidently posted the armed forces at the places in the city most favorable for keeping guard.

[45] Now when the beasts had been brought virtually to a state of madness, so to speak, by the very fragrant draughts of wine mixed with frankincense and had been equipped with frightful devices, the elephant keeper

[46] entered at about dawn into the courtyard -- the city now being filled with countless masses of people crowding their way into the hippodrome -- and urged the king on to the matter at hand.

[47] So he, when he had filled his impious mind with a deep rage, rushed out in full force along with the beasts, wishing to witness, with invulnerable heart and with his own eyes, the grievous and pitiful destruction of the aforementioned people.

[48] And when the Jews saw the dust raised by the elephants going out at the gate and by the following armed forces, as well as by the trampling of the crowd, and heard the loud and tumultuous noise,

[49] they thought that this was their last moment of life, the end of their most miserable suspense, and giving way to lamentation and groans they kissed each other, embracing relatives and falling into one another's arms -- parents and children, mothers and daughters, and others with babies at their breasts who were drawing their last milk.

[50] Not only this, but when they considered the help which they had received before from heaven they prostrated themselves with one accord on the ground, removing the babies from their breasts,

[51] and cried out in a very loud voice, imploring the Ruler over every power to manifest himself and be merciful to them, as they stood now at the gates of death.

3Mac.6

[1] Then a certain Eleazar, famous among the priests of the country, who had attained a ripe old age and throughout his life had been adorned with every virtue, directed the elders around him to cease calling upon the holy God and prayed as follows:

[2] "King of great power, Almighty God Most High, governing all creation with mercy,

[3] look upon the descendants of Abraham, O Father, upon the children of the sainted Jacob, a people of your consecrated portion who are perishing as foreigners in a foreign land.

[4] Pharaoh with his abundance of chariots, the former ruler of this Egypt, exalted with lawless insolence and boastful tongue, you destroyed together with his arrogant army by drowning them in the sea, manifesting the light of your mercy upon the nation of Israel.

[5] Sennacherib exulting in his countless forces, oppressive king of the Assyrians, who had already gained control of the whole world by the spear and was lifted up against your holy city, speaking grievous words with boasting and insolence, you, O Lord, broke in pieces, showing your power to many nations.

[6] The three companions in Babylon who had voluntarily surrendered their lives to the flames so as not to serve vain things, you rescued unharmed, even to a hair, moistening the fiery furnace with dew and turning the flame against all their enemies.

[7] Daniel, who through envious slanders was cast down into the ground to lions as food for wild beasts, you brought up to the light unharmed.

[8] And Jonah, wasting away in the belly of a huge, sea-born monster, you, Father, watched over and restored unharmed to all his family.

[9] And now, you who hate insolence, all-merciful and protector of all, reveal yourself quickly to those of the nation of Israel -- who are being outrageously treated by the abominable and lawless Gentiles.

[10] Even if our lives have become entangled in impieties in our exile, rescue us from the hand of the enemy, and destroy us, Lord, by whatever fate you choose.

[11] Let not the vain-minded praise their vanities at the destruction of your beloved people, saying, `Not even their god has rescued them.'

[12] But you, O Eternal One, who have all might and all power, watch over us now and have mercy upon us who by the senseless insolence of the lawless are being deprived of life in the manner of traitors.

[13] And let the Gentiles cower today in fear of your invincible might, O honored One, who have power to save the nation of Jacob.

[14] The whole throng of infants and their parents entreat you with tears.

[15] Let it be shown to all the Gentiles that you are with us, O Lord, and have not turned your face from us; but just as you have said, `Not even when they were in the land of their enemies did I neglect them,' so accomplish it, O Lord."

[16] Just as Eleazar was ending his prayer, the king arrived at the hippodrome with the beasts and all the arrogance of his forces.

[17] And when the Jews observed this they raised great cries to heaven so that even the nearby valleys resounded with them and brought an uncontrollable terror upon the army.

[18] Then the most glorious, almighty, and true God revealed his holy face and opened the heavenly gates, from which two glorious angels of fearful aspect descended, visible to all but the Jews.

[19] They opposed the forces of the enemy and filled them with confusion and terror, binding them with immovable shackles.

[20] Even the king began to shudder bodily, and he forgot his sullen insolence.

[21] The beasts turned back upon the armed forces following them and began trampling and destroying them.

[22] Then the king's anger was turned to pity and tears because of the things that he had devised beforehand.

[23] For when he heard the shouting and saw them all fallen headlong to destruction, he wept and angrily threatened his friends, saying,

[24] "You are committing treason and surpassing tyrants in cruelty; and even me, your benefactor, you are now attempting to deprive of dominion and life by secretly devising acts of no advantage to the kingdom.

[25] Who is it that has taken each man from his home and senselessly gathered here those who faithfully have held the fortresses of our country?

[26] Who is it that has so lawlessly encompassed with outrageous treatment those who from the beginning differed from all nations in their goodwill toward us and often have accepted willingly the worst of human dangers?

[27] Loose and untie their unjust bonds! Send them back to their homes in peace, begging pardon for your former actions!

[28] Release the sons of the almighty and living God of heaven, who from the time of our ancestors until now has granted an unimpeded and notable stability to our government."

[29] These then were the things he said; and the Jews, immediately released, praised their holy God and Savior, since they now had escaped death.

[30] Then the king, when he had returned to the city, summoned the official in charge of the revenues and ordered him to provide to the Jews both wines and everything else needed for a festival of seven days, deciding that they should celebrate their rescue with all joyfulness in that same place in which they had expected to meet their destruction.

[31] Accordingly those disgracefully treated and near to death, or rather, who stood at its gates, arranged for a banquet of deliverance instead of a bitter and lamentable death, and full of joy they apportioned to celebrants the place which had been prepared for their destruction and burial.

[32] They ceased their chanting of dirges and took up the song of their fathers, praising God, their Savior and worker of wonders. Putting an end to all mourning and wailing, they formed choruses as a sign of peaceful joy.

[33] Likewise also the king, after convening a great banquet to celebrate these events, gave thanks to heaven unceasingly and lavishly for the unexpected rescue which he had experienced.

[34] And those who had previously believed that the Jews would be destroyed and become food for birds, and had joyfully registered them, groaned as they themselves were overcome by disgrace, and their fire-breathing boldness was ignominiously quenched.

[35] But the Jews, when they had arranged the aforementioned choral group, as we have said before, passed the time in feasting to the accompaniment of joyous thanksgiving and psalms.

[36] And when they had ordained a public rite for these things in their whole community and for their descendants, they instituted the observance of the aforesaid days as a festival, not for drinking and gluttony, but because of the deliverance that had come to them through God.

[37] Then they petitioned the king, asking for dismissal to their homes.

[38] So their registration was carried out from the twenty-fifth of Pachon to the fourth of Epeiph, for forty days; and their destruction was set for the fifth to the seventh of Epeiph, the three days

[39] on which the Lord of all most gloriously revealed his mercy and rescued them all together and unharmed.

[40] Then they feasted, provided with everything by the king, until the fourteenth day, on which also they made the petition for their dismissal.

[41] The king granted their request at once and wrote the following letter for them to the generals in the cities, magnanimously expressing his concern:

3Mac.7

[1] "King Ptolemy Philopator to the generals in Egypt and all in authority in his government, greetings and good health.

[2] We ourselves and our children are faring well, the great God guiding our affairs according to our desire.

[3] Certain of our friends, frequently urging us with malicious intent, persuaded us to gather together the Jews of the kingdom in a body and to punish them with barbarous penalties as traitors;

[4] for they declared that our government would never be firmly established until this was accomplished, because of the ill-will which these people had toward all nations.

[5] They also led them out with harsh treatment as slaves, or rather as traitors, and, girding themselves

with a cruelty more savage than that of Scythian custom, they tried without any inquiry or examination to put them to death.

[6] But we very severely threatened them for these acts, and in accordance with the clemency which we have toward all men we barely spared their lives. Since we have come to realize that the God of heaven surely defends the Jews, always taking their part as a father does for his children,

[7] and since we have taken into account the friendly and firm goodwill which they had toward us and our ancestors, we justly have acquitted them of every charge of whatever kind.

[8] We also have ordered each and every one to return to his own home, with no one in any place doing them harm at all or reproaching them for the irrational things that have happened.

[9] For you should know that if we devise any evil against them or cause them any grief at all, we always shall have not man but the Ruler over every power, the Most High God, in everything and inescapably as an antagonist to avenge such acts. Farewell."

[10] Upon receiving this letter the Jews did not immediately hurry to make their departure, but they requested of the king that at their own hands those of the Jewish nation who had willfully transgressed against the holy God and the law of God should receive the punishment they deserved.

[11] For they declared that those who for the belly's sake had transgressed the divine commandments would never be favorably disposed toward the king's government.

[12] The king then, admitting and approving the truth of what they said, granted them a general license so that freely and without royal authority or supervision they might destroy those everywhere in his kingdom who had transgressed the law of God.

[13] When they had applauded him in fitting manner, their priests and the whole multitude shouted the Hallelujah and joyfully departed.

[14] And so on their way they punished and put to a public and shameful death any whom they met of their fellow-countrymen who had become defiled.

[15] In that day they put to death more than three hundred men; and they kept the day as a joyful festival, since they had destroyed the profaners.

[16] But those who had held fast to God even to death and had received the full enjoyment of deliverance began their departure from the city, crowned with all sorts of very fragrant flowers, joyfully and loudly giving thanks to the one God of their fathers, the eternal Savior of Israel, in words of praise and all kinds of melodious songs.

[17] When they had arrived at Ptolemais, called "rose-bearing" because of a characteristic of the place, the fleet waited for them, in accord with the common desire, for seven days.

[18] There they celebrated their deliverance, for the king had generously provided all things to them for their journey, to each as far as his own house.

[19] And when they had landed in peace with appropriate thanksgiving, there too in like manner they decided to observe these days as a joyous festival during the time of their stay.

[20] Then, after inscribing them as holy on a pillar and dedicating a place of prayer at the site of the festival, they departed unharmed, free, and overjoyed, since at the king's command they had been brought safely by land and sea and river each to his own place.

[21] They also possessed greater prestige among their enemies, being held in honor and awe; and they were not subject at all to confiscation of their belongings by any one.

[22] Besides they all recovered all of their property, in accordance with the registration, so that those who held any restored it to them with extreme fear. So the supreme God perfectly performed great deeds for their deliverance.

[23] Blessed be the Deliverer of Israel through all times! Amen.

4 Maccabees

4Mac.1

[1] The subject that I am about to discuss is most philosophical, that is, whether devout reason is sovereign over the emotions. So it is right for me to advise you to pay earnest attention to philosophy.

[2] For the subject is essential to everyone who is seeking knowledge, and in addition it includes the praise of the highest virtue -- I mean, of course, rational judgment.

[3] If, then, it is evident that reason rules over those emotions that hinder self-control, namely, gluttony and lust,

[4] it is also clear that it masters the emotions that hinder one from justice, such as malice, and those that stand in the way of courage, namely anger, fear, and pain.

[5] Some might perhaps ask, "If reason rules the emotions, why is it not sovereign over forgetfulness and ignorance?" Their attempt at argument is ridiculous!

[6] For reason does not rule its own emotions, but those that are opposed to justice, courage, and self-control; and it is not for the purpose of destroying them, but so that one may not give way to them.

[7] I could prove to you from many and various examples that reason is dominant over the emotions,

[8] but I can demonstrate it best from the noble bravery of those who died for the sake of virtue, Eleazar and the seven brothers and their mother.

[9] All of these, by despising sufferings that bring death, demonstrated that reason controls the emotions.

[10] On this anniversary it is fitting for me to praise for their virtues those who, with their mother, died for the sake of nobility and goodness, but I would also call them blessed for the honor in which they are held.

[11] For all people, even their torturers, marveled at their courage and endurance, and they became the cause of the downfall of tyranny over their nation. By their endurance they conquered the tyrant, and thus their native land was purified through them.

[12] I shall shortly have an opportunity to speak of this; but, as my custom is, I shall begin by stating my main principle, and then I shall turn to their story, giving glory to the all-wise God.

[13] Our inquiry, accordingly, is whether reason is sovereign over the emotions.

[14] We shall decide just what reason is and what emotion is, how many kinds of emotions there are, and whether reason rules over all these.

[15] Now reason is the mind that with sound logic prefers the life of wisdom.

[16] Wisdom, next, is the knowledge of divine and human matters and the causes of these.

[17] This, in turn, is education in the law, by which we learn divine matters reverently and human affairs to our advantage.

[18] Now the kinds of wisdom are rational judgment, justice, courage, and self-control.

[19] Rational judgment is supreme over all of these, since by means of it reason rules over the emotions.

[20] The two most comprehensive types of the emotions are pleasure and pain; and each of these is by nature concerned with both body and soul.

[21] The emotions of both pleasure and pain have many consequences.

[22] Thus desire precedes pleasure and delight follows it.

[23] Fear precedes pain and sorrow comes after.

[24] Anger, as a man will see if he reflects on this experience, is an emotion embracing pleasure and pain.

[25] In pleasure there exists even a malevolent tendency, which is the most complex of all the emotions.

[26] In the soul it is boastfulness, covetousness, thirst for honor, rivalry, and malice;

[27] in the body, indiscriminate eating, gluttony, and solitary gormandizing.

[28] Just as pleasure and pain are two plants growing from the body and the soul, so there are many offshoots of these plants,

[29] each of which the master cultivator, reason, weeds and prunes and ties up and waters and thoroughly irrigates, and so tames the jungle of habits and emotions.

[30] For reason is the guide of the virtues, but over the emotions it is sovereign. Observe now first of all that rational judgment is sovereign over the emotions by virtue of the restraining power of self-control.

[31] Self-control, then, is dominance over the desires.

[32] Some desires are mental, others are physical, and reason obviously rules over both.

[33] Otherwise how is it that when we are attracted to forbidden foods we abstain from the pleasure to be had from them? Is it not because reason is able to rule over appetites? I for one think so.

[34] Therefore when we crave seafood and fowl and animals and all sorts of foods that are forbidden to us by the law, we abstain because of domination by reason.

[35] For the emotions of the appetites are restrained, checked by the temperate mind, and all the impulses of the body are bridled by reason.

4Mac.2

[1] And why is it amazing that the desires of the mind for the enjoyment of beauty are rendered powerless?

[2] It is for this reason, certainly, that the temperate Joseph is praised, because by mental effort he overcame sexual desire.

[3] For when he was young and in his prime for intercourse, by his reason he nullified the frenzy of the passions.

[4] Not only is reason proved to rule over the frenzied urge of sexual desire, but also over every desire.

[5] Thus the law says, "You shall not covet your neighbor's wife...or anything that is your neighbor's."

[6] In fact, since the law has told us not to covet, I could prove to you all the more that reason is able to control desires. Just so it is with the emotions that hinder one from justice.

[7] Otherwise how could it be that someone who is habitually a solitary gormandizer, a glutton, or even a drunkard can learn a better way, unless reason is clearly lord of the emotions?

[8] Thus, as soon as a man adopts a way of life in accordance with the law, even though he is a lover of money, he is forced to act contrary to his natural ways and to lend without interest to the needy and to cancel the debt when the seventh year arrives.

[9] If one is greedy, he is ruled by the law through his reason so that he neither gleans his harvest nor gathers the last grapes from the vineyard. In all other matters we can recognize that reason rules the emotions.

[10] For the law prevails even over affection for parents, so that virtue is not abandoned for their sakes.

[11] It is superior to love for one's wife, so that one rebukes her when she breaks the law.

[12] It takes precedence over love for children, so that one punishes them for misdeeds.

[13] It is sovereign over the relationship of friends, so that one rebukes friends when they act wickedly.

[14] Do not consider it paradoxical when reason, through the law, can prevail even over enmity. The fruit trees of the enemy are not cut down, but one preserves the property of enemies from the destroyers and helps raise up what has fallen.

[15] It is evident that reason rules even the more violent emotions: lust for power, vainglory, boasting, arrogance, and malice.

[16] For the temperate mind repels all these malicious emotions, just as it repels anger -- for it is sovereign over even this.

[17] When Moses was angry with Dathan and Abiram he did nothing against them in anger, but controlled his anger by reason.

[18] For, as I have said, the temperate mind is able to get the better of the emotions, to correct some, and to render others powerless.

[19] Why else did Jacob, our most wise father, censure the households of Simeon and Levi for their irrational slaughter of the entire tribe of the Shechemites, saying, "Cursed be their anger"?

[20] For if reason could not control anger, he would not have spoken thus.

[21] Now when God fashioned man, he planted in him emotions and inclinations,

[22] but at the same time he enthroned the mind among the senses as a sacred governor over them all.

[23] To the mind he gave the law; and one who lives subject to this will rule a kingdom that is temperate, just, good, and courageous.

[24] How is it then, one might say, that if reason is master of the emotions, it does not control forgetfulness and ignorance?

4Mac.3

[1] This notion is entirely ridiculous; for it is evident that reason rules not over its own emotions, but over those of the body.

[2] No one of us can eradicate that kind of desire, but reason can provide a way for us not to be enslaved by desire.

[3] No one of us can eradicate anger from the mind, but reason can help to deal with anger.

[4] No one of us can eradicate malice, but reason can fight at our side so that we are not overcome by malice.

[5] For reason does not uproot the emotions but is their antagonist.

[6] Now this can be explained more clearly by the story of King David's thirst.

[7] David had been attacking the Philistines all day long, and together with the soldiers of his nation had

581

slain many of them.

[8] Then when evening fell, he came, sweating and quite exhausted, to the royal tent, around which the whole army of our ancestors had encamped.

[9] Now all the rest were at supper,

[10] but the king was extremely thirsty, and although springs were plentiful there, he could not satisfy his thirst from them.

[11] But a certain irrational desire for the water in the enemy's territory tormented and inflamed him, undid and consumed him.

[12] When his guards complained bitterly because of the king's craving, two staunch young soldiers, respecting the king's desire, armed themselves fully, and taking a pitcher climbed over the enemy's ramparts.

[13] Eluding the sentinels at the gates, they went searching throughout the enemy camp

[14] and found the spring, and from it boldly brought the king a drink.

[15] But David, although he was burning with thirst, considered it an altogether fearful danger to his soul to drink what was regarded as equivalent to blood.

[16] Therefore, opposing reason to desire, he poured out the drink as an offering to God.

[17] For the temperate mind can conquer the drives of the emotions and quench the flames of frenzied desires;

[18] it can overthrow bodily agonies even when they are extreme, and by nobility of reason spurn all domination by the emotions.

[19] The present occasion now invites us to a narrative demonstration of temperate reason.

[20] At a time when our fathers were enjoying profound peace because of their observance of the law and were prospering, so that even Seleucus Nicanor, king of Asia, had both appropriated money to them for the temple service and recognized their commonwealth --

[21] just at that time certain men attempted a revolution against the public harmony and caused many and various disasters.

4Mac.4

[1] Now there was a certain Simon, a political opponent of the noble and good man, Onias, who then held the high priesthood for life. When despite all manner of slander he was unable to injure Onias in the eyes of the nation, he fled the country with the purpose of betraying it.

[2] So he came to Apollonius, governor of Syria, Phoenicia, and Cilicia, and said,

[3] "I have come here because I am loyal to the king's government, to report that in the Jerusalem treasuries there are deposited tens of thousands in private funds, which are not the property of the temple but belong to King Seleucus."

[4] When Apollonius learned the details of these things, he praised Simon for his service to the king and went up to Seleucus to inform him of the rich treasure.

[5] On receiving authority to deal with this matter, he proceeded quickly to our country accompanied by the accursed Simon and a very strong military force.

[6] He said that he had come with the king's authority to seize the private funds in the treasury.

[7] The people indignantly protested his words, considering it outrageous that those who had committed deposits to the sacred treasury should be deprived of them, and did all that they could to prevent it.

[8] But, uttering threats, Apollonius went on to the temple.

[9] While the priests together with women and children were imploring God in the temple to shield the holy place that was being treated so contemptuously,

[10] and while Apollonius was going up with his armed forces to seize the money, angels on horseback with lightning flashing from their weapons appeared from heaven, instilling in them great fear and trembling.

[11] Then Apollonius fell down half dead in the temple area that was open to all, stretched out his hands toward heaven, and with tears besought the Hebrews to pray for him and propitiate the wrath of the heavenly army.

[12] For he said that he had committed a sin deserving of death, and that if he were delivered he would praise the blessedness of the holy place before all people.

[13] Moved by these words, Onias the high priest, although otherwise he had scruples about doing so, prayed for him lest King Seleucus suppose that Apollonius had been overcome by human treachery and not by divine justice.

[14] So Apollonius, having been preserved beyond all expectations, went away to report to the king what had happened to him.

[15] When King Seleucus died, his son Antiochus Epiphanes succeeded to the throne, an arrogant and terrible man,

[16] who removed Onias from the priesthood and appointed Onias's brother Jason as high priest.

[17] Jason agreed that if the office were conferred upon him he would pay the king three thousand six hundred and sixty talents annually.

[18] So the king appointed him high priest and ruler of the nation.

[19] Jason changed the nation's way of life and altered its form of government in complete violation of the law,

[20] so that not only was a gymnasium constructed at the very citadel of our native land, but also the temple service was abolished.

[21] The divine justice was angered by these acts and caused Antiochus himself to make war on them.

[22] For when he was warring against Ptolemy in Egypt, he heard that a rumor of his death had spread and that the people of Jerusalem had rejoiced greatly. He speedily marched against them,

[23] and after he had plundered them he issued a decree that if any of them should be found observing the ancestral law they should die.

[24] When, by means of his decrees, he had not been able in any way to put an end to the people's observance of the law, but saw that all his threats and punishments were being disregarded,

[25] even to the point that women, because they had circumcised their sons, were thrown headlong from heights along with their infants, though they had known beforehand that they would suffer this --

[26] when, then, his decrees were despised by the people, he himself, through torture, tried to compel everyone in the nation to eat defiling foods and to renounce Judaism.

4Mac.5

[1] The tyrant Antiochus, sitting in state with his counselors on a certain high place, and with his armed soldiers standing about him,

[2] ordered the guards to seize each and every Hebrew and to compel them to eat pork and food sacrificed to idols.

[3] If any were not willing to eat defiling food, they were to be broken on the wheel and killed.

[4] And when many persons had been rounded up, one man, Eleazar by name, leader of the flock, was brought before the king. He was a man of priestly family, learned in the law, advanced in age, and known to many in the tyrant's court because of his philosophy.

[5] When Antiochus saw him he said,

[6] "Before I begin to torture you, old man, I would advise you to save yourself by eating pork,

[7] for I respect your age and your gray hairs. Although you have had them for so long a time, it does not seem to me that you are a philosopher when you observe the religion of the Jews.

[8] Why, when nature has granted it to us, should you abhor eating the very excellent meat of this animal?

[9] It is senseless not to enjoy delicious things that are not shameful, and wrong to spurn the gifts of nature.

[10] It seems to me that you will do something even more senseless if, by holding a vain opinion concerning the truth, you continue to despise me to your own hurt.

[11] Will you not awaken from your foolish philosophy, dispel your futile reasonings, adopt a mind appropriate to your years, philosophize according to the truth of what is beneficial,

[12] and have compassion on your old age by honoring my humane advice?

[13] For consider this, that if there is some power watching over this religion of yours, it will excuse you from any transgression that arises out of compulsion."

[14] When the tyrant urged him in this fashion to eat meat unlawfully, Eleazar asked to have a word.

[15] When he had received permission to speak, he began to address the people as follows:

[16] "We, O Antiochus, who have been persuaded to govern our lives by the divine law, think that there is no compulsion more powerful than our obedience to the law.

[17] Therefore we consider that we should not transgress it in any respect.

[18] Even if, as you suppose, our law were not truly divine and we had wrongly held it to be divine, not even so would it be right for us to invalidate our reputation for piety.

[19] Therefore do not suppose that it would be a petty sin if we were to eat defiling food;

[20] to transgress the law in matters either small or great is of equal seriousness,

[21] for in either case the law is equally despised.

[22] You scoff at our philosophy as though living by it were irrational,

[23] but it teaches us self-control, so that we master all pleasures and desires, and it also trains us in courage, so that we endure any suffering willingly;

[24] it instructs us in justice, so that in all our dealings we act impartially, and it teaches us piety, so that with proper reverence we worship the only real God.

[25] "Therefore we do not eat defiling food; for since we believe that the law was established by God, we know that in the nature of things the Creator of the world in giving us the law has shown sympathy toward us.

[26] He has permitted us to eat what will be most suitable for our lives, but he has forbidden us to eat

meats that would be contrary to this.

[27] It would be tyrannical for you to compel us not only to transgress the law, but also to eat in such a way that you may deride us for eating defiling foods, which are most hateful to us.

[28] But you shall have no such occasion to laugh at me,

[29] nor will I transgress the sacred oaths of my ancestors concerning the keeping of the law,

[30] not even if you gouge out my eyes and burn my entrails.

[31] I am not so old and cowardly as not to be young in reason on behalf of piety.

[32] Therefore get your torture wheels ready and fan the fire more vehemently!

[33] I do not so pity my old age as to break the ancestral law by my own act.

[34] I will not play false to you, O law that trained me, nor will I renounce you, beloved self-control.

[35] I will not put you to shame, philosophical reason, nor will I reject you, honored priesthood and knowledge of the law.

[36] You, O king, shall not stain the honorable mouth of my old age, nor my long life lived lawfully.

[37] The fathers will receive me as pure, as one who does not fear your violence even to death.

[38] You may tyrannize the ungodly, but you shall not dominate my religious principles either by word or by deed."

4Mac.6

[1] When Eleazar in this manner had made eloquent response to the exhortations of the tyrant, the guards who were standing by dragged him violently to the instruments of torture.

[2] First they stripped the old man, who remained adorned with the gracefulness of his piety.

[3] And after they had tied his arms on each side they scourged him,

[4] while a herald opposite him cried out, "Obey the king's commands!"

[5] But the courageous and noble man, as a true Eleazar, was unmoved, as though being tortured in a dream;

[6] yet while the old man's eyes were raised to heaven, his flesh was being torn by scourges, his blood flowing, and his sides were being cut to pieces.

[7] And though he fell to the ground because his body could not endure the agonies, he kept his reason upright and unswerving.

[8] One of the cruel guards rushed at him and began to kick him in the side to make him get up again after he fell.

[9] But he bore the pains and scorned the punishment and endured the tortures.

[10] And like a noble athlete the old man, while being beaten, was victorious over his torturers;

[11] in fact, with his face bathed in sweat, and gasping heavily for breath, he amazed even his torturers by his courageous spirit.

[12] At that point, partly out of pity for his old age,

[13] partly out of sympathy from their acquaintance with him, partly out of admiration for his endurance, some of the king's retinue came to him and said,

[14] "Eleazar, why are you so irrationally destroying yourself through these evil things?

[15] We will set before you some cooked meat; save yourself by pretending to eat pork."

[16] But Eleazar, as though more bitterly tormented by this counsel, cried out:

[17] "May we, the children of Abraham, never think so basely that out of cowardice we feign a role unbecoming to us!

[18] For it would be irrational if we, who have lived in accordance with truth to old age and have maintained in accordance with law the reputation of such a life, should now change our course

[19] become a pattern of impiety to the young, in becoming an example of the eating of defiling food.

[20] It would be shameful if we should survive for a little while and during that time be a laughing stock to all for our cowardice,

[21] and if we should be despised by the tyrant as unmanly, and not protect our divine law even to death.

[22] Therefore, O children of Abraham, die nobly for your religion!

[23] And you, guards of the tyrant, why do you delay?"

[24] When they saw that he was so courageous in the face of the afflictions, and that he had not been changed by their compassion, the guards brought him to the fire.

[25] There they burned him with maliciously contrived instruments, threw him down, and poured stinking liquids into his nostrils.

[26] When he was now burned to his very bones and about to expire, he lifted up his eyes to God and said,

[27] "You know, O God, that though I might have saved myself, I am dying in burning torments for the sake of the law.

[28] Be merciful to your people, and let our punishment suffice for them.

[29] Make my blood their purification, and take my life in exchange for theirs."

[30] And after he said this, the holy man died nobly in his tortures, and by reason he resisted even to the very tortures of death for the sake of the law.

[31] Admittedly, then, devout reason is sovereign over the emotions.

[32] For if the emotions had prevailed over reason, we would have testified to their domination.

[33] But now that reason has conquered the emotions, we properly attribute to it the power to govern.

[34] And it is right for us to acknowledge the dominance of reason when it masters even external agonies. It would be ridiculous to deny it.

[35] And I have proved not only that reason has mastered agonies, but also that it masters pleasures and in no respect yields to them.

4Mac.7

[1] For like a most skilful pilot, the reason of our father Eleazar steered the ship of religion over the sea of the emotions,

[2] and though buffeted by the stormings of the tyrant and overwhelmed by the mighty waves of tortures,

[3] in no way did he turn the rudder of religion until he sailed into the haven of immortal victory.

[4] No city besieged with many ingenious war machines has ever held out as did that most holy man. Although his sacred life was consumed by tortures and racks, he conquered the besiegers with the shield of his devout reason.

[5] For in setting his mind firm like a jutting cliff, our father Eleazar broke the maddening waves of the emotions.

[6] O priest, worthy of the priesthood, you neither defiled your sacred teeth nor profaned your stomach, which had room only for reverence and purity, by eating defiling foods.

[7] O man in harmony with the law and philosopher of divine life!

[8] Such should be those who are administrators of the law, shielding it with their own blood and noble sweat in sufferings even to death.

[9] You, father, strengthened our loyalty to the law through your glorious endurance, and you did not abandon the holiness which you praised, but by your deeds you made your words of divine philosophy credible.

[10] O aged man, more powerful than tortures; O elder, fiercer than fire; O supreme king over the passions, Eleazar!

[11] For just as our father Aaron, armed with the censer, ran through the multitude of the people and conquered the fiery angel,

[12] so the descendant of Aaron, Eleazar, though being consumed by the fire, remained unmoved in his reason.

[13] Most amazing, indeed, though he was an old man, his body no longer tense and firm, his muscles flabby, his sinews feeble, he became young again

[14] in spirit through reason; and by reason like that of Isaac he rendered the many-headed rack ineffective.

[15] O man of blessed age and of venerable gray hair and of law-abiding life, whom the faithful seal of death has perfected!

[16] If, therefore, because of piety an aged man despised tortures even to death, most certainly devout reason is governor of the emotions.

[17] Some perhaps might say, "Not every one has full command of his emotions, because not every one has prudent reason."

[18] But as many as attend to religion with a whole heart, these alone are able to control the passions of the flesh,

[19] since they believe that they, like our patriarchs Abraham and Isaac and Jacob, do not die to God, but live in God.

[20] No contradiction therefore arises when some persons appear to be dominated by their emotions because of the weakness of their reason.

[21] What person who lives as a philosopher by the whole rule of philosophy, and trusts in God,

[22] and knows that it is blessed to endure any suffering for the sake of virtue, would not be able to overcome the emotions through godliness?

[23] For only the wise and courageous man is lord of his emotions.

4Mac.8

[1] For this is why even the very young, by following a philosophy in accordance with devout reason, have prevailed over the most painful instruments of torture.

[2] For when the tyrant was conspicuously defeated in his first attempt, being unable to compel an aged man to eat defiling foods, then in violent rage he commanded that others of the Hebrew captives be brought, and that any who ate defiling food should be freed after eating, but if any were to refuse, these should be tortured even more cruelly.

[3] When the tyrant had given these orders, seven brothers -- handsome, modest, noble, and accomplished in every way -- were brought before him along with their aged mother.

[4] When the tyrant saw them, grouped about their mother as if in a chorus, he was pleased with them. And struck by their appearance and nobility, he smiled at them, and summoned them nearer and said,

[5] "Young men, I admire each and every one of you in a kindly manner, and greatly respect the beauty and the number of such brothers. Not only do I advise you not to display the same madness as that of the old man who has just been tortured, but I also exhort you to yield to me and enjoy my friendship.

[6] Just as I am able to punish those who disobey my orders, so I can be a benefactor to those who obey me.

[7] Trust me, then, and you will have positions of authority in my government if you will renounce the ancestral tradition of your national life.

[8] And enjoy your youth by adopting the Greek way of life and by changing your manner of living.

[9] But if by disobedience you rouse my anger, you will compel me to destroy each and every one of you with dreadful punishments through tortures.

[10] Therefore take pity on yourselves. Even I, your enemy, have compassion for your youth and handsome appearance.

[11] Will you not consider this, that if you disobey, nothing remains for you but to die on the rack?"

[12] When he had said these things, he ordered the instruments of torture to be brought forward so as to persuade them out of fear to eat the defiling food.

[13] And when the guards had placed before them wheels and joint-dislocators, rack and hooks and catapults and caldrons, braziers and thumbscrews and iron claws and wedges and bellows, the tyrant resumed speaking:

[14] "Be afraid, young fellows, and whatever justice you revere will be merciful to you when you transgress under compulsion."

[15] But when they had heard the inducements and saw the dreadful devices, not only were they not afraid, but they also opposed the tyrant with their own philosophy, and by their right reasoning nullified his tyranny.

[16] Let us consider, on the other hand, what arguments might have been used if some of them had been cowardly and unmanly. Would they not have been these?

[17] "O wretches that we are and so senseless! Since the king has summoned and exhorted us to accept kind treatment if we obey him,

[18] why do we take pleasure in vain resolves and venture upon a disobedience that brings death?

[19] O men and brothers, should we not fear the instruments of torture and consider the threats of torments, and give up this vain opinion and this arrogance that threatens to destroy us?

[20] Let us take pity on our youth and have compassion on our mother's age;

[21] and let us seriously consider that if we disobey we are dead!

[22] Also, divine justice will excuse us for fearing the king when we are under compulsion.

[23] Why do we banish ourselves from this most pleasant life and deprive ourselves of this delightful world?

[24] Let us not struggle against compulsion nor take hollow pride in being put to the rack.

[25] Not even the law itself would arbitrarily slay us for fearing the instruments of torture.

[26] Why does such contentiousness excite us and such a fatal stubbornness please us, when we can live in peace if we obey the king?"

[27] But the youths, though about to be tortured, neither said any of these things nor even seriously considered them.

[28] For they were contemptuous of the emotions and sovereign over agonies,

[29] so that as soon as the tyrant had ceased counseling them to eat defiling food, all with one voice together, as from one mind, said:

4Mac.9

[1] "Why do you delay, O tyrant? For we are ready to die rather than transgress our ancestral commandments;

[2] we are obviously putting our forefathers to shame unless we should practice ready obedience to the law and to Moses our counselor.

[3] Tyrant and counselor of lawlessness, in your hatred for us do not pity us more than we pity ourselves.

[4] For we consider this pity of yours which insures our safety through transgression of the law to be more grievous than death itself.

[5] You are trying to terrify us by threatening us with death by torture, as though a short time ago you learned nothing from Eleazar.

[6] And if the aged men of the Hebrews because of their religion lived piously while enduring torture, it would be even more fitting that we young men should die despising your coercive tortures, which our

aged instructor also overcame.

[7] Therefore, tyrant, put us to the test; and if you take our lives because of our religion, do not suppose that you can injure us by torturing us.

[8] For we, through this severe suffering and endurance, shall have the prize of virtue and shall be with God, for whom we suffer;

[9] but you, because of your bloodthirstiness toward us, will deservedly undergo from the divine justice eternal torment by fire."

[10] When they had said these things the tyrant not only was angry, as at those who are disobedient, but also was enraged, as at those who are ungrateful.

[11] Then at his command the guards brought forward the eldest, and having torn off his tunic, they bound his hands and arms with thongs on each side.

[12] When they had worn themselves out beating him with scourges, without accomplishing anything, they placed him upon the wheel.

[13] When the noble youth was stretched out around this, his limbs were dislocated,

[14] and though broken in every member he denounced the tyrant, saying,

[15] "Most abominable tyrant, enemy of heavenly justice, savage of mind, you are mangling me in this manner, not because I am a murderer, or as one who acts impiously, but because I protect the divine law."

[16] And when the guards said, "Agree to eat so that you may be released from the tortures,"

[17] he replied, "You abominable lackeys, your wheel is not so powerful as to strangle my reason. Cut my limbs, burn my flesh, and twist my joints.

[18] Through all these tortures I will convince you that sons of the Hebrews alone are invincible where virtue is concerned."

[19] While he was saying these things, they spread fire under him, and while fanning the flames they tightened the wheel further.

[20] The wheel was completely smeared with blood, and the heap of coals was being quenched by the drippings of gore, and pieces of flesh were falling off the axles of the machine.

[21] Although the ligaments joining his bones were already severed, the courageous youth, worthy of Abraham, did not groan,

[22] but as though transformed by fire into immortality he nobly endured the rackings.

[23] "Imitate me, brothers," he said. "Do not leave your post in my struggle or renounce our courageous brotherhood.

[24] Fight the sacred and noble battle for religion. Thereby the just Providence of our ancestors may become merciful to our nation and take vengeance on the accursed tyrant."

[25] When he had said this, the saintly youth broke the thread of life.

[26] While all were marveling at his courageous spirit, the guards brought in the next eldest, and after fitting themselves with iron gauntlets having sharp hooks, they bound him to the torture machine and catapult.

[27] Before torturing him, they inquired if he were willing to eat, and they heard this noble decision.

[28] These leopard-like beasts tore out his sinews with the iron hands, flayed all his flesh up to his chin, and tore away his scalp. But he steadfastly endured this agony and said,

[29] "How sweet is any kind of death for the religion of our fathers!"

[30] To the tyrant he said, "Do you not think, you most savage tyrant, that you are being tortured more than I, as you see the arrogant design of your tyranny being defeated by our endurance for the sake of religion?

[31] I lighten my pain by the joys that come from virtue,

[32] but you suffer torture by the threats that come from impiety. You will not escape, most abominable tyrant, the judgments of the divine wrath."

4Mac.10

[1] When he too had endured a glorious death, the third was led in, and many repeatedly urged him to save himself by tasting the meat.

[2] But he shouted, "Do you not know that the same father begot me and those who died, and the same mother bore me, and that I was brought up on the same teachings?

[3] I do not renounce the noble kinship that binds me to my brothers."

[4]

[5] Enraged by the man's boldness, they disjointed his hands and feet with their instruments, dismembering him by prying his limbs from their sockets,

[6] and breaking his fingers and arms and legs and elbows.

[7] Since they were not able in any way to break his spirit, they abandoned the instruments and scalped him with their fingernails in a Scythian fashion.

[8] They immediately brought him to the wheel, and while his vertebrae were being dislocated upon it

he saw his own flesh torn all around and drops of blood flowing from his entrails.

[9] When he was about to die, he said,

[10] "We, most abominable tyrant, are suffering because of our godly training and virtue,

[11] but you, because of your impiety and bloodthirstiness, will undergo unceasing torments."

[12] When he also had died in a manner worthy of his brothers, they dragged in the fourth, saying,

[13] "As for you, do not give way to the same insanity as your brothers, but obey the king and save yourself."

[14] But he said to them, "You do not have a fire hot enough to make me play the coward.

[15] No, by the blessed death of my brothers, by the eternal destruction of the tyrant, and by the everlasting life of the pious, I will not renounce our noble brotherhood.

[16] Contrive tortures, tyrant, so that you may learn from them that I am a brother to those who have just been tortured."

[17] When he heard this, the bloodthirsty, murderous, and utterly abominable Antiochus gave orders to cut out his tongue.

[18] But he said, "Even if you remove my organ of speech, God hears also those who are mute.

[19] See, here is my tongue; cut it off, for in spite of this you will not make our reason speechless.

[20] Gladly, for the sake of God, we let our bodily members be mutilated.

[21] God will visit you swiftly, for you are cutting out a tongue that has been melodious with divine hymns."

4Mac.11

[1] When this one died also, after being cruelly tortured, the fifth leaped up, saying,

[2] "I will not refuse, tyrant, to be tortured for the sake of virtue.

[3] I have come of my own accord, so that by murdering me you will incur punishment from the heavenly justice for even more crimes.

[4] Hater of virtue, hater of mankind, for what act of ours are you destroying us in this way?

[5] Is it because we revere the Creator of all things and live according to his virtuous law?

[6] But these deeds deserve honors, not tortures."

[7]

[9] While he was saying these things, the guards bound him and dragged him to the catapult;

[10] they tied him to it on his knees, and fitting iron clamps on them, they twisted his back around the wedge on the wheel, so that he was completely curled back like a scorpion, and all his members were disjointed.

[11] In this condition, gasping for breath and in anguish of body,

[12] he said, "Tyrant, they are splendid favors that you grant us against your will, because through these noble sufferings you give us an opportunity to show our endurance for the law."

[13] After he too had died, the sixth, a mere boy, was led in. When the tyrant inquired whether he was willing to eat and be released, he said,

[14] "I am younger in age than my brothers, but I am their equal in mind.

[15] Since to this end we were born and bred, we ought likewise to die for the same principles.

[16] So if you intend to torture me for not eating defiling foods, go on torturing!"

[17] When he had said this, they led him to the wheel.

[18] He was carefully stretched tight upon it, his back was broken, and he was roasted from underneath.

[19] To his back they applied sharp spits that had been heated in the fire, and pierced his ribs so that his entrails were burned through.

[20] While being tortured he said, "O contest befitting holiness, in which so many of us brothers have been summoned to an arena of sufferings for religion, and in which we have not been defeated!

[21] For religious knowledge, O tyrant, is invincible.

[22] I also, equipped with nobility, will die with my brothers,

[23] and I myself will bring a great avenger upon you, you inventor of tortures and enemy of those who are truly devout.

[24] We six boys have paralyzed your tyranny!

[25] Since you have not been able to persuade us to change our mind or to force us to eat defiling foods, is not this your downfall?

[26] Your fire is cold to us, and the catapults painless, and your violence powerless.

[27] For it is not the guards of the tyrant but those of the divine law that are set over us; therefore, unconquered, we hold fast to reason."

4Mac.12

[1] When he also, thrown into the caldron, had died a blessed death, the seventh and youngest of all came forward.

[2] Even though the tyrant had been fearfully reproached by the brothers, he felt strong compassion for this child when he saw that he was already in fetters. He summoned him to come nearer and tried to console him, saying,

[3] "You see the result of your brothers' stupidity, for they died in torments because of their disobedience.

[4] You too, if you do not obey, will be miserably tortured and die before your time,

[5] but if you yield to persuasion you will be my friend and a leader in the government of the kingdom."

[6] When he had so pleaded, he sent for the boy's mother to show compassion on her who had been bereaved of so many sons and to influence her to persuade the surviving son to obey and save himself.

[7] But when his mother had exhorted him in the Hebrew language, as we shall tell a little later,

[8] he said, "Let me loose, let me speak to the king and to all his friends that are with him."

[9] Extremely pleased by the boy's declaration, they freed him at once.

[10] Running to the nearest of the braziers,

[11] he said, "You profane tyrant, most impious of all the wicked, since you have received good things and also your kingdom from God, were you not ashamed to murder his servants and torture on the wheel those who practice religion?

[12] Because of this, justice has laid up for you intense and eternal fire and tortures, and these throughout all time will never let you go.

[13] As a man, were you not ashamed, you most savage beast, to cut out the tongues of men who have feelings like yours and are made of the same elements as you, and to maltreat and torture them in this way?

[14] Surely they by dying nobly fulfilled their service to God, but you will wail bitterly for having slain without cause the contestants for virtue."

[15] Then because he too was about to die, he said,

[16] "I do not desert the excellent example of my brothers,

[17] and I call on the God of our fathers to be merciful to our nation;

[18] but on you he will take vengeance both in this present life and when you are dead."

[19] After he had uttered these imprecations, he flung himself into the braziers and so ended his life.

4Mac.13

[1] Since, then, the seven brothers despised sufferings even unto death, everyone must concede that devout reason is sovereign over the emotions.

[2] For if they had been slaves to their emotions and had eaten defiling food, we would say that they had been conquered by these emotions.

[3] But in fact it was not so. Instead, by reason, which is praised before God, they prevailed over their emotions.

[4] The supremacy of the mind over these cannot be overlooked, for the brothers mastered both emotions and pains.

[5] How then can one fail to confess the sovereignty of right reason over emotion in those who were not turned back by fiery agonies?

[6] For just as towers jutting out over harbors hold back the threatening waves and make it calm for those who sail into the inner basin,

[7] so the seven-towered right reason of the youths, by fortifying the harbor of religion, conquered the tempest of the emotions.

[8] For they constituted a holy chorus of religion and encouraged one another, saying,

[9] "Brothers, let us die like brothers for the sake of the law; let us imitate the three youths in Assyria who despised the same ordeal of the furnace.

[10] Let us not be cowardly in the demonstration of our piety."

[11] While one said, "Courage, brother," another said, "Bear up nobly,"

[12] and another reminded them, "Remember whence you came, and the father by whose hand Isaac would have submitted to being slain for the sake of religion."

[13] Each of them and all of them together looking at one another, cheerful and undaunted, said, "Let us with all our hearts consecrate ourselves to God, who gave us our lives, and let us use our bodies as a bulwark for the law.

[14] Let us not fear him who thinks he is killing us,

[15] for great is the struggle of the soul and the danger of eternal torment lying before those who transgress the commandment of God.

[16] Therefore let us put on the full armor of self-control, which is divine reason.

[17] For if we so die, Abraham and Isaac and Jacob will welcome us, and all the fathers will praise us."

[18] Those who were left behind said to each of the brothers who were being dragged away, "Do not put us to shame, brother, or betray the brothers who have died before us."

[19] You are not ignorant of the affection of brotherhood, which the divine and all-wise Providence has bequeathed through the fathers to their descendants and which was implanted in the mother's womb.

[20] There each of the brothers dwelt the same length of time and was shaped during the same period of time; and growing from the same blood and through the same life, they were brought to the light of day.

[21] When they were born after an equal time of gestation, they drank milk from the same fountains. For such embraces brotherly-loving souls are nourished;

[22] and they grow stronger from this common nurture and daily companionship, and from both general education and our discipline in the law of God.

[23] Therefore, when sympathy and brotherly affection had been so established, the brothers were the more sympathetic to one another.

[24] Since they had been educated by the same law and trained in the same virtues and brought up in right living, they loved one another all the more.

[25] A common zeal for nobility expanded their goodwill and harmony toward one another,

[26] because, with the aid of their religion, they rendered their brotherly love more fervent.

[27] But although nature and companionship and virtuous habits had augmented the affection of brotherhood, those who were left endured for the sake of religion, while watching their brothers being maltreated and tortured to death.

4Mac.14

[1] Furthermore, they encouraged them to face the torture, so that they not only despised their agonies, but also mastered the emotions of brotherly love.

[2] O reason, more royal than kings and freer than the free!

[3] O sacred and harmonious concord of the seven brothers on behalf of religion!

[4] None of the seven youths proved coward or shrank from death,

[5] but all of them, as though running the course toward immortality, hastened to death by torture.

[6] Just as the hands and feet are moved in harmony with the guidance of the mind, so those holy youths, as though moved by an immortal spirit of devotion, agreed to go to death for its sake.

[7] O most holy seven, brothers in harmony! For just as the seven days of creation move in choral dance around religion,

[8] so these youths, forming a chorus, encircled the sevenfold fear of tortures and dissolved it.

[9] Even now, we ourselves shudder as we hear of the tribulations of these young men; they not only saw what was happening, yes, not only heard the direct word of threat, but also bore the sufferings patiently, and in agonies of fire at that.

[10] What could be more excruciatingly painful than this? For the power of fire is intense and swift, and it consumed their bodies quickly.

[11] Do not consider it amazing that reason had full command over these men in their tortures, since the mind of woman despised even more diverse agonies,

[12] for the mother of the seven young men bore up under the rackings of each one of her children.

[13] Observe how complex is a mother's love for her children, which draws everything toward an emotion felt in her inmost parts.

[14] Even unreasoning animals, like mankind, have a sympathy and parental love for their offspring.

[15] For example, among birds, the ones that are tame protect their young by building on the housetops,

[16] and the others, by building in precipitous chasms and in holes and tops of trees, hatch the nestlings and ward off the intruder.

[17] If they are not able to keep him away, they do what they can to help their young by flying in circles around them in the anguish of love, warning them with their own calls.

[18] And why is it necessary to demonstrate sympathy for children by the example of unreasoning animals,

[19] since even bees at the time for making honeycombs defend themselves against intruders as though with an iron dart sting those who approach their hive and defend it even to the death?

[20] But sympathy for her children did not sway the mother of the young men; she was of the same mind as Abraham.

4Mac.15

[1] O reason of the children, tyrant over the emotions! O religion, more desirable to the mother than her children!

[2] Two courses were open to this mother, that of religion, and that of preserving her seven sons for a time, as the tyrant had promised.

[3] She loved religion more, religion that preserves them for eternal life according to God's promise.

[4] In what manner might I express the emotions of parents who love their children? We impress upon the character of a small child a wondrous likeness both of mind and of form. Especially is this true of mothers, who because of their birthpangs have a deeper sympathy toward their offspring than do the fathers.

[5] Considering that mothers are the weaker sex and give birth to many, they are more devoted to their children.

[6] The mother of the seven boys, more than any other mother, loved her children. In seven pregnancies she had implanted in herself tender love toward them,

[7] and because of the many pains she suffered with each of them she had sympathy for them;

[8] yet because of the fear of God she disdained the temporary safety of her children.

[9] Not only so, but also because of the nobility of her sons and their ready obedience to the law she felt a greater tenderness toward them.

[10] For they were righteous and self-controlled and brave and magnanimous, and loved their brothers and their mother, so that they obeyed her even to death in keeping the ordinances.

[11] Nevertheless, though so many factors influenced the mother to suffer with them out of love for her children, in the case of none of them were the various tortures strong enough to pervert her reason.

[12] Instead, the mother urged them on, each child singly and all together, to death for the sake of religion.

[13] O sacred nature and affection of parental love, yearning of parents toward offspring, nurture and indomitable suffering by mothers!

[14] This mother, who saw them tortured and burned one by one, because of religion did not change her attitude.

[15] She watched the flesh of her children consumed by fire, their toes and fingers scattered on the ground, and the flesh of the head to the chin exposed like masks.

[16] O mother, tried now by more bitter pains than even the birth-pangs you suffered for them!

[17] O woman, who alone gave birth to such complete devotion!

[18] When the first-born breathed his last it did not turn you aside, nor when the second in torments looked at you piteously nor when the third expired;

[19] nor did you weep when you looked at the eyes of each one in his tortures gazing boldly at the same agonies, and saw in their nostrils the signs of the approach of death.

[20] When you saw the flesh of children burned upon the flesh of other children, severed hands upon hands, scalped heads upon heads, and corpses fallen on other corpses and when you saw the place filled with many spectators of the torturings, you did not shed tears.

[21] Neither the melodies of sirens nor the songs of swans attract the attention of their hearers as did the voices of the children in torture calling to their mother.

[22] How great and how many torments the mother then suffered as her sons were tortured on the wheel and with the hot irons!

[23] But devout reason, giving her heart a man's courage in the very midst of her emotions, strengthened her to disregard her temporal love for her children.

[24] Although she witnessed the destruction of seven children and the ingenious and various rackings, this noble mother disregarded all these because of faith in God.

[25] For as in the council chamber of her own soul she saw mighty advocates -- nature, family, parental love, and the rackings of her children --

[26] this mother held two ballots, one bearing death and the other deliverance for her children.

[27] She did not approve the deliverance which would preserve the seven sons for a short time,

[28] but as the daughter of God-fearing Abraham she remembered his fortitude.

[29] O mother of the nation, vindicator of the law and champion of religion, who carried away the prize of the contest in your heart!

[30] O more noble than males in steadfastness, and more manly than men in endurance!

[31] Just as Noah's ark, carrying the world in the universal flood, stoutly endured the waves,

[32] so you, O guardian of the law, overwhelmed from every side by the flood of your emotions and the violent winds, the torture of your sons, endured nobly and withstood the wintry storms that assail religion.

4Mac.16

[1] If, then, a woman, advanced in years and mother of seven sons, endured seeing her children tortured to death, it must be admitted that devout reason is sovereign over the emotions.

[2] Thus I have demonstrated not only that men have ruled over the emotions, but also that a woman has despised the fiercest tortures.

[3] The lions surrounding Daniel were not so savage, nor was the raging fiery furnace of Mishael so intensely hot, as was her innate parental love, inflamed as she saw her seven sons tortured in such varied ways.

[4] But the mother quenched so many and such great emotions by devout reason.

[5] Consider this also. If this woman, though a mother, had been fainthearted, she would have mourned over them and perhaps spoken as follows:

[6] "O how wretched am I and many times unhappy! After bearing seven children, I am now the mother

of none!

[7] O seven childbirths all in vain, seven profitless pregnancies, fruitless nurturings and wretched nursings!

[8] In vain, my sons, I endured many birth-pangs for you, and the more grievous anxieties of your upbringing.

[9] Alas for my children, some unmarried, others married and without offspring. I shall not see your children or have the happiness of being called grandmother.

[10] Alas, I who had so many and beautiful children am a widow and alone, with many sorrows.

[11] Nor when I die, shall I have any of my sons to bury me."

[12] Yet the sacred and God-fearing mother did not wail with such a lament for any of them, nor did she dissuade any of them from dying, nor did she grieve as they were dying,

[13] but, as though having a mind like adamant and giving rebirth for immortality to the whole number of her sons, she implored them and urged them on to death for the sake of religion.

[14] O mother, soldier of God in the cause of religion, elder and woman! By steadfastness you have conquered even a tyrant, and in word and deed you have proved more powerful than a man.

[15] For when you and your sons were arrested together, you stood and watched Eleazar being tortured, and said to your sons in the Hebrew language,

[16] "My sons, noble is the contest to which you are called to bear witness for the nation. Fight zealously for our ancestral law.

[17] For it would be shameful if, while an aged man endures such agonies for the sake of religion, you young men were to be terrified by tortures.

[18] Remember that it is through God that you have had a share in the world and have enjoyed life,

[19] and therefore you ought to endure any suffering for the sake of God.

[20] For his sake also our father Abraham was zealous to sacrifice his son Isaac, the ancestor of our nation; and when Isaac saw his father's hand wielding a sword and descending upon him, he did not cower.

[21] And Daniel the righteous was thrown to the lions, and Hananiah, Azariah, and Mishael were hurled into the fiery furnace and endured it for the sake of God.

[22] You too must have the same faith in God and not be grieved.

[23] It is unreasonable for people who have religious knowledge not to withstand pain."

[24] By these words the mother of the seven encouraged and persuaded each of her sons to die rather than violate God's commandment.

[25] They knew also that those who die for the sake of God live in God, as do Abraham and Isaac and Jacob and all the patriarchs.

4Mac.17

[1] Some of the guards said that when she also was about to be seized and put to death she threw herself into the flames so that no one might touch her body.

[2] O mother, who with your seven sons nullified the violence of the tyrant, frustrated his evil designs, and showed the courage of your faith!

[3] Nobly set like a roof on the pillars of your sons, you held firm and unswerving against the earthquake of the tortures.

[4] Take courage, therefore, O holy-minded mother, maintaining firm an enduring hope in God.

[5] The moon in heaven, with the stars, does not stand so august as you, who, after lighting the way of your star-like seven sons to piety, stand in honor before God and are firmly set in heaven with them.

[6] For your children were true descendants of father Abraham.

[7] If it were possible for us to paint the history of your piety as an artist might, would not those who first beheld it have shuddered as they saw the mother of the seven children enduring their varied tortures to death for the sake of religion?

[8] Indeed it would be proper to inscribe upon their tomb these words as a reminder to the people of our nation:

[9] "Here lie buried an aged priest and an aged woman and seven sons, because of the violence of the tyrant who wished to destroy the way of life of the Hebrews.

[10] They vindicated their nation, looking to God and enduring torture even to death."

[11] Truly the contest in which they were engaged was divine,

[12] for on that day virtue gave the awards and tested them for their endurance. The prize was immortality in endless life.

[13] Eleazar was the first contestant, the mother of the seven sons entered the competition, and the brothers contended.

[14] The tyrant was the antagonist, and the world and the human race were the spectators.

[15] Reverence for God was victor and gave the crown to its own athletes.

[16] Who did not admire the athletes of the divine legislation? Who were not amazed?

[17] The tyrant himself and all his council marveled at their endurance,

[18] because of which they now stand before the divine throne and live through blessed eternity.

[19] For Moses says, "All who are consecrated are under your hands."

[20] These, then, who have been consecrated for the sake of God, are honored, not only with this honor, but also by the fact that because of them our enemies did not rule over our nation,

[21] the tyrant was punished, and the homeland purified -- they having become, as it were, a ransom for the sin of our nation.

[22] And through the blood of those devout ones and their death as an expiation, divine Providence preserved Israel that previously had been afflicted.

[23] For the tyrant Antiochus, when he saw the courage of their virtue and their endurance under the tortures, proclaimed them to his soldiers as an example for their own endurance,

[24] and this made them brave and courageous for infantry battle and siege, and he ravaged and conquered all his enemies.

4Mac.18

[1] O Israelite children, offspring of the seed of Abraham, obey this law and exercise piety in every way,

[2] knowing that devout reason is master of all emotions, not only of sufferings from within, but also of those from without.

[3] Therefore those who gave over their bodies in suffering for the sake of religion were not only admired by men, but also were deemed worthy to share in a divine inheritance.

[4] Because of them the nation gained peace, and by reviving observance of the law in the homeland they ravaged the enemy.

[5] The tyrant Antiochus was both punished on earth and is being chastised after his death. Since in no way whatever was he able to compel the Israelites to become pagans and to abandon their ancestral customs, he left Jerusalem and marched against the Persians.

[6] The mother of seven sons expressed also these principles to her children:

[7] "I was a pure virgin and did not go outside my father's house; but I guarded the rib from which woman was made.

[8] No seducer corrupted me on a desert plain, nor did the destroyer, the deceitful serpent, defile the purity of my virginity.

[9] In the time of my maturity I remained with my husband, and when these sons had grown up their father died. A happy man was he, who lived out his life with good children, and did not have the grief of bereavement.

[10] While he was still with you, he taught you the law and the prophets.

[11] He read to you about Abel slain by Cain, and Isaac who was offered as a burnt offering, and of Joseph in prison.

[12] He told you of the zeal of Phineas, and he taught you about Hananiah, Azariah, and Mishael in the fire.

[13] He praised Daniel in the den of the lions and blessed him.

[14] He reminded you of the scripture of Isaiah, which says, `Even though you go through the fire, the flame shall not consume you.'

[15] He sang to you songs of the psalmist David, who said, `Many are the afflictions of the righteous.'

[16] He recounted to you Solomon's proverb, `There is a tree of life for those who do his will.'

[17] He confirmed the saying of Ezekiel, `Shall these dry bones live?'

[18] For he did not forget to teach you the song that Moses taught, which says,

[19] `I kill and I make alive: this is your life and the length of your days.'"

[20] O bitter was that day -- and yet not bitter -- when that bitter tyrant of the Greeks quenched fire with fire in his cruel caldrons, and in his burning rage brought those seven sons of the daughter of Abraham to the catapult and back again to more tortures,

[21] pierced the pupils of their eyes and cut out their tongues, and put them to death with various tortures.

[22] For these crimes divine justice pursued and will pursue the accursed tyrant.

[23] But the sons of Abraham with their victorious mother are gathered together into the chorus of the fathers, and have received pure and immortal souls from God,

[24] to whom be glory for ever and ever. Amen.

Letter (Epistle) of Jeremiah

EpJer.6

[1] A copy of a letter which Jeremiah sent to those who were to be taken to Babylon as captives by the king of the Babylonians, to give them the message which God had commanded him.

[2] Because of the sins which you have committed before God, you will be taken to Babylon as captives by Nebuchadnezzar, king of the Babylonians.

[3] Therefore when you have come to Babylon you will remain there for many years, for a long time, up to seven generations; after that I will bring you away from there in peace.

[4] Now in Babylon you will see gods made of silver and gold and wood, which are carried on men's shoulders and inspire fear in the heathen.

[5] So take care not to become at all like the foreigners or to let fear for these gods possess you, when you see the multitude before and behind them worshiping them.

[6] But say in your heart, "It is thou, O Lord, whom we must worship."

[7] For my angel is with you, and he is watching your lives.

[8] Their tongues are smoothed by the craftsman, and they themselves are overlaid with gold and silver; but they are false and cannot speak.

[9] People take gold and make crowns for the heads of their gods, as they would for a girl who loves ornaments;

[10] and sometimes the priests secretly take gold and silver from their gods and spend it upon themselves,

[11] and even give some of it to the harlots in the brothel. They deck their gods out with garments like men -- these gods of silver and gold and wood,

[12] which cannot save themselves from rust and corrosion. When they have been dressed in purple robes,

[13] their faces are wiped because of the dust from the temple, which is thick upon them.

[14] Like a local ruler the god holds a scepter, though unable to destroy any one who offends it.

[15] It has a dagger in its right hand, and has an axe; but it cannot save itself from war and robbers.

[16] Therefore they evidently are not gods; so do not fear them.

[17] For just as one's dish is useless when it is broken, so are the gods of the heathen, when they have been set up in the temples. Their eyes are full of the dust raised by the feet of those who enter.

[18] And just as the gates are shut on every side upon a man who has offended a king, as though he were sentenced to death, so the priests make their temples secure with doors and locks and bars, in order that they may not be plundered by robbers.

[19] They light lamps, even more than they light for themselves, though their gods can see none of them.

[20] They are just like a beam of the temple, but men say their hearts have melted, when worms from the earth devour them and their robes. They do not notice

[21] when their faces have been blackened by the smoke of the temple.

[22] Bats, swallows, and birds light on their bodies and heads; and so do cats.

[23] From this you will know that they are not gods; so do not fear them.

[24] As for the gold which they wear for beauty -- they will not shine unless some one wipes off the rust; for even when they were being cast, they had no feeling.

[25] They are bought at any cost, but there is no breath in them.

[26] Having no feet, they are carried on men's shoulders, revealing to mankind their worthlessness.

[27] And those who serve them are ashamed because through them these gods are made to stand, lest they fall to the ground. If any one sets one of them upright, it cannot move itself; and if it is tipped over, it cannot straighten itself; but gifts are placed before them just as before the dead.

[28] The priests sell the sacrifices that are offered to these gods and use the money; and likewise their wives preserve some with salt, but give none to the poor or helpless.

[29] Sacrifices to them may be touched by women in menstruation or at childbirth. Since you know by these things that they are not gods, do not fear them.

[30] For why should they be called gods? Women serve meals for gods of silver and gold and wood;

[31] and in their temples the priests sit with their clothes rent, their heads and beards shaved, and their heads uncovered.

[32] They howl and shout before their gods as some do at a funeral feast for a man who has died.

[33] The priests take some of the clothing of their gods to clothe their wives and children.

[34] Whether one does evil to them or good, they will not be able to repay it. They cannot set up a king or depose one.

[35] Likewise they are not able to give either wealth or money; if one makes a vow to them and does not keep it, they will not require it.

[36] They cannot save a man from death or rescue the weak from the strong.

[37] They cannot restore sight to a blind man; they cannot rescue a man who is in distress.

[38] They cannot take pity on a widow or do good to an orphan.

[39] These things that are made of wood and overlaid with gold and silver are like stones from the mountain, and those who serve them will be put to shame.

[40] Why then must any one think that they are gods, or call them gods? Besides, even the Chaldeans themselves dishonor them;

[41] for when they see a dumb man, who cannot speak, they bring him and pray Bel that the man may speak, as though Bel were able to understand.

[42] Yet they themselves cannot perceive this and abandon them, for they have no sense.

[43] And the women, with cords about them, sit along the passageways, burning bran for incense; and when one of them is led off by one of the passers-by and is lain with, she derides the woman next to her, because she was not as attractive as herself and her cord was not broken.

[44] Whatever is done for them is false. Why then must any one think that they are gods, or call them gods?

[45] They are made by carpenters and goldsmiths; they can be nothing but what the craftsmen wish them to be.

[46] The men that make them will certainly not live very long themselves; how then can the things that are made by them be gods?

[47] They have left only lies and reproach for those who come after.

[48] For when war or calamity comes upon them, the priests consult together as to where they can hide themselves and their gods.

[49] How then can one fail to see that these are not gods, for they cannot save themselves from war or calamity.

[50] Since they are made of wood and overlaid with gold and silver, it will afterward be known that they are false.

[51] It will be manifest to all the nations and kings that they are not gods but the work of men's hands, and that there is no work of God in them.

[52] Who then can fail to know that they are not gods?

[53] For they cannot set up a king over a country or give rain to men.

[54] They cannot judge their own cause or deliver one who is wronged, for they have no power; they are like crows between heaven and earth.

[55] When fire breaks out in a temple of wooden gods overlaid with gold or silver, their priests will flee and escape, but the gods will be burnt in two like beams.

[56] Besides, they can offer no resistance to a king or any enemies. Why then must any one admit or think that they are gods?

[57] Gods made of wood and overlaid with silver and gold are not able to save themselves from thieves and robbers.

[58] Strong men will strip them of their gold and silver and of the robes they wear, and go off with this booty, and they will not be able to help themselves.

[59] So it is better to be a king who shows his courage, or a household utensil that serves its owner's need, than to be these false gods; better even the door of a house that protects its contents, than these false gods; better also a wooden pillar in a palace, than these false gods.

[60] For sun and moon and stars, shining and sent forth for service, are obedient.

[61] So also the lightning, when it flashes, is widely seen; and the wind likewise blows in every land.

[62] When God commands the clouds to go over the whole world, they carry out his command.

[63] And the fire sent from above to consume mountains and woods does what it is ordered. But these idols are not to be compared with them in appearance or power.

[64] Therefore one must not think that they are gods nor call them gods, for they are not able either to decide a case or to do good to men.

[65] Since you know then that they are not gods, do not fear them.

[66] For they can neither curse nor bless kings;

[67] they cannot show signs in the heavens and among the nations, or shine like the sun or give light like the moon.

[68] The wild beasts are better than they are, for they can flee to cover and help themselves.

[69] So we have no evidence whatever that they are gods; therefore do not fear them.

[70] Like a scarecrow in a cucumber bed, that guards nothing, so are their gods of wood, overlaid with gold and silver.

[71] In the same way, their gods of wood, overlaid with gold and silver, and like a thorn bush in a garden, on which every bird sits; or like a dead body cast out in the darkness.

[72] By the purple and linen that rot upon them you will know that they are not gods; and they will finally themselves be consumed, and be a reproach in the land.

[73] Better therefore is a just man who has no idols, for he will be far from reproach.

Prayer of Azariah – Song of the Three Children

1

[1] And they walked in the midst of the fire, praising God, and blessing the Lord.

[2] Then Azariah stood and offered this prayer; in the midst of the fire he opened his mouth and said:

[3] "Blessed art thou, O Lord, God of our fathers, and worthy of praise; and thy name is glorified for ever.

[4] For thou art just in all that thou hast done to us, and all thy works are true and thy ways right, and all thy judgments are truth.

[5] Thou hast executed true judgments in all that thou hast brought upon us and upon Jerusalem, the holy city of our fathers, for in truth and justice thou hast brought all this upon us because of our sins.

[6] For we have sinfully and lawlessly departed from thee, and have sinned in all things and have not obeyed thy commandments;

[7] we have not observed them or done them, as thou hast commanded us that it might go well with us.

[8] So all that thou hast brought upon us, and all that thou hast done to us, thou hast done in true judgment.

[9] Thou hast given us into the hands of lawless enemies, most hateful rebels, and to an unjust king, the most wicked in all the world.

[10] And now we cannot open our mouths; shame and disgrace have befallen thy servants and worshipers.

[11] For thy name's sake do not give us up utterly, and do not break thy covenant,

[12] and do not withdraw thy mercy from us,

for the sake of Abraham thy beloved and for the sake of Isaac thy servant and Israel thy holy one,

[13] to whom thou didst promise to make their descendants as many as the stars of heaven and as the sand on the shore of the sea.

[14] For we, O Lord, have become fewer than any nation, and are brought low this day in all the world because of our sins.

[15] And at this time there is no prince, or prophet, or leader, no burnt offering, or sacrifice, or oblation, or incense, no place to make an offering before thee or to find mercy.

[16] Yet with a contrite heart and a humble spirit may we be accepted, as though it were with burnt offerings of rams and bulls, and with tens of thousands of fat lambs;

[17] such may our sacrifice be in thy sight this day, and may we wholly follow thee, for there will be no shame for those who trust in thee.

[18] And now with all our heart we follow thee, we fear thee and seek thy face.

[19] Do not put us to shame, but deal with us in thy forbearance and in thy abundant mercy.

[20] Deliver us in accordance with thy marvelous works, and give glory to thy name, O Lord! Let all who do harm to thy servants be put to shame;

[21] let them be disgraced and deprived of all power and dominion, and let their strength be broken.

[22] Let them know that thou art the Lord, the only God, glorious over the whole world."

[23] Now the king's servants who threw them in did not cease feeding the furnace fires with naphtha, pitch, tow, and brush.

[24] And the flame streamed out above the furnace forty-nine cubits,

[25] and it broke through and burned those of the Chaldeans whom it caught about the furnace.

[26] But the angel of the Lord came down into the furnace to be with Azariah and his companions, and drove the fiery flame out of the furnace,

[27] and made the midst of the furnace like a moist whistling wind, so that the fire did not touch them at all or hurt or trouble them.

[28] Then the three, as with one mouth, praised and glorified and blessed God in the furnace, saying:

[29] "Blessed art thou, O Lord, God of our fathers, and to be praised and highly exalted for ever; [30] And blessed is thy glorious, holy name and to be highly praised and highly exalted for ever; [31] Blessed art thou in the temple of thy holy glory and to be extolled and highly glorified for ever. [32] Blessed art thou, who sittest upon cherubim and lookest upon the deeps, and to be praised and highly exalted for ever. [33] Blessed art thou upon the throne of thy kingdom and to be extolled and highly exalted for ever. [34] Blessed art thou in the firmament of heavenand to be sung and glorified for ever.

[35] "Bless the Lord, all works of the Lord, sing praise to him and highly exalt him for ever. [36] Bless the Lord, you heavens, sing praise to him and highly exalt him for ever. [37] Bless the Lord, you angels of the Lord, sing praise to him and highly exalt him for ever. [38] Bless the Lord, all waters above the heaven, sing praise to him and highly exalt him for ever. [39] Bless the Lord, all powers, sing praise to him and highly exalt him for ever. [40] Bless the Lord, sun and moon, sing praise to him and highly exalt him for ever. [41] Bless the Lord, stars of heaven, sing praise to him and highly exalt him for ever. [42] Bless the Lord, all rain and dew, sing praise to him and highly exalt him for ever. [43] Bless the Lord, all winds, sing praise to him and highly exalt him for ever. [44] Bless the Lord, fire and heat, sing praise to him and highly exalt him for ever. [45] Bless the Lord, winter cold and summer heat, sing praise to him and highly exalt him for ever. [46] Bless the Lord, dews and snows, sing praise to him and highly exalt him for ever. [47] Bless the Lord, nights and days, sing praise to him and highly exalt him for ever. [48] Bless the Lord, light and darkness, sing praise to him and highly exalt him for ever. [49] Bless the Lord, ice and cold, sing praise to him and highly exalt him for ever. [50] Bless the Lord, frosts and snows, sing praise to him and highly exalt him for ever. [51] Bless the Lord, lightnings and clouds, sing praise to him and highly exalt him for ever. [52] Let the earth bless the Lord; let it praise to him and highly exalt him for ever. [53] Bless the Lord, mountains and hills, sing praise to him and highly exalt him for ever. [54] Bless the Lord, all things that grow on the earth, sing praise to him and highly exalt him for ever. [55] Bless the Lord, you springs, sing praise to him and highly exalt him for ever. [56] Bless the Lord, seas and rivers, sing praise to him and highly exalt him for ever. [57] Bless the Lord, you whales and all creatures that move in the waters, sing praise to him and highly exalt him for ever. [58] Bless the Lord, all birds of the air, sing praise to him and highly exalt him for ever. [59] Bless the Lord, all beasts and cattle, sing praise to him and highly exalt him for ever. [60] Bless the Lord, you sons of men, sing praise to him and highly exalt him for ever. [61] Bless the Lord, O Israel, sing praise to him and highly exalt him for ever. [62] Bless the Lord, you priests of the Lord, sing praise to him and highly exalt him for ever. [63] Bless the Lord, you servants of the Lord sing praise to him and highly exalt him for ever. [64] Bless the Lord, spirits and souls of the righteous, sing praise to him and highly exalt him for ever. [65] Bless the Lord, you who are holy and humble in heart, sing praise to him and highly exalt him for ever. [66] Bless the Lord, Hananiah, Azariah, and Mishael, sing praise to him and highly exalt him for ever; for he has rescued us from Hades and saved us from the hand of death, and delivered us from the midst of the burning fiery furnace; from the midst of the fire he has delivered us. [67] Give thanks to the Lord, for he is good, for his mercy endures for ever. [68] Bless him, all who worship the Lord, the God of gods, sing praise to him and give thanks to him, for his mercy endures for ever."

Baruch

Bar.1

[1] These are the words of the book which Baruch the son of Neraiah, son of Mahseiah, son of Zedekiah, son of Hasadiah, son of Hilkiah, wrote in Babylon,

[2] in the fifth year, on the seventh day of the month, at the time when the Chaldeans took Jerusalem and burned it with fire.

[3] And Baruch read the words of this book in the hearing of Jeconiah the son of Jehoiakim, king of Judah, and in the hearing of all the people who came to hear the book,

[4] and in the hearing of the mighty men and the princes, and in the hearing of the elders, and in the hearing of all the people, small and great, all who dwelt in Babylon by the river Sud.

[5] Then they wept, and fasted, and prayed before the Lord;

[6] and they collected money, each giving what he could;

[7] and they sent it to Jerusalem to Jehoiakim the high priest, the son of Hilkiah, son of Shallum, and to the priests, and to all the people who were present with him in Jerusalem.

[8] At the same time, on the tenth day of Sivan, Baruch took the vessels of the house of the Lord, which had been carried away from the temple, to return them to the land of Judah -- the silver vessels which Zedekiah the son of Josiah, king of Judah, had made,

[9] after Nebuchadnezzar king of Babylon had carried away from Jerusalem Jeconiah and the princes and the prisoners and the mighty men and the people of the land, and brought them to Babylon.

[10] And they said: "Herewith we send you money; so buy with the money burnt offerings and sin offerings and incense, and prepare a cereal offering, and offer them upon the altar of the Lord our God;

[11] and pray for the life of Nebuchadnezzar king of Babylon, and for the life of Belshazzar his son, that their days on earth may be like the days of heaven.

[12] And the Lord will give us strength, and he will give light to our eyes, and we shall live under the protection of Nebuchadnezzar king of Babylon, and under the protection of Belshazzar his son, and we shall serve them many days and find favor in their sight.

[13] And pray for us to the Lord our God, for we have sinned against the Lord our God, and to this day the anger of the Lord and his wrath have not turned away from us.

[14] And you shall read this book which we are sending you, to make your confession in the house of the Lord on the days of the feasts and at appointed seasons.

[15] "And you shall say: `Righteousness belongs to the Lord our God, but confusion of face, as at this day, to us, to the men of Judah, to the inhabitants of Jerusalem,

[16] and to our kings and our princes and our priests and our prophets and our fathers,

[17] because we have sinned before the Lord,

[18] and have disobeyed him, and have not heeded the voice of the Lord our God, to walk in the statutes of the Lord which he set before us.

[19] From the day when the Lord brought our fathers out of the land of Egypt until today, we have been disobedient to the Lord our God, and we have been negligent, in not heeding his voice.

[20] So to this day there have clung to us the calamities and the curse which the Lord declared through Moses his servant at the time when he brought our fathers out of the land of Egypt to give to us a land flowing with milk and honey.

[21] We did not heed the voice of the Lord our God in all the words of the prophets whom he sent to us, but we each followed the intent of his own wicked heart by serving other gods and doing what is evil in the sight of the Lord our God.

Bar.2

[1] "`So the Lord confirmed his word, which he spoke against us, and against our judges who judged Israel, and against our kings and against our princes and against the men of Israel and Judah.

[2] Under the whole heaven there has not been done the like of what he has done in Jerusalem, in accordance with what is written in the law of Moses,

[3] that we should eat, one the flesh of his son and another the flesh of his daughter.

[4] And he gave them into subjection to all the kingdoms around us, to be a reproach and a desolation among all the surrounding peoples, where the Lord has scattered them.

[5] They were brought low and not raised up, because we sinned against the Lord our God, in not heeding his voice.

[6] "`Righteousness belongs to the Lord our God, but confusion of face to us and our fathers, as at this day.

[7] All those calamities with which the Lord threatened us have come upon us.

[8] Yet we have not entreated the favor of the Lord by turning away, each of us, from the thoughts of his wicked heart.

[9] And the Lord has kept the calamities ready, and the Lord has brought them upon us, for the Lord is righteous in all his works which he has commanded us to do.

[10] Yet we have not obeyed his voice, to walk in the statutes of the Lord which he set before us.

[11] "`And now, O Lord God of Israel, who didst bring thy people out of the land of Egypt with a mighty hand and with signs and wonders and with great power and outstretched arm, and hast made thee a name, as at this day,

[12] we have sinned, we have been ungodly, we have done wrong, O Lord our God, against all thy ordinances.

[13] Let thy anger turn away from us, for we are left, few in number, among the nations where thou hast scattered us.

[14] Hear, O Lord, our prayer and our supplication, and for thy own sake deliver us, and grant us favor in the sight of those who have carried us into exile;

[15] that all the earth may know that thou art the Lord our God, for Israel and his descendants are called by thy name.

[16] O Lord, look down from thy holy habitation, and consider us. Incline thy ear, O Lord, and hear;

[17] open thy eyes, O Lord, and see; for the dead who are in Hades, whose spirit has been taken from their bodies, will not ascribe glory or justice to the Lord,

[18] but the person that is greatly distressed, that goes about bent over and feeble, and the eyes that are failing, and the person that hungers, will ascribe to thee glory and righteousness, O Lord.

[19] For it is not because of any righteous deeds of our fathers or our kings that we bring before thee our prayer for mercy, O Lord our God.

[20] For thou hast sent thy anger and thy wrath upon us, as thou didst declare by thy servants the prophets, saying:

[21] "Thus says the Lord: Bend your shoulders and serve the king of Babylon, and you will remain in the land which I gave to your fathers.

[22] But if you will not obey the voice of the Lord and will not serve the king of Babylon,

[23] I will make to cease from the cities of Judah and from the region about Jerusalem the voice of mirth and the voice of gladness, the voice of the bridegroom and the voice of the bride, and the whole land will be a desolation without inhabitants."

[24] "`But we did not obey thy voice, to serve the king of Babylon; and thou hast confirmed thy words, which thou didst speak by thy servants the prophets, that the bones of our kings and the bones of our fathers would be brought out of their graves;

[25] and behold, they have been cast out to the heat of day and the frost of night. They perished in great misery, by famine and sword and pestilence.

[26] And the house which is called by thy name thou hast made as it is today, because of the wickedness of the house of Israel and the house of Judah.

[27] "`Yet thou hast dealt with us, O Lord our God, in all thy kindness and in all thy great compassion,

[28] as thou didst speak by thy servant Moses on the day when thou didst command him to write thy law in the presence of the people of Israel, saying,

[29] "If you will not obey my voice, this very great multitude will surely turn into a small number among the nations, where I will scatter them.

[30] For I know that they will not obey me, for they are a stiff-necked people. But in the land of their exile they will come to themselves,

[31] and they will know that I am the Lord their God. I will give them a heart that obeys and ears that hear;

[32] and they will praise me in the land of their exile, and will remember my name,

[33] and will turn from their stubbornness and their wicked deeds; for they will remember the ways of their fathers, who sinned before the Lord.

[34] I will bring them again into the land which I swore to give to their fathers, to Abraham and to Isaac and to Jacob, and they will rule over it; and I will increase them, and they will not be diminished.

[35] I will make an everlasting covenant with them to be their God and they shall be my people; and I will never again remove my people Israel from the land which I have given them."

Bar.3

[1] "`O Lord Almighty, God of Israel, the soul in anguish and the wearied spirit cry out to thee.

[2] Hear, O Lord, and have mercy, for we have sinned before thee.

[3] For thou art enthroned for ever, and we are perishing for ever.

[4] O Lord Almighty, God of Israel, hear now the prayer of the dead of Israel and of the sons of those who sinned before thee, who did not heed the voice of the Lord their God, so that calamities have clung to us.

[5] Remember not the iniquities of our fathers, but in this crisis remember thy power and thy name.

[6] For thou art the Lord our God, and thee, O Lord, will we praise.

[7] For thou hast put the fear of thee in our hearts in order that we should call upon thy name; and we will praise thee in our exile, for we have put away from our hearts all the iniquity of our fathers who sinned before thee.

[8] Behold, we are today in our exile where thou hast scattered us, to be reproached and cursed and punished for all the iniquities of our fathers who forsook the Lord our God.'"

[9] Hear the commandments of life, O Israel; give ear, and learn wisdom!

[10] Why is it, O Israel, why is it that you are in the land of your enemies, that you are growing old in a foreign country, that you are defiled with the dead,

[11] that you are counted among those in Hades?

[12] You have forsaken the fountain of wisdom. [13] If you had walked in the way of God, you would be dwelling in peace for ever. [14] Learn where there is wisdom, where there is strength, where there is understanding, that you may at the same time discern where there is length of days, and life, where there is light for the eyes, and peace. [15] Who has found her place? And who has entered her storehouses? [16] Where are the princes of the nations, and those who rule over the beasts on earth; [17] those who have sport with the birds of the air, and who hoard up silver and gold, in which men trust, and there is no end to their getting? [18] those who scheme to get silver, and are anxious, whose labors are beyond measure? [19] They have vanished and gone down to Hades, and others have arisen in their place. [20] Young men have seen the light of day, and have dwelt upon the earth; but they have not learned the way to knowledge, nor understood her paths, nor laid hold of her. [21] Their sons have strayed far from her way. [22] She has not been heard of in Canaan, nor seen in Teman; [23] the sons of Hagar, who seek for understanding on the earth, the merchants of Merran and Teman, the story-tellers and the seekers for understanding, have not learned the way to wisdom, nor given thought to her paths. [24] O Israel, how great is the house of God! And how vast the territory that he possesses! [25] It is great and has no bounds; it is high and immeasurable. [26] The giants were born there, who were famous of old, great in stature, expert in war. [27] God did not choose them, nor give them the way to knowledge; [28] so they perished because they had no wisdom, they perished through their folly. [29] Who has gone up into heaven, and taken her, and brought her down from the clouds? [30] Who has gone over the sea, and found her, and will buy her for pure gold? [31] No one knows the way to her, or is concerned about the path to her. [32] But he who knows all things knows her, he found her by his understanding. He who prepared the earth for all time filled it with four-footed creatures; [33] he who sends forth the light, and it goes, called it, and it obeyed him in fear; [34] the stars shone in their watches, and were glad; he called them, and they said, "Here we are!" They shone with gladness for him who made them. [35] This is our God; no other can be compared to him! [36] He found the whole way to knowledge, and gave her to Jacob his servant and to Israel whom he loved. [37] Afterward she appeared upon earth and lived among men.

Bar.4

[1] She is the book of the commandments of God, and the law that endures for ever. All who hold her fast will live, and those who forsake her will die.

[2] Turn, O Jacob, and take her; walk toward the shining of her light.

[3] Do not give your glory to another, or your advantages to an alien people.

[4] Happy are we, O Israel, for we know what is pleasing to God.

[5] Take courage, my people, O memorial of Israel!

[6] It was not for destruction that you were sold to the nations, but you were handed over to your enemies because you angered God.

[7] For you provoked him who made you, by sacrificing to demons and not to God.

[8] You forgot the everlasting God, who brought you up, and you grieved Jerusalem, who reared you.

[9] For she saw the wrath that came upon you from God, and she said: "Hearken, you neighbors of Zion, God has brought great sorrow upon me;

[10] for I have seen the captivity of my sons and daughters, which the Everlasting brought upon them.

[11] With joy I nurtured them, but I sent them away with weeping and sorrow.

[12] Let no one rejoice over me, a widow and bereaved of many; I was left desolate because of the sins of my children, because they turned away from the law of God.

[13] They had no regard for his statutes; they did not walk in the ways of God's commandments, nor tread the paths of discipline in his righteousness.

[14] Let the neighbors of Zion come; remember the capture of my sons and daughters, which the Everlasting brought upon them.

[15] For he brought against them a nation from afar, a shameless nation, of a strange language, who had no respect for an old man, and had no pity for a child.

[16] They led away the widow's beloved sons, and bereaved the lonely woman of her daughters.

[17] "But I, how can I help you?

[18] For he who brought these calamities upon you will deliver you from the hand of your enemies.

[19] Go, my children, go; for I have been left desolate.

[20] I have taken off the robe of peace and put on the sackcloth of my supplication; I will cry to the Everlasting all my days.

[21] "Take courage, my children, cry to God, and he will deliver you from the power and hand of the enemy.

[22] For I have put my hope in the Everlasting to save you, and joy has come to me from the Holy One, because of the mercy which soon will come to you from your everlasting Savior.

[23] For I sent you out with sorrow and weeping, but God will give you back to me with joy and gladness for ever.

[24] For as the neighbors of Zion have now seen your capture, so they soon will see your salvation by God, which will come to you with great glory and with the splendor of the Everlasting.

[25] My children, endure with patience the wrath that has come upon you from God. Your enemy has overtaken you, but you will soon see their destruction and will tread upon their necks.

[26] My tender sons have traveled rough roads; they were taken away like a flock carried off by the enemy.

[27] "Take courage, my children, and cry to God, for you will be remembered by him who brought this upon you.

[28] For just as you purposed to go astray from God, return with tenfold zeal to seek him.

[29] For he who brought these calamities upon you will bring you everlasting joy with your salvation."

[30] Take courage, O Jerusalem, for he who named you will comfort you.

[31] Wretched will be those who afflicted you and rejoiced at your fall.

[32] Wretched will be the cities which your children served as slaves; wretched will be the city which received your sons.

[33] For just as she rejoiced at your fall and was glad for your ruin, so she will be grieved at her own desolation.

[34] And I will take away her pride in her great population, and her insolence will be turned to grief.

[35] For fire will come upon her from the Everlasting for many days, and for a long time she will be inhabited by demons.

[36] Look toward the east, O Jerusalem, and see the joy that is coming to you from God!

[37] Behold, your sons are coming, whom you sent away; they are coming, gathered from east and west, at the word of the Holy One, rejoicing in the glory of God.

Bar.5

[1] Take off the garment of your sorrow and affliction, O Jerusalem, and put on for ever the beauty of the glory from God.

[2] Put on the robe of the righteousness from God; put on your head the diadem of the glory of the Everlasting.

[3] For God will show your splendor everywhere under heaven.

[4] For your name will for ever be called by God, "Peace of righteousness and glory of godliness."

[5] Arise, O Jerusalem, stand upon the height and look toward the east, and see your children gathered from west and east, at the word of the Holy One, rejoicing that God has remembered them.

[6] For they went forth from you on foot, led away by their enemies; but God will bring them back to you, carried in glory, as on a royal throne.

[7] For God has ordered that every high mountain and the everlasting hills be made low and the valleys filled up, to make level ground, so that Israel may walk safely in the glory of God.

[8] The woods and every fragrant tree have shaded Israel at God's command.

[9] For God will lead Israel with joy, in the light of his glory, with the mercy and righteousness that come from him.

Prayer of Manasseh

PrMan.1

[1] O Lord, Almighty God of our fathers, Abraham, Isaac, and Jacob, and of their righteous seed;

[2] thou who hast made heaven and earth with all their order;

[3] who hast shackled the sea by thy word of command, who hast confined the deep and sealed it with thy terrible and glorious name;

[4] at whom all things shudder, and tremble before thy power,

[5] for thy glorious splendor cannot be borne, and the wrath of thy threat to sinners is irresistible;

[6] yet immeasurable and unsearchable is thy promised mercy,

[7] for thou art the Lord Most High, of great compassion, long-suffering, and very merciful, and repentest over the evils of men. Thou, O Lord, according to thy great goodness hast promised repentance and forgiveness to those who have sinned against thee; and in the multitude of thy mercies thou hast appointed repentance for sinners, that they may be saved.

[8] Therefore thou, O Lord, God of the righteous, hast not appointed repentance for the righteous, for Abraham and Isaac and Jacob, who did not sin against thee, but thou hast appointed repentance for me, who am a sinner.

[9] For the sins I have committed are more in number than the sand of the sea; my transgressions are multiplied, O Lord, they are multiplied! I am unworthy to look up and see the height of heaven because of the multitude of my iniquities.

[10] I am weighted down with many an iron fetter, so that I am rejected because of my sins, and I have no relief; for I have provoked thy wrath and have done what is evil in thy sight, setting up abominations and multiplying offenses.

[11] And now I bend the knee of my heart, beseeching thee for thy kindness.

[12] I have sinned, O Lord, I have sinned, and I know my transgressions.

[13] I earnestly beseech thee, forgive me, O Lord, forgive me! Do not destroy me with my transgressions! Do not be angry with me for ever or lay up evil for me; do not condemn me to the depths of the earth. For thou, O Lord, art the God of those who repent,

[14] and in me thou wilt manifest thy goodness; for, unworthy as I am, thou wilt save me in thy great mercy,

[15] and I will praise thee continually all the days of my life. For all the host of heaven sings thy praise, and your is the glory for ever. Amen.

Bel and the Dragon

Bel.1

[1] When King Astyages was laid with his fathers, Cyrus the Persian received his kingdom.

[2] And Daniel was a companion of the king, and was the most honored of his friends.

[3] Now the Babylonians had an idol called Bel, and every day they spent on it twelve bushels of fine flour and forty sheep and fifty gallons of wine.

[4] The king revered it and went every day to worship it. But Daniel worshiped his own God.

[5] And the king said to him, "Why do you not worship Bel?" He answered, "Because I do not revere man-made idols, but the living God, who created heaven and earth and has dominion over all flesh."

[6] The king said to him, "Do you not think that Bel is a living God? Do you not see how much he eats and drinks every day?"

[7] Then Daniel laughed, and said, "Do not be deceived, O king; for this is but clay inside and brass outside, and it never ate or drank anything."

[8] Then the king was angry, and he called his priests and said to them, "If you do not tell me who is eating these provisions, you shall die.

[9] But if you prove that Bel is eating them, Daniel shall die, because he blasphemed against Bel." And Daniel said to the king, "Let it be done as you have said."

[10] Now there were seventy priests of Bel, besides their wives and children. And the king went with Daniel into the temple of Bel.

[11] And the priests of Bel said, "Behold, we are going outside; you yourself, O king, shall set forth the food and mix and place the wine, and shut the door and seal it with your signet.

[12] And when you return in the morning, if you do not find that Bel has eaten it all, we will die; or else Daniel will, who is telling lies about us."

[13] They were unconcerned, for beneath the table they had made a hidden entrance, through which they used to go in regularly and consume the provisions.

[14] When they had gone out, the king set forth the food for Bel. Then Daniel ordered his servants to bring ashes and they sifted them throughout the whole temple in the presence of the king alone. Then they went out, shut the door and sealed it with the king's signet, and departed.

[15] In the night the priests came with their wives and children, as they were accustomed to do, and ate and drank everything.

[16] Early in the morning the king rose and came, and Daniel with him.

[17] And the king said, "Are the seals unbroken, Daniel?" He answered, "They are unbroken, O king."

[18] As soon as the doors were opened, the king looked at the table, and shouted in a loud voice, "You are great, O Bel; and with you there is no deceit, none at all."

[19] Then Daniel laughed, and restrained the king from going in, and said, "Look at the floor, and notice whose footsteps these are."

[20] The king said, "I see the footsteps of men and women and children."

[21] Then the king was enraged, and he seized the priests and their wives and children; and they showed him the secret doors through which they were accustomed to enter and devour what was on the table.

[22] Therefore the king put them to death, and gave Bel over to Daniel, who destroyed it and its temple.

[23] There was also a great dragon, which the Babylonians revered.

[24] And the king said to Daniel, "You cannot deny that this is a living god; so worship him."

[25] Daniel said, "I will worship the Lord my God, for he is the living God.

[26] But if you, O king, will give me permission, I will slay the dragon without sword or club." The king said, "I give you permission."

[27] Then Daniel took pitch, fat, and hair, and boiled them together and made cakes, which he fed to the dragon. The dragon ate them, and burst open. And Daniel said, "See what you have been worshiping!"

[28] When the Babylonians heard it, they were very indignant and conspired against the king, saying, "The king has become a Jew; he has destroyed Bel, and slain the dragon, and slaughtered the priests."

[29] Going to the king, they said, "Hand Daniel over to us, or else we will kill you and your household."

[30] The king saw that they were pressing him hard, and under compulsion he handed Daniel over to them.

[31] They threw Daniel into the lions' den, and he was there for six days.

[32] There were seven lions in the den, and every day they had been given two human bodies and two sheep; but these were not given to them now, so that they might devour Daniel.

[33] Now the prophet Habakkuk was in Judea. He had boiled pottage and had broken bread into a bowl, and was going into the field to take it to the reapers.

[34] But the angel of the Lord said to Habakkuk, "Take the dinner which you have to Babylon, to Daniel, in the lions' den."

[35] Habakkuk said, "Sir, I have never seen Babylon, and I know nothing about the den."

[36] Then the angel of the Lord took him by the crown of his head, and lifted him by his hair and set him down in Babylon, right over the den, with the rushing sound of the wind itself.

[37] Then Habakkuk shouted, "Daniel, Daniel! Take the dinner which God has sent you."

[38] And Daniel said, "Thou hast remembered me, O God, and hast not forsaken those who love thee."

[39] So Daniel arose and ate. And the angel of God immediately returned Habakkuk to his own place.

[40] On the seventh day the king came to mourn for Daniel. When he came to the den he looked in, and there sat Daniel.

[41] And the king shouted with a loud voice, "Thou art great, O Lord God of Daniel, and there is no other besides thee."

[42] And he pulled Daniel out, and threw into the den the men who had attempted his destruction, and they were devoured immediately before his eyes.

Wisdom of Jesus Son of Sirach

Sir.0

[1-14] Whereas many great teachings have been given to us through the law and the prophets and the others that followed them, on account of which we should praise Israel for instruction and wisdom; and since it is necessary not only that the readers themselves should acquire understanding but also that those who love learning should be able to help the outsiders by both speaking and writing, my grandfather Jesus, after devoting himself especially to the reading of the law and the prophets and the other books of our fathers, and after acquiring considerable proficiency in them, was himself also led to write something pertaining to instruction and wisdom, in order that, by becoming conversant with this also, those who love learning should make even greater progress in living according to the law.

[15-26] You are urged therefore to read with good will and attention, and to be indulgent in cases where, despite our diligent labor in translating, we may seem to have rendered some phrases imperfectly. For what was originally expressed in Hebrew does not have exactly the same sense when translated into another language. Not only this work, but even the law itself, the prophecies, and the rest of the books differ not a little as originally expressed.

[27-36] When I came to Egypt in the thirty-eighth year of the reign of Euergetes and stayed for some time, I found opportunity for no little instruction. It seemed highly necessary that I should myself devote some pains and labor to the translation of the following book, using in that period of time great watchfulness and skill in order to complete and publish the book for those living abroad who wished to gain learning, being prepared in character to live according to the law.

Sir.1

[1] All wisdom comes from the Lord and is with him for ever.
[2] The sand of the sea, the drops of rain, and the days of eternity -- who can count them?
[3] The height of heaven, the breadth of the earth, the abyss, and wisdom -- who can search them out?
[4] Wisdom was created before all things, and prudent understanding from eternity.
[5] The root of wisdom -- to whom has it been revealed? Her clever devices -- who knows them?
[6] There is One who is wise, greatly to be feared, sitting upon his throne.
[7] The Lord himself created wisdom; he saw her and apportioned her, he poured her out upon all his works.
[8] She dwells with all flesh according to his gift, and he supplied her to those who love him.
[9] The fear of the Lord is glory and exultation, and gladness and a crown of rejoicing.
[10] The fear of the Lord delights the heart, and gives gladness and joy and long life.
[11] With him who fears the Lord it will go well at the end; on the day of his death he will be blessed.
[12] To fear the Lord is the beginning of wisdom; she is created with the faithful in the womb.
[13] She made among men an eternal foundation, and among their descendants she will be trusted.
[14] To fear the Lord is wisdom's full measure; she satisfies men with her fruits;
[15] she fills their whole house with desirable goods, and their storehouses with her produce.
[16] The fear of the Lord is the crown of wisdom, making peace and perfect health to flourish.
[17] He saw her and apportioned her; he rained down knowledge and discerning comprehension, and he exalted the glory of those who held her fast.
[18] To fear the Lord is the root of wisdom, and her branches are long life.
[22] Unrighteous anger cannot be justified, for a man's anger tips the scale to his ruin.
[23] A patient man will endure until the right moment, and then joy will burst forth for him.
[24] He will hide his words until the right moment, and the lips of many will tell of his good sense.
[25] In the treasuries of wisdom are wise sayings, but godliness is an abomination to a sinner.
[26] If you desire wisdom, keep the commandments, and the Lord will supply it for you.
[27] For the fear of the Lord is wisdom and instruction, and he delights in fidelity and meekness.
[28] Do not disobey the fear of the Lord; do not approach him with a divided mind.
[29] Be not a hypocrite in men's sight, and keep watch over your lips.

[30] Do not exalt yourself lest you fall, and thus bring dishonor upon yourself. The Lord will reveal your secrets
and cast you down in the midst of the congregation, because you did not come in the fear of the Lord, and your heart was full of deceit.

Sir.2

[1] My son, if you come forward to serve the Lord, prepare yourself for temptation.
[2] Set your heart right and be steadfast, and do not be hasty in time of calamity.
[3] Hold fast to him and do not depart, that you may be honored at the end of your life.
[4] Accept whatever is brought upon you, and in changes that humble you be patient.
[5] For gold is tested in the fire, and acceptable men in the furnace of humiliation.
[6] Trust in him, and he will help you; make your ways straight, and hope in him.
[7] You who fear the Lord, wait for his mercy; and turn not aside, lest you fall.
[8] You who fear the Lord, trust in him, and your reward will not fail;
[9] you who fear the Lord, hope for good things, for everlasting joy and mercy.
[10] Consider the ancient generations and see: who ever trusted in the Lord and was put to shame? Or who ever persevered in the fear of the Lord and was forsaken? Or who ever called upon him and was overlooked?
[11] For the Lord is compassionate and merciful; he forgives sins and saves in time of affliction.
[12] Woe to timid hearts and to slack hands, and to the sinner who walks along two ways!
[13] Woe to the faint heart, for it has no trust! Therefore it will not be sheltered.
[14] Woe to you who have lost your endurance! What will you do when the Lord punishes you?
[15] Those who fear the Lord will not disobey his words, and those who love him will keep his ways.
[16] Those who fear the Lord will seek his approval, and those who love him will be filled with the law.
[17] Those who fear the Lord will prepare their hearts, and will humble themselves before him.
[18] Let us fall into the hands of the Lord, but not into the hands of men; for as his majesty is, so also is his mercy.

Sir.3

[1] Listen to me your father, O children; and act accordingly, that you may be kept in safety.
[2] For the Lord honored the father above the children, and he confirmed the right of the mother over her sons.
[3] Whoever honors his father atones for sins,
[4] and whoever glorifies his mother is like one who lays up treasure.
[5] Whoever honors his father will be gladdened by his own children, and when he prays he will be heard.
[6] Whoever glorifies his father will have long life, and whoever obeys the Lord will refresh his mother;
[7] he will serve his parents as his masters.
[8] Honor your father by word and deed, that a blessing from him may come upon you.
[9] For a father's blessing strengthens the houses of the children, but a mother's curse uproots their foundations.
[10] Do not glorify yourself by dishonoring your father, for your father's dishonor is no glory to you.
[11] For a man's glory comes from honoring his father, and it is a disgrace for children not to respect their mother.
[12] O son, help your father in his old age, and do not grieve him as long as he lives;
[13] even if he is lacking in understanding, show forbearance; in all your strength do not despise him.
[14] For kindness to a father will not be forgotten, and against your sins it will be credited to you;
[15] in the day of your affliction it will be remembered in your favor; as frost in fair weather, your sins will melt away.
[16] Whoever forsakes his father is like a blasphemer, and whoever angers his mother is cursed by the Lord.
[17] My son, perform your tasks in meekness; then you will be loved by those whom God accepts.
[18] The greater you are, the more you must humble yourself; so you will find favor in the sight of the Lord.

[20] For great is the might of the Lord; he is glorified by the humble.

[21] Seek not what is too difficult for you, nor investigate what is beyond your power.

[22] Reflect upon what has been assigned to you, for you do not need what is hidden.

[23] Do not meddle in what is beyond your tasks, for matters too great for human understanding have been shown you.

[24] For their hasty judgment has led many astray, and wrong opinion has caused their thoughts to slip.

[26] A stubborn mind will be afflicted at the end, and whoever loves danger will perish by it.

[27] A stubborn mind will be burdened by troubles, and the sinner will heap sin upon sin.

[28] The affliction of the proud has no healing, for a plant of wickedness has taken root in him.

[29] The mind of the intelligent man will ponder a parable, and an attentive ear is the wise man's desire.

[30] Water extinguishes a blazing fire: so almsgiving atones for sin.

[31] Whoever requites favors gives thought to the future; at the moment of his falling he will find support.

Sir.4

[1] My son, deprive not the poor of his living, and do not keep needy eyes waiting.

[2] Do not grieve the one who is hungry, nor anger a man in want.

[3] Do not add to the troubles of an angry mind, nor delay your gift to a beggar.

[4] Do not reject an afflicted suppliant, nor turn your face away from the poor.

[5] Do not avert your eye from the needy, nor give a man occasion to curse you;

[6] for if in bitterness of soul he calls down a curse upon you, his Creator will hear his prayer.

[7] Make yourself beloved in the congregation; bow your head low to a great man.

[8] Incline your ear to the poor, and answer him peaceably and gently.

[9] Deliver him who is wronged from the hand of the wrongdoer; and do not be fainthearted in judging a case.

[10] Be like a father to orphans, and instead of a husband to their mother; you will then be like a son of the Most High,

and he will love you more than does your mother.

[11] Wisdom exalts her sons and gives help to those who seek her.

[12] Whoever loves her loves life, and those who seek her early will be filled with joy.

[13] Whoever holds her fast will obtain glory, and the Lord will bless the place she enters.

[14] Those who serve her will minister to the Holy One; the Lord loves those who love her.

[15] He who obeys her will judge the nations, and whoever gives heed to her will dwell secure.

[16] If he has faith in her he will obtain her; and his descendants will remain in possession of her.

[17] For at first she will walk with him on tortuous paths, she will bring fear and cowardice upon him, and will torment him by her discipline until she trusts him, and she will test him with her ordinances.

[18] Then she will come straight back to him and gladden him, and will reveal her secrets to him.

[19] If he goes astray she will forsake him, and hand him over to his ruin.

[20] Observe the right time, and beware of evil; and do not bring shame on yourself.

[21] For there is a shame which brings sin, and there is a shame which is glory and favor.

[22] Do not show partiality, to your own harm, or deference, to your downfall.

[23] Do not refrain from speaking at the crucial time, and do not hide your wisdom.

[24] For wisdom is known through speech, and education through the words of the tongue.

[25] Never speak against the truth, but be mindful of your ignorance.

[26] Do not be ashamed to confess your sins, and do not try to stop the current of a river.

[27] Do not subject yourself to a foolish fellow, nor show partiality to a ruler.

[28] Strive even to death for the truth and the Lord God will fight for you.

[29] Do not be reckless in your speech, or sluggish and remiss in your deeds.

[30] Do not be like a lion in your home, nor be a faultfinder with your servants.

[31] Let not your hand be extended to receive, but withdrawn when it is time to repay.

Sir.5

[1] Do not set your heart on your wealth, nor say, "I have enough."

[2] Do not follow your inclination and strength, walking according to the desires of your heart.

[3] Do not say, "Who will have power over me?" for the Lord will surely punish you.

[4] Do not say, "I sinned, and what happened to me?" for the Lord is slow to anger.

[5] Do not be so confident of atonement that you add sin to sin.

[6] Do not say, "His mercy is great, he will forgive the multitude of my sins," for both mercy and wrath are with him,

and his anger rests on sinners.

[7] Do not delay to turn to the Lord, nor postpone it from day to day; for suddenly the wrath of the Lord will go forth,

and at the time of punishment you will perish.

[8] Do not depend on dishonest wealth, for it will not benefit you in the day of calamity.

[9] Do not winnow with every wind, nor follow every path: the double-tongued sinner does that.

[10] Be steadfast in your understanding, and let your speech be consistent.

[11] Be quick to hear, and be deliberate in answering.

[12] If you have understanding, answer your neighbor; but if not, put your hand on your mouth.

[13] Glory and dishonor come from speaking, and a man's tongue is his downfall.

[14] Do not be called a slanderer, and do not lie in ambush with your tongue; for shame comes to the thief, and severe condemnation to the double-tongued.

[15] In great and small matters do not act amiss,

Sir.6

[1] and do not become an enemy instead of a friend; for a bad name incurs shame and reproach: so fares the double-tongued sinner.

[2] Do not exalt yourself through your soul's counsel, lest your soul be torn in pieces like a bull.

[3] You will devour your leaves and destroy your fruit, and will be left like a withered tree.

[4] An evil soul will destroy him who has it, and make him the laughingstock of his enemies.

[5] A pleasant voice multiplies friends, and a gracious tongue multiplies courtesies.

[6] Let those that are at peace with you be many, but let your advisers be one in a thousand.

[7] When you gain a friend, gain him through testing, and do not trust him hastily.

[8] For there is a friend who is such at his own convenience, but will not stand by you in your day of trouble.

[9] And there is a friend who changes into an enemy, and will disclose a quarrel to your disgrace.

[10] And there is a friend who is a table companion, but will not stand by you in your day of trouble.

[11] In prosperity he will make himself your equal, and be bold with your servants;

[12] but if you are brought low he will turn against you, and will hide himself from your presence.

[13] Keep yourself far from your enemies, and be on guard toward your friends.

[14] A faithful friend is a sturdy shelter: he that has found one has found a treasure.

[15] There is nothing so precious as a faithful friend, and no scales can measure his excellence.

[16] A faithful friend is an elixir of life; and those who fear the Lord will find him.

[17] Whoever fears the Lord directs his friendship aright, for as he is, so is his neighbor also.

[18] My son, from your youth up choose instruction, and until you are old you will keep finding wisdom.

[19] Come to her like one who plows and sows, and wait for her good harvest. For in her service you will toil a little while, and soon you will eat of her produce.

[20] She seems very harsh to the uninstructed; a weakling will not remain with her.

[21] She will weigh him down like a heavy testing stone, and he will not be slow to cast her off.

[22] For wisdom is like her name, and is not manifest to many.

[23] Listen, my son, and accept my judgment; do not reject my counsel.

[24] Put your feet into her fetters, and your neck into her collar.

[25] Put your shoulder under her and carry her, and do not fret under her bonds.

[26] Come to her with all your soul, and keep her ways with all your might.

[27] Search out and seek, and she will become known to you; and when you get hold of her, do not let her go.

[28] For at last you will find the rest she gives, and she will be changed into joy for you.

[29] Then her fetters will become for you a strong protection, and her collar a glorious robe.

[30] Her yoke is a golden ornament, and her bonds are a cord of blue.

[31] You will wear her like a glorious robe, and put her on like a crown of gladness.

[32] If you are willing, my son, you will be taught, and if you apply yourself you will become clever.

[33] If you love to listen you will gain knowledge, and if you incline your ear you will become wise.

[34] Stand in the assembly of the elders. Who is wise? Hold fast to him.

[35] Be ready to listen to every narrative, and do not let wise proverbs escape you.
[36] If you see an intelligent man, visit him early; let your foot wear out his doorstep.
[37] Reflect on the statutes of the Lord, and meditate at all times on his commandments. It is he who will give insight to your mind, and your desire for wisdom will be granted.

Sir.7

[1] Do no evil, and evil will never befall you.
[2] Stay away from wrong, and it will turn away from you.
[3] My son, do not sow the furrows of injustice, and you will not reap a sevenfold crop.
[4] Do not seek from the Lord the highest office, nor the seat of honor from the king.
[5] Do not assert your righteousness before the Lord, nor display your wisdom before the king.
[6] Do not seek to become a judge, lest you be unable to remove iniquity, lest you be partial to a powerful man, and thus put a blot on your integrity.
[7] Do not offend against the public, and do not disgrace yourself among the people.
[8] Do not commit a sin twice; even for one you will not go unpunished.
[9] Do not say, "He will consider the multitude of my gifts, and when I make an offering to the Most High God he will accept it."
[10] Do not be fainthearted in your prayer, nor neglect to give alms.
[11] Do not ridicule a man who is bitter in soul, for there is One who abases and exalts.
[12] Do not devise a lie against your brother, nor do the like to a friend.
[13] Refuse to utter any lie, for the habit of lying serves no good.
[14] Do not prattle in the assembly of the elders, nor repeat yourself in your prayer.
[15] Do not hate toilsome labor, or farm work, which were created by the Most High.
[16] Do not count yourself among the crowd of sinners; remember that wrath does not delay.
[17] Humble yourself greatly, for the punishment of the ungodly is fire and worms.
[18] Do not exchange a friend for money, or a real brother for the gold of Ophir.
[19] Do not deprive yourself of a wise and good wife, for her charm is worth more than gold.
[20] Do not abuse a servant who performs his work faithfully, or a hired laborer who devotes himself to you.
[21] Let your soul love an intelligent servant; do not withhold from him his freedom.
[22] Do you have cattle? Look after them; if they are profitable to you, keep them.
[23] Do you have children? Discipline them, and make them obedient from their youth.
[24] Do you have daughters? Be concerned for their chastity, and do not show yourself too indulgent with them.
[25] Give a daughter in marriage; you will have finished a great task. But give her to a man of understanding.
[26] If you have a wife who pleases you, do not cast her out; but do not trust yourself to one whom you detest.
[27] With all your heart honor your father, and do not forget the birth pangs of your mother.
[28] Remember that through your parents you were born; and what can you give back to them that equals their gift to you?
[29] With all your soul fear the Lord, and honor his priests.
[30] With all your might love your Maker, and do not forsake his ministers.
[31] Fear the Lord and honor the priest, and give him his portion, as is commanded you: the first fruits, the guilt offering, the gift of the shoulders, the sacrifice of sanctification, and the first fruits of the holy things.
[32] Stretch forth your hand to the poor, so that your blessing may be complete.
[33] Give graciously to all the living, and withhold not kindness from the dead.
[34] Do not fail those who weep, but mourn with those who mourn.
[35] Do not shrink from visiting a sick man, because for such deeds you will be loved.
[36] In all you do, remember the end of your life, and then you will never sin.

Sir.8

[1] Do not contend with a powerful man, lest you fall into his hands.

[2] Do not quarrel with a rich man, lest his resources outweigh yours; for gold has ruined many, and has perverted the minds of kings.
[3] Do not argue with a chatterer, nor heap wood on his fire.
[4] Do not jest with an ill-bred person, lest your ancestors be disgraced.
[5] Do not reproach a man who is turning away from sin; remember that we all deserve punishment.
[6] Do not disdain a man when he is old, for some of us are growing old.
[7] Do not rejoice over any one's death; remember that we all must die.
[8] Do not slight the discourse of the sages, but busy yourself with their maxims; because from them you will gain instruction and learn how to serve great men.
[9] Do not disregard the discourse of the aged, for they themselves learned from their fathers; because from them you will gain understanding and learn how to give an answer in time of need.
[10] Do not kindle the coals of a sinner, lest you be burned in his flaming fire.
[11] Do not get up and leave an insolent fellow, lest he lie in ambush against your words.
[12] Do not lend to a man who is stronger than you; but if you do lend anything, be as one who has lost it.
[13] Do not give surety beyond your means, but if you give surety, be concerned as one who must pay.
[14] Do not go to law against a judge, for the decision will favor him because of his standing.
[15] Do not travel on the road with a foolhardy fellow, lest he be burdensome to you; for he will act as he pleases, and through his folly you will perish with him.
[16] Do not fight with a wrathful man, and do not cross the wilderness with him; because blood is as nothing in his sight,
and where no help is at hand, he will strike you down.
[17] Do not consult with a fool, for he will not be able to keep a secret.
[18] In the presence of a stranger do nothing that is to be kept secret, for you do not know what he will divulge.
[19] Do not reveal your thoughts to every one, lest you drive away your good luck.

Sir.9

[1] Do not be jealous of the wife of your bosom, and do not teach her an evil lesson to your own hurt.
[2] Do not give yourself to a woman so that she gains mastery over your strength.
[3] Do not go to meet a loose woman, lest you fall into her snares.
[4] Do not associate with a woman singer, lest you be caught in her intrigues.
[5] Do not look intently at a virgin, lest you stumble and incur penalties for her.
[6] Do not give yourself to harlots lest you lose your inheritance.
[7] Do not look around in the streets of a city, nor wander about in its deserted sections.
[8] Turn away your eyes from a shapely woman, and do not look intently at beauty belonging to another; many have been misled by a woman's beauty, and by it passion is kindled like a fire.
[9] Never dine with another man's wife, nor revel with her at wine; lest your heart turn aside to her, and in blood you be plunged into destruction.
[10] Forsake not an old friend, for a new one does not compare with him. A new friend is like new wine; when it has aged you will drink it with pleasure.
[11] Do not envy the honors of a sinner, for you do not know what his end will be.
[12] Do not delight in what pleases the ungodly; remember that they will not be held guiltless as long as they live.
[13] Keep far from a man who has the power to kill, and you will not be worried by the fear of death. But if you approach him, make no misstep, lest he rob you of your life. Know that you are walking in the midst of snares, and that you are going about on the city battlements.
[14] As much as you can, aim to know your neighbors, and consult with the wise.
[15] Let your conversation be with men of understanding, and let all your discussion be about the law of the Most High.
[16] Let righteous men be your dinner companions, and let your glorying be in the fear of the Lord.
[17] A work will be praised for the skill of the craftsmen; so a people's leader is proved wise by his words.
[18] A babbler is feared in his city, and the man who is reckless in speech will be hated.

Sir.10

[1] A wise magistrate will educate his people, and the rule of an understanding man will be well ordered.

[2] Like the magistrate of the people, so are his officials; and like the ruler of the city, so are all its inhabitants.

[3] An undisciplined king will ruin his people, but a city will grow through the understanding of its rulers.

[4] The government of the earth is in the hands of the Lord, and over it he will raise up the right man for the time.

[5] The success of a man is in the hands of the Lord, and he confers his honor upon the person of the scribe.

[6] Do not be angry with your neighbor for any injury, and do not attempt anything by acts of insolence.

[7] Arrogance is hateful before the Lord and before men, and injustice is outrageous to both.

[8] Sovereignty passes from nation to nation on account of injustice and insolence and wealth.

[9] How can he who is dust and ashes be proud? for even in life his bowels decay.

[10] A long illness baffles the physician; the king of today will die tomorrow.

[11] For when a man is dead, he will inherit creeping things, and wild beasts, and worms.

[12] The beginning of man's pride is to depart from the Lord; his heart has forsaken his Maker.

[13] For the beginning of pride is sin, and the man who clings to it pours out abominations. Therefore the Lord brought upon them extraordinary afflictions, and destroyed them utterly.

[14] The Lord has cast down the thrones of rulers, and has seated the lowly in their place.

[15] The Lord has plucked up the roots of the nations, and has planted the humble in their place.

[16] The Lord has overthrown the lands of the nations, and has destroyed them to the foundations of the earth.

[17] He has removed some of them and destroyed them, and has extinguished the memory of them from the earth.

[18] Pride was not created for men, nor fierce anger for those born of women.

[19] What race is worthy of honor? The human race. What race is worthy of honor? Those who fear the Lord. What race is unworthy of honor? The human race. What race is unworthy of honor? Those who transgress the commandments.

[20] Among brothers their leader is worthy of honor, and those who fear the Lord are worthy of honor in his eyes.

[22] The rich, and the eminent, and the poor -- their glory is the fear of the Lord.

[23] It is not right to despise an intelligent poor man, nor is it proper to honor a sinful man.

[24] The nobleman, and the judge, and the ruler will be honored, but none of them is greater than the man who fears the Lord.

[25] Free men will be at the service of a wise servant, and a man of understanding will not grumble.

[26] Do not make a display of your wisdom when you do your work, nor glorify yourself at a time when you are in want.

[27] Better is a man who works and has an abundance of everything, than one who goes about boasting, but lacks bread.

[28] My son, glorify yourself with humility, and ascribe to yourself honor according to your worth.

[29] Who will justify the man that sins against himself? And who will honor the man that dishonors his own life?

[30] A poor man is honored for his knowledge, while a rich man is honored for his wealth.

[31] A man honored in poverty, how much more in wealth! And a man dishonored in wealth, how much more in poverty!

Sir.11

[1] The wisdom of a humble man will lift up his head, and will seat him among the great.

[2] Do not praise a man for his good looks, nor loathe a man because of his appearance.

[3] The bee is small among flying creatures, but her product is the best of sweet things.

[4] Do not boast about wearing fine clothes, nor exalt yourself in the day that you are honored; for the works of the Lord are wonderful, and his works are concealed from men.

[5] Many kings have had to sit on the ground, but one who was never thought of has worn a crown.

[6] Many rulers have been greatly disgraced, and illustrious men have been handed over to others.

[7] Do not find fault before you investigate; first consider, and then reprove.

[8] Do not answer before you have heard, nor interrupt a speaker in the midst of his words.

[9] Do not argue about a matter which does not concern you, nor sit with sinners when they judge a case.

[10] My son, do not busy yourself with many matters; if you multiply activities you will not go unpunished, and if you pursue you will not overtake, and by fleeing you will not escape.

[11] There is a man who works, and toils, and presses on, but is so much the more in want.

[12] There is another who is slow and needs help, who lacks strength and abounds in poverty; but the eyes of the Lord look upon him for his good; he lifts him out of his low estate

[13] and raises up his head, so that many are amazed at him.

[14] Good things and bad, life and death, poverty and wealth, come from the Lord.

[17] The gift of the Lord endures for those who are godly, and what he approves will have lasting success.

[18] There is a man who is rich through his diligence and self-denial, and this is the reward allotted to him:

[19] when he says, "I have found rest, and now I shall enjoy my goods!" he does not know how much time will pass until he leaves them to others and dies.

[20] Stand by your covenant and attend to it, and grow old in your work.

[21] Do not wonder at the works of a sinner, but trust in the Lord and keep at your toil; for it is easy in the sight of the Lord to enrich a poor man quickly and suddenly.

[22] The blessing of the Lord is the reward of the godly, and quickly God causes his blessing to flourish.

[23] Do not say, "What do I need, and what prosperity could be mine in the future?"

[24] Do not say, "I have enough, and what calamity could happen to me in the future?"

[25] In the day of prosperity, adversity is forgotten, and in the day of adversity, prosperity is not remembered.

[26] For it is easy in the sight of the Lord to reward a man on the day of death according to his conduct.

[27] The misery of an hour makes one forget luxury, and at the close of a man's life his deeds will be revealed.

[28] Call no one happy before his death; a man will be known through his children.

[29] Do not bring every man into your home, for many are the wiles of the crafty.

[30] Like a decoy partridge in a cage, so is the mind of a proud man, and like a spy he observes your weakness;

[31] for he lies in wait, turning good into evil, and to worthy actions he will attach blame.

[32] From a spark of fire come many burning coals, and a sinner lies in wait to shed blood.

[33] Beware of a scoundrel, for he devises evil, lest he give you a lasting blemish.

[34] Receive a stranger into your home and he will upset you with commotion, and will estrange you from your family.

Sir.12

[1] If you do a kindness, know to whom you do it, and you will be thanked for your good deeds.

[2] Do good to a godly man, and you will be repaid --if not by him, certainly by the Most High.

[3] No good will come to the man who persists in evil or to him who does not give alms.

[4] Give to the godly man, but do not help the sinner.

[5] Do good to the humble, but do not give to the ungodly; hold back his bread, and do not give it to him, lest by means of it he subdue you; for you will receive twice as much evil for all the good which you do to him.

[6] For the Most High also hates sinners and will inflict punishment on the ungodly.

[7] Give to the good man, but do not help the sinner.

[8] A friend will not be known in prosperity, nor will an enemy be hidden in adversity.

[9] A man's enemies are grieved when he prospers, and in his adversity even his friend will separate from him.

[10] Never trust your enemy, for like the rusting of copper, so is his wickedness.

[11] Even if he humbles himself and goes about cringing, watch yourself, and be on your guard against him; and you will be to him like one who has polished a mirror, and you will know that it was not hopelessly tarnished.

[12] Do not put him next to you, lest he overthrow you and take your place; do not have him sit at your right, lest he try to take your seat of honor, and at last you will realize the truth of my words, and be

stung by what I have said.

[13] Who will pity a snake charmer bitten by a serpent, or any who go near wild beasts?

[14] So no one will pity a man who associates with a sinner and becomes involved in his sins.

[15] He will stay with you for a time, but if you falter, he will not stand by you.

[16] An enemy will speak sweetly with his lips, but in his mind he will plan to throw you into a pit; an enemy will weep with his eyes, but if he finds an opportunity his thirst for blood will be insatiable.

[17] If calamity befalls you, you will find him there ahead of you; and while pretending to help you, he will trip you by the heel;

[18] he will shake his head, and clap his hands, and whisper much, and change his expression.

Sir.13

[1] Whoever touches pitch will be defiled, and whoever associates with a proud man will become like him.

[2] Do not lift a weight beyond your strength, nor associate with a man mightier and richer than you. How can the clay pot associate with the iron kettle? The pot will strike against it, and will itself be broken.

[3] A rich man does wrong, and he even adds reproaches; a poor man suffers wrong, and he must add apologies.

[4] A rich man will exploit you if you can be of use to him, but if you are in need he will forsake you.

[5] If you own something, he will live with you; he will drain your resources and he will not care.

[6] When he needs you he will deceive you, he will smile at you and give you hope. He will speak to you kindly and say, "What do you need?"

[7] He will shame you with his foods, until he has drained you two or three times; and finally he will deride you. Should he see you afterwards, he will forsake you, and shake his head at you.

[8] Take care not to be led astray, and not to be humiliated in your feasting.

[9] When a powerful man invites you, be reserved; and he will invite you the more often.

[10] Do not push forward, lest you be repulsed; and do not remain at a distance, lest you be forgotten.

[11] Do not try to treat him as an equal, nor trust his abundance of words; for he will test you through much talk, and while he smiles he will be examining you.

[12] Cruel is he who does not keep words to himself; he will not hesitate to injure or to imprison.

[13] Keep words to yourself and be very watchful, for you are walking about with your own downfall.

[15] Every creature loves its like, and every person his neighbor;

[16] all living beings associate by species, and a man clings to one like himself.

[17] What fellowship has a wolf with a lamb? No more has a sinner with a godly man.

[18] What peace is there between a hyena and a dog? And what peace between a rich man and a poor man?

[19] Wild asses in the wilderness are the prey of lions; likewise the poor are pastures for the rich.

[20] Humility is an abomination to a proud man; likewise a poor man is an abomination to a rich one.

[21] When a rich man totters, he is steadied by friends, but when a humble man falls, he is even pushed away by friends.

[22] If a rich man slips, his helpers are many; he speaks unseemly words, and they justify him. If a humble man slips, they even reproach him; he speaks sensibly, and receives no attention.

[23] When the rich man speaks all are silent, and they extol to the clouds what he says. When the poor man speaks they say, "Who is this fellow?" And should he stumble, they even push him down.

[24] Riches are good if they are free from sin, and poverty is evil in the opinion of the ungodly.

[25] A man's heart changes his countenance, either for good or for evil.

[26] The mark of a happy heart is a cheerful face, but to devise proverbs requires painful thinking.

Sir.14

[1] Blessed is the man who does not blunder with his lips and need not suffer grief for sin.

[2] Blessed is he whose heart does not condemn him, and who has not given up his hope.

[3] Riches are not seemly for a stingy man; and of what use is property to an envious man?

[4] Whoever accumulates by depriving himself, accumulates for others; and others will live in luxury on his goods.

[5] If a man is mean to himself, to whom will he be generous? He will not enjoy his own riches.

[6] No one is meaner than the man who is grudging to himself, and this is the retribution for his baseness;

[7] even if he does good, he does it unintentionally, and betrays his baseness in the end.

[8] Evil is the man with a grudging eye; he averts his face and disregards people.

[9] A greedy man's eye is not satisfied with a portion, and mean injustice withers the soul.

[10] A stingy man's eye begrudges bread, and it is lacking at his table.

[11] My son, treat yourself well, according to your means, and present worthy offerings to the Lord.

[12] Remember that death will not delay, and the decree of Hades has not been shown to you.

[13] Do good to a friend before you die, and reach out and give to him as much as you can.

[14] Do not deprive yourself of a happy day; let not your share of desired good pass by you.

[15] Will you not leave the fruit of your labors to another, and what you acquired by toil to be divided by lot?

[16] Give, and take, and beguile yourself, because in Hades one cannot look for luxury.

[17] All living beings become old like a garment, for the decree from of old is, "You must surely die!"

[18] Like flourishing leaves on a spreading tree which sheds some and puts forth others, so are the generations of flesh and blood: one dies and another is born.

[19] Every product decays and ceases to exist, and the man who made it will pass away with it.

[20] Blessed is the man who meditates on wisdom and who reasons intelligently.

[21] He who reflects in his mind on her ways will also ponder her secrets.

[22] Pursue wisdom like a hunter, and lie in wait on her paths.

[23] He who peers through her windows will also listen at her doors;

[24] he who encamps near her house will also fasten his tent peg to her walls;

[25] he will pitch his tent near her, and will lodge in an excellent lodging place;

[26] he will place his children under her shelter, and will camp under her boughs;

[27] he will be sheltered by her from the heat, and will dwell in the midst of her glory.

Sir.15

[1] The man who fears the Lord will do this, and he who holds to the law will obtain wisdom.

[2] She will come to meet him like a mother, and like the wife of his youth she will welcome him.

[3] She will feed him with the bread of understanding, and give him the water of wisdom to drink.

[4] He will lean on her and will not fall, and he will rely on her and will not be put to shame.

[5] She will exalt him above his neighbors, and will open his mouth in the midst of the assembly.

[6] He will find gladness and a crown of rejoicing, and will acquire an everlasting name.

[7] Foolish men will not obtain her, and sinful men will not see her.

[8] She is far from men of pride, and liars will never think of her.

[9] A hymn of praise is not fitting on the lips of a sinner, for it has not been sent from the Lord.

[10] For a hymn of praise should be uttered in wisdom, and the Lord will prosper it.

[11] Do not say, "Because of the Lord I left the right way"; for he will not do what he hates.

[12] Do not say, "It was he who led me astray"; for he had no need of a sinful man.

[13] The Lord hates all abominations, and they are not loved by those who fear him.

[14] It was he who created man in the beginning, and he left him in the power of his own inclination.

[15] If you will, you can keep the commandments, and to act faithfully is a matter of your own choice.

[16] He has placed before you fire and water: stretch out your hand for whichever you wish.

[17] Before a man are life and death, and whichever he chooses will be given to him.

[18] For great is the wisdom of the Lord; he is mighty in power and sees everything;

[19] his eyes are on those who fear him, and he knows every deed of man.

[20] He has not commanded any one to be ungodly, and he has not given any one permission to sin.

Sir.16

[1] Do not desire a multitude of useless children, nor rejoice in ungodly sons.

[2] If they multiply , do not rejoice in them, unless the fear of the Lord is in them.

[3] Do not trust in their survival, and do not rely on their multitude; for one is better than a thousand, and to die childless is better than to have ungodly children.

[4] For through one man of understanding a city will be filled with people, but through a tribe of lawless men it will be made desolate.

[5] Many such things my eye has seen, and my ear has heard things more striking than these.

[6] In an assembly of sinners a fire will be kindled, and in a disobedient nation wrath was kindled.

[7] He was not propitiated for the ancient giants who revolted in their might.

[8] He did not spare the neighbors of Lot, whom he loathed on account of their insolence.

[9] He showed no pity for a nation devoted to destruction, for those destroyed in their sins;

[10] nor for the six hundred thousand men on foot, who rebelliously assembled in their stubbornness.

[11] Even if there is only one stiff-necked person, it will be a wonder if he remains unpunished. For mercy and wrath are with the Lord; he is mighty to forgive, and he pours out wrath.

[12] As great as his mercy, so great is also his reproof; he judges a man according to his deeds.

[13] The sinner will not escape with his plunder, and the patience of the godly will not be frustrated.

[14] He will make room for every act of mercy; every one will receive in accordance with his deeds.

[17] Do not say, "I shall be hidden from the Lord, and who from on high will remember me? Among so many people I shall not be known, for what is my soul in the boundless creation?

[18] Behold, heaven and the highest heaven, the abyss and the earth, will tremble at his visitation.

[19] The mountains also and the foundations of the earth shake with trembling when he looks upon them.

[20] And no mind will reflect on this. Who will ponder his ways?

[21] Like a tempest which no man can see, so most of his works are concealed.

[22] Who will announce his acts of justice? Or who will await them? For the covenant is far off."

[23] This is what one devoid of understanding thinks; a senseless and misguided man thinks foolishly.

[24] Listen to me, my son, and acquire knowledge, and pay close attention to my words.

[25] I will impart instruction by weight, and declare knowledge accurately.

[26] The works of the Lord have existed from the beginning by his creation, and when he made them, he determined their divisions.

[27] He arranged his works in an eternal order, and their dominion for all generations; they neither hunger nor grow weary, and they do not cease from their labors.

[28] They do not crowd one another aside, and they will never disobey his word.

[29] After this the Lord looked upon the earth, and filled it with his good things;

[30] with all kinds of living beings he covered its surface, and to it they return.

Sir.17

[1] The Lord created man out of earth, and turned him back to it again.

[2] He gave to men few days, a limited time, but granted them authority over the things upon the earth.

[3] He endowed them with strength like his own, and made them in his own image.

[4] He placed the fear of them in all living beings, and granted them dominion over beasts and birds.

[6] He made for them tongue and eyes; he gave them ears and a mind for thinking.

[7] He filled them with knowledge and understanding, and showed them good and evil.

[8] He set his eye upon their hearts to show them the majesty of his works.

[10] And they will praise his holy name, to proclaim the grandeur of his works.

[11] He bestowed knowledge upon them, and allotted to them the law of life.

[12] He established with them an eternal covenant, and showed them his judgments.

[13] Their eyes saw his glorious majesty, and their ears heard the glory of his voice.

[14] And he said to them, "Beware of all unrighteousness." And he gave commandment to each of them concerning
his neighbor.

[15] Their ways are always before him, they will not be hid from his eyes.

[17] He appointed a ruler for every nation, but Israel is the Lord's own portion.

[19] All their works are as the sun before him, and his eyes are continually upon their ways.

[20] Their iniquities are not hidden from him, and all their sins are before the Lord.

[22] A man's almsgiving is like a signet with the Lord and he will keep a person's kindness like the apple of his eye.

[23] Afterward he will arise and requite them, and he will bring their recompense on their heads.

[24] Yet to those who repent he grants a return, and he encourages those whose endurance is failing.

[25] Turn to the Lord and forsake your sins; pray in his presence and lessen your offenses.

[26] Return to the Most High and turn away from iniquity, and hate abominations intensely.

[27] Who will sing praises to the Most High in Hades, as do those who are alive and give thanks?

[28] From the dead, as from one who does not exist, thanksgiving has ceased; he who is alive and well sings the Lord's praises.

[29] How great is the mercy of the Lord, and his forgiveness for those who turn to him!

[30] For all things cannot be in men, since a son of man is not immortal.

[31] What is brighter than the sun? Yet its light fails. So flesh and blood devise evil.

[32] He marshals the host of the height of heaven; but all men are dust and ashes.

Sir.18

[1] He who lives for ever created the whole universe;

[2] the Lord alone will be declared righteous.

[4] To none has he given power to proclaim his works; and who can search out his mighty deeds?

[5] Who can measure his majestic power? And who can fully recount his mercies?

[6] It is not possible to diminish or increase them, nor is it possible to trace the wonders of the Lord.

[7] When a man has finished, he is just beginning, and when he stops, he will be at a loss.

[8] What is man, and of what use is he? What is his good and what is his evil?

[9] The number of a man's days is great if he reaches a hundred years.

[10] Like a drop of water from the sea and a grain of sand so are a few years in the day of eternity.

[11] Therefore the Lord is patient with them and pours out his mercy upon them.

[12] He sees and recognizes that their end will be evil; therefore he grants them forgiveness in abundance.

[13] The compassion of man is for his neighbor, but the compassion of the Lord is for all living beings. He rebukes and trains and teaches them, and turns them back, as a shepherd his flock.

[14] He has compassion on those who accept his discipline and who are eager for his judgments.

[15] My son, do not mix reproach with your good deeds, nor cause grief by your words when you present a gift.

[16] Does not the dew assuage the scorching heat? So a word is better than a gift.

[17] Indeed, does not a word surpass a good gift? Both are to be found in a gracious man.

[18] A fool is ungracious and abusive, and the gift of a grudging man makes the eyes dim.

[19] Before you speak, learn, and before you fall ill, take care of your health.

[20] Before judgment, examine yourself, and in the hour of visitation you will find forgiveness.

[21] Before falling ill, humble yourself, and when you are on the point of sinning, turn back.

[22] Let nothing hinder you from paying a vow promptly, and do not wait until death to be released from it.

[23] Before making a vow, prepare yourself; and do not be like a man who tempts the Lord.

[24] Think of his wrath on the day of death, and of the moment of vengeance when he turns away his face.

[25] In the time of plenty think of the time of hunger; in the days of wealth think of poverty and need.

[26] From morning to evening conditions change, and all things move swiftly before the Lord.

[27] A wise man is cautious in everything, and in days of sin he guards against wrongdoing.

[28] Every intelligent man knows wisdom, and he praises the one who finds her.

[29] Those who understand sayings become skilled themselves, and pour forth apt proverbs.

[30] Do not follow your base desires, but restrain your appetites.

[31] If you allow your soul to take pleasure in base desire, it will make you the laughingstock of your enemies.

[32] Do not revel in great luxury, lest you become impoverished by its expense.

[33] Do not become a beggar by feasting with borrowed money, when you have nothing in your purse.

Sir.19

[1] A workman who is a drunkard will not become rich; he who despises small things will fail little by little.

[2] Wine and women lead intelligent men astray, and the man who consorts with harlots is very reckless.

[3] Decay and worms will inherit him, and the reckless soul will be snatched away.

[4] One who trusts others too quickly is lightminded, and one who sins does wrong to himself.

[5] One who rejoices in wickedness will be condemned,

[6] and for one who hates gossip evil is lessened.

[7] Never repeat a conversation, and you will lose nothing at all.

[8] With friend or foe do not report it, and unless it would be a sin for you, do not disclose it;

[9] for some one has heard you and watched you, and when the time comes he will hate you.

[10] Have you heard a word? Let it die with you. Be brave! It will not make you burst!

[11] With such a word a fool will suffer pangs like a woman in labor with a child.

[12] Like an arrow stuck in the flesh of the thigh, so is a word inside a fool.

[13] Question a friend, perhaps he did not do it; but if he did anything, so that he may do it no more.

[14] Question a neighbor, perhaps he did not say it; but if he said it, so that he may not say it again.

[15] Question a friend, for often it is slander; so do not believe everything you hear.

[16] A person may make a slip without intending it. Who has never sinned with his tongue?

[17] Question your neighbor before you threaten him; and let the law of the Most High take its course.

[20] All wisdom is the fear of the Lord, and in all wisdom there is the fulfilment of the law.

[22] But the knowledge of wickedness is not wisdom, nor is there prudence where sinners take counsel.

[23] There is a cleverness which is abominable, but there is a fool who merely lacks wisdom.

[24] Better is the God-fearing man who lacks intelligence, than the highly prudent man who transgresses the law.

[25] There is a cleverness which is scrupulous but unjust, and there are people who distort kindness to gain a verdict.

[26] There is a rascal bowed down in mourning, but inwardly he is full of deceit.

[27] He hides his face and pretends not to hear; but where no one notices, he will forestall you.

[28] And if by lack of strength he is prevented from sinning, he will do evil when he finds an opportunity.

[29] A man is known by his appearance, and a sensible man is known by his face, when you meet him.

[30] A man's attire and open-mouthed laughter, and a man's manner of walking, show what he is.

Sir.20

[1] There is a reproof which is not timely; and there is a man who keeps silent but is wise.

[2] How much better it is to reprove than to stay angry! And the one who confesses his fault will be kept from loss.

[4] Like a eunuch's desire to violate a maiden is a man who executes judgments by violence.

[5] There is one who by keeping silent is found wise, while another is detested for being too talkative.

[6] There is one who keeps silent because he has no answer, while another keeps silent because he knows when to speak.

[7] A wise man will be silent until the right moment, but a braggart and fool goes beyond the right moment.

[8] Whoever uses too many words will be loathed, and whoever usurps the right to speak will be hated.

[9] There may be good fortune for a man in adversity, and a windfall may result in a loss.

[10] There is a gift that profits you nothing, and there is a gift that brings a double return.

[11] There are losses because of glory, and there are men who have raised their heads from humble circumstances.

[12] There is a man who buys much for a little, but pays for it seven times over.

[13] The wise man makes himself beloved through his words, but the courtesies of fools are wasted.

[14] A fool's gift will profit you nothing, for he has many eyes instead of one.

[15] He gives little and upbraids much, he opens his mouth like a herald; today he lends and tomorrow he asks it back;

such a one is a hateful man.

[16] A fool will say, "I have no friend, and there is no gratitude for my good deeds; those who eat my bread speak unkindly."

[17] How many will ridicule him, and how often!

[18] A slip on the pavement is better than a slip of the tongue; so the downfall of the wicked will occur speedily.

[19] An ungracious man is like a story told at the wrong time, which is continually on the lips of the ignorant.

[20] A proverb from a fool's lips will be rejected, for he does not tell it at its proper time.

[21] A man may be prevented from sinning by his poverty, so when he rests he feels no remorse.

[22] A man may lose his life through shame, or lose it because of his foolish look.

[23] A man may for shame make promises to a friend, and needlessly make him an enemy.

[24] A lie is an ugly blot on a man; it is continually on the lips of the ignorant.

[25] A thief is preferable to a habitual liar, but the lot of both is ruin.

[26] The disposition of a liar brings disgrace, and his shame is ever with him.

[27] He who speaks wisely will advance himself, and a sensible man will please great men.

[28] Whoever cultivates the soil will heap up his harvest, and whoever pleases great men will atone for injustice.

[29] Presents and gifts blind the eyes of the wise; like a muzzle on the mouth they avert reproofs.

[30] Hidden wisdom and unseen treasure, what advantage is there in either of them?

[31] Better is the man who hides his folly than the man who hides his wisdom.

Sir.21

[1] Have you sinned, my son? Do so no more, but pray about your former sins.

[2] Flee from sin as from a snake; for if you approach sin, it will bite you. Its teeth are lion's teeth, and destroy the souls of men.

[3] All lawlessness is like a two-edged sword; there is no healing for its wound.

[4] Terror and violence will lay waste riches; thus the house of the proud will be laid waste.

[5] The prayer of a poor man goes from his lips to the ears of God, and his judgment comes speedily.

[6] Whoever hates reproof walks in the steps of the sinner, but he that fears the Lord will repent in his heart.

[7] He who is mighty in speech is known from afar; but the sensible man, when he slips, is aware of it.

[8] A man who builds his house with other people's money is like one who gathers stones for his burial mound.

[9] An assembly of the wicked is like tow gathered together, and their end is a flame of fire.

[10] The way of sinners is smoothly paved with stones, but at its end is the pit of Hades.

[11] Whoever keeps the law controls his thoughts, and wisdom is the fulfilment of the fear of the Lord.

[12] He who is not clever cannot be taught, but there is a cleverness which increases bitterness.

[13] The knowledge of a wise man will increase like a flood, and his counsel like a flowing spring.

[14] The mind of a fool is like a broken jar; it will hold no knowledge.

[15] When a man of understanding hears a wise saying, he will praise it and add to it; when a reveler hears it, he dislikes it
and casts it behind his back.

[16] A fool's narration is like a burden on a journey, but delight will be found in the speech of the intelligent.

[17] The utterance of a sensible man will be sought in the assembly, and they will ponder his words in their minds.

[18] Like a house that has vanished, so is wisdom to a fool; and the knowledge of the ignorant is unexamined talk.

[19] To a senseless man education is fetters on his feet, and like manacles on his right hand.

[20] A fool raises his voice when he laughs, but a clever man smiles quietly.

[21] To a sensible man education is like a golden ornament, and like a bracelet on the right arm.

[22] The foot of a fool rushes into a house, but a man of experience stands respectfully before it.

[23] A boor peers into the house from the door, but a cultivated man remains outside.

[24] It is ill-mannered for a man to listen at a door, and a discreet man is grieved by the disgrace.

[25] The lips of strangers will speak of these things, but the words of the prudent will be weighed in the balance.

[26] The mind of fools is in their mouth, but the mouth of wise men is in their mind.

[27] When an ungodly man curses his adversary, he curses his own soul.

[28] A whisperer defiles his own soul and is hated in his neighborhood.

Sir.22

[1] The indolent may be compared to a filthy stone, and every one hisses at his disgrace.

[2] The indolent may be compared to the filth of dunghills; any one that picks it up will shake it off his

hand.

[3] It is a disgrace to be the father of an undisciplined son, and the birth of a daughter is a loss.

[4] A sensible daughter obtains her husband, but one who acts shamefully brings grief to her father.

[5] An impudent daughter disgraces father and husband, and will be despised by both.

[6] Like music in mourning is a tale told at the wrong time, but chastising and discipline are wisdom at all times.

[7] He who teaches a fool is like one who glues potsherds together, or who rouses a sleeper from deep slumber.

[8] He who tells a story to a fool tells it to a drowsy man; and at the end he will say, "What is it?"

[11] Weep for the dead, for he lacks the light; and weep for the fool, for he lacks intelligence; weep less bitterly for the dead, for he has attained rest; but the life of the fool is worse than death.

[12] Mourning for the dead lasts seven days, but for a fool or an ungodly man it lasts all his life.

[13] Do not talk much with a foolish man, and do not visit an unintelligent man; guard yourself from him to escape trouble,

and you will not be soiled when he shakes himself off; avoid him and you will find rest, and you will never be wearied by his madness.

[14] What is heavier than lead? And what is its name except "Fool"?

[15] Sand, salt, and a piece of iron are easier to bear than a stupid man.

[16] A wooden beam firmly bonded into a building will not be torn loose by an earthquake; so the mind firmly fixed on a reasonable counsel will not be afraid in a crisis.

[17] A mind settled on an intelligent thought is like the stucco decoration on the wall of a colonnade.

[18] Fences set on a high place will not stand firm against the wind; so a timid heart with a fool's purpose will not stand firm against any fear.

[19] A man who pricks an eye will make tears fall, and one who pricks the heart makes it show feeling.

[20] One who throws a stone at birds scares them away, and one who reviles a friend will break off the friendship.

[21] Even if you have drawn your sword against a friend, do not despair, for a renewal of friendship is possible.

[22] If you have opened your mouth against your friend, do not worry, for reconciliation is possible; but as for reviling, arrogance, disclosure of secrets, or a treacherous blow -- in these cases any friend will flee.

[23] Gain the trust of your neighbor in his poverty, that you may rejoice with him in his prosperity; stand by him in time of affliction, that you may share with him in his inheritance.

[24] The vapor and smoke of the furnace precede the fire; so insults precede bloodshed.

[25] I will not be ashamed to protect a friend, and I will not hide from him;

[26] but if some harm should happen to me because of him, whoever hears of it will beware of him.

[27] O that a guard were set over my mouth, and a seal of prudence upon my lips, that it may keep me from falling, so that my tongue may not destroy me!

Sir.23

[1] O Lord, Father and Ruler of my life, do not abandon me to their counsel, and let me not fall because of them!

[2] O that whips were set over my thoughts, and the discipline of wisdom over my mind! That they may not spare me in my errors, and that it may not pass by my sins;

[3] in order that my mistakes may not be multiplied, and my sins may not abound; then I will not fall before my adversaries, and my enemy will not rejoice over me.

[4] O Lord, Father and God of my life, do not give me haughty eyes,

[5] and remove from me evil desire.

[6] Let neither gluttony nor lust overcome me, and do not surrender me to a shameless soul.

[7] Listen, my children, to instruction concerning speech; the one who observes it will never be caught.

[8] The sinner is overtaken through his lips, the reviler and the arrogant are tripped by them.

[9] Do not accustom your mouth to oaths, and do not habitually utter the name of the Holy One;

[10] for as a servant who is continually examined under torture will not lack bruises, so also the man who always swears and utters the Name will not be cleansed from sin.

[11] A man who swears many oaths will be filled with iniquity, and the scourge will not leave his house; if he offends, his sin remains on him, and if he disregards it, he sins doubly; if he has sworn needlessly, he will not be justified, for his house will be filled with calamities.

[12] There is an utterance which is comparable to death; may it never be found in the inheritance of

Jacob! For all these errors will be far from the godly, and they will not wallow in sins.

[13] Do not accustom your mouth to lewd vulgarity, for it involves sinful speech.

[14] Remember your father and mother when you sit among great men; lest you be forgetful in their presence, and be deemed a fool on account of your habits; then you will wish that you had never been born, and you will curse the day of your birth.

[15] A man accustomed to use insulting words will never become disciplined all his days.

[16] Two sorts of men multiply sins, and a third incurs wrath. The soul heated like a burning fire will not be quenched until it is consumed; a man who commits fornication with his near of kin will never cease until the fire burns him up.

[17] To a fornicator all bread tastes sweet; he will never cease until he dies.

[18] A man who breaks his marriage vows says to himself, "Who sees me? Darkness surrounds me, and the walls hide me, and no one sees me. Why should I fear? The Most High will not take notice of my sins."

[19] His fear is confined to the eyes of men, and he does not realize that the eyes of the Lord are ten thousand times brighter than the sun; they look upon all the ways of men, and perceive even the hidden places.

[20] Before the universe was created, it was known to him; so it was also after it was finished.

[21] This man will be punished in the streets of the city, and where he least suspects it, he will be seized.

[22] So it is with a woman who leaves her husband and provides an heir by a stranger.

[23] For first of all, she has disobeyed the law of the Most High; second, she has committed an offense against her husband; and third, she has committed adultery through harlotry and brought forth children by another man.

[24] She herself will be brought before the assembly, and punishment will fall on her children.

[25] Her children will not take root, and her branches will not bear fruit.

[26] She will leave her memory for a curse, and her disgrace will not be blotted out.

[27] Those who survive her will recognize that nothing is better than the fear of the Lord, and nothing sweeter than to heed the commandments of the Lord.

Sir.24

[1] Wisdom will praise herself, and will glory in the midst of her people.

[2] In the assembly of the Most High she will open her mouth, and in the presence of his host she will glory:

[3] "I came forth from the mouth of the Most High, and covered the earth like a mist.

[4] I dwelt in high places, and my throne was in a pillar of cloud.

[5] Alone I have made the circuit of the vault of heaven and have walked in the depths of the abyss.

[6] In the waves of the sea, in the whole earth, and in every people and nation I have gotten a possession.

[7] Among all these I sought a resting place; I sought in whose territory I might lodge.

[8] "Then the Creator of all things gave me a commandment, and the one who created me assigned a place for my tent.
And he said, `Make your dwelling in Jacob, and in Israel receive your inheritance.'

[9] From eternity, in the beginning, he created me, and for eternity I shall not cease to exist.

[10] In the holy tabernacle I ministered before him, and so I was established in Zion.

[11] In the beloved city likewise he gave me a resting place, and in Jerusalem was my dominion.

[12] So I took root in an honored people, in the portion of the Lord, who is their inheritance.

[13] "I grew tall like a cedar in Lebanon, and like a cypress on the heights of Hermon.

[14] I grew tall like a palm tree in En-ge'di, and like rose plants in Jericho; like a beautiful olive tree in the field, and like a plane tree I grew tall.

[15] Like cassia and camel's thorn I gave forth the aroma of spices, and like choice myrrh I spread a pleasant odor, like galbanum, onycha, and stacte, and like the fragrance of frankincense in the tabernacle.

[16] Like a terebinth I spread out my branches, and my branches are glorious and graceful.

[17] Like a vine I caused loveliness to bud, and my blossoms became glorious and abundant fruit.

[19] "Come to me, you who desire me, and eat your fill of my produce.

[20] For the remembrance of me is sweeter than honey, and my inheritance sweeter than the honeycomb.

[21] Those who eat me will hunger for more, and those who drink me will thirst for more.

[22] Whoever obeys me will not be put to shame, and those who work with my help will not sin."
[23] All this is the book of the covenant of the Most High God, the law which Moses commanded us as an inheritance for the congregations of Jacob.
[25] It fills men with wisdom, like the Pishon, and like the Tigris at the time of the first fruits.
[26] It makes them full of understanding, like the Euphrates, and like the Jordan at harvest time.
[27] It makes instruction shine forth like light, like the Gihon at the time of vintage.
[28] Just as the first man did not know her perfectly, the last one has not fathomed her;
[29] for her thought is more abundant than the sea, and her counsel deeper than the great abyss.
[30] I went forth like a canal from a river and like a water channel into a garden.
[31] I said, "I will water my orchard and drench my garden plot"; and lo, my canal became a river, and my river became a sea.
[32] I will again make instruction shine forth like the dawn, and I will make it shine afar;
[33] I will again pour out teaching like prophecy, and leave it to all future generations.
[34] Observe that I have not labored for myself alone, but for all who seek instruction.

Sir.25

[1] My soul takes pleasure in three things, and they are beautiful in the sight of the Lord and of men; agreement between brothers, friendship between neighbors, and a wife and a husband who live in harmony.
[2] My soul hates three kinds of men, and I am greatly offended at their life: a beggar who is proud, a rich man who is a liar, and an adulterous old man who lacks good sense.
[3] You have gathered nothing in your youth; how then can you find anything in your old age?
[4] What an attractive thing is judgment in gray-haired men, and for the aged to possess good counsel!
[5] How attractive is wisdom in the aged, and understanding and counsel in honorable men!
[6] Rich experience is the crown of the aged, and their boast is the fear of the Lord.
[7] With nine thoughts I have gladdened my heart, and a tenth I shall tell with my tongue: a man rejoicing in his children;
a man who lives to see the downfall of his foes;
[8] happy is he who lives with an intelligent wife, and he who has not made a slip with his tongue, and he who has not served a man inferior to himself;
[9] happy is he who has gained good sense, and he who speaks to attentive listeners.
[10] How great is he who has gained wisdom! But there is no one superior to him who fears the Lord.
[11] The fear of the Lord surpasses everything; to whom shall be likened the one who holds it fast?
[13] Any wound, but not a wound of the heart! Any wickedness, but not the wickedness of a wife!
[14] Any attack, but not an attack from those who hate! And any vengeance, but not the vengeance of enemies!
[15] There is no venom worse than a snake's venom, and no wrath worse than an enemy's wrath.
[16] I would rather dwell with a lion and a dragon than dwell with an evil wife.
[17] The wickedness of a wife changes her appearance, and darkens her face like that of a bear.
[18] Her husband takes his meals among the neighbors, and he cannot help sighing bitterly.
[19] Any iniquity is insignificant compared to a wife's iniquity; may a sinner's lot befall her!
[20] A sandy ascent for the feet of the aged -- such is a garrulous wife for a quiet husband.
[21] Do not be ensnared by a woman's beauty, and do not desire a woman for her possessions.
[22] There is wrath and impudence and great disgrace when a wife supports her husband.
[23] A dejected mind, a gloomy face, and a wounded heart are caused by an evil wife. Drooping hands and weak knees
are caused by the wife who does not make her husband happy.
[24] From a woman sin had its beginning, and because of her we all die.
[25] Allow no outlet to water, and no boldness of speech in an evil wife.
[26] If she does not go as you direct, separate her from yourself.

Sir.26

[1] Happy is the husband of a good wife; the number of his days will be doubled.
[2] A loyal wife rejoices her husband, and he will complete his years in peace.

[3] A good wife is a great blessing; she will be granted among the blessings of the man who fears the Lord.
[4] Whether rich or poor, his heart is glad, and at all times his face is cheerful.
[5] Of three things my heart is afraid, and of a fourth I am frightened: The slander of a city, the gathering of a mob, and false accusation -- all these are worse than death.
[6] There is grief of heart and sorrow when a wife is envious of a rival, and a tongue-lashing makes it known to all.
[7] An evil wife is an ox yoke which chafes; taking hold of her is like grasping a scorpion.
[8] There is great anger when a wife is drunken; she will not hide her shame.
[9] A wife's harlotry shows in her lustful eyes, and she is known by her eyelids.
[10] Keep strict watch over a headstrong daughter, lest, when she finds liberty, she use it to her hurt.
[11] Be on guard against her impudent eye, and do not wonder if she sins against you.
[12] As a thirsty wayfarer opens his mouth and drinks from any water near him, so will she sit in front of every post and open her quiver to the arrow.
[13] A wife's charm delights her husband, and her skill puts fat on his bones.
[14] A silent wife is a gift of the Lord, and there is nothing so precious as a disciplined soul.
[15] A modest wife adds charm to charm, and no balance can weigh the value of a chaste soul.
[16] Like the sun rising in the heights of the Lord, so is the beauty of a good wife in her well-ordered home.
[17] Like the shining lamp on the holy lampstand, so is a beautiful face on a stately figure.
[18] Like pillars of gold on a base of silver, so are beautiful feet with a steadfast heart.
[28] At two things my heart is grieved, and because of a third anger comes over me: a warrior in want through poverty,
and intelligent men who are treated contemptuously; a man who turns back from righteousness to sin -- the Lord will prepare him for the sword!
[29] A merchant can hardly keep from wrongdoing, and a tradesman will not be declared innocent of sin.

Sir.27

[1] Many have committed sin for a trifle, and whoever seeks to get rich will avert his eyes.
[2] As a stake is driven firmly into a fissure between stones, so sin is wedged in between selling and buying.
[3] If a man is not steadfast and zealous in the fear of the Lord, his house will be quickly overthrown.
[4] When a sieve is shaken, the refuse remains; so a man's filth remains in his thoughts.
[5] The kiln tests the potter's vessels; so the test of a man is in his reasoning.
[6] The fruit discloses the cultivation of a tree; so the expression of a thought discloses the cultivation of a man's mind.
[7] Do not praise a man before you hear him reason, for this is the test of men.
[8] If you pursue justice, you will attain it and wear it as a glorious robe.
[9] Birds flock with their kind; so truth returns to those who practice it.
[10] A lion lies in wait for prey; so does sin for the workers of iniquity.
[11] The talk of the godly man is always wise, but the fool changes like the moon.
[12] Among stupid people watch for a chance to leave, but among thoughtful people stay on.
[13] The talk of fools is offensive, and their laughter is wantonly sinful.
[14] The talk of men given to swearing makes one's hair stand on end, and their quarrels make a man stop his ears.
[15] The strife of the proud leads to bloodshed, and their abuse is grievous to hear.
[16] Whoever betrays secrets destroys confidence, and he will never find a congenial friend.
[17] Love your friend and keep faith with him; but if you betray his secrets, do not run after him.
[18] For as a man destroys his enemy, so you have destroyed the friendship of your neighbor.
[19] And as you allow a bird to escape from your hand, so you have let your neighbor go, and will not catch him again.
[20] Do not go after him, for he is too far off, and has escaped like a gazelle from a snare.
[21] For a wound may be bandaged, and there is reconciliation after abuse, but whoever has betrayed secrets is without hope.
[22] Whoever winks his eye plans evil deeds, and no one can keep him from them.
[23] In your presence his mouth is all sweetness, and he admires your words; but later he will twist his speech and with your own words he will give offense.

[24] I have hated many things, but none to be compared to him; even the Lord will hate him.

[25] Whoever throws a stone straight up throws it on his own head; and a treacherous blow opens up wounds.

[26] He who digs a pit will fall into it, and he who sets a snare will be caught in it.

[27] If a man does evil, it will roll back upon him, and he will not know where it came from.

[28] Mockery and abuse issue from the proud man, but vengeance lies in wait for him like a lion.

[29] Those who rejoice in the fall of the godly will be caught in a snare, and pain will consume them before their death.

[30] Anger and wrath, these also are abominations, and the sinful man will possess them.

Sir.28

[1] He that takes vengeance will suffer vengeance from the Lord, and he will firmly establish his sins.

[2] Forgive your neighbor the wrong he has done, and then your sins will be pardoned when you pray.

[3] Does a man harbor anger against another, and yet seek for healing from the Lord?

[4] Does he have no mercy toward a man like himself, and yet pray for his own sins?

[5] If he himself, being flesh, maintains wrath, who will make expiation for his sins?

[6] Remember the end of your life, and cease from enmity, remember destruction and death, and be true to the commandments.

[7] Remember the commandments, and do not be angry with your neighbor; remember the covenant of the Most High, and overlook ignorance.

[8] Refrain from strife, and you will lessen sins; for a man given to anger will kindle strife,

[9] and a sinful man will disturb friends and inject enmity among those who are at peace.

[10] In proportion to the fuel for the fire, so will be the burning, and in proportion to the obstinacy of strife will be the burning; in proportion to the strength of the man will be his anger, and in proportion to his wealth he will heighten his wrath.

[11] A hasty quarrel kindles fire, and urgent strife sheds blood.

[12] If you blow on a spark, it will glow; if you spit on it, it will be put out; and both come out of your mouth.

[13] Curse the whisperer and deceiver, for he has destroyed many who were at peace.

[14] Slander has shaken many, and scattered them from nation to nation, and destroyed strong cities, and overturned the houses of great men.

[15] Slander has driven away courageous women, and deprived them of the fruit of their toil.

[16] Whoever pays heed to slander will not find rest, nor will he settle down in peace.

[17] The blow of a whip raises a welt, but a blow of the tongue crushes the bones.

[18] Many have fallen by the edge of the sword, but not so many as have fallen because of the tongue.

[19] Happy is the man who is protected from it, who has not been exposed to its anger, who has not borne its yoke,
and has not been bound with its fetters;

[20] for its yoke is a yoke of iron, and its fetters are fetters of bronze;

[21] its death is an evil death, and Hades is preferable to it.

[22] It will not be master over the godly, and they will not be burned in its flame.

[23] Those who forsake the Lord will fall into its power; it will burn among them and will not be put out. It will be sent out against them like a lion; like a leopard it will mangle them.

[24] See that you fence in your property with thorns, lock up your silver and gold,

[25] make balances and scales for your words, and make a door and a bolt for your mouth.

[26] Beware lest you err with your tongue, lest you fall before him who lies in wait.

Sir.29

[1] He that shows mercy will lend to his neighbor, and he that strengthens him with his hand keeps the commandments.

[2] Lend to your neighbor in the time of his need; and in turn, repay your neighbor promptly.

[3] Confirm your word and keep faith with him, and on every occasion you will find what you need.

[4] Many persons regard a loan as a windfall, and cause trouble to those who help them.

[5] A man will kiss another's hands until he gets a loan, and will lower his voice in speaking of his neighbor's money;
but at the time for repayment he will delay, and will pay in words of unconcern, and will find fault with the time.

[6] If the lender exert pressure, he will hardly get back half, and will regard that as a windfall. If he does not, the borrower has robbed him of his money, and he has needlessly made him his enemy; he will repay him with curses and reproaches,
and instead of glory will repay him with dishonor.

[7] Because of such wickedness, therefore, many have refused to lend; they have been afraid of being defrauded needlessly.

[8] Nevertheless, be patient with a man in humble circumstances, and do not make him wait for your alms.

[9] Help a poor man for the commandment's sake, and because of his need do not send him away empty.

[10] Lose your silver for the sake of a brother or a friend, and do not let it rust under a stone and be lost.

[11] Lay up your treasure according to the commandments of the Most High, and it will profit you more than gold.

[12] Store up almsgiving in your treasury, and it will rescue you from all affliction;

[13] more than a mighty shield and more than a heavy spear, it will fight on your behalf against your enemy.

[14] A good man will be surety for his neighbor, but a man who has lost his sense of shame will fail him.

[15] Do not forget all the kindness of your surety, for he has given his life for you.

[16] A sinner will overthrow the prosperity of his surety,

[17] and one who does not feel grateful will abandon his rescuer.

[18] Being surety has ruined many men who were prosperous, and has shaken them like a wave of the sea; it has driven men of power into exile, and they have wandered among foreign nations.

[19] The sinner who has fallen into suretyship and pursues gain will fall into lawsuits.

[20] Assist your neighbor according to your ability, but take heed to yourself lest you fall.

[21] The essentials for life are water and bread and clothing and a house to cover one's nakedness.

[22] Better is the life of a poor man under the shelter of his roof than sumptuous food in another man's house.

[23] Be content with little or much.

[24] It is a miserable life to go from house to house, and where you are a stranger you may not open your mouth;

[25] you will play the host and provide drink without being thanked, and besides this you will hear bitter words:

[26] "Come here, stranger, prepare the table, and if you have anything at hand, let me have it to eat."

[27] "Give place, stranger, to an honored person; my brother has come to stay with me; I need my house."

[28] These things are hard to bear for a man who has feeling: scolding about lodging and the reproach of the moneylender.

Sir.30

[1] He who loves his son will whip him often, in order that he may rejoice at the way he turns out.

[2] He who disciplines his son will profit by him, and will boast of him among acquaintances.

[3] He who teaches his son will make his enemies envious, and will glory in him in the presence of friends.

[4] The father may die, and yet he is not dead, for he has left behind him one like himself;

[5] while alive he saw and rejoiced, and when he died he was not grieved;

[6] he has left behind him an avenger against his enemies, and one to repay the kindness of his friends.

[7] He who spoils his son will bind up his wounds, and his feelings will be troubled at every cry.

[8] A horse that is untamed turns out to be stubborn, and a son unrestrained turns out to be wilful.

[9] Pamper a child, and he will frighten you; play with him, and he will give you grief.

[10] Do not laugh with him, lest you have sorrow with him, and in the end you will gnash your teeth.

[11] Give him no authority in his youth, and do not ignore his errors.

[12] Bow down his neck in his youth, and beat his sides while he is young, lest he become stubborn and disobey you,

and you have sorrow of soul from him.

[13] Discipline your son and take pains with him, that you may not be offended by his shamelessness.

[14] Better off is a poor man who is well and strong in constitution than a rich man who is severely afflicted in body.

[15] Health and soundness are better than all gold, and a robust body than countless riches.

[16] There is no wealth better than health of body, and there is no gladness above joy of heart.

[17] Death is better than a miserable life, and eternal rest than chronic sickness.

[18] Good things poured out upon a mouth that is closed are like offerings of food placed upon a grave.

[19] Of what use to an idol is an offering of fruit? For it can neither eat nor smell. So is he who is afflicted by the Lord;

[20] he sees with his eyes and groans, like a eunuch who embraces a maiden and groans.

[21] Do not give yourself over to sorrow, and do not afflict yourself deliberately.

[22] Gladness of heart is the life of man, and the rejoicing of a man is length of days.

[23] Delight your soul and comfort your heart, and remove sorrow far from you, for sorrow has destroyed many, and there is no profit in it.

[24] Jealousy and anger shorten life, and anxiety brings on old age too soon.

[25] A man of cheerful and good heart will give heed to the food he eats.

Sir.31

[1] Wakefulness over wealth wastes away one's flesh, and anxiety about it removes sleep.

[2] Wakeful anxiety prevents slumber, and a severe illness carries off sleep.

[3] The rich man toils as his wealth accumulates, and when he rests he fills himself with his dainties.

[4] The poor man toils as his livelihood diminishes, and when he rests he becomes needy.

[5] He who loves gold will not be justified, and he who pursues money will be led astray by it.

[6] Many have come to ruin because of gold, and their destruction has met them face to face.

[7] It is a stumbling block to those who are devoted to it, and every fool will be taken captive by it.

[8] Blessed is the rich man who is found blameless, and who does not go after gold.

[9] Who is he? And we will call him blessed, for he has done wonderful things among his people.

[10] Who has been tested by it and been found perfect? Let it be for him a ground for boasting. Who has had the power to transgress and did not transgress, and to do evil and did not do it?

[11] His prosperity will be established, and the assembly will relate his acts of charity.

[12] Are you seated at the table of a great man? Do not be greedy at it, and do not say, "There is certainly much upon it!"

[13] Remember that a greedy eye is a bad thing. What has been created more greedy than the eye? Therefore it sheds tears from every face.

[14] Do not reach out your hand for everything you see, and do not crowd your neighbor at the dish.

[15] Judge your neighbor's feelings by your own, and in every matter be thoughtful.

[16] Eat like a human being what is set before you, and do not chew greedily, lest you be hated.

[17] Be the first to stop eating, for the sake of good manners, and do not be insatiable, lest you give offense.

[18] If you are seated among many persons, do not reach out your hand before they do.

[19] How ample a little is for a well-disciplined man! He does not breathe heavily upon his bed.

[20] Healthy sleep depends on moderate eating; he rises early, and feels fit. The distress of sleeplessness and of nausea
and colic are with the glutton.

[21] If you are overstuffed with food, get up in the middle of the meal, and you will have relief.

[22] Listen to me, my son, and do not disregard me, and in the end you will appreciate my words. In all your work be industrious, and no sickness will overtake you.

[23] Men will praise the one who is liberal with food, and their testimony to his excellence is trustworthy.

[24] The city will complain of the one who is niggardly with food, and their testimony to his niggardliness is accurate.

[25] Do not aim to be valiant over wine, for wine has destroyed many.

[26] Fire and water prove the temper of steel, so wine tests hearts in the strife of the proud.

[27] Wine is like life to men, if you drink it in moderation. What is life to a man who is without wine? It has been created to make men glad.

[28] Wine drunk in season and temperately is rejoicing of heart and gladness of soul.

[29] Wine drunk to excess is bitterness of soul, with provocation and stumbling.

[30] Drunkenness increases the anger of a fool to his injury, reducing his strength and adding wounds.

[31] Do not reprove your neighbor at a banquet of wine, and do not despise him in his merrymaking; speak no word of reproach to him, and do not afflict him by making demands of him.

Sir.32

[1] If they make you master of the feast, do not exalt yourself; be among them as one of them; take good care of them and then be seated;

[2] when you have fulfilled your duties, take your place, that you may be merry on their account and receive a wreath for your excellent leadership.

[3] Speak, you who are older, for it is fitting that you should, but with accurate knowledge, and do not interrupt the music.

[4] Where there is entertainment, do not pour out talk; do not display your cleverness out of season.

[5] A ruby seal in a setting of gold is a concert of music at a banquet of wine.

[6] A seal of emerald in a rich setting of gold is the melody of music with good wine.

[7] Speak, young man, if there is need of you, but no more than twice, and only if asked.

[8] Speak concisely, say much in few words; be as one who knows and yet holds his tongue.

[9] Among the great do not act as their equal; and when another is speaking, do not babble.

[10] Lightning speeds before the thunder, and approval precedes a modest man.

[11] Leave in good time and do not be the last; go home quickly and do not linger.

[12] Amuse yourself there, and do what you have in mind, but do not sin through proud speech.

[13] And for these things bless him who made you and satisfies you with his good gifts.

[14] He who fears the Lord will accept his discipline, and those who rise early to seek him will find favor.

[15] He who seeks the law will be filled with it, but the hypocrite will stumble at it.

[16] Those who fear the Lord will form true judgments, and like a light they will kindle righteous deeds.

[17] A sinful man will shun reproof, and will find a decision according to his liking.

[18] A man of judgment will not overlook an idea, and an insolent and proud man will not cower in fear.

[19] Do nothing without deliberation; and when you have acted, do not regret it.

[20] Do not go on a path full of hazards, and do not stumble over stony ground.

[21] Do not be overconfident on a smooth way,

[22] and give good heed to your paths.

[23] Guard yourself in every act, for this is the keeping of the commandments.

[24] He who believes the law gives heed to the commandments, and he who trusts the Lord will not suffer loss.

Sir.33

[1] No evil will befall the man who fears the Lord, but in trial he will deliver him again and again.

[2] A wise man will not hate the law, but he who is hypocritical about it is like a boat in a storm.

[3] A man of understanding will trust in the law; for him the law is as dependable as an inquiry by means of Urim.

[4] Prepare what to say, and thus you will be heard; bind together your instruction, and make your answer.

[5] The heart of a fool is like a cart wheel, and his thoughts like a turning axle.

[6] A stallion is like a mocking friend; he neighs under every one who sits on him.

[7] Why is any day better than another, when all the daylight in the year is from the sun?

[8] By the Lord's decision they were distinguished, and he appointed the different seasons and feasts;

[9] some of them he exalted and hallowed, and some of them he made ordinary days.

[10] All men are from the ground, and Adam was created of the dust.

[11] In the fullness of his knowledge the Lord distinguished them and appointed their different ways;

[12] some of them he blessed and exalted, and some of them he made holy and brought near to himself; but some of them he cursed and brought low, and he turned them out of their place.

[13] As clay in the hand of the potter -- for all his ways are as he pleases -- so men are in the hand of him who made them, to give them as he decides.

[14] Good is the opposite of evil, and life the opposite of death; so the sinner is the opposite of the

godly.

[15] Look upon all the works of the Most High; they likewise are in pairs, one the opposite of the other.

[16] I was the last on watch; I was like one who gleans after the grape-gatherers; by the blessing of the Lord I excelled,

and like a grape-gatherer I filled my wine press.

[17] Consider that I have not labored for myself alone, but for all who seek instruction.

[18] Hear me, you who are great among the people, and you leaders of the congregation, hearken.

[19] To son or wife, to brother or friend, do not give power over yourself, as long as you live; and do not give your property to another, lest you change your mind and must ask for it.

[20] While you are still alive and have breath in you, do not let any one take your place.

[21] For it is better that your children should ask from you than that you should look to the hand of you sons.

[22] Excel in all that you do; bring no stain upon your honor.

[23] At the time when you end the days of your life, in the hour of death, distribute your inheritance.

[24] Fodder and a stick and burdens for an ass; bread and discipline and work for a servant.

[25] Set your slave to work, and you will find rest; leave his hands idle, and he will seek liberty.

[26] Yoke and thong will bow the neck, and for a wicked servant there are racks and tortures.

[27] Put him to work, that he may not be idle, for idleness teaches much evil.

[28] Set him to work, as is fitting for him, and if he does not obey, make his fetters heavy.

[29] Do not act immoderately toward anybody, and do nothing without discretion.

[30] If you have a servant, let him be as yourself, because you have bought him with blood.

[31] If you have a servant, treat him as a brother, for as your own soul you will need him. If you ill-treat him, and he leaves and runs away, which way will you go to seek him?

Sir.34

[1] A man of no understanding has vain and false hopes, and dreams give wings to fools.

[2] As one who catches at a shadow and pursues the wind, so is he who gives heed to dreams.

[3] The vision of dreams is this against that, the likeness of a face confronting a face.

[4] From an unclean thing what will be made clean? And from something false what will be true?

[5] Divinations and omens and dreams are folly, and like a woman in travail the mind has fancies.

[6] Unless they are sent from the Most High as a visitation, do not give your mind to them.

[7] For dreams have deceived many, and those who put their hope in them have failed.

[8] Without such deceptions the law will be fulfilled, and wisdom is made perfect in truthful lips.

[9] An educated man knows many things, and one with much experience will speak with understanding.

[10] He that is inexperienced knows few things, but he that has traveled acquires much cleverness.

[11] I have seen many things in my travels, and I understand more than I can express.

[12] I have often been in danger of death, but have escaped because of these experiences.

[13] The spirit of those who fear the Lord will live, for their hope is in him who saves them.

[14] He who fears the Lord will not be timid, nor play the coward, for he is his hope.

[15] Blessed is the soul of the man who fears the Lord! To whom does he look? And who is his support?

[16] The eyes of the Lord are upon those who love him, a mighty protection and strong support, a shelter from the hot wind and a shade from noonday sun, a guard against stumbling and a defense against falling.

[17] He lifts up the soul and gives light to the eyes; he grants healing, life, and blessing.

[18] If one sacrifices from what has been wrongfully obtained, the offering is blemished; the gifts of the lawless are not acceptable.

[19] The Most High is not pleased with the offerings of the ungodly; and he is not propitiated for sins by a multitude of sacrifices.

[20] Like one who kills a son before his father's eyes is the man who offers a sacrifice from the property of the poor.

[21] The bread of the needy is the life of the poor; whoever deprives them of it is a man of blood.

[22] To take away a neighbor's living is to murder him; to deprive an employee of his wages is to shed blood.

[23] When one builds and another tears down, what do they gain but toil?

[24] When one prays and another curses, to whose voice will the Lord listen?

[25] If a man washes after touching a dead body, and touches it again, what has he gained by his washing?

[26] So if a man fasts for his sins, and goes again and does the same things, who will listen to his prayer? And what has he gained by humbling himself?

Sir.35

[1] He who keeps the law makes many offerings; he who heeds the commandments sacrifices a peace offering.

[2] He who returns a kindness offers fine flour, and he who gives alms sacrifices a thank offering.

[3] To keep from wickedness is pleasing to the Lord, and to forsake unrighteousness is atonement.

[4] Do not appear before the Lord empty-handed,

[5] for all these things are to be done because of the commandment.

[6] The offering of a righteous man anoints the altar, and its pleasing odor rises before the Most High.

[7] The sacrifice of a righteous man is acceptable, and the memory of it will not be forgotten.

[8] Glorify the Lord generously, and do not stint the first fruits of your hands.

[9] With every gift show a cheerful face, and dedicate your tithe with gladness.

[10] Give to the Most High as he has given, and as generously as your hand has found.

[11] For the Lord is the one who repays, and he will repay you sevenfold.

[12] Do not offer him a bribe, for he will not accept it; and do not trust to an unrighteous sacrifice; for the Lord is the judge, and with him is no partiality.

[13] He will not show partiality in the case of a poor man; and he will listen to the prayer of one who is wronged.

[14] He will not ignore the supplication of the fatherless, nor the widow when she pours out her story.

[15] Do not the tears of the widow run down her cheek as she cries out against him who has caused them to fall?

[16] He whose service is pleasing to the Lord will be accepted, and his prayer will reach to the clouds.

[17] The prayer of the humble pierces the clouds, and he will not be consoled until it reaches the Lord; he will not desist until the Most High visits him, and does justice for the righteous, and executes judgment.

[18] And the Lord will not delay, neither will he be patient with them, till he crushes the loins of the unmerciful and repays vengeance on the nations; till he takes away the multitude of the insolent, and breaks the scepters of the unrighteous;

[19] till he repays the man according to his deeds, and the works of men according to their devices; till he judges the case of his people and makes them rejoice in his mercy.

[20] Mercy is as welcome when he afflicts them as clouds of rain in the time of drought.

Sir.36

[1] Have mercy upon us, O Lord, the God of all, and look upon us,

[2] and cause the fear of thee to fall upon all the nations.

[3] Lift up thy hand against foreign nations and let them see thy might.

[4] As in us thou hast been sanctified before them, so in them be thou magnified before us;

[5] and let them know thee, as we have known that there is not God but thee, O Lord.

[6] Show signs anew, and work further wonders; make thy hand and thy right arm glorious.

[7] Rouse thy anger and pour out thy wrath; destroy the adversary and wipe out the enemy.

[8] Hasten the day, and remember the appointed time, and let people recount thy mighty deeds.

[9] Let him who survives be consumed in the fiery wrath, and may those who harm thy people meet destruction.

[10] Crush the heads of the rulers of the enemy, who say, "There is no one but ourselves."

[11] Gather all the tribes of Jacob, and give them their inheritance, as at the beginning.

[12] Have mercy, O Lord, upon the people called by thy name, upon Israel, whom thou hast likened to a first-born son.

[13] Have pity on the city of thy sanctuary, Jerusalem, the place of thy rest.

[14] Fill Zion with the celebration of thy wondrous deeds, and thy temple with thy glory.

[15] Bear witness to those whom thou didst create in the beginning, and fulfil the prophecies spoken in thy name.

[16] Reward those who wait for thee, and let thy prophets be found trustworthy.

[17] Hearken, O Lord, to the prayer of thy servants, according to the blessing of Aaron for thy people, and all who are on the earth will know that thou art the Lord, the God of the ages.

[18] The stomach will take any food, yet one food is better than another.

[19] As the palate tastes the kinds of game, so an intelligent mind detects false words.

[20] A perverse mind will cause grief, but a man of experience will pay him back.

[21] A woman will accept any man, but one daughter is better than another.

[22] A woman's beauty gladdens the countenance, and surpasses every human desire.

[23] If kindness and humility mark her speech, her husband is not like other men.

[24] He who acquires a wife gets his best possession, a helper fit for him and a pillar of support.

[25] Where there is no fence, the property will be plundered; and where there is no wife, a man will wander about and sigh.

[26] For who will trust a nimble robber that skips from city to city? So who will trust a man that has no home,

and lodges wherever night finds him?

Sir.37

[1] Every friend will say, "I too am a friend"; but some friends are friends only in name.

[2] Is it not a grief to the death when a companion and friend turns to enmity?

[3] O evil imagination, why were you formed to cover the land with deceit?

[4] Some companions rejoice in the happiness of a friend, but in time of trouble are against him.

[5] Some companions help a friend for their stomach's sake, and in the face of battle take up the shield.

[6] Do not forget a friend in your heart, and be not unmindful of him in your wealth.

[7] Every counselor praises counsel, but some give counsel in their own interest.

[8] Be wary of a counselor, and learn first what is his interest -- for he will take thought for himself -- lest he cast the lot against you

[9] and tell you, "Your way is good," and then stand aloof to see what will happen to you.

[10] Do not consult the one who looks at you suspiciously; hide your counsel from those who are jealous of you.

[11] Do not consult with a woman about her rival or with a coward about war, with a merchant about barter or with a buyer about selling, with a grudging man about gratitude or with a merciless man about kindness, with an idler about any work or with a man hired for a year about completing his work, with a lazy servant about a big task -- pay no attention to these in any matter of counsel.

[12] But stay constantly with a godly man whom you know to be a keeper of the commandments, whose soul is in accord with your soul, and who will sorrow with you if you fail.

[13] And establish the counsel of your own heart, for no one is more faithful to you than it is.

[14] For a man's soul sometimes keeps him better informed than seven watchmen sitting high on a watchtower.

[15] And besides all this pray to the Most High that he may direct your way in truth.

[16] Reason is the beginning of every work, and counsel precedes every undertaking.

[17] As a clue to changes of heart

[18] four turns of fortune appear, good and evil, life and death; and it is the tongue that continually rules them.

[19] A man may be shrewd and the teacher of many, and yet be unprofitable to himself.

[20] A man skilled in words may be hated; he will be destitute of all food,

[21] for grace was not given him by the Lord, since he is lacking in all wisdom.

[22] A man may be wise to his own advantage, and the fruits of his understanding may be trustworthy on his lips.

[23] A wise man will instruct his own people, and the fruits of his understanding will be trustworthy.

[24] A wise man will have praise heaped upon him, and all who see him will call him happy.

[25] The life of a man is numbered by days, but the days of Israel are without number.

[26] He who is wise among his people will inherit confidence, and his name will live for ever.

[27] My son, test your soul while you live; see what is bad for it and do not give it that.

[28] For not everything is good for every one, and not every person enjoys everything.

[29] Do not have an insatiable appetite for any luxury, and do not give yourself up to food;

[30] for overeating brings sickness, and gluttony leads to nausea.

[31] Many have died of gluttony, but he who is careful to avoid it prolongs his life.

Sir.38

[1] Honor the physician with the honor due him, according to your need of him, for the Lord created him;

[2] for healing comes from the Most High, and he will receive a gift from the king.

[3] The skill of the physician lifts up his head, and in the presence of great men he is admired.

[4] The Lord created medicines from the earth, and a sensible man will not despise them.

[5] Was not water made sweet with a tree in order that his power might be known?

[6] And he gave skill to men that he might be glorified in his marvelous works.

[7] By them he heals and takes away pain;

[8] the pharmacist makes of them a compound. His works will never be finished; and from him health is upon the face of the earth.

[9] My son, when you are sick do not be negligent, but pray to the Lord, and he will heal you.

[10] Give up your faults and direct your hands aright, and cleanse your heart from all sin.

[11] Offer a sweet-smelling sacrifice, and a memorial portion of fine flour, and pour oil on your offering, as much as you can afford.

[12] And give the physician his place, for the Lord created him; let him not leave you, for there is need of him.

[13] There is a time when success lies in the hands of physicians,

[14] for they too will pray to the Lord that he should grant them success in diagnosis and in healing, for the sake of preserving life.

[15] He who sins before his Maker, may he fall into the care of a physician.

[16] My son, let your tears fall for the dead, and as one who is suffering grievously begin the lament. Lay out his body with the honor due him, and do not neglect his burial.

[17] Let your weeping be bitter and your wailing fervent; observe the mourning according to his merit, for one day, or two, to avoid criticism; then be comforted for your sorrow.

[18] For sorrow results in death, and sorrow of heart saps one's strength.

[19] In calamity sorrow continues, and the life of the poor man weighs down his heart.

[20] Do not give your heart to sorrow; drive it away, remembering the end of life.

[21] Do not forget, there is no coming back; you do the dead no good, and you injure yourself.

[22] "Remember my doom, for yours is like it: yesterday it was mine, and today it is yours."

[23] When the dead is at rest, let his remembrance cease, and be comforted for him when his spirit is departed.

[24] The wisdom of the scribe depends on the opportunity of leisure; and he who has little business may become wise.

[25] How can he become wise who handles the plow, and who glories in the shaft of a goad, who drives oxen and is occupied with their work, and whose talk is about bulls?

[26] He sets his heart on plowing furrows, and he is careful about fodder for the heifers.

[27] So too is every craftsman and master workman who labors by night as well as by day; those who cut the signets of seals, each is diligent in making a great variety; he sets his heart on painting a lifelike image, and he is careful to finish his work.

[28] So too is the smith sitting by the anvil, intent upon his handiwork in iron; the breath of the fire melts his flesh, and he wastes away in the heat of the furnace; he inclines his ear to the sound of the hammer, and his eyes are on the pattern of the object. He sets his heart on finishing his handiwork, and he is careful to complete its decoration.

[29] So too is the potter sitting at his work and turning the wheel with his feet; he is always deeply concerned over his work, and all his output is by number.

[30] He moulds the clay with his arm and makes it pliable with his feet; he sets his heart to finish the glazing, and he is careful to clean the furnace.

[31] All these rely upon their hands, and each is skilful in his own work.

[32] Without them a city cannot be established, and men can neither sojourn nor live there.

[33] Yet they are not sought out for the council of the people, nor do they attain eminence in the public assembly.

They do not sit in the judge's seat, nor do they understand the sentence of judgment; they cannot expound discipline or judgment, and they are not found using proverbs.

[34] But they keep stable the fabric of the world, and their prayer is in the practice of their trade.

Sir.39

[1] On the other hand he who devotes himself to the study of the law of the Most High will seek out the wisdom of all the ancients, and will be concerned with prophecies;

[2] he will preserve the discourse of notable men and penetrate the subtleties of parables;

[3] he will seek out the hidden meanings of proverbs and be at home with the obscurities of parables.

[4] He will serve among great men and appear before rulers; he will travel through the lands of foreign nations, for he tests the good and the evil among men.

[5] He will set his heart to rise early to seek the Lord who made him, and will make supplication before the Most High; he will open his mouth in prayer and make supplication for his sins.

[6] If the great Lord is willing, he will be filled with the spirit of understanding; he will pour forth words of wisdom and give thanks to the Lord in prayer.

[7] He will direct his counsel and knowledge aright, and meditate on his secrets.

[8] He will reveal instruction in his teaching, and will glory in the law of the Lord's covenant.

[9] Many will praise his understanding, and it will never be blotted out; his memory will not disappear, and his name will live through all generations.

[10] Nations will declare his wisdom, and the congregation will proclaim his praise;

[11] if he lives long, he will leave a name greater than a thousand, and if he goes to rest, it is enough for him.

[12] I have yet more to say, which I have thought upon, and I am filled, like the moon at the full.

[13] Listen to me, O you holy sons, and bud like a rose growing by a stream of water;

[14] send forth fragrance like frankincense, and put forth blossoms like a lily. Scatter the fragrance, and sing a hymn of praise; bless the Lord for all his works;

[15] ascribe majesty to his name and give thanks to him with praise, with songs on your lips, and with lyres; and this you shall say in thanksgiving:

[16] "All things are the works of the Lord, for they are very good, and whatever he commands will be done in his time."

[17] No one can say, "What is this?" "Why is that?" for in God's time all things will be sought after. At his word the waters stood in a heap, and the reservoirs of water at the word of his mouth.

[18] At his command whatever pleases him is done, and none can limit his saving power.

[19] The works of all flesh are before him, and nothing can be hid from his eyes.

[20] From everlasting to everlasting he beholds them, and nothing is marvelous to him.

[21] No one can say, "What is this?" "Why is that?" for everything has been created for its use.

[22] His blessing covers the dry land like a river, and drenches it like a flood.

[23] The nations will incur his wrath, just as he turns fresh water into salt.

[24] To the holy his ways are straight, just as they are obstacles to the wicked.

[25] From the beginning good things were created for good people, just as evil things for sinners.

[26] Basic to all the needs of man's life are water and fire and iron and salt and wheat flour and milk and honey, the blood of the grape, and oil and clothing.

[27] All these are for good to the godly, just as they turn into evils for sinners.

[28] There are winds that have been created for vengeance, and in their anger they scourge heavily; in the time of consummation they will pour out their strength and calm the anger of their Maker.

[29] Fire and hail and famine and pestilence, all these have been created for vengeance;

[30] the teeth of wild beasts, and scorpions and vipers, and the sword that punishes the ungodly with destruction;

[31] they will rejoice in his commands, and be made ready on earth for their service, and when their times come they will not transgress his word.

[32] Therefore from the beginning I have been convinced, and have thought this out and left it in writing:

[33] The works of the Lord are all good, and he will supply every need in its hour.

[34] And no one can say, "This is worse than that," for all things will prove good in their season.

[35] So now sing praise with all your heart and voice, and bless the name of the Lord.

Sir.40

[1] Much labor was created for every man, and a heavy yoke is upon the sons of Adam, from the day they come forth from their mother's womb till the day they return to the mother of all.

[2] Their perplexities and fear of heart -- their anxious thought is the day of death,

[3] from the man who sits on a splendid throne to the one who is humbled in dust and ashes,

[4] from the man who wears purple and a crown to the one who is clothed in burlap;

[5] there is anger and envy and trouble and unrest, and fear of death, and fury and strife. And when one rests upon his bed, his sleep at night confuses his mind.

[6] He gets little or no rest, and afterward in his sleep, as though he were on watch, he is troubled by the visions of his mind like one who has escaped from the battle-front;

[7] at the moment of his rescue he wakes up, and wonders that his fear came to nothing.

[8] With all flesh, both man and beast, and upon sinners seven times more,

[9] are death and bloodshed and strife and sword, calamities, famine and affliction and plague.

[10] All these were created for the wicked, and on their account the flood came.

[11] All things that are from the earth turn back to the earth, and what is from the waters returns to the sea.

[12] All bribery and injustice will be blotted out, but good faith will stand for ever.

[13] The wealth of the unjust will dry up like a torrent, and crash like a loud clap of thunder in a rain.

[14] A generous man will be made glad; likewise transgressors will utterly fail.

[15] The children of the ungodly will not put forth many branches; they are unhealthy roots upon sheer rock.

[16] The reeds by any water or river bank will be plucked up before any grass.

[17] Kindness is like a garden of blessings, and almsgiving endures for ever.

[18] Life is sweet for the self-reliant and the worker, but he who finds treasure is better off than both.

[19] Children and the building of a city establish a man's name, but a blameless wife is accounted better than both.

[20] Wine and music gladden the heart, but the love of wisdom is better than both.

[21] The flute and the harp make pleasant melody, but a pleasant voice is better than both.

[22] The eye desires grace and beauty, but the green shoots of grain more than both.

[23] A friend or a companion never meets one amiss, but a wife with her husband is better than both.

[24] Brothers and help are for a time of trouble, but almsgiving rescues better than both.

[25] Gold and silver make the foot stand sure, but good counsel is esteemed more than both.

[26] Riches and strength lift up the heart, but the fear of the Lord is better than both. There is no loss in the fear of the Lord, and with it there is no need to seek for help.

[27] The fear of the Lord is like a garden of blessing, and covers a man better than any glory.

[28] My son, do not lead the life of a beggar; it is better to die than to beg.

[29] When a man looks to the table of another, his existence cannot be considered as life. He pollutes himself with another man's food, but a man who is intelligent and well instructed guards against that.

[30] In the mouth of the shameless begging is sweet, but in his stomach a fire is kindled.

Sir.41

[1] O death, how bitter is the reminder of you to one who lives at peace among his possessions, to a man without distractions, who is prosperous in everything, and who still has the vigor to enjoy his food!

[2] O death, how welcome is your sentence to one who is in need and is failing in strength, very old and distracted over everything; to one who is contrary, and has lost his patience!

[3] Do not fear the sentence of death; remember your former days and the end of life; this is the decree from the Lord for all flesh,

[4] and how can you reject the good pleasure of the Most High? Whether life is for ten or a hundred or a thousand years,

there is no inquiry about it in Hades.

[5] The children of sinners are abominable children, and they frequent the haunts of the ungodly.

[6] The inheritance of the children of sinners will perish, and on their posterity will be a perpetual reproach.

[7] Children will blame an ungodly father, for they suffer reproach because of him.

[8] Woe to you, ungodly men, who have forsaken the law of the Most High God!

[9] When you are born, you are born to a curse; and when you die, a curse is your lot.

[10] Whatever is from the dust returns to dust; so the ungodly go from curse to destruction.

[11] The mourning of men is about their bodies, but the evil name of sinners will be blotted out.

[12] Have regard for your name, since it will remain for you longer than a thousand great stores of gold.

[13] The days of a good life are numbered, but a good name endures for ever.

[14] My children, observe instruction and be at peace; hidden wisdom and unseen treasure, what advantage is there in either of them?

[15] Better is the man who hides his folly than the man who hides his wisdom.

[16] Therefore show respect for my words: For it is good to retain every kind of shame, and not everything is confidently esteemed by every one.

[17] Be ashamed of immorality, before your father or mother; and of a lie, before a prince or a ruler;

[18] of a transgression, before a judge or magistrate; and of iniquity, before a congregation or the people; of unjust dealing, before your partner or friend;

[19] and of theft, in the place where you live. Be ashamed before the truth of God and his covenant. Be ashamed of selfish behavior at meals, of surliness in receiving and giving,

[20] and of silence, before those who greet you; of looking at a woman who is a harlot,

[21] and of rejecting the appeal of a kinsman; of taking away some one's portion or gift, and of gazing at another man's wife;

[22] of meddling with his maidservant -- and do not approach her bed; of abusive words, before friends -- and do not upbraid after making a gift;

[23] of repeating and telling what you hear, and of revealing secrets. Then you will show proper shame, and will find favor with every man.

Sir.42

[1] Of the following things do not be ashamed, and do not let partiality lead you to sin:

[2] of the law of the Most High and his covenant, and of rendering judgment to acquit the ungodly;

[3] of keeping accounts with a partner or with traveling companions, and of dividing the inheritance of friends;

[4] of accuracy with scales and weights, and of acquiring much or little;

[5] of profit from dealing with merchants, and of much discipline of children, and of whipping a wicked servant severely.

[6] Where there is an evil wife, a seal is a good thing; and where there are many hands, lock things up.

[7] Whatever you deal out, let it be by number and weight, and make a record of all that you give out or take in.

[8] Do not be ashamed to instruct the stupid or foolish or the aged man who quarrels with the young. Then you will be truly instructed, and will be approved before all men.

[9] A daughter keeps her father secretly wakeful, and worry over her robs him of sleep; when she is young, lest she do not marry, or if married, lest she be hated;

[10] while a virgin, lest she be defiled or become pregnant in her father's house; or having a husband, lest she prove unfaithful, or, though married, lest she be barren.

[11] Keep strict watch over a headstrong daughter, lest she make you a laughingstock to your enemies, a byword in the city and notorious among the people, and put you to shame before the great multitude.

[12] Do not look upon any one for beauty, and do not sit in the midst of women;

[13] for from garments comes the moth, and from a woman comes woman's wickedness.

[14] Better is the wickedness of a man than a woman who does good; and it is a woman who brings shame and disgrace.

[15] I will now call to mind the works of the Lord, and will declare what I have seen. By the words of the Lord his works are done.

[16] The sun looks down on everything with its light, and the work of the Lord is full of his glory.

[17] The Lord has not enabled his holy ones to recount all his marvelous works, which the Lord the Almighty has established that the universe may stand firm in his glory.

[18] He searches out the abyss, and the hearts of men, and considers their crafty devices. For the Most High knows all that may be known, and he looks into the signs of the age.

[19] He declares what has been and what is to be, and he reveals the tracks of hidden things.

[20] No thought escapes him, and not one word is hidden from him.

[21] He has ordained the splendors of his wisdom, and he is from everlasting and to everlasting. Nothing can be added or taken away, and he needs no one to be his counselor.

[22] How greatly to be desired are all his works, and how sparkling they are to see!

[23] All these things live and remain for ever for every need, and are all obedient.

[24] All things are twofold, one opposite the other, and he has made nothing incomplete.

[25] One confirms the good things of the other, and who can have enough of beholding his glory?

Sir.43

[1] The pride of the heavenly heights is the clear firmament, the appearance of heaven in a spectacle of glory.

[2] The sun, when it appears, making proclamation as it goes forth, is a marvelous instrument, the work of the Most High.

[3] At noon it parches the land; and who can withstand its burning heat?

[4] A man tending a furnace works in burning heat, but the sun burns the mountains three times as much; it breathes out fiery vapors, and with bright beams it blinds the eyes.

[5] Great is the Lord who made it; and at his command it hastens on its course.

[6] He made the moon also, to serve in its season to mark the times and to be an everlasting sign.

[7] From the moon comes the sign for feast days, a light that wanes when it has reached the full.

[8] The month is named for the moon, increasing marvelously in its phases, an instrument of the hosts on high shining forth in the firmament of heaven.

[9] The glory of the stars is the beauty of heaven, a gleaming array in the heights of the Lord.

[10] At the command of the Holy One they stand as ordered, they never relax in their watches.

[11] Look upon the rainbow, and praise him who made it, exceedingly beautiful in its brightness.

[12] It encircles the heaven with its glorious arc; the hands of the Most High have stretched it out.

[13] By his command he sends the driving snow and speeds the lightnings of his judgment.

[14] Therefore the storehouses are opened, and the clouds fly forth like birds.

[15] In his majesty he amasses the clouds, and the hailstones are broken in pieces.

[16] At his appearing the mountains are shaken; at his will the south wind blows.

[17] The voice of his thunder rebukes the earth; so do the tempest from the north and the whirlwind. He scatters the snow like birds flying down, and its descent is like locusts alighting.

[18] The eye marvels at the beauty of its whiteness, and the mind is amazed at its falling.

[19] He pours the hoarfrost upon the earth like salt, and when it freezes, it becomes pointed thorns.

[20] The cold north wind blows, and ice freezes over the water; it rests upon every pool of water, and the water puts it on like a breastplate.

[21] He consumes the mountains and burns up the wilderness, and withers the tender grass like fire.

[22] A mist quickly heals all things; when the dew appears, it refreshes from the heat.

[23] By his counsel he stilled the great deep and planted islands in it.

[24] Those who sail the sea tell of its dangers, and we marvel at what we hear.

[25] for in it are strange and marvelous works, all kinds of living things, and huge creatures of the sea.

[26] Because of him his messenger finds the way, and by his word all things hold together.

[27] Though we speak much we cannot reach the end, and the sum of our words is: "He is the all."

[28] Where shall we find strength to praise him? For he is greater than all his works.

[29] Terrible is the Lord and very great, and marvelous is his power.

[30] When you praise the Lord, exalt him as much as you can; for he will surpass even that. When you exalt him, put forth all your strength, and do not grow weary, for you cannot praise him enough.

[31] Who has seen him and can describe him? Or who can extol him as he is?

[32] Many things greater than these lie hidden, for we have seen but few of his works.

[33] For the Lord has made all things, and to the godly he has granted wisdom.

Sir.44

[1] Let us now praise famous men, and our fathers in their generations.

[2] The Lord apportioned to them great glory, his majesty from the beginning.

[3] There were those who ruled in their kingdoms, and were men renowned for their power, giving counsel by their understanding, and proclaiming prophecies;

[4] leaders of the people in their deliberations and in understanding of learning for the people, wise in their words of instruction;

[5] those who composed musical tunes, and set forth verses in writing;

[6] rich men furnished with resources, living peaceably in their habitations --

[7] all these were honored in their generations, and were the glory of their times.

[8] There are some of them who have left a name, so that men declare their praise.

[9] And there are some who have no memorial, who have perished as though they had not lived; they

have become as though they had not been born, and so have their children after them.

[10] But these were men of mercy, whose righteous deeds have not been forgotten;

[11] their prosperity will remain with their descendants, and their inheritance to their children's children.

[12] Their descendants stand by the covenants; their children also, for their sake.

[13] Their posterity will continue for ever, and their glory will not be blotted out.

[14] Their bodies were buried in peace, and their name lives to all generations.

[15] Peoples will declare their wisdom, and the congregation proclaims their praise.

[16] Enoch pleased the Lord, and was taken up; he was an example of repentance to all generations.

[17] Noah was found perfect and righteous; in the time of wrath he was taken in exchange; therefore a remnant was left to the earth when the flood came.

[18] Everlasting covenants were made with him that all flesh should not be blotted out by a flood.

[19] Abraham was the great father of a multitude of nations, and no one has been found like him in glory;

[20] he kept the law of the Most High, and was taken into covenant with him; he established the covenant in his flesh, and when he was tested he was found faithful.

[21] Therefore the Lord assured him by an oath that the nations would be blessed through his posterity; that he would multiply him like the dust of the earth, and exalt his posterity like the stars, and cause them to inherit from sea to sea and from the River to the ends of the earth.

[22] To Isaac also he gave the same assurance for the sake of Abraham his father.

[23] The blessing of all men and the covenant he made to rest upon the head of Jacob; he acknowledged him with his blessings, and gave him his inheritance; he determined his portions, and distributed them among twelve tribes.

Sir.45

[1] From his descendants the Lord brought forth a man of mercy, who found favor in the sight of all flesh and was beloved by God and man, Moses, whose memory is blessed.

[2] He made him equal in glory to the holy ones, and made him great in the fears of his enemies.

[3] By his words he caused signs to cease; the Lord glorified him in the presence of kings. He gave him commands for his people, and showed him part of his glory.

[4] He sanctified him through faithfulness and meekness; he chose him out of all mankind.

[5] He made him hear his voice, and led him into the thick darkness, and gave him the commandments face to face, the law of life and knowledge, to teach Jacob the covenant, and Israel his judgments.

[6] He exalted Aaron, the brother of Moses, a holy man like him, of the tribe of Levi.

[7] He made an everlasting covenant with him, and gave him the priesthood of the people. He blessed him with splendid vestments, and put a glorious robe upon him.

[8] He clothed him with superb perfection, and strengthened him with the symbols of authority, the linen breeches, the long robe, and the ephod.

[9] And he encircled him with pomegranates, with very many golden bells round about, to send forth a sound as he walked, to make their ringing heard in the temple as a reminder to the sons of his people;

[10] with a holy garment, of gold and blue and purple, the work of an embroiderer; with the oracle of judgment, Urim and Thummim;

[11] with twisted scarlet, the work of a craftsman; with precious stones engraved like signets, in a setting of gold, the work of a jeweler, for a reminder, in engraved letters, according to the number of the tribes of Israel;

[12] with a gold crown upon his turban, inscribed like a signet with "Holiness," a distinction to be prized, the work of an expert, the delight of the eyes, richly adorned.

[13] Before his time there never were such beautiful things. No outsider ever put them on, but only his sons and his descendants perpetually.

[14] His sacrifices shall be wholly burned twice every day continually.

[15] Moses ordained him, and anointed him with holy oil; it was an everlasting covenant for him and for his descendants all the days of heaven, to minister to the Lord and serve as priest and bless his people in his name.

[16] He chose him out of all the living to offer sacrifice to the Lord, incense and a pleasing odor as a memorial portion, to make atonement for the people.

[17] In his commandments he gave him authority and statutes and judgments, to teach Jacob the testimonies, and to enlighten Israel with his law.

[18] Outsiders conspired against him, and envied him in the wilderness, Dathan and Abiram and their men and the company of Korah, in wrath and anger.

[19] The Lord saw it and was not pleased, and in the wrath of his anger they were destroyed; he wrought wonders against them to consume them in flaming fire.

[20] He added glory to Aaron and gave him a heritage; he allotted to him the first of the first fruits, he prepared bread of first fruits in abundance;

[21] for they eat the sacrifices to the Lord, which he gave to him and his descendants.

[22] But in the land of the people he has no inheritance, and he has no portion among the people; for the Lord himself is his portion and inheritance.

[23] Phinehas the son of Eleazar is the third in glory, for he was zealous in the fear of the Lord, and stood fast, when the people turned away, in the ready goodness of his soul, and made atonement for Israel.

[24] Therefore a covenant of peace was established with him, that he should be leader of the sanctuary and of his people,

that he and his descendants should have the dignity of the priesthood for ever.

[25] A covenant was also established with David, the son of Jesse, of the tribe of Judah: the heritage of the king is from son to son only; so the heritage of Aaron is for his descendants.

[26] May the Lord grant you wisdom in your heart to judge his people in righteousness, so that their prosperity may not vanish, and that their glory may endure throughout their generations.

Sir.46

[1] Joshua the son of Nun was mighty in war, and was the successor of Moses in prophesying. He became, in accordance with his name, a great savior of God's elect, to take vengeance on the enemies that rose against them, so that he might give Israel its inheritance.

[2] How glorious he was when he lifted his hands and stretched out his sword against the cities!

[3] Who before him ever stood so firm? For he waged the wars of the Lord.

[4] Was not the sun held back by his hand? And did not one day become as long as two?

[5] He called upon the Most High, the Mighty One, when enemies pressed him on every side,

[6] and the great Lord answered him with hailstones of mighty power. He hurled down war upon that nation, and at the descent of Beth-horon he destroyed those who resisted, so that the nations might know his armament, that he was fighting in the sight of the Lord; for he wholly followed the Mighty One.

[7] And in the days of Moses he did a loyal deed, he and Caleb the son of Jephunneh: they withstood the congregation,

restrained the people from sin, and stilled their wicked murmuring.

[8] And these two alone were preserved out of six hundred thousand people on foot, to bring them into their inheritance,

into a land flowing with milk and honey.

[9] And the Lord gave Caleb strength, which remained with him to old age, so that he went up to the hill country, and his children obtained it for an inheritance;

[10] so that all the sons of Israel might see that it is good to follow the Lord.

[11] The judges also, with their respective names, those whose hearts did not fall into idolatry and who did not turn away from the Lord -- may their memory be blessed!

[12] May their bones revive from where they lie, and may the name of those who have been honored live again in their sons!

[13] Samuel, beloved by his Lord, a prophet of the Lord, established the kingdom and anointed rulers over his people.

[14] By the law of the Lord he judged the congregation, and the Lord watched over Jacob.

[15] By his faithfulness he was proved to be a prophet, and by his words he became known as a trustworthy seer.

[16] He called upon the Lord, the Mighty One, when his enemies pressed him on every side, and he offered in sacrifice a sucking lamb.

[17] Then the Lord thundered from heaven, and made his voice heard with a mighty sound;

[18] and he wiped out the leaders of the people of Tyre and all the rulers of the Philistines.

[19] Before the time of his eternal sleep, Samuel called men to witness before the Lord and his anointed: "I have not taken any one's property, not so much as a pair of shoes." And no man accused him.

[20] Even after he had fallen asleep he prophesied and revealed to the king his death, and lifted up his voice out of the earth in prophecy, to blot out the wickedness of the people.

Sir.47

[1] And after him Nathan rose up to prophesy in the days of David.

[2] As the fat is selected from the peace offering, so David was selected from the sons of Israel.

[3] He played with lions as with young goats, and with bears as with lambs of the flock.

[4] In his youth did he not kill a giant, and take away reproach from the people, when he lifted his hand with a stone in the sling and struck down the boasting of Goliath?

[5] For he appealed to the Lord, the Most High, and he gave him strength in his right hand to slay a man mighty in war, to exalt the power of his people.

[6] So they glorified him for his ten thousands, and praised him for the blessings of the Lord, when the glorious diadem was bestowed upon him.

[7] For he wiped out his enemies on every side, and annihilated his adversaries the Philistines; he crushed their power even to this day.

[8] In all that he did he gave thanks to the Holy One, the Most High, with ascriptions of glory; he sang praise with all his heart, and he loved his Maker.

[9] He placed singers before the altar, to make sweet melody with their voices.

[10] He gave beauty to the feasts, and arranged their times throughout the year, while they praised God's holy name, and the sanctuary resounded from early morning.

[11] The Lord took away his sins, and exalted his power for ever; he gave him the covenant of kings and a throne of glory in Israel.

[12] After him rose up a wise son who fared amply because of him;

[13] Solomon reigned in days of peace, and God gave him rest on every side, that he might build a house for his name and prepare a sanctuary to stand for ever.

[14] How wise you became in your youth! You overflowed like a river with understanding.

[15] Your soul covered the earth, and you filled it with parables and riddles.

[16] Your name reached to far-off islands, and you were loved for your peace.

[17] For your songs and proverbs and parables, and for your interpretations, the countries marveled at you.

[18] In the name of the Lord God, who is called the God of Israel, you gathered gold like tin and amassed silver like lead.

[19] But you laid your loins beside women, and through your body you were brought into subjection.

[20] You put stain upon your honor, and defiled your posterity, so that you brought wrath upon your children and they were grieved at your folly,

[21] so that the sovereignty was divided and a disobedient kingdom arose out of Ephraim.

[22] But the Lord will never give up his mercy, nor cause any of his works to perish; he will never blot out the descendants of his chosen one, nor destroy the posterity of him who loved him; so he gave a remnant to Jacob, and to David a root of his stock.

[23] Solomon rested with his fathers, and left behind him one of his sons, ample in folly and lacking in understanding,

Rehoboam, whose policy caused the people to revolt. Also Jeroboam the son of Nebat, who caused Israel to sin and gave to Ephraim a sinful way.

[24] Their sins became exceedingly many, so as to remove them from their land.

[25] For they sought out every sort of wickedness, till vengeance came upon them.

Sir.48

[1] Then the prophet Elijah arose like a fire, and his word burned like a torch.

[2] He brought a famine upon them, and by his zeal he made them few in number.

[3] By the word of the Lord he shut up the heavens, and also three times brought down fire.

[4] How glorious you were, O Elijah, in your wondrous deeds! And who has the right to boast which you have?

[5] You who raised a corpse from death and from Hades, by the word of the Most High;

[6] who brought kings down to destruction, and famous men from their beds;

[7] who heard rebuke at Sinai and judgments of vengeance at Horeb;

[8] who anointed kings to inflict retribution, and prophets to succeed you.

[9] You who were taken up by a whirlwind of fire, in a chariot with horses of fire;

[10] you who are ready at the appointed time, it is written, to calm the wrath of God before it breaks out in fury, to turn the heart of the father to the son, and to restore the tribes of Jacob.

[11] Blessed are those who saw you, and those who have been adorned in love; for we also shall surely live.

[12] It was Elijah who was covered by the whirlwind, and Elisha was filled with his spirit; in all his days he did not tremble before any ruler, and no one brought him into subjection.

[13] Nothing was too hard for him, and when he was dead his body prophesied.

[14] As in his life he did wonders, so in death his deeds were marvelous.

[15] For all this the people did not repent, and they did not forsake their sins, till they were carried away captive from their land and were scattered over all the earth; the people were left very few in number, but with rulers from the house of David.

[16] Some of them did what was pleasing to God, but others multiplied sins.

[17] Hezekiah fortified his city, and brought water into the midst of it; he tunneled the sheer rock with iron and built pools for water.

[18] In his days Sennacherib came up, and sent the Rabshakeh; he lifted up his hand against Zion and made great boasts in his arrogance.

[19] Then their hearts were shaken and their hands trembled, and they were in anguish, like women in travail.

[20] But they called upon the Lord who is merciful, spreading forth their hands toward him; and the Holy One quickly heard them from heaven, and delivered them by the hand of Isaiah.

[21] The Lord smote the camp of the Assyrians, and his angel wiped them out.

[22] For Hezekiah did what was pleasing to the Lord, and he held strongly to the ways of David his father, which Isaiah the prophet commanded, who was great and faithful in his vision.

[23] In his days the sun went backward, and he lengthened the life of the king.

[24] By the spirit of might he saw the last things, and comforted those who mourned in Zion.

[25] He revealed what was to occur to the end of time, and the hidden things before they came to pass.

Sir.49

[1] The memory of Josiah is like a blending of incense prepared by the art of the perfumer; it is sweet as honey to every mouth, and like music at a banquet of wine.

[2] He was led aright in converting the people, and took away the abominations of iniquity.

[3] He set his heart upon the Lord; in the days of wicked men he strengthened godliness.

[4] Except David and Hezekiah and Josiah they all sinned greatly, for they forsook the law of the Most High; the kings of Judah came to an end;

[5] for they gave their power to others, and their glory to a foreign nation,

[6] who set fire to the chosen city of the sanctuary, and made her streets desolate, according to the word of Jeremiah.

[7] For they had afflicted him; yet he had been consecrated in the womb as prophet, to pluck up and afflict and destroy,

and likewise to build and to plant.

[8] It was Ezekiel who saw the vision of glory which God showed him above the chariot of the cherubim.

[9] For God remembered his enemies with storm, and did good to those who directed their ways aright.

[10] May the bones of the twelve prophets revive from where they lie, for they comforted the people of Jacob and delivered them with confident hope.

[11] How shall we magnify Zerubbabel? He was like a signet on the right hand,

[12] and so was Jeshua the son of Jozadak; in their days they built the house and raised a temple holy to the Lord,

prepared for everlasting glory.

[13] The memory of Nehemiah also is lasting; he raised for us the walls that had fallen, and set up the gates and bars and rebuilt our ruined houses.

[14] No one like Enoch has been created on earth, for he was taken up from the earth.

[15] And no man like Joseph has been born, and his bones are cared for.

[16] Shem and Seth were honored among men, and Adam above every living being in the creation.

Sir.50

[1] The leader of his brethren and the pride of his people was Simon the high priest, son of Onias, who in his life repaired the house, and in his time fortified the temple.

[2] He laid the foundations for the high double walls, the high retaining walls for the temple enclosure.

[3] In his days a cistern for water was quarried out, a reservoir like the sea in circumference.

[4] He considered how to save his people from ruin, and fortified the city to withstand a siege.

[5] How glorious he was when the people gathered round him as he came out of the inner sanctuary!

[6] Like the morning star among the clouds, like the moon when it is full;

[7] like the sun shining upon the temple of the Most High, and like the rainbow gleaming in glorious clouds;

[8] like roses in the days of the first fruits, like lilies by a spring of water, like a green shoot on Lebanon on a summer day;

[9] like fire and incense in the censer, like a vessel of hammered gold adorned with all kinds of precious stones;

[10] like an olive tree putting forth its fruit, and like a cypress towering in the clouds.

[11] When he put on his glorious robe and clothed himself with superb perfection and went up to the holy altar, he made the court of the sanctuary glorious.

[12] And when he received the portions from the hands of the priests, as he stood by the hearth of the altar with a garland of brethren around him, he was like a young cedar on Lebanon; and they surrounded him like the trunks of palm trees,

[13] all the sons of Aaron in their splendor with the Lord's offering in their hands, before the whole congregation of Israel.

[14] Finishing the service at the altars, and arranging the offering to the Most High, the Almighty,

[15] he reached out his hand to the cup and poured a libation of the blood of the grape; he poured it out at the foot of the altar, a pleasing odor to the Most High, the King of all.

[16] Then the sons of Aaron shouted, they sounded the trumpets of hammered work, they made a great noise to be heard

for remembrance before the Most High.

[17] Then all the people together made haste and fell to the ground upon their faces to worship their Lord, the Almighty, God Most High.

[18] And the singers praised him with their voices in sweet and full-toned melody.

[19] And the people besought the Lord Most High in prayer before him who is merciful, till the order of worship of the Lord was ended; so they completed his service.

[20] Then Simon came down, and lifted up his hands over the whole congregation of the sons of Israel, to pronounce the blessing of the Lord with his lips, and to glory in his name;

[21] and they bowed down in worship a second time, to receive the blessing from the Most High.

[22] And now bless the God of all, who in every way does great things; who exalts our days from birth, and deals with us according to his mercy.

[23] May he give us gladness of heart, and grant that peace may be in our days in Israel, as in the days of old.

[24] May he entrust to us his mercy! And let him deliver us in our days!

[25] With two nations my soul is vexed, and the third is no nation:

[26] Those who live on Mount Seir, and the Philistines, and the foolish people that dwell in Shechem.

[27] Instruction in understanding and knowledge I have written in this book, Jesus the son of Sirach, son of Eleazar, of Jerusalem, who out of his heart poured forth wisdom.

[28] Blessed is he who concerns himself with these things, and he who lays them to heart will become wise.

[29] For if he does them, he will be strong for all things, for the light of the Lord is his path.

Sir.51

[1] I will give thanks to thee, O Lord and King, and will praise thee as God my Savior. I give thanks to thy name,

[2] for thou hast been my protector and helper and hast delivered my body from destruction and from the snare of a slanderous tongue, from lips that utter lies. Before those who stood by thou wast my helper,

[3] and didst deliver me, in the greatness of thy mercy and of thy name, from the gnashings of teeth about to devour me,

from the hand of those who sought my life, from the many afflictions that I endured,

[4] from choking fire on every side and from the midst of fire which I did not kindle,

[5] from the depths of the belly of Hades, from an unclean tongue and lying words --

[6] the slander of an unrighteous tongue to the king. My soul drew near to death, and my life was very near to Hades beneath.

[7] They surrounded me on every side, and there was no one to help me; I looked for the assistance of men, and there was none.

[8] Then I remembered thy mercy, O Lord, and thy work from of old, that thou do deliver those who wait for thee and do save them from the hand of their enemies.

[9] And I sent up my supplication from the earth, and prayed for deliverance from death.

[10] I appealed to the Lord, the Father of my lord, not to forsake me in the days of affliction, at the time when there is no help against the proud.

[11] I will praise thy name continually, and will sing praise with thanksgiving. My prayer was heard,

[12] for thou didst save me from destruction and rescue me from an evil plight. Therefore I will give thanks to thee and praise thee, and I will bless the name of the Lord.

[13] While I was still young, before I went on my travels, I sought wisdom openly in my prayer.

[14] Before the temple I asked for her, and I will search for her to the last.

[15] From blossom to ripening grape my heart delighted in her; my foot entered upon the straight path; from my youth I followed her steps.

[16] I inclined my ear a little and received her, and I found for myself much instruction.

[17] I made progress therein; to him who gives wisdom I will give glory.

[18] For I resolved to live according to wisdom, and I was zealous for the good; and I shall never be put to shame.

[19] My soul grappled with wisdom, and in my conduct I was strict; I spread out my hands to the heavens, and lamented my ignorance of her.

[20] I directed my soul to her, and through purification I found her. I gained understanding with her from the first,

therefore I will not be forsaken.

[21] My heart was stirred to seek her, therefore I have gained a good possession.

[22] The Lord gave me a tongue as my reward, and I will praise him with it.

[23] Draw near to me, you who are untaught, and lodge in my school.

[24] Why do you say you are lacking in these things, and why are your souls very thirsty?

[25] I opened my mouth and said, Get these things for yourselves without money.

[26] Put your neck under the yoke, and let your souls receive instruction; it is to be found close by.

[27] See with your eyes that I have labored little and found myself much rest.

[28] Get instruction with a large sum of silver, and you will gain by it much gold.

[29] May your soul rejoice in his mercy, and may you not be put to shame when you praise him.

[30] Do your work before the appointed time, and in God's time he will give you your reward.

Wisdom of Solomon

Wis.1

[1] Love righteousness, you rulers of the earth, think of the Lord with uprightness, and seek him with sincerity of heart;

[2] because he is found by those who do not put him to the test, and manifests himself to those who do not distrust him.

[3] For perverse thoughts separate men from God, and when his power is tested, it convicts the foolish;

[4] because wisdom will not enter a deceitful soul, nor dwell in a body enslaved to sin.

[5] For a holy and disciplined spirit will flee from deceit, and will rise and depart from foolish thoughts, and will be ashamed at the approach of unrighteousness.

[6] For wisdom is a kindly spirit and will not free a blasphemer from the guilt of his words; because God is witness of his inmost feelings, and a true observer of his heart, and a hearer of his tongue.

[7] Because the Spirit of the Lord has filled the world, and that which holds all things together knows what is said;

[8] therefore no one who utters unrighteous things will escape notice, and justice, when it punishes, will not pass him by.

[9] For inquiry will be made into the counsels of an ungodly man, and a report of his words will come to the Lord, to convict him of his lawless deeds;

[10] because a jealous ear hears all things, and the sound of murmurings does not go unheard.

[11] Beware then of useless murmuring, and keep your tongue from slander; because no secret word is without result, and a lying mouth destroys the soul.

[12] Do not invite death by the error of your life, nor bring on destruction by the works of your hands;

[13] because God did not make death, and he does not delight in the death of the living.

[14] For he created all things that they might exist, and the generative forces of the world are wholesome, and there is no destructive poison in them; and the dominion of Hades is not on earth.

[15] For righteousness is immortal.

[16] But ungodly men by their words and deeds summoned death; considering him a friend, they pined away, and they made a covenant with him, because they are fit to belong to his party.

Wis.2

[1] For they reasoned unsoundly, saying to themselves, Short and sorrowful is our life, and there is no remedy when a man comes to his end, and no one has been known to return from Hades.

[2] Because we were born by mere chance, and hereafter we shall be as though we had never been; because the breath in our nostrils is smoke, and reason is a spark kindled by the beating of our hearts.

[3] When it is extinguished, the body will turn to ashes, and the spirit will dissolve like empty air.

[4] Our name will be forgotten in time and no one will remember our works; our life will pass away like the traces of a cloud, and be scattered like mist that is chased by the rays of the sun and overcome by its heat.

[5] For our allotted time is the passing of a shadow, and there is no return from our death, because it is sealed up and no one turns back.

[6] "Come, therefore, let us enjoy the good things that exist, and make use of the creation to the full as in youth.

[7] Let us take our fill of costly wine and perfumes, and let no flower of spring pass by us.

[8] Let us crown ourselves with rosebuds before they wither.

[9] Let none of us fail to share in our revelry, everywhere let us leave signs of enjoyment, because this is our portion, and this our lot.

[10] Let us oppress the righteous poor man; let us not spare the widow nor regard the gray hairs of the aged.

[11] But let our might be our law of right, for what is weak proves itself to be useless.

[12] "Let us lie in wait for the righteous man, because he is inconvenient to us and opposes our actions; he reproaches us for sins against the law, and accuses us of sins against our training.

[13] He professes to have knowledge of God, and calls himself a child of the Lord.

[14] He became to us a reproof of our thoughts;

[15] the very sight of him is a burden to us, because his manner of life is unlike that of others, and his ways are strange.

[16] We are considered by him as something base, and he avoids our ways as unclean; he calls the last end of the righteous happy, and boasts that God is his father.

[17] Let us see if his words are true, and let us test what will happen at the end of his life;

[18] for if the righteous man is God's son, he will help him, and will deliver him from the hand of his adversaries.

[19] Let us test him with insult and torture, that we may find out how gentle he is, and make trial of his forbearance.

[20] Let us condemn him to a shameful death, for, according to what he says, he will be protected."

[21] Thus they reasoned, but they were led astray, for their wickedness blinded them,

[22] and they did not know the secret purposes of God, nor hope for the wages of holiness, nor discern the prize for blameless souls;

[23] for God created man for incorruption, and made him in the image of his own eternity,

[24] but through the devil's envy death entered the world, and those who belong to his party experience it.

Wis.3

[1] But the souls of the righteous are in the hand of God, and no torment will ever touch them.

[2] In the eyes of the foolish they seemed to have died, and their departure was thought to be an affliction,

[3] and their going from us to be their destruction; but they are at peace.

[4] For though in the sight of men they were punished, their hope is full of immortality.

[5] Having been disciplined a little, they will receive great good, because God tested them and found them worthy of himself;

[6] like gold in the furnace he tried them, and like a sacrificial burnt offering he accepted them.

[7] In the time of their visitation they will shine forth, and will run like sparks through the stubble.

[8] They will govern nations and rule over peoples, and the Lord will reign over them for ever.

[9] Those who trust in him will understand truth, and the faithful will abide with him in love, because grace and mercy are upon his elect, and he watches over his holy ones.

[10] But the ungodly will be punished as their reasoning deserves, who disregarded the righteous man and rebelled against the Lord;

[11] for whoever despises wisdom and instruction is miserable. Their hope is vain, their labors are unprofitable, and their works are useless.

[12] Their wives are foolish, and their children evil;

[13] their offspring are accursed. For blessed is the barren woman who is undefiled, who has not entered into a sinful union; she will have fruit when God examines souls.

[14] Blessed also is the eunuch whose hands have done no lawless deed, and who has not devised wicked things against the Lord; for special favor will be shown him for his faithfulness, and a place of great delight in the temple of the Lord.

[15] For the fruit of good labors is renowned, and the root of understanding does not fail.

[16] But children of adulterers will not come to maturity, and the offspring of an unlawful union will perish.

[17] Even if they live long they will be held of no account, and finally their old age will be without honor.

[18] If they die young, they will have no hope and no consolation in the day of decision.

[19] For the end of an unrighteous generation is grievous.

Wis.4

[1] Better than this is childlessness with virtue, for in the memory of virtue is immortality, because it is known both by God and by men.

[2] When it is present, men imitate it, and they long for it when it has gone; and throughout all time it marches crowned in triumph, victor in the contest for prizes that are undefiled.

[3] But the prolific brood of the ungodly will be of no use, and none of their illegitimate seedlings will

strike a deep root or take a firm hold.

[4] For even if they put forth boughs for a while, standing insecurely they will be shaken by the wind, and by the violence of the winds they will be uprooted.

[5] The branches will be broken off before they come to maturity, and their fruit will be useless, not ripe enough to eat, and good for nothing.

[6] For children born of unlawful unions are witnesses of evil against their parents when God examines them.

[7] But the righteous man, though he die early, will be at rest.

[8] For old age is not honored for length of time, nor measured by number of years;

[9] but understanding is gray hair for men, and a blameless life is ripe old age.

[10] There was one who pleased God and was loved by him, and while living among sinners he was taken up.

[11] He was caught up lest evil change his understanding or guile deceive his soul.

[12] For the fascination of wickedness obscures what is good, and roving desire perverts the innocent mind.

[13] Being perfected in a short time, he fulfilled long years;

[14] for his soul was pleasing to the Lord, therefore he took him quickly from the midst of wickedness.

[15] Yet the peoples saw and did not understand, nor take such a thing to heart, that God's grace and mercy are with his elect, and he watches over his holy ones.

[16] The righteous man who had died will condemn the ungodly who are living, and youth that is quickly perfected will condemn the prolonged old age of the unrighteous man.

[17] For they will see the end of the wise man, and will not understand what the Lord purposed for him, and for what he kept him safe.

[18] They will see, and will have contempt for him, but the Lord will laugh them to scorn. After this they will become dishonored corpses, and an outrage among the dead for ever;

[19] because he will dash them speechless to the ground, and shake them from the foundations; they will be left utterly dry and barren, and they will suffer anguish, and the memory of them will perish.

[20] They will come with dread when their sins are reckoned up, and their lawless deeds will convict them to their face.

Wis.5

[1] Then the righteous man will stand with great confidence in the presence of those who have afflicted him, and those who make light of his labors.

[2] When they see him, they will be shaken with dreadful fear, and they will be amazed at his unexpected salvation.

[3] They will speak to one another in repentance, and in anguish of spirit they will groan, and say,

[4] "This is the man whom we once held in derision and made a byword of reproach -- we fools! We thought that his life was madness and that his end was without honor.

[5] Why has he been numbered among the sons of God? And why is his lot among the saints?

[6] So it was we who strayed from the way of truth, and the light of righteousness did not shine on us, and the sun did not rise upon us.

[7] We took our fill of the paths of lawlessness and destruction, and we journeyed through trackless deserts, but the way of the Lord we have not known.

[8] What has our arrogance profited us? And what good has our boasted wealth brought us?

[9] "All those things have vanished like a shadow, and like a rumor that passes by;

[10] like a ship that sails through the billowy water, and when it has passed no trace can be found, nor track of its keel in the waves;

[11] or as, when a bird flies through the air, no evidence of its passage is found; the light air, lashed by the beat of its pinions and pierced by the force of its rushing flight, is traversed by the movement of its wings, and afterward no sign of its coming is found there;

[12] or as, when an arrow is shot at a target, the air, thus divided, comes together at once, so that no one knows its pathway.

[13] So we also, as soon as we were born, ceased to be, and we had no sign of virtue to show, but were consumed in our wickedness."

[14] Because the hope of the ungodly man is like chaff carried by the wind, and like a light hoarfrost driven away by a storm; it is dispersed like smoke before the wind, and it passes like the remembrance of a guest who stays but a day.

[15] But the righteous live for ever, and their reward is with the Lord; the Most High takes care of them.

[16] Therefore they will receive a glorious crown and a beautiful diadem from the hand of the Lord, because with his right hand he will cover them, and with his arm he will shield them.

[17] The Lord will take his zeal as his whole armor, and will arm all creation to repel his enemies;

[18] he will put on righteousness as a breastplate, and wear impartial justice as a helmet;

[19] he will take holiness as an invincible shield,

[20] and sharpen stern wrath for a sword, and creation will join with him to fight against the madmen.

[21] Shafts of lightning will fly with true aim, and will leap to the target as from a well-drawn bow of clouds,

[22] and hailstones full of wrath will be hurled as from a catapult; the water of the sea will rage against them, and rivers will relentlessly overwhelm them;

[23] a mighty wind will rise against them , and like a tempest it will winnow them away. Lawlessness will lay waste the whole earth, and evil-doing will overturn the thrones of rulers.

Wis.6

[1] Listen therefore, O kings, and understand; learn, O judges of the ends of the earth.

[2] Give ear, you that rule over multitudes, and boast of many nations.

[3] For your dominion was given you from the Lord, and your sovereignty from the Most High, who will search out your works and inquire into your plans.

[4] Because as servants of his kingdom you did not rule rightly, nor keep the law, nor walk according to the purpose of God,

[5] he will come upon you terribly and swiftly, because severe judgment falls on those in high places.

[6] For the lowliest man may be pardoned in mercy, but mighty men will be mightily tested.

[7] For the Lord of all will not stand in awe of any one, nor show deference to greatness; because he himself made both small and great, and he takes thought for all alike.

[8] But a strict inquiry is in store for the mighty.

[9] To you then, O monarchs, my words are directed, that you may learn wisdom and not transgress.

[10] For they will be made holy who observe holy things in holiness, and those who have been taught them will find a defense.

[11] Therefore set your desire on my words; long for them, and you will be instructed.

[12] Wisdom is radiant and unfading, and she is easily discerned by those who love her, and is found by those who seek her.

[13] She hastens to make herself known to those who desire her.

[14] He who rises early to seek her will have no difficulty, for he will find her sitting at his gates.

[15] To fix one's thought on her is perfect understanding, and he who is vigilant on her account will soon be free from care,

[16] because she goes about seeking those worthy of her, and she graciously appears to them in their paths, and meets them in every thought.

[17] The beginning of wisdom is the most sincere desire for instruction, and concern for instruction is love of her,

[18] and love of her is the keeping of her laws, and giving heed to her laws is assurance of immortality,

[19] and immortality brings one near to God;

[20] so the desire for wisdom leads to a kingdom.

[21] Therefore if you delight in thrones and scepters, O monarchs over the peoples, honor wisdom, that you may reign for ever.

[22] I will tell you what wisdom is and how she came to be, and I will hide no secrets from you, but I will trace her course from the beginning of creation, and make knowledge of her clear, and I will not pass by the truth;

[23] neither will I travel in the company of sickly envy, for envy does not associate with wisdom.

[24] A multitude of wise men is the salvation of the world, and a sensible king is the stability of his people.

[25] Therefore be instructed by my words, and you will profit.

Wis.7

[1] I also am mortal, like all men, a descendant of the first-formed child of earth; and in the womb of a mother I was molded into flesh,

[2] within the period of ten months, compacted with blood, from the seed of a man and the pleasure of marriage.

[3] And when I was born, I began to breathe the common air, and fell upon the kindred earth, and my first sound was a cry, like that of all.

[4] I was nursed with care in swaddling cloths.

[5] For no king has had a different beginning of existence;

[6] there is for all mankind one entrance into life, and a common departure.

[7] Therefore I prayed, and understanding was given me; I called upon God, and the spirit of wisdom came to me.

[8] I preferred her to scepters and thrones, and I accounted wealth as nothing in comparison with her.

[9] Neither did I liken to her any priceless gem, because all gold is but a little sand in her sight, and silver will be accounted as clay before her.

[10] I loved her more than health and beauty, and I chose to have her rather than light, because her radiance never ceases.

[11] All good things came to me along with her, and in her hands uncounted wealth.

[12] I rejoiced in them all, because wisdom leads them; but I did not know that she was their mother.

[13] I learned without guile and I impart without grudging; I do not hide her wealth,

[14] for it is an unfailing treasure for men; those who get it obtain friendship with God, commended for the gifts that come from instruction.

[15] May God grant that I speak with judgment and have thought worthy of what I have received, for he is the guide even of wisdom and the corrector of the wise.

[16] For both we and our words are in his hand, as are all understanding and skill in crafts.

[17] For it is he who gave me unerring knowledge of what exists, to know the structure of the world and the activity of the elements;

[18] the beginning and end and middle of times, the alternations of the solstices and the changes of the seasons,

[19] the cycles of the year and the constellations of the stars,

[20] the natures of animals and the tempers of wild beasts, the powers of spirits and the reasonings of men, the varieties of plants and the virtues of roots;

[21] I learned both what is secret and what is manifest,

[22] for wisdom, the fashioner of all things, taught me. For in her there is a spirit that is intelligent, holy, unique, manifold, subtle, mobile, clear, unpolluted, distinct, invulnerable, loving the good, keen, irresistible,

[23] beneficent, humane, steadfast, sure, free from anxiety, all-powerful, overseeing all, and penetrating through all spirits

that are intelligent and pure and most subtle.

[24] For wisdom is more mobile than any motion; because of her pureness she pervades and penetrates all things.

[25] For she is a breath of the power of God, and a pure emanation of the glory of the Almighty; therefore nothing defiled gains entrance into her.

[26] For she is a reflection of eternal light, a spotless mirror of the working of God, and an image of his goodness.

[27] Though she is but one, she can do all things, and while remaining in herself, she renews all things; in every generation she passes into holy souls and makes them friends of God, and prophets;

[28] for God loves nothing so much as the man who lives with wisdom.

[29] For she is more beautiful than the sun, and excels every constellation of the stars. Compared with the light she is found to be superior,

[30] for it is succeeded by the night, but against wisdom evil does not prevail.

Wis.8

[1] She reaches mightily from one end of the earth to the other, and she orders all things well.

[2] I loved her and sought her from my youth, and I desired to take her for my bride, and I became enamored of her beauty.

[3] She glorifies her noble birth by living with God, and the Lord of all loves her.

[4] For she is an initiate in the knowledge of God, and an associate in his works.

[5] If riches are a desirable possession in life, what is richer than wisdom who effects all things?

[6] And if understanding is effective, who more than she is fashioner of what exists?

[7] And if any one loves righteousness, her labors are virtues; for she teaches self-control and prudence, justice and courage; nothing in life is more profitable for men than these.

[8] And if any one longs for wide experience, she knows the things of old, and infers the things to come; she understands turns of speech and the solutions of riddles; she has foreknowledge of signs and wonders and of the outcome of seasons and times.

[9] Therefore I determined to take her to live with me, knowing that she would give me good counsel and encouragement in cares and grief.

[10] Because of her I shall have glory among the multitudes and honor in the presence of the elders, though I am young.

[11] I shall be found keen in judgment, and in the sight of rulers I shall be admired.

[12] When I am silent they will wait for me, and when I speak they will give heed; and when I speak at greater length

they will put their hands on their mouths.

[13] Because of her I shall have immortality, and leave an everlasting remembrance to those who come after me.

[14] I shall govern peoples, and nations will be subject to me;

[15] dread monarchs will be afraid of me when they hear of me; among the people I shall show myself capable, and courageous in war.

[16] When I enter my house, I shall find rest with her, for companionship with her has no bitterness, and life with her has no pain, but gladness and joy.

[17] When I considered these things inwardly, and thought upon them in my mind, that in kinship with wisdom there is immortality,

[18] and in friendship with her, pure delight, and in the labors of her hands, unfailing wealth, and in the experience of her company, understanding, and renown in sharing her words, I went about seeking how to get her for myself.

[19] As a child I was by nature well endowed, and a good soul fell to my lot;

[20] or rather, being good, I entered an undefiled body.

[21] But I perceived that I would not possess wisdom unless God gave her to me -- and it was a mark of insight to know whose gift she was -- so I appealed to the Lord and besought him, and with my whole heart I said:

Wis.9

[1] "O God of my fathers and Lord of mercy, who hast made all things by thy word,

[2] and by thy wisdom hast formed man, to have dominion over the creatures thou hast made,

[3] and rule the world in holiness and righteousness, and pronounce judgment in uprightness of soul,

[4] give me the wisdom that sits by thy throne, and do not reject me from among thy servants.

[5] For I am thy slave and the son of thy maidservant, a man who is weak and short-lived, with little understanding of judgment and laws;

[6] for even if one is perfect among the sons of men, yet without the wisdom that comes from thee he will be regarded as nothing.

[7] Thou hast chosen me to be king of thy people and to be judge over thy sons and daughters.

[8] Thou hast given command to build a temple on thy holy mountain, and an altar in the city of thy habitation, a copy of the holy tent which thou didst prepare from the beginning.

[9] With thee is wisdom, who knows thy works and was present when thou didst make the world, and who understand what is pleasing in thy sight and what is right according to thy commandments.

[10] Send her forth from the holy heavens, and from the throne of thy glory send her, that she may be with me and toil,

and that I may learn what is pleasing to thee.

[11] For she knows and understands all things, and she will guide me wisely in my actions and guard me with her glory.

[12] Then my works will be acceptable, and I shall judge thy people justly, and shall be worthy of the throne of my father.

[13] For what man can learn the counsel of God? Or who can discern what the Lord wills?

[14] For the reasoning of mortals is worthless, and our designs are likely to fail,

[15] for a perishable body weighs down the soul, and this earthy tent burdens the thoughtful mind.

[16] We can hardly guess at what is on earth, and what is at hand we find with labor; but who has traced out what is in the heavens?

[17] Who has learned thy counsel, unless thou hast given wisdom and sent thy holy Spirit from on high?

[18] And thus the paths of those on earth were set right, and men were taught what pleases thee, and were saved by wisdom."

Wis.10

[1] Wisdom protected the first-formed father of the world, when he alone had been created; she delivered him from his transgression,

[2] and gave him strength to rule all things.

[3] But when an unrighteous man departed from her in his anger, he perished because in rage he slew his brother.

[4] When the earth was flooded because of him, wisdom again saved it, steering the righteous man by a paltry piece of wood.

[5] Wisdom also, when the nations in wicked agreement had been confounded, recognized the righteous man and preserved him blameless before God, and kept him strong in the face of his compassion for his child.

[6] Wisdom rescued a righteous man when the ungodly were perishing; he escaped the fire that descended on the Five Cities.

[7] Evidence of their wickedness still remains: a continually smoking wasteland, plants bearing fruit that does not ripen,

and a pillar of salt standing as a monument to an unbelieving soul.

[8] For because they passed wisdom by, they not only were hindered from recognizing the good, but also left for mankind a reminder of their folly, so that their failures could never go unnoticed.

[9] Wisdom rescued from troubles those who served her.

[10] When a righteous man fled from his brother's wrath, she guided him on straight paths; she showed him the kingdom of God, and gave him knowledge of angels; she prospered him in his labors, and increased the fruit of his toil.

[11] When his oppressors were covetous, she stood by him and made him rich.

[12] She protected him from his enemies, and kept him safe from those who lay in wait for him; in his arduous contest she gave him the victory, so that he might learn that godliness is more powerful than anything.

[13] When a righteous man was sold, wisdom did not desert him, but delivered him from sin. She descended with him into the dungeon,

[14] and when he was in prison she did not leave him, until she brought him the scepter of a kingdom and authority over his masters. Those who accused him she showed to be false, and she gave him everlasting honor.

[15] A holy people and blameless race wisdom delivered from a nation of oppressors.

[16] She entered the soul of a servant of the Lord, and withstood dread kings with wonders and signs.

[17] She gave holy men the reward of their labors; she guided them along a marvelous way, and became a shelter to them by day, and a starry flame through the night.

[18] She brought them over the Red Sea, and led them through deep waters;

[19] but she drowned their enemies, and cast them up from the depth of the sea.

[20] Therefore the righteous plundered the ungodly; they sang hymns, O Lord, to thy holy name, and praised with one accord thy defending hand,

[21] because wisdom opened the mouth of the dumb, and made the tongues of babes speak clearly.

Wis.11

[1] Wisdom prospered their works by the hand of a holy prophet.

[2] They journeyed through an uninhabited wilderness, and pitched their tents in untrodden places.

[3] They withstood their enemies and fought off their foes.

[4] When they thirsted they called upon thee, and water was given them out of flinty rock, and slaking of thirst from hard stone.

[5] For through the very things by which their enemies were punished, they themselves received benefit in their need.

[6] Instead of the fountain of an ever-flowing river, stirred up and defiled with blood

[7] in rebuke for the decree to slay the infants, thou gavest them abundant water unexpectedly,

[8] showing by their thirst at that time how thou didst punish their enemies.

[9] For when they were tried, though they were being disciplined in mercy, they learned how the ungodly were tormented

when judged in wrath.

[10] For thou didst test them as a father does in warning, but thou didst examine the ungodly as a stern king does in condemnation.

[11] Whether absent or present, they were equally distressed,

[12] for a twofold grief possessed them, and a groaning at the memory of what had occurred.

[13] For when they heard that through their own punishments the righteous had received benefit, they perceived it was the Lord's doing.

[14] For though they had mockingly rejected him who long before had been cast out and exposed, at the end of the events they marveled at him, for their thirst was not like that of the righteous.

[15] In return for their foolish and wicked thoughts, which led them astray to worship irrational serpents and worthless animals, thou didst send upon them a multitude of irrational creatures to punish them,

[16] that they might learn that one is punished by the very things by which he sins.

[17] For thy all-powerful hand, which created the world out of formless matter, did not lack the means to send upon them a multitude of bears, or bold lions,

[18] or newly created unknown beasts full of rage, or such as breathe out fiery breath, or belch forth a thick pall of smoke, or flash terrible sparks from their eyes;

[19] not only could their damage exterminate men, but the mere sight of them could kill by fright.

[20] Even apart from these, men could fall at a single breath when pursued by justice and scattered by the breath of thy power. But thou hast arranged all things by measure and number and weight.

[21] For it is always in thy power to show great strength, and who can withstand the might of thy arm?

[22] Because the whole world before thee is like a speck that tips the scales, and like a drop of morning dew that falls upon the ground.

[23] But thou art merciful to all, for thou canst do all things, and thou do overlook men's sins, that they may repent.

[24] For thou lovest all things that exist, and hast loathing for none of the things which thou hast made, for thou wouldst not have made anything if thou hadst hated it.

[25] How would anything have endured if thou hadst not willed it? Or how would anything not called forth by thee

have been preserved?

[26] Thou sparest all things, for they are your, O Lord who lovest the living.

Wis.12

[1] For thy immortal spirit is in all things.

[2] Therefore thou do correct little by little those who trespass, and do remind and warn them of the things wherein they sin, that they may be freed from wickedness and put their trust in thee, O Lord.

[3] Those who dwelt of old in thy holy land

[4] thou didst hate for their detestable practices, their works of sorcery and unholy rites,

[5] their merciless slaughter of children, and their sacrificial feasting on human flesh and blood. These initiates from the midst of a heathen cult,

[6] these parents who murder helpless lives, thou didst will to destroy by the hands of our fathers,

[7] that the land most precious of all to thee might receive a worthy colony of the servants of God.

[8] But even these thou didst spare, since they were but men, and didst send wasps as forerunners of thy army, to destroy them little by little,

[9] though thou wast not unable to give the ungodly into the hands of the righteous in battle, or to destroy them at one blow by dread wild beasts or thy stern word.

[10] But judging them little by little thou gavest them a chance to repent, though thou wast not unaware that their origin was evil and their wickedness inborn, and that their way of thinking would never change.

[11] For they were an accursed race from the beginning, and it was not through fear of any one that thou didst leave them unpunished for their sins.

[12] For who will say, "What hast thou done?" Or will resist thy judgment? Who will accuse thee for the destruction of

nations which thou didst make? Or who will come before thee to plead as an advocate for unrighteous men?

[13] For neither is there any god besides thee, whose care is for all men, to whom thou shouldst prove that thou hast not judged unjustly;

[14] nor can any king or monarch confront thee about those whom thou hast punished.

[15] Thou art righteous and rulest all things righteously, deeming it alien to thy power to condemn him who does not deserve to be punished.

[16] For thy strength is the source of righteousness, and thy sovereignty over all causes thee to spare all.

[17] For thou do show thy strength when men doubt the completeness of thy power, and do rebuke any insolence among those who know it.

[18] Thou who art sovereign in strength do judge with mildness, and with great forbearance thou do govern us; for thou hast power to act whenever thou do choose.

[19] Through such works thou has taught thy people that the righteous man must be kind, and thou hast filled thy sons with good hope, because thou givest repentance for sins.

[20] For if thou didst punish with such great care and indulgence the enemies of thy servants and those deserving of death,

granting them time and opportunity to give up their wickedness,

[21] with what strictness thou hast judged thy sons, to whose fathers thou gavest oaths and covenants full of good promises!

[22] So while chastening us thou scourgest our enemies ten thousand times more, so that we may meditate upon thy goodness when we judge, and when we are judged we may expect mercy.

[23] Therefore those who in folly of life lived unrighteously thou didst torment through their own abominations.

[24] For they went far astray on the paths of error, accepting as gods those animals which even their enemies despised;

they were deceived like foolish babes.

[25] Therefore, as to thoughtless children, thou didst send thy judgment to mock them.

[26] But those who have not heeded the warning of light rebukes will experience the deserved judgment of God.

[27] For when in their suffering they became incensed at those creatures which they had thought to be gods, being punished by means of them, they saw and recognized as the true God him whom they had before refused to know.

Therefore the utmost condemnation came upon them.

Wis.13

[1] For all men who were ignorant of God were foolish by nature; and they were unable from the good things that

are seen to know him who exists, nor did they recognize the craftsman while paying heed to his works;

[2] but they supposed that either fire or wind or swift air, or the circle of the stars, or turbulent water, or the luminaries of heaven were the gods that rule the world.

[3] If through delight in the beauty of these things men assumed them to be gods, let them know how much better than these is their Lord, for the author of beauty created them.

[4] And if men were amazed at their power and working, let them perceive from them how much more powerful is he who formed them.

[5] For from the greatness and beauty of created things comes a corresponding perception of their Creator.

[6] Yet these men are little to be blamed, for perhaps they go astray while seeking God and desiring to find him.

[7] For as they live among his works they keep searching, and they trust in what they see, because the things that are seen are beautiful.

[8] Yet again, not even they are to be excused;

[9] for if they had the power to know so much that they could investigate the world, how did they fail to find sooner the Lord of these things?

[10] But miserable, with their hopes set on dead things, are the men who give the name "gods" to the works of men's hands, gold and silver fashioned with skill, and likenesses of animals, or a useless

stone, the work of an ancient hand.

[11] A skilled woodcutter may saw down a tree easy to handle and skilfully strip off all its bark, and then with pleasing workmanship make a useful vessel that serves life's needs,

[12] and burn the castoff pieces of his work to prepare his food, and eat his fill.

[13] But a castoff piece from among them, useful for nothing, a stick crooked and full of knots, he takes and carves with care in his leisure, and shapes it with skill gained in idleness; he forms it like the image of a man,

[14] or makes it like some worthless animal, giving it a coat of red paint and coloring its surface red and covering every blemish in it with paint;

[15] then he makes for it a niche that befits it, and sets it in the wall, and fastens it there with iron.

[16] So he takes thought for it, that it may not fall, because he knows that it cannot help itself, for it is only an image and has need of help.

[17] When he prays about possessions and his marriage and children, he is not ashamed to address a lifeless thing.

[18] For health he appeals to a thing that is weak; for life he prays to a thing that is dead; for aid he entreats a thing that is utterly inexperienced; for a prosperous journey, a thing that cannot take a step;

[19] for money-making and work and success with his hands he asks strength of a thing whose hands have no strength.

Wis.14

[1] Again, one preparing to sail and about to voyage over raging waves calls upon a piece of wood more fragile than the ship which carries him.

[2] For it was desire for gain that planned that vessel, and wisdom was the craftsman who built it;

[3] but it is thy providence, O Father, that steers its course, because thou hast given it a path in the sea, and a safe way through the waves,

[4] showing that thou canst save from every danger, so that even if a man lacks skill, he may put to sea.

[5] It is thy will that works of thy wisdom should not be without effect; therefore men trust their lives even to the smallest piece of wood, and passing through the billows on a raft they come safely to land.

[6] For even in the beginning, when arrogant giants were perishing, the hope of the world took refuge on a raft, and guided by thy hand left to the world the seed of a new generation.

[7] For blessed is the wood by which righteousness comes.

[8] But the idol made with hands is accursed, and so is he who made it; because he did the work, and the perishable thing was named a god.

[9] For equally hateful to God are the ungodly man and his ungodliness,

[10] for what was done will be punished together with him who did it.

[11] Therefore there will be a visitation also upon the heathen idols, because, though part of what God created, they became an abomination, and became traps for the souls of men and a snare to the feet of the foolish.

[12] For the idea of making idols was the beginning of fornication, and the invention of them was the corruption of life,

[13] for neither have they existed from the beginning nor will they exist for ever.

[14] For through the vanity of men they entered the world, and therefore their speedy end has been planned.

[15] For a father, consumed with grief at an untimely bereavement, made an image of his child, who had been suddenly

taken from him; and he now honored as a god what was once a dead human being, and handed on to his dependents secret rites and initiations.

[16] Then the ungodly custom, grown strong with time, was kept as a law, and at the command of monarchs graven images were worshiped.

[17] When men could not honor monarchs in their presence, since they lived at a distance, they imagined their appearance far away, and made a visible image of the king whom they honored, so that by their zeal they might flatter the absent one as though present.

[18] Then the ambition of the craftsman impelled even those who did not know the king to intensify their worship.

[19] For he, perhaps wishing to please his ruler, skilfully forced the likeness to take more beautiful form,

[20] and the multitude, attracted by the charm of his work, now regarded as an object of worship the one whom shortly before they had honored as a man.

[21] And this became a hidden trap for mankind, because men, in bondage to misfortune or to royal authority, bestowed on objects of stone or wood the name that ought not to be shared.

[22] Afterward it was not enough for them to err about the knowledge of God, but they live in great strife due to ignorance, and they call such great evils peace.

[23] For whether they kill children in their initiations, or celebrate secret mysteries, or hold frenzied revels with strange customs,

[24] they no longer keep either their lives or their marriages pure, but they either treacherously kill one another, or grieve one another by adultery,

[25] and all is a raging riot of blood and murder, theft and deceit, corruption, faithlessness, tumult, perjury,

[26] confusion over what is good, forgetfulness of favors, pollution of souls, sex perversion, disorder in marriage, adultery, and debauchery.

[27] For the worship of idols not to be named is the beginning and cause and end of every evil.

[28] For their worshipers either rave in exultation, or prophesy lies, or live unrighteously, or readily commit perjury;

[29] for because they trust in lifeless idols they swear wicked oaths and expect to suffer no harm.

[30] But just penalties will overtake them on two counts: because they thought wickedly of God in devoting themselves to idols, and because in deceit they swore unrighteously through contempt for holiness.

[31] For it is not the power of the things by which men swear, but the just penalty for those who sin, that always pursues the transgression of the unrighteous.

Wis.15

[1] But thou, our God, art kind and true, patient, and ruling all things in mercy.

[2] For even if we sin we are your, knowing thy power; but we will not sin, because we know that we are accounted your.

[3] For to know thee is complete righteousness, and to know thy power is the root of immortality.

[4] For neither has the evil intent of human art misled us, nor the fruitless toil of painters, a figure stained with varied colors,

[5] whose appearance arouses yearning in fools, so that they desire the lifeless form of a dead image.

[6] Lovers of evil things and fit for such objects of hope are those who either make or desire or worship them.

[7] For when a potter kneads the soft earth and laboriously molds each vessel for our service, he fashions out of the same clay both the vessels that serve clean uses and those for contrary uses, making all in like manner; but which shall be the use of each of these the worker in clay decides.

[8] With misspent toil, he forms a futile god from the same clay -- this man who was made of earth a short time before
and after a little while goes to the earth from which he was taken, when he is required to return the soul that was lent him.

[9] But he is not concerned that he is destined to die or that his life is brief, but he competes with workers in gold and silver, and imitates workers in copper; and he counts it his glory that he molds counterfeit gods.

[10] His heart is ashes, his hope is cheaper than dirt, and his life is of less worth than clay,

[11] because he failed to know the one who formed him and inspired him with an active soul and breathed into him a living spirit.

[12] But he considered our existence an idle game, and life a festival held for profit, for he says one must get money however one can, even by base means.

[13] For this man, more than all others, knows that he sins when he makes from earthy matter fragile vessels and graven images.

[14] But most foolish, and more miserable than an infant, are all the enemies who oppressed thy people.

[15] For they thought that all their heathen idols were gods, though these have neither the use of their eyes to see with, nor nostrils with which to draw breath, nor ears with which to hear, nor fingers to feel with, and their feet are of no use for walking.

[16] For a man made them, and one whose spirit is borrowed formed them; for no man can form a god which is like himself.

[17] He is mortal, and what he makes with lawless hands is dead, for he is better than the objects he worships, since he has life, but they never have.

[18] The enemies of thy people worship even the most hateful animals, which are worse than all others, when judged by their lack of intelligence;

[19] and even as animals they are not so beautiful in appearance that one would desire them, but they have escaped both the praise of God and his blessing.

Wis.16

[1] Therefore those men were deservedly punished through such creatures, and were tormented by a multitude of animals.

[2] Instead of this punishment thou didst show kindness to thy people, and thou didst prepare quails to eat, a delicacy to satisfy the desire of appetite;

[3] in order that those men, when they desired food, might lose the least remnant of appetite because of the odious creatures sent to them, while thy people, after suffering want a short time, might partake of delicacies.

[4] For it was necessary that upon those oppressors inexorable want should come, while to these it was merely shown how their enemies were being tormented.

[5] For when the terrible rage of wild beasts came upon thy people and they were being destroyed by the bites of writhing serpents, thy wrath did not continue to the end;

[6] they were troubled for a little while as a warning, and received a token of deliverance to remind them of thy law's command.

[7] For he who turned toward it was saved, not by what he saw, but by thee, the Savior of all.

[8] And by this also thou didst convince our enemies that it is thou who deliverest from every evil.

[9] For they were killed by the bites of locusts and flies, and no healing was found for them, because they deserved to be punished by such things;

[10] but thy sons were not conquered even by the teeth of venomous serpents, for thy mercy came to their help and healed them.

[11] To remind them of thy oracles they were bitten, and then were quickly delivered, lest they should fall into deep forgetfulness and become unresponsive to thy kindness.

[12] For neither herb nor poultice cured them, but it was thy word, O Lord, which heals all men.

[13] For thou hast power over life and death; thou do lead men down to the gates of Hades and back again.

[14] A man in his wickedness kills another, but he cannot bring back the departed spirit, nor set free the imprisoned soul.

[15] To escape from thy hand is impossible;

[16] for the ungodly, refusing to know thee, were scourged by the strength of thy arm, pursued by unusual rains and hail and relentless storms, and utterly consumed by fire.

[17] For -- most incredible of all -- in the water, which quenches all things, the fire had still greater effect, for the universe defends the righteous.

[18] At one time the flame was restrained, so that it might not consume the creatures sent against the ungodly, but that seeing this they might know that they were being pursued by the judgment of God;

[19] and at another time even in the midst of water it burned more intensely than fire, to destroy the crops of the unrighteous land.

[20] Instead of these things thou didst give thy people food of angels, and without their toil thou didst supply them
from heaven with bread ready to eat, providing every pleasure and suited to every taste.

[21] For thy sustenance manifested thy sweetness toward thy children; and the bread, ministering to the desire of the one who took it, was changed to suit every one's liking.

[22] Snow and ice withstood fire without melting, so that they might know that the crops of their enemies were being destroyed by the fire that blazed in the hail and flashed in the showers of rain;

[23] whereas the fire, in order that the righteous might be fed, even forgot its native power.

[24] For creation, serving thee who hast made it, exerts itself to punish the unrighteous, and in kindness relaxes on behalf of those who trust in thee.

[25] Therefore at that time also, changed into all forms, it served thy all-nourishing bounty, according to the desire of those who had need,

[26] so that thy sons, whom thou didst love, O Lord, might learn that it is not the production of crops that feeds man, but that thy word preserves those who trust in thee.

[27] For what was not destroyed by fire was melted when simply warmed by a fleeting ray of the sun,

[28] to make it known that one must rise before the sun to give thee thanks, and must pray to thee at the dawning of the light;

[29] for the hope of an ungrateful man will melt like wintry frost, and flow away like waste water.

Wis.17

[1] Great are thy judgments and hard to describe; therefore unintructed souls have gone astray.
[2] For when lawless men supposed that they held the holy nation in their power, they themselves lay as captives of darkness and prisoners of long night, shut in under their roofs, exiles from eternal providence.
[3] For thinking that in their secret sins they were unobserved behind a dark curtain of forgetfulness, they were scattered, terribly alarmed, and appalled by specters.
[4] For not even the inner chamber that held them protected them from fear, but terrifying sounds rang out around them,
and dismal phantoms with gloomy faces appeared.
[5] And no power of fire was able to give light, nor did the brilliant flames of the stars avail to illumine that hateful night.
[6] Nothing was shining through to them except a dreadful, self-kindled fire, and in terror they deemed the things which they saw to be worse than that unseen appearance.
[7] The delusions of their magic art lay humbled, and their boasted wisdom was scornfully rebuked.
[8] For those who promised to drive off the fears and disorders of a sick soul were sick themselves with ridiculous fear.
[9] For even if nothing disturbing frightened them, yet, scared by the passing of beasts and the hissing of serpents,
[10] they perished in trembling fear, refusing to look even at the air, though it nowhere could be avoided.
[11] For wickedness is a cowardly thing, condemned by its own testimony; distressed by conscience, it has always exaggerated the difficulties.
[12] For fear is nothing but surrender of the helps that come from reason;
[13] and the inner expectation of help, being weak, prefers ignorance of what causes the torment.
[14] But throughout the night, which was really powerless, and which beset them from the recesses of powerless Hades,
they all slept the same sleep,
[15] and now were driven by monstrous specters, and now were paralyzed by their souls' surrender, for sudden and unexpected fear overwhelmed them.
[16] And whoever was there fell down, and thus was kept shut up in a prison not made of iron;
[17] for whether he was a farmer or a shepherd or a workman who toiled in the wilderness, he was seized, and endured the inescapable fate; for with one chain of darkness they all were bound.
[18] Whether there came a whistling wind, or a melodious sound of birds in wide-spreading branches, or the rhythm of violently rushing water,
[19] or the harsh crash of rocks hurled down, or the unseen running of leaping animals, or the sound of the most savage roaring beasts, or an echo thrown back from a hollow of the mountains, it paralyzed them with terror.
[20] For the whole world was illumined with brilliant light, and was engaged in unhindered work,
[21] while over those men alone heavy night was spread, an image of the darkness that was destined to receive them;
but still heavier than darkness were they to themselves.

Wis.18

[1] But for thy holy ones there was very great light. Their enemies heard their voices but did not see their forms, and counted them happy for not having suffered,
[2] and were thankful that thy holy ones, though previously wronged, were doing them no injury; and they begged their pardon for having been at variance with them.
[3] Therefore thou didst provide a flaming pillar of fire as a guide for thy people's unknown journey, and a harmless sun for their glorious wandering.
[4] For their enemies deserved to be deprived of light and imprisoned in darkness, those who had kept thy sons imprisoned, through whom the imperishable light of the law was to be given to the world.

[5] When they had resolved to kill the babes of thy holy ones, and one child had been exposed and rescued, thou didst in punishment take away a multitude of their children; and thou didst destroy them all together by a mighty flood.
[6] That night was made known beforehand to our fathers, so that they might rejoice in sure knowledge of the oaths in which they trusted.
[7] The deliverance of the righteous and the destruction of their enemies were expected by thy people.
[8] For by the same means by which thou didst punish our enemies thou didst call us to thyself and glorify us.
[9] For in secret the holy children of good men offered sacrifices, and with one accord agreed to the divine law, that the saints would share alike the same things, both blessings and dangers; and already they were singing the praises of the fathers.
[10] But the discordant cry of their enemies echoed back, and their piteous lament for their children was spread abroad.
[11] The slave was punished with the same penalty as the master, and the common man suffered the same loss as the king;
[12] and they all together, by the one form of death, had corpses too many to count. For the living were not sufficient even to bury them, since in one instant their most valued children had been destroyed.
[13] For though they had disbelieved everything because of their magic arts, yet, when their first-born were destroyed,
they acknowledged thy people to be God's son.
[14] For while gentle silence enveloped all things, and night in its swift course was now half gone,
[15] thy all-powerful word leaped from heaven, from the royal throne, into the midst of the land that was doomed,
a stern warrior
[16] carrying the sharp sword of thy authentic command, and stood and filled all things with death, and touched heaven while standing on the earth.
[17] Then at once apparitions in dreadful dreams greatly troubled them, and unexpected fears assailed them;
[18] and one here and another there, hurled down half dead, made known why they were dying;
[19] for the dreams which disturbed them forewarned them of this, so that they might not perish without knowing
why they suffered.
[20] The experience of death touched also the righteous, and a plague came upon the multitude in the desert, but the wrath did not long continue.
[21] For a blameless man was quick to act as their champion; he brought forward the shield of his ministry, prayer and propitiation by incense; he withstood the anger and put an end to the disaster, showing that he was thy servant.
[22] He conquered the wrath not by strength of body, and not by force of arms, but by his word he subdued the punisher,
appealing to the oaths and covenants given to our fathers.
[23] For when the dead had already fallen on one another in heaps, he intervened and held back the wrath, and cut off its way to the living.
[24] For upon his long robe the whole world was depicted, and the glories of the fathers were engraved on the four rows of stones, and thy majesty on the diadem upon his head.
[25] To these the destroyer yielded, these he feared; for merely to test the wrath was enough.

Wis.19

[1] But the ungodly were assailed to the end by pitiless anger, for God knew in advance even their future actions,
[2] that, though they themselves had permitted thy people to depart and hastily sent them forth, they would change their minds and pursue them.
[3] For while they were still busy at mourning, and were lamenting at the graves of their dead, they reached another foolish decision, and pursued as fugitives those whom they had begged and compelled to depart.
[4] For the fate they deserved drew them on to this end, and made them forget what had happened, in order that they might fill up the punishment which their torments still lacked,
[5] and that thy people might experience an incredible journey, but they themselves might meet a strange death.

[6] For the whole creation in its nature was fashioned anew, complying with thy commands, that thy children might be kept unharmed.

[7] The cloud was seen overshadowing the camp, and dry land emerging where water had stood before, an unhindered way out of the Red Sea, and a grassy plain out of the raging waves,

[8] where those protected by thy hand passed through as one nation, after gazing on marvelous wonders.

[9] For they ranged like horses, and leaped like lambs, praising thee, O Lord, who didst deliver them.

[10] For they still recalled the events of their sojourn, how instead of producing animals the earth brought forth gnats,

and instead of fish the river spewed out vast numbers of frogs.

[11] Afterward they saw also a new kind of birds, when desire led them to ask for luxurious food;

[12] for, to give them relief, quails came up from the sea.

[13] The punishments did not come upon the sinners without prior signs in the violence of thunder, for they justly suffered because of their wicked acts; for they practiced a more bitter hatred of strangers.

[14] Others had refused to receive strangers when they came to them, but these made slaves of guests who were their benefactors.

[15] And not only so, but punishment of some sort will come upon the former for their hostile reception of the aliens;

[16] but the latter, after receiving them with festal celebrations, afflicted with terrible sufferings those who had already shared the same rights.

[17] They were stricken also with loss of sight -- just as were those at the door of the righteous man -- when, surrounded by yawning darkness, each tried to find the way through his own door.

[18] For the elements changed places with one another, as on a harp the notes vary the nature of the rhythm, while each note remains the same. This may be clearly inferred from the sight of what took place.

[19] For land animals were transformed into water creatures, and creatures that swim moved over to the land.

[20] Fire even in water retained its normal power, and water forgot its fire-quenching nature.

[21] Flames, on the contrary, failed to consume the flesh of perishable creatures that walked among them, nor did they melt the crystalline, easily melted kind of heavenly food.

[22] For in everything, O Lord, thou hast exalted and glorified thy people; and thou hast not neglected to help them at all times and in all places.

Additions to the Book of Esther

AddEsth.11

[2] In the second year of the reign of Artaxerxes the Great, on the first day of Nisan, Mordecai the son of Jair, son of Shimei, son of Kish, of the tribe of Benjamin, had a dream.

[3] He was a Jew, dwelling in the city of Susa, a great man, serving in the court of the king.

[4] He was one of the captives whom Nebuchadnezzar king of Babylon had brought from Jerusalem with Jeconiah king of Judea. And this was his dream:

[5] Behold, noise and confusion, thunders and earthquake, tumult upon the earth!

[6] And behold, two great dragons came forward, both ready to fight, and they roared terribly.

[7] And at their roaring every nation prepared for war, to fight against the nation of the righteous.

[8] And behold, a day of darkness and gloom, tribulation and distress, affliction and great tumult upon the earth!

[9] And the whole righteous nation was troubled; they feared the evils that threatened them, and were ready to perish.

[10] Then they cried to God; and from their cry, as though from a tiny spring, there came a great river, with abundant water; [11] light came, and the sun rose, and the lowly were exalted and consumed those held in honor.

[12] Mordecai saw in this dream what God had determined to do, and after he awoke he had it on his mind and sought all day to understand it in every detail.

AddEsth.12

[1] Now Mordecai took his rest in the courtyard with Gabatha and Tharra, the two eunuchs of the king who kept watch in the courtyard.

[2] He overheard their conversation and inquired into their purposes, and learned that they were preparing to lay hands upon Artaxerxes the king; and he informed the king concerning them.

[3] Then the king examined the two eunuchs, and when they confessed they were led to execution.

[4] The king made a permanent record of these things, and Mordecai wrote an account of them.

[5] And the king ordered Mordecai to serve in the court and rewarded him for these things.

[6] But Haman, the son of Hammedatha, a Bougaean, was in great honor with the king, and he sought to injure Mordecai and his people because of the two eunuchs of the king.

AddEsth.13

[1] This is a copy of the letter: "The Great King, Artaxerxes, to the rulers of the hundred and twenty-seven provinces from India to Ethiopia and to the governors under them, writes thus:

[2] "Having become ruler of many nations and master of the whole world, not elated with presumption of authority but always acting reasonably and with kindness, I have determined to settle the lives of my subjects in lasting tranquillity and, in order to make my kingdom peaceable and open to travel throughout all its extent, to re-establish the peace which all men desire.

[3] "When I asked my counselors how this might be accomplished, Haman, who excels among us in sound judgment, and is distinguished for his unchanging good will and steadfast fidelity, and has attained the second place in the kingdom,

[4] pointed out to us that among all the nations in the world there is scattered a certain hostile people, who have laws contrary to those of every nation and continually disregard the ordinances of the kings, so that the unifying of the kingdom which we honorably intend cannot be brought about.

[5] We understand that this people, and it alone, stands constantly in opposition to all men, perversely following a strange manner of life and laws, and is ill-disposed to our government, doing all the harm they can so that our kingdom may not attain stability.

[6] "Therefore we have decreed that those indicated to you in the letters of Haman, who is in charge of affairs and is our second father, shall all, with their wives and children, be utterly destroyed by the sword of their enemies, without pity or mercy, on the fourteenth day of the twelfth month, Adar, of this present year,

[7] so that those who have long been and are now hostile may in one day go down in violence to Hades, and leave our government completely secure and untroubled hereafter."

[8] Then Mordecai prayed to the Lord, calling to remembrance all the works of the Lord. He said:

[9] "O Lord, Lord, King who rulest over all things, for the universe is in thy power and there is no one who can oppose thee if it is thy will to save Israel.

[10] For thou hast made heaven and earth and every wonderful thing under heaven,

[11] and thou art Lord of all, and there is no one who can resist thee, who art the Lord.

[12] Thou knowest all things; thou knowest, O Lord, that it was not in insolence or pride or for any love of glory that I did this, and refused to bow down to this proud Haman.

[13] For I would have been willing to kiss the soles of his feet, to save Israel!

[14] But I did this, that I might not set the glory of man above the glory of God, and I will not bow down to any one but to thee, who art my Lord; and I will not do these things in pride.

[15] And now, O Lord God and King, God of Abraham, spare thy people; for the eyes of our foes are upon us to annihilate us, and they desire to destroy the inheritance that has been your from the beginning.

[16] Do not neglect thy portion, which thou didst redeem for thyself out of the land of Egypt.

[17] Hear my prayer, and have mercy upon thy inheritance turn our mourning into feasting, that we may live and sing praise to thy name, O Lord; do not destroy the mouth of those who praise thee."

[18] And all Israel cried out mightily, for their death was before their eyes.

AddEsth.14

[1] And Esther the queen, seized with deathly anxiety, fled to the Lord;

[2] she took off her splendid apparel and put on the garments of distress and mourning, and instead of costly perfumes she covered her head with ashes and dung, and she utterly humbled her body, and every part that she loved to adorn she covered with her tangled hair.

[3] And she prayed to the Lord God of Israel, and said: Lord, thou only art our King; help me, who am alone and have no helper but thee,

[4] for my danger is in my hand.

[5] Ever since I was born I have heard in the tribe of my family that thou, O Lord, didst take Israel out of all the nations, and our fathers from among all their ancestors, for an everlasting inheritance, and that thou didst do for them all that thou didst promise.

[6] And now we have sinned before thee, and thou hast given us into the hands of our enemies,

[7] because we glorified their gods. Thou art righteous, O Lord!

[8] And now they are not satisfied that we are in bitter slavery, but they have covenanted with their idols

[9] to abolish what thy mouth has ordained and to destroy thy inheritance, to stop the mouths of those who praise thee and to quench thy altar and the glory of thy house,

[10] to open the mouths of the nations for the praise of vain idols, and to magnify for ever a mortal king.

[11] O Lord, do not surrender thy scepter to what has no being; and do not let them mock at our downfall; but turn their plan against themselves, and make an example of the man who began this against us.

[12] Remember, O Lord; make thyself known in this time of our affliction, and give me courage, O King of the gods and Master of all dominion!

[13] Put eloquent speech in my mouth before the lion, and turn his heart to hate the man who is fighting against us, so that there may be an end of him and those who agree with him.

[14] But save us by thy hand, and help me, who am alone and have no helper but thee, O Lord.

[15] Thou hast knowledge of all things; and thou knowest that I hate the splendor of the wicked and abhor the bed of the uncircumcised and of any alien.

[16] Thou knowest my necessity -- that I abhor the sign of my proud position, which is upon my head on the days when I appear in public. I abhor it like a menstruous rag, and I do not wear it on the days when I am at leisure.

[17] And thy servant has not eaten at Haman's table, and I have not honored the king's feast or drunk the wine of the libations.

[18] Your servant has had no joy since the day that I was brought here until now, except in thee, O Lord God of Abraham.

[19] O God, whose might is over all, hear the voice of the despairing, and save us from the hands of

evildoers. And save me from my fear!"

AddEsth.15

[1] On the third day, when she ended her prayer, she took off the garments in which she had worshiped, and arrayed herself in splendid attire.
[2] Then, majestically adorned, after invoking the aid of the all-seeing God and Savior, she took her two maids with her,
[3] leaning daintily on one,
[4] while the other followed carrying her train.
[5] She was radiant with perfect beauty, and she looked happy, as if beloved, but her heart was frozen with fear.
[6] When she had gone through all the doors, she stood before the king. He was seated on his royal throne, clothed in the full array of his majesty, all covered with gold and precious stones. And he was most terrifying.
[7] Lifting his face, flushed with splendor, he looked at her in fierce anger. And the queen faltered, and turned pale and faint, and collapsed upon the head of the maid who went before her.
[8] Then God changed the spirit of the king to gentleness, and in alarm he sprang from his throne and took her in his arms until she came to herself. And he comforted her with soothing words, and said to her,
[9] "What is it, Esther? I am your brother. Take courage;
[10] you shall not die, for our law applies only to the people. Come near."
[11] Then he raised the golden scepter and touched it to her neck;
[12] and he embraced her, and said, "Speak to me."
[13] And she said to him, "I saw you, my lord, like an angel of God and my heart was shaken with fear at your glory.
[14] For you are wonderful, my lord, and your countenance is full of grace."
[15] But as she was speaking, she fell fainting.
[16] And the king was agitated, and all his servants sought to comfort her.

AddEsth.16

[1] The following is a copy of this letter: "The Great King, Artaxerxes, to the rulers of the provinces from India to Ethiopia, one hundred and twenty-seven satrapies, and to those who are loyal to our government, greeting.
[2] "The more often they are honored by the too great kindness of their benefactors, the more proud do many men become.
[3] They not only seek to injure our subjects, but in their inability to stand prosperity they even undertake to scheme against their own benefactors.
[4] They not only take away thankfulness from among men, but, carried away by the boasts of those who know nothing of goodness, they suppose that they will escape the evil-hating justice of God, who always sees everything.
[5] And often many of those who are set in places of authority have been made in part responsible for the shedding of innocent blood, and have been involved in irremediable calamities, by the persuasion of friends who have been entrusted with the administration of public affairs,
[6] when these men by the false trickery of their evil natures beguile the sincere good will of their sovereigns.
[7] "What has been wickedly accomplished through the pestilent behavior of those who exercise authority unworthily, can be seen not so much from the more ancient records which we hand on as from investigation of matters close at hand.
[8] For the future we will take care to render our kingdom quiet and peaceable for all men,
[9] by changing our methods and always judging what comes before our eyes with more equitable consideration.
[10] For Haman, the son of Hammedatha, a Macedonian (really an alien to the Persian blood, and quite devoid of our kindliness), having become our guest,
[11] so far enjoyed the good will that we have for every nation that he was called our father and was

continually bowed down to by all as the person second to the royal throne.
[12] But, unable to restrain his arrogance, he undertook to deprive us of our kingdom and our life,
[13] and with intricate craft and deceit asked for the destruction of Mordecai, our savior and perpetual benefactor, and of Esther, the blameless partner of our kingdom, together with their whole nation.
[14] He thought that in this way he would find us undefended and would transfer the kingdom of the Persians to the Macedonians.
[15] "But we find that the Jews, who were consigned to annihilation by this thrice accursed man, are not evildoers but are governed by most righteous laws
[16] and are sons of the Most High, the most mighty living God, who has directed the kingdom both for us and for our fathers in the most excellent order.
[17] "You will therefore do well not to put in execution the letters sent by Haman the son of Hammedatha,
[18] because the man himself who did these things has been hanged at the gate of Susa, with all his household. For God, who rules over all things, has speedily inflicted on him the punishment he deserved.
[19] "Therefore post a copy of this letter publicly in every place, and permit the Jews to live under their own laws.
[20] And give them reinforcements, so that on the thirteenth day of the twelfth month, Adar, on that very day they may defend themselves against those who attack them at the time of their affliction.
[21] For God, who rules over all things, has made this day to be a joy to his chosen people instead of a day of destruction for them.
[22] "Therefore you shall observe this with all good cheer as a notable day among your commemorative festivals,
[23] so that both now and hereafter it may mean salvation for us and the loyal Persians, but that for those who plot against us it may be a reminder of destruction.
[24] "Every city and country, without exception, which does not act accordingly, shall be destroyed in wrath with spear and fire. It shall be made not only impassable for men, but also most hateful for all time to beasts and birds."

AddEsth.10

[1] And Mordecai said, "These things have come from God.
[2] For I remember the dream that I had concerning these matters, and none of them has failed to be fulfilled.
[3] The tiny spring which became a river, and there was light and the sun and abundant water -- the river is Esther, whom the king married and made queen.
[4] The two dragons are Haman and myself.
[5] The nations are those that gathered to destroy the name of the Jews.
[6] And my nation, this is Israel, who cried out to God and were saved. The Lord has saved his people; the Lord has delivered us from all these evils; God has done great signs and wonders, which have not occurred among the nations.
[7] For this purpose he made two lots, one for the people of God and one for all the nations.
[8] And these two lots came to the hour and moment and day of decision before God and among all the nations.
[9] And God remembered his people and vindicated his inheritance.
[10] So they will observe these days in the month of Adar, on the fourteenth and fifteenth of that month, with an assembly and joy and gladness before God, from generation to generation for ever among his people Israel."

AddEsth.11

[1] In the fourth year of the reign of Ptolemy and Cleopatra, Dositheus, who said that he was a priest and a Levite, and Ptolemy his son brought to Egypt the preceeding Letter of Purim, which they said was genuine and had been translated by Lysimachus son of Ptolemy, one of the residents of Jerusalem.

Tobit

Tob.1

[1] The book of the acts of Tobit the son of Tobiel, son of Ananiel, son of Aduel, son of Gabael, of the descendants of Asiel and the tribe of Naphtali,

[2] who in the days of Shalmaneser, king of the Assyrians, was taken into captivity from Thisbe, which is to the south of Kedesh Naphtali in Galilee above Asher.

[3] I, Tobit, walked in the ways of truth and righteousness all the days of my life, and I performed many acts of charity to my brethren and countrymen who went with me into the land of the Assyrians, to Nineveh.

[4] Now when I was in my own country, in the land of Israel, while I was still a young man, the whole tribe of Naphtali my forefather deserted the house of Jerusalem. This was the place which had been chosen from among all the tribes of Israel, where all the tribes should sacrifice and where the temple of the dwelling of the Most High was consecrated and established for all generations for ever.

[5] All the tribes that joined in apostasy used to sacrifice to the calf Baal, and so did the house of Naphtali my forefather.

[6] But I alone went often to Jerusalem for the feasts, as it is ordained for all Israel by an everlasting decree. Taking the first fruits and the tithes of my produce and the first shearings, I would give these to the priests, the sons of Aaron, at the altar.

[7] Of all my produce I would give a tenth to the sons of Levi who ministered at Jerusalem; a second tenth I would sell, and I would go and spend the proceeds each year at Jerusalem;

[8] the third tenth I would give to those to whom it was my duty, as Deborah my father's mother had commanded me, for I was left an orphan by my father.

[9] When I became a man I married Anna, a member of our family, and by her I became the father of Tobias.

[10] Now when I was carried away captive to Nineveh, all my brethren and my relatives ate the food of the Gentiles;

[11] but I kept myself from eating it,

[12] because I remembered God with all my heart.

[13] Then the Most High gave me favor and good appearance in the sight of Shalmaneser, and I was his buyer of provisions.

[14] So I used to go into Media, and once at Rages in Media I left ten talents of silver in trust with Gabael, the brother of Gabrias.

[15] But when Shalmaneser died, Sennacherib his son reigned in his place; and under him the highways were unsafe, so that I could no longer go into Media.

[16] In the days of Shalmaneser I performed many acts of charity to my brethren.

[17] I would give my bread to the hungry and my clothing to the naked; and if I saw any one of my people dead and thrown out behind the wall of Nineveh, I would bury him.

[18] And if Sennacherib the king put to death any who came fleeing from Judea, I buried them secretly. For in his anger he put many to death. When the bodies were sought by the king, they were not found.

[19] Then one of the men of Nineveh went and informed the king about me, that I was burying them; so I hid myself. When I learned that I was being searched for, to be put to death, I left home in fear.

[20] Then all my property was confiscated and nothing was left to me except my wife Anna and my son Tobias.

[21] But not fifty days passed before two of Sennacherib's sons killed him, and they fled to the mountains of Ararat. Then Esarhaddon, his son, reigned in his place; and he appointed Ahikar, the son of my brother Anael, over all the accounts of his kingdom and over the entire administration.

[22] Ahikar interceded for me, and I returned to Nineveh. Now Ahikar was cupbearer, keeper of the signet, and in charge of administration of the accounts, for Esarhaddon had appointed him second to himself. He was my nephew.

Tob.2

[1] When I arrived home and my wife Anna and my son Tobias were restored to me, at the feast of Pentecost, which is the sacred festival of the seven weeks, a good dinner was prepared for me and I sat down to eat.

[2] Upon seeing the abundance of food I said to my son, "Go and bring whatever poor man of our brethren you may find who is mindful of the Lord, and I will wait for you."

[3] But he came back and said, "Father, one of our people has been strangled and thrown into the market place."

[4] So before I tasted anything I sprang up and removed the body to a place of shelter until sunset.

[5] And when I returned I washed myself and ate my food in sorrow.

[6] Then I remembered the prophecy of Amos, how he said, "Your feasts shall be turned into mourning, and all your festivities into lamentation." And I wept.

[7] When the sun had set I went and dug a grave and buried the body.

[8] And my neighbors laughed at me and said, "He is no longer afraid that he will be put to death for doing this; he once ran away, and here he is burying the dead again!"

[9] On the same night I returned from burying him, and because I was defiled I slept by the wall of the courtyard, and my face was uncovered.

[10] I did not know that there were sparrows on the wall and their fresh droppings fell into my open eyes and white films formed on my eyes. I went to physicians, but they did not help me. Ahikar, however, took care of me until he went to Elymais.

[11] Then my wife Anna earned money at women's work.

[12] She used to send the product to the owners. Once when they paid her wages, they also gave her a kid;

[13] and when she returned to me it began to bleat. So I said to her, "Where did you get the kid? It is not stolen, is it? Return it to the owners; for it is not right to eat what is stolen."

[14] And she said, "It was given to me as a gift in addition to my wages." But I did not believe her, and told her to return it to the owners; and I blushed for her. Then she replied to me, "Where are your charities and your righteous deeds? You seem to know everything!"

Tob.3

[1] Then in my grief I wept, and I prayed in anguish, saying,

[2] "Righteous art thou, O Lord; all thy deeds and all they ways are mercy and truth, and thou do render true and righteous judgment for ever.

[3] Remember me and look favorably upon me; do not punish me for my sins and for my unwitting offences and those which my fathers committed before thee.

[4] For they disobeyed thy commandments, and thou gavest us over to plunder, captivity, and death; thou madest us a byword of reproach in all the nations among which we have been dispersed.

[5] And now thy many judgments are true in exacting penalty from me for my sins and those of my fathers, because we did not keep thy commandments. For we did not walk in truth before thee.

[6] And now deal with me according to thy pleasure; command my spirit to be taken up, that I may depart and become dust. For it is better for me to die than to live, because I have heard false reproaches, and great is the sorrow within me. Command that I now be released from my distress to go to the eternal abode; do not turn thy face away from me."

[7] On the same day, at Ecbatana in Media, it also happened that Sarah, the daughter of Raguel, was reproached by her father's maids,

[8] because she had been given to seven husbands, and the evil demon Asmodeus had slain each of them before he had been with her as his wife. So the maids said to her, "Do you not know that you strangle your husbands? You already have had seven and have had no benefit from any of them.

[9] Why do you beat us? If they are dead, go with them! May we never see a son or daughter of yours!"

[10] When she heard these things she was deeply grieved, even to the thought of hanging herself. But she said, "I am the only child of my father; if I do this, it will be a disgrace to him, and I shall bring his old age down in sorrow to the grave.

[11] So she prayed by her window and said, "Blessed art thou, O Lord my God, and blessed is thy holy and honored name for ever. May all thy works praise thee for ever.

[12] And now, O Lord, I have turned my eyes and my face toward thee.

[13] Command that I be released from the earth and that I hear reproach no more.

[14] Thou knowest, O Lord, that I am innocent of any sin with man,

[15] and that I did not stain my name or the name of my father in the land of my captivity. I am my father's only child, and he has no child to be his heir, no near kinsman or kinsman's son for whom I should keep myself as wife. Already seven husbands of mine are dead. Why should I live? But if it be not pleasing to thee to take my life, command that respect be shown to me and pity be taken upon me, and that I hear reproach no more."

[16] The prayer of both was heard in the presence of the glory of the great God.
[17] And Raphael was sent to heal the two of them: to scale away the white films of Tobit's eyes; to give Sarah the daughter of Raguel in marriage to Tobias the son of Tobit, and to bind Asmodeus the evil demon, because Tobias was entitled to possess her. At that very moment Tobit returned and entered his house and Sarah the daughter of Raguel came down from her upper room.

Tob.4

[1] On that day Tobit remembered the money which he had left in trust with Gabael at Rages in Media, and he said to himself;
[2] "I have asked for death. Why do I not call my son Tobias so that I may explain to him about the money before I die?"
[3] So he called him and said, "My son, when I die, bury me, and do not neglect your mother. Honor her all the days of your life; do what is pleasing to her, and do not grieve her.
[4] Remember, my son, that she faced many dangers for you while you were yet unborn. When she dies bury her beside me in the same grave.
[5] "Remember the Lord our God all your days, my son, and refuse to sin or to transgress his commandments. Live uprightly all the days of your life, and do not walk in the ways of wrongdoing.
[6] For if you do what is true, your ways will prosper through your deeds.
[7] Give alms from your possessions to all who live uprightly, and do not let your eye begrudge the gift when you make it. Do not turn your face away from any poor man, and the face of God will not be turned away from you.
[8] If you have many possessions, make your gift from them in proportion; if few, do not be afraid to give according to the little you have.
[9] So you will be laying up a good treasure for yourself against the day of necessity.
[10] For charity delivers from death and keeps you from entering the darkness;
[11] and for all who practice it charity is an excellent offering in the presence of the Most High.
[12] "Beware, my son, of all immorality. First of all take a wife from among the descendants of your fathers and do not marry a foreign woman, who is not of your father's tribe; for we are the sons of the prophets. Remember, my son, that Noah, Abraham, Isaac, and Jacob, our fathers of old, all took wives from among their brethren. They were blessed in their children, and their posterity will inherit the land.
[13] So now, my son, love your brethren, and in your heart do not disdain your brethren and the sons and daughters of your people by refusing to take a wife for yourself from among them. For in pride there is ruin and great confusion; and in shiftlessness there is loss and great want, because shiftlessness is the mother of famine.
[14] Do not hold over till the next day the wages of any man who works for you, but pay him at once; and if you serve God you will receive payment. "Watch yourself, my son, in everything you do, and be disciplined in all your conduct.
[15] And what you hate, do not do to any one. Do not drink wine to excess or let drunkenness go with you on your way.
[16] Give of your bread to the hungry, and of your clothing to the naked. Give all your surplus to charity, and do not let your eye begrudge the gift when you made it.
[17] Place your bread on the grave of the righteous, but give none to sinners.
[18] Seek advice from every wise man, and do not despise any useful counsel.
[19] Bless the Lord God on every occasion; ask him that your ways may be made straight and that all your paths and plans may prosper. For none of the nations has understanding; but the Lord himself gives all good things, and according to his will he humbles whomever he wishes. "So, my son, remember my commands, and do not let them be blotted out of your mind.
[20] And now let me explain to you about the ten talents of silver which I left in trust with Gabael the son of Gabrias at Rages in Media.
[21] Do not be afraid, my son, because we have become poor. You have great wealth if you fear God and refrain from every sin and do what is pleasing in his sight."

Tob.5

[1] Then Tobias answered him, "Father, I will do everything that you have commanded me;

[2] but how can I obtain the money when I do not know the man?"
[3] Then Tobit gave him the receipt, and said to him, "Find a man to go with you and I will pay him wages as long as I live; and go and get the money."
[4] So he went to look for a man; and he found Raphael, who was an angel,
[5] but Tobias did not know it. Tobias said to him, "Can you go with me to Rages in Media? Are you acquainted with that region?"
[6] The angel replied, "I will go with you; I am familiar with the way, and I have stayed with our brother Gabael."
[7] Then Tobias said to him, "Wait for me, and I shall tell my father."
[8] And he said to him, "Go, and do not delay." So he went in and said to his father, "I have found some one to go with me." He said, "Call him to me, so that I may learn to what tribe he belongs, and whether he is a reliable man to go with you."
[9] So Tobias invited him in; he entered and they greeted each other.
[10] Then Tobit said to him, "My brother, to what tribe and family do you belong? Tell me. "
[11] But he answered, "Are you looking for a tribe and a family or for a man whom you will pay to go with your son?" And Tobit said to him, "I should like to know, my brother, your people and your name."
[12] He replied, "I am Azarias the son of the great Ananias, one of your relatives."
[13] Then Tobit said to him, "You are welcome, my brother. Do not be angry with me because I tried to learn your tribe and family. You are a relative of mine, of a good and noble lineage. For I used to know Ananias and Jathan, the sons of the great Shemaiah, when we went together to Jerusalem to worship and offered the first-born of our flocks and the tithes of our produce. They did not go astray in the error of our brethren. My brother, you come of good stock.
[14] But tell me, what wages am I to pay you -- a drachma a day, and expenses for yourself as for my son?
[15] And besides, I will add to your wages if you both return safe and sound." So they agreed to these terms.
[16] Then he said to Tobias, "Get ready for the journey, and good success to you both." So his son made the preparations for the journey. And his father said to him, "Go with this man; God who dwells in heaven will prosper your way, and may his angel attend you." So they both went out and departed, and the young man's dog was with them.
[17] But Anna, his mother, began to weep, and said to Tobit, "Why have you sent our child away? Is he not the staff of our hands as he goes in and out before us?
[18] Do not add money to money, but consider it as rubbish as compared to our child.
[19] For the life that is given to us by the Lord is enough for us."
[20] And Tobit said to her, "Do not worry, my sister; he will return safe and sound, and your eyes will see him.
[21] For a good angel will go with him; his journey will be successful, and he will come back safe and sound." Tob 5:[22] So she stopped weeping.

Tob.6

[1] Now as they proceeded on their way they came at evening to the Tigris river and camped there.
[2] Then the young man went down to wash himself. A fish leaped up from the river and would have swallowed the young man;
[3] and the angel said to him, "Catch the fish." So the young man seized the fish and threw it up on the land.
[4] Then the angel said to him, "Cut open the fish and take the heart and liver and gall and put them away safely."
[5] So the young man did as the angel told him; and they roasted and ate the fish. And they both continued on their way until they came near to Ecbatana.
[6] Then the young man said to the angel, "Brother Azarias, of what use is the liver and heart and gall of the fish?"
[7] He replied, "As for the heart and liver, if a demon or evil spirit gives trouble to any one, you make a smoke from these before the man or woman, and that person will never be troubled again.
[8] And as for the gall, anoint with it a man who has white films in his eyes, and he will be cured."
[9] When they approached Ecbatana,
[10] the angel said to the young man, "Brother, today we shall stay with Raguel. He is your relative, and he has an only daughter named Sarah. I will suggest that she be given to you in marriage,

[11] because you are entitled to her and to her inheritance, for you are her only eligible kinsman.

[12] The girl is also beautiful and sensible. Now listen to my plan. I will speak to her father, and as soon as we return from Rages we will celebrate the marriage. For I know that Raguel, according to the law of Moses, cannot give her to another man without incurring the penalty of death, because you rather than any other man are entitled to the inheritance."

[13] Then the young man said to the angel, "Brother Azarias, I have heard that the girl has been given to seven husbands and that each died in the bridal chamber.

[14] Now I am the only son my father has, and I am afraid that if I go in I will die as those before me did, for a demon is in love with her, and he harms no one except those who approach her. So now I fear that I may die and bring the lives of my father and mother to the grave in sorrow on my account. And they have no other son to bury them."

[15] But the angel said to him, "Do you not remember the words with which your father commanded you to take a wife from among your own people? Now listen to me, brother, for she will become your wife; and do not worry about the demon, for this very night she will be given to you in marriage.

[16] When you enter the bridal chamber, you shall take live ashes of incense and lay upon them some of the heart and liver of the fish so as to make a smoke.

[17] Then the demon will smell it and flee away, and will never again return. And when you approach her, rise up, both of you, and cry out to the merciful God, and he will save you and have mercy on you. Do not be afraid, for she was destined for you from eternity. You will save her, and she will go with you, and I suppose that you will have children by her." When Tobias heard these things, he fell in love with her and yearned deeply for her.

Tob.7

[1] When they reached Ecbatana and arrived at the house of Raguel, Sarah met them and greeted them. They returned her greeting, and she brought them into the house.

[2] Then Raguel said to his wife Edna, "How much the young man resembles my cousin Tobit!"

[3] And Raguel asked them, "Where are you from, brethren?" They answered him, "We belong to the sons of Naphtali, who are captives in Nineveh."

[4] So he said to them, "Do you know our brother Tobit?" And they said, "Yes, we do." And he asked them, "Is he in good health?"

[5] They replied, "He is alive and in good health." And Tobias said, "He is my father."

[6] Then Raguel sprang up and kissed him and wept.

[7] And he blessed him and exclaimed, "Son of that good and noble man!" When he heard that Tobit had lost his sight, he was stricken with grief and wept.

[8] And his wife Edna and his daughter Sarah wept. They received them very warmly; and they killed a ram from the flock and set large servings of food before them. Then Tobias said to Raphael, "Brother Azarias, speak of those things which you talked about on the journey, and let the matter be settled."

[9] So he communicated the proposal to Raguel. And Raguel said to Tobias, "Eat, drink, and be merry;

[10] for it is your right to take my child. But let me explain the true situation to you.

[11] I have given my daughter to seven husbands, and when each came to her he died in the night. But for the present be merry." And Tobias said, "I will eat nothing here until you make a binding agreement with me."

[12] So Raguel said, "Take her right now, in accordance with the law. You are her relative, and she is yours. The merciful God will guide you both for the best."

[13] Then he called his daughter Sarah, and taking her by the hand he gave her to Tobias to be his wife, saying, "Here she is; take her according to the law of Moses, and take her with you to your father." And he blessed them.

[14] Next he called his wife Edna, and took a scroll and wrote out the contract; and they set their seals to it.

[15] Then they began to eat.

[16] And Raguel called his wife Edna and said to her, "Sister, make up the other room, and take her into it."

[17] so she did as he said, and took her there; and the girl began to weep. But the mother comforted her daughter in her tears, and said to her,

[18] "Be brave, my child; the Lord of heaven and earth grant you joy in place of this sorrow of yours. Be brave, my daughter."

Tob.8

[1] When they had finished eating, they escorted Tobias in to her.

[2] As he went he remembered the words of Raphael, and he took the live ashes of incense and put the heart and liver of the fish upon them and made a smoke.

[3] And when the demon smelled the odor he fled to the remotest parts of Egypt, and the angel bound him.

[4] When the door was shut and the two were alone, Tobias got up from the bed and said, "Sister, get up, and let us pray that the Lord may have mercy upon us."

[5] And Tobias began to pray, "Blessed art thou, O God of our fathers, and blessed be thy holy and glorious name for ever. Let the heavens and all thy creatures bless thee.

[6] Thou madest Adam and gavest him Eve his wife as a helper and support. From them the race of mankind has sprung. Thou didst say, `It is not good that the man should be alone; let us make a helper for him like himself.'

[7] And now, O Lord, I am not taking this sister of mine because of lust, but with sincerity. Grant that I may find mercy and may grow old together with her."

[8] And she said with him, "Amen."

[9] Then they both went to sleep for the night. But Raguel arose and went and dug a grave,

[10] with the thought, "Perhaps he too will die."

[11] Then Raguel went into his house

[12] and said to his wife Edna, "Send one of the maids to see whether he is alive; and if he is not, let us bury him without any one knowing about it."

[13] So the maid opened the door and went in, and found them both asleep.

[14] And she came out and told them that he was alive.

[15] Then Raguel blessed God and said, "Blessed art thou, O God, with every pure and holy blessing. Let thy saints and all thy creatures bless thee; let all thy angels and thy chosen people bless thee for ever.

[16] Blessed art thou, because thou hast made me glad. It has not happened to me as I expected; but thou hast treated us according to thy great mercy.

[17] Blessed art thou, because thou hast had compassion on two only children. Show them mercy, O Lord; and bring their lives to fulfilment in health and happiness and mercy."

[18] Then he ordered his servants to fill in the grave.

[19] After this he gave a wedding feast for them which lasted fourteen days.

[20] And before the days of the feast were over, Raguel declared by oath to Tobias that he should not leave until the fourteen days of the wedding feast were ended,

[21] that then he should take half of Raguel's property and return in safety to his father, and that the rest would be his "when my wife and I die."

Tob.9

[1] Then Tobias called Raphael and said to him,

[2] "Brother Azarias, take a servant and two camels with you and go to Gabael at Rages in Media and get the money for me; and bring him to the wedding feast.

[3] For Raguel has sworn that I should not leave;

[4] but my father is counting the days, and if I delay long he will be greatly distressed."

[5] So Raphael made the journey and stayed over night with Gabael. He gave him the receipt, and Gabael brought out the money bags with their seals intact and gave them to him.

[6] In the morning they both got up early and came to the wedding feast. And Gabael blessed Tobias and his wife.

Tob.10

[1] Now his father Tobit was counting each day, and when the days for the journey had expired and they did not arrive,

[2] he said, "Is it possible that he has been detained? Or is it possible that Gabael has died and there is no one to give him the money?"

[3] And he was greatly distressed.

[4] And his wife said to him, "The lad has perished; his long delay proves it." Then she began to mourn for him, and said,

[5] "Am I not distressed, my child, that I let you go, you who are the light of my eyes?"

[6] But Tobit said to her, "Be still and stop worrying; he is well."

[7] And she answered him, "Be still and stop deceiving me; my child has perished." And she went out every day to the road by which they had left; she ate nothing in the daytime, and throughout the nights she never stopped mourning for her son Tobias, until the fourteen days of the wedding feast had expired which Raguel had sworn that he should spend there. At that time Tobias said to Raguel, "Send me back, for my father and mother have given up hope of ever seeing me again."

[8] But his father-in-law said to him, "Stay with me, and I will send messengers to your father, and they will inform him how things are with you."

[9] Tobias replied, "No, send me back to my father."

[10] So Raguel arose and gave him his wife Sarah and half of his property in slaves, cattle, and money.

[11] And when he had blessed them he sent them away, saying, "The God of heaven will prosper you, my children, before I die."

[12] He said also to his daughter, "Honor your father-in-law and your mother-in-law; they are now your parents. Let me hear a good report of you. " And he kissed her. And Edna said to Tobias, "The Lord of heaven bring you back safely, dear brother, and grant me to see your children by my daughter Sarah, that I may rejoice before the Lord. See, I am entrusting my daughter to you; do nothing to grieve her."

Tob.11

[1] After this Tobias went on his way, praising God because he had made his journey a success. And he blessed Raguel and his wife Edna. So he continued on his way until they came near to Nineveh.

[2] Then Raphael said to Tobias, "Are you not aware, brother, of how you left your father?

[3] Let us run ahead of your wife and prepare the house.

[4] And take the gall of the fish with you." So they went their way, and the dog went along behind them.

[5] Now Anna sat looking intently down the road for her son.

[6] And she caught sight of him coming, and said to his father, "Behold, your son is coming, and so is the man who went with him!"

[7] Raphael said, "I know, Tobias, that your father will open his eyes.

[8] You therefore must anoint his eyes with the gall; and when they smart he will rub them, and will cause the white films to fall away, and he will see you."

[9] Then Anna ran to meet them, and embraced her son, and said to him, "I have seen you, my child; now I am ready to die." And they both wept.

[10] Tobit started toward the door, and stumbled. But his son ran to him

[11] and took hold of his father, and he sprinkled the gall upon his father's eyes, saying, "Be of good cheer, father."

[12] And when his eyes began to smart he rubbed them,

[13] and the white films scaled off from the corners of his eyes.

[14] Then he saw his son and embraced him, and he wept and said, "Blessed art thou, O God, and blessed is thy name for ever, and blessed are all thy holy angels!

[15] For thou hast afflicted me, but thou hast had mercy upon me; here I see my son Tobias!" And his son went in rejoicing, and he reported to his father the great things that had happened to him in Media.

[16] Then Tobit went out to meet his daughter-in-law at the gate of Nineveh, rejoicing and praising God. Those who saw him as he went were amazed because he could see.

[17] And Tobit gave thanks before them that God had been merciful to him. When Tobit came near to Sarah his daughter-in-law, he blessed her, saying, "Welcome, daughter! Blessed is God who has brought you to us, and blessed are your father and your mother." So there was rejoicing among all his brethren in Nineveh.

[18] Ahikar and his nephew Nadab came,

[19] and Tobias' marriage was celebrated for seven days with great festivity.

Tob.12

[1] Tobit then called his son Tobias and said to him, "My son, see to the wages of the man who went with you; and he must also be given more."

[2] He replied, "Father, it would do me no harm to give him half of what I have brought back.

[3] For he has led me back to you safely, he cured my wife, he obtained the money for me, and he also healed you."

[4] The old man said, "He deserves it."

[5] So he called the angel and said to him, "Take half of all that you two have brought back."

[6] Then the angel called the two of them privately and said to them: "Praise God and give thanks to him; exalt him and give thanks to him in the presence of all the living for what he has done for you. It is good to praise God and to exalt his name, worthily declaring the works of God. Do not be slow to give him thanks.

[7] It is good to guard the secret of a king, but gloriously to reveal the works of God. Do good, and evil will not overtake you.

[8] Prayer is good when accompanied by fasting, almsgiving, and righteousness. A little with righteousness is better than much with wrongdoing. It is better to give alms than to treasure up gold.

[9] For almsgiving delivers from death, and it will purge away every sin. Those who perform deeds of charity and of righteousness will have fulness of life;

[10] but those who commit sin are the enemies of their own lives.

[11] "I will not conceal anything from you. I have said, `It is good to guard the secret of a king, but gloriously to reveal the works of God.'

[12] And so, when you and your daughter-in-law Sarah prayed, I brought a reminder of your prayer before the Holy One; and when you buried the dead, I was likewise present with you.

[13] When you did not hesitate to rise and leave your dinner in order to go and lay out the dead, your good deed was not hidden from me, but I was with you.

[14] So now God sent me to heal you and your daughter-in-law Sarah.

[15] I am Raphael, one of the seven holy angels who present the prayers of the saints and enter into the presence of the glory of the Holy One."

[16] They were both alarmed; and they fell upon their faces, for they were afraid.

[17] But he said to them, "Do not be afraid; you will be safe. But praise God for ever.

[18] For I did not come as a favor on my part, but by the will of our God. Therefore praise him for ever.

[19] All these days I merely appeared to you and did not eat or drink, but you were seeing a vision.

[20] And now give thanks to God, for I am ascending to him who sent me. Write in a book everything that has happened."

[21] Then they stood up; but they saw him no more.

[22] So they confessed the great and wonderful works of God, and acknowledged that the angel of the Lord had appeared to them.

Tob.13

[1] Then Tobit wrote a prayer of rejoicing, and said:

"Blessed is God who lives for ever, and blessed is his kingdom. [2] For he afflicts, and he shows mercy; he leads down to Hades, and brings up again, and there is no one who can escape his hand. [3] Acknowledge him before the nations, O sons of Israel; for he has scattered us among them. [4] Make his greatness known there, and exalt him in the presence of all the living; because he is our Lord and God, he is our Father for ever. [5] He will afflict us for our iniquities; and again he will show mercy, and will gather us from all the nations among whom you have been scattered. [6] If you turn to him with all your heart and with all your soul, to do what is true before him, then he will turn to you and will not hide his face from you. But see what he will do with you; give thanks to him with your full voice. Praise the Lord of righteousness, and exalt the King of the ages. I give him thanks in the land of my captivity, and I show his power and majesty to a nation of sinners. Turn back, you sinners, and do right before him; who knows if he will accept you and have mercy on you? [7] I exalt my God; my soul exalts the King of heaven, and will rejoice in his majesty. [8] Let all men speak, and give him thanks in Jerusalem. [9] O Jerusalem, the holy city, he will afflict you for the deeds of your sons, but again he will show mercy to the sons of the righteous. [10] Give thanks worthily to the Lord, and praise the King of the ages, that his tent may be raised for you again with joy. May he cheer those within you who are captives, and love those within you who are distressed, to all generations for ever. [11] Many nations

627

will come from afar to the name of the Lord God, bearing gifts in their hands, gifts for the King of heaven. Generations of generations will give you joyful praise. [12] Cursed are all who hate you; blessed for ever will be all who love you. [13] Rejoice and be glad for the sons of the righteous; for they will be gathered together, and will praise the Lord of the righteous. [14] How blessed are those who love you! They will rejoice in your peace. Blessed are those who grieved over all your afflictions; for they will rejoice for you upon seeing all your glory, and they will be made glad for ever. [15] Let my soul praise God the great King. [16] For Jerusalem will be built with sapphires and emeralds, her walls with precious stones, and her towers and battlements with pure gold. [17] The streets of Jerusalem will be paved with beryl and ruby and stones of Ophir; [18] all her lanes will cry `Hallelujah!' and will give praise, saying, `Blessed is God, who has exalted you for ever.'"

Tob.14

[1] Here Tobit ended his words of praise.

[2] He was fifty-eight years old when he lost his sight, and after eight years he regained it. He gave alms, and he continued to fear the Lord God and to praise him.

[3] When he had grown very old he called his son and grandsons, and said to him, "My son, take your sons; behold, I have grown old and am about to depart this life.

[4] Go to Media, my son, for I fully believe what Jonah the prophet said about Nineveh, that it will be overthrown. But in Media there will be peace for a time. Our brethren will be scattered over the earth from the good land, and Jerusalem will be desolate. The house of God in it will be burned down and will be in ruins for a time.

[5] But God will again have mercy on them, and bring them back into their land; and they will rebuild the house of God, though it will not be like the former one until the times of the age are completed. After this they will return from the places of their captivity, and will rebuild Jerusalem in splendor. And the house of God will be rebuilt there with a glorious building for all generations for ever, just as the prophets said of it.

[6] Then all the Gentiles will turn to fear the Lord God in truth, and will bury their idols.

[7] All the Gentiles will praise the Lord, and his people will give thanks to God, and the Lord will exalt his people. And all who love the Lord God in truth and righteousness will rejoice, showing mercy to our brethren.

[8] "So now, my son, leave Nineveh, because what the prophet Jonah said will surely happen.

[9] But keep the law and the commandments, and be merciful and just, so that it may be well with you.

[10] Bury me properly, and your mother with me. And do not live in Nineveh any longer. See, my son, what Nadab did to Ahikar who had reared him, how he brought him from light into darkness, and with what he repaid him. But Ahikar was saved, and the other received repayment as he himself went down into the darkness. Ahikar gave alms and escaped the deathtrap which Nadab had set for him; but Nadab fell into the trap and perished.

[11] So now, my children, consider what almsgiving accomplishes and how righteousness delivers." As he said this he died in his bed. He was a hundred and fifty-eight years old; and Tobias gave him a magnificent funeral.

[12] And when Anna died he buried her with his father. Then Tobias returned with his wife and his sons to Ecbatana, to Raguel his father-in-law.

[13] He grew old with honor, and he gave his father-in-law and mother-in-law magnificent funerals. He inherited their property and that of his father Tobit.

[14] He died in Ecbatana of Media at the age of a hundred and twenty-seven years.

[15] But before he died he heard of the destruction of Nineveh, which Nebuchadnezzar and Ahasuerus had captured. Before his death he rejoiced over Nineveh.

Judith

Jdt.1

[1] In the twelfth year of the reign of Nebuchadnezzar, who ruled over the Assyrians in the great city of Nineveh, in the days of Arphaxad, who ruled over the Medes in Ecbatana --

[2] he is the king who built walls about Ecbatana with hewn stones three cubits thick and six cubits long; he made the walls seventy cubits high and fifty cubits wide;

[3] at the gates he built towers a hundred cubits high and sixty cubits wide at the foundations;

[4] and he made its gates, which were seventy cubits high and forty cubits wide, so that his armies could march out in force and his infantry form their ranks --

[5] it was in those days that King Nebuchadnezzar made war against King Arphaxad in the great plain which is on the borders of Ragae.

[6] He was joined by all the people of the hill country and all those who lived along the Euphrates and the Tigris and the Hydaspes and in the plain where Arioch ruled the Elymaeans. Many nations joined the forces of the Chaldeans.

[7] Then Nebuchadnezzar king of the Assyrians sent to all who lived in Persia and to all who lived in the west, those who lived in Cilicia and Damascus and Lebanon and Antilebanon and all who lived along the seacoast,

[8] and those among the nations of Carmel and Gilead, and Upper Galilee and the great Plain of Esdraelon,

[9] and all who were in Samaria and its surrounding towns, and beyond the Jordan as far as Jerusalem and Bethany and Chelous and Kadesh and the river of Egypt, and Tahpanhes and Raamses and the whole land of Goshen,

[10] even beyond Tanis and Memphis, and all who lived in Egypt as far as the borders of Ethiopia.

[11] But all who lived in the whole region disregarded the orders of Nebuchadnezzar king of the Assyrians, and refused to join him in the war; for they were not afraid of him, but looked upon him as only one man, and they sent back his messengers empty-handed and shamefaced.

[12] Then Nebuchadnezzar was very angry with this whole region, and swore by his throne and kingdom that he would surely take revenge on the whole territory of Cilicia and Damascus and Syria, that he would kill them by the sword, and also all the inhabitants of the land of Moab, and the people of Ammon, and all Judea, and every one in Egypt, as far as the coasts of the two seas.

[13] In the seventeenth year he led his forces against King Arphaxad, and defeated him in battle, and overthrew the whole army of Arphaxad, and all his cavalry and all his chariots.

[14] Thus he took possession of his cities, and came to Ecbatana, captured its towers, plundered its markets, and turned its beauty into shame.

[15] He captured Arphaxad in the mountains of Ragae and struck him down with hunting spears; and he utterly destroyed him, to this day.

[16] Then he returned with them to Nineveh, he and all his combined forces, a vast body of troops; and there he and his forces rested and feasted for one hundred and twenty days.

Jdt.2

[1] In the eighteenth year, on the twenty-second day of the first month, there was talk in the palace of Nebuchadnezzar king of the Assyrians about carrying out his revenge on the whole region, just as he said.

[2] He called together all his officers and all his nobles and set forth to them his secret plan and recounted fully, with his own lips, all the wickedness of the region;

[3] and it was decided that every one who had not obeyed his command should be destroyed.

[4] When he had finished setting forth his plan, Nebuchadnezzar king of the Assyrians called Holofernes, the chief general of his army, second only to himself, and said to him,

[5] "Thus says the Great King, the lord of the whole earth: When you leave my presence, take with you men confident in their strength, to the number of one hundred and twenty thousand foot soldiers and twelve thousand cavalry.

[6] Go and attack the whole west country, because they disobeyed my orders.

[7] Tell them to prepare earth and water, for I am coming against them in my anger, and will cover the whole face of the earth with the feet of my armies, and will hand them over to be plundered by my troops,

[8] till their wounded shall fill their valleys, and every brook and river shall be filled with their dead, and overflow;

[9] and I will lead them away captive to the ends of the whole earth.

[10] You shall go and seize all their territory for me in advance. They will yield themselves to you, and you shall hold them for me till the day of their punishment.

[11] But if they refuse, your eye shall not spare and you shall hand them over to slaughter and plunder throughout your whole region.

[12] For as I live, and by the power of my kingdom, what I have spoken my hand will execute.

[13] And you -- take care not to transgress any of your sovereign's commands, but be sure to carry them out just as I have ordered you; and do not delay about it."

[14] So Holofernes left the presence of his master, and called together all the commanders, generals, and officers of the Assyrian army,

[15] and mustered the picked troops by divisions as his lord had ordered him to do, one hundred and twenty thousand of them, together with twelve thousand archers on horseback,

[16] and he organized them as a great army is marshaled for a campaign.

[17] He collected a vast number of camels and asses and mules for transport, and innumerable sheep and oxen and goats for provision;

[18] also plenty of food for every man, and a huge amount of gold and silver from the royal palace.

[19] So he set out with his whole army, to go ahead of King Nebuchadnezzar and to cover the whole face of the earth to the west with their chariots and horsemen and picked troops of infantry.

[20] Along with them went a mixed crowd like a swarm of locusts, like the dust of the earth -- a multitude that could not be counted.

[21] They marched for three days from Nineveh to the plain of Bectileth, and camped opposite Bectileth near the mountain which is to the north of Upper Cilicia.

[22] From there Holofernes took his whole army, his infantry, cavalry, and chariots, and went up into the hill country

[23] and ravaged Put and Lud, and plundered all the people of Rassis and the Ishmaelites who lived along the desert, south of the country of the Chelleans.

[24] Then he followed the Euphrates and passed through Mesopotamia and destroyed all the hilltop cities along the brook Abron, as far as the sea.

[25] He also seized the territory of Cilicia, and killed every one who resisted him, and came to the southern borders of Japheth, fronting toward Arabia.

[26] He surrounded all the Midianites, and burned their tents and plundered their sheepfolds.

[27] Then he went down into the plain of Damascus during the wheat harvest, and burned all their fields and destroyed their flocks and herds and sacked their cities and ravaged their lands and put to death all their young men with the edge of the sword.

[28] So fear and terror of him fell upon all the people who lived along the seacoast, at Sidon and Tyre, and those who lived in Sur and Ocina and all who lived in Jamnia. Those who lived in Azotus and Ascalon feared him exceedingly.

Jdt.3

[1] So they sent messengers to sue for peace, and said,

[2] "Behold, we the servants of Nebuchadnezzar, the Great King, lie prostrate before you. Do with us whatever you will.

[3] Behold, our buildings, and all our land, and all our wheat fields, and our flocks and herds, and all our sheepfolds with their tents, lie before you; do with them whatever you please.

[4] Our cities also and their inhabitants are your slaves; come and deal with them in any way that seems good to you."

[5] The men came to Holofernes and told him all this.

[6] Then he went down to the seacoast with his army and stationed garrisons in the hilltop cities and took picked men from them as his allies.

[7] And these people and all in the country round about welcomed him with garlands and dances and tambourines.

[8] And he demolished all their shrines and cut down their sacred groves; for it had been given to him to destroy all the gods of the land, so that all nations should worship Nebuchadnezzar only, and all their tongues and tribes should call upon him as god.

[9] Then he came to the edge of Esdraelon, near Dothan, fronting the great ridge of Judea;
[10] here he camped between Geba and Scythopolis, and remained for a whole month in order to assemble all the supplies for his army.

Jdt.4

[1] By this time the people of Israel living in Judea heard of everything that Holofernes, the general of Nebuchadnezzar the king of the Assyrians, had done to the nations, and how he had plundered and destroyed all their temples;
[2] they were therefore very greatly terrified at his approach, and were alarmed both for Jerusalem and for the temple of the Lord their God.
[3] For they had only recently returned from the captivity, and all the people of Judea were newly gathered together, and the sacred vessels and the altar and the temple had been consecrated after their profanation.
[4] So they sent to every district of Samaria, and to Kona and Beth-horon and Belmain and Jericho and to Choba and Aesora and the valley of Salem,
[5] and immediately seized all the high hilltops and fortified the villages on them and stored up food in preparation for war -- since their fields had recently been harvested.
[6] And Joakim, the high priest, who was in Jerusalem at the time, wrote to the people of Bethulia and Betomesthaim, which faces Esdraelon opposite the plain near Dothan,
[7] ordering them to seize the passes up into the hills, since by them Judea could be invaded, and it was easy to stop any who tried to enter, for the approach was narrow, only wide enough for two men at the most.
[8] So the Israelites did as Joakim the high priest and the senate of the whole people of Israel, in session at Jerusalem, had given order.
[9] And every man of Israel cried out to God with great fervor, and they humbled themselves with much fasting.
[10] They and their wives and their children and their cattle and every resident alien and hired laborer and purchased slave -- they all girded themselves with sackcloth.
[11] And all the men and women of Israel, and their children, living at Jerusalem, prostrated themselves before the temple and put ashes on their heads and spread out their sackcloth before the Lord.
[12] They even surrounded the altar with sackcloth and cried out in unison, praying earnestly to the God of Israel not to give up their infants as prey and their wives as booty, and the cities they had inherited to be destroyed, and the sanctuary to be profaned and desecrated to the malicious joy of the Gentiles.
[13] So the Lord heard their prayers and looked upon their affliction; for the people fasted many days throughout Judea and in Jerusalem before the sanctuary of the Lord Almighty.
[14] And Joakim the high priest and all the priests who stood before the Lord and ministered to the Lord, with their loins girded with sackcloth, offered the continual burnt offerings and the vows and freewill offerings of the people.
[15] With ashes upon their turbans, they cried out to the Lord with all their might to look with favor upon the whole house of Israel.

Jdt.5

[1] When Holofernes, the general of the Assyrian army, heard that the people of Israel had prepared for war and had closed the passes in the hills and fortified all the high hilltops and set up barricades in the plains,
[2] he was very angry. So he called together all the princes of Moab and the commanders of Ammon and all the governors of the coastland,
[3] and said to them, "Tell me, you Canaanites, what people is this that lives in the hill country? What cities do they inhabit? How large is their army, and in what does their power or strength consist? Who rules over them as king, leading their army?
[4] And why have they alone, of all who live in the west, refused to come out and meet me?"
[5] Then Achior, the leader of all the Ammonites, said to him, "Let my lord now hear a word from the mouth of your servant, and I will tell you the truth about this people that dwells in the nearby mountain district. No falsehood shall come from your servant's mouth.
[6] This people is descended from the Chaldeans.
[7] At one time they lived in Mesopotamia, because they would not follow the gods of their fathers who were in Chaldea.
[8] For they had left the ways of their ancestors, and they worshiped the God of heaven, the God they had come to know; hence they drove them out from the presence of their gods; and they fled to Mesopotamia, and lived there for a long time.
[9] Then their God commanded them to leave the place where they were living and go to the land of Canaan. There they settled, and prospered, with much gold and silver and very many cattle.
[10] When a famine spread over Canaan they went down to Egypt and lived there as long as they had food; and there they became a great multitude -- so great that they could not be counted.
[11] So the king of Egypt became hostile to them; he took advantage of them and set them to making bricks, and humbled them and made slaves of them.
[12] Then they cried out to their God, and he afflicted the whole land of Egypt with incurable plagues; and so the Egyptians drove them out of their sight.
[13] Then God dried up the Red Sea before them,
[14] and he led them by the way of Sinai and Kadesh-barnea, and drove out all the people of the wilderness.
[15] So they lived in the land of the Amorites, and by their might destroyed all the inhabitants of Heshbon; and crossing over the Jordan they took possession of all the hill country.
[16] And they drove out before them the Canaanites and the Perizzites and the Jebusites and the Shechemites and all the Gergesites, and lived there a long time.
[17] As long as they did not sin against their God they prospered, for the God who hates iniquity is with them.
[18] But when they departed from the way which he had appointed for them, they were utterly defeated in many battles and were led away captive to a foreign country; the temple of their God was razed to the ground, and their cities were captured by their enemies.
[19] But now they have returned to their God, and have come back from the places to which they were scattered, and have occupied Jerusalem, where their sanctuary is, and have settled in the hill country, because it was uninhabited.
[20] Now therefore, my master and lord, if there is any unwitting error in this people and they sin against their God and we find out their offense, then we will go up and defeat them.
[21] But if there is no transgression in their nation, then let my lord pass them by; for their Lord will defend them, and their God will protect them, and we shall be put to shame before the whole world."
[22] When Achior had finished saying this, all the men standing around the tent began to complain; Holofernes' officers and all the men from the seacoast and from Moab insisted that he must be put to death.
[23] "For," they said, "we will not be afraid of the Israelites; they are a people with no strength or power for making war.
[24] Therefore let us go up, Lord Holofernes, and they will be devoured by your vast army."

Jdt.6

[1] When the disturbance made by the men outside the council died down, Holofernes, the commander of the Assyrian army, said to Achior and all the Moabites in the presence of all the foreign contingents:
[2] "And who are you, Achior, and you hirelings of Ephraim, to prophesy among us as you have done today and tell us not to make war against the people of Israel because their God will defend them? Who is God except Nebuchadnezzar?
[3] He will send his forces and will destroy them from the face of the earth, and their God will not deliver them -- we the king's servants will destroy them as one man. They cannot resist the might of our cavalry.
[4] We will burn them up, and their mountains will be drunk with their blood, and their fields will be full of their dead. They cannot withstand us, but will utterly perish. So says King Nebuchadnezzar, the lord of the whole earth. For he has spoken; none of his words shall be in vain.
[5] "But you, Achior, you Ammonite hireling, who have said these words on the day of your iniquity, you shall not see my face again from this day until I take revenge on this race that came out of Egypt.
[6] Then the sword of my army and the spear of my servants shall pierce your sides, and you shall fall among their wounded, when I return.

[7] Now my slaves are going to take you back into the hill country and put you in one of the cities beside the passes,

[8] and you will not die until you perish along with them.

[9] If you really hope in your heart that they will not be taken, do not look downcast! I have spoken and none of my words shall fail."

[10] Then Holofernes ordered his slaves, who waited on him in his tent, to seize Achior and take him to Bethulia and hand him over to the men of Israel.

[11] So the slaves took him and led him out of the camp into the plain, and from the plain they went up into the hill country and came to the springs below Bethulia.

[12] When the men of the city saw them, they caught up their weapons and ran out of the city to the top of the hill, and all the slingers kept them from coming up by casting stones at them.

[13] However, they got under the shelter of the hill and they bound Achior and left him lying at the foot of the hill, and returned to their master.

[14] Then the men of Israel came down from their city and found him; and they untied him and brought him into Bethulia and placed him before the magistrates of their city,

[15] who in those days were Uzziah the son of Micah, of the tribe of Simeon, and Chabris the son of Gothoniel, and Charmis the son of Melchiel.

[16] They called together all the elders of the city, and all their young men and their women ran to the assembly; and they set Achior in the midst of all their people, and Uzziah asked him what had happened.

[17] He answered and told them what had taken place at the council of Holofernes, and all that he had said in the presence of the Assyrian leaders, and all that Holofernes had said so boastfully against the house of Israel.

[18] Then the people fell down and worshiped God, and cried out to him, and said,

[19] "O Lord God of heaven, behold their arrogance, and have pity on the humiliation of our people, and look this day upon the faces of those who are consecrated to thee."

[20] Then they consoled Achior, and praised him greatly.

[21] And Uzziah took him from the assembly to his own house and gave a banquet for the elders; and all that night they called on the God of Israel for help.

Jdt.7

[1] The next day Holofernes ordered his whole army, and all the allies who had joined him, to break camp and move against Bethulia, and to seize the passes up into the hill country and make war on the Israelites.

[2] So all their warriors moved their camp that day; their force of men of war was one hundred and seventy thousand infantry and twelve thousand cavalry, together with the baggage and the foot soldiers handling it, a very great multitude.

[3] They encamped in the valley near Bethulia, beside the spring, and they spread out in breadth over Dothan as far as Balbaim and in length from Bethulia to Cyamon, which faces Esdraelon.

[4] When the Israelites saw their vast numbers they were greatly terrified, and every one said to his neighbor, "These men will now lick up the face of the whole land; neither the high mountains nor the valleys nor the hills will bear their weight."

[5] Then each man took up his weapons, and when they had kindled fires on their towers they remained on guard all that night.

[6] On the second day Holofernes led out all his cavalry in full view of the Israelites in Bethulia,

[7] and examined the approaches to the city, and visited the springs that supplied their water, and seized them and set guards of soldiers over them, and then returned to his army.

[8] Then all the chieftains of the people of Esau and all the leaders of the Moabites and the commanders of the coastland came to him and said,

[9] "Let our lord hear a word, lest his army be defeated.

[10] For these people, the Israelites, do not rely on their spears but on the height of the mountains where they live, for it is not easy to reach the tops of their mountains.

[11] Therefore, my lord, do not fight against them in battle array, and not a man of your army will fall.

[12] Remain in your camp, and keep all the men in your forces with you; only let your servants take possession of the spring of water that flows from the foot of the mountain --

[13] for this is where all the people of Bethulia get their water. So thirst will destroy them, and they will give up their city. We and our people will go up to the tops of the nearby mountains and camp there to keep watch that not a man gets out of the city.

[14] They and their wives and children will waste away with famine, and before the sword reaches them they will be strewn about in the streets where they live.

[15] So you will pay them back with evil, because they rebelled and did not receive you peaceably."

[16] These words pleased Holofernes and all his servants, and he gave orders to do as they had said.

[17] So the army of the Ammonites moved forward, together with five thousand Assyrians, and they encamped in the valley and seized the water supply and the springs of the Israelites.

[18] And the sons of Esau and the sons of Ammon went up and encamped in the hill country opposite Dothan; and they sent some of their men toward the south and the east, toward Acraba, which is near Chusi beside the brook Mochmur. The rest of the Assyrian army encamped in the plain, and covered the whole face of the land, and their tents and supply trains spread out in great number, and they formed a vast multitude.

[19] The people of Israel cried out to the Lord their God, for their courage failed, because all their enemies had surrounded them and there was no way of escape from them.

[20] The whole Assyrian army, their infantry, chariots, and cavalry, surrounded them for thirty-four days, until all the vessels of water belonging to every inhabitant of Bethulia were empty;

[21] their cisterns were going dry, and they did not have enough water to drink their fill for a single day, because it was measured out to them to drink.

[22] Their children lost heart, and the women and young men fainted from thirst and fell down in the streets of the city and in the passages through the gates; there was no strength left in them any longer.

[23] Then all the people, the young men, the women, and the children, gathered about Uzziah and the rulers of the city and cried out with a loud voice, and said before all the elders,

[24] "God be judge between you and us! For you have done us a great injury in not making peace with the Assyrians.

[25] For now we have no one to help us; God has sold us into their hands, to strew us on the ground before them with thirst and utter destruction.

[26] Now call them in and surrender the whole city to the army of Holofernes and to all his forces, to be plundered.

[27] For it would be better for us to be captured by them; for we will be slaves, but our lives will be spared, and we shall not witness the death of our babes before our eyes, or see our wives and children draw their last breath.

[28] We call to witness against you heaven and earth and our God, the Lord of our fathers, who punishes us according to our sins and the sins of our fathers. Let him not do this day the things which we have described!"

[29] Then great and general lamentation arose throughout the assembly, and they cried out to the Lord God with a loud voice.

[30] And Uzziah said to them, "Have courage, my brothers! Let us hold out for five more days; by that time the Lord our God will restore to us his mercy, for he will not forsake us utterly.

[31] But if these days pass by, and no help comes for us, I will do what you say."

[32] Then he dismissed the people to their various posts, and they went up on the walls and towers of their city. The women and children he sent home. And they were greatly depressed in the city.

Jdt.8

[1] At that time Judith heard about these things: she was the daughter of Merari the son of Ox, son of Joseph, son of Oziel, son of Elkiah, son of Ananias, son of Gideon, son of Raphaim, son of Ahitub, son of Elijah, son of Hilkiah, son of Eliab, son of Nathanael, son of Salamiel, son of Sarasadai, son of Israel.

[2] Her husband Manasseh, who belonged to her tribe and family, had died during the barley harvest.

[3] For as he stood overseeing the men who were binding sheaves in the field, he was overcome by the burning heat, and took to his bed and died in Bethulia his city. So they buried him with his fathers in the field between Dothan and Balamon.

[4] Judith had lived at home as a widow for three years and four months.

[5] She set up a tent for herself on the roof of her house, and girded sackcloth about her loins and wore the garments of her widowhood.

[6] She fasted all the days of her widowhood, except the day before the sabbath and the sabbath itself, the day before the new moon and the day of the new moon, and the feasts and days of rejoicing of the house of Israel.

[7] She was beautiful in appearance, and had a very lovely face; and her husband Manasseh had left her gold and silver, and men and women slaves, and cattle, and fields; and she maintained this estate.

[8] No one spoke ill of her, for she feared God with great devotion.

[9] When Judith heard the wicked words spoken by the people against the ruler, because they were

faint for lack of water, and when she heard all that Uzziah said to them, and how he promised them under oath to surrender the city to the Assyrians after five days,

[10] she sent her maid, who was in charge of all she possessed, to summon Chabris and Charmis, the elders of her city.

[11] They came to her, and she said to them, "Listen to me, rulers of the people of Bethulia! What you have said to the people today is not right; you have even sworn and pronounced this oath between God and you, promising to surrender the city to our enemies unless the Lord turns and helps us within so many days.

[12] Who are you, that have put God to the test this day, and are setting yourselves up in the place of God among the sons of men?

[13] You are putting the Lord Almighty to the test -- but you will never know anything!

[14] You cannot plumb the depths of the human heart, nor find out what a man is thinking; how do you expect to search out God, who made all these things, and find out his mind or comprehend his thought? No, my brethren, do not provoke the Lord our God to anger.

[15] For if he does not choose to help us within these five days, he has power to protect us within any time he pleases, or even to destroy us in the presence of our enemies.

[16] Do not try to bind the purposes of the Lord our God; for God is not like man, to be threatened, nor like a human being, to be won over by pleading.

[17] Therefore, while we wait for his deliverance, let us call upon him to help us, and he will hear our voice, if it pleases him.

[18] "For never in our generation, nor in these present days, has there been any tribe or family or people or city of ours which worshiped gods made with hands, as was done in days gone by --

[19] and that was why our fathers were handed over to the sword, and to be plundered, and so they suffered a great catastrophe before our enemies.

[20] But we know no other god but him, and therefore we hope that he will not disdain us or any of our nation.

[21] For if we are captured all Judea will be captured and our sanctuary will be plundered; and he will exact of us the penalty for its desecration.

[22] And the slaughter of our brethren and the captivity of the land and the desolation of our inheritance -- all this he will bring upon our heads among the Gentiles, wherever we serve as slaves; and we shall be an offense and a reproach in the eyes of those who acquire us.

[23] For our slavery will not bring us into favor, but the Lord our God will turn it to dishonor.

[24] "Now therefore, brethren, let us set an example to our brethren, for their lives depend upon us, and the sanctuary and the temple and the altar rest upon us.

[25] In spite of everything let us give thanks to the Lord our God, who is putting us to the test as he did our forefathers.

[26] Remember what he did with Abraham, and how he tested Isaac, and what happened to Jacob in Mesopotamia in Syria, while he was keeping the sheep of Laban, his mother's brother.

[27] For he has not tried us with fire, as he did them, to search their hearts, nor has he taken revenge upon us; but the Lord scourges those who draw near to him, in order to admonish them."

[28] Then Uzziah said to her, "All that you have said has been spoken out of a true heart, and there is no one who can deny your words.

[29] Today is not the first time your wisdom has been shown, but from the beginning of your life all the people have recognized your understanding, for your heart's disposition is right.

[30] But the people were very thirsty, and they compelled us to do for them what we have promised, and made us take an oath which we cannot break.

[31] So pray for us, since you are a devout woman, and the Lord will send us rain to fill our cisterns and we will no longer be faint."

[32] Judith said to them, "Listen to me. I am about to do a thing which will go down through all generations of our descendants.

[33] Stand at the city gate tonight, and I will go out with my maid; and within the days after which you have promised to surrender the city to our enemies, the Lord will deliver Israel by my hand.

[34] Only, do not try to find out what I plan; for I will not tell you until I have finished what I am about to do."

[35] Uzziah and the rulers said to her, "Go in peace, and may the Lord God go before you, to take revenge upon our enemies."

[36] So they returned from the tent and went to their posts.

Jdt.9

[1] Then Judith fell upon her face, and put ashes on her head, and uncovered the sackcloth she was wearing; and at the very time when that evening's incense was being offered in the house of God in Jerusalem, Judith cried out to the Lord with a loud voice, and said,

[2] "O Lord God of my father Simeon, to whom thou gavest a sword to take revenge on the strangers who had loosed the girdle of a virgin to defile her, and uncovered her thigh to put her to shame, and polluted her womb to disgrace her; for thou hast said, `It shall not be done' -- yet they did it.

[3] So thou gavest up their rulers to be slain, and their bed, which was ashamed of the deceit they had practiced, to be stained with blood, and thou didst strike down slaves along with princes, and princes on their thrones;

[4] and thou gavest their wives for a prey and their daughters to captivity, and all their booty to be divided among thy beloved sons, who were zealous for thee, and abhorred the pollution of their blood, and called on thee for help -- O God, my God, hear me also, a widow.

[5] "For thou hast done these things and those that went before and those that followed; thou hast designed the things that are now, and those that are to come. Yea, the things thou didst intend came to pass,

[6] and the things thou didst will presented themselves and said, `Lo, we are here'; for all thy ways are prepared in advance, and thy judgment is with foreknowledge.

[7] "Behold now, the Assyrians are increased in their might; they are exalted, with their horses and riders; they glory in the strength of their foot soldiers; they trust in shield and spear, in bow and sling, and know not that thou art the Lord who crushest wars; the Lord is thy name.

[8] Break their strength by thy might, and bring down their power in thy anger; for they intend to defile thy sanctuary, and to pollute the tabernacle where thy glorious name rests, and to cast down the horn of thy altar with the sword.

[9] Behold their pride, and send thy wrath upon their heads; give to me, a widow, the strength to do what I plan.

[10] By the deceit of my lips strike down the slave with the prince and the prince with his servant; crush their arrogance by the hand of a woman.

[11] "For thy power depends not upon numbers, nor thy might upon men of strength; for thou art God of the lowly, helper of the oppressed, upholder of the weak, protector of the forlorn, savior of those without hope.

[12] Hear, O hear me, God of my father, God of the inheritance of Israel, Lord of heaven and earth, Creator of the waters, King of all thy creation, hear my prayer!

[13] Make my deceitful words to be their wound and stripe, for they have planned cruel things against thy covenant, and against thy consecrated house, and against the top of Zion, and against the house possessed by thy children.

[14] And cause thy whole nation and every tribe to know and understand that thou art God, the God of all power and might, and that there is no other who protects the people of Israel but thou alone!"

Jdt.10

[1] When Judith had ceased crying out to the God of Israel, and had ended all these words,

[2] she rose from where she lay prostrate and called her maid and went down into the house where she lived on sabbaths and on her feast days;

[3] and she removed the sackcloth which she had been wearing, and took off her widow's garments, and bathed her body with water, and anointed herself with precious ointment, and combed her hair and put on a tiara, and arrayed herself in her gayest apparel, which she used to wear while her husband Manasseh was living.

[4] And she put sandals on her feet, and put on her anklets and bracelets and rings, and her earrings and all her ornaments, and made herself very beautiful, to entice the eyes of all men who might see her.

[5] And she gave her maid a bottle of wine and a flask of oil, and filled a bag with parched grain and a cake of dried fruit and fine bread; and she wrapped up all her vessels and gave them to her to carry.

[6] Then they went out to the city gate of Bethulia, and found Uzziah standing there with the elders of the city, Chabris and Charmis.

[7] When they saw her, and noted how her face was altered and her clothing changed, they greatly admired her beauty, and said to her,

[8] "May the God of our fathers grant you favor and fulfil your plans, that the people of Israel may glory and Jerusalem may be exalted." And she worshiped God.

[9] Then she said to them, "Order the gate of the city to be opened for me, and I will go out and accomplish the things about which you spoke with me." So they ordered the young men to open the

gate for her, as she had said.

[10] When they had done this, Judith went out, she and her maid with her; and the men of the city watched her until she had gone down the mountain and passed through the valley and they could no longer see her.

[11] The women went straight on through the valley; and an Assyrian patrol met her

[12] and took her into custody, and asked her, "To what people do you belong, and where are you coming from, and where are you going?" She replied, "I am a daughter of the Hebrews, but I am fleeing from them, for they are about to be handed over to you to be devoured.

[13] I am on my way to the presence of Holofernes the commander of your army, to give him a true report; and I will show him a way by which he can go and capture all the hill country without losing one of his men, captured or slain."

[14] When the men heard her words, and observed her face -- she was in their eyes marvelously beautiful -- they said to her,

[15] "You have saved your life by hurrying down to the presence of our lord. Go at once to his tent; some of us will escort you and hand you over to him.

[16] And when you stand before him, do not be afraid in your heart, but tell him just what you have said, and he will treat you well."

[17] They chose from their number a hundred men to accompany her and her maid, and they brought them to the tent of Holofernes.

[18] There was great excitement in the whole camp, for her arrival was reported from tent to tent, and they came and stood around her as she waited outside the tent of Holofernes while they told him about her.

[19] And they marveled at her beauty, and admired the Israelites, judging them by her, and every one said to his neighbor, "Who can despise these people, who have women like this among them? Surely not a man of them had better be left alive, for if we let them go they will be able to ensnare the whole world!"

[20] Then Holofernes' companions and all his servants came out and led her into the tent.

[21] Holofernes was resting on his bed, under a canopy which was woven with purple and gold and emeralds and precious stones.

[22] When they told him of her he came forward to the front of the tent, with silver lamps carried before him.

[23] And when Judith came into the presence of Holofernes and his servants, they all marveled at the beauty of her face; and she prostrated herself and made obeisance to him, and his slaves raised her up.

Jdt.11

[1] Then Holofernes said to her, "Take courage, woman, and do not be afraid in your heart, for I have never hurt any one who chose to serve Nebuchadnezzar, the king of all the earth.

[2] And even now, if your people who live in the hill country had not slighted me, I would never have lifted my spear against them; but they have brought all this on themselves.

[3] And now tell me why you have fled from them and have come over to us -- since you have come to safety.

[4] Have courage; you will live, tonight and from now on. No one will hurt you, but all will treat you well, as they do the servants of my lord King Nebuchadnezzar."

[5] Judith replied to him, "Accept the words of your servant, and let your maidservant speak in your presence, and I will tell nothing false to my lord this night.

[6] And if you follow out the words of your maidservant, God will accomplish something through you, and my lord will not fail to achieve his purposes.

[7] Nebuchadnezzar the king of the whole earth lives, and as his power endures, who had sent you to direct every living soul, not only do men serve him because of you, but also the beasts of the field and the cattle and the birds of the air will live by your power under Nebuchadnezzar and all his house.

[8] For we have heard of your wisdom and skill, and it is reported throughout the whole world that you are the one good man in the whole kingdom, thoroughly informed and marvelous in military strategy.

[9] "Now as for the things Achior said in your council, we have heard his words, for the men of Bethulia spared him and he told them all he had said to you.

[10] Therefore, my lord and master, do not disregard what he said, but keep it in your mind, for it is true: our nation cannot be punished, nor can the sword prevail against them, unless they sin against their God.

[11] "And now, in order that my lord may not be defeated and his purpose frustrated, death will fall upon them, for a sin has overtaken them by which they are about to provoke their God to anger when they do what is wrong.

[12] Since their food supply is exhausted and their water has almost given out, they have planned to kill their cattle and have determined to use all that God by his laws has forbidden them to eat.

[13] They have decided to consume the first fruits of the grain and the tithes of the wine and oil, which they had consecrated and set aside for the priests who minister in the presence of our God at Jerusalem -- although it is not lawful for any of the people so much as to touch these things with their hands.

[14] They have sent men to Jerusalem, because even the people living there have been doing this, to bring back to them permission from the senate.

[15] When the word reaches them and they proceed to do this, on that very day they will be handed over to you to be destroyed.

[16] "Therefore, when I, your servant, learned all this, I fled from them; and God has sent me to accomplish with you things that will astonish the whole world, as many as shall hear about them.

[17] For your servant is religious, and serves the God of heaven day and night; therefore, my lord, I will remain with you, and every night your servant will go out into the valley, and I will pray to God and he will tell me when they have committed their sins.

[18] And I will come and tell you, and then you shall go out with your whole army, and not one of them will withstand you.

[19] Then I will lead you through the middle of Judea, till you come to Jerusalem; and I will set your throne in the midst of it; and you will lead them like sheep that have no shepherd, and not a dog will so much as open its mouth to growl at you. For this has been told me, by my foreknowledge; it was announced to me, and I was sent to tell you."

[20] Her words pleased Holofernes and all his servants, and they marveled at her wisdom and said,

[21] "There is not such a woman from one end of the earth to the other, either for beauty of face or wisdom of speech!"

[22] And Holofernes said to her, "God has done well to send you before the people, to lend strength to our hands and to bring destruction upon those who have slighted my lord.

[23] You are not only beautiful in appearance, but wise in speech; and if you do as you have said, your God shall be my God, and you shall live in the house of King Nebuchadnezzar and be renowned throughout the whole world."

Jdt.12

[1] Then he commanded them to bring her in where his silver dishes were kept, and ordered them to set a table for her with some of his own food and to serve her with his own wine.

[2] But Judith said, "I cannot eat it, lest it be an offense; but I will be provided from the things I have brought with me."

[3] Holofernes said to her, "If your supply runs out, where can we get more like it for you? For none of your people is here with us."

[4] Judith replied, "As your soul lives, my lord, your servant will not use up the things I have with me before the Lord carries out by my hand what he has determined to do."

[5] Then the servants of Holofernes brought her into the tent, and she slept until midnight. Along toward the morning watch she arose

[6] and sent to Holofernes and said, "Let my lord now command that your servant be permitted to go out and pray."

[7] So Holofernes commanded his guards not to hinder her. And she remained in the camp for three days, and went out each night to the valley of Bethulia, and bathed at the spring in the camp.

[8] When she came up from the spring she prayed the Lord God of Israel to direct her way for the raising up of her people.

[9] So she returned clean and stayed in the tent until she ate her food toward evening.

[10] On the fourth day Holofernes held a banquet for his slave only, and did not invite any of his officers.

[11] And he said to Bagoas, the eunuch who had charge of his personal affairs, "Go now and persuade the Hebrew woman who is in your care to join us and eat and drink with us.

[12] For it will be a disgrace if we let such a woman go without enjoying her company, for if we do not embrace her she will laugh at us."

[13] So Bagoas went out from the presence of Holofernes, and approached her and said, "This beautiful maidservant will please come to my lord and be honored in his presence, and drink wine and be merry with us, and become today like one of the daughters of the Assyrians who serve in the house of

Nebuchadnezzar."

[14] And Judith said, "Who am I, to refuse my lord? Surely whatever pleases him I will do at once, and it will be a joy to me until the day of my death!"

[15] So she got up and arrayed herself in all her woman's finery, and her maid went and spread on the ground for her before Holofernes the soft fleeces which she had received from Bagoas for her daily use, so that she might recline on them when she ate.

[16] Then Judith came in and lay down, and Holofernes' heart was ravished with her and he was moved with great desire to possess her; for he had been waiting for an opportunity to deceive her, ever since the day he first saw her.

[17] So Holofernes said to her. "Drink now, and be merry with us!"

[18] Judith said, "I will drink now, my lord, because my life means more to me today than in all the days since I was born."

[19] Then she took and ate and drank before him what her maid had prepared.

[20] And Holofernes was greatly pleased with her, and drank a great quantity of wine, much more than he had ever drunk in any one day since he was born.

Jdt.13

[1] When evening came, his slaves quickly withdrew, and Bagoas closed the tent from outside and shut out the attendants from his master's presence; and they went to bed, for they all were weary because the banquet had lasted long.

[2] So Judith was left alone in the tent , with Holofernes stretched out on his bed, for he was overcome with wine.

[3] Now Judith had told her maid to stand outside the bedchamber and to wait for her to come out, as she did every day; for she said she would be going out for her prayers. And she had said the same thing to Bagoas.

[4] So every one went out, and no one, either small or great, was left in the bedchamber. Then Judith, standing beside his bed, said in her heart, "O Lord God of all might, look in this hour upon the work of my hands for the exaltation of Jerusalem.

[5] For now is the time to help thy inheritance, and to carry out my undertaking for the destruction of the enemies who have risen up against us."

[6] She went up to the post at the end of the bed, above Holofernes' head, and took down his sword that hung there.

[7] She came close to his bed and took hold of the hair of his head, and said, "Give me strength this day, O Lord God of Israel!"

[8] And she struck his neck twice with all her might, and severed it from his body.

[9] Then she tumbled his body off the bed and pulled down the canopy from the posts; after a moment she went out, and gave Holofernes' head to her maid,

[10] who placed it in her food bag. Then the two of them went out together, as they were accustomed to go for prayer; and they passed through the camp and circled around the valley and went up the mountain to Bethulia and came to its gates.

[11] Judith called out from afar to the watchmen at the gates, "Open, open the gate! God, our God, is still with us, to show his power in Israel, and his strength against our enemies, even as he has done this day!"

[12] When the men of her city heard her voice, they hurried down to the city gate and called together the elders of the city.

[13] They all ran together, both small and great, for it was unbelievable that she had returned; they opened the gate and admitted them, and they kindled a fire for light, and gathered around them.

[14] Then she said to them with a loud voice, "Praise God, O praise him! Praise God, who has not withdrawn his mercy from the house of Israel, but has destroyed our enemies by my hand this very night!"

[15] Then she took the head out of the bag and showed it to them, and said, "See, here is the head of Holofernes, the commander of the Assyrian army, and here is the canopy beneath which he lay in his drunken stupor. The Lord has struck him down by the hand of a woman.

[16] As the Lord lives, who has protected me in the way I went, it was my face that tricked him to his destruction, and yet he committed no act of sin with me, to defile and shame me."

[17] All the people were greatly astonished, and bowed down and worshiped God, and said with one accord, "Blessed art thou, our God, who hast brought into contempt this day the enemies of thy people."

[18] And Uzziah said to her, "O daughter, you are blessed by the Most High God above all women on earth; and blessed be the Lord God, who created the heavens and the earth, who has guided you to strike the head of the leader of our enemies.

[19] Your hope will never depart from the hearts of men, as they remember the power of God.

[20] May God grant this to be a perpetual honor to you, and may he visit you with blessings, because you did not spare your own life when our nation was brought low, but have avenged our ruin, walking in the straight path before our God." And all the people said, "So be it, so be it!"

Jdt.14

[1] Then Judith said to them, "Listen to me, my brethren, and take this head and hang it upon the parapet of your wall.

[2] And as soon as morning comes and the sun rises, let every valiant man take his weapons and go out of the city, and set a captain over them, as if you were going down to the plain against the Assyrian outpost; only do not go down.

[3] Then they will seize their arms and go into the camp and rouse the officers of the Assyrian army; and they will rush into the tent of Holofernes, and will not find him. Then fear will come over them, and they will flee before you,

[4] and you and all who live within the borders of Israel shall pursue them and cut them down as they flee.

[5] But before you do all this, bring Achior the Ammonite to me, and let him see and recognize the man who despised the house of Israel and sent him to us as if to his death."

[6] So they summoned Achior from the house of Uzziah. And when he came and saw the head of Holofernes in the hand of one of the men at the gathering of the people, he fell down on his face and his spirit failed him.

[7] And when they raised him up he fell at Judith's feet, and knelt before her, and said, "Blessed are you in every tent of Judah! In every nation those who hear your name will be alarmed.

[8] Now tell me what you have done during these days." Then Judith described to him in the presence of the people all that she had done, from the day she left until the moment of her speaking to them.

[9] And when she had finished, the people raised a great shout and made a joyful noise in their city.

[10] And when Achior saw all that the God of Israel had done, he believed firmly in God, and was circumcised, and joined the house of Israel, remaining so to this day.

[11] As soon as it was dawn they hung the head of Holofernes on the wall, and every man took his weapons, and they went out in companies to the passes in the mountains.

[12] And when the Assyrians saw them they sent word to their commanders, and they went to the generals and the captains and to all their officers.

[13] So they came to Holofernes' tent and said to the steward in charge of all his personal affairs, "Wake up our lord, for the slaves have been so bold as to come down against us to give battle, in order to be destroyed completely."

[14] So Bagoas went in and knocked at the door of the tent, for he supposed that he was sleeping with Judith.

[15] But when no one answered, he opened it and went into the bedchamber and found him thrown down on the platform dead, with his head cut off and missing.

[16] And he cried out with a loud voice and wept and groaned and shouted, and rent his garments.

[17] Then he went to the tent where Judith had stayed, and when he did not find her he rushed out to the people and shouted,

[18] "The slaves have tricked us! One Hebrew woman has brought disgrace upon the house of King Nebuchadnezzar! For look, here is Holofernes lying on the ground, and his head is not on him!"

[19] When the leaders of the Assyrian army heard this, they rent their tunics and were greatly dismayed, and their loud cries and shouts arose in the midst of the camp.

Jdt.15

[1] When the men in the tents heard it, they were amazed at what had happened.

[2] Fear and trembling came over them, so that they did not wait for one another, but with one impulse all rushed out and fled by every path across the plain and through the hill country.

[3] Those who had camped in the hills around Bethulia also took to flight. Then the men of Israel, every one that was a soldier, rushed out upon them.

[4] And Uzziah sent men to Betomasthaim and Bebai and Choba and Kola, and to all the frontiers of Israel, to tell what had taken place and to urge all to rush out upon their enemies to destroy them.

[5] And when the Israelites heard it, with one accord they fell upon the enemy, and cut them down as far as Choba. Those in Jerusalem and all the hill country also came, for they were told what had happened in the camp of the enemy; and those in Gilead and in Galilee outflanked them with great slaughter, even beyond Damascus and its borders.

[6] The rest of the people of Bethulia fell upon the Assyrian camp and plundered it, and were greatly enriched.

[7] And the Israelites, when they returned from the slaughter, took possession of what remained, and the villages and towns in the hill country and in the plain got a great amount of booty, for there was a vast quantity of it.

[8] Then Joakim the high priest, and the senate of the people of Israel who lived at Jerusalem, came to witness the good things which the Lord had done for Israel, and to see Judith and to greet her.

[9] And when they met her they all blessed her with one accord and said to her, "You are the exaltation of Jerusalem, you are the great glory of Israel, you are the great pride of our nation!

[10] You have done all this singlehanded; you have done great good to Israel, and God is well pleased with it. May the Almighty Lord bless you for ever!" And all the people said, "So be it!"

[11] So all the people plundered the camp for thirty days. They gave Judith the tent of Holofernes and all his silver dishes and his beds and his bowls and all his furniture; and she took them and loaded her mule and hitched up her carts and piled the things on them.

[12] Then all the women of Israel gathered to see her, and blessed her, and some of them performed a dance for her; and she took branches in her hands and gave them to the women who were with her;

[13] and they crowned themselves with olive wreaths, she and those who were with her; and she went before all the people in the dance, leading all the women, while all the men of Israel followed, bearing their arms and wearing garlands and with songs on their lips.

Jdt.16

[1] Then Judith began this thanksgiving before all Israel, and all the people loudly sang this song of praise.

[2] And Judith said, Begin a song to my God with tambourines, sing to my Lord with cymbals. Raise to him a new psalm; exalt him, and call upon his name.

[3] For God is the Lord who crushes wars; for he has delivered me out of the hands of my pursuers, and brought me to his camp, in the midst of the people.

[4] The Assyrian came down from the mountains of the north; he came with myriads of his warriors; their multitude blocked up the valleys, their cavalry covered the hills.

[5] He boasted that he would burn up my territory, and kill my young men with the sword, and dash my infants to the ground and seize my children as prey, and take my virgins as booty.

[6] But the Lord Almighty has foiled them by the hand of a woman.

[7] For their mighty one did not fall by the hands of the young men, nor did the sons of the Titans smite him, nor did tall giants set upon him; but Judith the daughter of Merari undid him with the beauty of her countenance.

[8] For she took off her widow's mourning to exalt the oppressed in Israel. She anointed her face with ointment and fastened her hair with a tiara and put on a linen gown to deceive him.

[9] Her sandal ravished his eyes, her beauty captivated his mind, and the sword severed his neck.

[10] The Persians trembled at her boldness, the Medes were daunted at her daring.

[11] Then my oppressed people shouted for joy; my weak people shouted and the enemy trembled; they lifted up their voices, and the enemy were turned back.

[12] The sons of maidservants have pierced them through; they were wounded like the children of fugitives, they perished before the army of my Lord.

[13] I will sing to my God a new song: O Lord, thou are great and glorious, wonderful in strength, invincible.

[14] Let all thy creatures serve thee, for thou didst speak, and they were made. Thou didst send forth thy Spirit, and it formed them; there is none that can resist thy voice.

[15] For the mountains shall be shaken to their foundations with the waters; at thy presence the rocks shall melt like wax, but to those who fear thee thou wilt continue to show mercy.

[16] For every sacrifice as a fragrant offering is a small thing, and all fat for burnt offerings to thee is a very little thing, but he who fears the Lord shall be great for ever.

[17] Woe to the nations that rise up against my people! The Lord Almighty will take vengeance on them in the day of judgment; fire and worms he will give to their flesh; they shall weep in pain for ever.

[18] When they arrived at Jerusalem they worshiped God. As soon as the people were purified, they offered their burnt offerings, their freewill offerings, and their gifts.

[19] Judith also dedicated to God all the vessels of Holofernes, which the people had given her; and the canopy which she took for herself from his bedchamber she gave as a votive offering to the Lord.

[20] So the people continued feasting in Jerusalem before the sanctuary for three months, and Judith remained with them.

[21] After this every one returned home to his own inheritance, and Judith went to Bethulia, and remained on her estate, and was honored in her time throughout the whole country.

[22] Many desired to marry her, but she remained a widow all the days of her life after Manasseh her husband died and was gathered to his people.

[23] She became more and more famous, and grew old in her husband's house, until she was one hundred and five years old. She set her maid free. She died in Bethulia, and they buried her in the cave of her husband Manasseh,

[24] and the house of Israel mourned for her seven days. Before she died she distributed her property to all those who were next of kin to her husband Manasseh, and to her own nearest kindred.

[25] And no one ever again spread terror among the people of Israel in the days of Judith, or for a long time after her death.

Susanna

Sus.1

[1] A man named Joacim lived in Babylon

[2] And he took a wife named Susanna, the daughter of Hilkiah, a very beautiful woman and one who feared the Lord.

[3] Her parents were righteous, and had taught their daughter according to the law of Moses.

[4] Joakim was very rich, and had a spacious garden adjoining his house; and the Jews used to come to him because he was the most honored of them all.

[5] In that year two elders from the people were appointed as judges. Concerning them the Lord had said: "Iniquity came forth from Babylon, from elders who were judges, who were supposed to govern the people."

[6] These men were frequently at Joakim's house, and all who had suits at law came to them.

[7] When the people departed at noon, Susanna would go into her husband's garden to walk.

[8] The two elders used to see her every day, going in and walking about, and they began to desire her.

[9] And they perverted their minds and turned away their eyes from looking to Heaven or remembering righteous judgments.

[10] Both were overwhelmed with passion for her, but they did not tell each other of their distress,

[11] for they were ashamed to disclose their lustful desire to possess her.

[12] And they watched eagerly, day after day, to see her.

[13] They said to each other, "Let us go home, for it is mealtime."

[14] And when they went out, they parted from each other. But turning back, they met again; and when each pressed the other for the reason, they confessed their lust. And then together they arranged for a time when they could find her alone.

[15] Once, while they were watching for an opportune day, she went in as before with only two maids, and wished to bathe in the garden, for it was very hot.

[16] And no one was there except the two elders, who had hid themselves and were watching her.

[17] She said to her maids, "Bring me oil and ointments, and shut the garden doors so that I may bathe."

[18] They did as she said, shut the garden doors, and went out by the side doors to bring what they had been commanded; and they did not see the elders, because they were hidden.

[19] When the maids had gone out, the two elders rose and ran to her, and said:

[20] "Look, the garden doors are shut, no one sees us, and we are in love with you; so give your consent, and lie with us.

[21] If you refuse, we will testify against you that a young man was with you, and this was why you sent your maids away."

[22] Susanna sighed deeply, and said, "I am hemmed in on every side. For if I do this thing, it is death for me; and if I do not, I shall not escape your hands.

[23] I choose not to do it and to fall into your hands, rather than to sin in the sight of the Lord."

[24] Then Susanna cried out with a loud voice, and the two elders shouted against her.

[25] And one of them ran and opened the garden doors.

[26] When the household servants heard the shouting in the garden, they rushed in at the side door to see what had happened to her.

[27] And when the elders told their tale, the servants were greatly ashamed, for nothing like this had ever been said about Susanna.

[28] The next day, when the people gathered at the house of her husband Joakim, the two elders came, full of their wicked plot to have Susanna put to death.

[29] They said before the people, "Send for Susanna, the daughter of Hilkiah, who is the wife of Joakim."

[30] So they sent for her. And she came, with her parents, her children, and all her kindred.

[31] Now Susanna was a woman of great refinement, and beautiful in appearance.

[32] As she was veiled, the wicked men ordered her to be unveiled, that they might feed upon her beauty.

[33] But her family and friends and all who saw her wept.

[34] Then the two elders stood up in the midst of the people, and laid their hands upon her head.

[35] And she, weeping, looked up toward heaven, for her heart trusted in the Lord.

[36] The elders said, "As we were walking in the garden alone, this woman came in with two maids, shut the garden doors, and dismissed the maids.

[37] Then a young man, who had been hidden, came to her and lay with her.

[38] We were in a corner of the garden, and when we saw this wickedness we ran to them.

[39] We saw them embracing, but we could not hold the man, for he was too strong for us, and he opened the doors and dashed out.

[40] So we seized this woman and asked her who the young man was, but she would not tell us. These things we testify."

[41] The assembly believed them, because they were elders of the people and judges; and they condemned her to death.

[42] Then Susanna cried out with a loud voice, and said, "O eternal God, who do discern what is secret, who art aware of all things before they come to be,

[43] thou knowest that these men have borne false witness against me. And now I am to die! Yet I have done none of the things that they have wickedly invented against me!"

[44] The Lord heard her cry.

[45] And as she was being led away to be put to death, God aroused the holy spirit of a young lad named Daniel;

[46] and he cried with a loud voice, "I am innocent of the blood of this woman."

[47] All the people turned to him, and said, "What is this that you have said?"

[48] Taking his stand in the midst of them, he said, "Are you such fools, you sons of Israel? Have you condemned a daughter of Israel without examination and without learning the facts?

[49] Return to the place of judgment. For these men have borne false witness against her."

[50] Then all the people returned in haste. And the elders said to him, "Come, sit among us and inform us, for God has given you that right."

[51] And Daniel said to them, "Separate them far from each other, and I will examine them."

[52] When they were separated from each other, he summoned one of them and said to him, "You old relic of wicked days, your sins have now come home, which you have committed in the past,

[53] pronouncing unjust judgments, condemning the innocent and letting the guilty go free, though the Lord said, `Do not put to death an innocent and righteous person.'

[54] Now then, if you really saw her, tell me this: Under what tree did you see them being intimate with each other?" He answered, "Under a mastic tree."

[55] And Daniel said, "Very well! You have lied against your own head, for the angel of God has received the sentence from God and will immediately cut you in two."

[56] Then he put him aside, and commanded them to bring the other. And he said to him, "You offspring of Canaan and not of Judah, beauty has deceived you and lust has perverted your heart.

[57] This is how you both have been dealing with the daughters of Israel, and they were intimate with you through fear; but a daughter of Judah would not endure your wickedness.

[58] Now then, tell me: Under what tree did you catch them being intimate with each other?" He answered, "Under an evergreen oak."

[59] And Daniel said to him, "Very well! You also have lied against your own head, for the angel of God is waiting with his sword to saw you in two, that he may destroy you both."

[60] Then all the assembly shouted loudly and blessed God, who saves those who hope in him.

[61] And they rose against the two elders, for out of their own mouths Daniel had convicted them of bearing false witness;

[62] and they did to them as they had wickedly planned to do to their neighbor; acting in accordance with the law of Moses, they put them to death. Thus innocent blood was saved that day.

[63] And Hilkiah and his wife praised God for their daughter Susanna, and so did Joakim her husband and all her kindred, because nothing shameful was found in her.

[64] And from that day onward Daniel had a great reputation among the people.

THE BOOK OF ENOCH

[Chapter 1]

1 The words of the blessing of Enoch, with which he blessed the elect and righteous, who will be living in the day of tribulation, when all the wicked and godless are to be removed.

2 And he began his story saying: Enoch a righteous man, whose eyes were opened by God, saw the vision of the Holy One in heaven, which the angels showed me, and I heard everything from them, and I saw and understood, but it was not for this generation, but for a remote one which is to come.

3 Concerning the elect I said, as I began my story concerning them: The Holy Great One will come out from His dwelling,

4 And the eternal God will tread on the earth, (even) on Mount Sinai, and appear in the strength of His might from heaven.

5 And all shall be very afraid, And the Watchers shall shake, And great fear and trembling shall seize them to the ends of the earth.

6 And the high mountains shall be shaken, and the high hills shall be laid low, and shall melt like wax in the flame.

7 And the earth shall be wholly torn apart, and all that is on the earth shall be destroyed, And there shall be a judgment on all.

8 But with the righteous He will make peace; and will protect the elect and mercy shall be on them. And they shall all belong to God, and they shall prosper, and they shall be blessed. And the light of God shall shine on them.

9 And behold! He comes with ten thousand of His holy ones (saints) to execute judgment on all, and to destroy all the ungodly (wicked); and to convict all flesh of all the works of their ungodliness which they have ungodly committed, and of all the hard things which ungodly sinners have spoken against Him.

[Chapter 2]

1 Observe everything that takes place in the sky, how the lights do not change their orbits, and the luminaries which are in heaven, how they all rise and set in order each in its season (proper time), and do not transgress against their appointed order.

2 Consider the earth, and give understanding to the things which take place on it from start to finish, how steadfast they are, how none of the things on the earth change, but all the works of God appear to you.

3 Behold the summer and the winter, how the whole earth is filled with water, and clouds and dew and rain lie on it.

[Chapter 3]

1 Observe and see how (in the winter) all the trees seem as though they had withered and shed all their leaves, except fourteen trees, which do not lose their foliage but retain the old foliage from two to three years until the new comes.

[Chapter 4]

1 And again, observe the days of summer how the sun is above the earth. And you seek shade and shelter because of the heat of the sun, and the earth also burns with growing heat, and so you cannot walk on the earth, or on a rock because of its heat.

[Chapter 5]

1 Observe how the trees are covered with green leaves and how they bear fruit. Understand, know, and recognize that He that lives for ever made them this way for you.

2 And all His works go on before Him from year to year for ever, and all the work and the tasks which they accomplish for Him do not change, and so is it done.

3 Consider how the sea and the rivers in like manner accomplish their course do not change because of His commandments.

4 But you, you have neither held to nor have you done the commandments of the Lord, But you have turned away and spoken proud and hard words with your unclean mouths against His greatness. Oh, you hard-hearted, you shall find no peace.

5 Therefore shall you curse your days, and the years of your life shall perish, and the years of your destruction shall be multiplied and in an eternal curse you shall find no mercy.

6 In those days you shall make your names an eternal curse to all the righteous, and by you shall all who curse, curse, and all the sinners and godless shall curse you forever. And for you the godless there shall be a curse.

7 And all the elect shall rejoice, and there shall be forgiveness of sins, and mercy and peace and forbearance and joy. There shall be salvation for them, (like/and) a good light. And for all of you sinners there shall be no salvation, but on you all shall abide a curse.

8 But for the elect there shall be light and joy and peace, and they shall inherit the earth.

9 And then wisdom shall be given to the elect, and they shall all live and never again sin, either through forgetfulness or through pride: But those who are given wisdom shall be humble.

10 And they shall not again transgress, Nor shall they sin all the days of their life, Nor shall they die of the anger or wrath of God, But they shall complete the number of the days of their lives. And their lives shall be increased in peace, and their years will grow in joy and eternal gladness and peace, all the days of their lives.

[Chapter 6]

1 And it came to pass when the children of men had multiplied that in those days were born to them beautiful and fair daughters.

2 And the angels, the sons of heaven, saw and lusted after them, and said to one another: 'Come, let us choose us wives from among the children of men

3 And have children with them.' And Semjaza, who was their leader, said to them: 'I fear you will not agree to do this deed,

4 And I alone shall have to pay the penalty of this great sin.'

5 And they all answered him and said: 'Let us all swear an oath, and all bind ourselves by mutual curses so we will not abandon this plan but to do this thing.' Then they all swore together and bound themselves by mutual curses.

6 And they were in all two hundred who descended in the days of Jared in the summit of Mount Hermon, and they called it Mount Hermon, because they had sworn and bound themselves by mutual curses on the act.

7 And these are the names of their leaders: Samlazaz, their leader, Araklba, Rameel, Kokablel, Tamlel, Ramlel, Danel, Ezeqeel, Baraqijal,

(Author's note: Samlazaz could be another spelling of Semjaza, and possibly be the same entity.)

8 Asael, Armaros, Batarel, Ananel, Zaqiel, Samsapeel, Satarel, Turel, Jomjael, Sariel. These are their chiefs of tens.

[Chapter 7]

1 And all of them together went and took wives for themselves, each choosing one for himself, and they began to go in to them and to defile themselves with sex with them,

2 And the angels taught them charms and spells, and the cutting of roots, and made them acquainted with plants.

3 And the women became pregnant, and they bare large giants, whose height was three thousand cubits (ells).

4 The giants consumed all the work and toil of men. And when men could no longer sustain them, the giants turned against them and devoured mankind.

5 And they began to sin against birds, and beasts, and reptiles, and fish, and to devour one another's flesh, and drank the blood.

6 Then the earth laid accusation against the lawless ones.
[Chapter 8]

1 And Azazel taught men to make swords, and knives, and shields, and breastplates, and taught them about metals of the earth and the art of working them, and bracelets, and ornaments, and the use of antimony, and the beautifying of the eyelids, and all kinds of precious stones, and all coloring and dyes.

2 And there was great impiety, they turned away from God, and committed fornication, and they were led astray, and became corrupt in all their ways.

3 Semjaza taught the casting of spells, and root-cuttings, Armaros taught counter-spells (release from spells), Baraqijal taught astrology, Kokabel taught the constellations (portents), Ezeqeel the knowledge of the clouds, Araqiel the signs of the earth, Shamsiel the signs of the sun, and Sariel the course of the moon. And as men perished, they cried, and their cry went up to heaven.

[Chapter 9]

1 And then Michael, Uriel, Raphael, and Gabriel looked down from heaven and saw much blood being shed on the earth, and all lawlessness being done on the earth.

2 And they said to each other: 'Let the cries from the destruction of Earth ascend up to the gates of heaven.

3 And now to you, the holy ones of heaven, the souls of men make their petition, saying, "Bring our cause before the Most High."'

4 And they said to the Lord of the ages: 'Lord of lords, God of gods, King of kings, and God of the ages, the throne of your glory endures through all the generations of the ages, and your name holy and glorious and blessed to all the ages!

5 You have made all things, and you have power over all things: and all things are revealed and open in your sight, and you see all things, and nothing can hide itself from you.

6 Look at what Azazel has done, who has taught all unrighteousness on earth and revealed the eternal secrets which were made and kept in heaven, which men were striving to learn:

7 And Semjaza, who taught spells, to whom you gave authority to rule over his associates.

8 And they have gone to the daughters of men on the earth, and have had sex with the women, and have defiled themselves, and revealed to them all kinds of sins.

9 And the women have borne giants, and the whole earth has thereby been filled with blood and unrighteousness.

10 And now, behold, the souls of those who have died are crying out and making their petition to the gates of heaven, and their lament has ascended and cannot cease because of the lawless deeds which are done on the earth.

11 And you know all things before they come to pass, and you see these things and you have permitted them, and say nothing to us about these things. What are we to do with them about these things?'

[Chapter 10]

1 Then said the Most High, the Great and Holy One, "Uriel, go to the son of Lamech.

2 Say to him: 'Go to Noah and tell him in my name "Hide yourself!" and reveal to him the end that is approaching: that the whole earth will be destroyed, and a flood is about to come on the whole earth, and will destroy everything on it.'

3 'And now instruct him as to what he must do to escape that his offspring may be preserved for all the generations of the world.'

.

4 And again the Lord said to Raphael: 'Bind Azazel hand and foot, and cast him into the darkness and split open the desert, which is in Dudael, and cast him in.

5 And fill the hole by covering him rough and jagged rocks, and cover him with darkness, and let him live there for ever, and cover his face that he may not see the light.

6 And on the day of the great judgment he shall be hurled into the fire.

7 And heal the earth which the angels have ruined, and proclaim the healing of the earth, for I will restore the earth and heal the plague, that not all of the children of men may perish through all the secret things that the Watchers have disclosed and have taught their sons.

8 The whole earth has been corrupted through the works that were taught by Azazel: to him ascribe ALL SIN.'

9 To Gabriel said the Lord: 'Proceed against the bastards and the reprobates, and against the children of fornication and destroy the children of fornication and the children of the Watchers. Cause them to go against one another that they may destroy each other in battle: Shorten their days.

10 No request that (the Watchers) their fathers make of you shall be granted them on their behalf; for they hope to live an eternal life, and that each one of them will live five hundred years.'

11 And the Lord said to Michael: 'Go, bind Semjaza and his team who have associated with women and have defiled themselves in all their uncleanness.

12 When their sons have slain one another, and they have seen the destruction of their beloved ones, bind them fast for seventy generations under the hills of the earth, until the day of the consummation of their judgment and until the eternal judgment is accomplished.

(Author's note: 70 generations of 500 years = 3500 years.)

13 In those days they shall be led off to the abyss of fire and to the torment and the prison in which they shall be confined for ever.'

14 Then Semjaza shall be burnt up with the condemned and they will be destroyed, having been bound together with them to the end of all generations.

15 Destroy all the spirits of lust and the children of the Watchers, because they have wronged mankind.

16 Destroy all wrong from the face of the earth and let every evil work come to an end and let (the earth be planted with righteousness) the plant of righteousness and truth appear; and it shall prove a blessing, the works of righteousness and truth shall be planted in truth and joy for evermore.

17 And then shall all the righteous survive, and shall live until they beget thousands of children, and all the days of their youth and their old age shall they complete in peace.

18 And then shall the whole earth be untilled in righteousness and shall be planted with trees and be full of blessing. And all desirable trees shall be planted on it, and they shall plant vines on it.

19 And the vine which they plant shall yield fruit in abundance, and as for all the seed which is sown, each measurement (of it) shall bear a thousand, and each measurement of olives shall yield ten presses of oil.

20 You shall cleanse the earth from all oppression, and from all unrighteousness, and from all sin, and from all godlessness, and all the uncleanness that is brought on the earth you shall destroy from off the earth.

21 All the children of men shall become righteous, and all nations shall offer adoration and shall praise Me,

22 And all shall worship Me. And the earth shall be cleansed from all defilement, and from all sin, and from all punishment, and from all torment, and I will never again send another flood from this generation to all generations and for ever.

[Chapter 11]

1 And in those days I will open the storehouse of blessings in heaven, and rain down blessings on the earth and over the work and labor of the children of men.

2 Truth and peace shall be united throughout all the days of the world and throughout all the generations of men.'

[Chapter 12]

1 Then Enoch disappeared and no one of the children of men knew where he was hidden, and where he abode;

2 And what had become of him. And his activities were with the Holy Ones and the Watchers.

3 And I, Enoch, was blessing the Lord of majesty and the King of the ages, and lo! the Watchers called me, Enoch the scribe, and said to me:

4 'Enoch, you scribe of righteousness, go, tell the Watchers of heaven who have left the high heaven, the holy eternal place, and have defiled themselves with women, and have done as the children of earth do, and have taken to themselves wives:

5 "You have done great destruction on the earth: And you shall have no peace nor forgiveness of sin:

6 Since they delight themselves in their children, They shall see the murder of their beloved ones, and the destruction of their children shall and they shall lament, and shall make supplication forever, you will receive neither mercy or peace."

[Chapter 13]

1 And Enoch went and said: 'Azazel, you shall have no peace: a severe sentence has been passed against you that you should be bound:

2 And you shall not have rest or mercy (toleration nor request granted), because of the unrighteousness which you have taught, and because of all the works of godlessness,

3 And unrighteousness and sin which you have shown to men.

4 Then I went and spoke to them all together, and they were all afraid, and fear and trembling seized them.

5 And they asked me to write a petition for them that they might find forgiveness, and to read their petition in the presence of the Lord of heaven. They had been forbidden to speak (with Him) nor were they to lift up their eyes to heaven for shame of their sins because they had been condemned.

6 Then I wrote out their petition, and the prayer in regard to their spirits and their deeds individually and in regard to their requests that they should obtain forgiveness and forbearance.

7 And I went off and sat down at the waters of Dan, in the land of Dan, to the southwest of Hermon: I read their petition until I fell asleep.

8 And I had a dream, and I saw a vision of their chastisement, and a voice came to me that I would reprimand (reprove) them.

9 And when I awoke, I came to them, and they were all sitting gathered together, weeping in Abelsjail, which is between Lebanon and Seneser, with their faces covered.
10 And I recounted to them all the visions which I had seen when I was asleep, and I began to speak the words of righteousness, and to reprimand heavenly Watchers.

[Chapter 14]

1 This is the book of the words of righteousness, and of the reprimand of the eternal Watchers in accordance with the command of the Holy Great One in that vision I saw in my sleep.

2 What I will now say with a tongue of flesh and with the breath of my mouth: which the Great One has given to men to speak with it and to understand with the heart.

3 As He has created and given to man the power of understanding the word of wisdom, so has He created me also and given me the power of reprimanding the Watchers, the children of heaven.

4 I wrote out your petition, and in my vision it appeared that your petition will not be granted to you throughout all the days of eternity, and that judgment has been finally passed on you:

5 Your petition will not be granted. From here on you shall not ascend into heaven again for all eternity, and you will be bound on earth for all eternity.

6 Before this you will see the destruction of your beloved sons and you shall have no pleasure in them, but they shall fall before you by the sword.
7 Your petition shall not be granted on their behalf or on yours, even though you weep and pray and speak all the words contained in my writings.

8 In the vision I saw clouds that invited me and summoned me into a mist, and the course of the stars and the flashes of lightning and hurried me and drove me,

9 And the winds in the vision caused me to fly and lifted me up, and bore me into heaven. And I went in until I drew near to a wall which was built out of crystals and surrounded by tongues of fire, and it began to frighten me.

10 I went into the tongues of fire and drew near a large house which was built of crystals: and the walls of the house were like a mosaic of hailstones and the floor was made of crystals like snow.

11 Its ceiling was like the path of the stars and lightning flashes, and between them were fiery cherubim,

12 Their sky was clear as water. A flaming fire surrounded the walls, and its doors blazed with fire.

13 I entered that house, and it was hot as fire and cold as ice; there were no pleasures or life therein: fear covered me, and trembling got hold of me.

14 As I shook and trembled, I fell on my face.

15 And I saw a vision, And lo! there was a second house, greater than the first,

16 And the all the doors stood open before me, and it was built of flames of fire. And in every respect it was splendid and magnificent to the extent that I cannot describe it to you.

17 Its floor was of fire, and above it was lightning and the path of the stars, and its ceiling also was flaming fire.

18 And I looked and saw a throne set on high, its appearance was like crystal, and its wheels were like a shining sun, and there was the vision of cherubim.

19 And from underneath the throne came rivers of fire so that I could not look at it.

20 And He who is Great in Glory sat on the throne, and His raiment shone more brightly than the sun and was whiter than any snow.

21 None of the angels could enter or could behold His face because of the magnificence and glory and no flesh could behold Him.

22 The sea of fire surrounded Him, and a great fire stood in front of Him, and no one could draw close to Him: ten thousand times ten thousand stood before Him, but He needed no Holy council.

23 The most Holy Ones who were near to Him did not leave night or day.

24 And until then I had been prostrate on my face, trembling, and the Lord called me with His own mouth, and said to me:

25 'Come here, Enoch, and hear my word.' And one of the Holy Ones came to me picked me up and brought me to the door: and I bowed down my face.

[Chapter 15]

1 And He answered and said to me, and I heard His voice: 'Do not be afraid, Enoch, you righteous man and scribe of righteousness.

2 Approach and hear my voice. Go and say to the Watchers of heaven, for whom you have come to intercede: "You should intercede for men, and not men for you."

3 Why and for what cause have you left the high, holy, and eternal heaven, and had sex with women, and defiled yourselves with the daughters of men and taken to yourselves wives, and done like the children of earth, and begotten giants (as your) sons?

4 Though you were holy, spiritual, living the eternal life, you have defiled yourselves with the blood of women, and have begotten children with the blood of flesh, and, as the children of men, you have lusted after flesh and blood like those who die and are killed.

5 This is why I have given men wives, that they might impregnate them, and have children by them, that deeds might continue on the earth.

6 But you were formerly spiritual, living the eternal life, and immortal for all generations of the world.

7 Therefore I have not appointed wives for you; you are spiritual beings of heaven, and in heaven was your dwelling place.

8 And now, the giants, who are produced from the spirits and flesh, shall be called evil spirits on the earth,

9 And shall live on the earth. Evil spirits have come out from their bodies because they are born from men and from the holy Watchers, their beginning is of primal origin;

10 They shall be evil spirits on earth, and evil spirits shall they be called spirits of the evil ones. [As for the spirits of heaven, in heaven shall be their dwelling, but as for the spirits of the earth which were born on the earth, on the earth shall be their dwelling.] And the spirits of the giants afflict, oppress, destroy, attack, war, destroy, and cause trouble on the earth.

11 They take no food, but do not hunger or thirst. They cause offences but are not observed.

12 And these spirits shall rise up against the children of men and against the women, because they have proceeded from them in the days of the slaughter and destruction.'

[Chapter 16]

1 'And at the death of the giants, spirits will go out and shall destroy without incurring judgment, coming from their bodies their flesh shall be destroy until the day of the consummation, the great judgment in which the age shall be consummated, over the Watchers and the godless, and shall be wholly consummated.'

2 And now as to the Watchers who have sent you to intercede for them, who had been in heaven before,

3 (Say to them): "You were in heaven, but all the mysteries of heaven had not been revealed to you, and you knew worthless ones, and these in the hardness of your hearts you have made known to the women, and through these mysteries women and men work much evil on earth."

4 Say to them therefore: " You have no peace."'

[Chapter 17]

1 And they took me to a place in which those who were there were like flaming fire,

2 And, when they wished, they made themselves appear as men. They brought me to the place of darkness, and to a mountain the point of whose summit reached to heaven.

3 And I saw the lighted places and the treasuries of the stars and of the thunder and in the uttermost depths, where were

4 A fiery bow and arrows and their quiver, and a fiery sword and all the lightning. And they took me to the waters of life, and to the fire of the west, which receives every setting of the sun.

5 And I came to a river of fire in which the fire flows like water into the great sea towards the west.
6 I saw the great rivers and came to the great darkness, and went to the place where no flesh walks.

7 I saw the mountains of the darkness of winter and the place from where all the waters of the deep flow.

640

8 I saw the mouths of all the rivers of the earth and the mouth of the deep.

[Chapter 18]

1 I saw the storehouse of all the winds: I saw how He had adorned the whole creation with them and the firm foundations of the earth.

2 And I saw the corner-stone of the earth: I saw the four winds which support the earth and the firmament of the heaven.

3 I saw how the winds stretch out the height of heaven, and have their station between heaven and earth; these are the pillars of heaven.

4 I saw the winds of heaven which turn and bring the sky and the sun and all the stars to their setting place.

5 I saw the winds on the earth carrying the clouds: I saw the paths of the angels. I saw at the end of the earth the firmament of heaven above.

6 And I continued south and saw a place which burns day and night, where there are seven mountains of magnificent stones, three towards the east, and three towards the south.

7 And as for those towards the east, they were of colored stone, and one of pearl, and one of jacinth (a stone of healing), and those towards the south of red stone.

8 But the middle one reached to heaven like the throne of God, and was made of alabaster.

9 And the summit of the throne was of sapphire.

10 And I saw a great abyss of the earth, with pillars of heavenly fire, and I saw among them fiery pillars of Heaven, which were falling,

11 And as regards both height and depth, they were immeasurable.

12 And beyond that abyss I saw a place which had no firmament of heaven above, and no firmly founded earth beneath it: there was no water on it, and no birds,

13 But it was a desert and a horrible place. I saw there seven stars like great burning mountains,

14 And an angel questioned me regarding them. The angel said: 'This place is the end of heaven and earth.

15 This has become a prison for the stars and the host of heaven. And the stars which roll over the fire are they which have transgressed the commandment of the Lord in the beginning of their rising, because they did not come out at their proper times.

16 And He was angry with them, and bound them until the time when their guilt should be consummated even for ten thousand years.'

[Chapter 19]

1 And Uriel said to me: 'The angels who have had sex with women shall stand here, and their spirits, having assumed many different forms, are defiling mankind and shall lead them astray into sacrificing to demons as gods, here shall they stand, until the day of the great judgment in which they shall be judged and are made an end of.

2 And the women also of the angels who went astray shall become sirens (other versions read 'shall become peaceful' also, another version reads, 'shall salute them').'

3 And I, Enoch, alone saw the vision, the ends of all things: and no man shall see as I have seen.

[Chapter 20]

1 These are the names of the holy angels who watch.

2 Uriel, one of the holy angels, who is over the world, turmoil and terror.

3 Raphael, one of the holy angels, who is over the spirits of men.

4 Raguel, one of the holy angels who takes vengeance on the world of the luminaries.

5 Michael, one of the holy angels, set over the virtues of mankind and over chaos.

6 Saraqael, one of the holy angels, who is set over the spirits, who sin in the spirit.

7 Gabriel, one of the holy angels, who is over Paradise and the serpents and the Cherubim.

8 Remiel, one of the holy angels, whom God set over those who rise.

[Chapter 21]

1 Then, I proceeded to where things were chaotic and void.

2 And I saw there something horrible: I saw neither a heaven above nor a firmly founded earth, but a place chaotic and horrible.

3 And there I saw seven stars of heaven bound together in it, like great mountains and burning with fire.

4 Then I said: 'For what sin are they bound, and on why have they been cast in here?'

5 Then said Uriel, one of the holy angels, who was with me, and was chief over them: 'Enoch, why do you ask, and why art you eager for the truth?

6 These are some of the stars of heaven, which have transgressed the commandment of the Lord, and are bound here until ten thousand years, the time entailed by their sins, are consummated.'

7 And I went out from there to another place, which was still more horrible than the former, and I saw a terrible thing: a great fire there which burnt and blazed, and the place was cleft as far as the abyss, full of great falling columns of fire:

8 Neither its width or breadth could I see, nor could I see its source.

9 Then I said: 'I am afraid of this place and cannot stand to look at it.!' Then Uriel, one of the holy angels who was with me, answered and said to me: 'Enoch, why are you so afraid?'

10 And I answered: 'Because of this fearful place, and because of the spectacle of the pain.' And he said to me: 'This place is the prison of the angels, and here they will be imprisoned for ever.'

[Chapter 22]

1 And I went out to another place west where there was a mountain and hard rock.

2 And there was in it four hollow places, deep and wide and very smooth. How smooth are the hollow places and looked deep and dark.

3 Then Raphael answered, one of the holy angels who was with me, and said to me: 'These hollow places have been created for this very purpose, that the spirits of the souls of the dead should be gathered here, that all the souls of the children of men should brought together here. And these places have been made to receive them until the day of their judgment and until the period appointed, until the great judgment comes on them.'

4 I saw the spirit of a dead man, and his voice went out to heaven and made petitions.

5 And I asked Raphael the angel who was with me, and I said to him: 'This spirit which petitions,

6 Whose is it, whose voice goes up and petitions heaven?'

7 And he answered me saying: 'This is the spirit which went out from Abel, whom his brother Cain slew, and he makes his suit against him until his offspring is destroyed from the face of the earth, and his offspring are annihilated from among the children of men.'

8 Then I asked, regarding all the hollow places: 'Why is one separated from the other?'

9 And he answered me and said to me: 'These three have been made that the spirits of the dead might be separated. Divisions have been made for the spirits of the righteous, in which there is the bright spring of water.

10 And one for sinners when they die and are buried in the earth and judgment has not been executed on them in their lifetime.

11 Here their spirits shall be set apart in this great pain until the great day of judgment and punishment and torment of those who curse for ever and retribution for their spirits.

12 There He shall bind them for ever. And such a division has been made for the spirits of those who make their petitions, who make disclosures concerning their destruction, when they were slain in the days of the sinners.

13 Such has been made for the spirits of men who were not righteous but sinners, who were complete in transgression, and of the transgressors they shall be companions, but their spirits shall not be destroyed in the day of judgment nor shall they be raised from here.'

14 Then I blessed the Lord of glory and said: 'Blessed be my Lord, the Lord of righteousness, who rules for ever.'

[Chapter 23]

1 From here I went to another place to the west of the ends of the earth.

2 And I saw a burning fire which ran without resting, and never stopped from its course day or night but flowed always in the same way.

3 And I asked saying: 'What is this which never stops?'

4 Then Raguel, one of the holy angels who was with me, answered me and said to me: 'This course of fire which you have seen is the fire in the west and is the fire of all the lights of heaven.'

[Chapter 24]

1 And from here I went to another place on the earth, and he showed me a mountain range of fire which burned day and night.

2 And I went beyond it and saw seven magnificent mountains, all differing from each other, and their stones were magnificent and beautiful, and their form was glorious: three towards the east, one founded on the other, and three towards the south, one on the other, and deep rough ravines, no one of which joined with any other.

3 And the seventh mountain was in the midst of these, and it was higher than them, resembling the seat of a throne.

4 And fragrant trees encircled the throne. And among them was a tree such as I had never smelled, nor was any among them or were others like it; it had a fragrance beyond all fragrance, and its leaves and blooms and wood would not ever wither:

5 And its fruit is beautiful, and its fruit resembles the dates of a palm. Then I said: 'How beautiful is this tree, and fragrant, and its leaves are fair, and its blooms very delightful in appearance.'

6 Then Michael, one of the holy and honored angels who was with me, and was their leader, spoke.

[Chapter 25]

1 And he said to me: 'Enoch, why do you ask me about the fragrance of the tree, and why do you wish to learn the truth?'

2 Then I answered him saying: 'I wish to know about everything, but especially about this tree.'

3 And he answered saying: 'This high mountain which you have seen, whose summit is like the throne of God, is His throne, where the Holy Great One, the Lord of Glory, the Eternal King, will sit, when He shall come down to visit the earth with goodness.

4 And as for this fragrant tree, no mortal is permitted to touch it until the great judgment, when He shall take vengeance on all and bring everything to its completion for ever.

5 It shall then be given to the righteous and holy. Its fruit shall be for food to the Elect: it shall be transplanted to the holy place, to the temple of the Lord, the Eternal King.

6 Then they shall rejoice and be glad, and enter into the holy place; And its fragrance shall enter into their bones, And they shall live a long life on earth, as your fathers lived. And in their days there will be no sorrow or pain or torment or toil.'

7 Then I blessed the God of Glory, the Eternal King, who has prepared such things for the righteous, and has created them and promised to give to them.

[Chapter 26]

1 And I went from there to the middle of the earth, and I saw a blessed place in which there were trees with branches alive and blooming on a tree that had been cut down.

2 And there I saw a holy mountain,

3 And underneath the mountain to the east there was a stream and it flowed towards the south. And I saw towards the east another mountain higher than this, and between them a deep and narrow valley.

4 In it ran a stream underneath the mountain. And to the west of it there was another mountain, lower than the former and of small elevation, and a dry, deep valley between them; and another deep and dry valley was at the edge of the three mountains.

5 And all the valleys were deep and narrow, being formed from hard rock, and there were no trees planted on them.

6 And I was very amazed at the rocks in the valleys.

[Chapter 27]

1 Then I said: 'What is the purpose of this blessed land, which is entirely filled with trees, and what is the purpose of this accursed valley between them?'

2 Then Uriel, one of the holy angels who was with me, answered and said: 'This accursed valley is for those who are cursed for ever: Here shall all the accursed be gathered together who utter with their lips words against the Lord not befitting His glory or say hard things against Him. Here shall they be gathered together, and here shall be their place of judgment.

3 In the last days there shall be the spectacle of righteous judgment on them in the presence of the righteous for ever: here shall the merciful bless the Lord of glory, the Eternal King.

4 In the days of judgment they shall bless Him for the mercy in that He has shown them.'

5 Then I blessed the Lord of Glory and set out His glory and praised Him gloriously.

[Chapter 28]

1 Then, I went towards the east, into the midst of the mountain range in the desert, and I saw a wilderness.

2 And it was solitary, full of trees and plants. And water gushed out from above.

3 Rushing like a torrent which flowed towards the north-west it caused clouds and dew to fall on every side.

[Chapter 29]

1 Then I went to another place in the desert, and approached to the east of this mountain range.

2 And there I saw aromatic trees exuding the fragrance of frankincense and myrrh, and the trees also were similar to the almond tree.

[Chapter 30]

1 Beyond these, I went far to the east,

2 And I saw another place, a valley full of water like one that would not run dry.

3 And there was a tree, the color of fragrant trees was that of mastic. And on the sides of those valleys I saw fragrant cinnamon. And beyond these I proceeded to the east.

[Chapter 31]

1 And I saw other mountains, and among them were groves of trees, and there was nectar that flowed from them, which is named Sarara and Galbanum.

2 And beyond these mountains I saw another mountain to the east of the ends of the earth, on which there were aloe trees, and all the trees were full of fruit, being like almond trees.

3 And when it was burned it smelled sweeter than any fragrant odor.

[Chapter 32]

1 And after I had smelled these fragrant odors, I looked towards the north over the mountains I saw seven mountains full of fine nard and fragrant trees of cinnamon and pepper.

2 And then I went over the summits of all these mountains, far towards the east of the earth, and passed over the Red Sea and went far from it, and passed over the angel Zotiel.

3 And I came to the Garden of Righteousness. I saw far beyond those trees more trees and they were numerous and large. There were two trees there, very large, beautiful, glorious, and magnificent. The tree of knowledge, whose holy fruit they ate and acquired great wisdom.

4 That tree is in height like the fir, and its leaves are like those of the Carob tree,

5 And its fruit is like the clusters of the grapes, very beautiful: and the fragrance of the tree carries far.

6 Then I said: 'How beautiful is the tree, and how attractive is its look!' Then Raphael the holy angel, who was with me, answered me and said: 'This is the tree of wisdom, of which your father of old and your mother of old, who were your progenitors, have eaten, and they learned wisdom and their eyes were opened, and they knew that they were naked and they were driven out of the garden.'

[Chapter 33]

1 And from there I went to the ends of the earth and saw there large beasts, and each differed from the other; and I saw birds also differing in appearance and beauty and voice, the one differing from the other.

2 And to the east of those beasts I saw the ends of the earth where heaven rests on it, and the doors of heaven open. And I saw how the stars of heaven come out, and I counted the gates from which they came out,

3 And wrote down all their outlets, of each individual star by their number and their names, their courses and their positions, and their times and their months, as Uriel the holy angel who was with me showed me.

4 He showed me all things and wrote them down for me; also their names he wrote for me, and their laws and their functions.

[Chapter 34]

1 From there I went towards the north to the ends of the earth, and there I saw a great and glorious device at the ends of the whole earth.

2 And here I saw three gates of heaven open : through each of them proceed north winds: when they blow there is cold, hail, frost, snow, dew, and rain.

3 And out of one gate they blow for good: but when they blow through the other two gates, it is for violence and torment on the earth, and they blow with force.

[Chapter 35]

1 Then I went towards the west to the ends of the earth, and saw there three gates of heaven open such as I had seen in the east, the same number of gates, and the same number of outlets.

[Chapter 36]

1 And from there I went to the south to the ends of the earth, and saw there three open gates of heaven.

2 And from them come dew, rain, and wind. And from there I went to the east to the ends of heaven, and saw here the three eastern gates of heaven open and small gates above them.

3 Through each of these small gates pass the stars of heaven and they run their course to the west on the path which is shown to them.

4 And as often as I saw I blessed always the Lord of Glory, and I continued to bless the Lord of Glory who has done great and glorious wonders, who has shown the greatness of His work to the angels and to spirits and to men, that they might praise His work and all His creation: that they might see the power of His might and praise the great work of His hands and bless Him for ever.

[Chapter 37]

1 The second vision which he saw, the vision of wisdom which Enoch the son of Jared, the son of Mahalalel,

2 The son of Cainan, the son of Enos, the son of Seth, the son of Adam, saw. And this is the beginning of the words of wisdom which I lifted up my voice to speak and say to those which dwell on earth: Hear,

you men of old time, and see, you that come after, the words of the Holy One which I will speak before the Lord of spirits.

3 The words are for the men of old time, and to those that come after. We will not withhold the beginning of wisdom from this present day. Such wisdom has never been given by the Lord of spirits as I have received according to my insight, according to the good pleasure of the Lord of spirits by whom the lot of eternal life has been given to me.

4 Now three Parables were imparted to me, and I lifted up my voice and recounted them to those that dwell on the earth.

[Chapter 38]

1 The first Parable: When the congregation of the righteous shall appear, and sinners shall be judged for their sins, and shall be driven from the face of the earth;

2 And when the Righteous One shall appear before the eyes of the elect righteous ones, whose works are weighed by the Lord of spirits, light shall appear to the righteous and the elect who dwell on the earth. Where will there be the dwelling for sinners, and where the will there be a resting-place for those who have denied the Lord of spirits? It had been good for them if they had not been born.

3 When the secrets of the righteous shall be revealed and the sinners judged, and the godless driven from the presence of the righteous and elect,

4 From that time those that possess the earth shall no longer be powerful and mighty: And they shall not be able to look at the face of the holy ones, because the Lord of spirits has caused His light to appear on the face of the holy, righteous, and elect.

5 Then the kings and the mighty shall be destroyed and be turned over into the hands of the righteous and holy.

6 And from then on none shall seek mercy from the Lord of spirits for themselves for their life is at an end.

[Chapter 39]

1 And it shall come to pass in those days that elect and holy children will descend from the high heaven, and their offspring will become one with the children of men.

2 And in those days Enoch received books of indignation and wrath, and books of turmoil and confusion. There will be no mercy for them, says the Lord of spirits.

3 And in those days a whirlwind carried me off from the earth, And set me down at the end of heaven.

4 There I saw another vision, the dwelling-places of the holy, and the resting-places of the righteous.

5 Here my eyes saw the dwelling places of His righteous angels, and the resting-places of the Holy Ones. And they petitioned and interceded and prayed for the children of men, and righteousness flowed before them like water, and mercy fell like dew on the earth: Thus it is among them for ever and ever.

6 And in that place my eyes saw the Elect One of righteousness and of faith,

7 And I saw his dwelling-place under the wings of the Lord of spirits.

8 And righteousness shall prevail in his days, and the righteous and elect shall be innumerable and will be before Him for ever and ever.

9 And all the righteous and elect ones before Him shall be as bright as fiery lights, and their mouth shall be full of blessing, and their lips shall praise the name of the Lord of spirits. Righteousness and truth before Him shall never fail.

10 There I wished to dwell, and my spirit longed for that dwelling-place; and thus it was decided and my portion was assigned and established by the Lord of spirits.

11 In those days I praised and exalted the name of the Lord of spirits with blessings and praises, because He had destined me for blessing and glory according to the good pleasure of the Lord of spirits.

12 For a long time my eyes looked at that place, and I blessed Him and praised Him, saying: 'Blessed is He, and may He be blessed from the beginning and for evermore. And in His presence there is no end.

13 He knows before the world was created what is for ever and what will be from generation to generation.

14 Those who do not sleep bless you, they stand before your glory and bless, praise, and exalt you, saying: "Holy, holy, holy, is the Lord of spirits: He fills the earth with spirits."'

15 And here my eyes saw all those who do not sleep: they stand before Him and bless Him saying: 'Blessed be you, and blessed be the name of the Lord for ever and ever.'

16 And my face was changed; for I could no longer see.

[Chapter 40]

1 And after that I saw thousands of thousands and ten thousand times ten thousand,

2 I saw a multitude beyond number and reckoning, who stood before the Lord of spirits. And on the four sides of the Lord of spirits I saw four figures, different from those that did not sleep, and I learned their names; for the angel that went with me told me their names, and showed me all the hidden things.

3 And I heard the voices of those four presences as they uttered praises before the Lord of glory.

4 The first voice blessed the Lord of spirits for ever and ever.

5 The second voice I heard blessing the Elect One and the elect ones who depend on the Lord of spirits.

6 And the third voice I heard pray and intercede for those who live on the earth and pray earnestly in the name of the Lord of spirits.

7 And I heard the fourth voice fending off the Satans (advisories or accusers) and forbidding them to come before the Lord of spirits to accuse them who dwell on the earth.

8 After that I asked the angel of peace who went with me, who showed me everything that is hidden: 'Who are these four figures which I have seen and whose words I have heard and written down?'

9 And he said to me: 'This first is Michael, the merciful and long-suffering; and the second, who is set over all the diseases and all the wounds of the children of men, is Raphael; and the third, who is set over all the powers, is Gabriel' and the fourth, who is set over the repentance and those who hope to inherit eternal life, is named Phanuel.'

10 And these are the four angels of the Lord of spirits and the four voices I heard in those days.

[Chapter 41]

1 And after that I saw all the secrets of heavens, and how the kingdom is divided, and how the actions of men are weighed in the balance.

2 And there I saw the mansions of the elect and the mansions of the holy, and my eyes saw all the sinners being driven from there which deny the name of the Lord of spirits, and they were being dragged off; and they could not live because of the punishment which proceeds from the Lord of spirits.

3 And there my eyes saw the secrets of the lightning and of the thunder, and the secrets of the winds, how they are divided to blow over the earth, and the secrets of the clouds and dew,

4 And there I saw where they came from and how they saturate the dusty earth.

5 And there I saw closed storehouses out of which the winds are divided, the storehouse of the hail and winds, the storehouse of the mist, and of the clouds, and the cloud thereof hovers over the earth from the beginning of the world.

6 And I saw the storehouses of the sun and moon, where they go and where they come, and their glorious return, and how one is superior to the other, and their stately orbit, and how they do not leave their orbit, and they add nothing to their orbit and they take nothing from it, and they keep faith with each other, in accordance with the oath by which they are bound together.

7 And first the sun goes out and traverses his path according to the commandment of the Lord of spirits, and mighty is His name for ever and ever. And after that I saw the invisible and the visible path of the moon, and she accomplishes the course of her path in that place by day and by night-the one holding a position opposite to the other before the Lord of spirits. And they give thanks and praise and rest not; but their thanksgiving is for ever and ever.

8 For the sun makes many revolutions for a blessing or a curse, and the course of the path of the moon is light to the righteous and darkness to the sinners in the name of the Lord, who made a separation between the light and the darkness, and divided the spirits of men and strengthened the spirits of the righteous, in the name of His righteousness.

9 For no angel hinders and no power is able to hinder; for He appoints a judge for them all and He judges them all Himself.

[Chapter 42]

1 Wisdom found no place where she might dwell; then a dwelling-place was assigned her in heavens.

2 Wisdom went out to make her dwelling among the children of men, and found no dwelling-place. Wisdom returned to her place, and took her seat among the angels.

3 And unrighteousness went out from her storehouses. She found those she did not seek, and dwelt with them, (she sought no one in particular but found a place...); as rain in a desert and dew on a thirsty land.

[Chapter 43]

1 And I saw other lightning and the stars of heaven, and I saw how He called them all by their names and they obeyed Him.

2 And I saw how they are weighed in a righteous balance according to their proportions of light: I saw the width of their spaces and the day of their appearing, and how their revolution produces lightning:

3 And I saw their revolution according to the number of the angels, and how they keep faith with each other. And I asked the angel who went with me who showed me what was hidden:

4 'What are these?' And he said to me: 'The Lord of spirits has shown you their parable: these are the names of the holy who dwell on the earth and believe in the name of the Lord of spirits for ever and ever.'

[Chapter 44]

1 Also another phenomenon I saw in regard to the lightning: how some of the stars arise and become lightning and cannot part with their new form.

[Chapter 45]

1 And this is the second Parable: concerning those who deny the name of the dwelling of the holy ones and the Lord of spirits.

2 They shall not ascend to heaven, and they shall not come on the earth: Such shall be the lot of the sinners who have denied the name of the Lord of spirits, who are preserved for the day of suffering and tribulation.

3 On that day My Elect One shall sit on the throne of glory and shall try the works of the righteous, and their places of rest shall be innumerable. And their souls shall grow strong within them when they see My Elect One, And those who have called on My glorious name:

4 Then will I cause My Elect One to dwell among them. I will transform heaven and make it an eternal blessing and light,

5 And I will transform the earth and make it a blessing, and I will cause My elect ones to dwell on it. But the sinners and evil-doers shall not set foot on it.

6 For I have seen and satisfied My righteous ones with peace and have caused them to dwell before Me, but for the sinners there is judgment impending with Me, so that I shall destroy them from the face of the earth.

[Chapter 46]

1 And there I saw One whose face looked ancient. His head was white like wool, and with Him was another being whose countenance had the appearance of a man, and his face was full of graciousness, like one of the holy angels.

2 And I asked the angel who went with me and showed me all the hidden things, concerning that Son of Man, who he was, and where came from, and why he went with the Ancient One? And he answered and said to me:

3 "This is the son of Man who has righteousness, with whom dwells righteousness, and who reveals all the treasures of that which is hidden, because the Lord of spirits has chosen him, and whose lot has preeminence before the Lord of spirits in righteousness and is for ever.

4 And this Son of Man whom you have seen shall raise up the kings and the mighty from their seats, and the strong from their thrones and shall loosen the reins of the strong, and break the teeth of the sinners.

5 And he shall put down the kings from their thrones and kingdoms because they do not exalt and praise Him, nor humbly acknowledge who bestowed their kingdom on them.

6 And he shall make the strong hang their heads, and shall fill them with shame. And darkness shall be their dwelling, and worms shall be their bed, and they shall have no hope of rising from their beds, because they do not exalt the name of the Lord of spirits."

7 They raise their hands against the Most High and tread on the earth and dwell on it and all their deeds manifest unrighteousness. Their power rests on their riches, and their faith is in the gods which they have made with their hands. They deny the name of the Lord of spirits,

8 And they persecute the houses of His congregations, and the faithful who depend on the name of the Lord of Spirits.

[Chapter 47]

1 In those days the prayer of the righteous shall have ascended, and the blood of the righteous from the earth shall be before the Lord of spirits.

2 In those days the holy ones who dwell above in heavens shall unite with one voice and supplicate and pray and praise, and give thanks and bless the name of the Lord of spirits on behalf of the blood of the righteous which has been shed, that the prayer of the righteous may not be in vain before the Lord of spirits, that they may have justice, and that they may not have to wait for ever.

3 In those days I saw the "Head of Days" when He seated himself on the throne of His glory, and the books of the living were opened before Him; and all His host which is in heaven above and His counselors stood before Him,

4 And the hearts of the holy were filled with joy because the number of the righteous had been offered, and the prayer of the righteous had been heard, and the blood of the righteous not been required before the Lord of spirits.

[Chapter 48]

1 And in that place I saw the spring of righteousness which was inexhaustible. And around it were many springs of wisdom. And all the thirsty drank of them, and were filled with wisdom, and their dwellings were with the righteous and holy and elect.

2 And at that hour that Son of Man was named in the presence of the Lord of spirits, And his name was brought before the Head of Days.

3 Even before the sun and the signs were created, before the stars of heaven were made, His name was named before the Lord of spirits.

4 He shall be a staff to the righteous and they shall steady themselves and not fall. And he shall be the light of the Gentiles, and the hope of those who are troubled of heart.

5 All who dwell on earth shall fall down and worship before him, and will praise and bless and sing and celebrate the Lord of spirits.

6 And for this reason he has been chosen and hidden in front of (kept safe by) Him, before the creation of the world and for evermore.

7 And the wisdom of the Lord of spirits has revealed him to the holy and righteous; For he has preserved the lot of the righteous, because they have hated and rejected this world of unrighteousness, and have hated all its works and ways in the name of the Lord of spirits. For in his name they are saved, and according to his good pleasure and it is He who has regard to their life.

8 In these days the kings of the earth and the strong who possess the land because of the works of their hands will be shamed, because on the day of their anguish and affliction they shall not be able to save themselves. And I will give them over into the hands of My elect.

9 As straw in the fire so shall they burn before the face of the holy; as lead in the water shall they sink before the face of the righteous, and no trace of them shall be found anymore.

10 And on the day of their affliction there shall be rest on the earth (because the evil ones will be destroyed), and before Him they shall fall down and not rise again, and there shall be no one to take them with his hands and raise them up; for they have denied the Lord of spirits and His Anointed. The name of the Lord of spirits be blessed.

[Chapter 49]

1 For wisdom is poured out like water, and glory will not fail before him ever.

2 For he is mighty in all the secrets of righteousness, and unrighteousness shall disappear like a shadow, and will no longer exist; because the Elect One stands before the Lord of spirits, and his glory is for ever and ever, and his might for all generations.

3 In him dwells the spirit of wisdom, and the spirit which gives insight, and the spirit of understanding and of might, and the spirit of those who have fallen asleep in righteousness.

4 And he shall judge the secret things, and no one shall be able to utter a lying or idle word before him, for he is the Elect One before the Lord of spirits according to His good pleasure.

[Chapter 50]

1 And in those days a change shall take place for the holy and elect, and the light of days shall abide on them, and glory and honor shall turn to the Holy.

2 On the day of trouble, affliction will be heaped on the evil. And the righteous shall be victorious in the name of the Lord of spirits. For He will this to others that they may repent and turn away from the works of their hands.

3 They shall have no honor through the name of the Lord of spirits, but through His name they shall be saved, and the Lord of spirits will have compassion on them, for His mercy is great.

4 He is righteous also in His judgment, and in the presence of His glory unrighteousness also shall not stand: At His judgment the unrepentant shall perish before Him.

5 And from now on I will have no mercy on them, says the Lord of spirits.

[Chapter 51]

1 And in those days shall the earth also give back that which has been entrusted to it, and Sheol (the grave) also shall give back that which it has received, and hell shall give back that which it owes. For in those days the Elect One shall arise,

2 And he shall choose the righteous and holy from among them. For the day has drawn near that they should be saved.

3 And in those days the Elect One shall sit on His throne, and all the secrets of wisdom and counsel shall pour from His mouth, for the Lord of spirits has given them to Him and has glorified Him.

4 In those days shall the mountains leap like rams, and the hills shall skip like lambs satisfied with milk, and the faces of all the angels in heaven shall be lighted up with joy.

5 And the earth shall rejoice, and the righteous shall dwell on it, and the elect shall walk on it.

[Chapter 52]

1 And after those days in that place where I had seen all the visions of that which is hidden, for I had been carried off in a whirlwind and they had borne me towards the west.

2 There my eyes saw all the secret things of heaven that shall be, a mountain of iron, and a mountain of copper, and a mountain of silver, and a mountain of gold, and a mountain of soft metal, and a mountain of lead.

3 And I asked the angel who went with me, saying, 'What things are these which I have seen in secret?'

4 And he said to me: 'All these things which you have seen shall serve the authority of His Messiah that he may be powerful and mighty on the earth.'

5 The angel of peace answered me saying: 'Wait a little while, and all secret things shall be revealed to you, things which surround the Lord of spirits.

6 And these mountains which your eyes have seen, the mountain of iron, and the mountain of copper, and the mountain of silver, and the mountain of gold, and the mountain of soft metal, and the mountain of lead, all of these shall be like wax before a fire in the presence of the Elect One. Like the water which streams down from above on those mountains, and they shall be weak under his feet.

7 And it shall come to pass in those days that none shall be saved, either by gold or by silver, and none will be able to save themselves or escape.

8 And there shall be no iron for war, nor materials for breastplates. Bronze shall be of no use, tin shall be worthless, and lead shall not be desired.

9 All these things shall be destroyed from the face of the earth, when the Elect One appears before the Lord of spirits.'

[Chapter 53]

1 There my eyes saw a deep valley with its mouth open, and all who dwell on the earth and sea and islands shall bring gifts and presents and tokens of homage to Him, but that deep valley shall not become full.

2 And their hands commit lawless deeds, and everything the righteous work at the sinners devour. The sinners shall be destroyed in front of the face of the Lord of spirits, and they shall be banished from off the face of His earth, and they shall perish for ever and ever.

3 For I saw all the angels of punishment abiding there and preparing all the instruments of Satan.

4 And I asked the angel of peace who went with me: 'For whom are they preparing these instruments?'

5 And he said to me: 'They prepare these for the kings and the powerful of this earth, that they may with them they be destroyed.

6 After this the Righteous and Elect One shall cause the house of His congregation to appear and from then on they shall hinder no more, in the name of the Lord of spirits.

7 And these mountains shall not stand as solid ground before His righteousness, but the hills shall be like springs of water, and the righteous shall have rest from the oppression of sinners.'

[Chapter 54]

1 And I looked and turned to another part of the earth, and saw there a deep valley with burning fire.

2 And they brought the kings and the powerful, and began to cast them into this deep valley.

3 And there my eyes saw how they made their instruments for them, iron chains of immeasurable weight.

4 And I asked the angel of peace who was with me, saying: 'For whom are these chains being prepared ?'

5 And he said to me: 'These are being prepared for the hosts of Azazel, so that they may take them and throw them into the bottom of the pit of hell, and they shall cover their jaws with rough stones as the Lord of spirits commanded.

6 And Michael, and Gabriel, and Raphael, and Phanuel shall take hold of them on that great day, and throw them into the burning furnace on that day, that the Lord of spirits may take vengeance on them for their unrighteousness in becoming servants to Satan and for leading astray those who live on the earth.'

7 And in those days punishment will come from the Lord of spirits, and he will open all the storehouses of waters above heavens, and of the fountains which are under the surface of the earth.

8 And all the waters shall be come together (flow into or be joined) with the waters of heaven (above the sky), that which is above heavens is the masculine, and the water which is beneath the earth is the feminine.

9 And they shall destroy all who live on the dry land and those who live under the ends of heaven.

(Author's note: The previous verse refers to Noah's flood).

10 And when they have acknowledged the unrighteousness which they have done on the earth, by these they shall perish.

[Chapter 55]

1 And after that the Head of Days repented and said: 'I have destroyed all who dwell on the earth to no avail.'

2 And He swore by His great name: 'From now on I will not do this to all who dwell on the earth again, and I will set a sign in heaven: and this shall be a covenant of good faith between Me and them for ever, so long as heaven is above the earth. And this is in accordance with My command.

(Author's note: The previous verse refers to the rainbow).

3 When I have desired to take hold of them by the hand of the angels on the day of tribulation, anger, and pain because of this, I will cause My punishment and anger to abide on them, says God, the Lord of spirits.

4 You mighty kings who live on the earth, you shall have to watch My Elect One, sit on the throne of glory and judge Azazel, and all his associates, and all his hosts in the name of the Lord of spirits.'

[Chapter 56]

1 And I saw there the hosts of the angels of punishment going, and they held scourges and chains of iron and bronze.

2 And I asked the angel of peace who went with me, saying: 'To whom are these who hold the scourges going?'
3 And he said to me: 'Each one to the ones they have chosen and to their loved ones, that they may be cast into the chasm of the abyss in the valley.

4 And then that valley shall be filled with ones they chose and their loved ones, and the days of their lives shall be at an end, and the days of their leading astray shall no longer be remembered (counted).

5 In those days the angels shall return and gather together and throw themselves to the east on the Parthians and Medes. They shall stir up the kings, so that a spirit of unrest and disturbance will come on them, and they shall drive them from their thrones, that they may rush out like lions from their lairs, and as hungry wolves among their flocks.

(Author's note: The names of certain countries help set the date of the manuscript. Scholars believe, based on the names of the countries mentioned in Enoch that the book could not have been written prior to 250 B.C. since some countries did not exist before that date. One could add that the particular part of Enoch is the only thing dated, since the book consists of several disjointed parts.)

6 And they shall go up and trample the lands of My elect ones, and the land of His elect ones shall be before them a threshing-floor (trampled, barren ground and a highway).

7 But the city of my righteous ones shall be a hindrance to their horses, and they shall begin to fight among themselves, and their own right hand shall be strong against themselves, and a man shall not know his brother, nor a son his father or his mother, until there will be innumerable corpses because of their slaughter, and their punishment shall be not in vain.

8 In those days hell (Sheol) shall open its jaws, and they shall be swallowed up. Their destruction shall be final. Hell (Sheol) shall devour the sinners in the presence of the elect.'

[Chapter 57]

1 And it came to pass after this that I saw another host of chariots, and men riding on them. They were coming on the winds from the east, and from the west to the south.

2 The noise of their chariots was heard, and when this turmoil took place the holy ones from heaven watched it, and the pillars of the earth were shaken and moved, and the sound of it was heard from the one end of heaven to the other, in one day.

3 And all shall fall down and worship the Lord of spirits. This is the end of the second Parable.

[Chapter 58]

1 And I began to speak the third Parable concerning the righteous and elect.

2 Blessed are you, you righteous and elect, for glorious shall be your lot.

3 And the righteous shall be in the light of the sun, and the elect will be in the light of eternal life. The days of their life shall be unending, and the days of the holy will be without number.

4 And they shall seek the light and find righteousness with the Lord of spirits. Peace to the righteous in the name of the Eternal Lord!

5 And after this it shall be said to the holy in heaven that they should seek secrets of righteousness, and the destiny of faith. For it has become bright as the sun on earth, and the darkness is passed away.

6 And there shall be a light that never ends, and to a number of days they shall not come, for the darkness shall first have been destroyed, [And the light established before the Lord of spirits] and the light of righteousness established for ever before the Lord of spirits.

[Chapter 59]

1 In those days my eyes saw the secrets of the lightning, and of the lights, and they judge and execute their judgment, and they illuminate for a blessing or a curse as the Lord of spirits wills.

2 And there I saw the secrets of the thunder, and how when it resounds above in heaven, the sound thereof is heard, and he caused me to see the judgments executed on the earth, whether they are for well-being and blessing, or for a curse according to the word of the Lord of spirits.

3 And after that all the secrets of the lights and lightning were shown to me, and they lighten for blessing and for satisfying.

[Chapter 60] - Noah's Vision

1 In the year 500, in the seventh month, on the fourteenth day of the month in the life of Enoch, in that parable I saw how a mighty quaking made the heaven of heavens to quake, and the host of the Most High, and the angels, a thousand thousands and ten thousand times ten thousand, were disquieted with great foreboding.

2 And the Head of Days sat on the throne of His glory, and the angels and the righteous stood around Him.

3 And a great trembling seized me, and fear took hold of me, and my legs gave way, and I melted with weakness and fell on my face.

4 And Michael sent another angel from among the holy ones and he raised me up, and when he had raised me up my spirit returned; for I had not been able to endure the look of this host, and the disturbance and the shaking of heaven.

5 And Michael said to me: 'Why are you upset with such a vision? Until this day, His mercy and long-suffering has lasted toward those who dwell on the earth.'

6 And when the day, and the power, and the punishment, and the judgment come, which the Lord of spirits has prepared for those who worship not the righteous law, and for those who deny the righteous judgment, and for those who take His name in vain, that day is prepared. It will be a covenant for the elect, but for sinners an inquisition. When the punishment of the Lord of spirits shall rest on them, it will not come in vain, and it shall slay the children with their mothers and the children with their fathers.

7 And on that day two monsters were separated from one another, a female monster named Leviathan, to dwell in the abyss of the ocean over the fountains of the waters;

8 And the male is named Behemoth, who occupied with his breast a wasted wilderness named Duidain, on the east of the garden where the elect and righteous dwell, where my (great) grandfather was taken up, the seventh from Adam, the first man whom the Lord of spirits created.

9 And I asked the other angel to show me the might of those monsters, how they were separated on one day and thrown, the one into the abyss of the sea, and the other to the earth's desert.

10 And he said to me: ' Son of man, you wish to know what is kept secret.'

11 And the other angel who went with me and showed me what was kept secret; told me what is first and last in heaven in the sky, and beneath the earth in the depth, and at the ends of heaven, and on the foundation of heaven.

12 And the storehouse of the winds, and how the winds are divided, and how they are weighed, and how the doors of the winds are calculated for each according to the power of the wind, and the power of the lights of the moon according to the power that is fitting; and the divisions of the stars according to their names, and how all the divisions are divided.

13 And the thunder according to the places where they fall, and all the divisions that are made among the lightning that it may light, and their host that they may at once obey.

14 For the thunder has places of rest which are assigned while it is waiting for its peal; and the thunder and lightning are inseparable, and although not one and undivided, they both go together in spirit and are not separate.

15 For when the lightning flashes, the thunder utters its voice, and the spirit enforces a pause during the peal, and divides equally between them; for the treasury of their peals is like the sand (of an hourglass), and each one of them as it peals is held in with a bridle, and turned back by the power of the spirit, and pushed forward according to the many parts of the earth.

16 And the spirit of the sea is masculine and strong, and according to the might of His strength He draws it back with a rein, and in like manner it is driven forward and disperses in the midst of all the mountains of the earth.

17 And the spirit of the hoar-frost is his own angel, and the spirit of the hail is a good angel. And the spirit of the snow has forsaken his storehouse because of his strength.

18 There is a special spirit there, and that which ascends from it is like smoke, and its name is frost. And the spirit of the mist is not united with them in their storehouse, but it has a special storehouse; for its course is glorious both in light and in darkness, and in winter and in summer, and in its storehouse is an angel.

19 And the spirit of the dew has its dwelling at the ends of heaven, and is connected with the storehouse of the rain, and its course is in winter and summer; and its clouds and the clouds of the mist are connected, and the one gives to the other.

20 And when the spirit of the rain goes out from its storehouse, the angels come and open the storehouse and lead it out, and when it is diffused over the whole earth it unites with the water on the earth.

21 And whenever it unites with the water on the earth, (for the waters are for those who live on the earth), they are (become) nourishment for the earth from the Most High who is in heaven.

22 Therefore there is a measurement for the rain, and the angels are in charge of it. And these things I saw towards the Garden of the Righteous.

23 And the Angel of Peace who was with me, said to me:

24 "These two monsters, prepared in accordance with the greatness of the Lord, will feed them the punishment of the Lord. And children will be killed with their mothers, and sons with their fathers.

[Chapter 61]

1 And I saw in those days that long cords were given to those angels, and they took to themselves wings and flew, and they went towards the north.

2 I asked the angel, saying to him: 'Why have those angels who have cords taken flight?' And he said to me: 'They have gone to take measurements.'

3 And the angel who went with me said to me: 'These shall bring the measurements of the righteous, and the cords of the righteous to the righteous, that they may rely on the name of the Lord of spirits for ever and ever.

4 The elect shall begin to dwell with the elect, and those are the measurements which shall be given to faith and which shall strengthen righteousness.

5 And these measurements shall reveal all the secrets of the depths of the earth, and those who have been destroyed by the desert, and those who have been devoured by the beasts, and those who have been devoured by the fish of the sea, that they may return and rely on the day of the Elect One. For none shall be destroyed before the Lord of spirits, and none can be destroyed.

6 And all who dwell in heaven received a command and power and one voice and one light like to fire.

7 And they blessed Him with their first words and exalted and praised Him in their wisdom. And they were wise in utterance and in the spirit of life.

8 And the Lord of spirits placed the Elect One on the throne of glory. And he shall judge all the works of the holy above in heaven, and in the balance their deeds shall be weighed.

9 And when he shall lift up his face to judge their secret ways according to the word of the name of the Lord of spirits, and their path according to the way of the righteous judgment of the Lord of spirits; then they shall all speak with one voice and bless and glorify and exalt the name of the Lord of spirits.

10 And He will summon all the host of heavens, and all the holy ones above, and the host of God, the cherubim, seraphim and ophannim, and all the angels of power, and all the angels of principalities (angels that rule over other angels), and the Elect One, and the other powers on the earth and over the water. On that day shall raise one voice, and bless and glorify and exalt in the spirit of faith, and in the spirit of wisdom, and in the spirit of patience, and in the spirit of mercy, and in the spirit of judgment and of peace, and in the spirit of goodness, and shall all say with one voice: "Blessed is He, and may the name of the Lord of spirits be blessed for ever and ever."

11 All who do not sleep above in heaven shall bless Him. All the holy ones who are in heaven shall bless Him; and all the elect who dwell in the garden of life, and every spirit who is able to bless, and glorify, and exalt, and praise Your blessed name, and to the extent of its ability all flesh shall glorify and bless Your name for ever and ever.

12 For great is the mercy of the Lord of spirits. He is long-suffering, and all His works and all that He has created He has revealed to the righteous and elect, in the name of the Lord of spirits.

[Chapter 62]

1 Thus the Lord commanded the kings and the mighty and the exalted, and those who dwell on the earth, and said: 'Open your eyes and lift up your horns if you are able to recognize the Elect One.'

2 And the Lord of spirits seated Him on the throne of His glory, and the spirit of righteousness was poured out on Him, and the word of His mouth slays all the sinners, and all the unrighteous are destroyed from in front of His face.

3 And in that day all the kings and the mighty, and the exalted and those who hold the earth shall stand up and shall see and recognize that He sits on the throne of His glory, and that righteousness is judged before Him, and no lying word is spoken before Him.

4 Then pain will come on them as on a woman in labor, and she has pain in giving birth when her child enters the mouth of the womb, and she has pain in childbirth.

5 And one portion of them shall look at the other, and they shall be terrified, and they shall look downcast, and pain shall seize them, when they see that Son of Man sitting on the throne of His glory.

6 And the kings and the mighty and all who possess the earth shall bless and glorify and exalt Him who rules over all, who was hidden.

7 For from the beginning the Son of Man was hidden, and the Most High preserved Him in the presence of His might, and revealed Him to the elect.

8 And the congregation of the elect and holy shall be sown, and all the elect shall stand before Him on that day.

9 And all the kings and the mighty and the exalted and those who rule the earth shall fall down before Him on their faces, and worship and set their hope on that Son of Man, and petition Him and supplicate for mercy at His hands.

10 Nevertheless that Lord of spirits will so press them that they shall heavily go out from His presence, and their faces shall be filled with shame, and the darkness grows deeper on their faces.

11 And He will deliver them to the angels for punishment, to execute vengeance on them because they have oppressed His children and His elect.

12 And they shall be a spectacle for the righteous and for His elect. They shall rejoice over them, because the wrath of the Lord of spirits rests on them, and His sword is drunk with their blood.

13 The righteous and elect shall be saved on that day, and they shall never again see the face of the sinners and unrighteous.

14 And the Lord of spirits will abide over them, and they shall eat, lie down and rise up with the Son of Man for ever and ever.

15 The righteous and elect shall have risen from the earth, and ceased to be downcast and they will have been clothed with garments of life.

16 And these shall be the garments of life from the Lord of spirits; they shall not wear out nor will your glory pass away from before the Lord of spirits.

[Chapter 63]

1 In those days shall the mighty and the kings who possess the earth beg Him to grant them a little respite from His angels of punishment to whom they were delivered, that they might fall down and worship before the Lord of spirits, and confess their sins before Him.

2 And they shall bless and glorify the Lord of spirits, and say: 'Blessed is the Lord of spirits and the Lord of kings, and the Lord of the mighty and the Lord of the rich, and the Lord of glory and the Lord of wisdom,

3 And every secret is revealed in front of you. Your power is from generation to generation, and your glory for ever and ever. Deep and innumerable are all your secrets, and your righteousness is beyond reckoning.

4 We have now learned that we should glorify and bless the Lord of kings and Him who is King over all kings.'

5 And they shall say: 'Would that we had a respite to glorify and give thanks and confess our faith before His glory!

6 And now we long for a little respite but find it not. We are driven away and obtain it not: And light has vanished from before us, and darkness is our dwelling-place for ever and ever;

7 Because we have not believed in Him nor glorified the name of the Lord of spirits, but our hope was in the scepter of our kingdom, and in our own glory.

8 In the day of our suffering and tribulation He does not save and we find no respite for confession that our Lord is true in all His works, and in His judgments and His justice, and His judgments have no respect of persons.

9 We pass away from before His face on account of our works, and all our sins are judged in (in comparison to) righteousness.'

10 Now they shall say to themselves: 'Our souls are full of unrighteous gain, but what we have gained does not prevent us from descending from the midst of our worldly gain into the torment (burden) of Hell (Sheol).'

11 And after that their faces shall be filled with darkness and shame before that Son of Man, and they shall be driven from His presence, and the sword shall abide before His face in their midst.

12 Thus spoke the Lord of spirits: 'This is the ordinance and judgment with respect to the mighty and the kings and the exalted and those who possess the earth before the Lord of spirits.'

[Chapter 64]

1 And other forms I saw hidden in that place.

2 I heard the voice of the angel saying: 'These are the angels who descended to the earth, and revealed what was hidden to the children of men and seduced the children of men into committing sin.'

[Chapter 65]

1 And in those days Noah saw the earth that it had sunk down and its destruction was near.

2 And he arose from there and went to the ends of the earth, and cried aloud to his grandfather, Enoch.

3 And Noah said three times with an embittered voice: "Hear me, hear me, hear me." And I said to him: 'Tell me what it is that is falling out on the earth that the earth is in such evil plight and shaken, lest perchance I shall perish with it?'

4 And there was a great disturbance on the earth, and a voice was heard from heaven, and I fell on my face. And Enoch my grandfather came and stood by me, and said to me: 'Why have you cried to me with a bitter cry and weeping?'

5 A command has gone out from the presence of the Lord concerning those who dwell on the earth that their ruin is accomplished because they have learned all the secrets of the angels, and all the violence of the Satans (deceivers, accusers);

6 And all their powers - the most secret ones - and all the power of those who practice sorcery, and the power of witchcraft, and the power of those who make molten images for the whole earth.

7 And how silver is produced from the dust of the earth, and how soft metal originates in the earth.

8 For lead and tin are not produced from the earth like the first; it is a fountain that produces them;

9 And an angel stands in it, and that angel is preeminent.' And after that my grandfather Enoch took hold of me by my hand and lifted me up, and said to me:

10 'Go, for I have asked the Lord of spirits about this disturbance on the earth. And He said to me: "Because of their unrighteousness their judgment has been determined and shall not be withheld by Me for ever. Because of the sorceries which they have searched out and learned, the earth and those who dwell on it shall be destroyed."

11 And from these, they have no place of repentance forever, because they have shown them what was hidden, and they are the damned. But as for you, my son, the Lord of spirits knows that you are pure and guiltless of this reproach concerning the secrets.

12 And He has destined your name to be among the holy, and will preserve you among those who dwell on the earth; and has destined your righteous seed both for kingship and for great honors, and from your seed shall proceed a fountain of the righteous and holy without number for ever.

[Chapter 66]

1 And after that he showed me the angels of punishment who are prepared to come and let loose all the powers of the waters which are beneath in the earth in order to bring judgment and destruction on all who dwell on the earth.

2 And the Lord of spirits gave commandment to the angels who were going out, that they should not cause the waters to rise but should hold them in check; for those angels were in charge of the forces of the waters.

3 And I went away from the presence of Enoch.

[Chapter 67]

1 And in those days the word of God came to me, and He said to me: 'Noah, your lot has come up before Me, a lot without blame, a lot of love and righteousness.

2 And now the angels are making a wooden structure, and when they have completed that task I will place My hand on it and preserve it (keep it safe), and there shall come out of it the seed of life, and a change shall set in so that the earth will not remain without inhabitants.

3 And I will establish your seed before me for ever and ever, and I will spread abroad those who dwell with you; and the face of the earth will be fruitful. They shall be blessed and multiply on the earth in the name of the Lord.'

4 And He will imprison those angels, who have shown unrighteousness, in that burning valley which my grandfather Enoch had formerly shown to me in the west among the mountains of gold and silver and iron and soft metal and tin.

5 And I saw that valley in which there was a great earth quake and a tidal waves of the waters.

6 And when all this took place, from that fiery molten metal and from the convulsion thereof in that place, there was a smell of sulfur produced, and it was connected with those waters, and that valley of the angels who had led mankind astray burned beneath that ground.

7 And there were streams of fire throughout the valley, where these angels are punished who had led astray those who dwell on the earth.

8 But those waters shall in those days serve for the kings and the mighty and the exalted, and those who dwell on the earth, for the healing of the body, but for the punishment of the spirit. Their spirit is full of lust, that they will be punished in their body, for they have denied the Lord of spirits. They will see their punishment daily, and yet, they believe not in His name.

9 There will be a relationship between the punishment and change. As their bodies burn, a change will take place in their spirit for ever and ever; for before the Lord of spirits none shall utter an idle word.

10 For the judgment shall come on them, because they believe in the lust of their body and deny the Spirit of the Lord.

11 And the waters will change in those days; for when those angels are punished in these waters, the springs shall change, and when the angels ascend, this water of the springs shall change their temperature and become cold.

12 And I heard Michael answering and saying: 'This judgment in which the angels are judged is a testimony for the kings and the mighty who possess the earth.'

13 Because these waters of judgment minister to the healing of the body of the kings and the lust of their bodies; therefore they will not see and will not believe that those waters will change and become a fire which burns for ever.

[Chapter 68]

1 And after that my grandfather Enoch gave me the explanations of all the secrets in the book of the Parables which had been given to him, and he put them together for me in the words of the book of the Parables.

2 And on that day Michael answered Raphael and said: 'The power of the spirit grips me and makes me tremble because of the severity of the judgment of the secrets, and the judgment of the angels. Who can endure the severe judgment which has been executed, and before which they melt away?'

3 And Michael answered again, and said to Raphael: 'Who would not have a softened heart concerning it, and whose mind would not be troubled by this judgment against them because of those who have led them out?'

4 And it came to pass when he stood before the Lord of spirits, Michael said thus to Raphael: 'I will not defend them under the eye of the Lord; for the Lord of spirits has been angry with them because they act as if they were the Lord.

5 Therefore all that is hidden shall come on them for ever and ever; for no other angel or man shall have his portion in this judgment, but they alone have received their judgment for ever and ever.

[Chapter 69]

1 And after this judgment I will terrify and make them tremble because they have shown this to those who dwell on the earth.

2 And behold the names of those angels: the first of them is Samjaza; the second Artaqifa; and the third Armen, the fourth Kokabe, the fifth Turael; the sixth Rumjal; the seventh Danjal; the eighth Neqael; the ninth Baraqel; the tenth Azazel; the eleventh Armaros; the twelfth Batarjal; the thirteenth Busasejal; the

fourteenth Hananel; the fifteenth Turel; and the sixteenth Simapesiel; the seventeenth Jetrel; the eighteenth Tumael; the nineteenth Turel; the twentieth Rumael; the twenty-first Azazyel;

3 And these are the chiefs of their angels and their names, and their leaders over hundreds, and leaders over fifties, and leaders over tens.

4 The name of the first Jeqon, that is, the one who led astray the sons of God, and brought them down to the earth, and led them astray through the daughters of men.

5 And the second was named Asbeel; he imparted to the holy sons of God evil counsel, and led them astray so that they defiled their bodies with the daughters of men.

6 And the third was named Gadreel; it is he who showed the children of men all the blows of death, and he led astray Eve, and showed the weapons of death to the sons of men; the shield and the coat of mail, and the sword for battle, and all the weapons of death to the children of men.

7 And from his hand they have proceeded against those who dwell on the earth from that day and for evermore.

8 And the fourth was named Penemue; he taught the children of men the bitter and the sweet, and he taught them all the secrets of their wisdom.

9 And he instructed mankind in writing with ink and paper, and thereby many sinned from eternity to eternity and until this day.

10 For men were not created for the purpose of confirming their good faith with pen and ink.

11 For men were created exactly like the angels, to the intent that they should continue pure and righteous; and death, which destroys everything, should not have taken hold of them, but through this their knowledge they are perishing, and through this power consumes them.

12 And the fifth was named Kasdeja; this is he who showed the children of men all the wicked smitings (blows) of spirits and demons, and the smitings (blows) of the embryo in the womb, that it may pass away, and the smitings (blows) of the soul the bites of the serpent, and the smitings (blows) which befall through the midday heat, the son of the serpent named Taba'et.

13 And this is the task of Kasbeel, the chief of the oath which he showed to the holy ones when he dwelt high above in glory, and its name is Biqa.

14 This (angel) requested Michael to show him the hidden name, that he might enunciate it in the oath,

15 So that those might quake before that name and oath who revealed all that was in secret to the children of men. And this is the power of this oath, for it is powerful and strong, and he placed this oath Akae in the hand of (under the control of) Michael.

16 And these are the secrets of this oath (God's promise, word) that heaven was suspended before the world was created, and for ever, and they are strong through his oath (word, promise).

17 And through it the earth was founded on the water, and from the secret recesses of the mountains come beautiful waters, from the creation of the world and to eternity.

18 And through that oath the sea was created, and as its foundation He set for it the sand against the time of its anger (rage) that it dare not pass beyond it from the creation of the world to eternity.

19 And through that oath are the depths made fast, and abide and stir not from their place from eternity to eternity.

20 And through that oath the sun and moon complete their course, and deviate not from their ordinance from eternity to eternity.

21 And through that oath the stars complete their course, and He calls them by their names, and they answer Him from eternity to eternity.

22 [And in like manner the spirits of the water, and of the winds, and of all kinds of spirits, and (their) paths from all the quarters of the winds respond to His command.]

(Author's note: Verse 22 is not complete in some translations.)

23 And there are preserved the voices of the thunder and the light of the lightning: and there are preserved the storehouses of the hail and the storehouses of the hoarfrost,

24 And the storehouses of the mist, and the storehouses of the rain and the dew. And all these believe and give thanks before the Lord of spirits, and glorify (Him) with all their power, and their food is in every act of thanksgiving; they thank and glorify and exalt the name of the Lord of spirits for ever and ever.

25 And this oath is mighty over them and through it they are preserved and their paths are preserved, and their course is not destroyed.

26 And there was great joy among them, and they blessed and glorified and exalted because the name of that Son of Man had been revealed to them.

27 And he sat on the throne of his glory, and the sum of judgment was given to the Son of Man. And he caused the sinners and all those who led the world astray to pass away and be destroyed from off the face of the earth.

28 They shall be bound with chains, and shut up and imprisoned in their place of assembly, and all their works vanish from the face of the earth.

29 And from that time forward, there shall be nothing corruptible; for that Son of Man has appeared, and has seated himself on the throne of his glory. And all evil shall pass away before his face, and the word of that Son of Man shall go out and be strong before the Lord of spirits.

[Chapter 70]

1 And it came to pass after this that during His lifetime His name was raised up to the Son of Man, and to the Lord of spirits from among those who dwell on the earth.

2 And He was raised aloft on the chariots of the spirit and His name vanished among them. And from that day I was no longer numbered among them; and He placed me between the two winds, between the North and the West, where the angels took the cords to measure the place for the elect and righteous for me.

3 And there I saw the first fathers and the righteous who dwell in that place from the beginning.

[Chapter 71]

1 And it came to pass after this that my spirit was translated (carried off) and it ascended into heaven; and I saw the sons of the holy angels (sons) of God. They were walking on flames of fire; their garments were white, and their faces shone like snow.

2 And I saw two rivers of fire, and the light of that fire shone like hyacinth, and I fell on my face before the Lord of spirits.

3 And the angel Michael, one of the archangels, seized me by my right hand, and lifted me up and led me out into all the secrets, and he showed me all the secrets of righteousness.

4 And he showed me all the secrets of the ends of heaven, and all the storehouses of all the stars, and all the lights, from where they proceed before the face of the holy ones.

5 And he translated (carried) my spirit into heaven of heavens, and I saw there as it were built of crystals, and between those crystals tongues of living fire.

6 My spirit saw circle of fire binding around the house of fire, and on its four sides were rivers full of living fire, and they encircled that house.

7 And round about were seraphim, cherubim, and ophannim; and these are they who sleep not and guard the throne of His glory.

8 And I saw angels who could not be counted, a thousand thousands, and ten thousand times ten thousand, encircling that house. And Michael, and Raphael, and Gabriel, and Phanuel, and the holy angels who are in heaven above, go in and out of that house.

9 And they came out from that house, and Michael and Gabriel, Raphael and Phanuel, and many holy angels without number.

10 And with them the Head of Days, His head white and pure as wool, and His raiment indescribable.

11 And I fell on my face, and my whole body melted, and my spirit was (transformed) transfigured. And I cried with a loud voice in the spirit of power, and I blessed and glorified and exalted.

12 And these blessings which came from my mouth were very pleasing before that Head of Days.

13 And the Head of Days came with Michael and Gabriel, Raphael and Phanuel, and thousands and ten thousands of angels without number.

14 And the angel came to me and greeted me with his voice, and said to me 'This is the Son of Man who is born to righteousness, and righteousness abides over him, and the righteousness of the Head of Days forsakes him not.'

15 And he said to me: 'He proclaims to you peace in the name of the world to come; for from there peace has proceeded since the creation of the world, and it shall be with you for ever and for ever and ever.

JOH 17:24 Father, I will that they also, whom thou hast given me, be with me where I am; that they may behold my glory, which thou hast given me: for thou lovest me before the foundation of the world.

16 And all shall walk in His ways since righteousness never forsook Him. Their dwelling-place shall be with Him and it will be their heritage, and they shall not be separated from Him for ever and ever and ever.

17 And so there shall be length of days with the Son of Man, and the righteous shall have peace and an upright way in the name of the Lord of spirits for ever and ever.'

HEB 4:3 For we which have believed do enter into rest, as he said, As I have sworn in my wrath, if they shall enter into my rest: although the works were finished from the foundation of the world.

Chapter 72

1 The book of the courses of the luminaries of heaven, the relations of each, according to their name, origin, and months (dominion and seasons) which Uriel, the holy angel who was with me, who is their guide, showed me; and he showed me all their laws (regulations) exactly as they are, and how it is with each of the years of the world and to eternity, until the new creation is accomplished which endures until eternity.

2 And this is the first law of the luminaries: the luminary the Sun has its rising in the eastern doors of heaven, and its setting in the western doors of heaven.

3 And I saw six doors in which the sun rises, and six doors in which the sun sets and the moon rises and sets in these doors, and the leaders of the stars and those whom they lead: six in the east and six in the west, and all following each other in accurately corresponding order.

4 There were also many windows to the right and left of these doors. And first there goes out the great luminary, named the Sun, and his sphere (orbit, disc) is like the sphere (orbit, disc) of heaven, and he is quite filled with illuminating and heating fire.

5 The chariot on which he ascends, the wind drives, and the sun goes down from heaven and returns through the north in order to reach the east, and is so guided that he comes to the appropriate door and shines in the face of heaven.

6 In this way he rises in the first month in the great door, which is the fourth.

7 And in that fourth door from which the sun rises in the first month are twelve windows, from which proceed a flame when they are opened in their season.

8 When the sun rises in heaven, he comes out through that fourth door, thirty mornings in succession, and sets accurately in the fourth door in the west of the heaven.

9 And during this period the day becomes daily longer and nights grow shorter to the thirtieth morning.

10 On that day the day is longer than the night by a ninth part, and the day amounts exactly to ten parts and the night to eight parts.

11 And the sun rises from that fourth door, and sets in the fourth and returns to the fifth door of the east thirty mornings, and rises from it and sets in the fifth door.

12 And then the day becomes longer by two parts and amounts to eleven parts, and the night becomes shorter and amounts to seven parts.

13 And it returns to the east and enters into the sixth door, and rises and sets in the sixth door one-and-thirty mornings on account of its sign.

14 On that day the day becomes longer than the night, and the day becomes double the night, and the day becomes twelve parts, and the night is shortened and becomes six parts.

15 And the sun mounts up to make the day shorter and the night longer, and the sun returns to the east and enters into the sixth door, and rises from it and sets thirty mornings.

16 And when thirty mornings are accomplished, the day decreases by exactly one part, and becomes eleven parts, and the night seven.

17 And the sun goes out from that sixth door in the west, and goes to the east and rises in the fifth door for thirty mornings, and sets in the west again in the fifth western door.

18 On that day the day decreases by two parts, and amounts to ten parts and the night to eight parts.

19 And the sun goes out from that fifth door and sets in the fifth door of the west, and rises in the fourth door for one-and-thirty mornings on account of its sign, and sets in the west.

20 On that day the day becomes equal with the night in length, and the night amounts to nine parts and the day to nine parts.

21 And the sun rises from that door and sets in the west, and returns to the east and rises thirty mornings in the third door and sets in the west in the third door.

22 And on that day the night becomes longer than the day, and night becomes longer than night, and day shorter than day until the thirtieth morning, and the night amounts exactly to ten parts and the day to eight parts.

23 And the sun rises from that third door and sets in the third door in the west and returns to the east, and for thirty mornings rises in the second door in the east, and in like manner sets in the second door in the west of heaven.

24 And on that day the night amounts to eleven parts and the day to seven parts.

25 And the sun rises on that day from that second door and sets in the west in the second door, and returns to the east into the first door for one-and-thirty mornings, and sets in the first door in the west of heaven.

26 And on that day the night becomes longer and amounts to the double of the day: and the night amounts exactly to twelve parts and the day to six.

(Author's note: The day is divided into 18 sections of 90 minutes each.)

27 And the sun has traversed the divisions of his orbit and turns again on those divisions of his orbit, and enters that door thirty mornings and sets also in the west opposite to it.

28 And on that night has the night decreased in length by a ninth part, and the night has become eleven parts and the day seven parts.

29 And the sun has returned and entered into the second door in the east, and returns on those his divisions of his orbit for thirty mornings, rising and setting.

30 And on that day the night decreases in length, and the night amounts to ten parts and the day to eight.

31 And on that day the sun rises from that door, and sets in the west, and returns to the east, and rises in the third door for one-and-thirty mornings, and sets in the west of heaven.

32 On that day the night decreases and amounts to nine parts, and the day to nine parts, and the night is equal to the day and the year is exactly as to its days three hundred and sixty-four.

33 And the length of the day and of the night, and the shortness of the day and of the night arise through the course of the sun these distinctions are separated'.

34 So it comes that its course becomes daily longer, and its course nightly shorter.

35 And this is the law and the course of the great luminary which is named the sun, and his return as often as he returns sixty times and rises, for ever and ever.

36 And that which rises is the great luminary, and is so named according to its appearance, according as the Lord commanded.

37 As he rises, so he sets and decreases not, and rests not, but runs day and night, and his light is sevenfold brighter than that of the moon; but in regard to size, they are both equal.

[Chapter 73]

1 And after this law I saw another law dealing with the smaller luminary, which is named the Moon.

653

2 And her orbit is like the sphere (orbit, disc) of heaven, and her chariot in which she rides is driven by the wind, and light is given to her in measurement.

3 And her rising and setting change every month and her days are like the days of the sun, and when her light is uniformly (completely) full it amounts to the seventh part of the light of the sun.

4 And thus she rises. And her first phase in the east comes out on the thirtieth morning and on that day she becomes visible, and constitutes for you the first phase of the moon on the thirtieth day together with the sun in the door where the sun rises.

5 And the one half of her goes out by a seventh part, and her whole disc is empty, without light, with the exception of one-seventh part of it, and the fourteenth part of her light.

6 And when she receives one-seventh part of the half of her light, her light amounts to one-seventh part and the half thereof.

7 And she sets with the sun, and when the sun rises the moon rises with him and receives the half of one part of light, and in that night in the beginning of her morning in the beginning of the lunar day the moon sets with the sun, and is invisible that night with the fourteen parts and the half of one of them.

8 And she rises on that day with exactly a seventh part, and comes out and recedes from the rising of the sun, and in her remaining days she becomes bright in the remaining thirteen parts.

[Chapter 74]

1 And I saw another course, a law for her, and how according to that law she performs her monthly revolution.

2 And all these Uriel, the holy angel who is the leader of them all, showed to me, and their positions, and I wrote down their positions as he showed them to me, and I wrote down their months as they were, and the appearance of their lights until fifteen days were accomplished.

3 In single seventh parts she accomplishes all her light in the east, and in single seventh parts accomplishes all her darkness in the west.

4 And in certain months she alters her settings, and in certain months she pursues her own peculiar course.

5 In two months the moon sets with the sun: in those two middle doors the third and the fourth.

6 She goes out for seven days, and turns about and returns again through the door where the sun rises, and all her light is full; and she recedes from the sun, and in eight days enters the sixth door from which the sun goes out.

7 And when the sun goes out from the fourth door she goes out seven days, until she goes out from the fifth and turns back again in seven days into the fourth door and accomplishes all her light; and she recedes and enters into the first door in eight days.

8 And she returns again in seven days into the fourth door from which the sun goes out.

9 Thus I saw their positions, how the moons rose and the sun set in those days.

10 And if five years are added together the sun has an excess of thirty days, and all the days which accrue to it for one of those five years, when they are full, amount to 364 days.

11 And an excess of the sun and of the stars amounts to six days; in five years six days every year come to 30 days, and the moon falls behind the sun and stars to the number of 30 days.

12 And the sun and the stars bring in all the years exactly, so that they do not advance or delay their position by a single day to eternity; but complete the years with perfect justice in 364 days.

13 In three years there are 1,092 days, and in five years 1,820 days, so that in eight years there are 2,912 days.

14 For the moon alone the days amount in three years to 1,062 days, and in five years she falls 50 days behind to the sum of 1,770 there is five to be added 1,000 and 62 days.

15 And in five years there are 1,770 days, so that for the moon the days six in eight years amount to 21,832 days.

16 For in eight years she falls behind to the amount of 80 days, all the days she falls behind in eight years are 80.

17 And the year is accurately completed in conformity with their world-stations and the stations of the sun, which rise from the doors through which the sun rises and sets 30 days.

[Chapter 75]

1 And the leaders of the heads of the (ten) thousands, who are in charge of the whole creation and over all the stars, have also to do with the four days of the year which are not counted in the yearly calendar, being not separated from their office, according to the reckoning of the year, and these render service on the four days which are not counted in the reckoning of the year.

2 And because of them men go wrong in them, for those luminaries truly render service to the stations of the world, one in the first door, one on the third door of heaven, one in the fourth door, and one in the sixth door, and the exactness of the year is accomplished through its separate three hundred and sixty-four stations.

3 For the signs and the times and the years and the days the angel Uriel showed to me, whom the Lord of glory has set for ever over all the luminaries of heaven, in heaven and in the world, that they should rule on the face of heaven and be seen on the earth, and be leaders for the day via the sun and the night via the moon, and stars, and all the ministering creatures which make their revolution in all the chariots of heaven.

4 In like manner, twelve doors Uriel showed me, open in the sphere (disc) of the sun's chariot in heaven, through which the rays of the sun break out; and from them is warmth diffused over the earth, when they are opened at their appointed seasons.

5 And there are openings for the wind and the spirit of dew that when they are opened, stand open in heaven at the ends of the earth.

6 As for the twelve doors in the heaven, at the ends of the earth, out of which go out the sun, moon, and stars, and all the works of heaven in the east and in the west; there are many windows open to the left and right of them,

7 And one window at its appointed season produces warmth, corresponding to the doors from which the stars come out as He has commanded them; and in which they are set, corresponding to their number.

8 And I saw chariots in heaven, running in the world, above those doors in which the stars that never set.

9 And one is larger than all the rest, and it is that that makes its course through the entire world.

[Chapter 76]

1 At the ends of the earth I saw twelve doors open to all quarters of heaven, from which the winds go out and blow over the earth.

2 Three of them are open on the face of heaven, and three in the west; and three on the right of heaven, and three on the left.

3 And the three first are those of the east, and three are of the north, and three, after those on the left, of the south, and three of the west.

4 Through four of these come winds of blessing and prosperity (peace), and from those eight come hurtful winds; when they are sent, they bring destruction on all the earth and the water on it, and on all who dwell on it, and on everything which is in the water and on the land.

5 And the first wind from those doors, called the east wind, comes out through the first door which is in the east, inclining towards the south; from it desolation, drought, heat, and destruction come out .

6 And through the second door in the middle comes what is fitting (right, correct), and there come rain and fruitfulness and prosperity and dew. And through the third door which lies toward the north comes cold and drought.

7 And after these, comes out the south winds through three doors; through the first door of them inclining to the east comes out a hot wind.

8 And through the middle door next to it there comes out fragrant smells, and dew and rain, and prosperity and health.

9 And through the third door which lies to the west dew comes out and also rain, locusts and desolation.

10 And from the seventh door in the east comes the north winds, and dew, rain, locusts and desolation.

11 And from the center door come health and rain and dew and prosperity; and through the third door in the west come cloud and hoar-frost, and snow and rain, and dew and locusts.

12 And after these came the four west winds; through the first door adjoining the north come out dew and hoar-frost, and cold and snow and frost.

13 And from the center door come out dew and rain, and prosperity and blessing.

14 And through the last door which adjoins the south, come drought and desolation, and burning and destruction. And the twelve doors of the four quarters of heaven are therewith completed, and all their laws and all their plagues and all their benefactions have I shown to you, my son Methuselah.

[Chapter 77]

1 And the first quarter is called the east, because it is the first; and the second, the south, because the Most High will descend there. From there will He who is blessed for ever descend.

2 And the west quarter is named the diminished, because there all the luminaries of the heaven wane and go down.

3 And the fourth quarter, named the north, is divided into three parts: the first of them is for the dwelling of men; and the second contains seas of water, and the abyss (deep) and forests and rivers, and darkness and clouds; and the third part contains the garden of righteousness.

4 I saw seven high mountains, higher than all the mountains which are on the earth: and from here comes hoar-frost, and days, seasons, and years pass away.

5 I saw seven rivers on the earth larger than all the rivers. One of them coming from the west pours its waters into the Great Sea.

6 And these two come from the north to the sea and pour their waters into the Erythraean Sea in the east.

7 And the remaining four come out on the side of the north to their own sea, two of them to the Erythraean Sea, and two into the Great Sea and some say they discharge themselves there into the desert.

8 I saw seven great islands in the sea and in the mainland, two in the mainland and five in the Great Sea.

[Chapter 78]

1 And the names of the sun are the following: the first Orjares, and the second Tomas.

2 And the moon has four names: the first name is Asonja, the second Ebla, the third Benase, and the fourth Erae.

3 These are the two great luminaries; their spheres (disc) are like the sphere (disc) of the heaven, and the size of the spheres (disc) of both is alike.

4 In the sphere (disc) of the sun there are seven portions of light which are added to it more than to the moon, and in fixed measurements it is transferred until the seventh portion of the sun is exhausted.

5 And they set and enter the doors of the west, and make their revolution by the north, and come out through the eastern doors on the face of heaven.

6 And when the moon rises one-fourteenth part appears in heaven, and on the fourteenth day the moon's light becomes full.

7 And fifteen parts of light are transferred to her until the fifteenth day when her light is full, according to the sign of the year, and she becomes fifteen parts, and the moon grows by an additional fourteenth parts.

8 And as the moon's waning decreases on the first day to fourteen parts of her light, on the second to thirteen parts of light, on the third to twelve, on the fourth to eleven, on the fifth to ten, on the sixth to nine, on the seventh to eight, on the eighth to seven, on the ninth to six, on the tenth to five, on the eleventh to four, on the twelfth to three, on the thirteenth to two, on the fourteenth to the half of a seventh, and all her remaining light disappears wholly on the fifteenth.

9 And in certain months the month has twenty-nine days and once twenty-eight.

10 And Uriel showed me another law: when light is transferred to the moon, and on which side it is transferred to her by the sun.

11 During all the period during which the moon is growing in her light, she is transferring it to herself when opposite to the sun during fourteen days her light is full in heaven, and when she is ablaze throughout, her light is full in heaven.

12 And on the first day she is called the new moon, for on that day the light rises on her.

13 She becomes full moon exactly on the day when the sun sets in the west, and from the east she rises at night, and the moon shines the whole night through until the sun rises over against her and the moon is seen over against the sun.

14 On the side whence the light of the moon comes out, there again she wanes until all the light vanishes and all the days of the month are at an end, and her sphere (disc) is empty, void of light.

15 And three months she makes of thirty days, and at her time she makes three months of twenty-nine days each, in which she accomplishes her waning in the first period of time, and in the first door for one hundred and seventy-seven days.

16 And in the time of her going out she appears for three months consisting of thirty days each, and she appears for three months consisting of twenty-nine each.

17 By night she looks like a man for twenty days each time, and by day she appears like heaven, and there is nothing else in her save her light.

[Chapter 79]

1 And now, my son Methuselah, I have shown you everything, and the law of all the stars of heaven is completed.

2 And he showed me all the laws of these for every day, and for every season of every rule, and for every year, and for its going out, and for the order prescribed to it every month and every week.

3 And the waning of the moon which takes place in the sixth door, for in this sixth door her light is accomplished, and after that there is the beginning of the waning.

4 And the waning which takes place in the first door in its season, until one hundred and seventy-seven days are accomplished, calculated according to weeks, twenty-five weeks and two days.

5 She falls behind the sun and the order of the stars exactly five days in the course of one period, and when this place which you see has been traversed.

6 Such is the picture and sketch of every luminary which Uriel the archangel, who is their leader, showed to me.

[Chapter 80]

1 And in those days the angel Uriel answered and said to me: 'Behold, I have shown you everything, Enoch, and I have revealed everything to you that you should see this sun and this moon, and the leaders of the stars of heaven and all those who turn them, their tasks and times and departures.

2 And in the days of the sinners the years shall be shortened, and their seed shall be tardy on their lands and fields, and all things on the earth shall alter, and shall not appear in their time. And the rain shall be kept back, and heaven shall withhold it.

3 And in those times the fruits of the earth shall be backward, and shall not grow in their time, and the fruits of the trees shall be withheld in their time.

4 And the moon shall alter her customs, and not appear at her time.

5 And in those days the sun shall be seen and he shall journey in the evening on the extremity of the great chariot in the west and shall shine more brightly than accords with the order of light.

6 And many rulers of the stars shall transgress their customary order. And these shall alter their orbits and tasks, and not appear at the seasons prescribed to them.

7 And the whole order of the stars shall be concealed from the sinners, and the thoughts of those on the earth shall err concerning them, and they shall be altered from all their ways, they shall err and take them to be gods.

8 And evil shall be multiplied on them, and punishment shall come on them so as to destroy all.'

[Chapter 81]

1 And he said to me: 'Enoch, look at these heavenly tablets and read what is written on them, and mark every individual fact.'

2 And I looked at the heavenly tablets, and read everything which was written on it and understood everything, and read the book of all the deeds of mankind, and of all the children of flesh; that shall be on the earth to the end of generations.

3 And I blessed the great Lord the King of glory for ever, in that He has made all the works of the world, and I exalted the Lord because of His patience, and blessed Him because of the children of men (sons of Abraham).

4 And then I said: 'Blessed is the man who dies in righteousness and goodness, concerning whom there is no book of unrighteousness written, and against whom no day of judgment shall be found.'

5 And the seven holy ones brought me and placed me on the earth before the door of my house, and said to me: 'Declare everything to your son Methuselah, and show to all your children that no flesh is righteous in the sight of the Lord, for He is their Creator.

6 For one year we will leave you with your son, until you give your last commands, that you may teach your children and record it for them, and testify to all your children; and in the second year they shall take you from their midst.

7 Let your heart be strong, for the good shall proclaim righteousness to the good; the righteous shall rejoice with the righteous, and shall wish one another well.

8 But the sinners shall die with the sinners, and the apostate shall go down with the apostate.

9 And those who practice righteousness shall die on account of the deeds of men, and be taken away on account of the deeds of the godless.'

10 And in those days they finished speaking to me, and I came to my people, blessing the Lord of the world.

[Chapter 82]

1 And now, my son Methuselah, all these things I am recounting to you and writing down for you! And I have revealed to you everything, and given you books concerning all these; so, my son Methuselah, preserve the books from your father's hand, and see that you deliver them to the generations of the world.

2 I have given wisdom to you and to your children, and those children to come, that they may give it to their children for generations. This wisdom namely that passes their understanding.

3 And those who understand it shall not sleep, but shall listen that they may learn this wisdom, and it shall please those that eat thereof better than good food.

4 Blessed are all the righteous, blessed are all those who walk in the way of righteousness and sin not as the sinners, in the numbering of all their days in which the sun traverses heaven, entering into and departing from the doors for thirty days with the heads of thousands of the order of the stars, together with the four which are within the calendar which divide the four portions of the year, which lead them and enter with them four days.

5 Owing to them men shall be at fault and not count them in the whole number of days of the year. Men shall be at fault, and not recognize them accurately.

6 For they belong to the calculations of the year and are truly recorded therein for ever, one in the first door and one in the third, and one in the fourth and one in the sixth, and the year is completed in three hundred and sixty-four days.

7 And the account of it is accurate and the recorded counting thereof is exact; for the luminaries, and months and festivals, and years and days, has Uriel shown and revealed to me, to whom the Lord of the whole creation of the world has subjected the host of heaven.

8 And he has power over night and day in heaven to cause the light to shine on men via the sun, moon, and stars, and all the powers of the heaven which revolve in their circular chariots. And these are the orders of the stars, which set in their places, and in their seasons and festivals and months.

9 And these are the names of those who lead them, who watch that they enter at their times, in their orders, in their seasons, in their months, in their periods of dominion, and in their positions.

10 Their four leaders who divide the four parts of the year enter first; and after them the twelve leaders of the orders who divide the months; and for the three hundred and sixty days there are heads over thousands who divide the days; and for the four days in the calendar there are the leaders which divide the four parts of the year.

11 And these heads over thousands are interspersed between leader and leader, each behind a station, but their leaders make the division.

12 And these are the names of the leaders who divide the four parts of the year which are ordained:

13 Milki'el, Hel'emmelek, and Mel'ejal, and Narel. And the names of those who lead them: Adnar'el, and Ijasusa'el, and 'Elome'el.

14 These three follow the leaders of the orders, and there is one that follows the three leaders of the orders which follow those leaders of stations that divide the four parts of the year. In the beginning of the year Melkejal rises first and rules, who is named Tam'aini and sun, and all the days of his dominion while he bears rule are ninety-one days.

15 And these are the signs of the days which are to be seen on earth in the days of his dominion: sweat, and heat; and calms; and all the trees bear fruit, and leaves are produced on all the trees, and the harvest of wheat, and the rose-flowers, and all the flowers which come out in the field, but the trees of the winter season become withered.

16 And these are the names of the leaders which are under them: Berka'el, Zelebs'el, and another who is added a head of a thousand, called Hilujaseph: and the days of the dominion of this leader are at an end.

17 The next leader after him is Hel'emmelek, whom one names the shining sun, and all the days of his light are ninety-one days.

18 And these are the signs of his days on the earth: glowing heat and dryness, and the trees ripen their fruits and produce all their fruits ripe and ready, and the sheep pair and become pregnant, and all the fruits of the earth are gathered in, and everything that is in the fields, and the winepress: these things take place in the days of his dominion.

19 These are the names, and the orders, and the leaders of those heads of thousands: Gida'ljal, Ke'el, and He'el, and the name of the head of a thousand which is added to them, Asfa'el: and the days of his dominion are at an end.

[Chapter 83]

1 And now, my son Methuselah, I will show you all my visions which I have seen, recounting them before you.

2 I saw two visions before I got married (took a wife), and the one was quite unlike the other: the first when I was learning to write: the second before I married (took) your mother, was when I saw a terrible vision.

3 And regarding them I prayed to the Lord. I had laid down in the house of my grandfather Mahalalel, when I saw in a vision how heaven collapsed and was carried off (removed, torn down) and fell to the earth.

4 And when it fell to the earth I saw how the earth was swallowed up in a great abyss, and mountains were suspended on mountains, and hills sank down on hills, and high trees were ripped from their stems, and hurled down and sunk in the abyss.

5 And then a word fell into my mouth, and I lifted up my voice to cry aloud, and said:

6 'The earth is destroyed.' And my grandfather Mahalalel woke me as I lay near him, and said to me: 'Why do you cry so, my son, and why do you make such moaning (lamentation)?'

7 And I recounted to him the whole vision which I had seen, and he said to me: 'You have seen a terrible thing , my son. Your dream (vision) is of a grave time and concerns the secrets of all the sin of the earth: it must sink into the abyss and be totally destroyed.

8 And now, my son, arise and pray to the Lord of glory, since you are a believer, that a remnant may remain on the earth, and that He may not destroy the whole earth.

9 My son, from heaven all this will come on the earth, and on the earth there will be great destruction.

10 After that I arose and prayed and implored and besought (God), and wrote down my prayer for the generations of the world, and I will show everything to you, my son Methuselah.

11 And when I had gone out below and seen the heaven, and the sun rising in the east, and the moon setting in the west, and a few stars, and the whole earth, and everything as He had known it in the beginning, then I blessed the Lord of judgment and exalted Him because He had made the sun to go out from the windows of the east, and he ascended and rose on the face of heaven, and set out and kept traversing the path shown to it.

[Chapter 84]

1 And I lifted up my hands in righteousness and blessed the Holy and Great One, and spoke with the breath of my mouth, and with the tongue of flesh, which God has made for the children of the flesh of men, that they should speak therewith, and He gave them breath and a tongue and a mouth that they should speak therewith:

2 Blessed be you, O Lord, King, Great and mighty in your greatness, Lord of the whole creation of heaven, King of kings and God of the whole world. And your power and kingship and greatness abide for ever and ever, and throughout all generations your dominion and all heavens are your throne for ever, and the whole earth your footstool for ever and ever.

3 For you have made and you rule all things, and nothing is too hard for you, wisdom never departs from the place of your throne, nor turns away from your presence. You know and see and hear everything, and there is nothing hidden from you for you see everything.

4 And now the angels of your heavens are guilty of trespass, and on the flesh of men abide your wrath until the great day of judgment.

5 And now, O God and Lord and Great King, I implore and beseech you to fulfill my prayer, to leave me a posterity on earth, and not destroy all the flesh of man, and make the earth without inhabitant, so that there should be an eternal destruction.

6 And now, my Lord, destroy from the earth the flesh which has aroused your wrath, but the flesh of righteousness and uprightness establish as an eternal plant bearing seed forever, and hide not your face from the prayer of your servant, O Lord.'

[Author's note: In chapter 85 and following, a series of animals is mentioned. These seem to refer to nations or ethnicities. For example, the eagles may refer to the Roman empire, the Islamic nation is represented by the asses, Abraham may be the white bull, Jacob is a sheep, Egyptians are wolves, and so on. See Daniel Chapter 10 for other like imagery.

Other writers have attempted to be more specific. Starting with the concept of Noah's three sons, Shem, Ham and Japheth, giving rise to all the animals or nations in Chapter 89, they link the white bull to Abraham; Abraham's son, Ishmael, to the wild ass; Isaac to the white bull; Esau to the wild boar; Jacob to the white sheep; the Assyrians to lions; The small lambs with open eyes to the Essenes; Jesus to the "sheep with the big horn"; and in 90.17, the final twelve shepherds represent the Christian era.]

[Chapter 85]

1 And after this I saw another dream, and I will show the whole dream to you, my son.

2 And Enoch lifted up his voice and spoke to his son Methuselah: 'I will speak to you, my son, hear my words. Incline your ear to the dream (vision) of your father.

3 Before I married (took) your mother Edna, I saw in a vision on my bed, and behold a bull came out from the earth, and that bull was white.

4 And after it came out a heifer, and along with this later came out two bulls, one of them black and the other red.

5 And that black bull gored the red one and pursued him over the earth, and then I could no longer see that red bull. But that black bull grew and that heifer went with him, and I saw that many oxen proceeded from him which resembled and followed him.

6 And that cow, that first one, went from the presence of that first bull in order to seek that red one, but found him not, and mourned with a great lamentation and sought him.

7 And I looked until that first bull came to her and quieted (calmed) her, and from that time onward she cried no more.

8 And after that she bore another white bull, and after him she bore many bulls and black cows.

9 And I saw in my sleep that white bull likewise grew and became a great white bull, and from him proceeded many white bulls, and they resembled him. And they began to father many white bulls, which resembled them, one following another.

[Chapter 86]

1 And again I looked with my eyes as I slept, and I saw the heaven above, and behold a star fell from heaven, and it arose and ate and pastured among those oxen (bulls).

2 And after that I saw the large and the black oxen (bulls), and behold they all changed their stalls and pastures and their heifers (cattle) , and began to live with each other.

3 And again I saw in the vision, and looked towards heaven, and behold I saw many stars descend and cast themselves down from heaven to that first star, and they became bulls among those cattle and pastured with them.

4 And I looked at them and saw they all let out their private (sexual) members, like horses, and began to mount the cows of the bulls (oxen), and they all became pregnant and bore elephants, camels, and asses.

5 And all the bulls (oxen) feared them and were frightened of them, and began to bite with their teeth and to devour, and to gore with their horns.

6 And, moreover, they began to devour those oxen; and behold all the children of the earth began to tremble and shake before them and to flee from them.

[Chapter 87]

1 And again I saw how they began to gore each other and to devour each other, and the earth began to cry aloud.

2 And I raised my eyes again to heaven, and I saw in the vision, and behold there came out from heaven beings who were like white men, and four went out from that place and three others with them.

3 And those three that had come out last grasped me by my hand and took me up, away from the generations of the earth, and raised me up to a high place, and showed me a tower raised high above the earth, and all the hills were lower.

4 And one said to me: 'Remain here until you see everything that befalls those elephants, camels, and asses, and the stars and the oxen, and all of them.'

[Chapter 88]

1 And I saw one of those four who had come out first, and he seized that first star which had fallen from heaven, and bound it hand and foot and cast it into an abyss; now that abyss was narrow and deep, and horrible and dark.

2 And one of them drew a sword, and gave it to those elephants and camels and asses then they began to smite each other, and the whole earth shook because of them.

3 And as I was beholding in the vision one of those four who had come out stoned them from heaven, and gathered and took all the great stars whose private (sexual) members were like those of horses, and bound them all hand and foot, and threw them in an abyss of the earth.

[Chapter 89]

1 And one of those four went to that white bull and instructed him in a secret, and he was terrified: he was born a bull and became a man, and built for himself a great vessel and dwelt on it.

2 And three bulls dwelt with him in the vessel and they were covered over. And again I raised my eyes towards heaven and saw a high roof, with seven water torrents on it, and those torrents flowed with much water into an enclosure. And I looked again, and behold fountains were opened on the surface of that great enclosure, and the water began to bubble and swell and rise on the surface, and I saw that enclosure until all its surface was covered with water.

3 And the water, the darkness, and mist increased on it; and as I looked at the height of that water, the water had risen above the height of the enclosure, and was streaming over the enclosure, and it stood on the earth.

4 And all the cattle of the enclosure were gathered together until I saw how they sank and were swallowed up and perished in that water.

5 But that vessel floated on the water, while all the oxen (bulls) and elephants and camels and asses sank to the bottom with all the animals, so that I could no longer see them, and they were not able to escape, but perished and sank into the depths.

6 And again I watched in the vision until those water torrents were removed from that high roof, and the chasms of the earth were leveled up and other abysses were opened.

7 Then the water began to run down into these abysses, until the earth became visible; but that vessel settled on the earth, and the darkness retired and light appeared.

8 But that white bull which had become a man came out of that vessel, and the three bulls with him, and one of those three was white like that bull, and one of them was red as blood, and one black; and that white bull departed from them.

9 And they began to bring out beasts of the field and birds, so that there arose different genera: lions, tigers, wolves, dogs, hyenas, wild boars, foxes, squirrels, swine, falcons, vultures, kites, eagles, and ravens; and among them was born a white bull.

10 And they began to bite one another; but that white bull which was born among them fathered a wild ass and a white bull with it, and the wild asses multiplied.

11 But that bull which was born from him fathered a black wild boar and a white sheep; and the former fathered many boars, but the sheep gave birth to twelve sheep.

12 And when those twelve sheep had grown, they gave up one of them to the asses, and the asses again gave up that sheep to the wolves, and that sheep grew up among the wolves.

13 And the Lord brought the eleven sheep to live with it and to pasture with it among the wolves and they multiplied and became many flocks of sheep.

14 And the wolves began to fear them, and they oppressed them until they destroyed their little ones, and they threw their young into a deep river, but those sheep began to cry aloud on account of their little ones, and to complain to their Lord.

15 And a sheep which had been saved from the wolves fled and escaped to the wild asses; and I saw the sheep how they lamented and cried, and besought their Lord with all their might, until that Lord of the sheep descended at the voice of the sheep from a high abode, and came to them and pastured them.

16 And He called that sheep which had escaped the wolves, and spoke with it concerning the wolves that it should admonish them not to touch the sheep.

17 And the sheep went to the wolves according to the word of the Lord, and another sheep met it and went with it, and the two went and entered together into the assembly of those wolves, and spoke with them and admonished them not to touch the sheep from then on.

18 And on it I saw the wolves, and how they more harshly oppressed the sheep with all their power; and the sheep cried aloud.

19 And the Lord came to the sheep and they began to beat those wolves, and the wolves began to make lamentation; but the sheep became quiet and ceased to cry out.

20 And I saw the sheep until they departed from among the wolves; but the eyes of the wolves were blinded, and the wolves departed in pursuit of the sheep with all their power.

21 And the Lord of the sheep went with them, as their leader, and all His sheep followed Him.

22 And his face was dazzling and glorious and terrible to behold. But the wolves began to pursue those sheep until they reached a sea of water.

23 And that sea was divided, and the water stood on this side and on that before their face, and their Lord led them and placed Himself between them and the wolves.

24 And as those wolves had not yet seen the sheep, they proceeded into the midst of that sea, and the wolves followed the sheep, and those wolves ran after them into that sea.

25 And when they saw the Lord of the sheep, they turned to flee before His face, but that sea gathered itself together, and became as it had been created, and the water swelled and rose until it covered the wolves.

26 And I watched until all the wolves who pursued those sheep perished and were drowned.

27 But the sheep escaped from that water and went out into a wilderness, where there was no water and no grass; and they began to open their eyes and to see;

28 And I saw the Lord of the sheep pasturing them and giving them water and grass, and that sheep going and leading them.

29 And the sheep ascended to the summit of that high rock, and the Lord of the sheep sent it to them. And after that I saw the Lord of the sheep who stood before them, and His appearance was great and terrible and majestic, and all those sheep saw Him and were afraid before His face.

30 And they all feared and trembled because of Him, and they cried to that sheep which was among them:

31 'We are not able to stand before our Lord or to behold Him.' And that sheep which led them again ascended to the summit of that rock, but the sheep began to be blinded and to wander from the way which he had showed them, but that sheep did not realize it.

32 And the Lord of the sheep was very angry with them, and that sheep discovered it, and went down from the summit of the rock, and came to the sheep, and found the greatest part of them blinded and fallen away.

33 And when they saw it they feared and trembled at its presence, and desired to return to their folds. And that sheep took other sheep with it, and came to those sheep which had fallen away, and began to slay them; and the sheep feared its presence, and thus that sheep brought back those sheep that had fallen away, and they returned to their folds.

34 And I saw in this vision until that sheep became a man and built a house for the Lord of the sheep, and placed all the sheep in that house.

35 And I saw until this sheep which had met that sheep which led them fell asleep (died); and I saw until all the great sheep perished and little ones arose in their place, and they came to a pasture, and approached a stream of water.

36 Then that sheep, their leader which had become a man, withdrew from them and fell asleep (died), and all the sheep looked for it (sought it) and cried over it with a great crying.

37 And I saw until they left off crying for that sheep and crossed that stream of water, and there arose the two sheep as leaders in the place of those which had led them and fallen asleep.

38 And I saw until the sheep came to a good place, and a pleasant and glorious land, and I saw until those sheep were satisfied; and that house stood among them in the (green) pleasant land.

39 And sometimes their eyes were opened, and sometimes blinded, until another sheep arose and led them and brought them all back, and their eyes were opened.

40 And the dogs and the foxes and the wild boars began to devour those sheep until the Lord of the sheep raised up another sheep, a ram from their midst, which led them.

41 And that ram began to butt on either side those dogs, foxes, and wild boars until he had destroyed them all.

42 And that sheep whose eyes were opened saw that ram, which was among the sheep, until it forsook its glory and began to butt those sheep, and trampled on them, and behaved itself unseemly.

43 And the Lord of the sheep sent the lamb to another lamb and raised it to being a ram and leader of the sheep instead of that ram which had forsaken its glory.

44 And it went to it and spoke to it alone, and raised it to being a ram, and made it the prince and leader of the sheep; but during all these things those dogs oppressed the sheep.

45 And the first ram pursued the second ram, and the second ram arose and fled before it; and I saw until those dogs pulled down the first ram.

46 And that second ram arose and led the little sheep. And those sheep grew and multiplied; but all the dogs, and foxes, and wild boars feared and fled before it, and that ram butted and killed the wild beasts, and those wild beasts had no longer any power among the sheep and robbed them no more of anything.

47 And that ram fathered many sheep and fell asleep; and a little sheep became ram in its place, and became prince and leader of those sheep.

48 And that house became great and broad, and it was built for those sheep: and a high and great tower was built on the house for the Lord of the sheep, and that house was low, but the tower was elevated and high, and the Lord of the sheep stood on that tower and they offered a full table before him.

49 And again I saw those sheep that they again erred and went many ways, and forsook that their house, and the Lord of the sheep called some from among the sheep and sent them to the sheep, but the sheep began to slay them.

50 And one of them was saved and was not slain, and it sped away and cried aloud over the sheep; and they sought to slay it, but the Lord of the sheep saved it from the sheep, and brought it up to me, and caused it to live there.

51 And many other sheep He sent to those sheep to testify to them and lament over them.

52 And after that I saw that when they forsook the house of the Lord and His tower they fell away entirely, and their eyes were blinded; and I saw the Lord of the sheep how He worked much slaughter among them in their herds until those sheep invited that slaughter and betrayed His place.

53 And He gave them over into the hands of the lions and tigers, and wolves and hyenas, and into the hand of the foxes, and to all the wild beasts, and those wild beasts began to tear in pieces those sheep.

54 And I saw that He forsook their house and their tower and gave them all into the hand of the lions, to tear and devour them, into the hand of all the wild beasts.

55 And I began to cry aloud with all my power, and to appeal to the Lord of the sheep, because the sheep were being devoured by all the wild beasts.

56 But He remained unmoved, though He saw it, and rejoiced that they were devoured and swallowed and robbed, and left them to be devoured in the hand of all the beasts.

57 And He called seventy shepherds, and gave those sheep to them that they might pasture them, and He spoke to the shepherds and their companions: 'Let each individual of you pasture the sheep from now on, and everything that I shall command you that do you.

58 And I will deliver them over to you duly numbered, and tell you which of them are to be destroyed- and them you will destroy.' And He gave over to them those sheep.

59 And He called another and spoke to him: 'Observe and mark everything that the shepherds will do to those sheep; for they will destroy more of them than I have commanded them.

60 And every excess and the destruction which will be done through the shepherds, record how many they destroy according to my command, and how many according to their own caprice; record against every individual shepherd all the destruction he effects.

61 And read out before me by number how many they destroy, and how many they deliver over for destruction, that I may have this as a testimony against them, and know every deed of the shepherds, that I may comprehend and see what they do, whether or not they abide by my command which I have commanded them.

62 But they shall not know it, and you shall not declare it to them, nor admonish them, but only record against each individual all the destruction which the shepherds effect each in his time and lay it all before me.'

63 And I saw until those shepherds pastured in their season, and they began to slay and to destroy more than they were bidden, and they delivered those sheep into the hand of the lions.

64 And the lions and tigers ate and devoured the greater part of those sheep, and the wild boars ate along with them; and they burned that tower and demolished that house.

65 And I became very sorrowful over that tower because that house of the sheep was demolished, and afterwards I was unable to see if those sheep entered that house.

66 And the shepherds and their associates delivered over those sheep to all the wild beasts, to devour them, and each one of them received in his time a definite number, it was written by the other in a book how many each one of them destroyed of them.

67 And each one slew and destroyed many more than was prescribed; and I began to weep and lament on account of those sheep.

68 And thus in the vision I saw that one who wrote, how he wrote down every one that was destroyed by those shepherds, day by day, and carried up and laid down and showed actually the whole book to the Lord of the sheep - everything that they had done, and all that each one of them had made away with, and all that they had given over to destruction.

69 And the book was read before the Lord of the sheep, and He took the book from his hand and read it and sealed it and laid it down.

70 And I saw how the shepherds pastured for twelve hours, and behold three of those sheep turned back and came and entered and began to build up all that had fallen down of that house; but the wild boars tried to hinder them, but they were not able.

71 And they began again to build as before, and they raised up that tower, and it was named the high tower; and they began again to place a table before the tower, but all the bread on it was polluted and not pure.

72 And as touching all this the eyes of those sheep were blinded so that they saw not, and the eyes of their shepherds likewise were blinded; and they delivered them in large numbers to their shepherds for destruction, and they trampled the sheep with their feet and devoured them.

73 And the Lord of the sheep remained unmoved until all the sheep were dispersed over the field and mingled with the beasts, and the shepherds did not save them out of the hand of the beasts.

74 And this one who wrote the book carried it up, and showed it and read it before the Lord of the sheep, and implored Him on their account, and besought Him on their account as he showed Him all the doings of the shepherds, and gave testimony before Him against all the shepherds.

75 And he took the actual book and laid it down beside Him and departed.

[Chapter 90]

1 And I saw until that in this manner thirty-five shepherds undertook the pasturing of the sheep, and they completed their periods as did the first; and others received them into their hands, to pasture them for their period, each shepherd in his own period.

2 And after that I saw in my vision all the birds of heaven coming, the eagles, the vultures, the kites, the ravens; but the eagles led all the birds; and they began to devour those sheep, and to pick out their eyes and to devour their flesh.

3 And the sheep cried out because their flesh was being devoured by the birds, and as for me I looked and lamented in my sleep over that shepherd who pastured the sheep.

4 And I saw until those sheep were devoured by the dogs and eagles and kites, and they left neither flesh nor skin nor sinew remaining on them until only their bones stood there; and their bones too fell to the earth and the sheep became few.

5 And I saw until that twenty-three had undertaken the pasturing and completed in their many periods fifty-eight times.

6 But behold lambs were borne by those white sheep, and they began to open their eyes and to see, and to cry to the sheep.

7 They cried to them, but they did not hearken to what they said to them, but were very deaf, and their eyes were very blinded.

8 And I saw in the vision how the ravens flew on those lambs and took one of those lambs, and dashed the sheep in pieces and devoured them.

9 And I saw until horns grew on those lambs, and the ravens cast down their horns; and I saw until there sprouted a great horn of one of those sheep, and their eyes were opened.

10 And it looked at them and their eyes opened, and it cried to the sheep, and the rams saw it and all ran to it.

11 And notwithstanding all this, those eagles and vultures and ravens and kites kept on tearing the sheep and swooping down on them and devouring them until the sheep remained silent, but the rams lamented and cried out.

12 And those ravens fought and battled with it and sought to lay low its horn, but they had no power over it.

13 All the eagles and vultures and ravens and kites were gathered together, and there came with them all the sheep of the field, they all came together, and helped each other to break that horn of the ram.

14 And I saw that man, who wrote down the names of the shepherds and brought them up before the Lord of the sheep, came, and he helped that ram and showed it everything; its help was coming down.

15 And I looked until that Lord of the sheep came to them angry, all those who saw him ran, and they all fell into the shadow in front of Him.

16 All the eagles and vultures and ravens and kites, gathered together and brought with them all the wild sheep, and they all came together and helped one another in order to dash that horn of the ram in pieces.

17 And I looked at that man, who wrote the book at the command of the Lord, until he opened that book of the destruction that those last twelve shepherds had done. And he showed, in front of the Lord of the sheep, that they had destroyed even more than those before them had.

18 And I looked and the Lord of the sheep came to them and took the Staff of His Anger and struck the Earth. And the Earth was split. And all the animals, and the birds of the sky, fell from those sheep and sank in the earth, and it closed over them.

19 And I saw until a great sword was given to the sheep, and the sheep proceeded against all the beasts of the field to slay them, and all the beasts and the birds of the heaven fled before their face. And I saw that man, who wrote the book according to the command of the Lord, until he opened that book concerning the destruction which those twelve last shepherds had wrought, and showed that they had destroyed much more than their predecessors, before the Lord of the sheep. And I saw until the Lord of the sheep came to them and took in His hand the staff of His wrath, and smote the earth, and the earth clave asunder, and all the beasts and all the birds of heaven fell from among those sheep, and were swallowed up in the earth and it covered them.

20 And I saw until a throne was erected in the pleasant land, and the Lord of the sheep sat Himself on it, and the other took the sealed books and opened those books before the Lord of the sheep.

21 And the Lord called those men, the seven first white ones, and commanded that they should bring before Him, beginning with the first star which led the way, all the stars whose private members were like those of horses, and they brought them all before Him.

22 And He said to that man who wrote before Him, being one of those seven white ones, and said to him: 'Take those seventy shepherds to whom I delivered the sheep, and who taking them on their own authority slew more than I commanded them.'

23 And behold they were all bound, I saw, and they all stood before Him.

24 And the judgment was held first over the stars, and they were judged and found guilty, and went to the place of condemnation, and they were cast into an abyss, full of fire and flaming, and full of pillars of fire.

25 And those seventy shepherds were judged and found guilty, and they were cast into that fiery abyss.

26 And I saw at that time how a like abyss was opened in the midst of the earth, full of fire, and they brought those blinded sheep, and they were all judged and found guilty and cast into this fiery abyss, and they burned; now this abyss was to the right of that house.

27 And I saw those sheep burning and their bones burning.

28 And I stood up to see until they folded up that old house; and carried off all the pillars, and all the beams and ornaments of the house were at the same time folded up with it, and they carried it off and laid it in a place in the south of the land.

29 And I saw until the Lord of the sheep brought a new house greater and loftier than that first, and set it up in the place of the first which had been folded up; all its pillars were new, and its ornaments were new and larger than those of the first, the old one which He had taken away, and all the sheep were within it.

30 And I saw all the sheep which had been left, and all the beasts on the earth, and all the birds of heaven, falling down and doing homage to those sheep and making petition to and obeying them in every thing.

31 And thereafter those three who were clothed in white and had seized me by my hand [who had taken me up before], and the hand of that ram also seizing hold of me, they took me up and set me down in the midst of those sheep before the judgment took place.

32 And those sheep were all white, and their wool was abundant and clean.

33 And all that had been destroyed and dispersed, and all the beasts of the field, and all the birds of heaven, assembled in that house, and the Lord of the sheep rejoiced with great joy because they were all good and had returned to His house.

34 And I saw until they laid down that sword, which had been given to the sheep, and they brought it back into the house, and it was sealed before the presence of the Lord, and all the sheep were invited into that house, but it held them not.

35 And the eyes of them all were opened, and they saw the good, and there was not one among them that did not see.

36 And I saw that the house was large and broad and very full.

37 And I saw that a white bull was born, with large horns and all the beasts of the field and all the birds of the air feared him and made petition to him all the time.

38 And I saw until all their generations were transformed, and they all became white bulls; and the first among them became a lamb, and that lamb became a great animal and had great black horns on its head; and the Lord of the sheep rejoiced over it and over all the oxen.

39 And I slept in their midst: And I awoke and saw everything.

40 This is the vision which I saw while I slept, and I awoke and blessed the Lord of righteousness and gave Him glory.

41 Then I wept greatly and my tears ceased not until I could no longer endure it; when I saw, they flowed on account of what I had seen; for everything shall come and be fulfilled, and all the deeds of men in their order were shown to me.

42 On that night I remembered the first dream, and because of it I wept and was troubled-because I had seen that vision.

[Author's note: As this section was interpreted from a Jewish point of reference, many have assumed the 'large horn' was Judas Maccabee. In the Christian frame of reference, the same symbol was Jesus Christ.]

[Note from editor: at this point, the time frame and text flow becomes non sequitur. It appears the codex was not kept in sequence here. Thus, the translated pages are out of sequence. The flow of time and occurrences seems to follow the pattern listed:

91:6 to 92.1 through 92:5 then jumps to 93:1. The flow then continues from 93:1 to 93:10 and then jumps to 91:7. From 91:7 the text continues to 91:19. It then picks up again at 93:11 and continues.

If one were to attempt to put this section into a time line, the interval would link together in some fashion resembling the following:

Ten Weeks of Judgment

WEEK 1	Judgment & righteousness	93.3	Enoch's time	Antediluvian
WEEK 2	Judgment & cleansing 93.4 Noah's time and the great flood			
WEEK 3	Righteousness is planted 93.5 Abraham's time			
WEEK 4	Law for all generations 93.6 Moses' time			
WEEK 5	House of Glory 93.7 Solomon's time			
WEEK 6	Jesus ascends, temple burned, elect scattered 93.8 Jesus' time			
WEEK 7	Apostate generation Judgment of Fire 93.9 - 91.11 Our time			
WEEK 8	A sword 91.12–13 New house, new heaven & earth Future time			
WEEK 9	The righteous judgment revealed 91.14 The judgment time			
WEEK 10	God's power is forever 91.15-16 Eternal time			

When reading the text from this point to the end of chapter 93 one should keep this flow in mind.]

[Chapter 91]

1 And now, my son Methuselah, call to me all your brothers and gather together to me all the sons of your mother; for the word calls me, and the spirit is poured out on me, that I may show you everything that shall befall you for ever.'

2 And thereon Methuselah went and summoned to him all his brothers and assembled his relatives.

3 And he spoke to all the children of righteousness and said: 'Hear, you sons of Enoch, all the words of your father, and hearken, as you should, to the voice of my mouth; for I exhort you and say to you, beloved:

4 Love righteousness and walk in it, and draw near to righteousness without a double heart, and do not associate with those of a double heart, but walk in righteousness, my sons. And it shall guide you on good paths. And righteousness shall be your companion.'

5 'For I know that violence must increase on the earth, and a great punishment will be executed on the earth, it shall be cut off from its roots, and its whole construct will be destroyed.

6 And unrighteousness shall again be complete on the earth, and all the deeds of unrighteousness and of violence and sin shall prevail a second time.

7 And when sin and unrighteousness and blasphemy and violence in all kinds of deeds increase, and apostasy and transgression and uncleanness increase; a great chastisement shall come from heaven on all these, and the holy Lord will come out with wrath and chastisement to execute judgment on earth.

8 In those days violence shall be cut off from its roots, and the roots of unrighteousness together with deceit, and they shall be destroyed from under heaven.

9 And all the idols of the heathen shall be abandoned. And the temples burned with fire, and they shall remove them from the whole earth; and the heathen shall be cast into the judgment of fire, and shall perish in wrath and in grievous judgment for ever.

10 And the righteous shall arise from their sleep, and wisdom shall arise and be given to them.

11 And after that the roots of unrighteousness and those who plan violence and those who commit blasphemy shall be cut off, and the sinners shall be destroyed by the sword.

12 And after this there will be another week; the eighth, that of righteousness, and a sword will be given to it so that the Righteous Judgment may be executed on those who do wrong, and the sinners will be handed over into the hands of the righteous.

13 And, at its end, they will acquire Houses because of their righteousness, and a House will be built for the Great King in Glory, forever.

14 And after this, in the ninth week, the Righteous Judgment will be revealed to the whole world. And all the deeds of the impious will vanish from the whole Earth. And the world will be written down for destruction and all men will look to the Path of Uprightness.

15 And, after this, in the tenth week, in the seventh part, there will be an Eternal Judgment that will be executed on the Watchers and the Great Eternal Heaven that will spring from the midst of the Angels.

16 And the First Heaven will vanish and pass away and a New Heaven will appear, and all the Powers of Heaven will shine forever, with light seven times as bright.

17 And after this, there will be many weeks without number, forever, in goodness and in righteousness. And from then on sin will never again be mentioned.

18 And now I tell you, my sons, and show you, the paths of righteousness and the paths of violence. I will show them to you again that you may know what will come to pass.

19 And now, hearken to me, my sons, and walk in the paths of righteousness, and walk not in the paths of violence; for all who walk in the paths of unrighteousness shall perish for ever.'

[Chapter 92]

1 The book written by Enoch {Enoch indeed wrote this complete doctrine of wisdom, (which is) praised of all men and a judge of all the earth} for all my children who shall live on the earth. And for the future generations who shall observe righteousness and peace.

2 Let not your spirit be troubled on account of the times; for the Holy and Great One has appointed days for all things.

3 And the righteous one shall arise from sleep, [Shall arise] and walk in the paths of righteousness, and all his path and conversation shall be in eternal goodness and grace.

4 He will be gracious to the righteous and give him eternal righteousness, and He will give him power so that he shall be (endowed) with goodness and righteousness. And he shall walk in eternal light.

5 And sin shall perish in darkness for ever, and shall no more be seen from that day for evermore.

[Chapter 93]

(Author's Note: Chapters 91 – 93 recount and expand on the events listed in the following weeks of prophecy. The explanation of the event are scattered in chapters 91 – 93, however, the list of events are stated clearly in the following list of week in chapter 93).

1 And after that Enoch both gave and began to recount from the books. And Enoch said:

2 'Concerning the children of righteousness and concerning the elect of the world, and concerning the plant of righteousness, I will speak these things. I Enoch will declare (them) to you, my sons, according to that which appeared to me in heavenly vision, and which I have known through the word of the holy angels, and have learned from heavenly tablets.'

3 And Enoch began to recount from the books and said: 'I was born the seventh in the first week, able judgment and righteousness still endured.

4 And after me there shall arise in the second week great wickedness, and deceit shall have sprung up; and in it there shall be the first end.

5 And in it a man shall be saved; and after it is ended unrighteousness shall grow up, and a law shall be made for the sinners. And after that in the third week at its close a man shall be elected as the plant of righteous judgment, and his posterity shall become the plant of righteousness for evermore.

6 And after that in the fourth week, at its close, visions of the holy and righteous shall be seen, and a law for all generations and an enclosure shall be made for them.

7 And after that in the fifth week, at its close, the house of glory and dominion shall be built for ever.

8 And after that in the sixth week, all who live in it shall be blinded, and the hearts of all of them shall godlessly forsake wisdom. And in it a man shall ascend; and at its close the house of dominion shall be burned with fire, and the whole race of the chosen root shall be dispersed.

9 And after that in the seventh week shall an apostate generation arise, and many shall be its deeds, and all its deeds shall be apostate.

10 And at its end shall be elected, the elect righteous of the eternal plant of righteousness shall be chosen to receive sevenfold instruction concerning all His creation.

11 For who is there of all the children of men that is able to hear the voice of the Holy One without being troubled? And who can think His thoughts? Who is there that can behold all the works of heaven?

12 And how should there be one who could behold heaven, and who is there that could understand the things of heaven and see a soul or a spirit and could tell of it, or ascend and see all their ends and think them or do like them?

13 And who is there of all men that could know what is the breadth and the length of the earth, and to whom has the measurement been shown of all of them?

14 Or is there any one who could discern the length of the heaven and how great is its height, and on what it is founded, and how great is the number of the stars, and where all the luminaries rest?

[Chapter 94]

1 And now I say to you, my sons, love righteousness and walk in it; because the paths of righteousness are worthy of acceptation, but the paths of unrighteousness shall suddenly be destroyed and vanish.

2 And to certain men of a generation shall the paths of violence and of death be revealed, and they shall hold themselves afar from them, and shall not follow them.

3 And now I say to you, the righteous, walk not in the paths of wickedness, nor in the paths of death, and draw not near to them, lest you be destroyed.

4 But seek and choose for yourselves righteousness and an elect life, and walk in the paths of peace, and you shall live and prosper.

5 And hold (keep) my words in the thoughts of your hearts, and permit them not to be erased from your hearts; for I know that sinners will tempt men to evilly entreat wisdom, so that no place may be found for her, and temptation will increase.

6 Woe to those who build unrighteousness and oppression and lay deceit as a foundation; for they shall be suddenly overthrown, and they shall have no peace.

7 Woe to those who build their houses with sin; for from all their foundations shall they be overthrown, and by the sword shall they fall. And those who acquire gold and silver shall suddenly perish in the judgment.

8 Woe to you, you rich, for you have trusted in your riches, and from your riches shall you depart, because you have not remembered the Most High in the days of your riches.

9 You have committed blasphemy and unrighteousness, and have become ready for the day of slaughter, and the day of darkness and the day of the great judgment.

10 Thus I speak and tell you: He who has created you will overthrow you, and for your fall there shall be no compassion, and your Creator will rejoice at your destruction.

11 And your righteousness shall be a reproach to the sinners and the godless in those days.

[Chapter 95]

1 Would that my eyes were rain clouds of water that I might weep over you, and pour down my tears as a cloud of water, that I might rest from my trouble of heart!

2 Who has permitted you to practice reproaches and wickedness? And so judgment shall overtake you, sinners.

3 You, righteous! Fear not the sinners, for again the Lord will deliver them into your hands, that you may execute judgment on them according to your desires.

4 Woe to you who speak against God (fulminate anathemas) which cannot be removed (reversed) - healing shall be far from you because of your sins.

5 Woe to you who repay your neighbor with evil; for you shall be repaid according to your works.

6 Woe to you, lying witnesses, and to those who weigh out injustice, for you shall suddenly perish.

7 Woe to you, sinners, for you persecute the righteous; for you shall be delivered up and persecuted because of injustice, and your yoke shall be heavy on you.

[Chapter 96]

1 Be hopeful, you righteous; for suddenly shall the sinners perish before you, and you shall have lordship over them, according to your desires.

2 And in the day of the tribulation of the sinners, your children shall mount and rise as eagles, and your nests shall be higher than the vultures'. You shall ascend as badgers and enter the crevices of the earth, and the clefts of the rock for ever before the unrighteous. And the satyrs (sirens) shall sigh and weep because of you.

3 Wherefore fear not, you that have suffered, for healing shall be your portion, and a bright light shall enlighten you, and the voice of rest you shall hear from heaven.

4 Woe to you, you sinners, for your riches make you appear like the righteous, but your hearts convict you of being sinners, and this fact shall be a testimony against you for a memorial of your evil deeds.

5 Woe to you who devour the finest of the wheat, and drink wine in large bowls (the best of waters), and tread under foot the lowly (humble) with your might.

6 Woe to you who drink water from every fountain (drink water all the time), for suddenly shall you be consumed and wither away, because you have forsaken the fountain of life.

(Author's note: the above reference is a euphemism for promiscuity.)

7 Woe to you who work unrighteousness and deceit and blasphemy; it shall be a memorial against you for evil.

8 Woe to you, you mighty, who with might oppress the righteous; for the day of your destruction is coming. Many and good days shall come to the righteous in those days - in the day of your judgment.

[Chapter 97]

1 Believe, you righteous, that the sinners will become a shame and perish in the day of unrighteousness.

2 Be it known to you, you sinners, that the Most High is mindful of your destruction, and the angels of heaven rejoice over your destruction.

3 What will you do, you sinners, and where shall you flee on that day of judgment, when you hear the voice of the prayer of the righteous?

4 You shall fare like to them, against whom these words shall be a testimony: "You have been companions of sinners."

5 And in those days the prayer of the righteous shall reach to the Lord, and for you the days of your judgment shall come.

6 And all the words of your unrighteousness shall be read out before the Great Holy One, and your faces shall be covered with shame, and He will reject every work which is grounded on unrighteousness.

7 Woe to you, you sinners, who live on the middle of the ocean and on the dry land, whose remembrance is evil against you.

8 Woe to you who acquire silver and gold in unrighteousness and say: "We have become rich with riches and have possessions; and have acquired everything we have desired.

9 And now let us do what we purposed, for we have gathered silver, and many are the servants in our houses and our granaries are full to the brim as if with water."

10 Yea, and like water your lies shall flow away; for your riches shall not abide but quickly depart (go up) from you, for you have acquired it all in unrighteousness, and you shall be given over to a great curse.

[Chapter 98]

1 And now I swear to you, to the wise and to the foolish, that you shall see (have) many experiences on the earth.

2 For you men shall put on more adornments than a woman, and colored garments more than a young woman, like royalty and in grandeur and in power, and in silver and in gold and in purple, and in splendor and in food they shall be poured out as water.

3 Therefore they shall have neither knowledge nor wisdom, and because of this they shall die together with their possessions; and with all their glory and their splendor, and in shame and in slaughter and in great destitution, their spirits shall be thrown into the furnace of fire.

4 I have sworn to you, you sinners, as a mountain has not become a slave, and a hill does not become the servant of a woman, even so sin has not been sent on the earth, but man of himself has created it, and they that commit it shall fall under a great curse.

5 And barrenness has not been given to the woman, but on account of the deeds of her own hands she dies without children.

6 I have sworn to you, you sinners, by the Holy Great One, that all your evil deeds are revealed in heaven, and that none of your wrong deeds (of oppression) are covered and hidden.

7 And do not think in your spirit nor say in your heart that you do not know and that you do not see that every sin is recorded every day in heaven in the presence of the Most High.

8 From now on, you know that all your wrongdoing that you do will be written down every day, until the day of your judgment.

9 Woe to you, you fools, for through your folly you shall perish; and you do not listen to the wise so no good will come to you against the wise,

10 And so and now, know you that you are prepared for the day of destruction. Therefore do not hope to live, you sinners, but you shall depart and die; for there will be no ransom for you; because you are prepared for the day of the great judgment, for the day of tribulation and great shame for your spirits.

11 Woe to you, you obstinate of heart, who work wickedness and eat blood. Where do you have good things to eat and to drink and to be filled? From all the good things which the Lord the Most High has placed in abundance on the earth; therefore you shall have no peace.

(Author's note: The above reference to eating blood may indicate cannibalism.)

12 Woe to you who love the deeds of unrighteousness; wherefore do you hope for good for yourselves? You know that you shall be delivered into the hands of the righteous, and they shall cut off your necks and slay you, and have no mercy on you.

13 Woe to you who rejoice in the distress of the righteous; for no grave shall be dug for you.

14 Woe to you who say the words of the wise are empty; for you shall have no hope of life.

15 Woe to you who write down lying and godless words; for they write down their lies so that men may hear them and act godlessly towards their neighbor. Therefore they shall have no peace but die a sudden death.

[Chapter 99]

1 Woe to you who do godless acts, and praise and honor lies; you shall perish, and no happy life shall be yours.

2 Woe to them who pervert the words of righteousness, and transgress the eternal law, and count themselves as sinless. They shall be trodden under foot on the earth.

3 In those days make ready, you righteous, to raise your prayers as a memorial, and place them as a testimony before the angels, that they may place the sin of the sinners for a reminder before the Most High.

4 In those days the nations shall be stirred up, and the families of the nations shall arise on the day of destruction.

5 And in those days the destitute shall go and throw their children out, and they shall abandon them, so that their children shall perish because of them. They shall abandon their children that are still babies (sucklings), and not return to them, and shall have no pity on their loved ones.

6 Again, I swear to you, you sinners, that sin is prepared for a day of unceasing bloodshed.

7 And they who worship stones, and carved images of gold and silver and wood and stone and clay, and those who worship impure spirits and demons, and all kinds of idols not according to knowledge, shall get no manner of help from them.

8 And they shall become godless by reason of the folly of their hearts, and their eyes shall be blinded through the fear of their hearts and through visions in their ambitions (dreams).

9 Through these they shall become godless and fearful; for they shall have done all their work with lies, and shall have worshiped a stone, therefore in an instant shall they perish.

10 But in those days blessed are all they who accept the words of wisdom, and understand them, and observe the paths of the Most High, and walk in the path of His righteousness, and become not godless with the godless, for they shall be saved.

11 Woe to you who spread evil to your neighbors, for you shall be slain in Hell.

12 Woe to you who make your foundation that of deceitful (sin) and lies, and who cause bitterness on the earth; for they shall thereby be utterly consumed.

13 Woe to you who build your houses through the hard labor of others, and all their building materials are the bricks and stones of sin; I tell you, you shall have no peace.

14 Woe to them who reject the measure and eternal inheritance of their fathers and whose souls follow after idols; for they shall have no rest.

15 Woe to them who do unrighteous acts and help oppression, and kill their neighbors until the day of the great judgment, for He will throw down your glory.

16 For He shall throw down your glory, and bring affliction on your hearts, and shall arouse His fierce anger, and destroy you all with the sword; and all the holy and righteous shall remember your sins.

[Chapter 100]

1 And in those days in one place the fathers together with their sons shall kill one another and brothers shall fall in death together until the streams flow with their blood.

2 For a man shall not withhold his hand from killing his sons and his sons' sons, and the sinner shall not withhold his hand from his honored brother, from dawn until sunset they shall kill one another.

3 And the horse shall walk up to the breast in the blood of sinners, and the chariot shall be submerged to its height.

REV 14:20 And the winepress was trodden without the city, and blood came out of the winepress, even unto the horse bridles, by the space of a thousand and six hundred furlongs.

4 In those days the angels shall descend into the secret places and gather together into one place all those who brought down sin and the Most High will arise on that day of judgment to execute great judgment among sinners.

5 And over all the righteous and holy He will appoint guardians from among the holy angels to guard them as the apple of an eye, until He makes an end of all wickedness and all sin, and even if the righteous sleep a long sleep, they have nothing to fear.

6 And the wise men will seek the truth and they and their sons will understand the words of this book, and recognize that their riches shall not be able to save them or overcome their sins.

7 Woe to you sinners, on the day of strong anguish, you who afflict the righteous and burn them with fire; you shall be requited according to your works.

8 Woe to you, you obstinate of heart, who watch in order to devise wickedness; therefore shall fear come on you and there shall be none to help you.

9 Woe to you, you sinners, on account of the words of your mouth, and on account of the deeds of your hands which your godlessness as caused, in blazing flames burning worse than fire shall you burn.

10 And now, know that the angels will ask Him in heaven about your deeds and from the sun and from the moon and from the stars they will ask about your sins because on the earth you execute judgment on the righteous.

11 And He will summon to testify against you every cloud and mist and dew and rain; for they shall all be withheld from falling on you, and they shall be mindful of your sins.

12 And now give gifts to the rain that it cease not from falling on you, nor the dew, when it has received gold and silver from you that it may fall. When the hoar-frost and snow with their chilliness, and all the snow storms with all their plagues fall on you, in those days you shall not be able to stand before them.

[Chapter 101]

1 Observe heaven, you children of heaven, and every work of the Most High, and fear Him and work no evil in His presence.

2 If He closes the windows of heaven, and withholds the rain and the dew from falling on the earth on your account, what will you do then?

3 And if He sends His anger on you because of your deeds, you cannot petition Him; for you spoke proud and arrogant words against His righteousness, therefore you shall have no peace.

4 Don't you see the sailors of the ships, how their ships are tossed back and forth by the waves, and are shaken by the winds, and are in great trouble?

5 And therefore they are afraid because all their nice possessions go on the sea with them, and they have bad feelings in their heart that the sea will swallow them and they will perish therein.

6 Are not the entire sea and all its waters, and all its movements, the work of the Most High, and has He not set limits to its actions, and confined it throughout by the sand?

7 And at His reproof it fears and dries up, and all its fish die and all that is in it; but you sinners that are on the earth fear Him not.

8 Has He not made heaven and the earth, and all that is in it ? Who has given understanding and wisdom to everything that moves on the earth and in the sea?

9 Do not the sailors of the ships fear the sea? Yet you sinners do not fear the Most High.

[Chapter 102]

1 In those days if He sent a horrible fire on you, where will you flee, and where will you find deliverance? And when He launches out His Word against you will you not be shaken and afraid?

2 And all the luminaries shall be shaken with great fear, and all the earth shall be afraid and tremble and be alarmed.

3 And all the angels shall execute their commands and shall seek to hide themselves from the presence of He who is Great in Glory, and the children of earth shall tremble and shake; and you sinners shall be cursed for ever, and you shall have no peace.

4 Fear you not, you souls of the righteous, and fear not you who have died in righteousness.

5 And don't grieve if your soul has descended in to the grave in grief, and that in your life you were not rewarded according to your goodness, but wait for the day of the judgment of sinners and for the day of cursing and chastisement.

6 And when you die the sinners will say about you: "As we die, so die the righteous, and what benefit do they reap for their deeds?

7 See, even as we, so do they die in grief and darkness, and what have they more than we? From now on we are equal.

8 And what will they receive and what will they see for ever? Look, they too have died, and from now on for ever shall they see no light."

9 I tell you, you sinners, you are content to eat and drink, and rob and sin, and strip men naked, and acquire wealth and see good days.

10 Have you seen the righteous how their end was peace, that no violence is found in them until their death?

11 Nevertheless they died and became as though they had not been, and their spirits descended into Hell in tribulation.

[Chapter 103]

1 Now, therefore, I swear to the righteous, by the glory of the Great and Honored and Mighty One who reigns, I swear to you, I know this mystery.

2 I have read the heavenly tablets, and have seen the holy books, and have found written in it and inscribed regarding them.

3 That all goodness and joy and glory are prepared for them, and written down for the spirits of those who have died in righteousness, and that much good shall be given to you in reward for your labors, and that your lot is abundant beyond the lot of the living.

4 And the spirits of you who have died in righteousness shall live and rejoice, and your spirits shall not perish, nor shall your memory from before the face of the Great One to all the generations of the world, therefore no longer fear their abuse.

5 Woe to you, you sinners, when you have died, if you die in the abundance of your sins, and woe to those who are like you and say regarding you: "Blessed are the sinners, they have seen all their days.

6 And how they have died in prosperity and in wealth, and have not seen tribulation or murder in their life; and they have died in honor, and judgment has not been executed on them during their life."

7 You know that their souls will be made to descend into Hell and they shall be wracked in great tribulation.

8 And into darkness and chains and a burning flame where there is harsh judgment your spirits shall enter, and the great judgment shall be for all the generations of the world. Woe to you, for you shall have no peace.

9 The righteous and good who are alive, do not say: "In our troubled days we have worked hard and experienced every trouble, and met with much evil and been afflicted, and have become few and our spirit small.

10 And we have been destroyed and have not found any to help us even with a word. We have been tortured and destroyed, and not expect to live from day to day.

11 We hoped to be the head and have become the tail. We have worked hard and had no satisfaction in our labor; and we have become the food of the sinners and the unrighteous, and they have laid their yoke heavily on us.

12 They have ruled over us and hated us and hit us, and to those that hated us we have bowed our necks but they pitied us not.

13 We desired to get away from them that we might escape and be at rest, but found no place where we should flee and be safe from them.

14 We complained to the rulers in our tribulation, and cried out against those who devoured us, but they did not pay attention to our cries and would not listen to our voice.

15 And they helped those who robbed us and devoured us and those who made us few; and they concealed their oppression (wrongdoing), and they did not remove from us the yoke of those that devoured us and dispersed us and murdered us, and they concealed their murder, and did not remember that they had lifted up their hands against us."

[Chapter 104]

1 I swear to you, that in heaven the angels remember you for good before the glory of the Great One.

2 And your names are written before the glory of the Great One. Be hopeful; for before you were put to shame through sickness and affliction; but now you shall shine as the lights of heaven,

3 You shall shine and you shall be seen, and the doors of heaven shall be opened to you. And in your cry, cry for judgment, and it shall appear to you; for all your tribulation shall be visited on the rulers, and on all who helped those who plundered you.

4 Be hopeful, and do not throw away your hopes for you shall have great joy as the angels of heaven.

5 What will you have to do ? You shall not have to hide on the day of the great judgment and you shall not be found as sinners, and the eternal judgment shall not come to you for all the generations, eternally.

6 And now fear not, you righteous, when you see the sinners growing strong and prospering in their ways; do not be their companions, but keep away from their violence.

7 For you shall become companions of the hosts of heaven. And, although you sinners say: "All our sins shall not be found out and be written down," nevertheless they shall write down all your sins every day.

8 And now I show to you that light and darkness, day and night, see all your sins.

9 Do not be godless in your hearts, and do not lie and do not change the words of righteousness, nor say that the words of the Holy Great One are lies, nor praise or rely on your idols; for all your lying and all your godlessness (leads not to) come not from righteousness but (leads to) from great sin.

10 And now I know this mystery, that sinners will alter and pervert the words of righteousness in many ways, and will speak wicked words, and lie, and practice great deceits, and write books concerning their words.

11 But when they write down all my words truthfully in their languages, and do not change or omit any of my words but write them all down truthfully - all that I first testified concerning them.

12 Then, I know another mystery, that books will be given to the righteous and the wise to produce joy and righteousness and much wisdom.

13 And to them the books shall be given, and they shall believe them and rejoice over them, and then all the righteous who have learned from them all the paths of righteousness shall be paid back.'

[Chapter 105]

1 In those days the Lord called them (the wise and righteous) to testify to the children of earth concerning their wisdom: Show it to them; for you are their guides, and a recompense over the whole earth.

2 For I and my son will be united with them for ever in the paths of righteousness in their lives; and you shall have peace: rejoice, you children of righteousness. Amen.

[Chapter 106]

Fragment of the Book of Noah

1 And after some days my son Methuselah took a wife for his son, Lamech, and she became pregnant by him and bore a son. And his body was white as snow and red as the blooming of a rose, and the hair of his head and his long curls were white as wool, and his eyes beautiful.

2 And when he opened his eyes, he lit up the whole house like the sun, and the whole house was very bright.

3 And on it he levitated (arose) in the hands of the midwife, opened his mouth, and conversed with the Lord of righteousness.

4 And his father, Lamech, was afraid of him and fled, and came to his father Methuselah. And he said to him: 'I have begotten a strange son, different and unlike man, and resembling the sons of the God of heaven; and his nature is different and he is not like us, and his eyes are as the rays of the sun, and his face is glorious.

5 And it seems to me that he did not spring from me but from the angels, and I fear that in his days a wonder may be performed on the earth.

6 And now, my father, I am here to ask you and beg you that you may go to Enoch, our father, and learn from him the truth, for his dwelling-place is among the angels."

7 And when Methuselah heard the words of his son, he came to me to the ends of the earth; for he had heard that I was there, and he cried aloud, and I heard his voice and I came to him. And I said to him: 'Behold, here am I, my son, why have you come to me? '

8 And he answered and said: 'Because of a great cause of anxiety have I come to you, and because of a disturbing vision have I approached.

9 And now, my father, hear me. To Lamech, my son, there has been born a son, the like of whom there is none other, and his nature is not like man's nature, and the color of his body is whiter than snow and redder than the bloom of a rose, and the hair of his head is whiter than white wool, and his eyes are like the rays of the sun, and he opened his eyes and the whole house lit up.

10 And he levitated (arose) in the hands of the midwife, and opened his mouth and blessed the Lord of heaven.

11 And his father Lamech became afraid and fled to me, and did not believe that he was sprung from him, but that he was in the likeness of the angels of heaven; and now I have come to you that you may make known to me the truth.'

12 And I, Enoch, answered and said to him: 'The Lord will do a new thing on the earth, and this I have already seen in a vision, and make known to you that in the generation of my father Jared some of the angels of heaven violated the word of the Lord. And they commit sin and broke the law, and have had sex (united themselves) with women and committed sin with them, and have married some of them, and have had children by them.

13 And they shall produce on the earth giants not according to the spirit, but according to the flesh, and there shall be a great punishment on the earth, and the earth shall be cleansed from all impurity.

14 There shall come a great destruction over the whole earth, and there shall be a flood (deluge) and a great destruction for one year.

15 And this son who has been born to you shall be left on the earth, and his three children shall be saved with him: when all mankind that are on the earth shall die, he and his sons shall be saved.

16 And now make known to your son, Lamech, that he who has been born is in truth his son, and call his name Noah; for he shall be left to you, and he and his sons shall be saved from the destruction, which shall come on the earth on account of all the sin and all the unrighteousness, which shall be full (completed) on the earth in his days.

17 And after that (flood) there shall be more unrighteousness than that which was done before on the earth; for I know the mysteries of the holy ones; for He, the Lord, has showed me and informed me, and I have read (them) in heavenly tablets.

[Chapter 107]

1 And I saw written about them that generation after generation shall transgress, until a generation of righteousness arises, and transgression is destroyed and sin passes away from the earth, and all manner of good comes on it.

2 And now, my son, go and make known to your son Lamech that this son, which has been born, is in truth his son, and this is no lie.'

3 And when Methuselah had heard the words of his father Enoch, for he had shown to him everything in secret, he returned and showed those things to him and called the name of that son Noah; for he will comfort the earth after all the destruction.

[Chapter 108]

1 Another book which Enoch wrote for his son Methuselah and for those who will come after him, and keep the law in the last days.

2 You who have done good shall wait for those days until an end is made of those who work evil; and an end of the power of the wrongdoers.

3 And wait until sin has passed away indeed, for their names shall be blotted out of the book of life and out of the holy books, and their (children) seed shall be destroyed for ever, and their spirits shall be killed, and they shall cry and lament in a place that is a chaotic desert, and they shall be burned in the fire; for there is no earth there.

4 I saw something there like an invisible cloud; because it was so deep I could not look over it, and I saw a flame of fire blazing brightly, and things like shining mountains circling and sweeping back and forth.

5 And I asked one of the holy angels who was with me and said to him: 'What is this bright thing (shining)? For it is not heaven but there was only the flame of a blazing fire, and the voice of weeping and crying and moaning, lamenting, and agony.'

6 And he said to me: 'This place which you see are where the spirits of sinners and blasphemers, and of those who work wickedness, are cast and the spirits of those who pervert everything that the Lord has spoken through the mouth of the prophets and even the prophecies (things that shall be).

7 For some of them are written and inscribed above in heaven, in order that the angels may read them and know that which shall befall the sinners, and the spirits of the humble, and of those who have afflicted their bodies, and been recompensed by God; and of those who have been abused (put to shame) by wicked men:

8 Who love God and loved neither gold nor silver nor any of the good things which are in the world, but gave over their bodies to torture.

9 Who, since they were born, longed not after earthly food, but regarded everything as a passing breath, and lived accordingly, and the Lord tried them much, and their spirits were found pure so that they should bless His name.

10 And all the blessings destined for them I have recounted in the books. And he has assigned them their reward, because they have been found to love heaven more than their life in the world, and though they were trodden under foot by wicked men, and experienced abuse and reviling from them and were put to shame, they blessed Me.

11 And now I will summon the spirits of the good who belong to the generation of light, and I will transform those who were born in darkness, who in the flesh were not rewarded with such honor as their faithfulness deserved.

12 And I will bring out in shining light those who have loved My holy name, and I will seat each on the throne of his honor.

MAT 19:28 And Jesus said unto them, Verily I say unto you, That you which have followed me, in the regeneration when the Son of man shall sit in the throne of his glory, you also shall sit upon twelve thrones, judging the twelve tribes of Israel.

13 And they shall shine for time without end; for righteousness is the judgment of God; because to the faithful He will give faithfulness in the habitation of upright paths.

14 And they shall see those who were born in darkness led into darkness, while the righteous shall shine. And the sinners shall cry aloud and see them shining, and they indeed will go where days and seasons are written down (prescribed) for them.

THE BOOK OF JUBILEES
THE LITTLE GENESIS, THE APOCALYPSE OF MOSES

This is the history of how the days were divided and of the days of the law and of the testimony, of the events of the years, and of the weeks of years, of their Jubilees throughout all the years of the world, as the Lord spoke to Moses on Mount Sinai when he went up to receive the tablets of the law and the commandment, according to the voice of God when he said to him, "Go up to the top of the Mount."

[Chapter 1]

1 It happened in the first year of the exodus of the children of Israel out of Egypt, in the third month, on the sixteenth day of the month, that God spoke to Moses, saying, "Come up to Me on the Mountain, and I will give you two tablets of stone of the law and the commandment, which I have written, that you may teach them."

2 Moses went up into the mountain of God, and the glory of the Lord rested on Mount Sinai, and a cloud overshadowed it six days.

3 He called to Moses on the seventh day out of the middle of the cloud, and the appearance of the glory of the Lord was like a flame on the top of the mountain.

4 Moses was on the mountain forty days and forty nights, and God taught him the earlier and the later history of the division of all the days of the law and of the testimony.

5 He said, "Open your heart to every word which I shall speak to you on this mountain, and write them in a book in order that their generations may see how I have not forsaken them for all the evil which they have committed when they transgressed the covenant which I establish between Me and you for their generations this day on Mount Sinai.

6 It will come to pass when all these things come on them, that they will recognize that I am more righteous than they in all their judgments and in all their actions, and they will recognize that I have truly been with them.

7 Write all these words for yourself which I speak to you today, for I know their rebellion and their stubbornness, before I brought them into the land of which I swore to their fathers, to Abraham and to Isaac and to Jacob, saying, " Unto your offspring will I give a land flowing with milk and honey.

8 They will eat and be satisfied, and they will turn to strange gods, to gods that cannot deliver them from any of their tribulation, and this witness shall be heard for a witness against them.

9 They will forget all My commandments, even all that I command them, and they will walk in the ways of the Gentiles, and after their uncleanness, and after their shame, and will serve their gods, and these will prove to them an offence and a tribulation and an sickness and a trap.

10 Many will perish and they will be taken captive, and will fall into the hands of the enemy, because they have forsaken My laws and My commandments, and the festivals of My covenant, and My sabbaths, and My holy place which I have made holy for Myself in their presence, and My tabernacle, and My sanctuary, which I have made holy for Myself in the midst of the land, that I should set My name on it, that it should reside there.

11 They will make themselves high places and places of worship and graven images. Each will worship graven images of his own making, Thus they will go astray. They will sacrifice their children to demons, and to all errors their hearts can work.

12 I will send witnesses to them that I may testify against them, but they will not hear. They will kill the witnesses. They will persecute those who seek the law, and they will abolish and change everything (in the Law) so as to work evil before My eyes.

13 I will hide My face from them. I will deliver them into the hand of the Gentiles. They will be captured like prey for their eating. I will remove them from the out of the land. I will scatter them among the Gentiles.

14 And they will forget My law and all My commandments and all My judgments. They will go astray regarding the observance of new moons, and sabbaths, and festivals, and jubilees, and laws.

15 After this they will turn to Me from among the Gentiles with all their heart and with all their soul and with all their strength, and I will gather them from among all the Gentiles, and they will seek me. I shall be found by them when they seek me with all their heart and with all their soul.

16 I will allow them to see abounding peace with righteousness. I will remove them, the plant of uprightness, with all My heart and with all My soul, and they shall be for a blessing and not for a curse, and they shall be the head and not the tail.

17 I will build My sanctuary among them, and I will dwell with them, and I will be their God and they shall be My people in truth and righteousness.

18 I will not forsake them nor fail them; for I am the Lord their God."

19 Moses fell on his face and prayed and said, 'O Lord my God, do not forsake Your people and Your inheritance, so that they should wander in the error of their hearts, and do not deliver them into the hands of their enemies, the Gentiles, so that they should rule over them and cause them to sin against You.

20 Let your mercy, O Lord, be lifted up on Your people, and create in them an upright spirit, and let not the spirit of Beliar rule over them to accuse them before You, and to ensnare them from all the paths of righteousness, so that they may perish from before Your face.

21 But they are Your people and Your inheritance, which You have delivered with Your great power from the hands of the Egyptians, create in them a clean heart and a holy spirit, and let them not be ensnared in their sins from now on until eternity."

22 The Lord said to Moses, "I know their contrariness and their thoughts and their stubbornness, and they will not be obedient until they confess their own sin and the sin of their fathers.

23 After this they will turn to Me in all uprightness and with all their heart and with all their soul, and I will circumcise the foreskin of their heart and the foreskin of the heart of their offspring, and I will create in them a holy spirit, and I will cleanse them so that they shall not turn away from Me from that day to eternity.

24 And their souls will cling to Me and to all My commandments, and they will fulfill My commandments, and I will be their Father and they shall be My children.

25 They all shall be called children of the living God, and every angel and every spirit shall know, yes, they shall know that these are My children, and that I am their Father in uprightness and righteousness, and that I love them.

26 Write down for yourself all these words which I say to you on this mountain, from the first to the last, which shall come to pass in all the divisions of the days in the law and in the testimony and in the weeks and the jubilees to eternity, until I descend and dwell with them throughout eternity."

27 He said to the angel of the presence (of the Lord), "Write for Moses from the beginning of creation until My sanctuary has been built among them for all eternity.

28 The Lord will appear to the eyes of all, and all shall know that I am the God of Israel and the Father of all the children of Jacob, and King on Mount Zion for all eternity. And Zion and Jerusalem shall be holy."

29 The angel of the presence (of the Lord) who went before the camp of Israel took the tables of the divisions of the years, written from the time of the creation, concerning the law and the testimony of the weeks of the jubilees, according to the individual years, according to the numbering of all the jubilees, from the day of the new creation when the heavens and the earth shall be renewed and all their creation according to the powers of the heaven, and according to all the creation of the earth, until the sanctuary of the Lord shall be made in Jerusalem on Mount Zion, and all the stars and planets be renewed for healing, peace, and blessing for all the elect of Israel, and that this is the way it may be from that day and to all the days of the earth.

[Chapter 2]

1 The angel of the presence (of the Lord) spoke to Moses according to the word of the Lord, saying, "Write the complete history of the creation, how in six days the Lord God finished all His works and all that He created, and kept Sabbath on the seventh day and made it holy for all ages, and appointed it as a sign for all His works.

2 For on the first day He created the heavens which are above and the earth and the waters and all the spirits which serve before him which are the angels of the presence (of the Lord), and the angels of sanctification, and the angels of the spirit of fire, and the angels of the spirit of the winds, and the angels of the spirit of the clouds, and of darkness, and of snow and of hail and of white frost, and the angels of the voices and of the thunder and of the lightning, and the angels of the spirits of cold and of heat, and of winter and of spring and of autumn and of summer and of all the spirits of his creatures which are in the heavens and on the earth, He created the bottomless pit and the darkness, evening and night, and the light, dawn and day, which He has prepared in the knowledge of His heart.

3 When we saw His works, we praised Him, and worshiped before Him because of all His works; for seven great works did He create on the first day.

4 On the second day He created the sky between the waters (above and below), and the waters were divided on that day. Half of them went up above the sky and half of them went down below the sky that was in the middle over the face of the whole earth. And this was the only work God created on the second day.

5 On the third day He commanded the waters to pass from off the face of the whole earth into one place, and the dry land to appear.

6 The waters did as He commanded them, and they receded from off the face of the earth into one place, and the dry land appeared.

7 On that day He created for them all the seas according to their separate gathering-places, and all the rivers, and the gatherings of the waters in the mountains and on all the earth, and all the lakes, and all the dew of the earth, and the seed which is sown, and all sprouting things, and fruit-bearing trees, and trees of the wood, and the garden of Eden, in Eden and throughout. These four great works God created on the third day.

8 On the fourth day He created the sun and the moon and the stars, and set them in the sky of the heaven, to give light on all the earth, and to rule over the day and the night, and divide the light from the darkness.

9 God appointed the sun to be a great sign on the earth for days and for sabbaths and for months and for feasts and for years and for sabbaths of years and for jubilees and for all seasons of the years.

10 And it divides the light from the darkness for prosperity that all things may prosper which sprout and grow on the earth. These three kinds He made on the fourth day.

11 On the fifth day He created great sea monsters in the depths of the waters, for these were the first things of flesh that were created by his hands, the fish and everything that moves in the waters, and everything that flies, the birds and all their kind.

12 And the sun rose above them to make them prosper, and the sun rose above everything that was on the earth, everything that sprouts out of the earth, and all fruit-bearing trees, and all flesh.

13 He created these three kinds on the fifth day. On the sixth day He created all the animals of the earth, and all cattle, and everything that moves on the earth.

14 After all this He created mankind. He created a man and a woman, and gave him dominion over all that is on the earth, and in the seas, and over everything that flies, and over beasts, and over cattle, and over everything that moves on the earth, and over the whole earth, and over all this He gave him dominion.

15 He created these four kinds on the sixth day. And there were altogether two and twenty kinds.

16 He finished all his work on the sixth day. That is all that is in the heavens and on the earth, and in the seas and in the abysses, and in the light and in the darkness, and in everything.

17 He gave us a great sign, the Sabbath day, that we should work six days, but keep Sabbath on the seventh day from all work.

18 All the angels of the presence (of the Lord), and all the angels of sanctification, these two great types of angels He has told to tell us to keep the Sabbath with Him in heaven and on earth.

19 And He said to us, "Look, I will separate to Myself a people from among all the peoples, and these shall keep the Sabbath day, and I will sanctify them to Myself as My people, and will bless them; as I have sanctified the Sabbath day and do sanctify it to Myself, even so will I bless them, and they shall be My people and I will be their God.

20 I have chosen the offspring of Jacob from among all that I have seen, and have written him down as My first-born son, and have sanctified him to Myself forever and ever; and I will teach them the Sabbath day, that they may keep Sabbath on it from all work."

21 He created in it a sign in accordance with which they should keep Sabbath with us on the seventh day, to eat and to drink, and to bless Him who has created all things as He has blessed and sanctified to Himself a particular, exclusive people above all peoples, and that they should keep Sabbath together with us.

22 He caused His commands to rise up as a sweet odor acceptable before Him all the days.

23 There were two and twenty heads (representatives) of mankind from Adam to Jacob, and two and twenty kinds of work (creation) were made until the seventh day; this is blessed and holy; and the former also is blessed and holy; and this one serves with that one for sanctification and blessing.

24 Jacob and his offspring were granted that they should always be the blessed and holy ones of the first testimony and law, even as He had sanctified and blessed the Sabbath day on the seventh day.

25 He created heaven and earth and everything that He created in six days, and God made the seventh day holy, for all His works; therefore He commanded on its behalf that, whoever does any work on it shall die, and that he who defiles it shall surely die.

26 Because of this, command the children of Israel to observe this day that they may keep it holy and not do on it any work, and not to defile it, as it is holier than all other days.

27 And whoever profanes it shall surely die, and whoever does any work on it shall surely die eternally, that the children of Israel may observe this day throughout their generations, and not be rooted out of the land; for it is a holy day and a blessed day.

28 Every one who observes it and keeps Sabbath on it from all his work will be holy and blessed throughout all days as we are blessed.

29 Declare and say to the children of Israel the law of this day that they should keep Sabbath on it, and that they should not forsake it in the error of their hearts; and that it is not lawful to do any work on it which is not suitable, to do their own pleasure on it, and that they should not prepare anything to be eaten or drunk on it, and that it is not lawful to draw water, or bring in or take out through their gates any burden which they had not prepared for themselves on the sixth day in their dwellings.

30 They shall not bring or take anything from house to house on that day; for that day is more holy and blessed than any jubilee day of the jubilees; on this we kept Sabbath in the heavens before it was made known to any flesh to keep Sabbath on the earth.

31 The Creator of all things blessed it, but He did not sanctify all peoples and nations to keep Sabbath, but Israel alone, them alone He permitted to eat and drink and to keep Sabbath on the earth.

32 And the Creator of all things blessed this day which He had created for blessing and holiness and glory above all days.

33 This law and testimony was given to the children of Israel as a law forever to their generations.

[Chapter 3]

1 On the sixth day of the second week, according to the word of God, we brought to Adam all the beasts, and all the cattle, and all the birds, and everything that moves on the earth, and everything that moves in the water, according to their kinds, and according to their types, the beasts on the first day; the cattle on the second day; the birds on the third day; and all that moves on the earth on the fourth day; and that moves in the water on the fifth day.

2 And Adam named them all by their respective names. As he called them, so was their name.

3 On these five days Adam saw all these, male and female, according to every kind that was on the earth, but he was alone and found no helpmate.

4 The Lord said to us, "It is not good that the man should be alone, let us make a helpmate for him."

5 And the Lord our God caused a deep sleep to fall on him, and he slept, and He took from Adam a rib from among his ribs for the woman, and this rib was the origin of the woman. And He built up the flesh in its place, and built the woman.

6 He awakened Adam out of his sleep and on awakening he rose on the sixth day, and He brought her to him, and he knew her, and said to her, "This is now bone of my bones and flesh of my flesh; she shall be called my wife; because she was taken from her husband."

7 Therefore shall man and wife become one and therefore shall a man leave his father and his mother, and cling to his wife, and they shall be one flesh.

8 In the first week Adam was created, and from his rib, his wife. In the second week God showed her to him, and for this reason the commandment was given to keep in their defilement. A male should be purified in seven days, and for a female twice seven days.

9 After Adam had completed forty days in the land where he had been created, we brought him into the garden of Eden to till and keep it, but his wife we brought in on the eightieth day, and after this she entered into the garden of Eden.

10 And for this reason the commandment is written on the heavenly tablets in regard to her that gives birth, "If she bears a male, she shall remain unclean for seven days according to the first week of days, and thirty-three days shall she remain in the blood of her purifying, and she shall not touch any holy thing, nor enter into the sanctuary, until she completes these days which are decreed in the case of a male child.

11 But in the case of a female child she shall remain unclean two weeks of days, according to the first two weeks, and sixty-six days in the blood of her purification, and they will be in all eighty days."

12 When she had completed these eighty days we brought her into the Garden of Eden, for it is holier than all the earth besides and every tree that is planted in it is holy.

13 Therefore, there was ordained regarding her who bears a male or a female child the statute of those days that she should touch no holy thing, nor enter into the sanctuary until these days for the male or female child are completed.

14 This is the law and testimony that was written down for Israel, in order that they should observe it all the days.

15 In the first week of the first jubilee, Adam and his wife were in the garden of Eden for seven years tilling and keeping it, and we gave him work and we instructed him to do everything that is suitable for tillage.

16 And he tilled the garden, and was naked and did not realize it, and was not ashamed. He protected the garden from the birds and beasts and cattle. He gathered its fruit, and ate, and put aside that which was left over for himself and for his wife.

17 After the completion of exactly seven years there, and in the second month, on the seventeenth day of the month, the serpent came and approached the woman, and the serpent said to the woman, "Has God commanded you saying, you shall not eat of every tree of the garden?"

18 She said to it, God said to us, of all the fruit of the trees of the garden, eat; but of the fruit of the tree which is in the middle of the garden God said to us, you shall not eat of it, neither shall you touch it, or you shall die."

19 The serpent said to the woman, "You shall not surely die. God does know that on the day you shall eat of it, your eyes will be opened, and you will be as gods, and you will know good and evil.

20 And the woman saw the tree that it was beautiful and pleasant to the eye, and that its fruit was good for food, and she took of it and ate.

21 First, she covered her shame with fig leaves and then she gave the fruit to Adam and he ate, and his eyes were opened, and he saw that he was naked.

22 He took fig leaves and sewed them together, and made an apron for himself, and covered his shame.

23 God cursed the serpent, and was very angry at it forever.

24 And He was very angry with the woman, because she listened to the voice of the serpent, and ate; and He said to her, "I will vastly multiply your sorrow and your pains, in sorrow you will bring forth children, and your master shall be your husband, and he will rule over you."

25 To Adam also he said, " Because you have listened to the voice of your wife, and have eaten of the tree of which I commanded you not to eat, cursed be the ground for your sake, thorns and thistles shall it produce for you, and you will eat your bread in the sweat of your face, until you return to the earth from where you were taken; for earth you are, and to earth will you return."

26 And He made for them coats of skin, and clothed them, and sent them out from the Garden of Eden.

27 On that day on which Adam went out from the Garden, he offered as a sweet odor an offering, frankincense, incense, and sweet spice, and spices in the morning with the rising of the sun from the day when he covered his shame.

28 On that day was closed the mouth of all beasts, and of cattle, and of birds, and of whatever walks, and of whatever moves, so that they could no longer speak, for they had all spoken one with another with one dialect and with one language.

29 All flesh that was in the Garden of Eden He sent out of the Garden of Eden, and all flesh was scattered according to its kinds, and according to its types to the places that had been created for them.

30 Of all the beasts and cattle only to Adam alone He gave the ability to cover his shame.

31 Because of this, it is prescribed on the heavenly tablets as touching all those who know the judgment of the law, that they should cover their shame, and should not uncover themselves as the Gentiles uncover themselves.

32 On the new moon of the fourth month, Adam and his wife went out from the Garden of Eden, and they dwelt in the land of Elda in the land of their creation.

33 And Adam called the name of his wife Eve.

34 And they had no son until the first jubilee, and after this he knew her.

35 Now he tilled the land as he had been instructed in the Garden of Eden.

[Chapter 4]

1 In the third week in the second jubilee she gave birth to Cain, and in the fourth week she gave birth to Abel, and in the fifth week she gave birth to her daughter Awan. (A week is seven years.)

2 In the first year of the third jubilee, Cain killed Abel because God accepted the sacrifice of Abel, and did not accept the offering of Cain.

3 And he killed him in the field, and his blood cried from the ground to heaven, complaining because he had killed him.

4 The Lord blamed Cain, because he had killed Abel, and He made him a fugitive on the earth because of the blood of his brother, and He cursed him on the earth.

5 Because of this it is written on the heavenly tablets, "Cursed is he who kills his neighbor treacherously, and let all who have seen and heard say, 'So be it', and the man who has seen and not reported it, let him be accursed as the one committing it."

6 For this reason we announce when we come before the Lord our God all the sin that is committed in heaven and on earth, and in light and in darkness, and everywhere.

7 And Adam and his wife mourned for Abel four weeks of years, and in the fourth year of the fifth week they became joyful, and Adam knew his wife again, and she gave birth to a son, and he called his name Seth, for he said "God has raised up a second offspring to us on the earth instead of Abel; for Cain killed him."

8 In the sixth week he begat his daughter Azura.

9 And Cain took Awan his sister to be his wife and she gave birth to Enoch at the close of the fourth jubilee.

10 In the first year of the first week of the fifth jubilee, houses were built on the earth, and Cain built a city, and called its name after the name of his son Enoch.

11 Adam knew Eve his wife and she gave birth to a total of nine sons. In the fifth week of the fifth jubilee Seth took Azura his sister to be his wife, and in the fourth year of the sixth week she gave birth to Enos.

12 He began to call on the name of the Lord on the earth.

13 In the seventh jubilee in the third week Enos took Noam his sister to be his wife, and she gave birth to a son in the third year of the fifth week, and he called his name Kenan.

14 At the close of the eighth jubilee Kenan took Mualeleth his sister to be his wife, and she gave birth to a son in the ninth jubilee, in the first week in the third year of this week, and he called his name Mahalalel.

15 In the second week of the tenth jubilee Mahalalel took to him to wife Dinah, the daughter of Barakiel the daughter of his father's brother, and she gave birth to a son in the third week in the sixth year, and he called his name Jared, for in his days the angels of the Lord descended on the earth, those who are named the Watchers, that they should instruct the children of men, and that they should do judgment and uprightness on the earth.

16 In the eleventh jubilee Jared took to himself a wife, and her name was Baraka, the daughter of Rasujal, a daughter of his father's brother, in the fourth week of this jubilee, and she gave birth to a son in the fifth week, in the fourth year of the jubilee, and he called his name Enoch.

17 He was the first among men that are born on earth who learned writing and knowledge and wisdom and who wrote down the signs of heaven according to the order of their months in a book, that men might know the seasons of the years according to the order of their separate months.

18 He was the first to write a testimony and he testified to the sons of men among the generations of the earth, and recounted the weeks of the jubilees, and made known to them the days of the years, and set in order the months and recounted the Sabbaths of the years as we made them, known to him.

19 And what was and what will be he saw in a vision of his sleep, as it will happen to the children of men throughout their generations until the day of judgment; he saw and understood everything, and wrote his testimony, and placed the testimony on earth for all the children of men and for their generations.

20 In the twelfth jubilee, in the seventh week of it, he took to himself a wife, and her name was Edna, the daughter of Danel, the daughter of his father's brother, and in the sixth year in this week she gave birth to a son and he called his name Methuselah.

21 He was with the angels of God these six jubilees of years, and they showed him everything that is on earth and in the heavens, the rule of the sun, and he wrote down everything.

22 And he testified to the Watchers, who had sinned with the daughters of men; for these had begun to unite themselves, so as to be defiled with the daughters of men, and Enoch testified against them all.

23 And he was taken from among the children of men, and we conducted him into the Garden of Eden in majesty and honor, and there he wrote down the condemnation and judgment of the world, and all the wickedness of the children of men.

24 Because of it God brought the waters of the flood on all the land of Eden; for there he was set as a sign and that he should testify against all the children of men, that he should recount all the deeds of the generations until the day of condemnation.

25 He burnt the incense of the sanctuary, even sweet spices acceptable before the Lord on the Mount.

26 For the Lord has four places on the earth, the Garden of Eden, and the Mount of the East, and this mountain on which you are this day, Mount Sinai, and Mount Zion which will be sanctified in the new creation for a sanctification of the earth; through it will the earth be sanctified from all its guilt and its uncleanness throughout the generations of the world.

27 In the fourteenth jubilee Methuselah took to himself a wife, Edna the daughter of Azrial, the daughter of his father's brother, in the third week, in the first year of this week, and he begat a son and called his name Lamech.

28 In the fifteenth jubilee in the third week Lamech took to himself a wife, and her name was Betenos the daughter of Baraki'il, the daughter of his father's brother, and in this week she gave birth to a son

and he called his name Noah, saying, "This one will comfort me for my trouble and all my work, and for the ground which the Lord has cursed."

29 At the close of the nineteenth jubilee, in the seventh week in the sixth year of it, Adam died, and all his sons buried him in the land of his creation, and he was the first to be buried in the earth.

30 He lacked seventy years of one thousand years, because one thousand years are as one day in the testimony of the heavens. Therefore was it written concerning the tree of knowledge, "On the day that you eat of it you shall die." Because of this he did not complete the one thousand years but instead he died during it.

31 At the close of this jubilee Cain was killed after him in the same year; because his house fell on him and he died in the middle of his house, and he was killed by its stones. With a stone he had killed Abel, and by a stone he was killed in righteous judgment.

32 For this reason it was ordained on the heavenly tablets, with the instrument with which a man kills his neighbor with the same shall he be killed. In the same manner that he wounded him, in like manner shall they deal with him."

33 In the twenty-fifth jubilee Noah took to himself a wife, and her name was Emzara, the daughter of Rake'el, the daughter of his father's brother, in the first year in the fifth week, and in the third year of it she gave birth to Shem, in the fifth year of it she gave birth to Ham, and in the first year in the sixth week she gave birth to Japheth.

[Chapter 5]

1 When the children of men began to multiply on the face of the earth and daughters were born to them, and the angels of God saw them on a certain year of this jubilee, that they were beautiful, and they took themselves wives of all whom they chose, and they gave birth to their sons and they were giants.

2 Because of them lawlessness increased on the earth and all flesh corrupted its way. Men and cattle and beasts and birds and everything that walked on the earth were all corrupted in their ways and their orders, and they began to devour each other. Lawlessness increased on the earth and the imagination and thoughts of all men were continually, totally evil.

3 God looked on the earth, and saw it was corrupt, and all flesh had corrupted its orders, and all that were on the earth had committed all manner of evil before His eyes.

4 He said that He would destroy man and all flesh on the face of the earth that He had created.

5 But Noah found grace before the eyes of the Lord.

6 And against the angels whom He had sent on the earth, He had boiling anger, and He gave commandment to root them out of all their dominion, and He commanded us to bind them in the depths of the earth, and look, they are bound in the middle of the earth, and are kept separate.

7 And against their sons went out a command from His mouth that they should be killed with the sword, and be left under heaven.

8 He said, "My spirit shall not always abide on man; for they also are flesh and their days shall be one hundred and twenty years."

9 He sent His sword into their presence that each should kill his neighbor, and they began to kill each other until they all fell by the sword and were destroyed from the earth.

10 And their fathers were witnesses of their destruction, and after this they were bound in the depths of the earth forever, until the day of the great condemnation, when judgment is executed on all those who have corrupted their ways and their works before the Lord.

11 He destroyed all wherever they were, and there was not one left of them whom He judged according to all their wickedness.

12 Through His work He made a new and righteous nature, so that they should not sin in their whole nature forever, but should be all righteous each in his own way always.

13 The judgment of all is ordained and written on the heavenly tablets in righteousness, even the judgment of all who depart from the path that is ordained for them to walk; and if they do not walk it, judgment is written down for every creature and for every kind.

14 There is nothing in heaven or on earth, or in light or in darkness, or in the abode of the dead or in the depth, or in the place of darkness that is not judged. All their judgments are ordained and written and engraved.

15 He will judge all, the great according to his greatness, and the small according to his smallness, and each according to his way.

16 He is not one who will regard the position of any person, nor is He one who will receive gifts, if He says that He will execute judgment on each.

17 If one gave everything that is on the earth, He will not regard the gifts or the person of any, nor accept anything at his hands, for He is a righteous judge.

18 Of the children of Israel it has been written and ordained, if they turn to him in righteousness He will forgive all their transgressions and pardon all their sins. It is written and ordained that He will show mercy to all who turn from all their guilt once each year.

19 And as for all those who corrupted their ways and their thoughts before the flood, no person was acceptable to God except Noah. His sons were saved in deference to him, and these God kept from the waters of the flood on his account; for Noah's heart was righteous in all his ways. He upheld the laws and did as God commanded him and he had not departed from anything that was ordained for him.

20 The Lord said that he would destroy everything on the earth, both men and cattle, and beasts, and birds of the air, and that which moves on the earth.

21 And He commanded Noah to make an ark, so that he might save himself from the waters of the flood.

22 And Noah made the ark in all respects as He commanded him, in the twenty-seventh jubilee of years, in the fifth week in the fifth year on the new moon of the first month.

23 He entered in the sixth year of it, in the second month, on the new moon of the second month, until the sixteenth; and he entered, and all that we brought to him, into the ark, and the Lord closed it from the outside on the seventeenth evening.

24 And the Lord opened seven floodgates of heaven, and He opened the mouths of the fountains of the great deep, seven mouths in number.

25 And the floodgates began to pour down water from the heaven forty days and forty closets, And the fountains of the deep also sent up waters, until the whole world was full of water.

26 The waters increased on the earth, by fifteen cubits (a cubit is about 18 inches) the waters rose above all the high mountains. And the ark was lift up from the earth. And it moved on the face of the waters.

27 And the water covered the face of the earth five months, which is one hundred and fifty days.

28 And the ark went and rested on the top of Lubar, one of the mountains of Ararat.

29 On the new moon in the fourth month the fountains of the great deep were closed and the floodgates of heaven were restrained; and on the new moon of the seventh month all the mouths of the bottomless gulfs of the earth were opened, and the water began to flow down into the deep below.

30 On the new moon of the tenth month the tops of the mountains were seen, and on the new moon of the first month the earth became visible.

31 The waters disappeared from the earth in the fifth week in the seventh year of it, and on the seventeenth day in the second month the earth was dry.

32 On the twenty-seventh of it he opened the ark, and sent out beasts, and cattle, and birds, and every moving thing.

[Chapter 6]

1 On the new moon of the third month he went out of the ark, and built an altar on that mountain.

2 And he made atonement for the earth, and took a kid and made atonement by its blood for all the guilt of the earth; for every thing that had been on it had been destroyed, except those that were in the ark with Noah.

3 He placed the fat of it on the altar, and he took an ox, and a goat, and a sheep and kids, and salt, and a turtle-dove, and the young of a dove, and placed a burnt sacrifice on the altar, and poured on it an offering mingled with oil, and sprinkled wine and sprinkled frankincense over everything, and caused a good and pleasing odor to arise, acceptable before the Lord.

4 And the Lord smelled the good and pleasing odor, and He made a covenant with Noah that there should not be any more floods to destroy the earth; that all the days of the earth seed-time and harvest should never cease; cold and heat, and summer and winter, and day and night should not change their order, nor cease forever.

5 "Increase and multiply on the earth, and become many, and be a blessing on it. I will inspire the fear of you and the dread of you in everything that is on earth and in the sea.

6 Look, I have given you all beasts, and all winged things, and everything that moves on the earth, and the fish in the waters, and all things for food; as the green herbs, I have given you all things to eat.

7 But you shall not eat anything live or with blood in it, for the life of all flesh is in the blood, or your blood of your lives will be required. At the hand of every man, at the hand of every beast will I require the blood of man.

8 Whoever sheds man's blood by man shall his blood be shed, for in the image of God He made man.

9 Increase, and multiply on the earth."

10 Noah and his sons swore that they would not eat any blood that was in any flesh, and he made a covenant before the Lord God forever throughout all the generations of the earth in this month.

11 Because of this He spoke to you that you should make a covenant with the children of Israel with an oath. In this month, on the mountain you should sprinkle blood on them because of all the words of the covenant, which the Lord made with them forever.

12 This testimony is written concerning you that you should observe it continually, so that you should not eat on any day any blood of beasts or birds or cattle during all the days of the earth, and the man who eats the blood of beast or of cattle or of birds during all the days of the earth, he and his offspring shall be rooted out of the land.

13 And you will command the children of Israel to eat no blood, so that their names and their offspring may be before the Lord our God continually.

14 There is no limit of days, for this law. It is forever. They shall observe it throughout their generations, so that they may continue supplicating on your behalf with blood before the altar; every day and at the time of morning and evening they shall seek forgiveness on your behalf perpetually before the Lord that they may keep it and not be rooted out.

15 And He gave to Noah and his sons a sign that there should not again be a flood on the earth.

16 He set His bow (a rainbow) in the cloud as a sign of the eternal covenant that there should never again be a flood on the earth to destroy it for all the days of the earth.

17 For this reason it is ordained and written on the heavenly tablets, that they should celebrate the feast of weeks in this month once a year, to renew the covenant every year.

18 This whole festival was celebrated in heaven from the day of creation until the days of Noah, which were twenty-six jubilees and five weeks of years. Noah and his sons observed it for seven jubilees and one week of years, until the day of Noah's death. From the day of Noah's death his sons did away with it until the days of Abraham, and they ate blood.

19 But Abraham observed it, and Isaac and Jacob and his children observed it up to your days, and in your days the children of Israel forgot it until you celebrated it anew on this mountain.

20 Command the children of Israel to observe this festival in all their generations for a commandment to them, one day in the year in this month they shall celebrate the festival.

21 For it is the feast of weeks and the feast of first-fruits, this feast is twofold and of a double nature, according to what is written and engraved concerning it, celebrate it.

22 For I have written in the book of the first law, in that which I have written for you, that you should celebrate it in its season, one day in the year, and I explained to you its sacrifices that the children of Israel should remember and should celebrate it throughout their generations in this month, the same day in every year.

23 On the new moon of the first month, and on the new moon of the fourth month, and on the new moon of the seventh month, and on the new moon of the tenth month are the days of remembrance, and the days of the seasons in the four divisions of the year. These are written and ordained as a testimony forever.

24 Noah ordained them for himself as feasts for the generations forever, so that they have become a memorial to him.

25 On the new moon of the first month he was told to make for himself an ark, and on that day the earth was dry and he saw from the opened ark, the earth. On the new moon of the fourth month the mouths of the depths of the bottomless pit beneath were closed.

26 On the new moon of the seventh month all the mouths of the abysses of the earth were opened, and the waters began to descend into them.

27 On the new moon of the tenth month the tops of the mountains were seen, and Noah was glad.

28 Because of this he ordained them for himself as feasts for a memorial forever, and thus are they ordained.

29 And they placed them on the heavenly tablets, each had thirteen weeks; from one to another passed their memorial, from the first to the second, and from the second to the third, and from the third to the fourth.

30 All the days of the commandment will be two and fifty weeks of days, and these will make the entire year complete. Thus it is engraved and ordained on the heavenly tablets.

31 And there is no neglecting this commandment for a single year or from year to year.

32 Command the children of Israel that they observe the years according to this counting, three hundred and sixty-four days, and these will constitute a complete year, and they will not disturb its time from its days and from its feasts; for every thing will fall out in them according to their testimony, and they will not leave out any day nor disturb any feasts.

33 But if they neglect and do not observe them according to His commandment, then they will disturb all their seasons and the years will be dislodged from this order, and they will neglect their established rules.

34 And all the children of Israel will forget and will not find the path of the years, and will forget the new moons, and seasons, and sabbaths and they will wrongly determine all the order of the years.

35 For I know and from now on will I declare it to you, and it is not of my own devising; for the book lies written in the presence of me, and on the heavenly tablets the division of days is ordained, or they forget the feasts of the covenant and walk according to the feasts of the Gentiles after their error and after their ignorance.

36 For there will be those who will assuredly make observations of the moon and how it disturbs the seasons and comes in from year to year ten days too soon.

37 For this reason the years will come upon them when they disturb (misinterpret) the order, and make an abominable day the day of testimony, and an unclean day a feast day, and they will confound all the days, the holy with the unclean, and the unclean day with the holy; for they will go wrong as to the months and sabbaths and feasts and jubilees.

38 For this reason I command and testify to you that you may testify to them; for after your death your children will disturb them, so that they will not make the year three hundred and sixty-four days only, and for this reason they will go wrong as to the new moons and seasons and sabbaths and festivals, and they will eat all kinds of blood with all kinds of flesh.

[Chapter 7]

1 In the seventh week in the first year of it, in this jubilee, Noah planted vines on the mountain on which the ark had rested, named Lubar, one of the Ararat Mountains, and they produced fruit in the fourth year, and he guarded their fruit, and gathered it in that year in the seventh month.

2 He made wine from it and put it into a vessel, and kept it until the fifth year, until the first day, on the new moon of the first month.

3 And he celebrated with joy the day of this feast, and he made a burnt sacrifice to the Lord, one young ox and one ram, and seven sheep, each a year old, and a kid of the goats, that he might make atonement thereby for himself and his sons.

4 He prepared the kid first, and placed some of its blood on the flesh that was on the altar that he had made, and all the fat he laid on the altar where he made the burnt sacrifice, and the ox and the ram and the sheep, and he laid all their flesh on the altar.

5 He placed all their offerings mingled with oil on it, and afterwards he sprinkled wine on the fire which had previously been made on the altar, and he placed incense on the altar and caused a sweet odor to rise up which was acceptable before the Lord his God.

6 And he rejoiced and he and his children drank the wine with joy.

7 It was evening, and he went into his tent, and being drunken he lay down and slept, and was uncovered in his tent as he slept.

8 And Ham saw Noah his father naked, and went out and told his two brothers (ridiculed his father to his two brothers) who were outside.

9 Shem took his garment and arose, he and Japheth, and they placed the garment on their shoulders and went backward and covered the shame of their father, and their faces were backward.

10 Noah awoke from sleep and knew all (abuse) that his younger son had done to him. He cursed him saying, "Cursed be Canaan; an enslaved servant shall he be to his brothers."

11 And he blessed Shem, and said, "Blessed be the Lord God of Shem, and Canaan shall be his servant.

12 God shall enlarge Japheth, and God shall dwell in the dwelling of Shem, and Canaan shall be his servant."

13 Ham knew that his father had cursed, him, his younger son, and he was displeased that he had cursed him, his son. And Ham parted from his father, he and his sons with him, Cush and Mizraim and Put and Canaan.

14 And he built for himself a city and called its name after the name of his wife Ne'elatama'uk.

15 Japheth saw it, and became envious of his brother, and he too built for himself a city, and he called its name after the name of his wife Adataneses.

16 Shem dwelt with his father Noah, and he built a city close to his father on the mountain, and he too called its name after the name of his wife Sedeqetelebab.

17 These three cities are near Mount Lubar; Sedeqetelebab in front of the mountain on its east; and Na'eltama'uk on the south; Adatan'eses towards the west.

18 These are the sons of Shem, Elam, and Asshur, and Arpachshad who was born two years after the flood, and Lud, and Aram.

19 The sons of Japheth, Gomer, Magog, Madai, Javan, Tubal and Meshech and Tiras, these are the descendants of Noah.

20 In the twenty-eighth jubilee Noah began to direct his sons in the ordinances and commandments, and all the judgments that he knew, and he exhorted his sons to observe righteousness, and to cover the shame of their flesh, and to bless their Creator, and honor father and mother, and love their neighbor, and guard their souls from fornication and uncleanness and all iniquity.

21 Because of these three things came the flood on the earth, namely, the fornication that the Watchers committed against the law of their ordinances when they went whoring after the daughters of men, and took themselves wives of all they chose, and they made the beginning of uncleanness.

22 And they begat sons, the Naphilim (Naphidim), and they were all dissimilar, and they devoured one another, and the Giants killed the Naphil, and the Naphil killed the Eljo, and the Eljo killed mankind, and one man killed one another.

23 Every one committed himself to crime and injustice and to shed much blood, and the earth was filled with sin.

24 After this they sinned against the beasts and birds, and all that moved and walked on the earth, and much blood was shed on the earth, and men continually desired only what was useless and evil.

25 And the Lord destroyed everything from the face of the earth. Because of the wickedness of their deeds, and because of the blood they had shed over all the earth, He destroyed everything. "

26 We were left, I and you, my sons, and everything that entered with us into the ark, and behold I see your works before me that you do not walk in righteousness, for in the path of destruction you have begun to walk, and you are turning one against another, and are envious one of another, and so it comes that you are not in harmony, my sons, each with his brother.

27 For I see the demons have begun their seductions against you and against your children and now I fear on your behalf, that after my death you will shed the blood of men on the earth, and that you, too, will be destroyed from the face of the earth.

28 For whoever sheds man's blood, and who ever eats the blood of any flesh, shall all be destroyed from the earth.

29 There shall be no man left that eats blood, or that sheds the blood of man on the earth, nor shall there be left to him any offspring or descendants living under heaven. Into the abode of the dead shall they go, and into the place of condemnation shall they descend, and into the darkness of the deep shall they all be removed by a violent death.

30 Do not smear blood on yourself or let it remain on you. Out of all the blood there shall be shed and out of all the days in which you have killed any beasts or cattle or whatever flies on the earth you must do a good work to your souls by covering that which has been shed on the face of the earth.

31 You shall not be like him who eats blood, but guard yourselves that none may eat blood before you, cover the blood, for thus have I been commanded to testify to you and your children, together with all flesh.

32 Do not permit the soul (life) to be eaten with the flesh, that your blood, which is your life, may not be required at the hand of any flesh that sheds it on the earth.

33 For the earth will not be clean from the blood that has been shed on it, for only through the blood of him that shed it will the earth be purified throughout all its generations.

34 Now, my children, listen, have judgment and righteousness that you maybe planted in righteousness over the face of the whole earth, and your glory lifted up in the presence of my God, who spared me from the waters of the flood.

35 Look, you will go and build for yourselves cities, and plant in them all the plants that are on the earth, and moreover all fruit-bearing trees.

36 For three years the fruit of everything that is eaten will not be gathered, and in the fourth year its fruit will be accounted holy, offered as first fruit, acceptable before the Most High God, who created heaven and earth and all things.

37 Let them offer in abundance the first of the wine and oil as first-fruits on the altar of the Lord, who receives it, and what is left let the servants of the house of the Lord eat before the altar which receives it.

38 In the fifth year make the release so that you release it in righteousness and uprightness, and you shall be righteous, and all that you plant shall prosper. For this is how Enoch did it, the father of your father commanded Methuselah, his son, and Methuselah commanded his son Lamech, and Lamech commanded me all the things that his fathers commanded him.

39 I also will give you commandment, my sons, as Enoch commanded his son in the first jubilees, while still living, the seventh in his generation, he commanded and testified to his son and to his son's sons until the day of his death.

[Chapter 8]

1 In the twenty-ninth jubilee, in the beginning of first week, Arpachshad took to himself a wife and her name was Rasu'eja, the daughter of Susan, the daughter of Elam, and she gave birth to a son in the third year in this week, and he called his name Kainam.

2 The son grew, and his father taught him writing, and he went to seek for himself a place where he might seize a city for himself.

3 He found writing which former generations had carved on a rock, and he read what was on it, and he transcribed it and sinned because of it, for it contained the teaching of the Watchers, which they had used to observe the omens of the sun and moon and stars in all the signs of heaven.

4 He wrote it down and said nothing of it, for he was afraid to speak to Noah about it or he would be angry with him because of it.

5 In the thirtieth jubilee, in the second week, in the first year of it, he took to himself a wife, and her name was Melka, the daughter of Madai, the son of Japheth, and in the fourth year he begat a son, and called his name Shelah; for he said, "Truly I have been sent."

6 Shelah grew up and took to himself a wife, and her name was Mu'ak, the daughter of Kesed, his father's brother, in the one and thirtieth jubilee, in the fifth week, in the first year of it.

7 And she gave birth to a son in the fifth year of it, and he called his name Eber, and he took to himself a wife, and her name was Azurad, the daughter of Nebrod, in the thirty-second jubilee, in the seventh week, in the third year of it.

8 In the sixth year of it, she gave birth to a son, and he called his name Peleg, for in the days when he was born the children of Noah began to divide the earth among themselves, for this reason he called his name Peleg.

9 They divided it secretly among themselves, and told it to Noah.

10 In the beginning of the thirty-third jubilee they divided the earth into three parts, for Shem and Ham and Japheth, according to the inheritance of each, in the first year in the first week, when one of us (angels) who had been sent, was with them.

11 He called his sons, and they drew close to him, they and their children, and he divided the earth into the lots, which his three sons were to take in possession, and they reached out their hands, and took the writing out of the arms of Noah, their father.

12 There came out on the writing as Shem's lot the middle of the earth that he should take as an inheritance for himself and for his sons for the generations of eternity. From the middle of the mountain range of Rafa, from the mouth of the water from the river Tina, and his portion goes towards the west through the middle of this river, and it extends until it reaches the water of the abysses, out of which this river goes out and pours its waters into the sea Me'at, and this river flows into the great sea.

13 All that is towards the north is Japheth's, and all that is towards the south belongs to Shem. And it extends until it reaches Karaso, this is in the center of the tongue of land that looks towards the south.

14 His portion extends along the great sea, and it extends in a straight line until it reaches the west of the tongue that looks towards the south, for this sea is named the tongue of the Egyptian Sea.

15 And it turns from here towards the south towards the mouth of the great sea on the shore of its waters, and it extends to the west to Afra, and it extends until it reaches the waters of the river Gihon, and to the south of the waters of Gihon, to the banks of this river.

16 It extends towards the east, until it reaches the Garden of Eden, to the south of it and from the east of the whole land of Eden and of the whole east, it turns to the east and proceeds until it reaches the east of the mountain named Rafa, and it descends to the bank of the mouth of the river Tina.

17 This portion came out by lot for Shem and his sons, that they should possess it forever to his generations forever.

18 Noah rejoiced that this portion came out for Shem and for his sons, and he remembered all that he had spoken with his mouth in prophecy; for he had said, "Blessed be the Lord God of Shem and may the Lord dwell in the dwelling of Shem."

19 He knew that the Garden of Eden is the holy of holies, and the dwelling of the Lord, and Mount Sinai the center of the desert, and Mount Zion which is the center of the navel of the earth, these three were created as holy places facing each other.

20 And he blessed the God of gods, who had put the word of the Lord into his mouth, and the Lord forever.

21 And he knew that a blessed portion and a blessing had come to Shem and his sons and to their generations forever which was the whole land of Eden and the whole land of the Red Sea, and the whole land of the east and India, and on the Red Sea and the mountains of it, and all the land of Bashan, and all the land of Lebanon and the islands of Kaftur, and all the mountains of Sanir and Amana, and the mountains of Asshur in the north, and all the land of Elam, Asshur, and Babel, and Susan and Ma'edai,

and all the mountains of Ararat, and all the region beyond the sea, which is beyond the mountains of Asshur towards the north, a blessed and spacious land, and all that is in it is very good.

22 Ham received the second portion, beyond the Gihon towards the south to the right of the Garden, and it extends towards the south and it extends to all the mountains of fire, and it extends towards the west to the sea of 'atel and it extends towards the west until it reaches the sea of Ma'uk which was that sea into which everything that is not destroyed descends.

23 It goes out towards the north to the limits of Gadir, and it goes out to the coast of the waters of the sea to the waters of the great sea until it draws near to the river Gihon, and goes along the river Gihon until it reaches the right of the Garden of Eden.

24 This is the land that came out for Ham as the portion which he was to occupy forever for himself and his sons to their generations forever.

25 Japheth received the third portion beyond the river Tina to the north of the outflow of its waters, and it extends north-easterly to the whole region of Gog, and to all the country east of it.

26 It extends northerly, and it extends to the mountains of Qelt towards the north, and towards the sea of Ma'uk, and it goes out to the east of Gadir as far as the region of the waters of the sea.

27 It extends until it approaches the west of Fara and it returns towards Aferag, and it extends easterly to the waters of the sea of Me'at.

28 It extends to the region of the river Tina in a northeasterly direction until it approaches the boundary of its waters towards the mountain Rafa, and it turns round towards the north.

29 This is the land that came out for Japheth and his sons as the portion of his inheritance that he should possess five great islands, and a great land in the north, for himself and his sons, for their generations forever.

30 But it is cold, and the land of Ham is hot, and the land of Shem is neither hot nor cold, but it is of blended cold and heat.

[Chapter 9]

1 Ham divided among his sons, and the first portion came out for Cush towards the east, and to the west of him for Mizraim, and to the west of him for Put, and to the west of him on the sea for Canaan.

2 Shem also divided among his sons, and the first portion came out for Elam and his sons, to the east of the river Tigris until it approaches the east, the whole land of India, and on the Red Sea on its coast, and the waters of Dedan, and all the mountains of Mebri and Ela, and all the land of Susan and all that is on the side of Pharnak to the Red Sea and the river Tina.

3 Asshur received the second Portion, all the land of Asshur and Nineveh and Shinar and to the border of India, and it ascends and skirts the river.

4 Arpachshad received the third portion, all the land of the region of the Chaldees to the east of the Euphrates, bordering on the Red Sea, and all the waters of the desert close to the tongue of the sea which looks towards Egypt, all the land of Lebanon and Sanir and Amana to the border of the Euphrates.

5 Aram received the fourth portion, all the land of Mesopotamia between the Tigris and the Euphrates to the north of the Chaldees to the border of the mountains of Asshur and the land of Arara.

6 Lud got the fifth portion, the mountains of Asshur and all surrounding to them until it reaches the Great Sea, and until it reaches the east of Asshur his brother.

7 Japheth also divided the land of his inheritance among his sons.

8 The first portion came out for Gomer to the east from the north side to the river Tina, and in the north there came out for Magog all the inner portions of the north until it reaches to the sea of Me'at.

9 Madai received as his portion that he should possess from the west of his two brothers to the islands, and to the coasts of the islands.

10 Javan got the fourth portion, every island and the islands that are towards the border of Lud.

11 For Tubal there came out the fifth portion in the middle of the tongue that approaches towards the border of the portion of Lud to the second tongue, to the region beyond the second tongue to the third tongue.

12 Meshech received the sixth portion, that is the entire region beyond the third tongue until it approaches the east of Gadir.

13 Tiras got the seventh portion, four great islands in the middle of the sea, which reach to the portion of Ham, and the islands of Kamaturi came out by lot for the sons of Arpachshad as his inheritance.

14 Thus the sons of Noah divided to their sons in the presence of Noah their father, and he bound them all by an oath, and invoked a curse on every one that sought to seize any portion which had not fallen to him by his lot.

15 They all said, "so be it; so be it " (amen and amen) for themselves and their sons forever throughout their generations until the day of judgment, on which the Lord God shall judge them with a sword and with fire for all the unclean wickedness of their errors, that they have filled the earth with, which are transgression, uncleanness and fornication and sin.

[Chapter 10]

1 In the third week of this jubilee the unclean demons began to lead astray the children of the sons of Noah, and to make them sin and to destroy them.

2 The sons of Noah came to Noah their father, and they told him about the demons that were leading astray and blinding and slaying his sons' sons.

3 And he prayed before the Lord his God, and said,
"God of the spirits of all flesh, who have shown mercy to me and have spared me and my sons from the waters of the flood,
and have not caused me to die as You did the sons of perdition; For Your grace has been great toward me,
and great has been Your mercy to my soul. Let Your grace be lifted up on my sons, and do not let the wicked spirits rule over them or they will destroy them from the earth.

4 But bless me and my sons, so that we may increase and multiply and replenish the earth.

5 You know how Your Watchers, the fathers of these spirits, acted in my day, and as for these spirits which are living, imprison them and hold them fast in the place of condemnation, and let them not bring destruction on the sons of your servant, my God; for these are like cancer and are created in order to destroy.

6 Let them not rule over the spirits of the living; for You alone can exercise dominion over them. And let them not have power over the sons of the righteous from now and forever."

7 And the Lord our God commanded us (angels) to bind all of them.

8 The chief of the spirits, Mastema, came and said, "Lord, Creator, let some of them remain before me, and let them listen to my voice, and do all that I shall say to them; for if some of them are not left to me, I shall not be able to execute the power of my will on the sons of men, for these are for corruption and leading astray before my judgment, for great is the wickedness of the sons of men."

9 He said, "Let one-tenth of them remain before him, and let nine-tenths of them descend into the place of condemnation."

10 He commanded one of us to teach Noah all their medicines, for He knew that they would not walk in uprightness, nor strive in righteousness.

11 We did according to all His words, all the malignant evil ones we bound in the place of condemnation and a tenth part of them we left that they might be subject in the presence of Satan on the earth.

12 We explained to Noah all the medicines of their diseases, together with their seductions, how they might heal them with herbs of the earth.

13 Noah wrote down all things in a book as we instructed him concerning every kind of medicine. Thus the evil spirits were precluded from hurting the sons of Noah.

14 He gave all that he had written to Shem, his eldest son, for he loved him greatly above all his sons.

15 And Noah slept with his fathers, and was buried on Mount Lubar in the land of Ararat.

16 Nine hundred and fifty years he completed in his life, nineteen jubilees and two weeks and five years.

17 In his life on earth he was greater than all the children of men except Enoch because of his righteousness he was perfect. For Enoch's office was ordained for a testimony to the generations of the world, so that he should recount all the deeds of generation to generation, until the day of judgment.

18 In the three and thirtieth jubilee, in the first year in the second week, Peleg took to himself a wife, whose name was Lomna the daughter of Sina'ar, and she gave birth to a son for him in the fourth year of this week, and he called his name Reu, for he said, "Look the children of men have become evil because the building a city and a tower in the land of Shinar was for an evil purpose."

19 For they departed from the land of Ararat eastward to Shinar, for in his days they built the city and the tower, saying, "Come, let us rise up by the tower into heaven."

20 They began to build, and in the fourth week they made brick with fire, and the bricks served them for stone,
and the clay with which they cemented them together was asphalt which comes out of the sea, and out of the fountains of water in the land of Shinar.

21 They built it, forty-three years were they building it. Its breadth was 203 bricks, and the height of a brick was the third of one; its height amounted to 5433 cubits and 2 palms, and the extent of one wall was thirteen times 600 feet and of the other thirty times 600 feet.

22 And the Lord our God said to us, "Look, they are one people, and they begin to do this, and now nothing will be withheld from them. Let us go down and confound their language, that they may not understand one another's speech, and they may be dispersed into cities and nations, and they will not be in agreement together with one purpose until the day of judgment."

23 And the Lord descended, and we descended with him to see the city and the tower that the children of men had built.

24 He confounded their language, and they no longer understood one another's speech, and they then ceased to build the city and the tower.

25 For this reason the whole land of Shinar is called Babel, because the Lord confounded all the language of the children of men there, and from that place they were dispersed into their cities, each according to his language and his nation.

26 Then, the Lord sent a mighty wind against the tower and it fell to the earth, and behold it was between Asshur and Babylon in the land of Shinar, and they called its name "Overthrow."

27 In the fourth week in the first year in the beginning of it in the four and thirtieth jubilee, were they dispersed from the land of Shinar.

28 Ham and his sons went into the land that he was to occupy, which he acquired as his portion in the land of the south.

29 Canaan saw the land of Lebanon to the river of Egypt was very good, and he did not go into the land of his inheritance to the west that is to the sea, and he dwelt in the land of Lebanon, eastward and westward from the border of Jordan and from the border of the sea.

30 Ham, his father, and Cush and Mizraim, his brothers, said to him, "You have settled in a land which is not yours, and which did not fall to us by lot, do not do so. If you do you and your sons will be conquered in the land and be accursed through a war. By war you have settled, and by war will your children fall, and you will be rooted out forever.

31 Do not live in the land of Shem, for to Shem and to his sons did it come by their lot.

32 Cursed are you, and cursed will you be beyond all the sons of Noah, by the curse by which we bound ourselves by an oath in the presence of the holy judge, and in the presence of Noah our father."

33 But he did not listen to them, and settled in the land of Lebanon from Hamath to the border of Egypt, he and his sons until this day. For this reason that land is named Canaan. And Japheth and his sons went towards the sea and settled in the land of their portion, and Madai saw the land of the sea and it did not please him, and he begged Ham and Asshur and Arpachshad, his wife's brother for a portion, and he dwelt in the land of Media, near to his wife's brother until this day.

34 And he called his and his son's dwelling-place, Media, after the name of their father Madai.

[Chapter 11]

1 In the thirty-fifth jubilee, in the third week, in the first year of it, Reu took to himself a wife, and her name was 'Ora, the daughter of 'Ur, the son of Kesed, and she gave birth to a son, and he called his name Seroh, in the seventh year of this week in this jubilee.

2 The sons of Noah began to war with each other, to take captives and kill each other, and to shed the blood of men on the earth, and to eat blood, and to build strong cities, and walls, and towers, and individuals began to exalt themselves above the nation, and to establish kingdoms, and to go to war, people against people, and nation against nation, and city against city, and all began to do evil, and to acquire arms, and to teach their sons war, and they began to capture cities, and to sell male and female slaves.

3 Ur, the son of Kesed, built the city of Ara of the Chaldees, and called its name after his own name and the name of his father.

4 And they made themselves molten images, and they worshipped the idols and the molten image they had made for themselves, and they began to make graven images and unclean and shadowy presence, and malevolent and malicious spirits assisted and seduced them into committing transgression and uncleanness.

5 Prince Mastema exerted himself to do all this, and he sent out other spirits, which were put under his control, to do all manner of wrong and sin, and all manner of transgression, to corrupt and destroy, and to shed blood on the earth.

6 For this reason he called the name of Seroh, Serug, for every one turned to do all manner of sin and transgression.

7 He grew up, and dwelt in Ur of the Chaldees, near to the father of his wife's mother, and he worshipped idols, and he took to himself a wife in the thirty-sixth jubilee, in the fifth week, in the first year of it, and her name was Melka, the daughter of Kaber, the daughter of his father's brother.

8 She gave birth to Nahor, in the first year of this week, and he grew and dwelt in Ur of the Chaldees, and his father taught him the sciences of the Chaldees to divine and conjure, according to the signs of heaven.

9 In the thirty-seventh jubilee in the sixth week, in the first year of it, he took to himself a wife, and her name was 'Ijaska, the daughter of Nestag of the Chaldees.

10 And she gave birth to Terah in the seventh year of this week.

11 Prince Mastema sent ravens and birds to devour the seed that was sown in the land, in order to destroy the land, and rob the children of men of their labors. Before they could plow in the seed, the ravens picked it from the surface of the ground.

12 This is why he called his name Terah because the ravens and the birds reduced them to destitution and devoured their seed.

13 The years began to be barren, because of the birds, and they devoured all the fruit of the trees from the trees, it was only with great effort that they could harvest a little fruit from the earth in their days.

14 In this thirty-ninth jubilee, in the second week in the first year, Terah took to himself a wife, and her name was 'Edna, the daughter of Abram, the daughter of his father's sister.

15 In the seventh year of this week she gave birth to a son, and he called his name Abram, by the name of the father of his mother, for he had died before his daughter had conceived a son.

16 And the child began to understand the errors of the earth that all went astray after graven images and after uncleanness,

and his father taught him writing, and he was two weeks of years old, and he separated himself from his father, that he might not worship idols with him.

17 He began to pray to the Creator of all things that He might spare him from the errors of the children of men, and that his portion should not fall into error after uncleanness and vileness.

18 The time came for the sowing of seed in the land, and they all went out together to protect their seed against the ravens, and Abram went out with those that went, and the child was a lad of fourteen years.

19 A cloud of ravens came to devour the seed, and Abram ran to meet them before they settled on the ground, and cried to them before they settled on the ground to devour the seed, and said, "Descend not, return to the place from where you came," and they began to turn back.

20 And he caused the clouds of ravens to turn back that day seventy times, and of all the ravens throughout all the land where Abram was there settled not so much as one.

21 All who were with him throughout all the land saw him cry out, and all the ravens turn back, and his name became great in all the land of the Chaldees.

22 There came to him this year all those that wished to sow, and he went with them until the time of sowing ceased, and they sowed their land, and that year they brought enough grain home to eat and they were satisfied.

23 In the first year of the fifth week Abram taught those who made implements for oxen, the artificers in wood, and they made a vessel above the ground, facing the frame of the plow, in order to put the seed in it, and the seed fell down from it on the share of the plow, and was hidden in the earth, and they no longer feared the ravens.

24 After this manner they made vessels above the ground on all the frames of the plows, and they sowed and tilled all the land, according as Abram commanded them, and they no longer feared the birds.

[Chapter 12]

1 In the sixth week, in the seventh year of it, that Abram said to Terah his father, saying, "Father!"

2 He said, "Look, here am I, my son." He said, "What help and profit have we from those idols which you worship, and in the presence of which you bow yourself?

3 For there is no spirit in them. They are dumb forms, and they mislead the heart.

4 Do not worship them, Worship the God of heaven, who causes the rain and the dew to fall on the earth and does everything on the earth, and has created everything by His word, and all life is from His presence.

5 Why do you worship things that have no spirit in them?

For they are the work of men's hands, and you bear them on your shoulders, and you have no help from them, but they are a great cause of shame to those who make them, and they mislead the heart of those who worship them. Do not worship them."

6 His father said to him, "I also know it, my son, but what shall I do with a people who have made me serve them?

7 If I tell them the truth, they will kill me, because their soul clings to them so they worship them and honor them.

8 Keep silent, my son, or they will kill you." And these words he spoke to his two brothers, and they were angry with him and he kept silent.

9 In the fortieth jubilee, in the second week, in the seventh year of it, Abram took to himself a wife, and her name was Sarai, the daughter of his father, and she became his wife.

10 Haran, his brother, took to himself a wife in the third year of the third week, and she gave birth to a son in the seventh year of this week, and he called his name Lot.

11 Nahor, his brother, took to himself a wife.

12 In the sixtieth year of the life of Abram, that is, in the fourth week, in the fourth year of it, Abram arose in the night and burned the house of the idols, and he burned all that was in the house and no man knew it.

13 And they arose and sought to save their gods from the fire.

14 Haran hasted to save them, but the fire flamed over him, and he was burnt in the fire, and he died in Ur of the Chaldees before Terah his father, and they buried him in Ur of the Chaldees.

15 Terah went out from Ur of the Chaldees, he and his sons, to go into the land of Lebanon and into the land of Canaan, and he dwelt in the land of Haran, and Abram dwelt with Terah his father in Haran two weeks of years.

16 In the sixth week, in the fifth year of it, Abram sat up all night on the new moon of the seventh month to observe the stars from the evening to the morning, in order to see what would be the character of the year with regard to the rains, and he was alone as he sat and observed.

17 And a word came into his heart and he said, "All the signs of the stars, and the signs of the moon and of the sun are all in the hand of the Lord. Why do I search them out?

18 If He desires, He causes it to rain, morning and evening, and if He desires, He withholds it, and all things are in his hand."

19 He prayed in the night and said, "My God, God Most High, You alone are my God, and You and Your dominion have I chosen. And You have created all things, and all things that are the work of Your hands.

20 Deliver me from the hands of evil spirits who have dominion over the thoughts of men's hearts, and let them not lead me astray from You, my God. And establish me and my offspring forever so that we do not go astray from now and forever."

21 He said, "Shall I return to Ur of the Chaldees who are trying to find me? Should I return to them? Am I to remain here in this place? The right path is before You. Make it prosper in the hands of your servant that he may fulfill it and that I may not walk in the deceitfulness of my heart, O my God."

22 He stopped speaking and stopped praying, and then the word of the Lord was sent to him through me, saying, "Get out of your country, and from your kindred and from the house of your father and go to a land which I will show you, and I shall make you a great and numerous nation.

23 And I will bless you and I will make your name great,

and you will be blessed in the earth, and in You shall all families of the earth be blessed, and I will bless them that bless you, and curse them that curse you.

24 I will be a God to you and your son, and to your son's son, and to all your offspring, fear not, from now on and to all generations of the earth I am your God."

25 The Lord God said, "Open his mouth and his ears, that he may hear and speak with his mouth, with the language which has been revealed," for it had ceased from the mouths of all the children of men from the day of the overthrow of Babel.

26 And I opened his mouth, and his ears and his lips, and I began to speak with him in Hebrew in the tongue of the creation.

27 He took the books of his fathers, and these were written in Hebrew, and he transcribed them, and he began from then on to study them, and I made known to him that which he could not understand, and he studied them during the six rainy months.

28 In the seventh year of the sixth week he spoke to his father and informed him, that he would leave Haran to go into the land of Canaan to see it and return to him.

29 Terah his father said to him; "Go in peace. May the eternal God make your path straight. And the Lord be with you, and protect you from all evil, and grant to you grace, mercy and favor before those who see you, and may none of the children of men have power over you to harm you. Go in peace.

30 If you see a land pleasant to your eyes to dwell in, then arise and take me with you and take Lot with you, the son of Haran your brother as your own son, the Lord be with you.

31 Nahor your brother leave with me until you return in peace, and we go with you all together."

[Chapter 13]

1 Abram journeyed from Haran, and he took Sarai, his wife, and Lot, his brother Haran's son and they went to the land of Canaan, and he came into Asshur, and proceeded to Shechem, and dwelt near a tall oak.

2 He saw the land was very pleasant from the border of Hamath to the tall oak.

3 The Lord said to him, "To you and to your offspring I will give this land."

4 He built an altar there, and he offered on it a burnt sacrifice to the Lord, who had appeared to him.

5 He left from that place and went to the mountain Bethel on the west and Ai on the east, and pitched his tent there.

6 He saw the land was very wide and good, and everything grew on it, vines, and figs, and pomegranates, oaks, and ilexes, and turpentine and oil trees, and cedars and cypresses, and date trees, and all trees of the field, and there was water on the mountains.

7 And he blessed the Lord who had led him out of Ur of the Chaldees, and had brought him to this land.

8 In the first year, in the seventh week, on the new moon of the first month, he built an altar on this mountain, and called on the name of the Lord and said, "You, the eternal God, are my God."

9 He offered on the altar a burnt sacrifice to the Lord that He should be with him and not forsake him all the days of his life.

10 He left that place and went toward the south, and he came to Hebron and Hebron was built at that time, and he lived there two years, and he went from that place into the land of the south, to Bealoth, and there was a famine in the land.

11 Abram went into Egypt in the third year of the week, and he dwelt in Egypt five years before his wife was torn away from him.

12 Now, Tanais in Egypt was built seven years after Hebron.

13 When Pharaoh seized Sarai, the wife of Abram the Lord plagued Pharaoh and his house with great plagues because of Sarai, Abram's wife.

14 Abram was celebrated and admired because of his great possessions of sheep, and cattle, and donkeys, and horses, and camels, and menservants, and maidservants, and in silver and gold. Lot and his brother's son were also wealthy.

15 Pharaoh gave back Sarai, the wife of Abram, and he sent him out of the land of Egypt, and he journeyed to the place where he had pitched his tent at the beginning, to the place of the altar, with Ai on the east, and Bethel on the west, and he blessed the Lord his God who had brought him back in peace.

16 In the forty-first jubilee in the third year of the first week, that he returned to this place and offered on it a burnt sacrifice, and called on the name of the Lord, and said, "You, the most high God, are my God forever and ever."

17 In the fourth year of this week Lot parted from him, and Lot lived in Sodom, and the men of Sodom sinned greatly.

18 It grieved him in his heart that his brother's son had parted from him because Abram had no children.

19 After Lot had parted from him, in the fourth year of this week. In that year when Lot was taken captive, the Lord said to Abram, "Lift up your eyes from the place where you are dwelling, northward and southward, and westward and eastward.

20 All the land that you see I will give to you and to your offspring forever, and I will make your offspring as the sand of the sea, though a man may number the dust of the earth, yet your offspring shall not be numbered.

21 Arise, walk through the land in the length of it and the breadth of it, and see it all. To your offspring will I give it." And Abram went to Hebron, and lived there.

22 And in this year came Chedorlaomer, king of Elam, and Amraphel, king of Shinar, and Arioch king of Sellasar, and Tergal, king of nations, and killed the king of Gomorrah, and the king of Sodom fled, and many fell through wounds in the valley of Siddim, by the Salt Sea.

23 They took captive Sodom and Adam and Zeboim, and they took Lot captive, the son of Abram's brother, and all his possessions, and they went to Dan.

24 One who had escaped came and told Abram that his brother's son had been taken captive.

25 And Abram equipped his household servants for Abram, and for his offspring, a tenth of the first-fruits to the Lord, and the Lord ordained it as a law forever that they should give it to the priests who served before Him, that they should possess it forever.

26 There is no limit of days to this law, for He has ordained it for the generations forever that they should give to the Lord the tenth of everything, of the seed and of the wine and of the oil and of the cattle and of the sheep.

27 He gave it to His priests to eat and to drink with joy before Him.

28 The king of Sodom came and bowed down to him, and said, "Our Lord Abram, give to us the souls which you have rescued, but let the booty be yours."

29 And Abram said to him, "I lift up my hands to the Most High God, that from a thread to a shoe-latchet I shall not take anything that is yours so that you could never say, I have made Abram rich, except only what the young men, Aner and Eschol, and Mamre have eaten, and the portion of the men who went with me. These shall take their portion."

[Chapter 14]

1 After these things, in the fourth year of this week, on the new moon of the third month, the word of the Lord came to Abram in a dream, saying, "Fear not, Abram, I am your defender, and your reward will be very great."

2 He said, "Lord, Lord, what will you give me, seeing I go from here childless, and the son of Maseq, the son of my handmaid, Eliezer of Damascus, he will be my heir, and to me you have given no offspring."

3 He said to him, "This man will not be your heir, but one that will come out of your own bowels. He will be your heir."

4 And He brought him out abroad, and said to him, "Look toward heaven and number the stars if you are able to number them."

5 He looked toward heaven, and beheld the stars. And He said to him, "so shall your offspring be."

6 And he believed in the Lord, and it was counted to him as righteousness.

7 God said to him, "I am the Lord that brought you out of Ur of the Chaldees, to give you the land of the Canaanites to possess it forever, and I will be God to you and to your offspring after you."

8 He said, "Lord, Lord, how shall I know that I shall inherit it?"

9 God said to him, "Take Me a heifer of three years, and a goat of three years, and a sheep of three years, and a turtle-dove, and a pigeon."

10 And he took all these in the middle of the month and he dwelt at the oak of Mamre, which is near Hebron.

11 He built an altar there, and sacrificed all these. He poured their blood on the altar, and divided them in half, and laid them over against each other, but the birds he did not divide.

12 Birds came down on the pieces, and Abram drove them away, and did not permit the birds to touch them.

13 It happened, when the sun had set, that an ecstasy fell on Abram, and such a horror of great darkness fell on him, and it was said to Abram, "Know of a surety that your offspring shall be a stranger in a land that is not theirs, and they shall be brought into bondage, and afflicted for four hundred years.

14 The nation also to whom they will be in bondage will I judge, and after that they shall come out from that place with many possessions.

15 You will go to your fathers in peace, and be buried in a good old age.

16 But in the fourth generation they shall return here, for the iniquity of the Amorites is not yet full."

17 And he awoke from his sleep, and he arose, and the sun had set; and there was a flame, and a furnace was smoking, and a flame of fire passed between the pieces.

18 On that day the Lord made a covenant with Abram, saying, "To your offspring will I give this land, from the river of Egypt to the great river, the river Euphrates, the Kenites, the Kenizzites, the Kadmonites, the Perizzites, and the Rephaim, the Phakorites, and the Hivites, and the Amorites, and the Canaanites, and the Girgashites, and the Jebusites.

19 The day passed, and Abram offered the pieces, and the birds, and their fruit offerings, and their drink offerings, and the fire devoured them.

20 On that day we made a covenant with Abram, in the same way we had covenanted with Noah in this month; and Abram renewed the festival and laws for himself forever.

21 Abram rejoiced, and made all these things known to Sarai his wife. He believed that he would have offspring, but she did not bear.

22 Sarai advised her husband Abram, and said to him, "Go in to Hagar, my Egyptian maid, it may be that I shall build up offspring to you by her."

23 Abram listened to the voice of Sarai his wife, and said to her, "Do so." And Sarai took Hagar, her maid, the Egyptian, and gave her to Abram, her husband, to be his wife.

24 He went in to her, and she conceived and gave birth to a son, and he called his name Ishmael, in the fifth year of this week; and this was the eighty-sixth year in the life of Abram.

[Chapter 15]

1 In the fifth year of the fourth week of this jubilee, in the third month, in the middle of the month, Abram celebrated the feast of the first-fruits of the grain harvest.

2 And he made new offerings on the altar, the first-fruits of the produce to the Lord, a heifer, and a goat, and a sheep on the altar as a burnt sacrifice to the Lord; their fruit offerings and their drink offerings he offered on the altar with frankincense.

3 The Lord appeared to Abram, and said to him, "I am God Almighty. Examine yourself and demonstrate yourself before me and be perfect.

4 I will make My covenant between Me and you, and I will multiply you greatly."

5 Abram fell on his face, and God talked with him, and said, "My law is with you, and you will be the father of many nations.

6 Neither shall your name any more be called Abram, but your name from now on, even forever, shall be Abraham.

7 For I have made you the father of many nations.

8 I will make you very great, and I will make you into nations, and kings shall come forth from you.

9 I shall establish My covenant between Me and you, and your offspring after you, throughout their generations, for an eternal covenant, so that I may be a God to you, and to your offspring after you.

10 You may possess the land where you have been a sojourner, the land of Canaan, and you will possess it forever, and I will be their God."

11 The Lord said to Abraham, "Keep my covenant, you and your offspring after you, and circumcise every male among you, and circumcise your foreskins, and it shall be a token of an eternal covenant between Me and you.

12 And the eighth day you shall circumcise the child, every male throughout your generations, him that is born in the house, or whom you have bought with money from any stranger, whom you have acquired who is not of your offspring.

13 He that is born in your house shall surely be circumcised, and those whom you have bought with money shall be circumcised, and My covenant shall be in your flesh for an eternal ordinance.

14 The uncircumcised male who is not circumcised in the flesh of his foreskin on the eighth day, that soul will be cut off from his people, for he has broken My covenant."

15 God said to Abraham, "As for Sarai your wife, her name shall no more be called Sarai, but Sarah shall be her name.

16 I will bless her, and give you a son by her, and I will bless him, and he shall become a nation, and kings of nations shall proceed from him."

17 Abraham fell on his face, and rejoiced, and said in his heart, "Shall a son be born to him that is a hundred years old, and shall Sarah, who is ninety years old, bring forth?"

18 Abraham said to God, "Oh, that Ishmael might live before you!"

19 God said, "Yea, and Sarah also shall bear you a son, and you will call his name Isaac, and I will establish My covenant with him, an everlasting covenant, and for his offspring after him.

20 And as for Ishmael also have I heard you, and behold I will bless him, and make him great, and multiply him greatly, and he shall beget twelve princes, and I will make him a great nation.

21 But My covenant will I establish with Isaac, whom Sarah shall bear to you this time next year."

22 God ceased speaking with him, and God went up from Abraham.

23 Abraham did according as God had said to him, and he took Ishmael his son, and all that were born in his house, and whom he had bought with his money, every male in his house, and circumcised the flesh of their foreskin.

24 On that same day was Abraham circumcised, and all the men of his house, and all those whom he had bought with money from the children of the stranger were circumcised with him.

25 This law is for all the generations forever, and there is no variance of days, and no omission of one day out of the eight days, for it is an eternal law, ordained and written on the heavenly tablets.

26 Every one that is born, the flesh of whose foreskin is not circumcised on the eighth day, does not belong to the children of the covenant which the Lord made with Abraham, but instead they belong to the children of destruction; nor is there any other sign on him that he is the Lord's, but he is destined to be destroyed and killed from the earth, and to be rooted out of the earth, for he has broken the covenant of the Lord our God.

27 All the angels of the presence (of the Lord) and all the angels of sanctification have been created already circumcised from the day of their creation, and before the angels of the presence (of the Lord) and the angels of sanctification He has sanctified Israel, that they should be with Him and with His holy angels.

678

28 Command the children of Israel and let them observe the sign of this covenant for their generations as an eternal law, and they will not be rooted out of the land.

29 For the command is ordained for a covenant, that they should observe it forever among all the children of Israel.

30 For Ishmael and his sons and his brothers, and Esau, the Lord did not cause them to come to Him, and he did not choose them. Although they are the children of Abraham, He knew them, but He chose Israel to be His people.

31 He sanctified them, and gathered them from among all the children of men; for there are many nations and many peoples, and all are His, and over all nations He has placed spirits in authority to lead them astray from Him.

32 But over Israel He did not appoint any angel or spirit, for He alone is their ruler, and He will preserve them and require them at the hand of His angels and His spirits, and at the hand of all His powers in order that He may preserve them and bless them, that they may be His and He may be theirs from now on forever.

33 I announce to you that the children of Israel will not keep true to this law, and they will not circumcise their sons according to all this law; for in the flesh of their circumcision they will omit this circumcision of their sons, and all of the sons of Beliar will leave their sons uncircumcised as they were born.

34 There will be great wrath from the Lord against the children of Israel because they have forsaken His covenant and turned aside from His word, and provoked (God) and blasphemed, because they do not observe the ordinance of this law; for they have treated their genitalia like the Gentiles, so that they may be removed and rooted out of the land. And there will no more be pardon or forgiveness to them for all the sin of this eternal error.

[Chapter 16]

1 On the new moon of the fourth month we appeared to Abraham, at the oak of Mamre, and we talked with him, and we announced to him that Sarah, his wife, would give him a son.

2 And Sarah laughed, for she heard that we had spoken these words to Abraham. We warned her, and she became afraid, and denied that she had laughed because of the words.

3 We told her the name of her son, as his name is ordained and written in the heavenly tablets and it is Isaac.

4 We told her that when we returned to her at a set time, she would have conceived a son.

5 In this month the Lord executed his judgments on Sodom, and Gomorrah, and Zeboim, and all the region of the Jordan, and He burned them with fire and brimstone, and destroyed them and they are destroyed until this day, because of all their works. They are wicked and vast sinners, and they defile themselves and commit fornication in their flesh, and work uncleanness on the earth as I have told you.

6 In like manner, God will execute judgment on the places where they have done similar to the uncleanness of the Sodomites, and they will suffer a judgment like that of Sodom.

7 But for Lot, we made an exception, for God remembered Abraham, and sent him out from the place of the overthrow.

8 And he and his daughters committed sin on the earth, such as had not been on the earth since the days of Adam until his time, for the man had sex with his daughters.

9 It was commanded and engraved concerning all his offspring, on the heavenly tablets, to remove them and root them out, and to execute judgment on them like the judgment of Sodom, and to leave no offspring of that man on earth on the day of condemnation.

10 In this month Abraham moved from Hebron, and departed and lived between Kadesh and Shur in the mountains of Gerar.

11 In the middle of the fifth month he moved from that place, and lived at the Well of the Oath.

12 In the middle of the sixth month the Lord visited Sarah and did to her as He had spoken and she conceived.

13 And she gave birth to a son in the third month. In the middle of the month, at the time of which the Lord had spoken to Abraham, on the festival of the first-fruits of the harvest, Isaac was born.

14 Abraham circumcised his son on the eighth day, he was the first that was circumcised according to the covenant that is ordained forever.

15 In the sixth year of the fourth week we came to Abraham at the Well of the Oath, and we appeared to him.

16 We returned in the seventh month, and found Sarah with child before us and we blessed him, and we announced to him all the things that had been decreed concerning him, so that he should not die until he should beget six more sons and saw them before he died.

17 But in Isaac should his name and offspring be called, and that all the offspring of his sons should be Gentiles, and be counted with the Gentiles; but from the sons of Isaac one should become a holy offspring, and should not be counted among the Gentiles.

18 For he should become the portion (dowry) of the Most High, and all his offspring had fallen into the possession of God, that they should be to the Lord a people for His possession above all nations and that they should become a kingdom and priests and a holy nation.

19 We went our way, and we announced to Sarah all that we had told him, and they both rejoiced with very great joy.

20 He built there an altar to the Lord who had delivered him, and who was causing him to rejoice in the land of his sojourning, and he celebrated a festival of joy in this month for seven days, near the altar which he had built at the Well of the Oath.

21 He built tents for himself and for his servants on this festival, and he was the first to celebrate the feast of tabernacles on the earth.

22 During these seven days he brought a burnt offering to the Lord each day to the altar consisting of two oxen, two rams, seven sheep, one male goat, for a sin offering that he might atone thereby for himself and for his offspring.

23 As an offering of thanks he brought, seven rams, seven kids, seven sheep, and seven male goats, and their fruit offerings and their drink offerings; and he burnt all the fat of it on the altar, a chosen offering to the Lord for a sweet smelling odor.

24 Morning and evening he burnt fragrant substances, frankincense and incense, and sweet spice, and nard, and myrrh, and spice, and aromatic plants; all these seven he offered, crushed, mixed together in equal parts and pure.

25 And he celebrated this feast during seven days, rejoicing with all his heart and with all his soul, he and all those who were in his house, and there was no stranger with him, nor any that was uncircumcised.

26 He blessed his Creator who had created him in his generation, for He had created him according to His good pleasure. God knew and perceived that from him would arise the plant of righteousness for the eternal generations, and from him a holy offspring, so that it should become like Him who had made all things.

27 He blessed and rejoiced, and he called the name of this festival the festival of the Lord, a joy acceptable to the Most High God.

28 And we blessed him forever, and all his offspring after him throughout all the generations of the earth, because he celebrated this festival in its season, according to the testimony of the heavenly tablets.

29 For this reason it is ordained on the heavenly tablets concerning Israel, that they shall celebrate the feast of tabernacles seven days with joy, in the seventh month, acceptable before the Lord as a statute forever throughout their generations every year.

30 To this there is no limit of days; for it is ordained forever regarding Israel that they should celebrate it and dwell in tents, and set wreaths on their heads, and take leafy boughs, and willows from the brook.

31 Abraham took branches of palm trees, and the fruit of good and pleasing trees, and every day going round the altar with the branches seven times a day in the morning, he praised and gave thanks to his God for all things in joy.

[Chapter 17]

1 In the first year of the fifth week Isaac was weaned in this jubilee, and Abraham made a great banquet in the third month, on the day his son Isaac was weaned.

2 Ishmael, the son of Hagar, the Egyptian, was in front of Abraham, his father, in his place, and Abraham rejoiced and blessed God because he had seen his sons and had not died childless.

3 He remembered the words which He had spoken to him on the day that Lot had departed from him, and he rejoiced because the Lord had given him offspring on the earth to inherit the earth, and he blessed with all his mouth the Creator of all things.

4 Sarah saw Ishmael playing and dancing, and Abraham rejoicing with great joy, and she became jealous of Ishmael and said to Abraham, "Throw out this bondwoman and her son. The son of this bondwoman will not be heir with my son, Isaac."

5 And the situation was troubling to Abraham, because of his maidservant and because of his son, because he did not want to drive them from him.

6 God said to Abraham "Let it not be troubling in your sight, because of the child and because of the bondwoman. Listen to Sarah and to all her words and do them, for in Isaac shall your name and offspring be called.

7 But as for the son of this bondwoman I will make him a great nation, because he is of your offspring."

8 Abraham got up early in the morning, and took bread and a bottle of water, and placed them on the shoulders of Hagar and the child, and sent her away.

9 And she departed and wandered in the wilderness of Beersheba, and the water in the bottle was spent, and the child was thirsty, and was not able to go on, and fell down.

10 His mother took him and laid him under an olive tree, and went and sat her down over away from him at the distance of a bow-shot; for she said, "Let me not see the death of my child," and she sat and wept.

11 An angel of God, one of the holy ones, said to her, "Why do you weep, Hagar? Stand. Take the child, and hold him in your hand, for God has heard your voice, and has seen the child."

12 She opened her eyes, and she saw a well of water, and she went and filled her bottle with water, and she gave her child a drink, and she arose and went towards the wilderness of Paran.

13 And the child grew and became an archer, and God was with him, and his mother took him a wife from among the daughters of Egypt.

14 She (the wife) gave birth to a son, and he called his name Nebaioth; for she said, "The Lord was close to me when I called on him."

15 In the seventh week, in the first year of it, in the first month in this jubilee, on the twelfth of this month, there were voices in heaven regarding Abraham, that he was faithful in all that He told him, and that he loved the Lord, and that in every affliction he was faithful.

16 Prince Mastema came and said before God, "Look, Abraham loves Isaac his son, and he delights in him above all things, tell him to offer him as a burnt-offering on the altar, and You will see if he will do this command, and You will know if he is faithful in everyway that You test him.

17 The Lord knew that Abraham was faithful throughout all his afflictions, for He had tried him through his country and with famine, and had tried him with the wealth of kings, and had tried him again through his wife, when she was torn from him, and with circumcision; and had tried him through Ishmael and Hagar, his maid-servant, when he sent them away.

18 In everything that He had tried him, he was found faithful, and his soul was not impatient, and he was not slow to act, because he was faithful and a lover of the Lord.

[Chapter 18]

1 God said to him, "Abraham. Abraham." and he said, "Look, here am I."

2 He said, "Take your beloved son, Isaac, whom you love, and go to the high country, and offer him on one of the mountains which I will point out to you."

3 He got early in the morning and saddled his donkey, and took two young men with him, and Isaac his son, and split the wood of the burnt offering, and he went to the place on the third day, and he saw the place afar off.

4 He came to a well of water (near Mount Moriah), and he said to his young men, "You stay here with the donkey, and I and the lad shall go yonder, and when we have worshiped we shall come back to you."

5 He took the wood of the burnt-offering and laid it on Isaac his son, and he took the fire and the knife, and they went both of them together to that place.

6 Isaac said to his father, "Father" and he said, "Here am I, my son." He said to him, "Look, we have the fire, and the knife, and the wood, but where is the sheep for the burnt-offering, father?"

7 He said, "God will provide for himself a sheep for a burnt-offering, my son." And he neared the place of the mountain of God.

8 He built an altar, and he placed the wood on the altar, and bound Isaac his son, and placed him on the wood that was on the altar, and stretched out his hand to take the knife to kill Isaac, his son.

9 I stood in the presence of him, and before prince Mastema, (and the holy angels stood and wept over the altar as prince Mastema and his angels rejoiced and said "Isaac will be destroyed and we will see if Abraham is faithful), and the Lord said, "Command him not to lay his hand on the lad, nor to do anything to him, for I have shown that he fears the Lord."

10 I called to him from heaven, and said to him, "Abraham, Abraham." and he was terrified and said, "Here am I."

11 I said to him, "Lay not your hand on the lad, neither do anything to him; for now I have shown that you fear the Lord, and have not withheld your son, your first-born son, from me."

12 Prince Mastema was put to shame (and was bound by the angels); and Abraham lifted up his eyes and looked and saw a ram caught by his horns, and Abraham went and took the ram and offered it as a burnt-offering in place of his son.

13 Abraham called that place "The Lord has seen," so that it is said the Lord has seen. This is Mount Zion.

14 The Lord called Abraham by his name a second time from heaven, as he caused us to appear to speak to him in the name of the Lord.

15 He said, "By Myself have I sworn," said the Lord, "Because you have done this thing, and have not withheld your son, your beloved son, from Me, that in blessing I will bless you, and in multiplying I will multiply your offspring as the stars of heaven, and as the sand which is on the seashore.

16 Your offspring shall inherit the cities of their enemies, and in your offspring shall all nations of the earth be blessed. Because you have obeyed My voice, and I have shown to all that you are faithful to Me in all that I have said to you, "Go in peace."

17 Abraham went back to his young men, and they stood and went back together to Beersheba, and Abraham lived by the Well of the Oath.

18 And he celebrated this festival every year, seven days with joy, and he called it the festival of the Lord according to the seven days during which he went and returned in peace.

19 Accordingly, it has been ordained and written on the heavenly tablets regarding Israel and its children that they should observe this festival seven days with the joy of festival.

[Chapter 19]

1 In the first year of the first week in the forty-second jubilee, Abraham returned and lived across from Hebron, in Kirjath Arba for two weeks of years.

2 In the first year of the third week of this jubilee the days of the life of Sarah were completed, and she died in Hebron.

3 Abraham went to mourn over her and bury her, and we tested him to see if his spirit was patient and he had neither anger nor contempt in the words of his mouth, and he was found patient in this and was not disturbed.

4 In patience of spirit he discussed with the children of Heth that they should give him a place in which to bury his dead.

5 And the Lord gave him grace before all who saw him, and he asked the sons of Heth in gentleness, and they gave him the land of the double cave over beside Mamre, that is Hebron, for four hundred pieces of silver.

6 They said to him, "We shall give it to you for nothing," but he would not take it from them for nothing, for he gave the price of the place and paid the money in full. And he bowed down before them twice, and after this he buried his dead in the double cave.

7 All the days of the life of Sarah were one hundred and twenty-seven years, that is, two jubilees and four weeks and one year, these are the days of the years of the life of Sarah.

8 This is the tenth trial with which Abraham was tested, and he was found faithful and patient in spirit.

9 He did not say a single word regarding the rumor in the land of how God had said that He would give it to him and to his offspring after him, but instead he begged for a place there to bury his dead. Because he was found faithful, it was recorded on the heavenly tablets that he was the friend of God.

10 In the fourth year of it (this jubilee) he took a wife for his son Isaac and her name was Rebecca the daughter of Bethuel, the son of Nahor, the brother of Abraham the sister of Laban and daughter of Bethuel; and Bethuel was the son of Melca, who was the wife of Nahor, the brother of Abraham.

11 Abraham took to himself a third wife from among the daughters of his household servants, for Hagar had died before Sarah, and her name was Keturah,. And she gave birth to six sons, Zimram, and Jokshan, and Medan, and Midian, and Ishbak, and Shuah, in the two weeks of years.

12 In the sixth week, in the second year of it, Rebecca gave birth to two sons of Isaac, Jacob and Esau.

13 And Jacob had no beard and was a straight and tall man who dwelt in tents, and Esau was a powerful a man of the field, and was hairy.

14 The youths grew, and Jacob learned to write, but Esau did not learn, for he was a man of the field and a hunter, and he learned war, and all his deeds were fierce.

15Abraham loved Jacob, but Isaac loved Esau.

16 And Abraham saw the deeds of Esau, and he knew that in Jacob should his name and offspring be called. He called Rebecca and gave commandment regarding Jacob, for he knew that she too loved Jacob much more than Esau.

17 He said to her, "My daughter, watch over my son Jacob, for he shall take my place on the earth. He shall be a blessing throughout the children of men and for the glory of all the offspring of Shem.

18 I know that the Lord will choose him to be a people (nation) and a possession to Himself, above all peoples that are on the face of the earth.

19 Isaac, my son, loves Esau more than Jacob, but I see that you truly love Jacob.

20 Add still further to your kindness to him, and regard him in love, for he shall be a blessing to us on the earth from now on to all generations of the earth.

21 Let your hands be strong and let your heart rejoice in your son Jacob, for I have loved him far beyond all my sons. He shall be blessed forever, and his offspring shall fill the whole earth.

22 If a man can number the sand of the earth, his offspring also shall be numbered.

23 And all the blessings with which the Lord has blessed me and my offspring shall belong to Jacob and his offspring always.

24 In his offspring shall my name be blessed, and the name of my fathers, Shem, Noah, Enoch, Mahalalel, Enos, Seth, and Adam. And these shall serve to lay the foundations of the heaven, and to strengthen the earth, and to renew all the stars and planets which are in the sky.

27 He called Jacob and kissed him in front of Rebecca, his mother, and blessed him, and said, "Jacob, my beloved son, whom my soul loves, may God bless you from above the sky, and may He give you all the blessings with which He blessed Adam, Enoch, Noah, and Shem; and all the things of which He told me, and all the things which He promised to give me, may He cause to be yours and your offspring forever, according to the days of heaven above the earth.

28 And the Spirits of Mastema shall not rule over you or over your offspring or turn you from the Lord, who is your God from now on forever.

29 May the Lord God be a father to you and may you be like His first-born son, and to the people always. Go in peace, my son."

30 And they both went out together from Abraham.

31 Rebecca loved Jacob, with all her heart and with all her soul, very much more than Esau, but Isaac loved Esau much more than Jacob.

[Chapter 20]

1 In the forty-second jubilee, in the first year of the seventh week, Abraham called Ishmael, and his twelve sons, and Isaac and his two sons, and the six sons of Keturah, and their sons.

2 And he commanded them that they should observe the way of the Lord, that they should work righteousness, and love each his neighbor, and act in this manner among all men, that they should each walk with regard to the ways of the Lord to do judgment and righteousness on the earth.

3 He also commanded them that they should circumcise their sons, according to the covenant, which God had made with them, and not deviate to the right or the left of all the paths which the Lord had commanded us, and that we should keep ourselves from all fornication and uncleanness.

4 He said, "If any woman or maid commits fornication among you, burn her with fire. And do not let them commit fornication with her with their eyes or their heart; and do not let them take to themselves wives from the daughters of Canaan, because the offspring of Canaan will be rooted out of the land."

5 He told them about the judgment on the giants, and the judgment on the Sodomites, how they had been judged because of their wickedness, and had died because of their fornication and uncleanness, and corruption through fornication together.

6 He said, "Guard yourselves from all fornication and uncleanness, and from all pollution of sin, or you will make our name a curse, and your whole life a shame, and all your sons to be destroyed by the sword, and you will become accursed like Sodom, and all that is left of you shall be as the sons of Gomorrah.

7 I implore you, my sons, love the God of heaven and cling to all His commandments.

8 Do not walk after their idols and after their ways of uncleanness, and do not make yourselves molten or graven gods. They are empty, and there is no spirit in them, for they are work of men's hands, and all who trust in them, trust in nothing.

9 Do not serve them, nor worship them, but serve the most high God, and worship Him continually, and hope for His presence always, and work uprightness and righteousness before Him, that He may have pleasure in you and grant you His mercy, and send rain on you morning and evening, and bless all your works which you have performed on the earth, and bless your bread and your water, and bless the fruit of your womb and the fruit of your land, and the herds of your cattle, and the flocks of your sheep.

10 You will be for a blessing on the earth, and all nations of the earth will desire you, and bless your sons in my name, that they may be blessed as I am."

11 He gave to Ishmael and to his sons, and to the sons of Keturah, gifts, and sent them away from Isaac his son, and he gave everything to Isaac his son.

12 Ishmael and his sons, and the sons of Keturah and their sons, went together and settled from Paran to the border of Babylon in all the land that is toward the East facing the desert.

13 These mingled (intermarried) with each other, and their names were called Arabs, and Ishmaelites.

[Chapter 21]

1 In the sixth year of the seventh week of this jubilee Abraham called Isaac his son, and commanded him, saying, "I have become old. I do not know the day of my death but I am full of my days.

2 I am one hundred and seventy-five years old, and throughout all the days of my life I have remembered the Lord, and sought with all my heart to do His will, and to walk uprightly in all His ways.

3 My soul has hated idols. I have given my heart and spirit to the observance of the will of Him who created me.

4 For He is the living God, and He is holy and faithful, and He is righteous beyond all, and He is no respecter of men or of their gifts, for God is righteous, and executes judgment on all those who transgress His commandments and despise His covenant.

5 My son, observe His commandments and His law and His judgments, and do not walk after the abominations and after the graven images and after the molten images.

6 And eat no blood at all of animals or cattle, or of any bird that flies in the heaven.

7 If you kill a sacrificial animal as an acceptable peace offering, kill it, and pour out its blood on the altar. Place all the fat of the offering on the altar with fine flour and the meat offering mingled with oil with its drink offering. Place them all together on the altar of burnt offering. It is a sweet odor before the Lord.

8 You will offer the fat of the sacrifice of thanks offerings on the fire which is on the altar, and the fat which is on the belly, and all the fat on the inside, behind the two kidneys, and all the fat that is on them, and lobes of the liver you will remove, together with the kidneys.

9 Offer all these for a sweet odor acceptable before the Lord, with its meat-offering and with its drink-offering, and the bread of the offering to the Lord.

10 Eat its meat on that day and on the second day, but do not let the sun go down on it until it is eaten. Let nothing be left over for the third day, for it is not acceptable. Let it no longer be eaten, and all who eat of it will bring sin on themselves, for thus I have found it written in the books of my forefathers, and in the words of Enoch, and in the words of Noah.

11 On all your offerings you will scatter salt, and do not let the salt of the covenant be lacking in all your offerings before the Lord.

12 As regards the wood of the sacrifices, beware to bring only these and no other wood to the altar in addition to these, cypress, bay, almond, fir, pine, cedar, savin, fig, olive, myrrh, laurel, and aspalathus.

13 Of these kinds of wood lay on the altar under the sacrifice, such as have been tested as to their appearance, and do not lay on it any split or dark wood, but only hard and clean wood, without fault, a healthy, new growth. Do not lay old wood on it, because there is no longer fragrance in it as before.

14 Besides these kinds of wood there is none other that you will place on the altar, for the fragrance is dispersed, and the smell of its fragrance will not go up to heaven.

15 Observe this commandment and do it, my son, that you may be upright in all your deeds.

16 Be clean in your body at all times. Wash yourself with water before you approach to offer on the altar. Wash your hands and your feet before you draw near to the altar, and when you are done sacrificing, wash your hands and feet again.

17 Let no blood appear on you or on your clothes. Be on your guard against blood, my son. Be on your guard continually and cover it with dust.

18 Do not eat any blood for it is the soul. Eat no blood whatsoever.

19 Take no payment for shedding the blood of man, or it will cause it to be shed without fear of punishment, without judgment. It is the blood that is shed that causes the earth to sin, and the earth cannot be cleansed from the blood of man except by the blood of he who shed it.

20 Take no present or gift for the blood of man, blood for blood, that you may be accepted before the Lord, the Most High God. He is the defense of the good, so that you may be preserved from all evil, and that He may withhold you from every kind of death.

21 I see, my son, all the works of the children of men are sin and wickedness, and all their deeds are uncleanness and an abomination and a pollution, and there is no righteousness in them.

22 Beware, or you will walk in their ways and tread in their paths, and commit a sin worthy of death before the Most High God. He will hide His face from you and give you back into the hands of your transgression, and root you out of the land, and your offspring likewise from under heaven, and your name and your offspring shall perish from the whole earth.

23 Turn away from all their deeds and all their uncleanness, and observe the laws of the Most High God, and do His will and be upright in all things.

24 If you do this, He will bless you in all your deeds, and will raise up from you a plant of righteousness through all the earth, throughout all generations of the earth, and my name and your name shall not be forgotten under heaven forever.

25 Go, my son in peace. May the Most High God, my God and your God, strengthen you to do His will, and may He bless all your offspring and the remainder of your offspring for the generations forever, with all righteous blessings, that you may be a blessing on all the earth."

26 And he went out from him rejoicing.

[Chapter 22]

1 In the first week in the forty-fourth jubilee, in the second year, that is, the year in which Abraham died, Isaac and Ishmael came from the Well of the Oath to celebrate the feast of weeks which is the feast of the first-fruits of the harvest to Abraham, their father, and Abraham rejoiced because his two sons had come.

2 Isaac had many possessions in Beersheba, and Isaac desired to go and see his possessions and to return to his father.

3 In those days Ishmael came to see his father, and they both came together, and Isaac offered a sacrifice for a burnt offering, and presented it on the altar of his father that he had made in Hebron.

4 He offered a thanks offering and made a feast of joy in the presence of Ishmael, his brother, and Rebecca made new cakes from the new grain, and gave them to Jacob, her son, to take them to Abraham, his father, from the first-fruits of the land, that he might eat and bless the Creator of all things before he died.

5 Isaac, also, sent Jacob to Abraham with an offering of his best for thanks so that he might eat and drink.

6 He ate and drank, and blessed the Most High God, who has created heaven and earth, who has made all the fat things of the earth, and given them to the children of men that they might eat and drink and bless their Creator.

7 "And now I give thanks to You, my God, because you have caused me to see this day, behold, I am one hundred three score and fifteen years, an old man and full of days, and all my days have been peace to me.

8 The sword of the adversary has not overcome me in all that You have given me and my children all the days of my life until this day.

9 My God, may Your mercy and Your peace be on Your servant, and on the offspring of his sons, that they may be to You a chosen nation and an inheritance from among all the nations of the earth from now on to all the days of the generations of the earth, to all the ages."

10 He called Jacob and said, "My son Jacob, may the God of all bless you and strengthen you to do righteousness, and His will before Him, and may He choose you and your offspring that you may become a people for His inheritance according to His will always.

11 My son, Jacob, draw near and kiss me." And he drew near and kissed him, and he said, "Blessed be my son Jacob and all the sons of God Most High, to all the ages. May God give to you an offspring of righteousness; and some of your sons may He sanctify throughout the whole earth. May nations serve you, and all the nations bow themselves before your offspring.

12 Be strong in the presence of men, and exercise authority over all the offspring of Seth. Then your ways and the ways of your sons will be justified, so that they shall become a holy nation.

13 May the Most High God give you all the blessings with which He has blessed me and He blessed Noah and Adam. May they rest on the sacred head of your offspring from generation to generation forever.

14 May He cleanse you from all unrighteousness and impurity so that you may be forgiven all the transgressions, which you have committed ignorantly. May He strengthen you, and bless you.

15 May you inherit the whole earth, and may He renew His covenant with you so that you may be to Him a nation for His inheritance for all the ages, and so that He may be to you and to your offspring a God in truth and righteousness throughout all the days of the earth.

16 My son Jacob, remember my words. Observe the commandments of Abraham, your father, separate yourself from the nations (gentiles), and do not eat with them. Do not emulate their works, and do not associate with them because their works are unclean, and all their ways are a pollution and an abomination and uncleanness.

17 They offer their sacrifices to the dead and they worship evil spirits, and they eat over the graves, and all their works are empty and nothingness.

18 They have no heart to understand and their eyes do not see what their works are, and how they go astray by saying to a piece of wood, "You are my God," and to a stone, "You are my Lord and you are my deliverer," because the stone and wood have no heart.

19 And as for you, my son Jacob, may the Most High God help you and the God of heaven bless you and remove you from their uncleanness and from all their error.

20 Jacob, be warned. Do not take a wife from any offspring of the daughters of Canaan, for all his offspring are to be rooted out of the earth.

21 Because of the transgression of Ham, Canaan erred, and all his offspring shall be destroyed from the earth including any remnant of it, and none springing from him shall exist except on the day of judgment.

22 And as for all the worshippers of idols and the profane, there shall be no hope for them in the land of the living, and no one on earth will remember them, for they shall descend into the abode of the dead, and they shall go into the place of condemnation. As the children of Sodom were taken away from the earth, so will all those who worship idols be taken away.

23 Fear not, my son Jacob. Be not dismayed, son of Abraham. May the Most High God preserve you from destruction, and may He deliver you from all the paths of error.

24 This house have I built for myself that I might put my name on it in the earth. It is given to you and to your offspring forever, and it will be named the house of Abraham. It is given to you and your offspring forever, for you will build my house and establish my name before God forever. Your offspring and your name will stand throughout all generations of the earth."

25 He ceased commanding him and blessing him.

26 The two lay together on one bed, and Jacob slept in the embracing arms of Abraham, his father's father, and he kissed him seven times, and his affection and his heart rejoiced over him.

27 He blessed him with all his heart and said, "The Most High God, the God of all, and Creator of all, who brought me out from Ur of the Chaldees that He might give me this land to inherit forever, that I might establish a holy offspring.

28 Blessed be the Most High forever."

29 And he blessed Jacob and said, "May Your grace and Your mercy be lift up on my son, over whom I rejoice with all my heart and my affection and on his offspring always.

30 Do not forsake him, nor diminish him from now to the days of eternity, and may Your eyes be opened on him and on his offspring, that You may preserve him, and bless him, and may sanctify him as a nation for Your inheritance. Bless him with all Your blessings from now to all the days of eternity, and renew Your covenant and Your grace with him and with his offspring according to all Your good pleasure to all the generations of the earth."

[Chapter 23]

1 He placed Jacob's two fingers on his eyes, and he blessed the God of gods, and he covered his face and stretched out his feet and slept the sleep of eternity, and was gathered to his fathers.

2 In spite of all this, Jacob was lying in his embracing arms, and knew not that Abraham, his father's father, was dead.

3 Jacob awoke from his sleep, and realized Abraham was cold as ice, and he said, "Father, father," but there was no answer, and he knew that he was dead.

4 He arose from his embracing arms and ran and told Rebecca, his mother, and Rebecca went to Isaac in the night, and told him and they went together, and Jacob with them, and a lamp was in his hand, and when they had gone in they found Abraham lying dead.

5 Isaac fell on the face of his father and wept and kissed him.

6 Ishmael, his son, heard the voices in the house of Abraham, and he arose, and went to Abraham his father, and wept over Abraham his father, he and all the house of Abraham, and they wept greatly.

7 His sons, Isaac and Ishmael, buried him in the double cave, near Sarah his wife, and all the men of his house, and Isaac and Ishmael, and all their sons, and all the sons of Keturah in their places wept for him forty days and then the days of weeping for Abraham were ended.

8 He lived three jubilees and four weeks of years, one hundred and seventy-five years, and completed the days of his life, being old and full of days.

9 For the days of the lives of their forefathers were nineteen jubilees; and after the Flood they began to grow less than nineteen jubilees, and to decrease in jubilees, and to grow old quickly, and to be full of their days because of the many types of hardships and the wickedness of their ways, with the exception of Abraham.

10 For Abraham was perfect in all his deeds with the Lord, and well-pleasing in righteousness all the days of his life. Yet, he did not complete four jubilees in his life, when he had grown old because of the wickedness in the world, and was full of his days.

11 All the generations which shall arise from this time until the day of the great judgment shall grow old quickly, before they complete two jubilees, and their knowledge shall forsake them because of their old age and all their knowledge shall vanish away.

12 In those days, if a man lives a jubilee and a-half of years, they shall say regarding him, "He has lived long," and the greater part of his days are pain and sorrow and hardship, and there is no peace. For calamity follows on calamity, and wound on wound, and hardship on hardship, and evil deeds on evil deeds, and illness on illness, and all judgments of destruction such as these, piled one on another, illness and overthrow, and snow and frost and ice, and fever, and chills, and mental and physical incapacity, and famine, and death, and sword, and captivity, and all kinds of calamities and pains.

13 All of these shall come on an evil generation, which transgresses on the earth. Their works are uncleanness and fornication, and pollution and abominations.

14 Then they shall say, "The days of the forefathers were many, lasting a thousand years, and were good; but the days of our lives, if a man lives a long life are three score years and ten, and, if he is strong, four score years, and those evil, and there is no peace in the days of this evil generation."

15 In that generation the sons shall convict their fathers and their elders of sin and unrighteousness, and of the words of their mouths and the great wickedness which they perform, and concerning their forsaking the covenant which the Lord made between them and Him. They should observe and do all His commandments and His ordinances and all His laws, without departing either to the right hand or the left.

16 For all have done evil, and every mouth speaks sinfully and all their works are unclean and an abomination, and all their ways are pollution, uncleanness, and destruction.

17 The earth shall be destroyed because of all their works, and there shall be no fruit (seed) of the vine, and no oil; for their actions are altogether faithless, and they shall all perish together, beasts and cattle and birds, and all the fish of the sea, because of the children of men.

18 They shall quarrel with one another, the young with the old, and the old with the young, the poor with the rich, the lowly with the great, and the beggar with the prince, because of the law and the covenant; for they have forgotten the commandments, and covenant, and feasts, and months, and Sabbaths, and jubilees, and all judgments.

19 They shall use swords and war to turn them back to the way, but they shall not return until much blood has been shed on the earth, one by another.

20 Those who have escaped shall not return from their wickedness to the way of righteousness, but they shall all raise themselves to a high status through deceit and wealth, that they may each steal all that belongs of his neighbor, and they shall name the great name (of God), but not in truth and not in righteousness, and they shall defile the holy of holies with their uncleanness and the corruption of their pollution.

21 A great punishment shall come because of the deeds of this generation, and the Lord will give them over to the sword and to judgment and to slavery, and to be plundered and consumed.

22 And He will arouse the Gentile sinners against them, who have neither mercy nor compassion, and who shall respect no one, neither old nor young, nor any one, for they are more wicked, strong, and evil than all the children of men.

23 They shall use violence against Israel and shall violate Jacob, and much blood shall be shed on the earth, and there shall be none to gather the dead and none to bury them.

24 In those days they shall cry aloud, and call and pray that they may be saved from the hand of the sinners, the Gentiles. But none shall be excluded (none shall be saved).

25 The heads of the children shall be white with grey hair, and a child of three weeks shall appear old like a man of one hundred years, and their work and worth shall be destroyed by hardship and oppression.

26 In those days the children shall begin to study the laws, and to seek the commandments, and to return to the path of righteousness.

27 The days shall begin to grow many and increase among those children of men until their days draw close to one thousand years, and to a greater number of years than before age was recorded.

28 There shall be neither old man nor one who is aged, for all shall be as children and youths.

29 All their days shall be full and they shall live in peace and in joy, and there shall be neither Satan nor any evil destroyer because all their days shall be days of blessing and healing.

30 And at that time the Lord will heal His servants, and they shall rise up and see great peace, and drive out their adversaries. The righteous shall understand and be thankful, and rejoice with joy forever and ever, and they shall see all their judgments and all their curses enacted on their enemies.

31 Their bones shall rest in the earth, and their spirits shall have much joy, and they shall know that it is the Lord who executes judgment, and shows mercy to hundreds and thousands and to all that love Him.

32 Moses, write down these words. Write them and record them on the heavenly tablets for a testimony for the generations forever.

[Chapter 24]

1 It happened after the death of Abraham, that the Lord blessed Isaac his son, who arose from Hebron and went and dwelt at the Well of the Vision in the first year of the third week of this jubilee, seven years.

2 In the first year of the fourth week a famine began in the land, besides the first famine, which had been in the days of Abraham.

3 Jacob made lentil soup, and Esau came from the field hungry. He said to Jacob his brother, "Give me some of this red soup."

4 Jacob said to him, "Sell to me your birthright and I will give you bread, and also some of this lentil soup." And Esau said in his heart, "If I shall die what good is my birthright to me?"

5 He said to Jacob, "I give it to you." And Jacob said, "Swear to me, this day," and he swore to him.

6 And Jacob gave his brother Esau bread and soup, and he ate until he was satisfied, and Esau despised his birthright. For this reason was Esau's name called Edom (red), because of the red soup which Jacob gave him for his birthright.

7 And Jacob became the elder, and Esau was brought down from his dignity.

8 The famine covered the land, and Isaac departed to go down into Egypt in the second year of this week, and went to the king of the Philistines to Gerar, into the presence of Abimelech.

9 The Lord appeared to him and said to him, "Do not go down into Egypt. Dwell in the land that I shall tell you of, and sojourn in this land, and I will be with you and bless you.

10 For to you and to your offspring will I give all this land, and I will establish My oath which I swore to Abraham your father, and I will multiply your offspring as the stars of heaven, and will give to your offspring all this land.

11 And in your offspring shall all the nations of the earth be blessed, because your father obeyed My voice, and kept My ways and My commandments, and My laws, and My ordinances, and My covenant; and now do as you are told and dwell in this land."

12 And he dwelt in Gelar three weeks of years. And Abimelech commanded concerning him, and concerning all that was his, saying, "Any man that shall touch him or anything that is his shall surely die."

13 Isaac grew strong among the Philistines, and he got many possessions, oxen and sheep and camels and donkeys and a great household.

14 He sowed in the land of the Philistines and brought in a hundred-fold, and Isaac became very great, and the Philistines envied him.

15 Now all the wells that the servants of Abraham had dug during the life of Abraham, the Philistines had stopped them after the death of Abraham, and filled them with dirt.

16 Abimelech said to Isaac, "Go from us, for you are much mightier than we." Isaac departed from that place in the first year of the seventh week, and sojourned in the valleys of Gerar.

17 And they dug the wells of water again which the servants of Abraham, his father, had dug, and which the Philistines had filled after the death of Abraham his father, and he called their names as Abraham his father had named them.

18 The servants of Isaac dug a well in the valley, and found fresh, flowing water, and the shepherds of Gerar bickered with the shepherds of Isaac, saying, "The water is ours." Isaac called the name of the well "Perversity," because they had been perverse with us.

19 And they dug a second well, and they fought for that also, and he called its name "Enmity."

20 He left that place and they dug another well, and for that they did not fight, and he called the name of it "Room," and Isaac said, "Now the Lord has made room for us, and we have increased in the land."

21 And he went up from that place to the Well of the Oath in the first year of the first week in the forty-fourth jubilee.

22 The Lord appeared to him in the night of the new moon of the first month, and said to him, "I am the God of Abraham your father; fear not, for I am with you, and shall bless you and shall surely multiply your offspring as the sand of the earth, for the sake of Abraham my servant."

23 And he built an altar there, which Abraham his father had first built, and he called on the name of the Lord, and he offered sacrifice to the God of Abraham his father.

24 They dug a well and they found fresh, flowing water.

25 The servants of Isaac dug another well and did not find water, and they went and told Isaac that they had not found water, and Isaac said, "I have sworn this day to the Philistines and this thing has been announced to us."

26 And he called the name of that place the Well of the Oath, because there he had sworn to Abimelech and Ahuzzath, his friend, and also to Phicol, who was the commander and his host.

27 Isaac knew that day that he had sworn to them under pressure to make peace with them.

28 On that day Isaac cursed the Philistines and said, "Cursed be the Philistines to the day of wrath and indignation from among all nations. May God make them a disdain and a curse and an object of anger and indignation in the hands of the Gentile sinners and in the hands of the Kittim.

29 Whoever escapes the sword of the enemy and the Kittim, may the righteous nation root them out in judgment from under heaven. They shall be the enemies and foes of my children throughout their generations on the earth.

30 No part of them will remain. Not even one shall be spared on the day of the wrath of judgment. The offspring of the Philistines will experience destruction, rooting out, and expulsion from the earth and this is all that is in store for them. There shall not be a name or an offspring left on the earth for these Caphtorim (the seat of the Philistine state).

31 For though he rises up to heaven, he shall be brought down, and though he makes himself strong on earth, from there shall he be dragged out, and though he hide himself among the nations, even from that place shall he be rooted out.

32 Though he descends into the abode of the dead, his condemnation shall be great, and he shall have no peace there.

33 If he goes into captivity by the hands of those that seek his life they shall kill him on the way (to his imprisonment), and neither his name nor offspring shall be left on all the earth. Into an eternal curse shall he depart."

34 It is written and engraved concerning him on the heavenly tablets, that on the day of judgment he will be rooted out of the earth.

[Chapter 25]

1 In the second year of this week in this jubilee, Rebecca called Jacob her son, and spoke to him, saying, "My son, do not take a wife from the daughters of Canaan as Esau, your brother, who took two wives of the daughters of Canaan, and they have made my soul bitter with all their unclean acts, for all their actions are fornication and lust, and there is no righteousness in them, because their deeds are evil.

2 I love you greatly, my son, and my heart and my affection bless you every hour of the day and in every night.

3 Now, my son, listen to my voice, and do the will of your mother, and do not take a wife of the daughters of this land, but only from the house of my father, and of those related to my father.

4 If you will take you a wife of the house of my father, the Most High God will bless you, and your children shall be a righteous generation and a holy offspring." And then spoke Jacob to Rebecca, his mother, and said to her, "Look, mother, I am nine weeks of years old, and I have neither been with nor have I touched any woman, nor have I engaged myself to any, nor I have even thought of taking me wife of the daughters of Canaan.

5 For I remember, mother, the words of Abraham, our father, for he commanded me not to take a wife of the daughters of Canaan, but to take me a wife from the offspring of my father's house and from my kind folks.

6 I have heard before that daughters have been born to Laban, your brother, and I have set my heart on them to take a wife from among them.

7 For this reason I have guarded myself in my spirit against sinning or being corrupted in any way throughout all the days of my life; for with regard to lust and fornication, Abraham, my father, gave me many commands.

8 Despite all that he has commanded me, these two and twenty years my brother has argued with me, and spoken frequently to me and said, "My brother, take a wife that is a sister of my two wives," but I refused to do as he has done.

9 I swear before you mother, that all the days of my life I will not take me a wife from the daughters of the offspring of Canaan, and I will not act wickedly as my brother has done.

10 Do not be afraid mother, be assured that I shall do your will and walk in uprightness, and not corrupt my ways forever."

11 When she heard this, she lifted up her face to heaven and extended the fingers of her hands, and opened her mouth and blessed the Most High God, who had created the heaven and the earth, and she gave Him thanks and praise.

12 She said, "Blessed be the Lord God, and may His holy name be blessed forever and ever. He has given me Jacob as a pure son and a holy offspring; for he is Yours, and Yours shall his offspring be continually, throughout all the generations forever.

13 Bless him, O Lord, and place in my mouth the blessing of righteousness, that I may bless him."

14 At that hour, when the spirit of righteousness descended into her mouth, she placed both her hands on the head of Jacob, and said, "Blessed are You, Lord of righteousness and God of the ages, and may You bless him beyond all the generations of men.

15 My Son, may He give you the path of righteousness, and reveal righteousness to your offspring.

16 May He make your sons many during your life, and may they arise according to the number of the months of the year. And may their sons become many and great beyond the stars of heaven, and may their numbers be more than the sand of the sea.

17 May He give them this good and pleasing land, as He said He would give it to Abraham and to his offspring after him always, and may they hold it as a possession forever.

18 My son, may I see blessed children born to you during my life, and may all your offspring be blessed and holy.

19 And as you have refreshed your mother's spirit during her life, the womb of her that gave birth to you blesses you now. My affection and my heart (breasts) bless you and my mouth and my tongue greatly praise you.

20 Increase and spread over the earth. May your offspring be perfect in the joy of heaven and earth forever. May your offspring rejoice, and on the great day of peace may they have peace.

21 May your name and your offspring endure to all the ages, and may the Most High God be their God, and may the God of righteousness dwell with them, and may His sanctuary be built by you all the ages.

22 Blessed be he that blesses you, and all flesh that curses you falsely, may it be cursed."

23 And she kissed him, and said to him, "May the Lord of the world love you as the heart of your mother and her affection rejoice in you and bless you." And she ceased from blessing.

[Chapter 26]

1 In the seventh year of this week Isaac called Esau, his elder son, and said to him, " I am old, my son, and my sight is dim, and I do not know the day of my death.

2 Now, take your hunting weapons, your quiver, and your bow, and go out to the field, and hunt and catch me venison, my son, and make me flavorful meat, like my soul loves, and bring it to me that I may eat, and that my soul may bless you before I die."

3 But Rebecca heard Isaac speaking to Esau.

4 Esau went out early to the field to hunt and catch and bring home meat to his father.

5 Rebecca called Jacob, her son, and said to him, "Look, I heard Isaac, your father, speak to Esau, your brother, saying, "Hunt for me, and make me flavorful meat, and bring it to me that I may eat and bless you before the Lord before I die."

6 Now, my son, do as you are told and do as I command you. Go to your flock and fetch me two good kids of the goats, and I will make them good tasting meat for your father, like he loves, and you will bring it to your father that he may eat and bless you to the Lord before he dies."

7 Jacob said to Rebecca his mother, "Mother, I shall not withhold anything which my father would eat and which would please him, but I am afraid that he will recognize my voice and wish to touch me.

8 And you know that I am smooth, and Esau, my brother, is hairy, and I he will see me an evildoer because I am doing something that he has not told me to do and he will be very angry with me, and I shall bring on myself a curse, and not a blessing."

9 Rebecca, his mother, said to him, "Your curse be on me, my son, just do as you are told."

10 Jacob obeyed the voice of Rebecca, his mother, and went and brought back two good and fat goat kids, and brought them to his mother, and his mother made them tasty meat like he loved.

11 Rebecca took the good and pleasing clothes of Esau, her elder son, which was with her in the house, and she clothed Jacob, her younger son, with them, and she put the skins of the kids on his hands and on the exposed parts of his neck.

12 And she gave the meat and the bread, which she had prepared, to her son Jacob.

13 Jacob went in to his father and said, "I am your son. I have done as you asked me. Arise and sit and eat of that which I have caught, father, that your soul may bless me."

14 Isaac said to his son, "How have you found game so quickly, my son?"

15 Jacob said, "Because the Lord your God caused me to find."

16 Isaac said to him, "Come closer, that I may feel you, my son, and know if you are my son Esau or not."

17 Jacob went near to Isaac, his father, and he felt him and said, "The voice is Jacob's voice, but the hands are the hands of Esau," and he did not recognize him, because it was a decision from heaven to remove his power of perception and Isaac discerned not, because his hands were hairy as his brother Esau's, so Isaac blessed him.

18 He said, "Are you my son Esau?" and Jacob said, "I am your son," and Isaac said, "Bring it to me that I may eat of that which you have caught, my son, that my soul may bless you."

19 And Jacob brought it to him, and he ate, and Jacob brought him wine and he drank.

20 Isaac, his father, said to him, "Come close and kiss me, my son."

21 He came close and kissed Isaac. And he smelled the smell of his raiment, and he blessed Jacob and said, "Look, the smell of my son is as the smell of a full field which the Lord has blessed.

22 May the Lord give you of the dew of heaven and of the dew of the earth, and plenty of corn and oil. Let nations serve you and peoples bow down to you.

23 Be ruler over your brothers, and let your mother's sons bow down to you; and may all the blessings that the Lord has blessed me and blessed Abraham, my father, be imparted to you and to your offspring forever. Cursed be he that curses you, and blessed be he that blesses you."

24 It happened as soon as Isaac had made an end of blessing his son Jacob, that Jacob had went away from Isaac his father and hid himself.

25 Esau, his brother, came in from his hunting. And he also made flavorful meat, and brought it to his father and Esau said to his father, "Let my father arise, and eat of my venison that your soul may bless me."

26 Isaac, his father, said to him, "Who are you?" Esau said to him, "I am your first born, your son Esau. I have done as you have commanded me."

27 Isaac was very greatly surprised, and said, "Who is he that has hunted and caught and brought it to me, and I have eaten of all before you came, and have blessed him, and he shall be blessed, and all his offspring forever."

28 It happened when Esau heard the words of his father Isaac that he cried with a very loud and bitter cry, and said to his father, "Bless me also, father!"

29 Isaac said to him, "Your brother came with trickery, and has taken away your blessing."

30 He said, "Now I know why his name is Jacob. Behold, he has supplanted me these two times, he took away my birth-right, and now he has taken away my blessing."

31 Esau said, "Have you not reserved a blessing for me, father?" and Isaac answered and said to Esau, "Look, I have made him your lord, and all his brothers have I given to him for servants. I have strengthened him with plenty of corn and wine and oil. Now what shall I do for you, my son?"

32 Esau said to Isaac, his father, "Have you only one blessing, father? Please. Bless me, also, father."

33 Esau lifted up his voice and wept. And Isaac answered and said to him, "Far from the dew of the earth shall be your dwelling, and far from the dew of heaven from above.

34 By your sword will you live, and you will serve your brother.

35 It shall happen that when you become great, and do shake his yoke from off your neck, you will sin completely and commit a sin worthy of death, and your offspring shall be rooted out from under heaven."

36 Esau kept threatening Jacob because of the blessing his father blessed him with, and he said in his heart, "May the days of mourning for my father come now, so that I may kill my brother Jacob."

[Chapter 27]

1 Rebecca was told Esau's words in a dream, and Rebecca sent for Jacob her younger son, and said to him, "Look, Esau, your brother, will take vengeance on you and kill you.

2 Now, therefore, my son, do as you are told, and get up and flee to Laban, my brother, to Haran, and stay with him a few days until your brother's anger fades away, and he removes his anger from you, and forgets all that you have done. Then I will send for you to come from that place."

3 Jacob said, "I am not afraid. If he wishes to kill me, I will kill him."

4 But she said to him, "Let me not be bereft of both my sons on one day."

5 Jacob said to Rebecca, his mother, "Look, you know that my father has become old, and does not see because his eyes are dull. If I leave him he will think it is wrong. If I leave him and go away from you, my father will be angry and will curse me.

6 I will not go. When he sends me, only then will I go."

7 Rebecca said to Jacob, "I will go in and speak to him, and he will send you away."

8 Rebecca went in and said to Isaac, "I hate my life because of the two daughters of Heth, whom Esau has taken as wives. If Jacob take a wife from among the daughters of the land such as these, I could not live with it, because the daughters of Canaan are evil."

9 Isaac called Jacob and blessed him, and warned him and said to him, "Do not take you a wife of any of the daughters of Canaan. Arise and go to Mesopotamia, to the house of Bethuel, your mother's father, and take a wife from that place of the daughters of Laban, your mother's brother.

10 And God Almighty bless you and increase and multiply you that you may become a company of nations, and give you the blessings of my father, Abraham, to you and to your offspring after you, that you may inherit the land that you travel in and all the land which God gave to Abraham. Go in peace, my son."

11 Isaac sent Jacob away, and he went to Mesopotamia, to Laban the son of Bethuel the Syrian, the brother of Rebecca, Jacob's mother.

12 It happened after Jacob had departed to Mesopotamia that the spirit of Rebecca was grieved for her son, and she wept.

13 Isaac said to Rebecca, "My sister, weep not because of Jacob, my son, for he goes in peace, and in peace will he return.

14 The Most High God will preserve him from all evil and will be with him. He will not forsake him all his days, for I know that his ways will be made to prosper in all things wherever he goes, until he return in peace to us, and we see him in peace. Fear not on his account, my sister, for he is on the upright path and he is a perfect man, and he is faithful and will not perish. Weep not."

15 Isaac comforted Rebecca because of her son Jacob, and blessed him.

16 Jacob went from the Well of the Oath to go to Haran on the first year of the second week in the forty-fourth jubilee, and he came to Luz on the mountains, that is, Bethel, on the new moon of the first month of this week, and he came to the place at dusk and turned from the way to the west of the road that is close, and that night he slept there, for the sun had set.

17 He took one of the stones of that place (as a pillow) and laid down under the tree, and he was journeying alone, and he slept.

18 Jacob dreamt that night, and saw a ladder set up on the earth, and the top of it reached to heaven, and he saw the angels of the Lord ascended and descended on it, and behold, the Lord stood on it.

19 And He spoke to Jacob and said, "I am the Lord God of Abraham, your father, and the God of Isaac. The land you are sleeping on I will give to you and to your offspring after you.

20 Your offspring shall be as the dust of the earth, and you will increase to the west and to the east, to the north and the south, and in you and in your offspring shall all the families of the nations be blessed.

21 Behold, I will be with you, and will keep you wherever you go. I will bring you into this land again in peace. I will not leave you until I do everything that I told you."

22 Jacob awoke from his sleep and said, "Truly this place is the house of the Lord, and I did not know it."

23 He was afraid and said, "I am afraid because this place is none other than the house of God, and this is the gate of heaven, and I did not know it."

24 Jacob got up early in the morning, and took the stone that he had placed under his head and set it up as a pillar for a sign. And he poured oil on the top of it. And he called the name of that place Bethel, but the name of the place was previously Luz.

25 And Jacob vowed a vow to the Lord, saying, "If the Lord will be with me, and will keep me in the way that I go, and give me bread to eat and clothes to put on, so that I come again to my father's house in peace, then the Lord shall be my God, and this stone which I have set up as a pillar for a sign in this place shall be the Lord's house, and of all that you gave me, I shall give the tenth to you, my God."

[Chapter 28]

1 He went on his journey, and came to the land of the east, to Laban, the brother of Rebecca, and he was with him, and Jacob served Laban for Rachel his daughter one week of years. In the first year of the third week of years he said to him, "Give me my wife, for whom I have served you seven years ," and Laban said to Jacob, "I will give you your wife."

2 Laban made a feast, and took Leah his elder daughter, and gave her to Jacob as a wife, and gave Leah Zilpah for a handmaid; and Jacob did not know, for he thought that she was Rachel.

3 He went in to her, and saw she was Leah; and Jacob was angry with Laban, and said to him, "Why have you done this to me?

4 Did I not serve you for Rachel and not for Leah? Why have you wronged me?

5 Take your daughter, and I will go. You have done evil to me." For Jacob loved Rachel more than Leah because Leah's eyes were weak, but her form was very beautiful. Rachel had beautiful eyes and a beautiful and very voluptuous form.

6 Laban said to Jacob, "It is not done that way in our country, we do not to give the younger before the elder." And it is not right to do this; for thus it is ordained and written in the heavenly tablets, that no one should give his younger daughter before the elder; but the elder one is given first and after her the younger. The man who does so will have guilt placed against him in heaven, and none is righteous that does this thing, for this deed is evil before the Lord.

7 Command the children of Israel that they not do this thing. Let them neither take nor give the younger before they have given the elder, for it is very wicked."

8 And Laban said to Jacob, "Let the seven days of the feast pass by, and I shall give you Rachel, that you may serve me another seven years, that you may pasture my sheep as you did in the former week (of years)."

9 On the day when the seven days of the feast of Leah had passed, Laban gave Rachel to Jacob, that he might serve him another seven years, and he gave Rachel, Bilhah, the sister of Zilpah, as a handmaid.

10 He served yet other seven years for Rachel, for Leah had been given to him for nothing, since it was Rachel he wanted.

11 And the Lord opened the womb of Leah, and she conceived and gave birth to a son for Jacob, and he called his name Reuben, on the fourteenth day of the ninth month, in the first year of the third week.

12 But the womb of Rachel was closed, for the Lord saw that Leah was hated and Rachel loved.

13 Again Jacob went in to Leah, and she conceived, and gave birth to a second son for Jacob, and he called his name Simeon, on the twenty-first of the tenth month, and in the third year of this week.

14 Again Jacob went in to Leah, and she conceived, and gave birth to a third son, and he called his name Levi, in the new moon of the first month in the sixth year of this week.

15 Again Jacob went in to her, and she conceived, and gave birth to a fourth son, and he called his name Judah, on the fifteenth of the third month, in the first year of the fourth week.

16 Because of all this Rachel envied Leah, for she did not bear a child, and she said to Jacob, "Give me children;" and Jacob said, "Have I withheld from you the fruits of your womb? Have I left you?"

17 And when Rachel saw that Leah had given birth to four sons for Jacob: Reuben and Simeon and Levi and Judah, she said to him, "Go in to Bilhah my handmaid, and she will conceive, and bear a son for me."

18 She gave him Bilhah, her handmaid, to wife. And he went in to her, and she conceived, and gave birth to a son, and he called his name Dan, on the ninth of the sixth month, in the sixth year of the third week.

19 Jacob went in again to Bilhah a second time, and she conceived, and gave birth to another son for Jacob, and Rachel called his name Napthali, on the fifth of the seventh month, in the second year of the fourth week.

20 When Leah saw that she had become sterile and could no longer have children, she envied Rachel, and she also gave her handmaid Zilpah to Jacob to wife, and she conceived, and gave birth to a son, and Leah called his name Gad, on the twelfth of the eighth month, in the third year of the fourth week.

21 He went in to her again, and she conceived and gave birth to a second son, and Leah called his name Asher, on the second of the eleventh month, in the fifth year of the fourth week.

22 Jacob went in to Leah, and she conceived, and gave birth to a son, and she called his name Issachar, on the fourth of the fifth month, in the fourth year of the fourth week, and she gave him to a nurse.

23 Jacob went in again to her, and she conceived, and gave birth to two children, a son and a daughter, and she called the name of the son Zabulon, and the name of the daughter Dinah, in the seventh day of the seventh month, in the sixth year of the fourth week.

24 The Lord was gracious to Rachel, and opened her womb, and she conceived, and gave birth to a son, and she called his name Joseph, on the new moon of the fourth month, in the sixth year in this fourth week.

25 In the days when Joseph was born, Jacob said to Laban, "Give me my wives and sons, and let me go to my father Isaac, and let me make a household for myself; for I have completed the years in which I have served you for your two daughters, and I will go to the house of my father."

26 Laban said to Jacob, "Stay with me and I will pay you wages, and pasture my flock for me again, and take your wages."

27 They agreed with one another that he should give him as his wages those of the lambs and kids which were born spotted black and white, these were to be his wages.

28 All the sheep brought out spotted and speckled and black, variously marked, and they brought out again lambs like themselves, and all that were spotted were Jacob's and those which were not spotted were Laban's.

29 Jacob's possessions multiplied greatly, and he possessed oxen and sheep and donkeys and camels, and men-servants and maid-servants.

30 Laban and his sons envied Jacob, and Laban took back his sheep from him, and he envied him and watched him for an opportunity to do evil.

[Chapter 29]

1 It happened when Rachel had given birth to Joseph, that Laban went to shear his sheep; for they were distant from him, a three-day journey.

2 Jacob saw that Laban was going to shear his sheep, and Jacob called Leah and Rachel, and spoke sweetly to them in order to convince them to come with him to the land of Canaan.

3 For he told them how he had seen everything in a dream. All that God had spoken to him that he should return to his father's house, and they said, "To every place where you go we will go with you."

4 Jacob blessed the God of Isaac his father, and the God of Abraham his father's father, and he arose and placed his wives and his children on donkeys, and took all his possessions and crossed the river, and came to the land of Gilead, and Jacob hid his intention from Laban and did not tell him.

5 In the seventh year of the fourth week Jacob turned his face toward Gilead in the first month, on the twenty-first of it.

6 Laban pursued and overtook Jacob in the mountain of Gilead in the third month, on the thirteenth of it. And the Lord did not permit him to injure Jacob for he appeared to him in a dream by night.

7 Laban spoke to Jacob. On the fifteenth of those days Jacob made a feast for Laban, and for all who came with him, and Jacob swore to Laban that day, and Laban also swore to Jacob, that neither should cross the mountain of Gilead to do evil to the other.

8 He made a heap (of stones) for a witness there; wherefore the name of that place is called, "The Heap of Witness," after this heap.

9 But before they used to call the land of Gilead the land of the Rephaim. The Rephaim were born giants whose height was ten, nine, eight, down to seven cubits.

10 Their dwelling place was from the land of the children of Ammon to Mount Hermon, and the seats of their kingdom were Karnaim and Ashtaroth, and Edrei, and Misur, and Beon.

11 The Lord destroyed them because of the evil of their deeds, for they were malevolent, and the Amorites were wicked and sinful. There is no people today which has committed the full range of their sins, and their life on the earth was shortened.

12 Jacob sent Laban away, and he departed into Mesopotamia, the land of the East, and Jacob returned to the land of Gilead.

13 He passed over the Jabbok in the ninth month, on the eleventh of it. On that day Esau, his brother, came to him, and he was reconciled to him, and departed from him to the land of Seir, but Jacob dwelt in tents.

14 In the first year of the fifth week in this jubilee he crossed the Jordan, and dwelt beyond the Jordan. He pastured his sheep from the sea of the heap to Bethshan, and to Dothan and to the forest of Akrabbim.

15 He sent his father Isaac all of his possessions such as clothing, and food, and meat, and drink, and milk, and butter, and cheese, and some dates of the valley.

16 Four times a year, he sent gifts to his mother Rebecca who was living at the tower of Abraham. He sent the gifts between the times of the months between plowing and reaping, and between autumn and the rain season, and between winter and spring.

17 For Isaac had returned from the Well of the Oath and gone up to the tower of his father Abraham, and he dwelt there apart from his son Esau.

18 For in the days when Jacob went to Mesopotamia, Esau took to himself a wife Mahalath, the daughter of Ishmael,

and he gathered together all the flocks of his father and his wives, and went up and dwelt on Mount Seir, and left Isaac his father at the Well of the Oath alone.

19 And Isaac went up from the Well of the Oath and dwelt in the tower of Abraham his father on the mountains of Hebron, and that is where Jacob sent all that he did send to his father and his mother from time to time, all they needed, and they blessed Jacob with all their heart and with all their soul.

[Chapter 30]

1 In the first year of the sixth week he went up to Salem, to the east of Shechem, in the fourth month, and he went in peace. Shechem, the son of Hamor, the Hivite, the prince of the land carried off Dinah, the daughter of Jacob, into the house, and he had sex with her and defiled her. She was a little girl, a child of twelve years.

2 He begged his father and her brothers that she might be given to him as a wife.

3 Jacob and his sons were very angry because of the men of Shechem, for they had defiled Dinah, their sister. They spoke to them while planning evil acts and they dealt deceitfully with them and tricked them.

4 Simeon and Levi came unexpectedly to Shechem and executed judgment on all the men of Shechem, and killed all the men whom they found in it. They did not leave a single one remaining in it. They killed all in hand to hand battle because they had dishonored their sister Dinah.

5 Let it not again be done from now on that a daughter of Israel be defiled. Judgment is ordained in heaven against them that they should destroy all the men of the Shechemites with the sword because they had committed shame in Israel.

6 The Lord delivered them into the hands of the sons of Jacob that they might exterminate them with the sword and execute judgment on them. That it might not again be done in Israel that a virgin of Israel should be defiled.

7 If there is any man in Israel who wishes to give his daughter or his sister to any man who is of the offspring of the Gentiles he shall surely die. They shall stone him, for he has committed shame in Israel. They shall burn the woman with fire, because she has dishonored the name of the house of her father, and she shall be rooted out of Israel.

8 Do not let an adulteress and let no uncleanness be found in Israel throughout all the days of the generations of the earth. For Israel is holy to the Lord, and every man who has defiled it shall surely die. They shall stone him.

9 For it has been ordained and written in the heavenly tablets regarding all the offspring of Israel. He who defiles it shall surely die. He shall be killed by stoning. There is no limit of days for this law. There is no remission, and no atonement.

10 The man who has defiled his daughter shall be rooted out from every corner of all Israel, because he has given of his offspring to Moloch (a pagan God, the worship of which involved burning the child alive), and committed impurity and defiled his child.

11 Moses, command the children of Israel and exhort them not to give their daughters to the Gentiles, and not to take for their sons any of the daughters of the Gentiles, for this is abominable before the Lord.

12 It is because of this that I have written all the deeds of the Shechemites, which they committed against Dinah, and placed them in the words of the Law for you. I have also written how the sons of Jacob spoke, saying, "We will not give our daughter to a man who is uncircumcised, for that is a reproach to us."

13 It is a reproach to Israel that anyone take the daughters of the Gentiles, for this is unclean and abominable to Israel.

14 Israel will not be free from this uncleanness if it has a wife of the daughters of the Gentiles, or has given any of its daughters to a man who is of any of the Gentiles.

15 There will be plague upon plague, and curse upon curse, and every judgment and plague and curse will come if he does this thing, or if they ignore those who commit uncleanness, or defile the sanctuary of the Lord, or those who profane His holy name. If any of these happen the whole nation together will be judged for all the uncleanness and profanation of this man.

16 There will be no judging people by their position and no receiving fruits, or offerings, or burnt-offerings, or fat, or the fragrance of sweet odor from his hands. It will be unacceptable and so warn every man and woman in Israel who defiles the sanctuary.

17 For this reason I have commanded you, saying, "Give this testimony to Israel, see how the Shechemites and their sons fared? See how they were delivered into the hands of two sons of Jacob, and they killed them under torture? It was counted to them for righteousness, and it is written down to them for righteousness.

18 The offspring of Levi were chosen for the priesthood, and to be Levites, that they might minister before the Lord, as we do, continually. Levi and his sons will be blessed forever, for he was zealous to execute righteousness and judgment and vengeance on all those who arose against Israel.

19 So they wrote a testimony in his favor of blessing and righteousness on the heavenly tablets in the presence of the God of all.

20 We remember the righteousness that the man fulfilled during his life, throughout the years, until a thousand generations they will record it. It will come to him and to his descendants after him, and he has been recorded on the heavenly tablets as a friend and a righteous man.

21 All this account I have written for you, and have commanded you to tell the children of Israel, so that they will not commit sin nor transgress the laws nor break the covenant which has been ordained for them. They should fulfill it and be recorded as friends (of God).

22 But if they transgress and work uncleanness in any way, they will be recorded on the heavenly tablets as adversaries (of God), and they will be blotted out of the book of life. Instead, they will be recorded in the book of those who will be destroyed and with those who will be rooted out of the earth.

23 On the day when the sons of Jacob killed Shechem it was written in the record in their favor in heaven that they had executed righteousness and uprightness and vengeance on the sinners, and it was written for a blessing.

24 They brought Dinah, their sister, out of the house of Shechem. They took everything that was in Shechem captive. They took their sheep and their oxen and their donkeys, and all their wealth, and all their flocks, and brought them all to Jacob their father.

25 He reproached them because they had put the city to the sword for he feared those who dwelt in the land, the Canaanites and the Perizzites.

26 The dread of the Lord was on all the cities that are near Shechem. They did not fight or chase after the sons of Jacob, for terror had fallen on them.

[Chapter 31]

1 On the new moon of the month, Jacob spoke to all the people of his house, saying, "Purify yourselves and change your clothes, and let us get up and go to Bethel where I vowed a vow to Him on the day when I fled from Esau my brother. Let us do this because God has been with me and brought me into this land in peace. You must put away the strange gods that you raise among you."

2 They gave up the strange gods and that which was in their ears and which was on their necks and the idols which Rachel stole from Laban her father she gave wholly to Jacob. And he burnt and broke them to pieces and destroyed them, and hid them under an oak, which is in the land of Shechem.

3 He went up on the new moon of the seventh month to Bethel. And he built an altar at the place where he had slept, and he set up a pillar there, and he sent word to his father, Isaac, and his mother, Rebecca. He asked to come to Isaac. There, Jacob wished to offer his sacrifice.

4 Isaac said, "Let my son, Jacob, come, and let me see him before I die."

5 Jacob went to his father, Isaac, and his mother, Rebecca, to the house of his father Abraham, and he took two of his sons with him, Levi and Judah.

6 Rebecca came out from the tower to the front of it to kiss Jacob and embrace him, for her spirit had revived when she heard, "Look Jacob your son has come," and she kissed him.

7 She saw his two sons and she recognized them. She said to him, "Are these your sons, my son?" and she embraced them and kissed them, and blessed them, saying, "In you shall the offspring of Abraham become illustrious, and you shall prove a blessing on the earth."

8 Jacob went in to Isaac his father, to the room where he lay, and his two sons were with him. He took his father's hand, stooped down, he kissed him. Isaac held on to the neck of Jacob his son, and wept on his neck.

9 The darkness left the eyes of Isaac, and he saw the two sons of Jacob, Levi, and Judah. And he said, "Are these your sons, my son? Because they look like you."

10 He said to Isaac, "They were truly my sons, and you have clearly seen that they are truly my sons."

11 They came near to him, and he turned and kissed them and embraced them both together.

12 The spirit of prophecy came down into his mouth, and he took Levi by his right hand and Judah by his left.

13 He turned to Levi first, and began to bless him first, and said to him, "May the God of all, the very Lord of all the ages, bless you and your children throughout all the ages.

14 May the Lord give to you and your offspring greatness and great glory from among all flesh. May the Lord cause you and your offspring to draw near to Him to serve in His sanctuary like the angels of the presence (of the Lord) and as the holy ones. The offspring of your sons shall be for the glory and greatness and holiness of God. May He make them great throughout all the ages. They shall be judges and princes, and chiefs of all the offspring of the sons of Jacob. They shall speak the word of the Lord in righteousness, and they shall judge all His judgments in righteousness.

15 They shall declare My ways to Jacob and My paths to Israel. The blessing of the Lord shall be given in their mouths to bless all the offspring of the beloved.

16 Your mother has called your name Levi, and rightly has she called your name. You will be joined to the Lord and be the companion of all the sons of Jacob. Let His table be your table, and let your sons eat from it. May your table be full throughout all generations, and let your food not fail in all the ages.

17 Let all who hate you fall down before you, and let all your adversaries be rooted out and perish. Blessed be he that blesses you, and cursed be every nation that curses you."

18 To Judah he said, "May the Lord give you strength and power to put all that hate you under your feet. You and one of your sons will be a prince over the sons of Jacob. May your name and the name of your sons go out across every land and region.

19 Then shall the Gentiles fear you, and all the nations and people shall shake (with fear of you). In you will be the help of Jacob, and in you will be found the salvation of Israel.

20 When you sit on the throne, which honors your righteousness, there shall be great peace for all the offspring of the sons of the beloved. Blessed be he that blesses you, and cursed be all that hate you, afflict you, or curse you. They shall be rooted out and destroyed from the earth."

21 He turned, kissed him again, and embraced him, and rejoiced greatly because he had seen the sons of his son, Jacob, clearly and truly.

22 He stepped out from between his feet and fell down. He bowed down to him, and blessed them. He rested there with Isaac, his father, that night, and they ate and drank with joy.

23 He made the two sons of Jacob sleep, the one on his right hand and the other on his left. It was counted to him for righteousness.

24 Jacob told his father everything during the night about how the Lord had shown him great mercy, and how he had caused him to prosper in all his ways, and how he protected him from all evil.

25 Isaac blessed the God of his father Abraham, who had not withdrawn his mercy and his righteousness from the sons of his servant Isaac.

26 In the morning, Jacob told his father, Isaac, the vow, which he had vowed to the Lord. He told him of the vision which he had seen, and that he had built an altar. He told him that everything was ready for the sacrifice to be made before the Lord as he had vowed. He had come to set him on a donkey.

27 Isaac said to Jacob his son, "I am not able to go with you, for I am old and not able to endure the way. Go in peace, my son. I am one hundred and sixty-five years this day. I am no longer able to journey. Set your mother on a donkey and let her go with you.

28 I know that you have come on my account, my son. May this day be blessed on which you have seen me alive, and I also have seen you, my son.

29 May you prosper and fulfill the vow that you have vowed. Do not put off your vow, for you will be called to account for the vow. Now hurry to perform it, and may He who has made all things be pleased. It is to Him you have vowed the vow."

30 He said to Rebecca, "Go with Jacob your son," and Rebecca went with Jacob her son, and Deborah with her, and they came to Bethel.

31 Jacob remembered the prayer with which his father had blessed him and his two sons, Levi and Judah. He rejoiced and blessed the God of his fathers, Abraham and Isaac.

32 He said, "Now I know that my sons and I have an eternal hope in the God of all." Thus is it ordained concerning the two. They recorded it as an eternal testimony to them on the heavenly tablets how Isaac blessed his sons.

[Chapter 32]

1 That night he stayed at Bethel, and Levi dreamed that they had ordained and made his sons and him the priests of the Most High God forever. Then he awoke from his sleep and blessed the Lord.

2 Jacob rose early in the morning, on the fourteenth of this month, and he gave a tithe for all that came with him, both of men and cattle, both of gold and every vessel and garment. Yes, he gave tithes of all.

3 In those days Rachel became pregnant with her son Benjamin. Jacob counted his sons starting from him and going to the oldest and Levi fell to the portion of the Lord. (Levi was the third son — three is the number of spiritual completeness.) His father clothed him in the garments of the priesthood and filled his hands.

4 On the fifteenth of this month, he brought fourteen oxen from among the cattle, and twenty-eight rams, and forty-nine sheep, and seven lambs, and twenty-one kids of the goats to the altar as a burnt-offering on the altar of sacrifice. The offering was well pleasing and a sweet odor before God.

5 This was his offering, done in acknowledgement of the vow in which he had promised that he would give a tenth, with their fruit-offerings and their drink- offerings.

6 When the fire had consumed it, he burnt incense over the fire, and for a thank-offering he sacrificed two oxen and four rams and four sheep, four male goats, and two sheep of a year old, and two kids of the goats. This he did daily for seven days.

7 He, his men, and all his sons were eating this with joy during seven days and blessing and thanking the Lord, who had delivered him out of all his tribulation and had given him His promise.

8 He tithed all the clean animals, and made a burnt sacrifice, but he did not give the unclean animals to Levi his son. He gave him (responsibility for) all the souls of the men. Levi acted in the priestly office at Bethel in the presence of Jacob his father, in preference to his ten brothers. He was a priest there, and Jacob gave his vow, and he gave a tithe to the Lord again and sanctified it, and it became holy to Him.

9 For this reason it is ordained on the heavenly tablets as a law for the offering of the tithe should be eaten in the presence of the Lord every year, in the place where it is chosen that His name should live and reside. This law has no limit of days forever.

10 This law is written so that it may be fulfilled every year. The second tithe should be eaten in the presence of the Lord, in the place where it has been chosen, and nothing shall be left over from it from this year to the following year.

11 In its year shall the seed be eaten until the days of the gathering of the seed of the year. The wine shall be consumed until the days of the wine, and the oil until the days of its season.

12 All that is left of it and all that becomes old will be regarded as spoiled, let it be burnt with fire, for it is unclean.

13 Let them eat it together in the sanctuary, and let them not permit it to become old.

14 All the tithes of the oxen and sheep shall be holy to the Lord, and shall belong to His priests. They will eat before Him from year to year, for thus is it ordained and written on the heavenly tablets regarding the tithe.

15 On the following night, on the twenty-second day of this month, Jacob resolved to build that place and to surround the court with a wall, and to sanctify it and make it holy forever, for himself and his children after him.

16 The Lord appeared to him by night and blessed him and said to him, "Your name shall not be called Jacob, but they will call your name Israel."

17 And He said to him again, "I am the Lord who created the heaven and the earth, and I will increase you and multiply you greatly, and kings shall come forth from you, and they shall be judges everywhere the foot of the sons of men have walked.

18 I will give to your offspring all the earth that is under heaven. They shall judge all the nations, as they desire. After that they shall possess the entire earth and inherit it forever."

19 And He finished speaking with him, and He went up from him.

20 Jacob watched until He had ascended into heaven.

21 In a vision at night he saw an angel descend from heaven with seven tablets in his hands, and he gave them to Jacob, and he read them and knew all that was written on it that would happen to him and his sons throughout all the ages.

22 He showed him all that was written on the tablets, and said to him, "Do not build on this place, and do not make it an eternal sanctuary, and do not live here. This is not the place. Go to the house of Abraham your father and live with Isaac, your father, until the day he dies.

23 For in Egypt you will die in peace, and in this land you will be buried with honor in the sepulcher of your fathers, with Abraham and Isaac.

24 Do not fear. As you have seen and read it shall all be. Write down everything that you have seen and read."

25 Jacob said, "Lord, how can I remember all that I have read and seen?" He said to him, "I will bring all things to your remembrance."

26 He ascended from Jacob, and Jacob awoke from his sleep. He remembered everything that he had read and seen, and he wrote down all the words.

27 He celebrated there yet another day, and he sacrificed on that day as he had sacrificed on all the former days. He called its name "Addition," because this day was added, and the former days he called "The Feast."

688

28 It was made known and revealed to him and it is written on the heavenly tablets that he should celebrate the day, and add it to the seven days of the feast.

29 Its name was called "Addition," because that it was recorded among the days of the feast days, according to the number of the days of the year.

30 In the night, on the twenty-third of this month, Deborah, Rebecca's nurse died, and they buried her beneath the city under the oak of the river. He called the name of this place, "The river of Deborah," and he called the oak, "The oak of the mourning of Deborah."

31 Rebecca departed and returned to her house, to his father Isaac. Jacob sent rams and sheep and male goats by her so that she should prepare a meal for his father such as he desired.

32 He followed his mother until he came to the land of Kabratan, and he lived there.

33 Rachel gave birth to a son in the night, and called his name "son of my sorrow", for she broke down while giving birth to him, but his father called his name Benjamin. This happened on the eleventh day of the eighth month in the first of the sixth week of this jubilee.

34 Rachel died there and she was buried in the land of Ephrath, the same is Bethlehem, and Jacob built a pillar on the grave of Rachel, on the road above her grave.

[Chapter 33]

1 Jacob went and lived to the south of Magdaladra'ef. He and Leah, his wife, went to his father, Isaac, on the new moon of the tenth month.

2 Reuben saw Bilhah, Rachel's maid, the concubine of his father, bathing in water in a secret place, and he loved her.

3 He hid himself at night, and he entered the house of Bilhah at night. He found her sleeping alone on a bed in her house.

4 He had sex with her. She awoke and saw that is was Reuben lying with her in the bed. She uncovered the border of her covering and grabbed him and cried out when she discovered that it was Reuben.

5 She was ashamed because of him and released her hand from him, and he fled.

6 Because of this, she mourned greatly and did not tell it to any one.

7 When Jacob returned and sought her, she said to him, "I am not clean for you. I have been defiled in regard to you. Reuben has defiled me, and has had sex with me in the night. I was asleep and did not realize he was there until he uncovered my skirt and had sex with me."

8 Jacob was very angry with Reuben because he had sex with Bilhah, because he had uncovered his father's skirt.

9 Jacob did not approach her again because Reuben had defiled her. And as for any man who uncovers his father's skirt his deed is greatly wicked, for he is disgusting to the Lord.

10 For this reason it is written and ordained on the heavenly tablets that a man should not lie with his father's wife, and should not uncover his father's skirt. This is unclean and they shall surely die together, the man who lies with his father's wife and the woman also, for they have committed uncleanness on the earth.

11 There shall be nothing unclean before our God in the nation that He has chosen for Himself as a possession.

12 Again, it is written a second time, "Cursed be he who lies with the wife of his father, for he has uncovered his father's shame." All the holy ones of the Lord said, "So be it. So be it."

13 "Moses, command the children of Israel so that they observe this word. It entails a punishment of death. It is unclean, and there is no atonement forever for the man who has committed this. He is to be put to death. Kill him by stoning. Root him out from among the people of our God.

14 No man who does so in Israel will be permitted to remain alive a single day on the earth. He is abominable and unclean.

15 Do not let them say, "Reuben was granted life and forgiveness after he had sex with his father's concubine, although she had a husband, and her husband, Jacob, his father, was still alive."

16 Until that time the ordinance and judgment and law had not been revealed in its completeness for all. In your days it has been revealed as a law of seasons and of days. It is an everlasting law for all generations forever. For this law has no limit of days, and no atonement for it.

17 They must both be rooted out of the entire nation. On the day they committed it they shall be killed.

18 Moses, write it down for Israel that they may observe it, and do according to these words, and not commit a sin punishable by death. The Lord our God is judge, who does not respect persons (position) and accepts no gifts.

19 Tell them these words of the covenant, that they may hear and observe, and be on their guard with respect to them, and not be destroyed and rooted out of the land; for an uncleanness, and an abomination, and a contamination, and a pollution are all they who commit it on the earth before our God.

20 There is no greater sin on earth than fornication that they commit. Israel is a holy nation to the Lord its God, and a nation of inheritance. It is a priestly and royal nation and for His own possession. There shall appear no such uncleanness among the holy nation.

21 In the third year of this sixth week, Jacob and all his sons went and lived in the house of Abraham, near Isaac his father and Rebecca his mother.

22 These were the names of the sons of Jacob, the first-born

Reuben, Simeon, Levi, Judah, Issachar, Zebulon, which are the sons of Leah. The sons of Rachel are Joseph and Benjamin. The sons of Bilhah are Dan and Naphtali; and the sons of Zilpah, Gad and Asher. Dinah is the daughter of Leah, the only daughter of Jacob.

23 They came and bowed themselves to Isaac and Rebecca. When they saw them they blessed Jacob and all his sons, and Isaac rejoiced greatly, for he saw the sons of Jacob, his younger son and he blessed them.

[Chapter 34]

1 In the sixth year of this week of the forty-fourth jubilee Jacob sent his sons and his servants to pasture their sheep in the pastures of Shechem.

2 The seven kings of the Amorites assembled themselves together (to fight) against them and kill them. They hid themselves under the trees, to take their cattle as booty.

3 Jacob, Levi, Judah and Joseph were in the house with Isaac their father, for his spirit was sorrowful, and they could not leave him. Benjamin was the youngest, and for this reason he remained with his father.

4 The king of Taphu, the king of Aresa, the king of Seragan, the king of Selo, the king of Ga'as, the king of Bethoron, the king of Ma'anisakir, and all those who dwell in these mountains and who dwell in the woods in the land of Canaan came.

5 They announced to Jacob saying, "Look, the kings of the Amorites have surrounded your sons, and plundered their herds."

6 And he left his house, he and his three sons and all the servants of his father, and his own servants, and he went against them with six thousand men, who carried swords.

7 He killed them in the pastures of Shechem, and pursued those who fled, and he killed them with the edge of the sword, and he killed Aresa and Taphu and Saregan and Selo and Amani sakir and Gaga'as, and he recovered his herds.

8 He conquered them, and imposed tribute on them that they should pay him five fruit products of their land. He built (the cities of) Robel and Tamnatares.

9 He returned in peace, and made peace with them, and they became his servants until the day that he and his sons went down into Egypt.

10 In the seventh year of this week he sent Joseph from his house to the land of Shechem to learn about the welfare of his brothers. He found them in the land of Dothan.

11 They dealt treacherously with him, and formed a plot against him to kill him, but they changed their minds and sold him to Ishmaelite merchants. They brought him down into Egypt, and they sold him to Potiphar, the eunuch of Pharaoh, the chief of the cooks and priest of the city of Elew."

12 The sons of Jacob slaughtered a kid, and dipped Joseph's coat in the blood and sent it to Jacob their father on the tenth of the seventh month.

13 They brought it to him in the evening and he mourned all that night. He became feverish with mourning for Joseph's death, and he said, "An evil beast has devoured Joseph". All the members of his house mourned and grieved with him that day.

14 His sons and his daughter got up to comfort him, but he refused to be comforted for his son.

15 On that day Bilhah heard that Joseph had perished, and she died mourning him. She was living in Qafratef, and Dinah, his daughter, died after Joseph had perished.

16 There were now three reasons for Israel to mourn in one month. They buried Bilhah next to the tomb of Rachel, and Dinah, his daughter. They were (all) buried there.

17 He mourned for Joseph one year, and did not cease, for he said, "Let me go down to my grave mourning for my son."

18 For this reason it is ordained for the children of Israel that they should remember and mourn on the tenth of the seventh month. On that day the news came which made Jacob weep for Joseph. On this day they should make atonement for their sins for themselves with a young goat on the tenth of the seventh month, once a year, for they had grieved the sorrow of their father regarding Joseph his son.

19 This day, once a year, has been ordained that they should grieve on it for their sins, and for all their transgressions and for all their errors, so that they might cleanse themselves.

20 After Joseph perished, the sons of Jacob took to themselves wives. The name of Reuben's wife is Ada; and the name of Simeon's wife is Adlba'a, a Canaanite. The name of Levi's wife is Melka, of the daughters of Aram, of the offspring of the sons of Terah. The name of Judah's wife is Betasu'el, a Canaanite. The name of Issachar's wife is Hezaqa, and the name of Zabulon's wife is Ni'iman. The name of Dan's wife is Egla. The name of Naphtali's wife is Rasu'u, of Mesopotamia. The name of Gad's wife is Maka. The name of Asher's wife is Ijona. The name of Joseph's wife is Asenath, the Egyptian. The name of Benjamin's wife is Ijasaka.

21 And Simeon repented, and took a second wife from Mesopotamia as his brothers had done.

[Chapter 35]

1 In the first year of the first week of the forty-fifth jubilee Rebecca called Jacob, her son, and commanded him regarding his father and regarding his brother, that he should honor them all the days of his life.

2 Jacob said, "I will do everything you have commanded. I will honor them. This will be honor and greatness to me, and righteousness before the Lord.

3 Mother, you know from the time I was born until this day, all my deeds and all that is in my heart. I always think good concerning all.

4 Why should I not do this thing which you have commanded me, that I should honor my father and my brother?

5 Tell me, mother, what perversity have you seen in me and I shall turn away from it, and mercy will be on me."

6 She said to him, "My son, in all my days I have not seen any perverseness in you, but only upright deeds. Yet, I will tell you the truth, my son, I shall die this year. I shall not survive this year in my life. I have seen the day of my death in a dream. I should not live beyond a hundred and fifty-five years. I have completed all the days that I am to live my life."

7 Jacob laughed at the words of his mother because his mother had said she should die. She was sitting across from him in possession of her strength, and she was still strong. She came and went (as she wished). She could see well, and her teeth were strong. No sickness had touched her all the days of her life.

8 Jacob said to her, "If my days of life are close to yours and my strength remains with me as your strength has, I would be blessed, mother. You will not die. You are simply joking with me regarding your death."

9 She went in to Isaac and said to him, " I make one request of you. Make Esau swear that he will not injure Jacob, nor pursue him with intent to harm him. You know Esau's thoughts have been perverse from his youth, and there is no goodness in him. He desires to kill him after you die.

10 You know all that he has done since the day Jacob, his brother, went to Haran until this day. He has forsaken us with his whole heart, and has done evil to us. He has stolen your flocks and carried off all your possessions while you watched.

11 When we asked him and begged him for what was our own, he did as a man (stranger) who was taking pity on us (giving a token like one giving alms to a beggar).

12 He is bitter against you because you blessed Jacob, your perfect and upright son. There is no evil but only goodness in Jacob. Since he came from Haran to this day he has not robbed us of anything. He always brings us everything in its season. He rejoices and blesses us with all his heart when we take his hands. He has not parted from us since he came from Haran until this day, and he remains with us continually at home honoring us."

13 Isaac said to her, "I also know and see the deeds of Jacob who is with us, how he honors us with all his heart. Before, I loved Esau more than Jacob because he was the first-born, but now I love Jacob more than Esau, for Esau has done many evil deeds, and there is no righteousness in him. All his ways are unrighteousness and violence.

14 My heart is troubled because of all his deeds. Neither he nor his offspring will be exempt because they are those who will be destroyed from the earth and who will be rooted out from under heaven. He and his children have forsaken the God of Abraham and gone after his wives (wives' gods) and after their uncleanness and after their error.

15 You told me to make him swear that he will not kill Jacob his brother, but even if he swears, he will not abide by his oath. He will not do good but evil only.

16 If he desires to kill Jacob, his brother, then into Jacob's hands he will be given. He will not escape from Jacob's hands.

17 Do not be afraid for Jacob, for the guardian of Jacob is great, powerful, honored, and praised more than the guardian of Esau."

18 Rebecca called for Esau and he came to her, and she said to him, "I have a request of you, my son. Promise to do it, my son."

19 He said, "I will do everything that you say to me, and I will not refuse your request."

20 She said to him, "I ask you that the day I die, you will take me in and bury me near Sarah, your father's mother, and that you and Jacob will love each other and that neither will desire evil against the other, but (have) mutual love only. Do this so you will prosper, my son, and be honored in the all of the land, and no enemy will rejoice over you. You will be a blessing and a mercy in the eyes of all those that love you."

21 He said, "I will do all that you have told me. I shall bury you on the day you die near Sarah, my father's mother, as you have desired that her bones may be near your bones.

22 Jacob, my brother, I shall love above all flesh. I have only one brother in all the earth but him. It is only what is expected of me. It is no great thing if I love him, for he is my brother, and we were sown together in your body, and together came we out from your womb. If I do not love my brother, whom shall I love?

23 I beg you to exhort Jacob concerning me and concerning my sons, for I know that he will assuredly be king over me and my sons, for on the day my father blessed him he made him the higher and me the lower.

24 I swear to you that I shall love him, and not desire evil against him all the days of my life but good only."

25 And he swore to her regarding all this matter. While Esau was there, she called Jacob and gave him her orders according to the words that she had spoken to Esau.

26 He said, "I shall do your pleasure, believe me that no evil will proceed from me or from my sons against Esau. I shall be first in nothing except in love only."

27 She and her sons ate and drank that night, and she died, three jubilees and one week and one year old on that night. Her two sons, Esau and Jacob, buried her in the double cave near Sarah, their father's mother.

[Chapter 36]

1 In the sixth year of this week Isaac called his two sons Esau and Jacob, and they came to him, and he said to them, "My sons, I am going the way of my fathers, to the eternal house where my fathers are.

2 Bury me near Abraham my father, in the double cave in the field of Ephron the Hittite, where Abraham purchased a sepulcher to bury in. Bury me in the sepulcher I dug for myself.

3 I command you, my sons, to practice righteousness and uprightness on the earth, so that the Lord may do to you what he said he would do to Abraham and to his offspring.

4 Love one another. Love your brothers as a man who loves his own soul. Let each seek how he may benefit his brother, and act together on the earth. Let them love each other as their own souls.

5 I command and warn you to reject idols. Hate them, and do not love them. They are fully deceptive to those that worship them and for those that bow down to them.

6 Remember the Lord God of Abraham, your father, and how I worshipped Him and served Him in righteousness and in joy, that God might multiply you and increase your offspring as the multitude of stars in heaven, and establish you on the earth as the plant of righteousness, which will not be rooted out to all the generations forever.

7 And now I shall make you swear a great oath, for there is no oath which is greater than that which is by the name glorious, honored, great, splendid, wonderful and mighty, which created the heavens and the earth and all things together, that you will fear Him and worship Him.

8 Each will love his brother with affection and righteousness. Neither will desire to do evil against his brother from now on forever all the days of your life so that you may prosper in all your deeds and not be destroyed.

9 If either of you plans evil against his brother, know that he that plans evil shall fall into his brother's hand, and shall be rooted out of the land of the living, and his offspring shall be destroyed from under heaven.

10 But on that day there will be turbulence, curses, wrath, anger, and will He burn his land and his city and all that is his with a devouring fire like the fire He sent to burn Sodom and he shall be blotted out of the book of the discipline of the children of men, and he will not be recorded in the book of life. He shall

690

be added in the book of destruction. He shall depart into eternal curses. Their condemnation may be always renewed in hate and in curses and in wrath and in torment and in anger and in plagues and in disease forever.

11 My sons, this, I say and testify to you, will be the result according to the judgment which shall come on the man who wishes to injure his brother."

12 Then he divided all his possessions between the two on that day, and he gave the larger portion to him that was the first-born, and the tower and all that was around it, and all that Abraham possessed at the Well of the Oath.

13 He said, "This larger portion I will give to the first-born."

14 Esau said, "I have sold and relinquished my birthright to Jacob. Let it be given to him. I have nothing to say regarding it, for it is his."

15 Isaac said, "May a blessing rest on you, my sons, and on your offspring this day. You have given me rest, and my heart is not pained concerning the birthright, or that you should work wickedness because of it.

16 May the Most High God bless the man and his offspring forever that does righteousness."

17 He stopped commanding them and blessing them, and they ate and drank together in front of him, and he rejoiced because there was one mind between them, and they went out from him and rested that day and slept.

18 Isaac slept on his bed that day rejoicing. He slept the eternal sleep, and died one hundred and eighty years old. He lived twenty-five weeks and five years; and his two sons, Esau and Jacob, buried him.

19 After that Esau went to the land of Edom, to the mountains of Seir, and lived there.

20 Jacob lived in the mountains of Hebron, in the high place of the land in which his father Abraham had journeyed. He worshipped the Lord with all his heart. He had divided the days of his generations according to the commands he had seen.

21 Leah, his wife, died in the fourth year of the second week of the forty-fifth jubilee, and he buried her in the double cave near Rebecca his mother to the left of the grave of Sarah, his father's mother. All her sons and his sons came to mourn over Leah, his wife, with him and to comfort him regarding her. He was lamenting her for he loved her greatly after Rachel, her sister, died. She was perfect and upright in all her ways and she honored Jacob. All the days that she lived with him he did not hear from her mouth a harsh word, for she was gentle, peaceable, upright and honorable.

22 And he remembered all the deeds she had done during her life and he lamented her greatly. He loved her with all his heart and with all his soul.

[Chapter 37]

1 On the day that Isaac, the father of Jacob and Esau died, the sons of Esau heard that Isaac had given the elder's portion to his younger son, Jacob, and they were very angry.

2 They argued with their father, saying, "Why has your father given Jacob the portion of the elder and passed you over even though you are the elder and Jacob the younger?"

3 He said to them, "Because I sold my birthright to Jacob for a small portion of lentils (lentil soup), and on the day my father sent me to hunt, catch, and bring him something that he should eat and bless me, Jacob came with deceit and brought my father food and drink. My father blessed him and put me under his hand.

4 Now our father has caused Jacob and me to swear that we shall not devise evil plans against his brother (each other), and that we shall continue in love and in peace each with his brother and not make our ways corrupt."

5 They said to him, "We shall not listen to you to make peace with him. We are stronger than him and we are more powerful than he is. We shall depose him and kill him, and destroy him and his sons. If you will not go with us, we shall hurt you also.

6 Listen! Let us send to Aram, Philistia, Moab, and Ammon. Let us take chosen men who are trained in battle, and let us go against him and do battle with him. Let us exterminate him from the earth before he grows strong."

7 Their father said to them, "Do not go and do not make war with him or you shall fall before him."

8 They said to him, "This is how you have acted from your youth until this day. You have continued to put your neck under his yoke. We shall not listen to these words."

9 Then they sent to Aram, and to Aduram to the friend of their father, and they also hired one thousand chosen men of war.

10 And there came to them from Moab and from the children of Ammon, those who were hired, one thousand chosen men, and from Philistia, one thousand chosen warriors, and from Edom and from the Horites one thousand chosen warriors, and from the Kittim mighty warriors.

11 They said to their father, "Go out with them and lead them or else we shall kill you."

12 And he was filled with boiling anger on seeing that his sons were forcing him to go before them to lead them against Jacob, his brother.

13 But afterward he remembered all the evil that lay hidden in his heart against Jacob his brother, and he did not remember the oath he had sworn to his father and to his mother that he would plan no evil against Jacob, his brother, all his days.

14 Because Jacob was in mourning for his wife Leah, he did not know they were coming to battle against him until they approached the tower with four thousand soldiers and chosen warriors. The men of Hebron sent to him saying, "Look your brother has come against you to fight. He has with him four thousand men carrying swords, shields, and weapons." They told him this because they loved Jacob more than Esau.

15 So they told him, for Jacob was a more gracious and merciful man than Esau.

16 But Jacob would not believe until they came very near to the tower.

17 He closed the gates of the tower; and he stood on the battlements and spoke to his brother Esau and said, "Noble is the comfort you have come to give me concerning the death of my wife. Is this the oath that you swore to your father and again to your mother before they died? You have broken the oath, and on the moment that you swore to your father you were condemned."

18 Then Esau answered and said to him, "Neither the children of men nor the beasts of the earth have sworn an oath of righteousness and kept it forever. Every day they lay evil plans one against another regarding how they might kill their adversary or foe.

19 You will hate my children and me forever, so there is no observing the tie of brotherhood with you.

20 Hear these words that I declare to you. If the boar can change its skin and make its bristles as soft as wool, or if it can cause horns to sprout out on its head like the horns of a stag or of a sheep, then will I observe the tie of brotherhood with you. Like breasts separate themselves from their mother (and fight), you and I have never been brothers.

21 If the wolves make peace with the lambs and not devour or do them violence, and if their hearts are towards them for good, then there shall be peace in my heart towards you. If the lion becomes the friend of the ox and makes peace with him and if he is bound under one yoke with him and plows with him, then will I make peace with you.

22 When the raven becomes white as the raza (a white bird?), then know that I have loved you and shall make peace with you. You will be rooted out, and your sons shall be rooted out, and there shall be no peace for you."

23 Jacob saw that Esau had decided in his heart to do evil toward him, and that he desired with all his soul to kill him. Jacob saw that Esau had come pouncing like the wild boar which charges the spear that is set to pierce and kill it, and yet does not even slow down. Then he spoke to his own people and to his servants and told them that Esau and his men were going to attack him and all his companions.

[Chapter 38]

1 After that Judah spoke to Jacob, his father, and said to him, "Bend your bow, father, and send forth your arrows and bring down the adversary and kill the enemy. You have the power to do it. We will not kill your brother because he is your kin and he is like you, so we will honor his life."

2 Then Jacob bent his bow and sent forth the arrow and struck Esau, his brother, on the right side of his chest and killed him.

3 And again he sent forth an arrow and struck Adoran the Aramaean, on the left side of his chest, and it drove him backward and killed him. Then the sons of Jacob and their servants went out, dividing themselves into companies on the four sides of the tower.

4 Judah went out in front. Naphtali and Gad along with fifty servants went to the south side of the tower, and they killed all they found before them. Not one individual escaped.

5 Levi, Dan, and Asher went out on the east side of the tower along with fifty men, and they killed the warriors of Moab and Ammon.

6 Reuben, Issachar, and Zebulon went out on the north side of the tower along with fifty men and they killed the warriors of the Philistines.

7 Reuben's son, Simeon, Benjamin, and Enoch went out on the west side of the tower along with fifty men and they killed four hundred men, stout warriors of Edom and of the Horites. Six hundred fled, and four of the sons of Esau fled with them, and left their father lying killed, as he had fallen on the hill that is in Aduram.

8 And the sons of Jacob pursued them to the mountains of Seir. And Jacob buried his brother on the hill that is in Aduram, and he returned to his house.

9 The sons of Jacob crushed the sons of Esau in the mountains of Seir, and made them bow their necks so that they became servants of the sons of Jacob.

10 They sent a message to their father to inquire whether they should make peace with them or kill them.

11 Jacob sent word to his sons that they should make peace. They made peace with them but also placed the yoke of servitude on them, so that they paid tribute to Jacob and to his sons always.

12 And they continued to pay tribute to Jacob until the day that he went down to Egypt.

13 The sons of Edom have not escaped the yoke of servitude imposed by the twelve sons of Jacob until this day.

14 These are the kings that reigned in Edom before there was any king over the children of Israel (until this day) in the land of Edom.

15 And Balaq, the son of Beor, reigned in Edom, and the name of his city was Danaba. Balaq died, and Jobab, the son of Zara of Boser, ruled in his place.

16 Jobab died, and Asam, of the land of Teman, ruled in his place.

17 Asam died, and Adath, the son of Barad, who killed Midian in the field of Moab, ruled in his place, and the name of his city was Avith.

18 Adath died, and Salman, from Amaseqa, ruled in his place.

19 Salman died, and Saul of Ra'aboth by the river, ruled in his place. Saul died, and Ba'elunan, the son of Achbor, ruled in his place.

20 Ba'elunan, the son of Achbor died, and Adath ruled in his place, and the name of his wife was Maitabith, the daughter of Matarat, the daughter of Metabedza'ab. These are the kings who reigned in the land of Edom.

[Chapter 39]

1 Jacob lived in the land that his father journeyed in, which is the land of Canaan.

2 These are the generations of Jacob. Joseph was seventeen years old when they took him down into the land of Egypt, and Potiphar, a eunuch of Pharaoh, the chief cook, bought him.

3 He made Joseph the manager over Potiphar's entire house and the blessing of the Lord came on the house of the Egyptian because of Joseph. And the Lord caused him to prosper in all that he did.

4 The Egyptian turned everything over to the hands of Joseph because he saw that the Lord was with him, and that the Lord caused him to prosper him in all that he did.

5 Joseph's appearance was beautiful, and his master's wife watched Joseph, and she loved him and wanted him to have sex with her.

6 But he did not surrender his soul because he remembered the Lord and the words which Jacob, his father, used to read to him from the writings of Abraham, that no man should commit fornication with a woman who has a husband. For him the punishment of death has been ordained in the heavens before the Most High God, and the sin will be recorded against him in the eternal books, which are always in the presence of the Lord.

7 Joseph remembered these words and refused to have sex with her.

8 And she begged him for a year, but he refused and would not listen.

9 But while he was in the house she embraced him and held him tightly in order to force him to sleep with her. She closed the doors of the house and held on to him, but he left his garment in her hands and broke through the door and ran out from her presence.

10 The woman saw that he would not sleep with her, and she slandered him in the presence of his master, saying "Your Hebrew servant, whom you love, sought to force me to have sex with him. When I shouted for help he fled and left his garment in my hands. I tried to stop him but he broke through the door."

11 When the Egyptian saw Joseph's garment and the broken door, and heard the words of his wife, he threw Joseph into prison and put him in the place where the prisoners of the king were kept.

12 He was there in the prison, and the Lord gave Joseph favor in the sight of the chief of the prison guards and caused him to have compassion for Joseph, because he saw that the Lord was with him, and that the Lord made all that he did to prosper.

13 He turned over all things into his hands, and the chief of the prison guards knew of nothing that was going on in the prison, because Joseph did everything for him, and the Lord perfected it. He remained there two years.

14 In those days Pharaoh, king of Egypt, was very angry at his two eunuchs, the chief butler, and the chief baker. He put them in the prison facility of the house of the chief cook, where Joseph was kept.

15 The chief of the prison guards appointed Joseph to serve them, and he served them.

16 They both dreamed a dream, the chief butler and the chief baker, and they told it to Joseph.

17 As he interpreted to them so it happened to them, and Pharaoh restored the chief butler to his office and he killed the chief baker as Joseph had interpreted to them.

18 But the chief butler forgot Joseph was in the prison, although he had informed him of what would happen to him. He did not remember to inform Pharaoh of how Joseph had told him (about his dream), because he forgot.

[Chapter 40]

1 In those days Pharaoh dreamed two dreams in one night concerning a famine that was to be in all the land, and he awoke from his sleep and called all the magicians and interpreters of dreams that were in Egypt. He told them his two dreams but they were not able to tell him what they meant.

2 Then the chief butler remembered Joseph and told the king of him, and he brought him out from the prison, and the king told his two dreams to him.

3 He said before Pharaoh that his two dreams were one, and he said to him, "Seven years shall come in which there shall be plenty in all the land of Egypt, but after that, seven years of famine. Such a famine as has not been in all the land.

4 Now, let Pharaoh appoint administrators in all the land of Egypt, and let them store up food in every city throughout all the years of plenty, and there will be food for the seven years of famine, and those of the land will not perish through the famine, even though it will be very severe."

5 The Lord gave Joseph favor and mercy in the eyes of Pharaoh. Pharaoh said to his servants, "We shall not find such a wise and prudent man like this man, because the spirit of the Lord is with him."

6 And he appointed Joseph the second in command in his entire kingdom and gave him authority over all Egypt, and placed him on the second chariot of Pharaoh to ride.

7 And he clothed him with fine linen clothes, and he put a gold chain around his neck, and a crier proclaimed before him "El" "El wa Abirer," and he placed a ring on his hand and made him ruler over all his house, and lifted him up before the people, and said to him, "Only on the throne shall I be greater than you."

8 Joseph ruled over all the land of Egypt, and all the governors of Pharaoh, and all his servants, and all those who did the king's business loved him because he walked in uprightness, because he was without pride and arrogance. He did not judge people by their position, and did not accept gifts, but he judged all the people of the land in uprightness.

9 The land of Egypt was at peace before Pharaoh because of Joseph, because the Lord was with him, and the Lord gave him favor and mercy for all his generations before all those who knew him and those who heard of him, and Pharaoh's kingdom was run efficiently, and there was no Satan (adversary) and no evil person in it.

10 And the king called Joseph's name Sephantiphans, and gave Joseph the daughter of Potiphar, the daughter of the priest of Heliopolis, the chief cook to marry.

11 On the day that Joseph stood before Pharaoh he was thirty years old.

12 In that year Isaac died. Things transpired as Joseph had said in the interpretation of Pharaoh's dream and there were seven years of plenty over all the land of Egypt, and the land of Egypt abundantly produced, one measure producing eighteen hundred measures.

13 Joseph gathered food into every city until they were full of grain and they could no longer count or measure it because of its multitude.

[Chapter 41]

1 In the forty-fifth jubilee, in the second week, and in the second year, Judah took his first-born Er, a wife from the daughters of Aram, named Tamar.

2 But he hated her, and did not have sex with her, because her mother was of the daughters of Canaan, and he wished to take him a wife of the lineage of his mother, but Judah, his father, would not permit him to do that.

3 Er, the first-born of Judah, was wicked, and the Lord killed him.

4 And Judah said to Onan, his brother, "Go in to your brother's wife and perform the duty of a husband's brother to her, and raise up offspring to your brother."

5 Onan knew that the offspring would not be his, but his brother's only, and he went into the house of his brother's wife, and spilt his seed (ejaculates) on the ground, and he was wicked in the eyes of the Lord, and He killed him.

6 Judah said to Tamar, his daughter-in-law, "Remain in your father's house as a widow until Shelah, my son has grown up, and I shall give you to him to wife."

7 He grew up, but Bedsu'el, the wife of Judah, did not permit her son Shelah to marry. Bedsu'el, Judah's wife, died in the fifth year of this week.

8 In the sixth year Judah went up to shear his sheep at Timnah.

9 And they told Tamar, "Look, your father-in-law is going up to Timnah to shear his sheep." And she took off her widow's clothes, and put on a veil, and adorned herself, and sat in the gate connecting the road to Timnah.

10 As Judah was going along he saw her, and thought she was a prostitute, and he said to her, "Let me come in to you," and she said to him, "Come in," and he went in.

11 She said to him, "Give me my pay," and he said to her, "I have nothing with me except my ring that is on my finger, my necklace, and my staff which is in my hand."

12 She said to him, "Give them to me until you send me my pay." And he said to her, "I will send to you a kid of the goats", and he gave her his ring, necklace, and staff, and she conceived by him.

13 Judah went to his sheep, and she went to her father's house.

14 Judah sent a kid of the goats by the hand of his shepherd, an Adullamite, but he could not find her, so he asked the people of the place, saying, "Where is the prostitute who was here?"

15 They said to him, "There is no prostitute here with us." And he returned and informed Judah that he had not found her, "I asked the people of the place, and they said to me, "There is no prostitute here." "

16 He said, "If you see her give the kids to her or we become a cause of ridicule." And when she had completed three months, it was revealed that she was with child, and they told Judah, saying, "Look Tamar, your daughter-in-law, is with child by whoredom."

17 And Judah went to the house of her father, and said to her father and her brothers, "Bring her out, and let them burn her, for she has committed uncleanness in Israel."

18 It happened when they brought her out to burn her that she sent to her father-in-law the ring and the necklace, and the staff, saying, "Tell us whose are these, because by him am I with child."

19 Judah acknowledged, and said, "Tamar is more righteous than I am."

20 Do not let them burn her." For that reason she was not given to Shelah, and he did not again approach her and after that she gave birth to two sons, Perez and Zerah, in the seventh year of this second week.

21 At this time the seven years of fruitfulness were completed, of which Joseph spoke to Pharaoh.

22 Judah acknowledged the evil deed that he had done because he had sex with his daughter-in-law, and he hated himself for it.

23 He acknowledged that he had transgressed and gone astray, because he had uncovered the skirt of his son, and he began to lament and to supplicate before the Lord because of his transgression.

24 We told him in a dream that it was forgiven him because he supplicated earnestly, and lamented, and did not commit the act again.

25 And he received forgiveness because he turned from his sin and from his ignorance, because he transgressed greatly before our God. Every one that acts like this, every one who has sex with his mother-in-law, let them burn him alive with fire. Because there is uncleanness and pollution on them, let them burn them alive.

26 Command the children of Israel that there should be no uncleanness among them, because every one who has sex with his daughter-in-law or with his mother-in-law has committed uncleanness. Let them burn the man who has had sex with her with fire, and likewise burn the woman, so that God will turn away wrath and punishment from Israel.

27 We told Judah that his two sons had not had sex with her, and for this reason his offspring was established for a second generation, and would not be rooted out.

28 For in single-mindedness he had gone and sought for punishment, namely, according to the judgment of Abraham, which he had commanded his sons. Judah had sought to burn her alive.

[Chapter 42]

1 In the first year of the third week of the forty-fifth jubilee the famine began to come into the land, and the rain refused to be given to the earth. None whatsoever fell.

2 The earth became barren, but in the land of Egypt there was food, because Joseph had gathered the seed of the land in the seven years of plenty and had preserved it.

3 The Egyptians came to Joseph that he might give them food, and he opened the storehouses where the grain of the first year was stored, and he sold it to the people of the land for gold.

4 Jacob heard there was food in Egypt, and he sent his ten sons that they should procure food for him in Egypt, and they arrived among those that went there, but Benjamin he did not send.

5 Joseph recognized them, but they did not recognize him. He spoke to them and questioned them, and he said to them, "Are you not spies and have you not come to explore ways to enter this land?"

6 And he put them in custody.

7 After that, he set them free again, and detained Simeon alone and sent his nine brothers away.

8 He filled their sacks with corn, and he put their gold back in their sacks, and they did not know it. Joseph then commanded them to bring their younger brother, because they had told him their father was living and also their younger brother.

9 They went up from the land of Egypt and they came to the land of Canaan. There they told their father all that had happened to them, and how the ruler of the country had spoken rudely to them, and had seized Simeon until they should bring Benjamin.

10 Jacob said, "You have taken my children from me! Joseph is gone and Simeon also is gone, and now you will take Benjamin away. I am the victim of your wickedness."

11 He said, "My son will not go down with you because fate may have it that he would fall sick. Their mother gave birth to two sons, and one has died, and this one also you will take from me. If, by fate, he took a fever on the road, you would turn my old age to sorrow and death."

12 He saw that every man's money had been returned to him in his sack, and for this reason he feared to send him.

13 The famine increased and became grievous in the land of Canaan, and in all lands except in the land of Egypt. Egypt had food because many of the children of the Egyptians had stored up their seed for food from the time when they saw Joseph gathering seed together and putting it in storehouses and preserving it for the years of famine.

14 The people of Egypt fed themselves on it during the first year of their famine but when Israel saw that the famine was very serious in the land, and that there was no deliverance, he said to his sons, "Go again, and procure food for us so that we will not die."

15 They said, "We shall not go unless our youngest brother go with us!"

16 Israel saw that if he did not send Benjamin with them, they would all perish because of the famine.

17 Reuben said, "Give him to me, and if I do not bring him back to you, kill my two sons in payment for his soul." Israel said to Reuben, "He shall not go with you."

18 Judah came near and said, "Send him with me, and if I do not bring him back to you, let me bear your blame all the days of my life."

19 He sent him with them in the second year of this week on the first day of the month.

20 They all came to the land of Egypt, and they had presents in their hands of sweet spice, almonds, turpentine nuts, and pure honey.

21 And they went and stood before Joseph, and he saw Benjamin his brother, and he knew him, and said to them, "Is this your youngest brother?" They said to him, "It is he."

22 He said, "The Lord be gracious to you, my son!" And he sent Benjamin into his house and he brought out Simeon to them. Joseph made a feast for them, and they presented to him the gifts that they had brought in their hands.

23 They ate before Joseph and he gave them all a portion of food, but the portion of food given to Benjamin was seven times larger than any of theirs.

24 And they ate and drank and got up and remained with their donkeys.

25 Joseph devised a plan whereby he might learn their thoughts as to whether they desired peace or not. He said to the steward who was over his house, "Fill all their sacks with food. Place their money back in their vessels. Put my cup, the silver cup out of which I drink, in the sack of the youngest and send them away."

[Chapter 43]

1 He did as Joseph had told him, and filled all their sacks with food for them and put their money back into their sacks, and put the cup in Benjamin's sack.

2 Early in the morning they departed, and it happened that when they had gone from that place, Joseph said to the steward of his house, "Pursue them, run and seize them, and say, 'You have repaid my kindness with evil. You have stolen from me the silver cup out of which my lord drinks.'

3 Bring me back their youngest brother. Go! Get him quickly before I go to my seat of judgment (judge you guilt of disobeying an order). "

4 He ran after them and said the words as he was told. They said to him, "God forbid that your servants should do this thing, and steal any utensil or money from the house of your lord, like the things we found in our sacks the first time we, your servants, came back from the land of Canaan.

5 We have not stolen any utensil. How could we? Look here in our sacks and search, and wherever you find the cup in the sack of any man among us, let him be killed, and we and our donkeys will serve your lord."

6 He said to them, "Not so. If I find it, the man whose sack I find it in I shall take as a servant, and the rest of you shall return in peace to your house."

7 He was searching in their vessels, beginning with the eldest and ending with the youngest, when it was found in Benjamin's sack.

8 They ripped their garments in frustration, and placed their belongings back on their donkeys, and returned to the city and came to the house of Joseph. They all bowed themselves with their faces to the ground in front of him.

9 Joseph said to them, "You have done evil." They said, "What shall we say and how shall we defend ourselves? Our lord has discovered the transgression of his servants; and now we and our donkeys are the servants of our lord."

10 Joseph said to them, "I too fear the Lord. As for you, go to your homes and let your brother be my servant, because you have done evil. I delight in this cup as no one else delights in his cup and yet you have stolen it from me."

11 Judah said, "O my lord, I pray you to let your servant speak a word in my lord's ear. Your servant's mother had two sons for our father. One went away and was lost, and has not been found since. This one alone is left of his mother, and your servant our father loves him. He would die if the lad were lost to him.

12 When we go to your servant our father, and the lad is not with us, it will happen that he will die. We will have brought so much sorrow on our father it will bring his death.

13 Now rather let me, your servant, stay here as a bondsman to my lord instead of the boy. Let the lad go with his brothers, because I will stand in for him at the hand of your servant our father. If I do not bring him back, your servant will bear the blame of our father forever."

14 Joseph saw that they were all in accord in doing good to one another. Then, he could not refrain himself, and he told them that he was Joseph.

15 And he conversed with them in the Hebrew tongue and hugged their necks and wept.

16 At first they did not recognize him and then they began to weep. He said to them, "Do not weep for me, but hurry and bring my father to me. See, it is my mouth that speaks and the eyes of my brother Benjamin see me.

17 Pay attention. This is the second year of the famine, and there are still five years to come without harvest or fruit of trees or plowing.

18 You and your households come down quickly, so that you won't die because of the famine. Do not be grieved for your possessions, because the Lord sent me before you to set things in order that many people might live.

19 Tell my father that I am still alive. You see that the Lord has made me as a father to Pharaoh, and ruler over his house and over all the land of Egypt.

20 Tell my father of all my glory, and all the riches and glory that the Lord has given me."

21 By the command of Pharaoh's mouth, he gave them chariots and provisions for the way, and he gave them all multi-colored raiment and silver.

22 He sent corn, raiment, silver, and ten donkeys that carried all of this to his father, and he sent them away.

23 They went up and told their father that Joseph was alive, and was measuring out corn to all the nations of the earth, and that he was ruler over all the land of Egypt.

24 But their father did not believe it, because he was not in his right mind. But when he saw the wagons, which Joseph had sent, the life of his spirit revived, and he said, "It is enough for me if Joseph lives. I will go down and see him before I die."

[Chapter 44]

1 Israel took his journey from Haran's house on the new moon of the third month, and he stopped at the Well of the Oath on the way and he offered a sacrifice to the God of his father Isaac on the seventh of this month.

2 Jacob remembered the dream that he had at Bethel, and he feared to go down into Egypt.

3 He was thinking of sending word to Joseph to come to him because he did not want to go down. He remained there seven days, hoping fate would permit him to see a vision as to whether he should remain or go down.

4 He celebrated the harvest festival of the first-fruits with old grain, because in all the land of Canaan there was not a handful of seed in the ground because the famine was affecting all the beasts, and cattle, and birds, and all men.

5 On the sixteenth the Lord appeared to him, and said to him, "Jacob, Jacob," and he said, "Here I am."

6 And He said to him, "I am the God of your fathers, the God of Abraham and Isaac. Do not be afraid to go down into Egypt, because I will be there to make you a great nation. I will go down with you, and I will bring you up again. You will be buried in this land and Joseph will put his hands on your eyes (to close them in death). Do not be afraid. Go down into Egypt."

7 And his sons got up and placed their father and their possessions on wagons.

8 Israel got up from the Well of the Oath on the sixteenth of this third month, and he went to the land of Egypt.

9 Israel sent Judah before him to his son Joseph to examine the Land of Goshen, because Joseph had told his brothers that they should come and live there so they could be near him.

10 This was the best land in Egypt. It was near to him and suitable for all of the cattle they had.

11 These are the names of the sons of Jacob who went into Egypt with Jacob their father; Reuben, the First-born of Israel and his sons Enoch, and Pallu, and Hezron and Carmi, making five.

12 Simeon and his sons Jemuel, and Jamin, and Ohad, and Jachin, and Zohar, and Shaul, the son of the Zephathite woman, making seven.

13 Levi and his sons Gershon, and Kohath, and Merari, making four.

14 Judah and his sons Shela, and Perez, and Zerah, making four.

15 Issachar and his sons Tola, and Phua, and Jasub, and Shimron, making five.

16 Zebulon and his sons Sered, and Elon, and Jahleel, making four.

17 These are the sons of Jacob and their sons whom Leah bore to Jacob in Mesopotamia, six, and their one sister, Dinah and all the souls of the sons of Leah, and their sons, who went with Jacob their father into Egypt. Twenty-nine souls, and Jacob, making thirty, were the number of people that went into Egypt.

18 And the sons of Zilpah, Leah's handmaid, the wife of Jacob, who bore to Jacob Gad and Ashur and their sons who went with him into Egypt.

19 The sons of Gad are Ziphion, and Haggi, and Shuni, and Ezbon, and Eri, and Areli, and Arodi, which make eight souls in total. The sons of Asher are Imnah, and Ishvah, and Ishvi, and Beriah, and Serah, and their one sister, which makes six in total.

20 All the souls were fourteen, and all those of Leah were forty-four.

21 The sons of Rachel, the wife of Jacob are Joseph and Benjamin.

22 There were born to Joseph in Egypt before his father came into Egypt, those whom Asenath, daughter of Potiphar, priest of Heliopolis gave birth to him, Manasseh, and Ephraim. The wife and children of Joseph totaled three.

23 The sons of Benjamin, Bela and Becher and Ashbel, Gera, and Naaman, and Ehi, and Rosh, and Muppim, and Huppim, and Ard with Benjamin totaled eleven.

24 And all the souls of Rachel were fourteen.

25 And the sons of Bilhah, the handmaid of Rachel, the wife of Jacob, whom she gave birth to Jacob, were Dan and Naphtali. These are the names of their sons who went with them into Egypt.

26 The sons of Dan were Hushim, and Samon, and Asudi. and 'Ijaka, and Salomon, all totaling six.

27 All but one died the year in which they entered into Egypt, and there was left to Dan only Hushim.

28 These are the names of the sons of Naphtali: Jahziel, and Guni and Jezer, and Shallum, and 'Iv.

29 And 'Iv, who was born after the years of famine, died in Egypt.

30 All the souls (offspring) of Rachel were twenty-six.

31 All the souls (offspring) of Jacob, which went into Egypt, were seventy souls.

32 These are his children and his children's children, in all seventy, but five died in Egypt in the time of Joseph's rule and they had no children.

33 In the land of Canaan two sons of Judah died, Er and Onan, and they had no children, and the children of Israel buried those who died, and they were counted among the seventy Gentile nations.

[Chapter 45]

1 On the new moon of the fourth month, in the second year of the third week of the forty-fifth jubilee, Israel went into the country of Egypt, to the land of Goshen.

2 Joseph went to meet his father, Jacob, in the land of Goshen, and he hugged his father's neck and wept.

3 Israel said to Joseph, "Now that I have seen you let me die and may the Lord God of Israel, the God of Abraham, and the God of Isaac, who has not withheld His mercy and His grace from His servant Jacob, be blessed.

4 It is enough for me to have seen your face while I am yet alive. Yes, this is the true vision which I saw at Bethel.

5 Blessed be the Lord my God forever and ever, and blessed be His name."

6 Joseph and his brothers ate bread in the presence of their father and drank wine, and Jacob rejoiced with very great joy because he saw Joseph eating with his brothers and drinking in the presence of him, and he blessed the Creator of all things who had preserved him, and had preserved for him his twelve sons.

7 Joseph had given his father and his brothers as a gift the right of dwelling in the land of Goshen and in Rameses and the entire region around it, which he ruled over in the presence of Pharaoh.

8 Israel and his sons dwelt in the land of Goshen, the best part of the land of Egypt, and Israel was one hundred and thirty years old when he came into Egypt. Joseph nourished his father and his brothers and also their possessions (servants) with bread as much as they needed for the seven years of the famine.

9 The land of Egypt became available for purchase because of the famine, and Joseph acquired all the land of Egypt for Pharaoh in return for food, and he got possession of the people and their cattle and everything for Pharaoh.

10 The years of the famine were completed, and Joseph gave the people in the land seed and food that they might sow the land in the eighth year, because the river had overflowed all the land of Egypt.

11 For in the seven years of the famine it had not overflowed and had irrigated only a few places on the banks of the river, but now it overflowed and the Egyptians sowed the land, and it produced much corn that year.

12 This was the first year of the fourth week of the forty-fifth jubilee. Joseph took one-fifth of the corn of the harvest for the king and left four parts for them for food and for seed, and Joseph made it a law for Egypt until this day.

13 Israel lived in the land of Egypt seventeen years, and all the days which he lived were three jubilees, one hundred and forty-seven years, and he died in the fourth year of the fifth week of the forty-fifth jubilee.

14 Israel blessed his sons before he died and told them everything that they would go through in the land of Egypt. He revealed to them what they would live through in the last days, and he blessed them and gave Joseph two portions of the land.

15 He slept with his fathers, and he was buried in the double cave in the land of Canaan, near Abraham his father, in the grave which he dug for himself in the land of Hebron.

16 And he gave all his books and the books of his fathers to Levi, his son so that he might preserve them and replicate them for his children until this day.

[Chapter 46]

1 It happened that after the death of Jacob the children of Israel continued to multiply in the land of Egypt, and they became a great nation, and they were in one accord of heart, so that brother loved brother and every man helped his brother. They increased abundantly and multiplied greatly, ten weeks of years, all the days of the life of Joseph.

2 There was neither Satan nor any evil in all the days of the life of Joseph after his father, Jacob (had died), because all the Egyptians respected the children of Israel all the days of the life of Joseph.

3 Joseph died, being a hundred and ten years old. He lived seventeen years in the land of Canaan, and ten years he was a servant, and three years in prison, and eighty years he was under the king, ruling all the land of Egypt.

4 He died and so did all his brothers and all of that generation. But, he commanded the children of Israel before he died that they should carry his bones with them when they went out from the land of Egypt.

5 And he made them swear regarding his bones, because he knew that the Egyptians would not bring his bones out of Egypt or bury him in the land of Canaan, because while dwelling in the land of Assyria, king Makamaron, the king of Canaan, fought against Egypt in the valley and killed the king of Egypt there, and pursued the Egyptians to the gates of "Ermon.

6 But he was not able to enter, because another king, a new king, had become king of Egypt, and he was stronger than he (Makamaron), and he returned to the land of Canaan, and the gates of Egypt were closed so that none came or went from Egypt.

7 Joseph died in the forty-sixth jubilee, in the sixth week, in the second year, and they buried him in the land of Egypt, and all his brothers died after him.

8 The king of Egypt went to war against the king of Canaan in the forty-seventh jubilee, in the second week in the second year, and the children of Israel brought out all the bones of the children of Jacob except the bones of Joseph, and they buried them in the field in the double cave in the mountain.

9 Then, most of them returned to Egypt, but a few of them remained in the mountains of Hebron, and Amram your father remained with them.

10 The king of Canaan was victorious over the king of Egypt, and he closed the gates of Egypt.

11 He devised an evil plan against the children of Israel to afflict them. He said to the people of Egypt, "Look, the people of the children of Israel have increased and multiplied more than we.

12 Let us use wisdom and deal with them before they become too many. Let us make them our slaves before we go to war and they rise up against us on the side of our enemies. Before they leave and fight against us let us do this because their hearts and faces (allegiances) are towards the land of Canaan."

13 He set over them taskmasters to enforce slavery, and they built strong cities for Pharaoh, Pithom, and Raamses and they built all the walls and all the fortifications, which had fallen in the cities of Egypt.

14 They enslaved them with harshness, and the more they were evil toward them, the more they increased and multiplied.

15 And the people of Egypt despised the children of Israel.

[Chapter 47]

1 In the seventh week, in the seventh year, in the forty-seventh jubilee, your father went out from the land of Canaan, and you (Moses) were born in the fourth week, in the sixth year of it, in the forty-eighth jubilee; this was the time of tribulation for the children of Israel.

2 Pharaoh, the king of Egypt, issued a command ordering them to throw all their newborn male children into the river.

3 And they threw them into the river for seven months until the day that you were born. It is said that your mother hid you for three months.

4 She made an ark for you, and covered it with pitch and tar, and placed it in the reeds on the bank of the river. She placed you in it seven days. Your mother came by night and nursed you. By day Miriam, your sister, guarded you from the birds.

5 In those days Tharmuth, the daughter of Pharaoh, came to bathe in the river, and she heard you crying. She told her maids to bring you out, and they brought you to her.

6 She took you out of the ark, and she had compassion on you.

7 Your sister said to her, "Shall I go and call to you one of the Hebrew women to nurse this baby for you?" And she said to her, "Go."

8 Your sister went and called your mother, Jochebed, and Pharaoh's daughter gave her wages (employed her), and she nursed you.

9 Afterwards, when you grew up, they brought you to the daughter of Pharaoh, and you became her son. Amram, your father, taught you writing. After you had completed three weeks (twenty-seven years) they brought you into the royal court.

10 You were three weeks of years at court until the time when you went out from the royal court and saw an Egyptian beating your friend who was of the children of Israel, and you killed him and hid him in the sand.

11 On the second day you came across two children of Israel quarreling together, and you asked the one who was doing wrong, "Why did you hit your brother?"

12 He was angry and indignant, and said, "Who made you a prince and a judge over us?

13 Do you want to kill me like you killed the Egyptian yesterday?" You were afraid and you fled on because of these words.

[Chapter 48]

1 In the sixth year of the third week of the forty-ninth jubilee you fled and went to live in the land of Midian for five weeks and one year. You returned to Egypt in the second week in the second year in the fiftieth jubilee.

2 You know what He said to you on Mount Sinai, and what prince Mastema desired to do with you when you returned to Egypt.

3 Did he (Mastema) not seek to kill you with all his power and to deliver the Egyptians from your hand when he saw that you were sent to execute judgment and to take revenge on the Egyptians?

4 But I delivered you out of his hand, and you performed the signs and wonders which you were sent to perform in Egypt against Pharaoh, and against all of his household, and against his servants and his people.

5 The Lord exacted a great vengeance on them for Israel's sake, and struck them through the plagues of blood, frogs, lice, dog-flies, malignant boils, breaking out in pustules, the death of their cattle, and the plague of hailstones. He destroyed everything that grew from them by plagues of locusts, which devoured the remainder left by the hail, and by darkness, and by the death of the first-born of men and animals. The Lord took vengeance on all of their idols and burned them with fire.

6 Everything was sent through your hand, that you should declare these things before they were done. You spoke with the king of Egypt in the presence of all his servants and in the presence of his people and everything took place according to your words. Ten great and terrible judgments came on the land of Egypt so that you might execute vengeance on Egypt for Israel.

7 And the Lord did everything for Israel's sake according to His covenant, which he had ordained with Abraham. He took vengeance on them because they had brought them by force into bondage.

8 Prince Mastema stood against you, and sought to deliver you into the hands of Pharaoh. He helped the Egyptian sorcerers when they stood up and committed the evil acts they did in your presence. Indeed, we permitted them to work, but the remedies we did not allow to be worked by their hands.

9 The Lord struck them with malignant ulcers (hemorrhoids?), and they were not able to stand. They could not perform a single sign because we destroyed them.

10 Even after all of these signs and wonders, prince Mastema was not put to shame because he took courage and cried to the Egyptians to pursue you with all the power the Egyptians had, with their chariots, and with their horses, and with all the hosts of the peoples of Egypt.

11 But I stood between the Egyptians and Israel, and we delivered Israel out of his hand, and out of the hand of his people. The Lord brought them through the middle of the sea as if it were dry land.

12 The Lord our God threw all the people whom he (Mastema) brought to pursue Israel into the middle of the sea, into the depths of the bottomless pit, beneath the children of Israel, even as the people of Egypt had thrown their (Israel's) children into the river. He took vengeance on one million of them. In addition to one thousand strong and energetic men were destroyed because of the death of the suckling children of your people, which they had thrown into the river.

13 On the fourteenth day and on the fifteenth and on the sixteenth and on the seventeenth and on the eighteenth days, prince Mastema was bound and imprisoned and placed behind the children of Israel so that he might not accuse them.

14 On the nineteenth day we let them (Mastema and his demons) loose so that they might help the Egyptians pursue the children of Israel.

15 He hardened their hearts and made them stubborn, and the plan was devised by the Lord our God that He might strike the Egyptians and throw them into the sea.

16 On the fourteenth day we bound him that he might not accuse the children of Israel on the day when they asked the Egyptians for vessels and garments, vessels of silver, and vessels of gold, and vessels of bronze, in order to exact from the Egyptians a price in return for the bondage they had been forced to serve.

17 We did not lead the children of Israel from Egypt empty handed.

[Chapter 49]

1 Remember the commandment which the Lord commanded you concerning the Passover. You should celebrate it in its season on the fourteenth day of the first month. You should kill the sacrifice before evening. They should eat it by night on the evening of the fifteenth from the time of the setting of the sun.

2 Because on this night, at the beginning of the festival and the beginning of the joy, you were eating the Passover (lamb) in Egypt, when all the powers of Mastema had been let loose to kill all the first-born in the land of Egypt, from the first-born of Pharaoh to the first-born of the captive maid-servant in the mill, and even the first-born of the cattle.

3 This is the sign that the Lord gave them, in every house on the door post on which they saw the blood of a lamb of the first year they should not enter to kill, but should pass by it, that all those should be exempt that were in the house because the sign of the blood was on its door posts.

4 And the powers of the Lord did everything as the Lord commanded them, and they passed by all the children of Israel, and the plague did not come on them to destroy them, cattle, man, or dog.

5 The plague was oppressive in Egypt, and there was no house in Egypt where there was not one dead, and weeping, and lamentation.

6 All Israel was eating the flesh of the paschal lamb, and drinking the wine, and was praising, and blessing, and giving thanks to the Lord God of their fathers, and they were ready to get out from under the yoke of Egypt and the evil bondage.

7 Remember this day all the days of your life. Observe it from year to year all the days of your life, once a year, on its day, according to all the law of it. Do not forsake it from day to day, or from month to month.

8 It is an eternal law, and engraved on the heavenly tablets regarding all the children of Israel that they should observe it on its day once a year, every year, throughout all their generations. There is no limit of days, for this is a law forever.

9 The man who is free from uncleanness, and does not come to observe Passover on the occasion of its day and does not bring an acceptable offering before the Lord to eat and to drink before the Lord on the day of its festival will be guilty. If he is clean and close at hand (near the temple) and does not come, he shall be cut off because he did not offer the offering of the Lord in its appointed season. He shall take the guilt on himself.

10 Let the children of Israel come and observe the passover on the day of its fixed time, on the fourteenth day of the first month, between the evenings, from the third part of the day to the third part of the night, for two portions of the day are given to the light, and a third part to the evening.

11 The Lord commanded you to observe it between the evenings.

12 And it is not permissible to kill the sacrifice during any period of light, but only during the period bordering on the evening, and let them eat it at the time of the evening, until the third part of the night. Whatever is left over of all its flesh from the third part of the night and onwards is to be burned with fire.

13 They shall not cook it with water (boil or seethe), nor shall they eat it raw, but roast it on the fire. They shall eat it with care, making sure its head with the inwards and its feet are roasted with fire, and they shall not break any bone of it, for of the children of Israel no bone shall be crushed.

14 For this reason the Lord commanded the children of Israel to observe the passover on the day of its fixed time, and they shall not break a bone of it, because it is a festival day He commanded. There was no passing over from any other day or any other month, but on the exact day let the festival be observed.

15 Command the children of Israel to observe the passover throughout their days, every year, once a year on the day of its fixed time, and it shall be a memorial well pleasing in the presence of the Lord, and no plague shall come on them to kill or to strike in that year in which they celebrate the passover in its season in every respect according to His command.

16 And they shall not eat it outside the sanctuary of the Lord, but before the sanctuary of the Lord, and all the people of the congregation of Israel shall celebrate it in its appointed season.

17 Every man twenty years of age and upward, who has come on the day of the Passover shall eat it in the sanctuary of your God before the Lord. This is how it is written and ordained. They should eat it in the sanctuary of the Lord.

18 When the children of Israel come into the land of Canaan that they are to possess, set up the tabernacle (tent) of the Lord within the land occupied by one of their tribes until the sanctuary of the Lord has been built in the land. There, let them come and celebrate the passover at tabernacle of the Lord, and let them kill it before the Lord from year to year.

696

19 When the house of the Lord has been built in the land of their inheritance, they shall go there and kill the Passover (lamb) in the evening, at sunset, at the third part of the day.

20 They shall offer its blood on the threshold of the altar, and shall place its fat on the fire, which is on the altar, and they shall eat its flesh roasted with fire in the yard of the house, which has been sanctified in the name of the Lord.

21 They may not celebrate the passover in their cities, nor in any place except at the tabernacle of the Lord, or before His house where His name has dwelt. They shall not stray from the Lord.

22 Moses, command the children of Israel to observe the ordinances of the passover, as it was commanded to you. Declare to them every year the purpose and time of the festival of unleavened bread. They should eat unleavened bread seven days. They should observe its festival and bring an offering every day during those seven days of joy before the Lord on the altar of your God.

23 Celebrate this festival with haste as when you went out from Egypt and you entered into the wilderness of Shur, because on the shore of the sea you completed it (the exodus).

[Chapter 50]

1 I made this law known to you the days of the Sabbaths in the desert of Sinai, between Elim and Sinai.

2 I told you of the Sabbaths of the land on Mount Sinai, and I told you of the jubilee years in the sabbaths of years, but have I not told you the year of it until you enter the land which you are to possess.

3 Keep the sabbaths of the land while they live on it, and they shall know the jubilee year.

4 I have ordained for you the year of weeks and the years and the jubilees. There are forty-nine jubilees from the days of Adam until this day, and one week and two years, and there are forty years yet to come for learning the commandments of the Lord, until they pass over into the land of Canaan, crossing the Jordan to the west.

5 The jubilees shall pass by until Israel is cleansed from all guilt of fornication, and uncleanness, and pollution, and sin, and error, and it dwells with confidence in all the land. There shall be no more Satan or any evil one, and the land shall be clean from that time forever.

6 I have written down the commandment for them regarding the Sabbaths and all the judgments of its laws for you.

7 Six days will you labor, but the seventh day is the Sabbath of the Lord your God.

8 You shall do no manner of work in it, you and your sons, and your menservants and your maidservants, and all your cattle and travelers also who lodge with you. The man that does any work on it shall die. Whoever desecrates that day, whoever has sex with his wife, whoever says he will do something on it, or he that will set out on a journey on it in regard to any buying or selling, or whoever draws water on it which he had not prepared for himself on the sixth day, and whoever takes up any burden to carry it out of his tent or out of his house shall die.

9 You shall do no work whatsoever on the Sabbath day except what you have prepared for yourselves on the sixth day, so as to eat, and drink, and rest. Keep Sabbath free from all work on that day. It is to bless the Lord your God, who has given you a day of festival and a holy day, and a day of the holy kingdom. This is a day for Israel among all their days forever.

10 Great is the honor which the Lord has given to Israel that they should eat, drink, and be satisfied on this festival day. Rest on it from all labor, which belongs to the labor of the children of men, except burning frankincense and bringing offerings and sacrifices before the Lord for days and for Sabbaths.

11 Only this work shall be done on the Sabbath days in the sanctuary of the Lord your God so that they may atone for Israel with sacrifice continually from day to day for a memorial pleasing before the Lord, so that He may always receive them from day to day according to what you have been commanded.

12 Every man who does any work on it, or takes a trip, or tills his farm, whether in his house or any other place, and whoever lights a fire, or rides a beast, or travels by ship on the sea shall die. And whoever strikes or kills anything, or slaughters a beast or a bird, or whoever catches an animal or a bird or a fish, or whoever fasts or makes war on the Sabbaths, the man who does any of these things on the Sabbath shall die. This is done so that the children of Israel will observe the Sabbaths according to the commandments regarding the Sabbaths of the land. It is written in the tablets, which He gave into my hands that I should write out for you the laws of the seasons, and the seasons according to the division of their days.

This completes the account of the division of the days.

CLEMENT OF ROME

First Epistle

THE FIRST EPISTLE OF CLEMENT TO THE CORINTHIANS

1Clem prologue:1
The Church of God which sojourns in Rome to the Church of God which sojourns in Corinth, to them which are called and sanctified by the will of God through our Lord Jesus Christ. Grace to you and peace from Almighty God through Jesus Christ be multiplied.

1Clem 1:1
By reason of the sudden and repeated calamities and reverses which are befalling us, brethren, we consider that we have been somewhat tardy in giving heed to the matters of dispute that have arisen among you, dearly beloved, and to the detestable and unholy sedition, so alien and strange to the elect of God, which a few headstrong and self-willed persons have kindled to such a pitch of madness that your name, once revered and renowned and lovely in the sight of all men, has been greatly reviled.

1Clem 1:2
For who that had sojourned among you did not approve your most virtuous and steadfast faith? Who did not admire your sober and forbearing piety in Christ? Who did not publish abroad your magnificent disposition of hospitality? Who did not congratulate you on your perfect and sound knowledge?

1Clem 1:3
For you did all things without respect of persons, and you walked after the ordinances of God, submitting yourselves to your rulers and rendering to the older men among you the honor which is their due. On the young too you enjoined modest and seemly thoughts: and the women you charged to perform all their duties in a blameless and seemly and pure conscience, cherishing their own husbands, as is meet; and you taught them to keep in the rule of obedience, and to manage the affairs of their household in seemliness, with all discretion.

1Clem 2:1
And you were all lowly in mind and free from arrogance, yielding rather than claiming submission, more glad to give than to receive, and content with the provisions which God supplies. And giving heed unto His words, you laid them up diligently in your hearts, and His sufferings were before your eyes.

1Clem 2:2
Thus a profound and rich peace was given to all, and an insatiable desire of doing good. An abundant outpouring also of the Holy Spirit fell upon all;

1Clem 2:3
and, being full of holy counsel, in excellent zeal and with a pious confidence you stretched out your hands to Almighty God, supplicating Him to be propitious, if unwillingly you had committed any sin.

1Clem 2:4
you had conflict day and night for all the brotherhood, that the number of His elect might be saved with fearfulness and intentness of mind.

1Clem 2:5
You were sincere and simple and free from malice one towards another.

1Clem 2:6
Every sedition and every schism was abominable to you. you mourned over the transgressions of your neighbors: you judged their shortcomings to be your own.

1Clem 2:7
you repented not of any well-doing, but were ready unto every good work.

1Clem 2:8
Being adorned with a most virtuous and honorable life, you performed all your duties in the fear of Him. The commandments and the ordinances of the Lord were written on the tablets of your hearts.

1Clem 3:1
All glory and enlargement was given unto you, and that was fulfilled which is written My beloved ate and drank and was enlarged and waxed fat and kicked.

1Clem 3:2
Hence come jealousy and envy, strife and sedition, persecution and tumult, war and captivity.

1Clem 3:3
So men were stirred up, the mean against the honorable, the ill reputed against the highly reputed, the foolish against the wise, the young against the elder.

1Clem 3:4
For this cause righteousness and peace stand aloof, while each man has forsaken the fear of the Lord and become purblind in the faith of Him, neither walketh in the ordinances of His commandments nor liveth according to that which becometh Christ, but each goeth after the lusts of his evil heart, seeing that they have conceived an unrighteous and ungodly jealousy, through which also death entered into the world.

1Clem 4:1
For so it is written, And it came to pass after certain days that Cain brought of the fruits of the earth a sacrifice unto God, and Abel he also brought of the firstlings of the sheep and of their fatness.

1Clem 4:2
And God looked upon Abel and upon his gifts, but unto Cain and unto his sacrifices He gave no heed.

1Clem 4:3
And Cain was very sorrowful, and his countenance fell.

1Clem 4:4
And God said unto Cain, Wherefore art you very sorrowful and

wherefore did thy countenance fall? If you hast offered aright and hast not divided aright, didst you not sin? Hold thy peace.

1Clem 4:5
Unto you shall he turn, and you shall rule over him. {This last phrase has also been translated: Be at peace: your offering returns to thyself, and you shall again possess it.}

1Clem 4:6
And Cain said unto Abel his brother, Let us go over unto the plain. And it came to pass, while they Were in the plain, that Cain rose up against Abel his brother and slew him.

1Clem 4:7
you see, brethren, jealousy and envy wrought a brother's murder.

1Clem 4:8
By reason of jealousy our father Jacob ran away from the face of Esau his brother.

1Clem 4:And jealousy caused Joseph to be persecuted even unto death, and to come even unto bondage.

1Clem 4:10
Jealousy compelled Moses to flee from the face of Pharaoh king of Egypt while it was said to him by his own countryman, Who made you a judge or a decider over us, Would you slay me, even as yesterday you murdered the Egyptian?
1Clem 4:11
By reason of jealousy Aaron and Miriam were lodged outside the camp.

1Clem 4:12
Jealousy brought Dathan and Abiram down alive to hades, because they made sedition against Moses the servant of God.

1Clem 4:13
By reason of jealousy David was envied not only by the Philistines, but was persecuted also by Saul [king of Israel].

1Clem 5:1
But, to pass from the examples of ancient days, let us come to those champions who lived nearest to our time. Let us set before us the noble examples which belong to our generation.

1Clem 5:2
By reason of jealousy and envy the greatest and most righteous pillars of the Church were persecuted, and contended even unto death.

1Clem 5:3
Let us set before our eyes the good Apostles.

1Clem 5:4
There was Peter who by reason of unrighteous jealousy endured not one not one but many labors, and thus having borne his testimony went to his appointed place of glory.

1Clem 5:5
By reason of jealousy and strife Paul by his example pointed out the prize of patient endurance. After that he had been seven times in bonds, had been driven into exile, had been stoned, had preached in the East and in the West, he won the noble renown which was the

reward of his faith,

1Clem 5:6
having taught righteousness unto the whole world and having reached the farthest bounds of the West; and when he had borne his testimony before the rulers, so he departed from the world and went unto the holy place, having been found a notable pattern of patient endurance.

1Clem 6:1
Unto these men of holy lives was gathered a vast multitude of the elect, who through many indignities and tortures, being the victims of jealousy, set a brave example among ourselves.

1Clem 6:2
By reason of jealousy women being persecuted, after that they had suffered cruel and unholy insults as Danaids and Dircae, safely reached the goal in the race of faith, and received a noble reward, feeble though they were in body.

1Clem 6:3
Jealousy has estranged wives from their husbands and changed the saying of our father Adam, This now is bone of my bones and flesh of my flesh.

1Clem 6:4
Jealousy and strife have overthrown great cities and uprooted great nations.

1Clem 7:1
These things, dearly beloved, we write, not only as admonishing you, but also as putting ourselves in remembrance. For we are in the same lists, and the same contest awaits us.

1Clem 7:2
Wherefore let us forsake idle and vain thoughts; and let us conform to the glorious and venerable rule which has been handed down to us;

1Clem 7:3
and let us see what is good and what is pleasant and what is acceptable in the sight of Him that made us.

1Clem 7:4
Let us fix our eyes on the blood of Christ and understand how precious it is unto His Father, because being shed for our salvation it won for the whole world the grace of repentance.

1Clem 7:5
Let us review all the generations in turn, and learn how from generation to generation the Master has given a place for repentance unto them that desire to turn to Him.

1Clem 7:6
Noah preached repentance, and they that obeyed were saved.

1Clem 7:7
Jonah preached destruction unto the men of Nineveh; but they, repenting of their sins, obtained pardon of God by their supplications and received salvation, albeit they were aliens from God.

1Clem 8:1

The ministers of the grace of God through the Holy Spirit spoke concerning repentance.

1Clem 8:2

Yea and the Master of the universe Himself spoke concerning repentance with an oath:

1Clem 8:3

for, as I live says the Lord, I desire not the death of the sinner, so much as his repentance,

1Clem 8:4

and He added also a merciful judgment: Repent you, O house of Israel, of your iniquity; say unto the sons of My people, Though your sins reach from the earth even unto the heaven, and though they be redder than scarlet and blacker than sackcloth, and you turn unto Me with your whole heart and say Father, I will give ear unto you as unto a holy people.

1Clem 8:5

And in another place He said on this wise, Wash, be you clean. Put away your iniquities from your souls out of My sight. Cease from your iniquities; learn to do good; seek out judgment; defend him that is wronged: give judgment for the orphan, and execute righteousness for the widow; and come and let us reason together, said He; and though your sins be as crimson, I will make them white as snow; and though they be as scarlet, I will make them white as wool. And if you be willing and will hearken unto Me, you shall eat the good things of the earth; but if you be not willing, neither hearken unto Me, a sword shall devour you; for the mouth of the Lord has spoken these things.

1Clem 8:6

Seeing then that He desires all His beloved to be partakers of repentance, He confirmed it by an act of His almighty will.

1Clem 9:1

Wherefore let us be obedient unto His excellent and glorious will; and presenting ourselves as suppliants of His mercy and goodness, let us fall down before Him and betake ourselves unto His compassions, forsaking the vain toil and the strife and the jealousy which leads unto death.

1Clem 9:2

Let us fix our eyes on them that ministered perfectly unto His excellent glory.

1Clem 9:3

Let us set before us Enoch, who being found righteous in obedience was translated, and his death was not found.

1Clem 9:4

Noah, being found faithful, by his ministration preached regeneration unto the world, and through him the Master saved the living creatures that entered into the ark in concord.

1Clem 10:1

Abraham, who was called the 'friend,' was found faithful in that he rendered obedience unto the words of God.

1Clem 10:2

He through obedience went forth from his land and from his kindred and from his father's house, that leaving a scanty land and a feeble kindred and a mean house he might inherit the promises of God.

1Clem 10:3

For He said unto him Go forth from thy land and from thy kindred and from thy father's house unto the land which I shall show you, and I will make you into a great nation, and I will bless you and will magnify thy name, and you shall be blessed. And I will bless them that bless you, and I will curse them that curse you; and in you shall all the tribes of the earth be blessed.

1Clem 10:4

And again, when he was parted from Lot, God said unto him Look up with your eyes, and behold from the place where you now art, unto the north and the south and the sunrise and the sea; for all the land which you see, I will give it unto you and to thy seed for ever;

1Clem 10:5

and I will make thy seed as the dust of the earth. If any man can count the dust of the earth, then shall thy seed also be counted.

1Clem 10:6

And again He said; God led Abraham forth and said unto him, Look up unto the heaven and count the stars, and see whether you canst number them. So shall thy seed be. And Abraham believed God, and it was reckoned unto him for righteousness.

1Clem 10:7

For his faith and hospitality a son was given unto him in old age, and by obedience he offered him a sacrifice unto God on one of the mountains which He showed him.

1Clem 11:1

For his hospitality and godliness Lot was saved from Sodom, when all the country round about was judged by fire and brimstone; the Master having thus fore shown that He forsakes not them which set their hope on Him, but appoints unto punishment and torment them which swerve aside.

1Clem 11:2

For when his wife had gone forth with him, being otherwise minded and not in accord, she was appointed for a sign hereunto, so that she became a pillar of salt unto this day, that it might be known unto all men that they which are double-minded and they which doubt concerning the power of God are set for a judgment and for a token unto all the generations.

1Clem 12:1

For her faith and hospitality Rahab the harlot was saved.

1Clem 12:2

For when the spies were sent forth unto Jericho by Joshua the son of Nun, the king of the land perceived that they were come to spy out his country, and sent forth men to seize them, that being seized they might be put to death.

1Clem 12:3

So the hospitable Rahab received them and hid them in the upper chamber under the flax stalks.

1Clem 12:4

And when the messengers of the king came near and said, The spies of our land entered in unto you: bring them forth, for the king so ordereth: then she answered, The men truly, whom you seek, entered in unto me, but they departed forthwith and are sojourning on the way; and she pointed out to them the opposite road.

1Clem 12:5

And she said unto the men, Of a surety I perceive that the Lord your God delivered this city unto you; for the fear and the dread of you is fallen upon the inhabitants thereof. When therefore it shall come to pass that you take it, save me and the house of my father.

1Clem 12:6

And they said unto her, It shall be even so as you hast spoken unto us. Whensoever therefore you perceives that we are coming, you shall gather all thy folk beneath thy roof and they shall be saved; for as many as shall be found without the house shall perish.

1Clem 12:7

And moreover they gave her a sign, that she should hang out from her house a scarlet thread, thereby showing beforehand that through the blood of the Lord there shall be redemption unto all them that believe and hope on God.

1Clem 12:8

you see, dearly beloved, not only faith, but prophecy, is found in the woman.

1Clem 13:1

Let us therefore be lowly minded, brethren, laying aside all arrogance and conceit and folly and anger, and let us do that which is written. For the Holy Ghost said, Let not the wise man boast in his wisdom, nor the strong in his strength, neither the rich in his riches; but he that boasts let him boast in the Lord, that he may seek Him out, and do judgment and righteousness most of all remembering the words of the Lord Jesus which He spoke, teaching forbearance and long-suffering:

1Clem 13:2

for thus He spoke Have mercy, that you may receive mercy: forgive, that it may be forgiven to you. As you do, so shall it be done to you. As you give, so shall it be given unto you. As you judge, so shall you be judged. As you show kindness, so shall kindness be showed unto you. With what measure you mete, it shall be measured withal to you.

1Clem 13:3

With this commandment and these precepts let us confirm ourselves, that we may walk in obedience to His hallowed words, with lowliness of mind.

1Clem 13:4

For the holy word said, Upon whom shall I look, save upon him that is gentle and quiet and feared My oracles?

1Clem 14:1

Therefore it is right and proper, brethren, that we should be obedient unto God, rather than follow those who in arrogance and unruliness have set themselves up as leaders in abominable jealousy.

1Clem 14:2

For we shall bring upon us no common harm, but rather great peril, if we surrender ourselves recklessly to the purposes of men who launch out into strife and seditions, so as to estrange us from that which is right.

1Clem 14:3

Let us be good one towards another according to the compassion and sweetness of Him that made us. For it is written:

1Clem 14:4

The good shall be dwellers in the land, and the innocent shall be left on it but they that transgress shall be destroyed utterly from it.

1Clem 14:5

And again He said I saw the ungodly lifted up on high and exalted as the cedars of Lebanon. And I passed by, and behold he was not; and sought out his place, and I found it not. Keep innocence and behold uprightness; for there is a remnant for the peaceful man.

1Clem 15:1

Therefore let us cleave unto them that practice peace with godliness, and not unto them that desire peace with dissimulation.

1Clem 15:2

For He said in a certain place This people honored Me with their lips, but their heart is far from Me,

1Clem 15:3

and again, they blessed with their mouth, but they cursed with their heart.

1Clem 15:4

And again He said, They loved Him with their mouth, and with their tongue they lied unto Him; and their heart was not upright with Him, neither were they steadfast in His covenant.

1Clem 15:5

For this cause let the deceitful lips be made dumb which speak iniquity against the righteous. And again May the Lord utterly destroy all the deceitful lips, the tongue that speaks proud things, even them that say, Let us magnify our tongue; our lips are our own; who is lord over us?

1Clem 15:6

For the misery of the needy and for the groaning of the poor I will now arise, said the Lord. I will set him in safety; I will deal boldly by him.

1Clem 16:1

For Christ is with them that are lowly of mind, not with them that exalt themselves over the flock.

1Clem 16:2
The scepter of the majesty of God, even our Lord Jesus Christ, came not in the pomp of arrogance or of pride, though He might have done so, but in lowliness of mind, according as the Holy Spirit spoke concerning Him.

1Clem 16:3
For He said Lord, who believed our report? and to whom was the arm of the Lord revealed? We announced Him in His presence. As a child was He, as a root in a thirsty ground. There is no form in Him, neither glory. And we beheld Him, and He had no form nor comeliness, but His form was mean, lacking more than the form of men. He was a man of stripes and of toil, and knowing how to bear infirmity: for His face is turned away. He was dishonored and held of no account.

1Clem 16:4
He bore our sins and suffers pain for our sakes: and we accounted Him to be in toil and in stripes and in affliction.

1Clem 16:5
And He was wounded for our sins and has been afflicted for our iniquities. The chastisement of our peace is upon Him. With His bruises we were healed.

1Clem 16:6
We all went astray like sheep, each man went astray in his own path:

1Clem 16:7
and the Lord delivered Him over for our sins. And He opened not His mouth, because He is afflicted. As a sheep He was led to slaughter; and as a lamb before his shearer is dumb, so opened He not His mouth. In His humiliation His judgment was taken away.

1Clem 16:8
His generation who shall declare? For His life is taken away from the earth.

1Clem 16:9
For the iniquities of my people He is come to death.

1Clem 16:10
And I will give the wicked for His burial, and the rich for His death; for He wrought no iniquity, neither was guile found in His mouth. And the Lord desired to cleanse Him from His stripes.

1Clem 16:11
If you offer for sin, your soul shall see along lived seed.

1Clem 16:12
And the Lord desired to take away from the toil of His soul, to show Him light and to mould Him with understanding, to justify a Just One that is a good servant unto many. And He shall bear their sins.

1Clem 16:13
Therefore He shall inherit many, and shall divide the spoils of the strong; because His soul was delivered unto death, and He was reckoned unto the transgressors;

1Clem 16:14
and He bare the sins of many, and for their sins was He delivered up.

1Clem 16:15
And again He Himself said; But I am a worm and no man, a reproach of men and an outcast of the people.

1Clem 16:16
All they that beheld me mocked at me; they spoke with their lips; they wagged their heads, saying, He hoped on the Lord; let Him deliver him, or let Him save him, for He desired him.

1Clem 16:17
you see, dearly beloved, what is the pattern that has been given unto us; for, if the Lord was thus lowly of mind, what should we do, who through Him have been brought under the yoke of His grace?

1Clem 17:1
Let us be imitators also of them which went about in goatskins and sheepskins, preaching the coming of Christ. We mean Elijah and Elisha and likewise Ezekiel, the prophets, and besides them those men also that obtained a good report.

1Clem 17:2
Abraham obtained an exceeding good report and was called the friend of God; and looking steadfastly on the glory of God, he said in lowliness of mind, But I am dust and ashes.

1Clem 17:3
Moreover concerning Job also it is thus written; And Job was righteous and unblamable, one that was true and honored God and abstained from all evil.

1Clem 17:4
Yet he himself accused himself saying, No man from filth; no, not though his life be but for a day.

1Clem 17:5
Moses was called faithful in all His house, and through his ministration God judged Egypt with the plagues and the torments which befell them. Howbeit he also, though greatly glorified, yet spoke no proud words, but said, when an oracle was given to him at the bush, Who am I, that Thou send me?

1Clem 17:6
Nay, I am feeble of speech and slow of tongue. And again he said, But I am smoke from the pot.

1Clem 18:1
But what must we say of David that obtained a good report? of whom God said, I have found a man after My heart, David the son of Jesse: with eternal mercy have I anointed him.

1Clem 18:2
Yet he too said unto God Have mercy upon me, O God, according to Your great mercy; and according to the multitude of Your compassions, blot out mine iniquity.

1Clem 18:3
Wash me yet more from mine iniquity, and cleanse me from my sin.

For I acknowledge mine iniquity, and my sin is ever before me. Against Thee only did I sin, and I wrought evil in Your sight; that You may be justified in Your words, and may conquer in Your pleading.

1Clem 18:4
For behold, in iniquities was I conceived, and in sins did my mother bear me. For behold You hast loved truth: the dark and hidden things of Your wisdom hast You showed unto me.

1Clem 18:5
You shall sprinkle me with hyssop, and I shall be made clean. You shall wash me, and I shall become whiter than snow.

1Clem 18:6
You shall make me to hear of joy and gladness. The bones which have been humbled shall rejoice.

1Clem 18:7
Turn away Your face from my sins, and blot out all mine iniquities.

1Clem 18:8
Make a clean heart within me, O God, and renew a right spirit in mine inmost parts. Cast me not away from Your presence, and take not Your Holy Spirit from me.

1Clem 18:9
Restore unto me the joy of Your salvation, and strengthen me with a princely spirit.

1Clem 18:10
I will teach sinners Your ways, and godless men shall be converted unto Thee.

1Clem 18:11
Deliver me from blood guiltiness, O God, the God of my salvation. My tongue shall rejoice in Your righteousness.

1Clem 18:12
Lord, You shall open my mouth, and my lips shall declare Your praise.

1Clem 18:13
For, if You had desired sacrifice, I would have given it: in whole burnt offerings You wilt have no pleasure.

1Clem 18:14
A sacrifice unto God is a contrite spirit; a contrite and humbled heart God will not despise.

1Clem 19:1
The humility therefore and the submissiveness of so many and so great men, who have thus obtained a good report, has through obedience made better not only us but also the generations which were before us, even them that received His oracles in fear and truth.

1Clem 19:2
Seeing then that we have been partakers of many great and glorious doings, let us hasten to return unto the goal of peace which has been handed down to us from the beginning, and let us look steadfastly unto the Father and Maker of the whole world, and hold fast unto His splendid and excellent gifts of peace and benefits.

1Clem 19:3
Let us behold Him in our mind, and let us look with the eyes of our soul unto His long-suffering will. Let us note how free from anger He is towards all His creatures.

1Clem 20:1
The heavens are moved by His direction and obey Him in peace.

1Clem 20:2
Day and night accomplish the course assigned to them by Him, without hindrance one to another.

1Clem 20:3
The sun and the moon and the dancing stars according to His appointment circle in harmony within the bounds assigned to them, without any swerving aside.

1Clem 20:4
The earth, bearing fruit in fulfillment of His will at her proper seasons, puts forth the food that supplies abundantly both men and beasts and all living things which are thereupon, making no dissension, neither altering anything which He has decreed.

1Clem 20:5
Moreover, the inscrutable depths of the abysses and the unutterable statutes of the nether regions are constrained by the same ordinances.

1Clem 20:6
The basin of the boundless sea, gathered together by His workmanship into it's reservoirs, passes not the barriers wherewith it is surrounded; but even as He ordered it, so it doeth.

1Clem 20:7
For He said, So far shall you come, and thy waves shall be broken within you.

1Clem 20:8
The ocean which is impassable for men, and the worlds beyond it, are directed by the same ordinances of the Master.

1Clem 20:9
The seasons of spring and summer and autumn and winter give way in succession one to another in peace.

1Clem 20:10
The winds in their several quarters at their proper season fulfill their ministry without disturbance; and the ever flowing fountains, created for enjoyment and health, without fail give their breasts which sustain the life for men. Yea, the smallest of living things come together in concord and peace.

1Clem 20:11
All these things the great Creator and Master of the universe ordered to be in peace and concord, doing good unto all things, but far beyond the rest unto us who have taken refuge in His compassionate mercies through our Lord Jesus Christ,

1Clem 20:12
to whom be the glory and the majesty for ever and ever. Amen.

1Clem 21:1
Look you, brethren, lest His benefits, which are many, turn unto judgment to all of us, if we walk not worthily of Him, and do those things which are good and well pleasing in His sight with concord.

1Clem 21:2
For He said in a certain place, The Spirit of the Lord is a lamp searching the closets of the belly.

1Clem 21:3
Let us see how near He is, and how that nothing escapes Him of our thoughts or our devices which we make.

1Clem 21:4
It is right therefore that we should not be deserters from His will.

1Clem 21:5
Let us rather give offense to foolish and senseless men who exalt themselves and boast in the arrogance of their words, than to God.

1Clem 21:6
Let us fear the Lord Jesus [Christ], whose blood was given for us. Let us reverence our rulers; let us honor our elders; let us instruct our young men in the lesson of the fear of God. Let us guide our women toward that which is good:

1Clem 21:7
let them show forth their lovely disposition of purity; let them prove their sincere affection of gentleness; let them make manifest the moderation of their tongue through their silence; let them show their love, not in factious preferences but without partiality towards all them that fear God, in holiness. Let our children be partakers of the instruction which is in Christ:

1Clem 21:8
let them learn how lowliness of mind prevailed with God, what power chaste love has with God, how the fear of Him is good and great and saved all them that walk therein in a pure mind with holiness.

1Clem 21:9
For He is the searcher out of the intents and desires; whose breath is in us, and when He listed, He shall take it away.

1Clem 22:1
Now all these things the faith which is in Christ confirmed: for He Himself through the Holy Spirit thus invite thus: Come, my children, hearken unto Me, I will teach you the fear of the Lord.

1Clem 22:2
What man is he that desired life and loved to see good days?

1Clem 22:3
Make thy tongue to cease from evil, and thy lips that they speak no guile.

1Clem 22:4
Turn aside from evil and do good.

1Clem 22:5
Seek peace and ensue it.

1Clem 22:6
The eyes of the Lord are over the righteous, and His ears are turned to their prayers. But the face of the Lord is upon them that do evil, to destroy their memorial from the earth.

1Clem 22:7
The righteous cried out, and the Lord heard him, and delivered him from all his troubles. Many are the troubles of the righteous, and the Lord shall deliver him from them all.

1Clem 22:8
And again Many are the stripes of the sinner, but them that set their hope on the Lord mercy shall compass about.

1Clem 23:1
The Father, who is pitiful in all things, and ready to do good, has compassion on them that fear Him, and kindly and lovingly bestowed His favors on them that draw nigh unto Him with a single mind.

1Clem 23:2
Therefore let us not be double-minded, neither let our soul indulge in idle humors respecting His exceeding and glorious gifts.

1Clem 23:3
Let this scripture be far from us where He said Wretched are the double-minded, Which doubt in their soul and say, These things we did hear in the days of our fathers also, and behold we have grown old, and none of these things has befallen us.

1Clem 23:4
you fools, compare yourselves unto a tree; take a vine. First it sheds its leaves, then a shoot cometh, then a leaf, then a flower, and after these a sour berry, then a full ripe grape. you see that in a little time the fruit of the tree attained unto mellowness.

1Clem 23:5
Of a truth quickly and suddenly shall His will be accomplished, the scripture also bearing witness to it, saying He shall come quickly and shall not tarry; and the Lord shall come suddenly into His temple, even the Holy One, whom you expect.

1Clem 24:1
Let us understand, dearly beloved, how the Master continually showed unto us the resurrection that shall be hereafter; whereof He made the Lord Jesus Christ the firstfruit, when He raised Him from the dead.

1Clem 24:2
Let us behold, dearly beloved, the resurrection which happened at its proper season.

1Clem 24:3
Day and night show unto us the resurrection. The night fell asleep, and day arose; the day departed, and night cometh on.

1Clem 24:4

Let us mark the fruits, how and in what manner the sowing took place.

1Clem 24:5

The sower went forth and casted into the earth each of the seeds; and these falling into the earth dry and bare decay: then out of their decay the mightiness of the Master's providence raised them up, and from being one they increase manifold and bear fruit.

1Clem 25:1

Let us consider the marvelous sign which is seen in the regions of the east, that is, in the parts about Arabia.

1Clem 25:2

There is a bird, which is named the phoenix. This, being the only one of its kind, lived for five hundred years; and when it has now reached the time of its dissolution that it should die, it made for itself a coffin of frankincense and myrrh and the other spices, into the which in the fullness of time it entered, and so it died.

1Clem 25:3

But, as the flesh rotted, a certain worm is engendered, which is nurtured from the moisture of the dead creature and put forth wings. Then, when it is grown lusty, it took up that coffin where are the bones of its parent, and carrying them journeyed from the country of Arabia even unto Egypt, to the place called the City of the Sun;

1Clem 25:4

and in the daytime in the sight of all, flying to the altar of the Sun, it bathed them thereupon; and this done, it set forth to return.

1Clem 25:5

So the priests examine the registers of the times, and they find that it has come when the five hundredth year is completed.

1Clem 26:1

Do we then think it to be a great and marvelous thing, if the Creator of the universe shall bring about the resurrection of them that have served Him with holiness in the assurance of a good faith, seeing that He showed to us even by a bird the magnificence of His promise?

1Clem 26:2

For He said in a certain place And You shall raise me up, and I will praise Thee; and; I went to rest and slept, I was awaked, for You art with me.

1Clem 26:3

And again Job said And You shall raise this my flesh which has endured all these things.

1Clem 27:1

With this hope therefore let our souls be bound unto Him that is faithful in His promises and that is righteous in His judgments.

1Clem 27:2

He that commanded not to lie, much more shall He Himself not lie:

for nothing is impossible with God save to lie.

1Clem 27:3

Therefore let our faith in Him be kindled within us, and let us understand that all things are nigh unto Him.

1Clem 27:4

By a word of His majesty He compacted the universe; and by a word He can destroy it.

1Clem 27:5

Who shall say unto Him, What hast you done? or who shall resist the might of His strength? When He listeth, and as He listeth, He will do all things; and nothing shall pass away of those things that He has decreed.

1Clem 27:6

All things are in His sight, and nothing escaped His counsel,

1Clem 27:7

seeing that The heavens declare the glory of God, and the firmament proclaimed His handiwork. Day uttered word unto day, and night proclaimed knowledge unto night; and there are neither words nor speeches, whose voices are not heard.

1Clem 28:1

Since therefore all things are seen and heard, let us fear Him and forsake the abominable lusts of evil works, that we maybe shielded by His mercy from the coming judgments.

1Clem 28:2

For where can any of us escape from His strong hand? And what world will receive any of them that desert from His service?

1Clem 28:3

For the holy writing said in a certain place Where shall I go, and where shall I be hidden from Your face? If I ascend into the heaven, You art there; if I depart into the farthest parts of the earth, there is Your right hand; if I make my bed in the depths, there is Your Spirit.

1Clem 28:4

Whither then shall one depart, or where shall one flee, from Him that embraced the universe?

1Clem 29:1

Let us therefore approach Him in holiness of soul, lifting up pure and undefiled hands unto Him, with love towards our gentle and compassionate Father who made us an elect portion unto Himself.

1Clem 29:2

For

thus it is written: When the Most High divided the nations, when He dispersed the sons of Adam, He fixed the boundaries of the nations according to the number of the angels of God. His people Jacob became the portion of the Lord, and Israel the measurement of His inheritance.

1Clem 29:3

And in another place He said, Behold, the Lord took for Himself a nation out of the midst of the nations, as a man took the first

fruits of his threshing floor; and the holy of holies shall come
forth from that nation.

1Clem 30:1
    Seeing then that we are the special portion of a Holy God, let us do
all things that pertain unto holiness, forsaking evil speakings,
abominable and impure embraces, drunkennesses and tumults and hateful
lusts, abominable adultery, hateful pride.

1Clem 30:2
For God, He said, resisted the proud, but gave grace to the
lowly.

1Clem 30:3
Let us therefore hold fast unto those to whom grace is given from God.
Let us clothe ourselves in concord, being lowly-minded and temperate,
holding ourselves aloof from all back biting and evil speaking, being
justified by works and not by words.

1Clem 30:4
For He said, He that said much shall hear also again. Doth the
ready talker think to be righteous?

1Clem 30:5
Blessed is the offspring of a woman that lived but a short time.
Be not you abundant in words.

1Clem 30:6
Let our praise be with God, and not of ourselves: for God hated
them that praise themselves.

1Clem 30:7
Let the testimony to our well doing be given by others, as it was
given unto our fathers who were righteous.

1Clem 30:8
Boldness and arrogance and daring are for them that are accursed of
God; but forbearance and humility and gentleness are with them that
are blessed of God.

1Clem 31:1
    Let us therefore hold fast unto His blessing, and let us see what are
the ways of blessing. Let us study the records of the things that
have happened from the beginning.

1Clem 31:2
Wherefore was our father Abraham blessed? Was it not because he
wrought righteousness and truth through faith?

1Clem 31:3
Isaac with confidence, as knowing the future, was led a willing
sacrifice.

1Clem 31:4
Jacob with humility departed from his land because of his brother,
and went unto Laban and served; and the twelve tribes of Israel were
given unto him.

1Clem 32:1
    If any man will consider them one by one in sincerity, he shall
understand the magnificence of the gifts that are given by Him.

1Clem 32:2
For of Jacob are all the priests and Levites who minister unto the
altar of God; of him is the Lord Jesus as concerning the flesh; of
him are kings and rulers and governors in the line of Judah; yea and
the rest of his tribes are held in no small honor, seeing that God
promised saying, Your seed shall be as the stars of heaven.

1Clem 32:3
They all therefore were glorified and magnified, not through
themselves or their own works or the righteous doing which they
wrought, but through His will.

1Clem 32:4
And so we, having been called through His will in Christ Jesus, are
not justified through ourselves or through our own wisdom or
understanding or piety or works which we wrought in holiness of
heart, but through faith, whereby the Almighty God justified all men
that have been from the beginning; to whom be the glory for ever and
ever. Amen.

1Clem 33:1
    What then must we do, brethren? Must we idly abstain from doing
good, and forsake love? May the Master never allow this to befall us
at least; but let us hasten with urgency and zeal to accomplish
every good work.

1Clem 33:2
For the Creator and Master of the universe Himself rejoiced in His
works.

1Clem 33:3
For by His exceeding great might He established the heavens, and in
His incomprehensible wisdom He set them in order. And the earth He
separated from the water that surrounded it, and He set it firm on
the sure foundation of His own will; and the living creatures which
walk upon it He commanded to exist by His ordinance. Having before
created the sea and the living creatures therein, He enclosed it by
His own power.

1Clem 33:4
Above all, as the most excellent and exceeding great work of His
intelligence, with His sacred and faultless hands He formed man in
the impress of His own image.

1Clem 33:5
For thus said God Let us make man after our image and after our
likeness. And God made man; male and female made He them.

1Clem 33:6
So having finished all these things, He praised them and blessed them
and said, Increase and multiply.

1Clem 33:7
We have seen that all the righteous were adorned in good works. Yea,
and the Lord Himself having adorned Himself with worlds rejoiced.

1Clem 33:8
Seeing then that we have this pattern, let us conform ourselves with
all diligence to His will; let us with all our strength work the work
of righteousness.

1Clem 34:1

The good workman received the bread of his work with boldness, but the slothful and careless dared not look his employer in the face.

1Clem 34:2

It is therefore needful that we should be zealous unto well doing, for of Him are all things:

1Clem 34:3

since He forewarned us saying, Behold, the Lord, and His reward is before His face, to recompense each man according to his work.

1Clem 34:4

He exhorted us therefore to believe on Him with our whole heart, and to be not idle nor careless unto every good work.

1Clem 34:5

Let our boast and our confidence be in Him: let us submit ourselves to His will; let us mark the whole host of His angels, how they stand by and minister unto His will.

1Clem 34:6

For the scripture said, Ten thousands of ten thousands stood by Him, and thousands of thousands ministered unto Him: and they cried aloud, Holy, holy, holy is the Lord of Sabaoth; all creation is full of His glory.

1Clem 34:7

Yea, and let us ourselves then, being gathered together in concord with intentness of heart, cry unto Him as from one mouth earnestly that we may be made partakers of His great and glorious promises.

1Clem 34:8

For He said, Eye has not seen and ear has not heard, and it has not entered into the heart of man what great things He has prepared for them that patiently await Him.

1Clem 35:1

How blessed and marvelous are the gifts of God, dearly beloved!!

1Clem 35:2

Life in immortality, splendor in righteousness, truth in boldness, faith in confidence, temperance in sanctification! And all these things fall under our apprehension.

1Clem 35:3

What then, think you, are the things preparing for them that patiently await Him? The Creator and Father of the ages, the All holy One Himself knew their number and their beauty.

1Clem 35:4

Let us therefore contend, that we may be found in the number of those that patiently await Him, to the end that we may be partakers of His promised gifts.

1Clem 35:5

But how shall this be, dearly beloved? If our mind be fixed through faith towards God; if we seek out those things which are well pleasing and acceptable unto Him; if we accomplish such things as beseem His faultless will, and follow the way of truth, casting off from ourselves all unrighteousness and iniquity, covetousness, strifes, malignity and deceits, whisperings and backbitings, hatred of God, pride and arrogance, vainglory and inhospitality.

1Clem 35:6

For they that do these things are hateful to God; and not only they that do them, but they also that consent unto them.

1Clem 35:7

For the scripture said, But unto the sinner said God, Wherefore do you declare Mine ordinances, and take My covenant upon thy lips?

1Clem 35:8

Yet You didst hate instruction and didst cast away My words behind you. If you saw a thief you didst keep company with him, and with the adulterers you didst set thy portion. Your mouth multiplied wickedness and thy tongue wove deceit. You sat and spoke against thy brother, and against the son of thy mother you didst lay a stumbling block.

1Clem 35:9

These things You hast done, and I kept silence. You thought unrighteous man, that I should be like unto you.

1Clem 35:10

I will convict you and will set you face to face with thyself.

1Clem 35:11

Now understand you these things, you that forget God, lest at any time He seize you as a lion, and there be none to deliver.

1Clem 35:12

The sacrifice of praise shall glorify Me, and there is the way wherein I will show him the salvation of God.

1Clem 36:1

This is the way, dearly beloved, wherein we found our salvation, even Jesus Christ the High priest of our offerings, the Guardian and Helper of our weakness.

1Clem 36:2

Through Him let us look steadfastly unto the heights of the heavens; through Him we behold as in a mirror His faultless and most excellent visage; through Him the eyes of our hearts were opened; through Him our foolish and darkened mind sprung up unto the light; through Him the Master willed that we should taste of the immortal knowledge Who being the brightness of His majesty is so much greater than angels, as He has inherited a more excellent name.

1Clem 36:3

For so it is written Who made His angels spirits and His ministers aflame of fire

1Clem 36:4

but of His Son the Master said thus, You art My Son, I this day have begotten you. Ask of Me, and I will give Thee the Gentiles for Your inheritance, and the ends of the earth for Your possession.

1Clem 36:5
And again He said unto Him Sit You on My right hand, until I make
Your enemies a footstool for Your feet.

1Clem 36:6
Who then are these enemies? They that are wicked and resist His
will.

1Clem 37:1
Let us therefore enlist ourselves, brethren, with all earnestness in
His faultless ordinances.

1Clem 37:2
Let us mark the soldiers that are enlisted under our rulers, how
exactly, how readily, how submissively, they execute the orders given
them.

1Clem 37:3
All are not prefects, nor rulers of thousands, nor rulers of
hundreds, nor rulers of fifties, and so forth; but each man in his
own rank executed the orders given by the king and the governors.

1Clem 37:4
The great without the small cannot exist, neither the small without
the great. There is a certain mixture in all things, and therein is
utility.

1Clem 37:5
Let us take our body as an example. The head without the feet is
nothing; so likewise the feet without the head are nothing: even the
smallest limbs of our body are necessary and useful for the whole
body: but all the members conspire and unite in subjection, that the
whole body maybe saved.

1Clem 38:1
So in our case let the whole body be saved in Christ Jesus, and let
each man be subject unto his neighbor, according as also he was
appointed with his special grace.

1Clem 38:2
Let not the strong neglect the weak; and let the weak respect the
strong. Let the rich minister aid to the poor; and let the poor give
thanks to God, because He has given him one through whom his wants
may be supplied. Let the wise display his wisdom, not in words, but
in good works. He that is lowly in mind, let him not bear testimony
to himself, but leave testimony to be borne to him by his neighbor.
He that is pure in the flesh, let him be so, and not boast, knowing
that it is Another who bestowed his continence upon him.

1Clem 38:3
Let us consider, brethren, of what matter we were made; who and what
manner of beings we were, when we came into the world; from what a
sepulchre and what darkness He that molded and created us brought us
into His world, having prepared His benefits aforehand ere ever we
were born.

1Clem 38:4
Seeing therefore that we have all these things from Him, we ought in
all things to give thanks to Him, to whom be the glory for ever and
ever. Amen.

1Clem 39:1
Senseless and stupid and foolish and ignorant men jeer and mock at
us, desiring that they themselves should be exalted in their
imaginations.

1Clem 39:2
For what power has a mortal? or what strength has a child of earth?

1Clem 39:3
For it is written; There was no form before mine eyes; only I heard
a breath and a voice.

1Clem 39:4
What then? Shall a mortal be clean in the sight of the Lord; or
shall a man be unblamable for his works? seeing that He is
distrustful against His servants and noted some perversity against
His angels.

1Clem 39:5
Nay, the heaven is not clean in His sight. Away then, you that dwell
in houses of clay, whereof, even of the same clay, we ourselves are
made. He smote them like a moth, and from morn to even they are no
more. Because they could not succor themselves, they perished.

1Clem 39:6
He breathed on them and they died, because they had no wisdom.

1Clem 39:7
But call you, if perchance one shall obey you, or if you shall
see one of the holy angels. For wrath killed the foolish man, and
envy slayed him that has gone astray.

1Clem 39:8
And I have seen fools throwing out roots, but forthwith their
habitation was eaten up.

1Clem 39:9
Far be their sons from safety. May they be mocked at the gates of
inferiors, and there shall be none to deliver them. For the things
which are prepared for them, the righteous shall eat; but they
themselves shall not be delivered from evils.

1Clem 40:1
Forasmuch then as these things are manifest beforehand, and we have
searched into the depths of the Divine knowledge, we ought to do all
things in order, as many as the Master has commanded us to perform
at their appointed seasons.

1Clem 40:2
Now the offerings and ministrations He commanded to be performed with
care, and not to be done rashly or in disorder, but at fixed times
and seasons.

1Clem 40:3
And where and by whom He would have them performed, He Himself fixed
by His supreme will: that all things being done with piety according
to His good pleasure might be acceptable to His will.

1Clem 40:4
They therefore that make their offerings at the appointed seasons are

acceptable and blessed: for while they follow the institutions of the Master they cannot go wrong.

1Clem 40:5
For unto the high priest his proper services have been assigned, and to the priests their proper office is appointed, and upon the Levites their proper ministrations are laid. The layman is bound by the layman's ordinances.

1Clem 41:1
Let each of you, brethren, in his own order give thanks unto God, maintaining a good conscience and not transgressing the appointed rule of his service, but acting with all seemliness.

1Clem 41:2
Not in every place, brethren, are the continual daily sacrifices offered, or the freewill offerings, or the sin offerings and the trespass offerings, but in Jerusalem alone. And even there the offering is not made in every place, but before the sanctuary in the court of the altar; and this too through the high priest and the afore said ministers, after that the victim to be offered has been inspected for blemishes.

1Clem 41:3
They therefore who do any thing contrary to the seemly ordinance of His will receive death as the penalty.

1Clem 41:4
you see, brethren, in proportion as greater knowledge has been vouchsafed unto us, so much the more are we exposed to danger.

1Clem 42:1
The Apostles received the Gospel for us from the Lord Jesus Christ; Jesus Christ was sent forth from God.

1Clem 42:2
So then Christ is from God, and the Apostles are from Christ. Both therefore came of the will of God in the appointed order.

1Clem 42:3
Having therefore received a charge, and having been fully assured through the resurrection of our Lord Jesus Christ and confirmed in the word of God with full assurance of the Holy Ghost, they went forth with the glad tidings that the kingdom of God should come.

1Clem 42:4
So preaching everywhere in country and town, they appointed their firstfruits, when they had proved them by the Spirit, to be bishops and deacons unto them that should believe.

1Clem 42:5
And this they did in no new fashion; for indeed it had been written concerning bishops and deacons from very ancient times; for thus said the scripture in a certain place, I will appoint their bishops in righteousness and their deacons in faith.

1Clem 43:1
And what marvel, if they which were entrusted in Christ with such a work by God appointed the aforesaid persons? seeing that even the blessed Moses who was a faithful servant in all His house recorded for a sign in the sacred books all things that were enjoined upon

him. And him also the rest of the prophets followed, bearing witness with him unto the laws that were ordained by him.

1Clem 43:2
For he, when jealousy arose concerning the priesthood, and there was dissension among the tribes which of them was adorned with the glorious name, commanded the twelve chiefs of the tribes to bring to him rods inscribed with the name of each tribe. And he took them and tied them and sealed them with the signet rings of the chiefs of the tribes, and put them away in the tabernacle of the testimony on the table of God.

1Clem 43:3
And having shut the tabernacle he sealed the keys and likewise also the doors.

1Clem 43:4
And he said unto them, Brethren, the tribe whose rod shall bud, this has God chosen to be priests and ministers unto Him.

1Clem 43:5
Now when morning came, he called together all Israel, even the six hundred thousand men, and showed the seals to the chiefs of the tribes and opened the tabernacle of the testimony and drew forth the rods. And the rod of Aaron was found not only with buds, but also bearing fruit.

1Clem 43:6
What think you, dearly beloved? Did not Moses know beforehand that this would come to pass? Assuredly he knew it. But that disorder might not arise in Israel, he did thus, to the end that the Name of the true and only God might be glorified: to whom he the glory for ever and ever. Amen...

1Clem 44:1
And our Apostles knew through our Lord Jesus Christ that there would be strife over the name of the bishop's office.

1Clem 44:2
For this cause therefore, having received complete foreknowledge, they appointed the aforesaid persons, and afterwards they provided a continuance, that if these should fall asleep, other approved men should succeed to their ministration. Those therefore who were appointed by them, or afterward by other men of repute with the consent of the whole Church, and have ministered unblamably to the flock of Christ in lowliness of mind, peacefully and with all modesty, and for long time have borne a good report with all these men we consider to be unjustly thrust out from their ministration.

1Clem 44:3
For it will be no light sin for us, if we thrust out those who have offered the gifts of the bishop's office unblamably and holily.

1Clem 44:4
Blessed are those presbyters who have gone before, seeing that their departure was fruitful and ripe: for they have no fear lest any one should remove them from their appointed place.

1Clem 44:5
For we see that you have displaced certain persons, though they were living honorably, from the ministration which had been respected by

them blamelessly.

1Clem 45:1
Be you contentious, brethren, and jealous about the things that pertain unto salvation.

1Clem 45:2
you have searched the scriptures, which are true, which were given through the Holy Ghost;

1Clem 45:3
and you know that nothing unrighteous or counterfeit is written in them. you will not find that righteous persons have been thrust out by holy men.

1Clem 45:4
Righteous men were persecuted, but it was by the lawless; they were imprisoned, but it was by the unholy. They were stoned by transgressors: they were slain by those who had conceived a detestable and unrighteous jealousy.

1Clem 45:5
Suffering these things, they endured nobly.

1Clem 45:6
For what must we say, brethren? Was Daniel cast into the lions' den by them that feared God?

1Clem 45:7
Or were Ananias and Azarias and Misael shut up in the furnace of fire by them that professed the excellent and glorious worship of the Most High? Far be this from our thoughts. Who then were they that did these things? Abominable men and full of all wickedness were stirred up to such a pitch of wrath, as to bring cruel suffering upon them that served God in a holy and blameless purpose, not knowing that the Most High is the champion and protector of them that in a pure conscience serve His excellent Name: unto whom be the glory for ever and ever. Amen.

1Clem 45:8
But they that endured patiently in confidence inherited glory and honor; they were exalted, and had their names recorded by God in their memorial for ever and ever. Amen.

1Clem 46:1
To such examples as these therefore, brethren, we also ought to hold fast.

1Clem 46:2
For it is written; Hold fast unto the saints, for they that hold fast unto them shall be sanctified.

1Clem 46:3
And again He said in another place; With the guiltless man you shall be guiltless, and with the elect you shall be elect, and with the crooked you shall deal crookedly.

1Clem 46:4
Let us therefore hold fast to the guiltless and righteous: and these are the elect of God.

1Clem 46:5
Wherefore are there strifes and wraths and factions and divisions and war among you?

1Clem 46:6
Have we not one God and one Christ and one Spirit of grace that was shed upon us? And is there not one calling in Christ?

1Clem 46:7
Wherefore do we tear and rend asunder the members of Christ, and stir up factions against our own body, and reach such a pitch of folly, as to forget that we are members one of another?

1Clem 46:8
Remember the words of Jesus our Lord: for He said, Woe unto that man; it were good for him if he had not been born, rather than that at he should offend one of Mine elect. It were better for him that a millstone were hanged about him, and be cast into the sea, than that he should pervert one of Mine elect.

1Clem 46:9
Your division has perverted many; it has brought many to despair, many to doubting, and all of us to sorrow. And your sedition still continued.

1Clem 47:1
Take up the epistle of the blessed Paul the Apostle.

1Clem 47:2
What wrote he first unto you in the beginning of the Gospel?

1Clem 47:3
Of a truth he charged you in the Spirit concerning himself and Cephas and Apollos, because that even then you had made parties.

1Clem 47:4
Yet that making of parties brought less sin upon you; for you were partisans of Apostles that were highly reputed, and of a man approved in their sight.

1Clem 47:5
But now mark you, who they are that have perverted you and diminished the glory of your renowned love for the brotherhood.

1Clem 47:6
It is shameful, dearly beloved, yes, utterly shameful and unworthy of your conduct in Christ, that it should be reported that the very steadfast and ancient Church of the Corinthians, for the sake of one or two persons, made sedition against its presbyters.

1Clem 47:7
And this report has reached not only us, but them also which differ from us, so that you even heap blasphemies on the Name of the Lord by reason of your folly, and moreover create peril for yourselves.

1Clem 48:1
Let us therefore root this out quickly, and let us fall down before the Master and entreat Him with tears, that He may show Himself propitious and be reconciled unto us, and may restore us to the seemly and pure conduct which belonged to our love of the brethren.

1Clem 48:2

For this is a gate of righteousness opened unto life, as it is written; Open me the gates of righteousness, that I may enter in thereby and preach the Lord.

1Clem 48:3

This is the gate of the Lord; the righteous shall enter in thereby.

1Clem 48:4

Seeing then that many gates are opened, this is that gate which is in righteousness, even that which is in Christ, whereby all are blessed that have entered in and direct their path in holiness and righteousness, performing all things without confusion.

1Clem 48:5

Let a man be faithful, let him be able to expound a deep saying, let him be wise in the discernment of words, let him be strenuous in deeds, let him be pure;

1Clem 48:6

for so much the more ought he to be lowly in mind, in proportion as he seemed to be the greater; and he ought to seek the common advantage of all, and not his own.

1Clem 49:1

Let him that has love in Christ fulfill the commandments of Christ.

1Clem 49:2

Who can declare the bond of the love of God?

1Clem 49:3

Who is sufficient to tell the majesty of its beauty?

1Clem 49:4

The height, where unto love exalted, is unspeakable.

1Clem 49:5

Love joined us unto God; love covered a multitude of sins; love endured all things, is long-suffering in all things. There is nothing coarse, nothing arrogant in love. Love has no divisions, love made no seditions, love doeth all things in concord. In love were all the elect of God made perfect; without love nothing is well pleasing to God:

1Clem 49:6

in love the Master took us unto Himself; for the love which He had toward us, Jesus Christ our Lord has given His blood for us by the will of God, and His flesh for our flesh and His life for our lives.

1Clem 50:1

you see, dearly beloved, how great and marvelous a thing is love, and there is no declaring its perfection.

1Clem 50:2

Who is sufficient to be found therein, save those to whom God shall vouchsafe it? Let us therefore entreat and ask of His mercy, that we may be found blameless in love, standing apart from the factiousness of men. All the generations from Adam unto this day have passed away: but they that by God's grace were perfected in love dwell in the abode of the pious; and they shall be made manifest in the visitation of the Kingdom of God.

1Clem 50:3

For it is written; Enter into the closet for a very little while until Mine anger and Mine wrath shall pass away, and I will remember a good day and will raise you from your tombs.

1Clem 50:4

Blessed were we, dearly beloved, if we should be doing the commandments of God in concord of love, to the end that our sins may through love be forgiven us.

1Clem 50:5

For it is written; Blessed are they whose iniquities are forgiven, and whose sins are covered. Blessed is the man to whom the Lord shall impute no sin, neither is guile in his mouth.

1Clem 50:6

This declaration of blessedness was pronounced upon them that have been elected by God through Jesus Christ our Lord, to whom be the glory for ever and ever. Amen.

1Clem 51:1

For all our transgressions which we have committed through any of the wiles of the adversary, let us entreat that we may obtain forgiveness. Yea and they also, who set themselves up as leaders of faction and division, ought to look to the common ground of hope.

1Clem 51:2

For such as walk in fear and love desire that they themselves should fall into suffering rather than their neighbors; and they pronounce condemnation against themselves rather than against the harmony which has been handed down to us nobly and righteously.

1Clem 51:3

For it is good for a man to make confession of his trespasses rather than to harden his heart, as the heart of those was hardened who made sedition against Moses the servant of God; whose condemnation was clearly manifest,

1Clem 51:4

for they went down to hades alive, and Death shall be their shepherd.

1Clem 51:5

Pharaoh and his host and all the rulers of Egypt, their chariots and their horsemen, were overwhelmed in the depths of the Red Sea, and perished for none other reason but because their foolish hearts were hardened after that the signs and the wonders had been wrought in the land of Egypt by the hand of Moses the servant of God.

1Clem 52:1

The Master, brethren, has need of nothing at all. He desired not anything of any man, save to confess unto Him.

1Clem 52:2

For the elect David said; I will confess unto the Lord, and it shall please Him more than a young calf that grew horns and hoofs. Let the poor see it, and rejoice.

1Clem 52:3

And again He said; Sacrifice to God a sacrifice of praise, and pay thy vows to the Most High: and call upon Me in the day of your affliction, and I will deliver you, and you shall glorify Me.

1Clem 52:4

For a sacrifice unto God is a broken spirit.

1Clem 53:1

For you know, and know well, the sacred scriptures, dearly beloved, and you have searched into the oracles of God. We write these things therefore to put you in remembrance.

1Clem 53:2

When Moses went up into the mountain and had spent forty days and forty nights in fasting and humiliation, God said unto him; Moses, Moses, come down , quickly hence, for My people whom you lead forth from the land of Egypt have wrought iniquity: they have transgressed quickly out of the way which you didst command unto them: they have made for themselves molten images.

1Clem 53:3

And the Lord said unto him; I have spoken unto you once and twice, saying, I have seen this people, and behold it is stiff-necked. Let Me destroy them utterly, and I will blot out their name from under heaven, and I will make of you a nation great and wonderful and numerous more than this.

1Clem 53:4

And Moses said; Nay, not so, Lord Forgive this people their sin, or blot me also out of the book of the living.

1Clem 53:5

O mighty love! O unsurpassable perfection! The servant is bold with his Master; he asked forgiveness for the multitude, or he demanded that himself also be blotted out with them.

1Clem 54:1

Who therefore is noble among you? Who is compassionate? Who is fulfilled with love?

1Clem 54:2

Let him say; If by reason of me there be faction and strife and divisions, I retire, I depart, whither you will, and I do that which is ordered by the people: only let the flock of Christ be at peace with its duly appointed presbyters.

1Clem 54:3

He that shall have done this, shall win for himself great renown in Christ, and every place will receive him: for the earth is the Lord's and the fullness thereof.

1Clem 54:4

Thus have they done and will do, that live as citizens of that kingdom of God which brings no regrets.

1Clem 55:1

But, to bring forward examples of Gentiles also; many kings and rulers, when some season of pestilence pressed upon them, being taught by oracles have delivered themselves over to death, that they might rescue their fellow citizens through their own blood. Many

have retired from their own cities, that they might have no more seditions.

1Clem 55:2

We know that many among ourselves have delivered themselves to bondage, that they might ransom others. Many have sold themselves to slavery, and receiving the price paid for themselves have fed others.

1Clem 55:3

Many women being strengthened through the grace of God have performed many manly deeds.

1Clem 55:4

The blessed Judith, when the city was beleaguered, asked of the elders that she might be suffered to go forth into the camp of the aliens.

1Clem 55:5

So she exposed herself to peril and went forth for love of her country and of her people which were beleaguered; and the Lord delivered Holophernes into the hand of a woman.

1Clem 55:6

To no less peril did Esther also, who was perfect in faith, expose herself, that she might deliver the twelve tribes of Israel, when they were on the point to perish. For through her fasting and her humiliation she entreated the all seeing Master, the God of the ages; and He, seeing the humility of her soul, delivered the people for whose sake she encountered the peril.

1Clem 56:1

Therefore let us also make intercession for them that are in any transgression, that forbearance and humility may be given them, to the end that they may yield not unto us, but unto the will of God. For so shall the compassionate remembrance of them with God and the saints be fruitful unto them, and perfect.

1Clem 56:2

Let us accept chastisement, whereat no man ought to be vexed, dearly beloved. The admonition which we give one to another is good and exceeding useful; for it joined us unto the will of God.

1Clem 56:3

For thus said the holy word; The Lord has indeed chastened me, and has not delivered me over unto death.

1Clem 56:4

For whom the Lord loved He chastened, and scourged every son whom He received.

1Clem 56:5

For the righteous, it is said, shall chasten me in mercy and shall reprove me, but let not the mercy of sinners anoint my head.

1Clem 56:6

And again He said; Blessed is the man whom the Lord has reproved, and refuse not you the admonition of the Almighty. For He caused pain, and he restored again:

1Clem 56:7

He has smitten, and His hands have healed.

1Clem 56:8

Six times shall He rescue you from afflictions and at the seventh
no evil shall touch you.

1Clem 56:9

In famine he shall deliver you from death, and in war He shall
release you from the arm of the sword.

1Clem 56:10

And from the scourge of the tongue He shall hide you and you
shall not be afraid when evils approach.

1Clem 56:11

You shall laugh at the unrighteous and wicked, and of the wild
beasts you shall not be afraid.

1Clem 56:12

For wild beasts shall be at peace with you.

1Clem 56:13

Then shall you know that thy house shall be at peace: and the
abode of thy tabernacle shall not go wrong,

1Clem 56:14

and you shall know that thy seed is many, and thy children as the
plenteous herbage of the field.

1Clem 56:15

And you shall come to the grave as ripe corn reaped in due season,
or as the heap of the threshing floor gathered together at the
right time.

1Clem 56:16

you see, dearly beloved, how great protection there is for them that
are chastened by the Master: for being a kind father He chastened
us to the end that we may obtain mercy through His holy chastisement.

1Clem 57:1

you therefore that laid the foundation of the sedition, submit
yourselves unto the presbyters and receive chastisement unto
repentance, bending the knees of your heart.

1Clem 57:2

Learn to submit yourselves, laying aside the arrogant and proud
stubbornness of your tongue. For it is better for you to be found
little in the flock of Christ and to have your name on God's roll,
than to be had in exceeding honor and yet be cast out from the hope
of Him.

1Clem 57:3

For thus said the All virtuous Wisdom; Behold I will pour out for
you a saying of My breath, and I will teach you My word.

1Clem 57:4

Because I called and you obeyed not, and I held out words and you
heeded not, but made My councils of none effect, and were
disobedient unto My reproofs; therefore I also will laugh at your
destruction, and will rejoice over you when ruin cometh upon you,
and when confusion overtook you suddenly, and your overthrow is
at hand like a whirlwind,

1Clem 57:5

or when you call upon Me, yet will I not here you. Evil men shall
seek me and not find me: for they hated wisdom, and chose not the
fear of the Lord, neither would they give head unto My councils,
but mocked at My reproofs.

1Clem 57:6

Therefore they shall eat the fruits of their own way, and shall be
filled with their own ungodliness.

1Clem 57:7

For because they wronged babes, they shall be slain, and
inquisition shall destroy the ungodly. But he that heard Me shall
dwell safely trusting in hope, and shall be quiet from all fear of
all evil.

1Clem 58:1

Let us therefore be obedient unto His most holy and glorious Name,
thereby escaping the threatenings which were spoken of old by the
mouth of Wisdom against them which disobey, that we may dwell safely,
trusting in the most holy Name of His majesty.

1Clem 58:2

Receive our counsel, and you shall have no occasion of regret. For as
God lived, and the Lord Jesus Christ lived, and the Holy Spirit,
who are the faith and the hope of the elect, so surely shall he, who
with lowliness of mind and instant in gentleness has without
regretfulness performed the ordinances and commandments that are
given by God, be enrolled and have a name among the number of them
that are saved through Jesus Christ, through whom is the glory unto
Him for ever and ever. Amen.

1Clem 59:1

But if certain persons should be disobedient unto the words spoken
by Him through us, let them understand that they will entangle
themselves in no slight transgression and danger;

1Clem 59:2

but we shall be guiltless of this sin. And we will ask, with
insistency of prayer and supplication, that the Creator of the universe
may guard intact unto the end the number that has been numbered of
His elect throughout the whole world, through His beloved Son Jesus
Christ, through whom He called us from darkness to light, from
ignorance to the full knowledge of the glory of His Name.

1Clem 59:3

[Grant unto us, Lord,] that we may set our hope on Your Name which is
the primal source of all creation, and open the eyes of our hearts,
that we may know Thee, who alone abide Highest in the lofty, Holy
in the holy; who lays low in the insolence of the proud, who
set the lowly on high, and brings the lofty low; who
makes rich and makes poor; who kills and makes alive; who
alone art the Benefactor of spirits and the God of all flesh; who
looks into the abysses, who sees the works of man; the rescuer
of them that are in peril, the Savior of them that are in
despair; The Creator and Overseer of every spirit; who multiplies
the nations upon earth, and hast chosen out from all men those that
love Thee through Jesus Christ, Your beloved Son, through whom You
didst instruct us, didst sanctify us, didst honor us.

1Clem 59:4

We beseech Thee, Lord and Master, to be our help and succor. Save those among us who are in tribulation; have mercy on the lowly; lift up the fallen; show Thyself unto the needy; heal the ungodly; convert the wanderers of Your people; feed the hungry; release our prisoners; raise up the weak; comfort the fainthearted. Let all the Gentiles know that You art the God alone, and Jesus Christ is Your Son, and we are Your people and the sheep of Your pasture.

1Clem 60:1

You through Your operations didst make manifest the everlasting fabric of the world. You, Lord, didst create the earth. You that art faithful throughout all generations, righteous in Your judgments, marvelous in strength and excellence, You that art wise in creating and prudent in establishing that which You hast made, that art good in the things which are seen and faithful with them that trust on Thee, pitiful and compassionate, forgive us our iniquities and our unrighteousnesses and our transgressions and shortcomings.

1Clem 60:2

Lay not to our account every sin of Your servants and Your handmaids, but cleanse us with the cleansing of Your truth, and guide our steps to walk in holiness and righteousness and singleness of heart and to do such things as are good and well pleasing in Your sight and in the sight of our rulers.

1Clem 60:3

Yea, Lord, make Your face to shine upon us in peace for our good, that we may be sheltered by Your mighty hand and delivered from every sin by Your uplifted arm. And deliver us from them that hate us wrongfully.

1Clem 60:4

Give concord and peace to us and to all that dwell on the earth, as You gave to our fathers, when they called on Thee in faith and truth with holiness, [that we may be saved,] while we render obedience to Your almighty and most excellent Name, and to our rulers and governors upon the earth.

1Clem 61:1

You, Lord and Master, hast given them the power of sovereignty through Your excellent and unspeakable might, that we knowing the glory and honor which You hast given them may submit ourselves unto them, in nothing resisting Your will. Grant unto them therefore, O Lord, health peace, concord, stability, that they may administer the government which You hast given them without failure.

1Clem 61:2

For You, O heavenly Master, King of the ages, give to the sons of men glory and honor and power over all things that are upon the earth. Do You, Lord, direct their counsel according to that which is good and well pleasing in Your sight, that, administering in peace and gentleness with Godliness the power which You hast given them, they may obtain Your favor.

1Clem 61:3

O You, who alone art able to do these things and things far more exceeding good than these for us, we praise Thee through the High priest and Guardian of our souls, Jesus Christ, through whom be the glory and the majesty unto Thee both now and for all generations and for ever and ever. Amen.

1Clem 62:1

As touching those things which befit our religion and are most useful for a virtuous life to such as would guide [their steps] in holiness and righteousness, we have written fully unto you, brethren.

1Clem 62:2

For concerning faith and repentance and genuine love and temperance and sobriety and patience we have handled every argument, putting you in remembrance, that you ought to please Almighty God in righteousness and truth and long suffering with holiness, laying aside malice and pursuing concord in love and peace, being instant in gentleness; even as our fathers, of whom we spoke before, pleased Him, being lowly minded toward their Father and God and Creator and towards all men.

1Clem 62:3

And we have put you in mind of these things the more gladly, since we knew well that we were writing to men who are faithful and highly accounted and have diligently searched into the oracles of the teaching of God.

1Clem 63:1

Therefore it is right for us to give heed to so great and so many examples and to submit the neck and occupying the place of obedience to take our side with them that are the leaders of our souls, that ceasing from this foolish dissension we may attain unto the goal which lies before us in truthfulness, keeping aloof from every fault.

1Clem 63:2

For you will give us great joy and gladness, if you render obedience unto the things written by us through the Holy Spirit, and root out the unrighteous anger of your jealousy, according to the entreaty which we have made for peace and concord in this letter.

1Clem 63:3

And we have also sent faithful and prudent men that have walked among us from youth unto old age unblamably, who shall also be witnesses between you and us.

1Clem 63:4

And this we have done that you might know that we have had, and still have, every solicitude that you should be speedily at peace.

1Clem 64:1

Finally may the All seeing God and Master of spirits and Lord of all flesh, who chose the Lord Jesus Christ, and us through Him for a peculiar people, grant unto every soul that is called after His excellent and holy Name faith, fear, peace, patience, long-suffering, temperance, chastity and soberness, that they may be well pleasing unto His Name through our High priest and Guardian Jesus Christ, through whom unto Him be glory and majesty, might and honor, both now and for ever and ever. Amen.

1Clem 65:1

Now send you back speedily unto us our messengers Claudius Ephebus and Valerius Bito, together with Fortunatus also, in peace and with joy, to the end that they may the more quickly report the peace and concord which is prayed for and earnestly desired by us, that we also may the more speedily rejoice over your good order.

1Clem 65:2

The grace of our Lord Jesus Christ be with you and with all men in all places who have been called by God and through Him, through whom be glory and honor, power and greatness and eternal dominion, unto Him, from the ages past and forever and ever. Amen.

The Ascension of Isaiah

CHAPTER 1

AND it came to pass in the twenty-sixth year of the reign of Hezediah king of Judah that he called Manasseh his son. Now he was his only one.

2. And he called him into the presence of Isaiah the son of Amoz the prophet, and into the presence of Josab the son of Isaiah, in order to deliver unto him the words of righteousness which the king himself had seen:

3. And of the eternal judgments and torments of Gehenna, and of the prince of this world, and of his angels, and his authorities and his powers.

4. And the words of the faith of the Beloved which he himself had seen in the fifteenth year of his reign during his illness.

5. And he delivered unto him the written words which Samnas the scribe had written, and also those which Isaiah, the son of Amoz, had given to him, and also to the prophets, that they might write and store up with him what he himself had seen in the king's house regarding the judgment of the angels, and the destruction of this world, and regarding the garments of the saints and their going forth, and regarding their transformation and the persecution and ascension of the Beloved.

6. In the twentieth year of the reign of Hezekiah, Isaiah had seen the words of this prophecy and had delivered them to Josab his son. And whilst he (Hezekiah) gave commands, Josab the son of Isaiah standing by.

7. Isaiah said to Hezekiah the king, but not in the presence of Manasseh only did he say unto him: `As the Lord liveth, and th3e Spirit which speaketh in me liveth, all these commands and these words will be made of none effect by Manasseh thy son, and through the agency of his hands I shall depart mid the torture of my body.

8. And Sammael Malchira will serve Manasseh, and execute all his desire, and he will become a follower of Beliar rather than of me:

9. And many in Jerusalem and in Judea he will cause to abandon the true faith, and Beliar will dwell in Manasseh, and by his hands I shall be sawn asunder.'

10. And when Hezekiah heard these words he wept very bitterly, and rent his garments, and placed earth upon his head, and fell on his face.

11. And Isaiah said unto him: `The counsel of Sammael against Manasseh is consummated: nought will avail thee."

12. And on that day Hezekiah resolved in his heart to slay Manasseh his son.

13. And Isaiah said to Hezekiah: `The Beloved hath made of none effect thy design, and the purpose of thy heart will not be accomplished, for with this calling have I been called and I shall inherit the heritage of the Beloved.'

CHAPTER 2

AND it came to pass after that Hezekiah died and Manasseh became king, that he did not remember the commands of Hezekiah his father, but forgat them, and Sammael abode in Manasseh and clung fast to him.

2. And Manasseh forsook the service of the God of his father, and he served Satan and his angels and his powers.

3. And he turned aside the house of his father, which had been before the face of Hezekiah (from) the words of wisdom and from the service of God.

4. And Manasseh turned aside his heart to serve Beliar; for the angel of lawlessness, who is the ruler of this world, is Beliar, whose name is Mantanbuchus. and he delighted in Jerusalem because of Manasseh, and he made him strong in apostatizing (Israel) and in the lawlessness which were spread abroad in Jerusalem.

5. And witchcraft and magic increased and divination and auguration, and fornication, a [and adultery], and the persecution of the righteous by Manasseh and [Belachira, and] Tobia the Canaanite, and John of Anathoth, an by (Zadok) the chief of the works.

6. And the rest of the acts, behold they are written in the book of the Kings of Judah and Israel.

7. And, when Isaiah, the son of Amoz, saw the lawlessness which was being perpetrated in Jerusalem and the worship of Satan and his wantonness, he withdrew from Jerusalem and settled in Bethlehem of Judah.

8. And there also there was much lawlessness, and withdrawing from Bethlehem he settled on a mountain in a desert place.

9. And Micaiah the prophet, and the aged Ananias, and Joel and Habakkuk, and his son Josab, and many of the faithful who believed in the ascension into heaven, withdrew and settled on the mountain.

10. They were all clothed with garments of hair, and they were all prophets. And they had nothing with them but were naked, and they all lamented with a great lamentation because of the going astray of Israel.

11. And these eat nothing save wild herbs which they gathered on the mountains, and having cooked them, they lived thereon together with Isaiah the prophet. And they spent two years of days on the mountains and hills.

12. And after this, whilst they were in the desert, there was a certain man in Samaria named Belchira, of the family of Zedekiah, the son of Chenaan, a false prophet, whose dwelling was in Bethlehem. Now Hezekiah the son of Chanani, who was the brother of his father, and in the days of Ahab, king of Israel, had been the teacher of the 400. prophets of Baal, had himself smitten and reproved Micaiah the son of Amada the prophet.

13. And he, Micaiah, had been reproved by Ahab and cast into prison. (And he was) with Zedekiah the prophet: they were with Ahaziah the son of Ahab, king in Samaria.

14. And Elijah the prophet of Tebon of Gilead was reproving Ahaziah and Samaria, and prophesied regarding Ahaziah that he should die on his bed of sickness, and that Samaria should be delivered into the had of Leba Nasr because he had slain the prophets of God.

15. And when the false prophets, who were with Ahaziah the son of Ahab and their teacher Jalerjas of Mount Joel, had heard-

16. Now he was a brother of Zedekiah - when they persuaded Ahaziah the king of Aguaron and (slew) Micaiah.

CHAPTER 3

AND Belchira recognized and saw the place of Isaiah and the prophets who were with him; for he dwelt in the region of Bethlehem, and was an adherent of Manasseh. And he prophesied falsely in Jerusalem, and many belonging to Jerusalem were confederate with him, and he was a Samaritan.

2. And it came to pass when Alagar Zagar, king of Assyria, had come and captive, and led them away to the mountains of the medes and the rivers of Tazon;

3. This (Belchira), whilst still a youth, had escaped and come to Jerusalem in the days of Hezekiah king of Judah, but he walked not in the ways of his father of Samaria; for he feared Hezekiah.

4. And he was found in the days of Hezekiah speaking words of lawlessness in Jerusalem.

5. And the servants of Hezekiah accused him, and he made his escape to the region of Bethlehem. And they persuaded...

6. And Belchira accused Isaiah and the prophets who were with him, saying: `Isaiah and those who are with him prophesy against Jerusalem and against the cities of Judah that they shall be laid waste and (against the children of Judah and) Benjamin also that they shall go into captivity, and also against thee, O lord the king, that thou shalt go (bound) with hooks and iron chains':

7. But they prophesy falsely against Israel and Judah.

8. And Isaiah himself hath said: `I see more than Moses the prophet.'

9. But Moses said: `No man can see God and live'; and Isaiah hath said: `I have seen God and behold I live.'

10. Know, therefore, O king, that he is lying. And Jerusalem also he hath called Sodom, and the princes of Judah and Jerusalem he hath declared to be the people of Gomorrah. And he brought many accusations against Isaiah and the prophets before Manasseh.

11. But Beliar dwelt in the heart of Manasseh and in the heart of the princes of Judah and Benjamin and of the eunuchs and of the councillors of the king.

12. And the words of Belchira pleased him [exceedingly], and he sent and seized Isaiah.

13. For Beliar was in great wrath against Isaiah by reason of the vision, and because of the exposure wherewith he had exposed Sammael, and because through him the going forth of the Beloved from the seventh heaven had been made known, and His transformation and His descent and the likeness into which He should be transformed (that is) the likeness of man, and the persecution wherewith he should be persecuted, and the torturers wherewith the children of Israel should torture Him, and the coming of His twelve disciples, and the teaching, and that He should before the sabbath be crucified upon the tree, and should be crucified together with wicked men, and that He should be buried in the sepulchre,

14. And the twelve who were with Him should be offended because of Him: and the watch of those who watched the sepulchre:

15. And the descent of the angel of the Christian Church, which is in the heavens, whom He will summon in the last days.

16. And that (Gabriel) the angel of the Holy Spirit, and Michael, the chief of the holy angels, on the third day will open the sepulchre:

17. And the Beloved sitting on their shoulders will come forth and send out His twelve disciples;

18. And they will teach all the nations and every tongue of the resurrection of the Beloved, and those who believe in His cross will be saved, and in His ascension into the seventh heaven whence He came:

19. And that many who believe in Him will speak through the Holy Spirit:

20. And many signs and wonders will be wrought in those days.

21. And afterwards, on the eve of His approach, His disciples will forsake the teachings of the Twelve Apostles, and their faith, and their love and their purity.

22. And there will be much contention on the eve of [His advent and] His approach.

23. And in those days many will love office, though devoid of wisdom.

24. And there will be many lawless elders, and shepherds dealing wrongly by their own sheep, and they will ravage (them) owing to their not having holy shepherds.

25. And many will change the honour of the garments of the saints for the garments of the covetous, and there will be much respect of persons in those days and lovers of the honour of this world.

26. And there will be much slander and vainglory at the approach of the Lord, and the Holy Spirit will withdraw from many.

27. And there will not be in those days many prophets, nor those who speak trustworthy words, save one here and there in divers places,

28. On account of the spirit of error and fornication and of vainglory, and of covetousness, which shall be in those, who will be called servants of that One and in those who will receive that One.

29. And there will be great hatred in the shepherds and elders towards each other.

30. For there will be great jealousy in the last days; for every one will say what is pleasing in his own eyes.

31. And they will make of none effect the prophecy of the prophets which were before me, and these my visions also will they make of none effect, in order to speak after the impulse of their own hearts.

CHAPTER 4

AND now Hezekiah and Josab my son, these are the days of the completion of the world.

2. After it is consummated, Beliar the great ruler, the king of this world, will descend, who hath ruled it since it came into being; yea, he will descend from his firmament in the likeness of a man, a lawless king, the slayer of his mother: who himself (even) this king.

3. Will persecute the plant which the Twelve Apostles of the Beloved have planted. Of the Twelve one will be delivered into his hands.

4. This ruler in the form of that king will come and there will come and there will come with him all the powers of this world, and they will hearken unto him in all that he desires.

5. And at his word the sun will rise at night and he will make the moon to appear at the sixth hour.

6. And all that he hath desired he will do in the world: he will do and speak like the Beloved and he will say: "I am God and before me there has been none."

7. And all the people in the world will believe in him. 8. And they will sacrifice to him and they will serve him saying: "This is God and beside him there is no other."

9. And they greater number of those who shall have been associated together in order to receive the Beloved, he will turn aside after him.

10. And there will be the power of his miracles in every city and region.

11. And he will set up his image before him in every city.

12. And he shall bear sway three years and seven months and twenty-seven days.

13. And many believers and saints having seen Him for whom they were hoping, who was crucified, Jesus the Lord Christ, [after that I, Isaiah, had seen Him who was crucified and ascended] and those also who were believers in Him - of these few in those days will be left as His servants, while they flee from desert to desert, awaiting the coming of the Beloved.

14. And after (one thousand) three hundred and thirty-two days the Lord will come with His angels and with the armies of the holy ones from the seventh heaven with the glory of the seventh heaven, and He will drag Beliar into Gehenna and also his armies.

15. And He will give rest of the godly whom He shall find in the body in this world, [and the sun wil be ashamed]:

16. And to all who because of (their) faith in Him have execrated Beliar and his kings. But the saints will come with the Lord with their garments which are (now) stored up on high in the seventh heaven: with the Lord they will come, whose spirits are clothed, they will descend and be present in the world, and He will strengthen those, who have been found in the body, together with the saints, in the garments of the saints, and the Lord will minister to those who have kept watch in this world.

17. And afterwards they will turn themselves upward in their garments, and their body will be left in the world.

18. Then the voice of the Beloved will in wrath rebuke the things of heaven and the things of earth and the things of earth and the mountains and the hills and the cities and the desert and the forests and the angel of the sun and that of the moon, and all things wherein Beliar manifested himself and acted openly in this world, and there will be [a resurrection and] a judgment in their midst in those days, and the Beloved will cause fire to go forth from Him, and it will consume all the godless, and they will be as though they had not been created.

19. And the rest of the words of the vision is written in the vision of Babylon.

20. And the rest of the vision regarding the Lord, behold, it is written in three parables according to my words which are written in the book which I publicly prophesied.

21. And the descent of the Beloved into Sheol, behold, it is written in the section, where the Lord says: "Behold my Son will understand." And all these things, behold they are written [in the Psalms] in the parables of David, the son of Jesse, and in the Proverbs of Solomon his son, and in the words of Korah, and Ethan the Israelite, and in the words of Asaph, and in the rest of the Psalms also which the angel of the Spirit inspired.

22. (Namely) in those which have not the name written, and in the words of my father Amos, and of Hosea the prophet, and of Micah and Joel and Nahum and Jonah and Obadiah and Habakkuk and Haggai and Malachi, and in the words of Joseph the Just and in the words of Daniel.

CHAPTER 5

ON account of these visions, therefore, Beliar was wroth with Isaiah, and he dwelt in the heart of Manasseh and he sawed him in sunder with a wooden saw.

2. And when Isaiah was being sawn in sunder, Belchira stood up, accusing him, and all the false prophets stood up, laughing and rejoicing because of Isaiah.

3. And Belchira, with the aid of Mechembechus, stood up before Isaiah, [laughing] deriding;

4. And Belchira said to Isaiah: 'Say, "I have lied in all that I have spoken, and likewise the ways of Manasseh are good and right.

5. And the ways also of Belchira and of his associates are good."

6. And this he said to him when he began to be sawn in sunder.

7. But Isaiah was (absorbed) in a vision of the Lord, and though his eyes were open, he saw them (not).

8. And Belchira spake thus to Isaiah: "Say what I say unto thee and I will turn their hearts, and I will compel Manasseh and the princes of Judah and the people and all Jerusalem to reverence thee.

9. And Isaiah answered and said: "So far as I have utterance (I say): Damned and accused be thou and all they powers and all thy house.

10. For thou canst not take (from me) aught save the skin of my body."

11. And they seized and sawed in sunder Isaiah, the son of Amoz, with a wooden saw.

12. And Manasseh and Belchira and the false prophets and the princes and the people [and] all stood looking on.

13. And to the prophets who were with him he said before he had been sawn in sunder: "Go ye to the region of Tyre and Sidon; for for me only hath God mingled the cup."

14. And when Isaiah was being sawn in sunder, he neither cried aloud nor wept, but his lips spake with the Holy Spirit until he was sawn in twain.

15. This, Beliar did to Isaiah through Belchira and Manasseh; for Sammael was very wrathful against Isaiah from the days of Hezekiah, king of Judah, on account of the things which he had seen regarding the Beloved.

16. And on account of the destruction of Sammael, which he had seen through the Lord, while Hezekiah his father was still king. And he did according to the will of Satan.

CHAPTER 6

The Vision Which Isaiah the Son of Amoz Saw:

In the twentieth year of the reign of Hezekiah, king of Judah, came Isaiah the son of Amoz, and Josab the son of Isaiah to Hezekiah to Jerusalem from Galgala.

2. And (having entered) he sat down on the couch of the king, and they brought him a seat, but he would not sit (thereon).

3. And when Isaiah began to speak the words of faith and truth with King Hezekiah, all the princes of Israel were seated and the eunuchs and the councillors of the king. And there were there forty prophets and sons of the prophets: they had come from the villages and from the mountains and the plains when they had heard that Isaiah was coming from Galgala to Hezekiah.

4. And they had come to salute him and to hear his words.

5. And that he might place his hands upon them, and that they might prophesy and that he might hear their prophecy: and they were all before Isaiah.

6. And when Isaiah was speaking to Hezekiah the words of truth and faith, they all heard a door which one had opened and the voice of the Holy Spirit.

7. And the king summoned all the prophets and all the people who were found there, and they came. and Macaiah and the aged Ananias and Joel and Josab sat on his right hand (and on the left).

8. And it came to pass when they had all heard the voice of the Holy Spirit, they all worshipped on their knees, and glorified the God of truth, the Most High who is in the upper world and who sits on High the Holy One and who rest among His holy ones.

9. And they gave glory to Him who had thus bestowed a door in an alien world had bestowed (it) on a man.

10. And as he was speaking in the Holy Spirit in the hearing of all, he became silent and his mind was taken up from him and he saw not the men that stood before him.

11. Though his eyes indeed were open. Moreover his lips were silent and the mind in his body was taken up from him.

12. But his breath was in him; for he was seeing a vision.

13. And the angel who was sent to make him see was not of this firmament, nor was he of the angels of glory of this world, but he had come from the seventh heaven.

14. And the people who stood near did (not) think, but the circle of the prophets (did), that the holy Isaiah had been taken up.

15. And the vision which the holy Isaiah saw was not from this world but from the world which is hidden from the flesh.

16. And after Isaiah had seen this vision, he narrated it to Hezekiah, and to Josab his son and to the other prophets who had come.

17. But the leaders and the eunuchs and the people did not hear, but only Samna the scribe, and Ijoaqem, and Asaph the recorder; for these also were doers of righteousness, and the sweet smell of the Spirit was upon them. But the people had not heard; for Micaiah and Josab his son had caused them to go forth, when the wisdom of this world had been taken form him and he became as one dead.

CHAPTER 7

AND the vision which Isaiah saw, he told to Hezekiah and Josab his son and Micaiah and the rest of the prophets, (and) said:

2. At this moment, when I prophesied according to the (words) heard which ye heard, I saw a glorious angel not like unto the glory of the angels which I used always to see, but possessing such glory ad position that I cannot describe the glory of that angel.

3. And having seized me by my hand he raised me on high, and I said unto him: "Who art thou, and what is thy name, and whither art thou raising me on high? for strength was given me to speak with him."

4. And he said unto me: "When I have raised thee on high [though the (various) degrees] and made thee see the vision, on account of which I have been sent, then thou wilt understand who I am: but my name thou dost not know.

5. Because thou wilt return into this thy body, but whither I am raising thee on high, thou wilt see; for for this purpose have I been sent."

6. And I rejoiced because he spake courteously to me.

7. And he said unto me: "Hast thou rejoiced because I have spoken courteously to thee?" And he said: "And thou wilt see how a grater also that I am will speak courteously and peaceably with thee."

8. And His Father also who is greater thou wilt see; for for this purpose have I been sent from the seventh heaven in order to explain all these things unto thee."

9. And we ascended to the firmament, I and he, and there I saw Sammael and his hosts, and there was great fighting therein and the angels of Satan were envying one another.

10. And as above so on the earth also; for the likeness of that which is in the firmament is here ont he earth.

11. And I said unto the angel (who was with me): "(What is this war and) what is this envying?"

12. And he said unto me: "So has it been since this world was made until now, and this war (will continue) till He, whom thou shalt see will come and destroy him."

13. And afterwards he caused me to ascend (to that which is) above the firmament: which is the (first) heaven.

14. And there I saw a throne in the midst, and on his right and on his left were angels.

15. And (the angels on the left were) not like unto the angels who stood on the right, but those who stood on the right had the greater glory, and they all praised with one voice, and there was a throne in the midst, and those who were out he left gave praise after them; but their voice was not such as the voice of those on the right, nor their praise like the praise of those.

16. And I asked the angel who conducted me, and I said unto him: "To whom is this praise sent?"

17. And he said unto me: "(it is sent) to the praise of (Him who sitteth in) the seventh heaven: to Him who rests in the holy world, and to His Beloved, whence I have been sent to thee. [Thither is it sent.]"

18. And again, he made me to ascend to the second heaven. now the height of that heaven is the same as from the haven to the earth [and to the firmament].

19. And (I saw there, as) in the first heaven, angels on the right and on the left, and a throne in the midst, and the praise of the angels in the second heaven; and he who sat on the throne in the second heaven was more glorious than all (the rest).

20. And there was great glory in the second heaven, and the praise also was not like the praise of those who were in the first heaven.

21. And I fell on my face to worship him, but he angel who conducted me did not permit me, but said

unto me: "Worship neither throne nor angel which belongs to the six heavens - for for this cause I was sent to conduct thee j- until I tell thee in the seventh heaven.

22. For above all the heavens and their angels has thy throne been placed, and thy garments and thy crown which thou shalt see."

23. And I rejoiced with great joy, that those who love the Most High and His Beloved will afterwards ascend thither by the angel of the Holy Spirit.

24. And he raise me to the third heaven, and in like manner I saw those upon the right and upon the left, and there was a throne there in the midst; but the memorial of this world is there unheard of.

25. And I said to the angel who was with me; for the glory of my appearance was undergoing transformation as I ascended to each heaven in turn: "Nothing of the vanity of that world is here named."

26. And he answered me, and said unto me: "Nothing is named on account of its weakness, and nothing is hidden there of what is done."

27. And I wished to learn how it is know, and he answered me saying: "When I have raised thee to the seventh heaven whence I was sent, to that which is above these, then thou shalt know that there is nothing hidden from the thrones and from those who dwell in the heavens and from the angels. And the praise wherewith they praised and glory of him who sat on the throne was great, and the glory of the angels on the right hand and on the left was beyond that of the heaven which was below them.

28. And again he raised me to the fourth heaven, and the height from the third to the height from the third to the forth heaven was greater than from the earth to the firmament.

29. And there again I saw those who were on the right hand and those who were on the left, and him who sat on the throne was in the midst, and there also they were praising.

30. And the praise and glory of the angels on the right was greater than that of those on the left.

31. And again the glory of him who sat on the throne was greater than that of the angels on the right, and their glory was beyond that of those who were below.

32. And he raised me to the fifth heaven.

33. And again I saw those upon the right hand and on the left, and him who sat on the throne possessing greater glory that those of the forth heaven.

34. And the glory of those on the right hand was greater than that of those on the left [from the third to the fourth].

35. And the glory of him who was on the throne was greater than that of the angels on the right hand.

36. And their praise was more glorious than that of the fourth heaven.

37. And I praised Him, who is not named and the Only-begotten who dwelleth in the heavens, whose name is not known to any flesh, who has bestowed such glory on the several heaves, and who makes great the glory of the angels, and more excellent the glory of Him who sitteth on the throne.

CHAPTER 8

AND again he raised me into the air of the sixth heaven, and I saw such glory as I had not seen in the five heavens.

2. For I saw angels possessing great glory.

3. And the praise there was holy and wonderful.

4. And I said to the angel who conducted me: "What is this which I see, my Lord?"

5. And he said: "I am not thy lord, but thy fellow servant."

6. And again I asked him, and I said unto him: "Why are there not angelic fellow servants (on the left)?"

7. And he said: "From the sixth heaven there are no longer angels on the left, nor a throne set in the midst, but (they are directed) by the power of the seventh heaven, where dwelleth He that is not named and the Elect One, whose name has not been made known, and none of the heavens can learn His name.

8. For it is He alone to whose voice all the heavens and thrones give answer. I have therefore been empowered and sent to raise thee here that thou mayest see this glory.

9. And that thou mayest see the Lord of all those heavens and these thrones.

10. Undergoing (successive) transformation until He resembles your form and likeness.

11. I indeed say unto thee, Isaiah; No man about to return into a body of that world has ascended or seen what thou seest or perceived what thou hast perceived and what thou wilt see.

12. For it has been permitted to thee in the lot of the Lord to come hither. [And from thence comes the power of the sixth heaven and of the air]."

13. And I magnified my Lord with praise, in that through His lot I should come hither.

14. And he said: "Hear, furthermore, therefore, this also from thy fellow servant: when from the body by the will of God thou hast ascended hither, then thou wilt receive the garment which thou seest, and likewise other numbered garments laid up (there) thou wilt see.

15. And then thou wilt become equal to the angels of the seventh heaven.

16. And he raised me up into the sixth heaven, and there were no (angels) on the left, nor a throne in

the midst, but all had one appearance and their (power of) praise was equal.

17. And (power) was given to me also, and I also praised along with them and that angel also, and our praise was like theirs. 18. And there they all named the primal Father and His Beloved, the Christ, and the Holy Spirit, all with one voice.

19. And (their voice) was not like the voice of the angels in the five heavens.

20. [Nor like their discourse] but the voice was different there, and there was much light there.

21. And then, when I was in the sixth heaven I thought the light which I had seen in the five heavens to be but darkness.

22. And I rejoiced and praised Him who hath bestowed such lights on those who wait for His promise.

23. And I besought the angel who conducted me that I should not henceforth return to the carnal world.

24. I say indeed unto you, Hezekiah and Josab my son and Micaiah, that there is much darkness here.

25. And the angel who conducted me discovered what I thought and said: "If in this light thou dost rejoice, how much more wilt thou rejoice, when in the seventh heaven thou seest the light where is the Lord and His Beloved [whence I have been sent, who is to be called "Son" in this world.

26. Not (yet) hath been manifested he shall be in the corruptible world] and the garments, and the thrones, and the crowns which are laid up for the righteous, for those who trust in that Lord who will descend in your form. For the light which is there is great and wonderful.

27. And as concerning thy not returning into the body thy days are not yet fulfilled for coming here."

28. And when I heard (that) I was troubled, and he said: "Do not be troubled."

CHAPTER 9
AND he took me into the air of the seventh heaven, and moreover I heard a voice saying: "How far will he ascend that dwelleth in the flesh?" And I feared and trembled.

2. And when I trembled, behold, I heard from hence another voice being sent forth, and saying: "It is permitted to the holy Isaiah to ascend hither; for here is his garment."

3. And I asked the angel who was with me and said: "Who is he who forbade me and who is he who permitted me to ascend?"

4. And he said unto me: "He who forbade thee, is he who is over the praise-giving of the sixth heaven.

5. And He who permitted thee, this is thy Lord God, the Lord Christ, who will be called "Jesus" in the world, but His name thou canst not hear till thou hast ascended out of thy body."

6. And he raised me up into the seventh heaven, and I saw there a wonderful light and angels innumerable.

7. And there I saw the holy Abel and all the righteous.

8. And there I saw Enoch and all who were with him, stript of the garments of the flesh, and I saw them in their garments of the upper world, and they were like angels, standing there in great glory.

9. And there I saw Enoch and all who were with him, stript of the garments of the flesh, and I saw them in their garments of the upper world, and they were like angels, standing there in great glory.

10. But they sat not on their thrones, nor were their crowns of glory on them.

11. And I asked the angel who was with me: "How is it that they have received the garments, but have not the thrones and the crowns?"

12. And he said unto me: "Crowns and thrones of glory they do not receive, till the Beloved will descend in the form in which you will see Him descend [will descend, I say] into the world in the last days the Lord, who will be called Christ.

13. Nevertheless they see and know whose will be thrones, and whose the crowns when He has descended and been made in your form, and they will think that He is flesh and is a man.

14. And the god of that world will stretch forth his hand against the Son, and they will crucify Him on a tree, and will slay Him not knowing who He is.

15. And thus His descent, as you will see, will be hidden even from the heavens, so that it will not be known who He is.

16. And when He hath plundered the angel of death, He will ascend on the third day, [and he will remain in that world five hundred and forty-five days].

17. And then many of the righteous will ascend with Him, whose spirits do not receive their garments till the Lord Christ ascend and they ascend with Him.

18. Then indeed they will receive their [garments and] thrones and crowns, when He has ascended into the seventh heaven."

19. And I said unto him that which I had asked him in the third heaven:

20. "Show me how everything which is done in that world is here made known."

21. And whilst I was still speaking with him, behold one of the angels who stood nigh, more glorious than the glory of that angel, who had raised me up from the world.

22. Showed me a book, [but not as a book of this world] and he opened it, and the book was written, but not as a book of this world. And he gave (it) to me and I read it, and lo! the deeds of the children of Israel were written therein, and the deeds of those whom I know (not), my son Josab.

23. And I said: "In truth, there is nothing hidden in the seventh heaven, which is done in this world."

24. And I saw there many garments laid up, and many thrones and many crowns.

25. And I said to the angel: "Whose are these garments and thrones and crowns?"

26. And he said unto me: "These garments many from that world will receive, believing in the words of That One, who shall be named as I told thee, and they will observe those things, and believe in them, and believe in His cross: for them are these laid up."

27. And I saw a certain One standing, whose glory surpassed that of all, and His glory was great and wonderful.

28. And after I had seen Him, all the righteous whom I had seen and also the angels whom I had seen came to Him. And Adam and Abel and Seth and all the righteous first drew near and worshipped Him, and they all praised Him with one voice, and I myself also gave praise with them, and my giving of praise was as theirs.

29. And then all the angels drew nigh and worshipped and gave praise.

30. And I was (again) transformed and became like an angel.

31. And thereupon the angel who conducted me said to me: "Worship this One," and I worshipped and praised.

32. And the angel said unto me: "This is the Lord of all the praise-givings which thou hast seen."

33. And whilst he was still speaking, I saw another Glorious One who was like Him, and the righteous drew nigh and worshipped and praised, and I praised together with them. But my glory was not transformed into accordance with their form.

34. And thereupon the angels drew near and worshipped Him.

35. And I saw the Lord and the second angel, and they were standing.

36. And the second whom I saw was on he left of my Lord. And I asked: "Who is this?" and he said unto me: "Worship Him, for He is the angel of the Holy Spirit, who speaketh in thee and the rest of the righteous."

37. And I saw the great glory, the eyes of my spirit being open, and I could not thereupon see, nor yet could the angel who was with me, nor all the angels whom I had seen worshipping my Lord.

38. But I saw the righteous beholding with great power the glory of that One.

39. And my Lord drew nigh to me and the angel of the Spirit and He said: "See how it is given to thee to see God, and on thy account power is given to the angel who is with thee."

40. And I saw how my Lord and the angel of the Spirit worshipped, and they both together praised God.

41. And thereupon all the righteous drew near and worshipped.

42. And the angels drew near and worshipped and all the angels praised.

CHAPTER 10
AND thereupon I heard the voices and the giving of praise, which I had heard in each of the six heavens, ascending and being heard there:

2. And all were being sent up to that Glorious One whose glory I could not behold.

3. And I myself was hearing and beholding the praise (which was given) to Him.

4. And the Lord and the angel of the Spirit were beholding all and hearing all.

5. And all the praises which are sent up from the six heavens are not only heard, but seen.

6. And I heard the angel who conducted me and he said: "This is the Most High of the high ones, dwelling in the holy world, and resting in His holy ones, who will be called by the Holy Spirit through the lips of the righteous the Father of the Lord."

7. And I heard the voice of the Most High, the Father of my Lord, saying to my Lord Christ who will be called Jesus:

8. "Go forth and descent through all the heavens, and thou wilt descent to the firmament and that world: to the angel in Sheol thou wilt descend, but to Haguel thou wilt not go.

9. And thou wilt become like unto the likeness of all who are in the five heavens.

10. And thou wilt be careful to become like the form of the angels of the firmament [and the angels also who are in Sheol].

11. And none of the angels of that world shall know that Thou art with Me of the seven heavens and of their angels.

12. And they shall not know that Thou art with Me, till with a loud voice I have called (to) the heavens, and their angels and their lights, (even) unto the sixth heaven, in order that you mayest judge and destroy the princes and angels and gods of that world, and the world that is dominated by them:

13. For they have denied Me and said: "We alone are and there is none beside us."

14. And afterwards from the angels of death Thou wilt ascend to Thy place. And Thou wilt not be transformed in each heaven, but in glory wilt Thou ascend and sit on My right hand.

15. And thereupon the princes and powers of that world will worship Thee."

16. These commands I heard the Great Glory giving to my Lord.

17. And so I saw my Lord go forth from the seventh heaven into the sixth heaven.

18. And the angel who conducted me [from this world was with me and] said unto me: "Understand, Isaiah, and see the transformation and descent of the Lord will appear."

19. And I saw, and when the angels saw Him, thereupon those in the sixth heaven praised and lauded Him; for He had not been transformed after the shape of the angels there, and they praised Him and I also praised with them.

20. And I saw when He descended into the fifth heaven, that in the fifth heaven He made Himself like unto the form of the angels there, and they did not praise Him (nor worship Him); for His form was like unto theirs.

21. And then He descended into the forth heaven, and made Himself like unto the form of the angels there.

22. And when they saw Him, they did not praise or laud Him; for His form was like unto their form.

23. And again I saw when He descended into the third heaven, and He made Himself like unto the form of the angels in the third heaven.

24. And those who kept the gate of the (third) heaven demanded the password, and the Lord gave (it) to them in order that He should not be recognized. And when they saw Him, they did not praise or laud Him; for His form was like unto their form.

25. And again I saw when He descended into the second heaven, and again He gave the password there; those who kept the gate proceeded to demand and the Lord to give.

26. And I saw when He made Himself like unto the form of the angels in the second heaven, and they saw Him and they did not praise Him; for His form was like unto their form.

27. And again I saw when He descended into the first heaven, and there also He gave the password to those who kept the gate, and He made Himself like unto the form of the angels who were on the left of that throne, and they neither praised nor lauded Him; for His form was like unto their form.

28. But as for me no one asked me on account of the angel who conducted me.

29. And again He descended into the firmament where dwelleth the ruler of this world, and He gave the password to those on the left, and His form was like theirs, and they did not praise Him there; but they were envying one another and fighting; for here there is a power of evil and envying about trifles.

30. And I saw when He descended and made Himself like unto the angels of the air, and He was like one of them.

31. And He gave no password; for one was plundering and doing violence to another.

CHAPTER 11

AFTER this I saw, and the angel who spoke with me, who conducted me, said unto me: "Understand, Isaiah son of Amoz; for for this purpose have I been sent from God."

2. And I indeed saw a woman of the family of David the prophet, named Mary, and Virgin, and she was espoused to a man named Joseph, a carpenter, and he also was of the seed and family of the righteous David of Bethlehem Judah.

3. And he came into his lot. And when she was espoused, she was found with child, and Joseph the carpenter was desirous to put her away.

4. But the angel of the Spirit appeared in this world, and after that Joseph did not put her away, but kept Mary and did not reveal this matter to any one.

5. And he did not approach May, but kept her as a holy virgin, though with child.

6. And he did not live with her for two months.

7. And after two months of days while Joseph was in his house, and Mary his wife, but both alone.

8. It came to pass that when they were alone that Mary straight-way looked with her eyes and saw a small babe, and she was astonished.

9. And after she had been astonished, her womb was found as formerly before she had conceived.

10. And when her husband Joseph said unto her: "What has astonished thee?" his eyes were opened and he saw the infant and praised God, because into his portion God had come.

11. And a voice came to them: "Tell this vision to no one."

12. And the story regarding the infant was noised broad in Bethlehem.

13. Some said: "The Virgin Mary hath borne a child, before she was married two months."

14. And many said: "She has not borne a child, nor has a midwife gone up (to her), nor have we heard the cries of (labour) pains." And they were all blinded respecting Him and they all knew regarding Him, though they knew not whence He was.

15. And they took Him, and went to Nazareth in Galilee.

16. And I saw, O Hezekiah and Josab my son, and I declare to the other prophets also who are standing by, that (this) hath escaped all the heavens and all the princes and all the gods of this world.

17. And I saw: In Nazareth He sucked the breast as a babe and as is customary in order that He might not be recognized.

18. And when He had grown up he worked great signs and wonders in the land of Israel and of Jerusalem.

19. And after this the adversary envied Him and roused the children of Israel against Him, not knowing who He was, and they delivered Him to the king, and crucified Him, and He descended to the angel (of Sheol).

20. In Jerusalem indeed I was Him being crucified on a tree:

21. And likewise after the third day rise again and remain days.

22. And the angel who conducted me said: "Understand, Isaiah": and I saw when He sent out the Twelve Apostles and ascended.

23. And I saw Him, and He was in the firmament, but He had not changed Himself into their form, and all the angels of the firmament and the Satans saw Him and they worshipped.

24. And there was much sorrow there, while they said: "How did our Lord descend in our midst, and we perceived not the glory [which has been upon Him], which we see has been upon Him from the sixth heaven?"

25. And He ascended into the second heaven, and He did not transform Himself, but all the angels who were on the right and on the left and the throne in the midst.

26. Both worshipped Him and praised Him and said: "How did our Lord escape us whilst descending, and we perceived not?"

27. And in like manner He ascended into the third heaven, and they praised and said in like manner.

28. And in the fourth heaven and in the fifth also they said precisely after the same manner.

29. But there was one glory, and from it He did not change Himself.

30. And I saw when He ascended into the sixth heaven, and they worshipped and glorified Him.

31. But in all the heavens the praise increased (in volume).

32. And I saw how He ascended into the seventh heaven, and all the righteous and all the angels praised Him. And then I saw Him sit down on the right hand of that Great Glory whose glory I told you that I could not behold.

33. And also the angel of the Holy Spirit I saw sitting on the left hand.

34. And this angel said unto me: "Isaiah, son of Amoz, it is enough for thee;... for thou hast seen what no child of flesh has seen.

35. And thou wilt return into thy garment (of the flesh) until thy days are completed. Then thou wilt come hither."

36. These things Isaiah saw and told unto all that stood before him, and they praised. And he spake to Hezekiah the King and said: "I have spoken these things."

37. Both the end of this world;

38. And all this vision will be consummated in the last generations.

39. And Isaiah made him swear that he would not tell (it) to the people of Israel, nor give these words to any man to transcribe.

40. ...such things ye will read. and watch ye in the Holy Spirit in order they ye may receive your garments and thrones and crowns of glory which are laid up in the seventh heaven.

41. On account of these visions and prophecies Sammael Satan sawed in sunder Isaiah the son of Amoz, the prophet, by the hand of Manasseh.

42. And all these things Hezekiah delivered to Manasseh in the twenty-sixth year.

43. But Manasseh did not remember them nor place these things in his heart, but becoming the servant of Satan he was destroyed. Here endeth the vision of Isaiah the prophet with his ascension.

The Shepherd of Hermas

Vision 1

1:1 The master, who raised me sold me to a lady, Rhoda in Rome. After many years, I met her again, and began to love her as a sister.

1:2 After a period of time I saw her bathing in the river Tiber; and I gave her my hand, and led her out of the river. When I saw her beauty, I thought to myself, "I would be happy if I had such a one as a wife both because of her beauty and character." I merely thought about this and nothing more.

1:3 After a while, as I was travelling to Cumae, and praising God because of his creatures, for their greatness and beauty and power. As I walked I fell asleep. And a Spirit took me, and lifted me away through a land that had no path and through which no man could pass. The place has cliffs, and was broken into clefts by rivers. When I had crossed the river, I came into the level country, and knelt down, and began to pray to the Lord and to confess my sins.

1:4 Now, while I prayed, heaven was opened, and I saw the lady, whom I had desired, greeting me from heaven, saying, "Good day, Hermas."

1:5 And, looking at her, I said to her, "Lady, what are you doing here?" Then she answered me, "I was taken up, that I might convict you of your sins before the Lord."

1:6 I said to her, "Dost you now convict me?" "Nay, not so," said she, "but hear the words, that I shall say to you. God, Who dwelled in the heavens, and created out of nothing the things which are, and increased and multiplied them for His holy Church's sake, is wroth with you, for that you didst sin against me."

1:7 I answered her and said, "Sin against you? In what way? Did I ever speak an unseemly word unto you? Did I not always regard you as a goddess? Did I not always respect you as a sister? How couldst you falsely charge me, lady, with such villainy and uncleanness?

1:8 "Laughing she said unto me, "The desire after evil entered into your heart. No, think you not that it is an evil deed for a righteous man, if the evil desire should enter into his heart? It is indeed a sin and a great one too," said she; "for the righteous man entertained righteous purposes. While then his purposes are righteous, his repute stands steadfast in the heavens, and he finds the Lord easily propitiated in all that he does. But they that entertain evil purposes in their hearts, bring upon themselves death an captivity, especially they that claim for themselves this present work and boast in its riches, and hold fast not to the good things that are to come.

1:9 Their souls shall rue it, seeing that they have no hope, but have abandoned themselves and their life. But do you pray unto God and He shall heal your own sins, and those of thy whole house, and of all the saints."

2:1 As soon as she had spoken these words the heavens were shut and I was given over to horror and grief Then I said within myself "If this sin is recorded against me, how can I be saved? Or how shall I propitiate God for my sins which are full-blown? Or with which words shall I entreat the Lord that He may be propitious unto me?

2:2 While I was advising and discussing these matters in my heart, I see, before me a great white chair of snow-white wool; and there came an aged lady in glistening raiment, having a book in her hands, and she sat down alone, and she saluted me, "Good morrow, Hermas." Then I grieved and weeping, said, "Good morrow, lady."

2:3 And she said to me "Why so gloomy, Hermas, you that art patient and good-tempered and art always smiling? Why so downcast in thy looks, and far from cheerful?" And I said to her, "Because of an excellent lady's saying that I had sinned against her."

2:4 Then she said, "Far be this thing from the servant of God! Nevertheless the thought did enter into thy heart concerning her. Now to the servants of God such a purpose brings sin. For it is an evil and mad purpose to overtake a devout spirit that has been already approved, that it should desire an evil deed, and especially if it be Hermas the temperate, who abstained from every evil desire, and is full of all simplicity and of great guilelessness.

3:1 "Yet it is not for this that God is wroth with you, but that you may convert thy family, that has done wrong against the Lord and against you their parents. But out of fondness for thy children you didst not admonish thy family, but didst suffer it to become fearfully corrupt. Therefore the Lord is wroth with you. But He will heal all thy past sins, which have been committed in thy family; for by reason of their sins and iniquities you hast been corrupted by the affairs of this world.

3:2 But the great mercy of the Lord had pity on you and thy family, and will strengthen you, and establish you in His glory. Only be not you careless, but take courage, and strengthen thy family. For as the smith hammering his work conquers the task which he wills, so also doth righteous discourse repeated daily conquer all evil. Cease not therefore to reprove thy children; for I know that if they shall repent with all their heart, they shall be written in the books of life with the saints."

3:3 After these words of hers had ceased, she said unto me, "Wilt you listen to me as I read?" Then say I, "Yes, lady." She said to me, "Be attentive, and hear the glories of God" I listened with attention and with wonder to that which I had no power to remember; for all the words were terrible, such as man cannot bear. The last words however I remembered, for they were suitable for us and gentle.

3:4 "Behold, the God of Hosts, Who by His invisible and mighty power and by His great wisdom created the world, and by His glorious purpose clothed His creation with comeliness, and by His strong word fixed the heaven, and founded the earth upon the waters, and by His own wisdom and providence formed His holy Church, which also He blessed-behold, He removed the heavens and the mountains and the hills and the seas, and all things are made level for His elect, that He may fulfill to them the promise which He promised with great glory and rejoicing, if so be that they shall keep the ordinances of God, which they received, with great faith."

4:1 When then she finished reading and arose from her chair, there came four young men, and they took away the chair, and departed towards the East.

4:2 Then she called me unto her, and she touched my breast, and said to me, "Did my reading please you?" And I say unto her, "Lady, these last words please me, but the former were difficult and hard." Then she spoke to me, saying, "These last words are for the righteous, but the former are for the heathen and the rebellious."

4:3 While she yet spoke with me, two men appeared, and took her by the arms, and they departed, whither the chair also had gone, towards the East. And she smiled as she departed and, as she was going, she said to me, "Play the man, Hermas."

Vision 2

1[5]:1 I was on the way to Cumae, at the same season as last year, and called to mind my last year's vision as I walked; and again a Spirit took me, and carried me away to the same place as last year.

1[5]:2 When then I arrived at the place, I fell upon my knees, and began to pray to the Lord, and to glorify His name, for that he counted me worthy, and made known unto me my former sins.

1[5]:3 But after I had risen up from prayer, I behold before me the aged lady, whom also I had seen last year, walking and reading a little book. And she said to me, "Canst you report these things to the elect of God?" I say unto her, "Lady, I cannot recollect so much; but give me the little book, that I may copy it." "Take it," said she, "and be sure and return it to me."

1[5]:4 I took it, and retiring to a certain spot in the country I copied it letter for letter: for I could not make out the syllables. When then I had finished the letters of the book, suddenly the book was snatched out of my hand; but by whom I did not see.

2[6]:1 Now after fifteen days, when I had fasted and entreated the Lord earnestly, the knowledge of the writing was revealed to me. And this is what was written:--

2[6]:2 "Your seed, Hermas, have sinned against God, and have blasphemed the Lord, and have betrayed their parents through great wickedness, yea, they have got the name of betrayers of parents, and yet they did not profit by their betrayal; and they still further added to their sins wanton deeds and reckless wickedness; and so the measure of their transgressions was filled up.

2[6]:3 But make these words known to all thy children, and to thy wife who shall be as thy sister; for she too refrained not from using her tongue, wherewith she doeth evil. But, when she hears these words, she will refrain, and will find mercy.

2[6]:4 After that you hast made known unto them all these words, which the Master commanded me that they should be revealed unto you, then all their sins which they sinned aforetime are forgiven to them; yea, and to all the saints that have sinned unto this day, if they repent with their whole heart, and remove double-mindedness from their heart.

2[6]:5 For the Master swore by His own glory, as concerning His elect; that if, now that this day has been set as a limit, sin shall hereafter be committed, they shall not find salvation; for repentance for the righteous has an end; the days of repentance are accomplished for all the saints; whereas for the Gentiles there is repentance until the last day.

2[6]:6 You shall therefore say unto the elders of the Church, that they direct their paths in righteousness, that they may receive in full the promises with abundant glory.

2[6]:7 you therefore that work righteousness be steadfast, and be not double-minded, that you may have admission with the holy angels. Blessed are you, as many as endure patiently the great tribulation that cometh, and as many as shall not deny their life.

2[6]:8 For the Lord swear concerning His Son, that those who denied their Lord should be rejected from their life, even they that are now about to deny Him in the coming days; but to those who denied Him aforetime, to them mercy was given of His great loving kindness.

3[7]:1 "But do you, Hermas, no longer bear a grudge against thy children, neither suffer thy sister to have her way, so that they may be purified from their former sins. For they shall be chastised with a righteous chastisement, unless you bear a grudge against them thyself. The bearing of a grudge worked death. But you, Hermas, hast had great tribulations of your own, by reason of the transgressions of thy family, because you had no care for them. For you was neglectful of them, and was mixed up with your evil transactions.

3[7]:2 But herein is thy salvation, in that you didst not depart from the living God, and in thy simplicity and thy great continence. These have saved you, if you abide therein; and they save all who do such things, and walk in guilelessness and simplicity. These men prevail over all wickedness, and continue unto life eternal.

3[7]:3 Blessed are all they that work righteousness. They shall never be destroyed.

3[7]:4 But you shall say to Maximus, "Behold tribulation cometh (upon you), if you think fit to deny a second time. The Lord is nigh unto them that turn unto him, as it is written in Eldad and Modat, who prophesied to the people in the wilderness."

4[8]:1 Now, brethren, a revelation was made unto me in my sleep by a youth of exceeding fair form, who said to me, "Whom think you the aged woman, from whom you received the book, to be?" I say, "The Sibyl" "You art wrong," said he, "she is not." "Who then is she?" I say. "The Church," said he. I said unto him, "Wherefore then is she aged?" "Because," said he, "she was created before all things; therefore is she aged; and for her sake the world was framed."

4[8]:2 And afterwards I saw a vision in my house. The aged woman came, and asked me, if I had already given the book to the elders. I said that I had not given it. "You hast done well," she said, "for I have words to add. When then I shall have finished all the words, it shall be made known by thy means to all the elect.

4[8]:3 You shall therefore write two little books, and shall send one to Clement, and one to Grapte. So Clement shall send to the foreign cities, for this is his duty; while Grapte shall instruct the widows and the orphans. But you shall read (the book) to this city along with the elders that preside over the Church.

Vision 3

1[9]:1 The third vision, which I saw, brethren, was as follows.

1[9]:2 After fasting often, and entreating the Lord to declare unto me the revelation which He promised to show me by the mouth of the aged woman, that very night the aged woman was seen of me, and she said to me, "Seeing that you art so importunate and eager to know all things, come into the country where you abide, and about the fifth hour I will appear, and will show you what you ought to see."

1[9]:3 I asked her, saying, "Lady, to what part of the country?" "Where you wilt," said she. I selected a beautiful and retired spot; but before I spoke to her and named the spot, she said to me, "I will come, whither you will."

1[9]:4 I went then, brethren, into the country, and I counted up the hours, and came to the place where I appointed her to come, and I see an ivory couch placed there, and on the couch there lay a linen cushion, and on the cushion was spread a coverlet of fine linen of flax.

1[9]:5 When I saw these things so ordered, and no one in the place, I was amazed, and a fit of trembling seized me, and my hair stood on end; and a fit of shuddering came upon me, because I was alone. When then I recovered myself, and remembered the glory of God, and took courage, I knelt down and confessed my sins to the Lord once more, as I had done on the former occasion.

1[9]:6 Then she came with six young men, the same whom I had seen before, and she stood by me, and listened attentively to me, as I prayed and confessed my sins to the Lord. And she touched me, and said: "Hermas, make an end of constantly entreating for thy sins; entreat also for righteousness, that you may take some part forthwith to thy family."

1[9]:7 Then she raised me by the hand, and led me to the couch, and said to the young men, "Go you, and build."

1[9]:8 And after the young men had retired and we were left alone, she said to me, "Sit down here." I say to her, "Lady, let the elders sit down first." "Do as I bid you," said she, "sit down."

1[9]:9 When then I wanted to sit down on the right side, she would not allow me, but beckoned me with her hand that I should sit on the left side. As then I was musing thereon, and was sad because she would not permit me to sit on the right side, she said to me, "Art you sad, Hermas? The place on the right side is for others, even for those who have already been well-pleasing to God, and have suffered for the Name's sake. But you lack much that you should sit with them; but as you abide in thy simplicity, even so, and you shall sit with them, you and as many as shall have done their deeds, and have suffered what they suffered."

2[10]:1 "What did they suffer?" say I. "Listen," said she. "Stripes, imprisonments, great tribulations, crosses, wild beasts, for the Name's sake. Therefore to them belongs the right side of the Holiness--to them, and to all who shall suffer for the Name. But for the rest is the left side. Howbeit, to both, to them that sit on the right, and to them that sit on the left, are the same gifts, and the same promises, only they sit on the right and have a certain glory.

2[10]:2 You indeed art very desirous to sit on the right with them, but thy shortcomings are many; yet you shall be purified from thy shortcomings; yea, and all that are not double-minded shall be purified from all their sins unto this day."

2[10]:3 When she had said this, she wished to depart; but, falling at her feet, I entreated her by the Lord that she would show me the vision which she promised.

2[10]:4 Then she again took me by the hand, and raised me, and seated me on the couch at the left hand, while she herself sat on the right. And lifting up a certain glistening rod, she said to me, "See you a great thing?" I say to her, "Lady, I see nothing." She said to me, "Look you; do you not see in front of you a great tower being built upon the waters, of glistening square stones?"

2[10]:5 Now the tower was being built foursquare by the six young men that came with her. And countless other men were bringing stones, some of them from the deep, and others from the land, and were handing them to the six young men. And they took them and built.

2[10]:6 The stones that were dragged from the deep they placed in every case, just as they were, into the building, for they had been shaped, and they fitted in their joining with the other stones; and they adhered so closely one with another that their joining could not possibly be detected; and the building of the tower appeared as if it were built of one stone.

2[10]:7 But of the other stones which were brought from the dry land, some they threw away, and some they put into the building; and others they broke in pieces, and threw to a distance from the tower.

2[10]:8 Now many other stones were lying round the tower, and they did not use them for the building; for some of them were mildewed, and others had cracks in them, and others were too short, and others were white and round, and did not fit into the building.

2[10]:9 And I saw other stones thrown to a distance from the tower, and coming to the way, and yet not staying in the way, but rolling to where there was no way; and others falling into the fire and burning there; and others falling near the waters, and yet not able to roll into the water, although they desired to roll and to come to the water.

3[11]:1 When she had shown me these things, she wished to hurry away. I say to her, "Lady, what advantage is it to me to have seen these things, and yet not to know what the things mean? "She answered and said unto me, "You art an over-curious fellow, in desiring to know all that concerns the tower." "Yea, lady," I said, "that I may announce it to my brethren, and that they [may be the more gladdened and] when they hear [these things] they may know the Lord in great glory." Then said she,

3[11]:2 "Many shall hear; but when they hear, some of them shall be glad, and others shall weep. Yet even these latter, if they hear and repent, shall likewise be glad. Hear you therefore the parables of the tower; for I will reveal all things unto you. And trouble me no more about revelation; for these revelations have an end, seeing that they have been completed. Nevertheless you wilt not cease asking for revelations; for you art shameless."

3[11]:3 The tower, which you see building, is myself, the Church, which was seen of you both now and aforetime. Ask, therefore, what you will concerning the tower, and I will reveal it unto you, that you may rejoice with the saints."

3[11]:4 I say unto her, "Lady, since you didst hold me worthy once for all, that you should reveal all things to me, reveal them." Then she said to me, "Whatsoever is possible to be revealed to you, shall be revealed. Only let thy heart be with God, and doubt not in thy mind about that which you sees."

3[11]:5 I asked her, "Wherefore is the tower built upon waters, lady?" "I told you so before," said she, "and indeed you do enquire diligently. So by thy enquiry you discovered the truth. Hear then why the tower is built upon waters; it is because your life is saved and shall be saved by water. But the tower has been founded by the word of the Almighty and Glorious Name, and is strengthened by the unseen power of the Master."

4[12]:1 I answered and said unto her, "Lady, this thing is great and marvelous. But the six young men that build, who are they, lady?" "These are the holy angels of God, that were created first of all, unto whom the Lord delivered all His creation to increase and to build it, and to be masters of all creation. By their hands therefore the building of the tower will be accomplished."

4[12]:2 "And who are the others who are bringing the stones in?" "They also are holy angels of God; but these six are superior to them. The building of the tower then shall be accomplished, and all alike shall rejoice in the (completed) circle of the tower, and shall glorify God that the building of the tower was accomplished."

4[12]:3 I enquired of her, saying, "Lady, I could wish to know concerning the end of the stones, and their power, of what kind it is." She answered and said unto me, "It is not that you of all men art especially worthy that it should be revealed to you; for there are others before you, and better than you art, unto whom these visions ought to have been revealed. But that the name of God may be glorified, it has been revealed to you, all shall be revealed, for the sake of the doubtful-minded, who question in their hearts whether these things are so or not. Tell them that all these things are true, and that there is nothing beside the truth, but that all are steadfast, and valid, and established on a firm foundation.

5[13]:1 "Hear now concerning the stones that go to the building The stones that are squared and white, and that fit together in their joints, these are the apostles and bishops and teachers and deacons, who walked after the holiness of God, and exercised their office of bishop and teacher and deacon in purity and sanctity for the elect of God, some of them already fallen on sleep, and others still living. And because they always agreed with one another, they both had peace among themselves and listened one to another. Therefore their joinings fit together in the building of the tower."

5[13]:2 "But they that are dragged from the deep, and placed in the building, and that fit together in their joinings with the other stones that are already built in, who are they?" "These are they that suffered for the name of the Lord."

5[13]:3 "But the other stones that are brought from the dry land, I would fain know who these are, lady." She said, "Those that go to the building, and yet are not hewn, these the Lord has approved because they walked in the uprightness of the Lord, and rightly performed His commandments."

5[13]:4 "But they that are brought and placed in the building, who are they?" "They are young in the faith, and faithful; but they are warned by the angels to do good, because wickedness was found in them."

5[13]:5 "But those whom they rejected and threw away, who are they?" "These have sinned, and desire to repent, therefore they were not cast to a great distance from the tower, because they will be useful for the building, if they repent. They then that shall repent, if they repent, will be strong in the faith, if they repent now while the tower is building. But if the building shall be finished, they have no more any place, but shall be castaways. This privilege only they have, that they lie near the tower.

5[13]:1 But wouldst you know about them that are broken in pieces, and cast away far from the tower? These are the sons of lawlessness. They received the faith in hypocrisy, and no wickedness was absent from them. Therefore they have not salvation, for they are not useful for building by reason of their wickednesses. Therefore they were broken up and thrown far away by reason of the wrath of the Lord, for they excited Him to wrath.

5[13]:2 But the rest whom you hast seen lying in great numbers, not going to the building, of these they that are mildewed are they that knew the truth, but did not abide in it, nor hold fast to the saints. Therefore they are useless."

5[13]:3 "But they that have the cracks, who are they?" "These are they that have discord in their hearts against one another, and are not at peace among themselves; who have an appearance of peace, but when they depart from one another, their wickednesses abide in their hearts. These are the cracks which the stones have.

5[13]:4 But they that are broken off short, these have believed, and have their greater part in righteousness, but have some parts of lawlessness; therefore they are too short, and are not perfect."

5[13]:5 "But the white and round stones, which did not fit into the building, who are they, lady?" She answered and said to me, "How long art you foolish and stupid, and enquire everything, and understand nothing? These are they that have faith, but have also riches of this world. When tribulation cometh, they deny their Lord by reason of their riches and their business affairs."

5[13]:6 And I answered and said unto her, "When then, lady, will they be useful for the building?" "When," she replied, "their wealth, which led their souls astray, shall be cut away, then will they be useful for God. For just as the round stone, unless it be cut away, and lose some portion of itself, cannot become square, so also they that are rich in this world, unless their riches be cut away, cannot become useful to the Lord.

5[13]:7 Learn first from thyself When you had riches, you was useless; but now you art useful and profitable unto life. Be you useful unto God, for you thyself also art taken from the same stones.

7[15]:1 "But the other stones which you saw cast far away from the tower and falling into the way and rolling out of the way into the regions where there is no way, these are they that have believed, but by reason of their double heart they abandon their true way. Thus thinking that they can find a better way, they go astray and are sore distressed, as they walk about in the regions where there is no way.

7[15]:2 But they that fall into the fire and are burned, these are they that finally rebelled from the living God, and it no more entered into their hearts to repent by reason of the lusts of their wantonness and of the wickednesses which they wrought.

7[15]:3 But the others, which are near the waters and yet cannot roll into the water, would you know who are they? These are they that heard the word, and would be baptized unto the name of the Lord. Then, when they call to their remembrance the purity of the truth, they change their minds, and go back again after their evil desires."

7[15]:4 So she finished the explanation of the tower.

7[15]:5 Still importunate, I asked her further, whether for all these stones that were rejected and would not fit into the building of the tower that was repentance, and they had a place in this tower. "They can repent," she said, "but they cannot be fitted into this tower.

7[15]:6 Yet they shall be fitted into another place much more humble, but not until they have undergone torments, and have fulfilled the days of their sins. And they shall be changed for this reason, because they participated in the Righteous Word; and then shall it befall them to be relieved from their torments, if the evil deeds, that they have done, come into their heart; but if these come not into their heart, they are not saved by reason of the hardness of their hearts."

8[16]:1 When then I ceased asking her concerning all these things, she said to me; "Would you see something else?" Being very desirous of beholding, I was greatly rejoiced that I should see it.

8[16]:2 She looked upon me, and smiled, and she said to me, "See you seven women round the tower?" "I see them, lady," say I. "This tower is supported by them by commandment of the Lord.

8[16]:3 Hear now their employments. The first of them, the woman with the strong hands, is called Faith; through her are saved the elect of God.

8[16]:4 And the second, that is girded about and looked like a man, is called Continence; she is the daughter of Faith. Whosoever then shall follow her, becomes happy in his life, for he shall refrain from all evil deeds, believing that, if he refrain from every evil desire, he shall inherit eternal life."

8[16]:5 "And the others, lady, who be they?" "They are daughters one of the other. The name of the one is Simplicity, of the next, Knowledge, of the next, Guilelessness, of the next, Reverence, of the next, Love. When then you shall do all the works of their mother, you canst live."

8[16]:6 "I would fain know, lady," I say, "what power each of them possessed." "Listen then," said she, "to the powers which they have.

8[16]:7 Their powers are mastered each by the other, and they follow each other, in the order in which they were born. From Faith is born Continence, from Continence Simplicity, from Simplicity Guilelessness, from Guilelessness Reverence, from Reverence Knowledge, from Knowledge Love. Their works then are pure and reverent and divine.

8[16]:8 Whosoever therefore shall serve these women, and shall have strength to master their works, shall have his dwelling in the tower with the saints of God."

8[16]:9 Then I asked her concerning the seasons, whether the consummation is even now. But she cried aloud, saying, "Foolish man, see you not that the tower is still a-building? Whenever therefore the tower shall be finished building, the end cometh; but it shall be built up quickly. Ask me no more questions: this reminder is sufficient for you and for the saints, and is the renewal of your spirits.

8[16]:10 But it was not revealed to thyself alone, but in order that you might show these things unto all. After three days--

8[16]:11 for you must understand first, and I charge you, Hermas, first with these words, which I am about to speak to you--(I charge you to) tell all these things into the ears of the saints, that hearing them and doing them they may be purified from their wickednesses, and thyself also with them."

9[17]:1 "Hear me, my children. I brought you up in much simplicity and guilelessness and reverence, through the mercy of the Lord, Who instilled righteousness into you, that you might be justified and sanctified from all wickedness and all crookedness. But you will not to cease from your wickedness.

9[17]:2 Now then hear me and be at peace among yourselves, and have regard one to another, and assist one another, and do not partake of the creatures of God alone in abundance, but share them also with those that are in want.

9[17]:3 For some men through their much eating bring weakness on the flesh, and injure their flesh: whereas the flesh of those who have nought to eat is injured by their not having sufficient nourishment, and their body is ruined.

9[17]:4 This exclusiveness therefore is hurtful to you that have and do not share with them that are in want.

9[17]:5 Look you to the judgment that cometh. you then that have more than enough, seek out them that are hungry, while the tower is still unfinished; for after the tower is finished, you will desire to do good, and will find no place for it.

9[17]:6 Look you therefore, you that exult in your wealth, lest they that are in want shall moan, and their moaning shall go up unto the Lord, and you with your [abundance of good things be shut outside the door of the tower.

9[17]:7 Now therefore I say unto you that are rulers of the Church, and that occupy the chief seats; be not you like unto the sorcerers. The sorcerers indeed carry their drugs in boxes, but you carry your drug and your poison in your heart.

9[17]:8 you are case-hardened, and you will not cleanse your hearts and mix your wisdom together in a clean heart, that you may obtain mercy from the Great King.

9[17]:9 Look you therefore, children, lest these divisions of yours deprive you of your life.

9[17]:10 How is it that you wish to instruct the elect of the Lord, while you yourselves have no instruction? Instruct one another therefore, and have peace among yourselves, that I also may stand gladsome before the Father, and give an account concerning you all to your Lord."

10[18]:1 When then she ceased speaking with me, the six young men, who were building, came, and took her away to the tower, and other four lifted the couch, and took it also away to the tower. I saw not the face of these, for they were turned away.

10[18]:2 And, as she went, I asked her to reveal to me concerning the three forms, in which she had appeared to me. She answered and said to me; "As concerning these things you must ask another, that they may be revealed to you."

10[18]:3 Now she was seen of me, brethren, in my first vision of last year, as a very aged woman and seated on a chair.

10[18]:4 In the second vision her face was youthful, but her flesh and her hair were aged, and she spoke to me standing; and she was more gladsome than before.

10[18]:5 But in the third vision she was altogether youthful and of exceeding great beauty, and her hair alone was aged; and she was gladsome exceedingly and seated on a couch. Touching these things I was very greatly anxious to learn this revelation.

10[18]:6 And I see the aged woman in a vision of the night, saying to me, "Every enquiry needs humility. Fast therefore, and you shall receive what you ask from the Lord."

10[18]:7 So I fasted one day; and that very night there appeared unto me a young man, and he said to me, "Seeing that you ask me revelations offhand with entreaty, take heed lest by thy much asking you injure thy flesh.

10[18]:8 Sufficient for you are these revelations. Canst you see mightier revelations than those you hast seen?"

10[18]:9 I say unto him in reply, "Sir, this one thing alone I ask, concerning the three forms of the aged woman, that a complete revelation may be vouchsafed me." He said to me in answer, How long are you without understanding? It is your double-mindedness that made you of no understanding, and because your heart is not set towards the Lord."

10[18]:10 I answered and said unto him again, "From you, Sir, we shall learn the matters more accurately."

11[19]:1 Listen," said he, "concerning the three forms, of which you enquire.

11[19]:2 In the first vision wherefore did she appear to you an aged woman and seated on a chair? Because your spirit was aged, and already decayed, and had no power by reason of your infirmities and acts of double-mindedness.

11[19]:3 For as aged people, having no longer hope of renewing their youth, expect nothing else but to fall asleep, so you also, being weakened with the affairs of this world gave yourselves over to repining, and cast not your cares on the Lord; but your spirit was broken, and you were aged by your sorrows."

11[19]:4 "Wherefore then she was seated on a chair, I would fain know, Sir." "Because every weak person sits on a chair by reason of his weakness, that the weakness of his body may be supported. So you hast the symbolism of the first vision."

12[20]:1 "But in the second vision you saw her standing, and with her countenance more youthful and more gladsome than before; but her flesh and her hair aged. Listen to this parable also," said he.

12[20]:2 "Imagine an old man, who has now lost all hope of himself by reason of his weakness and his poverty, and expected nothing else save the last day of his life. Suddenly an inheritance is left him. He heard the news, rose up and full of joy clothes himself with strength, and no longer lied down, but stood up, and his spirit, which was now broken by reason of his former circumstances, is renewed again, and he no longer sat, but took courage; so also was it with you, when you heard the revelation which the Lord revealed unto you.

12[20]:3 For He had compassion on you, and renewed your spirits, and you laid aside your maladies, and strength came to you, and you were made powerful in the faith, and the Lord rejoiced to see you put on your strength. And therefore He showed you the building of the tower; yea, and other things also shall He show you, if with your whole heart you be at peace among yourselves.

13[21]:1 But in the third vision you saw her younger and fair and gladsome, and her form fair.

13[21]:2 For just as when to some mourner cometh some piece of good tidings, immediately he forgot his former sorrows, and admitted nothing but the tidings which he has heard, and is strengthened thenceforth unto that which is good, and his spirit is renewed by reason of the joy which he has received; so also you have received a renewal of your spirits by seeing these good things.

13[21]:3 And whereas you saw her seated on a couch, the position is a firm on; for the couch has four feet and stood firmly; for the world too Is upheld by means of four elements.

13[21]:4 They then that have fully repented shall be young again, and founded firmly, seeing that they have repented with their whole heart. There you hast the revelation entire and complete. You shall ask nothing more as touching revelation-- but if anything be lacking still, it shall be revealed unto you."

Vision 4

1[22]:1 The fourth vision which I saw, brethren, twenty days after the former vision which came unto me, for a type of the impending tribulation.

1[22]:2 I was going into the country by the Companion Way. From the high road, it is about ten stades; and the place is easy for traveling.

1[22]:3 While then I am walking alone, I entreat the Lord that He will accomplish the revelations and the visions which He showed me through His holy Church, that He may strengthen me and may give repentance to His servants which have stumbled, that His great and glorious Name may be glorified, for that He held me worthy that He should show me His marvels.

1[22]:4 And as I gave glory and thanksgiving to Him, there answered me as it were the sound of a voice, "Be not of doubtful mind, Hermas." I began to question in myself and to say, "How can I be of doubtful mind, seeing that I am so firmly founded by the Lord, and have seen glorious things?"

1[22]:5 And I went on a little, brethren, and behold, I see a cloud of dust rising as it were to heaven, and I began to say within myself, "Can it be that cattle are coming, and raising a cloud of dust?" for it was just about a stade from me.

1[22]:6 As the cloud of dust waxed greater and greater, I suspected that it was something supernatural. Then the sun shone out a little, and behold, I see a huge beast like some sea-monster, and from its mouth fiery locusts issued forth. And the beast was about a hundred feet in length, and its head was as it were of pottery.

1[22]:7 And I began to weep, and to entreat the Lord that He would rescue me from it. And I remembered the word which I had heard, "Be not of doubtful mind, Hermas."

1[22]:8 Having therefore, brethren, put on the faith of the Lord and called to mind the mighty works that He had taught me, I took courage and gave myself up to the beast. Now the beast was coming on with such a rush, that it might have ruined a city.

1[22]:9 I come near it, and, huge monster as it was, it stretched itself on the ground, and merely put forth its tongue, and stirred not at all until I had passed by it.

1[22]:10 And the beast had on its head four colors; black then fire and blood color, then gold, then white.

2[23]:1 Now after I had passed the beast, and had gone forward about thirty feet, behold, there met me a virgin arrayed as if she were going forth from a bridal-chamber all in white and with white sandals, veiled up to her forehead, and her head-covering consisted of a turban, and her hair was white.

2[23]:2 I knew from the former Visions that it was the Church, and I became more cheerful. She saluted me, saying, "Good morrow, my good man"; and I saluted her in turn, "Lady, good morrow."

2[23]:3 She answered and said unto me, "Did nothing meet you?" I say unto her, Lady, such a huge beast, that could have destroyed whole peoples: but, by the power of the Lord and by His great mercy, I escaped it."

2[23]:4 "You didst escape it well," said she, "because you didst cast thy care upon God, and didst open thy heart to the Lord, believing that you can be saved by nothing else but by His great and glorious Name. Therefore the Lord sent His angel, which is over the beasts, whose name is Segri, and shut his mouth that it might not hurt you. You hast escaped a great tribulation by reason of thy faith, and because, though you saw so huge a beast, you didst not doubt in thy mind.

2[23]:5 Go therefore, and declare to the elect of the Lord His mighty works, and tell them that this beast is a type of the great tribulation which is to come. If therefore you prepare yourselves beforehand, and repent (and turn) unto the Lord with your whole heart, you shall be able to escape it, if your heart be made pure and without blemish, and if for the remaining days of your life you serve the Lord blamelessly. Cast your cares upon the Lord and He will set them straight.

2[23]:6 Trust you in the Lord, you men of doubtful mind, for He can do all things, yea, He both turned away His wrath from you, and again He sent forth His plagues upon you that are of doubtful mind. Woe to them that hear these words and are disobedient; it were better for them that they had not been born."

3[24]:1 I asked her concerning the four colors, which the beast had upon its head. Then she answered me and said, "Again you art curious about such matters." "Yes, lady," said I, "make known unto me what these things are."

3[24]:2 "Listen," said she; "the black is this world in which you dwell;

3[24]:3 and the fire and blood color showed that this world must perish by blood and fire;

3[24]:4 and the golden part are you that has escaped from this world. For as the gold is tested by the fire and is made useful, so you also [that dwell in it] are being tested in yourselves. you then that abide and pass through the fire will be purified by it. For as the old loses its dross. so you also shall cast away all sorrow and tribulation, and shall be purified, and shall be useful for the building of the tower.

3[24]:5 But the white portion is the coming age, in which the elect of God shall dwell; because the elect of God shall be without spot and pure unto life eternal.

3[24]:6 Wherefore cease not you to speak in the ears of the saints. you have now the symbolism also of the tribulation which is coming in power. But if you be willing, it shall be nothing. Remember you the things that are written beforehand."

3[24]:7 With these words she departed, and I saw not in what direction she departed; for a noise was made: and I turned back in fear, thinking that the beast was coming.

Vision 5

5[25]:1 As I prayed in the house, and sat on the couch, there entered a man glorious in his visage, in the garb of a shepherd, with a white skin wrapped about him, and with a wallet on his shoulders and a staff in his hand. And he saluted me, and I saluted him in return.

5[25]:2 And he immediately sat down by my side, and he said unto me, "I was sent by the most holy angel, that I might dwell with you the remaining days of thy life."

5[25]:3 I thought he came to tempt me, and I say unto him, "Why, who art you? For I know," say I, "unto whom I was delivered." He said to me, "Dost you not recognize me?" "No," I say. "I," said he, "am the shepherd, unto whom you were delivered."

5[25]:4 While he was still speaking, his form was changed, and I recognized him as being the same, to whom I was delivered; and straightway I was confounded, and fear seized me, and I was altogether overwhelmed with distress that I had answered him so wickedly and senselessly.

5[25]:5 But he answered and said unto me, "Be not confounded, but strengthen thyself in my commandments which I am about to command you. For I was sent," said he, "that I might show you again all the things which you didst see before, merely the heads which are convenient for you. First of all, write down my commandments and my parables; and the other matters you shall write down as I shall show them to you. The reason why," said he, "I command you to write down first the commandments and parables is, that you may read them off-hand, and may be able to keep them."

5[25]:6 So I wrote down the commandments and parables, as he commanded me.

5[25]:7 If then, when you hear them, you keep them and walk in them, and do them with a pure heart, you shall receive from the Lord all things that He promised you; but if, when you hear them, you do not repent, but still add to your sins, you shall receive from the Lord the opposite. All these the shepherd, the angel of repentance commanded me to write.

Mandate 1

1[26]:1 "First of all, believe that God is One, even He who created all things and set them in order, and brought all things from non-existence into being, Who comprehends all things, being alone incomprehensible.

1[26]:2 Believe Him therefore, and fear Him, and in this fear be continent. Keep these things, and you shall cast off all wickedness from thyself, and shall clothe thyself with every excellence of righteousness, and shall live unto God, if you keep this commandment."

Mandate 2

1[27]:1 He said to me; "Keep simplicity and be guileless, and you shall be as little children, that know not the wickedness which destroyed the life of men.

1[27]:2 First of all, speak evil of no man, neither take pleasure in listening to a slanderer. Otherwise you that hear too shall be responsible for the sin of him that speaks the evil, if you believe the slander, which you hear; for in believing it you thyself also wilt have a grudge against thy brother. So then shall you be responsible for the sin of him that speaks the evil.

1[27]:3 Slander is evil; it is a restless demon, never at peace, but always having its home among factions. Refrain from it therefore, and you shall have success at all times with all men.

1[27]:4 But clothe thyself in reverence, wherein is no evil stumbling-block, but all things are smooth and gladsome. Work that which is good, and of thy labors, which God gives you, give to all that are in want freely, not questioning to whom you shall give, and to whom you shall not give. Give to all; for to all God desires that there should be given of His own bounties.

1[27]:5 They then that receive shall render an account to God why they received it, and to what end; for they that receive in distress shall not be judged, but they that receive by false pretence shall pay the penalty.

1[27]:6 He then that gives is guiltless; for as he received from the Lord the ministration to perform it, he has performed it in sincerity, by making no distinction to whom to give or not to give. This ministration then, when sincerely performed, becomes glorious in the sight of God. He therefore that ministered thus sincerely shall live unto God.

1[27]:7 Therefore keep this commandment, as I have told you, that your own repentance and that of thy household may be found to be sincere, and [thy] heart pure and undefiled."

Mandate 3

1[28]:1 Again he said to me; "Love truth, and let nothing but truth proceed out of thy mouth, that the Spirit which God made to dwell in this flesh, may be found true in the sight of all men; and thus shall the Lord, Who dwelt in you, be glorified; for the Lord is true in every word, and with Him there is no falsehood.

1[28]:2 They therefore that speak lies set the Lord at nought, and become robbers of the Lord, for they do not deliver up to Him the deposit which they received. For they received of Him a spirit free from lies. This if they shall return a lying spirit, they have defiled the commandment of the Lord and have become robbers."

1[28]:3 When then I heard these things, I wept bitterly. But seeing me weep he said, "Why weep you?" "Because, Sir," say I "I know not if I can be saved." "Why so?" said he. "Because, Sir," I say, "never in my life spoke I a true word, but I always lied deceitfully with all men and dressed up my falsehood as truth before all men; and no man ever contradicted me, but confidence was placed in my word. How then, Sir," say I, "can I live, seeing that I have done these things?"

1[28]:4 "Your supposition," he said, "is right and true, for it behooved you as a servant of God to walk in truth, and no complicity with evil should abide with the Spirit of truth, nor bring grief to the Spirit which is holy and true." "Never, Sir," say I, "heard I clearly words such as these."

1[28]:5 "Now then," said he, "you heard Guard them, that the former falsehoods also which you spake in thy business affairs may themselves become credible, now that these are found true; for they too can become trustworthy. If you keep these things, and from henceforward speak nothing but truth, you shall be able to secure life for thyself And whosoever shall hear this command, and abstain from falsehood, that most pernicious habit, shall live unto God."

Mandate 4

1[29]:1 "I charge you, "said he, "to keep purity, and let not a thought enter into thy heart concerning another's wife, or concerning fornication, or concerning any such like evil deeds; for in so doing you commit a great sin. But remember your own wife always, and you shall never go wrong.

1[29]:2 For should this desire enter into your heart, you wilt go wrong, and should any other as evil as this, you commit sin. For this desire in a servant of God is a great sin; and if any man doeth this evil deed, he worked out death for himself.

1[29]:3 Look to it therefore. Abstain from this desire; for, where holiness dwells, there lawlessness ought not to enter into the heart of a righteous man."

1[29]:4 I say to him, "Sir, permit me to ask you a few more questions" "Say on," said he. "Sir," say I, "if a man who has a wife that is faithful in the Lord detect her in adultery, doth the husband sin in living with her?"

1[29]:5 "So long as he is ignorant," said he, "he sinned not; but if the husband know of her sin, and the wife repent not, but continue in her fornication, and her husband live with her, he makes himself responsible for her sin and an accomplice in her adultery."

1[29]:6 "What then, Sir," say I, "shall the husband do, if the wife continue in this case?" "Let him divorce her," said he, "and let the husband abide alone: but if after divorcing his wife he shall marry another, he likewise commits adultery."

1[29]:7 "If then, Sir," say I, "after the wife is divorced, she repent and desire to return to her own husband, shall she not be received?"

1[29]:8 "Certainly," said he, "if the husband received her not, he sinned and brings great sin upon himself; nay, one who has sinned and repented must be received, yet not often; for there is but one repentance for the servants of God. For the sake of her repentance therefore the husband ought not to marry. This is the manner of acting enjoined on husband and wife.

1[29]:9 Not only," said he, "is it adultery, if a man pollute his flesh, but whosoever doeth things like unto the heathen commits adultery. If therefore in such deeds as these likewise a man continue and repent not, keep away from him, and live not with him. Otherwise, you also art a partaker of his sin.

1[29]:10 For this cause you were enjoined to remain single, whether husband or wife; for in such cases repentance is possible.

1[29]:11 I," said he, "am not giving an excuse that this matter should be concluded thus, but to the end that the sinner should sin no more. But as concerning his former sin, there is One Who is able to give healing; it is He Who has authority over all things."

2[30]:1 I asked him again, saying, "Seeing that the Lord held me worthy that you should always dwell with me, suffer me still to say a few words, since I understand nothing, and my heart has been made dense by my former deeds. Make me to understand, for I am very foolish, and I apprehend absolutely nothing."

2[30]:2 He answered and said unto me, "I," said he, "preside over repentance, and I give understanding to all who repent. No, think you not," said he, "that this very act of repentance is understanding? To repent is great understanding," said he. "For the man that has sinned understands that he has done evil before the Lord, and the deed which he has done enters into his heart, and he repents, and doeth no more evil, but doeth good lavishly, and humbles his own soul and puts it to torture because it sinned. You see then that repentance is great understanding."

2[30]:3 "It is on this account therefore, Sir," say I, "that I enquire everything accurately of you; first, because I am a sinner; secondly, because I know not what deeds I must do that I may live, for my sins are many and various."

2[30]:4 "You shall live," said he, "if you keep my commandments and walk in them and whosoever shall hear these commandments and keep them, shall live unto God."

3[31]:1 "I will still proceed, Sir," say I, "to ask a further question." "Speak on," said he. "I have heard, Sir," say I, "from certain teachers, that there is no other repentance, save that which took place when we rent down into the water and obtained remission of our former sins."

3[31]:2 He said to me; "You hast well heard; for so it is. For he that has received remission of sins ought no longer to sin, but to dwell in purity.

3[31]:3 But, since you enquire all things accurately, I will declare unto you this also, so as to give no excuse to those who shall hereafter believe or those who have already believed, on the Lord. For they that have already believed, or shall hereafter believe, have not repentance for sins, but have only remission of their former sins.

3[31]:4 To those then that were called before these days the Lord has appointed repentance. For the Lord, being a discerner of hearts and foreknowing all things, perceived the weakness of men and the manifold wiles of the devil, how that he will be doing some mischief to the servants of God, and will deal wickedly with them.

3[31]:5 The Lord then, being very compassionate, had pity on His handiwork, and appointed this (opportunity of) repentance, and to me was given the authority over this repentance.

3[31]:6 But I say unto you," said he, "if after this great and holy calling any one, being tempted of the devil, shall commit sin, he has only one (opportunity of) repentance. But if he sin off-hand and repent, repentance is unprofitable for such a man; for he shall live with difficulty."

3[31]:7 I say unto him, "I was quickened unto life again, when I heard these things from you so precisely. For I know that, if I shall add no more to my sins, I shall be saved." "You shall be saved," he said, "you and all, as many as shall do these things."

4[32]:1 I asked him again, saying, "Sir, since once you do bear with me, declare unto me this further matter also." "Say on," said he. "If a wife, Sir," say I, "or, it may be, a husband fall asleep, and one of them marry, doth the one that marries sin?"

4[32]:2 "He sins not," said he, "but if he remain single, he invests himself with more exceeding honor and with great glory before the Lord; yet even if he should marry, he sins not.

4[32]:3 Preserve purity and holiness therefore, and you shall live unto God. All these things, which I speak and shall hereafter speak unto you, guard from this time forward, from the day when you was committed unto me, and I will dwell in thy house.

4[32]:4 But for thy former transgressions there shall be remission, if you keep my commandments. Yea, and all shall have remission, if they keep these my commandments, and walk in this purity."

Mandate 5

1[33]:1 "Be you long-suffering and understanding," he said, "and you shall have the mastery over all evil deeds, and shall work all righteousness.

1[33]:2 For if you art long-suffering, the Holy Spirit that abides in you shall be pure, not being darkened by another evil spirit, but dwelling in a large room shall rejoice and be glad with the vessel in which he dwells, and shall serve God with much cheerfulness, having prosperity in himself.

1[33]:3 But if any angry temper approach, forthwith the Holy Spirit, being delicate, is straitened, not having [the] place clear, and seeks to retire from the place; for he is being choked by the evil spirit, and has no room to minister unto the Lord, as he desires, being polluted by angry temper. For the Lord dwells in long-suffering, but the devil in angry temper.

1[33]:4 Thus that both the spirits then should be dwelling together is inconvenient and evil for that man in whom they dwell.

1[33]:5 For if you take a little wormwood, and pour it into a jar of honey, is not the whole of the honey spoiled, and all that honey ruined by a very small quantity of wormwood? For it destroyed the sweetness of the honey, and it no longer has the same attraction for the owner, because it is rendered bitter and has lost its use. But if the wormwood be not put into the honey, the honey is found sweet and becomes useful to its owner.

1[33]:6 You see [then] that long-suffering is very sweet, beyond the sweetness of honey, and is useful to the Lord, and He dwells in it. But angry, temper is bitter and useless. If then angry temper be mixed with long-suffering, long-suffering is polluted and the man's intercession is no longer useful to God."

1[33]:7 "I would fain know, Sir," say I, "the working of angry temper, that I may guard myself from it." "Yea, verily," said he, "if you guard not thyself from it--you and thy family--you hast lost all thy hope. But guard thyself from it; for I am with you. Yea, and all men shall hold aloof from it, as many as have repented with their whole heart. For I will be with them and will preserve them; for they all were justified by the most holy angel.

2[34]:1 "Hear now," said he, "the working of angry temper, how evil it is, and how it subverts the servants of God by its own working, and how it leads them astray from righteousness. But it doth not lead astray them that are full in the faith, nor can it work upon them, because the power of the Lord is with them; but them that are empty and double-minded it leads astray.

2[34]:2 For when it sees such men in prosperity it insinuates itself into the heart of the man, and for no cause whatever the man or the woman is embittered on account of worldly matters, either about meats, or some triviality, or about some friend, or about giving or receiving, or about follies of this kind. For all these things are foolish and vain and senseless and inexpedient for the servants of God.

2[34]:3 But long-suffering is great and strong, and has a mighty and vigorous power, and is prosperous in great enlargement, gladsome, exultant, free from care, glorifying the Lord at every season, having no bitterness in itself, remaining always gentle and tranquil. This long-suffering therefore dwells with those whose faith is perfect.

2[34]:4 But angry temper is in the first place foolish, fickle and senseless; then from foolishness is engendered bitterness, and from bitterness wrath, and from wrath anger, and from anger spite; then spite being composed of all these evil elements becomes a great sin and incurable.

2[34]:5 For when all these spirits dwell in one vessel, where the Holy Spirit also dwells, that vessel cannot contain them, but overflows.

2[34]:6 The delicate spirit therefore, as not being accustomed to dwell with an evil spirit nor with harshness, departs from a man of that kind, and seeks to dwell with gentleness and tranquility.

2[34]:7 Then, when it has removed from that man, in whom it dwells, that man becomes emptied of the righteous spirit, and henceforward, being filled with the evil spirits, he is unstable in all his actions, being dragged about hither and thither by the evil spirits, and is altogether blinded and bereft of his good intent. Thus then it happens to all persons of angry temper.

2[34]:8 Refrain therefore from angry temper, the most evil of evil spirits. But clothe thyself in long-suffering, and resist angry temper and bitterness, and you shall be round in company with the holiness which is beloved of the Lord. See then that you never neglect this commandment; for if you master this commandment, you shall be able likewise to keep the remaining commandments, which I am about to give you. Be strong in them and endowed with power; and let all be endowed with power, as many as desire to walk in them."

Mandate 6

1[35]:1 I charged you," said he, "in my first commandment to guard faith and fear and temperance." "Yes, Sir," say I. "But now," said he, "I wish to show you their powers also, that you mayest understand what is the power and effect of each one of them. For their effects are two fold. Now they are prescribed alike to the righteous and the unrighteous.

1[35]:2 Do you therefore trust righteousness, but trust not unrighteousness; for the way of righteousness is straight, but the way of unrighteousness is crooked. But walk you in the straight [and level] path, and leave the crooked one alone.

1[35]:3 For the crooked way has no tracks, but only pathlessness and many stumbling stones, and is rough and thorny. So it is therefore harmful to those who walk in it.

1[35]:4 But those who walk in the straight way walk on the level and without stumbling: for it is neither rough nor thorny. You seest then that it is more expedient to walk in this way."

1[35]:5 "I am pleased, Sir," say I, "to walk in this way." "You shall walk," he said, "yea, and whosoever shall turn unto the Lord with his whole heart shall walk in it.

2[36]:1 "Hear now," said he, "concerning faith. There are two angels with a man, one of righteousness and one of wickedness."

2[36]:2 "How then, Sir," say I, "shall I know their workings, seeing that both angels dwell with me?"

2[36]:3 "Hear," said he, "and understand their workings. The angel of righteousness is delicate and bashful and gentle and tranquil. When then this one enters into thy heart, forthwith he speaketh with you of righteousness, of purity, of holiness, and of contentment, of every righteous deed and of every glorious virtue. When all these things enter into thy heart, know that the angel of righteousness is with you. [These then are the works of the angel of righteousness.] Trust him therefore and his works.

2[36]:4 Now see the works of the angel of wickedness also. First of all, he is quick tempered and bitter and senseless, and his works are evil, overthrowing the servants of God. Whenever then he entereth into thy heart, know him by his works."

2[36]:5 "How I shall discern him, Sir," I reply, "I know not." Listen," said he. "When a fit of angry temper or bitterness comes upon you, know that he is in you. Then the desire of much business and the costliness of many viands and drinking bouts and of many drunken fits and of various luxuries which are unseemly, and the desire of women, and avarice, and haughtiness and boastfulness, and whatsoever things are akin and like to these--when then these things enter into thy heart, know that the angel of wickedness is with you.

2[36]:6 Do you therefore, recognizing his works, stand aloof from him, and trust him in nothing, for his works are evil and inexpedient for the servants of God. Here then you hast the workings of both the angels. Understand them, and trust the angel of righteousness.

2[36]:7 But from the angel of wickedness stand aloof, for his teaching is evil in every matter; for though one be a man of faith, and the desire of this angel enter into his heart, that man, or that woman, must commit some sin.

2[36]:8 And if again a man or a woman be exceedingly wicked, and the works of the angel of righteousness come into that man's heart, he must of necessity do something good.

2[36]:9 You see then," said he, "that it is good to follow the angel of righteousness, and to bid farewell to the angel of wickedness.

2[36]:10 This commandment declares what concerns faith, that you may trust the works of the angel of righteousness, and doing them may live unto God. But believe that the works of the angel of wickedness are difficult; so by not doing them you shall live unto God."

Mandate 7

1[37]:1 "Fear the Lord," said he, "and keep His commandments. So keeping the commandments of God you shall be powerful in every deed, and thy doing shall be incomparable. For whilst you fear the Lord, you shall do all things well. But this is the fear wherewith you ought to be afraid, and you shall be saved.

1[37]:2 But fear not the devil; for, if you fear the Lord, you shall be master over the devil, for there is no power in him. [For] in whom is no power, neither is there fear of him; but in whom power is glorious, of him is fear likewise. For every one that has power has fear, whereas he that has no power is despised of all.

1[37]:3 But fear you the works of the devil, for they are evil. While then you fear the Lord, you wilt fear the works of the devil, and wilt not do them, but abstain from them.

1[37]:4 Fear therefore is of two kinds. If you desire to do evil, fear the Lord, and you shall not do it. If again you desire to do good, fear the Lord and you shall do it. Therefore the fear of the Lord is powerful and great and glorious. Fear the Lord then, and you shall live unto Him; yea, and as many of them that keep His commandments as shall fear Him, shall live unto God."

1[37]:5 "Wherefore, Sir," say I, "didst you say concerning those that keep His commandments, "They shall live unto God"?" "Because," said he, "every creature fears the Lord, but not every one keeps His commandments. Those then that fear Him and keep His commandments, they have life unto God; but they that keep not His commandments have no life in them."

Mandate 8

1[38]:1 "I told you," said he, "that the creatures of God are twofold; for temperance also is twofold. For in some things it is right to be temperate, but in other things it is not right."

1[38]:2 "Make known unto me, Sir," say I, "in what things it is right to be temperate, and in what things it is not right." "Listen," said he. "Be temperate as to what is evil, and do it not; but be not temperate as to what is good, but do it. For if you be temperate as to what is good, so as not to do it, you commits a great sin; but if you be temperate as to what is evil, so as not to do it, you doest great righteousness. Be temperate therefore in abstaining from all wickedness, and do that which is good."

1[38]:3 "What kinds of wickedness, Sir," say I, "are they from which we must be temperate and abstain?" "Listen," said he; "from adultery and fornication, from the lawlessness of drunkenness, from wicked luxury, from many viands and the costliness of riches, and vaunting and haughtiness and pride, and from falsehood and evil speaking and hypocrisy, malice and all blasphemy.

1[38]:4 These works are the most wicked of all in the life of men. From these works therefore the servant of God must be temperate and abstain; for he that is not temperate so as to abstain from these cannot live unto God. Listen then to what follows upon these."

1[38]:5 "Why, are there still other evil deeds, Sir?" say I. "Aye, said he, "there are many, from which the servant of God must be temperate and abstain; theft, falsehood, deprivation, false witness, avarice, evil desire, deceit, vain-glory, boastfulness, and whatsoever things are like unto these.

1[38]:6 Think you not that these things are wrong, yea, very wrong," [said he,] "for the servants of God? In all these things he that serves God must exercise temperance. Be you temperate, therefore, and refrain from all these things, that you may live unto God, and be enrolled among those who exercise self-restraint in them. These then are the things from which you should restrain thyself

1[38]:7 Now hear," said he, "the things, in which you should not exercise self restraint, but do them. Exercise no self-restraint in that which is good, but do it."

1[38]:8 "Sir," say I, "show me the power of the good also, that I may walk in them and serve them, that doing them it may be possible for me to be saved." "Hear," said he, "the works of the good likewise, which you must do, and towards which you must exercise no self-restraint.

1[38]:9 First of all, there is faith, fear of the Lord, love, concord, words of righteousness, truth, patience; nothing is better than these in the life of men. If a man keep these, and exercise not self-

restraint from them, he becomes blessed in his life.

1[38]:10 Hear now what follow upon these; to minister to widows, to visit the orphans and the needy, to ransom the servants of God from their afflictions, to be hospitable (for in hospitality benevolence from time to time has a place), to resist no man, to be tranquil, to show yourself more submissive than all men, to reverence the aged, to practice righteousness, to observe brotherly feeling, to endure injury, to be long-suffering, to bear no grudge, to exhort those who are sick at soul, not to cast away those that have stumbled from the faith, but to convert them and to put courage Into them, to reprove sinners, not to oppress debtors and indigent persons, and whatsoever actions are like these.

1[38]:11 Do these things," said he, "seem to you to be good?" "Why, what, Sir," say I, "can be better than these?" "Then walk in them," said he, "and abstain not from them, and you shall live unto God.

1[38]:12 Keep this commandment therefore. If you do good and abstain not from it, you shall live unto God; yea, and all shall live unto God who act so. And again if you do not evil, and abstain from it, you shall live unto God; yea, and all shall live unto God, who shall keep these commandments, and walk in them."

Mandate 9

1[39]:1 He said to me; "Remove from thyself a doubtful mind and doubt not at all whether to ask of God, saying within thyself, "How can I ask thing of the Lord and receive it, seeing that I have committed so many sins against Him?"

1[39]:2 Reason not thus, but turn to the Lord with thy whole heart, and ask of Him nothing wavering, and you shall know His exceeding compassion, that He will surely not abandon you, but will fulfill the petition of thy soul.

1[39]:3 For God is not as men who bear a grudge, but Himself is without malice and has compassion on His creatures.

1[39]:4 Do you therefore cleanse thy heart from all the vanities of this life, and from the things mentioned before; and ask of the Lord, and you shall receive all things, and shall lack nothing of all thy petitions, if you ask of the Lord nothing wavering.

1[39]:5 But if you waver in thy heart, you shall surely receive none of thy petitions. For they that waver towards God, these are the doubtful-minded, and they never obtain any of their petitions.

1[39]:6 But they that are complete in the faith make all their petitions trusting in the Lord, and they receive, because they ask without wavering, nothing doubting; for every doubtful-minded man, if he repent not, shall hardly be saved.

1[39]:7 Cleanse therefore thy heart from doubtful-mindedness, and put on faith, for it is strong, and trust God that you wilt receive all thy petitions which you ask; and if after asking anything of the Lord, you receive thy petition somewhat tardily, be not of doubtful mind because you didst not receive the petition of thy soul at once. For assuredly it is by reason of some temptation or some transgression, of which you art ignorant, that you receive thy petition so tardily.

1[39]:8 Do you therefore cease not to make thy soul's petition, and you shall receive it. But if you grow weary, and doubt as you ask, blame yourself and not Him that gave unto you. See to this doubtful-mindedness; for it is evil and senseless, and uproots many from the faith, yea, even very faithful and strong men. For indeed this doubtful-mindedness is a daughter of the devil, and works great wickedness against the servants of God.

1[39]:9 Therefore despise doubtful-mindedness and gain the mastery over it in everything, clothing yourself with faith which is strong and powerful. For faith promises all things, accomplishes all things; but doubtful-mindedness, as having no confidence in itself, fails in all the works which it doeth.

1[39]:10 You see then," said he, "that faith is from above from the Lord, and has great power; but doubtful-mindedness is an earthly spirit from the devil, and has no power.

1[39]:11 Do you therefore serve that faith which has power, and hold aloof from the doubtful-mindedness which has no power; and you shall live unto God; yea, and all those shall live unto God who are so minded."

Mandate 10

1[40]:1 "Put away sorrow from yourself," said he, "for she is the sister of doubtful-mindedness and of angry temper."

1[40]:2 "How, Sir," say I, "is she the sister of these? For angry temper seems to me to be one thing, doubtful-mindedness another, sorrow another." "You art a foolish fellow," said he, "[and] perceives not that sorrow is more evil than all the spirits, and is most fatal to the servants of God, and beyond all the spirits destroys a man, and crushes out the Holy Spirit and yet again saves it."

1[40]:3 "I, Sir," say I, "am without understanding, and I understand not these parables. For how it can crush out and again save, I do not comprehend."

1[40]:4 "Listen," said he. "Those who have never investigated concerning the truth, nor enquired concerning the deity, but have merely believed, and have been mixed up in business affairs and riches and heathen friendships, and many other affairs of this world--as many, I say, as devote themselves to these things, comprehend not the parables of the deity; for they are darkened by these actions, and are corrupted and become barren.

1[40]:5 As good vineyards, when they are treated with neglect, are made barren by the thorns and weeds of various kinds, so men who after they have believed fall into these many occupations which were mentioned before, lose their understanding and comprehend nothing at all concerning righteousness; for if they hear concerning the deity and truth, their mind is absorbed in their occupations, and they perceive nothing at all.

1[40]:6 But they that have the fear of God, and investigate concerning deity and truth, and direct their heart towards the Lord, perceive and understand everything that is said to them more quickly, because they have the fear of the Lord in themselves; for where the Lord dwells, there too is great understanding. Hold fast therefore unto the Lord, and you shall understand and perceive all things.

2[41]:1 "Hear now, senseless man," said he, "How sorrow crushes out the Holy Spirit, and again saves it.

2[41]:2 When the man of doubtful mind sets his hand to any action, and fails in it owing to his doubtful-mindedness, grief at this enters into the man, and grieves the Holy Spirit, and crushes it out.

2[41]:3 Then again when angry temper cleaves to a man concerning any matter, and he is much embittered, again sorrow enters into the heart of the man that was ill-tempered, and he is grieved at the deed which he has done, and repents that he did evil.

2[41]:4 This sadness therefore seems to bring salvation, because he repented at having done the evil. So both the operations sadden the Spirit; first, the doubtful mind saddens the Spirit, because it succeeded not in its business, and the angry temper again, because it did what was evil. Thus both are saddening to the Holy Spirit, the doubtful mind and the angry temper.

2[41]:5 Put away therefore from yourself sadness, and afflict not the Holy Spirit that dwells in you, lest haply He intercede with God [against you], and depart from you.

2[41]:6 For the Spirit of God, that was given unto this flesh, endures not sadness neither constraint.

3[42]:1 "Therefore clothe yourself in cheerfulness, which has favor with Cod always, and is acceptable to Him, and rejoice in it. For every cheerful man works good, and thinks good, and despises sadness;

3[42]:2 but the sad man is always committing sin. In the first place he commits sin, because he grieves the Holy Spirit, which was given to the man being a cheerful spirit; and in the second place, by grieving the Holy Spirit he doeth lawlessness, in that he doth not intercede with neither confess unto God. For the intercession of a sad man has never at any time power to ascend to the altar of God."

3[42]:3 "Wherefore," say I, "doth not the intercession of him that is saddened ascend to the altar?" "Because," said he, "sadness is seated at his heart. Thus sadness mingled with the intercession doth not suffer the intercession to ascend pure to the altar. For as vinegar when mingled with wine in the same (vessel) has not the same pleasant taste, so likewise sadness mingled with the Holy Spirit has not the same intercession.

3[42]:4 Therefore cleanse yourself from this wicked sadness, and you shall live unto God; yea, and all they shall live unto God, who shall cast away sadness from themselves and clothe themselves in all cheerfulness."

Mandate 11

1[43]:1 He showed me men seated on a couch, and another man seated on a chair. And he said to me, "See you those that are seated on the couch?" "I see them, Sir," say I. "These," said he, "are faithful, but he that sits on the chair is a false prophet who destroys the mind of the servants of God--I mean, of the doubtful-minded, not of the faithful.

1[43]:2 These doubtful-minded ones then come to him as to a soothsayer and enquire of him what shall befall them. And he, the false prophet, having no power of a divine Spirit in himself, speaks with them according to their enquiries [and according to the lusts of their wickedness], and fills their souls as they themselves wish.

1[43]:3 For being empty himself he gives empty answers to empty enquirers; for what-ever enquiry may be made of him, he answers according to the emptiness of the man. But he speaks also some true words; for the devil fills him with his own spirit, if so be he shall be able to break down some of the righteous.

1[43]:4 So many therefore as are strong in the faith of the Lord, clothed with the truth, hold fast not to such spirits, but hold aloof from them; but as many as are doubters and frequently change their minds, practice soothsaying like the Gentiles, and bring upon themselves greater sin by their idolatries. For he that consults a false prophet on any matter is an idolater and emptied of the truth, and senseless.

1[43]:5 For no Spirit given of God needs to be consulted; but, having the power of deity, speaks all things of itself, because it is from above, even from the power of the divine Spirit.

1[43]:6 But the spirit which is consulted, and speaks according to the desires of men, is earthly and fickle, having no power; and it speaks not at all, unless it be consulted."

1[43]:7 "How then, Sir," say I, "shall a man know who of them is a prophet, and who a false prophet?" "Hear," said he, "concerning both the prophets; and, as I shall tell you, so shall you test the prophet and the false prophet. By his life test the man that has the divine Spirit.

1[43]:8 In the first place, he that has the [divine] Spirit, which is from above, is gentle and tranquil and humble-minded, and abstains from all wickedness and vain desire of this present world, and holds himself inferior to all men, and gives no answer to any man when enquired of, nor speaks in solitude (for neither doth the Holy Spirit speak when a man wishes Him to speak); but the man speaks then when God wishes him to speak.

1[43]:9 When then the man who has the divine Spirit cometh into an assembly of righteous men, who have faith in a divine Spirit, and intercession is made to God by the gathering of those men, then the angel of the prophetic spirit, who is attached to him, fills the man, and the man, being filled with the Holy Spirit, speaks to the multitude, according as the Lord wills.

1[43]:10 In this way then the Spirit of the deity shall be manifest. This then is the greatness of the power as touching the Spirit of the deity of the Lord.

1[43]:11 Hear now," said he, "concerning the earthly and vain spirit, which has no power but is foolish.

1[43]:12 In the first place, that man who seems to have a spirit exalts himself, and desires to have a chief place, and straight-way he is impudent and shameless and talkative and conversant in many luxuries and in many other deceits and receives money for his prophesying, and if he receives not, he prophesies not. Now can a divine Spirit receive money and prophesy? It is not possible for a prophet of God to do this, but the spirit of such prophets is earthly.

1[43]:13 In the next place, it never approaches an assembly of righteous men; but avoids them, and clings to the doubtful-minded and empty, and prophesies to them in corners, and deceives them, speaking all things in emptiness to gratify their desires; for they too are empty whom it answers. For the empty vessel placed together with the empty is not broken, but they agree one with the other.

1[43]:14 But when he comes into an assembly full of righteous men who have a Spirit of deity, and intercession is made from them, that man is emptied, and the earthly spirit flees from him in fear, and that man is struck dumb and is altogether broken in pieces, being unable to utter a word.

1[43]:15 For, if you pack wine or oil into a closet, and place an empty vessel among them, and again desire to unpack the closet, the vessel which you place there empty, empty in like manner you will find it. Thus also the empty prophets, whenever they come unto the spirits of righteous men, are found just such as they came.

1[43]:16 I have given you the life of both kinds of prophets. Therefore test, by his life and his works, the man who says that he is moved by the Spirit.

1[43]:17 But do you trust the Spirit that cometh from God, and has power; but in the earthly and empty spirit put no trust at all; for in it there is no power, for it cometh from the devil.

1[43]:18 Listen [then] to the parable which I shall tell you. Take a stone, and throw it up to heaven--see if you can reach it; or again, take a squirt of water, and squirt it up to heaven--see if you can bore through the heaven."

1[43]:19 "How, Sir," say I, "can these things be? For both these things which you hast mentioned are beyond our power." "Well then," said he, "just as these things are beyond our power, so likewise the earthly spirits have no power and are feeble.

1[43]:20 Now take the power which cometh from above. The hail is a very, small grain, and yet, when it falls on a man's head, what pain it causes! Or again, take a drop which falls on the ground from the tiles, and bores through the stone.

1[43]:21 You see then that the smallest things from above falling on the earth have great power. So likewise the divine Spirit coming from above is powerful. This Spirit therefore trust, but from the other hold aloof."

Mandate 12

1[44]:1 He said to me; "Remove from yourself all evil desire, and clothe yourself in the desire which is good and holy; for clothed with this desire you shall hate the evil desire, and shall bridle and direct it as you wilt.

1[44]:2 For the evil desire is wild, and only tamed with difficulty; for it is terrible, and by its wildness is very costly to men; more especially if a servant of God get entangled in it, and have no understanding, he is put to fearful costs by it. But it is costly to such men as are not clothed in the good desire, but are mixed up with this life "These men then it hands over to death."

1[44]:3 "Of what sort, Sir," say I, "are the works of the evil desire, which hand over men to death? Make them known to me, that I may hold aloof from them." Listen," [said he,] "through what works the evil desire brings death to the servants of God.

2[45]:1 "Before all is desire for the wife or husband of another, and for extravagance of wealth, and for many needless dainties, and for drinks and other luxuries, many and foolish. For even luxury is foolish and vain for the servants of God.

2[45]:2 These desires then are evil, and bring death to the servants of God. For this evil desire is a daughter of the devil. you must, therefore, abstain from the evil desires, that so abstaining you may live unto God.

2[45]:3 But as many as are mastered by them, and resist them not, are done to death utterly; for these desires are deadly.

2[45]:4 But do you clothe yourself in the desire of righteousness, and, having armed yourself with the fear of the Lord, resist them. For the fear of God dwells in the good desire. If the evil desire shall see you armed with the fear of God and resisting itself, it shall flee far from you, and shall no more be seen of you, being in fear of your arms.

2[45]:5 Do you therefore, when you art crowned for thy victory over it, come to the desire of righteousness, and deliver to her the victor's prize which you hast received, and serve her, according as she herself desires. If you serve the good desire, and art subject to her, you shall have power to master the evil desire, and to subject her, according as you wilt."

3[46]:1 "I would fain know, Sir," say I, "in what ways I ought to serve the good desire." "Listen," said he; "practice righteousness and virtue, truth and the fear of the Lord, faith and gentleness, and as many good deeds as are like these. Practicing these you shall be well-pleasing as a servant of God, and shall live unto Him; yea, and every one who shall serve the good desire shall live unto God."

3[46]:2 So he completed the twelve commandments, and he said to me; You hast these commandments; walk in them, and exhort thy hearers that their repentance may become pure for the rest of the days of their life.

3[46]:3 This ministration, which I give you, fulfill you with all diligence to the end, and you shall effect much. For you shall find favor among those who are about to repent, and they shall obey thy words. For I will be with you, and will compel them to obey you."

3[46]:4 I say to him; "Sir, these commandments are great and beautiful and glorious, and are able to gladden the heart of the man who is able to observe them. But I know not whether these commandments can be kept by a man, for they are very hard."

3[46]:5 He answered and said unto me; "If you set it before yourself that they can be kept, you wilt easily keep them, and they will not be hard; but if it once enter into thy heart that they cannot be kept by a man, you wilt not keep them.

3[46]:6 But now I say unto you; if you keep them not. but neglect them you shall not have salvation, neither thy children nor thy household, since you hast already pronounced judgment against yourself that these commandments cannot be kept by a man."

4[47]:1 And these things he said to me very angrily, so that I was confounded, and feared him exceedingly; for his form was changed, so that a man could not endure his anger.

4[47]:2 And when he saw that I was altogether disturbed and confounded, he began to speak more kindly [and cheerfully] to me, and he said; "Foolish fellow, void of understanding and of doubtful mind, perceives you not the glory of God, how great and mighty and marvelous it is, how that He created the world for man's sake, and subjected all His creation to man, and gave all authority to him, that he should be master over all things under the heaven?

4[47]:3 If then," [he said,] "man is lord of all the creatures of God and masters all things, cannot he also master these commandments Aye," said he, "the man that has the Lord in his heart can master [all things and] all these commandments.

4[47]:4 But they that have the Lord on their lips, while their heart is hardened, and are far from the Lord, to them these commandments are hard and inaccessible.

4[47]:5 Therefore do you, who are empty and fickle in the faith, set your Lord in your heart, and you shall perceive that nothing is easier than these commandments, nor sweeter, nor more gentle.

4[47]:6 Be you converted, you that walk after the commandments of the devil, (the commandments which are so) difficult and bitter and wild and riotous; and fear not the devil, for there is no power in him against you.

4[47]:7 For I will be with you, I, the angel of repentance, who have the mastery over him. The devil has fear alone, but his fear has no force. Fear him not therefore; and he will flee from you."

5[48]:1 I say to him, "Sir, listen to a few words from me." "Say what you wilt," said he. "Man, Sir," I say, "is eager to keep the commandments of God, and there is no one that asks not of the Lord that he may be strengthened in His commandments, and be subject to them; but the devil is hard and overmasters them."

5[48]:2 "He cannot," said he, "overmaster the servants of God, who set their hope on Him with their whole heart. The devil can wrestle with them, but he cannot overthrow them. If then you resist him, he will be vanquished and will flee from you disgraced. But as many," said he, "as are utterly empty, fear the devil as if he had power.

5[48]:3 When a man has filled amply sufficient jars with good wine, and among these jars a few are quite empty, he comes to the jars, and does not examine the full ones, for he knows that they are full; but he examines the empty ones, fearing lest they have turned sour. For empty jars soon turn sour, and the taste of the wine is spoilt.

5[48]:4 So also the devil cometh to all the servants of God tempting them. As many then as are complete in the faith, oppose him mightily, and he departs from them, not having a place where he can find an entrance. So he cometh next to the empty ones, and finding a place goes into them, and further he doeth what he wills in them, and they become submissive slaves to him.

6[49]:1 "But I, the angel of repentance, say unto you; Fear not the devil; for I was sent," said he, "to be with you who repent with your whole heart, and to strengthen you in the faith.

6[49]:2 Believe, therefore, on God, you who by reason of your sins have despaired of your life, and are adding to your sins, and weighing down your life; for if you turn unto the Lord with your whole heart, and work righteousness the remaining days of your life, and serve Him rightly according to His will, He will give healing to your former sins, and you shall have power to master the works of the devil. But of the threatening of the devil fear not at all; for he is unstrung, like the sinews of a dead man.

6[49]:3 Hear me therefore, and fear Him, Who is able to do all things, to save and to destroy, and observe these commandments, and you shall live unto God."

6[49]:4 I say to him, "Sir, now am I strengthened in all the ordinances of the Lord, because you art with me; and I know that you wilt crush all the power of the devil, and we shall be masters over him, and shall prevail over all his works. And I hope, Sir, that I am now able to keep these commandments which you hast commanded, the Lord enabling me."

6[49]:5 "You shall keep them," said he, "if thy heart be found pure with the Lord; yea, and all shall keep them, as many as shall purify their hearts from the vain desires of this world, and shall live unto God."

Parables Which He spoke With Me

Parable 1

1[50]:1 He said to me; "you know that you, who are the servants of God, are dwelling in a foreign land; for your city is far from this city. If then you know your city, in which you shall dwell, why do you here prepare fields and expensive displays and buildings and dwelling-chambers which are superfluous?

1[50]:2 He, therefore, that prepares these things for this city does not purpose to return to his own city.

1[50]:3 O foolish and double-minded and miserable man, perceives you not that all these things are foreign, and are under the power of another For the lord of this city shall say, "I do not wish you to dwell in my city; go forth from this city, for you do not conform to my laws."

1[50]:4 You, therefore who hast fields and dwellings and many other possessions, when you art cast out by him, what wilt you do with thy field and thy house am all the other things that you prepared for yourself? For the lord of this country said to you justly, "Either conform to my laws, or depart from my country."

1[50]:5 What then shall you do, who art under law in your own city? For the sake of thy fields and the rest of thy possessions wilt you altogether repudiate thy law, and walk according to the law of this city? Take heed, lest it be inexpedient to repudiate the law; for if you should desire to return again to thy city, you shall surely not be received [because you didst repudiate the law of the city], and shall be shut out from it.

1[50]:6 Take heed therefore; as dwelling in a strange land prepare nothing more for yourself but a competency which is sufficient for you, and make ready that, whenever the master of this city may desire to cast you out for your opposition to his law, you may go forth from his city and depart into your own city and use your own law joyfully, free from all insult.

1[50]:7 Take heed therefore, you that serve God and have Him in your heart: work the "works of God being mindful of His commandments and of the promises which He made, and believe Him that He will perform them, if His commandments be kept.

1[50]:8 Therefore, instead of fields buy you souls that are in trouble, as each is able, and visit widows and orphans, and neglect them not; and spend your riches and all your displays, which you received from God, on fields and houses of this kind.

1[50]:9 For to this end the Master enriched you, that you might perform these ministrations for Him. It is much better to purchase fields [and possessions] and houses of this kind, which you wilt find in your own city, when you visit it.

1[50]:10 This lavish expenditure is beautiful and joyous, not bringing sadness or fear, but bringing joy. The expenditure of the heathen then practice not you; for it is not convenient for you the servants of God.

1[50]:11 But practice your own expenditure, in which you can rejoice; and do not corrupt, neither touch that which is another man's, nor lust after it for it is wicked to lust after other men's possessions. But perform your own task, and you shall be saved."

Parable 2

1[51]:1 As I walked in the field, and noticed an elm and a vine, and was distinguishing them and their fruits, the shepherd appears to me and said; "What art you meditating within yourself?" "I am thinking, [Sir,]" say I, "about the elm and the vine, that they are excellently suited the one to the other."

1[51]:2 "These two trees," said he, "are appointed for a type to the servants of God." "I would fain know, [Sir,]" say I, "the type contained in these trees, of which you speak." "See you," said he, "the elm and the vine ?" "I see them, Sir," say I.

1[51]:3 "This vine," said he, "bears fruit, but the elm is an unfruitful stock. Yet this vine, except it climb up the elm, cannot bear much fruit when it is spread on the ground; and such fruit as it bears is rotten, because it is not suspended upon the elm. When then the vine is attached to the elm, it bears fruit both from itself and from the elm.

1[51]:4 You see then that the elm also bears [much] fruit, not less than the vine, but rather more." How more, Sir?" say I. "Because," said he, "the vine, when hanging upon the elm, bears its fruit in abundance, and in good condition; but, when spread on the ground, it bears little fruit, and that rotten. This parable therefore is applicable to the servants of God, to poor and to rich alike."

1[51]:5 "How, Sir?" say I; "instruct me." "Listen," said he; the rich man has much wealth, but in the things of the Lord he is poor, being distracted about his riches, and his confession and intercession with the Lord is very scanty; and even that which he gives is mall and weak and has not power above. When then the rich man goes up to the poor, and assists him in his needs, believing that for what he doth to the poor man he shall be able to obtain a reward with God--because the poor man is rich in intercession [and confession], and his intercession has great power with God--the rich man then supplies all things to the poor man without wavering.

1[51]:6 But the poor man being supplied by the rich makes intercession for him, thanking God for him that gave to him. And the other is still more zealous to assist the poor man, that he may be continuous in his life: for he knows that the intercession of the poor man is acceptable and rich before God.

1[51]:7 They both then accomplish their work; the poor man makes intercession, wherein he is rich [which he received of the Lord]; this he renders again to the Lord Who supplies him with it. The rich man too in like manner furnishes to the poor man, nothing doubting, the riches which he received from the Lord. And this work great and acceptable with God, because (the rich man) has understanding concerning his riches, and works for the poor man from the bounties of the Lord, and accomplishes the ministration of the Lord rightly.

1[51]:8 In the sight of men then the elm seems not to bear fruit, and they know not, neither perceive, that if there cometh a drought the elm having water nurtures the vine, and the vine having a constant supply of water bears fruit two fold, both for itself and for the elm. So likewise the poor, by interceding with the Lord for the rich, establish their riches, and again the rich, supplying their needs to the poor, establish their souls.

1[51]:9 So then both are made partners in the righteous work. He then that doeth these things shall not be abandoned of God, but shall be written in the books of the living.

1[51]:10 Blessed are the rich, who understand also that they are enriched from the Lord. For they that have this mind shall be able to do some good work."

Parable 3

1[52]:1 He showed me many trees which had no leaves, but they seemed to me to be, as it were, withered; for they were all alike. And he said to me; "See you these trees?" "I see them, Sir," I say, "they are all alike, and are withered." He answered and said to me; "These trees that you see are they that dwell in this world."

1[52]:2 "Wherefore then, Sir," say I, "are they as if they were withered, and alike?" "Because," said he, "neither the righteous are distinguishable, nor the sinners in this world, but they are alike. For this world is winter to the righteous, and they are not distinguishable, as they dwell with the sinners.

1[52]:3 For as in the winter the trees, having shed their leaves, are alike, and are not distinguishable, which are withered, and which alive, so also in this world neither the just nor the sinners are distinguishable, but they are all alike."

Parable 4

1[53]:1 He showed me many trees again, some of them sprouting, and others withered, and he said to me; "See you," said he, "these trees?" "I see them, Sir," say I, "some of them sprouting, and others withered."

1[53]:2 "These trees," said he, "that are sprouting are the righteous, who shall dwell in the world to come; for the world to come is summer to the righteous, but winter to the sinners. When then the mercy of the Lord shall shine forth, then they that serve God shall be made manifest; yea, and all men shall be made manifest.

1[53]:3 For as in summer the fruits of each several tree are made manifest, and are recognized of what sort they are, so also the fruits of the righteous shall be manifest, and all [even the very smallest] shall be known to be flourishing in that world.

1[53]:4 But the Gentiles and the sinners, just as you saw the trees which were withered, even such shall they be found, withered and unfruitful in that world, and shall be burnt up as fuel, and shall be manifest, because their practice in their life has been evil. For the sinners shall be burned, because they sinned and repented not; and the Gentiles shall be burned, because they knew not Him that created them.

1[53]:5 Do you therefore bear fruit, that in that summer thy fruit may be known. But abstain from overmuch business, and you shall never fill into any sin. For they that busy themselves overmuch, sin much also, being distracted about their business, and in no wise serving their own Lord.

1[53]:6 How then," said he, "can such a man ask anything of the Lord and receive it, seeing that he serves not the Lord? [For] they that serve Him, these shall receive their petitions, but they that serve not the Lord, these shall receive nothing.

1[53]:7 But if any one work one single action, he is able also to serve the Lord; for his mind shall not be corrupted from (following) the Lord, but he shall serve Him, because he keeps his mind pure.

1[53]:8 If therefore you doest these things, you shall be able to bear fruit unto the world to come; yea, and whosoever shall do these things, shall bear fruit."

Parable 5

1[54]:1 As I was fasting and seated on a certain mountain, and giving thanks to the Lord for all that He had done unto me, I see the shepherd seated by me and saying; "Why hast you come hither in the early morn?" "Because, Sir," say I, "I am keeping a station."

1[54]:2 "What," said he, "is a station?" "I am fasting, Sir," say I. "And what," said he, "is this fast [that you are fasting]?" "As I was accustomed, Sir," say I, "so I fast."

1[54]:3 "you know not," said he, "how to fast unto the Lord, neither is this a fast, this unprofitable fast which you make unto Him." "wherefore, Sir," say I, "say you this?" "I tell you," said he, "that this is not a fast, wherein you think to fast; but I will teach you what is a complete fast and acceptable to the Lord. Listen," said he;

1[54]:4 "God desires not such a vain fast; for by so fasting unto God you shall do nothing for righteousness. But fast you [unto God] such a fast as this;

1[54]:5 do no wickedness in thy life, and serve the Lord with a pure heart; observe His commandments and walk in His ordinances, and let no evil desire rise up in thy heart; but believe God. Then, if you shall do these things, and fear Him, and control yourself from every evil deed, you shall live unto God; and if you do these things, you shall accomplish a great fast, and one acceptable to God.

2[55]:1 "Hear the parable which I shall tell you relating to fasting.

2[55]:2 A certain man had an estate, and many slaves, and a portion of his estate he planted as a vineyard; and choosing out a certain slave who was trusty and well-pleasing (and) held in honor, he called him to him and said unto him; "Take this vineyard [which I have planted], and fence it [till I come], but do nothing else to the vineyard. Now keep this my commandment, and you shall be free in my house." Then the master of the servant went away to travel abroad.

2[55]:3 When then he had gone away, the servant took and fenced the vineyard; and having finished the fencing of the vineyard, he noticed that the vineyard was full of weeds.

2[55]:4 So he reasoned within himself, saying, "This command of my lord I have carried out I will next dig this vineyard, and it shall be neater when it is dug; and when it has no weeds it will yield more fruit, because not choked by the weeds." He took and dug the vineyard, and all the weeds that were in the vineyard he plucked up. And that vineyard became very neat and flourishing, when it had no weeds to choke it.

2[55]:5 After a time the master of the servant [and of the estate] came, and he went into the vineyard. And seeing the vineyard fenced neatly, and dug as well, and [all] the weeds plucked up, and the vines flourishing, he rejoiced [exceedingly] at what his servant had done.

2[55]:6 So he called his beloved son, who was his heir, and the friends who were his advisers, and told them what he had commanded his servant, and how much he had found done. And they rejoiced with the servant at the testimony which his master had borne to him.

2[55]:7 And he said to them; "I promised this servant his freedom, if he should keep the commandment which I commanded him; but he kept my commandment and did a good work besides to my vineyard, and pleased me greatly. For this work therefore which he has done, I desire to make him joint-heir with my son, because, when the good thought struck him, he did not neglect it, but fulfilled it."

2[55]:8 In this purpose the son of the master agreed with him, that the servant should be made joint-heir with the son.

2[55]:9 After some few days, his master made a feast, and sent to him many dainties from the feast. But when the servant received [the dainties sent to him by the master], he took what was sufficient for him, and distributed the rest to his fellow servants.

2[55]:10 And his fellow-servants, when they received the dainties, rejoiced, and began to pray for him, that he might find greater favor with the master, because he had treated them so handsomely.

2[55]:11 All these things which had taken place his master heard, and again rejoiced greatly at his deed. So the master called together again his friends and his son, and announced to them the deed that he had done with regard to his dainties which he had received; and they still more approved of his resolve, that his servant should be made joint-heir with his son."

3[56]:1 I say, "Sir, I understand not these parables, neither can I apprehend them, unless you explain them for me."

3[56]:2 "I will explain everything to you," said he; "and will show you whatsoever things I shall speak with you. Keep the commandments of the Lord, and you shall be well-pleasing to God, and shall be enrolled among the number of them that keep His commandments.

3[56]:3 But if you do any good thing outside the commandment of God, you shall win for yourself more exceeding glory, and shall be more glorious in the sight of God than you would otherwise have been. If then, while you keep the commandments of God, you add these services likewise, you shall rejoice, if you observe them according to my commandment."

3[56]:4 I say to him, "Sir, whatsoever you command me, I will keep it; for I know that you art with me." "I will be with you," said he, "because you hast so great zeal for doing good; yea, and I will be with all," said he, "whosoever have such zeal as this.

3[56]:5 This fasting," said he, "if the commandments of the Lord are kept, is very good. This then is the way, that you shall keep this fast which you art about to observe].

3[56]:6 First of all, keep yourself from every evil word and every evil desire, and purify thy heart from all the vanities of this world. If you keep these things, this fast shall be perfect for you.

3[56]:7 And thus shall you do. Having fulfilled what is written, on that day on which you fastest you shall taste nothing but bread and water; and from thy meats, which you would have eaten, you shall reckon up the amount of that day's expenditure, which you would have incurred, and shall give it to a widow, or an orphan, or to one in want, and so shall you humble thy soul, that he that has received from thy humiliation may satisfy his own soul, and may pray for you to the Lord.

3[56]:8 If then you shall so accomplish this fast, as I have commanded you, thy sacrifice shall be acceptable in the sight of God, and this fasting shall be recorded; and the service so performed is beautiful and joyous and acceptable to the Lord.

3[56]:9 These things you shall so observe, you and thy children and thy whole household; and, observing them, you shall be blessed; yea, and all those, who shall hear and observe them, shall be blessed, and whatsoever things they shall ask of the Lord, they shall receive."

4[57]:1 I entreated him earnestly, that he would show me the parable of the estate, and of the master, and of the vineyard, and of the servant that fenced the vineyard, [and of the fence,] and of the weeds which were plucked up out of the vineyard, and of the son, and of the friends, the advisers. For I understood that all these things are a parable.

4[57]:2 But he answered and said unto me; "You art exceedingly importunate in enquiries. You ought not," [said he,] "to make any enquiry at all; for if it be right that a thing be explained unto you, it shall be explained." I say to him; "Sir, whatsoever things you show unto me and do not explain, I shall have seen them in vain, and without understanding what they are. In like manner also, if you speak parables to me and interpret them not, I shall have heard a thing in vain from you."

4[57]:3 But he again answered, and said unto me; "Whosoever," said he, "is a servant of God, and has his own Lord in his heart, asks understanding of Him, and receives it, and interprets every parable, and the words of the Lord which are spoken in parables are made known unto him. But as many as are sluggish and idle in intercession, these hesitate to ask of the Lord.

4[57]:4 But the Lord is abundant in compassion, and gives to them that ask of Him without ceasing. But you who hast been strengthened by the holy angel, and hast received from him such (powers of intercession and art not idle, wherefore do you not ask understanding of the Lord, and obtain it from Him)."

4[57]:5 I say to him, "Sir, I that have you with me have (but) need to ask you and enquire of you; for you show me all things, and speak with me; but if I had seen or heard them apart from you I should have asked of the Lord, that they might be shown to me."

5[58]:1 "I told you just now," said he, "that you art unscrupulous and importunate, in enquiring for the interpretations of the parables. But since you art so obstinate, I will interpret to you the parable of the estate and all the accompaniments thereof, that you may make them known unto all. Hear now," said he, "and understand them.

5[58]:2 The estate is this world, and the lord of the estate is He that created all things, and set them in order, and endowed them with power; and the servant is the Son of God, and the vines are this people whom He Himself planted;

5[58]:3 and the fences are the [holy] angels of the Lord who keep together His people; and the weeds, which are plucked up from the vineyard, are the transgressions of the servants of God; and the dainties which He sent to him from the feast are the commandments which He gave to His people through His Son; and the friends and advisers are the holy angels which were first created; and the absence of the master is the time which remains over until His coming."

5[58]:4 I say to him; "Sir, great and marvelous are all things and all things are glorious; was it likely then," say I, "that I could have apprehended them?" "Nay, nor can any other man, though he be full of understanding, apprehend them." "Yet again, Sir," say I, "explain to me what I am about to enquire of you."

5[58]:5 "Say on," he said, "if you desire anything." "Wherefore, Sir,]" say I, "is the Son of God represented in the parable in the guise of a servant?"

6[59]:1 "Listen," said he; "the Son of God is not represented in the guise of a servant, but is represented in great power and lordship." "How, Sir?" say I; "I comprehend not."

6[59]:2 "Because," said he, "God planted the vineyard, that is, He created the people, and delivered them over to His Son. And the Son placed the angels in charge of them, to watch over them; and the Son Himself cleansed their sins, by laboring much and enduring many toils; for no one can dig without toil or labor.

6[59]:3 Having Himself then cleansed the sins of His people, He showed them the paths of life, giving them the law which He received from His Father. You see," said he, "that He is Himself Lord of the people, having received all power from His Father.

6[59]:4 But how that the lord took his son and the glorious angels as advisers concerning the inheritance of the servant, listen.

6[59]:5 The Holy Pre-existent Spirit. Which created the whole creation, God made to dwell in flesh that He desired. This flesh, therefore, in which the Holy Spirit dwelt, was subject unto the Spirit, walking honorably in holiness and purity, without in any way defiling the Spirit.

6[59]:6 When then it had lived honorably in chastity, and had labored with the Spirit, and had cooperated with it in everything, behaving itself boldly and bravely, He chose it as a partner with the Holy Spirit; for the career of this flesh pleased [the Lord], seeing that, as possessing the Holy Spirit, it was not defiled upon the earth.

6[59]:7 He therefore took the son as adviser and the glorious angels also, that this flesh too, having served the Spirit unblamably, might have some place of sojourn, and might not seem to hare lost the reward for its service; for all flesh, which is found undefiled and unspotted, wherein the Holy Spirit dwelt, shall receive a reward.

6[59]:8 Now you hast the interpretation of this parable also."

7[60]:1 "I was right glad, Sir," say I, "to hear this interpretation." "Listen now," said he, "Keep this thy flesh pure and undefiled, that the Spirit which dwells in it may bear witness to it, and thy flesh may be justified.

7[60]:2 See that it never enter into your heart that this flesh of your is perishable, and so you abuse it in some defilement. [For] if you defile thy flesh, you shall defile the Holy Spirit also; but if you defile the flesh, you shall not live."

7[60]:3 "But if, Sir," say I, "there has been any ignorance in times past, before these words were heard, how shall a man who has defiled his flesh be saved?" "For the former deeds of ignorance," said he, "God alone has power to give healing; for all authority is His.

7[60]:4 [But now keep yourself, and the Lord Almighty, Who is full of compassion, will give healing for thy former deeds of ignorance,] if henceforth you defile not thy flesh, neither the Spirit; for both share in common, and the one cannot be defiled without the other. Therefore keep both pure, and you shall live unto God."

Parable 6

1[61]:1 As I sat in my house, and glorified the Lord for all things that I had seen, and was considering concerning the commandments, how that they were beautiful and powerful and gladsome and glorious and able to save a man's soul, I said within myself; "Blessed shall I be, if I walk in these commandments; yea, and whosoever shall walk in them shall be blessed."

1[61]:2 As I spoke these things within myself, I see him suddenly seated by me, and saying as follows; "Why art you of a doubtful mind concerning the commandments, which I commanded you? They are beautiful. Doubt not at all; but clothe yourself in the faith of the Lord, and you shall walk in them. For I will strengthen you in them.

1[61]:3 These commandments are suitable for those who meditate repentance; for if they walk not in them, their repentance is in vain.

1[61]:4 you then that repent, cast away the evil doings of this world which crush you; and, by putting on every excellence of righteousness, you shall be able to observe these commandments, and to add no more to your sins. If then you add no further sin at all, you will depart from your former sins. Walk then in these my commandments, and you shall live unto God. These things have [all] been told you from me."

1[61]:5 And after he had told these things to me, he said to me, "Let us go into the country, and I will show you the shepherds of the sheep." "Let us go, Sir," say I. And we came to a certain plain, and he shows me a young man, a shepherd, clothed in a light cloak, of saffron color;

1[61]:6 and he was feeding a great number of sheep, and these sheep were, as it were, well fed and very frisky, and were gladsome as they skipped about hither and thither; and the shepherd himself was all gladsome over his flock; and the very visage of the shepherd was exceedingly gladsome; and he ran about among the sheep.

2[62]:1 And he said to me; "See you this shepherd?" "I see him Sir," I say. "This," said he, "is the angel of self-indulgence and of deceit. He crushes the souls of the servants of God, and perverts them from the truth, leading them astray with evil desires, wherein they perish.

2[62]:2 For they forget the commandments of the living God, and walk in vain deceits and acts of self-indulgence, and are destroyed by this angel, some of them unto death, and others unto corruption."

2[62]:3 I say to him, "Sir, I comprehend not what means "unto death," and what "unto corruption". "Listen," said he; "the sheep which you saw gladsome and skipping about, these are they who have been turned asunder from God utterly, and have delivered themselves over to the lusts of this world. In these, therefore, there is not repentance unto life. For the Name of God is being blasphemed through them. The life of such persons is death.

2[62]:4 But the sheep, which you saw not skipping about, but feeding in one place, these are they that have delivered themselves over to acts of self-indulgence and deceit, but have not uttered any blasphemy against the Lord. These then have been corrupted from the truth. In these there is hope of repentance, wherein they can live. Corruption then has hope of a possible renewal, but death has eternal destruction."

2[62]:5 Again we went forward a little way, and he showed me a great shepherd like a wild man in appearance, with a white goatskin thrown about him; and he had a kind of wallet on his shoulders, and a staff very hard and with knots in it, and a great whip. And his look was very sour, so that I was afraid of him because of his look.

2[62]:6 This shepherd then kept receiving from the young man, the shepherd, those sheep that were frisky and well fed, but not skipping about, and putting them in a certain spot, which was precipitous and covered with thorns and briars, so that the sheep could not disentangle themselves from the thorns and briars, but [became entangled among the thorns and briars.

2[62]:7 And so they] pastured entangled in the thorns and briars, and were in great misery with being beaten by him; and he kept driving them about to and fro, and giving them no rest, and all together those sheep had not a happy time.

3[63]:1 When then I saw them so lashed with the whip and vexed, I was sorry for their sakes, because they were so tortured and had no rest at all.

3[63]:2 I say to the shepherd who was speaking with me; "Sir, who is this shepherd, who is [so] hard-hearted and severe, and has no compassion at all for these sheep?" "This," said he, "is the angel of punishment, and he is one of the just angels, and presides over punishment.

3[63]:3 So he receives those who wander away from God, and walk after the lusts and deceits of this life, and punishes them, as they deserve, with fearful and various punishments."

3[63]:4 "I would fain learn, Sir," said I, "of what sort are these various punishments." "Listen," said he; "the various tortures and punishments are tortures belonging to the present life; for some are punished with losses, and others with want, and others with divers maladies, and others with [every kind] of unsettlement, and others with insults from unworthy persons and with suffering in many other respects.

3[63]:5 For many, being unsettled in their plans, set their hands to many things, and nothing ever goes forward with them. And then they say that they do not prosper in their doings, and it doth not enter into their hearts that they have done evil deeds, but they blame the Lord.

3[63]:6 When then they are afflicted with every kind of affliction, then they are delivered over to me for good instruction, and are strengthened in the faith of the Lord, and serve the Lord with a pure heart the remaining days of their life. But, if they repent, the evil works which they have done rise up in their hearts, and then they glorify God, saying that He is a just Judge, and that they suffered justly each according to his doings. And they serve the Lord thenceforward with a pure heart, and are prosperous in all their doings, receiving from the Lord whatsoever things they may ask; and then they glorify the Lord because they were delivered over unto me, and they no longer suffer any evil thing."

3[63]:1 I say unto him; "Sir, declare unto me this further matter." "What enquire you yet?" said he. "Whether, Sir," say I, "they that live in self-indulgence and are deceived undergo torments during the same length of time as they live in self-indulgence and are deceived." He said to me, "They undergo torments for the same length of time."

3[63]:2 "Then, Sir," say I, "they undergo very slight torments; for those who are living thus in self-indulgence and forget God ought to have been tormented seven-fold."

3[63]:3 He said to me, "You art foolish, and comprehend not the power of the torment" "True," say I, "for if I had comprehended it, I should not have asked you to declare it to me." "Listen," said he, "to the power of both, [of the self-indulgence and of the torment].

3[63]:4 The time of the self-indulgence and deceit is one hour. But an hour of the torment has the power of thirty days. If then one live in self indulgence and be deceived for one day, and be tormented for one day, the day of the torment is equivalent to a whole year. For as many days then as a man lives in self-indulgence, for so many years is he tormented. You see then," said he, "that the time of the self-indulgence and deceit is very short, but the time of the punishment and torment is long."

5[65]:1 "Inasmuch, Sir," say I, "as I do not quite comprehend concerning the time of the deceit and self-indulgence and torment, show me more clearly."

5[65]:2 He answered and said unto me; "Your stupidity clings to you; and you wilt not cleanse thy heart and serve God Take heed," [said he,] "lest haply the time be fulfilled, and you be found in thy foolishness. Listen then," [said he,] "even as you wish, that you may comprehend the matter.

5[65]:3 He that lives in self-indulgence and is deceived for one day, and doeth what he wishes, is clothed in much folly and comprehended not the thing which he doeth; for on the morrow he forgets what he did the day before. For self-indulgence and deceit have no memories, by reason of the folly, wherewith each is clothed; but when punishment and torment cling to a man for a single day, he is punished and tormented for a whole year long; for punishment and torment have long memories.

5[65]:4 So being tormented and punished for the whole year, the man remembers at length the self-indulgence and deceit, and perceives that it is on their account that he is suffering these ills. Every man, therefore, that lives in self-indulgence and is deceived, is tormented in this way because, though possessing lire, they have delivered themselves over unto death."

5[65]:5 "What kinds of self-indulgence, Sir," say I, "are harmful?" "Every action," said he, "is self-indulgence to a man, which he does with pleasure; for the irascible man, when he gives the reins to his passion, is self-indulgent; and the adulterer and the drunkard and the slanderer and the liar and the miser and the defrauder and he that doeth things akin to these, gives the reins to his peculiar passion; therefore he is self-indulgent in his action.

5[65]:6 All these habits of self-indulgence are harmful to the servants of God; on account of these deceits therefore they so suffer who are punished and tormented.

5[65]:7 But there are habits of self-indulgence like-wise which save men; for many are self-indulgent in doing good, being carried away by the pleasure it gives to themselves. This self-indulgence then is expedient for the servants of God, and brings life to a man of this disposition; but the harmful self-indulgences afore-mentioned bring to men torments and punishments; and if they continue in them and repent not, they bring death upon themselves."

Parable 7

1[66]:1 After a few days I saw him on the same plain, where also I had seen the shepherds, and he said to me, "What seek you?" "I am here, Sir," say I, "that you may bid the shepherd that punishes go out of my house; for he afflicts me much." "It is necessary for you," said he, "to be afflicted; for so," said he, "the glorious angel ordered as concerning you, for he wishes you to be proved." "Why, what so evil thing have I done, Sir," say I, "that I should be delivered over to this angel?"

1[66]:2 "Listen," said he. "Your sins are many, yet not so many that you should be delivered over to this angel; but thy house has committed great iniquities and sins, and the glorious angel was embittered at their deeds, and for this cause he bade you be afflicted for a certain time, that they also might repent and cleanse themselves from every lust of this world. When therefore they shall repent and be cleansed, then shall the angel of punishment depart."

1[66]:3 I say to him; "Sir, if they perpetrated such deeds that the glorious angel is embittered, what have I done?" "They cannot be afflicted otherwise," said he, "unless you, the head of the [whole] house, be afflicted; for if you be afflicted, they also of necessity will be afflicted; but if you be prosperous, they can suffer no affliction."

1[66]:4 "But behold, Sir," say I, "they have repented with their whole heart." "I am quite aware myself," said he, "that they have repented with their whole heart; well, think you that the sins of those who repent are forgiven forthwith? Certainly not; but the person who repents must torture his own soul, and must be thoroughly humble in his every action, and be afflicted with all the divers kinds of affliction; and if he endure the afflictions which come upon him, assuredly He Who created all things and endowed them with power will be moved with compassion and will bestow some remedy.

1[66]:5 And this (will God do), if in any way He perceive the heart of the penitent pure from every evil thing. But it is expedient for you and for thy house that you should be afflicted now. But why speak I many words to you? You must be afflicted as the angel of the Lord commanded, even he that delivered you unto me; and for this give thanks to the Lord, in that He deemed you worthy that I should reveal unto you beforehand the affliction, that foreknowing it you might endure it with fortitude."

1[66]:6 I say to him; "Sir, be you with me, and I shall be able to endure all affliction [easily]." "I will be with you," said he; "and I will ask the angel that punishs to afflict you more lightly; but you shall be afflicted for a short time, and you shall be restored again to thy house. Only continue to be humble and to minister unto the Lord with a pure heart, you and thy children and thy house, and walk in my commandments which I command you, and thus it will be possible for thy repentance to be strong and pure.

1[66]:7 And if you keep these commandments with thy household, all affliction shall hold aloof from you; yea, and affliction," said he, "shall hold aloof from all whosoever shall walk in these my commandments."

Parable 8

1[67]:1 He showed me a [great] willow, overshadowing plains and mountains, and under the shadow of the willow all have come who are called by the name of the Lord.

1[67]:2 And by the willow there stood an angel of the Lord, glorious and very tall, having a great sickle, and he was lopping branches from the willow, and giving them to the people that sheltered beneath the willow; and he gave them little rods about a cubit long.

1[67]:3 And after all had taken the rods, the angel laid aside the sickle, and the tree was sound, just as I had seen it.

1[67]:4 Then I marveled within myself, saying, "How is the tree sound after so many branches have been lopped off?" The shepherd said to me, "Marvel not that the tree remained sound, after so many branches were lopped off but wait until you see all things, and it shall be shown to you what it is."

1[67]:5 The angel who gave the rods to the people demanded them back from them again, and according as they had received them, so also they were summoned to him, and each of them returned the several rods. But the angel of the Lord took them, and examined them.

1[67]:6 From some he received the rods withered and eaten as it were by grubs: the angel ordered those who gave up rods like these to stand apart.

1[67]:7 And others gave them up withered, but not grub-eaten; and these again he ordered to stand apart.

1[67]:8 And others gave them up half-withered; these also stood apart.

1[67]:9 And others gave up their rods half-withered and with cracks; these also stood apart.

1[67]:10 And others gave up their rods green and with cracks; these also stood apart. And others gave up their rods one half withered and one half green; these also stood apart.

1[67]:11 And others brought their rods two parts of the rod green, and the third part withered; these also stood apart. And others gave them up two parts withered, and the third part green; these also stood apart.

1[67]:12 And others gave up their rods nearly all green, but a very small portion of their rods was withered, just the end; but they had cracks in them; these also stood apart.

1[67]:13 And in those of others there was a very small portion green, but the rest of the rods was withered; these also stood apart.

1[67]:14 And others came bringing their rods green, as they received them from the angel; and the most part of the multitude gave up their rods in this state; and the angel rejoiced exceedingly at these; these also stood apart.

1[67]:15 And others gave up their rods green and with shoots, these also stood apart; and at these again the angel rejoiced exceedingly.

1[67]:16 And others gave up their rods green and with shoots; and their shoots had, as it were, a kind of fruit. And those men were exceeding gladsome, whose rods were found in this state. And over them the angel exulted, and the shepherd was very gladsome over them.

2[68]:1 And the angel of the Lord commanded crowns to be brought. And crowns were brought, made as it were of palm branches; and he crowned the men that had given up the rods which had the shoots and some fruit, and sent them away into the tower.

2[68]:2 And the others also he sent into the tower, even those who had given up the rods green and with shoots, but the shoots were without fruit; and he set a seal upon them.

2[68]:3 And all they that went into the tower had the same raiment, white as snow.

2[68]:4 And those that had given up their rods green as they received them, he sent away, giving them a [white] robe, and seals.

2[68]:5 After the angel had finished these things, he said to the shepherd; "I go away; but these you shall send away to (their places within) the walls, according as each deserves to dwell; but examine their rods carefully, and so send them away. But be careful in examining them. Take heed lest any escape you," said he. "Still if any escape you, I will test them at the altar." When he had thus spoken to the shepherd, he departed.

2[68]:6 And, after the angel had departed, the shepherd said to me; "Let us take the rods of all and plant them, to see whether any of them shall be able to live." I say unto him, "Sir, these withered things, how can they live?"

2[68]:7 He answered and said unto me; "This tree is a willow, and this class of trees clings to life. If then the rods shall be planted and get a little moisture, many of them will live. And afterwards let us try to pour some water also over them. If any of them shall be able to live, I will rejoice with it; but if it live not, I at least shall not be found neglectful."

2[68]:8 So the shepherd bade me call them, just as each one of them was stationed. And they came row after row, and they delivered up the rods to the shepherd. And the shepherd took the rods, and planted them in rows, and after he had planted them, he poured much water over them, so that the rods could not be seen for the water.

2[68]:9 And after he had watered the rods, he said to me; "Let us go now. and after days let us return and inspect all the rods; for He Who created this tree wills that all those who have received rods from this tree should live. And I myself hope that these little rods, after they have got moisture and been watered, will live the greater part of them."

3[69]:1 I say to him; "Sir, inform me what this tree is. For I am perplexed herewith, because, though so many branches were cut off, the tree is sound, and nothing appears to have been cut from it; I am therefore perplexed thereat."

3[69]:2 "Listen," said he; "this great tree which overshadows plains and mountains and all the earth is the law of God which was given to the whole world; and this law is the Son of Cod preached unto the ends of the earth. But the people that are under the shadow are they that have heard the preaching, and believed on Him;

3[69]:3 but the great and glorious angel is Michael, who has the power over this people and is their captain. For this is he that puts the law into the hearts of the believers; therefore he himself inspects them to whom he gave it, to see whether they have observed it.

3[69]:4 But you see the rods of every one; for the rods are the law. You see these many rods rendered useless, and you shall notice all those that have not observed the law, and shall see the abode of each severally."

3[69]:5 I say unto him; "Sir, wherefore did he send away some into the tower, and leave others for you?" "As many," said he, "as transgressed the law which they received from him, these he left under my authority for repentance; but as many as already satisfied the law and have observed it, these he has under his own authority."

3[69]:6 "Who then, Sir," say I, "are they that have been crowned and go into the tower?" ["As many," said he, "as wrestled with the devil and overcame him in their wrestling, are crowned:] these are they that suffered for the law.

3[69]:7 But the others, who likewise gave up their rods green and with shoots, though not with fruit, are they that were persecuted for the law, but did not suffer nor yet deny their law.

3[69]:8 But they that gave them up green just as they received them, are sober and righteous men, who walked altogether in a pure heart and have kept the commandments of the Lord. But all else you shall know, when I have examined these rods that have been planted and watered."

4[70]:1 And after a few days we came to the place, and the shepherd sat down in the place of the angel, while I stood by him. And he said to me; "Gird yourself with a garment of raw flax, and minister to me." So I girded myself with a clean garment of raw flax made of coarse material.

4[70]:2 And when he saw me girded and ready to minister to him "Call," said he, "the men whose rods have been planted, according to the rank as each presented their rods." And I went away to the plain, and called them all; and they stood all of them according to their ranks.

4[70]:3 He said to them; "Let each man pluck out his own rod, and bring it to me." Those gave them up first, who had the withered and chipped rods, and they were found accordingly withered and chipped. He ordered them to stand apart.

4[70]:4 Then those gave them up, who had the withered but not chipped; and some of them gave up the rods green, and others withered and chipped as by grubs. Those then that gave them up green he ordered to stand apart; but those that gave them up withered and chipped he ordered to stand with the first.

4[70]:5 Then those gave them up who had the half-withered and with cracks; and many of them gave them up green and without cracks; and some gave them up green and with shoots, and fruits on the shoots, such as those had who went into the tower crowned; and some gave them up withered and eaten, and some withered and uneaten, and some such as they were, half-withered and with cracks. He ordered them to stand each one apart, some in their proper ranks, and others apart.

5[71]:1 Then those gave them up who had their rods green, but with cracks. These all gave them up green, and stood in their own company. And the shepherd rejoiced over these, because they all were changed and had put away their cracks.

5[71]:2 And those gave them up likewise who had the one half green and the other half withered. The rods of some were found entirely green, of some half-withered, of some withered and eaten, and of some green and with shoots. These were all sent away each to his company.

5[71]:3 Then those gave them up who had two parts green and the third withered; many of them gave them up green, and many half-withered, and others withered and eaten. These all stood in their own company.

5[71]:4 Then those gave them up who had two parts withered and the third part green. Many of them gave them up half-withered, but some withered and eaten, others half-withered and with cracks, and a few green. These all stood in their own company.

5[71]:5 Then those gave them up who had their rods green, but a very small part [withered] and with cracks. Of these some gave them up green, and others green and with shoots. These also went away to their own company.

5[71]:6 Then those gave them up who had a very small part green and the other parts withered. The rods of these were found for the most part green and with shoots and fruit on the shoots, and others altogether green. At these rods the shepherd rejoiced very [greatly], because they were found so. And these went away each to his own company.

6[72]:1 After [the shepherd] had examined the rods of all, he said to me, "I told you that this tree clings to life. See you," said he, "how many repented and were saved?" "I see, Sir," say I. "It is," said he, that you may see the abundant compassion of the Lord, how great and glorious it is, and He has given (His) Spirit to those that are worthy of repentance."

6[72]:2 "Wherefore then, Sir," say I, "did they not all repent?" "To those, whose heart He saw about to become pure and to serve Him with all the heart, to them He gave repentance; but those whose craftiness and wickedness He saw, who intend to repent in hypocrisy, to them He gave not repentance, lest haply they should again profane His name."

6[72]:3 I say unto him, "Sir, now then show me concerning those that have given up their rods, what manner of man each of them is, and their abode, that when they hear this, they that believed and have received the seal and have broken it and did not keep it sound may fully understand what they are doing, and repent, receiving from you a seal, and may glorify the Lord, that He had compassion upon them and sent you to renew their spirits."

6[72]:4 "Listen," said he; "those whose rods were found withered and grub-eaten, these are the renegades and traitors to the Church, that blasphemed the Lord in their sins, and still further were ashamed of the Name of the Lord, which was invoked upon them. These then perished altogether unto God. But you see how not one of them repented, although they heard the words which you spoke to them, which I commanded you. From men of this kind life departed.

6[72]:5 But those that gave up the withered and undecayed (rods), these also are near them; for they were hypocrites, and brought in strange doctrines, and perverted the servants of God, especially them that had sinned, not permitting them to repent, but persuading them with their foolish doctrines. These then have hope of repenting.

6[72]:6 But you see that many of them have indeed repented from the time when you speak to them my commandments; yea, and (others) still will repent. And as many as shall not repent, have lost their life; but as many of them as repented, became good; and their dwelling was placed within the first walls, and some of them even ascended into the tower. You see then," [said he,] "that repentance from sins brings life, but not to repent brings death.

7[73]:1 "But as many as gave up (the rods) half-withered, and with cracks in them, hear also concerning these. Those whose rods were half-withered throughout are the double-minded; for they neither live nor are dead.

7[73]:2 But those that have them half-withered and cracks in them, these are both double-minded and slanderers, and are never at peace among themselves but always causing dissensions. Yet even to these," [said he,] "repentance is given. You see," [said he,] "that some of them have repented; and there is still," said he, "hope of repentance among them.

7[73]:3 And as many of them," said he, "as have repented, have their abode within the tower; but as many of them as have repented tardily shall abide within the walls; and as many as repent not, but

continue in their doings, shall die the death.

7[73]:4 But they that have given up their rods green and with cracks, these were found faithful and good at all times, [but] they have a certain emulation one with another about first places and about glory of some kind or other; but all these are foolish in having (emulation) one with another about first places.

7[73]:5 Yet these also, when they heard my commandments, being good, purified themselves and repented quickly. They have their habitation, therefore, within the tower. But if any one shall again turn to dissension, he shall be cast out from the tower and shall lose his life.

7[73]:6 Life is for all those that keep the commandments of the Lord. But in the commandments there is nothing about first places, or about glory of any kind, but about long-suffering and humility in man. In such men, therefore, is the life of the Lord, but in factious and lawless men is death.

8[74]:1 "But they that gave up their rods half green and half withered, these are they that are mixed up in business and hold fast not to the saints. Therefore the one half of them lives , but the other half is dead.

8[74]:2 Many then when they heard my commandments repented. As many then as repented, have their abode within the tower. But some of them altogether stood aloof These then have no repentance; for by reason of their business affairs they blasphemed the Lord and denied Him. So they lost their life for the wickedness that they committed.

8[74]:3 But many of them were doubtful-minded. These still have place for repentance, if they repent quickly, and their dwelling shall be within the tower; and if they repent tardily, they shall dwell within the walls; but if they repent not, they too have lost their life.

8[74]:4 But they that have given up two parts green and the third part withered, these are they that have denied with manifold denials.

8[74]:5 Many of them therefore repented and departed to dwell inside the tower; but many utterly rebelled from God; these lost their life finally. And some of them were double-minded and caused dissensions. For these then there is repentance, if they repent speedily and continue not in their pleasures; but if they continue in their doings, they likewise procure for themselves death.

9[75]:1 "But they that have given up their rods two thirds withered and one third green, these are men who have been believers, but grew rich and became renowned among the Gentiles. They clothed themselves with great pride and became high-minded, and abandoned the truth and did not hold fast to the righteous, but lived together after the manner of the Gentiles, and this path appeared the more pleasant unto them; yet they departed not from God, but continued in the faith, though they wrought not the works of the faith.

9[75]:2 Many of them therefore repented, and they had their habitation within the tower.

9[75]:3 But others at the last living with the Gentiles, and being corrupted by the vain opinions of the Gentiles, departed from God, and worked the works of the Gentiles. These therefore were numbered with the Gentiles.

9[75]:4 But others of them were doubtful-minded, not hoping to be saved by reason of the deeds that they had done; and others were double-minded and made divisions among themselves. For these then that were double-minded by reason of their doings there is still repentance; but their repentance ought to be speedy, that their dwelling may be within the tower; but for those who repent not, but continue in their pleasures, death is nigh.

10[76]:1 "But they that gave up their rods green, yet with the extreme ends withered and with cracks; these were found at all times good and faithful and glorious in the sight of God, but they sinned to a very slight degree by reason of little desires and because they had somewhat against one another. But, when they heard my words, the greater part quickly repented, and their dwelling was assigned within the tower.

10[76]:2 But some of them were double-minded, and some being double-minded made a greater dissension. In these then there is still a hope of repentance, because they were found always good; and hardly shall one of them die.

10[76]:3 But they that gave up their rods withered, yet with a very small part green, these are they that believed, but practiced the works of lawlessness. Still they never separated from God, but bore the Name gladly, and gladly received into their houses the servants of God. So hearing of this repentance they repented without wavering, and they practice all excellence and righteousness.

10[76]:4 And some of them even suffer persecution willingly, knowing the deeds that they did. All these then shall have their dwelling within the tower."

11[77]:1 And after he had completed the interpretations of all the rods, he said unto me; "Go, and tell all men to repent, and they shall live unto God; for the Lord in His compassion sent me to give repentance to all, though some of them do not deserve it for their deeds; but being long-suffering the Lord wills them that were called through His Son to be saved."

11[77]:2 I say to him; "Sir, I hope that all when they hear these words will repent; for I am persuaded that each one, when he fully knows his own deeds and fears God, will repent."

11[77]:3 He answered and said unto me; "As many," [said he,] "as [shall repent] from their whole heart [and] shall cleanse themselves from all the evil deeds aforementioned, and shall add nothing further to their sins, shall receive healing from the Lord for their former sins, unless they be double-minded concerning these commandments, and they shall live unto God. [But as many," said he, "as shall add to their sins and walk in the lusts of this world, shall condemn themselves to death.]

11[77]:4 But do you walk in my commandments, and live [unto God; yea, and as many as shall walk in them and shall do rightly, shall live unto God."]

11[77]:5 Having shown me all these things [and told me them] he said to me; "Now the rest will I declare (unto you) after a few days."

Parable 9

1[78]:1 After I had written down the commandments and parables of the shepherd, the angel of repentance, he came to me and said to me; "I wish to show you all things that the Holy Spirit, which spoke with you in the form of the Church, showed unto you. For that Spirit is the Son of God.

1[78]:2 For when you was weaker in the flesh, it was not declared unto you through an angel; but when you was enabled through the Spirit, and didst grow mighty in thy strength so that you could even see an angel, then at length was manifested unto you, through the Church, the building of the tower. In fair and seemly manner hast you seen all things, (instructed) as it were by a virgin; but now you see (being instructed) by an angel, though by the same Spirit;

1[78]:3 yet must you learn everything more accurately from me. For to this end also was I appointed by the glorious angel to dwell in thy house, that you might see all things mightily, in nothing terrified, even as before."

1[78]:4 And he took me away into Arcadia, to a certain rounded mountain, and set me on the top of the mountain, and showed me a great plain, and round the plain twelve mountains, the mountains having each a different appearance.

1[78]:5 The first was black as soot; the second was bare, without vegetation; the third was thorny and full of briars;

1[78]:6 the fourth had the vegetation half-withered, the upper part of the grass green, but the part by the roots withered, and some of the grass became withered, whenever the sun had scorched it;

1[78]:7 the fifth mountain had green grass and was rugged; the sixth mountain was full with clefts throughout, some small and some great, and the clefts had vegetation, but the grass was not very luxuriant, but rather as if it had been withered;

1[78]:8 the seventh mountain had smiling vegetation, and the whole mountain was in a thriving condition, and cattle and birds of every kind did feed upon that mountain; and the more the cattle and the birds did feed, so much the more did the herbage of that mountain flourish. The eighth mountain was full of springs, and every kind of creature of the Lord did drink of the springs on that mountain.

1[78]:9 the ninth mountain had no water at all, and was entirely desert; and it had in it wild beasts and deadly reptiles, which destroy mankind. The tenth mountain had very large trees and was umbrageous throughout, and beneath the shade lay sheep resting and feeding.

1[78]:10 the eleventh mountain was thickly wooded all over, and the trees thereon were very productive, decked with divers kinds of fruits, so that one seeing them would desire to eat of their fruits. The twelfth mountain was altogether white and its aspect was cheerful; and the mountain was most beauteous in itself.

2[79]:1 And in the middle of the plain he showed me a great white rock, rising up from the plain. The rock was loftier than the mountains, being four-square, so that it could contain the whole world.

2[79]:2 Now this rock was ancient, and had a gate hewn out of it; but the gate seemed to me to have been hewed out quite recently. And the gate glistened beyond the brightness of the sun, so that I marveled at the brightness of the gate.

2[79]:3 And around the gate stood twelve virgins. The four then that stood at the corners seemed to me to be more glorious (than the rest); but the others likewise were glorious; and they stood at the four quarters of the gate, and virgins stood in pairs between them.

2[79]:4 And they were clothed in linen tunics and girt about in seemly fashion, having their right shoulders free, as if they intended to carry some burden. Thus were they prepared, for they were very cheerful and eager.

2[79]:5 After I had seen these things, I marveled in myself at the greatness and the glory of what I was seeing And again I was perplexed concerning the virgins, that delicate as they were they stood up like men, as if they intended to carry the whole heaven.

2[79]:6 And the shepherd said unto me; "Why question you within yourself and art perplexed, and bring sadness on yourself? For whatsoever things you can not comprehend, attempt them not, if you art prudent; but entreat the Lord, that you may receive understanding to comprehend them.

2[79]:7 What is behind you you can not see, but what is before you you behold. The things therefore which you can not see, let alone, and trouble not yourself (about them; but the things which you see, these master, and be not over curious about the rest; but I will explain unto you all things whatsoever I shall show you. Have an eye therefore to what remains."

3[80]:1 I saw six men come, tall and glorious and alike in appearance and they summoned a multitude of men. And the others also which came were tall men and handsome and powerful. And the six men ordered them to build a tower above the gate. And there arose a great noise from those men who had come to build the tower, as they ran hither and thither round the gate.

3[80]:2 For the virgins standing round the gate told the men to hasten to build the tower. Now the virgins had spread out their hands, as if they would take something from the men.

3[80]:3 And the six men ordered stones to come up from a certain deep place, and to go to the building of the tower. And there went up ten stones square and polished, [not] hewn from a quarry.

3[80]:4 And the six men called to the virgins, and ordered them to carry all the stones which should go unto the building of the tower, and to pass through the gate and to hand them to the men that were about to build the tower.

3[80]:5 And the virgins laid the first ten stones that rose out of the deep on each other, and they carried them together, stone by stone.

4[81]:1 And just as they stood together around the gate, in that order they carried them that seemed to be strong enough and had stooped under the corners of the stone, while the others stooped at the sides of the stone. And so they carried all the stones. And they carried them right through the gate, as they were ordered, and handed them to the men for the tower; and these took the stones and built.

4[81]:2 Now the building of the tower was upon the great rock and above the gate. Those ten stones then were joined together, and they covered the whole rock. And these formed a foundation for the building of the tower. And [the rock and] the gate supported the whole tower.

4[81]:3 And, after the ten stones, other twenty-five stones came up from the deep, and these were fitted into the building of the tower, being carried by the virgins, like the former. And after these thirty-five stones came up. And these likewise were fitted into the tower. And after these came up other forty stones. and these all were put into the building of the tower. So four rows were made in the foundations of the tower.

4[81]:4 And (the stones) ceased coming up from the deep, and the builders likewise ceased for a little. And again the six men ordered the multitude of the people to bring in stones from the mountains for the building of the tower.

4[81]:5 They were brought in accordingly from all the mountains, of various colors, shaped by the men, and were handed to the virgins; and the virgins carried them right through the gate, and handed them in for the building of the tower. And when the various stones were placed in the building, they became all alike and white, and they lost their various colors.

4[81]:6 But some stones were handed in by the men for the building, and these did not become bright; but just as they were placed, such likewise were they found; for they were not handed in by the virgins, nor had they been carried in through the gate. These stones then were unsightly in the building of the tower.

4[81]:7 Then the six men, seeing the stones that were unsightly in the building, ordered them to be removed and carried [below] into their own place whence they were brought.

4[81]:8 And they say to the men who were bringing the stones in; "Abstain for your parts altogether from handing in stones for the building; but place them by the tower, that the virgins may carry them through the gate, and hand them in for the building. For if," [say they,] they be not carried in through the gate by the hands of these virgins, they cannot change their colors. Labor not therefore," [say they,] "in vain."

5[82]:1 And the building was finished on that day, yet was not the tower finally completed, for it was to be carried up [still] higher; and there was a cessation in the building. And the six men ordered the builders to retire for a short time [all of them], and to rest; but the virgins they ordered not to retire from the tower. And I thought the virgins were left to guard the tower.

5[82]:2 And after all had retired Land rested], I say to the shepherd; "How is it, Sir," say I, "that the building of the tower was not completed?" "The tower," he said, "cannot yet be finally completed, until its master come and test this building, that if any stones be found crumbling, he may change them; for the tower is being built according to His will."

5[82]:3 "I would fain know, Sir," say I, "what is this building of this tower, and concerning the rock and gate, and the mountains, and the virgins, and the stones that came up from the deep, and were not shaped, but went just as they were into the building;

5[82]:4 and wherefore ten stones were first placed in the foundations, then twenty-five, then thirty-five, then forty, and concerning the stones that had gone to the building and were removed again and put away in their own place--concerning all these things set my soul at rest, Sir, and explain them to me."

5[82]:5 "If," said he, "you be not found possessed of an idle curiosity, you shall know all things. For after a few days we shall come here, and you shall see the sequel that overtakes this tower and shall understand all the parables accurately."

5[82]:6 And after a few days we came to the place where we had sat, and he said to me, "Let us go to the tower; for the owner of the tower cometh to inspect it." And we came to the tower, and there was no one at all by it, save the virgins alone.

5[82]:7 And the shepherd asked the virgins whether the master of the tower had arrived. And they said that he would be there directly to inspect the building.

6[83]:1 And, behold, after a little while I see an array of many men coming, and in the midst a man of such lofty stature that he overtopped the tower.

6[83]:2 And the six men who superintended the building walked with him on the right hand and on the left, and all they that worked at the building were with him, and many other glorious attendants around him. And the virgins that watched the tower ran up and kissed him, and they began to walk by his side round the tower.

6[83]:3 And that man inspected the building so carefully, that he felt each single stone; and he held a rod in his hand and struck each single stone that was built in.

6[83]:4 And when he smote, some of the stones became black as soot, others mildewed, others cracked, others broke off short, others became neither white nor black, others rough and not fitting in with the other stones, and others with many spots; these were the varied aspects of the stones which were found unsound for the building.

6[83]:5 So he ordered all these to be removed from the tower, and to be placed by the side of the tower, and other stones to be brought and put into their place.

6[83]:6 And the builders asked him from what mountain he desired stones to be brought and put into their place. And he would not have them brought from the mountains, but ordered them to be brought from a certain plain that was nigh at hand.

6[83]:7 And the plain was dug, and stones were found there bright and square, but some of them too were round. And all the stones which there were anywhere in that plain were brought every one of them, and were carried through the gate by the virgins.

6[83]:8 And the square stones were hewed, and set in the place of those which had been removed; but the round ones were not placed in the building, because they were too hard to be shaped, and to work on them was slow. So they were placed by the side of the tower, as though they were intended to be shaped and placed in the building; for they were very bright.

7[84]:1 So then, having accomplished these things, the glorious man who was lord of the whole tower called the shepherd to him, and delivered unto him all the stones which lay by the side of the tower, which were cast out from the building, and said unto him;

7[84]:2 "Clean these stones carefully, and set them in the building of the tower, these, I mean, which can fit with the rest; but those which will not fit, throw far away from the tower."

7[84]:3 Having given these orders to the shepherd, he departed from the tower with all those with whom he had come. And the virgins stood round the tower watching it.

7[84]:4 I say to the shepherd, "How can these stones go again to the building of the tower, seeing that they have been disapproved?" He said unto me in answer; "See you", said he, "these stones ?" I see them, Sir," say I. "I myself," said he, "will shape the greater part of these stones and put them into the building, and they shall fit in with the remaining stones."

7[84]:5 "How, Sir," say I, "can they, when they are chiseled, fill the same space?" He said unto me in answer, "As many as shall be found small, shall be put into the middle of the building; but as many as are larger, shall be placed nearer the outside, and they will bind them together."

7[84]:6 With these words he said to me, "Let us go away, and after two days let us come and clean these stones, and put them into the building; for all things round the tower must be made clean, lest haply the master come suddenly and find the circuit of the tower dirty, and he be wroth, and so these stones shall not go to the building of the tower, and I shall appear to be careless in my master's sight."

7[84]:7 And after two days we came to the tower, and he said unto me; "Let us inspect all the stones, and see those which can go to the building." I say to him, "Sir, let us inspect them."

8[85]:1 And so commencing first we began to inspect the black stones; and just as they were when set aside from the building, such also they were found. And the shepherd ordered them to be removed from the tower and to be put on one side.

8[85]:2 Then he inspected those that were mildewed, and he took and shaped many of them, and ordered the virgins to take them up and put them into the building. And the virgins took them up and placed them in the building of the tower in a middle position. But the rest he ordered to be placed with the black ones; for these also were found black.

8[85]:3 Then he began to inspect those that had the cracks; and of these he shaped many, and he ordered them to be carried away by the hands of the virgins for the building. And they were placed towards the outside, because they were found to be sounder. But the rest could not be shaped owing to the number of the cracks. For this reason therefore they were cast aside from the building of the tower.

8[85]:4 Then he proceeded to inspect the stunted (stones), and many among them were found black, and some had contracted great cracks; and he ordered these also to be placed with those that had been cast aside. But those of them which remained he cleaned and shaped, and ordered to be placed in the building So the virgins took them up, and fitted them into the middle of the building of the tower; for they were somewhat weak.

8[85]:5 Then he began to inspect those that were half white and half black, and many of them were (now) found black; and he ordered these also to be taken up with those that had been cast aside. But all the rest were [found white, and were] taken up by the virgins; for being white they were fitted by [the

virgins] them[selves] into the building. But they were placed towards the outside, because they were found sound, so that they could hold together those that were placed in the middle; for not a single one of them was too short.

8[85]:6 Then he began to inspect the hard and rough; and a few of them were cast away, because they could not be shaped; for they were found very hard. But the rest of them were shaped [and taken up by the virgins] and fitted into the middle of the building of the tower; for they were somewhat weak.

8[85]:7 Then he proceeded to inspect those that had the spots, and of these some few had turned black and were cast away among the rest; but the remainder were found bright and sound, and these were fitted by the virgins into the building; but they were placed towards the outside, owing to their strength.

9[86]:1 Then he came to inspect the white and round stones, and he said unto me; "What shall we do with these stones?" "How do I know, Sir?" say I [And he said to me,] "Perceives you nothing concerning them?"

9[86]:2 "I, Sir," say I, "do not possess this art, neither am I a mason, nor can I understand." See you not," said he, "that they are very round; and if I wish to make them square, very much must needs be chiseled off from them? Yet some of them must of necessity be placed into the building."

9[86]:3 "If then, Sir," say I, "it must needs be so, why distress yourself, and why not choose out for the building those you will, and fit them into it?" He chose out from them the large and the bright ones, and shaped them; and the virgins took them up, and fitted them into the outer parts of the building.

9[86]:4 But the rest, which remained over, were taken up, and put aside into the plain whence they were brought; they were not however cast away, "Because," said he, there remains still a little of the tower to be built And the master of the tower is exceedingly anxious that these stones be fitted into the building, for they are very bright."

9[86]:5 So twelve women were called, most beautiful in form, clad in black, [girded about and having the shoulders bare,] with their hair hanging loose. And these women, I thought, had a savage look. And the shepherd ordered them to take up the stones which had been cast away from the building, and to carry them off to the same mountains from which also they had been brought;

9[86]:6 and they took them up joyfully, and carried away all the stones and put them in the place whence they had been taken. And after all the stones had been taken up, and not a single stone still lay round the tower, the shepherd said unto me; "Let us go round the tower, and see that there is no defect in it." And I proceeded to go round it with him.

9[86]:7 And when the shepherd saw that the tower was very comely in the building, he was exceedingly glad; for the tower was so well built, that when I saw it I coveted the building of it; for it was built, as it were, of one stone, having one fitting in it. And the stone-work appeared as if hewn out of the rock; for it seemed to me to be all a single stone.

10[87]:1 And I, as I walked with him, was glad to see so brave a sight. And the shepherd said to me; "Go and bring plaster and fine clay, that I may fill up the shapes of the stones that have been taken up and put into the building; for all the circuit of the tower must be made smooth."

10[87]:2 And I did as he bade, and brought them to him. "Assist me," said he, "and the work will speedily be accomplished." So he filled in the shapes of the stones which had gone to the building, and ordered the circuit of the tower to be swept and made clean.

10[87]:3 And the virgins took brooms and swept, and they removed all the rubbish from the tower, and sprinkled water, and the site of the tower was made cheerful and very seemly.

10[87]:4 The shepherd said unto me, "All," said he, "has now been cleaned. If the lord come to inspect the tower, he has nothing for which to blame us." Saying this, he desired to go away.

10[87]:5 But I caught hold of his wallet, and began to adjure him by the Lord that he would explain to me [all] what he had showed me. He said to me; "I am busy for a little while, and then I will explain everything to you. Await me here till I come."

10[87]:6 I say to him; "Sir, when I am here alone what shall I do?" "You art not alone," said he; "for these virgins are here with you." "Commend me then to them," say I. The shepherd calls them to him and said to them; "I commend this man to you till I come," and he departed.

10[87]:7 So I was alone with the virgins; and they were most cheerful, and kindly disposed to Me especially the four of them that were the more glorious in appearance.

11[88]:1 The virgins say to me; "Today the shepherd cometh not here." "What then shall I do?" say I. "Stay for him," say they, "till eventide; and if he come, he will speak with you; but if he come not, you shall stay here with us till he cometh."

11[88]:2 I say to them; "I will await him till evening, and if he come not, I will depart home and return early in the morning." But they answered and said unto me; "To us you were entrusted; you can not depart from us."

11[88]:3 "Where then," say I, "shall I remain?" "You shall pass the night with us," say they as a brother, not as a husband; for you art our brother, and henceforward we will dwell with you; for we love you dearly." But I was ashamed to abide with them.

11[88]:4 And she that seemed to be the chief of them began to kiss and to embrace me; and the others seeing her embrace me, they too began to kiss me, and to lead me round the tower, and to sport with me.

11[88]:5 And I had become as it were a younger man, and I commenced myself likewise to sport with them. For some of them began to dance, [others to skip,] others to sing. But I kept silence and walked with them round the tower, and was glad with them.

11[88]:6 But when evening came I wished to go away home; but they would not let me go, but detained me. And I stayed the night with them, and I slept by the side of the tower.

11[88]:7 For the virgins spread their linen tunics on the ground, and made me lie down in the midst of them, and they did nothing else but pray; and I prayed with them without ceasing, and not less than they. And the virgins rejoiced that I so prayed. And I stayed there with the virgins until the morning till the second hour.

11[88]:8 Then came the shepherd, and said to the virgins; "Have you done him any injury?" "Ask him," say they. I say to him, "Sir, I was rejoiced to stay with them." "On what didst you sup?" said he "I supped, Sir," say I, "on the words of the Lord the whole night through." "Did they treat you well?" said he. "Yes, Sir," say I.

11[88]:9 "Now," said he, "what would you hear first?" "In the order as you showed to me, Sir, from the beginning," say I; "I request you, Sir, to explain to me exactly in the order that I shall enquire of you." According as you desire," said he, "even so will I interpret to you, and I will conceal nothing whatever from you."

12[89]:1 "First of all, Sir," say I, "explain this to me. The rock and the gate, what is it?" "This rock," said he, "and gate is the Son of God." "How, Sir," say I, "is the rock ancient, but the gate recent?" "Listen," said he, "and understand, foolish man.

12[89]:2 The Son of God is older than all His creation, so that He became the Father's adviser in His creation. Therefore also He is ancient." "But the gate, why is it recent, Sir?" say I.

12[89]:3 "Because," said he, "He was made manifest in the last days of the consummation; therefore the gate was made recent, that they which are to be saved may enter through it into the kingdom of God.

12[89]:4 Didst you see," said he, "that the stones which came through the gate have gone to the building of the tower, but those which came not through it were cast away again to their own place?" "I saw, Sir," say I. "Thus," said he, "no one shall enter into the kingdom of God, except he receive the name of His Son.

12[89]:5 For if you wish to enter into any city, and that city is walled all round and has one gate only, can you enter into that city except through the gate which it has?" "Why, how, Sir," say I, "is it possible otherwise?" "If then you can not enter into the city except through the gate itself, even so," said he, "a man cannot enter into the kingdom of God except by the name of His Son that is beloved by Him.

12[89]:6 Didst you see," said he, "the multitude that is building the tower?" "I saw it, Sir," say I. "They," said he, are all glorious angels. With these then the Lord is walled around. But the gate is the Son of God; there is this one entrance only to the Lord. No one then shall enter in unto Him otherwise than through His Son.

12[89]:7 Didst you see," said he, "the six men, and the glorious and mighty man in the midst of them, him that walked about the tower and rejected the stones from the building?" "I saw him, Sir," say I.

12[89]:8 "The glorious man," said he, "is the Son of God, and those six are the glorious angels who guard Him on the right hand and on the left. Of these glorious angels not one," said he, "shall enter in unto God without Him; whosoever shall not receive His name, shall not enter into the kingdom of God."

13[90]:1 "But the tower," say I, "what is it?" "The tower," said he, "why, this is the Church.

13[90]:2 "And these virgins, who are they?" "They," said he, "are holy spirits; and no man can otherwise be found in the kingdom of God, unless these shall clothe him with their garment; for if you receive only the name, but receive not the garment from them, you profit nothing. For these virgins are powers of the Son of God. If [therefore] you bear the Name, and bear not His power, you shall bear His Name to none effect.

13[90]:3 And the stones," said he, "which you didst see cast away, these bare the Name, but clothed not themselves with the raiment of the virgins." "Of what sort, Sir," say I, "is their raiment?" "The names themselves," said he, "are their raiment. Whosoever bears the Name of the Son of God, ought to bear the names of these also; for even the Son Himself bears the names of these virgins.

13[90]:4 As many stones," said he, "as you saw enter into the building of the tower, being given in by their hands and waiting for the building, they have been clothed in the power of these virgins.

13[90]:5 For this cause you see the tower made a single stone with the rock. So also they that have believed in the Lord through His Son and clothe themselves in these spirits, shall become one spirit and one body, and their garments all of one color. But such persons as bear the names of the virgins have their dwelling in the tower."

13[90]:6 "The stones then, Sir," say I, "which are cast aside, wherefore were they cast aside? For they passed through the gate and were placed in the building of the tower by the hands of the virgins." "Since all these things interest you," said he, "and you enquire diligently, listen as touching the stones that have been cast aside.

13[90]:7 These all," [said he,] "received the name of the Son of God, and received likewise the power of these virgins. When then they received these spirits, they were strengthened, and were with the servants of God, and they had one spirit and one body [and one garment]; for they had the same mind, and they wrought righteousness.

13[90]:8 After a certain time then they were persuaded by the women whom you saw clad in black raiment, and having their shoulders bare and their hair loose, and beautiful in form. When they saw them they desired them, and they clothed themselves with their power, but they stripped off from themselves the power of the virgins.

13[90]:9 They then were cast away from the house of God, and delivered to these (women). But they that were not deceived by the beauty of these women remained in the house of God. So you hast," said he, "the interpretation of them that were cast aside."

13[90]:1 What then, Sir," say I, "if these men, being such as they are, should repent and put away their desire for these women, and return unto the virgins, and walk in their power and in their works? Shall they not enter into the house of God?"

13[90]:2 "They shall enter," said he, "if they shall put away the works of these women, and take again the power of the virgins, and walk in their works. For this is the reason why there was also a cessation in the building, that, if these repent, they may go into the building of the tower; but if they repent not, then others will go, and these shall be cast away finally."

13[90]:3 For all these things I gave thanks unto the Lord, because He had compassion on all that called upon His name, and sent forth the angel of repentance to us that had sinned against Him, and refreshed our spirit, and, when we were already ruined and had no hope of life, restored our life.

13[90]:4 "Now, Sir," say I, "show me why the tower is not built upon the ground, but upon the rock and upon the gate." "Because you art senseless," said he, "and without understanding [you ask the question]." "I am obliged, Sir," say I, "to ask all questions of you, because I am absolutely unable to comprehend anything at all; for all are great and glorious and difficult for men to understand."

13[90]:5 "Listen," said he. "The name of the Son of God is great and incomprehensible, and sustains the whole world. If then all creation is sustained by the Son [of God], what think you of those that are called by Him, and bear the name of the Son of God, and walk according to His commandments?

13[90]:6 See you then what manner of men He sustains? Even those that bear His name with their whole heart. He Himself then is become their foundation, and He sustains them gladly, because they are not ashamed to bear His name."

15[92]:1 "Declare to me, Sir," say I, "the names of the virgins, and of the women that are clothed in the black garments." "Hear," said he, "the names of the more powerful virgins, those that are stationed at the corners.

15[92]:2 The first is Faith, and the second, Continence, and the third, Power, and the fourth, Long-suffering. But the others stationed between them have these names--Simplicity, Guilelessness, Purity, Cheerfulness, Truth, Understanding, Concord, Love. He that bears these names and the name of the Son of God shall be able to enter into the kingdom of God.

15[92]:3 Hear," said he, "likewise the names of the women that wear the black garments. Of these also four are more powerful than the rest; the first is Unbelief; the second, Intemperance; the third, Disobedience; the fourth, Deceit; and their followers are called, Sadness, Wickedness, Wantonness, Irascibility, Falsehood, Folly, Slander, Hatred. The servant of God that bears these names shall see the kingdom of God, but shall not enter into it."

15[92]:4 "But the stones, Sir," say I, "that came from the deep, and were fitted into the building, who are they?" "The first," said he, "even the ten, that were placed in the foundations, are the first generation; the twenty-five are the second generation of righteous men; the thirty-five are God's prophets and His ministers; the forty are apostles and teachers of the preaching of the Son of God."

15[92]:5 "Wherefore then, Sir," say I, "did the virgins give in these stones also for the building of the tower and carry them through the gate?"

15[92]:6 "Because these first," said he, "bore these spirits, and they never separated the one from the other, neither the spirits from the men nor the men from the spirits, but the spirits abode with them till they fell asleep; and if they had not had these spirits with them, they would not have been found useful for the building of this tower."

15[92]:1 "Show me still further, Sir," say I. "What desire you to know besides?" said he. "Wherefore, Sir," say I, "did the stones come up from the deep, and wherefore were they placed into the building, though they bore these spirits?"

15[92]:2 "It was necessary for them," said he, "to rise up through water, that they might be made alive; for otherwise they could not enter into the kingdom of God, except they had put aside the deadness of their [former] life.

15[92]:3 So these likewise that had fallen asleep received the seal of the Son of God and entered into the kingdom of God. For before a man," said he, "has borne the name of [the Son of] God, he is dead; but when he has received the seal, he lays aside his deadness, and resumes life.

15[92]:4 The seal then is the water: so they go down into the water dead, and they come up alive. "thus to them also this seal was preached, and they availed themselves of it that they might enter into the kingdom of God."

15[92]:5 "Wherefore, Sir," say I, "did the forty stones also come up with them from the deep, though they had already received the seal?" "Because," said he, "these, the apostles and the teachers who preached the name of the Son of God, after they had fallen asleep in the power and faith of the Son of God, preached also to them that had fallen asleep before them, and themselves gave unto them the seal of the preaching.

15[92]:6 Therefore they went down with them into the water, and came up again. But these went down alive [and again came up alive]; whereas the others that had fallen asleep before them went down dead and came up alive.

15[92]:7 So by their means they were quickened into life, and came to the full knowledge of the name of the Son of God. For this cause also they came up with them, and were fitted with them into the building of the tower and were built with them, without being shaped; for they fell asleep in righteousness and in great purity. Only they had not this seal. You hast then the interpretation of these things also." "I have, Sir," say I.

17[94]:1 "Now then, Sir, explain to me concerning the mountains. Wherefore are their forms diverse the one from the other, and various?" "Listen," said he. "These twelve mountains are [twelve] tribes that inhabit the whole world. To these (tribes) then the Son of God was preached by the Apostles."

17[94]:2 But explain to me, Sir, why they are various--these mountains--and each has a different appearance." "Listen," said he. "These twelve tribes which inhabit the whole world are twelve nations; and they are various in understanding and in mind. As various, then, as you saw these mountains to be, such also are the varieties in the mind of these nations, and such their understanding. And I will show unto you the conduct of each."

17[94]:3 "First, Sir," say I, "show me this, why the mountains being so various, yet, when their stones were set into the building, became bright and of one color, just like the stones that had come up from the deep."

17[94]:4 "Because," said he, "all the nations that dwell under heaven, when they heard and believed, were called by the one name of [the Son of] God. So having received the seal, they had one understanding and one mind, and one faith became theirs and [one] love, and they bore the spirits of the virgins along with the Name; therefore the building of the tower became of one color, even bright as the sun.

17[94]:5 But after they entered in together, and became one body, some of them defiled themselves, and were cast out from the society of the righteous, and became again such as they were before, or rather even worse."

18[95]:1 "How, Sir," say I, "did they become worse, after they had fully known God?" "He that knows not God," said he, "and commits wickedness, has a certain punishment for his wickedness; but he that knows God fully ought not any longer to commit wickedness, but to do good.

18[95]:2 If then he that ought to do good commits wickedness, does he not seem to do greater wickedness than the man that knows not God? Therefore they that have not known God, and commit wickedness, are condemned to death; but they that have known God and seen His mighty works, and yet commit wickedness, shall receive a double punishment, and shall die eternally. In this way therefore shall the Church of God be purified.

18[95]:3 And as you saw the stones removed from the tower and delivered over to the evil spirits, they too shall be cast out; and there shall be one body of them that are purified, just as the tower, after it had been purified, became made as it were of one stone. Thus shall it be with the Church of God also, after she has been purified, and the wicked and hypocrites and blasphemers and double-minded and they that commit various kinds of wickedness have been cast out.

18[95]:4 When these have been cast out, the Church of God shall be one body, one understanding, one mind, one faith, one love. And then the Son of God shall rejoice and be glad in them, for that He has received back His people pure." "Great and glorious, Sir," say I, "are all these things.

18[95]:5 Once more, Sir," [say I,] "show me the force and the doings of each one of the mountains, that every soul that trusts in the Lord, when it hears, may glorify His great and marvelous and glorious name." "Listen," said he, "to the variety of the mountains and of the twelve nations.

19[96]:1 "From the first mountain, which was black, they that have believed are such as these; rebels and blasphemers against the Lord, and betrayers of the servants of God. For these there is no repentance, but there is death. For this cause also they are black; for their race is lawless.

19[96]:2 And from the second mountain, the bare one, they that believed are such as these; hypocrites and teachers of wickedness. And these then are like the former in not having the fruit of righteousness. For, even as their mountain is unfruitful, so likewise such men as these have a name indeed, but they are void of the faith, and there is no fruit of truth in them. For these then repentance is offered, if they repent quickly; but if they delay, they will have their death with the former."

19[96]:3 "Wherefore, Sir," say I, "is repentance possible for them, but not for the former ? For their doings are almost the same." "On this account," he said, "is repentance offered for them, because they blasphemed not their Lord, nor became betrayers of the servants of God; yet from desire of gain they played the hypocrite, and taught each other [after] the desires of sinful men. But they shall pay a certain penalty; yet repentance is ordained for them, because they are not become blasphemers or betrayers.

20[97]:1 "And from the third mountain, which had thorns and briars, they that believed are such as these; some of them are wealthy and others are entangled in many business affairs. The briars are the wealthy, and the thorns are they that are mixed up in various business affairs.

20[97]:2 These [then, that are mixed up in many and various business affairs,] hold fast [not] to the servants of God, but go astray, being choked by their affairs, but the wealthy unwillingly hold fast to the servants of God, fearing lest they may be asked for something by them. Such men therefore shall hardly enter into the kingdom of God.

20[97]:3 For as it is difficult to walk on briars with bare feet, so also it is difficult for such men to enter the kingdom of God.

20[97]:4 But for all these repentance is possible, but it must be speedy, that in respect to what they omitted to do in the former times, they may now revert to (past) days, and do some good. If then they shall repent and do some good, they shall live unto God; but if they continue in their doings, they shall be delivered over to those women, the which shall put them to death.

20[97]:1 "And from the fourth mountain, which had much vegetation, the upper part of the grass green and the part towards the roots withered, and some of it dried up by the sun, they that believed are such as these; the double-minded, and they that have the Lord on their lips, but have Him not in their heart.

20[97]:2 Therefore their foundations are dry and without power, and their words only live, but their works are dead. Such men are neither alive nor dead. They are, therefore, like unto the double-minded; for the double-minded are neither green nor withered; for they are neither alive nor dead.

20[97]:3 For as their grass was withered up when it saw the sun, so also the double-minded, when they hear of tribulation, through their cowardice worship idols and are ashamed of the name of their Lord.

20[97]:4 Such are neither alive nor dead. Yet these also, if they repent quickly, shall be able to live; but if they repent not, they are delivered over already to the women who deprive them of their life.

22[99]:1 "And from the fifth mountain, which had green grass and was rugged, they that believed are such as these; they are faithful, but slow to learn and stubborn and self-pleasers, desiring to know all things, and yet they know nothing at all.

22[99]:2 By reason of this their stubbornness, understanding stood aloof from them, and a foolish senselessness entered into them; and they praise themselves as having understanding, and they desire to be self-appointed teachers, senseless though they are.

22[99]:3 Owing then to this pride of heart many, while they exalted themselves, have been made empty; for a mighty demon is stubbornness and vain confidence. Of these then many were cast away, but some repented and believed, and submitted themselves to those that had understanding, having learnt their own senselessness.

22[99]:4 Yea, and to the rest that belong to this class repentance is offered; for they did not become wicked, but rather foolish and without understanding. If these then shall repent, they shall live unto God; but if they repent not, they shall have their abode with the women who work evil against them.

23[100]:1 "But they that believed from the sixth mountain, which had clefts great and small, and in the clefts herbage withered, are such as these;

23[100]:2 they that have the small clefts, these are they that have aught against one another, and from their backbitings are withered in the faith; but many of these repented Yea, and the rest shall repent, when they hear my commandments; for their backbitings are but small, and they shall quickly repent.

746

23[100]:3 But they that have great clefts, these are persistent in their backbitings and bear grudges, nursing wrath against one another. These then were thrown right away from the tower and rejected from its building. Such persons therefore shall with difficulty live.

23[100]:4 If God and our Lord, Who rules over all things and has the authority over all His creation, bears no grudge against them that confess their sins, but is propitiated, doth man, who is mortal and full of sins, bear a grudge against man, as though he were able to destroy or save him?

23[100]:5 I say unto you--I, the angel of repentance--unto as many as hold this heresy, put it away from you and repent, and the Lord shall heal your former sins, if you shall purify yourselves from this demon; but if not, you shall be delivered unto him to be put to death.

24[101]:1 " And from the seventh mountain, on which was herbage green and smiling, and the whole mountain thriving, and cattle of every kind and the fowls of heaven were feeding on the herbage on that mountain, and the green herbage, on which they fed, only grew the more luxuriant, they that believed are such as these;

24[101]:2 they were ever simple and guileless and blessed, having nothing against one another, but rejoicing always in the servants of God, and clothed in the Holy Spirit of these virgins, and having compassion always on every man, and out of their labors they supplied every man's need without reproach and without misgiving.

24[101]:3 The Lord then seeing their simplicity and entire childishness made them to abound in the labors of their hands, and bestowed favor on them in all their doings.

24[101]:4 But I say unto you that are such--I, the angel of repentance--remain to the end such as you are, and your seed shall never be blotted out. For the Lord has put you to the proof, and enrolled you among our number, and your whole seed shall dwell with the Son of God; for of His Spirit did you receive.

25[102]:1 "And from the eighth mountain, where were the many springs, and all the creatures of the Lord did drink of the springs, they that believed are such as these;

25[102]:2 apostles and teachers, who preached unto the whole world, and who taught the word of the Lord in soberness and purity, and kept back no part at all for evil desire, but walked always in righteousness and truth, even as also they received the Holy Spirit. Such therefore shall have their entrance with the angels.

26[103]:1 "And from the ninth mountain, which was desert, which had [the] reptiles and wild beasts in it which destroy mankind, they that believed are such as these;

26[103]:2 they that have the spots are deacons that exercised their office ill, and plundered the livelihood of widows and orphans, and made gain for themselves from the ministrations which they had received to perform. If then they abide in the same evil desire, they are dead and there is no hope of life for them; but if they turn again and fulfill their ministrations in purity, it shall be possible for them to live.

26[103]:3 But they that are mildewed, these are they that denied and turned not again unto their Lord, but having become barren and desert, because they hold fast not unto the servants of God but remain alone, they destroy their own souls.

26[103]:4 For as a vine left alone in a hedge, if it meet with neglect, is destroyed and wasted by the weeds, and in time becomes wild and is no longer useful to its owner, so also men of this kind have given themselves up in despair and become useless to their Lord, by growing wild.

26[103]:5 To these then repentance cometh, unless they be found to have denied from the heart; but if a man be found to have denied from the heart, I know not whether it is possible for him to live.

26[103]:6 And this I say not in reference to these days, that a man after denying should receive repentance; for it is impossible for him to be saved who shall now deny his Lord; but for those who denied Him long ago repentance seems to be possible. If a man therefore will repent, let him do so speedily before the tower is completed; but if not, he shall be destroyed by the women and put to death.

26[103]:7 And the stunted, these are the treacherous and backbiters; and the wild beasts which you saw on the mountain are these. For as wild beasts with their venom poison and kill a man, so also do the words of such men poison and kill a man.

26[103]:8 These then are broken off short from their faith through the conduct which they have in themselves; but some of them repented and were saved; and the rest that are of this kind can be saved, if they repent; but if they repent not, they shall meet their death from those women of whose power they are possessed.

27[104]:1 "And from the tenth mountain, where were trees sheltering certain sheep, they that believed are such as these;

27[104]:2 bishops, hospitable persons, who gladly received into their houses at all times the servants of God without hypocrisy. [These bishops] at all times without ceasing sheltered the needy and the widows in their ministration and conducted themselves in purity at all times.

27[104]:3 These [all] then shall be sheltered by the Lord for ever. They therefore that have done these things are glorious in the sight of God, and their place is even now with the angels, if they shall continue unto the end serving the Lord.

27[104]:1 "And from the eleventh mountain, where were trees full of fruit, decked with divers kinds of fruits, they that believed are such as these;

27[104]:2 they that suffered for the Name [of the Son of God], who also suffered readily with their whole heart, and yielded up their lives."

27[104]:3 "Wherefore then, Sir," say I, "have all the trees fruits, but some of their fruits are more beautiful than others?" "Listen," said he; "all as many as ever suffered for the Name's sake are glorious in the sight of God, and the sins of all these were taken away, because they suffered for the name of the Son of God. Now here why their fruits are various, and some surpassing others.

27[104]:4 "As many," said he, "as were tortured and denied not, when brought before the magistracy, but suffered readily, these are the more glorious in the sight of the Lord; their fruit is that which surpasses. But as many as become cowards, and were lost in uncertainty, and considered in their hearts whether they should deny or confess, and yet suffered, their fruits are less, because this design entered into their heart; for this design is evil, that a servant should deny his own lord.

27[104]:5 See to it, therefore, you who entertain this idea, lest this design remain in your hearts, and you die unto God. But you that suffer for the Name's sake ought to glorify God, because God deemed you worthy that you should bear this name, and that all your sins should be healed.

27[104]:6 Reckon yourselves blessed therefore; yea, rather think that you have done a great work, if any of you shall suffer for God's sake. The Lord bestowed life upon you, and you perceived it not; for your sins weighed you down, and if you had not suffered for the Name [of the Lord], you had died unto God by reason of your sins.

27[104]:7 These things I say unto you that waver as touching denial and confession. Confess that you have the Lord, lest denying Him you be delivered into prison.

27[104]:8 If the Gentiles punish their slaves, if any one deny his lord, what think you the Lord will do unto you, He who has authority over all things? Away with these designs from your hearts, that you may live forever unto God."

27[104]:1 "And from the twelfth mountain, which was white, they that believed are such as these; they that are as very babes, into whose heart no guile entered, neither learned they what wickedness is, but they remained as babes forever.

27[104]:2 Such as these then dwell without doubt in the kingdom of God, because they defiled the commandments of God in nothing, but continued as babes all the days of their life in the same mind.

27[104]:3 As many of you therefore as shall continue," said he, "and shall be as infants not having guile, shall be glorious [even] than all them that have been mentioned before; for all infants are glorious in the sight of God, and stand first in His sight. Blessed then are you, as many as have put away wickedness from you, and have clothed yourselves in guilelessness: you shall live unto God cheifest of all."

27[104]:4 After he had finished the parables of the mountains, I say unto him, "Sir, now explain to me concerning the stones that were taken from the plain and placed in the building in the room of the stones that were taken from the tower, and concerning the round (stones) which were placed in the building, and concerning those that were still round".

27[104]:1 "Hear," said he, "likewise concerning all these things. The stones which were taken from the plain and placed in the building of the tower in the room of those that were rejected, are the roots of this white mountain.

27[104]:2 When then they that believed from this mountain were all found guiltless, the lord of the tower ordered these from the roots of the mountain to be put into the building of the tower. For He knew that if these stones should go into the building [of the tower], they would remain bright and not one of them would turn black.

27[104]:3 But if he added (stones) from other mountains, he would have been obliged to visit the tower again, and to purify it. Now all these have been found white, who have believed and who shall believe; for they are of the same kind. Blessed is this kind, for it is innocent!

27[104]:4 Hear now likewise concerning those round and bright stones. All these are from the white mountain. Now here wherefore they have been found round. Their riches have darkened and obscured them a little from the truth.

27[104]:5 When therefore the Lord perceived their mind, *that they could favor the truth,* and likewise remain good, He commanded their possessions to be cut off from them, yet not to be taken away altogether, so that they might be able to do some good with that which has been left to them, and might live unto God for that they come of a good kind. So therefore they have been cut away a little, and placed in the building of this tower".

27[104]:1 "But the other (stones), which have remained round and have not been fitted into the building, because they have not yet received the seal, have been replaced in their own possession, for they were found very round.

27[104]:2 For this world and the vanities of their possessions must be cut off from them, and then they will fit into the kingdom of God. For it is necessary that they should enter into the kingdom of God; because the Lord has blessed this innocent kind. Of this kind then not one shall perish. Yea, even though any one of them being tempted by the most wicked devil have committed any fault, he shall

return speedily unto his Lord.

27[104]:3 Blessed I pronounced you all to be--I the angel of repentance--whoever of you are guileless as infants, because your part is good and honorable in the sight of God.

27[104]a:4 Moreover I bid all of you, whoever have received this seal, keep guilelessness, and bear no grudge, and continue not in your wickedness nor in the memory of the offenses of bitterness; but become of one spirit, and heal these evil clefts and take them away from among you, that the owner of the flocks may rejoice concerning them.

27[104a]:5 For he will rejoice, if he find all things whole. But if he find any part of the flock scattered, woe unto the shepherds.

27[104a]:6 For if the shepherds themselves shall have been found scattered, how will they answer for the flocks? Will they say that they were harassed by the flock? No credence will be given them. For it is an incredible thing that a shepherd should be injured by his flock; and he will be punished the more because of his falsehood. And I am the shepherd, and it behooved me most strongly to render an account for you.

32[109]:1 "Amend yourselves therefore, while the tower is still in course of building.

32[109]:2 The Lord dwells in men that love peace; for to Him peace is dear; but from the contentious and them that are given up to wickedness He kept afar off. Restore therefore to Him your spirit whole as you received it.

32[109]:3 For suppose you hast given to a fuller a new garment whole, and desired to receive it back again whole, but the fuller give it back to you torn, wilt you receive it thus? Wilt you not at once blaze out and attack him with reproaches, saying; "The garment which I gave you was whole; wherefore hast you rent it and made it useless? See, by reason of the rent, which you hast made in it, it cannot be of use." Wilt you not then say all this to a fuller even about a rent which he has made in thy garment?

32[109]:4 If therefore you art thus vexed in the matter of thy garment, and complained because you received it not back whole, what think you the Lord will do to you, He, Who gave you the spirit whole, and you hast made it absolutely useless, so that it cannot be of any use at all to its Lord? For its use began to be useless, when it was corrupted by you. Will not therefore the Lord of this spirit for this thy deed punish [you with death]?"

32[109]:5 "Certainly," I said, "all those, whomsoever He shall find continuing to bear malice, He will punish." "Trample not," said he, "upon His mercy, but rather glorify Him, because He is so long-suffering with your sins, and is not like unto you. Practice then repentance which is expedient for you.

33[110]:1 "All these things which are written above I, the shepherd, the angel of repentance, have declared and spoken to the servants of God. If then you shall believe and hear my words, and walk in them, and amend your ways, you shall be able to live. But if you continue in wickedness and in bearing malice, no one of this kind shall live unto God. All things which were to be spoken by me have (now) been spoken to you."

33[110]:2 The shepherd said to me, "Hast you asked all thy questions?" And I said, "Yes, Sir." "Why then hast you not enquired of me concerning the shape of the stones placed in the building, in that we filled up their shapes?" And I said, "I forgot, Sir."

33[110]:3 "Listen now," said he, "concerning them. These are they that have heard my commandments now, and have practiced repentance with their whole heart. So when the Lord saw that their repentance was good and pure, and that they could continue therein, he ordered their former sins to be blotted out. These shapes then were their former sins, and they have been chiseled away that they

748

might not appear."

Parable 10

1[111]:1 After I had written out this book completely, the angel who had delivered me to the shepherd came to the house where I was, and sat upon a couch, and the shepherd stood at his right hand. Then he called me, and spoke thus unto me;

1[111]:2 "I delivered you," said he, "and thy house to this shepherd, that you might be protected by him." "True, Sir," I said "If therefore," said he, "you desire to be protected from all annoyance and all cruelty, to have also success in every good work and word, and all the power of righteousness, walk in his commandments, which I have given you, and you shall be able to get the mastery over all wickedness.

1[111]:3 For if you keep his commandments, all evil desire and the sweetness of this world shall be subject unto you; moreover success shall attend you in every good undertaking. Embrace his gravity and self-restraint, and tell it out unto all men that he is held in great honor and dignity with the Lord, and is a ruler of great authority, and powerful in his office. To him alone in the whole world has authority over repentance been assigned. Seemed he to you to be powerful? Yet you despise the gravity and moderation which he used towards you."

2[112]:1 I say unto him; "Ask him, Sir, himself, whether from the time that he has been in my house, I have done ought out of order, whereby I have offended him."

2[112]:2 "I myself know," said he, "that you hast done nothing out of order, nor art about to do so. And so I speak these things unto you, that you may persevere. For he has given a good account of you unto me. You therefore shall speak these words to others, that they too who have practiced or shall practice repentance may be of the same mind as you art; and he may give a good report of them to me, and I unto the Lord."

2[112]:3 "I too, Sir," I say, "declare to every man the mighty works of the Lord; for I hope that all who have sinned in the past, if they hear these things, will gladly repent and recover life."

2[112]:4 "Continue therefore," said he, "in this ministry, and complete it unto the end. For whosoever fulfill his commandments shall have life; yea such a man (shall have) great honor with the Lord. But whosoever keep not his commandments, fly from their life, and oppose him, and follow not his commandments, but deliver themselves over to death; and each one becomes guilty of his own blood. But I bid you obey these commandments, and you shall have a remedy for thy sins.

3[113]:1 "Moreover, I have sent these virgins unto you, that they may dwell with you; for I have seen that they are friendly towards you. You hast them therefore as helpers, that you may be the better able to keep his commandments; for it is impossible that these commandments be kept without the help of these virgins. I see too that they are glad to be with you. But I will charge them that they depart not at all from thy house.

3[113]:2 Only do you purify thy house; for in a clean house they will gladly dwell. For they are clean and chaste and industrious, and have favor in the sight of the Lord. If, therefore, they shall find thy house pure, they will continue with you; but if the slightest pollution arise, they will depart from thy house at once. For these virgins love not pollution in any form."

3[113]:3 I said unto him, "I hope, Sir, that I shall please them, so that they may gladly dwell in my house for ever; and just as he to whom you didst deliver me makes no complaint against me, so they likewise shall make no complaint."

3[113]:4 He said unto the shepherd, "I perceive," said he, "that he wishes to live as the servant of God, and that he will keep these commandments, and will place these virgins in a clean habitation."

3[113]:5 With these words he again delivered me over to the shepherd, and called the virgins, and said to them; "Inasmuch as I see that you are glad to dwell in this man's house, I commend to you him and his house, that you depart not at all from his house." But they heard these words gladly.

4[114]:1 He said then to me, "Quit you like a man in this ministry; declare to every man the mighty works of the Lord, and you shall have favor in this ministry. Whosoever therefore shall walk in these commandments, shall live and be happy in his life; but whosoever shall neglect them, shall not live, and shall be unhappy in his life.

4[114]:2 Charge all men who are able to do right, that they cease not to practice good works; for it is useful for them. I say moreover that every man ought to be rescued from misfortune; for he that has need, and suffered misfortune in his daily life, is in great torment and want.

4[114]:3 Whosoever therefore rescued from penury a life of this kind, wins great joy for himself. For he who is harassed by misfortune of this sort is afflicted and tortured with equal torment as one who is in chains. For many men on account of calamities of this kind, because they can bear them no longer, lay violent hands on themselves. He then who knows the calamity of a man of this kind and rescues him not, commits great sin, and becomes guilty of the man's blood.

4[114]:4 Do therefore good works, whoever of you have received (benefits) from the Lord, lest, while you delay to do them, the building of the tower be completed. For it is on your account that the work of the building has been interrupted. Unless then you hasten to do right, the tower will be completed, and you shut out."

4[114]:5 When then he had finished speaking with me, he rose from the couch and departed, taking with him the shepherd and the virgins. He said however unto me, that he would send the shepherd and the virgins back again to my house. . .

The Didache or Teaching of the Apostles
APOSTOLIC FATHERS

1:1 There are two ways, one of life and one of death, and there is a great difference between the two ways. 1:2 The way of life is this. 1:3 First of all, you shall love the God that made you; 1:4 secondly, your neighbor as yourself. 1:5 And all things whatsoever you would not have befall yourself neither do you unto another. 1:6 Now of these words the doctrine is this. 1:7 Bless them that curse you, and pray for your enemies and fast for them that persecute you; 1:8 for what thank is it, if you love them that love you? Do not even the Gentiles the same? But do you love them that hate you, and you shall not have an enemy. 1:9 Abstain from fleshly and bodily lusts. 1:10 If any man give you a blow on your right cheek, turn to him the other also, and you shall be perfect; 1:11 if a man impress you to go with him, one mile, go with him two; 1:12 if a man take away your cloak, give him your coat also; 1:13 if a man take away from you that which is your own, ask it not back, for neither are you able. 1:14 To every man that asks of you give, and ask not back; 1:15 for the Father desires that gifts be given to all from His own bounties. 1:16 Blessed is he that gives according to the commandment; 1:17 for he is guiltless. 1:18 Woe to him that receives; 1:19 for, if a man receives having need, he is guiltless; 1:20 but he that had no need shall give satisfaction why and wherefore he received; 1:21 and being put in confinement he shall be examined concerning the deeds that he has done, and he shall not come out thence until he has given back the last farthing. 1:22 Yes, as touching this also it is said; 1:23 Let your alms sweat into your hands, until you shall have learned to whom to give.

2:1 And this is the second commandment of the teaching. 2:2 You shall do no murder, you shall not commit adultery, you shall not corrupt boys, you shall not commit fornication, you shall not steal, you shall not deal in magic, you shall do no sorcery, you shall not murder a child by abortion nor kill them when born, you shall not covet your neighbor's goods, you shall not perjure yourself, you shall not bear false witness, you shall not speak evil, you shall not cherish a grudge, you shall not be double-minded nor double-tongued; 2:3 for the double tongue is a snare of death. 2:4 Your word shall not be false or empty, but fulfilled by action. 2:5 You shall not be materialistic nor a plunderer nor a hypocrite nor ill-tempered nor proud. 2:6 You shall not entertain an evil design against your neighbor. 2:7 You shall not hate any man, but some you shall reprove, and for others you shall pray, and others you shall love more than your life.

3:1 My child, flee from every evil and everything that resembles it. 3:2 Be not angry, for anger leads to murder, nor jealous nor contentious nor wrathful; 3:3 for from all these things murders are engendered. 3:4 My child, be not lustful, for lust leads to fornication, neither foul-speaking neither with uplifted eyes (pride); 3:5 for of all these things adulteries are engendered. 3:6 My child, be no dealer in omens, since it leads to idolatry, nor an enchanter nor an astrologer nor a magician, neither be willing to look at them; 3:7 for from all these things idolatry is engendered. 3:8 My child, be not a liar, since lying leads to theft, neither avaricious neither vainglorious; 3:9 for from all these things thefts are engendered. 3:10 My child, be not a complainer, since it leads to blasphemy, neither self-willed neither a thinker of evil thoughts; 3:11 for from all these things blasphemies are engendered. 3:12 But be meek, since the meek shall inherit the earth. 3:13 Be long-suffering and pitiful and guileless and quiet and kindly and always fearing the words which you have heard. 3:14 You shall not exalt yourself, neither shall you admit boldness into your soul. 3:15 Your soul shall not cleave together with the lofty, but with the righteous and humble shall you walk. 3:16 The accidents that befall you, you shall receive as good, knowing that nothing is done without God.

4:1 My child, you shall remember him that speaks unto you the word of God night and day, and shall honor him as the Lord; 4:2 for from where ever the Lordship speaks, there is the Lord. 4:3 Moreover you shall seek out day by day the persons of the saints, that you may find rest in their words. 4:4 You shall not make a schism, but you shall pacify them that contend; 4:5 you shall judge righteously, you shall not make a difference in a person to reprove him for transgressions. 4:6 You shall not doubt whether a thing shall be or not be. 4:7 Be not found holding out your hands to receive, but drawing them in as to giving. 4:8 If you have ought passing through your hands, you shall give a ransom for your sins. 4:9 You shall not hesitate to give, neither shall you complain when giving; 4:10 for you shall know who is the good paymaster of your reward. 4:11 You shall not turn away from him that is in want, but shall make your brother partaker in all things, and shall not say that anything is your own. 4:12 For if you are fellow-partakers in that which is imperishable, how much rather in the things which are perishable? You shall not withhold your hand from your son or from your daughter, but from their youth you shall teach them the fear of God. 4:13 You shall not command your bondservant or your handmaid in your bitterness, who trust in the same God as yourself, lest haply they should cease to fear the God who is over both of you; 4:14 for He comes, not to call men with respect of persons, but He comes to those whom the Spirit has prepared. 4:15 But you, servants, shall be subject unto your masters, as to a type of God, in shame and fear. 4:16 You shall hate all hypocrisy, and everything that is not pleasing to the Lord. 4:17 You shall never forsake the commandments of the Lord; 4:18 but shall keep those things which you have received, neither adding to them nor taking away from them. 4:19 In church you shall confess your transgressions, and shall not betake yourself to prayer with an evil conscience. 4:20 This is the way of life.

5:1 But the way of death is this. 5:2 First of all, it is evil and full of a curse murders, adulteries, lusts, fornications, thefts, idolatries, magical arts, witchcrafts, plunderings, false witnessings, hypocrisies, doubleness of heart, treachery, pride, malice, stubbornness, covetousness, foul-speaking, jealousy, boldness, exaltation, boastfulness; 5:3 persecutors of good men, hating truth, loving a lie, not perceiving the reward of righteousness, not cleaving to the good nor to righteous judgment, wakeful not for that which is good but for that which is evil; 5:4 from whom gentleness and forbearance stand aloof; 5:5 loving vain things, pursuing a recompense, not pitying the poor man, not toiling for him that is oppressed with toil, not recognizing Him that made them, murderers of children, corrupters of the creatures of God, turning away from him that is in want, oppressing him that is afflicted, advocates of the wealthy, unjust judges of the poor, altogether sinful. 5:6 May you be delivered, my children, from all these things.

6:1 See lest any man lead you astray from this way of righteousness, for he teaches you apart from God. 6:2 For if you are able to bear the whole yoke of the Lord, you shall be perfect; 6:3 but if you are not able, do that which you are able. 6:4 But concerning eating, bear that which you are able; 6:5 yet abstain by all means from meat sacrificed to idols; 6:6 for it is the worship of dead gods.

7:1 But concerning baptism, thus shall you baptize. 7:2 Having first recited all these things, baptize in the name of the Father and of the Son and of the Holy Spirit in living (running) water. 7:3 But if you have not living (running) water, then baptize in other water; 7:4 and if you are not able in cold, then in warm. 7:5 But if you have neither, then pour water on the head thrice in the name of the Father and of the Son and of the Holy Spirit. 7:6 But before the baptism let him that baptize and him that is baptized fast, and any others also who are able; 7:7 and you shall order him that is baptized to fast a day or two before.

8:1 And let not your fastings be with the hypocrites, for they fast on the second and the fifth day of the week; 8:2 but do you keep your fast on the fourth and on the preparation (the sixth) day. 8:3 Neither pray you as the hypocrites, but as the Lord commanded in His Gospel, thus pray you. 8:4 Our Father, which are in heaven, hallowed be Your name; 8:5 Your kingdom come; 8:6 Your will be done, as in heaven, so also on earth; 8:7 give us this day our daily bread; 8:8 and forgive us our debt, as we also forgive our debtors; 8:9 and lead us not into temptation, but deliver us from the evil one; 8:10 for Yours is the power and the glory for ever and ever. 8:11 Three times in the day pray you so.

9:1 But as touching the eucharistic thanksgiving give you thanks thus. 9:2 First, as regards the cup: 9:3 We give You thanks, O our Father, for the holy vine of Your son David, which You made known unto us through Your Son Jesus; 9:4 Yours is the glory for ever and ever. 9:5 Then as regards the broken bread: 9:6 We give You thanks, O our Father, for the life and knowledge which You did make known unto us through Your Son Jesus; 9:7 Yours is the glory for ever and ever. 9:8 As this broken bread was scattered upon the mountains and being gathered together became one, so may Your Church be gathered together from the ends of the earth into Your kingdom; 9:9 for Yours is the glory and the power through Jesus Christ for ever and ever. 9:10 But let no one eat or drink of this eucharistic thanksgiving, but they that have been baptized into the name of the Lord; 9:11 for concerning this also the Lord has said: 9:12 Give not that which is holy to the dogs.

10:1 And after you are satisfied thus give you thanks: 10:2 We give You thanks, Holy Father, for Your holy name, which You have made to tabernacle in our hearts, and for the knowledge and faith and immortality, which You have made known unto us through Your Son Jesus; 10:3 Yours is the glory for ever and ever. 10:4 You, Almighty Master, did create all things for Your name's sake, and did give food and drink unto men for enjoyment, that they might render thanks to You; 10:5 but did bestow upon us spiritual food and drink and eternal life through Your Son. 10:6 Before all things we give You thanks that You are powerful; 10:7 Yours is the glory for ever and ever. 10:8 Remember, Lord, Your Church to deliver it from all evil and to perfect it in Your love; 10:9 and gather it together from the four winds--even the Church which has been sanctified--into Your kingdom which You have prepared for it; 10:10 for Yours is the power and the glory for ever and ever. 10:11 May grace come and may this world pass away. 10:12 Hosanna to the God of David. 10:13 If any man is holy, let him come; 10:14 if any man is not, let him repent. Maran Atha (Come Lord). Amen. 10:15 But permit the prophets to offer thanksgiving as much as they desire.

11:1 Whosoever therefore shall come and teach you all these things that have been said before, receive him; 11:2 but if the teacher himself be perverted and teach a different doctrine to the destruction thereof, hear him not; 11:3 but if to the increase of righteousness and the knowledge of the Lord, receive him as the Lord. 11:4 But concerning the apostles and prophets, so do you according to the ordinance of the Gospel. 11:5 Let every apostle, when he comes to you, be received as the Lord; 11:6

but he shall not abide more than a single day, or if there be a need, 11:7 but if he abide three days, he is a false prophet. 11:8 And when he departs let the apostle receive nothing save bread, until he finds shelter; 11:9 but if he ask money, he is a false prophet. 11:10 And any prophet speaking in the Spirit you shall not try neither discern; 11:11 for every sin shall be forgiven, but this sin shall not be forgiven. 11:12 Yet not every one that speaks in the Spirit is a prophet, but only if he have the ways of the Lord. 11:13 From his ways therefore the false prophet and the prophet shall be recognized. 11:14 And no prophet when he orders a table in the Spirit shall eat of it; 11:15 otherwise he is a false prophet. 11:16 And every prophet teaching the truth, if he does not what he teaches, is a false prophet. 11:17 And every prophet approved and found true, if he does ought as an outward mystery typical of the Church, and yet teaches you not to do all that he himself does, shall not be judged before you; 11:18 he has his judgment in the presence of God; 11:19 for in like manner also did the prophets of old time. 11:20 And whosoever shall say in the Spirit, Give me silver or anything else, you shall not listen to him; 11:21 but if he tell you to give on behalf of others that are in want, let no man judge him.

12:1 But let every one that comes in the name of the Lord be received; 12:2 and then when you have tested him you shall know him, for you shall have understanding on the right hand and on the left. 12:3 If the one who comes is a traveler, assist him, so far as you are able; 12:4 but he shall not stay with you more than two or three days, if it be necessary. 12:5 But if he wishes to settle with you, being a craftsman, let him work for and eat his bread. 12:6 But if he has no craft, according to your wisdom provide how he shall live as a Christian among you, but not in idleness. 12:7 If he will not do this, he is trafficking upon Christ. 12:8 Beware of such men.

13:1 But every true prophet desiring to settle among you is worthy of his food. 13:2 In like manner a true teacher is also worthy, like the workman, of his food. 13:3 Every firstfruit then of the produce of the wine-vat and of the threshing-floor, of your oxen and of your sheep, you shall take and give as the firstfruit to the prophets; 13:4 for they are your chief-priests. 13:5 But if you have not a prophet, give them to the poor. 13:6 If you make bread, take the firstfruit and give according to the commandment. 13:7 In like manner, when you open a jar of wine or of oil, take the firstfruit and give to the prophets; 13:8 yea and of money and raiment and every possession take the firstfruit, as shall seem good to you, and give according to the commandment.

14:1 And on the Lord's own day gather yourselves together and break bread and give thanks, first confessing your transgressions, that your sacrifice may be pure. 14:2 And let no man, having his dispute with his fellow, join your assembly until they have been reconciled, that your sacrifice may not be defiled; 14:3 for this sacrifice it is that was spoken of by the Lord; 14:4 In every place and at every time offer Me a pure sacrifice; 14:5 for I am a great king, says the Lord and My name is wonderful among the nations.

15:1 Appoint for yourselves therefore bishops and deacons worthy of the Lord, men who are meek and not lovers of money, and true and approved; 15:2 for unto you they also perform the service of the prophets and teachers. 15:3 Therefore despise them not; 15:4 for they are your honorable men along with the prophets and teachers. 15:5 And reprove one another, not in anger but in peace, as you find in the Gospel; 15:6 and let no one speak to any that has gone wrong towards his neighbor, neither let him hear a word from you, until he repent. 15:7 But your prayers and your almsgivings and all your deeds so do you as you find it in the Gospel of our Lord.

16:1 Be watchful for your life; 16:2 let your lamps not be quenched and your loins not ungirded, but be you ready; 16:3 for you know not the hour in which our Lord comes. 16:4 And you shall gather yourselves together frequently, seeking what is fitting for your souls; 16:5 for the whole time of your faith shall not profit you, if you be not perfected at the last season. 16:6 For in the last days the false prophets and corrupters shall be multiplied, and the sheep shall be turned into wolves, and love shall be turned into hate. 16:7 For as lawlessness increases, they shall hate one another and shall persecute and betray. 16:8 And then the world-deceiver shall appear as a son of God; 16:9 and shall work signs and wonders, and the earth shall be delivered into his hands; 16:10 and he shall do unholy things, which have never been since the world began. 16:11 Then all created mankind shall come to the fire of testing, and many shall be offended and perish; 16:12 but they that endure in their faith shall be saved by the Curse Himself. 16:13 And then shall the signs of the truth appear; 16:14 first a sign of a rift in the heaven, then a sign of a voice of a trumpet, and thirdly a resurrection of the dead; 16:15 yet not of all, but as it was said: 16:16 The Lord shall come and all His saints with Him. 16:17 Then shall the world see the Lord coming in the clouds of heaven.

Apocalypse of Baruch
2 Baruch

Chapter 1

1 And it happened in the twenty-fifth year of Jeconiah, king of Judah, that the word of the Lord came to Baruch, the son of Neriah, and said to him:

2 Have you seen all that this nation (people) are doing to Me, that the evils which these two tribes which remained have done are greater than (those of) the ten tribes which were carried away captive?

3 For the former tribes were forced by their kings to commit sin, but these two of themselves have been forcing and compelling their kings to commit sin.

4 For this reason, I bring evil upon this city, and upon its inhabitants, and it will be removed from before Me for a time, and I will scatter these people among the Gentiles that they may do good to the Gentiles. And My people will be chastened, and the time will come when they will seek the prosperity of this period (their times.)

Chapter 2

1 For I have said these things to you that you may tell Jeremiah, and all those that are like you, to leave this city.

2 For your works are to this city as a firm pillar, and your prayers as a strong wall.

Chapter 3

1 And I said: O Lord, my Lord, have I come into the world for this purpose that I might see the evils of my mother?

2 Not so, my Lord. If I have found grace in Your sight, first take my spirit that I may go to my father's and not witness the destruction of my mother.

3 For two things vehemently constrain me: for I cannot resist You, and my soul cannot behold the evils of my mother.

4 But one thing I will ask in Your presence, O Lord.

5 What will there be after these things? If You destroy Your city and deliver up Your land to those that hate us, how will the name of Israel be remembered?

6 Or how will one speak of Your praises?

7 Or to whom will Your law be explained and all things therein?

8 Or will the world return to the nature it had before, and the age revert to primeval silence?

9 And will the multitude of souls be taken away, and the nature of man not again be named? And where is all that which You said to Moses regarding us?

Chapter 4

1 And the Lord said to me: This city will be delivered up for a time, and the people will be chastened during a time, And the world will not be given over to oblivion.

2 Do you think that this is that city of which I said: On the palms of My hands have I graven you?

3 This building now built in your midst is not that which is revealed with Me, that which was prepared beforehand here from the time when I took counsel to make Paradise, and showed it to Adam before he sinned, but when he transgressed the commandment it was removed from him, as also Paradise.

4 And after these things I showed it to My servant Abraham by night among the allotted victims.

5 And again also I showed it to Moses on Mount Sinai when I showed him the likeness of the tabernacle and all its vessels.

6 And now, behold, it is preserved with Me, as also is Paradise.

7 Go, therefore, and do as I command you."

Chapter 5

1 And I answered and said: So then I am destined to grieve for Zion, For your enemies will come to this place and pollute your sanctuary, and lead your inheritance into captivity; And make themselves masters of those whom You have loved. They will depart again to the place of their idols, and will boast before them: And what will You do for Your great name?

2 And the Lord said to me: My name and My glory are to all eternity; And My judgment will maintain its right in its own time.

3 You will see with your eyes that the enemy will not overthrow Zion, nor will they burn Jerusalem, but be the ministers of the Judge for the time.

4 Now go and do what I have said to you.

5 And I went and took Jeremiah, and Adu, and Seriah, and Jabish, and Gedaliah, and all the honorable men of the people, and I led them to the valley of Cedron, and I explained to them all that had been said to me.

7 And they lifted up their voices, and they all wept.

8 And we sat there and fasted until the evening.

Chapter 6

1 And it came to pass the next day that the army of the Chaldees surrounded the city, and at the time of the evening, I, Baruch, left the people and I went out and stood by the oak.

2 And I was grieving over Zion, and lamenting over the captivity which had come upon the people.

3 Suddenly a strong spirit raised me, and carried me aloft over the wall of Jerusalem.

4 And I saw four angels standing at the four corners of the city, each of them holding a torch of fire in his hands.

5 And another angel began to descend from heaven, and said to them: Hold your lamps, and do not light them till I tell you.

6 For I am first sent to speak a word to the earth, and to place in it what the Lord the Most High has commanded me.

7 And I saw him descend into the Holy of holies, and take from there the veil, and the holy ark, and the mercy-seat, and the two tables, and the holy raiment of the priests, and the altar of incense, and the forty-eight precious stones, wherewith the priest was adorned and all the holy vessels of the tabernacle.

8 And he spoke to the earth with a loud voice: Earth, earth, earth, hear the word of the mighty God, And receive what I commit to you, And guard them until the last times so that when you are ordered you may restore them, so that strangers may not get possession of them.

9 For the time comes when Jerusalem also will be delivered for a time, until it is said, that it is again restored for ever.

10 And the earth opened its mouth and swallowed them up.

Chapter 7

1 And after these things I heard that angel saying to those angels who held the lamps. Destroy it and overthrow its wall to its foundations so that the enemy should not boast and say: We have overthrown the wall of Zion, and we have burnt the place of the mighty God.

2 And you have seized the place where I had been standing before.

Chapter 8

1 Now the angels did as he had commanded them, and when they had broken up the corners of the walls, a voice was heard from the interior of the temple, after the wall had fallen, saying:

2 Enter, you enemies. Come, you adversaries; For he who kept the house has forsaken it.

3 And I, Baruch, departed.

4 And after these things happened the army of the Chaldees entered and seized the house and all that was around it.

5 And they led the people away captive, and killed some of them, and bound Zedekiah the King, and sent him to the King of Babylon.

Chapter 9

1 And I, Baruch, came, and Jeremiah, whose heart was found pure from sins, who had not been captured in the seizure of the city.

2 And we ripped our garments, we wept, and mourned, and fasted seven days.

Chapter 10

1 After seven days the word of God came to me, and said to me:

2 Tell Jeremiah to go and support the people who are led captive in to Babylon.

3 But you remain here amid the desolation of Zion, and I will show you after these days what will occur at the end of days.

4 And I said to Jeremiah as the Lord commanded me.

5 And he indeed, departed with the people; but I, Baruch, returned and sat before the gates of the temple, and I lamented with the following lamentation over Zion and said:

6 Blessed is he who was not born, or he, who having been born, has died.

7 But as for us who live, woe to us, Because we see the afflictions of Zion, and what has befallen Jerusalem.

8 I will call the Sirens from the sea, And you Lilin, (Lilin, in Jewish myth, was the daughter of Lilith, Adam's first wife, and the demon Samael who is often identified with Satan) come from the desert. And you Shedim and dragons from the forests: Awake and prepare yourselves for mourning; and take up with me the dirges, and make lamentation with me.

9 You husbandmen, sow not again; and, O earth, wherefore gives you your harvest fruits? Keep within you the sweets of your sustenance.

10 And you, vine, why further do you give your wine; for an offering will not again be made there from in Zion. Nor will the first-fruits again be offered.

11 And do you, O heavens, withhold your dew, and open not the treasuries of rain?

12 And do you, O sun, withhold the light of your rays? And do you, O moon, extinguish the multitude of your light? For why should light rise again where the light of Zion is darkened?

13 And you, you bridegrooms, enter not in. And let not the brides adorn themselves with garlands. And you women, pray not that you may bear.

14 For the barren will above all rejoice, And those who have no sons will be glad, and those who have sons will have anguish.

15 For why should they bear in pain, only to bury in grief?

16 Why again should mankind have sons? Why should the offspring of their kind again be named; where this mother is desolate, and her sons are led into captivity?

17 From this time forward speak not of beauty, and do not discuss gracefulness.

18 Moreover, you priests, take you the keys of the sanctuary and cast them into the height of heaven; and give them to the Lord and say: Guard Your house Yourself. For we are found to be false stewards.

19 And you virgins who weave fine linen and silk with gold of Ophir (the place from where the fleets of Solomon brought gold), take with haste all (these) things and cast (them) into the fire, that it may carry them to Him who made them. And the flame send them to Him who created them, lest the enemy get possession of them.

Chapter 11

1 Moreover, I, Baruch, say this against you, Babylon: If you had prospered, and Zion had dwelt in her glory, the grief to us would have been great because you would be equal to Zion.

2 But now, the grief is infinite; and the lamentation measureless because you are prospered and Zion desolate.

3 Who will be judge regarding these things? Or to whom will we complain regarding that which has befallen us? O Lord, how have You borne (it)?

4 Our fathers went to rest without grief and the righteous sleep in the earth in tranquility.

5 For they knew not this anguish, nor yet had they heard of that which had befallen us.

6 Would that you had ears, O earth, and that you had a heart, O dust. That you might go and announce in Sheol (hell / place of the dead) and say to the dead: Blessed are you more than we who live.

Chapter 12

1 But I will say what I think and I will speak against you, O land, which are prospering.

2 The noonday does not always burn, nor do the rays of the sun constantly give light.

3 Do not expect [and hope] that you will always be prosperous and rejoicing. Do not be not greatly arrogant and boastful.

4 For certainly in its own season the divine rage will awake against you, even though now in long-suffering it is held in as it were by reins.

5 And when I had said these things, I fasted seven days.

Chapter 13

1 After these things I, Baruch, was standing upon Mount Zion, and a voice came from the height and said to me:

2 Stand up on your feet, Baruch, and hear the word of the mighty God.

3 Because you have been amazed at what has befallen Zion, you will therefore be certainly preserved to the conclusion of the times, that you may be for a testimony.

4 If ever those prosperous cities say: Why has the mighty God brought upon us this retribution?

5 You say to them: You and those like you who will have seen this evil; (This is the evil) and retribution which is coming upon you and upon your people in its (destined) time that the nations may be thoroughly beaten (smitten.)

6 And then they will be in anguish.

7 And if they say at that time: For how long? You will say to them: You who have drunk the strained wine, drink also of its dregs, the judgment of the Lofty One Who has no respect of persons.

8 On this account before he had no mercy on His own sons, but afflicted them as His enemies, because they sinned, then they were disciplined so that they might be sanctified.

9 But now, you peoples and nations, you are guilty because you have always trodden down the earth, and used the creation sinfully and wrongfully.

10 For I have always benefited you and you have always been ungrateful for the beneficence.

Chapter 14

1 And I answered and said: You have shown me the method (behavior / procedure) of the times, and that which will alter these things, and You have said to me that the retribution, which has been spoken of by You, will come upon the nations.

2 And now I know that those who have sinned are many, and they have lived in prosperity, and left the world, but few nations will be left in those times, to whom those words will be said which You have said.

3 For what advantage is there in this, or what evil, worse than what we have seen happen us can we expect to see?

4 But again I will speak in Your presence: What have they profited who had knowledge before You and have not walked in vanity as the rest of the nations, and have not said to the dead: "Give us life," but always feared You, and have not left Your ways?

5 They have been carried off, nor on their account have You had mercy on Zion.

6 And if others did evil, it was due to Zion, that on account of those who do good works should be forgiven, and should not be overwhelmed on account of the works of those who practice unrighteousness.

7 But who, O Lord, my Lord, will understand Your judgment, or who will search out the profoundness of Your way?

8 Or who will think out the weight of Your path?

9 Or who will be able to think out Your incomprehensible counsel?

10 Or who of those that are born has ever found the beginning or end of Your wisdom?

11 For we have all been made like a breath. For as the breath ascends involuntarily and again dies, so it is with the nature of men, who depart not according to their own will, and know not what will befall them in the end.

12 For the righteous justly hope for the end, and without fear leave this habitation, because they have with You a store of works preserved in treasuries.

13 On this account also these without fear leave this world, and trusting with joy they hope to receive the world which You have promised them.

14 But as for us --- woe to us, who also are now shamefully treated, and at that time look forward (only) to evil.

15 But You know accurately what You have done by means of Your servants; for we are not able to understand that which is good as You are, our Creator.

16 But again I will speak in Your presence, O LORD, my Lord.

17 In ancient times there was no world with its inhabitants, You did devise and speak with a word, and with that the works of creation stood before You.

18 And You did say that You would make man the administrator of Your works, that it might be known that he was by no means made on account of the world, but the world on account of him.

19 And now I see that as the world was made on account of us, and it abides, but we, on account of whom it was made, depart.

Chapter 15

1 And the Lord answered and said to me: You are rightly amazed regarding the departure of man, but you have not judged well regarding the evils which befall those who sin.

2 And as regards what you have said, that the righteous are carried off and the impious are prospered.

3 And as regards what you have said, "Man knows not Your judgment," on this account hear, and I will speak to you, and listen, and I will cause you to hear My words.

4 Man would not rightly have understood My judgment, unless he had accepted the law, and I had instructed him in understanding.

5 But now, because he transgressed knowingly on this ground that he worked, he will be tormented.

6 And as regards what you did say regarding the righteous, that on account of them has this world come, so also again will that which is to come, come on their account.

7 For this world is to them a strife and a labor with much trouble; and that accordingly which is to come, a crown with great glory.

Chapter 16

1 And I answered and said: O LORD, my Lord, the years of this time are few and evil, and who is able in his little time to acquire that which is measureless?

Chapter 17

1 And the Lord answered and said to me: With the Most High account is not taken of much time nor of a few years.

2 For what did it profit Adam that he lived nine hundred and thirty years, and transgressed that which he was commanded?

3 Therefore the multitude of time that he lived did not profit him, but brought death and cut off the years of those who were born from him.

4 Or wherein did Moses suffer loss in that he lived only one hundred and twenty years, and inasmuch as he was subject to Him who formed him, brought the law to the seed of Jacob, and lighted a lamp for the nation of Israel?

Chapter 18

1 And I answered and said: He that lighted has taken from the light, and there are but few that have imitated him.

2 But those many whom he has lighted have taken from the darkness of Adam and have not rejoiced in the light of the lamp.

Chapter 19

1 And He answered and said to me: So it was at that time he appointed for them a covenant. And He said to them: Behold I have placed before you life and death, and he called heaven and earth to witness against them.

2 For he knew that his time was but short, but that heaven and earth endure always.

3 But after his death they sinned and transgressed, though they knew that they had the law reproving them, and the light in which nothing could err, also the spheres (planets and stars?) which testify, and Me.

4 Now regarding everything that is, it is I that judge, but do not you take counsel in your soul regarding these things, nor afflict yourself because of those which have been.

5 For now it is the consummation of time that should be considered, whether of business, or of prosperity, or of shame, and not the beginning thereof.

6 Because if a man be prospered in his beginnings and shamefully treated in his old age, he forgets all the prosperity that he had.

7 And again, if a man is shamefully treated in his beginnings, and at his end is prospered, he remembers not again his evil treatment.

8 And again listen; though each one were prospered all that time all the time from the day on which death was decreed against those who transgress, and in his end was destroyed, everything would have been in vain.

Chapter 20

1 Therefore, behold! The days come, and the times will hasten more than the former, and the seasons will speed on more than those that are past, and the years will pass more quickly than the present (years).

2 Therefore have I now taken away Zion, that I may the more speedily visit the world in its season.

3 Therefore hold fast in your heart everything that I command you, and seal it in the recesses of your mind.

4 And then I will show you the judgment of My might, and My ways which cannot be known.

5 Go and sanctify yourself seven days, and eat no bread, nor drink water, nor speak to anyone.

6 Afterwards come to that place and I will reveal Myself to you, and speak true things with you, and I will give you commandment regarding the method (procedure / system) of the times; for they are coming and tarry not.

Chapter 21

1 And I went thence and sat in the valley of Cedron in a cave of the earth, and I sanctified my soul there, and I ate no bread, yet I was not hungry, and I drank no water, yet I thirsted not, and I was there till the seventh day, as He had commanded me.

2 And afterwards I came to that place where He had spoken with me.

3 And it came to pass at sunset that my soul (mind) took much thought, and I began to speak in the presence of the Mighty One, and said:

4 O You that made the earth, hear me; you that have fixed the firmament by the word, and have made firm the height of the heaven by the spirit, that have called from the beginning of the world that which did not yet exist, and they obey You.

5 You that have commanded the air by Your nod, and have seen those things which are to be as those things which You are (now) doing.

6 You that rule with great thought the hosts that stand before You; also the countless holy beings which You made from the beginning from the flame and fire, which stand around Your throne where You rule with indignation.

7 To You only does this belong that You should do whatsoever You wish.

8 Who causes the drops of rain to rain by number upon the earth, and alone know the conclusion of the times before they come; have respect to my prayer.

9 For You alone are able to sustain all who are, and those who have passed away, and those who are to be, those who sin, and those who are righteous as living and being past finding out.

10 For You alone live immortal and past finding out, and know the number of mankind.

11 And if in time many have sinned, yet others not a few have been righteous.

12 You know where You preserve the end of those who have sinned, or the conclusion of those who have been righteous.

13 For if there were this life only, which belongs to all men, nothing could be more bitter than this.

14 For of what profit is strength that turns to sickness, or fullness of food that turns to famine, or beauty that turns to ugliness?

15 For the nature of man is always changeable.

16 For what we were formerly now we no longer are, and what we now are we will not afterwards continue to be.

17 For if a conclusion had not been prepared for all, then their beginning would have been in vain.

18 Everything that comes from You, You informed me, and regarding everything about which I ask You, You enlighten me?

19 How long will that which is corruptible remain, and how long will the time of mortals succeed, and until what time will those who transgress in the world be polluted with much wickedness?

20 Command in mercy and accomplish all that You said You would bring, that Your might may be made known to those who think that Your long-suffering is weakness.

21 Show to those who do not recognize it, that everything that has befallen us and our city until now has been according to the long-suffering of Your power, because on account of Your name You have called us a beloved people.

22 Bring mortality to an end. Reprimand the angel of death, and let Your glory appear, and let the might of Your beauty be known, and let Sheol be sealed so that from this time forward it may not receive the dead, and let the treasuries of souls (the chamber of Guf, in Jewish mythology) restore those which are enclosed in them.

23 For there have been many years like those that are desolate from the days of Abraham and Isaac and Jacob, and of all those who are like them, who sleep in the earth, on whose account You did say that You had created the world.

24 And now quickly show Your glory, and do not put off what has been promised by You. When I had completed this prayer I was greatly weakened.

Chapter 22

1 After these things the heavens were opened, and I saw, and power was given to me, and a voice was heard from on high, and it said to me:

2 Baruch, Baruch, why are you troubled?

3 He who travels by a road but does not complete it, or who departs by sea but does not arrive at the port, can he be comforted?

4 Or he who promises to give a present to another, but does not fulfill it, is it not robbery?

5 Or he who sows the earth, but does not reap its fruit in its season, does he not lose everything?

6 Or he who plants a plant unless it grows till the time suitable to it, does he who planted it expect to receive fruit from it?

7 Or a woman who has conceived, if she bring forth untimely, does she not certainly kill her infant?

8 Or he who builds a house, if he does not roof it and complete it, can it be called a house? Tell Me that first.

Chapter 23

1, And I answered and said: "Not so, O LORD, my Lord."

2 And He answered and said to me: Why are you troubled about that which you know not, and why are you ill at ease about things of which you are ignorant?

3 You have not forgotten the people who now are and those who have passed away, so I remember those who are appointed to come.

4 Because when Adam sinned and death was the judgment against those who should be born, then the multitude of those who should be born was numbered, and for that number a place was prepared where the living might dwell and the dead might be guarded.

5 Before the appointed number is fulfilled, the creature will not live again for My spirit is the creator of life, and Sheol will receive the dead.

6 It is given to you to hear what things are to come after these times.

7 For truly My redemption has drawn near, and is not as distant as it was.

Chapter 24

1 The days come and the books will be opened in which are written the sins of all those who have sinned, and also the treasuries in which the righteousness of all those who have been righteous in creation is gathered.

2 For it will come to pass at that time that you will see, and the many that are with you, the long-suffering of the Most High, which has been throughout all generations, who has been long-suffering towards all who are born, like those who sin and those who are righteous."

3 And I answered and said: But Lord, no one knows the number of those things which have passed nor yet of those things which are to come.

4 For I know indeed that which has befallen us, but what will happen to our enemies I know not, and when You will visit Your works.

Chapter 25

1 And He answered and said to me: You too will be preserved till that time till that sign which the Most High will work for the inhabitants of the earth in the end of days.

2 This therefore will be the sign:

3 When a stupor will seize the inhabitants of the earth, and they will fall into many tribulations, and again when they will fall into great torments.

4 And it will come to pass when they say in their thoughts because of their much tribulation: The Mighty One doth no longer remember the earth yea, it will come to pass when they abandon hope, that the time will then awake.

Chapter 26

1 And I answered and said: Will that tribulation which is to be, continue a long time, and will it necessitate many years?

Chapter 27

1 And He answered and said to me: Into twelve parts (pieces or section) is that time divided, and each one of them is reserved for that which is appointed for it.

2 In the first section (piece) there will be the beginning of commotions.

3 And in the second section (piece) slayings of the great ones.

4 And in the third section (piece) the fall of many by death.

5 And in the fourth section (piece) the sending of the sword.

6 And in the fifth section (piece) famine and the withholding of rain.

7 And in the sixth section (piece) earthquakes and terrors and wanting (need for food, water, and shelter).

8 And in the eighth section (piece) a multitude of specters and attacks of the Shedim.

9 And in the ninth section (piece) the fall of fire.

10 And in the tenth section (piece) rapine and much oppression.

11 And in the eleventh section (piece) wickedness and hedonism.

12 And in the twelfth section (piece) confusion from the mingling together of all those things aforesaid.

13 For these slices of that time are reserved, and will be mingled one with another and reinforce one another.

14 For some will leave out some of their own, and receive (in its stead) from others, and some complete their own and that of others, so that those may not understand who are upon the earth in those days that this is the consummation of the times.

Chapter 28

1 Nevertheless, whosoever understands will then be wise.

2 For the measure and reckoning of that time are two parts (pieces or section) a week of seven weeks.

3 And I answered and said: It is good for a man to come and behold, but it is better that he should not come lest he fall.

4 But I will ask this also: Will he who is incorruptible despise those things which are corruptible? What happens in the case of those things which are corruptible, so that he might look only to those things which are not corruptible?

5 But if, O Lord, those things will certainly come to pass which You have foretold to me, show this to me also if indeed I have found grace in Your sight.

6 Is it in one place or in one of the sections of the earth that those things are come to pass, or will the whole earth experience them?

Chapter 29

1 And He answered and said to me: Whatever will befall the whole earth all who live will experience.

2 For at that time I will protect only those who are found in those same days in this land.

3 And when all is accomplished that was to come to pass in those sections, that the Messiah will then begin to be revealed.

4 And Behemoth will be revealed from his place and Leviathan will ascend from the sea, those two great monsters which I created on the fifth day of creation, and will have kept until that time; and then they will be food for all that are left.

5 The earth also will yield its fruit ten thousand fold and on each vine there will be a thousand branches, and each branch will produce a thousand clusters, and each cluster produces a thousand grapes, and each grape produces a cor (a unit of measure approximately 517 pints) of wine.

6 And those who have hungered will rejoice, moreover, they will behold marvels every day.

7 For winds will go forth from before Me to bring every morning the fragrance of aromatic fruits, and at the close of the day clouds distilling the dew of health.

8 And it will come to pass at that same time that the treasury of manna will again descend from on high, and they will eat of it in those years, because these are they who have come to the end of time.

Chapter 30

1 And it will come to pass after these things, when the time of the advent of the Messiah is fulfilled, that He will return in glory.

2 Then all who have fallen asleep in hope of Him will rise again.

3 And it will come to pass at that time that the treasuries will be opened in which is preserved the number of the souls of the righteous, and they will come forth, and a multitude of souls will be seen together in one assemblage of one thought, and the first will rejoice and the last will not be grieved. For they know that the time has come of which it is said, that it is the consummation of the times.

4 But the souls of the wicked, when they behold all these things, will then waste away the more.

5 For they will know that their torment has come and their perdition has arrived."

Chapter 31

1 And after these things I went to the people and said to them:

2 Assemble to me all your elders and I will speak words to them.

3 And they all assembled in the valley of the Cedron. And I answered and said to them: Hear, O Israel, and I will speak to you, And give ear, O seed of Jacob, and I will instruct you.

4 Forget not Zion, But hold in remembrance the anguish of Jerusalem.

5 For the days come, when everything exists will become the prey of corruption and will be as though it had not been.

Chapter 32

1 But if you prepare your hearts, so as to sow in them the fruits of the law, it will protect you in that time in which the Mighty One is to shake the whole creation.

2 Because after a little time the building of Zion will be shaken in order that it may be built again.

3 But that building will not remain, but will again after a time be pulled up by the roots, and will remain desolate until the time.

4 And afterwards it must be renewed in glory, and perfected for evermore.

5 Therefore we should not be distressed so much over the evil which has now come as over that which is still to be.

6 For there will be a greater trial than these two tribulations when the Mighty One will renew His creation.

7 And now do not draw near to me for a few days, nor seek me till I come to you.

8 And when I had spoken to them all these words, that I, Baruch, went my way, and when the people saw me leaving, they lifted up their voice and lamented and said: To what place do you depart from us, Baruch, and forsake us as a father who forsakes his orphan children, and departs from them?

Chapter 33

1 Are these the commands which your companion, Jeremiah the prophet, commanded you, and said to you:

2 Look to this people till I go and make ready the rest of the brethren in Babylon, against whom has gone forth the sentence that they should be led into captivity?

3 And now if you also forsake us, it were good for us all to die before you withdraw from us.

Chapter 34

1 And I answered and said to the people: Far be it from me to forsake you or to withdraw from you, but I will only go to the Holy of Holies to inquire of the Mighty One concerning you and concerning Zion; in the hopes I should receive more illumination and after these things I will return to you.

Chapter 35

1 And I, Baruch, went to the holy place, and sat down upon the ruins and wept, and said:

2 O that mine eyes were springs, and mine eyelids a spring of tears.

3 For how will I lament for Zion, and how will I mourn for Jerusalem?

4 Because in that place where I am now prostrate, of old the high priest offered holy sacrifices; and placed thereon an incense of fragrant odors.

5 But now our glorying has been made into dust, And the desire of our soul into sand.

Chapter 36

1 And when I had said these things I fell asleep there, and I saw a vision in the night.

2 I saw a forest of trees planted on the plain, and lofty and rugged rocky mountains surrounded it, and that forest occupied much space.

3 And over beside it arose a vine, and from under it there went forth a peaceful fountain.

4 Now that fountain came to the forest and was agitated into great waves, and those waves submerged that forest, and suddenly they pulled up by the roots the greater section (area) of that forest, and overthrew all the mountains which were around it.

5 And the height of the forest began to be made low, and the top of the mountains was made low and that fountain greatly overtook it, so that it left nothing of that great forest save one cedar only.

6 Also when it had cast it down and had destroyed and pulled up by the roots the greater part of that forest, so that nothing was left of it, nor could its place be recognized, then that vine began to come with the fountain in peace and great tranquility, and it came to a place which was not far from that cedar, and they brought the cedar which had been cast down to it.

7 And I saw that vine opened its mouth and spoke and said to that cedar: Are you not that cedar which was left of the forest of wickedness, and by whose means wickedness persisted, and did evil all those years, and goodness never?

8 And you kept conquering that which was not yours, and to that which was yours you never showed compassion, and you kept extending your power over those who were far from you, and those who ventured near to you held tightly in the toils of your wickedness, and you lifted yourself up always as one that could not be pulled up by the roots!

9 But now your time has sped by and your hour is come. Do you also therefore depart O cedar, after the forest, which departed before you, and become dust with it, and let your ashes be mingled together?

10 And now lay down in anguish and rest in torment till your last time comes, in which you will come again and be tormented still more.

Chapter 37

1 And after these things I saw that cedar burning, and the vine glowing and all around it the plain was full of unfading flowers. And I awoke and arose.

Chapter 38

1 And I prayed and said: O LORD, my Lord, You always enlighten those who are led by understanding.

2 Your law is life, and Your wisdom is right guidance.

3 Make known to me the interpretation of this vision.

4 For You know that my soul has always walked in Your law, and from my earliest days I departed not from Your wisdom.

Chapter 39

1 And He answered and said to me: Baruch, this is the interpretation of the vision which you have seen.

2 As you have seen the great forest which lofty and rugged mountains surrounded, this is the word.

3 The days come, and this kingdom will be destroyed which once destroyed Zion, and it will be subjected to that which comes after it.

4 After a time the kingdom will be destroyed, and another, a third, will arise, and that also will have dominion for its time, and will be destroyed.

5 And after these things a fourth kingdom will arise, whose power will be harsh and evil far beyond those which were before it, and it will rule many times as the forests on the plain, and it will hold firmly for a time, and will exalt itself more than the cedars of Lebanon.

6 And by it the truth will be hidden, and all those who are polluted with sinfulness will flee to it, as evil beasts flee and creep into the forest.

7 And when the time of its end and fall has approached, then the kingdom of My Messiah will be revealed, which is like the fountain and the vine, and when it is revealed it will root out the multitude of its host.

8 And concerning that which you have seen, the lofty cedar, which was left out of that forest, and the fact, that the vine spoke those words with it which you did hear, this is the word.

Chapter 40

1 The last leader of that time will be left alive, when the multitude of his hosts will be put to the sword, and he will be bound, and they will take him up to Mount Zion, and My Messiah will convict him of all his unlawful deeds, and will gather and set before him all the works of his hosts.

2 And afterwards he will put him to death, and protect the rest of My people which will be found in the place which I have chosen.

3 And his kingdom will stand for ever, until the world of corruption is at an end, and until the times aforesaid are fulfilled.

4 This is your vision, and this is its interpretation.

Chapter 41

1 And I answered and said: For whom and for how many will these things be or who will be worthy to live at that time?

2 I will speak to you everything that I think, and I will ask of You regarding those things about which I think.

3 I see many of Your people who have withdrawn from Your covenant, and cast from them the yoke of Your law.

4 But I have seen others who have forsaken their vanity, and fled for refuge beneath Your wings.

5 What will become of them or how will the last time receive them?

6 Or perhaps the time of these will certainly be weighed, and as the beam inclines will they be judged accordingly?

Chapter 42

1 And He answered and said to me: "I will show you these things also.

2 To whom will these things be, and how many will they be?"

3 To those who have believed there will be the good which was spoken of before, and to those who despise there will be the contrary.

4 And regarding those who have drawn near (to Me) and those who have withdrawn (from Me) this is the word. As for those who were before subject (to Me), and afterwards withdrew and mingled themselves with the seed of mingled peoples, the time of these was the former, and was accounted as something exalted.

5 As for those who before knew (Me) not but afterwards knew life, and mingled (only) with the seed of the people which had separated itself the time of these (is) the latter, and is accounted as something exalted.

6 Time will succeed to (advance) time and season to season, and one will receive from another, and then with a view to the conclusion everything will be compared according to the measure of the times and the hours of the seasons.

7 Corruption will take those that belong to it, and life will take those that belong to it.

8 And the dust will be called, and there will be said to it: Give back that which is not yours, and raise up all that you have kept until its time.

Chapter 43

1 But, do you, Baruch, direct your heart to that which has been said to you, and understand those things which have been shown to you? For there are many eternal comforts for you.

2 You will leave this place, and you will pass from the regions which you see now, and you will forget whatever is corruptible, and will not again recall those things which happen among mortals.

3 Go and command your people, and come to this place, and afterwards fast seven days, and then I will come to you and speak with you.

Chapter 44

1 And I, Baruch, went from that place and came to my people, and I called my first-born son and the Gedaliahs my friends, and seven of the elders of the people, and I said to them:

2 I go to my fathers according to the way of all the earth.

3 But you should not withdraw from the way of the law, but guard and admonish the people which remain;

4 that they should not withdraw from the commandments of the Mighty One, for you see that He whom we serve is just, and our Creator is no respecter of persons.

5 And see what has happened to Zion, and what has happened to Jerusalem.

6 For the judgment of the Mighty One will be made known, and His ways, which, though past finding out, are right.

7 For if you endure and persevere in fear (respect / awe) of Him, and do not forget His law, the times will change over you for good. And you will see the consolation (reward) of Zion.

8 Because whatever exists now is nothing, but that which will be is very great. For everything that is corruptible will pass away, and everything that dies will depart, and all the present time will be forgotten, nor will there be any remembrance of the present time, which is defiled with evil.

9 That which runs now runs to vanity, and that which prospers will quickly fall and be humiliated.

10 That which is to come will be the object of desire, and for that which comes afterwards will we hope.

11 For it is a time that will not pass, and the hour comes which abides for ever.

12 And the new world (comes) which is blessedness and does not turn to corruption for those who depart to it, but it has no mercy on those who depart to torment, and it leads to perdition those who live in it.

13 For these are they who will inherit that time which has been spoken of, and theirs is the inheritance of the promised time.

14 These are they who have acquired for themselves treasures of wisdom, and with them are found stores of understanding, and they have not withdrawn from mercy and the truth of the law have they preserved.

15 For to them will be given the world to come, but the dwelling of the rest, who are many, will be in the fire."

Chapter 45

1 Instruct the people as far as you are able, for that labor is ours. For if you teach them, you will quicken them.

Chapter 46

1 And my son and the elders of the people answered and said to me: Has the Mighty One humiliated us to such a degree as to take you from us quickly?

2 We will truly be in darkness, and there will be no light to the people who are left For where again will we seek the law, or who will distinguish for us between death and life?

3 And I said to them: I cannot resist the throne of the Mighty One; nevertheless, there will not be wanting in Israel for a wise man, nor a son of the law to the race of Jacob.

4 But only prepare your hearts, that you may obey the law, and be subject to those who in fear are wise and understanding;

5 And prepare your souls that you may not leave them.

6 For if you do these things, good things will come to you., which I before told you of; nor will you fall into the torment, of which I testified to you before.

7 But with regard to the word that I was to be taken I did not make it known to them or to my son.

Chapter 47

1 And when I had gone out and dismissed them, I went from there and said to them:

2 I go to Hebron: for that is where the Mighty One has sent me. And I came to that place where the word had been spoken to me, and I sat there, and fasted seven days.

Chapter 48

1 And it came to pass after the seventh day, that I prayed before the Mighty One and said, O my Lord, You summon the advent of the times and they stand before You;

2 You cause the power of the ages to pass away, and they do not resist You; You arrange the method (progress / procedures) of the seasons, and they obey You.

3 You alone know the duration of the generations, and You do not reveal Your mysteries to many.

4 You make known the multitude of the fire, and You weigh the lightness of the wind.

5 You explore the limit of the heights, and You scrutinize the depths of the darkness.

6 You care for the number which pass away that they may be preserved and You prepare an habitation (abode) for those that are to be.

7 You remember the beginning which You have made, and the destruction that is to be You do not forget.

8 With nods of fear and indignation You command the flames, and they change into spirits, and with a word You quicken that which was not, and with mighty power You hold that which has not yet come.

9 You instruct created things in the understanding of You, and You make wise the spheres (orbs / heavenly bodies) so as to minister in their orders.

10 Armies innumerable stand before You and minister in their orders quietly at Your nod.

11 Hear Your servant and give ear to my petition.

12 For in a little time are we born, and in a little time do we return.

13 But with You hours are as a time (an age / eon) , and days as generations.

14 Be not angry with man; for he is nothing and take not account of our works; for what are we?

15 For by Your gift we come into the world, and we depart not of our own will.

16 For we said not to our parents, Beget us, Nor did we send to Sheol (place of the dead) and say, Receive us.

17 What therefore is our strength that we should bear Your rage or what are we that we should endure Your judgment?

18 Protect us in Your compassions, and in Your mercy help us.

19 Behold the little ones that are subject to You, and save all that draw near to You: Do not destroy the hope of our people, and do not cut short the times (occurrences) of our aid.

20 For this is the nation which You have chosen, and these are the people, to whom You find no equal.

21 But I will speak now before You, and I will say as my heart thinks.

22 In You do we trust, for Your law is with us and we know that we will not fall so long as we keep Your statutes.

23 To all time are we blessed at all events in this that we have not mingled with the Gentiles.

24 For we are all one celebrated people, who have received one law from One:

25 And the law which is among us will aid us, and the surpassing wisdom which is in us will help us.

26 And when I had prayed and said these things, I was greatly weakened. And He answered and said to me: You have prayed simply, O Baruch, and all your words have been heard.

27 But My judgment exacts its own and My law exacts its rights.

28 For from your words I will answer you, and from your prayer I will speak to you.

29 For this is as follows: he that is corrupted is not at all (is as though he does not exist);

30 He has acted sinfully in any way he could and has not remembered my goodness, and has not remembered My goodness, nor accepted My long-suffering.

31 Therefore you will surely be taken up, as I before told you.

32 For that time will arise which brings affliction; for it will come and pass by with quick vehemence, and it will be turbulent coming in the heat of indignation.

33 And it will come to pass in those days that all the inhabitants of the earth will be moved one against another, because they do not know that My judgment has drawn near.

34 For there will not be found many wise at that time, and the intelligent will be but a few. Moreover, even those who know will most of all be silent.

35 And there will be many rumors and tidings, not just a few. And the actions and deeds of spirits (phantoms) will be manifest, and many promises will be recounted. Some of them (will prove) idle, and some of them will be confirmed.

36 And honor will be turned into shame, and strength will be humiliated into contempt, and decency will be destroyed, and beauty will become ugliness.

37 And many will say to many at that time: "Where has the multitude of intelligence hidden itself, and to what place has the multitude of wisdom removed itself?"

38 And while they are thinking on these things, envy will arise in those who had not thought highly of themselves, and passion will seize him that is peaceful, and many will be stirred up in anger to injure many, and they will rouse up armies in order to shed blood, and in the end they will perish together with them.

39 And it will come to pass at the same time, that a change of times will manifestly appear to every man, because in all those times they polluted themselves. and they practiced oppression, and walked every man in his own works, and remembered not the law of the Mighty One.

40 Therefore a fire will consume their thoughts, and in flame will the control of their thoughts be tested; for the Judge will come and will not tarry, because each of the inhabitants of the earth knew when he was transgressing. But because of their pride they did not know My Law.

41 But many will certainly weep over the living more than over the dead.

42 And I answered and said: O Adam, what have you done to all those who are born from you? And what will be said to the first Eve who hearkened to the serpent?

43 For all this multitude are going to corruption, nor is there any numbering of those whom the fire will devour.

44 But again I will speak in Your presence.

45 You, O LORD, my Lord, know what is in Your creature.

46 Long ago You command the dust to produce Adam, and You know the number of those who are born from him, and how far they have sinned before You, who have existed and not confessed You as their Creator.

47 Their end will convict all of them, and Your law which they have transgressed will reward (revenge) them on Your day.

48 But now let us dismiss the wicked and inquire about the righteous.

49 And I will recount their blessedness and not be silent in celebrating their glory, which is reserved for them.

50 This transitory world which you live, has made you endured much labor in a short time, so in that world to which there is no end you will receive great light.

Chapter 49

1 Nevertheless, I will again ask mercy from You, O Mighty One, who made all things.

2 In what shape will those live who live in Your day? Or how will the splendor of those who are after that time continue?

3 Will they then resume this form of the present, and put on these members which hold us back, impeded us, and are now involved in evils, and in which evils are consummated, or will You possibly change these things which have been in the world as You also change the world?

Chapter 50

1 And He answered and said to me: "Hear, Baruch, this word, and write the remembrance of all that you will learn in your heart.

2 The earth will certainly return the dead, which it now receives in order to preserve them. It will not change their form, but it will return them in the same form it received them, and as I delivered them to it, so will it raise them.

3 Then it will be necessary to show the living that the dead have come to life again, and that those who had departed have returned again.

4 And when they have recognized those whom they now know, then judgment will grow strong, and those things which were spoken of prior will come to be.

Chapter 51

1 When that appointed day has passed, the appearance of those who are condemned will be changed and the glory of those who are justified will be shown.

2 For the appearance of those who act wickedly will become worse because they will suffer torment.

3 But the glory of those who have now been justified in My law, who have had understanding in their life, and who have planted the root of wisdom in their heart, their splendor for their face will be changed and glorified. Their face will be turned into the light of their beauty, that they may be able to take and receive the world which does not die, which is promised to them at that time.

4 Those that rejected My law, and stopped their ears that they might not hear wisdom or receive understanding will lament their actions over and above all things.

5 When they see those they were exalted over but who will be exalted and glorified more than they, they will both be transformed, the latter into the splendor of angels, and the former will waste away more as they wonder at the visions when they see the angelic forms.

6 For they will first see these things and afterwards depart to be tormented.

7 But those who have been saved by their works, and to whom the law has been a hope and understanding, and an expectation, and wisdom, and a confidence, will have wonders appear in their time.

8 For they will behold the world which is now invisible to them, and they will behold the time which is now hidden from them:

9 And time will no longer cause them to age.

10 For they will dwell in the high places of that world and they will be made like the angels and they will be made equal to the stars, and they will be changed into every form they desire from beauty to loveliness and from light to glorious splendor.

11 Before them the borders of Paradise will be spread out, and the beauty and majesty of the living creatures which are beneath the throne will be shown to them. They will see the armies of the angels who are held fast by My word, lest they should appear and are held fast by a command, that they may stand in their places until the time of their appearance comes.

12 There will be righteous excellence surpassing that of the angels.

13 For the first will receive the last. Those who have passed away will receive whom they were expecting. Those who had passed away and who we had head of we should expect to see.

14 For they have been delivered from the tribulation of this world and laid down their burden of anguish.

15 For what have men lost their life, and for what have those who were on the earth exchanged their soul?

16 They did not choose the time which is beyond the reach of anguish. But they chose that time whose results are full of lamentations and evils, and they denied the world which does make those who come to it grow old, but they rejected the time of glory. Thus that they will not have the honor of which I told you before."

Chapter 52

1 And I asked: How can we forget those whom are destined for sorrow?

2 Why do we mourn for those who die? Why do we weep for those who depart to Sheol?

3 Lamentations should be reserved for the beginning of the torment to come. Let tears be stored up for the time of destruction.

4 But even in the face of these things will I speak. What will the righteous do now?

5 Rejoice in the suffering which you now suffer. Why do you look for the decline of your enemies?

6 Make your soul ready for what is reserved for you, and prepare your souls for the reward which is stored up for you.

Chapter 53

1 And when I had said these things I fell asleep and I saw a vision. A cloud was ascending from a very large sea, and I kept looking at it and I saw it was full of black and white waters, and there were many colors in those same waters, and it looked like powerful lightning as seen from a summit.

2 And I saw the cloud passing quickly in short courses, and it covered all the earth.

3 Then, after these things that cloud began to pour all the waters that were in it upon the earth.

4 And I saw that all the waters which fell from it looked different.

5 To begin with, the waters were black and there was a lot for a time, and afterwards I saw that the waters became bright, but they were not as much, and after that I again saw black waters, and after these things again bright, and again black and again bright how this was done twelve times, but the black were always more numerous than the bright.

6 At the end of the cloud it rained black waters, and they were darker than had been all those waters that were before, and fire was mingled with them, and where those waters descended, they work devastation and destruction.

7 And after all of this I saw that lightning I had seen on the summit of the cloud seized hold of it and hurled it to the earth.

8 Now that lightning shone very brightly so that it illuminated the whole earth, and it healed those regions where the last waters had descended and work devastation.

9 And it took hold of the whole earth, and had dominion over it.

10 After these things I saw the twelve rivers were ascending from the sea, and they began to surround that lightning and to become subject to it.

11 And because of my fear I awoke.

Chapter 54

1 And I besought the Mighty One, and said: You alone, O Lord, know the deep things of the world before they happen. The things which occur in their times You bring about by Your word. You speed the beginning of these times against the works of the inhabitants of the earth, and the end of the seasons You alone know.

2 For You nothing is too hard. You do everything easily by a nod.

3 You, to whom the depths come as the heights, and whose word the beginnings of the ages serve;

4 You, who reveal to those who fear what You prepared for them so that they may be comforted.

5 You show great acts to those who do not know You. You break down the walls of those who are ignorant, and You light up what is dark, and You reveal what is hidden to the pure, who have submitted themselves to You and in Your law.

6 You have shown your servant this vision. Reveal its interpretation to me.

7 I know that for those things I have asked You about, I have received and answer. You have revealed to me with what voice I should praise You, and with what members of mine I should praises You and cause hallelujahs to ascend to You.

8 If my members were mouths and the hairs of my head were voices, I could not give you adequate food of praise, nor could I worship you as is befitting. I could never tell the glory of your beauty or praise you enough.

9 For what am I among men? Why am I counted among those who are more excellent than I that I have heard all these marvelous things from the Most High and numberless promises from Him who created me?

10 Blessed be my mother among those that bear, and let she that bare me be praised among women.

11 For I will not be silent in praising the Mighty One, and with the voice of praise I will tell His marvelous deeds.

12 For who does deeds like Your marvelous deeds, O God? Who comprehends Your deep thought of life?

13 With Your counsel You govern all the creatures which Your right hand has created. You have established every fountain of light beside You, and You have prepared the treasures of wisdom beneath Your throne.

14 Those who do not love your law perish justly. The torment of judgment awaits those who have not submitted themselves to Your power.

15 For though Adam first sinned and untimely brought death upon all, yet each of those who were born from him has prepared his own soul for the torment to come, and each one of them has chosen for himself glories to come.

16 It is certain that he who believes will receive reward.

17 But now, you wicked are bond for destruction because you will quickly be visited because you have rejected the understanding of the Most High.

18 His works have not taught you, and you have not been convinced by the skill of His creation which argued with you continually.

19 Adam is therefore not the cause, except for only his own soul, but each of us has been the Adam (man) of his own soul.

20 But You, O Lord, explain (open) to me those things which You have revealed to me, and inform me regarding that which I besought You.

21 For at the creation and until the end of the world, vengeance will be taken upon those who have done wickedness according to the wickedness in them, and You will glorify the faithful according to their faithfulness.

22 For those who are among Your own You rule, and those who sin You blot out from among Your own.

Chapter 55

1 Then, when I had finished speaking the words of this prayer I sat there under a tree that I might rest in the shade of the branches.

2 And I wondered and was amazed as I pondered the multitude of goodness which sinners who are upon the earth have rejected, and the tremendous torment they have hated, though they knew that they would be tormented because of the sin they had committed.

3 And when I was thought about these things the angel Ramiel, who presides over visions of truth, was sent to me, and he said to me:

4 Why does your heart trouble you, Baruch, and why do you have disturbing thoughts?

5 If the report you have only heard regarding judgment moved you so much what will you do when you see it manifest before yours eyes?

6 And if you expect day of the Mighty One and you are so overcome just by the expectation, what will you do when you come to its actual occurrence?

7 If at the mention of the announcement of the torment of those who have done foolishly, you are so completely upset, how much more will you be when the event reveals astonishing things? And if you have heard announcements of the good and evil things which are coming and are grieved, what will you do when you behold the majesty that will be revealed, which will convict some and cause others to rejoice.

Chapter 56

1 Nevertheless, because you have asked the Most High to reveal to you the interpretation of the vision you have seen, I have been sent to tell you.

2 And the Mighty One has certainly made known to you the arrangement of the times which have passed, and are destined to pass in His world regarding those of deceit and of those of truth from the beginning of its creation to its end.

3 As you saw, a tremendous cloud ascended from the sea, and covered the earth. This is the duration of the world which the Mighty One made when he thought to make the world.

4 And when the world came into being and had left His presence (area of the throne), the time of the world was short, and was established according to the vast intelligence of Him who sent it.

5 And as you saw before on the summit of the cloud, black waters descended previously on the earth. This is the transgression that Adam the first man committed.

6 For since the time he transgressed, (early) untimely death came. Grief was named and anguish was prepared, pain was created, and trouble was born, disease took hold, and Sheol kept demanding to be renewed in blood The birth of children was brought about, and the passion of parents was its fruit, and the greatness of humanity was humiliated, and goodness died.

7 What can be blacker or darker than these things?

8 This is the beginning of the black waters which you have seen.

9 From these black waters, black was derived, and from the darkness, darkness was produced.

10 For he became a danger to his own soul and even to the angels.

11 At the time when he was created, they (the angels) enjoyed liberty.

12 But some of them descended, and mingled with the women.

13 And those who did so were tormented in chains.

14 But the rest of the multitude of the angels, of which there is no number, restrained themselves.

15 Those who lived on the earth perished together with them (the fallen angels) through the waters of the flood.

16 These are the first black waters.

Chapter 57

1 And after these waters you saw bright waters. This is the spring of Abraham and his generations and the birth of his son and his son's son and of those like them.

2 Because at that time the unwritten law was named among them. The words of the commandments were then fulfilled. Belief in the coming judgment was then born and hope of the world that was to be renewed was then created. The promise of life to come was began.

3 These are the bright waters, which you have seen.

Chapter 58

1 The third black waters you have seen are the mingling of all sins, which the nations committed after the death of those righteous men in the wickedness of the land of Egypt where they did unrighteousness. And they made their sons serve unrighteousness.

2 However, these also perished in the end.

Chapter 59

1 And the fourth bright waters you have seen are the birth of Moses, Aaron, Miriam, and Joshua the sons of Nun and Caleb and of all those like them.

2 For at that time the lamp of the eternal law shone on all those who sat in darkness, which announced to them that believe the promise of their reward, and to them that deny, the torment of fire which is reserved for them.

3 But also the heavens at that time were shaken from their place, and those who were under the throne of the Mighty One were disturbed, when He was taking Moses to Himself For He showed him many reproofs along with the principles of the law and the completion of the times, as He also showed to you. He also showed the pattern of Zion and its size, in the pattern of which the sanctuary of the present time was to be made.

4 But then also He showed him the size of the fire, the depths of the abyss, the weight of the winds, the number of the drops of rain,

5 How much of (His) anger (He) holds back, and the amount of long-suffering (He has), and the truth of (His) judgment,

6 And the origin of wisdom, the wealth of understanding, the wellspring of knowledge,

7 The height of the air, and the greatness of Paradise, the end of the ages, and the beginning of the day of judgment,

8 The amount of the offerings, the earths which are yet to come,

9 The mouth of Gehenna (hell), the place of vengeance, the place of faith, and the place of hope,

10 The visions of future torment, the multitude of angelic hosts, the flaming hosts, the splendor of the lightning and the voice of the thunders, the orders of the captains of the angels, the treasuries of light, and the changing of times, and the searching of the law.

11 These are the bright fourth waters which you have seen.

Chapter 60

1 The fifth black waters you have seen raining are the deeds the Amorites committed, and the spells of their incantations which they performed, and the unrighteousness contained in their mysteries, and the pollutions they mixed.

2 Even Israel was polluted by sins in the days of the judges, though they saw many slip from Him who made them.

Chapter 61

1 And the sixth bright waters you saw is the time in which David and Solomon were born.

2 That was the time of the building of Zion, the dedication of the sanctuary, the shedding of much blood of the nations that sinned, and many offerings which were given in the dedication of the sanctuary.

3 Peace and tranquility existed at that time, And wisdom was heard in the congregation.

4 The wealth of understanding was magnified in the congregations, and the holy feasts and ceremonies were carried out in blessings and great joy.

5 The judgment of the rulers was without guile and it was witnessed as such. The righteous law of the Mighty One was accomplished with truth.

6 And the land was then loved by the Lord because its inhabitants sinned not and it was glorified beyond all lands. At that time the city Zion ruled over all lands and regions.

7 These are the bright waters which you have seen.

Chapter 62

1 And the seventh black waters which you have seen is the perversion brought about by the counsel of Jeroboam, who decided to make two calves of gold:

2 And all the iniquities which kings who were after him sinfully worked,

3 And the curse of Jezebel and the worship of idols which Israel practiced at that time.

4 The withholding of rain, and the famines which occurred until women ate the fruit of their wombs,

5 And the time of their captivity which came upon the nine tribes and a half tribe because they were in many sins.

6 Then, Salmanasar, King of Assyria, came and led them away captive.

7 But regarding the Gentiles, how they always were sinful and wicked, and always unrighteousness would be wearisome to tell

8 These are the seventh black waters which you have seen.

Chapter 63

1 And the eighth bright waters you have seen is the correction and uprightness of Hezekiah King of Judah and the grace of God which came upon him.

2 When Sennacherib was aggressing in order to kill Hezekiah the deadly rage of Sennacherib troubled Hezekiah because a great population of the nations were with him .

3 When Hezekiah the king heard those things which the king of Assyria was devising and how he planned to come and seize him and destroy his people, the two and a half tribes which remained and how he wished to overthrow Zion Hezekiah trusted in his works, and had hope in his righteousness, and spoke with the Mighty One and said:

4 "Look! Sennacherib is prepared to destroy us, and he will boast and strut when he has destroyed Zion."

5 And the Mighty One heard him because Hezekiah was wise and so He listened to his prayer because he was righteous.

6 Then the Mighty One commanded Ramiel, His angel, who speaks with you.

7 And I went out and destroyed their population, whose count of their chiefs alone was a hundred and eighty-five thousand, and each one of them had an equal number that he commanded.

8 And at that time I burned their bodies from the inside out, but their clothing and weapons I preserved outwardly so that more wonderful deeds of the Mighty One might be seen, and that because of this His name might be spoken of throughout the whole earth.

9 And Zion was saved and Jerusalem delivered and Israel was freed from tribulation.

10 And all those who were in the holy land rejoiced, and the name of the Mighty One was mentioned and glorified.

11 These are the bright waters which you have seen.

Chapter 64

1 "The ninth black waters which you saw was all the wickedness which was in the days of Manasseh the son of Hezekiah.

2 His deed showed that he had no regard for God. He killed the righteous people, and he forcibly stole away judgment. He shed the blood of the innocent. He violently raped women, he overturned the altars and destroyed their offerings. He drove out their priests so that they could not minister in the sanctuary.

3 He made an image with five faces: four of them looked to the four winds, and the fifth on the top of the image was a passionate enemy of the Mighty One.

4 Then rage went out from the presence of the Mighty One to the intent that Zion should be pulled up by its roots, just like it happened in your days.

5 A decree went out from God against the two tribes and a half tribe that they should also be led away captive, as you have now seen.

6 The impiety of Manasseh increased greatly to the point that it removed the praise of the Most High from the sanctuary.

7 Because of this Manasseh was then named "the impious", and finally his dwelling was in the fire.

8 For though his prayer was heard by the Most High, finally, when he was thrown into the brass horse and the brass horse was then melted, it was meant as a sign to him for that time.

9 He had not lived perfectly. He was not worthy but this was done so that he might know by whom he should be tormented in the end.

10 For He who is able to reward is also able to torment.

Chapter 65

1 Manasseh acted without regard for God, and thought that in his time the Mighty One would not look into these things.

2 These are the ninth black waters which you saw.

Chapter 66

1 "And the tenth bright waters which you have seen is the purity of the generations of Josiah King of Judah, who was the only one at the time who submitted himself to the Mighty One with all his heart and with all his soul.

2 He cleansed the land from idols, and sanctified all the vessels which had been polluted, and restored the offerings to the altar, and the horn of the holy was lifted, and he exalted the righteous, and honored all that were wise in understanding, and brought back the priests to their ministry, and destroyed and removed the magicians and enchanters and necromancers from the land.

3 He killed the sinners that were living and they also took from the sepulchers the bones of the dead and burned them with fire.

4 He established the festivals and the Sabbaths in their sanctity. He burned their polluted ones in the fire and the lying prophets which deceived the people were also burned in the fire, and the people who listened to them when they were living, he threw them into the brook Cedron, and heaped stones upon them.

5 And he was zealous with passion for the Mighty One with all his soul. He alone was steadfast in the law at that time, so that he left none that was uncircumcised, or that sinned in all the land, all the days of his life.

6 Therefore he will receive an eternal reward, and he will be glorified with the Mighty One beyond many at a later time.

7 For on his account and on account of those who are like him were the honorable glories, of which you was told before, created and prepared.

8 These are the bright waters which you have seen.

Chapter 67

1 "And the eleventh black waters which you have seen is the calamity which is now befalling Zion.

2 Do you think that there is no anguish to the angels in the presence of the Mighty One because Zion was delivered up in such a way or that the Gentiles boast in their hearts, and amass before their idols? The gentiles say, 'she who so often trod down is now trodden down and she who reduced others to slavery is now a slave herself.

3 Do you think that in these things the Most High rejoices, or that His name is glorified?

4 But how will it effect His righteous judgment?

5 Yet after these things the gentile will seize and scatter them in the tribulation and they will dwell in shame in every place.

6 Because Zion is delivered up and Jerusalem has been laid waste, idols prosper in the cities of the Gentiles, and the cloud of smoke from the incense of the righteousness which the commands is now extinguished in Zion. In every place in and surrounding Zion there is the smoke of sin.

7 The King of Babylon who has now destroyed Zion will arise, and he will boast about being ruler over the people, and he will speak great things in his heart in the presence of the Most High.

8 But he will fall in the end. These are the black waters.

Chapter 68

1 The twelfth bright waters which you have seen is the word.

2 After these things occur a time will come when your people will fall into distress, so that they will all run the risk of perishing together.

3 Nevertheless, they will be saved, and their enemies will fall in their presence.

4 In time they will have much joy.

5 After a little space of time Zion will be built again, and its offerings will be restored again, and the priests will return to their ministry, and the Gentiles will come to glorify it, but not as fully as they did in the beginning.

6 After these things there will be the fall of many nations.

8 These are the bright waters which you have seen."

Chapter 69

1 The last waters which you have seen were darker than all that were before them. Those were after the twelfth number were collected together. They belong to the entire world.

2 The Most High made division from the beginning, because He alone knows what will happen due to the depth and breadth of the sin which will be committed before Him. He foresaw six kinds of them.

5 He also foresaw six kinds of good works of the righteous which will be accomplished before Him. They will go beyond those which He will work at the end and conclusion of the age.

6 For Him there were not black waters with black, nor bright with bright; because it is the end.

Chapter 70

1 Hear the interpretation of the last black waters which are to come after the all other black waters. This is the word.

2 The days will come when the time of the age is ripe that is the harvest of evil and good seeds. This is what the Mighty One will bring upon the earth and its inhabitants and upon its rulers. It is disturbing to the spirit and lethargy of heart.

3 They will hate one another, and provoke one another to fight, and the cruel will rule over the honorable, and those of low status will be honored above the famous.

4 Many will be delivered into the hands of the few, and those who were nothing will rule over the strong. The poor will have abundance beyond the rich, and the wicked will exalt themselves above the heroic.

5 The wise will be silent, and the foolish will speak. The ideas of men will not be heeded, nor will the counsel of the mighty. The hope of those who hope be will not be rewarded.

6 And when those things which were predicted have come to pass confusion will fall upon all men. Some of them will fall in battle, some of them will die in torment and pain, and some of them will be destroyed by their own people.

7 Then the Most High will reveal those peoples whom He has prepared from before and they will come and make war with the leaders that will be left.

8 And whosoever survives the war will die in the earthquake, and whosoever survives the earthquake will be burned by the fire, and whosoever survives the fire will be destroyed by famine.

9 But whosoever of the victors and the vanquished survives and escapes all these things mentioned before will be delivered into the hands of My servant Messiah.

10 For all the earth will devour its inhabitants.

Chapter 71

1 And the holy land will have mercy on its own, and it will protect its inhabitants at that time.

2 This is the vision you have seen and this is the interpretation.

3 I have come to tell you these things because your prayer has been heard by the Most High.

Chapter 72

1 Listen, regarding the bright lightning which is to come at the end, after the black waters. This is the word.

2 After the signs which you were told of before, when the nations become turbulent, and the time of My Messiah is come, he will summon all the nations. Some of them he will spare, and some of them he will kill.

3 These things will come upon the nations which are spared by Him.

4 Every nation which does not know Israel and has not trodden down the seed of Jacob will be spared.

5 This is because some out of every nation will be subjected to your people.

6 But all those who have ruled over you or have known you will be given up to the sword.

Chapter 73

1 When He has brought everything that is in the world low and has sat down on the throne of His kingdom in peace for the dispensation, joy will be revealed and rest will appear.

2 Healing will descend in the dew and disease will go away and anxiety, pain and sorrow will vanish from among men. Gladness will go forth through the whole earth.

3 And no one will again die before his time (young) nor will adversity suddenly befall any.

4 Judgments, reproach, arguments, revenge, spilling of blood, passions, envy, hatred, and things like these will be condemned when they are removed.

5 For it is these very things which have filled this world with evils. On account of these the life of man has been greatly troubled.

6 Wild beasts will come from the forest and minister to men, asps and dragons (serpents) will come out from their holes to submit themselves to a little child.

7 Women will no longer then have pain when they bear children or suffer torment when they yield the fruit of the womb.

Chapter 74

1 In those days the reapers will not grow weary, nor those that build be weary from work. The works will quicken itself and speed those who doe the work and give them much tranquility.

2 That which is corruptible will be destroyed. It is the beginning of that which is not corruptible.

3 Those things predicted will belong to this age. It is far removed from evil and near to things eternal.

4 This is the bright lightning which came after the last dark waters."

Chapter 75

1 And I asked: Lord, Who can understand Your goodness? For it is incomprehensible.

2 Who can look into your compassions, which are infinite?

3 Who can understand Your intelligence?

4 Who is able to explain the thoughts of Your mind?

5 Who of those born can hope to attain those things unless to him are merciful and gracious?

6 Certainly if You did not have compassion on those who are under Your right hand they could not come to those things. Only those who are in the numbers you named can be called.

7 We who exist know why we have come and so we submit ourselves to Him who brought us out of Egypt. We will come again and remember those things which have passed. We will rejoice in what has been.

8 But if we do not know why we have come and if we do not recognize the kingdom of Him who brought us up out of Egypt, we will have to come again and seek after those things which have been now. We will be grieved with pain again because of those things which have befallen.

Chapter 76

1 And He answered and said to me: This vision has been revealed and interpreted to you as you asked me to do, now hear the word of the Most High that you may know what is to befall you after these things.

2 You will surely leave this earth, but not by death, but you will be preserved until the end of the age (times).

3 Go up to the top of that mountain, and all the regions of that land, and the figure of the inhabited world, and the tops of the mountains, and the depth of the valleys, and the depths of the seas, and the number of the rivers will pass before you so that you may see what you are leaving, and to what place you are going. Now this will happen after forty days.

4 Go now during these days and teach the people as much as you are able so that they may learn and not die at the last age but they may learn in order that they may live at the last age."

Chapter 77

1 And I, Baruch, went from there and came to the people, and assembled them together from the greatest to the least, and said to them:

2 Hear, children of Israel! See how many of you are who remain of the twelve tribes of Israel.

3 To you and to your fathers the Lord gave a law more excellent than to all peoples.

4 Because your brethren transgressed the commandments of the Most High, He brought vengeance upon you and upon them. He did not spare the former, and the latter also He gave into slavery.

5 He did not leave a trace of them. But you are here with me.!

6 If you direct your ways correctly you will not depart as your brethren departed, but they will come back to you.

7 You worship He who is full of mercy. Your hope is in Him who is gracious and true. He will do good and not evil.

8 Have you not seen what has befallen Zion?

9 Do you think that the place (area/location) had sinned and that is why it was overthrown? Did you think that the land had performed foolishness and that because of this it was delivered up?

10 Don't you know it was because of you who sinned, that those things which did not sin were overthrown? It was because of you who performed wickedness that those thing which did not do foolish acts were delivered up to its enemies?

11 All the people answered and said to me, We can recall the good things which the Mighty One has done for (to) us. We do recall them. There are these things and those things which we do not remember that He in His mercy knows.

12 In spite of this, please do this for us, your people, write to our brethren in Babylon an letter of (religious) teaching and a scroll containing hope so that you may confirm them before you leave us.

13 The religious leaders (shepherds) of Israel have died, and the lamps which gave light are extinguished, and the fountains from which we drank have withheld their stream.

14 We are left in the darkness among the trees of the forest, the thirst of the wilderness."

15 And I answered and said to them: Shepherds and lamps and fountains come from the law: And though we leave, yet the law remains.

16 If you have respect for the law, and are determined to become wise, a lamp will not be lacking, and a shepherd (religious leader) will not fail, and a fountain will not dry up.

17 I will write also to your brethren in Babylon, and I will send by means of men, and I will write in like manner to the nine tribes and a half, and send by means of a bird.

18 And on twenty-first day in the eighth month that I, Baruch, came and sat down under the oak under the shadow of the branches, and no man was with me, but I was alone.

19 And I wrote these two letters; one I sent by an eagle to the nine and a half tribes;

20 And the other I sent to those that were at Babylon by means of three men.

21 And I called the eagle and spoke these words to it: The Most High has made you that you should be higher than all birds.

22 Now go and do not stop in any place, nor enter a nest, nor settle upon any tree, till you have passed over the breadth of the many waters of the river Euphrates, and have gone to the people that dwell there, and drop down to them this letter.

23 Remember that at the time of the deluge Noah received the fruit of the olive from a dove when he sent it out from the ark.

24 The ravens also ministered to Elijah, bringing him food as they had been commanded.

25 Solomon, in the time of his kingdom, when he wished to send or seek for anything, commanded a bird to go out and it obeyed him as he commanded it.

26 So do not tire, and do not turn to the right hand nor the left, but fly and go by a direct way, that you may preserve the command of the Mighty One, according as I said to you.

Chapter 78

1 These are the words of that letter which Baruch the son of Neriah sent to the nine and a half tribes, which were across the river Euphrates, in which these things were written.

2 Baruch the son of Neriah says to the brethren carried into captivity: "Mercy and peace."

3 I bear in mind, my brethren, the love of Him who created us, who loved us from ancient times, and never hated us, but above all taught us.

4 And truly I know that all of us in the twelve tribes are bound by one bond, inasmuch as we are born from one father.

5 Because of this I have been the more diligent to leave you the words of this letter before I die, so that you may be comforted regarding the evils which have come upon you, and also that you may be grieved regarding the evil that has befallen your brethren; and also that you may justify (understand and accept) His judgment which He has decreed against you that you should be carried away captives. What you have suffered is a sentence disproportionibly greater than what you have done. But this was done in order that, at the last times, you may be found worthy of your fathers.

6 So, if you consider that you have now suffered those things for your good, that you may not be condemned and tormented in the end, then you will receive eternal hope. But you must remove from your heart all error and vanity, for it was because of this you departed from here.

7 If you so do these things He will never forget you. He who gave His promise to those greater than us but on our behalf, that He will never forget or forsake us, but will gather together again those who were dispersed with much mercy.

Chapter 79

1 Now, my brethren, learn first what befell Zion and how Nebuchadnezzar King of Babylon came up against us.

2 For we have sinned against Him who made us, and we have not kept the commandments which he ordered us to keep. Yet he has not chastened us as we deserved.

3 For what befell you we also suffer in a the highest degree, for it happened to us also.

Chapter 80

1 And now, my brethren, I reveal to you that when the enemy had surrounded the city the angels of the Most High were sent, and they collapsed the fortifications of the strong wall and they destroyed the solid iron corners, which could not be pulled up.

2 Nevertheless, they hid all the vessels of the sanctuary, to prevent the enemy from possessing them.

3 And when they had done these things, they delivered to the enemy the collapsed wall, and the plundered house, and the burnt temple, and the people who were overcome because they were delivered up. They did this so the enemy could not boast and say: " In war. by force have we been able to lay waste to the house of the Most High."

4 They also have bound your brethren and led away them to Babylon, and have forced them to live there.

5 But we, being very few, have been left here..

6 This is the tribulation about which I wrote to you.

7 And certainly I know that alleviation of the pain of the inhabitants of Zion consoles you. You knew that they prospered so your consolation was greater than the tribulation which you endured in having to leave it.

Chapter 81

1 But regarding consolation, listen to my word.

2 I was grieving regarding Zion, and I prayed for mercy from the Most High, and I said:

3 How long will these things last for us? Will we always have these evils on us?"

4 The Mighty One acted according out of the multitude of His mercies and according to the vastness of His compassion. He revealed to me His word so that my suffering would be relieved. He showed me visions that I should not again endure anguish. He made known to me the mystery of the times. And the advent of the hours he showed me.

Chapter 82

1 Therefore, my brethren, I have written to you, that you may comfort yourselves regarding the multitude of tribulations.

2 You know that our Maker will certainly avenge us and do to our enemies according to all that they have done to us. The end, which the Most High will make is very near will bring His mercy and the final result of His judgment is by no means far off.

3 For now we see the numerous prosperity of the Gentiles, even though they act sinfully and they are like a vapor.

4 We see their great power, even though they act wickedly, But they will become like a drop (of water).

5 We see the strength of their might, even though they resist the Mighty One every hour. But they will be considered as spittle.

6 We consider the glory of their greatness, though they do not keep the statutes of the Most High. But as smoke will they pass away.

7 And we think about the beauty of theirs gracefulness, even though they give it with pollutions. But as grass that withers will they fade away.

8 And we consider the strength of their cruelty, though they do not remember what it brought or how it ended. But as a wave that passes (through them) they will be broken.

9 And we remark about how the brag about being mighty although they deny that it was God that gave it to them. But they will disappear like a passing cloud.

Chapter 83

1 Most High will certainly speed up His times, and He will bring on His hours.

2 He will judge those who are in His world with certainty, and visit truth on all their hidden works.

3 He will examine the secret thoughts, and those things of all the members of man which they laid up in the secret chambers. He will make them appear in the presence of all with reproof.

4 Allow none of these present things to ascend into your hearts, but above all let us be expectant because that which is promised to us will come.

5 Do not let us look to the delights of the Gentiles now but let us remember what has been promised to us in the end.

6 For the end of the times and of the seasons and whatever is with them will cease together.

7 The conclusion of the age will show the tremendous strength of its ruler, when all things come to judgment.

8 Prepare your hearts for that which you have believed or you will be in bondage in both worlds and you be led away captive here and be tormented there.

9 That which is now or which was, or which will come, is the evil fully evil, nor the good fully good.

10 For all your health of this time are turning into sickness, and all strength of this time is turning into weakness, and all the power of this time is turning into impotence, and the energy of youth is turning into old age and death.

11 Every beauty of gracefulness of this time is becoming faded and hateful, and every prideful kingdom of this time is turning into humiliation and shame, and every praise of the glory of this time is turning into the embarrassment of silence, and every empty bragging insult of this time is turning into a mute ruin.

12 Every delight and joy of this time is turning to worms and decay, and every noise of the proud of this time is turning into dust and lethargy.

13 Every possession of riches of this time is being turned into Sheol (hell) alone, and all the yearning of passion of this time is turning into death, and every lustful desire of this time is turning into judgment with torment.

14 Every trick and craftiness of this time is turning into a proof of the truth. Every sweet ointment of this time is turning into judgment and condemnation, and every love of lying is turning to rudely to the truth.

15 Since all these things are done now does anyone think that they will not be avenged? The consummation of all things will come to the truth.

Chapter 84

1 Because of these things I have revealed to you this while I am still alive. I have said these things that you should learn the things that are excellent, for the Mighty One has commanded me to instruct you. So I will set before you some of the commandments of His judgment before I die.

2 Do not forget that Moses called heaven and earth to witness against you and said:

3 If you transgress the law you will be dispersed, but if you keep it you will be kept." He also used to say these things to you when you, the twelve tribes, were together in the desert.

4 After his death you threw them away from you and because of this there came upon you what had been predicted.

5 Moses used to tell you tell you what would befall you, and now you see they have befallen you because you have forsaken the law.

6 Now, I also say to you after you have suffered, that if you obey those things which have been said to you, you will receive from the Mighty One whatever has been laid up and waiting for you.

7 Let this letter be for a testimony between me and you so that you may remember the commandments of the Mighty One and that there may be to me a defense in the presence of Him who sent me.

8 And remember the law and Zion, the holy land, your brethren, and the covenant of your fathers. Do not forget the festivals and the sabbaths.

9 Deliver this letter and the traditions of the law to your sons after you, as also your fathers delivered them to you.

10 At all times make requests and pray diligently and unceasingly with your whole heart that the Mighty One may hold nothing against you, and that He may not count the multitude of your sins, but instead remember the rectitude of your fathers.

11 If He doe not judges us according to the multitude of His mercies, woe to all us who are born.

Chapter 85

1 Do you not know that in the past and in the generations of old our fathers had helpers? They were righteous men and holy prophets.

2 We were in our own land and they helped us when we sinned, and they interceded for us with Him who made us, because they trusted in their works, and the Mighty One heard their prayer and forgave us.

3 But now the righteous have been gathered and the prophets have fallen asleep, and we also have gone out from the land, and Zion has been taken from us, and we have nothing now except the Mighty One and His law.

4 If therefore we direct and commit our hearts we will receive everything that we lost, and much better things than we lost by many times.

5 For what we have lost would decay, but what we will receive will not be corruptible.

6 Also, I have written to our brethren to Babylon that to them also I may testify to these very things.

7 Let all those things I said before be always before your eyes, because we are still in the spirit and the power of our liberty.

8 The Most High is long-suffering towards us here, and He has shown us what is to be, and has not concealed from us what will happen in the end.

9 Before judgment takes its own (costs), and truth that which is its due, let us prepare our souls so that we may possess and not be taken as a possession and that we may hope and not be put to shame, and that we may rest with our fathers, and not be tormented with our enemies.

10 For the youth of the world is past, and the strength of the creation already exhausted, and the occurrence of the times is very short because they have already passed by. The pitcher is near to the cistern, and the ship to the port, and the course of the journey nears the city, and life to its conclusion.

11 Prepare your souls, so that when you sail and ascend from the ship you may have rest and not be condemned when you depart.

12 When the Most High will bring about all these things there will not be a place left for repentance, nor a limit to the times or a duration for the hours, or a change of ways, or a place to pray, or a way to send pleas, or to receive knowledge, or give of love. There will be no place of repentance for the soul, nor prayers for offences, nor intercession of the fathers, nor prayer of the prophets, nor help of the righteous.

13 There is the sentence of decay, the way of fire, and the path which leads to Gehenna (place of burning/hell/destruction).

14 There is one law (made) by one. There is one age and an end for all who are in it.

15 Then He will save those whom He can forgive, and at the same time destroy those who are polluted with sins.

Chapter 86

1 When you receive this, my letter, read it in your congregations with care.

2 Meditate on it, and above all do this on the days of your fasts.

3 Keep me in mind by means of this letter, as I also keep you in mind in it, always. Fare you well.

Chapter 87

1 And when I had ended all the words of this letter, and had written it without tiring to its close, that I folded it, and sealed it carefully, and bound it to the neck of the eagle, and dismissed it and sent it.

Josephus' Wars Of The Jews
Or
The History Of The Destruction Of Jerusalem
Book VI

CONTAINING THE INTERVAL OF ABOUT ONE MONTH. FROM THE GREAT EXTREMITY TO WHICH THE JEWS WERE REDUCED TO THE TAKING OF JERUSALEM BY TITUS.

CHAPTER 1.

THAT THE MISERIES STILL GREW WORSE; AND HOW THE ROMANS MADE AN ASSAULT UPON THE TOWER OF ANTONIA.

1. THUS did the miseries of Jerusalem grow worse and worse every day, and the seditious were still more irritated by the calamities they were under, even while the famine preyed upon themselves, after it had preyed upon the people. And indeed the multitude of carcasses that lay in heaps one upon another was a horrible sight, and produced a pestilential stench, which was a hinderance to those that would make sallies out of the city, and fight the enemy: but as those were to go in battle-array, who had been already used to ten thousand murders, and must tread upon those dead bodies as they marched along, so were not they terrified, nor did they pity men as they marched over them; nor did they deem this affront offered to the deceased to be any ill omen to themselves; but as they had their right hands already polluted with the murders of their own countrymen, and in that condition ran out to fight with foreigners, they seem to me to have cast a reproach upon God himself, as if he were too slow in punishing them; for the war was not now gone on with as if they had any hope of victory; for they gloried after a brutish manner in that despair of deliverance they were already in. And now the Romans, although they were greatly distressed in getting together their materials, raised their banks in one and twenty days, after they had cut down all the trees that were in the country that adjoined to the city, and that for ninety furlongs round about, as I have already related. And truly the very view itself of the country was a melancholy thing; for those places which were before adorned with trees and pleasant gardens were now become a desolate country every way, and its trees were all cut down: nor could any foreigner that had formerly seen Judea and the most beautiful suburbs of the city, and now saw it as a desert, but lament and mourn sadly at so great a change: for the war had laid all the signs of beauty quite waste: nor if any one that had known the place before, had come on a sudden to it now, would he have known it again; but though he were at the city itself, yet would he have inquired for it notwithstanding.

2. And now the banks were finished, they afforded a foundation for fear both to the Romans and to the Jews; for the Jews expected that the city would be taken, unless they could burn those banks, as did the Romans expect that, if these were once burnt down, they should never be able to take it; for there was a mighty scarcity of materials, and the bodies of the soldiers began to fail with such hard labors, as did their souls faint with so many instances of ill success; nay, the very calamities themselves that were in the city proved a greater discouragement to the Romans than those within the city; for they found the fighting men of the Jews to be not at all mollified among such their sore afflictions, while they had themselves perpetually less and less hopes of success, and their banks were forced to yield to the stratagems of the enemy, their engines to the firmness of their wall, and their closest fights to the boldness of their attack; and, what was their greatest discouragement of all, they found the Jews' courageous souls to be superior to the multitude of the miseries they were under, by their sedition, their famine, and the war itself; insomuch that they were ready to imagine that the violence of their attacks was invincible, and that the alacrity they showed would not be discouraged by their calamities; for what would not those be able to bear if they should be fortunate, who turned their very misfortunes to the improvement of their valor! These considerations made the Romans to keep a stronger guard about their banks than they formerly had done.

3. But now John and his party took care for securing themselves afterward, even in case this wall should be thrown down, and fell to their work before the battering rams were brought against them. Yet did they not compass what they endeavored to do, but as they were gone out with their torches, they came back under great discouragement before they came near to the banks; and the reasons were these: that, in the first place, their conduct did not seem to be unanimous, but they went out in distinct parties, and at distinct intervals, and after a slow manner, and timorously, and, to say all in a word, without a Jewish courage; for they were now defective in what is peculiar to our nation, that is, in boldness, in violence of assault, and in running upon the enemy all together, and in persevering in what they go about, though they do not at first succeed in it; but they now went out in a more languid manner than usual, and at the same time found the Romans set in array, and more courageous than ordinary, and that they guarded their banks both with their bodies and their entire armor, and this to such a degree on all sides, that they left no room for the fire to get among them, and that every one of their souls was in such good courage, that they would sooner die than desert their ranks; for besides their notion that all their hopes were cut off, in case these their works were once burnt, the soldiers were greatly ashamed that subtlety should quite be too hard for courage, madness for armor, multitude for skill, and Jews for Romans. The Romans had now also another advantage, in that their engines for sieges co-operated with them in throwing darts and stones as far as the Jews, when they were coming out of the city; whereby the man that fell became an impediment to him that was next to him, as did the danger of going farther make them less zealous in their attempts; and for those that had run under the darts, some of them were terrified by the good order and closeness of the enemies' ranks before they came to a close fight, and others were pricked with their spears, and turned back again; at length they reproached one another for their cowardice, and retired without doing any thing. This attack was made upon the first day of the month Panemus [Tamuz.] So when the Jews were retreated, the Romans brought their engines, although they had all the while stones thrown at them from the tower of Antonia, and were assaulted by fire and sword, and by all sorts of darts, which necessity afforded the Jews to make use of; for although these had great dependence on their own wall, and a contempt of the Roman engines, yet did they endeavor to hinder the Romans from bringing them. Now these Romans struggled hard, on the contrary, to bring them, as deeming that this zeal of the Jews was in order to avoid any impression to be made on the tower of Antonia, because its wall was but weak, and its foundations rotten. However, that tower did not yield to the blows given it from the engines; yet did the Romans bear the impressions made by the enemies' darts which were perpetually cast at them, and did not give way to any of those dangers that came upon them from above, and so they brought their engines to bear. But then, as they were beneath the other, and were sadly wounded by the stones thrown down upon them, some of them threw their shields over their bodies, and partly with their hands, and partly with their bodies, and partly with crows, they undermined its foundations, and with great pains they removed four of its stones. Then night came upon both sides, and put an end to this struggle for the present; however, that night the wall was so shaken by the battering rams in that place where John had used his stratagem before, and had undermined their banks, that the ground then gave way, and the wall fell down suddenly.

4. When this accident had unexpectedly happened, the minds of both parties were variously affected; for though one would expect that the Jews would be discouraged, because this fall of their wall was unexpected by them, and they had made no provision in that case, yet did they pull up their courage, because the tower of Antonia itself was still standing; as was the unexpected joy of the Romans at this fall of the wall soon quenched by the sight they had of another wall, which John and his party had built within it. However, the attack of this second wall appeared to be easier than that of the former, because it seemed a thing of greater facility to get up to it through the parts of the former wall that were now thrown down. This new wall appeared also to be much weaker than the tower of Antonia, and accordingly the Romans imagined that it had been erected so much on the sudden, that they should soon overthrow it: yet did not any body venture now to go up to this wall; for that such as first ventured so to do must certainly be killed.

5. And now Titus, upon consideration that the alacrity of soldiers in war is chiefly excited by hopes and by good words, and that exhortations and promises do frequently make men to forget the hazards they run, nay, sometimes to despise death itself, got together the most courageous part of his army, and tried what he could do with his men by these methods. "O fellow soldiers," said he, "to make an exhortation to men to do what hath no peril in it, is on that very account inglorious to such to whom that exhortation is made; and indeed so it is in him that makes the exhortation, an argument of his own cowardice also. I therefore think that such exhortations ought then only to be made use of when affairs are in a dangerous condition, and yet are worthy of being attempted by every one themselves; accordingly, I am fully of the same opinion with you, that it is a difficult task to go up this wall; but that it is proper for those that desire reputation for their valor to struggle with difficulties in such cases will then appear, when I have particularly shown that it is a brave thing to die with glory, and that the courage here necessary shall not go unrewarded in those that first begin the attempt. And let my first argument to move you to it be taken from what probably some would think reasonable to dissuade you, I mean the constancy and patience of these Jews, even under their ill successes; for it is unbecoming you, who are Romans and my soldiers, who have in peace been taught how to make wars, and who have also been used to conquer in those wars, to be inferior to Jews, either in action of the hand, or in courage of the soul, and this especially when you are at the conclusion of your victory, and are assisted by God himself; for as to our misfortunes, they have been owing to the madness of the Jews, while their sufferings have been owing to your valor, and to the assistance God hath afforded you; for as to the seditions they have been in, and the famine they are under, and the siege they now endure, and the fall of their walls without our engines, what can they all be but demonstrations of God's anger against them, and of his assistance afforded us? It will not therefore be proper for you, either to show yourselves inferior to those to whom you are really superior, or to betray that Divine assistance which is afforded you. And, indeed, how can it be esteemed otherwise than a base and unworthy thing, that while the Jews, who need not be much ashamed if they be deserted, because they have long learned to be slaves to others, do yet despise death, that they may be so no longer; and do make sallies into the very midst of us frequently, no in hopes of conquering us, but merely for a demonstration of their courage; we, who have gotten possession of almost all the world that belongs to either land or sea, to whom it will be a great shame if we do not conquer them, do not once undertake any attempt against our enemies wherein there is much danger, but sit still idle, with such brave arms as we have, and only wait till the famine and fortune do our business themselves, and this when we have it in our power, with some small hazard, to gain all that we desire! For if we go up to this tower of Antonia, we gain the city; for if there should be any more occasion for fighting against those within the city, which I do not suppose there will, since we shall then be upon the top of the hill (1) and be upon our enemies before they can have taken breath, these advantages promise us no less than a certain and sudden victory. As for myself, I shall at present wave any commendation of those who die in war, (2) and omit to speak of the immortality of those men who are slain in the midst of their martial bravery; yet cannot I forbear to imprecate upon those who are of a contrary disposition, that they may die in time of peace, by some distemper or other, since their souls are condemned to the grave, together with their bodies. For what man of virtue is there who does not know, that those souls which are severed from their fleshly bodies in battles by the sword are received by the ether, that purest of elements, and joined to that company which are placed among the stars; that they become good demons, and propitious heroes, and show themselves as such to their posterity afterwards? while upon those souls that wear away in and with their distempered bodies comes a subterranean night to dissolve them to nothing, and a deep oblivion to take away all the remembrance of them, and this notwithstanding they be clean from all spots and defilements of this world; so that, in this ease, the soul at the same time comes to the utmost bounds of its life, and of its body, and of its memorial also. But since he hath determined that death is to come of necessity upon all men, a sword is a better instrument for that purpose than any disease whatsoever. Why is it not then a very mean thing for us not to yield up that to the public benefit which we must yield up to fate? And this discourse have I made, upon the supposition that those who at first attempt to go upon this wall must needs be killed in the attempt, though still men of true courage have a chance to escape even in the most hazardous undertakings. For, in the first place, that part of the former wall that is thrown down is easily to be ascended; and for the new-built wall, it is easily destroyed. Do you, therefore, many of you, pull up your courage, and set about this work, and do you mutually encourage and assist

one another; and this your bravery will soon break the hearts of your enemies; and perhaps such a glorious undertaking as yours is may be accomplished without bloodshed. For although it be justly to be supposed that the Jews will try to hinder you at your first beginning to go up to them; yet when you have once concealed yourselves from them, and driven them away by force, they will not be able to sustain your efforts against them any longer, though but a few of you prevent them, and get over the wall. As for that person who first mounts the wall, I should blush for shame if I did not make him to be envied of others, by those rewards I would bestow upon him. If such a one escape with his life, he shall have the command of others that are now but his equals; although it be true also that the greatest rewards will accrue to such as die in the attempt." (3)

6. Upon this speech of Titus, the rest of the multitude were aftrighted at so great a danger. But there was one, whose name was Sabinus, a soldier that served among the cohorts, and a Syrian by birth, who appeared to be of very great fortitude, both in the actions he had done, and the courage of his soul he had shown; although any body would have thought, before he came to his work, that he was of such a weak constitution of body, that he was not fit to be a soldier; for his color was black, his flesh was lean and thin, and lay close together; but there was a certain heroic soul that dwelt in this small body, which body was indeed much too narrow for that peculiar courage which was in him. Accordingly he was the first that rose up, when he thus spake: "I readily surrender up myself to thee, O Caesar; I first ascend the wall, and I heartily wish that my fortune may follow my courage and my resolution And if some ill fortune grudge me the success of my undertaking, take notice that my ill success will not be unexpected, but that I choose death voluntarily for thy sake." When he had said this, and had spread out his sheild over his head with his left hand, and hill, with his right hand, drawn his sword, he marched up to the wall, just about the sixth hour of the day. There followed him eleven others, and no more, that resolved to imitate his bravery; but still this was the principal person of them all, and went first, as excited by a divine fury. Now those that guarded the wall shot at them from thence, and cast innumerable darts upon them from every side; they also rolled very large stones upon them, which overthrew some of those eleven that were with him. But as for Sabinus himself, he met the darts that were cast at him and though he was overwhelmed with them, yet did he not leave off the violence of his attack before he had gotten up on the top of the wall, and had put the enemy to flight. For as the Jews were astonished at his great strength, and the bravery of his soul, and as, withal, they imagined more of them had got upon the wall than really had, they were put to flight. And now one cannot but complain here of fortune, as still envious at virtue, and always hindering the performance of glorious achievements: this was the case of the man before us, when he had just obtained his purpose; for he then stumbled at a certain large stone, and fell down upon it headlong, with a very great noise. Upon which the Jews turned back, and when they saw him to be alone, and fallen down also, they threw darts at him from every side. However. be got upon his knee, and covered himself with his shield, and at the first defended himself against them, and wounded many of those that came near him; but he was soon forced to relax his right hand, by the multitude of the wounds that had been given him, till at length he was quite covered over with darts before he gave up the ghost. He was one who deserved a better fate, by reason of his bravery; but, as might be expected, he fell under so vast an attempt. As for the rest of his partners, the Jews dashed three of them to pieces with stones, and slew them as they were gotten up to the top of the wall; the other eight being wounded, were pulled down, and carried back to the camp. These things were done upon the third day of the month Panemus [Tamuz].

7. Now two days afterward twelve of those men that were on the forefront, and kept watch upon the banks, got together, and called to them the standard-bearer of the fifth legion, and two others of a troop of horsemen, and one trumpeter; these went without noise, about the ninth hour of the night, through the ruins, to the tower of Antonia; and when they had cut the throats of the first guards of the place, as they were asleep, they got possession of the wall, and ordered the trumpeter to sound his trumpet. Upon which the rest of the guard got up on the sudden, and ran away, before any body could see how many they were that were gotten up; for, partly from the fear they were in, and partly from the sound of the trumpet which they heard, they imagined a great number of the enemy were gotten up. But as soon as Caesar heard the signal, he ordered the army to put on their armor immediately, and came thither with his commanders, and first of all ascended, as did the chosen men that were with him. And as the Jews were flying away to the temple, they fell into that mine which John had dug under the Roman banks. Then did the seditious of both the bodies of the Jewish army, as well that belonging to John as that belonging to Simon, drive them away; and indeed were no way wanting as to the highest degree of force and alacrity; for they esteemed themselves entirely ruined if once the Romans got into the temple, as did the Romans look upon the same thing as the beginning of their entire conquest. So a terrible battle was fought at the entrance of the temple, while the Romans were forcing their way, in order to get possession of that temple, and the Jews were driving them back to the tower of Antonia; in which battle the darts were on both sides useless, as well as the spears, and both sides drew their swords, and fought it out hand to hand. Now during this struggle the positions of the men were undistinguished on both sides, and they fought at random, the men being intermixed one with another, and confounded, by reason of the narrowness of the place; while the noise that was made fell on the ear after an indistinct manner, because it was so very loud. Great slaughter was now made on both sides, and the combatants trod upon the bodies and the armor of those that were dead, and dashed them to pieces. Accordingly, to which side soever the battle inclined, those that had the advantage exhorted one another to go on, as did those that were beaten make great lamentation. But still there was no room for flight, nor for pursuit, but disorderly revolutions and retreats, while the armies were intermixed one with another; but those that were in the first ranks were under the necessity of killing or being killed, without any way for escaping; for those on both sides that came behind forced those before them to go on, without leaving any space between the armies. At length the Jews' violent zeal was too hard for the Romans' skill, and the battle already inclined entirely that way; for the fight had lasted from the ninth hour of the night till the seventh hour of the day, While the Jews came on in crowds, and had the danger the temple was in for their motive; the Romans having no more here than a part of their army; for those legions, on which the soldiers on that side depended, were not come up to them. So it was at present thought sufficient by the Romans to take possession of the tower of Antonia.

8. But there was one Julian, a centurion, that came from Eithynia, a man he was of great reputation, whom I had formerly seen in that war, and one of the highest fame, both for his skill in war, his strength of body, and the courage of his soul. This man, seeing the Romans giving ground, and ill a sad condition, (for he stood by Titus at the tower of Antonia,) leaped out, and of himself alone put the Jews to flight, when they were already conquerors, and made them retire as far as the corner of the inner court of the temple; from him the multitude fled away in crowds, as supposing that neither his strength nor his violent attacks could be those of a mere man. Accordingly, he rushed through the midst of the Jews, as they were dispersed all abroad, and killed those that he caught. Nor, indeed, was there any sight that appeared more wonderful in the eyes of Caesar, or more terrible to others, than this. However, he was himself pursued by fate, which it all not possible that he, who was but a mortal man, should escape; for as he had shoes all full of thick and sharp nails (4) as had every one of the other soldiers, so when he ran on the pavement of the temple, he slipped, and fell down upon his back with a very great noise, which was made by his armor. This made those that were running away to turn back; whereupon those Romans that were in the tower of Antonia set up a great shout, as they were in fear for the man. But the Jews got about him in crowds, and struck at him with their spears and with their swords on all sides. Now he received a great many of the strokes of these iron weapons upon his shield, and often attempted to get up again, but was thrown down by those that struck at him; yet did he, as he lay along, stab many of them with his sword. Nor was he soon killed, as being covered with his helmet and his breastplate in all those parts of his body where he might be mortally wounded; he also pulled his neck close to his body, till all his other limbs were shattered, and nobody durst come to defend him, and then he yielded to his fate. Now Caesar was deeply affected on account of this man of so great fortitude, and especially as he was killed in the sight of so many people; he was desirous himself to come to his assistance, but the place would not give him leave, while such as could have done it were too much terrified to attempt it. Thus when Julian had struggled with death a great while, and had let but few of those that had given him his mortal wound go off unhurt, he had at last his throat cut, though not without some difficulty, and left behind him a very great fame, not only among the Romans, and with Caesar himself, but among his enemies also; then did the Jews catch up his dead body, and put the Romans to flight again, and shut them up in the tower of Antonia. Now those that most signalized themselves, and fought most zealously in this battle of the Jewish side, were one Alexas and Gyphtheus, of John's party, and of Simon's party were Malachias, and Judas the son of Merto, and James the son of Sosas, the commander of the Idumeans; and of the zealots, two brethren, Simon and Judas, the sons of Jairus.

CHAPTER 2.

HOW TITUS GAVE ORDERS TO DEMOLISH THE TOWER OF ANTONIA AND THEN PERSUADED JOSEPHUS TO EXHORT THE JEWS AGAIN [TO A SURRENDER].

1. AND now Titus gave orders to his soldiers that were with him to dig up the foundations of the tower of Antonia, and make him a ready passage for his army to come up; while he himself had Josephus brought to him, (for he had been informed that on that very day, which was the seventeenth day (5) of Panemus, [Tamuz,] the sacrifice called "the Daily Sacrifice" had failed, and had not been offered to God, for want of men to offer it, and that the people were grievously troubled at it,) and commanded him to say the same things to John that he had said before, that if he had any malicious inclination for fighting, he might come out with as many of his men as he pleased, in order to fight, without the danger of destroying either his city or temple; but that he desired he would not defile the temple, nor thereby offend against God. That he might, if he pleased, offer the sacrifices which were now discontinued by any of the Jews whom he should pitch upon. Upon this Josephus stood in such a place where he might be heard, not by John only, but by many more, and then declared to them what Caesar had given him in charge, and this in the Hebrew language. (6) So he earnestly prayed them to spare their own city, and to prevent that fire which was just ready to seize upon the temple, and to offer their usual sacrifices to God therein. At these words of his a great sadness and silence were observed among the people. But the tyrant himself cast many reproaches upon Josephus, with imprecations besides; and at last added this withal, that he did never fear the taking of the city, because it was God's own city. In answer to which Josephus said thus with a loud voice: "To be sure thou hast kept this city wonderfully pure for God's sake; the temple also continues entirely unpolluted! Nor hast thou been guilty of ally impiety against him for whose assistance thou hopest! He still receives his accustomed sacrifices! Vile wretch that thou art! if any one should deprive thee of thy daily food, thou wouldst esteem him to be an enemy to thee; but thou hopest to have that God for thy supporter in this war whom thou hast deprived of his everlasting worship; and thou imputest those sins to the Romans, who to this very time take care to have our laws observed, and almost compel these sacrifices to be still offered to God, which have by thy means been intermitted! Who is there that can avoid groans and lamentations at the amazing change that is made in this city? since very foreigners and enemies do now correct that impiety which thou hast occasioned; while thou, who art a Jew, and wast educated in our laws, art become a greater enemy to them than the others. But still, John, it is never dishonorable to repent, and amend what hath been done amiss, even at the last extremity. Thou hast an instance before thee in Jechoniah, (7) the king of the Jews, if thou hast a mind to save the city, who, when the king of Babylon made war against him, did of his own accord go out of this city before it was taken, and did undergo a voluntary captivity with his family, that the sanctuary might not be delivered up to the enemy, and that he might not see the house of God set on fire; on which account he is celebrated among all the Jews, in their sacred memorials, and his memory is become immortal, and will be conveyed fresh down to our posterity through all ages. This, John, is an excellent example in such a time of danger, and I dare venture to promise that the Romans shall still forgive thee. And take notice that I, who make this exhortation to thee, am one of thine own nation; I, who am a Jew, do make this promise to thee. And it will become thee to consider who I am that give thee this counsel, and whence I am derived; for while I am alive I shall never be in such slavery, as to forego my own kindred, or forget the laws of our forefathers. Thou hast indignation at me again, and makest a clamor at me, and reproachest me; indeed I cannot deny but I am worthy of worse treatment than all this amounts to, because, in opposition to fate, I make this kind invitation to thee, and endeavor to force deliverance upon those whom God hath condemned. And who is there that does not know what the writings of the ancient prophets contain in them, - and particularly that oracle which is just now going to be fulfilled upon this miserable city? For they foretold that this city should be then taken when somebody shall begin the slaughter of his own countrymen. And are not both the city and the entire temple now full of the dead bodies of your countrymen? It

is God, therefore, it is God himself who is bringing on this fire, to purge that city and temple by means of the Romans, (8) and is going to pluck up this city, which is full of your pollutions."

2. As Josephus spoke these words, with groans and tears in his eyes, his voice was intercepted by sobs. However, the Romans could not but pity the affliction he was under, and wonder at his conduct. But for John, and those that were with him, they were but the more exasperated against the Romans on this account, and were desirous to get Josephus also into their power: yet did that discourse influence a great many of the better sort; and truly some of them were so afraid of the guards set by the seditious, that they tarried where they were, but still were satisfied that both they and the city were doomed to destruction. Some also there were who, watching a proper opportunity when they might quietly get away, fled to the Romans, of whom were the high priests Joseph and Jesus, and of the sons of high priests three, whose father was Ishmael, who was beheaded in Cyrene, and four sons of Matthias, as also one son of the other Matthias, who ran away after his father's death, (9) and whose father was slain by Simon the son of Gioras, with three of his sons, as I have already related; many also of the other nobility went over to the Romans, together with the high priests. Now Caesar not only received these men very kindly in other respects, but, knowing they would not willingly live after the customs of other nations, he sent them to Gophna, and desired them to remain there for the present, and told them, that when he was gotten clear of this war, he would restore each of them to their possessions again; so they cheerfully retired to that small city which was allotted them, without fear of any danger. But as they did not appear, the seditious gave out again that these deserters were slain by the Romans, which was done in order to deter the rest from running away, by fear of the like treatment. This trick of theirs succeeded now for a while, as did the like trick before; for the rest were hereby deterred from deserting, by fear of the like treatment.

3. However, when Titus had recalled those men from Gophna, he gave orders that they should go round the wall, together with Josephus, and show themselves to the people; upon which a great many fled to the Romans. These men also got in a great number together, and stood before the Romans, and besought the seditious, with groans and tears in their eyes, in the first place to receive the Romans entirely into the city, and save that their own place of residence again; but that, if they would not agree to such a proposal, they would at least depart out of the temple, and save the holy house for their own use; for that the Romans would not venture to set the sanctuary on fire but under the most pressing necessity. Yet did the seditious still more and more contradict them; and while they cast loud and bitter reproaches upon these deserters, they also set their engines for throwing of darts, and javelins, and stones upon the sacred gates of the temple, at due distances from one another, insomuch that all the space round about within the temple might be compared to a burying-ground, so great was the number of the dead bodies therein; as might the holy house itself be compared to a citadel. Accordingly, these men rushed upon these holy places in their armor, that were otherwise unapproachable, and that while their hands were yet warm with the blood of their own people which they had shed; nay, they proceeded to such great transgressions, that the very same indignation which Jews would naturally have against Romans, had they been guilty of such abuses against them, the Romans now had against Jews, for their impiety in regard to their own religious customs. Nay, indeed, there were none of the Roman soldiers who did not look with a sacred horror upon the holy house, and adored it, and wished that the robbers would repent before their miseries became incurable.

4. Now Titus was deeply affected with this state of things, and reproached John and his party, and said to them, "Have not you, vile wretches that you are, by our permission, put up this partition-wall before your sanctuary? Have not you been allowed to put up the pillars thereto belonging, at due distances, and on it to engrave in Greek, and in your own letters, this prohibition, that no foreigner should go beyond that wall. (10) Have not we given you leave to kill such as go beyond it, though he were a Roman? And what do you do now, you pernicious villains? Why do you trample upon dead bodies in this temple? and why do you pollute this holy house with the blood of both foreigners and Jews themselves? I appeal to the gods of my own country, and to every god that ever had any regard to this place; (for I do not suppose it to be now regarded by any of them;) I also appeal to my own army, and to those Jews that are now with me, and even to yourselves, that I do not force you to defile this your sanctuary; and if you will but change the place whereon you will fight, no Roman shall either come near your sanctuary, or offer any affront to it; nay, I will endeavor to preserve you your holy house, whether you will or not." (11)

5. As Josephus explained these things from the mouth of Caesar, both the robbers and the tyrant thought that these exhortations proceeded from Titus's fear, and not from his good-will to them, and grew insolent upon it. But when Titus saw that these men were neither to be moved by commiseration towards themselves, nor had any concern upon them to have the holy house spared, he proceeded unwillingly to go on again with the war against them. He could not indeed bring all his army against them, the place was so narrow; but choosing thirty soldiers of the most valiant out of every hundred, and committing a thousand to each tribune, and making Cerealis their commander-in-chief, he gave orders that they should attack the guards of the temple about the ninth hour of that night. But as he was now in his armor, and preparing to go down with them, his friends would not let him go, by reason of the greatness of the danger, and what the commanders suggested to them; for they said that he would do more by sitting above in the tower of Antonia, as a dispenser of rewards to those soldiers that signalized themselves in the fight, than by coming down and hazarding his own person in the forefront of them; for that they would all fight stoutly while Caesar looked upon them. With this advice Caesar complied, and said that the only reason he had for such compliance with the soldiers was this, that he might be able to judge of their courageous actions, and that no valiant soldier might lie concealed, and miss of his reward, and no cowardly soldier might go unpunished; but that he might himself be an eye-witness, and able to give evidence of all that was done, who was to be the disposer of punishments and rewards to them. So he sent the soldiers about their work at the hour forementioned, while he went out himself to a higher place in the tower of Antonia, whence he might see what was done, and there waited with impatience to see the event.

6. However, the soldiers that were sent did not find the guards of the temple asleep, as they hoped to have done; but were obliged to fight with them immediately hand to hand, as they rushed with violence upon them with a great shout. Now as soon as the rest within the temple heard that shout of those that were upon the watch, they ran out in troops upon them. Then did the Romans receive the onset of those that came first upon them; but those that followed them fell upon their own troops, and many of them treated their own soldiers as if they had been enemies; for the great confused noise that was made on both sides hindered them from distinguishing one another's voices, as did the darkness of the night hinder them from the like distinction by the sight, besides that blindness which arose otherwise also from the passion and the fear they were in at the same time; for which reason it was all one to the soldiers who it was they struck at. However, this ignorance did less harm to the Romans than to the Jews, because they were joined together under their shields, and made their sallies more regularly than the others did, and each of them remembered their watch-word; while the Jews were perpetually dispersed abroad, and made their attacks and retreats at random, and so did frequently seem to one another to be enemies; for every one of them received those of their own men that came back in the dark as Romans, and made an assault upon them; so that more of them were wounded by their own men than by the enemy, till, upon the coming on of the day, the nature of the right was discerned by the eye afterward. Then did they stand in battle-array in distinct bodies, and cast their darts regularly, and regularly defended themselves; nor did either side yield or grow weary. The Romans contended with each other who should fight the most strenuously, both single men and entire regiments, as being under the eye of Titus; and every one concluded that this day would begin his promotion if he fought bravely. What were the great encouragements of the Jews to act vigorously were, their fear for themselves and for the temple, and the presence of their tyrant, who exhorted some, and beat and threatened others, to act courageously. Now, it so happened, that this fight was for the most part a stationary one, wherein the soldiers went on and came back in a short time, and suddenly; for there was no long space of ground for either of their flights or pursuits. But still there was a tumultuous noise among the Romans from the tower of Antonia, who loudly cried out upon all occasions to their own men to press on courageously, when they were too hard for the Jews, and to stay when they were retiring backward; so that here was a kind of theater of war; for what was done in this fight could not be concealed either from Titus, or from those that were about him. At length it appeared that this fight, which began at the ninth hour of the night, was not over till past the fifth hour of the day; and that, in the same place where the battle began, neither party could say they had made the other to retire; but both the armies left the victory almost in uncertainty between them; wherein those that signalized themselves on the Roman side were a great many, but on the Jewish side, and of those that were with Simon, Judas the son of Merto, and Simon the son of Josas; of the Idumeans, James and Simon, the latter of whom was the son of Cathlas, and James was the son of Sosas; of those that were with John, Gyphtheus and Alexas; and of the zealots, Simon the son of Jairus.

7. In the mean time, the rest of the Roman army had, in seven days' time, overthrown [some] foundations of the tower of Antonia, and had made a ready and broad way to the temple. Then did the legions come near the first court, (12) and began to raise their banks. The one bank was over against the north-west corner of the inner temple (13) another was at that northern edifice which was between the two gates; and of the other two, one was at the western cloister of the outer court of the temple; the other against its northern cloister. However, these works were thus far advanced by the Romans, not without great pains and difficulty, and particularly by being obliged to bring their materials from the distance of a hundred furlongs. They had further difficulties also upon them; sometimes by their over-great security they were in that they should overcome the Jewish snares laid for them, and by that boldness of the Jews which their despair of escaping had inspired them withal; for some of their horsemen, when they went out to gather wood or hay, let their horses feed without having their bridles on during the time of foraging; upon which horses the Jews sallied out in whole bodies, and seized them. And when this was continually done, and Caesar believed what the truth was, that the horses were stolen more by the negligence of his own men than by the valor of the Jews, he determined to use greater severity to oblige the rest to take care of their horses; so he commanded that one of those soldiers who had lost their horses should be capitally punished; whereby he so terrified the rest, that they preserved their horses for the time to come; for they did not any longer let them go from them to feed by themselves, but, as if they had grown to them, they went always along with them when they wanted necessaries. Thus did the Romans still continue to make war against the temple, and to raise their banks against it.

8. Now after one day had been interposed since the Romans ascended the breach, many of the seditious were so pressed by the famine, upon the present failure of their ravages, that they got together, and made an attack on those Roman guards that were upon the Mount of Olives, and this about the eleventh hour of the day, as supposing, first, that they would not expect such an onset, and, in the next place, that they were then taking care of their bodies, and that therefore they should easily beat them. But the Romans were apprized of their coming to attack them beforehand, and, running together from the neighboring camps on the sudden, prevented them from getting over their fortification, or forcing the wall that was built about them. Upon this came on a sharp fight, and here many great actions were performed on both sides; while the Romans showed both their courage and their skill in war, as did the Jews come on them with immoderate violence and intolerable passion. The one part were urged on by shame, and the other by necessity; for it seemed a very shameful thing to the Romans to let the Jews go, now they were taken in a kind of net; while the Jews had but one hope of saving themselves, and that was in case they could by violence break through the Roman wall; and one whose name was Pedanius, belonging to a party of horsemen, when the Jews were already beaten and forced down into the valley together, spurred his horse on their flank with great vehemence, and caught up a certain young man belonging to the enemy by his ankle, as he was running away; the man was, however, of a robust body, and in his armor; so low did Pedanius bend himself downward from his horse, even as he was galloping away, and so great was the strength of his right hand, and of the rest of his body, as also such skill had he in horsemanship. So this man seized upon that his prey, as upon a precious treasure, and carried him as his captive to Caesar; whereupon Titus admired the man that had seized the other for his great strength, and ordered the man that was caught to be punished [with death] for his attempt against the Roman wall, but betook himself to the siege of the temple, and to pressing on the raising of the banks.

9. In the mean time, the Jews were so distressed by the fights they had been in, as the war advanced higher and higher, and creeping up to the holy house itself, that they, as it were, cut off those limbs of their body which were infected, in order to prevent the distemper's spreading further; for they set the north-west cloister, which was joined

to the tower of Antonia, on fire, and after that brake off about twenty cubits of that cloister, and thereby made a beginning in burning the sanctuary; two days after which, or on the twenty-fourth day of the forenamed month, [Panemus or Tamuz,] the Romans set fire to the cloister that joined to the other, when the fire went fifteen cubits farther. The Jews, in like manner, cut off its roof; nor did they entirely leave off what they were about till the tower of Antonia was parted from the temple, even when it was in their power to have stopped the fire; nay, they lay still while the temple was first set on fire, and deemed this spreading of the fire to be for their own advantage. However, the armies were still fighting one against another about the temple, and the war was managed by continual sallies of particular parties against one another.

10. Now there was at this time a man among the Jews, low of stature he was, and of a despicable appearance; of no character either as to his family, or in other respects: his flame was Jonathan. He went out at the high priest John's monument, and uttered many other insolent things to the Romans, a challenged the best of them all to a single combat.But many of those that stood there in the army huffed him, and many of them (as they might well be) were afraid of him. Some of them also reasoned thus, and that justly enough: that it was not fit to fight with a man that desired to die, because those that utterly despaired of deliverance had, besides other passions, a violence in attacking men that could not be opposed, and had no regard to God himself; and that to hazard oneself with a person, whom, if you overcome, you do no great matter, and by whom it is hazardous that you may be taken prisoner, would be an instance, not of manly courage, but of unmanly rashness. So there being nobody that came out to accept the man's challenge, and the Jew cutting them with a great number of reproaches, as cowards, (for he was a very haughty man in himself, and a great despiser of the Romans,) one whose name was Pudens, of the body of horsemen, out of his abomination of the other's words, and of his impudence withal, and perhaps out of an inconsiderate arrogance, on account of the other's lowness of stature, ran out to him, and was too hard for him in other respects, but was betrayed by his ill fortune; for he fell down, and as he was down, Jonathan came running to him, and cut his throat, and then, standing upon his dead body, he brandished his sword, bloody as it was, and shook his shield with his left hand, and made many acclamations to the Roman army, and exulted over the dead man, and jested upon the Romans; till at length one Priscus, a centurion, shot a dart at him as he was leaping and playing the fool with himself, and thereby pierced him through; upon which a shout was set up both by the Jews and the Romans, though on different accounts. So Jonathan grew giddy by the pain of his wounds, and fell down upon the body of his adversary, as a plain instance how suddenly vengeance may come upon men that have success in war, without any just deserving the same.

CHAPTER 3.

CONCERNING A STRATAGEM THAT WAS DEVISED BY THE JEWS, BY WHICH THEY BURNT MANY OF THE ROMANS; WITH ANOTHER DESCRIPTION OF THE TERRIBLE FAMINE THAT WAS IN THE CITY.

1. BUT now the seditious that were in the temple did every day openly endeavor to beat off the soldiers that were upon the banks, and on the twenty-seventh day of the forenamed month [Panemus or Tamuz] contrived such a stratagem as this: They filled that part of the western cloister (14) which was between the beams, and the roof under them, with dry materials, as also with bitumen and pitch, and then retired from that place, as though they were tired with the pains they had taken; at which procedure of theirs, many of the most inconsiderate among the Romans, who were carried away with violent passions, followed hard after them as they were retiring, and applied ladders to the cloister, and got up to it suddenly; but the prudent part of them, when they understood this unaccountable retreat of the Jews, stood still where they were before. However, the cloister was full of those that were gone up the ladders; at which time the Jews set it all on fire; and as the flame burst out every where on the sudden, the Romans that were out of the danger were seized with a very great consternation, as were those that were in the midst of the danger in the utmost distress. So when they perceived themselves surrounded with the flames, some of them threw themselves down backwards into the city, and some among their enemies [in the temple]; as did many leap down to their own men, and broke their limbs to pieces; but a great number of those that were going to take these violent methods were prevented by the fire; though some prevented the fire by their own swords. However, the fire was on the sudden carried so far as to surround those who would have otherwise perished. As for Caesar himself, he could not, however, but commiserate those that thus perished, although they got up thither without any order for so doing, since there was no way of giving the many relief. Yet was this some comfort to those that were destroyed, that every body might see that person grieve, for whose sake they came to their end; for he cried out openly to them, and leaped up, and exhorted those that were about him to do their utmost to relieve them; So every one of them died cheerfully, as carrying along with him these words and this intention of Caesar as a sepulchral monument. Some there were indeed who retired into the wall of the cloister, which was broad, and were preserved out of the fire, but were then surrounded by the Jews; and although they made resistance against the Jews for a long time, yet were they wounded by them, and at length they all fell down dead.

2. At the last a young man among them, whose name was Longus, became a decoration to this sad affair, and while every one of them that perished were worthy of a memorial, this man appeared to deserve it beyond all the rest. Now the Jews admired this man for his courage, and were further desirous of having him slain; so they persuaded him to come down to them, upon security given him for his life. But Cornelius his brother persuaded him on the contrary, not to tarnish his own glory, nor that of the Roman army. He complied with this last advice, and lifting up his sword before both armies, he slew himself. Yet there was one Artorius among those surrounded by the fire who escaped by his subtlety; for when he had with a loud voice called to him Lucius, one of his fellow soldiers that lay with him in the same tent, and said to him, "I do leave thee heir of all I have, if thou wilt come and receive me." Upon this he came running to receive him readily; Artorius then threw himself down upon him, and saved his own life, while he that received him was dashed so vehemently against the stone pavement by the other's weight, that he died immediately. This melancholy accident made the Romans sad for a while, but still it made them more upon their guard for the future, and was of advantage to them against the delusions of the Jews, by which they were greatly damaged through their unacquaintedness with the places, and with the nature of the inhabitants. Now this cloister was burnt down as far as John's tower, which he built in the war he made against Simon over the gates that led to the Xystus. The Jews also cut off the rest of that cloister from the temple, after they had destroyed those that got up to it. But the next day the Romans burnt down the northern cloister entirely, as far as the east cloister, whose common angle joined to the valley that was called Cedron, and was built over it; on which account the depth was frightful. And this was the state of the temple at that time.

3. Now of those that perished by famine in the city, the number was prodigious, and the miseries they underwent were unspeakable; for if so much as the shadow of any kind of food did any where appear, a war was commenced presently, and the dearest friends fell a fighting one with another about it, snatching from each other the most miserable supports of life. Nor would men believe that those who were dying had no food, but the robbers would search them when they were expiring, lest any one should have concealed food in their bosoms, and counterfeited dying; nay, these robbers gaped for want, and ran about stumbling and staggering along like mad dogs, and reeling against the doors of the houses like drunken men; they would also, in the great distress they were in, rush into the very same houses two or three times in one and the same day. Moreover, their hunger was so intolerable, that it obliged them to chew every thing, while they gathered such things as the most sordid animals would not touch, and endured to eat them; nor did they at length abstain from girdles and shoes; and the very leather which belonged to their shields they pulled off and gnawed: the very wisps of old hay became food to some; and some gathered up fibres, and sold a very small weight of them for four Attic [drachmae]. But why do I describe the shameless impudence that the famine brought on men in their eating inanimate things, while I am going to relate a matter of fact, the like to which no history relates, (15) either among the Greeks or Barbarians? It is horrible to speak of it, and incredible when heard. I had indeed willingly omitted this calamity of ours, that I might not seem to deliver what is so portentous to posterity, but that I have innumerable witnesses to it in my own age; and besides, my country would have had little reason to thank me for suppressing the miseries that she underwent at this time.

4. There was a certain woman that dwelt beyond Jordan, her name was Mary; her father was Eleazar, of the village Bethezob, which signifies the *house of Hyssop*. She was eminent for her family and her wealth, and had fled away to Jerusalem with the rest of the multitude, and was with them besieged therein at this time. The other effects of this woman had been already seized upon, such I mean as she had brought with her out of Perea, and removed to the city. What she had treasured up besides, as also what food she had contrived to save, had been also carried off by the rapacious guards, who came every day running into her house for that purpose. This put the poor woman into a very great passion, and by the frequent reproaches and imprecations she east at these rapacious villains, she had provoked them to anger against her; but none of them, either out of the indignation she had raised against herself, or out of commiseration of her case, would take away her life; and if she found any food, she perceived her labors were for others, and not for herself; and it was now become impossible for her any way to find any more food, while the famine pierced through her very bowels and marrow, when also her passion was fired to a degree beyond the famine itself; nor did she consult with any thing but with her passion and the necessity she was in. She then attempted a most unnatural thing; and snatching up her son, who was a child sucking at her breast, she said, "O thou miserable infant! for whom shall I preserve thee in this war, this famine, and this sedition? As to the war with the Romans, if they preserve our lives, we must be slaves. This famine also will destroy us, even before that slavery comes upon us. Yet are these seditious rogues more terrible than both the other. Come on; be thou my food, and be thou a fury to these seditious varlets, and a by-word to the world, which is all that is now wanting to complete the calamities of us Jews." As soon as she had said this, she slew her son, and then roasted him, and eat the one half of him, and kept the other half by her concealed. Upon this the seditious came in presently, and smelling the horrid scent of this food, they threatened her that they would cut her throat immediately if she did not show them what food she had gotten ready. She replied that she had saved a very fine portion of it for them, and withal uncovered what was left of her son. Hereupon they were seized with a horror and amazement of mind, and stood astonished at the sight, when she said to them, "This is mine own son, and what hath been done was mine own doing! Come, eat of this food; for I have eaten of it myself! Do not you pretend to be either more tender than a woman, or more compassionate than a mother; but if you be so scrupulous, and do abominate this my sacrifice, as I have eaten the one half, let the rest be reserved for me also." After which those men went out trembling, being never so much affrighted at any thing as they were at this, and with some difficulty they left the rest of that meat to the mother. Upon which the whole city was full of this horrid action immediately; and while every body laid this miserable case before their own eyes, they trembled, as if this unheard of action had been done by themselves. So those that were thus distressed by the famine were very desirous to die, and those already dead were esteemed happy, because they had not lived long enough either to hear or to see such miseries.

5. This sad instance was quickly told to the Romans, some of whom could not believe it, and others pitied the distress which the Jews were under; but there were many of them who were hereby induced to a more bitter hatred than ordinary against our nation. But for Caesar, he excused himself before God as to this matter, and said that he had proposed peace and liberty to the Jews, as well as an oblivion of all their former insolent practices; but that they, instead of concord, had chosen sedition; instead of peace, war; and before satiety and abundance, a famine. That they had begun with their own hands to burn down that temple which we have preserved hitherto; and that therefore they deserved to eat such food as this was. That, however, this horrid action of eating an own child ought to be covered with the overthrow of their very country itself, and men ought not to leave such a city upon the habitable earth to be seen by the sun, wherein mothers are thus fed, although such food be fitter for the fathers than for the mothers to eat of, since it is they that continue still in a state of war against us, after they have undergone such miseries as these. And at the same time that he said this, he reflected on the desperate condition these men must be in; nor could he expect that such men could be recovered to sobriety of mind, after they had endured those very sufferings, for the avoiding whereof it only was probable they might have repented.

CHAPTER 4.

WHEN THE BANKS WERE COMPLETED AND THE BATTERING RAMS BROUGHT, AND COULD DO NOTHING, TITUS GAVE ORDERS TO SET FIRE TO THE GATES OF THE TEMPLE;

IN NO LONG TIME AFTER WHICH THE HOLY HOUSE ITSELF WAS BURNT DOWN, EVEN AGAINST HIS CONSENT.

1. AND now two of the legions had completed their banks on the eighth day of the month Lous [Ab]. Whereupon Titus gave orders that the battering rams should be brought, and set over against the western edifice of the inner temple; for before these were brought, the firmest of all the other engines had battered the wall for six days together without ceasing, without making any impression upon it; but the vast largeness and strong connexion of the stones were superior to that engine, and to the other battering rams also. Other Romans did indeed undermine the foundations of the northern gate, and after a world of pains removed the outermost stones, yet was the gate still upheld by the inner stones, and stood still unhurt; till the workmen, despairing of all such attempts by engines and crows, brought their ladders to the cloisters. Now the Jews did not interrupt them in so doing; but when they were gotten up, they fell upon them, and fought with them; some of them they thrust down, and threw them backwards headlong; others of them they met and slew; they also beat many of those that went down the ladders again, and slew them with their swords before they could bring their shields to protect them; nay, some of the ladders they threw down from above when they were full of armed men; a great slaughter was made of the Jews also at the same time, while those that bare the ensigns fought hard for them, as deeming it a terrible thing, and what would tend to their great shame, if they permitted them to be stolen away. Yet did the Jews at length get possession of these engines, and destroyed those that had gone up the ladders, while the rest were so intimidated by what those suffered who were slain, that they retired; although none of the Romans died without having done good service before his death. Of the seditious, those that had fought bravely in the former battles did the like now, as besides them did Eleazar, the brother's son of Simon the tyrant. But when Titus perceived that his endeavors to spare a foreign temple turned to the damage of his soldiers, and then be killed, he gave order to set the gates on fire.

2. In the mean time, there deserted to him Ananus, who came from Emmaus, the most bloody of all Simon's guards, and Archelaus, the son of Magadatus, they hoping to be still forgiven, because they left the Jews at a time when they were the conquerors. Titus objected this to these men, as a cunning trick of theirs; and as he had been informed of their other barbarities towards the Jews, he was going in all haste to have them both slain. He told them that they were only driven to this desertion because of the utmost distress they were in, and did not come away of their own good disposition; and that those did not deserve to be preserved, by whom their own city was already set on fire, out of which fire they now hurried themselves away. However, the security he had promised deserters overcame his resentments, and he dismissed them accordingly, though he did not give them the same privileges that he had afforded to others. And now the soldiers had already put fire to the gates, and the silver that was over them quickly carried the flames to the wood that was within it, whence it spread itself all on the sudden, and caught hold on the cloisters. Upon the Jews seeing this fire all about them, their spirits sunk together with their bodies, and they were under such astonishment, that not one of them made any haste, either to defend himself or to quench the fire, but they stood as mute spectators of it only. However, they did not so grieve at the loss of what was now burning, as to grow wiser thereby for the time to come; but as though the holy house itself had been on fire already, they whetted their passions against the Romans. This fire prevailed during that day and the next also; for the soldiers were not able to burn all the cloisters that were round about together at one time, but only by pieces.

3. But then, on the next day, Titus commanded part of his army to quench the fire, and to make a road for the more easy marching up of the legions, while he himself gathered the commanders together. Of those there were assembled the six principal persons: Tiberius Alexander, the commander [under the general] of the whole army; with Sextus Cerealis, the commander of the fifth legion; and Larcius Lepidus, the commander of the tenth legion; and Titus Frigius, the commander of the fifteenth legion: there was also with them Eternius, the leader of the two legions that came from Alexandria; and Marcus Antonius Julianus, procurator of Judea: after these came together all the rest of the procurators and tribunes. Titus proposed to these that they should give him their advice what should be done about the holy house. Now some of these thought it would be the best way to act according to the rules of war, [and demolish it,] because the Jews would never leave off rebelling while that house was standing; at which house it was that they used to get all together. Others of them were of opinion, that in case the Jews would leave it, and none of them would lay their arms up in it, he might save it; but that in case they got upon it, and fought any more, he might burn it; because it must then be looked upon not as a holy house, but as a citadel; and that the impiety of burning it would then belong to those that forced this to be done, and not to them. But Titus said, that "although the Jews should get upon that holy house, and fight us thence, yet ought we not to revenge ourselves on things that are inanimate, instead of the men themselves;" and that he was not in any case for burning down so vast a work as that was, because this would be a mischief to the Romans themselves, as it would be an ornament to their government while it continued. So Fronto, and Alexander, and Cerealis grew bold upon that declaration, and agreed to the opinion of Titus. Then was this assembly dissolved, when Titus had given orders to the commanders that the rest of their forces should lie still; but that they should make use of such as were most courageous in this attack. So he commanded that the chosen men that were taken out of the cohorts should make their way through the ruins, and quench the fire.

4. Now it is true that on this day the Jews were so weary, and under such consternation, that they refrained from any attacks. But on the next day they gathered their whole force together, and ran upon those that guarded the outward court of the temple very boldly, through the east gate, and this about the second hour of the day. These guards received that their attack with great bravery, and by covering themselves with their shields before, as if it were with a wall, they drew their squadron close together; yet was it evident that they could not abide there very long, but would be overborne by the multitude of those that sallied out upon them, and by the heat of their passion. However, Caesar seeing, from the tower of Antonia, that this squadron was likely to give way, he sent some chosen horsemen to support them. Hereupon the Jews found themselves not able to sustain their onset, and upon the slaughter of those in the forefront, many of the rest were put to flight. But as the Romans were going off, the Jews turned upon them, and fought them; and as those Romans came back upon them, they retreated again, until about the fifth hour of the day they were overborne, and shut themselves up in the inner [court of the] temple.

5. So Titus retired into the tower of Antonia, and resolved to storm the temple the next day, early in the morning, with his whole army, and to encamp round about the holy house. But as for that house, God had, for certain, long ago doomed it to the fire; and now that fatal day was come, according to the revolution of ages; it was the tenth day of the month Lous, [Ab,] upon which it was formerly burnt by the king of Babylon; although these flames took their rise from the Jews themselves, and were occasioned by them; for upon Titus's retiring, the seditious lay still for a little while, and then attacked the Romans again, when those that guarded the holy house fought with those that quenched the fire that was burning the inner [court of the] temple; but these Romans put the Jews to flight, and proceeded as far as the holy house itself. At which time one of the soldiers, without staying for any orders, and without any concern or dread upon him at so great an undertaking, and being hurried on by a certain divine fury, snatched somewhat out of the materials that were on fire, and being lifted up by another soldier, he set fire to a golden window, through which there was a passage to the rooms that were round about the holy house, on the north side of it. As the flames went upward, the Jews made a great clamor, such as so mighty an affliction required, and ran together to prevent it; and now they spared not their lives any longer, nor suffered any thing to restrain their force, since that holy house was perishing, for whose sake it was that they kept such a guard about it.

6. And now a certain person came running to Titus, and told him of this fire, as he was resting himself in his tent after the last battle; whereupon he rose up in great haste, and, as he was, ran to the holy house, in order to have a stop put to the fire; after him followed all his commanders, and after them followed the several legions, in great astonishment; so there was a great clamor and tumult raised, as was natural upon the disorderly motion of so great an army. Then did Caesar, both by calling to the soldiers that were fighting, with a loud voice, and by giving a signal to them with his right hand, order them to quench the fire. But they did not hear what he said, though he spake so loud, having their ears already dimmed by a greater noise another way; nor did they attend to the signal he made with his hand neither, as still some of them were distracted with fighting, and others with passion. But as for the legions that came running thither, neither any persuasions nor any threatenings could restrain their violence, but each one's own passion was his commander at this time; and as they were crowding into the temple together, many of them were trampled on by one another, while a great number fell among the ruins of the cloisters, which were still hot and smoking, and were destroyed in the same miserable way with those whom they had conquered; and when they were come near the holy house, they made as if they did not so much as hear Caesar's orders to the contrary; but they encouraged those that were before them to set it on fire. As for the seditious, they were in too great distress already to afford their assistance [towards quenching the fire]; they were every where slain, and every where beaten; and as for a great part of the people, they were weak and without arms, and had their throats cut wherever they were caught. Now round about the altar lay dead bodies heaped one upon another, as at the steps (16) going up to it ran a great quantity of their blood, whither also the dead bodies that were slain above [on the altar] fell down.

7. And now, since Caesar was no way able to restrain the enthusiastic fury of the soldiers, and the fire proceeded on more and more, he went into the holy place of the temple, with his commanders, and saw it, with what was in it, which he found to be far superior to what the relations of foreigners contained, and not inferior to what we ourselves boasted of and believed about it. But as the flame had not as yet reached to its inward parts, but was still consuming the rooms that were about the holy house, and Titus supposing what the fact was, that the house itself might yet he saved, he came in haste and endeavored to persuade the soldiers to quench the fire, and gave order to Liberalius the centurion, and one of those spearmen that were about him, to beat the soldiers that were refractory with their staves, and to restrain them; yet were their passions too hard for the regards they had for Caesar, and the dread they had of him who forbade them, as was their hatred of the Jews, and a certain vehement inclination to fight them, too hard for them also. Moreover, the hope of plunder induced many to go on, as having this opinion, that all the places within were full of money, and as seeing that all round about it was made of gold. And besides, one of those that went into the place prevented Caesar, when he ran so hastily out to restrain the soldiers, and threw the fire upon the hinges of the gate, in the dark; whereby the flame burst out from within the holy house itself immediately, when the commanders retired, and Caesar with them, and when nobody any longer forbade those that were without to set fire to it. And thus was the holy house burnt down, without Caesar's approbation.

8. Now although any one would justly lament the destruction of such a work as this was, since it was the most admirable of all the works that we have seen or heard of, both for its curious structure and its magnitude, and also for the vast wealth bestowed upon it, as well as for the glorious reputation it had for its holiness; yet might such a one comfort himself with this thought, that it was fate that decreed it so to be, which is inevitable, both as to living creatures, and as to works and places also. However, one cannot but wonder at the accuracy of this period thereto relating; for the same month and day were now observed, as I said before, wherein the holy house was burnt formerly by the Babylonians. Now the number of years that passed from its first foundation, which was laid by king Solomon, till this its destruction, which happened in the second year of the reign of Vespasian, are collected to be one thousand one hundred and thirty, besides seven months and fifteen days; and from the second building of it, which was done by Haggai, in the second year of Cyrus the king, till its destruction under Vespasian, there were six hundred and thirty-nine years and forty-five days.

CHAPTER 5.

THE GREAT DISTRESS THE JEWS WERE IN UPON THE CONFLAGRATION OF THE HOLY HOUSE. CONCERNING A FALSE PROPHET, AND THE SIGNS THAT PRECEDED THIS DESTRUCTION.

1. WHILE the holy house was on fire, every thing was plundered that came to hand, and ten thousand of those that were caught were slain; nor was there a commiseration of any age, or any reverence of gravity, but children, and old men, and profane persons, and priests were all slain in the same manner; so that this war went round all sorts of men, and brought them to destruction, and as well those that made supplication for their lives, as those that defended themselves by fighting. The flame was also carried a long way, and made an echo, together with the groans of those that were slain; and because this hill was high, and the works at the temple were very great, one would have thought the whole city had been on fire. Nor can one imagine any thing either greater or more terrible than this noise; for

there was at once a shout of the Roman legions, who were marching all together, and a sad clamor of the seditious, who were now surrounded with fire and sword. The people also that were left above were beaten back upon the enemy, and under a great consternation, and made sad moans at the calamity they were under; the multitude also that was in the city joined in this outcry with those that were upon the hill. And besides, many of those that were worn away by the famine, and their mouths almost closed, when they saw the fire of the holy house, they exerted their utmost strength, and brake out into groans and outcries again: Pera (17) did also return the echo, as well as the mountains round about [the city,] and augmented the force of the entire noise. Yet was the misery itself more terrible than this disorder; for one would have thought that the hill itself, on which the temple stood, was seething hot, as full of fire on every part of it, that the blood was larger in quantity than the fire, and those that were slain more in number than those that slew them; for the ground did no where appear visible, for the dead bodies that lay on it; but the soldiers went over heaps of those bodies, as they ran upon such as fled from them. And now it was that the multitude of the robbers were thrust out [of the inner court of the temple by the Romans,] and had much ado to get into the outward court, and from thence into the city, while the remainder of the populace fled into the cloister of that outer court. As for the priests, some of them plucked up from the holy house the spikes (18) that were upon it, with their bases, which were made of lead, and shot them at the Romans instead of darts. But then as they gained nothing by so doing, and as the fire burst out upon them, they retired to the wall that was eight cubits broad, and there they tarried; yet did two of these of eminence among them, who might have saved themselves by going over to the Romans, or have borne up with courage, and taken their fortune with the others, throw themselves into the fire, and were burnt together with the holy house; their names were Meirus the son of Belgas, and Joseph the son of Daleus.

2. And now the Romans, judging that it was in vain to spare what was round about the holy house, burnt all those places, as also the remains of the cloisters and the gates, two excepted; the one on the east side, and the other on the south; both which, however, they burnt afterward. They also burnt down the treasury chambers, in which was an immense quantity of money, and an immense number of garments, and other precious goods there reposited; and, to speak all in a few words, there it was that the entire riches of the Jews were heaped up together, while the rich people had there built themselves chambers [to contain such furniture]. The soldiers also came to the rest of the cloisters that were in the outer [court of the] temple, whither the women and children, and a great mixed multitude of the people, fled, in number about six thousand. But before Caesar had determined any thing about these people, or given the commanders any orders relating to them, the soldiers were in such a rage, that they set that cloister on fire; by which means it came to pass that some of these were destroyed by throwing themselves down headlong, and some were burnt in the cloisters themselves. Nor did any one of them escape with his life. A false prophet (19) was the occasion of these people's destruction, who had made a public proclamation in the city that very day, that God commanded them to get upon the temple, and that there they should receive miraculous signs of their deliverance. Now there was then a great number of false prophets suborned by the tyrants to impose on the people, who denounced this to them, that they should wait for deliverance from God; and this was in order to keep them from deserting, and that they might be buoyed up above fear and care by such hopes. Now a man that is in adversity does easily comply with such promises; for when such a seducer makes him believe that he shall be delivered from those miseries which oppress him, then it is that the patient is full of hopes of such his deliverance.

3. Thus were the miserable people persuaded by these deceivers, and such as belied God himself; while they did not attend nor give credit to the signs that were so evident, and did so plainly foretell their future desolation, but, like men infatuated, without either eyes to see or minds to consider, did not regard the denunciations that God made to them. Thus there was a star (20) resembling a sword, which stood over the city, and a comet, that continued a whole year. Thus also before the Jews' rebellion, and before those commotions which preceded the war, when the people were come in great crowds to the feast of unleavened bread, on the eighth day of the month Xanthicus, (21) [Nisan,] and at the ninth hour of the night, so great a light shone round the altar and the holy house, that it appeared to be bright day time; which lasted for half an hour. This light seemed to be a good sign to the unskillful, but was so interpreted by the sacred scribes, as to portend those events that followed immediately upon it. At the same festival also, a heifer, as she was led by the high priest to be sacrificed, brought forth a lamb in the midst of the temple. Moreover, the eastern gate of the inner (22) [court of the] temple, which was of brass, and vastly heavy, and had been with difficulty shut by twenty men, and rested upon a basis armed with iron, and had bolts fastened very deep into the firm floor, which was there made of one entire stone, was seen to be opened of its own accord about the sixth hour of the night. Now those that kept watch in the temple came hereupon running to the captain of the temple, and told him of it; who then came up thither, and not without great difficulty was able to shut the gate again. This also appeared to the vulgar to be a very happy prodigy, as if God did thereby open them the gate of happiness. But the men of learning understood it, that the security of their holy house was dissolved of its own accord, and that the gate was opened for the advantage of their enemies. So these publicly declared that the signal foreshowed the desolation that was coming upon them. Besides these, a few days after that feast, on the one and twentieth day of the month Artemisius, [Jyar,] a certain prodigious and incredible phenomenon appeared: I suppose the account of it would seem to be a fable, were it not related by those that saw it, and were not the events that followed it of so considerable a nature as to deserve such signals; for, before sun-setting, chariots and troops of soldiers in their armor were seen running about among the clouds, and surrounding of cities. Moreover, at that feast which we call Pentecost, as the priests were going by night into the inner [court of the temple,] as their custom was, to perform their sacred ministrations, they said that, in the first place, they felt a quaking, and heard a great noise, and after that they heard a sound as of a great multitude, saying, "Let us remove hence." But, what is still more terrible, there was one Jesus, the son of Ananus, a plebeian and a husbandman, who, four years before the war began, and at a time when the city was in very great peace and prosperity, came to that feast whereon it is our custom for every one to make tabernacles to God in the temple, (23) began on a sudden to cry aloud, "A voice from the east, a voice from the west, a voice from the four winds, a voice against Jerusalem and the holy house, a voice against the bridegrooms and the brides, and a voice against this whole people!" This was his cry, as he went about by day and by night, in all

the lanes of the city. However, certain of the most eminent among the populace had great indignation at this dire cry of his, and took up the man, and gave him a great number of severe stripes; yet did not he either say any thing for himself, or any thing peculiar to those that chastised him, but still went on with the same words which he cried before. Hereupon our rulers, supposing, as the case proved to be, that this was a sort of divine fury in the man, brought him to the Roman procurator, where he was whipped till his bones were laid bare; yet he did not make any supplication for himself, nor shed any tears, but turning his voice to the most lamentable tone possible, at every stroke of the whip his answer was, "Woe, woe to Jerusalem!" And when Albinus (for he was then our procurator) asked him, Who he was? and whence he came? and why he uttered such words? he made no manner of reply to what he said, but still did not leave off his melancholy ditty, till Albinus took him to be a madman, and dismissed him. Now, during all the time that passed before the war began, this man did not go near any of the citizens, nor was seen by them while he said so; but he every day uttered these lamentable words, as if it were his premeditated vow, "Woe, woe to Jerusalem!" Nor did he give ill words to any of those that beat him every day, nor good words to those that gave him food; but this was his reply to all men, and indeed no other than a melancholy presage of what was to come. This cry of his was the loudest at the festivals; and he continued this ditty for seven years and five months, without growing hoarse, or being tired therewith, until the very time that he saw his presage in earnest fulfilled in our siege, when it ceased; for as he was going round upon the wall, he cried out with his utmost force, "Woe, woe to the city again, and to the people, and to the holy house!" And just as he added at the last, "Woe, woe to myself also!" there came a stone out of one of the engines, and smote him, and killed him immediately; and as he was uttering the very same presages he gave up the ghost.

4. Now if any one consider these things, he will find that God takes care of mankind, and by all ways possible foreshows to our race what is for their preservation; but that men perish by those miseries which they madly and voluntarily bring upon themselves; for the Jews, by demolishing the tower of Antonia, had made their temple four-square, while at the same time they had it written in their sacred oracles, "That then should their city be taken, as well as their holy house, when once their temple should become four-square." But now, what did the most elevate them in undertaking this war, was an ambiguous oracle that was also found in their sacred writings, how," about that time, one from their country should become governor of the habitable earth." The Jews took this prediction to belong to themselves in particular, and many of the wise men were thereby deceived in their determination. Now this oracle certainly denoted the government of Vespasian, who was appointed emperor in Judea. However, it is not possible for men to avoid fate, although they see it beforehand. But these men interpreted some of these signals according to their own pleasure, and some of them they utterly despised, until their madness was demonstrated, both by the taking of their city and their own destruction.

CHAPTER 6.

HOW THE ROMANS CARRIED THEIR ENSIGNS TO THE TEMPLE, AND MADE JOYFUL ACCLAMATIONS TO TITUS. THE SPEECH THAT TITUS MADE TO THE JEWS WHEN THEY MADE SUPPLICATION FOR MERCY. WHAT REPLY THEY MADE THERETO; AND HOW THAT REPLY MOVED TITUS'S INDIGNATION AGAINST THEM.

1. AND now the Romans, upon the flight of the seditious into the city, and upon the burning of the holy house itself, and of all the buildings round about it, brought their ensigns to the temple (24) and set them over against its eastern gate; and there did they offer sacrifices to them, and there did they make Titus imperator (25) with the greatest acclamations of joy. And now all the soldiers had such vast quantities of the spoils which they had gotten by plunder, that in Syria a pound weight of gold was sold for half its former value. But as for those priests that kept themselves still upon the wall of the holy house, (26) there was a boy that, out of the thirst he was in, desired some of the Roman guards to give him their right hands as a security for his life, and confessed he was very thirsty. These guards commiserated his age, and the distress he was in, and gave him their right hands accordingly. So he came down himself, and drank some water, and filled the vessel he had with him when he came to them with water, and then went off, and fled away to his own friends; nor could any of those guards overtake him; but still they reproached him for his perfidiousness. To which he made this answer: "I have not broken the agreement; for the security I had given me was not in order to my staying with you, but only in order to my coming down safely, and taking up some water; both which things I have performed, and thereupon think myself to have been faithful to my engagement." Hereupon those whom the child had imposed upon admired at his cunning, and that on account of his age. On the fifth day afterward, the priests that were pined with the famine came down, and when they were brought to Titus by the guards, they begged for their lives; but he replied, that the time of pardon was over as to them, and that this very holy house, on whose account only they could justly hope to be preserved, was destroyed; and that it was agreeable to their office that priests should perish with the house itself to which they belonged. So he ordered them to be put to death.

2. But as for the tyrants themselves, and those that were with them, when they found that they were encompassed on every side, and, as it were, walled round, without any method of escaping, they desired to treat with Titus by word of mouth. Accordingly, such was the kindness of his nature, and his desire of preserving the city from destruction, joined to the advice of his friends, who now thought the robbers were come to a temper, that he placed himself on the western side of the outer [court of the] temple; for there were gates on that side above the Xystus, and a bridge that connected the upper city to the temple. This bridge it was that lay between the tyrants and Caesar, and parted them; while the multitude stood on each side; those of the Jewish nation about Sinran and John, with great hopes of pardon; and the Romans about Caesar, in great expectation how Titus would receive their supplication. So Titus charged his soldiers to restrain their rage, and to let their darts alone, and appointed an interpreter between them, which was a sign that he was the conqueror, and first began the discourse, and said, "I hope you, sirs, are now satiated with the miseries of your country, who have not bad any just notions, either of our great power, or of your own great weakness, but have, like madmen, after a violent and inconsiderate manner, made such attempts, as have brought your people, your city, and your holy house to destruction. You have been the men that have never left off rebelling since Pompey first conquered you, and have, since that time, made open war with the Romans. Have you

depended on your multitude, while a very small part of the Roman soldiery have been strong enough for you? Have you relied on the fidelity of your confederates? And what nations are there, out of the limits of our dominion, that would choose to assist the Jews before the Romans? Are your bodies stronger than ours? nay, you know that the [strong] Germans themselves are our servants. Have you stronger walls than we have? Pray, what greater obstacle is there than the wall of the ocean, with which the Britons are encompassed, and yet do adore the arms of the Romans. Do you exceed us in courage of soul, and in the sagacity of your commanders? Nay, indeed, you cannot but know that the very Carthaginians have been conquered by us. It can therefore be nothing certainly but the kindness of us Romans which hath excited you against us; who, in the first place, have given you this land to possess; and, in the next place, have set over you kings of your own nation; and, in the third place, have preserved the laws of your forefathers to you, and have withal permitted you to live, either by yourselves, or among others, as it should please you: and, what is our chief favor of all we have given you leave to gather up that tribute which is paid to God (27) with such other gifts that are dedicated to him; nor have we called those that carried these donations to account, nor prohibited them; till at length you became richer than we ourselves, even when you were our enemies; and you made preparations for war against us with our own money; nay, after all, when you were in the enjoyment of all these advantages, you turned your too great plenty against those that gave it you, and, like merciless serpents, have thrown out your poison against those that treated you kindly. I suppose, therefore, that you might despise the slothfulness of Nero, and, like limbs of the body that are broken or dislocated, you did then lie quiet, waiting for some other time, though still with a malicious intention, and have now showed your distemper to be greater than ever, and have extended your desires as far as your impudent and immense hopes would enable you to do it. At this time my father came into this country, not with a design to punish you for what you had done under Cestius, but to admonish you; for had he come to overthrow your nation, he had run directly to your fountain-head, and had immediately laid this city waste; whereas he went and burnt Galilee and the neighboring parts, and thereby gave you time for repentance; which instance of humanity you took for an argument of his weakness, and nourished up your impudence by our mildness. When Nero was gone out of the world, you did as the wickedest wretches would have done, and encouraged yourselves to act against us by our civil dissensions, and abused that time, when both I and my father were gone away to Egypt, to make preparations for this war. Nor were you ashamed to raise disturbances against us when we were made emperors, and this while you had experienced how mild we had been, when we were no more than generals of the army. But when the government was devolved upon us, and all other people did thereupon lie quiet, and even foreign nations sent embassies, and congratulated our access to the government, then did you Jews show yourselves to be our enemies. You sent embassies to those of your nation that are beyond Euphrates to assist you in your raising disturbances; new walls were built by you round your city, seditions arose, and one tyrant contended against another, and a civil war broke out among you; such indeed as became none but so wicked a people as you are. I then came to this city, as unwillingly sent by my father, and received melancholy injunctions from him. When I heard that the people were disposed to peace, I rejoiced at it; I exhorted you to leave off these proceedings before I began this war; I spared you even when you had fought against me a great while; I gave my right hand as security to the deserters; I observed what I had promised faithfully. When they fled to me, I had compassion on many of those that I had taken captive; I tortured those that were eager for war, in order to restrain them. It was unwillingly that I brought my engines of war against your walls; I always prohibited my soldiers, when they were set upon your slaughter, from their severity against you. After every victory I persuaded you to peace, as though I had been myself conquered. When I came near your temple, I again departed from the laws of war, and exhorted you to spare your own sanctuary, and to preserve your holy house to yourselves. I allowed you a quiet exit out of it, and security for your preservation; nay, if you had a mind, I gave you leave to fight in another place. Yet have you still despised every one of my proposals, and have set fire to your holy house with your own hands. And now, vile wretches, do you desire to treat with me by word of mouth? To what purpose is it that you would save such a holy house as this was, which is now destroyed? What preservation can you now desire after the destruction of your temple? Yet do you stand still at this very time in your armor; nor can you bring yourselves so much as to pretend to be supplicants even in this your utmost extremity. O miserable creatures! what is it you depend on? Are not your people dead? is not your holy house gone? is not your city in my power? and are not your own very lives in my hands? And do you still deem it a part of valor to die? However, I will not imitate your madness. If you throw down your arms, and deliver up your bodies to me, I grant you your lives; and I will act like a mild master of a family; what cannot be healed shall be punished, and the rest I will preserve for my own use."

3. To that offer of Titus they made this reply: That they could not accept of it, because they had sworn never to do so; but they desired they might have leave to go through the wall that had been made about them, with their wives and children; for that they would go into the desert, and leave the city to him. At this Titus had great indignation, that when they were in the case of men already taken captives, they should pretend to make their own terms with him, as if they had been conquerors. So he ordered this proclamation to be made to them, That they should no more come out to him as deserters, nor hope for any further security; for that he would henceforth spare nobody, but fight them with his whole army; and that they must save themselves as well as they could; for that he would from henceforth treat them according to the laws of war. So he gave orders to the soldiers both to burn and to plunder the city; who did nothing indeed that day; but on the next day they set fire to the repository of the archives, to Acra, to the council-house, and to the place called Ophlas; at which time the fire proceeded as far as the palace of queen Helena, which was in the middle of Acra; the lanes also were burnt down, as were also those houses that were full of the dead bodies of such as were destroyed by famine.

4. On the same day it was that the sons and brethren of Izates the king, together with many others of the eminent men of the populace, got together there, and besought Caesar to give them his right hand for their security; upon which, though he was very angry at all that were now remaining, yet did he not lay aside his old moderation, but received these men. At that time, indeed, he kept them all in custody, but still bound the king's sons and kinsmen, and led them with him to Rome, in order to make them hostages for their country's fidelity to the Romans.

CHAPTER 7.

WHAT AFTERWARD BEFELL THE SEDITIOUS WHEN THEY HAD DONE A GREAT DEAL OF MISCHIEF, AND SUFFERED MANY MISFORTUNES; AS ALSO HOW CAESAR BECAME MASTER OF THE UPPER CITY,

1. AND now the seditious rushed into the royal palace, into which many had put their effects, because it was so strong, and drove the Romans away from it. They also slew all the people that had crowded into it, who were in number about eight thousand four hundred, and plundered them of what they had. They also took two of the Romans alive; the one was a horseman, and the other a footman. They then cut the throat of the footman, and immediately had him drawn through the whole city, as revenging themselves upon the whole body of the Romans by this one instance. But the horseman said he had somewhat to suggest to them in order to their preservation; whereupon he was brought before Simon; but he having nothing to say when he was there, he was delivered to Ardalas, one of his commanders, to be punished, who bound his hands behind him, and put a riband over his eyes, and then brought him out over against the Romans, as intending to cut off his head. But the man prevented that execution, and ran away to the Romans, and this while the Jewish executioner was drawing out his sword. Now when he was gotten away from the enemy, Titus could not think of putting him to death; but because he deemed him unworthy of being a Roman soldier any longer, on account that he had been taken alive by the enemy, he took away his arms, and ejected him out of the legion whereto he had belonged; which, to one that had a sense of shame, was a penalty severer than death itself.

2. On the next day the Romans drove the robbers out of the lower city, and set all on fire as far as Siloam. These soldiers were indeed glad to see the city destroyed. But they missed the plunder, because the seditious had carried off all their effects, and were retired into the upper city; for they did not yet at all repent of the mischiefs they had done, but were insolent, as if they had done well; for, as they saw the city on fire, they appeared cheerful, and put on joyful countenances, in expectation, as they said, of death to end their miseries. Accordingly, as the people were now slain, the holy house was burnt down, and the city was on fire, there was nothing further left for the enemy to do. Yet did not Josephus grow weary, even in this utmost extremity, to beg of them to spare what was left of the city; he spake largely to them about their barbarity and impiety, and gave them his advice in order to their escape; though he gained nothing thereby more than to be laughed at by them; and as they could not think of surrendering themselves up, because of the oath they had taken, nor were strong enough to fight with the Romans any longer upon the square, as being surrounded on all sides, and a kind of prisoners already, yet were they so accustomed to kill people, that they could not restrain their right hands from acting accordingly. So they dispersed themselves before the city, and laid themselves in ambush among its ruins, to catch those that attempted to desert to the Romans; accordingly many such deserters were caught by them, and were all slain; for these were too weak, by reason of their want of food, to fly away from them; so their dead bodies were thrown to the dogs. Now every other sort of death was thought more tolerable than the famine, insomuch that, though the Jews despaired now of mercy, yet would they fly to the Romans, and would themselves, even of their own accord, fall among the murderous rebels also. Nor was there any place in the city that had no dead bodies in it, but what was entirely covered with those that were killed either by the famine or the rebellion; and all was full of the dead bodies of such as had perished, either by that sedition or by that famine.

3. So now the last hope which supported the tyrants, and that crew of robbers who were with them, was in the caves and caverns under ground; whither, if they could once fly, they did not expect to be searched for; but endeavored, that after the whole city should be destroyed, and the Romans gone away, they might come out again, and escape from them. This was no better than a dream of theirs; for they were not able to lie hid either from God or from the Romans. However, they depended on these under-ground subterfuges, and set more places on fire than did the Romans themselves; and those that fled out of their houses thus set on fire into the ditches, they killed without mercy, and pillaged them also; and if they discovered food belonging to any one, they seized upon it and swallowed it down, together with their blood also; nay, they were now come to fight one with another about their plunder; and I cannot but think that, had not their destruction prevented it, their barbarity would have made them taste of even the dead bodies themselves.

CHAPTER 8.

HOW CAESAR RAISED BANKS ROUND ABOUT THE UPPER CITY [MOUNT ZION] AND WHEN THEY WERE COMPLETED, GAVE ORDERS THAT THE MACHINES SHOULD BE BROUGHT. HE THEN POSSESSED HIMSELF OF THE WHOLE CITY.

1. NOW when Caesar perceived that the upper city was so steep that it could not possibly be taken without raising banks against it, he distributed the several parts of that work among his army, and this on the twentieth day of the month Lous [Ab]. Now the carriage of the materials was a difficult task, since all the trees, as I have already told you, that were about the city, within the distance of a hundred furlongs, had their branches cut off already, in order to make the former banks. The works that belonged to the four legions were erected on the west side of the city, over against the royal palace; but the whole body of the auxiliary troops, with the rest of the multitude that were with them, [erected their banks] at the Xystus, whence they reached to the bridge, and that tower of Simon which he had built as a citadel for himself against John, when they were at war one with another.

2. It was at this time that the commanders of the Idumeans got together privately, and took counsel about surrendering up themselves to the Romans. Accordingly, they sent five men to Titus, and entreated him to give them his right hand for their security. So Titus thinking that the tyrants would yield, if the Idumeans, upon whom a great part of the war depended, were once withdrawn from them, after some reluctancy and delay, complied with them, and gave them security for their lives, and sent the five men back. But as these Idumeans were preparing to march out, Simon perceived it, and immediately slew the five men that had gone to Titus, and took their commanders, and put them in prison, of whom the most eminent was Jacob, the son of Sosas; but as for the multitude of the Idumeans, who did not at all know what to do, now their commanders were taken from them, he had them watched, and secured the walls by a more numerous garrison, Yet could not that garrison resist those that were deserting; for although a great number of them were slain, yet were the deserters many more in number. They were all received by the Romans, because Titus himself grew negligent as to his former orders for killing them, and because the very soldiers

grew weary of killing them, and because they hoped to get some money by sparing them; for they left only the populace, and sold the rest of the multitude, (28) with their wives and children, and every one of them at a very low price, and that because such as were sold were very many, and the buyers were few: and although Titus had made proclamation beforehand, that no deserter should come alone by himself, that so they might bring out their families with them, yet did he receive such as these also. However, he set over them such as were to distinguish some from others, in order to see if any of them deserved to be punished. And indeed the number of those that were sold was immense; but of the populace above forty thousand were saved, whom Caesar let go whither every one of them pleased.

3. But now at this time it was that one of the priests, the son of Thebuthus, whose name was Jesus, upon his having security given him, by the oath of Caesar, that he should be preserved, upon condition that he should deliver to him certain of the precious things that had been reposited in the temple (29) came out of it, and delivered him from the wall of the holy house two candlesticks, like to those that lay in the holy house, with tables, and cisterns, and vials, all made of solid gold, and very heavy. He also delivered to him the veils and the garments, with the precious stones, and a great number of other precious vessels that belonged to their sacred worship. The treasurer of the temple also, whose name was Phineas, was seized on, and showed Titus the coats and girdles of the priests, with a great quantity of purple and scarlet, which were there reposited for the uses of the veil, as also a great deal of cinnamon and cassia, with a large quantity of other sweet spices, (30) which used to be mixed together, and offered as incense to God every day. A great many other treasures were also delivered to him, with sacred ornaments of the temple not a few; which things thus delivered to Titus obtained of him for this man the same pardon that he had allowed to such as deserted of their own accord.

4. And now were the banks finished on the seventh day of the month Gorpieus, [Elul,] in eighteen days' time, when the Romans brought their machines against the wall. But for the seditious, some of them, as despairing of saving the city, retired from the wall to the citadel; others of them went down into the subterranean vaults, though still a great many of them defended themselves against those that brought the engines for the battery; yet did the Romans overcome them by their number and by their strength; and, what was the principal thing of all, by going cheerfully about their work, while the Jews were quite dejected, and become weak. Now as soon as a part of the wall was battered down, and certain of the towers yielded to the impression of the battering rams, those that opposed themselves fled away, and such a terror fell upon the tyrants, as was much greater than the occasion required; for before the enemy got over the breach they were quite stunned, and were immediately for flying away. And now one might see these men, who had hitherto been so insolent and arrogant in their wicked practices, to be cast down and to tremble, insomuch that it would pity one's heart to observe the change that was made in those vile persons. Accordingly, they ran with great violence upon the Roman wall that encompassed them, in order to force away those that guarded it, and to break through it, and get away. But when they saw that those who had formerly been faithful to them had gone away, (as indeed they were fled whithersoever the great distress they were in persuaded them to flee,) as also when those that came running before the rest told them that the western wall was entirely overthrown, while others said the Romans were gotten in, and others that they were near, and looking out for them, which were only the dictates of their fear, which imposed upon their sight, they fell upon their face, and greatly lamented their own mad conduct; and their nerves were so terribly loosed, that they could not flee away. And here one may chiefly reflect on the power of God exercised upon these wicked wretches, and on the good fortune of the Romans; for these tyrants did now wholly deprive themselves of the security they had in their own power, and came down from those very towers of their own accord, wherein they could have never been taken by force, nor indeed by any other way than by famine. And thus did the Romans, when they had taken such great pains about weaker walls, get by good fortune what they could never have gotten by their engines; for three of these towers were too strong for all mechanical engines whatsoever, concerning which we have treated above.

5. So they now left these towers of themselves, or rather they were ejected out of them by God himself, and fled immediately to that valley which was under Siloam, where they again recovered themselves out of the dread they were in for a while, and ran violently against that part of the Roman wall which lay on that side; but as their courage was too much depressed to make their attacks with sufficient force, and their power was now broken with fear and affliction, they were repulsed by the guards, and dispersing themselves at distances from each other, went down into the subterranean caverns. So the Romans being now become masters of the walls, they both placed their ensigns upon the towers, and made joyful acclamations for the victory they had gained, as having found the end of this war much lighter than its beginning; for when they had gotten upon the last wall, without any bloodshed, they could hardly believe what they found to be true; but seeing nobody to oppose them, they stood in doubt what such an unusual solitude could mean. But when they went in numbers into the lanes of the city with their swords drawn, they slew those whom they overtook without and set fire to the houses whither the Jews were fled, and burnt every soul in them, and laid waste a great many of the rest; and when they were come to the houses to plunder them, they found in them entire families of dead men, and the upper rooms full of dead corpses, that is, of such as died by the famine; they then stood in a horror at this sight, and went out without touching any thing. But although they had this commiseration for such as were destroyed in that manner, yet had they not the same for those that were still alive, but they ran every one through whom they met with, and obstructed the very lanes with their dead bodies, and made the whole city run down with blood, to such a degree indeed that the fire of many of the houses was quenched with these men's blood. And truly so it happened, that though the slayers left off at the evening, yet did the fire greatly prevail in the night; and as all was burning, came that eighth day of the month Gorpieus [Elul] upon Jerusalem, a city that had been liable to so many miseries during this siege, that, had it always enjoyed as much happiness from its first foundation, it would certainly have been the envy of the world. Nor did it on any other account so much deserve these sore misfortunes, as by producing such a generation of men as were the occasions of this its overthrow.

CHAPTER 9.

WHAT INJUNCTIONS CAESAR GAVE WHEN HE WAS COME WITHIN THE CITY. THE NUMBER OF THE CAPTIVES AND OF THOSE THAT PERISHED IN THE SIEGE; AS ALSO

CONCERNING THOSE THAT HAD ESCAPED INTO THE SUBTERRANEAN CAVERNS, AMONG WHOM WERE THE TYRANTS SIMON AND JOHN THEMSELVES.

1. Now when Titus was come into this [upper] city, he admired not only some other places of strength in it, but particularly those strong towers which the tyrants in their mad conduct had relinquished; for when he saw their solid altitude, and the largeness of their several stones, and the exactness of their joints, as also how great was their breadth, and how extensive their length, he expressed himself after the manner following: "We have certainly had God for our assistant in this war, and it was no other than God who ejected the Jews out of these fortifications; for what could the hands of men or any machines do towards overthrowing these towers?" At which time he had many such discourses to his friends; he also let such go free as had been bound by the tyrants, and were left in the prisons. To conclude, when he entirely demolished the rest of the city, and overthrew its walls, he left these towers as a monument of his good fortune, which had proved his auxiliaries, and enabled him to take what could not otherwise have been taken by him.

2. And now, since his soldiers were already quite tired with killing men, and yet there appeared to be a vast multitude still remaining alive, Caesar gave orders that they should kill none but those that were in arms, and opposed them, but should take the rest alive. But, together with those whom they had orders to slay, they slew the aged and the infirm; but for those that were in their flourishing age, and who might be useful to them, they drove them together into the temple, and shut them up within the walls of the court of the women; over which Caesar set one of his freed-men, as also Fronto, one of his own friends; which last was to determine every one's fate, according to his merits. So this Fronto slew all those that had been seditious and robbers, who were impeached one by another; but of the young men he chose out the tallest and most beautiful, and reserved them for the triumph; and as for the rest of the multitude that were above seventeen years old, he put them into bonds, and sent them to the Egyptian mines (31) Titus also sent a great number into the provinces, as a present to them, that they might be destroyed upon their theatres, by the sword and by the wild beasts; but those that were under seventeen years of age were sold for slaves. Now during the days wherein Fronto was distinguishing these men, there perished, for want of food, eleven thousand; some of whom did not taste any food, through the hatred their guards bore to them; and others would not take in any when it was given them. The multitude also was so very great, that they were in want even of corn for their sustenance.

3. Now the number (32) of those that were carried captive during this whole war was collected to be ninety-seven thousand; as was the number of those that perished during the whole siege eleven hundred thousand, the greater part of whom were indeed of the same nation [with the citizens of Jerusalem], but not belonging to the city itself; for they were come up from all the country to the feast of unleavened bread, and were on a sudden shut up by an army, which, at the very first, occasioned so great a straitness among them, that there came a pestilential destruction upon them, and soon afterward such a famine, as destroyed them more suddenly. And that this city could contain so many people in it, is manifest by that number of them which was taken under Cestius, who being desirous of informing Nero of the power of the city, who otherwise was disposed to contemn that nation, entreated the high priests, if the thing were possible, to take the number of their whole multitude. So these high priests, upon the coming of that feast which is called the Passover, when they slay their sacrifices, from the ninth hour till the eleventh, but so that a company not less than ten (33) belong to every sacrifice, (for it is not lawful for them to feast singly by themselves,) and many of us are twenty in a company, found the number of sacrifices was two hundred and fifty-six thousand five hundred; which, upon the allowance of no more than ten that feast together, amounts to two millions seven hundred thousand and two hundred persons that were pure and holy; for as to those that have the leprosy, or the gonorrhea, or women that have their monthly courses, or such as are otherwise polluted, it is not lawful for them to be partakers of this sacrifice; nor indeed for any foreigners neither, who come hither to worship.

4. Now this vast multitude is indeed collected out of remote places, but the entire nation was now shut up by fate as in prison, and the Roman army encompassed the city when it was crowded with inhabitants. Accordingly, the multitude of those that therein perished exceeded all the destructions that either men or God ever brought upon the world; for, to speak only of what was publicly known, the Romans slew some of them, some they carried captives, and others they made a search for under ground, and when they found where they were, they broke up the ground and slew all they met with. There were also found slain there above two thousand persons, partly by their own hands, and partly by one another, but chiefly destroyed by the famine; but then the ill savor of the dead bodies was most offensive to those that lighted upon them, insomuch that some were obliged to get away immediately, while others were so greedy of gain, that they would go in among the dead bodies that lay on heaps, and tread upon them; for a great deal of treasure was found in these caverns, and the hope of gain made every way of getting it to be esteemed lawful. Many also of those that had been put in prison by the tyrants were now brought out; for they did not leave off their barbarous cruelty at the very last: yet did God avenge himself upon them both, in a manner agreeable to justice. As for John, he wanted food, together with his brethren, in these caverns, and begged that the Romans would now give him their right hand for his security, which he had often proudly rejected before; but for Simon, he struggled hard with the distress he was in, fill he was forced to surrender himself, as we shall relate hereafter; so he was reserved for the triumph, and to be then slain; as was John condemned to perpetual imprisonment. And now the Romans set fire to the extreme parts of the city, and burnt them down, and entirely demolished its walls.

CHAPTER 10.

THAT WHEREAS THE CITY OF JERUSALEM HAD BEEN FIVE TIMES TAKEN FORMERLY, THIS WAS THE SECOND TIME OF ITS DESOLATION. A BRIEF ACCOUNT OF ITS HISTORY.

1. AND thus was Jerusalem taken, in the second year of the reign of Vespasian, on the eighth day of the month Gorpeius [Elul]. It had been taken five (34) times before, though this was the second time of its desolation; for Shishak, the king of Egypt, and after him Antiochus, and after him Pompey, and after them Sosius and Herod, took the city, but still preserved it; but before all these, the king of Babylon conquered it, and made it desolate, one thousand four hundred and sixty-eight years and six months after it was built. But he who first built it. Was a potent man among the Canaanites, and is in our own tongue called [Melchisedek], the Righteous King, for such he really

was; on which account he was [there] the first priest of God, and first built a temple [there], and called the city Jerusalem, which was formerly called Salem. However, David, the king of the Jews, ejected the Canaanites, and settled his own people therein. It was demolished entirely by the Babylonians, four hundred and seventy-seven years and six months after him. And from king David, who was the first of the Jews who reigned therein, to this destruction under Titus, were one thousand one hundred and seventy-nine years; but from its first building, till this last destruction, were two thousand one hundred and seventy-seven years; yet hath not its great antiquity, nor its vast riches, nor the diffusion of its nation over all the habitable earth, nor the greatness of the veneration paid to it on a religious account, been sufficient to preserve it from being destroyed. And thus ended the siege of Jerusalem.

1.1

It came to pass, when the children of Israel were taken captive by
the king of the Chaldeans, that God spoke to Jeremiah saying:
Jeremiah, my chosen one, arise and depart from this city, you and
Baruch, since I am going to destroy it because of the multitude of
the sins of those who dwell in it.

1.2

For your prayers are like a solid pillar in its midst, and like an
indestructible wall surrounding it.

1.3

Now, then, arise and depart before the host of the Chaldeans
surrounds it.

1.4

And Jeremiah answered, saying:
I beseech you, Lord, permit me, your
servant, to speak in your presence.

1.5

And the Lord said to him:
Speak, my chosen one Jeremiah.

1.6

And Jeremiah spoke, saying:
Lord Almighty, would you deliver the
chosen city into the hands of the Chaldeans, so that the king with
the multitude of his people might boast and say: "I have prevailed
over the holy city of God"?

1.7

No, my Lord, but if it is your will, let it be destroyed by your
hands.

1.8

And the Lord said to Jeremiah:
Since you are my chosen one, arise and
depart form this city, you and Baruch, for I am going to destroy it
because of the multitude of the sins of those who dwell in it.

1.9

For neither the king nor his host will be able to enter it unless I
first open its gates.

1.10

Arise, then, and go to Baruch, and tell him these words.

1.11

And when you have arisen at the sixth hour of the night, go out on
the city walls and I will show you that unless I first destroy the
city, they cannot enter it.

1.12

When the Lord had said this, he departed from Jeremiah.

2.1

And Jeremiah ran and told these things to Baruch; and as they went
into the temple of God, Jeremiah tore his garments and put dust on
his head and entered the holy place of God.

2.2

And when Baruch saw him with dust sprinkled on his head and his
garments torn, he cried out in a loud voice, saying:
Father Jeremiah, what are you doing?
What sin has the people committed?

2.3

(For whenever the people sinned, Jeremiah would sprinkle dust on his
head and would pray for the people until their sin was forgiven.)

2.4

So Baruch asked him, saying:
Father, what is this?

2.5

And Jeremiah said to him:
Refrain from rending your garments --
rather, let us rend our hearts! And let us not draw water for the
trough, but let us weep and fill them with tears! For the Lord will
not have mercy on this people.

2.6

And Baruch said:

Father Jeremiah, what has happened?

2.7

And Jeremiah said:
God is delivering the city into the hands of the
king of the Chaldeans, to take the people captive into Babylon.

2.8

And when Baruch heard these things, he also tore his garments and
said:
Father Jeremiah, who has made this known to you?

2.9

And Jeremiah said to him:
Stay with me awhile, until the sixth hour
of the night, so that you may know that this word is true.

2.10

Therefore they both remained in the altar-area weeping, and their
garments were torn.

3.1

And when the hour of the night arrived, as the Lord had told Jeremiah
they came up together on the walls of the city, Jeremiah and Baruch.

3.2

And behold, there came a sound of trumpets; and angels emerged from
heaven holding torches in their hands, and they set them on the walls
of the city.

3.3

And when Jeremiah and Baruch saw them, they wept, saying:
Now we know that the word is true!

3.4

And Jeremiah besought the angels, saying:
I beseech you, do not
destroy the city yet, until I say something to the Lord.

3.5

And the Lord spoke to the angels, saying:
Do not destroy the city
until I speak to my chosen one, Jeremiah.

3.6

Then Jeremiah spoke, saying:
I beg you, Lord, bid me to speak in your presence.

3.7

And the Lord said:
Speak, my chosen one Jeremiah.

3.8

And Jeremiah said:
Behold, Lord, now we know that you are delivering
the city into the hands of its enemies, and they will take the people
away to Babylon. What do you want me to do with the holy vessels of
the temple service?

3.10

And the Lord said to him:
Take them and consign them to the earth, saying:
Hear, Earth, the voice of your creator
who formed you in the abundance of waters,
who sealed you with seven seals for seven epochs,
and after this you will receive your ornaments (?) --

3.11

Guard the vessels of the temple service until the gathering of the
beloved.

3.12

And Jeremiah spoke, saying:
I beseech you, Lord, show me what I
should do for Abimelech the Ethiopian, for he has done many
kindnesses to your servant Jeremiah.

3.13

For he pulled me out of the miry pit; and I do not wish that he
should see the destruction and desolation of this city, but that you
should be merciful to him and that he should not be grieved.

3.14

And the Lord said to Jeremiah:
Send him to the vineyard of Agrippa,
and I will hide him in the shadow of the mountain until I cause the

people to return to the city.

3.15

And you, Jeremiah, go with your people into Babylon and stay with them, preaching to them, until I cause them to return to the city.

3.16

But leave Baruch here until I speak with him.

3.17

When he had said these things, the Lord ascended from Jeremiah into heaven.

3.18

But Jeremiah and Baruch entered the holy place, and taking the vessels of the temple service, they consigned them to the earth as the Lord had told them.

3.19

And immediately the earth swallowed them.

3.20

And they both sat down and wept.

3.21

And when morning came, Jeremiah sent Abimelech, saying:
Take a basket
and go to the estate of Agrippa by the mountain road, and bring back some figs to give to the sick among the people; for the favor of the Lord is on you and his glory is on your head.

3.22

And when he had said this, Jeremiah sent him away; and Abimelech went as he told him.

4.1

And when morning came, behold the host of the Chaldeans surrounded the city.

4.2

And the great angel trumpeted, saying:
Enter the city, host of the Chaldeans;
for behold, the gate is opened for you.

4.3

Therefore let the king enter, with his multitudes, and let him take all the people captive.

4.4

But taking the keys of the temple, Jeremiah went outside the city and threw them away in the presence of the sun, saying:
I say to you, Sun,
take the keys of the temple of God and guard them until the day in which the Lord asks you for them.

4.5

For we have not been found worthy to keep them, for we have become unfaithful guardians.

4.6

While Jeremiah was still weeping for the people, they brought him out with the people and dragged them into Babylon.

4.7

But Baruch put dust on his head and sat and wailed this lamentation, saying:
Why has Jerusalem been devastated? Because of the sins of the beloved people she was delivered into the hands of enemies -- because of our sins and those of the people.

4.8

But let not the lawless ones boast and say:
"We were strong enough to
take the city of God by our might;"
but it was delivered to you because of our sins.

4.9

And God will pity us and cause us to return to our city, but you will not survive!

4.10

Blessed are our fathers, Abraham, Isaac and Jacob, for they departed from this world and did not see the destruction of this city.

4.11

When he had said this, Baruch departed from the city, weeping and saying:
Grieving because of you, Jerusalem, I went out from you.

4.12

And he remained sitting in a tomb, while the angels came to him and explained to him everything that the Lord revealed to him through them.

5.1

But Abimelech took the figs in the burning heat; and coming upon a tree, he sat under its shade to rest a bit.

5.2

And leaning his head on the basket of figs, he fell asleep and slept for 66 years; and he was not awakened from his slumber.

5.3

And afterward, when he awoke from his sleep, he said:
I slept sweetly for a little while,
but my head is heavy because I did not get enough sleep.

5.4

Then he uncovered the basket of figs and found them dripping milk.

5.5

And he said:
I would like to sleep a little longer, because my head
is heavy. But I am afraid that I might fall asleep and be late in awakening and my father Jeremiah would think badly of me; for if he were not in a hurry, he would not have sent me today at daybreak.

5.6

So I will get up, and proceed in the burning heat; for isn't there heat, isn't there toil every day?

5.7

So he got up and took the basket of figs and placed it on his shoulders, and he entered into Jerusalem and did not recognize it -- neither his own house, nor the place -- nor did he find his own family or any of his acquaintances.

5.8

And he said:
The Lord be blessed, for a great trance has come over me today!

5.9

This is not the city Jerusalem -- and I have lost my way because I came by the mountain road when I arose from my sleep; and since my head was heavy because I did not get enough sleep, I lost my way.

5.10

It will seem incredible to Jeremiah that I lost my way!

5.11

And he departed from the city; and as he searched he saw the landmarks of the city, and he said:
Indeed, this is the city; I lost my way.

5.12

And again he returned to the city and searched, and found no one of his own people; and he said:
The Lord be blessed, for a great trance
has come over me!

5.13

And again he departed from the city, and he stayed there grieving, not knowing where he should go.

5.14

And he put down the basket, saying:
I will sit here until the Lord
takes this trance from me.

5.15

And as he sat, he saw an old man coming from the field; and Abimelech said to him:
I say to you, old man, what city is this?

5.16

And he said to him:
It is Jerusalem.

5.17

And Abimelech said to him:
Where is Jeremiah the priest, and Baruch the secretary, and all the people of this city, for I could not find them?

5.18

And the old man said to him:
Are you not from this city, seeing that

you remember Jeremiah today, because you are asking about him after such a long time?

5.19

For Jeremiah is in Babylon with the people; for they were taken captive by king Nebuchadnezzar, and Jeremiah is with them to preach the good news to them and to teach them the word.

5.20

As soon as Abimelech heard this from the old man, he said:
If you were not an old man,
and if it were not for the fact that it is not
lawful for a man to upbraid one older than himself, I would laugh at you and say that you are out of your mind -- since you say that the people have been taken captive into Babylon.

5.21

Even if the heavenly torrents had descended on them, there has not yet been time for them to go into Babylon!

5.22

For how much time has passed since my father Jeremiah sent me to the estate of Agrippa to bring a few figs, so that I might give them to the sick among the people?

5.23

And I went and got them, and when I came to a certain tree in the burning heat, I sat to rest a little; and I leaned my head on the basket and fell asleep.

5.24

And when I awoke I uncovered the basket of figs, supposing that I was late; and I found the figs dripping milk, just as I had collected them.

5.25

But you claim that the people have been taken captive into Babylon.

5.26

But that you might know, take the figs and see!

5.27

And he uncovered the basket of figs for the old man, and he saw them dripping milk.

5.28

And when the old man saw them, he said:
O my son, you are a righteous man,
and God did not want you to see the desolation of the city, so he brought this trance upon you.

5.29

For behold it is 66 years today since the people were taken captive into Babylon.

5.30

But that you might learn, my son, that what I tell you is true -- look into the field and see that the ripening of the crops has not appeared.

5.31

And notice that the figs are not in season, and be enlightened.

5.32

Then Abimelech cried out in a loud voice, saying:
I bless you, God of heaven and earth,
the Rest of the souls of the righteous in every place!

5.33

Then he said to the old man:
What month is this?

5.34

And he said:
Nisan (which is Abib).

5.35

And taking some of figs, he gave them to the old man and said to him:
May God illumine your way to the city above, Jerusalem.

6

6.1

After this, Abimelech went out of the city and prayed to the Lord.

6.2

And behold, an angel of the Lord came and took him by the right hand and brought him back to where Baruch was sitting, and he found him in a tomb.

6.3

And when they saw each other, they both wept and kissed each other.

6.4

But when Baruch looked up he saw with his own eyes the figs that were covered in Abimelech's basket.

6.5

And lifting his eyes to heaven, he prayed, saying:

6.6

You are the God who gives a reward to those who love you. Prepare yourself, my heart, and rejoice and be glad while you are in your tabernacle, saying to your fleshly house, "your grief has been changed to joy;" for the Sufficient One is coming and will deliver you in your tabernacle -- for there is no sin in you.

6.7

Revive in your tabernacle, in your virginal faith, and believe that you will live!

6.8

Look at this basket of figs -- for behold, they are 66 years old and have not become shrivelled or rotten, but they are dripping milk.

6.9

So it will be with you, my flesh, if you do what is commanded you by the angel of righteousness.

6.10

He who preserved the basket of figs, the same will again preserve you by his power.

6.11

When Baruch had said this, he said to Abimelech:
Stand up and let us pray
that the Lord may make known to us how we shall be able to send to Jeremiah in Babylon the report about the shelter provided for you on the way.

6.12

And Baruch prayed, saying:
Lord God, our strength is the elect light
which comes forth from your mouth.

6.13

We beseech and beg of your goodness -- you whose great name no one is able to know -- hear the voice of your servants and let knowledge come into our hearts.

6.14

What shall we do, and how shall we send this report to Jeremiah in Babylon?

6.15

And while Baruch was still praying, behold an angel of the Lord came and said all these words to Baruch:
Agent of the light, do not be
anxious about how you will send to Jeremiah; for an eagle is coming to you at the hour of light tomorrow, and you will direct him to Jeremiah.

6.16

Therefore, write in a letter:
Say to the children of Israel: Let the
stranger who comes among you be set apart and let 15 days go by; and after this I will lead you into your city, says the Lord.

6.17

He who is not separated from Babylon will not enter into the city; and I will punish them by keeping them from being received back by the Babylonians, says the Lord.

6.18

And when the angel had said this, he departed from Baruch.

6.19

And Baruch sent to the market of the gentiles and got papyrus and ink and wrote a letter as follows:
Baruch, the servant of God, writes to
Jeremiah in the captivity of Babylon:

6.20

Greetings! Rejoice, for God has not allowed us to depart from this body grieving for the city which was laid waste and outraged.

6.21

Wherefore the Lord has had compassion on our tears, and has remembered the covenant which he established with our fathers Abraham, Isaac and Jacob.

6.22

And he sent his angel to me, and he told me these words which I send to you.

6.13

These, then, are the words which the Lord, the God of Israel, spoke, who led us out of Egypt, out of the great furnace:
Because you did
not keep my ordinances, but your heart was lifted up, and you were haughty before me, in anger and wrath I delivered you to the furnace in Babylon.

6.24

If, therefore, says the Lord, you listen to my voice, from the mouth of Jeremiah my servant, I will bring the one who listens up from Babylon; but the one who does not listen will become a stranger to Jerusalem and to Babylon.

6.25

And you will test them by means of the water of the Jordan; whoever does not listen will be exposed -- this is the sign of the great seal.

7.1

And Baruch got up and departed from the tomb and found the eagle sitting outside the tomb.

7.2

And the eagle said to him in a human voice:
Hail, Baruch, steward of the faith.

7.3

And Baruch said to him:
You who speak are chosen from among all the birds of heaven, for this is clear from the gleam of your eyes; tell me, then, what are you doing here?

7.4

And the eagle said to him:
I was sent here so that you might through me send whatever message you want.

7.5

And Baruch said to him:
Can you carry this message to Jeremiah in Babylon?

7.6

And the eagle said to him:
Indeed, it was for this reason I was sent.

7.7

And Baruch took the letter, and 15 figs from Abimelech's basket, and tied them to the eagle's neck and said to him:
I say to you, king of
the birds, go in peace with good health and carry the message for me.

7.8

Do not be like the raven which Noah sent out and which never came back to him in the ark; but be like the dove which, the third time, brought a report to the righteous one.

7.9

So you also, take this good message to Jeremiah and to those in bondage with him, that it may be well with you-take this papyrus to the people and to the chosen one of God.

7.10

Even if all the birds of heaven surround you and want to fight with you, struggle -- the Lord will give you strength.

7.11

And do not turn aside to the right or to the left, but straight as a speeding arrow, go in the power of God, and the glory of the Lord will be with you the entire way.

7.12

Then the eagle took flight and went away to Babylon, having the letter tied to his neck; and when he arrived he rested on a post outside the city in a desert place.

7.13

And he kept silent until Jeremiah came along, for he and some of the people were coming out to bury a corpse outside the city.

7.14

(For Jeremiah had petitioned king Nebuchadnezzar, saying: "Give me a place where I may bury those of my people who have died;" and the king gave it to him.)

7.15

And as they were coming out with the body, and weeping, they came to where the eagle was.

7.16

And the eagle cried out in a loud voice, saying:
I say to you,
Jeremiah the chosen one of God, go and gather together the people and come here so that they may hear a letter which I have brought to you from Baruch and Abimelech.

7.17

And when Jeremiah heard this, he glorified God; and he went and gathered together the people along with their wives and children, and he came to where the eagle was.

7.18

And the eagle came down on the corpse, and it revived.

7.19

(Now this took place so that they might believe.)

7.20

And all the people were astounded at what had happened, and said:
This is the God who appeared to our fathers in the wilderness through Moses, and now he has appeared to us through the eagle.

7.21

And the eagle said:
I say to you, Jeremiah, come, untie this letter
and read it to the people --
So he untied the letter and read it to the people.

7.22

And when the people heard it, they wept and put dust on their heads, and they said to Jeremiah:
Deliver us and tell us what to do that we
may once again enter our city.

7.23

And Jeremiah answered and said to them:
Do whatever you heard from
the letter, and the Lord will lead us into our city.

7.24

And Jeremiah wrote a letter to Baruch, saying thus:
My beloved son,
do not be negligent in your prayers, beseeching God on our behalf, that he might direct our way until we come out of the jurisdiction of this lawless king.

7.25

For you have been found righteous before God, and he did not let you come here, lest you see the affliction which has come upon the people at the hands of the Babylonians.

7.26

For it is like a father with an only son, who is given over for punishment; and those who see his father and console him cover his face, lest he see how his son is being punished, and be even more ravaged by grief.

7.27

For thus God took pity on you and did not let you enter Babylon lest you see the affliction of the people.

7.28

For since we came here, grief has not left us, for 66 years today.

7.29

For many times when I went out I found some of the people hung up by king Nebuchadnezzar, crying and saying:
"Have mercy on us, God-ZAR!"

7.30

When I heard this, I grieved and cried with two-fold mourning, not only because they were hung up, but because they were calling on a foreign God, saying "Have mercy on us."

7.31

But I remembered days of festivity which we celebrated in Jerusalem

before our captivity; and when I remembered, I groaned, and returned
to my house wailing and weeping.

7.32
Now, then, pray in the place where you are -- you and Abimelech -- for
this people, that they may listen to my voice and to the decrees of
my mouth, so that we may depart from here.

7.33
For I tell you that the entire time that we have spent here they have
kept us in subjection, saying:
Recite for us a song from the songs of
Zion [see Ps 136.3c/4] -- the song of your God.

7.34
And we reply to them:
How shall we sing for you
since we are in a foreign land? [Ps 136.4]

7.35
And after this, Jeremiah tied the letter to the eagle's neck, saying:
Go in peace, and may the Lord watch over both of us.

7.36
And the eagle took flight and came to Jerusalem and gave the letter
to Baruch; and when he had untied it he read it and kissed it and
wept when he heard about the distresses and afflictions of the people.

7.37
But Jeremiah took the figs and distributed them to the sick among the
people, and he kept teaching them to abstain from the pollutions of
the gentiles of Babylon.

6

8.1
And the day came in which the Lord brought the people out of Babylon.

8.2
And the Lord said to Jeremiah:
Rise up -- you and the people -- and come
to the Jordan and say to the people:
Let anyone who desires the Lord
forsake the works of Babylon.

8.3
As for the men who took wives from them and the women who took
husbands from them -- those who listen to you shall cross over, and you
take them into Jerusalem; but those who do not listen to you, do not
lead them there.

8.4
And Jeremiah spoke these words to the people, and they arose and came
to the Jordan to cross over.

8.5
As he told them the words that the Lord had spoken to him, half of
those who had taken spouses from them did not wish to listen to
Jeremiah, but said to him:
We will never forsake our wives,
but we will bring them back with us into our city.

8.6
So they crossed the Jordan and came to Jerusalem.

8.7
And Jeremiah and Baruch and Abimelech stood up and said:
No man joined with Babylonians shall enter this city!

8.8
And they said to one another:
Let us arise and return to Babylon to our place --
And they departed.

8.9
But while they were coming to Babylon, the Babylonians came out to
meet them, saying:
You shall not enter our city, for you hated us and
you left us secretly; therefore you cannot come in with us.

8.10
For we have taken a solemn oath together in the name of our god to
receive neither you nor your children, since you left us secretly.

8.11
And when they heard this, they returned and came to a desert place
some distance from Jerusalem and built a city for themselves and

named it 'SAMARIA.'

8.12
And Jeremiah sent to them, saying:
Repent, for the angel of
righteousness is coming and will lead you to your exalted place.

6

9.1
Now those who were with Jeremiah were rejoicing and offering
sacrifices on behalf of the people for nine days.

9.2
But on the tenth, Jeremiah alone offered sacrifice.

9.3
And he prayed a prayer, saying:
Holy, holy, holy, fragrant aroma of the living trees,
true light that enlightens me until I ascend to you;

9.4
For your mercy, I beg you --
for the sweet voice of the two seraphim, I beg --
for another fragrant aroma.

9.5
And may Michael, archangel of righteousness, who opens the gates to
the righteous, be my guardian (?) until he causes the righteous to
enter.

9.6
I beg you, almighty Lord of all creation, unbegotten and
incomprehensible, in whom all judgment was hidden before these things
came into existence.

9.7
When Jeremiah had said this, and while he was standing in the
altar-area with Baruch and Abimelech, he became as one whose soul had
departed.

9.8
And Baruch and Abimelech were weeping and crying out in a loud voice:
Woe to us! For our father Jeremiah has left us -- the priest of God has
departed!

9.9
And all the people heard their weeping and they all ran to them and
saw Jeremiah lying on the ground as if dead.

9.10
And they tore their garments and put dust on their heads and wept
bitterly.

9.11
And after this they prepared to bury him.

9.12
And behold, there came a voice saying:
Do not bury the one who yet lives,
for his soul is returning to his body!

9.13
And when they heard the voice they did not bury him, but stayed
around his tabernacle for three days saying, "when will he arise?"

9.14
And after three days his soul came back into his body and he raised
his voice in the midst of them all and said:
Glorify God with one voice!
All of you glorify God and the son of God who awakens us --
messiah Jesus -- the light of all the ages, the inextinguishable
lamp, the life of faith.

9.15
But after these times there shall be 477 years more and he comes to
earth.

9.16
And the tree of life planted in the midst of paradise
will cause all the unfruitful trees to bear fruit,
and will grow and sprout forth.

9.17
And the trees that had sprouted and became haughty and said:
"We have supplied our power (?) to the air,"
he will cause them to wither, with the grandeur of their branches,
and he will cause them to be judged -- that firmly rooted tree!

9.18
And what is crimson will become white as wool --
  the snow will be blackened --
  the sweet waters will become salty, and the salty sweet,
  in the intense light of the joy of God.
9.19
And he will bless the isles
  so that they become fruitful by the word of the mouth of his messiah.
9.20
For he shall come,
  and he will go out and choose for himself twelve apostles
    to proclaim the news among the nations--
  he whom I have seen adorned by his father
    and coming into the world on the Mount of Olives --
  and he shall fill the hungry souls.
9.21
When Jeremiah was saying this concerning the son of God -- that he is
coming into the world -- the people became very angry and said:
This is a repetition of the words spoken by Isaiah son of Amos,
when he said:
  I saw God and the son of God.
9.22
Come, then, and let us not kill him by the same sort of death with
which we killed Isaiah, but let us stone him with stones.
9.23
  And Baruch and Abimelech were greatly grieved because they wanted to
hear in full the mysteries that he had seen.
9.24
But Jeremiah said to them:
Be silent and weep not, for they cannot kill me
until I describe for you everything I saw.
9.25
And he said to them:
Bring a stone here to me.
9.26
And he set it up and said:
Light of the ages,
  make this stone to become like me in appearance,
    until I have described to Baruch and Abimelech everything I saw.
9.27
Then the stone, by God's command, took on the appearance of Jeremiah.
9.28
And they were stoning the stone, supposing that it was Jeremiah!
9.29
  But Jeremiah delivered to Baruch and to Abimelech all the mysteries
he had seen, and forthwith he stood in the midst of the people
desiring to complete his ministry.
9.30
Then the stone cried out, saying:
O foolish children of Israel,
  why do you stone me, supposing that I am Jeremiah?
Behold, Jeremiah is standing in your midst!
9.31
And when they saw him, immediately they rushed upon him with many
stones, and his ministry was fulfilled.
9.32
  And when Baruch and Abimelech came, they buried him, and taking the
stone they placed it on his tomb and inscribed it thus:
This is the stone that was the ally of Jeremiah.

//end of Longer Version//

THAT WHICH THE LORD SPOKE TO JEREMIAH BEFORE THE CAPTURE OF JERUSALEM AND HOW THE CAPTURE HAPPENED

1.1
  In those days the Lord spoke to Jeremiah, saying: Arise,
depart from this city with Baruch, since I am going to destroy
it because of the multitude of the sins of those who dwell in it.
1.2

For your prayers are like solid pillars in its midst, and like an
indestructible wall surrounding it.
  1.3
Now, then, depart from it before the host of the Chaldeans
surrounds it.
  1.4
And Jeremiah spoke, saying: I beseech you, Lord, permit me,
your servant, to speak in your presence.
  1.5
And the Lord said: Speak.
  1.6
And Jeremiah said: Lord, would you deliver this city into
the hands of the Chaldeans, so that they might boast that they
had prevailed against it?
  1.7
My Lord, if it is your will, rather let it be destroyed by
your hands and not by the Chaldeans.
  1.8
And God said: You, arise, depart.
  1.9
But they will not boast. Unless I open (the gates), they are
not able to enter.
  1.10
Therefore go to Baruch and tell him.
  1.11
And at the sixth hour of the night go up on the city walls
and see that unless I open (the gates), they are not able to
enter.
  1.12
And when he had said these things he departed from him.
  2.1
  And Jeremiah departed and told Baruch; and as they went into
the temple they tore their garments and mourned much.
  3.1
  And at the sixth hour when they had gone up on the city
walls, they heard the sound of trumpets.
  3.2
And the angels came from heaven, holding torches in their
hands, and they set them on the walls of the city.
  3.3
And when they saw them they wept and said: Now we know that
the word that God spoke is true.
  3.4
And they besought the angels, saying: We beseech (you) not
to destroy the city until we speak to God.
  3.6
Then Jeremiah spoke, saying: I beg you, Lord, bid me to
speak in your presence.
  3.7
And the Lord said: Speak.
  3.8
And Jeremiah said: Behold, Lord, we know that you are
delivering the city into the hands of its enemies, and your
people depart for Babylon.
  3.9
What then will we do with your holy vessels?
  3.10
And God said: Consign them to the earth, saying: Hear,
earth, the voice of your creator, who founded you upon the
waters, who sealed you with seven seals for seven epochs, and
after this you will receive your ornaments.
  3.11
Guard the vessels of the temple service until the gathering
of the beloved.
  3.12
And Jeremiah spoke again, saying: I beseech you, Lord, what
should I do for Abimelech the Ethiopian, for he has done many
kindnesses to your servant?
  3.13

For he drew me up out of the miry pit where they threw me, and I do not wish that he should see the destruction and spoiling of the city because he is little-souled.
3.14
And the Lord said to Jeremiah: Send him to the vineyard of Agrippa, and I will hide him in the shadow of the mountain until the people are about to return from the captivity.
3.15
And you, Jeremiah, go with your people into Babylon and stay with them, preaching to them, until I cause them to return.
3.16
But leave Baruch here.
3.18
Then they went into the temple, and taking the vessels of the temple service, they consigned them to the earth as the Lord had told them.
3.21
And at morning, Jeremiah said to Abimelech: Take a basket, child, and go to the estate of Agrippa by the mountain road, and bring back figs to the sick of the people; for their favor is on you, and glory is on your head.
3.22
And immediately he went to the field.
4.1
And when he had departed and the sun had appeared at dawn, behold, the host of the Chaldeans, having arrived, had surrounded the city of Jerusalem.
4.2
And the great angel trumpeted, saying: Enter the city, the entire host of the Chaldeans; for behold, the gates are opened for you.
4.4
Then Jeremiah, taking the keys of the temple, went outside the city and throwing them away in the presence of the sun, said: Take them and guard (them) until the day in which the Lord asks you for them.
4.5
For we have not been found worthy to keep them.
4.6
And Jeremiah went with the people into captivity in Babylon.
4.11"-12"
But Baruch departed from the city and remained sitting in a tomb.
5.1
And Abimelech, taking the figs in the burning heat and coming upon a tree, sat under its shade to rest a bit.
5.2
And leaning his head on the basket, he fell asleep for seventy times. And this happened according to the commandment of God because of the word which he spoke to Jeremiah: I will hide him.
5.3
And after awakening he said: I slept sweetly for a little while, and because of this my head is heavy because I did not get enough sleep.
5.4
And uncovering the figs, he found them dripping milk, as if he had gathered them shortly before.
5.5
And he said: I would like to sleep a little longer, but since Jeremiah sent me in much haste, if I do this I will be late and he will be distressed.
5.6
For isn't there toil and heat every day? Rather, I should leave quickly, and I will heal him and then I can sleep.
5.7
And taking the figs, he went into Jerusalem and he did not recognize either his house or that of his relatives or of his friends.

5.8
And he said: The Lord be blessed, a trance came over me today!
5.9
This is not the city. Lacking sleep, I have gone astray.
5."11"z"1"
And he departed from (the city) and searching for the landmarks he said: Indeed, this is the city; I went astray.
5.12
And entering again and searching, he found no one of his relatives or of his friends; and he said: The Lord be blessed, a great trance has come over me!
5.13
And going out, he stayed there grieving, not knowing what he should do.
5.14
And putting down the basket, he said: I must sit here until the Lord takes the trance from me.
5.15
And as he was sitting, behold, an old man was coming from the field, and he said to him: I say to you, old man, what city is this?
5.16
And he said: It is Jerusalem, child.
5.17
And Abimelech said: And where is Jeremiah the priest of God, and Baruch the secretary, and all the people of the city, for I could not find them?
5.18
And the old man said to him: Are you not from this city? Today you remembered Jeremiah and asked about him.
5.19
Jeremiah has been in Babylon with the people since they were made captives by Nebuchadnezzar the king seventy times ago; and how is it that you, being a young man and never having been (old), then, are asking about the things which I have never seen?
5.20
And when he had heard these things, Abimelech said to him: If you were not an old man, and if it were not for the fact that it is not lawful for a man of God to upbraid one older than himself, I would laugh at you and say that you are out of your mind for saying that the people went captive into Babylon.
5.21
Even if the heavenly torrents had opened, and the angels of God came to take them with power and authority, not yet would they have (time) to go into Babylon!
5.22
For how much time has passed since my father Jeremiah sent me to the estate of Agrippa because of a few (figs), so that I might give them to the sick of the people?
5.23
And coming to a tree from out of the heat, I fell asleep for a little bit.
5.24
Supposing that I was late, I uncovered the figs and found them dripping milk just as I had collected (them).
5.25
And you say that the people were taken captive into Babylon.
5.26
But that you might know, and not account me a liar, take the figs and see.
5.28
And when the old man saw these things he said: O child, you are the son of a righteous man, and God did not want to show you the desolation of this city and he brought this trance upon you.
5.29
Behold, it is seventy times (since) the people were taken

captive into Babylon with Jeremiah from this day.

5.30

But so that you may learn, my child, that what I tell you
is true, look into the field and see that the ripening of the
crops has not yet appeared.

5.31

And notice that the figs are not in season, and be
enlightened and be persuaded that I am telling the truth.

5.32

Then Abimelech, just as from great sobriety and observing
the land accurately, and the trees in it, said: Blessed be the
God of heaven and earth, the Rest of the souls of the righteous.

5.33

And he said to the old man: What month is this?

5.34

And the old man said: The twelfth.

5.35

And giving some figs to the old man, he departed when he
had blessed him.

6.1

And rising up, Abimelech prayed that it might be revealed to
him what he should do.

6.2

And behold, an angel of the Lord came and took him by the
right hand and brought him safely to the tomb in which Baruch
was sitting.

6.3

And seeing one another, they wept much, and then they prayed
to God and rejoiced, glorifying and praising him.

6.4

And Baruch, seeing the figs which were picked seventy times
before still dripping milk, was astonished, and said:

6.11

Let us pray to God that the Lord may make known to us how,
then, we will give knowledge to Jeremiah concerning the shelter
made for you, and now (your) incredible awakening.

6.15

And while they were doing this, they heard an angel which
was sent to them:

6.16

Write a letter to Jeremiah (saying) what he must do unto
the people as I say to you. And he told them everything that
they should write, and he also delivered over this: Behold, in a
few days God will lead you out of Babylon into Jerusalem. And
early tomorrow when an eagle comes, bind the letter and a few
figs on its neck so that it may carry these things to Jeremiah
in Babylon.

6.18

And when he had said these things he departed from them.

6.19

And immediately taking papyrus Baruch sat down and wrote
the things which he heard from the angel.

7.1

And coming early, the eagle cried out. And going out, they
praised God.

7.7

And when they had prayed they bound the letter and ten figs
on its neck.

7.8

And when they had prayed for it they sent it away, having
commanded it to return to them again.

7.12

And it went away to Babylon (and having arrived) it sat on
a pillar outside the city.

7.13

And according to the stewardship of God, Jeremiah was going
out of the city with all the people to bury a corpse.

7.14"-15"

And they were mourning and were about to bury it in the

place which Jeremiah received from Nebuchadnezzar which he
yielded for the burying of dead Jews.

7.16

And the eagle cried out with the voice of a man and said: I
say to you Jeremiah, take the letter which I have brought to you
from Baruch and Abimelech and let all the people of Jerusalem
hear it.

7.17

And when Jeremiah heard, he glorified God.

7.18

And the eagle sat on the corpse and immediately it arose.

7.20

Everyone seeing this knew that the letter was sent from
God. And when all had glorified God at what had happened,

7.21

Jeremiah untied the letter and read it before all.

7.22

And when they heard it they shouted out and rejoiced
greatly.

7.24

And Jeremiah also wrote on papyrus of all the tribulations
and misfortunes that had happened to them.

7.35

And he tied it to the neck of the eagle and blessing it, he
sent it off.

7.36

And again it took this letter to Baruch and Abimelech, and
when they had read it they wept and with thanks they glorified
God because they had not been tested with such tribulations.

7.37

But Jeremiah gave the figs to the sick of the people, and
they were all healed, as many as ate of them.

8.1

And when the appointed day had been attained,

8.2

God said to Jeremiah: Take the entire night and go out of
Babylon and come to the Jordan.

8.3

And there you will separate the rulers of the Babylonians
who took wives from your nation and the women of the Babylonians
who joined together with your people. And those who do not hear
you the Jordan will separate. They will not cross with you.

8.4

And Jeremiah did as God commanded him.

8.5

And in separating them at the Jordan, most of those who had
joined (with the Babylonians) did not wish to listen to
Jeremiah, but said: It is better for us to return to Babylon
than to forsake our wives.

8.8

And they departed for Babylon.

8.9

But they were not welcomed by the Babylonians who said:
Because you left us and departed secretly,

8.10

We have sworn an oath among ourselves not to receive you or
your children.

8.11

But these who were not received, either by Jeremiah or by
the Babylonians departed into a desert place some distance from
Jerusalem and built for themselves a city which is called
Samaria, which is what they named it.

9.1

And Jeremiah with the people went into Jerusalem and they
rejoiced, bringing up their sacrifices for nine days.

9.2

And on the tenth day Jeremiah offered his sacrifice to God.

9.3

And he prayed

9.7

until his soul went up and his body fell down dead in the altar-area.

9.8

Then Baruch and Abimelech came to mourn Jeremiah.

9.9

And when all the people heard they ran to them and saw Jeremiah lying on the ground dead.

9.10

And they tore their garments and put dust on their heads and they all wept bitterly.

9.11

And after this they prepared to bury him.

9.12

And behold, there was a voice from heaven saying: Do not bury the one who yet lives.

9.13

And when they heard the voice they stayed beside him, praying for three days.

9.14

And after three days his soul came back into his body and he raised his voice in the midst of them all, saying: With one voice all of you glorify God and his son who awakens us, messiah Jesus, the light of all the ages, the inextinguishable lamp, the life of our nature.

9.15

For after these times there shall be 377 years more.

9.21

And as he preached the good news of the messiah to them as he saw and heard enigmatically when his soul went up, all the people shouted: These are the words which Isaiah of old spoke to our fathers: I saw God and his son.

9.22

And they killed him with a wooden saw, sawing him asunder. Come then, let us stone him.

9.23

And when they heard these things, Baruch and Abimelech were greatly grieved because of the death of Jeremiah and had not heard in full the mysteries which the prophet who had gone up had seen and heard.

9.24

And he, knowing their thoughts, said: Be silent; they will not kill me until everything which I saw and heard I describe for you.

9.25

And he said to them: Bring a great stone to me. And they brought it to him.

9.26

And the prophet said: Lord, make this stone like me in appearance so that the people will stone it until I tell my brothers the things which I saw and heard.

9.27

Then, by the commandment of God, the stone took on the appearance of the prophet,

9.28

And they stoned it instead of him.

9.29

And he told them everything that he saw and heard. Desiring to complete his ministry, he went into the midst of the people.

9.30

And by the command of God the stone went up and cried out in the voice of a man, saying: O foolish children of Israel, why do you stone me, supposing that I am Jeremiah, who is standing in your midst?

9.31

Then, out of great sobriety, they saw the holy one, and taking up stones they killed him. And he was stoned by his fellow captives of Jerusalem who owed him much good, and he did not speak against them neither was he angry, but thus he

received the overpowering of the stones, as through them he went up into heaven.

9.32

And when Baruch and Abimelech came, they buried him, and taking the stone they placed it on his tomb, inscribing on it: This is the stone that was the ally of Jeremiah.

9.33

And the sacred vessels Jeremiah laid away according to the command of God, sealed in this stone by his finger in the name of God. Through the writing of iron, the imprint has become on the stone a shadowy cloud, because it is indistinguishable. And the stone is in the desert where formerly the ark was prepared with the others. And this Jeremiah spoke: The Lord went up to heaven from Zion, but he will come again to visit Zion, and the coming of the messiah will be the sign whenever every nation worships the cross, glorifying and praising God, to whom becomes all glory forever and ever, Amen.

Printed in the USA
CPSIA information can be obtained
at www.ICGtesting.com
LVHW070756311223
767720LV00081B/2554

9 781933 580937